PUBLIC PAPERS OF THE PRESIDENTS
OF THE
UNITED STATES

William J. Clinton

1993

(IN TWO BOOKS)

BOOK I—JANUARY 20 TO JULY 31, 1993

UNITED STATES GOVERNMENT PRINTING OFFICE
WASHINGTON : 1994

Published by the
Office of the Federal Register
National Archives and Records Administration

PUBLIC PAPERS OF THE PRESIDENTS
OF THE
UNITED STATES

Foreword

In my inaugural address, I declared: "Our democracy must be not only the envy of the world but the engine of our own renewal. There is nothing wrong with America that cannot be cured by what is right with America."

In the first 6 months of our Administration, we called upon America's historic strengths to revitalize the economy, restore the middle class, rebuild our national security for a new era, and renew the people's sense of national community and their faith in public institutions.

We built upon the entrepreneurial energy of our free enterprise system with an economic plan that cut the Federal deficit, invested in our workers' skills, expanded college opportunity for the sons and daughters of the middle class, rewarded the efforts of the working poor, and helped businesses expand and create new jobs. We strengthened American families with the Family and Medical Leave Act, which helps Americans be good parents and good workers. We enhanced America's world leadership with efforts to open foreign markets, ensure the readiness of our military forces, promote democracy abroad, preserve our planet's natural environment, and advance regional security in Europe, Asia, the Mideast, and throughout the world. We strengthened America's sense of community with initiatives here at home to encourage young people to serve their country, to protect our people from violent crime and drug abuse, and to reinvent government to make it reflect American values. And we began the work of preserving what is right, and fixing what is wrong, with America's health care system.

Most of all, this volume is a testimonial to those who embody what is best about America, the citizens of our country. The American people called for the changes chronicled in this volume; they held the President and the Congress accountable for achieving these changes; and, in countless actions in their own lives—from raising their children with values of responsibility and faith to helping to keep their own neighborhoods safe from crime and violence—they are continuing the work of renewing our democracy.

Preface

This book contains the papers and speeches of the 42d President of the United States that were issued by the Office of the Press Secretary during the period January 20–July 31, 1993. The material has been compiled and published by the Office of the Federal Register, National Archives and Records Administration.

The material is presented in chronological order, and the dates shown in the headings are the dates of the documents or events. In instances when the release date differs from the date of the document itself, that fact is shown in the textnote. Every effort has been made to ensure accuracy: Remarks are checked against a tape recording, and signed documents are checked against the original. Textnotes and cross references have been provided by the editors for purposes of identification or clarity. Speeches were delivered in Washington, DC, unless indicated. The times noted are local times. All materials that are printed full-text in the book have been indexed in the subject and name indexes, and listed in the document categories list.

The Public Papers of the Presidents series was begun in 1957 in response to a recommendation of the National Historical Publications Commission. An extensive compilation of messages and papers of the Presidents covering the period 1789 to 1897 was assembled by James D. Richardson and published under congressional authority between 1896 and 1899. Since then, various private compilations have been issued, but there was no uniform publication comparable to the Congressional Record or the United States Supreme Court Reports. Many Presidential papers could be found only in the form of mimeographed White House releases or as reported in the press. The Commission therefore recommended the establishment of an official series in which Presidential writings, addresses, and remarks of a public nature could be made available.

The Commission's recommendation was incorporated in regulations of the Administrative Committee of the Federal Register, issued under section 6 of the Federal Register Act (44 U.S.C. 1506), which may be found in title 1, part 10, of the Code of Federal Regulations.

A companion publication to the Public Papers series, the Weekly Compilation of Presidential Documents, was begun in 1965 to provide a broader range of Presidential materials on a more timely basis to meet the needs of the contemporary reader. Beginning with the administration of Jimmy Carter, the Public Papers series expanded its coverage to include additional material as printed in the Weekly Compilation. That coverage provides a listing of the President's daily schedule and meetings, when announced, and other items of general interest issued by the Office of the Press Secretary. Also included are lists of the President's nominations submitted to the Senate, materials released by the Office of the Press Secretary that are not printed full-text in the book, and proclamations, Executive orders, and other Presidential documents released by the Office of the Press Secretary and published in the *Federal Register*. This information appears in the appendixes at the end of the book.

Volumes covering the administrations of Presidents Hoover, Truman, Eisenhower, Kennedy, Johnson, Nixon, Ford, Carter, Reagan, and Bush are also available.

The Public Papers of the Presidents publication program is under the direction of Frances D. McDonald, Director of the Presidential Documents and Legislative Division. The series is produced by the Presidential Documents Unit, Gwen H. Estep, Chief. The Chief Editor of this book was Karen Howard Ashlin, assisted by Margaret A. Hastings, Carolyn W. Hill, Susannah C. Hurley, Rachel Rondell, Cheryl E. Sirofchuck, Michael J. Sullivan, and Elizabeth N. Thomas.

The frontispiece and photographs used in the portfolio were supplied by the White House Photo Office. The typography and design of the book were developed by the Government Printing Office under the direction of Michael F. DiMario, Public Printer.

Martha L. Girard
Director of the Federal Register

Trudy Huskamp Peterson
Acting Archivist of the United States

Contents

Cabinet

Secretary of State .... Warren M. Christopher

Secretary of the Treasury .... Lloyd Bentsen

Secretary of Defense .... Les Aspin

Attorney General .... Janet Reno

Secretary of the Interior .... Bruce Babbitt

Secretary of Agriculture .... Mike Espy

Secretary of Commerce .... Ronald H. Brown

Secretary of Labor .... Robert B. Reich

Secretary of Health and Human Services .... Donna E. Shalala

Secretary of Housing and Urban
Development .... Henry G. Cisneros

Secretary of Transportation .... Federico Peña

Secretary of Energy .... Hazel Rollins O'Leary

Secretary of Education .... Richard W. Riley

Secretary of Veterans Affairs .... Jesse Brown

United States Representative to the
United Nations .... Madeleine Korbel Albright

Administrator of the Environmental
Protection Agency .... Carol M. Browner

United States Trade Representative .... Michael Kantor

Director of the Office of Management
and Budget .... Leon E. Panetta

Assistant to the President and
Chief of Staff .... Thomas F. McLarty III

Chair of the Council of Economic
Advisers .... Laura D'Andrea Tyson

Director of National Drug
Control Policy .... Lee Patrick Brown

Administration of William J. Clinton

1993

Inaugural Address
January 20, 1993

My fellow citizens, today we celebrate the mystery of American renewal. This ceremony is held in the depth of winter, but by the words we speak and the faces we show the world, we force the spring, a spring reborn in the world's oldest democracy that brings forth the vision and courage to reinvent America. When our Founders boldly declared America's independence to the world and our purposes to the Almighty, they knew that America, to endure, would have to change; not change for change's sake but change to preserve America's ideals: life, liberty, the pursuit of happiness. Though we marched to the music of our time, our mission is timeless. Each generation of Americans must define what it means to be an American.

On behalf of our Nation, I salute my predecessor, President Bush, for his half-century of service to America. And I thank the millions of men and women whose steadfastness and sacrifice triumphed over depression, fascism, and communism.

Today, a generation raised in the shadows of the cold war assumes new responsibilities in a world warmed by the sunshine of freedom but threatened still by ancient hatreds and new plagues. Raised in unrivaled prosperity, we inherit an economy that is still the world's strongest but is weakened by business failures, stagnant wages, increasing inequality, and deep divisions among our own people.

When George Washington first took the oath I have just sworn to uphold, news traveled slowly across the land by horseback and across the ocean by boat. Now, the sights and sounds of this ceremony are broadcast instantaneously to billions around the world. Communications and commerce are global. Investment is mobile. Technology is almost magical. And ambition for a better life is now universal.

We earn our livelihood in America today in peaceful competition with people all across the Earth. Profound and powerful forces are shaking and remaking our world. And the urgent question of our time is whether we can make change our friend and not our enemy. This new world has already enriched the lives of millions of Americans who are able to compete and win in it. But when most people are working harder for less; when others cannot work at all; when the cost of health care devastates families and threatens to bankrupt our enterprises, great and small; when the fear of crime robs law-abiding citizens of their freedom; and when millions of poor children cannot even imagine the lives we are calling them to lead, we have not made change our friend.

We know we have to face hard truths and take strong steps, but we have not done so; instead, we have drifted. And that drifting has eroded our resources, fractured our economy, and shaken our confidence. Though our challenges are fearsome, so are our strengths. Americans have ever been a restless, questing, hopeful people. And we must bring to our task today the vision and will of those who came before us. From our Revolution to the Civil War, to the Great Depression, to the civil rights movement, our people have always mustered the determination to construct from these crises the pillars of our history. Thomas Jefferson believed that to preserve the very foundations of our Nation, we would need dramatic change from time to time. Well, my fellow Americans, this is our time. Let us embrace it.

Our democracy must be not only the envy of the world but the engine of our own renewal. There is nothing wrong with America that cannot be cured by what is right with America. And so today we pledge an end to the era of deadlock and drift, and a new season of American renewal has begun.

To renew America, we must be bold. We must do what no generation has had to do before. We must invest more in our own people, in their jobs, and in their future, and at the same time cut our massive debt. And we must do so in a world in which we must compete for every opportunity. It will not be easy. It will require sacrifice, but it can be done and done fairly, not choosing sacrifice for its own sake but for our own sake. We must provide for our Nation the way a family provides for its children.

Our Founders saw themselves in the light of posterity. We can do no less. Anyone who has ever watched a child's eyes wander into sleep knows what posterity is. Posterity is the world to come: the world for whom we hold our ideals, from whom we have borrowed our planet, and to whom we bear sacred responsibility. We must do what America does best: offer more opportunity to all and demand more responsibility from all. It is time to break the bad habit of expecting something for nothing from our Government or from each other. Let us all take more responsibility not only for ourselves and our families but for our communities and our country.

To renew America, we must revitalize our democracy. This beautiful Capital, like every capital since the dawn of civilization, is often a place of intrigue and calculation. Powerful people maneuver for position and worry endlessly about who is in and who is out, who is up and who is down, forgetting those people whose toil and sweat sends us here and pays our way. Americans deserve better. And in this city today there are people who want to do better. And so I say to all of you here: Let us resolve to reform our politics so that power and privilege no longer shout down the voice of the people. Let us put aside personal advantage so that we can feel the pain and see the promise of America. Let us resolve to make our Government a place for what Franklin Roosevelt called bold, persistent experimentation, a Government for our tomorrows, not our yesterdays. Let us give this Capital back to the people to whom it belongs.

To renew America, we must meet challenges abroad as well as at home. There is no longer a clear division between what is foreign and what is domestic. The world economy, the world environment, the world AIDS crisis, the world arms race: they affect us all. Today, as an older order passes, the new world is more free but less stable. Communism's collapse has called forth old animosities and new dangers. Clearly, America must continue to lead the world we did so much to make.

While America rebuilds at home, we will not shrink from the challenges nor fail to seize the opportunities of this new world. Together with our friends and allies, we will work to shape change, lest it engulf us. When our vital interests are challenged or the will and conscience of the international community is defied, we will act, with peaceful diplomacy whenever possible, with force when necessary. The brave Americans serving our Nation today in the Persian Gulf, in Somalia, and wherever else they stand are testament to our resolve. But our greatest strength is the power of our ideas, which are still new in many lands. Across the world we see them embraced, and we rejoice. Our hopes, our hearts, our hands are with those on every continent who are building democracy and freedom. Their cause is America's cause.

The American people have summoned the change we celebrate today. You have raised your voices in an unmistakable chorus. You have cast your votes in historic numbers. And you have changed the face of Congress, the Presidency, and the political process itself. Yes, you, my fellow Americans, have forced the spring. Now we must do the work the season demands. To that work I now turn with all the authority of my office. I ask the Congress to join with me. But no President, no Congress, no Government can undertake this mission alone.

My fellow Americans, you, too, must play your part in our renewal. I challenge a new generation of young Americans to a season of service: to act on your idealism by helping troubled children, keeping company with those in need, reconnecting our torn communities. There is so much to be done; enough, indeed, for millions of others who are still young in spirit to give of themselves in service, too. In serving, we recognize a simple but powerful truth: We need each other, and we must care for one another.

Today we do more than celebrate America. We rededicate ourselves to the very idea of America, an idea born in revolution and renewed through two centuries of challenge; an idea tempered by the knowledge that, but for fate, we, the fortunate, and the unfortunate might have been each other; an idea ennobled by the faith that our Nation can summon from its myriad diversity the deepest measure of unity; an idea infused with the conviction that America's long, heroic journey must go forever upward.

And so, my fellow Americans, as we stand at the edge of the 21st century, let us begin anew with energy and hope, with faith and discipline. And let us work until our work is done.

The Scripture says, "And let us not be weary in well doing: for in due season we shall reap, if we faint not." From this joyful mountaintop of celebration we hear a call to service in the valley. We have heard the trumpets. We have changed the guard. And now, each in our own way and with God's help, we must answer the call.

Thank you, and God bless you all.

NOTE: The President spoke at 12:01 p.m. at the West Front of the Capitol. Prior to the address, Chief Justice William H. Rehnquist administered the oath of office.

Remarks at the Inaugural Luncheon
January 20, 1993

Thank you very much, Senator Ford, Mr. Speaker, Majority Leader Gephardt, Senator Mitchell, Senator Dole, Representative Michel. I'd like to begin by saying I didn't get much sleep last night, and if I get through this it will be tour de force. Al Gore and I stayed up a long time talking last night about this day and this country and what we hoped that we could do.

I want to say first how very grateful I am to the Congress for the exertions here to make this Inaugural Day such a meaningful and wonderful one. I would like to especially thank Senator Ford who worked so hard to make sure everything went off without a hitch. And he did.

I also thank you for the wonderful gift of crystal, the letter opener, which I will treasure always, that proved that we did get enough electoral votes to be here today.

And Mr. Speaker, I'm delighted to have that key. However, with all respect, I can't believe you were fully briefed about my proclivities in lobbying legislators to let me come up here without an invitation. I may be here all the time. [*Laughter*] Why, just when you said you wished me well in untangling my relationships with Congress, my head, almost as if by magic, tilted in Senator Dole's direction. [*Laughter*]

I make two serious points. Once in a generation we really are called upon to redefine the public interests and the common ground. I honestly do believe much of what we have to do today is work that knows no necessary partisan label and does not fall easily within the conventional divisions of liberal and conservative or Republican and Democrat.

The second point I wish to make is that I cannot succeed as President unless Congress itself succeeds and the American people like the Congress again, too. For I seek to do, and to do we have to work together and move forward together.

So I would like, in gratitude and respect, to propose a toast to a new partnership in America's Government.

NOTE: The President spoke at 2:20 p.m. in Statuary Hall at the Capitol. Prior to his remarks, Thomas S. Foley, Speaker of the House of Representatives, presented the President with a key to the Capitol.

Message to the Congress on Adjustment of the National Deficit
January 21, 1993

To the Congress of the United States:

Pursuant to section 254(c) of the Balanced Budget and Emergency Deficit Control Act of 1985, as amended ("Act") (2 U.S.C. 904(c)), notification is hereby provided of my decision that the adjustment of the maximum deficit amount, as allowed under section 253(g)(1)(B) of the Act (2 U.S.C. 903(g)(1)(B)), shall be made.

WILLIAM J. CLINTON

The White House,
January 21, 1993.

NOTE: The White House released the following statement by the Director of Communications George Stephanopoulos on adjustment of the national deficit:

As provided by the law, the President has today notified the congressional leadership of technical adjustments to be made in calculating the national deficit. This procedure, which occurred automatically under the previous administration for 3 fiscal years, prevents across-the-board budget reductions in accounts such as national defense that could equal 11 percent in the beginning of the next fiscal year. A failure to make this adjustment would also undermine the credibility of economic and budget estimates.

President Clinton will soon put before the Congress a real economic program aimed at reducing the deficit and providing long-term economic growth.

Remarks to Inaugural Parade Groups
January 21, 1993

The President. Thank you. One of the first lessons that I was told to learn about becoming President is that the President could not fix all the problems in America. [*Laughter*] But this is pretty close to fixing the float breaking down, don't you think?

I want to make sure that I have properly acknowledged all the groups that are here, so I want to call your names, and you raise your hand if you're in one of these groups. Who's here from the Sounds of Silence in Canton, Ohio? [*Applause*] Thank you. I'd also like to say I'm glad to see Senators Glenn and Metzenbaum here. Give them a hand. [*Applause*] Who's here from the Boy Singers of Maine? [*Applause*] From my alma mater, the Georgetown Chimes? [*Applause*] And the Georgetown Grace Notes?

[*Applause*] And from Hillary's alma mater, the Wellesley Widows? [*Applause*]

Hillary Clinton. Just two left. They all had to go back to school.

The President. Two hung in there to be represented tonight. [*Laughter*] I'm very sorry about what happened yesterday, but I'm glad you're all here today.

Anybody want to sing me a quick song?

Hillary Clinton. Let's start in order.

The President. All right, we'll start in order. The Sounds of Silence go first.

NOTE: The President spoke at 6:45 p.m. on the State Floor at the White House. A tape was not available for verification of the content of these remarks.

Memorandum on Review of Regulations
January 21, 1993

Memorandum for the Acting Director
Office of Management and Budget

The Council on Competitiveness, established March 31, 1989, terminated on January 20, 1993.

Pending completion of a review, existing Executive orders on regulatory management will continue to apply. You are directed to request the agencies described in section 1(d) of Executive Order 12291 to assure that in publishing regulations, and subject to such exceptions as the Director or the Acting Director of the Office of Management and Budget determines to be appropriate, all regulations must first be approved by an agency head or the designee of an agency head who, in either case, is a person appointed by me and confirmed by the Senate.

WILLIAM J. CLINTON

NOTE: This memorandum was released by the Office of the Press Secretary on January 22.

Statement on Withdrawal of the Nomination of Zoe Baird To Be Attorney General
January 22, 1993

Tonight I received a letter from my Attorney-General-designate, Ms. Zoe Baird, asking that I withdraw her nomination to lead the United States Department of Justice from further consideration by the Senate.

Ms. Baird is a gifted attorney and a woman of decency and integrity. She responded to the call to public service with energy and a firm dedication to the mission of the Justice Department. Her candid disclosure of the child care matter to officials of my transition and to the Senate Judiciary Committee led to the circumstances we face today.

Clearly, our review process prior to her selection failed to evaluate this issue completely. For that, I take full responsibility. I hold Zoe Baird in the highest regard, and I believe she has much to give to her profession and to our country. I hope to continue to seek her advice and counsel. With sadness, I have accepted her request that the nomination be withdrawn and have so informed the Senate majority leader, George Mitchell.

Letter on Withdrawal of the Nomination of Zoe Baird To Be Attorney General
January 22, 1993

Dear Zoe:

I have received your letter asking that I withdraw your nomination as Attorney General of the United States from further consideration by the Senate. With sadness, I accept your request that the nomination be withdrawn.

You are an exceptionally gifted attorney, and a person of great decency and integrity. You have responded to the call of public service with energy and a firm dedication to the mission of the Justice Department. I realize that it was your candid disclosure of the child care matter that led to the circumstances we face today. I believe that the concerns raised about your child care situation were unique to the position of Attorney General.

You are highly qualified to be Attorney General. Your stated goals for a nonpartisan, independent and strongly managed Department of Justice were fully in accord with my own. I believe you would have been a fine Attorney General.

Hillary and I value your and Paul's friendship. We look forward to seeing you often. I hope that you will be available for other assignments for your country in my Administration.

Sincerely,

BILL CLINTON

NOTE: The White House also made available Ms. Baird's letter requesting that her nomination to be Attorney General be withdrawn.

Remarks on the Swearing-In of Cabinet Members
January 22, 1993

The President. Good morning, ladies and gentlemen. Today I am proud to present to you and to the American people a Cabinet of talented, diverse, and seasoned leaders.

I'm deeply gratified to the United States Senate for their quick confirmation of 18 nominees only 2 days after the Inauguration. The Senate acted with historic dispatch because it recognizes that our Nation needs action now on our problems. I very much appreciate that, and like them I am ready to get to work.

Ladies and gentlemen, I would like to now present the Chief Justice to administer the oath of office. Mr. Chief Justice.

Chief Justice Rehnquist. Would you each raise your right hands and repeat after me. And the first phrase is "I, blank," and obviously there you insert your name—[*laughter*]—"do solemnly swear."

[*At this point, the Chief Justice administered the oath of office.*]

The President. Let me, first of all, say I'm glad no one said "I, blank." [*Laughter*] There will be time enough for those blanks in the days ahead. [*Laughter*]

I think now we're supposed to adjourn to the State Dining Room, is that correct? Is that right?

I also want to recognize my Ambassador to the United Nations-designate, Madeleine Albright, who has not quite been confirmed by the Senate, but I think she will be soon. Because she teaches at my alma mater, I thought she ought to have a separate swearing-in ceremony. [*Laughter*]

So I think that's it. Let's adjourn, please, to the reception in the State Dining Room. Thank you.

NOTE: The President spoke at 10:22 a.m. in the East Room at the White House.

Remarks at a Cabinet Meeting
January 22, 1993

I'd like to open our first meeting with a brief prayer.

Our Heavenly Father, we thank you for the unique opportunity which has been given to us to serve our country to thy ends. Please be with us and guide us. Keep us humble and eager. And help us to proceed with wisdom. Amen.

Well, good morning. I want to say again how very proud I am of all of you and how pleased I am to be off to what I think is quite a good start. And I think we have an enormous reservoir of good will out in the country and a fair amount of elbow room to face the issues that are before us. In the next several days we will have to make a lot of tough economic decisions that some of you have been more involved in than others—that everybody will be involved in.

This should be a fairly good meeting today. I just wanted to make a few remarks and then introduce Mack McLarty and let him talk a little bit. First of all, we're going to have this Cabinet retreat, as you know, in a few days. And some of the issues that we might ordinarily hash out here over an hour or two I think would be better put off until that retreat. If I might begin with sort of a major substantive decision. I basically very much believe in teamwork. And I think that over time you make better decisions if you get good input from a reasonable number of people who have different perspectives. Therefore, for example, when I was Governor, I didn't have a lot of Cabinet meetings, but I had a fair number in which people had the opportunity to comment on matters of public interest that were sometimes outside the narrow confines of what they were doing.

NOTE: The President spoke at 11:08 a.m. in the Cabinet Room at the White House. A tape was not available for verification of the content of these remarks.

Exchange With Reporters Following a Cabinet Meeting
January 22, 1993

Withdrawal of Nomination for Attorney General

Q. Mr. President, how difficult was the Zoe Baird decision? How agonizing was it for you?

The President. I'm sad about it. But it wasn't agonizing. I'm sad about it, and I take full responsibility, as I said in my statement, for the way the evaluation was done. I still have a very high regard for her. She is an extraordinary person. And I feel very badly about it, but I'm responsible for it, and I'm going to start this afternoon looking for an Attorney General. And

I have the process set up, and we're going to begin as soon as the lunch hour is over, working on the future. And that's what I intend to focus on.

Q. Will it be a woman?

The President. I have nothing else to say. I'm going to start this afternoon. Thanks.

NOTE: The exchange began at 11:15 a.m. in the Cabinet Room at the White House. A tape was not available for verification of the content of this exchange.

Remarks on Signing Memorandums on Medical Research and Reproductive Health and an Exchange With Reporters
January 22, 1993

The President. Please sit down, ladies and gentlemen. Today I am acting to separate our national health and medical policy from the divisive conflict over abortion. This conflict, which stems from the *Roe* v. *Wade* decision of 20 years ago, has brought to a halt promising research on treatment for serious conditions and diseases that affect millions of Americans, millions of American men, women, and children who include the members of my family and friends of mine and I'm sure virtually every other set of family and friends in the United States. We must free science and medicine from the grasp of politics and give all Americans access to the very latest and best medical treatments.

Today I am directing Secretary of Health and Human Services Shalala immediately to lift the moratorium on Federal funding for research involving transplantation of fetal tissue. This moratorium, which was first imposed in 1988, was extended indefinitely in 1989 despite the recommendation of a blue ribbon National Institutes of Health advisory panel that it be ended. Five years later, the evidence is overwhelming. The moratorium has dramatically limited the development of possible treatment for millions of individuals who suffer from serious disorders, including Parkinson's disease, Alzheimer's dis-

ease, diabetes, and leukemia. We must let medicine and science proceed unencumbered by anti-abortion politics.

Today also marks the beginning of a new national reproductive health policy that aims to prevent unintended pregnancies. Our administration is committed to providing the kind of prenatal care, child care, and family and medical leave that will lead to healthy childbearing and support America's families. As a nation, our goal should be to protect individual freedom while fostering responsible decisionmaking, an approach that seeks to protect the right to choose while reducing the number of abortions. Our vision should be of an America where abortion is safe and legal, but rare.

Let me also say that our administration is particularly concerned with the epidemic of teenage pregnancy. The greatest human cost of our continuing national debate over reproductive policy is borne by our children and by their children. A few teenagers choose to have and raise children, and we must help them to succeed. But for millions a teen pregnancy is unintended, leaving the young woman and her partner totally unprepared for the responsibilities of parenthood. The social and economic price paid today and for the last several years by our Nation is enormous.

So today I am also directing Secretary Shalala to act immediately to implement her intended suspension of the Title X family planning regulations that are also known as the "gag rule." For almost 5 years, HHS has prohibited Title X recipients from providing their patients with full information and counseling concerning pregnancy. This dangerous restriction censors the medical information and advice that health care professionals can give their patients. As a result of today's action, every woman will be able to receive medical advice and referrals that will not be censored or distorted by ideological arguments that should not be a part of medicine.

I'm also ordering today the Director of the Agency for International Development to repeal immediately what has become known as the Mexico City policy, that has effectively applied the "gag rule" to organizations that receive United States funding, even when those organizations use non-AID funds for those activities. Today's actions will allow organizations that received AID funds to provide information regarding all family planning options to individuals in foreign nations. It will reverse a policy that has seriously undermined much-needed efforts to promote safe and effective family planning programs abroad and will allow us to once again provide leadership in helping to stabilize world population. Many believe that this is one of the most important environmental steps we can take.

Today I am also directing Secretary of Defense Aspin to lift immediately the near-total ban on abortions at United States military facilities and to permit them to be performed at those facilities provided that the procedure is paid for entirely with private funds. This action will allow military hospitals to perform abortions and reverse a ban that has adversely affected the lives of scores of men and women who serve our Nation around the world, or members of their families.

Finally, I am directing Secretary Shalala to instruct the Food and Drug Administration to determine whether the current import ban on the drug Mifepristine, commonly known as RU–486, is justified and to rescind the ban if there is no basis for it. Here in the United States, RU–486 has been held hostage to politics. It is time to learn the truth about what the health and safety risks of the drug really are. If the FDA removes the ban, Americans will be able to bring the drug into the country for their personal use consistent with existing FDA policies that govern drugs not approved for distribution.

I've also ordered HHS to immediately explore the propriety of promoting testing in the United States as well as the possibility of licensing and manufacturing according to the standards which govern all other drugs so reviewed by our Government.

Taken as a group, today's actions will go a long way toward protecting vital medical and health decisions from ideological and political debate. The American people deserve the best medical treatment in the world. We're committed to providing them with nothing less.

I'd like to say in closing a special word of personal thanks to the unbelievable number of Americans from all walks of life and all different political perspectives who have children with diabetes or who, like me, have lost relatives to Alzheimer's or have friends suffering with Parkinson's and other diseases who came up to me over the last year and made a personal plea on the fetal tissue issue. Their statements to me and their life stories had a far greater impact on me even than the actions of the United States Congress, which included, as you know, a very broad spectrum of Republicans and Democrats on this issue.

I'd like now to sign these directives.

[*At this point, the President signed the five memorandums.*]

Thank you very much.

President's Signature

Q. Mr. President, was it "William J." or "Bill"?

The President. After a considered policy debate—[*laughter*]—we decided that I should sign my full name to all official documents of the Government, and I'll continue to sign all my non—my letters "Bill Clinton."

Withdrawal of Nomination for Attorney General

Q. Let me ask you: George was having a really hard time explaining to us what you knew about Zoe Baird's problem, when you knew it.

Press aide. Thank you.

Q. Can you please explain——

The President. No, I want to answer this.

Q. ——that to us, so that the American public would really know?

The President. I think the American people

are entitled to know that. If you go back to my statement, I acknowledged that there were errors in the evaluation process, for which I take full responsibility. What happened was this. She voluntarily disclosed that; it was not in any way picked up in the vetting. It was, as you know, we were trying to make a Christmas deadline, which was probably my error again, on this.

So just before she was announced, but after I had discussed the appointment with her, I was told that this matter had come up. Nobody said anything to me about the taxes. And what I was told was what you heard, in a very cursory way, was that an error had been made in the hiring of an illegal alien; that it had been made after consulting a lawyer who was an expert in this area, so basically they had acted on counsel's advice, but they were wrong; that they moved immediately to try to correct it, and the status had been corrected in terms of the legality of the person; and that the vettor's conclu-

sion was there would be no problem.

I have to tell you that during the course of these inquiries, I received other weightier warnings, if you will, of things which had to be worked through with other potential nominees. In retrospect, what I should have done is to basically delay the whole thing for a couple of days and look into it in greater depth.

But I take full responsibility for that. This process is in no way a reflection on her. We would not have known any of this had she not disclosed it to us and to the United States Senate subsequently. So I will say again what I said this morning: I'm sorry about this. I still think she is an extraordinary person and a very able person who will have a rich and successful career, and I take full responsibility for what happened in the review process.

Thank you.

NOTE: The President spoke at 3:22 p.m. in the Roosevelt Room at the White House.

Memorandum on Fetal Tissue Transplantation Research
January 22, 1993

Memorandum for the Secretary of Health and Human Services

Subject: Federal Funding of Fetal Tissue Transplantation Research

On March 22, 1988, the Assistant Secretary for Health of Health and Human Services ("HHS") imposed a temporary moratorium on Federal funding of research involving transplantation of fetal tissue from induced abortions. Contrary to the recommendations of a National Institutes of Health advisory panel, on November 2, 1989, the Secretary of Health and Human Services extended the moratorium indefinitely.

This moratorium has significantly hampered the development of possible treatments for individuals afflicted with serious diseases and disorders, such as Parkinson's disease, Alzheimer's disease, diabetes, and leukemia. Accordingly, I hereby direct that you immediately lift the moratorium.

You are hereby authorized and directed to publish this memorandum in the *Federal Register.*

WILLIAM J. CLINTON

[Filed with the Office of the Federal Register, 1:17 p.m., February 3, 1993]

Memorandum on the Title X "Gag Rule"
January 22, 1993

*Memorandum for the Secretary of Health and
Human Services*

Subject: The Title X "Gag Rule"

Title X of the Public Health Services Act provides Federal funding for family planning clinics to provide services for low-income patients. The Act specifies that Title X funds may not be used for the performance of abortions, but places no restrictions on the ability of clinics that receive Title X funds to provide abortion counseling and referrals or to perform abortions using non-Title X funds. During the first 18 years of the program, medical professionals at Title X clinics provided complete, uncensored information, including nondirective abortion counseling. In February 1988, the Department of Health and Human Services adopted regulations, which have become known as the "Gag Rule," prohibiting Title X recipients from providing their patients with information, counseling, or referrals concerning abortion. Subsequent attempts by the Bush Administration to modify the Gag Rule and ensuing litigation have created confusion and uncertainty about the current legal status of the regulations.

The Gag Rule endangers women's lives and health by preventing them from receiving complete and accurate medical information and interferes with the doctor-patient relationship by prohibiting information that medical professionals are otherwise ethically and legally required to provide to their patients. Furthermore, the Gag Rule contravenes the clear intent of a majority of the members of both the United States Senate and House of Representatives, which twice passed legislation to block the Gag Rule's enforcement but failed to override Presidential vetoes.

For these reasons, you have informed me that you will suspend the Gag Rule pending the promulgation of new regulations in accordance with the "notice and comment" procedures of the Administrative Procedure Act. I hereby direct you to take that action as soon as possible. I further direct that, within 30 days, you publish in the *Federal Register* new proposed regulations for public comment.

You are hereby authorized and directed to publish this memorandum in the *Federal Register.*

WILLIAM J. CLINTON

[Filed with the Office of the Federal Register, 1:16 p.m., February 3, 1993]

Memorandum on the Mexico City Policy
January 22, 1993

*Memorandum for the Acting Administrator of
the Agency for International Development*

Subject: AID Family Planning Grants/Mexico City Policy

The Foreign Assistance Act of 1961 prohibits nongovernmental organizations ("NGO's") that receive Federal funds from using those funds "to pay for the performance of abortions as a method of family planning, or to motivate or coerce any person to practice abortions." (22 U.S.C. 2151b(f)(1)). The August 1984 announcement by President Reagan of what has become know as the "Mexico City Policy" directed the Agency for International Development ("AID")

to expand this limitation and withhold AID funds from NGO's that engage in a wide range of activities, including providing advice, counseling, or information regarding abortion, or lobbying a foreign government to legalize or make abortion available. These conditions have been imposed even where an NGO uses non-AID funds for abortion-related activities.

These excessively broad anti-abortion conditions are unwarranted. I am informed that the conditions are not mandated by the Foreign Assistance Act or any other law. Moreover, they have undermined efforts to promote safe and efficacious family planning programs in foreign nations. Accordingly, I hereby direct that AID remove the conditions not explicitly mandated by the Foreign Assistance Act or any other law from all current AID grants to NGO's and exclude them from future grants.

WILLIAM J. CLINTON

Memorandum on Abortions in Military Hospitals
January 22, 1993

Memorandum for the Secretary of Defense

Subject: Privately Funded Abortions at Military Hospitals

Section 1093 of title 10 of the United States Code prohibits the use of Department of Defense ("DOD") funds to perform abortions except where the life of a woman would be endangered if the fetus were carried to term. By memoranda of December 21, 1987, and June 21, 1988, DOD has gone beyond what I am informed are the requirements of the statute and has banned all abortions at U.S. military facilities, even where the procedure is privately funded. This ban is unwarranted. Accordingly, I hereby direct that you reverse the ban immediately and permit abortion services to be provided, if paid for entirely with non-DOD funds and in accordance with other relevant DOD policies and procedures.

You are hereby authorized and directed to publish this memorandum in the *Federal Register*.

WILLIAM J. CLINTON

[Filed with the Office of the Federal Register, 11:50 a.m., January 27, 1993]

Memorandum on Importation of RU–486
January 22, 1993

Memorandum for the Secretary of Health and Human Services

Subject: Importation of RU–486

In Import Alert 66–47, the Food and Drug Administration ("FDA") excluded the drug Mifepristine—commonly known as RU–486—from the list of drugs that individuals can import into the United States for their "personal use," although the drugs have not yet been approved for distribution by the FDA. (*See* FDA Regulatory Procedures Manual, Chapter 9–71.) Import Alert 66–47 effectively bans the importation into this Nation of a drug that is used in other nations as a nonsurgical means of abortion.

I am informed that in excluding RU–486 from the personal use importation exemption, the FDA appears to have based its decision on factors other than an assessment of the possible health and safety risks of the drug. Accordingly, I hereby direct that you promptly instruct the FDA to determine whether there is sufficient evidence to warrant exclusion of RU–486 from the list of drugs that qualify for the personal use importation exemption. Furthermore, if the FDA concludes that RU–486 meets the criteria for the personal use importation exemption, I direct that you immediately take steps to rescind Import Alert 66–47.

In addition, I direct that you promptly assess initiatives by which the Department of Health and Human Services can promote the testing, licensing, and manufacturing in the United States of RU–486 or other antiprogestins.

You are hereby authorized and directed to publish this memorandum in the *Federal Register*.

WILLIAM J. CLINTON

[Filed with the Office of the Federal Register, 1:20 p.m., February 3, 1993]

Exchange With Reporters
January 23, 1993

Oval Office

Q. How do you like your new office, Mr. President?

The President. I like it a lot. It's a wonderful office.

Q. Did you read the note that President Bush left for you?

The President. I did.

Q. What did that say?

The President. I think we should leave it between the two of us, but it was a very generous note and a very encouraging one.

Attorney General Nomination

Q. Mr. President, what are you doing in pursuit of a new nominee for the attorney generalship? How are you going about this?

The President. I did some work on it yesterday afternoon and had several extended conversations with people about potential nominees and gave my staff some instructions to go do some work on three or four folks.

Q. Three or four—men?

The President. Three or four people. [*Laughter*] I'm not going to say who——

Q. Have you talked to any prospective nominees directly?

Q. How's it gone so far?

The President. So far I've liked it very much.

Q. ——surprises so far?

The President. We just got started, you know. I've got a lot——

Q. Will you be keeping Mr. Sessions on?

The President. I don't want to talk about——

President's Schedule

Q. What are you going to do for the rest of the day, Mr. President?

The President. Work.

Q. Not jogging?

The President. No, I'm going to go out for a jog later. And I'm going to do a little work, and I'm trying to get the house acclimated, get organized.

NOTE: The exchange began at 12:08 p.m. in the Oval Office at the White House. A tape was not available for verification of the content of this exchange.

Statement on the Death of Justice Thurgood Marshall
January 24, 1993

I am deeply saddened by the passing of Justice Thurgood Marshall. He was a giant in the quest for human rights and equal opportunity in this century. Every American should be grateful for the contributions he made as an advocate and Justice of the United States Supreme Court.

NOTE: The related proclamation is listed in Appendix D at the end of this volume.

Remarks on the Establishment of the National Economic Council and an Exchange With Reporters
January 25, 1993

The President. This is the Executive order which establishes the National Economic Council and which brings into the economic policymaking of the Federal Government not just the traditional Secretaries of Treasury, the OMB, the Council of Economic Advisers but also the Departments of Commerce, Labor, Agriculture, HUD, Transportation, Energy, EPA, as well as the Trade Office, State, so that we can all work together. I want to thank all of the people around this table for all the work they've done on this and especially Mr. Rubin for the work that he's done to try to reconcile all these things. I believe that this will enable us to make economic policy in a much more specific, clear, and effective way than the Federal Government has in quite a long while.

[*At this point, the President signed the Executive order.*]

Homosexuals in the Military

Q. If the Joint Chiefs oppose this lifting of the ban on gays in the military, are you still going to go ahead with that?

The President. I'm going to meet with them and discuss it this afternoon. But I intend to keep my commitment. I want their input on how we should do it, however. I think they're entitled to really be listened to on a lot of the practical issues.

Q. Is this part of what you said in your Inaugural Address, that it will require sacrifice?

The President. I think everybody wants to make a contribution to solving these problems, and we're going to give everyone the opportunity to do that.

Q. How quickly will you lift this ban, Mr.

President?

The President. I don't have anything else to say about it right now. We're going to have a meeting——

Q. Are you going to have a meeting on it?

The President. I want to talk to the Joint Chiefs about that, and then I'll have a statement to make later.

Q. Today?

The President. I don't know. We've got a lot of other things to do today. Maybe; I don't know.

Taxes

Q. Mr. President, can you say anything about the consumption tax that Senator Bentsen addressed yesterday?

The President. No. I thought he did a very good job on television. I wasn't sure that I was reading about the same interview in the press this morning. He said that no decision had been made, and no decision has been made. We have a lot of options under consideration, but no decision has been made.

NOTE: The President spoke at 11:30 a.m. in the Roosevelt Room at the White House. The Executive order is listed in Appendix D at the end of this volume.

Remarks and an Exchange With Reporters on Health Care Reform
January 25, 1993

I want to say good afternoon to members of the press. We have just finished a very lively discussion about the massive task before us in health care. Vice President Gore and I made a strong commitment to the American people during the last election that we would present to the United States Congress, within 100 days, a plan that would take strong action to control health care costs in America and to begin to provide for the health care needs of all Americans.

As I traveled across the country last year, no stories moved me more than the health care stories. As I think all of you know, many of the people in our Faces of Hope luncheon last week during the Inaugural were people who were struggling to overcome incredible adversity occasioned by their health care problems. We've met elderly people choosing every week between medicine and food; we've met people forced to leave their jobs to get on public assistance to deal with children with terrific problems; we've met countless people who can't change their jobs because they or someone in their family have had health care problems.

You will all remember, at the economic conference that we sponsored in Little Rock, perhaps the overwhelming concern of the business people there, of all sizes, was doing something about the cost and the availability of health care. When the Vice President and I met with the big three auto makers and the president of the United Auto Workers, once again they said, if you want to do something to help rebuild the auto industry, do something to control health care costs. And as Mr. Panetta just said again in a rather plaintive way before you came in, there is no way we will ever get control of the Federal budget deficit unless we do something about health care.

The message is pretty simple. It's time to make sense of America's health care system. It's time to bring costs under control and to make our families and businesses secure. It's time to make good on the American promise that too many people have talked about for too long, while we have continued to spend more than 30 percent more of our income on health care than any other nation in the world, get less for it, and see 100,000 Americans a month losing their health insurance.

As a first step in responding to the demands of literally millions of Americans, today I am announcing the formation of the President's Task Force on National Health Reform. Although the issue is complex, the task force's mission is simple: Build on the work of the campaign and the transition, listen to all parties, and prepare health care reform legislation to be submitted to Congress within 100 days of our taking office.

This task force will be chaired by the First Lady, Hillary Rodham Clinton, and will include the Secretaries of Health and Human Services, Treasury, Defense, Veterans Affairs, Commerce, Labor, as well as the Director of the Office of Management and Budget and senior White House staff members.

I am grateful that Hillary has agreed to chair this task force and not only because it means she'll be sharing some of the heat I expect to generate. As many of you know, while I was Governor of my State, Hillary chaired the Arkansas Education Standards Committee, which created public school accreditation standards that have since become a model for national reform. She served as my designee on the Southern Regional Task Force on Infant Mortality, was also chair of our State's rural health committee in 1979 and 1980, a time in which we initiated a number of health care reforms that benefit the people of my State to the present day. And on the board of the Arkansas Children's Hospital, she helped to establish our State's first neonatal unit.

I think that in the coming months the American people will learn, as the people of our State did, that we have a First Lady of many talents, who most of all can bring people together around complex and difficult issues to hammer out consensus and get things done.

Here in the White House, Hillary will work with my Domestic Policy Adviser, Carol Rasco; my Senior Policy Adviser, Ira Magaziner; and the head of our health care transition team, Judy Feder. I've asked all of them to be as inclusive as possible. And as a part of that, we are inviting the American public to write us here at the White House with their suggestions. All of them should be sent to the Task Force on National Health Care Reform at the White House in Washington, DC 20500.

We will no doubt be criticized by some for undertaking something very, very ambitious. But as I said in my Inaugural Address, we're going to have to make some tough choices in order to control health care costs, to bring them down within inflation, and to provide health care for all. In order to preserve the vitality of the American private sector, in order to keep the American people's budget here at this national level from going totally bankrupt, we are going to have to make some tough choices. Powerful lobbies and special interests may seek to derail our efforts, and we may make some people angry. But we are determined to come up with the best possible solution.

And in my lifetime, at least, there has never been so much consensus that something has to be done. We have a plan from the American Nurses Association, from the American Academy of Physicians, from the American Academy of Family Practice, from the health insurance industry itself. We have a plan uniting business and labor. There is an overwhelming knowledge that we have to move and move now. We are going to do our best to reform our system. We are going to do our best to meet the human needs of the people of this country.

There are all kinds of problems that have to be dealt with that we haven't even discussed yet: access to care in inner cities and rural areas, coverage for little children, dealing with the AIDS crisis adequately, still unmet needs in the area of women's health care, the problem of the veterans in this country who don't have access to care, even as their own network goes broke. All these issues will be dealt with in this task force. This is going to be an unprecedented effort. And let me just say, in general, we're going to set up a workroom, kind of like the war room we had in the campaign, over in the Executive Office Building. And all of the departments you see here represented and leaders you see represented around this table will be represented in that room. And we are going to work constantly, day and night, until we have a health care plan ready to submit to the Congress that we believe we can pass.

Finally, let me say I am committed to doing this in a partnership with the Congress. I will ask the leadership of the Congress to work with me on a bipartisan basis and to do whatever we can to make sure that as we present the plan, we have also maximized its chances of early passage in the Congress.

I thank all these people for their willingness to serve and to work together. I hope the American people will see just how passionately I personally am committed to doing something about health care reform. We've talked about it long enough. The time has come to act, and I have chosen the course that I think is most likely to lead to action that will improve the lives of millions of Americans.

Q. Mr. President, can you provide universal coverage without driving up the deficit?

The President. I think you can do it if you control the cost of health care. You have to really—let me just—I don't want to get into one of these things that provoke a lot of cartoons about my policy wonk weakness, but we're at 14 percent of our income on health care now. The next most expensive health care system in the world is Canada's. It's at about 9.2 percent of income. That is a huge difference, massive. And yet, every other major country with which we compete provides some basic health care to everybody, something we don't do. So the answer to your question is, in my judgment, if we do this right over the next 8 years, you're going to see huge savings in tax dollars and even bigger savings, more than twice the savings, in private dollars that will free up hundreds of billions of dollars literally between now and the end of the decade to reinvest in economic growth and opportunity.

In the short run, our tough call will be, how do you take the savings and phase in universal coverage, or should there be some other way to pay for that? We've got some short-term calls to make. But there's no question that in the medium term, 5 to 8 years, you're looking at massive savings with universal coverage, in both tax dollars and private sector dollars, if we do

it right.

Q. Mr. President, do you intend to pay the First Lady for her efforts?

The President. No. No. I never have paid her for her public service efforts. I don't want to start now.

Q. Is 100 days hard and fast, or are you willing to be flexible on that if it's not quite ready?

The President. If it were 101 days I wouldn't have a heart attack, but I don't want to—I want it done now. I think we know what the major alternatives are. What we have to do now is something nobody's done, and that is to meld them into the best possible legislation, taking account of some of the problems that exist with every course.

And let me make one acknowledgment on the front end about this. Legitimate objections can be raised to any course of action in this area. That is, there is no such thing as a perfect solution. So whatever course we choose to take, somebody can say, "Well, it's not perfect for these reasons." To that, I have two answers, and I'm going to say this until I'm blue in the face for this entire year until we get action. Number one, the worst thing we can do is keep on doing what we're doing now, because more and more people are falling out of the system and the cost is becoming more and more burdensome to those who are still bearing it. So whatever course we take, we will preserve what is best about American health care, some consumer choice and the quality of care. So whatever problems we have, they won't be as bad as the ones we've got now. Number two, this is not going to be the end of the line. Whatever problems are there can be fixed later. But we will never, never get anywhere if we stand paralyzed, because there's no such thing as a perfect alternative.

Q. What factors did you consider in giving this high-profile position to Mrs. Clinton?

The President. Of all the people I've ever worked with in my life, she's better at organizing and leading people from a complex beginning to a certain end than anybody I've ever worked with in my life. And that's what I want done here.

NOTE: The President spoke at 2:02 p.m. in the Roosevelt Room at the White House at a meeting of the Health Care Working Group.

Exchange With Reporters Prior to a Meeting with Congressional Leaders
January 26, 1993

Q. Mr. President, are you going to have a policy statement on gays in the military by the end of the week?

The President. I'm going to talk to the leadership of Congress about our legislative agenda.

Q. How do you feel your meeting with the Joint Chiefs went yesterday, Mr. President?

The President. It was a very good meeting. I was very impressed by them. The country's well served.

NOTE: The President spoke at 9:38 a.m. in the Cabinet Room at the White House.

Nomination for Ambassador to Russia
January 26, 1993

The President announced today that he intends to nominate Thomas R. Pickering as Ambassador of the United States of America to the Russian Federation.

In making this announcement, President Clinton said, "It is essential that we continue to expand and develop our relationship with Russia. I want to do everything I can to support democratic and economic reform there and want an experienced and dedicated Ambassador to represent our Nation in Moscow. Ambassador Pickering has demonstrated throughout his career that he has the ability and wisdom to carry out this important assignment. I have full confidence in him."

NOTE: A biography of the nominee was made available by the Office of the Press Secretary.

Nomination for Director of the Office of Personnel Management
January 26, 1993

The President today announced that he intends to nominate Jim King as Director of the Office of Personnel Management.

"Jim King will bring invaluable expertise, knowledge, and enthusiasm to the Office of Personnel Management," said President Clinton.

NOTE: A biography of the nominee was made available by the Office of the Press Secretary.

Exchange With Reporters Prior to a Meeting With Congressional Leaders
January 27, 1993

Q. Mr. President, would you consider backing down on your lifting the ban on gays in the military because of the opposition?

The President. We're not here to discuss that. We're here to discuss the economy, which is all I discussed yesterday with congressional leadership, contrary to——

Q. But would you consider——

The President. We're here to discuss the economy.

Q. Have you decided on a consumption tax yet?

The President. No——

Q. Are you closer to a decision——

The President. I'm going to give a speech to the joint session February 17th, and we'll lay out my program then. But I've not made any decisions yet. This is the first opportunity I've had to meet with the economic leadership of Congress.

Q. [*Inaudible*]—you decide, or announce what you've decided on a consumption tax in your—a joint address——

The President. [*Inaudible*]

Q. Is this gay-in-the-military issue distracting you at all, sir, from the——

The President. No, it's distracting you, it's not distracting—[*laughter*].

Q. Can you reach $145 billion in deficit reductions without a consumption tax?

The President. I don't know the answer to that. We're working on it.

NOTE: The exchange began at 2:10 p.m. in the Oval Office at the White House. A tape was not available for verification of the content of this exchange.

Exchange With Reporters Prior to a Meeting With Federal Reserve Chairman Alan Greenspan
January 28, 1993

Q. Mr. President, what's the principle you're fighting for in sticking with your plan not to ban gays in the military? What's the principle that you believe in that makes you want to stick with that?

The President. I came here to talk about the economy today with Mr. Greenspan. If he wants to express his opinion on that subject, I'll be glad to hear it. Most people with whom I talk, except you folks, never discuss that. We have other things we're trying to deal with.

Q. Sir, there was good news about the economy—[*inaudible*]

The President. I think that there's a lot of response to the efforts we're making now, but there's also a lot of troubling news about lost jobs. And we've got a lot of work to do, a lot of work to do.

NOTE: The exchange began at 9:37 a.m. in the Oval Office at the White House.

Remarks Honoring the School Principal of the Year and an Exchange With Reporters
January 28, 1993

The President. This is Janie Hatton from Milwaukee, and she is the School Principal of the Year. You can tell she's from Wisconsin because Senator Kohl is here, but I have to tell you she also grew up in my hometown of Hot Springs, Arkansas. We grew up in the same town. She's younger than I am. [*Laughter*]

That's her husband, Isaac, who also comes from Arkansas. And these other three gentlemen are with the National Association of School Principals.

Janie Hatton. And MetLife.

The President. And MetLife, which sponsors this award. She gave me two paperweights for my wife and daughter, and now you're going to give me something, right?

Mrs. Hatton. Right. This is a hat for you to jog in, as well as, when the days are cold, the long jogging pants, "Tech has style." And the mornings when it's kind of warm, you can wear the short ones that says "Tech, Milwaukee." This is the one that we're most proud of because '93 Tech and when you have said Milwaukee Tech, you've said it all. And we invite you to Tech at all times, any time. We're building a referendum issue February 16. We want you to think thumbs up because that style is really good. So wear it with pride. And Tech is an important——

The President. I think it's going to fit, don't you? That's great.

Mrs. Hatton. Thank you so much, Mr. President.

The President. I'm proud of you.

Mrs. Hatton. And I'm proud of you. Great things happen to great people.

The President. Thank you.

Meetings With Members of Congress

Q. Mr. President, are you building incentives to help the economy and working with Congress? Are you getting momentum having all these meetings with the Hill, with Chairman Greenspan?

The President. Well, I think so. You know, we've got a lot more meetings ahead. I'm going to have a huge number of meetings, I hope, next week with Members. I needed this first week just to kind of get our feet on the ground here and get organized and get ready. But I have held a lot of meetings with Congress, and I'll do many more next week. I'll do as many as I can leading up to the February 17 address to the joint session. And after that I'll do as many more as I can.

Homosexuals in the Military

Q. Mr. President, are you confident that you'll ever get the ban on gays in the military lifted?

The President. Well, we're working on the resolution in the Senate, as you know. And I've been working mostly on economic issues today, so I just heard from my staff. But they seem to think we're pretty close to——

Q. Are you satisfied with 6 months down the road?

The President. I'm satisfied with what I hope the resolution will be. You'll have to come back to me when there's final language there.

I think the Joint Chiefs should have 6 months to deal with the practical issues involved. This is not free of difficulty. There are certain factual problems involved.

But the principle—let me answer the question Mark [Mark Halperin, ABC News] asked me this morning about the principle. The principle behind this for me is that Americans who are willing to conform to the requirements of conduct within the military services, in my judgment, should be able to serve in the military and that people should be disqualified from serving in the military based on something they do, not based on who they are. That is the elemental principle.

There is actually an enormous amount of agreement on this. The Joint Chiefs agree, for example, that we should not anymore ask people about their sexual orientation when they enlist. And I believe that any sort of improper conduct should result in severance. The narrow issue on which there is disagreement is whether people should be able to say that they're homosexual—and do nothing else—without being severed. But there are a whole lot of very complicated practical questions that flow from that very narrow issue. And that's what I want to have 6 months to give them a chance to work on. So, I hope we can.

NOTE: The President spoke at 4:50 p.m. in the Oval Office at the White House.

Exchange With Reporters Prior to a Meeting With Representatives of the Close-Up Foundation
January 29, 1993

Homosexuals in the Military

Q. Mr. President, when are you going to announce your policy on gays in the military? What time today?

The President. Well, we're waiting for an analysis of the court decision now and how it affects what we would have to do anyway. So, that sort of—we were here, as you know, last night with Senator Nunn, and I thought it was quite close to an agreement that would give the military what I think ought to be done without anybody agreeing to change their position now—give them a chance to look into what the practical problems are. But this court decision may change that, and we are looking at it. And I will probably have something to say later today.

Q. But do you—[*inaudible*]—decision because—[*inaudible*]—get through now?

The President. Well, we talked about it a little last night, but I wanted to—the staff stayed here quite late. I thought they ought to get a chance to get a little sleep and then think through it. So, as you know, there is virtual agreement on everything but one issue anyway. So, you are trying to figure out how this court case fits, that and whether it changes anything for either side.

So, we'll talk about it this morning and then try to resolve it soon.

Q. Are you concerned, Mr. President, that this controversy this week has given the American people the wrong idea of what your priorities are?

The President. Yes, I do. Of course, I didn't bring it up; people in the Senate did. I just tried—I have not, frankly, spent very much time on it compared to the time I'm spending on the economy, which is what I was elected to do. And we've been working on that hard. So, I'm just going to keep doing what I was elected to do and try to stick up for what I believe and see if we can work through this.

NOTE: The President spoke at 8:37 a.m. in the Oval Office at the White House. A tape was not available for verification of the content of these remarks.

Teleconference Remarks on Family and Medical Leave Legislation
January 29, 1993

The President. Thank you very much, Al. And hello, ladies and gentlemen. I want to thank you for agreeing to join us on this telephone call today and through this telephone call to speak to the people in your own State and throughout the United States.

One of the things that we are determined to do here in Washington is open the Government to you and never let people forget, who are here making decisions, that you and lives are at stake and that these matters that we discuss and vote upon here really do affect real people out in our country.

So with that, let me just now go from one person to the next and let each of you say something about how this family and medical leave act might affect your life in the future or could have affected your life in the past or the fact that we didn't have it affected you.

[*At this point, the President took a series of telephone calls from people who described their personal experiences.*]

The President. Ladies and gentlemen, I know I speak for Vice President Gore when I thank all of you for your courage and your support on behalf of your own children and your own families and working families all across this country. We believe that next week, the Congress and the leaders who have worked on this in both parties will help our Nation join the 72 other countries who already have family and medical leave. And if it happens, it will be because of people like you and for people like you.

I think a lot of you said this, but I just want to close with this: It's easy for people to talk about family values, but it's also important for us to value families. And your Government is going to be given a chance to value the American family next week. We hope and pray they'll do it. And if it does happen, you all can claim a lot of the credit.

Thank you so much for being with us today, and have a wonderful time. And keep those kids making that good noise. I like to hear it.

Bless you all. Goodbye.

NOTE: The President spoke at approximately 11:42 a.m. from the Oval Office at the White House. He was introduced by the Vice President.

The President's News Conference
January 29, 1993

Homosexuals in the Military

The President. Good afternoon, ladies and gentlemen. I'm sorry, we had a last-minute delay occasioned by another issue, not this one.

The debate over whether to lift the ban on homosexuals in the military has, to put it mildly, sparked a great deal of interest over the last few days. Today, as you know, I have reached an agreement, at least with Senator Nunn and Senator Mitchell, about how we will proceed in the next few days. But first I would like to explain what I believe about this issue and why, and what I have decided to do after a long conversation, and a very good one, with the Joint Chiefs of Staff and discussions with several Members of Congress.

The issue is not whether there should be homosexuals in the military. Everyone concedes that there are. The issue is whether men and women who can and have served with real distinction should be excluded from military service solely on the basis of their status. And I believe they should not.

The principle on which I base this position is this: I believe that American citizens who want to serve their country should be able to do so unless their conduct disqualifies them from doing so. Military life is fundamentally different from civilian society; it necessarily has a different and stricter code of conduct, even a different code of justice. Nonetheless, individuals who are prepared to accept all necessary restrictions on their behavior, many of which would be intolerable in civilian society, should be able to serve their country honorably and well.

I have asked the Secretary of Defense to submit by July the 15th a draft Executive order, after full consultation with military and congressional leaders and concerned individuals outside of the Government, which would end the present policy of the exclusion from military service solely on the basis of sexual orientation and at the same time establish rigorous standards regarding sexual conduct to be applied to all military personnel.

This draft order will be accompanied by a study conducted during the next 6 months on the real, practical problems that would be involved in this revision of policy, so that we will have a practical, realistic approach consistent with the high standards of combat effectiveness and unit cohesion that our armed services must maintain. I agree with the Joint Chiefs that the highest standards of conduct must be required.

The change cannot and should not be accomplished overnight. It does require extensive consultation with the Joint Chiefs, experts in the Congress and in the legal community, joined by my administration and others. We've consulted closely to date and will do so in the future. During that process, interim measures will be placed into effect which, I hope, again, sharpen the focus of this debate. The Joint Chiefs of Staff have agreed to remove the question regarding one's sexual orientation from future versions of the enlistment application, and it will not be asked in the interim.

We also all agree that a very high standard of conduct can and must be applied. So the single area of disagreement is this: Should someone be able to serve their country in uniform if they say they are homosexuals, but they do nothing which violates the code of conduct or undermines unit cohesion or morale, apart from that statement? That is what all the furor of the last few days has been about. And the practical and not insignificant issues raised by that issue are what will be studied in the next 6 months.

Through this period ending July 15th, the Department of Justice will seek continuances in pending court cases involving reinstatement. And administrative separation under current Department of Defense policies based on status alone will be stayed pending completion of this review. The final discharge in cases based only on status will be suspended until the President has an opportunity to review and act upon the final recommendations of the Secretary of Defense with respect to the current policy. In the meantime, a member whose discharge has been suspended by the Attorney General will be separated from active duty and placed in standby reserve until the final report of the Secretary of Defense and the final action of the President. This is the agreement that I have reached with Senator Nunn and Senator Mitchell.

During this review process, I will work with the Congress. And I believe the compromise announced today by the Senators and by me shows that we can work together to end the gridlock that has plagued our city for too long.

This compromise is not everything I would have hoped for or everything that I have stood for, but it is plainly a substantial step in the right direction. And it will allow us to move forward on other terribly important issues affecting far more Americans.

My administration came to this city with a mission to bring critical issues of reform and renewal and economic revitalization to the public debate, issues that are central to the lives of all Americans. We are working on an economic reform agenda that will begin with an address to the joint session of Congress on February 17th. In the coming months the White House Task Force on Health Care, chaired by the First Lady, will complete work on a comprehensive health care reform proposal to be submitted to Congress within 100 days of the commencement of this administration. We will be designing a system of national service to begin a season of service in which our Nation's unmet needs are addressed and we provide more young people the opportunity to go to college. We will be proposing comprehensive welfare reform legislation and other important initiatives.

I applaud the work that has been done in the last 2 or 3 days by Senator Nunn, Senator Mitchell, and others to enable us to move forward on a principle that is important to me without shutting the Government down and running the risk of not even addressing the family and medical leave issue, which is so important to America's families, before Congress goes into its recess. I am looking forward to getting on with this issue over the next 6 months and with these other issues which were so central to the campaign and, far more importantly, are so important to the lives of all the American people.

Q. Mr. President, yesterday a Federal court in California said that the military ban on homosexuals was unconstitutional. Will you direct the Navy and the Justice Department not to appeal that decision? And how does that ruling strengthen your hand in this case?

The President. Well, it makes one point. I think it strengthens my hand, if you will, in two ways. One, I agree with the principle embodied in the case. I have not read the opinion, but as I understand it, the opinion draws the distinction that I seek to draw between conduct and status. And secondly, it makes the practical point I have been making all along, which is that there is not insignificant chance that this matter would ultimately be resolved in the courts in a way that would open admission into the military without the opportunity to deal with this whole range of practical issues, which everyone who has ever thought about it or talked it through concedes are there. So I think it can—it strengthens my hand on the principle as well as on the process.

Q. Mr. President, there's a glass of water there, by the way, while I ask the question. Do you think, since you promised during the campaign—your literature put out a very clear statement: lift the ban on homosexuals in the military immediately—do you think you didn't think through these practical problems? What have you learned from this experience in dealing with powerful members of the Senate and the Joint Chiefs? And how much of a problem is this for you to accept a compromise which doesn't meet your real goals?

The President. Well, I haven't given up on my real goals. I think this is a dramatic step forward. Normally, in the history of civil rights advancements, Presidents have not necessarily been in the forefront in the beginning. So I think the fact that we actually have the Joint Chiefs of Staff agreeing that it's time to take this question off the enlistment form, that there ought to be a serious examination of how this would be done, even though they haven't agreed that it should be done; that the Senate, if they vote for the motion advocated by Senators Nunn and Mitchell, will agree; Senators who don't agree that the policy should be changed are agreeing that we ought to have a chance to work through this for 6 months and persuade them of that, I think, is very, very significant.

Now, I would remind you that any President's Executive order can be overturned by an act of Congress. The President can then veto the act of Congress and try to have his veto sustained if the act stands on its own as a simple issue that could always be vetoed. But I always knew that there was a chance that Congress would disagree with my position. I can only tell you that I still think I'm right; I feel comfortable about the way we have done this; and I'm going to maintain the commitment that I have.

Q. But do you think that you hadn't examined the practical problems——

Q. Sir, I just wonder, do you think in retrospect that—obviously, you didn't intend the first week—I'm sorry, you want to——

The President. No, I had always planned to allow some period of time during which policies would be developed to deal with what I think are the significant practical problems. This, in effect, may reverse the process over what I intended to do, but there has to be a time in which these issues, these practical issues are developed and policies are developed to deal with them.

Q. Obviously, you didn't intend the first week of your administration, given your promise to have the laser focus on the economy, to be seen around the country as military gay rights week. I wonder if in retrospect you think you could have done things differently to have avoided that happening?

The President. I don't know how I could have done that. The Joint Chiefs asked for a meeting about a number of issues, in which this was only one. We spent a lot of time talking about other things. This issue was not put forward in this context by me; it was put forward by those in the United States Senate who sought to make it an issue early on. And I don't know how I could have stopped them from doing that.

Q. You don't think that in making the promise and then in promising to follow through on it early that you might have given rise to this, do you, sir?

The President. Well, I think it was pretty clear to me that we were talking about some sort of 6-month process days and days ago. And the people who wanted it debated now were not deterred by that, and probably a lot of them won't be deterred by the agreement announced today. I think that we must—they have the perfect right to do this. But the timing of this whole issue was clearly forced by the people in the Senate who were opposed to any change of the policy no matter what the facts are. And I think that was their right to do, but they control the timing of this, not me.

Q. Two questions. First of all, just to make sure that we're clear on this: July 15th this happens, period, regardless of what comes out at these hearings, is that correct? The ban will be issued, or will be lifted, rather?

The President. That is my position. My position is that I still embrace the principle, and I think it should be done. The position of those who are opposed to me is that they think that the problems will be so overwhelming everybody with good sense will change their position. I don't expect to do that.

Q. So you definitely expect to do it. And secondly——

The President. I don't expect to change my position, no.

Q. What do you think is going to happen in the military? There have been all sorts of dire predictions of violence, of mass comings-out, whatever. What do you think the impact of this is going to be, practically?

The President. For one thing, I think if you look at the last 10 years of experience here, according to the reports we have, this country spent $500 million in tax dollars to separate something under 16,500 homosexuals from the service and has dealt with complaints, at least, of sexual abuse, heterosexual abuse, largely against women, far greater volumes. But during this period, we have plainly had the best educated, best trained, most cohesive military force in the history of the United States. And everybody, ask anybody, and the Joint Chiefs will tell you that.

They agreed that we should stop asking the question. This single thing that is dividing people on this debate, I want to make it very clear that this is a very narrow issue. It is whether a person, in the absence of any other disqualifying conduct, can simply say that he or she is homosexual and stay in the service. I do not expect that to spark this kind of problem. And I certainly think in the next 6 months, as people start to work it through and talk it through, a lot of legitimate, practical issues will be raised and dealt with in a more rational environment that is less charged. That is certainly what I hope will happen.

Thank you.

Q. Want to tell us what the other problem was you were working on, Mr. President, on the Middle East, sir?

The President. No, tomorrow or the next day.

NOTE: The President's first news conference began at 1:44 p.m. in the Briefing Room at the White House.

Memorandum on Ending Discrimination in the Armed Forces
January 29, 1993

Memorandum for the Secretary of Defense

Subject: Ending Discrimination on the Basis of Sexual Orientation in the Armed Forces

I hereby direct you to submit to me prior to July 15, 1993, a draft of an Executive order ending discrimination on the basis of sexual orientation in determining who may serve in the Armed Forces of the United States. The draft of the Executive order should be accompanied by the results of a study to be conducted over the next six months on how this revision in policy would be carried out in a manner that is practical, realistic, and consistent with the high standards of combat effectiveness and unit cohesion our Armed Forces must maintain.

In preparing the draft, I direct you to consult fully with the Joint Chiefs of Staff and the military services, with other Departments affected by the order, with the Congress, and with concerned individuals and organizations outside the executive branch.

WILLIAM J. CLINTON

Nomination for Deputy Secretary of Commerce
January 29, 1993

The President today nominated John A. Rollwagen, the head of the world's largest manufacturer of supercomputers, to be the Deputy Secretary of Commerce. Rollwagen is the chairman and CEO of Cray Research, Inc.

"The Department of Commerce will play a leading role in the development of a high skill, high wage economy," President Clinton said. "Having presided over a high skill, high wage corporation for 15 years, John Rollwagen can help us bring this about. As a proven CEO of a high technology company, Rollwagen is an innovative thinker and highly respected manager. He combines business savvy, international experience, and high technology knowledge. I'm convinced that he is the best choice to work together with Secretary Ron Brown to make the Commerce Department a powerful part of our administration's work of restoring the competitiveness of American business," said the President.

NOTE: A biography of the nominee was made available by the Office of the Press Secretary.

Remarks at a State Dinner for the Nation's Governors
January 31, 1993

You ever had the feeling you've been here before? [*Laughter*]

Governor and Mrs. Romer and distinguished Governors and spouses and our very special guests from around the Nation, Hillary and I are delighted to welcome all of you here to our first state dinner. This is something that I have looked forward to for some time, and as I'm sure you know, I am delighted that this is the first official dinner we're having in the White House. I couldn't be more pleased to see you here.

Many of you were kind enough to come to the luncheon that I hosted, along with Hillary and Vice President Gore and Tipper, for all the Governors and former Governors with whom I had the honor to serve. And I would just like to say tonight on this occasion that I'm looking forward to getting to work with you tomorrow.

This country needs your involvement and your support to deal with the health care crisis, which is threatening to bankrupt many of you; to deal with the budget crisis, which is undermining the economic stability of every State in America; and to seize the opportunities that are out there.

The time I spent as a Governor and the time I spent working with you and those who preceded you was some of the best time I ever spent in my life. I look back on it with great pride and gratitude. And to all of you I say that I honor the work that you must do, and I look forward to being a real partner.

I'm delighted that you're here, and I hope you have a great time tonight as we move from the dinner into the entertainment. I want to say that I expect to have a special treat tonight for you in the entertainment. I think you'll all enjoy it very much.

But please know here that this house is your house, that I am well aware of the fact that I am just a temporary tenant, and that while here I intend to do my very best to be faithful to the lessons that I learned as a Governor that most of what you do ought to be done by you and not by us. And I will try to be a good partner, and I hope you will be mine, as we get this country to face its problems and seize its promise.

I now propose a toast to the Governors and their spouses, friends, and family members.

NOTE: The President spoke at 9:13 p.m. in the State Dining Room at the White House.

Remarks in a Telephone Conversation Congratulating the Super Bowl Champion Dallas Cowboys
January 31, 1993

The President. Jerry?

Jerry Jones. Mr. President.

The President. How are you doing, man?

Mr. Jones. Bill, I'm telling you, I appreciate this call so much.

The President. Congratulations.

Mr. Jones. Thank you.

The President. I'll tell you what, this is a lot bigger deal at home than me getting elected President. [*Laughter*]

Mr. Jones. I'll tell you this right now, you were an inspiration to us.

The President. Great.

Mr. Jones. I saw how to get out on a knee and come back up swinging.

The President. Thanks, man. This is great.

Mr. Jones. Well, I really appreciate this call. And I've got Jimmy standing by me.

The President. Thanks. I've got somebody who wants to say hi to you, and then I want to talk to Jimmy.

Mr. Jones. Okay, fine.

Gov. Ann Richards. Jerry, it's Ann Richards. Listen, I got to watch the ball game in the White House with Mario Cuomo.

Mr. Jones. Ann, you are wonderful for calling us.

Governor Richards. It was absolutely wonderful. And let me tell you, we gave him the hardest time in the world.

Mr. Jones. Well, you've answered my question: You didn't go easy on him then, did you?

Governor Richards. No, darlin', we did not let our foot off his neck.

Mr. Jones. Did you tell him you hadn't been to one we lost? [*Laughter*]

Governor Richards. Here's the President. We're so proud of you. You tell Emmitt Smith that he's number one for me.

Mr. Jones. Thank you, Governor. Thank you. Hey, Mr. President.

The President. Yes, yes.

Mr. Jones. Thank you so much for calling. I can't tell you what it means.

The President. Thanks, Jerry.

Mr. Jones. And here's Jimmy. Here's Jimmy.

Jimmy Johnson. Hello, Mr. President.

The President. Jimmy, how are you doing? Congratulations.

Mr. Johnson. Well, thank you. I think you understand how much we put into this thing and where we are. I'll tell you, it's a great feeling for all of our guys.

The President. Well, you've come a long way in a short time and with a lot of courage. And I'll tell you, I watched your team all year long just basically wear everybody down by hanging in there, and it was amazing what you did.

Mr. Johnson. Well, you know a little bit about perseverance yourself, so I understand.

The President. Well, I really admire what you did. And this is a great night for you, and I want you to get back to your players. I just wanted to say hello and we're proud of you.

Mr. Johnson. Thank you a lot, Mr. President.

The President. Goodbye, Jimmy.

NOTE: The President spoke at 9:59 p.m. from the State Floor at the White House. In his remarks, he referred to Dallas Cowboys owner Jerry Jones and head coach Jimmy Johnson.

Remarks Following Entertainment at a State Dinner for the Nation's Governors
January 31, 1993

The President. Ladies and gentlemen, first I think we ought to acknowledge the musicians: Peter Howard, John Beal, Martin Erskine, John Redsecker, and Wally Harper. Let's give them a hand. [*Applause*] I'd also like to thank the people who put this wonderful program together: Marty Bell, Beverly Camhe, Phyllis Newman, and my good friend Bobbie Handman, who's here with her husband, Len, tonight and whose daughter and son-in-law have been so instrumental in our political life, Harold Ickes and Laura Handman. Let's give all of them a hand. [*Applause*] I want to thank Ms. Handman and Ms. Newman, in particular, for writing this; and for Peter Howard for his musical direction tonight.

And now let me say that I hope that we can take good care of this house and that this house will always be a house of America's family. I can't help but note, I don't want to embarrass Phyllis, but Phyllis and her husband, Adolph Green, who sang a little tonight—stand up, Adolph—[*applause*]—they're celebrating their 33d wedding anniversary. As you can see, he had to get not only her parents' permission but the law's as well to marry her at that young age.

[*Laughter*]

Phyllis Newman. That's the nicest thing you've said. [*Laughter*]

The President. I understand that this is Governor Dean's wedding anniversary tonight, too, and I want to acknowledge that. This is Governor Mickelson's birthday.

This is also a very important birthday: Tonight is Carol Channing's birthday. I want all of us to sing "Happy Birthday" to her in just a moment, but I want to tell you that she performed here with George Burns for President and Mrs. Kennedy. She performed here when President Johnson was here. She made President Nixon's hate list, so she didn't perform then. [*Laughter*] We all knew about her in "Hello Dolly" and "Gentlemen Prefer Blondes," where she immortalized that song that you heard about being a little girl from Little Rock. I wish she had been.

I'd like to ask us all now to stand and sing "Happy Birthday" to her. George, you come up here to lead the singing.

NOTE: The President spoke at 11:45 p.m. in the State Dining Room at the White House.

Remarks Following a Meeting With the Nation's Governors
February 1, 1993

The President. Well, I want to say good morning to the members of the press who are here from Washington and many of you from around the Nation.

I'd like to read a statement and then call on the Governors, Romer and Campbell, to make a statement about the meeting we had here today and the actions which I will take today as a result of this meeting and the work that I have been doing over the last couple of months.

The day before my Inauguration, on one of the last days people called me Governor, I had lunch with many of the Governors here and many others with whom I have served over the past 14 years. I pledged to them a partnership between the country's Governors and this administration, rooted in our common experience on the front lines of people's lives.

I've told my friends, my colleagues, that the one thing I hoped that I could actually demand from them was a commitment to keep me rooted in that common experience and the real problems of real people. The White House, after all, only works when it is the people's house.

Today we have continued our partnership in earnest. We agreed to challenge together the one obstacle that could keep us from success in virtually every arena of national endeavor: the twin monsters of spiraling health care costs and the agony of having no access to health care, no health care coverage, or living in fear of losing it.

Left unaddressed, the health care crisis has had devastating impacts on families, businesses, the fiscal conditions of State and local government, and the economic performance of the United States. For 12 years our national Government has ignored the problem, partisan gridlock has prevented action, and Americans are paying the price. The amount we spend on health care has more than tripled. Now we spend far more than any other nation on Earth, about 30 percent more of our income, and we get less for it.

We send American companies out into the world with this 30 percent handicap simply because of high health care costs. The average American car alone includes over $1,000 in health care costs, twice as much as its Japanese competitor. You know as well as I do that the real people of this country are paying the price: working families who live in fear of losing their insurance; small businesses who have to choose between dropping coverage or going broke; State and local governments who have to balance their books every year and are now choosing between cutting education, raising taxes, or cutting other needed investments just to pay more for the same health care bills.

If every person striving to overcome this challenge will bring to that work the same depth of drive and determination that our Nation's Governors have brought here to the White House today with their policy position, the American people will have the commitment it takes to solve this problem.

This meeting was a model of everything I want my relationship with our Governors to be. It wasn't scripted or staged. It was simply an honest discussion where real work was done, real opinions were argued and a room filled with women and men who left their partisan banners outside the door. And in that spirit and what I hope is the first of a series of announcements we will make together, I want to announce that I am taking the following steps to help them meet the health care needs of their people in their States.

For years the Nation's Governors have been arguing that the process through which waivers from the Medicaid mandates imposed on them by the Federal Government is Byzantine and counterproductive. They are right. I have today directed the Department of Health and Human Services and its Health Care Financing Agency to take immediately a series of actions designed to streamline the Medicaid waiver process to enable the States of our country to serve more people at lower costs. These include a requirement that from now on the Health Care Financing Agency and its regional centers will have only one opportunity to ask for additional information and clarifications on States' waiver requests. I also want the Health Care Financing Agency to examine the development of a list of standard initiatives for automatic approval for State action.

In consultation with the National Governors' Association, I want a rapid review of the entire waiver request process that produces a list of additional streamlining recommendations within 60 days. And I am directing the Health Care Financing Agency to reopen negotiations with the National Governors' Association to issue new regulations related to how they can use provider taxes and disproportionate share reimbursement to meet the needs of the people in their State.

Finally, I am directing the Department of Health and Human Services to conduct a similar review of the non-Medicaid waiver submissions not addressed in the matters I have just discussed.

I'm also happy to announce that Hillary and the leadership of the National Governors' Association have agreed on a formal process for the Governors to have input into the Health Care Task Force. Their input, their advice, their perspective is essential to our success. When all this is said and done, the health care problems of this country can only be met if we have a good partnership.

And for those of you in the press and the general public who may not understand all the language that I have used about Medicaid and waivers, if I could put it in simple terms, it amounts to this: The Federal Government requires the States to provide a certain number of health services in a certain way to people who are poor enough to qualify for Medicaid. The States very often believe that they can provide more services at lower cost if we don't impose our rules and regulations on them.

For years and years and years, Governors have been screaming for relief from the cumbersome process by which the Federal Government has micromanaged the health care system affecting poor Americans. We are going to try to give them that relief so that for lower costs we can

do more good for more people. This will be one big step on a long road to giving this country the kind of health care system it needs.

Governor Romer.

[*At this point, Gov. Roy Romer and Gov. Carroll Campbell made statements on cooperation with the administration on health care reform.*]

The President. That's our statement. I know a lot of you here want to take pictures of your Governors, so have at it.

Governor King, of all of the people of America, they know you from behind as well as from the front, but turn around. I think you ought to turn around. How about giving them a profile, at least, that sort of tough western profile? [*Laughter*]

Thank you all very much.

NOTE: The President spoke at 11:23 a.m. in the East Room at the White House.

Statement on Revocation of Certain Executive Orders Concerning Federal Contracting
February 1, 1993

Today I am taking two actions to restore a needed balance in America's workplace. I believe that these steps, by reducing unnecessary Federal Government intrusion into workplace relations, ultimately will promote the shared goals of American workers and management and strengthen the ability of this country's businesses and industry to compete in the world economy.

First, I am revoking Executive Order No. 12818. This order, issued on October 23, 1992 by President Bush, prohibits contractors that have entered into project agreements with unions from bidding on Federal construction contracts. American taxpayers and the Federal Government are not well-served by this restriction. Such agreements establish labor standards for work early in the process. They reduce instances of cost overruns by permitting contract bidders to make more reliable cost estimates before bidding. They promote completion of projects in a timely manner by assuring a stable supply of skilled workers. And they promote safe working conditions. By revoking Executive Order No. 12818 today, such project agreements

will again be allowed in Federal construction contracts.

Second, I am revoking Executive Order No. 12800, issued on April 13, 1992. This order required unionized Federal contractors to post a notice in the workplace that workers are not required to join or support a union and threatened sanctions against contractors who did not comply. The effect of this order was distinctly antiunion as it did not require contractors to notify workers of any of their other rights protected by the National Labor Relations Act, such as the right to organize and bargain collectively. By revoking this order, I today end the Government's role in promoting this one-sided version of workplace rights.

WILLIAM J. CLINTON

The White House,
February 1, 1993.

NOTE: The Executive order revoking Executive Orders 12800 and 12818 is listed in Appendix D at the end of this volume.

Message on National African-American History Month
February 1, 1993

This February we rediscover, celebrate, and honor the history and achievements of African-Americans during National African-American History Month.

In 1993, I am proud to recognize that more African-Americans serve in the President's Cabinet than ever before in the history of our country. We are nearing the day when we will have built a new home for America, a home where all Americans will have a place at the table.

Understanding our past makes us aware of how far we have come and how far we have to go. Last month, for the first time in many years, our National Archives displayed for the public the Emancipation Proclamation. That document, signed by President Abraham Lincoln on January 1, 1863, launched the beginning of a life of freedom for millions of African-American people.

For several months last year, individuals and groups of citizens had been writing to the National Archives to inquire whether the historic document would be exhibited over the new year holiday in honor of its anniversary. After considering the matter, the National Archives decided to arrange an exhibit.

The fragile document was shown in our Nation's Capital for five days adjacent to the original Charters of Freedom—the Declaration of Independence, the Constitution of the United States, and the Bill of Rights. The exhibit reminded America of how liberty had once been denied to a particular segment of our population. The diverse backgrounds of the people in those lines each day, however, showed how the history of African-Americans touches all of us.

The public response was overwhelming. People came from all walks of life, with their children or their friends, from every corner of our country, to see for themselves the pieces of paper that meant for millions the difference between slavery and freedom. Each night at closing time, the National Archives had to extend the visiting hours to accommodate people who had waited in line for nearly three hours. Indeed, the efforts of the few citizens that gave birth to the exhibit brought to life for thousands the story of freedom in America.

I invite all Americans to rediscover that story and others as our Nation observes National African-American History Month.

WILLIAM J. CLINTON

Nomination for President and Chairman of the Export-Import Bank of the United States
February 1, 1993

The President today announced his intention to nominate Kenneth D. Brody as President and Chairman of the Export-Import Bank of the United States.

"I'm very pleased to make this announcement today," said the President. "Having someone with Ken Brody's experience and knowledge at the helm of the Export-Import Bank will help to ensure the orderly flow of trade and the promotion of American exports, a vital part of our Nation's economy."

NOTE: A biography of the nominee was made available by the Office of the Press Secretary.

Remarks at the Democratic Governors' Association Dinner
February 1, 1993

Thank you very much, Governor Walters. And thank you, ladies and gentlemen, for that wonderful welcome.

I am full of gratitude tonight as I remember that just a year ago when I was at this banquet, I came in from the cold of New Hampshire, cold in more ways than one—*[laughter]*—and received from the leadership of this organization a white scarf, which I wore for the remainder of the campaign in New Hampshire to stay warm, a cap which I still have, and a renewed sense that the battle in which I was engaged was worth the effort.

I want to thank every one of you who had anything to do with that. I noticed in the audience tonight the Secretary of Commerce, Ron Brown, who did such a brilliant job as the head of our party and keeping us going; representatives of many groups, teachers, working people, and others out here in this audience, that have worked so hard to give us a chance to put our children first in this country again; and many others who raised money, knocked on doors, and walked along roads.

I want to pay a particular tribute tonight to my good friend the Governor of Hawaii, not only for his leadership as the chair of the Democratic Governors' Association but for being my friend and supporter and for giving us a model of what an aggressive, active Democratic leader ought to be. Under John's leadership, the Democratic Governors' Association had one of its busiest and most successful years. There are now two more Democratic Governors. The DGA worked closely with our campaign, and largely as a result of that teamwork we won 8 of the 12 races in which we were engaged last year, the best showing by the Democratic Governors since 1982 when I, as the youngest ex-Governor in the history of America, made my comeback. *[Laughter]* Now we have Democratic Governors in 30 of the 50 States, our best margin since 1985.

I've also been impressed by John's extraordinary political leadership in Hawaii. When he was supporting me in the primary campaign last year, I kept angling for an invitation to Hawaii. I kept saying, "You know, I need to carry Hawaii. I haven't carried any western States. Don't

you think I ought to show up out there?" And he said, "If I can't carry Hawaii for you without your presence, I shouldn't be the Governor out here." And sure enough, we did. I think it has something to do with his native Hawaiian heritage. We were playing golf once together in Hawaii, John and I, and we played on a course on which there were no sand traps; there were only lava flows—*[laughter]*—so that the ball simply disappeared, never to be seen again. And we both hit long drives that sliced slightly into the lava flows. Mine disappeared; his hit a rock and bounced into the middle of the fairway. He informed me that his ancestors, who included King Kamehameha, who united the Hawaiian Islands, believed in a form of ancestor worship. And now, surely I can see the ultimate truth of his faith. Anyway, I think John and Lynne are great, and I hope that they will have many more years in public service. This country would be a lot better off if that happens.

I also want to salute the new chair of the DGA, my friend David Walters from Oklahoma. He and Rhonda were among those who were in the snows of New Hampshire with me. I told them the other day when I saw them that I just looked at a picture of us a year ago; here we are now in Washington celebrating a new inauguration. A year ago, I have a picture of us with Mike Sullivan; the former Governor of Vermont, Madeleine Kunin; and the former Governor of Michigan, Jim Blanchard, standing at the Super 8 Motel in Manchester. *[Laughter]* And it's a great commentary on how we get things done in this country. I think David Walters and Ann Richards will be a great team; that is, if Ann Richards is not too boastful about the Super Bowl victory last night. *[Laughter]*

I remember last fall when the Democratic Governors joined me in a western fly-around and a campaign we called "Winning the West." Most people thought the Democrats had no chance in the West. We traveled to seven States and won six, in no small measure because of the inordinate support that the western Democratic Governors gave the Clinton-Gore campaign.

Democratic Governors from the South participated—*[applause]*—clap, Governor Roberts.

That's good. You can clap for yourself. Democratic Governors in the South participated in a fly-around and campaigned for me in a region in which we invested relatively small amounts of money. They went to six States, and for the first time in 12 years we carried three of them.

As someone who answered to the term "Governor" until just 12 days ago, I'm proud to be here with the men and women who have been my friends and colleagues in the struggle to deal with the legacy of the 1980's, people who deal with the real problems of real people, who can't make excuses or print money when there's no money there, who struggle with health care and welfare and jobs and education and the ways that national economic trends and international development actually touch people's lives for good or ill.

As you and I learned from the elections last year, the American people want their political system and their Government to end gridlock, to face problems, and to make progress. They're tired of a process that's been too divided by partisanship or dominated by special interests or driven by short-term advantage of politicians instead of the long-term interests of people. They sent us to the statehouse and to the White House to change America. And they want action now. That is our mandate, and we must never forget it.

We have a chance to create a new Democratic majority in this country, rooted in the experience of governing and living. But we must never forget some basic things. First of all, we have to do this together: the Congress and the President, the States and the communities and the National Government.

I see in the audience a person who ran for President last year and turned out to be the best supporter I ever had in the Presidential campaign, Senator Tom Harkin from Iowa, and I want to thank him. After a tough primary campaign, when he began to work for me, even in the primary when it was still going, I realized that he had gotten into this race for the same reason I had: He believed that we had to change this country. And the changes were more important than him or me or anybody else. Well, I still believe that. And if we remember that, we can succeed.

I think that you might be interested to know that there were some surveys conducted after the Inaugural week. After the television ratings turned out to be very high and there were huge

crowds at all the events, the people had watched the gala all over America, and they'd watched that magnificent service at the Lincoln Memorial, and they'd watched our church service, and 800,000 people showed up at the Inaugural. But you know what people in America remembered most about the Inaugural week? That on the day after the Inauguration, we opened the White House to ordinary Americans. That is what registered out in the country.

I say that because somehow we've all got to find a way to remember every day that the people who can't come to these dinners are the people we hold these dinners for. We also have to remember we got elected to try a new approach, to expand opportunity, not Government, to increase investment, and to show literally that we can reinvent Government.

I was amazed, you know, the other crowd's had the White House for 12 years, and they have presented themselves as businesslike and modern, you know, and tried to make the Democrats look like yesterday's crowd. Well, when I got to the White House, guess what I found? Same phone system Jimmy Carter had, with technology that was put in during Kennedy's time and changed only to put pushbuttons instead of dials. No E-mail, no conference calls, but anybody could pick up the button I was talking on anywhere in the White House and listen in on the conversation. [*Laughter*] So we could have the conference call we didn't want, but we couldn't have the one we did.

People said last week, "Well, you know, when you're going to do controversial things, you need to gin up your operation again and send the talking points out and communicate with people." There's not even any E-mail in the office. It's a yesterday place, and we need to make it a tomorrow place.

I also want you to know that two of my Cabinet members have already met with every employee in their Departments, in their national headquarters, and were told, both of them, that they were the first Secretaries in 12 years to meet with all the employees in their Departments. The leadership of one of our Cabinet agencies abolished the executive dining room and saved $125,000 or $150,000 and brought the career employees up to the executive suite, and there were people who worked there for 25 years and had never seen where the bosses work. We are going to change the culture of the way this Federal Government works. We are going to reinvent it, and we're going to make it work again.

We are going to try to do what our adversaries always talked about, and that is to empower people, not entitle them. Whether it's welfare or trade or industrial policy or technology policy, what the American people want is a hand up, not a handout, and we're going to give it to them, if we can get the kind of support we need across the country to support these changes.

And most importantly, we're going to try to recreate a sense of partnership and community in America again, an America in which we don't have a person to waste. I believe as strongly as I can say that if we could create in this country a feeling burning in the heart of every American, that it was simply unacceptable to let one life go that could be saved, we could solve virtually every problem we have. Because if you look at every place where the system has broken down, the manifestation of that breakdown is somebody's life that is less than it ought to be. These children being shot in the streets—we're in Somalia, debating how we can keep peace in Somalia when the mortality rate is greater in some neighborhoods in the United States of America.

The immunization initiative that you've read about that we're going to be announcing in the next few days, you know, we were actually criticized in a story in the New York Times for the idea that the National Government might use its purchasing power to buy enough vaccines to immunize all the kids in the country. And people say, well, that would be bad if we did that. It would be better if we don't and we let these kids get sick?

All the factory workers in this country that are losing their jobs because we have no real strategy to create jobs, let me just say in parentheses here: As Democrats, we ought not ever to forget that there is a big difference between economic measurements of progress and whether that progress is manifested in the real lives of people. In the 1980's, the stock market tripled, but the Fortune 500 companies reduced employment. And the difference was made up by small business. So we can have a strong economy on the surface where the stock market is booming, but if small business people can't get bank loans at the local bank, jobs won't be created for all these people that are losing their

big employee jobs. And we have to remember things like that. With all this so-called economic recovery of the last 6 months, we're not creating jobs yet. And we've got to find a way to put people back to work. That is the ultimate and first test of whether life is working in America.

Finally, let me reiterate a line that I borrowed from President Roosevelt for the Inaugural speech. We learned in the 1980's that we had to be about bold, persistent experimentation. That is what I want to try to convince Congress and the country we ought to do. It means that we will try some things that will not work. And when we do, we have to have the courage to quit. One of the weaknesses of our Government is that when we start something that doesn't work, or whether we start something that does, we keep on doing it. We have to have the courage to experiment, to try, to stop, to start again. I am convinced that if we do that, we can deal with the health care crisis; we can deal with the deficit; we can deal with all these problems, but ultimately, we can change the shape of people's lives. And if I might say—I know that it defies the momentary conventional wisdom—I think we're off to a pretty good start.

The United States Congress in the next few days—maybe both Houses after the recess—will pass the new budget for the National Institutes of Health. And now we'll be able to go back to doing research, including fetal tissue, that offers great progress in dealing with children with diabetes and Parkinson's and Alzheimer's problems and other problems. I think that is progress.

The United States Senate was good enough to confirm every one of my Cabinet members, save one, on the day after I became President, the first time in longer than a generation that that had happened. And I did get into a controversy. But you know something? If you just want me to do things that are easy, you should have elected somebody else President.

When we deal with things that are hard, there ought to be debate. There ought to be discussion. People ought to say they disagree. They ought to call the White House and jam the phone lines. And by the way, there's a 1964 switchboard in the White House. That's one reason that the phone lines are jammed. But I'm just telling you, I think this is exciting. We need to shake things up. We need to have a debate in this country again. We need to do things and talk about things, get them out and let people argue.

I think together we can do what we were hired to do. But remember: I think we are about the business of creating a new Democratic majority if, but only if, we go to where the people are, lift them up, bring them with us, and change their lives. That requires a decent attention to the opinions of Republicans who want to help in change, too, and most importantly, a passionate determination never to forget that there is a real reason that most Americans remembered—2,000 of their number who won a lottery to come to the White House. They haven't felt like it was their house in a long time. You help me give it back to them, and we'll have a bright future.

Thank you, and God bless you all.

NOTE: The President spoke at 9:21 p.m. at the National Building Museum. In his remarks, he referred to Gov. Michael J. Sullivan of Wyoming and Gov. Ann Richards of Texas.

Remarks to the National Governors' Association
February 2, 1993

Thank you very much. Thank you very much, Governor Romer, ladies and gentlemen. I felt pretty good sitting at that table although that's my real place over there. [*Laughter*] We had a wonderful meeting yesterday, I thought, for a long time, maybe the longest time a President has ever met with a group of Governors, but we were discussing a terribly important issue: health care. And then we also got to discuss the deficit crisis and the budget problems a little bit.

I wanted to come here today, as you prepare to leave, to once again reaffirm my commitment to working in partnership with the Governors. You deal with real people in a more immediate way than, unfortunately, the President often gets to do. When I was a Governor, every day I would hear directly from people or see people who had suffered from layoffs or had their businesses closed down or who were afraid of losing their health coverage or who desperately wanted to improve their schools.

As you and I learned from last year's elections, the only pattern was not a partisan one. It was a pattern of determination on the part of the American people to have their political system and their Government address their real concerns. They don't want our process divided by partisanship or dominated by special interest or driven by short-term advantage. They know things that have too often been forgotten here over the last dozen years. The values that are central to our country's character must be central to our Government: work, family, faith, opportunity, responsibility, and community.

What I appreciated about this meeting is that no matter what our region or our party, we've always gotten together and tried to pay serious attention to our problems. I think the Governors have exemplified for the last dozen years the bold, persistent experimentation that President Roosevelt called for at the beginning of the Great Depression when he took office. And I'm here to tell you that I'm going to do everything I can to work with you in partnership to share ideas and resources and energy to try to do what we can to move this country forward.

As we discussed health care, economic policy, and the deficit yesterday, I'd like to spend just a few moments today talking about something that many of us have been working on since the middle 1980's, the issue of welfare reform.

I've often spoken with many of you about the need to end welfare as we know it, to make it a program that supports people who have fallen on hard times or who have difficulties that can be overcome, but eventually and ultimately a program that helps people to get on their feet through health care, child care, job training, and ultimately a productive job.

No one likes the welfare system as it currently exists, least of all the people who are on it. The taxpayers, the social service employees themselves don't think much of it either. Most people on welfare are yearning for another alternative, aching for the chance to move from dependence to dignity. And we owe it to them to give them that chance.

In the middle 1980's, when I was a Governor here, I worked with Governor Castle, now a

Member of the Congress—he and Governor Carper changed jobs, and in 6 months they're going to have a vote to see who won and who lost—[*laughter*]—to try to work with the Congress to develop a national welfare reform program. With the support of people in the House and the Senate, with the particular help of Senator Moynihan, now the chairman of the Senate Finance Committee, and with the support of the White House, the Governors had an unprecedented role in writing the Family Support Act of 1988, which President Reagan signed into law shortly before he left office and which Senator Moynihan said was the most significant piece of social reform in this area in the last generation.

The Family Support Act embodies a principle which I believe is the basis of an emerging consensus among people without regard to party or without regard to their traditional political philosophies. We must provide people on welfare with more opportunities for job training, with the assurance that they will receive the health care and child care they need when they go to work, and with all the opportunities they need to become self-sufficient. But then we have to ask them to make the most of these opportunities and to take a job.

As all of you know, the States never had the chance to fully implement the Welfare Reform Act of 1988 for two reasons: first, because over the last 4 years the welfare rolls have exploded everywhere and health care costs have gone up as the job market has declined and the economy has grown at the slowest rate in half a century; secondly, because of the economic problems, Government revenues have been down and the Congress and the administration were never able to fully fund the education and training portion of the act. This was clearly manifested not only in the growth of welfare rolls but in the fact that last year, for the first time since the program began, 1 in 10 Americans were on food stamps. So as the weak economy left millions of more in poverty, and the welfare rolls increased 5 times greater during the last 4 years than under the previous two administrations combined, it made it more difficult to make welfare reform work.

In spite of that, I think it would be a great mistake to conclude that that act was of no significance or that nothing good has occurred. Bipartisan efforts in State after State from New Jersey to Georgia, to Wisconsin, and many others all across the country, have resulted in innovative approaches to help move people off welfare rolls and onto payrolls.

In our State, through the program we call Project Success, more than 17,000 people moved from welfare to work. And more importantly, at a time when the rolls were exploding, our rolls grew much more slowly than the national average. Many of you have your own successes to report, and I had the opportunity to visit, in many of the States here represented, projects that were terribly impressive to me.

I say this to make the following point: The bill that is on the books will work, given the right economy and the right kind of support systems, but we need to do more than fully implement it; we need to do that and go beyond.

I salute you for forming a State officials advisory group on welfare reform with Governors and legislators and health and welfare directors from 10 States. I want to tell you today that within the next 10 days I will announce a welfare reform group to work with you. I will ask top officials from the White House, the Health and Human Services, and other agencies involved to sit down with Governors and congressional leaders and develop a welfare reform plan that will work. I have asked the best people in the Nation on this subject to come and help me do this.

The day I took office I promised the American people I would fight for more opportunity for all and demand more responsibility from all. And that is a commitment I am determined to keep, with your help, by putting an end to welfare as we know it.

Our working group will learn from and work with State officials, business and labor folks, and leaders from every walk of life who care about this issue. On welfare reform, as on health care reform, there are no top-down, made-in-Washington solutions that will work for everyone. The problems and the progress are to be found in the communities of this country.

But I do want to tell you the principles this morning that will guide my administration as we work with you to reform welfare. First, welfare should be a second chance, not a way of life. I want to give people on welfare the education and training and the opportunities they need to become self-sufficient. To make sure they can do it after they go to work, they must still have access to health care and to child care. So many people stay on welfare not because of the checks; the benefit levels, as many of you know, in real dollar terms are lower than they were 20 years ago. They do it solely because they do not want to put their children at risk of losing health care or because they do not have the money to pay for child care out of the meager wages they can earn coming from a low education base. We have got to deal with that.

I believe 2 years after a training program is completed, you have to ask people to take a job ultimately, either in the private sector or in public service. There must be, in addition to the full implementation of the welfare reform act of 1988, in my opinion, a time-certain beyond which people don't draw a check for doing nothing when they can do something. And there is a lot of work out there to be done.

Senator Boren and Senator Wofford have offered a bill to try to recreate on a very limited basis a pilot project that would take the best of what was done with the work programs of the thirties and try to throw them into the context of the nineties. We must begin now to plan for a time when people will ultimately be able to work for the check they get, whether the check comes from a private employer or from the United States taxpayers.

Today, about half the people on welfare are just the people welfare was meant to help. They fall on hard times, and they have to have public assistance. They're eager to move on with their lives. And after 5 or 6 months or 8 months they're right back at work again, struggling to make their way in the American way. About half the people on welfare stay on for over 2 years. But one in four persons, the people that we really need to try to help to break the cycle that is gripping their children and grandchildren, about one in four stays a recipient for 8 years or longer. Those are the folks that Governor Wilder I know is now working on, that many of you have tried to address the problems of, and I want to help you with that.

Second, we need to make work pay. We have to make sure that every American who works full-time, with a child in the home, does not live in poverty. If there is dignity in all work, there must be dignity for every worker. Therefore, I will propose an expansion in the earned-income tax credit which supplements the income of the working poor.

We can do that. We ought to be able to lift people who work 40 hours a week, with kids in their home, out of poverty. And we will remove the incentive for staying in poverty. It will be much less expensive than to have Government direct supplements to pay people to remain idle. And it will reinforce the work ethic. If we can do that and at the same time do what we discussed yesterday, control health care costs and expand coverage so that no one has to stay on welfare just to take care of their children's medical needs, I think you will see a dramatic breakthrough in our efforts to liberate people from their dependency.

Third, we need tougher child support enforcement. An estimated 15 million children have parents who could pay child support but don't. We need to make sure that they do. Parents owe billions of dollars in child support that is unpaid, money that could go a long way toward cutting the welfare rolls and lifting single parents out of poverty and money that could go a long way toward helping us control Government expenditures and reducing that debt. We're going to toughen child support enforcement by creating a national databank to track down deadbeat parents, by having the States go as far as they possibly can to establish paternity at the hospital when children are born, and if I can prevail up here, by using the IRS to collect unpaid support in seriously delinquent cases. I've said it before because it's the simple truth: Governments don't raise children, people do. And even people who aren't around ought to do their part to raise the children they bring into this world.

Fourth, we need to encourage experimentation in the States. I will say again what you know so well: There are many promising initiatives right now at the State and local level, and we will work with you to encourage that kind of experimentation. I do not want the Federal Government, in pushing welfare reforms based on these general principles, to rob you of the ability to do more, to do different things. And I want to try to flesh out a little bit of the idea we discussed yesterday about the waivers. My view is that we ought to give you more elbow room to experiment.

I know I was perplexed during the recent campaign when I tried to make a statement that some people in the press said reflected waffling, and it seemed to me to express the real genius of the federal system. I said that if I were President I would approve waivers of experiments that I did not necessarily agree with. And they said, "You're trying to have it both ways." I said, "No, I'm not. I'm trying to honor the Founding Fathers." If we didn't disagree on anything, what would be the need for experiments? That is the nature of the experiment, is that one person has an idea different from another person.

So I will encourage all of us to work together to try things that are different. And the only thing I want to ask you in return is, let us measure these experiments and let us measure them honestly, so that if they work, we can make them the rule, we can all adopt things that work. And if they don't, we can stop and try something else. That's the only thing I ask of you. If we say, okay, we're going to have more waivers and you're going to be able to experiment in projects that use Federal dollars, let's measure the experiment, let's be honest about it. And if it works, let's tell everybody it works so we can all do it. And if it doesn't, let's have the courage to quit and admit it didn't.

I think all of us want what most people on welfare want, a country that gives you a hand up, not a handout. We don't have a person to waste. We need the talent, the energy, the skills of every man and woman, every boy and girl in this country.

Of all the problems we have with competitiveness, whether it is the deficit or the level of investment or anything else, I think all of us know in our heart of hearts America's biggest problem today is that too many of our people never get a shot at the American dream and that if all of our people were living up to the fullest of their potential, we would surely have a much easier path in solving all the issues that we constantly debate about at these meetings.

Of all my moments as Governor, one I remember with the most pride occurred here at a National Governors' Association meeting during that 2-year period when we were working on welfare reform. Governor Castle and I sponsored a panel, and I think 40 Governors attended. And we had welfare recipients from all over the country come in and talk to the Governors about what it was like to be on welfare.

A woman from Arkansas who was there, whom I knew but had not vetted for this conversation, started talking about her program and how she'd gone into a training program and she had gotten a job, all of that. And I did something lawyers are told never to do: I asked a question without knowing the answer. I said, "Do you think this program ought to be mandatory? Should everybody have to participate in this?" She said, "I sure do." And I said, "Why?" And she said, "Well, because if it wasn't, there would be a lot of people like me home watching the soaps because we don't believe we can make anything of ourselves anymore. So you've got to make it mandatory." And I said, "What's the best thing about having a job?" She said, "When my boy goes to school, and they say, 'What does your mama do for a living?', he can give an answer."

I think that moment says more than I will ever be able to say about why this is important, not just important for the poor but important for the rest of us. We must end poverty for Americans who want to work. And we must do it on terms that dignify all of the rest of us, as well as help our country to work better. I need your help, and I think we can do it.

Thank you very much.

NOTE: The President spoke at 10 a.m. at the J.W. Marriott Hotel.

Letter to Federal Emergency Management Agency Acting Director William C. Tidball on Disaster Assistance for Louisiana
February 2, 1993

Dear Mr. Tidball:

I have determined that the damage in certain areas of the State of Louisiana, resulting from severe storms and flooding on January 20 through January 25, 1993, is of sufficient severity and magnitude to warrant a major disaster declaration under the Robert T. Stafford Disaster Relief and Emergency Assistance Act ("the Stafford Act"). I, therefore, declare that such a major disaster exists in the State of Louisiana.

In order to provide Federal assistance, you are hereby authorized to allocate from funds available for these purposes, such amounts as you find necessary for Federal disaster assistance and administrative expenses.

You are authorized to provide Individual Assistance in the designated areas. Public Assistance may be added at a later date, if requested and warranted. Consistent with the requirement that Federal assistance be supplemental, any Federal funds provided under the Stafford Act for Public Assistance will be limited to 75 percent of the total eligible costs.

Sincerely,

WILLIAM J. CLINTON

NOTE: This letter was made available by the Office of the Press Secretary but was not issued as a White House press release.

Letter to Governor Edwin W. Edwards on Disaster Assistance for Louisiana
February 2, 1993

Dear Governor Edwards:

As requested, I have declared a major disaster under the Robert T. Stafford Disaster Relief and Emergency Assistance Act (the Stafford Act) for the State of Louisiana due to damage resulting from severe storms and flooding on January 20 through January 25, 1993. I have authorized Federal relief and recovery assistance in the affected area.

Individual Assistance will be provided. Public Assistance may be added at a later date, if requested and warranted. Consistent with the requirement that Federal assistance be supplemental, any Federal funds provided under the Stafford Act for Public Assistance will be limited to 75 percent of the total eligible costs in the designated areas.

The Federal Emergency Management Agency ("FEMA") will coordinate Federal assistance efforts and designate specific areas eligible for such assistance. The Federal Coordinating Officer will be Mr. Leland R. Wilson of FEMA. He will consult with you and assist in the execution of the FEMA-State Disaster Assistance Agreement governing the expenditure of Federal Funds.

Sincerely,

BILL CLINTON

NOTE: This letter was made available by the Office of the Press Secretary but was not issued as a White House press release.

Nomination for Deputy Secretary and Assistant Secretaries of Housing and Urban Development
February 2, 1993

The President today nominated four recognized leaders in the housing field to work with Secretary Henry Cisneros as top officials at the Department of Housing and Urban Development. The nominees for Deputy Secretary and three Assistant Secretary positions are recognized and experienced leaders in the housing field.

As Deputy Secretary, the President nominated Terry Duvernay, executive director of the Geor-gia Housing and Finance Authority, and HUD Chief of Staff under Secretary Moon Landrieu. Also nominated were Andrew Cuomo, the founder and president of an innovative and successful New York area housing organization, to be Assistant Secretary for Community Planning and Development; San Francisco Board of Supervisors member Roberta Achtenberg, to be Assistant Secretary for Fair Housing and Equal Opportunity; and Jean Nolan, formerly director of communications for The Enterprise Foundation, a national foundation that works to provide housing for low-income people, to be Assistant Secretary for Public Affairs.

"I am committed," said the President, "as is Secretary Cisneros, to turning the Department of Housing and Urban Development into a center for action and a home for innovation. Terry Duvernay, Andrew Cuomo, Roberta Achtenberg, and Jean Nolan have a big task ahead of them—rebuilding housing opportunity for all Americans and repairing the torn fabric of our nation's urban communities. These four outstanding individuals have the experience, the knowledge, and the ability to make that happen. They will be an essential part of my team."

NOTE: Biographies of the nominees were made available by the Office of the Press Secretary.

Remarks to Office of Management and Budget Employees
February 3, 1993

Thank you very much, Mr. Vice President. Mr. Panetta, Ms. Rivlin, ladies and gentlemen. I'm really sorry to know that the Vice President has a lavish office in this building. If it gets any hotter over at the White House he may want to occupy it. [*Laughter*]

I want to tell you how very proud I am to be here today, how grateful I am for the enormous amount of work I know all of you have been doing because of the tight timetables we have set on ourselves leading up to the February 17th address to Congress. Nobody in this country is working any harder than you are to give the promises I made to the American people a chance to take life. And I just wanted to come by here today and say a simple thank you.

For years politicians have run for President and Governor and other offices by running against the Government. And to be sure, there is a lot to run against; there is a lot which needs to be changed. There are people here in this room today that know more specifically about what needs to be changed than those of us who give speeches about it. But I think it is terribly important, in the midst of all that rhetoric, not to forget that behind that Government that needs to be changed there are people who have decided to give their lives to the interest of the United States and its citizens. And they deserve to be honored. And I do appreciate that.

I wanted to tell you today a little bit about why I think I got elected to this job and what I hope, together, we can do, and most importantly, what's behind the enormous and increasingly complex challenges facing this country.

Let me begin by relating a simple experience I had a few months ago which affected me deeply, involving a man named Benjamin Edwards, a 52-year-old man who lived in Philadelphia. The night of the first Presidential debate, he had a viewing party at his house, but it was a highly unusual viewing party. He was out of work, and his electricity had been turned off because he couldn't pay the bills. So his neighbors brought over television sets and lamps and ran extension cords from a nearby apartment because that's the only way they could watch it. About 100 of them did. And the next day Benjamin Edwards took a bus 15 miles to attend one of our campaign rallies. As I came down the line, he grabbed my hand and told me to win the election because he had to have a job. I told him that if I won the election I'd try to get him a job. Well, he's got a job now because he became somewhat famous as a result of this incident. [*Laughter*]

But there are millions and millions of other Americans who still don't. I read an article yesterday in the paper about another unemployed person who had voted for me who had only gotten a form response from the White House. And I told somebody today to pick up the phone and call him and talk to him and try to make him feel connected to his Government again.

I say this to reiterate something that I think most of you already know, but it's easy to forget here working in the splendid isolation of the Capital City. Budgets are not about numbers; they're about people. They mean jobs and health care, education or training. We can't ever afford to let our people get lost in a blizzard of statistics.

Since the election we've learned even more about the difficulty of the budgets and the difficulty of putting together an economic program that puts people to work in the short run and deals with the long-term problems of this economy.

Just today we got the news about the economic indicators for the month of December being the best in 10 years and yet the disturbing prospect that a lot of new jobs are not being created. How could this be so? Well, partly because there's been no inflation in the economy and interest rates have been down for some while; people are now beginning to refinance their home, debts, or buy and sell new homes, so that generates a lot of economic activity. And partly because we have an inordinate number of companies in our free enterprise system who have gotten more and more productive and therefore earning more money. The problem is that a lot of them are doing what we need to do, which is to gradually downsize. A lot of them are not hiring new people, even though their incomes are going way up.

Now, during the eighties that happened to the Fortune 500 companies, which reduced employment by over a couple hundred thousand a year all during the eighties. But all those jobs were made up for in the eighties by small businesses hiring new people. And yet, now small business hiring is dropping, too, as small businesses are loathe to hire new people because they can't afford to pay for health care or because they can't get credit from their local banks.

So we have this anomalous situation where the economy seems to be growing but employment is not, and where more and more middle-income workers are working harder and harder every year but their wages aren't keeping up with inflation, and the costs of health care and education are outstripping inflation.

So we have this perplexing dilemma. How can we build on what the free enterprise system is doing that is good, get small business growth going again, and increase investment so that we generate more high-wage jobs, so that the economy can grow, not just in the overall statistics but in the real lives of real people? That's important to you, not only because of your mission at OMB but because how you do is a reflection of how the taxpayers do, since they pay your bill.

So you have an immediate as well as a long-range interest in the success of what is our economic commitment: to do something which the American people have never before had to do, to increase investment and bring down the deficit at the same time. That is our challenge.

And on February 17 we're going to start anew in an effort to meet that challenge. We've got to turn this country around to build a long-term stable growth of jobs and income. We cannot go 10 more years with insufficient jobs and insufficient income growth for people who are working hard, playing by the rules, willing to become educated and trained in ever-new skills, meeting ever-new challenges.

That is our challenge. And we are doing our best to meet it. Since no one has ever tried to do both these things at once, to get the job base going, which we want to do with a modest stimulus program in the beginning, increase permanently investment in people and jobs and growth, and reduce the deficit, it is not always clear exactly what specific decisions we must make. But the general path we have to follow is clear, because if we don't do something about investment, we won't have the kind of high-wage jobs that will shape a good future for ourselves and our children. If we don't do something about the deficit, it will eventually overwhelm our ability to borrow money at affordable rates and to have any money left in the public purse to take care of people in need and to invest in our future.

So we have no choice but to embark on this course, but it is an uncharted course. No one has ever tried to do both things at the same time before. President Roosevelt elected to pursue investments in putting the American people back to work; deflation was so bad he didn't have to worry about the deficit. And before he had to deal with it, we were in a world war with full production and a massive deficit that then dropped dramatically as a percentage of our income for the next 35 years for the simple reason that we were growing so fast we didn't have to worry about it. Now we need a new commitment to investment, but we cannot ignore our debt.

We have to remember a few basic things, I think, in putting this program together. The first is that while every American is willing to make a contribution, the contribution we ask of every American must be viewed against what happened to them in the 1980's. In the 1980's, the middle class paid the bill while the wealthiest Americans enjoyed the fruits of their labors. Taxes went up on middle class Americans while their real incomes went down. Taxes went down on upper income Americans while their real incomes went up.

The expansion of Government services, the expansion of all the public programs was basically done on the backs of the people who weren't having any income growth. That means before we ask them to do more, we have to demand that Government do everything it can to do with less. Before I ask working Americans to work harder and pay more, I will ask the economic elite, who made more money and paid less in taxes, to pay their fair share. We have to literally be about the business, as Vice President Gore said first, of reinventing Government.

I have been very careful, I will say again, to honor the contribution of public employees. I know that to a major degree, I cannot succeed as President unless you and the people who work in all these other departments believe in our common mission.

I know that for every subject I could bring up that I want do do something about, there are 10 employees in this city of the Federal Government who know more about the details of what ought to be done than I do. I need your ideas and your energy. When I say we're going to reinvent Government, we're going to downsize some things; we're going to stop doing other things. We're going to do it in a way that lifts up the influence, the energy, and values the ideas of our best employees, not that grinds them down or uses them as political footballs. I have no interest in doing that to you or to anybody else. I think the American people know you want a change, too.

But let me just give you two or three examples. When I took office, the Labor Department had a nice executive dining room for its Secretary but not enough money to train unemployed workers. I'm going to propose a stimulus package that has some more money to train unemployed workers, and the Secretary of Labor is now eating in the dining room with the employees.

When I took office, the White House had a telephone system that had been there since President Carter and a switchboard that has been there since the 1960's. They talk about jamming the White House switchboards—you

can do it tomorrow if you want to; it's not hard. I could not have a conference call in my office on my telephone, except an unwanted one. Anybody in the central office could punch a lighted button and listen to what I had to say. [*Laughter*] The American people, I think, would be pretty surprised and disappointed that after a dozen years of people who promised to run the Government like a business—they meant a business in the 1950's, not for the 21st century. [*Laughter*]

So we are committed to making the kinds of structural changes that every major organization in this country has had to make in order to survive. It is not right for us to spend taxpayers' money on antiquated communications systems, on unjustifiable perks, and on a system that cannot be, cannot be justified to the American people, given the times that they're having and the sacrifices we're going to ask of them.

In the next several days, I will be finalizing and announcing plans which will demonstrate a substantial reduction in spending at the White House, reversing many years of growth in services and personnel provided to the President. We're going to rely more on help from people in the departments to run the Government and on a new partnership to move the country forward. And we're going to set an example by saving money for the taxpayers, which will then have to be followed by everybody else in the executive branch and I hope in the legislative branch as well.

Second, I'm going to ask, as I said, those who made more money in the eighties and paid fewer taxes to pay their fair share before I ask anyone in the working middle class to pay more. But we have to recognize that together we have to find a way to change the mix of Government spending away from so much consumption toward more investment and, at the same time, to reduce the deficit so we can bring interest rates down and bring up long-term living standards. We have no right, frankly, to continue to finance a Government budget that is 20 percent debt-financed, and will be more debt-financed in the years ahead, and leave it to our children to figure out how to live with lower incomes than they otherwise would have. And believe me, it isn't just our children. We're going to be living with the consequences in the very near future.

And I might add something that all of you who work on budgets know, which is that one of the huge dilemmas we face—and that can't be resolved today in this speech, but I just want to lay it out there—is one that all of you know. And that is we are spending 14 percent of our income on health care. No other country except Canada spends more than 9, and they're just a little above 9.

And every day we read in the paper another expert, just like there's one today, saying, well, you certainly can't save any money on health care costs in this country. God forbid that you should put any of that in there; you can't do that. If we can't do that, we can't fix the deficit; we can't fix the economy; we can't turn America around. And if we could lower the rate of health care spending increase, we would save more than twice as much money in the private sector and in the public sector, unleashing more money for investment than anything we can do in terms of tax cuts, spending increases, or anything else to turn this economy around. So there's plenty for us to do.

What I want you to know is that I do not believe our problems are insoluble. And one of my major goals is to leave the next President with a new set of things to worry about. [*Laughter*] I'm getting bored reading the same problems in the paper, decade after decade. I want people to have to deal with new problems.

I am asking you today to do two things: First of all, to personally invest yourself in this great mission. It is our job in this generation to deal with these problems so that the American dream

can endure. Ultimately, that is why everybody should come to work for the Federal Government and why everyone's job counts. And I am asking you to remember how terribly difficult life is for many people who pay our bills and pay your salary and mine.

I got an incredibly moving call the other day from a friend of mine, shortly before I took office, in which he said he had just talked to a person who worked in his office who said that—in bad grammar but compelling truth— he said, "This woman came up to me and said, 'You know, it's scary to be a little people.' " And it really is.

I want to send a signal to this country that I may not do everything right, and I can't do everything that's just popular in the short run, but every day in every way we're trying to set an example for the people that sent us here. We don't want the people to sacrifice their income before the Government sacrifices everything it can. We don't want the people who bore the burden in the eighties to make any contributions before people who reaped the benefits of the eighties do their fair share, and that together we really do believe we can make a difference. If you help me and we work together, I'm confident that we can.

Thank you, and bless you all.

NOTE: The President spoke at 11:02 a.m. in the New Executive Office Building.

Exchange With Reporters Prior to a Meeting With Economic Advisers
February 3, 1993

Q. Mr. President, while we have you, why do Social Security recipients in the middle class appear to be getting a little bit more nervous as your economic plan unfolds? Should they be?

The President. Well, the way you folks were leaking the story today—[*laughter*].

The people of this country ought to know that I'm going to do my best to be fair to the people that I ran to represent and to get the job machine of this country moving again and bring the deficit down. And I think the people will believe that I've been fair and comprehensive when the plan comes out. But you

know, it's very difficult for us to make decisions in an environment where we have no control over who says what, about what really comes out, and half the stuff that comes out is not even accurate. So all I can tell you is I'm not going to comment on the specifics until I settle on the plan, and then I'll come forward with it. But it will be consistent with what I said today to the employees over at the OMB.

Thank you.

NOTE: The President spoke at 2:25 p.m. in the Roosevelt Room at the White House.

Exchange With Reporters Prior to Meeting With Democratic Congressional Leaders
February 3, 1993

Q. Mr. President, when do you want campaign's finance reforms to go into effect?

The President. We're here to talk about what's going to be in the bill. I want to pass a bill early this year, as early as we can, and we're going to talk about that.

There was a good bill last year—it had a lot of good features in it—which was vetoed by President Bush. And I guess we'll start talking about that and see where we go from there.

But I hope we can get a good bill.

In terms of when it goes into effect, and the last bill skipped an election cycle and was widely applauded by all the public interest groups as a great advance over where we are now. I think when it goes into effect is a subject of discussion here. But I want to pass a good bill. That's my concern.

NOTE: The President spoke at 3:49 p.m. in the Cabinet Room at the White House.

Letter to Federal Emergency Management Agency Acting Director William C. Tidball on Disaster Assistance for California
February 3, 1993

Dear Mr. Tidball:

I have determined that the damage in certain areas of the State of California, resulting from severe winter storms, mud and rock slides, and flooding on January 5–22, 1993, is of sufficient severity and magnitude to warrant a major disaster declaration under the Robert T. Stafford Disaster Relief and Emergency Assistance Act ("the Stafford Act"). I, therefore, declare that such a major disaster exists in the State of California.

In order to provide Federal assistance, you are hereby authorized to allocate from funds available for these purposes, such amounts as you find necessary for Federal disaster assistance

and administrative expenses.

You are authorized to provide Individual Assistance and Public Assistance in the designated areas. Consistent with the requirement that Federal assistance be supplemental, any Federal funds provided under the Stafford Act for Public Assistance will be limited to 75 percent of the total eligible costs.

Sincerely,

BILL CLINTON

NOTE: This letter was made available by the Office of the Press Secretary but was not issued as a White House press release.

Letter to Governor Pete Wilson on Disaster Assistance for California
February 3, 1993

Dear Governor Wilson:

As requested, I have declared a major disaster under the Robert T. Stafford Disaster Relief and Emergency Assistance Act (the Stafford Act) for the State of California due to damage resulting from severe winter storms, mud and rock

slides, and flooding on January 5–22, 1993. I have authorized Federal relief and recovery assistance in the affected area.

Individual Assistance and Public Assistance will be provided. Consistent with the requirement that Federal assistance be supplemental, any Federal funds provided under the Stafford Act for Public Assistance will be limited to 75 percent of the total eligible costs in the designated areas.

The Federal Emergency Management Agency ("FEMA") will coordinate Federal assistance efforts and designate specific areas eligible for such assistance. The Federal Coordinating Officer will be Mr. Frank Kishton of FEMA. He will consult with you and assist in the execution of the FEMA-State Disaster Assistance Agreement governing the expenditure of Federal Funds.

Sincerely,

BILL CLINTON

NOTE: This letter was made available by the Office of the Press Secretary but was not issued as a White House press release.

Nomination for Deputy Secretary of Defense
February 3, 1993

The President today nominated William J. Perry, a highly respected expert on military technology, to serve as Deputy Secretary of Defense under Secretary Les Aspin.

"William Perry is a sound and sophisticated adviser whose expertise on military technology and policy is unmatched," said President Clinton. "Secretary Aspin and I will rely heavily on his knowledge, imagination, and judgment as we work to keep our military the strongest in the world in a time of budgetary constraints."

NOTE: A biography of the nominee was made available by the Office of the Press Secretary.

Remarks at the National Prayer Breakfast
February 4, 1993

Thank you very much. Congressman Emerson and distinguished guests at the head table; to my friend Reverend Billy Graham and Ruth; and to all those who have given such moving presentations. This has been a wonderful morning, I think, for all of us.

When I heard Wentley Phipps recounting our first, rather awkward meeting, I thought that I would admit to being Governor of Alabama just to hear him sing. [*Laughter*]

My mind has been full of memories this morning. I helped to start the first Governor's prayer breakfast in my State; it became a very important part of our life there. And every year I had the pleasure of delegating two Arkansans, one a clergyman or -woman and one a citizen, to come to this wonderful event.

I thought about the first time I ever saw Billy Graham—appropriate to mention now. He came in the 1950's, in the heat of all our racial trouble, to Arkansas to have a crusade. And the white citizens council tried to get him, because of the tensions of the moment, to agree to segregate his crusade in the fifties in the South. And he said, "If I have to do that, I'm not coming." And I remember I got a Sunday school teacher in my church—and I was about 11 years old—to take me 50 miles to Little Rock so I could hear a man preach who was trying to live by what he said. And then I remember, for a good while thereafter, trying to send a little bit of my allowance to the Billy Graham crusade because of the impression he made on me then.

I am honored that all of you are here not for a political purpose. We come here to seek the help and guidance of our Lord, putting aside our differences, as men and women who freely acknowledge that we don't have all the answers. And we come here seeking to restore and renew and strengthen our faith.

In this town, as much as any place on the face of the Earth, we need that. We need faith as a source of strength. "The assurance of things hoped for, the conviction of things unseen," the Scripture says. What it means to me is that here, if we have enough faith, in spite of all the pressures to the contrary, we can define ourselves from the inside out, in a town where everybody tries to define you from the outside in.

We need our faith as a source of hope because it teaches us that each of us is capable of redemption and, therefore, that progress is possible—not perfection, for all the reasons Reverend Graham said, but progress. We need our faith as a source of challenge because if we read the Scriptures carefully, it teaches us that all of us must try to live by what we believe or, in more conventional terms, to live out the admonition of President Kennedy that here on Earth God's work must truly be our own.

But perhaps most important of all for me, we need our faith, each of us, President, Vice President, Senator, Congressman, General, Justice, as a source of humility, to remember that, as Bishop Sheen said, we are all sinners. St. Paul once said in an incredibly moving Scripture in the Bible, "The very thing which I would not do, that I do, and that which I would, that I do not." And even more, not only because we do wrong but because we don't always know what is right.

In funerals and weddings and other important ceremonies, you often hear that wonderful verse from Corinthians cited: "Now abideth faith, hope, and love, but the greatest of these is love." But the important thing is often left out, which is the verse above. Why is the greatest of these love? Because "now I see through a glass, darkly . . . now I know only in part." None of us know all that we need to know to do what we need to do.

I have always been touched by the living example of Jesus Christ and moved particularly by all the religious leaders of His day who were suspicious of Him and always trying to trap Him because He was so at ease with the hurting and the hungry and the lonely and, yes, the sinners. And in one of those marvelous attempts to trick Christ, He was asked, "What is the greatest Commandment?" And He answered, quoting Moses, "You shall love the Lord, your God, with all your heart and with all your soul and with all your mind." And then He added, as we should add, "This is the great and foremost Commandment. And the second is like it: You shall love your neighbor as yourself."

Just 2 weeks and a day ago, I took the oath of office as President. You know the last four words, for those who choose to say it in this way, are "so help me God." And the Chief Justice was giving me the oath, and I was trying to remember the words. And I said, you know, when I get to the end I'm going to think of the ringing voice of Washington and Jefferson and Lincoln and the Roosevelts and Kennedy and all the other great Presidents through the ages, and I will say "so help me God" with all the strength at my command. And I did. But deep down inside I wanted to say it the way I was thinking it, which was, "So, help me, God." [*Laughter*]

So today my prayer for you as we begin this great new adventure, and I pray that your prayer for me, will be that God will help us to have the strength to define ourselves from the inside out, not the outside in, to have the hope that it takes never to give up and the determination it takes always to make progress in an imperfect world and the humility to walk by faith and not by sight.

Thank you very much.

NOTE: The President spoke at 9:30 a.m. at the Washington Hilton.

Exchange With Reporters During a Luncheon With the Vice President
February 4, 1993

The Economy and Job Creation

Q. Mr. President, with productivity soaring and factory orders up, does this mean it's a strong recovery and you might have to adjust your economic plan?

The President. Well, we haven't—it could mean that more evidence will come in the deficit will be smaller. But there's no—it could mean that we'll have more jobs, which is the real issue. But we don't see it yet.

I think the real issue—what appears to be the case is that American productivity is up and that a lot of Americans are refinancing their homes or buying new homes because of low interest rates. But so far, we're not adding jobs to the economy. That's the critical thing.

I think it means we need to take a real close look at the credit crunch for small business. I think it means we need to redouble our efforts on health care cost restraints because that's one of the things that's preventing small business from hiring more people. But if you look at the downsizing going on in a lot of these big companies, we still need a program which will help us to generate jobs and higher income jobs. And that's the focus that I had for several months now.

I'm happy that the productivity rates picked up, and I'm glad that people are able to finance their homes at lower interest rates. But I'm still not convinced that this country is yet set on the right course in terms of generating the jobs.

And that's the key thing: jobs.

Q. What if the markets, which seem encouraged by your commitment to deficit reduction, go down if you don't live up to your promise of 145,000 jobs?

The President. I think they want us to have a steady, disciplined, downward path on the deficit. But I also would point out that sometimes when the markets have been up, the job market has been down. The market that counts is the market that affects ordinary Americans. Do they have jobs? Are their incomes going up? And that's why I think we have to increase investment for jobs and decrease the debt. And we're going to do our best to do both. On February 17th I'm going to——

NOTE: The exchange began at 12:30 p.m. in the Oval Office at the White House. A tape was not available for verification of the content of this exchange.

Statement on Secretary of State Warren M. Christopher's Trip to the Middle East
February 4, 1993

In accord with my pledge to maintain continuity in the Arab-Israeli peace negotiations, I have decided to dispatch Secretary of State Christopher to the Middle East. His purpose will be to convey to all the parties my commitment to advance the peace negotiations. He will elicit their views on how best to promote progress, and he will discuss bilateral issues and regional problems, including Iraq.

This will be Secretary Christopher's first mission abroad. It is an indication of the priority my administration attaches to peacemaking in the Middle East. It also presents an opportunity for the parties to focus their energies on the formidable challenge of achieving peace in a strife-torn region.

With violence engulfing so much of the world, it is striking that in the Middle East a process of direct negotiations has begun. Israel, all its Arab neighbors, and the Palestinians have been

engaged in a common endeavor to achieve a just, lasting, and comprehensive peace based on U.N. Security Council Resolutions 242 and 338.

The United States, together with our Russian cosponsor, played a critical role in launching these negotiations. It is my intention to see that we continue that role.

We cannot impose a solution on the Middle East. Only the leaders of the region can make peace. Theirs is an awesome responsibility. Those who oppose the process, who seek to subvert it through violence and intimidation, will find no tolerance here for their methods. But those who are willing to make peace will find in me and my administration a full partner. This is an historic moment. It can slip away all too easily. But if we seize the opportunity, we can begin now to construct a peaceful Middle East for future generations.

Exchange With Reporters Prior to Discussions With Foreign Minister Klaus Kinkel of Germany
February 4, 1993

National Service Plan

Q. Mr. President, are you disappointed that you've had to scale back your national service plan? You've scaled it back to a pilot program, and is that a big disappointment to you?

The President. No, I haven't. That article was a complete surprise to me this morning.

Q. How so?

The President. I haven't made any decision to scale it back to a pilot program. I had a meeting just yesterday on national service, and I'm working on funding it just as close to what I recommended in the campaign book, "Putting People First," as possible. We always knew that we would phase it in to some extent in the sense that there would be a limited number of young people in the early years that would be in the service programs, and that it would build up over a 6-year period. That's what we proposed all last year. But I'm not at all sure that we're going to cut back much from what we recommended.

Q. So you think it will take 6 years to fully fund it and have every American have an opportunity for a college education?

The President. No, no. I think it will take 6 years before the number of young people who choose the service option as opposed to the repayment option hits its maximum number. That's what we calculated last year in the campaign and what we put out in our book. But unless the mechanics are such that we can't implement the service program, which I don't believe is the case, I would expect us to be well beyond what you would call a pilot program as soon as we implement it. I was surprised by the slant of the Post story this morning, because I think we'll do more than that.

Bosnia

Q. Mr. President, can you think of anything positive to say about the Bosnian peace plan that has been offered?

The President. Yes, I think anything, any effort that increases the chance of some ultimately peaceful solution is important. But I think the United States has under review now all of its options in that area. And I think at this time

the position that the Secretary of State has taken is the one that we have agreed on and the one that I think is proper.

Q. Are you close to an announcement, though?

Q. When will you have something more to say about that, Mr. President?

Q. Sprechen Sie deutsch, Mr. President?

Q. Are you practicing your German?

The President. I haven't been conversational in 24 years. Maybe I can brush up on it.

Q. But you read it?

The President. Yes, I can still read pretty well.

Foreign Minister Kinkel. Do you know our country?

The President. Yes, I've been there several times. When I was at Georgetown, I took 3 years of German. And I was in Germany in '69 and '70, and I've been back a few times since. And then I was in Baden-Baden in 1991 at the Bilderberg meeting.

Foreign Minister Kinkel. Oh, I see. For some days?

The President. For several days. The Bilderberg meeting was 3 or 4 days, I would guess.

Foreign Minister Kinkel. That means that you understand a little bit German?

The President. A little, yes. I haven't spoken it, literally, in 24 years. But when I was in the country, I heard the people talking, and usually I know a lot of what they're saying.

Foreign Minister Kinkel. You can read a newspaper, perhaps?

The President. I can read quite a bit of the newspaper. I ran—I was in—where was I—in the English gardens in Munich. I ran in a 10K race there a couple of years ago when I was over there on a trade mission. And they wrote it up in the newspaper. And someone sent me the article, and I read the whole article. I could read that. So I can read a little bit. And my daughter goes to German camp every summer.

Foreign Minister Kinkel. Yes, I read it in my paper. This is important because these are my press people from Germany. And they are interested especially in this, your relations to our country.

The President. Oh, I've been there many times. I first went in '69, and I've been going a lot since then. And my daughter, as I said, goes to this German village in Minnesota, language camp, every year now for 5 years.

Foreign Minister Kinkel. And she speaks our language?

The President. Well, a little bit. You know, it's a children's camp. They send the kids to the camp, and the camp is built like a German village. And they give them German names, German money, a German passport, and they have to speak conversational German.

But next year, when she moves into high school, she will go for a month and begin an academic study. And then she will get, and each year she goes for the next 4 years, a year's academic credit for studying it. So by the time she finishes in high school she should be pretty close to conversational.

NOTE: The exchange began at 4:20 p.m. in the Oval Office at the White House.

Remarks at a Dinner Honoring the New Jersey Congressional Delegation
February 4, 1993

Good evening. Thank you. I know we're not really, but it feels like it's nice to be back in New Jersey. And I'm glad to have you here in the Nation's Capital. You may or may not be able to see this, but on the way in tonight, Bill Faherty gave me a New Jersey tie, which I have proudly donned. They even had a mirror outside for me to be able to tie it in a straight and appropriate fashion. [*Laughter*]

I want to tell you how very glad I am to be here tonight with the State chamber, how much I want to welcome you to our Nation's Capital. I've just been here as President 2 weeks and a day, and I'm already hoping we can keep an infusion of people from the heartland coming in to keep us in touch with reality.

I'm glad to see all the Members of the House here. Senator Bradley and Senator Lautenberg are voting tonight as the United States Senate attempts to work out the family leave bill. I do want to say a special word of appreciation to both of them in front of their constituents for not only the support they have given me but for the genuinely good advice across a whole wide range of issues. I have the sort of relationship with them which I really respect and which I hope the Members of Congress here will take to heart. Either one of them is liable to call me at any time of the day or night from places unknown. Always all right places, but—[*laughter*]—I mean, when they're around, you know. And I'm very, very grateful to both of them not only for their support in the recent election but for their involvement in the great issues of this time.

I've been working hard for the last 2 weeks to try to be worthy of the trust of the voters of this country who gave me a chance to become President, including the people of New Jersey who voted for a Democrat for the first time in 28 years. I know you haven't always been able to tell it from the news, but I spent virtually all of my time working on the economy, the jobs issues, the deficit, meeting in long periods with my staff, with people from around the country who know about these matters, with Members of the United States Congress, working with people in both parties to try to end the gridlock and to reach agreement so that we can move forward.

We've had, as all of you know now, an economic upturn in the last few months, and we hope that we are coming out firmly of the longest recession we've had in a good long while. There is much to be encouraged about in two or three areas. First of all, interest rates have been down for a good long while now, and millions of Americans have refinanced their homes or been able to buy new homes in ways that have generated significant economic activity. Second, and even more encouraging over the long run, there has been a big increase in the productivity of American businesses and workplaces. That is, after all, the key to our economic future. And finally, beginning in December with a little bit in November, but a big increase in December in consumer confidence, which has strengthened the consumer market in our country, something we hope will carry through for the next few months.

Still, there are clear challenges before us. With all these good numbers coming in, very few new jobs have been created in America yet in this recovery. Most big businesses that are doing better are still downsizing; it's a part of their productivity. That happened all during the 1980's, when in every year of the 1980's the Fortune 500 companies reduced employment in total by more than a quarter of a million in the United States. But throughout much of the eighties, that reduction was more than offset by the creation of jobs in the small business sector.

In the last couple of years and regrettably even in the last few months, small business is not taking up the slack because of the crushing burden of health care costs and because of the credit crunch, which is much more severe in some States and regions than others but which is a very serious problem for our economy.

We also have a deficit that next year is projected to be $50 billion bigger as of December than we were told in August and is growing exponentially, even though the Congressmen who are here can tell you that they made a good faith effort in 1990 to rein the deficit in with spending cuts and tax increases they thought would do it. It didn't happen because the taxes didn't bring in as much money as they thought, but even more importantly because health care costs have continued unabated, rising at breathtaking rates. So that at the end of this year—those of you who pay health insurance will know this—but we now, alone of all the advanced countries in the world, are spending 14 percent of our income on health care. No other country except Canada is over 9.

That is a terrific competitive disadvantage. It is costing you a great deal of money not only as taxpayers, for what you pay for Government health care, but in the private sector. And the hemorrhage is such that about 100,000 Americans a month are now losing their health insurance, many of them finding their way onto the public rolls and leading to explosive increases in the Government's health care burden.

So as we look ahead to our challenges and as I look ahead to this speech I have to give on February 17th to the joint session of Congress, I still believe in the fundamental themes on which I ran for President: We have to in-

crease job growth and income growth without increasing inflation. We have to face the serious problems of our urban areas and the serious problems of the underclass in ways that liberate the ability of all people to perform at high levels in this economy if we want to continue the increase in productivity. That means that we have to shift away in the money that you give us to spend, away from consumption, more toward investment. We have to increase investment in new technologies and education and training, in infrastructure and the things that will grow this economy. It also means that we have to provide more incentives in our Tax Code for investment in the private sector. And it means we have to act at long last to bring health care costs in line with inflation. If we did that, it would do more to free up private sector dollars to invest in economic growth than any tax cut I could sign into law or any spending increase that Congress and I together can enact.

So we will begin in earnest as soon as this break is over to do those things that your National Government has never had to do simultaneously before: We will attempt to increase investment and reduce the deficit at the same time. It will require an enormous amount of discipline and a willingness to try some new things and to cut some things in ways that we have not done before.

I hope you will all wish us well, and I hope you will tell every Member of your congressional delegation up here, without regard to party, that you know they're going to have to cast some difficult votes in order for this country to face its problems, and if they do it in good conscience and explain to you why you did it, you will not hold it against them. That's what they were hired to do, and you'll stick with them if they can do it.

You know, when I was Governor—and I did that job for a dozen years, and I had a good time doing it—there were many times when I had to cut spending five or six times in a given year. And people would be a little disconcerted at first, but we never got in debt. And I was always proud of the fact that my State had such a disciplined system. We paid a terrible price for it during the eighties when times were tough. But because we rode them out, last year we ranked first or second in job growth in virtually every month when I was off running for President, not because of anything that happened last year but because of the foundations that were laid in investments, in being competitive, and in fiscal integrity, in keeping those books balanced. Those are the kind of difficult decisions we're going to have to make now.

Not so long ago, you elected a Governor who had to make some of those decisions. And let me say that, again without attempting to be too partisan, the truth is that if you live in a State, you don't get to print your own money. You can't get in the mess that your National Government is in because you can't run that long without having the brakes come on, without throwing people through the collective windshield that keeps us all in the same boat. And I have to tell you that for all the pain that the decisions made by Governor Florio and the legislature then caused him and them, the truth is that your house is in order now. New Jersey is going to have a balanced budget without a tax increase, and you even have a rainy day fund at a time when many States are going bankrupt.

Sooner or later, we all have to face the music. And when we do, we are normally rewarded. So New Jersey is being rewarded. Look at your credit rating. Look at the overall health of the economy. Look at the trends in the State. I hope that together with the Senate and the House, with the Republicans and the Democrats in this great Capital of yours, we can come to grips with our problems in ways that the American people will understand and embrace, perhaps with less political fallout, but I hope in the end with the same sort of stability and success that you have achieved with Governor Florio. And I hope you're proud of it, because I am.

Let me just mention one other thing. I happened to think of this—it really hadn't occurred to me, but I think I ought to mention it. I asked Governor Florio, through the Trade Ambassador, Mickey Kantor, to serve on our intergovernmental advisory committee, because there's so much relationship now between our national trade policies and the policies followed at the State and local level for growth. I think he'll do a good job on that, but I wanted to emphasize it because a big part of our economic strength is in our capacity to export.

While our administration has found it necessary to take some pretty tough positions on trade issues in the last 2 weeks, I want to emphasize to you I do not take those positions in the hope of provoking a trade war or raising trade barriers in this country but only so that we can have expanded trade on fair terms for ourselves and for all nations. We cannot grow this economy, and no wealthy nation can grow, unless there is global economic growth. And I want to pledge to you that I will do my best to help all the world-class companies headquartered in New Jersey have an environment in which they can grow and flourish in the international economy, with a trade system that is constantly expanding, but expanding on terms that are genuinely fair not only to ourselves but to our trading partners as well.

I ask you all without regard to your party to wish us well. And I ask you one more time to give the Members of Congress here a pat on the back at the end of the dinner tonight. We're going to have a very challenging few months ahead of us. But it is an exciting time, and it is a fabulous opportunity for us to put our house in order and to deal with these problems and to move this country ahead.

We are now positioned better than we have been in more than a decade to reassert the leadership of the United States economically and politically in the world in a way that is very positive if we will ensure future growth, get job growth along with economic growth, and put our financial house in order. I think we can do it if all the American people, again without regard to party, agree generally on the goal. We will disagree on the details, but in the end we will come to the people's business with a resolution. That's what you need, and most importantly, it's what your children need. We cannot afford to permit the Government to go on out of control, leaving our children with a legacy of debt and diminished living standards, when we can do so much better now.

I want to thank you for what you have done, all of you in the private sector, to restore America's productivity to the breathtaking rates we've seen in this last quarter. We're going to try to give you that kind of productivity in your National Government. Thank you very much.

[At this point, the President was presented with a gift.]

I just want to say, if I ever heard a chamber of commerce speech in my life, it was that. He said, "This is a Parker pen; it's for your wife. It's the nicest one they make." And then he said, "And this other one's for you." [Laughter]

[*At this point, the President was presented with a second gift.*]

Let me say, I wish she were here to thank her personally. But this is a gift for the White House, for the American people. And I hope a lot of you from New Jersey will see this when you come in and know that it is yours. We'll leave it there for all time from the people of New Jersey.

Thank you.

NOTE: The President spoke at 7:43 p.m. at the Washington Sheraton Hotel. In his remarks, he referred to William H. Faherty, president, New Jersey Chamber of Commerce.

Remarks on Signing the Family and Medical Leave Act of 1993
February 5, 1993

Mrs. Yandle, I never had a better introduction. Before we thank anyone else, I think all of us should acknowledge that it was America's families who have beaten the gridlock in Washington to pass family leave, people like this fine woman all over America who talked to Members of Congress, both Democrat and Republican, who laid their plight out, who asked that their voices be heard. When Senator Gore and I ran in the election last year, we published a book called "Putting People First." I'm very proud that the first bill I am to sign as President truly puts people first.

I do want to thank the United States Congress for moving expeditiously on this matter and for doing it before their first recess so that every Member of Congress who voted for this bill can go home and say, "We are up there working on your problems and your promise, trying to make a better future for you." This sends a clearer signal than any words any of us could utter, that we have tried to give this Government back to the American people. And I am very appreciative that the Congress has moved so rapidly on this bill.

There are many, many Members of Congress here and many others who are not here who played a major role in this legislation. Time does not permit me to mention them all, but I do want to thank the Senate majority leader for his heroic efforts in the 11th hour to make sure we passed this bill; Senator Kennedy and Senator Dodd for their passionate and years-long commitment to this effort. I want to thank the Speaker, Speaker Foley, and Congressman Ford, the chairman of the committee that had jurisdiction over this bill, and Congresswoman Pat Schroeder and all the other Democrats who worked on this bill.

But I want to acknowledge, too, consistent with the promise I made in my Inaugural to reach out to members of both parties who would try to push for progress, that this bill also had passionate support among Republicans. My old colleague in the Governors' Association, Senator Kit Bond from Missouri, I thank you for your leadership. Senator Jeffords and Senator Coats I don't believe are here, but they supported this bill strongly; and Congresswoman Marge Roukema from New Jersey, her commitment on this was unwavering; Congresswoman Susan Molinari from New York and many other Republicans voted for, spoke for, and worked for this bill. I thank them, the subcommittee chairs who are here, and all the others who worked so hard to make this bill a real live promise kept for the Congress to the people of the United States.

Family medical leave has always had the support of a majority of Americans, from every part of the country, from every walk of life, from both political parties. But some people opposed it. And they were powerful, and it took 8 years and two vetoes to make this legislation the law of the land. Now millions of our people will no longer have to choose between their jobs and their families.

The law guarantees the right of up to 12 weeks of unpaid leave per year when it's urgently needed at home to care for a newborn child or an ill family member. This bill will strengthen our families, and I believe it will strengthen our businesses and our economy as well.

I have spent an enormous amount of time in the last 12 years in the factories and businesses of this country talking to employers and employees, watching the way people work, often working with them. And I know that men and women are more productive when they are sure they won't lose their jobs because they're trying to be good parents, good children. Our businesses should not lose the services of these dedicated Americans. And over the long run, the lessons of the most productive companies in the world, here at home and around the world, are that those who put their people first are those who will triumph in the global economy. The business leaders who have already instituted family and medical leave understand this, and I'm very proud of some of the business leaders who are here today who represent not only themselves but others all across America who were ahead of all of us who make laws in doing what is right by our families.

Family and medical leave is a matter of pure common sense and a matter of common decency. It will provide Americans what they need most: peace of mind. Never again will parents have to fear losing their jobs because of their families.

Just a week ago, I spoke to 10 people in families who had experienced the kinds of problems Mrs. Yandle has talked about today. Vice President Gore and I talked to people all across America who moved us deeply. We were saddened to hear their stories, but today all of us can be happy to think of their future.

Now that we have won this difficult battle, let me ask all of you to think about what we must do ahead to put the public interest ahead of special interest, to pass a budget which will grow this economy and shrink our deficit, and to go on about the business of putting families first. There's a lot more we need to do to help people trapped in welfare move to work and independence; to strengthen child support enforcement; to reward those who work 40 hours a week and have children at home with an increase in the earned-income tax credit so we can really say we're rewarding work instead of dependence; to immunize all the children of this country so more parents won't have to take advantage of family leave because their children will be well and strong and healthy.

Let all of us who care about our families, our people, the strength of our economy, and the future of our Nation put our partisan and other interests aside and be inspired by this great victory today to have others when Congress returns to this city and we go on about the people's business.

Thank you very much.

NOTE: The President spoke at 9:22 a.m. in the Rose Garden at the White House. In his remarks, he referred to Vicki Yandle, whose daughter's illness had resulted in both parents losing their jobs. H.R. 1, approved February 5, was assigned Public Law No. 103–3.

Statement on Signing the Family and Medical Leave Act of 1993
February 5, 1993

Today, I am pleased to sign into law H.R. 1, the "Family and Medical Leave Act of 1993." I believe that this legislation is a response to a compelling need—the need of the American family for flexibility in the workplace. American workers will no longer have to choose between the job they need and the family they love.

This legislation mandates that public and private employers with at least fifty workers provide their employees with family and medical leave. At its core is the provision for employees to take up to 12 weeks of unpaid leave for the care of a newborn or newly adopted child, for the care of a family member with a serious medical condition, or for their own illness. It also requires employers to maintain health insurance coverage and job protection for the duration of the leave. It sets minimum length of service and hours of work requirements before employees become eligible.

The need for this legislation is clear. The American workforce has changed dramatically in recent years. These changes have created a substantial and growing need for family and medical leave for working Americans.

In 1965, about 35 percent of mothers with children under 18 were labor force participants. By 1992, that figure had reached 67 percent.

By the year 2005, one of every two people entering the workforce will be women.

The rising cost of living has also made two incomes a necessity in many areas of this country, with both parents working or looking for work in 48 percent, or nearly half, of all two parent families with children in the United States.

Single parent families have also grown rapidly, from 16 percent of all families with children in 1975 to 27 percent in 1992. Finally, with America's population aging, more working Americans have to take time off from work to attend to the medical needs of elderly parents.

As a rising number of American workers must deal with the dual pressures of family and job, the failure to accommodate these workers with adequate family and medical leave policies has forced too many Americans to choose between their job security and family emergencies. It has also resulted in inadequate job protection for working parents and other employees who have serious health conditions that temporarily prevent them from working. It is neither fair nor necessary to ask working Americans to choose between their jobs and their families—between continuing their employment and tending to their own health or to vital needs at home.

Although many enlightened companies have recognized the benefits to be realized from a system providing for family and medical leave, not all do. We all as a nation must join hands and extend the ethic of long-term workplace relationships and reciprocal commitment between employer and employee. It is only when workers can count on a commitment from their employer that they can make their own full commitments to their jobs. We must extend the success of those forward-looking workplaces where high-performance teamwork has already begun to take root and where family and medical leave already is accepted.

Data from the Bureau of Labor Statistics support the conclusion that American business has been fully responsive to the need of workers for family and medical leave. This data showed that, in 1991, for private business establishments with 100 workers or more, 37 percent of all full-time employees (and 19 percent of all part-time employees) had unpaid maternity leave available to them, and only 26 percent of all full-time employees in such establishments had unpaid paternity leave available. The most recently available data for smaller business establishments (those with fewer than 100 workers) are for 1990, and show that only 14 percent of all these employees had unpaid maternity leave available, and only 6 percent had unpaid paternity leave available.

The insufficient response to the family and medical leave needs of workers has come at a high cost to both the American family and to American business. There is a direct correlation between health and job security in the family home and productivity in the workplace. When businesses do not give workers leave for family needs, they fail to establish a working environment that can promote heightened productivity, lessened job turnover, and reduced absenteeism.

We all bear the cost when workers are forced to choose between keeping their jobs and meeting their personal and family obligations. When they must sacrifice their jobs, we all have to pay more for the essential but costly safety net. When they ignore their own health needs or their family obligations in order to keep their jobs, we all have to pay more for social services and medical care as neglected problems worsen.

The time has come for Federal legislation to bring fair and sensible family and medical leave policies to the American workplace. Currently, the United States is virtually the only advanced industrialized country without a national family and medical leave policy. Now, with the signing of this bill, American workers in all 50 States will enjoy the same rights as workers in other nations. This legislation balances the demands of the workplace with the needs of families. In supporting families, it promotes job stability and efficiency in the American workplace.

The Family and Medical Leave Act of 1993 sets a standard that is long overdue in working America. I am very pleased to sign this legislation into law.

WILLIAM J. CLINTON

The White House,
February 5, 1993.

NOTE: H.R. 1, approved February 5, was assigned Public Law No. 103–3.

Exchange With Reporters Prior to Discussions With Prime Minister Brian Mulroney of Canada
February 5, 1993

The President. Hi, Helen [Helen Thomas, United Press International].

Q. Hi.

Prime Minister Mulroney. Hi, Helen. How are you?

Unemployment

Q. What's your reaction to the unemployment numbers, Mr. President?

The President. Better, but still too high: you know, at the trough of the recession, unemployment was 6.8 percent, lower than it is now. And now we've had 14 months over 7 percent, and I hope it's going down. But until we get it way down, there will still be a lot of unused capacity in the country and a lot of idle people.

Bosnia

Q. Are you going to have a statement soon on Bosnia, Mr. President?

The President. Well, Mr. Christopher is working on it, and we're working on it. I've spent a good deal of time on it in the last 2 weeks. But I don't have anything to say yet. It's a very difficult problem, I'm very concerned about it, and I have spent a good deal of time on it. When I have something to say, I will.

Q. Will that be a topic for this meeting, sir?

The President. We're going to talk about a lot of things. We don't have a typed agenda.

Q. This isn't the first time you've met, is it?

The President. Yes, but we've talked before several times.

Q. On the phone, but not——

The President. This is our first meeting.

Prime Minister Mulroney. And you were probably mentioned in those conversations. [*Laughter*]

[*At this point, one group of reporters left the room, and another group entered.*]

Trade

Q. Prime Minister, will you be seeking some assurances against the winds of protectionism in Congress you mentioned yesterday?

Prime Minister Mulroney. Yes, I will. I think that any time protectionism takes hold in the United States or Canada or elsewhere, it's bad for prosperity. It cripples growth everywhere. And so the President's a free trader, and so am I. And so I expect that we'll resolve the difficulties that we have, not in today's meeting but over a period of time. And so I look forward to the meeting. I have been very encouraged by my earlier telephone conversations with the President in regard to trade and other matters.

[*At this point, a question was asked and answered in French, and a translation was not provided.*]

Q. Mr. President, what do you think about the free trade of Canada? Is it important for U.S., do you think?

The President. I think it's very important for both of us. And I think it will have real benefits over the long run. As a Governor, I was one of those who took responsibility for trying to lobby the original agreement through the Congress here. And I hope we can complete the North American Free Trade Agreement, bringing in Mexico, making some changes that I think will be good for the Mexicans and good for the Canadians and the Americans.

But I think that if you just look at the last 50 years, the only way you can have growth within advanced countries over the long run is to have global growth. The only way you can have global growth is to expand trade.

This is a difficult time. Europe is in distress economically. Japan is having some difficulties. And of course, there will always be discussions among us about whether the rules of trade are fair or not. But our goal must continue to be the opening of trade and the increase in volume of trade.

Q. So do you want to reassure Canadians? Because there's a little fear in Canada about U.S. protectionism.

The President. Oh, I think Canada is our most important trading partner. I hope that we can do some things that will improve the economy of Canada. I'm very concerned that—our economy has started to pick up now. And normally when it does, Canada follows behind just by a few months. I want some of that growth to come back into Canada now.

One of the reasons I want to try to generate more jobs here is I think that would create more jobs in Canada. The more people we have with incomes and the more consumers we will have, the more economic impact we'll be able to have in Canada to bring that unemployment down there.

Q. What are the problems, if any, in the relationship?

The President. Well, let me say, this is our first conversation face to face. I don't want to dwell on the problems. The opportunities overwhelm the problems. And I'm sure we'll work through the problems.

Prime Minister Mulroney. Maybe I could just say, Mr. President, in regard to that, that our total trade, all in, is in Canadian dollars about $275 billion a year. It dwarfs anything that the United States has anywhere in the world. But more importantly, at the end of the year when

you factor everything in, from interest payments to dividends, our trade is in rough balance. It is extraordinary that the largest trading relationship between two nations in history is in rough balance at the end of the year, which means that with the imperfections that we have, that we've got a pretty good system that is self-governing. And from time to time, the President and the Prime Minister of Canada have to intervene to make sure that this really remarkably productive relationship with both countries is preserved and strengthened.

That's what President Clinton did. He was selling the free trade agreement when he was Governor of Arkansas throughout the United States. So I'm very encouraged by his attitudes and his record in regard to developing world trade.

NOTE: The exchange began at 11:38 a.m. in the Oval Office at the White House.

The President's News Conference With Prime Minister Brian Mulroney of Canada
February 5, 1993

Canada-U.S. Relations

The President. Good afternoon. I'm delighted that my first meeting as President with a foreign leader is with the Prime Minister of Canada, Brian Mulroney. On the day after I was elected, I spoke of the essential continuity of our country's foreign policy. Our steadfast relationship with Canada is an indispensable element of that continuity. Prime Minister Mulroney and the people of Canada should know that the United States is still their friend and their partner.

It is worth noting that the United States and Canada share the world's longest undefended border and that we haven't had a battle between us since the War of 1812. Now having said that, Mr. Prime Minister, I will tell you that I look forward to winning back the World Series. [*Laughter*]

Canada has long stood as our partner in promoting democracy and human rights around the world. Today Canada is demonstrating her international leadership for peace and freedom through her commitment of troops in peacekeeping efforts around the world, in Somalia,

in Bosnia, and elsewhere. Canada is our largest trading partner. Both our nations benefit enormously from the immense river of goods and services flowing across our border, with an increase of $30 billion just since the free trade agreement went into effect.

It is remarkable how relatively few disputes have attended the vigorous trading between us. Yet it is inevitable that there will be some disagreements even among close partners. And we agreed today to maintain high-level attention to that trading relationship, to ensure that the problems are addressed before they become crises.

The Prime Minister and I discussed the North American Free Trade Agreement. I assured him that my administration intends to move forward with NAFTA while establishing a process to provide adequate protection to workers, to farmers, and to the environment. Canada was our partner in working with Mexico to negotiate NAFTA, and Canada will be our partner as we move forward to put it and its related agreements into effect. We've made a good start here today in setting the stage for working together.

We also discussed the GATT agreement, and I reassured the Prime Minister that the United States will do what it can to secure an agreement at GATT that all the world can be proud of and can be a prosperous part of.

We reviewed a broad range of global issues, including the developments in Russia and elsewhere in the former Soviet Union, the crisis in the Balkans, the situation in Somalia and Haiti. We also discussed our participation in the Group of Seven and what the United States and Canada might hope to achieve this year, and especially this summer when the G–7 meets in Tokyo, to help move the global economy out of recession and into a strong recovery.

This was a very good beginning. I want to thank Prime Minister Mulroney for coming down from Canada and tell him that he'll always be welcome here. And I look forward to visiting you on your home turf soon.

Prime Minister Mulroney. Thank you, Mr. President. I'll simply say that, as the President indicated, we had a very full review of quite a large number of items in the few hours we spent together and a very productive working lunch. I thought it was a very good meeting and a very good beginning of the relationship of Canada with the new administration.

The President has indicated the complex issues that we've touched on, tried to deal with, principally, of course, and I think you'll understand, the relationship between Canada and the United States itself. The relationship is by far the most important one the United States has in the world. This is the biggest trading relationship ever between two nations. And at the end of the year the important thing is it tends to be in rough balance, which indicates that you can have free trade and prosper.

And so we're very concerned about the GATT, and we're very concerned about trading currents generally and very reassured by the President's strong commitments and strong positions in respect of the manner in which you bring back and reenergize prosperity around the world.

So we covered our bilateral arrangements, and we covered a lot of the hot spots around the world. And I'm sure that the President and I would be happy to take a few questions.

[*At this point, the Prime Minister repeated his statement in French.*]

Thank you very much, Mr. President.

NAFTA

Q. Mr. Prime Minister, what do you think of the changes the President wants to make in the NAFTA agreement?

Prime Minister Mulroney. Well, Helen [Helen Thomas, United Press International], the changes that the—the President doesn't—he indicated—he will, himself, I'm sure, but the President has indicated many times that he is going to sign the NAFTA agreement as it is but that he proposes to bring in supplemental agreements with Mexico, particularly in regard to some of the points that he has mentioned, that do not impact on the NAFTA agreement as concluded. That may change. If it does, I'm sure we'll hear from the President. But our information is that, by and large, that the NAFTA agreement with those supplemental accords is something that he could promote and defend very vigorously.

I think, Mr. President, that's the position.

The President. That's right. And I might add that the Prime Minister's administration in Canada has had a strong record on the environment, something that we want to try to beef up in a supplemental agreement, and that Canada would be, I think, more or less in line with the United States in terms of its impact on any supplemental labor accord we might reach.

So we certainly intend to work with them. After all, this is a three-way agreement, not a two-way agreement. But I still believe, as I said many weeks ago, that we can negotiate these agreements without reopening the NAFTA itself.

Bosnia

Q. [*Inaudible*]—the best way to proceed is to attempt to modify the U.N. plan? And how long do you think that negotiations can be relied on before stronger action is taken?

The President. Perhaps the best way to answer your question would be to let the Prime Minister communicate his views, which he communicated to me, and then let me tell you what my response is. Shall we do that?

Prime Minister Mulroney. In regard to the Bosnian situation, we think, Susan [Susan Spencer, CBS News], that the elements of an agreement—there's been a lot of constructive work done, but that there are inadequacies in it that can be corrected at the Security Council by the involvement, a greater degree of involvement by the United States in terms of the accord itself and also the involvement of President Yeltsin.

We believe that the elements of an agreement, impacted by the concern of the United States and Canada in the area of human rights, in the area of war crimes, for example, can be—these amendments can be of significant substance without altering a lot of the hard and constructive work that has taken place so far by Cy Vance and David Owen.

But it would be important that in this process at the Security Council there be greater involvement by Russia and by President Yeltsin. And I took the liberty of making some recommendations along those lines to the President, and he'll reflect upon them and probably have something to say.

The President. Let me answer now to just reaffirm what our present posture is. We have given the Bosnian situation urgent consideration. We have reviewed a wide range of options. We certainly will take into account what the Prime Minister has said. Our reluctance on the Vance-Owen proposals, while I applaud the effort both personally and as President, is that the United States at the present time is reluctant to impose an agreement on the parties to which they do not agree, especially when the Bosnian Muslims might be left at a severe disadvantage if the agreement is not undertaken in good faith by the other parties and cannot be enforced externally.

So we are looking at that. I think one of the things the Prime Minister said is absolutely right: If there is to be a diplomatic political solution to this over the long run, we very much need President Yeltsin involved and the support of Russia. He reaffirmed to me just a few days ago in our telephone conversation his general support for the policy that we have outlined. But I'm sure you can understand why with a problem this difficult, we would like a few days longer just to seriously review this to come up with what our policy is going to be. Then we'll announce it as clearly and forcefully and follow it as strongly as we possibly can.

Haiti

Q. [*Inaudible*]—is it time to strengthen pressure on Haiti? Do think we should have stronger action——

[*At this point, a question was asked and answered in French, and a translation was not provided.*]

Q. Mr. President, the same question, please.

The President. As the Prime Minister has said, our Secretary of State met today with President Aristide and discussed a wide range of issues with him as well as what our efforts have been, the progress and the lack of progress of Mr. Caputo's efforts. We talked about where we're going with this relationship in the future.

Let me say that I am committed to restoring democracy to Haiti. I am doing my best to work through the U.N. and the OAS with Mr. Caputo. I am, frankly, disappointed that the Prime Minister in Haiti has apparently backed off a little bit of his original willingness to let us send in some third-party observers, not just to protect the petitions for refugee status but also to try to stabilize conditions leading toward a restoration of democracy there. And we're going to talk to Mr. Caputo, see where he thinks things are, and then reassess our position.

But I share the Prime Minister's determination. The United States and Canada should be and are one in our commitment to restoring democracy to Haiti. And we will continue to push ahead either on the course we're now on, or if that fails, on a more vigorous course toward that end.

Israel

Q. What did you tell the President on the deportees in Israel?

Prime Minister Mulroney. We touched peripherally on the Middle East because the Secretary of State is going to, I gather, to the Middle East at an early moment. The position of Canada, my own view is that we tend not to try and give Israel lessons in regard to the determinations it has to make about its own national security. Israel's entitled to make some important value judgments about itself.

That being said, I congratulated the President and the Secretary of State for their leadership in bringing about the first step of the return of the hundred deportees, which I think was an excellent example of diplomacy and international leadership by the President.

It's the first step. It's not the whole answer. And it's a complicated matter which I think will be resolved—where the resolution of which will be clearer after Secretary of State Christopher has had an opportunity to visit the region. But I think that we're supportive of the U.N. resolutions, but I'm always very concerned when people start to lecture Israel on the manner in which it has to look after its own internal security, because for very important historical reasons, Israel, of course, is better qualified than most to make determinations about its own well-being.

Bosnia

Q. Mr. President, on Bosnia, do you expect that there would be an American diplomatic initiative to replace what you see as the flaws in the Vance-Owen initiative?

The President. I can't say that at this time. As I say, I applaud the efforts that have been made by Lord Owen and by Secretary Vance. I think that they have done the very best they could. And I don't criticize the details so much as—it's not a criticism so much as a reluctance on the part of the United States to impose on parties an agreement which they do not freely accept themselves, particularly one that might work to the immediate and to the long-term further disadvantage of the Bosnian Muslims.

But I would not rule out any option at this time. We have a wide range of options under consideration. We are working very hard on this. We will settle on a course and then do our best to consult with our allies and win broad support for it. You heard the Prime Minister say that over the long run we need President Yeltsin's involvement in this, and I agree. You heard me say that we hardly ever do anything in foreign policy that we don't have Canada's support in, and we'll need that.

So we've got a lot of work to do on this. We've been working very hard and we'll try to bring it to a quick closure.

Q. There seems to be disagreement, though, in that the Prime Minister seems to think that that can be built upon—

Q. ——come up with some agreement.

The President. I hope we can revive them. Our biggest problem in this country is the expiration of fast track authority. But we have begun a lot of talks in earnest within the administration about that. I've done my best to send a signal

to our trading partners and to the parties to GATT that we very much want a successful agreement. And I'll have more to say about that in the days ahead.

Thank you.

Haiti

[*At this point, a question was asked and answered in French, and a translation was not provided.*]

The President. Let me answer that also. I take it by what I believe was your French, of what then was a good translation I got, that you mean by complexity of the situation in Haiti the fact that Father Aristide was plainly elected by an overwhelming majority and is plainly still—has the support of an overwhelming majority of the people; but while, in the brief period when he was in authority, made some statements which caused people in the military and others to have fear for their security, their personal security, in ways that are inconsistent with running a democracy, which has to recognize human rights—does that present the complexity? Yes, that is the nub of the issue.

We have to be able to restore democracy in a way that convinces everybody that their human rights will be respected and, for an interim period, protected. And obviously, that's what the Caputo mission is designed to do.

But the complexity of the issue cannot deter us from the fundamental mission, which is to restore a democratically elected government that will not abuse the human rights of ordinary Haitians. And I agree with the Prime Minister, we certainly ought to be able to do that here in our backyard, and we're going to work hard on it.

Thank you very much.

Prime Minister Mulroney. Thank you very much.

NOTE: The President's second news conference began at 1:44 p.m. on the South Lawn of the White House. In his remarks, he referred to Lord David Owen and Cyrus Vance, Cochairmen of the International Conference on the former Yugoslavia, and Dante Caputo, U.N./OAS Special Envoy to Haiti.

Remarks to the National Conference of Mayors
February 5, 1993

Let me say, first of all, welcome to the White House.

Mayor Jackson, I saw your brother earlier today at the signing of the Family and Medical Leave Act, and he was bragging on you, said you're now as thin as he is. I assured him I would still be able to recognize you when I saw you. [*Laughter*]

This has been a wonderful day here at the White House. Congress adjourned—[*laughter*]—but only after passing the Family and Medical Leave Act. We had a great signing this morning. It was a great bipartisan effort; about a third of the Republicans in the Senate voted for it. And it was a really good, good way to start the day.

I'm glad you're here. I know you've been meeting with Secretary Cisneros, who's one of your own. There are times when we meet when I can't tell whether he's changed positions or not—[*laughter*]—which I suppose from your point of view is a good thing.

Most of you in this room I know well. I've spent a lot of time in your communities, and you have played a major role in my political education. I assure you that I think every day about many of the places we've been and the things we've seen and the things that I have learned from you. I think that the time I spent in our country's cities in this last election, that was in many ways the most instructive time that I spent. And one of the things that impressed me so much is that so many things, against all the odds, are being done that work. And I want you to help me now figure out how to make those things that work the rule rather than the exception in American life.

I told the Governors when they came in here and spent some time with me earlier this week on the subject of health care that if somebody asked me to name my greatest failing as a Governor after 12 years, it was that I never could quite figure out a way to make the exception the rule, to take those things that worked and make them work everywhere.

In that connection, I have been working with Secretary Cisneros and have sent, after working it out with him, a directive to him today to deal with a number of specific things that I know are important to all of you:

First, to establish a weekly mechanism for communication with the State and local leaders of our country on issues of housing and urban development. And I hope we'll have a chance to talk about both of them because they are related, but they aren't the same.

Second, to try to expedite the programs that are already there now, to unclog some $6 billion that have been inexplicably tied up in the pipeline of the Federal Government that have already been appropriated; to speed up by 3 to 4 months the processing of the over $3 billion in public housing funds that are available and to try to accelerate the real implementation of the HOME Program where there's $2.5 billion in largely unmoved funds because the administrative system of this Department has been largely paralyzed.

I told Henry when I asked him to take this position that there was some risk because of the pall which had been cast over HUD and the problems of past years and because there had been a lot of rhetoric but not enough action out of the Department in recent years. We're going to do what we can to marry rhetoric and action. We don't promise to shut up, but we promise to try to do some things.

I also want to tell you that I'm going to do the best I can in this upcoming stimulus and economic package to do what I said I would do: to bring down the deficit but to increase investment at the same time in ways that will make available more funds for the cities.

I remember, Mayor White, when we were in Cleveland with Congressman Stokes, you said you thought we ought to increase the community development block grant funds because you could move those more quickly to create jobs. And there will be a fairly sizable increase in that in the proposed stimulus package to try to help you create jobs.

Let me just make a couple of general remarks about where we are on this whole economic approach, and then I'd like to hear from you, and I'd like to just be as informal and conversational as possible.

The economic news is good but mixed and incomplete. That is, starting in the last quarter we have begun to have two pieces of good economic news. One is that productivity is increasing, and that's good. Companies are making more money. They're figuring out how to compete in a tough international environment. Two is that there's a lot more economic activity around housing as low interest rates finally are letting millions of Americans refinance their home mortgages, others get into buying homes, and that's all been good.

Then since the election, there have been two good pieces of economic news that I think the election can fairly claim some credit for. One is that consumer confidence started going up in November and exploded in December, and it's going to be strong in January. The second is that the financial markets generally are upbeat about the direction that our administration has outlined, which means they take us seriously that we're going to try to do what many say is impossible, which is to increase investment and reduce the debt at the same time.

So, that's the good news. The bad news is that in this economy, the downsizing of big firms is continuing apace. It started in the 1980's, when every year of the 1980's the Fortune 500 together reduced employment in the United States by about 400,000 people per year, big, big reductions in employment. In most years, that was offset by job increases in small and medium-sized companies. Now that is not happening, even though this recovery is in place. So you have this strange thing where the economic indicators are going up in the last quarter like crazy, but the unemployment rate is higher than it was at the depth of the recession. And for 14 months we've had a national unemployment rate over 7 percent. Why is that?

I think there are several reasons, but let me just say there are plainly three. One is that small business cannot afford to hire new workers and make up the slack from big business cuts because of the exploding costs of health care. Two is that the small businesses that want to hire workers can't get credit because of the credit crunch, which is more heavily concentrated in some places than others and particularly in California and southern Florida—Mayor Lanier, still in Texas—but generally across the country. The third is that the defense cutbacks have accelerated the loss of high-wage manufacturing jobs without any offsetting industrial strategy or conversion strategy in America, which has been particularly devastating for

southern California, for Connecticut, and for one or two other places, but has been generally felt across the country.

So the first thing I've got to try to figure out how to do is how to keep this economic recovery with all these big numbers going but to actually help real people out of it. How are we going to generate some more jobs? One way is to put some more money into basic construction, which would affect you. We're going to try to accelerate the funding of ISTEA, which would help you. We're going to try to put some money into this stimulus package. It will be modest because we don't want to be accused of ignoring the economic indicators, but it will be substantial to several areas.

And the other is to outline a 5-year investment plan which will increase our investment in infrastructure, which will have a defense conversion plan, and which will attempt to address these very serious problems that are killing small business, namely controlling health costs and providing basic health care to all Americans and trying to break open the credit crunch.

If you think about it, two best things I could do for you are both indirect. If we could bring health costs in line with inflation and get banks to lending again, economic activity would pick up among people who would then pay taxes to your local government, and you could take that money and do what you need to do.

The best thing I could do for the private sector, if we could bring health costs in line with inflation between now and the year 2000, we would save the private sector 2½ times as much as the public purse, freeing hundreds of billions of dollars a year to be reinvested in the economies of this country.

So, what I'm going to try to do is just that. It's never been done before in this country, having to bring down the deficit and increase investment at the same time. It's going to require some very tough choices. I spent 2 hours yesterday trying to cut the budget in areas that I thought were inessential in order to free up monies that would be invested. And obviously most of our investment money goes directly back to State and local government.

I'm sure that a lot of you will wish we were spending more. But let me say that it is critical, I'm convinced, that we show some discipline in bringing down this deficit, because every point we drop long-term interest rates frees up $50 billion for new investment in this economy.

So I'm going to try to spend more in terms of investment and reduce the deficit, which means I'm going to have to cut consumption even more. And we're working on it. And I hope that we can work together closely, and we can do a very good job together.

One of the things that I've been impressed with—Secretary Cisneros' work over at the Department—is he came back saying what a lot of our Secretaries have said. He said, "This thing's not working very well when we've got all this money out there that's not even being spent." We've got $6 billion in the pipeline. We got $3.1 billion that's been approved that's

going to take 4 months too long to get out there. We've got this HOME Program; nobody can access the money because of the administrative problems. So, we can keep you busy for a year or so if we just run the Department right. And we're going to do our best to do that.

I think the floor is now yours. Thank you.

NOTE: The President spoke at 3:26 p.m. in the State Dining Room at the White House. In his remarks, he referred to Mayor Maynard Jackson of Atlanta, GA, and Mayor Bob Lanier of Houston, TX.

Letter to Congressional Leaders on Certification of Major Narcotics Producing and Transit Countries
February 5, 1993

Dear Mr. Chairman:

In accordance with section 490(h) of the Foreign Assistance Act of 1961, as amended (FAA), I am submitting a list of countries which, as of January 1, 1993, have been determined to be major illicit drug producing and drug transit countries. These countries have been selected on the basis of information from the March 1, 1992, International Narcotics Control Strategy Report (INCSR) and from other U.S. Government sources. The list of countries is identical to the one submitted by the Secretary of State on October 1, 1992, pursuant to the provisions of section 481(k)(3) (now repealed) of the FAA and using the definition of a major illicit drug producing country and a major drug transit country given in sections 481(i) (2) and (5) of the same law.

The International Narcotics Control Act of 1992 (INCA) amended the FAA on November 2, 1992, by changing the reporting date to January 1, 1993, and by suspending the sections 481(i) (2) and (5) definitions for fiscal years 1993 and 1994. In fiscal year 1995 the section 481(i) definitions will again apply. Since the section 481(i) definitions, however, have provided a generally sound and consistent basis for classifying major drug producing and transit countries, we will continue to use them with some practical adjustments to take into account more accurate measurement techniques and the effect on the

illicit U.S. drug market. We will not add or remove countries to or from the major drug producers list until we have our own confirmation that conditions in the country so warrant.

We expect to revise the list during 1993 based on information in the next International Narcotics Control Strategy Report and survey information. At this time, there are reports that there may be significant illicit cultivation of opium poppies in Vietnam and in the former Soviet Central Asian republics. When we complete the relevant surveys of these countries, we will decide whether the data justify their inclusion on the list.

The following countries are subject to certification on narcotics cooperation: The Bahamas, Belize, Bolivia, Brazil, Colombia, Ecuador, Guatemala, Jamaica, Mexico, Panama, Paraguay, Peru, Venezuela, Afghanistan, India, Iran, Lebanon, Morocco, Nigeria, Pakistan, Syria, Burma, China, Hong Kong, Laos, Malaysia, and Thailand.

Sincerely,

BILL CLINTON

NOTE: Identical letters were sent to William H. Natcher, chairman, House Committee on Appropriations; Robert C. Byrd, chairman, Senate Committee on Appropriations; Claiborne Pell, chairman, Senate Committee on Foreign Relations; and Lee H. Hamilton, chairman, House Committee on Foreign Affairs. The related Presidential determination of March 31 is listed in Appendix D at the end of this volume.

Statement on the Withdrawal of Kimba Wood as a Candidate for Attorney General
February 5, 1993

I understand and respect Judge Wood's decision not to proceed further with the possibility of being nominated as Attorney General. I was greatly impressed with her as a lawyer, a judge, and a person. I respect her legal talents, judicial record, and integrity. I wish her well.

The President's Radio Address
February 6, 1993

Good morning. This is Bill Clinton. And this morning, on my first radio address, I want to talk with you about the most important challenge facing our country and the challenge that has consumed almost all my time since I became your President on January 20th: how we can build a strong and growing economy for ourselves and for our children.

Lately we've had some good news about our economy. Our business productivity is up. Our people are producing more at lower cost. And lower interest rates are giving people the opportunity to refinance their home mortgages and to show more activity in the housing market. Now that change is in the air, people have more hope. Consumer confidence is up, and the financial markets are performing well. And all of that is good news for the economy.

But chances are, you're not satisfied. And neither am I, because our economy isn't numbers, it's people and how their lives are affected. And still today, all across America, more than 16 million of us are looking for full-time jobs and can't find them. Our unemployment rate, at 7.1 percent, is over 7 percent for 14 months now and still higher than it was at what we thought was the bottom of the recession. Our country is simply not producing enough new jobs, even in the recovery. And we're having a harder time hanging on to the good jobs that give people a good standard of living and give their children a good future. Too many people are working

longer and harder just to stay even, living in fear that their families will be devastated by a serious illness. And too many parents are wondering if their children will live as well as they have or even if they'll be able to afford a college education.

As I traveled across our country last year, I spoke with many thousands of you about my ideas for creating new jobs and increasing our families' incomes. Now, in my first weeks as President, I've learned, as you have, that the economic situation has some greater problems than we thought. Shortly after the election, the Federal Government announced that the proposed deficit for next year and the year after that and the year after that was about $50 billion more than we'd been told last August. The difference between what the Government spends and what the Government takes in is much larger than we had thought before and poses new challenges for our administration.

For the past 12 years, our leaders haven't completely leveled with us. They loved to tell us how much they cared about us and how much they hated big Government. But Government kept spending more money, and the deficit kept growing. And even worse, all the time Government took care of a privileged elite while our country's real problems kept worsening.

So today we have to do something no generation has ever had to do before. We have to build a high-growth, high-skilled, high-wage economy by investing in the health, the education, the job training, and the technologies of our people and their future. And at the same time, we have to cut that enormous Federal deficit before it chokes off our ability to invest in our future and undermines your living standards and those of your children. When the Government keeps borrowing more and more money, it becomes more difficult for business and Government and for our own families to make the investments we all need. Today the government is spending about a $1.20 for every $1.00 it takes in taxes. We've got to act and act now. There is simply no alternative.

In the days ahead, I'll be discussing with you in greater detail my plan to put our economy back on track. But this morning I just want to tell you about my guiding principles. They are the same ones that got me into this campaign well over a year ago, that kept me going all through the year 1992, and that I carry with me to work every morning in the Oval Office.

We have to ask everyone to contribute something to get the job done. But we're going to ask the most from those who have got the most and gave the least during the past dozen years, those at the top of the ladder. And we're going to do everything we can to protect people who are suffering the most from declining incomes and vanishing jobs, the middle class and the working poor.

First, we've got to control the cost of Government, starting with my own people. I'll be making big cuts in the White House staff, cutting payrolls and perks and privileges. I want to set an example so that I can take the fight to the rest of the Government to eliminate unnecessary commissions, to reduce the Federal payroll, to

get rid of needless luxuries like posh dining rooms. And we're going to take on the lobbyists for the special interests that have grown used to getting special favors from our Government.

Then we'll ask the people who have benefited most from the eighties to give something back to their country. While most Americans paid higher taxes on lower real incomes, the privileged few paid lower taxes on much higher real incomes. We're going to ask them now to pay their fair share, along with corporations whose tax burden has been dramatically reduced in the last 12 years. I'm going to cut the cost of our Government and get rid of windfalls for the wealthy before I ask any of the rest of the American people to make a contribution that is fair and essential to grow our economy.

I'd ask you to remember that we didn't get into this mess overnight. In the last 12 years, our debt has grown to 4 times what it was before. We're now spending 14 cents of every tax dollar paying interest on past debt, almost as much as we're spending on our social services and our defense budget. We can't get out of this overnight, but we have to make a beginning.

Together we can return to the time-honored American values of rewarding work, offering opportunity, demanding responsibility, and providing for our future as a community. We're all in this together. We're going up or down together. I'm convinced we're going up, if we have the courage to invest, if we have the courage to reduce our deficit, and if we have the courage to do it in a fair way.

Thank you, and good morning.

NOTE: The President spoke at 9:06 a.m. from the Oval Office at the White House.

Statement on the Death of Arthur Ashe
February 7, 1993

I am deeply saddened by the death last night of Arthur Ashe. The embodiment of true sportsmanship, Arthur rose from the segregated courts of Richmond, VA, to the championship at Wimbledon displaying grace, strength, and courage every step of the way.

Arthur Ashe never rested with fame. He used

the strength of his voice and the power of his example to open the doors of opportunity for other African-Americans, fighting discrimination in America and around the world.

In the last years of his life he continued his tenacious battle for others in the face of a disease he could not beat. He was a true American hero and a great example to us all.

Letter to Representative William F. Clinger, Jr., on the President's Task Force on National Health Care Reform
February 5, 1993

Dear Congressman Clinger:

Thank you for your letter of February 1 concerning my health care task force. I appreciate your support of my efforts to formulate a national health care policy. It is my intention to develop a plan for high quality, affordable health care for all Americans, and I have asked the health care task force to help me develop legislation for comprehensive health care reform.

I have referred your questions concerning the Federal Advisory Committee Act to Bernard Nussbaum, the White House Counsel. Mr. Nussbaum has prepared a letter addressing your concerns, which he will deliver to you under separate cover. I have also asked Mr. Nussbaum and his staff to be available to answer any further questions you may have on legal issues relating to the health care task force.

With best wishes,

Sincerely,

BILL CLINTON

NOTE: The President's letter was made available by the Office of the Press Secretary on February 8 but was not issued as a White House press release. The White House Counsel's letter was attached to the President's letter.

Remarks Announcing the Creation of the White House Office on Environmental Policy
February 8, 1993

Good morning. I want to make a statement this morning and then turn the microphone over to the Vice President to discuss the environmental issues. And then he will take questions on the matter.

Today I am announcing the creation of a White House Office on Environmental Policy, keeping a commitment that both the Vice President and I made to the American people to bring new leadership and new energy to these issues. And I am today reinforcing my intention to work with the Congress for legislation that will make the Environmental Protection Agency a part of my Cabinet.

We face urgent environmental and economic challenges that demand a new way of thinking and a new way of organizing our efforts here in the White House and in the National Government. This Office represents in action our commitment to confront these challenges in a new, more effective way, recognizing the connection between environmental protection and economic growth and our responsibility to provide real leadership on global environmental issues.

We must move in a new direction to recognize that protecting the environment means strengthening the economy and creating new jobs for Americans. And we must be ready to take advantage of the absolutely enormous business opportunities that exist both here and around the world for new environmental technologies that protect the environment and increase business profits and jobs.

The days of photo-op environmentalism are over. The Competitiveness Council is closed and so is the back door the polluters used to be able to use to get out from under our laws. This Office represents our commitment to the environment and to a new, more efficient and effective way to craft policies that work, policies that recognize that protecting the environment, strengthening the economy, promoting the global environment, and dealing with global environmental problems have all too often been relegated to the bottom of the agenda. These are policies that will renew for the American people a genuine commitment to their health, their safety, and their jobs.

This Office will be responsible for coordinating environmental policy. The Director of the Office will participate in the National Security Council, the National Economic Council, and the Domestic Policy Council and will work with all the relevant agencies. I am pleased to announce today that Kathleen McGinty will lead this Office and its efforts.

We are today changing the way Government works, replacing the Council on Environmental Quality with a new office that will have broader influence and a more effective and focused mandate to coordinate environmental policy. The American people look to us to make Government work better and more efficiently and more effectively for them. We are taking an important step in that direction today. The American people, our economy, and our environment will benefit as a result of this.

And I'd like to say a special word of thanks to Vice President Gore for the work that he has done on this since the election. We have been working hard now for more than 2 months to determine exactly how we ought to reorganize our environmental efforts and how we could integrate the environment, for the first time really, into national security policy, national economic policy, and other domestic policies. I think we've taken a long step in that direction. I thank the Vice President for his leadership, and I turn the microphone over to him.

NOTE: The President spoke at 11 a.m. in the Roosevelt Room at the White House.

Exchange With Reporters Prior to Discussions With President Turgut Ozal of Turkey
February 8, 1993

Tax Payment for Domestic Help

Q. Mr. President, are you now going to ask all of your Cabinet Secretaries and Deputy Secretaries whether they have paid Social Security taxes and whether they ever had hired any illegal domestic help?

The President. I've handled that through the White House Legal Counsel. I think Mr. Stephanopoulos has already given a statement about it.

Q. Do you feel confident that everyone will now pay back taxes?

The President. I do. I think everybody will do what they're supposed to do.

Q. Sir, when are you going to——

Bosnia

Q. Sir, when do you expect to have a statement on Bosnia?

The President. We're very close. I don't want to give you a specific time, but we're very close. As you know, we've done an awful lot of work on it. I spent a lot of time on it last week and a considerable amount of time today. So we're quite close.

Q. Do you think this week you might have a diplomatic initiative?

The President. I think we might be prepared to make a statement in the next few days, yes.

NOTE: The President spoke at 2:04 p.m. in the Oval Office at the White House.

Remarks and an Exchange With Reporters Prior to a Meeting With Economic Advisers
February 8, 1993

Stimulus Package

Q. Mr. President, do you have any response to the Republican letter? Did they say that they will not support your economic plan unless you do more on the spending side?

The President. They said they were against the stimulus program, and that's basically a statement that they think things are fine in the economy now, and I just disagree with that.

I'd like to read this statement, and then I'll

be glad to answer it. That reflects the old way of thinking, you know, we're coming out of a recession, therefore we don't need a stimulus package. It overlooks the fact that there are now 3 million jobs less in this economy than there would be if we were in a normal recovery, that we now have fewer nonfarm payroll jobs today than we did 2 years ago—3 years ago, 646,000 fewer jobs than in January of 1990.

Let me make this announcement about unemployment, and then I'll answer a couple of more questions on this.

Unemployment

You all know that we've been here working every day for hours and hours, putting together this economic package designed to increase income and generate jobs and reduce the deficit.

Before we begin our next meeting, I have two things that I want to say: First, despite these encouraging statistics about the increased productivity, there are still millions of Americans who want to go to work to support their families, but they can't find jobs. The unemployment rate, indeed, is 7.1 percent. It's been above 7 percent for 14 months and is now higher than it was at the so-called bottom of this recession.

Secondly, no short-term solution to the problems of the unemployed is adequate. Many unemployed workers are what we call "permanently displaced." And they need much better access to reemployment services that will provide them the information and the changing skills necessary to compete in the changing world. The old ways of doing business are simply not good enough anymore. Unemployment compensation must now be both a short-term lifeline for workers and a long-term link to the skills that it will take for them to get where they want to be, back in the work force.

Interestingly enough, Secretary of Labor Reich just showed me this little chart which makes the point painfully well. In the last four recessions, 56 percent of the workers laid off did not think they would get their jobs back; 44 percent did. In this recession, 86 percent of the workers don't believe they're going to get their jobs back, and only 14 percent think they will. That means that we need a much stronger plan to create new jobs and an aggressive effort at unemployment compensation that does more than just pay.

Today I want to announce a two-part initiative. First, I'm directing the Department of Labor to pursue legislation to extend the emergency unemployment compensation program for 7 months beyond March 6th, the date set for its expiration. I'm very pleased to also announce that this package will include reforms to the unemployment insurance program that will dramatically improve reemployment services available to structurally unemployed workers.

The first step is to provide the critical link between permanently displaced workers and services to help them find the jobs. Using the data that is now routinely collected when an unemployed worker files a claim, individuals can be profiled by the 5th week of their unemployment to determine their need for reemployment assistance, and a referral for appropriate services can then be made. Recently, a number of demonstration projects, particularly the New Jersey Re-Employment Project, showed that this kind of work and referral can significantly reduce the time that workers spend unemployed, as well as raise their earnings once they do go back to work. And of course, that means that that will reduce State unemployment insurance costs and costs to the Federal Treasury.

I will say again: I know the economic upturn looks good in terms of the big statistics, but the unemployment rate is higher than it was at the bottom of the recession. There are fewer jobs than there were 3 years ago this month. We are 3 million jobs below where we would be in a normal recovery at this time. So we need this unemployment extension, and we need the economic stimulus program that I will propose when the Congress comes back into session.

Stimulus Package

Q. Have you made your decision on that stimulus program, and have you ruled out anything except the COLA on the Social Security?

The President. I have made the decision on the general outline of the stimulus program, and I have made a lot of the specific decisions within it, but we're going to go back over it all one more time to refine it. I have worked very hard on the deficit reduction package, and I'll have more to say about that on the 17th.

Kimba Wood

Q. Mr. President, a lot of groups feel that there is a double standard here on the gender issue, because Kimba Wood was disqualified even though she had paid Social Security, but members of your Cabinet have not paid Social Security and are now trying to catch up. Are women being treated unfairly?

The President. Absolutely not. For one thing, this issue was never an issue, and it never occurred to anyone to make it an issue, until Zoe Baird voluntarily disclosed it. So, no one knew, so no one was subjected to a double standard. Since that time—the Attorney General, which should be held to a higher standard than other Cabinet members on matters of this kind—all of our interviews, for men and women alike, have been conducted in a totally evenhanded fashion.

And finally, I think Judge Wood has been somewhat unfairly treated inasmuch as what happened to her happened in the ordinary course of the vetting process. It's happened to many other people in the months that we have been working on this. She was singled out only because it was wrongly reported that she had been offered a job that she had not been offered by me or anybody else. I'm sorry that happened, and some say that a leak inside this administration caused that. If I knew who did it, they wouldn't be here.

Q. What about the leak about the——

Q. Playboy bunny girls, and——

Q. ——Playboy Club?

The President. That did not come out of here. Absolutely!

Q. Where did——

The President. It categorically did not come out of here, and I thought whoever leaked it, it was outrageous. But it did not come out of here.

Q. When do you hope to have a decision on Attorney General, sir?

The President. I have nothing else to say.

NOTE: The President spoke at 3:15 p.m. in the Roosevelt Room at the White House.

Statement on Signing Legislation Designating the Thurgood Marshall Federal Judiciary Building
February 8, 1993

Today, I am signing into law, S. 202, which designates the newly-completed Federal Judiciary Building in Washington, D.C. as the "Thurgood Marshall Federal Judiciary Building."

It is fitting that a building which houses the work of more than 2000 judicial employees be named after a man who dedicated more than six decades of his life to public service in the judicial arena. Leading the legal arm of the National Association for the Advancement of Colored People, Thurgood Marshall worked tirelessly for more than a quarter century to dismantle racial segregation in all manner of human endeavor. His twenty-nine victories before the U.S. Supreme Court serve as a reminder to the American people of our individual potential to have a dramatic impact in our service to others.

Marshall brought the same fervent commitment to social equality to his work as an appeals court judge, the Solicitor General of the United States and Associate Justice of the United States Supreme Court. His insistent vision for America is a legacy which I hope we will cherish and strive to fulfill.

WILLIAM J. CLINTON

The White House,
February 8, 1993.

NOTE: S. 202, approved February 8, was assigned Public Law No. 103–4.

Remarks on Reduction and Reorganization of the White House Staff
February 9, 1993

Good morning. Next week I will outline our new economic plan to create jobs, to raise incomes, to reduce the deficit, and to lay the foundation for long-term economic growth for this country. Twelve years of denial and delay have left a legacy that will take years to overcome. Economic renewal will require tough choices from every American. But we have to ask the most of those who got the most and gave the least during the last decade, those at the top of the ladder, and those who have the levers of Government.

We in Government cannot ask the American people to change if we will not do the same. Most families in this country have had to adjust their priorities and tighten their belts in the last decade. Just about every American business from the smallest hardware store to the largest conglomerate has had to change to meet increased competition. And so, too, the Government must do more and make do with less.

During the recent campaign I pledged to reduce the White House staff by 25 percent below the size left by my predecessor. Today I am announcing a reorganization of the White House that keeps that commitment to the American people. Our White House will be leaner but more effective, and designed to work both hard and smart for the changes we seek in America.

These cuts come as part of a quite significant reorganization of the Office of the President. The reorganization will reduce the size of the President's Office including the White House and the Executive Office of the President by some 350 people from its staffing at the end of the Bush administration, not counting, of course, OMB and the Trade Representative's Office, nor part of the Cabinet.

This reduction will be implemented in the next fiscal year—that is, the one that begins with the new budget—not at some distant date in the future. And these cuts will come at all levels of our operations. I should point out that this is one of the few times in this century that any President has actually shrunk the size of the White House staff.

In addition, we'll be cutting back on some of the perks that can too often delude public servants into thinking that the people work for them instead of the other way around. And the salaries of many top White House staff have been reduced also.

I take these steps not simply to save the taxpayers' money but also because I believe this smaller White House will actually work better and serve the American people better. We have begun a process of revitalization and reorganization that must consume our entire Government and not simply its most visible symbol here on Pennsylvania Avenue.

Over the past decade the best American businesses have had to reorder themselves and revitalize themselves. They've had to reduce layers of bureaucracy, give people on the front lines the freedom to innovate, and do more with less to better serve their customers. Well, the taxpayers of this country are our customers, and we intend to follow those methods of modernization to increase our services to them and to do it at an affordable cost so that this money can be put to more productive purposes.

Millions of dollars will be saved by this reorganization. But we will do more in the other Cabinet Departments, throughout the Government, and not just in this year but in the years ahead. Too often in recent years our Government has been on automatic pilot. People do things today just because that's the way they were done yesterday. It has grown to satisfy not only the needs of the people but its own needs. America has changed, but Washington hasn't. Now, as have so many businesses before, our Government must reform itself and to be able to take the lead in the challenging decisions which lie ahead of us.

Now Mr. McLarty, my Chief of Staff, will explain the details of the reorganization.

NOTE: The President spoke at 11:34 a.m. in the Briefing Room at the White House.

Exchange With Reporters During a Meeting With Boy Scouts
February 9, 1993

White House Staff Reduction

Q. Mr. President, are you going to share in the sacrifice, giving up perks?

Q. Mr. President, will you raise the corporate tax rate to 36 percent?

Q. Were you a Boy Scout, Mr. President?

The President. I gave up 350 staff members, a remarkable accomplishment. And Mr. McLarty answered the other question.

NOTE: The exchange began at 2:14 p.m. in the Oval Office at the White House.

Remarks at a Meeting With Cabinet Members
February 10, 1993

The President. Ladies and gentlemen, I'm going to sign these Executive orders, and then I will go over to the microphone and make a statement about each one.

The first order requires by attrition a reduction in Federal positions of 100,000. The second order is a reduction in the administrative costs of the present Federal Government by 3 percent per year on average leading up to 5 percent in the 4th year of this 4-year term and abolishing several boards and commissions. The third order deals with the commissions.

These are memoranda to the Department heads. One deals with perks; one deals with Government vehicles; one deals with aircraft.

[*At this point, the President signed the documents.*]

Members of the Cabinet and staff, tonight I will be going to Michigan and the Vice President will be going to California to hold town meetings with American citizens to talk to them about the economic problems and the budget mess that we have inherited and the priorities and principles we intend to bring to our efforts to change the country and bring about recovery.

The people demand and deserve an active Government on their side. But they don't want a Government that wastes money, a Government that costs more and does less. They voted for change. They wanted a literal revolution in the way Government operates, and now you and I must deliver.

Yesterday I announced the reorganization of the White House staff that will reduce our staff by 25 percent and cut costs by $10 million per year. Today I have called you, the Members of the Cabinet, together to take the next step, to begin the overhaul of Government as a whole. The steps we're taking today will save the American taxpayer $9 billion. They won't be easy, but they will make a difference. We have an obligation and an opportunity to change the way Government works and to show that Government can do more with less.

Our Government needs change. For the last dozen years I've heard our leaders call loudly for less Government while giving people more Government and, perhaps more importantly, while giving almost no attention to better or different Government, to new ways in which partnerships could be made with people in the private sector and in State and local governments. Too often in the last decade people have rushed to defend the power of the few at the top and privileges of the elite, not just in the private sector but also in Government. Too often when economic security of ordinary Americans has been threatened, Government has sat still, refused to lead; not even follow, just get in the way. That era has come to an end with our coming to office.

Today the Cabinet and I are taking several steps to show that we intend to change the way that Government works. But I want to make it clear this is only a beginning, not the end of the process.

First, I am ordering a reduction of the Federal bureaucracy by at least 100,000 positions over the next 4 years. At least 10 percent of these cuts must come from senior management. The cuts can come from attrition; I see no need for layoffs. These cuts will make our Government more efficient and more effective. The Government is full of dedicated people whose hard work is being choked off by our own bureaucracy.

Second, I'm ordering each Federal department and agency to reduce its administrative, as opposed to its program, costs by 12 percent over the next 4 years. With better planning and innovation we can make better use of the money we already have. In many agencies overhead is too high, redtape is too thick, and the day-to-day operations of the agencies have not been reexamined in a very long time. I believe Government can both care about people and be careful with their money.

Third, I am today ordering the elimination of hundreds of unproductive and duplicative advisory commissions that have spread across this Government like kudzu. I'm asking the Office of Management and Budget to eliminate at least one-third of the 700 advisory boards and commissions that were not created by Congress. From now on agencies and departments will not be allowed to create new commissions without permission from OMB. We simply cannot allow the Federal bureaucracy to beget more bureaucracy.

Finally, we have to shrink the gulf between Government and the average citizen. Too often success in Washington is measured not by results but by perks. Today I've issued three directives that will begin to limit perks and privileges that have driven a wedge between Washington and the public: First, an end to widespread use of home-to-office limousines by top officials and a reduction in the limousine fleets overall by half. Second, I'm tightening the rules for using Government airplanes and ordering an inventory of the airplane fleet with an eye toward eliminating unnecessary planes. Many people believe that there are substantial savings here. Finally, I'm ordering the elimination of such perks as below-cost executive dining rooms and free membership in private health clubs.

However, I do want to say to you, as I just told the Cabinet before we came in, this administration was also elected to provide a health care plan for the American people, including setting a good example. And one of the ways I want to do that is to keep people healthier. So, I will also encourage every Government agency to provide health facilities in any building of any size, as long as they are provided on equal terms to all employees from the building maintenance people to the Secretary of the Department.

These Executive orders are just a beginning, but they're a good beginning. We will now move on to really try to find ways to reinvent the way Government works and relates to people: how we can empower people more and entitle them less, how we can have more effective partnerships with the private sector and with State and local government, how we can find some of the dramatic productivity innovations that have characterized our finest companies over the last few years.

I'd like to now call upon a few of our Cabinet Secretaries to discuss some of the things that they have been doing in their agencies, beginning with the Labor Secretary, Secretary Reich.

[At this point, Secretary Reich discussed how eliminating executive perks improves management-labor relations.]

The President. Secretary O'Leary.

[Secretary O'Leary discussed the example set by staff reductions in her own office.]

The President. I also appreciate what you've done to make the building more accessible over there.

Secretary O'Leary. Thank you.

The President. Secretary Cisneros.

[Secretary Cisneros discussed HUD cost-cutting measures and management improvement efforts.]

The President. Secretary Babbitt.

[Secretary Babbitt discussed Interior Department management improvement and elimination of perks.]

The President. Well, thank you. One of us has had a big problem to deal with in the last few days, and my impression is that he's done quite well. I'd like to ask Secretary Espy just to give a report about the crisis he's been dealing with and what his recommendation has been.

[Secretary Espy discussed plans for improvement of the meat inspection program in response to reported cases of E. coli bacterial contamination.]

The President. Anybody else like to be heard?

Bosnia

Q. Mr. President, changing the subject, since

Secretary Christopher is going to talk about Bosnia this afternoon, could you at least tell us are U.S. troops a part of the initiative that will be unveiled this afternoon?

The President. I think I should let Secretary Christopher give his speech first. We have all worked very hard on this Bosnia policy ever since we took office and even before, trying to find a way to do more but do it with the support of our allies and through the United Nations. I think I'll let him give his speech, and then I'll be glad to answer questions about the policies after he does.

Q. Do you think the public——

The President. I think the public will support the policy that he will outline today, yes. I think they will want us to do more and want us to do it in a prudent way. And I think that they will support this policy.

NOTE: The President spoke at 10:33 a.m. in the Cabinet Room at the White House. The Executive orders are listed in Appendix D at the end of this volume.

Memorandum on Fiscal Responsibility
February 10, 1993

Memorandum for the Heads of Executive Departments and Agencies and Employees of the Executive Office of the President

Subject: Government Fiscal Responsibility and Reducing Perquisites

To promote Government fiscal responsibility by cutting the perquisites and excesses of Government office, it is hereby ordered as follows:

Section 1. Executive Dining Facilities

Executive dining facilities in the executive departments and agencies and the White House Executive Mess will not be permitted hereafter to provide below-cost meals. The Office of Management and Budget, after consultation with the agencies as needed, will develop promptly a plan and issue any directives required to recover the costs of meals served in these executive dining rooms.

I strongly support the decision of those Secretaries who have concluded that they do not need an executive dining room for the conduct of their agencies' business and have closed and converted them to other uses. I therefore am requesting the other heads of agencies to review their official needs and close voluntarily executive dining facilities that are not essential for the regular conduct of Government business.

Section 2. Conferences

The public interest requires that agencies exercise strict fiscal responsibility when selecting conference sites. Accordingly, agencies are not to select conference sites without evaluating the cost differences of prospective locations. When agency representatives attend conferences sponsored by others, the agency must keep its representation to a minimum consistent with serving the public's interest. The Office of Management and Budget, after consultation with the agencies, will issue further directives necessary to implement this requirement.

WILLIAM J. CLINTON

Memorandum on Restriction of Government Aircraft
February 10, 1993

Memorandum for the Heads of Executive Departments and Agencies and Employees of the Executive Office of the President

Subject: Restricted Use of Government Aircraft

The taxpayers should pay no more than absolutely necessary to transport Government officials. The public should only be asked to fund necessities, not luxuries, for its public servants. I describe in this memorandum the limited circumstances under which senior executive branch officials are authorized to use Government aircraft.

In general, Government aircraft (either military or owned and operated by a particular agency) shall not be used for nongovernmental purposes. Uses other than those that constitute the discharge of an agency's official responsibilities are nongovernmental.

The Secretary of State, Secretary of Defense, Attorney General, Director of the Federal Bureau of Investigation, and the Director of Central Intelligence may use Government aircraft for nongovernmental purposes, but only upon reimbursement at "full coach fare" and with my authorization (or that of my designated representative) on the grounds that a threat exists which could endanger lives or when continuous 24-hour secure communication is required.

When travel is necessary for governmental purposes, Government aircraft shall not be used if commercial airline or aircraft (including charter) service is reasonably available, i.e., able to meet the traveler's departure and/or arrival requirements within a 24-hour period, unless highly unusual circumstances present a clear and present danger, an emergency exists, use of Government aircraft is more cost-effective than commercial air, or other compelling operational considerations make commercial transportation unacceptable. Such authorization must be in accordance with the May 22, 1992, Office of Management and Budget Circular A–126, "Improving the Management and Use of Government Aircraft." (The provisions and definitions of this Circular are to supplement but not replace the provisions in this memorandum.) In addition, Government funds shall not be used to pay for first-class travel, unless no other commercial service is reasonably available, or such travel is necessary for reasons of disability or medical condition.

In order to assist the Administrator of General Services oversight of agency aircraft, all use of Government aircraft by senior executive branch officials shall be documented and such documentation shall be disclosed to the public upon request unless classified. Each agency and the Executive Office of the President shall report semiannually to the General Services Administration and the Office of Management and Budget data relating to the amount of travel on Government aircraft by such officials at Government expense and the amount of reimbursements collected for travel for nongovernmental purposes.

In addition, all agencies are directed to report to OMB within 60 days of this memorandum on their continuing need for aircraft configured for passenger use in their inventories. OMB, in turn, shall evaluate the sufficiency and effectiveness of current policies. Such review should include a public comment process.

This memorandum shall apply solely to senior executive branch officials. For purposes of this memorandum, senior executive branch officials are civilian officials appointed by the President with the advice and consent of the Senate, as well as civilian employees of the Executive Office of the President.

Thank you for your assistance in implementing these restrictions.

WILLIAM J. CLINTON

Memorandum on Use of Government Vehicles
February 10, 1993

Memorandum for the Heads of Executive Departments and Agencies

Subject: Use of Government Vehicles

The use of Government vehicles for daily home-to-work transportation of high-level executive branch officials is a privilege designed to facilitate the efficient operation of the Government and to provide security to key Government employees with substantial military and national security responsibilities. In the past, however, this privilege has been abused by certain executive branch officials and has come to exemplify a Government out of touch with the American people. Using such perquisites of office outside of the scope of our mission to serve the public is unacceptable. Accordingly, I believe that there must be a strong presumption against the general granting of this privilege absent security concerns or compelling operational necessity.

The law authorizes me to designate up to

six employees in the Executive Office of the President to receive daily home-to-work transportation in Government vehicles. In addition, the law allows me to designate up to 10 additional employees of Federal agencies to receive this benefit. However, for the reasons stated above, in my Administration, no officer or employee of the Executive Office of the President or any other Federal agency is authorized by me to receive use of a Government vehicle for daily home-to-work transportation pursuant to 31 U.S.C. 1344(b)(1)(B)&(C). The only exceptions, for compelling national security reasons, are the Assistant to the President for National Security Affairs, the Deputy Assistant to the President for National Security Affairs, and the Chief of Staff of the White House.

The law also allows Cabinet Secretaries and other Executive Level I officials to authorize one principal deputy to use a Government vehicle for daily home-to-work transportation. The use of Government vehicles for this purpose is simply not appropriate for Government officials at this level absent security or operational requirements. Accordingly, by this memorandum I am instructing you to refrain from authorizing the use of Government vehicles for your deputies for daily home-to-work transportation. This memorandum does not prevent you from authorizing the temporary use of Government vehicles in accordance with the requirements of the law.

I further direct each executive department or agency to reduce the number of executive motor vehicles (except armored vehicles) that it owns or leases by at least 50 percent by the end of fiscal year 1993. Each agency will report on its compliance to the Director of the Office of Management and Budget at that time. I order the Director of the Office of Management and Budget, in consultation with the Administrator of General Services, to issue any further directives necessary to implement this memorandum and to monitor compliance.

Finally, I urge the head of each agency to strictly enforce the Governmentwide regulations prohibiting the unauthorized use of Government vehicles, including the use of corrective or disciplinary action where appropriate.

WILLIAM J. CLINTON

Remarks on Arrival in Detroit, Michigan
February 10, 1993

Thank you very, very much. Thank you for coming out on this cold day to make me feel warmly welcome to Michigan. I want to say how grateful I am to be back here again. This is my first trip out of the Nation's Capital as your President. The first time I've ever been on Air Force One, I flew here to Michigan.

I want to say a word of thanks to Chairman Dingell and your wonderful Congressman from this district, David Bonior, and all the Members of Congress who are here, and Senator Levin and Senator Riegle. I want to thank my good friend Governor Blanchard, who flew here with me from Washington. I want to thank all of you who are here, and I'd like to say a special word of thanks to the men and women in uniform who are here in this crowd who serve our Nation every day. I know you're grateful to them. I want to thank the people of Michigan, without whom I might well not be here as President today, for your support in November and your support in March, and, more importantly, maybe, for all the things that I learned here in Michigan.

When I was a boy, the first thing I ever knew about Michigan, growing up in Arkansas, was it was sort of the land of opportunity for our people who couldn't make a living on the farm anymore. They came here and became middle class citizens by working in the auto plants or by other industries that were successful. When I came here as a candidate for President, I didn't know whether I could do very well. And after I came home the first time, I called my wife. I said, "Every other person I met was from Arkansas; we're going to do all right up here." [*Laughter*]

People came here because Michigan was the American dream. When I came back to Michigan in this Presidential campaign I found a different picture, not all bad by any means but much more mixed. I saw in Michigan people

71

who were developing new industries and new technologies and new hope for the future. I saw people working together across racial lines. But I also saw industries dying on the vine and people who had worked all their lives losing jobs and losing their health care. And I saw people divided by race, too.

I saw everything about America writ large here in this State: all that is best, all that is most troubling. But I saw an awful lot of hope, too. Today when I left the White House to come here, we had a crowd of folks come out on the lawn to say goodbye, and when I knew that we'd bring in some folks just from the public who were there and some people who work in the White House, many of whom had never met the President before. And I had so many people who work in correspondence who were telling me that the letters are coming in at record rates here, massive numbers of letters for me, for my wife, for my daughter, people writing us about their hopes, their dreams, their new ideas.

I'm going to do a town hall meeting tonight, a televised meeting connecting four cities, not just Detroit but three others, too, and all across the country. You know, between June and November I did nine of those. But I started a year ago in New Hampshire doing them, because I believe that people like me shouldn't hide from the people who elected them. I think we ought to be accountable.

There will be many difficult and challenging days ahead. But if you'll stay in touch with me, if you'll let me hear the truth of your feelings and your ideas, when you agree and when you disagree, I think we can change this country. And if you will give courage to your elected officials and tell them that that's what you voted for, for a change, that as difficult as it may be to change, staying where we are is the most expensive course of all, we can do it.

You know, shortly after you elected me to President, I was given my first piece of good news and my first piece of bad news. The good news was that consumer confidence was up and people were feeling better and people thought we could change the economy; that American companies, in a tough global environment, were becoming more productive; that interest rates had come down some and people were financing their home loans. The bad news was that no new jobs were being created in our economy and that incomes were not going up and that

after the election it was announced that the Government deficit was going to be $50 billion higher next year and just about that high every year thereafter during my term of office. And so I had to go back to the drawing board and figure out how we were going to put the American people first, take on the special interests, invest in jobs and incomes and deal with the health care crisis and still bring the deficit down, as I promised to do, and to do it in a way that is fair to the middle class, people who've worked hard and paid the bills for 12 years. It isn't easy, I'll tell you that. But I'm doing my best.

We have spent literally hours and hours and hours, the administration people and I, and I've met with large numbers of people in Congress, many people many times, since I became President just 3 weeks ago, doing almost nothing but focusing on this economy. And I am telling you I am confident that if we'll make some challenging decisions now and put this country on the right path, we can lift this economy up, we can create jobs, we can deal with the health care crisis and have a bright future.

But remember: Everywhere I went in this election I said, "Do not vote for me if you're going to quit on election day. Do not come to the Inaugural and celebrate the victory unless you're going to help us make the victory good." I need your help. I didn't see a single soul all those thousands of miles I traveled on those buses, stopping on the country roads and going to the big cities, I never did see a person holding up a sign saying, "Everything's just fine. Leave well enough alone." Not the first sign. Even the people who honestly disagreed with me on a whole range of issues never said they believed that we didn't have to have the courage to change.

And so tonight I ask you, watch what we do closely. If you think I'm wrong, call or write and tell me. But continue to support me with your prayers and your voice and your conviction, and give the Members of Congress the courage to change. That is what the election was all about. And we are going to try to make good on it.

Thank you, and God bless you all.

NOTE: The President spoke at 5:10 p.m. at the Selfridge Air National Guard Base. In his remarks, he referred to John D. Dingell, chairman, House Energy and Commerce Committee.

Remarks at a Town Meeting in Detroit
February 10, 1993

The President. Thank you, thank you very much. Let me, first of all, thank all of you for being here in Michigan, and thank our audiences in Washington and Georgia and Florida for joining us, and all the people across this country who are watching this event.

I started doing these televised town meetings a year ago in New Hampshire. Between June and November I did nine that were televised alone, including one here at this station. And I wanted to come out of the White House 3 weeks to the day after I became President because I can see now, after only 3 weeks, how easy it is for a President to get out of touch, to be caught up in the trappings of Washington, and basically to be told by people that nothing needs to be changed or you can't change things.

Let me just briefly say, I want to take as much time as possible for questions, but I want to say one or two things real quickly. I believe I got elected on a commitment to change America, to create jobs, try to raise incomes, to face the health care crisis, to try to liberate the Government from special interests and turn it back to the people, and to try to reduce the deficit and put America on a path to long-term health and recovery, bringing the American people together.

There's been some good news and bad news since I won the election. The good news is that productivity of American firms is up. People are buying houses because interest rates are down. Consumer confidence is up since the election. I like that. People think things are going to be better.

There's been some bad news. With all these economic improvements, we aren't generating new jobs. And the deficit of this country is about $50 billion a year bigger than I was told it was going to be before the election.

So we have to put together a plan that keeps my commitments to you, invest in you, in your jobs, in your education, your health care, and your future; that brings that debt down; that deals with the health care crisis; and that does it in a way that's fair to all Americans.

I've been working almost exclusively on the economic issues of the country since I became President. I've got another week to put it together. And I wanted to come up here tonight and just listen to your questions, answer them as candidly as I could, and share with you as much as I can my feelings about where we're going to go.

But I'll say this: All the hundreds of thousands and maybe a million miles that I've traveled, I never saw one person along the highway with a sign that said, "Things are just fine the way they are. Don't change anything." So I'm going to keep trying to change, and I'm going to try to stay in touch with you this whole 4 years so that you can honestly tell me what you think.

I'm really proud of the fact that the voter turnout was not only up, we not only had the biggest crowd for the Inauguration in history, but the mail and the phone calls in the White House are running at record levels, some good, some critical. But that's good. That's democracy. And it proves that people really feel, at least so far, that I'm going to listen and try to move forward. And that's what we're here to do tonight. So let's begin.

Bill Bonds. Thank you very much, Mr. President. You know, in reality there are several town meetings tonight besides our audience here at WXYZ. The President is going to be taking questions from people in three other major American cities. From the far northwest, we welcome the people at station KOMO in Seattle, Washington. Ken Schramm will be the moderator, bringing us questions from the people of that Evergreen State; Ann Bishop, our moderator from station WPLG in Miami, Florida; from our station in Atlanta, Georgia, Bill Nigut taking questions from the people visiting him at station WSB.

The response from the people in these American cities has been overwhelming. And we'll begin right now by taking a question from a member of the audience here at WXYZ in Detroit and see if this bird's going to fly tonight.

Our first question is from Susan Esser. Susan Esser was the political coordinator for the Ross Perot campaign for the Presidency in the State of Michigan. I suspect this is going to be about—well, it's "the economy, stupid," as we heard—the economy.

Balancing the Budget

Q. The American people, Mr. President, feel that Congress does not have the political will to balance the budget. If this is true, and as you say, if the economy is your priority, will you support a strong balanced budget amendment, one that is not watered down, and with us send a signal to Congress that we need them to face the issue? And when can we expect Washington to start to solve this enormous problem of ours?

The President. I think you can—first of all, I'm not for any version of the balanced budget amendment that I have seen because I think it is basically a gimmick and a way of putting the decision off that would give us 5 years to deal with it. Secondly, if we balanced the budget tomorrow, we'd drive unemployment up because it would require such terrible sacrifices.

I hate to say this again, but if you look at what the Japanese did, they had a huge deficit in the 1970's, about as big, even a little bigger than ours is now. And they brought it down over about a 10-year period until, in 1990, they were the only major industrial country with a balanced budget; one reason, they had low unemployment and high growth.

Let me just tell you what I'm going to do, and I wouldn't rule out other measures later. I'm going to try to get the Congress to pass the modified line-item veto bill that the House passed the last time and the Senate didn't. I strongly support it. I'm going to try to pass a strong campaign finance reform law and a lobby reform law to free the Congress of undue influence of special interests. I'm going to ask them to cut spending, and dramatically, across a broad range of areas, and to raise some more money to try to bring this deficit down in a dramatic way that will send a signal that we're in control of our own house again. And we're going to lower interest rates as a result of it and get this economy going again. I think that's what we want.

The important thing is not to balance the budget overnight but to put it on a steady and decided downward tack. If we don't do it— let me just say, there's no virtue in any of this unless it helps you.

Let me just answer this. A lot of people say to me, "Why do you want to balance the budget?" It's no fun cutting spending or raising more money to balance the budget or reduce the defi-

cit. If you reduce the deficit, the United States doesn't borrow so much money. We have more of your tax money to spend on the education of your children or on developing new jobs or on health care. We keep interest rates down, and it's easier for you to borrow money in the private sector. So you create more jobs. If the deficit gets bigger and bigger and bigger every year, it weakens the economy.

So we have to do two things at once that no Government in your country's history has ever done. We've got to increase investment in jobs and reduce the deficit, and we're going to do it. And I think we can start next week. Look at my plan. See how you like it and see if the Congress responds. I predict to you that they will respond in a bipartisan fashion and reduce the debt for the first time in a long time.

Mr. Bonds. Mr. President, we've kicked it off with that first question. Thank you, Susan. We're going to keep this moving right along. Let me throw it now and link up with Ann Bishop from station WPLG in Miami.

Ann Bishop. Thank you very much, Bill. And with me is Kelly Kaprin, an attorney, and she has a question for the President. Kelly.

Family Leave and Homosexuals in the Military

Q. Why did you choose to tackle the gays in the military and the family leave bill first versus getting right to the economy and the Federal deficit?

The President. I didn't—I did choose the family leave bill first. Let me answer the question separately. I chose to deal with the family leave bill because I knew there was a majority support in both Houses for it and because I thought it was a pro-family bill. I thought it was a bill that would be helpful to strengthen the American family with so many people forcibly in the work force. It contained an exemption for small business. It had been passed twice by the Congress before and vetoed. I thought it would help families and illustrate we had ended gridlock.

I tried to put off the gays in the military issue for 6 months. Senators in the other party wanted it dealt with now. They saw it as a way to delay family leave and to throw the whole Federal Government into debating that. I actually spent very little time on the issue myself. I met with the Joint Chiefs on a number of issues, including that; met with the Senate Democrats on the Armed Services Committee.

But I was, frankly, appalled that we spent so much time the first week talking about that instead of how to get the economy going again. It wasn't my idea. My agreement with the Joint Chiefs was to study the issue for 6 months, so we could focus immediately on the economy. Thank goodness that's what we're now doing.

Mr. Bonds. Some people say you probably would have been better off if you had sat down with Sam Nunn and maybe somebody like Admiral Crowe, a couple of the heavyweights in the U.S. Senate and say, "Look, how do I approach this thing with the Joint Chiefs of Staff?" and not get the mess that we got into.

The President. That's just what we did do. The Joint Chiefs wanted to meet with me on that and other issues. I met with them. Senator Nunn got into this because I asked him to. I hate that it was written, particularly in Georgia, that there was some conflict between us. I asked him to help me craft a resolution to do what the Joint Chiefs asked, which was to review it for 6 months and to put it off. We did our best, but there were others in the Senate, mostly Republicans, who just wanted to debate it to death because they thought it was hurting the other efforts we were making. And now we're on the economy, and that's where we ought to stay.

Mr. Bonds. Mr. President, we're going to switch now to Atlanta, a little bit closer to your hometown part of the country. Bill Nigut, WSB. Bill.

Tax Increases

Bill Nigut. Mr. President, we're glad that you could join us by satellite from Detroit. We're going to start with Katie Rapkin, who works here for the Atlanta Symphony and who is a bit concerned about at least one of the campaign promises that she believes you made and yet she feels—you're not quite sure he's going to follow through on it.

Q. I'm concerned about your campaign promise to not raise the taxes for the middle class, how you intend to keep that promise.

Mr. Nigut. Did you vote for President Clinton?

Q. Yes, I did.

Mr. Nigut. Was that one reason you did?

Q. Yes, I did.

The President. Well, first of all, I did put out a plan which didn't contain a middle class tax increase, but I also repeatedly said, and I said in the debates in front of 100 million people, I refuse to say "read my lips." That's not responsible.

Now, what's happened since the election? We have been told since the election that the Federal debt every year is going to be $50 billion bigger than we were told it was before the election. I wish I could promise you that I won't ask you to pay any more. But I can tell you this: Look what I'm doing. I'm doing my best to keep my campaign commitments.

I have, first of all, started by cutting the Government. I cut the White House staff by 25 percent yesterday. I bet that's never happened in the lifetime of anybody in this audience. And it's real cuts. Today I announce $9 billion in cuts in the central administration of the Federal Government, $9 billion. I have also said that before I ask the middle class to pay, I'm going to ask the wealthiest Americans and companies who made money in the eighties and had their taxes cut to pay their fair share. And I'm going to cut more Government spending. But I cannot tell you that I won't ask you to make any contribution to the changes we have to make.

We have got to do two things at the same time. We've got to bring the debt down for the reasons that the first questioner so clearly articulated. And secondly, we've got to invest more in creating new jobs, in educating people, and providing health care for all Americans and controlling cost.

I'm doing my best to do that in a way that is fairest to middle class America. But I have to be honest with you: The debt is $50 billion a year bigger than we were told it was before the election. I'm doing my best. I have done nothing almost for 3 weeks but wrestle with this budget, try to cut costs, and find ways to finance what we have to do. But we've got to change what we're doing.

Let me say I do have an alternative. I could play the same kind of games with you that have been played for the last 10 or 12 years. And this is not a partisan comment. This happened out of Washington. I could give you a bunch of smoke and mirrors and pretend the deficit is not there, and then 3 or 4 years from now we'd be spending 20 cents of every tax dollar paying off the debt. And it's not right.

So I'm going to do the best I can. Listen to what I say next week. Decide whether you think it's fair, and tell me and your Senators and Congressmen whether you think I'm right or wrong.

Crime and Gun Control

Mr. Bonds. Mr. President, there are a lot of people who are convinced that the Federal Government doesn't spend enough money battling crime. I don't have to tell you about the mean streets of America. This man is John Marbury. His son was killed in the city of Detroit for a leather jacket. Right, Mr. Marbury?

Q. Yes. I would like to ask Mr. Clinton what advice would he give to the administrations of these large urban areas of how to get rid of these illegal handguns and curbing the violence with an immediate impact?

The President. I wish I knew how to have an immediate impact. And I thank you for having the courage to come here tonight, with all the pain you must feel.

Let me tell you where I think we ought to begin. We ought to begin by passing the crime bill that nearly passed last year, which does two things: It gives the urban areas of this country more police officers for the streets. I have been in areas that were dominated by drugs, by weapons, and by murders, which are now virtually crime-free because they have enough policemen. They have neighborhood policemen walking the streets on every block, working with their neighbors. That's the first thing.

The second thing that bill has is the Brady bill that would require a waiting period before people could buy handguns.

And the third thing we probably ought to do is do what Governor Wilder in Virginia is trying to do. It takes a lot of guts to do that, but he's trying to pass a law which says that you can't buy a handgun more than once a month. Try to stop all these people that go to legal gun stores and buy guns and then turn around and just give them to kids like they're going out of style.

So those are three places that I think we ought to start. And if you've got any other ideas, I'd like to have them. I think the problem of violence among young people, particularly in our inner cities and not all big cities, is maybe the biggest problem we've got today in terms of their future and the future of our cities.

I'm now preparing a jobs package for the Congress that I want to try to boost the job-creating capacity of the economy for the next year or so while we bring the deficit down, because I don't want unemployment to go up.

And one of the things I want to do is give extra incentives for companies to invest in inner cities. But they're not going to do it if they think it's not safe. You can't have a job in a place where people can't walk to work safely.

Mr. Bonds. The most powerful lobby perhaps in the U.S. Congress is the NRA, and they don't want gun control. How are you going to overcome that?

The President. We're going to fight to change. All I can tell you is, that's what I hired on to do. I may not win every battle I fight, but that's one of the changes we ought to make. And let me say, I live in a State where more than half the people have a hunting or fishing license or both. I believe in the right to keep and bear arms. I believe in the right to hunt. I believe in all this. I do not believe that we're well served by having a bunch of 14- or 15-year-old kids out there with handguns shooting each other because of blood battles between gangs or because they're mad or because they're high on drugs. It's wrong. We've got to do something about it.

Mr. Bonds. We've had some difficulty linking up with our station out in Seattle. We switch there now to Ken Schramm, KOMO.

Aerospace Industry

Ken Schramm. Thanks, Bill. I'd like to introduce Larry Brown, who is a machinist with the Boeing Company. I'm going to go out on a limb here and suggest that perhaps you have a question concerning the economy.

Q. I certainly do. Good evening, Mr. President.

The President. Good evening, Larry.

Q. Yesterday the Boeing Company announced that there would be 16,000 layoffs here in Seattle. Recently, Pratt Whitney announced 10,000 layoffs, and over 200,000 aerospace workers have lost their jobs in southern California. At last report, the governments in Europe involved with the airbus consortium have subsidized their industry to a tune of $26 billion. My question is, how can America meet the challenge of maintaining our leadership in the very important aerospace industry?

The President. The answer, I think, is twofold: First, a lot of those aerospace workers who lost their jobs, lost their jobs because of cutbacks in defense which had to come at the end of the cold war. That is, we couldn't keep spending so much more than all of our competitors in these high-wage countries on defense without paying an economic price for it. But we shouldn't have cut defense as much as we did in terms of high-tech, high-wage employment without a plan to reinvest in other industries, in other technologies, to put those people to work. So the first thing we have to do is to invest more in converting these high-wage jobs to other technologies.

The second thing we need to do, frankly, is to take a serious look at the aerospace industry itself. The Congress passed a bill last year that was never enacted that we're now trying to get up and going, where I will appoint someone and they will appoint some people to a commission to focus on how to rebuild the aviation industry in our country in two ways: Number one, people who work for Boeing, McDonnell Douglas, and other subsidiary companies—how can we get more jobs in making these planes and selling them at home and around the world. And number two, how can we do something about the commercial airlines themselves to avoid further bankruptcies and massive layoffs like—we've got a Florida station here with us tonight. Miami has been devastated by layoffs at Eastern and Pan Am.

So we are going to work on that. And I assure you that I'm going to have a strategy to try to invest in commercial aviation. And we're also going to either have to—either the Europeans are going to have to quit subsidizing airbus and trying to deny us access to those contracts, which is something else that's going on now, or we're going to have to meet the competition. I am not going to roll over and play dead.

Seven, seven technologies are going to shape the high-wage jobs of the future. And one of the biggest is commercial aviation. The United States has a lead there. We are losing it because we have not fought to maintain it. And I assure you, as soon as I get this budget and this investment plan, this jobs program sent up to the Congress, we're going to start working on defense conversion and aerospace.

Mr. Bonds. We're going to switch now to Ann Bishop, WPLG, Miami.

Florida Disaster Assistance and Military Base Closings

Ms. Bishop. Thank you very much, Bill. And of course, we've not only had the devastation of the air industry but also Hurricane Andrew. And I want you to meet now the Reverend Walter Richardson, who certainly lives in the area that was hardest hit.

Q. Good evening, Mr. President. On August 24th, many of the things that we had in the south Florida area were gone. One of the things that was gone because of Hurricane Andrew was Homestead Air Force Base. What plans do you have for the restoration of Homestead Air Force Base?

The President. Well, first of all, let me talk generally about the hurricane. There is a lot of aid left to go to south Florida which has been approved but not spent, that's tied up in various Government pipelines. Some of it was not pushed through under the previous administration. But I have to say, frankly, some of it was slowed down because of the transition, the change of governments. That happens. And I'm going to put someone on that next week because of something Governor Chiles said to me. I want to put one person in charge of making sure that all the assistance that's supposed to go to south Florida for Hurricane Andrew actually goes there as quickly as possible. We'll run through all those Departments and try to push it out.

On Homestead Air Force Base: In the campaign, President Bush said that he would just rebuild it while we were closing a lot of other air force bases. The Congress voted against that and said Homestead had to be considered along with all other bases. I agree with that; I think we have to consider Homestead along with all other air bases. There's a base commission, and they will evaluate the needs for it.

But let me say what I believe, based on having spent an enormous amount of time in south Florida and having talked to your congressional delegation about it and others. I think that is an invaluable asset. I think it is important to rebuild enough support systems so that all the retired military personnel, around the air base at least, don't lose the dependence they had on it and turn around and leave your community, which would be bad for you.

I think it's important to find a mission for Homestead. And I believe that there are a number of multiple use missions which are potential. We may even have joint use between military and commercial uses. I've given a good deal of thought to it, and it's one of the things that I want to talk to you folks about. Now, if it clears the base closing commission, it will just be rebuilt with its mission. If it doesn't, then

I think we need to look at whether there is a mixed use for it as both a military and commercial mission.

It's an incredible resource for south Florida, and it has to be used as a part of the rebuilding process. So if the base is not rebuilt because the base closing commission doesn't recommend it, then I'll help you do something else with it to generate an equal amount of jobs.

Q. Thank you, Mr. President.

Ms. Bishop. Thank you, Mr. President. We'll throw it back to you, Bill, now in Detroit.

Mr. Bonds. Okay, thank you very much Ann. We switch now to Bill Nigut, WSB, in Atlanta, Georgia. Bill.

Homosexuals in the Military

Mr. Nigut. Bill Bonds, as you know, the issue of lifting the ban on gays in the military has been a particularly heated one here in the South. Roger Turner wants to ask you, Mr. President, why you want to do it. Tell the President why you don't want him to lift the ban and see if he can respond to that.

Q. Having served in the United States Navy for 5 years aboard a guided missile destroyer and also doing isolated duty in Alaska and as a Christian and having the opportunity to minister to a number of men in the Navy, I believe it would just add continued undue pressure on the situation that's already pressure-packed to begin with. And I want to know, why do you want to lift the ban, and what impact do you see the ban having on the military?

Mr. Bonds. Mr. President, does it surprise you to hear a minister—we also have a minister standing here who very much wants the ban lifted. Does it surprise you to hear a minister say we should keep the ban in place or continue a discriminatory pattern?

The President. Absolutely not, because a lot of ministers of the gospel believe that homosexuality is morally wrong and, therefore, that ground alone is enough to justify the ban.

Let me tell you why I favor lifting it very briefly. We have now and everyone concedes we have always had homosexual men and women in the military service. I received a letter from a retired officer, a woman, the other day who told me she left the service because she could not be honest about her sexual orientation, even though she was a distinguished officer with a remarkable service record, one of many such letters I have received. Your Government spent $500 million to get rid of about 16,300 homosexuals from the service in the 1980's.

Now, here's my position. If there are homosexual men and women in the service anyway, if we know they have served with distinction and they have always been there, the issue is should you be able to say what you are and not be kicked out. This is not about conduct. This is about status. I believe there ought to be the strictest code of behavioral conduct applicable here. I also believe there ought to be an even stricter code applicable to sexual harassment, whether homosexual or heterosexual. The biggest sexual problem in the armed services, according to the men and women who talked to me, involves heterosexual harassment.

I think there ought to be a tough code of conduct. If people do wrong, they ought to be gotten out. But I think people should not be asked to lie if they're going to be allowed to serve, because the question is not whether they should be there or not. They are there. So the narrow question of this debate is should you be able to stay and admit it.

The military itself has admitted they should stop asking people when they join. That's the position of the Joint Chiefs. So the only question here is should you be able to say that you're a homosexual if you do nothing wrong. I say yes. Others say no. The military is studying the practical problems about duty assignments and other things, and we'll revisit this in about 6 months.

Mr. Bonds. I want to advise my stations along the link-up that it's time for us to take a break here. They'll be taking a break. Speaking about the military, we have military forces in the Persian Gulf. We have military forces still in the Kuwait area. Are we going over to Bosnia-Herzegovina? And we'll be back with that question for you, Mr. President, in just a moment.

[*At this point, the television stations took a commercial break.*]

Mr. Bonds. I appreciate your enthusiasm. I think we'd save a little time if we'd hold the applause to the end so that you could get more questions in, the President of the United States could get more answers in. So you do what you want to do, but we feel it would be better that way.

We have troops in the Middle East; we have troops in Somalia. Are we going to go into Yugoslavia? That's this young lady's question.

Bosnia

Q. Good evening, Mr. President. Serbian death camps and rape camps have shocked the world. And today we have heard Mr. Warren Christopher stating that he supports negotiated settlement in Bosnia. How does one negotiate with war criminals without a clear enforcement to let them know that they have to stop with the atrocity? And how does one ensure that the Serbs will not continue with their atrocities and that they will negotiate in good faith and that they will lay down the arms? Will you ask NATO for their enforcement of the terms of agreement and give them the authority to use force in this case? And will you also help Croatia regain its sovereignty on the territories it's lost so that 700,000 people can return to their homes? Thank you.

The President. I'm glad you asked the question in the way you did. I was afraid you were going to ask me why we agreed to get involved in this process today.

Just for the benefit of the people who don't know as much about it as you, let me tell you what happened today. Today the Secretary of State announced a new policy by our Government that we would agree to become more involved in what is going on in Bosnia, not in committing our ground troops now or anything like that but in trying to get involved in these negotiations to protect the rights and the integrity of the Bosnians, the Croatians, and others who have been basically subject to the assaults of the Serbs; that we would be in a position to say we're not going to enforce a peace agreement on the Croatians or the Bosnians that they don't believe in, but that if we could get an agreement, then the United States would participate, not alone but with the United Nations and with Europe, in guaranteeing that the agreement would protect the basic human rights of the people involved and the terms of the agreement.

Now, people say, "So we are not committing today to make war in the former Yugoslavia." We are committing to try to help get a peace and then to enforce it. Why is that? Because if we don't, number one, the terrible principle of ethnic cleansing will be validated, that one ethnic group can butcher another if they're strong enough to do it, at the end of the cold war; number two, that problem could spread to other republics and nations near there. Never

forget, it's no accident that World War I started in this area. There are ancient ethnic hatreds that have consumed people and led to horrible abuses. You know about it, the rapes of the women, the murders of the children, all these things you have read about. We've got to try to contain it.

And I think we have to be very much stronger standing up to aggression. We've got to get the heavy weapons out of utilization; you implied that. We've got to toughen the embargo against the Serbs. We ought to open a United Nations war crimes inquiry, and we ought to enforce the no-fly zone against Serbian aircraft, strongly. Those are the things that I think we should do.

I do not believe that the military of the United States should get involved unilaterally there now. We have to work with these other countries. And I might say that that's the position that General Powell and our foreign policy folks have taken. But this is a much more aggressive position than the United States has taken.

But I can tell you, folks: We're not going to make peace over there in a way that's fair to the minorities that are being abused unless we get involved. And if we don't get involved and the thing spreads all over creation over there, then we'll be pulled into it in horrible ways that could be very dangerous to our people. So we ought to do what is right now. It's also what is safest for the United States.

Mr. Bonds. But isn't it a reality, Mr. President, that if the United States doesn't get involved and doesn't lead, nothing is going to change?

The President. I think that it is reality that if we don't get involved, either nothing will change or the Bosnians will be wrecked and the Croatians will be hurt badly.

Mr. Bonds. And it could still spread after that.

The President. And it could go into Kosovo, which is next door; it could go into Macedonia. You could involve the Turks. You could involve the Greeks. We could have a serious problem.

Mr. Bonds. Then you've got a major policy decision to make.

The President. I just did it. [*Laughter*] We're going to get involved.

Mr. Bonds. I don't think she thinks you did make it.

The President. Let me just say, the United States has learned one thing: When we operate—look at the Gulf War. If we operate with the support of the United Nations and with the support of Europe and with the support of our allies, we can do a lot of things at an acceptably low cost of life, and get something done. If we go off on our own and everybody else is over here, we can't get it done.

I have to deal with the fact that Europe believes today that negotiations are possible, that Russia wants negotiations from a different point of view. And even though they've been historically sympathetic to the Serbs, they have supported our position that we ought to toughen the embargo and stand up to aggression.

And if I go in there, the United States now takes a leadership role, I think there's a real chance we can stop some of the killing, stop the ethnic cleansing, and get a peace agreement. And then we'll have to help enforce it. She's absolutely right. If we don't have an enforcement mechanism, you won't be able to do it. But I believe this is the best thing to do for the Croatians and for the Bosnians and for humanity at large in the former Yugoslavia. I think it's the right thing to do.

Health Care Reform and Meat Inspection

Mr. Bonds. Thank you, Mr. President. Ken Schramm, KOMO in Seattle.

Mr. Schramm. Thank you. Mr. President, my understanding is that while you were en route to tonight's program, while aboard Air Force One you called an area hospital because you were concerned and wanted to speak to some parents and some children who have been affected by the *E. coli* bacteria contamination in this area. I'd like to introduce Vicky and Darrin Detweiler, whose 16-month-old son remains in critical condition at Tacoma's Mary Bridge Hospital. And they have a question concerning health care.

Q. Mr. President, actually our child is at Children's Hospital in Seattle, but he is in intensive care, in critical condition. And only 2 days prior to him going in there with *E. coli* poisoning from tainted meat, my husband lost his job, and we were left without medical coverage.

I'm Canadian originally and always took comfort in the medical system there and in knowing that my children would be taken care of. My question to you now is: What are you prepared to do in regards to the tainted meat problem, and is there any hope in the near future of seeing universal health care so no one else has to go through what we've gone through?

The President. Let me, first of all, say I thank you for being on the program, and I hope your child will be well. I did call two other sets of parents who are in the hospital with their children, on the way out here, just to inquire about that and to get their ideas about what we should do.

Let me answer your second question first. As I'm sure you know, I've asked my wife to head a task force to come up with a bill within 100 days which will bring a new system of health care to America which offers us the chance to provide basic health coverage to everybody, to stop people from losing their health coverage when they lose a job, to stop people from their inability to change jobs because they've had someone in their family sick, and to bring the cost of health care in line with inflation. I think we can do that. And if we don't do it, we'll never balance the budget, and we'll never restore health to this economy. Fifty percent of the projected deficit growth between now and the year 2000 is all in health care costs. So it is a terrific human issue, but it's a big economic issue for Americans. And the answer to your question is: Within 100 days of my becoming President, we're going to have a bill to the Congress to do just what you've said.

Now, the second thing, this *E. coli* thing—have you all been following it up in Washington? I asked the Secretary of Agriculture, Mike Espy, who is responsible for the regulation of the slaughterhouses and the meat before it comes to a restaurant, to go up there and look into the situation. And we think there are two things that have to be done.

First of all, we've got to make it clear to people who are providing the fast food that they've got to do everything they can to comply with our cooking regulations. Some of these viruses would have clearly died had the heat been observed. On the other hand, we've got to find ways to do more inspections and to try to do them in a more effective way. And so we are reviewing now the possibility of not only hiring more inspectors, which I've already agreed to do, but secondly, seeing if there is some way we can do a better job of actually inspecting the meat, empowering the inspectors to do some more things.

We have got to do that. And I can tell you, if you have any more ideas, I'd like to have them. The parents that I talked to today had some, actually, some quite good ideas that we're going to pursue. And I want to invite you and any others who are listening who have other ideas to let me know. But you can look forward to more inspectors, and we're looking for ways to inspect better as well.

Mr. Bonds. In that case, you're increasing Government.

The President. We are there. But that's a direct service to people. That's not a waste of bureaucracy. I think the American people want us to make sure they're safe if we can.

Job Retraining

Q. Mr. President, I'm a former Pan American Airline employee, and I'm still unemployed at this time. And I would like to know if you have any new provisions for people who suffer from big industries' traumas.

The President. Let me tell you, we're going to try to do two things. One is to provide a much more comprehensive program of retraining and job placement; and secondly is to try to have a strategy available when we know that major, major industries are going to shut down, to try to do conversion, to try to provide investment opportunities for new kinds of economic activities.

I said earlier something that I probably should have broadened. This is not just a problem in defense industries. It's also a problem in other big employers. As we're in Michigan tonight, as the people in Michigan know, the biggest companies in America did nothing but basically lay off people in the 1980's and the early nineties. Even when they were making more money, they restructured.

For the last 10 years, until 2 or 3 years ago, a lot of the jobs that were lost by big companies were made up by jobs that were created by small companies. About 2 or 3 years ago, that process slowed to a halt because of the cost of health care to small business, because of the general recession, because of the credit crunch.

So my answer to your question is: We're going to be much more aggressive than American governments have been in the past in trying to find ways to deal with these problems when we know in advance they're coming, and go in and give people the chance to restructure their lives, to rebuild them, and try to create other kinds of economic activities with new partnerships in the private sector.

We're also going to try to change the tax system to favor investment more. That is, we want to raise the corporate tax rate some. But then we want to say, if you want to lower your taxes, invest more. And you can lower your taxes if you invest to create jobs. And I think that will help a lot. We're going to try to do that.

Q. I have a followup on Homestead and some of that training. We obviously have plenty of space down here to have it done. But what kind of training are you going to give someone who's middle-aged or even older but who still needs to work?

The President. Well, I think that is both the burden and the excitement of the time in which we live. That is, there is nothing I or any public official can do about the fact that the average 18-year-old American today will change jobs about eight times in a lifetime. Even if you keep working for the same company, if you're lucky enough never to be laid off, in order to keep a job, an 18-year-old today will have to be retrained to do eight different jobs. So whether we like it or not, middle-aged people will have to keep learning new things, developing new skills.

Now, that will be very exciting and interesting for people in their middle and later years if we can spare them of the gnawing insecurity of thinking they're going to be thrown onto the scrap heap of history, they're going to lose their job and never get another one, or they're going to lose their job and then getting another one making one-third of what they used to make. That's our great challenge. And we are working on it. That is something that I think America ought to be able to lead the world in, and now we're behind some of our other countries.

Health Care Reform

Q. Mr. President, is it possible to pay them and give them benefits as well, like health benefits, while they're learning?

The President. Oh, I think so. What we're going to try to do with this health care plan is to make sure that everybody, whether employed or unemployed, has access to a basic package of comprehensive benefits. Every other country in the world, advanced country, does this. Every industrialized country but South Africa does this, everybody. And yet we spend 30 percent more of our income on health care than anybody else.

Now, if you have access to health care in America it's the best in the world—and a lot of good things about it. But there are ways to give people a choice of doctors, high quality care, and do it for lower cost if we're willing to take on the insurance cost, if we're willing to take on a lot of the other waste in this system, the phenomenal waste. The paperwork in the American health care system alone is enough to cover virtually everybody without health insurance.

Let me just give you an example. In most hospitals in America today for the last 5 years have hired clerical workers at 4 times the rate of health caregivers like nurses, even though there's been a national nursing shortage. Why? Because we're the only country in the world with 1,500 separate health insurance companies writing thousands of different policies, covering small, small groups with a blizzard of rules that would choke a horse. Plus the Government makes it worse by the way we run Medicare and Medicaid.

And we're going to try to fix it. It's the most complicated problem I've ever messed with. But if we don't fix it, we can't control the deficit, we can't restore health to the economy, and most important, we can't restore security to the lives of people like those who've asked these questions tonight.

Child Care

Mr. Bonds. Child care and the terrible dilemma that so many working parents have had finding competent child care has obviously been in the news a great deal recently, Mr. President. Hattie Henry lives in a community just north of Atlanta. She is a first-time mother with a 6-week-old baby. And you want to go back to your job as a nurse. You're struggling with that dilemma. Is there something that you think that the President can do to help ease this terrible child care crisis out there?

Q. That's what I want to know. I'm obviously going to be a working mother, and I'm very concerned about the child care crisis, which has finally been thrown into the spotlight with "Nannygate." And I would like to know what your first thing is that you're going to do to address the child care issue, to make it affordable and reasonable.

The President. Let me ask you—can you hear me?

Q. Yes, go ahead, Mr. President.

The President. Bill, I'd like to ask your questioner a question first. As you contemplate going back to work, is your biggest concern the cost of child care or the availability of quality care?

Q. The quality of the care. The quality of what I can get for the affordability of what I can get; if it is even worth it to go back to work with what we have available. And what about working mothers who don't have any choice about going back to work? Where can they take their children and have it be affordable and quality care, where they're sure their children are safe and getting good care?

The President. Well, I think there are two or three things we can do that we're working on now. First is to work in partnerships with States to help them to develop high standards for child care but also quality care at affordable prices. And one of the things that we did in my State when I was Governor is to spend a good deal bit of our training money. For example, training people who are on welfare but who were quite intelligent and capable of—for taking care of their own children—to work in child care facilities and moving them from welfare to work in ways that took maximum advantage of money the taxpayers are spending already and lower the cost of child care. And we often put these child care facilities in and around job training facilities to help working mothers and working parents that were going back to school. Sometimes they were going to school and working at the same time. I think we can do that.

The second thing we can do is to increase the earned-income tax credit for working Americans, especially middle to lower middle income working Americans, so that they will have more disposable income to pay their child care expenses.

The third thing we can do is simply to increase the child care credit itself. We basically have got to make the economics of this work. And I think there are lots of other things that can be done, but they won't affect the population as a whole. The population as a whole needs to be helped by making sure you've got a steady stream of trained quality child care workers and then more income for middle-class people, either through the child care tax credit or through the general earned-income tax credit, which basically says if you work 40 hours a week and you've got kids in the house, you shouldn't be put into poverty because of your other expenses, including child care. The Government ought to reduce your tax burden, if necessary even give you money back, as long as you're working hard and playing by the rules and you need to take care of your kids.

Kimba Wood

Mr. Bonds. Mr. President, as long as we're on the subject, let me come in the back door on it and ask you the same question that many Americans apparently have felt, and that is, Judge Kimba Wood certainly did everything she could legally to attain child care. Why was she penalized, punished by being eliminated as a candidate for Attorney General if, in fact, she dealt with this rather difficult problem in a perfectly legal way?

The President. Well, first of all, I never selected her to be Attorney General. There was a press report that she was, and I regret—I think she was treated quite unfairly in this whole thing. I have high regard for her, but she was one of three or four people I was considering.

Secondly, the facts of her case was that she did not violate the law, because in 1986 the law was changed to say if you knowingly hire an illegal alien, you're violating the law, but if you did it before the law became into effect, you're not violating the law. So a few months before the law was passed, she knowingly hired an illegal alien.

Now, I think—and she did not do anything illegal. She knew the person providing child care was doing something illegal, but she didn't. But the question there that you can ask or answer, that I would have had to answer had I decided to put her up for Attorney General, is whether the Attorney General, who runs the Immigration and Naturalization Service, has a special standard to meet in this area that other Cabinet members might not have to meet. And that's a question that I would have had to resolve, had I decided to nominate her.

One of the things that I think has been very good in this whole business is that we've now taken a lot of these issues out. They're now the subject of public debate, and I hope that we will be able to resolve some of them, including—you would be amazed how many people who come to my attention as potential candidates for various positions in Government honestly did not know that they had to take out withholding on anybody who worked for them if they spent more than $50 on them every 3 months. They just didn't know. And that's something that I think has really been raised on the public agenda. I think people are so

much more aware of that than they were. You know, some people don't think that ought to be the law, but that's what the law is.

Health Care Reform

Mr. Bonds. Mr. President, a lot of people wonder if when your wife speaks on health care reform she is speaking directly for you and if that is the message that you're sending to the American people. Here's a young woman by the name of Marcie Hoffmaster; she's 17. She's going to be graduating soon. And you've got a tough future in front of you.

Q. Yes, I do. I suffer from a chronic illness called systemic lupus, and I've already discovered that it will be almost impossible for me to get health care. I'd like to know what you're going to do ensure that people with a preexisting condition can get health care. And also, if the Government decides to regulate health insurance and prioritize illnesses, where will long-term, incurable illnesses, such as lupus and cancer and AIDS, stand on that list of priorities?

The President. Let me answer your first question first. The reason so many people with preexisting conditions can't get health insurance is because people are so often insured in very small pools. Like, look around here, suppose there are about 60 people in this room. Suppose all of us belong to a group health insurance, and suppose we have the standard array of illnesses and problems. And a couple of us have cancer, and you have lupus, and maybe one person has HIV, and all the rest of us are healthy as can be, right? It only takes one or two people in a group that small to bankrupt the pool.

But in most countries, and in a few States in America, insurance companies are required to rate people for insurance according to huge community pools with hundreds of thousands of people in them, so that the risk of your care is spread across large numbers of people. And insurance companies make money the way grocery stores do, a little bit of money on a lot of people, instead of a lot of money on a few people. So the short answer to your question is, the way to keep preexisting conditions from barring people from getting health insurance is, number one, to make it illegal and, number two, to make it possible for the insurance pools to be big enough so that they don't go broke taking people like you.

The second answer is, I believe, if you look

at how much money we're spending on health care, if we can redirect a lot of the money that would be saved from administrative costs and from insurance overcharges per person, because of the system we have, if we could do more preventive and primary health care, if we can, in short, maximize the money we're now spending and keep people like you in big pools, I believe there would be enough money to cover your care. If that is not true, what the Government will have to do is to develop a Government long-term care program, because you cannot abandon people who have AIDS or who have prolonged bouts with cancer. In fact, a lot of cancer survivors, as you know, are living now for 10, 15, 20 years and during most of that time, even when there's a recurrence, are serving quite productively. So I think we have to do that.

I just approved, by the way, a strategy to fully fund the Ryan White Act for the care of AIDS patients over the next couple of years, because I think that's an important issue. But we'll never do it, you won't be treated right until we have a national program that covers everybody.

Mr. Bonds. Mr. President, we're going to move into kind of a roundrobin here. We're going to throw it now to Seattle. Ken Schramm, KOMO.

Antidrug Program

Mr. Schramm. Thank you. I've got two quick questions for you here, Mr. President. The first one is from Rochelle Pinrod, who is 9 years old, has never spoken to a President before, but she has written you a letter.

Q. Mr. President, how will you help make a drug-free America so I can feel safe walking out on the streets, so that no one's going to come up and ask me, "Would you like to buy some drugs?"

The President. Good for you. There's no easy answer to your question. One thing I can do is to speak out. Another thing I can do is to hire a person to be our national drug czar, the developer of, the leader of our drug policy, who understands that you have to have a combination of things. You have to have a strong education program in the schools. You have to have a strong program in the communities to keep the streets safe and to protect the children and to give them something to do. And you have to have a strong enforcement program designed

to break those people who are bringing drugs into our country in large quantities. I went to college with a person who's done a lot of very serious prosecution of people involved in and around drug transactions. And he tells me one big mistake we've made, for example, over the years, is not to go after people who make big money at it by chasing the money instead of the drugs.

So all I can tell you is that drugs have affected my family. I hate what they are doing to America and to children's future. And I'm going to do what I can to fight it through education, through treatment, through opportunities for safety on the streets, and through trying to go after the people who are really causing the problems.

Who's next, Bill?

Mr. Bonds. Well, I have a young man here in the studio, but I think we're going to throw it to Miami. Ann Bishop, WPLG.

Ms. Bishop. Thank you very much, Bill. We have with us Marlene Bashin, who has a question for you. Marlene.

Haiti

Q. President Clinton, during the Presidential campaign, you severely criticized George Bush's policy on Haitian refugees, but now you're not only carrying that same policy, you also place a naval blockade against Haiti, giving these frightened people no chance to escape. How do you explain these actions, especially at a time when the situation in Haiti is as bad as possible?

The President. Well, for one thing, the situation in Haiti is getting better. But let me tell you, I explain the action in the following ways: My policy is not the same as President Bush's policy because I'm trying to bring democracy back, because I am committed to putting more resources there to process people who want to be political refugees and can meet the standards and bringing them safely to the United States.

And let me tell you why I did what I did. I did what I did because of the evidence that people in Haiti were taking the wood off the roofs of their houses to make boats that were of questionable safety, to pour in thousands of numbers to come to this country, when we knew for sure hundreds of them would die on the high seas coming here in a human tragedy of monumental proportions; and that if they came here, they would all come to south Florida, where the unemployment rate is high, the government is strapped, they don't have any money. And the Federal Government has constantly broken their commitment to the people of south Florida to help them deal with the immigrant problem.

I decided that the better course was to launch an aggressive effort to restore democracy to Haiti and to launch an aggressive effort to protect people who want to apply to be political refugees in this country, in Haiti, and to process their applications all over the island, which is what we are doing now. And I might say, the ultimate proof that my policy is different is that President Aristide himself asked the Haitians to stay home and work with him to restore democracy. And if you noticed, just in the last day, the present rump government in Haiti has agreed to let us send observers there. And I look forward to fully changing the policy and in restoring democracy in Haiti. But I could not, in good conscience, let hundreds of people die on the high seas and create an enormous problem simply because the United States has not used its muscle to restore democracy to Haiti. That's the problem, and that's the one I'm trying to tackle.

Mr. Bonds. But Mr. President, if you place or slap an embargo on Haiti, you don't hurt the people at the top, you hurt even more severely the people at the bottom.

The President. The embargo was there all along, and I support it.

Mr. Bonds. Yes, but I mean, it gets worse.

The President. Look, if we lift the embargo, then what incentive does the government have to change? That is an unelected government there. The man who was elected President, ev-

erybody down there concedes, if he were on the ballot again today would win overwhelmingly. And we have got to try to restore democracy there. I want to lift the embargo very badly. I want to do more than lift the embargo; I want to help rebuild the economy of Haiti. That would be good for America. They could be good partners for us. A lot of the Haitians who are in south Florida would dearly love to go home. But I am not going to lift the embargo as long as there is a government down there oppressing the people.

Media Relations

Mr. Bonds. You can't do a town meeting every month, Mr. President, and many people in the White House press corps are saying, "He's going to have to come and answer our questions." You've got about 50 seconds left to answer that question. How are your relationships with the White House press corps?

The President. I think they're all right.

Mr. Bonds. They'd like to talk to you.

The President. I answer their questions just about every day. They come in and ask me questions, and I answer them. We don't see the world the same way.

Mr. Bonds. Well, I think the point is, are there going to be many more of these?

The President. Oh, I hope there will be a lot of these.

Mr. Bonds. Thanks, Mr. President.

The President. I hope there will be a lot of these.

NOTE: The town meeting began at 8 p.m. at the WXYZ–TV studios in Southfield, MI.

Remarks to Business Leaders
February 11, 1993

Thank you very much. I would like to thank all of you ladies and gentlemen for coming here to join me today. I would like to say a special word of thanks to the leaders of various organizations and sectors of our economy who came in a little earlier for a briefing. And thanks to the members of the administration who are here, who have been working so hard for the last 3 weeks on our economic program, and

to the Vice President who went all the way to California last night to do a town meeting and came in about 5 o'clock this morning. He's the only person here who's had less sleep than I have. That's what Vice Presidents are for. [*Laughter*]

I have asked you to come here today because we have to meet a challenge together. Many of you have been my friends for some time, and you have worked with me in this campaign and in others. Many of you are members of the other party who love your country and care very deeply about the health of our economy. It doesn't matter. If you look at the history of our country, whenever the chips have been down, the private sector, the business community has rallied to help America meet its challenges in war and in peace. In two World Wars, business men and women were among the leaders in our great national mobilizations, putting aside narrow interests for the national interest. When our Nation faced challenges from civil rights to the energy crisis, businesses have taken the lead in coping with change. Americans are at their best answering alarm bells in the night.

But I think every one of you know that today we face a crisis which, while quieter, is every bit as profound as those we have faced in our past. We risk losing the standard of living that we have taken for granted for so many years as Americans. Too many middle class Americans have already suffered through a decade or more of declining real wages and rising basic costs. Now, even though it is said we are in a recovery and the overall economic indicators are quite impressive, the job creation that normally accompanies a recovery is not in evidence. Small businesses are having trouble creating jobs because of the lack of the availability of credit or because of the costs of health care. Big businesses are continuing to restructure, not just manufacturing businesses now but service organizations, too, because of the demands of the global economy.

Business people have to deal with the realities they face, and they often make annual plans and 5-year forecasts, based on the best numbers they can get. Your Government for the last several years has either not been making annual plans or 5-year forecasts, or they've been based on numbers which aren't real and plans which were never intended to be carried out.

Early in my campaign for President I did what I had always done when running for Governor: I put out a plan which, as nearly as I could, set forth what I thought we ought to do as a country to increase jobs and incomes, to reduce the national debt, to restore the health of our economy, and to deal with the long-term problems we face. I wanted to increase investment, reduce consumption, restore fairness to the Tax Code and growth to the incomes of America, deal with the structural problems of this economy like health care and the credit crunch, and to do it in a context that would enable us to have long-term health by reducing the national debt considerably.

I did it last year based on the numbers that were then available. I revised the plan again in late spring. In August the Government said that the deficit was going to be bigger than we had anticipated. Then, still, I thought we could do essentially what we had outlined. But after the election, the Government revised the deficit figures upward again, this time by as much as $50 billion per year in each of the next 4 years.

Now I have a choice. I can do what has been done by people in both parties for the last several years and has certainly been done by administrations unwilling to give up the rhetoric of low taxes and less Government, even though costs were exploding: I can sort of deny the problem and finesse the numbers. Or I can tell you what I think is the truth. I think I should follow the latter course.

I believe that given the size of this deficit, given the burden it will put on today and tomorrow in terms of higher interest rates, given the fact that we also have a plain investment deficit in the education and training of our people and the investment in our infrastructure and those things that are critical to building high-wage, high-growth jobs, we have to take even more dramatic action than I had previously thought to increase investment for jobs and incomes, restrain unnecessary Government spending, raise revenues in a fair way, and reduce the national debt so we can have long-term growth.

I think if we do not do these things, we will pay for it. I think the cost of the status quo is far, far higher than facing our problems and moving forward. Business people have known for years that something had to be done about our deficit. The national debt has quadrupled since 1980. Even more disturbing, unless present trends are altered, the debt on an annual basis will explode in the years ahead with 50 percent of it coming from increases in health care costs.

I want to reduce this deficit, not as an end in itself but because I think it is a critical part of a strategy to build jobs and growth for America today and over the long run. In order to do that, I need your support and your contribution. Everyone will have to pay their fair share. But if you do, we will all be better off, and the business community will be stronger in the years ahead.

Government has an obligation to provide the proper environment in which business can prosper, but the private sector drives the economy. If interest rates are too high, if the financial system is in disarray, if health care costs are crushing out discretionary income which can be put into new plant and equipment or hiring additional workers, the environment in which we operate will be crippled because the private sector cannot work. I want to be a better partner than that to you so that you can do your job.

Productivity has gone up at an astonishing rate in many sectors of the American economy in the 1980's and in the early nineties. This recovery, indeed, that we now see underway seems to be based on three things: home mortgages going down enough for people to refinance their homes and buy new homes; consumer confidence coming up since the election—I hope I can keep it up; but most important, dramatic increases in productivity in the private sector. Those productivity increases are not yet manifest in more jobs for the American people or higher incomes, and they won't be until we do something about health care, about the deficit, and about doing the things it takes to make our country as a whole competitive over the long run. That is what I am trying to grapple with as your President, and what I need your support beginning next Wednesday in the Congress with, so that we can make progress on these great issues.

If we don't reform our economic policies, I'm convinced eventually we will fall further and further behind. Ten years from now we won't even recognize the country that we all grew up in. Ten years from now, if we don't change present policies, the following things will happen: The deficit will be $653 billion in a given year. The national debt will be 78 percent of our gross domestic product. Health care costs will take up almost 20 percent of GDP. They are at 14 percent today. Only one other advanced nation in the entire world, Canada, is above 9, and they're just a little bit above 9 today. Medicare and Medicaid costs will triple for taxpayers and people less able to bear the burden.

We have got to change. The short-term pain of making changes now is so much less than the long-term cost of continuing to do things the way we're doing them. So next week I will try to propose an economic package that will give the American people fundamental change. A goal is an economy that faces the world without fear and not only meets but beats our rivals in economic competition around the world; an economy that is growing, that provides jobs to everyone willing and able to work, that does not rest until the great American middle class that built this country once again feels that people who work hard and play by the rules will be rewarded and not punished.

The broad outlines of this plan are no secret, but I'd like to restate them. First, to ensure that we do not lose the momentum and the new confidence that we have seen among consumers and in the markets and to finally get sustainable job growth, I believe strongly that we need an investment-led jobs package. But all of us here know that our problems go beyond the business cycle. More importantly, we need a long-term plan to increase investment in the American people and their future. We will put in place a program of investment in the physical infrastructure that is a precondition for prosperity and productivity. Finally, we will reduce our deficit, not as an end in itself, as I said, but as a means to achieve higher incomes and more jobs. This will require tough choices from all Americans. And before I turn to the middle class for help I have to turn to people who did well in the last decade.

This past week we began with the Government, where we ought to begin, setting our own house in order. Too often in recent years our Government has been on automatic pilot. And believe me, it's been a very long time since the kind of searching reexamination of the mission of Government has been undertaken that you do all the time, that you do just to survive. And so we are beginning a process of literally trying to reinvent your National Government so that we can increase its productivity, its effectiveness, and its ability to be a partner with you in the great enterprise on which we now embark.

I believe that Washington has to change before we can ask America to change. On Tuesday I kept my campaign pledge to cut the White House staff by 25 percent below the level that I found it. That was a significant cut, but I want to emphasize to you I did it the way most of you would have done it. I didn't just slash the numbers. We have reorganized the White

House staff, and I believe this smaller group will increase its ability to serve the American people.

We now have an Economic Security Council to go with our National Security Council and our domestic policy operation. We're going to have a smaller drug policy operation, but it's finally going to have something to do with the rest of the Government. It's not going to be politics and speeches and posturing; it's going to be affecting the policies of every department of the National Government. We are going to have a smaller, but more importantly, far more productive White House.

And on yesterday, we extended those measures to the entire Government, ordering a reduction in Federal bureaucracy by 100,000 people by attrition over the next 4 years, with at least 10 percent of those cuts to come from senior management, and ordering agency and department costs to be reduced by between 3 and up to 5 percent over the next 4 years, for savings in excess of $9 billion by administrative actions alone—and again, not cutting for cuts' sake but to redirect those monies to more productive purposes and leaving those departments not only leaner but more efficient than they were before.

This is just the beginning. We are going to reexamine whether you're getting your money's worth. One of the people I spoke with already this morning said, "I can give you some examples of things that work and things that don't in the National Government." I'll just mention one publicly because we all know it doesn't work: The Superfund has been a disaster. All the money goes to lawyers, and none of the money goes to clean up the problems that it was designed to clean up. Those are the kinds of challenges we expect to do a better job of meeting, perhaps with fewer people whenever possible, but with greater productivity.

Now I ask you to do your part. We have to replace this social contract that somehow crept into our thinking in the 1980's, that somehow we had to have greater inequality in this country to get prosperity. That was the idea. Even in the years in which we created jobs, income inequality was exacerbated in America.

Now I think we need a new compact. Everybody does his or her part, pays their fair share, joins our national effort, and garners the rewards of a growing economy. The plan I will offer will give a climate in which you can grow, investing in people and the best trained work force in the world, giving us the kind of flexible employees that we all need. That is Government's responsibility to work with you to do and one that we have not done a very good job of in the past.

We want to lower the cost of capital through long-term reductions in the deficit. We want to provide special incentives to new enterprises with long-term capital gains treatment. We want to provide some changes in the Tax Code that will plainly reward investment as opposed to consumption in the business sector. But we also have to face the fact that the deficit will not vanish in a flash. We will cut it, and we will cut it as much as we reasonably can. And if our plan is adopted, it will be the first time since the 1940's that the Government has succeeded in dramatically slashing the debt. And I might add, it was inevitable then at the end of World War II, when the debt was running at about 120 percent of gross national product.

We are going to work as hard as we can, and we desperately need your support to do it, to bring health care costs under control. I have to say this: If you want this deficit brought down, not for 4 years but for 8 or 10 years until we can do away with it, it will never, ever be done until we pass a national health plan to control costs and provide a basic health system for all Americans and to stop shifting costs onto you for people who aren't insured. It will never happen unless we do that.

Fifty percent—let me reiterate—fifty percent of the projected growth in this debt between now and the year 2000 is in health care costs. And we only pay 33 percent of the national health care bill. More than two-thirds of it is being paid by you. And the same thing will happen to your cost. The best thing the President and the Congress could do for the American economy over the next decade is to bring health costs in line with inflation. It would free up hundreds of billions of dollars to reinvest in new jobs and higher incomes and greater productivity and growth. And we must not delay that.

So I implore you not only to feel that you can be involved in our deliberations on what should be in the national health strategy but also to help us pass that, along with this budget, in Congress this year.

I want to also do something the governments of our competitors do without apology. I think we ought to have pragmatic partnerships with the private sector to strengthen our technological leadership. Research and development resources should shift toward technologies that will translate into commercial successes. And we must work together to create a national information infrastructure.

One of the things I've been determined to do in all these budget meetings we've been having for the last 3 weeks is to make sure that every dollar by which we reduce research and development in the defense budget finds itself into an increase in the domestic research and development budget of this country, and more. We have got to do that. We also should give you more incentives to invest, as I said. I want to reform the corporate tax system to ensure that it rewards and encourages those who invest in productivity: in plant, equipment, research and development, in people who will create the jobs and the markets of tomorrow.

And in return, we must ask your contribution to bringing the deficit down. Let me say something I haven't said yet. We did not just cut the White House staff and the executive administrative costs of this budget. You will see there are a lot of other very real cuts in Federal spending—and they will be real, definable and measurable, not imaginary—that will be laid on the table before the Congress and the American people.

Once we do that, we must ask for greater contributions to close this deficit. And we should begin with those whose taxes were reduced and whose incomes went up in the 1980's, the wealthiest Americans and corporations. I will ask for an increase, as I said in the campaign, on the income tax for the wealthiest Americans and corporations, along with the incentives that I have recommended to get people—lower their tax burden if, but only if, they make investments in this country.

Our situation is worsened, and we may have to broaden the range of revenues which we seek. But we should begin by asking those who can most afford to pay to do so.

I have also been persuaded by my Treasury Secretary that it is unwise, indeed impossible, to raise the individual income tax rate unless there is a corresponding increase in the corporate tax rate to avoid tax shifting. But the corporations should also have incentives to reinvest as their rates are raised. And so we have done both things in the plan we will recommend.

I talked a lot in the campaign about an issue which has relatively small dollar impact but great significance to the American working people, and that is the enormously increased rate of executive compensation in the last 12 years as compared with the compensation of workers. I want to make a proposal that deals with the fact that the Tax Code should no longer subsidize excessive pay of chief executives and other high executives, excessive defined as unrelated to the productivity of the enterprise.

I believe, finally, that if all of us do what we're supposed to do, if I can ask every American honestly to look in the mirror and say, "What do I want this country to look like in 4 years? What do I want this country to look like in 10 years? What do I want this country to look like when my children are my age? Do I really want to let yet another opportunity go by when we just wander through a year instead of really investing in our people and our future, instead of really having a technology policy, instead of really having an economic strategy, instead of really doing something about the credit crunch, instead of really doing something about health care, instead of really doing something about the deficit, just because I wish I didn't have to change my ways?"—I think almost every American will look in the mirror and say no, no, this year we'll pull together and do our part.

If the business community leads the way, Congress will follow. I need your help. I hope you'll be there.

Thank you very much.

NOTE: The President spoke at 11:49 a.m. in the East Room at the White House.

Exchange With Reporters at a Meeting With Arkansas High School Students
February 11, 1993

The President. This is the Close-Up program, but they're not close up. [*Laughter*]

Did you hear what I said today, Helen? [Helen Thomas, United Press International]

Q. What?

The President. When I went in from the run? I said you had a great voice. It pierced the atmosphere.

Q. Yes, but you didn't answer any questions.

The President. I know, all your questions— have any answer——

Attorney General

Q. Got a woman for Attorney General?

Q. Mr. President, are you not committed to an across-the-board business tax increase?

Q. Which one's going to be President someday?

Q. You've got 14 lawyers in the Cabinet. Which one's going to be Attorney General?

The President. Well, we thought it would be part of my productivity in Government. We have so many lawyers in the Cabinet—something I didn't know, actually, until someone pointed it out to me—that we could just rotate the job once a month among the lawyers. [*Laughter*]

Town Meetings and Media Relations

Q. Mr. President, you had some tough words for the businessmen today. Will there be similarly tough words for middle class taxpayers come next week?

The President. I talked to them last night. I think they got the message. I was really pleased with that last night. I liked it because the people who were asking questions, basically, they talked to me just like they did when I was a candidate. I was glad there was no dif-

ference in their——

Q. Why do you think we're different?

The President. ——questions to challenge me, I like it.

Q. Why do you think the press is not with you?

The President. Why what?

Q. You said the press is not in your world.

The President. Why, what do you mean?

Q. We think differently or something?

Q. You said we think differently.

The President. No, no, I said just on—what was I talking about? [*Laughter*]

Q. Washington.

Q. Press corps.

The President. No, no, no, there was a specific question.

Q. Press conferences among the White House press corps. And you said, I answered that question——

The President. [*Inaudible*]—the question was about. You've got to get—before you lay that on me, you've got to put it in proper context now. What was——

Q. Okay, you said we see the world differently.

The President. Well, I think sometimes you do, but that's what you're hired to do. That's your job.

Attorney General

Q. Is it a man for Attorney General, sir?

The President. It's a lawyer. How's that?

NOTE: The exchange began at 1:50 p.m. in the Rose Garden at the White House. A tape was not available for verification of the content of this exchange.

Exchange With Reporters Following Discussions With Foreign Minister Michio Watanabe of Japan
February 11, 1993

The President. We just had a very serious trade talk here. We decided that when all the

people came in and took all the pictures that I was contributing to the Japanese trade surplus because of all the film that was being shot.

Q. Are you relieved, sir, that you have finally settled upon an Attorney General?

The President. I'll discuss that at 4:30 p.m.

Q. Are you asking for greater access for American goods in Japan?

The President. This is just the beginning of our relationship. We had a little talk about trade. And Minister Watanabe said that he thought that we shouldn't become protectionist in our relationship. And I agreed, but I said I thought we had to bring the trade deficit down and that I would be working with him on it very firmly.

Q. Did he agree to that?

The President. Yes, he agreed. As a matter of fact, he discussed some things that he thought would be done. So we had a good talk. But it was very preliminary. You shouldn't attach any burden on him because he came to see me today.

Q. So you're going to be friends?

The President. Well, I think we'll be friends and we'll have a few disagreements and a lot of agreements.

Q. So is this lawyer you mentioned a woman?

The President. At 4:30 p.m.

Q. At each photo op you go a little bit further.

Q. Will we see her on the way out?

The President. I hope not.

[*At this point, one group of reporters left the room, and another group entered.*]

Q. Mr. President, will you meet with the Japanese Prime Minister by the end of March? Have any plans?

The President. I don't think a specific date has been set yet, but I want very much to meet with him in the near future. The Japanese-American relationship is very important, not only to Japan and to America but to the rest of the world. And I think it's important that we meet pretty soon, and I'm trying to set it up now.

Q. Was there a big agenda for this meeting, today's meeting?

The President. Was there a big agenda? Well, we talked for a good while, as you probably know, about a wide range of things, everything from the AIDS crisis to the situation in Russia, to the GATT round, to the necessity of resolving the trade differences between our two countries. It was a good first meeting. I thought it was a good first meeting.

Q. [*Inaudible*]—diplomatic?

The President. It's my job.

NOTE: The exchange began at 2:35 p.m. in the Oval Office at the White House.

The President's News Conference With Attorney-General-Designate Janet Reno
February 11, 1992

Nomination of Janet Reno To Be Attorney General

The President. Good afternoon. One of my central missions as President is to reconnect the Government of the American people with the people who sent us here. Government cannot be an abstract, distant entity. It must be directly linked to the real lives of real people. I pledged when I ran to reach beyond Washington to bring the best from America's statehouses and courthouses to our Government. And I believe that my Cabinet and other appointees have fulfilled that pledge so far.

No agency needs an injection of innovative spirit more than the Department of Justice.

Americans demand and deserve freedom from crime in their homes, at their schools, and on the streets. Talking tough is easy. Actually getting results is much more difficult and much more rare. Thousands of prosecutors and police across America have been developing successful ways to fight crime and, just as important, to restore the sense of security that makes community possible in our Nation. I expect my Justice Department to take those lessons and apply them nationally, to be an innovator for law enforcement.

After years of political controversy and abuse, the Justice Department also needs an Attorney General who will bring a sense of pride, integrity, and new energy to that agency. The Department's dedicated career staff need leadership to help the Department pull together to focus on the urgent interests and issues of justice and law that brought the employees of the Justice Department into public service in the first place. They need an administrator schooled in the management of tough and complex problems and difficult-to-call legal cases, things that affect matters in the office and on the streets of America.

I am proud to announce today that I intend to nominate Janet Reno, the State attorney from Miami and Dade County, Florida, to be our next Attorney General. She is a front-line crime fighter and a caring public servant. She has devoted her life to making her community safer, keeping children out of trouble, reducing domestic violence, and helping families. She has truly put people first.

She grew up as the daughter of two respected Florida journalists. She worked her way through Cornell University, graduating in 1960. Three years later, in 1963, she was one of a handful of women to graduate from the Harvard Law School, a year behind her distinguished Senator, Bob Graham. After a decade in the private practice of law, she was appointed the State attorney in 1978.

Janet Reno is ready to tackle the Justice Department's problems. Serving successfully as the chief prosecutor in a complex, diverse urban community is a really tough job. And she has done that job and done it well. She supervises an office of 900, including 230 attorneys. Her office handles over 120,000 cases per year, 40,000 of them felonies, and has won 80 capital punishment convictions for first degree murderers since she became prosecutor.

She has pioneered innovative programs to reduce crime, violence, and drug abuse. She launched a drug court program that has become nationally acclaimed that gets young first-time offenders back on track. She's piloted a community policing program, helping to reduce crime in blighted urban areas, something we want to do all across America. She began one of the first and best domestic violence programs combating spousal and child abuse. She runs a tough child support program that is at the leading edge of making deadbeat parents pay up.

She has been a fair-minded and effective prosecutor. Her balanced approach has won wide praise from across the community, from

law enforcement, the bar, community leaders, civil rights leaders. People from all walks of life have hailed her achievements and her remarkable dedication to public service. She has won election five times and is the single biggest votegetter in Dade County. The overwhelming support of the people who know her best is the most telling testament to her skills that I know of.

As an experienced law enforcement leader, she will be an effective voice in our fight against violent crime, spearheading our efforts to put 100,000 new police officers on the street, to keep dangerous weapons out of the hands of criminals, to make greater use of boot camps and other alternative means of service for young offenders, to increase aid to local law enforcement, to expand the use of community policing and to tackle the problems of violence against women and the need for tougher child support enforcement.

She will join with local leaders and environmental advocates to make sure that those who pollute our air and our water pay for their actions and take responsibility for the needed clean-up. She will work to invigorate our civil rights laws and to ensure that every person has an equal chance to contribute to and to participate in all our country has to offer. And she'll lead the fight against crime in the suites, as well as crime in the streets, ensuring that every possible penny is recovered from people who have bilked the S&L's and other white-collar criminals.

Finally, I want to say to you that every one I know who knows and has worked with Janet Reno agrees that she possesses one quality most essential to being Attorney General: unquestioned integrity. She's demonstrated throughout her career a commitment to principles that I want to see enshrined at the Justice Department. No one is above the law. Our legal system must protect the innocent and punish the wrongdoers. That the promise of equal justice under law must be a reality for every American.

This remarkable public servant still lives in a house in Florida that her mother built with her own hands. She has a listed phone number, and she's told me many times that people who find that their ex-spouses are delinquent in their child support call her at home because they believe that she can go collect their child support. She has lived the kind of life, in real contact with the toughest problems of this country, that I think will serve her very well as the Nation's chief law enforcement officer.

Janet Reno.

I want her to give a statement first.

[*At this point, Attorney-General-designate Reno made a statement.*]

FBI Director William Sessions

Q. Does this mean you're going to have a house-cleaning of the Justice Department, and that Sessions is on his way out as FBI Director?

The President. Well, first of all, I think it's important that we put the new Attorney General in and get our leadership team in at Justice. And I don't want to speak for her, but I think the appropriate thing is to wait until the final report is in on the FBI Director and give the Attorney-General-designate a chance to review that before we say anything else about that.

Q. Do you have any ideas on that subject?

Selection Process

Q. Mr. President, how much was your selection guided by a determination to have a woman as the first Attorney General?

The President. Somewhat, but not entirely. I also reviewed a large number of men for this position. And in the last several weeks, actually, I decided that I would just do it as if I were doing it all over again. I would go back to ground one. I reviewed a large number of potential candidates, both men and women.

I have to tell you, if I might be permitted a little personal moment, I've had a high regard for Janet Reno for some time because my brother-in-law is the defense attorney in the drug court about which I spoke so I've known about her exploits for some time. And I considered her even in the beginning, even though she and I never had a conversation. So I think it's fair to say that in my mind at least she prevailed in a fleet of very fine candidates, both men and women.

Q. Mr. President, can you tell us what role Mrs. Clinton had in this selection because we know that Janet Reno has a great deal of experience in child issues and that she's come to Mrs. Clinton's attention last year at least?

The President. None except to say that she liked her a lot. I mean, that she knew her and liked her a lot. And of course, Hillary's brother had been in the drug court. So I knew that from my own direct knowledge, though she didn't even talk to me about that.

Q. Did she participate in the interviewing?

The President. No, not at all.

Inslaw Case

Q. Mr. President, will she clean up the Inslaw case, that case where Meese and others stole a great system for using computers and didn't pay for it, and the House Judiciary Committee has recommended that there be an independent counsel to clean this up? It's a scandal on the face of the United States Government.

Attorney-General-Designate Reno. What I will do is what I do in each of these instances. I'll make sure that we review it carefully, look at the evidence, look at what should be done based on the evidence and the law, and take appropriate action.

Death Penalty

Q. Ms. Reno, could we get your views on the death penalty, and is there a difference between your view and the President's view? And if there is, is that significant, and how will that affect your policy at the Justice Department?

Attorney-General-Designate Reno. I'm personally opposed to the death penalty, as I've told the President, but I've probably asked for it as much as many prosecutors in the country and have secured it. And when the evidence and the law justify the death penalty, I will ask for it as I have consistently. I will advocate for it as the law of the land in particular situations if we can secure such penalties.

Q. Will you move to reverse the death penalty?

Nominee's Qualifications

Q. Mr. President, can you assure us today, sir, that of all the candidates you either reviewed or could have reviewed for this job, that the one you have chosen is the absolute best qualified person possible?

The President. I can assure you that based on my criteria I think she's the best. Somebody else might have other criteria. My criteria were the ones that I outlined. I wanted to bring someone to the Justice Department who had had both management experience and legal experience. I want to bring someone to the Justice Department who had dealt with a wide range of real-world problems and who had a keen eye for excellence and talent, to restore a sense of movement and energy and vitality. There are an awful lot of good people at the Justice Department who want to be part of a Department on the move and feel good about it.

And the one thing I thought—I can tell you this—this is ironic since I'm now naming Janet Reno. I want to be forthright and answer the question fully.

In the beginning of my deliberations weeks ago, the one reason that I did not pursue this more was because Janet Reno had always been a State prosecutor and not a Federal U.S. attorney or not a higher Justice Department official. But the more I dug into it and the more I talked to people about it, the more I realized that you couldn't be the State's attorney in Dade County for 15 years without having enormous exposure to a wide range of issues that the Justice Department deals with and without working with the United States attorney. You might want to ask her for some specifics.

So finally, I said, well, why don't I just call and explore this. And I did, and I was fully satisfied that she had more than enough familiarity with the Federal system to do the job.

Q. Mr. President, can you outline for us, when you say "somewhat," that her gender was somewhat of a factor, can you explain to us how big a role that played, and why? And I'd like to ask Ms. Reno how she feels about taking a position that seems to have been set aside for a woman.

The President. It was not set aside. I'll tell you again, I considered a significant number of men for this position. And as I said before— someone asked me about this double standard issue—there were also a significant number of men who couldn't go forward in this process because of some of the same problems that you all have written about.

I thought it was important not to disqualify women just because of what happened before. And I really believe—I'm not sure you could find anybody around the country that would get any more favorable and broad-based support than I have been given in spontaneous comments. I just left a Member of the House of Representatives who doesn't live within 200 miles of Janet Reno, who heard that I was going to name her and just went out of his way to tell me that it was a great appointment, what a wonderful thing it was that I had done. I feel very comfortable with this appointment on the merits.

Law Enforcement

Q. Mr. President, given the tight budget constraints that you have been focusing on over the past weeks, how do you and this Attorney General plan to go about fulfilling your campaign promise to hire 100,000 police officers for this country?

The President. Well, I think there are three things that I would point you to, and keep in mind we don't have to do it in the first year. We have—when you all talk to me about my campaign commitments, remember I've got a 4-year term—[*laughter*]—at least that.

I want to do that from three sources. Number one, I hope we can bring that crime bill back up that almost passed but didn't last time and have some funds for local law enforcement to hire more police officers. Number two, I want to proceed at a pace with the national service program, which will give priority in every State to people who want to pay their college loans back by working as police officers. Number three, I want to pursue the idea that Senator Nunn first raised, at least he was the first one I ever heard raise it, of helping people who are going to be mustered out of the military service to qualify to move quickly into careers as police officers or teachers.

And so, we believe from those three sources, with the funding that I have set aside in the budget I will recommend, and the other things that we will do over the next 4 years, we will be able to meet that goal.

Susan [Susan Spencer, CBS News].

Selection Process

Q. Is it safe to assume that Ms. Reno has (a) never hired an illegal alien, legally or illegally; (b) paid all her Social Security taxes? And finally, as you look back on the soap opera that has led to this, how do you assess whatever political damage you may or may not have incurred?

The President. Oh, I don't think there is much. I think what happened—I just would remind you, though, I nominated one other person for this, Zoe Baird, and I took responsibility for that fact that our vetting procedure was inadequate. It was my personal responsibility. Since then, all the other things that you have written about are things that you found out about in ways that I don't know, but our procedure worked and worked quite well. And I didn't discuss anybody or anything until I got ready to nominate somebody else. So I think they did a good job.

If there were any mistakes made in the interim, it was people who worked here, worked around here, or were talked to by us who said things to you they shouldn't have. But otherwise, the system worked pretty well as it was supposed to have worked.

Q. First question: we can assume that all of these other matters are not a problem?

The President. Well, why don't you ask her?

Attorney-General-Designate Reno. I've never hired any illegal aliens, and I think I've paid all my Social Security taxes. Certainly in the vetting process in the last week we've covered everything.

The Vice President. She made sure that a lot of others have, too.

Q. Mr. President, to the extent that you wanted to fulfill these commitments, did you feel hamstrung by the pledge or the perception of a pledge that you had set aside this job for a woman?

The President. No.

Q. And part two, if we can ask Ms. Reno, we never got an answer to Ruth's question about how she feels about being appointed to a job in which there is that perception of a pledge.

The President. No. As I said, I interviewed— I even talked to—I don't know how it didn't get into the paper, but it didn't—both men as well as women about this job. And I seriously considered, seriously considered, at least four men for this job. I really concluded in the end that Janet Reno would be best. I never felt hamstrung by any commitment, even though I did want to name a woman Attorney General. I thought it would be a good thing. There are a lot of women lawyers in the country, a lot of women judges in the country, a lot of women prosecutors in the country. And I thought it would be a good and interesting thing to do. But I never felt hamstrung by the commitment.

Attorney-General-Designate Reno. I think this is one of the greatest challenges that any lawyer could have in America. And I want to try my level-best. I have been so impressed with members of the administration and with the vetting team and with the approach to Government, the approach that Government can work to put people first. And I'm just delighted to be here, and I'm going to try my level-best.

Nominee's Qualifications

Q. Are you a feminist?

The President. You want to answer that?

Q. Are you a feminist?

Attorney-General-Designate Reno. The question is whether I'm a feminist. My mother always told me to do my best, to think my best, and to do right and consider myself a person.

The President. I do think I need to make one factual disclosure and then I promise to call on Mr. Lauter [David Lauter, Los Angeles Times]. There was one factor which affected me about Janet Reno, which is that Senator Gore and I, when he was Senator and I was Governor, we carried Dade County in the Presidential election by 4 percentage points. The last time Janet Reno had an opponent, she carried it by 40 percentage points. [*Laughter*] That had a lot more to do than gender with convincing me that she could handle things at the Justice Department. If you know anything about Dade County, you know that is a truly astonishing achievement.

Q. If I could ask Ms. Reno, the President mentioned that he was attracted to your experience as a State prosecutor which gave you a lot of experience on the criminal law side. But you obviously haven't had direct experience with a number of Federal issues that will come up, constitutional issues that will come up. Do you feel that you'll have a substantial learning curve that you'll have to get over in order to be able to deal with those Federal law issues that you haven't been dealing with in your career, certainly for the last 15 years?

Attorney-General-Designate Reno. I think one of the splendors of the law is that it covers so many areas and that if you're going to be Attorney General, it's going to be very difficult for any one person to be skilled and to be experienced in every area that the Attorney General must cover. I think I can do the job, and I think I can do it by building a team dedicated to excellence, to professionalism, a team where the hallmark is integrity. And using the base of the tremendous career lawyers that exist in the Department of Justice, I think we're going to have a great team.

Q. Mr. President, this has been a frustrating process for you in some ways. If you had it to do all over again, what would you do differently?

The President. Oh, I would have called Janet

Reno on November 5th. [*Laughter*]

Immigration Law

Q. Ms. Reno lives in an area which is full of immigrants, legal and illegal, and a lot of things about the confusing laws of immigration came out in the past few weeks, as we all know. What will she do to clear up all these problems?

Attorney-General-Designate Reno. Again, what I would like to do is work with members of the administration, members of the Department of Justice, to look at the problem, to consult with the President, and to make recommendations based on a thorough study of the matter.

Abortion

Q. Can you tell us your views on freedom of choice?

Attorney-General-Designate Reno. I am pro-choice.

Florida Corruption Investigation

Q. Ms. Reno, could I ask a question? The county—Dade County—some of the critics have said that you have passed along questions of local corruption, government corruption, to the Federal courts and the Federal system. The question is why did you choose to do that?

Attorney-General-Designate Reno. Let me give you a classic example. My office was responsible for investigating and putting together a case against a significant number of corrupt officials. Florida has very liberal discovery rules that give defense attorneys the right to question all the witnesses, somewhat far more liberal than Federal court. The Federal authorities also have the Internal Revenue Service. It seemed to us as the case progressed that it would be best handled in Federal court. I didn't ship the case over there. I shipped the case with my prosecutors, who were cross-designated to the Federal court.

One of the things that interested me when I asked the U.S. Attorney to work with us in this effort is that he said, "Janet, that's political suicide. People will think you're ducking." And I said, "Mr. Kellner, I want to do what's right for the case and right to see that justice is secured." Our prosecutors participated in that prosecution. I think it gave me an understanding of Federal process, Federal procedure, Federal law. And I think it's an example of what State and Federal officials can do working together, without everybody being concerned about turf

and taking credit for something.

Confirmation

Q. Mr. President, how long do you think it's going to take to get this nominee confirmed?

The President. Well, I talked to Senator Biden today, and he said that he would proceed in an expeditious way. So I think that you should ask Senator Biden about that. I think that the committee will take it up in an appropriate fashion. I don't expect them to race it through or anything, but I think they will do it in a prompt way when they come back.

Q. Can you think of any issues at all that might complicate the confirmation process? Anything that will have to be explained?

The President. I don't. I think that she may have to—she just explained one issue here. I can tell you this: If you've been a prosecutor for 15 years, it's like if you've been a Governor for 12 years. Not every call you make is right; not every case you pursue is won. But I can just tell you, I have been literally amazed at the quality of the recommendations that I received for Janet Reno.

Justice Department Staff

Q. Mr. President, have you make any decisions yet on any other top positions at Justice, and what is Webb Hubbell's role going to be at Justice?

The President. Well, we'll have to discuss that with the Attorney General now. But I will say this for the hometown press: He has done a magnificent job for the last 3 weeks under rather adverse circumstances, just trying to keep things together there and to keep the morale up and help at least to do the things that had to be done. I hope he will be staying there. And the answer to your other question is, as you might imagine, we have done an enormous amount of work on top-flight candidates for other positions, and I would expect that if this nomination goes as I expect it to, we will be able to fill out the Justice Department with first-class lawyers very, very quickly. Thank you.

Q. Are you sure you're not troubled by the fact that her parents were both journalists? [*Laughter*]

The President. No, actually, I thought the fact that her parents were both journalists and she still was a surviving elected politician made her doubly qualified to be Attorney General. [*Laughter*]

NOTE: The President's third news conference began at 4:40 p.m. in the Rose Garden at the White House. In the news conference, he referred to Webster Hubbell, Acting Assistant to the Attorney General.

Remarks and an Exchange With Reporters on Child Immunization at the Fenwick Center in Arlington, Virginia
February 12, 1993

The President. Thank you. We are delighted to be here today. I want to thank all of you for hosting us and coming out in such wonderful numbers, and I want to especially thank the young people who are here.

I want to begin my introducing the First Lady, my wife, Hillary. As many of you know, she is the chair of the President's Task Force on Health Care and came today to review the work of this wonderful clinic in anticipation of our presenting to the Congress a program to provide affordable health care for all Americans in the next several weeks.

We've had a wonderful time here today. And I want to introduce the person to my left who will speak in a moment, the Secretary of Health and Human Services, Donna Shalala. I also want to introduce two United States Senators who came with us today: first, the chair of the Senate Committee on Labor and Human Resources, Senator Edward Kennedy of Massachusetts; and Senator Don Riegle of Michigan.

I'd like to thank Jim Hunter, the Arlington County Board chair, for meeting us here. I know we have members of the Virginia Senate and House here, and the school board chair, Frank Wilson. I thank all of them for being here. But the two people I'd like to thank most today are the two fine public servants who showed us around. I'd like to ask them to stand and be recognized: Dr. Susan Allan, the Arlington County health director—where is Susan?—and Sue Adams, the Family Health Bureau chief. Thank you, Sue.

We've had a wonderful time today. We got to walk through the process of what it was like for a parent to have a child immunized here. We saw the good news, which is that this place is doing a wonderful job of reaching people. We also saw some of the bad news, which is it's still pretty cumbersome to have a child immunized. And we did get to see a young woman of 20 months, get her a polio vaccine, which is an oral vaccine. So it was nice to see someone be vaccinated without pain. [*Laughter*]

We came here today to make this day a landmark and to fight to protect the health of millions of our children. I can think of no better place to announce a new immunization policy than right here on the front lines of the fight to provide accessible, affordable health care to every family in this area.

I'm pleased to be joined here by the children's advocates whom I have introduced. And I do want to say again our thanks to Sue Adams, the director of this clinic, and all the wonderful staff that came out and said hello to us and encouraged us along the way.

This week I was startled to read of the case of a young boy named Rodney Miller, a 20-month-old child who lives in Miami, currently being treated for meningitis in the Jackson Memorial Hospital. He's there because he did not receive a meningitis vaccine that cost $21.48. The bill for his stay in the hospital has already topped $46,500.

In the health care policy that our national task force is developing, nothing will be more important than preventive care. Today, American taxpayers are being hit with $10 in avoidable health care costs, avoidable health care costs, for every $1 we could be spending on immunizing our young people. The recent resurgence of measles in our country afflicted over 55,000 people, most of whom were children. The epidemic cost this country $20 million in avoidable hospital costs alone. Prevention would have cost $1 million. And those figures don't begin to take into account the terrible human cost, the agony of a young man like Rodney Miller with his joints swollen, with his ankles so swollen they have to be relieved with needling to get the pus out, that the pain and problems that he and many others will take throughout their lives simply because we don't immunize our children.

Lest you think that this is a problem that every country has, I want you to know in this beautiful health care building that the United States has the third worst immunization record in this hemisphere. Of all the nations in this hemisphere, only Bolivia and Haiti have lower immunization rates for their children than the United States of America.

Over the past 10 years, while immunization rates have been declining in many important areas, the price of vaccine has risen at 6 times the rate of inflation. Immunizing a child cost about $23 10 years ago; it costs more than $200 today. In a public clinic, the cost of fully immunizing a child has leapt from $7 to more than $90. Manufacturers of these vaccines cite the cost of research and development to defend the rising prices. Well, nobody wants research to slow down, but let's look at what's really happening.

The pharmaceutical industry is spending $1 billion more each year on advertising and lobbying than it does on developing new and better drugs. Meanwhile, its profits are rising at 4 times the rate of the average Fortune 500 company. Compared to other countries, our prices are shocking. Listen to this: The polio vaccine in the United States currently costs close to $10. In England, the same drug is available for $1.80. In Belgium, it costs 77 cents. The problems of having an adequate delivery system, plus the spiraling costs, are putting America's children and America's future in jeopardy.

To make matters worse, the makers of these vaccines have refused to make their products available to States at more affordable cost. I should tell you, those of you who don't know, that the Federal Government buys vaccines from the manufacturer and distributes it through the States and ultimately the people through the Center for Disease Control. We buy the vaccines at a much lower cost than a doctor can. The States often directly buy vaccines. They buy the vaccines at a higher cost than the Federal Government, but still at a lower cost than doctors. States can order large quantities and therefore should receive lower prices.

But listen to this: While 10 States have succeeded in negotiating agreements with the vaccine manufacturers that allow them to immunize all the children they can reach, manufacturers are now balking at starting talks with other

States. In fact, just recently Texas, South Carolina, and Hawaii were all turned away. They were told that their efforts to get cheaper vaccines for their children were against public policy.

Today we must tell the drug companies to change those priorities. We cannot have profits at the expense of our children. These practices have got to stop.

But I want to make it clear: Dealing with the cost of vaccines will not be enough. We also have to improve the delivery of preventive care. I want to say to the members of the press and to all the people who are here, we should be under no illusion that every family and every child in America has access to a health clinic as good as this one. We should be under no illusion that every family and every child in America has access to a health clinic that opens at 7 a.m. in the morning and closes at 7 p.m. at night so that working families can bring their children.

Even here, where there has been a dramatic increase in the number of children immunized, we are still seeing rates of 70 percent immunization when the national goal, and what is necessary to assure that there will be no outbreak of communicable diseases, is 90 percent. Without an outreach program to go out and reach people where they are, in the languages they speak, in the homes and in the neighborhoods and in the organizations that they frequent, we will not be able to reach this goal.

So today I am announcing a three-part policy to protect our children's future and to save the taxpayers millions of dollars. It will require changes on the part of all of us. And as I have in the last 3 weeks, I want to begin with the Government so that we do our job first before we ask anyone else to change what they are doing.

I am pleased to announce that the job stimulus program that I will outline on Wednesday evening to the Congress will include $300 million to make vaccination services more widely available to all Americans. These funds will help public programs buy more vaccines. They will improve community services and personal outreach efforts. They will mean extended clinic hours all across America, more staff, and increased education efforts in conjunction with the Department of Education and the Department of Health and Human Services, and the resources necessary to create a national tracking system so we know what is happening to these children. These folks here are having a terrible time getting good and accurate records because we don't have a national tracking system.

These are the kinds of things that the National Government owes the American people and owes these fine public health professionals if we're going to do what we should be doing to help protect our children. And we will begin with that.

Second, I'm directing Secretary Shalala to begin negotiations with our drug manufacturers to assure that other States who do not have the arrangements that 10 do can buy the vaccines they need at affordable prices. There is no reason in the world why a child in Texas is unable to receive vaccination while a child in Massachusetts can. We can't stand this kind of inequality simply because of the economic priorities of the manufacturers of the vaccine. It's wrong.

Finally, the administration will prepare an initiative for my review, in cooperation with key congressional health leaders such as Senator Kennedy, Senator Riegle, Senator Bumpers, Senator Pryor, Congressmen Dingell, Waxman, and others, that will guarantee the immunization of every child in America.

And I want to challenge the manufacturers of these vaccines to work with us. We cannot possibly justify financing research and development in future vaccines based on prices that will assure that children will not receive the vaccines that are available today. We can do better than that, and we have to.

Our Nation is the only industrialized nation in the entire world that does not guarantee childhood vaccination for all children. It ought to be like clean water and clean air; it ought to be a part of the fabric of our life. Look at these children. We should not risk losing one of them, and we should not waste one dollar on our already over-bloated health care system that we could do away with vaccinations.

The cruel irony is that we are the Nation that develops and produces the majority of the world's vaccines. But we don't have an effective or an affordable mechanism for distributing them, and we charge more for vaccines in this country than are charged in other countries for the same vaccines that are manufactured here. That is an irony that we cannot permit to continue.

So the steps we're taking today will go a long

way towards solving that dilemma. We'll make sure that excessive profits do not stand in the way of children's health. And I want you to know that we will not stop until preventable childhood diseases no longer threaten the families, the children, and the future of the United States.

[*At this point, Secretary of Health and Human Services Donna E. Shalala made brief remarks.*]

The President. Thank you very much. Thank you very much. We're going to shake hands, but I promised the press we'd answer a couple of questions. Does anybody have one? Where are they? I was listening for a familiar voice. Go ahead.

Q. Mr. President, can you tell us what you hope to achieve? What makes you think that the health costs——

The President. Well, for one thing, the drug companies are used to selling drugs on a bulk basis at a discount rate to the Federal Government and to some of the States. I think that the position they have taken, that we should continue the status quo, is untenable. But if they have legitimate arguments on research and development, maybe there's some other ways we can try to address those.

I think we ought to let Secretary Shalala and the White House folks meet and deal with them and see what position they take. I cannot believe that anyone seriously believes that America should manufacture vaccines for the world, sell them cheaper in foreign countries, and immunize fewer kids as a percentage of the population than any nation in this hemisphere but Bolivia and Haiti. I can't believe that that is their position. But that is the inevitable consequence of what we have not done.

Yes?

Q. [*Inaudible*]—Congress is going to go along with any——

The President. Well, I'm going to present a program to the Congress to provide for the immunization of all children at a reasonable price. I hope they will be a part of developing that program. Whether they are or not is up to them. But this is unconscionable. We are running the risk of new epidemics spreading out in this country. We cannot do it. We were supposed to have 90 percent of our kids immunized in 1990. That's what Dr. Koop wanted when he was Surgeon General. We missed the deadline. They put it off to the year 2000. And unless we do something about the delivery system and the price, we're not going to get there in the year 2000. I want to get there sooner, and I think we can. I believe they'll be a part of this. I think the public outpouring on this is going to be so strong that they'll come along and do it.

I'm still going to try to pass a bill that will permit us to immunize all the children of the country.

Q. [Inaudible]

The President. Well, let me say, in my State the public health department does 85 percent of the immunizations done. I'm very proud of that. And there are a lot of Southern States that, because of our legacy of poverty, have had to develop very elaborate public health networks. So this is something that we've been sensitive to for a long time.

I've also been interested in buying the vaccinations. But everything that I've done on public health since—well, ever since we got into public life, Hillary's been a part of. So she's been pushing this, but so has Secretary Shalala. I don't know who to give credit to. But I don't care who you give credit to, as long as we get it done.

Thank you very much.

NOTE: The President spoke at 11:07 a.m. at the Arlington County Career Center.

Exchange With Reporters Prior to a Meeting With Congressional Leaders
February 12, 1993

Q. Mr. President, what kind of feedback have you been getting, sir? What kind of feedback you've been getting from the Congressmen and——

The President. Very helpful.

Q. Do you think the Republicans will go along with you?

The President. Well, I don't know. Right now, I'm gathering their ideas and opinions, and we'll see. I hope so.

Q. Are you going to cut spending, sir, on the space station and the super collider?

The President. Tune in Wednesday.

Q. Have you started writing the speech?

The President. I've started putting the elements of it together. It may not be as much of a speech as a talk.

NOTE: The exchange began at 3:08 p.m. in the State Dining Room at the White House. A tape was not available for verification of the content of this exchange.

Nomination for Under Secretary and Assistant Secretaries of Commerce
February 12, 1993

The President today announced his choices for four top leadership positions at the Department of Commerce, expressing his intention to nominate James Baker to be Under Secretary for Oceans and Atmosphere, Doug Hall to be Assistant Secretary for Oceans and Atmosphere, Sheila Anthony to be Assistant Secretary for Legislative and Intergovernmental Affairs, and Larry Irving to be Assistant Secretary for Communications and Information.

Baker and Hall will serve as the Director and Deputy Director of the National Oceanic and Atmospheric Administration (NOAA), one of the Federal Government's key environmental research agencies.

"Secretary Ron Brown is putting together a superb leadership team at the Department of Commerce," said President Clinton. "I am looking forward to working with them to turn Commerce into one of our administration's most vital agencies."

"We have found the perfect balance to lead NOAA," the President added. "With Jim Baker and Doug Hall, we have a team that will bring great scientific skills, laboratory management experience, a strong commitment to environmental protection, and the savvy required to deal effectively with sensitive issues."

As Assistant Secretary for Communications and Information, Clarence L. (Larry) Irving will direct the National Telecommunications and Information Administration (NTIA). "One of the most important missions that I have charged the Commerce Department with is nurturing the key industries of the future, in areas like telecommunications," said the President. "Larry Irving has a clear vision for turning telecommunications innovations into high skill, high wage jobs."

"In addition," said President Clinton, "with his experience on Capitol Hill, Larry will be invaluable in moving legislation swiftly through the Congress.' He will be joined in that effort by Sheila Anthony, someone with the political and management experience to strengthen the lines of communication between Commerce and Capitol Hill. I am so pleased to have a native of Hope, Arkansas, working closely with Congress to get our plans enacted."

NOTE: Biographies of the nominees were made available by the Office of the Press Secretary.

Nomination for Director of the Federal Emergency Management Agency
February 12, 1993

The President today announced his intention to nominate James Lee Witt, the head of Arkansas' State Office of Emergency Management and a former county judge, as Director of the Nation's Federal Emergency Management Agency. "The devastation wrought by Hurricane Andrew last year was a sober reminder that we need to provide strong, organized, and effective help to American families whose lives are dramatically affected by disaster," President Clinton said. "James Lee has done an outstanding job in Arkansas, and I am confident he will do the same for the country in his new role."

NOTE: A biography of the nominee was made available by the Office of the Press Secretary.

Exchange With Reporters Prior to a Meeting With the Economic Policy Group
February 13, 1993

Q. What's on the agenda, Mr. President?

The President. We're working on the budget. You know what we're doing. [*Laughter*]

Q. Still?

Q. [*Inaudible*]—all the decisions, sir?

The President. No, otherwise I wouldn't be asking them to meet on Saturday.

Q. Mr. President, have you heard anything from the lawmakers that would cause you to change your mind on any policies that you intend to propose?

The Vice President. That's kind of a broad question anyway. [*Laughter*]

The President. I've gotten a lot of good advice from them, a lot of good ideas. I've basically just been asking them for their ideas, not only in the meetings here but in telephone calls. And I've gotten some good suggestions, some of which we've been able to incorporate.

Q. How long do you think you're going to have to work?

The President. I'm going to work a while today and a while tomorrow and a while——

Q. You playing golf today?

The President. It doesn't look like it. It's warmer today, though, isn't it?

Q. A little wet.

The President. I knew as soon as I decided not to play golf it would warm up.

NOTE: The exchange began at 9:35 a.m. in the Roosevelt Room at the White House.

Exchange With Reporters Prior to a Meeting With Democratic Congressional Leaders
February 13, 1993

Economic Program

Q. Mr. President, what kind of concerns are you hearing from congressional leaders?

The President. I think they want me to give them a good, credible program, and one that will get the economy——

Space Program

Q. Will you be cutting the space station, Mr. President?

The President. Tune in Wednesday. Before I discuss any specifics—I support—I think you all know I've always been a big supporter of NASA and the space program and the technologies it can represent. I think that people who care about that will be pleased by the recommendations we make.

Somalia

Q. Will the troops be coming home from Somalia?

The Vice President. Thanks for coming to the photo op. [*Laughter*]

Q. Will the troops be coming home from Somalia, sir, by April?

The President. Well, I'm encouraged by what the Secretary-General said today. This does need to go from a U.S. mission from a U.N. mission. I never thought we could do it. Even though I think President Bush hoped we could, I never thought we could do it by the end of January. And I'm hopeful, by the timetable he has suggested today. And I'll do some work on that Monday.

NOTE: The exchange began at 10:25 a.m. in the Cabinet Room at the White House. A tape was not available for verification of the content of this exchange.

The President's Radio Address
February 13, 1993

Good afternoon, my fellow Americans. On Wednesday night I will present my plan to generate jobs and increase the incomes of the American people. This morning I want to talk with you for a few moments about that program, its goals, and the thinking that went into it.

As I have traveled our country over the last year and a half, a single theme has emerged repeatedly from all of you in every region and from every walk of life. That theme is the need for change: bold, comprehensive change to reverse the trickle-down policies of the 1980's and restore the vitality of the American dream.

Over the last 12 years, while the middle class saw their tax burdens rise and their incomes go down, the wealthiest Americans, whose incomes went up, often by paperwork manipulation and moving jobs overseas, saw their taxes go down. Higher deficits came with lower taxes on the wealthy. And those deficits forced Government to cut back on essential services to

the middle class, the working poor, and the neediest Americans. Good families in embattled neighborhoods saw their children getting by with outdated school books, going to school in neighborhoods that were ever more dangerous, while the wealthiest Americans in protected communities watched their bankbooks grow. Our economy suffered through two grinding recessions, and our job-creating engine stalled. The status quo simply isn't working for working families anymore.

The experts say we're in a robust economic recovery. And to be fair, there are some good signs: our best companies doing better, people being able to refinance their homes, and consumer confidence on the upswing since the election.

But the jobs just aren't there yet. The unemployment rate has been over 7 percent for 14 months now, and we're 3 million jobs behind where we ordinarily would be in a real economic recovery. That's why change is so important. And the risk of doing the same old thing is far higher than the cost of change. If we don't change, the American economy and the living standards of our broad middle class will continue to decline, and many of us and most of our children will not enjoy the standard of living that past Americans have.

Change is never easy. It requires us to forsake the old order and to embrace a new one. Change means asking everyone to pull his or her own weight for the common good. But change is our only choice.

Under my economic program, we will build an America where even the most privileged pay their fair share, not because we want to soak the rich but because we want to stop soaking the middle class and ask everybody to bear a fair share of the load; an America where the most impoverished move off welfare and go back to work; an America where middle class families who work hard and play by the rules are rewarded in their own lives and can pass on to their children a more prosperous future than they inherited from their parents; and yes, an America where Government is not immune from the sacrifices it asks of our people.

Just this week I cut the White House staff by 25 percent and saved $10 million compared to the budgets of my predecessors. I've ordered further administrative cuts in Federal departments and agencies of $9 billion over the next 4 years, with more to follow from tough and smart management.

I'm also ordering an investigation into the enormous cash bonuses paid to officials of the departing administration. In some cases it was done just minutes before I was sworn into office. While I deeply admire the dedicated members of our Federal services, we simply cannot have extravagant payments made to departing bureaucrats and political cronies at a time when most people are tightening their belts.

If Government is going to ask the American people to contribute, it must lead by example and learn to do more while spending less. That is a challenge I have embraced and one I will present to the Congress on Wednesday.

Next, we will take the battle to the special interests. We will demand that those who see the Tax Code as a table game to be won rather than a social compact to be respected pay their fair share of taxes. I will keep my pledge to restore fairness to the Tax Code. We will raise taxes on the wealthiest individuals and companies in our society. That will be one of their contributions to create the high-skill, high-wage economy that we seek. And I will say to the drug companies, the insurance companies, and the others who profit from the status quo, they must join our cause to make comprehensive reforms in our medical care system. The time has come for all Americans to have affordable health care, a real chance at a healthy life.

In return for these contributions, we are determined to create long-term, good-paying private sector jobs. We will encourage the development of new technologies and find markets for them all across America and around the world. We will provide special incentives to new businesses and small businesses to create the jobs of the future. We will lower their costs of capital so they can expand and succeed. We will upgrade the skills of the long-term unemployed and the rest of our work force. And when military cutbacks hurt our enterprises, we'll help defense workers to find new careers and to continue productive lives.

That's what my plan is all about: a leaner, more efficient, more responsive Government; a ladder of contribution that demands the most from those who have the most; investment incentives to help businesses build for the future and create jobs for all Americans; education and training to prepare workers and students for new jobs in a new economy; a reformed medical system that restores peace of mind to family life; an America where every citizen has a right to a prosperous economy and a shared patriotic stake in the work to make it grow.

That is a program for economic change you have justly demanded. Now it's time for all Americans to join the cause and embrace the change. It is time to restore the American dream.

Thank you, and God bless you.

NOTE: The President spoke at 12:06 p.m. from the Oval Office at the White House.

Exchange With Reporters Prior to a Meeting With Democratic Congressional Leaders
February 15, 1993

Economic Program Presentation

Q. Are you going to appear before Congress, Mr. President, in parliamentary-style Q&A?

The President. That hasn't been resolved yet. I'm interested in it, but we haven't finally resolved that.

Q. What would determine it?

The President. We just haven't resolved it yet. We'll probably know by the end of the day.

Q. Is Wednesday night's speech shaping up as the most important of your life?

The President. Well, I don't—[*inaudible*]. In the sense that every one—the ones that are ahead are more important than the ones that are behind.

I think tonight is important. I think Wednesday night is important. But you know, we're trying to change a direction of 12 years and take a new course. I'm going to offer a program that will create half a million or more jobs in the short run, that is highly progressive, that is very well-balanced, that is faithful to the great middle class of this country and good for the things that we care about, jobs and education and health care. But I think it's going to be very important that I sell it to the Congress and to the American people and that we have a partnership here. So yes, it'll be big.

NOTE: The exchange began at 11:22 a.m. in the Roosevelt Room at the White House.

Exchange With Reporters Prior to a Meeting With Democratic Congressional Leaders
February 15, 1993

Energy Tax

Q. Mr. President, if I could ask a specific question. What is——

The President. I may not give you a specific answer. [*Laughter*]

Q. You don't have to get into too much detail, but from your perspective what's more progressive, a broad-based energy tax based on Btu's or an ad valorem type of energy tax? What would be more progressive for the middle class?

The President. Well, I think, first of all, you can't evaluate one of these things without seeing the whole package. But I think a Btu tax is,

because an ad valorem tax reinforces price changes. In other words, if you have an ad valorem tax and the price of one fuel goes up, then the tax rate goes up. So, it would aggravate whatever price changes are out there in the market, and that would hurt the consumers more.

Q. Have you settled on a Btu tax?

The President. I answered a very specific question in a photo op. [*Laughter*]

NOTE: The exchange began at 1:45 p.m. in the Roosevelt Room at the White House.

Address to the Nation on the Economic Program
February 15, 1993

Good evening. I have chosen this day on which we honor two great Presidents to talk with you about the serious problems and the

great promise of our country and the absolute necessity for change if we're to secure a better future for ourselves and for our children. On

Wednesday evening I'll address the Congress about the specifics of my plan, but first I turn to you for your strength and support, to enlist you in the cause of changing our course.

This is a momentous time for our Nation. We stand at the end of the cold war and on the edge of the 21st century. For two decades we've moved steadily toward a global economy in which we must compete with people around the world, a world which requires us to work hard and smart, a world in which putting people first is more than a political slogan, it's a philosophy of governing and the only path to prosperity.

For 12 years we've followed a very different philosophy. It declared that Government is the problem, that fairness to the middle class is less important than keeping taxes low on the wealthy, that Government can do nothing about our deepest problems: lost jobs, declining wages, increasing inequality, inadequate educational opportunity, and a health care system that costs a fortune but does too little.

During those 12 years as Governor of Arkansas, I followed a very different course, more like what you've done at home and at work. I invested in the future of our people and balanced a State budget with honesty and fairness and without gimmicks. It's just common sense. But in the 26 days I've been your President, I've already learned that here in Washington, common sense isn't too common. And you've paid a lot for that loss of common sense.

The typical middle class family is working harder for less. Despite the talk of a recovery, more than 9 million of our fellow citizens are still out of work. And as this chart indicates, if this were a real, normal recovery, 3 million more Americans would already be back at work by now. In fact, there are more jobless people now than there were at what the experts call the bottom of this recession.

All during this last 12 years the Federal deficit has roared out of control. Look at this: The big tax cuts for the wealthy, the growth in Government spending, and soaring health care costs all caused the Federal deficit to explode. Our debt is now 4 times as big as it was in 1980. That's right. In the last 12 years we piled up 4 times as much debt as in the previous 200.

Now, if all that debt had been invested in strengthening our economy, we'd at least have something to show for our money: more jobs, better educated people, a health care system

that works. But as you can see, while the deficit went up, investments in the things that make us stronger and smarter, richer and safer, were neglected: less invested in education, less in our children's future, less in transportation, less in local law enforcement. An awful lot of that money was just wasted.

This matters. When you don't invest in jobs and education and economic opportunity, unemployment goes up and our incomes go down. And when the deficit gets bigger and bigger and bigger, the Government takes more of your money just for interest payments. And then it's harder for you to borrow money for your own business or to afford a new home or to send a child to college.

That's exactly what's been happening. Once our living standards doubled every 25 years. But at the rate we're going today our living standard won't double for another 100 years, until our grandchildren's grandchildren are born. That's too long. We must act now to restore the American dream.

Despite the enormity of this crisis, believe it or not, the status quo still has its defenders, people who point to hopeful statistics like the recent increase in productivity and consumer confidence and say we should do nothing. Well, American business has been forced to become more competitive in this global economy. And I'm glad that consumers' confidence is up since the election. But we're not generating jobs or making headway on these other long-term problems.

My message to you is clear: The price of doing the same old thing is far higher than the price of change. After all, that's why you sent me here: not to keep this seat warm but to work for fundamental change, to make Washington work for all Americans, not just the special interests, and to chart a course that will enable us to compete and win in this new world.

Here's the challenge I will offer the Congress and the country on Wednesday. We'll invest in our future by nurturing our children and supporting their education, by rewarding work and family, by creating the jobs of the future and training our people to fill them. Our every effort will reflect what President Franklin Roosevelt called bold, persistent experimentation, a willingness to stay with things that work and stop things that don't.

Change must begin at the top. That's why I cut the White House staff by 25 percent and ordered Federal agencies to cut billions of dollars in administrative costs and to trim 100,000 Federal positions by attrition. And in my budget there will be more than 150 specific cuts in Government spending programs. Then I'll ask the wealthiest Americans to pay their fair share.

That brings us to those of you who gave the most in the 1980's. I had hoped to invest in your future by creating jobs, expanding education, reforming health care, and reducing the debt [deficit] [1] without asking more of you. And I've worked harder than I've ever worked in my life to meet that goal. But I can't because the deficit has increased so much beyond my earlier estimates and beyond even the worst official Government estimates from last year. We just have to face the fact that to make the changes our country needs, more Americans must contribute today so that all Americans can do better tomorrow. But I can assure you of this: You're not going alone anymore. You're not going first. And you're no longer going to pay more and get less. Seventy percent of the new taxes I'll propose, 70 percent, will be paid by those who make more than $100,000 a year. And for the first time in more than a decade, we're all in this together.

More important, here's the payoff: Our comprehensive plan for economic growth will create millions of long-term, good-paying jobs, including a program to jumpstart our economy with another 500,000 jobs in 1993 and 1994. And as we make deep cuts in existing Government programs, we'll make new investments where they'll do the most good: incentives to business to create new jobs; investments in education and training; special efforts for displaced defense workers; a fairer tax system to ensure that parents who work full-time will no longer raise their children in poverty; welfare reform to move people from welfare to work; vaccinations and Head Start opportunities for all children who need them; and a system of affordable quality health care for all Americans. Our na-

tional service plan will throw open the doors of college opportunity to the daughters and sons of the middle class. Then we'll challenge them to give something back to our country as teachers, police officers, community service workers, taking care of our own right here at home. And we'll do it all while reducing our debt [deficit].[1]

Change this fundamental will not be easy, nor will it be quick. But at stake is the control of our economic destiny. Within minutes of the time I conclude my address to Congress Wednesday night, the special interests will be out in force. Those who profited from the status quo will oppose the changes we seek, the budget cuts, the revenue increases, the new investment priorities. Every step of the way they'll oppose it. Many have already lined the corridors of power with high-priced lobbyists. They are the defenders of decline. And we must be the architects of the future.

I'm confident in our cause because I believe in America, and I know we have learned the hard lessons of the 1980's. This is your country. You demonstrated the power of the people in the last election. I urge you to stay informed and to stay involved. If you're vigilant and vocal, we can do what we have to do.

On this Presidents' Day, we recall the many times in our history when past Presidents have challenged this Nation from this office in times of crisis. If you will join with me, we can create an economy in which all Americans work hard and prosper. This is nothing less than a call to arms to restore the vitality of the American dream.

When I was a boy, we had a name for the belief that we should all pull together to build a better, stronger nation. We called it patriotism. And we still do.

Good night, and God bless America.

NOTE: The President spoke at 9 p.m. from the Oval Office at the White House.

---

[1] White House correction.

Exchange With Reporters Prior to a Meeting With Democratic Congressional Leaders
February 16, 1993

Economic Program

Q. Mr. President, are you going to expand the millionaires surtax and apply it to everyone earning more than $250,000——

The President. Stay tuned.

Q. ——as has been reported?

Q. Mr. President, Senator Gramm says this isn't contributions from everybody, it's just raw pain.

Q. Which Gramm? [*Laughter*]

The President. I think when you see the whole program, it won't be raw pain. I think most middle class Americans, when you look at the costs plus the benefits, are going to be much, much better off. It's a very progressive program. And a lot of the wealthiest American business leaders I've talked to believe that their businesses will be much better off with stable long-term low interest rates and the availability to invest and grow. And they think that the price is a small one compared to the long-term economic health of their own businesses as well as the economy.

Q. Are you going to have a second round of tax increases to pay for health care, as a memo advising your task force——

The President. Tune in.

Q. But will that be necessary——

The President. Depends on how you do it.

Q. Is it harder to cut spending than you thought it would be? Is it more difficult?

The President. We've cut quite a bit of spending. I think it is difficult to justify cutting big health care spending unless it is in the context of providing affordable health care to everybody, because you don't want to do it in a way that's really burdensome on the consumers with health care. The people we help now with Government money in health care are elderly and the poor. So we can control that spending in the years ahead but only in the context of an overall health care program. So if you take health care off the books and you take interest on the debt off the books, it's more difficult to get big spending cuts. But I think we've done a pretty good job, and tomorrow night we'll outline it.

NOTE: The exchange began at 9:50 a.m. in the Cabinet Room at the White House.

Exchange With Reporters Prior to a Meeting With Democratic Congressional Leaders
February 16, 1993

Economic Program

Q. Mr. President, do you think you can get Ross Perot to at least not criticize this economic plan?

The President. I don't know——

Q. Have you been in touch with him or anybody on your staff been in touch with him to try to get him on board?

Q. Do they treat you like this all the time?

The President. Tomorrow night, all the time. [*Laughter*] All the time.

Q. What a job. [*Laughter*]

Q. Mr. President, what——

The President. ——budget practices—it's truth in budgeting, truth in budgeting. We're using objective numbers, the most conservative revenue estimates. It'll be the most candid budget Congress has received in a long time. And I think there will be a lot of people who understand it and will respond very positively to it.

Q. Well, the markets are down sharply this morning. Do you think that's an immediate reaction to your——

The President. No. Look, the bond market's a better indicator, because they—and that response has been very positive. And I think when the business community, those people who come in here from the business community who actually know pretty well what's in this program, have responded very positively to it. So I wouldn't say that.

NOTE: The exchange began at 11:25 a.m. in the Roosevelt Room at the White House. A tape was not available for verification of the content of this exchange.

Teleconference Remarks to the California Economic Conference
February 16, 1993

Thank you very much, Willie Brown. And thank you, ladies and gentlemen, for letting me join you by high-tech communications for just a few minutes.

First of all, let me say how very impressed I was by the comment of the previous speaker. He may not have been in California very long, but I think his prescription for how to solve our Nation's problems, concentrating on investment and achieving consensus, is what we all have to focus on.

I wish I could be with you in person today. You know, I have spent a great deal of time in California in the last 16 months talking to people about the problems and the promise of your State. I don't believe for a moment that America's economy can recover until California recovers, and I applaud what you are doing in this economic summit.

I understand the economic summit that I sponsored down in Little Rock for our Nation may have been part of the inspiration for this meeting, and if so, I'm very grateful. I applaud Willie Brown and Senator Roberti and Governor Wilson for cosponsoring this, and all the rest of you who are part of it.

Let me get to the point very quickly because I think that these summits work so much better when there is interaction, so I don't want to intrude on what I think is going very well. First, I want to reaffirm my commitment to the economic revitalization of California. Californians played a major role in my election as President and play a very major role in my Presidency now, people who are important to your future. Our Trade Ambassador, Mickey Kantor, has already spoken this morning; you know he's from California. The Secretary of State, Warren Christopher, is from California, and we're increasingly involving the State Department in the revitalization of the American economy. Our Budget Director, the Director of the Office of

Management and Budget, Leon Panetta, was a Congressman from northern California and is here with me; I'm in his building as we speak today. And of course, the Chair of the Council of Economic Advisers, Laura Tyson, is from northern California. All of these people are in a position to bring their experience and knowledge to bear on what we in the National Government can do.

In addition to that, I've already had an extensive visit with Senator Feinstein. I've talked with Senator Boxer. I've talked with many members of your congressional delegation about the issues that they have brought to my attention. And as I said, the time I spent there taught me a lot about the problems in California that are caused by reducing employment in the defense industry, by the collapse of real estate, by the problems in the financial institutions, by the general manufacturing difficulties, and by the increased costs brought on by immigration as well as the population increase generally in California.

Let me say first that I'm convinced we're going to have to solve this problem by partnership. I am offering the American people a program which will reverse three big trends in our country which have affected California. We built an American dream, especially after World War II, based on increasing economic prosperity in a high-wage, high-growth economy, increasing equality among our working people, and making more and more strength out of our diversity. The economic and social difficulties we have faced in the last few years threaten to reverse all those trends. Wages are stagnant. Inequality has increased over the last decade, and our diversity has often been a source of great tension and division in California and elsewhere throughout the country.

I'm convinced that in order to change this, the National Government has to take the lead, first of all in investing in our people, their jobs, their technology, and their future; secondly, in dealing with the health care crisis; thirdly, in reducing the enormous Federal debt to stabilize long-term interest rates and free up more money for investment in the private sector; and finally, by developing economic policies in partnership with the private sector which encourage more investment in the private sector and which enable us to work together to create that high-wage, high-growth economy again.

As that applies to California, it means we will be doing the following things: First of all, in my economic program there's a plan to jumpstart the economy, to create another half-million jobs in the near future. California will receive a significant number of those jobs.

Secondly, I intend to follow through on the technology policy I announced in California in the last campaign. That means we'll be providing more incentives to start new enterprises and to expand existing enterprises and to build on the job-generating capacity of the technology-leading companies that are in your State.

Thirdly, I want to invest in our children and their future and our educational system. I want to do what I can at the national level to alleviate some of the problems caused by the financial conditions you have there.

Fourthly, I'll ask the Congress to change some of the tax rules involving passive losses in hope of alleviating some of the real estate problems in California, as well as giving industry more incentive to invest in the next couple of years.

Next, Mr. Panetta and I have worked hard on trying to figure out how we can redesign some of these Federal programs so that the Federal Government can keep its commitment to the States that have been overwhelmed by immigration problems, California most of all, but also Texas and Florida and some other States who should have been helped more by the National Government because of the burdens they bear due to a national policy on immigration.

Finally, let me just say, if I might harken back again to the last person who spoke before I did, California has some challenges that will have to be met by Californians. You will have to take the lead in improving your education system. I'm going to give you a good Department of Education that will help to reform the practices in education and to make education work again. But some of the premier reformers in America are right there in California now. You have to find a way to make their exceptions the rule in California education.

And next, you will have to take the lead in making sure your manufacturing and production environment is at least competitive with other States in the United States, not by driving down wages but by changing the environment so that you can be competitive. I'll do whatever I can to support you. The best thing we could do here to help you with that is to solve the health care crisis: to bring health care costs in line with inflation; to make basic, affordable health care available to all; and therefore, to stop whatever incentives there are for people to move across State lines or to move their plants because they've got high embedded health care costs. But a lot of these productivity issues are going to have to be faced, and faced squarely, by the people of California and every other State.

We're prepared to do our part. I'll say again: This country cannot rise again to its full potential until California is on the move again. I'm going to do what I can to help. I ask you for your support in my aggressive plan to reduce the debt and to increase investment in education and training, in new technologies, in new jobs, and in dealing with the health care crisis. I'll do what I can to support you. Together, we can turn this country around. We can lift California up, and California can once again be the beacon of hope for America and for the world.

Thank you very much.

NOTE: The President spoke at 2:38 p.m. via satellite from Room 459 of the Old Executive Office Building to the conference in Los Angeles. In his remarks, he referred to Willie L. Brown, Jr., California State Assembly speaker, and David Roberti, California State Senate president pro tempore.

Exchange With Reporters Prior to a Meeting With Democratic Congressional Leaders
February 16, 1993

Economic Program

Q. Mr. President, your spokesman says there would be no negative effects on the economy from the tax portion of your stimulus plan and your economic plan, and that the stock market's reaction today is just a simple stock market cycle that has nothing to do with your program. Do you agree?

The President. I do. I mean, the people in the stock market know, have known in general all along what was going to be in the program, and the stock market has gone up markedly since the election. The stock market's been going up since the election.

Q. Do you agree there will be no negative effects on the economy from taxes?

The President. Absolutely, I do. I believe if we reduce the deficit it will stabilize long-term interest rates, free up money for growth and increase jobs——

Q. Your spokesman also said that the middle class tax increase could also touch those making $30,000 and more. Is that breaking the faith with the middle class, Mr. President?

The President. Tune in tomorrow night.

NOTE: The exchange began at 3:08 p.m. in the State Dining Room at the White House.

Message to the Congress Reporting on the National Emergency With Respect to Iraq
February 16, 1993

To the Congress of the United States:

I hereby report to the Congress on the developments since the last report of August 3, 1992, concerning the national emergency with respect to Iraq that was declared in Executive Order No. 12722 of August 2, 1990. This report is submitted pursuant to sections 401(c) of the National Emergencies Act ("NEA"), 50 U.S.C. 1641(c), and section 204(c) of the International Emergency Economic Powers Act ("IEEPA"), 50 U.S.C. 1703(c).

Executive Order No. 12722 ordered the immediate blocking of all property and interests in property of the Government of Iraq (including the Central Bank of Iraq) then or thereafter located in the United States or within the possession or control of a U.S. person. That order also prohibited the importation into the United States of goods and services of Iraqi origin, as well as the exportation of goods, services, and technology from the United States to Iraq. The order prohibited travel-related transactions to or from Iraq and the performance of any contract in support of any industrial, commercial, or governmental project in Iraq. U.S. persons were

also prohibited from granting or extending credit or loans to the Government of Iraq.

The foregoing prohibitions (as well as the blocking of Government of Iraq property) were continued and augmented on August 9, 1990, by Executive Order No. 12724, which was issued in order to align the sanctions imposed by the United States with United Nations Security Council Resolution 661 of August 6, 1990.

This report discusses only matters concerning the national emergency with respect to Iraq that was declared in Executive Order No. 12722 and matters relating to Executive Orders Nos. 12724 and 12817 (the "Executive Orders"). The report covers events from August 2, 1992, through February 1, 1993.

1. On October 21, 1992, President Bush issued Executive Order No. 12817, implementing in the United States measures adopted in United Nations Security Council Resolution ("UNSCR") No. 778 of October 2, 1992. UNSCR No. 778 requires U.N. member states temporarily to transfer to a U.N. escrow account up to $200 million apiece in Iraqi oil proceeds paid by the purchaser after the imposition of

U.N. sanctions on Iraq. These funds finance Iraq's obligations for U.N. activities with respect to Iraq, including expenses to verify Iraqi weapons destruction and to provide humanitarian assistance in Iraq on a nonpartisan basis. A portion of the escrowed funds will also fund the activities of the U.N. Compensation Commission in Geneva, which will handle claims from victims of the Iraqi invasion of Kuwait. The funds placed in the escrow account are to be returned, with interest, to the member states that transferred them to the U.N., as funds are received from future sales of Iraqi oil authorized by the United Nations Security Council. No member state is required to fund more than half of the total contributions to the escrow account.

Executive Order No. 12817 authorized the Secretary of the Treasury (the "Secretary") to identify the proceeds of the sale of Iraqi petroleum or petroleum products paid for by or on behalf of the purchaser on or after August 6, 1990, and directed United States financial institutions holding such funds to transfer them to the Federal Reserve Bank of New York ("FRBNY") in the manner required by the Secretary. Executive Order No. 12817 further directs the FRBNY to receive, hold, and transfer funds in which the Government of Iraq has an interest at the direction of the Secretary to fulfill U.S. rights and obligations pursuant to UNSCR No. 778.

2. The economic sanctions imposed on Iraq by the Executive orders are administered by the Treasury Department's Office of Foreign Assets Control ("FAC") pursuant to the Iraqi Sanctions Regulations, 31 CFR Part 575 ("ISR"). The ISR were amended on September 1, 1992, to revoke section 575.603, which had required U.S. financial institutions to file monthly reports regarding certain bank accounts in which the Government of Iraq has an interest. While this information was needed during the early implementation of the regulations and for a period thereafter, it is no longer required on a monthly basis and can be obtained by FAC on a case-by-case basis as required. The amendment is in harmony with President Bush's Regulatory Initiative.

3. Investigations of possible violations of the Iraqi sanctions continue to be pursued and appropriate enforcement actions taken. These are intended to deter future activities in violation of the sanctions. Additional civil penalty notices were prepared during the reporting period for violations of the IEEPA and ISR with respect to transactions involving Iraq. Penalties were collected, principally from financial institutions which engaged in unauthorized, albeit apparently inadvertent, transactions with respect to Iraq.

4. Investigation also continues into the roles played by various individuals and firms outside Iraq in Saddam Hussein's procurement network. These investigations may lead to additions to the FAC listing of individuals and organizations determined to be Specially Designated Nationals ("SDNs") of the Government of Iraq.

5. Pursuant to Executive Order No. 12817 implementing UNSCR No. 778, on October 26, 1992, FAC directed the FRBNY to establish a blocked account for receipt of certain post-August 6, 1990, Iraqi oil sales proceeds, and to hold, invest, and transfer these funds as required by the order. On the same date, FAC directed the eight United States financial institutions holding the affected oil proceeds, on an allocated, pro rata basis, to transfer a total of $200 million of these blocked Iraqi assets to the FRBNY account. On December 15, 1992, following the payment of $20 million by the Government of Kuwait and $30 million by the Government of Saudi Arabia to a special United Nations-controlled account, entitled UNSCR No. 778 Escrow Account, the FRBNY was directed to transfer a corresponding amount of $50 million from the blocked account it holds to the United Nations-controlled account. Future transfers from the blocked FRBNY account will be made on a matching basis up to the $200 million for which the United States is potentially obligated pursuant to UNSCR No. 778.

6. Since the last report, one case filed against the Government of Iraq has gone to judgment. *Consarc Corporation* v. *Iraqi Ministry of Industry and Minerals et al.*, No. 90–2269 (D.D.C., filed December 29, 1992), arose out of a contract for the sale of furnaces by plaintiff to the Iraqi Ministry of Industry and Minerals ("MIM"), an Iraqi governmental entity. In connection with the contract, the Iraqi defendants opened an irrevocable letter of credit with an Iraqi bank in favor of Consarc, which was advised by Pittsburgh National Bank ("PNB"), with the Bank of New York ("BoNY") entering into a confirmed reimbursement agreement with the advising bank. Funds were set aside at BoNY, in an account of the Iraqi bank, for reimbursement of BoNY if PNB made a payment to Consarc on the letter of credit and sought reim-

bursement from BoNY. Consarc received a down payment from the Iraqi MIM and manufactured the furnaces. No goods were shipped prior to imposition of sanctions on August 2, 1990, and the United States claimed that the funds on deposit in the Iraqi bank account at BoNY were blocked, as well as the furnaces manufactured for the Iraqi Government or the proceeds of the sale of the furnaces to third parties. The district court ruled that the furnaces or their sales proceeds were properly blocked pursuant to the declaration of the national emergency and blocking of Iraqi Government property interests, but that, due to fraud on MIM's part in concluding the sales contract, the funds on deposit in an Iraqi bank account at BoNY were not the property of the Government of Iraq, and ordered FAC to unblock these funds. FAC has noted its appeal of this ruling.

7. FAC has issued a total of 337 specific licenses regarding transactions pertaining to Iraq or Iraqi assets since August 1990. Since the last report, 49 specific licenses have been issued. Licenses were issued for transactions such as the filing of legal actions involving Iraqi interests, for legal representation of Iraq, and the exportation to Iraq of donated medicine, medical supplies, and food intended for humanitarian relief purposes.

To ensure compliance with the terms of the licenses which have been issued, stringent reporting requirements have been imposed that are closely monitored. Licensed accounts are regularly audited by FAC compliance personnel and deputized auditors from other regulatory agencies. FAC compliance personnel continue to work closely with both State and Federal bank regulatory and law enforcement agencies in conducting special audits of Iraqi accounts subject to the ISR.

8. The expenses incurred by the Federal Government in the 6-month period from August 2, 1992, through February 1, 1993, that are directly attributable to the exercise of powers and authorities conferred by the declaration of a national emergency with respect to Iraq are estimated at about $2 million, most of which represents wage and salary costs for Federal personnel. Personnel costs were largely centered in the Department of the Treasury (particularly in FAC, the U.S. Customs Service, the Office of the Assistant Secretary for Enforcement, the Office of the Assistant Secretary for International Affairs, and the Office of the General Counsel), the Department of State (particularly the Bureau of Economic and Business Affairs, the Bureau of Near East and South Asian Affairs, the Bureau of International Organizations, and the Office of the Legal Adviser), the Department of Transportation (particularly the U.S. Coast Guard), and the Department of Commerce (particularly in the Bureau of Export Administration and the Office of the General Counsel).

9. The United States imposed economic sanctions on Iraq in response to Iraq's invasion and illegal occupation of Kuwait, a clear act of brutal aggression. The United States, together with the international community, is maintaining economic sanctions against Iraq because the Iraqi regime has failed to comply fully with United Nations Security Council resolutions, including those calling for the elimination of Iraqi weapons of mass destruction, the inviolability of the Iraq-Kuwait boundary, the release of Kuwaiti and other third country nationals, compensation for victims of Iraqi aggression, long-term monitoring of weapons of mass destruction (WMD) capabilities, and the return of Kuwaiti assets stolen during its illegal occupation of Kuwait. The U.N. sanctions remain in place; the United States will continue to enforce those sanctions.

The Saddam Hussein regime continued to violate basic human rights by repressing the Iraqi civilian population and depriving it of humanitarian assistance. The United Nations Security Council passed resolutions that permit Iraq to sell $1.6 billion of oil under U.N. auspices to fund the provision of food, medicine, and other humanitarian supplies to the people of Iraq. Under the U.N. resolutions, the equitable distribution within Iraq of this assistance would be supervised and monitored by the United Nations. The Iraqi regime continued to refuse to accept these resolutions and has thereby chosen to perpetuate the suffering of its civilian population.

The regime of Saddam Hussein continues to pose an unusual and extraordinary threat to the national security and foreign policy of the United States, as well as to regional peace and security. Because of Iraq's failure to comply fully with United Nations Security Council resolutions, the United States will therefore continue to apply economic sanctions to deter Iraq from threatening peace and stability in the region, and I will continue to report periodically to the Congress on significant developments, pursuant to 50 U.S.C. 1703(c).

WILLIAM J. CLINTON

The White House,
February 16, 1993.

Exchange With Reporters Prior to a Meeting With Congressional Leaders
February 17, 1993

Economic Program

Q. Mr. President, if you count Social Security as a tax increase, you don't have a one-to-one ratio. Are you going to have enough cuts in this program to be able to sell this thing?

The President. I think so. There are 150 specific ones, and I'll be glad to entertain some more if anybody's got any specific ideas.

The Vice President. At this point——

Q. Can you honestly say, as Senator Dole has asked, that you have made all the cuts you could possibly make in this program?

The President. I can honestly say I've made more specific cuts that affect me personally than I can think that any of my predecessors have made and that I intend to find more as I go along. I've just been here 4 weeks, and I'll continue to work on it. But I've made an awful lot of cuts; I'm going to make some more.

Q. Have you convinced Senator Dole and Michel and all of the other Republican leaders? And did you call Ross Perot?

The President. My duty is to try to convince them that I will.

The Vice President. In the words of the old hymn, they're "almost persuaded."

The President. I thought that was a country and western song. [*Laughter*]

Q. They don't look it.

Q. How about Ross Perot, Mr. President?

White House Jogging Track

Q. Why build a jogging track when you're making cuts across the board in Government?

The President. I thought the thing was going to be paid for with contributions; that's what I was told. I think it would be a good thing to have, but I think if we can pay for it with contributions; otherwise, I don't think we ought to spend any tax money on it.

Q. You don't have an alternative way to pay for it?

The President. I was told that the stuff had been donated already. I told them if it was all going to be donated, it was fine with me if it was built. That's what I was told from the very beginning, so that's all I know about it.

NOTE: The exchange began at 2:22 p.m. in the Cabinet Room at the White House.

Address Before a Joint Session of Congress on Administration Goals
February 17, 1993

Mr. President, Mr. Speaker, Members of the House and the Senate, distinguished Americans here as visitors in this Chamber, as am I. It is nice to have a fresh excuse for giving a long speech. [*Laughter*]

When Presidents speak to Congress and the Nation from this podium, typically they comment on the full range in challenges and opportunities that face the United States. But this is not an ordinary time, and for all the many tasks that require our attention, I believe tonight one calls on us to focus, to unite, and to act. And that is our economy. For more than anything else, our task tonight as Americans is to make our economy thrive again.

Let me begin by saying that it has been too long, at least three decades, since a President has come and challenged Americans to join him on a great national journey, not merely to consume the bounty of today but to invest for a much greater one tomorrow.

Like individuals, nations must ultimately decide how they wish to conduct themselves, how they wish to be thought of by those with whom they live, and later, how they wish to be judged by history. Like every individual man and woman, nations must decide whether they are prepared to rise to the occasions history presents them.

We have always been a people of youthful energy and daring spirit. And at this historic moment, as communism has fallen, as freedom is spreading around the world, as a global economy is taking shape before our eyes, Americans have called for change. And now it is up to those of us in this room to deliver for them.

Our Nation needs a new direction. Tonight I present to you a comprehensive plan to set our Nation on that new course. I believe we will find our new direction in the basic old values that brought us here over the last two centuries: a commitment to opportunity, to individual responsibility, to community, to work, to family, and to faith. We must now break the habits of both political parties and say there can be no more something for nothing and admit frankly that we are all in this together.

The conditions which brought us as a nation to this point are well-known: two decades of low productivity, growth, and stagnant wages; persistent unemployment and underemployment; years of huge Government deficits and declining investment in our future; exploding health care costs and lack of coverage for millions of Americans; legions of poor children; education and job training opportunities inadequate to the demands of this tough, global economy. For too long we have drifted without a strong sense of purpose or responsibility or community.

And our political system so often has seemed paralyzed by special interest groups, by partisan bickering, and by the sheer complexity of our problems. I believe we can do better because we remain the greatest nation on Earth, the world's strongest economy, the world's only military superpower. If we have the vision, the will, and the heart to make the changes we must, we can still enter the 21st century with possibilities our parents could not even have imagined and enter it having secured the American dream for ourselves and for future generations.

I well remember 12 years ago President Reagan stood at this very podium and told you and the American people that if our national debt were stacked in thousand-dollar bills, the stack would reach 67 miles into space. Well, today that stack would reach 267 miles. I tell you this not to assign blame for this problem. There is plenty of blame to go around in both branches of the Government and both parties. The time has come for the blame to end. I did not seek this office to place blame. I come here tonight to accept responsibility, and I want you to accept responsibility with me. And if we do right by this country, I do not care who gets the credit for it.

The plan I offer you has four fundamental components. First, it shifts our emphasis in public and private spending from consumption to investment, initially by jumpstarting the economy in the short term and investing in our people, their jobs, and their incomes over the long run. Second, it changes the rhetoric of the past into the actions of the present by honoring work and families in every part of our public decisionmaking. Third, it substantially reduces the Federal deficit honestly and credibly by using in the beginning the most conservative estimates of Government revenues, not, as the executive branch has done so often in the past, using the most optimistic ones. And finally, it seeks to earn the trust of the American people by paying for these plans first with cuts in Government waste and efficiency; second, with cuts, not gimmicks, in Government spending; and by fairness, for a change, in the way additional burdens are borne.

Tonight I want to talk with you about what Government can do because I believe Government must do more. But let me say first that the real engine of economic growth in this country is the private sector, and second, that each of us must be an engine of growth and change. The truth is that as Government creates more opportunity in this new and different time, we must also demand more responsibility in turn.

Our immediate priority must be to create jobs, create jobs now. Some people say, "Well, we're in a recovery, and we don't have to do that." Well, we all hope we're in a recovery, but we're sure not creating new jobs. And there's no recovery worth its salt that doesn't put the American people back to work.

To create jobs and guarantee a strong recovery, I call on Congress to enact an immediate package of jobs investments of over $30 billion to put people to work now, to create a half a million jobs: jobs to rebuild our highways and airports, to renovate housing, to bring new life to rural communities, and spread hope and opportunity among our Nation's youth. Especially I want to emphasize, after the events of last year in Los Angeles and the countless stories of despair in our cities and in our poor rural communities, this proposal will create almost 700,000 new summer jobs for displaced, unemployed young people alone this summer. And tonight I invite America's business leaders to join us in this effort so that together we can provide over one million summer jobs in cities and poor rural areas for our young people.

Second, our plan looks beyond today's business cycle because our aspirations extend into the next century. The heart of this plan deals with the long term. It is an investment program designed to increase public and private investment in areas critical to our economic future. And it has a deficit reduction program that will increase the savings available for the private sector to invest, will lower interest rates, will decrease the percentage of the Federal budget claimed by interest payments, and decrease the risk of financial market disruptions that could adversely affect our economy.

Over the long run, all this will bring us a higher rate of economic growth, improved productivity, more high-quality jobs, and an improved economic competitive position in the world. In order to accomplish both increased investment and deficit reduction, something no American Government has ever been called upon to do at the same time before, spending must be cut and taxes must be raised.

The spending cuts I recommend were carefully thought through in a way to minimize any adverse economic impact, to capture the peace dividend for investment purposes, and to switch the balance in the budget from consumption to more investment. The tax increases and the spending cuts were both designed to assure that the cost of this historic program to face and deal with our problems will be borne by those who could readily afford it the most. Our plan is designed, furthermore, and perhaps in some ways most importantly, to improve the health of American business through lower interest rates, more incentives to invest, and better trained workers.

Because small business has created such a high percentage of all the new jobs in our Nation over the last 10 or 15 years, our plan includes the boldest targeted incentives for small business in history. We propose a permanent investment tax credit for the smallest firms in this country, with revenues of under $5 million. That's about 90 percent of the firms in America, employing about 40 percent of the work force but creating a big majority of the net new jobs for more than a decade. And we propose new rewards for entrepreneurs who take new risks. We propose to give small business access to all the new technologies of our time. And we propose to attack this credit crunch which has denied small business the credit they need to flourish and prosper.

With a new network of community development banks and $1 billion to make the dream of enterprise zones real, we propose to bring new hope and new jobs to storefronts and factories from south Boston to south Texas to south central Los Angeles. This plan invests in our roads, our bridges, our transit systems, in high-speed railways and high-tech information systems. And it provides the most ambitious environmental cleanup in partnership with State and local government of our time, to put people to work and to preserve the environment for our future.

Standing as we are on the edge of a new century, we know that economic growth depends as never before on opening up new markets overseas and expanding the volume of world trade. And so, we will insist on fair trade rules in international markets as a part of a national economic strategy to expand trade, including the successful completion of the latest round of world trade talks and the successful completion of a North American Free Trade Agreement with appropriate safeguards for our workers and for the environment.

At the same time—and I say this to you in both parties and across America tonight, all the people who are listening—it is not enough to pass a budget or even to have a trade agreement. This world is changing so fast that we must have aggressive, targeted attempts to create the high-wage jobs of the future. That's what all our competitors are doing. We must give special attention to those critical industries that are going to explode in the 21st century but that are in trouble in America today, like aerospace. We must provide special assistance to areas and to workers displaced by cuts in the defense budget and by other unavoidable economic dislocations.

And again I will say we must do this together. I pledge to you that I will do my best to see that business and labor and Government work together for a change.

But all of our efforts to strengthen the economy will fail—let me say this again; I feel so strongly about this—all of our efforts to strengthen the economy will fail unless we also take this year, not next year, not 5 years from now but this year, bold steps to reform our health care system.

In 1992, we spent 14 percent of our income on health care, more than 30 percent more than any other country in the world, and yet we were the only advanced nation that did not provide a basic package of health care benefits to all of its citizens. Unless we change the present pattern, 50 percent of the growth in the deficit between now and the year 2000 will be in health care costs. By the year 2000 almost 20 percent of our income will be in health care. Our families will never be secure, our businesses will never be strong, and our Government will never again be fully solvent until we tackle the health care crisis. We must do it this year.

The combination of the rising cost of care and the lack of care and the fear of losing care are endangering the security and the very lives of millions of our people. And they are weakening our economy every day. Reducing health care costs can liberate literally hundreds of billions of dollars for new investment in growth and jobs. Bringing health costs in line with inflation would do more for the private sector in this country than any tax cut we could give and any spending program we could promote. Reforming health care over the long run is critically essential to reducing not only our deficit but to expanding investment in America.

Later this spring, after the First Lady and the many good people who are helping her all across the country complete their work, I will deliver to Congress a comprehensive plan for health care reform that finally will bring costs under control and provide security to all of our families, so that no one will be denied the coverage they need but so that our economic future will not be compromised either. We'll have to root out fraud and overcharges and make sure that paperwork no longer chokes your doctor. We'll have to maintain the highest American standards and the right to choose in a system that is the world's finest for all those who can access it. But first we must make choices. We must choose to give the American people the quality they demand and deserve with a system that will not bankrupt the country or further drive more Americans into agony.

Let me further say that I want to work with all of you on this. I realize this is a complicated issue. But we must address it. And I believe if there is any chance that Republicans and Democrats who disagree on taxes and spending or anything else could agree on one thing, surely we can all look at these numbers and go home and tell our people the truth. We cannot continue these spending patterns in public or private dollars for health care for less and less and less every year. We can do better. And I will work to do better.

Perhaps the most fundamental change the new direction I propose offers is its focus on the future and its investment which I seek in our children. Each day we delay really making a commitment to our children carries a dear cost. Half of the 2-year-olds in this country today don't receive the immunizations they need against deadly diseases. Our plan will provide them for every eligible child. And we know now that we will save $10 later for every $1 we spend by eliminating preventable childhood diseases. That's a good investment no matter how you measure it.

I recommend that the women, infants, and children's nutrition program be expanded so that every expectant mother who needs the help gets it. We all know that Head Start, a program that prepares children for school, is a success story. We all know that it saves money. But today it just reaches barely over one-third of all the eligible children. Under this plan, every eligible child will be able to get a head start. This is not just the right thing to do; it is the smart thing to do. For every dollar we invest today, we'll save $3 tomorrow. We have to start thinking about tomorrow. I've heard that somewhere before. [*Laughter*]

We have to ask more in our schools of our students, our teachers, our principals, our parents. Yes, we must give them the resources they need to meet high standards, but we must also use the authority and the influence and the funding of the Education Department to promote strategies that really work in learning. Money alone is not enough. We have to do what really works to increase learning in our schools.

We have to recognize that all of our high school graduates need some further education in order to be competitive in this global economy. So we have to establish a partnership between businesses and education and the Government for apprenticeship programs in every State in this country to give our people the skills they need. Lifelong learning must benefit not just young high school graduates but workers, too, throughout their career. The average 18-year-old today will change jobs seven times in a lifetime. We have done a lot in this country on worker training in the last few years, but the system is too fractured. We must develop a unified, simplified, sensible, streamlined worker-training program so that workers receive the training they need regardless of why they lost their jobs or whether they simply need to learn something new to keep them. We have got to do better on this.

And finally, I propose a program that got a great response from the American people all across this country last year: a program of national service to make college loans available to all Americans and to challenge them at the same time to give something back to their country as teachers or police officers or community service workers; to give them the option to pay the loans back, but at tax time so they can't beat the bill, but to encourage them instead to pay it back by making their country stronger and making their country better and giving us the benefit of their knowledge.

A generation ago when President Kennedy proposed and the United States Congress embraced the Peace Corps, it defined the character of a whole generation of Americans committed to serving people around the world. In this national service program, we will provide more than twice as many slots for people before they go to college to be in national service than ever served in the Peace Corps. This program could do for this generation of Members of Congress what the land grant college act did and what the GI bill did for former Congressmen. In the future, historians who got their education through the national service loan will look back on you and thank you for giving America a new lease on life, if you meet this challenge.

If we believe in jobs and we believe in learning, we must believe in rewarding work. If we believe in restoring the values that make America special, we must believe that there is dignity in all work, and there must be dignity for all workers. To those who care for our sick, who tend our children, who do our most difficult and tiring jobs, the new direction I propose will make this solemn, simple commitment: By expanding the refundable earned-income tax credit, we will make history. We will reward the work of millions of working poor Americans by realizing the principle that if you work 40 hours a week and you've got a child in the house, you will no longer be in poverty.

Later this year, we will offer a plan to end welfare as we know it. I have worked on this issue for the better part of a decade. And I know from personal conversations with many people that no one, no one wants to change the welfare system as badly as those who are trapped in it. I want to offer the people on welfare the education, the training, the child care, the health care they need to get back on their feet, but say after 2 years they must get back to work, too, in private business if possible, in public service if necessary. We have to end welfare as a way of life and make it a path to independence and dignity.

Our next great goal should be to strengthen our families. I compliment the Congress for passing the Family and Medical Leave Act as a good first step, but it is time to do more. This plan will give this country the toughest child support enforcement system it has ever had. It is time to demand that people take responsibility for the children they bring in this world.

And I ask you to help to protect our families against the violent crime which terrorizes our people and which tears our communities apart. We must pass a tough crime bill. I support not only the bill which didn't quite make it to the President's desk last year but also an initiative to put 100,000 more police officers on the street, to provide boot camps for first-time nonviolent offenders for more space for the hardened criminals in jail. And I support an initiative to do what we can to keep guns out of the hands of criminals. Let me say this. I will make you this bargain: If you will pass the Brady bill, I'll sure sign it.

Let me say now, we should move to the harder parts.

I think it is clear to every American, including every Member of Congress of both parties, that the confidence of the people who pay our bills in our institutions in Washington is not high.

We must restore it. We must begin again to make Government work for ordinary taxpayers, not simply for organized interest groups. And that beginning must start with real political reform. I am asking the United States Congress to pass a real campaign finance reform bill this year. I ask you to increase the participation of the American people by passing the motor voter bill promptly. I ask you to deal with the undue influence of special interests by passing a bill to end the tax deduction for lobbying and to act quickly to require all the people who lobby you to register as lobbyists by passing the lobbying registration bill.

Believe me, they were cheering that last section at home. I believe lobby reform and campaign finance reform are a sure path to increased popularity for Republicans and Democrats alike because it says to the voters back home, "This is your House. This is your Senate. We're your hired hands, and every penny we draw is your money."

Next, to revolutionize Government we have to ensure that we live within our means, and that should start at the top and with the White House. In the last few days I have announced a cut in the White House staff of 25 percent, saving approximately $10 million. I have ordered administrative cuts in budgets of agencies and departments. I have cut the Federal bureaucracy, or will over the next 4 years, by approximately 100,000 positions, for a combined savings of $9 billion. It is time for Government to demonstrate, in the condition we're in, that we can be as frugal as any household in America.

And that's why I also want to congratulate the Congress. I noticed the announcement of the leadership today that Congress is taking similar steps to cut its costs. I think that is important. I think it will send a very clear signal to the American people.

But if we really want to cut spending, we're going to have to do more, and some of it will be difficult. Tonight I call for an across-the-board freeze in Federal Government salaries for one year. And thereafter, during this 4-year period, I recommend that salaries rise at one point lower than the cost of living allowance normally involved in Federal pay increases.

Next, I recommend that we make 150 specific budget cuts, as you know, and that all those who say we should cut more be as specific as I have been.

Finally, let me say to my friends on both sides of the aisle, it is not enough simply to cut Government; we have to rethink the whole way it works. When I became President I was amazed at just the way the White House worked, in ways that added lots of money to what taxpayers had to pay, outmoded ways that didn't take maximum advantage of technology and didn't do things that any business would have done years ago to save taxpayers' money.

So I want to bring a new spirit of innovation into every Government Department. I want to push education reform, as I said, not just to spend more money but to really improve learning. Some things work, and some things don't. We ought to be subsidizing the things that work and discouraging the things that don't. I'd like to use that Superfund to clean up pollution for a change and not just pay lawyers.

In the aftermath of all the difficulties with the savings and loans, we must use Federal bank regulators to protect the security and safety of our financial institutions, but they should not be used to continue the credit crunch and to stop people from making sensible loans.

I'd like for us to not only have welfare reform but to reexamine the whole focus of all of our programs that help people, to shift them from entitlement programs to empowerment programs. In the end we want people not to need us anymore. I think that's important.

But in the end we have to get back to the deficit. For years there's been a lot of talk about it but very few credible efforts to deal with it. And now I understand why, having dealt with the real numbers for 4 weeks. But I believe this plan does; it tackles the budget deficit seriously and over the long term. It puts in place one of the biggest deficit reductions and one of the biggest changes in Federal priorities, from consumption to investment, in the history of this country at the same time over the next 4 years.

Let me say to all the people watching us tonight who will ask me these questions beginning tomorrow as I go around the country and who've asked it in the past: We're not cutting the deficit just because experts say it's the thing to do or because it has some intrinsic merit. We have to cut the deficit because the more we spend paying off the debt, the less tax dollars we have to invest in jobs and education and the future of this country. And the more money we take out of the pool of available savings, the harder it is for people in the private sector to borrow money at affordable interest rates for a college loan for their children, for a home mortgage, or to start a new business.

That's why we've got to reduce the debt, because it is crowding out other activities that we ought to be engaged in and that the American people ought to be engaged in. We cut the deficit so that our children will be able to buy a home, so that our companies can invest in the future and in retraining their workers, so that our Government can make the kinds of investments we need to be a stronger and smarter and safer nation.

If we don't act now, you and I might not even recognize this Government 10 years from now. If we just stay with the same trends of the last 4 years, by the end of the decade the deficit will be $635 billion a year, almost 80 percent of our gross domestic product. And paying interest on that debt will be the costliest Government program of all. We'll still be the world's largest debtor. And when Members of Congress come here, they'll be devoting over 20 cents on the dollar to interest payments, more than half of the budget to health care and to other entitlements. And you'll come here and deliberate and argue over 6 or 7 cents on the dollar, no matter what America's problems are. We will not be able to have the independence we need to chart the future that we must. And we'll be terribly dependent on foreign funds for a large portion of our investment.

This budget plan, by contrast, will by 1997 cut $140 billion in that year alone from the deficit, a real spending cut, a real revenue increase, a real deficit reduction, using the independent numbers of the Congressional Budget Office. [*Laughter*] Well, you can laugh, my fellow Republicans, but I'll point out that the Congressional Budget Office was normally more conservative in what was going to happen and closer to right than previous Presidents have been.

I did this so that we could argue about priorities with the same set of numbers. I did this so that no one could say I was estimating my way out of this difficulty. I did this because if we can agree together on the most prudent revenues we're likely to get if the recovery stays and we do right things economically, then it will turn out better for the American people than we say. In the last 12 years, because there were differences over the revenue estimates, you and I know that both parties were given greater elbow room for irresponsibility. This is tighten-

ing the rein on the Democrats as well as the Republicans. Let's at least argue about the same set of numbers so the American people will think we're shooting straight with them.

As I said earlier, my recommendation makes more than 150 difficult reductions to cut the Federal spending by a total of $246 billion. We are eliminating programs that are no longer needed, such as nuclear power research and development. We're slashing subsidies and canceling wasteful projects. But many of these programs were justified in their time, and a lot of them are difficult for me to recommend reductions in, some really tough ones for me personally. I recommend that we reduce interest subsidies to the Rural Electric Administration. That's a difficult thing for me to recommend. But I think that I cannot exempt the things that exist in my State or in my experience, if I ask you to deal with things that are difficult for you to deal with. We're going to have to have no sacred cows except the fundamental abiding interest of the American people.

I have to say that we all know our Government has been just great at building programs. The time has come to show the American people that we can limit them too; that we can not only start things, that we can actually stop things.

About the defense budget, I raise a hope and a caution. As we restructure our military forces to meet the new threats of the post-cold-war world, it is true that we can responsibly reduce our defense budget. And we may all doubt what that range of reductions is, but let me say that as long as I am President, I will do everything I can to make sure that the men and women who serve under the American flag will remain the best trained, the best prepared, the best equipped fighting force in the world. And every one of you should make that solemn pledge. We still have responsibilities around the world. We are the world's only superpower. This is still a dangerous and uncertain time, and we owe it to the people in uniform to make sure that we adequately provide for the national defense and for their interests and needs. Backed by an effective national defense and a stronger economy, our Nation will be prepared to lead a world challenged as it is everywhere by ethnic conflict, by the proliferation of weapons of mass destruction, by the global democratic revolution, and by challenges to the health of our global environment.

I know this economic plan is ambitious, but I honestly believe it is necessary for the continued greatness of the United States. And I think it is paid for fairly, first by cutting Government, then by asking the most of those who benefited the most in the past, and by asking more Americans to contribute today so that all of us can prosper tomorrow.

For the wealthiest, those earning more than $180,000 per year, I ask you all who are listening tonight to support a raise in the top rate for Federal income taxes from 31 to 36 percent. We recommend a 10 percent surtax on incomes over $250,000 a year, and we recommend closing some loopholes that let some people get away without paying any tax at all.

For businesses with taxable incomes in excess of $10 million, we recommend a raise in the corporate tax rate, also to 36 percent, as well as a cut in the deduction for business entertainment expenses. Our plan seeks to attack tax subsidies that actually reward companies more for shutting their operations down here and moving them overseas than for staying here and reinvesting in America. I say that as someone who believes that American companies should be free to invest around the world and as a former Governor who actively sought investment of foreign companies in my State. But the Tax Code should not express a preference to American companies for moving somewhere else, and it does in particular cases today.

We will seek to ensure that, through effective tax enforcement, foreign corporations who do make money in America simply pay the same taxes that American companies make on the same income.

To middle class Americans who have paid a great deal for the last 12 years and from whom I ask a contribution tonight, I will say again as I did on Monday night: You're not going alone any more, you're certainly not going first, and you're not going to pay more for less as you have too often in the past. I want to emphasize the facts about this plan: 98.8 percent of America's families will have no increase in their income tax rates, only 1.2 percent at the top.

Let me be clear: There will also be no new cuts in benefits for Medicare. As we move toward the 4th year, with the explosion in health care costs, as I said, projected to account for 50 percent of the growth of the deficit between now and the year 2000, there must be planned cuts in payments to providers, to doctors, to

hospitals, to labs, as a way of controlling health care costs. But I see these only as a stopgap until we can reform the entire health care system. If you'll help me do that, we can be fair to the providers and to the consumers of health care. Let me repeat this, because I know it matters to a lot of you on both sides of the aisle. This plan does not make a recommendation for new cuts in Medicare benefits for any beneficiary.

Secondly, the only change we are making in Social Security is one that has already been publicized. The plan does ask older Americans with higher incomes, who do not rely solely on Social Security to get by, to contribute more. This plan will not affect the 80 percent of Social Security recipients who do not pay taxes on Social Security now. Those who do not pay tax on Social Security now will not be affected by this plan.

Our plan does include a broad-based tax on energy, and I want to tell you why I selected this and why I think it's a good idea. I recommend that we adopt a Btu tax on the heat content of energy as the best way to provide us with revenue to lower the deficit because it also combats pollution, promotes energy efficiency, promotes the independence, economically, of this country as well as helping to reduce the debt, and because it does not discriminate against any area. Unlike a carbon tax, that's not too hard on the coal States; unlike a gas tax, that's not too tough on people who drive a long way to work; unlike an ad valorem tax, it doesn't increase just when the price of an energy source goes up. And it is environmentally responsible. It will help us in the future as well as in the present with the deficit.

Taken together, these measures will cost an American family with an income of about $40,000 a year less than $17 a month. It will cost American families with incomes under $30,000 nothing because of other programs we propose, principally those raising the earned-income tax credit.

Because of our publicly stated determination to reduce the deficit, if we do these things, we will see the continuation of what's happened just since the election. Just since the election, since the Secretary of the Treasury, the Director of the Office of Management and Budget, and others who have begun to speak out publicly in favor of a tough deficit reduction plan, interest rates have continued to fall long-term. That means that for the middle class who will pay something more each month, if they had any credit needs or demands, their increased energy costs will be more than offset by lower interest costs for mortgages, consumer loans, credit cards. This can be a wise investment for them and their country now.

I would also point out what the American people already know, and that is, because we're a big, vast country where we drive long distances, we have maintained far lower burdens on energy than any other advanced country. We will still have far lower burdens on energy than any other advanced country. And these will be spread fairly, with real attempts to make sure that no cost is imposed on families with incomes under $30,000 and that the costs are very modest until you get into the higher income groups where the income taxes trigger in.

Now, I ask all of you to consider this: Whatever you think of the tax program, whatever you think of the spending cuts, consider the cost of not changing. Remember the numbers that you all know. If we just keep on doing what we're doing, by the end of the decade we'll have a $650-billion-a-year deficit. If we just keep on doing what we're doing, by the end of the decade 20 percent of our national income will go to health care every year, twice as much as any other country on the face of the globe. If we just keep on doing what we're doing, over 20 cents on the dollar will have to go to service the debt.

Unless we have the courage now to start building our future and stop borrowing from it, we're condemning ourselves to years of stagnation interrupted by occasional recessions, to slow growth in jobs, to no more growth in income, to more debt, to more disappointment. Worse, unless we change, unless we increase investment and reduce the debt to raise productivity so that we can generate both jobs and incomes, we will be condemning our children and our children's children to a lesser life than we enjoyed. Once Americans looked forward to doubling their living standards every 25 years. At present productivity rates, it will take 100 years to double living standards, until our grandchildren's grandchildren are born. I say that is too long to wait.

Tonight the American people know we have to change. But they're also likely to ask me tomorrow and all of you for the weeks and months ahead whether we have the fortitude to make the changes happen in the right way. They know that as soon as I leave this Chamber and you go home, various interest groups will be out in force lobbying against this or that piece of this plan, and that the forces of conventional wisdom will offer a thousand reasons why we well ought to do this but we just can't do it.

Our people will be watching and wondering, not to see whether you disagree with me on a particular issue but just to see whether this is going to be business as usual or a real new day, whether we're all going to conduct ourselves as if we know we're working for them. We must scale the walls of the people's skepticisms, not with our words but with our deeds. After so many years of gridlock and indecision, after so many hopeful beginnings and so few promising results, the American people are going to be harsh in their judgments of all of us if we fail to seize this moment.

This economic plan can't please everybody. If the package is picked apart, there will be something that will anger each of us, won't please anybody. But if it is taken as a whole, it will help all of us. So I ask you all to begin by resisting the temptation to focus only on a particular spending cut you don't like or some particular investment that wasn't made. And nobody likes the tax increases, but let's just face facts. For 20 years, through administrations of both parties, incomes have stalled and debt has exploded and productivity has not grown as it should. We cannot deny the reality of our condition. We have got to play the hand we were dealt and play it as best we can.

My fellow Americans, the test of this plan cannot be "what is in it for me." It has got to be "what is in it for us." If we work hard and if we work together, if we rededicate ourselves to creating jobs, to rewarding work, to strengthening our families, to reinventing our Government, we can lift our country's fortunes again.

Tonight I ask everyone in this Chamber and every American to look simply into your heart, to spark your own hopes, to fire your own imagination. There is so much good, so much possibility, so much excitement in this country now that if we act boldly and honestly, as leaders should, our legacy will be one of prosperity and progress. This must be America's new direction.

Let us summon the courage to seize it.

Thank you. God bless America.

NOTE: The President spoke at 9:10 p.m. in the House Chamber of the Capitol.

Remarks on the Economic Program in St. Louis, Missouri
February 18, 1993

Thank you. I love these signs: "Our children's future starts today." "Health care for all." "No guts, no glory: Stop gridlock." "The Devil's in the details." That's right, too. [*Laughter*] "Divided we'll go down the tubes." "We want real recovery." I love these signs, and I thank you all for being here today.

Let me begin by saying how much I enjoyed flying down here with Congressman Clay and Congressman Gephardt and with Congressman Volkmer and Congresswoman Danner; they're here, too. They are part of the engine for change that you're going to see move through our Congress. I thank Bill Clay for hosting us in his district, and I want to congratulate him on the passage and this time the signing, not the veto, of the Family and Medical Leave Act.

I want to say how glad I am to be back in St. Louis with your Governor, my longtime friend and early supporter. And I know that he will be a great success, and I'm going to do what I can to be his partner in Washington. I know from clear experience that we don't have all the answers, and I'll do what I can to see that we make as many decisions as possible out here in the Governor's offices where the rubber meets the road. And I thank him for being here.

I want to recognize two of the groups that performed, the Fox High School Band and Harris-Stowe College Choir.

Let me say a word if I might about our majority leader, Dick Gephardt. There is no way that I can convey to the people of St. Louis and Missouri how important he is to the Nation. But I can tell you this: I'm not sure we could do any of the things we have to do if it were not for his leadership. If you knew all the times that he had brought together the other Members of the House of Representatives on the Democratic side and told them they were going to have to cut spending as well as raise money, told them we were going to have to change our priorities, told them we were going to have

to stick together to turn this country around, and been a force for moral leadership within the United States Congress, the heart of every person not just in his district but this whole State would swell with pride to know that you're represented by somebody like that.

If you knew all the times that I heard him stick up in private for the men and women who build the cars and build the airplanes and brew the beer and provide the backbone of America, you would know that he doesn't just say things in public and then behave differently in private. He is the same everywhere. And I am very glad that he is my full partner in this crusade to change our country.

You know, St. Louis is a special place for me. It's here where we ended the first of our wonderful bus trips across America and where we had a rally of about 40,000 people. It was the biggest crowd we'd had at that time in the campaign. And we started our second bus trip over in east St. Louis. And then we had the first Presidential debate here. So I think it's only fitting that I would come to my neighboring State in the heartland of America to start day one of America's new direction.

I was in Missouri on the other side of the State on Labor Day, and I went to Harry Truman's home town. I guess in some ways the talk I gave to Congress last night was like one of President Truman's talks. Some of it was just off the top of my head and from the bottom of my heart. It was sort of plain spoken, and I couldn't figure out how else to say what I think is the plain truth about where we are.

This is a country of enormous promise, of unlimited potential, of a great future burdened by big problems. I think everybody knows that. And we also know, I think, that some mistakes have been made in the course we have taken. The fundamental problems we have are because of big, sweeping changes in history: America being pushed into a global economy, all of us being subject to changes at a far more rapid rate than ever before.

But we know that the responses we have taken have not worked. There are too many people who are unemployed. There are too many people who are underemployed. There are too many people who have lost good jobs, that cannot get jobs at that income left. There are too many people with no health insurance and too many others terrified of losing it. There are too many people who don't have access to the education over a lifetime that they need to continually be retrained. There are too many places where we are not investing in the future. There are too many industries, like the aerospace industry in Missouri and throughout the country, that we know will produce a huge portion of the high-wage jobs of the future all over the world, and yet, they're dying on the vine here in America. These things don't make sense.

What we have been doing has not worked. We need to take a new direction that will build a high-wage, high-growth, secure future where people can be educated, where there is affordable health care for all, and where Americans have a fair chance to compete and win. That's what this is all about.

I want to repeat to you what I said to the Congress last night. I remember in 1981 when President Reagan said if you stacked 1,000-dollar bills on top of each other, our national debt would go 67 miles into the sky. If you did it today, it would go 267 miles into the sky. I say that not to blame him, not to blame my predecessor, not to blame anybody. Goodness knows, there's enough blame to go around, both parties and the Presidency and the Congress, but what good is it going to do us? Let us forget about blame and take responsibility for our future. Let's do it together. I don't care who gets the credit, I just want us to go forward.

There are already people who are saying that we really can't make fundamental changes. There are people who are saying, "Well, you can't bring the deficit down," or "Well, nobody will hang in there and make these tough budget cuts the President's proposing," or "Well, you can't really reform the health care system," even though we're paying more and getting less for ours than any country on the face of the Earth. I'm tired of all the nay-sayers. I think we can make some changes. But we need your help.

We need your help in two ways: Number one, we need you to show up like this, and we need you to tell your Members of Congress that we will support you if you make the honest, tough, hard decisions. We know we didn't get into this mess overnight. We're not going to get out of it overnight. But we cannot keep doing the same old thing. The price of doing the same thing is higher than the price of change.

The second thing you can do is to support your Members of Congress by demanding real political reform that will protect them in making courageous changes. Tell them you want a campaign finance reform bill that will limit the cost of congressional campaigns, limit the influence of special interests, and open this process to all people.

Tell them you want something done to make sure all of the lobbyists in Washington have to register and report on their activities; two-thirds of them don't. Tell them you support our bill to remove the tax deduction for lobbying activities. You are subsidizing interests that together undermine your future. Individually they've all got a good story to tell, but collectively they help to paralyze the political process. And you, at least, should not subsidize it with your tax dollars because you don't have comparable deductions.

My fellow Americans, last night I tried to lay out to the Congress and to the American people a plan that will change the direction of this country and give us a genuine economic strategy, a plan to produce more jobs, higher income, deal with the health care crisis, provide a lifetime system of education, and reduce the national debt. We have to begin with the Government, and at the top with the President.

So I have tried to set an example. I have cut the White House staff by 25 percent. That will be in my budget for the White House. I have cut the administrative costs of the executive branch in my budget 14 percent over the next 4 years, over and above the cuts in the White House, and we'll reduce employment, not by firing people but by attrition, by 100,000 over the next 4 years. That will save $9 billion. And yesterday the leaders of the House and the Senate announced that the Congress would follow our lead and cut their budgets by that much, which I think is good.

There are 150 other specific cuts in this budget, including some that were very tough for me to recommend, some in programs that don't make any sense anymore. For example, do you remember when we had the Bicentennial celebration in 1976? There is still a Bicentennial Commission. Our Government's great at starting things and not very good at stopping things. So we eliminated a lot of things that ought to be stopped.

The second thing we did was to reduce our investment in programs that have done a lot of good, but where the amount you're spending can't be justified anymore, including one that was really close to my heart. We recommended a reduction in the Federal subsidy to the Rural Electric Administration, something that serves a lot of people in my State and yours. But America is 100 percent electrified now, and we ought not to have the full subsidy continued from all of the rest of the people who get their electricity from someplace else.

We recommended some unwarranted subsidies be eliminated because the need for the work is much less or nonexistent anymore. For example, we recommended a big cutback in a lot of programs related to the nuclear industry and the elimination of a nuclear research program that is inconsistent with our new energy future.

We recommended some big changes in the environmental Superfund program: one, to make the polluters pay more and the taxpayers pay less and the second, to get the money freed up so that we can use the money to clean up pollution. It's all going to lawyer fees now, because people don't want anything to happen. We're going to try to make it work.

Finally, I recommended—and this was difficult for me because I can't do anything as your President in the end without the support of the fine people in the Federal work force—but we recommended a freeze on Federal pay raises for a year and modest pay raises for the next 3, because that saves billions of dollars that we don't have to take out of the rest of the people in taxes to reduce the deficit.

So there are 150 tough cuts. Now, let me say I've already heard some people on the other side of the aisle say, "Well, he should have cut more." And my answer is: Show me where, but be specific. No hot air. Show me where, and be specific.

And since I am here in Missouri, I think I will repeat that. Show me. And I say that not in the spirit of partisanship but in the spirit of genuine challenge. I know there is more that we can eliminate. I am honestly looking. I've just been there 4 weeks and a day, and I'm

nowhere near through. And I want you to help me, and I want them to help me.

Let me say also, the burdens in terms of taxes I think are imposed in a fair way. The rates of 98.9 percent of Americans will not be raised. Late in the last election, the New York Times carried a front-page story showing that 70 percent of the gains of the 1980's had been reaped by the top one percent of the people. This plan asked the top 1.2 percent of the people to have an income tax increase. This plan asked companies with incomes of over $10 million to match that income tax increase.

This plan raises over 70 percent of the funds from people with incomes above $100,000. This plan raises no money from people with incomes below $30,000. And indeed, because we increased the refundable income tax credit, this plan, if it passes, will enable us to do something I would think every American would be proud of. For the first time ever, if this plan passes, we can say to the people of this country: Look, we are rewarding work and family. If you work full-time and you've got a kid in your house, you won't live in poverty because of the changes we're going to have in the tax system.

People making $40,000, $50,000, in that range, will pay about $17 a month under this plan. But let me tell you, a lot of those people, many of whom are in this station today, may wind up not being out any more money for this reason: Just since the election, since I said we're going to have a tough plan to reduce this debt, long-term interest rates have gone down. If you take only the reduction in interest rates which have occurred from the election day until this day, for everybody who gets the benefit of those lower interest rates in a home mortgage, a car payment, consumer credit, you will make more in lower interest rates than you'll pay in the energy tax if we can show that we're serious about cutting spending and cutting this deficit. We've got to do it.

One final thing which you'll also hear about from people who oppose this plan: I do propose to spend some more money, but not in the old way. Look at what we spend it for. We have reduced Government consumption. We have reduced inessential programs. But we increase spending on jobs: a jobs program to create a half a million jobs starting right now in building roads, repairing streets, fixing airports, cleaning up the environment with water systems and sewer systems; a million summer jobs for young people, if I could get the private sector to contribute to the 700,000 we're going to create in the Government.

This program invests in opening the doors of college education to all people and giving them a chance to pay the loan back on favorable terms or to pay it back with service to our country. This plan will put 100,000 police officers on the streets of America over the next 4 years. This plan will give us a chance to invest in the new technologies that will create jobs for the people who have lost their jobs in the defense industries and in other big industries that have been downscaling.

We have got to create some new jobs in this country, for goodness sakes. You can have all the other programs in the world, and unless we do it, we're going to be in trouble.

And this plan will reduce the deficit by hundreds of billions of dollars over the next 5 years. And I ask you, I ask you to support it not just for you but for us, not just for narrow interest but for the national interest. I believe it will be good for virtually every American.

Today as we speak, a lot of big corporate executives are endorsing this plan, even though their income tax bills will go up, their companies' bills will go up, because they want a healthy, strong, well-educated, vibrant America with an investment climate that's good, with stable interest rates, with a declining deficit, with a health care issue addressed, and with a country that can grow into the 21st century. So a lot of the people who are paying this bill are going to support it because they trust us.

And let me say this: We need you to hold our feet to the fire. No raising taxes unless we cut spending.

We've got to do this in a package, and we've got to do it together. I need your help. I'm delighted to see you here today. With your help we can make the spirit of St. Louis the spirit of America.

Thank you, and God bless you all.

NOTE: The President spoke at 2:59 p.m. at Union Station. In his remarks, he referred to Gov. Mel Carnahan of Missouri.

Remarks and a Question-and-Answer Session on the Economic Program in Chillicothe, Ohio
February 19, 1993

The President. Thank you very much. Let me say, first of all, what a wonderful time I have had in your community since I arrived last night. I have seen a lot of your fellow citizens who did not win the lottery. [*Laughter*] They were out by the Comfort Inn where we stayed last night, and they were around the city park where—the Mayor and I went jogging this morning around the city park. It was 3 degrees, which I suppose means I don't have enough sense to be President. [*Laughter*] But we had a wonderful time. We ran around the park three times and saw some students from the school, and we saw some city employees and others. I flew in here with Congressman Strickland last night, and we had a great visit on the way in. I'm glad to see him over here.

And so between the two of them I know a lot about this congressional district and a good deal about this community. I know it has a lot of beautiful old buildings—I saw them this

morning—and was the first capital of Ohio. I also know it has a nice new McDonald's— [*laughter*]—because I went there this morning. Good to see you. [*Applause*] How embarrassing.

Let me say, too, I want to thank your school officials, Superintendent Cline and your principal, Rod Jenkins. And Melissa Hagen did a good job, don't you think? I thought she did a really good job. Maybe she'll be coming back here someday to hold a town meeting like this; you can't tell.

I also want to say—I just have a couple of notes. Normally I don't use them, and I want to put them down, but I asked for some notes about some people in the crowd because they illustrate what to me this effort that I have undertaken as your President is all about.

Is John Cochran here? Is he here anywhere? John, are you here? Stand up there. Now, my notes say that he has 16 children—and you're one of them—[*laughter*]—that he has the largest family-owned farm in town. And important to me, he owns the bowling alley. [*Laughter*] And I want to thank him. He was unable to come to the Inauguration.

I want to say—is 8-year-old Tiffany Sexton here? Stand up here, Tiffany. Now, these are her parents, Sgt. Anthony and Jerry Sexton; is that right? All of you stand up. I want you to see them. Now, she invited me to dinner and promised to cook—Tiffany—so I had to take a raincheck, and I asked them to come today.

Is Cindy Baker here? Stand up. Cindy Baker has three children, one of whom is a student in this school. She wrote me a half a dozen times in the election, pleading with me to come to Chillicothe. So I thought since she was the first person who invited me, she should be here at this meeting.

I also want you to know, you know, we had those famous bus tours, you remember, Hillary and I and Al and Tipper Gore. What you may not know is the people who owned the bus company that we used all during the bus tours all across America are from Ohio. They're from Columbus, and they are here: Barbara and Tom Sabatino and Kerwin and Regina Elmers. Would they stand? They're here somewhere, I think. Yes, in the back. There's Tom, my bus driver. Give him a hand. [*Applause*] Thanks. If it hadn't been for them, we might not have won the election. [*Laughter*]

Now, let me just make a couple of introductory remarks, and then we'll get right to the questions, because I want to just restate very briefly how I came to the plan that I announced to the Congress a couple of nights ago.

First, let me say that I was Governor for 12 years of a State with a lot of towns like this one, a lot of counties like Ross County, a lot of manufacturing facilities like the Mead Paper facility here that worked our people and a lot of people who worked on the farm. And we had a pretty tough time in the eighties. We lost a lot of manufacturing jobs, a lot of farm jobs. A lot of our small towns got in trouble. And I was forced to spend a lot of time trying to figure out how we could change things to make a better future for the hard-working good people of my State. So a lot of what I believe about all this goes directly to the experience that I've had for many years working with people like you.

If I might, let me just mention one or two

things. A lot of our problems stem from all the pressures we're having now in a global economy and stem from the fact that we've got some problems here at home which make it difficult for us to compete in that economy. We have a higher percentage of poor children. We have much more diversity than many of the countries with which we compete. And historically, we have never had the kind of partnership between Government and business and working people that some other countries have. So, for example, if you read yesterday Boeing is laying off a lot of employees in the airline manufacturing business—not affecting Ohio, but it's a big thing for America, in part because of defense cuts but in part because Europe put $26 billion into the airbus project, a direct taxpayer investment, to make sure they could make airplanes that would compete with Boeing, something that we haven't historically done.

So we have a new global economy in which there are great opportunities but new challenges. We have some problems here at home that make it hard for us to compete. We have to educate a higher percentage of our people at a higher level. We have to provide basic health care to everybody but control health care costs. All of our major manufacturers are spending 30 percent more for health care than all their competitors around the world, and that puts them in a real bind. And we have many other challenges of this kind that we have to face.

Now, for the last 12 years we have followed a certain approach there. We have said as a nation our policy is to keep taxes low on the wealthiest Americans in the hope that they will invest in our economy and make it grow. And that worked. In the last 12 years, the tax burden basically went up on the middle class, went down on the wealthiest Americans, and according to a study released last year, about 70 percent of the economic gains of the last decade went to the top 1 or 2 percent of the people in the country. That was a deliberate decision that was made to try to free up that money in the hope that it would be invested to create new jobs for everybody else.

Also, our theory was that the Government should not be too active. So we didn't deal with a lot of the issues that other Governments around the world were dealing with, in Japan, in Germany and other countries, for example. And we actually reduced our investment of your money in a lot of things that make jobs, like the Community Development Block Grant program, which cities in Ohio like because they provide funds not only to do things like repair your parks but also to build roads and rail networks and other support systems for new industry if you're trying to get them into a community. We sort of held the lid on that on the theory that we should just put a big bind on the Government, and all Government spending was bad, and all Government activity should be discouraged, and we'll just see what happens.

Well, there have been some not-too-bad years in the last 12. But overall, we've still got a lot of problems. Unemployment's too high. Most people are working harder for lower wages. Health care costs are exploding, but fewer people have health care coverage in this country than any other major country in the world. And the insecurity of losing health insurance is one of the major problems for many, many American families. And we are not educating a high enough percentage of our people at very high levels to compete in this global economy. And because we lowered taxes a lot on the wealthy but could not control the health care costs the Government was spending, we starting running bigger deficits. So that even though we reduced our investment in things like aid for small cities to create jobs, the cost of health care and the cost of interest on our debt exploded, so we've got a huge Government deficit. Our national debt is now 4 times as big as it was in 1980.

So when I got elected President, I did it with a conviction that we needed to do the following things: We needed to emphasize investment for jobs and for incomes—that means investments in new technologies, investments in things like highways and bridges and airports and water systems and sewer systems, investments in the areas that will create jobs for the future, and investments in education of our children all the way from Head Start to college loans, to investments for adults to become retrained if they lose their jobs; second, that we needed to provide affordable health care for all Americans and bring the cost in line with inflation before it bankrupts the country with nothing to show for it; third, that we had to bring down the national debt; and fourth, that we needed a national economic strategy where the American people could work in partnership again to try to grow this economy.

Now, we have a lot of tough decisions to make to try to pursue all these objectives at once. The plan I announced to the Congress relies on the following things.

Number one, we cut spending, 150 different specific spending cuts, putting a lid on Federal pay increases, cutting the White House staff by 25 percent, cutting the administrative costs of the Federal Government by 14 percent over 4 years, saving billions and billions of dollars.

Number two, we raise funds in taxes in a way that I think is fair, with 70 percent of the money coming from people whose incomes are above $100,000 and with a broad-based energy tax that would affect a little bit on oil, a little bit on natural gas, a little bit on coal, so we wouldn't hit any region of the country too much.

Thirdly, we increase dramatically something that a lot of you may not know about that's one of the best things in the Tax Code—it's called the refundable earned-income tax credit—so that no one with an income of $30,000 a year or less would pay any new money under this plan, and so that people who work 40 hours a week and have children in their home would be lifted above poverty for the first time for working, not for welfare but for working.

The other thing that you will hear from some of my critics, and so I want to tell you it's true, is that we did actually increase some funds: in the short run, with a plan to jumpstart the economy by creating a half million new jobs; and over the long run, with increases in education programs from Head Start to worker retraining, to apprenticeship programs for high school grads who don't go on to college, to increased access to college loans, to retraining for workers who lose their jobs when there are defense cuts or other cuts in our industry. We have to do that because that's what determines what people's incomes are and whether you can keep people working. We also did increase funds in direct aid to things that create jobs: new technologies and investments to put people to work.

So it's a balanced program: deep spending cuts, tax increases fairly applied, and new investments in the areas that create jobs. That's what I'm trying to do. The Congress will decide to vote for it in part based on whether people in towns like Chillicothe all over America think it's a good deal.

I can tell you this: The price of doing the same thing is higher than the price of my program. And I'll just give you one example and open the floor to questions. Just since the election, since we made it absolutely clear that we were determined to bring down the deficit, interest rates, long term, have begun to drop. If you look at the difference in long-term interest rates on election day and where they were after I made my speech to Congress, a lot of the people who might have spent $10 or $12 or $15 more per month in energy costs, directly and indirectly, will save much more than that if they're paying a home mortgage, a note on a car, they've got consumer credit, or they otherwise have to borrow money.

That's because if you bring the deficit down, you not only free up tax dollars to spend on education and other things, you free up money in the private sector to borrow at lower interest rates. So an awful lot of people are going to save a lot of money on this program immediately. It will create jobs immediately. And the price of it, I am confident, is lower than the price of doing the same old thing.

So I thank you for being here. I want to say a special word of thanks to all these Ohio elected officials who are here. I presume they've all been introduced, but I saw Senator Glenn and Senator Metzenbaum and Speaker Riffe, a lot of others here. I thank them for being here. And we're here for you. So thank you very much, and I'll take questions.

Social Security

Q. I get Social Security disability, a little over $6,000 a year. And if that is willing to help bring the economy up to shape, I am willing to let some of my Social Security go for that economy. And I was wondering if that will affect my Social Security disability any.

The President. The short answer to that is it depends on whether you pay any tax now on your income. Let me explain what that means.

The only people on Social Security who will pay any more tax are those who pay some tax on it now. That is, in America today, if you drew a Social Security check, and in addition to the Social Security check you have an income of $25,000 a year or more, or if you're a married couple, $32,000 a year or more, one-half of that income is subject to income tax at whatever rate your total income is.

We propose to go from half of that to 85 percent, because that is about the amount that the average Social Security recipient should pay taxes on if they get the rest of it for a lifetime. The rest of it, that is, that 15 percent, will equal about what they paid in plus interest. So they get back what they paid in plus interest without taxation on average, and the rest of it would be subject to tax.

So the answer is, if you draw Social Security and you pay some tax now, you would pay some more. If you don't pay any tax now, you won't pay any more because your income is too low to be subject to it.

Student Loans

Q. Hi. My name is Greg Gilmore, and I'm a senior here at Chillicothe High School. How will the new program for college loans and community service be handled? And, to clarify, what process will students have to go through to receive the college loans?

The President. Well, we're working out the details now. But let me tell you how I want it to work, okay? And it will be pretty close to this, I think. First of all, let me tell you how it works today. You know, there is a student loan program today, and the more you borrow, the more you have to pay back in short order. And you get the money through your bank, and there's a Government guarantee.

Today, that program costs the taxpayers about $4 billion a year: $3 billion in busted loans where people don't pay back the money they owe and $1 billion in transaction fees to the bank. What I hope to be able to do is to have people borrow the money directly from the Government and pay it back at tax time so they can't beat the bill. That will save a huge amount of money. And I want to take the savings and do two things:

One is to say to young people, you must pay the money back, but you can pay the money back as a percentage of your income. So that if you make less money, you pay less, and we'll string it out over longer periods of time. So we'll never discourage anybody from being a teacher or working in some other kind of public work just because the salary is low.

The second thing we want to do is give people the option either to earn credits against this loan before they go to college, or to do community service after they get out, as teachers or police officers or in other public service. And the way I'm trying to set it up, if you borrowed the maximum amount of money we'd make available and then you worked for 2 years at roughly half pay as a teacher or police officer, that would wipe off your obligation. And you'd pay your loan back by giving something back to your country. And so that's how it's supposed to work.

Now, that's more Government spending all right, but see, that's a direct investment in you. That's not expanding some Government program. That's putting the money direct into you. That's cutting the cost of a program and increasing investment in your future.

Youth Apprenticeship Program

Q. Mr. President, I'm a student member from Pickley Ross Vocational Center. Since there is a critical need in this country for skilled workers, I'm excited about your youth apprenticeship program. My question is what role will public vocational education play in your youth apprenticeship program?

The President. The short answer is, a big one. The longer answer is, here's how I want to set it up. What we're trying to do at the national level is to come up with enough funds to match with local funds and to encourage private sector people to get into an apprenticeship program which will be an American version of what the Europeans have done for years.

I've asked the Labor Secretary, Bob Reich, to work with the Education Department, the vocational people in the private sector to try to set up a framework within which every State in America would be able to design a program that a person, a young man or woman, could enter in high school if they wanted, and they would continue for at least 2 years after high school.

Let me tell you why we have to do that very quickly. If you look at the income charts on American earnings from, oh, let's say for the last 20 years, for the last 20 years you see a bigger and bigger and bigger gap every year between the earnings of young people with college degrees and young people who drop out of high school or young people who had only a high school diploma. However, if you look at the earnings of young people who get at least 2 years of training after high school in a vocational institution, the community colleges, in the service, or on the job, if it is high-quality training, a great deal of that job gap is closed, and the young person moreover acquires the ability to continue to learn new things through-

out a lifetime.

The best programs are those which start in the high schools and run with some continuity for 2 years thereafter. And so there is no magic answer. We're going to have to design these sector by sector in the economy, and the National Government can't do it. We can just set up a framework and standards and provide some of the funds, but we're going to have to do it on a State-by-State and sector-by-sector basis.

But that's what we have to do. We need to get—first of all, my dream would be no high school dropouts, and then for 100 percent of the high school graduates to have at least 2 years of some kind of very high-quality training that is approved by both education and the private sector. Some would be delivered in schools; some would be delivered in the job place.

Health Care

Q. My name is Karen Ritinger. Mr. President, once reimbursement for Medicare is reduced, what actions will be implemented to prevent health care providers from shifting costs to the private sector?

The President. Well, first of all, that is a bigger problem with Medicaid than Medicare, as you know, I'm sure. The budget that I introduced to do that, to cut down on Medicare reimbursement, is a budget that assumes we're not going to do anything else about health care. Within 100 days of my taking office, we're going to present a plan to the Congress to try to deal with the cost shifting problem.

The question she asked indicates a real understanding of the problem. If all you do is to cut what the Government pays to doctors and hospitals, if you cut it below their real costs, then the medical providers will find a way to recover their real costs from people who pay directly or through private insurance, and the insurance premiums will go up more.

So what we have to do is to do what every other country in the world but America has done and develop some sort of all-payer system where the reimbursement levels are pretty much the same and where you have real efforts to eliminate unnecessary duplication and waste and paperwork that benefit the private sector along with the public sector, and that's what we're going to do.

In other words, I just presented the best budget I could with the system we've got, but what we need is a comprehensive system which eliminates the cost shifting from the Medicare and Medicaid to the private sector and has some cost reduction mechanisms that benefit everybody.

Let me say—I don't know, there must be some people that work at the factories in town or work in other manufacturing facilities. Our program has some significant tax incentives over the next 5 years for businesses big and small to reinvest, to create jobs, and to become more productive. But the best thing we could do, better than an investment tax credit, better than the tax changes for big manufacturers, the best thing we could do is to find a way to get health costs in line with inflation and still take care of everybody in America. If you did that, you'd free up hundreds of billions of dollars to make America compete again. And so that's a very good question.

Yes, let's take one over here. We haven't taken any over here.

NAFTA

Q. Mr. President, as a member of the UAW and local union president, I'm concerned about the loss of American jobs to foreign countries. What impact will the North American Free Trade Act have on the economy and the budget deficit?

The President. The North American Free Trade Agreement, in my opinion, will help the economy and reduce the budget deficit if, but only if, it is implemented in a way that protects us from unfair practices.

What I want to do is to get the North American Free Trade Agreement ratified, if we can also get an agreement that requires the Mexican Government and private sector to invest in environmental investments to get their environmental cost up to ours, so we don't have people just running down there so they can evade all the Clean Air Act and all those other acts in America. And I want to have some labor standards agreements that will reassure us that the Mexican Government will enforce even their own labor laws.

One of the things that—I don't know if you all remember one of the television ads I ran in the last campaign about an American program where we were actually subsidizing companies that would move their plants overseas, and some of them went to Central America and lowered wages. They didn't raise wages down there; they went down there and lowered wages. So what

we have to know is that we are actually strengthening the Mexican economy so they will buy more.

Now, let me say this in defense of President Salinas. In the last 5 years, our trade deficit with Mexico has gone from a huge deficit to a slight surplus, and our volume has gone way up. So they bought a lot more from us than we sold to them relative to where we were 5 or 6 years ago.

But this agreement, I'm convinced, needs some strengthening in order to avoid hurting the American work force. I do think, if you look at it over the long run, a country like ours can only get wealthier by selling more to other countries. And it's easier to sell to your neighbors than it is to people far away. And so far, Mexico has not been wealthy enough to buy a significant volume of our goods.

Let me give you an example. Our biggest trading partner by far is Canada, even though it's a tiny country; it's a big country geographically, but in terms of population they only have about 30 million people. But they buy a huge amount of our stuff, by far our biggest trading partner.

So we would be better off—one of the reasons the Japanese and the Germans have gotten so much richer so much quicker in the last 10 years is that they've been selling more stuff overseas. So I've got to try to make that a market. It's good for us over the long run, but I'm going to try to do it in a way that builds up the American manufacturing base, not tears it down.

Abortion

Q. I know the discussion so far has been centered around the economy, but personally I feel I must address a different issue. The Senate Report, 97th Congress, S. 158, concludes that, "Physicians, biologists and other scientists agree that conception marks the beginning of the life of the human being." And it goes on to say, "There's overwhelming agreement on this point in countless medical, biological, and scientific writings." The Constitution of the United States guarantees life, liberty, and the pursuit of happiness. My question for you, Mr. President, is deep down inside do you believe that life begins at conception? And if so, why are we denying the right to life for the 4,400 human beings a day and 1.6 million human beings a year in the murder of an abortion?

The President. Wait a minute. Okay. My question for you is do you believe that women who have abortions should be tried for first degree murder?

Q. Yes, I do.

The President. Good. At least you have a consistent position. He said yes. That was his answer. His answer was yes.

Then that brings me to the question—there are two different issues here, not one. One is the biological question: Is a cell a living thing? Answer? If two cells join in the process that begins to make a human being, are they living? Answer? No one disputes that. That's not the issue.

The issue is a much deeper one, and one over which people have argued for a long time, one over which Christians have argued for a long time: When does the soul enter the body so that to terminate the living organism amounts to killing a person? That is the question. It is a deep, moral question over which serious Christians disagree.

I have heard—you may smile with all your self-assurance, young man, but there are many Christian ministers who disagree with you. And the question is—and let me say, I honor your convictions. I worked very hard in my State to reduce the number of abortions. I don't like abortion. The question for policymakers on the issue of whether *Roe* v. *Wade* should be repealed is the question of whether we really are prepared to go all the way and make women and their doctors criminals because we believe we know that.

Now, you are. But here's the problem. In a great democratic society, you have to be very careful what you apply the criminal law to. For example, we make drugs criminal, right? And we throw a lot of people in jail, and our jails are full and they're just doubling all the time because they're so full. And 90 percent of us agree that drug use should be criminal, and we've still got the jails full. You have to be very careful when you know that there is a difference that splits the American people right down the middle.

Very few Americans believe that all abortions all the time are all right. Almost all Americans believe that abortion should be illegal when the children can live without the mother's assistance, when the children can live outside the mother's womb. There is about a 50–50 split in our country of honest conviction about whether terminat-

ing a baby in the mother's womb before the baby can live outside the mother's womb amounts to what you say it does, which is first degree murder.

So the reason I support *Roe* v. *Wade* and the reason I signed a bill to make abortion illegal in the third trimester is because I think that the Government of this country should not make criminal activities over which even theologians are in serious disagreement. That's how I feel.

Employment

Q. My name is Melissa Zangree. Mr. President, I'm a sophomore here at Chillicothe High School. Will there be jobs for me when I graduate college?

The President. There will be if my economic program has a chance to be put in, I think. But let me say this: The most maddening thing in the world for me as a public servant is to see people who want to work, who don't have jobs.

A year ago yesterday we celebrated the first anniversary of the first primary in our Presidential campaign in New Hampshire. And so I made a few calls there, and I was reminiscing yesterday about going into New Hampshire, a State that tripled the unemployment rate in 3 years, and listening to young people like you tell me that the worst thing about their lives was going home at night when their parents, who had lost their jobs through no fault of their own, and they couldn't even bear to talk at the dinner table anymore.

But it is the big challenge. What is happening is all these big companies are restructuring. They're trying to be more competitive in a global economy, and they're laying people off. And small companies have to make up the difference, and a lot of them can't borrow money from the bank, and there aren't markets there.

All I can tell you is I'm doing the very best I can to make sure that there will be jobs available for you. That is the issue. If we cannot maintain America's position and the American dream unless we are able to create a higher number of jobs every year. This is amazing. We're supposed to be coming out of this recession we've been in, and unemployment's higher now than it was at the bottom of the recession. So the answer to your question is, I honestly believe that if my program is given a chance to work, it will create jobs for young people like you. That's what I honestly believe. I believe that.

Taxes

Q. Welcome, Mr. President. My name is Barbara Smith, and I'm a concerned citizen. And my question is, instead of imposing an energy tax which would unequally affect consumers, why not develop a national sales tax which would be equal to all consumers, or even a national lottery, to help with the deficit?

The President. A lottery is a different issue. I doubt it would raise a great deal of money, and I've always been opposed to them, because lotteries tend to have an unequal effect, taking a disproportionate amount of money from lower income people. So I've always been opposed to that.

But let's talk about the national sales tax. Almost every country that I know of that we compete with, advanced countries, all the European countries and Japan and Canada, have a national sales tax. They call it a value-added tax. Most of them—if you go to Canada you see it on your bill—you know, they separate it out, just like the sales tax.

But most countries just put the value-added tax into the wholesale price, and you don't even see it on your bill. And a lot of those countries like that because what they do is they tax things sold in their country. Now, what's good about that? That means that—let's take, again, your plant here—if Mead Paper makes, let's say, stationery and sells 15 percent of its products overseas, those products would not be subject to the VAT tax. Or, you're in the UAW, if you make an automobile, and any automobile you sold in another country would be subject to no tax at all. Then, when another country's car came in here, it would be subject to the tax.

So a lot a people in manufacturing like this national sales tax because it helps your exports, and it puts a burden on imports coming in, supports the job base of the country. It's perfectly legal; all our other competitors do it.

Now, here's why I didn't propose it right now. That is a radical change in the tax system of the United States. It is something I think we may well have to look at in the years ahead. But I did not want to confuse two different things: One is the imperative of getting the deficit down, with the need to maybe change our tax system. I mean, there's only so much change a country can accommodate at the same time.

Also, the energy tax equals about 1.5 percent of total Federal revenues, or 1.6 percent. And it will have a very modest impact on energy, and it is pretty equal throughout the regions of the country, actually.

If you take a farmer, you might argue that a farmer might pay a little more directly or indirectly because if you buy fuel it's about 2 cents a gallon, but then if you buy fertilizer, that's got a lot of fuel in it. So the only people who will be unevenly affected are people who buy things that have a lot of fuel component.

But I thought, and by the way, we still have the lowest energy cost by far of any of our competitors, and our energy taxes are very low. If it were to put us out of compliance, I might have thought of that. But I do believe that America, at another time, and maybe not too long in the future, will debate whether we want to shift the nature of our tax system because we're in a global economy.

But let me say one other thing. If you do a value-added tax, if you do a national sales tax, you have to be really careful to be fair to people. You have to exempt food; you have to exempt maybe clothing or a certain amount of allowance. You've got to be careful how you do it so you don't make it a regressive tax. But they can be designed that way, and we're the only major nation without one.

Prescription Drug Costs

Q. Mr. President, my name is Cathy Dunn. My mother's monthly prescription drug cost exceeds her monthly income on retirement. What, if anything, can be done about the rising cost of drugs in this country?

The President. Well, one problem is that older people who are eligible for Medicare, but not poor enough to be on Medicaid, don't have their prescription drugs covered. So you have this ironic development that older people who have serious medical problems and require expensive medicine who are on Medicare might actually have lower incomes—real incomes—than some people on Medicaid. And it's a big gap in our health care system, and it's one that I'm going to try to see that we address now.

Let me say, you may have seen on the other end of the age spectrum, I've been in somewhat of a dispute with some of the drug companies because I want to immunize all the children in our country. But only about half of our 2-year-olds are immunized against serious diseases.

That's a very serious thing. And I'm coming back to the drug problem. Let me bring you back around to this, because it's very important that you understand this. And we save $10 later for every $1 we invest now in immunizations of children for preventable diseases. And yet, a lot of vaccines made in America sell for lower prices overseas than they sell in America.

Now, if you look at the price of vaccines— for a lot of these vaccines, the most expensive price goes to the family doctor who buys them. That's why the cost of getting your shots has gone from about, oh, $10 to over $200 if you just go to a family doctor and get all the baby's shots. Right?

Next cheapest is, State government can buy vaccines in bulk. The next cheapest is, the Federal Government can buy even bigger—vaccines—and we buy through a Federal agency about 40 percent of the vaccines in the country, and then we give them out to the States. And then the States that have good public health networks, they give them out, and those shots are the cheapest of all. But even cheaper than that are some of these same vaccines made by American companies sold in foreign countries.

Now, that all sounds terrible. Let me say one or two things, since I've been fighting with the drug companies, in defense of them. They're a very important part of our economy. They do a wonderful job in finding new drugs to solve problems. They have to spend a fortune to do all the research and development. The problem is that to sell those vaccines in other countries, these other countries are tougher on them, and because they want everybody immunized, they drive down the cost of the vaccines. So Americans are paying the whole research and development costs for people who benefit from these drugs all over the world, because the companies can't collect other places.

Another problem is that we have more lawsuits in this country, so we add about $4 a vial to the vaccines to put into a fund against the possibility that some child might have a reaction. So they would always be somewhat more expensive.

But we have got to find a way to work with the drug companies. They do very well, I want to emphasize. They are some of our best companies. But we've got to find a way to deal with these two huge problems. One is older people, particularly, paying huge prices for drugs that have been developed for some time, that are not experimental drugs. I think we'd all admit we should pay more for experimental drugs; that's got all the research cost in it. And the second is children in America paying more for vaccines than children in other countries, even though they were made here. And we're trying to work through that, and I think we're going to make some progress on it.

Health Care Reform

Q. Mr. President, I am one of those family doctors who you were speaking about, and I have a couple of questions. One is, in your address to the joint session of Congress, nothing was mentioned about tort reform. And I'm very concerned about that because of the malpractice crisis and the liability costs in malpractice insurance. The second thing is, our local medical society has reviewed at least four plans put forward by organized medicine, the American Academy of Family Physicians and so on. Are you going to look at those programs and incorporate physicians' ideas as you're formulating the policies?

The President. Absolutely. And we will also bring doctors into the process. But let me answer the second question first. Last year there were two major suggestions made for health care reform by physicians groups, the American College of Physicians and the American Academy of Family Practice. A more modest but still significant program was offered by the American Medical Association. And the American Nurses Association put out a very interesting plan. And I think all of those things should have a big influence on what we do, because in the end it's the doctors and the other health care providers that have to live with whatever system we put out. So the answer to your question is yes, those suggestions, and in particular the two you mentioned, are being taken very seriously.

Second, on cutting the cost of malpractice, that's a big issue with me. I'm proud of the fact that my State had the second lowest malpractice rates in the country. And one of the things we did was to pass a law enabling the court to fine anyone who brought a frivolous tort suit, if it was judged to be frivolous, that the lawyer himself or herself could actually be fined. Not a big fine, but it had a real impact.

The other thing I think that has real promise is an experiment that I believe is now being tried in Maine and one or two other places which really relates to family practitioners, because we cannot get medical reform in this country unless family practitioners, family doctors, feel freer to set simple fractures, to get back into the business of delivering babies, to do that whole range of things. The thing that a lot of people are working on now is being able to say to doctors in small towns and rural areas, for example, here are a set of accepted practice guidelines for this procedure or that procedure. If you can show that you have followed these guidelines, that will raise a presumption against malpractice for you. I think that has real promise.

The third thing in really expensive areas is, we might all look at what's been done in the vaccine area. That really worked, where people just pay a fee into a fund and a big national fund is set up. And if there's a problem, you go against that fund; you don't have to go through a whole prolonged lawsuit with an insurance company, a lawyer, a doctor, and all the lawyers and all that. That's something else that I think we need to look at to see if that might have more general application.

Economic Program

Q. During the campaign, Ross Perot spoiled me with flip charts, pointers, and poster board. I'm a simple woman. What I need to hear from you is, over the next 4 years, how much spending cuts, dollar-wise, will we see? How much total revenue will be brought through our taxes, through the increase in our taxes? And what percentage of that is going towards new programs? In other words, we're hearing "tax and spend," the old Republican motto about the Democrats. I want you to show me in a simple manner exactly the dollar figures that we'll look at over the next 4 years.

The President. I don't know if I can do the math in my head right now for 4 years, but I will tell you, basically, the tax bill goes from about $20 billion to about $75 billion over the next 4 years; the spending cuts go up to more than that in the fourth year. In the early years there are more tax increases than spending cuts; in the later years there are far more spending cuts than tax increases. At the end, they're about the same. The net aggregate reduction in the deficit over 4 years is about $320 billion, over 5 years is at $475 billion less debt than we would otherwise have.

In the fourth year of the budget, which is

the one that we all target on under the Federal system, the deficit will go down $140 billion a year in that year. Essentially, there will be a net increase in that fourth year in spending of about $26 billion a year. That is, there's about $40 billion more in spending, net new spending, all targeted toward things like the college loan program, Head Start, new technologies, and jobs and about $15 billion in additional tax incentives to businesses to reinvest in new jobs. So that's what the net new spending is. But if you look at it total in the first 4 years, the spending cuts and the revenue increases are about equal. If you string it out for 4 more years, if we really change the spending habits of the country, the spending cuts are far greater than the tax increases. And I've got a little chart. I'll send it to you, and you can see exactly how much year by year in each of the three categories.

Let me just make this point on the spending cuts. I have spent a month during which we have worked almost around the clock trying to get a handle on this budget. The Federal budget is put together in a way that I don't think is very good, and it doesn't resemble any business budget or any State or local budget you have ever seen.

Let me give you an example. I wrote a letter to the Agency that is supposed to be helping me put together the budget—a memo—and I said, here are about 30 questions I want answered. One question was, how much more money are we collecting a day than we were 5 years ago in tax money, and how much of revenue has grown in each of the last 5 years? You know what the answer was that I got back from the Agency? "Federal revenues as a percentage of our gross national product are slightly smaller than they were 5 years ago." So help me, that was the answer I got back, I promise. In other words, just to your point, we were taking more money in, and tax revenues had grown less fast than the economy, but what difference did that make; we had more money. They didn't even answer the questions.

I'll send you the exact chart. But it's basically 50–50 spending cuts, revenue increases for the first 4 years. Spending cuts swamped revenue increases in the second 4 years and will go much more if we adopt a new health care control plan. And the investment increases are significant but modest. They reflect a big change in the spending priorities.

One of the things I'm trying to do is change;

Government is great at starting things and bad at stopping things. So we're still, believe it or not, you're still paying for a bicentennial commission. That was over in 1976. And there are lots of things. It's a little bit of money, but you can't justify it. It's just terrible. And there's a lot of stuff in there like that. So what I'm trying to do is to flush that out, reduce consumption, and increase investment so that we can put some people to work. That's what I'm trying to do. And I'll send you the chart.

When I spoke on Thursday night I tried to give the exact numbers in the last, but I will be glad to—I mean, that chart was in the book that we presented to the Congress. And I was hoping that it would be run in all the newspapers in the country, because there is a chart in the book we released to the press on Thursday morning. Anybody who wants that chart, I'll be glad to give it to you.

Let me make one final point about that: I have no interest in raising a penny in taxes if we're not going to do the cuts. I don't want to get a deal where we're going to raise the money and not do the cuts. Not a penny.

The second point is, I don't have any pride of authorship in this. I've been working on this like crazy for 4 weeks. There must be people who know more about some of these things than I do. And I have invited all the people in the Congress, Republicans as well as Democrats, and all the people in the country to help us find more. I'm more than open to it.

But I have to say, too, there are some tough decisions involved in the cuts. As you know, there is a uranium enrichment facility in this congressional district not far from here. And one of the things we've concluded is that there are only two in the country, and both are running at about half capacity—with the projected need going down—is that we will have to close one of those. So there are tough decisions involved in this. There are a lot of tough decisions that have to be made in this cut area. But if anybody's got any more ideas about how we can cut more, I'd like to have them.

Health Care Reform

Q. Mr. President, I'm Mayor of a small town. We have two employees. About the last 8 years, health insurance went from $400 a month to $1,500 a month for two employees. If you can have Hillary get this health insurance in line, it will help our little village. Plus, I'm on economic development in our county, and our biggest employer makes television sets. And if that health care comes down, it will sure help those stay in business, too. So tell Hillary to keep on it. And if you get that down, we'll send her a big thanks.

The President. Thank you. Let me say, this is a subject, probably a whole subject for another town meeting. But let me say that one of my biggest problems with a lot of you in dealing with health care is this: If you ask the American people a question about health care, are we spending too much or too little, a lot of people will say we're spending too little. Why? Because they feel insecure about losing their health insurance. Or because, like your mother, they're spending too much out of pocket. So if you ask the American people, are we spending too much or too little, a lot of people say too little. That's wrong. We're spending too much and on the wrong things.

That young doctor that stood up here, I'll bet you anything more than 30 percent of his gross income goes to paperwork. Right? We are the only country in the world where you have 1,500 separate health insurance companies writing thousands of policies with every doctor's office and every hospital in America having to keep up with them.

Just for example, the average country we complete with, of every dollar people spend on health care, 95 cents on the dollar goes to health care, a nickel to run the administrative programs. In America, it's more like 86 cents. You figure out what 9 cents on the dollar is—or 11 cents on the dollar—for an $840 billion health bill, or if you take the Government out of it, about $600 billion. You just figure it out. It's lots of money.

Tuition Tax Credits

Q. Yes, Mr. President. I'm John Cooper, and I go to a private school. And in years past we have not had any support from the Government with funds. And I was just wondering if you had a plan that will help pay for some of the taxes that we have. And I was wondering, if you don't have one, why not?

The President. I'll tell you why not. I don't, and I'll tell you why not. When I was a boy, I went 2 years to a private school, to a wonderful Catholic school. And we paid tuition. And my folks were not wealthy. They were working people when we did it. And I was living way out in the country, and we moved to a new community, and we just didn't know anything about the school. And I've always treasured that experience. But I don't believe, particularly right now, that we can afford to give tuition tax credits or other breaks to fund private schools, even though I support the competition private schools give to public schools. And I'll tell you why.

Q. Mr. President——

The President. Let me tell you why. Even though I'll bet you anything you've raised more money in this State to put into this school system we're in right now, the United States today is behind at least eight of its major competitors in the percentage of our income we spend on kindergarten through 12th grade education. And we have more problems in our schools than most of our competitors because we have more income diversity and more racial and ethnic diversity, and a lot of our schools are located in places where there are a lot of tough economic problems. So I don't think we can afford to do that now. I wish I could tell you what you want to hear, but I just don't agree with it.

Mayor Joe Sulzer. Mr. President, I'm sorry, but we have time for only one more question over here, and then we'll have a special presentation. And then we would ask everyone to remain seated as the President leaves. Thank you.

Participation in Government

The President. May I ask a question? May I ask you something before we get off, Mayor? These things always work like this. We could stay here till the cows come home to do this. And I love this. And you've been great. But I want to—[*applause*]—I want to say—wait a minute. I want to make two points, and then I'll answer the last question, whichever, whoever the Mayor designates to be the last question.

The first is that one of the things I've been really proud of in the last month—it proved the election worked, it proved all the town meetings worked, it proved the Ross Perot charts worked, it proved the whole thing worked—is that the volume of our mail and telephone calls is running at historic highs in the White House. That means the American people—a lot of its people who disagree with me, a lot of its people who agree, a lot of its people who are just asking honest questions—but my point is, it means people believe maybe their Government can be made to work

for them again and maybe we can be accountable again.

So a lot of you have questions you haven't gotten answered today. I would encourage you to write to us. I have reorganized the White House Correspondence Office. I've tried to put a number of people there who really understand the issues that I believe in and the things that we care about. We're trying to minimize the number of just formal responses we give—unless people send us a form letter; that's different—but I mean people that really write us. So I would encourage you to do that.

The second thing I want to do is to say that I want to encourage you to continue to hold me and everybody else accountable and ask the tough questions. I don't think it was all that easy for that young man to stand up there and ask the question he asked on abortion because he knew he had a different position than I did. And I was proud of him for doing that, and I think you should be, too.

And believe me, none of us have all of the answers. This is a new and uncharted time. And I want to encourage you to continue to believe in your country and to participate in this. Hold our feet to the fire, but try to make it a constructive thing. This is an exciting time for this country and it's sort of a make-or-break time, I think, and I'm doing the best I can and I think you are, too. And if we keep doing that, I think the chances are we're going to come out okay.

I think I can say for the other elected officials here, I'll bet you they're pretty proud of their constituents in Ohio after this town meeting. Who is last, Mayor? Who did you select, Mayor?

Mayor Sulzer. Right over there, Mr. President.

Education Reform

Q. Mr. President, I'm a sixth grader at Smith Middle School, and I'm wondering, do any parts of your education plan deal with children my age?

The President. Good for you. Okay. The answer is yes, but most of them don't. And let me tell you why—the answer is yes, they do. We emphasize more funds and more efforts in math and science education, for example. And I have asked the Congress to give the Education Department some funds that will enable us to target learning strategies in elementary and junior high and high school that work, and try to get schools to repeat them.

Do you know that every problem in American education has been solved by somebody, somewhere? I mean, this is not like looking for a cure for some disease we haven't found a cure for yet. What we are not good at in American education is taking what works in one place and putting it in place another. So the two major things are, we're trying to repeat education strategies that have given young people in the sixth grade great performance in some places; we want to try to put them in all the schools in the country. And secondly, we're going to make a special effort on math and science education.

Now, let me answer the other question. Most of the funds that I have recommended in education, most of the effort will be going to try to make sure kids get off to an equal start in school: fully funding the Head Start program, supporting schools and their preschool programs, trying to make sure that child nutrition and child health care is good, and then when children leave school, trying to make sure that they have a vocational program, a job training program, a college program to go to.

Why? Because over 90 percent of the cost of the public schools, kindergarten through 12th grade, comes from the State and local level. I can have an impact on your education only if we focus on a few issues where we can really help, like how do you get more computers in schools, how do you do better with math and science. But most of the money comes from the State and local level. Whereas, a lot of what we have to do for children before they start school and after they graduate from high school has to come from the national level, and that's why we do it that way.

Thank you very much. You were great.

NOTE: The President spoke at 9 a.m. at Chillicothe High School. In his remarks, he referred to Mayor Joe Sulzer; Richard Cline, superintendent of schools; Vernal G. Riffe, speaker, Ohio House of Representatives; and Melissa Hagen, high school student council president.

Remarks on the Economic Program in Hyde Park, New York
February 19, 1993

Thank you very much, my good friend James Roosevelt, who has likewise been an inspiration to me over the years, and who knows and cares a great deal about a subject that we must all come to grips with this year, the crisis in health care; to Senator Pat Moynihan, one of the most productive people in public life in the 20th century in America.

And Mrs. Cuomo, I'm delighted to see you here, and we wish Governor Cuomo good health. He might have thought to himself, on deciding whether to do the responsible thing and take to his sick bed today, that he's probably heard this speech before and he's probably given it before. [*Laughter*] I can't tell you how grateful I am to your Governor for his support and his wise counseling. We had a delightful time in the White House, Hillary and I and Governor and Mrs. Cuomo, not very long ago. It's something I will treasure for a long time.

I'm glad to see Lieutenant Governor Lundine and Attorney General Abrams and Members of the Congress, and members of both parties from the New York Assembly and State Senate, and people here who are here because you are Americans. You're Republicans, Democrats, independents. I am glad to see you all here in this monument to America's possibility.

I wanted to come here for a thousand reasons, some of which are obvious. During the New York primary, which was successful in its conclusion but rather rough in its prelude on me— [*laughter*]—I was absolutely enthralled by a book about President Roosevelt called "The First Class Temperament" written by a man named Jeffrey Ward. And I read a lot about Hyde Park. And the thing that moved me most was the way President Roosevelt came to grips with the fact of his polio and learned to live with it and learned to triumph over it and learned to use it to make himself stronger inside and not to be defeated by it. And ever since, I have been transformed from someone who had a mild interest in coming here to someone who had a burning passion to see this place. And I am honored to be here today.

I want to say one more word, if I might, about Senator Moynihan because we've worked together over the years on a lot of things. I helped him to rewrite the welfare laws of our Nation in the late eighties and what he said was the most significant social welfare reform in 30 years, if only we could implement it. And one of the reasons I ran for President is to try to change the welfare system as we know it. I have watched him over more than two decades personally warn us about the decline of America's families, the development of a new and possibly permanent underclass in America, the importance of restoring the value of work to our social programs, a decade ago warning about the breakup of what was then the Soviet Union when most people thought that he was speaking a foreign language. And I can tell you that with leadership like his we can solve the problems this country faces today.

I think of that because—[*applause*]—yes, you can give him a hand. That's good. We were about 45 or 50 minutes away from here when we landed in the airplane, and all along the way there were people, school children, hundreds of them, lining the way with their signs, and the young people at Marist College having even printed signs. Many people were young; some were older. A lot of them were terribly young. Most of them were, I'd say, between 20 and 50, anyway. [*Laughter*] That's young to me, you know. I find myself redefining that word every year. And there are all kinds of incredible things: "Get the U.S. fit," one sign said. "I want to give something to my country," another said. One I might have to give a trip to the doctor. It said, "I want to pay more taxes." I couldn't believe that. [*Laughter*] One sign said, "Shake 'em up, Bill." One sign said, "Give Bill a chance." One said, "Turn my country around." Another said, "I've got a B.A. and no job; I'm ready to change." Another said, "Just do something."

Then, of course, there were a few that weren't so favorable, but that's all right. That's what this country's all about, too. But I couldn't believe the number of people who were there. And I say that because as much as anything else, I think our country now is infused with a new sense of possibility.

One of the things that really used to depress me as I crossed America last year was the look

I saw in so many people's eyes of skepticism, almost a painful unwillingness to believe that we can make things better, that we could change, that we could come to grips with the challenges of our time and overcome them and move forward.

One of the things that I think—perhaps the most important thing that was achieved in the last election year was we had a huge increase in turnout, an even bigger increase among younger people. And now every day the White House switchboard and the mailroom are fuller than they have been in decades and decades because people believe that it matters again.

This country has been kept going through two centuries now because of the peculiar mix of the energy of its people at the grassroots level and the vision of its leaders. But if you have one without the other, the country can't go forward. There have been times in the past when leaders have foreseen the future and known what needed to be done, but there was no connection with the people and so nothing could happen. There have been many times, I'm convinced, when the people have been ahead of their leaders. But if they had no visionary leaders, nobody to put all that energy together with the levers of public authority, nothing happened. We all hope, I think, from whatever perspective we come, that we now have a moment in our history where we have the energy of the people and a direction we can take.

I ran for President because I believe this was a critical moment in our country's history. And there have been many over the last two centuries. I think of the Founding Fathers, who actually welded a nation out of 13 independent colonies when many people—maybe if you'd even taken a poll, a majority of the people would have said, "Who wants one army? Who wants one currency? Who wants to really give up all this independence we have in New York or South Carolina? What do we have in common with those people down there?"

I think of Thomas Jefferson. Some people thought he was crazy when he ponied up $15 million to buy something then called the Louisiana Purchase, which most Americans could not even imagine and hardly anyone had ever seen. And if he hadn't done it, since I live on the edge of the Louisiana Purchase, you'd be listening to somebody from somewhere else give this speech today.

I think of Abraham Lincoln. We now take

it for granted that the Union would be preserved, that the slaves would be freed, that all this would happen. The truth is that a great many people thought there was no way to hold this Nation together. And a great deal of what did it was his vision and his sheer will.

I think of President Roosevelt in the depths of the Depression, having gone through his personal journey to cope with his personal problems, summoning interior strength and reserve to lift the Nation's vision and to make people believe again that by taking one step at a time, by coming and building a beautiful school like this with the WPA—that if you did enough things like this and you just kept trying long enough, sooner or later we would go forward, we would work our way out of it by what he called then bold, persistent experimentation.

Today, I think we need that kind of experimentation based on the plain evidence that we are in a rut. What we have been doing is not working to deal with the problems we face.

For about two decades, through administrations of both parties' Presidents, we've been steadily moving into a global economy which is much more competitive, where other countries have been growing more rapidly than we and moving toward our standard of living, where we have to compete in all forms of economic life in ways that can force us to endure real pain, as you folks in this part of the country have seen recently with the difficulties that a magnificent company, IBM, has been forced to come to grips with. This is not an isolated event. This is part of the passage of time and the economic realities in which we live.

That global economy abroad has presented us with a lot of challenges and a lot of opportunities here. But our ability to deal with it has been limited by a lot of the educational and training and social problems we have here at home, our racial and ethnic and income diversity, the high rates of violence and the whole pockets of poverty we have in this country, and lack of investment. We have seen that there are a lot of things that are just not quite fitting very well.

And now we've had two decades in which the wages of most Americans have been stagnant compared to inflation. And when you look at the rising cost of education, health care, housing, the tax burden, most Americans are working harder today than they were 10 years ago for real, disposable income that is less, because of

these sweeping trends.

For 12 years, we have tried a clear approach to our country's problems. When President Reagan was elected in 1980, he ran with a clear sense of what he wished to do. He said, "The Government is the problem here. It causes inflation. It causes middle-class people to have trouble. What we need is a very restricted role for Government. And we will also lower taxes on everybody, but most of all on the wealthiest Americans. Because if we give them their money back, they will invest it in America, create jobs, drive up incomes, increase jobs, and we will be the most prosperous country in the world."

Well, I believe that free enterprise is the engine of growth in America. We are fundamentally a conservative, private, capitalist free enterprise country. But every other nation with which we compete decided to take a slightly different course. They said to themselves in Germany and Japan: Well, we're in a global economy in which the government and the people in the private sector have to work together. We've got to work together to train and educate our people as well as possible. We've got to work together to have economic policies that encourage investment over consumption so we can always be competitive. We've got to have a good trade policy, and we've got to do things that make it possible to create high-wage, high-growth jobs so that all the students who go to school here will have a future, and so that America will be strong. That's what I think we have to do.

In other words, that is my vision. That is not what we have done. What we have done is to try for 12 years to cramp the role of Government. Now, look what's happened in practice. In practice, we have lowered taxes on the wealthiest Americans. Taxes on the middle class have actually gone up in the last 12 years. We have run a horrendous Government deficit. The deficit is now 4 times as big as it was in 1980.

We have seen spending go up in areas that the Government would have to move to control, mostly health care and then interest on the debt, because when the deficit gets bigger and bigger and bigger, you spend more money on the debt. So we have reduced investment, increased the debt, moved money upward so that there's been much more inequality of income distribution, but we have not seen the kind of investment that creates high-wage, high-growth jobs in the emerging technologies that guarantee a future for all the young people that live here and throughout our land.

So I ran for President because I really believe we ought to try a different course. Not to blame past Presidents; if you look at what's happened in Washington, none of it could have happened if there hadn't been bipartisan support for the course and support in Congress as well as in the White House. This is not about blame.

I want to simply take responsibility. And as I told the Congress the other night, if we turn this country around, I don't care who gets the credit for it, either. I just think the time has come to make a change. We have tried one thing 12 years. It obviously has problems. It is time to change.

Now, what does that mean? Change for change sake is not good. What does it mean? It means to me that we should do the following things. First of all, the Government should pursue a policy of increasing investment in those things which contribute to a growing economy. What are those things? We should invest more than we are now and more toward what our competitors do, in the infrastructure of the country, in transportation and communications, in environmental cleanup, in those things which increase productivity and put people to work.

It means we should do whatever it takes to educate people for a lifetime at very high levels, because the skill level of the work force is the single most important determinant of income and the capacity to grow new jobs rapidly as new areas of opportunity open up. It means that we should invest in partnership with the private sector in new technologies which will determine the future of the country. And it means we should not give up on those areas where we have a lead. And let me just give you two examples:

One is in computer technology and information technology. That's why what's happening to some of our big companies is very disturbing and why I'm going to California this weekend to announce a new technology policy to try to revitalize this whole sector of our economy.

I'll give you another example which doesn't affect New York much, but it affects our country desperately, and that is aerospace. Boeing just announced 23,000 layoffs when we know that aerospace jobs are growing in number worldwide, high-wage jobs. And we sat here for 10 years and let Europe put $26 billion into an airbus program, direct government subsidies, to throw Boeing workers, McDonnell-Douglas workers, and other aerospace workers in America out of work because we said, "Well, we don't practice those kind of partnerships." So we have got to face the fact that we've taken a new direction.

And finally, it means that we must reduce the Government's debt. Why? Because if the debt gets bigger and bigger and bigger, two bad things happen: Bad thing number one is the Congress spends more of your tax money every year paying interest on the debt rather than investing in your future. It's now up to 15 cents on the dollar. If we do not change present spending patterns—when you hear people oppose the program I outline, ask them what the cost of the status quo is.

If we behave for 4 more years like we have for the last 12, here's what will happen: By the end of the decade, the deficit will be $650 billion a year, and we'll be spending about 22 cents of every one of your tax dollars just paying interest on the debt. We'll be spending by then, because of the growth of health care costs, about 65 cents of your tax dollars on entitlements, and being in Congress will be a matter of how you spend 5 or 6 cents on every dollar. The rest of this will be just be rubber stamped. You can just have a computer instead of Congress.

I know what you're thinking. Please don't say that. [*Laughter*] So, forgive me, Senator Moynihan, I had to say that. [*Laughter*] But you get it. I mean, it's squeezing the life out of the money you're giving up in taxes.

The second reason, even more important, is the more money the Government borrows every year, the less money there is for people to borrow in the private sector and the higher the cost of the money is. Just since the election, since we made it clear that there was going to be a determined effort to lower the deficit, interest rates long-term have dropped considerably. I'll come back to this in a moment.

But if you think about it, this year if we pass this budget, everybody in America who borrows long-term to finance a business, to finance a car, to finance a home, to finance credit card purchases, everybody that has access to variable interest rates will have those interest rates go down. And in my judgment, virtually everybody who has credit will save more money in lower interest costs than they will pay in higher taxes. Now, that's very, very important.

Now, how are we going to do this? The first thing we have to do, and I mean the first, is to cut inessential Government spending. I've been President 4 weeks, and I've found things that I wouldn't have believed. The White House, when I became President, was running on Jimmy Carter's telephone system and Lyndon Johnson's switchboard in this—true—high-wage, this high-technology era, with a procurement system that would have broken Einstein's brain. [*Laughter*]

There were a lot of things that needed to be changed in the Federal Government, and there still are. But in 4 weeks, we have cut the White House staff by 25 percent, starting at the beginning of the next fiscal year, and reorganized the White House so it will work more efficiently; not just cut but serve better. We have authorized in this budget administrative cuts in every Government Department, totaling 14 percent over the next 4 years for a savings of $9 billion. And there have been 150 specific cuts in Government programs, including programs that help a lot of good people but that I don't think we can afford at the present level anymore, programs like the two uranium enrichment facilities we have when we now know we only need one. And I was in one congressional district where one of those two facilities are this morning.

You can say these cuts are not difficult, but when you look into the eyes of people who may be personally affected by them, they are, including reductions in the interest subsidies to the Rural Electrification Authority, something that brought electricity to my relatives in my State and which is still a very major force. Things that have some good in them, but we simply can't afford them.

We've cut things out that have no good purpose anymore as far as I can tell, including a whole slew of commissions. Do you remember when we had the tall ships come into New York Harbor for the Bicentennial? That was a long time ago. Remember that? There's still a bicentennial commission. [*Laughter*] That's just one example. It's the funniest, but not the most costly. There are a lot of others.

We have cut back on programs that involve subsidizing activities more than we should. The Superfund, for example, has, in my judgment, too much contribution from the taxpayer, too little from those who are responsible for the problem, and none of the money is being spent right. So far it's all going to lawyers. It's all going to lawyers.

There is a program that I think helps a lot of wonderful people. It's a subsidy to sheep growers. You laugh. I asked Senator Moynihan if anybody in New York still raised sheep. We had sheep on the farm when I was a boy, so I'm more sensitive to this than some are.

But when I got to studying this, we started to subsidize the sheep growers in World War I because we needed plenty of wool for uniforms. But the program is still on the books exactly as it was, not designed to help the small farmers stay in business, necessarily, but an across-the-board subsidy of that kind. So I recommended cutting it back. All these things have constituencies. But I can tell you, we are going to have to prove that we can cut things.

When Roosevelt talked about bold, persistent experimentation, you know what an experiment is in science. It is trying out a new thesis. If it works, you incorporate it. You build on it. You go on to the next experiment. If it doesn't work, you quit. Government has a one-way experiment. We're very good at starting things and absolutely terrible at stopping them.

So what we're going to try to do is start some new things. I want to fully fund Head Start. I want a big, new technology initiative. I want a big, new technology issue. I want to make it possible for every student in this country to borrow the money to go to college and then pay it back on favorable terms or work it off in national service, as teachers or police officers or working with kids in trouble.

But we can't do that if we keep on doing everything we used to do. We have to stop doing some things we used to do to free up some money for things we should do. And we have to cut more in the past than we're going to spend in the future, because we have to use some of that money to reduce the deficit, too. So I ask you to support that.

Now, in 4 weeks we found 150 specific cuts. As I said to the Congress the other night, in all good conscience to both the Republicans and the Democrats, I've just been there 4 weeks. Some of them have been there a lot longer than I have, and if anybody's got any other ideas, I'd like to have them. I just got started. You can look forward to more.

I also think as I said in the campaign that we have to raise some more money. I now believe what I said might be true in the campaign, but I didn't think it was, that we have to raise it from a broader base than just people that make over $100,000, and I want to deal with that.

After the election in December, the Government increased its estimates of our deficit by about $50 billion a year over the next 4 years. Now, if I had stayed with exactly the same plan that I recommended in the campaign, the first thing my critics who now attack me for raising taxes would say is, "Oh, he's going to increase the deficit. Oh, he's being too optimistic."

I decided that when they revised deficit figures up one more time $50 billion a year, that somebody had to take this thing and shake it up and say, "We are definitely going to have a plan of spending cuts, new investments, and revenue increases that will bring this debt down." And I plead guilty to doing that.

And I think almost any of you, if you had been in my circumstance, would have done the same thing if you were thinking about what was in the long-term best interest of the country. And you can see it by how much interest rates have come down just since the election. People who control these things desperately want to believe that our Government can exercise some discipline again, that we can have some focus, that we can show some restraint as well as some activity.

Now, the taxes that I propose to raise—let me just basically go through them—are essentially three. There are more minor ones, but the big-ticket items are as follows:

Number one, an increase in the income tax on the top 1.2 percent of income earners; an increase in the corporate income tax on corporations that have income in excess of $10 million a year.

Number two, an increase in the income subject to taxation of people who draw Social Security but also have other income in excess of $32,000 a year if they're couples, or individuals in excess of $25,000 a year. In other words, anyone who is not paying tax on Social Security now will not pay tax under my plan. That's 80 percent of the Social Security recipients. The upper 20 percent will be asked to pay taxes on a higher percentage of their income, but we will still leave enough of that income free so that almost all of them will get back what they put into the Social Security system plus interest without taxation. The rest will be subject to the income tax. I think that is fair.

Since 1985—I'm very proud of this—since 1985—as an American, you should be proud

of it—the people of this country over 65 have had a lower poverty rate than people under 65. That's the good news. The bad news is that one in five American kids is living in poverty. So it seems to me that this is a fair thing to do under these circumstances.

And then the third thing I recommended was an energy tax that will raise $20 billion a year and will help us to clean up the environment, promote conservation, and make us more independent of foreign oil. It is a broad-based tax to try to be fair to every part of the country.

And I want to deal with this because I'm in New York now. There were some who said tax carbon, that's a fancy way of saying tax coal, which is very tough on West Virginia, Virginia, Ohio, Pennsylvania, coal States that have been very hard hit. So I said no. There were others who said put a huge tax on gasoline, which is good for city dwellers but tough on people that live in the country and that live in those big western States where they have to drive very long distances and a carpool is not an option. So we said no. And some said tax the value of energy, which sounds great, except whenever one source of energy goes up the taxes go up. So you reinforce price increases. So we decided the most environmentally responsible and regionally fair way to do it was to tax the heat content of energy, oil, gas, coal in a very modest way, and then to have an offset over the next 4 years where any disproportionate impact in the Northeast for home heating oil, and real incentives for conversion.

Now finally, let me say this program exacts no new taxes for the 40-plus percent of our income tax payers whose taxable income is under $30,000; about $20 a year for people at $30,000; goes up to something between $10 and $15 a month, depending on what your purchasing habits are, for people at $40,000. Seventy percent of it comes from people whose incomes exceed $100,000.

There are also some other things here I want you to know about. This program has some tax incentives, which is a fancy way for saying tax cuts for people who invest their money: for the next 2 years, an investment tax credit for all businesses in America large and small who increase their rate of investment; then after that, some tax changes asked for by the manufacturing community for bigger businesses that will always encourage investment; and, for the first time, I think, ever, a small business investment tax credit that is a permanent 7-percent invest-ment tax credit for the 90-plus percent of our businesses that operate on $5 million or less in revenues but create most of our new jobs.

This is a very significant thing that will en-courage the private sector to invest in job-gener-ating activities and very important, because in every year of the 1980's, big business lost em-ployment and small business overcame it with more new jobs; but for the last 2½ years small business has not been creating enough jobs to offset the losses in big business. So we've got to reverse that.

There's one final point I want to make as strongly as I can about this. Our plan will bring the deficit down dramatically over the next 4 years. In the 4th year, it will be $140 billion a year lower than it would otherwise be. But unless we also tackle the health care crisis this year, the deficits will start going up after that no matter what we do, because the cost of health care is going to overtake every other thing in the budget and swallow it whole, and not for new health care. We will be paying more for the same health care. So there is no more urgent item on our national agenda than getting all the people involved in health care together and trying to hammer it out.

I asked the First Lady, as all of you know, to head a task force on this. She is increasingly less grateful to me for having asked her to do that. [*Laughter*] But she's very good at bringing people together on a complex matter and bring-ing them to conclusions and coming to a clear plan. And we have got to do that, or we can't turn this country's economic health around.

You talk to any major manufacturer and ask them what their biggest problem is. Nine out of ten of them will tell you, "my health care costs." You talk to the steel people and the auto people and ask them, and a lot of them will tell you, "just paying the health care costs of our retirees." So we have to face that.

Now, that's all of the bad news. Now, what's the good news? What are you going to get out of this? A half a million new jobs in the next year and a half in a job stimulus program, and a long-term program to raise our levels of invest-ment and our quality of education and training, to be fairer to the lower income working people and create an environment that moves people from welfare to work, to have policies that really support families who are working and trying to raise children, and to have an investment pro-gram that breaks the barriers of new tech-nologies and actually tries to create more new jobs than we are losing every year.

No one can promise you, nobody, to stop anything bad from happening in this world. The world you're living in is so dynamic; there's going to be so many changes; no one can repeal the law of change. But change has been too many enemies for too many people. I seek to make change the friend of the American people. That's what this program does. It will make change our friend instead of our enemy. But we first have the courage. We must have the courage to seize control of our own destiny.

So I want to say to you, just as I said to Congress the other night, I need your help. I can't do this alone. If you think there's some-thing wrong with my program, fine. Come up with an alternative. But I promise you, the cost of the status quo is the most expensive course of all. Staying with what we've been doing is plainly unacceptable. Every American ought to be able to see that. The price is entirely too high. The price of my program is far lower with far higher results.

I ask people of good will all across this coun-try, just as I asked the Congress: If you can think of more things we can cut in spending that are really good for this economy and the American people over the long run, have at it. Let's go. I'm just getting started. I will not, I will not support any tax increase without the spending cuts. I'm not for that. I think we would also be very foolish to say that we don't need to invest more in our children and in our tech-nology and in our economic future in putting the American people back to work. After all, the bottom line of all this is the chance that Americans need to have a dignified life.

We are here in this beautiful school building today. It still looks fabulous after all these years because President Roosevelt knew it was wrong to let all those energetic, hard-working, family-oriented, God-fearing craftsmen and people who could work, sit idle month after month, year after year, when they had a contribution to make that would be good for themselves and good for the country.

I ask you now to give me your support so that we can mobilize the energies of a whole generation of Americans. It will be good for you, but more important, it will be good for the country.

Thank you very much.

NOTE: The President spoke at 3:46 p.m. in the auditorium of Haviland Middle School. In his remarks, he referred to Lt. Gov. Stan Lundine and attorney general Robert Abrams of New York.

Nomination for Deputy Director for Management at the Office of Management and Budget
February 19, 1993

The President today appointed Phil Lader, a South Carolina businessman and educator, to be the Office of Management and Budget's Deputy Director for Management. As the senior administration official directly responsible for cutting waste and inefficiency in Government operations, Lader will play a key role in the President's efforts to reinvent Government.

"We must streamline the operations of the Federal Government," said President Clinton.

"We must squeeze every penny that we have out of the Government before we ask ordinary Americans to contribute to deficit reduction. Phil Lader has my complete confidence. I trust his ability to find every way possible to carry out my mandate of slashing the executive costs of Government."

NOTE: A biography of the nominee was made available by the Office of the Press Secretary.

Nomination for Deputy Secretary of Labor
February 19, 1993

The President announced today his intention to nominate Thomas Glynn of Belmont, Massachusetts for the post of Deputy Secretary of Labor. Glynn is currently Brown University's senior vice president for finance and administration.

"One of the most important things we need to do in this administration is learn how to manage the Government better," said President Clinton. "I've pledged to save $9 billion by controlling administrative costs. Thomas Glynn has the kind of experience managing large institutions, both public and private, that is needed to make that happen."

NOTE: A biography of the nominee was made available by the Office of the Press Secretary.

Nomination for an Assistant Secretary of the Treasury
February 19, 1993

The President announced today that he intends to nominate Leslie Samuels, a highly respected tax attorney, as Assistant Secretary for Tax Policy at the Department of Treasury.

"As I take the case for my economic plan to the people of this country," said the President, "I am very pleased to know that someone of Leslie Samuels' caliber will be watching over tax policy at Treasury. He will do an excellent job at keeping my commitment to a tax system that is fair to all Americans."

NOTE: A biography of the nominee was made available by the Office of the Press Secretary.

The President's Radio Address
February 20, 1993

This is Bill Clinton. As you know, this week I sent Congress my economic plan to create new jobs and to lift the living standards of Americans and their children. This morning I want to talk with you directly about it.

Let's begin with the children. If you're on your way to soccer practice or to take your children to a grocery store, if you can see from the window of your apartment children riding bikes or tossing a snowball, you know why we care so much about our schools and our neighborhoods and why we feel so strongly about being able to give our children what they need in life. We've always been a strong and caring nation where families worked hard to pass on something better to their children, and where government accepted the responsibility to support the efforts of families and the futures of our kids. But for too many years, our families have struggled without the help they need.

Our Federal Government in Washington has spent more than it had, run up huge deficits, and yet done nothing during difficult economic times to help families and their children. We neglected our economy and those very efforts like education, health care, training, and nutrition where national investments today pay big dividends in the future. Gridlock here in our Capital between the parties and among all the special interests has simply blocked progress, leading us to the politics of least resistance. A lot of people talked about change, but it never came. I hope those days of business as usual are over.

This year can be different with your help. I've presented a plan to grow this economy, a plan that takes America in historic new directions to improve the lives of our workers, our businesses, and our families. We can cut the deficit and increase investment if we have the courage to make changes.

Let's begin with investment. My proposal invests in infants and young children in programs that guarantee big returns for every dollar spent. For example, I've asked Congress to approve an immunization program to reach all children under the age of 2 with the shots they need to fight preventable diseases like polio, measles, tetanus, and the mumps. Every $1 invested today saves $10 in the future in preventable childhood diseases. But today, of all the countries in our hemisphere, only Haiti and Bolivia have lower immunization rates than the United States. We can do better.

I've also recommended a maximum effort for nutrition programs to help pregnant mothers have healthy babies, and full funding for the Head Start program, the most successful early education program our country has ever seen. Again, we know now that $1 invested today will save $3 in avoidable health and education problems for these children in the future.

I believe our families must also again enjoy the rewards that come with productive work. Under our new direction, the working poor will rise out of poverty. Welfare recipients will be trained for work, not welfare. And because families must also take responsibility for their own children, there will be tougher requirements for parents to pay their own child support, including stiffening our collection procedures and identifying parents when the child is born.

And to restart America's economic engine, our primary and principal goal, we'll take several historic steps. We'll reward investments in small business with a permanent tax credit and fund new research and development. We'll create new incentives for bigger business to always be investing in high quality equipment and the best training and jobs for their workers. We'll create a better environment for all of the private sector, both business and agriculture and self-employed people, through deficit reduction, lower interest rates, and better trained workers. We'll build enterprise zones and community development banks across the country so that investment capital can flow to people and to forgotten neighborhoods desperate for the chance to grow. And I'd like to put hundreds of thousands of idle people back to work right now, repairing our public works and building the new infrastructure of tomorrow. As our plan restores the economy to health, millions more jobs will be created. These are the values and goals our plan is designed to accomplish. They reflect an economy that puts people first.

But you must all be wondering how we'll provide the means to reach our goals. First, we'll cut wasteful or inessential Government spending. I've cut the White House staff by 25 percent and told the Federal agencies they must cut $9 billion in administrative waste and to reduce personnel slots by 100,000. I've asked Congress to freeze the salaries paid by Federal Government workers next year and to match the administrative cuts that I've proposed for the Government agencies. They've agreed to match those administrative cuts, and I hope they'll agree to the other budget cuts, too. I don't like asking for these contributions, but I have to deliver to you a leaner Government and a more vibrant economy in return.

I do propose to raise income tax rates, but only for the top 1.2 percent of taxpayers, those taxpayers whose taxes went down in the 1980's while their incomes went way up. And our overall tax proposal will cost a family of four with an income of $40,000 less than $17 a month.

Finally, I will cut almost $250 billion from more than 150 domestic programs, many of them with some merit, and from the defense budget.

Now a lot of interests will argue that these cuts are too steep. Still others will say they're not enough or demand that we protect their pet projects while cutting someone else. To all, I say the same thing: Give me real cuts; don't waste the people's time anymore. I'm committed to cutting every bit of spending we can from programs we don't need or can't afford. And I won't raise taxes without cutting spending. But tell us exactly where you want to cut, and I'll gladly listen.

It's time to put politics aside and put America first. It's been years since our Government fought for working families and gave them a system where they could thrive and pass the American dream on to their children. It's time to include all Americans again, to build a new prosperity, not because we want new wealth for the Government but because we want to renew the dreams of our children, all of them.

I'm determined to take us in a new direction, and I ask you to join me in this fight for the future. Support your elected Representatives who are demonstrating the courage to change. If you do, we can write the next great chapter in the history of the greatest country the world has ever known. Thank you, and good morning.

NOTE: The President spoke at 10:06 a.m. from the Oval Office at the White House.

Remarks at the Children's Town Meeting
February 20, 1993

The White House

Peter Jennings. Mr. President, one of my first impressions here is that this is an awful lot bigger than what you were used to living in Arkansas.

The President. It's bigger than almost anybody in America lives in, but it's a beautiful house. You know it was started in 1792. President Washington authorized it to be built, and then before it was finished, actually, President Adams and his wife moved in here. So it's been here a long time.

Mr. Jennings. Right behind us here, of course, we can't go in this morning, but it's really one of the most beautiful rooms, the Blue Room, looking out onto the Jefferson Memorial.

The President. It's very beautiful. And upstairs, just above it, there's another big oval room which President Franklin Roosevelt used as his office during World War II. And now we use it for formal receiving of foreign dignitaries. And it also looks directly out on the Jefferson Memorial. And there's a porch there that President Harry Truman put on, so I can go out at night now and look at the lights shining down on Thomas Jefferson's head. It's a wonderful sight.

Mr. Jennings. You know the White House staff is very discreet. When I asked them if you sneaked around, sticking your heads in various rooms at night, they said, "Ask him." Do you wander around at night?

The President. I do a little, not so much down here but up on the second and third floor. And I spent a lot of time working, in this last month, over around the Oval Office, so I'm in the Cabinet Room a lot and in the Roosevelt Room, which is the President's big staff room. And

I'm just trying to learn what all the pictures are and where all the things are and learn the history of the place. I'm very interested in it.

The Presidency

Mr. Jennings. I just have one question before we go and actually meet the children. There's the President's seal up there, the President of the United States, just above the door of the Blue Room. And it reminds me of Teddy White, the political writer, who said there is a moment when the man stops being the man and becomes the President. Was there such a moment for you, do you remember?

The President. I think there was a moment when I realized I was going to be President, and it was different after that. And it was not at the election. It was a couple of weeks after the election when I was planning the Inaugural and they asked me what I wanted to do. And we decided that I would start at Thomas Jefferson's home at Monticello and then go to the Lincoln Memorial, and then the next morning I would go to the graves of President Kennedy and his brother, Senator Robert Kennedy. And I realized, in describing that that's what I would do, that I was becoming a part of our history.

Mr. Jennings. Well, you indeed—and these young boys and girls, between about 8 and 15, from Washington and other parts around the country, are very interested in you and history.

Good morning, everybody. You welcome the President? Nice to have him, isn't it? Well, I think they have a lot of questions. Who wants to ask the first question?

School Integration in Little Rock

Q. I would like to ask you a question that goes back to about 30, 40 years ago, back in Little Rock, Arkansas. If you were in the same position that you are now, and during the time of the occurrence of the Little Rock Nine, how would you take forth the matters about them going into the school? Would you go with the community, or would you go with your heart?

The President. I would have gone with my heart and with the law of the United States, which was that the children had a right to go to the school without regard to their race. I would have done what President Eisenhower did. I would have sent troops there and done whatever it took to give the children the right to go to school.

One of the people who was part of the Little Rock Nine, Earnest Green, is now a business executive here in Washington and a good friend of mine. And I'm glad he had a chance to do that.

Mr. Jennings. Mr. President, excuse me, I don't think everybody knows who the Little Rock Nine were.

The President. Oh, what he's asking about— about 40 years ago, a lot of the schools, public schools, in our country were still segregated by race. Virtually all the schools in the southern part of the United States were segregated by race. Young black and white children went to different schools. Forty years ago, the courts ruled that we could no longer segregate schools by race. In my hometown of Little Rock, in the capital city, the Governor and the local school board tried to keep them separate. President Eisenhower then ordered troops there to open the schools so that the schools could be integrated. He was asking me if I would do the same thing, and I said I would.

Good for you. Great question.

Mr. Jennings. There's a stool behind you, Mr. President, if you feel like sitting on it. Who else had got a—we kind of broke it down into fun questions and serious questions. Who had a fun question they wanted to start with?

Chelsea Clinton

Q. Do you help Chelsea with her homework?

The President. I do. I do math with her quite often. I took a lot of algebra and advanced mathematics in high school, and then I didn't take any more after I went to college. So when Chelsea got into algebra, she started asking me to help. And so I've used it sort of to learn algebra again. It's been a lot of fun for me. I enjoy it a lot. We do it quite often at night or early in the morning.

Mr. Jennings. Now, Mr. President, people all over the country who I know want to ask you questions, we have an 800 number which we'll put on the screen. It's been up for a while, and people have been trying to call in. So take a look, 1–800–648–8094. And I know we have a call from Kim in Minnesota. Go ahead, Kim.

Women in Political Office

Q. My question is, why can't women be President? Why is it just men?

The President. Women can be President, Kim. No woman has been elected President yet, but we now have a significant number of women in the United States Senate. We've had a good number of women Governors. We have a large number of women in the House of Representatives. And I think that there will be a woman elected President in the not too distant future.

I think that the American people used to be prejudiced against women in public life, and women didn't even have the right to vote guaranteed until, well, less than a hundred years ago. But it's been done now in every other political office in the country. And I think you'll see a woman President before long. Maybe it will be you, if you work hard and do what you can to get involved in public affairs.

Mr. Jennings. I wonder if we can test the confidence level on that statement in here. How many of you girls, or young women, think a woman will be President in your lifetime? Oh, confidence level is very high.

Who's got the next question? How about you, Shannon?

Los Angeles Civil Disturbances

Q. Since the L.A. riots, we have a lot of empty buildings, and a lot of people in our neighborhood want to open businesses. I want to know how can we have low-interest loans to help minorities build shops and buildings?

Mr. Jennings. Mr. President, before you answer that question of Shannon's—I forgot for a second—would you like to see a little bit of where she comes from?

The President. Sure, I would.

Mr. Jennings. Shannon has come here to us from Los Angeles today. How many kids have come from different parts of the country? Just give the President some indications. We have a large contingent from other parts of the country. And Shannon comes from Los Angeles, and here's a little bit about the way she lives. You can look at the monitors.

[*At this point, a short film was shown in which Shannon described life in Los Angeles after the civil disturbances.*]

Mr. Jennings. Sir, her question about low-interest loans for minorities makes a lot of sense.

The President. Good for you; it does. Let me tell you the two or three things we're working on here. First of all, I'm trying to set up, in all the big cities throughout the country, a financial institution that will make low-interest loans to people who live in those communities. There is such a bank in Chicago that's done a very

good job of rebuilding some of the poor communities through setting up businesses.

The second thing that I want to do is to get the Congress to pass a bill which will give people special incentives to invest funds in communities like south central Los Angeles, that you put money in places where there's a lot of unemployment, a lot of empty buildings, you get a special tax break for doing it.

And the third thing I have asked Congress to do is to pass a bill to benefit small business people so that as long as they keep investing money to create jobs, they'll have their taxes lowered for doing that. And I think these things are very important, and I'm glad you asked.

Let me just mention one other thing. One of the provisions of the economic plan I sent to Congress would also permit us to create about 700,000 summer jobs this summer for young people, which would get them active. And then they could be used to clean up the area and to help people make the parks more attractive and to do things to make those areas better and make people want to invest in them more. We've got a lot of work to do, and I'm glad you asked the question.

Health Care Reform

Mr. Jennings. We have a question down here in the front row.

Q. I would like to ask, if we start health care programs, when we start them, who is going to pay for them? Who is going to fund them?

The President. First of all, we're already paying a lot of money on health care. Your country, believe it or not, has the most expensive health care system in the world. We spend much more for health care than any other country, but a lot of Americans don't have health insurance. You know that, don't you? A lot of Americans don't have health care.

So what I think will happen is that we will have a health care system which will be paid for partly by the Government and partly by people who are employers and partly by the people who work for them. And we'll pay for it in three ways. But what we've got to do is to find a way to provide basic health care to all Americans, including people who have serious health problems—I know there are some people in this audience today who have members of your family with serious health problems—and to keep the cost down, more like what it costs in other countries. Because otherwise, we're going to be hurt very bad economically.

One of the reasons we're having trouble generating a lot of new jobs in this country is that our businesses are spending so much more money for health care than any other businesses anywhere in the world, that they have less money to invest to put people to work. So my job is to do two things that are hard to do: get health care for everybody, and then to bring the costs down.

The Presidency

Mr. Jennings. We have a phone call from Connecticut. Go ahead, Connecticut.

Q. I was wondering what made you have the burden to become the President?

The President. You mean, why did I want to become President?

Q. Yes.

The President. That's a good question, Andrea. I decided to run for President in 1991 because I was concerned that there were too many people in America who were out of work; there were too many people who were losing their jobs; there were too many people who had problems with health care; there was too much of an indication that we weren't building a future so that young people like you would be able to grow up and have a better life than your parents did. And I was afraid that the American dream was in danger. I thought I had some good ideas about how to turn it around and how to make life better for the American people, and that's why I ran. I asked the American people to listen to my ideas, and they were good enough to vote for me and give me a chance to serve.

The White House

Mr. Jennings. Now, I know a lot of you have questions about exactly how the President spends his day. Who's got a question about what the President does in the White House?

Q. I just wanted to know—I mean, you were just coming down the hall in the Oval Office showing us how nice, you know, everything around here is, just look around the room and—I don't know, personally if I lived here I would feel constrained to actually live, you know? I mean, it's just so nice, everything is so perfect, I would not—I mean, I don't know. So how do you feel about——

The President. I feel a little that way, too,

sometimes. But let me say that upstairs, on the second floor, there are some nice formal guestrooms but there also is—Chelsea has a bedroom and a little room where she can study and do her work. And Hillary and I have a bedroom and a little family room, and they're not quite so formal. So the rooms that we have are much more like regular rooms in a house, and you don't have to worry so much about breaking an expensive piece of china or something like that.

Mr. Jennings. But it wasn't always so formal here, was it, Mr. President? The East Room, they used to hang laundry in the East Room.

The President. Oh, absolutely. It wasn't always so formal at all. It's probably as formal now as it's ever been, but there are some more informal rooms. And then there's a third floor, a floor two floors up from here, which has some other rooms and a little hallway where we have our rocking chairs and our family books and all kind of stuff like that, which is really much more homey. So we spend a lot of our time in places where we don't have to go on tiptoes all around.

Mr. Jennings. We said we were going to test you on some of the questions here. Do you know the children of which President rollerskated in here, in the East Room? Who remembers that?

Q. Roosevelt.

Mr. Jennings. Which Roosevelt?

Q. Teddy.

Mr. Jennings. Exactly. President Theodore Roosevelt's children used to roller-skate here in the East Room. And of course, maybe you'd like to point out to the kids the famous painting.

The President. Yes. That's a picture of who? Who is that?

The Children. George Washington.

The President. That's right. That's President Washington, painted by Gilbert Stuart. And it is an absolutely invaluable piece of art. Gilbert Stuart was a very famous artist. I think it was offered to the United States first for about $500. He painted it in 1797. That was a lot of money back then. It's worth millions of dollars today. It's a priceless picture.

Mr. Jennings. And who saved it?

The President. Excuse me?

Mr. Jennings. Who saved it?

The President. Who saved it?

Mr. Jennings. Dolley Madison, right?

The President. Yes, Dolley Madison saved it.

Mr. Jennings. When there was——

The President. ——from the fire.

Mr. Jennings. She wouldn't leave the White House until the——

The President. Yes, during the War of 1812 the British marched on Washington and tried to burn the city, and the White House caught fire. There's still some char marks actually out on the front of the White House. And Dolley Madison would not leave the White House until the precious treasures were preserved, including that.

There's also a picture back there of President Theodore Roosevelt, painted when he was a year younger than I am now. Theodore Roosevelt was the youngest person ever to become President. He was elected President at the age—well, he became President when President McKinley died; he was 42. And President Kennedy was elected when he was 43, and I was elected when I had just turned 46. So I'm the third youngest person to be President.

Mr. Jennings. But not—[*inaudible*]. You probably need a bit of rest for the moment, though, sir, as you're the third youngest, so we'll go away for a commercial and be right back.

The President. I feel like the oldest some days. [*Laughter*]

[*The television stations took a commercial break.*]

President's Pastimes

Mr. Jennings. Welcome back to the East Room of the White House. Let's go straight to you, Jared, you have a question.

Q. What do you do for fun around here? [*Laughter*]

The President. I like to play golf. I've only gotten to do it one time since I've been President, but I like to do that. And I like to play cards and games with Hillary and Chelsea. We play pinochle; we play a game that Chelsea taught me called Hungarian rummy. I like to play Trivial Pursuit. That's pretty much what I do.

Q. Are you a good Trivial Pursuit player?

The President. Sometimes. I'm better on some subjects than others, but I like it a lot.

Somalia

Mr. Jennings. Way over there in the corner.

Q. About Somalia and the United States, are we going to help the United States or Somalia first? Because Somalia has been in trouble for years, but we haven't done anything. We've done something, but not that much. So are you going to start helping Somalia first or getting the United States their jobs back first?

The President. Well, my most important job is to try to help people in the United States get their jobs back, because I was elected first and most importantly to help the people here with jobs and education and health care.

But I think the United States has a responsibility in Somalia. And I supported it when we sent our troops over there to try to stop the fighting and to try to bring some safety and food and medicine and education back to the children there. And I think that what we will be doing in Somalia is trying to work with other countries to always keep enough soldiers there to try to keep the peace, but there won't be so many Americans there. And then we can support others and try to make sure that we restore peace on a long-term basis and try to make sure that the people always had enough food and medicine and shelter to do well. I think we do have a responsibility there, but as President my first responsibility is to all of you.

The Presidency

Mr. Jennings. Behind you here, Mr. President. Jeannie has a question. Jeannie Lee.

Q. Hi. How do you feel, like, now that you're the President of the United States?

The President. It's an incredible honor. And every day I still get up and I feel a lot of gratitude just for having the chance to serve. I also feel a big sense of responsibility. I don't want to let you down, all of you and all the people all over the country, the people who voted for me and those who didn't. I hope I can do a good job to help solve our problems and move us forward.

Mr. Jennings. Jeannie, what do you think is probably the best thing about being President? If you were him, what would you guess?

Q. I think I would have a lot of responsibility, too, because I've got to take care of the whole United States and I've got to help others. And you've got to help the people of the United States fight their enemies and crime and riots and gangs.

President's Education

Mr. Jennings. Right behind you, Willie.

Q. When you were in, like, our grade, what was your hardest subject in school?

The President. When I was in your—when I was your age? How old are you?

Q. Nine.

The President. Nine. You're in the fourth grade? I made my lowest grades in conduct—[*laughter*]—because I talked too much in school and the teachers were always telling me to stop talking. I did best in math. I did well in reading. I had some trouble spelling, interestingly enough, when I was young, because I'd get excited and I would go too fast. And sometimes I wouldn't spell so well.

Q. What are you going to do about the environment?

Violence in Schools

Mr. Jennings. Well, let me hold the President on the environment for just a second, if that's okay with you, because I think touching on education is really interesting.

Mr. President, I'd like you to meet Michael Cruz here. We met Michael out in the country, and we did a little film about him which I'd like you to see, because I know he has a question. And it's something I know that he cares a lot about and he'd like to ask you about. So let's, first of all, look at where Michael goes to school.

[*A short film was shown in which Michael described the effect of the violence in his school on his education.*]

Mr. Jennings. Well, Michael goes to the Roberto Clemente High School in Chicago, Illinois. Have you got a question for the President, Michael?

Q. How are you going to make my school safer to get a better education?

The President. I have an answer to that, but let me ask you first so I won't prejudice your answer: If you were in my position, what would you do to make the school safer?

Q. I would try to get as much teachers and, mainly, security guards in there to keep the violence, because now there's not so many security guards and there's too many students. I would just try to control the school first. And then once they control the school, then I'll throw the education on their lap.

The President. Let me tell you what we're going to try to do. First of all, as part of the economic program I sent to Congress there is a safe schools initiative which, if it passes, would enable us to help schools with more security

guards and with more, like metal detectors and things like that, to try to make sure kids don't come to school with weapons.

Secondly, I have offered a program that would permit us to put another 100,000 police officers on the street in America in the next couple of years, including people who could be stationed in around schools. The third thing I think we ought to do is to pass a bill which says that nobody can buy a handgun unless there's a waiting period, during which time you can check their criminal history and see if they've been in any trouble before, because you don't have to sell them guns if they have been in trouble before. But if you don't check, you don't know. I think that's a good place to start.

But let me also say, you're from Chicago, right? I was in a junior high school in Chicago not very long ago called the Beasley Academic Center. It's a public school in Chicago. Do you know where it is? It's in a neighborhood with a very high crime rate. And they have police outside the school. Now, I know it's not a high school, it's a junior high school. There are police outside the school, but not in the school, because the teacher has to deal with—she's got 75 fathers a week coming to the school, 150 mothers a week coming to the school, and the kids have a whole strict code of conduct. They ask to go there, but there's no academic requirement. You know, if everybody asks to go and if there are too many who ask, then they do it by lottery. But the kids that go there really help to keep the peace in their own school, supporting the principal. And with the parents involved, I think that's real important, too.

I can provide extra help for law enforcement, but we've got to get more grassroots community people involved. I loved seeing you in that class. And I just hope that a year or two from now, all those other desks will be full, too. And don't you give up on your education, because—don't let anybody else, no matter what their problems are, take your future away from you. Only you can do that.

Mr. Jennings. You know, there's something else about Michael, which I'm not sure I'm right about. Michael, did I hear that some of the kids in your school teased you badly about coming to see the President?

Q. Yes.

The President. Why? Why did they do that?

Q. Because people don't believe that. People don't want to believe it.

The President. They don't believe that I care anything about them?

Q. Yes, in a way, you can say like that.

Mr. Jennings. Do you think the President's answer to you is—did it give you some satisfaction?

Q. Yes, it gave me a lot.

The President. Look, you know, when I was your age it was a lot easier to be young than it is now. We worried about liquor and cigarettes. Nobody worried about drugs and guns. And I know it's hard to be young now. But I also know that if you get a good education, nobody can take that away from you. You can still have a good life. And there are people there who care about your education. And I'm going to do what I can to support them.

Home Schooling

Q. I'm home schooled; I don't go to school. And I was wondering what you thought about home schooling and what you were going to do about it, or if there was anything you were going to do?

Mr. Jennings. Can you explain what home schooling is?

Q. Yes, my parents teach me at home, so I don't go to school. They don't really believe some of the stuff that's being taught and done in the schools.

The President. I can tell you what I have done about it. Let me tell all of you this, just by way of background. The public schools of our country are largely run at the local level by school boards and school administrators. And the money for them and the rules by which they are run are largely set at the State level, by the State governments throughout the country. So you're from Virginia, right?

Q. Yes.

The President. So the State government in Richmond largely makes the rules for the public schools. I was a Governor before I became President. And while I was Governor, I supported and passed a law through our legislature which made home schooling legal and which supported home schooling and parents and children making the decision to be educated at home, as long as the children were willing to take examinations every year and prove that they were learning what they should be learning for people their age. And that's the way I feel. I think that your parents and you, as a family, should have the right to do this as long as you're

learning. And if you can demonstrate that you're learning, I think you should have the right to do it.

Mr. Jennings. Can I interrupt, sir, because I don't think people really understand why many parents want to teach or insist on teaching their children at home. A lot of it has to do with sex education, doesn't it?

The President. It's different for different people. I think there—and Katie, you can interrupt me or say what you think—but I have talked to a lot of parents and children who have been in the home schooling movement, and normally they fall into two groups. There is one group, perhaps the smaller one, who believe that they just give their kids a better education, that their kids learn more and more quickly. Then there's a second set of concerns which revolve around values. A lot of parents are really upset by what Michael just said, that kids go to school, they have to worry about being exposed to violence, to premature sex, to drugs, to things that they may not agree with. So there are what you might call the values objections, to things that children are exposed to, and then the academic objections.

Is that a fair statement?

Q. Yes.

White House Meals

Mr. Jennings. Who has got—somebody's got some questions about the White House. I want to make sure that I don't lose who has got questions about the White House.

Q. Does Hillary ever cook for you?

The President. Does Hillary ever cook for me? Sometimes.

Mr. Jennings. Do you ever cook?

The President. Believe it or not, sometimes we cook for each other. But we've been so busy lately we haven't had a chance to do it since we've been here. But Hillary's actually a pretty good cook. And I like to cook, but what I like to do is to make things like omelets. I love to make omelets. And sometimes on Sunday nights, Hillary and Chelsea and I will go into the kitchen, and I'll make everybody omelets and we'll sit around and talk.

So both of us like to cook, but we've been—you know, I asked Hillary to take charge of the health care problem and try to come up with a solution to it. And I've been working real hard on the economic problems, so neither of us has had much time to cook. And they have wonderful cooks here. As a matter of fact, Chelsea can tell you there is a whole little kitchen where they don't do anything but make pastry and sweet things and desserts.

Mr. Jennings. They'd all hate that here, sir.

The President. Oh. [*Laughter*] So I've been mostly relying on those folks. But, yes, she does cook for me sometimes.

Mr. Jennings. What about Ellie, way at the back.

Q. My question is sort of serious.

Mr. Jennings. Well, if it's serious, let's hold it for one second, and we'll go to a commercial and come right back.

The President. Okay.

Mr. Jennings. Okay? My apologies.

[*The television stations took a commercial break.*]

Mr. Jennings. But you have to work on Omar here, because he told me he's a Republican. [*Laughter*] When we were away for a commercial, some of these kids said you look a lot better in person than you do on television.

The President. Well, that's good news.

Mr. Jennings. You want to deal with that?

The President. Well, sometimes I have these big bags under my eyes when I don't get any sleep the night before if I work late, or when my allergies are bad. So I'm glad you think I look better. I feel better today.

Mr. Jennings. Carlos, what did you want to know? You want to know where Socks was?

Q. Yes.

The President. Socks is just around the corner and downstairs. He's here all the time.

DC School Closings

Q. Well, I also want to know something else. What are you going to do about what the school board is doing about closing 10 schools in every ward?

The President. Here?

Q. In DC.

The President. That's a different question because the Washington, DC, government does get some money directly from the Congress and the President. I can't answer that question today because I don't know whether they're closing down the schools because they don't have enough money to run them or because they have too many schools for the kids that are there now. That is, a lot of school districts in

America are losing school populations.

But I'll tell you what I'll do, I'll look into it. And I've got your address, and I'll write you a letter about it. Okay?

Q. There's a little more I need to tell you. Can you at least talk to them to not close the good ones? Because they might close my school, and my school is the only elementary school that's bilingual in all DC.

The President. You don't want them to do that, do you? Because we have a lot of bilingual kids in DC, don't we, now? Thank you. I'll look into that, and I'll get back in touch with you.

Proposed Handgun Legislation

Mr. Jennings. Okay. We have a phone call, Mr. President, and I think from Texas. Go ahead, Allison.

Q. What is the Brady bill?

Mr. Jennings. What is the Brady bill?

The President. Oh, what is the Brady bill? The Brady bill is the bill I was just actually talking about. It's a bill that would require people who want to buy handguns to wait for a few days while the people who sell the handguns check to see if they have committed a crime or if they have a mental health history or some other problem which would make it dangerous for them to get the handgun. And the Brady bill would require people to wait just a few days until that check is done.

I strongly support the Brady bill. Some people are against it. But I think it's a good idea just to wait a couple of days. I don't think it's much of an inconvenience for people who want to buy guns to ask them to wait so we can check their criminal history.

Homosexuals in the Military

Mr. Jennings. I almost forgot you, Ellie. I'm sorry.

Q. The opposition to your recent attempt to lift the ban on the homosexuals in the military shows that as a society we're still very biased towards homosexuals. What are you going to do to help America as a nation accept them?

The President. Well, I think what's important about that issue to me is not that Americans agree with the lifestyle but that they accept the fact that there are citizens in the United States who are homosexual, who work hard, who don't break laws, who pay their taxes, don't bother other people, who ought to have a chance to serve. And I just say that at every chance I get. And I have also been involved in giving some people the chance to serve who are homosexual, and I think that's important. I think that there are a lot of people whose religious beliefs dictate that the homosexual lifestyle is wrong. I don't ask them to give up their religious beliefs but simply to accept other people as people and give them a chance to be citizens as long as they're not doing anything wrong. That's my position on it.

Special Education

Mr. Jennings. Anastasia, you've had your hand up a lot. Maybe, Mr. President, you'd like to come and sit down for a second.

The President. Hi, Anastasia.

Mr. Jennings. Excuse me for one second for reaching over you. Come and sit here. Sara, you come and sit here if you would and let the President sit down.

The President. Okay.

Q. I have a twin sister and we go to the same school. But she can't speak. So because she can't speak, they've put her in a special class. But she uses computers to speak. And I would like her to be in a regular class just like me.

The President. Wow. And you think your sister could do just as well as you in a regular class?

Q. Yes.

The President. As long as she can use her computer. And her computer is on a little top just like this, isn't it?

Q. Yes. Well, you can put it on here and you can put it on regular tables also if—because you can carry it around. It's a little computer.

The President. And she talks to you by using it?

Q. Yes.

The President. Why do you think they put her in the special education class?

Q. I think it's because she couldn't talk. And they thought—the principal thinks that she can't do it because she can't use her hands and she can't speak.

The President. But you think that she could learn just as quickly if she were in a regular class?

Q. Yes.

The President. Have your parents asked the principal to put her in a regular class?

Q. Yes.

The President. And they said no?

Q. The principal said no.

The President. Well, you know, as President I can't do anything about that except to speak about it. But I'll tell you this, I have a friend named Hamp Rasco whose mother works for me here. And he's now 18 years old. He has cerebral palsy. And he doesn't speak quite as well as you, but he can probably speak a little more than your sister. And I watched him go all the way through high school and graduate from high school and get his graduation degree. And he lives out on his own now. And I'm going to do what I can to help people let all Americans go as far as they can. And I think young people who are working hard to prove they can do this kind of work ought to be given a chance to do it. And I think your sister should be given a chance to show whether she can work in the class or not.

That's what you think then? You just want her to have a chance to prove whether she can do it or not, right?

Q. Yes.

The President. And if she tried and she couldn't do it, then would you support her being in another class?

Q. Yes.

The President. So you just want your sister to have a chance.

Q. Yes.

The President. Good for you. Maybe she'll get it because we were here talking about this.

Mr. Jennings. I have a feeling. Thanks very much.

Q. You're welcome.

The President. Give her a hand. Wasn't that great? Thanks for sticking up for your sister. That's wonderful.

The Environment

Mr. Jennings. We have a phone call from Ian. Go ahead.

Q. President Clinton, how will you stop pollution in the United States?

Mr. Jennings. Just like that. [*Laughter*]

The President. Well, it's not quite that simple because you know we make pollution every day, Ian. When we drive our cars, we make pollution; when we run our factories, we make pollution. But there are two or three things we can do. Let me just mention them.

Number one, we have a Clean Air Act in the United States, designed to reduce the amount of pollution that goes into the air in the first place. I want to enforce that. Number two, I want to support clean water. We put a lot of stuff in our water. I want to reduce that. Number three, I want to try to do things that will help preserve the quality of the environment in the first place, like planting more trees and reforesting the land and building up the soil of the United States. I think we want to clean up the things that are being polluted, but we want to stop things from being polluted as much as possible. And then, finally, I'm trying to promote more energy conservation and cleaner energy. Like natural gas, for example, is the cleanest form of energy that we can burn. So I'm trying to promote the use of natural gas. Those are the things that I think we should do in the beginning.

Mr. Jennings. I don't think anybody in the East Room, Mr. President, feels as strongly about that as Pernell does. And I know he has a question to ask you, but before you ask your question, let's show the President a little bit about where you live.

[*A short film was shown in which Pernell described the effect of environmental pollution on his family's health.*]

Mr. Jennings. Pernell comes from Garyville, Louisiana, and it's about a hundred miles' trip between New Orleans and Baton Rouge, right, Pernell?

Q. Yes.

Mr. Jennings. Where there are about a hundred petrochemical plants.

Q. Yes, Garyville, the small town that I live in, is right between the chemical corridor, which is the area between Baton Rouge and New Orleans. And Mr. President, I'd like to ask if restrictions can be put on the amount of carelessly handled hazardous waste and air pollution, such as smoke, and if the health care system can get into this somewhat and help the cancer victims, which this cancer may have resulted from this environmental contamination.

The President. Why don't you tell these folks how many relatives in your family have had cancer.

Q. Well, I'm not exactly sure, but I know my 10-year-old brother died of something that even the experts—experts across the country came over to Children's Hospital in New Orleans to look at this. They could not—they were just stumped. My brother, Charlie, was either

the 10th or the 11th person in recorded history ever to catch this. Through all the other patients that caught this, the experts could never figure it out. And they checked into just about every condition that could have caused it, with the exception of the environment.

The President. Let me say that this young man lives in Louisiana, which is just to the south of my home State of Arkansas, so I know quite a bit about where you live and I've been in that alley between Baton Rouge and New Orleans many, many times. The cancer rate there is way above the national average.

I think there are two things we should be doing. One is, we should be doing a lot more medical research to try to find out what causes these cancers. And the second thing we ought to be doing is to invest more money there to do environmental cleanup.

In the election campaign that I went through to be elected President, I said many times that I thought we ought to take some of the money that we're reducing the defense budget by and putting it into cleaning up the environment here at home. Because I think there are now all kinds of health hazards that we never knew about before that we're now learning about in some of the things we've done. And we need to do a lot of environmental cleanup in that part of Louisiana where you live and throughout the country. And I'm going to do my best to do it.

Mr. Jennings. It's interesting, sir, that a lot of people were playing the budget game earlier, helping how to spend your money for you. And an awful lot of kids, both last night and tonight, all of them putting their money into cleaning up the environment.

The President. How many of you think we should spend more money on the environment, cleaning it up?

Q. We've only got one planet. If we don't preserve it, you know, there's no other place we can go to. And everyone from my area and the surrounding areas, most of them voted for you, you know. We all believe very strongly that you, as an individual, do have the know-how and the courage to go about and tackle this problem and many others, and we do have faith in you.

The President. We'll do it for your brother, okay?

Q. Okay. Thank you.

Mr. Jennings. We'll be back in just a moment.

[*The television stations took a commercial break.*]

Economic Legislation

Mr. Jennings. Well, I haven't had a chance to ask you kids this question yet, but how—you've all heard President Clinton—put down your hands for just a second—you all have heard President Clinton say many things he'd like to do. Now, he's a very powerful individual, as I think we all agree, but he can't do it all by himself. You have to get bill through Congress.

The President. That's right.

Mr. Jennings. Your budget bill's up there now. You're going to have a real tough time——

The President. A real tough time.

Mr. Jennings. Right. How many of you would like to know how to get a bill through Congress? Do you think that would be useful in order to find out how you get it done?

The President. I'd like to know that. [*Laughter*]

Mr. Jennings. Well, we've enlisted the help of Steven Urkel, who's a great, great pal, I guess, of all yours, to tell us how you actually get a bill through the Congress. Let's watch.

[*A short film was shown on the legislative process.*]

Mr. Jennings. Isn't that great?

The President. That was great.

Mr. Jennings. I have a present for you, Mr. President, the Urkel clean air act of 1993, like all Government bills today, on recycled paper.

The President. That's good. That's right. We use a lot of recycled paper.

Mr. Jennings. So you have a chance now to sign that bill or you can veto that bill, right?

The President. That's right. I have to act within 10 days of getting it, and I can sign it or veto it. I think I'd better sign, don't you?

Mr. Jennings. I think you'd better. Do you think he should sign it? Okay.

Let's go back to questions. Venus, you have a question.

Homelessness

Q. As a new President, how are you going to end homelessness, or what are you going to do to end homelessness in the world?

The President. Do you want to say anything about Venus before I answer the question?

Mr. Jennings. Yes, I do. I do. It's a tough question for Venus, and we told the President before that Venus had come to us from the west coast, and I think it would help if the rest of you kids here and the audience at home saw a little bit about the circumstances in which she lives.

[*A short film was shown in which Venus described the difficulties of living in a homeless shelter.*]

The President. Good for you.

Mr. Jennings. What's your question then, Venus? Again, would you repeat it.

Q. As the new President, what are you going to try to do or how are you going to do—what are you going to do to end homelessness in our world?

The President. May I ask you a question? How did you become homeless?

Q. I came from New York around 5 months ago, and we didn't have an exact place to go to. So we went to social services and from there on, it was homeless until we can get an apartment.

The President. I think there are two or three things we should do. And I asked her this question because over one-third of the homeless people in America now are families with children. And a lot of them are people who moved from one town to another, and they have no savings; they have no money in the bank.

I met a homeless couple in my hometown about a year ago. It was kind of like you. They had come down from Chicago. And they actually had jobs, but they hadn't drawn a paycheck yet and they had no place to live.

So here are the things that we're going to try to do. First of all, we're going to try to build more housing for low-income working people. We haven't had much of a housing program for a long time. Secondly, I'm going to have an inventory done—an inventory means a list done—of all the housing in America which exists today that belongs to the Government which is boarded up or closed down, and see whether or not we can't give a lot of that housing back to churches or community groups or other groups and let people work on repairing it. And if they do work on repairing it, they should be able to live in it. I met a woman and her children in Philadelphia who were doing a lot of their own work on a home, an old home that had been boarded up. And they were going to get to move in it and live there because of the work they had done to do it.

The third thing we have to do is to create more jobs because a lot of the homeless people wouldn't be homeless if they had jobs.

Mr. Jennings. One of the things about all your answers, Mr. President—and I don't want to take time away from them—is that they all seem to be long-term. And Venus has a short-term problem, and Pernell has a short-term problem, and Shannon has a short-term problem.

The President. Well, I think to be fair, though, if you look at Venus' problem, it wouldn't necessarily be a long-term problem if we increase the capacities of cities throughout this country to move people directly into more stable environments. I know in San Francisco there was a real detailed homeless program that I saw there that the administration wanted to put in that they just didn't have the money to put in because there was no partnership with the National Government. And my feeling on the homeless issue is that a lot of Americans who have money and homes really want us to do something about it and would really support our doing more about it. I don't think Americans like the fact that children like you, your mother are in homeless shelters just because you happen to move from one town to the other.

Now, on your problem——

Mr. Jennings. Pernell.

The Environment

The President. On Pernell's problem, it's a little different because you have to do a lot of medical research to find out exactly what's causing this. But I think you will see this year, greater efforts in environmental cleanup all over the country if our program passes this year. It's not too late.

But as Pernell probably knows, since you studied your brother's problem, a lot of times these cancers develop over 2 or 5 or 10 and sometimes even over 20 years. So they are long-term problems. And we did a lot of things to our environment in the past because we didn't know what it was doing. And I think now we just have to turn it around; we just have to start cleaning up more. And I think most Americans want to do that.

Mr. Jennings. We have an awful lot of questions, obviously. We're going to go away for just a minute.

[*The television stations took a commercial break.*]

Chelsea Clinton and Socks the Cat

Mr. Jennings. Well, Mr. President, I must tell you, as impressed as we all are to have you here, and as good as they think you've been so far, there's somebody else they'd like to meet more, and you know that. So we do have a bit of a surprise for you. Chelsea, would you come and join us for a second?

These are the two people that you've all been asking about. Do you want to sit on the stool?

Chelsea Clinton. Sure.

Mr. Jennings. Two people that the boys and girls have all been asking about this morning, Chelsea and Socks. You all had questions about Socks. Who wants to go?

Q. Why did you call your cat "Socks"?

The President. Who knows—guess? Why did we call him "Socks"? Hold him up, Chelsea. Why did we call him "Socks"? Because he has white paws. He's a black cat with white paws, that's right. Good for you.

Mr. Jennings. And he's very restless, right?

Chelsea Clinton. Yes, I had to wake him up.

Mr. Jennings. Does he really have the run of the White House?

Chelsea Clinton. Yes, basically, he can go wherever he wants.

Mr. Jennings. Who else has a question? Jamie in St. Louis has a question for Chelsea. Go ahead, Jamie.

Q. I wanted to know, does Chelsea have to take Secret Service guards to school with her?

Chelsea Clinton. Yes, I do.

Mr. Jennings. What's that like?

Chelsea Clinton. It's okay. They stay out of the way. They do. They have an office up on the third floor of my school, and they sit there most of the day. Or when I'm in gym, they come outside and just sit on the bleachers or just watch my soccer practice.

Q. What kind of cat food do you feed Socks?

Chelsea Clinton. What kind of cat food? Dry cat food. I don't know the brand.

Mr. Jennings. Nor should you, probably. [*Laughter*]

Q. How old is Socks?

Chelsea Clinton. Socks is almost 3 years old. He'll be 3 years old in July.

Q. Does Socks—who trains him? Is he trained?

Chelsea Clinton. Yes.

Q. Like, do you guys play? Also, do you ever

have to talk to her about playing with her when she's supposed to do her homework?

The President. Never. She's very good about that. She does her homework pretty well.

Mr. Jennings. Christine in Fulton, Mississippi, has a question for you.

Q. Mr. President, how do you and Mrs. Clinton punish Chelsea when she doesn't listen?

Chelsea Clinton. I didn't hear that.

Mr. Jennings. How do they punish you?

The President. How do I punish you when you don't listen?

Chelsea Clinton. I always listen.

The President. Chelsea's a pretty good girl. We don't have much of that. Sometimes we have to—the number one thing we have to do is to make her go to bed earlier. She has a fault that her father has, which is that she would stay up too late at night if I let her do that. So the number one thing we have to do is to make her go to bed earlier.

Mr. Jennings. And one more question for Chelsea.

Q. Is Chelsea single? *[Laughter]*

The President. She better be. *[Laughter]*

Chelsea Clinton. Do you want to keep Socks?

The President. No, you take him.

Mr. Jennings. You're really nice to come by, Chelsea. Thanks very much.

Chelsea Clinton. Thank you very much.

Mr. Jennings. Isn't that nice to have her come by?

All right, now let's get back to you, sir. You got off the hook there for a few minutes.

The President. I loved it.

Health Care Reform

Q. I have a question about health insurance.

Mr. Jennings. Would you speak a little closer to your microphone, Kevin?

Q. I have a big brother named Jason, and he's 17 now and will be graduating high school soon. Will you have a health insurance program in place so that people like my brother and my twin sister can buy health insurance? If so, how will it work? Will we be able to afford it?

The President. Good for you. Is there anything you want to say about Kevin, Peter, before——

Mr. Jennings. Not just yet.

The President. Okay. The answer to your question is we're going to present a program to the Congress. And if they adopt it, then every American will be able to get health insurance, either from the Government or from their place of employment. And they will be able to afford it because, for people with lower incomes, the premiums will be less. But everybody, pretty much, will have to pay something for it. And I think that's important. But we want to make it possible for people all over the country to have some health insurance. There are over 35 million people in America today that don't have any health insurance and many others who can't change their jobs because if they change jobs they would lose it.

Mr. Jennings. On Monday night, when you were speaking—or Wednesday night when you were speaking to the Congress, you ad-libbed; you took off talking about health care as if you think there's no more complicated problem in the country.

The President. It's the most complicated problem I've ever dealt with, but also the most important. I mean, American families, millions of them, are so insecure about their health care. And yet I say again, we're spending 30 percent more than any other country on Earth, and we have less to show for it. We can do better. We have to.

Homelessness

Mr. Jennings. Bernice. You had your hand up there, like, for a week. *[Laughter]*

The President. She wore her arm out, she's been up there so long.

Q. This is a question that refers to what Venus said. You said that instead of—the best way to end homelessness is to—you said to build houses. Well, you don't really need to build any houses, referring to DC and over the U.S., because there are more than 3,000 houses and apartments that are boarded up with no use. Do you plan to fix any of them up?

The President. Yes. I'm sorry, that's the second point I made: that in the places where we have a lot of boarded-up and vacant buildings, I think what we should do is to try to provide some funds to local communities to fix those up first because that's cheaper and quicker.

But we just don't invest as much money as we did 12 years ago. Twelve years ago we were investing more money on building homes for the homeless than we are now. And as I said, I think most Americans are really concerned that so many people—there are people who sleep on the sidewalk within two blocks of the

White House every night. And I'd like to see us do something about it, and I think most Americans would. And I agree with you, we should start with the structures that are already there.

Antidrug Program

Q. Governor Clinton, I was just wondering— I come from a drug rehab over in Fort Pierce, Florida, and I was wondering how—why is it that we always spend all this money on the supply of drugs coming in, like trying to cut it down, you know? Like down in Miami, there's a $50 million operation down there that doesn't even work, trying to—like planes that fly in where the cocaine——

The President. Trying to stop the planes from flying in.

Q. Right. What are you going to do about the, like, the demand? How are you going to cut that down? You know, you can never cut down the supply, but you can always cut down the demand. How are you going to do that?

The President. You know that from your own personal experience, don't you?

Mr. Jennings. She does, yes.

The President. I appreciate—you're a brave girl, and I'm glad you're here. And the reason I said that is because my brother is also a recovering drug user. And I believe that's right. And I have a brother-in-law who is a defense lawyer in the drug court in Miami that keeps people out of jail if they'll go into rehab. And I think— I can tell you what we're going to try to do. We're going to try to shift some of the money that used to be spent on excessive expenditures in some kinds of enforcement and do more to do rehab and education and treatment for people because I believe that rehabilitation works.

I think that if we have drug treatment on demand, that is without delay for people who want it, we could cut down on the costs of the courts, we could cut down on a lot of our criminal problems, and we could rescue a lot of young people's lives. We don't invest enough money in that now. So we're trying to change the priorities a little bit to put some more money into rehab.

Health Insurance and Defense Conversion

Mr. Jennings. In just a moment, Mr. President, I'd like you to meet Shana because we've done a little bit of filming out where she lives. But before that, I'd like to tell our stations all over the country that President Clinton has agreed to stay on for half an hour more and answer more questions, so we're going to go a half an hour longer. We thank you for that, sir.

Now, let's take a look at how Shana lives. Because I think you probably have as representative a problem in your family as almost anybody here today. Let's look.

[*A short film was shown in which Shana described her parents' medical problems and concerns about employment.*]

Mr. Jennings. So Shana, what's your question?

Q. As you know, my mom was laid off, and my dad presently works for the same aerospace company. And they've both been treated for cancer, but now they're in remission, thank God. And I was just wondering, because due to her history with the cancer, she's having a hard time with finding a job. And I was wondering what your administration can do in regard to paying health coverage with their preexisting illnesses.

Mr. Jennings. One of the things you're doing—excuse me, sir, before you answer—is, you're cutting back on, you want to cut back on jobs in the defense industry, right—or, you'll have to cut back. Which is it?

The President. Can I ask you a question first? Does your mother—is she covered by your father's insurance policy at Rockwell?

Q. No, her own, I think. I'm pretty sure. I'm not sure.

The President. They paid individually, they were covered individually? Let me talk about the health insurance, and then I'd like to talk about your parents' jobs.

One of the changes we want to make in the health insurance system of America is to say that all Americans will be insured in huge, big pools of people, so that there are a large number of people insured. And if one or two of them get cancer, like your mother, that their cost of care will then be spread over a very large number of other people who don't have that problem. That will lower the risk of any insurance policy causing the company to go broke. And it will mean that we can pass a law which says that you can't refuse to hire somebody just because they've been sick before. In other words, I want to pass a law saying that you can't refuse to hire somebody because they've been sick before, but first I have to make sure that the companies themselves won't go broke if they do it. So we're going to do that.

Now, let me make a comment about your parents' jobs. Your father still works for Rockwell, and your mother used to. We had to reduce the defense budget at the end of the cold war when the Soviet Union broke up because we were spending so much more money on the military than any other country. We had to invest it in other things here at home.

But we need people working in aerospace. There are about—I don't know what kind of lives you all want to have now, but there are about seven or eight major areas of technology which will produce a lot of the high-wage jobs of the future, and aerospace is one of them. The United States has not done a very good job of trying to build up aerospace jobs in nondefense areas. And next week we're going to start on a major effort, working with the Congress, to do that. I'm going out to California and to Washington State where Boeing is headquartered, and they just announced 23,000 layoffs, to talk about this. So we're going to start trying to figure out what we can do to save the jobs in the aerospace industry and maybe to start building them up again.

Spotted Owl Habitat Protection

Mr. Jennings. Oh, my goodness. Go ahead, Elizabeth.

Q. I live in northern California in a town called Hayfork. And we live in the forests. And my Dad, he had a logging business. And he had to shut it down because they're setting aside the forest for the spotted owl. And this is my school yearbook, and I've highlighted the names of the people—of the kids like me whose parents will lose their job because of the spotted owl. And I just wanted to know what you're going to do to try to help people get their jobs back.

The President. Can you all see this?

Mr. Jennings. It was not a set-up, I wish to assure you, Mr. President.

The President. No. Did you all see this, all the yellow names here highlighted? Does anybody else here know what she's talking about, the spotted owl controversy? David, do you understand it?

Q. Yes.

The President. What is it? What's the issue?

Q. Well, the spotted owl's natural habitat in the wildlife is being threatened by loggers who

cut down the trees. It's like in the northwest of the United States. It's like—that's a lot of people's living. And they take the trees and produce timber that all of us use every day. And now since the owl's habitat was being threatened, environmental groups got the forest to be set aside as a preserve for the owl. But then when that happened, it hurt a lot of loggers who make their living off of that. So it's kind of a tough situation.

The President. Do you think that's a good description, Elizabeth, of what happened?

Yes? Let me say that in northern California and in Washington and in Oregon in the Pacific Northwest of the United States where Elizabeth lives and where her father works, a lot of people make their living in the forests. Part of the forests are called old-growth forests. They're very, very old trees. And most of the old-growth forest has all been cut down, but a little of it is left. And there's some logging in that. And then, as Elizabeth can tell you, there are forests sort of rimming the old-growth forest where the trees are newer where some of the land is being ordered to be set aside for the spotted owl.

We have a law in the United States called the Endangered Species Law which says that if an animal is placed on that list, then it has to be protected, even if it costs some jobs to protect it. So there's been a big fight going on for the last few years about how much land should be set aside to preserve the spotted owl and how much land should be left alone to log in the forest.

I want to make two points to you. First of all—and let me say, I live in—my State, Arkansas, has—over half the land is covered with timber, so I have a lot of personal friends who make their living the same way your father did. First of all, the problem has been made worse because the United States Government has not come up with a solution. So that as you may know, the courts have stopped logging all over northern California and Washington and Oregon, including some places where people should be allowed to log. So I have committed myself to organize, along with Vice President Gore, a forest summit. And the Secretary of the Interior, Bruce Babbitt, in particular, is doing a lot of work on that now. We're trying to set up a forest summit out there to bring all the people together to try to come up with the best compromise that will permit us to save not just the spotted owl but this other point

I wanted to make is the old-growth forest that remains, and still let people log.

Let me say it to you in another way: We could remove all the restrictions on logging tomorrow and even put more people to work; not only secure your father's business, but we could put more people to work. But then in a few years we'd have no trees at all to log. So the issue is, how can we have a stable logging environment and keep a significant number of people working and still preserve the old-growth forest, and by the way, the spotted owl.

I think we can do a much better job if we can just get this out of the courts and start— there is a lot of land available, that should be available for logging that's been tied up in the courts that our Government does not want to tie up anymore. So what I'm going to try to do is put a group of people together to come out to Washington, Oregon, and northern California and sit down and go through all this and see if we can't resolve it so we can keep the largest number of people working and still preserve the forests.

Q. But the land that they set aside, like there's lots of lightning up where we live, and there's lots of dead trees. And if we don't go in there and cut the dead trees down, it will start a fire and burn it all down.

The President. That's right, there are a lot of problems. I agree with you, there are a lot of practical problems with what has been done. And that's why I want to try to bring, now that there's been a change in the administration, I want to try to bring our people out there and sit down with all the parties involved and try to hammer this out and resolve it. Unfortunately, it's been all tied up in the courts. And a lot of things have been done which should not have been done.

I believe—all I can tell you, is I'm going to do the best I can to preserve the diversity of the forests, the old forests up there, because most of it's already gone, and we can't afford to let it all go and still provide a stable logging environment. As I said, we could build it up, but if we built it up too much, we'd cut all the trees down; and if we shut it down too much, we'll throw everybody out of work. So the question is, we have to find some way to find the right balance, and we're going to try to do it.

Mr. Jennings. We'll stay on the President's case and make sure that you know particularly when the forest summit comes——

The President. Yes, I'd like for you—will you come and bring your parents when we do it?

AIDS

Mr. Jennings. Mr. President, I know you feel the weight of problems in the country in this room, and there's one other person here I'd like to introduce you to and tell you a little bit about his life, because I know he's been wanting very much to ask you a question. His name is Joey. Meet Joey.

[*A short film was shown in which Joey described how he contracted AIDS and how his illness affected his family.*]

Mr. Jennings. So what's your question, Joey?

Q. That President Bush, he took $350 million away from AIDS research. I want to know if you're going to put that back.

Mr. President. Oh yes, and then some. Right now we're working on a bill for the National Institutes of Health that will increase funding for cancer research, for AIDS research, for health research generally. And I think you'll be pleased with that. In addition to that, in this budget that I have presented to Congress, I've asked them to fully fund the Ryan White Health Care Act so that we can deal with the health care costs of people with AIDS and the burdens that it puts on families.

Meanwhile, you hang in there. We'll keep working until we find a cure.

Mr. Jennings. Is that a good answer, Joey?

Q. Yes.

Mr. Jennings. Something else, Mr. President. Joey, do you ever feel discriminated against because you have AIDS?

Q. Not a lot anymore.

Mr. President. You think people are kind of over their fears, irrational fears of it now?

Q. They don't care about it anymore. No, I mean, they care about it, but it's like they're not afraid of people. I hope not.

Mr. President. Okay, thanks, Joey. Thanks for coming.

Foreign Assistance

Q. A lot of people across the world are fighting and killing each other. I want to know if there's anything America can do to stop it?

Mr. President. The answer is, there are some things we can do and some things we can't. Let's just take some specific examples, and then maybe you can ask me some specific examples.

Somalia: a lot of people were fighting and killing each other. Our country led a group of forces, but most of them were Americans, into Somalia. And because the armies weren't big and the weapons weren't great and because a lot of the people wanted us to come there, we were able to stop a lot of the fighting and provide for safety for people.

Bosnia: you saw the young girl in Bosnia. A much tougher problem, because there were more weapons involved, the land is more difficult, the people have been fighting each other there for centuries, except when they have been stopped by government authority there. And we're trying to find ways to increase humanitarian aid to Bosnia and to push for a peace settlement which, if the parties down there will agree, the people who are doing all the killing, we could then come in and help to enforce.

Haiti: a country in our own hemisphere where the elected president was kicked out after he had threatened some of the people in the army and the government in Haiti. We're doing our best to try to stop any repression there and then to restore the elected government there. That might not be as hard for us because it's a smaller population, a smaller army, and because it's right here next to us, and we can do things with and for them.

So it's different in different places. But I think the United States has a responsibility to try to stop that. There are some places a long—I don't know if you saw the religious fighting in India recently—that's a long way from us, and it's very hard for us to have any influence there. So we're doing the best we can. Let me just say, it works better when the United Nations will do it, when other nations will go along with us. And it works better if there is some support for a solution short of war. So I'm going to do what I can to stop the fighting and killing.

Mr. Jennings. I read in the paper this morning, I think, Mr. President, that you are considering making air drops of food to people in Bosnia who can't get it. Do you think you'll go ahead with that?

The President. Actually, after I leave you today I'm going to go discuss it with our aides and consider that as one option. There are a lot of children in Bosnia who now can't get food and medicine because, I don't know if you've been seeing it on the news, but the trucks which have been delivering those supplies have been stopped. So we have an agreement tentatively to try to start the trucks up again, but we may have to go in and drop some aid into them.

Fast Food and Advertisements

Mr. Jennings. We have a question from Georgia.

Q. Hello. Mr. President, when you go to McDonald's, do you have to pay? Do they accept, or do they say you're the President so you don't have to pay?

The President. Usually I pay. I have—in my neighborhood McDonald's at home when I would go running every morning, they would often give me a cup of coffee. But if I go into McDonald's and buy food, I try to pay. I try not to have anybody give me food when I go in a place.

Mr. Jennings. We had a—is Basil here? Where's Basil? Basil, you wanted to say something to the President about junk food, you told me earlier.

Q. I'm Basil Jeheen. I'm vice president of Kids Against Junk Food. President Clinton, I know that you have received some bad press from an occasional trip to a fast food restaurant. My question is, how are you going to protect kids from being bombarded with junk food advertisements during their TV shows?

Mr. Jennings. Whoo! [*Laughter*]

The President. I'm going to ask Mr. Jennings——

Mr. Jennings. I'm leaving.

The President. I'm going to ask Mr. Jennings not to take any more advertisement from junk food manufacturers.

Let me say, if you look at what the fast food chains—this is not McDonald's—if you look at Burger King, if you look at Wendy's, if you look at Taco Bell—look at a lot of these fast food places, in the last few years, a lot of them have made a real effort to reduce the junk food content of the food they sell. They're offering more lean chicken; they're offering more fish; they're offering more salads and vegetables. I think a lot of the fast food places are trying to increase the nutritional content of what they sell.

Let me just say this: About 40 percent of American food dollars are now spent in fast food places, because so many mothers and fathers work—parents work. And it's very important that you keep the pressure up, through

Kids Against Junk Food, to keep the pressure up to say, "Okay, a lot of people work. They're busy. They have to buy food at fast food places. But increase the nutritional content of the food." I think that's what you ought to do, and I think that's the position I ought to take.

Mr. Jennings. Go ahead.

Q. What I mean is, all right, say you're watching a cartoon and something—they interrupt and then they have an advertisement for junk food. I mean, they interrupt what you want to do, like——

The President. Let me tell you what the Government does and can do. The Government can require the people who sell this food to publish on a fairly large sign like the cereals do now what the real nutritional content of the food is and how much stuff that's not so good for you is in it. But right now we don't have the authority to stop it from being advertised at all. Do you think there should be a law saying you can't even advertise junk food?

Q. No. What I mean is there should be a limit. Like so many advertisements per hour, because they just throw in advertisements. And you pay for it, and throw in advertisements.

The President. What you need to do is to write the networks, ABC and CBS and NBC, and maybe all the other smaller networks that advertise, and tell them to reduce advertisements of junk food—limit to a certain number of hours on Saturday morning, especially.

Mr. Jennings. Basil, one of the things—I'll tell you two things. First of all, when you write to a network like that, if enough of you write they listen to you. And the other thing I'll tell you about the President which I think you'll find encouraging, though I hope it wasn't just a political statement, sir—the President very kindly had a number of reporters in the other day to have lunch with him, and he served us broccoli. [*Laughter*]

At any rate, we're going to go to a commercial now, which makes me just little nervous. [*Laughter*] We'll be right back.

[*The television stations took a commercial break.*]

Support for the President's Program

Mr. Jennings. We have a question from California on the telephone. Go ahead.

Q. I'd like to know, as children, how we can help you achieve your goals you have set?

The President. Oh, thank you, Byron.

Mr. Jennings. Paid political announcement.

The President. Thank you very much. Isn't that nice?

Mr. Jennings. Yes.

The President. Well, I'll tell you what you can do. You can, as a student you can write to your Congressman and to your two Senators and ask them to support the program that I've talked about today. You can try to get your fellow classmates and your schools, your teachers, and others to get in touch with the people in Congress and ask them to vote for this program. And then at home, in your communities, if we pass the program you can try to make sure that we do it right; that we actually spend some of this money, for example, to recover houses for homeless people, or that we put more young people to work in the summertime—that we do these things. But the first thing we've got to do is pass the program. So I would ask you, starting Monday, try to get your classmates to write your Member of Congress and your Senators and ask them to vote for the program.

Mr. Jennings. On the other hand, they could also write you in the White House and tell you that they think you're wrong so far.

The President. Sure, they could. If you think I'm wrong, write me and tell me that.

Mr. Jennings. Now, a couple of kids who aren't here today but asked me before, which I think is on these kids' mind, are you going to keep your promises?

The President. I'm sure doing my best. The most important thing I can do, I think, is to try to give these young people a future by creating these jobs and dealing with their educational issues, and try to do all the things that I talked about in the campaign. Sometimes circumstances change and you can't do everything you want. I'm not investing as much money as I wanted to in jobs and I'm raising a little more than I wanted to in taxes because the deficit of our country is bigger than I thought it was. But, in general, I'm right on track to try to do what I wanted to do when I ran for President.

Endangered Species

Q. Well, I would like to know what are you going to do to help endangered species?

The President. Well, we were talking about that before, you know, with the spotted owl. There is a law which requires us to protect endangered species and I support the law. I don't want to see it repealed, but I want to see it administered in a way that doesn't throw a large number of Americans out of work. And I think most people feel that way. They feel we ought to have an Endangered Species Act, but there ought to be a procedure to try to have a balance between preserving those species and not hurting families too much. But I support the Endangered Species Act.

Hillary Clinton's Role

Mr. Jennings. Another telephone call. Go ahead.

Q. Do you feel uneasy about Mrs. Clinton taking such an active role in the Government because if something goes wrong both of you would be blamed?

The President. No, I don't feel uneasy about it at all. I think it's a good thing. She is a very able person. This is the first time since we've been married that she hasn't had a full-time job in addition to everything else, that she's got a lot of time. And she wants to be part of my administration. She's the most talented person that I've ever worked with on a lot of the issues that I care about. And I think she'll be great on this health care thing, and if it doesn't work, I'm going to be blamed anyway.

Native Americans

Q. Mr. President, I'm here today as a Lumbee Indian of North Carolina. Yet under the law, I'm not an Indian. What are you going to do to resolve this problem?

The President. Why is that? I don't understand it. You mean you're not a recognized Native American under the law?

Q. Exactly.

The President. Why?

Q. Because the rules and regulations say that if a tribe is not recognized, you're not an Indian.

The President. And why is your tribe not recognized?

Q. They're still trying to prove that we are Indian with the Department of Interior and the BIA process.

Mr. Jennings. Bureau of Indian Affairs.

The President. Yes.

Q. Yes.

The President. You've asked me a question I don't know the answer to. But I'll tell you what I'll do. If you make sure—I guess Peter's got your address—I will put somebody to work

on it the first of the week and I'll try to figure out if there is anything we can do. I wish I could answer your question, but I didn't know that there were Native American tribes that hadn't been formally recognized.

Q. Yes, there are lots.

Mr. Jennings. Nor did I. We'll find out for you. Right next to you, Isaac.

The President. Thank you very much.

Teacher Furloughs

Q. President Clinton, what are you going to do about furloughs?

The President. About what?

Q. Furloughs.

The President. You mean from prisons?

Q. No, I mean from teachers getting out of work.

The President. Oh. You mean, teachers being laid off?

Q. Yes.

The President. Well, where do you live?

Q. I live in Washington.

The President. In Washington. This is a problem around the country because a lot of State and local governments haven't had enough money to fund their school budgets. I think you asked me about that, too, earlier.

There is nothing I can do about it directly, because the United States Government, the President and the Congress don't hire teachers; they're all hired at local school district level. But there are two things that I can do to help indirectly. One is to try to get the economy going again, because if people are working, they'll be paying taxes, and the school districts will have more money. That's the most important thing I could do.

The second thing is to try to have the National Government help our schools a little more than they have for the last 12 years, and the budget that I gave to the Congress does ask us to put more money into education. And that should help some of the school districts around the country.

The most important thing I can do is give them a healthy economy, because most of the money to run the school district comes from the local level. It doesn't come here to Washington.

Child Support Enforcement and Tax Reform

Q. Yes. I was just wondering: How can you help the families where there's a mom and she's taking care of a kid or kids, and the father isn't willing or isn't able to pay child support.

Mr. Jennings. And you have about 30 seconds, Mr. President.

The President. If he's not willing, we can have much tougher child support enforcement. I feel very strongly about it, and I've got a good program to strengthen it. If he's not able and the mother is working and taking care of the kids, I think the tax system should actually give the mother money back, if necessary. I think any parent that's working 40 hours a week with children in the home should not live in poverty. I think we should change the tax system so that people who work with children should be lifted out of poverty.

Mr. Jennings. That's a good question, Jordan. In fact, you know where you can watch for something on that? In the confirmation hearings for your new Attorney General.

The President. That's right.

Mr. Jennings. ——because she has quite a reputation in Florida on that particular subject.

We could go on. You've been very gracious to stay the extra half-hour.

Did you enjoy yourselves this morning? Was he good? Yes? He was okay?

The President. I loved it.

Mr. Jennings. Satisfied with all the answers?

The President. No. [*Laughter*] Thank you.

Mr. Jennings. Well, Mr. President, you know as well as I do it's a rare treat for any of us to be able to come in here and to see you. Thank you very much for having us. Thank you all.

The President. You're terrific; our country's in good hands, all of you. I feel good about our future just listening to you.

Mr. Jennings. Have a good weekend, everybody. Thank you very much, and goodbye from the East Room at the White House.

The President. Thank you.

NOTE: The town meeting began at 11:30 a.m. in the East Room at the White House. Peter Jennings, ABC News, was the moderator for the program. During the meeting, Mr. Jennings referred to Stephen Urkel, the character on ABC's television program "Family Matters" played by actor Jalleel White. Prior to the town meeting, the President conducted a brief tour of the White House.

Remarks on the Economic Program in Santa Monica, California
February 21, 1993

The President. Thank you very much, President Moore, and ladies and gentlemen. This is a wonderful welcome on a Sunday afternoon, and I'm very grateful to you.

I was honored to fly out here today with two of your Members of Congress: Congressman Waxman and his wife, I know we're in Henry's district, he's here; Senator Barbara Boxer and her husband down there. And I think we have four or five other Members of Congress here. Where are they all? Here they are, Maxine Waters, Jane Harman, Howard Berman.

We have a lot of your State officials here and mayors. Mayor Bradley I think is here. He met me at the airport. I resent Mayor Bradley. He looks 10 years younger than me. [*Laughter*] I see a lot of my old friends here, a lot of members of your legislature. If I start introducing people I will never quit. But I do want to say a special word of appreciation to Speaker Willie Brown and Senator Roberti and those who invited me. They sponsored, along with Governor Wilson, that economic summit for California, and they invited me to call in, and I appreciate that. And I am glad to see—I have to say a few things—I see your Lieutenant Governor, Leo McCarthy; and March Fong Yu here, secretary of state; and Gray Davies, your comptroller; Tom Hayden and Diane Watson; and Yvonne Burke. I'm pretty good at this, don't you think? I mean, just for a guy who walked in. And I still think John Garamendi's health care plan may wind up being the model for what we do in the country. It's got a lot to recommend it. Is the Mayor of Santa Monica here? Judy Abdo, stand up here. How are you? And we're in Terry Friedman's district. Is he here? There he is. Marguerite Archie Hudson, is she here? That's right. And we've got a lot of L.A. council members here. I see several here, Zev and others. Now we have—Santa Monica council.

Now, I'm leading up to something here which is that I want to introduce two other people. One is a good friend of mine, someone who helped me with higher education issues in the transition, and one of America's most distinguished educators: Dr. Johnetta Cole, the president of Spelman College, is over here. Then I want to introduce someone who sort of played a hobo in my Inaugural gala and who makes me the second most famous person in the room, Mr. Bill Cosby, who just came in over here.

Ladies and gentlemen, I wanted to come out to California, which was so good to me and to Al Gore, a State that did so much to give us a chance to serve and to try to turn our country around, to talk about the economic plan that I have presented to the Congress, the challenge that it presents to the country, and the help that all of us need from you to have any hope of its passage.

I have embraced as my cause the idea that every person in this country ought to be able to live up to the fullest of their God-given potential. If it can happen anywhere, it must happen in California. Unless California is revived, the Nation cannot recover economically. And unless the people who live here in this State, indeed in this county, with all of its multiracial and multiethinic and multireligious implications, unless you can draw strength out of your diversity, the Nation cannot bring strength out of its diversity and out of the challenges we face today.

The problems you have here are familiar to you and, I guess, to the rest of the country. But since we are here in an event that is not only in Santa Monica but that will beam out to the Nation, I think it is worth reaffirming that for so many years California led the country in economic growth and now is having difficulties for some reasons that affect every American.

First of all, for two decades through the administrations of Democratic and Republican Presidents alike, the productivity rate of our country, the output per worker, has been slowing down. And that has led to diminished wages and more and more families being forced to have extra earners just to make ends meet. And some good things have happened. The enrollment at community colleges has exploded, simply because people recognize that they need more skills and they have to keep learning things

over and over again. The average age here is now 27. Fifteen years from now I predict to you the average age here will be about 35, just because people will have to keep learning for a lifetime, in a global economy in which what we earned is a function of what we can learn.

But in addition to that, California has been especially hard hit by some other things: by reducing the defense budget, something we all celebrate as a move toward world peace at the end of cold war but something which has led to big dislocations, especially among high-wage factory workers, because our country began a few years ago to reduce defense with no plan to convert our massive human capital from producing instruments of war to using the technologies of peace to clean up the environment and to improve the quality of our lives and to go forward. And so we have to do that. But because we haven't, California suffers today.

California suffers because all big operations in this country, and indeed to some extent throughout the world, are undergoing a massive reorganization. But for the last couple of years, as big companies lay off people, small companies are not hiring because of the credit crunch, the cost of health care, the lack of a market, things that we have to face everywhere but that have been particularly painful here.

Finally, we find that a lot of the areas that are critical to our future, the high technologies of the future, are not being seized by this country because we don't have the partnership we need between the Government, business, and labor to break the barriers of the future. And other countries are doing better.

After I leave this State tomorrow, I'm flying on to Washington State to meet with representatives of Boeing. Boeing just announced laying off 23,000 workers. Now, part of that is defense cuts, but after all, Boeing makes a lot of other kinds of planes, too. And for the last several years, we have stood by while Europe invested $26 billion in taxpayer money to build the airbus to push American people out of work, not because they won any sort of free market competition but because Europe had a theory about how to get high-wage jobs going into the 21st century in aerospace. And we were in the grip of a theory that said, oh, that's industrial policy; we don't do that.

So this whole part of our country, which has been the beacon of hope for decades for Americans, is now under great stress. And the economic problems aggravate the underlying social difficulties that you find in every big city in America: more and more poor people, more and more single parent households, more and more children forgotten and left behind—things that we have to do.

Overhanging all of this is the idea which has dominated our Government for the last 12 years, which is that if we just kept taxes low on the wealthiest Americans and got out of the way, the economy would flourish. Well, what has happened is that because we had a theory of Government nonintervention, the deficit has exploded as taxes were lowered on the wealthiest Americans, but health care costs exploded; interest on the debt exploded; the cost of Government continued to increase, and now I find myself being elected President, knowing we have to invest more in the new technologies of the future, knowing we have to invest more in helping people to convert from a defense base to a domestic economy, knowing we have to invest more in early childhood health problems and early childhood education and the education of our people, and knowing that we have a huge deficit that is going to be next year $50 billion bigger than we were told during the election. In December, the deficit numbers were revised upward $50 billion a year roughly for every year of my term.

So here is the dilemma: We have to do something no Americans have had to do before. We have to increase investment in our people and our future and reduce our debt at the same time. And to do it, we have to make some difficult choices, some that are more difficult even than I thought during the campaign because the debt has gotten bigger. And yes, those choices carry a pricetag. But if I have one message to you today it is this: The price of doing the same old thing is far higher than the price of change. And that is why we have to have the courage to change.

If we do not change, then the good things that are happening today will not translate into jobs and opportunity for America. Here's something good that is going on today. The productivity of American firms is rising at a rapid rate. All this global competition has forced many millions of our businesses to produce more with less and to generate more wealth. That's good. But it will only really be good if that money is then taken and invested in this country to put people to work or to raise people's wages.

And if we don't do something about the cost of health care, if we don't do something about the productivity of the work force, if we don't do something to make America a better place to invest money to generate jobs, if we don't have incentives that say reinvest your money here and put our people to work, if we don't help people control their health care costs, then all that increased productivity may result in opportunities elsewhere, but it won't result in bringing America back to where it ought to be.

If we don't change, if we just keep on doing what we've been doing for the last 8 or 12 years, by the end of the decade our Government's deficit will be over $650 billion a year. Over 20 cents of every dollar you pay in taxes will go to interest on the debt. About 65 cents of all the money you pay will go to entitlements in health care. The rest will go to defense. And every Member of Congress, all these people that I recognize, they'll be going to Washington to figure out how to spend 3 or 4 cents on the dollar. Because they will be paralyzed because we refused at this moment to face up to our responsibilities to change this country. And I don't think you want that.

If we keep on going like we've been going, by the end of the decade we'll be spending 20 percent of our income on health care, and yet, we'll have over 40 million of our people without any health insurance. We'll be spending twice as much by then as any country on Earth and have so much less to show for it because our Government refused to work with the people of this country to find a solution to the health care crisis. And so I say again, the price of doing the same old thing is a whole lot higher than the price of change.

What I have challenged the Congress, Republicans as well as Democrats, to do, is to join me in this crusade for change. And I said I will set an example. We have to cut spending, raise taxes, and then increase investment, the things that will make people better able to live and grow this economy. We've got to do both: cut spending, raise taxes. And then we have to increase our investment in the things that will grow the economy.

We should begin with the cuts. I set an example. I cut the staff of the White House by 25 percent below what my predecessor had. You know, it's one thing to talk like a conservative, and another thing altogether to live like one. And I'll tell you something, and I believe the

White House staff will work better. I believe it will be more efficient. I believe we will serve more people. And I believe we'll be able to do what needs to be done.

We're going to cut $9 billion out of the administrative costs of the Federal Government. We're going to cut subsidies to programs, including some that I like that help people where I came from. I have recommended reducing the interest subsidies, for example, to the rural electric association. And that's something that's tough for me. I grew up in the South where a lot of my folks wouldn't have any electricity if it weren't for the REA. But most everybody's got electricity now, and I think it's fair to say we're going to cut spending across the board, they should bear a share of that cut.

We're going to eliminate things that don't need to exist anymore, including a third of the Government commissions you're paying for. We celebrated the Bicentennial—listen to this—we celebrate the Bicentennial of the Constitution in 1987, right? Guess what? There's still a Constitutional Bicentennial Commission you're paying for—[*laughter*]—not to mention the Tea Tasters Board. Now, I say that not because there's a lot of money here, but when you add them all up, it's a whole lot of money. Not any one is a lot of money.

We're going to cut some subsidies that I think ought to be cut. For example, the Superfund was held up as the salvation of the American people for environmental cleanup. But if you look at what's happened to it, it's operated as a big tax subsidy to people who have polluted, and yet most of the money in the Superfund is going to lawyers for lawsuits and legal fees instead of to clean up pollution. We're going to make people pay their fair share and use it to clean up pollution.

I'll tell you something else that wasn't easy to meet or ask for. I know it's popular, and it's also the right thing to do under these circumstances, but I've asked all the Federal employees to take a freeze in pay for a year, and then for the next 3 years to have their pay increased by less than the cost of the living allowance they would otherwise get. And that will save billions of dollars.

I have offered 150 specific spending cuts, 150. And these aren't gimmicks. These aren't the kind of things that we used to have where the President will say, "Well, I just want to cap expenditures, and I'll let the Congress figure out how to distribute the pain." These are 150 specific cuts. Now, that's not bad for 4 weeks on the job. I think we can do better. I think we can do better. But I think that what we ought to do is to do better and not talk about doing better. So I have challenged everybody who wants to say to me—every time I go someplace they say, "Cut more, tax less." I say, "Tell me where." Starting in the Congress, tell me where. I'll be glad to listen.

Audience member. Star Wars.

The President. Everything—everything. We did cut Star Wars quite a lot, as a matter of fact, a whole lot.

I want you to know something else: I will not support a tax increase, even a tax increase, even a tax increase on the wealthiest 1.2 percent of the American people, who are the only people whose rates are being raised, I won't support that until I know we have the spending cuts, too. I don't think anybody should pay more until we cut more.

And I did ask a broad base of the American people to pay a modest energy tax, and I want to talk about that. I did it because the deficit was bigger than I thought and because I knew we had to bring down interest rates, and if we did, it would save money for the American people. And let me just tell you what's happened.

Since the election, just since the election, since it was clear we were going to finally tackle this debt, interest rates have dropped seven-tenths of one percent. If every one of you— I want you to think about it—every one of you who has a variable interest rate on a home mortgage, a car payment, a credit card payment, you're going to make more money in the next year than you'll pay in this energy tax if we can keep the interest rates down. So it's good in the short run but it will also be good in the long run for America.

But I want to talk a little about the energy tax, because that's what most of you will pay. People have been arguing for years that America ought to have a big increase in the gas tax, because we have the lowest gas tax in the world. Then they argue we ought to have a big increase in the carbon tax because we use a lot of coal, and that's polluting.

I concluded that we shouldn't do either one of those because it wouldn't be fair to the American people. A carbon tax would hit those States with high unemployment in the East, like Ohio and West Virginia, where people earn their livings in the coal mines that are around them. We've already got a tough Clean Air Act that's going to require them to pay more, and I didn't think that was fair. And I didn't want a big increase in the gas tax because I didn't think that was fair to people who lived in rural areas or people who had long commuting times and no options for mass transit. It's great if you live in the city and get on the subway every day, but if you have to drive to and from work and you drive long distances, it can be very burdensome.

So we decided—and I might say I want to compliment him; the Vice President had a lot to do with this decision—that we ought to go with a Btu tax based on the health—excuse me, the heat component, the energy component of natural gas, of oil, and of coal, to spread it broadly across energy sources so that the whole thing would encourage conservation, would encourage renewable resources, would encourage less reliance on foreign oil, and would help us to bring down the debt. I think it is the fairest way to go, and it's a balanced thing to do.

Let me say, having done that, I also believe there are some things we must spend more on, because the only reason for reducing the deficit is not just to prove you can bring it down but because it's better for the people of this country. And if we reduce the deficit, it means we spend more of your money on education and jobs and less paying interest on the debt. And if we reduce the debt, it means that you'll be able to borrow more money privately and at lower interest rates. But we still have to spend some more money, and let me tell you where. The first thing we need to do is to adopt a jumpstart program that I have recommended that will create a half a million jobs in this country to try to take advantage of this economic recovery with new jobs over the next year.

The second thing we need to do is to focus closely on the cities and the problems they have with some specific efforts. And let me just mention a few. Our program will invest more money in the cities, in street projects, park projects, water projects, sewer projects, environmental cleaning projects. It will provide for the young people of this country who live in depressed areas, not just big cities but poor rural areas, 680,000 new summer jobs this summer, something that is needed here.

I am going to challenge the business community to join with me to create more than a million new summer jobs this summer so we won't have to worry about what the kids are doing. If we give them something to say yes to, we won't have to spend so much time telling them to say no to things.

We're also going to do some other things that we know work. There's been a lot of people talking about it. This budget, for the first time, fully funds the Head Start program that gives every child a chance to go to Head Start. It fully funds the nutrition program for women and infant children. It will give us the mechanism to immunize every child in this country against preventable childhood diseases.

Now, there will be those who say, "Well, just don't spend any new money." But let me say, we have been closing the barn door after the cow's out, as we say in my home State, for decades on these problems. You spend $1 on Head Start and WIC, you save $3 down the road in problems kids are going to have. If you spend $1 on childhood immunizations, you save $10 down the road in preventable childhood diseases. You tell me how we can defend having the finest pharmaceutical companies in the world in this country, still the richest on Earth, and yet, only Haiti and Bolivia have lower childhood immunization rates in this hemisphere than the United States. It's inexcusable, and we're going to change it. We can do better.

Education works. And I intend to follow through on my pledge to make college loans available to all Americans based on their ability to repay when they take a job and giving a huge number of Americans the right to earn their way out of their college loan, either before or after they go to college, with national service as police officers or teachers or in community youth programs. These are the kinds of things that can turn this country around.

Let me just mention two other things. The people of our country have elected politicians for years who have always talked tough about crime. It's sort of like being for motherhood and apple pie; you've got to be against crime. And I don't mean to trivialize this; no one is for crime. But there are some things, you know, that work. Drug treatment works. Jobs work. And there are law enforcement strategies that work. And unfortunately, most cities don't have enough money to implement them, because they require you to put police back in the same communities working with their neighbors. One part of our plan will put another 100,000 police officers on the street in this country over the next 3 to 4 years, and that will make a difference.

There are some things in this plan that will be especially good for this State, one of which is full funding of the Ryan White Act to care for people with AIDS. Another is that we will spend almost $5 billion over the next 4 years retraining workers and reinvesting in communities who have been hurt by defense closings. It's time to stop talking about conversion and start doing something about it.

Last year the Congress—I have to say something to take up for your congressional delegation here—the United States Congress appropriated $1.7 billion for defense conversion, to go into communities that have been hurt, to educate people again who'd lost their jobs, to give communities incentives to find new kinds of peacetime investments to build for a better future. And the administration which preceded me released zero dollars of that $1.7 billion. I just talked to my Budget Director, Leon Panetta, who's up in northern California today, and confirmed that we will shortly release $500 million of that fund, a lot of which will go to the State of California to put people back to work.

Today when I leave you, I'm going to northern California, and tomorrow morning there I will announce a new technology policy. And I don't want to go through all of it now, but just let me say this: One of the things that I'm proudest of about this budget is that we reinvest more money than we cut in defense research in domestic research. We are trying to find answers to the profound environmental difficulties we face today. We believe we can create jobs in saving America's environment and the global environment. We believe they can be created in the most sophisticated research and our most advanced labs that used to worry about how to find new ways to destroy massive populations. And we believe we can create them in the national forests of our country and throughout the land with reforestation projects to clean up the air and put people back to work, and in all manner of ways in between.

I need your support for this program. The Members of Congress can only be expected to do what they think the people back home will stick by them in doing. We've got to cut spending. We've got to increase some taxes. We've got to invest some in America. We need an economic program that really recognizes that we

live in a world where the capacity of our people and their ability to work together, their ability to learn new things, their ability to have access to investment capital, and their ability to live together so that they draw strength from one another is the critical element in our future. We cannot continue to go on with the kind of paralysis and division and just ignoring our problems that has ripped us for too long.

Nobody wants to talk about half the things that I tried to deal with in this budget because they're too painful. But if only you worry about what's happening today and tomorrow, you never really look beyond that. And I tell you, this is a historic moment for us. We have an inordinately great opportunity to fashion a whole new future for America if we have the courage to seize it. But let me say to all of you, I want to make two points to every one of you here. And since so many of you here are students here, at least one of these will be preaching to the choir:

Point number one, the President and the Congress, working with the people of this country, can create a framework of opportunity, but that is all. Seizing the opportunity depends upon the individual initiative of people in every community in this country. And making it really work depends upon decisions made by people at the grassroots level. You have to make these things work by taking advantage of them. If we pass these programs, for goodness sakes, seize them; make them work. Rededicate yourselves to the proposition that you'll do your part to solve the problems of your community and your country.

The second point I plead with you to communicate to the Members of the House and the Senate is that you understand you can't just have the sweet parts of this program; you've got to have the tough parts too. You know, if you, for example, are feeling pretty good and you're in a business that's doing pretty well, it's easy for you to say, "Well, the only thing I care about is the budget cuts. Just let them cut the budgets." Or if you're not doing very well, you might say, "The only thing I care about is the spending increases and taxing those rich folks, because I don't have that kind of money." Or if you're sort of in the middle, you might say, "I like the budget cuts and the taxes, but I don't want the spending. I'd just as soon have the deficit down, and then I wouldn't have to pay the energy taxes." In other words, every one of you, if you look just at your own interests, could find one part of this program that is not in your interest today.

So we have to ask ourselves the question I put to the Congress and to you, the American people, on Wednesday night. You can't just say, "What's in it for me?" You have to ask, "What's in it for us?"

Let me close with just this story. I left my wife and my daughter at the White House this morning, and I walked across the lawn to get on the helicopter to come to the plane to come out here, and it was snowing and cold. And I said, boy, am I glad to be in California, when I got off the plane. But at least it was 20 degrees or 30 or whatever it was this morning. But a couple of days ago, I got up in the morning in Chillicothe, Ohio, the first capital of the State of Ohio, and I went running in the city park with the Mayor. It was 3 degrees, 3. But all along the road coming in there, there were hundreds and hundreds of people standing out there in the dark when I'd come in the night before in 3-degree temperature, saying, "We want our country back. We want our country to work again."

And then I flew to New York and I had a 50-minute drive to Franklin Roosevelt's home in Hyde Park, New York, where we went to a school that was built during the WPA which is still a functioning school, a beautiful school, proving that work is better than idleness when

you can put people to work. And all along the way it was 8 degrees, and all along the way hundreds and hundreds of people along the way with their signs up. They weren't all friendly, but—[*laughter*]—and by the way, that's good, too. That's another thing we've done: People are debating these issues now and at least participating. But 9 out of 10, 9 out of 10 of them were favorable. And there was this incredible sign standing there in the cold. I mean, 8 degrees; we were in single digits and out there on the highway. Nobody was going to stop—these people—and in the middle, there was this one guy on this sign that says, "Do something. Just do something." [*Laughter*] Let's do something, and we'll all win.

God bless you, and thank you.

NOTE: The President spoke at 1:25 p.m. at Santa Monica College. In his remarks, he referred to Richard Moore, president of the college; David Roberti, president pro tempore, California State Senate; Willie Brown, speaker, California State Assembly; Lt. Gov. Leo McCarthy of California; March Fong Yu, California secretary of state; Tom Hayden and Diane Watson, California State senators; Yvonne Burke, former U.S. Representative; John Garamendi, California insurance commissioner; Terry B. Friedman and Marguerite Archie Hudson, California State Assembly representatives; and Zev Yaroslavsky, Los Angeles city councilman.

Remarks and a Question-and-Answer Session With Silicon Graphics Employees in Mountain View, California
February 22, 1993

The President. First of all, I want to thank you all for the introduction to your wonderful company. I want to thank Ed and Ken. We saw them last night with a number of other of the executives from Silicon Valley, people, many of them with whom I've worked for a good length of time, many of whom the Vice President's known for a long time in connection with his work on supercomputing and other issues.

We came here today for two reasons, and since mostly we just want to listen to you, I'll try to state this briefly. One reason was to pick

this setting to announce the implementation of the technology policy we talked about in the campaign, as an expression of what we think the National Government's role is in creating a partnership with the private sector to generate more of these kinds of companies, more technological advances to keep the United States always on the cutting edge of change and to try to make sure we'll be able to create a lot of good new jobs for the future.

The second reason—can I put that down? We're not ready yet for this. The second reason I wanted to come here is, I think the Government ought to work like you do. And before that can ever happen we have to be able to get the people, the Congress, and the press, who have to interpret all this to the people, to imagine what we're talking about.

I have, for example, the first State government in the country that started a total quality management program in all the departments of government, trying to figure out how we could reinvent the government. And I basically believe my job as President is to try to adjust America in good ways so that we can win in the 21st century, so that we can make change our friend and not our enemy.

Ed said that you plan your new products knowing they'll be obsolete within 12 to 18 months, and you want to be able to replace them. We live in an era of constant change. And America's biggest problem, if you look at it through that lens, is that for too many people change is an enemy, not a friend. I mean, one reason you're all so happy is you found a way to make change your friend, right? Diversity is a strength, not a source of division, right? Change is a way to make money, not throw people out of work, right?

If you decentralize and push decisions made down to the lowest possible level, you enable every employee to live up to the fullest of their ability. By giving them a 6-week break every 4 years, you don't force them to make these sharp divisions between your work life and your private life. It's sort of a seamless web. These are things we need to learn in America and we need to incorporate even into more traditional workplaces.

So I'd like to start—we'll talk about the technology policy later, and the Vice President, who had done so much work, will talk a lot about the details at the end of this meeting. But I just want to start by telling you that one of our missions—in order to make this whole thing work we're going to have to make the Government work differently.

Example: We cut the White House staff by 25 percent to set a standard for cutting inessential spending in the Government. But the work load of the White House is way up. We're getting all-time record telephone calls and letters coming in, and we have to serve our customers, too. Our customers are the people that put us there, and if they have to wait 3 months for an answer to a letter, that's not service.

But when we took office, I walked into the Oval Office—it's supposed to be the nerve center of the United States—and we found Jimmy Carter's telephone system. [Laughter] All right. No speaker phone, no conference calls, but anybody in the office could punch the lighted button and listen to the President talk, so that I could have the conference call I didn't want but not the one I did. [Laughter]

Then we went down into the basement where we found Lyndon Johnson's switchboard— [laughter]—true story—where there were four operators working from early morning till late at night. Literally, when a phone would come and they'd say, "I want to talk to the Vice President's office," they would pick up a little cord and push it into a little hole. [Laughter] That's today, right?

We found procedures that were so bureaucratic and cumbersome for procurement that Einstein couldn't figure them out. And all the offices were organized in little closed boxes, just the opposite of what you see.

In our campaign, however, we ran an organization in the Presidential campaign that was very much like this. Most decisions were made in a great big room in morning meetings that we had our senior staff in, but any 20-year-old volunteer who had a good idea could walk right in and say, "Here's my idea." Some of them were very good, and we incorporated them.

And we had a man named Ellis Mottur who helped us to put together our technology policy. He was one of our senior citizens; he was in his fifties. And he said, "I've been writing about high-performance work organizations all my life. And this is the first one I've ever worked in, and it has no organizational chart. I can't figure out what it looks like on paper, but it works."

The Vice President was making fun of me when we were getting ready for the speech I gave Wednesday night to the Congress; it was like making sausage. People were running in and out saying, "Put this in, and take this out." [Laughter] But it worked. You know, it worked.

So I want to hear from you, but I want you to know that we have hired a person at the Office of Management and Budget who has done a lot of work in creating new businesses and turning businesses around, to run the management part of that. We're trying to review all these indictments that have been issued over the last several years about the way the Federal Government is run. But I want you to know that I think a major part of my mission is to literally change the way the National Government works, spends your tax dollars, so that we can invest more and consume less and look toward the future. And that literally will require rethinking everything about the way the Government operates.

The Government operates so much to keep bad things from happening that there's very little energy left in some places to make good things happen. If you spend all your time trying to make sure nothing bad happens, there's very little time and money and human energy left to make good things happen. We're going to try to pare away a lot of that bureaucracy and speed up the decisionmaking process and modernize it. And I know a lot of you can help. Technology is a part of that, but so is organization and empowerment, which is something you've taught us again today. And I thank you very much.

We want to do a question and answer now, and then the Vice President is going to talk in more detail about our technology policy later. But that's what we and Ed agreed to do. He's my boss today; I'm doing what he —[laughter]. So I wonder if any of you have a question you want to ask us or a comment you want to make.

Yes, go ahead.

Export Control Policy

Q. Now that Silicon Graphics has entered the supercomputer arena, supercomputers are subject to very stringent and costly export controls. Is part of your agenda to review the export control system, and can industry count on export regulations that will keep pace with technology advances in our changing world?

The Vice President. Let me start off on that. As you may know, the President appointed as the Deputy Secretary of Commerce John Rollwagen, who was the CEO at Cray. And he and Ron Brown, the Secretary of Commerce, have been reviewing a lot of procedures for stimulating U.S. exports around the world. And we're going to be a very export-oriented administration. However, we are also going to keep a close eye on the legitimate concerns that have in the past limited the free export of some technologies that can make a dramatic difference in the ability of a Qadhafi or a Saddam Hussein to develop nuclear weapons or ICBM's.

Now, in some cases in the past, these legitimate concerns have been interpreted and implemented in a way that has frustrated American

business unnecessarily. There are, for example, some software packages that are available off the shelf in stores here that are nevertheless prohibited from being exported. And sometimes that's a little bit unrealistic. On the other hand, there are some in business who are understandably so anxious to find new customers that they will not necessarily pay as much attention as they should to what the customer might use this new capacity for. And that's a legitimate role for Government, to say, hold on, the world will be a much more dangerous place if we have 15 or 20 nuclear powers instead of 5 or 6, and if they have ICBM's and so forth.

So it's a balance that has to be struck very carefully. And we're going to have a tough nonproliferation strategy while we promote more exports.

The President. If I might just add to that, the short answer to your question, of course, is yes, we're going to review this. And let me give you one example: Ken told me last night at dinner, he said, "If we export substantially the same product to the same person, if we have to get one permit to do it, we'll have to get a permit every time we want to do the same thing, over and over again. They always give it to us, but we have to wait 6 months, and it puts us behind the competitive arc." Now, that's something that ought to be changed, and we'll try to change that.

We also know that some of our export controls, rules and regulations, are a function of the realities of the cold war which aren't there anymore. But what the Vice President was trying to say, and he said so well—I just want to reemphasize—our biggest security problem in the future may well be the proliferation of nuclear and nonnuclear, like biological and chemical, weapons of mass destruction to small, by our standards, countries with militant governments who may not care what the damage to their own people could be. So that's something we have to watch very closely.

But apart from that, we want to move this much more quickly, and we'll try to slash a lot of the time delays where we ought to be doing these things.

Scientific Visualization

Q. Mr. President, Mr. Vice President, you've seen scientific visualization in practice here. As a company we're also very interested in ongoing research in high-performance computing and scientific visualization. Can we expect to see a change in the national scientific agenda that includes scientific visualization? Right now I don't see the scientific visualization as being represented, for example, on the FCCSET committee.

The Vice President. It is a good question. One of the people who flew out here with us for this event and for the release of the technology policy in just a few minutes is Dr. Jack Gibbons, who is in the back of the room, the President's science adviser and head of the Office of Science and Technology Policy. And he will be in charge of the FCCSET process. That's an acronym that—what does it stand for, Jack— the Federal Coordinating Council on Science and Engin—what is it?

Jack Gibbons. Federal Coordinating Council for Science, Engineering, and Technology.

The Vice President. Right. And visualization will play a key role in the deliberations of the FCCSET.

We were actually, believe it or not, talking about this a little bit with Dr. Gibbons on the way over here. I had hearings one time where a scientist used sort of technical terms that he then explained. It made an impression on me. He said, "If you tried to describe the human mind in terms applicable to a computer, you'd say we have a low bit rate but high resolution." Meaning—this is one of the few audiences I can use that line with. [*Laughter*]

But he went on to explain what that means. When we try to absorb information bit by bit, we don't have a huge capacity to do it. That's why the telephone company, after extensive studies, decided that seven numbers were the most that we could keep in short-term memory. And then they added three more. [*Laughter*] But if we can see lots of information portrayed visually in a pattern or mosaic, where each bit of data relates to all of the others, we can instantly absorb a lot of information. We can all recognize the Milky Way, for example, even though there are trillions of points of light, stars, and so forth.

And so the idea of incorporating visualization as a key component of this strategy is one that we recognize as very important, and we're going to pursue it.

The President. Let me just add one thing to that. First of all, I told the crowd last night that the Vice President was the only person ever to hold national office in America who knew what the gestalt of the gigabit is. [*Laughter*] But anyway—and now we're going to get some very funny articles out of this. They're going to make fun of us for being policy wonks. [*Laughter*]

Let me say something to sort of take this one step further. This whole visualization movement that you have been a part of in your line of work is going to merge in a very short time with the whole business in traditional education theory called applied academics. We're now finding, with just sort of basic computer work in the elementary schools of our country, dramatic differences in learning curves among people who can see the work they're doing as opposed to people who are supposed to read it. And we're now finding that the IQ's of young people who might take a vocational track in school may not be all that different from kids that would stay in a traditional academic track and wind up at Stanford, but their learning patterns are dramatically different. And there are some people—this is a huge new discovery, basically, that's coming into the whole business of traditional educational theory.

So someday what you're doing here will revolutionize the basic teaching in our schools, starting at kindergarten and going forward, so that the world of work and the world of education will begin to be merged backwards all the way to the beginning. And it's going to be, I think, the most important thing we've ever done and very important for proving that in a diverse population all people can reach very high levels of achievement.

Ed McCracken. The President and Vice President have also come here today to present a new national technology policy for the country. Do you want to——

The President. We'll answer some more questions. I'm going to forego my time and just let him announce the policy, so we can hear some more questions. Got to give the man equal time, I know. [*Laughter*]

Economic Program

Q. I'd just like to say, I didn't vote for you; I wish I had. [*Laughter*]

The President. I hope you feel that way 4 years from now. [*Laughter*]

Q. Well, that's actually why I'm standing up. I really see a possibility in what you stand for, and I really think this is why you were elected, that you say you stand for change. You said that during your campaign. I think the company believed that. They're counting on you—I'm nervous—and I just want to say we're really, as a country, behind you. I think that's why the statistics are saying that we're willing to have our taxes increased; we're willing to have cuts, because you say you're really going to do it this time and decrease the deficit. I hope to God that you do. We need it not just for this present time, but by your actually fulfilling on this it will make a major change in how we feel about Government; that when Government says they're going to make a difference and they really come through, it will make a huge impact for the future. And I'm really personally behind you all the way. I wish I'd voted for you.

The President. Thank you. I really appreciate that. Let me make one comment in response, if I might. I think it's important, and you can help others understand this, to understand why we have to reduce the deficit, which is something that is normally not done when unemployment is high. And unemployment is still too high. Even though we're in an economic recovery, most of our recovery is due to higher productivity from firms that, in turn, this time are not hiring new people for all kinds of reasons.

And we have to reduce the deficit for two reasons: Number one, we're already spending 15 percent of your tax money just to pay interest on past debt. If we don't change present patterns, we'll be over 20 cents by the year 2000. That's money we should be spending on education and technology in the future.

Number two, the more money we take out of the pool of funds for borrowing, the more expensive it is for companies like this and other companies that have to go into the markets and borrow to borrow. Just since the election, since we made it clear we were going to try to bring the deficit down, long-term interest rates have dropped seven-tenths of one percent. That is a huge savings for everybody that is going to borrow money or that has a variable interest rate on a loan, whether it's a home mortgage or a business loan or a car loan or whatever. That's important.

The second thing we're trying to do that I know you will also appreciate is to shift the balance of the money we do spend more away from consumption toward investment, investments in education, technology, environmental cleanup, and converting from a defense to a domestic economy. One of the bizarre things

that happened to us in the eighties is that we increased the deficit first through defense expenses and then through exploding health care costs and increasing interest payments. But we reduced our investments in the future and the things that make us richer.

So those are the changes we're trying to effect. Let me just make one other point. I will not support raising anybody's taxes unless budget cuts also pass.

Foreign Trade

Q. One of the things that Silicon Graphics has been really successful in is selling into the international markets. Approximately 50 percent of our revenues come internationally, including a substantial market in Japan. What types of programs does your administration plan to help the high-growth companies of the nineties sell to the international markets?

The President. Two things. First of all, we intend to try to open new markets and new markets in our region. That is, to keep America growing, I believe high-growth companies are going to have to sell south of the border more. And to do that we have to negotiate trade agreements that will help to raise incomes in those countries even as we are growing. That's why I support, with some extra agreements, the NAFTA agreement and why I hope we can have an agreement with Chile and hope we can have an agreement with other countries like Argentina that are making a serious effort to build market economies: because we want to build new markets for all of you.

With Japan, I think what we have to do is to try to continue to help more companies figure out how to do business there and keep pushing them to open their markets. I don't want to close American markets to Japanese products, but it is the only nation with which we have a persistent and unchanging structural deficit. The product deficit with Japan is not $43 billion, which is our overall trade deficit, it is actually about $60 billion in product, in manufactured production. So we've got a lot of problems we have to work out there.

With Europe, we sometimes are in surplus; we're sometimes in deficit. But it's a floating thing, so it's more or less in balance. With developing nations like Taiwan and Korea, those countries had big surpluses with us, but as they became richer they brought them down, so that we're more or less in balance. We have our biggest trade relationship with Canada, and we're more or less in balance.

So we have to work on this Japanese issue while trying to help more of you get involved. Let me make one final comment on that. I think we should devote more Government resources to helping small and medium-size companies figure out how to trade, because that's what the Germans do with such great success and why they're one of the great exporters of the world. They don't waste a lot of money on the real big companies that have already figured it out, but they have extra efforts for small and medium-size companies to get them to think global from the beginning of their endeavors. And I think we're going to have to do more of that.

The Environment

Q. In addition to concerns about the economy, Silicon Graphics employees are also concerned about the environment. Your economic plan does a great job of promoting R&D investment. Are there any elements that are specifically targeted to promote the application of Silicon Graphics technology to environmental-friendly initiatives such as the electric car or the mag-lev train?

The President. I think I should let the Vice President answer that since it's his consuming passion. And if I do it, his book sales will go up again. [*Laughter*]

We devoted a lot of time and attention to that for two reasons. One is the environment needs it. Secondly, we think it's wonderful economics, because I believe that all these environmental opportunities that are out there for us represent a major chunk of what people who used to be involved in defense technologies could be doing in the future if we're going to maintain a high wage base in America.

So I'd like for the Vice President to talk a little about the specifics that we're working on.

The Vice President. That goal is integrated into the technology plan as one of our key objectives. The Japanese and the Germans are now openly saying that the biggest new market in the history of world business is the market for the new products, technologies, and processes that foster economic progress without environmental destruction.

Some have compared the drive for environmental efficiency to the movement for quality control and the quality revolution in the sixties and seventies. At that time, you know, many companies in the United States felt that the existing level of product quality was more or less ordained by the forces of supply and demand and it couldn't be improved without taking it out of the bottom line. But the Japanese, taking U.S. innovations from Dr. Deming and others, began to introduce a new theory of product quality and simultaneously improved quality, profits, wages, and productivity.

The environmental challenge now presents us with the same opportunity. By introducing new attention to environmental efficiency at every step along the way, we can simultaneously reduce the impact of all our processes on the environment, improve environmental efficiency, and improve productivity at the same time. We need to set clear, specific goals in the technology policy, in the economic plan.

And you know, both the stimulus package and the investment package focus a great deal on environmental cleanup and environmental innovation. And whereas we've talked a lot about roads and bridges in the past, and they're a big part of this plan also, we're putting relatively more emphasis as well on water lines and sewer lines and water treatment plants and renovating the facilities in the national parks and cleaning up trails, taking kids from inner cities and putting them to work cleaning up trails in national parks, for example, as part of the summer jobs program.

So you'll find when you look at both the technology plan and the economic plan an enormous emphasis on the environment.

The President. Go ahead, sir. They say we have to quit in a minute. I'll take one more question after this.

The Economy

Q. Mr. President, Mr. Vice President, the news stories and articles that the public has access to regarding the budget and the economy are very often confusing and contradictory. I might explain it in the same terms that you used: The information is delivered low bit rate, but the problem is huge and requires the high-res view. So my question is: I wonder if you're using Lyndon Johnson's computer to analyze the budget and the economy, or whether or not you might be open to using some of the things you've seen here to get the bigger picture and also communicate that to us?

The President. Thank you. There are two

things I'd like to respond to on that, and I'd like to invite you to help. [*Laughter*] I'd like to invite you to help, and I'd like to invite you to help on two grounds: One is the simple ground of helping to decide which visual images best capture the reality of where we are and where we're going.

Senator Moynihan and I went to Franklin Roosevelt's home in Hyde Park, New York, just a couple of days ago. You may have seen the press on it. And on the way back he said to me that the challenges that we face are different from those that Roosevelt faced but just as profound. Unemployment was higher and America was more devastated when he took office, he said, but everybody knew what the problem was. Therefore, he had a lot of leeway working with the Congress in the beginning to work toward a solution. Now, he said, we are facing severe challenges to a century of economic leadership, and it's not clear to every American exactly what the dimensions of the problem are. The capacity you have to help me help the American people conceptualize this is quite significant: showing the trends in the deficit, showing the trends in the investment, showing how the money is spent now and how we propose to spend it.

The second big problem we have you can see if you look at the front page of USA Today today, which shows a traditional analysis, yesterday's analysis—of the business section—of the economic program. It basically says, "Oh, it will bring unemployment down a little and it will increase economic growth a little if we do this, but not all that much." Now, why is that? That's because traditional economic analysis says that the only way the Government can ever help the economy grow is by spending more money and taxing less. In other words, traditional Keynesian economics: Run a bigger deficit. But we can't do that. The deficit's already so big, I can't run the risk to the long-term stability of this country by going in and doing that.

This analysis doesn't really make a distinction between investment and consumption, doesn't take any account of what we might do with a technology policy or a trade policy to make the economy grow faster, has no way of factoring in what other good things could happen in the private market if you brought long-term interest rates down through the deficit. So you could also help us to reconceptualize this. A lot of the models that dominate policymaking are yesterday's models, too.

I'll give you just one example. The Japanese had a deficit about as big as ours, and they were increasing spending at 19 percent a year, government spending, back in the early seventies when the oil prices went way up and they were more energy-dependent than we were on foreign oil. And they just decided they had to change it, but they couldn't stop investing. So they had a budget which drew a big distinction, a literal distinction, legal distinction, between investment and consumption, and they embarked on a 10 or 11 year effort to bring the budget into balance. And during that time they increased investment and lowered unemployment and increased growth through the right kind of spending and investment.

And I want to lead in, if I might, and ask the Vice President before we go to give you some of the specifics of this technology policy, by making one more pitch to you about this whole economic plan. This plan has 150 specific budget cuts. And I'm welcome to more. I told the Republican leadership if they had more budget cuts that didn't compromise our economy, if they helped us, I would be glad to embrace them. I'm not hung up about that. But I did pretty good in 4 weeks to find 150, and I'll try to find some more on my own.

It also has the revenue increases that you know about. It also has some spending increases, and there will be debate about that. There will be people who say, "Well, just don't spend this new money. Don't immunize all the kids. Don't fully fund Head Start. Don't pay for this technology policy. Don't invest in all these environmental cleanup things, and that way you won't have to raise taxes so much."

The problem is, if you look at the historic spending trends, we are too low on investment and too high on the deficit, and both are problems. And secondly, we've got to have some of these economic cooperations in order to move the economy forward.

So I want you to listen to what the Vice President says in that context. Because what you will hear is, we don't need to do what we think we should do in this area. If we don't, I think we'll be out of competition. People like you will do fine because you've got a good company here, but the country as a whole will fall behind. And you can help on both those points.

So would you proceed?

NOTE: The President spoke at 10 a.m. at Silicon Graphics. In his remarks, he referred to company officers Ed McCracken, founder and president, and Ken Coleman, senior vice president.

At the conclusion of the question-and-answer session, the Vice President made the following statement on the new technology policy:

I want to give you just a few of the details of this technology policy. There will be a printed copy available, and you will be able to see for yourself all of the goals and all of the elements of it.

But I want to start by describing how it fits into the President's economic plan. You know, some of the special interests who oppose the President's plan are saying to the American people, "Don't pass this plan because everything's fine just the way it is." Well, anybody who says everything's fine with our economy hasn't been to California lately. We need some change. We can't stand the status quo.

California has to participate in the recovery in order for America to have a recovery that is worth the name "recovery," so that we can start creating new jobs. And many of the high-skill, high-wage jobs of the future are in technology areas. And that's why a key component of the President's economic plan is the technology policy that we're announcing here today.

It starts with an appreciation of the importance of continuing basic R&D because that's the foundation for all of the exciting products that this company and others like this company come up with. It continues with an emphasis on improving education because in order for companies like this one to survive and prosper in the world economy, we as a nation have to have highly educated, well-trained young men and women coming out of colleges on to campuses like this. You call it a campus, right? That's the term that's very common now.

We also have to pay attention to the financial environment in which companies like this have to exist. In order for this company to attract investors for the kind of products that you are building here, you have got to be able to tell them that the interest rates are not going to be too high if they're borrowing money to invest; you've got to be able to tell them, look, President Clinton is making permanent the R&E tax credit, for example, and there are going to be specific new provisions in the law to encourage investment in high-risk ventures that are very common in the high-technology area.

And then this plan makes specific investments in something called the national information infrastructure. Now, infrastructure is a five-dollar word that used to describe roads, bridges, water lines, and sewer lines. But if we're going to compete in the 21st century, we have to invest in a new kind of infrastructure.

During the Industrial Revolution, the nations that competed most successfully were often ones that did the best job of building deep-water ports, those that did the best job of putting in good railway systems to carry the coal and the products to the major centers where they were going to be sold and consumed. But now we are seeing a change in the definition of commerce. Technology plays a much more important role. Information plays a much more important role. And one of the things that this plan calls for is the rapid completion of a nationwide network of information super-highways so that the kind of demonstrations that we saw upstairs will be accessible in everybody's home. We want to make it possible for a school child to come home after class and, instead of just playing Nintendo, to plug into a digital library that has color moving graphics that respond interactively to that child's curiosity.

Now, that's not the only reason to have such a network or a national information infrastructure. Think about the importance of software. If we could make it possible for talented young software writers here in Silicon Valley and elsewhere in the United States to sell their latest product by downloading it from their desk into a nationwide network that represented a marketplace with an outlet right there in that person's home or business, we would make it possible for the men and women who are interested in technology jobs here in the United States to really thrive and prosper.

In keeping with one of the questions that was asked earlier about how we can export more into the world marketplace and how we can be more successful in world competition, one way is by making our own domestic market the most challenging, most exciting, with the most exacting standards and levels of quality of any nation in the world. And then we will naturally roll out of our domestic marketplace into the world marketplace and compete successfully with our counterparts everywhere in the world.

Now, there are some other specific elements of this package which you can read for yourself when you see the formal package. Let me just list them very briefly: A permanent extension of the research and experimentation tax credit; completion of the national information infrastructure; specific investments in advanced manufacturing technology. And in response to one of the questions that was asked over here, there is a specific program on high-speed rail to do the work necessary to lay the foundation for a nationwide network of high-speed rail transportation, and a specific project to work cooperatively with the automobile companies in the United States of America to facilitate the more rapid development of a new generation of automobiles that will beat all the world standards and position our automobile industry to dominate the automobile industry of the future in the world.

We also have a specific goal to apply technology to education and training. Dr. Gibbons and others have given a tremendous amount of thought to this because, after all of the dashed hopes and false expectations for computers in schools, ironically, we now have a new generation of educational hardware and software that really can make a revolutionary difference in the classroom, and it's time to use it.

And we are going to save billions of dollars each year part way through this decade with the full implementation of environmental technologies and energy efficiency technologies, starting with Federal buildings. We're going to save a billion dollars a year in 1997 just in the energy costs of Federal buildings around the United States by using off-the-shelf technology that has a 4-year payback on the investment. And then we're going to encourage the use of those technologies around the country, and we're going to invest in the more rapid creation of new generations of that technology.

Now, the other details of this technology program will be available in the handout that's going to be passed out here. And any of you who have ideas on how we can improve it and make better use of technology, we invite you to contact us and let us know how we can improve this program as we go along.

But one final word: The President's economic program is based, as he said, on cutting spending; reducing the deficit over time, including with some revenue increases that are progressive and fair; and also investing in those things which we know will create good, high-wage, high-skill jobs here in the United States. You all are pioneers in a sense, showing how that can be accomplished. We want to make it easier for working men and women throughout this country and other companies to follow your example and to create more jobs in high technology. And that is the focus of this technology policy, which is part of the overall plan to create more jobs for the American people and get our economy moving again.

The Office of the Press Secretary also released a summary of the technology initiative.

Remarks in a Telephone Conversation With Larry Villella
February 22, 1993

The President. Larry, it's President Clinton. How are you?

Larry. Great. Nice to talk to you.

The President. It's nice to hear your voice. I just heard about you sending me this $1,000 check on CBS Radio. We just heard it over the radio this morning, and I really appreciate it.

Larry. Okay. I hope that you can use it towards the economy.

The President. Well, I think we can. One of the things that I've asked our staff to do, since citizens are not in the habit of sending money like this, is to see whether we can legally receive it and spend it just the way you want. And I'm going to also see whether or not your suggestion can be carried out in terms of involving other people doing the same thing you did.

But I think it's a remarkable thing for a 14-year-old young American to do. And it's very impressive that you have a business that's so successful that you can afford to do this.

How long have you been doing that?

Larry. I've been doing it for 3 years now.

The President. And do you do it year-round?

Larry. It's pretty much year-round, except during the wintertime we have a few less sales of the sprinkler.

The President. And what's your annual— what's your sales, your volume of sales? How much do you sell every year?

Larry. Well, so far we've sold 3,000, and it's been divided between the 3 years since I'm just starting out.

The President. I think that's pretty good.

Larry. Thank you.

The President. Pretty impressive. What do you want to do when you get out of high school?

Larry. I want to go to college and then medical school.

The President. Do you want to be a doctor?

Larry. I'm hoping to be a cardiologist.

The President. That's great. Well, by the time you can get out of medical school and be a cardiologist the American people will be living much longer, but they'll all be worried about their hearts. There will be a big demand for what you do.

Larry. I hope so.

The President. Well, I certainly hope that I get to meet you sometime. And I'm really, really impressed that you did this. I think you're really a symbol of what's best in this country, and I'm proud of you, and I thank you for doing this. And I'm going to be back in touch with you about exactly what we can do with your money and whether we can adopt your suggestion.

Larry. Okay. Thank you. I'd really like to meet you, too.

The President. That's great. Tell your family hello, and you have a good day, okay?

Larry. Okay. Thank you.

The President. Bye-bye.

Larry. Bye.

NOTE: The President spoke at 12:52 p.m. aboard Air Force One while he was en route to Everett, WA.

Remarks to Boeing Employees in Everett, Washington
February 22, 1993

Thank you very much, Chairman Shrontz, Speaker Foley, Senator Murray, Governor Lowrey, and Member of the congressional delegation, and most of all to the men and women of Boeing. I have looked forward to coming here for a long time. And I guess what I ought to begin by saying is, thank you for Air Force One.

You know, everywhere I go in that airplane, I am the second most important celebrity. People really just want to see the plane. [*Laughter*] And I know I can make all my friends and supporters happy, even my mother, just by taking them on the plane and letting them look at your magnificent work.

You should also know that it enables me on these flights across the country and going across the world to continue to work with a full staff almost as if I had never left the office. And it is a real tribute to all of you, and a magnificent set of planes—you know, there are two of them. I know a lot of you made them both, so you know that. But I'm grateful to you for that.

I also think you may know, but I should say that after this meeting with you, I'm going to go to another room and meet with a lot of folks who have come here to meet with me and with our national leaders about the health of the airline industry, about the commercial airline companies themselves, and about the airline manufacturers, the chief of which obviously is Boeing, but including other companies as well. So when I leave you, I'm going to go and meet with them for about an hour to talk about where we're going from here.

I want to begin by saying that there's an interesting book, which has been written by a very famous economics writer named Lester Thurow called "Head to Head." And Thurow's argument in this book is—it affects your lives, so I'm going to tell you about it—his argument is that there may be a limited number of highway jobs available over the next 20 years, and that seven major technologies will provide most of the growth in those jobs, a lot of them are, as you might suspect, in the computer and electronics field.

I was just down in Silicon Valley before I came here at a magnificent little company named Silicon Graphics that does some work for you, to talk about a technology policy to accelerate the growth in areas where we're doing well. But one of those seven areas is aeronautics and the manufacturer of airplanes and in the provision of airline services to commercial travelers.

It is indeed ironic that the United States which, for so long has led the world in the production of airplanes and in the development of sophisticated consumer-oriented services through commercial carriers, has had 3 years in which more money has been lost than was made in the previous history of the airline industry. And I can tell you from my study, very little of that is your fault. A lot of it has to do with the fact that other nations follow targeted strategies of partnerships to pierce markets which you had dominated under a free market system but with which you could not compete in Europe's subsidized airbus to the tune of $26 billion, for example.

I want to talk to you today about the whole economic plan, the tough parts as well as the good parts. But I want you to know that one big part of my economic strategy is to try to identify all those areas that can really provide high-wage, high-growth futures for Americans and their families and make sure that we are there, competing and winning, that people have a chance to work and make a living. And we can't begin by giving up on the production of aircraft, which is what we have come dangerously close to doing by sitting by and letting our competitors do things that we did not do to meet the competition. And I believe we can do better. I hope this meeting today is the first step in that regard.

I also want to say a special word of appreciation to the Speaker and to the leaders of Congress. In the next few days, the Congress will produce a bill establishing a national commission on the condition of the airlines industries in America; one that will require the House and the Senate to appoint five members each and the President to appoint five members; and unlike a lot of commissions, will require them to report back within 90 days with a tight time table with a specific set of recommendations to take to the country to preserve and promote the economic health of the industry that you've done so much to make the world's best.

The second thing I want to say is that my trade ambassador, Mickey Kantor, will be closely monitoring the agreement which was made finally last year with regard to limiting European subsidies to airbus to allow a level playing field. We'll be seeking tough new discipline on those subsidies, both in our attempts to get an agreement on the general agreement on trade, as well as the specific aircraft code.

You know, I've seen these agreements made for years. I've seen people promise us they'd do this, that, and the other thing, and then nothing ever happens. And I think you and I know deep in our heart that most of these layoffs—maybe not all, because the airline industry itself has problems which are bleeding back on to you, the commercial carriers—but a lot of these layoffs would not have been announced had it not been for the $26 billion that the United States sat by and let Europe plow into airbus over the last several years. So we're going to try to change the rules of the game.

I can't promise you overnight miracles. We didn't get into this fix overnight. But I can say that we have to turn the direction of this country around, and we need a commitment, not to shield ourselves from competition but to reward ourselves when we fairly compete and win.

We need a commitment to meet the competition around the world in a global economy in which the things that really pay off are high levels of education and skills, high levels of investment in appropriate technologies, a very close amount of cooperation within each workplace among workers and between workers and management, and in the national sense between Government and business and labor. The countries which do that win; those which don't are punished. And we can no longer afford to wait for 10 years while someone does something to us that we do not respond to. And I want to turn that around, not with overnight miracles but with a disciplined approach to put the American people and their economic future first in the policymaking of the United States Government. It's your country, and I'm doing my best to give it back to you.

I ask each of you to express to your Congressmen and your Senators support for the national economic plan which I announced to the Congress on last Wednesday. It is a plan which seeks to do two things that we've never done in the history of America before at the same time. It seeks to reduce this awful Government debt and to increase investment in our future at the same time. And it's hard to cut your debts and increase your investment at the same time. It's hard if you're Boeing. It's hard if you're the United States Government.

But we have no choice, because in the last

12 years, we have quadrupled the debt of the Government, which means we're spending 15 cents of every dollar you give us in taxes right now just paying interest on yesterday's debt, 15 cents of every dollar you pay in taxes that we can't put into an investment incentive for an airline company, for an education for your children, for better health care for America.

It also means we're taking so much money out of the pool of money available that if Boeing or a small business or somebody wanting to buy a car or a home has to borrow money, their interest rates are higher than they otherwise would be. So we've got to bring the debt down, but we also have to look over the last 12 years. Your country has reduced its investment while our competitors have increased their investments in critical areas of education and training and new technologies and in building the kinds of things that put people to work and make a country rich. So to do it, we have to cut spending, raise some more tax money, and target some new investments, not in consuming things but in things that will build jobs and incomes in the years ahead.

I have offered the Congress in good faith an honest spending cut program with 150 specific reductions in spending cuts, including a 25 percent cut in my own staff, the biggest, as far as I can tell, in the history of the Republic, certainly in the 20th century, and a $9 billion cut in the administrative costs to the Federal Government, and asking the Federal employees who work for you to have a pay freeze this year and to have their pay go up at less than the rate of inflation for the next 3 years, which will save that much again. We are cutting spending where we can.

I have also made it clear that I don't want to raise one penny of tax dollars until I know those cuts are in effect. We shouldn't raise money until we cut spending. We should do them together.

Seventy percent of the burden of this tax program will fall on people whose taxable income, not net income, taxable income is above $100,000. But some of it will fall on people with incomes of between $30,000 and $100,000, and I want to level with you about that. For years there have been those who say we ought to reduce the deficit by raising the gas tax a whole lot. That's fine if you live in the city and ride mass transit to work. It's not so good if you live in the country and drive yourself

to work. There are a lot of working people in America today that have no access to mass transit and can't carpool; so I rejected a big gas tax.

Then there were people who said, "Well, the best thing to do environmentally is to tax carbon." That's a funny way of saying coal. The problem with that is, there's a lot of people just like you in Pennsylvania and West Virginia and places like that who make their livings in and around the coal mines. And it didn't seem fair to me to put such a burden on them that they would be in trouble.

So we decided to pick what seems to be the environmentally best thing that doesn't hurt so many people, and that is a tax on the energy capacity of all forms of fuel, of gas and oil and coal, called a BTU tax, which amounts to about 2 cents on a gallon of gasoline, and will cost the average family with an income of $50,000 about 15 bucks a month at the outside if they have a family of four and drive a lot. And I think that is a fair way to go.

I didn't want to even do that, but after the election I was told that the Government deficit was going to be about $50 billion a year bigger than we had been told before the election. And so my choice was not to ask for an additional contribution from the middle class, let the deficit get out of hand, and have your interest rates go up, or try to deal with this debt and try to face the fact that we need to invest some more money too. I hope you'll support that.

But I also hope you will support spending some more money in the areas that will create jobs. And let me just mention two or three. This plan contains tax incentives to business and direct investments in things like roads and environmental cleanup and airport construction that will create a half a million jobs in the next year and a half. This plan contains $8 billion in new investments in aeronautics, in technology, in research and development, the development of new products over the next 5 years. It contains a major new general technology initiative that the Vice President and I announced today in Silicon Valley to create high-wage jobs. It contains $9 billion in new investments in high-tech products all across the Government, including the attempt to develop an environmentally clean car and new high speed rail technology that could dramatically alter the economics of living on the Pacific Rim of our country. It contains new incentives to businesses to create jobs and especially to small business.

Let me tell you that all the big companies in the country together reduced jobs all during the 1980's, but little companies created more jobs than big companies lost until about 2 years ago when the cost of health care, the unavailability of credit, and the decline of the economy stopped small business in its tracks. So we have to not only help big manufacturing operations; we've got to have a climate where people can start small businesses and keep them going. Because we know that even if we do very well in the aerospace industry, for example, there will be other very big companies that will have to downsize and restructure. And we've got to do something for small business to try to help them to go and to grow.

These things are very important. And let me say one other thing that affects Boeing, at least a little bit, and that is we propose to put a lot more money into the space program, but to restructure it so that we not only have a space station but we also have a lot of new investments in other kinds of aeronautics research that will generate even more jobs in America in the years ahead. And we've proposed to spend more money on domestic research and development than we reduce in defense research and development.

These are the things that made your company great, and these are the kinds of things that will make America great again. And so I ask you to support not just the spending cuts, the revenue increases, and the deficit reduction but also these very targeted investments in our future.

I also ask you to support immunizing every child before the age of 2 in America, for a change, Head Start for the kids that need it, and making college loans available to all middle class, as well as low-income people, and letting them pay those loans off as a percentage of their income.

Now, a lot of people will say—there's a lot of ways you can debate this—a lot of people will say, I didn't cut spending enough. To them, I say give me more spending cuts. I've just been there 4 weeks, and I'm sure there are more, and I'll find more. Then there will be those that say we cut too much. Some will say we didn't raise enough money. Some will say we've raised too much. And then some will say you shouldn't spend any new money.

But remember what I said: A country now is like a big company in the global economy. If you don't invest in the right things, you don't grow. So we not only have to reduce this deficit; we've got to turn our spending priorities on their head. We've got to invest more and consume less so the country can grow, just like you want this company to grow.

I believe with all my heart that the years ahead can still be the best years this country ever had. But you know what you're going through now. Just look at it. We are living in a world where change is the law of life, where the average 18-year-old will change work eight times in a lifetime. And we will be judged harshly by our children if we permit the kinds of things to go on that are happening today, which make change our enemy and not our friend.

My whole goal in this economic program is to try to change the priorities of this country so people can pursue what the Founding Fathers wanted, life, liberty, the pursuit of happiness, by making change our friend. I can't promise you and no politician can, to repeal the laws of global competition. I can't promise you that you won't have to work not only harder but smarter than ever before. Nobody can do that.

But I think you know that your Government has been inadequate to the task of preparing you to win if you play by the rules, if you do your part, if you're highly productive. That's my job. That's what this plan's designed to do. I hope you will support it. I think it will secure the American dream for you and your children.

Thank you very much, and God bless you all.

[At this point, the President was presented with a gift.]

Thank you.

I want to say two things. First of all, it was very diplomatic of you not to give me a bigger shirt than you gave Vice President Gore. *[Laughter]* And secondly, I don't think anyone who sees me running in this will really believe I'm about to fly. *[Laughter]* But I will wear it and enjoy it every day.

Thank you very much.

NOTE: The President spoke at 2:02 p.m. in Hangar 40–23 at Boeing. In his remarks, he referred to Frank Shrontz, company president and chief executive officer.

Remarks Following a Meeting With Airline Industry Leaders and an Exchange With Reporters in Everett
February 22, 1993

The President. I would like to thank Frank Shrontz and the good people at Boeing for hosting representatives of the major airline companies in the United States, as well as manufacturers of airplanes and airplane engines, along with the Secretary of Transportation, the Speaker of the House, and the distinguished Members of the Washington congressional delegation along with the Governor of this State.

We have had a very good meeting about the problems of the manufacturers of airlines and the airline companies themselves, airplanes and airline companies. We talked a lot about the proposal now in the Congress, which is soon to be passed, to create a national commission to ensure a strong, competitive airline industry. That commission will require five appointments from the House, five appointments from the Senate, and five appointments from the President. I assured the representatives here, as did the Speaker, that we had no desire other than to find the 15 best people in America immediately to work on this issue, without regard to party or region. We just want to work together to appoint people who will come back within 90 days and give us some concrete suggestions to revitalize this very important part of our economic future.

I thought it was a terrific meeting. We went around the table. Everyone who was at the meeting made a very constructive set of comments about what they thought we ought to do. And I look forward to the legislation passing, to signing it, and to immediately making the appointments and to going to work.

Q. What do you think, Mr. President, that will mean for the worker who is laid off here? What will be the direct——

The President. Well, if we do a good job, we'll be able to find more business and bring some of them back to work. That's what we want to do.

I'd like to ask the Speaker and the Secretary and Mr. Shrontz and anybody else who is here who wants to make a comment to make some comments, and then we'll answer a couple of more questions.

*[At this point, Speaker of the House of Rep-*resentatives Thomas S. Foley, Secretary of Transportation Federico Peña, and Frank Shrontz, president and CEO, Boeing Co., made brief remarks.]*

Q. Mr. President—*[inaudible]*——

The President. If you guys would talk, I wouldn't have to answer so many questions. *[Laughter]*

Bosnia

Q. Mr. President, are we going to airdrop supplies in to the besieged people in Bosnia?

The President. It's a possibility. I want to wait a couple of more days before I announce a policy on it.

Economic Program

Q. Mr. President, you said in your speech that you wanted spending cuts first and then invest in programs you call investments. Given that your spokespeople had said you're going to pass an authorization for short-term stimulus spending and that the rest of the package has come down the line, and given that most of the spending comes in the early years and the taxes would come in the out-years, in what sense do you want the spending cuts first?

The President. Well, I want an omnibus program passed which has all the spending cuts mandated along with the tax increases. I don't want to raise taxes and then sit around waiting to see whether the spending cuts are going to be enacted. I think that we ought to pass a package which includes the spending cuts at the same time we raise revenues.

Q. Will you still be—to do your new spending first?

European Airline Subsidies

Q. *[Inaudible]*—the airbus?

The President. Well, you may know that last year our Government signed an agreement, which had the support of the airline industry, which got a commitment out of Europe to dramatically reduce the subsidies to airbus. What I seek to do, number one, is to review it as to its adequacy and, number two, to make sure it's enforced. But I think we made a huge mistake permitting it to happen with no response. And I hope that it's not too late to have an appropriate response to maintain our position in this global marketplace.

U.S. Trade Policy

Q. Do you think you need a tougher trade policy, in general, Mr. President?

The President. No, not necessarily. I think we need a different trade policy. Let me say that the linchpin of our policy still must be to expand trade. A wealthy country cannot grow wealthier by hunkering down within its own borders. We have to be a great trading nation, and we have to help other nations to grow wealthier in order for them to buy more of our products. So our goal still has to be to expand trade.

But we no longer have the luxury, with other nations having grown so much more rapidly than we for 20 years, other nations being about as wealthy as we are—we no longer have the luxury of being the only country in the world that can ignore certain problems in terms of trade fairness that other countries don't ignore. We have to make sure that we are treated in these market-opening measures with the requisite amount of fairness. And so I think we may have a firmer trade policy in some respects than we've had in the past, but our allies will be under no illusions. I do not want a protectionist trade policy; I want to expand trade. But I want to do it in ways that preserves America as a high-wage country. Otherwise, we won't be very good trading partners for a lot of these nations over the long run.

Thank you very much.

NOTE: The President spoke at 3:57 p.m. in Hangar 40–22 at Boeing.

Remarks to the U.S. Chamber of Commerce National Business Action Rally
February 23, 1993

Thank you very much. Chairman Gorr, President Lesher, Vice Chairman Marcil, ladies and gentlemen, I thank you for that warm welcome. And I welcome you to your Nation's Capital and to this magnificent old hall.

I was glad to be here early enough to hear at least some of the Marine Band warming you up. That should put us all in a better frame of mind.

I thank you all for your concern for your country and for the contribution you make every year and every day to make America work. I want to say a special word of appreciation for the people from my native State who even hung a sign up there so I could find them.

As you know, if you've been following the news, I have been out on the road discussing with the American people the economic plan I have presented to the Congress. Yesterday I had a particularly amazing day, seeing everything that is best about our economy and some of the most profound challenges we face. I began at an interesting firm called Silicon Graphics in California's Silicon Valley, where I spent a goodly amount of time visiting with the employees and watching what they do.

The Vice President and I went there to outline our technology policy. But afterward we just talked to the employees and listened to them. I was amazed to see that this company, as so many others in this country, has really succeeded in making the changes going on in our world friendly to the company, its employees, its owners, and its customers, not the enemy. As I have said so many times across this country, I think one of my primary jobs as President now is to try to figure out a way to make these turning changes in the global environment our friend and not our enemy.

Silicon Graphics have unleashed the creative energy of their most talented people. They've made a strength of the diversity that is so prominent throughout the State of California. They reduced bureaucracy to make it virtually nonexistent, pushed decisions down to the lowest level, and succeeded in creating products that are displaced every 12 to 18 months with their own products.

Then I flew up to Washington to meet with the employees at the Boeing Corporation, our

Nation's largest exporter, a company that, as you know, is in some trouble now. It just announced 23,000 layoffs. And after I met with several thousand of the employees there, I had an hour private meeting with the heads of all the major American airplane companies: with Boeing, then with McDonnell-Douglas, with Pratt-Whitney, those who manufacture the airplanes and the component parts that are an important part of our economy.

They're facing some very tough competition. They have some structural problems in the market here, and I think have been subjected to some fairly unfair competition abroad, principally from airbus, a consortium of European efforts that has benefited from $26 billion in direct Government subsidies in the last year few years.

I spent a lot of my adult life dealing with large organizations in times of challenge and change. I had the great privilege to be Governor of my State for a dozen years. And I have acquired an enormous respect for people in the private sector and what they've had to cope with in this country over the last 12 to 15 years, some of you over the last 20 years, as we have moved inexorably into a very different global economy.

I came here today to ask for your support for my economic plan to take this country in a new direction because I believe it will make business more competitive and workers more productive and will help us to deal with some of the principal problems that we have faced over the last several years: high levels of unemployment periodically, stagnant wages among workers, lower levels of overall productivity than many of our major competitors.

In the news today, there are things which are good news. We know that in the last quarter, American productivity jumped to almost a 20-year high as more and more American businesses have come to grips with the challenges they face. We know that the housing markets are beginning to pick up, and that's good news. We know that in the last 2 months of the last quarter, consumer confidence took a big jump, and that's good news.

But we also know that there are still very serious problems in this economy with creating new jobs, serious problems with stagnant incomes, and enormous problems that have led to dampening the growth of new jobs in the small business sector. The restructuring of big

business, which has been going on now for more than a decade, led to a reduction in employment in every year of the 1980's in larger businesses. But in most of that decade, the reduction in employment in big business was more than offset by the creation of new jobs in small businesses. In the last couple of years, that trend has not been able to continue.

There are lots of reasons why. Clearly, the exploding cost of health care is one. The credit crunch that exists in much of our country is another, and we're trying to address that. And there are many other reasons. But it is plain that the lack of a clear national economic strategy to deal with our long-term problems has played a central role.

My goal in this economic program is to follow a strategy which will, short- and long-term, increase jobs, increase incomes, and increase productivity. That means, in my judgment, we have to increase investment, both public and private; we have to do more to educate and train our people so that they can produce at high levels; we have to take far better advantage of technology in the world, especially in the commercial sector.

In the 1980's, the most successful industrial strategy we had was our defense budget which kept our lead in international defense technologies while we were losing our lead in many commercial technologies.

We have to have a strategy for preserving our environment that makes that an engine of economic growth, not a burden on business and a drag on the economy. We have to reduce our inordinate Government deficit. We have to deal with the health care crisis. And we have to change the way Government operates and relates to the private sector in very fundamental ways.

There has not been a serious reexamination of the structure, the role, and the function of the Federal Government in some sort of comprehensive way in a generation. And because we have guaranteed claim on revenues and guaranteed claim on some customers, we have not been under the same pressures that many of you have to undergo, the kind of searching reexamination that the international economy has imposed on all of you. And I am committed to doing that.

I ask you before we get into the details to look at just two things: First of all, if we do not think to change the fundamental pattern of the way your National Government works, if we just keep on doing what we've been doing and argue around the edges, the Republicans winning a little here, the Democrats winning a little there, everybody chipping around, but basically we keep on the same course, here is what will happen. By the end of the decade the annual deficit will be $653 billion. About 22 cents of every dollar you pay to the United States Government will go to pay interest on past debt. We'll be up to about 60 cents on entitlements by then because of the exploding cost of health care and more people retiring. We will be spending a certain amount of money that we have to spend on the national defense, and people in the Congress will come to this city having made great campaign commitments to all of you out in the country and without regard to their party, they'll be arguing over how they're going to spend 3 or 4 cents on the dollar because we will be paralyzed in the expenditure of the public money, and we'll have less money to spend on investment in our future.

We'll be spending 20 percent of the gross national product on health care. And no other country, if present trends continue, will be above 10, which means every productive enterprise in the country will be spotting its international competitors 10 cents on the dollar in health care alone. If we continue the present patterns, that is what we have to look forward to.

We have no alternative but to change. We should begin with a program that increases public investment in technology and education and in people and bring this deficit down at the same time. That's hard to do. This country has never tried to do that before. We've had times past when times were good and the deficit was brought down. And in times past when things were tough, the deficit has been increased to increase investment. Our Nation has never before tried to increase investment and reduce the debt at the same time. It is not easy to do.

I have offered a plan to do that that cuts spending with real specific cuts, not rhetoric about overall caps; with tax increases that I believe are progressive, although none are free of pain; and with targeted, specific investments to grow this economy.

Now, already we're beginning to see some impact. Just since the election, since the Sec-

retary of the Treasury and other people on our economic team and the President have been able to send clear signals to the market that we are going to bring down this deficit, there has been a seven-tenths of one percent drop in long-term interest rates.

Just yesterday, due to increased confidence in the plan in the bond market, long-term interest rates fell to a 16-year low. As a result, over the last several days mortgage rates have begun another significant decline. The serious drop in interest rates is already providing a major stimulus to economic growth and major savings to millions of American families.

As interest rates fall more people will be able to save money on business loans, home loans, car loans, credit card transactions; all these things will free up cash to get the economy moving again. If we do it right and deliberately, the vast majority of Americans will save more money on lower interest rates than they will pay in the higher energy tax. Many businesses will save more money on lower interest rates than they will pay in the other tax increases. By increasing the pool of available investments through debt reduction, we can free up tax money away from interest on the debt to invest in education in our future, and we can free up major sources of funds in the private sector.

We have to do this together. The reason the debt portion of the package is important is that many of the changes which happen in America that are good, by definition, have to happen outside Washington. Generations of experience has taught us that the private sector functions best when the Government supports it but does not direct it; frames environment but does not intrude upon it; when the climate is stable and sustaining but when you can create jobs and grow the economy through your own enterprise.

For many years I was charged with being the chief advocate for the business community of my State. I went around the world trying to sell our products and increase investment in our State. We worked on a long-term strategy under the most difficult imaginable circumstances. When I took office in 1983, our unemployment rate was in double digits and most of our counties had unemployment rates not only in double digits but in the high unemployment counties in the State we had several counties with unemployment rates in excess of 20 percent. And we set about to increase investment, increase competitiveness, improve the

187

education and training of our work force. Last year we ranked second in the country in job growth, and for the last 5 years have been in the top 10, not because of anything I did but because of what we did.

There has to be a clear partnership here that empowers the private sector to grow jobs by having the right kind of environment, the right kind of incentives, and the right kind of long-term commitments. This is the sort of commitment that I seek to bring to the Nation with this national economic program.

I think it is impossible to underestimate the importance of any particular element although there are those who will. If we don't reduce the deficit, long-term interest rates don't go down, and the Government spends more of your money paying interest. If we don't cut spending, the deficit reduction package has no credibility. And besides that, a lot of this spending really needs to be cut. If we don't raise some revenues, we won't really cut the deficit as much as we should. And if we don't have some targeted investments, we will ignore the fact for the last 12 years, while other countries have been putting more into infrastructure, into technology, and into education and training, relative to the efforts of our competitors, we have been declining. And in absolute dollars, our Federal effort has declined in many critical areas.

So I would argue that we need a comprehensive approach. But let me be clear again: This administration understands clearly that the private sector is the central engine of economic growth. I have tried to put together a plan that will enable you to succeed.

I hope that this plan and this speech, frankly, is just the beginning of a continuing dialog between us. I don't accept the conventional wisdom that a President has about 6 months, and after that everybody's running for reelection and everything's over and the political climate takes over. The truth is that we have been going in a certain direction economically for 2 decades, and we have been in the grip of a partisan and interest-dominated gridlock for a long time, and it is not going to turn around overnight. And a lot of the things that I have to do here with our business cannot be done overnight. And so we need a dialog, a set of continuous changes.

If it is true that business has to manage change on a constant basis, surely it must also be true of Government. We can no longer afford the luxury of being told that the President has a year to work and after that everybody just waits around until the next election. That is a highly unproductive way to spend your money. And I believe we can do better.

Every one of you who's ever run any sort of enterprise knows that there comes a time in the life of any organization when the person in charge has to face facts and change or just let the thing drift into decline, maybe sudden loss. I sought this office because I became convinced that the classic American idea of progress, the idea that if we worked hard, played by the rules, made the necessary adjustments, we'd all do a little better, and we could certainly leave a better life to our children. And that idea had been imperiled by our failure to face many of the fundamental realities about which I have already spoken.

Our Government has responsibilities which have been too long neglected: to run a balanced economy, to invest in our people, to support business ability, to create wealth. In this city, people are very good at blaming one another for who did the wrong thing and pointing the finger at one another, but we've not been very good in the last few years at forgetting about blame and assuming responsibility.

Last Wednesday when I gave my State of the Union speech to Congress, I said to the Republicans and the Democrats in the audience, and I say to you, that I don't much care anymore whose fault our problems are. I do think we should all be willing to assume responsibility for improving the situation. And if it gets better, I could care less who gets credit for it. But the time has come to go to work.

I think that, to be fair, before I ask any of you to change anything, I need to set an example with the Federal Government. Let me begin by saying there are an awful lot of good people who work for you everyday in the Federal Government, people of astonishing dedication. And like any other business, there are a lot of people who are out there in the Federal Government who know a lot more than I do about what we could do to change it, to save you money, and to make it work. But as an institution, our system has become too large, too slow, too unresponsive.

The Government accepts, even when it's doing things that you would all agree with, is often locked into a style of management and outmoded priorities on spending and regulation and rulemaking that hamper even the best of intentions. Really, if this Government were a business, it would have gone under a long time ago. And again I say, not because of the people working here—most of the people who work for you decided to do this because they love their country, and they believe in public service—but because we have simply not been forced to undergo the discipline of reexamining how we do our business.

And so it is time to take stock of Government, not just from the point of view of cutting but from the point of view of how it can be made to work. We have to look through every program and ask if it works. I've said this before, but I'll say it to you in case any of you missed it, I felt enormous sympathy for all my predecessors when I walked into the Oval Office and found that I had Jimmy Carter's phone system operating with Lyndon Johnson's switchboard. [*Laughter*] It was a metaphor for how business is done: when you call into the White House, there's someone actually there picking up a wire and hooking it into the extension. [*Laughter*] And I might say, they're some of the most valuable people we have, because they do something that every modern organization needs: They can find anybody in the country when they need to. [*Laughter*] And we certainly need those operators to do that. But the point is that that really is a metaphor for the fact that Government often feels that it doesn't need to reexamine it.

I found that I could not have a conference call as the President of the United States in the Oval Office—[*Laughter*]—except for one: anybody in the central office who wanted to hear what I was saying could punch the lighted button and listen. [*Laughter*] We also found, interestingly enough, that while it cost money to change the technology on telephones, we were actually spending more money than we should be on monthly service charges and operating charges because we had an antiquated system. It was amazing.

Well, anyway, I think the Government has to set an example. So I have submitted to the Congress a budget that, in the coming fiscal year, will cut the White House staff by 25 percent below what it was when my predecessor left office, and not only cutting it but reorganizing it so that it will function better. We'll have a smaller drug policy office with more influence and more impact. We'll have an Economic Pol-

icy Council for only the second time in our country's history to go with the Domestic Policy Council and the National Security Council so that we can bring all the people who have an influence on economic policy together and focus on every aspect of it so that the right hand knows what the left hand is doing, and so that, hopefully, we can do a better job of anticipating the real consequences of any decisions which are made.

I've also asked the Congress to cancel next year's pay raise for Federal employees and to reduce their raises in each of the following 3 years, not because I want to hurt those people—they make this Government go—but because we have to tighten our belts before we ask Americans to tighten theirs.

I have submitted a budget that reduces the administrative costs of every Federal Agency in the next 4 years by 3 percent, 3 percent, 3 percent, and 5 percent, a total of 14; and which will reduce by attrition, not by firing, the Federal work payroll by 100,000, for savings in excess of $9 billion.

I was pleased the other night when I went up to the Congress to deliver my talk that the leadership told me they were going to reduce the staffs of Congress by the same amount that we reduced the administrative budget of the Federal Government, which is a real change and a welcome one.

We have also tried to reduce a lot of the executive perks to set an example. A lot of our Secretaries are now eating in the dining room with their employees, and they're finding they're learning more during the lunch hour about how we can improve the Agency than they could have in all the meetings that have been scheduled.

But these things are the tip of the iceberg. We have really got to find a way to reinvent the way the Government works, to bring modern technology and modern management practices to the workplace, to speed the flow of information, streamline decisions, and empower people at the grassroots level. I want you to be able to look at your National Government a couple of years from now as a model for customer service, not a bureaucratic monstrosity.

As an indication of that commitment, I have appointed as the Deputy Director of the Office of Management and Budget for Management, my friend Phil Lader, a remarkable businessman from South Carolina, who understands these concepts and will be able for the first time to make the management part of the Office of Management and Budget as important as the budget part. It's not just important to cut the spending; it's important that whatever you give us we spend right. And I think we can.

Let me just give you one example. We have contributed an inordinate amount of money to the Superfund to clean up sites which need to be cleaned up. The money is being used to pay lawyers' fees instead to clean up the sites. We might as well have just have been crass and said, "We don't care about the environmental consequences. We're not going to raise this money. We're not going to have a fund." Then we could pat ourselves on the back and say, "We're really concerned about this environmental problem of toxic waste sites, and so we raised the Superfund." Except the Fund's not being spent to clean up the sites. We're going to find a way to spend that money cleaning up pollution not paying for lawyers. That's the kind of thing we have to do if we're going to run this Government right.

There are also 150 very specific budget cuts in this budget. And to people who say to me, "Well, you ought to be able to find more, "I say, "that's right, but there's 150 I found in 4 weeks that haven't been there in 12 years." So I feel that we're doing pretty good.

I'm more than happy to do more. But since the first budget President Reagan submitted in 1981, which did have a lot of very specific budget cuts, this budget is the one that has the most specific cuts. Not saying to the Congress, "Well, let's put a cap on this or a lid on that and you all figure out how to distribute the pain," but saying, "I'll take responsibility for angering these constituencies by cutting this spending."

Can we do more? Of course we can. But we had to get off to a fast start. And I have made a good-faith offer to Republicans as well as Democrats, and to the Congress, and to people around the country to talk about how we can do that. It is very, very important.

The second thing I want to say to you, however, is that there is a big structural deficit which it is difficult to overcome by budget cuts alone, for this reason: Every year we grant cost-of-living increases to people on Social Security, and we should. There is a surplus in the Social Security tax fund which is being used to make the deficit look smaller. And that is very hard

on small business in America, by the way, that we finance so much of our Government through the payroll tax. We'll need those payroll taxes later, but not now.

We have increases in health care for the same reasons you do, that is, the cost of health care is rising faster than the rate of inflation. That drives up the cost of Medicare for the elderly and Medicaid for low-income people.

And then we have another problem aggravated by the flaws in our system, which is that every month in this country 100,000 Americans lose their health insurance and some of them are eligible for the Medicaid programs for the working poor. So our costs go up as private sector folks can't afford to cover people with health insurance anymore, and they get pushed onto the Government payroll. So those increases occur and will continue to occur until we reform structurally the health care system. And I'll come back to that in a moment. So those increases are there.

Then there are some programs that I think are quite central to our economy that require us to continue to fund them. Many are controversial with those who don't benefit from them, but I believe in some of them. I'll tell you a couple I believe in. I think that we should continue to fund the superconducting super collider because I think it's good science, even though it's expensive. We are going to create a lot of jobs in the future through investments in technology and science.

I believe that we cannot afford the space station design we have been operating on. And it hasn't been properly funded for years, and it's having huge costs overruns. But I think there should be a space station program that supports our shuttle program and supports the kinds of technological benefits that space has produced for the American economy here down on the ground over the last several years. And so I will support that, though we will not increase that spending as rapidly as it would take to support the old design. But we will do enough to keep all the people that are working, working in this area that I think is important. And that means we'll spend more money on that, and I think that's significant. But there still will be net budget cuts that are very deep, and I'm looking for more.

I also want to say that I intend to make reports to you on that, and before we get to any tax increases I want to know that the spending cuts are going to be there. I will not sign a tax increase without the spending cuts.

The tax problem, as you know, is highly progressive. And some say that it is so progressive that it will discourage people from reinvesting. I would just ask you to study the whole thing. We provide for the first time in the history of the country a permanent investment tax credit for small businesses for 90 percent of the employers who have 40 percent of the workers but create a majority of the jobs in this country.

We provided alternative minimum tax relief for the big capital-intensive businesses of this country, who have told us repeatedly that the alternative minimum tax treatment in the present Tax Code actually discourages people from making investments. We have provided some relief from the passive-loss provisions of the income Tax Code for people who are in the real estate business, because I think that has aggravated the condition not only of real estate but of some of our banks and contributed to the credit crunch. So I think there will be both direct benefits to real estate and indirect benefits to people who had to get bank financing by changing this passive-loss provision.

There are lots of other things in this bill which I think are important to the creation of jobs. So I ask you to look at it as a whole package and to recognize that we have to, again, move away from a tax system that is based too much on fixed-rate taxes, like excise and payroll taxes, more toward income taxes that have also offsetting incentives to invest. I believe that that is the proper direction to go.

I know there is also some controversy over the energy tax. And I'd like to talk about that for just a moment. If we are to find more revenue, I would rather not tax work and effort of working people. I would instead rather have some tax that operates on consumption and promotes energy efficiency in the development of alternative energy technologies. We have the lowest energy taxes in the world by far. And there was an enormous consensus among the deficit-reducing folks all over the country that there ought to be an energy tax but a big difference about what kind it ought to be.

There were those, principally in the East, who said we needed a huge gas tax. I can hear the groan from my folks up there in the gallery. It's tough on people who live in the West or who have to drive long distances to work where there's no public transport, where there's no

practical carpooling. It really could have an adverse impact on sectors of our transportation economy.

Then there were those who if you want only to clean up the environment, you should have a carbon tax. The problem is, that's pretty rough if you're from Pennsylvania or Ohio or West Virginia or someplace where coal is important to the economy and where you're already bearing the enormous burden of the enforcement of the Clean Air Act.

So this Btu tax, taxing the heat content of energy, seemed to be a fair way of spreading the burden in a limited way across all energy sources, in a way that would still do what I think needs to be done, which is to promote conservation and not undermine something else that I strongly support, which is the increased production of natural gas in America. It's our fuel. It's clean, and it will create enormous economic opportunities in the future.

I want to say again, I don't want to raise one penny of this money unless we have the spending cuts. Not a penny. And I am sure, after now almost 5 weeks in office, that there are more cuts coming. I can tell you I will find more. And I think we have gotten everybody in the National Government interested in finding more. And I encourage you to give us more. Nothing is off the table, except those things that reflect the fundamental interest of the American people.

But remember, we don't want to do anything that will further erode our investment in our children and their future in programs that are working. Indeed, we need to do more there. And we cannot afford to break the fragile bond of responsibility we have with elderly people who live on Social Security for all their income and who need Medicare for their health care. We can reduce further health care expenditures of the Government but only in the context of an overall resolution of the health care crisis.

The plan I have presented will reduce the deficit substantially and fairly. And if we do, it will mean lower interest rates. You can see that already by this historic low in long-term interest rates coming out today.

I also want to say, however, that in my judgment, there are some things we should invest in, not just the things I've mentioned for business: the permanent investment tax credit for small business, the targeted capital gains tax, the technology extension center, the manufacturing changes in the alternative minimum tax, the incremental investment tax credit that will be available to every business in America over the next couple of years. But there are also some things that we need to invest in our people. And I'd like just to mention one or two of them.

Another change in this tax system is one that I will hope you will all support, and it is the one that enables us to hold harmless to 40-plus percent of the taxpayers with incomes of $30,000 or less. This is a dramatic increase in the refundable earned-income tax credit for working people. This mechanism in this plan will enable us to say for the first time in the history of the country, "If you are a full-time worker with a child in your house, you will not live in poverty." Let me say why I think that is so important.

One of the things we have to deal with in America to make ourselves more productive is how we can reduce the volume of the large underclass we have: the people who are permanently trapped in poverty, the children living in the big cities. And we have to think of strategies to deal with that. Some of those things are things that I think you can do. I have proposed, for example, urban enterprise zones which give huge incentives for private sector investment in depressed areas.

But we have to break the psychology of poverty and dependence on the Government. I will come forward later this year with a welfare-reform proposal that will literally end welfare as we know it, will say we'll have education and training and child care and health care. After 2 years you've either got to go to work or do public service work to draw an income tax from the Government.

But consider this: We also need to build in incentives. You know as well as I do from the people you work with that an incentive system is better most of the time than a rulemaking system. So we can have a welfare rulemaking system, but you've got to change the incentives. How many working women are there in America today who barely make ends meet because of the cost of child care? I mean, an enormous number.

So what this refundable earned-income tax credit will do is to change the economic system. It will say: We are going to reward work. You put in your 40 hours; you've got a kid in the house. If we need to, we will refund money

through the tax system, but we're going to lift you above the poverty line so no one will ever have that as an excuse not to be a productive citizen. If everybody in this country were working, we wouldn't have half the problems that the Government wrestles with here all day, every day. And I hope you can support that.

Now, let me just make another couple of comments that relate to this. In the next few days we will be announcing some initiatives that we're going to take from a regulatory point of view to try to deal with the credit crunch, to try to make it possible for banks to loan money to businesses again, to try to release the energies for the old-fashioned character of small business loans, to try to reduce the fear that a lot of banks have that if they make sensible loans, the Government will come down on them.

I think that the improvement in the books that will come from changing the passive-loss provision, plus the regulatory changes we make, will really make a dent in this credit crunch problem, especially in the areas of our country where it has been so profound. And if it isn't, you let me know about it in a few months, and we'll do something else. We have got to deal with this problem for small business to grow again.

Now, let me talk just very briefly about what I think will become very quickly a controversial part of this program. There will be those who want to cut spending and wish we didn't have to raise any taxes, who will say, "You wouldn't have to raise so many taxes if you didn't spend any new money on anything." And that is absolutely true. I admit that is absolutely true. I want you to know what I propose to spend new money on and why, in addition to the tax incentives I've already discussed.

First of all, I want to increase research and development in new technologies that will create new jobs and new economic opportunities, dramatically. Not only by making the research and experimentation tax credit permanent, but by increasing commercial R&D by more than we reduce defense R&D, and by emphasizing dual-use technologies in defense research and development.

It is killing me to look at the numbers when you compare the percentage of our income we're spending on research and development in America compared to our competitors. Five years, 10 years, 20 years from now, that means more high-wage jobs somewhere else and fewer high-wage jobs here. And we cannot tolerate it. We must again achieve competitive levels of R&D, and that is a worthy expenditure of your tax money. We have good people who will do that right and spend it efficiently, and I would hope you would support it.

There is no way the private sector can equal the aggregate efforts in Germany, Japan, or any other rich country, provided there by enormous public sector investment to support the private sector. So I hope you'll be for that.

Secondly, I think we have to invest more in our infrastructure, in our roads, our bridges, our airports, in high-speed rail, in water projects, in sewer projects, in environmental cleanup. We are again spending a much lower percentage of our income on that than all of our major competitors. And that bears a direct relationship to productivity, to wealth generation, and to the cost of doing business in the private sector. So we propose to fully fund the surface transportation act and to do a lot of things in this area.

Third, we propose to really invest some money in targeted people investments that will increase productivity. Let me just mention three or four. Number one, we want to spend some new money to set up a network that will permit us to immunize every child in America by the age of two for preventable childhood diseases. For every dollar we spend on that today, we will save $10 in the future in preventable diseases. We are dangerously at risk of new outbreaks of diseases because our immunization levels have fallen so low.

Most of the controversy you've seen in the press is about the price of vaccines, and that's a legitimate issue. But it is also true that we don't have the delivery network in this country we need. And as a result, we have the appalling statistic that in America, which produces vaccines for the world, we have the third-lowest immunization rate in this hemisphere. Only Bolivia and Haiti are lower. It is unconscionable. We can't justify it. For a little bit of money today we can save big bucks tomorrow.

Secondly, we ought to fully fund the Head Start program, because it is a proven success that will save us $3 tomorrow for every dollar we spend today.

Those are among the things that I think we should do. Let me just mention two others. We ought to have an apprenticeship program in America that guarantees every high school graduate access to 2 years of further quality education in the workplace, in a community college, in a vocational institution. The Federal Government's responsibility here is basically to help States in the private sector create networks and to fill the funding gap. For next to no money we could bring our 2-year education program up to where it is universally accessible to all Americans and it is at a level of quality comparable to our competitors. We are not there today. For not very much money, we can do that.

The next thing I think we really ought to do is to open the doors to college education to all Americans. Not just open them, but keep them open. The college drop-out rate today is two and a half times the high school drop-out rate. And one reason is that a college education is about the only thing that increased more rapidly than health care costs in the 1980's.

Now, all of you need to think about this as this is something you can do that I can't since all these colleges—none of them are Federal institutions. Something needs to be done to contain the rising costs of those colleges. But in the meantime, we need to make sure that young Americans are not dropping out just because they can't afford to go.

The student loan program today is wildly expensive. It costs $4 billion a year, $3 billion in defaulted loans alone. And what we need to do is to set up an income-contingent repayment plan so everybody can pay back as a percentage of their income, which will reduce the incentive to default; really stiffen the collection measures, including involving the IRS in it. I'm tired of people making money and defaulting on their loans; that's not right. But we also should make available the opportunity for many young Americans to pay back their student loans by serving their country, by going home and working as teachers or police officers, or doing things that need to be done in the community.

We can rescue a lot of these kids out of inner cities by letting them work before they go to college and put in time in building up credits so that they then turn their loans into scholarships before they even go. These are things that ought to be done.

You know, when President Kennedy started the Peace Corps, it shaped the imagination of a whole generation. We need a peace corps here at home to deal with our problems here at home, and it needs to be much bigger than the Peace Corps ever was.

Finally, let me just make this point: If we cut spending, increase revenues, target investments, we'll have a Government that will go in the right direction for the next 4 years with real discipline. If you want to get to the end of the decade with a healthy American economy, we have to do something else. We've got to reform the health care system.

In 5 years, projected Government expenditures on health care would go from $210 billion to $350 billion, a two-thirds increase, annualized increase of 12 percent per year. We are already spending, as of the end of 1992, 14 percent of our gross domestic product on health care. No other nation in the world except Canada is over nine, and they're just barely over nine. And our health indicators are not all that much better. In fact, they're quite worse in some areas.

Now, this is not a simple problem. This is the most complex issue with which I have ever tried to come to grips. But one thing is pretty clear: If present spending trends continue, we'll be bumping 20 percent of GDP by the end of the decade, and you can forget about our being competitive in manufacturing.

At our economic conference in Little Rock, Red Poling, the chairman of Ford Motor Company, pointed out how Ford's health care costs had risen by 800 percent in the last 20 years, and now they spend as much on health care for workers as on steel for cars. Almost $1,100 of the price of each American car is in health care. Our competitors in Japan have only $550 in a car; hard to be price competitive and make money.

Small businesses are hit even harder by health care costs. And for many self-employed people and farmers, it's impossible to get health care. As I said earlier, 100,000 Americans a month are losing their health insurance. Seventy percent of the small businesses in this country are still providing health care to their employees, but they're hurt very badly by insurance-rating practices in most States. And workers are terrorized by the fact that if they or someone in their family has ever been sick, they have a preexisting condition which locks them into a job.

I had dinner the other night with a high school friend of my wife who is a wonderful small business guy with four employees. And one of his employees just had a child with Down's syndrome. And he told me, he said,

"You know, that guy and I, we're partners for life now." And he said, "He really can do better. He's a gifted person. I want him to be able to go on and move, and he can't."

And more and more businesses are having to give up their health insurance every year or run the co-pay so high they might as well be giving up on it. And that, as I said earlier, is driving some people back down into the Federal Government's and the State government's health care system.

What I want to do is to find a way to preserve what is best about American health care—the right to choose your doctor, the technology that we have—and stop the incredible waste on paperwork, which means that clerical workers are being hired at 4 times the rate of health care providers in hospitals and doctors' offices, on unnecessary technology, on the absence of preventive and primary care, on all the things that we know that are wrong.

And some time in the next several weeks, within 100 days after the time I took office, we'll be presenting a plan to the Congress and the American people to deal with that. But I want to be up-front about this. The economic plan I have presented will bring that debt down for 4 years. If we don't deal with the health care crisis, it's going to turn around and go right back up in the next 4 years, just like your costs are going to.

We have got to face this. Every other advanced country in the world has devised some system which works better than ours does to keep costs closer to inflation while providing a basic package of benefits to all Americans. We cannot fix this economy over the long run unless we do that. It is inhumane. It is also very bad business to let the status quo persist.

Let me close just by saying that if every American looks at my proposal in terms of what is best for him or her, at least one-third of it will seem unattractive. That is, if you're an upper-income person who has to pay the income taxes, you would say, "Give me the budget cuts and don't increase spending." Unless you're in a technology-related business in which you might say, "Give me the budget cuts and the new investments, but forget about the tax increases." Or if you're an educator, you might say, "Fund Head Start." A middle-class person might say, "Tax the rich and spend the money on new jobs. Cut the budget, but forget about the energy tax." A lower-income person might say, "Tax the wealthy. Give me the new spending, but forget about the budget cuts."

In other words, if everybody looks at this just through the prism of how it will immediately affect you, it's a nonstarter, because there's no way you can bat three for three. We can't get there.

And that's why I say to all of you what I have asked the American people to do; I invite your efforts to improve this, to say what's wrong with it, to say how we can make it better. That's fine. But ask the question, not just what's in it for me, but what's in it for us. This country has got to change. We know we cannot stay on the present course. We know we cannot stay on the present course.

We also know if we look ahead to the future that the next 20 years could be the best years this country ever had. But we've got to increase productivity. We've got to increase job generation. We've got to increase income, and we've got to increase our ability to rely on all the American people. We do not have a person to waste. I believe this program achieves those objectives, and I ask for your support.

Thank you very much, and God bless you.

NOTE: The President spoke at 11:15 a.m. at DAR Constitution Hall. In his remarks, he referred to U.S. Chamber of Commerce officers Ivan Gorr, chairman of the board; Richard Lesher, president; and William Marcil, vice chairman of the board.

Exchange With Reporters Prior to Discussions With United Nations Secretary-General Boutros Boutros-Ghali
February 23, 1993

Bosnia

Q. Mr. President, is an airdrop enough to relieve the suffering? Will that do the job of getting food to people?

The President. Well, if we can reach an agreement, it will help, I think.

Q. How close are you to an agreement, Mr. President?

The President. I don't know. We can't talk until you leave. [*Laughter*]

Q. Do you think that there is some risk, though, of this being the first step to an engagement that we won't be able to get out of?

The President. Not necessarily, no. Not at all.

Q. Why not?

The President. Because what we're discussing is very different. It has no combat connotations whatever, and it's purely humanitarian and quite limited.

Q. Isn't there a risk of people being shot at by antiaircraft artillery?

The President. Well, if we do it, we'll have an announcement that deals with that. We think the risks are quite small.

NOTE: The exchange began at 4:10 p.m. in the Oval Office at the White House.

Exchange With Reporters Prior to Discussions With Prime Minister John Major of the United Kingdom
February 24, 1993

Bosnia

Q. Mr. President, are you going to make an announcement on Bosnia today? On the airdrop?

The President. I don't think we'll have a final announcement today. But the Prime Minister

and I certainly are going to discuss that along with a number of other things.

Q. Mr. Prime Minister, are you concerned that American airdrops might endanger British troops on the ground, put them subject to Serbian——

Prime Minister Major. No, I'm not remotely concerned about that. We'll discuss the airdrops. I think, as a humanitarian initiative that's very welcome. And it'll have our support. I don't think it is going to endanger British troops.

Q. What is holding you up, Mr. President, in your decision?

The President. Just going through the procedures we have to go through to discuss this with our allies.

News Conference

Q. When are you going to announce a press conference?

The President. You know, I didn't realize it had been so long since I had one. I really didn't, Helen [Helen Thomas, United Press International], until you mentioned it the other day. I need to give you one. I'll get——

Q. When?

The President. I'm going to take it up with our folks. I didn't even know it had been a long time, since I answer these questions all the time.

The Vice President. It seems like there is a press conference every day.

Q. That's not a press conference.

The Vice President. Oh, I know. I know.

The President. I'll do better on that.

Q. You promise?

[*At this point, one group of reporters left the room, and another group entered.*]

Prime Minister Mulroney of Canada

Q. Do you gentlemen have anything to say about Brian Mulroney in his resignation today?

The President. I wish him well. I talked to him. We had a nice visit. And I don't think that I can add anything to the statement that was made. But I was very appreciative of the conversation we had, and I wish him well.

United Kingdom-U.S. Relations

Q. Can we ask how the special relationship is, Mr. President?

The President. Excuse me?

Q. Can we ask how the special relationship between the U.S. and Britain is?

The President. Absolutely.

Prime Minister Major. You have got the British press. [*Laughter*]

The President. Absolutely. It's special to me personally, and it's special to the United States, and I think it will be as long as I'm sitting here in this office.

NOTE: The exchange began at 3:10 p.m. in the Oval Office at the White House.

The President's News Conference With Prime Minister John Major of the United Kingdom
February 24, 1993

The President. Good afternoon, ladies and gentlemen. I want to formally welcome Prime Minister Major to the White House and to the United States. We are delighted to have him here. As I'm sure you know, he has already met earlier today with people on the Hill and with members of my Cabinet. We have just finished the first of two meetings. We talked for about an hour, and then this evening we'll have a working dinner.

About the conversations we've had so far, I'd just like to make two points. First, we covered a wide range of topics. We talked about Bosnia, as you might imagine we would. We talked about the Middle East. And then the rest of our time was spent virtually exclusively talking about economic matters, about the upcoming meeting of the G-7; about the importance of trying to get an agreement under GATT and my commitment to that; about the absolute necessity of the United States, Europe, and Japan working together during this difficult time to try to prevent a contraction of the global economy and instead to hopefully promote growth, not only here at home but throughout the world. And we talked about that at some considerable detail.

The Prime Minister, as you know, has been in office a lot longer than I have. And I asked him for his advice about a number of things and his opinion about others. And we had a very, very good meeting. And I'm looking forward to our dinner tonight.

A second point I would like to make is to reaffirm something that some of you asked me during the photo op, and that is whether the United States will continue to have a very special relationship with Great Britain. The answer to that from my point of view is an unqualified yes. I think that only two Presidents ever lived in England. I think I'm one of only two. There may have been more somewhere in the past centuries. But this is a very important relationship to me, and I think it's off to a very good start. And I would like to say again how much I appreciate the candor with which the Prime Minister has approached the issues, with which we've discussed our mutual interests.

Mr. Prime Minister.

Prime Minister Major. Mr. President, firstly, thank you for your welcome today. And I've found our meeting extremely useful, and I look forward to continuing it this evening. And I certainly had some very useful meetings this morning on the Hill and with other members of your Cabinet earlier this morning, with Lloyd Bentsen, and of course over lunch as well with some of your colleagues.

It's nice, having had a number of telephone conversations over the last few months, to actually see a face across the table rather than just hear a voice across the phone. And I look forward to continuing that dialog this evening.

You set out some of the things that we were able to discuss over the last hour or so. I was particularly pleased we were able to reach such a meeting of minds on the importance of reaching an agreement to the Uruguay round as speedily as possible. I think we share the view that for a raft of reasons it's important to get a satisfactory and fair agreement to the GATT round, not just because of the impetus that will give to trade growth and hopefully to prosperity and job growth as well but also because of the very remarkable advantage that will give not just to the industrialized but to the nonindustrialized world with the many difficulties that are faced economically at the moment. So I was particularly pleased at our meeting of minds on that particular subject.

We found also a complete agreement about the need for the Security Council resolutions that have been imposed in respect to Iraq to be fully met and to be fully honored in the future. I had the pleasure of being able to welcome the President's initiative, humanitarian airdrops in Bosnia. The United Kingdom—we've got a number of thousands of troops actually delivering humanitarian aid in central Bosnia. They've been doing that for some time. I think as a result of their activities, many people who otherwise might not have lived through this winter have done. And I think this new initiative by the President is thoroughly welcome. So it's been a very worthwhile and a very enjoyable meeting thus far, and I look forward to continuing it this evening.

The President. Thank you.

Northern Ireland

Q. Mr. President, do you still want a U.S. envoy—[*inaudible*]—Northern Ireland——

The President. Well, let me answer the first question. If the United States can in some way make a constructive contribution to a political settlement, of course, we'd be interested in doing that. But that is not a subject we have discussed in any way so far. And I think I'd rather wait to make further comments until after we have a chance to discuss it.

As far as the campaign, the campaign is over. You're a good one to ask that question, since you know that compared to previous campaigns I've been in, this was just sort of another day at the office. And once you achieve the responsibilities of office, that's what you have to do. I told the Prime Minister today that I was just grateful that I got through this whole campaign with most of my time in England still classified. [*Laughter*]

Bosnia

Q. [*Inaudible*]—on Bosnia. I'd like to ask both you and the Prime Minister, what do you think can be accomplished in the airdrops, since many in the military believe that it will not be terribly effective or efficient? And what other steps do you think need to be taken, military steps, in particular, such as some that were discussed during the campaign, in order to inflict enough pressure on the Serbs?

The President. Let me deal with the airdrops first. General Powell came over here last weekend, and we talked for a very extended period of time about this operation and about how we can maximize the safety to United States pilots and other personnel on the planes who'd be involved in this and minimize the prospect that any humanitarian relief operation could be drawn into the politics and the military operations of this area.

We know that if we are high enough to virtually assure the complete safety of the people who will participate in the airlift, that a percentage of the packages we drop will be outside the more or less half-mile circle that we would be trying to hit. We also know that if we leaflet the area in advance, if we notify the people about what we're dropping and how to use the medicine and what kind of food will be there, to whatever extent people need it, they'll be on the lookout for it. And if they have to walk a mile instead of a half-mile for it, we think they will. So we believe that, A, there is a need in some of the remote areas, and B, we can do this with quite an effective but safe mission.

Now, insofar as other actions, I think there are a number of things that we're looking at. I'm encouraged by the United Nations interest in the war crimes issue. I'm encouraged by the conversation the Prime Minister and I had about the importance of trying to make the sanctions that are now in force actively be more effective.

But I would remind you that our policy is that we want to try to have a good faith in negotiations with all the parties there. We are committed to doing what we can to encourage the Bosnians to engage in negotiations within the Vance-Owen framework. And President Yeltsin has been very forthcoming on his part in trying to help get the negotiations back on track, too.

So, I think we should look at it just from that point of view. It would be a great mistake to read this humanitarian relief operation as some initial foray toward a wider military role.

Prime Minister Major. Can I just add something to that, as you requested. We're able, at the moment, to deliver a substantial amount of aid in central Bosnia by land. But the natural terrain of Bosnia, as a whole, means that isn't practicable for a raft of reasons, not least geographical reasons, at the moment in all parts of Bosnia. I think, therefore, you do have to look at imaginative ways of actually getting food aid and medicine aid through. And I think the prospect that the President is exploring is an imaginative one, and I hope it will prove successful. There are a number of logistics to be worked out.

On sanctions, one of the things we have been discussing in the last half an hour or so is the prospects of enhanced sanctions, and I think there clearly are opportunities there that we'll need to examine.

Q. Such as?

Prime Minister Major. Well, I think we can improve the sanctions over the Danube, for example. I don't think they're being enforced very effectively.

Russia

Q. I would like to direct my question to both of you. Do you think that Yeltsin, President Yeltsin, is so politically weakened that his days are numbered? Also, what can the U.S. and the allies do to prop him up, to prevent another Communist takeover that could lead to another cold war? And are you going to meet President Yeltsin in March at any point?

Prime Minister Major. I don't think President Yeltsin is weakened by his present conflict to the extent that he's not going to continue. Clearly there are difficulties in the disputes he's had with Congress and, in particular, the Speaker. But I expect President Yeltsin to be there and to continue. I think he's the best hope for the Russians, and I think the policies and the movements towards reform that he has in mind and continues to have in mind are the right ways forward.

I think there are two things we can do to help Russia in general and President Yeltsin. One is the economic assistance that's been provided, and there's a great deal of discussion to be had about whether we're directing that in the right way and in the right volume.

And secondly, I think also there's the political messages of support to the reformers and to the reform policies, personified at the moment in the person of President Yeltsin. But the underlying purpose of the assistance is to assist the reformers and to assist the reform policies in Russia. I think we ought to give them political support as well as the practical and economic support that we've been giving them.

The President. I believe that President Yeltsin has not been paralyzed by what's happened. I support him and his role and what he's trying to do. I have not established a definite date for a meeting with him yet, but I do hope to meet with him soon personally.

I know he's having some trouble with his Congress, but that's part of being in a democratic society with an elected President separate from the Congress. He may just be learning what it's like in our system. I don't want to minimize that, but I think it is a grave error to assume that he cannot continue and do well. I believe he can.

And I think that in terms of what we ought to be doing about it, I think the Prime Minister has pretty well laid out the kind of political and economic support we ought to be giving. But let me say that as all of you know, I have placed a great priority on this. The State Department will now have an ambassador at large whose job it is to coordinate a response not only to Russia but to all the Republics of the former Soviet Union. And we have a very distinguished American, Thomas Pickering, nominated to be our Ambassador to Moscow. We are putting a lot of effort into trying to support democracy and trying to support economic recovery there.

Multilateral Trade Negotiations

Q. [*Inaudible*]—I don't have a word count, sir, but it's interesting that Prime Minister Major here may have said more about the importance of the Uruguay round than you have here in the White House. I wonder, do you take away from your meeting with him any renewed sense of the importance of that round, and if so, how you plan now to approach it?

The President. Well, we're going to ask for an extension of fast track authority. And we're going to really put a real effort into a successful conclusion of the round. I advocated that in 1991 at the beginning of my race for President, and I still feel very strongly that it's important.

I think if you look at the press response around the world to the economic plan I've presented to Congress, it's been very positive because our trading partners have been asking us for years to make a real effort to reduce the debt. And so we're doing that. And I think that sparks hope not only here at home but around the world. And I think if we were to successfully conclude the Uruguay round, that would also spark hope that we will be expanding trade on terms that are fair to everyone. So I'm very hopeful that we can get a trade agreement.

Northern Ireland

Q. Did you raise today the question of human rights in Northern Ireland, and did you get to discuss it with him——

The President. We haven't discussed Northern Ireland at all. And after we do, I'll be happy to answer your questions.

Bosnia

Q. Mr. Prime Minister, you expressed earlier—said that you are not remotely concerned about the British troops, that they will be in any danger because—[*inaudible*]—defense against these deliveries, and the President has said—[*inaudible*]—slight risk. And I'm wondering, beyond your saying you have this policy, if both of you could give some idea of why you sound so confident there will be no attempts to stop this—[*inaudible*]. There's been a lot of effort to block it so far.

The President. Well, all I can tell you is General Powell has been—let me answer, and then he'll answer—has been asked to design the mission in such a way that we would minimize risk to our folks. And we have obviously engaged in an extensive consultation, which is not over. Helen's [Helen Thomas, United Press International] been asking me every day when I was ready to make this announcement. The consultations aren't over. And one of the things that we want, we want everybody to know that this is a humanitarian mission, that we're prepared to help anybody who needs the food and medicine. And we want the broadest possible support for this. And we want all the people on the ground in the various factions to know that this is not a political issue with us. We're very encouraged by the responses we've gotten so far to all the elements with whom we have discussed this plan. That's all I can tell you.

Q. Mr. Prime Minister, could you answer, please?

Prime Minister Major. I don't think there's a great deal to add to it. As I indicated earlier, there's a twin-track approach. We're providing aid by land. The President has in mind aid delivered by air to areas where we can't reach it by land. I've no reason to suppose that that is going to put at risk the lives of the British soldiers in central Bosnia.

Q. But you're in an area where they have a fighter capability and an antiaircraft weapon. If they don't want this material to be delivered, they have to use that.

Prime Minister Major. Well, you asked the question. I've given you the judgment I make.

Middle East Peace Talks

Q. Mr. President, you said you discussed the Middle East. Did you reach any conclusion, and do you favor returning to the peace talks even if the Palestinians do not?

The President. We talked mostly about the importance of adhering to the United Nations resolutions as they apply to Iraq and the aftermath of the Gulf war and about our general support for the peace process continuing. We didn't deal with that issue, and I think I ought to wait until the Secretary of State returns from his mission before I discuss it further.

Bosnia

Q. You talk about consultations on Bosnia. Is there any realistic expectations at this point that any other country except for the United States will be involved in this airdrop?

The President. Yes, we might have some other countries involved in it. I don't think it would be—I believe the Prime Minister made his statement. I think he's done his part. His troops are on the ground there. But I think there is a chance that we will have support from other nations.

Q. [*Inaudible*]—ask Great Britain to participate in the airdrop as well?

The President. No.

Q. [*Inaudible*]—question to both leaders. Do you think that the current Vance-Owen map forms the fair basis for a settlement of the crisis in the former Yugoslavia?

Prime Minister Major. Well, that's the matter that has to be negotiated between the parties. And I don't think I'm going to express a view on whether that is the right map. I think the process of seeking a negotiated settlement and trying to reach by agreement between the three parties, an agreement on the map that will enable a political settlement to be reached is the right way. But I don't think it's for me to judge whether the map is right.

Clearly, the views of the participants at the moment is that the map isn't right. But that is the purpose of negotiations. That is why I was delighted to hear this morning that Karadzic and Izetbegovic will be joining talks again with Boban so that they can actually talk to Cy Vance and David Owen and see if they can reach an agreement. The first prize is clearly an agreement that is reached voluntarily and willingly and as speedily as possible.

The President. The only thing I would say, just to add to that, is that I agree with what the Prime Minister has said. As you know, the United States feels very strongly that this agreement must be just that, an agreement that must not be shoved down the throat of the Bosnians or anyone else if it's going to work. We also feel strongly that all the parties should negotiate in good faith.

And therefore, I agree with what he said about the map. I would make this further point: The United States has made it clear in our statement of policy that if an agreement is reached in good faith, that we would be prepared to be part of a NATO or United Nations effort to monitor or support the agreement, and that map would be difficult to monitor and support, I think.

But I think we're going to have to—before we make any final judgments, we need to give the parties a chance to reach their accord.

Spending Cuts

Q. Mr. President, on—[*inaudible*]—economics, you indicated you will find more spending cuts. Will you give a sense of when? And are you really talking about a new round of cuts or just——

The President. Oh well, what I said was, I have invited the Members of the Congress to present them to me and instructed our people to continue to look for them. And I presume as we define things that we're willing to put on the table, we will continue to do it. We don't have any orchestrated theory about how to do that now. But I'd be surprised if there aren't some more coming.

Airbus

Q. Mr. Prime Minister, were you disappointed or taken aback by what the President said the other day about the airbus, and were you reassured by your conversations today?

Prime Minister Major. There's an agreement over the degree of subsidies for projects like airbus. And that agreement continues into July, and I think there is no proposition in what the President said to change that particular agreement.

Northern Ireland

Q. Mr. President, you said you may discuss Northern Ireland this evening. Would you expect to discuss both the—[*inaudible*]—issue and the human rights issue? And do you share the view expressed by some Members of Congress, Senators and Representatives, that there are abuses to human rights in Northern Ireland that need to be addressed? And perhaps the Prime Minister would like to address that allegation.

Prime Minister Major. Well, I'll address that point first. The real abuse of human rights in Northern Ireland is the abuse of human rights of people who find bombs in shopping malls when they're going about their ordinary, everyday business. I think that is the abuse of human rights that is overwhelmingly the concern of everybody in Northern Ireland on both sides of the sectarian divide.

Over the past 2 or 3 years, the British Government with the Taoiseach and with the political parties in Northern Ireland, have been engaged on talks to try and find a political settlement to a problem that has existed in Northern Ireland for generations. We are seeking that agreement. Those talks, I believe it is fair to say, have made more progress than most people believed was possible.

Talks came to a halt with the general election in the Republic of Ireland and the forthcoming local elections in Northern Ireland. But it is the policy of my government to resume those talks, to resume those talks with all the parties in Northern Ireland and try and reach a satisfactory political settlement and remove many of the disputes and hatreds that have existed for generations.

Those disputes and hatreds are worsened by violence, whether it is the IRA violence or whether it is the response to IRA violence which has also been prevalent over the last year or so. I condemn both unreservedly and without any distinction.

Q. Mr. President—[*inaudible*]—respond to that.

The President. I believe that obviously there has to be a political solution there, or there will be no solution at all, and that the human rights issues will have to be addressed in that context. Whether the United States can play any sort of constructive role is something that we want to discuss later this evening.

Press Secretary Myers. Last question.

Economic Program

Q. Mr. President, here just one week after your speech announcing your budget and economic plan, Senator Bob Dole is pronouncing it in trouble. What's your read on that, and do you think this is the start of a war of words that's going to slow down the whole process?

The President. Well, I think you have to ex-

pect that there would be some trouble. And the Senate Minority Leader can say that. But he was here during the last 12 years when other Presidents and the Congress quadrupled the national debt. I'm trying to do something about it and turn it around and go in the opposite direction. The surveys show that a big majority of the American people support my initiative. The response from people and governments around the world, it's been almost uniformly positive that America's trying to change the nature of its economic policy, reduce its debt, increase investment in high growth items. And I never expected this to be easy. This is a fundamental change. I don't expect it to be easy. But I hope that I'll be working with Senator Dole and with others to bring it to a successful conclusion.

Q. Can I follow up on that, Mr. President?

Prime Minister Mulroney of Canada

Q. [*Inaudible*]—Canada? Have you spoken to the Prime Minister?

The President. Yes, I spoke to the Prime Minister of Canada. We had a very nice conversation, which was mostly personal. And I thanked him for his kindness to me. And he assured me that his country would continue to work with me and that he would personally until his tenure in office was over. I wish him well. He seemed to be a person who had worked through this and was very much at peace with himself today.

Prime Minister Major. Can I just answer that point as well? I regard Brian as an old friend and a good friend. I shall miss him. He's been a very good friend to the United Kingdom and a very good friend to the Commonwealth. So I'm sad to hear of his decision today. It must be his decision. I wish him well in the future, and I look forward to seeing him in the United Kingdom in a few weeks' time.

Northern Ireland

Q. Mr. Prime Minister, do you think there's any constructive role the United States can play in solving the Northern Ireland problem?

Prime Minister Major. I think from time to time distinguished visitors from the United States in Northern Ireland have come back to the United States, and they have actually explained the remarkable changes that have taken part in Belfast. There was a delegation that was there recently. And the reality is that anyone who knew the place 10 years ago and knows the place today will see there is an absolute and total sea change. And I think the fact that there is a great knowledge about the willful peace amongst people in Northern Ireland and especially the ordinary people of Northern Ireland of both sides of the sectarian divide, the more that is understood, the better. And what is actually needed in Northern Ireland to help speed that is more understanding of the process, more support for the talks, more investment for job creation, and less money to fund terrorism.

And the more people know about that, the nearer we come to a solution.

Press Secretary Myers. Thank you.

NOTE: The President's fourth news conference began at 4:32 p.m. in the East Room at the White House. In his remarks, the Prime Minister referred to Lord David Owen and Cyrus Vance, Cochairmen of the International Conference on the former Yugoslavia; Alija Izetbegovic, President, Republic of Bosnia-Herzegovina; Radovan Karadzic, Bosnian Serb leader; and Mate Boban, Bosnian Croat leader.

Statement on the Planned Resignation of Prime Minister Brian Mulroney of Canada
February 24, 1993

Prime Minister Mulroney and I had a good conversation following his announcement that he is stepping down as Prime Minister of Canada. Prime Minister Mulroney has been a good friend and partner of the United States, and I wish him well. The Free Trade Agreement, the NAFTA, and Canada's voice in helping to move the world into a more hopeful era are all testimony to his leadership and courage.

It was a pleasure to meet with the Prime Minister earlier this month and to speak with him several times since my election. I greatly appreciated the Prime Minister's insight and wise counsel in tackling the common challenges of promoting world economic growth and peace. My meeting with him reinforced my conviction that Canadian engagement in world affairs remains as vital as ever. That our meeting was my first as President underscores the close rela-tionship between our two countries. Our enduring friendship is based on the common vision we share of peace and democratic principles. From peacekeepers in Bosnia and Somalia to partnership in the G–7 and in NATO, Canada has been a true global ally. Both our people benefit from our important trading relationship, with $200 billion in goods and services alone exchanged each year.

Our steadfast relationship with Canada is an indispensable element in the essential continuity of American foreign policy. As the Prime Minister and the people of Canada prepare for the road ahead, I want them to know that the United States is and will remain their friend and partner. Our cooperation will continue to grow in the years ahead.

Remarks to Business and Labor Leaders and an Exchange With Reporters on the Economic Program
February 25, 1993

The President. Thank you very much. To all the business and the labor leaders who are here, and to Representative Clayton and the many Members of the House whom she represents so ably. Let me begin with a simple thank you to all of you for your support of our common efforts to turn our country around and put our Nation on the right track.

For too long we have seen business and labor divided over more issues than we see them united on. Part of that has been occasioned by the incredible difficulties of our economy. When people believe there is a shrinking pie, they're more likely to be fighting over that. Part of that has been occasioned by the fact that we have not been on a great national journey together in which we could all feel that we were a part, making our equal contributions, reaping our equal rewards.

I'm very encouraged by the business-labor partnership that we see manifested here today, by the fact that it represents a commitment to ending gridlock and to beginning change, and deeply impressed by the letter which Representative Clayton has brought here today by the people whom I think in many ways are most representatives of the American people: this new big class of freshmen Congress men and women who are out there, just as Vice President Gore and I were last year, criss-crossing the country in a beginning effort, listening to people and their concerns and their hopes. So I'm very, very happy about that.

If I might, I'd like to close just by emphasizing three or four of the critical elements of this economic plan and why I think they are worthy of the support of this distinguished group of Americans. Everyone knows we have to bring the deficit down; it has become the dominant fact of all the budgeting of the Federal Government. But there are those who say, "Well, how can you do that. You're just coming out of a recession, and traditional economic theory holds that the last thing you want to do is to slow down a recovery by closing a deficit."

That is, ever since the Depression, our country has operated on an economic theory that said when times were slow, there should be more Government spending; when times were great, then you could bring our accounts into balance. The problem is that for more than 20 years we have been building in a structural deficit into our Government, one that robbed the National Government of that flexibility, the flexibility to tighten up in good times to slow down inflation, and to invest more in bad times to put people back to work.

And our strategy now, I think, is actually supporting an economic recovery in bringing this deficit down because you can see the decline in long-term interest rates which means that borrowing is cheaper and which means that mil-lions of Americans in their personal capacities and as business persons are going to refinance their debt which will free up cash to be reinvested in economic growth. So I believe this strategy is expansionary.

I also would make a couple of other points if I might. We are changing fundamentally the direction of Government spending itself, moving away from spending for consumption towards spending a higher percentage of the people's tax dollars on investment. It is simply not true that all Government spending is equal. Some investment will have a much bigger reward in terms of jobs and incomes than spending more money on the same program.

Finally, we are looking at ways to basically make the Government itself work in a very different and more efficient way. One of them has already been alluded to by Kathryn Thompson. We will be announcing in the near future some efforts by this administration to ease the credit crunch on small business. We are also trying to change the way the Government itself operates and the regulatory framework to do things that will achieve objectives in a better way.

We believe we can promote a clean environment and economic growth with the right kind of regulatory and investment climate. We believe by changing the way the Government itself does business, we can give the American people a much leaner Government. We think that the White House staff cuts and the reorganization are simply an example of what we can do throughout the Government, given time.

So I appreciate the support for this program. And let me reiterate, I am not simply interested in raising more revenues. I don't want new taxes unless we're going to have spending cuts, unless we are going to change the nature of Government spending toward more investment, and unless we're going to change the way the Government itself operates.

This is a whole program that will fundamentally give us an end to gridlock and the change we need. And I thank these people who are here. They are reflective of the kind of unity we need in America to move this country forward. Thank you very much.

Q. How committed, sir, are you to the stimulus part of your package? It's now been delayed another month, perhaps; your budget is not even going up until April 5th. A lot of economists say that if it gets delayed much longer, it won't even help the economy. Only one of the preceding speakers even mentioned this stimulus package. Just how important is this?

The President. Yes, that's not true. At least one of them did mention it first. And secondly, I think it is quite important. I think it would be a big mistake—let me just give you—it will do what it's designed to do later in time for everything except those things that have to be in place this summer. And I'm hoping that we can get the kind of—a lot of the Members of Congress are looking for a way to demonstrate to the country that they don't want to raise more taxes without cutting spending. And we're working on giving them an opportunity to do that. I agree with that. I think that's fine.

But there are some things that are time-sensitive in this stimulus package. The most obvious and apparent one is the summer jobs program. Nearly every person I know, including an enormous number of business people who are in and around cities like Los Angeles or Chicago or New York or other cities, believe that the prospect of being able to provide nearly 700,000 summer jobs in a framework in which we can then get business people together to work to provide more jobs—and one of the people here on this platform today has already told me that he wanted to get involved in that—could be a major statement this summer that we are trying to turn some things around in the more depressed areas of our country.

There are some other things that are somewhat time sensitive, but the main thing is we need to be investing more money at the same time that we are bringing down this deficit so that we'll be creating some jobs. The traditional economic theory is that if you reduce the deficit, you're going to slow down the economy and undermine the ability to create jobs. I just can convince—that's wrong now because of the vast accumulated debt. If you can keep interest rates down, you're going to speed up the economy by putting more money out there.

But I think the stimulus is important, and I intend to continue to support it.

Q. Mr. President, I was struck by the fact that of all your speakers here, they all said, "We support the package, but we'd like changes in the area that affects us." Isn't that what you've been warning against? That the tax increase——

The President. That's not what they said. That's not what—only one of them said that, I think. And I think that, for one thing, the very fact that they're here supporting it, knowing that they'd all like changes in something that affects them, is the very point I've been trying to make to the American people.

If you look at this, if you look at this, if every person looks at this through the mirror of what is best for you today, there will always be something in here that doesn't quite work. The thing that makes this work is that it is a package in which everybody forgoes something they would like and gets something that they would like, but that in the main it moves the country in the right direction.

The Vice President. Could I add something to that?

The President. Yes.

The Vice President. You know, Lod Cook started off by singling out the two provisions which you would expect him to oppose in the old model. And he singled those out as things that he supported. And many of the others have said, privately and publicly, that they strongly support the package in spite of the fact that it contains elements that they would not like to necessarily single out by themselves but as part of a package it makes sense for the country.

Q. Would you be willing to put forth more spending cuts before your budget goes up? I know you called for the Republicans——

The President. Like what? Like what? I mean, unlike a lot of these other people, I worked for weeks and weeks and weeks on this budget. What I said was, if they had more spending cuts they thought were good ideas, I'd be happy to embrace them, that I intended for the entire duration of my term here to continue to look for more spending cuts. If I find more that I think are worthy, I'll be glad to incorporate them.

But let me just say, I have a difficult time taking these people seriously, who say we should have more spending cuts, who were here for the last 12 years. Where were they? I don't mind; anybody can say whatever they want about more spending cuts, but why are you asking me? Why don't you ask them? They're going around saying, "I have the list of spending cuts that I will discuss with somebody at some later date."

Q. They're saying that you're suggesting many spending cuts which have been up on the Hill for years and that these aren't any new cuts and these are——

The President. If we pass them, it will be new. [*Laughter*] They've been up there. If we pass them, they will be new.

Q. You said earlier you obviously don't like to raise taxes. Are you ready to acknowledge at this point that you will have to go back to Congress and ask for more tax increases for the health care reform package? And would you also comment on a report that you've dropped the idea of taxing benefits?

The President. I haven't picked any tax up, so how could I drop—you can't drop something you didn't pick up. So I won't comment on something—if I pick something, I'll tell you.

I can say this: I'm not ready to admit that I think that the people who have paid the bill for health care in the 1980's should turn around and pay more right now. We're spending 14 percent of gross national product. You do have to find some way to recover some revenues to cover people who now don't have coverage, if the Government pays for the coverage. And that's an important part of stopping the cost shifting, which has led to so much increase in private insurance.

But there are lots of options we are looking at now which wouldn't necessarily increase middle class tax burdens. There are a whole range of options for dealing with this, which is why I asked you to let us finish this process of review before we try to pick it apart.

There was a huge transfer of wealth in America in the 1980's away from everything else to health care, to pay more for the same health care. Most of it went into paperwork, insurance costs, extra procedures by providers, and duplication of expensive equipment, and emergency care, partly due to the absence of primary and preventive care. If you correct all those things and you don't change the present spending patterns, that will create a huge windfall to people whose pricing structures have all that built in. There are all kinds of things that we might be able to do to solve this problem, short of having health care become even more expensive for people who are paying 30 percent more for it than anybody else on Earth.

Q. [*Inaudible*]—that burden middle class. Does that rule out sin taxes then?

The President. I think health-related taxes are different. I think cigarette taxes, for example, are different.

Q. Why?

The President. Why? Because I think that we are spending a ton of money in private insurance and in Government tax payments to deal with the health care problems occasioned by bad health habits, and particularly smoking, which is costing us a lot of money.

Q. [*Inaudible*]—you stand on the cuts? What kind of cuts would be considered? I know you're hearing a lot of input. You stressed the importance of input. In that input——

The President. I haven't really been getting a lot of input. That's the thing. A lot of people keep talking about it; I haven't been getting a lot of specific input. A lot of folks say they want overall caps. Overall caps are another way of saying, let's take Social Security benefits away from people even though Social Security is producing a $70 billion—$60 billion-plus surplus in taxes. Or let's take Medicare benefits away from middle class Medicare beneficiaries instead of reforming the health care system.

That's basically the only things I've heard since then. If somebody wants to come forward with something else specific—now, there are some people who—let me just be also fair. Some of the people in my party have been somewhat more specific about some of the cuts they want that I honestly disagree with, and there ought to be a debate on that in Congress. Some of them want me to cut defense more. I've already had to cut defense more than I pledged to do in the campaign because it appears that the last budget which was adopted by Congress had defense cuts in it which weren't real. So I don't think I can cut any more right now. The Congress will be free to debate that.

Some people think that we should abolish the superconducting super collider or end the space station program, but I honestly don't agree with that. I thought about those programs and I debated them, but at least those are specific, and they can be debated on the floor of Congress. But these general "cap this, blanket that," I think people ought to say what the cut is and who will be affected by it and be very specific.

Thank you.

NOTE: The President spoke at 11:02 a.m. in Room 450 of the Old Executive Office Building. In his remarks, he referred to Representative Eva M. Clayton, who represented the newly elected Democratic Representatives, and Kathryn G. Thompson, chairman and chief executive officer, Kathryn G. Thompson Development Co.

Statement Announcing Airdrops To Provide Humanitarian Aid to Bosnia-Herzegovina
February 25, 1993

The war that has raged in Bosnia-Herzegovina over the past year has taken a staggering toll: Thousands have been killed or imprisoned, thousands more are at risk due to hunger and exposure, and over 2 million people have been forced from their homes. The humanitarian need is particularly great in eastern Bosnia, where areas have been denied basic food and medicines.

In view of the emergency humanitarian need, I am announcing today that in coordination with the United Nations and UNHCR, the United States will conduct humanitarian airdrops over Bosnia. The airdrops are an extension of the airlift currently underway into Sarajevo. Their purpose is to supplement land convoys. This is a temporary measure designed to address the immediate needs of isolated areas that cannot be reached at this time by ground. Regular overland deliveries are the best means to ensure that the long-term needs of the Bosnian population are met, and the United States calls on the parties to guarantee the safe passage of the humanitarian convoys throughout Bosnia.

The priority for air deliveries will be determined without regard to ethnic or religious affiliation. These airdrops are being carried out strictly for humanitarian purposes; no combat aircraft will be used in this operation. The Department of Defense will be working with the UNHCR to determine the timing and locations for the airdrops.

I am grateful for the considerable international support given to this initiative.

Exchange With Reporters at a Meeting With Close-Up Foundation Students From Arkansas
February 25, 1993

Bosnia

Q. Mr. President, do you care to say any more about the operational details of the airlift?

The President. No.

Q. How about explaining to the American people why it's an important issue for the United States to undertake?

The President. What?

Q. Why is it an important mission for us to put people at risk for that?

The President. Well, I'll say again, General Powell believes the risk is quite limited and not appreciably more than many training flights that our airmen do every year. It's important because we believe if—number one, there are a lot of people over there who need the food and can't get it by road, so it's a humanitarian gesture. And secondly, we think if we do it, we will be able to create a somewhat better climate for negotiations, and we're pushing to try to have good-faith negotiations. So we're hoping it works out.

NOTE: The President spoke at 4:01 p.m. in the Oval Office at the White House.

Remarks at the American University Centennial Celebration
February 26, 1993

Thank you very much, President Duffey, distinguished members of the board of trustees, and faculty and patrons of American University, and Members of Congress, members of the diplomatic corps, and my fellow citizens, and especially to the students here today. I am very honored to be here today at this wonderful school on the occasion of your centennial, at the dawn of a new era for our Nation and for our world, and deeply honored to receive this honorary degree, although I almost choked on it here. [*Laughter*]

My mind is full of many memories today, looking at all of you in your youthful enthusiasm and your hope for the future. I'd like to say a special word of thanks to all of you for the warm reception you gave to the person to whom I owe more than anybody else in this audience, Senator Fulbright.

When I was barely 20 years old, Senator Fulbright's administrative assistant called me one morning in Arkansas and asked me if I wanted a job working for the Senate Foreign Relations Committee as an assistant clerk. Since I couldn't really afford the cost of my education to Georgetown, I told him I was interested. And he said, "Well, you can have a part-time job at $3,500 a year or a full-time job at $5,000 a year." I said, "How about two part-time jobs." [*Laughter*] He replied that I was just the sort of mathematician they were looking for and would I please come. [*Laughter*] The next week, literally a day and a half later, I was there working for a person I had admired all my life, and the rest of it is history. But Senator Fulbright, now 88 years young, taught me a lot about the importance of our connections to the rest of the world, and that even in our small landlocked State of Arkansas, we were bound up inextricably with the future, with the passions and the promise of people all across this globe. And it is about that which I come to speak today.

I also want to say a special word of thanks to your president, Joe Duffey, and to his wonderful wife, Anne Wexler, who have been my friends for many years. When I was a young man at Yale Law School, I went to work for Joe Duffey in his campaign for the Senate. His wife was then his campaign manager. I enjoyed working for a woman. I learned a lot about equal opportunity, which I have tried to live out in my own life. Well, Joe Duffey didn't win that race for the Senate. And 4 years later I went home to Arkansas, and I ran for Congress, and I lost my race, too. And I thought how ironic it is that our failed efforts to get to Congress made us both President. [*Laughter*]

Finally, let me say that in my senior year at Georgetown, in the winter, on a day very much like today, I had a date with a girl from American University. I didn't think about this until I got in the car to come up here today, but it was snowing like crazy that night, just like it was today. And I creeped along in my car from Georgetown to American with this fellow who was in my class. And we picked up these two fine women from American University. And we went to the movie, and then we went to dinner. We went to a movie, we took them home, and then we were driving home. As we were driving home it was very slick, just like it is today. And I put my brakes on when I was almost home, and my car went into a huge spin. And it missed this massive pole on which the stoplight was by about 2 inches. And I couldn't help thinking after my speech last week how many more people would have been happy in America if I'd been a little bit closer to that pole 25 years ago. [*Laughter*]

Thirty years ago in the last year of his short but brilliant life, John Kennedy came to this university to address the paramount challenge of that time: the imperative of pursuing peace in the face of nuclear confrontation. Many Americans still believe it was the finest speech he ever delivered. Today I come to this same place to deliver an address about what I consider to be the great challenge of this day: the imperative of American leadership in the face of global change.

Over the past year I have tried to speak at some length about what we must do to update our definition of national security and to promote it and to protect it and to foster democracy and human rights around the world. Today, I want to allude to those matters, but to focus on the economic leadership we must exert at home and abroad as a new global economy unfolds before our eyes.

Twice before in this century, history has asked the United States and other great powers to provide leadership for a world ravaged by war. After World War I, that call went unheeded. Britain was too weakened to lead the world to reconstruction. The United States was too unwilling. The great powers together turned inward as violent, totalitarian power emerged. We raised trade barriers. We sought to humiliate rather than rehabilitate the vanquished. And the result was instability, inflation, then depression and ultimately a Second World War.

After the Second War, we refused to let history repeat itself. Led by a great American President, Harry Truman, a man of very common roots but uncommon vision, we drew together with other Western powers to reshape a new era. We established NATO to oppose the aggression of communism. We rebuilt the American economy with investments like the GI bill and a national highway system. We carried out the Marshall plan to rebuild war-ravaged nations abroad. General MacArthur's vision prevailed in Japan, which built a massive economy and a remarkable democracy. We built new institutions to foster peace and prosperity: the United Nations, the International Monetary Fund, the World Bank, the General Agreement on Tariffs and Trade, and more.

These actions helped to usher in four decades of robust economic growth and collective security. Yet the cold war was a draining time. We devoted trillions of dollars to it, much more than many of our more visionary leaders thought we should have. We posted our sons and daughters around the world. We lost tens of thousands of them in the defense of freedom and in the pursuit of a containment of communism.

We, my generation, grew up going to school assemblies learning about what we would do in the event a nuclear war broke out. We were taught to practice ducking under our desks and praying that somehow they might shield us from nuclear radiation. We all learned about whether we needed a bomb shelter in our neighborhood to which we could run in the event that two great superpowers rained nuclear weapons on one another. And that fate, frankly, seemed still frighteningly possible just months before President Kennedy came here to speak in 1963. Now, thanks to his leadership and that of every American President since the Second World War from Harry Truman to George Bush, the cold war is over.

The Soviet Union itself has disintegrated. The nuclear shadow is receding in the face of the START I and START II agreements and others that we have made and others yet to come. Democracy is on the march everywhere in the world. It is a new day and a great moment for America.

Yet, across America I hear people raising central questions about our place and our prospects in this new world we have done so much to make. They ask: Will we and our children really have good jobs, first-class opportunities, world-class education, quality affordable health care, safe streets? After having fully defended freedom's ramparts, they want to know if we will share in freedom's bounty.

One of the young public school students President Duffey just introduced was part of the children's program that I did last Saturday with children from around America. If you saw their stories, so many of them raised troubling questions about our capacity to guarantee the fruits of the American dream to all of our own people.

I believe we can do that, and I believe we must. For in a new global economy, still recovering from the after-effects of the cold war, a prosperous America is not only good for Americans, as the Prime Minister of Great Britain reminded me just a couple of days ago, it is absolutely essential for the prosperity of the rest of the world.

Washington can no longer remain caught in the death grip of gridlock, governed by an outmoded ideology that says change is to be resisted, the status quo is to be preserved. Like King Canute ordering the tide to recede, we cannot do that. And so, my fellow Americans, I submit to you that we stand at the third great moment of decision in the 20th century. Will we repeat the mistakes of the 1920's or the 1930's by turning inward, or will we repeat the successes of the 1940's and the 1950's by reaching outward and improving ourselves as well? I say that if we set a new direction at home, we can set a new direction for the world as well.

The change confronting us in the 1990's is in some ways more difficult than previous times because it is less distinct. It is more complex and in some ways the path is less clear to most of our people still today, even after 20 years of declining relative productivity and a decade or more of stagnant wages and greater effort.

The world clearly remains a dangerous place. Ethnic hatreds, religious strife, the proliferation of weapons of mass destruction, the violation of human rights flagrantly in altogether too many places around the world still call on us to have a sense of national security in which our national defense is an integral part. And the world still calls on us to promote democracy, for even though democracy is on the march in many places in the world, you and I know that it has been thwarted in many places, too. And yet we still face, overarching everything else, this amorphous but profound challenge in the way humankind conducts its commerce.

We cannot let these changes in the global economy carry us passively toward a future of insecurity and instability. For change is the law of life. Whether you like it or not, the world will change much more rapidly in your lifetime than it has in mine. It is absolutely astonishing the speed with which the sheer volume of knowledge in the world is doubling every few years. And a critical issue before us and especially before the young people here in this audience is whether you will grow up in a world where change is your friend or your enemy.

We must challenge the changes now engulfing our world toward America's enduring objectives of peace and prosperity, of democracy and human dignity. And we must work to do it at home and abroad.

It is important to understand the monumental scope of these changes. When I was growing up, business was mostly a local affair. Most farms and firms were owned locally; they borrowed locally; they hired locally; they shipped most of their products to neighboring communities or States within the United States. It was the same for the country as a whole. By and large, we had a domestic economy.

But now we are woven inextricably into the fabric of a global economy. Imports and exports, which accounted for about $1 in $10 when I was growing up, now represent $1 in every $5. Nearly three-quarters of the things that we make in America are subject to competition at home or abroad from foreign producers and foreign providers of services. Whether we see it or not, our daily lives are touched everywhere by the flows of commerce that cross national borders as inexorably as the weather.

Capital clearly has become global. Some $3 trillion of capital race around the world every day. And when a firm wants to build a new factory, it can turn to financial markets now open 24 hours a day, from London to Tokyo, from New York to Singapore. Products have clearly become more global. Now if you buy an American car, it may be an American car built with some parts from Taiwan, designed by Germans, sold with British-made advertisements, or a combination of others in a different mix.

Services have become global. The accounting firm that keeps the books for a small business in Wichita may also be helping new entrepreneurs in Warsaw. And the same fast food restaurant that your family goes to or at least that I go to—[*laughter*]—also may well be serving families from Manila to Moscow and managing its business globally with information technologies, and satellites.

Most important of all, information has become global and has become king of the global economy. In earlier history, wealth was measured in land, in gold, in oil, in machines. Today, the principal measure of our wealth is information: its quality, its quantity, and the speed with which we acquire it and adapt to it. We need more than anything else to measure our wealth and our potential by what we know and by what we can learn and what we can do with it. The value and volume of information has soared; the half-life of new ideas has trumped.

Just a few days ago, I was out in Silicon Valley at a remarkable company called Silicon Graphics that has expanded exponentially, partly by developing computer software with a life of 12 to 18 months, knowing that it will be obsolete after that and always being ready with a new product to replace it.

We are in a constant race toward innovation that will not end in the lifetime of anyone in this room. What all this means is that the best investment we can make today is in the one resource firmly rooted in our own borders. That is, in the education, the skills, the reasoning capacity, and the creativity of our own people.

For all the adventure and opportunity in this global economy, an American cannot approach it without mixed feelings. We still sometimes wish wistfully that everything we really want, particularly those things that produce good wages, could be made in America. We recall simpler times when one product line would be made to endure and last for years. We're angry when we see jobs and factories moving overseas or across the borders or depressing wages here at home when we think there is nothing we can do about it. We worry about our own prosperity being so dependent on events and forces beyond our shores. Could it be that the world's most powerful nation has also given up a significant measure of its sovereignty in the quest to lift the fortunes of people throughout the world?

It is ironic and even painful that the global village we have worked so hard to create has done so much to be the source of higher unemployment and lower wages for some of our people. But that is no wonder. For years our leaders have failed to take the steps that would harness the global economy to the benefit of all of our people, steps such as investing in our people and their skills, enforcing our trade laws, helping communities hurt by change; in short, putting the American people first without withdrawing from the world and people beyond our borders.

The truth of our age is this and must be this: Open and competitive commerce will enrich us as a nation. It spurs us to innovate. It forces us to compete. It connects us with new customers. It promotes global growth without which no rich country can hope to grow wealthier. It enables our producers who are themselves consumers of services and raw materials to prosper. And so I say to you in the face of all the pressures to do the reverse, we must compete, not retreat.

Our exports are especially important to us. As bad as the recent recession was, it would have gone on for twice as long had it not been for what we were able to sell to other nations. Every billion dollars of our exports creates nearly 20,000 jobs here, and we now have over 7 million export-related jobs in America. They tend to involve better work and better pay. Most are in manufacturing, and on average, they pay almost $3,500 more per year than the average American job. They are exactly the kind of jobs we need for a new generation of Americans.

American jobs and prosperity are reason enough for us to be working at mastering the essentials of the global economy. But far more is at stake, for this new fabric of commerce will also shape global prosperity or the lack of it, and with it, the prospects of people around the world for democracy, freedom, and peace.

We must remember that even with all our problems today, the United States is still the world's strongest engine of growth and progress. We remain the world's largest producer and its largest and most open market. Other nations, such as Germany and Japan, are moving rapidly. They have done better than we have in certain areas. We should respect them for it, and where appropriate, we should learn from that. But we must also say to them, "You, too, must act as engines of global prosperity." Nonetheless, the fact is that for now and for the foreseeable future, the world looks to us to be the engine of global growth and to be the leaders.

Our leadership is especially important for the world's new and emerging democracies. To grow and deepen their legitimacy, to foster a middle class and a civic culture, they need the ability to tap into a growing global economy. And our security and our prosperity will be greatly affected in the years ahead by how many of these nations can become and stay democracies.

All you have to do to know that is to look at the problems in Somalia, to look at Bosnia, to look at the other trouble spots in the world. If we could make a garden of democracy and prosperity and free enterprise in every part of this globe, the world would be a safer and a better and a more prosperous place for the United States and for all of you to raise your children in.

Let us not minimize the difficulty of this task. Democracy's prospects are dimmed, especially in the developing world, by trade barriers and slow global growth. Even though 60 developing nations have reduced their trade barriers in recent years, when you add up the sum of their collective actions, 20 of the 24 developed nations have actually increased their trade barriers in recent years. This is a powerful testament to the painful difficulty of trying to maintain a high-wage economy in a global economy where production is mobile and can quickly fly to a place with low wages.

We have got to focus on how to help our people adapt to these changes, how to maintain a high-wage economy in the United States without ourselves adding to the protectionist direction that so many of the developed nations have taken in the last few years. These barriers in the end will cost the developing world more in lost exports and incomes than all the foreign assistance that developed nations provide, but after that they will begin to undermine our economic prosperity as well.

It's more than a matter of incomes. I remind you: It's a matter of culture and stability. Trade, of course, cannot ensure the survival of new democracies, and we have seen the enduring power of ethnic hatred, the incredible power of ethnic divisions, even among people literate and allegedly understanding, to splinter democracy and to savage the nation's state.

But as philosophers from Thucydides to Adam Smith have noted, the habits of commerce run counter to the habits of war. Just as neighbors who raise each other's barns are less likely to become arsonists, people who raise each other's living standards through commerce are less likely to become combatants. So if we believe in the bonds of democracy, we must resolve to strengthen the bonds of commerce.

Our own Nation has the greatest potential to benefit from the emerging economy, but to do so we have to confront the obstacles that stand in our way. Many of our trading partners cling to unfair practices. Protectionist voices here at home and abroad call for new barriers. And different policies have left too many of our workers and communities exposed to the harsh winds of trade without letting them share in the sheltering prosperity trade has also brought and without helping them in any way to build new ways to work so they can be rewarded for their efforts in global commerce.

Cooperation among the major powers toward world growth is not working well at all today. And most of all, we simply haven't done enough to prepare our own people and to produce our own resources so that we can face with success the rigors of the new world. We can change all that if we have the will to do it. Leonardo da Vinci said that God sells all things at the price of labor. Our labor must be to make this change.

I believe there are five steps we can and must take to set a new direction at home and to help create a new direction for the world. First, we simply have to get our own economic house in order. I have outlined a new national economic strategy that will give America the new direction we require to meet our challenges. It seeks to do what no generation of Americans has ever been called upon to do before: to increase investment in our productive future and to reduce our deficit at the same time.

We must do both. A plan that only plays down the deficit without investing in those things that make us more productive will not make us stronger. A plan that only invests more money without bringing down the deficit will weaken the fabric of our overall economy such that even educated and productive people cannot succeed in it.

It is more difficult to do both. The challenges are more abrasive. You have to cut more other spending and raise more other taxes. But it is essential that we do both: invest so that we can compete; bring down the debt so that we can compete. The future of the American dream and the fate of our economy and much of the world's economy hangs in the balance on what happens in this city in the next few months. Already the voices of inertia and self-interest

have said, well, we shouldn't do this or this, or that detail is wrong with that plan. But almost no one has taken up my original challenge that anyone who has any specific ideas about how we can cut more should simply come forward with them. I am genuinely open to new ideas to cut inessential spending and to make the kinds of dramatic changes in the way Government works that all of us know we have to make. I don't care whether they come from Republicans or Democrats, or I don't even care whether they come from at home or abroad. I don't care who gets the credit, but I do care that we not vary from our determination to pass a plan that increases investment and reduces the deficit.

I think every one of you who is a student at this university has a far bigger stake in the future than I do. I have lived in all probability more than half my life with benefits far beyond anything I ever dreamed or deserved because my country worked. And I want my country to work for you.

The plan I have offered is assuredly not perfect, but it's an honest and bold attempt to honestly confront the challenges before us, to secure the foundations of our economic growth, to expand the resources, the confidence and the moral suasion we need to continue our global leadership into the next century. And I plead with all of you to do everything you can to replace the blame game that has dominated this city too long with the bigger game of competing and winning in the global economy.

Second, it is time for us to make trade a priority element of American security. For too long, debates over trade have been dominated by voices from the extremes. One says Government should build walls to protect firms from competition. Another says Government should do nothing in the face of foreign competition, no matter what the dimension and shape of that competition is, no matter what the consequences are in terms of job losses, trade dislocations, or crushed incomes. Neither view takes on the hard work of creating a more open trading system that enables us and our trading partners to prosper. Neither steps up to the task of empowering our workers to compete or of ensuring that there is some compact of shared responsibility regarding trade's impact on our people or of guaranteeing a continuous flow of investment into emerging areas of new technology which will create the high-wage jobs of

211

the 21st century.

Our administration is now developing a comprehensive trade policy that will step up to those challenges. And I want to describe the principles upon which it will rest. It will not be a policy of blame but one of responsibility. It will say to our trading partners that we value their business, but none of us should expect something for nothing.

We will continue to welcome foreign products and services into our markets but insist that our products and services be able to enter theirs on equal terms. We will welcome foreign investment in our businesses knowing that with it come new ideas as well as capital, new technologies, new management techniques, and new opportunities for us to learn from one another and grow. But as we welcome that investment, we insist that our investors should be equally welcome in other countries.

We welcome the subsidiaries of foreign companies on our soil. We appreciate the jobs they create and the products and services they bring. But we do insist simply that they pay the same taxes on the same income that our companies do for doing the same business.

Our trade policy will be part of an integrated economic program, not just something we use to compensate for the lack of a domestic agenda. We must enforce our trade laws and our agreements with all the tools and energy at our disposal. But there is much about our competitive posture that simply cannot be straightened out by trade retaliation. Better educated and trained workers, a lower deficit, stable, low interest rates, a reformed health care system, world-class technologies, revived cities: These must be the steel of our competitive edge. And there must be a continuing quest by business and labor and, yes, by Government for higher and higher and higher levels of productivity.

Too many of the chains that have hobbled us in world trade have been made in America. Our trade policy will also bypass the distracting debates over whether efforts should be multilateral, regional, bilateral, unilateral. The fact is that each of these efforts has its place. Certainly we need to seek to open other nations' markets and to establish clear and enforceable rules on which to expand trade.

That is why I'm committed to a prompt and successful completion of the Uruguay round of the GATT talks. That round has dragged on entirely too long. But it still holds the potential,

if other nations do their share and we do ours, to boost American wages and living standards significantly and to do the same for other nations around the world.

We also know that regional and bilateral agreements provide opportunities to explore new kinds of trade concerns, such as how trade relates to policies affecting the environment and labor standards and the antitrust laws. And these agreements, once concluded, can act as a magnet including other countries to drop barriers and to open their trading systems.

The North American Free Trade Agreement is a good example. It began as an agreement with Canada, which I strongly supported, which has now led to a pact with Mexico as well. That agreement holds the potential to create many, many jobs in America over the next decade if it is joined with others to ensure that the environment, that living standards, that working conditions, are honored, that we can literally know that we are going to raise the condition of people in America and in Mexico. We have a vested interest in a wealthier, stronger Mexico, but we need to do it on terms that are good for our people.

We should work with organizations, such as the Asian-Pacific Economic Cooperation Forum, to liberalize our trade across the Pacific as well.

And let me just say a moment about this: I am proud of the contribution America has made to prosperity in Asia and to the march of democracy. I have seen it in Japan after World War II. I have seen it then in Taiwan, as a country became more progressive and less repressive at the same time. I have seen it in Korea, as a country has become more progressive and more open. And we are now making a major contribution to the astonishing revitalization of the Chinese economy, now growing at 10 percent a year, with the United States buying a huge percentage of those imports. And I say, I want to continue that partnership, but I also think we have a right to expect progress in human rights and democracy as we support that progress.

Third, it is time for us to do our best to exercise leadership among the major financial powers to improve our coordination on behalf of global economic growth. At a time when capital is mobile and highly fungible, we simply cannot afford to work at cross-purposes with the other major industrial democracies. Our major partners must work harder and more closely with us to reduce interest rates, stimulate investment, reduce structural barriers to trade, and to restore robust global growth. And we must look anew at institutions we use to chart our way in the global economy and ask whether they are serving our interest in this new world or whether we need to modify them or create others.

Tomorrow our Treasury Secretary, Secretary Bentsen, and the Federal Reserve Board Chairman, Alan Greenspan, will meet with their counterparts from these Group of Seven nations to begin that work. And I look forward to meeting with the G–7 heads of state and the representatives of the European Community at our Tokyo summit in July. I am especially hopeful that by then our economic package here at home will have been substantially enacted by the Congress. And if that is so, I will be able to say to my counterparts, you have been telling us for years that America must reduce its debt and put its own house in order. You have been saying to us for years we must increase investment in our own education and technology to improve productivity. We have done it. We have done it for ourselves. We have done it for you. Now you must work with us in Germany and Japan and other nations to promote global growth.

We have to work with these nations. None of us are very good at it. America doesn't want to give up its prerogatives. The Japanese don't want to give up theirs. The Germans don't want to give up theirs. There are deep and ingrained traditions in all these nations. But the fact is that the world can't grow if America is in recession, but it will be difficult for us to grow coming out of this recovery unless we can spark a renewed round of growth in Europe and in Japan. We have got to try to work more closely together.

Fourthly, we need to promote the steady expansion of growth in the developing world, not only because it's in our interest but because it will help them as well. These nations are a rapidly expanding market for our products. Some three million American jobs flow from exports to the developing world. Indeed, because of unilateral actions taken by Mexico over the last few years, the volume of our trade has increased dramatically, and our trade deficit has disappeared.

Our ability to protect the global environment and our ability to combat the flow of illegal narcotics also rests in large measure on the relationships we develop commercially with the developing world.

There is a great deal that we can do to open the flow of goods and services. Our aid policies must do more to address population pressures; to support environmentally responsible, sustainable development; to promote more accountable governance; and to foster a fair distribution of the fruits of growth among an increasingly restive world population where over one billion people still exist on barely a dollar a day. These efforts will reap us dividends of trade, of friendship, and peace.

The final step we must take, my fellow Americans, is toward the success of democracy in Russia and in the world's other new democracies. The perils facing Russia and other former Soviet republics are especially acute and especially important to our future. For the reductions in our defense spending that are an important part of our economic program over the long run here at home are only tenable as long as Russia and the other nuclear republics pose a diminishing threat to our security and to the security of our allies and the democracies throughout the world. Most worrisome is Russia's precarious economic condition. If the economic reforms begun by President Yeltsin are abandoned, if hyperinflation cannot be stemmed, the world will suffer.

Consider the implications for Europe if millions of Russian citizens decide they have no alternative but to flee to the West where wages are 50 times higher. Consider the implication for the global environment if all the Chernobyl-style nuclear plants are forced to start operating there without spare parts, when we should be in a phased stage of building them down, closing them up, cleaning them up. If we are willing to spend trillions of dollars to ensure communism's defeat in the cold war, surely we should be willing to invest a tiny fraction of that to support democracy's success where communism failed.

To be sure, the former Soviet republics and especially Russia, must be willing to assume most of the hard work and high cost of the reconstruction process. But then again, remember that the Marshall plan itself financed only a small fraction of postwar investments in Europe. It was a magnet, a beginning, a confidence-building measure, a way of starting a process that turned out to produce an economic miracle.

Like Europe then, these republics now have a wealth of resources and talent and potential. And with carefully targeted assistance, conditioned on progress toward reform and arms control and nonproliferation, we can improve our own security and our future prosperity at the same time we extend democracy's reach.

These five steps constitute an agenda for American action in a global economy. As such, they constitute an agenda for our own prosperity as well. Some may wish we could pursue our own domestic effort strictly through domestic policies, as we have understood them in the past. But in this global economy, there is no such thing as a purely domestic policy. This thing we call the global economy is unruly. It's a bucking bronco that often lands with its feet on different sides of old lines and sometimes with its whole body on us. But if we are to ride the bronco into the next century, we must harness the whole horse, not just part of it.

I know there are those in this country in both political parties and all across the land who say that we should not try to take this ride, that these goals are too ambitious, that we should withdraw and focus only on those things which we have to do at home. But I believe that would be a sad mistake and a great loss. For the new world toward which we are moving actually favors us. We are better equipped than any other people on Earth by reason of our history, our culture, and our disposition, to change, to lead, and to prosper. The experience of the last few years where we have stubbornly refused to make the adjustments we need to compete and win are actually atypical and unusual seen against the backdrop of our Nation's history.

Look now at our immigrant Nation and think of the world toward which we are tending. Look at how diverse and multiethnic and multilingual we are, in a world in which the ability to communicate with all kinds of people from all over the world and to understand them will be critical. Look at our civic habits of tolerance and

respect. They are not perfect in our own eyes. It grieved us all when there was so much trouble a year ago in Los Angeles. But Los Angeles is a country with 150 different ethnic groups of widely differing levels of education and access to capital and income. It is a miracle that we get along as well as we do. And all you have to do is to look at Bosnia, where the differences were not so great, to see how well we have done in spite of all of our difficulties.

Look at the way our culture has merged technology and values. This is an expressive land that produced CNN and MTV. We were all born for the information age. This is a jazzy nation, thank goodness, for my sake. It created be-bop and hip-hop and all those other things. We are wired for real time. And we have always been a nation of pioneers. Consider the astonishing outpouring of support for the challenges I laid down last week in an economic program that violates every American's narrow special interest if you just take part of it out and look at it.

And yet, here we are again, ready to accept a new challenge, ready to seek new change because we're curious and restless and bold. It flows out of our heritage. It's ingrained in the soul of Americans. It's no accident that our Nation has steadily expanded the frontiers of democracy, of religious tolerance, of racial justice, of equality for all people, of environmental protection and technology and, indeed, the cosmos itself. For it is our nature to reach out. And reaching out has served not only ourselves but the world as well.

Now, together, it is time for us to reach out again: toward tomorrow's economy, toward a better future, toward a new direction, toward securing for you, the students at American University, the American dream.

Thank you very much.

NOTE: The President spoke at 10:44 a.m. at Bender Arena. In his remarks, he referred to Joseph Duffey, president of the university.

Message to the Congress Reporting Budget Deferrals
February 26, 1993

To the Congress of the United States:

In accordance with the Congressional Budget and Impoundment Control Act of 1974, I herewith report three new deferrals of budget authority, totaling $354.0 million.

These deferrals affect Funds Appropriated to the President and the Department of Agriculture. The details of these deferrals are contained in the attached report.

WILLIAM J. CLINTON

The White House,
February 26, 1993.

NOTE: The report detailing the deferrals was published in the *Federal Register* on April 1.

Nomination for Posts at the Defense and Treasury Departments
February 26, 1993

President Clinton today announced his intention to nominate Jamie Gorelick to be General Counsel of the Department of Defense and Jean Hanson to be General Counsel of the Treasury Department.

"Jamie Gorelick and Jean Hanson are two of the most qualified people in the country for these important positions," said the President. "Each of them combines impressive legal expertise and private sector experience with a demonstrable commitment to public service."

NOTE: Biographies of the nominees were made available by the Office of the Press Secretary.

The President's Radio Address
February 27, 1993

Good morning. Before I talk with you about our economic program this morning, I want to say a word to the good people of New York City and to all Americans who have been so deeply affected by the tragedy that struck Manhattan yesterday. A number of innocent people lost their lives, hundreds were injured, and thousands were struck with fear in their hearts when an explosion rocked the basement of the World Trade Center.

To their families, you are in the thoughts and prayers of my family. And in the synagogues and churches last night, today, and tomorrow you will be remembered and thought of again and again. My thoughts are also with the police, the firefighters, the emergency response teams, and the citizens whose countless acts of bravery averted even more bloodshed. Their reaction and their valor reminds us of how often Americans are at their best when we face the worst.

I thank all the people who reached out to the injured and the frightened amid the tumult that shook lower Manhattan.

Following the explosion I spoke with New York's Governor Mario Cuomo and New York City Mayor David Dinkins to assure them that the full measure of Federal law enforcement resources will be brought to bear on this investigation. Just this morning I spoke with FBI Director Sessions, who assured me that the FBI and the Treasury Department are working closely with the New York City police and fire departments. Working together we'll find out who was involved and why this happened. Americans should know we'll do everything in our power to keep them safe in their streets, their offices, and their homes. Feeling safe is an essential part of being secure, and that's important to all of us.

I also want to take this opportunity this morning to talk about another crucial aspect of our security, our economic security. Ten days ago I asked for your help to bring bold changes to our economy. I said it would be a challenge and that our plan would require every one of us to contribute and that the price of doing nothing is far, far higher for all of us than the price of change. Most of all, our work together will bring us important returns: more jobs, more growth, better incomes, and a better future for our children.

Your response to this plan has been overwhelming to me. Business and labor leaders have made a rare alliance on behalf of a program that offers lower interest rates and investment incentives for private enterprise and modern skills and opportunities for working people. Citizens from cities all across the country have looked at our plan and concluded that the changes we ask are right in the short term and for the long-term health of the economy. I think you know that we can no longer deny that our huge national deficit drains our economic health and that our investment deficit will smother our hopes for economic growth.

There is an alternative: our plan for a new direction. It provides retraining to Americans for better jobs, incentives for small businesses to invest, and a head start, better nutrition and superior schools for our children. Our plan will cut the deficit as a percentage of our national income in half between now and 1997, so we can put our resources to work for all of us. What is happening in this Nation is historic. After many years of drift and division and gridlock, the American people are uniting behind this call for a new direction. In recent days the White House has been flooded with letters. You've sent along moving stories about how you've been affected by the hard economic times, and we've received several contributions to reduce the debt.

Many of you who have written are single parents. You're worried about paying your own bills today, but you're also worried about the lives of your children tomorrow. Your support is a symbol of selflessness, of the foresight and determination now catching fire across our Nation.

I received one letter from Rachel Nunamaker of San Jose, California. She's 83 years old, and she wrote, "Stick to your guns, you're on the right track." Well, I think Mrs. Nunamaker is right; we are on the right track. Already mortgage rates have fallen to their lowest level in

20 years, 20 years. With falling interest rates more people can afford loans to build their businesses, buy cars, or purchase houses. This is good news for everyone but especially for the young adults and middle class families who thought they would never be able to afford their own homes. That's an essential part of the American dream we're working hard to restore. And it can be restored.

Our plan will work. It cuts waste and inessential Government spending, and it increases public and private investments to create more jobs and rising incomes and to educate and train people better. It spreads the burden as fairly as possible, and the opportunity it promises will pay us back many times over. If we get America moving again, I don't care who gets the credit. Ultimately the credit will go to you, the American people. As a patriot once said to the citizens of our democracy, You are the beginning and the end. This is an exciting time to be an American, and we must not let this historic moment pass. We are rebuilding the American community and the American economy together.

On March the first we'll mark an anniversary that is especially significant to my generation. Thirty-two years ago President Kennedy inspired Americans to serve in the Peace Corps. On Monday I will discuss my proposal for a new form of voluntary national service. It's a plan to invest in our country's future, a call to action and to responsibility that will involve one of our most precious national resources, our young people. With national service, hundreds of thousands of students will have a chance to pursue higher education. Everyone with the desire to serve will have the opportunity and will meet social needs that for too long have gone unaddressed. National service will be a great gift for the next generation of Americans.

In closing today, let me share with you another letter I received that arrived with an extraordinary gift. They come from George L. Baker of Sherwood, Arkansas, a retired Air Force major. After serving his country under extreme danger, Major Baker was awarded the Distinguished Flying Cross for heroism. It is a recognition that George Baker should have kept for the rest of his life. But Major Baker sent that medal to me as a sign of his support for our economic program and to encourage me in this "quest for sanity in our national direction." And he closed his letter, "Godspeed, Mr. President." From the bottom of my heart, Major

Baker, thank you for this most inspirational gift. With your help and with the help of Americans just like you all across this country, we will restore the vitality of the American economy and enjoy a nation united by the dreams we all share.

Thanks for listening.

NOTE: The President spoke at 10:06 a.m. from the Oval Office at the White House.

Remarks and a Question-and-Answer Session at the Adult Learning Center in New Brunswick, New Jersey
March 1, 1993

Judy Kesin. Welcome, Mr. President. We are so thrilled and pleased and honored to have you with us today. And we also would like to welcome Governor Florio, the attorney general Del Tufo, Eli Segal from your office who works with national community service. This is just such a treat. My name is Judy Kesin, and I am the principal of the Adult Learning Center of the New Brunswick Public Schools. We are so thrilled you could visit our program.

[*At this point, Ms. Kesin described the center's educational and community service programs and the involvement of Rutgers University students and then presented the President with a gift. Several participants then discussed the effect of education and involvement in community service on their lives.*]

The President. Well, first of all, I want to thank everyone who spoke. And maybe in a minute I could give some of you who haven't spoken a chance to say something, if you want to say something.

Let me tell you why I came here today. First of all, I've been very impressed by a lot of the efforts that the State of New Jersey has already made to serve people who need an education and need a second chance and to give people a chance to serve their communities.

Secondly, this center reflects two very important things that I'm trying to do in my national economic program that I'm asking the Congress to pass. The first is what I came here to talk about, and I'm going over to Rutgers to talk to the students about in a few moments, and that is the idea of giving people a chance to serve their country in their community, and in return, giving them the opportunity to further their education.

I've got the gentleman who was introduced here a minute ago with me to my right. Eli Segal and I have been friends since we were about your age, since we were very young. And I've asked him to head up our national and community service program. What we want to do is to provide young people the opportunity to do the following things.

Number one, if you go to college and you have loans outstanding, we want to give people the opportunity to go out in the community and do community service work, work as teachers or police officers or work with the homeless or work in hospitals or work on immunizing children who need it, and doing that for a lower rate of pay for a couple of years and then pay off their college loans by doing the same. Number two, we want to give people some credit for community service they do while they're in college. And number three, we want to give people like you the opportunity to earn some credits to get college or job training by doing community service before you go. So the idea is to make higher education available to more people, in return for the service they give to the community.

Now, in addition to all that, we're going to change the way young people pay their college loans back. We're going to make it possible for people who get out of college to pay their loans back as a percentage, a limited percentage, of their income. Because what happens now is a lot of young people get out of college, they have big college loans. Because they have to pay the loans back, they might want to get out, let's say, and do community service work which doesn't pay very much, but instead they may take a job paying a higher salary just to make their loan repayment. So we're going to try to restructure the college loan program so that if people want to serve over a long period of time, they won't be discouraged from taking community service type jobs just because they pay less. They'll be able to pay their loans back as a percentage of their income.

Now, the other thing I want to emphasize is there's also an investment in this education program that helps centers like this: more money for adult education for people who come back after dropping out of school, more money to help welfare mothers move from dependence to independence, more money to help young people who drop out of school and come back. When I was Governor of my State over the period of about 1983 to 1992, we increased by about 6 times the amount of investment in remaking education programs like this. It just exploded the number of people in it.

Now, why is that an important economic investment? Because this lady with her three children—it wasn't her fault that her husband, first of all, is out of the service and then gets hurt, right? She can either draw taxpayer dollars by taking public assistance, or get an education and pay taxes to educate other people's children. One of the things we have to realize in this country is that an economic investment is not just building an airport or a road or investing in new technology. It's also investing in people who are prepared to help themselves, to make sure that all of you can contribute in a world that is dominated by knowledge, in a world in which the living you make depends on what you know and what you can learn.

And if every person, if every single mother in the United States could stand up and give the speech you just gave with the determination you just gave, it would not only help people like you but you'd be helping people like me. Right? I mean, we're all better off, right? We are. And if you look at our country, if you look at all the different racial and ethnic groups in our country, all the different levels of education, if you look at all the different levels of income, if you look at all the problems we've got, you just think about it—if everybody in our country had a chance to get a really good high school diploma or a GED and then get at least 2 years of education and training beyond that in some way or another, and if all the while they were doing it they were doing community service work, we'd have about half as many problems than we've got, wouldn't we?

So that's why I wanted to come here today, to emphasize that this economic program that

I'm trying to persuade the Congress to pass will help people to do what you've been doing in service, will help people who do it to pile up education credits, and will invest more money in programs like those here at this center.

Developing the capacity of the American people to be all they can be is perhaps the most important job that I have as President. And people now all across America will see you today, and you may have no idea how many people you will inspire today because you had the courage to do what you did; you, or you, or you, or all of you for being here. And I really— I thank you very much. You were great.

Would anybody else like to say anything or ask a question? I can't believe you have nine children. You're a beautiful mother to have nine children. Were one of you going to talk? Yes, go ahead. Tell us your name and how you happen to be here.

[*A Rutgers student presented the President with a sweatshirt.*]

The President. I wish I had this this morning in Washington. [*Laughter*] The wind chill factor was 13 when I was on my jog this morning. Thank you very much. It's beautiful.

Funding for Arts Programs

Q. My name is Shantel Ehrenberg. I'm a dance major at the School of the Arts, and I'm originally from Minnesota. I have a question as during our program with the children and teaching them about art and through art, eliminating the prejudices and educating them on something that they find kind of foreign to them. I was wondering what you were going to do, if you have any plans for the arts, funding the arts?

The President. Programs like the one you're in will be funded basically based on the initiative of people at the local level. So if there's a program like this one at the local level which you're participating in, then it will be eligible to get community service funding.

So the answer is maybe yes, maybe no. And let me tell you why that's important. We don't want to set up a big new national bureaucracy to tell every State and every community what they should teach and what they should do. What we want to do is to build on the strengths of existing community programs like the one you're involved in. In other words, why should we come into New Jersey and create some big bureaucracy and waste a lot of money hiring people to administer programs when you've got a perfectly good program here who can access the money and use it all to put people to work teaching art or whatever else you're doing.

So the answer is that the people who are interested in arts education throughout America, once this national program is passed, should make sure that that is an important part of the community service efforts in every State and every community. Because they will be certainly eligible for it, but we're not going to tell people what to do.

As a matter of fact, we'll have relatively few mandates in this program. The two things we are going to do is to require every State to try to provide opportunities for college graduates to be either teachers or police officers, because we know we've got a shortage of both of them in every State. But otherwise, particularly with the college students themselves or with young people who are like you, who are in school and may be earning credit toward going to college or getting job training, we're going to let that be highly decentralized so that you can meet the needs in each community and State.

National and Community Service Program

Q. I'm a Rutgers College graduating senior in May. And I was wondering when you think that law you're trying to instate or whatever is going to come into effect. I'm worrying, like, when I graduate in May, whether I'm going to go pursue chiropractic college, or because I may not have the money for it, I may have to get a job or get in more debt to try to get into chiropractic school. And I think it's a good program that you're trying to instate, but how soon would it come that we would have a chance to excel?

The President. It's up to the Congress. We'll present the law, the bill, soon. And I'm hoping it will pass this year and become immediately effective.

[*A participant explained how improving her education would enable her to pass the citizenship test. Another participant said how happy she was to meet the President.*]

The President. Anybody else want to say anything?

[*A participant presented the President with a gift from the New Jersey Youth Corps.*]

Q. It's my pleasure to have you here, not only because you're the President but because you're a President we all like. [*Laughter*] And I just wanted to ask you one question. As a minority student in the United States I have experience of some kind of prejudice in the country, and how we have to struggle a little bit harder than everyone else. And I just wanted to tell you that all this that you're doing is great, especially for Hispanics, Latinos, blacks. We all recognize how you're trying to make it seem that this is not only a white country anymore but all a mixture of all different cultures. And one of the groups that I've seen that has not been seen and they are a minority group, and there has not been putting any attention toward the handicapped people. I think that I wanted to ask you are you thinking of doing anything for them, because I think that they're there, and we should put some kind of value to them and some kind importance. I'm very close to one family that they have experienced with their handicapped child many different problems. And one of the things was the Reagan administration; they always had been cutting down on those programs, especially for the handicapped. And they had to have been placed in different schools, which is not appropriate for handicapped people. And they have, you know, have many problems because it's not where they should be. Do you plan to do anything for them?

The President. Yes, I'm glad you brought that up. Let's talk about two or three things. Let me say, first of all, a lot of people with disabilities have problems that aren't easy to solve, as you know. But they also have enormous potential to contribute to this country. I can make the same argument for people with disabilities I made for all of you: that it is in our interest to see that everyone develops to the maximum of his or her capacity and serves to the maximum of his or her capacity.

Let me just mention two or three things: Number one, last year before I became President, the Congress passed and President Bush signed a bill called the Americans with Disabilities Act. It has not been fully implemented. One of the commitments I made in this campaign is to try to bring that law to life for Americans with disabilities. It provides all kinds of extra effort to make America accessible and to invest in the potential of people with disabilities.

The second thing is, I hope that a lot of these service programs will involve special services to people with disabilities working toward independence, not dependence. There are a lot of Government programs now which if you know someone with disabilities, you know it's basically—it favors funding that is designed almost to keep disabled people dependent instead of independent. And more and more disabled people want to and are able to, given technological supports, to live on their own, to work on their own, to live in at least assisted-living environments. And this is a very big deal for me and for my administration. My Domestic Policy Adviser has a child, whom I've known since he was a little boy, who had cerebral palsy and is now living out on his own in an assisted-living environment. And he will soon get his high school diploma. So I believe in that.

The third thing I would say is we're going to do a lot of work through the Department of Education to try to make sure that children get appropriate placements and at least have the chance that they need to get a public education.

I don't know if you've noticed this but, not this Saturday, the Saturday before last, I did a little town meeting like this with children. And there was a 9-year-old child with cerebral palsy who was very eloquent on the show. And she said she had a twin sister who was also in a wheelchair, but her twin sister couldn't speak except with the use of a computer, which is not uncommon. And she said because she could speak, she was in a regular classroom; because her sister had to use the computer to speak, she was in a special ed classroom. And she felt that they had the same mental capacity. So she said, "Can you help get my sister in my classroom?" And I asked—it was an interesting thing to question—I asked her, I said, "Would you, if your sister couldn't do the work, would you then favor her getting special assistance?" And she said, "Yes." And I said, "What you really want is for your sister just to have a chance to do what you do?" And she said, "That's what I want. I just want her to have a chance." It was very moving.

But a lot of schools and school districts are just now learning what they can do. And we're always learning more and more about proper placements of these children. So anyway, those are some of the things that I will work on for persons with disabilities.

I appreciate the other comment you made, because I am trying to demonstrate to the American people that we are all one country. We have to live together not only with tolerance for one another but with absolute appreciation for one another's differences. We shouldn't just put up with one another; we should actually enjoy the fact that this is a country of people of different racial and ethnic backgrounds.

When you look at what's going on today in the former Yugoslavia with the ethnic hatred—the Serbs and the Croatians and the Bosnian Muslims shooting and killing each other and starving each other, with differences, cultural and historic differences that are deep and long-lasting but, at least to the naked eye, not near as different as the cultural differences represented just in this room—for all of the problems we have in this country, we are moving forward on that. And I really believe that a great test of whether we will go into the next century and maintain our position as the greatest and strongest nation in the world may well be whether we can learn to live together across racial and ethnic lines, and not just put up with one another but absolutely enjoy the fact and make the most of it.

One of our counties, Los Angeles County in California, has 150 different racial and ethnic groups within one county. I once spoke at a university there that had students from 122 different countries. You know what that meant. This can be an enormous strength of us in a world that is getting smaller and smaller and smaller. If you look around this room, the fact that some of you can come from such different cultures is a very big positive in a world that's getting smaller. The fact that we have a huge Hispanic population, for example, will be an enormous asset to us as more and more of our trade goes to Mexico, Central America, and South America to try to build up their economy. That's just one example. If you look at the fact that we have a substantial Asian population, it can be an enormous strength to us with the fastest growing economies in the world being in Asia. There are lots of examples. The fact that we have a big African-American population will be an enormous strength to us when 20 years from now we might find out that Africa then has the fastest growing economy in the world, if they can solve some of their political problems. So America is in an incredible position to have another great century as a nation if we can learn to really build on the strength of our diversity.

Oh, yes. I want you all to be—you've been invited to ride a bus over to the speech. And I'm going to go with you. Do you want to go? Ready?

World Trade Center Bombing

Q. Mr. President, I have a question before you go, if you don't mind. It's not directly related to this event. But if you could, I know the American public is really interested in knowing what is going on with the World Trade Center explosion. Was it a terrorist incident?

The President. I'm not in a position to say that now, and I don't mean because I know something that I'm not telling you. I think you know that there was severe structural damage done to the World Trade Center. And as I think Governor Cuomo has already announced, you know the Federal and State and local people have been working together ever since the incident occurred. It took a substantial amount of time just to get people down in the crater that the bomb made to begin the analysis. I can tell you this: that we have put the full, full resources, the Federal law enforcement agencies, all kinds of agencies, all kinds of access to information at the service of those who are working to figure out who did this and why and what the facts are. But I cannot answer your question yet.

National and Community Service Program

Q. Mr. President, on national service, you campaigned on the promise that anybody who wanted to go to school could go and then repay their loans in national service. I think in your economic plan, under investment, there's $3 billion allotted for national service.

The President. More now.

Q. Which would not be enough to provide this to everyone. How long would it take to phase it in? And do you think that you're not really fulfilling your campaign promise?

The President. No. As a matter of fact, in the campaign, we only talked about making it available as an option. We talked about making it available for everybody to pay off their loans as a percentage of their income, and then the funding of national service slots will be college graduates. That's all we talked about in the campaign. Now, we're actually going to start funding slots for people before they go to high school.

And we think we'll start—we think we'll have 35,000 of them, which is twice as many people as were ever in the Peace Corps in any given year, in addition to those coming out of college.

What we don't know, and we may have to modify the funding I asked for from Congress over the next 4 years, but it is impossible to know how many people will choose the service option. So the funding we asked for is based on our best available effort to estimate how many people will choose the service option. All the students will be able to choose to pay their loans back as a percentage of their income immediately. And we think we'll be able to accommodate over the next 4 years, everybody who chooses the service option. We think we will.

But we have to build it up a little in the first year or two so we learn how to do it. There has been a pilot project going, as you probably know, under legislation that was sponsored in the previous Congress by, I think, Senator Nunn, Senator Wofford, and others. And we're going to expand it just as quickly as we can, and we're going to do our level-best, once we get the system worked out over the next year or so, to make service available to everybody who wants it. We think their numbers are about right. We think we have funded it about the level of maximum participation for college graduates. But we're adding on pre-college students, which we think is a good thing. This is something I had not planned to do basically until I kept seeing programs like the L.A. Conservation Corps, City Year, programs like the ones the young people are involved in here.

Q. Are you concerned, sir, that it may become a kind of new entitlement, that it will grow beyond the ability to fund and out of control?

The President. No, if we can't fund it, the entitlement will be access to a loan you can pay back based on a percentage of your income, which will be a huge—we're going to strengthen collection procedures, cut defaults, cut the cost of administering the program until we can fund a lot of that.

The service issue cannot become an entitlement. If all of a sudden in one year a million people want to convert from a loan to service, we won't be able to afford that. But based on the experiences we have seen in the past, we think that this will be, by far, the biggest service program in the history of America. And we think we'll be able to take everybody who will choose the service option. We're just going on historical precedents now. We think we can more than fund the people who will choose the service option in the first 4 years. If they don't, I would consider going back. But we can't let that become an absolute entitlement.

World Trade Center Bombing

Q. [*Inaudible*]—economic aid, sir, to New York, and are you prepared to do that? Governor Cuomo has asked for it.

The President. This morning I got a report on that, and it's my understanding that we are going through the regular agencies and that the request will be processed promptly. I don't think that there is any problem with the request that he made as far as I understand it. And we're giving that a high priority.

Rutgers University and Community Service

Q. Mr. President, why did you choose Rutgers for this announcement? And what impressed you about their community service program here?

The President. I chose Rutgers because, first of all, the university was involved with this facility and because I want to keep highlighting adult education, education of welfare recipients, education of kids that drop out of school, and because I like this New Jersey Youth Program here. Under Governor Florio's administration, they started, I think, 9, 10, 11 of these, something like that. Again, I do not want this to be a bureaucratic program. I want to encourage kind of an entrepreneurial spirit out there at the State and local level. I want States to be encouraged to set up Youth Corps. I want comprehensive community service centers like this to be able to get people doing national service.

So I wanted to come here to say I really appreciate what these folks are doing, but also to give the rest of America an idea of what we mean by community service, what we mean by national service, and how it can embrace people of different ages and different backgrounds with different needs; because it's very important that to make this work, we're going to have to rely on the creativity of people at the grassroots level. And the last thing I want is another centralized bureaucracy telling people how to serve.

As I said, right now, the only decisions we have made for categories of service that have to be approved in every State are in the area of police and teaching, because we know as a practical matter we need more community polic-

ing in high-crime areas where we can reduce crime and work with kids and not just be there after it happens. And we know we need more teachers in a lot of core areas to reduce the student-teacher ratio and increase learning. So we've done that. But otherwise, this program is not going to have a huge set of national requirements or bureaucracy.

Neighborhood Corps Legislation

Q. Mr. President, how closely, if at all, did you work with Senator Bradley's neighborhood corps bill?

The President. We reviewed it very closely. I think he's going to meet us over at Rutgers today. I was very impressed by it. And as a matter of fact, I had a personal conversation with him about it. That's one of the reasons we wanted to come up here, too. And I invited him to come today, and I think he's going to be over there.

Terrorism

Q. Mr. President, do you fear that a fear of terrorism in America might change the way of life that most Americans have, if this bombing proves to be terrorism?

The President. I certainly hope not. We've been very blessed in this country to have been free of the kind of terrorist activity that has gripped other countries. Even a country like Great Britain, that has a much lower general crime rate, has more of that sort of activity because of the political problems that it has been involved in.

I don't want the American people to overreact to this at this time. I can tell you, I have put the—I will reiterate—I have put the full resources of the Federal Government, every conceivable law enforcement information resource we could put to work on this, we have. I'm very concerned about it. But I think it's also important that we not overreact to it. After all, sometimes when an incident like this happens, people try to claim credit for it who didn't do it. Sometimes if folks like that can get you to stop doing what you're doing, they've won half the battle. If they get you ruffled, if they get us to change the way we live and what we do, that's half the battle.

I would discourage the American people from overreacting to this. It's a very serious thing. And I'm heartbroken for the people who were killed and their families and those who were injured. There was some significant business disruptions, too, as you probably know and as I'm afraid we'll find out more about in the next day or two, just by shutting down the World Trade Center and all the activities that go on there. But I would plead with the American people and the good people of New York to right now keep your courage up, go on about your lives. And we're working as hard as we can to get to the bottom of this.

[*A student expressed appreciation and support for community service ideals.*]

Gun Control Legislation

Q. The National Rifle Association right now, in New Jersey, is actively seeking to overturn the assault weapons ban that Governor Florio put on the books in 1990. They say if they're successful, then no other State will be able to enact rigid gun control and that you'll have a very tough time getting the Brady bill through Congress. Are you concerned about that?

The President. I think Governor Florio is right. And I'm going to sure try to pass the Brady bill. I think Americans who want safer streets and still want people to be able to hunt and fish and pursue their sporting activities should take a lot of heart in the success that Governor Wilder had in Virginia recently. And Virginia, it has become a source, as you know, of weapons for a lot of illegal activity all up and down the Atlantic seaboard. And they've gone to that once-a-month limitation on the purchase of guns.

You know, we can't be so fixated on our desire to preserve the rights of ordinary Americans to legitimately own handguns and rifles—it's something I strongly support—we can't be so fixated on that that we are unable to think about the reality of life that millions of Americans face on streets that are unsafe, under conditions that no other nation—no other nations—has permitted to exist. And at some point, I still hope that the leadership of the National Rifle Association will go back to doing what it did when I was a boy and which made me want to be a lifetime member because they put out valuable information about hunting and marksmanship and safe use of guns. But just to know of the conditions we face today in a lot of our cities and other places in this country and the enormous threat to public safety is amazing.

I've got young Americans now in Somalia trying to create conditions of peaceful existence there in a country where it is difficult. But there are a lot of young Americans who are living in neighborhoods today that are about as dangerous or worse than what kids are facing in Somalia in terms of shots, not in terms of hunger and access to medicine and shelter, that's different.

But I have to tell you I think that Governor Florio did a gusty thing here. I think Governor Wilder did a brave thing. I had my own encounters back home in Arkansas, and I just hope to be able to pass the Brady bill and do some other sensible things that do not unduly infringe on the right of the law-abiding citizen to keep and bear arms, but will help make these children's future safer. And I think we ought to do that.

Q. Do you think that the NRA's contributing to that threat that you just talked about because it is opposing these gun control measures?

The President. Well, I don't want to get into character. I think that it is an error for them to oppose every attempt to bring some safety and some rationality into the way we handle some of the most serious criminal problems we have. And these things do not unduly affect the right to keep and bear arms. It's not going to kill anybody to wait a couple of days to get a handgun while we do a background check on somebody that wants to buy a gun.

I have personal experience with this. I live in a State where half the people have a hunting or a fishing license. I know somebody who once sold a weapon to a person who went out and killed a bunch of people because he was an escapee from a mental hospital. And the guy liked to never got over it. And if he had just had a law where he was supposed to wait 2 or 3 days to check, they would have found that out. I know that happens. I don't believe that everybody in America needs to be able to buy a semiautomatic or an automatic weapon, built only for the purpose of killing people, in order to protect the right of Americans to hunt and to practice marksmanship and to be secure in their own homes and own a weapon to be secure. I just don't believe that.

So I hope that this is a debate that will continue. And I think, as I said, what Governor Florio did and what Governor Wilder did, I think will contribute to Americans facing this and trying to reconcile our absolute obligation under the Constitution to give people the right to handle a firearm responsibly and our obligation to try to preserve peace and keep these kids alive in our cities.

NOTE: The President spoke at 11:20 a.m. at the center.

Remarks on National Service at Rutgers University in New Brunswick
March 1, 1993

Thank you, Nakia Tomlinson, for that fine introduction. I wish I could take you with me everywhere. We'd make a great duo there. Let's give her another hand. I thought she was great. [*Applause*]

I'd like to thank President Frank Lawrence— Francis Lawrence—for his fine speech. Does anybody call him Frank? I should have asked. [*Laughter*] I want to compliment Professor Benjamin Barber for his leadership and service here. And I want to thank all of you here in the Rutgers community for coming out for what I hope will be a truly historic moment in our Nation's history.

In addition to the people who have been introduced here, there are a host of mayors and members of the assembly and county officials here from your State. We have two former Governors, both of whom I served with, Brendan Byrne and Tom Kean, who are out there. I'm glad to see them, my friends. We have a distinguished array of Members of the House from New Jersey, Herb Klein, Bob Menendez, Frank Pallone, Donald Payne.

But you have some Members of the Congress from all over America here, and I want to introduce them, too, because they have taken a lot of trouble to come to Rutgers and because without them and without the people who represent you, the proposal I make today has no hope of passage. Many Members of the Congress for years have believed we ought to do more in national service, and some of them are here today.

I'd like to begin by introducing your Senator, Bill Bradley, who's behind me. I must say, when I walked into this arena, I turned around and asked Bill Bradley if he'd ever shot any baskets in here. I'd be intimidated to be the opposing team in here. Senator Bradley sponsored legisla-

tion to establish neighborhood corps and self-reliance scholarships, things that are forebears of the proposal I came to make.

I'd like to recognize the presence on the platform of Senator Ted Kennedy from Massachusetts who chairs the Senate Committee on Human Resources and Education, which shepherded the pilot national and community service bill through the Congress in the last session, along with his counterpart who is out here in the audience somewhere. I'd like to ask him to stand up, the chairman of the House committee, Congressman Bill Ford, who came all the way from Michigan to be with us. Congressman, would you stand up.

I'd like to recognize in the audience the presence of Senator Chris Dodd from Connecticut, who was one of the first Peace Corps volunteers in the United States.

The Member of Congress who introduced many, many years ago the first piece of national service legislation ever introduced, the chairman of the Foreign Relations Committee, Senator Claiborne Pell from Rhode Island is here.

I'd also like to introduce the only person in this audience, at least of our crowd, who doesn't have to look up to Senator Bradley, Senator Jay Rockefeller from West Virginia, an early VISTA volunteer in the United States.

And finally, I would like to recognize two other people, one a Member of the United States Senate and one a distinguished American citizen, the first boss of the Peace Corps, Sargent Shriver, who's up here with me, and his deputy, Senator Harris Wofford, from Pennsylvania, and Mrs. Wofford, I'm glad to see you.

Now, I was involved before I became President in a group called the Democratic Leadership Council, and we made one of the central parts of our platform to reclaim a new majority of Americans for our party the establishment of a system of national service to help people to finance education. And one of our founding members and guiding lights is here, Representative Dave McCurdy from Oklahoma. I'd like for him to stand up.

Let me make this last point, if I might, by way of beginning. None of these things happen at the national level. We empower them to happen, and then people have to do things here at the grassroots. And I want to say a special word of thanks to your Governor for supporting the New Jersey Youth Corps and several other projects like it around the State, because if nobody's here to believe in this, it can't happen. And I thank Governor Florio for his support for these things.

I came here to ask all of you to join me in a great national adventure, for in the next few weeks I will ask the United States Congress to join me in creating a new system of voluntary national service, something that I believe in the next few years will change America forever and for the better.

My parents' generation won new dignity working their way out of the Great Depression through programs that provided them the opportunity to serve and to survive. Brave men and women in my own generation waged and won peaceful revolutions here at home for civil rights and human rights and began service around the world in the Peace Corps and here at home in VISTA.

Now, Americans of every generation face profound challenges in meeting the needs that have been neglected for too long in this country, from city streets plagued by crime and drugs, to classrooms where girls and boys must learn the skills they need for tomorrow, to hospital wards where patients need more care. All across America we have problems that demand our common attention.

For those who answer the call and meet these challenges, I propose that our country honor your service with new opportunities for education. National service will be America at its best, building community, offering opportunity, and rewarding responsibility. National service is a challenge for Americans from every background and walk of life, and it values something far more than money. National service is nothing less than the American way to change America.

It is rooted in the concept of community: the simple idea that none of us on our own will ever have as much to cherish about our own lives if we are out here all alone as we will if we work together; that somehow a society really is an organism in which the whole can be greater than the sum of its parts, and every one of us, no matter how many privileges with which we are born, can still be enriched by the contributions of the least of us; and that we will never fulfill our individual capacities until, as Americans, we can all be what God meant for us to be.

If that is so, if that is true, my fellow Americans, and if you believe it, it must therefore follow that each of us has an obligation to serve. For it is perfectly clear that all of us cannot be what we ought to be until those of us who can help others, and that is nearly all of us, are doing something to help others live up to their potential.

The concept of community and the idea of service are as old as our history. They began the moment America was literally invented. Thomas Jefferson wrote in the Declaration of Independence, "With a firm reliance on the protection of Divine Providence, we mutually pledge to each other our lives, our fortune, and our sacred honor."

In the midst of the Civil War, President Lincoln signed into law two visionary programs that helped our people come together again and build America up. The Morrill Act helped States create new land grant colleges. This is a land grant university. The university in my home State was the first land grant college west of the Mississippi River. In these places, young people learn to make American agriculture and industry the best in the world. The legacy of the Morrill Act is not only our great colleges and universities like Rutgers but the American tradition that merit and not money should give people a chance for a higher education.

Mr. Lincoln also signed the Homestead Act that offered 100 acres of land for families who had the courage to settle the frontier and farm the wilderness. Its legacy is a nation that stretches from coast to coast. Now we must create a new legacy that gives a new generation of Americans the right and the power to explore the frontiers of science and technology and space. The frontiers of the limitations of our knowledge must be pushed back so that we can do what we need to do. And education is the way to do it, just as surely as it was more than 100 years ago.

Seven decades after the Civil War, in the midst of the Great Depression, President Roosevelt created the Civilian Conservation Corps, which gave 2½ million young people the opportunity to support themselves while working in disaster relief and maintaining forests, beaches, rivers, and parks. Its legacy is not only the restoration of our natural environment but the restoration of our national spirit. Along with the Works Products Administration, the WPA, the Civilian Conservation Corps symbolized Government's effort to provide a nation in depression with the opportunity to work, to build the American community through service. And all over America today you can see projects, even today in the 1990's, built by your parents or your grandparents with the WPA plaque on it, the CCC plaque on it, the idea that people should be asked to serve and rewarded for doing it.

In the midst of World War II, President Roosevelt proposed the GI bill of rights, which offered returning veterans the opportunity for education in respect to their service to our country in the war. Thanks to the GI bill, which became a living reality in President Truman's time, more than 8 million veterans got advanced education. And half a century later, the enduring legacy of the GI bill is the strongest economy in the world and the broadest, biggest middle class that any nation has ever enjoyed.

For many in my own generation, the summons to citizenship and service came on this day 32 years ago, when President Kennedy created the Peace Corps. With Sargent Shriver and Harris Wofford and other dedicated Americans, he enabled thousands of young men and women to serve on the leading edge of the new frontier, helping people all over the world to become what they ought to be, and bringing them the message by their very lives that America was a great country that stood for good values and human progress. At its height, the Peace Corps enrolled 16,000 young men and women. Its legacy is not simply good will and good works in countries all across the globe but a profound and lasting change in the way Americans think about their own country and the world.

Shortly after the Peace Corps, Congress, under President Johnson, created the Volunteers In Service To America. Senator Jay Rockefeller, whom I introduced a moment ago, and many thousands of other Americans went to the hills and hollows of poor places, like West Virginia and Arkansas and Mississippi, to lift up Ameri-

cans through their service.

The lesson of our whole history is that honoring service and rewarding responsibility is the best investment America can make. And I have seen it today. Across this great land, through the Los Angeles Conservation Corps, which took the children who lived in the neighborhoods where the riots occurred and gave them a chance to get out into nature and to clean up their own neighborhoods and to lift themselves and their friends in the effort; in Boston with the City Year program; with all these programs represented here in this room today, the spirit of service is sweeping this country and giving us a chance to put the quilt of America together in a way that makes a strength out of diversity, that lifts us up out of our problems, and that keeps our people looking toward a better and brighter future.

National service recognizes a simple but powerful truth, that we make progress not by governmental action alone, but we do best when the people and their Government work at the grassroots in genuine partnership. The idea of national service permeates many other aspects of the programs I have sought to bring to America. The economic plan that I announced to Congress, for example, will offer every child the chance for a healthy start through immunization and basic health care and a head start. But still it depends on parents doing the best they can as parents and children making the most of their opportunities.

The plan can help to rebuild our cities and our small communities through physical investments that will put people to work. But Americans still must work to restore the social fabric that has been torn in too many communities. Unless people know we can work together in our schools, in our offices, in our factories, unless they believe we can walk the streets safely together, and unless we do that together, governmental action alone is doomed to fail.

The national service plan I propose will be built on the same principles as the old GI bill. When people give something of invaluable merit to their country, they ought to be rewarded with the opportunity to further their education. National service will challenge our people to do the work that should and indeed must be done and cannot be done unless the American people voluntarily give themselves up to that work. It will invest in the future of every person who serves.

As we rekindle the spirit of national service, I know it won't disappoint many of the students here to know that we also have to reform the whole system of student loans. We should begin by making it easier for young people to pay back their student loans and enabling them to hold jobs that may accomplish much but pay little.

Today, when students borrow money for an education, the repayment plan they make is based largely on how much they have to repay, without regard to what the jobs they take themselves pay. It is a powerful incentive, therefore, for young college graduates to do just the reverse of what we might want them to do, to take a job that pays more even if it is less rewarding because that is the job that will make the repayment of the loans possible. It is also, unfortunately, a powerful incentive for some not to make the payments at all, which is unforgivable.

So what we seek to do is to enable the American students to borrow the money they need for college and pay it back as a small percentage of their own income over time. This is especially important after a decade in which the cost of a college education has gone up even more rapidly than the cost of health care, making a major contribution to one of the more disturbing statistics in America today, which is that the college dropout rate in this country is now 2½ times the high school dropout rate. We can do better than that through national service and adequate financing.

The present system is unacceptable, not only for students but for the taxpayers as well. It's complicated, and it's expensive. It costs the taxpayers of our country about $4 billion every year to finance the student loan program because of loan defaults and the cost of administering the program. And I believe we can do better.

Beyond reforming this system for financing higher education, the national service program more importantly will create new opportunities for Americans to work off outstanding loans or to build up credits for future education and training opportunities.

We'll ask young people all across this country, and some who aren't so young who want to further their college education, to serve in our schools as teachers or tutors in reading and mathematics. We'll ask you to help our police forces across the Nation, training members for a new police corps that will walk beats and work with neighborhoods and build the kind of community ties that will prevent crime from happening in the first place so that our police officers won't have to spend all their time chasing criminals.

We'll ask young people to work, to help control pollution and recycle waste, to paint darkened buildings and clean up neighborhoods, to work with senior citizens and combat homelessness and help children in trouble get out of it and build a better life.

And these are just a few of the things that you will be able to do, for most of the decisions about what you can do will be made by people like those in this room, people who run the programs represented by all of those wearing these different kinds of tee-shirts. We don't seek a national bureaucracy. I have spoken often about how we need to reinvent the Government to make it more efficient and less bureaucratic, to make it more responsive to people at the grassroots level, and I want national service to do just that. I want it to empower young people and their communities, not to empower yet another Government bureaucracy in Washington. This is going to be your programs at your levels with your people.

And as you well know, that's what's happening all across America today. People are already serving their neighbors in their neighborhoods. Just this morning, I was inspired to see and to speak with students from Rutgers serving their community, from mentoring young people as Big Sisters to helping older people learn new skills. I met a lady today who has 13 grandchildren and 5 great-grandchildren who dropped out of school the year before I was born, who's about to become a high school graduate shortly because of the efforts of this program. You back there? Stand up.

I'm impressed by the spirit behind the Rutgers Civic Education and Community Service Program, the understanding that community service enriches education, that students should not only take the lessons they learn in class out into the community but bring the lessons they learn in the community back into the classroom. In that spirit, during this academic year alone, more than 800 students from Rutgers are contributing more than 60,000 hours of community service in New Brunswick, in Camden, in Newark, throughout this State.

This morning I also met with members of

the New Jersey Youth Corps—here they are; see them? Stand up—young people who are looking for a second chance at school and who, when coming back to finish their high school degrees, also serve in their communities. Through this program, more than 6,500 young adults have contributed over 900,000 hours of service to the State of New Jersey. They've done everything from paint senior citizens' homes to tutor and mentor children in after-school programs. For the future of our State and Nation, we need more young people like those in the New Jersey Youth Corps who exemplify the spirit of service.

That spirit also moves people all across the Nation. In my State, there's a young woman named Antoinette Jackson, who's a senior in a small community called Gould, Arkansas. She's a member of the Delta Service Corps. The rural Mississippi Delta is still the poorest place in America. And in that area, she works with a "lend-a-hand" program which runs a thrift shop to provide hungry and homeless people with food and clothing. And in return, the Delta Corps is going to help her attend college so that she can make an even greater contribution.

The spirit of service also moves a young man I met about a year ago named Stephen Spalos, who works with the City Year program in Boston. At age 23, he's had some hard times in his life. But as he puts it, City Year gave him a place and the tools to be able to start over. He works as a team leader, a mentor, a tutor, a project manager for a bunch of young people who restore senior citizens' homes. Last year when I visited his project, he literally took his sweatshirt off his back and gave it to me so that I would never forget the kids at City Year. And I still wear it when I go jogging, always remembering what they're doing in Boston to help those kids.

The spirit of service moves Orah Fireman, a graduate of Wesleyan College. As a sophomore in high school, she worked with disadvantaged children in upstate New York. That experience changed her life. And during her high school and college years, she continued to work with children. And now that she is out of college, she has begun what will probably be a lifetime of service by working at a school for emotionally disturbed children in Boston. She wants other people to have the opportunity to serve, and she wrote this: "Service work teaches responsibility and compassion. It fights alienation by

proving to young people that they can make a difference. There is no lesson more important than that."

Well, there are stories like this in this room and all across America. And we're going to create thousands of more of them through national service. We'll work with groups with proven track records to serve their community, giving them the support they need. And if you have more good ideas, if you're entrepreneurs of national service, we'll let you compete for our form of venture capital, to develop new programs to serve your neighbors. That's how we want the national service program to grow every year, rewarding results, building on success, and bubbling up from the grassroots energy and compassion and intellect of America.

I don't want service to wait while this potential is wasted. That's why I want to make this summer a summer of service when young people can not only serve their communities but build a foundation for a new national effort. I've asked Congress to invest in and I'm asking young people to participate in a special effort in national service and leadership training just this summer. We are going to recruit about 1,000 young people from every background, from high school dropouts to college graduates, to send to an intensive leadership training program for national service at the beginning of the summer.

Then we'll ask them to work on one of our country's most urgent problems, helping our children who are in danger of losing their God-given potential. Some of them will tutor. Some will work on programs to immunize young children from preventible childhood diseases. Some will help to develop and run recreational centers or reclaim urban parks from dealers and debris. Some will counsel people a few years younger than themselves to help keep them out of gangs and into good activities. And everyone will learn about serving our country and helping our communities.

At the end of this summer, we'll bring all these people together for several days of debriefing and training, and then they'll all join in a youth service summit. I will attend the meeting, and I expect to listen a lot more than I talk. I'll ask leaders from Congress, from business, labor, religious, and community groups to attend the youth service summit too. We'll give those who serve the honor they deserve, and we'll learn a lot more about how to build this national service program. And from the thousand pioneers of this summer, I want the national service to grow 100-fold in the next 4 years.

But even when hundreds of thousands are serving, I want to maintain the pioneer spirit of this first few months, because national service can make America new again. It can help solve our problems, educate our people, and build our communities back together. So if anybody here would like to be one of those 1,000 or if anybody who is listening to this speech by radio or television or reads about it would like to be one of those 1,000, drop me a card at the White House and just mark it "national service." We're going to pick them, and I can't promise you'll be selected, but I promise you'll be considered. I want to engage the energies of America in this effort.

I also want to say that you shouldn't wait for the summer or for a new program. We need to begin now. We are going to be looking for the kinds of ideas that we ought to be funding. This is Monday. I ask you by Friday, every one of you, to think about what you think you can do and what we should do to be agents of renewal; to talk with your parents, your clergy, your friends, your teachers; to join the effort to renew our community and to rebuild our country; and to write to me about what you are doing. It's time for millions of us to change our country block by block, neighborhood by neighborhood; time to return to our roots an excitement, an idealism, and an energy.

I have to tell you that there are some among us who do not believe that young Americans will answer a call to action, who believe that our people now measure their success merely in the accumulation of material things. They believe this call to service will go unanswered. But I believe they are dead wrong.

And so, especially to the young Americans here, I ask you to prove that those who doubt you are wrong about your generation. And today I ask all of you who are young in spirit, whether you are a 10-year-old in a service program in our schools who reads to still younger children or a 72-year-old who has become a foster grandparent, I ask you all to believe that you can contribute to your community and your country. And in so doing, you will find the best in yourself.

You will learn the lessons about your life that you might not ever learn any other way. You

will learn again that each of us has the spark of potential to accomplish something truly and enduringly unique. You will experience the satisfaction of making a connection in a way with another person that you could do in no other way. You will learn that the joy of mastering a new skill or discovering a new insight is exceeded only by the joy of helping someone else do the same thing. You will know the satisfaction of being valued not for what you own or what you earn or what position you hold but just because of what you have given to someone else. You will understand in personal ways the wisdom of the words spoken years ago by Martin Luther King, who said, "Everybody can be great because everybody can serve."

I ask you all, my fellow Americans, to support our proposal for national service and to live a proposal for national service, to learn the meaning of America at its best, and to recreate for others America at its best. We are not just another country. We have always been a special kind of community, linked by a web of rights and responsibilities and bound together not by bloodlines but by beliefs. At an age in time when people all across the world are being literally torn apart by racial hatreds, by ethnic hatreds, by religious divisions, we are a nation, with all of our problems, where people can come together across racial and religious lines and hold hands and work together not just to endure our differences but to celebrate them. I ask you to make America celebrate that again.

I ask you, in closing, to commit yourselves to this season of service because America needs it. We need every one of you to live up to the fullest of your potential, and we need you to reach those who are not here and who will never hear this talk and who will never have the future they could otherwise have if not for something that you could do. The great challenge of your generation is to prove that every person here in this great land can live up to the fullest of their God-given capacity. If we do it, the 21st century will be the American century. The American dream will be kept alive if you will today answer the call to service.

Thank you, and God bless you all.

NOTE: The President spoke at 1:15 p.m. at Rutgers University. In his remarks, he referred to Nakia Tomlinson, a Rutgers student, and Benjamin Barber, founder of the Rutgers Civic Education and Community Service Program.

Exchange With Reporters Prior to a Meeting With Democratic Congressional Leaders
March 2, 1993

Spending Cuts

Q. Mr. President, we hear you're not going to ask for any more spending cuts. Is that right?

The President. Where did you hear that?

Q. Well, there's a little piece in the paper that says somebody on your staff admitted that, well, they didn't really think you'd be able to find any more spending cuts.

The President. Well, I expect there will be a lot more as we go along. I just don't think we should shut the Congress down while we all look for them. Keep in mind that we've got more than they've had in a long time, and we need to go forward with this program. But I think you'll see a continuous stream of them coming out as we go along.

Q. From you?

The President. From me and from others.

Bosnia

Q. Mr. President, are you satisfied with the airdrops in Bosnia, the success of the airdrops?

The President. Well, the last report I got this morning was pretty good, based on the last information I had. And I haven't talked directly to General Powell today, but he thinks they've gone pretty well, and I have to rely partly on— largely on his judgment.

Q. How long do you think they need to go on there?

The President. I don't have an answer to that now.

NOTE: The exchange began at 10:19 a.m. in the Cabinet Room at the White House.

Exchange With Reporters Prior to Discussions With Secretary General Manfred Woerner of the North Atlantic Treaty Organization
March 2, 1993

Branch Davidian Religious Sect Standoff

Q. Mr. President, the incident in Waco appears to be ending. Do you have any misgivings at all about how that was executed?

The President. I don't think now is the time to discuss that. I'm pleased that it's ending. I think it's ending in a way that's very consistent with a similar incident that occurred in my State, very similar, when I was Governor there many years ago.

Q. Are you satisfied that the appropriate action was taken in the first place?

The President. I don't think this is the time for me to comment on that. It's not appropriate at this time for me to comment on it.

Haiti

Q. Are you having any second thoughts about your criticism of George Bush's Haiti policy during the campaign, given that today you went to court to essentially support his position?

The President. But our position is different.

Our position now is that there's a difference if there are extreme circumstances, and I think there are. You know, maybe I was too harsh in my criticism of him, but I still think there's a big difference between what we're doing in Haiti and what they were doing in Haiti. And there's a big difference between the kinds of problems that are created by the Haitian circumstance. I mean, something that was never brought up before but is now painfully apparent is that if we did what the plaintiffs in the court case want, we would be consigning a very large number of Haitians, in all probability, to some sort of death warrant. I mean, if you look at how many people have been lost at sea, look at the number of people who died not even trying to come to the United States in a much shorter trip recently, given the means they had to get here, the kinds of boats they have and all of that.

We have now cut from 2 months down to 1 week the amount of time it takes to process people who want to be considered to be refugees in Haiti. When we bring people back, we meet them there now. We don't just let them get dispersed into the country. We're going out into the country and doing the refugee handling. So it's a very different set of circumstances than it was.

NOTE: The exchange began at 4:25 p.m. in the Oval Office at the White House. A tape was not available for verification of the content of this exchange.

Statement by the Director of Communications on the Situation in Haiti
March 2, 1993

Today the Supreme Court heard arguments concerning the current repatriation policy regarding Haitian asylum-seekers. At that time, the Justice Department supported the President's legal authority to carry out the practice of direct return. The President believes it is essential that he retain the ability to implement such measures when exceptional circumstances demand.

The current practice of direct returns is based on the President's conviction that it is necessary to avert a humanitarian tragedy that could result from a large boat exodus. Hundreds, if not thousands, could lose their lives in overloaded, unseaworthy vessels if the United States reversed the practice of direct return precipitously.

At the same time, the President regards the current practice of direct return as a policy for exceptional circumstances. It is continually under review and will be adjusted when conditions permit.

In addition, the President is taking a series of initiatives to promote human rights and democratization in Haiti and to enhance the safety and well-being of those who have reason to fear persecution.

First, the Clinton administration strongly has supported the negotiating process undertaken by the United Nations and the Organization of American States (U.N./OAS) and has urged other nations, both within and outside the hemisphere, to provide diplomatic and financial support to the U.N./OAS effort. A U.N./OAS civilian monitoring team now is being deployed in Haiti. We hope and expect that their presence will create an atmosphere conducive to respect for human rights and political dialog, including progress on a settlement to this crisis.

The President will continue efforts to move the negotiating process forward as expeditiously as possible, leading to the restoration of constitutional government and the return of President Aristide. President Clinton will meet with President Aristide on March 16 to review the progress that has been achieved and the challenges that lie ahead.

Second, the President is committed to enhancing the safety and well-being of those in Haiti who have reason to fear reprisal for their political activities and affiliations, and has taken a number of actions to improve in-country processing of Haitian refugees, the procedures by which Haitians may apply in Haiti for refugee status and resettlement in the United States.

Shortly after January 20, the President directed that U.S. officials double our capacity for the interviewing of refugee applicants in Haiti by officials of the Immigration and Naturalization Service. The President also directed the State Department to send a technical mission to Haiti to develop detailed proposals for:

—more rapid refugee processing;

—making it easier for Haitians outside of Port-au-Prince to apply for refugee status and U.S. resettlement; and

—enhancing the safety of the repatriation process for returnees.

Since return of the technical team, we have streamlined procedures and added staff in Port-au-Prince and have reduced considerably the processing time for refugee applications in Haiti. We have already developed the capacity to reduce processing time for high priority cases from 2 months or more to about 7 working days.

The technical team, which also included congressional staff and representatives from the INS, made a series of additional recommendations for improvements in procedures, including the addition of personnel at the U.S. Refugee Processing Center in Haiti to serve as liaison with human rights groups and as a resource for INS adjudicators; procedures for identifying those who may be especially at risk; and the establishment of processing centers outside of Port-au-Prince to enhance access to the program for Haitians throughout Haiti.

Based on these and other recommendations made by the team, the President has directed

that U.S. officials implement further improvements in the process. To accomplish these goals, the President is authorizing expenditure of up to $5 million from the Emergency Refugee and Migration Assistance Fund (ERMA).

The United States has been in the forefront of refugee protection around the world. We will continue to play this important role in the years to come.

Nomination for Posts at the State and Education Departments and the Environmental Protection Agency
March 2, 1993

The President announced today his intention to nominate a total of 11 officials for senior sub-Cabinet jobs at the Department of State, the Environmental Protection Agency, and the Department of Education.

"This group of nominations continues the process of filling our Government with top-flight public servants," said the President. "I am proud that they have agreed to join my administration."

The individuals named today are:

State Department

Patrick Kennedy, Assistant Secretary for Administration

Elinor Constable, Assistant Secretary for International Environmental and Scientific Affairs

Alexander Watson, Assistant Secretary for Inter-American Affairs

John Shattuck, Assistant Secretary for Human Rights and Humanitarian Affairs

Mary Ryan, Assistant Secretary for Consular Affairs

Wendy Sherman, Assistant Secretary for Legislative Affairs

Environmental Protection Agency

Robert Sussman, Deputy Administrator

Bailus Walker, Jr., Assistant Administrator for the Office of Research and Development

Steve Herman, Assistant Administrator for Enforcement

David Gardiner, Assistant Administrator for Policy Planning and Evaluation

Education Department

Kay Casstevens, Assistant Secretary for Legislation and Congressional Affairs

NOTE: Biographies of the nominees were made available by the Office of the Press Secretary.

Exchange With Reporters Prior to a Meeting With Democratic Congressional Leaders
March 3, 1993

Texas Senatorial Campaign

Q. When are you going to Texas to campaign for Mr. Krueger?

The President. I don't know. I want to go. I haven't been invited yet. I imagine I'll get a way down there.

The Vice President. I'm going next week, aren't I?

The President. You're going——

The Vice President. I'll be there next week, Carl [Carl Leubsdorf, Dallas Morning News]. You didn't ask, but that's the answer.

Senator Krueger. Don't insult the Vice President, Carl.

Q. Will you?

The Vice President. Next week.

Bosnia

Q. [*Inaudible*]—situation on the Bosnian airlift? Is it on or off?

The President. No, it's——

Q. [*Inaudible*]—Aspin off the reservation?

The President. No, we're continuing the airlift plan. This phase of it's going forward just as planned. And it's under continuous review, but we're going forward with the phase just as it's planned.

Q. There's no pause at all in relief efforts, in flying it in?

The President. We're going forward with the phase as we had planned. As you know, for obvious reasons we don't want to discuss specifi-

cally when we're doing what. But the initial phase of the airlift is going forward just as——

Q. Why did Secretary Aspin indicate that——

The President. I don't know exactly what he said. I haven't had a chance to talk to him about it.

Q. He said it was symbolic.

Q. Was there ever a time when it was going to be off?

The Vice President. No, no. What he meant by that was that it accomplished not only the result of getting the relief but also getting the convoys a little freer access. That's what he meant by that word.

Q. And has it done that?

The Vice President. Yes, it has.

NOTE: The exchange began at 9:45 a.m. in the Oval Office at the White House.

Remarks Announcing the National Performance Review
March 3, 1993

Ladies and gentlemen, I think you all know we are here to announce a terribly important initiative in this administration to bring about greater efficiency and lower cost of Government.

I want to begin by saying that we intend for this to be a bipartisan and a citizen Government effort. And I'm delighted by the concerned Members of Congress who are here today with the Vice President and me, people who have already worked on this issue. I'd like to begin just by acknowledging the presence here of Senators Glenn and Levin, Senator Cohen, Senator Dorgan, Senator Lieberman, Senator Roth, and Senator Krueger; and in the House, Congressman Conyers, Congressman Clinger, Congressman Gordon, Congressman Laughlin, and Congresswoman Pryce and Congresswoman Slaughter. All of them have manifested an interest in the issues we are here to discuss today.

I also want to especially thank the distinguished comptroller of the State of Texas, John Sharp, who's to my right here, for the work that he did with us to put this project together and for coming all the way from Texas to be with us and with his Senator.

Today I am taking what I hope and believe will be a historic step in reforming the Federal

Government by announcing the formation of a national performance review. Our goal is to make the entire Federal Government both less expensive and more efficient, and to change the culture of our national bureaucracy away from complacency and entitlement toward initiative and empowerment. We intend to redesign, to reinvent, to reinvigorate the entire National Government.

Working under the direction of the Vice President for the next 6 months, we'll conduct an intensive national review of every single Government agency and service. We'll enlist citizens and Government workers and leaders from the private sector in a search not only for ways to cut wasteful spending but also for ways to improve services to our citizens and to make our Government work better.

I'll ask every member of our Cabinet to assign their best people to this project, managers, auditors, and frontline workers as well. And to put the "M" back in the OMB, I've asked Phil Lader, who is to my far left, the new Deputy Director for Management at OMB and a person who has spent his life solving difficult and challenging management and people problems, to take the lead in making our Government work better, not only during this 6-month period but permanently for as long as I am President.

We will turn first to Federal employees for help. They know better than anyone else how to do their jobs if someone will simply ask them and reward them for wanting to do it better. We'll ask the public to help us improve services and cut waste by calling an 800 number or by writing to the Vice President, because no one deserves a bigger say in the services Government provides than Government's customers, the American people. We'll look for ways to streamline our own organizations to reduce unnecessary layers and to improve services to the better uses of technology by giving managers more flexibility and by giving frontline workers more decisionmaking power. Just as we're trying to do that in the White House, we will try to do that throughout the National Government.

When I was the Governor of Arkansas, our State became the first in the Nation to institute a governmentwide total quality management program. And I can tell you, it works. It isn't easy. It isn't quick. It can make a huge difference, not only to the people but also to the people who work for the Government as well.

We'll look at the good work that has already been done, including many thoughtful reforms proposed by Members of the Congress, including the work last year by the House Task Force on Government Waste, chaired by then Congressman and now Senator Byron Dorgan. They discovered, among other things, that the Pentagon had stockpiled 1.2 million bottles of nasal spray. Even with my allergies, I only need half that many. [*Laughter*] As we locate such waste and wipe it out, it will be a breath of fresh air to the American taxpayers.

Cutting spending will be a priority. But so is making the system work better for the people who work in Government and the people who pay the bills and are served by it. The truth is we can't achieve the savings we want simply by cutting funds. We must also use the remaining funds in a much wiser way. We'll challenge the basic assumptions of every program, asking does it work; does it provide quality service; does it encourage innovation and reward hard work? If the answer is no or if there's a better way to do it or if there's something that the Federal Government is doing it should simply stop doing, we'll try to make the changes needed.

Many good programs began for a good reason:

to serve a national purpose or to give the States time to develop an institutional capacity to administer them. But times change, and in many cases State and local governments are now better suited to handle these programs. The Federal Government simply can't do everything, and there are many things the States or the private sector could do better.

This performance review will not produce another report just to gather dust in some warehouse. We have enough of them already. That's why I am asking for a list of very specific actions we can take now, agency by agency, program by program. This is hard work. We've been a long time getting to this spot, and we can't change the Government overnight. But we can continuously improve our operations in ways that reap dramatic results for the people of this country.

Two years ago, when the State of Texas faced an enormous budget shortfall, they launched a performance review under the leadership of John Sharp that saved the taxpayers billions of dollars over the ensuing years, made government work better at the same time.

Last month, Senator Bob Krueger took out an ad in the Washington Post just inviting the public to call a waste hotline to help make Government work and to help make it 100 percent fat-free. He got 200 calls the first day.

Vice President Gore and I think a national performance review is an absolutely necessary beginning, because we have too much to do that a wasteful and mismanaged Government will not be able to do. We have to cut and invest at the same time, something that's never been done before. We have to reduce the cost of health care and meet the challenges of an intensely competitive global economy. And we have to do those things with less money than we're spending in many areas today. We have to reduce the largest deficit in our history, as we do in our economic program, or it will literally rob us of our ability to solve problems, invest in the future, or thrive economically.

And most important, the American people deserve a Government that is both honest and efficient, and for too long they haven't gotten it. For most Americans, a college loan or a Social Security check represents a common border with the best ideals and goals of our country. We all count to some extent on our Government to protect the environment, to provide education and health care and other basic needs. But democracy can become quickly an empty phrase, if those who are elected to serve cannot meet the needs of the people except with Government that costs too much or is too slow or too arrogant or too unresponsive.

Finally, let me stress that this performance review, as I said at the beginning, is not about politics. Programs passed by both Democratic Presidents and Republican Presidents, voted on by Members of Congress of both parties, and supported by the American people at the time are being undermined by an inefficient and outdated bureaucracy and by our huge debt. For too long the basic functioning of the Government has gone unexamined. We want to make improving the way Government does business a permanent part of how Government works, regardless of which party is in power.

It isn't written anywhere that government can't be thrifty or flexible or entrepreneurial. Increasingly, most government is, and it is time the Federal Government follows the example set by the most innovative State and local leaders and by the many huge private sector companies that have had to go through the same sort of searching reexamination over the last decade, companies that have downsized and streamlined and become more customer friendly and, as a result, have had much, much more success.

In short, it's time our Government adjusted to the real world, tightened its belt, managed its affairs in the context of an economy that is information based, rapidly changing, and puts a premium on speed and function and service, not rules and regulations.

Americans voted for a change last November. They want better schools and health care and better roads and more jobs, but they want us to do it all with a Government that works better on less money and is more responsive. The American people may not know specifically how to do it, although many of them have good particular ideas, but I'm confident our people are willing to try new ways and they want us to experiment. They want us to do things that have worked in other contexts now in the National Government, and that's what we are here to do today.

I thank the Vice President for his willingness to lead this effort. I thank the Members of Congress who are here and those who are not who are supporting us. And I earnestly enlist the support of the American people and especially the employees of the United States Government in this important effort.

I'd like now to introduce the Vice President, who will be in charge of this effort of performance review for the next 6 months, for his statement.

NOTE: The President spoke at 10:07 a.m. in Room 450 of the Old Executive Office Building.

Statement on the Death of Albert Sabin
March 3, 1993

I was saddened to learn of the passing this morning of Dr. Albert Sabin, one of the great heroes of American medicine. The oral polio vaccine that he developed has saved countless lives and provided millions more with the comfort of security.

I have made a commitment to work towards the goal of ensuring that all of our Nation's children receive proper immunizations. This loss today reminds us all of the seriousness with which that task must be taken. We must continue the battle which Albert Sabin so nobly waged.

Remarks on Receiving the Rotary International Award of Honor and an Exchange With Reporters
March 4, 1993

Award of Honor

Clifford Dochterman. Mr. President, as the former president of Rotary International, I have the occasion on several occasions to present an award called the Rotary International Award of Honor presented to selected heads of state. We've only presented this on about 12 occasions. This award is given for humanitarian service. And the service that you're giving for Rotary International's programs of support for immunization of children in the world, as well as our programs of humanitarian aid in Bosnia and Croatia, gives me the opportunity—if you would accept this award on behalf of 1,100,000 Rotarians of the world in 187 countries—it would be a great pleasure—to accept this award.

The President. Thank you for your good work, and thank you for the award. I appreciate that.

Mr. Dochterman. It has a ribbon there, but I'll not be so presumptuous to put it over your——

The President. Isn't it beautiful? Thank you.

Mr. Dochterman. This award has been presented on selected occasions on behalf of those who support humanitarian efforts throughout the world.

The President. I'm deeply honored.

World Trade Center Bombing

Q. Excuse me, Mr. President, can you tell us anything about the arrest and whether the American people can now believe that they are secure in that someone has been arrested?

The President. I can tell you that I was informed this morning about it. And the authorities are still working on a statement that I think will be issued to you later this afternoon. I think they'll be able to give you some more information later this afternoon.

Q. Now the suspect though is linked to terrorism, should Americans feel less secure about their safety?

The President. I think you should wait until the—I think, first of all, the American people should be very proud of the work done by the law enforcement authorities. They worked hard together. They worked aggressively. They worked without stopping until they made, I think, a very quick arrest. But I'd like for you to wait until the proper authorities have a chance to make their statement to you later this afternoon. And then tomorrow I will have a chance to make some more comments on it.

Q. Can we assume that it's terrorism?

The President. I don't think you should assume anything until you hear the statement today. I know that an arrest was made. I know who was arrested. I think that at the time I was informed this morning there were a lot of other questions we did not know the answers to. And they're trying to get as much information together as possible to give you later this afternoon.

NOTE: The presentation began at 3:07 p.m. in the Oval Office at the White House.

Exchange With Reporters Following a Meeting With Tilden Middle School Students
March 4, 1993

Health Care Task Force

Q. Mr. President, can you explain to us why your health care task force won't be open to the public?

The President. No working group of the Government before they have a proposal—that would be like opening the White House at every staff meeting we have. We can't do that. I mean, they've got 400 people over there, working continuously on thousands of different issues. Nobody ever does that. We would never—we can't get anything done.

Also, what we've done has been publicly reported. Most of the papers have been released or leaked. But they have to be able to work. It's an ongoing project. It's like any other staff work the White House does.

Q. But how do we know that there is no conflict of interest since we don't know who is working on it and we can't attend any of the meetings, the public meetings?

The President. It's just like any other—how do you know that about anything we do here at the White House?

World Trade Center Bombing

Q. Can you be any more reassuring on the whole terrorism question, sir? This is obviously what people are going to be most worried about.

The President. I think that people should be very reassured by the incredibly rapid work done by the law enforcement officials involved. It is very impressive. All resources were put into this from the moment the explosion occurred, and I think they did a remarkable job. I don't think I should say more than I know now. And I think you should wait until the statement is made tonight by the appropriate officials, and I'll be glad to give you further comments. But I think the American people should be very much reassured by the speed with which the law enforcement folks responded to this circumstance.

NOTE: The exchange began at 3:25 p.m. in the North Foyer at the White House. A portion of this exchange could not be verified because the tape was incomplete.

Remarks on Signing the Emergency Unemployment Compensation Amendments of 1993 and an Exchange With Reporters
March 4, 1993

The President. I want to, first of all, acknowledge the presence here of Senators Mitchell, Moynihan, Riegle, Sarbanes, Sasser, Hatfield, and Durenberger; the Speaker and Congressman Matsui and Congressman Fish. I would also like to acknowledge the Labor Secretary and two of his employees whom I will recognize formally in just a moment.

Today I am signing important legislation to extend unemployment benefits long term. I want to thank the Congress for passing this bill, which is the first provision in the economic package I recommended to them in my joint address.

The bill reforms existing law. It symbolizes the success of a new management style we are bringing to the Government. And it reminds us of how critical it is to adopt the rest of our economic plan, to increase investment, reduce the deficit, create private-sector jobs, and increase the incomes of working Americans.

We have extended unemployment benefits. Now it's time to extend jobs. It's been less than a month since I asked the Secretary of Labor to prepare the emergency legislation. I want to commend the leadership of the Congress, of those who are here and those who are not, who made rapid action possible. Thanks to them, the benefits of millions of Americans will proceed without interruption. More important, this legislation takes an existing pilot program and applies it nationally in ways that I am convinced will help tens of thousands of workers immediately. This reform was brought to the attention of Secretary Reich by line workers at the Department of Labor, and it reflects the kind of innovation and imagination we must bring to the entire Federal Government. It is at the core of the national performance review initiative that the Vice President and I announced yesterday.

The Department of Labor funds a demonstration project in New Jersey that matches up workers who are permanently displaced with training and reemployment services. They use existing data to provide services to people in need. Once they're identified, the workers receive the kind of counseling, training, and retraining that gets them back to work faster and often at higher wages than would have otherwise been the case.

Secretary of Labor Reich held a town meeting in his Department of Labor to break down the walls that too often have existed between senior management and Federal employees. Because two dedicated public employees brought this successful innovation to his attention, today it is becoming the law of the land everywhere, thanks to the Congress. It's a great example of what we can and must do throughout the Government.

And the people who made it happen have joined us here for this important moment. With this bill becoming law, 1½ million unemployed Americans who need help making the rent and buying groceries and paying for school clothes will receive it. I hope they will also recognize the efforts of the two gentlemen to my left with the Secretary of Labor, Steve Wandner and Steve Marler, the Labor Department employees who brought the profiling reform to the Secretary's attention. Thank you very much.

Some of the indicators are that we are coming out of a long and deep recession. But, as all of you know, this has been a slow, anemic recovery when it comes to job growth especially. It is time now to get on to the important work of stimulating our economy and putting the American people back to work, to creating the conditions that will allow the private sector to create jobs, and to create jobs at good wages. I hope that this is a good first step.

There are those who say we don't need to do anything else to our economy, but I would remind you all that we are 3 million jobs behind where we would be at this point in an ordinary American recovery. Claims for unemployment benefits are up again this week, and there are still deep structural changes going on in this economy as well as a recession in Europe and a very difficult economic problem in Japan, all of these things affecting our future prospects. I think we can grow our economy, and we can create jobs. But we have to be committed, as I said, to a long-term program to create jobs and raise incomes. That is what our economic plan seeks to do.

As I said, we're now extending unemployment benefits, and that's a good thing to do. We are recognizing the fact that more and more Americans who lose their jobs now don't expect to go back to those old jobs. There's been a stunning increase in the number of people who say when they lose their jobs today, I don't expect to get this job back. And the reform brought to our attention by these two fine gentlemen will help us to help those people. But in the end, what we have to do is to extend jobs and not unemployment. That is our next great test,

and I think we're off to a good beginning today.

[At this point, the President signed the bill.]

Bosnia

Q. Mr. President, do you have any response to Mr. Karadzic, who had an implied threat of violence against the United States because of its policy of airdrops?

The President. Well, if that's what he meant to do, he made a terrible mistake, and it was something that I viewed with grave concern and real disapproval.

World Trade Center Bombing

Q. Do you think that the incident in New York and the arrest today should make Americans afraid about foreign policy decisions that might affect us domestically through terrorism?

The President. No, I don't think the American people can afford to be afraid. I think we all have to be concerned about any risks to our people's safety. But I would say again what I said to you earlier: My feeling now is one of real gratitude to the law enforcement officials at every level who worked together and moved quickly to try to resolve this matter and who did make an arrest.

I think we should wait until the formal statement is issued, until we know more facts before we can draw any conclusions about anything other than the fact that an arrest was undertaken. When I know more facts I'll be glad to answer more questions and say more. But I think that today we ought to be very impressed that the law enforcement authorities in this country moved so quickly to make an arrest. And I'm grateful to them.

Q. Why would it be a grave mistake for him to make implications?

Q. Based on what you know, sir, do you think they'll be able to crack the bombing case?

Deficit Reduction

Q. What does this say about your commitment to cutting the deficit?

The President. It says I've done more about it than anybody in recent history. And I intend to keep on.

Thank you.

NOTE: The President spoke at 4:33 p.m. in the Roosevelt Room at the White House. H.R. 920, approved March 4, was assigned Public Law No. 103–6.

Statement on Signing the Emergency Unemployment Compensation Amendments of 1993
March 4, 1993

Today I am pleased to sign into law H.R. 920, the "Emergency Unemployment Compensation Amendments of 1993." This legislation will provide critical assistance to the unemployed and their families by extending the Emergency Unemployment Compensation (EUC) program—which is scheduled to expire March 6—through October 2, 1993. In addition, the legislation includes an innovative worker profiling program to encourage States to use the Unemployment Insurance system to link permanently displaced workers to reemployment services early in their period of unemployment and facilitate their transition to new jobs.

With the EUC program due to expire this Saturday, I commend the Congress for its swift action to ensure that there will be continued help for millions of jobless Americans who want to work to support their families but cannot find jobs. I believe that, as a Nation, we have a moral obligation, as well as an economic interest, to help these families stay afloat while they attempt to find jobs.

While there have been recent signs of improvement in the economy, this improvement has regrettably not extended to the area of employment. The unemployment rate has been over 7 percent for 14 consecutive months and the current rate is higher than the rate that existed when the EUC program was originally enacted. Moreover, the current labor market is, in many respects, weaker than it was at what was considered the worst point of the recession. For example, the rates at which the unemployed are now exhausting their regular State benefits and the average length of time the unemployed are now receiving benefits are significantly higher than they were at the bottom of the recession.

H.R. 920 combines compassion with a healthy dose of common sense. It not only provides extended income support to help the unemployed with grocery bills, mortgages, car and tuition payments, and other expenses, but also offers a means to help target reemployment services to the structurally unemployed so they can get back to work.

Enactment of this bill is an important first step. While there are funds available to pay EUC benefits for a few more weeks, the funds for the balance of the extension are included as part of my economic stimulus package. The EUC extension will help sustain the unemployed until we are successful in creating more jobs. It is therefore also imperative that we now work together to enact quickly the stimulus package, as well as the long-term public investment and deficit reduction proposals I have presented. These actions will ensure strong, sustained economic growth and significantly increase the job opportunities available to the American people.

WILLIAM J. CLINTON

The White House,
March 4, 1993.

NOTE: H.R. 920, approved March 4, was assigned Public Law No. 103–6.

Letter to the Acting Director of the Federal Emergency Management Agency on Disaster Assistance for Washington
March 4, 1993

Dear Mr. Tidball:

I have determined that the damage in certain areas of the State of Washington, resulting from severe storms and high winds on January 20–21, 1993, is of sufficient severity and magnitude to warrant a major disaster declaration under the Robert T. Stafford Disaster Relief and Emergency Assistance Act ("the Stafford Act"). I, therefore, declare that such a major disaster exists in the State of Washington.

In order to provide Federal assistance, you are hereby authorized to allocate from funds available for these purposes, such amounts as you find necessary for Federal disaster assistance and administrative expenses.

You are authorized to provide Public Assistance in the designated areas. Consistent with the requirement that Federal assistance be supplemental, any Federal funds provided under the Stafford Act for Public Assistance will be limited to 75 percent of the total eligible costs.

Sincerely,

BILL CLINTON

NOTE: This letter was made available by the Office of the Press Secretary but was not issued as a White House press release.

Letter to Governor Mike Lowry on Disaster Assistance for Washington
March 4, 1993

Dear Governor Lowry:

As requested, I have declared a major disaster under the Robert T. Stafford Disaster Relief and Emergency Assistance Act (the Stafford Act) for the State of Washington due to damage resulting from severe storms and high winds on January 20–21, 1993. I have authorized Federal relief and recovery assistance in the affected area.

Public Assistance will be provided. Consistent with the requirement that Federal assistance be supplemental, any Federal funds provided under the Stafford Act for Public Assistance will be limited to 75 percent of the total eligible costs in the designated areas.

The Federal Emergency Management Agency ("FEMA") will coordinate Federal assistance efforts and designate specific areas eligible for such assistance. The Federal Coordinating Officer will be Mr. John Kainrad of FEMA. He will consult with you and assist in the execution of the FEMA-State Disaster Assistance Agreement governing the expenditure of Federal Funds.

Sincerely,

BILL CLINTON

NOTE: This letter was made available by the Office of the Press Secretary but was not issued as a White House press release.

Nomination for an Associate Judge of the Superior Court of the District of Columbia
March 4, 1993

The President has nominated Russell F. Canan to be an Associate Judge of the Superior Court of the District of Columbia. In doing so, the President discharged his responsibility under local law to select a nominee from a list of candidates originally submitted last year by the District of Columbia Judicial Nominating Commission.

"I was impressed with all of the candidates," said the President, "but Russ Canan stood out because of his broad support within the District of Columbia legal community, including Mayor Kelly's personal recommendation, and because of the impressive track record he has accumulated in 16 years of law practice in Washington. Above all, we heard nothing but the highest praise for Mr. Canan's professional skills and talents from those who know his work the best: the many judges on the Superior Court before whom he has practiced."

NOTE: A biography of the nominee was made available by the Office of the Press Secretary.

Remarks on Mayoral Support for the Economic Program and an Exchange With Reporters
March 5, 1993

The President. I want to thank all of the mayors who spoke, and all the ones who are here who have not spoken, for their strong support without regard to party or region or the size of the communities from which they come. As a matter of fact, when I heard the Mayor of York, Pennsylvania, speak, I was trying to decide whether his tie was a Republican or a Democratic tie. I think it is really an all-American tie. It's a bold tie, the Vice President said. [*Laughter*]

I want to say a special word of thanks, too, to the Secretary of the Department of Housing and Urban Development, Henry Cisneros, who is with us, who has worked very closely with the mayors.

I have just a few things I want to say about this. First of all, any mayor who has served for any length of time has been compelled to make the kinds of choices that are embodied in this economic program. If you look at the budgets of the cities of this country or the budgets of the States of this country over the last decade you will see the choices that have been imposed in order to balance books and keep the functions of our cities running, in order to deal with relative reductions in Federal assistance and all the economic crises that have ripped our communities. Mayors have learned to cut budgets and to shift funds away from inessential things toward investments in our futures.

I know that that is one reason that mayors intuitively and without regard to party have responded to my efforts to increase investment and reduce the deficit at the same time. We have to do both. Today there was a report that the unemployment rate in February dropped to 7 percent, one-tenth of 1 percent, and that 365,000 jobs were created, an estimated 365,000 jobs. That is good news. But if you look behind the numbers, it also reveals the stark challenges before us, for most of those jobs were part-time jobs, and we are still about 3 million jobs behind where we would ordinarily be in a recovery.

Indeed, we are, according to the aggregate economic statistics, in a recovery in which, ironically, the unemployment rate is still higher than it was at the very bottom of the recession. That shows you that there is a fundamental restructuring going on in the American economy which requires an extraordinary approach to the creation of jobs in the short and in the long term.

That's why these investments in repairing our streets and bridges, renovating our housing, rebuilding our water and sewer lines, improving mass transit, retooling our industrial parks, and protecting our environment are important parts of the larger plan also to invest in our people and their economic, educational, and technological futures.

Through $3 billion in additional funding for highways, airports, and mass transit, $2.5 billion in community development block grants, which can be used to create new jobs and improve the quality of life, communities will be able to complete projects they've needed for years but haven't been able to finance. They will create new jobs today, but they will also build the foundations for broader economic growth in the private sector tomorrow.

This plan also will create almost 700,000 new jobs this summer for unemployed young people, something that will be profoundly important again in sending the right signals. We all know, for example, that the financial markets, as Mayor Dinkins said, respond to the right signals, interest rates are down almost one full point now. And if we can keep them down for several months, we may well put another $100 billion in refinancing back into this economy for investment and growth. Why? Because the markets have responded to a signal.

Well, people respond to signals, too. People in San Diego, where the unemployment has been so high, will respond to a signal. Will this stimulus program give a job to every person in San Diego? Of course not, but it will send a signal that America is on the move again. Will this stimulus program provide a summer job for every young person in south central Los Angeles that Mayor Bradley is so concerned about? Of course not, but it will sure send a signal that America is on the move again and coming together again.

Will it in the beginning provide enough funds for everybody to do in every city what Mayor Lanier and Mayor Freedman and others have done in parts of their communities with community policing? Of course not, but it will provide a beginning, and it will send a signal that we are moving in the right direction. And it will actually have an economic impact that is positive. These things are very important.

I also don't want to forget the fact that a significant percentage, almost half, of this stimulus package is as incentives to the private sector for private investment in these same communities. Small businesses have created virtually all of the new jobs in our country in the last 10 years. Their inability to create more jobs than larger employers have been shedding is the central cause of stagnant employment in America. So the small business tax credit that we offer, the new business long-term capital gains tax, and the other incentives for businesses, both small and large, to create new jobs is very important.

This plan is based on the idea that we all have to work together to build our future; the idea that we have to look at the long-run needs for the 365,000 or so kids that will be in Head Start, for the millions of young people who we want to provide for education and training, for all the people who have lost their jobs because of defense cutbacks or other industrial relocations; that they need intense efforts to reinvest in their community as well as to retraining opportunities; that we need to couple those long-term efforts with the short-term stimulus that will send the right signal, spark this economy, and get some job growth back into this recovery.

This is not, as so many have said, a partisan issue. It is not a small town or a large city issue. It is something that we all have to face to get the job done. And I'm very grateful for the support that's been given.

Meeting With Russian President Yeltsin

Now, before I answer questions, I'd like to make just a very brief announcement that I think the press here already knows about. But I want to formally announce that in Vancouver, Canada, on April 3d and 4th, I will meet with President Yeltsin of Russia to explore what the United States can do to support his efforts to strengthen democracy and to create a vibrant market economy, and to support our common interests in solving crises around the world in maintaining a general march toward peace and freedom and democracy.

I will try to be rather specific at that time in terms of what the United States will be prepared to do, and we will try to offer some innovative solutions to the difficulties faced by the President and by the Russian people.

I hope that this will be a very productive thing. I look forward to it. I'll be glad to answer a few questions about that, but I hope, too, that you recognize that the significance of this action today is that if we can have enough bipartisan support to pass an economic program in the Congress that will strengthen America. America, in turn, will be better able to deal with the problems that we face beyond our borders. Unless we're strong here, it's going to be very difficult for us to meet our responsibilities around the world.

Q. Mr. President, the Soviets or the Russians have made it clear that what they need most at this point is U.S. financial aid. Are you planning to bring anything like that to the Vancouver summit?

The President. There will be—obviously, money will be discussed, but it is not just a question of money, and it's certainly not money alone. I don't want to put a figure on it yet. We've made no decisions. But I can tell you we've discussed some rather innovative things that have not yet been on the table in these discussions in the past. This will not be a meet-and-greet meeting with President Yeltsin. We have met before, and we have talked several times since I have been in office. I am going there to try to have a very businesslike meeting. And as we get closer to the meeting, we'll be able to discuss more specifics.

Stimulus Package

Q. Several economists already this morning were jumping on the unemployment figures to say that, no, in fact, the stimulus package isn't needed, despite your interpretation of these numbers. What does this do to the political environment that you face in getting this through as quickly as you need to?

The President. That in part depends on whether the Members of the Congress listen to economists who have good jobs—*[laughter]*—and who have not had declining incomes, by and large, for the last 12 years, or whether they listen to people like the folks who are up here with me, without regard to party, who know what's happening on the streets out there.

The assumption is—look, nothing would make me happier than to know that just the efforts to bring interest rates down and the extraordinary efforts by American business-people in the private sector to increase productivity would generate 365,000 jobs a month for 2 or 3 years. That would be a wonderful thing.

But I would say again, the unemployment rate in this country is 7 percent. That is very high in our economy because it's an open economy without the sort of huge support you have in some of the European economies that are built for higher unemployment rates in a way. And a lot of those jobs were part-time jobs. That, again, speaks to the need to address the health care issue because one of the reasons so many of these jobs are part-time jobs is that employers can't afford to hire full-time employees because they can't pay the health care bill.

But I just simply don't agree. I mean, there are people who see one month of—the employment rate dropped one-tenth of a point. That is not an enormous drop. These jobs were not all, or even most, full-time jobs. I am very grateful for it, but it seems to me that, if anything, the continued persistence of relatively high unemployment is a good argument for the stimulus package.

Q. Politically, you are trying to buck a trend here, right? I mean, the political indicators are going the other way.

The President. The economic indicators are not. I think the political indicators are going the other way because I have challenged the Congress to cut spending. And so since there hasn't been a response in terms of "Here's our list," the easiest thing to do is to say, "Well, let's just don't hire any kids this summer in Los Angeles or New York or Cincinnati or Cleveland or whatever."

You know, this is about jobs. This economic recovery is about jobs. How anybody could go to any State in this country, and particularly to some of those in real duress, and say that we're in the midst of a strong recovery is a mystery to me.

Aid to Russia

Q. One of the things that's plagued the U.S.-Russia relationship when it comes to this aid question for the last couple of years has been this kind of chicken and egg situation: We want Yeltsin to make the reforms, and we'll give him

the aid. He says, "I need the aid first. Then I'll make the reforms." How can we get out of that situation? And is it time for the West to maybe consider lowering the goalpost a little bit in terms of the prior conditions he has to implement before we come through with our aid?

The President. Let me try to answer the question in this way: I believe that he is a man of real courage and real commitment to democracy. I believe, indeed, even his parliamentary opponents, who often say things with which I disagree, are engaged in the messy process of democracy which many other countries trying to move to a market economy, for example, have decided to postpone until they get the market reforms underway.

So I believe that they've made enough effort for us to try to engage them in specific actions that will produce economic results. Now, I don't want to make any sweeping commitments that would indicate that I would disregard a move toward reform or disregard issues that have been at play before, proliferation issues and others. But I'm going there to this meeting with the intention of trying to more aggressively engage the United States in the economic and political revitalization of Russia. I agree, frankly, with the general thrust of President Nixon's article in the New York Times today.

Mayoral Support

Q. Mr. President, why would you expect Members of Congress to be swayed by this event here today when big-city mayors would obviously support your package? It's a veritable goody basket for them.

The President. A veritable what?

Q. Goody basket.

The President. Well, I disagree with that. It is not nearly as much money as most of them believe we should need. And not all of them here are big-city mayors.

The fundamental issue is really here whether you believe there is a distinction between investing in infrastructure and technology, in people, and just continuing present Government spending patterns and whether you really believe that 7 percent unemployment and another decade of stagnant wages is an acceptable economic course for America. I just think that this notion that—let me tell you what I really think is going on. [*Laughter*] Let me tell you what I really think is going on, and I say this to compliment the Congress to some extent on this issue.

I think the American people liked it when I offered 150 specific spending cuts, and they said they wanted more. But if you do a poll, the people are still trying to come to grips with the reality of the budget. They'll also say, do you want us to spend more on jobs, education, and health care? Eighty percent will say yes. Do you want Congress to find more budget cuts? Eighty percent will say yes.

So the issue is not whether there should be more budget cuts. Indeed, the process that I announced, the 6-month process that I announced for the national performance review that the Vice President is overseeing, will produce more reductions in spending. There is no question about it. The issue is whether under the general shield of saying we need to reduce spending, we'll step away from investment. Just because a mayor wants to do it doesn't make it wrong, doesn't make it pork, and doesn't make it useless. I mean, we have tried ignoring the cities for 12 years, and it has not been a very successful economic strategy for the country.

Bosnia

Q. Are you concerned, sir, at all by indications that your mercy flights to Bosnia are actually increasing the violence there, increasing the ethnic cleansing? And if so, what could you do about it, sir? Any thought of——

The President. Well, first of all, let me say, both at the national security meeting and again that morning at our morning briefing I asked and pressed this question that's being asserted in the press. And it is true—I mean, we knew when we dropped food into a contested area in eastern Bosnia where there had been a build-up of fighting over time that we were dropping food to people who were at risk. That's precisely one of the reasons that that's an area we were asked to look at for airlift because the cars couldn't get in there. I mean the trucks couldn't get in there.

But all I can tell you is the people I have asked in the privacy of the Oval Office and the privacy of the national security meetings, frankly, just dispute that assertion. They do not believe that the airlift has exposed the Bosnians to any more danger than they otherwise would have been exposed to. And the surveillance we've done indicates that there has been actually slightly more accuracy in the drops from the altitude we chose for safety for our pilots than

we thought there would be.

So would I reexamine it if I thought they were doing more harm than good? Of course, I would. But I can tell you that I have pressed that point very hard in our meetings, and our people simply dispute the proposition.

Q. Mr. President, following up on that, what more can be done to tighten the embargo on oil and other supplies? The leakage to the Danube is quite clear. Is a naval blockade the way to go?

The President. Let me say we are exploring and, indeed, are in the process of implementing ways to tighten the embargo, which we will announce very shortly. And I think there are other things we can do. There are two constraints on our field of action that I would ask all of you to remember. Apart from my concern that we not commit the United States to a quagmire where our efforts would be frustrated but where I could put a lot of Americans at risk, but apart from that, apart from the whole issue of ground forces which is not on the table at all, there are two other constraints on our action which I ask you all to consider.

One is the need to proceed with the cooperation of our European allies, who have been reluctant to do certain things because the French and the British actually have forces on the ground who would be at risk if there were a reaction to whatever else we did. And those forces have been superintending the delivery of humanitarian aid, and most people there believe that their presence has saved more lives than their absence and tougher action would have saved.

The other is, of course, the not insignificant difficulties that further confrontation might depose to the cooperation we have enjoyed so far in that region with the Russians, given the internal political conflicts in Russia based on their historic ties to Serbia.

Now, notwithstanding those two things, we want to find ways to tighten the embargo, and we are moving on that right now. Even as we speak we are moving on that. And we're moving on some other options that might be available to us that I wouldn't rule out. But I do need to proceed here. The United States cannot proceed here unilaterely. We need the support of the Europeans, who are much closer to the situation and who will be much more immediately impacted by any further adverse instability in the Balkans than we would.

Q. But does this 24-hour incidence indicate to you that the ethnic cleansing is succeeding, that the policy of the Serbs——

The President. I don't think there's any question that when the Serbs take an area and then run all the Bosnian Muslims out, then that means that they are succeeding. They have succeeded in running some people out of communities.

Now, the people on the ground, the United Nations, I think still have to be defended for trying to facilitate their escape, not for supporting ethnic cleansing but because it is below freezing, it is in the snow, those people are at risk, and the United Nations operation there is now simply trying to save their lives.

There is some indication that there may be some break in the negotiations and some willingness on the part of some of the parties to compromise in the Vance-Owen process. And I think it will be very interesting for the world to look and see if the Serbians are willing to negotiate in good faith in a process that they have embraced when it suited their short-term strategic interests. I hope that they will support it over a longer term. We'll see.

Press Secretary Myers. Last question.

World Trade Center Bombing

Q. Mr. President, I'm wondering if you and perhaps Mayor Dinkins could update us on the investigation in New York of the World Trade Center bombing. Yesterday you indicated you'd have more to say after the arraignment of this one suspect.

The President. Anything else I can say is something I've already read in the morning press. You now know more about the profile of the person who was arrested, and you've seen the speculation about it. I do not want to feed that speculation. I will say again I am very impressed with the work done by the law enforce-

ment officials. They got on this. They did it in a hurry. They would admit there was a break or two in their inquiry, but they also, I think, did a very commendable job.

I think it is very important not to rush the judgment here, not to reach ahead of the facts which are known to reach broad conclusions about who was behind this or what happened. When I know who was behind this and what happened, I will then determine what the appropriate course for the United States is, and I will say it. But I think it is very, very important, and this is a delicate matter, that we reassure the American people in terms of what law enforcement did in response to the incident.

But we ask them not to jump to conclusions. We have massive resources at work on this case, massive. And we are doing everything we can to get as many facts as quickly as we can. When we know the facts and when I can state them to you with real confidence so that it's not conjecture or opinion, I will be glad to make a very forthright statement about it.

Thank you.

Dave, do you want to say anything else?

Mayor David Dinkins. The President has said it all. As a matter of fact, the Department of Justice has requested that the New York City Police Department and all others involved in this effort stay within the confines of the complaint. And while it is easy to go a little beyond that because you think it won't be harmful, you really get to a slippery slope situation, and some unfortunate comment can impede an otherwise very successful investigation.

NOTE: The President spoke at 10:46 a.m. in Room 450 of the Old Executive Office Building. In his remarks, he referred to the following Mayors: Bill Althaus, York, PA; David Dinkins, New York City; Bob Lanier, Houston, TX; and Sandra Freedman, Tampa, FL.

Exchange With Reporters on Bosnia
March 5, 1993

Q. Mr. President, can you tell us any more about the Bosnian sanctions that you're putting on today?

The President. No, we'll have more to say.

Q. Are these going to be unilateral or through the United Nations?

The President. We'll put it out—I'm not— everything we've done on the sanctions so far is, and all of the things I've explored with our allies has pretty well been supported by everyone.

Q. Are the Russians sending arms to Serbia, sir?

The President. I'm in a photo op. [*Laughter*]

NOTE: The exchange began at 11:21 a.m. in the Oval Office at the White House, prior to a meeting with Roman Catholic bishops.

Remarks Congratulating the Super Bowl Champion Dallas Cowboys
March 5, 1993

The President. It's about time we had somebody with real popularity in here. [*Laughter*] I want to say it is a great pleasure and honor for all of us to have the Dallas Cowboys in the East Room. Four years ago they were about 1 and 15, and 4 years later they won the Super Bowl. In the parlance of Washington we call that deficit reduction. [*Laughter*]

I want to say a special word of appreciation to Jimmy Johnson and Jerry Jones. I watched them win a national championship for Arkansas 30 years ago, before most of the players were born, and I've been cheering them on ever since. Most of the people in our State were Cowboy fans even before Arkansas got its hands on the Cowboys.

I also want to say something very serious. I watched this team over the last year win the way I think Americans win best. They hung in there. They were strong. They were dedicated. They started a lot of games slow, and they always finished fast. And that's what we have to do as a country. We have to endure. We have to never quit, and we have to finish fast. And I think that the country was very thrilled just to watch the renaissance of the Cowboys over the last couple of years.

Let me also say I had a very great political dilemma because the Super Bowl occurred the night I hosted the state dinner for the Governors. So, I had the Governor of New York and the Governor of Texas sitting on either side of me in the beginning of the game before it was obvious what the outcome would be. I was tested as never before in trying to maintain a poker face about the game. [*Laughter*] But

you made it easy for us after a couple of quarters.

Let me say again on behalf of the Vice President and myself to you, Jerry, and to you, Jimmy, and to all the Cowboys, we're grateful to have you here.

And I understand that this is Michael Irving's birthday, is that right?

Jimmy Johnson. He probably just made that up. [*Laughter*]

The President. Is that right? Is that right? Is it your birthday? Come up here. How old are you? I said, "How old are you?" He said, "27, but tell them 24." Have you ever considered running for office? [*Laughter*] Can you imagine that, 27 years old and wealthy enough to retire the national debt. [*Laughter*] Well, happy birthday. I hope you'll have many more. You may not be able to have any years better than this one, but I hope you have many more at least as good.

[*At this point, Dallas Cowboys owner Jerry Jones made a statement.*]

Mr. Johnson. Mr. President, it is a tremendous thrill and tremendous honor for all of us to make you an official member of the Dallas Cowboys as a reserve quarterback.

The President. Thank you. I'm just going to sit around now and wait for my number to be called. [*Laughter*] I'm going to start practicing this afternoon. You know, it's never too late.

Thank you very much.

NOTE: The President spoke at 3:20 p.m. in the East Room at the White House.

Nomination for Posts at the Departments of Health and Human Services and Education
March 5, 1993

The President today announced his intention to nominate Bruce Vladeck to be Administrator of the Health Care Financing Administration at the Department of Health and Human Services and Norma Cantu to be Assistant Secretary for Civil Rights at the Department of Education.

"I am very pleased to make these nominations today to two extremely important positions," said the President. "Bruce Vladeck and Norma Cantu are highly talented individuals with unique qualifications for the leadership roles that I have asked them to take."

NOTE: Biographies of the nominees were made available by the Office of the Press Secretary.

Nomination for Posts at the Department of State
March 5, 1993

The President today expressed his intention to nominate Douglas Bennet, the president and CEO of National Public Radio, to be the Assistant Secretary of State for International Organization Affairs; Eric James Boswell to be the Director of the Office of Foreign Missions; and Conrad Harper to be the State Department's Legal Adviser.

"These three positions are essential to the smooth workings of State Department operations," said the President. "Douglas Bennet, Eric James Boswell, and Conrad Harper will fill them with talent, dedication, and the steady hands that are needed to get the job done."

NOTE: Biographies of the nominees were made available by the Office of the Press Secretary.

The President's Radio Address
March 6, 1993

Good morning. We've come a long way together in the last few weeks. You've had the opportunity to look over my plan to give America a new direction. And from what I've heard all across the country, you like what you see, not because you agree with all of the details but because you know that this program is a fundamental departure from business as usual in Washington. It makes dramatic reductions in deficit spending, over 150 specific cuts in domestic programs, and asks a contribution from every American based on his or her ability to pay, all to get the deficit down.

I've challenged the critics of our plan to help me find more spending cuts that reduce the deficit for real, not the kind of gimmicks and not the delays of tough choices we've seen in the past. Previously, when Washington has talked about cutting the deficit tomorrow, it was a tomorrow that never comes. We're going to change that. But perhaps the biggest change we're offering is a national investment strategy to create jobs and grow our economy. Every investment we make is paid for, dollar for dollar, by spending cuts in existing programs. Every investment is designed to make us smarter, safer, and more secure, now and in the long term. These investments embraced old-fashioned ideas like education and work and self-reliance, but they meet the challenges of the new economy with an arsenal of new ideas.

But we begin by making an ironclad commitment to the safety and well-being of our families: First, to immunize every American against

247

avoidable, preventable childhood diseases. For every $1 we spend today, we'll save $10 in the future. Then, to fully fund the Head Start program to give all of our children a chance to start school ready to learn. That will save $3 for every $1 we invest. And then, to open the doors to college education to tens of thousands of promising young students in exchange for their work in a program of national service. In every case, they are investments that will pay dividends and strengthen our economy for years to come. We can't afford to do less.

At a time of immense global change, the price of doing nothing is persistent unemployment, shrinking wages, and workers unable to fulfill their potential. But with the advantages of intelligent investment, our workers can compete and win in this global economy. For example, changes are coming for communities and companies which defended America during the cold war. As the defense industry shrinks and adjusts to the new world, we must make offsetting investments in civilian research. And if your job has been threatened by the end of the cold war or by changes in world trade or by changes in the way we build products or provide services here in America, the United States shouldn't let you down.

This investment program includes a bold new initiative to ensure that every worker has the training to get a good job in the new economy. And the plan contains the boldest national apprenticeship program our country has ever had, so that all high school graduates who don't go to college can receive the skills and the encouragement they need to find good jobs.

For all these workers and students, their lives and livelihoods depend upon the power of investment. Overall, this plan will create more than 8 million public and private sector jobs over the next 4 years. It'll put people back to work in building roads and bridges and creating the new technologies that will employ our people and bolster our profits well into the 21st century.

We also propose the boldest package of incentives targeted to small business: a $3 billion-per-year permanent investment tax credit, targeted to the small businesses that promote job growth in this country, and tax initiatives for small companies who will start new enterprises so that we can reward entrepreneurs who take risks to build new businesses. And next week we'll go further by announcing regulatory changes to expand the availability of credit for small- and medium-sized businesses seeking loans, without sacrificing our abiding commitment to the safety and security of our financial system.

By making more capital available to the private sector and by lowering its costs, business will be able to expand, grow, and create jobs again. All of these investments, the new policies, and the new ideas reflect my belief, and I think yours, that the status quo isn't good enough and that we can do better.

Yesterday we saw figures showing a slight improvement in the Nation's jobless rate. We're happy whenever fewer Americans are out of work. But we certainly can't declare victory now. For while employment is edging up, unemployment is still higher than it was at the depths of this recession. And most of the new jobs being created pay part-time wages and rarely provide workers with the health care coverage families need. If this anemic recovery is the best we can do, it's further proof that real changes are needed to produce a better economy and a better life for our people.

There are those who actually lack the vision to support these investments because they say that we shouldn't spend any new money trying to grow this economy. It's not that they have a plan to make the economy grow, but they just dismiss the investment portion of our program by calling it more Government spending.

There is a profound difference between spending and investment. It's the difference between the status quo and change. And clearly, we have to change. We have to have the courage to cut spending and the wisdom to invest our new resources wisely. We can't do nothing, but we shouldn't do one without the other. The program I've offered to Congress is the only one which will offer a balanced approach to turn the economy around, and we have to do it now.

I hope you'll join me in this call for a new direction. I hope you'll enlist your Representatives and Senators in the critical cause of change. This is the American way, taking charge of our destiny, working hard, and investing today so that we might build a better tomorrow.

Thanks for listening.

NOTE: The President spoke at 10:06 a.m. from the Oval Office at the White House.

Letter to Representative Robert H. Michel on Justice Department Action on the Trial of Representative Harold Ford
March 6, 1993

Dear Mr. Leader:

This is in response to the March 2 letter from you and four of your colleagues. In that letter you express concern about the process which led the Department of Justice to object to the impaneling of a virtually all-white jury brought in from Jackson, Tennessee to try Congressman Harold Ford in Memphis, Tennessee.

Please be informed that when the White House received inquiries concerning this jury issue, they were referred, at the direction of my Counsel, to the Department of Justice for whatever action the Department deemed proper. I have been informed by Counsel that the White House made no recommendation to anyone at the Department of Justice as to how this issue should be resolved.

The Acting Attorney General, Stuart Gerson (who, as you know, was a senior member of the prior Administration and will be leaving office when a new Attorney General is confirmed), has informed us that he personally made the decision to object to the impaneling of the jury and that he did so strictly on the merits. When he made his decision, Mr. Gerson wrote that he was motivated by "a desire to achieve a principle of fairness and uniformity that reflects on far more than this case" and his decision was based on an "[un]willing[ness] to say on behalf of the United States, that justice cannot be obtained from a Memphis jury or, indeed, from the jury in any city." I am attaching a copy of his written statement.

I have no reason to question this statement by Mr. Gerson or his explicit assurance that political considerations played no role in his decision.

Sincerely,

BILL CLINTON

NOTE: This letter was made available by the Office of the Press Secretary but was not issued as a White House press release.

Remarks to the Legislative Conference of the National League of Cities
March 8, 1993

The President. Thank you very much, Mayor Fraser, ladies and gentlemen. It's a great honor for me to be here. This is a pretty rowdy bunch. [*Laughter*] A vital group, a group more interested in change than in more of the status quo, I think. I look around this audience today, and already, just walking in and looking in the crowd and saying hello to people here at the head table, I see people without whom I would not be standing here today. I thank those of both parties and those who run as independents for your support of this plan. And I say again what I always feel when I'm with a group of people from America's cities and small communities or from the States, and that is I feel very much at home.

A lot of times my friends ask me what's the difference from being President and having any other kind of job or the life you used to have.

The following thing occurred to me the other day in the White House. I was down on the ground floor; I had been out running or something, and I was going back up to get ready to start the day's work. And a group of people were coming out who had been at a meeting there, at another meeting with other people. And I ran into them and stopped and shook hands with them. It was totally an impromptu thing. And this man who worked at the White House said, "Mr. President, I'm really sorry that you had to confront those people." And I said, "That's all right. I used to be one once." [*Laughter*] I look forward to being one again someday. [*Laughter*]

The work of this White House has been very much influenced by many of you in this group. And I assure you that you will be represented in the future. We have a strong intergovernmental affairs group that works every day with leaders at the city and county and State level, including Regina Montoya and Loretta Avent, who used to work for you. [*Applause*] Now, we had a bet coming over here. I said, "Loretta, if I mention your name, will they boo or clap?" She won. [*Laughter*]

I came here today to ask you to translate the support you have given to the program I have presented to the Congress and to the American people from support to a commitment to secure its approval in the Congress and to make the change that we seek inevitable and return to the status quo impossible.

All of you are on the frontlines of change. Every day in every way you have to struggle with the things which now confront me as your President. For a long time you've been making tough choices, struggling to balance your books, trying to spend less on yesterday's mistakes and more on tomorrow's needs. You try to put common sense into practice. And now I would like you to ask to help make common sense more common here in your Nation's Capital.

I think everyone now recognizes that we cannot continue on the past course. If we keep on doing just what we've been doing with no fundamental changes, then by the end of the decade the Government's annual deficit will be $650 billion a year. We will be spending 20 percent of our Nation's income every year on health care, and our nearest competitor will be spending about 10 percent, and we'll be insuring fewer people than any country with which we compete. And over 20 cents of every dollar the American people pay in taxes to the United States Government will be expended just paying interest on the vastly accumulated debt.

We've been spending too much and investing too little for quite a long while now. And the result has been slow growth and weak job creation. We've had our private sector handcuffed by high interest rates and inadequate investment, a work force inadequate to the needs of the 21st century and an economic program equally inadequate. If we keep on doing business as usual, we'll just stumble into the next century burdened by the baggage of the past. But if we have the courage to change, the next 20 years could be the best in our Nation's history.

When I introduced my plan to the Congress just 19 days ago, I asked all of us to ask of this plan not what's in it for me but what's in it for us. And people have responded in astonishing ways but I suppose predictable ways if you look at the history of the American people. All across this country people have been taking off their special interest hats and putting on their thinking caps. Business and labor, Republicans and Democrats, people from every walk of life and all points on the political spectrum have rallied behind this plan as a vehicle to move this country forward. I think everybody who seriously thinks about it understands that the great issue now is no longer Republican versus Democrat, urban versus rural, liberal versus conservative. It is whether we will stay in this gridlock that you have buttons campaigning against, or have the courage to change in ways that allow all our people to live up to the fullest of their potential. Even if I start preaching, I promise not to pass the plate. [*Laughter*]

You would be amazed how many times in the last year I would be in a little town or along some country crossroads and people would say to me they were worried about what happened in Los Angeles. You would be amazed how many times I was in a community that was 99 percent one ethnic group and somebody would say they wished that we could work out a way for the ethnic diversity of America to be a source of our strength. You would be amazed how many times I was in groups of people, all of whom had incomes above $150,000 a year, when they said to me, isn't there something we can do about homelessness in America. I think the people of this country are dying to come together again and make this country work again.

Nonetheless, let us be clear on this: There are people who are honestly debating whether this three-pronged plan is the right thing to do for the country. There are some who say, "Well, of course, I want you to cut spending. And as a matter of fact, if you'll cut her spending, you could cut mine a little less." [*Laughter*] And there are others who say, "Well, I know you have to raise taxes, but I wish you wouldn't raise this one or that one so much. Raise the upper income taxes less," or "Do away with the energy tax," or "Put it all on gasoline," which is harder on the rural States and the western States, "but let natural gas and oil off the hook."

And then there are those—and I want to talk to you about them today because you are not among them, but I need your help to deal with it—who say, "Well, if you cut the spending and raise the taxes and didn't invest any new money in anything, you'd have more deficit reduction," or "If you cut the spending and didn't invest any new money in anything, you wouldn't have to raise quite so many taxes," and "After all, if the Government spends a dollar, it's Government spending."

One of the central debates now raging in this Capital is whether there is any difference in the kinds of Government spending. Is there a distinction to be made between, for example, spending more for the same health care every year and accelerating the funding of the Surface Transportation Act? Is there a distinction to be made between a subsidy that was justified 50 years ago because we needed more wool in our uniforms and a subsidy that might be justified tomorrow to give to people who start new businesses and new high-tech enterprises to grow jobs for the future?

The people who say we do not need this economic stimulus plan and we do not need so much investment either argue one of two points. They either say, "All Government spending is bad, and there is no distinction to be made," something until recent times every Republican and Democratic officeholder in America, from the top to the bottom, would have disagreed with. Dwight Eisenhower knew there was a difference between the interstate highway system and paying to maintain the status quo of Government programs that didn't work. Everybody always recognized that distinction before, but there are a lot of people who have had a lot of sway in this town for years now who really argued that there are no distinctions to be made. There are others who say, "Well, the economy is recovering anyway and everything is going to be hunky-dory. So all you have to do is worry about reducing the deficit." Now, their view of what we ought to do might be characterized as "status quo lite." [*Laughter*] That is, "Yeah, I know you've got to change on the cutting side, and maybe we have to have a little tax increase, but there is no distinction between kinds of Government spending. And besides, the economy is in great shape. We just don't know it yet." [*Laughter*]

Now, let's be candid. We do have some good economic news in the aggregate. And last month, for the first time really in a very, very long time, we had a significant number of new jobs. But if you look behind those numbers,

you see that while employment is edging up, an awful lot of those jobs were part-time jobs with part-time wages which rarely provide the health care benefits that families so desperately need today.

To build a stronger recovery with real jobs and rising incomes, we'll have to break the gridlock that has paralyzed public action, cut the deficit, and invest more in the future. If you look at our economic performance over the last dozen years and you say, describe the ways in which America has not been competitive with other nations that are growing faster, and you had to list them, you just think of what you would list. You would say, well, the deficit grew more rapidly than it did in Japan, for example. And America spent a higher percentage of its income on health care than any other country in the world by far, even though we did less with it in terms of covering people.

You'd also have to say, however, our investment in the things that make a country rich and strong actually went down in several areas, in our infrastructure, in K-through-12 education. Nine nations in the world invest a higher percentage of their income in K-through-12 education than we do, even though we have more diversity by race and income, which would argue for greater efforts in our Nation.

If you look at the United States budget just over the last 4 years, you will see we spent more on Medicaid and Medicare and food stamps, with over 1 in 10 Americans on food stamps, and more on interest in the debt, and relatively less on everything else, the investments which would make us richer as a country, which will grow the economy, which will put people back to work, which will reduce our reliance on public assistance and increase our ability to support each other.

So I would argue to you, my fellow Americans, that we have to argue in this community where the ultimate decision will be made: number one, that we need to pass the whole program; number two, there are jobs still begging to be created out there; number three, there are differences in the quality and character of government spending, whether it is in the smallest community of this country or the United States budget. There are differences.

The stimulus plan I have asked the Congress to adopt, along with the spending cuts, the investment increase, and the tax increase itself, will create a half a million new jobs in the short run. The economic program, if it is fully enacted, will create 8 million jobs over the long run—that is, in this 4 year period—the vast majority of them in the private sector.

This plan is based on values that are central to what makes America work and what has always made America work: work and family and faith, responsibility and community and opportunity. I think the change obviously has to start at the top. I have presented a budget which in the next fiscal year will cut the White House staff by 25 percent and save $10 million in privileges and perks and payroll. I have reduced the administrative costs of the executive branch by 14 percent over 4 years and, by attrition, payroll, 100,000 over 4 years, saving $9 billion.

I have asked the Congress to freeze the pay of Federal employees next year and then to lower it by one percent less than would otherwise be the cost of living for the succeeding 3 years, saving billions more dollars and asking a substantial, a very substantial sacrifice from the Federal work force because I thought that was important before I could ask the taxpayers to contribute more.

And last Wednesday, I asked the Vice President to head a national performance review of every Government agency and every Government program, not simply to identify more specific spending cuts but also to identify services that don't work and things that can be done better, to do what the smartest private companies and the best local governments are already doing: streamlining operations, eliminating unnecessary layers of management, empowering frontline workers in holding our investments up to the clear light of day to see whether they make sense.

I have proposed already 150 specific spending cuts, saving $247 billion. And that's much more than the cost of the net new investments I have proposed. I ask you to join me now in fighting for these investments and in cutting back the spending, but not in doing one without the other.

For example, our plan calls for ending the designated project program at the Department of Housing and Urban Development. It spends over $100 million a year without any published selection criteria or competitive procedures or basic accountability. But if you join me in cutting that program, I also ask that you support what I know you believe in and what we have to say to the Congress is worth doing: doubling

the number of housing vouchers for working people on moderate incomes, creating a network of community development banks, bringing new opportunities to our communities through enterprise zones, and doing something to reinvigorate the housing programs of this country. These things can be done together.

I ask you to help me reduce low-priority highway demonstration projects by $1 billion; but also for calling in the new investments we need, we ought to fully fund the Surface Transportation Act, and do it quickly. And we should recognize that transportation offers enormous economic opportunities to increased productivity and jobs. So we have to look at mass transit, high-speed rails, smart cars, smart highways, and commercial aviation as we move toward the 21st century. If we want this economy to grow, we have to do those things.

This plan calls for cutting $300 million in earmarked small business loans but also calls for the most dramatic effort in the history of America that I can determine, at least, from our research, to help small business create jobs: a permanent investment tax credit for small businesses, 90 percent of the employers in this country with 40 percent of the employees creating the vast majority of the new jobs; a new venture capital gains tax for people who will start new businesses and have the courage to begin being on the cutting edge of change; and real steps which we will announce in a couple of days to try to end the credit crunch and the lack of availability of credit to small businesses who have to provide the jobs of today and tomorrow.

In short, we have to cut, and we have to invest. We have to reject trickle-down economics, and we have to reject tax-and-spend economics. We have to stop spending money on things that don't work, but we have to continue to invest in things that do.

A lot of the things that we propose to do are literally direct investment incentives to the private sector. I mentioned a couple already: the $3 billion permanent small business investment tax credit; some significant changes in the way taxes are computed for our larger businesses so that when they do invest in new plant and new equipment and new jobs for our people, they will be rewarded, not punished, by the tax system. If people do what's right, they should be supported. We should make a distinction between how private companies spend their money. And when they invest to grow and to create jobs, they should be rewarded for that. And that's what we're trying to do in the tax system.

In addition to those things I have already mentioned, I recommended a significant increase, about $2.5 billion—the first one in a very long time, as all of you know—in the community development block grant program. I can say with confidence as a Governor that that program was absolutely critical to helping many of the smaller and moderate-sized communities in my State attract new jobs in the tough decade of the 1980's and that without it I do not know if we would have been able to do so. There are people in this audience from my State who know that is true because they have personally experienced it. And I think that is true all across the country.

We simply cannot afford not to invest what it takes to make our communities attractive to new businesses and new jobs. And if anyone here in this community tells you that the economy is fine in America, tell them where you live there's still a little work to be done.

I want to hammer this home as hard as I can. This is the first recovery, economic recovery, in my lifetime where if you look at the overall numbers, it really does look like a recovery is underway. Productivity is increasing. American businesses are doing a better job. A lot of things are going on, but the jobs themselves are not yet being created. And we are facing other problems which may further put pressure on some communities, including the imperative of continuing to reduce the defense budget. We have got to follow a jobs strategy. We have got to do that.

Now, one of the things that I've tried to do, as all of you know, is to reduce the deficit, because if we do we'll reduce interest rates. And if you keep interest rates down and people go out and refinance their businesses, their homes, their cars, their credit cards, they'll have more cash. They can invest it and make this economy grow. That is also happening.

Interest rates just since the election have gone down, long term, almost one full point. If we can keep them down and everybody, all of you and all of the people you represent, will go out and refinance all the debt they've piled up in the 1980's, that will free up another $80 billion to $90 billion to $100 billion this next year to grow this economy. That's important,

but we also have to get some real investment incentives, public and private. Unless we create jobs, we cannot claim to have done anything to promote an economic recovery that affects the lives of the people that you see on the street every day.

Let me also say, in addition to creating an economic environment in which there is investment, we also have to do what we can in common to prepare our people for those challenges. And we have to recognize the fact that, in many ways, America has not done a good job of preparing its people. Example number one, to begin with children, all the nations in this hemisphere, only two, only two, Haiti and Bolivia, have lower immunization rates against preventable childhood diseases than the United States of America, where all of the vaccine is made. Only two. We have proposed in this program, starting with the stimulus package, an effort that will permit us over the next few years to immunize all the kids in this country against preventable childhood diseases.

The estimates are that for every $1 we spend immunizing children against those diseases, we'll save $10 down the road in the care that will otherwise be spent on them. But in order to make those estimates right, you have to have a critical core threshold of young children who are immunized. And we are running the risk of falling dangerously below that threshold in many areas and having new epidemics of disease break out among our children simply because we do not provide either the infrastructure in order to do that or the affordability and availability of the vaccines. We must do that.

Let me give you one other example. The Head Start program, where it is fully and firmly implemented along with other support services, plainly saves more money than it costs in the terms of keeping kids in school and making them successful, in helping them to graduate and do well. And yet for years we've all talked about fully funding the Head Start program and supporting other efforts like in-school preschool programs or parent-based preschool programs, yet we've never really done it. Congress and the previous administration did expand the Head Start program some, but there are still enormous numbers of children who are not able to access those services. This budget starting this summer fully funds the Head Start program. And we ought to pass that.

If we begin this summer and we work for

the next 3 years, just think what it will be like. Wouldn't it be nice to be able to say we've actually done something so we can go and work on a new problem? Wouldn't it be nice if in the next election cycle in 1996, no one could argue about Head Start or immunization; they had to argue about something else? [*Laughter*] I mean, somebody asked me one time what my goal as President was, and I said that I'd like to leave my successor a new set of problems. [*Laughter*] You think about it.

This plan will create about 700,000 summer jobs for people in this country. And we are attempting to mobilize private sector employers to match what we're doing with the goal of creating over a million jobs. Think about it. Think about how many young people in this country have been surrounded by devastating economic conditions year in and year out for the last several years. They flip on the television, and they see another ad telling them what they ought to say no to. Well, I'm all for telling them what they ought to say no to. But I think we should set an example and give them something to say yes to as well.

This plan will give our country the most ambitious system of lifelong learning we have ever had: programs for high school dropouts and others to learn to read adequately and get their high school equivalency; programs for young people to be able to borrow the money they need to go to college and pay it back on far more favorable terms or with service to our country here at home as police officers or teachers or in other forms of community service; programs for adults who lose their jobs because of defense cutbacks or because of sweeping changes in the global economy to get serious, serious opportunities to retrain in areas where there are jobs available, tied to incentives to getting investments for those new jobs in their communities. Not just talking about it; this plan gets serious about it. We have almost $5 billion for the retraining of adults in the work force alone in the next 4 years in this program, and it needs to pass.

And anybody who says that this recovery will just do fine without a serious attempt to retrain the work force has not been to California lately to see what's happened in the industries where the defense cuts occurred; have not been in the rural parts of America to see what has happened when a lot of those low-wage, low-skilled, high labor-intensive manufacturing plants closed

down and moved overseas with no plans to retrain or reinvest in those communities; or all the places in-between.

There is too much work to be done. We need a partnership, and it has to begin with making sure the people of this country can compete and win in the global economy. And that requires some investment. And there is a difference between whether you spend money making people stronger and smarter and safer and more secure and more able to compete, and whether you just keep spending more money on the same thing. There is a difference. And this program is different.

This plan will enable us over the next couple of years to work with you to put 100,000 more police officers on the streets of the cities of this country. There are cities which have actually seen a reduction in the crime rate, either in specific neighborhoods or in the cities as a whole, in the last few years, cities here represented in this room, when they've gone to community policing strategies. You know it works. I know it works. And we know most cities don't have enough money to do it right. We're going to help you through giving people incentives who are coming out of the service to be police officers, through giving people incentives to be police officers as a way of paying for their college education, and through, I hope and pray, passing the crime bill, which didn't quite make it through last year, to put these police officers on the street.

One of the most remarkable aspects of this program is one that hasn't received a great deal of attention and doesn't involve you directly, but it will shape the communities you lead and govern indirectly. And that is the astonishing increase in this program in the refundable earned income tax credit for working people, not only to offset the impacts of the energy tax on families with incomes under $30,000 but also so that we can finally say in this country, if this earned-income tax credit passes as it will be presented, that if you work 40 hours a week and you have children in the home, you should not be in poverty. And the tax system will lift you out and reward work. It will reward work. Imagine it! Just imagine, politicians for years have been saying they wanted to reward work, not welfare. Now, by adopting a simple bill that says the tax system will reward work, not welfare, we can give people something new to argue about. It would be a great thing to do.

I ask for your help again. The big issue is, should we do all these things: Should we cut spending; should we raise revenues; should we increase investment so that the deficit goes down while investment goes up. This country has never tried to do this before. You've got to be fair to the Members of the United States Congress. We are asking them to do something our country has never tried to do before, which is to hammer the deficit down and increase investment significantly at the same time. But you know where you live, you can see it every day that we have to do both. We have to do both.

And so I say again in closing, I thank you for your endorsement of this program. It made me feel great. I want every Member of the United States House and Senate to know that you not only endorsed it but that you believe in it, not just because of what you get out of it but——

Audience member. What about drugs?

The President. You want to talk? I'll be glad—this program has a lot in it, actually, about drugs. It has a significant increase in funds for drug treatments and gives you, through providing 100,000 more police officers, the power to combat drugs on the street. It does both things. It increases enforcement and treatment, which I would think you would want.

But that makes a good point: Is that spending, or is that an investment? You have to decide. But you have got to give the Congress courage to do this. And you have to help people understand that in this group there were Republicans and Democrats and city people and country people, people from the frost belt and the sun belt and the rust belt and the Bible belt, people like me that have to get bigger belts every year. [*Laughter*] You can do that. And if we can do that, we've got a real shot to sit here in honest discussion year in and year out and face these problems.

You know, how many years have you been coming up here and listening to this debate, and it doesn't bear any relationship to the life you live when you go back home? How many, really? I mean, whether it's a discussion about drugs where somebody just talks about getting tough on crime and nobody ever gets down to what they're going to do to help you deal with the problem where you live; or jobs, and somebody rails against taxes and the deficit, and then every year the deficit goes up and so do taxes. Or just how many years have you been coming here listening to these debates when nothing ever changed?

And I just want to tell you, as I said to the Congress, there is plenty of blame to go around; this is not about party. And I don't care who is to blame. I'm prepared to take responsibility. I'm more than willing to face the heat, and if something goes wrong, I'll take responsibility for that and change it. But let's do something, and let's do it now.

Thank you.

NOTE: The President spoke at 1:15 p.m. at the Washington Hilton. In his remarks, he referred to Donald M. Fraser, Mayor of Minneapolis, MN, and president of the National League of Cities; Regina Montoya, Assistant to the President for Intergovernmental Affairs; and Loretta Avent, Special Assistant to the President for Intergovernmental Affairs.

Exchange With Reporters Prior to a Meeting With the Congressional Black Caucus
March 8, 1993

Spending Cuts

Q. Mr. President, do you agree to the extra $50 billion in cuts that the House and Senate leaders want?

The President. I agree that we will have a budget resolution which will be roughly conforming to the reestimates of the CBO in general terms and that will still contain the investment strategy that I want to pursue.

NOTE: The exchange began at 5:11 p.m. in the Roosevelt Room at the White House.

Nomination for Posts at the Housing and Urban Development, Commerce, and Agriculture Departments and the United Nations
March 8, 1993

The President continued the process of filling the sub-Cabinet today, expressing his intent to nominate eight senior officials at the Departments of Agriculture, Commerce, and Housing and Urban Development and at the U.S. Mission to the United Nations. Named today were:

Michael Stegman, Assistant Secretary for Policy Development and Research, Department of Housing and Urban Development

Everett Ehrlich, Under Secretary for Economic Affairs, Department of Commerce

Eugene Moos, Under Secretary for International Affairs and Commodity Programs, Department of Agriculture

Richard Rominger, Deputy Secretary of Agriculture

Wardell Townsend, Jr., Assistant Secretary for Administration, Department of Agriculture

Francis Vacca, Assistant Secretary for Congressional Relations, Department of Agriculture

Victor Marrero, U.S. Representative to the Economic and Security Council, United Nations

Karl F. (Rick) Inderfurth, U.S. Alternate Representative for Special Political Affairs, United Nations

"The people I am asking to serve in my administration today combine academic achievement with real world experience," said the President. "I am particularly pleased to be naming two family farmers to help run the Department of Agriculture."

NOTE: Biographies of the nominees were made available by the Office of the Press Secretary.

Exchange With Reporters Prior to a Meeting With the Senate Budget Committee
March 9, 1993

Q. Mr. President, are you going for nonmilitary domestic spending cuts across the board?

The President. Well, first of all, let me say I think both the Senate and the House committees deserve a lot of credit. They've come forward with further spending reductions consistent with what the CBO group calculations would indicate. They are consistent with the direction of my plan to reduce the deficit and increase investment. And I think that eventually all the committees will get together, and the two bodies will get together, and we will work out a budget that the American people can be proud of that

does the things that we're all trying to do. I'm encouraged by it.

Q. So you are going to accept the across-the-board cuts?

The President. We haven't worked out the details on how it's going to be done. The two committees have slightly different positions, as you probably know. But I think that in the end there will be further cuts and there will be, I'm convinced, a much more substantial reduction in the deficit than the estimates show. I feel good about it.

NOTE: The exchange began at 9:17 a.m. in the Old Family Dining Room at the White House.

Exchange With Reporters Prior to Discussions With President François Mitterrand of France
March 9, 1993

Russia

Q. Mr. President, are you going to accept Russia into the G–7 and hold an emergency summit meeting of heads of state involved also on the economy?

President Clinton. Well, I intend to discuss the Russian situation with President Mitterrand today. And obviously, whatever the United States does, we hope it will be part of a coordinated effort. But in terms of mechanics, no decision has been made.

Q. Do you think a compromise is possible on a special meeting of the G–7, discussing maybe Russia and the economy both together?

President Clinton. I don't think it's a—we're at a point even to make that decision yet. As you know, the Japanese have been somewhat reluctant to have any kind of special meeting, looking toward their own meeting they're hosting in Tokyo this summer. But I think that we will—let me say this, I think we will all, the G–7, be dealing with the issue of Russia before July in some form or fashion. How that will happen, I can't say yet. That's one of the reasons I was looking forward to this meeting with President Mitterrand.

Q. Did President Nixon talk you into talking Japan out of opposing Russia's participation?

President Clinton. No, we had a great meeting. But we were pretty much on the same wavelength. And we have been pretty much on the same wavelength on this issue for more than a year now. And he gave me a lot of very good ideas. It was a good meeting.

Q. Have you forgiven him for Watergate?

President Clinton. That was a long time ago. Is there another round?

Q. The French.

President Clinton. Now, Mr. President, it's your turn. I'm going to smile and look wise. [*Laughter*]

Q. Did you have a good trip?

President Mitterrand. All is well.

Q. How's the first contact going?

President Mitterrand. As you can see. You will know later.

President Clinton. He answers these questions better than I do.

Q. Do you speak some French, Mr. President?

President Clinton. No, but I understand a little. I can pick up the questions a little.

Q. What's the first order of business with President Mitterrand?

President Clinton. Well, we want to get acquainted and talk about some matters of mutual concerns. We'll discuss that later.

NOTE: The exchange began at 10:35 a.m. in the Oval Office at the White House.

The President's News Conference With President François Mitterrand of France
March 9, 1993

President Clinton. Good afternoon. It is a great pleasure for me to welcome President Mitterrand to the White House at this early date in our administration.

Our two nations share a friendship which dates back to the revolutionary birth of both countries, rooted in common values of equality, liberty, and democracy. These bonds of culture, of history, and of common purpose have made possible a remarkable amount of cooperation in recent days in meeting the challenges in Iraq and Somalia and Bosnia.

Today President Mitterrand and I discussed the global partnership that we must bring to the post-cold-war world, new uncertainties and new opportunities. Both our nations and both our continents are renewing institutions of security and economic growth for this era.

I salute President Mitterrand and the French people for their leadership. Their exemplary contribution to the United Nations peacekeeping operations around the globe is just one of many examples of the contributions they have and will continue to make.

This morning we discussed Russia, Bosnia, and the progress toward European union. Over lunch we will discuss other issues including the Uruguay round of trade talks. We have differences on some issues. Clearly, we need French leadership to resolve some outstanding differences but also to make common cause in the areas in which we agree.

Both our nations are great trading nations and have much to gain by resolving the differences between us and moving the world toward a growing global economy. I am very, very hopeful that the United States and France can be partners in updating our common interests and in leading the G–7 toward coordinated policies of global economic growth and especially toward action in dealing with Russia.

President Mitterrand is going to Russia soon, and he will be there and back before I have an opportunity to meet with President Yeltsin in April in Canada. I look forward to closely consulting with him about that again after his trip to Russia.

We talked a little bit about the Vance-Owen peace process today, and you might want to ask President Mitterrand about his views on that. Let me say that I have been very pleased with the comments that he has made today and with the possibilities that we might have toward working together to secure a peace in Bosnia.

There are many challenges facing the great democracies of the world today. We have to reaffirm our support for the difficult transformations to democracy now taking place in the former Soviet Union and in central and eastern Europe, to reaffirm our interest in closely cooperating to advance peace in the Middle East and elsewhere in the world, and to promote democracy and economic growth throughout the world.

We made a very good beginning this morning, and I want to publicly thank the President, as I have privately, for the enormously helpful conversations we had this morning. He has been at this work longer than I have by several years. I learned a lot today. I appreciated his candor and the insights which he brought to our discussion. I look forward to continuing over lunch

and to continue a long and significant relationship between the United States and France.

And I thank you, Mr. President. And the microphone is yours.

President Mitterrand. Ladies and gentlemen, I think everything that needs to be said has been said. At least everything has been said about what we talked about and about what we will be talking about during the time that remains for our meeting. So I haven't really anything to add, while waiting for questions that you may wish to ask.

On the other hand, I would like to recall, just as President Clinton has just done, I'd like to recall that for Frenchmen it's always a very important moment, it's a real event, and it's a very happy moment to be coming to Washington in order to meet with the President of the United States of America. And so it is with the same keen interest that today I'm here in this capital city in order to meet a President whose fame has already encompassed the world several times but whom I'd never met.

And now we have had useful conversations. And the subjects that we've talked about, as mentioned by President Clinton, these subjects have given us the opportunity of seeing that our positions were very similar. And it is pleasant to note, particularly as the subjects are very difficult subjects, Bosnia, former Yugoslavia, the revolution that is taking place in Russia and in all the countries of the former Soviet Union, and all this is very important.

President Clinton has shown a keen interest in the future of the European unity. And I gave him my feelings and what I was committed to myself. We still have matters to talk about. There are interests of which oppose us, which is perfectly natural, between our countries. That's in the nature of things. But there is a real determination to reach agreement. And that is, I think, which is the leitmotiv of all our conversations. And I'm delighted with the hospitality extended to me. I appreciate this very warmly, very much.

And I wish to express my warm thanks, at the same time, to the members of the press who have been good enough to be present here today. Now, I am at your disposal, as you are, doubtless, yourself, Mr. President, at the disposal of the curiosity of the ladies and gentlemen of the press. I'm sure they'll be very discreet. They won't ask much.

Bosnia

Q. President Clinton, did you discuss at all the specifics of a possible American contribution of ground troops in the enforcement phase of a peace agreement in Bosnia?

President Clinton. Only in the most general terms. I restated the position of the administration, which is now well-known in the public, that we were opposed to the introduction of American ground forces to try to mandate an agreement or to in any way engage in the present conflict, but that if an agreement could be reached, that the United States would be interested in being part of a United Nations effort to secure the agreement.

Q. Mr. President, you said that both of you have reached some sort of agreements on new efforts in Bosnia. Can you tell us what they are?

President Clinton. No.

Q. And also, I would like to ask President Mitterrand how can European leaders ban the slaughter, in view of the lead-up to World War I and World War II, similarities of the hatreds and abuses that have led now to these conflicts?

President Clinton. Shall I go first? The only agreement we made with regard to Bosnia was that it would be an error for France to increase its troops or for the United States to introduce troops to become embroiled in the conflict but that we both should be prepared to make our contributions to securing the agreement if the Vance-Owen process could produce one.

President Mitterrand. Madam, no more than you do, we just do not accept violence, violence of any kind, the violence that is taking place in particular in Bosnia. A problem for us—and we have the responsibility of defining the policies of our countries—our problem is to know how, by what means, what means do we have and what means should we employ in order to get the results that we all want, which is peace or at least the end of violence.

And in that respect, may I remind you that France is participating in the United Nations efforts. France is actually the country that is at present supplying the most numerous troops, military contribution to the U.N. efforts, more than—well, almost 5,000 men right now. And we already have lost 12 people killed and more than 100 wounded.

Our position is very simple to express but, of course, difficult to implement. We approve

the Vance-Owen plan. We want it to be successful. We see in what way it is not perfect, but this instrument, well, we know of none better. And as it is the best of the possible plans, right now, as of today, we support the Vance-Owen plan, and we want it to be the basis of an agreement.

So if it does succeed, if it gets the agreement of the three parties concerned—one might almost say four parties or five even—in other words, if you include the three countries which are Croatia, Serbia, and Bosnia, but there are also the Serbs in Bosnia and perhaps the Croats in Bosnia, et cetera. So if the agreement is reached—and for the moment it is under discussion, as you know, as a whole series of discussions that are taking place and will take place, and I'll have occasion to take part in them myself in the next few days. And the purpose of all these discussions is to get the Owen-Vance plan accepted, agreed. If it is agreed, thanks to discussions and possibly modifications, but if it ends up by being agreed, accepted, then we think that immediately it will be necessary to set up without the transition taking too long— and if it could be immediate transition, it would be even better—we think we must ensure military presence in order to ensure the full respect for the agreements reached, so that the passions and local animosities should not immediately prevail. And in that respect, France is prepared to participate in this force of peace under the authority of the United Nations.

Russia

Q. [*Inaudible*]—have an emergency meeting of the G–7 sometime before the July summit in order to deal at the clinical level the question of Russian aid? And, if not, how do you propose breaking what seems to be the gridlock between the Russian Government and the international lending institutions?

President Clinton. The short answer to your question, I suppose, is yes. I think it is entirely possible that such a meeting might be useful. Whether a meeting is possible or not depends in part on the response of the other members of the G–7. The Japanese, as you know, have territorial disputes outstanding and also have put a lot into the upcoming meeting in July. Perhaps there is some other way that we can engage the G–7 in trying to address the Russian situation.

I guess the important point I'd like to make

is, I don't believe we can wait until July for the major countries of the world who care about what happens in Russia and who would like very much to keep political and economic reform on track there to move. And President Mitterrand is going to Moscow, and then we'll talk when he gets back. Then I'm going to Canada. And at the conclusion of that meeting, if not before, I will try to move to mobilize others to act in this regard whether or not it is possible to have a formal G–7 meeting.

Bosnia

Q. Did you get the impression that President Clinton would be prepared to, in fact, move in, in former Yugoslavia once an agreement is reached?

President Mitterrand. Yes, well, he has just expressed himself on this a moment ago. He said that he did not want to engage in a military campaign on the basis of a disagreement among the parties concerned. And that is exactly the same position as France.

But the President also indicated that he was prepared to examine the possibility of having an American presence in the framework of all the steps that will be taken for the implementation of an agreement, once an agreement is reached, if the agreement is reached.

Russia

Q. Did you specifically talk about Russia?

President Mitterrand. Well, I am glad you asked me the question, too, because it was already a question for President Clinton. I'm in favor of what you are suggesting, an earlier G–7. I think it's even necessary, because there are problems specifically in Eastern Europe and in Russia that are urgent, quite apart from many other problems. I also know about the Japanese opposition to the idea. Perhaps Japan is not having sufficient regard in this respect to the importance of events that are taking place mainly in Europe. I have already given my agreement to Mr. Delors anyway.

Middle East Peace Talks

Q. Did you discuss with the French President at all the Middle East peace process? And are you optimistic, for the next round of talks, that Syria comes to an agreement with Israel?

President Clinton. We have not discussed the Middle East yet. We will over lunch. Yes, I am hopeful.

Health Care Reform

Q. Mr. President, may I ask, regarding your health care reform, now that you're so deeply involved in trying to find more budget cuts, what is your expectation for when you would start seeing some savings from health reform? And should Americans expect that they will have to settle for reduced core benefits unless they can pay more, of course——

President Clinton. No.

Q. ——for some sort of reduced services in order to achieve these savings?

President Clinton. No, I don't necessarily accept that. Of course, we have 400 people working on this now and consulting widely with all the people involved in the health care issue.

Let me answer your first question pointedly. I believe, under all the scenarios I have seen that I think are possible, we would see immediate savings in the private sector if we were to adopt a comprehensive health care reform package. That is, private employers and employees would see the rate of their insurance premium increases drop rather dramatically and there would be really significant savings immediately in the private sector.

Because those savings in the public sector would have to be used to provide some insurance at least to the unemployed uninsured, who are about 30 percent of the total population of uninsured—at least to them—it might take 4 years or so before we would start seeing significant taxpayer savings. But interestingly enough, that's about the time we need it. That is, if you look at all the scenarios, the deficit can be brought down under our plan for 4 years, and then if health care costs are not brought under control, it will start up again in the latter part of this decade. So we certainly believe that the health care plan would bring the deficit down virtually to zero over the next 8 to 10 years.

Now, will people have to accept a lower quality of health care? I just dispute that entirely. We're already spending 30 percent more of our income than any country in the world. I don't think that——

Steel Subsidies

Q. Yesterday the United States imposed some tithes, additional tithes on some products of steel. The argument is that the subsidies are unfair. But the other side says that the subsidies are not unfair. What is the middle ground?

What do you think can be negotiated? And, also, I would like to hear the response of President Mitterrand.

President Clinton. First of all, I want to make it very clear that the steel case was a case which was made on the basis of the facts, and waiting for me when I took office as President and waiting for our Trade Ambassador. So the real question was whether we would act consistent with the work that had been done before we took office, based on the evidence that had been amassed then. And we decided that we had to proceed with that to provide the continuity of the enforcement of our trade laws.

I think the ultimate resolution of all these things is to continue to work for a more open trading system. I am strongly committed to a successful completion of the Uruguay round this year and to taking other measures which will open markets all around the world and reduce trade barriers. And I'm going to do everything I can to be instrumental in that regard. In order to get there, every nation has to have some mechanism to protect itself if there is uneven treatment. And we'll always have factual arguments about what is even and uneven, but I think the key is, are we moving toward a more open trading system or not?

International Arms Sales

Q. How can we stop wars as long as the United States permits the sale of arms around the world by our CIA agents and by bringing in arms from China? And now, faced with the proposition from the Soviet—Russia that we let them sell conventional arms around the world to aid their economy, how can we get wars to stop under those conditions?

President Clinton. I think both of us should answer that question. President Mitterrand will be the company misery loves on that question. [*Laughter*]

I believe the United States has an obligation to try to stop the proliferation of weapons of mass destruction and to slow the proliferations of weapons generally throughout the world. It is not a simple or an easy thing to do. And our ability to do it is limited by the sovereignty of other nations and by the policies they pursue. But I can assure you just since I have been in office, and on more than one occasion, I have done what I could within the means available to me to try to limit proliferation, and I will continue to do that.

Since you brought up Russia, let me say again, one of the reasons I think it is so important for us to try to move aggressively to give the Russians the means to restore some economic growth and opportunity and preserve political liberty is that as other options close to them, they will be more and more and more forced to look upon their capacity to sell arms as the only way they can earn foreign currency, the only way they can keep the economy going, the only way they can keep a lot of their factories open. So I think the case you have made and the question is a powerful argument for the policies we are attempting to undertake with Russia.

Mr. President.

President Mitterrand. Well, I might simply recall to the lady who spoke that it was in Paris at the end of an international conference—well, it was the largest ever number of participants. It was in Paris, then, that there was the signature of the convention on the prohibition of chemical and biological weapons; furthermore, that France has always approved the various plans for limiting nuclear weaponry signed between the United States of America and the Soviet Union in the past and more recently with Russia. And France took the initiative of stopping nuclear testing precisely in order to give everyone time to reconsider the possibility of bringing them to a definitive end, with the end of over-armaments in this area.

So I think that there is a very favorable ground here. The reduction of armaments, though, can only be conceived with the ending of sales of armaments. This can only be conceived in the framework of an international negotiation. No country otherwise could afford to place itself in a situation of danger, in fact, if the other countries don't do likewise and make the same effort. But we're certainly prepared to move ahead in this direction.

Trade

Q. Mr. President, you heard President Clinton and his administration in recent months challenging Europe on steel, on agriculture, on civil aircraft. I know that that part of your discussion will be for lunch, but what is your viewpoint?

President Mitterrand. Well, we decided to talk about this later on, so it's difficult for me to accelerate things all alone just of my own accord. I can't jump the gun. But President Clinton probably knows as much as you do about my frame of mind and the frame of mind of France, in this respect, which can be summed up in a word: international negotiations of GATT is trade negotiation so as to eliminate protectionism, precisely. And it's an overall comprehensive negotiation, global negotiation which doesn't touch all sectors but many, many sectors and, therefore, not only farming and agriculture.

If one, therefore, looks at the discussion solely from the point of view of agriculture, then it can't work. If, however, it is looked at in the form of a balanced negotiation, covering the various sectors that are involved, of industries, services, intellectual property, and so on, then there's no reason not to be able to succeed. And in that respect, what France wants is that there should be a success of this, because I share the view expressed by President Clinton a moment ago which is that it is better we will be able to succeed in this respect, then the sooner we will get out of the present recession, the present crisis, the present problems. But at the same time, we mustn't isolate and separate off subjects and just deal with them piecemeal. No, we mustn't do that, which is what happens only too often nowadays.

Spending Cuts

Q. Several questions have been raised by your agreement to cut spending further here. First among them is why you've agreed to general budget cuts without the specifics when you have for so long been demanding specifics of others who wanted to cut the budget further. Also, Senator Sasser said outside that while you have not agreed to necessarily $90 billion in further cuts, that is about as far, he suggested, that you feel they could go without harming the economy. Is that the case, that $90 billion is it and no more suggestions need be made?

President Clinton. There are two different questions there. First of all, in this budget resolution there is an attempt to deal by both the Senate and the House Budget Committees, an honest attempt to deal with the so-called reestimates of the Congressional Budget Office; that is, to get even more deficit reduction. And I believe it will produce far more than we even estimate. They have to decide to get the budget resolution passed by category. But I assure you that we will be very specific before the process is over.

It is true that I think that we have cut the deficit in a 4-year period about as much as

we should with these new numbers. But that doesn't mean we don't need more specifics, because we have to define how we're going to cut. And since I also strongly believe we have to increase our investments in education and training and in new technologies and in the things which will make our economy grow, it means we need all the suggestions we can get about other places we can cut the budget, and we will need to do that until the budget is finally passed.

So I strongly support that. The Vice President, as you know, is heading the performance review audit of the entire Federal Government. And the more specific suggestions we can come up with that everyone agrees with, the fewer controversial and potentially damaging cuts we'll have.

Let me just make the economic argument. Our deficit reduction package—and Senator after Senator said today, you know, that this is the most credible budget I've seen in 15 or 17 or however many years—it is producing the desired results: low interest rates, stock market back up and doing well.

We have to deal with that against a backdrop of a Europe that's had slow growth, Japan with some serious economic problems and no political consensus about what to do about it in Japan. So we want to do what our European and Japanese friends have been telling us for years we should do, get our deficit under control. But we want to do it at a moderate pace so that we don't throw the United States back into recession and further complicate the economic problems of Europe, which will be helped by a growing American economy. So I think we've struck the right balance, and that was the point I was making to them.

Middle East Peace Talks

Q. President Clinton, concerning the Middle East, you said that your country intends to play the role of a full partner in the peace process. How do you intend to translate this? And what would you tell Israeli Prime Minister Rabin when you receive him next week so that to resume the talks, especially concerning the Palestinian deportees?

President Clinton. Well, I think that what we mean by a full partnership was evidenced by the fact that the Secretary of State's first trip abroad was to the Middle East and that he made aggressive efforts there to try to get the talks back on track and to involve as many parties as possible. In terms of what I will tell Prime Minister Rabin when he comes back, I won't say anything I haven't said in public about the deportee issue or anything else. We are working together. I feel comfortable and confident that he very much wants the peace process back on track, and I will support that.

Civil Aircraft Agreement

Q. What specific revisions do you want in the agreement on civil aircraft? And are you prepared to abrogate last year's agreement?

President Clinton. No, no, absolutely not. I think to some extent my remarks in that regard have been misunderstood, and they may be my fault. I support last year's agreement. The point I was trying to make is this: The United States had a big lead in civilian aircraft. Arguably, it was contributed to by the massive investments we made in defense and the spinoff benefits. That was always the European argument for their own direct subsidies in the airbus program, that we had indirectly done the same thing through defense.

It costs a great deal of money to develop new aircraft, to break into new markets, and to go forward. The argument I was trying to make to the Boeing workers last week, and I will restate it here, is that the adversity they have suffered in the market is through no fault of their own. That is, they have not failed by being unproductive or lazy or asking for too much but that Europe was able to penetrate

this market because of the airbus policy. And the blame I placed was on our Government for not responding, not Europe's for trying to get in. That was their right; it was legal under international law, and they did it. Now, we chose instead to try to convince them to stop doing as much as they were doing, which produced the agreement to which you just alluded. I strongly support that agreement. I do not want it abrogated; I want it enforced.

My policy now on this—and I don't want to prejudge the work that the commission we're about to appoint—Congress is going to pass a bill in the next few days—we're going to appoint a commission on the future of our commercial airlines company and our airline manufacturers. I don't want to prejudge that, but my policy basically has two points: Number one, the agreement must be honored and strictly adhered to. And, number two, the agreement leaves the United States as well as Europe the opportunity to significantly invest in the development of new technologies for new generations of aircraft, and we have to take that opportunity in order to be competitive. And I appreciate your asking the question because it gives me the opportunity to clarify my position.

Thank you very much.

NOTE: The President's fifth news conference began at 12:20 p.m. in the East Room at the White House. President Mitterrand spoke in French, and his remarks were translated by an interpreter.

Letter to Congressional Leaders on Nuclear Cooperation With EURATOM
March 9, 1993

Dear Mr. Speaker: (Dear Mr. President:)

The United States has been engaged in nuclear cooperation with the European Community for many years. This cooperation was initiated under agreements that were concluded over 3 decades ago between the United States and the European Atomic Energy Community (EURATOM) and that extend until December 31, 1995. Since the inception of this cooperation, the Community has adhered to all its obligations under those agreements.

The Nuclear Non-Proliferation Act of 1978 amended the Atomic Energy Act of 1954 to

establish new nuclear export criteria, including a requirement that the United States have a right to consent to the reprocessing of fuel exported from the United States. Our present agreements for cooperation with EURATOM do not contain such a right. To avoid disrupting cooperation with EURATOM, a proviso was included in the law to enable continued cooperation until March 10, 1980, if EURATOM agreed to negotiations concerning our cooperation agreements. EURATOM agreed in 1978 to such negotiations.

The law also provides that nuclear cooperation

with EURATOM can be extended on an annual basis after March 10, 1980, upon determination by the President that failure to cooperate would be seriously prejudicial to the achievement of U.S. non-proliferation objectives or otherwise jeopardize the common defense and security and after notification to the Congress. President Carter made such a determination 13 years ago and signed Executive Order No. 12193, permitting nuclear cooperation with EURATOM to continue until March 10, 1981. President Reagan made such determinations in 1981, 1982, 1983, 1984, 1985, 1986, 1987, and 1988, and signed Executive Orders Nos. 12295, 12351, 12409, 12463, 12506, 12554, 12587, and 12629 permitting nuclear cooperation to continue through March 10, 1989. President Bush made such determinations in 1989, 1990, 1991, and 1992, and signed Executive Orders Nos. 12670, 12706, 12753, and 12791 permitting nuclear cooperation to continue through March 10, 1993.

In addition to numerous informal contacts, the United States has engaged in frequent talks with EURATOM regarding the renegotiation of the U.S.-EURATOM agreements for cooperation. Talks were conducted in November 1978, September 1979, April 1980, January 1982, November 1983, March 1984, May, September, and November 1985, April and July 1986, September 1987, September and November 1988, July and December 1989, February, April, October, and December 1990, and September 1991.

Formal negotiations on a new agreement were held in April, September, and December 1992 and are expected to continue this year.

I believe that it is essential that cooperation between the United States and the Community continue, and likewise, that we work closely with our allies to counter the threat of proliferation of nuclear explosives. Not only would a disruption of nuclear cooperation with EURATOM eliminate any chance of progress in our negotiations with that organization related to our agreements, it would also cause serious problems in our overall relationships. Accordingly, I have determined that failure to continue peaceful nuclear cooperation with EURATOM would be seriously prejudicial to the achievement of U.S. non-proliferation objectives and would jeopardize the common defense and security of the United States. I therefore intend to sign an Executive order to extend the waiver of the application of the relevant export criterion of the Atomic Energy Act for an additional 12 months from March 10, 1993.

Sincerely,

BILL CLINTON

NOTE: Identical letters were sent to Thomas S. Foley, Speaker of the House of Representatives, and Albert Gore, Jr., President of the Senate. The Executive order is listed in Appendix D at the end of this volume.

Nomination for Posts at the Departments of Agriculture, Education, and Housing and Urban Development
March 9, 1993

The President made eight senior personnel announcements today, expressing his intention to nominate a group of experts from around the country to posts at the Departments of Agriculture, Education, and Housing and Urban Development.

Named today were the following:

Department of Agriculture

James Gilliland, General Counsel

James Lyons, Assistant Secretary (Natural Resources and Environment)

Bob Nash, Under Secretary for Small Community and Rural Development

Department of Education

Judith Heumann, Assistant Secretary for Special Education and Rehabilitative Services

Dr. Augusta Kappner, Assistant Secretary for Vocational and Adult Education

Dr. Thomas Payzant, Assistant Secretary for Elementary and Secondary Education

Dr. Marshall Smith, Under Secretary

Department of Housing and Urban Development

Nicolas Retsinas, Assistant Secretary (Federal Housing Commission)

"I am committed to bringing people into the Federal Government who've made a difference in States and communities around the country," said the President. "This is a group of people who truly meet that standard."

NOTE: Biographies of the nominees were made available by the Office of the Press Secretary.

Remarks Announcing the Initiative to Alleviate the Credit Crunch
March 10, 1993

Thank you very much. Thank you very much, Secretary Bentsen, other members of the Cabinet and distinguished Members of the House and Senate of both parties, and the business men and women and the bankers who are here today.

I am in debt to many people in this room and throughout this country who raised to me in many ways, over the 16 months in which I was engaged in the campaign for the Presidency, the question of the credit crunch. From the beginnings of that campaign in New Hampshire, across the country to Illinois and Michigan, down to Florida, across to California, and in all points in between, I repeatedly ran into small business men and women, I repeatedly met bankers themselves who said they wished that something could be done to open up credit again to creditworthy loans, to generate jobs in the private sector.

Today we are taking a step to speed the economic recovery that will increase jobs by increasing access to credit for the main engine of our economy, small and medium-sized businesses. At the same time, by strengthening our banking system, our plan will move us beyond the banking problems of the last decade. The initiative avoids the regulatory excess and duplication we've seen and focuses on real risks within our financial institutions and on fair lending, equal opportunity, and credit availability.

Every day, small business is a big part of all of our lives. It's the coffee shop on the corner, the florist down the street, the stationery store that carries office supplies, the dry cleaner, the contractor who will remodel a kitchen. Many are businesses with fewer than 100 employees. Many more employ fewer than 20 people. But they keep communities and neighborhoods vibrant and vital. They are the industry in a cottage, in a garage, in a spare bedroom. They are downtown in every town, and sometimes they grow into very large enterprises indeed.

Small business includes small farms, the agricultural community. Their contribution is evident every day on our tables. But it is much more. They are the cultivators of an essential part of our history, our heritage, our culture. Small business is also high tech, the industries of tomorrow, from computer software to communications, to biotechnology and environmental testing, all enterprises that create high-wage, high-skill jobs for Americans today, and they will be there tomorrow.

And small business has been the route to a better life for immigrants who set up a family business, for men and women who save as they work for others until they can venture off on their own. Often a small business is actually an outgrowth of the global economy. As larger firms downsize to remain competitive, they contract out to smaller firms. And many talented people who once worked for large companies are now going off on their own to seize opportunities in smaller enterprises, building businesses for themselves.

Owning one's own business is a cornerstone of the American dream, fortified by hard work, determination, and creativity. My first experience in life with business was in my grandfather's little grocery store. He was the symbol of hope and opportunity to many people with whom he dealt in many ways, 6 days a week at all hours of the day and night.

Today's small businesses are a barometer of the economic recovery. And as the strength of this recovery has been diluted by the inability to create jobs, it is clear that it's largely because small companies are still having a hard time. If you look at this chart here, you can see the number of small business failures, just since 1985: 119,000 in '85–'86; 118,000 the next year; 111,000 in the next 2-year period; but in '91–'92, almost 185,000 small business failures.

These businesses have been hit especially hard by the recession and by a problem not of their own making that can be summarized by two fearsome but now well-worn words: credit crunch. Small companies are simply unable in too many cases to get loans from banks. And I want to show this—they turned it, and I didn't see—if you look here, the growth in commercial and industrial loans, '85–'86, in billions of dollars; and the last 2 years, down to a negative $36 billion. Now, if these businesses can't begin or expand or try new ventures, that means stagnation for our economy, lost opportunity, and sometimes ruin for entrepreneurs. Indeed, I've met business people in this country in the last year and a half who've never missed a payment on a loan and still had the loans canceled.

These problems are America's problems. When small businesses aren't prospering, they create fewer jobs, and that means fewer jobs for America. If you look at this last chart, you will see the real essence of why this has turned out to be, so far, a jobless recovery. In '85–'86, there was a positive change in small business employment of 2.4 million; '87–'88, 2.8 million; '89–'90, 3.2 million; but down in '91–'92, 400,000. Now, in every year of the 1980's the Fortune 500 companies have reduced employment by several hundred thousand people a year in the United States. But all during the eighties that reduction was more than offset by the creation of new jobs in the small business sector, until the last couple of years.

If you had to put in a sentence why this has been a jobless recovery, it's because small business job creation hasn't offset big business job losses. And that is the central challenge we face. As we take advantage of the incredible things going on now in the big and small business sector with productivity increases, with the aggregate indications that we're in an economic recovery, we have to look for ways, all of us together, to try to help to spur small business and medium-size business job growth so that we can put some jobs back into these impressive economic figures of the last quarter.

Nearly two-thirds of all of our workers are employed by small businesses. And as I said, millions of jobs in the last decade were created by them, even as larger employers were downsizing, contracting out, or moving employment offshore. We cannot afford not to try to resume this trend in the 1990's. We know that if we create a reliable and secure system of credit for America's small businesses, they'll create jobs for Americans and profits for themselves. That's why we have offered incentives like investment tax credits for small employers, the new business capital gains tax, urban enterprise zones, and a network of small business community development banks.

In our country you can become successful if you have a better idea that you can turn into reality. But that reality can only occur if credit is available, for most Americans. And we think we have a better idea for getting lenders and creditworthy borrowers together. What we propose does not involve any changes in legislation. These steps can be taken quickly because they have been agreed to already by the four Federal bank and thrift regulatory agencies: the Comptroller of the Currency, the Federal Reserve, the Federal Deposit Insurance Corporation, and the Office of Thrift Supervision. Today I'll outline the basics of the plan, but the four bank and thrift regulators are issuing a joint interagency policy statement today that sets out more of the details. It will be available to all of you, and most of you will understand it. [*Laughter*] I don't know if I left the implication that I didn't. [*Laughter*]

What we have done, first of all, is to reexamine our examination system, a system that bankers often felt has become too excessive in the wake of the banking and savings and loan failures of the eighties. With this plan our examiners will be directed to do what they do best and not to spend endless hours on pointless paperwork. It will strengthen our oversight by shifting our regulatory attention from unproductive and repetitive procedures, redirecting our resources to better use so that bank examiners will be able to seek out the real risks in today's environment. They'll go after bad loans and troubled banks. That means improved safety and soundness. But they will reduce the credit crunch because they will reduce attention to things that do not deserve them.

We will not, I will say again, we will not reduce attention to important regulation or to proper reserves for problem loans. The plan will not lower the capital requirements established in accordance with international standards. It will not cause a single bank to fail. And it will not cost the deposit insurance funds one dollar.

Through a proper allocation of our regulatory resources, we will be able to focus more on examination procedures to further meaningful compliance with the Community Reinvestment Act and to promote fair opportunities for all of our people while reducing the hassles for all creditworthy loans.

Above all, borrowers can go to their banks expecting fair and equal treatment and a reasonable application process. Fairness is a goal for many good reasons, including the fact that women and other minorities have been very bullish for small business and for America. Female-owned companies now employ 11½ million Americans.

A side effect of the savings and loan disaster was a reaction that forced many banks into a thinking mode that didn't distinguish between a good risk and a bad risk where small businesses were concerned. They were afraid to. This was a problem, especially for community bankers who frequently had to decide whether they could loan money to other members in their own community. Even if a banker could personally vouch that an applicant was a person of good character with an unblemished credit record and a good business track record, a loan might still be turned down because the banker felt his hands were tied by tight restrictions.

So while we ask bankers to give the small business men and women credit, we'll give the bankers some credit too, as they consider loans to small and medium-size companies in their own communities and neighborhoods. They'll be encouraged to use their judgment to determine whether a borrower is creditworthy. And we're telling bankers that as long as their institutions and their practices are sound, they shouldn't be afraid of the regulator. If they disagree with a decision by a regulator, they'll now have a recourse, a workable and prompt appeals process.

To bankers across the Nation we say, you are a pillar of our neighborhoods and communities. We know the demands of rebounding from the last decade have often been painful for many of you. Your comeback has been nothing short of amazing. But there is more work to do. And we need you to get it done. And if it gets done, there will be something to show for it, the kind of broad-based economic growth that benefits all of us.

And we further say to bankers across the land that if you make sensible loans, the Government should not come down on you. That's why we're taking this action today. We want bankers to get back into the business of lending money,

and we're going to work with them to make it happen.

We're also making clear that taking collateral as part of a business loan should not be so burdensome or costly to discourage borrowers or lenders from making sound credit decisions. Often the only collateral a would-be borrower can offer is real estate. Of course, we learned the hard way in the eighties that we had to be careful where loans involving commercial real estate are concerned. But care has been confused with regulatory excess that has been too much of a burden for everyone. The changes we propose will strike a balance so that we can have both safety and credit availability.

These changes will also address the paper crunch in getting a small business loan. It simply shouldn't be as burdensome to get a $25,000 loan as it is to get a $25 million loan. It makes no sense for a small or medium-sized business borrower, or for an individual for that matter, to be required in every case to produce a pile of paper like this one—pretty thick—when a loan can be made safely in many cases, particularly by banks who have demonstrated judgment in their business practices, with merely a promissory note and a financial statement and possibly a short credit application like this.

So under the current system, the paperwork— and I expect every one of you to come back and show me your measured envelopes here. We've got to prove that the difference is what we're asserting it is today. [*Laughter*] Under the current system, the paperwork is often daunting to the applicant and discourages banks from making smaller loans. Streamlining the process will make it easier to free up credit without compromising security. This is action that everyone, conscientious regulators, community-conscious banks, and growing businesses, can embrace.

With this approach we want to marry the ingredients for a thriving business climate. Right now banks are healthier than they've been in years; 1990 was a record year for bank profitability. And these profits have been used to put banks in the strongest position they've been in, in a quarter of a century. At the same time, interest rates have gone down. Just 3 years ago the average interest rate on a small business loan was 12 percent. So far the average is 8 percent. The climate for business ventures has been made even sunnier by economic growth that we've seen in the last quarter. That's a byproduct of the optimism for the growth that we are pressing for now with all the economic initiatives that are before the Congress and the country.

So both supply and demand for business loans are there. And would-be small business owners are right to feel they have the wind at their backs. Now that we have banks in the strongest positions they've been in in a quarter century, they ought to be able to give us the strongest economic boost we've had for small business in a quarter century. Until now the problem has been that everyone has had to face a 10-foot wall called the credit crunch. This action that this administration is taking today should take a big chunk out of that wall. The result should be a flow of billions of dollars of economic stimulus that doesn't cost the American taxpayers one red cent. The payoff will be in new jobs and in reversing the charts that I have shown you today.

At the same time, by encouraging new small business ventures, we'll be laying the ground-work for a smarter work force that can compete more effectively in the global economy. Getting financing to these businesses is absolutely essential to the future growth of America. We'll see the benefits, and so will our children.

This administration is firmly and unequivocally committed to the private sector as the engine of economic growth in America. We have no illusions, no abstractions, no preoccupations; we know that this is what works in this country. In America we put people first, first by having a prosperous economy founded on a thriving private sector. What's good for America is good for business, and we are determined to make the climate for business and for growth better and better and better, beginning today where so many of you have told me for so long we ought to begin, with a real assault on the credit crunch.

Thank you very much.

NOTE: The President spoke at 1:43 p.m. in the East Room at the White House.

Exchange With Reporters Prior to a Meeting With California State Legislators
March 10, 1993

Health Care Task Force

Q. Mr. President, can your health care task force proceed in public?

The President. Well, I understand we got a good ruling from the judge today.

Q. The judge ruled that the meetings have to be open.

The President. He's ruled that they had to have some open meetings, but the briefing I got was that he ruled that some of the assertions that were made were absolutely unconstitutional. The briefing that I got was that we got a very good ruling from the judge today.

Military Base Closings

Q. Are the bases going to close in California, sir?

The President. I don't know. We don't know what's going to happen. I don't know what—you all have published lists. I've not seen the lists. You know how it works: The base closing commission has to make a recommendation. Then they give it to me, and I have to evaluate whether I think it's right or not. And then, after that, after those two things are reconciled, the Congress gets to vote up or down on it. So I don't know what's going to happen.

NOTE: The exchange began at 2:45 p.m. in the State Dining Room at the White House.

Statement on Announcing the Forest Conference
March 10, 1993

Planning and good long-term management can help us protect jobs and the unique old-growth forests that are as much a part of our national heritage as the Grand Canyon or Yosemite. It is time to break the gridlock that has blocked action and bring all sides together to craft a balanced approach to the economic and environmental challenges we face.

NOTE: The President's statement was included in a White House statement announcing the Forest Conference scheduled for April 2 in Portland, OR.

Remarks to Westinghouse Employees in Linthicum, Maryland
March 11, 1993

Thank you very much. I want to say a special word of thanks to the people from Westinghouse who greeted me when I arrived: Gary Clark, who introduced me, Dick Linder, Gladys Green, Rich O'Leary, and Gary Eder. And thank you to all of you who made this tour possible.

I want to thank the Members of the United States Congress who are here, who have worked very hard for a long time and before I became President to help to design a plan to strengthen our economy even as we reduce military spending. Your Senators, Barbara Mikulski and Paul Sarbanes, are here. Your Congressman, Ben Cardin, is here. Senator Jeff Bingaman of New Mexico; Senators Barbara Boxer and Dianne Feinstein of California; Senator Bill Cohen of Maine; Senator Claiborne Pell of Rhode Island; Congressman Martin Frost of Texas; Congresswoman Jane Harman of California; and Congressman Tom Foglietta of Pennsylvania. I think that is the entire delegation here, along with Mayor Kurt Schmoke of Baltimore and Governor Schaefer. I'm glad to see all of them. I have to note here, you can tell who the best politician is. Of all these people I've introduced, only Senator Mikulski found a seat. [*Laughter*]

I'd also like to thank the members of my Cabinet who have helped to work on the statement that I will announce today who are here: the Defense Secretary Les Aspin, Labor Secretary Bob Reich, Veterans Affairs Director Jesse Brown, Energy Secretary Hazel O'Leary, Commerce Secretary Ron Brown. I want to thank all of them for their work.

All of you know from personal experience how much American industry has been changed by the cutbacks in defense. Defense spending peaked in 1985. And by 1997, it will have been reduced approximately 40 percent, perhaps more, from its 1985 peak. These changes have led not only to reductions in military personnel abroad and closings of bases at home but dramatic changes in military contracting that have affected companies like this one and which have affected the economies of the States of California, Connecticut, Texas, and many others.

It has been said that while change is certain, progress is not. And that certainly is true when it comes to the challenge of meeting the national economic goals that we have in the face of cutbacks in military spending. As I said, these cutbacks have been made since 1985; more are to come. They are essential in a world in which we need funds to be reinvested in the domestic economy and in which the security threats we meet today, while very serious, are different and clearly less expensive than those we faced when the Soviet Union and the United States faced each other across the Berlin Wall with the barriers of the cold war and the imminent prospect of nuclear war. So these changes had to come. But if we do nothing in the face of change, we have learned the hard way that we are its victims. If we take bold action, we can be the beneficiaries of change.

All of you here at Westinghouse Electronic Systems Group are proof that you can make change your friend. In 1986, just 16 percent of the work done here was nondefense. Today, it's 27 percent. By 1995, half or more of your work will be nondefense. What you have done here is what I wish to do nationally: take some of the most talented people in the world who produce some of the most sophisticated military technology and put that to work in the civilian economy.

The military surveillance technology I have seen here can now be used to help commercial airlines avoid wind shears. Military security technology can now be used to help police officers on the streets and in their patrol cars to be safer and to solve crimes and to find missing children more rapidly. State-of-the-art batteries is helping here to develop an electric car which may well provide an enormous opportunity for America to become more energy-independent and to dramatically reduce the pollution of our atmosphere, at a time when we have been reminded anew that there really is a hole in the ozone layer and there really are problems with unlimited emissions of CO_2.

Clearly, defense conversion can be done and can be done well, making change our friend and not our enemy. But in order to do it we must act, act decisively, act intelligently, and not simply react years after the cuts occur.

Last year, when a candidate for President, I outlined a plan to create new jobs in the civilian economy. Anticipating this challenge, far-sighted Members of Congress appropriated approximately $1.5 billion for defense conversion last year, including ideas that literally came from the minds and the efforts of some of the Members of Congress who are here with us today. They've demonstrated aggressiveness in adapting to change. But until today, in spite of that act, none of the money appropriated by Congress was released, and there was no comprehensive plan for what to do with it.

Today I want to explain how we're going to put your money to work to put Americans to work and how we're planning for the future by investing in our people, encouraging our companies, and assisting our communities. Our first priority has to be investing in our people. Keep in mind, as you all know here, when the defense budget is reduced, that affects, obviously, contracts and therefore the jobs of people who work in the private sector. It also affects the size of the military force itself, the configuration of our defense forces abroad and here at home, and the people who will be affected by the reductions.

Our defense reinvestment and conversion initiative will rededicate $375 million right away to help working people affected by defense re-

ductions with employment services, job training, and transition assistance; $150 million of that will go to Government and employer-sponsored job training programs; $112 million will help members of the Guard and the Reserves make the transition to civilian life and to provide severance pay and health benefits to civilians who are leaving Government employment.

There's also initiative to provide early retirement benefits for military personnel with 15 years of service or more, to start a new program to encourage them to put their skills to work in vital areas like teaching, law enforcement, environmental restoration, and health care. Under a provision offered by Senator Sam Nunn of Georgia, any member of the military who is being mustered out with 15 years or more of service can go to work in law enforcement, for example, and earn a year of military retirement for every year they were in law enforcement, so that these people who have committed their lives to the service of our country and could not reasonably have known that this reduction would occur and would affect them can still earn their military retirement by serving their country here at home.

We must also recognize the ripple effect of defense adjustment and target assistance to our communities. In 1993 alone, we will triple the budget of the Defense Department's Office of Economic Adjustment. The $30 million we've committed to this task will be invested in helping our communities find the tools and the expertise to adjust to the changed nature of their local economy. It will be an investment that pays off in the long-term.

In addition, through the Commerce Department, we'll invest another $80 million in a revolving loan and grant program to directly and immediately aid communities hit hardest by defense cuts.

Finally, the Secretary of Defense has assured me that he will do everything he can to speed the environmental cleanup on bases that are closed so that they can be turned over either to commercial purposes or to local government at the earliest possible time so that there will be a minimum loss of economic activity in areas where bases are closed.

But all the worker training in the world and all the community assistance in the world will do no good if there are no jobs for those workers and no businesses for those communities. The private sector is the engine of lasting economic growth in our system, and therefore, our plan must help our companies to make these transitions to compete and to win.

We seek to go beyond the debate of the past in which some thought Government alone could do everything and others claimed Government could do nothing. In this area there are two things Government can do to aid companies like this one: promote dual use research and promote civilian use of technology that was formerly developed for military purposes. That is what you have done here. We want to speed and expand that process all across the United States.

One of the success stories of the cold war was the Defense Advanced Research Agency, or DARPA. DARPA helped keep America on the cutting edge of defense research. To meet the new challenges of the new world, we're giving DARPA a new mission and restoring its old name, because before 1972 that Agency was known simply as the Advanced Research Products Agency. By going back to that name and refocusing the Agency's efforts on dual use technologies, such as that which you have demonstrated to me here today, rather than strictly military applications, we'll be better able to integrate research to strengthen defense and to promote our economic security here at home.

Starting now, this Agency, ARPA, will allocate more than $500 million to technology and industrial programs like the ones we've seen here today. We'll support industry-led consortia and dual use technologies and promote efforts to break through with commercial uses of formerly defense technologies. Programs will be selected on the basis of merit and will require matching funds from the corporations affected. We're even going to set up a toll-free number to attract good ideas from good companies. And you will like this. The number is 1–800–DUAL–USE. The hotline will be hooked up tomorrow, so don't call today. [*Laughter*]

To help walk companies through their new opportunities, ARPA will provide them with this book, which puts together programs from the Defense Department, the Department of Commerce, the Department of Energy, NASA, and the National Science Foundation. It is a remarkable coalition of Agencies finally putting all the information together for defense technology conversion, reinvestment, and transition assistance.

To further coordinate assistance, ARPA will

work with four other Agencies, the ones I just mentioned. And we're going to have a series of regional outreach meetings all across this country, again, to try to mobilize other companies to get involved in this initiative so that they can save or create jobs instead of lose jobs in the face of defense reductions.

We want Government-industry partnerships to help develop advanced materials. We want companies to form regional technology alliances so they can share information and develop new products and new markets. Our manufacturing extension programs will help bring state-of-the-art technology to companies in much the same way as the Agricultural Extension Service helped our farmers more than two generations ago begin to become the most productive in the world. And through the Small Business Innovation Research Program, we'll help small businesses in their efforts to develop dual use technology.

But dual use technology is just the beginning. We have to explore also new opportunities in purely civilian technologies. This year alone, we'll invest $300 million in emerging nondefense technology. The Department of Energy will speed the transfer of technology to private industry from our national labs. And when Congress passes the stimulus package I have proposed, we'll have millions more to invest in research and development partnerships, in advanced technology programs, and in computer networks for schools and libraries around the country.

As with every aspect of the program for change I have asked the American people and the Congress to embrace, defense conversion will require us to literally reimagine and reinvent the way Government works. I've asked the National Economic Council to take the lead in our efforts to streamline and coordinate our conversion efforts so that you don't have to deal with a big bureaucracy where all the information is in many different places and sometimes seems to be operating at cross purposes.

Shifting to a civilian economy is of obvious concern to the Defense Department, but it's also the business of the Commerce Department, the Labor Department, the Energy Department, NASA, and many other agencies, including the Department of Veterans Affairs, which will have even more veterans now as people are coming out of the service and going into the civilian work force. Our National Economic Council will cut through redtape, break through turf battles, and help to deliver services to our customers quickly and efficiently.

I don't pretend that this will be easy, and all of it will take some time. But the choice we face is between bold action to build a stronger and safer and smarter America, or continuing to cut defense with no appropriate response or with one that is too localized and too limited.

The soldier-statesman Dwight Eisenhower once observed that the resourceful American makers of plowshares could, with time and as required, make swords as well. Our challenge is now to reverse the process. You have given us a stunning example of just how brilliantly that can be done here in this fine facility. I know today that the world's finest makers of swords can and will be the finest makers of plowshares, and they will lead America into a new century of strength, growth, and opportunity.

Thank you very much.

NOTE: The President spoke at 12:29 p.m. at Westinghouse Electric Corp. In his remarks, he referred to Dick Linder, president, Westinghouse Electronic Systems Group; Gary Clark, acting CEO, Westinghouse Electric Corp.; and union local presidents Gladys Green, IBEW, Rick O'Leary, IUE, and Gary Eder, Salaried Employees Association.

Remarks to the Children's Defense Fund Conference
March 11, 1993

The President. Thank you very much, ladies and gentlemen, distinguished members of the Children's Defense Fund board, Secretary Reich, and Secretary Riley. Did you see the way Secretary Reich rushed out when they said the President of the United States? [*Laughter*] That's not true. I pushed him through the door so I could get a laugh out of it. [*Laughter*]

My dear friend Marian Wright Edelman, as usual, your introduction has left me nothing to say. I will say this: I know a lot of people will come here and tell you how much they appreciate people who are children's advocates. Not very many people appreciate it enough to marry one, and I did. [*Laughter*] I also have savaged the ranks of the CDF board. My wife had to resign because she was married to a Presidential candidate. And then Donna Shalala had to resign because I gave her a job—[*laughter*]—which on Sunday she'd probably rather swap for being chair of the Children's Defense Fund board.

I am delighted to be here. I look out on this crowd and I see many old friends. You know, a lot of people ask me what it's like to be President. And I don't know if I can explain it, but it is different. People either want to walk around on tippy-toe or take a baseball bat and whack your head off. There seems to be nothing in between. The other day Hillary had a number of people into the White House on the first floor to some sort of meeting, and I got off on the floor, and I had to go someplace else. And all of a sudden, all these people were there. And I walked out into this crowd, and I started shaking their hands. And the guy who was with me said, "Oh, Mr. President, I'm so sorry that you had to deal with all those people." I said, "That's all right, I used to be one." [*Laughter*] I hope I will be again some day. Meanwhile, I'm going to depend on you and the American people to keep me just as close to humanity as I possibly can.

I've just come from a remarkable event in Maryland with a number of Members of the Congress who are friends of the Children's Defense Fund. We were there; Secretary Reich was there with me; we flew back. And we were at a plant that belongs to Westinghouse. It used to be a defense plant, and it is increasingly becoming a domestic technology plant. And we went there to announce an economic conversion program to try to help more people who are losing their jobs from military cutbacks either in the private or the public sector find new opportunities moving toward the economy of the 21st century.

This is a very important thing. We've been reducing defense since 1985, and no nation would so reduce one sector of its economy that provided so many high-wage, high-growth jobs, that was on the cutting edge of new technology—no other nation would ever have done what we've done with no clear strategy for what to do with all those resources, all those people, to try to help to build our economic base. So we will continue to reduce defense, as we must, but we're trying to plan for the future of those people and those incredible resources.

I saw military technology turn into an electric car that will drive over 80 miles an hour and which may hold the promise of ending our dependence on foreign oil and cleaning up our atmosphere. I saw a police car with a computer screen with visual imaging developed for defense technology, which can now be used immediately to transmit to police officers who have it pictures of missing children, immediately, while they're in their car. I saw a plane with radar technology which just came back from dealing with the difficult incident in Waco, Texas—defense technology—another plane with a different sort of technology now which can be put on all of our commercial air flights to detect wind shears, which is one of the major causes of airline misfortunes now among commercial airlines.

I say all this because everybody says, well, that's a great idea, and it's self-evident, and why haven't we been doing this? But it is simply reflective of a problem we have had in this country for some time, which is that we have undervalued the importance of increasing the capacity of our people. We have talked a lot about a lot of things in America. But when you strip it all away and you look at where we have been, sort of out of sync with many other countries and with where we have to go in the future, it is clear that on a broad range of areas, we have simply undervalued the importance of making a commitment to the idea that we don't have a person to waste, that everybody counts, and that what you can do affects not only your future but mine as well.

These, of course, are the arguments that the Children's Defense Fund has been making since its inception in its struggles to get a better deal for America's children. They have become far more important arguments in the last decade.

In 1985 a remarkable thing happened, a thing altogether laudatory in our country: Our senior citizens became less poor than the rest of us, a thing we can be proud of. People used to have to live in absolute agony wondering what would happen to their parents. You still do if you have long-term care problems. But most elderly people now, because of Social Security and supplemental security income and Medicare and because of the pension reforms of the last several years, can look forward to a security in their later years that 10 or 20 or 30 years ago was utterly unheard of. And it is really a testimony to the farsightedness of our country.

However, at the same time, in the same decade, we began to experience a new class of poor people who were dramatically undervalued. They were little children and their poor parents, usually their single poor parents. And they had no advocates in many councils of power. If it hadn't been for the Children's Defense Fund and a few others who walked with them through life, many of the good things which have been done would not have been done. And all the things which were done were not enough to reverse the trends of the 1980's, when the elderly became less poor and the children became more poor.

Now, because many of you in this room have continued this fight, and because of the decisions the American people made in the last election, we once again have a chance to invest in the hopes and the dreams of our children.

I have asked the United States Congress to embrace a program that recognizes, as was said earlier, that we have two big deficits in this country. We have a huge budget deficit, but we also have a huge investment deficit. It was a cruel irony of the last 12 years that we not only took the Government debt from $1 trillion to $4 trillion, with annual deficits now in excess of $300 million projected for the next few years unless we change it, but we found a way in all of that to actually reduce our investment in our future at the national level.

How could it happen? Well, it happened because of a big military buildup. It happened because of a big tax cut early. It happened because health care costs have been completely out of control. It happened because an underperforming economy didn't produce many revenues. But it happened also because there were not enough people who said we must constantly invest in the most important thing in a modern society, the capacity of the people to be healthy and strong and good.

So you have all these anomalies. The United States, the world's strongest economy, has the third worst record in the Western Hemisphere for immunizing its children against preventable childhood diseases. The United States, a country that has dominated the economy of the world for the last half a century, has higher rates of adult illiteracy and school dropout and dysfunction among adults than most of its major competitors, and the highest rate of incarceration of any country in the world, something we rank first in.

That bespeaks our inability to make the diversity of our country a source of strength instead of weakness, and to deal with the stark dilemmas of poverty in ways that at least give the children a chance to do better. Well, now we have a chance.

The good news is we know a lot about what works. We've known for years through clear studies that, though not perfect, Head Start and WIC and immunizations really do make a difference. We know that if you give children a better life and you strengthen their families, you make the economy stronger and you free up money to be spent on things like that economic conversion program I just visited today.

We know that if we focus on people and their capacities, it really does work. That's why I was really pleased that the first bill I signed was the Family and Medical Leave Act because it will, even to those who oppose it, make their businesses more productive, not less, by securing family life and making it possible for people to be good parents. That's why the long-term economic plan and the short-term economic stimulus I asked the Congress to embrace includes funds to put our people first: for 700,000 summer jobs for young people; for the beginnings of summer Head Start programs where they don't exist; for beginning to set up the infrastructure of immunization where it isn't, so that we can start to do the work that has to be done.

We have simply got to invest in our people in ways that work. Marian has already said it, but I will reiterate. This budget, if funded by the Congress, will fully fund Head Start and WIC, will create a network of immunization efforts which will permit us to finally immunize our little children against preventable childhood diseases, something that will save, over the long run, 10 bucks for every dollar we put into it. How do you explain, I mean, how can you possibly justify to anybody that our country, with the power of its economy, that produces the vast majority of vaccines produced anywhere in

the world, is better only than Bolivia and Haiti in this hemisphere in immunizing our children?

And you know, you have to have a certain core of immunization to make sure that there will be no outbreak of diseases. We are dangerously, perilously close to falling below that core of immunized children in many different areas. This is a big deal, folks.

So I hope that we will have this attitude now that we ought to invest as we cut the deficit. The plan that I presented to the Congress reduces the deficit dramatically, has 150 specific budget cuts, starts with an example from the White House staff. We cut the staff in the next fiscal year 25 percent below the staffing levels that I found when I came. We cut $9 billion out of the administrative costs of Federal agencies. And I mean they're real cuts; they're going into the budget. They cannot be escaped. [*Applause*] I'm glad you're clapping for that, you know, because the people that are attacking me act like anybody that wants any money from the Government just loves all that bureaucracy you have to put up with. I know better. [*Laughter*] It's good for you to clap. [*Applause*]

We also raised some tax money. I saw the proof of an article by David Stockman coming out in a magazine soon which talked about how the clear problem is that the tax base of this country was dramatically, fundamentally, and permanently eroded in 1981, that Social Security's about the same percentage of gross national product today it was back in 1981.

So we have to raise some more money if we want to reduce the debt. But we also try to reverse the investment gap in things that you didn't come here to talk about, like transportation and clean water and better sewage systems, in things that will strengthen the environment and put people to work and increase our productivity, in things like community development operations to add jobs to high unemployment areas, in national service, which Marian mentioned, and in other areas that will increase the capacity of people to work, to grow, to learn, to flourish.

Now, there are people, believe it or not, who, number one, don't want to pass a stimulus package at all because they say the economy's great—that's because most people in Washington are employed; talk to them about that, will you—[*laughter*]—and who think that this program would be even better if it didn't have any new investment at all.

Now, to be fair to those people, there are basically three lines of attack. You're going to the Hill. I want you to know I need your help. I need your help because there are a lot of people without jobs; there are a lot of people without adequate jobs. Most of the new jobs created in this last round—365,000 last month—hallelujah, that's great, but more than half of them were part-time jobs that don't have health care benefits for the kids and the families.

You need to know what they are saying, the people against whom you must argue. They will say, number one, "We can cut the deficit even more if we just didn't have any investment," or "If we didn't pass any of the President's spending programs, we could cut the deficit as much and raise taxes less."

The problem with that argument is those people think there is absolutely no difference between putting another child in Head Start and keeping somebody working in an agency when the job is no longer needed and can be phased out, in supporting a regulatory apparatus that has long since lost its justification, in funding a pork barrel project that can't possibly be justified. In other words, these people think anything the Government spends is equally bad. Educating a kid to go to college is the same as continuing the subsidy for sheep or any other program; no difference. Government spending is Government spending is Government spending. There is no difference.

Now, do you believe that in your own lives?

Audience members. No-o-o!

The President. No. I mean, in your lives, if you take home a check every month, is it the same whether you spend it on making a house payment, making a car payment, saving money for your child's education, or just paying for an extra helping at dinner? Of course not. There are distinctions in the relative impact of how you spend your pay, how your business invests its money, and how your Government invests your money. And so when people tell you there's no difference, tell them that's wrong.

And then there is a crowd that say, "Well, these programs don't really make any difference. Head Start doesn't work, and there's no proof Head Start works." Now, this is an interesting argument. Most of those who think there's no proof Head Start works still believe trickle-down economics did.

Until I proposed phasing in the full funding of this program, many of those who themselves objected had previously voted to expand it. To be fair, President Bush praised Head Start at every turn. A few years ago, Senator Dole introduced his own legislation to expand it. Sure, there are serious criticisms rooted in the fact that this is now not a new program. There are people who say it's not evenly good across the country. That is true. There are people who say it could be managed better. That's true. There are people who say that cognitive improvements don't always last more than 2 years after children stop attending, depending on where they are. That's true. One big deal is how strong the parents' involvement really is. There are those who say there ought to be more school-based programs or more home-based programs, and we've worked hard on that at home. All that's true. That is not an excuse not to fully fund Head Start.

Our program will serve more children, but it will also strengthen the quality of Head Start and put some flexibility back into the program so that it can meet the needs of the different communities that are served. But those who choose to ignore the overwhelming evidence of the program's success have an obligation to tell us why more children with high self-esteem and better grades and better thinking skills and better predictable long-term performance is such a bad idea. I think it's a great idea.

But we must, in fairness to the criticisms, become our own most severe critics. That's where you come in, because all of you live out there where these programs work. You could give a better criticism of what's wrong with most of these public programs than those who don't want to fund them. Most of you could. So tell them you know it is up to us to be our own most severe critics.

I just asked the Vice President to review every program in the Government, come back to me in 6 months with all kinds of other things that we can stop doing or that we can modify or that we can push back to people at the grassroots level. If we who believe in Government don't have the courage to change it, we cannot expect those who don't to help us in our efforts.

And this is just the beginning. Just 2 days ago I asked Secretary Shalala to draft a new child welfare initiative to combine family support and family preservation services, to do more to build on the work of Senator Rockefeller and Congressman Matsui and Congresswoman Schroeder and to do more for families at risk, especially those at risk of foster care placement, even as we try to strengthen our efforts to enforce child support enforcement for those who have been abandoned by one parent.

Now, there is a third argument against this effort. There are those who say, "Yes, Head Start's a good deal; WIC is a good deal; the immunization's a good deal. And yes, we ought to invest as opposed to consume. There is a distinction to be drawn in the way this money is spent, and investment is better, investment in our children, our future. But we still ought not to do it because we need even more deficit reduction."

And let me say, that is an argument you must treat with respect. We have gone from a $1 trillion deficit to a $4 trillion deficit in 12 years. We have imposed a crushing burden on the present and a bigger one on the future. And if you think about it, it's really an income transfer. Now that we're spending 15 cents of every dollar you pay the Government—most of you are middle class people, and we spend 15 cents of every dollar you pay the Government paying interest on the debt. Those bonds are largely held by upper income people. So there are now a lot of liberals in the Congress who are rethinking their old positions on things like the mechanisms by which we move to balance the budget on the theory that we're spending all this money having an income transfer from middle class taxpayers, lower income taxpayers to people who hold the bonds because we didn't have the discipline to run our budgets better.

And if we don't do something about the deficit, we just keep on spending like we are, by the end of the decade your annual debt will be $653 billion a year. The interest service will be about 22 cents of your tax dollar. Twenty cents on the dollar of every dollar in America, public and private, will go to health care. So we have to change.

But my answer to those who say, "Well, let's just don't invest because this deficit is such a big problem," is: Number one, we got into this mess over 12 years, and we have more than 4 years to get out of it. Number two, we are reaping the benefits of the clear and disciplined and determined effort that the congressional leadership has now agreed to make with me to bring the deficit down. We have interest rates at very, very low rates. We have the stock market back up. People say, "Hey, this thing is going to work." All of you can now look at

whether you should refinance your home or your car. Businesses should refinance their debt. If we get all this debt refinanced in the next year, that will add $80 to $100 billion back in our economy. We are reaping the benefits of a disciplined program to reduce the deficit today. But if we do not also at the same time recognize that for 12 years we have ignored our obligations to invest in our jobs, in our people, in our education, if we don't do that, we will pay for that neglect tomorrow, just like we're paying for yesterday's neglect today. We can do both things.

There's another argument you need to make—and I'm speaking for my wife now, as well as for me—which is that if you just cut out all these programs that we believe in, if you just cut them plumb out, you'll still have an increase in the deficit again, starting in about 5 years, because of the explosion in health care costs. The real, ultimate answer to the deficit problem is to bring health care cost in line with inflation and provide a decent system of health care for all Americans.

And we can do that. So, with discipline, with a willingness to both cut and tax, with a willingness to reduce consumption expenditures and increase investment in our future, we can do the things that we have to do. But we can't walk away from any of our challenges and expect the results America needs.

If we walk away from the health care challenge, it doesn't matter what they do on all these other cuts. You'll be swallowed up in debt in 5 or 6 years again if we walk away from the health care challenge.

If we walk away from the challenge to raise some more revenues and cut the spending we must, we'll lose control of our economic destiny even if we spend more money on the programs you want. You'll be raising and educating healthier, more well-educated kids to a weaker economy.

But if we reduce the deficit and we forget about the fact that in the world we live in the only thing that really counts is people—every factory can be moved overseas. Three trillion dollars in money crosses national lines every day. Everything else is mobile except us. We're here. We don't want to move. [*Laughter*]

All we've got's each other now in America. That's what we've got. And if we ignore that, we don't think those little kids that live in the Mississippi Delta, in my home State, many of whom never see a dentist the whole time of their childhood, need a better shot in life because of us as well as them; if we don't believe that those kids that are sitting out there in the barrios in Los Angeles, in the black community, in the Hispanic community, in the Asian-American community, waiting for the resolution of the Rodney King trial only because it stands for everything else that ever happened to them, not because of the trial but because of what it stands for; if we don't think that we need to prove that a county like Los Angeles County with people from 150 different racial and ethnic groups can live together and learn together and grow together and if they play by the rules can have the right to earn a decent living, and we don't think that affects the rest of us, we haven't learned very much in the last 12 years.

And so I ask you to do this: I ask you to go to the Congress and ask them to support this program. And go with respect, because I promise you most of these people are trying to come to grips with the dilemmas of this time. And they have gotten one big message: that is that we made a horrible mistake to let the deficit get out of hand like we did in the last 12 years. And they deserve respect for getting

that message. And they now have a President who will take the lead and fade some of the heat for the unpopularity of the decisions which have to be made. Go with respect for that. Say, "You had to do that, and we respect that."

But remind them that out in the country where you live, bringing down the deficit is important if it gives people jobs and raises people's incomes and if there are people out there who can seize the opportunities of the future. And what you represent is the future. You represent the needs of the people who will not be able to perform even with a sensible economic policy unless we do better in health care, in education, and in dealing with the needs of our poorest children. That is what you represent. None of this other stuff will amount to a hill of beans unless we put the American people first in all of these decisions. That is the message I plead with you to bring to the Congress.

Thank you, and God bless you all.

NOTE: The President spoke at 1:52 p.m. at the Washington Hilton. In his remarks, he referred to Marian Wright Edelman, president, Children's Defense Fund.

Exchange With Reporters Prior to a Meeting With the National Conference of State Legislatures
March 11, 1993

President Boris Yeltsin of Russia

Q. Mr. President, do you think Yeltsin's going to survive?

The President. I think that he is the duly elected President of Russia and a genuine democrat, small "d," and that he is leading a country that is trying bravely to do two things: one, escape from communism into market economics, a world they never lived in before; and second, to preserve real democracy. That's a tough job. It's pretty hard to do here. [*Laughter*]

I intend to do what I can to be supportive of that process and to be supportive of him while he serves as President of Russia. I don't know what else to tell you. I'm not a seer. I don't know what's going to happen to him

or to me tomorrow. But I've got confidence in him. I'm going to work with him as long as I can.

Attorney-General-Designate Janet Reno

Q. What about Janet Reno?

The President. I'm elated by that. I had some Senators in the office, and I said, "That may be the only vote I carry 98 to 0 this year." But I enjoyed it. She's an extraordinary person, and I think she will do well.

We've got to go. Thank you.

Q. When is she going to be sworn in?

The President. When?

Q. When?

The President. Soon, I hope. I've been waiting

for someone in the Justice Department for a while now.

NOTE: The exchange began at 4:15 p.m. in the State Dining Room at the White House.

Exchange With Reporters Prior to a Meeting With the Congressional Caucus for Women's Issues
March 11, 1993

Abortion Clinic Shooting

Q. Mr. President, do you have any reaction to the shooting of Dr. Gunn in Pensacola?

The President. Yes. I was outraged by it. We have got to create a climate in this country where people do not think that is acceptable. And I think that's—how could someone have thought that they could take civil disobedience and carry it one extra step? Dr. Gunn was exercising his constitutional rights. And what happened was awful.

President Boris Yeltsin of Russia

Q. [*Inaudible*]—Yeltsin apparently had informed you that he plans to dissolve or may have to dissolve the Parliament. Have you gotten word of that, and what's your reaction to it?

The President. I have had no communication from him today, or if it has, it hasn't been communicated to——

Q. Thank you.

Chancellor Helmut Kohl of Germany

Q. How about Mr. Kohl? Has Mr. Kohl called you about a summit?

The President. If he has, no one on my staff has told me he's called me today.

NOTE: The exchange began at 5:35 p.m. in the Roosevelt Room at the White House. A tape was not available for verification of the content of this exchange.

Statement on the Death of Dr. David Gunn
March 11, 1993

I was saddened and angered by the fatal shooting in Pensacola yesterday of Dr. David Gunn. The violence against clinics must stop. As a nation committed to rule of law, we cannot allow violent vigilantes to restrict the rights of American women. No person seeking medical care and no physician providing that care should have to endure harassment, threats, or intimidation.

Statement on Joint Production Venture Legislation
March 11, 1993

I want to commend Chairman Jack Brooks, Senator Pat Leahy, Chairman Joe Biden, and the bipartisan leadership of the House and Senate Judiciary Committees on the introduction today of an important new bill to help create jobs and build a more competitive, high-tech American economy. This bill, the National Cooperative Production Amendments of 1993, will pave the way for companies large and small to pool their resources and talents in new joint production ventures. It is just the kind of forward-thinking initiative we need to drive our economy toward a decade of creative change.

We live in a world in which our competitive advantage flows more and more from our command of high technology, but in which the development and production of high-tech products has become enormously expensive. It is altogether appropriate to lift the legal barriers that prevent good companies from playing to win in the global market, provided, of course, that our antitrust laws continue to prevent improper collusion. Now is the time, as we work together to turn this Nation in a new direction, to strip away outdated impediments to our growth and potential.

I look forward to working with Chairman Brooks, Chairman Biden, Senator Leahy, and their colleagues on this important legislation.

Announcement of the Continuation of Foreign Service Officers in Three State Department Posts
March 11, 1993

The President announced today that three career Foreign Service officers will continue serving in State Department positions that they currently hold. The three are Genta Hawkins Holmes, Director General of the Foreign Service and Director of Personnel, Robert Gallucci, Assistant Secretary for Politico-Military Affairs, and Anthony Quainton, Assistant Secretary, Bureau of Diplomatic Security.

"I am very pleased with the team that Secretary Christopher and I are assembling at the Department of State," said the President. "I am particularly gratified that we have been able to put a number of people into senior positions who have devoted their careers to the Foreign Service."

NOTE: Biographies were made available by the Office of the Press Secretary.

Remarks on the Swearing-In of Attorney General Janet Reno
March 12, 1993

Thank you very much. Please be seated. We are honored here in the White House to be joined today by distinguished Members of the Senate and the House: Senator Biden, Senator Hatch, Senator Kennedy, Senator Sarbanes, one of Janet Reno's Senators, Senator Connie Mack. Senator Graham called me last night. He's in Florida today with the First Lady at a health care hearing. And he said he had an excused absence from the Attorney General. [*Laughter*]

The Speaker and Congressman Edwards are here, and we're delighted to see all of them. I also would say we're delighted to be joined by Mr. Justice White and Mrs. White. Thank you very much for coming. Let me say that it is a great honor for me to be able to be here at this ceremony today with Janet Reno, her family, and a few of her many friends.

I'd like to say a special word of thanks to Stuart Gerson, who has served ably and honorably as Acting Attorney General since the Inau-

guration. I think we owe him a round of applause. [*Applause*]

Somehow I don't think any of my other proposals will pass the Senate by the same vote margin—[*laughter*]—that Janet's confirmation did. I especially want to thank Senator Biden and Senator Hatch and the members of the Judiciary Committee for waiving the normal waiting period between hearings and the confirmation vote, making this event possible today and making it possible for us to proceed immediately with the urgent tasks at hand.

But more than anything else, I think it is clear that Janet Reno made her own swift confirmation possible, showing the Senate and all who followed the hearings the qualities of leadership and integrity, intelligence, and humanity that those gathered in this room have recognized for a very long time.

You shared with us the life-shaping stories of your family and career that formed your deep sense of fairness and your unwavering drive to help others to do better. You showed us that your career in public service, working on the frontlines in your community, fighting crime, understanding the impact on victims and on neighborhoods, mending the gritty social fabric of a vibrant but troubled urban area, is excellent preparation for carrying forward the banner of justice for all the American people.

You'll help to guide the Federal Government to assist State and local law enforcement in ways that really count. You demonstrated that you will be a formidable advocate for the vulnerable people in our society and especially for our children.

Most of all, you proved to the Nation that you are a strong and an independent person who will give me your best legal judgment whether or not it's what I want to hear. [*Laugh-*

ter] It's an experience I've already had, I'm glad to say. That is the condition upon which you accepted my nomination and the only kind of Attorney General that I would want serving in this Cabinet.

As Janet Reno begins her work at the Justice Department, she will enter a building that symbolizes our Nation's commitment to justice, to equality, to the enforcement of our laws. On the side of that building, carved above one of the portals, is the inscription, "The halls of justice are a hallowed place." With Janet Reno serving as our Nation's Attorney General, those words will have great meaning for all Americans.

NOTE: The President spoke at 9:21 a.m. in the Roosevelt Room at the White House. Following the President's remarks, Justice Byron White administered the oath of office.

Remarks to the Crew of the U.S.S. *Theodore Roosevelt*
March 12, 1993

Thank you very much, Captain. I know that I won't be able to see all of you now, but I've seen as many as I could, and I've shaken hands with a lot of you. I've also reviewed your mission and been very impressed with it.

I want to recognize the presence on the ship of the 1992 Sailor of the Year, Donald Leroy Heffentrager; as well as the First Class Petty Officer of the Quarter, Gary Neff; the Senior Petty Officer of the Quarter, Gregory Ham; the Junior Petty Officer of the Quarter, Jason McCord; and the Blue Jacket of the Quarter, Airman Todd Pearson.

I've been very impressed with everything I've seen and with all the people I've met. As Com-

mander in Chief it's immensely reassuring to me to know that the United States is served by people of such high quality and such great dedication. The Secretary of Defense, Les Aspin, and the others who are here in my company have already learned a great deal and see a lot that we admire and that we like. I thank you for your service to the country, and I look forward to the remainder of my stay here. And I wish you well on your deployment.

NOTE: The President spoke at 1:40 p.m. in the Carrier Intelligence Center aboard the ship. A tape was not available for verification of the content of these remarks.

Remarks to the Crew of the U.S.S. *Theodore Roosevelt*
March 12, 1993

Thank you very much, Secretary Aspin, Admiral Miller, Admiral Johnson, Captain Bryant, Captain Moore, Colonel Schmidt, General Keys, and to all of you here on the crew of the *Theodore Roosevelt*. I think I can speak for the peo-

ple who came in my party, including the distinguished Members of the United States Congress who are here. This has been a wonderful day for us, and we thank you.

I am honored to be here. As many of you

know, it is a great blessing and a great honor to be elected President of the United States. But there is no greater honor in the office than being the Commander in Chief of the finest Armed Forces in the world today and the finest America has ever known.

Our Armed Forces are more than the backbone of our security. You are the shining model of our American values: dedication, responsibility, a willingness to sacrifice for the common good and for the interests and the very existence of this country. Our Armed Forces today stand as one of modern history's great success stories. Look at this crew, reflecting every color, every background, every region of our society. I might say it's been a special pleasure to me to meet at least six people from my home State of Arkansas here today. I'm sure there are more of you here that I haven't met.

The American military pioneered our Nation's progress toward integration and equal opportunity. It is America's most effective education and training system. It's constantly asked to adapt to change and always, always, you have risen to the challenge. All who wear America's uniforms are what makes the United States of America a true superpower and a genuine force for peace and democracy in the world.

Yes, this carrier can extend our reach. These planes can deliver our might. They are truly extraordinary tools, but only because they are in the hands of you. It is your skill, your professionalism, your courage, and your dedication to our country and to service that gives the muscle, sinew, and the soul of our strength. And today, I'm proud to be here to salute you. I want to say a word about the Navy and to tell you what it means to me to have a ready fleet.

When word of crisis breaks out in Washington, it's no accident that the first question that comes to everyone's lips is, where is the nearest carrier? This ship's namesake, President Theodore Roosevelt, once said, "The Navy of the United States is the right arm of the United States and is emphatically the peacemaker." Theodore Roosevelt took special pride in our Navy, and I do, too. All of you ought to know that he was the first American ever to win the Nobel Prize. He won the Nobel Peace Prize for his role in settling a war between Russia and Japan in the first decade of this century, in part due to the contributions of the United States Navy.

This impressive ship, not yet 10 years old,

already has an impressive history, serving with distinction during the Gulf war, where many of you served as well. And today we should recall that three of this ship's crew gave the last full measure of their devotion toward that victory.

But the *Theodore Roosevelt* was part of history even earlier. In 1988, it was here that an American Chairman of the Joint Chiefs of Staff first welcomed his Soviet counterpart to visit an American aircraft carrier. When my friend Admiral William Crowe and Marshal Sergey Akhromeyev stepped aboard this ship together to meet the crew and watch flight operations, as I have done here today, it was a key milestone on the road to the end of the cold war.

Now, less than 5 years later, the world has changed faster than anyone on board then could have possibly imagined. The cold war is over. The Soviet Union itself no longer exists. The Warsaw Pact is gone. The specter of Soviet tanks rolling westward across the north German plain no longer haunts the United States.

Yet this world remains a very dangerous place. Saddam Hussein confirmed that. The tragic violence in Bosnia today reminds us of that every day. The proliferation of nuclear and other weapons of mass destruction is a growing menace, unfortunately, not a receding one, to peaceful nations. And human suffering such as that now being endured by the people of Somalia may not threaten our shores, but still they require us to act.

Such challenges are new in many ways, but we dare not overlook the significance that they pose to our new world. Blinders never provide security. A changed security environment demands not less security but a change in our security arrangements.

What is happening on this ship proves that it can be done. On this deployment you are, as the Secretary of Defense noted, doing something new. You've changed your crew and your equipment to reflect the new challenges of the post-cold-war era. A squadron of sub-hunting planes is gone, giving room to carry a contingent of tough and versatile Marines, enabling you to address new potential challenges such as evacuations or taking control of troubled ports.

You have the services working together in new ways. That enables you to operate perhaps with fewer ships and personnel but with greater efficiency and effectiveness. This isn't downsizing for its own sake. It's rightsizing for security's sake.

The changes on board the *Theodore Roosevelt* preview the changes I believe we must pursue throughout our military. We must keep, however, a few core ideas in mind as we pursue those changes. Our military must be exceptionally mobile, with first-rate sealift, airlift, and the ability to project power. And there is no more awesome example of that than the fearsome striking power that can be launched from the deck of this mighty ship.

Our military must also be agile, with an emphasis on maneuver, on speed, on technological superiority. That's exactly what the special purpose Marine air ground task force you have on board is all about. Our fire power must be precise, so that we can minimize the exposure to harm for the men and women who wear our uniforms and reduce civilian casualties where we must act.

Our military increasingly needs to be flexible so that we can cooperate with diverse coalition partners in very different parts of the world. And we must be smart, with the intelligence and communications we need for the complex threats we face. And I might say I was deeply impressed with a wide array of communications equipment that many of you showed me today. Above all else, we must always be ready, given the unpredictability of new threats.

None of these goals are possible unless we have a quality force. You, the crew of this ship, exemplify that quality with your skills, your experience, your training, and your dedication, many of you at astonishingly young ages. You have shown me that you know how to get the job done. I know our Nation can now have confidence that America's vital interests are well protected.

While all of you from the grapes on the roof to the aviators in the ready rooms, to the snipes in the holes, while you carry out your missions so far from home over the next few months, we back at home will be engaged in a raging debate about defense policy. As you watch the news on CNN or read the newspapers that are delivered here to your ship, you will hear us talk of roles and missions. You will see news about bases and budgets. But as we reduce defense spending, we will not leave the men and the women who helped to win the cold war out in the cold. As bases close, and they must, we must not close our eyes and hearts to the need for new investments to create opportunities in the communities with the old bases.

Defense spending has been declining ever since 1986. But I believe we have not had a strong enough plan for what to do with the new defense we are building and with those who contributed to the old defense; an insufficient plan for military personnel who muster out; an insufficient plan for civilian workers who made the wonderful weapons that helped us to dominate the world who now have lost their jobs; an insufficient plan for the communities that have been devastated or for the companies that have been hurt.

We cannot repeal the laws of change. After all, you and those who preceded you in uniform worked so hard, fought so hard, and many died so that the cold war could be won and we could rely less on defense and focus more of our resources on building our economy here at home. But still, we must act boldly to deal with the consequences of the changes we face. That's why it's so important to make the investments we need in defense conversion and the education and training in new jobs and new industries but also to continue to make the investments we need in the defense that must be there for the United States and for the world tomorrow.

As you follow the news of these events during your voyage, while our voyage back home into this great debate is taking place, I ask you to remember this: As your Commander in Chief, I am immensely proud of who you are, what you stand for, and what you are doing. As these changes proceed, I pledge to you that as long as I am President, you and the other men and women in uniform of this country will continue to be the best trained, the best prepared, the best equipped, and the strongest supported fighting force in the world. There is no single decision I take more seriously than decisions involving the use of force. As I weigh crises that confront America around the world, you will be in my mind and in my heart.

This is a hopeful time, yet one still full of challenges. It is uncertain, and therefore, we are glad that missions such as this, while not darkly framed by the cold war confrontation with a nuclear adversary, are still smartly focused on the challenges we might face in the days ahead. Many new duties and dangers are taking place. And there is no clear direction for what things we all might have to face in the future. There is no sonar that can enable us to fathom all the changes in the terrain over which we are now setting sail.

Napoleon had a standing order to his corps commanders to, quote, "March to the sound of the guns." He meant that when the shooting starts on a battlefield, it is the soldier's obligation to move into the fight. Well, today, there are different security challenges into which we must march. And at times you who serve our Nation in uniform may be called upon to answer not only the sound of guns but also a call of distress, a summons to keep the peace, even a cry of starving children. The calls will be more diverse, but our values remain unchanged. Our purposes remain clear. And your commitment to serve remains the linchpin in every new and continuing effort.

I know this has been a difficult day for many of you. It can't be easy to leave family and friends for 6 months at sea, especially when the challenges before us seem unclear, and when you wonder whether world events may or may not place you in harm's way. But I hope you understand that your work is vitally important to the United States and to the Com-mander in Chief.

This is a new and hopeful world but one full of danger. I am convinced that your country, through you, has a historic role in trying to make sure that there is, after all, a new world order, rooted in peace, dedicated to prosperity and opportunity.

The American people have placed their faith in you, and you have placed your life at the service of your country. The faith is well placed, and I thank you.

NOTE: The President spoke at 2:25 p.m. in the hangar bay aboard the ship. In his remarks, he referred to Adm. Paul David Miller, USN, commander in chief, U.S. Atlantic Command; Adm. Jay L. Johnson, USN, commander, Carrier Group 8; Capt. Stanley W. Bryant, USN, commanding officer, U.S.S. *Theodore Roosevelt*; Capt. C.W. Moore, USN, commander, Carrier Air Wing 8; Col. John W. Schmidt, USMC, commander, Special Purpose Marine Air/Ground Task Force, U.S.S. *Theodore Roosevelt*; and Gen. William M. Keys, USMC, commander, Marine Forces Atlantic.

Radio Address to the Armed Forces
March 12, 1993

Good afternoon. I'm coming to you from aboard the United States ship *Theodore Roosevelt*, which left yesterday from Norfolk, Virginia, on a 6-month mission. What I've seen on this ship today only increases my pride not only in the sailors and marines I met but also in every soldier, every sailor, every airman, every marine who serves our Nation, from Rhein-Main Air Force Base in Germany, where Americans are leaving to airdrop lifesaving supplies into Bosnia, to Somalia, where our Armed Forces have served with great distinction and made every American proud.

I'm honored to join you on Armed Forces Radio. I've had many blessings this year: the privilege of meeting Americans all across our Nation, the opportunity to hear about their lives and their dreams for our future, and of course, the opportunity to become the President of the United States. But there is no greater honor than actually serving as America's Commander in Chief.

Your work is often dangerous, even when times are quiet. Your day at the office can be 6 months or longer. And it's not for the money, it's always for the country. Because America's Armed Forces are more than the backbone of our security, you're the shining model of our best values: dedication and responsibility and the willingness of you and your loved ones to bear a tremendous level of sacrifice. You commit your daily energies and even your lives to benefit your fellow Americans.

Our armed services stand as one of history's great successes. Every color, every background, every region of our society is represented in America's Armed Forces. The American military pioneered our Nation's progress toward integration and equal opportunity. It's America's most effective education and training system. It's constantly adapted to change and always rising to the challenge of change. You, and all who wear

America's uniforms, are what make the United States a true superpower. It is your skill, your professionalism, your courage, and your dedication to country and service that constitutes the muscle, the sinew, and the soul of our strength. And today I salute you.

I want to say a special word about the Navy since I'm on board this fine ship today. It means a lot to a Commander in Chief to have a ready fleet. When word of a crisis breaks out in Washington, it's no accident that the first question is: Where is the nearest carrier? This ship's namesake, President Theodore Roosevelt, once said, "The Navy of the United States is the right arm of the United States and is emphatically the peacemaker." Theodore Roosevelt was the first American ever to win the Nobel Peace Prize, in part with the help of the United States Navy.

We have a great stake, you and I, in maintaining a strong American defense and in working hard even at the end of the cold war. The *Theodore Roosevelt* played an important part in the end of the cold war. In 1988, it was here that an American Chairman of the Joint Chiefs of Staff first welcomed his Soviet counterpart to visit an American aircraft carrier. That was when my friend Admiral William Crowe and Marshal Sergey Akhromeyev stepped aboard this ship to meet the crew and watch flight operations just as I have done today. It was a key milestone on the path to the end of the cold war.

Less than 5 years later, the world has changed, faster than anyone could have possibly guessed. The cold war is over. The Soviet Union no longer exists. The Warsaw Pact is gone. The specter of Soviet tanks rolling westward across the northern German plains no longer haunts us. But the world remains a dangerous and increasingly an uncertain place. Saddam Hussein confirmed that. The tragic violence in Bosnia reminds us of that every day. The proliferation of nuclear and other weapons of mass destruction is unfortunately a growing, not a receding, menace. And human suffering, such as that in Somalia, may not threaten our shores but still requires us to act.

These challenges are new in many ways, but we dare not overlook their significance. Blinders never provide security. A changed security environment demands that we change our security arrangement. Yes, we are reducing the defense budget because of the end of the cold war, but we're not downsizing for its own sake, we're trying to rightsize our security for security's sake. And as we change, we must keep a few core ideas in mind: Our military first must be exceptionally mobile, with first-rate sealift, airlift, and ability to project power. Our military must be agile, with an emphasis on maneuver, on speed, and on technological superiority. Our firepower must be precise so that we can minimize the exposure to harm for men and women who wear our uniform and reduce civilian casualties. Our military must be flexible so that we can operate with diverse coalition partners in different parts of the world. Our forces must be smart with the intelligence and communications we need for complex threats. And above all, our military must be ever-ready, given the unpredictability of new threats.

None of these goals are possible without a quality force. The people on this ship and all of you who are listening to me exemplify that quality. It is your skills, your experience, your training, and your dedication that will get the job done for America and guarantee that our vital interests can be protected.

While all of you carry out your mission so far from home, we back home will be engaged in many debates on defense policy. I will tell you that there are changes which lie ahead. Defense cuts are, and have been for the last several years, a fact of life, an inescapable consequence of the new world you've worked so hard to create. As you watch the news or read newspapers, you will hear us talk of new roles and missions and you'll see news about bases and budget cuts. But as we reduce defense spending, we must not leave the men and women who won the cold war out in the cold. As these bases close, as close some of them must, we must not close our eyes and our hearts to the need for new investments and a need to create new jobs in communities with old bases.

Defense spending has been declining since 1986, but there's been no real plan about what to do on it, no real plan for military personnel mustered out, no real plan for civilian workers who have lost their jobs or for the communities who have been hurt or for the companies who have been devastated. We can't repeal the laws of change, but we do have a choice: We can be buffeted by change, or we can act boldly to use this change to make our country stronger and safer and smarter. That's why it's so important to make the investments we need in defense conversion, in education and training and new jobs in new industries. I want to help ensure that those of you who choose to leave the military in the years to come return to a nation of jobs and growth and opportunity.

As you follow the news of all these changes, I ask you to remember this: I am immensely proud of who you are and what you're doing. And as these changes proceed I pledge that as long as I am your President, you and the other men and women in uniform will continue to be the best trained, the best prepared, the best equipped fighting force in the world. There is no single decision I take more seriously than those involving the use of force. As I weigh crises that confront America around the world, you will be in my mind and in my heart.

This is, on balance, a very hopeful time. But still, it is full of challenges. We can be glad that your mission is not darkly framed by the cold war's confrontation with a nuclear adversary. But many new duties and dangers are taking the place of that single stark threat, some of them yet unknown. There is no sonar, no radar that can enable us to fathom all the changes in terrain over which we are about to set sail.

Napoleon had a standing order to his corps commanders to, quote, "March to the sound of the gun." He meant that when the shooting starts on a battlefield, it is the soldier's obligation to move into the fight. Today, there are many different security challenges into which we must all move. And at times, you who serve our Nation in uniform may be called upon to answer not only the sound of guns but also the call of distress, or a summons to keep the peace in a troubled part of the world, or even the cry of starving children. The cause may be more diverse, but our values must remain unchanged, our purposes clear. And your commitment to serve remains the linchpin in every new and continuing effort.

I know that for some of you listening to me today, this is a difficult time. You have left your family, your friends, your home. I hope you understand that your work is vitally important to your fellow Americans and to the President and to this very new and very hopeful world we are trying to nourish and to build. The American people have great faith in what you do. Their faith is well placed, and I thank you for your service.

NOTE: The President spoke at 3:03 p.m. from the U.S.S. *Theodore Roosevelt.*

The President's Radio Address
March 13, 1993

Good morning. I want to talk with you about a decision Americans will make very soon, one that will determine the future of our country, our communities, our companies, and our jobs.

All around us, we see changes transforming our economy. Global competition, new technologies, and the reductions in military spending after we won the cold war. We can't stop the world from changing, but there is one decision we can and must make. Will we leave our people and our Nation unprepared for changes that are remaking our world, or will we invest in our people's jobs, our education, our training, our technology to build a high-skilled, high-wage future for ourselves and for our children?

The choice is especially urgent because of the reductions in military spending here at home. Yesterday I visited the U.S.S. *Theodore*

Roosevelt. That aircraft carrier and its crew served with distinction during the Gulf war. There's no greater honor than serving as their Commander in Chief. As long as I'm President, the men and women who wear our Nation's uniforms will continue to be the best trained, best prepared, and best equipped fighting force in the world.

We must never forget that the world is still a dangerous place. Our military is continuing to change, not to downsize for its own sake but so that we can meet the challenges of the 21st century. In the post-cold-war era, our military can be cut even while we maintain the forces necessary to protect our interests and our people.

The preliminary announcements of base closings in this morning's paper are part of that process. What we need to decide is whether we will invest in the economic security of the people who defend our national security. For the past 4 years our Government has done essentially nothing. Since 1989, 300,000 soldiers, sailors, and flyers have been mustered out of the service. One hundred thousand civilian employees of the Defense Department have also lost their jobs. And 440,000 workers from defense industries have been laid off.

As the business magazine Fortune has reported, these cuts cost 840,000 jobs over the past 4 years. That's more than the combined total layoffs at GM, IBM, AT&T, and Sears. Too many of the men and women affected by defense cuts are still looking for full-time jobs or working at jobs that pay much lower wages and use fewer of their skills.

These Americans won the cold war. We must not leave them out in the cold. That's why I propose a new national strategy to make these Americans have the training, the skills, and the support they need to compete and win in the post-cold-war economy.

Last year the Congress appropriated $1.4 billion for defense conversion activities. But the previous administration did not put any of that money to work. Our administration's plan gets those funds moving immediately and calls for an additional $300 million in resources, for a total of $1.7 billion this year alone, and for nearly $20 billion over the next 5 years.

Our plan invests in job training and employment services for military personnel and defense workers who have been displaced by declining military spending. And we'll make sure that every community affected by a base closing will have the help they need right away to plan for new businesses and new jobs. It takes 3 to 5 years for a base to close. We need to use that time to be ready.

That's why I'm proposing a national strategy to make sure that all these communities and all these workers can use this valuable time to plan and to acquire the tools to build a new future.

Our plan also invests in dual use technologies, that is, those that have both civilian and military applications and in advanced civilian technologies as well. With these technologies, defense companies can create new products and new jobs.

Americans have the ingenuity to adapt to changing times. On Thursday I visited a defense plant just outside Baltimore that is using military technology to make products for commercial use. I wish you could have seen what I saw. Police cars with computer screens that display photographs of missing children and radar systems that warn the commercial airlines about sudden wind currents that cause accidents. I saw an electric car that will run 80 miles an hour, and run for more than 120 miles before being recharged.

With a national economic strategy, more companies will be able to make the most of changes that are affecting not only defense but every industry, and will be able to make products like these. Our economic plan cuts Government spending that we don't need and brings down the Federal deficit that threatens our future.

But just as important, our plan also makes the investments that we do need in our children's schools, our workers' skills, cutting-edge technologies, and our transportation and communications networks. This plan will create 8 million jobs, building the foundation for a new era where every American can profit, prosper, and produce.

In the days ahead you'll hear a great debate in Congress about this plan. Some will say, don't cut anything; some will say, don't invest in anything. But what many of them are really saying is, don't change anything, because failing to invest and failing to reduce the deficit means failing to change the status quo.

I'm confident that Congress and the country will choose a new direction for America, making our Government more effective and less expensive, and making the investments that make us smarter, stronger, and more secure. I ask you to express your support for this approach to Senators and Representatives. Those who support our entire plan should be supported. They're cutting spending that we don't need and investing more in what we do need.

It's been said that while change is certain, progress is not. Together, we can turn away from drift and decline and choose a new direction with hope and growth and opportunity for every American.

NOTE: The President spoke at 10:06 a.m. from the Oval Office at the White House.

Interview With the Southern Florida Media
March 13, 1993

The President. Good morning. Last August, Hurricane Andrew devastated south Florida. Essential services were wiped out, and although 6 months later basic services have been restored, the progress toward redevelopment has been minimal.

Two weeks ago I asked Secretary Cisneros to go to south Florida and assess the situation, to try to evaluate what was holding up Federal efforts, and report back to me. As a result of the initial work done by the Secretary, I have released a seven-point plan to ensure that the remainder of the Federal funds dedicated to hurricane relief can be used for long-term building efforts now needed for south Florida. That seven-point plan includes the following:

First, the Federal Emergency Management Agency will stay on the job in south Florida for as long as it takes to help the residents of south Dade. They will expedite removal of debris that litters the streets, keep the trailers in place as long as people need housing, and continue to promptly reimburse owners and assist renters.

Second, the physical and mental health of south Dade residents is critically important. The people of this community need help to cope with the problems that have loomed large in the last 6 months and that still lie ahead. Therefore, the Department of Health and Human Services will accelerate its efforts to inoculate residents against disease and, additionally, will fund crisis and counseling centers for the many children and adults now experiencing severe emotional problems as a result of the traumatic experiences they have undergone.

Third, housing continues to be the single largest need in south Dade. Thousands are homeless. Many more are living in tents, trailers, with friends and relatives, and other temporary quarters. As you know, they are under particular distress today because of the storm that is sweeping up our coast. The Department of Housing and Urban Development will put $100 million in reprogrammed funds in the most flexible programs available, such as home and community development block grants, to rebuild housing in south Dade. Additionally, HUD will open an office in south Dade with community

development, public housing, and fair housing capabilities to ease the rebuilding efforts.

Fourth, I have requested the Department of Defense to release the $76 million Congress appropriated to help facilitate the rebuilding of those facilities at Homestead Air Force Base that are critical to the future use of the base, to explore the possibility of joint military and civilian uses of the base, and to make sure we do everything we can in the transition period to serve the people who are in south Dade County.

Fifth, agriculture is a vital economic resource in south Florida. The Department of Agriculture will transfer several hundred million dollars to programs to assist with emergency conservation, debris removal on farmlands, and housing for migrant farm workers.

Sixth, recognizing the need to provide assistance to property owners who must comply with the Government's rebuilding requirements in flooded areas, we have made this one of our highest priorities, and we are looking for ways to address this issue.

And finally, in order to effectively coordinate our efforts, I believe we need local leadership and the Secretary does, too. As a result, Secretary Cisneros and I have asked Otis Pitts, Jr., a highly respected nonprofit developer of affordable housing in the Miami area to coordinate our efforts in south Dade. I met Otis last year on one of my many trips to the Miami area. I was very impressed with what he had done.

I think I want to emphasize to all of you that these actions, in my view, only constitute the beginning of our long-term commitment to south Florida. Through the leadership of Secretary Cisneros and Mr. Pitts and the coordinated efforts of the community, I believe we can find the resources, develop the solutions, and maintain the spirits and the commitment necessary to ensure the economic, political, social, and physical vitality of south Dade County.

I'd like now to ask the Secretary to make a few remarks and then to introduce Mr. Pitts for whatever he would like to say.

[*At this point, Secretary Cisneros and Mr. Pitts made brief statements.*]

The President. Let me just make one more

remark, and then we'll be available for questions. I also want to acknowledge the work of Jeff Watson, a valued member of the White House staff, who is a native of Florida and who has worked very, very hard on this with Secretary Cisneros and me. And again, I want to thank Otis for being willing to take on this task. We plan this to be a very long-term and intense effort, and I'm looking forward to producing some results.

Homestead Air Force Base

Q. Mr. President, on behalf of the people of south Florida, we all thank you for your efforts on the economic and emotional side. But there is also the perception of threat. We are going to be living with the closing of Homestead Air Force Base, closer to a Cuban military air force base than to an American Air Force base. And several years ago, a Cuban general said that the Cuban Government had a plan in case of a crisis, of attacking Turkey Point nuclear plant. Can you tell us if the Federal Government can tell the people of south Florida, yes, you are safe, yes, we're going to take care of you, that perception of threat?

The President. Yes, I can say that categorically. The Pentagon has considered very carefully what the possible threats to this country's security are and before making any of those recommendations. But let me also say one of the things that I have advocated very strongly—and just in the last couple of days I've talked to Senator Graham and Governor Chiles about this—is releasing the money that was approved last year by the Congress to rebuild Homestead for purposes that will permit us always to have access to joint use of that air base if we need it.

And let me just mention that Secretary Aspin and I had another long conversation yesterday morning about this. We want to rebuild the airstrip and make sure that it is adequate to take any kind of planes. We need to rebuild the control tower. We want the facility, during the transition period, at a minimum to be available for use for the Reserves, for the Guard, for the DEA, for any Coast Guard operations, all of the things that might make possible long-term dual use planning and would also make the base a valuable facility in the event that the community decided that they wanted to have it for some potential commercial use, or in the event that we can use it for both commer-

cial and Government uses. So in any case, we're going to rebuild the capacity of the air base to actually engage in operations, which I think is terribly important.

Federal Rebuilding Effort

Q. Mr. President, why do you think that the progress in the rebuilding effort has been so unsatisfactory so far? Do you think the Bush administration botched the job?

The President. I don't want to get into that. I don't know. All I know is that not long after I took office, the people I know in south Dade County reminded me of what I had seen there and talked to me about how important it was to get things moving. And I asked Secretary Cisneros to go down there and conduct a first-hand assessment of the operation. He said we needed someone on the ground who knew the community and could get things done, and that there were lots of things we could do to push the money through the pipeline that had already been approved that hadn't been done. And he came up with this plan, working with Jeff Watson, and Otis Pitts agreed to help us. So I don't want to go into what happened before, I just want to try to get things done now.

Homestead Air Force Base

Q. Mr. President, after you toured south Dade on September 3d, you said at a news conference, "It is my belief that there is a mission for Homestead. It is still the closest major airstrip to Cuba, and it still has the potential to play a major role in our effort to reduce drug trafficking." Now, do you think that your statement today and your seven-point plan is, in a sense, a fulfillment of what you had said September 3d, or do you think that in fact you would be willing to listen to Dante Fascell or people from south Florida who are going to try to tell you that Homestead should remain a functioning Air Force base?

The President. Well, let me tell you the decision I had to make on that. The series of base closings that were announced yesterday are the third of four series of base closings that will be announced. All the services did what they were required to do under the law. They assessed what they needed and what the infrastructure of the country was and what they thought ought to do done.

The Secretary of Defense then forwarded the list, after having tried to evaluate the aggregate economic impact of the past three base closings, and something only the Secretary can do, which is to evaluate the cumulative impact of the recommendations of the Air Force, the Army, and the Navy, since they didn't review each other's recommendations before they were made.

I did not believe that I should interfere in that process. I think that I am open to any arguments anybody wants to make, and I think the base commission will be, too. Keep in mind, this is the biggest round of base closings we've ever announced. The base closing commission did make adjustments, modest adjustments in previous recommendations coming out of the Pentagon, and they may well make some this time.

But the conclusion that I reached is that at this point, I should let the services make their recommendation, the Secretary do his economic evaluation, then let the recommendations go to the commission and try to get all these arguments out in the public. But in any case, if we can get the money released and we can rebuild the airstrip itself and the control tower and some of the facilities, then we will be able to meet at least the security needs of the area and also develop what could be an immensely valuable long-term economic resource to the people of south Dade County, something that has the potential, I think, of being a far bigger economic impact even than the base was.

Q. Mr. President, in south Florida there is a feeling among some people, a sense of betrayal. They thought they had tantamount to a promise that you would restore Homestead Air Force Base in some form or fashion. Long-range, what specifically will you do to blunt the economic impact? Because what you're saying sounds like it will help a little bit, but it won't replace——

The President. I disagree with that. First of all, I also made it clear to the people of south Florida that we had a base closing commission process and a United States Congress that had roles in this, and there is no prospect whatever that the Congress would have appropriated any money to fully rebuild that base with it on the base closing list until the commission ruled on it, one way or the other. I mean, that is just not an option. There wasn't a 10 percent, a 5 percent chance that that would be done, with the Air Force saying we don't need the base and it being submitted under law to the base closing commission.

I would remind you that the Congress appropriated $76 million to rebuild, to do rebuilding work at the base that the previous administration did not release. I support releasing the money. I'm going to aggressively work to rebuild the airstrips and to rebuild the control tower and to use the rest of that money to maximize the potential of both military and civilian uses of that airstrip. And I would say again to you, it is an enormous potential resource to south Dade County. If we handle this right, we can generate more jobs out of that facility over a period of a few years even than were presented by the Air Force.

Q. Mr. President, the joint use proposal you've talked about a number of times—not just Homestead, other bases you've mentioned—do you have something in the back of your mind, specifically, that you'd like to see there—you're talking about either a mega-airport, an industrial development zone, or something like that, or are you just waiting to hear ideas from the private sector of what could be done there? Do you have some——

The President. In the case of south Dade County, as you know, there have been people for years who thought that you could have a mega-port there, a big commercial airport, perhaps even a newer and bigger airport for passenger traffic, too. And what I think we need to do is to rebuild the infrastructure; that's what I'm saying. Try to maintain some basic functions there, the Guard function, the Reserve function, the DEA function. I hope I can get an approval to go along with that, and then see what happens as we explore possibilities with the people who live in south Dade County.

The only thing I want to point out to you is that it is an immensely valuable resource, and that one of the areas of our economy that everyone projects to grow in the next 10 years is the area of commercial aviation, not just passengers but also freight, mail, and other things. So I think that one of the things we know for sure is, if we don't rebuild the strip and we don't rebuild the control tower, nothing good can occur. We know that for sure.

We know, too, in my judgment that the Federal Government has an obligation to do that. Let me just give you—if you go back—even if let's say the whole thing were going to be shut down in 3 years under the base closing. No dual use, no nothing. Every other place in the country with a base that's about to be shut down has a resource right now that could be turned over to the local community that's worth a lot of money.

The Homestead base is not worth what it ought to be until it's rebuilt. So what I want to do is to focus on rebuilding it so that it is a valuable asset—the airstrip and the control tower, at least, and maybe some other facilities there—and then see what we can do, see what we can do in terms of joint use, and see what the community wants to do in terms of potential uses. I do have some specific ideas, but I think, frankly, that the people down there will have better ideas than I do.

Haiti

Q. I have two foreign questions. Yesterday in Haiti, the military arrested a man who was granted asylum by the United States and was at the airport with U.S. officials. What are you going to do about that? And second, Mr. Aristide, who was going to meet you next week, is urging you to set a date for his return. Is that feasible?

The President. First of all, I'm very upset about what happened to Haiti. The man was returned by error, frankly. He should be given status in this country. And this is a very serious thing. We are actually meeting on it today to see what our options are.

Q. Would that——

The President. But we believe that, strongly that the Haitian Government should release him so that he can be brought back here, and we believe it very strongly, and we are discussing it today.

As to your second question, I think that I should leave my conversations with President Aristide until we have them. But I am committed to the restoration of democracy in Haiti. It is the only thing that will fully resolve the economic problems and the enormous social dislocation and the enormous numbers of people who are willing to risk their lives to leave the island, hundreds of whom have lost their lives trying to leave the island, and I think you will see this administration taking a more active role.

I have tried to exercise some restraint in my remarks, because I believe it's important that

what we do, we do with the Organization of the American States and with the United Nations and in tandem with the Caputo mission to Haiti. I don't think it should look as if the United States is alone dictating policy there. But the people who have power now cannot hold it inevitably. They've got to recognize that the people of Haiti voted in overwhelming numbers for a democratic government, and they're entitled to it. They are entitled, those people, to human rights protections just like everybody else. They're entitled not to be subject to violence and abuse of their own rights and existence, and I think we can work out such an arrangement, and I think we can work it out in the not-too-distant future.

All I can tell you is, I've spent a lot of time on Haiti, I'm working hard on it. And the United States will become increasingly insistent that democracy be restored.

Cuba

Q. Some in Congress, including Congressman Torricelli, are asking for the U.S. to spearhead the internationalization of the U.S. embargo against Cuba, specifically going to the United Nations and the Security Council. What is your position?

The President. Well, first I'd like to talk to Congressman Torricelli about it. I'm not sure the Security Council is open to that, but I'll be glad to talk to—he may know more about it than I do, and I'll be glad to talk to him about it. But as you know, I supported the Cuban Democracy Act when he conceived it and pushed it, and I supported it all during last year. I was pleased when it was signed, and the United States intends to honor it. But just last week, one member of the Security Council strongly disagreed with our policy there, and so I think it's highly questionable that we could get the Security Council to go along.

NOTE: The President spoke at 11 a.m. via satellite from the Roosevelt Room at the White House. In his remarks, he referred to Jeffrey Watson, Deputy Assistant to the President and Deputy Director of Intergovernmental Affairs, and Dante Caputo, U.N./OAS Special Envoy to Haiti.

Interview With the Connecticut Media
March 13, 1993

East Coast Winter Storm

The President. I'm sorry I'm a little late, but I'm trying to make sure we're doing what we need to do about the storm, which, as you know, is moving up the coast with winds very heavy now in the South Carolina area. And the center of the storm is projected to reach here as late as 7 o'clock tonight, so it will come to you sometime in the middle of the night. And we're working hard, but I wanted to get an update and see what FEMA was doing. And we're going to be talking today about what other resources we ought to make available.

I think the only thing I would say is that we have shared all the information we have with all the State governments involved, and I think people should simply exercise caution, because it's easy to go from what seems to be a nice big snowstorm to these very rapid winds. And the more you can keep telling people when the winds are coming, I think the better off we'll be. Once you get north of Washington, most people are fairly well-prepared for heavy doses of snow, even if it's the biggest they've had in years. But the winds are of great concern. Whatever you can do to make sure your people know that there are winds coming—and unless this storm dissipates, that can be serious; that would call for them to exercise great caution as the center of the storm approaches, which will be sometime late, late tonight for you— I'd appreciate it. Questions?

Defense Conversion

Q. Yes, sir. Can we talk about the defense cutbacks in Connecticut?

The President. Sure.

Q. You have a $1.7 billion plan for retraining and dual use technology. You've got $350 billion set aside for FY '93. I guess the bottom line is, when we hear in Connecticut, for example Pratt & Whitney, they're going to be laying off 7,000 people, sir, for people that are facing unemployment, the people who are unemployed, when are they going to see some of that money come to them this year? And is the infrastructure already in place to see that those industries are targeted that need it and the money gets there?

The President. Well, let's back up a minute. The Congress appropriated this money months and months and months ago. There was a big debate, and the previous administration basically didn't believe that this was a big problem, so they never released any of the money. In the last few weeks, we have worked very hard to put together a plan that would release over $1 billion this year in defense conversion.

In addition to that, let me just say, apropos of the Connecticut economy specifically, if the Congress passes the stimulus plan that I have recommended to try to jumpstart the economies of the States with high unemployment rates, Connecticut should receive about $118 million, just out of the stimulus package, in funds for community development block grants and Federal highway construction and clean water and clean drinking water efforts and urban transit money. So all that will be coming into the State, and obviously that will create a lot of jobs. Some of those jobs will be created in the same areas where the defense jobs have been lost.

Now, to go back to your original question, we're going to move the job training money, the community assistance money, and the new technology money as quickly as we can. By and large, in most States there is a retraining infrastructure which will accommodate it. The infrastructure we need to create, frankly, is to make sure there's a good partnership between the Defense Department, the Commerce Department, and all the other Federal Agencies and communities, so that communities can take money and begin immediately planning to generate new jobs. And we need a better partnership between the Government and the private contractors to make sure that they have as much lead time as possible to plan to put new technologies into effect or to take their defense technologies and convert them into commercial products.

I'm sure all of you saw the press when I went to Baltimore to the Westinghouse plant. To assist in that regard, we're going to do two things. First, we've got all the Federal Agencies involved to put together a book which can be made available to every defense contractor in America, which shows the resources and the efforts that can be made by the Advanced Research Products Agency, the Commerce Department, the Energy Department, which controls the Federal labs where a lot of this research is done, the Defense Department, NASA, and others.

Secondly, we're going to go out across the country now and hold meetings that are literal workshops for defense contractors to try to get them involved in this process before the contracts run out. The thing that has bothered me about this all along is that these contracts have been canceled, and then someone comes along and says, well, why don't you think of something else to do? So what we're going to try to do is to develop an ongoing relationship with defense contractors which will permit them to plan for conversion, even as they're still producing whatever products they're contracted to produce by the Defense Department. And this whole thing has to be coordinated in a much more disciplined fashion than it has been in the past. And that's why I've set up this defense conversion group, to do.

Let me just make one other point, since the Department of Defense yesterday announced another round of base closings and realignments, which would be modest compared to the contracting losses you've had. There would be a reduction of 2200 jobs in Connecticut around the submarine operations. Here is the dilemma for us—and I want to just put that out here so you will be able to evaluate what happens in the future. We've had two rounds of base closings so far. They've been fairly modest. And this announcement from the Pentagon was pretty big. And there will be another one in 1995. Keep in mind, all these bases that were on that list, even if the commission approves them for closing or realignment, they won't be closed for 3 to 5 years. That gives us real time to plan, if we do it. If we really have an aggressive plan, it gives us time to plan the futures of the men and women in uniform who may be mustered out. It gives us time to plan for the futures of the communities and the civilian employees.

Let me ask you to consider what happens when you don't do this. On the plan we're on now, if we don't close any more bases, we will have by 1997 reduced defense by 40 percent, personnel in uniform by 35 percent, overseas deployments by 56 percent, and base structure by 9 percent. Now, what does that mean to Connecticut? It means that if you—because of

the incredible difficulty of closing domestic bases, it means if you don't close any of them and you have this defense budget going down, that means more reductions in contracts. It means it hurts the plants and where the high-tech production is done even more.

One of the reasons that we have to close some more bases is, with a reduced Armed Forces at the end of the cold war, we have got to maintain a very, very high level of technological superiority and military readiness, which means we still are going to have a very significant amount of military contracts out there in high technology areas. But you could argue that over the long run, the States that have a lot of the plants that do this work, like Connecticut, California, and others, would be better off if we can exercise the discipline to close the bases in a way that is humane and fair and economically advantageous. So that's what we're trying to do.

Sea Wolf Submarine Program

Q. Mr. President, John Baxter from Associated Press. As you know, I'm sure, part of your reputation in Connecticut regarding defense stems from your comments during the campaign in support of the Sea Wolf, and I'm sure you know what an important program that is in terms of jobs up there. I wonder if I could ask you if you could tell us at this point what your plans are for the Sea Wolf, and more generally, what your comments to the people of Connecticut would be now that we're beyond the campaign and into the administration and defense spending is going down sharply?

The President. Well, you remember what my position was on the Sea Wolf, which is that I thought at least one more ship should be completed than the administration said, and then we should, in effect, transform the operation to produce a smaller follow-on ship. That is what I believed, and interestingly enough, that's what I was advised by the people with whom I was consulting back in 1991 was the best policy. Contrary to a lot of the things which were written in and out of Connecticut, it didn't have much to do with the Connecticut primary. I didn't even know if I'd be politically alive in the Connecticut primary in November and December of 1991 when we were trying to evaluate these decisions. I see no reason in my own mind to change that position.

Now, what we are doing now with the Defense Department—let me tell you what we have to face. What we are doing now is to try to see what our options are for proceeding both with contracts and with personnel, with the new budget targets we're going to be required to meet. I'm hopeful that both the Senate and the House will adopt my defense budget cuts without cutting them anymore. And if so, then we may be able to pursue the course that I outlined in the campaign.

But let me tell you, there is one other problem. I just want to make you aware of this, and we won't know exactly what the end of it is until, oh, about 2 weeks from now. The budget that the Department of Defense has that was approved by the last Congress includes several billions of dollars in management savings in the Department of Defense which the Secretary of Defense, Mr. Cheney, offered and which the Congress accepted, which are now being questioned. That is, it's now being questioned about whether these management savings are real. And a special committee has been appointed to review the budget and to see whether or not, in effect, the Congress has approved a cut which can't be realized simply by reorganizing the Defense Department in management savings. We were advised to put another $10 billion in reduction on our defense budget at the end of this cycle, in fiscal year '97, as a hedge against the fact that as much as $30 billion of those management savings by FY '97 may not be real.

Now, let me tell you what that means practically since we're all committed to certain deficit reduction targets. What that means is that if these management savings which the Congress has already budgeted for from the previous administration don't turn out to be real, we'll have a very serious question to address. I am resisting further cuts in defense, apart from the $10 billion extra one I agreed to try to absorb at the end of this process. But I just want you to be aware of the fact that that is out there and that this is sort of an ongoing debate in-house here. We're trying to figure out—the Secretary of Defense is working with the services to see what they believe we should do and to work out the best possible result.

Q. But the Sea Wolf question relating to this upcoming budget remains an open question until notice——

The President. I think it is an open question, but I haven't changed my position on it. But

I cannot tell you it's a lock-cinch deal because of what's happened, because of this—this is sort of a wild card for us—and because I'm obviously involved with the Congress now in trying to work through this.

Q. Brian Thomas at WTIC in Hartford. General Dynamics as a corporation, producer of the Sea Wolf, as you know, openly is not embracing the dual use concept. They are staying with defense as a livelihood. Is this kind of approach in your view something that's viable, given this situation we have now, or will they sign on to this eventually?

The President. Well, it depends. Let me say what I mean by that. It depends on what General Dynamics or any other kind of company in this position projects will be the future demand for defense products that they can produce. Let me give you an example. For example, Sikorsky in Connecticut and another one of your helicopter companies I think is up in employment. And a lot of our allies may well be buying more short-haul aircraft and may be buying more helicopters in the future for more limited and different kinds of military operations. So there's no question that some military contractors will be able to continue to fully—or almost all military contractors—and do well. And there will be some things where the demand for products will actually increase. We, the United States, will be buying some new military products and technology that we have not purchased in the past. So some people will be there.

On the other hand, with the overall budget going down and, therefore, with both the size of the Armed Forces and at least the guaranteed replacement of old products being less, a number of these defense contractors are going to have to look for alternative products. And I don't know enough about what General Dynamics' options are to know whether that's the right or the wrong decision. All I can tell you is that we're prepared to assist with joint research and development efforts and everything else in our power. We're prepared to assist those companies that are serious about converting. The Westinghouse plant—let me just tell you, the one in Maryland I visited—5 years ago was 16 percent nondefense. Today it's 27 percent nondefense. By 1995 it'll be 50-plus percent nondefense. And what I think you're going to see—I'll just make a prediction where I think you're going to see in many areas—is a kind of a blending where the defense-nondefense line is regularly crossed and where the technology is being used for both civilian and military purposes. For example, at Westinghouse we saw some things making full circle. We saw military technology producing a civilian product; then we saw civilian technology being marketed back to the military for the first time. So I think that this will become a blurry line.

Now, submarines have few uses other than military. I mean, it's hard to imagine—you know, maybe some weather uses there, maybe nonmilitary uses for submarines in the environmental area, particularly around the poles and other things. But I just think—I wish I could give you a yes or no answer, but I'd have to know more about what their options are and what they project the products to be.

Q. When you say completion of another submarine, are you talking about the third or the second, since the second hasn't really started yet? And if the submarine fleet is to be reduced to 40 to 45 submarines, when do you envision funding for the next generation and what would it look like?

The President. I can't answer that yet because that's one of the things we have under review. But I will be glad to try to get you an answer from the Defense Department as quickly as I can. The last time I had a conversation about this, there was a general consensus that the design of the Sea Wolf was not necessary in terms of its size, bulk, given a declining Soviet threat and breathtaking drops in production there for their own capacity, but that we still needed and, in fact, were quite dependent on submarine technology to maintain our overall military superiority, but that there ought to be one designed that was smaller and quicker and could do more different things. And so we're working on that. But I don't have—I can't answer the specifics you've asked.

Russia

Q. [*Inaudible*]—the developments in the former Soviet Union right now with Boris Yeltsin, and how does that fit into your accounting strategy for defense?

The President. Well, obviously, we're all concerned about it. But, you know, I don't think you could have ever predicted an easy ride for democracy and for a market economy in a country which had never had a market economy and which had the courage to try to seek democracy

at the same time. So I view all these things with—I'm interested in it, I'm concerned about it, but as far as I'm concerned, he is still the only person who's been elected President of the country, and I believe he genuinely believes in economic reforms and political democracy. And I think we should support that. And I'm going to do what I can to be supportive.

I think that if the major countries, the G–7 countries that are in a position to support those movements would show a more coordinated and aggressive approach to the problems, it might be possible to build a consensus in Russia for how they would work with all of us. Every elected official has his or her political opponents. That's part of the way the system works. And an awful lot of the people that are in the Russian legislature were active members of the Communist Party. So you would expect it to be somewhat less reformist than he is. Plus a lot of them are responding to the cries of their own people for help. They're in deep trouble economically.

My own view is there are a lot of things that can be done, that that country can still have a bright future as part of a peaceful coalition of nations in the world. And I just hope that we'll have the opportunity to do it. I was encouraged in my meeting with President Mitterrand that he seemed very willing to adopt an aggressive posture toward trying to do more. And I'll do the best I can to be ready on April 4th, which is just a few days from now, with my meeting with President Yeltsin.

Q. Would you support him still if he suspends the Parliament? And also, if he calls in military force, would you support him? Also, what would you say to those who are saying you're relying too much on his survival?

The President. Well, first of all, I don't think that it would serve any useful purposes for me to try to interpret the Russian constitution right now and what it does or doesn't mean or what we would or wouldn't respond to. The United States supports democracy and economic reform in Russia.

Now, in terms of whether we're putting too much reliance on Yeltsin personally, my answer to that is, we will work with what we have to work with, whatever happens. But I think we should support him because he has been elected, after all. I mean, there was an election; the people voted for him. And he represents a passionate commitment to democracy and economic reform. And he's gotten, frankly, in my judgment, from the major countries of the world who have a stake, not just a political but an economic stake in Russia, an inadequate response to date.

So I'm trying to do what I can to muster the support to do more, because I think it's very much in America's interests, and he's the person that I think I should work with. He is the elected President of Russia. That is a fact. And I hope he will continue to be the elected President of Russia. But the United States has an interest in a Russia that is not hostile to us, that is not a military enemy, and that, frankly, has a whole lot more economic growth than the Russia that we know does now. And I'm just trying to respond to that. I think that working with him is the best way to do it at this time, and I believe—I'll say again—no one knows what's going to happen. But the man is an honest democrat—small "d"—and he's passionately committed to reform. And I want to keep working with him.

Defense Conversion

Q. Mr. President, diversification is a goal, but what can you do about the fact that so many defense manufacturers have been reluctant to diversify?

The President. All I can do is to try to make sure that they have the maximum number of options. Let me give you an example of what happened yesterday, or the day before yesterday at the Westinghouse plant. I talked to one of the people, a woman there who was in charge of marketing these new products, and I said, "Tell me what the problems are." She said, "Well, it's not so much that we can't ever think of what we could do that might have a nondefense application, but most of us have never contracted in the private sector before. We have never marketed in the private sector. And we're not sure that what we think will work, will work." Basically, I think what I have to do for these defense contractors is to try to create, through the enormous resources that the Federal Government has invested in them over time and has invested in technology research, an environment in which they can at least visualize and imagine all the potential that might be there and then the opportunity they have to make the connections with the private sector on the civilian side. So that's what we're going to try to do. I just would say every defense

contractor needs to think about it. The answer may be no in some cases, but everybody really needs to think about it and that the Government is going to be there in a consistent way to do it.

If you look at every projection of high technology, high-wage employment going well into the 21st century, the technologies that are there are things that have often been dealt with in defense; biotechnology, civilian aviation, computer software. Some of the most sophisticated imaging in the world is done by the Defense Department. Now, that's the only thing I would say. There may be some products which are not susceptible to civilian spinoffs, but most of them are.

Legalized Gambling

Q. I don't know if you're aware of it, but one of the things that's been talked about in Connecticut, to fill the gap with defense leaving, is casino gambling. And I wonder if you'd just share your thoughts with us on how you feel about legalized gambling coming to a State like Connecticut, if we should do it?

The President. I'm not the best person in the world to ask about that because I grew up in a town that had the largest illegal gambling operation in America—[*laughter*]—when I was a kid, until it was shut down in the mid-sixties.

First of all, I strongly believe it should remain a question of State law. That is, I don't think I should decide for you one way or the other—or the Congress. I think that it ought to be a local question. The second thing I would urge is that before you do it, you analyze very carefully what the benefits and the costs are, because it is not a free ride. That's the only thing I'll say. It is not an unmixed blessing. You may decide that it is, on balance, worth doing, but it is not an unmixed blessing. If you look at Nevada, for example, the fastest growing State in the country, one of the reasons they're growing fast is that they're diversifying away from gambling toward more broad-based convention work and other kinds of economic activity. So that would be my advice. Don't just take it at face value. And really think about it before you do it.

Thanks.

Military Base Closings

Q. [*Inaudible*]—reviewing and tinkering with

the base closing list?

The President. No. The Secretary of Defense had the list, and he made the decisions. The only thing I asked him to do was to make sure that he had really evaluated the economic impacts of it all. And he said that he would do that. The only—he made a point to me that under the law, the Defense Department is required to do that, and it really couldn't be done by the services because they made their recommendations based on their needs within their services. So the Air Force and the Army and the Navy couldn't have foreseen the cumulative impact on any given State of what they recommended. And that's why the Secretary of Defense went through the process he did. But he did it. I think it's very important that we leave the process in that way. And so that's what we did.

NOTE: The President spoke at 11:42 a.m. in the Cabinet Room at the White House.

Interview With the California Media
March 13, 1993

East Coast Winter Storm

The President. Hello, everybody. Welcome to sunny Washington. [*Laughter*] I want to basically just answer questions. I brought Mr. Panetta so he could help with any details of any questions you might have. I'm sorry we're a little late, but as you might imagine, I've had to take some time this morning to try to calculate what our response should be to this severe storm that is sweeping the east coast and that will move over Washington in its center not until about 7 o'clock tonight. So that's what I've been working on. And I know it doesn't concern you except you're here.

Yes.

Military Base Closings

Q. Mr. President, you got some of your highest vote totals from the San Francisco Bay area when you ran for President: San Francisco 78 percent, Alameda County. A lot of folks out there are wondering how you're letting them take such a big hit to lose five facilities when they're watching southern California facilities also, some of them being taken care of. What do you say to the people in the Bay area who supported you so strongly and now are looking at themselves taking a pretty big hit?

The President. Well, first of all, those decisions were not made on a political basis, and I did not intervene individually in those decisions, nor do I think I should have. I'll tell you what I did do. I asked the Secretary of Defense to be sure that he fulfilled his legal responsibility to consider the economic impact of every State, including California, and because it's so big, all parts of California, before sending the list on to the Congress. And he did that to the best of his ability.

There hadn't been a lot of naval closings in the first two rounds. The Navy strongly recommended all the sites, including the ones in the Bay area. I'm concerned about it. If you look at the whole country, the Bay area and perhaps Charleston, South Carolina, were the hardest hit, although the Charleston Yard won't close entirely.

But the way the process works, it seems to me, is the only way it can work. And that is for the services to make their recommendation and for the Secretary of Defense to try to evaluate the economic impact—something, by the way, that can't be done by the services because they don't know what each other is doing; so if the Secretary of Defense doesn't do it, no one can, because they've got the Navy, the Air Force, and the Army cumulatively coming in with these recommendations—and then to send it on to the Congress.

I believe that the Bay area ought to do— I think we ought to have two things to be sensitive to what's happened there. One is the base closing commission itself, which has in the two previous cases made modifications in the services' requests, should consider the strongest argument the Bay area can put together for some modification of it. But secondly, the areas that are disproportionately hit, it seems to me, should receive extra attention from this administration in the new conversion effort that we have announced just in the last couple of days. We are going to put into play this year over $1 billion in funds not only for worker retraining but also for community redevelopment and for the development of new technologies and new purposes for economic activity where there has been a severe dislocation.

So I am prepared to do that for the Bay area, to make a special effort to focus on their long-term needs so that—and keep in mind, this is not going to happen overnight, this is a longer term phaseout—so that by the time the jobs were actually lost there, we would be ready to move forward with new economic activity, perhaps even before that time.

Another issue that relates to all the bases in California, and indeed all the ones in the United States, is that the environmental cleanup at a lot of these bases, especially the air bases, has taken so long that by the time the bases close, they're not ready to be taken over by local community interests, even though if they were ready, economic activity would pick up almost immediately. So another thing we've really focused on is trying to make sure we are moving as aggressively, as quickly as possible on the environmental cleanup. I talked to the Secretary of Defense for an hour about that yesterday when we were on the helicopter going to visit the U.S.S. *Theodore Roosevelt.*

Q. Mr. President, how do you justify, although it's not your decision, but how would you justify spending $320 million to close a working capable home for three nuclear carriers in Alameda to build a facility in—[*inaudible*]—that was conceived as part of an outdated home-porting strategy that won't post its first carrier, nuclear carrier, until 1996, that will require by the Navy's own estimates at least another $140 million to complete, and that the GAO recommended closing 2 years ago on the grounds that it was a waste of money to duplicate facilities already present in Alameda?

The President. That's a question you should ask the Navy and the Secretary of Defense. As I said, I did not review that list. I didn't think I should. This law was established—this is the third round of base closings. The Navy's been pushing for base closings. I heard about the GAO report after the list was ultimately released yesterday, and that's one of the issues I think the base closing commission ought to be required to confront.

Q. Mr. President, you said politics didn't play

a role in this. Let's not talk politics, let's just talk simple fairness. Was this list fair to the Bay area?

The President. Well, let me answer you in this way. I think that the Secretary of Defense deleted a couple of the facilities in northern California because he thought the aggregate economic impact was too great. That's my impression of why he made the decision that he made. The Bay area still takes a big hit. The Navy was very adamant about the recommendations they made and pointed out that very few Navy installations had been closed previously. If the Navy can be proved wrong, I think that's something we ought to consider.

I believe that a couple of those facilities, the Treasure Island one, for example, I think that the potential of even more economic benefits by turning some of those facilities over to non-military uses are very great indeed. But again, I think that the people from the Bay area and the elected Representatives from California ought to make the strongest case they can to the base closing commission.

This is the public process. This sort of enables me in a way to discuss these things, to get involved, to evaluate them, because after the base closing commission makes their recommendations, they send it back to me so that there's no suggestion of closed doors or behind-the-scenes maneuvering. This is all out-in-the-open debating. And I think that the people in the Bay area ought to make the strongest case they can on all these things, including aggregate fairness, to the base closing commission. I'm going to review it very closely. I also think they ought to claim the right to have an extra intense effort in our conversion process if they're going to have to eat all these closings.

Q. Mr. President, the Naval Training Center in San Diego is now on the so-called hit list when it wasn't before. Do you have any insight as to why that changed?

The President. No, I don't. What do you mean it wasn't before?

Q. It never showed up on a list before, the Naval Training Center, and then it seemed to be on the list in the newspaper in the morning.

The President. No, because I didn't know whether the list that was in the press was right or not. You know, the Long Beach facility was on that list, and apparently it was not recommended for closing. So I can't comment on that. San Diego is going to net out a substantial increase in jobs in this. There will be a few thousand more people employed in the San Diego area when all these changes are made, I know that.

Q. Do you know why McClellan was removed from the list? It was the biggest one that was removed.

The President. You ought to ask the Secretary of Defense. The only thing I asked him to do was to realize that the law imposed on us the responsibility of seriously taking into account the aggregate economic impacts not only on this round of base closings but on the previous two as well. And I think you should ask him about that.

Q. Mr. President, the people of California, the people of Los Angeles understand that we've got to cut the deficit, so we've got to cut the defense budget, so we've got to cut bases. But given the fact that the recession in California is so deep, many people there feel the timing is poor to cut so deeply now. What's your view?

The President. If we were cutting now, I would agree with that. But keep in mind, these are bases that starting between 3 and 5 years from now will be closed. And I certainly hope that 3 years from now the California economy will be in much better shape than it is now.

Right now, what I'm trying to do is to get a big infusion of capital into California through this stimulus program that will put a lot of money to work in community development block grants and highway projects and clean water projects and through some changes in the Federal aid programs that Mr. Panetta and I have worked very hard on, to try to get several hundred million dollars a year more into California in recognition of the fact that you have a big problem with immigrants that the Federal Government has let you struggle with for too long without appropriate response.

And during this 3-year period, I plan to start an intense effort to diversify defense contractors' production, to intensely retrain men and women who might lose their jobs, and to put real funds into communities to develop new and different economic strategies. I think there is an enormous potential in California, if we do all these things, to rebuild the high-wage job base that has been so savaged by this.

And let me just make one other point I made to the State legislators who were here last week about the base closing issue. Now, this doesn't answer the Bay area question, I don't pretend.

But in the aggregate, let me make this point. We started reducing defense spending in 1986—topped out, and it started going down. And it's projected to go down until 1997. If we don't change anything else—let's say we hadn't made this announcement yesterday. It doesn't answer any of the detail questions. You may be right about the specific one. If no announcement had been made yesterday, here's what would have been the picture by 1997: a 40-percent reduction in the defense budget, a 35-percent reduction in personnel, a 56-percent reduction in our presence overseas, and a 9-percent reduction in bases.

Now, if we permitted that to happen, what State would be hurt worst? California. Why? Because California, with 12 percent of the Nation's population, received 21 percent of the total defense budget last year. Why? Because you have a lot of the plants that make the high-tech defense products that are a critical part of this country's economic strategy. So the more you keep bases that can't be justified for strategic purposes, if you keep the same defense cuts, the more you wind up cutting contracts and laying factory workers off and putting pressure on those companies.

So if we want a balanced approach that maintains a smaller but still the best trained and best equipped military force in the world, with unquestioned technological superiority, and if we keep in place an industrial infrastructure that can be called upon to meet those needs and to expand if necessary, that's another reason we have to proceed with discipline on the base closing, so we can build up and maintain the private sector industrial production we need that gives us our technological lead.

Q. Mr. President, you made this point a couple of times, and I just want to make sure that we get it nailed down. Some Members of Congress are pointing to the exclusion of McClellan Air Force Base as evidence that the whole process was contaminated by politics. And they're saying we're going to get a coalition together, we're going to kill the whole list. What would you say to those delegates?

The President. I would say to them that, first of all, they ought to talk to the Secretary of Defense before they do that. Secondly, if they didn't want the economic impact on States considered, then that shouldn't have been part of the legislation. Thirdly, that there is no way the aggregate economic—let me ask you this:

Add back in McClellan and the Defense Language Institute to the Bay area closings, and calculate the impact on northern California, and add that to the impact on California of the previous two rounds of base closings, and tell me that that is fair or takes into account the economic impact.

My view is that the Secretary of Defense basically took the list that was submitted to him by the separate services and did two things they did not do. He aggregated them together so he could calculate the cumulative impact of Navy, Air Force, and Army closings and then considered the cumulative impact of the previous two rounds of base closings. And I believe that was his legal responsibility. That is all I asked him to do. We didn't get into any specifics. I just said, you've got to—that's part of your job—do that. And I think he'll be able to do that with great credibility.

There was also a lot of effort made in other areas to minimize the economic impact by the services themselves. For example, they didn't entirely close the Charleston Navy Yard. They didn't entirely close up some other operations that people had feared that they would. So, to me, he did the best job he could with a very difficult circumstance. And even with this, this round of base closings is the biggest we've had. And even with this, California takes the biggest hit. I think that's going to be a pretty hard sell for those other Congressmen.

Q. Mr. President, someone in the California delegation said the military base closure list was actually left over from the Bush administration, that more time and thought should be given to it in terms of what combination of bases should be closed for the best cost-effectiveness and also more knowledge of the military economic impact. They think that it should be slowed down—the process, even a new list started. What would be your response to that?

The President. I think it would be a mistake to discard the list. I think that the people in California—it is true that this is left over from the Bush administration in the sense that the legislation requiring a list to be produced in 1993 was signed previously and that the services surely were doing this work last year, working on this. But, after all, this list was produced by the military services and only slightly modified by the Secretary of Defense under a discipline that has to be undertaken in this country.

I will say again, if you leave all these bases

open it means more contract cuts. We're taking the military force down to 1.4 million people and keeping a base structure that supported nearly twice that many. These things have to be done.

That does not mean that the services made the right decision in every case. But that's why we have a commission. In each of the two previous commission hearings, even though the aggregate base closings were much smaller, the commission made some minor modifications to the recommendations. And I would say to the people who make those arguments that they ought to go forthrightly with those arguments to the commission; they ought to make them in public. There are some things that I might want considered by the commission as I have time to evaluate this. And I will seriously consider those things as they're made.

But that's why we're moving now to the public part of this process, and that's the time for those arguments to be made. But the people in the services had a very difficult and heavy responsibility. I don't suppose that the Naval officers or the Air Force officers or the Army officers in charge relished making the recommendations they made. They did it because they think that that is best for the national security, given the reductions in the defense budget.

Defense Conversion

Q. Turning to your defense conversion program, a lot of what you say—a lot of your program involves having companies in California compete for partnerships. And I'm not sure exactly what your program involves concerning defense contractors, but the problem in California is that a lot of jobs, a lot of high-wage manufacturing jobs have moved out of State. Some have moved to Arkansas. You, in fact, helped negotiate one deal where a company moved from southern California to Arkansas. How do you safeguard against that, and do you want to safeguard against that? Do you want to keep high-wage manufacturing jobs in California?

The President. Oh, absolutely. Well, I think part of that work has to be done in California itself. That's why I was very enthusiastic when the leaders of the House and the Senate and the Governors co-sponsored that bipartisan economic conference recently that I spoke to by satellite technology. I think California needs a manufacturing base, in my judgment. And there needs to be a serious evaluation of where you are with regard to that competitively and what you have to do to rebuild it.

But I believe that most of the companies will stay where they are if they have enough work to keep them going. And we are allocating over the course of the next 4 or 5 years, if my budget passes, about $20 billion to help the private sector convert this economy and to deal with the dislocations caused by defense cutbacks and by other differences in the economy. And a lot of those companies are going to be able to—they will be competing with one another, but they'll be competing with one another for a much bigger economic pie in terms of the exploration of new technologies.

Let me just give you one example. There's an effort going on in California similar to the one I saw at the Westinghouse plant in Maryland 2 days ago to develop an electric car. There are now electric cars that run 80 miles or more an hour, that run over 100 miles without being recharged. You get up to about 200 miles without being recharged, and then you begin to talk about real commercial viability. That could put an unbelievable number of people to work in the State of California.

Q. But the problem with that is GM developed an electric car in southern California, and it is now building it elsewhere. With your technology partnerships and your other programs, are you going to have some sort of a safeguard to make sure that these companies keep these manufacturing jobs in California?

The President. Well, I don't think you can force—I don't think the national Government can force private companies not to cross State lines. I mean, that's almost a constitutional issue. I mean, under the commerce clause, that would be a hard sell.

Military Base Closings

Q. Mr. President, the reason there are so many political questions this morning—one of the reasons is that all the politicians in California are taking credit for saving a number of bases. The two Senators and the Governor have had press conferences and said, "We saved Long Beach." And they said, "We took a list that was 11 and took it down to 6." But when you check with the Pentagon, they say that's not true. There were only two changes from the original list: McClellan and Monterey. And all this other stuff is just smoke. And that's why we are confused here. Was there, in fact, only

those two adjustments in the list, or was there, in fact, a grand salvage effort here, successfully completed by the two people out there, the two Senators and the Governor?

The President. Well, I can say this: I know that the Secretary of Defense recommended—decided to delete the two facilities. I know that now. I don't know that there were any others that were deleted. Those were the only two that I know about. I know that your Senators and a number of the people in your congressional delegation made pleas to the Defense Department, contacted us, contacted others after the list was leaked. The list that was leaked was not accurate in some respects. The list that was leaked did have other facilities in California on it that I am not aware—that I don't know that the Secretary of Defense deleted, nor—I wouldn't say that wasn't done. I'm just telling you I don't know. I only know of two personally.

But I do think that at least the people who contacted him and contacted me probably had some impact on him. The only thing I said to him was that the law requires us to take into account economic impact, and I think you ought to do that.

I guess I ought to say one other thing. There were some people who weren't from California who urged the Secretary of Defense not to delete the Defense Language Institute, including Senator Simon from Illinois who made a public plea about it. So there was a lot of support around the country for not doing that. But I do think you've got to give credit to the people who made that intense plea. I mean, they may have had some impact on this. I'm sure they did in the sense that I told them that he should consider economic impact and he did and he made the decisions he did. But I don't know that the list was as long as has been speculated about.

Immigration

Q. Mr. President, may I change the subject for a moment? You mentioned immigration. I'm from San Diego. Our drought ended with millions of dollars in flood damage and a tremendous loss of life of people trying to cross the river to come to California. We're at a point now where the county, tragic in both senses, says it doesn't even have the money to pay for the medical examiner to deal with the loss of life amongst immigrants, both legal and illegal. How do you foresee dealing with some of our border problems—of dealing with the problem of immigration and the load on the county and the local jurisdictions, of issues that some would argue really are solely a Federal problem?

The President. Well, first of all, I think what I'd like to do is ask Leon Panetta to explain to you what we've got in this budget to deal with that, to deal with the whole immigration issue. But there's no question in my mind that, for years, the Federal Government's immigration policy or lack of it has had a profound impact on California and on Florida and on Texas, and that basically, immigration is a national policy, the lack of an immigration enforcement is a national responsibility, and that under the system we have for joint financing of all kinds of health and human services, California, Texas, and Florida, and to some extent New York— and to a much lesser extent some other States— have basically been unfairly financially burdened by Federal policy, and we're trying to offset that.

Since Leon worked up the budgets, I'd like for him to describe in more specific terms what we're trying to do. Would you do that? Let him answer that question first.

Director Panetta. We have been working on a program to try to target those States that are impacted by immigration, in part, legal immigration and refugee resettlement but also undocumented immigration as well. And the key to our program is to try to develop an approach that, first of all, tries to fully fund the immigration assistance, the so-called SLIAG provisions that flow to States like California, Texas, and Florida. That's the legalized immigration assistance grants. While those grants have been there, they've never been fully funded for various reasons. We intend to fully fund those. So, for example, in a State like California, we estimate that SLIAG funding will approach almost $600 million for '94.

Secondly, what we want to do is develop a program to expand refugee settlement assistance. That is a program that's in place. As a matter of fact, there were some cuts that were enacted in that program. There was an effort by the prior administration to, so-called, privatize it. Never worked, and as a consequence we're going to be asking for additional funds for refugee resettlement and a supplemental request that will follow the battle on the stimulus program; that's two.

Three, we're looking at additional funds for migrant education as well as Chapter I education. And then, fourthly, we're looking towards assistance, an assistance program to try to help those States that are providing health care to undocumented individuals.

Q. Is it realistic to assume that there might be Federal money for the hospital to treat so many, for all of the facilities that the county now pays for, to augment those with Federal dollars because——

Director Panetta. I can't tell you that there will be direct funding to that kind of hospital, but what we want to do is provide some assistance to the States that have to meet that responsibility, and that's what we're trying to fashion now. And there will be a program like this included in the budget presentation that we'll make at the end of this month.

Q. Mr. President, do you feel under siege on this issue from California?

Military Base Closings

The President. No, but I want to tell you that if you go back to the very first question I was asked, if this had been a purely political process, your question would have had a different answer. You know, this has been a very painful thing for me, seeing this thing happen to the Bay area. The chairman of the House Armed Services Committee, a man I very much respect and admire, has taken—his district has the biggest projected loss. But was there—do the people who speak for California deserve some credit for making sure that the Secretary of Defense did fulfill his legal obligation? I think that's probably yes. The answer to that is, yes, that they did.

But I will say again, this is not going to happen tomorrow; this is going to happen between 3 and 5 years from now. If we want to maintain our high-wage base and technological lead in defense, we will have an easier time doing that if we close appropriate bases and if we do it in a timely fashion. The difference between now and what has been done in defense cutbacks, both bases and defense contractors—and keep in mind, most of the losses California has endured in the last few years has come from the loss of private sector jobs because of contracting cuts. And we have not got an aggressive and a well-funded program which we will pursue, which has not been done for the last 3 or 4 years, to try to make sure that we find jobs and economic opportunities for the people in the communities involved.

So I don't feel under siege. I wanted to do this today. I think you could make a compelling case if it hadn't been for the people of California, I wouldn't be the President of the United States. And I told them that I would work on these problems, and I will. But I cannot walk away from my responsibilities to continue this base closing process. And in the end, California is going to be better off if we preserve the capacity for high-tech employment in the defense industries and if we speed up the diversification process.

Thank you.

East Coast Winter Storm

Q. [*Inaudible*]—about your response to the storm?

The President. What was that?

Director Panetta. There was a question on the storm.

The President. On the storm, we've got two FEMA people in every State now with a State operation. We're in touch with the State officials in every State involved, and we will be spending the remainder of the day trying to assess the damage that has been done, the damage that might be done, and what other resources we should perhaps bring into play. I don't want to say any more about it than that because we're monitoring it as it goes along.

I will say that I just came from a meeting with press people on the east coast, and I would just urge our people to exercise caution as the center of the storm moves closer to their community and because what looks like a very enjoyable late-winter snowstorm—and it's not enjoyable maybe if you're from the South and you're not used to seeing it. But as you move from here on up, a lot of people will be used to seeing snows of this magnitude. And I don't want them to get careless in it, because behind the snow are very, very high winds. And so that we're trying to do is just prepare as best we can and deal with it. And we may have more to say later today.

Defense Conversion

Q. Mr. President, laid-off workers in California think this is too little, too late.

The President. I just got here. It's not too little, too late. This is a good program. It is very aggressive. The Congress appropriated $1.4 billion last year, and none of it was spent. And we're going to spend it and move aggressively. Twenty billion dollars over 5 years is a lot of money to put into defense conversion.

Q. People will have lost their houses by then.

Q. [*Inaudible*]—in California.

The President. Well, maybe people who were affected by decisions made before I got here will be, but these decisions we announced yesterday are going to take effect 3 to 5 years from now and we will have our programs in place and we'll be working on it. And we're going to do our best to reach out to those who have already been adversely affected.

That's one of the reasons the stimulus package ought to pass. California will get more than a billion dollars worth of benefits out of this.

NOTE: The President spoke at 12:25 p.m. in Room 450 of the Old Executive Office Building. Following the interview, Office of Management and Budget Director Leon Panetta continued to answer questions from reporters.

Statement on Disaster Assistance for Florida
March 13, 1993

On March 12 and 13, excessive rainfall, tornadoes, flooding, high tides, and gale force winds caused death, serious personal injury, and property damage in the State of Florida.

In a telephone call to me today, Gov. Lawton Chiles requested individual assistance and public assistance from the Federal Emergency Management Agency (FEMA) for Alachua, Citrus, Columbia, Dade, Duval, Hamilton, Hendry, Hernando, Hillsborough, Lake, Levy, Manatee, Marion, Martin, Pasco, Pinellas, Polk, Putnam, Sarasota, Taylor, and Volusia Counties.

The situation is of such severity and magnitude that effective response is beyond the capabilities of the State of Florida and local governments. Therefore, I concur that supplemental

Federal assistance is necessary, and FEMA is directed to provide such assistance.

Individual assistance can include temporary housing, grants, low-cost loans to cover uninsured property losses, and other programs to help individuals and business owners recover

from the effects of the disaster. Public assistance is available to eligible local governments on a cost-sharing basis for the repair or replacement of public facilities damaged by the flooding.

Additional areas may be designated at a later date, if requested and warranted.

Exchange With Reporters Prior to Discussions With Prime Minister Yitzhak Rabin of Israel
March 15, 1993

Middle East Peace Talks

Q. Mr. President, what do you think are the chances of resuming the Middle East peace talks if deportees are not returned immediately?

The President. I think the Secretary of State's done a commendable job on his trip, and he's worked with the Prime Minister on that issue. And I think we've got a good chance to resume the talks. I certainly hope we will.

Q. Do you think all the parties will come back?

The President. I certainly hope so.

Q. Sir, as you prepare for the first peace talks under your guidance, what do you think the prospects are for a lasting peace in the Middle East?

The President. I think there are a lot of reasons to be hopeful. Obviously, there's difficulty, and there are those who would prefer that it not be done, but I think we have a real shot.

[*At this point, one group of reporters left the room, and another group entered.*]

Q. Mr. President, do you think the United States could be helpful in bringing peace between Israel and Syria? Are you optimistic that peace between these two countries can come during this year?

The President. Well, I hope that the peace process will resume shortly. And I'm hopeful that it can produce a good result. I think there's a chance.

Q. What is your reaction to terrorist action in Israel today and the day before? If you've heard about it, what do you think about it?

The President. Yes, I've heard about it, and I'm disturbed about it. I hope it won't deter any of the parties involved from seeking a genuine long-term peace. But the larger security interests of all the nations involved still argue for trying to have a good-faith effort at the peace process.

NOTE: The exchange began at 10:35 a.m. in the Oval Office at the White House.

The President's News Conference With Prime Minister Yitzhak Rabin of Israel
March 15, 1993

The President. Good afternoon. It's a great pleasure for me to welcome Prime Minister Rabin back to Washington. Since we first met here last August, much has changed. But one thing I can say definitely will never change is the unique bond that unites the United States and Israel. It is a bond that goes back to the founding of the state of Israel and beyond,

based on shared values and shared ideals.

Israel's democracy is the bedrock on which our relationship stands. It's a shining example for people around the world who are on the frontline of the struggle for democracy in their own lands. Our relationship is also based on our common interest in a more stable and peaceful Middle East, a Middle East that will finally accord Israel the recognition and acceptance that its people have yearned for so long and have been too long denied, a Middle East that will know greater democracy for all its peoples.

I believe strongly in the benefit to American interests from strengthened relationships with Israel. Our talks today have been conducted in that context. We have begun a dialog intended to raise our relationship to a new level of strategic partnership, partners in the pursuit of peace, partners in the pursuit of security.

We focused today on our common objective of turning 1993 into a year of peacemaking in the Middle East. Prime Minister Rabin has made clear to me today that pursuing peace with security is his highest mission. I have pledged that my administration will be active in helping the parties to achieve that end. At the same time, Prime Minister Rabin and I agree that our common objective should be real, lasting, just, and comprehensive peace, based on Resolutions 242 and 338. It must involve full normalization, diplomatic relations, open borders, commerce, tourism, the human bonds that are both the fruits and the best guarantee of peace. And Israel's security must be assured. The Israeli people cannot be expected to make peace unless they feel secure, and they cannot be expected to feel secure unless they come to know real peace.

Those like Prime Minister Rabin who genuinely seek peace in the Middle East will find in me and my administration a full partner. But those who seek to subvert the peace process will find zero tolerance here for their deplorable acts of violence and terrorism.

Prime Minister Rabin has told me that he is prepared to take risks for peace. He has told his own people the same thing. I have told him that our role is to help to minimize those risks. We will do that by further reinforcing our commitment to maintaining Israel's qualitative military edge.

Another way we can strengthen Israel and the United States is to combine the skills of its people with those of our own. I am pleased to announce today the establishment of a U.S.-Israel science and technology commission, chaired on the American side by our Secretary of Commerce, Ron Brown. The commission will enhance cooperation to create technology-based jobs for the 21st century in both Israel and the United States. Our economies will also benefit from a lifting of the Arab boycott. And I hope that this boycott can end soon.

Prime Minister Rabin, this year will be a year of enhanced relations between our countries. It should also be a year of peace in the Middle East, as you have declared. We have an historic responsibility and an historic opportunity. We stand here together today resolved not to let that opportunity pass.

Prime Minister Rabin. President Clinton, in just a few days I will return to Israel, but I know, and will tell everyone in my country, Israel has a friend in the White House. Our home is many miles away, but Mr. President, we feel very close. We thank you for the hours we spent with you and your team, for the atmosphere of friendship and the openness and the depth of our discussions. The leadership which you have displayed in coping with America's domestic problems is inspiring and stands out like a beacon in the night.

Today we were happy to learn that at the same time you are also willing to invest efforts in promoting peace and stability in the Middle East. In this effort, Mr. President, you will find us to be full partners. You are aware that no one wants peace more than us and that there is no country more resolved to defend itself when necessary. We are veterans of many wars. And today we say, no more blood and tears. We now wish to experience lasting and meaningful peace.

In our talks today, I presented to you Israel's approach to the peacemaking. And we are willing to take upon ourselves risks for peace. But we are determined to protect our security.

Peace has many enemies. Terror is used by the enemies of peace in our effort to undermine it. And we will combat it while we continue to seek a solution that will lead to peace.

Since the formation of my government, we have invested efforts in trying to advance towards peace in the framework of the Madrid formula. We introduced new ideas in the negotiation tracks with Syria, Lebanon, Jordan, and the Palestinians. Some progress has been made, but more is needed in order to come to agreement. We are ready for compromise, but compromises cannot be one-sided. We call on our partners, the Arab States, the Palestinians from the territories, to seize the moment, to return to the negotiating table so that we can use this historic opportunity. We call upon them to respond openly and willingly to our positions. Our children and grandchildren in Jerusalem and the Arab children and grandchildren in Damascus, Beirut, Amman, and elsewhere in the Arab world will not forgive us if we all fail to act now.

We have heard today with satisfaction, Mr. President, your concept of the role of the full partner as an intermediary. We shall continue our direct talks with our Arab neighbors. But in order to expedite the dialog between the parties, we welcome your good offices and hope to rely on your role as facilitator.

President Clinton, we are deeply indebted to you and to your predecessors who helped us in hours of need. We do appreciate and greatly value the decision to maintain the current level of aid to Israel. This decision will help us to integrate new immigrants into our society and to bear the heavy burden of our security.

You know, President, that we will not be able to win the battle for peace without a qualitative edge. Therefore, I wish to thank you and your colleagues on behalf of the Israeli soldiers and their parents and the citizens of Israel for your decision to help to maintain that edge. Moreover, such a qualitative edge enables the Israeli defense forces to contribute to the overall effort to maintain stability in our stormy region. The decision made today to raise the level of strategic dialog between our two countries will open new doors of opportunity. The fact that the next months we will renew the memorandum of agreement between us for 5 more years, and that we do it as a matter of course, is a proof of the kind of mutually beneficial relationships that we enjoy. The formation of new high-level forum for strategic dialog will further upgrade this relationship.

We will also have a turn in the near future with much urgency to address the struggle against various kinds of fanaticism which give birth to murderous terror, the kind that recently landed even on these shores. We must institutionalize our dialog and include all free countries in consultations on the ways to curb the threatening extremism.

We attach much importance to the decision made today to create the high-level joint commission for the development of projects of science and technology. The investment in research and industrial applications in Israel and in America will explore new frontiers of knowledge. And they are a telling example of how our two countries can mutually benefit from this cooperation.

President Clinton, thank you for your invitation and reception, for the warmth on a wintry day, and for your good will. I came from Jerusalem, the city of the prophets. I return to Jerusalem, the city that witnessed so many wars and wants so dearly peace because she knows that in war there are no winners and in peace no losers.

Thank you very much.

Palestinian Deportees

Q. President Clinton—[*inaudible*]—demands for the immediate repatriation of the Palestinian deportees, and where did you leave that subject?

The President. No, we did not discuss that. As far as I'm concerned, the Secretary of State and the Prime Minister reached an agreement on that. And I think that is the framework within which we are proceeding.

Middle East Peace Talks

Q. Mr. President——

The President. Yes. Go ahead.

Q. Mr. President, the last peace agreement between an Arab nation and Israel was, as you know, the Egyptian Peace Agreement. In that case, the President kept a very personal part as an intermediary. To what extent are you willing to become personally involved? And Mr. Prime Minister, to what extent are you willing to see the President become personally involved in this peace negotiation?

Prime Minister Rabin. Well, as you can expect, I cannot answer in the name of the President of the United States. But I believe, as it has happened whenever agreements were reached between the Arab countries and Israel from '74 to '79, and even the creation of the Madrid peace conference, could not be achieved without the United States being involved in encouraging the parties to do so. I believe that there was, there is a need of the United States' partnership to the peacemaking process. At what level, at what time, it's not up to me to answer.

The President. The answer to your question is that I would be prepared to commit the resources, the effort and the attention of this administration, of my Secretary of State, and my personal efforts to achieve lasting agreements.

We have, on the table, the potential of very significant bilateral agreements and the potential of some regional agreements that I think ought to be pursued. I feel very strongly about it, and I think the opportunities for progress are there. I don't want to minimize the difficulties, the obstacles, the years of frustration, but I think the fact that this Prime Minister, who became a hero as a warrior, is doing what he can and risking significantly to promote peace, is a good beginning. And I think there are other good indications in the region. And I'm prepared to personally do what I can to facilitate that.

Helen [Helen Thomas, United Press International].

West Bank and Gaza Strip

Q. Do you support the transitional—[*inaudible*]—policy of self-determination for the people on the West Bank and Gaza who have been living for years under military occupation? Mr. Prime Minister, do you think that during your regime there will be any measure of self-rule for the Palestinians while you are a leader?

Prime Minister Rabin. I don't want to give you a lengthy answer, but allow me to say, in 1967 we did not want war. It's more than that. Even when we found ourselves in a clash with the Egyptians, we offered to the Jordanians, stay out of the war and we'll keep your line with us without any change.

If you'll follow the history, we were always for compromise. U.N. decision, partition of Palestine to two states: We accepted; they rejected. They went to war to destroy us. It's bad luck to the Arabs. Whenever they go to war, they lose. We offer them this time, to the Palestinians in the territories, what no one offered them when the Arab countries were in occupation, Jordan of the West Bank, Egypt of the Gaza Strip, self-rule—run your own life by yourself— as an interim agreement for a transition period of not more than 5 years. Not later than the third year, we are ready to enter negotiations with them about a permanent solution based on Resolution 242 and 338.

What else can we do? By violence and terror no one will make us run. The solution should be around the negotiation table, by talks, not by weapons.

The President. The answer is the United States position has not changed. As I said in my statement, we support a solution based on the governing United Nations resolutions. But the important thing is that everything we say or do today sends a clear message, particularly to the other parties in the Middle East, that

the time has come to negotiate peace. And the United States is prepared to be involved all the way through the process.

Wolf [Wolf Blitzer, Cable News Network].

Syria

Q. [*Inaudible*]—both of you have addressed the question of bilateral arrangements between Israel and Syria. It seems that the Prime Minister in recent statements has backed away from some earlier statements that Israel would never go down from the Golan Heights. Is there a change? Would Israel be prepared to accept a complete withdrawal from the Golan Heights in exchange for complete peace with Syria, along the lines of the Israeli-Egyptian peace agreement? And would the United States welcome that kind of separate Israeli-Syrian agreement even in advance of a Palestinian agreement?

Prime Minister Rabin. Well, first, we are serious in our negotiations with every one of the Arab partners for the peace negotiations. We are ready to negotiate and reach agreement with every one of the partners that sit around the negotiation table with us.

Second, peace has to be negotiated not between me, as the Prime Minister of Israel, and you. After all, you don't represent Syria. We made it clear that we accept the principle of withdrawal of the armed forces of Israel on the Golan Heights, to secure the recognized boundaries, but we'll not enter negotiations on the dimension of the withdrawal without knowing what kind of peace Syria offers us. Is it a fully fledged peace, open boundaries for movement of people and goods, diplomatic relations including embassies, normalization of relations? Will they let that peace treaty stand on its own two feet, will not be influenced by what happens or doesn't happen in the negotiations with the other Arab partners?

Before we know that, why would I have to say how much we will withdraw once it is an issue to be agreed on between Syria and ourselves, with the assistance of the United States?

The President. The answer to your question, from my point of view, is that the United States believes that the full peace process should resume. We hope very much that the Palestinians will come to the table. We would like to see all the bilaterals go forward. But if the parties could reach an agreement consistent with security interests and the governing United Nations resolutions that was their genuine agreement, would I welcome that and be prepared to support it? Yes, I would.

The Peace Process

Q. Mr. President, the Arabs think that you favor Israel against them. What are you doing to balance this situation? We know that Secretary Christopher has gone there, but what specifically has been offered to them, and how would you see a confederation of Jordan with the Palestinians? And also I would like to ask the response to that from Prime Minister Rabin.

The President. Secretary Christopher went to the Middle East, and I can assure you, one of the things that he did was to say the same thing to everybody in every capital that he visited, to say that the United States wanted to be a partner in this process, but that we recognize we had to be a mediator, and that, in the end, the only thing that would make peace possible was the assurance of security that would come to the parties afterward.

I believe that the other nations involved know that the United States has had an historic relationship of friendship with Israel, but also know that we can be counted upon to keep our word and to do what we can to support the security of all the parties if an agreement can be reached.

Do you want to answer that?

Prime Minister Rabin. I can speak only as an Israeli, and in the name of Israel. I believe that the government that I serve as its Prime Minister is the first government that accepted the principle or the Resolutions 242 and 338 as applicable to the achievement of peace. No government in the past did so, which shows that we understand that in peace, compromises have to be made by both sides.

Security Issues

Q. Mr. President, Prime Minister Rabin today spoke about raising the level of strategic dialog; you spoke about strategic dialog. I was wondering if you could elaborate what that means more, and does this mean greater coordination between the two countries in terms of what approaches to take to peace, and then bringing that to the table? Are we talking about a whole new approach here?

The President. No, we're not talking about a whole new approach. Our two governments have some very gifted people who work on a continuous basis on security issues between us

and facing the region. Looking ahead 10 years down the road, we know that we have to pay greater attention to missile defenses; we know that we have to pay greater attention to the possibility of proliferation of weapons of mass destruction; we know that in order for any agreement in the Middle East to have lasting impact, there will be significant, and must be, significant security implications flowing out of any kind of arrangements which might be made. And we just want to make sure that beginning now we give those matters the most careful attention at the appropriate level.

This will not supplant anything that is now being done. We're very well satisfied with the work being done by our people now. But these three things, it seems to us, will shape a lot of our deliberations for a decade to come.

Russia

Q. Mr. President, can you clarify your administration's views on the situation in Russia today? In particular, do you believe that the Russian Parliament is a democratically elected institution? And if it is not a democratically elected institution, why would you object to its dissolution by Mr. Yeltsin—the rewriting of a new Russian Constitution—would that not be helpful?

The President. Mr. Friedman [Tom Friedman, New York Times], those are great questions. But I think any answer I'd give to them might only complicate the decisions I might have to make in the days ahead.

Q. It would be a great story. [*Laughter*]

The President. It will be a wonderful story, and I must say those are questions I have, we have all posed to ourselves. But let me say this: I hope that everybody in America, I hope everybody in Israel, is pulling for the triumph of freedom and market reform in Russia. Democracy is an uncertain process. The Prime Minister and I have been in and out of office. We know that. And I don't pretend to know everything that's going to happen in Russia in the days and weeks ahead, and I don't want to say anything now which might constrict my field of decision in ways that would not be in the interest of the United States or of freedom and market reform in Russia.

So I wish I could say more, but I can't. All I can tell you is I'm working like crazy to get ready for that meeting with President Yeltsin. I'm going to do what I can and mobilize what forces I can, public and private, in the United

States to support the march of progress in Russia. And I'm going to hope and pray that all those who want the same thing will be in there pushing with us.

Last question.

North Korea

Q. Can you give us any more insight into what the situation is in North Korea, whether you believe they do have nuclear capability? If so, where did they get it from, and what leverage the United States might have in addressing this issue?

The President. I cannot answer your exact question. I can tell you that I, personally, and speaking for the Government, the United States is very concerned and very disappointed that North Korea has at least for the time being chosen to eject the IAEA inspectors and to withdraw from the international regime of which they are part.

The board of directors of the IAEA is meeting on Wednesday. They will make a statement at that time, and I will make a response. There are 3 months still to go, and as you know, any country that wants to withdraw is bound for 3 months. I hope that North Korea will reconsider its decision. I think there is a genuine impulse among the peoples of North Korea and South Korea, among the peoples to see a reduction in tensions and an increase in commerce and communication and contact. And I'm very disturbed by this turn of events. But I'm hoping that it will not be a permanent thing. There are several weeks ahead when North Korea might reverse its decision. I hope they will do so, because we simply cannot back up on the determination to have the IAEA inspections proceed there.

The answers to your questions could only be found in complete and thorough and ongoing investigations by the IAEA, either in North Korea or any other country where these questions are asked. And I'm hoping very, very much that they will reconsider their decision and permit the inspectors to come again.

Thank you very much.

NOTE: The President's sixth news conference began at 2:02 p.m. in the East Room at the White House.

Nomination for Posts at the Office of Management and Budget and the Department of Veterans Affairs
March 15, 1993

The President announced today his intention to nominate Sally Katzen to be Administrator of the OMB's Office of Information and Regulatory Affairs, and James Allen, Yvonne Santa Anna, and Victor Raymond to be Assistant Secretaries of Veterans Affairs for Human Resources and Administration, Public and Intergovernmental Affairs, and Policy and Planning, respectively.

"Each of the individuals I am calling on today has had a distinguished career in which they have proven themselves in both private and public enterprises," said the President. "I am proud that they are joining me in the Federal Government."

NOTE: Biographies of the nominees were made available by the Office of the Press Secretary.

Exchange With Reporters Prior to a Meeting With Congressional Leaders
March 16, 1993

Q. Mr. President, do you think you can really afford to cut the defense budget with what's happening in Russia? Cut it as much as you want to?

The President. Well, I think we're going to have hearings about it. We're going to have to see. We'll have to cut it some. We can't meet the deficit reduction targets if we don't.

What's happening in Russia may or may not present an additional threat to our security, but what we hope we can do is to keep democracy and economic reform going. And I think there's an almost unanimous feeling in the Congress that we ought to do that. We're bipartisan, and that's one of the issues I want to discuss here today.

Q. Senator Dole said last night that instead of choosing Al Gore to reinvent Government, you should have chosen Ross Perot. What do you think of that?

The Vice President. I can't believe he'd say that. [*Laughter*]

The President. If I said what I thought, it would be a story. I don't want to do that. [*Laughter*]

NOTE: The exchange began at 9:47 a.m. in the Cabinet Room at the White House.

Remarks With President Jean-Bertrand Aristide of Haiti and an Exchange With Reporters
March 16, 1993

President Clinton. I'd like to make a brief statement and then invite President Aristide to make a statement. And then we'll answer questions.

It's been a great honor for all of us to have President Aristide and members of his government and the Ambassador from Haiti to the United States here in the Oval Office today. And we wanted to have the opportunity to speak to the American people and to the people of Haiti from the Oval Office to emphasize how important it is to me personally and to the United States to restore democracy in Haiti and to restore President Aristide as the elected leader of that country.

To those who have blocked the restoration of democracy, I want to make it clear in the strongest possible terms that we will not now or ever support the continuation of an illegal government in Haiti and that we want to step up dramatically the pace of negotiations to restore President Aristide under conditions of national reconciliation and mutual respect for human rights with a program of genuine economic progress.

The Secretary of State has named an experienced diplomat, Mr. Lawrence Pezzullo, who is here now, to be his special representative in Haiti, to work with the Caputo mission through the United Nations and the Organization of American States to push forward with a rapid settlement of these issues. I would urge the de facto government of Haiti and the military officials in that country and police officials

to support this process. Any opposition, any delay will only result in stronger measures taken by the United States and more difficulty and hardship for the people of Haiti, who have been the innocent sufferers in this whole sad saga.

I look forward to working with President Aristide. I look forward to the success of Mr. Pezzullo. And I want to make it clear that the United States is committed strongly to a much more aggressive effort to restore Mr. Aristide to his Presidency and to, over the long run, work with the people of Haiti to restore conditions of economic prosperity.

I am prepared to commit the United States to its fair portion of a 5-year, multinational $1 billion effort to rebuild the Haitian economy. And we are going to begin on this project in earnest now.

I'd like to now invite President Aristide to make whatever remarks he would like to make, and then open the floor for your questions.

President Aristide. Mr. President Clinton, we are delighted to be here with you, with the Vice President, Secretary of State, Ambassador Pezzullo. We want to thank you on behalf of the Haitian people for your support. We want to thank you for what you just said. That went directly to the heart of the Haitian people working peacefully for the restoration of democracy.

I grasp this opportunity to thank the American people for their solidarity, because with our American brothers and sisters, since 18 months we realize how beautiful it is to work in a nonviolent way for the restoration of democracy. The Haitian people today hear your voice, and on behalf of them, I can say, in the past we wanted to be with you; we are with you; in the future, we will be with you, and you will be welcome in Haiti when I will be there after the restoration of democracy.

We have a lot of people suffering since 18 months. And today I'm sure they are happy because they realize finally that day for the restoration of democracy will come, and since today they can continue to build but in a strongest way that democracy, always in a nonviolent way. The refugees can feel happy. Those who are in Guantanamo can feel happy. Those who are in Haiti working peacefully for that democracy can feel happy because that day is coming because of you, because of the American Government, because of the U.S., because of the OAS.

Thanks once again for that, and you are welcome to our land.

Q. Mr. President, in the past few days, President Aristide has called for a date certain for his return. He's called for tougher sanctions, a tougher enforcement of the embargo, a naval blockade, and for some action to relieve the suffering of those in Guantanamo. Are you prepared to take any of those steps?

President Clinton. Let me respond, if I might, to each in turn. And let me start with the middle suggestion, the question of whether the United States would take tougher action on the embargo. I wouldn't rule that out, but I think you shouldn't underestimate the impact of this diplomatic initiative, sending Mr. Pezzullo to Haiti, making the statements we're making today, sending the clear and unambiguous signal we're sending.

And I might note that just a few moments ago the person we had approved for refugee status who had been held illegally by the Haitian de facto Government was released to come to the United States as a refugee.

I think that the message we're sending out there is clear. So I think what we would like to do is to give Mr. Pezzullo a chance to go to Haiti, communicate strongly and directly to the appropriate people there what our position is and where we're going before we take actions, which at least in the short run will make life even more difficult for the Haitians. I wouldn't rule them out, but I think we ought to have it in an appropriate sequence of events.

As to the question of a date certain, I certainly think that we ought to return President Aristide in the near future. But I think that the date for the conclusion of the negotiations ought to come out of Mr. Caputo and his mission. And I think we ought to, in fairness, let him do that. It is a very grave thing for the United States alone to be setting a date certain in an endeavor that involves the United Nations and the Organization of the American States. So I think a date may well come out of the efforts of the Caputo mission, but we don't feel at this time it is the wisest thing for the long-term interests of President Aristide or Haiti for us to set the date on our own.

With regard to the refugees in Guantanamo, I'm going to do the following things: First of all, I'm going to send someone from our White House staff to Guantanamo to review the situation personally. Secondly, I'm going to take up the legal and human conditions of the refugees with the Attorney General, who has jurisdiction in these areas, now that we have a new Attorney General confirmed. I wanted to wait and have the opportunity to discuss that with her.

And then we will review the whole question and see whether or not there's anything else we should do. I expect all this would be done in the near future. I don't expect to take a good deal of time on this.

Q. President Aristide, is that satisfactory to you?

President Aristide. Totally.

Q. Can we expect or can any Haitian in Cap Haitien or elsewhere expect the early return, constitutional return of the constitutional President of Haiti?

President Aristide. Every Haitian should be extremely happy about what has happened today. I think that all Haitians can look with joy at the cooperation of myself and President Clinton, working hand in hand for all Haitians, looking forward to peace, to nonviolence, to economic development. I think everyone can feel great contentment and happy anticipation.

Q. Is there going to be a real celebration of the Constitution, the anniversary of the Constitution of Haiti?

President Aristide. Yes, with the help of President Clinton, all Haitians can feel comfortable and happy about celebrating March 29th as an anniversary for peace and respect of the law, the Constitution as a basis for the law, and for its respect for all Haitians.

Q. Mr. Clinton, would it be acceptable to you if the coup leaders left without being punished?

President Clinton. Well, it would be acceptable to me to restore President Aristide to power in Haiti under conditions which were safe for him and for all Haitians. He has spoken in the past about what his policies would be in that regard, and I presume that a lot of the details of this would be the subject of negotiations. And those are negotiations of which I do not believe I should engage, although I would say that I was very impressed with what President Aristide said today about the need for national reconciliation. And perhaps you'd want him to make a comment.

Q. Mr. President, you criticized——

President Clinton. Could we give him a chance to answer, please.

President Aristide. In Haiti we don't have an institution giving justice to people but unfortunately selling that justice. After 200 years, we realize we still have an army of 7,000 military and 40 percent of the national budget. So I used to ask the Haitians, do not go to any kind of violence or retaliation or vengeance. I will continue to do the same, because what we need is nonviolent reality, not violent.

That's why I'm not saying we want to see the coup leaders in jail and then to feel happy because we punished them. I'm saying, asking to all the Haitians to not go to vengeance, to wait for justice instead of doing justice for themselves out of institution. We can work peacefully to remove the coup leaders from the army and that way to free the army and let justice be done; not then to feel happy because we put them in jail, no; happy because we can that way make a balance in a country where we don't have yet institutions who give justice.

I would add this point: We want reconciliation. We want justice. We want peace. That's why through this process, by a dialog, we can reach that level where, finally, the Haitians will feel so happy to not go to vengeance and to not see the symbol of the coup in the same place, with the same weapons, doing the same repression. That's the way we are trying to go.

[*At this point, President Aristide repeated his answer in French, and it was then translated by an interpreter as follows.*]

President Aristide. There is no institution in Haiti which is in a position or able to give justice in Haiti at the present time. Justice is sold, and that has been the case for the last 200 years. We in Haiti are opting now for nonviolence, for peace for all the people of Haiti. Therefore, we must free the army from those who were responsible for the coup, asking at the same time all Haitians not to engage in vengeance, but rather to devote themselves to justice and to feel happy in the knowledge that justice will be done.

It is in that sense that we have asked for the departure of the coup leaders, that they no longer be the heads of the army, not necessarily that they either be in jail or have to leave the country, but that a solution be found via dialog which will lead to a truly balanced situation so that all can work together in this nonviolent context which will bring about a feeling of deepest joy in the hearts of all Haitians.

Q. Thank you.

President Clinton. I know we have to go. Let me just reaffirm two points, and I'm glad you said it the second time because that's exactly what came out of our meetings. That sort of attitude on the part of President Aristide is the very thing that should enable us to resolve this in a peaceful way. If the people of Haiti can live in peace and security, subsequent to an agreement, and begin once again to work for their own prosperity instead of living in ever-deepening misery, then I think that we will be well on the road to alleviating literally centuries of oppression in that beautiful country that has been so misgoverned for so long.

And I applaud his statement. It is in that spirit that I undertake this initiative. And I want to close by reaffirming the determination of the United States to restore democracy and President Aristide as soon as possible.

Thank you very much.

NOTE: The President spoke at 5 p.m. in the Oval Office at the White House.

Exchange With Reporters Prior to a Meeting With the Hispanic Caucus
March 16, 1993

Q. Mr. President, what are you doing in this meeting tonight, or this afternoon? Some special——

The President. Well, we're going to talk about a lot of things of interest to the caucus, and I'm going to listen. We're going to talk about the economic program, and they're going to talk about some things that they're interested in in the administration. And they can talk about it when the meeting is over. I'm listening today.

Surgeon General

Q. Mr. President, could you tell us why Dr. Novello is being asked to step down as Surgeon General before her term expires?

The President. I don't know what arrange-ments—she's going to continue in the Department of Health and Human Services, and I have a very high regard for her. And I told Donna Shalala when I appointed her Secretary of HHS that I had a very strong feeling about wanting my health department director from home to be the Surgeon General, but that I very strongly approved of the record Dr. Novello has made and I hoped that we could persuade her to stay on. And this is an arrangement they all worked out. I don't know the details and the timing. I can't comment on it. I just don't know anything about that.

NOTE: The exchange began at 5:51 p.m. in the Roosevelt Room at the White House.

Remarks at the American Ireland Fund Dinner
March 16, 1993

Thank you very much, Mr. Speaker, for once again participating in the great American charade designed to convince people that the President has more authority than the Speaker of the House. Now, if I were a prime minister, I wouldn't have to worry about that. [*Laughter*] Mr. Prime Minister, it's a delight to welcome you to our Nation's Capital, and I look forward to our visit tomorrow. I want to congratulate Chairman O'Reilly. Let me ask you: Do you like the purple? [*Laughter*] I want you to understand that is not royal purple. That is a substitute, because he made the ultimate sacrifice; he gave his President the green.

I want to thank all those who worked so hard to make this dinner successful. It's often remarked that on St. Patrick's Day we're all Irish, or we wish we were. I am actually part Irish, and I have often been accused of having a certain gift for blarney—[*laughter*]—although those were not the words used last year when that was said. I'm glad to see Senator Kennedy and Congressman Kennedy and Mrs. Smith in the audience. But, you know, President Kennedy was the first Irish Catholic to become President. But though a Baptist from Arkansas, I'm the first graduate of a Catholic university to become President. I'm glad to see Father O'Donovan out there, my president, of Georgetown. Thank you.

As a younger man, I went through a period of intense uncertainty about whether I should pursue a career in music or a career in politics. I was happy to learn that the Prime Minister, whom you affectionately called the Taoiseach— you know, I want the Members of the Congress to learn that. I like that, the chieftain. It has a good feeling. [*Laughter*] He's been an exponent of one of Ireland's most popular forms of native music, country and western. I'm glad he pursued his political career in Ireland, because if he had chosen to come to Arkansas, he might have defeated me with that sort of background. [*Laughter*] You know, Irish music has made almost as much of a contribution to modern life as Irish politicians, from the Chieftains to Phil Coulter to Van Morrison to that wonderful group U-2 that played such a major role in trying to get the young people in America to go and vote. The first time I heard that their lead singer was named Bono, I asked what his last name was. Then I found out he didn't have a last name. Then, after I spent an hour with him, I discovered he didn't need one. [*Laughter*]

You know, there are 44 million Americans of Irish descent, that is, those who are telling the truth and those who lie, which qualifies them—[*laughter*]—who have contributed immeasurably to every sphere of our life. In fact, the house that I now live in, which either makes me the resident of America's finest public housing or, as some of my critics say, the crown jewel of the Federal penal system, was designed by James Hoban, a famous Irishman who designed the White House based on a model of a magnificent house in Ireland.

I thought I would tell you this, for those of you who don't know, since President Kennedy once said at a dinner of Nobel laureates that it was the most distinguished array of brain-power ever gathered in the White House since Thomas Jefferson dined there alone. [*Laughter*] James Hoban defeated Thomas Jefferson for the design of the White House. Jefferson submitted anonymously a design for the White House, and the people making the decision, basically George Washington and a few of his friends, concluded that Hoban was superior to Jefferson. [*Laughter*]

President Kennedy said that "Here on Earth, God's work is truly our own." Whenever I'm asked to speak in a church I say that. It captured for me, more than anything else, what the essence of public service is about. The American Ireland Foundation embodies that phrase as well as any group of Americans: offering hope and opportunity to all the people of Ireland; promoting peace, reconciliation, and common enterprise between Catholics and Protestants, nationalists and unionists; and promoting cultural activities, community development, employment opportunities in health care and counseling. I am absolutely delighted, I must say, that the Government of Ireland is now providing a site, an historic castle, for the new Hole in the Wall Gang Camp for children with life-threatening diseases. I'm glad to see Paul Newman and Joanne Woodward here tonight, and I can tell you that Hillary and I visited the Hole in the Wall Gang Camp in Connecticut a couple of years ago, and I was moved beyond words by what I saw there. And I thank everyone who is responsible for giving the children of Ireland this remarkable opportunity.

The American Ireland Fund is doing in Ireland what we are trying to do here in the United States: to offer opportunity, to encourage responsibility, to reknit the social fabric badly frayed by the pressures of modern life, and to restore a sense of community without which it is difficult for people to proceed with their individual and family lives. I'm proud to support your work because it's important, it's an inspiration, it's a lesson for all of us, not only for those who are Irish all year long but for those who are just Irish for 24 hours a year.

I thank the Irish Americans who have worked with me, particularly in the last 16 months, to try to help me learn more about Ireland, as well as about the problems and promise of Irish Americans here at home, and I look forward to working with all of you in the days and weeks and years ahead. I hope that we will always be able to bring to our labors the remarkable spirit I sense in this room tonight, and never lose the sense of humor which has become so associated with this wonderful holiday.

Thank you very much.

NOTE: The President spoke at 6:43 p.m. at the Capital Hilton. In his remarks, he referred to Anthony J.F. O'Reilly, chairman, American Ireland Fund.

Nomination for Five Ambassadorial Posts
March 16, 1993

The President named five career Foreign Service officers to ambassadorial positions today. The President announced his intention to nominate Alvin Adams to be Ambassador to Peru; Harry Gilmore, Ambassador to Armenia; Mark Johnson, Ambassador to Senegal; Marilyn McAfee, Ambassador to Guatemala; and Allan Wendt, Ambassador to Slovenia.

"Secretary Christopher and I have pledged to name Ambassadors who meet the highest standards of excellence," the President said. "With these announcements today, we have done just that."

NOTE: Biographies of the nominees were made available by the Office of the Press Secretary.

Nomination for Small Business Administrator
March 16, 1993

The President today announced his intention to nominate North Carolina businessman Erskine Bowles to head the Small Business Administration.

"Small business is the engine that runs the American economy. We need to give a hand up to the new businesses and traditional mom-and-pop stores that provide the jobs in our cities and small towns," the President said. "Erskine Bowles will do an excellent job of making SBA a more efficient operation that works to strengthen the backbone of small business in this country."

NOTE: A biography of the nominee was made available by the Office of the Press Secretary.

Remarks at a Saint Patrick's Day Ceremony With Prime Minister Albert Reynolds of Ireland and an Exchange With Reporters
March 17, 1993

The President. Good day, ladies and gentlemen. On this St. Patrick's Day, I am delighted to welcome Prime Minister Reynolds, called Taoiseach in his country, to the White House. We both share a love of music and a love of Ireland, and I'm looking forward to working with him in the years ahead. I accept with honor this beautiful bowl of shamrocks he has presented from the people of Ireland to the people of the United States. And it will be proudly displayed in the White House as a symbol of our shared values and common heritage.

The Prime Minister's visit is an opportunity not only to recall our kinship but also to work together on issues of critical importance to both our nations. We just concluded a good meeting which covered many issues, and I benefited greatly from the Prime Minister's advice and counsel.

We discussed the importance of bringing the Uruguay round to a successful conclusion. We reviewed the humanitarian relief effort in Somalia, including the generous contributions of Irish citizens working in such organizations as CON-

CERN and UNICEF.

Let me take a moment here, Mr. Prime Minister, to extend to the families and friends of Valerie Place and Sean Devereux the heartfelt condolences of the American people over their tragic deaths and our gratitude for their service. Their dedication to the relief efforts in Somalia will serve as an inspiration to us as we seek to extend the hand of comfort to victims of strife.

The Prime Minister and I also discussed the continuing tragic conflict in Northern Ireland that has cost 3,000 lives over the last 2 decades. I congratulate both the Irish and the British Governments for their joint efforts to promote the necessary dialog to bring about a just and lasting peace. And I want to underscore my strong support for that important goal. We agree that such an outcome cannot be coerced or imposed, and that those who resort to violence must not be tolerated. Violence condemns generation to harvest the seeds of bitterness, not peace. Nor can the problem be resolved by the language of victories or defeats. It must be resolved in the language and spirit of compromise and conciliation.

I told the Prime Minister that the United States stands ready to do whatever we can to help in bringing peace to Northern Ireland. We are a nation of diversity. We are prepared to help in any way that we can. I think that it is important to say that the most significant thing I should be doing now is to encourage the resumption of the dialog between the Irish and the British Governments, which I think is a critical precondition to any establishment of a lasting peace. Our support for the International Fund for Ireland is an important demonstration of our commitment to encourage investment and economic growth and to advance the cause of peace and tolerance.

My discussions with Prime Minister Reynolds, as with Prime Minister Major, were the first of many that I think you will see our governments having as we offer our assistance in trying to end the troubles.

Let me close by saying that the ties of culture, history, and friendship between the United States and Ireland mean a great deal to me. Last night the Prime Minister and I joined together in singing "When Irish Eyes Are Smiling." He did a slightly better job than I did. [*Laughter*] Today we pause to renew our ties to Ireland and the challenges ahead. Let me add that Ireland will have a friend in the White House, Mr. Prime Minister, not just on St. Patrick's Day but on every day of the year.

I also want to take advantage of the Prime Minister's visit here to announce my intention to nominate as Ambassador to Ireland a distinguished individual, as Irish as Americans can be, Jean Kennedy Smith. I can think of no one who better captures the bonds between Ireland and the United States or who will work harder to advance our relationship. In many ways she's already been an unofficial international ambassador. Since she founded Very Special Arts two decades ago, she has traveled tirelessly throughout the United States and the world. Very Special Arts provides opportunities for the disabled in creative arts in all 50 States and over 50 countries, including Ireland. As a testament to her success, a play from her young playwrights program in Dublin will open shortly off Broadway.

I know firsthand Jean's achievements from the Arkansas Very Special Arts program and remember well when Hillary joined her in our State

for the competition to commemorate the 200th anniversary of the White House.

The people of the United States will be proud of our new Ambassador. I am proud of her, and I'm glad to have a couple of her relatives, the Senator from the State of Massachusetts and Congressman Kennedy, to join with us today. And Mr. Ambassador, let me say again how very grateful we are to you and offer you the opportunity to make a few remarks and then offer Mrs. Smith.

Ambassador-Designate Smith. Thank you very much. It is a great honor for me to be nominated as Ambassador to Ireland. And I'm extremely grateful to President Clinton for his confidence in me. I will do all I can to repay this confidence. It's a wonderful St. Patrick's Day. Thank you.

Prime Minister Reynolds. Thank you, President. And first of all, may I take the first opportunity of saying—[*at this point, Prime Minister Reynolds spoke in Gaelic*]—which is congratulations to Jean Kennedy Smith to be the U.S. Ambassador to Ireland. The U.S. is proud of her. We are more proud still to welcome home Jean Kennedy Smith. She has been a regular visitor to our shores. She has done marvelous work throughout the world, as the President has just said, in relation to her work for the disabled arts. And I know she'll get plenty of opportunity to continue that creative work in Ireland.

Thank you, President. St. Patrick's Day, Mr. President, is an occasion which bonds and brings together our two communities and peoples in a uniquely meaningful way. It is not simply about shamrock and symbols, important though these are; rather does it have as its core a deep, abiding, and shared belief in democracy and freedom and in the protection and extension of human rights.

It was because these values were incorporated in the foundation of the American republic that Thomas Jefferson could proclaim in his first Inaugural Address what might then have seemed a paradox, and I quote: "I believe this . . . the strongest Government on earth."

It is a day and this is a unique occasion, standing as we are here in the house which, as President Clinton remarked last night at that very enjoyable function, that this house was designed just over 200 years ago by an Irishman, James Hoban. That's one of the reasons why we are contemplating the extraordinary success of Irish America. You will have no difficulty,

Mr. President, if on this day I characterize you, you yourself, as reflecting on that Irish American success story. Like John F. Kennedy, Ronald Reagan, Andrew Jackson, Ulysses S. Grant, and other Presidents of Irish extraction before you, you have risen to the highest position in the land adopted by your ancestors and demonstrated again that the great American dream which inspired so many of your forbears is alive and well and in very good hands.

The success story that is Irish America today began as one of political, economic, and social struggle in the home country. It should not be surprising therefore that when the earlier waves of our immigrants reached these shores, they were to the forefront in the American War of Independence and in the drafting and promulgation of the American Declaration of Independence, and that later waves of immigrants quickly and enthusiastically embraced that declaration, to quote just one historian, "not as a tired formula, but as an ideal to be reached out for and grasped."

It is against that background, Mr. President, that I have always believed that the constructive interest and support of the United States has the potential to be uniquely helpful in finding a solution to the situation in Northern Ireland, that last residual problem of a long and often sad history between Ireland and Britain.

My government are determined not to allow another generation to suffer the scourge and savagery of violence or its demeaning and related manifestations: disadvantage, harassment, and discrimination.

There are no immediate answers, no simple solutions, but there is a way forward. It involves courage, commitment, and imagination. It will require, above all, the letting go of all vestiges of triumphalism on every side and replacing it with a willingness and a determination to work together in partnership within new structures which will embrace and seek to reconcile the two conflicting rights and aspirations in our small country.

We warmly welcome your concern, Mr. President, your commitment, and your active support as we take on this daunting but vital challenge. If we can succeed, Mr. President, in establishing in Ireland structures that achieve these goals, the benefits may not just be for Ireland alone. In a world where deeper ethnic divisions have assumed a new and violent prominence, it may well be that the model we create in Ireland will have application in similar conflict situations around the world.

So in conclusion, Mr. President, may I thank you again for the hospitable American reception you have given us here today at the White House. In so doing, you acknowledge and honor the contribution of the millions of fellow Irish who have made their homes and built their dreams in this great land. You make us all proud.

As we travel together now for a gathering on Capitol Hill hosted by another outstanding Irishman, Speaker Foley, may I extend to you, Mrs. Clinton, and your family our warmest best wishes on this very special day for all of us and convey our sincerest wish for the success of your administration.

I hope Americans of all ethnic backgrounds have a wonderful St. Patrick's Day. And what a day in which to celebrate it here with one of us as President, another, Albert here on my right, and the Kennedy family that are a legend in Ireland, the United States, and throughout the world.

The President. That was such an outstanding performance, I think the Prime Minister should have to answer all the questions.

Northern Ireland

Q. Have you decided, Mr. President, whether or not to send a peace envoy or to send a fact-finding mission to Northern Ireland? And could you give us some idea of a timeframe for that action, please?

The President. No, I discussed it with the Prime Minister. And we decided after our consultations that that is certainly an option that I should leave open, both of those options, and have under serious consideration.

As you know, talks began last year and then were suspended. I'm very hopeful that the British and the Irish Governments will get back together and begin a serious dialog soon. I think that is a precondition, as I said, for the other talks proceeding. And I'm going to stay in touch closely with Prime Minister Reynolds. We're going to talk frequently, and I expect to have an Ambassador in Ireland pretty soon. And I'll make those decisions at what seems to me to be the appropriate time. I have not made them now, and I don't think it would be appropriate to make a final decision on that at this time.

Q. Can we ask the Prime Minister if he likes the idea of a special envoy, opposes it, or would like to——

Prime Minister Reynolds. I think we had a very long and fruitful discussion, both the President and myself. I gave him a fairly quick synopsis of the whole situation: the relationship between the two Governments that are excellent, between Dublin and London; the talks that took place last year; the progress that was made there; the suspension of the talks. And I think the objective of both of us, and indeed, the British Government included, would be to get those talks resumed at an earlier stage.

We fully appreciate the keen interest and support of President Clinton in this regard and of his burning desire to have those talks recommenced. And he will keep in close consultation with all parties concerned so that we can get those talks resumed at the earliest possible date.

Q. You don't think that a special envoy at this point would be helpful?

Prime Minister Reynolds. As you have heard, the President just confirmed that both of those options are left open, and he will consult widely in the days and weeks and months ahead in relation to that. At the end of the day, it will be his decision.

Q. Mr. President, have you taken on board the unionists' concerns about—in Northern Ireland—the suggestions that you might send somebody who would attempt to mediate the peace situation?

President Clinton. Well, I don't think the United States can make peace in Northern Ireland, and I don't think that the unionists, the nationalists, anyone else would expect that. I think that we have a deep concern about the future of Ireland. We have a deep concern about ending the violence and the abuses of humanity which have been there. And I want to do whatever I can to support that process.

I do believe, I'll say again, I do believe that the dialog that was opened not all that long ago between these two Governments in Ireland and Great Britain offer the real chance of producing a framework within which peace could occur. And I am going to continue to stay on top of the situation, involved in it. I'll make those decisions at a later time when I think

they are appropriate. I think it is inappropriate now for me to do more than just to say that I think the Governments should in earnest embrace the opportunities that are before them. And I will be as supportive as I can. And whenever there seems to be something else I can do by taking further action, then I will do it. I don't want to do anything to undermine the peace process. I want to do something that will support it and reinforce it.

Secretary of Defense Les Aspin

Q. Mr. President, what about Secretary Aspin's health? Do you have to now consider, at least consider, having a new Secretary of Defense?

The President. No, people get pacemakers all the time. No. As far as I know he's just doing fine.

Northern Ireland

Q. Mr. President, do you still support the McBride principles which you said in your meeting with Irish leaders in New York——

The President. Yes, I do.

What did you say about Ray Flynn?

Mayor Raymond Flynn of Boston

Q. Aren't you concerned the country may be losing one of its better mayors?

The President. Yes, I am. [*Laughter*]

Press Secretary Myers. Thank you.

The President. It was a difficult decision for that reason. I think he's one of the best mayors to serve in the United States in my lifetime.

Q. Why did you offer him the job?

The President. Because I need him and because I think he'll do a great job in a whole wide range of areas. And he was willing to serve, and I want him in the administration.

Thank you.

NOTE: The President spoke at 12:07 p.m. in the Roosevelt Room at the White House. In his remarks, he referred to Valerie Place and Sean Devereux, Irish citizens who were killed in Somalia. He also referred to his intention to nominate Raymond Flynn to be Ambassador to the Holy See, which was formally announced on April 22.

Remarks to Treasury Department Employees
March 18, 1993

Thank you very much. Secretary Bentsen and ladies and gentlemen, thank you for that wonderful reception.

I have looked forward to this day when I might come to the Treasury for some time, and with somewhat mixed feelings. I read about this building since I was a boy. I remember, in the periods of my life when I was absolutely absorbed in the Civil War, reading about the trips that President Lincoln used to make across the street to come to the Treasury Department. I learned today from the Secretary that in 1830 the employees burned this building down. You know, I've done a lot to increase people's sense of empowerment, but I hope I didn't overdo it. [*Laughter*] I've also, quite frankly, heard that I would be humbled to the point of embarrassment if I walked into the offices of either the Secretary or the Deputy Secretary of the Treasury, that they would make the White House look like public housing. [*Laughter*] So I thought I'd show up and see.

Years ago, the whole Government used to be within walking distance of the White House, and I'm glad the Treasury still is. I'm glad that so many of you have worked so hard to help to put together the economic program that is now making its way through the Congress. And I want to thank you for that, and to echo what Secretary Bentsen said: that most Americans literally would have no idea, they would be staggered to know the hours that were put in by public servants in the preparation of this program and in the historic speed with which it was put together. I hope that you did it not only because you were here and it was your job but because you know what Americans feel, and that is that our national security today is tied as never before to our economic security, and that if we do not regain control of our economic destiny, we will soon lose the ability not only to provide for a future for our children but to lead the world that has come to look to us. That's why I asked the Secretary of the Treasury to serve on the National Security Council as well as on the National Economic Council; and why, when he met to meet with the leaders of the other G–7 nations and found himself treated with such respect, he helped

us in the conduct of American foreign policy as much as in the conduct of American domestic economic policy.

Our policy is a team effort. I tried to convince the White House staff and all of my Cabinet of that, and I say that to you. In Lloyd Bentsen, I think we have a Secretary of the Treasury with the unique capacity to command respect, not only in the halls of this building and among the financial leaders of the country but also in the Congress and in the world's financial and political capitals. And that is an invaluable asset. He's been my neighbor for a long time. I've known him for nearly 20 years and admired him for a long time. And when we were riding the bus on one of my numerous bus trips, this one across Texas, I made up my mind then that if the people elected me President of the United States that I would ask him to become Secretary of the Treasury. I think it's been a pretty good decision.

He has sought here in Deputy Secretary Altman, an old and trusted friend of mine of many, many years. We went to college together. He made money; I went into politics. [*Laughter*] Until I was elected President, my mother was absolutely convinced he had made the right decision. [*Laughter*] In Under-Secretary-designate Newman and Under-Secretary-designate Summers and so many others, I think we have a rare combination of intellect and experience, of people who are committed to making this country into the high-wage, high-growth nation that it ought to be.

In all the employees of the Treasury Department I have seen, I've noticed a rare commitment to serve this Nation conscientiously. And I must say, with the recent tragedies freshly in our minds, I think that we should all once again honor the plaque on the 4th floor of this building that notes more than 160 Treasury agents who have been killed in the line of duty in our Nation's history. From the Secret Service agents who protect our Presidents and who have a particular chore in me because I like to get out and see the people who put me in this job, to Customs agents who wage war on drugs, to the agents of the Bureau of Alcohol, Tobacco, and Firearms, many of the employees of this

Department risk their lives to protect the lives of the rest of us. My prayers and I'm sure yours are still with the families of all four of the Alcohol, Tobacco, and Firearms agents who were killed in Waco: Todd McKeehan and Conway Le Bleu of New Orleans, Steve Willis of Houston, and Robert Williams from my hometown of Little Rock. Three of those four were assigned to my security during the course of the primary or the general election. My gratitude is also with the Alcohol, Tobacco, and Firearms agents who helped to evacuate the World Trade Center in New York in the aftermath of the explosion and later, who helped to find the identification number of the van that led to the arrest of the first suspect in the bombing. I know that all of you join with me in praying for a peaceful and sure and quick conclusion to the events in Waco.

Here in this building, Treasury employees made extraordinary efforts—this has already been noted—in the preparation of the economic plan. And you are continuing to tackle some of the most important issues facing our country. I want to reemphasize what Secretary Bentsen said: The agenda that I have laid before the American people cannot be effective without the confident, committed, intense, consistent, and long-lasting efforts of the employees of the Department of the Treasury. From our efforts to find ways to control health care costs and provide coverage for every family, to our plan to ease the credit crunch on small businesses, to the plan to extend the earned-income tax credit to lift every working family out of poverty, to the proposal to create community development banks in the communities of this country where the poor are willing to work if they can access the free enterprise system, to our efforts to negotiate Russian debt relief and promote free institutions and free markets there and around the world, and to our effort to create a comprehensive strategy for global economic growth; all these things depend upon you and the employees of the Department of the Treasury. And every one of you, whether you consider your job large or small, is making an inestimable contribution to our efforts to adjust to the changes in the world that have dealt so much grief to the American people over the last several years that can bring so much hope and prosperity to the American people in the years ahead, if we can find a way to make these changes our friends and not our enemies. Indeed, I think you could make a very compelling case that the central challenge of this time is the challenge of making the changes that we cannot control, that are inevitably going to come anyway, the friends of the average American people instead of their enemy.

Even as we speak, the Congress is debating and deciding on the economic program, especially on the immediate jobs package. This economic stimulus will create a half a million jobs. It will create some jobs immediately that will build a foundation for more prosperity in the future. We have to start immediately investing in our children's schools, our workers' skills, our families' health, the transportation and communications networks that will make our communities more productive, our companies more profitable, and our people more secure over the long run. If we make these investments, we will create more jobs today and have a stronger economy tomorrow. Every element of this plan is designed to help Americans do better, to get the economy moving whether by generating jobs or increasing income, investing in the future or reducing the deficit that has so paralyzed our ability to control our own destiny. If we give the plan's elements a chance to work all together, we can make the changes we need. We can create a half a million new jobs in the short run, eight million during the term of this economic program, and make our next 20 years, most important of all, the best in our history.

There are those who still resist these changes, who prefer the status quo. They say we don't have to change anything. I say, just look around the world. Look at what happened in Europe for the last decade when they had two major economic recoveries that generated no new jobs. Look at what happened just last month, where our trade deficit went up, even though the American dollar went down because our trading partners, gripped in recession and without any new jobs and any incomes, couldn't buy any more of our products. Look at what has happened in this country, where the unemployment rate is higher today than it was at the depths of the recession, even though we just reported the biggest increase in productivity in 20 years in this country. It is clear that there needs to be a partnership between the private sector and the Government to get the economy going again in ways that generate incomes and jobs as well as show good economic statistics at the end of every month.

There are some who say, well, this program's all right, but we ought to do a little less of it. They are known affectionately as the "status quo lite" crowd over at the White House. [*Laughter*] Frankly, I think that if we do a little less of everything, we have a little less deficit reduction, a little less spending cuts, a little less tax increase, a little less investment, we'll get a lot less in results.

It is clear that the time has come to make a fundamental change in policy and direction in this country. We know that the things that we're doing will work. This plan contains an enormous incentive to increase private investment in the near-term in ways that will generate jobs. We know it contains a permanent investment incentive for small business, which until just a couple of years ago, had been the main generator of new jobs in this economy.

Indeed, you can make a compelling case that the recession we have endured in jobs is almost totally tied to the fact that the small business engine, that created more jobs than big business lost in the 1980's, came to a screeching halt in the last 2 years in the face of a recession, a credit crunch, the incredible burden of health care costs, and other costs on small business in adding new employees to their enterprises. We also have proposed some special incentives for new companies in high technology areas that will create the high-wage jobs of the future. All of these things should not be compromised. If you just take the last issue alone, the economist Lester Thurow has written a book called, "Head to Head," which estimates that most of the new high-wage jobs in the future will be created in seven areas of high technology, and that there is a limit to the total number of jobs the world can absorb in those areas, and that many of our competitors have planned for what will happen 10 years from now much better than we have.

We are playing catch-up in some areas where we appear to enjoy the lead. This program is designed to insure that we can keep that lead for 10 or 20 years, and that our economy and your future as public employees will be supported by that kind of technologically based job growth in the future. I believe that these things are critically important to our future. And I hope that the United States House of Representatives will vote today for new jobs and deficit reduction.

Let me also say that there are a lot of people programs that some question the value here of. But look at the plan for immunization. We know that if we immunize all children against the preventable childhood diseases, we would save over the course of their lives $10 in health care and lost economic benefits for every $1 we spend on immunization today. It works. We know that if we expand college opportunities to families of middle class people and low income people who otherwise couldn't afford to go to college or stay in college, we'll get more money back because of the earning power of college graduates and how much greater it is than the earning power of college dropouts or high school dropouts. We know that. And so when we invest in people in a world where what you earn depends so much on what you can learn, we know there will be a direct return to the taxpayers and to the rest of the people in this country.

These things are unobjectionable, but we've always found excuses not to make a full commitment. The toughest thing about this economic program is it requires so many difficult decisions, if you want to increase investment and reduce the deficit at the same time. That's never been done. We've reduced the deficit in times past, we've increased investment in times past, and we've had years where all we did was just let the present spending patterns spiral out of control, but we have never had a disciplined plan to reduce the debt and increase investment at the same time.

Look what this plan has produced in the markets. Look how much lower interest rates are just since the last election. I bet there are people in this room today who have refinanced a house or gotten the benefit of a variable interest rate on a credit card or gone out and bought a car at a lower interest rate because of the interest rates going down. There are Americans who have literally already gotten as much back in lower home mortgage payments, already, than they're going to pay in the energy tax for the next year or two. Because if you make real changes that are tangible, that people can see, they have real results.

So many times our Government has been burdened by blurring everything around the edges. I hope that today the House will make a clear statement to the American people that we're not going to blur this around the edges. We're going to have 150 and now, more cuts in specific spending programs. We're going to raise some taxes, even though they're tough, and make over

half of the money come from people who benefited most in the 1980's, those with incomes
above $200,000. We're going to have a balanced
program that also increases investment. And
we're going to say there really is a difference
in Government spending, that immunizing a
child or sending somebody to college is not the
same thing as spending more money every year
on the same health care. There is a real difference. There is a difference, and it matters.

Let me say, finally, that I appreciate, more
than I can say, the work that you have done
and the sacrifices that you will have to make
to make this economic program work. The Vice
President has been asked by me to head a program on reviewing the entire performance of
the Federal Government, trying to find ways
to, in effect, reinvent the way Government operates. And he told me right before I came over
here that he was well aware that Treasury had
been among the leading Departments in installing quality management techniques and doing
other things that would modernize the operations of Government. We have some money
in the stimulus package that will help you to
modernize the operations of Government further. And when he comes back I hope you will
be willing to meet with him and work with
him and, in the meanwhile, remember we have
6 months to try to get the best ideas we can
from all the Federal employees in the country
about how to save more money and increase
our ability to serve our customers, the American
people. So if you have those ideas I ask you
to give them to the Vice President.

Finally, let me say that the end result of all
of this has to be to help our country work better, has to be to improve the lives of the American people. I hope that by my coming here
today millions of Americans who never thought
about the Treasury Department will know that
you're here working for them. And I hope you
will know how very grateful I am for all you
have done and all you must do if this program
to turn America around is to succeed.

Thank you very much.

NOTE: The President spoke at 11:48 a.m. in the
Cash Room at the Treasury Department.

Nomination for Deputy Secretary of Transportation
March 18, 1993

The President today announced his intention
to nominate Mortimer L. Downey, the Executive Director and Chief Financial Officer of the
Metropolitan Transit Authority of New York
City, to be the Deputy Secretary of Transportation.

"There are few people in this country who
can match the experience or the expertise of
Mortimer Downey," said the President. "I am
very pleased that he is joining Secretary Peña
at a Department that will play a key role in
implementing my economic plan, as well as in
improving our Nation's transportation system."

NOTE: A biography of the nominee was made
available by the Office of the Press Secretary.

Nomination for the Office of the United States Trade Representative
March 18, 1993

The President announced today his intention
to nominate Rufus Yerxa and Charlene
Barshefsky as Deputy U.S. Trade Representatives, and his approval of the appointment by
Ambassador Mickey Kantor of the following:

Ira Shapiro, General Counsel

Nancy LeaMond, Assistant U.S. Trade Representative for Congressional Affairs
Anne Luzzatto, Assistant U.S. Trade Representative for Public Affairs
Debbie Shon, Assistant U.S. Trade Representative for Intergovernmental Affairs and

Public Liaison
Ellen Frost, Counselor
Howard Reed, Special Counsel for Financial and Investment Policy
Tom Nides, Special Counsel for Congressional and Intergovernmental Affairs

"We are at a key moment in the history of American trade policy," said the President.

"Rufus Yerxa, Charlene Barshefsky, and the outstanding team that Ambassador Kantor has put together will work hard to make sure that we do not miss the opportunities that lay ahead of us."

NOTE: Biographies of the nominees were made available by the Office of the Press Secretary.

Remarks at a Breakfast for Members of the House of Representatives
March 19, 1993

Last night I went to bed early—at 1:15 a.m.—for you, and I was taking odds on how many of you would actually be here this morning at 8:30 a.m. [*Laughter*] This may be a greater test of loyalty than the votes yesterday. [*Laughter*]

I want to say to you, Mr. Speaker, a special word of thanks, and in his absence, to Mr. Gephardt, to whom I talked last night sometime after midnight. I want to thank you, David Bonior, for your work. And I want to say a special word of thanks for the southern-drawled discipline of Butler Derrick, the fine job he did. I love to listen to Butler talk. He makes me sound like a Yankee. [*Laughter*] I'd also like to thank the other leaders up here on the platform but especially the two chairs who are here, Mr. Natcher and Mr. Sabo, for the work they did.

And I want to thank, of course, most of all, all of you for what you did yesterday. And I want to thank your constituents, the people who made this possible. If it hadn't been for the American people voting for a change in direction in this country, communicating that to you, and telling you that they would stay behind you if you made the tough decisions, none of this would have been possible.

Yesterday was a great day of victory for ordinary Americans and for the proposition that this Government can work for them again, that we don't have to be mired in gridlock, that we don't have to spend all of our time posturing and dividing and running for cover instead of moving into the future. It was a wonderful beginning. I think it's important to remember that it's just a beginning, that you now have to encourage your colleagues on the other side of

the Capitol to act and that we all have to continue to stay in touch with the people who sent us here. When I leave you today, I'm going to Atlanta to try to continue my dialog with the American people and to say we still have a great deal of work to do to create the jobs and invest in our people and reduce the deficit. But people know that it's working.

You know, this last week I have had to take a good deal of time off to deal with the foreign policy responsibilities of the President. But one of the most interesting things that happened during the last week is that every world leader with whom I met at some point during the conversation said that America seems to be on the move again, that it's exciting to see so much happening here.

I just want to say on behalf of all of you who were working last night, who missed the White House correspondents' dinner, I'll give you a list of my jokes on the way out—[*laughter*]—but you won't have to endure them again.

We are looking forward, the Vice President and I and all of our family, to working with you as we complete this work. This can be a historic year for this country. You acted with unbelievable dispatch. I don't think that a budget resolution has ever been passed so quickly and one has ever been this comprehensive and acted on this quickly. It is a wonderful beginning but is just the beginning. And let's, all of us, determine that we're not going to quit until our job is done. Let's urge the people, as I said, in the Senate to join hands with us and move forward quickly now. And let's stay in touch with the folks back home and tell them what we're really doing is giving the Government back to them.

Thank you very much, and God bless you.

NOTE: The President spoke at 8:55 a.m. in the East Room at the White House.

Remarks on the Retirement of Supreme Court Justice Byron R. White and an Exchange With Reporters
March 19, 1993

The President. Let me say, as all of you know, I received a letter not long ago from Justice White expressing his intention to resign from the Court at the end of this term and saying that he wanted to give me this much notice so that hopefully I could announce my intention to nominate someone and all the hearings could be concluded in time to really prepare someone to serve at the beginning of the October term of the Court.

I called Justice White just a few moments ago and had a fine conversation with him. I've known him for nearly 20 years, and I thanked him for his service to our country. He's had a truly remarkable life. And I appreciate the fact that he cared enough about the Court as an institution to offer me a significant period of time to deliberate and still to have plenty of time to have a nominee considered by the Senate and then confirmed well in advance of the beginning of the Court's next term.

So I will begin work on this tomorrow in earnest. And I will attempt to be faithful to my Constitutional duties and appoint a truly outstanding American in a timely fashion.

Potential Supreme Court Nominees

Q. [*Inaudible*]—you once mentioned Governor Cuomo before.

The President. I don't want to get into personalities now. This is Mr. Justice White's day. And as I said, I never will forget sitting in the Supreme Court as a young attorney general and having had him already tell me that the quality of representation by the States was pretty poor. And then I had worked very hard with a lawyer from my State who was making the argument, and he sent me a note, which I still have in my personal files 16 years later, saying that we

were doing better. So that's what I'm going to try to do every day.

Q. Do you have a long list of possible nominees?

The President. No. The list may get longer; it may get shorter. I did not anticipate having the opportunity to make an appointment at this early stage, so we don't have a big bank of potential nominees. I'll go to work on it tomorrow. I don't want to discuss any individuals at this point. I will do my best to pick a truly outstanding person just as soon as I can.

Bosnia

Q. [*Inaudible*]—is to get people out of Bosnia. Are you going to be able to comply with that request?

The President. President Mitterrand and I talked the other day, and he told me he was going to give some helicopters, which, as you know, he's done. And this morning was the first I have been informed of that. So we're going to discuss that today and make a decision.

Abortion

Q. Is abortion a litmus test for a Supreme Court nominee? Is that the whole issue?

The President. Now, the question as you ask it contains a thousand questions. And I wouldn't say no, and a thousand questions no. Do I believe that there is a constitutional right to privacy? Yes, I do.

Thank you.

NOTE: The President spoke at 9:55 a.m. on the South Lawn at the White House upon departure for Atlanta, GA. In his remarks, he referred to President François Mitterrand of France.

Statement on the Retirement of Supreme Court Justice Byron R. White
March 19, 1993

This morning I received a letter from Justice Byron White informing me that he intends to retire at the end of the current Supreme Court term.

He is a living example of the American dream fulfilled. He came from humble beginnings, was a star college and professional athlete, a Rhodes scholar, a prominent private attorney, and Deputy Attorney General at one of the most important times in our history before joining the Court in 1962. In his 31 years on the Supreme Court, Justice White served his country and our Constitution well. We are all more fortunate that he devoted the great portion of his life to public service.

Remarks at the Downtown Child Development Center in Atlanta, GA
March 19, 1993

Well, first of all, I would like to thank Cheryl and all the people at this wonderful center for giving me a few minutes' break out of my normal schedule. The Mayor and I talked about business on the way in from the airport, and then I got to help put a puzzle together and play a drum and do some things that are more fun than what I do most days. [*Laughter*]

Let me begin by saying that last night the House of Representatives cast an historic set of votes. Among those in the leadership was your Congressman, John Lewis, who is here with me now, a longtime friend of mine. The House voted to do something that our country, as far as I can tell from my reading of history, has never done before at the same time. They voted to make a drastic cut in the Federal deficit and at the same time to invest some new money in the children of the country, through preschool programs and nutrition programs and education programs, and in new jobs for the American people. And I wanted to come here to Atlanta today to talk about it and to try to help to keep the American people informed of what the House has done and what the Senate must now do and what we still have to do to pass this budget. I wanted to come here to this child care center because the children who are here, the children of working parents, desperately need the kinds of opportunities that are provided here and that we're trying to provide there.

Just on the way in something happened that we couldn't have organized, Cheryl, neither you nor I, if we tried to do this. A man was standing outside this center with a child in his arms saying, "If I could afford to get my child in a good center like this, then I could take a job even at minimum wages and support my child." It was very touching. He just happened to be in the crowd outside.

So I guess what I'd like to do is just to ask all of you to tell me what I, as President, can do to help to continue to support these kinds of projects, maybe get Federal Agencies in other cities to do the same thing you've done, perhaps work on enhancing the child care incentives in the Federal program. But I'd like to know what you think I can do to help to deal with this problem. Because as I go around the country, next to the cost of health care and the fear of losing health insurance, the availability and quality and affordability of child care are the things that working parents most often mention to me, after health care. So I just wanted to come here and listen for a while.

NOTE: The President spoke at 1:05 p.m. at the center. In his remarks, he referred to Cheryl Smith, director of the center, and Maynard Jackson, Mayor of Atlanta.

Exchange With Reporters in Atlanta
March 19, 1993

Potential Supreme Court Nominee

Q. Mr. President, excuse the interruption, sir, but could you give us some feel for what you'll be looking for in a replacement for Justice White?

The President. I already said that in Washington. I used to teach constitutional law, and I think that there are few decisions the President makes which are more weighty, more significant, or can have a greater impact on more Americans than an appointment to the Supreme Court. And I'm going to try to pick a person that has a fine mind, good judgment, wide experience in the law and in the problems of real people, and someone with a big heart.

NOTE: The exchange began at 1:10 p.m. at the Downtown Child Development Center.

Remarks to the Business Community in Atlanta
March 19, 1993

Thank you very much. Virgil, I'm glad I let you introduce me. [*Laughter*] I'm delighted to be here with so many distinguished Georgians, the people here on the platform with me today, including Virgil Williams, who really did do a good job. And there are some days I wish I were called Governor again. [*Laughter*]

People ask me all the time, is it different being President? And the truth is, it is, in ways that are wonderful and ways that aren't so good. But I had an encounter the other day which describes, better than any words I could say, what's right and what's wrong with it. I was up in the White House in the Residence part, and I had to go back down to the first floor to a big meeting. And my wife had been having a meeting there that I didn't know anything about. It wasn't public, you know. [*Laughter*] And anyway, so I got down to the first floor, and these throngs of people were there. And I just walked right out of the elevator into them, which was nice. They were people I didn't know, and I stopped, shook hands with them all, and talked to them. And this young man I was with, who had come to work at the White House during a previous administration, was just aghast. He said, "Oh, Mr. President, I'm so sorry that I got you in the middle of all these people." And I said, "That's okay, I used to be one." [*Laughter*]

I want to thank John Portman and Sam Williams and Peg Canter and Doug Miller for hosting me and welcoming me here to the Atlanta Apparel Mart. I want to say a special word of thanks to these distinguished business leaders who are up here on the platform; thank my good friend Governor Miller—I'm glad to see Governor and Mrs. Miller here—for meeting me outside; and for Mayor Jackson, who rode in with me and asked me to do more for Atlanta. [*Laughter*] You know, I don't know what I'd ever do if I came to Atlanta without a suit coat because I always have the Maynard Jackson memorial list. [*Laughter*] And I actually got gigged today in the office before I left the White House; they said, now be sure and remember to leave Maynard's list on the desk tonight when you get back so we can go to work on it. [*Laughter*]

I flew down here with a number of members of your congressional delegation who had a great, great night last night. I thank them for their presence here. And I'm glad to see many others in the audience, Andy Young and Max Cleland and others who are here. I thank you all for being here.

It was just a few days ago that I celebrated—and I did celebrate; I wrote Zell a note about it—the first anniversary of the Georgia Democratic primary, when all the experts were saying that if I didn't receive 40 percent of the vote here, I would have to pack up my tent and go home. And thanks to you, some of you, anyway, who voted in the primary, I got—[*laughter*]—57 percent, and I didn't have to pack up my tent and go home.

This is the first opportunity I've had to come back to Georgia since your State gave your electoral votes to the Clinton-Gore ticket in November. I want to tell you how very grateful I am for that and how much I enjoy working with your Representatives and how dedicated I think the people in Washington are now to break the gridlock that has gripped our country for too long. Not only did the folks in the House delegation who flew down with me today cast some historic votes last night, but there were also some attempts to derail our program in the United States Senate last night. And they too fell short, even though they were very carefully developed to be as attractive as possible. And I thank Senator Nunn for his help in maintaining the integrity of the program yesterday in the Senate, too.

When the House of Representatives acted last night to pass the budget resolution and to pass the emergency jobs program, they did something that our country, as nearly as I can tell from my study of our history, has never before done. They actually voted at the same time to reduce the national debt and to increase our investment in jobs and in education, in the new technologies of the future, and helping us to adjust to the defense cutbacks and to the rigors of the global economy. Reduce the deficit; increase investment. In order to do it, they had to take some very tough positions. They had to vote to reduce spending in very specific ways, not just general rhetoric but real specific commitments to reduce spending. They had to vote to raise taxes after more than a decade of being told that that was always a bad thing to do. And they had to draw clear distinctions between different kinds of Government spending.

As Virgil said in the introduction, here at the grassroots level of America, if you're running a business or if you're running a city or if you're running a State government, you know there is a difference between investing in education and job growth and infrastructure and the things that will increase productivity and wealth and employment, and just expanding programs that may or may not work or taking more people to do the same thing. For too long in Washington there has been no distinction, so we've had this unbelievable irony for 12 years in which the deficit has gone up, but our investment in the future has gone down. And we have paid a terrific price for it.

I hope and believe that the process of real renewal has begun, but only begun. On the 57th day of this administration, our economic plan is almost halfway home. The new direction is designed to meet the needs of the broad middle class of America again for jobs and for schools, for bringing a college education back within the reach of ordinary people, and bringing down the cost of health care and extending its reach. It's about giving the poor a chance to work their way out of poverty and welfare and dependence, about investing wisely again in our future, about helping all Americans and especially our children to be stronger and healthier and smarter so that they can realize their full potential and our country can maintain its economic superiority, without which we cannot hope to lead the world in this new era.

At the same time, we're actually wasting a lot less of the taxpayers' money. We've cut 150 specific programs, and there are more on the way. Tens of billions of dollars in spending have been cut. And under this budget resolution, not one penny in taxes can be raised unless we also cut spending in the amounts prescribed.

The new direction is also about changing the nature of the way Government works. The Government that I inherited, through no particular person or party's fault perhaps, is too large, too slow, too distant, and often too old in its approach to solving problems. I am committed to changing the way the Government operates, starting at the top with my own budget and taking a look at every program and every Agency. I have asked the Vice President to take 6 months to take advantage of the best talent we can find and to review the operations of every single Government Agency and program with a view toward not just cutting unnecessary spending but literally changing the whole way Government works: relying more on markets and incentives, eliminating unnecessary layers of management, pushing decisions down to the lowest possible level, taking full advantage of technology.

I discovered that in the White House alone, if we could invest $4.7 million in new technology, in communications technology and other technology, we could save over $10 million a year in payroll. And we could do it in spite of the fact that we are now getting 34,000 letters a day. And we are trying to set up a system where we can actually answer them. The White House operation historically has been so antiquated that at least two-thirds of the letters that came in never got answered at all. And usually they were those that, to keep faith with the American people, perhaps should have been answered first. Often letters that were critical were just thrown away as negative mail, because literally there was no capacity to handle it. Thousands of people every day want to call the White House, but the switchboard was put there when Lyndon Johnson was President, and people still pick up wires and plug them into holes when the calls are made. When I became President, I walked into the Oval Office and found the telephone system that President Jimmy Carter had operated with. And I found that I couldn't have a conference call, but when the light came on on my phone, anybody in the central office of the White House could push their lighted button down and have a conference call I didn't want. [*Laughter*]

Now, that's funny, but it says something about the tendency of Government to add layer upon layer upon layer to the way things used to be, when new things have to be done, rather than stopping old things while you start new things and changing the way things work. The longer you've got a monopoly on money and a monopoly on customers, there is very little incentive out there to change. But there is no real monopoly anymore because there's a limit to how much the Government can take out of the economy and we are constrained by what we have to spend on defense, on health care, on interest on the debt, and other things. So the Government is compelled to reexamine the way we do our business. And I think we're going to have some very exciting things to show for our efforts in the weeks and months ahead.

The plan I ask the American people to embrace and to support the Congress in embracing is a thoughtful one, built piece by piece, a strategy that looks at the entire picture of America and asks what we have to do to ensure growth. It's a plan for short-term job creation and long-term prosperity, a chance to invest and prosper in a free market system, to improve education and training for a lifetime, to make health care more affordable and accessible, to make our streets safer, and more importantly, to give our people a chance to be involved in the large work of keeping our country moving forward.

One of the most frustrating things to me about the year and a half that I crossed this country in the campaign was the number of people I met who had simply given up on the

system. Now if we get 34,000 letters a day and half of them are critical, I count that as a good day, because it means that people believe they can write their President and somebody will be there listening and paying attention. People believe the system will work again. There was a poll in New Jersey last week—one of two States that have elections for Governor in this off-year—saying that 18 percent of the people who are going to vote in this election this year voted for the very first time in the Presidential election in 1992. The Los Angeles Times poll said that 70 percent of the American people had actually discussed the economic plan I presented to the Congress and to the people with one of their friends or neighbors or family members. That means democracy is on the march again in America, and people believe the system can be made to work for them. And that is in itself a victory for the efforts that we are all making.

Make no mistake. I know that there are many roadblocks ahead. I know that I'll make some mistakes along the way. And I know, too, there are still guardians of gridlock in Washington who will fight fundamental change. There are those now who say that we ought to cut the investments that I propose to make in families and children, in jobs and education and health care, make them vulnerable, and then we won't have to ask as much from others in either tax increases or spending cuts in older programs.

There are about 80,000 lobbyists in and around Washington. By some estimates, they spend nearly $1 billion a year protecting the various interests they're hired to protect. They get a tax deduction to do it, for a while. But the kind of children I saw today in the joint public-private child care center I visited before coming over here don't have much of a lobby in Washington. Pregnant mothers or out of work or hard-working parents don't have a lot of time to hire people to roam the halls of Congress to stick up for them. Those who are neither wealthy nor organized, no matter what they're doing, are very often the most voiceless and powerless in our system, even though they may carry the day in whether our free enterprise system actually works or not. That's why it's the President's job to try to speak and fight for them. It's why we have to encourage those in Congress to stand ready to vote for change.

Yesterday's vote in the House is really a huge step in that direction. You ought to talk to John Lewis or the others who are here, Nathan Deal and Buddy Darden or Cynthia McKinney or Don Johnson, and ask them what it was like last night—Sanford Bishop—ask them what it was like when we get 218 votes and all of a sudden people say, "My God, we actually did something here for a change. We've got something to go home and talk about. Even if somebody jumps on us, at least they'll jump on us for doing something instead of for not doing something."

A few weeks ago I went with Senator Moynihan of New York to New York. We flew into an Air Force facility, and then we drove for about 50 minutes to Franklin Roosevelt's hometown in Hyde Park. There were hundreds of people along the way—8, 10 degrees outside, people standing outside holding their signs up. One person had a sign that I thought was pretty reflective of the American public mood. It said, "Just do something." [*Laughter*] Just do something.

Well, the Congress has acted in a fundamental departure from the status quo. They proved that change is possible. And let me just give you one example that has already taken place. Last year when this recession started going way, way too long and no new jobs were being created, the Federal Reserve Board began to lower the Government's rediscount rate in an earnest attempt to bring interest rates down. And interest rates came down some. But there was still a huge gap between the rate that the Government charged bankers and the long-term interest rates in this country. Just since the election, since this deficit reduction plan has come out, interest rates have been down between .8 percent and one full percentage point, floating back and forth more or less in that range.

I'll bet you if I ask for a show of hands in this room, there are a lot of people in this room that, in the last 4 months, have refinanced a house or have benefited from a changing interest rate on a business loan or a car loan or credit card purchases. There are millions and millions of Americans who, in the first 6 months of this year, will save more money in interest payments than they'll pay in the energy tax I propose for the full 4 years of this administration. That is what happens if you gain control of your economic destiny, if you keep interest rates down, if you bring this deficit down, and if you have a plan for long-term growth.

I've had to put on my foreign policy hat a little bit in the last 10 days, meeting with leaders around the world. I've seen in the last several weeks the Prime Ministers of Canada and Great Britain and then recently the President of France and the President of Haiti and the head of the European Community and the Prime Minister of Israel. And sooner or later, it always gets around to a conversation where they say, you know—particularly the Europeans say—America is on the move again. You've restored people's feeling that the Government can actually work with the people in a country and get something going again. It can make a difference again. And that is what I came here to ask for your support for today: Not to agree with everything I say or do; I'm sure I've made some mistakes, and I'll make some more. But I think we ought to get up and go to work every day, and I think we ought to make a difference.

We're working hard first to fix this economy, to bring the deficit down, and then to face the other problems ahead of us. We need to pass, and I want to emphasize this, we need to pass what is a modest but important stimulus program to create a half a million jobs in the short run. We need to do it for a couple of reasons. First of all, the program is targeted to give businesses that are creating jobs more incentive to invest to create more jobs, and secondly, to target public spending programs into projects that are ready to go and designed to be guaranteed to produce new jobs. And, secondly, in a larger sense, we need to do it because all the wealthier countries in the world, not just the United States, all of them are having great difficulty now, even in times of economic recovery, in creating new jobs. In the last decade, Europe had two big economic recovery periods, created virtually no new jobs, even though incomes were going up, profits were going up, new jobs were not coming into the economy.

In the last 2 or 3 years, that's started to happen in the United States. All during the 1980's, the largest companies in America downsized, just the way I'm trying to downsize the Federal Government. They had to do it to be more competitive. But in every year of the eighties, small business created more jobs than larger businesses lost. Then, the last couple of years, that whole trend came to a screeching halt. There were a lot of reasons: the recession, the cost of health care, the credit crunch, the enormous cumulative cost of adding a new employee to a small business work force.

In the last month, we had 365,000 new jobs.

That's the good news. The bad news is that more than half of them were part-time jobs, jobs that didn't contain a full income and couldn't provide for health care coverage for the family. Every month now, because of the changing mix in our economy, 100,000 Americans are losing their health insurance. So there are severe problems in this economy that we have to address to create the jobs. Let me just mention a couple of things that we're trying to do, particularly to focus on small business.

We have announced a Governmentwide program with every Agency that regulates our financial institutions to try to end the credit crunch on small business and give banks the flexibility they need to make good loans to worthy customers in the small business sector and to drastically, and I mean drastically, cut the paperwork required to access Government programs and to comply with the regulatory requirements.

We have proposed a program that would give small businesses—90 percent of the employers employing 40 percent of the people but providing way over half the new jobs—a permanent investment tax credit so that they'll always have more incentives to plow money back into the business.

We have taken steps to pass a budget which will contain billions of dollars in funds to help to deal with these terrible, terrible economic problems caused by defense cutbacks and base closings by not only retraining workers at very high levels but also providing joint ventures in new technologies so that defense contractors will have a fighting chance to get into technologies that have both civilian and defense uses, or entirely civilian uses, to create the jobs of the future.

These are just some of the things that have to be done to keep our eye on the ball. The purpose of bringing the deficit down is to make the economy work, which means we've got to both bring the deficit down and focus on these investments. We've got to change the nature of Federal spending: less consumption, more investment.

And finally, in order to get that done, we're going to have to face the health care crisis in America. It is projected that if we do nothing to change Government spending patterns on health care, listen to this, in 5 years, adding no new benefits—adding no new benefits—in 5 years, your tax bill for paying for Medicare and Medicaid will go from $210 billion to $350 billion, a 67 percent increase in 5 years with no new benefits, because of the explosion of health care costs and the explosion in the number of people who will be forced onto the public health care rolls as people cannot afford anymore to insure their employees.

This is a devastating blow to our efforts to reduce the deficit. If you want us to bring the budget into balance, you must insist that after we pass this budget, we move on to find a way to bring health costs in line with inflation and provide a basic package of health care to all of our people. Every other country in the world, except the United States, has figured out a way to do that. Let me tell you what will happen if we don't. By the end of the decade we'll be spending 20 percent of every dollar, 20 cents on the dollar, on health care. And none of our competitors will be over a dime, and we will be in a serious hole in terms of trying to be competitive. We also cannot balance the budget.

The flip side of that is if by working in partnership with providers, employers, and employee groups, we can bring health costs in line with inflation without sacrificing quality, we can emphasize preventive and primary care, we can provide a way for everybody to have basic coverage, we can guarantee people that they won't lose their health insurance if somebody in their family's been sick, or if their own business goes down, if we can do that, we can free up hundreds of billions of dollars.

If you look at the projected increases in health care costs, bringing health costs in line with inflation would do more to stimulate the private economy, even in keeping interest rates down, and much more than any tax cut or any Government spending program we can hope to put out there. So that is the next big challenge for us. But first we've got to pass the economic program.

So I ask all of you today to bring to your views of the National Government the spirit that I see in Atlanta: the idea that the Government and the business sector ought to be in a partnership, the idea that there's a difference between investment and consumption, the idea that you can't run from your problems so you might as well face them and try to do something about them and make progress on them. Those are the things that I saw in that child care center here today. That is the spirit that brought the Olympics to Atlanta. That is the spirit behind the old motto you had when my State had its misfortune in the racial crisis in 1957 and Atlanta called itself "the city that was too busy to hate."

That is what you have to do as a citizen of the United States: Support the Members of the Congress that are up there trying to get something done. Support the idea that we can reduce the deficit and increase investment and create jobs. Support the idea that gridlock is not good for anybody except people who like to hear the gears squeal. Support the idea that we have to change in order to renew the American dream.

We are moving in the right direction. Last night was an exhilarating first step. But believe me, you can ask any Member of the United States Congress, they did not count that a victory for themselves last night: It was a victory for you. They know that they will do only what they believe you want them to do. The people of this country are back in the driver's seat; it's time to put your foot on the accelerator and stay in the middle of the road.

Thank you, and God bless you all.

NOTE: The President spoke at 2:02 p.m. at the Apparel Mart. In his remarks, he referred to Virgil R. Williams, president and chief executive officer, Williams Communications, Inc.; John Portman, chairman, Portman Companies; Sam Williams, president, Atlanta Market Center; Peg Canter, general manager, Apparel Mart; Doug Miller, general manager, Atlanta Market Center Trade Shows; Zell Miller, Governor of Georgia; Andrew Young, chief executive officer, Law International, and former Mayor of Atlanta; and Max Cleland, Georgia Secretary of State.

Nomination for Posts at the Departments of Veterans Affairs, State, and Housing and Urban Development
March 19, 1993

The President announced today his choices for four senior positions at the Departments of Veterans Affairs, State, and Housing and Urban Development. He expressed his intention to nominate the following:

Jerry Bowen, Director, National Cemetery System, Department of Veterans Affairs

Mark Catlett, Assistant Secretary for Finance and Information Resources Management, Department of Veterans Affairs

Daniel Tarullo, Assistant Secretary for Economic and Business Affairs, Department of State

Susan Gaffney, Inspector General, Department of Housing and Urban Development

"I am very pleased with the pace of the nominations that we have been making," said the President. "This week alone, I have named more than 30 people to fill important positions in the day-to-day operations of the Federal Government," he added.

NOTE: Biographies of the nominees were made available by the Office of the Press Secretary.

The President's Radio Address
March 20, 1993

Good morning. Today I want to give you a progress report on our plans to get the country moving again. With the support of so many Americans, including many of you listening today, we won an important victory on Capitol Hill this week. The House of Representatives approved the economic package and with it an immediate crucial investment program to create jobs that will be like a booster rocket for our economy.

It was a week that reaffirmed why I came to Washington: to deliver the kind of change you demanded when you cast your ballots last November. It's significant, I think, that I can bring you this news on the first day of spring. It may be gloomy or even cold where you are right now, but the signs of the season are unmistakable. In Washington the snow is melting, trees are budding, and outside the window of the Oval Office birds are announcing their return. And there's something else in the air. Exactly 2 months ago at my Inauguration as your President, I said that together we could force a season of growth and renewal. I'm happy to tell you today that we're on our way to that kind of spring, too.

We thank all the Congressmen and Congresswomen who carried the day for all of us. But mostly the credit goes to you, the American people, because after all, you issued the challenge and demanded the change. Your message was loud and clear. You said no more status quo. And that message must continue to ring in the ears of all our lawmakers. It should drown out the drone of special interests who would decimate the plan bit by bit until we're back to where we began.

I know you don't want that. You didn't vote for half measures or excuses or business as usual. Because you demanded change, we've begun to turn our back on the long winter of trickle-down economics, moving toward investing in people and their jobs and education and health care and in the future. The price of doing nothing is too high. You've already seen what more than a decade of neglect can do. We're losing our competitive edge in the world. At home, our highways and mass transit systems were falling into disrepair; cities deteriorating; rural areas suffering; and most important, families, especially middle income families, were feeling enormous strains.

On all these fronts there is ground to be regained and advances to be made. Every part of our program is aimed at making lives better across the Nation. And it does it with investments paid for dollar by dollar by cuts in spending.

With our plan, we'll build up our job base. Small businesses, the source of more than half the jobs held by Americans, will get the help with freer access to credit, with investment tax credits and urban enterprise zones and special capital gains for new enterprises. At the same time, we'll invest more in research and development for new technologies and to convert defense technology. And that will help us stay competitive globally. With our investment in lifelong learning, we'll give Americans the tools they need to stay sharp in the changing job market.

Our plan takes care of our children, too. We want to immunize every child against infectious diseases, to get them off on the right foot with Head Start, to help mothers and infants to get the nutrition they need. It's the smart thing to do and the right investment to make. Every dollar we invest today will give us back many more dollars tomorrow. Just yesterday I saw what investments in children can bring. I was in Atlanta where parents, teachers, and business leaders have joined forces to create a Downtown Child Development Center. In every direction I looked, I saw small faces with big smiles. It's a nurturing environment that produces happy kids, productive parents, and satisfied employers. In many ways, it's a microcosm of what we want for America.

Our economic recovery package may be the boldest economic plan that Congress has ever seen. In addition to the investments, the plan passed by the House will reduce the Federal deficit by $510 billion in the next 5 years. If we can make these changes, our children will live better, more prosperous lives.

Make no mistake about it, this is a bold plan, because we need bold change. You know it; that's what you asked for. The American people are, by their very nature, people of action. It's been very frustrating to have more than a decade of policies that run up the deficit and ran down morale and investment. And it's been more frustrating still to see Government in gridlock where nothing profoundly important ever happens.

Our plan to cut spending and increase investment in the future of our country is now being considered in the United States Senate. In Washington, your voices are being heard, so I urge you to raise them. We need to enlist the Senators now in our cause to break gridlock and get the economy moving. Please encourage your Senators to support the economic plan, to create jobs and boost incomes and reduce our national debt.

The sooner our plan becomes a reality, the sooner we'll be shifting the gears of our economy out of neutral and into drive. You're in the driver's seat now. I urge you, make sure your foot's off the brake, step on the accelerator,

and help move this country forward.
   Thanks for listening.

NOTE: The President spoke at 10:10 a.m. from the Oval Office at the White House.

Letter to Congressional Leaders Reporting on Iraq's Compliance With United Nations Security Council Resolutions
March 22, 1993

Dear Mr. Speaker: (Dear Mr. President:)

Consistent with the Authorization for Use of Military Force Against Iraq Resolution (Public Law 102–1) and in an effort to keep the Congress fully informed, I am reporting on the status of efforts to obtain Iraq's compliance with the resolutions adopted by the U.N. Security Council.

Under my Administration, the United States will continue to lead international efforts aimed at ensuring that the Iraqi regime does not threaten international peace and security and at ending the Iraqi Government's brutal repression of its people. To that end, we will maintain our insistence on full Iraqi compliance with U.N. Security Council resolutions. We will work with the international community to ensure the integrity of the U.N. sanctions regime, which is the best means to promote Iraqi compliance.

In accordance with U.N. Security Council Resolution 687, the U.N. Special Commission on Iraq (UNSCOM) and the International Atomic Energy Agency (IAEA) have continued to investigate Iraq's weapons of mass destruction (WMD) programs and to verify the destruction of relevant facilities, equipment, and weapons. Destruction of chemical munitions at Al Muthanna has continued.

UNSCOM #48, a missile team, and UNSCOM #49/IAEA #17, a nuclear team, arrived in Iraq just a week after the cruise missile attack on the Al Zaafaraniyah nuclear-related facility. The nuclear team inspected the Al Zaafaraniyah site, confirmed that only buildings with technical functions had been hit, and verified the destruction of many highly sensitive machine tools. After initial resistance, Iraqi officials have permitted baseline inventories of the Ibn Al Haytham Research Center; this is an important but limited step in enabling UNSCOM to move toward comprehensive evaluation and long-term monitoring of Iraqi WMD capabilities.

The inspections were successful in eliciting new details of Iraqi WMD programs and an admission from Iraqi officials that they attempted to deceive a previous UNSCOM team.

A missile team designated as UNSCOM #50 discovered a small discrepancy in the inventory of missile propellant at one site. During this inspection, the Iraqi side argued that UNSCOM should not be permitted to use Global Positioning System equipment to identify the precise locations of sites visited. Iraq alleges inaccurately that such readings were used by the U.S. military to target the Al Zaafaraniyah site. UNSCOM rejected this argument. On February 22, the team was redesignated as UNSCOM #51 and searched for possible SCUD sites west of Baghdad.

Iraqi harassment of inspectors and interference with UNSCOM and IAEA activities have resumed, after a lull immediately following the attack on Al Zaafaraniyah. Iraqi authorities also threatened to shoot down a helicopter performing support for a ground inspection that UNSCOM #51 was carrying out. In early February, an Iraqi, possibly an official "minder" for the inspectors, threw a rock through the window of an UNSCOM vehicle.

Iraq continues to refuse to provide the United Nations and IAEA with a comprehensive list of the suppliers for its WMD programs. Moreover, it refuses to accept U.N. Security Council Resolution 715, which mandates the creation of a long-term monitoring regime for Iraq's WMD infrastructure. The international community must insist on such long-term monitoring.

The United Nations has continued its work to settle the Iraq-Kuwait border. The Iraq-Kuwait Boundary Demarcation Commission continues its work, without Iraqi participation. At its December meeting, the Commission agreed to begin to demarcate the offshore section of the boundary "with the principal purpose . . . being navigational access for both parties."

In response to continued Iraqi violations of the border and the demilitarized zone (DMZ), the U.N. Security Council adopted Resolution 806 on February 5. The Resolution clarified that the United Nations Iraq-Kuwait Observer Mission (UNIKOM) can take any necessary actions to prevent such violations and authorized a potential increase in UNIKOM forces from 250 to 3,600 troops. The United Nations is seeking to identify countries willing to contribute an armed battalion for this purpose.

Evidence continues to mount concerning the massive extent of the Iraqi Government's human rights violations, both before and after the Persian Gulf War. Max van der Stoel, Rapporteur of the U.N. Human Rights Commission, has produced compelling evidence of Iraqi atrocities against the civilian population in southern Iraq. We support the Rapporteur's proposal to place human rights monitors throughout Iraq.

Iraq's campaigns of repression against its own people underline the importance of international actions to protect Iraq's civilian populations. Acts of violence and terrorism continue at the behest of the Government of Iraq in violation of U.N. Security Council Resolutions 687 and 688. The "no-fly zones" over northern and southern Iraq seek to monitor Iraq's compliance with U.N. Security Council Resolution 688. Since the no-fly zone was instituted in southern Iraq last year, Iraq's use of aircraft in aggression against its population in the region has stopped. The no-fly zone in the north has also prevented use of fixed or rotary wing aircraft against the local population there. Other acts of repression continue, however, underscoring the need for U.N. monitors.

The international community has continued its efforts, consistent with Security Council resolutions, to alleviate suffering in Iraq. The United States is working closely with the United Nations and other organizations to provide humanitarian relief to the people of northern Iraq, in the face of Iraqi Government efforts to disrupt this assistance. We support new U.N. efforts to mount a relief program for persons in Baghdad and the south, but the United Nations must be able to prevent the Iraqi Government from diverting supplies.

The U.N. sanctions regime exempts medicine and requires only that the U.N. Sanctions Committee be notified of food shipments. In accordance with paragraph 20 of Resolution 687, the Committee received notices of 17 million tons of foodstuffs to be shipped to Iraq through January 1993. The Sanctions Committee also continues to consider and, when appropriate, approve requests to send to Iraq materials and supplies for essential civilian needs.

The Iraqi Government, in contrast, has for months maintained a full embargo against its northern provinces, in violation of U.N. Security Council Resolution 688, and has acted to distribute humanitarian supplies only to its supporters and to the military. It has also refused to utilize the opportunity under Resolutions 706 and 712 to sell up to $1.6 billion in oil, proceeds from which could be used by Iraq to purchase foodstuffs, medicines, materials, and supplies for essential civilian needs of its populations; the distribution of these supplies would be monitored by the United Nations. (These proceeds could also be used to finance essential U.N. activities concerning Iraq.) The Iraqi authorities bear full responsibility for any suffering in Iraq that results from their refusal to implement Resolutions 706 and 712.

The United States has recently transmitted to the United Nations a report on Iraqi violations of international humanitarian law committed during the Gulf War. This report provides the international community with a documented record of Iraqi crimes. We encourage others to transmit whatever information they have on Iraqi violations of international humanitarian law to the United Nations in accordance with U.N. Security Council Resolution 674.

Since January 19, the U.N. Compensation Commission has continued to prepare for the processing of claims from individuals, corporations, other entities, governments, and international organizations that suffered direct loss or damage as a result of Iraq's unlawful invasion and occupation of Kuwait. The Commission has received about 400,000 claims to date. The next session of the Governing Council of the Commission is scheduled to be held in Geneva March 29 to April 2, 1993, with another meeting in July 1993.

Iraq has not met its obligations concerning Kuwaitis and third-country nationals its detained during the war. The Government of Kuwait has compiled over 600 files on missing individuals. Although Iraq has received this information through the International Committee of the Red Cross (ICRC), it has taken no substantive steps to comply with Security Council Resolution 687, which requires that Iraq cooperate fully with the ICRS. Regional organizations have also been engaged—thus far to no avail—in trying to obtain Iraqi compliance on the issue of detainees. We continue to work for Iraqi compliance and the release of all those detained in Iraq.

The United States and out allies continue to press the Government of Iraq to return all property and equipment removed from Kuwait by Iraq. Iraq continues to withhold necessary cooperation on these issues and to resist unqualified ICRC access to detention facilities in Iraq.

We will continue to seek to maintain Iraq's territorial integrity. A future government that represents all the people of Iraq and that is committed to the territorial integrity and unity of Iraq would be a stabilizing force in the Gulf region. In this regard, we are encouraged by recent efforts of the Iraq National Congress (INC) to develop broad-based, indigenous opposition to the Baghdad regime. A democratic and pluralistic government would be the best guarantor of the future of the Iraqi people.

My Administration does not seek to use force, but we will not shrink from using force in self-defense or as authorized by U.N. Security Council resolutions to compel Iraq's compliance with their terms. I am grateful for the support of the Congress for these efforts.

Sincerely,

BILL CLINTON

NOTE: Identical letters were sent to Thomas S. Foley, Speaker of the House of Representatives, and Robert C. Byrd, President pro tempore of the Senate.

Nomination for Posts at the Treasury and Transportation Departments
March 22, 1993

The President announced today his intention to nominate George Weise, the staff director of the House Ways and Means Committee's Subcommittee on Trade, to be Commissioner of the U.S. Customs Service, Department of the Treasury; and Stephen Kaplan, the former city attorney of Denver, to be General Counsel for the Department of Transportation.

"George Weise," said the President, "is one of this country's leading experts on customs matters, with experience that few can match. I am confident that he will work to make the Customs Service a model of effectiveness and efficiency."

"As Denver's city attorney," the President added, "Stephen Kaplan served Federico Peña with unparalleled dedication and professionalism. He will, I am sure, do no less here in the Federal Government."

NOTE: Biographies of the nominees were made available by the Office of the Press Secretary.

The President's News Conference
March 23, 1993

Russian Reforms and U.S. Economy

The President. Good afternoon. Before taking your questions today I would like to speak very briefly about some foreign and domestic issues.

First, I want to reiterate that the United States supports the historic movement toward democratic political reform in Russia. President Yeltsin is the leader of that process. He is a democratically elected national leader, indeed, the first democratically elected President in a thousand years of Russian history. He has United States support, as do his reformed government and all reformers throughout Russia. At this moment, Russia is in a constitutional and political crisis. President Yeltsin proposes to break the logjam by letting the people of Russia decide on April 25th. That is an appropriate step in a democracy. Our interest is to see that this process unfolds peacefully.

We're encouraged that President Yeltsin is committed to defend civil liberties, to continue economic reform, to continue foreign policy cooperation toward a peaceful world. Russia is, and must remain, a democracy. Democratic reform in Russia is the basis for a better future for the Russian people, for continued United States-Russian partnership, and for the hopes of all humanity for a more peaceful and secure world.

The United States has great responsibilities abroad and at home. To meet these responsibilities, we must not only continue to support reform and change abroad but also the revitalization of our economy here at home. We need to fundamentally change as our times require it. On February 17th, I offered an economic plan to provide for that kind of fundamental change. Just 5 days ago, the House of Representatives took a giant step toward breaking the logjam and the gridlock here in Washington in approving the economic plan. And in just 1 or 2 days, the Senate will have the opportunity to demonstrate that it too has heard the people's call for change. Make no mistake about it, our people too have demanded a new direction in our economy: cutting the deficit, investing in our people, and creating high-skill, high-wage jobs for working men and women and for our children.

Our plan does reduce the Federal deficit now by about $500 billion over the next 5 years. And just as important, it will grow the economy by investing in our people, their skills, their technological future, their health, and by offering new incentives for businesses to create jobs. In helping the economy to create millions of new jobs, the great majority of them in private business, we are building the foundations of a future prosperity, from world-class transportation and communication networks to safer streets and smarter schools. Each of these elements, reducing the deficit, asking the wealthy to pay their fair share, investing in the future, and creating jobs, will work as a package, and Congress should pass the package.

Just as the best social program is a job, the best deficit reduction program is a growing economy. This plan sets our country on a new course that honors our oldest values, moving away from gridlock to action; away from a Government that serves only privileged interests to a Government that serves the public interest; away from paying for the mistakes of the past and the expediencies of the present toward investing in the needs of the future.

The work has only begun. The Vice President is heading our effort to reinvent Government. Cutting back programs that don't work or whose work is already done, we're going to do what the smartest companies have already done in our country: streamline our operations, eliminate wasteful levels of management, and empower our frontline workers to take initiative and to take us on a better course. We're going to make Government less expensive and more effective. And as we pursue fundamental change in our economy, our health care system, and our schools, we will ask all our people to do their part.

The change the American people voted for is now beginning. We have a rare moment in Washington's history when people's voices are being heard and a rare opportunity to get things done. With the continued involvement of our people and the support of Congress, we can deliver the changes the people demand here at home. We can give the country the best years it has ever had, and we can have the United States still on the side of freedom and democracy and market reform around the world. Those are the objectives of this administration.

And I'll be glad to answer your questions. Helen [Helen Thomas, United Press International].

Russia

Q. Mr. President, would you be willing to hold the summit meeting in Moscow if it would be best for President Yeltsin's political health? Have you spoken to President Yeltsin? And don't you think that if you did go to Moscow, it would engage the U.S. too closely in the power struggle in the capital?

The President. You've got me on both sides of the issue before I even started. Well, let me say, first, I have not talked to President Yeltsin, but I have sent him two letters, one in response to his statement and the other, of course, a letter of condolence on his mother's death. I am going to meet in the morning with Foreign Minister Kozyrev to get a direct first-hand appraisal of where we are, after which it might be appropriate for us to have a telephone conversation. But I thought I should have the Kozyrev meeting first.

As of this time, we have not received any indications that the Russians, specifically President Yeltsin and his government, have any desire to change the site of the meeting or the time. So we are working very hard; indeed, I'm going to have a long session tonight to try to prepare for the summit at the appropriate date in Vancouver. I expect to spend a good deal of time this week consulting with the congressional leaders of both parties and others who might have ideas about what we ought to put in our package. And I intend to go there with an aggressive and quite specific plan for American partnership. So that's where we are now.

Q. Would you go to Moscow if it was called for?

The President. Well, let me say this. If they were to express an interest in that, then it's obviously something that we would have to consider. But that has not been done yet. There were some conversations this morning between the Secretary of State and Mr. Kozyrev—that has not been done yet. If that were to happen, then we would cross that bridge when we come to it.

Q. Mr. President, what would the U.S. policy be if the Soviet legislature votes to impeach Mr. Yeltsin, as appears increasingly likely? Would you continue to view Mr. Yeltsin as the duly elected leader of Russia?

The President. Well, I view him as such now. He is the only person who has been elected. The others are proceeding under a constitution that goes back to the Communist era. What I would do under those circumstances, I don't want to speculate about.

First of all, let me say, we have to appreciate, I think, the unique character of the events going on in Russia. It is a Russian experience. I myself have been, I think, in a way, most interested by the television interviews of the people in the street in Russia. You know, just talking about it, they sound almost like our people might sound talking about some fight we were having here. They've been remarkably level-headed about it and of different opinions, obviously. I think we just have to let this play out. I don't want to speculate about what the position of the United States would be in a hypothetical situation.

Yes.

Q. Mr. President, have you received any assurances about the command and control of Russian nuclear weapons in this crisis?

The President. We are monitoring that very closely, and we will continue to monitor that

very closely. At the present time, we have no reason to be concerned that the command and control procedures that are appropriate have been interrupted or face any imminent threat of interruption. We feel good about it at this time, and we will continue to monitor it closely.

Brit [Brit Hume, ABC News].

Q. Mr. President, I wonder what your view of the American possibilities are. How do you see the U.S. role? Can the U.S. play a decisive role, or are we really just ultimately bystanders?

The President. I think somewhere in between. I think in the end the Russian people will have to resolve this for themselves, and I hope they'll be given the opportunity to do that in some appropriate fashion. I have only the same access, in a way, that you do in terms of all the possible developments that are in the air. I do not believe that we can be decisive in the sense that we can determine the course of events in Russia or, frankly, in the other Republics of the former Soviet Union, with which we also have a deep interest. But I do believe that we are not bystanders. For one thing, I don't think that this country can do what it needs to do in any acceptable timeframe in moving to a successful economy unless we move to act across a whole broad range of areas. And over the next few days, I should have more to say about that as I work hard on this package.

Wolf [Wolf Blitzer, Cable News Network].

Defense Budget Cuts

Q. Mr. President, the former Secretary of State, Dick Cheney, and the chairman of the Senate Armed Services Committee, Sam Nunn, have both suggested that your proposed Pentagon budget cuts would perhaps be inappropriate at this time of uncertainty in Russia and elsewhere around the world. Are you taking another look at all of those cuts to perhaps revisit the whole issue?

The President. I'm not taking another look at the cuts at this time. Let me remind you that basically I think we have still presented a responsible defense budget. But what I am doing is trying to make sure that we can fulfill the missions that we have to fulfill based on any projected developments within the confines of that budget as it's staged over the next 5 years. And we'll be able to constantly review that. Obviously, these budgets are passed every year for 5 years in the future. And I expect, to whatever extent the world is uncertain, we'll have to be more vigilant in reviewing what our commitments are.

Russia

Q. Mr. President, you've made clear that you support both Russian reform and Yeltsin as the embodiment of that reform movement. But if President Yeltsin is removed either constitutionally or unconstitutionally, would it affect the package of aid, both the size and the specific package that the United States would offer Russia, without a President Yeltsin? Should the conservatives, the nationalists in the Parliament be on notice that it could affect the kind of aid we'd contribute?

The President. Well, let me say again, I don't want to get into hypothetical situations because I don't want anything I say or do to either undermine or rigidify the situation there. I mean, this is something the Russians are going to have to develop.

The United States has three interests in our cooperation with Russia. One is to make the world a safer place, to continue to reduce the threat of nuclear war and the proliferation of nuclear weapons. Two is to support the development of democracy and freedom for the people of Russia—it is a vast and great country—and indeed, for all of the Commonwealth of Independent States. And three is to support the development of a market economy. At every step along the way, with or without President Yeltsin in authority, from now, I suppose, until the end of time or at least for the foreseeable future, the United States will have those interests, and we will be guided by those interests.

Homosexuals in the Military

Q. Mr. President, you seem to be having some difficulty with the Pentagon. When you went to the U.S.S. *Theodore Roosevelt*, the sailors there were mocking you before your arrival, even though you are the Commander in Chief. The services have been undercutting your proposal for permitting gays to be in the military. There's been no Pentagon creation of the task force that was supposed to be created. The hearings are to start a week from now, and Congress has not gotten any advice from the Pentagon or from the services as to what to propose. Do you have a problem, perhaps because of your lack of military service or perhaps because of issues such as gays in the military, in being effective in your role as Commander

in Chief, and what do you propose to do about it?

The President. No. No, I don't have a problem being Commander in Chief. You knew that a lot of the service officers disagreed with the position on gays in the military before I ever took office. The Secretary of Defense has not been in the best of health; I think he is either fully recovered now or on the verge of it. And I asked him to give me a report on June 15th. Senator Nunn said back in January that he would have hearings sometime probably in March, so I think we're at the outer limits of the time that he was going to have hearings. And his schedule to have hearings, in my view, has nothing to do with the fact that I asked the Secretary of Defense to present to me on June 15th a report, which I expect to receive.

Q. Can I follow, sir? The task force was supposed to be created by now. The Pentagon has not created the task force, and there has been no report to the Hill. And in fact, Senator Nunn has indicated that he thinks some of the compromises that might have been possible, such as not having gays go to sea or be in combat, are not constitutional. Does that give you pause?

The President. Not constitutional?

Q. Would not pass constitutional muster.

The President. Well, I don't want to get into a constitutional debate, but if you can discriminate against people in terms of whether they get into the service or not, based on not what they are but what they say they are, then I would think you could make appropriate distinctions on duty assignments once they're in. The courts have historically given quite wide berth to the military to make judgments of that kind in terms of duty assignments.

Yes.

Potential Supreme Court Nominee

Q. Mr. President, on another topic, you've laid out some of the criteria you're going to use to choose the next Supreme Court Justice: a fine mind, experience in the law, experience dealing with people, and a big heart. Does Governor Mario Cuomo fit that criteria, and do you think that he would make a good Supreme Court Justice?

The President. Well, I'm on record on that, but the last time I said it, he wound up in the midst of a lot of conversation that I don't think either he or I intended. I will stay with my criteria. I will make the appointment as soon as I reasonably can. Justice White, I think, tendered his letter at this time, before the end of this term of Court, in order to give me a significant amount of time to make a judgment. This is a very busy time around here, as you know, because of all the foreign and domestic activities, but I intend to spend a lot of time on that.

Yes?

FBI Director Sessions

Q. Mr. President, aides suggest that you've made a preliminary decision to remove William Sessions, the FBI Director, from office; you're only waiting for a recommendation from Janet Reno. Can you deny that?

The President. Yes, that's not correct. I've not had a decision about that. I have asked Janet Reno to look at it. My review of the Director and the issues surrounding his appointment is largely confined to what has already been in the press. I wanted to wait until I had an Attorney General and until she could make a review. I have not made a decision, and I am going to wait for her judgment on it.

Yes, Susan [Susan Spencer, CBS News].

Health Care Reform

Q. Americans are eagerly awaiting May 1st to find out what you have in mind for health care reform. Are you ready to stand here now and make a pledge that by the end of your first term all Americans will have health insurance? And how much latitude do you think you have politically to raise taxes to be sure that that happens before the end of your first term? And I have a followup.

The President. Well, I'm ready to tell you that I will present a plan which would provide the American people the opportunity to have the security of health care coverage by the end of my first term. Whether or not that plan will pass the Congress in the form I will propose it, you know, that's a matter for conjecture. But I think we've got an excellent chance of passing it. In terms of how it will be paid for, let me say that no decision has been made on that. All the surveys show lopsided majorities of the American people willing to pay somewhat more, a little more, if they were guaranteed the security of health care coverage when they change jobs, when someone in their family's been sick, when other things happen, when their company can no longer afford it under present cir-

cumstances.

But what I'm trying to do now is to reconcile—the key financial conflict in the health care issue is this: We've got to give the American people the right to know they're going to be covered with health insurance, that they're not going to have their costs going up 2 or 3 times the rate of inflation, and they're not going to lose the right to pick their doctor. And we know that if we do it in any one of three or four ways, it will save literally hundreds of billions of dollars, between now and the end of the decade, of tax money and more importantly of private money. Massive amounts of money will be saved. So the question is: How much do you have to raise now in order to save all that money later? Those are the judgments we'll be making in the next month. We've still got about 5 weeks to make the decisions.

You had a followup.

Q. I did. I wanted to ask you if long-term care would absolutely be included in that package of benefits that you're talking about everybody having by the end of the first term.

The President. To what extent it will be hasn't been resolved because of the cost questions there.

Mark [Mark Miller, Newsweek].

Homosexuals in the Military

Q. Are you prepared to support restrictions, to follow up on Andrea's [Andrea Mitchell, NBC News] question, prepared to support restrictions on the deployment of homosexual members of the service? And if you are, do you think that fulfills the criteria that you laid out that discrimination should be on the basis of conduct, not orientation?

The President. That depends on what the report says. That's why I'm waiting for the Secretary of Defense to issue the report. But I wouldn't rule that out, depending on what the grounds and arguments were.

Yes.

Health Care Reform

Q. Mr. President, your own advisers have said that your health care reform might cost from $30 billion to $90 billion more a year, cost the Government more. That's in addition to the tax hikes you proposed for your economic program. Are you saying you cannot tell the middle class and working people that you will not seek higher taxes for health care reform?

The President. I'm saying that I have not made a judgment yet about how to recover what monies it would take to provide the security to all families that they would have some health insurance. That's right, I have not made that decision yet. I have sat through now probably 10, 12 hours, maybe, of intense staff briefings on the health care issue, and I would say we have 12 to 15 hours to go before I will be in a position to make some of these calls.

I can tell you this: I will not ask the American people to pay for a health care plan until the people who will be making money out of the changes that we propose are asked to give back some of the money they will make. Keep in mind, these changes will save massive amounts of money immediately to some of the health care providers.

Yes.

Russia

Q. Thank you, sir. Mr. President, if I may return to Russia for a moment. As your spokespersons have told us over the past few days, there are other reformers there. Is there a danger in putting too much American weight behind Boris Yeltsin?

The President. I don't think so. Some people say, well, what's the difference in this and the Gorbachev situation before, and is this the same sort of problem? I tried to answer that question earlier about what the United States interests are and how we would pursue them. And I've tried to be supportive of reformers throughout Russia and, indeed, throughout all the former Communist countries and the former Republics of the Soviet Union. But he is, after all, the first elected President in a thousand years. He has the mandate of having been voted on in a free and open election where people were free to vote and free to stay home, something that was not true previously. And that is something you would expect me to do.

Let's put it in a different context. Well, we just had the Prime Minister of Great Britain here, right? And the United States and Great Britain have had historic ties and shared values. You expect me to work with the Prime Minister of Great Britain, even if he is of a party that was openly supportive of my opponent in the last election. [*Laughter*] Boris Yeltsin is the elected President of Russia, and he has shown a great deal of courage in sticking up for democracy and civil liberties and market reforms, and

I'm going to support that.

Yes, in the back.

Economic Program

Q. Mr. President, you congratulated the House of Representatives for a speedy action on your economic plan last week, but you face some tougher hurdles in the Senate in part because some members of your own party, like Senator Breaux, are not on board with you. Why haven't you been able to get some of these Democratic Senators on board, and are you prepared to make some compromises in breaking the gridlock there?

The President. Well, let me just answer you this way. There were two big problems that we confronted when we got here in terms of how the people's money was being spent. One problem was the deficit had exploded. It had gone from $1 trillion, the debt had, to $4 trillion in 12 years. The other problem was we'd managed to explode our national debt while reducing our investment in the future.

Now, there are a block of people in the Senate, including some Democrats, who believe that the only thing that matters is to reduce the deficit. Now, believe me, that's a big improvement over the past, but I just disagree with them. I don't think that's the only thing that matters. I believe that investing in the future matters, too. And I believe if we don't change the spending patterns of the Government and invest and put some of the American people back to work to create millions of jobs, that we're not going to have an economic recovery. So we just have a difference of opinion.

Now, Senator Breaux is much closer to me than many others are in the sense that he basically wants to phase in this spending. But the problem with phasing it in is if you delay the investment, you also delay the impact of the investment, which means you put off the effective date of the jobs being created. That's my only argument with him. He, to be fair to him, has said, "This is an acceptable stimulus package and an acceptable level of investment, but I think we should, in effect, slow down the rate of spending until we have the whole package passed." And my position is, if the United States Senate will adopt a budget resolution like the House did, the American people will know we are not going to raise their taxes until we cut spending, and we are going to create jobs. And this is a plan where 70 percent of it's paid by people with incomes above $100,000, $500 billion of deficit reduction, but millions of jobs over the next 4 years, including a half a million in this program. So that's my argument, and I hope I'll be able to persuade enough to get the vote.

Yes.

Russia

Q. Mr. President, could you explain, please, the situation on nuclear weapons in Russia?

The President. This is self-selection over here. It's impressive. [*Laughter*] Go ahead.

Q. Mr. President, given the fact that both the START I and the START II treaties are hostage to the political outcome in Moscow, and given also the potential for conflict, armed conflict between Russia and Ukraine, are you prepared to draft contingency plans, at least, that would either restore funding or add funding to the Strategic Defense Initiative, if not the space-based part, at least the ground-based element, as a hedge against the worst possible outcome?

The President. Well, we're not in a position to make a judgment about the worst possible outcome now. Let me say, I've talked to President Kravchuk twice about the Ukraine's position on START I, and I'm very concerned about the very issues you raised. But let me say that even as we speak I'm not ready to say that there is a strong likelihood that we can't proceed with both START I and START II and that we can't resolve the conflicts between Russia and Ukraine. If that becomes apparent that we can't, then we will obviously assess our position and all of our options.

North American Free Trade Agreement

Q. Mr. President, on April 2, the Free Trade Agreement negotiators are going to meet again to talk about the additional agreements. Now, there has been a lot of talk that your administration plans to be very tough. How do you characterize being tough? Do you agree with that statement, and is there any room for compromises? How are you seeing those negotiations?

The President. Well, I wouldn't call it being tough. I would say that I intend to try to get a trade agreement that will be in the best interest of both the United States and Mexico. And keep in mind, this is not simply a trade agreement, this is also an investment agreement. And the issue is whether, when we make it much

more attractive for the United States to invest in Mexico and much more secure, shouldn't we also, in the interest of both the economies of Mexico and the United States, see that basic environmental standards and labor standards are observed, and shouldn't we have some protections greater than those embodied in the present agreement in the event that there is severe economic dislocations because of unintended consequences? I believe that we should. And I believe that's in Mexico's interest. And I would just point you to a much smaller example. We had examples in our aid program where the United States spent taxpayers' money to encourage American companies to invest in Central America, who then went down there and actually lowered wages instead of raising them in the host country. So what I'm trying to do is to promote market reforms and the benefits of them to both countries.

Second thing, let me say, I have enormous admiration for President Salinas and for what he's doing. I want to support that. And I want to remind all of you that insofar as to the trade portion of the NAFTA agreement goes, just look at the unilateral reductions by the Salinas government in trade barriers; took the United States over the past 5 years from a $6 billion trade deficit to a $5 billion-plus trade surplus with Mexico. So I have no quarrel with the trade provisions. But the investment provisions need to be used in ways that will raise wages on both sides of the border instead of lower wages on both sides of the border and pollute the environment. That's what I want to avoid.

Cuba-U.S. Relations

Q. Among the people you have charmed, it seems you have charmed President Fidel Castro because—[*laughter*]—in a recent interview with a TV network, he wanted to meet with you. Would you be willing to meet with him? And a Democratic administration might change the approach towards Cuba, versus a Republican?

The President. I have no change in Cuba policy except to say that I supported the Cuban Democracy Act, and I hope someday that we'll all be able to travel to a democratic Cuba.

Debra [Debra Mathis, Gannett News Service]——

Q. Would you meet with President Castro?

The President. I said "democratic Cuba"—elections.

Go ahead.

Deaths in Mississippi Jails

Q. A totally different subject, although it is south of here. I wonder about, in Mississippi, where as you know, civil rights and human rights groups are asking for your help in investigating the 40-plus hangings, suicides supposedly, in Mississippi jails. Some of the civil rights groups say that they are asking you, in fact, to order a Justice Department investigation. Have you heard from them directly, and are you amenable to that request?

The President. Well, I'm very much concerned about the deaths in the jails. I have not had a—if they have communicated with me directly, my staff has not yet discussed it with me, although they may have done so. What I would always do in a situation like that is to first discuss it with the Attorney General after an assessment of the facts and to see whether it is appropriate. But obviously, if we were asked to look into it, I would certainly at least discuss it with the Attorney General.

Japan-U.S. Trade

Q. Mr. President, on another trade issue, during your campaign last year in Michigan and other States, you criticized a Bush administration decision which allowed foreign-made minivans, MPV's to come into the country at low tariff rates. This led the auto industry and auto workers to believe that you would take action early in your administration to do something about this. Have you changed your mind on that subject, or do you still intend to take action?

The President. No, I haven't changed my mind on that subject. That issue is now under review, along with a number of others relating to our trade relations with Japan. And let me just say this: I had hoped, and still hope, to engage the Japanese Government in an ongoing dialog across a whole broad range of these issues. If you look at the history of American trade relationships, the one that never seems to change very much is the one with Japan. That is, we're sometimes in a position of trade deficit, but we're often in a position of trade surplus with the European Community. We once had huge trade deficits with Taiwan and South Korea, but they've changed now quite a bit; they move up and down. But the persistence of the surplus the Japanese enjoy with the United States and with the rest of the devel-

oped world can only lead one to the conclusion that the possibility of obtaining real, even access to the Japanese market is somewhat remote. And I will say again, I was astonished that the Bush administration overruled its own customs office and gave a $300 million a year freebie to the Japanese for no apparent reason. And we got nothing, and I emphasize nothing, in return. So, no, I haven't changed my position about that. I did hope to put it in the context of a larger set of trade issues to be raised first with the Japanese Government before acting unilaterally. But my own opinion about that has not changed.

Yes, Randy [Randy Lilleston, Arkansas Democrat-Gazette], go ahead.

Q. Mr. President, you've been——

The President. I'm going to come back to the right. I'm left-handed, you know, and I—[*laughter*]—sometimes discriminate. No, go ahead.

Potential Supreme Court Nominee

Q. Mr. President, during the campaign you gave some pretty strong indications that your Supreme Court nominee—you would certainly consider their position on abortion. Is that still the case?

The President. Thank you for asking, because I want to emphasize what I said before. I will not ask any potential Supreme Court nominee how he or she would vote in any particular case. I will not do that. But I will endeavor to appoint someone who has certain deep convictions about the Constitution. I would not, for example, knowingly appoint someone that did not have a very strong view about the first amendment's freedom of religion, freedom of association, and freedom of speech provisions. And I strongly believe in the constitutional right to privacy. I believe it is one of those rights embedded in our Constitution which should be protected.

Yes.

Q. Mr. President, on the issue of the Supreme Court, is your commitment to a Government that looks like America, does that also extend to the Supreme Court to the extent you can influence that through your appointments? Will you be taking age into consideration? And given what you just said about the right to privacy, do you think it's appropriate and will you or members of your administration be asking potential nominees if they support the right to privacy and whether they think that right includes the right to abortion?

The President. I'll answer the question. I will not ask anybody how they will vote in a specific case. I will endeavor to appoint someone who has an attachment to, a belief in a strong and broad constitutional right to privacy. And on the age issue, I will not discriminate against people who are older than I am. [*Laughter*] Yes. I won't discriminate against people who are of a different gender, of a different racial or ethnic group.

Q. How about a Government and the Court that looks like America, sir—on diversity?

The President. I don't know how many appointments I'll get to the Supreme Court; I don't know what will happen there. I'm going to appoint someone I think will be a great Justice.

Go ahead.

Campaign Finance Reform

Q. Mr. President, on campaign finance reform, could you tell us how you plan to end soft money contributions to State and national parties?

The President. First let me say that I intend to come forward with a proposal that will end the use of soft money in Presidential campaigns in the next few days. We're working on it now. We're working on trying to hammer it out with the friends of campaign finance reform in both Houses of the Congress. I will attempt to do it in a different way that will at least enable the parties to raise sufficient funds to involve grassroots people and empower people to participate in the political process, but I think that we should do away with this soft money issue and make a lot of other changes as well, and we're working on it. We should have a bill out that has the support of the administration quite soon. We've been working very hard now for the last couple of weeks on it.

Press Secretary Myers. Last question.

Forest Conference

Q. Mr. President, you're going to the forest conference in a couple of weeks, looking for a solution to an issue that has dragged on for a long time partly because both sides are unwilling to compromise or share the pain and, some say, the previous administration's unwillingness to obey the law of the land. How do you propose to find a solution where so many have failed or been unwilling to find a solution?

The President. Let me say, I would like to begin by having the United States have one position, and let me come back to the larger issue. The forest summit involves, as you know, what will happen to the old growth forest and to adjacent forests in the Pacific Northwest which are the habitat of the spotted owl, but which also are now a very small part of what once was a massive old growth forest up there. Thousands of jobs are at stake, but the very ecostructure of the Pacific Northwest is also at stake. The parties on both sides have been paralyzed in court battles, and all timber sales have been frozen, including many timber sales that virtually all environmentalists think should go forward, because of the impasse. One of the problems has been that the United States itself has taken different positions across the Agencies. So the first thing I hope to do is to be able to at least adopt a uniform legal position for the United States.

The second thing I want to do is go out there along with the Vice President and listen, hammer out the alternatives, and then take a position that I think will break the logjam. The position—it may be like my economic program—it'll probably make everybody mad, but I will try to be fair to the people whose livelihoods depend on this and fair to the environment that we are all obligated to maintain. And let me say, I live in a State that's 53 percent timberland. I have dealt with a lot of these timber issues for many years. The issue is, in this case, what is the right balance, given some facts that are inevitable about what's going to happen. And I think we can hammer out a solution. And as I said, everybody may be somewhat disappointed, but the paralysis now gripping the lives of the people out there is totally unacceptable.

Stimulus Package

Q. Sir, did you screen those projects in the economy stimulus package before you sent them to the Hill? The Republicans are saying there are so many things in there that are totally unnecessary. I can't believe that you sent those up there; and maybe somebody did it for you. [*Laughter*] But there are—[*inaudible*]—in there and swimming pools and copying statues——

The President. No.

Q. ——and even a project on studying the religion in Sicily.

The President. No—[*laughter*]—let me say, you will read those bills for years in vain and not find those projects. The——

Q. Well, the——

The President. Let me say, I have a letter here, dated on March 22d, to Senator Byrd from Leon Panetta about those alleged projects. What Mr. Panetta points out is to say that none of the specific projects referenced are actually in the legislation proposed by me. What they have done is to go to these Departments and say, if you had this much more money, give me every absurd thing you could possibly spend the money on. I am not going to let those things be done.

The other thing they have done is to go to some isolated parts of the country and pick atypical examples of community development block grant funds. I would remind you that it was the Republicans who've always supported the community development block grant proposal on the theory that we ought to rely more on the States and local governments to make judgments about how best to create jobs. So, I will do everything I can to keep undue waste and abuse from coming into this process. I do not support it.

We've got to quit. Thank you. We'll do it again sometime. I like this. [*Laughter*]

NOTE: The President's seventh news conference began at 1:02 p.m. in the East Room at the White House.

Remarks to Democratic Governors Association Members and State and Business Leaders
March 23, 1993

Thank you very much. Governor Walters, thank you for that introduction. That was spoken with a fervor that could have only been mustered by someone who, a year and a month ago, was freezing to death in the Super 8 Motel in Manchester, New Hampshire. [*Laughter*]

I also want to tell you that we just had a press conference at the other end of the hall, and I was upstairs on the telephone, and I didn't know you were here yet. And I was told that I had been introduced, so I rushed downstairs, only to find that I would be introduced twice or thrice. [*Laughter*]

I'm delighted to see you all. I thank you for being here. I thank the leaders of business and labor and State and local government for coming along with my colleagues in the Democratic Governors group to endorse this program.

Last week was a remarkable week here in this Capital. The House of Representatives took a strong stand for the most credible deficit reduction program in anybody's memory. At their request and based on the Congressional Budget Office estimates and based on what the Governors asked, we took another $60 billion-plus in deficit reduction spending cuts so that now we'll have $500 billion in deficit reduction over 5 years; a significant amount of tax increases, most of them on upper income people whose incomes went up the most in the 1980's, but a broad-based Btu tax that we think will both preserve the environment, promote energy conservation, and raise money in a fair way; big spending cuts; and finally, some very significant but very targeted investment increases.

The debate moves to the Senate this week, and I want to tell you a little about that, because there is an honest philosophical debate going on, as well as an underlying political one that I need your help on. In the last 12 years I think you could argue that your Government had two big problems: one is that the deficit literally exploded, and the public debt quadrupled. We started the decade of 1980 with a $1 trillion debt; we in 1992 had it up to $4 trillion, with huge projected annual operating deficits. That is a massive problem. It led to a big gap between short- and long-term interest rates, and it clearly had a major contributing impact on our trade deficit, our ability to save and invest, and our long-term economic growth. We had to do something about it.

The other big problem was that we were actually seeing reductions in investment by the National Government even as all of our competitors were increasing their investment. And that may seem inconsistent. I mean, how could we be making a relatively smaller contribution at the national level to the education, for example, of people who graduate from high school but don't go to college and need apprenticeship programs? How could we be retrenching in our commitment to the education of our young children and to dealing with the problems of poor children? How could we be retrenching in our commitment to develop new technologies and new partnerships in the public-private sector and new partnerships for dual-use technologies between defense and domestic technologies?

Well, the answer is pretty clear. We're spending more and more money every year, first on defense in the first part of the 1980's. And then the latter half of the 1980's, while we have cut defense, we spend even more on interest on the debt and more money for the same health care. And then as all of you know, those of you who are employers in particular, about 100,000 Americans a month are actually losing their health insurance; and many of them, the lower wage working people, are coming onto the public rolls.

So that's what's happened to us. So we run the deficit up. We run investment down at the same time. That is a huge problem. Our plan seeks to address both of these.

There are those who really don't want a change. They don't want any tax increases, or they don't really want the cuts that I have offered. And they're going to maneuver this process for political paralysis.

But underneath that or over that, if you will, there are a group of people who do want to reduce the deficit but just don't agree that an investment strategy is important. And they are the people that I urge you to reach out to, because it is important to reduce the deficit. But it's also important to increase investment. And if you do one without the other, you won't get the full benefits of this plan.

I would argue to you that we have gotten a major benefit out of deficit reduction. Look what has happened to long-term interest rates: down almost a full point since the election. You have millions of Americans refinancing business debt, consumer debt, home mortgages, getting the benefit of variable interest rates on various kinds of debt payment. That will unleash billions of dollars, tens of billions of dollars into this economy this year, which in turn will be reinvested, which will create new jobs. That is very

important. I don't think the marginal amount of deficit reduction you would get by killing this investment package or killing our emergency jobs program would bring interest rates down any more. You just can't get them down much more. But we would, if we killed it, forgo the chance to jumpstart the job engine of this economy by half a million jobs. And that is a serious thing. That's about a half a percent on the unemployment rate. That's a very substantial impact.

Now, let me make one other comment that, again, the employers here as well as the employees will not find surprising. There has been a dramatic restructuring of our economy and of the global economy which has been going on for the better part of 20 years, and we've been clearly aware of it for a decade now, where the biggest companies in America have been forced to restructure their operations here, either because they're going global and they have to put production overseas or because they just have to increase productivity and do more with less through technology. But many of them have also provided for outsourcing or contracts with smaller businesses, and the American entrepreneurial economy for the entire decade of the 1980's was able to create more jobs in the small business sector and the medium-size business sector than big business lost.

Two years ago, it stopped. And it started slowing down about 4 years ago, so that over a 4-year period we had almost no net job growth in the private sector. Virtually all, not quite all but almost all the net job growth for the previous 4 years was, believe it or not, in State, local, and national government.

Job growth was canceled out by job reduction in the private sector. Now, why did that happen? The truth is, no one knows all of the answers. It's an international phenomenon. In Europe during the 1980's, where they didn't have the vital small business sector that we had and all the entrepreneurial culture, there were two major economic recoveries where the economy was growing like crazy and no new jobs were created. So this is a global phenomenon.

But we also know that part of the problem here has been the credit crunch, the general recession, the cost of hiring new workers because of the back-breaking costs of health care as well as other attendant costs. So more and more people are relying on part-time workers or asking their existing work force to work overtime.

I say that to make this point: We have gotten the maximum short-term benefits we can get now out of a very, very tough and vigorous deficit reduction program. We are going to get long-term benefits out of it. The time has come to put in the other piece to create jobs and to lay the foundation for an educated work force and for a high-technology future. And that is what the rest of this program does.

So I ask those of you who are living out there at the grassroots, in the private sector

or at the State and local level, to go make that honest policy argument in the United States Senate. We've done our work on deficit reduction. Let's do our work on investing in our people and putting them back to work, too.

Thank you very much.

NOTE: The President spoke at 2:38 p.m. in the State Dining Room at the White House. In his remarks, he referred to Gov. David Walters of Oklahoma, chairman, Democratic Governors Association.

Nomination for Ambassador to France
March 23, 1993

The President announced today his intention to nominate Pamela Harriman to be Ambassador to France.

"Anyone who has been involved with the Democratic Party for any length of time is certainly familiar with Mrs. Harriman's talent for diplomacy," said the President. "Her many years

of dedicated service to the United States and her unceasing devotion to the cause of world peace are only two of the many qualifications that she will bring with her to Paris."

NOTE: A biography of the nominee was made available by the Office of the Press Secretary.

Exchange With Reporters Prior to Discussions With Foreign Minister Andrey Kozyrev of Russia
March 24, 1993

Russia

Q. Will you answer a couple of questions? Do you have any reaction to what Mr. Kozyrev suggested this morning as to the future economic relations between us and Russia?

The President. Well, we haven't had a conversation about it yet. Let me just say that I'm delighted to have him here. I'm glad to have a firsthand account of what's going on in Russia. And I want to reaffirm my support for democracy and for reform and say I'm looking very much forward to the Vancouver summit with President Yeltsin.

Q. Mr. President, apparently you seem to oppose aiding Russia. What will you do to try to sell your program for Russian aid?

The President. Well, I would tell the American people what I've been saying for well over a year now, that it is very much in our interest

to keep Russia a democracy, to keep moving toward market reforms, and to keep moving toward reducing the nuclear threat. It will save the American people billions of dollars, in money we don't have to spend maintaining a nuclear arsenal, if we can continue to denuclearize the world. It will make the American people billions of dollars in future trade opportunities. And it will make the world a safer place. So, I think this is a good investment for America. I've always believed that. And I hope I can persuade the American people and the United States Congress that it is.

Q. Do you think there's still a chance for a compromise in Russia?

The President. That's something the Russians will have to work out among themselves. I presume there is, but that's obviously something that has to be decided by the Russian people.

The United States can't dictate that.

Q. Mr. Kozyrev, can you tell us, did the meetings go poorly this morning, because it seems as though the line was harder when they came out from those meetings?

Foreign Minister Kozyrev. [*Inaudible*]—well, I think the people will pass final judgment. As President just said, it is for Russians and Russian people to pass final judgment, and President calls for vote, popular vote. And I think this will be the decisive event. But on the—President, as always, is open to compromise where there are those political forces who are not apt to just reverse the reform and advance the democracy.

Q. Will you support the idea of Russia joining G–7 as soon as possible?

The President. I wouldn't rule out or in anything particular. We're going to be dealing with a whole broad range of issues between the United States and Russia and with the G–7. And let's just see what happens.

NOTE: The exchange began at 1:10 p.m. in the Oval Office at the White House. A tape was not available for verification of the content of this exchange.

Exchange With Reporters on Russia
March 24, 1993

Q. Mr. President, did you and Mr. Kozyrev reach any kind of agreement on the type of aid package that might be most helpful for Russia?

The President. No, we discussed what I was thinking about and what our people are working on. And I told him it would be a good and specific package, and I was looking forward to having the opportunity to discuss it with President Yeltsin.

Q. Did he give you any encouragement, sir, that the current political crisis could be resolved?

The President. I think he's hopeful.

Q. Any specifics as to how it might be resolved, sir?

The President. No, he's been here with me.

NOTE: The exchange began at 3:50 p.m. in the State Dining Room at the White House, prior to a meeting with members of the National Council of Churches. A tape was not available for verification of the content of this exchange.

Interview With Dan Rather of CBS News
March 24, 1993

President's Schedule

Mr. Rather. How's your golf game?

The President. Not very good. I've only played twice. The first time it was about 35 degrees with a whipping wind, and the second time, I had a very good second nine holes. But I haven't gotten to play very much.

Mr. Rather. We were talking about your sleep or lack of same over in the Oval Office. You mentioned something about a nap. Are you trying to nap these days?

The President. If I can take a nap, even 15 or 20 minutes in the middle of the day, it is really invigorating to me. On the days when I'm a little short of sleep, I try to work it out so that I can sneak off and just lie down for 15 minutes, a half an hour, and it really makes all the difference in the world.

The White House

Mr. Rather. We're in the Library now, where President Roosevelt made his fireside chats. Is this among your favorite rooms?

The President. I love this room. And this is a highly public room. It is actually a lending library. People who work around here can come in here and check out these books just like any other library. It's also a public room that's open to everyone who comes in the White House on a tour. So people get to see this wonderful library of America, great old portrait of George Washington, and as I was telling you a moment ago, the little-known anonymous design for the White House by Thomas Jefferson. He tried to become the architect of the White House anonymously, and his design was rejected in favor of this one.

Mr. Rather. You were mentioning that certain Presidents dominate this house, as opposed to how they may be viewed in history. What did you mean by that?

The President. What I meant was most of the Presidents who are dominant here were very important Presidents, or all of them. Lincoln is plainly the dominant presence here: a bedroom named for him, the room where he signed the Emancipation Proclamation, his statues and portraits everywhere. But Andrew Jackson is very important here. He put both of the round porches on the White House and changed the front to the back of the White House and the back to the front. Theodore Roosevelt built both the wings, and his portraits are everywhere and his vigor and youth. Franklin Roosevelt lived here longer than everyone else, but he has just a couple of portraits here in the house and a very modest presence, considering the fact that he was plainly the dominant personality in terms of the length of time that he dominated here. So it's just sort of interesting who dominates, because of the contributions they made to the house itself, I think.

Mr. Rather. What are the chances that Bill Clinton can be one of those dominant Presidents in this house?

The President. Well, I don't know. Probably not much. I think this house is in good shape; I don't know that I can do anything to it that would improve it. I imagine that I will enjoy living here and that I will revere the responsibility about as much as anybody who's ever been here.

The Presidency

Mr. Rather. What's been your biggest disappointment so far?

The President. How hard it is to do everything I want to do as quickly as I want to do it, that the pace of change, although they say we're keeping quite a brisk pace—the House of Representatives adopted the budget resolution and

my jobs stimulus package last week in record time—but I still get frustrated. I have a hard time keeping up with everything and keeping it going forward. I'm an impatient person by nature, and I want to do things. That's been disappointing.

But I've been pleased that my staff has worked like crazy, my Cabinet's worked hard. We've had a minimum so far of the kind of backbiting and factionalism and all that you hear about.

Economic Program

Mr. Rather. What would you count as your biggest success so far?

The President. I think moving the economic program as quickly as possible and developing a big consensus for the idea that we need to make a serious attempt to both reduce the deficit and increase investments in jobs and education and technology. We've got to do both at the same time.

I've been very worried that I wouldn't be able to convince the American people or the Congress to do both at the same time because we've never done it before in the history of the country. But the competition we're in in the world and the problems we've had for the last 12 years absolutely require us to invest in our people and their jobs and to reduce the deficit at the same time, I believe.

Stimulus Package

Mr. Rather. Now, it's my information, I want to check it with yours, that what you call the job stimulus part of your economic plan is in trouble in the Senate. One, you may not have the votes. Senator Byrd said this afternoon that he saw trouble on the horizon. Does that match your information?

The President. We plainly got the votes to pass it as it is or with very minor modifications. What most Americans don't know is that of the 100 Members of the Senate, if you have one more than 40 you can shut everything down. And you know, there's been some discussion that the Republicans may try to filibuster the stimulus program and may try to stop us from trying to create any new jobs. They have 43 Republican Senators, and they may be able to hold 41 of them. And if they do, you know, they can indefinitely postpone a vote. Well, there's some speculation about that. I would hate to see that happen, and I think it would not serve them well. The American people did not elect any of us to perpetuate the kind of partisan gridlock we've had for the last several years, and particularly to have a minority of one House do that. So, I'm hopeful that that won't occur. I do hear that.

You know there's some argument around the edges among the more pro-deficit reduction Democrats that we should make some minor changes in the jobs stimulus program, but they're not great, I don't think.

Mr. Rather. Two things strike me, not just about what you said but the way you said it. Correct me if I'm wrong, it sounds to me like you're really worried about the possibility that it will be slowed if not stopped, the stimulus part.

The President. I think in the end we will pass it because, first of all, I think the public would just be outraged at the thought that we have a chance here to create half a million new jobs and to do things that are good that need to be done and that it would be slowed up. I'm just pointing out that if the minority in the Senate can get 40 votes plus one, they can stop anything from happening.

And that's what happened when they tried to gut the motor voter bill last week. That would have really been a big—it's a major piece of political reform, makes it easier for all kinds of people to register and vote. And they were willing to pass the motor voter bill, which allowed people to register when they license their car but not allow people, low-income people, to register when they pick up their Medicaid or Social Security benefits or something else. I've seen it. It can happen. All I'm saying is it can happen. I hope it won't, and we'll do our best to avert it.

Mr. Rather. Mr. President, let me come to what I and, I think, a lot of Americans perceive to be the gut of this. The economic indicators are looking good. Do we really need this, what you call stimulus package now? Doesn't it or does it present a real threat to inflation and increasing the deficit? Why not either reduce it or call it off since the economy seems to be moving?

The President. Because we're not producing jobs and because it doesn't present a threat to inflation, nor does it present a threat to the deficit. I agreed over the next 5 years to reduce the deficit by 4 times as much as the stimulus package over and above the deficit reduction

that I've proposed, $500 billion of deficit reduction. So, we have blown away the amount of the stimulus package over the next 4 years in extra deficit reduction. So, we're not adding to the deficit.

Secondly, the financial markets have already discounted the prospects of this being inflationary.

Third, and most important of all, unemployment in America is too high. Unemployment in all the rich countries except Japan is too high. We have to prove that we can generate jobs in America again. And there is no indication that we are doing that. Now, last month we had a lot of new jobs, but way, way over half of them were part-time jobs with no health care benefits and no security of lasting. So, we need this to create jobs. This program invests in community, invests in people and their education. I think it's very important.

Mr. Rather. Mr. President, I want to talk to you about Russia. Time for us to take a break. Stay here with us for our special edition of 48 Hours, an interview with President Clinton. We'll continue with conversation about Russia in just a moment.

[At this point, the television stations took a commercial break.]

Russia

Mr. Rather. Mr. President, just right off the top of your head, what percentage of this day have you spent dealing with the problems in Russia?

The President. Probably 30 percent today.

Mr. Rather. That's a lot.

The President. A lot.

Mr. Rather. Why? And let me ask a specific question. If I'm a trying-to-do-right American, lost my job, trying to support my wife and kids, tell me why I should pay for spending foreign aid to help the Russians?

The President. Because it's in your interest. And let me tell you why it's in your interest. For one thing, America needs good customers for its products. And Russia, a free Russia with a free economy, would prefer to do business with America over any other country. And they prefer to buy our farm products and other products, and we have to look ahead. Every year we have to be looking ahead to find more and more markets for our products because as we get drawn into the global economy, we've got to sell more to other people to keep our incomes high.

Secondly, we have a real interest in keeping Russia democratic and keeping them committed to reducing their nuclear arsenals. Why? Because otherwise we have to turn right around and rebuild our defenses at very high levels, spend huge amounts of taxpayers' money on nuclear arsenals, raise our children in a more dangerous world, and divert needed resources which ought to be spent on education and training and investment here at home.

So a safe, a democratic, a free market-oriented Russia is in the immediate economic interest of every working American and very much in the interest of those folks and their children over the long run. If we let Russia revert to a country which will never be able to do business with us, that's bad business. If it reverts to a nationalist, even if not a Communist, a highly nationalist nuclear power that forces us to spend more of our money keeping our guard higher, then that's money that will be diverted from the future of the working families and their children.

Mr. Rather. What about the theory that whatever money we try to give to the Russians, it would be money down a black hole, just disappear because chaos and pandemonium are hour by hour?

The President. First of all, we don't have enough money to, on our own, affect the course of events. Ultimately the Russian people will have to work out their own future. But there are some specific things we can do which will not hurt us; in fact, will help us, and which will send a clear signal to the forces of freedom and democracy and market economics in Russia that we and the rest of the West will help them.

You know, for example, if we provide more food aid, that helps our farmers, and we can do it at relatively low cost to ourselves. If we can find a way to help to privatize more businesses and to make those work, that helps us. If we can find a way to help them run their energy business better so they don't lose as much of their oil or their gas in the pipeline, that helps them without hurting us. It gives us a market for our pipeline products. If we can find a way to help them convert their nuclear power plants that are built on the Chernobyl model to a different energy source, that could put a lot of our folks to work, put a lot of their people to work, and make them safer environmentally and economically. So there is a zillion things we can do.

Now, over the long run, they're going to have to do some things for themselves. They're going to have to get control of their rampant inflation. They're going to have to make sure that they can get out of the bureaucracies that don't work anymore, that clog up all reforms. They're going to have to make a lot of decisions themselves. But there are some targeted, limited commitments we can make that, no matter what happens, won't hurt us very much and carry the potential of helping us a great deal while helping to keep good things alive in Russia.

Mr. Rather. Now you've met with the Russian Foreign Minister this afternoon.

The President. I did.

Mr. Rather. Did you come out of that with increased confidence that Boris Yeltsin will survive?

The President. He's a very resilient fellow, you know. He's like all of us in public life; he's not perfect. I'm not perfect; we all have our problems. But he is a genuinely courageous man, genuinely committed to freedom and democracy, genuinely committed to reform. And I think now he is more open perhaps than in the past at trying to work out some kind of accommodation with others who would negotiate with him to keep reform going, even though they may have some different ideas. Well, that's what I have to do here. I have to work with the Senate and the House, the Democrats and the Republicans. I think he's got to work on all that. But I think he's got a fair chance to survive. And I think not only the United States but I think the major Western countries ought to do what they can to be supportive of his elected Presidency now because he represents the ideals and the interests of our Nation and our way of life.

Mr. Rather. Mr. President, correct me if I'm wrong, but you've said a couple of times, I think, recently that Boris Yeltsin is the only democratically elected leader in Russia. In fact, his Vice President——

The President. That's right.

Mr. Rather. ——Aleksandr Rutskoy is also democratically elected. I just want to go over that. If Boris Yeltsin is impeached because he's tried to suspend the constitution and Aleksandr Rutskoy, who has now broken with Yeltsin and is also committed to democratic reform, comes into power, would you, would the United States

Government consider him a democratically elected leader and swing in behind him?

The President. First of all, it is true that he was elected on the ticket with Yeltsin. But when Yeltsin was elected, he won an overwhelming popular victory. If you go back and look at the distribution of votes, there's no question that that's what happened.

I don't want to get into what might happen or what-if questions. The constitution under which these proceedings might take place was one that came in 1978 under the Communist government. The only popularly elected President ever is Yeltsin. Yeltsin and Rutskoy were elected together on a ticket. And we'll just have to see what happens. I think in the end the Russian people will resolve this one way or the other by what they do or don't do in the referendum in April.

Mr. Rather. Mr. President, I would love to spend hours talking foreign policy. We have such a short time here. Let me try to do something reasonably brief, and that is mention some countries and potential problems out on the horizon and just have you respond briefly.

The President. Sure.

Iran

Mr. Rather. Iran: Particularly if it is proven that Iranian-sponsored terrorists had anything to do with the World Trade Center bombing, would you be prepared to retaliate?

The President. First, let's note that even as we speak, we were just given notice that another major arrest was made and someone brought to the United States from Egypt where the apprehension was made. That's very good news. I don't want to speculate about who was behind it until I know. That would be a very dangerous thing to do.

Let me say that I'm more concerned about the Iranian government maintaining its militance, perhaps supporting, in general, terrorists organizations or engaging in unsafe proliferation of weapons of mass destruction for its own use or for the benefit of others. I wish Iran would come into the family of nations. They could have an enormous positive impact on the future of the Middle East in ways that would benefit the economy and the future of the people of Iran. I am very troubled that instead of trying to contribute to alleviating a lot of the problems of the Islamic people to the region, they are seeming to take advantage of them. I hope that they will moderate their course.

Mr. Rather. I want to move on, but I want to make sure that I understand. I asked the question, should it be proven they had anything to do with the World Trade, would you be prepared to retaliate? So far, you're on the record as not answering.

The President. That's right. I want to be on the record as not answering. I want to maintain all options in dealing with terrorists, but I want to be on the record as not answering because I don't want the inference to be there that I'm accusing them of something that I have no earthly idea whether they did or not.

Iraq and Saddam Hussein

Mr. Rather. I understand.

Iraq and Saddam Hussein: Just before you came into office, you were quoted as saying words to the effect, well, if Saddam Hussein goes a certain way, I, Bill Clinton, could see relations getting better. Do you regret having said that, or is that a fair quotation?

The President. I think the inference was wrong. What I said was, I cannot conceive of the United States ever having any kind of normal relationship with Iraq as long as Saddam Hussein is there. I can't conceive it. What I said was that I did not wish to demonize him; I want to judge him based on his conduct. And in that context, I will be very firm, and the United States will remain very tough on the proposition that he must fully comply with the United Nations requirements, which he has still not done, in order for us to favor any kind of relaxation of the restrictions now on him through the U.N. That's my position.

Bosnia

Mr. Rather. What used to be called the Balkans, what once was Yugoslavia, is now referred to in shorthand as Bosnia. You seem—and I say this respectfully, but I want to say it directly—you seem to have been all over the place in terms of policy toward Bosnia. One, tell us exactly what U.S. policy toward Bosnia is at the moment and what we can expect in the future.

The President. Well, first, let me respond to your general comment. And like most Americans, I am appalled by what has happened there; I am saddened; I am sickened. And I know that our ability to do anything about it is somewhat limited. I'm convinced that anything we do would have to be done through the United

Nations or through NATO or through some other collective action of nations. And I am limited also not only by what I think the United States can do or should do but by what our allies are willing to do.

Now, against that background, we have done a number of things. We have been instrumental in tightening the embargo against Serbia. It's much tighter than it was when I took office. We have pushed for enforcement of the no-fly zone against the Serbians. I think we will get that in the United Nations sometime in the next couple of weeks. We have begun the airlift operation, which was initially criticized and is now universally recognized as having done an awful lot to alleviate severe human suffering and to meet profound needs. We have determined that we should support the Vance-Owen peace process to try to bring an end to hostilities there. But we've also been very clear that if the Bosnians will sign off under the Vance-Owen plan and the Croatians sign off on it, and the Serbs don't, that we think that we're going to have to look at some actions to try to give the Bosnians a means to at least defend themselves. I'm very concerned about this.

But my view is that we ought to try to get the Vance-Owen peace process working. If the parties will good-faith agree to a peace process, then I would be willing to have the United States participate with other nations in trying to keep the peace in Bosnia.

[At this point, the television stations took a commercial break.]

North Korea

Mr. Rather. Mr. President, before I get away from foreign policy, very quickly—North Korea, nuclear proliferation: one of those things people's eyes glaze over. Important, of course, but is it something that consumes a lot of your time?

The President. Well, it's caused me a lot of concern in the last few days. Just for the benefit of our viewers, the North Koreans have refused to allow the International Atomic Energy Agency's inspectors to look into sites where they might be illegally producing nuclear weapons under the nonproliferation regime. And because they wouldn't allow our inspectors in and because the United Nations continued to insist that they do so, the North Koreans have now given us notice that they are going to withdraw, which means they're going to put themselves

outside the family of nations seeking to contain nuclear weapons. That would be a great mistake, and I hope they don't do it.

It's deeply troubling to us and to the South Koreans. You know, Seoul, which is now a teeming city of well over 8 million people, is very close to the 38th parallel, very close to North Korea. And over the last few years, relations between those two nations have been warming, and people began to dream of reunification in the same way that it happened in Germany. So this is a very sad and troubling development. I don't want to overreact to it. The North Koreans still have a couple of months to change their mind, and I hope and pray that they will change their mind and return to the family of nations committed to restraining nuclear proliferations.

Health Care Reform

Mr. Rather. There's no easy transition to make to health care, but we need to move on. So, if I may. As I understand it—correct me if I'm wrong—you are telling the American people that their health care coverage will be increased, that the deficit at the same time will be cut. The translation of that is that there's going to be yet another significant increase in taxes, isn't it? How can it be avoided?

The President. Not necessarily. And we're looking at the options to do it. If I might, let me try to describe the problem. And I know we don't have a lot of time, but let me be as brief as I can.

There are the following problems in health care: The average person who has health insurance is pretty satisfied with the quality of health care, but terrified of losing the health care coverage. They're just afraid that either through higher deductibles, higher copay, or just outright loss of the insurance, or they had to change jobs but they've had somebody in their family that's sick, they won't be able to keep their health insurance. That's one big problem. The average business is terrified about the cost of health care. We're spending 30 percent more than any other country and getting less for it. So more and more people lose their health insurance every year. And then there are a lot of people who don't even have access to health care. They never see doctors or dentists or go to a medical clinic.

So we've got the most expensive health care system in the world. For the people that can afford it and stay with it, you get to choose your doctor, choose your providers of all kinds, and it's good stuff. But millions of people live with insecurity, and the cost of it is really breaking the economy.

Now, here is the dilemma. In order to fix this cost problem and the security problem, you know, to tell people you can still choose your doctor but you're never going to have to worry about losing your health insurance, you have to find a way to pay, to cover everybody who doesn't now have health insurance, and to stop the loss of coverage for people that have it. That costs money.

But if you do it, that permits you to cut out literally tens of billions of dollars of excess paperwork and administrative cost, stop a lot of other things that are driving up costs in the system. And you literally save, between now and the end of this decade, hundreds of billions of dollars, of both private dollars and taxpayer dollars. So the issue is, how do we make people secure so you can still pick your doctor; you're never going to lose your health insurance, you're always going to have it, no matter whether you change jobs or lose your job; you're always going to have access to health care. It's going to be good. How do we do that? Bring the cost down, and do it within a time that is acceptable.

Mr. Rather. How are you going to pay for that?

The President. We are looking for a lot of different options, but the last thing I think we ought to do, the last place we ought to look, is to ask the employers and the employees of America who are paying too much for their health care right now to pay more to solve this short-term problem.

But the dilemma is this, quite simply—100 percent of the people who studied this problem say this—you may have to pay some more in the short run or find some more money in the short run, but over the long run it's going to save a massive amount of money. I can do more to save money on the Government deficit and to free up money in the private sector by bringing health costs in line with inflation and solving this problem than any other single thing I can do.

What we're trying to find a way to do is to cover all the people who don't have coverage and to guarantee the security to the working people who are afraid of losing it without raising their taxes. And we're looking for ways to do

it. And there may be some options. We've got 400 people, including doctors, nurses, health economists, experts from all over America working on this, and they've done good work. I think we've got a chance. And I've got another month to do it.

[*At this point, the television stations took a commercial break.*]

Homosexuals in the Military

Mr. Rather. Mr. President, at your news conference yesterday, correct me if I'm wrong, but I thought you got a little testy when you were asked about gays in the military, respect for you in the military. Am I wrong about that?

The President. No, I didn't feel testy. I thought it was an unusually worded question, but that's all part of it. No, I don't mind talking about it. Let me say, I talk on a regular basis with General Powell. I have met with the Joint Chiefs. I have a whole schedule of things that I'm working through now to continue to work with the military. This is a very difficult time for them.

Mr. Rather. Well, is it correct that you have reversed your position? You say we now——

The President. Absolutely wrong.

Mr. Rather. Did you misspeak yourself?

The President. No, I didn't misspeak myself. Nothing I said yesterday is in any way inconsistent with anything I've ever said before about this.

First, let's review this issue. Half the battle is over. Half the battle is over. The Joint Chiefs agree that they should stop asking enlistees whether or not they're gay. So they have already said, we won't ask you to lie, and we won't use your forms against you. And if you get in and you perform well, that's fine.

I agree and everybody else agrees that any kind of improper sexual conduct should be grounds for dismissal or other appropriate discipline. There's no difference in opinion on that. There is a very limited argument here, which is if you do not do anything wrong but you do acknowledge that you are gay, should you be able to stay in the military and, if so, should you be able to do anything anyone else can do?

The question I was asked yesterday was as follows: Would you consider any restrictions on duty assignments? And the answer is, I am waiting for the report of the Secretary of Defense made in conjunction with the Joint Chiefs. I think they're divided among themselves on this issue. Other nations which admit gays into the military, some of them have no differences in duty assignments, and some do. What I said was, if they made a recommendation to me, would I review it and consider it? Of course I would. I mean, I asked them to study this. I can't refuse then to get the results of the study and act like my mind's made up. This is not an area where I have expertise. I have to listen to what people say. I will consider the arguments. I have a presumption against any discrimination based on status alone, but I will listen to any report filed.

Potential Supreme Court Nominee

Mr. Rather. Mr. President, time is running out on us here. I want to give you an opportunity on this program before this tremendous audience to indicate who your choice on the Supreme Court is going to be. This is a great opportunity for you to do it. I want to give you an opportunity.

The President. I thought you'd never ask. [*Laughter*] I must tell you I have not reached a final decision. The problems in Russia and just the stuff I've been doing on the economy have kept me from spending quite as much time on it as I would have. But Justice White, to his everlasting credit, gave me his letter now for his resignation in June, and his successor can't take office until October, so he gave us some time.

I love the Constitution of the United States, and I believe in the Supreme Court as an institution. I used to teach constitutional law. There will be few things that I will do in this job that I will take more seriously, few responsibilities I will cherish more. And I will try to appoint someone that I think has the potential of being a magnificent Justice, someone who will be a defender of the Constitution, but someone who has good values and common sense and who understands the real life experiences of Americans as well as the law.

Mr. Rather. Let's talk about this for a moment. I think you were just starting college when the last Democratic President had a chance——

The President. That's right.

Mr. Rather. ——to choose someone for the Supreme Court. If you think about it, it's been a long time.

The President. A long time. President Johnson put Thurgood Marshall on the Court, and I just went to his funeral. It was a long time ago.

Mr. Rather. If you're not going to reveal who it's going to be—I'll give you another opportunity to do that—tell us in what directions you hope to take the Court? I mean, you make an appointee hoping that he will at least bump the Court in some other direction. Let's talk philosophically about the Court.

The President. Well, there was a lot of talk, as you know, during the last 12 years when the Republicans held the White House, about trying to move the Court in a sort of a rightward direction. Indeed, the political platforms of the Republicans were repeatedly filled with litmus tests and specific requirements and everything, and pushing the Court to the right. In fact, as has always been the experience with Presidents, some of the appointees did, in fact, move to the right. Others turned out to be much more complicated people. You know, they had different views. I would like to put someone on the Court who would make sure that there was a certain balance in the debate, that there was a real feeling for the rights of ordinary Americans under the Constitution, but that also someone who was hard-headed, who understood that the criminal law had to be enforced, that you didn't want to over-legalize the country. There's a nice balance to be formed.

I'd also like to put someone on there who was a very cogent and powerful arguer and who could show respect for the other Justices, who could be a good colleague, and who could engage people in honest dialog. I mean, I think the Supreme Court is no different, really, in that sense from a lot of other units. I can't help but believe that when they're all talking together and working together and honestly trying to pick each other's brains, that they're not only free to act on their own convictions but they'll learn from one another and maybe make better decisions.

Mr. Rather. During the campaign, you campaigned as one who would be a President tough on crime. There became this opening on the Supreme Court. You talked about wanting to appoint a Justice with a "big heart." What do you mean "big heart"? Does that mean trouble for prosecutors and law enforcement officers?

The President. No, not at all. As a matter of fact, I think—there may be differences about capital punishment, for example. I've supported capital punishment, and I still do. And I wouldn't necessarily make that a litmus test, because there's a big majority on the Supreme Court that support capital punishment. So whatever my appointee turns out to do on that, it won't change the majority. The majority agree with me on that issue.

But I think that being big-hearted is not the same thing as being soft-headed. I mean, we need an administration that takes an aggressive approach to the crime issue. But we need to be smarter about it. I mean, we can't talk tough on crime and make sentences tougher and refuse to pass the Brady bill and make people wait 7 days before criminals can buy handguns. We ought to take automatic weapons out of the hands of kids in the streets of our cities. If we're really going to be tough on crime, we ought to be not only tough in the traditional ways but also to change the environment some.

Academy Awards

Mr. Rather. Mr. President, it's my unfortunate duty now to ask the tough questions you don't want to hear. Number one, do you have a favorite in the Oscar race for the Academy Awards? Have you seen these movies? Which one do you favor?

The President. I haven't seen them all, so I can't say. The ones I have seen I enjoyed. I thought Clint Eastwood's western was very good, "The Unforgiven," and a remarkable departure from a lot of his past movies. I thought

Jack Nicholson was brilliant in "A Few Good Men." I try to see all the Oscar movies every year. I still haven't seen "Scent of a Woman." I'm working on that. I'm trying to have that brought into the White House. And when I see them all, then I'll have my favorite, but I don't think it's fair until I give them all a shot.

NCAA Basketball Championships

Mr. Rather. I know you don't follow basketball, but I'm willing to make you an offhand wager that North Carolina slaughters Arkansas.

The President. I bet they don't. I don't think they can slaughter them. We haven't lost too many games by a lot of points. Arkansas doesn't have any tall players. As you saw in the St. John's game where they played an incredibly talented, well-disciplined team, they often win by never quitting, a philosophy that I try to follow myself.

Mr. Rather. Mr. President, you're very generous. We appreciate your hospitality. Thank you very much.

The President. Thank you.

NOTE: The interview began at 5:25 p.m. in the Library at the White House, and it was broadcast nationwide at 10 p.m. In his remarks, the President referred to Gen. Colin Powell, Chairman of the Joint Chiefs of Staff. A tape was not available for verification of the content of this interview.

Nomination for Posts at the Housing and Urban Development and Transportation Departments
March 24, 1993

The President intends to nominate his long-time adviser Rodney Slater as Administrator of the Federal Highway Administration, San Francisco port executive Michael Huerta as Associate Deputy Secretary of Transportation for Intermodalism, and investment banker Aida Alvarez as Director of the Department of Housing and Urban Development's Office of Federal Housing Enterprise Oversight, the White House announced today.

In addition, the President announced his approval of the appointments by Transportation

Secretary Peña of Jane Garvey to be Deputy Administrator of the Federal Highway Administration; by Energy Secretary O'Leary of John Keliher to be Director of the Office of Intelligence and National Security; and by Health and Human Services Secretary Shalala of four officials: Wendell Primus, Deputy Assistant Secretary for Planning and Evaluation; Kimberly Parker, Deputy Assistant Secretary for Legislation (Congressional Liaison); Karen Pollitz, Deputy Assistant Secretary for Legislation (Health); and James O'Hara, Associate Commissioner for

Public Affairs, Food and Drug Administration. "Rodney Slater has been one of my most trusted advisers for many years and played a major role in getting me to this position," said the President. "Rodney, Michael Huerta, and Aida Alvarez are the kind of innovative leaders that we need in public service. I am very pleased that they and the people chosen by Secretaries Peña, O'Leary, and Shalala are joining me here in Washington."

NOTE: Biographies were made available by the Office of the Press Secretary.

Remarks in a Telephone Conversation With Senators George Mitchell and Jim Sasser and an Exchange With Reporters
March 25, 1993

Russia

Q. Does the situation now appear to have eased in Russia to you, Mr. President?

The Vice President. I don't think this is a press conference.

The President. I don't know. I hope so.

[*At this point, the telephone conversation began.*]

Senator Mitchell. Hello?

The President. Senator?

Senator Mitchell. Yes.

The President. How are you doing?

Senator Mitchell. We're doing fine. How are you doing?

The President. Well, I'm doing a lot better, thanks to you.

Senator Mitchell. No, thanks to Jim Sasser, who is sitting right here with me and on the line, too.

Senator Sasser. Hey, Mr. President, I'm on this party line, also.

The President. Hello, Senator Sasser.

Senator Sasser. How are you doing? We're doing terrific here.

The President. The Vice President's here with me, and we just wanted to thank you for the work you've done. This is a great, great day.

Senator Sasser. It certainly is. And we want to thank you, I do, particularly, for the help that you gave us in moving this resolution through the committee and off the floor. We had 56 amendments, and the truth is that not a single number changed in that budget resolution on any of those amendments. And we couldn't have done it without your help.

The President. Well, we were glad to do it. I believe, and I think the American people believe, that this is really an historic moment. Finally, we've done something to break the gridlock and to bring the deficit down and to create new jobs through investment. It's a remarkable achievement. And I know we've got a lot of work still to do, but the fact that the Senate and the House have both passed these budget resolutions, it's really astonishing this early. And I'm just amazed, because we all know what a hard road you had to hoe. I can't tell you how much I admire you and how grateful I am to both of you.

Senator Sasser. You're very kind to say that, and I very much appreciate it. I might say that this is the earliest time in my memory—the majority leader may know another time—but this is the earliest time in my memory that we passed a budget resolution here in the Senate. And we're proud of that and proud of your help on getting it done.

And tell the Vice President we sure appreciate him coming over here and giving us encouragement.

The Vice President. Well, I'm on the line, Jim, and thank you very much. You did a fantastic job. George, I think Jim is right. This is the earliest in history that a new budget has passed. And I've been hearing from a lot of people about how effective you all were in the caucus meeting in the conference a couple of days ago. The unity among Democratic Senators has been just remarkable and has made this whole thing possible. So, Mr. Leader, congratulations to you, and to you, Jim.

Senator Mitchell. Thank you very much, Mr. Vice President. We really do appreciate your help, not just your physical presence but the leadership you gave in talking to Democratic Senators. I know many of them were impressed with the fact that you took the time to come up here, meet with them, talk with them, express support for and explain the President's position. I think that was extremely helpful in getting that kind of unity. So we're very grateful to both of you.

And now, of course, there's no rest for the weary. I'll have a list of people for you to call on the supplemental——

The Vice President. I'm ready.

The President. We're ready to go. Give us our next assignment.

Senator Mitchell. Well, that's it. We've already started on it, and we'll be in touch with you on that later today.

The President. Thank you very much, George.

Senator Mitchell. Thank you. Bye, Mr. President.

[*At this point, the telephone conversation ended, and the President took questions from reporters.*]

Stimulus Package

Q. Do you feel you now have the votes on the stimulus package, Mr. President?

The President. Well, I haven't gotten a late count, but I feel good about it. We worked hard on it, and I feel good about it.

Q. What does it do to your package if Breaux and Boren were to prevail? Is that a killer amendment?

The President. All I can tell you is, we're going to try to pass it. Let's just see what happens. I feel pretty good about it. We're working hard

Russia

Q. Mr. President—contact of Boris Yeltsin today? Have you heard anything?

The President. No. I would say I've gotten reports and I've spent about, oh, I don't know, an hour and half on it this morning, working, trying to get ready for Vancouver and trying to make sure we know what's going on. But I don't have anything to add to what you already know.

NOTE: The President spoke at 2:22 p.m. in the Oval Office at the White House. A tape was not available for verification of the content of these remarks.

Exchange With Reporters Prior to a Meeting With Dorsey High School Students
March 25, 1993

Ukraine

Q. Mr. President, did anything come out of your meeting with the Ukrainian Foreign Minister as far as the START Treaty?

The President. I just told him how important it was to us, that I realize that there was some opposition at home in Ukraine because of uncertainty in Russia, but we had to have them sign on. And I would encourage them to go ahead and do it, while I realize there are some implementation issues that we would have to work with them on. And I was glad to work with him on that but that the United States wanted very much to be close to the Ukraine. We have a big stake in their success, and we've got a lot of commercial potential there and they here, as well as a lot of ties. We have a lot of Ukrainian-Americans, as you know.

But I think this START Treaty is a precondition to a long-term, successful relationship.

And I think they should go into the nonproliferation regime and give up nuclear weapons. We don't need any more nuclear states. The United States is trying to reduce our nuclear arsenals, and we need to continue to push in that direction.

It was a very good meeting. And I think over the long run, the United States will have a good relationship with Ukraine if we get the START issue resolved.

Q. Mr. President, did he say the crisis in Moscow is having repercussions back home for him?

The President. Well, he said it was adding to a sense of uncertainty in this country, which you would expect it would. I mean, they're right next door there. But I hope, of course, as every day goes by there seems to be an attempt by President Yeltsin and others, frankly, to confine the dimensions of the process, to regularize it and to let it play itself out in a vote of the people on April 25th. Of course that's the most democratic way you could do that to resolve that crisis.

Q. Did you get a sense——

The President. I don't know that. I know what you were going to say. I don't know that. I hope so. I feel better about it, but I don't know that for sure.

U.S. Attorneys

Q. Are you afraid that firing all the U.S. attorneys at once will be seen as political?

The President. Absolutely not. We waited longer than most of our predecessors have. Go back and look and see when they tried to replace them under Bush, under Reagan, under— particularly under Reagan. Anytime when you change parties—it took us longer to begin the process because of the delay in getting an Attorney General confirmed. But all those people are routinely replaced, and I have not done anything differently. The Justice Department is just proceeding from essentially a late start. And I think the blanket decision is less political than picking people out one by one.

Q. Do you think Jay Stephens should stay on at least to the end of the Rostenkowski——

The President. I support the Attorney General. She made the decision about what the best way to handle this was, since we were behind. And I support her decision.

NOTE: The exchange began at 4:10 p.m. in the Oval Office at the White House. Jay Stephens was the U.S. attorney for the District of Columbia. A tape was not available for verification of the content of this exchange.

Remarks on Signing the Greek Independence Day Proclamation
March 25, 1993

I just wanted to ask Mr. Stephanopoulos to come up here so I could remove all doubt about how I know what to do. [*Laughter*] Please sit, ladies and gentlemen, Archbishop.

I have a few remarks, but before I do, I want to formally sign this proclamation for Greek Independence Day and present it to the Archbishop.

[*At this point, the President signed the proclamation.*]

Thank you. Please be seated. I'd like to welcome all of you here to the White House and say a special word of welcome to Archbishop Iakovos, the spiritual leader of the Greek American community, with whom I have just had a wide-ranging discussion of many of the issues that I know that concern you. I'd also like to welcome the political leader of the Greek American community, my friend Senator Paul Sarbanes of Maryland, and to say how delighted I am to sign this proclamation recognizing Greek Independence Day and celebrating the democracy that we share in the United States with Greece.

It is particularly timely that we celebrate democracy today at the very moment that our friends around the world who have been deprived of democracy are working hard against great odds to bring it to full flower. And I know, Archbishop, that our prayers are with the people in Russia today and throughout the world who are working hard to preserve and enhance their own democracy.

Greece, the birthplace of democracy, and the United States have long had a history of friendship and cooperation. The authors of our Nation's Declaration of Independence and our Constitution were inspired by Greece's commitment to liberty, to freedom, and to democracy. Indeed, James Madison and Alexander Hamilton wrote in the Federalist Papers, and I quote, "Among the confederacies of antiquity, the most considerable was that of the Grecian republics." Today, those ideas continue to strengthen the United States. And working together, Greece and the United States have worked to advance the cause of freedom around the world.

It is against that backdrop of longstanding and close cooperation between the United States and Greece that I want to say a brief word about two issues that I know concern this audience greatly: Cyprus and the former Yugoslav Republic of Macedonia.

On Cyprus, I want to give you my personal

assurance that I and my administration will stay fully engaged in the U.N. process of negotiations, that we will give our full energies to helping reach a fair and permanent solution to the Cyprus dispute, and that we will not rest until a solution is found. Already, in the first 2 months of my Presidency, I have had the opportunity to raise the issue of Cyprus in serious discussions in person with President Özal of Turkey and by a long telephone conversation with Prime Minister Demirel. You can count on the United States to be there until this issue is resolved.

On Macedonia: Here, also, I take seriously the concerns that have been raised by Greece. Like Athens, we believe that a solution to the dispute over the name of the former Yugoslav Republic must be found rapidly to avoid the spread of further instability. I have admired the steady hand of Prime Minister Mitsotakis, and I want to work closely with him to find an appropriate solution to this problem. Progress has already been made on this issue, as I'm sure you know, and I believe we can find a just solution with broad vision and flexibility. Again, you can be sure that the United States will not allow the security of such a close friend and ally as Greece to be threatened in any way.

You know, I come from a State where Greek Americans make up only one-tenth of one percent of our population, and about half of them are in this room today. [*Laughter*] But their contributions to our State and to my life have been enormous.

Last night, my good friend from the time I was 9 years old, David Leopoulis, spent the night with me in the White House. He campaigned with me all over America. He became the symbol of an ordinary American who was for me. Think of it: Here I was, a WASP, not ordinary, supported by a Greek American who was ordinary. [*Laughter*] He appeared on television all over the country and worked with our campaign basically to talk about a lifetime of friendship and shared values. And our relationship, in that sense, is a mirror image of the relationship between the United States and Greece.

My personal health for many years has been in the hands of Dr. Drew Kampuris, whose father, Dr. Frank Kampuris, is an appointee of mine to the University of Arkansas board of trustees. There are others here in this audience and back home in Arkansas without whom I would not be here today.

My campaign and my administration have gained much from the talents of Greek Americans, including my close assistant and Director of Communications, George Stephanopoulos, who came up here a moment ago, who has become the heartthrob of the teen set of America. George's parents are in the audience today, and they did such a good job raising him I would like to ask them to stand up.

We did a little search for Greek Americans on the President's staff, and we discovered, notwithstanding some of their last names, the following fully qualify: my staff secretary, John Podesta; Sylvia Mathews, on the National Economic Commission staff—she hails from a little town in West Virginia, which just proves that you really are everywhere; Peter Pappas, my Associate Counsel; and George Tenet, my Special Assistant and Senior Director for Intelligence Programs at the National Security Council. Indeed, you might argue that I could have a reverse affirmative action suit for the overrepresentation of Greeks on the White House staff. [*Laughter*]

My good friend from New Jersey, Clay Constantinou, is here, who was with me from the beginning. There are others here in the audience who helped so much in the election. I want to note the presence of Angelo Zicapulous and many others who worked in the campaign for whom I'm very, very grateful.

And I also would like to ask us all to remember in our prayers my most formidable opponent in the Democratic primary, Paul Tsongas, as we pray for his recovery.

American politics has benefited greatly from the involvement of Greek Americans. In the Democratic Party, we had last year two great State party chairmen: Phil Angelides in California and Chris Spirou in New Hampshire. They each played an integral part in that election. And I can't help but say, and I hope the Republicans in the audience will forgive me, that it was rather unusual for a Democrat to carry either California or New Hampshire, and at least they think it was the Greek influence that put us over the top.

The Greek American community has always taken pride in and has been known for its commitment to the values that our country desperately needs more of today: commitment to family and neighborhood, to education and hard work, to freedom and the rule of law. These are the values that built America, shared still by the vast majority of Americans. But we know that for America to go where it needs to go, all Americans will have to embrace them again.

And so even as we look beyond our Nation's borders to the problems around the world, I ask those of you here in this wonderful house and those whom you represent throughout the country to lead our Nation in a re-embrace of these values born in the democracy of Greece, nourished in the democracy of the United States, now desperately needed in every city and hamlet in this country.

To Greece, the Nation that first shaped the political ideals we cherish, and to Greek Americans who help us every day, we are greatly indebted. And as I turn to the Archbishop for his remarks, let me say, courtesy of my distinguished language instructor, Mr. Stephanopoulos, *Zeto e Hellas.*

NOTE: The President spoke at 4:38 p.m. in the East Room at the White House. A tape was not available for verification of the content of these remarks. The proclamation is listed in Appendix D at the end of this volume.

Nomination for Posts at the Council of Economic Advisers and the Commerce and Housing and Urban Development Departments
March 25, 1993

The President added five senior members to his administration today, announcing his intention to nominate Alan Blinder and Joseph Stiglitz as members of the Council of Economic Advisers, Kathryn Sullivan as Chief Scientist at the Commerce Department's National Oceanic and Atmospheric Administration, Arati Prabhakar as Director of the National Institute of Standards and Technology at Commerce, and Marilynn Davis as the Assistant Secretary for Administration at the Department of Housing and Urban Development.

"I am asking these people today to fill roles

which are absolutely essential for the effective workings of this Government," said the President. "Providing sound economic advice, developing better models to understand environmental change, working to ensure an American edge in high technology, and finally bringing the operations of HUD under control are the kinds of actions that the American people need. The people that I am nominating will get the job done for them."

NOTE: Biographies of the nominees were made available by the Office of the Press Secretary.

Exchange With Reporters Prior to Discussions With Chancellor Helmut Kohl of Germany
March 26, 1993

Russia

Q. Mr. President, are you going to brief Mr. Kohl about your aid package, what your plans are?

The President. Well, we're going to discuss Russia and what we might both do. But we haven't met yet, so I can't say any more.

Q. Mr. President, have you received any word from Moscow how Yeltsin is doing? Are you further encouraged today, sir?

The President. Things look pretty good today. I think—they seem to be making progress toward——

Q. Are you comfortable speaking in German, Mr. President?

The President. No, but I understand a lot of what the Chancellor says. Perhaps not as much as what he understands what I say.

Bosnian Peace Agreement

Q. Mr. President, how long should the Serbs

be given before you push to lift the embargo?

The President. Well, let me say I just hope the Serbs will sign the agreement now.

NOTE: The exchange began at 10:40 a.m. in the Oval Office at the White House. A tape was not available for verification of the content of this exchange.

The President's News Conference With Chancellor Helmut Kohl of Germany
March 26, 1993

U.S.S. "Theodore Roosevelt"

The President. Good afternoon, ladies and gentlemen. Before we begin the press conference, I have a sad announcement to make. I have just been informed that five United States servicemen on a routine training flight with the United States ship *Theodore Roosevelt* have crashed at sea within a mile of the carrier. I want to express my deep concern over the accident. Just 2 weeks ago, I visited the U.S.S. *Theodore Roosevelt* and met the fine sailors and marines serving their Nation at sea there. I was profoundly impressed by their commitment, their dedication, and their professionalism. They made America proud. And I want to say that my thoughts and prayers are with the relatives and the shipmates of those five servicemen who are missing at sea.

Discussions With Chancellor Kohl

I want to begin by extending a warm welcome to Chancellor Kohl. We have had a wonderful visit. The personal chemistry between us, I think, was quite good. Helmut Kohl, over more than a decade of service in his present position, has proved himself time and again to be a true friend and staunch ally of the United States. Our peoples are closely linked with longstanding ties and common values. Our common bonds ensure that our two federal systems can learn much from each other. And indeed, I told the Chancellor that notwithstanding the persistent problems of cost in the German health care system, my wife had found a lot to learn from Germany.

We are working, our two countries, on the establishment of a project conceived by Chancellor Kohl and very close to his heart, the German American Academic Council, which will promote exchanges of people in the areas of science and technology and about which he might want to speak more in a moment.

During the cold war our two nations stood shoulder to shoulder in the common effort to contain communism in Europe. Today we must be leaders in the great crusade of the post-cold-war era to foster liberty, democracy, human rights, and free market economics throughout the world. If the world is to progress and prosper, the United States and Germany must work closely together. Our bilateral relationship is invaluable. Our relations are at the same time important in the context of the North Atlantic Alliance, the European Community, and the Conference on Security and Cooperation in Europe. In these three institutions, Germany serves as both an anchor of stability and a source of fresh initiatives to meet the challenges of our changing world.

A paramount challenge for the West in our generation is helping to ensure the survival of democracy and economic reform in Russia and the other republics of the former Soviet Union. Germany, as the largest single donor of assistance to Russia, has demonstrated its firm commitment to this historic cause. The United States and Germany must now strengthen our partnership on this effort and work both bilaterally and multilaterally to support Russian reform. The Chancellor and I discussed this issue at great length today.

I discussed with him the approach that I plan to take in the meeting with President Yeltsin at Vancouver. And I believe we are in agreement on the general approach. I know that we are committed to doing everything we possibly can to keep alive democracy and reform in Russia, and we believe it is in the immediate interests and the long-term interest of all of our people.

We also believe that the rest of the G–7 countries must cooperate with us and with each other to vigorously produce a program of support for Russia. We discussed in depth the troubling situations in Bosnia and elsewhere, and we conferred on trade and economics. We agreed that we must work hard to conclude the Uruguay GATT round this year, and we committed to work closely together in this endeavor.

As two of the world's leading exporting nations, the United States and Germany have a powerful interest in expanding global trade. I assured the Chancellor that the United States intends to remain politically and strategically engaged in Europe and to maintain a significant military presence on the Continent. The budget that I am fighting for in the Congress now would permit us to maintain a troop contingent on the order of 100,000 troops in Europe. We believe that American and European securities remain indivisible, and that the common threads of the post-cold-war era require common action. At the same time, we also recognize that each of us are reducing our defense budgets and must be increasingly responsible for our own defense needs.

Thirty years ago during his famous trip to Germany, President Kennedy toasted another great leader of the Christian Democratic Union and the German people, Konrad Adenauer, saying, "These are critical days." The President's pronouncement reflected his concern then for the survival of freedom and even humankind at the height of the cold war.

Today, thankfully the nuclear shadow is receding from both our lands. And the wall that divided the German people is gone. But I would say again, these are critical days, for the actions we take together now will help to determine the fate of democracy, the prosperity of our people, and the peace of the world. In that work I could not ask for a better partner than Chancellor Kohl or the German people. And I want to say to him, I am delighted with this first visit, and I look forward to working with you in the days ahead.

Chancellor Kohl. Mr. President, ladies and gentlemen. First, Mr. President, allow me to express my heartfelt sympathy on the loss and the fear, because we don't have any detailed information about the loss of life of five American officers. I hope very much that these soldiers may be able to return to their families safe and sound, because they serve the freedom and the security of their country, the United States of America. And without that service,

there would be no freedom and peace and no reunification for Germany. And this is why I am very sad about the things that you have just had to present to us. And I should like to ask you to convey to the families of the people concerned my feelings of sympathy.

Ladies and gentlemen, today I had my first meeting with the President of the United States of America. It was a friendly exchange of views. It is something that can be easily said in English; the chemistry is right. You said so, and I am pleased to take it up, indeed, the chemistry is right. We touched upon many issues, issues, many of which are very close to our hearts, at an important point in time of international politics, of European politics. And I was also able to present many things that are important to German politics.

American-German relations, to put it in a nutshell, are for us, Germans and for me personally, today equally important if not more important than 30 years ago. More than 30 years ago, when I was for the first time elected to the German Parliament, the alliance between the Americans and Germans, the European-American alliance, was much more matter of fact, because we lived under the threat and in the fear of the war. Remember the Berlin blockade, the Berlin Wall, many challenges that we had to master together, down to the things that happened under John F. Kennedy in Cuba.

Today, many of these people have been released. They're free again. But in Europe and in Germany, too, there are quite a few who believe that there were no dangers existent anymore now that the times are changed. For these reasons, American-German relations have become ever more important. The psychological environment has changed.

I said to you, Mr. President, and I should like to repeat this here and now, in this house of Europe that we are in the process of building right now—and I should like to go into greater detail on that later on—it is of existential importance for me, a German, that the Americans have a flat in this house; that the American soldiers and troops, the presence in Europe and in Germany, documents that they're not there for decorative purposes but to defend freedom and security of people. The fact that we can further develop the relations in the economic field, and that includes that despite the problems that we have, we bring about a speedy and successful conclusion of the GATT round.

This is something that we touched upon, too. We agreed on that we want to work on this.

You were so kind, Mr. President, to mention that in the cultural and scientific field, we have the intention to intensify relations between both our countries. You mentioned the German American Academic Council which is to be founded this year. I am very happy that you have agreed that once the necessary decisions have been taken in the next few weeks, we will found this economic council. This is important for the public in both our countries. It is for me very important that young Americans, that young Germans visit the other country, vice versa, that they get to know the people and their culture. To put it differently, Mr. President, that we plant many young trees so that we have a forest later on of things that we share, that we have in common.

I should also like to add for those who might have heard different reports on this here in the United States, there is no alternative for the Germans to a policy that makes progress with European unification—and we are the engine of this development—and at the same time, places great care and value on American-German relations. This is never an either-or; it has to be a this-as-well-as-the-other. Both include each other and do not exclude one another.

And I should like to say this. Because we are now confronted with a common challenge and major task, that is: We have to see to it that the spirit of reform, the willingness to establish democratic structures and a pleuralist society, market economic structures in Russia and the CIS, is continuing.

I'm very grateful to you personally, Mr. President, for the determination and the courage that you have documented in the last few weeks in standing by Boris Yeltsin. I underline and subscribe to every single word that you said on this one, that reforms are successful in Russia. And both of us are aware of the fact that any type of setback will in the end turn out to be much more expensive than any type of assistance we have the intention of granting right now.

We have discussed many issues and items on our plate. The members of our staff will continue prior to the meeting with President Yeltsin and the American President to continue to discuss these matters. Then we have the G–7 finance and foreign minister's meeting in Tokyo, the 14th and 15th of April. We want to send a message to the people of Russia that the West, under the leadership of the Americans and the American President, will do everything in its power to see to it that Russia and other successor states to the Soviet Union stand a chance to walk on their own path towards freedom.

We, the Germans, and I outlined this earlier on to you Mr. President, as far as this question is concerned, are very committed, not only because we are neighbors of the former Soviet Union and the threat, if there was a relapse to form a dictator structures, would effect us first and foremost, but we do so because we have made our own experiences.

We were standing in the Oval Office looking at the sculpture of Harry S. Truman, and I was reminded of the importance that the activities of George Marshall and Harry S. Truman had for Germany when the zero hour when we were outlawed in the world. These two stood up, stood by us, and assisted us. These were the fathers of the Marshall Plan, of a moral gesture of coexistence and cooperation. And this, to my mind, is fair to say: A flourishing industry and country has developed, the former Federal Republic of Germany.

And if the Americans at that point in time had stood back and said, "Well what do we care? The Germans shall see what will become of it. And if something good comes out of it, we'll be proud to say we assisted, and if not, we will say, we've always told you so didn't we, and therefore we stood back."

This kind of policy, a policy pursued by Harry S. Truman and George Marshall rules a successful recipe for the whole of Europe, West Europe. And this is why I should like to tell my American listeners here that you can learn lessons from history. And with a view to what is happening right now in Moscow, I think the message is what counts. The message indicating in what way the big countries of the western democracies and market economic systems feel committed to assist.

Allow me also to say that we discussed *in extenso*, Mr. President, the developments in the former Yugoslavia. The Bosnian President happened to be here this morning, and we met briefly in the White House. We would wish to see that use is being made of all opportunities to see to it that a cease-fire occurs, that then peace can be reached. What is happening to the people there, day-in, day-out, belongs in numbers amongst the most terrible experiences of this very century. And here again, I'm happy and grateful, Mr. President, that you and your administration have taken a clear position on this.

Once again, thank you very much for this friendly reception, for the friendly and open talks that we had.

May I perhaps just briefly announce, Mr. President, that I repeat my invitation to you and to your wife to come and to visit in Germany, and that you were so kind, Mr. President, to follow that invitation.

Russia

Q. Do you think that President Yeltsin emerges from the constitutional crisis that seems to be easing there, weakened or strengthened? And how would that affect the aid that you would propose to send to him?

The President. First of all, I think it's important that we not place too much importance on the momentary event, the day-to-day events, not because they're not heartening today, they are, but because it's difficult to know what's going to happen from day to day now. I have said always that I am proceeding to the summit with President Yeltsin with the firm intention of working with him and trying to propose some things that the United States can join with Germany and the other G–7 countries. And doing that will be helpful in the short run and in the long run in promoting democracy and market economics and an improvement in the difficult economic situation they face. So I feel pretty good about where we are with it now.

Bosnian Peace Agreement

Q. Mr. President, how long would you give the Serbs to respond to the peace overtures, to the peace pact that's been signed by the two other parties? Would you favor imposing a deadline prior to lifting an arms embargo? And given the carnage in this place and the amount of arms that are there already, why would you even consider that to be a good alternative?

The President. First, let me say that you heard the Chancellor say President Izetbegovic was here with us today. He met with the Vice President; then I went back to visit with him briefly. The Chancellor wanted to see him, too, so we just had an impromptu brief meeting.

This signing by the Bosnians has just occurred. We're going to do everything we can now to put on a full-court press, first diplomatically, to secure the agreement of the Serbs. We will do what we can if there is any delay whatever in trying to strengthen the embargo. The embargo has already been quite effective in causing some economic difficulty. We expect the United Nations to take up the enforcement of the no-fly zone within the next few days. We will discuss a number of other measures, including the arms embargo, with our allies. As you know, it's not simply a decision for the United States. But I think that the main thing is that we now have two of the three blocs having agreed that we ought to have this. The Croats have signed; the Bosnian Government has now signed. We need to keep the pressure on, and we will do what we can. I don't want to rule in or rule out a specific timetable or a specific action, because the developments are recent and the decision has not been made on the specific timetable.

Q. Mr. President, do you have any more reason to believe today than you might have earlier that our allies, particularly those who have troops on the ground there, would be more willing than they've been to see the arms embargo lifted?

The President. I'll say this. Our allies are now more eager to see the no-fly zone enforced. And I think that the international impatience is going to grow rather rapidly with the Serbs if they want to continue the carnage in Bosnia, when not very long ago they acted as if they thought this was a pretty good deal.

Aid to Russia

Q. Mr. Chancellor, you've seen or you've heard—the President presented his—or gave you a good idea what's going to be included in his Russian aid package. Do you see it as being adequate, sir, or do you think it will make a difference over there?

Chancellor Kohl. I think that indeed we have a possibility to cooperate. You may know that the Federal Republic of Germany has provided, by far, more than 50 percent of financial assistance to the states of the former Soviet Union. And I am very happy that the President has again taken a new initiative in the framework of the G–7, but going beyond that to wrap up a package of assistance to Boris Yeltsin and the reformist forces in the country.

And I believe that this package should contain three to four elements to put it in a general matter: bilateral assistance, multilateral assistance, then questions to provide relief goods to the country, but also specific types of assistance by way of providing help towards self-help. Let us think of the safety of civilian nuclear power plants in the former Soviet Union. In Munich, at the G–7 summit, we discussed that issue, too. And I'm very happy that the American President is taking up that idea to the question of the safety, you know, based on the experiences of Chernobyl, has turned out to be a central question touching each and every one of us; not a question that is restricted to Russia and the Ukraine but is addressed to all of us.

And if we take all these issues together and wrap them up in a package, I think we stand a good chance to be successful. And I would like to express my support to the President on this.

[*At this point, a question was asked in German, and a translation was not provided.*]

Chancellor Kohl. Well, the only thing that we did was that we exchanged the information on that—the Federal Government in case a decision of the Security Council will be taking— what the Federal Government will do.

German Constitutional Conflicts

Q. [*Inaudible*]—satisfied with that report to solve the German constitutional conflicts that way?

The President. I think he's been remarkably deft in his dealing with the issue so far.

Aid to Russia

Q. Thank you, Mr. President. Will you go further than President Bush did in your aid package to Russia, such as including long-term concessional financing or government guarantees? And can we expect the size of the package to be larger or less than the $24 billion that was attempted last year but not completed?

The President. Well, of course, the package was not quite a $24 billion package. It was in theory that, over a long period of years. But if you go back and look at what was actually released, the Congress specifically appropriated $650 million in aid and an $800 million appropriation under the Nunn-Lugar bill to help to denuclearize Russia and the other nuclear Republics. Most of that money has not been spent yet. And I say that not as a criticism.

Let me back up and say one of the places

where we started this discussion, in-house here, is to ask ourselves, what happened to the policy that was announced last year? What money has been appropriated and spent? What has been approved, but not spent? What are the problems? Are there any problems where the United States has not followed through? Are there problems where there are bottlenecks or failures in Russia? Are there problems because we said in theory we would support a few billion dollars in aid through international institutions, but Russia can't comply right now with the eligibility requirements for the IMF, for example? We analyzed all that.

And so, when we finally put together this package, which has not been done yet—I'm in the middle of congressional consultations and talking with people outside as well as inside the Government—we will have made an honest effort to assess what happened to the last proposal, what the problems were, how to get around them. And I can't yet tell you—we've not yet made a final decision on the dollar value, but I expect it will be broadbased and comprehensive.

Bosnian Peace Agreement

Q. The sanctions so far have just about wrecked the Serbian economy, yet there doesn't seem to be any deterrent effect on the military aggression. With the developments in Srebrenica and related communities, what makes the administration think that further sanctions will have any impact on Serbian behavior?

The President. I think the real issue is whether the cumulative impact of the events of the last few days will bring the Serbs to the signing table. That is, whether or not they really want so desperately to cleanse the Bosnian Muslims out of all their living space that they will defy now what is now for the first time, for the first time, the virtually unanimous opinion of all the governments that they will be in the wrong if they do not sign this agreement, which they had previously complimented. I don't know what's going to happen, Andrea [Andrea Mitchell, NBC News]. If I did, I would tell you.

But let me say I think we have a chance to get a good-faith signing. I think we have to try. We have to give that a few days before we up the ante again.

Q. Mr. President, well, what if the Serbs do sign this agreement? Are we still committed to sending U.S. ground forces in to enforce the agreement within 72 hours? And what happens if there are some Serbs who don't honor the agreement and U.S. troops and other troops, peacekeeping forces, get in the way? That sounds like it's a prescription for some potentially bloody fighting to continue.

The President. Well, all those decisions obviously would have to be made. We have not made those decisions yet. All I have said is that the United States would be prepared to participate in a multinational effort to help keep the peace. We believe that we'll be able to tell whether there is or is not a good-faith signing and whether there is or is not a peace. Of course, the whole reason you have peacekeeping forces is that from time to time the peace may be broken, but you hope it will be a general commitment to the peace. I still feel that that is an appropriate approach.

Multilateral Trade Negotiations

Q. Mr. President, both you gentlemen mentioned the GATT agreement and voiced optimism that a solution could be reached fairly shortly. As I recall, a little over a year ago, Chancellor Kohl was here and had been optimistic that perhaps it would be resolved before the Munich economic summit. Obviously that didn't happen. Currently there seems to be more tension between the U.S. and its trading partners than there was a year ago. What is it that makes you both optimistic that a breakthrough can be reached?

Chancellor Kohl. Well, for me, there's no doubt about the fact that it was a mistake not to conclude it prior to Munich. And then we had many reasons after the summit had taken place. But I said to the President today that there is a convincing argument when we meet in Tokyo and read to the public the final document of the G–7 meeting, and Prime Minister Miyazawa stands up in front of 1,800 journalists and reads to them that the G–7 participants' countries are convinced that the successful conclusion of the GATT Uruguay round is an important precondition for fighting the recession, there would be an uproar of laughter greeting him. And some of you will take up the document from London and the document from Munich and hold it up in the air and wave it at the gentlemen. And in describing this to you, I think, and I said luckily so, luckily you know in what position we find ourselves in.

But as I said, I have a serious argument in favor of a successful conclusion which people tend not to mention in the discussion. We all believe in a free international trade, and we need it if we want to get out of the recession. The Americans luckily are, as is clearly visible, on a good path out of it. But hardly ever do we talk about the third world countries. The economic situation in the third world countries is miserable. It is devastating, and the present recession affects the third world country far more than it affects the industrialized countries.

And in the talks that I had with the President and Vice President Gore, we talked about the work that has to follow the conference of Rio, the UNCED. One cannot expect from us that in the question of the damage done to the tropical rain forest that we make progress on these issues if countries who undergo recessionist development are not being assisted by opening up the GATT Uruguay round and bringing it to a successful conclusion.

I, however, do not believe that things have improved in the course of the last 2 years, and they will be even worsened if we wait another year for a conclusion. Therefore, I think that the Tokyo meeting and the threat of having about 2,000 journalists standing there laughing at us is quite a positive thing.

The President. Let me make one other point. It is true that there have been a couple of points of contention since I became President. Both of them arose out of cases which developed well before I took office. But I also think you have to look at the upside in terms of the last 10 years. Just take our relationship with Europe: We have an agreement now on agriculture, if it can be held. We have an agreement on airline manufacturing and to what extent subsidies can be permitted and what is it not, if it can be held. We have experience now of the last 2 years of what happened without a GATT agreement when we've had very low economic growth in Europe and a very persistent and lagging recession in the United States. And now with the United States making an effort to come out of this recession but the projected growth rates in Europe low, I think that there is an understanding that it is very difficult for one country to grow without more general growth throughout the world; and that Europe, the United States, and Japan, all in different ways, have a big stake in getting a GATT agreement that will set a framework that will permit us to promote global growth. That's why I think we've got a good chance to make it, and I hope we do.

Thank you very much.

NOTE: The President's eighth news conference began at 2:31 p.m. in the East Room at the White House. Chancellor Kohl spoke in German, and his remarks were translated by an interpreter.

Nomination for Three Ambassadorial Posts
March 26, 1993

The President named three senior Foreign Service officers to key Latin American ambassadorial posts today, announcing his intention to nominate John Maisto to be Ambassador to Nicaragua, James Cheek to be Ambassador to Argentina, and William Pryce to be Ambassador to Honduras.

"Our relationships with our Latin American neighbors are among the most important we have," said the President. "I am very glad to be putting them into steady hands today."

NOTE: Biographies of the nominees were made available by the Office of the Press Secretary.

The President's Radio Address
March 27, 1993

Good morning. Last November you demanded a new spirit of action and an end to gridlock in Washington. Well, what you demanded is finally taking hold. The House and the Senate are now completing work on the heart of our bold economic plan for new directions: to create jobs, to increase incomes, to bring down our terrible national debt.

The actions taking place in Congress are a welcome departure from the status quo of the past. For 12 years, our Government was paralyzed by partisan gridlock, our economy caught in the grip of powerful special interests who bent the system so that they could win at our expense. Our deficits went up, and the creation of high-paying jobs went down. And good families found themselves working harder, paying more in taxes, and bringing less money home.

When you sent me and our administration here, you wanted a plan of action, and we've provided it. Our plan is based on this simple principle: The best social program is a good job, and the best way to reduce the deficit is by cutting spending and making smart investments to grow the economy.

Last week, the House of Representatives endorsed this plan. And this week, the Senate did the same, approving our budget resolution in record time, just 36 days after we took it to you, the American people.

I salute our supporters on Capitol Hill for their outstanding work. And also I want to thank Vice President Gore, who's worked tirelessly to enlist lawmakers in the cause of change. We should all be pleased that we're on our way toward putting this plan in motion.

Before the Congress goes home for Easter recess, I'm counting on them to complete their work on the plan, to finish the budget and pass our proposals to create good jobs in the short term. The progress we've made shows we're beating the status quo. And you have given us the clout to do it.

We've come a long way in 9½ weeks. Interest rates are down. The power of investment is returning to the economy. Confidence is strong. But I won't rest until we right the economy and guarantee for future generations the prosperity that should be the birthright of every American.

We can begin with this program, because the best way to build the economy and lay the foundation for the future is to create 8 million jobs in the next 4 years and by adopting the immediate investments that will create a half a million jobs in the near term. That's what this plan does.

To create jobs and to make our economy more productive, we're planning to build and repair new roads and transit systems. We want to place hundreds of thousands of Americans in productive summer jobs and get young people the education they need while they're working. And we're challenging the private sector to create more and giving them the incentives to do it.

We want to fund future-oriented research and equip our Nation's young scientists and engineers with the skills to excel in high-technology fields. We want to convert military technology for peaceful uses that will benefit all of us and help communities hard hit by base closings and cutbacks on defense contracts. We want to retrain the defense workers put out of work by the end of the cold war. These people are patriots, and they deserve nothing less than a chance to work in civilian jobs that will earn them the kind of money they earned protecting our national defense.

Some people say these investments are unnecessary and costly. Their only alternative is to do nothing, accept things just the way they are, and hope, with no Government action in partnership with the private sector, somehow things will get better. These friends of the status quo have tried everything in recent days to show that we don't need new investments. But they've forgotten: We tried cutting investments for years. We forgot about the human equation, the necessity to train and educate people. And guess what? We didn't get jobs.

We still have a jobless economic recovery. If this were even an average recovery, we'd have 3 million more Americans working today. Many of the jobs that were created last month were part-time jobs. And the unemployment rate is still higher today than it was at the bottom of the recession.

This job drought has put individuals and families under great stress. Americans don't want handouts; they just want a hand up, a chance to work and to provide for their own. And our plan does just that. In doing so, we'll be on our way to a real job-creating recovery that gets the incomes of American workers growing again.

We have to raise the living standards of our people now and in the long run. To keep our preeminence in the world economy, we have to create a smarter work force, with lifelong learning that trains all our people for better, higher paying jobs. And we need to develop the new technologies that are farsighted, that will create the high-wage jobs of today and tomorrow. If we're shortsighted today, we'll be blindsided tomorrow.

That's why I'm working hard, not just on this economic plan, although it is the centerpiece of our efforts, but on other fronts too: from controlling health care costs and providing the security of health care to all Americans, to moving people from welfare into jobs, to correcting the way we finance campaigns to bring the people in and move the special interests out. Each step of the way, I'm trying to listen to you. What happens on the short stretch of road between 1600 Pennsylvania Avenue and Capitol Hill is only meaningful if we're acting for you and with you. This is the promise of our new plan for new directions.

Thanks for listening.

NOTE: The President spoke at 10:06 a.m. from the Oval Office at the White House.

Exchange With Reporters in Little Rock, Arkansas
March 29, 1993

Aid to Russia

Q. Sir, three-quarters of Americans say we're already giving enough aid to Russia.

The President. We give a lot more money than we give to Russia to smaller countries. We've got a big interest there. And I realize that the responsibility is on me to communicate to the American people any kind of pay package I propose and to justify it. That's my responsibility, and I intend to assume it.

Q. Where would you get another billion dollars, sir?

The President. We're working on the details of it. We'll be able to announce something——

Q. Are you concerned by these latest poll

figures, sir, that many Americans, 75 percent of the Americans, think we already give the Russians enough?

The President. Well, foreign aid is unpopular in every country in the world, and it's always been unpopular here. And I haven't really had a chance to talk much directly to the American people about what's going on there, what our stake in it and what their stake in it is, what the American people's stake in it. The American people are smart enough to know that we can't determine the course of events in Russia all by ourselves. They know that. But we can have an impact on it. And my job as President is to convince the citizens of this country that they have an immediate and personal interest in the outcome of events. I think I can do it, and I'm going to do my best.

NOTE: The exchange began at 11:05 a.m. outside the U.S. Male barbershop. A tape was not available for verification of the content of this exchange.

Nomination for Administrator of the Agency for International Development
March 29, 1993

The President announced his intention today to nominate Brian Atwood as Administrator of the Agency for International Development, U.S. International Development Cooperation Agency.

"Secretary Christopher and I have concluded that the skills that Brian Atwood brings to the State Department are greatly needed at AID," said the President. "I am confident that he will be the kind of effective administrator that our foreign assistance programs need at this time. His proven effectiveness and his commitment to democratic change make him an ideal choice."

NOTE: A biography of the nominee was made available by the Office of the Press Secretary.

Nomination for Assistant Secretaries of Education
March 29, 1993

The President named two national education leaders to key positions at the Department of Education today, expressing his intention to nominate Colorado education official David Longanecker to be Assistant Secretary for Postsecondary Education and education innovator Sharon Porter Robinson to be Assistant Secretary for Educational Research and Improvement.

"I have pledged to make the Department of Education a center for innovative policymaking," said the President. "David Longanecker and Sharon Porter Robinson will join with Secretary Riley and the rest of his team to bring the leadership that will make that happen."

NOTE: Biographies of the nominees were made available by the Office of the Press Secretary.

Nomination for Administrator of General Services
March 29, 1993

In a move designed to cut waste and promote efficiency in the Federal Government, the President today announced his intention to nominate Roger Johnson, chairman an CEO of Western Digital, to head the giant General Services Administration. The first Republican named to a top post in the new administration, Johnson served as an outspoken advocate for the Clinton-Gore ticket during the Presidential campaign, joining with other Orange County, CA, Republicans to endorse the Clinton-Gore plan to reinvest the Government and make it work for the American people.

"Roger Johnson's skills as a business leader and strong commitment to Government change will ensure that economy and efficiency are standard rule at the new GSA," said the President. "Partisan politics have no place at this crucial juncture of our history. We must all work together to get our Government back on track."

NOTE: A biography of the nominee was made available by the Office of the Press Secretary.

Nomination for President of the Overseas Private Investment Corporation
March 30, 1993

The President today announced his intention to nominate Ruth Harkin, a top corporate attorney with expertise in international trade and investment, as President of the Overseas Private Investment Corporation, U.S. International Development Cooperation Agency.

"Ruth Harkin has the experience, know-how and new ideas to make OPIC an innovative Agency that will work aggressively to increase American investment overseas while protecting jobs at home," the President said.

NOTE: A biography of the nominee was made available by the Office of the Press Secretary.

Nomination for Assistant Secretaries of Defense
March 30, 1993

The President announced his intention today to nominate Edward Warner to be Assistant Secretary of Defense for Strategy and Resources and Charles Freeman to be Assistant Secretary of Defense for Regional Security.

"Ted Warner and Charles Freeman are two of the most outstanding people working on defense issues today," said the President. "I am extremely pleased that they are joining Secretary Aspin at the Pentagon."

NOTE: Biographies of the nominees were made available by the Office of the Press Secretary.

Exchange With Reporters Prior to a Cabinet Meeting
March 31, 1993

Budget Resolution and Stimulus Package

Q. Mr. President, are you going to get a $1 billion package for the Russians in aid?

The President. I'll have more to say about that tomorrow in Annapolis. I'm going out there to speak.

Let me say in front of the whole Cabinet here, it was just 6 weeks ago that I presented my plan to the United States Congress. They are on the verge of adopting the budget resolution, which will drastically reduce the Federal deficit. The Senate, I believe, is on the verge of passing the jobs program to put a half-million jobs into this economy. Things are going well. We are moving with remarkable speed.

I do want to make one point, which was obscured a little in the news stories today. I say that not out of criticism, but on the issue of the drop in consumer confidence, the Wall Street Journal had a very detailed article which showed that the principal reason for it is the continuing worry of the American people that this economy is not producing jobs. And consumers without jobs don't have confidence because they don't have money with which to consume. So it is very important that this week, before the Congress goes home, that we pass the budget resolution to reduce the deficit and the jobs program to create jobs. If we can do that, this will be an historic 6 weeks in which we are moving at a very rapid pace.

Q. Do you think, Mr. President, that the Republicans will seek to filibuster against the stimulus package? And if they do, what's your strategy?

The President. Well, we're going to try to win. I don't think so. I believe some of the Republicans support this. As a matter of fact, I think a lot of them support it. Some of them may never vote for it because of partisan divisions. But I think they know that the American people will be very disappointed to find out that a half a million jobs went by the wayside because 41—not even a majority, but 41 Senators stopped a vote from occurring. I don't think that's going to happen. I would be very surprised.

NOTE: The exchange began at 10:12 a.m. in the Cabinet Room at the White House. A tape was not available for verification of the content of this exchange.

Nomination for Posts at the Department of Defense
March 31, 1993

The President will nominate Dr. Anita Jones to be Director of Defense Research and Engineering and Graham Allison, Edwin Dorn, and Morton Halperin to be Assistant Secretaries of Defense for Plans and Policy, Personnel and Readiness, and Democracy and Human Rights respectively, the White House announced today.

"At this time of change and uncertainty, it is imperative that we have a topflight team at the Pentagon," said the President. "These four people have what it takes to keep the Defense Department moving forward."

NOTE: Biographies of the nominees were made available by the Office of the Press Secretary.

Exchange With Reporters Prior to a Meeting With Congressional Leaders
April 1, 1993

Q. Mr. President, is your stimulus package in trouble? That's what we hear.

The President. Well, we just passed the budget, but I'm celebrating that right now. I think we can pass it. We'll keep working on it. We have to have 60 votes to pass it, but we'll keep

working on it.

We're here talking about Russia today.

NOTE: The exchange began at 10:30 a.m. in the Cabinet Room at the White House. A tape was not available for verification of the content of this exchange.

Remarks to Midshipmen at the United States Naval Academy in Annapolis, Maryland
April 1, 1993

Thank you very much, Admiral Lynch, men and women of the brigade. I'm delighted to be here. They say there's no such thing as a free lunch, but I thought as President I'd come here and test the theory.

In a few moments I am going to deliver a speech, as Admiral Lynch has already said, to the newspaper editors of our country about our Nation's purposes in the world and specifically about what we should be doing now to promote democracy in Russia and in the other Republics of the former Soviet Union. The struggle to build free societies in those new nations is probably the great security challenge of our age, one of the greatest opportunities the United States will have. And how we do this job, in many ways, will shape the future that you will have in our Armed Forces.

I believe we must do what we can to support the reform movement and to support democracy, a precious commodity anywhere in the world. And that is why my first trip out of the United States as President will be to Vancouver, Canada, this weekend to meet with the Russian President Boris Yeltsin.

The success of the changes that he and the other reformers are advancing will ultimately have an impact on the life of every American but especially an impact on your lives. If Russia can continue to be a partner with us addressing global concerns and dousing the flames of regional crises, then it is less likely that you and the men and women under your command will have to be sent into harm's way during my term or under some future President.

I respect the difficulty and the danger of the work that the men and women of our armed services perform. I understand that in a new way now, because last month I watched the flight operations on the deck of the United States ship *Theodore Roosevelt*. And I was deeply saddened a few days after I was there to learn that five naval aviators lost their lives returning to the *TR* from operations in support of our presence in the former Yugoslavia.

The conflict in that region and those we see elsewhere remind us that we have entered a new world that will test us in new ways. Our Navy will play an important role in getting us past those tests, as it has throughout our history. To help the men and women in our Navy perform effectively and safely, we will need talented, committed leadership as never before.

Leadership can take many forms. It can be command of a ship or a submarine, of an aviation squadron, or of a naval base. It can show itself in training commanders by teaching leadership to the next generation of midshipmen as your instructors are doing here at the Academy. Whatever form it takes, your leadership will make an important contribution not only to the Navy but to the security of our great Nation. This is a new and a hopeful world but also one where there is still danger. I want you to know that I'm proud of you and the work you do, and so is the Nation you have chosen to serve.

Finally, although I'm sure this doesn't apply to any of you here, I read this little sign. As you might imagine as I travel around the country, I'm used to seeing such signs. [*Laughter*] Some of them are not altogether favorable. That's a good part of our democracy, that people feel free to express their views.

One of the most compelling signs that I saw was on the way from the airport the other day in New York State to the home of President Franklin Roosevelt in Hyde Park. And there were hundreds of people standing along the road in 8 degree temperature, and one person was holding a sign that said, "Just do something." So that's what I'm going to do.

In the tradition followed by Commanders in Chief in visits to the service academy, I hereby grant amnesty to the members of the brigade—the last thing the Superintendent said before I got up here was to finish the sentence so that it would not be a total and complete amnesty—from all punishments for all 4000-level conduct offenses. And even though this is April Fools' Day, that's not April fools.

Thank you very much, and God bless you all.

NOTE: The President spoke at 1:03 p.m. in Bancroft Hall at the U.S. Naval Academy. In his remarks, he referred to Rear Adm. Thomas C. Lynch, USN, Superintendent of the U.S. Naval Academy.

Remarks to the American Society of Newspaper Editors in Annapolis
April 1, 1993

Thank you very much, Mr. Topping, distinguished guests at the head table, ladies and gentlemen. I want to say a special word of thanks and acknowledgement to the Superintendent of the Naval Academy, Admiral Lynch, who's here with us and who came up with me. He just gave me something I was told even a politician couldn't get in this country anymore, a free lunch. [*Laughter*]

I just had lunch with 4,000 of the finest young men and women in this country or in any country, who are here at the Naval Academy. I went around the table, the table where I was sitting, and I asked every one of the young men and women who were seated at my table why they decided to come to the Naval Academy. And I wish every one of you could have heard their answers. It would have moved you immensely.

And as I go now to meet with President Yeltsin in Vancouver, I will be even more freshly reminded about what the stakes are, because as much as any group of Americans, those young people about to enter our Nation's Armed Forces have a very great stake in what will occur.

I'm delighted to be here with all of you who do so much to shape what our people think and even to give them access to what they need to know about these and other important issues. Had we met last year, if my voice had been in full flower, we doubtless would have talked almost exclusively about the economic issues facing America. And I am quite mindful of the fact that I am the first member of my party for a very long time who received a majority of the editorial endorsements of America's newspapers. That is something that I took very seriously. I was honored to receive them. And I can only hope that a year or so from now, those of you who did it will still be glad you did. In my heart of hearts, I hope that those of you who didn't will be sorry you didn't. [*Laughter*] But today, in this magnificent place in this wonderful State, I might also say I'm delighted to be joined here by my former colleague in the Governors' Association and my friend Governor Don Schaefer, the Governor of Maryland. Thank you for being here.

I want to talk to you about the events in Russia, about our policies toward the newly independent states of the former Soviet Union, and about my meetings with President Boris Yeltsin this weekend. But first, I wish to speak about America's purposes in the world. That is not something we often examine, for it is human nature to focus on daily affairs most of the time. In our own lives, we do our jobs, we raise our children, we nurture our relationships, we struggle with the dilemmas of the moment one day at a time. Yet we are each guided by some sense of purpose, drawn from our families and our faith, which shapes the millions of small events of our life into a larger work that bears the imprint of our character.

And so it is in the life of a nation. Decisions command attention. Crises drive action. But it is only with an overriding sense of purpose, drawn from their history and their cultures, that great nations can rise above the daily tyranny of the urgent to construct their security, to build their prosperity, to advance their interests, and to reaffirm their values.

A clear sense of purpose is most essential, yet most elusive, at times of profound global change. A half a century ago, our Nation emerged victorious from the Second World War to discover itself in wholly unfamiliar terrain. The old empires of Europe and Asia were gone. A new Communist empire loomed. Ours was the only economy in the world still strong and dominant.

Former Secretary of State, the late Dean Acheson, later described it as a time of "great obscurity." Yet in that dim obscurity, he and George Marshall and President Harry Truman and other leaders in both political parties saw the stakes clearly enough. They acted decisively. They accepted the mantle of leadership. Their sense of purpose helped to rescue Europe, to rebuild Japan, to contain aggression, and to foster two generations of unprecedented prosperity and peace.

And now thanks in large measure to their vision, carried forward through succeeding generations, and thanks, too, to the enormous courage of the people of Russia and the other Republics of the former Soviet Union and the people of Eastern Europe, freedom has once again won a very great victory.

Over the past 4 years, the Berlin Wall crumbled. The cold war ended. The Soviet Union gave way to 15 sovereign states. Millions threw off the constricting yoke of communism so they could assume instead the ennobling burdens of democracy.

Yet these victories also confront us with a moment of profound change, a challenge. The collapse of the Soviet Union changed the international order forever. The emerging economic powerhouses of the Pacific are changing the financial order forever. The proliferation of demonic weapons of mass destruction threaten to change the distribution of military power forever. Resurgent ethnic conflict is challenging the very meaning of the nation state. The rise of a global economy has changed the linkages between our domestic and our foreign policies and, I would argue to you, has made them indivisible.

In a time of dramatic global change we must define America's broader purposes anew. And part of that purpose clearly consists of reviving economic opportunity and growth here at home, for the opportunity to do well here at home is the ultimate basis of our influence abroad.

Congress is acting this week to break the gridlock, to build our prosperity. Just today, the Congress passed the heart of my economic program, a long-term plan to drastically reduce the deficit and increase investment in our Nation's economic future. After years of policies that have diminished our future, Washington has finally realized that the best social program is a good job, and the best route to deficit reduction is a growing economy founded on a bold plan of change that will both cut spending and increase investment to empower the working people of this country.

Our program invests in people by changing the Tax Code to reward work and investment;

by working to ensure that anybody who works 40 hours a week and has children in the home won't have to live in poverty anymore; by providing our children with education and nutrition and the immunizations they need to start life successfully; by reinvesting the way we educate and train our workers to make it properly adequate for the new global economy; and by creating jobs now through investment in infrastructure and safe streets and community development in communities large and small all across this land.

The American people had the courage to call for change last November and gave me the awesome opportunity and responsibility to try to implement that change. I am hopeful that Congress will now have the courage to vote for all those changes this week. As I said, today they voted for a plan that both reduces the long-term deficit and increases our investment in the things that will grow this economy, in new jobs and new technologies and new education strategies.

I hope now they will adopt the short-term jobs program that will add a half a million new jobs to this country over the next 2 years. Let me say parenthetically that one of the great challenges of every wealthy country in the world today is not only to promote growth but to create jobs. There are many, many examples in the 1980's, when in Europe and elsewhere countries had great growth but produced no new jobs. That is what has happened here in the last year or so. And we must prove that we can do better.

As I have said so often over the last year and a half, in the global village, with this kind of global economy, there is simply no clear dividing line between domestic and foreign policy. We can't be strong abroad unless we're strong at home. And we cannot be strong at home unless we are actively engaged in the world which is shaping events for every American. There is a sense in which every one of the young people in this country today will live a life which is shaped by events beyond our borders as well as events within our borders.

And so today I say again we must have a clear sense of our purposes around the world. Everyone knows the world remains a dangerous place. And our preeminent imperative is to ensure our own security. That is why we're working to ensure that our military is not only the finest in the world but also specifically tailored for the challenges of this new era, for the central fronts of our fight for a safe world have moved from the plains of northern Europe to our efforts to stem weapons of mass destruction, to relieve ethnic turmoil, to promote democracy, to expand markets, and to protect the global environment.

During the cold war our foreign policies largely focused on relations among nations. Our strategies sought a balance of power to keep the peace. Today, our policies must also focus on relations within nations, on a nation's form of governance, on its economic structure, on its ethnic tolerance. These are of concern to us, for they shape how these nations treat their neighbors as well as their own people and whether they are reliable when they give their word. In particular, democracies are far less likely to wage war on other nations than dictatorships are.

Emphatically, the international community cannot seek to heal every domestic dispute or to resolve every ethnic conflict. Some are simply beyond our reach. But within practical bounds and with a sense of clear strategic priorities, we must do what we can to promote the democratic spirit and the economic reforms that can tip the balance for progress well into the next century.

From the first hours of my administration, several critical situations have demanded our attention, in Iraq, in Somalia, in Haiti, in the Middle East, in the former Yugoslavia, and elsewhere. We have sought to develop strategies to address these and other immediate challenges. And I'm encouraged by the progress which has been made in most of the areas of challenge.

Yet all of us must also focus on the larger questions that this new era presents. For if we act out of a larger sense of purpose and strategy, our work on the crises of the late 20th century can lay the basis for a more peaceful and democratic world at the start of the 21st century.

The end of the long, twilight struggle does not ensure the start of a long peace. Like a wise homeowner who recognizes that you cannot stop investing in your house once you buy it, we cannot stop investing in the peace now that we have obtained it. That recognition was a triumph of President Truman's era. But unlike then, we lack the specter of a menacing adversary to spur our efforts to engage other nations. Now, not fear but vision must drive our invest-

ment and our engagement in this new world.

Nowhere is that engagement more important than in our policies toward Russia and the newly independent states of the former Soviet Union. Their struggle to build free societies is one of the great human dramas of our day. It presents the greatest security challenge for our generation and offers one of the greatest economic opportunities of our lifetime. That's why my first trip out of the country will be to Vancouver, to meet with President Yeltsin.

Over the past month, we have seen incredibly tumultuous events in Russia. They've filled our headlines and probably confused our heads. President Yeltsin has been at loggerheads with the People's Congress of Deputies. Heated political standoffs have obstructed economic change. Meanwhile, neighboring states, such as Ukraine and the Baltic nations, have watched Russia anxiously while they grapple with their own reforms and while they deal with economic problems equally severe.

For most Americans, these events, while dramatic, are still very remote from their immediate concerns. After all, in every community we have our own problems. We've got our own needs. We face a stagnant economy and dislocations brought about by the end of the cold war and the downsizing of the military budget. We've got all these big companies restructuring themselves. And for the last 2 years small business has not created enough new jobs to offset that. It's projected that two-thirds of the growth of our income in the next 5 years, two-thirds, will be absorbed by health care cost increases. And 100 percent of the wage increases for the next 5 years will be absorbed by health care cost increases unless we act. We're worried about our cities, like Los Angeles, coming up on the anniversary of the disturbances there a year ago. And many people say, in the face of all this and with a huge budget deficit, why in the world should we help a distant people when times are so tough here at home?

Well, I know that we cannot guarantee the future of reform in Russia or any of the other newly independent states. I know and you know that ultimately, the history of Russia will be written by Russians and the future of Russia must be charted by Russians. But I would argue that we must do what we can. We must act now, not out of charity, but because it is a wise investment, a wise investment building on what has already been done and looking to our own future. While our efforts will entail new costs, we can reap even larger dividends for our safety and our prosperity if we act now.

To understand why, I think we must grasp the scope of the transformation now occurring in Russia and the other states. From Vilnius on the Baltic to Vladivostok on the Pacific, we have witnessed a political miracle, genuinely historic and heroic deeds without precedent in all of human history. The other two world-changing events of this century, World Wars I and II, exacted a price of over 60 million lives. By contrast, look at this world-changing event. It has been remarkably bloodless, and we pray that it remains so.

Now free markets and free politics are replacing repression. Central Europe is in command of its own fate. Lithuania, Latvia, and Estonia are again independent. Ukraine, Armenia, and other proud nations are free to pursue their own destinies.

The heart of it all is Russia. Her rebirth has begun. A great nation, rich in natural and human resources and unbelievable history, has once again moved to rejoin the political and economic cultures of the West. President Yeltsin and his fellow reformers throughout Russia are courageously leading three modern Russian revolutions at once to transform their country: from a totalitarian state into a democracy; from a command economy into a market; from an empire into a modern nation-state that freely let go of countries once under their control and now freely respect their integrity.

Russia's rebirth is not only material and political; it is genuinely spiritual. As the Librarian of Congress James Billington said, "Evil has been transcended by repentance without revenge. Innocent suffering in past gulags has been given redemptive value. And the amazingly nonviolent breakthrough of August 1991, which occurred on the Feast of the Transfiguration, was indeed a miracle through which ordinary people rediscovered a moral dimension to their own lives." Across what was the Soviet Union, the freedom to pray has been met by a resurgence of worship.

Nothing could contribute more to global freedom, to security, to prosperity than the peaceful progression of this rebirth of Russia. It could mean a modern state, at peace not only with itself but with the world. It could mean one productively and prosperously integrated into a global economy, a source of raw materials and manufactured products and a vast market for American goods and services. It could mean a populous democracy contributing to the stability of both Europe and Asia.

The success of Russia's renewal must be a first-order concern to our country because it confronts us with four distinct opportunities. First, it offers us an historic opportunity to improve our own security. The danger is clear if Russia's reforms turn sour, if it reverts to authoritarianism or disintegrates into chaos. The world cannot afford the strife of the former Yugoslavia replicated in a nation as big as Russia, spanning 11 time zones with an armed arsenal of nuclear weapons that is still very vast.

But there is great opportunity here. Across most of our history, our security was challenged by European nations, set on domination of their continent and the high seas that lie between us. The tragic violence in Bosnia reminds us again that Europe has not seen the end of conflict within its own borders.

Now, we could at last face a Europe in which no great power, not one, harbors continental designs. Think of it: Land wars in Europe cost hundreds of thousands of American lives in the 20th century. The rise of a democratic Russia, satisfied within her own boundaries, bordered by other peaceful democracies, could ensure that our Nation never needs to pay that kind of price again.

We also face the opportunity to increase our own security by reducing the chances of nuclear war. Russia still holds over 20,000 strategic and tactical nuclear warheads. Ukraine, Belarus, and Kazakhstan have nuclear weapons on their own soil as well. We are implementing historic arms control agreements that for the first time will radically reduce the number of strategic nuclear weapons. Now, by supporting Russia's reforms, we can help to turn the promise of those agreements into a reality for ourselves and for our children, and for the Russians and their children, too.

Second, Russia's reforms offer us the opportunity to complete the movement from having an adversary in foreign policy to having a partner in global problem solving. Think back to the cold war. Recall the arenas in which we played out its conflicts: Berlin, Korea, the Congo, Cuba, Vietnam, Nicaragua, Angola, Afghanistan. We competed everywhere. We battled the Soviets at the U.N. We tracked each other's movements around the globe. We lost tens of thousands of our finest young people to hold freedom's line. Those efforts were worthy. But their worth was measured in prevention more than in creation, in the containment of terror and oppression rather than the advancement of human happiness and opportunity.

Now reflect on what has happened just since Russia joined us in a search for peaceful solutions. We cooperated in the United Nations to defeat Iraqi aggression in Kuwait. We cosponsored promising peace talks in the Mideast. We worked together to foster reconciliation in Cambodia and El Salvador. We joined forces to protect the global environment. Progress of this kind strengthens our security and that of other nations. If we can help Russia to remain increasingly democratic, we can leave an era of standoff behind us and explore expanding horizons of progress and peace.

Third, Russia's reforms are important to us because they hold one of the keys to investing more in our own future. America's taxpayers have literally spent trillions of dollars to prosecute the cold war. Now we can reduce that pace of spending, and indeed, we have been able to reduce that pace of spending, not only because the arms of the former Soviet Union pose a diminishing threat to us and our allies. If Russia were to revert to imperialism or were to plunge into chaos, we would need to reassess all our plans for defense savings. We would have to restructure our defenses to meet a whole different set of threats than those we now think will occur. That means billions of dollars less for other uses: less for creating new businesses and new jobs; less for preparing our children for the future; less for the new technologies of the 21st century which our competitors in Germany, Japan, and elsewhere are pouring money into right now, hoping they can capture the high wage jobs of the future. Therefore, our ability to put people first at home requires that we put Russia and its neighbors first on our agenda abroad.

Fourth, Russia's reforms offer us an historic opportunity. Russia, after all, is in a profound economic crisis today. But it is still an inherently rich nation. She has a wealth of oil and gas and coal and gold and diamonds and timbers for her own people to develop. The Russian people are among the most well educated and highly skilled in the world. They are good people sitting on a rich land. They have been victimized by a system which has failed them. We

must look beyond the Russia of today and see her potential for prosperity. Think of it: a nation of 150 million people able to trade with us in a way that helps both our peoples. Russia's economic recovery may be slow, but it is in the interest of all who seek more robust global growth to ensure that, aided by American business and trade, Russia rises to her great economic potential.

The burning question today is whether Russia's economic progress, whether Russia's democratic progress will continue or be thwarted. I believe that freedom, like anything sweet, is hard to take from people once they have had a taste of it. The human spirit is hard to bottle up again, and it will be hard to bottle up again in Russia. Yet if we cannot be certain of how Russia's affairs will proceed, we are nonetheless certain of our own interests. The interest of all Americans lie with efforts that enhance our security and our prosperity. That's why our interests lie with Russian reform and with Russian reformers led by Boris Yeltsin.

America's position is unequivocal. We support democracy. We support free markets. We support freedom of speech, conscience, and religion. We support respect for ethnic minorities in Russia and for Russian and other minorities throughout the region.

I believe it is essential that we act prudently but urgently to do all that we can to strike a strategic alliance with Russian reform. My goal in Vancouver will be that. And that will be my message to the man who stands as the leader of reform, Russia's democratically elected President, Boris Yeltsin. I won't describe today all the specific ideas that I plan to discuss with him. And of course, I don't know all those that he will discuss with me. But I want to tell you the principles on which our efforts to assist reform will rest.

First, our investments in Russian reform must be tangible to the Russian people. Support for reform must come from the ground up. And that will only occur if our efforts are broadly dispersed and not focused just on Moscow. I plan to talk with President Yeltsin about measures intended to help promote the broad development of small businesses, to accelerate privatization of state enterprises, to assist local food processing and distribution efforts, and to ease the transition to private markets. Our goal must be to ensure that the Russian people soon come to feel that they are the beneficiaries of reform and not its victims. We must help them to recognize that their sufferings today are not the birth pangs of democracy and capitalism but the death throes of dictatorship and communism.

Second, our investments in Russian reform must be designed to have lasting impact. Russia's economic vessel is too large and leaky for us to bail it out. That's not what's at issue here. Our challenge is to provide some tools to help the Russians do things that work for themselves. A good example is Russia's energy sector. Russia is one of the world's largest oil producers; yet millions of barrels of the oil Russia pumps each month seep out of the system before ever reaching the market. Just the leakage from Russia's natural gas pipelines could supply the entire State of Connecticut. The Russians must make many reforms to attract energy investments. And by helping to introduce modern drilling practices and to repair Russia's energy infrastructure, we can help Russia regain a large and lasting source of hard currency. Over the long run, that effort can help to protect the environment as well and to moderate world energy prices. We have a direct interest in doing that.

Third, our people must do what we can to have people-to-people initiatives, not just government-to-government ones. We have entered a new era in which the best way to achieve many of our goals abroad is not through diplomats or dollars but through private citizens who can impart the skills and habits that are the lifeblood of democracy and free markets. We intend to expand efforts for retired American business executives to work with Russian entrepreneurs to start new businesses. We intend to work so that our farmers can teach modern farming practices; so that our labor leaders can share the basics of trade unionism; so that Americans experienced in grassroots activities can impart the techniques that ensure responsive government; so that our Armed Forces can engage in more exchanges with the Russian military; and so that thousands and thousands of young Russians who are reform's primary beneficiaries and reform's primary constituency—so that they can come to our country and study our government, our economy, and our society, not because it's perfect but because it's a great example of a democracy at work.

Fourth, our investments in reform must be part of a partnership among all the newly independent states and the international community.

They must be extended in concert with measures from our allies, many of whom have at least as much stake in the survival of Russian democracy as we do. Working through the international financial institutions, we can do great things together that none of us can do by ourselves.

This principle is especially important as we help Russia to stabilize its currency and its markets. Russia's central bank prints too many rubles and extends too many credits. The result is inflation that has been nearly one percent a day. Inflation at such levels gravely imperils Russia's emerging markets. In Vancouver, I plan to discuss the progress we are making among the major industrialized nations to help Russia make the leap to a stable currency and a market economy. While we cannot support this effort alone in the United States and while we must insist on reciprocal commensurate Russian reforms, American leadership to curb inflation and stabilize the currency is essential.

Fifth, we must emphasize investments in Russia that enhance our own security. I want to talk with President Yeltsin about steps we can take together to ensure that denuclearization continues in Russia and her neighboring states. We will explore new initiatives to reassure Ukraine so that it embraces the START Treaty, and to move toward the goal of the Lisbon Protocol agenda, which was intended to ensure that Russia is the only nuclear-armed successor state to the Soviet Union. Ukraine will play a special role in the realization of these objectives, and we recognize our interest in the success of reform in Ukraine and the other new states. I'll talk with President Yeltsin about new efforts to realize the two-thirds reduction in United States and Soviet strategic nuclear arsenals envisioned under START. And I'll suggest steps both of us can take to stem the proliferation of weapons of mass destruction, something that will be a major, major cause of concern for years to come.

Sixth, we must recognize that our policies toward Russia and the other states comprise a long-term strategy. It may take years to work completely. That was the key to our success in the cold war. We were in it for the long run, not to win every day, not to know what every development in every country would be. We had clear principles, clear interests, clear values, a clear strategy, and we were in it for the long run. As the Soviets veered from the terror of Stalin to the thaw of Khrushchev, to the gray days of Brezhnev, to the *perestroika* of Gorbachev, our purpose always remained constant: containment, deterrence, human freedom.

Our goals must remain equally fixed today: above all, our security and that of our allies but also democracy, market economies, human rights, and respect for international law. In this regard, I welcome President Yeltsin's assurance that civil liberties will be respected and continuity in Russia's foreign policy maintained as Russia strives to determine her own future.

The path that Russia and the other states take toward reform will have rough stretches. Their politics may seem especially tumultuous today, in part because it's so much more public than in decades past, thanks to the television and to the other mass media. Then, the ruler of the Kremlin had only subjects; now, the ruler of the Kremlin has constituents, just like me, and it's a lot more complicated. We must be concerned over every retreat from democracy but not every growing pain within democracy.

Let me remind you of our own early history. It was marked by revision of our governing charter and fistfights in Congress. Vaclav Havel has noted, "Democracy is not a destination, but it's a horizon toward which we make continual progress." Just remember how long it was from the signing of the Declaration of Independence to forging a real new Constitution to the election of the first President, and then you can't be so impatient about what's happened in the short stretch of time from Gorbachev to Yeltsin to the present crisis. As long as there are reformers in the Russian Federation and other states leading the journey toward democracy's horizon, our strategy must be to support them. And our place must be at their side.

Moreover, we and the Russian people must not give up on reform simply because of the slow pace of economic renewal. Recall for a moment how many of the world's economic success stories were written off too soon. Western visitors to Japan in 1915 dismissed its economic prospects as dismal. Korea's economy was described as a "hopeless case" by American experts in 1958, and look at them now. Many Germans after World War II anticipated decades of national poverty. A German Minister of Economic Affairs noted after the war, "Few realized that if people were allowed once more to become aware of the value and worth of freedom, dy-

namic forces would be released." The miracle of prosperity that Japan, Korea, and Germany have discovered awaits those who are willing to sustain democratic and economic reforms in Russia and in her neighboring states. I believe that, and I hope you do too.

Despite today's troubles, I have great faith that Russian reform will continue and eventually succeed. Let me here address directly the Russian people who will read or hear my words. You are a people who understand patriotic struggle. You have persevered through an unforgiving climate. Your whole history has been punctuated with suffering on a scale unknown to the American people. You heroically withstood murderous invasions by Napoleon and Hitler. Your great literature and your music, which has so enriched our own culture, were composed with the pen of longing and the ink of sorrow. Your accomplishments of education and science speak to your faith in progress. And now, as you seek to build a great tomorrow for Russia upon a foundation of democracy and commerce, I speak for Americans everywhere when I say, we are with you. For we share this bond: The key to each of our futures is not in clinging to the past but in having the courage to change.

As we look upon Russia's challenges, we should remember, all of us, that the American and Russian people have in common so much. We are both rooted deeply in our own land. We are both built of diverse heritage. We are both forever struggling with the responsibilities that come with vast territory and power. We both have had to deal with the dilemmas of human nature on an immense scale. That may be why there has been so little real hatred between our people, even across the decades when we pointed weapons of nightmarish destruction at each other's lands.

Now, as in the past, America's future is tied in important ways to Russia's. During the cold war, it was tied in negative ways. We saw in each other only danger. Now that the walls have come down, we can see hope and opportunity.

In the end, our hope for the future of Russian reform is rooted simply in our faith in the institutions that have secured our own freedom and prosperity. But it is also rooted in the Russian people. The diversity of their past accomplishments gives us hope that there are diverse possibilities for the future. The vitality of Russian journalism and public debate today gives us hope that the great truth-seeking traditions of Russian culture will endure and that Russia's antidemocratic demagogs will not, indeed, must not in the long run prevail. And the discipline of Russia's military, which has proved itself anew in August of 1991 and since, that discipline gives us hope that Russia's transition can continue to be peaceful.

Fifty years ago, in a different period of historic challenge for Russia, the great Russian poet Anna Akhmatova wrote, "We know what lies in the balance at this moment and what is happening right now. The hour for courage strikes upon our clocks, and the courage will not desert us."

The opportunity that lies before our Nation today is to answer the courageous call of Russian reform, as an expression of our own values, as an investment in our own security and prosperity, as a demonstration of our purpose in a new world.

Thank you very much.

NOTE: The President spoke at 1:26 p.m. in Dahlgren Hall at the U.S. Naval Academy. In his remarks, he referred to Seymour Topping, president of the society.

Question-and-Answer Session With the American Society of Newspaper Editors in Annapolis
April 1, 1993

Bosnia

Q. Mr. President, I support your vision and am grateful to be here for this historic speech. As a journalist and a citizen I am deeply anguished over the reports from Bosnia: deliberate, premeditated rape, the shelling of innocent civilians, families forced from their homes, children crushed to death in desperate attempts to escape. I'd like to ask two brief questions. Do we have a national interest in checking the spread of greater Serbian ethnic cleansing in the Balkans? And are we losing our credibility as a nation as this horrifying aggression in a sovereign state continues without your unrestrained, forceful, and public condemnation of it?

The President. Yes, we have a national interest in limiting ethnic cleansing. I disagree with you that I have not given a forceful and public condemnation of it. I think the issue is whether you think the United States is capable of doing what Europe has not in somehow forcing its will upon Bosnia and the former Yugoslavia. Since I have become President we have dramatically stiffened the embargo on Serbia. We have hurt them very badly economically, but the war continues. We do not have the votes in the United Nations at the present time to lift the embargo on arms to the Bosnians. If we did, it would endanger the humanitarian mission there carried on by the French and British, who oppose lifting the embargo, and they have kept many people alive.

I decided that I would support the Vance-Owen peace process when it was clear that that was what our European allies wanted to do and that that was the best vehicle for a potential peace. Now, the Bosnians and the Croats have signed on to that, the Muslims and the Croats in Bosnia. We are waiting to see whether the Serbs will. If they do not, we will then have to contemplate where we go from there. But I would remind you that when I became President the situation there was already grave. We had a policy through the United Nations which I think was of limited effectiveness, which I have tried to stiffen as well as I could.

But the United States has many commitments and many interests, and I would just remember that the thing that I have not been willing to do is to immediately take action the end of which I could not see. Whatever I want to do, I want to do it with vigor and wholeheartedly. I want it to have a reasonable prospect of success. And I have done the best I could with the cards that I found on the table when I became President. If you have other ideas about what you think I ought to do that would minimize the loss of life, I would be glad to have them.

Q. Sir, do you condemn it here today?

The President. Absolutely. I condemn it, and

I have condemned it repeatedly and thoroughly. And I have done everything I could to increase the pressure of the international community on the outrages perpetrated in Bosnia by the aggressors and to get people to stand up against ethnic cleansing. The question is what are we capable of doing about it from the United States. If you look at the responses that have been mustered so far from the European states that are even closer and that have a memory of what happened when Hitler, who was not shy about using his power, had hundreds of thousands of people in the former Yugoslavia and even then was unable to subdue it entirely.

I think you have to look at what our realistic options are for action. The question is not whether we condemn what's going on. Ethnic cleansing is an outrage, and it is an idea which should die, which should not be able to be expanded. The question is, what can we do?

Now, I have said that the United States would be prepared to join with a United Nations effort in supporting a peacekeeping process that was entered into in good faith. If the Serbs refuse to do that, then we will all have to reassess our position. But we must be careful not to use words that will outstrip our capacity to back them up. That is a grave error for any great nation, and one I will try not to commit.

Freedom of the Press

Q. This is—[*inaudible*]—he is one of the leading editors at Izvestia, Moscow—[*inaudible*]—I hope you will take a question from him. My question, Mr. President: His newspaper in Russia has had deep trouble because of its criticisms of Parliament and Parliament's reaction to that. You in this country have taken some hits, some heavy hits in the campaign and as President from a critical, probative, intrusive, at times abusive press. I wonder if you could give us your feelings, perhaps, words of philosophy as to how you view press freedom given its critical and at times abusive nature?

The President. If you have in a democratic society any freedom enshrined in the Constitution, it is as certain as the Sun rising in the morning that the freedom will be abused. Think of any freedom enshrined in the Constitution. They are all capable of abuse, some in different ways than others. The freedom of speech is abused every day in the country. The freedom of the press, of course, can be abused. Other freedoms can be. People can claim to be practic-

ing religion when perhaps they aren't. That is the price we pay for freedom, and we are stronger because of it.

I think that no one has done better for 200 years than Thomas Jefferson did when he said—and Thomas Jefferson got a pretty rough press, too, from time to time if you go back and read how people worked on him. My consolation is no one remembers the people who falsely blasphemed him in print. [*Laughter*] But Thomas Jefferson said that if he had to choose between maintaining the Government and the freedom of the press, he would choose the freedom of the press because democracy could not exist without it. And I agree with that. And Government restraint in the face of criticism is in some ways the most important test of a true democracy.

Trade Negotiations and Russia

Q. I wish to welcome you to the Free State of Maryland. Four times during the term of your predecessor the leaders of the Group of Seven industrial democracies assembled in early July, and each time they pledged their personal prestige to a GATT agreement, the new world reform of trade regulations. Each time they failed. My question is this: When you go to the Group of Seven summit in July, are you going to renew that pledge? And secondly, and this is pertinent to what you've been talking about, if we don't have a new GATT agreement, is there any way Russia will be able to enter the world trading system in a way that will lead to its evolution from its present situation?

The President. Well, as you know—first let me answer the first question. Yes, I will renew the pledge, and I will hope to do it without having the international press corps laugh since they've now heard it four times. We got an agreement on agriculture, so-called Blair House accord, which I hope will stand up in the wake of the recent elections in Europe. If it does, I am frankly optimistic that we will be able to proceed to a GATT agreement. There are other outstanding issues, but on balance the United States would be much better off with it.

We need to maintain a commitment to global economic growth in ways that are good for the wealthy countries of the world. As I said in my speech, one of the great challenges is for a wealthy country not only to maintain its technological lead and its capacity to generate growth but also its capacity to generate jobs.

In the 1980's Europe had at least two significant economic recoveries and generated no jobs. That's the thing that's bothering me now. This recovery allegedly started a long time ago, but the unemployment rate is higher than it was at the depth of the recession, and that's because we are now finding some of the same difficulties. So, I think the GATT agreement can help that, and I will do what I can to get it.

The answer to your second question is not so simple. I believe Russia would be better off if it could be brought into the international trading system with a new GATT agreement, but the leaders of the G–7 this year obviously are the Japanese. This is Japan's turn to lead, and the Government of Japan has issued an invitation to President Yeltsin to attend the G–7 meeting. And as you know, on April 14th and 15th the foreign ministers and finance ministers of the G–7 are meeting in Tokyo to talk about what we can do in multilateral ways to help the process of Russian reform.

So, I believe a lot can be done even if there's no new GATT agreement. Indeed, I would argue that for the kinds of things which need to be worked out for Russia to really benefit from trade and for the rest of us to benefit from it, involve more either ad hoc relationships between businesses and governments dealing with Russia or changes within Russia itself relating to property rights, privatization, the reliability of contracts, the freeing up of the ability to contract in the energy area, and things of that kind.

I should have let you answer that question.

Q. Mr. President, I am absolutely sure that millions and millions of Russians would be really proud to listen to the words you have just said about my country. Unfortunately, we have not a lot of politicians who are able to do the same. Let me just add one thing. Russians are not just settling from new changes. There are millions and millions of young people who don't care about communism at all, and they enjoy new freedom and new situations. Many of them don't know who was Stalin or who was Lenin, but they do know who is William Clinton. And so here is my question: If a future friend shows once again that the great majority of Russians are committed to democracy and free market economy, can we expect this year your visit to Russia?

The President. If I gave you the answer that

I want to give you, half of my Cabinet would have a heart attack—*[laughter]*—simply because I haven't discussed it with anyone. Let me say that I think I should follow the same practice I always do. I can't commit to a specific date, but if the process of reform stays alive in Russia, I want very much to go back there.

I had the honor to be in your country, briefly, 3 days before Boris Yeltsin was elected, as a completely anonymous citizen who was invited to come just for a few days. So I was able to walk the streets, to talk to people, to observe what was going on. I was immensely impressed. I had not been in Russia for over 20 years. Everybody in America now knows I went to Russia. We found that out in the Presidential campaign. I enjoyed that trip, too. *[Laughter]*

I would very much like to go back, very much.

Ross Perot

Q. I'd like to head back to the domestic front, if I could. Ross Perot spoke to us yesterday, and he said as he travels around the country he finds his supporters asking him about and upset about two recent events in Washington. I'd like to ask you about both of them. One is the dismissal of Jay Stephens as District attorney as he was pursuing the Rostenkowski case in the postage stamp for cash case. And the other was the story about the general who was supposedly told at the White House that he should leave quickly because the White House staff was not comfortable with uniformed military personnel. Could you comment on both of those?

The President. I will, and then I want to ask you a question. First of all, the United States attorney in Washington, DC, was not dismissed. They were all replaced, and they will all be replaced just like the Republicans replaced them all when President Carter was defeated by President Reagan. And in fact, many of them got, including the United States attorney in Washington, DC, got to serve extra time because of the difficulty in getting a new Attorney General. We did not replace any of them until we had a new Attorney General.

There is a provision now for appointing interim U.S. attorneys from people who are of long service within each office. There is no reason to believe that any particular case will be pursued in a different manner. But I think you could make a very compelling case that that

United States attorney and others served longer than they would have normally because there was not an Attorney General confirmed on the day I became President. Everybody else in my Cabinet was confirmed. So to say that that person was singled out is absurd.

The real flip side is some of the people in the other party are saying, why didn't we leave him in there all by himself because this is the most important case in America and no one else can pursue it. I just dispute that. I just don't agree with that. There is no evidence to support that. We followed a uniform policy that was exactly like the one followed by previous administrations, except we started later in time.

Secondly, the other story, like all those military stories, was an abject lie. And thank God some people in the press have finally started pointing it out and have even expressed some shame that they were guilty of printing those kinds of rumors. Some of the press have begun to print letters from people at the Pentagon who have been disputing some of these specific stories like the lieutenant general that was allegedly told by someone on the White House staff that she didn't speak to people in the military. Those kinds of stories, they are all just made up out of whole cloth. And people who run them based on gossip or people who talk about them from podiums ought to be ashamed of themselves, without knowing they're true.

You know, Mr. Perot came to Washington the other day and attacked my Chief of Staff as not being a real business person, and he had to call him on the phone and personally apologize the next day. I mean, people can say anything from the podium. I'd be more interested in why my economic program, which is 85 percent what Ross Perot recommended in the campaign, except we raised taxes less on the middle class, more on the wealthy, and don't have unspecified health care savings, hasn't been endorsed since it's almost identical to the one he ran on.

I don't think we ought to be out here rumormongering myself. I think it does very little to support the public interest.

Public-Private Partnership

Q. Mr. President, in your speech you alluded to a global economy and also to the Marshall plan in the days in which this country stood alone as an economic power without competition. What, sir, do you feel is your responsibility and that of the Federal Government in assuring that this country's industrial might remains competitive in an intensely competitive environment in which competitors enjoy a different and more supportive relationship with their government?

The President. Well, I'm trying to change that in this country, as you know, by changing the whole nature of the relationship between Government and business. I want to have a Tax Code which rewards investment more. I want to have a strategy of partnership in the new technologies which will produce the lion's share of the jobs for the 21st century.

I think that it is imperative. If you look at what works, if you look at the high-wage, high-growth economies, Government must be a partner with the private sector. There should be limitations on the partnership. The Government can't pick winners and losers, but there are plainly some functions that if not embraced by Government will not be done properly.

And I might point out that most of the countries of the world with advanced economies are governed by what would be called their Republican Parties, if we used the Democratic-Republican parlance in other countries. And yet, every one of them has a more aggressive public-private partnership than we do when it comes to educating and training the work force, when it comes to investing in civilian technologies for jobs for the 21st century, when it comes to maintaining competitive policies that will guarantee at least that they'll have a chance to generate high-wage, high-growth jobs. And I think my responsibility is to try to implement an American version of that kind of policy.

Media Coverage

Q. Mr. President, how would you assess the coverage of your administration by the Nation's news media, particularly newspapers?

The President. Good. *[Laughter]*

Q. It doesn't have to be that short an answer. *[Laughter]*

The President. Well, first of all, it's different in different places, but let me say on balance I think it's been remarkably fair and thorough. The only frustrations that I feel since I've been President relate far more to what I would call almost the commercial imperatives that are on the press that have nothing to do with anybody trying to be unfair in their coverage. If I might, let me just give you one example.

I saw a survey recently that was reported

somewhere, I'm embarrassed I don't remember where. They were asking the American people, this survey, is the President spending enough time on the economy, is the President spending enough time on health care, and a bunch of other questions. Only half the people said I was spending enough time on the economy even though that's what I spend all my time on. By two to one the people said I was spending enough time on health care. Why is that? Because the effort of the health care task force, chaired by my wife, to come up with a health care program is the subject of intense speculation because it hasn't been presented yet. So, given the propensity of people in Washington to leak, there's a new story every day about some little paper or another that's come out and all that. And then they have these public hearings, so there's a lot of anticipation.

The economic program was announced one month into my Presidency, and then I went to work on it in Congress. And what really is news is sort of around the edges; is he losing this or winning that or whatever. It becomes a process debate, and the American people tend to lose sight of what is the major focus of my every day, which is how to pass that jobs pro-

gram and the economic program. That is simply a function of the way the news works.

The other thing I think is different about the news today than maybe 20 years ago, particularly for the coverage around Washington, is this: Because of CNN and others who now give virtually continuous direct access to the facts of whatever is going on to wide numbers of people, there is even more pressure than there used to be on everybody in the media to find an angle to the story, a unique angle, an insight, you know, a twist. And sometimes that's good, and sometimes it's not. But it always presents a different challenge to me than perhaps the President might have had 20 years ago in trying to keep the focus of the public on the big issues that I'm trying to deal with.

But I say that not as a criticism but simply as an observation. That is simply the way things are. On balance we're better off. People are getting more information more quickly than ever before, but it's changed the dynamics of how we relate to each other.

Thank you very much.

NOTE: The President spoke at 2:07 p.m. in Dahlgren Hall at the U.S. Naval Academy.

Message to the Congress Transmitting Proposed Child Immunization Legislation
April 1, 1993

To the Congress of the United States:

I am pleased to transmit for your immediate consideration and enactment the "Comprehensive Child Immunization Act of 1993". Also transmitted is a section-by-section analysis.

This legislation launches a new partnership among parents and guardians; health care providers; vaccine manufacturers; and Federal, State, and local governments to protect our Nation's children from the deadly onslaught of infectious diseases. The legislation is a comprehensive initiative to remove existing barriers to immunization. It will ensure that all children in the United States are immunized against vaccine-preventable diseases by their second birthday. Because of the importance of this initiative to the health of our children, I am transmitting this legislation in advance of my proposal for

comprehensive reform of the Nation's health care system, which I expect to submit to the Congress in May.

Beginning in fiscal year 1995, the bill would authorize the Secretary of Health and Human Services to purchase and provide childhood vaccines in quantities sufficient to meet the immunization needs of children in the United States. It would also institute a national immunization tracking system through grants to the States to establish State immunization registries. In addition, the bill contains provisions to ensure that the National Vaccine Injury Compensation Program, an essential link in our Nation's immunization system, remains operational. Funding for the program of vaccine purchase and distribution will be identified in my legislation for broad-based reform of the national health care system and made available beginning in fiscal year 1995 from the Comprehensive Child Immunization Account in the United States Treasury.

Immunizations are cost-effective. For example, the measles vaccine saves over $10 in health care costs for every $1 invested in prevention. We know that children are most vulnerable before their second birthday and that approximately 80 percent of vaccine doses should be given before then. Many children, however, do not receive even their basic immunizations by that age. We must remove the financial barriers to immunization that impede children from being vaccinated on time, and facilitate development of a national tracking system to ensure children are immunized at the earliest appropriate age.

The problem posed by soaring vaccine costs is exacerbated by a deteriorating immunization infrastructure. This legislation continues the rebuilding of our capacity to deliver vaccines and educate parents started in my economic stimulus package.

This proposal would direct the Secretary to purchase and provide vaccine without charge to health care providers who serve children and are located in a State that participates in the State registry grant program. In nonparticipating States, free vaccine would be distributed to Federal health care centers and providers, including those serving Indian populations. Health care providers could not charge patients for the cost of the vaccine. They could, however, impose

a fee for its administration, unless such a fee would result in the denial of vaccine to someone unable to pay. The authority of the Secretary established under this legislation, to purchase and provide vaccines, shall cease to be in effect beginning on such date as may be specified in a Federal law providing for immunization services for all children as part of a broad-based reform of the national health care system.

In addition, the bill would provide for a collaborative Federal and State effort to track the immunization status of the Nation's children. It would authorize the Secretary to make grants to States to establish and operate State immunization registries containing specific information for each child in the State. Entering infant birth and immunization data into registries will enable identification of children who need vaccinations and will help parents and providers ensure that children are appropriately immunized.

A keystone of the Nation's vaccine immunization effort is the National Vaccine Injury Compensation Program. This legislation would authorize payments from the Vaccine Injury Compensation Trust Fund for compensable injuries from vaccines administered on or after October 1, 1992, and would reinstate and permanently extend the vaccine excise tax.

I urge the Congress to take prompt and favorable action on this legislation.

WILLIAM J. CLINTON

The White House,
April 1, 1993.

Nomination for Inspector General of the Department of Health and Human Services
April 1, 1993

The President announced today that he will nominate June Gibbs Brown, a former Inspector General at the Department of Defense, NASA, and the Department of the Interior, to be Inspector General of the Department of Health and Human Services.

"HHS is the biggest civilian Agency of the Federal Government," said the President, "and it is imperative that it be managed as efficiently

as possible. That is one of the central tasks that Secretary Shalala has taken on, and I am very pleased to be nominating someone of June Gibbs Brown's stature as Inspector General."

NOTE: A biography of the nominee was made available by the Office of the Press Secretary.

Remarks on Opening the Forest Conference in Portland, Oregon
April 2, 1993

Good morning. I want to thank every one of you who are in the room today and also all of those who are outside—and there are certainly many who have come here—for caring enough to be here. We're here to discuss issues whose seriousness demands that we respect each other's concerns, each other's experiences, and each other's views. Together we can move beyond confrontation to build a consensus on a balanced policy to preserve jobs and to protect our environment.

I want to say a special word of thanks to Governor Roberts and Mayor Katz for hosting this conference, and Governors Lowry, Wilson, and Andrus for attending.

As you can see, the Vice President and I are here with representatives from our administration who deal every day with virtually every issue which will be discussed. With us here today are the Interior Secretary, Bruce Babbitt; the Agriculture Secretary, Mike Espy; Labor Secretary Bob Reich, all of whom have been meeting with people here in the Northwest in recent weeks. We also have the Commerce Secretary, Ron Brown; Environmental Protection Administrator Carol Browner; the Deputy Budget Director, Alice Rivlin; and our Science and Technology Adviser, Dr. John Gibbons.

We're all here to listen and to learn from you. We're here to discuss issues about which people feel strongly, believe deeply, and often disagree vehemently. That's because the issues are important and are related and intrinsic to the very existence of the people who live here in the Pacific Northwest.

We're discussing how people earn their livelihoods. We're discussing the air, the water, the forests that are important to your lives. And we're addressing the values that are at the core of those lives. From the trailblazers and the pioneers to the trapper and the hunters, the loggers and the mill workers, the people of the Northwest have earned their livings from the land and have lived in awe of the power, the majesty, and the beauty of the forests, the rivers, and the streams.

Coming from a State, as I do, that was also settled by pioneers and which is still 53 percent timberland—we have an important timber industry and people who appreciate the beauty and the intrinsic value of our woodlands—I've often felt at home here in the Northwest. I'll never forget the people I've met here over the last year-and-a-half whose lives have been touched by the issues that we're here to discuss. I remember the timber industry workers with whom I spoke at a town hall meeting in Seattle last July who invited me to come to their communities and learn about their problems.

I remember the families from the timber industry whom I met last September in Max Groesbeck's backyard in Eugene, Oregon. I was moved beyond words by the stories that people told me there and by their determination to fight for their communities and their companies and their families.

I was also inspired by Frank Henderson, who had lost his job as a timber worker and gone through retraining to learn thermoplastic welding and now owns a plastics welding business of his own. He was a guest of mine at the Inaugural, and I'm glad to have him here with us today.

And I remember Elizabeth Bailey of Hayfork, California. She's 11 years old and she was one of the girls and boys who visited me at the White House a few Saturdays ago to participate in our televised townhall meeting for children. Her parents, Willie and Nadine Bailey, have had to close their timber business because, in the past, politics seemed to matter more than people or the environment. And I'm glad that Nadine Bailey, a dedicated spokesperson for loggers, is also here with us today.

As I've spoken with people who work in the timber industry I've been impressed by their love of the land. As one worker told me at our meeting in the Groesbecks' backyard, "I care about Oregon a lot, the beauty of the country."

We're fortunate to have people with us today who bring not only a variety of experiences but a variety of views to the questions before the conference: How can we achieve a balanced and comprehensive policy that recognizes the importance of the forests and timber to the economy and jobs of this region? And how can we preserve our precious old-growth forests which are part of our national heritage and that, once destroyed, can never be replaced?

For too long, the National Government has done more to confuse the issues than to clarify them. In the absence of real leadership, at least six different Federal Agencies have hooked their horses to different sides of the cart, and then they've wondered why the cart wouldn't move forward. To make things worse, the rhetoric from Washington has often exaggerated and exacerbated the tensions between those who speak about the economy and those who speak about the environment.

Not surprisingly, these issues have very often ended up in court while the economy, the environment, and the people have all suffered. That's why it's so important that the people here today are meeting in a conference room, not a courtroom. Whatever your views, everyone who will speak today comes from the Northwest and will have to live with the results of whatever decisions we all make.

We're here to begin a process that will help ensure that you will be able to work together in your communities, for the good of your businesses, your jobs, and your natural environment. The process we begin today will not be easy. Its outcome cannot possibly make everyone happy. Perhaps it won't make anyone completely happy. But the worst thing we can do is nothing. As we begin this process, the most important thing we can do is to admit, all of us to each other, that there are no simple or easy answers.

This is not about choosing between jobs and the environment but about recognizing the importance of both and recognizing that virtually everyone here and everyone in this region cares about both. After all, nobody appreciates the natural environment more than the working people who depend upon it for fishing, for boating, for teaching their children to respect the land, the rivers, and the forests. And most environmentalists are working people and business peo-

ple themselves, and understand that only an economically secure America can have the strength and confidence necessary to preserve our land, our water and our forests, as you can see in how badly they're despoiled in nations that are not economically secure.

A healthy economy and a healthy environment are not at odds with each other. They are essential to each other. Here in the Northwest, as in my own home State, people understand that healthy forests are important for a healthy forest-based economy; understand that if we destroy our old growth forest, we'll lose jobs in salmon fishing and tourism and, eventually, in the timber industry as well. We'll destroy recreational opportunities in hunting and fishing for all and eventually make our communities less attractive.

We all understand these things. Let's not be afraid to acknowledge them and to recognize the simple but powerful truth that we come here today less as adversaries than as neighbors and coworkers. Let's confront problems, not people.

Today I ask all of you to speak from your hearts, and I ask you to listen and strive to understand the stories of your neighbors. We're all here because we want a healthy economic environment and a healthy natural environment, because we want to end the divisions here in the Northwest and the deadlock in Washington.

If we commit today to move forward together, we can arrive at a balanced solution and put the stalemate behind us. Together, we can make a new start.

Thank you very much.

NOTE: The President spoke at 10:38 a.m. at the Oregon Convention Center. In his remarks, he referred to Gov. Barbara Roberts of Oregon, Mayor Vera Katz of Portland, Gov. Mike Lowry of Washington, Gov. Pete Wilson of California, and Gov. Cecil D. Andrus of Idaho.

Remarks Concluding the First Roundtable Discussion of the Forest Conference in Portland
April 2, 1993

I'm going to refrain until the afternoon session from getting into the specifics of what we ought to do. But I'd like to say something to the people who were on this panel that talked about the human impact of the present conditions.

Mr. Espy and I are neighbors, and we share a border of the Mississippi River. For almost all the history of this country our two States were the poorest States in America. When agriculture collapsed there in and after the Great Depression, the people who loved my State more than life were forced to leave in huge numbers. As a matter of fact, it's the only way I got elected President. Every third voter in Illinois and Michigan and in the inland empire in California was from Arkansas. [*Laughter*] But it bespoke a terrible inability to manage a process of change so that people could stay with their roots and their culture and their lives.

Then we got everything going again. And then when he and I came of age in the early eighties and began to assume positions of responsibility, we had another horrible structural collapse in the rural areas and the small towns along the Mississippi River because agriculture and the labor-intensive, low-scale, low-wage industries both collapsed at the same time. And our little towns were turned into ghost towns. We had whole counties, county after county after county, with 20, 25 percent unemployment.

What we found was when we talk about managing the process of change, it was like a lot of what Nadine and others have said. Mike, you showed us those pictures. You had people who knew they had to change or they ought to change, but they had a relatively low skill level. They had limits on what kind of opportunities you could immediately put in the small towns, what the Mayor talked about, and they had a horrendous aversion to moving because their life was more than their livelihood. And then it all became complicated by the incredible

pressures on family life, which led more and more families to disintegrate under the burden. And Mike and I literally began our careers dealing with the broken pieces of people's lives against that background.

I say that only to make this point: I cannot repeal the laws of change. In every State in every area of this country the average 18-year-old will change the nature of work seven or eight times in a lifetime now, in a global economy. People who take jobs as bank tellers, for example, even if they keep working for the banks, 10 years after they started what they do will be different because of technology and because of the changes in the economy.

But what we have to find a way to do is to try to make it possible for more people to be faithful to their cultural roots and their way of life and to work through this process in a human way. And if you look at it, there's a lot of analogy here to all these defense workers that are on the food lines in southern California now. I mean, they did what they thought they were supposed to do. They won the cold war, and then we just cut back on defense spending. There they were in the street; nobody had even a theory about how they might go through the kind of process Larry described and be given the opportunity to reclaim their own destiny.

I don't pretend that any of this is easy, but I want you to know that at least some of us have a feel for what this must be like in those little towns. And we'll do what we can.

Thank you very much.

NOTE: The President spoke at 12:57 p.m. at the Oregon Convention Center. In his remarks, he referred to Secretary of Agriculture Mike Espy and timber business owner Nadine Bailey.

Remarks at the Conclusion of the Forest Conference in Portland
April 2, 1993

I want to thank all of you for being here and for sitting through this long day, and all of the participants for everything you've done. I'd like to thank the Cabinet for coming and participating and the Vice President and our staff for all the work they did to put this meeting together.

One of the things that has come out of this meeting to me loud and clear is that you want us to try to break the paralysis that presently controls the situation, to move and to act. I hope that as we leave here we are more committed to working together to move forward than perhaps we were when we came.

I tell you, I'll never forget what I've heard today, the stories, the pictures, the passion from all of you. In a funny way, even when you were disagreeing, every one of you was a voice for change. Every one of you was saying we can't possibly do any worse than to stay within the framework which has now undermined our ability to work together and to build a sense of common community. Too many people are being hurt, and too many resources are being threatened. And we're going to do our best to turn this away from at least the short-term politics of just trying to avoid the tough decisions.

I intend to direct the Cabinet and the entire administration to begin work immediately to craft a balanced, a comprehensive, a long-term policy. And I will direct the Cabinet to report back to me within 60 days to have a plan to end this stalemate.

In the meanwhile, I want each of our Cabinet to look within the departments to determine which policies are at odds with each other. It is true, as I've said many times, that I was mortified when I began to review the legal documents surrounding this controversy to see how often the departments were at odds with each other, so that there was no voice of the United States. I want the Cabinet members to talk with each other to try to bring these conflicts to an end, which at their extreme have had our own agencies suing one another in courts, often over issues which are hard to characterize as monumental. I want everyone to examine his or her approach to existing legal and administrative proceedings to see if inadvertently any of us are hampering the march toward a solution of the larger issues or even toward the particular ones now in litigation.

Regardless of what we are doing, our efforts must be guided, it seems to me, by five fundamental principles: First, we must never forget the human and the economic dimensions of these problems. Where sound management policies can preserve the health of forest lands, sales should go forward. Where this requirement cannot be met, we need to do our best to offer new economic opportunities for year-round, high-wage, high-skill jobs.

Second, as we craft a plan, we need to protect the long-term health of our forests, our wildlife, and our waterways. They are, as the last speaker said, a gift from God, and we hold them in trust for future generations.

Third, our efforts must be, insofar as we are wise enough to know it, scientifically sound, ecologically credible, and legally responsible.

Fourth, the plan should produce a predictable and sustainable level of timber sales and non-timber resources that will not degrade or destroy our forest environment.

And, fifth, to achieve these goals, we will do our best, as I said, to make the Federal Government work together and work for you. We may make mistakes, but we will try to end the gridlock within the Federal Government. And we will insist on collaboration, not confrontation. We will do our best to do our part. We will act with a single purpose and a single agenda once we have a chance to get all these departments working on their respective responsibilities.

But I want to say, too, that all of you have demonstrated to me today your willingness to do your part. I ask you not to let this be the end of it. This conference has established a dialog. Even when it was somewhat funny between Mr. Kerr and Miss Mater, it was still a dialog. And it's got to continue between us and you, and among yourselves. You have got to be a part of this solution. Even if we make the most enlightened possible decisions under the circumstances, they will be all the more resented if they seem to be imposed, without a continuing mechanism for people whose lives will be affected here to be involved.

So when you leave here today, I ask you to keep working for a balanced policy that promotes the economy, preserves jobs, and protects the environment even as you may disagree, as Mr. Thomas said, over how the word "balance" should be defined. When you hit an impasse, I plead with you not to give up. And don't turn against your neighbors. You don't have to fight in a court of law anymore. You can work with us to try to have a long-term solution. If you feel frustrated at times—all of us will— I ask you to stay at the table and to keep talking and keep trying to find common ground. I don't want this situation to go back to posturing, to positioning, to the politics of division that has characterized this difficult issue in the past. I hope we can stay in the conference room and stay out of the courtroom. If we don't give up or give in to deadlock or divisiveness or despair, I think we can build a more prosperous and a more secure future for our communities and for our children. And I think we'll be proud years from now that we were here today.

I thank you for caring and for coming, for speaking out and for reaching out. And I ask you to continue to work with us so that this Forest Conference is the beginning, not the end, of a solution. But we will move. We will move. And I will do my best to assume the responsibility the American people have given me to try to break this deadlock in a responsible way. I just ask you to remember that this listening cannot be a one-shot deal. We've got to continue to work together. And I think, if we do, we'll all be pleased with the results.

Thank you very much.

NOTE: The President spoke at 6:10 p.m. at the Oregon Convention Center. In his remarks, he referred to Andy Kerr, conservation director, Oregon Natural Resources Council, and Jack Ward Thomas, scientist, U.S. Forest Service Pacific Northwest Research Station, La Grande, OR.

Nomination for Posts at the Department of Justice
April 2, 1993

The President announced his choices today for several senior positions at the Department of Justice. He intends to nominate Philip Heymann to be Deputy Attorney General. He is nominating Webster Lee Hubbell to be Associate Attorney General and Drew S. Days III to be Solicitor General.

"The team that Attorney General Reno and I are putting together at the Justice Department is talented, strong, and ready to move forward quickly to tackle the many difficult issues the Department faces." said the President. "With this core group in place, we can move forward to make an independent, aggressive force working to achieve justice for all Americans and safe streets across our country. I hope that the Senate will quickly confirm these outstanding individuals."

NOTE: Biographies of the nominees were made available by the Office of the Press Secretary.

The President's Radio Address
April 3, 1993

Good morning. There's much wisdom in these words from the Scriptures, "Come, let us reason together." This week we've seen a good example of what happens when people talk to each other instead of shout at each other. And unfortunately, we've also seen what happens when some people go to unreasonable lengths to prevent reasonable discussion and decisionmaking.

I'm speaking to you from the Pacific Northwest where we've just concluded the Forest Conference. For years, the good people of the Northwest have been divided by a difficult argument over important values: how best to preserve jobs and protect the forests in this beautiful and productive region of our great Nation.

Yesterday in Portland, Oregon, timber workers, business people, environmentalists, and community leaders sat down together in a conference room, not a courtroom. We discussed how to achieve a healthy economy and a healthy environment. And I directed my Cabinet to come back within 60 days with a plan for a balanced policy.

Grassroots Americans want to end the gridlock and get the economy moving. They want to follow the same practice that we followed in Oregon yesterday. Unfortunately, some people in Washington, DC, haven't gotten the message that the people want fundamental change. Yesterday the minority party in the Senate used procedural tactics to prevent the entire Senate from voting on our jobs and economic recovery package, which has already been passed overwhelmingly by the House of Representatives.

Yesterday we also learned why our jobs package is even more urgent than ever. After 3 years, when America lost one million jobs in the private sector, the unemployment rate remained unchanged in March, and the total number of jobs in our economy actually declined. Now, some folks in Washington may think everything is fine, but all across America the people understand there won't be a real recovery until our working men and women can look forward to a secure, high-wage future for themselves and their children. The people know that America needs our plan to put 500,000 Americans back to work by beginning the investments we need in a stronger, smarter economy.

It's time to move beyond the old politics of partisanship, posturing, and procedural delays and start working together to solve problems. Good things can be accomplished when we reason together. And just as this works in our own country, so too can it work between ourselves and other nations.

That's why I'm taking my first trip out of the country today to meet with Russia's democratically elected President, Boris Yeltsin. Nowhere is progress toward democracy and free markets more important to us than in Russia and the new independent states of the former Soviet Union. Their progress presents a great security challenge and offers great economic opportunities. Russia's rebirth is in the economic interests of American taxpayers, workers, and businesses and the security interests of all of us.

We spent over $4 trillion to wage the cold war. Now we can reduce that spending because the arms and armies of the former Soviet Union pose a greatly reduced threat to us and to our allies. If Russia were to revert to its old ways or plunge into chaos, we would need to reassess our plans for defense savings. That could mean less money for creating new businesses and new jobs, less for preparing our children for the future, less for education. Our economic program at home, more jobs and greater incomes for Americans, could be jeopardized if the reforms in Russia fail.

My discussions with President Yeltsin involve measures intended to help the Russian people make the difficult transition to a market economy by helping themselves. I want America to act, but America cannot and should not act alone. Just as we mobilized the world on behalf of war in the Gulf, we must now mobilize the world on behalf of peace and reform in Russia. Most of this effort will have to come from the Russian people themselves. They will chart the path to their own future. These efforts to offer an historic chance to improve our own security, however, require some action by ourselves, too.

Russia still holds over 20,000 strategic and tactical nuclear warheads. We are implementing historic arms control agreements that for the first time will actually reduce the level of strategic nuclear weapons. By supporting Russia's reforms we can help turn the promise of those agreements into reality for ourselves and for our children and for the Russian people and their children as well. And we can make life in America more safe and prosperous.

For too long, work in Washington on issues like economics, the environment, and foreign policy took place in isolation. The interests of the American people weren't amply protected because their voices weren't adequately heard. The change we want is this: to bring men and women of good will together so that we can put people, the American people, first. We need you to stay active and informed and involved.

Now, I ask you to call or write your Senators. Ask them to take action on our jobs and economic recovery package. I ask for your best wishes as I go into this meeting with President Yeltsin and your understanding that here there is no clear line between our interests at home and our interests abroad. We cannot withdraw from the world even as we work to make America stronger. Together we can change America and change the world.

Thank you for listening.

NOTE: The address was recorded at 8 p.m. on April 2 at the Benson Hotel in Portland, OR, for broadcast at 10:06 a.m. on April 3.

Remarks and an Exchange With Reporters in Vancouver, Canada
April 3, 1993

The President. Thank you very much. I want to begin by thanking the Prime Minister and Canada for hosting this meeting between President Yeltsin and me. I want to thank also the Prime Minister for his leadership in support of the process of democracy and reform in Russia and the Canadian effort to support that process, which has recently been announced. We have worked together very, very closely in the last few weeks to mobilize support among the G–7 for the process of democracy and reform. And he deserves a good share of credit for many of the positive actions which will be taken in the days and weeks ahead. I thank him for that and for hosting this. And I look forward to the meeting with President Yeltsin.

Aid to Russia

Q. Mr. President, there's some concern that any U.S. aid or any Western aid that may pour into Russia now could be wasted. Is there a danger at this point that you could actually give Russia too much Western aid?

The President. Well, I guess there are two concerns that you might have. One is that any aid itself might not be well spent. The other is that future political events might undermine the impact of the aid. As far as the second risk is concerned, that is there, it is clear. But you could say that about any effort we might make anywhere, including in our own country, that future events might undermine the impact of present action. We are proposing to take action to support democracy and to support economic reform.

Now, in terms of making sure the money is spent properly, that it's the right kind of aid, I have spent a significant amount of time on this. We have put together a very good team. I will be consulting in significant detail with President Yeltsin about this. I think that the kinds of things we propose to do are likely to have lasting and tangible impact, and the way we propose to do it will minimize the chance that the money will be squandered.

Q. Does that mean control, sir, control on how the money is spent?

The President. No. You'll see. We're working on it. I think you'll like it.

Q. Mr. President, on the way over here, President Yeltsin mentioned a figure of $100 billion in connection with the cost that Germany had to pay for East Germany. Is that a realistic figure in your mind?

The President. Well, he didn't mention it. I know what he said when he got here, and he went out of his way to say that the amount of money wasn't as important as the kind of support. Germany had to spend a lot of money on Germans to integrate their country. It's a different and I don't think entirely analogous situation.

I believe what you will see building up over the next few weeks is a very significant effort by the G–7 and perhaps by other countries as well to support a long-term process of development in Russia. To go back to the first question, it is important that the efforts that are made be targeted and be designed to produce and support reform and lasting and tangible benefits to the people in Russia in ways that help the security and the economy of all the countries that are helping. So I think I look at this as a long-term effort, and I think it would be a mistake to put a short-term dollar figure on it.

Yes, Mark [Mark Miller, Newsweek].

Q. How much pressure do you feel under going into this 2-day event? And what are the big unanswered questions in your mind, the things that, despite all your preparation, you still don't know the answers to?

The President. I don't feel under any pressure. I'm glad that this day has arrived. I welcome the chance that the United States has to support the millions of courageous people in Russia who have stood up for democracy and have had the courage to go through some very difficult times and, I might add, to support the people in the other newly independent states of the former Soviet Union who are going through equally difficult economic times and striving hard for democracy. I welcome that opportunity.

The only unanswered questions I have are the same ones that you have. I don't know what's going to happen. None of us do. But I think that, I would just remind you all—it's something I said in my speech at Annapolis— in 1776 the United States adopted the Declaration of Independence. It was well over a decade before we actually settled on a Constitution and got around to electing a President.

And the Russians are trying to undertake three fundamental changes at once: moving from a Communist to a market economy; moving from a tyrannical dictatorship to a democracy; and moving to an independent nation state away from having a great empire. And these are very difficult and unsettling times. But I think that the direction is clear, the direction that they ought to take, and I think we ought to support the direction. And I'm not troubled by the fact that I can't control that process or that I don't know the outcome of it. We just need to weigh in and do what we can to do what's right.

Q. Mr. President, why don't the majority of Americans think we should be sending more aid to Russia?

The President. I think there are probably two or three reasons. First of all, historically in our country, foreign aid has never been popular. And that's why I have gone out of my way to show that this is the establishment of a partnership which will be mutually beneficial. This is not in any way an act of charity that we are engaged in. It doesn't have anything to do with that.

Secondly, the American people are preoccupied with their own problems. We've got one million fewer jobs in the private sector than we had 3 years ago. Unemployment is high. Incomes have been stagnant for years. We have serious challenges at home, and they want to know that we're putting those first.

Then I think the third thing is the question that you asked in the beginning. They want to know that if we are going to do something, they want us at least to go to extra efforts to make sure that the money is well spent and is in the long-term benefit of both countries.

Yes.

Japan

Q. Are both of you confident that you can get Japan on side with some big bucks for this venture and to ignore the Northern Islands issue?

The President. Well, let me say this. I had a very good talk with Prime Minister Miyazawa last night. The Japanese have been very forthcoming as the leaders of the G–7. This is their year to lead, and they are leading. They are hosting this meeting of the finance and foreign ministers on the 14th and 15th, and I believe that they will fulfill their leadership role. I'm encouraged.

Thank you very much.

NOTE: The President spoke at 11:39 a.m. at the Mackenzie House at the University of British Columbia.

Exchange With Reporters With President Boris Yeltsin of Russia in Vancouver
April 3, 1993

Russia–U.S. Relations

Q. President Yeltsin, will American aid make a difference to the political situation in Russia?

President Yeltsin. You know, it's always useful to help a friend, especially if a friend goes through a difficult period. And we are partners, and we are friends.

Q. Go ahead, Mr. President, you can talk.

President Clinton. I just was going to say, I don't view this as a—this is not a talk about aid; this is a talk about a long-term partnership. The United States has a great deal to gain from a strong, successful, democratic Russia. It is in our interest. And I'm very encouraged by the things that President Yeltsin has stood for, and the fight that he's waging now.

President Yeltsin. And the rest of the world, too.

NOTE: The exchange began at 1:55 p.m. at the MacKenzie House at the University of British Columbia. President Yeltsin spoke in Russian, and his remarks were translated by an interpreter. A tape was not available for verification of the content of this exchange.

The President's News Conference With President Boris Yeltsin of Russia in Vancouver
April 4, 1993

President Clinton. Good afternoon. I have just completed 2 days of intensely productive discussions with President Boris Yeltsin. I want to join him in thanking Prime Minister Mulroney and the people of Canada for their hospitality. The beauty of Vancouver has inspired our work here, and this weekend I believe we have laid the foundation for a new democratic partnership between the United States and Russia.

The heroic deeds of Boris Yeltsin and the Russian people launched their reforms toward democracy and market economies and defended them valiantly during the dark days of August of 1991. Now it is the self-interest and the high duty of all the world's democracies to stand by Russia's democratic reforms in their new hour of challenge.

The contrast between our promising new partnership and our confrontational past underscores the opportunities that hang in the balance today. For 45 years we pursued a deadly competition in nuclear arms. Now we can pursue a safe and steady cooperation to reduce the arsenals that have haunted mankind. For 45 years our Nation invested trillions of dollars to contain and deter Soviet communism. Now the emergence of a peaceful and democratic Russia can enable us to devote more to our own domestic needs.

The emergence of a newly productive and prosperous Russia could add untold billions in new growth to the global economy. That would mean new jobs and new investment opportunities for Americans and our allies around the world. We are investing today not only in the future of Russia but in the future of America as well.

Mr. President, our Nation will not stand on the sidelines when it comes to democracy in Russia. We know where we stand. We are with Russian democracy. We are with Russian reforms. We are with Russian markets. We support freedom of conscience and speech and religion. We support respect for ethnic minorities. We actively support reform and reformers and you in Russia.

The ultimate responsibility for the success of Russia's new course, of course, rests with the people of Russia. It is they who must support economic reforms and make them work. But Americans know that our Nation has a part to play, too, and we will do so.

In our discussions, President Yeltsin and I reached several important agreements on the ways in which the United States and the other major industrialized democracies can best support Russian reforms. First are programs that can begin immediately. I discussed with President Yeltsin the initiatives totaling $1.6 billion intended to bolster political and economic reforms in Russia. These programs already are funded. They can provide immediate and tangible results for the Russian people.

We will invest in the growth of Russia's private sector through two funds to accelerate privatization and to lend to new small private businesses. We will resume grain sales to Russia and extend $700 million in loans for Russia to purchase American grain. We will launch a pilot project to help provide housing and retraining for the Russian military officers as they move into jobs in the civilian economy.

Because the momentum for reform must come upward from the Russian people, not down from their government, we will expand exchanges between American farmers, business people, students, and others with expertise working directly with the Russian people. And we agreed to make a special effort to promote American investment, particularly in Russia's oil and gas sectors. To give impetus to this effort, we will ask Vice President Gore and Russian Prime Minister Chernomyrdin to chair a new commission on energy and space.

Second, beyond these immediate programs, the President and I agreed that our partnership requires broader perspectives and broader cooperative initiatives, which I will discuss with the Congress when I return home. We expect to do more than we are announcing today in housing and technical assistance, in nuclear safety and cooperation on the environment, and in important exchanges.

Third, this challenge we face today is clearly not one for the United States and Russia alone. I have asked our allies in the G-7 to come forward with their own individual bilateral initiatives. Canada and Britain have already done so, and I expect others to follow.

President Yeltsin and I also discussed plans for the G–7 nations to act together in support of Russia's reforms. The foreign and finance ministers of the G–7 are meeting in Tokyo on April 14th and 15th. Coordinated efforts are required to help Russia stabilize its economy and its currency. The President and I agreed that Russia and the G–7 nations must take mutually reinforcing steps to strengthen reform in Russia. And those will be announced on the 14th and 15th in Tokyo.

Beyond these economic initiatives, the President and I discussed a broad agenda of cooperation in foreign affairs. We reaffirmed our commitment to safe dismantlement and disposal of nuclear weapons. We discussed the need to strengthen the Non-Proliferation Treaty and to assure that Ukraine along with Belarus and Kazakhstan ratify the START Treaty and accede to the NPT as non-nuclear-weapons states. I stress that we want to expand our relationships with all the new independent states.

We also agreed to work in concert to help resolve regional crises, to stem weapons of proliferation, to protect the global environment, and to address common challenges to international peace, such as the tragic violence in Bosnia, advancing the promising peace talks we have cosponsored in the Mideast, and continuing our cooperation to end the regional conflicts of the cold war era.

Many of the dreams Americans and Russians hold for their children and for generations to come rest on the long-term success of Russia's reforms and, thus, on the long-term partnerships between our two nations. Our new democratic partnership can make an historic contribution for all humanity well into the next century. Both of us know that it requires effort and vigilance to make progress along the path toward democracy's ideal. And I believe we both see those ideas as rooted deeply in the human spirit.

I think of the words of one of the great poets of democracy within our own country, Walt Whitman. In a poem about crossing the East River in New York where the Brooklyn Bridge now stands, he commands, "Flow on, river; flow on." Of course, the river hardly required his permission. It has flowed on for centuries and will continue to, whether old Walt Whitman decreed it or not. Yet, he bellowed his enthusiastic support for the river's timeless journey.

Russia's struggle for democracy and America's support are much the same. We know that the attraction to freedom that animates democracy flows powerfully through the human spirit like a river. Our words do not cause that river to flow, and history has now proven that in the long run no tyrant can cause the river to stop. Yet, we bellow our support because it is right and because democracy's river can carry both our nations toward a better future.

As we have looked out across the Pacific to the shores of Russia and its far east over the last 2 days, we have committed ourselves anew to that journey. I now return to the United States with a reaffirmed commitment to that course and a determination to engage Members of Congress in both parties and the American people in a rededication to the prospect that a successful and strong and democratic Russia is very much in the best interest of America and the world.

President Yeltsin. First of all, I should like to thank you, Mr. President, for your kind words addressed to Russia. I should like to thank Canada's Prime Minister, Mr. Mulroney, for the excellent way in which this summit of two Presidents of two great powers was organized. I'd like to thank the people of Vancouver for being so hospitable, for having so warmly welcomed our delegations and us personally, the Presidents. I should like to thank the journalists, who, it seems to me, kept a round-the-clock watch at their posts.

I am fully satisfied by the results and by the spirit and atmosphere of my encounter with President Bill Clinton. It was in all senses out of the ordinary. But it was made extraordinary by processes transpiring in the United States and Russia, conditioned by very special relationships developing between ourselves and Mr. Bill Clinton. We met for the first time but yesterday, but became partners back at that meeting in Washington.

When Bill Clinton became President, we rapidly established good working contacts over the telephone. We candidly discussed the most intricate issues and stated at the outset that there would be no pauses in our dialog and that we would rapidly manage to find time to meet and established that right at the beginning, as I say, several months ago.

We had no right to further postpone personal encounter in the face of this world emerging from a wounded past, its thoughts preoccupied by what has occurred in two great countries, the United States and Russia. We immediately found common language in Vancouver, probably because we're both businesslike people and at the same time, to some extent, idealists, both.

We also believe that freedom, democracy, and freedom of choice for people are not mere words and are prepared to struggle for our beliefs. We understand that everything that happens in the world is interlinked, that cooperation is not concession-making but a vital necessity, a contribution to our future.

At previous meetings, the nations' leaders discussed primarily the disassembly of confrontational structures, but here in Vancouver, we talked about building the new, laying the foundations of a future economy. This was the first economically oriented meeting of the meeting of the two great powers. We adopted some signal decisions in the interests of the people of the Russian Federation, in the interests of the people of the United States of America, in the interests of the world's people.

We decided to eliminate discriminatory limitations on trade with Russia. We, in fact, said that we were simply hurt. Russia had embarked upon the path of democracy, whereas America was still treating us as though we were a Communist country. In fact, we're struggling against communism. I stated that quite clearly, and Bill Clinton agreed. We are prepared to compete but compete honestly. We decided to alter our approach to trade in Russian uranium, space technology, access to Russian military technology. We decided to do away with the Jackson-Vanik amendment and to resolve other legislative issues. There is considerably greater interest on the part of American investors in the fuel sector, in Russia space technology. We decided to cooperate in this area and decided to join forces, the U.S. and Russian administrations.

The economic package of Bill Clinton—this is what it's going to be called from here on in—Bill Clinton's economic package is predicated on the fact that America wishes to see Russia prosper with a blooming economy. America intends to support Russian entrepreneurs, particularly small and medium farmers, Russia's youth. It's going to cooperate in housing construction for the military and in other areas. All of this is in support of Russian reforms, a part of the strategic form of cooperation be-

tween us, stressed Bill Clinton. Now, that figure, the figure that reflects that cooperation is a $1.6 billion. We're looking forward to other steps to be undertaken by the United States of America and other major industrial countries to support real reform in Russia.

The linkage between that set of measures and other political measures was avoided. Of course, military and political problems could not be skirted. We discussed what might be done to see to it that all participants in the Bosnian conflict support the U.N. position. Here, our positions match as to the main points. We devoted quite a lot of attention to problems of nonproliferation. We decided to extend our agreements on the avoidance of accidents, such as the near accident involving submarines very recently. We decided to strengthen cooperation between various areas of the military. All of this is reflected in the Vancouver declaration, some of the principal elements of that declaration.

Members of our delegation felt that the U.S. side did appreciate that support for Russia had to be timely. Our partners make it their goal to support Russia's reforms, which are not yet yielding major results as far as ordinary Russians are concerned.

The meeting in Vancouver signals a shift from general assurances of support to Russia to pragmatic, specific, nitty-gritty projects. What we see dominating here are economic and not military strategic issues dominant.

Another very important result is that we, with President Bill Clinton, did establish some pretty close personal contacts. Bill Clinton is a serious partner. He is prepared to tackle the major problems confronting our two countries in the interest of our two countries, in the interest of all free people throughout the world. I have invited Bill Clinton to visit Moscow, to render us an official visit at a time convenient to himself.

Thank you very much.

Nuclear Disarmament

Q. President Clinton, after 45 years of deadly competition in nuclear arms and now a new spirit of democratic partnership, in this new spirit of democratic partnership, did you discuss whether Russia and the United States—[*inaudible*]——

President Clinton. We did discuss that, and we discussed that within the framework of the

START agreements and the timetables established—[*inaudible*]—and we agreed that we would reexamine that at an early, early time. We did not resolve that issue, but we agreed to take it up again.

Aid to Russia

Q. A question, Mr. President, for you and President Yeltsin. Much of Bill Clinton's economic package is old wine in new bottles, and it's money that was previously authorized and appropriated by Congress. Why will it make a difference now, more of a difference now than it would have when it was approved last year? And what guarantees are there that it will be delivered this time, when it was not, when originally approved?

President Clinton. I'd like to make two points. First of all, the nature of this package is, I think, somewhat different than the one which was discussed last year. First, three-quarters, three-quarters of this money will be distributed not government to government but will go to benefit the private sector, the emerging private sector in Russia, and will go outside of the central apparatus in terms of supporting privatization, helping to start new businesses, establishing a democracy corps at a really significant level.

If you look at all the things that are down here, they are very specific; they are tangible; they are designed to develop concrete benefits for the people who will be involved. And as President Yeltsin reiterated to me in our last meeting, in each of these categories we have a proven mechanism for distributing the assistance so that we know how to get the money to its intended purpose.

The second point I would like to make is that we intend for this to be leveraged in two ways: first, because I intend now to go back to the Congress, to the leaders of both parties with whom I met extensively before I came here, and discuss a second package of bilateral assistance which will be more aggressive in the areas of energy and environmental cleanup, areas which will be dramatically helpful in supporting the economy of Russia, and more aggressive in the whole issue of housing for returning soldiers, which is a very important issue socially and politically as well as economically in the country, and in several other areas. And we have asked the other G–7 countries each to do something on their own. And those messages are coming in now.

And finally, I would remind you that we want a different kind of multilateral agreement to come out of Tokyo. That is, last year when the figure $24 billion was floated all across the United States and the world and Russia, a lot of it was contingent on all kinds of things which never happened and could not reasonably have been expected to happen. We are going to try to make sure that anything we say will be done, in fact, will be done. And that will be a big difference.

President Yeltsin. I should like to stress a major difference between that which was decided upon in the past and that which was decided upon, economically speaking, in Bill Clinton's economic package: first, a close linkage to specific sectors in terms of sums earmarked, which will enable us to monitor the expenditure of each and every line item; second, a close connection to deadlines, which had never been done in the past. The figure of $24 billion was moot at, say, by the year 2000, but now we've stated the 25th of April, 27th of April, 1st of May, the month of May, the month June, the month of September, the month of October, and throughout the remainder of 1993. That is the principal set of differences.

Q. You somewhat anticipated what I had intended to ask. I see here a clear break in the type of assistance being rendered to reform, about which so much had been said by way of lipservice in the past. So what do you expect of the G–7 meeting in Tokyo, then?

President Yeltsin. Reform, of course, is proceeding, but it's a young reform process. It's really only a year old. It's only for a year that we have reform underway in Russia. Now, in that one year we have had 60,000 private enterprises set up. In over 70 years not a single one was established. We must remember that over 50,000 major stockholding companies in that one year. These are perhaps minor successes, but they are signal successes nonetheless.

But of course, certain quarters are putting on brakes on the process. Russia tends to run out of breath from time to time. It needs a transition period, a breather of, say, 2 years. And in that period of breather, we need this kind of support; not aid, I would stress, not in assistance but support, because in supplying food, technologies, goods, et cetera, et cetera, you do create additional workplaces, additional jobs in the United States of America, additional use of American industrial plant capacity, a fuller use of U.S. economic potential. So these are not Christmas presents, I put it to you, not at all. This is policy and major policymaking, I put it to you. Thank you.

Q. President Yeltsin, President Clinton, you've all indicated your devotion to democracy, but that you're both idealists at the same time. But what we're hearing about right now is a very pragmatic, a very down-to-earth set of measures, a very down-to-earth program. Now, President Yeltsin, how is this assistance to be rendered to particular sectors? You've indicated that there is a definite time, a place for delivery of the assistance. Now, you've also indicated that jobs will be created in America. But what will actually happen on the ground, so to speak, in Russia?

President Yeltsin. Let's say we're going to spend 300 billion rubles on health in Russia, that will reach every single Russian—100 million in medicines that will reach every Russian. Technology—after all, new technologies will generate new consumer goods for each and every Russian. Everything is people oriented. This is Bill Clinton's policy. It is Yeltsin's policy. That is, that we work for people's benefit, for the benefit of each and every free individual.

Aid Coordination and Trade Restrictions

Q. What assurances do you have from President Yeltsin that this medicine, this food, these housing guarantees, that any of this can really be delivered through a system that we've been told is very bureaucratic and somewhat corrupt? What assurances have you given him that there won't be logjams on the American side? And could you tell us, do you agree with his opening statement that there is agreement here between the two leaders about ending the Jackson-Vanik amendment and about the technology transfers through COCOM?

President Clinton. Let me answer the first question first. On the delivery systems, we have reached a tentative agreement, pending the acquiescence by other G–7 countries—I say that because I have not had a chance to discuss this with any of them—that there were logjams in the past, both within the government agencies of the United States and other countries and within Russia itself, and that we have now asked in a very carefully coordinated fashion all the G–7 to do two things: to commit to more bilateral assistance in terms of development and

partnership and to work for a multilateral development package.

So we have tentatively agreed, the two of us have—but again, I say nobody else has agreed to this—that we should establish a coordinating office in Moscow to make sure, number one, that each of us in the G–7 does what we promise to do on time, without delay, and number two, that our efforts are coordinated within Russia, both so that we are not in conflict with each other and so that the money can actually go where it's supposed to go. So we devoted quite a bit of time to the whole business of implementation.

As to your second question, we discussed Jackson-Vanik, COCOM, and a number of other issues. And I told President Yeltsin that in my meetings with the Congress before I left, we agreed that certain Members of Congress with an interest in this—I might add, in both parties—would actually compile a list of every one of the cold war legislative and other restrictions that are still being applied to Russia, even though it is now a democratic state, that I would listen to President Yeltsin on these issues, and that I would then return home and we would make as many changes as we could.

But with regard specifically to Jackson-Vanik, I think the issue there is whether—it's a fact question from my point of view: Are there any more people who wish to emigrate who have not been allowed to? The President says he doesn't think so. He's going to look into that. I'm going to go back and raise that issue with Congress, along with the COCOM issue and a whole range of others. And I would expect within a matter of a few days, we'll be able to give to the American press and public a comprehensive answer to what the position of the administration on that will be.

Q. COCOM?

President Clinton. Including that. We are reviewing that, too.

Go ahead.

Areas of Cooperation

Q. My question is directed both to President Yeltsin and to President Clinton. It goes as follows: The elimination of restrictions on trade with Russia, if that does happen, what perhaps should be the harbinger of the establishment of those relations of partnership which we've been talking about for so long. Now, I'd like to ask you, gentlemen, what particular priority areas are up for partnership and cooperation? And President Clinton, how do you feel? Are there particular areas which the U.S. might like to stress in building up business cooperation with the Russians?

President Yeltsin. On that first point, I should like to say that we discussed something like 50 issues yesterday and today, and practically all of those issues had to do with partnership. We would not manage to tackle any one of those issues if we were not partners, if we were rivals in each other's eyes, adversaries in each other's eyes. No, we are partners and future allies. That was the way our relationship unfolded. That's the way the negotiations went. That's the way we went about resolving issues. And in discussing those approximately 50 issues, we didn't sweep anything under the table; we didn't set anything aside. We decided either to pass them on for further investigation and analysis, or else we resolved them on the spot.

President Clinton. I'd like to answer the question also, and respond to what President Yeltsin said. Among the areas in which the United States sees real opportunities for joint activity are energy, space, the environment, nuclear safety. These are some of the areas that we believe we can work together on in ways that would benefit Russia economically in a very short time and also be beneficial for the United States. Over and above that, we discussed but did not settle on a range of possible actions that we could take to make private investment in Russia more attractive to American investors because, after all, in the end a market economy is built by private investment and not just public investment alone.

The second point I'd like to make in response to the comment by President Yeltsin: We did discuss a phenomenal number of issues. I think it's fair to say we discussed more issues than either one of us thought we would when we came here. We did not agree on everything. You would not expect the leaders of two great nations, even in partnership, to have total agreement. But we did come to agreement on how we would handle these issues, how we would try to work through our disagreements, and what we would do in the future. And I appreciated the extreme candor with which President Yeltsin treated all our discussions, including those areas where there is still some gap between our two positions.

Submarine Incident and Baltic States

Q. I have a two-part question, one for each of you. Mr. President, on another irritant in the U.S.-Russian relationship that was pointed out to us yesterday by your Communications Director, George Stephanopoulos, the patrolling off the Russian coast by U.S. submarines: What have you agreed to now to prevent these kinds of accidents from recurring down the road? Is this another case of old habits dying hard, that the U.S. still finds a need to keep these kinds of submarines off the Russian coast?

And for President Yeltsin: An irritant in the U.S.-Russian relationship is the slow withdrawal of Russian troops from the Baltic States and from Eastern Europe. Are you committed to withdrawing the Russian soldiers as quickly as possible from those independent nations?

President Clinton. Let me answer first. I don't mind saying to this whole assemblage that I told President Yeltsin I very much regretted the submarine incident, and that I had ordered a thorough review of the incident as well as the policy of which the incident happened to be an unintended part, and that as soon as that review was completed, I would engage Russia at the appropriate levels to discuss whether the policy should be changed and where we should go from here. That was a regrettable thing, and I don't want it to ever happen again.

President Yeltsin. On the first point I'd add just a couple of words. We did agree that somewhere late in May or early in June the Minister of Defense of the Russian Federation, Grachev, would visit the United States of America to discuss the entire gamut of issues of this sort, including close passage of submarines, so that such incidents might be avoided in the future.

Now, with regard to withdrawal of troops from the Baltic States, we are adhering very closely to the schedule on troop withdrawals from Lithuania, and we are completing work on that schedule since Lithuania does not violate human rights and treats the Russian-speaking population fairly. If Latvia and Estonia violate human rights, if their laws are presently so structured that in fact some national minorities continue to be persecuted, and that involves basically Russians, we have, on the whole, adopted a political decision, a policy decision to withdraw troops from those states. We will be scheduling the actual withdrawal in line with what they decide in the human rights area.

Russian Referendum

Q. I have a question that I would like to address to President Yeltsin and also to President Clinton.

President Yeltsin, you indicated that Bill Clinton's economic package lays the groundwork for partnership between the United States of America and Russia and will provide considerable impetus to the reform process in Russia. In April, we're going to have a referendum in Russia. How, here today in Vancouver, would you forecast the situation unfolding on the basis of agreements reached here in Canada?

Now, President Clinton, the personal factor is a major element in politics. Now, what would you indicate by way of your personal contact with President Yeltsin in regard to the referendum?

President Yeltsin. That's our internal domestic issue. Whether it will be impacted directly or indirectly is another issue, but it's up to us to deal with the referendum issue. It's up to us to work with our people. It's up to us to persuade the citizens of the Russian Federation that if they do not vote in favor of confidence on the 25th of April, they will be dealing a major blow not only upon Russia but also upon the United States of America, upon the other countries of the world. This would be a loss to democracy, a loss to freedom, a rollback to the past, a return to the Communist yokes, something which is entirely inadmissible.

President Clinton. My personal reaction to President Yeltsin based on these 2 days is, first, that he is very much what he seems to be—he's a person who rose from humble beginnings, who has never forgotten where he came from—and second, that his enduring virtue is that he trusts the Russian people.

The great courage involved in all democracies is that in the end you have to trust the people, including you have to trust the people if they decide to throw you out. You have to trust the people.

Boris Yeltsin has put the fate of the Government of Russia into the hands of the people of Russia. That is a unique thing in your history. There are few nations in the world that have the spirit, the culture, the richness that the Russian people can claim. And yet, for too long, they were never given control over their own destiny. My belief is that deep down inside he actually does trust all the people who live in

those communities in the 12 time zones that make up Russia. And that is a very great thing. Yes.

Exchange Programs

Q. Mr. President and Mr. President, definitely we are interested if there is any part of the package which deals with Russia's far east and Pacific Northwest of the United States of America as far as economic reform and development is concerned and people-to-people relationships in particular.

President Clinton. Yes, we agreed to have a substantial increase in the exchanges of people, particularly in the area of increasing the number of people we might bring to this country for training in business management, and big increases in student exchanges and a whole range of other things, including agriculture and other areas that we are still going to identify.

Let me say that it is easy to minimize such things because they often do not cost as much money as some other parts of a long-term development package. But no one who has lived through the second half of the 20th century could possibly be blind to the enormous impact of exchange programs on the future of the countries.

You know, when I was a young man I worked for the chairman of the Senate Foreign Relations Committee, Senator Fulbright. There is a scholarship program that carries his name that, literally, in my judgment, has changed the whole direction of policy in country after country after country. So I believe this is a very important thing, and I'm going to do everything I can to see that there is a major, major increase in the number of broad-gauged exchanges. And I might say I think that has great support in the United States Congress.

President Yeltsin. I'd like to add a few words to that. This package, which I would like to call a very large and wise package which is going to make history, involves yet another question mark, and that is that of assisting the native populations in the northern reaches of Russia. It's a very, very important issue to tackle that one.

Russian Referendum

Q. I would like to know what is your deep feeling, because everybody tries to help you, and I think everybody is right to help you because you represent democracy. But the question I will ask you is that, after you, do you think there is an alternative that maybe our American friends, President Clinton, has been obliged to think about in case your enemies, your adversary oust you from power after the referendum on the 25th of April?

President Yeltsin. My first point to that would be this: I intend to do everything I can in my power—and, by the way, I do believe in the Russian people making its proper choice on the 25th of April. At the moment, today I say there is no alternative to Yeltsin. Perhaps there will be one tomorrow, but certainly not one today.

President Clinton. If I were on the ballot, I would make exactly the statement. The answer to your question is simple, I think. I have made it clear that the United States is committed to democracy, to human rights, to market economics, to reducing the nuclear threat, to respecting national sovereignty of the other newly independent states. We have interests and values. They are embodied by the policies and the direction of President Yeltsin. They are enduring. He is the duly elected President of Russia. And as long as he is, I intend to work with him and support him because he reflects those enduring values.

Aid to Russia

Q. I have a question to the President of Russia. The overall sum of this is that this is perhaps not so great. For example, when we had the Los Angeles riots we had a package twice that size set up. Now, what sort of projects in Russia do you think will yield the most immediate results and will have the greatest impact socially in the short run?

President Yeltsin. I feel that we do not need astronomical figures, headline-making figures. What we need are real figures. These are real figures which are do-able, which are implementable in terms of things that we can do.

Q. Well, what specific projects would you regard as the most effective ones?

President Yeltsin. Well, the first priority would be fuel, which would enable us to replenish, to top off our hard-currency reserves. I'm talking about oil and gas, its revitalization, and we addressed that topic in very specific terms. The next issue would be immediate delivery of goods to the people.

Cuba

Q. I have a two-part question, one for Mr. Clinton and one for Mr. Yeltsin, please. Before leaving the United States, Hispanic Congressmen requested that you talk about the nuclear plant of Cienfuegos in Cuba, trying to get the commitment of Mr. Yeltsin not to continue or not to help in continuing the construction of that plant. Did you get that commitment?

And for Mr. Yeltsin: I would like to know if you have a timetable for finishing the withdrawal of troops, Soviet troops, from Cuba?

President Clinton. First of all, let me say that the day of massive subsidies between Russia and the Government of Cuba is over. The lion's share of the trade which exists now between Russia and Cuba is a market-based trade. There is a nuclear facility being constructed there. The United States is concerned about it. We've expressed our concern about it. That was basically the extent of our discussions here at this meeting.

President Yeltsin. In regard to troop withdrawals, we have already initiated that withdrawal and are now finalizing a schedule for the final withdrawal of troops; nothing in terms of a specific timetable.

Characterization of Summit

Q. I have a question for President Clinton. Mr. President, even today, I think we can foretell that President Yeltsin's opponents will certainly be accusing him of making unilateral political concessions in exchange for Clinton's package. Perhaps we could anticipate their commentary and respond to that question even today.

President Clinton. First of all, I do not believe it would be fair to say that President Yeltsin made a lot of political concessions in return for the commitments made by the United States. We did clarify some positions on some issues. And I felt better about it. But basically everything President Yeltsin said in our private meetings was consistent with the direction in which he has tried to lead Russia since he has been President.

Secondly, I would remind you that the United States also has taken some steps that have nothing to do with money to try to reinforce the fact that we consider this a partnership of two great nations, that we want to work in partnerships. That's why I agreed to a comprehensive review of all the cold war statutes and other limitations on our relationships with Russia. That's why I went out of my way to tell the President in our very first meeting how much I regretted the incident of the submarine bumping and how I was committed to reviewing our policy and to getting back with him on that.

So I would say that President Yeltsin's opponents might want to characterize this meeting in that way, but it would not be a fair characterization. In fact, it would be a distortion of the conversation that we had.

President Yeltsin. I am not frightened of possible reprimands or reproaches from the opposition because I see no single matter upon which it could hang such an accusation. There's nothing in any of the documents; there's nothing in what was said between us.

President Clinton. Thank you very much.

NOTE: The President's ninth news conference began at 1:45 p.m. at Canada Place. President Yeltsin spoke in Russian, and his remarks were translated by an interpreter.

Question-and-Answer Session With Russian Reporters in Vancouver
April 4, 1993

Aid to Russia

Q. I had two questions for both Presidents, so you could probably answer for Boris, too. [*Laughter*]

The President. I'll give you my answer, then I'll give you Yeltsin's answer. [*Laughter*]

Q. The first is that this is the meeting of the Presidents. So the money that's being promised is Government money, and naturally it's going to be distributed through the Government. But you've indicated that three-quarters are going to be going to businesses. So the question is how the Russian businesses themselves are going to be consulted, if ever? What are the priorities, because there are several association of Russian businessmen existing already. So will they be invited to participate in setting up priorities for investment? This is the first.

And second, to you: We know that polls, public polls in America do not show that Americans are very enthusiastic about giving this aid. Like Newsweek polls say that about 75 percent don't approve it, and New York Times published that 52 percent support if it just prevents civil war, 42 percent if it fosters democratic reform, and only 29 percent if it just personally supports Yeltsin. How are you going to sort of handle this problem that Americans themselves are not very enthusiastic?

Thank you.

Q. I have a question. I'm sorry, is there going to be a translation of everything into Russian? No, just the answers. Just the answers. Okay.

The President. The answer to the first question is, it depends on what kind of aid we're discussing. For example, the funds that will be set up for financing new businesses will obviously go to those businesses who apply and who seem to be good risks and make the application. The privatization fund will be used to support the privatization of existing public enterprises. Then there are some other general funds in the Democracy Corps and other things which people in Russia will have some influence over the distribution of.

With regard to your second question, let me say that I would think that there would be people in both countries who would not feel too warmly toward simply the American Government giving money to the Russian Government. There's opposition to that in Russia. And in our country, throughout our whole history, there has been an opposition to foreign aid of all kinds. That is, this has nothing to do with Russia. If you look at the whole history of America, any kind of aid program has always been unpopular.

What I have tried to tell the American people is, this is not an aid program, this is an investment program; that this is an investment in our future. We spent $4 trillion, trillion, on armaments, on soldiers, and other investments because of the cold war. Now, with a democratic government in Russia, with the newly independent states, the remainder of them, working on a democracy and struggling to get their economies going, it seems to me very much in our interest to make it possible to do whatever we can for democracy to survive, for the economy of Russia to grow because of the potential for trade and investment there, and for us to continue the effort to reduce nuclear weapons and other elements of hostility on both sides, on our side and on the Russian side. So I don't see this as an aid program. This is an investment for the United States. This is very much in the interest of the United States. The things I announced today, the second stage of the program which I hope to put together next week, in my view are things that are good for my country and for the taxpayers and workers of my country.

Russia is a very great nation that needs some partnership now, some common endeavor with other people who share her goals. But it would be a great mistake for anyone to view this as some sort of just a charity or an aid issue. That's not what it is. It's an investment for America, and it's a wonderful investment. Like all investments, there is some risk. But there's far less risk with a far greater potential of return than the $4 trillion we spend looking at each other across the barrier of the cold war.

Ukraine and Trade Restrictions

Q. Mr. President, first of all, thank you very much indeed for coming here and talking to us. In the memory of the living correspondents, this is the first time an American President is doing this to the Russian press corps, so it's kind of a very measured breakthrough.

I have two questions. One, in your introductory remarks of the other press conference, you mentioned in brief that you discussed the START II and START I issues. Could you tell us, did you reach an agreement with President Yeltsin as to what might be done in order to have Ukraine join the ratification of START I and the NPT regime? And my second question is, how confident you are that the United States Congress would be eager to support you in lifting Jackson-Vanik and other restrictions inherited from the cold war?

The President. First, we discussed the issue of Ukraine with regard to START I and NPT and generally with regard to the need to proceed to have the other independent states all be non-nuclear but also to have the United States develop strong relationships with them. We know that one thing that we could do that would increase, I think, the willingness of the Ukraine to support this direction is to success-

fully conclude our own negotiations on highly enriched uranium, because that would provide not only an important economic opportunity for Russia but also for Ukraine, and it would show some reaching out on our part. But we agreed that basically the people who signed off on the Lisbon Protocol have got to honor what they did, and we agreed to continue to press that.

I, myself, have spent a good deal of time trying to reassure Ukraine's leaders, specifically the President and the Foreign Minister, that I want strong ties with Ukraine, that the United States very much wants a good relationship with Ukraine, but that in order to do what we need to do together to strengthen the economy of Ukraine and to have the United States be fully supportive, the commitment to ratify START I and to join the NPT regime is critical.

With regard to Jackson-Vanik and COCOM, I would make two points: First, I have agreed with the Republican and Democratic leaders in the Congress that we will, as soon as I return, have a list of all the legislative and other restrictions—some of them are regulatory in nature—imposed on relations between the United States and Russia, that are legacies of the cold war. And we will see how many of them we could agree to do away with right now, at least among the leadership of the Congress.

With regard to Jackson-Vanik, I think there will be an openness to change the law if the Congress is convinced there are, in fact, no more refuseniks, no more people who wish to emigrate who are not being allowed to. If the fact is that there is no one there who the law was designed to affect, then I think that the desire to keep the law will be much less.

With regard to COCOM, my guess is, and it's nothing more than a guess, that the leadership of Congress and indeed my own advisers might prefer to see some sort of phased movement out of the COCOM regime. But I think they would be willing to begin it in the fairly near future.

President's Interest in Russia

Q. Mr. Clinton, when I read your speech in Annapolis, I got the impression that you have a completely different personal—and I stress that, personal, not political—approach towards Russia, compared to the approach of Mr. Bush. Could you formulate in a few words what is the difference between you as a personality and your approach, the difference between your approach to Russia and the approach of Mr. Bush? And why did you cite Akhmatova in the last part of your speech?

The President. Let me say, first, I do not wish to compare myself with President Bush or anyone else. I can't say what was in his heart about Russia. I can say that since I was a boy, I have been personally fascinated with the history, the music, and the culture and the literature of Russia. I have been thrilled by Russian music since I was a serious student of music, for more than 30 years now. I have read major Russian novelists and many of your poets and followed your ballet and tried to know as much as I could about your history.

And I went to the Soviet Union, but it was then the Soviet Union—you may know, it was a big issue in the last Presidential campaign that I spent the first week of 1970 alone in Moscow—and did not return again until 3 days before Mr. Yeltsin was elected President. But all that time I was away, I was following events there very closely and hoping for the day when we could be genuine partners. So I have always had a personal feeling about Russia.

I remember, for example—a lot of you know I like music very much—one of the most moving experiences for me as a musician was when Leonard Bernstein took the New York Philharmonic to Moscow and played Shostakovich's Fifth Symphony to the Russians. And he played the last movement more rapidly than anyone had ever played it before because it was technically so difficult. That is something I followed very closely when it occurred.

These are things that have always had a big impact on my life. And I had just always hoped that someday, if I ever had the chance to, I could play a role in seeing our two countries become closer partners.

NOTE: The question-and-answer session began at 2:46 p.m. at Canada Place.

Exchange With Reporters En Route to the Opening Day Baseball Game in Baltimore, Maryland
April 5, 1993

Affirmative Action in Baseball

Q. Mr. President, what do you think of Jesse Jackson's protest today?

The President. I think it's an informational protest. I think it's fine. The owners put out a statement a few days ago which they say was the first step in, you know, efforts to increase minority ownership and minority increases in management. I think we should. I'm encouraged by Don Baylor's appointment out in Colorado. And I think it's time to make a move on that front. So, I think it's a legitimate issue, and I think it's, like I said, it's an informational picket and not an attempt to get people not to go to the game. So, I think it's good.

Q. Do you think they're moving fast enough?

The President. Well, I think that it was a good first step. And I think you'll see some movement now. And I think it's an issue that deserves some attention, and they're obviously going to give it some. And I think that Reverend Jackson being out there will highlight the issue. So I think it's fine.

Stimulus Package

Q. Mr. President, how about the logjam in the Senate on the economic stimulus plan? Do you think they'll be able to break that and get cloture?

The President. I don't know. We're working at it. I mean, it's a classic—there was an article in the paper today, one of the papers I saw, which pretty well summed it up. They said, you know, it's just a political power play. In the Senate the majority does not rule. It's not like the country. It's not like the House. If the minority chooses, they can stop majority rule. And that's what they're doing. There are a lot of Republican Senators who have told people that they might vote for the stimulus program but there's enormous partisan political pressure not to do it.

And of course, what it means is that in this time when no new jobs are being created even though there seems to be an economic recovery, it means that for political purposes they're willing to deny jobs to places like Baltimore and

Dallas and Houston and Pittsburgh and Philadelphia and Portland and Seattle. It's very sad. I mean, the block grant program was designed to create jobs in a hurry based on local priorities, and it's one that the Republicans had always championed. Just about the only Democrat champions of the program were people like me who were out there at the grassroots level, Governors and Senators. I just think it's real sad

that they have chosen to exert the minority muscle in a way that will keep Americans out of work. I think it's a mistake.

NOTE: The exchange began at 11:45 a.m. aboard the MARC train en route to Oriole Park at Camden Yards. In his remarks, the President referred to civil rights leader Jesse Jackson. A tape was not available for verification of the content of this exchange.

Message to the Congress Transmitting a Report on Hazardous Materials Transportation
April 5, 1993

To the Congress of the United States:

In accordance with the requirements of section 109(e) of the Hazardous Materials Transportation Act (Public Law 93–633); 49 U.S.C. 108(e)), I transmit herewith the Annual Report

on Hazardous Materials Transportation for calendar year 1991.

WILLIAM J. CLINTON

The White House,
April 5, 1993.

Nomination for Posts at the Departments of Defense and Labor
April 5, 1993

The President today announced his intention to nominate two more Assistant Secretaries at the Department of Defense and an Administrator at the Department of Labor. Additionally, the President announced the nomination of five other men and women to Defense and Labor posts.

The President announced his intention to nominate Lt. Gen. Emmett Paige, Jr., as Assistant Secretary for Command, Control and Communications at the Department of Defense, Deborah Lee as Assistant Secretary for Reserve Affairs at the Department of Defense, and Maria Echaveste as Administrator of the Wage and Hour Division at the Department of Labor. In addition, the President announced the following appointments: Colleen Preston, Deputy Under Secretary for Acquisition, Department of

Defense; Sherri Wasserman Goodman, Deputy Under Secretary for Environmental Security, Department of Defense; William Lynn, Director, Program Analysis and Evaluation, Department of Defense; Joyce Miller, Executive Director, Glass Ceiling Commission, Department of Labor; and Charles Richards, Director, Office of the New American Workplace, Department of Labor.

"These men and women, with their collective experience, intelligence, and commitment to making Government work for the American people, will add to the excellent staffs already at work with both Secretaries Aspin and Reich," the President said.

NOTE: Biographies of the nominees were made available by the Office of the Press Secretary.

Exchange With Reporters Prior to Discussions With President Hosni Mubarak of Egypt
April 6, 1993

World Trade Center Bombing

Q. President Mubarak, did you give the United States a specific warning about the World Trade Center bombing?

President Mubarak. Let me tackle this problem in the press conference, if you don't mind.

Stimulus Package

Q. Mr. President, do you think you'll get your stimulus package intact after the recess?

President Clinton. Well, let me say this: We're going to give the Senate a chance to prove that the stated objections to some of the programs were their real objections. I mean, the American people, I'm sure, are disappointed to find that a program that would put a half-million people to work and that has the support of a majority of the United States Senate cannot be brought to a vote in the Senate, because democracy and the majority rule is being undermined.

The whole purpose of the Senate's debating rules is to allow all amendments to be offered. We've had amendment after amendment after amendment after amendment, and the Republican minority is just trying to keep it from being voted on. So we're going to give them a chance to see if they were serious about their specific concerns and if they really want to put the American people back to work or not. This is a big issue, and we'll just see what happens.

Q. You are going to have to compromise, though, aren't you?

Q. [*Inaudible*]—frustrated about the delay?

President Clinton. Of course. I think that we ought to be—I can't imagine how they could be satisfied with the condition of this economy. I can't imagine how they could be satisfied with it. They were here, many of them, while we increased the national debt by 4 times, while we exploded the deficit, we drove down employment and drove up unemployment. And I've given them a plan to bring down the deficit and increase employment, put people back to work, and I think they ought to be for it. And we'll see if they will be.

Q. How much are you willing to cut——

President Clinton. As soon as the thing is over—when they come back, we'll see whether they really care about putting people to work or whether this is all just political posturing to prove that a minority can paralyze the Federal Government. It's just more gridlock, and I think the people will rebel against it.

You can count how many people they're going to keep out of work. You will know job by job how many they'll be responsible for not putting to work. We'll see.

Q. You sound pretty passionate on the subject.

Serbia

President Clinton. What did you say about Milosevic?

Q. How do you feel—[*inaudible*]—by his message?

President Clinton. Oh, that was like the Iraqi charm offensive. He's just trying to head off tougher sanctions if the Vance-Owen plan is not embraced.

Q. Is it going to work?

President Clinton. No, it won't. Of course not.

Q. Do you think he's getting the wrong message, though, sir? I mean——

President Clinton. It's pure politics. He's trying to head off tougher sanctions in the U.N. if the Serbs don't sign off on Vance-Owen. That's all that's going on there. And it won't work.

Q. Don't you think he's sending a message saying it's actually—this is great, you're not going to hound us?

President Clinton. Well, we are going to press for tougher sanctions. We'll see.

Q. You don't want any compliments from him, huh?

Q. [*Inaudible*]—are you rethinking the arms embargo?

President Clinton. I'm always rethinking that. There's never been a day when I haven't rethought that. But I can't do that by myself.

[*At this point, one group of reporters left the room, and another group entered.*]

Meeting With President Mubarak

Q. How about your first impression, Mr. President?

President Clinton. Very good. I'm glad to see President Mubarak. He and I have talked on the phone and worked on some things together, but this is our first personal meeting. And we'll have a press conference in a few minutes—in a couple of hours, I guess. We'll answer your questions.

NOTE: The exchange began at 9:45 a.m. in the Oval Office at the White House. In his remarks, President Clinton referred to President Slobodan Milosevic of Serbia. A tape was not available for verification of the content of this exchange.

The President's News Conference With President Hosni Mubarak of Egypt
April 6, 1993

President Clinton. Good morning. Today I have the great pleasure of welcoming President Mubarak to Washington and to the White House. We have had an excellent meeting, and I look forward to more in the coming years, as well as to a successful conclusion of our first meeting here at lunch after this press conference.

For nearly 2 decades, Egypt and the United States have worked together in a special relationship to bring peace and stability to the Middle East. American and Egyptian soldiers have served side by side in defeating aggression in the Gulf and in bringing humanitarian relief in Somalia. American and Egyptian diplomats have worked side by side to pioneer peace with Israel and lately to bring others to the negotiating table. And after our discussions today, I am convinced that we share a common vision of a more peaceful Middle East, and we are determined to see that vision realized.

Egypt has long experience in peacemaking and knows that only negotiations can resolve longstanding grievances. The Egyptian-Israeli treaty stands as a cornerstone of our common efforts to attain a just and lasting and comprehensive settlement based upon U.N. Security Council Resolutions 242 and 338. Our challenge is now to broaden the circle of peace, recognizing the principles that underlie the peace process: territory for peace, realization of the legitimate rights of the Palestinian people, security for all parties, and full and real peace.

As I have made clear, the United States is prepared to assume the role of full partner when the parties themselves return to the negotiating table for serious discussions. We both feel deeply that there is an historic opportunity to achieve real progress in the Arab-Israeli peace process in 1993. This opportunity must not be missed. And all parties must live up to their responsibilities for making peace.

We discussed the need to ensure stability in the Gulf. We're determined that the hard-won achievements of Desert Storm will be protected and that Iraq will comply fully with all relevant U.N. Security Council resolutions. We're also determined to counter Iran's involvement in terrorism and its active opposition to the Middle East peace process.

Both our nations have suffered from the tragic consequences of terrorism. Both are absolutely determined to oppose the cowardly cruelty of terrorists wherever we can. We reviewed the common danger presented by religious extremism which promotes an intolerant agenda through violent means. We discussed ways of strengthening our cooperation in countering this and other forms of terrorism. We know that all Americans, including Americans of all races and all faiths, join us in strongly condemning such terrorism.

Mr. President, I know that you have undertaken the difficult task of reforming and restructuring your nation's economy to provide for the needs of tomorrow. We have a similar challenge here in the United States. We appreciate the gains that have been made in Egypt, as well as the bridges that remain to be crossed. We are impressed by your courage and your efforts.

We will continue to work together to stimulate trade, investment, and cooperation. Our economic assistance will continue to support Egypt's economic reform program, including privatization and Egypt's cooperation with international financial institutions.

We are fast approaching a new century. This is perhaps less of a milestone for Egypt, which has, after all, 7,000 years of recorded history, than it is for our relatively young country. I told the President on the way up that every President of the United States since 1800 had lived in the White House, and he looked at me as if it were a drop in the bucket of time. [*Laughter*]

But even taking the longest view, this is a critical period for the Middle East, the crucible of much of our common spiritual heritage. For the Middle East, the year 1993 can determine whether the new century is consumed by old enmities or used to unlock the human and material potential of the people. Our historic mission is to make this a year of peace. And I am delighted to have President Mubarak as a partner in pursuing this mission.

The microphone is yours.

President Mubarak. Thank you, Mr. President.

I was very pleased to meet with President Clinton today. Our meeting was very positive and productive. In a spirit of friendship and mutual confidence, we explored the problems and opportunities our two nations are facing. I emphasized to the President that it is of utmost importance to our region to reach a just and comprehensive settlement between Israel and all her Arab neighbors, including the Palestinian people.

Such a settlement should be based on Security Council Resolution 242 and 338 and the principle of land for peace and realizing the national rights of the Palestinians. We believe that Egypt and the United States have a crucial role to play in order to allow the peace negotiations to reach a successful conclusion. Together we can make the ends meet and bridge the existing gaps.

Equally important is the task of removing the remaining obstacles, especially that of the deportees. I was pleased to hear from President Clinton that significant progress has been on this issue and that he recognizes the importance of the Middle East peace talks. He is committed to use the influence of the United States to achieve meaningful progress in these talks when they are resumed on April 20th. We are confident that the negotiations will proceed smoothly and successfully.

Beyond the peace process, we discussed a wide range of regional issues of common concern to our two countries. We stressed our concern for the stability of the Gulf region and the need for full compliance with the relevant Security Council resolutions. No country of that region should doubt our firm commitment to help preserve the security, stability, and territorial integrity of all friendly states. Similarly, we are doing all what we can to stop the spread of weapons of mass destruction in the Middle East. As you are certainly aware, Egypt has submitted a plan for making the area free of all weapons of mass destruction. We shall pursue this goal with vigor and determination.

On the global front, I offered to work closely with the President for the purpose of making the world more humane and equitable, a world where opportunity and hope exist for all and where people learn to accept divergences and employ diversity for the benefit of mankind.

I am making this appeal because I am alarmed by the refusal of some elements in the different societies to accept the diversity and the coexistence. This has resulted in unprecedented atrocities and suffering in Bosnia and Herzegovina. The world cannot tolerate the savage practices which are committed under the ugly slogan of ethnic cleansing and purification. It is against all human values to see such claims emerge at the threshold of the 21st century.

Unfortunately, violence is increasingly being used by certain misguided elements in many parts of the world, including the Middle East. Acute social and economic problems are being exploited in order to breed violence and anarchy. At the same time, foreign countries are interfering in the domestic affairs of other nations under false pretexts. All civilized nations are called upon to fight the spirit of violence and terrorism everywhere, for this is a threat to the existence and future of humanity. No country is immune or distant from that danger.

In Egypt, we are coping with the phenomena through a comprehensive program which deals with the roots and the causes of the problem. We have embarked on an ambitious economic reform program. Parallel with this, we are enforcing our democratic system, solidifying the protection of the human rights. Our goal is to improve the quality of life for every Egyptian with equal determination. We are confronting foreign plots and attempted intervention.

Having said this, I would like to assure you all that Egypt is not in danger. The image which has been projected by the media lately is rather exaggerated. As well as all know, violence makes instant news, but the real story is our confidence, our unity, and our growing success in facing this problem. The Egyptian people will not accept any challenge to their tradition of friendship with other nations and hospitality to our visitors. We will remain true to our culture of resolving problems peacefully and defeating the forces of violence and aggression. Let the whole world know that Egypt is as strong as ever and that its leadership is firm and confident.

Mr. President, as I told you, Egypt is a country which values its excellent relations with the United States. Let me take this opportunity to express our deep appreciation for the support and assistance we are receiving from the United States. This aid is crucial to the success of our reform program.

We would like to assure a friendly welcome to all Americans who visit us. We encourage the American business community to invest in our economy. The climate for investment has become very favorable following the steps we took in the past few years on the road to economic reform. Our budget deficit has been reduced from 18 percent of the GDP in 1990 to 3.5 percent this year. The foreign exchange market has been deregulated, and our foreign currency reserves have reached record levels. Trade is being liberalized, and the balance of payment is showing steady improvement. After registering a deficit of $2.6 billion in 1990, it now shows a surplus of about $3 billion.

President Clinton, our discussion today affirmed a broad identity of interest over a wide range of issues. We have developed a full agenda of cooperation for the future. I want to thank you for your understanding and your enthusiastic response. I fully appreciate your warm welcome and extend to the American people my best wishes for success and fulfillment. I look forward to working closely with you during the months ahead for our common goals. And I extend to you an invitation to visit Egypt at your earliest convenience.

Thank you.

President Clinton. Helen [Helen Thomas, United Press International]?

Middle East Peace Process

Q. Mr. President, in view of the rising violence in the Middle East and elsewhere, what is the cause of your optimism? And this question's for both of you: What can you both do to promote peace this year, in the future?

President Clinton. The cause of my optimism, in terms of peace in the Middle East, is the extraordinary efforts that Prime Minister Rabin is making and my belief that the peace talks will reconvene in April, as well as some encouraging comments that have been made by Mr. Assad, the leader of Syria, recently in Egypt and publicly. He said he wanted a full peace, peace in all of its aspects, I think on Egyptian television. I think there is reason to believe that we can make real headway.

President Mubarak might want to answer the question.

President Mubarak. Really, I could tell you very frankly, I have met so many leaders in the area, not only the President of Syria, the Palestinians and the other Arab leaders. All of them want to reach peace as quickly as possible. The Syrian leader, he said it publicly and clearly, "I'm very keen on peace." Peace will help every leader to raise the standard of the living of the people in the area. The Palestinians also are fed up from the present situation, being denied from everything. So I think this is very important, and I have great hopes that the negotiations will start on the 20th of April. And I may say much more, I hope and we are going to work closely on that to get an end to the problem by the end of this year, if it is possible.

Terrorism

Q. [*Inaudible*]—what's new happening in Egypt is Muslim and Muslim which is not really Islam. What is your policy in confronting this exported terrorism to Egypt and get Egypt back where it was and where it is: love, peace, happiness, pleasure with Egypt?

President Mubarak. Look, the majority of the Egyptian people are supporting me and any measures I am taking to put an end to this kind of terrorism. Copts, Muslims, any kind of religion in Egypt, they are all Egyptians. We expect that this small minority was trying to make use of the economic problems. You know we are going through economic reform in our country; the reform has its side-effects. It makes a burden on some groups of the people. Some foreign forces, like the Iranians, let me mention the name, making use of this to try to destabilize the country. But be sure we are very firm with that by law, and we are not going to violate the law. And the Copts and the Muslims are very good friends. And I could tell you, the best friends I had all my life were all Copts.

Stimulus Package

Q. Mr. President, on another subject, the Republicans have been delaying action on your $1 billion jobs stimulus bill, and now the Senate has gone out. Are there areas where you would be willing to compromise, cut spending in order to win Republican votes?

President Clinton. Well, I'm going to work on a proposal that I think will address some of the legitimate expressed objections. And we will see when Congress comes back whether the Republicans are committed to putting the American people back to work or just playing politics.

You know, we have a system in this country where people, all of whom have jobs—a minority of the Senators, who all have jobs—can literally thwart majority rule; where a rule designed to guarantee that all possible amendments can be offered can be used to stop all decisions. Now, the American people now are learning that again, that—and if they want to stop the Government, they can do it.

But I don't think that it's going to be very defensible when they come back to say, "The economy is fine in America. There are enough jobs. We don't have to do this." And I'll give them a chance to show their real motives, and I trust that they'll do the right thing.

Andrea [Andrea Mitchell, NBC News]?

Palestinians

Q. Mr. President, President Mubarak has been quoted as saying he wants you to press Mr. Rabin on the issues of the deportees. When Mr. Rabin was here, you said that you didn't raise that issue with him. Are you now prepared to——

President Clinton. We had discussed that in great detail before he came here; that's what I said.

Q. Are you now prepared to take more steps to press Mr. Rabin? And Mr. Mubarak, I'd like to know whether you feel that the President is doing enough to resolve that issue.

President Clinton. I believe that Israel has been quite forthcoming in trying to give the reassurance that the Palestinians need to come to the talks. President Mubarak is going to have further discussions, I think, with all the parties and certainly with Israel about it. We will see what will be done. But President Rabin has taken a very forthright and open stand in trying to reach out to the Palestinians and to the other

parties, and I believe that it's enough to get people back to the table. I hope it is.

President Mubarak. Really I didn't use the word "press" on Mr. Rabin. We have good contacts with Mr. Rabin. I'm used to exchange views with him, and where it was convenient to help the peace process to start and the negotiations to continue, I am doing it. I sent him a message when I was in London before I come here and am intending to meet with him. And I have discussed all these points with the President, and I am going to continue that with Mr. Rabin whenever I go back.

Q. Is there anything more that the United States should be doing regarding Israel?

President Mubarak. I think that the United States is a full partner and she's doing its maximum in that sense. She has good dialog with Prime Minister Rabin, and he was here. And I'm going to continue with Mr. Rabin so as to persuade the Palestinians to start negotiations on the fixed date.

President Clinton. There is someone from the Egyptian press——

Q. I would like to address to President Clinton, please, the human rights President: How far are you ready to go to help the human rights of the Palestinians in the occupied territories? Would you like to comment on the ideas expressed by President Mubarak to remove the obstacles so that they can come to the table?

President Clinton. Well, the human rights issues obviously will be discussed as a part of the peace process. They are very important to me, and I think they will be at the forefront of the process. And President Mubarak and I have discussed that, and I think that there won't be peace in the Middle East unless those issues are addressed.

Tom [Tom Friedman, New York Times]?

Palestine Liberation Organization

Q. When the United States broke off the dialog with the PLO 2 years ago, it did so leaving three conditions behind that if the PLO met, the dialog would be resumed: that they forswear terrorism, expel those involved, and condemn the act involved. Does your administration stand by those conditions? That is, if the PLO now fulfills those conditions, would you be willing to resume the U.S.-PLO dialog? And to President Mubarak: Do you think the resumption of the U.S.-PLO dialog would be helpful to the peace process at this time?

President Clinton. Let me say this: There has been no change in the policy of the United States, but the focus of my efforts has been toward getting the peace process started again. I still believe that that is the best way to proceed.

President Mubarak. The PLO we consider in the Arab world is the representative of the Palestinians. We have very good contacts with them, and we convey whatever we needed to President Clinton and even to the Israelis. I think at this present time we are going to concentrate on the negotiations to start. And you know, the PLO is everywhere. So many people of the delegation are from the PLO. So I don't think that there is any problem at the time being for that.

Serbia

Q. [*Inaudible*]—the situation in Bosnia. I know that earlier today you dismissed the comments of President Milosevic about your policy there as a charm offensive. But I wonder, sir, if you don't think, nonetheless, that he wouldn't have said such things if he was finding the actions you've taken so far very bothersome and perhaps whether you think now that they would ever be sufficient to deter?

President Clinton. I don't know. I've done everything that I know to do, consistent with the possibilities we have for further action in the United Nations with our European allies and the members of the Security Council. As you know, I think the sanctions should be strengthened if the Bosnians don't sign the Vance-Owen agreement. We obviously have made life more difficult for the people in Serbia, and I think there are other things that we can do. I wouldn't rule out or in anything. But it's plain that what Milosevic was trying to do was to essentially head off further efforts to toughen the sanctions or to take further actions. That will not be successful.

Q. [*Inaudible*]—that he may not feel that, not ruling out anything, that he may indeed feel that the use, for example, of American military force has in effect been ruled out?

President Clinton. It's never been ruled in. The United States is not capable of solving that problem alone. I don't think anyone expects us to do that. We have been, in many cases, more aggressive in what we were willing to do than the European neighbors of the former Yugoslavia. I still believe there is some chance that

we can make this peace process work, and I still think there are lots of other things we can do to make life more uncomfortable for the Serbs. And I wouldn't rule those out.

Libya

Q. This is a question to President Clinton, please. Owing to the new——

President Clinton. Oh, I recognized you hoping you would ask President Mubarak a question. [*Laughter*]

Q. Egyptians want to ask you——

President Clinton. Please, go ahead.

Q. Owing to the new liberal view that you represent now in being the President of the United States, to what limits have you arrived to an agreement with Mr. Mubarak, President Mubarak, about the cries of Libya with the West?

President Clinton. The question was about our policies with regard to Libya.

Well, as you know, we have one huge barrier that overrides everything else right now, and that is the determination of the United States to see that the people who have been charged with the Pan Am 103 disaster are released from Libya and subject to a legitimate trial. And that has to be resolved in a way that is legal and appropriate before any other issues with regard to Libya can be raised.

The President and I discussed this today. I think that it is inevitable that we will press for tougher sanctions if the Government of Libya does not release the people that have been charged. There's a lot of evidence against them. They should go on trial. They should be punished if they're found guilty. It should be a real and legitimate trial. It is an enormous issue in the United States, and nothing else really can be resolved with regard to Libya until that issue is resolved.

World Trade Center Bombing

Q. Could the United States have made better use of the information which was given to us by Egypt before the bombing of the World Trade Center? President Mubarak, why do you believe, as you said in an interview, that the bombing might have been prevented if the U.S. had used the information differently?

President Clinton. The short answer to your question is I don't know yet. I have ordered a complete review of what the United States was told last year and when we were told it.

I think President Mubarak would support my contention that we have tried to step up our cooperation with the Egyptians in combating international terrorism since I've been President. In February we sent American officials to Egypt, and they stayed there about a week working on cooperative exchanges and information. And we talked today about what we could do to do more. Whether there was something given to us that we could have acted on that might have changed the shape of future events, I cannot answer that yet. But since the statements that President Mubarak has made, I have ordered a review of what we knew, when we knew it, what was done. And I don't know yet what the answer to that is.

I think the important thing is we do know that there was nothing specific related to the World Trade Center bombing that was given to the United States. We know we have stepped up cooperation, and we know we intend to do more in the future. And the United States has to review a lot of its policies in view of what happened at the World Trade Center to try to make sure we are doing everything we can to minimize the impact of terrorism in this country.

President Mubarak. I would like, if the President would permit me, we had no definite information about what happened in the World Trade Center. We were making good cooperation with the United States in the direction of fighting terrorism. But nobody knows, or knew beforehand that something was going to happen to the World Trade Center.

We are exchanging information about any kind of terrorism which takes place here or there. But different information, of course, we haven't. Otherwise, we would have told very clearly to the Americans, there is something going to happen in this or that place.

Iran

Q. Mr. President, it was mentioned the question of the threat of regional security in the Gulf. Can you be more specific what these threats are at present, and are you putting the threats from Iran and Iraq on an equal footing?

President Mubarak. It's for me?

President Clinton. Both.

President Mubarak. Look, Iraq now is in a position not to have the ability to threaten any of the—[*inaudible*—that Kuwait is ours, but there are so many measures being taken. But

Iran, Iran now, because it's the only country on the theater—you know the Iranians and Kuwaitis were competing each other. Nowadays, the Iranians are stronger. They are trying to find a way to destabilize the security in some countries, mainly Egypt. And we are working hard for that. And this was the main cause of making some explosions, some instance in our country. I think Iran now is trying to create problems. And we are very firm with them. We are capable to do so many things, but we are not a country to interfere in any internal affair of any other.

Q. You mentioned that you and President Mubarak were agreed on the need to counter Iran's support for terrorism and its opposition to the Middle East peace process. What specific steps are you considering and have you discussed with President Mubarak?

President Clinton. I don't think it would be appropriate for us to discuss that at this time.

Serbia

Q. I couldn't help but notice in your answer to Brit's [Brit Hume, ABC News] question that you sounded frustrated about the situation in Bosnia and that if there is no change in the position of European governments, that if they can withstand sanctions, the Serbians will essentially be able to get what they want.

President Clinton. That is what I am concerned about. You got it. That's about as good a statement as I could have made myself. [*Laughter*]

Q. Are you putting, then, the onus on the European governments to take this a further step, or is there some other step the U.S. can——

President Clinton. No. No, my point is, though, that the United States—if you believe that we should engage these problems in a multilateral way, if you believe, for example, in what happened in a good way in Operation Desert Storm, then the reverse has to be true, too. The United States has got to work through the United Nations, and all of our views may not always prevail. Look how long it took us to just secure the approval of enforcement of the no-fly zone.

Also it is, frankly, a very difficult situation. The Europeans remember how many German troops were once in what became Yugoslavia and then came apart. It is a difficult situation. It is the most difficult, the most frustrating problem in the world today.

The only point I was trying to make is I have proceeded all along on the assumption that whatever we did and whatever we could do, we would and should act through the United Nations in a multilateral way. I have done my best to continue to stiffen the sanctions, to continue to push for more action, to push for the enforcement of the no-fly zone, to push all the countries involved to do what we could to try to bring this to a successful conclusion so that the principle of ethnic cleansing is not rewarded in Bosnia and, therefore, encouraged in other countries.

I have not thought that the United States should or could successfully take unilateral ac-

tion. And I know that a lot of things that we could do to inflict some pain might also entail a great deal of cost and might not change the ultimate outcome of how the Bosnian people have to live.

So it is a very frustrating and difficult circumstance. And I can't really add to the way you captured the question; you said it very well.

Thank you.

President Mubarak. Thank you.

NOTE: The President's 10th news conference began at 11:35 a.m. in the Briefing Room at the White House. In the news conference, he referred to Prime Minister Yitzhak Rabin of Israel.

Nomination for Posts at the Energy and Interior Departments and the Office of Personnel Management
April 6, 1993

The President today named three deputies to the Departments of Energy and the Interior and the Office of Personnel Management. The President announced his intention to nominate William H. White as Deputy Secretary at the Department of Energy and Lorraine A. Green as Deputy Director of the Office of Personnel Management. In addition, the President approved Allen P. Stayman as Deputy Assistant Secretary for Territorial and International Affairs

at the Department of the Interior.

"The field experience, technical know-how, and commitment to excellence these three individuals have demonstrated in the past will serve them well as they join our teams already in place at Energy, OPM, and Interior," the President said. "I have full confidence they will work hard to reinvent the way Government works."

NOTE: Biographies of the nominees were made available by the Office of the Press Secretary.

Remarks on Signing Enabling Legislation for the National Commission to Ensure a Strong Competitive Airline Industry and an Exchange With Reporters
April 7, 1993

The President. Good morning, everybody. As you know, the bill I have just signed is the aviation commission legislation. It enables us to start planning the revitalization of one of our country's most important industries, one of our most important exporters, one of our most important employers: the aircraft manufacturers and carriers that have been the pride of the

United States and the world's leaders since the beginning of aviation.

But we're also here because our National Government has failed to create the economic climate necessary for this leading edge industry to thrive at home and in an increasingly competitive global economy. The condition of the domestic aviation industry has been spiraling downward for some time. Unemployment in the industry has reached record levels over the past few years. Recent layoffs have been severe. New orders for aircraft have shrunk, along with the demand for airline service, leading to unemployment in the aircraft manufacturing industry as well.

When I visited with managers and employees at the Boeing Corporation in Everett, Washington, they described for me in very personal terms the devastating impact of these developments in their lives and the lives of their co-workers. The legislation I sign today, providing for the creation of a National Commission to Ensure a Strong Competitive Airline Industry, commits us, on behalf of the industry and the workers whose livelihoods depend on its health, to search for real answers.

Some of the answers may lie in a more aggressive trade policy. Others may come from keeping the global marketplace freer from unfair competition. More may stem from the supporting role of aviation in preserving our national security. In any case, I want to commend the strong bipartisan effort that was shown in passing this legislation on such a fast track. This bill creates the Commission that will enable me and the House and the Senate leadership to appoint a knowledgeable and diverse group of people to review these complex issues and make recommendations back to the President and the Congress within 90 days of the appointment of the Commission. This is a fast-track operation.

I've been working closely with both parties in the House and the Senate, and I anticipate that the Commission will be appointed very soon after Congress returns from its recess. As I think all of you know, the minority leader, Bob Michel, is in Russia now on a mission. He has two voting and two ex officio members who he must appoint. We are, for our part, ready to go here in the White House, and I think the Commission will be appointed very soon.

I also want to make it clear that I will detail whatever staff is necessary from the National Economic Council, from the Council of Economic Advisers, from Commerce, from the Trade Representative's Office, wherever we need it.

The problems facing this industry are quite complex, and it's important that we build a consensus as quickly as possible. I assure you that when that is done, I will move rapidly with Congress to take whatever action is appropriate

based on the recommendations of the Commission.

But ultimately, no industry in our country flourishes in isolation. The health of each sector depends at least in some measure on the overall health of the American economy. And no one can look at this economy and say that we are satisfied with things just the way they are. We are in the midst of the weakest recovery since World War II. The March unemployment report failed to show any improvement in the labor market. Unemployment is stuck at 7 percent of the labor force. While the economy supposedly has been in recovery for a year now, manufacturing employment has continued to decline. This recovery is like a fire starving for oxygen. Jobs, and the incomes, profits, and consumer spending jobs produce, are the oxygen this recovery needs.

Investment and deficit reduction are long-term ingredients for making the recovery durable, and we've gone a long way toward doing that over the long run. Our economic plan addresses these objectives and addresses them very well. Long-term help is on the way. The Congress has agreed to provide the broad outlines of our budget package, paving the way for real deficit reduction and a high-investment, high-productivity, high-wage economy. The plan also increases investment by the Federal Government in our physical infrastructure and the human capital of our citizens. This shift in the spending priorities of the Government will help make us competitive again in the global economy.

While the budget plan will provide long-term benefits for the economy, the jobs plan now is needed to ensure a sustained recovery. As it is written, the job stimulus package will provide about 500,000 full-time jobs this year and next year: real jobs, repairing and rebuilding highways and bridges, creating new mass transit and clean water projects, rebuilding our communities. Passage of the bill will mean youths in our cities and rural communities can make their passage from idleness to a meaningful work experience, boosting their incomes and educational achievements, learning as they earn. The jobs plan is carefully targeted and will be followed by real and enforceable budget cuts, now more than 200 specific budget cuts contained in the investment and deficit reduction package Congress has approved.

In my view, the message of the last election

was to break the gridlock and grow the economy, because Americans are tired of a system that doesn't work and a recovery that doesn't produce new jobs. We know what works. We'll only be able to reduce the deficit and increase investment in the long term if we guarantee the strength of the recovery by building jobs in the short run. Passing the jobs plan following the adoption of deficit reduction and increased investment by Congress is the best way to accomplish those objectives. This will strengthen not only the aviation industry but every industry at a time when workers, firms, and average citizens are looking to us here in Washington for leadership.

I want to commend Secretary Peña, the House and Senate leadership, and all the others who have supported this legislation. I look forward to announcing the Commission membership. I also hope very much that we can break this deadlock and create some jobs for this economy beginning immediately.

Stimulus Package

Q. Mr. President, the Republicans have legitimate concerns about your stimulus package, and what would they be?

The President. Well, the only legitimate concerns I cited were the ones that were cited by the Democrats, too. What they did, and you can see this in the amendment that the House decided not to adopt and the amendment Mr. Brown offered in the Senate, was to take hypotheticals from what could be funded through the community development block grant program and in the Economic Development Administration, and come up in a multibillion dollar jobs package with a couple of hundred million dollars of things that they thought were wrong. I had assured them that I would take executive steps to stop that. That is not what is going on here. The kinds of cuts the Republican Senators are talking about are cuts designed to keep people out of the work force. And so that was a tempest in a teapot. That's the only point I was making.

And I will say again, a lot of the things that were cited amaze me. It was the Republicans and the Democrats at the State and local level all these years who came out for greater flexibility for the States and the localities. Now the Republican Senators are saying they don't trust Republican Governors to spend the money in a way that will create jobs in their own States.

I find that an amazing argument and a 20-year departure from their stated position.

Economic Initiatives

Q. Mr. President, you just named an airline commission. You've asked for a timber report. You've got the health care commission. You've got the budget coming out tomorrow. Have you too much on your plate? Some critics are saying that you're spreading yourself too thin and missing what happened to Jimmy Carter.

The President. Well, if you look at what we're doing, though, it all relates to the economy. It all comes back to the economy. The health care issue is an issue of personal security to Americans and American families who've been badly battered by the economic developments of the last decade or more. But it also is critical to the long-term deficit reduction, to balancing the Federal budget, and to strengthening the health of the American economy. The timber issue is not just an environmental issue; it's an economic issue. We have to resolve the deadlock out there so people can get on with their lives. Every other issue you've mentioned is an economic issue.

We may not get 100 percent of everything we're trying to do in every area. But I do think the American people will see that the focus of all of this is to guarantee a healthy economy and a growing jobs market to try to turn this around. There are many things which need attention in the economic area, I think we have to be active in all of them. I don't want to spread myself personally too thin, but we have, after all, a large number of people working in this Government and a lot of work to do. And I think I have to keep pushing on the economic front.

Potential Supreme Court Nominee

Q. [*Inaudible*]—Cuomo decided not—no to being a justice?

The President. Excuse me?

Q. Has Governor Cuomo decided not to be a Supreme Court Justice?

Q. And are you disappointed about it?

The President. Well, you know, I think he's terrific. I think you need to talk to him for anything on that.

Q. Did he pull out?

The President. I'm not going to discuss the appointments until I make them. Justice White was kind enough to give me a considerable amount of time. And given the economic issues before the Congress and the summit I had with President Yeltsin, I appreciated that because I couldn't devote immediate time to it. But I don't think I should comment on any individuals. You know about my regard for Governor Cuomo. He would have to say anything that would be said on this.

Q. But you want someone like Governor Cuomo, now that he has withdrawn.

The President. I didn't say he had. You'll have to ask him about that.

Stimulus Package

Q. Mr. President, during your administration the American people seem to be really engaged. There were telephone calls flooding Washington on various issues, yet they seem to be largely silent on the deadlock over the jobs program. To what do you attribute the gridlock in that case?

The President. Well, I think first of all, I don't think they've tuned out but, to go back to Andrea's [Andrea Mitchell, NBC News] question, there's a lot going on here. And I think that one of the things that I hope will happen during the break here is that we can somehow bring all these disparate activities back into sharp focus. I also, to be fair, have not been out in the country much in the last few weeks discussing this. I've been here working at the job. And one of the toughest decisions, when you talk about spreading myself too thin, one of the toughest decisions I have to make every week is to balance between staying here and meeting with the Congress and doing the job that I have to do here, and going out into the country and continuing to engage the people.

I think they know that the broad outlines of the economic program have passed, and I think there was an enormous amount of support for that. I think a lot of people thought that the whole thing passed when the economic program passed, and I have to just try to bring this jobs program into sharp focus and explain to everybody why I think we need to create some jobs now and bring the unemployment rate down now.

And as I have pointed out again and again, this is not a uniquely American problem. Every major economic power is facing this. The Japanese are about to adopt a much bigger stimulus package than we have to drive their unemployment rate down and generate domestic eco-

nomic development. And I think we ought to do the same thing. It is going to be critical, in my view, to try and keep faith with the American people, especially during the upcoming summer.

Q. How much are you willing to cut on the stimulus?

The President. All I can tell you is I'm going to try to get action here. I think it is a shame to rob anybody of the right to have a job. And a lot of the objections which have been raised, I think, are somewhat spurious. I mean, the attack on building swimming pools, let's just take that one, for example. You know, if you put people to work in a city or a suburb or a small town building a city park which gives people, kids a chance to have recreational opportunities in the summertime, and you create jobs doing it, is that a waste of money? I don't really think it is. I mean, the Senate's got a swimming pool, doesn't it? [*Laughter*] Doesn't it? And, it was built with taxpayers' money, and somebody worked; somebody had a job building it. And so, you know——

Q. How much are you going to cut?

The President. No more than I have to, to get the thing passed. I just—I want some action. I want those kids in this country to have jobs this summer. I want them to have the first summer jobs program that includes a strong educational component. I want these places where they have not seen any jobs in years to have a chance to have them. And I'm going to create as many as I can, but I want to get some action. I want to do something, and I'll do the very best I can.

Q. Are you going to go to the country?

The President. Excuse me?

Q. Are you going to the country during the recession on this issue?

The President. I haven't made a decision what to do yet, about how to do it. I'm going to reassess all that today. As you pointed out, I've been dealing with a lot of different issues, and this morning I've got to try to put it into focus. Again, let me say, I think some of this is politics. It's, you know, just pure gridlock politics. Some of it is the continuing debate over what is the best economic policy. But in terms of the minor objections that have been raised to things in this bill, those can be taken care of rather easily.

The real thing we've got to decide is whether the United States Government has a responsibility to try to help start the jobs machine again, and I believe we do. There is obviously a difference in the United States and every other wealthy country in the world between what looks like an economic recovery and creating jobs. That is the big idea we've got to come to grips with. It goes way beyond sort of traditional politics. There is a difference now. This is a problem that all these countries are having. I do not want to see the United States go the way of the European countries that are now living with 10 percent unemployment. And by the way, we can't afford to do it, because we don't provide health care. We don't provide the supports they do. It's tougher for people in this country when they're unemployed than it is in Europe or Japan. So we don't provide that kind of support services. And the Japanese unemployment rate, I might say, is still about half what ours is, actually slightly less than half.

We have got to do something to create the jobs. And I'm just going to do the very best job I can. And in terms of how to spend my time and how to do it, I'm going to have to assess that over the next couple of days.

Thank you.

Q. Speaking of cuts, what kind of razor are you using?

The President. I got this playing with my daughter, I'm ashamed to say, rolling around acting like a child again. I reaffirm that I'm not a kid anymore.

Thank you.

NOTE: The President spoke at 10:40 a.m. in the Oval Office at the White House. H.R. 904, approved April 7, was assigned Public Law No. 103–13. A tape was not available for verification of the content of these remarks.

Statement on Signing Enabling Legislation for the National Commission to Ensure a Strong Competitive Airline Industry
April 7, 1993

Today I am signing into law H.R. 904, a bill providing for appointments to the "National Commission to Ensure a Strong Competitive Airline Industry." I am pleased to have the opportunity to join with the Congress so quickly in the new session in this effort to gain a fuller understanding of the difficulties facing the Nation's aviation industry—both airlines and aircraft manufacturing.

The recent experience of the aviation industry has not been good. Unemployment in the airline industry has reached record levels over the past few years. The backlog of new orders for aircraft has shrunk, leading to unemployment in the aircraft manufacturing industry as well. When I visited the Boeing Corporation in Everett, Washington, managers and employees alike described the personal impact of these developments.

The issues facing the industry have an international dimension. In recent remarks at the American University here in Washington, I stressed that our Nation is ready to compete in the world economy fairly and squarely. In our bilateral and multilateral aviation negotiations, my Administration will promote fair competition in international trade and airline routes.

I asked Secretary of Transportation Peña to join with the Congress to develop a process for addressing the industry's problems, and I am pleased by this strong bipartisan result. The aviation industry is important not only to our economy, but (as Operation Desert Storm demonstrated just 2 years ago) to our national defense as well. The information and recommendations developed by the Commission will assist us in building a consensus from the many competing views on how government and industry can best work together to address the aviation industry's current difficulties.

I am pleased that this legislation accelerates the deadline for the Commission's report. I have asked Secretary Peña, working with the rest of the Cabinet, to do everything possible to get the Commission up and running quickly. I look forward to receiving the Commission's report within 90 days after appointments to the Commission are completed.

I note that the House Subcommittee on Aviation has already begun to assemble a record of the relevant issues during its hearings in February. With concerted effort by all parties, this

Commission can provide valuable, timely answers.

WILLIAM J. CLINTON

The White House,
April 7, 1993.

NOTE: H.R. 904, approved April 7, was assigned Public Law No. 103–13.

Nomination for Ambassadorial Posts
April 7, 1993

The President announced today his nomination of Marshall McCallie to be Ambassador to Namibia, and his intention to nominate John Schmidt to the rank of Ambassador during his tenure of service as the Uruguay Round Coordinator. In that position, Mr. Schmidt will be the chief U.S. negotiator for the Uruguay round of the General Agreement on Tariffs and Trade.

"These are two key appointments," said the President. "The Uruguay round of the GATT talks is vital to our hopes for freer and fairer trade in the world. Likewise, our relationship with Namibia is key as we seek to promote democracy in southern Africa. I am very happy with the choices of John Schmidt and Marshall McCallie to fill those roles."

NOTE: Biographies of the nominees were made available by the Office of the Press Secretary.

Nomination for Posts at the Department of the Treasury
April 8, 1993

The President intends to nominate George Munoz to be Assistant Secretary of the Treasury for Management and Chief Financial Officer, the White House announced today. The President also expressed his approval of Secretary Bentsen's choices for three positions. Joyce Carrier, Joan Logue-Kinder, and Marina Weiss will serve as Deputy Assistant Secretaries with responsibility for Public Liaison, Public Affairs, and Health, respectively.

"George Munoz has excelled in a variety of ways in both the private and public sectors," said the President. "I am confident that he and the rest of Lloyd Bentsen's team at Treasury will keep that key Department running smoothly."

NOTE: Biographies of the nominees were made available by the Office of the Press Secretary.

Nomination for an Assistant to the Secretary of Defense
April 9, 1993

The President will nominate Harold Palmer Smith to be Assistant to the Secretary of Defense for Atomic Energy. Mr. Smith, a trained nuclear engineer, has advised the Defense Department in a variety of capacities since the late 1960's.

"Through his long career of public and private sector service, Harold Palmer Smith has distinguished himself with sound scientific advice," said the President. "I am glad to have him joining Secretary Aspin at the Pentagon."

NOTE: A biography of the nominee was made available by the Office of the Press Secretary.

Remarks on Preschool Immunization and an Exchange With Reporters
April 12, 1993

The President. This is a proclamation in support of Preschool Immunization Week. I'd like to read a statement about it, and then I'll be glad to answer some questions, along with Secretary Shalala who also has a few remarks to make.

This proclamation in support of Preschool Immunization Week gives us all a chance to promote our best ideals in the Nation and to prove that we can make a difference in the lives of our children. In fact, the $300 million in our stimulus program will help us to immunize one million children this summer and to show that this is a campaign of words and deeds.

Studies under all administrations have shown that vaccines are the most cost-effective way to prevent human suffering and to reduce the economic cost that result from vaccine-preventable diseases. But because we've gotten away from preventive care and because immunizations have become unaffordable or unavailable, millions of infants and toddlers are at risk of completely preventable diseases like polio, mumps, and measles; children like Rodney Miller, a 20-month-old in Miami who had meningitis that could have been prevented with a vaccine that costs $21.48, instead had a hospital stay that cost in excess of $46,000.

Through public investment and leadership we can do better. It's a miracle of our system and our ingenuity that we can prevent the worst infectious diseases of children with vaccines and save $10 for every $1 invested. But things started to go sour in the eighties. We had the third worst immunization rate in this hemisphere. Ten years ago, immunizations cost $23. Now they cost $200. We're the only industrialized nation that does not immunize all children, although we develop and produce a majority of the vaccines. As a result, we've had thousands of new cases of measles. Immunization rates have not improved, and in the case of some, diseases have actually gone down. We have seen and predict what this will mean in terms of suffering and human costs.

Our plan will allow us to purchase vaccine and conduct outreach programs in the appropriate language and at the appropriate neighborhood venues, to reach those who'd been shut out of this part of our system. It will allow us to extend clinic hours, expand education efforts, create a national tracking system so that we know what's happening to our children. It will give us the resources to help those in the public health system and in advocacy groups who are already working heroically to bring this simple technology to all of our children.

Today we will begin what will become, with later legislation, a comprehensive program to support community based immunization projects and to lower vaccine costs with the goal of having the best, not the worst rate in the hemisphere. There are great coalitions working on making this effort successful and fun and a model of what we can do again to make this Government work.

I just want to say that today we're having the Easter egg roll on the White House lawn. You can look out there at those kids. They are the hostages of the Senate filibuster on the program. They are the hostages of the Senate filibuster on the stimulus program. All this hot air rhetoric about how this money is being wasted and that money is being wasted. These people, most of them have been here for the last 12 years while we have run immunization into the ground, while we have developed the third worst rate in the hemisphere. And they've always got some excuse, some of them, for not doing anything.

Now, what are we going to do for those children? That ought to be the question of the week. When I go out there on the lawn, and I think about those kids picking up Easter eggs, I want to be able to think about them all being immunized and all those children coming along behind them being immunized. There is no excuse for this. And it is time that we broke the gridlock and stopped making excuses for not doing anything.

Secretary Shalala.

[At this point, Secretary of Health and Human Services Donna E. Shalala spoke on the preschool immunization program.]

The President. Thank you.

Stimulus Package

Q. Mr. President, in order to save the $300

million immunization program, are you prepared to compromise with the Republicans in the Senate to scale back the stimulus package to something a lot less than you had originally hoped for?

The President. Well, I think, I'd like to know how many more Americans they want to keep out of work. I mean, what is their position? That's basically what it amounts to. I mean, all this business about there being the potential for abuse in the community development block grant program, that is a smoke screen, and this is politics. So they're going to have to decide. I want to put as many people to work as I can. They're going to have to decide how many people they're determined to keep out of work. And I'll do everything I can to pass the best bill I can.

But let's not talk about compromise. Let's strip all this rhetoric away. This is about whether you want to reduce the unemployment rate in America by another half a percentage point for a very modest amount. And they don't. For whatever reason, they don't. They want more people to stay out of work. So they just have to decide, I guess, how many people we can put to work and what we can do. And I'm going to do the best I can to get the best program I can. I'll be discussing it this week.

Whenever we use the word compromise, let's talk about what's really at stake. The Republicans had 12 years in which unemployment went down only when they were exploding the deficit and increasing the defense budget. Now we're reducing the defense budget. What is it that we propose to replace it with? We must have some investment. We must have some jobs. We must have primarily the overall program that we've already passed. But I think we need to strike a match to the job engine in America,

and that's what I'm trying to do. And I'll do the best I can. I'm going to create as many jobs as I can.

Q. Well, Mr. President, what are you prepared to do to make sure that your program gets through Congress?

The President. We're working—look, we've got a majority in both Houses. The American people, I think, are astonished to find out that 41 Senators, 41 percent of the Senate can shut the whole place down. And they've just got to decide, as I said, how many people they want to keep out of work and how many people we want to put to work. And I think we can work something out. I'm hopeful that we can. I know that there are people in that Republican Senate bloc that want to vote for a good stimulus program. I know they do. I hope they'll be released to do it.

Bosnia

Q. Mr. President, have you rejected the recommendation of your commission that force be used in Bosnia?

The President. I saw that story. That commission has not made a report to me yet. We didn't ask anybody not to talk to the Congress. We just asked that policy recommendations not be made to the Congress before a commission that came out of the executive branch made final recommendations to me. We have not received a final report from them.

NOTE: The President spoke at 10:07 a.m. in the Oval Office at the White House. The National Preschool Immunization Week proclamation of April 9 is listed in Appendix D at the end of this volume. A tape was not available for verification of the content of these remarks.

Remarks at the White House Easter Egg Roll
April 12, 1993

Good morning, everybody. I want to welcome all of you here to the White House for the Easter egg roll and the Easter egg hunt. I want to say a special word of thanks to the sponsors who made this possible and say how wonderful it is for all of us here to see the children,

especially for me and for Hillary.

And I want now to introduce the First Lady, who is the hostess for this event, to say a few more words about it. But let me again say how very, very grateful we are to see all of you here. This is a children's day for America at the White House, and I'm glad you're here to make it so special. Please welcome the First Lady.

NOTE: The President spoke at 10:48 a.m. on the South Lawn at the White House. Following his remarks, Hillary Clinton welcomed the participants to the annual White House Easter egg roll. A tape was not available for verification of the content of these remarks.

Remarks at the Technology Reinvestment Project Conference
April 12, 1993

I want to welcome you to the first of five White House briefings on the Technology Reinvestment Project, a key part of my defense reinvestment and conversion initiative. I'd like to thank the organizations that are hosting this event, the Northeast Midwest Institute and the New York Academy of Sciences, as well as the 10 States that are participating. You're in good hands today with Energy Secretary Hazel O'Leary and our science adviser, Jack Gibbons. They're here to kick off the event. A superb team lead by Gary Denman, the Director of the Advanced Research Projects Agency, or ARPA, and Fred Bernthal, Acting Director of the National Science Foundation, will fully brief you on the Technology Reinvestment Project and answer all your questions.

With the collapse of the former Soviet Union and the end of the cold war, we've been undertaking substantial cuts in defense expenditures, and they will continue while still maintaining a flexible and effective military force. Now we can turn our attention to other national needs.

But the adjustment to lower defense spending is still painful for many communities and workers and firms. An estimated 60 percent of the total loss in defense-related jobs between 1991 and 1997 will occur in only 10 States. Those of you here today represent communities and companies that face the challenges of moving to a civilian economy.

Defense conversion is one of my highest priorities. It's one of the reasons I ran for President in 1992. We simply must act to ease the pain of defense downsizing, while capturing the great potential that defense workers and firms offer to meet pressing national economic needs. And we have to do it quickly.

Last month, I announced a $20 billion 5-year initiative to reinvest in workers, communities, and companies harmed by cuts in military spending. The plan provides immediate help for hard-hit defense workers and communities, as well as long-term investment in our Nation's industrial technology infrastructure. The reinvestment and conversion initiative will rededicate $375 million this year alone to helping defense workers and military personnel hurt by cuts. They'll receive job training, employment services, and transition assistance to help them put their skills to work in a new setting.

We're also targeting assistance to communities that are hard hit by defense drawdown. Through programs in the Department of Commerce and the Department of Defense that provide grants and revolving loans, we're helping these communities identify new sources of economic strength that will create new jobs. These defense workers and the communities will succeed in adapting only if we have an expanding industrial base. The Technology Reinvestment Project, a key component of my conversion plan, will play a vital role in helping defense companies adjust and compete.

I've given this project another name, Operation Restore Jobs, to signify its ultimate mission, namely, to expand high quality employment opportunities and to enhance demonstrably our Nation's competitiveness. This project has generated enormous interest in the 4 weeks since I announced it at a Westinghouse plant outside Baltimore. More than 8,000 people have called our 1–800–DUAL–USE hotline. Many of you who have placed those calls are here today. Others plan to attend one of the briefings to be held later this week in Detroit, Orlando, Dallas, and Los Angeles.

As this enthusiastic response demonstrates, the Technology Reinvestment Project marks a new way of doing business. First, it begins a new partnership between Government and industry aimed at making American companies more competitive. Industry must take the lead and share the cost. But, in return, the Federal Government will directly support commercial technology through industry consortia, regional technology alliances, and other collaborative activities. This approach rejects the reliance on defense spinoffs that has been the core of the Federal Government's technology strategy for more than 40 years. It recognizes that in the years ahead a growing number of defense needs can be met most efficiently by commercial products and commercial technology.

Second, the Technology Reinvestment Project marks a new partnership between the Federal and State governments. The States have pioneered programs to apply technology to industrial needs, and these programs often provide the most effective way to help smaller defense firms adjust and compete in commercial markets. By supporting industry-led consortia through this project, we'll nurture technologies with the potential to become commercial products and processes within 5 years. By funding regional technology alliances, we'll encourage companies in defense-dependent regions to share information and technology in order to develop new products and new markets. By supporting innovative manufacturing extension programs run by States and universities, we'll help small defense firms make the transition to commercial production.

The Technology Reinvestment Project will provide matching funds for efforts such as New York's defense diversification program, which has worked closely with more than 100 small and medium-size defense firms just in the last 2 years. For example, the EDO Corporation, which some of you visited this morning in Queens, makes antisubmarine warfare and aircraft armament. With help from the State's diversification program, this company is moving into the market for natural gas fueling stations. New York is also working with defense-dependent regions, particularly Long Island and the southern tier, to develop regional strategies for diversification and economic growth.

Our past experience with defense conversion yields two lessons. The first is that the process of defense conversion can be improved by government policies designed to help companies and workers make the transition to new forms of production. The Technology Reinvestment Project, Operation Restore Jobs, is a model of how that can work. Lesson two is that conversion proceeds more smoothly if the domestic economy is growing rapidly. That's why it's so important for Congress to enact my whole economic program, including the stimulus package, which will help put Americans back to work and provide the kind of short-term boost that New York and New England so desperately need.

If you want this program to go forward, if you believe in the need for conversion, I need your help. While Congress has passed the broad outlines of our economic program, it will be considering the specifics in the next couple of weeks. And if you've been following the filibuster in the Senate, you know that just a few people can stop action on important economic legislation by talking and talking and talking. You've got to remind them that they can save jobs, indeed, create new jobs if they'll just save their breath, stop playing politics, and start responding to the needs of the American people for a change.

My mission is simple and straightforward. I want to create a healthy economic climate for all Americans and all businesses in all regions. I want to create a program of economic conversion for your businesses. I believe in jobs. I believe in the private sector, and I believe in you.

Thank you for attending this conference. And thank you for your work in creating profits, products, and opportunities for our economy and our people.

NOTE: The President spoke at 1:20 p.m. in Room 459 of the Old Executive Office Building.

Nomination for Administrator of the Federal Railroad Administration
April 12, 1993

The President will nominate Jolene Molitoris to be the Administrator of the Federal Railroad Administration, Department of Transportation, the White House announced today. Ms. Molitoris served for more than a decade with the Ohio Department of Transportation and Ohio Rail Transportation Authority.

"One of the most important things we can do to improve our overall transportation system and to create high-wage manufacturing jobs is to improve and expand our Nation's rail system," said the President. "Jolene Molitoris is a seasoned executive with direct experience in doing the kinds of things we need to be doing."

NOTE: A biography of the nominee was made available by the Office of the Press Secretary.

Nomination for Commissioners of the Federal Energy Regulatory Commission
April 12, 1993

The President announced his intention today to nominate four experts on energy regulation, Bill Massey, Donald Santa, James Hoecker, and Vicky Bailey, to be Commissioners of the Federal Energy Regulatory Commission. He also announced his intention to designate Elizabeth Anne "Betsy" Moler as the Commission's Chair, a position she has held on an interim basis since February.

"I have called for a sensible, comprehensive energy policy that serves our future energy needs, protects our precious environment, and helps to build a growing economy," said the President. "This experienced and talented group of Commissioners will help to meet those goals."

NOTE: Biographies of the nominees were made available by the Office of the Press Secretary.

Remarks on the Observance of the 250th Anniversary of the Birth of Thomas Jefferson
April 13, 1993

Thank you very much, Colonel McCarty, General Streeter, my fellow Americans. I want to begin by offering my compliments to the United States Marine Band and the Virginia Glee Club, who have entertained us so well today. I think we should give them another hand. [*Applause*]

Today we observe the birthday of perhaps the most brilliant of our Founding Fathers in a setting Thomas Jefferson would have very much approved: one that joins the beauty of human architecture with the rapturous side of nature, with the cherry blossoms bursting all around us in a wreath.

Mr. Jefferson used to say with some pride that the Sun never found him in bed, that he always rose early, and he was very proud of the fact that well into his seventies, he could ride a horse several miles a day without tiring. Well, in honor of his birthday, I rose early this morning and finding no horses around the White House, I ran over here and jogged around this magnificent Tidal Basin, seeing many of my fellow citizens who were here even before me, at the dawn, to see this magnificent sight.

Today we have come to lay our wreaths in honor of Thomas Jefferson, as his likeness towers behind us. And yet, no amount of bronze can capture the measure of the man who helped to cut a path for our Nation, who personally forged the principles that continue to guide us as Americans and as lovers of freedom.

As has already been said, this monument was dedicated a half a century ago, on the 200th anniversary of Jefferson's birthday by President Franklin Roosevelt, a worthy heir to the spirit of Jefferson. Were Jefferson here today, I think he would not want very much to talk about the America of his time; instead, he would be talking about the America of our time. He would certainly not be at a loss for ideas about what we ought to be doing, for he was a man blessed with an eye for invention, an ear for music, the hands of a farmer, the mind of a philosopher, the voice of a statesman, and the soul of a searcher for truth.

The genius of Thomas Jefferson was his ability to get the most out of today while never taking his eye off tomorrow, to think big while enjoying the little things of daily life. Perhaps most important, he understood that in order for us to preserve our timeless values, people have to change. And free people need to devise means by which they can change profoundly and still peacefully. If you go back to this monument after the ceremony, you will see on the wall in part the following quotation: "Laws and institutions must go hand-in-hand with the progress of the human mind as that becomes more developed, more enlightened, as new discoveries are made and new truths discovered, and manners and opinions change. With the change of circumstances, institutions must advance also to keep pace with the times."

A very modern statement from our third President. In his own time, the pace of change was enormous. Just think back, during Jefferson's Presidency the steamboat made its debut, revolutionizing travel. The importing of slaves was banned, paving the way toward emancipation and the realignment of society. And he acquired the Louisiana Purchase for the then massive sum of $15 million. Turns out it was an awfully sound investment. It doubled the size of our Nation, it opened up a new frontier, and it enabled me to be born in the United States of America, and many of you as well, I suspect.

But believe it or not, every step along the way, Thomas Jefferson was opposed. There were people who opposed the Louisiana Purchase, people who opposed his then radical conception of human liberty, and both the power of individuals and the limitations of the Government. He fought, and he prevailed.

I wonder what he would say about our time, in which the pace of change is even greater. I think he would take great pride in the fact that we have now found ways to literally double the volume of knowledge every few years. But I think he would be terribly disappointed that our understanding in this country of the science and mathematics that he loved so much is still so limited and so inadequate when compared to that of many other nations.

I think he would be delighted that the principles of freedom for which he stood all his life finally resulted in the end of the cold war and the demise of communism. But I think he would be deeply disappointed that ethnic and racial and other hatreds had kept this world such a dangerous and unstable place, in ways that are blatantly unreasonable, as he defined reason.

I think he would be proud of the technological and economic advances of this time, of the increasing interconnection of peoples across national borders in a global economy. But I think he would be profoundly disturbed that even the richest countries are now having enormous difficulty in finding enough jobs for their people, including his own beloved United States, and that so much technological advance seems to bring the destruction of much of the environment, about which he cared so deeply.

I think Jefferson would be impressed at the enormous advances in health care. He cared a lot about his health, and he lived to be 83 largely by taking good care of himself. And I think he would be a little disappointed that more of us don't take better care of ourselves and appalled to think that the United States is the only advanced country where every person doesn't have access to affordable health care, something I hope we can change before long.

If you go up there and read what's on those walls, there is an incredibly moving statement where Jefferson said, he trembles to think that God is just when he considers the real meaning of the institution of slavery. So I think he would be delighted at the progress we have made in human rights and living together across racial lines. Because he had such a passionate belief in individual liberty, I think he would be delighted by the range of personal choices and freedom of speech that the American people enjoy today, even to say things that he would find offensive, for he understood the clear meaning of the First Amendment.

But I think he would be appalled at the lack of self-respect and self-control and respect for others which manifests itself in the kind of mindless violence to which this city and others have been subject for the last several years, and appalled at the millions of young people who will never know the full measure of their freedom because they have been raised without order, without love, without family, without even the basic safety which people need to be able almost to take for granted in order to be citizens of a real democracy. In short, I think Thomas Jefferson would tell us that this is one of those times when we need to change.

Clearly, the call for change that Jefferson made, he intended to be echoed generation after generation after generation. He believed if we set up the Constitution in the way that it was set up, that Americans of courage and good sense would always, always find themselves in the majority for change when they needed to be there. He believed in Government constantly being reformed by reason and popular will.

That is what this administration is trying to do now. We know that we have an economy that, even in growth, does not produce new jobs. We know that we have increased by 4 times the debt of this Nation over the last 12 years, and we don't have much to show for it. We know that the people have now courageously asked us to take on the problems of jobs and the deficit, the environment and education and health care, to try to put our people first again and make Government work for them.

The American people, deep in their bones, without even thinking about it, are the agents of change that Thomas Jefferson sought to write in perpetuity into our Constitution. For in the end, Thomas Jefferson understood that no politician, no government, no piece of paper could do for the American people what they would have to do for themselves. He understood better perhaps than any of his colleagues that the people of this country would always have to be not only the protectors of their own liberty but the agents of their own transformation and change. But he also knew that Government must be willing to supply the tools of that change.

And that, very simply, is our task today. After all, what is a good education but a tool to a better life. What is a job but a tool to build self-sufficiency, self-esteem, and dignity for a worker and a family.

As I look around this Nation, I know that Thomas Jefferson would be very proud and pleased by much of what has happened here. I suspect it would amuse and surprise him and make him very proud to think that for most Americans, on most days, people from 150 and more racial and ethnic groups live together in not only peace and law abidingness but also mutual respect and reinforcing strength. I think that would make him proud. I think he would be proud of the generosity of spirit that characterizes our people and manifests itself most clearly at a time of national crisis and national tragedy. After all, in Jefferson's time people gave food and shelter to travelers who came to their doors at night, even when they were total strangers. Jefferson himself, at Monticello, often offered his home over the years to bone-weary travelers.

Today many of our people would do the same thing. But together, together, we have not faced the problems of the bone-weary travelers in our own land, nor have we faced the problems that we all share in common. We cannot turn the problems away. It is time for reasonable change. It is time for the Americans in our time to live up to the principles etched in stone in this magnificent memorial.

Just look at the beauty around us today. Do you know that in Mr. Jefferson's time almost all of this was a swamp? People avoided this place like the plague, because they were afraid of the plague. But with a plan, with investment, with effort, with vision, Americans transformed it. And from this inhospitable terrain rose the city before us, one of the most magnificent capitals in the history of the world. But the structures around us are simply buildings. They come to life only when they shake from the will of the people. That is what Thomas Jefferson knew.

We are the inheritors of Jefferson's rich legacy. On this the 200th anniversary of his birth, we can honor him best by remembering our own role in governing ourselves and our Nation: to speak, to move, to change, for it is only in change that we preserve the timeless values for which Thomas Jefferson gave his life, over two centuries ago.

Thank you, and God bless you all.

NOTE: The President spoke at 12:42 p.m. at the Jefferson Memorial.

Remarks at a Town Meeting on Goals 2000
April 13, 1993

The President. Thank you very much, Mr. Secretary.

I'm glad to be here with my friends Dick Riley and Bob Reich, also members of my Cabinet, at the headquarters of the Chamber of Commerce to support the effort that the chamber is making, along with its Center for Work Force Preparation, to help to examine tonight the whole critical question of how to move our young people from school to the workplace.

I want to compliment the chamber on all their efforts, recognizing that without an educated work force we can't grow this economy or remain competitive and recognizing that we all have to work together, business and Government, labor and educators, to make things happen. This satellite town meeting is a good example of that kind of working together. And if you'll forgive me a little home State pride, I want to say a special word of thanks to the Wal-Mart Corporation, headquartered in Bentonville, Arkansas, for providing several hundred of the sites for this town meeting tonight. I appreciate that a lot, as well as the sites that are provided for all the rest of you.

I have tried as hard as I could to move toward constructive change for this country. Secretary Riley talked about this being Thomas Jefferson's 250th birthday. If Thomas Jefferson believed in anything, he believed in these three things: first, in education; second, in real personal liberty, freedom of religion, freedom of speech, freedom of association, freedom of the press; and third, in the absolute imperative of changing as times change.

If you go to the Jefferson Memorial here in this beautiful city, which is now bedecked with all of its wonderful cherry blossoms, you will see Jefferson saying that we have to change with changing times. For us here in America that means reducing our deficit and increasing our investment and putting our people first so that we can compete in the world. We're here to talk about that tonight, about what we can do

to educate and train our people better. Unless we do that, none of the efforts that all the rest of us make in Government, even to bring the budget into balance, even to increase our investment in other things which will grow jobs, will last in the long run.

We also have to have people who can carry their load. And in a world where the average young person will change jobs seven or eight times in a lifetime, that begins with the education system and continues into the work force where education must go on for a lifetime. It's not just important what you know but what you can learn.

And if I might, I'd like to close just by emphasizing we're doing our best to try to have the most innovative partnership between the Labor Department and the Education Department and the private sector to build a good school-to-work transition. And we're trying to get off to a good start this summer with a program that would create more than 700,000 new summer jobs, including many thousands that have a strong education component so our young people can be learning and working at the same time.

Dick, I think I ought to stop there. That's a good place we can begin, I think, the discussion.

[At this point, Secretary of Education Richard W. Riley discussed the Summer Youth Challenge program and asked the President to explain the importance of educational enrichment in summer jobs.]

The President. I think it's important for two reasons. First of all, a lot of the young people we're trying to reach may have had trouble adjusting to school and learning. And while we want them to have a good experience with a real job, we also want them to continue to learn during the summer because we know from a lot of research that a lot of kids that have trouble learning in school may forget as much as 30 percent of what they learned the previous year over the summertime. And that is a very unproductive thing for schools, to have to take up a lot of time teaching what they already taught before. Secondly, we want to help these young people progress, not only in terms of work but in terms of learning. We want to abolish the artificial dividing line between what is work and what is learning because we think that the best and most productive workers will have to be lifetime learners. And we think that this experience could maybe drive that point home and prepare these young people to succeed in school or at work or in college as they go on.

[*Secretary Riley and Secretary of Labor Robert B. Reich discussed the importance of on-the-job experience combined with education. Secretary Riley then asked the President to discuss his apprenticeship proposal.*]

The President. Well, first of all, let's talk about why it's important. Most new jobs that will be created in this decade will not require a 4-year college degree, but most of them will require some learning and skills that go well beyond what most people get in a high school diploma.

If you look at the last 10 years, the average salaries of young people that had at least 2 years of good post-high school education was a good salary that went up over the decade. The young people who had less than that tended to have lower wages that did not go up and, in many cases, in real terms, fell over the decade because they weren't productive, they weren't more valuable to their employers.

So we think America has a big economic interest in trying to ensure that all the young people who get out of high school but don't go on to college make a transition to work, which includes 2 years of further training either in a community college, a vocational setting, or perhaps on the job. And what I have done in this budget, as you know, is to give you and Secretary Reich some funds and some incentives to try to work in partnership with States and with the private sector to build these programs State-by-State in a way that would be customized essentially by the business community, based on the needs of the economy in any given area. It could revolutionize long term the quality of the American work force and the earnings of American workers.

[*Secretary Reich and Secretary Riley discussed community involvement, academic excellence, and skills development as necessary components of school-to-work transition programs.*]

The President. I think—if I might just interject one point based on my personal experience at home—the business community has a critical role to play, not simply in saying, "Here are the job skills that are needed, and here's what ought to be taught," but also in monitoring that excellence. If you have the right sort of partnership there, the people who are paying the taxes and who are going to then be hiring the workers are not going to permit the second-rate programs to survive if they have any way to shape and influence them. So I think that's very important.

And when we try to, if you will, fill in the blanks at the Federal level, trying to set some standards and provide some funds, one of the things that we want to be sure and do is to make sure that the employer has a heavy amount of influence over the quality of these programs, because that's really what's going to determine whether the whole thing is worthwhile.

[*Secretary Riley asked the President about long-term school reform proposals.*]

The President. Well, as you know, back when you and I were both Governors, we spent a lot of time working on our public schools, and we tried to be very candid with our people in saying that a lot of these things were going to take some time to materialize.

I had a hand in writing the national education goals that the Governors drafted, along with representatives of President Bush's administration back in 1989. And what we're going to try to do this year with your leadership is to introduce legislation in Congress that will actually define the things that the National Government ought to do to try to help the local schools and the children of this country and the adult learners, too, meet those goals: making sure that by 2000, people show up for school ready to learn; that we get a 90 percent on-time high school graduation rate; that children at the 4th, 8th, and 12th grades are confident in the subjects they're supposed to know; that they are second to none in math and science; that our schools are safe, disciplined, and drug-free. And of course, the fifth goal—I took them out of line to say this the last—is that we have a system of lifelong learning in this country.

And each one of those goals, there's a national role, a State role, a school role, school district role, and a private sector role. And what you've attempted to do in this bill you're going to introduce with me in the next few weeks is to define what our job is and then to give the rest of America a way of defining what their job is and seeing whether we're actually meeting the standards of quality that we need to meet.

It's very exciting. So far as I know, nothing quite like it has ever been done in the form of Federal legislation before. Not mandating and telling people what they have to do with their money, but actually setting up a framework for excellence and partnerships so that we can do our job. I'm really excited about it.

[*Secretary Riley and Secretary Reich discussed the development of national skills standards. Mayor Bruce Todd of Austin, TX, then asked a question via satellite about Federal initiatives for school-to-work transition programs.*]

Secretary Riley. Mr. President.

The President. I think I'll give everybody a chance to answer the question, Bruce, but let me first thank you for calling and thank you for all the great work that you're doing in Austin. I've see some of it, and I've always been very impressed.

First, with regard to the summer program, we hope we can structure it in a way that will enable us to continue the summer program and that will move a lot of these young people back into schools under circumstances that might allow them to do some work in the private sector, too. Secretary Reich is going to try to set up a system where we create a lot of private sector jobs to be matched with the public sector jobs this summer, and we're working on that.

Secondly, in the program that I have presented to the Congress over the next 5 years, what we are attempting to do is to build in an amount of investment that's quite substantial for job training programs, for school-to-work programs, all of which give heavy, heavy weight to local community input—just the question you

asked—but do provide some Federal investment dollars, which we hope you can put with local dollars to keep people working and being trained on a year-round basis.

And I will say again, to echo what Secretary Reich said a moment ago, to try to break down the barrier between what is seen as work and what is seen as learning. An awful lot of young people actually have quite high IQ's, but actually learn so much better when they're doing than when they're reading or just listening. So we hope that the community involvement part of it will be permanent. And we hope that if the whole budget passes—and we do have 200 budget cuts, and more than 200, actually, in the budget and some revenue raisers and some new money for education and training—that we'll be able to do just what you seem to want based on your question.

Bob, do you want to say anything?

[*Secretary Reich stressed the need for job creation as a prerequisite for the success of the program. Secretary Riley stated that the Goals 2000 program will involve individual State action plans. Dr. Harry Heinemann, special assistant to the president of LaGuardia Community College, Long Island City, NY, then asked a question via satellite about closer integration of school curricula with the transition to work.*]

The President. I'd just like to say, if I might, one thing. I want to reemphasize this, and I don't think I'm being as clear about it as I'd like, although I think at least one of the people who will be on the second panel will be able to say it more explicitly than I. I think this whole concept of applied academics is very important. And I think that we have to basically abolish what I consider to be a very artificial distinction between what is vocational learning and what is academic learning. I think we should keep the liberal arts going. I think we should have a strong component for people who are in the vocational program.

NOTE: The town meeting began at 8:30 p.m. The President spoke via satellite from the U.S. Chamber of Commerce Building.

Letter to Congressional Leaders on Trade With Ecuador
April 13, 1993

Dear Mr. Speaker: *(Dear Mr. President:)*

Pursuant to section 203 of the Andean Trade Preference Act (ATPA) (19 U.S.C. 3202), I wish to inform you of my intent to designate Ecuador as a beneficiary of the trade-liberalizing measures provided for in this Act. Designation will entitle the products of Ecuador, except for products excluded statutorily, to duty-free treatment for a period ending on December 4, 2001.

Designation is an important step for Ecuador in its effort to fight against narcotics production and trafficking. The enhanced access to the U.S. market provided by the ATPA will encourage the production of and trade in legitimate products.

My decision to designate Ecuador results from consultations concluded in January 1993 between my Administration and the Government of Ecuador regarding the designation criteria set forth in section 203 of the ATPA. Ecuador has demonstrated to my satisfaction that its laws, practices, and policies are in conformity with the designation criteria of the ATPA. The Government of Ecuador has communicated on these matters by letter to the Office of the United States Trade Representative and in so doing has indicated its desire to be designated as a beneficiary.

On the basis of the statements and assurances in Ecuador's letter, and taking into account information developed by the United States Embassy and through other sources, I have concluded that designation is appropriate at this time.

I am mindful that under section 203(e) of the ATPA, I retain the authority to suspend, withdraw, or limit the application of ATPA benefits from any designated country if a beneficiary's laws, policies, or practices are no longer in conformity with the designation criteria. The United States will keep abreast of developments in Ecuador that are pertinent to the designation criteria.

My Administration looks forward to working closely with the Government of Ecuador and with the private sectors of the United States and Ecuador to ensure that the wide-ranging opportunities opened by the ATPA are fully utilized.

Sincerely,

BILL CLINTON

NOTE: Identical letters were sent to Thomas S. Foley, Speaker of the House of Representatives, and Albert Gore, Jr., President of the Senate. The related proclamation is listed in Appendix D at the end of this volume.

Letter to Congressional Leaders Transmitting the Report on the North Atlantic Treaty
April 13, 1993

Dear Mr. Speaker: *(Dear Mr. President:)*

As requested in section 1314 of the National Defense Authorization Act for Fiscal Year 1993 (Public Law 102–484), I am forwarding the "Report on the North Atlantic Treaty of 1949."

Sincerely,

WILLIAM J. CLINTON

NOTE: Identical letters were sent to Thomas S. Foley, Speaker of the House of Representatives, and Albert Gore, Jr., President of the Senate.

Nomination for Posts at the National Endowment for the Humanities
April 13, 1993

The President announced his intention to nominate Sheldon Hackney to be Chair of the National Endowment for the Humanities, National Foundation on the Arts and the Humanities, today. He will also name Michael Shapiro to be the Endowment's General Counsel.

"The National Endowment for the Humanities plays a vital role in encouraging and enhancing a better understanding of our country's rich heritage," said the President. "Doing just that has been the work of Sheldon Hackney's life. Likewise, Michael Shapiro has demonstrated true ability in the management of cultural institutions. I am confident that the NEH will flourish in their hands."

NOTE: Biographies of the nominees were made available by the Office of the Press Secretary.

Nomination for an Assistant Secretary of Defense
April 13, 1993

The President announced today that he intends to nominate Ashton Carter, the director of Harvard's Center for Science and International Affairs, to be Assistant Secretary of Defense for Nuclear Security and Counter-Proliferation.

"One of the key national security challenges of the post-cold-war era is containing the spread of nuclear arms and other weapons of mass destruction," said the President. "In Ashton Carter we will have an experienced and expert Assistant Secretary focusing on the problems and seeking solutions."

NOTE: A biography of the nominee was made available by the Office of the Press Secretary.

Letter to Congressional Leaders Reporting on the No-Fly Zone Over Bosnia
April 13, 1993

Dear Mr. Speaker: (Dear Mr. President:)

As part of my continuing effort to keep the Congress fully informed, I am providing this report, consistent with section 4 of the War Powers Resolution, to advise you of actions that I have ordered in support of the United Nations efforts in Bosnia-Herzegovina.

Beginning with U.N. Security Council Resolution 713 of September 25, 1991, the United Nations has been actively addressing the crisis in the former Yugoslavia. The Security Council acted in Resolution 781 to establish a ban on all unauthorized military flights over Bosnia-Herzegovina. There have, however, been blatant violations of the ban, and villages in Bosnia have been bombed.

In response to these violations, the Security Council decided, in Resolution 816 of March 31, 1993, to extend the ban to all unauthorized flights over Bosnia-Herzegovina and to authorize Member States, acting nationally or through regional organizations, to take all necessary measures to ensure compliance. NATO's North Atlantic Council (NAC) agreed to provide NATO air enforcement for the no-fly zone. The U.N. Secretary General was notified of NATO's decision to proceed with Operation DENY FLIGHT, and an activation order was delivered to participating allies.

The United States actively supported these decisions. At my direction, the Joint Chiefs of Staff sent an execute order to all U.S. forces participating in the NATO force, for the conduct of phased air operations to prevent flights not authorized by the United Nations over Bosnia-Herzegovina. The U.S. forces initially assigned to this operation consist of 13 F–15 and 12 F–18A fighter aircraft and supporting tanker aircraft. These aircraft commenced enforcement operations at 8:00 a.m. e.d.t. on April 12, 1993. The fighter aircraft are equipped for combat to accomplish their mission and for self-defense.

NATO has positioned forces and has established combat air patrol (CAP) stations within the control of Airborne Early Warning (AEW) aircraft. The U.S. CAP aircraft will normally operate from bases in Italy and from an aircraft carrier in the Adriatic Sea. Unauthorized aircraft entering or approaching the no-fly zone will be identified, interrogated, intercepted, escorted/monitored, and turned away (in that order). If these steps do not result in compliance with the no-fly zone, such aircraft may be engaged on the basis of proper authorization by NATO military authorities and in accordance with the approved rules of engagement, although we do not expect such action will be necessary. The

Commander of UNPROFOR (the United Nations Protection Force currently operating in Bosnia-Herzegovina) was consulted to ensure that his concerns for his force were fully considered before the rules of engagement were approved.

It is not possible to predict at this time how long such operations will be necessary. I have directed U.S. armed forces to participate in these operations pursuant to my constitutional authority as Commander in Chief. I am grateful for the continuing support that the Congress has given to this effort, and I look forward to continued cooperation as we move forward toward attainment of our goals in this region.

Sincerely,

WILLIAM J. CLINTON

NOTE: Identical letters were sent to Thomas S. Foley, Speaker of the House of Representatives, and Robert C. Byrd, President pro tempore of the Senate. This letter was released by the Office of the Press Secretary on April 14.

Remarks at the Summer Jobs Conference in Arlington, Virginia
April 14, 1993

Thank you very much. The speech that Octavius gave says more than anything I will be able to say today about why it's important to give all of our young people a chance to get a work experience and to continue to learn, to merge the nature of learning and work; why it's important to honor the efforts of people like Jerry Levin and Nancye Combs and Pat Irving and all of those who are here.

I want to thank the Secretaries of Labor and Education and all the people who work with them for sponsoring this; my good friend, Governor Wilder, for being here and for speaking; and all of the business and local community leaders from the city and county and State level from around America who are here.

This has been a pretty fun day. I loved hearing the young people sing. It was music to my ears because it is their future that we are really struggling about. A year and a half ago I began the quest to seek the Presidency because I was concerned about their future, because I believe that our country, which had always been a bea-

con of hope for the young, had too little opportunity, was too divided among ourselves across lines of income and race and region and other ways, without a vision to take us into the future.

I entered with the hope that together we could create more opportunity and insist on much more responsibility from all of our people. But in the process we might recreate the best of America's community, knowing that together we could always do more than we could individually and that we might secure our future.

All of you here today are committed to that. The 1,000 jobs that Jerry Levin has committed Time-Warner to is symbolic of the commitments made by many of the private sector people who are here, and those who are around the country. The work that Nancye Combs does, and the successes of all the young people like those on this stage, and especially the eloquent statement by Octavius Jeffers, all those things show that together we know what we need to do, and we're on the right track.

Last July when I was traveling across America's heartland in my luxurious bus, I visited Seneca High School in Louisville, Kentucky. And there I met young people and business people who were participating in the Louisville Education and Employment Partnership. I saw what Nancye Combs talked about today. I saw how the young people were making an extra effort to succeed both in school and at work. I saw, as I have seen many times in my own State, the principle illustrated that Octavius talked about: that for millions of American young people it is really an impediment to both their learning and their ability to be good workers, to draw a sharp dividing line between what is work and what is learning.

In the world in which we are living, the average young person will change the nature of work seven or eight times in a lifetime. We must learn to merge the work world and the learning world much better. And we must determine that all of our young people see the opportunities that some of them have had showcased here today.

Whether you're in business or in government or in education, you know that we have a big job to do when it comes to building a future that really, honestly includes opportunity for all of our people. There are still a lot of people who say, "Well, things are pretty good here in Washington. Everything's fine. The best thing we can do about this whole thing is nothing." They all have jobs, all the people who say that. They all have health insurance. They all have a pretty good education. And they all have a pretty secure knowledge that they'll be okay no matter what happens. I say that not to be either political or unduly critical but to point out that one of the great challenges of this age for every advanced nation, everyone, is to fully develop the capacities of all of its people and then find work for them to do.

All the European countries have higher unemployment rates than we do but also stronger support systems for the unemployed. The Japanese unemployment rate has been going up. They're going to adopt a stimulus that, even if you count it in its most rigorous terms, is 3 or 4 times bigger than the one that I have proposed to create jobs. In West Germany alone, the unemployment rate is now about as high as ours.

This is a big problem for advanced nations. It costs a lot of money to add an extra employee, with a lot of pressure from low-wage producers in other countries that are growing their own economies and trying to provide new opportunity for their people. But it is especially important for America for two reasons. One is, we have a whole lot of folks who, unless we move aggressively, will not have the education and skills we need to be competitive and productive in a nation like this. The second is, even if we educate them all, if there aren't jobs, they will be robbed of the fruits of their educational labors. People need to be able to work in this country.

We have always had some unemployment, and indeed, some of it is normal. You've always got some people leaving jobs and moving around the country and doing first one thing and another. We have now, at this moment in our history, the necessity for all big organizations, including the Government, to reexamine the way they are organized and to ask whether there are too many people working at some kinds of jobs. But in the whole, we must still be able to create jobs in a country like America, to provide people with the chance to work.

It's going to be difficult for me to make the welfare reform proposals that I will make to Congress in the next couple of months. It's going to be hard for me to make those work if at the end of all this work to get off welfare, there isn't a job.

So we have two tasks. One is to develop the capacity of the American people to perform without regard to race or income or the circumstances of their birth. The other is to make sure that there are some opportunities for them to bring to bear for their talent and to be rewarded with a paycheck. It is a great challenge. I do not pretend that all of the answers are simple. But I know if you want to ask the American people, all of them, to be more responsible, if you want to recreate a sense of community in this country that bridges the lines of race and income and region, you have got to have opportunity in that mix.

A part of our vision for America has to be a future for every young person in this country who's willing to play by the rules and work hard and strive for the end of the rainbow. There has to be something at the end of that rainbow. And that is what we are basically here to talk about today: What can we all do as partners, recognizing none of us can do it alone, to develop the capacities of our people to succeed wherever they live and whatever their background. And then, what can we do to make sure that there's something there for them to do?

The summer jobs program we're discussing today is an integral part of that plan, because it will promote the values of work and opportunity and fairness, community. It will put the people first, and it does have a partnership between the public and private sector.

I said when I addressed the United States Congress in February on this program that I would seek to create about 700,000 extra summer jobs from Government sources and then challenge the American business community to meet that target so that we can create more than a million new summer jobs over and above what had been created before.

Many, many people have responded to that challenge. And Jerry is just a shining example of that which has been replicated in this room and around the country, people who are going to do more than they otherwise would in the private sector to give young people a work experience. And it is terribly important.

I want to emphasize that this summer jobs program is part of an overall commitment to increase the capacity of the American people, from retraining defense workers who lose their jobs and other adults who need to acquire new skills, to improving the transition from school to work for young people who don't go to college but do need at least 2 years of post-high school training either on the job or in a community college or a vocational setting, so that they can be competitive workers, making it possible for more people to go on to college who do want to go. All these things are part and parcel of a comprehensive plan.

It's also important, as I said, that we create more jobs. The emergency jobs program that I asked the Congress to adopt would create a half a million extra jobs over the next year and a half, and that would reduce the unemployment rate by a half a percent. It would also enable us to absorb more young people coming into the work force in jobs that otherwise will not be created. It also will help a lot of cities and counties to invest in things that need to be done at the grassroots level: projects long delayed, water projects, sewer projects, park projects, new industries and particularly in small- and medium-size communities, a whole range of things that will improve the economy and improve the environment.

The summer jobs program is an important part of that because we have tried for the first time, through the work of the Labor Department and the Education Department and through reaching out to people like you, to make this more than just a one-shot summer jobs program; to integrate it with private sector efforts; to hopefully replicate it in each coming summer; to move these young people into further educational opportunities and to further job opportunities; and to have a strong, meaningful education component to these summer jobs, something that the United States Government has never fully emphasized before.

A lot of these young people, as you well know, because they come from difficult backgrounds, because they go to school in difficult and challenging circumstances, need extra help in building their basic skills in math and language, reasoning, and in other areas. And a lot of educational studies show that young people who have difficulty in school often forget as much as 30 percent of what they learn over the summer and then that has to be repeated the next year.

What we are trying to do here is to give people the opportunity to learn good work habits and to reinforce their learning skills and to put them together, and then, hopefully, over the next couple of years, if our entire program passes, to give every school in this country the opportunity to have a good work and learning environment.

There will be more applied academics, more opportunities for people to learn and work during the school year, so that this will not simply be an isolated moment for these young folks but will be a part of building a whole new educational experience, a whole new work experience, and moving on a pathway to a better future.

The summer jobs programs are not designed to be make-work jobs. They're designed to make a future for the people holding the job. And that's what they will do. In the process, they'll help to build local communities, to strengthen local economies, to solve local problems—real jobs renovating housing, repairing public buildings, doing clerical work, providing nursing assistance in hospitals, supervising and training children at child care centers, and learning all the way, challenging young people to learn while they earn but letting them earn.

You know, it's very difficult to make a case

to people who have never seen opportunity on their own street that they should do this, that, or the other thing if there's no evidence of the opportunity that's at the end of the effort. I have not been sparing in going for the last year-and-a-half into places where it isn't exactly popular to say it and say I wanted to reform the welfare system; I wanted to toughen child support; I wanted to require people to work; I was sick and tired of people being irresponsible in the use of guns on the streets, and I wanted to change all that. But if you're going to summon people to greater responsibility, you have to reward them when they do the right thing with opportunity.

The young people we propose to put to work under our program will spend 90 hours learning basic skills, such as math, reading, writing, either on the job or in the classroom. They will stretch their minds as well as work up a sweat. They will have a sense of accomplishment. It will literally be a summer challenge but a challenge that will take them into a different life.

So I want to ask all of you to support this effort even as I, as your President, support your effort. At the end of the summer we will evaluate all the young people who participate. We'll see whether they, instead of falling behind over the summer academically as too many young people do, they stayed even or moved ahead. I suspect that they will.

This summer, Secretary Reich and Secretary Riley and I will be visiting many of your communities. We'll really try to learn from you which of these efforts are working, what we should do next summer, how we can build it in to what goes on during the school year, how we can build in our job training efforts and the works that we do with your companies to make sense of this whole thing, so that we maximize the impact of the taxpayer dollar and your private investments as well.

We want to honor the companies and the communities, the business leaders and the young people who do the very best jobs this summer. And again, I want to say to all of you in private business who have matched our effort, I thank you. And to all of you who haven't and those across the country who may listen or learn about this event today, I want to implore other private employers to stretch a little bit to give other young people a chance to work this summer. I'm telling you, we cannot go through another 10 years when we don't give these children any-

thing to say yes to. If we exhort them to do right, we've got to be able to reward them.

When the other speakers were talking, I was sitting up here on the platform, listening and reveling. And they got talking about work, and I got to thinking about all the different things I've done to make a living in my life. When I was 13, I made a very foolish short-term business investment: I set up a comic book stand and sold two trunks full of comic books. Made more money than I had ever had in my life. But if I had saved those trunks, they'd be worth $100,000 today. [*Laughter*] That does not mean young people should not be entrepreneurial. It just means that you can't foresee a generation ahead. I have mowed yards and cleared land and built houses and worked in body shops and the parts departments of a car dealership. And I've done a lot of different things for a living. Some people say I got into politics to escape work. [*Laughter*]

I learned something from every job I ever had. But I grew up in a generation where I literally did not know a living soul, without regard to race or income, who wanted to work who didn't have a job. I grew up in a generation when all you had to really say to people is, get an education, and you'll be all right. You'll get a job, and you'll make more money next year than you did this year. Now I live in a generation full of people, most of whom don't make any more money in real dollars than they did 10 years ago, and they're working longer hours, and they're paying more for the basics of life. And we are now wondering whether we can create the jobs that these young people want.

Now, I want to close by reemphasizing these two things: It doesn't matter what kind of economic policies this administration pursues or how much productivity increases there are in the private sector. If young Americans don't get a good education, don't learn how to work, and can't be productive, those jobs will not be created in this country. Machines will do the work, or the work will be done off-shore by people who have the same skill levels and can work for a third or a fourth or a fifth the wages. So nothing we can do economically will matter unless we build the skills and capacities of America's work force. And anybody that pretends otherwise is just kidding.

On the other hand, we need to be honest. Every wealthy country in the world, including the United States, is having difficulty creating jobs. If I knew everything that needs to be done, I'd be glad to tell you, and we could just call off the whole deliberations of Congress and everything else. I don't have all the answers. But I know this: Doing nothing is not the answer.

And so the jobs program that I have presented to Congress, with the summer jobs, with the money for the cities and the counties, through the community development program, with the infrastructure money, is a small part of a big budget. It is an attempt to engage in an experiment to see whether or not, with the economy recovering in terms of corporate profit, we can give a little boost to it, give opportunities to young people, create a half a million jobs, and maybe get the engine going again.

Most of the jobs in this program are going to be jobs in the private sector, not Government jobs, even though it's Government money. And the lion's share of the work in rebuilding the American economy obviously will come from the private sector. That's the kind of system we have, and it works pretty well.

But this is the challenge we have. So I ask all of you here today to support the summer jobs program, to ask your friends and neighbors to support it, to go back home and ask your employers to make a little extra effort, to do what you can to help me pass the funds to create the 700,000 jobs that the United States Government should create this summer, so that together we can have this partnership. Because more than anything else, we have to give a future, a future that our young people can believe in.

We need to send them a message that here in America if you study hard and work hard, if you obey the law and contribute something to your community, you will be rewarded by your country. You can build a future from your own dreams.

That has always been the promise of America. Together that's what this summer of challenge needs to be: a reaffirmation of the promise of America for so many young people to whom that promise has been an illusion. We can make it a reality.

Thank you very much.

NOTE: The President spoke at 11:22 a.m. in the Regency Ballroom at the Hyatt Regency Hotel. In his remarks, he referred to Octavius Jeffers, 1992 Summer Youth Program participant; Jerry Levin, chairman of the board, Time-Warner, Inc.; Nancye Combs, chair, Private Industry Council; and Patricia Irving, president and chief executive officer, Private Industry Council of Philadelphia.

Nomination for Posts at the Transportation, Commerce, and Defense Departments and the Overseas Private Investment Corporation
April 14, 1993

The President announced his intention today to nominate Albert Herberger to be Administrator of the Federal Maritime Administration, Department of Transportation; Loretta Dunn to be Assistant Secretary of Commerce for Import Administration; and Christopher Finn to be Executive Vice President of the Overseas Private Investment Corporation, U.S. International Development Cooperation Agency.

Additionally, he has approved the appointments of Joan Yim to be Deputy Administrator of the Federal Maritime Administration, Alice Maroni to be Principal Deputy Comptroller of the Department of Defense, and Deborah Castleman to be Deputy Assistant Secretary of Defense for Command, Control, and Communications.

"We are continuing to move forward with putting together a Government of excellent, diverse Americans who share my commitment to changing the way that Washington works," said the President. "These six people I am naming today fit that bill."

NOTE: Biographies of the nominees were made available by the Office of the Press Secretary.

Appointment of White House Liaison to the Metropolitan Washington Council of Governments
April 14, 1993

The President has named Loretta Avent, his Special Assistant for Intergovernmental Affairs, to be the White House Liaison to the Metropolitan Washington Council of Governments, the White House announced today.

"Too often in the past, the Federal Government has not been a very good neighbor to the rest of the Washington area," said the President. "I am committed to changing that relationship and have full confidence in Loretta's ability to act effectively to make the White House a full partner in the affairs of the region where we live."

NOTE: A biography of the nominee was made available by the Office of the Press Secretary.

Remarks to Law Enforcement Organizations and an Exchange With Reporters
April 15, 1993

The President. Good afternoon. Ladies and gentlemen, 2 months ago I presented a comprehensive plan to reduce our national deficit and to increase our investment in the American people, their jobs, and their economic future. The Federal budget plan passed Congress in record time and created a new sense of hope and opportunity in the country. Then the short-term jobs plan I presented to Congress, which would create a half a million jobs in the next 2 years, passed the House of Representatives 2 weeks ago. It now has the support of a majority of the United States Senate.

All of these Members of Congress know it's time to get the economy moving again, to get job growth going again, to get a fast start on the investments we need to build a lasting prosperity. Unfortunately, a minority of the Members of the United States Senate have used gridlock tactics to prevent their colleagues from working the will of the majority on the jobs bill.

When Congress returns, I ask every Senator from every State and from both parties to remember what is at stake. The issue is not politics, it's people. Sixteen million of them are looking for full-time jobs and can't find them. These men and women don't care about who's up or down in Washington. They care about paying the rent and meeting the mortgage payment, about putting food on the table and buying shoes for their children, about regaining a sense of dignity that comes from doing a day's work and supporting their families and drawing a paycheck. They're asking those of us who have the privilege of serving to put aside politics and do something now to move our economy forward.

I am prepared to do that. And I have been working with the Senate to come up with an adjusted package that meets some of the concerns of those who've been blocking action on the jobs plan. I'm willing to compromise, so long as we keep the focus on jobs, keep the focus on growth, and keep the focus on meeting unmet national needs.

Our opponents have been asking for a smaller package. Today I ask them to join me in determining exactly what kind and what size package Congress can approve that actually meets the needs of the American people.

But even as we make those reductions, and the package will be smaller, I believe we must address problems that are on the minds of millions of Americans, and one in particular, and that is the need to toughen law enforcement in our society to deal with the dramatic rise in violent crime.

So I will ask, even in this reduced package, for an additional $200 million in Federal funding to help local communities to rehire police officers who have been laid off because of the fiscal problems caused by the national recession. Together with a matching effort by local governments, this could put as many as 10,000 police officers back on the job and back on the beat in communities all across our Nation. At a time when too many of our people live in fear of violent crime, when too many businesses have closed and too many people have lost their jobs because people are afraid to leave their homes, rehiring thousands of officers is one of the best investments America can make. And I ask both Houses of Congress to make that investment in our people's safety and in their peace of mind.

I believe in the need for strong Federal action to keep the economy going toward recovery and to create jobs. Make no mistake about it: I will fight for these priorities as hard as I ever have. I will never forget that the people sent me here to fight for their jobs, their future, and for fundamental change.

I want to thank the police officers who are here today and tell you that not a single one of them knew before they came here that I had determined to ask for more money in this jobs bill to rehire police officers. They came here because they believe in the summer jobs portion of the package. And I want them to be free to talk about that. They came here not out of any law enforcement concern other than the fact that they wanted the kids in this country to have a chance to have jobs this summer, to have safer streets and a brighter and more peaceful future.

I say what I say today not just because it's good for law enforcement but because it's good for the people who live in these communities. I have always supported community policing, not only because it helps to prevent crime and to lower the crime rate but because it cements better relationships between people in law enforcement and the people that they're hired to protect. It reduces the chances of abusive action by police officers and increases the chances of harmony and safe streets at the same time.

These are the kinds of things that we are trying to do. I promised in my campaign that I'd do everything I could to put another 100,000 police officers on the street over the next 4 years. This makes a good downpayment on that. This keeps in mind the core of the jobs package. And this will help us to move forward.

So I ask the people in the Senate who have blocked the jobs bill, let's work together. I can accept a reduced package if you will increase your commitment to safe streets. I do not accept the fact that we should reduce our commitment to summer jobs or to building our infrastructure or to doing those other things that will create real and lasting prosperity for our people. I have done my part now to end the gridlock; I ask you to do yours.

I want now to give the people who are here with me on the platform a chance to make some remarks and to be heard by the American people, beginning with Janet Reno, the distinguished Attorney General.

[At this point, Attorney General Reno spoke, followed by Robert T. Scully, executive director, National Association of Police Organizations; Raymond McGrath, president, International Brotherhood of Police Officers; Robert B. Kliesmet, president, International Union of Police Associations; and Dewey R. Stokes, national president, Fraternal Order of Police.]

Value Added Tax

Q. Mr. President, can you tell us, do you think that the jobs package could be put in further jeopardy by controversy over the suggestion of a VAT tax at this point in the congressional dialog?

The President. Oh, no, not at all. I think it should have—they wouldn't have any relationship one to the other. First of all, I've made absolutely no decision on that. You should know that there's a lot of support in the business community and the labor community. People have asked us to consider that because of the enormous burden of the present system on many of our major employers, particularly many of those that we depend upon to generate jobs and to carry the strength of this economy. But I have made absolutely no decision that would even approach that, on that or any other kind of general tax.

Q. Do you personally believe that the American public is ready to have another tax to pay for health care? I mean, apart from what business and labor leaders have said——

The President. I'm not going to speculate on that. I will say this: The real issue is how quickly we could recycle the benefits of all the savings to cover the cost. Everyone knows that if you do what we're proposing to do, if you streamline the insurance system, if you fix the system so that there's no longer an enormous economic incentive to overutilize or overprovide certain services, if you provide primary and preventive care in places where it isn't now, every single analysis shows absolutely massive savings to the health care system. The real question is whether you can transfer those savings to cover those who have no coverage now or those who have virtually no coverage so that you provide people the security.

I have no idea. The polls say that, but I don't know. All I know is the polls that I see in the press, that many of you have commissioned, they say overwhelmingly the American people want the security of an affordable health care system.

But I don't think that has anything to do with this stimulus, and it certainly shouldn't have. People want a job first and foremost. They want that more than anything else.

Yes.

Stimulus Package

Q. Now that you've announced your willingness to compromise on the stimulus package, can you tell us what parts of your package you consider vital and uncompromisable? I assume summer jobs is one.

The President. I want the summer jobs, I want the highway program, and I want the police program. Let me say this: I still intend to fully and aggressively push the crime bill, which did not pass the Congress last year. This is a supplement to that, not a substitute for it in any way. But I think we need to do that.

I think we need the Ryan White funds because of the enormous health care burdens to the communities that are inordinately and disproportionately affected by the problems of caring for people with AIDS. And there are several other things that I think should be done. We

have to do the Agriculture Department meat inspectors; the safety of the public depends on that.

I don't think any of it should be cut, but I have given Senator Mitchell and Senator Byrd—I've talked to them. And Senator Dole called me yesterday to discuss this, and I told him that I would call him back. I called him back last night in New Hampshire, and we discussed this. And I basically asked them to talk today and said that I would not make any statements about any specifics until at least they had a chance to talk to see whether or not they could reach some accord.

So I don't want to be any more specific than I have been already. And let's see if they can talk it out.

Yes.

Q. When you talked to Senator Dole and Senator Mitchell did you tell them about your—[*inaudible*]—increase also, that $200 million, that you want that as part of the package?

The President. I did. I left word for Senator Mitchell last night about it. When I talked to Senator Dole—I don't remember for sure—I do not believe I mentioned it. But I did tell him that I was prepared to reduce the package and I wanted to break the gridlock. And I told him that I was working on a reformulation of it in the hope that it would become even more focused on jobs and the kinds of issues that I thought the American people wanted us to address. And this is certainly consistent with that.

Thank you.

NOTE: The President spoke at 2:52 p.m. in the Rose Garden at the White House.

Nomination for Posts at the United States Information Agency and the Board for International Broadcasting
April 15, 1993

The President today announced his intention to nominate American University president and former State Department Assistant Secretary Joseph Duffey to be Director of the United States Information Agency. The President also designated Daniel Mica Chairman of the Board for International Broadcasting.

"Joe Duffey's expertise in the fields of education, communications, and foreign affairs is vast and will serve him well as he takes the helm at USIA and works to promote the ideals of democracy and freedom abroad," the President said.

Mr. Mica becomes Chairman of the Board

for International Broadcasting after serving as a member of the board since 1991.

"Dan Mica has done an excellent job on the Board of International Broadcasting, and I expect he will continue as Chairman to promote the cause of democracy abroad," the President said.

NOTE: Biographies of the nominees were made available by the Office of the Press Secretary.

Exchange With Reporters Prior to Discussions With Prime Minister Kiichi Miyazawa of Japan
April 16, 1993

Bosnia

Q. Mr. President, we understand that Srebrenica is about to fall and some 60,000 Bosnian Muslims may be evacuated or surrender on your watch. That must be pretty painful.

The President. I regret that it's happening. We met and discussed this morning what our other options are and whether our allies might now be willing to take further action. We may know some more before the end of the day.

Q. Do you expect some military action to do something about this?

The President. We're looking at a number of options. I don't want to rule in or out any, except that we've never considered the introduction of American ground forces as you know. But I hope that the gravity of the situation will develop a consensus among the United Nations partners. We'll see.

Japan-U.S. Trade

Q. Has the widening of the trade deficit with Japan—does that add importance to this meeting today, sir?

The President. Sure. Of course.

[At this point, one group of reporters left the room, and another group entered.]

Japan's Support for Aid to Russia

Q. Mr. President, would you mind explaining to us what you meant when you said to President Yeltsin, Japanese yes often means no?

The President. I don't know whether to say yes or no.

Prime Minister Miyazawa. Remember the song "Yes, We Have No Bananas"? The idea is, I think——

The President. Bananas. Yes. That's it.

Prime Minister Miyazawa. ——every language has its own peculiarity.

Japan-U.S. Discussions

Q. President, are you talking about the exchange rate today with Mr. Miyazawa?

The President. We haven't had a chance to start our conversation. I think we'll talk about a lot of things today, many things.

Q. What kind of talks do you think are top priority at this meeting with Mr. Prime Minister Miyazawa?

Prime Minister Miyazawa. You'll know in 2 hours. *[Laughter]*

NOTE: The exchange began at 10:33 a.m. in the Oval Office at the White House. A tape was not available for verification of the content of this exchange.

The President's News Conference With Prime Minister Kiichi Miyazawa of Japan
April 16, 1993

The President. Good afternoon. I'm delighted to welcome Prime Minister Miyazawa to Washington and the White House. I especially appreciate his making this very long journey so soon after he hosted the foreign and finance ministers of the G–7 in Tokyo in discussing aid to Russia.

There is no more important relationship for the United States than our alliance with Japan. We are the world's largest economies, with 40 percent of the world's GNP between us. Our security ties have fostered a generation of peace in the Asia-Pacific region and remain critical to the region's continued stability and prosperity.

As we survey the key security challenges of this decade—supporting reform in Russia, advancing the Middle East peace process, efforts toward reconciliation and peacekeeping from Somalia to Cambodia—it is clear that there must be sustained cooperation between the United States and Japan. To help us meet these challenges I have stressed with the Prime Minister the need for some change in our relations. The cold war partnership between our two countries is outdated. We need a new partnership based on a longer term vision and, above all, based on mutual respect and responsibility.

There have always been three elements to our relationship with Japan: our economic dealings, our security alliance, and our cooperative efforts on global problems. Each is essential to our relationship, and each must serve our mutual self-interests. But during the cold war, security relations often overshadowed other considerations, especially economic concerns. In today's world, as I have often said, the United States cannot be strong abroad unless it is strong at home. And our strength at home depends increasingly on open and equitable engagement with our major trading partners. That requires that we now pay special attention to the economic side of our relationship.

Our security partnership is strong. That relationship has been an anchor for Pacific stability for two generations. It remains fundamental to both our interests. The United States intends to remain fully engaged in Asia and committed to our strategic alliance and our political partnership with Japan.

The Prime Minister and I discussed a range of security matters in the Pacific region that concern both of us, including efforts to gain the fullest possible accounting of our POW's and MIA's in Vietnam and North Korea's refusal to comply with the international nuclear inspections and standards, which causes us serious concern. Because of the importance of our security relationship, we will maintain close working ties between our two defenses. And I am

pleased that the Prime Minister will be meeting later today with Defense Secretary Les Aspin.

We also reviewed many global issues that challenge both our nations. In particular, we talked about the extraordinary meeting of G–7 foreign and finance ministers just completed in Tokyo to provide mutual support for Russian economic and democratic reforms. I appreciate the Prime Minister's leadership in convening that meeting. We agreed that the success of these reforms is critical to world peace and prosperity. I believe both our nations understand the stakes and stand ready to work in partnership with President Yeltsin and Russia's other reformers. We look forward to the G–7 summit this July in Tokyo and to Russian participation in the G–7-plus meeting.

But economics were at the heart of our discussions. I stressed that the rebalancing of our relationship in this new era requires an elevated attention to our economic relations. That must begin with an honest appraisal of each country and our mutual responsibilities. The fact is that I have enormous admiration for Japan's economic performance. The Japanese have been pioneers in high quality manufacturing. Their record of innovation and prosperity has been built on hard work and social cooperation. But we and many countries have other concerns as well. I stressed to the Prime Minister that I am particularly concerned about Japan's growing global current account and trade surpluses and deeply concerned about the inadequate market access for American firms, products, and investors in Japan.

I recognize that these are complex issues. But the simple fact is that it is harder to sell in Japan's market than in ours. America is accepting the challenge of change, and so, too, must Japan.

For our part, the United States is making economic renewal over the long term our highest priority. And we are not making the hard decisions many of our trading partners have urged us for years to make, required to put our economic house in order. Our good friends, like Japan, for some time have urged us to do this, and we are attempting to do it, by bringing down our deficit through a combination of spending cuts and tax increases and committing ourselves to long-term investment.

It is important that Japan lead the way to global economic growth. The Prime Minister's newly announced stimulus program is a very good first step toward stronger domestic growth in Japan. But as in America, it must be part of a continued and sustained effort. Japan's goal must be to become one of the engines of growth that creates jobs not only in Japan but throughout the world.

In addition, the Prime Minister and I reaffirmed our commitment to lead the Uruguay round to an early and successful conclusion. We are committed to making the Asia-Pacific Economic Cooperation Organization a vehicle for trade liberalization in the region. And I look forward to the United States hosting that organization in Seattle later this year.

Robust economic growth in America and Japan is in everyone's interest. That's why I hope our own Congress will pass our jobs package and the budget, just as I hope Japan will continue taking steps to boost its own economic growth. But macroeconomic action alone is not enough. I am concerned not only about how much we sell but about what we sell. Our companies that manufacture high-quality, high-wage goods are among the most competitive in the world. If their products are to be a greater part of our exports to Japan, if our workers are to receive their fair share of the benefits of trade, Japan's markets must be more open. United States companies bear the responsibility for providing high-quality and competitively priced goods, but when they do, as increasingly they do today, Japan's markets must receive them.

When our two nations take these economic steps individually and together, we will be the two strongest drivers of global economic growth. That growth is essential not only for our own prosperity but also for the success of the world's many new and emerging democracies.

In order to take these steps, we also need to develop a new framework for our two nations to address concretely our economic agenda, the structural and sectoral issues that can expand growth and increase trade and investment flows in key industries. This framework should also enable us to discuss other issues in which we can cooperate, such as technology and the environment. Within the next 3 months, the Prime Minister and I expect to have a plan for specific negotiations that can then occur on an expedited basis in these areas. The Prime Minister and I also agreed to meet twice annually, including during the G–7 annual summit. We have agreed to do this because we believe this new partnership deserves our highest priority from the high-

est levels of our Government.

I view today's discussion with the Prime Minister as a very positive step in our effort to begin a new and mutually beneficial stage in the long and productive friendship between the United States and Japan. Each spring, all who reside here in the Nation's Capital have a wonderful reminder of that friendship. Just blocks from here at the Tidal Basin, the circle of flowering cherry trees, begun as a gift from the people of Japan, are the uplifting image that defines the start of our season of hope.

Today I believe the new partnership we are forging between our nations can help to usher in a season of hope not only for ourselves but for the world as well, the season when we restore economic growth, when we expand economic opportunities in our own countries and elsewhere, when we help to fuel the worldwide movement toward democracy, and when we help to lay the foundation for peace and progress in the next century. I look forward to working with Prime Minister Miyazawa in the coming months as we join together to build that new partnership.

Mr. Prime Minister.

Prime Minister Miyazawa. Mr. President, thank you for your kind words, and thank you also for your very warm welcome today.

I have been looking forward to this important meeting. May I say that I have a sense of accomplishment in that we have built a personal relationship of mutual trust. I am convinced that our new partnership can respond to the needs of a new era. Our partnership is crucial for making the world more peaceful and prosperous. The President and I have, therefore, agreed to meet at least once every year, separate from the G–7 process.

Let me comment briefly on four areas of our discussions today. First, we affirmed the continuing importance of Japan-U.S. security treaty in the post-cold-war era. Second, on the economy, I welcome the President's leadership in tackling the budget deficit problem head on. On our part, Japan's new '93 fiscal budget is geared to stimulating domestic demand. And 3 days ago, my government decided on an additional package of expansionary measures totaling $116 billion to further stimulate our domestic demand. This will certainly accelerate our economic growth.

I also stressed our continuing efforts to increase market access. I further explained to the

President that my government has decided to undertake a new funds for development initiative to facilitate financial flow from Japan to developing countries. These respective efforts by both Japan and the United States are critically important for ensuring world economic growth. They are also vital for strengthening the foundation of our partnership.

In the area of our bilateral trade and economic relations, I stressed to the President that our economic prosperity is founded on our deep economic interdependence. We must nurture this relationship with a cooperative spirit based upon the principle of free trade. This cannot be realized with managed trade nor under the threat of unilateralism.

Our relationship must be a plus-sum relationship, not a zero-sum one. It is in this context that I expressed serious concern over some trends in the United States. I explained my government's policy to continue efforts to increase our market access. But this must be done with parallel efforts of the United States to strengthen competitiveness, export promotion under the free trade system.

On the Uruguay round negotiations, we cannot allow them to fail. And after 7 years, we must reach a realistic agreement through further negotiations.

Recognizing the importance of advancing our new economic partnership, we need to develop a new framework for our two nations to address the structural and sectoral issues of both countries that can promote trade and the investment flows in key industries, as well as enhance our cooperation in such areas as environment, technology, and development of human resources. Within the next 3 months, the President and I expect to create such a new framework.

Third, on Russia, Japan chaired the meeting of foreign and finance ministers of G-7 countries, subsequently joined by the Russian ministers, which ended yesterday in Tokyo. I cooperated closely with President Clinton on the preparations for this meeting, talking over the phone a few times. I believe the joint ministerial meeting sent a strong message of support for Russia's efforts for democratic and economic reform, and its law and justice foreign policy. At the opening session of that meeting, I announced a $1,820,000,000 package of Japan's bilateral assistance to Russia. Today the President and I discussed how we would follow up and build on the results of that meeting as Russia undergoes a delicate period of transition.

Fourth, the dynamic growth of the Asia-Pacific region promises benefits for the entire world. But we must bear in mind that the region is undergoing changes with risks and instabilities. American presence and Japan-U.S. security treaty are indispensable, stabilizing elements for the region. I assured the President that Japan would continue to provide host nation support which amounts to $4,600,000,000 in the year 1993. Japan will also work together with the United States to build more cohesiveness and the feeling of reassurance through regional dialog and cooperation.

Finally, let me make a personal observation. For half a century, I have been involved in bilateral regulations in one way or another. Now, talking to the youthful new leader of this great nation, who has emerged at an historic time of changes in the world, I have felt optimism for the unbounded possibilities of our two nations working together in our new partnership to bring a better world for all of us.

Thank you very much.

Bosnia

Q. Mr. President, if all bets are off now, are you seriously considering the use of air power in Bosnia against the Serbs and also lifting the arms embargo? Have you given any kind of ultimatum to the Serbs? And what kind of a feedback are you getting from Russia and the allies for stronger action?

The President. Let me try to answer some of those, anyway. We began this morning with a discussion of the situation in Bosnia. And the Secretary of State has been on the phone quite a bit today, consistent with his obligation to be part of the meeting with the Prime Minister. All I can tell you is that, at this point, I would not rule out any option except the option that I have never ruled in, which was the question of American ground troops.

I would also remind all of you that I have operated from the beginning under the assumption that whatever is done must be done within the framework of a multilateral cooperation, that this was not something the United States could effectively do alone.

Since we decided to become involved there after the situation was already quite severe, we have dramatically increased the availability of humanitarian aid, secured a resolution to enforce the no-fly zone, become involved in the

Vance-Owen negotiations in a way that got the Bosnians to agree, and have worked on strengthening the sanctions which, while not doing much to stem the violence in Bosnia, certainly have exacted a price from the Serbians economically.

Those are the things that I have been able to do, taking a situation that was in quite bad shape when I found it and within the limits of multilateralism. I wouldn't rule out other steps. I wouldn't rule them in. All I can tell you is that I'm going to be spending a lot of time on this today, and I'm very concerned about it. And I'm outraged that the Serbians, when given the opportunity, did not sign on to the Vance-Owen process.

Japan-U.S. Trade

Q. I would like to ask to the President—[*inaudible*]—tough talk with the Prime Minister regarding trading issue, do you think this is the right way for the United States to get along with Japan? And my other question is do you have—[*inaudible*]—a substantial result from this meeting regarding trading?

The President. First of all, let me reiterate what I said. Our relationship is built on shared values and a commitment to democracy. It has a security aspect. It has an aspect of cooperation on global affairs—and we discussed those in great detail—and it has a bilateral economic aspect. Two nations can be great friends and can admire each other greatly and still not agree on every issue.

We have had a long and substantial trade deficit with Japan, which is highly concentrated in manufacturing and in certain sectors of manufacturing where we now believe we are competitive in price and quality: Autos, auto parts, electronics, supercomputers, semiconductors—you know the list—agriculture—as well as I do.

The difference—I don't want to characterize the issue as tough or not tough. I want it to be different. I want our relationship now to focus on the specific sectors in which there are problems and on the kind of structural difference which makes it difficult for us to ever meet. We have differences in patent law, differences in antitrust law, differences in the way our financial services and our other services sector works. And what I asked the Prime Minister for was a change in the direction of our relationship so we could focus on specific sectors and specific structures, with the view toward getting results.

I would just say that we have gotten some results in the semiconductor area where there was a specific agreement. But there's also been some progress in the auto parts area where there was a more general agreement. I think when we focus on specific areas, even though we may differ about specifically how we should do that, we tend to make progress. And I say this in a way of hoping that will lead us to greater cooperation.

The world needs a strong Japan. The world needs a strong United States. The world needs these two countries to cooperate. And it can only happen if we are making real progress on this trade deficit.

Q. The trade deficit has been stubborn for many years. It just went up again today, the Commerce Department reported. Why do you think that you can do something different now that your predecessors couldn't do? The Prime Minister just said that access for American products to Japanese markets would have to go along the lines of free trade. Would you like to see specific help for specific industries and targets?

The President. Well, let me reiterate what I said. I would like to have a focus on specific sectors of the economy, and I would like to obviously have specific results. We had a semiconductor agreement which gave some hope that this approach could work. There was also a more general commitment in the area of auto parts which has shown some progress.

Let me say that I think there are three or four things working today which may give us more results: Number one, the appreciation of the Japanese yen; number two, the stimulus program, which the Prime Minister has talked about—the last time we had a measurable drop in our trade deficit with Japan, it was after Japan adopted a stimulus program; number three, a breathtaking increase in productivity and quality by American manufacturers over the last several years, which makes us the low cost producer in many of these areas now; and number four, a different approach, commitment to focus sector by sector. The Prime Minister—let's not paper this over—there are some differences still between the Prime Minister and me about what kinds of agreements we should make, sector by sector, on these structural issues. But if we focus on them and talk about them specifically, honestly, and openly, I believe this is very different from what has happened in the past.

Japan's Support for Aid to Russia

Q. Mr. President, what is it that you really wanted to convey to President Yeltsin in Vancouver when you reportedly told him that when Japanese say yes, they often mean no? And secondly, using probably the same degree of candid description, would you care to characterize the Japanese economic activities in the arena of international trade and the economy?

The President. You know, let me say first of all, the world would be a sad place if people could never say anything in an offhand manner without having it turn into an international incident. I remember when I was elected, someone in your country suggested that Presidents always spoke a lot of hot air once they got elected. I took no offense at that. That's a part of the daily life.

I think your Prime Minister made the best statement of all when he said it reminded him of that old American song "Yes, We Have No Bananas." You asked me a question, what I meant; I don't know whether to tell you yes or no. I don't know what I meant anymore. [*Laughter*]

I will say, let me make the real point: The Prime Minister answered the question with a resounding yes by agreeing, number one, to host the meeting of foreign and finance ministers in Tokyo to discuss Russian aid and, number two, to a very aggressive commitment of $1.8 billion to help to alleviate the situation and to support Russian reform.

So Japan's answer to this problem was clearly yes, capital Y-E-S, yes.

Stimulus Package

Q. Mr. President, you mentioned the stimulus program that Miyazawa's government has put forward and described it as a good first step. If that's a good first step, sir, is it really reasonable to argue that your own stimulus program, less than a seventh of that, is a first step of any significance at all?

The President. I think it is because the circumstances are different. Let's go back to the mid-seventies, and perhaps Prime Minister Miyazawa could fill in the blanks, but if my memory is right, Japan had a very large budget deficit about 15 years ago, which they then set about to erase. And they worked very hard to do it. They are in a surplus position now if you take all their government budgets together, social insurance and all of that. They're in a

surplus position. So they're in a position to have a bigger stimulus. Also, they have a big trade surplus with the rest of the world, so the economic prescription to get growth back in their country and also to reduce the trade surplus would be to dramatically expand domestic demand.

We have a large trade deficit, and we are in an economic recovery, that is, our projected growth rate, economic growth rate is larger than the Japanese projected rate before their stimulus. But our problem is that even in recovery we, like the Europeans, weren't generating any new jobs. So what I am trying to do here is to fire not a shotgun, but a rifle to try to take advantage of the economic recovery and the fact that I do have a long-term dramatic reduction of the deficit which more than covers the cost of this modest stimulus to create new jobs. So, there are two different programs with two different objectives. I think both of them are quite well-founded.

North Korea

Q. Did you discuss options against North Korea with Prime Minister Miyazawa? Also, could you tell us which is the United States policy, sanctions or direct talk with North Korea?

The President. We discussed the situation in North Korea and what our options were and what could be done within the next couple of months to try to persuade North Korea, number one, not to withdraw from the NPT regime and, number two, not to pursue an aggressive development program for nuclear weapons. And we talked about the relative merits of both sanctions and persuasion and who might be able to talk to North Korea and what might be able to be done to convince them that this was not the way to go. We discussed the whole range of options.

Gay Rights

Q. Mr. President, in an hour or so you're going to meet with gay rights leaders in the Oval Office—the first time in history, apparently, that this has happened—a meeting that mysteriously is closed to television cameras. Would you (a) like to reconsider that in that it appears that you're trying to make this a very low-key exercise? And secondly, what do you say to the gay rights leaders who regard your decision to skip their march next weekend as something of a snub?

The President. Well, let me first of all answer—I didn't know about the thing being closed. I can't comment on it because I haven't thought about it.

But I don't see how any serious person could claim that I have snubbed the gay community in this country, having taken the position I have not only on the issue of the military but of participation in the Government. I have, I believe it's clear, taken a stronger position against discrimination than any of my predecessors. And it is a position that I believe in very deeply, one that I took publicly in 1991 before there was any organized political support for me in the gay community. It had nothing to do with politics and has everything to do with the fact that I grew up in a segregated society and have very strong feelings about the right of everybody who is willing to work hard and play by the rules to participate in American life.

During the time of the—on Saturday, I'm going to be with the Senate. On Sunday, I'm going to meet with the newspaper publishers. I mean no snub. But Presidents usually don't participate in marches. That has nothing to do with my commitment on the fundamental issue of being antidiscrimination.

Yes, in the back.

Japan-U.S. Trade and Japan's Economy

Q. Mr. President, I know the United States is seeking the result-oriented trade policy. So my question is that the U.S. is also seeking a visible result in the area of macroeconomic problems, such as a sharp decline of the Japanese trade surplus or something?

And that the next question is for Prime Minister Miyazawa. Did you make any commitment in the future of the Japanese economy, such as the 1994 growth rate or a trade surplus or something?

The President. You want me to go first? I'm not sure I entirely understood your question, but let me answer you in this way: When the Prime Minister and I were discussing this meeting in our private one-on-one meeting, he pointed out quite accurately that the last time there was a reduction in the trade deficit that the U.S. has with Japan was after a significant economic stimulus program was adopted several years ago in the eighties which he helped to engineer in a previous capacity.

And then he said, but still we may not get the trade deficit down low enough for the United States purposes, and so perhaps we should examine these things sector by sector as well as some of the structural problems relating to the differences in our laws and the way they operate and some of the way we're organized. Obviously, beyond that in terms of how you get those results, there are still things to be hashed out and differences. But I consider that to be a significant move forward, that we at least have agreed on the conceptual framework in which we will deal with these problems.

Prime Minister Miyazawa. The $116 billion is a sizable amount of money, particularly on top of the $86 billion we committed over this last year. These two stimulus measures are bound to affect the Japanese economy; no doubt about it. By this time of the year, we feel the Japanese economy has picked up, recovering slow but steady, and I am sure that the government-forecasted 3.3 percent growth is, I think, within our reach.

Bosnia

Q. On Bosnia, do you feel that this is a time for American leadership, that sanctions have obviously not had any effect on the Serbian behavior, even though they've had an effect on the Serbian economy? Are you trying to persuade our allies to lift the arms embargo, to take other steps including possibly air strikes? Or do you feel that this is something where your hands are tied by our European partners?

The President. I think all I should say now, because we are engaged in rather intense discussions about this, is that I think the time has come for the United States and Europe to look honestly at where we are and what our options are and what the consequences of various courses of action will be. And I think we have to consider things which at least previously have been unacceptable to some of the Security Council members and some of those in NATO and in other common security arrangements of which the United States is a part.

I do think that the United States, as I have said for a long time now and said during my campaign, has an interest in what happens in Bosnia. I think we have an interest in standing up against the principle of ethnic cleansing. If you look at the turmoil all through the Balkans, if you look at the other places where this could play itself out in other parts of the world, this is not just about Bosnia.

On the other hand, there is reason to be humble when approaching anything dealing with the former Yugoslavia. Everyone remembers the experience of the German army there during World War II. You have only to look at the topography of the country to realize the limits of outside action there. So, we have to be humble in the face of it, and we haven't had a very good hand to play, at least in the last 2½

months since I've been looking closely at this.

But I do think the United States at least has an obligation to force the consideration by all the parties of all responsible options and try to come to the best possible result. And that's what I intend to do.

NOTE: The President's 11th news conference began at 1:59 p.m. in the East Room at the White House.

Letter to Senate Majority Leader George J. Mitchell on the Stimulus Package
April 16, 1993

Dear Mr. Leader:

As the Senate prepares to return Monday to consideration of the pending appropriations bill to create jobs, to boost the economy, and to meet pressing human needs, it is important that we renew our commitment to breaking gridlock and to making government work.

To help accomplish those goals, I recommend you consider changes in the pending legislation to reduce its scope, while leaving unaffected certain key programs in the bill. I understand the procedural situation permits you and Senator Byrd to offer a substitute amendment when the Senate reconvenes. Unfortunately, the rules of the Senate have enabled a minority to block the will of the majority. That makes it necessary for us to step forward and modify the bill in order to meet our objectives. Therefore I recommend you consider offering a substitute that includes these components:

—Leave in place the proposed funding levels for these essential programs to create jobs and to meet human needs: highway construction, summer jobs for young people, childhood immunization, the Ryan White program for AIDS victims, construction of wastewater treatment facilities, hiring meat inspectors, and assistance to small business. Of course, the $4 billion for extended unemployment compensation benefits would be left in place.

—Reduce proportionately the other programs in the bill to bring budget authority down from $16.2 billion to $12 billion. This will require an across-the-board cut in other programs of about 44 percent.
—Target $200 million for grants to local governments to hire police as a means of helping to fight crime and to offset layoffs resulting from the fiscal constraints on local government.

This approach would reduce the budget authority in this bill by approximately 25 percent, but it would create only 18 percent fewer jobs in this fiscal year.

I make this recommendation reluctantly, and regret the unwillingness of the minority to let the Senate act on the original legislation. But our mandate is to achieve change, to move the country forward, and to end business as usual in Washington. By taking the initiative in the face of an unrelenting filibuster I believe we can respond to that mandate and achieve a significant portion of our original goals.

Your advice and counsel, and persistent hard work for the working people of this country are greatly appreciated. You have my respect and the thanks of the millions of Americans in the cities, towns and rural communities across the nation who you are trying to help.

Sincerely,

BILL CLINTON

Nomination for Posts at the Departments of Energy and Education
April 16, 1993

The President announced his intention to nominate two senior officials at the Department of Energy today and one at the Department of Education. At Energy, William Taylor will be Assistant Secretary for Congressional and Legislative Affairs and Tara O'Toole will be Assistant Secretary for Environment, Safety, and Health. Judith Winston will be the General Counsel at the Department of Education.

"I am very pleased that William Taylor, Tara O'Toole, and Judith Winston will be taking positions in my administration," said the President. "All three of these people have distinguished themselves through public service throughout their careers."

NOTE: Biographies of the nominees were made available by the Office of the Press Secretary.

The President's Radio Address
April 17, 1993

Good morning. My voice is coming to you this morning through the facilities of the oldest radio station in America, KDKA in Pittsburgh. I'm visiting the city to meet personally with citizens here to discuss my plans for jobs, health care, and the economy. But I wanted first to do my weekly broadcast with the American people.

I'm told this station first broadcast in 1920 when it reported that year's Presidential elections. Over the past seven decades Presidents have found ways to keep in touch with the people, from whistle-stop tours to fireside chats to the bus tour that I adopted, along with Vice President Gore, in last year's campaign.

Every Saturday morning I take this time to talk with you, my fellow Americans, about the problems on your minds and what I'm doing to try and solve them. It's my way of reporting to you and of giving you a way to hold me accountable. You sent me to Washington to get our Government and economy moving after years of paralysis in policy and a bad experiment with trickle-down economics. You know how important it is for us to make bold, comprehensive changes in the way we do business.

We live in a competitive global economy. Nations rise and fall on the skills of their workers, the competitiveness of their companies, the imagination of their industries, and the cooperative experience and spirit that exists between business, labor, and government. Although many of the economies of the industrialized world are now suffering from slow growth, they've made many of the smart investments and the tough choices which our Government has for too long ignored. That's why many of them have been moving ahead and too many of our people have been falling behind.

We have an economy today that even when it grows is not producing new jobs. We've increased the debt of our Nation by 4 times over the last 12 years, and we don't have much to show for it. We know that wages of most working people have stopped rising, that most people are working longer work weeks, and that too many families can no longer afford the escalating cost of health care.

But we also know that, given the right tools, the right incentives, and the right encouragement, our workers and businesses can make the kinds of products and profits our economy needs to expand opportunity and to make our communities better places to live.

In many critical products today Americans are the low cost, high quality producers. Our task is to make sure that we create more of those kinds of jobs.

Just 2 months ago I gave Congress my plan for long-term jobs and economic growth. It changes the old priorities in Washington and puts our emphasis where it needs to be: on people's real needs, on increasing investments and jobs and education, on cutting the Federal deficit, on stopping the waste which pays no dividends, and redirecting our precious resources toward investment that creates jobs now and lays the groundwork for robust economic growth in the future.

These new directions passed the Congress in record time and created a new sense of hope and opportunity in our country. Then the jobs plan I presented to Congress, which would create hundreds of thousands of jobs, most of them in the private sector in 1993 and 1994, passed the House of Representatives. It now has the support of a majority of the United States Senate. But it's been held up by a filibuster of a minority in the Senate, just 43 Senators. They blocked a vote that they know would result in the passage of our bill and the creation of jobs.

The issue isn't politics. The issue is people. Millions of Americans are waiting for this legislation and counting on it, counting on us in Washington. But the jobs bill has been grounded by gridlock.

I know the American people are tired of business as usual and politics as usual. I know they don't want us to spin our wheels. They want the recovery to get moving. So I have taken a first step to break this gridlock and gone the extra mile. Yesterday I offered to cut the size of this plan by 25 percent, from $16 billion to $12 billion.

It's not what I'd hoped for. With 16 million Americans looking for full-time work, I simply can't let the bill languish when I know that even a compromise bill will mean hundreds of thousands of jobs for our people. The mandate is to act to achieve change and move the country forward. By taking this initiative in the face of an unrelenting Senate talkathon, I think we can respond to your mandate and achieve a significant portion of our original goals.

First, we want to keep the programs as much as possible that are needed to generate jobs and meet human needs, including highway and road construction, summer jobs for young people, immunization for children, construction of waste water sites, and aid to small businesses. We also want to keep funding for extended unemployment compensation benefits for people who have been unemployed for a long time because the economy isn't creating jobs.

Second, I've recommended that all the other programs in the bill be cut across-the-board by a little more than 40 percent.

And third, I've recommended a new element in this program to help us immediately start our attempt to fight against crime by providing $200 million for cities and towns to rehire police officers who lost their jobs during the recession and put them back to work protecting our people. I'm also going to fight for a tough crime bill because the people of this country need it and deserve it.

Now the people who are filibustering this bill, the Republican Senators, say they won't vote for it because it increases deficit spending, because there's extra spending this year that hasn't already been approved. That sounds reasonable, doesn't it? Here's what they don't say. This program is more than paid for by budget cuts over my 5-year budget, and this program is well within the spending limits already approved by the Congress this year.

It's amazing to me that many of these same Senators who are filibustering the bill voted during the previous administration for billions of dollars of the same kind of emergency spending, and much of it was not designed to put the American people to work.

This is not about deficit spending. We have offered a plan to cut the deficit. This is about where your priorities are, on people or on politics.

Keep in mind that our jobs bill is paid for dollar-for-dollar. It is paid for by budget cuts. And it's the soundest investment we can now make for ourselves and our children. I urge all Americans to take another look at this jobs and investment program, to consider again the benefits for all of us when we've helped make more American partners working to ensure the future of our Nation and the strength of our economy.

You know, if every American who wanted a job had one, we wouldn't have a lot of the other problems we have in this country today. This bill is not a miracle; it's a modest first step to try to set off a job creation explosion in this country again. But it's a step we ought to take. And it is fully paid for over the life of our budget.

Tell your lawmakers what you think. Tell them how important the bill is. If it passes, we'll all be winners.

Good morning, and thank you for listening.

NOTE: The President spoke at 10:06 a.m. in the USAir terminal at Pittsburgh International Airport.

Interview With Mike Whitely of KDKA Radio in Pittsburgh, Pennsylvania
April 17, 1993

Mr. Whitely. For everyone listening on KDKA Radio, I'm Mike Whitely, KDKA Radio News. We're here at the Pittsburgh International Airport and with me is the President of the United States, Bill Clinton.

And I'd like to welcome you to the area and to KDKA.

The President. Thank you, Mike. Glad to be here.

Los Angeles Police Trial Verdict

Mr. Whitely. There are a lot of things we'd like to talk about in the brief amount of time we have, but some news is just breaking from Los Angeles. I guess the entire country has been kind of holding their breath, wondering what's going to happen in the trial of the four Los Angeles police officers. We just heard that two of those officers—the sergeant, Sergeant Koon, and Officer Powell—have been found guilty, and two officers have been found not guilty.

It's a situation that's been building for over a year since the first trial and now this trial and this verdict. And I wonder what your thoughts are this morning on how you see the situation in Los Angeles in connection with your administration and what you're trying to do.

The President. Well, first of all, I think the American people should know that this trial, in my judgment, is a tribute to the work and judgment of the jury, as well as to the efforts of the Federal Government in developing the case.

The law under which the officers were tried is a complex one; the standards of proof are complicated. The jury decided that they would convict the sergeant who was responsible for supervising the officers and the officer who on the film did most of the beating. The jury acquitted an officer who kicked Rodney King, but also plainly tried to shield him from some blows, and another officer who was a rookie.

No one knows exactly why they did what they did, but it appears that they really tried to do justice here. They acknowledged that his civil rights were violated. And I think that the American people should take a lot of pride in that. But I hope now we can begin to look ahead and focus on three things: first of all, the importance of trying to bring this country together

and not violate the civil rights of any American; secondly, the importance of renewing our fight against crime.

I think it's important to recognize that in the poorest areas of Los Angeles and many other cities in this country, people may be worried about police abuse, but they're even more worried about crime. It's time that we renewed our efforts to go to community policing: put 100,000 more police officers on the street, pass the Brady bill that would require a waiting period before people could buy a handgun, and do some other things to reduce the vulnerability of our people to violence and drugs.

And the last point I'd like to make is it seems to me that we have got to rededicate ourselves to the economic revitalization of our cities and other economically distressed areas. If you just think about it, if everybody in Los Angeles who wanted a job had one, I don't think we'd have quite as many problems as we do.

I laid out a very ambitious program in the campaign to try to bring private investment and public investment to bear in our cities. I have dispatched the Commerce Secretary, Ron Brown, to California to try to come up with some strategies for that State, because it's our biggest State with our highest unemployment rate, which could then be applied around the country. I want to talk to him and to the Attorney General, to the new head of the NAACP, to Reverend Jackson, and to several other people, and then I'll decide where to go from here with regard to Los Angeles and the other cities of the country.

Stimulus Package

Mr. Whitely. Let's talk about what brings you to the Pittsburgh area today. I guess there's been a lot of discussion on Capitol Hill about your stimulus package. You've been locked in a battle with the GOP. Yesterday, as you said earlier in your radio address, you made some moves to break that gridlock. What brings you to Pittsburgh, in particular to Allegheny County, in particular to Pennsylvania, with that battle?

The President. Well, there are two reasons. First of all, Pittsburgh, Allegheny County, and Pennsylvania supported me in the last election because they wanted a new direction in economic policy. We have passed our overall economic plan. It gives the country a very different budget for the next 5 years than we've had in the previous 12. We reduced the deficit and, at the same time, increased investment in jobs and education and health care, in the things that will make us a stronger country.

But in addition to that, I asked the Congress in the short run to spend a little more money, a modest amount of money to create another half-million jobs in the next year and a half, to try to cut the unemployment rate by half a percent but also to try to spark job creation in the private sector more. The plan passed the House. It has the support of a majority of the Senate. At the present time, all the Republican Senators as a bloc are filibustering the bill. That is, they won't let it come to a vote.

I believe that Senator Specter would like to vote for the bill. And I believe that Senator Dole, the Republican leader, has put a lot of pressure on a lot of the Republicans to stay hitched. And they're all saying that this bill increases the deficit. It doesn't. This bill is well below the spending targets that Congress approved, including the Republicans, for this year. This bill is paid for by budget cuts in the next 5 years. This bill is designed to give a jumpstart to the economy. And I must say, a lot of the Republican Senators that are holding it up, when Mr. Bush was President, voted for billions of dollars of emergency spending of just this kind, much of it was totally unrelated to creating jobs.

So what I'm trying to do is to break this logjam. I've held out an olive branch; I've offered a compromise. But I think that we ought to try to put some more Americans to work right now to show that we're changing the direction of the country. And that's the purpose of the bill.

Mr. Whitely. Have you been in touch with Senator Specter or his office lately?

The President. Well, we've been trying to talk regularly, through my White House congressional liaison operation, to the Senators that we think are open to this, Senator Specter, Senator D'Amato from New York, Senator Jeffords from Vermont, Senator Hatfield from Oregon, and five or six others whom we believe know we need more jobs in this economy and know what we are paying for this with budget cuts over the life of the budget I presented.

You know, it has a lot of appeal to say, "Well, we've got a big deficit. We shouldn't increase it more." But the truth is that we are paying for this with budget cuts in the whole life of the budget over the next few years. And more importantly, we have this program well below the spending targets that Congress has already approved for this year. And they've done this for years, with the Republicans voting for it, many Republicans voting for it, for things that weren't nearly as important as putting the American people back to work.

So I just hope that this doesn't become a political issue. It ought to just be about the people of this country and the need for jobs.

Mr. Whitely. I have some questions from people who supported you, and some people who are skeptical about your administration. It has to do with their hopes and also with their fears. A lot of people who supported you and voted for you in Pennsylvania, I think some of them are now saying, "We're glad we got him in the White House, but now look at this incredible process he has to go through. Look at these problems. Look at this gridlock." And they're beginning to wonder: Is this going to work; can you pull it off? And of course, your skeptics are saying, "Well, I knew it was going to be like this."

The President. Well, I'd ask people, first of all, to remember that we are, frankly, moving very fast. The budget resolution that the Congress passed was the fastest they have ever passed a budget resolution, ever in history, setting out the next 5 year budget targets. So we are moving really rapidly. And we've got them working on political reform, welfare reform, health care reform, a whole wide range of things.

But it's a big operation. You can't expect to turn it around overnight. It took 12 years to produce the conditions which led to the victory I received from the people in November, and we can't turn it around in 90 days. But I think we're making real, real progress.

I would urge the people not to get discouraged. We're not going to win every battle, and not everything is going to happen overnight. But we are definitely moving and changing things.

NOTE: The interview began at 10:40 a.m. in the USAir terminal at Pittsburgh International Airport.

Remarks to the Community in Pittsburgh
April 17, 1993

Thank you so much, Senator Wofford, Governor Casey, Commissioner Foerster—happy birthday—and Commissioner Flaherty. I am so glad to be back in Pittsburgh, in Allegheny County.

Now, where's the band who played for us, up there? The Richland High Marching Band, thank you very much.

I want to say, Mayor, it's always good to be with you and be in your city. I want to also acknowledge the presence here today of Congressmen Coyne, Klink, Murphy, and Murtha, all of whom have supported this economic program to get our country moving again, and a person who has made some decisions that are very good for Pittsburgh and USAir and, I think, for the future of the country, the Transportation Secretary, Federico Peña, who is here with us.

I want to say a lot of things about the economic program, but before I do, let me say what—since all of you heard the radio address and the interview, you know that this morning the jury in Los Angeles handed down a verdict in the Rodney King case. You don't know that? I thought you heard it. Well, let me say that they did. The jury found two of the defendants guilty and two of the defendants not guilty. The jury convicted the officer, Officer Powell, who was shown on the film, who did most of the beating, and the sergeant who was in charge of the group of police officers who were there. The jury acquitted two of the other officers, including the one who was a rookie and the one who was on the film and, in part, trying to deflect some blows from Rodney King.

Now, I want to say just a few words about that, because I think, frankly, our attitude about each other may have as much to do with the progress we need to make in the future as any specific law we can pass. This verdict was a tribute to the work and the judgment of the jury and the efforts of the Federal Government in putting the case together. It was, once again, a reminder that our courts are the proper forum for the resolution of even our deepest legal disputes. And it did establish what a lot of people have felt in their hearts for 2 years, that the civil rights of Rodney King were violated.

But I ask you to think about the deeper meaning of this whole issue. All across the world today people are fighting with each other and killing each other because of their racial and religious differences. In eastern Bosnia, in the town of Srebrenica, Muslims and Serbs that lived together for centuries, and tens of thousands of the Muslims are now about to be forced from their homes through a process called ethnic cleansing and because the Serbs had decided that they just can't live unless they can live alone and without others who are different from them.

Our country has always been about something different from that. We see these kinds of racial and ethnic conflicts on every continent all across the globe. But we've always been about something different from that. I once gave a speech to a university in Los Angeles County where there were students from 122 different countries. There are now people from 150 different racial and ethnic groups in that county alone. And I say to you, my fellow Americans, unless we really do believe that underneath the differences of race and religion and ethnicity, underneath the differences of political party and political opinion, there is a core in each one of us, given us by God, in which we share in common, which obliges us to respect one another and to wish to live together in harmony and peace, none of the other things I came to talk to you about today can come to pass.

For the people of Los Angeles and the people of this country, all around the country, who need more opportunity, the time has come to go forward, to rededicate ourselves to the civil rights of all Americans, to rededicate ourselves to the fight against crime and drugs and violence, to put 100,000 more police officers on the street, to pass the Brady bill and try to reduce the vulnerability to violence and crimes by people, to commit ourselves to a new agenda of expanding opportunity and empowerment. But in the beginning must be the willingness of every American to assume a personal responsibility to respect the differences of his or her fellow Americans and rejoice in what unites us as human beings. Surely the lasting legacy of the Rodney King trial ought to be that, a determination to reaffirm our common humanity and to make a strength of our diversity. And if we can do that, then we can get on about the business of this great land.

I want to, before I talk a little bit about the stimulus program, also say a special word about the gentleman who introduced me and those of you who sent him to the Senate. When Pennsylvania elected Harris Wofford against all the odds less than 2 years ago, you started a movement not just that led to a change in Presidents but that led to a change in America. I'm here to tell you today that Pennsylvania sent shock waves to the country by electing Harris Wofford because Pennsylvania was saying we expect our Government to solve the health care crisis, we expect our Government to solve the jobs crisis.

I wonder how many people would have even taken seriously the campaign that I undertook to try to break the gridlock and change the whole way Washington works, to reduce the influence of special interests and put the American people, their jobs, their health care, their education first, to try to change the welfare system and start a system of national service so people could earn their way through college, I wonder if any of that could have happened if Pennsylvania hadn't said in a loud, screaming, clear voice by electing Harris Wofford, the time has come to change the direction of this country.

I also want to ask you for your understanding and your patience. Senator Wofford has been working hard on this health care issue ever since he got to the Senate, but you can't change the health care system unless the White House and the Congress are in harness. And I, my wife, and our administration are working on this health care issue to put the White House and the Congress in harness to ensure affordable health care to all Americans.

I also want to say, again, how much I appreciate USAir and the employees for giving us this wonderful terminal to meet in today.

And now let me talk about what Governor Casey spoke about. When I became President, I promised a long-term economic plan, no short-term miracles but a real effort to turn this country around. And I presented that plan to the Congress. They have to vote on it twice, first in broad outlines and then in the details. They adopted the outlines, the so-called budget resolution, in record time. They have never moved so rapidly.

It changes the whole way the Federal Government takes care of your money and has your priorities at stake. It emphasizes a dramatic reduction in the Federal deficit and, at the same time, increasing investment in jobs, in education and health care and communities and the things that will make the country grow over a 5-year period, not a one-shot deal, over 5 years. It does it by a combination of strict budget cuts and raising some more money. Seventy percent of it comes from people with incomes over $100,000 a year to try to restore some fairness to this Tax Code that has gotten so unfair in the last 12 years. This program is a good program. It is what I campaigned on.

Then I asked the Congress to do something I didn't really campaign on but that I decided was important, to adopt a short-term jobs program to immediately create a half a million jobs in this economy. And I'll tell you why I did it, even though we never talked about it in these rallies when I came here. Because I looked around the world and I saw that every advanced economy in the world is having trouble creating jobs, every one. Then I looked at America, and I saw that the economists were saying that we have been in an economic recovery for a year, and the unemployment rate is higher now than it was when we were in the depths of the recession.

So America is like a lot of these other countries. If you look at the overall figures—a lot of you are responsible for this, by the way—productivity, our output per working person, is up. Some profits of our corporations are up, stock market at record-high levels. Now interest rates are going down because we're committed to reducing the deficit. And a lot of you, as a result, have refinanced your homes or gotten a lower mortgage or interest rate on a car or other consumer interest rates. People have been able to get business loans or refinance them.

That's all good. But where are the jobs? This is a sweeping, worldwide problem for wealthier countries. But it is your problem and your community's problem if you or your neighbors don't have one. And as a result of the incredible pressures on business today, we see that even in this so-called recovery, we're having no new jobs created and we're having 100,000 Americans a month lose their health insurance. I say we can do better. And we have to try to do better.

So we came up with the idea of not having the Government create a job for everybody that's unemployed—you know we don't have enough money to do that with the deficit as high as it is—but of having a very carefully targeted jobs plan to create a half a million jobs and hope it would operate like striking a match, and then that would get the economy spurred, and other new jobs would be created. It was a disciplined, limited, targeted plan, clearly designed to get this economy going again in the short run. That is what I've asked the House and the Senate to adopt. The House adopted the plan right away. A majority of the Senate is for it. All the Republicans are filibustering it, which means they know it will pass, so they won't let it come to a vote.

Now, let me tell you what it will do. It will give communities a lift by putting thousands of police officers on the street to try to make the streets safer. It will invest in roads and streets and bridges and cleaner water and sewer systems and put people to work in construction work. That is important. It will give cities and counties and States some discretionary money to support projects like this one. It will create 700,000 jobs for young people who otherwise wouldn't have any work this summer to get them off the streets.

After trying for a long time to pass this program and getting no help from any of the Republican Senators—because we have to have at least three or four of them to help because it takes 60 people to shut off debate in the Senate, not a majority, 60 percent—I offered a compromise. Well, you've heard that old saying, it takes two to tango? It also takes two to untangle the gridlock in Washington. And I came here today asking you to ask Senator Specter to help me untangle this gridlock.

The Republicans say, "Well, maybe we ought to pay money to extend the unemployment benefits of people who are unemployed," but not a dime to create any jobs. We tried that for 12 years: Pay people to be unemployed; don't pay them to work. I say we should do both, take care of the unemployed but reduce the unemployed. Put people to work.

There are those who say, "Everything's fine. We don't need this." Everybody who says that has got a job. [*Laughter*] Everybody who says that has got health insurance. Everybody who says that has a good education and is going to do fine almost no matter what happens. They can take care of themselves. The people who know how many vulnerable people there are

in America know that we've got to try to do something to put the people to work. If it doesn't work, we'll do something else. But let's try this. It can work.

Let me say, in fairness to my opponents— I want you to know what their argument is. They say if the Congress passes an emergency jobs bill, that adds to the deficit, and we shouldn't do anything to make the deficit bigger, nothing, except maybe unemployment benefits. Now, that has a lot of appeal. Here's what they don't tell you. We could pass every dollar I've asked for in this jobs plan and still be below the total spending targets that this Congress established before I ever became President, for how much money was going to be spent this year. Right, Congressmen? Number one.

Number two, we have cut and cut and cut spending in this budget, over 200 specific spending cuts over the next 5 years that will blow away this extra spending. This spending is more than covered by budget cuts.

And third, and the most important thing of all you need to know, is that before I became President, just in the last 4 years, a lot of these same people voted for the same kind of emergency spending, billions and billions and billions of dollars of it, a lot of it for overseas spending or other things that didn't have anything to do with putting the people of Pennsylvania to work. So they did this before. Let's do it for the American people this time.

What's amazing to me, they also say, "Well, you can't trust the cities and counties with the money. You give these community development block grants to the cities, you can't ever tell. Well, they'll fool around and build a swimming pool with it." [*Laughter*] I have a couple of things to say about that. First of all, it was the Republicans in Washington that once championed these community development grants. Your late Senator from this State, John Heinz, was a great champion of the very thing I'm trying to do, increasing community development block grants.

Before I became President, I heard speech after speech out of the Republicans in Washington that I agreed with, saying that people at the local level have better sense than we do about how to spend this money. How many times did the Congress get that speech from the Republicans, "Let the mayors, let the Governors, let the county officials spend this money. They know how to do it." Well, funny enough,

I propose to expand that program, and all of a sudden they said, "Why, you can't trust those people. They'll squander the money. They might build a swimming pool." [*Laughter*]

Let me tell you something. I don't know how you feel, but in a lot of these cities and small towns and country places, I'd a lot rather those kids be at swimming pools this summer than some of the places they're going to be. You go to Washington. The President's got a swimming pool. The Senate has a swimming pool. Why shouldn't the people have a swimming pool? And what about all those people who are going to work building those kinds of things in our cities? I'm telling you, folks, every argument they've got still comes back to gridlock.

Now again, I'm going to tell you, this is not the end of the world, but we need to keep this country moving. And we need to create some jobs now. And we need to stop making excuses. We need to pull together. I have reached out the hand of compromise to the Republicans in the Senate. I did it all by myself. I didn't have any kind of deal from them. I just listened to them. I listened to all those speeches about how bad these programs were. So I said, "Okay, here's a different deal, and by the way, how about spending $200 million more to put police on the street? Why don't you do that?" Let's hear what their answer is. Why shouldn't we have police on the street where we need it in the cities, where we've have to cut back on law enforcement coverage? Why shouldn't we have more people working in this country?

I want to ask you to help us put America back to work. I want to ask you to help keep the movement going. I have been very honest with you. We don't have any magic bullets. We know there won't be any overnight successes. But we know that this economy, like so many countries in the world, is not creating jobs. And if people were working, you just think about it, if everybody in this country who wanted a job had one, we wouldn't have half the problems we've got now. Let's try to put America back to work.

By the end of this month, let me give you one more example, if we don't fund this program, the main loan program of the Small Business Administration will be shut down. The opposite party for years paraded as the champion of the small businesses of this country. That program can help start 25,000 small businesses. Small business is generating most of the new jobs in America today. That is the kind of thing we have done here.

I ask you, please, not in a spirit of partisanship, not in an atmosphere of hostility, not with political rhetoric, just for the benefit of the people of Pittsburgh and Allegheny County and Pennsylvania and the United States of America, ask your Senator and the Senators in the United States Senate to give us a chance to put this country back to work, starting Monday.

Thank you, and God bless you all.

NOTE: The President spoke at 11:16 a.m. in the USAir terminal at Pittsburgh International Airport. In his remarks, he referred to Tom Foerster and Pete Flaherty, Allegheny County commissioners, and Sophie Masloff, Mayor of Pittsburgh.

The Office of the Press Secretary also released a statement by the President on the jury verdict in the Rodney King case which was an excerpt from the President's remarks printed above.

Statement on the Death of President Turgut Ozal of Turkey
April 17, 1993

Mrs. Clinton and I are deeply saddened over the passing of President Turgut Ozal of Turkey. We have expressed our condolences to the Acting President of Turkey, Hussametin Cindoruk, and to Mrs. Semra Ozal at this difficult and sad time. Friends of Turkey everywhere mourn his passing.

President Ozal devoted his life to public serv-

ice, and Turkey is a stronger country because of his dedicated and visionary leadership. President Ozal's mark on the political life of Turkey, both at home and abroad, has been extraordinary. He crafted a new regional role for his country, stressing always the importance of democracy, trade, and peace. The alliance of Turkey and the United States is stronger today because of the personal leadership of the late President.

On behalf of all Americans, Mrs. Clinton and I extend our heartfelt sympathies to the people of Turkey and to the family and friends of President Ozal.

Remarks to the Champion University of Maine Ice Hockey Team and an Exchange With Reporters
April 19, 1993

The President. Good morning, ladies and gentlemen. It's an honor for me to welcome the University of Maine Black Bears, the winner of the NCAA Division I hockey national championship to the Rose Garden and the White House. I understand from Senator Mitchell that this is the first team from the University of Maine ever to win a national championship. And we're glad to have them here.

I'm inspired not only by how the team pulled together to win the championship but how the entire State pulled together to cheer them on to victory. Coming from a State that is also relatively small in size but also filled with pride and tradition and community, I can understand how the people of Maine must feel about the Black Bears. In our State, people are still talking about the time we won the Orange Bowl over the number one ranked football team, and that was back in 1978. I'm sure that 15 years from now the people of Maine will be as proud of this team as they are today.

You know, in my State football is a slightly more popular sport than hockey. We don't have a lot of ice. [*Laughter*] But after spending 3 months getting banged around in this town, I can understand a little more about hockey than I did before I came here. Hockey is a tough game; it's a hard-hitting sport. It does have one virtue though, there's a penalty for delay of game. I wish we had that rule in the Senate. [*Laughter*] In Government, as in hockey, leadership is important. In the United States Senate, our team has a great captain, the majority leader and the senior Senator from Maine, George Mitchell; junior Senator Cohen looks so young, I can't imagine. [*Laughter*] I'm actually bitter about Senator Cohen because he looks so much younger than me.

On your hockey team the captain, Jim Montgomery, has done a great job. He scored the winning goal late in the championship game, leading you to a come-from-behind victory, something else I know a little bit about. Sport brings out the best in individuals and in teams and in communities. I share the pride that Senator Mitchell and Senator Cohen and Congressman Andrews and all the people of Maine must feel for the Black Bears who have shown us all how to play as a team, how to bring out the best in one another, and how to come from behind. I think it's important, as I ask young people from around America who have achieved outstanding things in working together to come here to the White House to be recognized and appreciated by their country, to remember that those kinds of values and those kinds of virtues need to be ingrained in all of us for all of our lives. We now have another role model, and I'm glad to have them here today.

[*At this point, the President was presented with a team jersey.*]

The President. That's great. I love it. It's beautiful.

[*The President was then presented with an autographed hockey stick.*]

The President. Thank you. That's great.

Branch Davidian Religious Sect Standoff

Q. Mr. President, did you authorize the move on Waco this morning, sir?

The President. I was aware of it. I think the Attorney General made the decision. And I think I should refer all questions to her and to the FBI.

Q. Did you have any instructions for her as to how it should be executed?

The President. No, they made the tactical decisions. That was their judgment, the FBI.

Q. Is this a raid?

The President. I want to refer you to, talk to the Attorney General and the FBI. I knew it was going to be done, but the decisions were entirely theirs, all the tactical decisions.

Stimulus Package

Q. What did you and Senator Mitchell talk about this morning?

Q. Any chance for that stimulus package?

The President. Senator Mitchell ought to pay my quarter. I was in there—[*laughter*]——

Senator Mitchell. You have to pay that quarter.

The President. I was ready. [*Laughter*] Senator Mitchell, he's worth a quarter any day.

Q. Any chance for your bill, sir?

The President. We talked about what was going to happen this week in the Senate and about what other meetings we're going to have for the rest of the week. We only had about 5 minutes to talk, and we agreed we'd get back together later, around noon, and talk some more.

Q. Senator Dole said over the weekend that your compromise is no compromise.

The President. Well, I know he did, but look, Senator Dole and a lot of the other Republicans now in the Senate voted for the same kind of thing for Ronald Reagan in 1983. And our research indicates that a majority of them over time voted for a total of 28 emergency spending measures totaling over $100 billion when Reagan and Bush were President, in those administra-

tions. And many of those purposes were not nearly as worthy as putting the American people back to work. I don't want to go back and revisit every one, but you can do it. You can look at the research there. So this position they're taking is not credible. We have a very tough 5-year deficit reduction plan. All these costs are covered during that time and then some. And the very people that are saying this has all got to be paid for don't have much of a history on which to base their position. They've got 12 years of votes for stimulus measures of this kind that had very little to do with putting the American people back to work. So I think we've got a chance to work it out, and I'm hopeful. We'll see what happens today and tomorrow. I'm feeling pretty good about it.

NOTE: The President spoke at 9:58 a.m. in the Rose Garden at the White House. In his remarks, he referred to the assault by Federal agents with armored vehicles and tear gas on the Branch Davidian religious sect compound in Waco, TX. The action ended a 51-day standoff which began on February 28 when Federal agents raided the compound in an attempt to serve warrants for firearms violations on David Koresh, leader of the sect. A portion of these remarks could not be verified because the tape was incomplete.

Remarks to the Building and Construction Trades Department of the AFL–CIO
April 19, 1993

The President. Thank you very much, Bob. And thank you, ladies and gentlemen, for that wonderful, wonderful reception.

Audience member. My hero! [*Laughter*]

The President. I don't know about that, but I'm up here fighting for you every day, I'll tell you that.

I like looking out into a big crowd into the faces of people who have worked hard and played by the rules and tried to make this country work again. I thank you for the help you gave me last November when we said together we wanted to change this country; we wanted to break the gridlock in Washington; we wanted to change the priorities and put our people first

again; we wanted to develop a high-wage, high-growth economy.

We knew that to do it we'd have to do some very tough things. All of us knew that going in. We knew that these decisions would be difficult and that they wouldn't come overnight and that the country had been going in one direction for more than a decade and you couldn't turn it around overnight. But everyone knew that we had to reduce this awful Federal deficit, we had to increase our investment in our people and jobs, at the same time we had to address the health care crisis. Now, we're spending 15 percent of our national income on health care with 37 million people uninsured,

100,000 people a month losing their health insurance, and more and more money every year going to health care instead of investment in jobs and growth and the economy. We knew we had to make some changes.

I made some commitments to you, and I told you that if you'd vote for me, I'd try to bring fairness and growth and opportunity back to America. I tried to do everything that I said I'd do. I've confronted some different and difficult circumstances, but we are moving ahead.

I have been gratified, frankly, by most of what has happened here in the last 2½ months. Congress passed a resolution endorsing the budget plan I presented to reduce the deficit and increase investment in jobs and education and training, in record time. They have never passed a budget plan that fast.

And then I said, well, now I think we ought to have an emergency jobs plan to try to jumpstart this economy, to put a half a million more people back to work through direct investment in the public and private sector over the next year and a half because this economy doesn't seem to be creating any jobs, even though everybody tells us we're in a recovery.

And there was broad-based support for that, for creating jobs and using the money to immunize children and to rebuild our community and to rebuild our infrastructure. The bill swept through the House and is supported by a majority of the Senate.

A few weeks ago we had a meeting of business and labor leaders that included Bob Georgine and Lane Kirkland and some of the biggest business people in this country saying we need the jobs bill. And the labor movement has shown real leadership on this issue in working in partnership with business on the concept of investment.

I tried to look hard at this economy and ask what we can do. How can we move this economy forward? How can we do it in the short term and in the long term? Over the long term, we've got to bring the deficit down. That gets interest rates down. You've seen that already. Interest rates have come down since the election. And billions of dollars are being refinanced in homes, in car loans, in commercial loans, in business loans. And that's going to mean more jobs for people like you. But it also means that we have to have some direct investment to create jobs in this economy. We've got to get the economy moving. There are those who

say, well, we're in a recovery and things are going fine. Well, I don't know about you, but 16 months of 7 percent unemployment or more is not fine with me. I ran because I thought we could do better.

You know, people ask me all the time what is the real difference about being President? Is it really different? And I have to tell you, after just a couple of months, I've got an enormous amount of sympathy with every predecessor I ever had who got out of touch. [*Laughter*] You know, you live in the nicest public housing in America—[*laughter*]—and somebody drives you around everywhere, and you're always being protected because you are at some risk, and you've got the nicest airplane anybody ever saw—[*laughter*]—and nobody except your wife and your mama and your nearest family can call you by your first name anymore without violating protocol. Before you know it, you're just walking around in a bubble.

The other day—this is a true story—the other day I came down from the upper residence floor of the White House down to the first floor, the big floor, and I was going to a meeting. And I didn't know it but my wife had had a meeting with a bunch of other people, and when the elevator door opened I found myself standing in the midst of 20 or 30 people. I didn't know them, and I just shook hands with them, and said hello, and went on and—to give you an example of how bad it is—this very nice person working at the White House said, "Oh, Mr. President, I'm so sorry I let you out in the middle of those people." And so I looked at him and I said, "That's okay young man, I used to be one myself." [*Laughter*]

It's so easy for people who make decisions here to forget. You know, everybody that makes a decision here has got a job. Everybody that makes a decision here that affects your life got a good education. Everybody that makes a decision here has got a good health care plan and has pretty good security because we keep taking in tax dollars.

And it's important that we think about where other people are. Unemployment in building trades across the board is about 14 percent, about twice the national average. And yet we know we're spending much less of our income investing in building things, in the infrastructure and in construction and things that really make a country rich over the long run, than almost all of our competitors.

We also know that every wealthy country in the world is having trouble creating jobs. All the rich countries are. Even Japan's seen its unemployment rate go up some, and theirs is lower than everybody else's because their economy is more closed. But all the wealthy countries, including Japan, including Germany, are having difficulty creating jobs. This is not just an American problem. But we need to find the courage and the creativity to solve the problem. We're not like some of those countries who give you your wages for a year and a half and all of your benefits if you lose the job. In America, people need to work. And you just think about it, about half our problems would go away overnight if everybody in this country who wanted to work had a job.

There are more than a million fewer jobs in the private sector now than there were before this recession began. Virtually all the net growth in employment has come in local, State, and Federal Government. And if you will forgive me, that's not a very sound basis for long-term economic recovery, because their bills are all paid by somebody else. The somebody elses need the work. And that's what we're trying to do.

Last year, more businesses failed than at any time in memory. Last month, we lost a total of net 22,000 jobs, including 59,000 construction jobs. There are now 16 million Americans who are looking for the wages and dignity of full-time work. There may be more who aren't on the rolls who have just given up trying.

I've taken a lot of heat because I have cut Government programs that some people in my own party like a lot. I offered a program that had 200 specific budget cuts, a program that will reduce this deficit by about $500 billion over 5 years. I don't think the Government can do everything or should try to do everything. And a lot of what we used to do either doesn't need to be done or must be done by State and local government or the private sector. But I am not willing to say when 7 percent of our people are unemployed and have been for 16 months, when millions more are underemployed, when business is under so much pressure that 100,000 Americans a month are losing their health insurance, when city after city after city in this country is full of young people who won't have anything to do this summer and have never had a good job and need to have the experience of working, that we

shouldn't do more to create real opportunity and to have the dignity of work and to develop the capacity of our people.

I just think we can do better. I did not ask for this job for the honor, great as it is, of living in the White House and riding around in all the limousines and the airplanes. It is a very great honor to be President, but you can only do honor to the job if you get up every day and try to make things better and change things. That's why I asked you to give me the job.

Now I need your help today, because I know that the building trades have been willing in the past to endorse builders, whether they were Republicans or Democrats. And you have been willing to endorse people that you thought—Members of Congress and others at the State level who would help you to put people to work. Some of the people you endorsed are now involved in the Senate filibuster of the jobs plan.

Now this plan will create hundreds of thousands of jobs. Is it the answer to all our problems? No. Is it big enough? Probably not, but it's about as big as it can be given the size of the deficit and the fact that we've got to bring that down and keep interest rates down. Will it hurt the economy? No.

We want to put people to work in construction. We also want to rehire thousands of police officers who have lost their jobs so they can do a better job protecting people from crime. You know, there was a fascinating article on Los Angeles the other day before the verdict in the King case, which said that in all neighborhoods, without regard to race or income, people wanted more police officers. They wanted community policing. They knew it would reduce the possibility of abusive police power if they had enough police on the street so that they knew their neighbors. They worked together to prevent crime as well as to catch criminals. And people felt less tension and more community.

That's what's also in this jobs plan. In your industry, a $450 billion a year industry, we can create about 23,000 to 25,000 jobs directly, quickly, quickly, if this bill will pass. We can give 700,000 young people a chance to have a job this summer that will not only be a real job but will require them to do some more work on their education so that they will learn even as they earn.

We will provide some loans to small businesses where most of the new jobs are created.

The Republican Party has been a champion of this small business program in the past as they have been of the community development block grants, Republican Mayors all over America supporting my jobs program as the Republican Senators say how bad the community development block grant is. They used to trust Mayors and Governors when they had a Republican in the White House. I don't know what this has got to do with me. They've still got the same Mayors and Governors they had before.

It's time to stop playing politics and move forward. Many of the projects funded by this jobs plan have sat on the shelves for years while deficits exploded and investments in the things that make the economy strong and the people strong have been totally neglected.

Now what are my opponents saying? Why did they say it's okay for the minority to keep the majority from even voting on this bill? They say this bill adds to the deficit. Well, I'll give you four arguments against that. I want you to give it back to them before you leave town.

First, they're more than happy to pay for unemployment benefits to be extended. That is, they say, Okay, we'll vote for that in emergency funding. But they won't create any money to put people to work so they don't have to draw unemployment. Now, we tried it their way for 12 years. They always voted to extend unemployment benefits. I'd like to extend employment benefits. That's a lot better than unemployment benefits.

Second thing you need to know is, because of some savings in the defense budget, which have already occurred, we could pass every dollar in this jobs bill and still be below the target for total discretionary Federal spending set by these folks in Congress before I ever got here. They never tell you that.

Third thing you need to know, as I said, is that we have proposed 200 specific budget cuts that will more than pay for this modest amount of extra spending. And very often in the past, these same folks have voted to spend money this year and pay for it in the years ahead in a 5-year budget plan.

And finally, and maybe most importantly, many and perhaps most of the Senators who are blocking consideration of our plan have actually voted for emergency measure after emergency measure after emergency measure just like this for 12 years, often in legislation that wasn't paid for. And they didn't have much trouble with it then when their guys were in the White House.

This plan puts people to work. It's paid for. It doesn't shift jobs overseas, it puts jobs on the streets of America. Many of the people who are leading this filibuster voted for a stimulus plan like this under President Reagan back in 1983. We did some quick research over the weekend. It appears that 28 times in the last 12 years, many of the same people who are holding this bill up voted to do the same thing I'm asking for to the tune of over $100 billion, often for foreign aid and for other things that didn't have nearly as much to do with affecting the lives of the American people in Main Street America. And it's time to help Main Street America.

We had an election in November that said stop the gridlock, stop the partisan bickering, compromise, work together, move the country forward, and start by putting the American people back to work. That's what this is all about. Don't listen to those arguments.

So that's it. When they say, oh, we can't add to the deficit, say, well, you guys, you guys not the Democrats, you guys, you voted for 12 years for these kinds of things, often to help countries, why not help us? Two, you've got $500 billion in deficit reduction; it'll cover this real well. Three, you're still under the spending targets that you adopted before President Clinton ever got to town. And four, we need this jobs plan. We don't need to fund just unemployment benefits, we want to fund employment benefits.

This whole thing has got to be about enabling people to live up to their potential. I went on these buses all across the country with Hillary and Al and Tipper Gore, and we went into little towns and big cities. Over and over and over again, what I left those encounters with was the sense that Americans were yearning just to be themselves as fully as they could be. And you can't do that if you can't have a job. You can't do that if you can't get a decent education. You can't do that if you think no matter how hard you work, you can't take care of your family if they get sick. You can't do that if you think you can never change jobs without losing your health benefits.

If you think about it, we live in a world where the power of people is uppermost. We live in a country where, thank God, no one is a dictator. We have to work together. We have to be able to put aside our partisan labels and sometimes our personal prejudices and think about what it takes to pull people together and give everybody a chance to be the most they can be. That's what the whole purpose of politics is.

And when this bill was held up, I didn't like it, but I offered to compromise, to take some of the jobs out of it, though it grieves me, to try to respond to some of the specific speeches that were given by Republican Senators on the floor of the Senate.

And so far what have they said to my good faith offer? Same old thing: stonewall. This is the deficit; we can't add to the deficit. Folks, this is the crowd that had the Government for 12 years. They took the deficit from $1 trillion to $4 trillion. Have they no shame? How can they say this? What is going on? Sometimes I think the secret to success in this town is being able to say the most amazing things with a straight face.

We're going to get the deficit down. We're going to try to keep interest rates down. But we've got to invest in people, and we've got to try to create jobs. Will this work wonders? No. Will it work some good? Yes, you bet it will. It is an effort. Did I even campaign on this? No. You endorsed me without asking me to promise an emergency jobs program. I offered this program for the simple reason that I looked at the performance of this economy and its difficulty in creating jobs. Then I looked around the world and I saw all these other countries having the same exact problem we were

having, and I thought, we've got to try something else. And I'll tell you something, if we get this done and it doesn't work, I'll try something else. We're living in a new and different time where we've got to try.

I ask you, every one of you that ever had a chance to make it because you joined this union, because somebody invested in a project that gave you a chance to work, because you had the opportunity to raise a family and have a house, educate kids. Just take a little time now and ask the people you know in the United States Congress, who have all made it, to think about how together we can provide these opportunities for others. The arguments they are using just don't hold water. They don't measure against the facts of what they have done in the past and what the facts of this budget that I have presented are. This is a modest program to give hope and opportunity to people in this country who need it and to try to get the job engine going in America again.

I have compromised. I have held out my hand. I think it's time for somebody to reach back across the divide of party politics and put the American people first. And you can help get it done today. I hope you will.

Thank you, and God bless you.

NOTE: The President spoke at 11:53 a.m. at the Washington Hilton Hotel. In his remarks, he referred to Robert Georgine, president, Building and Construction Trades Department, and Lane Kirkland, president, AFL–CIO.

Statement on the Tragedy in Waco, Texas
April 19, 1993

I am deeply saddened by the loss of life in Waco today. My thoughts and prayers are with the families of David Koresh's victims.

The law enforcement agencies involved in the Waco siege recommended the course of action pursued today. The Attorney General informed

me of their analysis and judgment and recommended that we proceed with today's action given the risks of maintaining the previous policy indefinitely. I told the Attorney General to do what she thought was right, and I stand by that decision.

Nomination for Assistant Secretaries of Labor
April 19, 1993

The President today named California Chief Deputy Treasurer E. Olena Berg and former Michigan Department of Commerce Director Douglas Ross to senior positions at the Department of Labor. He intends to nominate Ms. Berg to be Assistant Secretary for Pension and Welfare Benefit Programs, Pension and Welfare Benefits Administration, and Mr. Ross to be Assistant Secretary for Employment and Training, Employment and Training Administration.

"Olena Berg and Doug Ross have been effective and innovative officials at the State government level," said the President. "Both have significant business experience as well. I am very pleased that they will be part of Secretary Reich's team at Labor."

NOTE: Biographies of the nominees were made available by the Office of the Press Secretary.

Remarks on Presenting the Teacher of the Year Award
April 20, 1993

The President. Good afternoon. Please be seated.

I want to say, first, how delighted I am to be here with Secretary Riley and with Senator Graham. The three of us served as Governors together during the 1980's when we worked constantly on strategies to improve our schools, when we led often difficult and long efforts to upgrade the standards in American education and to improve the quality of instruction our children were receiving.

There were no two Governors whom I admired more during that period than the two who now stand on this stage with the Teacher of the Year. And I think both of them would join me in saying that, after all the testimony has been heard and all the bills have been passed and the funds have been raised and allocated, it all comes down to what happens between the teacher and the students in the classroom.

That's why today's ceremony honoring the National Teacher of the Year is so important. Tracey Leon Bailey has won recognition all across our country for highly advanced and innovative science programs. He's developed and introduced into Florida's classrooms cutting-edge programs in molecular biology and DNA fingerprinting, subjects usually taught only in college and, I might add, probably only dimly understood here in the Nation's Capital.

Within 3 years of being hired by a satellite high school, Mr. Bailey's institution had one of the strongest science programs in the entire State of Florida, and it won numerous national and international awards. These advanced programs aren't just for a favored few. Tracey Bailey has inspired all kinds of students, including those previously known as low-achieving or at-risk, to reach for excellence and to attain it. This is what our students need and what our country needs.

Today, we know that a good future with high wages and rich opportunities rests on the foundation of quality education for a lifetime. The basics aren't enough anymore. All our kids need competence in math and science and advanced problemsolving. That's why Tracey Bailey's accomplishments are so important and why I am so pleased and proud to participate in recognizing and honoring these accomplishments.

Tracey, you represent the best in the United States. I'm glad to recognize you today and to formally present you with this apple award as the Teacher of the Year for 1993.

[*At this point, the President presented the award, and Mr. Bailey made a brief statement of appreciation.*]

The President. In closing, I would like to also welcome the education leaders from Florida who are here, those representing the national education groups who have also come. I'd like to recognize Tracey's Congressman, Representative Jim Bacchus in the back, himself a great advocate of education. And I'd like to remind all of you that the ultimate purpose of the National Teacher of the Year Award is to find a way for the rest of us to express our appreciation to people all across this country who give their lives to our children, all of the teachers of this country who get up every day and do their best to try to advance the cause of learning for all the children of America. They are, in so many ways, our most important public servants.

Thank you very much.

NOTE: The President spoke at 1:25 p.m. in the Rose Garden at the White House.

The President's News Conference
April 20, 1993

Tragedy in Waco

The President. On February the 28th, four Federal agents were killed in the line of duty trying to enforce the law against the Branch Davidian compound, which had illegally stockpiled weaponry and ammunition and placed innocent children at risk. Because the BATF operation had failed to meet its objective, a 51-day standoff ensued.

The Federal Bureau of Investigation then made every reasonable effort to bring this perilous situation to an end without bloodshed and further loss of life. The Bureau's efforts were ultimately unavailing because the individual with whom they were dealing, David Koresh, was dangerous, irrational, and probably insane. He engaged in numerous activities which violated both Federal law and common standards of decency. He was, moreover, responsible for the deaths and injuries which occurred during the action against the compound in February. Given his inclination towards violence and in an effort to protect his young hostages, no provocative actions were taken for more than 7 weeks by Federal agents against the compound.

This weekend I was briefed by Attorney General Reno on an operation prepared by the FBI, designed to increase pressure on Koresh and persuade those in the compound to surrender peacefully. The plan included a decision to withhold the use of ammunition, even in the face of fire, and instead to use tear gas that would not cause permanent harm to health but would, it was hoped, force the people in the compound to come outside and to surrender.

I was informed of the plan to end the siege. I discussed it with Attorney General Reno. I asked the questions I thought it was appropriate for me to ask. I then told her to do what she thought was right, and I take full responsibility for the implementation of the decision.

Yesterday's action ended in a horrible human tragedy. Mr. Koresh's response to the demands for his surrender by Federal agents was to destroy himself and murder the children who were his captives, as well as all the other people who were there who did not survive. He killed those he controlled, and he bears ultimate responsibility for the carnage that ensued.

Now we must review the past with an eye toward the future. I have directed the United States Departments of Justice and Treasury to undertake a vigorous and thorough investigation to uncover what happened and why and whether anything could have been done differently. I have told the Departments to involve independent professional law enforcement officials in the investigation. I expect to receive analysis and answers in whatever time is required to complete the review. Finally, I have directed the Departments to cooperate fully with all congressional inquiries so that we can continue to be fully accountable to the American people.

I want to express my appreciation to the Attorney General, to the Justice Department, and to the Federal agents on the frontlines who did the best job they could under deeply difficult circumstances.

Again I want to say, as I did yesterday, I am very sorry for the loss of life which occurred at the beginning and at the end of this tragedy in Waco. I hope very much that others who will be tempted to join cults and to become involved with people like David Koresh will be deterred by the horrible scenes they have seen over the last 7 weeks. And I hope very much that the difficult situations which Federal agents confronted there and which they will be doubtless required to confront in other contexts in the future will be somewhat better handled and better understood because of what has been learned now.

Q. Mr. President, can you, first of all, tell us why after 51 days you decided——

Q. Mr. President, can you describe for us what it is that Janet Reno outlined to you in your 15-minute phone conversation with——

The President. I can't hear you both. If one will go first and then the other.

Q. Sorry. Can you describe what Janet Reno——

Q. Mr. President——

The President. I'll answer both your questions, but I can't do it at once.

Q. Can you describe what she told you on Sunday about the nature of the operation and how much detail you knew about it?

The President. Yes. I was told by the Attorney General that the FBI strongly felt that the time had come to take another step in trying to dislodge the people in the compound. And she described generally what the operation would be, that they wanted to go in and use tear gas which had been tested not to cause permanent damage to adults or to children but which would make it very difficult for people to stay inside the building. And it was hoped that the tear gas would permit them to come outside.

I was further told that under no circumstances would our people fire any shots at them, even if fired upon. They were going to shoot the tear gas from armored vehicles which would protect them, and there would be no exchange of fire. In fact, as you know, an awful lot of shots were fired by the cult members at the Federal officials. There were no shots coming back from the Government side.

I asked a number of questions. The first question I asked is, why now? We have waited 7 weeks; why now? The reasons I was given were the following:

Number one, that there was a limit to how long the Federal authorities could maintain with their limited resources the quality and intensity of coverage by experts there. They might be needed in other parts of the country.

Number two, that the people who had reviewed this had never seen a case quite like this one before, and they were convinced that no progress had been made recently and no

progress was going to be made through the normal means of getting Koresh and the other cult members to come out.

Number three, that the danger of their doing something to themselves or to others was likely to increase, not decrease, with the passage of time.

And number four, that they had reason to believe that the children who were still inside the compound were being abused significantly, as well as being forced to live in unsanitary and unsafe conditions.

So for those reasons, they wanted to move at that time.

The second question I asked the Attorney General is whether they had given consideration to all of the things that could go wrong and evaluated them against what might happen that was good. She said that the FBI personnel on the scene and those working with them were convinced that the chances of bad things happening would only increase with the passage of time.

The third question I asked was, has the military been consulted? As soon as the initial tragedy came to light in Waco, that's the first thing I asked to be done, because it was obvious that this was not a typical law enforcement situation. Military people were then brought in, helped to analyze the situation and some of the problems that were presented by it. And so I asked if the military had been consulted. The Attorney General said that they had and that they were in basic agreement, that there was only one minor tactical difference of opinion between the FBI and the military, something that both sides thought was not of overwhelming significance.

Having asked those questions and gotten those answers, I said that if she thought it was the right thing to do, that she should proceed and that I would support it. And I stand by that today.

Q. Mr. President——

The President. Wait. Go ahead.

Q. Can you address the widespread perception, reported widely—television, radio, and newspapers—that you were trying somehow to distance yourself from this disaster?

The President. No, I'm bewildered by it. The only reason I made no public statement yesterday, let me say, the only reason I made no public statement yesterday is that I had nothing to add to what was being said, and I literally did not know until rather late in the day whether anybody was still alive other than those who had been actually seen and taken to the hospital or taken into custody. It was purely and simply a question of waiting for events to unfold.

I can't account for why people speculated one way or the other, but I talked to the Attorney General on the day before the action took place. I talked to her yesterday. I called her again late last night after she appeared on the Larry King show, and I talked to her again this morning. It is not possible for a President to distance himself from things that happen when the Federal Government is in control.

I will say this, however. I was, frankly, "surprised" would be a mild word, to say that anyone that would suggest that the Attorney General should resign because some religious fanatics murdered themselves.

I regret what happened, but it is not possible in this life to control the behavior of others in every circumstance. These people killed four Federal officials in the line of duty. They were heavily armed. They fired on Federal officials yesterday repeatedly, and they were never fired back on. We did everything we could to avoid the loss of life. They made the decision to immolate themselves. And I regret it terribly, and I feel awful about the children.

But in the end, the last comment I had from Janet Reno is when—and I talked to her on Sunday—I said, "Now, I want you to tell me once more why you believe, not why they believe, why you believe we should move now rather than wait some more." And she said, "It's because of the children. They have evidence that those children are still being abused and that they're in increasingly unsafe conditions, and that they don't think it will get any easier with the passage of time. I have to take their word for that. So that is where I think things stand."

Q. Can we assume then that you don't think this was mishandled in view of the outcome, that you didn't run out of patience? And if you had it to do over again, would you really decide that way?

The President. No—well, I think what you can assume is just exactly what I announced today. The FBI has done a lot of things right for this country over a long period of time. This is the same FBI that found the people that bombed the World Trade Center in lickety-split, record time. We want an inquiry to analyze

the steps along the way. Is there something else we should have known? Is there some other question they should have asked? Is there some other question I should have asked? Can I say for sure that we could have done nothing else to make the outcome different? I don't know that. That's why I want the inquiry and that's why I would like to make sure that we have some independent law enforcement people, not political people but totally nonpolitical, outside experts who can bring to bear the best evidence we have.

There is, unfortunately, a rise in this sort of fanaticism all across the world. And we may have to confront it again. And I want to know whether there is anything we can do, particularly when there are children involved. But I do think it is important to recognize that the wrongdoers in this case were the people who killed others and then killed themselves.

Q. Mr. President, were there any other options presented to you for resolving this situation at any point from February 28th until yesterday?

The President. Well, yes, I got regular reports all along the way. There were lots of other options pursued. If you go back—you all covered it very well. You did a very good job of it. I mean, the FBI and the other authorities there pursued any number of other options all along the way, and a lot of them early on seemed to be working. Some of the children got out. Some of the other people left. At one point, there seemed to be some lines of communication opening up between Koresh and the authorities. And then he would say things and not do them, and things just began to spin downward.

In terms of what happened yesterday, the conversation I had with the Attorney General did not involve other options except whether we should take more time with the present strategy we were pursuing because they said they wanted to do this, because they thought this was the best way to get people out of the compound quickly before they could kill themselves. That's what they thought.

Q. Did the government know that the children did not have gas masks?

Q. [*Inaudible*]—congressional hearings once the situation—are you in agreement with that?

The President. That's up to the Congress. They can do whatever they want. But I think it's very important that the Treasury and Justice Departments launch this investigation and bring in some outside experts. And as I said in my statement, if any congressional committees want to look into it, we will fully cooperate. There is nothing to hide here. This was probably the most well-covered operation of its kind in the history of the country.

Go ahead, Sarah [Sarah McClendon, McClendon News Service].

Q. There are two questions I want to ask you. The first is, I think that they knew very well that the children did not have gas masks while the adults did, so the children had no chance because this gas was very—she said it was not lethal, but it was very dangerous to the children, and they could not have survived without gas masks. And on February 28th—let's go back—didn't those people have a right to practice their religion?

The President. They were not just practicing their religion. The Treasury Department believed that they had violated Federal laws, any number of them.

Q. What Federal laws?

The President. Let me go back and answer that. I can't answer the question about the gas masks, except to tell you that the whole purpose of using the tear gas was that it had been tested; they were convinced that it wouldn't kill either a child or an adult, but it would force anybody that breathed it to run outside. And one of the things that I've heard—I don't want to get into the details of this because I don't know— but one of the things that they were speculating about today was that the wind was blowing so fast that the windows might have been opened and some of the gas might have escaped, and that may be why it didn't have the desired effect.

They also knew, Sarah, that there was an underground compound, a bus buried underground, where the children could be sent. I think they were hoping very much that if the children were not released immediately outside, that the humane thing would be done and that the children would be sent someplace where they could be protected.

In terms of the gas masks themselves, I learned yesterday—I did not ask this fact question before—that the gas was supposed to stay active in the compound longer than the gas masks themselves were to work. So that it was thought that even if they all had gas masks, that eventually the gas would force them out in a nonviolent, nonshooting circumstance.

Press Secretary Myers. Last question.

Q. Mr. President, why are you still saying that——

Q. Could you tell us whether or not you ever asked Janet Reno about the possibility of a mass suicide? And when you learned about the actual fire and explosion what went through your mind during those horrendous moments?

The President. What I asked Janet Reno is if they had considered all the worst things that could happen. And of course, the whole issue of suicide had been raised in the public—he had—that had been debated anyway. And she said that the people who were most knowledgeable about these kinds of issues concluded that there was no greater risk of that now than there would be tomorrow or the next day or the day after that or at anytime in the future. That was the judgment they made. Whether they were right or wrong, of course, we will never know.

What happened when I saw the fire, when I saw the building burning? I was sick. I felt terrible. And my immediate concern was whether the children had gotten out and whether they were escaping or whether they were inside trying to burn themselves up. That's the first thing I wanted to know.

Thank you.

Q. Mr. President, why are you still saying it was a Janet Reno decision? Isn't it, in the end, your decision?

The President. Well, what I'm saying is that I didn't have a 4- or 5-hour detailed briefing from the FBI. I didn't go over every strategic part of it. It is a decision for which I take responsibility. I'm the President of the United States, and I signed off on the general decision and giving her the authority to make the last call. When I talked to her on Sunday, some time had elapsed. She might have made a decision to change her mind. I said, "If you decide to go forward with this tomorrow, I will support you." And I do support her.

She is not ultimately responsible to the American people; I am. But I think she has conducted her duties in an appropriate fashion, and she has dealt with this situation, I think, as well as she could have.

Thank you.

NOTE: The President's 12th news conference began at 1:36 p.m. in the Rose Garden at the White House.

Exchange With Reporters Prior to Discussions With President Václav Havel of the Czech Republic
April 20, 1993

Bosnia

Q. Mr. President, President Havel is here for the Holocaust Museum opening, and you toured the museum last night. All this focus on the Holocaust, how does that weigh on your decisionmaking process as far as Bosnia is concerned?

The President. Well, I think the Holocaust is the most extreme example the world has ever known of ethnic cleansing. And I think that even in its more limited manifestations, it's an idea that should be opposed. You couldn't help thinking about that. That's not to compare the two examples. They're not identical. Everyone knows that. But I think that the United States should always seek an opportunity to stand up against— at least to speak out against inhumanity.

Q. Sir, how close are you to a decision on more sanctions on Bosnia?

The President. Well, of course, we've got the U.N. vote. Ambassador Albright was instrumental in the U.N. vote to strengthen the sanctions, and they are quite tough. And we now are putting our heads at the business of implementing them and looking at what other options we ought to consider. And I don't have anything else to say, except to tell you that I spent quite a bit of time on it and will continue to over the next several days.

Q. Following your meeting today, sir, are you any closer to some sort of U.S. military presence there?

The President. I have not made any decisions.

[At this point, one group of reporters left the room, and another group entered.]

Meeting With President Havel

Q. President Clinton, why have you decided to meet with Mr. Havel?

The President. Well, I'm just honored that he would come and see me. I'm glad he's here in the United States for the dedication of the Holocaust Museum. He is a figure widely admired in our country and around the world and a very important person in Europe and a very important person to the United States. So I'm hoping that we'll have a chance to talk about the new Czech Republic and what kinds of things we can do together to support the causes we believe in.

NOTE: The exchange began at 5 p.m. in the Oval Office at the White House. A tape was not available for verification of the content of this exchange.

Message to the Congress Reporting Budget Rescissions and Deferrals
April 20, 1993

To the Congress of the United States:

In accordance with the Congressional Budget and Impoundment Control Act of 1974, I herewith report one proposed rescission in budget authority, totaling $180.0 million, and one revised deferral of budget authority, totaling $7.3 million.

The proposed rescission affects the Board for International Broadcasting. The deferral affects the Department of Health and Human Services.

The details of the proposed rescission and the revised deferral are contained in the attached reports.

WILLIAM J. CLINTON

The White House,
April 20, 1993.

NOTE: The report detailing the rescissions and deferral was published in the *Federal Register* on May 6.

Message to the Senate Transmitting the Protocol to the International Convention on Atlantic Tunas
April 20, 1993

To the Senate of the United States:

I transmit herewith, for the advice and consent of the Senate to ratification, the Protocol adopted June 5, 1992, by the Conference of Plenipotentiaries of the Contracting Parties to the International Convention for the Conservation of Atlantic Tunas (ICCAT) to amend paragraph 2 of Article X of ICCAT. The Protocol was signed by the United States on October 22, 1992. Also transmitted for the information of the Senate is the report of the Department of State with respect to the Protocol.

The Protocol would amend the subject Convention to modify the formula used to calculate the budgetary obligations of the parties to the Convention. The ICCAT, which establishes a Commission to address the conservation and management of highly migratory fisheries stocks in the Atlantic Ocean, has an accumulated debt of over $700,000 due to the inability of some of its very poor member states to meet their obligations to contribute to the annual budget of the Commission. At a Conference of Plenipotentiaries of the States Party to the Conven-

tion, held in Madrid June 4 through 5, 1992, a Protocol was adopted which, along with a new financial contribution scheme to be set forth in the ICCAT Financial Regulations, amends the Convention in such a way as to reduce the contributions of the developing countries to make it easier for them to meet their assessments. The Protocol and the new financial contribution scheme will base assessments on the GNP per capita and on tuna production.

The Protocol amending the budget scheme is necessary to ensure the continued viability of ICCAT, which is responsible for the conservation of highly migratory fisheries stocks of great value to the United States. Ratification by the United States will be necessary before the Protocol can enter into force. I recommend that the Senate give early consideration to the Protocol and give its advice and consent to ratification.

WILLIAM J. CLINTON

The White House,
April 20, 1993.

Message to the Senate Transmitting the Protocol to the Caribbean Environmental Convention
April 20, 1993

To the Senate of the United States:

I transmit herewith, for the advice and consent of the Senate to ratification, the Protocol Concerning Specially Protected Areas and Wildlife to the Convention for the Protection and Development of the Marine Environment of the Wider Caribbean Region, done at Kingston on January 18, 1990. Included for the information of the Senate is a Procès-verbal of Rectification correcting technical errors in the English and Spanish language texts. I also transmit, for the information of the Senate, the Annexes to the Protocol which were adopted at Kingston June 11, 1991, and the report of the Department of State with respect to the Protocol.

The Protocol elaborates and builds on the general obligation in the Convention for the Protection and Development of the Marine Environment of the Wider Caribbean Region, which calls for parties to establish specially protected areas in order to protect and preserve rare or fragile ecosystems, as well as the habitats of threatened or endangered species of fauna and flora. Species of plants and animals that the parties believe require international cooperation to provide adequate protection are listed in three Annexes developed in implementation of the Protocol. The initial version of the Annexes was adopted in 1991. Annexes I and II list species of special concern, including endangered and threatened species, subspecies, and their populations of plants (Annex I) and animals (Annex II). Species included in these Annexes are to receive protection within the geographic area of the Protocol comparable to that for species listed as endangered or threatened under the Endangered Species Act, or protected under the Marine Mammal Protection Act. Annex III lists plants and animals requiring some management, but not necessarily full protection.

The Protocol is considered a major step forward in protecting wildlife and habitats of spe-

cial concern in the Caribbean. Early ratification will demonstrate our continued commitment to the goal of sound regional environmental management and protection. I recommend that the Senate give early and favorable consideration to the Protocol and give its advice and consent to ratification, subject to the understanding and reservations described in the accompanying report of the Secretary of State.

WILLIAM J. CLINTON

The White House,
April 20, 1993.

Message to the Congress Transmitting Reports on Highway and Motor Vehicle Safety
April 20, 1993

To the Congress of the United States:

I transmit herewith the 1991 calendar year reports as prepared by the Department of Transportation on activities under the Highway Safety Act and the National Traffic and Motor

Vehicle Safety Act of 1966, as amended (23 U.S.C. 401 note and 15 U.S.C. 1408).

WILLIAM J. CLINTON

The White House,
April 20, 1993.

Message to the Congress Transmitting the Railroad Safety Report
April 20, 1993

To the Congress of the United States:

I transmit herewith the 1991 annual report on the Administration of the Federal Railroad Safety Act of 1970, pursuant to section 211 of

the Act (45 U.S.C. 440(a)).

WILLIAM J. CLINTON

The White House,
April 20, 1993.

Nomination for Director of the Women's Bureau
April 20, 1993

The President will nominate Karen Nussbaum, who holds leadership positions in several women's and workers' organizations, to be Director of the Department of Labor's Women's Bureau, the White House announced today. The Women's Bureau is responsible for programs aimed at meeting the needs of working women.

"Karen Nussbaum has been organizing working women for two decades," said the President. "She is uniquely qualified for this important job."

NOTE: A biography of the nominee was made available by the Office of the Press Secretary.

Remarks on Earth Day
April 21, 1993

Thank you very much, ladies and gentlemen, for being here in the wonderful Botanical Gardens. I must say there's a lot I have to learn about this town, as you can tell if you follow events from day to day. And I didn't know that the Botanical Gardens was a branch of the Congress until I showed up here. [*Laughter*] Just one more thing I'm not responsible for. I'm glad to be here.

I also think that we should introduce a guest from another country who is here with us, the Environmental Minister from Australia, Roz Kelly. Would you stand up? We're glad to have you here.

Al Gore introduced Katie McGinty, and you were all good enough to clap. And I don't know if you could hear through the clapping that her parents are here. And what you may not know is that the real reason we appointed her is that she's one of 10 children, and we'd like to carry Pennsylvania in 1996. [*Laughter*] We think that there's a significant likelihood now because of that.

I want to say a special word of thanks to the Vice President for two things: first of all, for the wonderful trip that he has just concluded, going to Poland to represent our country on the occasion of the 50th anniversary of the Warsaw Uprising, and the wonderful remarks he gave in New York on the eve of that departure and the way that he represented the United States in Poland. And secondly, notwithstanding what he said in the introduction, which was true, one of the reasons I did ask him to join the ticket is that he knew more about the subject of the environment than I did, and I thought I had something to learn from him. And I have learned a great deal, and it has been an immensely rewarding experience and one which I hope will benefit the United States in many ways over the course of the next 4 years. That's worth clapping for. I agree with that, Nancy, thank you. [*Applause*]

It's a good thing to have this celebration in the springtime, a time when our spirits are renewed and we are reminded by nature of new beginnings and forgotten beauty. This has been an astonishingly beautiful spring in Washington, DC, and something for which I will always be grateful, my first springtime here that I see every morning as I go out and jog around in it and try to breath in it, something that is a continuing challenge. [*Laughter*]

A little more than a week ago, most Americans celebrated holy days of freedom and renewal. Today, we still nurture the faith that helps us to understand more clearly that we can do better. This is a time of new beginnings, a time when there is anguish and anxiety all around us, but we still must yearn once again to succeed in our common purposes to reach our deepest goals.

For all of our differences, I think there is an overwhelming determination to change our course, to offer more opportunity, to assume more responsibility, to restore the larger American community, and to achieve things that are larger than ourselves and more lasting than the present moment. We seek to set our course by the star of age-old values, not short-term expediencies; to waste less in the present and provide more for the future; to leave a legacy that keeps faith with those who left the Earth to us. That is the American spirit. It moves us not only in great gatherings but also when we stand silently all alone in the presence only of nature and our Creator.

If there is one commitment that defines our people, it is our devotion to the rich and expansive land we have inherited. From the first Americans to the present day, our people have lived in awe of the power, the majesty, and the beauty of the forest, the rivers, and the streams of America. That love of the land, which flows like a mighty current through this land and through our character, burst into service on the first Earth Day in 1970.

When I traveled the country last year, I saw and spoke of how much had been accomplished by the environmental movement since then and how much still remains to be done. For all that has been done to protect the air and the water, we haven't halted the destruction of wetlands at home and the rain forest abroad. For all that has been learned, we still struggle to comprehend such dangers to our planet's delicate environment as the shroud of greenhouse gases and the dangerous thinning of the ozone layer. We haven't done nearly enough to protect our forest communities from the hazards, such as lead poisoning, which is believed to cause mental retardation, learning disabilities, and impaired growth.

Unless we act and act now, we face a future where our planet will be home to 9 billion people within our lifetime, but its capacity to support and sustain our lives will be very much diminished. Unless we act, we face the extinction of untold numbers of species that might support our livelihoods and provide medication to save our very lives. Unless we act now, we face a future in which the sun may scorch us, not warm us; where the change of season may take on a dreadful new meaning; and where our children's children will inherit a planet far less hospitable than the world in which we came of age. I have a faith that we will act, not from fear but from hope and through vision.

All across this country, there is a deep understanding rooted in our religious heritage and renewed in the spirit of this time that the bounty of nature is not ours to waste. It is a gift from God that we hold in trust for future generations. Preserving our heritage, enhancing it, and passing it along is a great purpose worthy of a great people. If we seize the opportunity and shoulder the responsibility, we can enrich the future and ennoble our own lives.

Just as we yearn to come together as a people, we yearn to move beyond the false choices that the last few years have imposed upon us. For too long we have been told that we have to choose between the economy and the environment, between our jobs, between our obligations to our own people and our responsibilities to the future and to the rest of the world, between public action and private economy.

I am here today in the hope that we can together take a different course of action, to offer a new set of challenges to our people. Our environmental program is based on three principles.

First, we think you can't have a healthy economy without a healthy environment. We need not choose between breathing clean air and bringing home secure paychecks. The fact is, our environmental problems result not from robust growth but from reckless growth. The fact is that only a prosperous society can have the confidence and the means to protect its environment. And the fact is healthy communities and environmentally sound products and services do

best in today's economic competition. That's why our policies must protect our environment, promote economic growth, and provide millions of new high-skill, high-wage jobs.

Second, we want to protect the environment at home and abroad. In an era of global economics, global epidemics, and global environmental hazards, a central challenge of our time is to promote our national interest in the context of its connectedness with the rest of the world. We share our atmosphere, our planet, our destiny with all the peoples of this world. And the policies I outline today will protect all of us because that is the only way we can protect any of us.

And third, we must move beyond the antagonisms among business, Government, and individual citizens. The policies I outlined today are part of our effort to reinvent Government, to make it your partner and not your overseer, to lead by example and not by bureaucratic fiat.

In the face of great challenges, we need a Government that not only guards against the worst in us but helps to bring out the best in us. I know we can do this because our administration includes the best team of environmental policy makers who have ever served the United States: the Vice President, Interior Secretary Babbitt, EPA Administrator Browner—and I hope that the EPA will soon, by the grace of Congress, be a Cabinet-level Department—and Energy Secretary O'Leary, Commerce Secretary Brown, Transportation Secretary Peña, the Agriculture Secretary Mike Espy, our Environmental Policy Director Katie McGinty, and our Science and Technology Adviser Jack Gibbons. All of them share an unshakable commitment to a healthy environment, a growing economy, and a responsive Government.

Our economic plan will create new job opportunities and new business opportunities, protecting our natural environment. The reductions in the interest rates which we have seen already will free up tens of billions of dollars for responsible investments in this year alone.

The jobs package I have asked the Congress to pass contains—this has hardly been noticed, but it actually contains green jobs from waste water treatment to energy efficiency, to the restoration of our national parks, to investments in new technologies designed to create the means by which we can solve the problems of the future and create more jobs for Americans.

Our long-term strategy invests more in pollution prevention, energy efficiency, in solar energy, in renewable energy, and environmental restoration, and water treatment, all of which can be found in the 5-year budget that we have presented to the Congress.

These investments will create tens of thousands of new jobs, and they will save tens of thousands more. Because when we save energy and resources, we will have more to invest in creating new jobs and providing better living standards. Today every other advanced nation is more energy efficient than we are. That is one of the reasons why over the last couple of years, for example, the average German factory worker has come to make over 20 percent more than his American counterpart; that German workers, while having higher wages, also have more secure and better health care. That's because that economy uses one-half the energy we do to produce the same amount of goods. We can do better, and we will.

I believe we can develop the know-how to out-conserve and out-compete anyone else on Earth. All over the world, people are buying products that help them to protect their environment. There's a $200 billion market today for environmental technologies, and by the turn of the decade and the century, it will be $300 billion.

Let me just share one example with you. Something we all know and use and something some of us are still trying to learn how to replace: light bulbs. Long-lasting, energy-saving light bulbs didn't even exist in 1985. Now American companies sell over $500 million worth of these products, with sales expected to reach $2 billion by 1995 and $10 billion by the year 2000, creating thousands of new jobs. American scientists have taken the lead in developing these technologies, and it's time to help our companies take the lead in bringing our products and services to market.

I've asked the Energy Department, the Commerce Department, and the EPA to assess current environmental technologies and create a strategic plan to give our companies the trade development, promotional efforts, and technical assistance they need to turn these advances into jobs here in America, as well as to help promote a better environment. America can maintain our lead in the world economy by taking the lead to preserve the world environment.

Last year, the nations of the world came together at the Earth Summit in Rio to try to find a way to protect the miraculous diversity of plant and animal life all across the planet. The biodiversity treaty which resulted had some flaws, and we all knew that. But instead of fixing them, the United States walked away from the treaty. That left us out of a treaty that is critically important not only to our future but to the future of the world, and not only because of what it will do to preserve species but because of opportunities it offers for cutting-edge companies whose research creates new medicines, new products, and new jobs.

Again, just one recent example makes the point. A tree that was thought to have no value, the Pacific Yew, used to be bulldozed and burned. Now we know that that tree contains one of our most promising potential cures for ovarian cancer, breast cancer, and other forms of cancer. We cannot walk away from challenges like those presented by the biodiversity treaty. We must step up to them.

Our administration has worked with business and environmental groups toward an agreement that protects both American interests and the world environment. And today, I am proud to announce the United States' intention to sign the biodiversity treaty.

This is an example of what you can do by bringing business and environmentalists together, instead of pitting them against each other. We can move forward to protect critical natural resources and critical technologies. I'm also directing the State Department to move ahead with our talks with other countries which have signed the convention so that the United States can move as quickly as possible toward ratification.

To learn more about where we stand in protecting all our biological resources here at home, I'm asking the Interior Department to create a national biological survey to help us protect endangered species and, just as importantly, to help the agricultural and biotechnical industries of our country identify new sources of food, fiber, and medication.

We also must take the lead in addressing the challenge of global warming that could make our planet and its climate less hospitable and more hostile to human life. Today, I reaffirm my personal and announce our Nation's commitment to reducing our emissions of greenhouse gases to their 1990 levels by the year 2000.

I am instructing my administration to produce a cost-effective plan by August that can continue the trend of reduced emission. This must be a clarion call, not for more bureaucracy or regulation or unnecessary costs but, instead, for American ingenuity and creativity, to produce the best and most energy-efficient technology.

After the cold war, we face the challenge of helping Russia achieve a healthy democracy, a healthy economy, and a healthy environment. Our Russian aid package includes $38 million to clean up pollution and promote better uses of energy. As with the full range of our investments in Russia, this is truly an investment not only in promoting our own values but in protecting our national security. To protect the environment at home and abroad, I am committed to a Government that leads by example, brings people together, and brings out the best in everyone. For too long our Government did more to inflame environmental issues than to solve them. Different Agencies pursued conflicting policies. National leaders polarized people. And problems wound up in the courts or in the streets instead of being solved.

We seek to bring a new spirit to these difficult issues. Three weeks ago in Portland, Oregon, we brought together business people, timber workers, and environmentalists from throughout the Northwest to discuss how best to preserve jobs and to protect the old-growth forests and the species which inhabit them. People sat down in a conference room, not a court room, and in the words of Archbishop Thomas Murphy of Seattle, we tried to find common ground for a common good. At the close of that forest conference, I asked my Cabinet and our entire administration to begin work immediately to craft a balanced, comprehensive long-term policy that is also comprehensible.

Before I ask our companies and our communities and our families to meet any challenge, it seems to me we have to set that standard for the Government. The American people are entitled to know where the United States stands on this issue and many other issues. And it is time to bring an end to the time when issues like this wind up in court and there are five different positions from the United States Government itself. We can never solve problems in that fashion. We can only undermine the security and stability of people's lives.

That's one reason I am proud that yesterday the United States Army announced its plan to clean up a large number of sites where we learned recently that chemical weapons mate-

rials may be buried, in some places from as long ago as World War I. Working with the EPA, the Army will clean up this problem safely and in an environmentally sound manner.

This is a legacy of America's efforts to defend our people and the community of free nations. Now, we are taking steps to defend our people and our environment and the environment of the world. In that same spirit, I plan to sign an Executive order requiring Federal facilities that manufacture, process, or use toxic chemicals, to comply with the Federal right-to-know laws and publicly report what they are doing.

I might add that it is time that the United States Government begins to live under the laws it makes for other people. With this Executive order, I ask all Federal facilities to set a voluntary goal to reducing their release of toxic pollutants by 50 percent by 1999. This will reduce toxic releases, control costs associated with cleanups, and promote clean technologies. And it will help make our Government what it should be, a positive example for the rest of the country.

Poor neighborhoods in our cities suffer most often from toxic pollution. Cleaning up the toxic wastes will create new jobs in these neighborhoods for those people and make them safer places to live, to work, and to do business.

Today I am also signing an Executive order that directs Federal agencies to make preliminary changes in their purchasing policies, to use fewer substances harmful to the ozone layer. Here, too, we must put our actions where our values are. Our Government is a leading purchaser of goods and services. And it's time to stop not only the waste of taxpayers' money but the waste of our natural resources.

Today I am signing an Executive order which commits the Federal Government to buy thousands more American made vehicles, using clean, domestic fuels such as natural gas, ethanol, methanol, and electric power. This will reduce our demand for foreign oil, reduce air pollution, promote promising technologies, promote American companies, create American jobs, and save American tax dollars. To demonstrate my commitment to this issue, Energy Secretary O'Leary is creating a task force led by the land commissioner of Texas, Garry Mauro, who is here in the audience today, who has headed a successful effort in his own State. I hope we can do as well in America as they have done in Texas.

In that same spirit, I plan to sign an Executive order committing every agency of the National Government to do more than ever to buy and use recycled products. This will provide a market for new technologies, make better use of recycled materials, and encourage the creation of new products that can be offered to the Government, to private companies, and to consumers. And again, it will create jobs through the recycling process.

We must keep finding new ways to be a force for positive change. For example, the Federal Government is the largest purchaser of computer equipment in the world, and computers are the fastest growing area of electricity use. That's why I am also signing an Executive order today requiring the Federal Government to purchase energy-efficient computers. We're going to expand the market for a technology where America pioneered and still leads the world, and we'll save energy, saving the taxpayers $40 million a year, and set an example for our country and for the world.

For as long as I live and work in the White House, I want Americans to see it not only as a symbol of clean Government but also a clean environment. That's why I'm announcing an energy and environmental audit of the White House. We're going to identify what it takes to make the White House a model for efficiency and waste reduction. It might mean fewer memos and less paper. [*Laughter*] And then we're going to get the job done. I want to make the White House a model for other Federal agencies, for State and local governments, for business, and for families in their homes. Before I ask you to do the best you can in your house, I ought to make sure I'm doing the best I can in my house.

I ask that all of us today reaffirm our willingness to assume responsibility for our common environment and to do it willingly, hopefully, and joyously. We are challenged here today not so much to sacrifice as to celebrate and create.

I've challenged Americans who are young in years or young in spirit to offer their time and their talent to serve their communities and their country. I've asked them to help in teaching our children, healing the sick, policing our streets. But equally important are efforts to protect our environment, from our largest cities to our smallest towns to our suburbs. Our national service plan will ask thousands of Americans to do their part, from leading recycling drives to preventing lead poisoning.

The challenge to shoulder responsibility and seize opportunity extends to each of us in businesses, communities, and homes. In our own lives, in our own ways, each of us has something to offer to the work of cleaning up America's environment. And each of us surely has something very personal to gain.

On a colder day in the middle of winter, just 3 months ago, a poet asked us to celebrate not only the marvelous diversity of our people but the miraculous bounty of our land. "Here on the pulse of this new day," Maya Angelou challenged us to look at "the rock, the river, the tree, your country." Now, it is a season of new hope and new beginnings. And as we look anew at our neighbors, our children, and our own communities, as well as the world around us, we must seize the possibilities inherent in this exhilarating moment, to face our challenges, to exercise our responsibilities, and to rejoice in them.

Thank you very much.

NOTE: The President spoke at 11:50 a.m. at the U.S. Botanic Gardens. The Executive orders of April 21 on ozone-depleting substances, alternative fueled vehicles, and energy efficient computer equipment are listed in Appendix D at the end of this volume. Later in the year, the President signed Executive orders on compliance with right-to-know laws (August 3, 58 FR 41981) and recycling (October 20, 58 FR 54911).

Remarks at a Reception for the Opening of the United States Holocaust Memorial Museum
April 21, 1993

Thank you so much for that magnificent statement and for the kind introduction. Ladies and gentlemen, Hillary and I and the Vice President and Mrs. Gore are deeply honored to welcome all of you here to the White House this afternoon to mark the opening of the United States Holocaust Memorial Museum.

All of us are honored to be joined by the heads of state of so many distinguished nations: of Israel and Portugal, Croatia and Romania, Bulgaria and Hungary, Poland, Slovenia, the Czech Republic, the Slovak Republic, Albania and Moldova. These fine people, as you heard, and I had a lot of conversations this afternoon and we are a little late, and for that I apologize. I do want to say that for a while some of my friends in the audience were speculating, as Mandy had to stand up and sing again and again, that I was really testing the proposition that he has not only the best voice but the strongest lungs in the United States of America.

This afternoon I was interrupted on a couple of occasions to go back and work with the Congress in our attempt to create more jobs for the American people, but I spent a great deal of time talking to these world leaders about things that concern us all and that are very relevant to the occasion which has brought all of you here today. I was honored to see the President of Israel on this day when we announce the resumption of peace talks in the Middle East starting next week. We know this is the beginning, not the end of the process; but what a fine day it is to begin.

I was honored to talk with the leaders of these other nations about things of profound concern to the Jewish community in America. How can we keep democracy alive in Russia and the other republics of the former Soviet Union and throughout Eastern Europe? How can we stand against the awful principle of ethnic cleansing which has too much currency in the world today, given the experiences of so many people in a world so recently gone by?

I want to thank Benjamin Meed, not only for what he said but for what he has done. I want to thank Bud Meyerhoff and Bill Lowenberg who made a very significant contribution to this week's events through their services as Chair and Vice Chair of the Museum Council. I understand that we have here in this audience two half-siblings of Raoul Wallenberg, Nina Lager and Guy von Dardel. And I want to recognize them and all the rest of you whose generosity and dedication and determination never to forget has helped make this day a reality. I want to recognize the members of the Cabinet and the distinguished Members of the United States Congress who are here and thank them for their presence and their dedication. Finally, there are many friends of the Gores and the Clintons who are here tonight whom I've not seen since the election. And I want to thank you and say that we're going to take more time shaking hands on the way out than we did on the way in, and I hope we'll be able to see all of you.

We've gathered here to mark the opening of this Holocaust Museum. We do so to help ensure that the Holocaust will remain ever a sharp thorn in every national memory, but especially in the memory of the United States, which has such unique responsibilities at this moment in history. We do so to redeem in some small measure the deaths of millions whom our nations did not, or would not, or could not save. We do so to help teach new generations the dangers of antidemocratic despots, racist ideologies, and ethnic hatreds.

Late Monday night, I walked through the museum with the museum's Director, Jeshajahu Weinberg. He did a brilliant job of telling me about the incredible work in the relatively brief time of 2 hours and 10 minutes. And I say that in all seriousness. When the Vice President went through the museum, he said, if you go back there you ought to allow at least 2 hours so that you can really absorb what you will see and feel. I can personally now attest to how darkly it teaches and how deeply it moves all who step inside with their ears, their eyes, and their hearts open. It is the testament not only to the worst and most depraved examples of human conduct but also to the best, the bravest, and the most loving in the human soul. I hope that all of you who are here and all of the many visitors who come to Washington from now on will take the opportunity to visit and be touched by this wonderful place.

Many of the leaders who join us today are from countries now making bold transitions toward democracy, as I have said. As a Nation that's been struggling with it for more than 200 years now, we understand some of the challenges of that transition. Even after 200 years there are parts of it we have trouble getting right. The Holocaust Museum will stand as a stark reminder that, of the many tasks of democracy, the most imperative perhaps, are those of fostering tolerance for ethnic and religious and racial differences, of fostering religious freedom and individual right and civic responsibility; each of us to take responsibility for the welfare of all of us.

The event we have joined to commemorate is one of immeasurable sorrow; yet today we speak of hope, as others have said. For while the faces pictured within the museum remind us of the worst of an old Europe, the faces I see within this tent suggest the best of a new Europe and a new world: a Europe no longer divided by ideology, no longer braced for all-consuming war, where freedom is replacing repression, where people can devote less of their resources to preparation for hostilities and more for investment for prosperity. We know, of course, that the new Europe is not yet free of old cruelties and that contemporary horrors like the slaughter of innocents in Bosnia have not disappeared. Indeed, one of the eternal lessons to which this museum bears strong witness is that the struggle against darkness will never end and the need for vigilance will never fade away.

Still, we have grounds to hope that the seeds of democracy in Europe will one day soon bear the fruit of a more peaceful civic culture in which neighbor no longer lifts up sword against neighbor, within countries or across national borders. Our own people have long waited and too often have had to fight for that kind of Europe. Now that these historic transitions are underway, I want you to know that the United States will remain fully engaged in Europe and in its transitions toward a new and better future. For, as we vow never to forget the dark days of a half-century ago when all humanity fell apart, we can also celebrate in this event the process of coming together by rededicating ourselves to making sure that the process works, that this time all of us will get it right. It is a coming together of Israel and those nations that saw much of the worst persecution of the Jews. A coming together of Western Europe and Central Europe and Eastern Europe and, indeed, the first coming together of those regions ever as democratic states. It is a coming together among free peoples determined to confront and remember the horrors that befell past generations so that we can create a world of justice and peace for our generation and for the children to come.

I thank all of you for coming here today. But more than that, I thank you for living the lives that brought you here today. God bless you all.

NOTE: The President spoke at 6:43 p.m. on the South Lawn at the White House. In his remarks, he referred to entertainer Mandy Patinkin and Benjamin Meed, president, American Gathering of Jewish Holocaust Survivors.

Exchange With Reporters on the Stimulus Package
April 21, 1993

Q. Mr. President, any reaction to the——

The President. Well, I'm disappointed. But I knew when I came here that we'd have to change some things in Washington and that the American people won't be surprised, I guess, to think that a minority of one House could keep several hundred thousand people out of work this year. I think it's a mistake, but I'm not done. I'm going to come back next week and regroup and go forward.

We've had a real good success getting our budget plan through. We've kept interest rates down. There's going to be $100 billion in refinancing this year as a result of that. So I think that things are going basically in the right direction, but I'm very disappointed about this. And frankly, I'm a little surprised about it. It doesn't make a lot of sense. A lot of the Republican Senators told me they wanted us to work something out, and I went out of my way to meet them halfway, and then some. I don't know. But I just think that we've got to keep fighting for jobs.

I think it's so easy for people who are here, who have not been out in the country, who make these decisions, who all have jobs, to be willing to pay for unemployment but not want to invest in employment, not want to put people to work. And I just think we've got to keep fighting for it. So next week I'll regroup and try to do something else.

Q. What do you come back with next week?

The President. I don't know. We'll see. This country went in one direction solid for more than a decade. I've been here about 90 days; it's going to take a little while to turn it around. But I'm not too disheartened. I'm disappointed in this particular thing and surprised by it, genuinely surprised, but I think we can regroup and go forward.

Q. If you can't get a $16-billion stimulus package through Congress, what does it say for some of your more ambitious proposals, health care reform and the price tag that that carries with it?

The President. Well, we'll just have to see. I think that depends on, always, whether there is a majority for a proposition and then whether the minority will keep it from even being voted on. I think the American people need to know that we had a majority in both Houses of Congress, but the minority kept the issue from being voted on. I feel pretty good about it.

We passed the budget resolution, and we got the 60 votes necessary to break the debate in the Senate there, so I think we've got a real shot at a lot of reform. But it's going to be hard. And as I said, look at what's happened in the last 12 years: the deficit goes up, jobs go down, and no investment in our people. Congress passes laws it doesn't live under. We're trying to change this. And a lot of the Members of Congress have been willing to support this process of reform. This is, I hope and believe, an aberration where a minority stubbornly refused to let an issue get voted on. I'm just not going to be discouraged by it; we're just going to go on.

Q. Let me ask you, when you come back next week, are you coming back with a scaled-down jobs bill or what are you——

The Vice President. Stay tuned.

The President. I've got to talk to a lot of people, see where we are, and go forward. We've got lots of other issues we need to put out there in the Congress and, you know, we may not win them all. But I'm going to keep fighting for jobs. I'm going to wake up tomorrow knowing that I'm waging a fight to put the American people back to work and lift this economy up, and that's what I was hired to do. I'm just going to keep doing it.

Q. Is this a pretty big defeat for you, Mr. President? Isn't this a big defeat?

The President. Not a big defeat. For me, it's a big disappointment to the hundreds of thousands of Americans who would have had jobs. But I don't have to explain it; I fought for it. The people who have voted for this sort of spending repeatedly to help other countries and wouldn't do it to help their own folks and did it when the deficit was going up, and I'm bringing the deficit down, they may have to explain some things, but that's the way Washington's worked for too long. We're going to lift this thing up and change it. We've just got to get people focused on the American people and their needs and put aside all the petty politics and all the maneuvering and start thinking about what's best for the American people. I think we can change it, and I'm upbeat about it. We've just been here 90 days. And basically, the big part of the plan, the budget resolution, passed. We've just got to keep fighting it.

NOTE: The exchange began at 7:42 p.m. in the North Portico at the White House. A tape was not available for verification of the content of this exchange.

Letter to Congressional Leaders Reporting on Panamanian Government Assets
April 21, 1993

Dear Mr. Speaker: *(Dear Mr. President:)*

1. I hereby report on developments since the last Presidential report on October 5, 1992, concerning the continued blocking of Panamanian government assets. This report is submitted pursuant to section 207(d) of the International Emergency Economic Powers Act, 50 U.S.C. 1706(d).

2. On April 5, 1990, President Bush issued Executive Order No. 12710, terminating the na-

tional emergency declared on April 8, 1988, with respect to Panama. While this order terminated the sanctions imposed pursuant to that declaration, the blocking of Panamanian government assets in the United States was continued in order to permit completion of the orderly unblocking and transfer of funds that the President directed on December 20, 1989, and to foster the resolution of claims of U.S. creditors involving Panama, pursuant to 50 U.S.C. 1706(a). The termination of the national emergency did not affect the continuation of compliance audits and enforcement actions with respect to activities taking place during the sanctions period, pursuant to 50 U.S.C. 1622(a).

3. Of the approximately $6.3 million remaining blocked at this time (which includes approximately $100,000 in interest credited to the accounts since the last report), some $5.7 million is held in escrow by the Federal Reserve Bank of New York at the request of the Government of Panama. Additionally, approximately $600,000

is held in commercial bank accounts for which the Government of Panama has not requested unblocking. A small residual in blocked reserve accounts established under section 565.509 of the Panamanian Transactions Regulations, 31 CFR 565.509, remains on the books of U.S. firms pending the final reconciliation of accounting records involving claims and counterclaims between the firms and the Government of Panama.

4. I will continue to report periodically on the exercise of authorities to prohibit transactions involving property in which the Government of Panama has an interest, pursuant to 50 U.S.C. 1706(d).

Sincerely,

WILLIAM J. CLINTON

NOTE: Identical letters were sent to Thomas S. Foley, Speaker of the House of Representatives, and Albert Gore, Jr., President of the Senate.

Letter to Congressional Leaders Reporting on the Cyprus Conflict
April 21, 1993

Dear Mr. Speaker: (*Dear Mr. Chairman:*)

In accordance with Public Law 95–384 (22 U.S.C. 2373(c)), I am submitting to you this bimonthly report on progress toward a negotiated settlement of the Cyprus question. The previous report, sent to you by President Bush, covered September, October, and part of November 1992. The current report covers the remainder of November 1992 through February 14, 1993.

There were no further face-to-face negotiating sessions on the Cyprus issue from the time of the October 12, 1992, recess of the New York talks through February 14, 1993. During this period, which coincided with the campaign and Presidential election in the Republic of Cyprus, the U.N. Secretary General's negotiators and the U.S. Special Cyprus Coordinator, Ambassador John Maresca, and other U.S. officials remained in contact with the two Cypriot communities and the Governments of Greece and Turkey.

The previous report on this subject included Secretary General Boutros-Ghali's report on the October-November U.N. negotiating session and

U.N. Security Council Resolution 789, which unanimously endorsed the Secretary General's report, including the confidence-building measures suggested therein. On November 24, 1992, President Vassiliou notified the Secretary General by letter that the Greek-Cypriot side accepted the Secretary General's report, including the confidence-building measures. The Turkish-Cypriot side reacted negatively to both the Secretary General's report and to Security Council Resolution 789.

On November 22, between the time of the issuance of the Secretary General's report and the passage of Security Council Resolution 789, U.S. Special Cyprus Coordinator Maresca visited Ankara and Athens and discussed the report and the resolution that was then being drafted in New York. Ambassador Maresca had further discussions in Washington with representatives of the two Cypriot sides as well as with the Turkish Embassy. Ambassador Maresca informed all concerned that he would not visit Cyprus during the Cypriot election campaign.

In early December, during a regular visit to

the Eastern Mediterranean area, the Director of the State Department's European Bureau, Office of Southern European Affairs, discussed the Cyprus negotiations with the leaders of both Cypriot communities on the island and with officials of the Governments of Greece and Turkey.

The election campaign in Cyprus continued into February 1993. On February 7, the first round of the election did not produce a majority for any candidate. One week later, on February 14, the last day covered by this report, the two candidates with the most votes in the first round—the incumbent, President George Vassiliou, and Mr. Glafcos Clerides—faced each other in a runoff election. Mr. Clerides won the runoff by about 2,000 votes.

I would like to take the opportunity of my first letter on the Cyprus dispute to reiterate my strong commitment to press hard for a lasting solution to the tragedy of Cyprus. I intend to give that goal a high priority in my Adminis-

tration. The U.N. "set of ideas" for a bizonal and bicommunal federation with a single national sovereignty and identity continues to offer the best chance for a peaceful resolution of this dispute. I urge both President Clerides, in his new capacity as the leader of the Greek-Cypriot community, and Mr. Denktash, the leader of the Turkish-Cypriot community, to continue their participation in the U.N.-sponsored negotiations and to be ready when the talks resume to make the political decisions necessary to resolve this long-standing dispute in a way that is acceptable and beneficial to all Cypriots.

Sincerely,

BILL CLINTON

NOTE: Identical letters were sent to Thomas S. Foley, Speaker of the House of Representatives, and Claiborne Pell, Chairman of the Senate Committee on Foreign Relations.

Message to the Congress Transmitting the "Goals 2000: Educate America Act"
April 21, 1993

To the Congress of the United States:

I am pleased to transmit today for your immediate consideration and enactment the "Goals 2000: Educate America Act."

This legislation strives to support States, local communities, schools, business and industry, and labor in reinventing our education system so that all Americans can reach internationally competitive standards, and our Nation can reach the National Education Goals. Also transmitted is a section-by-section analysis.

Education is and always has been primarily a State responsibility. States have always been the "laboratories of democracy." This has been especially true in education over the past decades. The lessons we have learned from the collective work of States, local education agencies, and individual schools are incorporated in Goals 2000 and provide the basis for a new partnership between the Federal Government, States, parents, business, labor, schools, communities, and students. This new partnership is not one of mandates, but of cooperation and leadership.

The "Goals 2000: Educate America Act" is designed to promote a long-term direction for the improvement of education and lifelong learning and to provide a framework and resources to help States and others interested in education strengthen, accelerate, and sustain their own improvement efforts. Goals 2000 will:

• Set into law the six National Education Goals and establish a bipartisan National Education Goals Panel to report on progress toward achieving the goals;
• Develop voluntary academic standards and assessments that are meaningful, challenging, and appropriate for all students through the National Education Standards and Improvement Council;
• Identify the conditions of learning and teaching necessary to ensure that all students have the opportunity to meet high standards;
• Establish a National Skill Standards Board to promote the development and adoption of occupational standards to ensure that American workers are among the best

trained in the world;

- Help States and local communities involve public officials, teachers, parents, students, and business leaders in designing and reforming schools; and
- Increase flexibility for States and school districts by waiving regulations and other requirements that might impede reforms.

Though voluntary, the pursuit of these goals must be the work of our Nation as a whole.

Ten years ago this month, *A Nation At Risk* was released. Its warnings still ring true. It is time to act boldly. It is time to rekindle the dream that good schools offer.

I urge the Congress to take prompt and favorable action on this legislation.

WILLIAM J. CLINTON

The White House,
April 21, 1993.

Nomination for Secretary of the Navy
April 21, 1993

The President announced today that he intends to nominate John Dalton, an Annapolis graduate and former Chairman of the Federal Home Loan Bank Board, to be Secretary of the Navy.

"Throughout his distinguished Navy career and his equally distinguished civilian career in public service and private industry, John Dalton has displayed true leadership ability," said the President. "I am proud that he has agreed to serve with me and confident that he will work with Secretary Aspin and the Navy to adjust to the new security realities that we face."

NOTE: A biography of the nominee was made available by the Office of the Press Secretary.

Remarks at the Dedication of the United States Holocaust Memorial Museum
April 22, 1993

Thank you very much, Mr. Vice President, Mrs. Gore, President and Mrs. Herzog, distinguished leaders of nations from around the world who have come here to be with us today, the leaders of our Congress, and the citizens of America, and especially to Mr. Meyerhoff and all of those who worked so hard to make this day possible, and even more to those who have spoken already on this program, whose lives and words bear eloquent witness to why we have come here today.

It is my purpose on behalf of the United States to commemorate this magnificent museum, meeting as we do among memorials, within the sight of the memorial to Thomas Jefferson, the author of our freedom, near where Abraham Lincoln is seated, who gave his life so that our Nation might extend its mandate of freedom to all who live within our borders. We gather near the place where the legendary

and recently departed Marian Anderson sang songs of freedom and where Martin Luther King summoned us all to dream and work together. Here on the town square of our national life, on this 50th anniversary of the Warsaw Uprising, at Eisenhower Plaza on Raoul Wallenberg Place, we dedicate the United States Holocaust Museum and so bind one of the darkest lessons in history to the hopeful soul of America.

As we have seen already today, this museum is not for the dead alone nor even for the survivors who have been so beautifully represented; it is perhaps most of all for those of us who were not there at all, to learn the lessons, to deepen our memories and our humanity, and to transmit these lessons from generation to generation.

The Holocaust, to be sure, transformed the entire 20th century, sweeping aside the Enlightenment hope that evil somehow could be permanently vanished from the face of the Earth, demonstrating there is no war to end all war, that the struggle against the basest tendencies of our nature must continue forever and ever.

The Holocaust began when the most civilized country of its day unleashed unprecedented acts of cruelty and hatred, abetted by perversions of science, philosophy, and law. A culture, which produced Goethe, Schiller, and Beethoven, then brought forth Hitler and Himmler, the merciless hordes, who themselves were educated, as others who were educated stood by and did nothing. Millions died for who they were, how they worshiped, what they believed, and who they loved. But one people, the Jews, were immutably marked for total destruction. They who were among their nation's most patriotic citizens, whose extinction served no military purpose nor offered any political gain, they who threatened no one were slaughtered by an efficient, unrelenting bureaucracy, dedicated solely to a radical evil with a curiously antiseptic title: The Final Solution.

The Holocaust reminds us forever that knowledge divorced from values can only serve to deepen the human nightmare, that a head without a heart is not humanity. For those of us here today representing the nations of the West, we must live forever with this knowledge. Even as our fragmentary awareness of crimes grew into indisputable facts, far too little was done. Before the war even started, doors to liberty were shut. And even after the United States and the Allies attacked Germany, rail lines to the camps within miles of military-significant targets were left undisturbed.

Still there were, as has been noted, many deeds of singular courage and resistance: the Danes and the Bulgarians, men like Emmanuel Ringelbaum, who died after preserving in metal milk cans the history of the Warsaw ghetto; Janusz Korczak, who stayed with children until their last breaths at Treblinka; and Raoul Wallenberg, who perhaps rescued as many as 100,000 Hungarian Jews; and those known and those never to be known, who manned the thin line of righteousness, who risked and lost their lives to save others, accruing no advantage to themselves but nobly serving the larger cause of humanity.

As the war ended, these rescuers were joined by our military forces who, alongside the allied armies, played the decisive role in bringing the Holocaust to an end. Overcoming the shock of discovery, they walked survivors from those dark, dark places into the sweet sunlight of redemption, soldiers and survivors being forever joined in history and humanity. This place is their place, too, for them as for us, to memorialize the past and steel ourselves for the challenges of tomorrow.

We must all now frankly admit that there will come a time in the not too distant future when the Holocaust will pass from living reality and shared experience to memory and to history. To preserve this shared history of anguish, to keep it vivid and real so that evil can be combated and contained, we are here to consecrate this memorial and contemplate its meaning for us. For more than any other event, the Holocaust gave rise to the universal declaration of human rights, the charter of our common humanity. And it contributed, indeed made certain, the long overdue creation of the nation of Israel.

Now, with the demise of communism and the rise of democracy out of the ashes of former Communist states, with the end of the cold war, we must not only rejoice in so much that is good in the world but recognize that not all in this new world is good. We learn again and again that the world has yet to run its course of animosity and violence.

Ethnic cleansing in the former Yugoslavia is but the most brutal and blatant and ever-present manifestation of what we see also with the oppression of the Kurds in Iraq, the abusive treatment of the Baha'i in Iran, the endless race-based violence in South Africa. And in many other places we are reminded again and again how fragile are the safeguards of civilization. So do the depraved and insensate bands now loose in the modern world. Look at the liars and the propagandists among us, the skinheads and the Liberty Lobby here at home, the Afrikaaners resistance movement in South Africa, the Radical Party of Serbia, the Russian blackshirts. With them we must all compete for the interpretation and the preservation of history, of what we know and how we should behave.

The evil represented in this museum is incontestable. But as we are its witness, so must we remain its adversary in the world in which we live; so we must stop the fabricators of history and the bullies as well. Left unchallenged, they would still prey upon the powerless, and we must not permit that to happen again.

To build bulwarks against this kind of evil,

we know there is but one path to take. It is the direction opposite that which produced the Holocaust; it is that which recognizes that among all our differences, we still cannot ever separate ourselves one from another. We must find in our diversity our common humanity. We must reaffirm that common humanity, even in the darkest and deepest of our own disagreements.

Sure, there is new hope in this world. The emergence of new, vibrant democratic states, many of whose leaders are here today, offers a shield against the inhumanity we remember. And it is particularly appropriate that this museum is here in this magnificent city, an enduring tribute to democracy. It is a constant reminder of our duty to build and nurture the institutions of public tranquility and humanity.

It occurs to me that some may be reluctant to come inside these doors because the photographs and remembrance of the past impart more pain than they can bear. I understand that. I walked through the museum on Monday night and spent more than 2 hours. But I think that our obligations to history and posterity alike should beckon us all inside these doors. It is a journey that I hope every American who comes to Washington will take, a journey I hope all the visitors to this city from abroad will make.

I believe that this museum will touch the life of everyone who enters and leave everyone forever changed: a place of deep sadness and a sanctuary of bright hope, an ally of education

against ignorance, of humility against arrogance, an investment in a secure future against whatever insanity lurks ahead. If this museum can mobilize morality, then those who have perished will thereby gain a measure of immortality.

I know this is a difficult day for those we call survivors. Those of us born after the war cannot yet fully comprehend their sorrow or pain. But if our expressions are inadequate to this moment, at least may I share these words inscribed in the Book of Wisdom: "The souls of the righteous are in the hands of God, and no torment shall touch them. In the eyes of fools they seem to die. Their passing away was thought to be an affliction, and their going forth from us, utter destruction. But they are in peace."

On this day of triumphant reunion and celebration, I hope those who have survived have found their peace. Our task, with God's blessing upon our souls and the memories of the fallen in our hearts and minds, is to the ceaseless struggle to preserve human rights and dignity. We are now strengthened and will be forever strengthened by remembrance. I pray that we shall prevail.

NOTE: The President spoke at 12:43 p.m. at the Memorial. In his remarks, he referred to Chaim Herzog, President of Israel, and Harvey M. Meyerhoff, Chairman, U.S. Holocaust Memorial Council.

Remarks on Presenting the American Cancer Society Courage Awards and an Exchange With Reporters
April 22, 1993

The President. Ladies and gentlemen, these are the annual American Cancer Society Courage Awards. And the certificate salutes the two people I'll present the awards to for personal courage in the battle against cancer and for a message of hope and inspiration given to all Americans in the fight for life and health.

We have here to my right Dr. Reginald Ho, the president of the American Cancer Society; Stanley Shmichkiss, who is the chairman of the board of the Cancer Society; Dr. John Seffrin, the national executive vice president and chief

staff officer of the Cancer Society.

The young gentleman to my right is Mr. Jeremy Fleury, who is here with his mother, Sharon. And I want to tell you a little about him. He is 13, same age as my daughter. He's undergone treatment for non-Hodgkin's lymphoma way back in 1989, and since then he's been in clinical remission. He's a very brave young man, and he's from Clovis, New Mexico.

So I want to give you this. I'll let you hold it so everyone can see it.

And further to the left is Matilda Goodridge,

from New York, New York, who has been enrolled since 1981 in the Breast Examination Center of Harlem, located at the Harlem Hospital, which I have visited. She kept annual visits for a mammogram and in 1991 was diagnosed with a localized breast cancer. She's undergone surgery and treatment, and she's doing quite well. And I want to recognize her.

Both these folks have had a lot of personal difficulties because of the absence of medical coverage and some other economic problems, and they're carrying on with a lot of real courage. I also want to compliment Ms. Goodridge, as the son of a breast cancer survivor, for being enrolled in the breast examination program for over a decade. I think that example will help to save the lives of many women in this country who will see this ceremony recorded in the news media.

So I congratulate both of you. Let me give this to you. And thank you very much for being here.

[*At this point, the President presented the awards.*]

If I might point out, this young man and his mother—if she remains unemployed, they can be covered through Medicaid. But if she were to take another job, it would be very difficult, because of his treatment and past condition, even though he's in remission, for her to get a job with health insurance.

If we can pass reforms which will guarantee coverage to all Americans and which will provide a broad-based community base for any insurance against risks so that there will be no economic advantage or disadvantage to employers for hiring the parents or the people who suffer from disease, this country will be a long way down the road toward dealing with this problem. And I think that that clearly will be a part of the health program that we come out with, something that will guarantee coverage to all Americans and will enable people to leave their jobs to care for sick family members and then resume employment when possible without having the employer suffer economically crippling con-

sequences or forcing the people to choose between staying unemployed to get Government health care or taking a job and losing health coverage.

Health Care Reform

Q. Mr. President, have you decided on a way to finance health care reform? I mean, you're moving toward a deadline now. Have you made any decisions?

The President. We're moving toward a deadline, and we'll have the details for you. I've already told—those things will be in the program. Whatever options we decide, we'll do that.

Q. When do you think you'll make your mind up?

The President. Well, we're still well within our deadline. I think that—because of my father-in-law's illness my wife was out of pocket for about 3 weeks, and so we're going to be pushed back a little bit off the 100 days. But we're working very hard. I spent many, many hours on this myself and, indeed, this afternoon will be spending another 2½ hours on it. So I think we're pretty well on schedule.

Bosnia

Q. [*Inaudible*]—Elie Wiesel's comments about Bosnia this morning, sir, as a challenge to you personally?

The President. I think it was a challenge to the United States and to me and to the West to take further initiatives in Bosnia. And I accepted it as such.

I was eager to have a few moments to speak with Elie Wiesel after the ceremony. We went back into a holding room, and I introduced him to my wife and my daughter, who wanted very much to meet him. And then we sat and talked for a while. We may talk again. But I welcomed his remarks this morning.

NOTE: The President spoke at 3:30 p.m. in the Oval Office at the White House. A tape was not available for verification of the content of these remarks.

Remarks at the National Volunteer Action Award Ceremony
April 22, 1993

Thank you very much. I want to thank, first of all, the people who have made possible this 12th annual National Volunteer Action Award event, begun in the early 1980's under President Reagan, people from the Points of Light Foundation and the folks from ACTION. I want to say, too, to all of you that this is a matter of great personal pride to me to be President and be a part of this today, because I have believed for a long time in grassroots community efforts and community service.

Last year, on the occasion of my birthday, which I share with the Vice President's wife, Tipper Gore, our two families went to Georgia and built a house with Habitat for Humanity, along with President and Mrs. Carter as a way of symbolizing our commitment to national service. And my daughter selected a school here in Washington in part because one of the requirements of being enrolled in the school was to do community service. Just a couple of days ago, she and her group went out and did one of their service projects, working to build some park facilities for young people who will come behind and use those facilities.

I can't help but say I'm especially proud today because one of the honorees today is the Arkansas Land and Farm Development Corporation from my home State. I should say, I had nothing to do with selecting any of these awards. [*Laughter*] But they will tell you that for well over a decade I have worked with them in many ways, watching them work against often enormous odds to empower poor people in rural areas to seize control of their own destinies. So I am especially proud of them as well as of all the other honorees.

I think all of you recognize the fundamental truth that as Americans and as human beings we can never be completely fulfilled unless we help each other. Just a few moments ago, I was over at the dedication of the Holocaust Museum. And we recognized, of course, the great losses of the Jewish people, of the Gypsies, and others who were systematically exterminated by the Nazis. But we also recognize the services of perhaps the most important volunteers in the 20th century, those who put their lives at risk to try to save large numbers of the Jews.

On that cold, wind-whipped occasion, I think it's fair to say that, by far, the most popular speaker at the event was a woman who put her life at risk to shield Jews from almost certain death and, in the process, found a person who became her husband. The Scriptures say that in giving we will receive. Perhaps not all of us will find a mate for life in our gifts, but all of us certainly will receive.

I think it has been recognized for a long time that service sustains and defines our democracy and helps us to understand that we are not brought together by race or religion or region but that we cannot be kept apart by those things if we have common values, common interests, and undertake common endeavors.

After all, volunteers won the American Revolution. And ever since, volunteers have been winning our wars and winning the battles of peacetime. Volunteers helped to get women the right to vote and helped to effect the civil rights revolution and help us even today to overcome the barriers that divide us.

All generations have been called upon to serve. And today, as people are living longer than ever before, every generation now living is called upon to serve, to deepen our lives and to strengthen the bonds of our communities. Today is so special to me because we are recognizing those of you who have risen to the challenge in particularly innovative and effective ways.

I hope that as we honor you today you will all join me in renewing our call for all Americans to embrace the spirit of service. We all have roles to play. Even those who are not in organizations represented here may be able to help to patrol this, police, and support the work of law enforcement officers in areas plagued by high crime, where children are unsafe, or may help to volunteer in a community health center where health care is available in theory but not in practice unless people can find their way to the clinic; or tutoring children after school; or being mentors to children who themselves would like to do better but don't have the role models they need.

We bring out the best in our country when we serve. I know that you know that I've tried to make sure our Government will do its part. And as Mr. Segal said, next week I intend to introduce the national service legislation that I hope will change our country for the better and forever to provide a revolution in the best sense of the word, bringing us back to our best values, offering opportunity, requiring responsibility, and creating a stronger sense of the American community.

Those are the things which drove me into this race for President well over a year ago and the things which I hope so deeply will be embodied in the national service movement. We want to make opportunity available by making it easier to get a loan to go to college and easier to pay it off through service, demanding responsibility by making sure that everybody who gets something from their Government finally gives something back, we hope in service but at least in dollars, and rebuilding communities all over this country through our civilian GI bill, with thousands of people paying their way to college either before or after they go by doing what their communities need.

We'll bring ourselves a little closer to that sacred day when all of our children can live up to their full potential by working together to make sure that we do that as well as the children we're trying to help. If these efforts are to succeed, the spirit of service must be renewed in the hearts of every American, not just in those who will be part of the national service movement. I hope that this movement will go well beyond party or any other political division in this country. I hope that everybody will embrace the cause and the spirit, because I believe we can change the country. If we can do it here in the Government, we can then challenge our corporations, our foundations, our schools, our nonprofits to follow the leads of those whom we honor here today. And if we're in it for the long haul because we know we all have a role to play, I really believe it means an America finally and fully living up to its potential, that is, being more like those of you whom we honor today.

Thank you very much.

NOTE: The President spoke at 3:47 p.m. in the East Room at the White House.

Nomination for Energy Department and Ambassadorial Posts
April 22, 1993

The President announced today that he will nominate Archer Durham, a retired Major General in the U.S. Air Force, to be Assistant Secretary of Energy for Human Resources and Administration. He also formally announced his intent to nominate Boston Mayor Raymond Flynn to be Ambassador to the Holy See.

"Through his long and exemplary career in the Air Force, Archer Durham had a reputation of being a hands-on manager who consistently led the Air Force in management efficiency indicators," said the President. "Secretary O'Leary has called for that kind of management at her Department, and I am glad that General Dur-ham will be providing it."

"I am also very pleased to be formally announcing my intention to nominate Mayor Flynn for the important post of Ambassador to the Holy See," the President added. "As I said on St. Patrick's Day here at the White House, he has been one of the best mayors to serve in my lifetime, and I think he'll do a great job in a wide range of areas."

NOTE: Biographies of the nominees were made available by the Office of the Press Secretary.

The President's News Conference
April 23, 1993

The President. Terry [Terence Hunt, Associated Press], do you have a question?

Bosnia

Q. Mr. President, there's a growing feeling that the Western response to bloodshed in Bosnia has been woefully inadequate. Holocaust survivor Elie Wiesel asked you yesterday to do something, anything to stop the fighting. Is the United States considering taking unilateral action such as air strikes against Serb artillery sites?

The President. Well, first let me say, as you know, for more than a week now we have been seriously reviewing our options for further action. And I want to say, too, let's look at the last 3 months. Since I became President, I have worked with our allies, and we have tried to move forward, first on the no-fly zone, on enforcement of it, on the humanitarian airdrops, on the war crimes investigation, on getting the Bosnian Muslims involved in the peace process. We have made some progress. And now we have a very much tougher sanctions resolution. And Leon Fuerth, who is the National Security Adviser to the Vice President, is in Europe now working on implementing that. That is going to make a big difference to Serbia.

And we are reviewing other options. I think we should act. We should lead. The United States should lead. We have led for the last 3 months. We have moved the coalition. And to be fair, our allies in Europe have been willing to do their part. And they have troops on the ground there.

But I do not think we should act alone, unilaterally, nor do I think we will have to. And in the next several days I think we will finalize the extensive review which has been going on and which has taken a lot of my time as well as the time of the administration, as it should have, over the last 10 days or so. I think we'll finish that in the near future, and then we'll have a policy, and we'll announce it and everyone can evaluate it.

Q. Can I follow up?

The President. Sure.

Q. Do you see any parallel between the ethnic cleansing in Bosnia and the Holocaust?

The President. I think the Holocaust is on a whole different level. I think it is without precedent or peer in human history. On the other hand, ethnic cleansing is the kind of inhumanity that the Holocaust took to the nth degree. The idea of moving people around and abusing them and often killing them solely because of their ethnicity is an abhorrent thing. And it is especially troublesome in that area where people of different ethnic groups live side by side for so long together. And I think you have to stand up against it. I think it's wrong.

We were talking today about all of the other troubles in that region. I was happy to see the violence between the Croats and the Muslims in Bosnia subside this morning, and I think we're making progress on that front. But what's going on with the Serbians and the ethnic cleansing is qualitatively different than the other conflicts, both within the former Yugoslavia and in other parts of the region.

Helen [Helen Thomas, United Press International]?

The First 100 Days

Q. Mr. President, by any count, you have not had a good week in your Presidency. The tragedy in Waco, the defeat of your stimulus bill, the standoff in Bosnia. What did you do wrong, and what are you going to do differently? How do you look at things? Are you reassessing?

The President. I don't really believe that the situation in Bosnia—it's not been a good week for the world, but I don't know that the administration could have made it different.

On the stimulus package, I'd like to put it into the larger context and remind you that in this 100 days we have already fundamentally changed the direction of an American Government. We have abandoned trickle-down economics. We've abandoned the policies that brought the debt of this country from $1 trillion to $4 trillion in only a decade.

The budget plan, which passed the Congress, which will reduce the deficit and increase investment, has led to a 20-year low in mortgage rates, dramatically lower interest rates. There are probably people in this room who have refinanced their home mortgages in the last 3 months or who have had access to cheaper credit. That's going to put tens of billion dollars coursing throughout this economy in ways that are very, very good for the country. And so we are moving in the right direction economically.

I regret that the stimulus did not pass, and I have begun to ask, and will continue to ask, not only people in the administration but people in the Congress whether there is something I could have done differently to pass that. Part of the reason it didn't pass was politics; part of it was a difference in ideas. There are really people still who believe that it's not needed. I just disagree with that.

I think the recovery—the economists say it's been underway for about 2 years, and we've still had 16 months of 7-percent unemployment, and all the wealthy countries are having trouble creating jobs. So I think there was an idea base, an argument there, that while we're waiting for the lower interest rates and the deficit reduction and the investments of the next 4 years to take effect, this sort of supplemental appropriation should go forward.

Now, I have to tell you, I did misgauge that because a majority of the Republican Senators now sitting in the Senate voted for a similar stimulus when Ronald Reagan was President in 1983 and voted 28 times for regular supplemental appropriations like this. I just misgauged it. And I hope that I can learn something. I've just been here 90 days. And you know, I was a Governor working with a contentious legislature for 12 years, and it took me a decade to get political reform there. So it takes time to change things. But I basically feel very good about what's happened in the first 100 days with regard to the Congress.

Tragedy in Waco

Q. Waco—[*inaudible*]——

The President. Well, with regard to Waco I don't have much to add to what I've already said. I want the situation looked into. I want us to bring in people who have any insights to bear on that. I think it's very important that the whole thing be thoroughly gone over. But I still maintain what I said from the beginning, that the offender there was David Koresh. And I do not think the United States Government is responsible for the fact that a bunch of fanatics decided to kill themselves. And I'm sorry that they killed their children.

Ross Perot

Q. Mr. President, to follow up partly on Helen, on your stimulus package and on your political approach to Capitol Hill, Ross Perot said today that you're playing games with the American people in your tax policy. He was strongly critical of your stimulus package. He said he's going to launch an advertising campaign against the North American Free Trade Agreement. How are you going to handle his political criticism? Will it complicate your efforts on the Hill with your economic plan? And do you plan to repackage some of the things that have been in your stimulus program and try to resubmit them to the Hill?

The President. Let me answer that question first. We're going to revisit all of that over the next few days. I'm going to be talking to Members of Congress and to others to see what we can do about that. With regard to the economic plan, I must say I found that rather amazing. I don't want to get into an argument with Mr. Perot. I'll be interested to hear what his specifics are, but I would—go back and read his book and his plan. There's a remarkable convergence except that we have more specific budget cuts. We raise taxes less on the middle class and more on the wealthy. But otherwise, the plans are remarkably similar.

So I think it would be—I'll be interested to see if maybe perhaps he's changed his position from his book last year, and he has some new ideas to bring to bear. I'll be glad to hear them.

Q. To follow up, sir, how do you plan to handle his political criticism? He's launched a campaign against you. Do you think you can sit back and just——

The President. Well, first of all, I will ask you to apply the same level of scrutiny to him as you do to me. And if he's changed his position from the positions he took in the campaign last year, then we need to know why and what his ideas are. Maybe he's got some constructive ideas.

I think the American people have shown that they're very impatient with people who don't want to produce results. And the one thing I think that everybody has figured out about me in the last—even if they don't agree with what I do—is that I want to get something done. I just came here to try to change things. I want to do things. And I want to do things that help people's lives. So my judgment is that if he makes a suggestion that is good, that is constructive, that takes us beyond some idea I've proposed that will change people's lives for the better, fine. But I think that that ought to be the test that we apply to everyone who weighs into this debate and not just to the President.

Bosnia

Q. Mr. President, to go back to Bosnia for a minute. You continue to insist that this has to be multilateral action, a criteria that seems to have hamstrung us when it comes to many options thus far and makes it look as if this is a state of paralysis. The United States is the last remaining superpower. Why is it not appropriate in this situation for the United States to act unilaterally?

The President. Well, the United States—surely you would agree, that the United States, even as the last remaining superpower, has to act consistent with international law under some mandate of the United Nations.

Q. But you have a mandate and——

The President. They do, and that is one of the things that we have under review. I haven't ruled out any option for action. I would remind all of you, I have not ruled out any option, except that we have not discussed and we are not considering the introduction of American forces in continuing hostilities there. We are not.

So we are reviewing other options. But I also would remind you that, to be fair, our allies have had—the French, the British, and the Canadians—have had troops on the ground there. They have been justifiably worried about those. But they have supported the airdrops, the toughening of the sanctions. They welcomed the American delegation now in Europe, working on how to make these sanctions really work and really bite against Serbia. And I can tell you that the other nations involved are also genuinely reassessing their position, and I would not rule out the fact that we can reach an agreement for a concerted action that goes beyond where we have been. I don't have any criticism of the British, the French, and others about that.

Q. Would that be military action?

Statements by Administration Officials

Q. Mr. President, several of the leading lights in your administration, ranging from your FBI Director to your U.N. Ambassador, to your Dep-

uty Budget Director, to your Health Services Secretary, have issued statements in the last couple of weeks which are absolutely contradictory to some of the positions you've taken in your administration. Why is that? Are you losing your political grip?

The President. Give me an example.

Q. Example? Judge Sessions said that there was no child abuse in Waco. Madeleine Albright has said in this morning's newspapers, at least, that she favors air strikes in Bosnia. All of these are things you said that you didn't support.

The President. First of all, I don't know what—we know that David Koresh had sex with children. I think that is undisputed, is it not? Is it not? Does anybody dispute that? Where I come from that qualifies as child abuse. And we know that he had people teaching these kids how to kill themselves. I think that qualifies as abuse. And I'm not criticizing Judge Sessions because I don't know exactly what he said.

In terms of Madeleine Albright, Madeleine Albright has made no public statement at all about air strikes. There is a press report that she wrote me a confidential letter in which she expressed her—or memos—in which she expressed her views about the new direction we should take in response to my request to all the senior members of my administration to let me know what they thought we ought to do next. And I have heard from her and from others about what they think we ought to do next. And I'm not going to discuss the recommendations they made to me, but in the next few days when I make a decision about what to do, then I will announce what I'm going to do. So I wouldn't say that either one of those examples qualifies speaking out of school.

Q. How about the value-added tax, Mr. President?

The President. What was that?

Q. The value-added tax, Mrs. Rivlin and Ms. Shalala both said that they thought that that was a good idea.

The President. I don't mind them saying they think it's a good idea. There are all kinds of arguments for it on policy grounds. That does not mean that we have decided to incorporate it in the health care debate. No decision has been made on that. And I have no objection to their expressing their views on that. We've had a lot of people from business and labor come to us saying that they thought that tax would help make their particular industries more competitive in the global economy. That wasn't taking a line against an administration policy.

Gay Rights

Q. Mr. President, a week ago a group of gay and lesbian representatives came out of a meeting with you and expressed in the most ringing terms their confidence in your understanding of them and their political aspirations, and their belief that you would fulfill those aspirations. Do you feel now that you will be able to meet their now-enhanced expectations?

The President. Well, I don't know about that. And I don't know what their—it depends on what the expectations are. But I'll tell you this: I believe that this country's policies should be heavily biased in favor of nondiscrimination. I believe when you tell people they can't do certain things in this country that other people can do, there ought to be an overwhelming and compelling reason for it. I believe we need the services of all of our people, and I have said that consistently and not as a political proposition. The first time this issue came up was in 1991 when I was in Boston. I was just asked the question about it.

And I might add, it's interesting that I have been attacked. Obviously, those who disagree with me here are primarily coming from the political right in America. When I was Governor, I was attacked from the other direction for sticking up for the rights of religious fundamentalists to run their child care centers and to practice home schooling under appropriate safeguards. I just have always had an almost libertarian view that we should try to protect the rights of American individual citizens to live up to the fullest of their capacities, and I'm going to stick right with that.

Q. Are you concerned, sir, that you may have generated expectations on their end and criticism among others that has hamstrung your administration in the sense of far too great emphasis on this issue?

The President. Yes, but I have not placed a great deal of emphasis on it. It's gotten a lot of emphasis in other quarters and in the press. I've just simply taken my position and tried to see it through. And that's what I do. It doesn't take a lot of my time as President to say what I believe in and what I intend to do, and that's what I'll continue to do.

Bosnia

Q. Mr. President, getting back to the situation in Bosnia—and we understand you haven't made any final decisions on new options previously considered unacceptable. But the two most commonly heard options would be lifting the arms embargo to enable the Bosnian Muslims to defend themselves and to initiate some limited air strikes, perhaps, to cut off supply lines. Without telling us your decision—presumably, you haven't made any final decisions on those two options—what are the pros and cons that are going through your mind right now and will weigh heavily on your final decision?

The President. I'm reluctant to get into this. Those are two of the options. There are some other options that have been considered. All have pluses and minuses; all have supporters and opponents within the administration and in the Congress, where, I would remind you, heavy consultations will be required to embark on any new policy.

I do believe that on the air strike issue, the pronouncements that General Powell has made generally about military action apply there. If you take action, if the United States takes action, we must have a clearly defined objective that can be met. We must be able to understand it, and its limitations must be clear. The United States is not, should not, become involved as a partisan in a war.

With regard to the lifting of the arms embargo, the question obviously there is if you widen the capacity of people to fight, will that help to get a settlement and bring about peace? Will it lead to more bloodshed? What kind of reaction can others have that would undermine the effectiveness of the policy?

But I think both of them deserve some serious consideration, along with some other options we have.

Q. Do you think that these people who are trying to get us into war in Bosnia are really remembering that we haven't taken care of hundreds of thousands of veterans from the last war and we couldn't take care of our prisoners and get them all home from Vietnam? And now many of them are coming up with bills for treatment of Agent Orange. How can we afford to go to any more of these wars?

The President. Well, I think that's a good argument against the United States itself becoming involved as a belligerent in a war there.

But we are, after all, the world's only super-power. We do have to lead the world, and there is a very serious problem of systematic ethnic cleansing in the former Yugoslavia, which could have not only enormous further humanitarian consequences, and goodness knows there have been many, but also could have other practical consequences in other nearby regions where the same sorts of ethnic tensions exist.

Q. Did you make any kind of agreement with Boris Yeltsin to hold off either on air strikes or any kind of aggressive action against the Serbs until after Sunday? And in general, how has his political situation affected your delibera-tion on Bosnia?

The President. No, I have not made any agreement, and he did not ask for that. We never even discussed that, interestingly enough. The Russians, I would remind you, in the mid-dle of President Yeltsin's campaign, abstained from our attempt to get tougher sanctions through the United Nations in what I thought was the proper decision for them and one that the United States and, I'm sure, the rest of the free world very much appreciated.

Tragedy in Waco

Q. Do you wish, Mr. President, that you'd become more involved in the planning of the Waco operation? And how would you handle that situation differently now?

The President. I don't think as a practical matter that the President should become in-volved in the planning of those kinds of things at that detail. One of the things that I'm sure will come out when we look into this is—the questions will be asked and answered: Did all of us who were up the line of command ask the questions we should have asked and get the answers we should have gotten? And I look forward to that. But at the time, I have to say as I did before, the first thing I did after the ATF agents were killed, once we knew that the FBI was going to go in, was to ask that the military be consulted because of the quasi-, as least, military nature of the conflict given the resources that Koresh had in his compound and their obvious willingness to use them. And then on the day before the action, I asked the questions of the Attorney General which I have reported to you previously and which at the time I thought were sufficient. As I said, I'm sure, I leave it to others to make the suggestions about whether there are other questions I should have asked.

FBI Director Sessions

Q. Mr. President, what is your assessment of Director Sessions' role in the Waco affair? And have you made a decision on his future? And if you haven't, will you give him a personal hearing before you do decide?

The President. Well, first of all, I have no assessment of his role since I had no direct contact with him. And I mean no negative or positive inference. I have no assessment there. I stand by what I said before about my general high regard for the FBI. And I'm waiting for a recommendation from the Attorney General about what to do with the direction of the FBI.

Bosnia

Q. Mr. President, since you said that one side in the Bosnia conflict represents inhumanity that the Holocaust carried to the nth degree, why do you then tell us that the United States cannot take a partisan view in this war?

The President. Well, I said that the principle of ethnic cleansing is something we ought to stand up against. That does not mean that the United States or the United Nations can enter a war, in effect, to redraw the lines, geographical lines of republics within what was Yugoslavia, or that that would ultimately be successful.

I think what the United States has to do is to try to figure out whether there is some way consistent with forcing the people to resolve their own difficulties we can stand up to and stop ethnic cleansing. And that is obviously the difficulty we are wrestling with. This is clearly the most difficult foreign policy problem we face and that all of our allies face. And if it were easy, I suppose it would have been solved be-fore. We have tried to do more in the last 90 days than was previously done. It has clearly not been enough to stop the Serbian aggression, and we are now looking at what else we can do.

Q. Yesterday you specifically criticized the Roosevelt administration for not having bombed the railroads to the concentration camps and things that were near military targets. Aren't there steps like that that would not involve con-flict, direct conflict or partisan belligerence, that you might consider?

The President. There may be. I would remind you that the circumstances were somewhat dif-ferent. We were then at war with Germany at the time, and that's what made that whole series of incidents so perplexing. But we have—as I say, we've got all of our options under review.

Haiti

Q. The diplomatic initiative on Haiti is on the verge of collapse. What can you do to salvage it short of a full-scale military operation?

The President. Well, you may know something I don't. That's not what our people tell me. I think Mr. Caputo and Ambassador Pezzullo have done together a good job. The thing keeps going back and forth because of the people who are involved with the de facto government there. It's obvious what their concerns are. They were the same concerns that led to the ouster of Aristide in the first place, and President Aristide, we feel, should be restored to power. We're working toward that. I get a report on that. We discuss it at least three times a week, and I'm convinced that we're going to prevail there and be successful.

I do believe that there's every reason to think that there will have to be some sort of multilateral presence to try to guarantee the security and the freedom from violence of people on both sides of the ledger while we try to establish the conditions of ongoing civilized society. But I believe we're going to prevail there.

The First 100 Days

Q. Mr. President, would you care to make your assessment of the first 100 days before we make one for you? [*Laughter*]

The President. Well, I'll say if—I believe, first of all, we passed the budget resolution in record time. That was the biggest issue. That confirmed the direction of the administration and confirmed the commitments of the campaign that we could both bring the deficit down and increase investment, and that we could do it by specific spending cuts and by raising taxes, almost all of which come from the highest income people in this society, reversing a 12-year trend in which most of the tax burdens were borne by the middle class, whose incomes were going down when their taxes were going up, while the deficit went from $1 trillion to $4 trillion, the total national debt, and the deficit continued to go up.

We have a 20-year low in interest rates from mortgages. We have lower interest rates across the board. We have tens of billions of dollars flooding back into this economy as people refi-

nance their debt. We have established a new environmental policy, which is dramatically different. The Secretary of Education has worked with me and with others and with the Governors to establish a new approach in education that focuses on tough standards as well as increasing opportunity. We have done an enormous amount of work on political reform, on campaign finance, and lobbying reform. And I have imposed tough ethics requirements on my own administration's officials. These things are consistent with not only what I said I'd do in the campaign but with turning the country around. The Vice President is heading a task force which will literally change the way the Federal Government operates and make it much more responsive to the citizens of this country.

We are working on a whole range of other things: the welfare reform initiative, to move people from welfare to work. And, of course, a massive amount of work has been done on the health care issue, which is a huge economic and personal security problem for millions of Americans.

So I think it is amazing how much has been done. More will be done. We also passed the family leave bill, a version of the motor voter bill that has not come out of conference back to me yet. And everything has been passed except the stimulus program. So I think we're doing fine, and we're moving in the right direction. I feel good about it.

Aid to Russia

Q. Sir, a followup. Wouldn't you say, though, that one of your biggest initiatives, aid to Soviet Russia, is now practically finished? If we can't pass a stimulus bill in our own country, how can we do it for them?

The President. Let me recast the question a little bit. It's a good question. [*Laughter*] It's a good question, but to be fair we've got to recast it. We have already—the first round of aid to non-Soviet Russia, to a democratic Russia, is plainly going to go through, the first $1.6 billion. The aid that we agreed with our partners in the G–7 to provide through the international financial institutions, which is a big dollar item, is plainly going to go through. The question is, can we get any more aid for Russia that requires a new appropriation by the United States Congress? And that is a question I think, Mary [Mary McGrory, Washington Post], that will be resolved in the weeks ahead, in part by what happens to the American workers and their jobs and their future. I think the two things will be tied by many Members of Congress.

Navy Sexual Harassment Investigation

Q. The Tailhook report came out this morning, documenting horrendous and nearly criminal conduct on the part of the Navy. How much did you discuss the incident, and what might be done about it with your nominee to be the Secretary of the Navy?

The President. First, let me comment a little on that. The Inspector General's report details conduct which is wrong and which has no place in the armed services. And I expect the report to be acted on in the appropriate way. I also want to say to the American people and to all of you that the report should be taken for what it is, a very disturbing list of allegations which will have to be thoroughly examined. It should not be taken as a general indictment of the United States Navy or of all the fine people who serve there. It is very specific in its allegations, and it will be pursued.

The only thing I said to the Secretary-designate of the Navy and the only thing I should have said to him, I think, is that I expected him to take the report and to do his duty. And I believe he will do that.

Russia

Q. Mr. President, to go back to Russia for just a minute. The latest polls show that Mr. Yeltsin will probably win his vote of confidence. But there seems to be a real toss-up on whether or not voters are going to endorse his economic reforms.

The President. I understand that.

Q. Can you live with a split decision, though, or do you need both passed in order to then build support for Russian aid?

The President. I believe—the answer to your question is, for the United States, the key question should be that which is posed to any democracy, which is who wins the election? If he wins the election, if he is ratified by the Russian people to continue as their President, then I think we should do our best to work with him toward reform.

You know, we had a lot of other countries here for the Holocaust Museum dedication; their leaders were here. Leaders from Eastern Europe, leaders from at least one republic of the former Soviet Union, all of them having terrible economic challenges as they convert from a Communist command-and-control economy to a market economy in a world where there's economic slowdown everywhere. And in a world in which there's economic slowdown and difficulty, all leaders will have trouble having their policies be popular in a poll because they haven't produced the results that the people so earnestly yearn for. You can understand that.

But if they have confidence in the leadership, I think that's all we can ask. And the United States will, if the Russian people ratify him as their President and stick with him, then the United States will continue to work with him. I think he is a genuine democrat—small "d"—and genuinely committed to reform. I think that we should support that.

NAFTA

Q. Mr. President, Mr. Perot has come out strongly in what is perceived behind the line against a free trade agreement, NAFTA. How hard are you going to fight for this free trade agreement, and when do you expect to see it accomplished?

The President. I think we'll have the agreement ready in the fairly near future. You know, our people are still working with the Mexican Government and with the Canadians on the side agreements. We're trying to work out what the environmental agreement will say, what the labor agreement will say, and then what the fairest way to deal with enforcement is.

The Mexicans say, and there is some merit to their position, that they're worried about transferring their sovereignty in enforcement to a multilateral commission. Even in the United States, to be fair, we have some folks who are worried about that, about giving that up. On the other hand, if we're going to have an environmental agreement and a labor standards agreement that means something, then there has to be ultimately some consequences for violating them. So what we're trying to do is to agree on an approach which would say that if there is a pattern of violations, if you keep on violating it past a certain point—maybe not an isolated incident, but a pattern of violation—there is going to be some enforcement. There must be consequences. And we're working out the details of that.

But I still feel quite good about it. And this

is just an area where I disagree with Mr. Perot and with others. I think that we will win big if we have a fair agreement that integrates more closely the Mexican economy and the American economy and leads us from there to Chile to other market economies in Latin America and gives us a bigger world in which to trade. I think that's the only way a rich country can grow richer. If you look at what Japan and other countries in the Pacific are doing to reach out in their own region, it's a pretty good lesson to us that we had better worry about how to build those bridges in our own area.

So this is an idea battle. You know, you've got a lot of questions, and I want to answer them all. But let me say not every one of these things can be distilled simply into politics, you know, who's for this and who's for that, and if this person is for this, somebody else has got to be for that. A lot of these things honestly involved real debates over ideas, over who's right and wrong about the world toward which we're moving. And the answers are not self-evident. And one of the reasons that I wanted to run for President is I wanted to sort of open the floodgates for debating these ideas so that we could try to change in the appropriate way. So I just have a difference of opinion. I believe that the concept of NAFTA is sound, even though, as you know, I thought that the details needed to be improved.

POW/MIA's

Q. Mr. President, there was a tremendous flurry of interest earlier this month in the Russian document that purported to show that the Vietnamese had held back American prisoners. General Vessey has now said publicly that while the document itself was authentic, he believes that it was incorrect. Do you have a personal view at this point about that issue? And more broadly, do you believe that, in fact, the Vietnamese did return all the American prisoners at the time of the Paris Peace Accord?

The President. First let me say, I saw General Vessey before he went to Vietnam and after he returned. And I have a high regard for him, and I appreciate his willingness to serve his country in this way. As to whether the document had any basis in fact, let me say that the Government of Vietnam was more forthcoming than it had been in the past and gave us some documents that would tend to undermine the validity of the Russian documents claim.

I do not know whether that is right or wrong. We are having it basically evaluated at this time, and when we complete the evaluation, we'll tell you. And of course, we want to tell the families of those who were missing in action or who were POW's. I think that we'll be able to make some progress in eliminating some of the questions about the outstanding cases as a result of this last interchange, but I cannot say that I'm fully satisfied that we know all that we need to know. There are still some cases that we don't know the answer to. But I do believe we're making some progress. I was encouraged by the last trip.

Q. I'd like to follow up on that. Before the U.S. normalizes relations, allows trade to go forward, do you have to be personally sure that every case has been resolved or would you be willing to go forward on the basis that while it may take years to resolve these cases, the Vietnamese have made sufficient offerings to us to confirm good faith?

The President. A lot of experts say you can never resolve every case, every one, that we couldn't resolve all the cases for them and that there are still some cases that have not been factually resolved, going back to the Second World War. But what I would have to be convinced of is that we had gone a long way toward resolving every case that could be resolved at this moment in time, and that there was a complete, open, and unrestricted commitment to continue to do everything that could be done always to keep resolving those cases. And we're not there yet.

Again, I have to be guided a little bit by people who know a lot about this. And I confess to being much more heavily influenced by the families of the people whose lives were lost there or whose lives remain in question than by the commercial interest and the other things which seem so compelling in this moment. I just am very influenced by how the families feel.

Legislative Agenda

Q. [*Inaudible*]—your economic stimulus package, are you doing some kind of reality check now and scaling back some of your plans, your legislative plans for the coming year, including the crime bill, the health care initiatives, and other things? Are there any plans to do that? And also, did you underestimate the power of Senator Bob Dole?

The President. No, what I underestimated was the extent to which what I thought was a fairly self-evident case, particularly after we stayed below the spending caps approved by this Congress, including the Republicans who were in this Congress last year, when we had already passed a budget resolution which called for over $500 billion in deficit reduction. When they had voted repeatedly for supplemental appropriations to help foreign governments, I thought at least four of them would vote to break cloture, and I underestimated that. I did not have an adequate strategy of dealing with that.

I also thought that if I made a good-faith effort to negotiate and to compromise, that it would not be rebuffed. Instead, every time I offered something they reduced the offer that they had previously been talking to the majority leader about. So it was a strange set of events. But I think what happened was what was a significant part of our plan, but not the major part of it, acquired a political connotation that got out of proportion to the merits, so that a lot of Republicans were saying to me privately, "Mr. President, I'd like to be for this, but I can't now. And we're all strung out, and we're divided."

I think we need to do a reality check. As I said, what I want to know—let me go back to what I said—what I want to know from our folks and from our friends in the Senate, and Republicans or Democrats, is what could I have done differently to make it come out differently, because the real losers here were not the President and the administration. The real losers were the hundreds of thousands of people who won't have jobs now. We could have put another 700,000 kids to work this summer. I mean, we could have done a lot of good things with that money. And I think that is very, very sad. And it became more political than it should have. But the underlying rationale I don't think holds a lot of water, that it was deficit spending. That just won't wash.

Q. [*Inaudible*]—and redo——

The President. No. I mean, you know, for example, you mentioned the crime bill. I think it would be a real mistake not to pass the crime bill. I mean, the crime bill was almost on the point of passage last year. And they were all fighting over the Brady bill. Surely, surely after what we have been through in this country just in the last 3 months, with the kind of mindless violence we have seen, we can pass a bill requir-

ing people to go through a waiting period before they buy a handgun. And surely we can see that we need more police officers on the street.

That's another thing that—I really believe that once we move some of that money, not all but some of it, up into this jobs package to make some of the jobs rehiring police officers on the street who'd been laid off, that would be a compelling case. I mean people are scared in this country, and I think we need to go forward. I feel very strongly that we need to go forward on the crime bill.

Navy Sexual Harassment Investigation

Q. Mr. President, back to the Tailhook report for a second. That report contained very strong criticism of the Navy's senior leadership in general but did not name any of the senior officers. Do you believe that the senior officers who are implicated in this, including Admiral Kelso who was there one night in Las Vegas, should they be disciplined, and do you believe the public has a right to know the names of the senior officers?

The President. You should know that under the rules of law which apply to this, I am in the chain of command. There is now an Inspector General's report, and the law must take its course. If I were to answer that question I might prejudice any decisions which might be later made in this case. I think all I can tell you is what I have already said. I was very disturbed by the specific allegations in the Inspector General's report, and I want appropriate action to be taken.

Until the proper procedures have a chance to kick in and appropriate action is taken, I have been advised that because I am the Commander in Chief I have to be very careful about what I say so as not to prejudice the rights of anybody against whom any action might proceed or to prejudice the case in any other way either pro or con. So I can't say any more except to say that I want this thing handled in an appropriate and thorough way.

Bosnia

Q. Mr. President, could I ask you for a clarification on Bosnia? You said that you were not considering introduction of American forces. Does that include any air forces as well as ground forces, sir?

The President. I said ground forces.

Q. You said ground forces. Could I ask you,

sir, if you fear that using U.S. air strikes might draw the United States into a ground war there?

The President. I just don't want to discuss our evaluation of the options anymore. I've told you that there's never been a serious discussion in this country about the introduction of ground forces into an ongoing conflict there.

Gay Rights March

Q. With hundreds of thousands of gays in Washington this weekend for the march, did you ever reconsider your decision to leave town for this weekend? Did you ever consider in any way participating in some of the activities?

The President. No.

Q. Why not?

The President. Because I—and, basically, I wouldn't participate in other marches. I think once you become President, on balance, except under unusual circumstances, that is not what should be done. But more importantly, I'm going to the American Society of Newspaper Editors, a trip that presumably most of you would want me to make, to try to focus anew on what I think are the fundamental issues at stake for our country right now. And I expect that I will say something about the fact that a lot of Americans have come here asking for a climate that is free of discrimination, asking basically to be able to work hard and live by the rules and be treated like other American citizens if they do that, and just that. And that's always been my position, not only for the gays who will be here but for others as well.

Thank you very much.

NOTE: The President's 13th news conference began at 1 p.m. in the East Room at the White House. During the news conference, the following persons were referred to: Elie Wiesel, Nobel laureate and concentration camp survivor; Dante Caputo, U.N./OAS Special Envoy to Haiti; Lawrence Pezzullo, Special Assistant to the Secretary of State on Haiti; and Adm. Frank B. Kelso II, USN, Chief of Naval Operations.

Statement on Advancing U.S. Relations With Russia and the Other New Independent States
April 23, 1993

Since my summit in Vancouver with Russian President Boris Yeltsin, I have pursued a number of measures to implement our policy of economic and strategic partnership between our two countries. These reflect my conviction that the movement toward political and economic reform in Russia and the other new states of the former Soviet Union is the greatest security challenge of our day and can fuel our own future prosperity as well.

It is time to put our relations with Russia and the other states on a new footing. As an important step in that process, we need to update the accumulated cold war vestiges that remain in U.S. laws and practices. Our statutes and regulations are filled with restrictions on a Communist Soviet Union, a nation that no longer exists. Many of those provisions needlessly impede our relations with the democratic states that replaced the Soviet Union.

Many in Congress have already taken the lead on re-examining these provisions. Today I have asked Ambassador-at-Large Strobe Talbott to coordinate our Executive review of these laws and statutes on an expedited basis, with the goal of revising or removing them where appropriate and consistent with our security and other national interests. Related to this process, our administration will also begin a thorough review, working with our allies, of how to reorient export controls on sensitive technology. I ask the bipartisan leaders in Congress to work with us to coordinate and expedite these reviews.

Today I am also announcing steps to help build a new security partnership with Russia and the other states. We will accelerate the deactivation of nuclear weapons systems already scheduled for elimination under the START I Treaty, while working to accelerate dismantlement in Russia and the three other states with nuclear weapons on their territory. We are beginning a comprehensive review of measures that could enhance strategic stability, including the possibility of each side reprogramming its nuclear missiles so they are not routinely aimed at each other. And we will be starting a consultative process within the next 2 months with Russia, our allies, and other states, aimed at commencing negotiations toward a multilateral nuclear test ban.

Finally, we are continuing our efforts to strike a partnership with political and economic reformers throughout Russia and the other states. We are continuing work with our G-7 partners to assemble the package of multilateral assistance that Secretaries Bentsen and Christopher recently negotiated in Tokyo. And I am continuing consultation with Congress over the further efforts our own Nation will take to assist Russia's reforms.

The hardest work of reform must be done by the people of Russia and the other states themselves, and we applaud the courageous steps they have taken. Yet we dare not miss opportunities to do what we can to bolster their processes of democratization and economic liberalization. The steps I am announcing today will advance those objectives.

Statement on the Death of Cesar Chavez
April 23, 1993

The labor movement and all Americans have lost a great leader with the death today of Cesar Chavez. An inspiring fighter for the cause to which he dedicated his life, Cesar Chavez was an authentic hero to millions of people throughout the world.

I share the sadness his family, friends, followers, and supporters all feel upon his passing away. We can be proud of his enormous accomplishments and the dignity and comfort he brought to the lives of so many of our country's least powerful and most dispossessed workers. He had a profound impact upon the people of the United States. My deepest sympathies go out to all his loved ones.

NOTE: The related proclamation of April 28 is listed in Appendix D at the end of this volume.

Statement on Signing Emergency Supplemental Appropriations Legislation
April 23, 1993

Today I have signed into law H.R. 1335, the "Emergency Supplemental Appropriations" Act of 1993. This Act provides $4 billion in emergency unemployment compensation to approximately 1.9 million unemployed American workers. This critical assistance will help the unemployed and their families with grocery bills, mortgage payments and other expenses while they seek new employment. I am disappointed that the job-producing elements of the original version of the legislation were forced to be removed from it.

Our efforts to create jobs, increase investment, and safeguard our communities and our children, were frustrated by the use of parliamentary tactics in the Senate in the furtherance of politics-as-usual. The losers, in the end, were jobless Americans looking for the dignity of employment, and communities across the United States looking forward to meeting unmet national needs through growth-oriented efforts provided by the legislation in its original form. It is my hope that the Congress will consider further legislation to produce the jobs that are needed to strengthen and sustain the current economic recovery.

WILLIAM J. CLINTON

The White House,
April 23, 1993.

NOTE: H.R. 1335, approved April 23, was assigned Public Law No. 103–24. This statement was released by the Office of the Press Secretary on April 24.

The President's Radio Address
April 24, 1993

Good morning. It's been said that to learn about democracy you can take a break from Plato and take the bus. I know firsthand that's good advice. It was on our bus tour last year that I met so many of the Americans who helped to chart our course toward tomorrow: fathers and mothers and children, citizens whose concerns are everyday concerns, the kind that unfortunately have been ignored for too long in this Capital City.

I heard worry in some of those voices and hope everywhere that new leadership could change our country for the better. That strengthened my resolve to beat back the status quo, to fight against special interest and politics as usual, to fight for the people who work hard and play by the rules. You put your faith in us so that we could put you, the American people, first. And that's what I try to do every day. In every battle I fight, I just try to keep you and your needs and the future of our great Nation in mind.

Even today I'm reminded of the work still to be done here. For many Americans the weekend is a time to unwind a bit, see friends, catch up with the family, do the shopping and other chores. Maybe some of you are out in the yard gardening or washing a car or tossing a softball or a frisbee.

I know there's been some good news lately. After about 100 days as President we've begun to change the direction of America. Our economic program has been adopted in its broad outlines by Congress. That's brought an end to trickle-down economics. The stock market is at an all-time high, and interest rates are very, very low, mortgages at a 20-year low. Many of you have already saved a lot of money just since the November election on these lower interest rates, with refinancing your home mortgages or getting car loans or consumer credit or perhaps business loans at lower rates. That's going to put billions and billions of dollars back into this economy, which will create jobs and opportunities for people for years to come. I'm excited about that. We're also lowering the deficit with over 200 specific cuts in Government spending and tax increases, almost all of which are coming on people with incomes above $100,000.

We're doing some other things, like taking steps to make more credit available to businesses and farms, supporting working families with children, developing a proposal to clean up our environment in a way that creates jobs rather than costs jobs, and working to invest for new jobs for those people who have been laid off by defense cuts.

These developments will all help to turn our country around and move us in the right direction. But still, for many Americans, this is just another day without a job and a cruel reminder that without gainful employment even the basics in life, including self-esteem, are hard to come by.

For those Americans I'll never stop fighting, because for all Americans the stakes go up whenever unemployment refuses to go down. Think about this: For 16 straight months the national unemployment rate has been 7 percent or higher. Just this week we saw the latest figures for unemployment claims, and it still wasn't good. There were 359,000 claims, an increase of 26,000.

And some say we're in a recovery. Well, the majority of the officials you elected to represent you in Washington know this is a serious situation. They know that every industrial nation in the world is having a big problem creating jobs. Most people understand we need action and bold changes to ensure that we get out of this cycle of job loss. How can anybody with a lick of sense think that we don't need more jobs?

Yet, still, this past week, a minority of the United States Senate, 43 Senators, played parliamentary games with our people's lives. They blocked an attempt to even vote on our plan to put Americans back to work. Instead of giving the majority the chance they wanted to pass the jobs bill, which would have put hundreds of thousands of Americans to work, they decided we should spend your tax dollars only to extend unemployment benefits.

I could think they don't understand. The 16 million Americans who want full-time jobs don't just want more handouts to get from week to week. They want work so they can support themselves and be independent and pay taxes instead of spending tax dollars.

The bill I proposed didn't create Democratic jobs or Republican jobs. And it certainly didn't create make-work jobs. It was a bill to create jobs building the fundamentals for long-term economic growth. It funded highway and mass transit constructions. It would have enabled inner-city and rural kids to get off the streets and go to work. It would have permitted hard-pressed communities to rehire as many as 10,000 police officers to enlist them in the fight against street crime. And these investments were paid for by more than 200 real spending cuts contained in the budget that Congress has already passed.

Of course, the best program is one that will help to generate jobs. That's the social program we really need. Think of it: If everybody in America who wanted a job had one, we wouldn't just be a more productive nation; we'd be a freer people, free of many of the problems in our society.

That's why I went the extra mile on this jobs program. I offered a compromise. I offered another compromise that met our opponents more than halfway, and why I still want to work with Congress, both Democrats and Republicans, to pass the details of our economic program and to create jobs.

Look what happened in the Senate. When the economy is looking weak, when the recovery isn't producing jobs, when you, the American people, are asking lawmakers to cut out the gridlock, the opponents of our program filibustered and literally prevented even a vote so that the majority could have worked its will. Well, a lot of those people think they've scored a victory by killing a chance to put nearly a half million Americans to work. I don't think that's much of a victory. I think that's letting the American people down. And I'm going to do my best not to let you down.

I've just been here in Washington a short time. We've made some big strides. Our budget blueprint has been approved by Congress in record time, and that's led to a record reduction in interest rates. As I said earlier, a lot of you have already benefited from that, and that's going to release tens of billions of dollars to invest in this economy.

We're not going to play business as usual here. We're going to shift the course of this economy from consumption and waste to investment and growth. We're taking on some of the hardest problems facing America, such as changing the health care system to make it work for you and trying to drive special interest out of politics through campaign finance and lobbying reform. We're asking everyone to take more responsibility by reforming welfare so it's a second chance, not a way of life, by making our education system live up to strong national standards, by offering students a chance to go to college in exchange for community service, by forcing Federal Agencies to do more with a lot less of your money.

These are big changes. We all know they won't happen overnight. But we're on our way, thanks to the support you've given us. I want our debate on key issues like creating jobs to rise above politics, to rise above party and up to the level of the American people. Our only agenda should be your needs, the kind of needs you've been telling us about for a long time.

I'm still listening to you. And I'll keep on doing it. But all the people here in Washington are going to have to get on the bus. We can't miss the bus this time. We've got to be out there working for you to make this country what it ought to be.

Thank you.

NOTE: The address was recorded at 7:30 p.m. on April 23 in Room 453 of the Old Executive Office Building for broadcast at 10:06 a.m. on April 24.

Remarks to the Newspaper Association of America in Boston, Massachusetts
April 25, 1993

Thank you very much. Frank, I am delighted to be here. You reminded me, when you said that I came last year to the Waldorf, that I was in Los Angeles last year on the day before this convention. And I was flying back, and I got somewhere around Las Vegas, and our plane malfunctioned. We had to go back to California, and I took the red-eye into the Waldorf. I've always thought that was why I was the first Democrat in 28 years to receive a majority of the newspaper endorsements in the last election. I was thinking today whether there was some stunt I could pull that would have the equal effect. [*Laughter*]

When Frank was giving me the introduction, he said it was just a year ago, and this young, charismatic Governor was out—I thought to myself, what happened to that guy? [*Laughter*] You know, people ask me all the time whether there's anything really different about being President, and is it different from being a Governor or some other job? And it really is.

One of the things is that people walk around on eggshells all the time, and they're always trying to protect you, even from things that aren't necessarily in need of protecting. The other day I came down from the residence floor at the White House to the first floor. And I didn't know this, but my wife was having a meeting with some women there, about 30 of them, talking about health care, and the meeting just let out as I got off on the floor. I was going around the corner to another little room, and all of a sudden I found myself in the middle of 30 people whom I had never met before. I literally just walked out into their midst. So I shook hands with them, said hello. It was quite pleasant. And this young aide who was working there, a man who's a full-time employee of the White House, said, "Oh, Mr. President, I'm so sorry that I let you out in the middle of all those people." And I looked at him, and I said, "That's all right, young man, I used to be one." [*Laughter*] That's the way I sort of feel sometimes.

I want to tell you how very proud I am to be here today with you, all of you who offer our fellow countrymen and women the information, the analysis, the range of opinions that they need to make decisions about their future.

I know that there's always a healthy tension between the people in public service and the press. And when I have bad days I remember that another President who had a few bad days with the press himself, Thomas Jefferson, said that if he had to choose between having a Government without newspapers or newspapers without a Government, that he would not hesitate for a moment to prefer the latter. I think that was on one of the days when he got a

good press. [*Laughter*]

I want to say, in all seriousness, that I've had the opportunity over the last several years to read a fairly large number of newspapers from around the country. As all of you know, I believe very strongly that over the last 10 to 12 years the political system, which includes both parties, in many important ways failed our people. And oftentimes, it was newspapers of our country who continued to put the human concerns of people back at the center stage of public debate, reporting on the stagnation of living standards that created so much anxiety for the middle class and so much despair for the poor.

I think, in particular, of the incredible series run by the Philadelphia Inquirer, called "America: What Went Wrong?", and the detail in which that series documented what happened to the middle class in America as most families worked harder for lower wages and had more insecurity in the fundamentals of their lives.

But many other papers, perhaps all of them all across the country, issued various reports on other problems that were neglected for too long: how we went from a $1 trillion to a $4 trillion deficit in national debt in 12 years; how most of the gains, the economic gains of the 1980's went to people in the top 3 to 4 percent of income brackets; how we came to spend over 33 percent more than any other country in the world on health care and still had over 35 million people without any health insurance and millions of others at risk of losing it at a moment's notice; the problems we had in our school systems, our welfare systems; the problems we had with drug abuse and crime; the problems we have in the rising tide of people in what may well be for them a permanent underclass, most of them young women and their little children or young, single, unemployed and uneducated men.

Editorial writers warned us about organized interest having too much dominance over public policy, and the slogans and the smears and the sound bites having too much dominance over public debate and election decisions. Newspaper after newspaper reported on the profound disaffection of so many of our people from the political process itself. When the political system seemed brain-dead and deadlocked, with so many people locked into yesterday's rhetoric and yesterday's policies, many in the newspapers helped to give the American people not only the information they need but the sense that with that information, something profound could be done to change the course of our Nation's history.

I don't think there's any question that the size of the turnout last November, the nature of the turnout, with so many people from traditionally underrepresented groups in the electorate, including so many millions of young people, indicated that the American people wanted some fundamental change in the way our Government does the people's business. And fortunately for me, I was given the opportunity to try to lead that change.

Now that we have taken office and had almost 100 days to work at it, I know that you are about the business of playing your roles, not as a cheering section for our administration but as a conscience for the Nation, measuring the deeds against the words, reminding us still, always, no matter what happens in Washington, of the hurts and the hopes and the capacities of the people who do the voting and who challenge us now to live up to the promise of America.

For those who serve in Government and for those who watch Government up close in Washington, it's all too easy to concentrate on the daily events and the inside stories, to worry about who's up or down or in or out, who won or who lost the moment's battle; too easy to forget about the real people whose real lives will be changed for better or worse by what we do or do not do: the unemployed people, the people who are afraid of losing their health insurance, the teenagers who wonder if they'll have a chance to work this summer, the families who feel less safe on their streets when we don't provide enough law enforcement officials, and on and on.

We can't forget, amidst all the gamesmanship of American political life which is a high form of entertainment, that there are real people with real stories, and they are what all of our efforts are ultimately about.

Every day, I try to devote some time to looking past the deadlines, to look ahead of the headlines, to look beyond the beltway, to go beyond the false choices and the failed policies and philosophies that still grip so much of the debate that I must confront every day, to go beyond the politics of abandonment or the politics of entitlement, to think about how we can all be in this together. No more every person for himself or herself, and no more something for nothing.

I am doing my best to offer every American an opportunity to succeed and to challenge every American to give something back to our country. Everyone who is willing to work hard and play by the rules ought to have a chance to be a part of this American community, and I think we all know that that is not the case today.

In the first 96 days of this administration, I think we have begun to fundamentally change the direction taken by the Government over the past decade, to go beyond trickle-down and tax-and-spend to a new approach to our deficit and to Government's role that reduces the deficit and increases investment in our future with an economic plan that reduces the deficit by over $500 billion in the next 5 years, has led to a 20-year low in mortgage rates, which the business writers say this year alone, if we can keep the interest rates down, will result in refinancings which will put over $100 billion back into this economy; an economic plan that includes an attempt to avoid the inevitable conflict between the environment and the economy by finding ways to create jobs with responsible environmental policy; an economic plan which tries to deal seriously with the enormous problems occasioned by the dramatic reductions in the defense budget and the impact that's had on high-tech, high-wage employment in the United States.

And I might add that tomorrow here in Boston we're going to have the first of five national conferences on that subject here to try to work in partnership with the private sector, to use the fact that the cold war is over and the defense budget is going down to find new ways for these people to work, to bring their talents and their knowledge and their enormous experience to bear.

We've tried to go, in the trade debate, beyond the old debate between free trade and protectionism to a new policy rooted in the notion that we ought to expand trade to grow our economy and to grow the economy of our trading partners. That is driving us as we seek to conclude a new agreement on the General Agreement on Tariffs and Trades, as we seek to conclude a treaty with Mexico and Canada to integrate our economies over the long run, and as we seek to redefine our relationship with Japan in the economic area.

We seek to go beyond inertia and ideology to experimentation and initiative and a reliance on more individual responsibility in social policy, with initiatives in welfare reform and national service and national health care and community policing. We seek to go beyond politics as usual to political reform with a serious effort to reduce the influence of lobbying in our political process, to reform the campaign finance system, to reduce the Federal bureaucracy and increase the amount of your tax dollars that can be invested in ways that directly promote the health and welfare and economic well-being of the American people. We seek to go beyond the divisive rhetoric of family values to an administration that values families, one that gives everybody a chance to be part of America's families. That's what the Family and Medical Leave Act was all about. That's what repealing the ban on fetal tissue research so that we could save the lives of children afflicted by diabetes and other dangerous diseases was all about. That's what the effort to immunize all of our children is all about.

There is such an incredible gulf in this country between what we say and what we do, it is an awful burden to bear if you're a serious American citizen. You hear all this talk about how much we care about our children. Well, I'll tell you something. We make over half the vaccines in the world in this country, and we have the third worst immunization record in the Western Hemisphere. And everybody goes around piously talking about how all this Government stimulus program I had was a bunch of pork barrel. It wouldn't have been pork barrel for the kids we would have immunized against preventable childhood diseases.

In the aftermath of the cold war, we are trying to fashion a new world rooted in democracy and human rights and economic reform, a world in which the United States will lead but in which we will continue to work with our allies. There is, as we speak now, a Russian election which has just concluded. We don't know how it came out. I can tell you that I know the polls show that the American people think that the President of the United States should not have spent time or their money on Russia. But I respectfully disagree.

I grew up in an age when the biggest threat to my future as a little child was whether there would be a nuclear war between the United States and what was then the Soviet Union. His-toric events in the former Soviet Union and in Eastern Europe have given democracy new hope. The START I and START II treaties, if they can both be implemented by all the nuclear powers, give our children new hope. We cannot afford to withdraw from the struggle of promoting democracy, human rights, market reforms, and an end to imperialism in that part of the world. And whatever happens today, we must engage the Russian people on those fronts, because my children and our country's future, all of our futures and all of our children's, are at stake there.

We have other interests as well, in Bosnia. The United States in the last 96 days has tried to increase the efforts of the West to bring about a settlement. We led the effort to put a no-fly zone and to enforce it through the United Nations. We started airlifts of supplies to people who were isolated. We got two of the three parties to sign on to the Vance-Owen peace process. We have dramatically increased the enforcement of tougher sanctions. It has not been enough, and now we are considering what our other options are. I say, frankly, it is the most difficult foreign policy problem this country faces, but we have to try to bring an end to the practice of ethnic cleansing and to bring a beginning of peaceful resolution of the conflict there.

We told the American people, I and the people who work with me, that we would restore real, not just rhetorical, responsibility to the actions of Government. That's what our education initiative to write the national education goals into the law of this country, to have real standards, is all about. That's what the initiatives that the HUD Secretary, Henry Cisneros, is undertaking to have certain strict rules of conduct for people who live in public housing is all about. That's what the initiatives we're taking to help people move from welfare to work is all about.

We told the American people we would try to accomplish what no other administration has ever been called up to do in the history of this country before. We would try to reduce this massive Federal deficit and increase investments in areas critical to our future, because, funny enough, in the last 12 years we exploded the deficit and reduced our investment in areas critical to our future. We have to do that because we have to free this economy of the burden of debt we are shouldering. And we have to invest because while we're doing it, we have to realize that we're in a competitive global economy, and we still have technologies and workers and students that have to have the benefit of appropriate investments in order to be fully competitive.

Doing these things will expand job opportunities and incomes for middle class people and help others to move into the middle class, something that has all but stopped in the last couple of years.

When I submitted to the Congress the core elements of my budget plan, designed to change these policies of debt and disinvestment and decline in return for thrift and investment and growth, the Congress adopted that budget plan in record time, the first time in 17 years a budget resolution has passed Congress on time.

When people say to me, "Well, what did you do in your first 100 days?" I say, "What did the other guys do in their first 100 days?" The United States Congress deserves a lot of credit for taking all the heat after all these years of antitax rhetoric, "No such thing as a good tax. Taxes are terrible." They adopted a budget with 200 specific budget cuts, over and above the last budget adopted under the previous administration, and some tax increases, 70 percent of which fall on people with incomes above $100,000, over 50 percent of which fall on people with incomes above $200,000; with an energy tax that the middle class will have to help pay that is good for conservation and good for the environment and good for the long-term direction this country needs to go in. Budget cuts and revenue increases.

We are already seeing the fruits of that. Because of interest rates going down, the deficit this year is going to be less than we thought it was going to be. This is something of very significant importance. The financial markets have clearly responded. Stock prices are at all-time highs, and many key interest rates, including home mortgage rates, are at 20-year lows. As I said, this means $100 billion more in money coming from refinancing of homes and businesses, credit card rates, and automobile interest rates going directly into the economy over the next year. And that's not my figure. Those are the figures of the business writers who have examined the circumstance that exists. These refinancing possibilities mean that farmers and small business people and homeowners are going to have a better deal in their ordinary

lives, but that money will then flow back to more productive purposes in the economy.

Along with the $514 billion deficit reduction program, we're also trying to confront the long-term economic problems of this country with a lifelong learning package that includes an attempt to devise apprenticeship opportunities of 2 years after high school for every American who does not go on to college, with initiatives to build a 21st-century infrastructure that focuses on technology as well as physical infrastructure, with efforts to revitalize our community and to strengthen our economy.

As I said, I think to get this done—and we're coming back now to try to pass the details of the budget—we will have to begin to see the world new, not as tax-and-spend, not as trickle-down, but as invest-and-grow. We'll have to think of Government not as the sole problem or the sole savior but as a partner with the private sector in trying to work our way out of the problems that we have. We'll have to think about new approaches based on old values like work and faith and family and opportunity, responsibility and community. Our success will ultimately be measured not by how many programs we've passed but by whether we improve the lives of our fellow Americans, not simply by what we do for people but by what we help people to do for themselves.

We start, I think as we must, with honoring and rewarding work. Just 17 days into this administration, we made family and medical leave the law of the land after 8 years of gridlock and delay and two vetoes. Hard-working men and women now can know that if they have to take a little time off for a genuine family problem, they can do it without losing their jobs.

Again I say, I heard all the clamor about what a terrible bill this was. And I looked around the world, and a hundred and some nations have found a way to give family leave that we just couldn't find it in our heart, our minds, a way to provide before we got around to doing it. It's time Americans put their actions where their rhetoric is, and that's what this administration is trying to do.

Forty-four days into the administration we were called upon to extend unemployment compensation to hundreds of thousands of jobless men and women, something now Congress will do as a matter of course without regard to party. Everybody is willing to pay people to remain unemployed. But this time we changed the law so that we spend a small portion of that money to offer the unemployed new opportunities for job training and counseling to try to move them back to work more quickly, based on a New Jersey experiment which shows clearly that we can do that if we don't just pay people to stay out of work but we take some of that money to get them back to work.

That's why we are trying to dramatically increase the earned-income tax credit to working poor people. It is a solemn commitment to those who work, who care for our sick or tend to our children or do our most difficult and tiring jobs, that we're going to do our best to enshrine in our tax law and in our country's life the principle that if you work for a living 40 hours a week and you've got children in the house, you should not live in poverty. I think that is an important principle and one that's worth fighting for.

That is why I tried for several weeks to pass an emergency jobs program through the Congress which, I want to point out, I did not campaign on in the campaign of 1992. I ran a fiscally responsible campaign. I did not offer to do anything that we did not pay for in the moment we did it. And this jobs program was a responsible approach based on the fact that the American economy was not producing new jobs, even though we were allegedly into the second year of a recovery.

We're supposed to be in the 24th month of a recovery, according to the economic statistics. But jobs have increased by only eight-tenths of one percent. And private sector jobs have not increased in that period. If we were following the trend of typical past recoveries, jobs would have grown by more than 7 percent. We are still 3.5 million jobs behind the rate generated in a normal economic recovery. And we have reclaimed only one-half the jobs we lost in the last recession. This past week, jobless claims went up yet again. At a time in which 16 million men and women are out of work or looking for full-time work with part-time jobs, I'm fighting to give them a chance to earn a paycheck, to do useful work, to support their families, to contribute to their communities.

Now, the stimulus package that I offered, the jobs plan, would not have revolutionized the economy. It was a $16 billion program in a $6 trillion economy. The purpose of it was to do just exactly what it would have done. It would have lowered the unemployment rate by half a percent. And it might have sparked a new round of job creation in other sectors of the economy.

I decided to do it, even though it was not part of my campaign, because the economy was sluggish and because as I looked around the rest of the world, I discovered that all of the advanced industrialized countries were having great difficulty creating jobs even in recovery. If you go back and look at what happened to Europe in the last decade, they had two different economic recoveries that have produced virtually no new jobs in many of those countries. And all I wanted to do was to try to find a way to deal with what I think is the number one problem. If everybody in this country who wanted a job had one, we wouldn't have half the other problems we've got. And I think every one of you, without regard to party or philosophy, would agree on that.

There were two objections raised to the program. Some said, "Well, you ought to pay for it all right now." Well, we had a 5-year deficit reduction plan that reduces the deficit by $514 billion. And Congress pays for things all the time over a multiyear period, number one. Number two, because of unpredicted reductions in defense, if we'd spent every penny I recommended, we'd still be under the spending levels approved by the Congress for this year.

The other thing people said, well, was, "There's a lot of pork in this plan." Well, I don't know how you define that. I think if you put 700,000 kids to work this summer, particularly under our plan, which for the first time said that the at-risk kids had to do some education as well as take jobs—we tried to take more pork out and put more standards in— it would be a good thing. I think if you open these immunization centers this summer, I think if you had more kids in summer Head Start and you paid people to work in that, I think if you rehired 20,000 of these police officers who were laid off because of tough economic times and made the streets safer, I think if we accelerated funding under the highway program, which has always had enormous support from the other party as well as from the Democrats, and I think if we gave some more money to the Mayors and the Governors of this country for job purposes, that would be a good thing. I don't think it would be a lot of pork.

It was amazing to me to listen to some of

the debate about the community development program. I was a Governor for 12 years. I used that program. You might quarrel with some of the things we did, but usually what we did was good for creating jobs in my State. And the Republican Party had always supported community development block grants before. They thought Mayors and Governors were smart enough to make the decisions. I wanted to give money to Governor Weld, a Republican Governor of Massachusetts—I thought he had enough sense to figure out how to best spend the money here for the Massachusetts economy—or the Republican Mayor of York, Pennsylvania, or the Republican Mayor from Indiana who's the head of the Republican Mayors Association. You know, all we did was change the occupants of the White House. We didn't change the party or the personality of the Governors and the Mayors. I don't know what happened that made that program such a bad idea all of a sudden. It was a good idea.

And again, I tell you that it is not nearly as important as the big picture budget that has already passed. But it is symbolic of the idea battle that we have to fight. We have to be prepared to think anew. Now, if no western country is creating jobs, even in the midst of economic recovery, it is not readily apparent that the $100 billion we're going to put back into the economy with lower interest rates are going to lead to a whole lot of new jobs. They may. It depends on how the money is invested.

That's the big deal, the fact that we've got interest rates down, we've passed the budget resolution, it's going. All I wanted to do was to strike a little match to that and see if we couldn't put several hundred thousand people back to work in useful places and see if that would help the economy to get going on the job machine. I think, still think, it was a worthwhile effort. And I'd a lot rather get beat trying to put people to work than get beat fighting putting people to work.

Let me also tell you that I regret the partisan tone of the rhetoric of the last several days, because a lot of the things that I support have a lot of support among Republicans. I'm for the line-item veto. There are Democrats that are against it and Republicans that are for it. I'm for the crime bill. I hope we can pass it with bipartisan support, the Brady bill and more police on the street. I'm for cuts in the budget that a lot of people in my own party won't

support. But a lot of them voted for cuts in the budget, because they thought it was a responsible way to go overall.

There are lots of things that I think we need to do that I hope we can get bipartisan support, toughening the child support system, having a national service program that will give every young person in this country a chance to borrow the money to go to college and pay it back, either as a percentage of their income at tax time so they can't beat the bill or by working it off and giving something to their country. These are things that ought to have bipartisan support. We cannot solve the problems of this country if every last issue that comes up, just because the President recommends it, becomes a source of a filibuster in the Senate or, frankly, attracts only members of my own party. I don't want that. I want us to debate these ideas anew, to look at them anew, to take our blinders off. And I'm not going to be right about everything I recommend, but at least I want us to be up there all working together fighting for change.

Let me say one thing in particular about the work that two very important people in my administration are doing, the Vice President and the First Lady. I met with a lot of you before I came out here, and several of you said, "Well, I generally support what you're doing, but you ought to bring that deficit down more." And I will say to you what I say to everybody: Send me a list of the things you want cut, because we found 200 things that we were cutting that weren't cut in the previous budget, and we're not done yet.

But I want you to know what this Government is like now. In my judgment, if you want further meaningful cuts, you have to do two things: You have to look at the whole way the Federal Government is organized, because there is a limit to how much you can get just out of cutting defense unless you deal with the way it is organized, like procurement and issues like that, structural things. And that's what the Vice President is involved in, this whole initiative to reinvent the Government. We've got hundreds of gifted people from all over America coming to work with us in Washington now, reexamining every last Government program, every last Government organization, committed to thinking about it anew.

This fall, when we come out with our program, we're going to ask the American people to think about the role of the Federal Government: What it should do; how it should be organized. And it's going to be a very challenging report. I hope all of you will read it and give it a lot of publicity. And on the tough things that we recommend, in terms of changes, I hope we can get some good support without regard to party, because a lot of the things that we have to do now require us to rethink how this whole thing is organized.

We've already cut 14 percent in administrative costs, 25 percent of the personnel in the White House, and a lot of other things that we can do symbolically and substantively that will save billions of dollars. But to get more, we're going to have to literally rethink the whole Government.

The second point I want to make is, you can do all that, and unless we address this health care crisis, the Government's deficit cannot be erased. Under every scenario we saw, from every political source—that is, the Republicans and the Democrats agreed, the bipartisan Congressional Budget Office agreed, everybody agreed—no matter how much we cut the deficit, we could bring it down for 5 years. But after that, it would start going right back up again because of the breathtaking increase in health care cost.

The estimates are now that over a 5-year period, Federal spending for Medicare and Medicaid alone will go up by 67 percent in 5 years. Taking away the defense cuts, taking away the interest savings, taking away the cuts in other Government programs, taking away the cuts in farm support programs, taking away, you name it, anything you want cut, you're just transferring the money to health care and not new health care, more money for the same health care. So that this is not only an incredibly compelling human issue—how do you give coverage to those who don't have it? How do you give courage to those who want to change jobs but can't because they had somebody in their family sick, and the preexisting condition keeps them from getting any health insurance? But how do you restore sanity to the Nation's budget? And by the way, how do you restore health to big chunks of our economy, a lot of our biggest and best companies striving to be more competitive. We say, "We desperately want you to start investing in America and stop investing so much of your money to create jobs somewhere else." And they say, "Give me a break. I'm spending

19 percent of payroll on health care."

This country is spending 15 percent of its income on health care. No other country is up to 10 percent. Only Canada is over 9 percent. So when people say—you'll hear it all—they'll say, oh, they're dealing with health care again, there they go again; it's all taxes and terrible and everything. You figure out what you're paying right now. Every one of you figure out what you're paying for health care, in taxes, premiums, uncompensated care that gets shifted on to your health insurance bills.

And so I say to you, we have got to face some other big fundamental issues. Not just this budget but how the Government is organized, what it delivers, whether it needs to deliver what it does, whether it needs to stop doing some things altogether. And then, what are we going to do about health care? We cannot go on ignoring the fundamental problems. If you've got it, it's still the best health care system in the world.

There are a lot of things about it that are wonderful. I want the delivery system to stay in private hands. I want people to still be able to pick their doctor. I want the best things about this health care system to stay just as it is. But you cannot look at it as long and hard as we have without concluding that we are spending a dime on the dollar on unnecessary paperwork and bureaucratic and regulatory expenses.

People say to me all the time, "You've got to do something about doctors' fees." Let me tell you just one little interest number. In 1980, the average doctor, working in a clinic, took home 75 percent of the money that came into the clinic. By 1990, that doctor was taking home 52 percent of the money coming into the clinic. Where did the rest of it go? Mostly to paper, to regulation, mostly from the proliferation of insurance policies, but some from what the Government did.

We can do better. We must. And we're going to bust a gut trying in this administration. We're going to do our best.

The last thing I want to say about this is, I ask for your scrutiny and your understanding as we get into the difficult business of political reform. I intend to ask the Congress to pass a tough campaign finance reform law. I intend to ask the Congress to adopt some restrictions on lobbying and some disclosure requirements that are not there now. We had the toughest ethics rules any President ever imposed on his appointee that prevent people from leaving my administration and going to work anytime in the near future to make money as lobbyists in the areas in which they worked for us.

These things are important. It may never be possible to be perfect, but it is important that we take these things on and that the voters of this country understand what is at stake as these matters begin to be debated.

And finally let me say—I think it's important to talk about today—I'm doing my best to restore a sense of real community in this country. As I said right when I came to you last year, we'd just seen Los Angeles racked by riots, and we were all talking about how we had to learn to live together without regard to race or income or region. I want to reiterate what I said to you a year ago: We don't have a person to waste in this country, and we're wasting them by the bucketful. We're letting people go, this way, that way, and the other way. And that's one of the reasons that I have said that we have to fight for a society that is not at all permissive but that is tolerant.

Today in Washington, many Americans came to demonstrate against discrimination based on their sexual orientation. A lot of people think that I did a terrible political thing—and I know I paid a terrible political price—for saying that I thought the time had come to end the categorical ban on gays and lesbians serving in our military service and that they should not be subject to other discrimination in governmental employment.

Let me tell you what I think. This is not about embracing anybody's lifestyle. This is a question of whether if somebody is willing to live by the strict code of military conduct, if somebody is willing to die for their country, should they have the right to do it? I think the answer is yes, if somebody is willing.

But in a larger sense, I want to say to you that I think the only way our country can make it is if we can find somehow strength out of our diversity, even with people with whom we profoundly disagree, as long as we can agree on how we're going to treat each other and how we're going to conduct ourselves in public forums. That is the real issue.

It's very ironic to me to see that the traditional attacks on the position I've taken on this issue have come from conservatives saying that I am a dangerous liberal. I took on two issues like this as Governor of Arkansas, and I was attacked by liberals for what I did, and I want to tell you what they were.

One was the leadership role I took in crafting a bill that permitted people to educate their children at home, consistent with their religious beliefs and their educational convictions, as long as the kids could take and pass a test every year. And people say, "Oh, that's a terrible thing. All those kids should be required to be in a school. How can you do that?" And I said, "Because at least these people have coherent families and that's still the most important unit of our society, and people ought to have a chance to try other things. And it wouldn't do the schools any harm to have a little competition, unsubsidized by the taxpayers, just letting people do it."

Two, when the fundamentalist religious groups in my State were confronting a legal issue that swept the country in the mid-eighties, a bunch of them came to me and said, "We do not mind having our child care centers subject to the same standards that everybody else is subject to. But it is a violation of our belief to have to get a State certificate to operate what we think is a ministry of our church. Don't make us do that." I don't know if you remember this, but in one or two States there were preachers that actually wound up going to jail over this issue, the certification of child care centers.

We sat down and worked out a law that permitted those churches to operate their child care centers without a certificate from the State as long as they were willing to be subject to investigation for health and fire safety, and as long as they agreed to be in substantial compliance with the rules and regulations that those who were certified observed. And people said, "How can you do that?" You know how many complaints we've had coming out of that, to the best of my knowledge? Zero. Not a one. Why? Because they were good people, and they were willing to play by the rules, and they wanted to have their religious convictions, and they wanted to stick up for their minister, and they desperately love the children that were in their charge. And we protected the public interest.

But all the criticism I got was from the left, not the right. This doesn't have anything to do with left or right. This is about whether we are going to live in a country free of unnecessary discrimination. You are free to discriminate in your judgments about any of us, how we look, how we behave, what we are. Make your judgments. But if we are willing to live together according to certain rules of conduct, we should be able to do so. That is the issue for America. And it has ever been unpopular at certain critical junctures. But just remember this: A whole lot of people came to this country because they wanted a good letting alone. And that's what we ought to be able to do today.

That's it. I've already talked longer than I meant to. I'll still stay and answer the questions for the allotted time. We've got to change the direction of the country. We've got to compete in a new world we don't understand all the dimensions of. But we ought to be guided by

three simple things: How can we create opportunity; how can we require all of us to behave more responsibly; and how can we build a stronger American community. And I don't believe that the answer necessarily has a partisan tinge. And I hope we can begin tomorrow the business of going forward with what this country urgently needs to do.

Thank you very much.

NOTE: The President spoke at 4:14 p.m. in the Grand Ballroom at the Marriott Copley Place Hotel.

Question-and-Answer Session With the Newspaper Association of America in Boston
April 25, 1993

Bosnia

Q. I'm director of the School of Journalism at Northeastern University here in Boston. I apologize for not being an actual member of NAA, but I guess I'm here as your guest.

Mr. President, you did refer to Bosnia. And I must say, as we look at that situation, it is horrifying; it is so reminiscent of what happened in Europe in the Second World War. I wonder if you would be able to explain to us why the West, which is possessed of imagination and technology, can stand idly by while these horrible things go on?

The President. Suppose you tell me what you think we ought to do, what the end of it will be?

Q. Well, you know, I could speculate, but I didn't come here to foist my ideas on other people. I'd be interested to hear what you have to say. It's obviously an immensely difficult question, because it could drag you into areas that you don't want to go, a Balkan war, an expanded—but let me quit. I'd like to hear your——

The President. All right. Let me just tell you that I think that the European countries, that are much closer to this than we, would like very much to find a way to put an end to the practice and to the principle of ethnic cleansing. They are very concerned about it, just as the United States has been.

The question is not simply how to stop the

Serbs from cleansing certain areas of Bosnia of all the Muslim inhabitants and killing and raping along the way, but also what the end of it is from a military and political point of view. That is, there is much more ethnic coherence, as you know, in the other republics of what used to be Yugoslavia. So the question is, what can we do that will actually achieve the objectives you seek? And secondly, who's going to live where, and how are they going to live when it's over?

Then there are all the tactical questions about whether, in fact, it could be done. Remember, in the Second War, Hitler sent tens of thousands of soldiers to that area and never was successful in subduing it, and they had people on the ground.

That does not mean that there is not anything else that we can do. I'm not prepared to announce my policy now. I can tell you I've asked myself the question you asked me a thousand times. I have spent immense amounts of time on this, talking to General Powell; talking to Reg Bartholomew, our Special Ambassador to the area; talking to the Secretaries of State and Defense and the Ambassador to the United Nations; and soliciting opinions from others in Congress and elsewhere. And I assure you that we are going to do everything we think we can to achieve those two objectives. One is to stand up against and stop the practice of ethnic cleansing. The second is to try to find some way

505

for the people who live in Bosnia and Herzegovina to live in peace. But I have to tell you, the more you look at it, it is by far the most difficult foreign policy problem we face, both in terms of the larger political issues and in the purely tactical questions to resolve it. I wish I could be more specific now, but if I were, I would be announcing a policy that has not been finalized.

Telecommunications

Q. My question has to do with telecommunications. Newspapers and others who wish to offer electronic information services can do so now only by using the local exchange monopolies of the telephone companies, principally the Bell operating companies. The telephone companies would like to be deregulated, and they would like to use those monopolies to offer those same services themselves. Would your administration support the establishment of competition for local exchange services before granting deregulation?

The President. I thought you'd never ask. [*Laughter*] I hesitate to give you the honest answer. The honest answer is, I'm not sure I still understand it well enough to give you an answer. We have a technology working group in the White House; there are about five issues that we're looking at, of which this is one. And no decision has been made yet, and I wish I could give you a more intelligent answer. I can tell you this: You have certainly rung my bell, and I will get on top of it next week. [*Laughter*] I didn't mean that, ring my bell. Hey, what can I tell you; it was a long week. [*Laughter*]

President Boris Yeltsin of Russia

Q. You mentioned the Russian election ongoing today. Could you tell us whether or not you have had any contact within the past 24 hours with President Yeltsin and, if so, what advice or counsel you may have given him?

The President. I haven't had any contact with him in the last 24 hours. And I haven't done it because he had no business talking to me because I couldn't vote for him. [*Laughter*] He needed to be out there stirring around. I also was, frankly, quite sensitive to the delicate tightrope that Yeltsin walks in our relationships together. That is, apparently the Russian people believe that it is, on balance, a good thing that we met in Canada and that we came forward with the aid package and that all of us in the

G–7 are trying to help them in ways that will be more real than the last aid package. And that's not a criticism of the previous administration so much as a criticism of the process which made Russia ineligible for a lot of the things that we said, the nations of the world said they were going to do for them. All that's been a plus.

On the other hand, the enemies of reform and the enemies of Yeltsin just beat him to death with me all the time. I don't know if you saw in one of the newspapers—maybe it was the Wall Street Journal that had a quote in the last day or two in Yeltsin's campaign where one of his enemies were saying: The only person for him is Bill Clinton. [*Laughter*] And so I have on purpose not had any personal and direct contact with him in the last few days because I didn't want to hurt him in the election. But I can tell you this: I think he's going to do pretty well today, and we need to be in this for the long term with him. And I intend to call him as soon as it's appropriate, when we have some sense of which way things are going.

Education Financing

Q. I'm a student at University of Massachusetts at Amherst. And I, with a lot of other students, because of tuition fees, may not be coming back next year. And I was wondering how your administration is going to try and step in and help public state colleges, help us students afford it, basically.

The President. We're trying to do two things. First of all, one of the things I attempted to do in the jobs program which didn't have anything to do with jobs—it was sort of like unemployment—was to deal with the problem left on the table last year, which is to replenish the Pell grant program, to try to get it ginned up.

And then, what I want to do with this national service proposal—it really has two components that are distinct but related. The one would make available, to all Americans who go to college, income-contingent loan repayment. Now, that's a brain-breaker of a phrase; I'm trying to think of some clever way to say that that makes common sense. But the idea is that any young American, or not-so-young American would be able to borrow the money to finance a college education and then pay the loan back, not based on so much just on how much you borrowed but also on a percentage of your income so that it would be affordable for everyone. And we could do it for a lower cost because we are proposing to cut the administrative costs of the program and to make people pay the loan back with some connection to the tax system so you can't beat the loan. An enormous number of college loans now are not repaid at all, putting enormous burdens on those who do repay. If we set this up the way we're trying to, that would mean no one would ever have to fear a loan again, because you would not start to repay it until you were employed. And your ability to repay would be secured by having the formula for repayment tied to your own salary. So if you made less, even though you borrowed more, you'd just pay at a smaller rate over a longer period of time.

The second thing we want to do is to give more young people like you the chance to actually earn your way through college through rendering service to your country, either before you go to college, after you get out, or while you're going, under the national service program. And if we could do those two things, I think we could lift the crushing burden of college costs off millions of young people. And we're going to introduce the national service program to do that on the 100th day of this administration. And I hope you will support it.

Media Credibility

Q. Mr. President, I'm a student at Boston College and a communications major. I'd like to ask you, do you think the news media today is too concerned with gossip and sensationalism?

The President. I don't know that I'm the one to answer that. [*Laughter*] I think the answer to that is, you can't generalize about it. I must say, I am stunned from time to time at the stuff I read in the papers now about things in the National Government that are just purely based on gossip. I mean, I think you can get a rumor into print a little too easy now, I do, and even in the news magazines, some of them, although there seem to be different standards for different ones. But I wouldn't generalize. I think, by and large, there are still quite high standards of proof and fact that most people in journalism require before they go with stories. But I am kind of amazed, actually, of the stuff—most of it doesn't affect me at all—but the things that will get into print if you just say it is a rumor or "it's alleged that" or "somebody

said that." I think there's a little too much of that in some places, but it would be unfair to generalize about it. And by and large, it occurs either in the tabloids, which are a different class, or in journalistic media that basically live and breathe with political gossip, where there's more pressure to do that all the time.

Congressional Budget Cuts

Q. Mr. President, I think many of us were very pleased to hear you say today that Vice President Gore has been put in charge of looking at ways of streamlining the budget. Of course, we all know that the Congress is in charge of the financial spending of the United States. Will there be any looking by Vice President Gore of the way Congress has increased its spending many times over the last few decades?

The President. Well, let me say two things. Number one, I think Congress has made a commendable beginning in cutting back its staff expenses, too. They've, I think, adopted a 12 percent cut, absolute cut target over the next couple of years, not quite as much as the administration has but not insignificant. And they deserve credit for that. Secondly, there's been a lot of pressure, because of the publicity that's been brought to bear on Congress, to scale down on some of the committee and subcommittee work for select committees that were recently abolished by the Congress. And let me just say this: There are a lot of Members of Congress who believe that they're on too many committees or subcommittees. There are a lot of them who don't feel they can do their best work. I don't think it is for the executive branch to tell the legislative branch how it should reorganize itself. We have a separation of powers clause in the Constitution which I think has a good purpose.

I think the best thing you could do, since you need to know—there are a lot of people in the Congress who are honestly asking these questions—the best thing you can do is to give the issues that you care about, all of you, in terms of congressional organization, a high level of visibility and make your suggestions about what should be done and go at them directly, because they are not reform averse. Now, I can tell you that the freshman legislators are certainly not. But believe me, I've got plenty to do reorganizing the executive branch, and there's more money there. And I think it would be inappropriate for me to tell them how to do it. I think it's better for you to tell them how to do it.

Stimulus Package

Q. Mr. President, some recent indicators suggest that the economic recovery may be slowing down. If that continues, will you take another run at a stimulus package? And what would have to be different about it this time?

The President. Well, I don't know. As I said in my press conference a couple of days ago, we've sat down at the White House, and we've tried to really reexamine how this whole thing was handled and what I could have done differently, how I could have done a better job in presenting this, because I'm sure that there were some mistakes made on our side, too, in terms of how it was done.

I can tell you this: There are people in the Republican Party, for example, in the Senate, who are generally sympathetic to this sort of thing—people who voted for these kind of supplemental appropriations over 25 times in the last 12 years—who voted against it because they basically thought that even if it wasn't increasing the deficit, this was another way certainly to reduce it—if you don't spend the money—and that we were in a recovery.

I think what I'm going to do is to just examine, with people who care about this, what we did that wasn't right the last time and how we could do it better and what our options are. Because as I said, I live in a State with perhaps the toughest balanced budget law in the country. I'm appalled by the size of the deficit. I can't stand it. I wouldn't spend a nickel to see the cow jump over the Moon if I didn't think it needed to be done. So the reason I asked for this package was because I saw it as a part of a big overall deficit reduction package that would maybe jumpstart this economy right now. And we're just going to have to revisit it.

Let me say that we had a huge increase in productivity in the fourth quarter, as all of you who follow this know, I know, and that's wonderful work. It means output per worker is escalating dramatically. The difference is that in the past when productivity went way up, it normally meant a reinvestment in the business which would lead to more people being hired.

Today—and I'll bet you a lot of newspapers can identify with this, I'll bet you a lot of you have gone through this—today, when you have

an increase in productivity, you may turn around and put it right back into what produced the productivity, which is new technology which may reduce the pressure to hire people. And small businesses, which hired almost all the new workers net in the eighties, have slowed down not only because they too are reaping the gains of technology and productivity but also because of the incredible extra costs it takes to hire a new worker in terms of health care costs, Social Security, workers' comp, and all the rest of it.

So, I know I haven't answered your question, but the short answer is this: If the economy slows down, we'll go back and try something different. And I don't know what it is, but we'll keep trying things that are different. Because keep in mind, one of the reasons the economy may be slowing down is that the economic growth rate is so low in Europe and that our friends in Japan are having a tough time. That's another reason: I thought if we could get this small stimulus out now, that the Japanese job stimulus package which is much larger would begin to bite about 6 or 7 months from now and that we might have some movement in Europe because the Germans continue to lower their interest rates, hoping, I think, trying to make an effort to stave off this slow growth. So what we do will depend on what happens in Europe, what happens in Japan, and what my options are if it becomes clear that the economy's really slowing down.

Moderator. Mr. President, unfortunately I'm going to have to interrupt and say we have time for just one more question. And there's a smile back on that lady's face. And I'd like all of you please to stay in place when the President is finished. You're going to do more than that, did you say?

The President. We ought to let those two young people back there——

Moderator. All right, fine. We're going to——

The President. You qualify——

Moderator. There's no question you're in charge here, so——*[laughter]*

The President. Nearly everybody looks young to me these days. Go ahead.

The First 100 Days

Q. Over the past week or so, I've been taking a poll for my radio class about your favorability with your first 100 days in office. It seems that you've started to fall out of grace with a lot of college students. And they were citing that you didn't keep the campaign promises. What would you say to boost the morale of our generation?

The President. Well, give me an example. One thing I'd say, you can't expect instant results. It took 12 years to get in the situation that I found when I took office. One of the things I would say to college students is you need to have a realistic expectation about what kind of time it takes to get anything done.

The second thing I would say is that what I promised college students was a national service bill, and we're introducing it on the 100th day. We're doing it. And we're also going to release a report which shows how many of my campaign commitments that I have kept. To the best of my knowledge, the only one I haven't been able to keep was to give some tax relief to the middle class because the deficit, the week after the election, was announced at being $50 billion bigger than I thought it was. And I can't responsibly offer to cut anybody's taxes when the deficit is going up instead of down. That's not right, and I can't do it. But the budget that was adopted by the Congress, in general, is completely consistent with my campaign commitments. I've got a national service program going, a health care program going. We're changing the way the Government operates—all the things that I promised to do. I have imposed tougher ethics guidelines than anybody else has ever imposed. I'm going to offer a campaign finance reform and a lobby restriction bill. Everything I talked about in the campaign is being done.

Now, if people thought that I'd be President and 90 days later every campaign commitment I made would be written into the law and everybody's life would be changed, I think that's just not realistic. You have to have a realistic feeling about how much time it takes to change and how long it takes to have an impact on it.

Another thing is, when you're not in a campaign, when you have to stay there and go to work, you're at the—and this is not a criticism of you, this is a fact—you are at the mercy of the press coverage. The defeat of the $16 billion stimulus package got 50 times the press coverage of the passage of the multitrillion-dollar budget resolution. Why? Because we won, and we won in record time and in short order. Again, I'm not being critical; that's just the way this whole deal works. And if somebody stands

up and criticizes me, that's good news. And I welcome that.

But I'm just telling you, I think that if you look at what's actually been done in this 100-day period and compare it to what has previously been done within 100 days, in a long time, I think you'll have a very difficult time saying that the actual accomplishments were, number one, not consistent with my campaign commitments—they were—and, number two, that they're not quite considerable. So what I've got to do is a better job communicating to the students you represent what has been done and what we're going to do and how much I need their help to fight for it. That's why you get a 4-year term, not a 3-month term.

Stimulus Package

Q. I don't know if I should be up here or not, but just to make sure that you're not guilty of age discrimination—[*laughter*]—I guess that I was ahead of the gentleman behind me. I have a question for you about what you refer to as gridlock in Congress, because it seemed to me that for the first time Congress did say no to some very good programs because of the fact that they would add to the deficit, and that this was in fact breaking a previous gridlock which existed when Congress, when they had good programs, would simply say, well, we've got to add to the deficit. And you campaigned on reducing the deficit. And why couldn't you—admittedly, that you have some very good programs in the stimulus bill—why couldn't you, say, cut tobacco subsidies or any of a number of other programs that weren't as necessary as what's in your stimulus package?

The President. I will answer that. First of all, I had 200 such cuts, 200 that were not adopted by the previous administration or the previous Congress in the previous budget, 200. I did not ask that stimulus bill to be voted on until the Congress had adopted the budget resolution committing itself to more than $500 billion of deficit reduction in the next 5 years, more than $500 billion, including this $16 billion. It was paid for by those budget cuts.

Secondly, as I said, even if it hadn't been paid for, all of the spending was under the spending limits that Congress had already adopted. It was paid for. And you know, I must tell you that I find it—I will say one more time, a majority of the Republican Senators voted under Presidents Reagan and Bush—not the Democrats, the Republicans—28 times for over $100 billion of exactly the same kind of spending, usually for foreign aid purposes, without blinking an eye. And so, do I think that it was a mistake that they didn't vote for it? I do.

Now, if I had just come up and said, how about adding $16 billion to the deficit this year, they should have voted against that. But I didn't ask them to vote on it until we had adopted a budget resolution in the Congress that reduced the deficit $514 billion over the next 5 years, including the $16 billion. I did not ask them to vote to spend until they had voted to cut. Now, I concede that I didn't do a great job of painting that picture, but that is a fact. And you ought to write those fellows and ask them how they'd feel about just the suggestion that you made. Tell them to come up with that program. We'll see what we can do with it.

Q. Thank you.

Law Enforcement

Q. Thank you for waiting, Mr. President. I'm a student journalist from Boston University. And you've mentioned so far, in a couple different contexts, that you're interested in putting more police officers on the streets. I was also concerned and wondering that, in the same notion, are you willing to create some kind of, I don't know—do you have a task force now that would look into community relations between police officers and the public? Because I'm from a city and a neighborhood where some people might feel safer with more police in the streets, but a lot of people would actually be terrified with more police in the streets.

The President. Well, I accept that. The answer to your question is no, I haven't thought about that. Maybe I should think about it, but I haven't. But let me answer you in this way: When I have talked about putting more police officers on the street, I've always talked about

it with two things in mind. First of all, keep in mind that in the last 30 years, there has been a dramatic worsening in the ratio of police to crime. Thirty-five years ago there were approximately three policemen for every serious crime, every felony reported. Now there are three felonies for every police officer. That puts enormous pressure on those police officers. I'm not justifying abuse. I'm just talking about the kinds of pressures in the day-to-day work of the cops on the beat, out there on the front line living with all this. So I believe that if you had more police officers who were well-trained, you would have a reduction in tensions.

But secondly and more importantly, I believe it's important to go to community based policing, where you have the same group of police officers, unless they're misbehaving, working in the communities month in and month out, year in and year out, establishing relationships with people in the communities so that you dramatically reduce the likelihood of abuse or fear, because people know each other. They've got people walking the beats. They know the first names of the police officers. They see them as friends. In the cities where I have seen that happen, I have seen not only a decline in crime but also an increase in mutual trust and understanding between folks in a community and folks in the uniforms.

So I think you've made a very good point. It's not just important that we have more police officers, but the structure of policing, in my judgment, has to be more rooted in particular communities. And I think if we did that, the crime rate would go down significantly. And by the way, there is a lot of evidence, probably in a lot of the cities in which you live here, that that would in fact occur.

Thank you very much.

NOTE: The President spoke at 4:56 p.m. at the Marriott Copley Place Hotel.

Statement to Participants in the March for Lesbian, Gay, and Bi Equal Rights and Liberation
April 25, 1993

Welcome to Washington, DC, your Nation's Capital.

During my campaign and since my election, I have said that America does not have a person to waste. Today I want you to know that I am still committed to that principle.

I stand with you in the struggle for equality for all Americans, including gay men and lesbians. In this great country, founded on the principle that all people are created equal, we must learn to put aside what divides us and focus on what we share. We all want the chance to excel in our work. We all want to be safe in our communities. We all want the support and acceptance of our friends and families.

Last November, the American people sent a message to make Government more accountable to all its citizens, regardless of race, class, gender, disability, or sexual orientation. I am proud of the strides we are making in that direction.

The Pentagon has stopped asking recruits about their sexual orientation, and I have asked the Secretary of Defense to determine how to implement an Executive order lifting the ban on gays and lesbians in the military by July 15.

My 1994 budget increases funding for AIDS research, and my economic plan will fully fund the Ryan White Act. Soon I will announce a new AIDS coordinator to implement the recommendations of the AIDS Commission reports.

I met 9 days ago with leaders of the gay and lesbian community in the Oval Office at the White House. I am told that this meeting marks the first time in history that the President of the United States has held such a meeting. In addition, members of my staff have been and will continue to be in regular communication with the gay and lesbian community.

I still believe every American who works hard and plays by the rules ought to be a part of the national community. Let us work together to make this vision real.

Thank you.

NOTE: Representative Nancy Pelosi read the statement to march participants assembled on The Mall.

Remarks to the Champion University of Arkansas Track Team
April 26, 1993

Thank you very much. Please be seated. As all of you know, as an ardent sports fan I have happily followed the practice of previous Presidents in welcoming to the White House various national championship teams in college and professional athletics. But this is a special honor for me today to welcome to the White House an historic team, the NCAA indoor track champions for the 10th year in a row, the Razorbacks from my home State and home university, the University of Arkansas.

I also want to extend a special welcome to my friend, who this year became the most successful coach in the history of intercollegiate athletics, John McDonnell. I'm sorry it's raining here today. I wanted the team to have a chance to try out the new jogging track on the South Lawn. [*Laughter*]

I also want to say that this team has done some amazing things. I would like to just say that it's really worth contemplating how it happened and what it means for the efforts they made and the kinds of things that ought to be done in intercollegiate athletics and at the

athletic events and teams of younger people, too. This is the first time that any team in any sport has ever won 10 national titles in a row. The Razorbacks, under coach McDonnell, have now won 18 national championships in cross-country and indoor and outdoor track, which makes him the winningest coach in history.

Just think of it, though, John: If you had come here last year they might have called you the failed coach from a small southern State. [*Laughter*] Before the coach came to the University of Arkansas we really had no history of track success there; football got all the attention. He left his native County Mayo in the west of Ireland and made his way to Arkansas, and he's been bringing our track teams the Irish luck ever since.

I am told now that every one of our school's indoor and outdoor track records is held by one of John's recruits. Over the last three decades, since he came to the university in the seventies, he's coached 10 Olympians in 4 games, including Mike Conley who won the gold in the triple jump last year in Barcelona. He's fostered 19 individual national champions in 39 different events.

I actually think that I might hire him to become my training coach. [*Laughter*] I read in Runner's World that I didn't have enough stamina, and they told me that I should run up the steps of the Capitol. And so, I've started running up the steps of the Capitol every morning, which is exhausting to the Secret Service but as yet is having no effect on the United States Congress. [*Laughter*] I thought about this all, and I've decided that I should instead prepare for a marathon and leave track and field to the University of Arkansas.

I want to say, too, that this team has twice won the triple crown, the combined championships in indoor, outdoor, and cross-country. And they're trying for a third triple crown at the NCAA outdoor competition in New Orleans in June, and I want to wish them well.

Again, I want to say that I am especially proud to welcome this team here, because I know something about the coach and his values and the way these things have been done over the years. You don't win this many times over this many years unless you're concerned about the character and well-being of your athletes, as well as just about whether you win one particular meet or another. And so I want to say to all of you, it's a great source of pride and pleasure for me to present to the United States this track team and this fine coach.

Coach, come up here and say a word.

[*At this point, the President was presented with a gift.*]

John, I have something I want to give you in honor of your historic achievement. I want to give you this Presidential commendation for doing something no one ever did before, one for you and one for the team.

I also want to point out that in your honor the First Lady made a rare appearance at one of my press conferences wearing Irish green.

At the end of the press conference, I'm going to shake hands with the team and take some pictures and say hello to all of you from home, but I do have to make a brief announcement about the election in Russia and then perhaps answer a couple of questions.

NOTE: The President spoke at 3:10 p.m. in the East Room at the White House.

Remarks on the Election in Russia and an Exchange With Reporters
April 26, 1993

The President. Not very long ago, perhaps about, oh, an hour ago now, I had a conversation with President Yeltsin. I called to congratulate him on his outstanding victory in the election and to reassure him that the United States continues to support him as the elected leader of Russia and continues to look forward to our partnership in working to reduce the threat of nuclear weapons, to increase trade and commerce, and to promote democracy. This is a very, very good day, not only for the people of Russia but for the people of the United States and all the people of the world.

I will say again I know that there have been times in the last 3 months when many Americans, troubled with their own economic difficulties, have asked why their President would be so involved in trying to support the process of democracy in Russia. And I want to say again why that is so. They are a huge country with vast natural resources, with enormous opportunities for Americans to create jobs and to earn income and to reap the benefits of trade. They still have thousands of nuclear weapons which we must proceed to reduce and to dismantle so that the world will be a safer place and so that we will no longer have to spend our investment dollars, that we need so desperately to rebuild our own economy, on maintaining a state of extreme readiness and large numbers of warheads positioned against Russia. And they are a great country that can be a symbol of democracy in a very troubled part of the world if democracy can stay alive there. They can prove that you can make three dramatic changes at once as they try to move from a Communist system to a democracy, from a controlled economy to a market economy, and to a nation state away from being an imperial power with occupying armies.

This is a victory that belongs to the Russian people and to the courage of Boris Yeltsin, but I am very glad that the United States supported steadfastly the process of democracy in Russia. I was glad to have a chance to talk to President Yeltsin. Needless to say, he was in a very good humor when I talked to him, and he had a good sense of humor. And he offered the United States a great Russian bear hug for their support for democracy in Russia and, actually, in the other republics of the former Soviet Union as well.

So, it was a very good conversation. But I do want to say that this is a good day, not just for the people of Russia but for the people of the United States as well.

Russia

Q. Mr. President, will this election result help you sell your aid package to Congress?

The President. I would hope so. I think it will validate the policy of the United States, which I might say has been by and large a completely bipartisan one. I want to say a special word of appreciation to all the living former Presidents who supported the position I took here: President Carter and President Reagan and President Ford, President Nixon and President Bush, all of them. They made it easier for all of us to maintain a united American front. And I want to say a special word of thanks to all the leaders in Congress on both sides of the aisle who supported this policy.

I do believe that we have to think of this as a long-term effort. We have to be in this for the long run. But I think it will be immensely beneficial to the United States.

Q. Mr. President, were you surprised by the results on all four questions?

The President. Well, I sort of thought he would win on all four. I thought there might be some difference, and as you know, there was a difference in the vote between the referendum on Yeltsin himself and his policies. But you would expect that in tough times. We've had a lot of Western leaders reelected in the last 3 or 4 years in the midst of economic difficulties where the people got reelected and there was still debate about their policy, because people are having a tough time, and people in Russia are having a very tough time. I think

the reaffirmation of his policies really is a tribute to the farsightedness of the Russian people. I think in the end what happened was they decided that as difficult as it is, that that is the only path they could take. And I think, again, it's a real tribute to his courage and to their common sense and ability to see the future. And it's very tough to do when you're going through what they're going through: terrible inflation, unemployment, all those dislocating problems. It is a real tribute to their maturity and to their courage and foresight.

Stimulus Package

Q. Mr. President, will you now break down your jobs stimulus bill and offer them one at a time on the meritorious projects?

The President. Sarah [Sarah McClendon, McClendon News Service], I thought they were all meritorious. I have not made a decision about what to do. I want to consult with the Members of Congress. I think it is imperative that we make some decisions along that line. Certainly the Russian issue, I think if it's going to be seriously addressed by Congress, has to be done in the context of what our first obligations are to the American people and their interests. And so we'll be talking about that. And I expect to make a decision in the fairly near future on that.

Bosnia

Q. Mr. President, do you now have a course of action that you're free to take by virtue of this result in Russia that you might have been inhibited in taking before, perhaps on Bosnia or perhaps on some other issue, perhaps on Russia itself?

The President. Well, what you say may be true in the sense that had there been a reversal there, the position of the Russian Government might have become much more intransigent. It is now, I think, clear that the United States and our allies need to move forward with a stronger policy in Bosnia, and I will be announcing the course that I hope we can take in the next several days. I want to do some serious consultations with the Congress and others, and I will be doing that in the next few days.

But now I think the time had come to focus on that problem and what it means for the United States and has for the rest of the world,

as well as for the people that are suffering there.
Thank you very much.

NOTE: The President spoke at 3:20 p.m. in the East Room at the White House.

Message to the Congress on Additional Measures With Respect to the Federal Republic of Yugoslavia (Serbia and Montenegro)
April 26, 1993

To the Congress of the United States:

On June 1, 1992, pursuant to section 204(b) of the International Emergency Economic Powers Act (50 U.S.C. 1703(b)) and section 301 of the National Emergencies Act (50 U.S.C. 1631), President Bush reported to the Congress by letters to the President of the Senate and the Speaker of the House, dated May 30, 1992, that he had exercised his statutory authority to issue Executive Order No. 12808 of May 30, 1992, declaring a national emergency and blocking "Yugoslav Government" property and property of the Governments of Serbia and Montenegro.

On June 5, 1992, pursuant to the above authorities as well as section 1114 of the Federal Aviation Act (49 U.S.C. App. 1514), and section 5 of the United Nations Participation Act (22 U.S.C. 287c), the President reported to the Congress by letters to the President of the Senate and the Speaker of the House that he had exercised his statutory authority to issue Executive Order No. 12810 of June 5, 1992, blocking property of and prohibiting transactions with the Federal Republic of Yugoslavia (Serbia and Montenegro). This latter action was taken to ensure that the economic measures taken by the United States with respect to the Federal Republic of Yugoslavia (Serbia and Montenegro) conform to U.N. Security Council Resolution No. 757 (May 30, 1992).

On January 19, 1993, pursuant to the above authorities, President Bush reported to the Congress by letters to the President of the Senate and the Speaker of the House that he had exercised his statutory authority to issue Executive Order No. 12831 of January 15, 1993, to impose additional economic measures with respect to the Federal Republic of Yugoslavia (Serbia and Montenegro) to conform to U.N. Security Council Resolution No. 787 (November 16, 1992). Those additional measures prohibited transactions related to transshipments through the Federal Republic of Yugoslavia (Serbia and Montenegro), as well as transactions related to vessels owned or controlled by persons or entities in the Federal Republic of Yugoslavia (Serbia and Montenegro).

On April 17, 1993, the U.N. Security Council adopted Resolution No. 820, calling on the Bosnian Serbs to accept the Vance-Owen peace plan for Bosnia-Hercegovina and, if they failed to do so by April 26, calling on member states to take additional measures to tighten the embargo against the Federal Republic of Yugoslavia (Serbia and Montenegro). Effective 12:01 a.m. EDT on April 26, 1993, I have taken additional steps pursuant to the above statutory authorities to enhance the implementation of this international embargo and to conform to U.N. Security Council Resolution No. 820 (April 17, 1993).

The order that I signed on April 25, 1993:

—blocks all property of businesses organized or located in the Federal Republic of Yugoslavia (Serbia or Montenegro), including the property of entities owned or controlled by them, wherever organized or located, if that property is in or later comes within the United States or the possession or control of U.S. persons, including their overseas branches;

—charges to the owners or operators of property blocked under that order or Executive Order No. 12808, 12810, or 12831 all expenses incident to the blocking and maintenance of such property, requires that such expenses be satisfied from sources other than blocked funds, and permits such property to be sold and the proceeds (after payment of expenses) placed in a blocked account;

—orders (1) the detention, pending investigation, of all nonblocked vessels, aircraft, freight vehicles, rolling stock, and cargo within the United States that are suspected of violating U.N. Security Council Resolution No. 713, 757, 787, or 820, and (2) the blocking of such conveyances or cargo if a violation is determined to have been committed, and permits the sale of such blocked conveyances or cargo and the placing of the net proceeds into a blocked account;

—prohibits any vessel registered in the United States, or owned or controlled by U.S. persons, other than a United States naval vessel, from entering the territorial waters of the Federal Republic of Yugoslavia (Serbia and Montenegro); and

—prohibits U.S. persons from engaging in any dealings relating to the shipment of goods to, from, or through United Nations Protected Areas in the Republic of Croatia and areas in the Republic of Bosnia-Hercegovina under the control of Bosnian Serb forces.

The order that I signed on April 25, 1993, authorizes the Secretary of the Treasury in consultation with the Secretary of State to take such actions, and to employ all powers granted to me by the International Emergency Economic Powers Act and the United Nations Participation

Act, as may be necessary to carry out the purposes of that order, including the issuance of licenses authorizing transactions otherwise prohibited. The sanctions imposed in the order apply notwithstanding any preexisting contracts, international agreements, licenses or authorizations. However, licenses or authorizations previously issued pursuant to Executive Order No. 12808, 12810, or 12831 are not invalidated by the order unless they are terminated, suspended or modified by action of the issuing federal agency.

The declaration of the national emergency made by Executive Order No. 12808 and the controls imposed under Executive Orders No. 12810 and 12831, and any other provisions of those orders not modified by or inconsistent with the April 25, 1993, order, remain in full force and are unaffected by that order.

WILLIAM J. CLINTON

The White House,
April 26, 1993.

NOTE: The Executive order of April 25 is listed in Appendix D at the end of this volume.

Nomination for Ambassador to the Organization for Economic Cooperation and Development
April 26, 1993

The President announced today that he intends to nominate David Aaron to be Ambassador to the Organization for Economic Cooperation and Development.

"David Aaron is an experienced and accomplished foreign policy hand, who has already been of great service to me as an adviser during

my campaign and an emissary in Europe before I was inaugurated," said the President. "I am confident he will serve our country capably at OECD."

NOTE: A biography of the nominee was made available by the Office of the Press Secretary.

Remarks to the National Realtors Association
April 27, 1993

The President. Thank you very much. And thank you, president Bill. [*Laughter*] I'm glad to be on your coattails today. [*Laughter*]

I'm glad to see all of you in a good humor, enthusiastic and, I hope, feeling very good about

your country. I'm glad to have you here today in our Nation's Capital. I saw some people from my home State out there in the crowd as I wandered around. I see them back there.

You know, in politics, you don't have a lot

of job security. And therefore, I've been a good customer for several realtors over the years. [*Laughter*] Even though I now live in America's finest public housing—[*laughter*]—I actually was a customer on several occasions.

I want to thank you at the outset for the support this organization has given to the economic program I have put before the Congress and to our efforts to put the American people back to work. I'm proud to be here with people who are on the frontlines of America's real economy, who understand the need for fundamental change in the way we promote growth and increase profits and generate jobs.

I believe we have begun to make those fundamental changes, but I think we can only see the job through if we have the help of you and millions of people like you who live in the economy beyond the beltway, where people are not guaranteed jobs and have an uncertain future.

I had an interesting encounter here just a couple of days ago. I was out on my morning run, and as is often the case, I just saw some people along the Mall out there. I was running up toward the Capitol the end of last week, and this young man asked if he could jog along with me. And he was visiting the Nation's Capital, and I asked him what he did for a living. And he said, "I'm in the real estate business in Texas." And he said, "I'm just telling you," he said, "I'm out there seeing it." He said, "It's just amazing how hard people work just to keep their heads above the water. And we need jobs and education in this country. We need to do something to make these cities safer. And we've got to turn these things around." And he said, "I just want you to know that." He said, "I have more awareness of it than I ever did since I've been in the real estate business, because I really see people and how they have to live and the struggles they endure." And I understand that about the work that you do. And I thank you for the support you've given to the efforts that we've made.

In the first 3 months of this administration, we have fundamentally changed the direction taken by our National Government over the previous decade. I've tried to overcome inertia, ideology, and indifference. I've tried to reach out a hand of partnership and to restore energy and experimentation to this Government.

Everybody knows we're living in a new and uncharted time. There is a global economy coming together in ways that are good and bad, opening all kinds of new opportunities for us but also affecting us. When there is a recession in Japan and recession in Germany and a recession in the rest of Europe, it affects the United States.

We are trying to figure out now how we should chart our course in the future. But we do know some things about what works and what doesn't and what has always worked in the American free enterprise system. The changes we have to make won't be easy. It hasn't been so far. It's not going to be easy in the future. But we have to do these things. One of the things that we know is the worst thing we can do in many cases is to stay on the path that we were on.

I submitted to the Congress a blueprint of a budget plan designed to change the policies of debt and disinvestment and decline, to bring a new spirit of investment and growth and thrift to the Government. Both Houses of Congress agreed to the budget plan in record time, a plan that will reduce the national deficit by over $500 billion in the next 5 years.

These votes are important because they're votes of confidence, and they illustrate that this town has finally gotten serious about cutting the deficit. That's one of the reasons we saw a big upturn in the stock market at the same time interest rates were hitting record lows. As you know better than anyone, these things can bring enormous long-term benefits to the economy.

Just look at this chart that I brought with me. I only brought one, but I wanted to show this one. My staff, they started letting me take charts around again. You know, I used to carry them all, and I used to get criticized for putting people to sleep with numbers and statistics and everything. So I quit for a while. But I just couldn't stand it anymore, I had to bring one. [*Laughter*]

This chart shows what has happened to 30 year fixed rate mortgages with a 20-percent downpayment since the election. Look at this. Six months prior to the election the average rate was 8.2 percent. Right after the election we announced that we were going to seriously work to bring this deficit down, and we began intense meetings in Little Rock with people who were part of our administration and people from around the country. We had the national economic summit. From election day to February 17th, the day on which I presented the plan, the average rate was 8.1 percent. Since February 17th the average rate has been 7.5 percent. Today the rate is the lowest it's been since August of 1972, the lowest in over 20 years.

These reductions have prompted, as you well know, a wave of refinancing which will put over $100 billion back into this economy in a 12 month period if we can keep these rates down. That is a huge boost to the economy.

Businesses will pay less to borrow. That will help them to make new investments and create new jobs. The Federal Government is already saving billions of dollars as we roll over the debt at each auction. Our national deficit this year in this budget is going to be much lower than it was thought to be because of the lower interest rates. And of course, as you well know, this means lower home mortgages for citizens, lower car payments, less expensive credit card payments at the end of each month, strengthened by our subsidiary efforts to attack the credit crunch, which are now getting underway in earnest, and working with community banks all across the country. This is liberating billions of dollars in capital. It means that farmers and small business people and others can look forward to a better future if we can keep the trend going. It means that there will be new confidence in the economy, and that can be a catalyst for economic growth. It means progress.

The question we now have to ask is: Will we continue this progress? How can we turn back? For in the next few days, Congress will begin to consider the legislation to turn the budget resolution, which adopted the form of budget cuts and revenue increases and deficit reduction and new investments, into very specific, specific budget items. And now the time has come to reinvigorate and reenergize our efforts to make sure that the budget steps that have been taken are going to be followed through on.

The process is kind of complicated, and it's known in the Congress as reconciliation. But it means that they have to reconcile all of the thousands and thousands and thousands of specific decisions on tax cuts, tax increases, spending decreases, spending increases into a final bill which reflects the budget resolution which was adopted several weeks ago and which you all supported. So it is very important that the final resolution be really a reconciliation; that is, that it is consistent with that first budget

resolution that the Congress courageously adopted.

It's important to realize what's at stake. We're supposed to be in the 24th month of an economic recovery. I bet if we took a poll among you, it would be hard to get a majority for that proposition. But the economists say, based on aggregate economic figures, we're in the 24th month of a recovery. Still, we have fewer private sector jobs than we did in 1990; 16 million men and women are looking for full-time jobs. This past week, jobless claims went up again. Housing starts and sales of existing homes are still on the decline. That's why I've been fighting so hard for some immediate action to get the economy moving and to create new jobs.

I want to stop here, just sort of create a parenthesis and say, when you see all these struggles going back and forth in Washington, and it may be reported to you that the President wins this battle and loses that battle, or somebody's up and somebody's down, it's very important for you to try to clear away the political smokescreen and ask yourself what is really at stake here. We are waging a great contest of ideas. And I ran for President in the hope that I could change the ideas that both parties had brought to the national debate. And there are, not surprisingly, people here who not only have different political agendas but who honestly have different ideas.

What I hope to do in the days and weeks and months ahead is to say, look, I don't have all the answers, but if we're going to fight, let's don't fight over this or that political advantage or some speculative impact on some future election. Let us wage an honest battle of ideas. And then we can find out what's best for the American people.

My belief is, if you look at the last 12 years, our country got in trouble because we did two things at the same time: We dramatically increased the Government's debt, going from $1 trillion in national debt to $4 trillion in debt. And believe it or not, we decreased at the same time the Nation's investment in many things that are critical to our future, the National Government's investment in many education and training areas, in nondefense technologies. We weren't keeping up with all of our competitors in the infrastructure that makes communities strong and growing and lifts incomes and opportunities. We weren't keeping up with our competitors. And we were actually spending a much smaller percentage of our budget in 1990 than we had in 1980 or 1975 in many of these critical areas. This had never happened before.

At the same time, because of these policies, because of tax policies, and because of global economic pressures, we saw most middle class people working longer weeks for lower wages than they had been drawing 10, 15 years before.

So it seemed to me what we needed to try to do was to turn both those things around, to try to decrease the Government's deficit and adopt a disciplined plan that would run not just 4 years, but 8 or 10 years, to bring this debt down to zero—the deficit down to zero, so we could turn—[*applause*]—so that we could reduce the percentage of our income that our national debt comprises.

In the early seventies the national debt got down to about, oh, 27 percent of annual income. It's now up to $4 trillion, which is about two-thirds of annual income. On the other hand, I want to emphasize, if you wanted to abolish it overnight, you could do it, but it would collapse the economy.

Again, this is a battle of ideas. Idea number one: Should we reduce the deficit? Everybody will say yes.

Audience member. Yes.

The President. Sure. [*Laughter*] Sure. Then the question is: How fast, how much, and on what kind of a timeframe? My objective has been to try to bring it down substantially but not so dramatically as to cause another recession in a difficult economic time but to do it with an 8 year plan in mind, not just 4, that will actually do away with it. So we can bring it down to zero so we can begin to stabilize the debt, because even as you reduce the deficit—that's what you're running in red ink every year—the debt will grow.

But if we do this for 8 years, we can bring it down to zero. We can then reduce dramatically the percentage of our income that the national debt represents, and we can strengthen the long-term health of the economy. And then we can have some money to invest in other things that we need to invest it in.

Second thing: Can we afford to put all of our investment programs on hold for 4 or 8 years and spend no new money on anything? Major idea: I would argue the answer to that is, no. Because we know that in the world in which we're living, in the global economy, what we earn depends on what we can learn; that

new technologies are the source of most new jobs that pay high wages and have enormous spin-off effects on people like realtors. You've got a growing economy in your area; you're going to do better. If you have a shrinking economy in your area, you won't do as well.

Thirdly, I would argue, you cannot afford to stop investing, because we have cut the defense budget so much in areas that cost jobs, not just base closings, the obvious things, but even more importantly, as anybody from California or Connecticut or Massachusetts can tell you, in areas related to research and development and production of weapons, which provided very high-wage jobs in manufacturing and in research.

So for all those reasons I don't think you can just put all your investments on hold. I think we've got to empower the American people to be able to compete in the global economy. So while we bring the deficit down, I would argue we need to have at least modest increases in some areas of investment.

That means, in my view, that you have to have very rigorous spending cuts in other areas, and you have to raise some more money, because we dramatically altered the tax base of the country back in 1981. That's why I presented the program that this organization endorsed.

Now, I welcome people who have different ideas. But I think it's very important to scrutinize them. Some will say, "Well, we can have the same deficit reduction with lower taxes if we have no new investments." That's true. They're right. That is an opposition idea that is absolutely true. But I think we would pay for it. So we could argue about that.

Others will say, "We ought to cut the deficit more, and I hate all taxes." They're not telling you the way it is. If that crowd wins this battle, the deficit will go up, not down. You mark my words.

There are others who say, "I wish they'd leave that health care thing alone." Let me tell you why I don't agree with that. The biggest spending increases in the first part of the last 12-year period were in defense. But defense peaked out in 1986, and it's been going down since. And my fellow Americans, without regard to party, respectfully, there is a limit to how much you can take it down, how fast. We still have responsibilities, and this is still a difficult world with a lot of unpredictable things out there.

And we have cut it a lot. I don't mean the rate eventually. It's been cut.

So you might say, "Well, what has happened? If defense has been going down for 5 years, how come this deficit keeps going up?" I'll tell you why. Because in the last 5 years the defense increases have been supplemented by explosive increases in health care costs and in interest payments on the debt.

So we're trying to get the interest payments down by bringing the interest rates down. But we have to address the health care issue. If we don't do anything to add a single new benefit, not anything to add a single new benefit, we'll have a 67-percent increase in outlays for Medicare and Medicaid in the next 5 years, going up at 12 percent a year, assuming an inflation rate in the economy as a whole of about 4 to 5 percent. And, of course, a lot of you who pay health insurance see the same thing in your own premiums.

The United States of America spends 15 percent of its income on health care. No other nation in the world is at 10. Only Canada is over 9. That means when our automotive companies or our airplane manufacturers or our major service sector people go into the global economy, they have spotted their competitors a one-third advantage on health care. And actually, it's worse than that because a lot of people don't pay anything, because they get uncompensated care at emergency rooms. So a lot of our bigger manufacturers actually pay more than 15 percent of their income for health care.

This is a very troubling thing. I don't mean to tell you there are easy answers, but the reason I asked my wife to take on this issue is, I could see that if you want an 8-year plan that brings this debt down to zero, you can never get there without health care reform. You can't get there without health care reform.

Another big idea: If you look at everybody's deficit reduction plan—it doesn't matter what party or what their ideas are—we can cut this budget and we can bring it down for 5 years. If my plan is adopted, the one I put before Congress or some reasonable facsimile of it, it will bring this debt down steeply for 5 years. And then the next year it goes right up again. Why? Because all the cuts we make and all the money we raise will be overcome by health care explosion.

If we don't change the way we're going by the end of this decade, we'll be spending 18 percent of our income on health care. No other country then will be over 10, and we will really be in the soup. Now, that's a big idea. You have to decide whether you agree with that or not, but I believe that. And that drives what I'm trying to do as your President.

So in summary, what I've tried to do is to put people and their needs first, build a foundation that invests in education and technology and the future economy and gets people out of an economy that is fast going away and has trapped them, to do what business people do for their companies, to put more investments into things that don't work, to try to reduce unnecessary debts and cut out a lot of things, put more investment in things that do work and cut out a lot of things that don't.

In this budget that I have presented to the Congress, there are over 200 specific budget cuts. I do want to restore responsibility in the way your money is spent. And I am appalled at this deficit. I live in a State which is in the bottom five in the percentage of income going to State and local taxes, had a tough balanced budget law, and permitted me to cut spending across the board every month when revenues were below spending. I don't like what's going on. But you cannot fix it overnight. We have to have a disciplined plan that will bring it down without endangering the economic recovery and recognizing the things that we ought to be investing in so we can compete with these other nations for the jobs of tomorrow.

I tried to set an example. We cut the size of the White House staff by 25 percent starting in the next budget year. It's already well below where it was when I took office. We cut across-the-board administrative expenditures of the Federal Government 14 percent over the next 5 years. The Congress has followed suit. They get a lot of criticism, but I will say this: They've followed suit. They've agreed to nearly that big an administrative cut in their staff. We've eliminated a lot of unnecessary perks and privileges. And most important of all, I've asked the Vice President to head up a task force on reinventing Government.

We now have several hundred people from all over this country coming to Washington to help us reexamine the way every last dollar of your tax money is spent. And in September when we come forward with that report and the Vice President's task force reports, I think we'll have a whole new round of changes in the way your money is spent that will not only save money but will treat taxpayers more like customers and try to make this Government a low-cost, high-quality producers of services for you. And we'll reexamine some things, believe me, that have not been examined in 60 years in the way things are done.

What I want to ask all of you to do is to ask the Members of Congress to help us make this street run two ways. Pennsylvania Avenue has to run two ways. And the dispute I had last week over the stimulus, all the people who disagreed with me were in the other party, in the Republican Party. I'm going to have disputes in the weeks ahead where the people who disagree with me, many of them will be in my own party. But again I say, let us keep this battle a battle of ideas. That's one I think I can win, because I told my ideas to the American people when they voted. But we cannot afford to have one day wasted on mindless maneuvering. We need to argue over the direction of the country.

I'd also like to ask for your help on a specific thing. When I was a Governor I had a line-item veto that I could use to wipe out unnecessary spending. Believe it or not, once I'd used it a little bit, I hardly ever had to use it again. The fact of having it even made a difference in disciplining spending.

I want to point out, it's not just about spending reduction, but it's about the quality of the overall budget. The legislative process is always and in every place a lot like making sausage, as some wise wag once said. That's just the nature of it. A lot of us in our different roles in life have probably contributed to that sausage slicing at some time or another.

It is important that someone who is accountable only to everyone can have some discipline over the process. We now have an opportunity to adopt a law that will provide the President not an identical but a similar means to cut wasteful spending.

This week the House of Representatives is considering, and I urge them to pass, a new law that would give the President the right to reject items in appropriations bills. This proposal is called enhanced rescission. Let me tell you what that means. I hate all these Washington words, don't you? It's kind of like the line-item veto and only slightly different. Let me tell you what it means. It means that the President is given the power to cut individual spending items, and the rest of the bill can go into effect. Once cut by the President, these items can only be restored unless Congress voted on them separately. Now it wouldn't require a two-thirds majority. It would only require a majority. I think that's probably all we can do under the Constitution of the United States.

But the difference is these items would be out there by themselves, not buried in some big bill. So that when the votes were taken, they would be taken in view of the press and the public, and you could draw your conclusions. And if they were areas where we had, again, a difference of ideas and they believed in the idea and thought it could be defended, then they could vote on it. And you could make your decision. It would give me the chance, and any future President, the chance to try to impose some budget discipline.

In the early seventies the Congress adopted a new budget control act. Before that, Presidents could regularly impound big amounts of spending in the budget, before 20 years ago. And Presidents of both parties regularly did that.

This would, at least, begin to move us in the direction of what I think of as an acceptable compromise. It respects the separation of powers. It ultimately respects the right of the United States Congress to do what the Constitution gives it and not the President the power to do. But it makes both of us more responsible in how your money is spent.

I hope you will ask your Senators and Representatives, without regard to party, to vote for this bill. It is a good idea. And it is a beginning of a reform agenda which I think we should see through.

In the next several days, as we consult with Republicans as well as Democrats, I hope to announce my support of a sweeping bill to reform the system of campaign finance that will reduce the influence of special interest and big money and open up the political process to challengers and also open up the airwaves a little bit so that people will have a chance for honest debate in elections, and they won't all be turned by expensive 30-second ads.

I hope we'll see the passage in this Congress of a bill requiring much more sweeping disclosure laws for lobbyists. I hope we will see more efforts to get the Federal Government to live within the laws it makes. For example, on Earth Day, the day before Earth Day when I gave my environmental speech, one of the things that I said we were going to do is to have the Federal Government, when we deal with toxic sites within our jurisdiction, start living by the right-to-know laws that were long ago imposed on private employers. I think if we're going to do that to people in the private sector, we ought to live within it.

And I think we have to constantly keep changing the Government. I am very excited about the work being done by the Vice President's Commission on Reinventing Government, and I think you will be, too. There are dramatic changes that can be made in the way we deliver the goods, in ways that will both save money and improve the quality of service.

But let's begin with what I call the Federal version of the line-item veto. Ask your Members of Congress to vote for this enhanced rescission bill. It can't do any harm, and it might do a whole lot of good. And I need it, and you need it.

I just want to say a couple of things that you already know, but they bear repeating. I don't just ask for, in this economic plan, to invest money publicly in things like Head Start and better standards for our schools and apprenticeship programs for young people who don't go to college and the national service program, which we will unveil in its details on Friday, to provide for college education loans for every young person who is willing to pay them back at tax time so they can't beat the bill or by working and paying off the loan by doing something for their country. I also recognize that the main engine of economic growth is you and people like you.

So I believe—and again, this is a battle of ideas. And you can read a lot about this since you're in this town. I believe that, while the '86 Tax Reform Act had some good provisions, the idea of simplifying the rate structure, lowering the rates, and eliminating some of the individual deductions and trying to simplify, that was basically good. I think the idea that you can have a tax system which has no incentives for investment at a time when you need to increase investment and reduce consumption is wrong. That's my view. That's my view.

Again, this is an honest contest of ideas. I recognize that anytime you fool with the Tax Code, if you're not careful, you just make more money for accountants and lawyers and open loopholes. You've got to be careful with that.

So let's recognize there are two sides to every argument on changing the Tax Code. I accept that. But what I have tried to do, based on my experience of a dozen years as a Governor, struggling to get people to invest in my State and grow our economy, and based on untold thousands of conversations over the years with people in the private sector, I tried to present a bill to the Congress that would strike the right balance between not just opening the Tax Code and having it riddled but having significant incentives, especially now, to boost investment.

There are a lot of people who don't think I struck the right balance. But as long as it's a battle of ideas, we can wage that. I just think there is a compelling case to be made that we have always benefited in the history of this country from investment incentives. At a time when there is too little investment and everybody can see that, I think it's something we ought to be sensitive to. So that's something else you'll see as we unfold this battle.

You know how I feel about the real estate issues. I recommended making permanent the low-income housing tax credit. And I recommended stopping the discrimination against people in real estate by changing the passive loss provisions. I feel strongly about it. But I also recommended a change in the alternative minimum tax, which would primarily benefit bigger businesses which invest.

Yes, I asked for the corporate rate on high income corporations to be raised to 36 percent. But I wanted to change those things which would reward investment. I think that's the right decision. I know it's the right direction. We can argue about the details. I know it's the right direction. So I ask you to help to get that passed.

Let me just say a personal word in closing. I've been very fortunate in my life. I've had a good family. I've had a good education. I've had good jobs. I got to live the American dream. And as I've already said, I've lived in the best public housing in Arkansas and Washington, DC. [*Laughter*]

I live by some values that I was raised with: the idea that everybody ought to have an opportunity to work hard; the idea that everybody who gets an opportunity has responsibility that goes with it; and the idea that we're all part of a bigger community, and if we have a chance in life, we ought to try to guarantee that same chance to everyone else. That's why I respect the work you do. There's no greater goal for America's families than to be able to live in their own homes and to help their children and their grandchildren and their neighbors to do it.

I respect you, too, because I know that you live with a certain amount of uncertainty in your own life. You live by your wits; you live by your efforts. You don't have a guaranteed income. How well you do depends on how hard and how smart you work, but it also depends on the decisions made by people in this town and by people all around the world that you don't know that impinge on your life and set the parameters in which you operate.

And so I ask you to help join me again in partnership on these issues, to make sure that the struggles that we have in the months ahead are great battles of ideas. It is an exciting time, after all. A lot of good things are going on. The cold war is over. The people of Russia stood up to the old guard and said, "We're going to stay with freedom. We're going to stay with free market economics. We don't want to go back to being an imperial power. We'd like to be part of the world," that you and I take for granted.

A lot of good things going on. Productivity in the private sector in this country increased by the highest rate in 20 years in the last quarter of last year, the American business sector trying to reinvest, trying to compete. A lot of good things going on, but a lot of profound chal-

lenges. Let these challenges be addressed in the spirit of partnership, and let the battles be battles of ideas, not politics.

I do not think we can be down about what's going on. These problems are big problems. They're the problems of our generation. We inherited them, and it's our job to deal with them, not to moan about them. That's our job, to roll up our sleeves and face them and deal with them.

One of the greatest poets that this country ever produced was Carl Sandburg. And I used to save a little quote by Carl Sandburg. I carried it with me for years and years when I was a young man. And it was—I believe I remember it, even though I haven't seen it in 15 years. Sandburg said, "A tough will counts. So does desire. So does a rich, soft wanting. Without rich wanting, nothing arrives. Without effort, nothing arrives." Sandburg said, "I see America not in the setting sun of black night of despair ahead of us. I see America in the crimson light of a rising sun, fresh from the burning, creative hand of God. I see great days ahead, great days possible to men and women of will and vision." I see that, and I think you do, too.

Thank you very much.

NOTE: The President spoke at 11:52 a.m. at the Sheraton Washington Hotel. In his remarks, he referred to Bill Chee, president, National Realtors Association.

Remarks to the NCAA Men's and Women's Basketball Champions and an Exchange With Reporters
April 27, 1993

The President. Good afternoon. I want to apologize to the people who are here from North Carolina and Texas. I have been inside in a meeting with some Members of the United States Congress of both parties, some of whom are also here in the crowd, talking about the situation in Bosnia. And I got away as quickly as I could. I thank all of you for coming here.

It's a great honor for me as an ardent basketball fan to welcome to the White House two proud new national champions, the Tarheels of North Carolina and the Lady Raiders of Texas

Tech, who won the men's and women's NCAA basketball championships.

The Lady Raiders have been stirring things up in West Texas for some time now, with back-to-back Southwest Conference titles, and this year, of course, they brought home Texas Tech's first national championship in any sport. It helps when you have a secret weapon in basketball whose name rhymes with "hoops." No doubt about it, Cheryl Swoopes turned in a tournament performance that was one for the ages. She averaged over 32 points a game and scored

47 points in the final, which is an all-time championship record for men or women in basketball finals. If anybody hasn't figured it out yet, I think women's basketball has arrived.

I'd also like to say that we have to make special mention of the coach of the Lady Raiders, coach Marcia Sharp, who is a four-time Southwest Conference Coach of the Year and who took a wonderful 11-year career at Texas Tech to new heights.

Then there are the Tarheels, one of whom had the grace to remind me that they waxed Arkansas in getting to the Sweet 16. [*Laughter*] There may not be many things you can depend upon in this world, but normally it is when "March Madness" rolls around, you can be sure that Dean Smith's Tarheels will be there at the final bell, with discipline and style as great as any you will ever see. Nineteen consecutive years in the NCAA, 13 trips to the Sweet 16, 9 times to the Final 4, 2 national championships. Even though I have to admit that I didn't pull for them in every game—[*laughter*]—I thought they were magnificent, true Carolina Blue champions.

I also want to say a special word of thanks to Eric Montross for not standing on the riser when I walked by. I felt small enough as it was. [*Laughter*] I want to congratulate him and Donald Williams for the three-pointers that they made, and George Lynch for muscling out his opposition on the inside. As a matter of fact, I was thinking of asking George to stay around here for a few days and help me. [*Laughter*]

I want to say again that the thing I like about basketball and the thing I think our country needs more of is that you can't just win with great players; you have to have great teamwork. People have to understand each other's strengths and weaknesses and learn to work together in a consistent way. These two teams have done it and have done it magnificently, and it's a great honor for me to welcome them to the White House today.

I'd like to now invite the coaches to come up and say a few words.

[*At this point, team members were introduced, and each team presented the President with a basketball.*]

The President. I want to invite all the people to come up here, and we'll all take a few pictures and everything. And I thank all of you for coming. I want to take a few minutes; then I've got to go back to my meeting. Thank you very much.

Congressional Meeting on Bosnia

Q. Have you talked to Biden about your decision, or is this just an information meeting?

The President. No. I have not made a final decision yet, and I am consulting with them and giving them a chance to tell me what they think we should do. And I think that's the appropriate thing to do. I've tried to proceed here, as I did in Russia, with bipartisan support. We're having a very good meeting, and I'm going to take a few minutes to shake hands, then go back to the meeting. We're in the middle of the meeting. I have no results to report, but I am just listening to them.

OMB Director Panetta

Q. What do you think about what Mr. Panetta said today?

Q. Are you taking Leon Panetta to the woodshed, Mr. President?

The President. No, I don't need to take him to the woodshed. I need for him to get his spirits up a little. You know, this is like a basketball game. You see, these guys, there were a lot of times that they were in close games; a lot of times they were in close games, they wound up winning.

I just think he's been working 60 to 70 hours a week, and he got discouraged. I need for him to sort of get his spirits up. He's done a wonderful job for this administration. He's got a lot of credibility, and I think every Member of Congress that's ever worked with Leon Panetta would say he's one of the most honest, competent people they've ever worked with. He had a bad day yesterday because he got his spirits down. I want to buck him up; I don't want to take him to the woodshed.

Thank you.

NOTE: The President spoke at 4:45 p.m. in the Rose Garden at the White House.

Message to the Congress Reporting on the Continuation of Export Control Regulations
April 27, 1993

To the Congress of the United States:

1. On September 30, 1990, in Executive Order No. 12730, President Bush declared a national emergency under the International Emergency Economic Powers Act ("IEEPA") (50 U.S.C. 1701 *et seq.*) to deal with the threat to the national security and foreign policy of the United States caused by the lapse of the Export Administration Act of 1979, as amended (50 U.S.C. App. 2401 *et seq.*), and the system of controls maintained under that Act. In that order, the President continued in effect, to the extent permitted by law, the provisions of the Export Administration Act of 1979, as amended, the Export Administration Regulations (15 C.F.R. 768 *et seq.*), and the delegations of authority set forth in Executive Order No. 12002 of July 7, 1977, Executive Order No. 12214 of May 2, 1980, and Executive Order No. 12131 of May 4, 1979, as amended by Executive Order No. 12551 of February 21, 1986.

2. President Bush issued Executive Order No. 12730 pursuant to the authority vested in him as President by the Constitution and laws of the United States, including IEEPA, the National Emergencies Act (NEA) (50 U.S.C. 1601 *et seq.*), and section 301 of title 3 of the United States Code. At that time, the President also submitted a report to the Congress pursuant to section 204(b) of IEEPA (50 U.S.C. 1703(b)). Section 204 of IEEPA requires follow-up reports, with respect to actions or changes, to be submitted every 6 months. Additionally, section 401(c) of the NEA requires that the President, within 90 days after the end of each 6-month period following a declaration of a national emergency, report to the Congress on the total expenditures directly attributable to that declaration. This report, covering the 6-month period from October 1, 1992, to March 31, 1993, is submitted in compliance with these requirements.

3. Since the issuance of Executive Order No. 12730, the Department of Commerce has continued to administer and enforce the system of export controls, including antiboycott provisions, contained in the Export Administration Regulations. In administering these controls, the Department has acted under a policy of conforming actions under Executive Order No. 12730 to those required under the Export Administration Act, insofar as appropriate.

4. Since the last report to the Congress, there have been several significant developments in the area of export controls:

—United States Government experts have continued their efforts to implement and strengthen export control systems, including pre-license inspections and post-shipment verifications, in the nations of Central Europe and the former Soviet Union—notably Belarus, Bulgaria, the Czech Republic, Hungary, Kazakhstan, Poland, Romania, Russia, the Slovak Republic, and Ukraine, as they continue their progress towards democracy and market economies. We anticipate that these developments will facilitate enhanced trade in high-technology items and other commodities in the region, while helping to prevent unauthorized shipments or uses of such items. A key element of these efforts continues to be the prevention of proliferation of weapons of mass destruction and corresponding technology.

—Working diligently with our Coordinating Committee (COCOM) partners to expand export control cooperation with the newly developing democracies of Central Europe and the former Soviet Union and to streamline multilateral national security controls, we are pleased to report the following important developments:

—In their November 1992 High-Level Meeting, the COCOM partners took action to significantly liberalize export controls on certain telecommunications exports to the newly independent states (NIS) of the former Soviet Union and other Central European nations, which should facilitate rapid and reliable telecommunications between these nations and the West, as well as modern, cost-effective domestic telecommunications systems. This action was soon thereafter reflected in corresponding amendments to the Export Administration Regulation. (57 F.R. 61259, December 24, 1992.)

—Also in November, at the first High-Level "COCOM Cooperation Forum" (CCF) Meeting, which included the 17 members of COCOM, most of the newly independent states of the former Soviet Union (NIS), and other Central European nations, the United States announced an $11 million technical assistance package to assist in the elimination of nuclear arms, enhanced nonproliferation efforts, and export control development. The United States, in cooperation with the CCF, hopes to engage these nations in further establishing controls for trade in sensitive goods and technologies, and to provide an impetus for wider access by those countries to controlled items.

—In the first 2 months of 1993, as a result of Bulgarian and Romanian commitments to undertake the establishment of effective export control systems, COCOM agreed to provide favorable consideration treatment for exports of strategic items to those countries. The Commerce Department is amending its regulations to reflect this development.

—We are also continuing our efforts to address the threat to the national security and foreign policy interests of the United States posed by the spread of weapons of mass destruction and missile delivery systems. As such, we continue to work with our major trading partners to strengthen export controls over goods, technology, and other forms of assistance that can contribute to the spread of nuclear, chemical, and biological weapons and missile systems:

—As of December 1992, the Australia Group (AG), a consortium of nations that seeks to prevent the proliferation of chemical and biological weapons (CBW), increased its membership to 24, with the admission of Iceland and Sweden in 1991 and Argentina and Hungary in 1992. In addition, the delegates agreed to increase from 50 to 54 the number of precursor chemicals subject to control and to adopt a common list of controlled biological items. The Commerce Department published a rule implementing these measures. (57 F.R. 60122, December 18, 1992.) As of December 1992, the delegates also agreed to a refined common control list of dual-use biological equipment. The Commerce Department is in the process of publishing a rule reflecting the changes to conform the U.S. list to the AG list.

—The United States was also a key partici-

pant in the Chemical Weapons Convention (CWC) negotiations in Geneva, Switzerland. On September 3, 1992, the Conference on Disarmament, which drafted the CWC, forwarded to the United Nations General Assembly a draft CWC, which includes a prohibition on the development, production, acquisition, stockpiling, use, or transfer of chemical weapons, as well as provides for destruction of chemical weapons production facilities and stockpiles. The Convention opened for signing in January of this year. The United States strongly supports these provisions and is working to implement them in harmony with our laws.

—In December 1992, the 27-nation Nuclear Suppliers Group (NSG), in which the United States participates, continued its discussions on nuclear-related dual-use controls. The NSG list is similar to the nuclear referral list currently administered by the Department of Commerce. The Department is working to publish a rule to conform the U.S. list with the NSG list. Also in December 1992, the NSG members agreed to procedures intended to standardize and improve the exchange of information among members.

—At the March plenary session in Canberra, the Missile Technology Control Regime (MTCR) members welcomed Iceland as the newest partner, bringing the total membership to 23 nations. Argentina and Hungary were also accepted as members, subject to final arrangements agreed to by the MTCR partners. A licensing and enforcement officers conference will be held in June 1993 to provide an information exchange forum for all partners on implementation of the new extended Guidelines, which now cover missiles capable of delivering all weapons of mass destruction. Previously, the regime covered only missiles capable of delivering nuclear weapons. The future of the MTCR is likely to be a main agenda item for the next plenary session to be held in November 1993.

—In the area of supercomputers, in 1991 the United States established a supercomputer safeguard regime with Japan. Since that time both countries have negotiated with European suppliers to expand this regime. Issues discussed at the March 1993 London meeting include the development of a common licensing policy and security safeguards.

—Finally, we continue to enforce export controls vigorously. The export control provisions of the Export Administration Regulations are enforced jointly by the Commerce Department's Office of Export Enforcement and the U.S. Customs Service. Both of these agencies investigate allegations and, where appropriate, refer them for criminal prosecution by the Justice Department. Additionally, the Commerce Department has continued its practice of imposing significant administrative sanctions for violations, including civil penalties and denial of export privileges.

—Commerce's Office of Export Enforcement (OEE) has continued its vital preventive programs such as pre-license checks and post-shipment verifications, export license review, and on-site verification visits by teams of enforcement officers in many countries. The OEE has also continued its outreach to the business community to assist exporters with their compliance programs and to solicit their help in OEE's enforcement effort. The OEE further continued its well-received Business Executive Enforcement Team (BEET) to enhance interaction between the regulators and the regulated.

—During this 6-month reporting period, OEE has continued its new program—the Strategic and Nonproliferation Enforcement Program (SNEP)—which targets critical enforcement resources on exports to countries of concern in the Middle East and elsewhere.

—Two particularly important enforcement efforts during the past 6 months in which OEE was involved resulted in the arrest and indictment of several individuals, including several foreign nationals. In one case, OEE special agents arrested an Iranian national, Reza Zandian, and an American citizen, Charles Regar, on charges that they conspired and attempted to export a computer to Iran without the required validated license. The computer, valued in excess of $2 million, was seized by the Commerce Department. The Department of Justice will seek forfeiture of the computer to the United States. In another case, a British citizen doing business in South Africa, David Brownhill, was arrested and charged with attempting to export polygraph and thermal imaging system equipment to South Africa without authorization. Both of these cases are currently pending trial.

—In the last 6 months, the Commerce Department has also continued to enforce the antiboycott law vigorously. The Office of Antiboycott Compliance (OAC) maintains 30 full-time staff positions, and OAC has doubled the level of civil penalties it seeks to impose within the statutory $10,000 per violation maximum. The total dollar amount of civil penalties imposed in fiscal year 1992 approaches $2,109,000, the second largest amount in the history of the program. This amount includes a civil penalty of $444,000 imposed in the first case alleging both antiboycott and export control violations.

—One particularly significant antiboycott compliance case was recently concluded by an order of February 11, 1993. Under that order, William Hardimon was assessed a civil penalty of $54,000, and his export privileges were denied for 6 months. Hardimon allegedly refused to do business with another person in order to comply with an illegal Saudi Arabian requirement, complied with an illegal Kuwaiti boycott request, and failed to report the receipt of the boycott requests.

5. The expenses incurred by the Federal Government in the 6-month period from October 1, 1992, to March 31, 1993, that are directly attributable to the exercise of authorities conferred by the declaration of a national emergency with respect to export controls were largely centered in the Department of Commerce, Bureau of Export Administration. Expenditures by the Department of Commerce are anticipated to be $17,897,000, most of which represents program operating costs, wage and salary costs for Federal personnel, and overhead expenses.

WILLIAM J. CLINTON

The White House,
April 27, 1993.

Nomination for Navy Department and Ambassadorial Posts
April 27, 1993

The President today announced his intention to nominate Steve Honigman to be General Counsel for the Department of the Navy, and his intention to make the following ambassadorial nominations:

Howard Jeter, Ambassador to the Republic of Botswana

William Ramsay, Ambassador to the People's Republic of the Congo

David Romero, Ambassador to the Republic of Ecuador

Alan Flanigan, Ambassador to the Republic of El Salvador

Andrew Winter, Ambassador to the Republic of Gambia

Aurelia Brazeal, Ambassador to the Republic of Kenya

William Dameron, Ambassador to the Republic of Mali

Dennis Jett, Ambassador to the Republic of Mozambique

John Davidson, Ambassador to the Republic of Niger

John Sprott, Ambassador to the Kingdom of Swaziland

David Rawson, Ambassador to the Republic of Rwanda

"These Ambassadors are a talented and experienced group who will, I am sure, represent our country's interests ably," said the President.

NOTE: Biographies of the nominees were made available by the Office of the Press Secretary.

Remarks Announcing the Appointment of the Director of the Office of National Drug Control Policy and an Exchange With Reporters
April 28, 1993

The President. Thank you very much, ladies and gentlemen. Please be seated. I want to thank the members of the Cabinet who are here and the Members of the Congress who are here and express my apologies for the Attorney General who is with the Congress. And that's why some of them and why she is not here.

I want to thank the representatives of law enforcement, people who are involved in drug treatment and drug education, and other citizens who are here with us today, as well as those who have been working in the office of drug policy who are here.

It is a great pleasure and honor for me today to announce the appointment of Lee Brown, the first police officer ever to hold the job of Director of the Office of National Drug Control Policy.

A few weeks ago I elevated this office to Cabinet-level status because I believe drug abuse is as serious a problem as we have in America and because I believe that this office cannot work effectively on its own, no matter how many people it might have. The real ability

of this office to make a difference in the lives of the American people is the ability to work with all the Departments of the National Government and with others who care about this issue to maximize our resources, to focus our efforts, and to make sure we're all working together. Lee Brown shares that view, and I am proud that he has agreed to join us in this administration.

As Americans who care about our future, we can't let drugs and drug-related crimes continue to ruin communities, threaten our children even in schools, and fill up our prisons with wrecked and wasted lives. We have to do a better job of preventing drug use and treating those who seek treatment, and we must do more to protect law-abiding citizens from those who victimize them in the pursuit of drugs or profits from drugs. I'm committed to winning this struggle, as all Americans are, and I'm convinced that there is no better American to lead this effort than Lee Brown. He's been the chief law enforcement officer in Atlanta, in Houston, and New York. He's a policeman with a Ph.D. in criminology who brings to this tough job a truly extraordinary record of innovation in crime reduction and a sensitivity to the problems of real people who want to walk home safe at night and who want to be free of the problems that we're trying to combat.

To reduce drug use and drug-related crimes we have to do many things at the same time. It has to start with community policing, with more police at the local level working with our neighbors and the children and the friends to prevent crime and to quickly punish criminals. There must be better education and prevention efforts starting at the earliest ages. These work; I know that. And there must be treatment for those who want to get better.

Dr. Brown knows a little something about community policing. It's nearly his invention. He turned the Houston police force into a model of community policing. And for many serious crimes, the crime rate there dropped. In New York he added thousands of officers to foot patrols; men and women whom he empowered to solve problems, not with the Federal program but with a commitment to a better life in a particular neighborhood. And reports of serious crime fell where that was done in New York. He's had the vision to seek conditions clearly and the courage to change what doesn't work. Most importantly, he gets results. And this is exactly what we need in the war against drugs.

I pledge to him and to the American people an exceptionally focused and carefully executed antidrug effort from the National Government. At the heart of our efforts will be more funds for local police officers, more for treatment and more for prevention. We will continue to work with other nations who have shown the political will to fight illegal drugs. They will continue to get our full support and our cooperation.

But it's time we turned our attention home and built a strategy to make the neighborhoods of America safer and more drug-free. We want to close the gap between those who want treatment and available treatment. Treating addiction is good urban policy and good anticrime policy and good health policy. We ask for a 10-percent increase in treatment funds for 1994. And we'll make drug treatment an important part of the national health care plan that will be presented to the Congress and the American people. Our goal is to work toward treatment on demand.

I believe the parents of America want and deserve more help in educating their children about drugs. We can prevent drug abuse. School programs work. Public service programs work. But they aren't miracles. They require a commitment and a consistency year in and year out. We've asked for a 16-percent increase in drug prevention funding.

Finally, we're determined to put more police officers on the street and to expand community policing. It's a local program, old-fashioned law enforcement, but it works. It means less crime. I think it's time to go back to the basics. I asked the Congress to approve $200 million in the jobs stimulus package for community policing. And I proposed almost $600 million in policing and other initiatives similar to that in 1994.

The most basic responsibility of the Government is to protect the American people. It's our sacred duty to do our best. I believe we have a good program. It can be a great program if it can come alive in America in every community in this country. It's basic: more officers, more education, more treatment. And with the leadership of Lee Brown it promises to be effective.

I look forward to working with him and with the other members of our Cabinet, administration to meet and to master the challenges ahead.

[*At this point, Dr. Brown expressed his appreciation to the President and his commitment to develop a national drug control strategy.*]

Drug Control Policy Director

Q. Mr. President, you talked about the need to give resources to education and treatment from some of the law enforcement efforts. Why then did you pick someone with a background in law enforcement?

The President. Because I don't think it's an either-or thing. I think having the right kind of community-based education and treatment programs, if they work, also requires having the right kind of community law enforcement strategy. One of the things that I have learned in the many years I served as attorney general and Governor, and talking to other people who have been involved in that, is that if you do it right, all these things go hand in hand.

I wish the Attorney General were here today to talk about the drug courts she started in Miami, and what the relationship of law enforcement there is to integrating a treatment and education program.

That's why I wanted someone who had a background in law enforcement and credibility on that issue, but who believed in innovation and education and treatment to do this job. I wanted someone who could put together a policy that makes sense. If you try to pick one or the other, you're never going to get the job done.

Wolf [Wolf Blitzer, CNN News]?

Bosnia

Q. Mr. President, you met last night with a bipartisan group of congressional leaders on the situation in Bosnia. And by all accounts, they seem to have given you some conflicting advice. Many of them appear to be more moved by the lessons of Vietnam than they are by the Holocaust. Did you emerge from that session more confused about what the United States should do as far as the situation in Bosnia is concerned?

The President. No, I didn't. I still believe the United States has to strengthen its response. But the meeting was helpful because of the practical issues which were raised and the specific suggestions I got from people, many of whom have different views. But some who were there last night are here today; they can make their own comments. But I think it was a very helpful meeting and there were a lot of very specific things that came out of that, and that I think will come out of our consultations over the next couple of days.

Andrea [Andrea Mitchell, NBC News]?

Q. Do you feel that you can continue, though, to consider military options now that so many Members of Congress have strongly expressed their objections? Would you proceed if you felt it was still the right thing to do and if you had allied support?

The President. Well, I will decide what I think the right thing to do is, and then see if I can persuade the Congress and the allies to go along. Right now, what I want to do is to hear what they think the right thing to do is, and the people with whom I consulted last night were good enough to tell me. And we agreed that they would set in motion a process to go back to their committees and try to solicit some more views.

Q. Mr. President, is it accurate——

Drug Control Policy

Q. [*Inaudible*]—plan to continue with the pol-

icy of hot pursuit like in the Machain case, or how are you going to deal with cases like that? Are you going to come to other countries and kidnap or bring to justice in this country a person suspected of a crime in a drug situation, like in the Machain case? How are you going to deal with that situation?

The President. I'm not sure I heard you— the plane flew over. But you asked about the abduction out of Mexico? Is that what you asked about?

Q. That's right—if you are going to continue with that type of policy.

The President. I think I've made my position clear on that. I think the present ruling of law is too broad there. I don't believe that the United States should be involved in that unless there is a clear and deliberate attempt by a government in another country to undermine extradition or undermine the enforcement of its own laws and our laws on that. So that's been my position for months and months; I haven't changed that.

Q. Mr. President, do you expect to get bipartisan support from Congress for the money you're going to need? The two predecessors of Mr. Brown accomplished certain things, but not much. How will you make sure that Mr. Brown has the money to accomplish——

The President. Well, I think there will be bipartisan support. Keep in mind this is partly a money problem and partly a resource problem. We're going to try to do some different things and attract people who have thought about this issue. I don't think this is a Republican or a Democratic issue. There's hardly a family in America that hasn't been touched directly or indirectly by this problem. So I feel very hopeful about it.

Q. [*Inaudible*]—in the budget, sir?

The President. Well, we recommended more funds in the budget, and it's very critical to the whole health reform area. I mean, a big part of our strategy in this is embodied in the proposals we'll make on health care to deal with the whole treatment issue.

Helen [Helen Thomas, United Press International]?

Bosnia

Q. When do you think you will have a decision? Do you have Yeltsin on board now to do more? And do you think the American people will support a military—[*inaudible*]—use of military force?

The President. Well, you asked me three questions. I think there will be a decision soon. We are working very hard on it. There are a lot of very practical questions that have to be asked and answered. As you know, it is a very difficult matter.

I believe that when we do make a decision, we will be, as we have been all along, consulting with our allies in the United Nations. And I think there is a fair chance that we'll be able to get the U.N. to go along with what we decide to do if we have some consultations as we go along; as we have.

I think President Yeltsin—I don't know what he will say. It depends in part, obviously, on what we recommend. But I'll tell you this: I've been very pleased by the positions that he has taken both publicly and privately recently. And even in the midst of his own election, when it might have hurt him politically, Russia did not veto our attempts to get much tougher sanctions. And I think he's been pretty clear since the election that he's not at all happy about the continuation of Serbian aggression and the refusal to negotiate in good faith and try to settle this war and stop the ethnic cleansing. So I feel pretty good about that.

Q. Mr. President, how are you going to tell the American people——

Drug Control Policy

Q. Mr. President, a former drug czar, Bill Bennett, said today that you have gutted the Office by cutting it down, cutting the personnel. How do you answer that?

The President. Well, my answer to that—maybe I should refer you to Congressman Rangel. I spoke with him when we were trying to figure out what to do about this budget. And what I perceived happened in that office before is that it was a large office that operated basically separate from the rest of the Government. It has no legal authority to compel the behavior of any law enforcement officials, and it obviously has no legal authority over all the State and local people and the nonprofit people who are involved in drug education and treatment. So the real issue is whether it has the mechanisms

necessary to pull all the levers in the Federal Government and pull people together.

And I think by putting the Office in the Cabinet, by coordinating all of our national policies throughout the Federal Government, and by having a staff that can support that function, it's much more likely that we're going to be effective.

And I also would tell you that I believe in rhetoric in the war against drugs. I know that works. I think the education programs work, the prevention programs work, but it needs to be more than rhetoric. And I think it will also be perceived that I have appointed the most experienced person with the best record and the least political person who ever held this job. And I think that will count for something, too, with the Republicans and the Democrats.

Take Our Daughters to Work Day

Q. Where's Chelsea?

The President. Well, we discussed it this morning and she said, "You know, it's easier for me; you work where you live. I know what it's like." She said, "I missed a lot of school last month, so I'm going to school."

Q. Would she have gone to work with you or Hillary?

The President. Actually, she thought it was just for mothers to take their daughters. I said, "No, no, fathers can, too." She said, "Well, you both work where you live. I'm going to school." But she's spent some time with us over here.

Health Care Reform

Q. Have you firmly decided not to delay health care because it might risk your budget proposal, sir?

The President. I think what we're talking about is not a risk.

Thank you very much.

NOTE: The President spoke at 12:30 p.m. in the Rose Garden at the White House. A biography of the nominee was made available by the Office of the Press Secretary. A portion of the exchange could not be verified because the tape was incomplete.

Exchange With Reporters Prior to a Meeting With National Governors' Association Representatives on Health Care Reform
April 28, 1993

Q. Mr. President, do you feel that you can extend health care to all the uninsured in the first——

The President. I think we're going to have a very successful health care program that will be very much like the one I talked about when I started the campaign. It will be very good. I think——

Q. But do you think you can do it?

The President. Wait until we come out with it; you'll see.

NOTE: The exchange began at 4:37 p.m. in the State Dining Room at the White House. A tape was not available for verification of the content of this exchange.

Letter to Congressional Leaders Transmitting a Report on Nonproliferation in South Asia
April 28, 1993

Dear Mr. Speaker: (Dear Mr. Chairman:)

As required under section 620F(c) of the Foreign Operations, Export Financing, and Related Programs Appropriations Act, 1993 (22 U.S.C. 2376(c)), I am transmitting a report entitled "Progress Toward Regional Nonproliferation in South Asia." The report is unclassified.

This is the first report required on this subject and reflects information available as of March 19, 1993. Events after March 18, 1993, will be included in the next report.

Sincerely,

WILLIAM J. CLINTON

NOTE: Identical letters were sent to Thomas S. Foley, Speaker of the House of Representatives; William H. Natcher, chairman, House Committee on Appropriations; Robert C. Byrd, chairman, Senate Committee on Appropriations; and Claiborne Pell, chairman, Senate Committee on Foreign Relations.

Statement by the Press Secretary on the President's Meeting With the Dalai Lama
April 28, 1993

The President and the Vice President met yesterday with His Holiness the Dalai Lama and discussed issues relating to Tibet.

"The Dalai Lama is internationally revered for his spiritual and moral leadership," the President said. "As a Nobel Peace Prize winner and committed advocate of nonviolent change and resolution of disputes, I deeply appreciated hearing the Dalai Lama's views on the situation in China, including Tibet. The administration continues to urge Beijing and the Dalai Lama to revive a dialog between them and presses China to address human rights abuses in Tibet."

Nomination for Posts at the Departments of Education and Energy
April 28, 1993

The President announced today that he intends to nominate former San Francisco superintendent of schools Ramon Cortines to be Assistant Secretary of Education for Intergovernmental and Interagency Affairs and Jay Hakes, a top aide to Senator Bob Graham of Florida, to be Administrator of the Energy Information Administration.

"Ramon Cortines and Jay Hakes have both distinguished themselves as public servants in their own States and at the national level," said the President. "I am grateful that they have agreed to continue their service as part of my administration."

NOTE: Biographies of the nominees were made available by the Office of the Press Secretary.

Nomination for Chairman of the Securities and Exchange Commission
April 28, 1993

The President today announced his intention to nominate Arthur Levitt, Jr., owner of the Capitol Hill newspaper Roll Call and formerly chairman of the American Stock Exchange, as a member of the Securities and Exchange Commission. Once Mr. Levitt is confirmed as a member, the President intends to designate him Chairman of the SEC.

"Backed by 20 years of experience in high finance and newly introduced to the workings of Capitol Hill, Arthur Levitt is well prepared to take the helm at the SEC," the President said. "I have full confidence he will use his office wisely to strengthen public confidence in our country's financial agencies."

NOTE: A biography of the nominee was made available by the Office of the Press Secretary.

Remarks Prior to a Meeting With Members of the House Ways and Means Committee and an Exchange With Reporters
April 29, 1993

The President. Let me just make a brief remark, and then I'll answer your questions.

First, I want to thank these members of the Ways and Means Committee for coming in for this meeting. This morning's economic figures on the performance of the United States economy in the first 3 months of the year clearly, I think, support the policies of this administration. They support filling out and implementing the budget commitment that the Congress has made to reduce the deficit and to increase targeted investments and to generate jobs.

It also plainly proves, I think, that the administration was right in trying to hedge against this economic slow growth by passing the jobs bill that the House of Representatives passed and that the Senate wanted to pass. It proves that we were right in both reducing the deficit and in trying to create some jobs right now in this economy. But it also proves that the long-term interests of the country will be served if we fulfill our commitments on the budget.

The budget, I think, is well under way. The Ways and Means Committee had a good day yesterday. And I think we can continue to show our commitment to bring the deficit down and to target our investments in areas that will create jobs. We'll have a long-term plan that's good. But it also proves, I think clearly, beyond any doubt, that the strategy of the administration to create some more jobs right now was the right strategy. The American people still need more employment, and we're going to do our best to give it to them.

The First 100 Days

Q. Mr. President, 100 days, have there been mistakes? Are there things you would do differently? What have you learned, what lessons?

The President. Well, I learned that things are not going to change quite as fast as I wanted them to. But I noticed there was—one columnist a day or two ago in one of the major papers pointed out that at least the American people know that the Democratic Party is serious and the President is serious about deficit reduction. They know we're going to do something about health care reform. They know we're going to try to be partners with the private sector in rebuilding the economy. And they know we're trying to make the Government work again, with the national service program that I will announce tomorrow and a whole other range of issues to try to give people educational and other opportunities. So I feel basically quite good about what's happened.

But this country has some serious problems, and we're going to have to get everybody serious about dealing with the problems. Now, I am very impressed so far with the work that we've been able to do with the House and with the majority in the Senate in getting the deficit down and in focusing on the investment needs of our people. But we've got a lot of work to do.

I don't know that 100 days is a rational category, but if you look at how much we've done and how much is well underway now as compared with most previous administrations in a similar time period, I think we're doing pretty well.

Q. Did you take on too much, Mr. President?

Bosnia

Q. Have you reached a decision on Bosnia yet, Mr. President?

The President. Helen [Helen Thomas, United Press International], I have not. As you probably know, General Powell was away for most of the week in Europe. And I want to see and talk with him personally and have some other consultations on some of the military issues. And I have not. But we will do so soon, and then we'll begin some pretty aggressive consultations with our allies.

President's Agenda

Q. [*Inaudible*]—took on too much, Mr. President? Do you have some concerns about that?

The President. No, I will. You know, it's a question of—the Vice President has a word for it, sequence and timing, I think he calls it. I believe I got hired to try to do something about the economy and the health care issue, and to try to promote political reform and many other things we're trying to do. When we put all these things out here, I don't expect them all to be resolved right away. But I think we're going to focus on the budget first. That's what we're doing today. Then we're going to take up, we're going to focus on health care.

But this country still needs to remember that we've got to do these things to put people back to work and to solve their economic problems. That is the issue, the economy. And that is what we are spending—I'm spending two-thirds of my time or more on the economy and health care. And that's what I hope we can do in the Congress in the few weeks ahead.

Q. So you're more optimistic than Mr. Panetta? You're more optimistic than Mr. Panetta?

The President. I have more faith in Mr. Panetta's colleagues than he does. [*Laughter*]

I think we're going to bring this deficit down, and I think we're going to get some investments passed. I think we're going to turn this economy around. I wish we could have done it faster. I still think we ought to create some jobs now. I think that was a mistake. But I think we just keep going. We'll make the progress we can and go on.

NOTE: The President spoke at 10:20 a.m. in the Roosevelt Room at the White House. A tape was not available for verification of the content of these remarks.

Remarks to Justice Department Employees
April 29, 1993

Thank you very much. When Janet Reno was confirmed, she said she never wanted to be called General, but only Janet. But somehow I feel I should call her General. She certainly seemed in command to me yesterday up on the Hill.

I want to say to all of you what an incredible honor it has been for me as a citizen of this country, as well as President, to be in the Justice Department for the first time, to walk down the halls and to see the wonderful work that was done more than 50 years ago now in building this great building during the Great Depression, when President Roosevelt was trying to lift the spirits of the country by putting the people to work—that's still a pretty good idea, I think; to walk into the Attorney General's office and see the magnificent portrait of Robert Kennedy, who was my favorite Attorney General from my childhood; and mostly just to shake hands with all the employees here. I think it is so easy for us to forget, in the ebb and flow of events when we were so focused on the moment, and easy for the American people to forget that every day there are so many Americans who could have chosen a different life, who get up every day and come to work in this building because they believe in simple justice and fairness and in doing right by the American people. And I want you to know that I appreciate that very, very much, and I thank you for your service.

After years of taking a different course, I am doing my best to turn this Government around, to change the way things operate here, to convince the American people that we are serious about the economy, serious about reducing the deficit, serious about investing in the real needs of our people, serious about providing fairness to the middle class and to others who are willing to work hard and play by the rules in America, and serious about trying to bring all the people of this country together again in a great national community in which we all recognize that we are in this together.

The changes we are making go well beyond policy and particular bills and, I hope, beyond politics to a whole new idea of hope in this country as we move toward the 21st century,

the idea that we can keep the American dream alive, preserve our basic values, and make the new future that all of you and your children deserve.

I thought about this a lot when I was attorney general, that when you work to ensure the full protection of the law for every citizen, you help to sustain the most fundamental values of democracy and, indeed, to provide for the freedom of all. I know most of you came here with similar feelings for the law. I have enormous respect for your motives. I come from a generation that revered the law because we believed it gave us the tools to help people and, in my part of the country, that it was the only instrument that would ever enable us all, black and white together, to live as equals.

I still believe those things. Today before I came over here, I had a whole string of people into my office who I had known for years and years and years, and they were laughing about how sometimes I may seem almost naive because I genuinely feel more idealism and hope today than I did in the first day I entered public life, than I did on the first day I cast a vote as a young man. I still believe that we can make a difference, that we can live up to the ideals enshrined in the Constitution, and that we have the obligation to do so. And I asked Janet Reno to become the Attorney General of the United States because I knew she believed that, too.

Since I became President I have spent a good deal of time trying to focus on law enforcement issues, because I saw all across this land in the last year and a half when I ran for President the enormous amount of insecurity and fear that so many Americans felt, living in their homes, walking on their streets. Many of you may have heard me tell this story, at least in the media, before, but one of the most gripping things that ever happened to me in the race for President occurred in a hotel in New York.

It was about a week before the New Hampshire primary. I looked like I was yesterday's news, to say the least. I was walking through this corridor to go to a big fundraiser full of people who wondered why they had bought tickets. I was feeling sorry for myself. And a man who worked in the hotel as a waiter stuck his hand out and grabbed my hand, and he said, "My 10-year-old boy studies the Presidential race in school, and he says you should be President, so I will be for you. I'm an immigrant from Greece." And he said, "I will be for you because my boy wants me to be." But he said, "You know, where I came from we were so much poorer, but at least we were free." And he said, "Now when my boy walks outside from our apartment, he cannot go across the street and play in the park unless I am with him because he won't be safe. We live only two blocks from the school, and he cannot walk to his school unless I am with him because he won't be safe. So if I do what my boy wants me to do and I vote for you, will you make my boy free?"

And all of a sudden I couldn't remember what I was feeling sorry for myself about. But I did remember one of the reasons that I wanted to be President and one of the solemn duties of the Government of the United States and every other law enforcement jurisdiction in this country. And I think it's time that we move from the incredible gulf between rhetoric and reality to doing some very specific things that will make the American people safer. We ought to pass and sign the Brady bill.

I will propose a major new safe schools program so that children at least can be drug free and safe in their schools. I have just appointed Lee Brown, who was the police chief of Atlanta, Houston, and New York City, to be the Director of the Drug Control Office, the first police officer ever to hold that position, a person who pioneered community policing and actually can show how the crime rate went down in communities where there were enough police officers on the street to walk the beat and know their neighbors and work to prevent crime, not just to catch criminals after crimes had occurred. I have asked for more resources for drug education programs and treatment programs. And I want to increase police presence in our communities, so I've asked for substantial new funding to eventually add up to 100,000 more police officers on our streets.

Some of them will come, I hope, through the crime bill that I hope we can pass this year that was filibustered last year. That's a thing, institution, I've learned to have less and less respect for as we go along. [*Laughter*] Some of them will come from incentives we give, from

people coming out of the service as we build down our armed services and give people incentives to move into police or teaching. Some of them will come from the national service corps, which we will announce tomorrow in New Orleans, as people who will pay off their college loans by working as police officers. I had hoped that some would come from the jobs program, which contained $200 million for more police officers. But we are going to work together to do this. When I sat in the Attorney General's office just a few moments ago, it's the second issue she brought up. She said, we've still got to deliver for the American people. We have to give them the police officers they need and the security they need. And we're going to do it.

I also want our Government to set an example. I want us to have a tougher child support enforcement program. I've asked my appointees to adhere to the strictest ethics law ever applied to executive branch appointees. I have cut my own White House staff and begun a Governmentwide review of every program we operate, so that we can show the American people we are trying to be accountable and responsible and effective and that we're trying to make sure that when we do something in Washington, it's for the good of the people out there who pay the bills and not just for ourselves.

Our country is great because we have succeeded over 200 years in providing opportunity to all, freedom of speech and worship and association to all, providing equal justice to all. We have become the custodian of freedom's dream for the entire world because people like you have decided to give your lives to this great call.

My goals for this Justice Department are simple. I want it to be free of political controversy and political abuse. I want it to be an innovator in crime reduction and in law enforcement. I want it to create a genuine partnership with those who work with us in State and local systems of justice. I want it to set an example in the practice of law and in the protection of civil rights that will make all Americans proud. And I want the American people to believe that you are their partners in making our communities, our children, and our families safe again.

In closing, let me say how very, very proud I am to name these seven Attorneys General, Assistant Attorneys General, to your Justice Department team. Some of them are new to me; some I have known and admired a very long time. At least one of them once sued me; shows you how broadminded I am. [*Laughter*] And I can tell you, I am very pleased that each of them has agreed to join our administration.

This may surprise you if you've been reading the press reports, but with these appointments, our administration has in 100 days nominated 172 people for consideration by the Senate. At the same point in their administrations, President Reagan had named 152 people, and President Bush had named 99. By any measure, we're doing a fairly good job in staffing up this administration with high-quality folks. And I might add, since I look across here I can't resist saying, a third of them are women, for a change.

Today when I walked through these halls and I went to the Attorney General's office, I couldn't help but remember that it was 25 years ago in this springtime when Robert Kennedy, by then a Senator from New York, was running for President and was subsequently killed, just 2 days before I graduated from college, with one of my roommates working in his office. It's impossible for me still, especially now as I think back across those 25 years, not to be moved by his memory and his work and the power of the example he set for all Americans, regardless of their gender or color or station in life.

I hope 25 years from now, another daughter or son of America will walk in here and remember what you have accomplished here and be moved. I believe the tradition of greatness here is still very much alive. I believe that Janet Reno and the team that she is assembling can bring it to life for all Americans. The American people want you to succeed in your work; I do, too. Working together, we can be proud to honor the tradition of the Justice Department by ensuring its great future.

Thank you all, and God bless you.

NOTE: The President spoke at 1:12 p.m. in the Courtyard at the Department of Justice.

The President named the following Assistant Attorneys General:

Walter Dellinger, Office of Legal Counsel
Lani Guinier, Civil Rights Division
Frank W. Hunger, Civil Division
Anne K. Bingaman, Antitrust Division
Eleanor Dean Acheson, Office of Policy Development
Sheila Foster Anthony, Office of Legislative Affairs
Gerald Torres, Environment and Natural Resources Division

Biographies of the nominees were made available by the Office of the Press Secretary.

Remarks at a Reception for the President's Health Care Task Force and an Exchange With Reporters
April 29, 1993

The President. Thank you very much. Let me say how pleased I am that one of the things that even people who care about health care can't control, the weather, cooperated with us today. How delighted we are to have you here to just say a simple thank you for all the work you've done.

I have a few other things I want to say, but I think I should begin by introducing the First Lady by way of saying that 10 years ago we tried this once before when I was Governor of our State. And it was obvious that we needed to dramatically overhaul our education system, and I asked her to chair this committee. And

she looked at me as if I had lost my mind because we knew we had to make everybody in the State mad to do what needed to be done. And it turned out to be all right. We had to change a lot of things, but it was one of those remarkable moments in history when all the people were ahead of all the policy-makers.

I think we may be there again with health care. And I think that if all of this works I will be once again indebted to my wonderful wife and all of you. And I just want you to know that she has sung your praises to the Moon from the beginning of this. And so I hope that you think that she did as good a job as she thinks you did, because I think you were both pretty great. Thank you very much.

[*At this point, Hillary Clinton and Tipper Gore made statements welcoming members of the task force and commending their efforts.*]

The President. Thank you very much. You know, I wish there were something more I could do for all of you. I think you deserve a medal just for putting up with Ira's tollgates. I can't believe Ira's hiding back there. He's probably sharpening darts or something. [*Laughter*]

I want to say a special word of thanks to Tipper Gore for her involvement and for the work that she's done to personally sensitize me to a lot of the mental health issues that I think all Americans need to know more about.

I want to say, too, that the Vice President is not here tonight because he is on an errand for our administration in Florida and could not be here. But he sat in all those meetings with me, that we had, long hours trying to make sure that we understood the implications of every issue and understood all the incredible work that all of you have done.

I want to say a special word of thanks to Ira. Hillary and I have known Ira a long time. Ira and I were at Oxford together back in the late sixties, and we always used to say when Ira walked into a room he doubled the IQ of whoever was in there, however many people were in there. [*Laughter*] I don't know how many of his brain cells he has departed forever in this endeavor, but—[*laughter*]—I hope that part of this endeavor will lead some of you to encourage him to take more care of his health. I don't think he's had any sleep since this whole thing started. He's really been a champ, and Hillary and I are very grateful for his efforts.

I want to say, too, that there are a lot of people who said, well—I mean, I never could believe this—for years and years and years we all complained of gridlock and do-nothing and nothing ever got done. And the last 5 days, I see all these articles complaining that I'm trying to do too much. [*Laughter*] I plead guilty to that.

But the overwhelming focus of this administration has been on the economy, jobs, deficit reduction, and investment in our people and on health care. That's what we have focused on, the things that will lift this country up again

and bring this country together again and give people some measure of security, even as they go out in the highly changed and charged world that we're moving toward.

I wish I could write a book. I wish I could even remember all the incredible stories I heard along this last year and a half when we were out on the campaign trail, related to health care.

I'll never forget the woman I met in Columbus, Ohio who had six or seven kids and had to give up a $50,000 a year job because one of her children was so sick, and the only way she could get any care was to become Medicaid eligible; the farmers that I met along the way who couldn't get health insurance, or if they did, it took up the whole profit from the farms in the average years; the small business person I met who had only four employees and was chagrined because of the exploding cost of insurance in his small group, he had to go to a $2,500 deductible, and how badly he felt for his own employees; the big businesses that told me about their inability to compete in a global economy because they had to spot their competitors so much; the doctors that I know who wanted to be good doctors and wanted to reach out to people who were spending more and more of their time and money on paperwork and regulation, and on and on and on.

The human dimension of this issue is utterly enormous. The economic dimension is also very great. We're here, struggling to really be serious about reducing the Government's deficit, and under every scenario we can cut it quite a bit in the next 5 years, and then it starts to go right up again because of health care costs. So there has rarely been a time in the history of this country when an economic issue and a social issue, when an issue that affects all the big people and all the little people and all the people in between has been so tightly joined, as this health care issue.

I know there are those who say, "Well, we shouldn't try to deal with this. It ought to be enough just to have a fundamental budget that dramatically changes the priorities of America." But if you want to get rid of the deficit and have any money left to invest in your children and your education, your economy and your future, we have to do both.

And so I just want to reaffirm to you that all of your efforts have not been in vain, and I'm going to do my best to give us a health care reform package that can pass the Congress this year. And I'm going to do my best to fight for it, and I hope you will, too.

It may be that we can only do one thing at a time in this town. That may be, but I'm not prepared to acknowledge that. Congress has worked out smaller bills, but they're all different. I mean, they've got an agreement on the family and medical leave, and now they're apparently going to send me the motor voter bill I've been working on. And today, they voted for a modified line-item veto in the House, which I thought was remarkable, the first bill we've had with real bipartisan support.

I think we can do more than one thing. And I think if people understand that you have to do both of these things—have a new budget and a new direction and a new approach to health care to get control of our deficit and our financial future and to have something left to invest in our people, our economy, and our own future, I think we can do it.

And I just have to ask all of you to be committed now to be agents of change. You've done all this work on this program. And you know, the final thing we come out with, none of you will agree with all of it. I won't agree with all of it. We're going to do the best we can to put something together that's good for America and that we can get through the United States Congress. And we're going to do our best to continue to reach out to both Democrats and Republicans as we have throughout this entire process, to try to make this an American effort, not a Bill Clinton effort, not a Democratic effort, not a Republican effort, but an American effort. America needs this.

I'll say this: You know, when this group began to get together, I kept reading all this stuff about secrecy. And you know, shoot, I've read more about everything you've done in the press than anything else I've seen. [*Laughter*] If you can't keep a secret in Washington with two people, you sure can't keep a secret with 1,000. [*Laughter*]

I think you've been great. I want to ask you to commit now to do what you can. A lot of you don't come from here. A lot of you live out in the country where a lot of these problems are being grappled with. When you go home, try to mobilize your friends to tell your Members of Congress that the time is now. The time is now to deal with this. And if you do

live here and you have even more contacts on the Hill or with others that can influence this process, use your time now to pass it. Don't let all your work have been in vain. This is a magic moment in the history of this issue. People have been working for decades just to have the circumstances which exist now. And I hardly see anybody who doesn't admit that the time has come to do something, to do something bold and do something substantial, to do something we can live with from years to come that will really make our country better off, our people more secure, healthier, and happier.

We're going to have enough insecurity as it is in America, and everybody is, with all the changes that are going on in this world. The least we can do is to join the mainstream of the world in taking care of our people better, providing a comprehensive, affordable, good, quality health care system. And it's good for the economy. If we can get that idea across, we can prevail.

I need your help now to carry the fight to the floors of the Congress, both Chambers and both parties. And let's lift this issue up. Let's keep it high in America's mind and heart, and let's make sure that all this work you have done will be rewarded for generations to come.

This is a real moment in the history of this country. You can be a part of it. Now the time has come to bring it home.

Thank you very much.

Bosnia

Q. Mr. President, does this reconvening of the peace talks take the pressure off you at all, sir?

The President. Well, let's see what happens there. Let's see what happens. Let's see how serious they are. You know, they've said things before and not meant it. If they mean it now, so much the better. I'll see.

Q. How are you going to know if they mean it, sir?

The President. We will know them by their deeds, not their words.

NOTE: The President spoke at 6:38 p.m. on the South Lawn at the White House. In his remarks, he referred to Ira Magaziner, Senior Adviser to the President for Policy Development.

Statement on the National Commission to Ensure a Strong Competitive Airline Industry
April 29, 1993

Today I am, in conjunction with the bipartisan congressional leadership, releasing the names of the members of the National Commission to Ensure a Strong and Competitive Airline Industry.

This Commission will enable us to start planning the revitalization of one of our country's most important industries, one of our most important exporters, one of our Nation's most important employers: the aircraft manufacturers and carriers that have been the pride of the United States and the world's leaders since the beginning of aviation. I pledge that this Commission will have the full resources of every Agency of the Federal Government at its disposal.

Each of the individuals on this Commission brings a strong record of accomplishment in his or her field, together with a keen sense of the importance of aviation in a global economy. Each of them has demonstrated the ability to look toward the future and the energy and intellect to shape the course of the current airline debate.

I would like to thank the bipartisan congressional leadership for their support and leadership in creating this Commission and in selecting persons of such high caliber.

The Chairman of the Commission will be an old friend and former colleague of mine, former Virginia Governor Gerald L. Baliles. Perhaps no other Governor in the past decade devoted more thought and attention to the global nature of the challenges facing his State. Governor Baliles always recognized that the nature of competition had changed fundamentally and that any strategy to shape that change must be rooted in a vision extending beyond our borders. He recognized that aviation is the lifeblood of commerce in a global economy and made it an important part of his State's competitiveness strategy. That is what we must do now at a national level.

As the legislation creating this Commission was debated in Congress, it became clear that there are many different explanations of why our airline carriers and manufacturers are facing such financial difficulty. And those issues will be debated. But it will be valuable for the Commission to take a step back from that debate and examine the context in which the aviation industry operates. To the extent the Commission can help us understand how we got to where we are today and provide a vision for a competitive future, it will have rendered an invaluable service. I look forward to receiving their report and pledge the full cooperation of my entire administration in their work.

NOTE: The Office of the Press Secretary announced the membership of the Commission as follows:

Members appointed by the President:
> Gerald L. Baliles, partner, Hunton & Williams, and former Governor of Virginia, Richmond, VA (Chair)
> Bette B. Anderson, president, Kelly, Anderson and Associates, Inc., Washington, DC
> Sylvia A. de Leon, partner, Akin, Gump, Strauss, Hauer and Feld, Washington, DC
> Herbert D. Kelleher, chief executive officer, Southwest Airlines, Dallas, TX
> Gina F. Thomas, managing attorney for international and regulatory affairs, Federal Express Corp., Memphis, TN

Members appointed by the Senate:
> Charles "Chip" M. Barclay, president, American Association of Airport Executives, Washington, DC
> Robert F. Daniell, chief executive officer, United Technologies, West Hartford, CT
> Felix G. Rohatyn, managing partner, Lazard Freres and Co., New York, NY
> Russell W. Meyer, Jr., chairman and chief executive officer, Cesna Aircraft Company, Wichita, KS
> Abraham D. Sofaer, partner, Hughes, Hubbard and Reed, Washington, DC

Members appointed by the House:
> Captain J. Randolph Babbitt, president, Airline Pilots Association (ALPA), Oakton, VA
> John Peterpaul, vice president, International Association of Machinists (IAM), Silver Spring, MD
> Sandra Pianalto, first vice president, Federal Reserve Bank, Cleveland, OH

John E. Robson, Lister Crown distinguished faculty fellow, Yale University, New Haven, CT

Daniel M. Kasper, director of transportation practice, Harbridge House, Inc., Boston, MA

Ex officio (nonvoting) members:
Laura D'Andrea Tyson, Chair, President's Council of Economic Advisers, CA

Senator J. James Exon, NE
Senator Ernest Hollings, SC
Senator Patty Murray, WA
Senator John Danforth, MO
Senator Slade Gorton, WA
Representative Richard Gephardt, MO
Representative Robert Borski, PA
Representative Maria Cantwell, WA
Representative Newt Gingrich, GA
Representative Bud Shuster, PA

Remarks and a Question-and-Answer Session on National Service in New Orleans, Louisiana
April 30, 1993

The President. Thank you. It's good to see you. How many of you are students here? Okay. And how many of you are in the Delta Service Corps? And then, who's here from Teach For America? That's good. I've got it.

Let me, first of all, say how delighted I am to be here and how much I appreciate all of you taking a little time out to talk with me. You probably know that I am going from here over to the University of New Orleans to speak about the national service plan and the new direct loan plan for college students that will be announced today and will be introduced shortly into the Congress.

I have with me today Senator Johnston and many Members of your congressional delegation and your Lieutenant Governor and many State officials here and some people who have come all the way from Washington to be with us, the Secretary of Education and Gen. David Jones, former Chairman of the Joint Chiefs of Staff, a lot of people who believe in you and your future and all the other young people in this country.

What I wanted to do today is to try to sort of set the stage for this speech that I'm going to go give and also to listen to you a little bit about the kinds of things that you do now: Why did you get into this service? Do you believe if there were more opportunities, more young people would do it?

This program we're going to propose will provide opportunities for tens of thousands of young people to work before, during, or after college to build up credit against a college education or, if they do it afterward, to pay off their college loans. It will also change the way young people borrow money to go to college so that you won't have to pay money back that you can't afford to pay back. Even if you borrow a lot of money to go to college, you'll always pay it back as a percentage of your income, so that people will be able to, and if you're not working, you don't have to pay it back. Then you pay it back as you work. But we're going to use the tax system and make sure that you have to pay it back if you can, so there won't be all the defaults we have now. That will lower the cost of and the threshold of going to college for every young person in America who wants to deal with it.

So I want to increase access to college, but also it's very important for me to increase the number of people, starting in our high schools, who will engage in some form of service.

So I think it would be helpful to me to know—we can maybe start with the high school students. If you could talk a little bit about the service projects you've been involved in and why you do it and whether you think we can get a lot more people involved.

Who wants to go first?

[At this point, a student discussed her experience as a volunteer with the Girl Scouts of America and the importance of being a role model.]

The President. You know, one of the things that I think is good about this program is we're going to build on the organizations at work now and set it up on a State-by-State basis. And a State can certify any program that's working in that State to be eligible to take young people for the national service program. So we're not going to create a whole new network of things. We're going to build on the programs that are working.

Anybody else? Anybody from the Delta Service Corps? Go ahead.

[*A National Summerbridge Program volunteer discussed that program.*]

The President. Anyone else?

[*A student discussed a volunteer program funded by the Nestle Corp.*]

The President. And how many young people were involved in the project?

Q. We started out with about 40, and then through attrition, we ended up with about 8 or 10 of us at the end. But it was just a great feeling to go down there and do that.

The President. What did you learn about homeless people?

Q. That they're just like us; that they're families and that they want to succeed as badly as we do and that there are more of them in the city than I ever thought possible. The line for that lunch just kept going forever.

[*A Delta Service Corps member then discussed that program.*]

The President. Do you have a feeling in the Teach For America program that you're actually helping people change their lives?

[*A teacher discussed how teachers and the Teach For America program can be a positive influence in a student's life.*]

The President. The Teach For America program has worked very well. This should help increase the recruitment, because you'll get some credit against whatever your accumulated college loans are to go do that.

What about you? What are you doing?

[*A VISTA volunteer stressed the importance of the literacy program.*]

The President. You know, one of the things that we discovered when we started trying to put this national service program together is that there were a whole lot of programs like that that had been funded at a very limited level in one Government agency or another. No one had ever put them all together and figured out how to get them all to work together. It's one

of the things we're trying to do.

Another thing I want to say about the literacy issue is that when I was Governor of my State, I devoted a lot of time to trying to dramatically increase the number of people who would go back to get their GED and get into adult literacy programs. We had a huge increase. And one of the things that we can now tell those folks, too, is if you're involved in any kind of service program, you can earn credit to go on after high school. But you can't get any money until you get your GED, which I think is important. You know, that will sort of reinforce that.

[*A participant stressed that local agencies should have a role in the national service program.*]

The President. That's great. Yes, sir?

[*A participant suggested that communities be given a leading role in the national service program and expressed concern about the motivation of some students in the program.*]

The President. You might, but first, you raise two issues. Let me respond to the first one. I, 100 percent, agree with you about having to be community-based. That's why we went out of our way not to create some big new Federal bureaucracy but to require the States to have community representatives on a board that can just certify a project in a community that's plainly working, because otherwise this whole thing is going to fail. There's no way we know what's good for your home town or mine or anybody else's of the Federal Government.

The second thing is: That may be right. You may have more young people—I hope you do have more young people coming into the service. It may be that some of them will be just doing it for the money. But frankly, if you look at, for example, the GI bill, there's a lot of evidence people enroll in the military service in part because of the benefits, but no evidence that they do it only because they think they're going to get money on the back end, because you have to make the effort, you have to go to it. And I think—or one of you alluded to this earlier, one of you has already talked— I don't think you can be in these service programs without being changed yourself. I think it's pretty hard to go all the way through one and not get connected to the people you're trying to help. I think it's worth the risk to get more people.

I may mess up the numbers here, but there's a man here with me from New Jersey who is very successful in business, named Ray Chambers, who has given the rest of his life to try to help the people in his community and other communities like his community all over the country, poor kids growing up with all kinds of problems. And we were talking about trying to get more mentors. And he said there's something like 15 million children who need these mentors and only 100,000, 150,000 of the mentors out there. So I think you have to take some risk if you put these incentives out that there will be some people doing it who may not care that much about it. But first of all, the benefit is not so great as to look like you're just giving somebody something. And secondly, I think most people will themselves be changed by this, will be reconnected to our country.

Go ahead.

Q. I'm a volunteer for Habitat. We help build homes for families who might otherwise not have an opportunity to own a home of their own.

The President. It's a great program.

[*The volunteer discussed both the Habitat for Humanity and Delta Service Corps experiences and the importance of giving people the opportunity to provide community service.*]

The President. You know, I'm really particularly proud of the Delta Service Corps because it grew out of the work that was done a few years ago by the States of Arkansas, Louisiana, Mississippi, and then Missouri, Kentucky, and Illinois and the parts that are right along the river. And we studied the conditions of the lower Mississippi Delta, and one of the things that we urged was that some way be found to bring young people in here to this area to work. And then the legislators and the Congressmen from our States sponsored this bill that's really been very impressive. I'm glad to see all of you here. Walter, did you have——

[*A Delta Service Corps member stressed the importance of making sure that the volunteers are suited for their jobs. Another volunteer then suggested that the Delta Service Corps become a nationwide program.*]

The President. I think it may. And certainly, things like it will. I think new organizations will spring up from the grassroots. Just to go back to the point you made about that, what's the

most likely thing that will happen is that there will be communities where there are people like you, but there's no organization. And when this thing comes out and young people start talking about it and thinking about it, it'll probably be much more likely that in every community in America there will be groups like this.

You know, when I hear all of you talk, one of the things that, as you know, I worry about most of the time is how to find enough jobs for the American people in a world in which we've had a difficult time in our country creating jobs, and other wealthy countries are having trouble creating jobs. And a lot of the good things that happen in the economy now—a lot of you can do this; most of you probably are proficient with computers and things like that—a lot of the things that happen in the economy now mean that people can do more with fewer workers, because they have all this technology.

But one of the things that you cannot substitute people for are the kind of human contacts that you all are engaged in. I mean, a lot of the people problems of America can only be solved by people in very small groups or one on one. So I think there will be a huge increase in the demand for folks like you to do what you're doing in the years ahead.

[*A student stated that the national service program will probably encourage more students to become involved in community service.*]

The President. That's a terrific point. I know we've got to quit in a minute, and I want to give you a chance to talk. But let me say that people say to me, "Well, can you afford this program, and what if 250,000, what if 500,000, what if a million young people want to do this?" Well, if you think about it, think what we're paying now for the failures of the present society, think what we're paying now for all the young people who drop out of school, who have children when they're children, who get involved in drugs, who wind up in prisons, who can't work and draw welfare or food stamps or unemployment or who wind up in homeless shelters, you think what it's cost us now to do that.

We're living in a world where we need every person. And I agree with you. I think when people like you get out of college, you get a world-class education in a place like Tulane, if you can get people like that who still are really aware of what is going on and who understand the point you made, that homeless people are just like us. There are a lot of kids out there in these homeless shelters. A lot of them can learn and do real well if they're given a chance. And if they do well, this is going to affect you much more than me. One in ten Americans now is on food stamps.

Now, you think about what your life is going to be like when you're my age, you have children getting ready to go to college, if we don't reverse these trends. What's the unemployment rate in America going to be? What's your tax burden going to be? What are you going to be paying it for? What's it going to be like to be in the streets of your country? This service thing has so much more to do with your future in a way than with mine. And I think the point you made is terrific.

I know we've got to quit, but I want to— go ahead.

[*A participant stated that working on community service projects fosters a desire to continue serving others.*]

The President. Good for you.

Q. Thank you for visiting.

The President. Thank you all very much. You're terrific. I feel a lot better about my country every time I see young people like you. We're going to be fine. Thank you.

NOTE: The President spoke at 11:52 a.m. in the courtyard at Benjamin Franklin High School. In his remarks, he referred to Lt. Gov. Melinda Schwegmann of Louisiana.

Exchange With Reporters in New Orleans
April 30, 1993

Bosnia

Q. [*Inaudible*]

The President. I'm going to have another meeting in the morning about it, do a little more work on the way back today, and then have another meeting in the morning. And then I may want to make another round of phone calls after we meet with the principals. And I expect then we'll be pretty close to deciding where we are. I want to get an updated report on the situation, and I'll ask a lot of questions

about it.

Q. Mr. President, has all this talk about military force already had an impact, sir? Do you think it's already had an impact?

The President. I hope so. I hope so. I think it may well have, and I certainly hope so.

NOTE: The exchange began at 1:35 p.m. in the Health and Physical Education Center at the University of New Orleans. A tape was not available for verification of the content of this exchange.

Remarks on the National Service Initiative at the University of New Orleans
April 30, 1993

Thank you very much. I ought to quit while I'm ahead. [*Laughter*] It is wonderful to be back in New Orleans and in Louisiana and to have the first chance I've had since the election to thank you for your support, your electoral votes, and the education you gave me on my many trips here during the campaign last year. I'm glad to be back on this campus. I want to thank your student body president, Robert Styron. I thought he gave a good speech. I think he's

got a future in politics, don't you? [*Applause*] And Chancellor O'Brien. I want to thank Senator Breaux for his kind remarks and for his leadership of the Democratic Leadership Council. I want to acknowledge the presence here of Senator Johnston and many members of the Louisiana House and many other Members of the United States Congress, along with many others who are here with the Democratic Leadership Council, including my good friend and former colleague, the Governor of New Mexico, Bruce King, who's here. There are two members of my Cabinet here, the Secretary of Education, Dick Riley, and the Secretary of Agriculture, Mike Espy, also a DLC Vice Chair.

I want to thank all the people who are here representing volunteer organizations. I met with some young people just before I came in here who are scattered around near me from Benjamin Franklin High School just across the way. [*Applause*] Absolutely no enthusiasm in that place. [*Laughter*] From the Delta Service Corps., from VISTA, from Summerbridge, from Teach for America, we also have some students here, apart from all of you from UNO, we have some students here who have worked in service projects at Xavier University and at Tulane. We also have people here who have been involved in service for a long time from ACTION, from the Older Americans Volunteer Program, from the National Association of Senior Companions and Foster Grandparents and the National Association of Retired Senior Volunteers. All these people I am very grateful to.

I'd like to just acknowledge in general the people who are here from law enforcement organizations and firefighters' organizations and public employees and teachers' groups who have helped us on this national service project. And I want to say a special word of thanks to three other people. First of all, Gen. David Jones, a former Chairman of the Joint Chiefs of Staff who has worked very hard helping us put together this program, who is here. General Jones, thank you for being here. Secondly, a remarkable gentleman from New Jersey, an immensely successful businessman who retired early and is devoting his entire life to community service to rebuild the lives and the neighborhoods of the people in his community in New Jersey and now helping others around the country, a founding Member of the Points of Light Foundation, Mr. Ray Chambers, who is here. And I'd like to pay a little special attention to two members of Congress who are not here and to one who is, for their long work on the whole idea of national service. The two in the Senate who are not here are Senator Harris Wofford from Pennsylvania and Senator Sam Nunn from Georgia. And then Representative Dave McCurdy from Oklahoma, thank you for all of the work you've done on this over the years.

I am glad to be here. You know, when I come down here I always sort of relax. I don't know why that is. I timed it just in time for the Jazz Festival, but I left my saxophone at the White House.

This is the 100th day of my administration. In Washington, some say it marks a milestone. But in many ways it's just another day at the office for what we're trying to do in changing America. In the last 99 days we have worked relentlessly to address the pressing and long-ignored needs of the American people and to bring to the Government something it has not seen in a long time: an acknowledgment that bold action is needed, and needed now, to secure and enlarge America's future, and that in order to do it we not only have to change programs, we have to change the way the Government works and engage the energies of the American people in the process.

In the last 100 days I think we have begun to change the direction in which our country has been going for a long time, and to go toward a new direction more like the one the American people demanded last November. We've also started an unprecedented debate in our Nation's capital about big ideas and better lives across our Nation, ideas that in many cases were shaped and nurtured by some of the people who are here today, as Senator Breaux said earlier, the members of the Democratic Leadership Council, of which I am proud to be a founding member. Unlike most organizations, the DLC has done more than just talk about the problems in our country. It has made an honest effort to develop real ideas about how to restore the American economy, and make the Government work, and rebuild the confidence and the link that exists between the American people and their Government when things are at their best here. And it's been a laboratory for experimentation and solutions.

During my years with the DLC we really tried to refine our philosophy of what it would mean to take not only the Democratic Party but the United States of America in a new direction, to make our country work again and to reward work and family, to encourage education and enterprise, to establish what I have often called a new covenant with the American people: Creating opportunity but demanding responsibility from all so that once again we could be a true American community where we know and believe and live as if we're all in this together. This group has conceived many of the ideas that I've advocated since I've been in

Washington from setting a limit on welfare and putting people to work to police reform and community policing to rewarding work of low-income working people by having an earned-income tax credit that would lift the working poor with children out of poverty. So we could say if you work 40 hours a week in this country, you have a child in the house, you ought not to be poor. These are the kinds of things that this organization has done. They helped to develop the idea I want to talk to you today about that has so much to do with the future of the young people here and throughout our country: national service. This is an organization about ideas.

Now in Washington, as you might imagine, we don't always agree with one another. And that is good—that's why we've got a system where the Government's divided up and we have two parties and we have people fighting all the time—as long as it's about ideas. But too often we've seen that the debate over big ideas gets mired in petty politics. I know one thing: The American people are tired of gridlock and petty politics. If we're going to fight, they want us to fight over ideas and the future of this country.

In the past 99 days we tried to address the problems the American people told me they wanted to be addressed. We focused more than anything else on the economy, passing the outline of a budget that will reduce the deficit by more than $500 billion, increase investment in education and technologies and the things that will create the economy of the 21st century that all of you need so that you'll have good and decent jobs and a decent future laying the groundwork for a more prosperous tomorrow.

Just in 100 days we've announced a policy to help to convert the defense cutbacks and the economic opportunities for people who are losing their jobs because of the military cutbacks; to take a new direction in technology to create more opportunities for our people; to be more aggressive in preserving the environment, but do it in a way that creates jobs, not a way that costs jobs; to have a trade policy that will really reflect our common interest with other nations and expanding jobs and opportunities everywhere. We've begun the long-overdue renovation of the American economic base. The question now, unlike 100 days ago, the question is now not whether we're going to reduce the deficit but how and how much. The question

now is not whether the Government will have a new partnership with the private sector to shape the economy but exactly what the details will be and how much our part will be.

We've also taken on the issue of health care, something million of Americans cried out for last year. I got a letter today from a young woman I shook hands with whose—literally, her life is on the line, and she cannot get health insurance. It is wrong that in this Nation—we are the only advanced country in the world with 34 million people without health insurance. It is wrong that millions of Americans cannot change their jobs without losing their health insurance because they or a child or a spouse has been sick. It is wrong that the price of health care goes up 2.5 times the rate of inflation every year. And it is wrong that we spend 30 percent more of our income than any other country on Earth on health care and have less to show for it. But it is also wrong to assume that there is some magic, quick answer. That's why we've been working with a task force headed by the First Lady and over 400 people from all aspects of health care to do something about this.

But now, for the American people the issue is no longer whether we're going to address the health care crisis, whether we're going to provide security to hard-working middle class Americans, whether we're going to cover the people who aren't covered, whether we're going to control costs, but how are we going to do it and how fast and when are we going to begin. I hope the answer is soon. And not too soon is soon enough for me.

There was a lot of discussion last year about how bad the Government was, and it didn't work, and it was bloated, it needed a change. Look at the last 100 days: I've tried to set an example by offering a budget to reduce the White House staff by 25 percent; by putting the lid on and reducing the Federal bureaucratic expenses, the administrative expenses of the Federal Government by over $10 billion; by moving dramatically to reduce the influence of special interests on Executive Branch appointments by having the toughest ethics laws and restrictions on people becoming lobbyists for other interests when they leave the payroll of the President of the United States; by asking the Vice President to share the most sweeping review of the way the Federal Government works in a generation, with a promise of real reform and reinventing Government, something else this organization has long believed in.

We are moving. And the Congress is moving to join. The Congress has voted to cut the administrative costs of running the Congress, something many of you never thought you would see happen. They did that. The House of Representatives voted yesterday to give the President of the United States a modified line-item veto, and I hope the Senate will follow their lead. I hope soon they will send to my desk the motor voter bill which will make it easier for young people and other people to vote and participate in their country's political process. And there will be campaign finance reform and lobby reform legislation and a crime bill that will put more police on the street and give us the capacity we need to take our communities back. These things are going on. The question is no longer whether we're going to reform the way Government works but how fast and how much and how well. And those are the right questions, my fellow Americans, good questions to ask.

And now I come to the last, and in many ways the most important issue that we have tried to address—the economy, yes; health care, yes; reform in the way the Government works, yes—but also what about the American people. How can each American make a contribution? How can each American do the work that all Americans must, taking responsibility for himself or herself and growing up into a vibrant community? We have tried to address those issues as well. The buzz word now people use is empowerment. I used to call it responsibility. I often have said, and I want to reiterate today, the United States Government cannot create an opportunity for anyone who will not be responsible enough to seize it. Opportunity is a two-way street and requires responsibility. That is the only way we'll ever rebuild the American community.

In the days and months ahead, you will see the Secretary of Education talk about his remarkable education program to provide tougher national standards in education but also to give people at the grassroots level more flexibility in making public education work. You will see the Secretary of Agriculture and the Secretary of Housing and Urban Development talk about how we can empower even the poorest Americans to start their own businesses, save their own money, and take control of their own fu-

ture. You will see other people talking about how we can reform the welfare system. All of these things are at the core of the notion that we ought to make it possible for every American to live up to the fullest of his or her God-given ability. And that is what in the end national service is all about: helping ourselves and helping each other at the same time.

On this 100th day of my administration I want to recommit myself and those who work with me to the values that have made our Nation without peer in all human history, those of opportunity, responsibility, community, and respect for one another. Today I want to propose applying those values to a revolution of opportunity for our hard-pressed families and for those who have been left out. As a first step we're going to ease the terms of college loans, helping students from middle and lower-middle income families to clear a major path to the American dream, the path of higher education. In return we'll demand responsibility from young people. We'll make it easier to borrow money and much easier to pay it off, but this time you have to pay it off. You can't just default on the loan. And we will also offer the young people of America the opportunity of paying their loans back by serving their communities in a new program of national service.

In just a few days I will send to the Congress two bills containing our proposals, first to strengthen college opportunity and to establish national service. Together they will revive America's commitment to community and make affordable the cost of a college education for every American. It's no secret that over the last 10 or 12 years the cost of a college education is about the only essential think that's gone up even more rapidly than health care costs. And middle class parents, and even upper middle class parents, not to mention lower income people, have borne the burden, paying now about five percent of median income just to put one child through a 4 year in-State public college. It costs an average of over $5,200 a year for that education. That means families are depleting savings and many students are faced with cutting back to a part-time course load or having to drop out simply because of the cost of a college education. A college dropout is now more than twice the high school dropout rate. We cannot afford that, and we can do better.

I propose a new way to finance college for millions of students who seek loans every year.

We call it an EXCEL account. With it, students can repay the loans they take out not with a percentage of the loan they borrowed but with a percentage of their actual earnings. Now think about that. For students driven by debt into careers with high pay and low satisfaction this can be very liberating. Take a student torn, for example, between pursuing a career in teaching and corporate law. This student now can at least make the career choice based on what he or she wants to do and not the size of the outstanding student loan, because we propose to let everybody have the option of paying the student loan back based on how much they earn not just how much they owe. That is an incredible incentive.

However, under the current system, as many of you know, students faced with big bills or just inconvenient responsibilities have too often taken the irresponsible route and defaulted on their loans or have been found in default because they couldn't find a job. Often times there's no serious effort to collect the loan because the Government guarantees 90 percent of it. So if the bank makes the loan, it costs more than 10 percent to go collect it. What's the result? The taxpayers every year pay about $3 billion on other people's loans, money that could be spent on your education, on the schools here, on the future of the children here, just for bad loans. It isn't right.

Under our system, the Department of Education would engage the Internal Revenue Service. We would have the payroll records. And you wouldn't be able to beat the bill because you would have to pay the loan back as a percentage of your income, if you choose, but you'd have to pay it because you pay taxes and because we have your records and because you won't be able to get out of it. And that is the right thing to do.

But these EXCEL accounts are just the beginning. We hope they will lead more and more Americans not only to seize the opportunity of a college education and to exert a stronger sense of responsibility but also to seek to serve their communities through a program of national service. It was Thomas Jefferson who first told the American people in essence that the more you know, the more you owe. In his words, and I quote, "A debt of service is due from every man to his country proportioned to the bounties which nature and fortune have measured to him." This statement reminds us that values

never go out of fashion, that civic responsibility is as good for democracy today as it was when Thomas Jefferson said that, and that if you really want to be the best citizen of your country, you have to give something back to your country. With national service, we can literally open a new world to a new generation of Americans where higher learning goes hand-in-hand with the higher purpose of addressing our unmet needs, our educational, our social, our environmental needs, to secure the future that we all will share. National service will mark the start of a new era for America in which every citizen, every one of you, can become an agent of change armed with the knowledge and experience that a college education brings, and ready to transform the world in which we live, city by city, community by community, block by block. I say to you, we need you.

You know, there's a lot of talk in America today, and I spend hours every week worrying about the effect that automation and technology is having on employment. Indeed, as we see the productivity of American enterprises rise, their need for workers goes down because they can do more with computes that they used to do with people. So people ask me all the time, where will we find the jobs for this new generation of Americans? How can we drive this unemployment rate down? But if you look around this country at all the human problems, all the homeless people, all the environmental waste dumps in our cities and our rural areas, all the problems that we've got in every community in America, and see all the kids that are in trouble—15 million of them at risk and needing somebody to pay attention to—you know where the work needs to be.

Late last night when I was preparing to come down here, I took a little time off at my desk and I read the letters that my staff had given me. And I got a letter from a woman who grew up with me. I've known here since we were in grade school. In this letter she said, "You know, someone asked me a couple of days ago: How are we going to save all these kids in this country that are in trouble?" And she said, "Without even thinking, I blurted out, the same way we lost them, one at a time." And so today my fellow Americans, I issue a call to national service, to Americans young and old, Democrats and Republicans, white, black, Hispanic, Asian and you name it, all of us that make up this great Nation. I call you to national service because it is only that together we can advance a tradition rooted in our people's history, helping our people to help themselves. And with national service we can rejoin the citizens in communities of this country, bonding each to the other with the glue of common purpose and real patriotism.

We have many young people here today, students of this place of higher learning where we're gathered. In you I know I see the builders of tomorrow. And I say to you, as good as the education is here and at the other great institutions represented here today and all across America, the power of academic learning is incomplete unless every American can share in it. That is the only way we can lift our whole country up. I say to you further that our country needs you. We need your knowledge and your initiative and your energy. We need you because you are still stripped and free of the cynicism that has paralyzed too many of your parents and your grandparents, and led us to spend too much time talking about what we can't do instead of seizing what we can. You are not afflicted by that, and I pray you never will be.

We need to make sure that we can use your energies and your talents. One way is by making sure that the low wages that public service often offers won't be a route to the poorhouse for someone with college loans. As I said, we're going to make it easier for you to pay off your college loan. But also, if you engage in national service, we'll make it easier for you to pay off a college debt or to earn credits toward it before you go to college, or while you're in college.

For each term of service, 1 or 2 years, participants in national service programs will receive benefits that can be used toward past, present, or future obligations, whether for college or advanced job training. You can get a college education and, in addition, through service, perhaps the best experience of your life. That's a pretty good investment.

I've talked a lot about the students here. And they do play a large part in this plan, but they're not alone. Here in New Orleans many of you already know what it means to make a difference in your community because you've just been doing that for a long time. And I'm very proud, as I said. I'm going to get another cheer about this, but one of the models that I had a little something to do with is the Delta Service Corps, and I appreciate what they're doing. [*Applause*]

There are people here working to restore housing. There are people here working in other ways. I just want to mention three: Lawrence Williams, a team leader in the Corps who has helped to restore housing for low-income people with the local Habitat for Humanity Project; Jane Sullivan, a retired public schoolteacher and a former VISTA volunteer who helps rural communities gain better access to health care, housing, and other assistance; and a young person I met just a few moments ago, Parris Moore-Brown, who works with parents in housing programs for drug awareness outreach and now plans to work with the physically challenged. She says that she has no tolerance for self-pity, and she lives what she preaches. She hasn't been slowed by what her birth dealt her, a brittle bone disorder that has left her as an adult, and by her own measure, 4 feet, 2¼ inches tall. Where are you? Stand up on here so we can see you. After my meeting with her and the other young people today, I'd say she stands about 10 feet tall in America today. There are tens of thousands of people like Parris and Jane and Lawrence and those of you who are here with these service programs who are dying to be called to a new season of service, and we want to do that.

Another part of our plan is to build on the National and Community Service Act that was passed in 1990, and the already flourishing programs that are started and up and going in every State in this country. National service is not going to be a Federal bureaucracy; it's going to operate at the grassroots with the real problems of real people and with the programs that work today. It will be locally driven because I trust the communities in this country to make decisions for themselves.

I also want to say that while we want very much to have young people in this program who are working toward earning credits for college or paying their college loans off through national service, we need so many other people in service projects. We need our older people who never will go back to college but have a lifetime of experience and energy to give to the young people of this country. We need young people who may not be old enough to drive a car or to qualify for this program but can have a dramatic impact on fellow students by helping them learn better study habits or just keeping them out of trouble. I've learned already that, as the parent of a teenager, that the peers can have a big impact on the shape and quality of a child's life. Even a child can serve in programs that now begin as early as kindergarten. We have no upper age limit in America, or lower age limit for being a good public servant.

To be successful, this national program will need the broad-based support of all the American people. Parents and children, churches and synagogues, colleges and universities and the potential providers and the beneficiaries of our services. In this vision of national service, everyone is a partner. And that includes, of course, the business community in this country. We need businesses to contribute to the effort, to match Federal money and local programs and to contribute at the national level, helping to make sure that the programs we choose are good ones indeed.

What will set this legislation apart from other similar efforts in the past that rewarded service to our country is that it will totally eliminate the Federal Government bureaucracy. And believe me, no one will miss that. We're going to set up a national service corporation that will run like a big venture capital outfit not like a bureaucracy. And communities, as I said, will have the flexibility to make their own programs work. I think that I've seen enough today and I've heard enough of your applause to know that the American people are hungry for a chance to serve their country and to reap the rewards of civic pride and education in the process.

In answering this call our people are following a proud history. More than a century ago President Abraham Lincoln signed the Homestead Act, and the frontier of this country was settled by countless families who took up the challenge in exchange for 100 acres to call their own. In the 1930's President Roosevelt enlisted millions of young people to restore the environment through the Civilian Conservation Corps. FDR gave others a chance to support themselves through the buildings made possible by the Works Project Administration. I was in the United States Justice Department just yesterday, a building built in 1934 by people who were giving service to their country, and it's still a beautiful monument to the legacy of that kind of service. The parents of the baby boom had the GI bill, which was one of the best investments our Government ever made. A generation ago, the young people of my generation saw suffering in Latin America, Asia, and Africa, and many rushed to the challenge laid down by President Kennedy when he created the Peace Corps, which became our country's greatest ambassador, building bridges of understanding to far off cultures. And now, three decades later, a challenge has been presented to all of you, a new challenge and an old one, as old as America and as new as your future.

A year ago when the Democratic Leadership Council met in New Orleans, I asked the following question: I said, I want you to think about what kind of citizens you're going to be—[*inaudible*]—administration that this was the day the American people were empowered to renew their Nation and their communities, to seize a better future for themselves, and to help all of us to be what the—[*inaudible*]—out of helping our fellow citizens and ourselves to become what we ought to be, this country will be all right.

Thank you very much, and God bless you all.

NOTE: The President spoke at 2:10 p.m. in the Health and Physical Education Center at the university. In his remarks, he referred to Gregory O'Brien, chancellor of the university.

Nomination for Chairman of the Merit Systems Protection Board
April 30, 1993

The President today declared his intention to nominate former Alabama Congressman Ben Erdreich as a member and Chairman of the Merit System Protection Board.

"I have full confidence Ben Erdreich will serve with distinction and dedication at the helm of the Merit Systems Protection Board," the

President said.

NOTE: A biography of the nominee was made available by the Office of the Press Secretary.

The President's Radio Address
May 1, 1993

Good morning. It's the first day of May, and for many of our high school seniors it's time to begin thinking about their last final exams, packing up their rooms, and setting out on the adventures that will come in the next stage of their lives. Whether they are heading to college or looking for their first jobs, these students are getting ready to cross a threshold that will shape them and their futures as people and citizens.

All of us have a big stake in whether these young people have opportunities for success. The great promise of American life has always been expanding opportunities for each succeeding generation, opportunities for education, for employment, for home ownership, for good health care for all those willing to work hard and play by the rules. I am determined that we won't ever lose that promise of American life.

I sought this office because the dreams of working Americans were in deep danger. And I promised all of you that I would work my heart out to restore them. All the work we do in this administration springs from that determination and is rooted in our values, the values that have strengthened our families and given generations of Americans brighter futures than their parents, values that have made this Nation without peer, those of opportunity, responsibility, and community. With them, we propose putting Government back on the side of America's hard-pressed families.

In the first 100 days of this administration we've tried to do that. We've worked hard to cut the big Government deficit, and interest rates are down, enabling millions of Americans to refinance their homes and get interest rates lower in business and consumer loans. We've made a long-term commitment to invest in jobs and education and technology. We've begun to reform the Government by cutting unnecessary spending and having tougher lobbying rules and moving to reinvent the whole way Government operates. And of course, we're facing the big crisis of health care, trying to guarantee security to all Americans and control costs so that we

can move forward with the kind of basic health care that other people in other countries take for granted but that threatens to bankrupt America.

In addition to that, I am determined to open the doors of college education and to give American students the opportunity to pay for it through a program of national service. In the last several years, the cost of a college education has become more important than ever before. And yet, those costs have gone up more than any other basic in American life, including health care. We've simply got to do something for all these high school seniors and all those coming along behind them to open the doors of college education and to help those now in college to stay in and to succeed.

As a first step, I will ask Congress to approve legislation changing the terms of college loans. By giving our students a new way to finance college, we will be able to ensure that many more go and stay. This new method will be called an EXCEL account. With it, students will be able to repay the loans on a schedule based on a percentage of their future earnings and not just on the amount they borrow, as is the case today. This will be nothing less than liberating for many students who drop out of college because of financial strains or who graduate with big debts and then feel driven into careers with higher pay but lower satisfaction. A student torn between pursuing a career in teaching or corporate law, for example, will be able to make a career choice based on what he or she wants to do, not how much he or she can earn to pay off college debt.

Another problem with the current student loan system is that far too many students default on their loans, costing taxpayers billions of dollars a year and adding to our deficit. Giving students the chance to pay their loans back as a small percentage of their incomes will reduce the default rate by making it possible for more students to repay. But we're also going to make it tougher for those who can repay the loans to avoid doing it by involving the IRS in the collection process so that those who work and pay taxes must also repay their loans. With this new opportunity must come new responsibility.

But these EXCEL accounts are just the beginning. I also want to give tens of thousands of young people the chance to pay for part of their college education or advanced job training through a program of national service. With national service, we can open a new world to a new generation, one where higher learning goes hand-in-hand with a higher purpose of addressing our Nation's unmet needs, educational, social, and environmental. Things that will secure the future, we will all share together.

Americans, without regard to age, will be able to earn credit against college costs before, during, or after college by working as tutors for children, volunteers at hospitals, as public safety officers, or in countless other grassroots community efforts that are working all across America today but need more help. College graduates can repay a portion of their loans by working as teachers or police officers in underserved areas. National service will mark the start of a new era for America, one in which every citizen can become an agent of change, armed with the knowledge and experience that a college education brings and ready to transform the world in which we live, city by city, community by community, block by block, person by person. National service will operate at the level Americans know best, the grassroots. Its programs will be locally driven, because we trust communities to know what works. And this program is designed and will succeed without a traditional Washington bureaucracy. And believe me, no one will miss that.

Expanding opportunity, restoring responsibility, reviving our sense of community: these are the values that have always made our country strong. America has always succeeded when we've understood that we're all in this together. With national service, Americans can help themselves by helping each other. It's the best investment we could ever make in our future.

Thank you.

NOTE: The President spoke at 10:06 a.m. from the Oval Office at the White House.

Statement on the Death of President Ranasinghe Premadasa of Sri Lanka
May 1, 1993

I am outraged by the assassination of President Ranasinghe Premadasa of Sri Lanka. I condemn this brutal act of terrorism.

President Premadasa served his country with great distinction. As Prime Minister and then as President, he worked tirelessly to promote his country's development and raise the standard of living of all Sri Lankans. His efforts made a real difference to his fellow citizens.

I hope that the people of Sri Lanka will join together at this difficult time to renew their commitment to the fight against terrorism and to underscore their support for their democratic institutions.

Hillary and I wish to extend the sympathy of the American people to the people of Sri Lanka at the loss of their leader. We send our sincere condolences to the family of President Premadasa at this tragic time.

Statement on the Prospects for Peace in Bosnia
May 2, 1993

The developments in the Vance-Owen process are a positive step, but we have yet to determine whether the Serbs are serious about peace. We will make that judgment based upon their actions on the ground in Bosnia. As Lord Owen said this morning, "We still have a long way to go."

Other agreements in this protracted war have raised hopes but not changed behavior. We will judge intentions by actions. Accordingly, I have instructed Secretary Christopher to continue as planned with his consultations through Europe on the measures we will take if the Serbs do not act in good faith.

I have spoken in the past 2 days with a number of congressional leaders as well as President Yeltsin, Prime Minister Major, Chancellor Kohl, President Mitterrand, Prime Minister Mulroney, and Prime Minister-designate Ciampi. I will continue such consultations.

We all hope for a true and just peace in Bosnia. It must include not only the provisions of peace on paper but also the practices of peace on the ground.

Exchange With Reporters Prior to Discussions With Governor Chris Patten of Hong Kong
May 3, 1993

Bosnia

Q. Mr. President, do you expect the Serbs to keep their word——

The President. The what?

Q. ——the Bosnian Serbs? Do you trust the Serbs at this point?

The President. Well, I want to reiterate what we've already said. I want to evaluate them by their actions. We'll see what they do. I hope the Serbian Assembly will support the decision to sign onto Vance-Owen, and we'll just see. We'll just have to measure it as we go along.

Q. Mr. President, are you still committed, as you said, to sending in ground troops to help enforce the peace if it does hold? Would there be American participation in a peacekeeping mission?

The President. We said several weeks ago that the United States would be prepared to support a United Nations effort, heavily engaged in by the Europeans, to help to enforce a peace if a peace was made that we would have no interest in. We were not interested in sending soldiers in there into combat, into a fighting situation but that we thought there would have to be a peacekeeping force there and that we would be prepared to participate.

Q. Well, if this peace holds, then, if Vance-Owen holds, you've got 10 provinces, wouldn't that be a very difficult and dangerous mission for American and United Nations forces?

The President. No, it depends entirely on what happens between now and then. And before I agree to put one American soldier there, we're going to watch events, and I will obviously speak not only to you but directly to the American people about it.

Q. How many do you contemplate sending in?

The President. I think it's very important now to point out—let me just restate what's at stake here—there has been enormous loss of life under especially brutal conditions there. And it is a very politically unstable part of the world, which has significant potential for a wider war.

So the United States has tried to work with our allies—Secretary Christopher, as you know, is on this mission now—in an attempt to get the parties together so that we can present a united front and so that we can keep the pressure up to end the killing but also to stop the prospect of a much wider war, which could cause much more trouble, much more instability. But there has been at this point no decision made on any of that, and I would not make any such decisions without further consultation with the Congress and discussing it directly with the American people.

Q. Why don't the allies agree with you?

Q. Are you getting cooperation from the allies——

The President. So far, the meetings are going great.

Q. Have you talked to Christopher?

The President. I have. I talked to him twice yesterday, talked to him twice.

Q. You mean, they have signed on your policy?

The President. I talked to Christopher, Prime Minister Major, President Mitterrand, the Prime Minister-designate of Italy, to President Yeltsin, and to Chancellor Kohl. I've talked to a lot of people——

Q. And they all agree——

The President. ——Prime Minister Mulroney. We have agreed that we're going to keep the pressure up and have a united front and move forward, and we're developing a policy now.

China

Q. Mr. President, can we ask you a question about——

The President. Sure.

Q. ——we're just trying find out—the Governor will be here to ask you not to renew MFN with conditions. You have said that you will have some conditions. Can you have any kind of a compromise here? And the other question was, if you do support the Governor's proposals, do you think that will upset the Chinese?

The President. Well, let me answer the first question first. We obviously hope that we can maintain the maximum good relationship with the Chinese. I have no interest in trying to isolate them. I'm encouraged by the successes of their economic reforms. And that's got to be in the interest of the whole world if it is accompanied with responsible behavior and respect for human rights and movement toward a more democratic society. There has been some encouraging news in China on a number of fronts in the last few weeks. I still think that more needs to be done. And I'm hopeful that

it will be. But we're not in the position to say finally what the condition of our relations will be—and next month when the time runs out because it's an evolving situation.

And secondly, I just have to say that I think that the democracy initiative in Hong Kong is a good thing. And I'm encouraged that the parties have agreed to talk about it. And it's one of the world's most vibrant, thriving important cities. It is an incredible center of commerce and haven of opportunity for millions of people who literally have—many of them have not a thing but the clothes on their back when they came there. And I think the idea of trying to keep it an open and free society after 1997 is in the best interest of the Chinese. I think it's clearly in the best interest of the Chinese. So I think this initiative is well-founded, and I support it. I hope it doesn't offend anybody, but how can the United States be against democracy? That's our job; get out there and promote it.

NOTE: The exchange began at 10:31 a.m. in the Oval Office at the White House. A tape was not available for verification of the content of this exchange.

Remarks on Signing the Asian/Pacific American Heritage Month Proclamation
May 3, 1993

Thank you very much. Let me begin by extending a warm welcome to all of you, especially those who have traveled very great distances, as many of you have, to help celebrate Asian Pacific American Heritage Month.

I'm pleased to be joined on the stage by Senator Dan Akaka, with whom I played golf last weekend—less well than he did, I might add— and Representatives Bob Matsui, Norm Mineta, Robert Underwood, Patsy Mink, Eni Faleomavaega—did I do a good job? Pretty good—and Jay Kim. And let us also honor the memory of the late Senator Spark Matsunaga, who left such a wonderful legacy as a true friend of the Asian Pacific community.

My campaign and my administration have gained so much from the talents of Asian Pacific Americans, and I'd like to recognize just a few

of them: Barbara Chow, my Special Assistant for Legislative Affairs; Neil Dhillon, at the Department of Transportation; Atul Gawande, who has been working on the Health Care Task Force; Maria Haley on our personal staff; Goody Marshall with the Vice President's staff; Doris Matsui in Public Liaison who did such a wonderful job with this event; Shirley Sagawa in Legislative Affairs; Debra Shon at the United States Trade Representative's Office; Melinda Yee at the Department of Commerce; and many others who are an essential part of our efforts every day.

Fifteen years ago, Representative Frank Horton introduced the first resolution proclaiming Asian Pacific American Heritage Week, honoring the significant contributions of Asian Pacific Americans in all walks of life. In 1990, Congress designated and President Bush proclaimed the month of May as Asian Pacific Heritage Month. And last year, with the help of Representative Horton and 106 of his colleagues, the designation of May as Asian Pacific Heritage Month each year became the law of the land.

The month of May was chosen because of its significance to Asian Pacific American history. In the first week of May in 1843, the first Japanese arrived in America. And on May 10, 1869, Golden Spike Day, the Transcontinental Railroad, built partly with Chinese labor, was completed. Today, 150 years after these historic events, nearly 8 million Asian Pacific Americans can trace their roots to Asia and the islands of the Pacific.

It is astonishing to realize the breadth of diversity among Americans of Asian Pacific heritage. The Asian Pacific community stretches across thousands of miles and encompasses millions of diverse people. In our country the Asian Pacific American community can trace its roots to at least 25 different nationalities, more than 75 different languages, and literally hundreds of different ethnic groups. Now, that's diversity.

And still Asian Pacific Americans have something in common and something to emulate, a commitment to strong families, to community, and to instilling in each new generation a respect for educational opportunity and hard work. These values have been an essential part of success in achieving the American dream, as so many Asian Pacific Americans know.

And while we realize all the rich opportunities America has given to all our people, we are aware also of how much Asian Pacific Americans have given back to this country. Immigrants from Asia and the Pacific helped build our country. Today their descendants are making us even better. They are prominent among our scientists, artists, doctors, teachers, and other professionals who have enriched the lives of all of us in America.

I want to talk for a moment about the importance of education. The Asian Pacific community has demonstrated that a commitment to education is truly the key to bettering our lives. Among Asian Pacific Americans 25 years old and over, 82 percent have had 4 years of high school or more; 39 percent have completed 4 years of college or more. For individuals, education is the key to economic parity and social mobility. But for America, it is the key to our strength and our competitiveness in the global economy.

I want to thank you all again for coming here today to recognize all the achievements and the contributions that Asian Pacific Americans have made to this great Nation. I hope that we can continue to come together as we have today to rejoice in our diversity as we renew the bonds of community that bring all Americans together. I believe that if we embrace those things which we share, if we embrace our common values and our common goals, we strengthen ourselves, our community, and our democracy, and we make ourselves free to celebrate the richness of our diversity.

Therefore, it is with great pride and admiration that I take this opportunity, my first one, to sign the proclamation proclaiming this Asian Pacific American Heritage Month.

Thank you very much.

NOTE: The President spoke at 5:40 p.m. in the East Room at the White House. The proclamation is listed in Appendix D at the end of this volume.

Nomination for Three Ambassadorial Posts
May 3, 1993

The President today announced his intention to nominate Laurence E. Pope II to be Ambassador to the Republic of Chad, Joseph A. Saloom to be Ambassador to the Republic of Guinea, and Steven E. Steiner to be U.S. Representative to the START Joint Compliance and Inspection Commission with the rank of Ambas-

sador. All three are career members of the U.S. Foreign Service.

"These three individuals will be excellent representatives of the United States and its interests," said the President. "They have served their country well throughout their careers, and I have confidence that they will continue to do so."

NOTE: Biographies of the nominees were made available by the Office of the Press Secretary.

Teleconference Remarks on Empowerment Zones and an Exchange With Reporters
May 4, 1993

The President. So we've got L.A., Kentucky, Chicago, Baltimore, York, and New York.

Q. Sounds like a good lineup.

The President. Sounds like a good lineup to me. I want to thank you all for joining me today. As you know, I have a new proposal we're going to be discussing this morning that I believe is a fundamental departure from traditional programs offered by Democratic administrations and fundamentally different from the previous enterprise zone proposals offered by recent Republican administrations.

All of you represent areas of the country that, while unique, are each joined together by a common need. The economic potential of your areas, like other urban and rural communities, is still stifled because you lack the investment capital you need and a comprehensive strategy for jobs and growth. What we want to do is to help you to revive your communities economically. And our proposals for empowerment zones and enterprise neighborhoods we believe is the right way to begin.

Federal aid to these areas is certainly not new, but in the past it hasn't always worked. There has often been no coordinated strategy for using the Federal money. Your growth has been restrained by a maze of Federal regulations and the need to appeal to an array of Federal Agencies. And these factors have contributed to an unwillingness on the part of too many companies to invest in your areas.

We're trying to change all of that. We begin with a challenge: Under our program not a single dollar will go out without a coordinated strategy developed at the grassroots level. Yet your communities enjoy immense and committed talent at that level. Our plan proposes a partnership between local organizations so that they can coordinate the use of Federal, State, and local resources.

I know that your areas need investment capital, both public and private. Our proposal provides targeted investment incentives to draw investment dollars into distressed urban and rural communities. Your areas deal with a confusing maze of Agencies and regulations. This proposal features a single point of contact so that the Federal Government contributes to rather than stifles the rebirth of your communities. We're going to streamline regulations, rules, and paperwork so that we reward initiative at the local level.

These are innovations and new approaches. They're going to result in new economic growth, opportunity, and hope in areas long denied their piece of the American dream. And just as your local communities will have a chance to participate in the planning of their economic revival, we also want to offer you a chance now to discuss the economic challenges you face, to discuss this new effort to participate in the revival of your communities.

I just want to emphasize two or three things here. First of all, we do propose to do something that I discussed with the Mayors a few months ago, or several weeks ago, and that is to focus the limited money we have to spend here in terms of tax incentives and investments on, first of all, 10 empowerment zones that will get an enormous amount of concentrated effort to see if it works, a wage credit, credits for equipment, credits for rehabilitating existing housing. With a bottom-up community-based strategy and with a lot of waiver authority, we're going to set up an enterprise board that will provide communities the opportunity to come and get waivers from all these Federal rules and regulations. I think that's very important.

In addition to that, we're going to have 100 more enterprise communities that will be targets for our other community investments, like the Federal funds we're going to spend on setting up community policing to make the streets safer, the initiative we're going to have in community development banks, and any number of other initiatives we're going to have coming out of this Government. Those 100 communities will be target areas for getting first crack at them.

So I think that this is the sort of thing that will really support what a lot of you have been doing for a long time, cutting out a lot of the Federal rules and regulations, letting you consolidate the funds that you're getting from these different Government Agencies, and getting you the chance to develop a plan to develop your communities.

I know it's consistent with what I always thought ought to be done when I was a Governor, and I think it will meet with a lot of support out in the country among Republicans and Democrats. And I hope we'll get that kind of bipartisan support here in the Congress. I think there's a good chance that we will.

Well, I've already said a little more than I meant to. I'd like to now go to our cities and hear from them one at a time, and of course, the State of Kentucky, too. But let's begin with Los Angeles.

Mayor Bradley?

[At this point, Los Angeles Mayor Tom Bradley stated his support for the program. Brenda Shockley of Community Build and Tony Salazar of Rebuild L.A. then discussed what empowerment zones would do to assist their organizations.]

The President. Thank you, Tom. And I want to thank Brenda and Tony for what they said. And I want to just emphasize that I think we've got the proper division of labor here. At the community level, you've got to provide for people who are chronically unemployed: job training, child care, and other supports. But those needs and the opportunity to meet them are going to be so different from community to community. And that's why I think it's so important that what we do here in terms not only of new investment but in letting you spend the money that is presently appropriated in the most flexible way will guarantee that that can be done.

Then the other thing that I want to say, particularly in response to what Tony said with the Rebuild L.A. effort, we can't expect, it seems to me, a lot of new investment in a lot of our difficult areas until we do a couple of things that send the right signals to the private sector, which this plan does: first of all, that we appreciate the people who are there now and we recognize that they have a potential to expand employment in distressed communities,

and we ought to take care of the people that are there now; and secondly, that the Government needs to take the lead in offering some significant tax incentives to people who will take an additional risk to try to give people a chance who haven't had a chance in a long time. And so those are the things that are part of this program. I'm very excited about it, and I'm glad you're so well organized to try to take advantage of it.

Let's go on now to Governor Jones in Kentucky. We asked the Governor to join us because we wanted to emphasize that rural areas will be eligible to participate in both the empowerment zones and in the enterprise areas. And I know that Kentucky, like my home State, has a lot of very poor rural communities, and I wanted Governor Jones to have a chance to comment on this.

Governor, can you hear us?

[Gov. Brereton C. Jones of Kentucky spoke in support of empowerment zones, streamlining Federal and State government operations, and the upcoming environmental conference, From Rio to the Capitals: State Strategies for Sustainable Development.]

The President. Well, thank you very much. I'd just like to make a couple of comments about what you said. First of all, most of our listeners may know, but some may not, that you had a very distinguished career in business before you became the Governor of Kentucky or got into Kentucky politics.

One of the things that I think all of us have noticed who have been Governors or Mayors is that an enormous amount of the money that's appropriated for special programs is often peeled off before it finally gets to its ultimate purpose by all the various administrative layers and regulatory requirements that are on the money. And one of the things that we're trying to do here by setting up this enterprise board and giving people the chance to come up with plans that would put a lot of these funds together is to make the money go a lot further. And it dovetails very well with what the Vice President is trying to do in looking at the whole structure of the Federal Government and how we can overhaul it.

And we're up here now trying to cut spending dramatically and find some money to increase targeted investments in areas where we need it, to create jobs and improve education and explore new technologies. And I am convinced that one of the ways we're going to be able to both cut the spending programs that ought to be cut and increase investment is to get rid of a lot of the layers of regulation and management that we've had.

The second point I want to make is about your conference coming up in May on sustainable development. One of our great challenges is to try to figure out how to improve the environment and improve the economy at the same time. And one of the clear areas of opportunity there that no one disagrees with is in the area of environmental cleanup in some of our most distressed urban and rural communities. And so I would hope that all the people on this telephone call today as well as all the people who will hear about this program and will file applications will look very closely at some of the environmental problems in their communities and at how many people can be put to work in cleaning those up and how that can be a part of the enterprise proposal, because that's clearly something that we need to do.

Let's go into Chicago now. Mayor Daley is in Washington today, isn't he?

[Valerie Jarrett, Chicago commissioner of planning and development, discussed the city's holistic community-based approach to planning and development and the adverse impact of Federal regulations. Ted Wysocki, Chicago Association of Neighborhood Development Organizations (CANDO), then advocated legislation for abandoned land reuse, corporate community involvement tax credits, and grants for community projects.]

The President. Thank you, Ted, and thank you, Valerie. Let me just respond to one or two of the things that you said. First of all, the comment Valerie made about diverse neighborhoods is clearly true. I have walked the streets in every community represented on this phone call today. And I remember being so impressed in Chicago more than a year ago at seeing some new housing construction in one of the Hispanic neighborhoods from a community group that was the lowest cost, highest efficiency housing I had ever seen in an urban area. And there are a lot of these things going on in our country today which need to be supported, not by uniform Federal programs.

Secondly, I want to say that Mayor Daley was the first big-city Mayor to tell me, again

more than a year ago, that an enormous amount of money being appropriated by the Congress was not being well spent because of all the rules and regulations and that we needed to focus first on getting more buying for the present dollar we're getting. And he cited me, chapter and verse, some of the things that you've mentioned today.

Secondly, I want to say to Ted, I think we have got in our economic program and in this proposal significant incentives from our equity financing for economic development. But I will look at the "Community Economic Partnership Act." And I do agree that we need to be actively involved in the cleanup of some of these sites that we can restore to industrial development in a lot of our urban areas if we can solve the environmental problems. I see this as a really big job generator for America over the next few years. It's a big problem just trying to find work for all of the people who want to go to work now in our country. It's a big problem worldwide. And the environmental cleanup and rehabilitation of a lot of these abandoned areas in our urban cities and in some of our small towns and rural areas, too, I think is very, very important. I thank you for that.

Let's go on to Baltimore now. Mayor?

Mayor Kurt Schmoke. Yes, sir. Good morning.

The President. Are you really at the Parks Sausage Company?

Mayor Schmoke. Absolutely. And Ray Haysbert, the chairman of Parks Sausage, is sitting right here next to me.

The President. I want you to send me some. I admit that I am hereby asking for my own pork. *[Laughter]* I plead guilty.

[Mayor Schmoke stated his support for waivers to provide flexibility at the local level and advocated greater involvement of the Justice Department in community policing as part of community development initiatives. Raymond Haysbert, chairman, Parks Sausage Co., then endorsed the President's community development strategy and his efforts to restructure Government.]

The President. Thank you, Raymond. I've been very impressed with the work that the Baltimore Economic Development Corporation has done there. And I know you've had a lot of attention to the work that's been done there over the last few years. It's evidence that if you've got some committed people and some land and some physical structures, that you can really do things to put people to work back in cities and in areas where others have given up.

I think that all anybody has to do is go out there and see—I think you've got, my staff has said, about 1,400 people working in the industrial park now, and all the different businesses generating taxes, attracting private investment. That's the sort of thing we're going to have to do. The Government doesn't have enough money to solve this problem. We've got to leverage what resources we have to get private sector people like you to come in and put folks to work. And I really thank you on that.

And Mayor Schmoke, I should have depended on you as an old prosecutor to mention the Justice Department, but I want to assure you that the Justice Department is an integral part of this project. These cities, both the empowerment zones and the enterprise cities, will be considered for priorities for community policing, for alternative punishments, for institutions like the drug court which Janet Reno helped to set up in Miami, all things which really help communities become safer and handle their crime and drug problems better, as well as for community development banks and some of the initiatives that we're going to have to try to bring capital into these areas.

But the Justice Department will be a big part of that. And she's very excited about it. You'll be able to talk to her about it today. But we think there are a lot of things the Justice Department can do to make both the perception and the reality of safer streets and safer communities a big asset in developing the economy and putting people to work.

Mayor Schmoke. Thanks, Mr. President.

The President. York? Mayor Althaus, are you on the phone?

Mayor Bill Althaus. I sure am, Mr. President.

The President. The first night I spent on my bus trip was York, Pennsylvania.

[*Mayor Althaus, chairman of U.S. Conference of Mayors, endorsed the President's urban strategy. Robert Simpson, executive director, Christmas Addicts Neighborhood Association, then advocated cutting redtape and implementing a grassroots approach to community development.*]

The President. Thank you, Robert. You know, I think you might be able to be a model for what we're trying to do in some other cities. But I'm sure that this works.

A few years ago as Governor, I set up a program quite similar to this in our poorest counties, and I required all of them to come up with community-based development plans and then we worked hard to try to make sure all the resources of the State were put at their disposal. And we even got the Federal Agencies involved. But I always had the feeling that we could have done so much more if the Federal Government had been able to fully join our efforts. But I'm very impressed by what you've done there.

I want to say a special word of thanks to you, Mayor Althaus. You know, we find, I think, that partisan differences tend to evaporate the further you get away from Washington. And when more people get down to the grassroots and have to face each other across the table and deal with real problems, it's obvious that there are certain things that work and certain things that don't, and people tend to work on what works.

I can't tell you how much respect I have for the leadership you've given the U.S. Conference of Mayors and the willingness that you have expressed to work with us in trying to find American solutions to these problems. I am convinced that at the very basic human level we need to make a departure from the approaches of the past. And you've been willing to do that, and I take my hat off to you. And I hope that we can do that more and more and more on all these problems, because a lot of these problems are America's problems, and they don't have a partisan label after them. And I think if all of us take our blinders off and roll our sleeves up, we'll get a lot further. And I really appreciate you.

Thank you.

Mayor Althaus. Mr. President, thank you. I have to say, the partisanship in Washington is not at your end of Pennsylvania Avenue right now. It's really not. It's been a joy working with you.

The President. Thank you, Mayor.

New York?

Mayor David Dinkins. Yes, sir.

The President. Hello, Mayor.

[*New York City Mayor Dinkins complimented the President on members of the administration, discussed the success of New York City's community policing effort, and stated his support for the empowerment initiative. David Jones,*] *president and chief executive officer of the Community Service Society, then stated his support for the President's approach to community development and administration initiatives on health care reform, job training, and voluntarism.*]

The President. Thank you, Mayor, and thank you, David Jones.

Let me just comment first on what Mr. Jones said. I think we do have to provide some assistance to build up these community-based, nonprofit organizations. And I do think the National Government has to take the lead in health care, in trying to put together the kind of system that will work on job training and apprenticeship programs, as well as trying to take a little different direction, as you know I feel we should, on the drug front. And that's one reason I asked Lee Brown to be the drug czar.

But I'm also convinced that if we do this, that building these things at the grassroots level and having everything driven by that is the only way to ever get anything done, in my opinion. You know, we've got to help people to help themselves, and that's what this whole thing is about.

The other point I wanted to make in response to what you said, Mayor Dinkins, is, first of all, thank you for the compliments on the people in my administration. Andrew Cuomo had a lot to do with putting this initiative together, and he's sitting here in the Oval Office with me. Actually, he's standing in the back, so he grew about 4 inches when you were bragging on him in front of America.

Mayor Dinkins. Very good.

The President. And I thank you for that. And let me again once again emphasize that I am convinced that the experience of New York in community policing demonstrates beyond anything I could say that if we can put these programs in place in all the major neighborhoods of this country that have crime problems, we would immediately make them not only more livable and more attractive, we would make them far more apt to get private investment.

This is a huge economic issue as well as a personal security issue. And that's why we've just got to wrap the Justice Department and crime control initiatives into this whole effort. If we don't do it, we can't be successful in some areas, and if we do, of course, the flip side is that we can.

I want to thank all of you so much for giving me a little of your time today and for your support of this initiative. I hope you'll talk to your colleagues across the country, to the Members of Congress, and again reach out across party and other lines and say this is something that will be good for America. I need your help now to pass it, and I'm ready to go to work to do that.

Thank you very, very much.

Mayor Dinkins. Thank you, Mr. President.

The President. Goodbye.

[*At this point, the teleconference ended, and the President took questions from reporters.*]

White House Staff

Q. Mr. President, now that you've had your— what changes do you plan in the White House staff to make your administration more effective?

The President. Keep in mind that, before you ask that question, this administration is the only one in 17 years to pass a budget resolution within the legal time limit. Nearly as I can tell, we have put more major initiatives out there in 100 days than any of my recent predecessors, and we're working on some very major problems. So I think, on balance, the staff has done a good job.

We've lost one initiative in the Congress that took way too long, dealing with a relatively small program to put some people to work. What I think we need to do, frankly, is to get the focus back on the things that I have been working on from the beginning, passing the major economic program, making sure the Congress will adopt the spending cuts, reaffirming that I have no interest in raising taxes until spending is cut—no tax increases without the spending cuts—getting the budget program so that we can keep interest rates down.

I talked to more people today, just people around here; I asked how many people have refinanced any housing loans or other loans that save money on that. That's going to be the biggest stimulus we can ever provide if we can keep the interest rates down with deficit reduction. And then going on to health care and passing these empowerment initiatives, that's the one we're here talking about today.

So will we make any changes in the way our process works, to try and improve it? I hope we can make some. We've got that under review. We've been discussing it for, oh, about

5 weeks now: What we can do to be more effective. After all, I just got here. I've never operated here before, and there are some things that are very different about the way Washington works, some good and some not so good.

But I think we're on the right track, and I just want to focus now on the work before us, which is passing this budget. If we don't pass the final budget with the spending cuts and the revenue increases and keep them focused on the people who got all the benefits out of the eighties, having the upper income people pay the vast bulk of the load but not taxing them until the spending cuts were in place, that's what I think we have to do now. And that's what I'm focusing on.

Q. Specifically, sir, will Mack McLarty be hiring a deputy to tighten things up in the operation?

The President. One of the things that we've looked at—keep in mind one of my first spending cuts was committing by the end of the next fiscal year to have a White House staff that was 25 percent smaller than my predecessor's. But when I got to looking at it, every other Chief of Staff has always had basically three major; the recent ones, at least have had three major aides, and Mack's been functioning with one. So I'm trying to figure out how to give him at least one more. He still wouldn't have as many—if he had two instead of three, he wouldn't have as many as most of his predecessors have.

But we think that there needs to be a little tighter coordination here to make sure that we've got our priorities straight and that those priorities are communicated all the way down to the staff, and a little better focus. One of the things that you risk when you try to get a lot of things going in a hurry—and we tried to get a lot of things going in a hurry because 4 years passes in a hurry—is that you wind up having people work very, very hard, but maybe getting a little out of focus. And I think we can tighten the focus a little, and I think that's what we ought to do.

The Economy

Q. Leading economic indicators are pretty grim. Do you think anything beyond what you've done, the empowerment zones, the economic stimulus package, has it got you thinking about either delaying the tax cuts further or any other kind of emergency push at this point?

The President. I'll answer the specific question first. The best thing we can do for the economy this year, this year, is to clearly pass a multiyear deficit reduction plan because of what it will do to interest rates. As Americans borrow money at lower rates or refinance their existing debt, the economists estimate that over the next year and a half, that will put $110 billion back into this economy if we can get the interest rates down. That's a huge stimulant to the economy, totally in private sector investment to refinancing debt.

So my present feeling is that we have got to pass the multiyear deficit reduction package, which requires the spending cuts first and the tax increases, focused on people who have basically benefited from the last 12 years of lower taxes. Now, I think we're going to have to—we need to pass that, keep the interest rates down, and see what happens.

What I tried to do was make a down payment on the jobs plan. And I still would say what I've been saying since—well, all last year and even after the election, I tried to say that we were part of a global economy, where there was a lot of economic slowdown in Europe and elsewhere, and that people could not expect immediate results, and we were going to have to really focus on what it took to create jobs.

I will say that again: My major focus—if I can pass the budget, then we will move on to health care and job creation. And I think that we may try a lot of things over the next 4 years because we're in a period of new and different economic forces which are all working to make it more challenging for us to create large numbers of new jobs.

But I'm not at all surprised. I started saying back in November that there's too much recession in the rest of the economy, and we have cut defense spending in America without offsetting investments in our people and new jobs on the civilian front. And we were being burdened by enormous debt. But I can't tell you that I think we ought to come off the deficit reduction. I think bringing that deficit down and keeping interest rates down is the best investment program we've got right now.

But we are going to have to keep our ears and eyes open, because this is a new and difficult and unprecedented time, and we've got to put the work of the American people first. So I wouldn't rule out anything down the road, but I'm confident we need to pass the budget first.

Bosnia

Q. Are there special forces in Bosnia on the ground?

The President. There aren't any. I saw the report, Ron [Ron Fournier, Associated Press]. I don't know what the basis of it is. I have not authorized that at all.

NOTE: The teleconference began at 10:30 a.m. The President spoke from the Oval Office at the White House. In his remarks, he referred to Andrew Cuomo, Assistant Secretary-designate for Community Planning and Development at HUD. A portion of the teleconference could not be verified because the tape was incomplete.

Nomination For Deputy Director of the United States Information Agency
May 4, 1993

The President today announced his intention to nominate Penn Kemble, Board for International Broadcasting member and a longtime advocate of democracy abroad, as Deputy Director of the United States Information Agency. Mr. Kemble will serve as Deputy to Joseph Duffey, recently named by the President as Director of USIA.

"Throughout his career, Penn Kemble has worked hard to promote the cause of freedom abroad," the President said. "I am certain he and Joe Duffey will work well together to use all of USIA's resources to continue pursuing that ideal."

NOTE: A biography of the nominee was made available by the Office of the Press Secretary.

Remarks at the Democratic Congressional Dinner
May 4, 1993

For a minute there, I thought I was at a meeting of the Republican Senate caucus. [*Laughter*] I'm so glad to see all of you. I can't tell you how much I appreciate that warm greeting, how very much I appreciate being here with Speaker Foley and Senator Mitchell and Majority Leader Gephardt and Senator Graham, Senator Boxer, Congressman Fazio, Congressman Torricelli, and all of you out in the audience tonight who did so much to make our victory possible last November and who have done so much to try to help us make a difference to America.

I also want to say a special word of thanks to the Vice President. We have developed a remarkable partnership. And you know, sometimes when I hear him introduce me, I really think he believes it. He almost convinced me, I believe it. [*Laughter*] I can tell you this, that when the record of this administration is written, one thing will go down in the history books:

There will never have been a Vice President in the history of the Republic who played such a constructive role in helping to advance the public interest.

I come here tonight on two missions: First and obviously, I want to support this fundraising effort. I want more Democrats to win in '94. I need every one of you. I want all of you to be reelected. And I know that in major part— [*applause*]—yes, that's worth clapping for. I'm in a little different position than a lot of Presidents; I got elected because I wanted to do something. If you don't want to do anything, you don't really need the Congress. If you want to do something, you have to have a partnership, an unprecedented one, to get things done and move things forward. But this is about more than winning elections. It's about what the elections themselves are for.

Today I had a wonderful experience. I invited the man who brought me into the Congress the first time when I was a college student, Senator J. William Fulbright, who will be 88 tomorrow, I invited him to come have lunch with me at the White House today. And he told me he had not been there since President Nixon was in office. It was wonderful. We had lunch there, and then we went up to the Oval Office and sat around, and we started talking about some of the great people who served our party and our country. And we got to talking about Senator Mike Mansfield, who as you probably know is 90 and walks 5 miles every day, one of our most distinguished Ambassadors to Japan ever. And he told me that he had dinner with Senator Mansfield about a month ago. And Mike looked at him and he said, "Now, Bill, how old are you?" He said, "I'm 87." And he said, "Oh, to be 87 again." [*Laughter*]

I say that to try to give some perspective beyond the moment to the work we are about. I ran for this job not just for the privilege of living in the White House and even for the wonderful privilege of being with all of you on a regular basis but because I thought together we could make a difference in the history of this country. If we live to be 87, 88, or 90 and we look back on our lives, we will doubtless measure the quality of those lives by whether we did something with the jobs we hold, or whether, if we are in the private sector, we did something to help affect and shape the public interest.

No one ever said this was going to be easy, but I think it is clear that fundamentally we have changed the direction of the Government. A few days ago there was a remarkable article in the Wall Street Journal by the political columnist who said that, beyond all the smoke and fight, look at what's happened in the last 100 days. The question used to be, would the Democrats ever really lower the Government deficit? Now the question is, how much and how fast? The question used to be, would we ever do anything about health care? And now the question is, what and how quickly? The question used to be whether the Government really had a role working with the private sector to help revitalize the economy in a tough global economy. Now the issue is, what is the nature of the partnership between Government and business to create jobs and help Americans compete again? The question used to be, the columnist went on, whether Government was intrinsically bad or whether it could be made to work for

people. And this crowd believes you can make Government work, believes it can be different, believes it can lead us into the future, believes we can work together. Now, I don't know about you, but I think that's a pretty good start.

And it is very easy, my fellow Americans, to say you want to put Government on the side of the middle class, and you want to reward the values of work and family, that you want to offer opportunity and demand responsibility and reestablish the bonds of American community. But I'll tell you something: It's a lot easier to say it than it is to do it.

Everybody knows the broad outlines of the last dozen years, that most working-class people have worked longer hours for lower pay to pay higher taxes; that there has been a dramatic increase in inequality; that there have been almost no private sector jobs created for the last 3 years; that even when we have increases in productivity, they don't yet manifest themselves in higher employment. Everybody knows that we had this gaping deficit that was caused by big tax cuts, big spending increases, first in defense and then when defense went down, exploding health care costs and costs to maintain interest on the debt.

The question is, will we do anything about it? Will we really move to deal with the enormous debt, to invest in our future and create jobs, to make the Government work again for ordinary people? Well, in the first 100 days, we've shown both the up and the down sides of that. We've shown what happens when the President and the Congress work together, and we've also seen a little bit of the hazards of gridlock.

I'm proud and grateful for those of you who stood with me in our efforts to change, because I think the people prefer action over inaction, innovation over inertia, and decision over delay. I believe more than anything else, two-thirds of the American people want us to do what I saw on a sign when I was on my way with Senator Moynihan up to Hyde Park to Franklin Roosevelt's home a few weeks ago. There was a guy standing out in the road—it was 8 degrees and several hundred people standing alongside the road—one guy had a sign that said, "Just do something." I believe the people want us to do something. I believe they're tired of do-nothing Government.

Thanks to the leadership of this Congress, just 17 days into this administration, after 8 years of gridlock and vetoes, we made the family and medical leave law the law of the land. That's something to be proud of. Because of innovations in the executive branch with people who never had their opinions asked before, just 44 days into this administration when we extended unemployment benefits, we did it for the first time with a program that provided new opportunities for job training for the unemployed. I don't know about you, but I'm tired of paying people to be out of work. I want to invest in putting them back to work. And that's what we're trying to do.

In record time and for the first time in 17 years within the legally mandated time, the Democratic leadership in the Congress passed a blueprint of our budget which, I want to remind you and all the American people tonight, reduces the deficit by over $500 billion over the next 5 years, with over 200 specific budget cuts—over 200 specific budget cuts—and tax increases, the overwhelming burden of which fall on people like us in this room, because we're Democrats and we want to relieve the middle class and the working people of the burdens of the last 12 years.

And you know, when I hear all this talk from the people who hear our adversaries talking about taxes, they say, no taxes without the spending cuts. I say, I agree, but that's what we're going to do. The Democrats are not about to raise taxes unless we cut spending. That's what we're about. But the difference between us and the other side is we asked them for their spending cuts and we're still waiting. We're the ones that are cutting unnecessary Government spending, and we're going to bring this deficit down. And it's time to tell the American people the truth.

The Vice President already mentioned it, but you look at what's happened to interest rates just since the election and we made clear that we were going to bring this deficit down. I don't know that they can get a lot lower than they are. The economists estimate that if we can keep interest rates at their present level for a year, that will put over $110 billion back into this economy as people refinance their homes and their businesses and are able to get credit who couldn't get it before. Just think of that.

Now, the other guys talked about it for 12 years, and they took our national debt from $1 trillion to $4 trillion. We've had 100 days, and

we've done something about it. And if we can keep these interest rates down and be serious about this budget, it's going to put $100 billion back into the pockets of ordinary Americans to invest in this economy and to grow it.

We also are working hard to deal with the health care crisis, without which we will never bring our budget into balance, we will never make our American industries fully competitive, and we will never restore real security to America's families. How can we, any of us, tolerate going on 1 more year, 2 more years, 3 more years with a health care system that costs a third more than any other system in the world, leaves 37 million of our people without insurance, and strikes terror into the hearts of millions of people who have health insurance but are so scared they're going to lose it because of problems with their business or because someone in their family will be sick and they'll never again be able to change jobs without losing their health insurance.

I believe we can do better. This is a problem others have solved. We are up to the task, and the time has come to do it, to liberate this country's economy and restore security to America's families.

This administration has proposed an education bill that will establish the national education goals as the law of the land, establish tough new standards for our schools, and give flexibility for people all over the country to try new experiments to see what can be done to make these schools work better. We're not just talking about it; we're trying to do it. We are trying to open the doors of college education to all Americans by making it possible for anybody to borrow money and pay it back as a small percentage of their income and by letting thousands and tens of thousands of young people do national service to pay off a part of their college loan or earn credit to go to college. That will be the best program we could ever pass for this country.

When I have heard the rhetoric of family values for years and years and years now, I see every year more pressure on families, less evidence we're valuing families. That's what the family and medical leave law was all about. You think people who have to work ought to be good parents. Give them the right to do it. And that's what we want to do. That's why our welfare reform program will move people from dependence to independence. That's why we want the earned-income tax credit to be increased, so we can say a simple thing to America's families: If you work 40 hours a week and you've got a child in your house, you shouldn't live in poverty. Your country is better than that, and the tax system ought to reflect it.

Now, you know it's a lot easier to talk about than it is to do, because we have to do in ways that require all of us to change. And now the United States Congress is getting to the hard part. They are going to be called upon to make the decisions on the budget to make good that commitment to reduce the deficit by over $500 billion without throwing large numbers of Americans out of work, because we have to continue to invest in education and technology and the things that will make us competitive in the future. That is the test. We know how to do it. It is hard to get from here to there. There will always be those who really don't have much of a stake in change and love to complain; who will say, well, we should do it this, that, or the other way. There will be those who sing the siren's song that there is somehow a painless way to change. I don't know about you folks, but I'm 46 years old; I've been trying to lose 15 pounds for 2 months. There's no painless way to do that. [*Laughter*] There is no painless way to do that.

This is a time not just for vision but for discipline and for maturity and for understanding that if we are going to turn this country around, as I have said so many times, we are not going to be able to ask, "What's in it for me?" We're going to have to say, what is in it for us? How can we all give something so we can all get something? How we can give today to get tomorrow, that is the test before us. So I ask all of you to support the Members of Congress with the budget cuts, with the revenue increases, with the targeted investments that will change this country and lift up this economy and keep going what has happened that is good already. We have got to have the courage to do it.

And finally, let me say that I think it is important that we do our best to reconnect people to the political process who voted in record numbers in November, could never afford to come to a dinner like this, but desperately care about their country. You would not believe the volume of letters we are getting in the White House. We've already gotten as much mail in the first 3 months, somebody told me yesterday, as my predecessor did in a whole year. And I say that not to criticize him or to laud myself. That has nothing to do with it. A lot of it's critical; that's good. We've opened the doors of possibility to people, and they think maybe, just maybe, their Government is going to listen to them again.

That's why I feel so strongly about all these political empowerment bills. That's why I believe in the motor voter bill—I'm glad we got a conference report on it—because it will say to kids, we want you to vote. That's why I believe in the work the Vice President is doing to literally not just save money but change the whole way Government operates and make it more friendly to people who want to access it. That's why I feel so strongly that the House did the right thing in passing that enhanced rescission bill. That's why I believe we ought to pass a campaign finance reform bill, not because I don't want you to give but because I want them to be able to give, too. And I want people to believe that everybody has got a stake in the system. Because if we can reconnect those people to the system, then they will understand that change is a long and hard road.

In 1918, the famous German sociologist Max Weber said that politics is the long and slow boring of hard boards. We have come to the hard part. Mario Cuomo used to say, "You campaign in poetry, and you have to govern in prose." The time has come for the prose. And people need to read it straight and clean and clear from the shoulder, with all the varnish off, as honestly as we can.

We are being called upon now to see whether we have the courage and the discipline and the will and the vision to change. I believe we do. And I came here tonight not only because I want you to keep your jobs but because I hope if we can live to be 88 or 90 years old, like Bill Fulbright and Mike Mansfield, we can look back and say this was a time when we lifted America to new heights, we met our challenges, and we did our jobs.

Thank you, and God bless you all.

NOTE: The President spoke at 8:50 p.m. at the Washington Hilton.

Remarks on Welcoming Military Personnel Returning From Somalia
May 5, 1993

To all of our distinguished guests from all the services, to General Powell and the Joint Chiefs, Secretary Aspin, Mr. Vice President, ladies and gentlemen, and especially to General Johnston and the men and women of the Unified Task Force in Somalia.

General Johnston has just reported to me: Mission accomplished. And so, on behalf of all the American people, I say to you, General, and to all whom you brought with you: Welcome home, and thank you for a job very, very well done.

You represent the thousands who served in this crucial operation, in the First Marine Expeditionary Force, in the Army 10th Mountain Division, aboard the Navy's Tripoli Amphibious Ready Group, in the Air Force and Air National Guard airlift squadrons, and in other units in each of our services. Over 30,000 American military personnel served at sometime in these last 5 months in Somalia. And serving alongside you were thousands of others from 20 nations.

Although your mission was humanitarian and not combat, you nonetheless faced difficult and dangerous conditions. You sometimes were subjected to abuse and forced to dodge rocks and even bullets. You saw firsthand the horror of hunger, disease, and death. But you pressed on with what you set out to do, and you were successful. You have served in the best tradition of the Armed Forces of the United States, and you have made the American people very, very proud.

In the weeks to come, we will formally recognize the contributions of those who participated in Operation Restore Hope. But earlier today, to honor their accomplishments and that of all who supported that effort, I awarded to General Johnston the Defense Distinguished Service Medal in recognition not only of his extraordinary service but also of all those who served with him so well. Thank you all for your dedicated work.

To understand the magnitude of what our forces in Somalia accomplished, the world need only look back at Somalia's condition just 6 months ago. Hundreds of thousands of people were starving; armed anarchy ruled the land and the streets of every city and town. Today, food is flowing; crops are growing; schools and hospitals are reopening. Although there is still much to be done if enduring peace is to prevail, one can now envision a day when Somalia will be reconstructed as a functioning civil society.

If all of you who served had not gone, it is absolutely certain that tens of thousands would have died by now. You saved their lives. You gave the people of Somalia the opportunity to look beyond starvation and focus on their future and the future of their children. Although you went on a mission of peace, eight Americans did not return. We salute each of them. We thank them and their families. America will never forget what they did or what they gave. To their loved ones we extend our hearts and our prayers.

As we honor the service of those who have returned and those who did not, it is fitting that we reflect on what the successful mission signifies for the future. This, the largest humanitarian relief operation in history, has written an important new chapter in the international annals of peacekeeping and humanitarian assistance.

You have shown that the work of the just can prevail over the arms of the warlords. You have demonstrated that the world is ready to mobilize its resources in new ways to face the challenges of a new age. And you have proved yet again that American leadership can help to mobilize international action to create a better world.

You also leave behind a U.N. peacekeeping force with a significant American component. This force is a reflection of the new era we have entered, for it has Americans participating in new ways. Just hours ago, General Johnston turned over command to General Bir of Turkey as UNTAF became UNOSOM II. You set the stage and made it possible for that force to do its mission and for the Somalis to complete the work of rebuilding and creating a peaceful, self-sustaining, and democratic civil society.

Your successful return reminds us that other missions lie ahead for our Nation. Some we can foresee, and others we cannot. As always we stand ready to defend our interests, working with others where possible and by ourselves where necessary. But increasingly in this new era, we will need to work with an array of multinational partners, often in new arrangements. You have proved again that that is possible. You have proved again that our involvement in multilateral efforts need not be open-ended or ill-defined, that we can go abroad and accomplish some distinct objectives, and then come home again when the mission is accomplished.

Some will ask why, if the cold war ended, we must still support the world's greatest military forces, the kind that General Johnston and his comrades represent. I say it is because we still have interests; we still face threats; we still have responsibilities. The world has not seen the end of evil, and America can lead other countries to share more of the responsibilities that they ought to be shouldering.

Some will ask why we must so often be the one to lead. Well, of course we cannot be the world's policeman, but we are, and we must continue to be, the world's leader. That is the job of the United States of America. And so today, America opens its arms in a hearty welcome home.

General, to you and all the men and women who served with you, you have the admiration of the world and the thanks of your country for continuing the tradition of our Armed Forces and the values that make us proud to be Americans and for proving that we can lead and serve in new ways in a new world.

In the words of the Scriptures: Blessed are the peacemakers. Thank you very much.

NOTE: The President spoke at 10:37 a.m. on the South Lawn at the White House. In his remarks, he referred to Lt. Gen. Robert B. Johnston, USMC, commander, Operation Restore Hope.

Exchange With Reporters Prior to a Meeting With Congressional Leaders
May 5, 1993

Bosnia

Q. Mr. President, will you be going to Congress to get authorization before any troops would be sent to Bosnia?

The President. We're here consulting about Bosnia today, and I have been extensively consulting, and no decision has been made by this administration about this yet. So when I do, then we'll continue to have proper process.

Q. Do you think the War Powers Act is constitutional?

The President. Ask my lawyer. I don't play lawyer. I think it's worked reasonably well.

Q. How do you think the vote will go in the Serb parliament?

The President. I don't know. I hope they'll not only vote for it, I hope they'll observe it, which is two different issues. We have to start our meeting here in a minute, but I think one of the things that we have to discuss is that we want an agreement in words and an agreement in fact. And that's what we've got to watch.

Q. Are you feeling any comfort in what Mr. Christopher is saying? It sounds as though he's running into roadblocks.

The President. No, I talked to him several times since he's been on the trip. I'm pretty pleased, actually, with the progress he's made. We're in a much different place and much nearer agreement than we were 10 or 12 days ago.

Q. Have you and Senator Dole made up?

The President. Absolutely. I agree with what he said yesterday.

NOTE: The exchange began at 11 a.m. in the Cabinet Room at the White House. A tape was not available for verification of the content of this exchange.

Remarks on the Observance of National Nurses Week and an Exchange With Reporters
May 5, 1993

The President. Thank you very much, Ginny, for that wonderful statement and the introduction. And thank you, Secretary Shalala, for everything you said. I noticed a few groans in the audience when you pointed out that Dorothea Dix worked for nothing. I don't think she was suggesting that you do that, I think she was volunteering to do that, don't you think? [*Laughter*]

I want to say, you know, I knew nurses were miracle workers, having been raised by one. But I don't see how you staved off the rain today. When I first heard 100 nurses were going to be here I thought to myself, what else can I do? I've given up junk food. I run every day. What more do you want of me? [*Laughter*] I'm doing my part.

I want to say a special word of acknowledgement, too, to the nurses who are in this audience who work here at the White House, who care for me and my family and are available to the other people who work here. They do a wonderful job, and I'm very grateful to them. And they're here and there and around, and I thank them for their presence here.

I'd also like to pay a special word of tribute to your president, Ginny Trotter Betts, for hanging it out there with us in the election and bringing the support for the American Nurses Association and also for being such a forceful advocate of sweeping reforms in our health care system. Hillary and I very much appreciate the work that she and the Nurses Association have done. And I know that she's also an old friend of Al and Tipper Gore's, and they're grateful, too, for her contributions.

I'd also like to recognize some of the other people who are here today, including a remarkable nurse whose presence in the Congress is a symbol of your political strength, Congresswoman Eddie Bernice Johnson from Dallas and my dear friend. She's really a tribute to the practice of good health. I've known her for 20 years, and I look much older, and she looks younger than she did the first time we met.

I also want to thank all the nurses who have advised our Health Care Reform Task Force and brought such a valuable perspective to that effort. You've really made a difference, and we're grateful to you.

We're here today to mark the beginning of National Nurses Week, a time for our country to recognize the services that you and your colleagues provide 24 hours a day, 7 days a week, 365 days a year. From inner city hospitals to rural clinics, from the Red Cross to the armed services, America's nurses always answer the call.

Today we're reminded that our Nation's 1.8 million working nurses are the backbone of a health care system, the largest single group of health care providers in America, and I might add, a group that will have to do more and should do more in primary and preventive care if we're going to bring the cost of medical care down.

You know better than anyone else what is wrong with this system. You see all the people who show up at the emergency room to get the most expensive care too late because they didn't have a basic primary and preventive health care package. You see the enormous burden of paperwork squandering more and more hours of nurses and doctors, requiring more and more precious health care dollars to be diverted to clerical expenses instead of to investing in the health of our people. Every day you see these kinds of problems as the Nation continues to wait for action on a health care front. I'm here today on this beginning of your week to reaffirm to you my commitment that now is the time to do something about health care and to do it right.

One of the most challenging things we have to do in this city at this time is to break a mindset that we have one problem at a time, and we'll get on it, and we'll only think about that. I believe that this country has at least three huge problems that relate one to the other. One is, there are too many people who are unemployed and too many people who are working harder with no gains in their incomes. And it's been that way for a long, long time. Two is, the cost of health care is exploding at an unacceptable rate, and yet, too few people have coverage, or their coverage is too limited.

Third is, we're absolutely being consumed by a massive national debt and a growing deficit. And these things are all related one to the other.

Now, people say to me, "Well, we just do one thing at a time." Well, look back over time where that's gotten us. People just say, "Well, we ought to just spend money and give it to people, and maybe that will work." That hasn't worked. Then for 12 years we heard the worst thing in the world is taxes; we'll just cut taxes, especially on wealthy people, and that will make everything wonderful. Well, that hasn't worked out very well either. So the guy said to me yesterday, "I know a bunch of people who got tax cuts last year, because they used to be making $40,000 a year, and now they're making $10,000. They all got a tax cut."

And what I say to you is that we don't want to just keep trying to give people things in a system that is broken. You can't give people Government money. You can't give people tax cuts if the system is broken. What we have to do is to attack all these problems at once and not keep giving people things but give them the means to take care of themselves and to create lives that are productive and good and strong for themselves and their families, their children. That's what we have to do.

That's why, yes, we have to reduce spending and increase taxes, mostly on wealthy people who got their taxes cut in the 1980's, to bring the deficit down. But we also have to invest carefully in programs that will create jobs and raise incomes, new technologies for the 21st century, and the kind of education and training that will give people work. If everybody in this country who wanted a good job had one, we wouldn't have half the problems we've got.

And then the third thing we have to do is to attack the health care crisis, because if we don't we will never get the Government deficit under control. We will never balance this budget, and more importantly, we will never provide the security that most families need and deserve in a rapidly changing and increasingly insecure world.

There are millions of Americans today who cannot change jobs, because somebody in their family has been sick. There are millions of others who have no health insurance. There are millions of others who have some health insurance but very little, because they work for small businesses who cannot afford a basic package of health care because of the insurance system that we have in this country. There are untold billions of dollars being spent that should not be spent by the people who pay the full price and more for health care because they have to pay for somebody else's health care who's not covered when it's too late and too expensive or because they're paying an unbelievable bureaucratic burden for the paperwork burdens of this system.

So I say to you, these are false choices. People cannot say to us you must choose between having a healthy country, an employed country, a country bringing its deficit down. We must do all three of those things because that's the only way we can—instead of trying to give people something that's not there to give, empower people to seize control of their destiny and bring this country back. That's what we've got to do.

There will always be defenders of the status quo. It is easy to say, "Well, let's just write somebody a check." Even easier to say, "Taxes are evil. They're out to get you."

Right now, you know as well as I do, the lobbyists are lining up strategizing about how they're going to pick this health care proposal to death. But I'll tell you something, the worst thing we could do, in my opinion, after 400-and-something people have worked their hearts out for months and months and months, is to take a dive on the health care thing, to turn away from it, to deal with the inconveniences of it.

People say, "Well, it may cost somebody else some money." Let me tell you something, all those people who don't have health insurance today, they're being paid for by everybody else who's paying the bill. What about fairness to them? Who's thinking about them? I'll tell you something else, we've been reducing defense spending quite steeply and about all we can for the last 5 years. And all the savings we hope to have in the peace dividend have been exploded away by rising health care costs and interest payments on this deficit.

So it is all related. You've got to have a job strategy. You've got to have a deficit reduction strategy. And you've got to have a health care strategy. Because if you don't have a health care strategy, the American people can't stay well, the American economy can't get well, and you cannot reduce the deficit to zero in this decade. Those things must be done together. We cannot be forced to make that false choice.

And so I ask you—you represent 1.8 million

people who know the heartache, the heartbreak, and the problems of this system, and who also know that that which is right about our system makes it the best in the world for those who can access it. We are determined to come forward to the Congress with a plan that keeps the best of America's health care system, keeps the private provider system, keeps a lot of choice in the system, but deals with the awful problems that you know better than anybody. And I ask you to commit today not to let the special interests tell us that we can't deal with health care, not to let the special interests spook and scare the Members of Congress away from doing what is our manifest duty to the people of this country who are working hard and playing by the rules and falling further behind, and instead, to give us all a chance to do the work of a generation.

And that is really what's being given us in this time, in this Congress: the opportunity to do something that comes along once in a generation to change the whole course of America's future. By dealing with these things together, providing security and quality and control of cost in this health care system, bringing this deficit down and pursuing a long-term strategy for a high-wage, high-growth, low-unemployment economy. And they're all together. If you'll help me take that message to the Congress, this will be one of the best years the American people ever had.

Thank you very much.

Bosnia

Q. Have you heard anything from Bosnia, sir?

The President. No.

Q. How quickly are you prepared to move once you do?

The President. Well, let's wait and see what they do first.

Q. Mr. President, there is word that the parliament has agreed to the peace agreement. Mr. President, there is——

The President. I hope they—I'm waiting for a call from Secretary Christopher right now. Let me go take the call, and I'll give you——

Q. And then what, sir?

Child Immunization

Q. Sir, what happened to your immunization program on the Hill? Why did you have to dog back on that?

The President. Well, Secretary Shalala says we're going to get a program that can immunize a lot more people. We did the best we could with the money we had. You know, a lot of these things are going to be a function of how much money we have. But I feel pretty good about it. I talked to her about it. She feels good about it. We think it's a big advance over where we are.

Thank you.

NOTE: The President spoke at 4:27 p.m. in the Rose Garden at the White House. A portion of the remarks could not be verified because the tape was incomplete.

Message to the Congress Transmitting a Report on the Canada-U.S. Free Trade Agreement
May 5, 1993

To the Congress of the United States:

Pursuant to section 304(f) of the United States-Canada Free-Trade Agreement Implementation Act of 1988 (Public Law 100–449; 102 Stat. 1875), I am pleased to transmit the attached biennial report regarding the actions taken by the United States and Canada to implement the Free-Trade Agreement.

WILLIAM J. CLINTON

The White House,
May 5, 1993.

Nomination for an Assistant Secretary of State
May 5, 1993

The President announced his intention today to nominate Robin Lynn Raphel to be Assistant Secretary of State for South Asian Affairs. Ms. Raphel is a career member of the Foreign Service.

"I am very glad that Robin Raphel has agreed to serve as Assistant Secretary for South Asian Affairs," said the President. "Having lived in the region as a diplomat and as a visiting teacher, she brings a tremendous understanding to the post."

NOTE: A biography of the nominee was made available by the Office of the Press Secretary.

Nomination for Director of the Office for Civil Rights at the Department of Health and Human Services
May 5, 1993

The President announced today the appointment of Asian-American civil rights attorney Dennis Hayashi to be Director of the Department of Health and Human Services' Office for Civil Rights.

"Dennis Hayashi has had a distinguished career of both legal and public advocacy for equal rights," said the President. "I am counting on him to continue his good work as part of Secretary Shalala's team at HHS. We need to continue to work for fair treatment for all Americans."

NOTE: A biography of the nominee was made available by the Office of the Press Secretary.

Remarks at the Tribute to Senator J. William Fulbright
May 5, 1993

Thank you very much. It's good to know that I did get a vote out of the press. [*Laughter*] Roger, I'm delighted to be here, and I'm so glad that you're here. I'm glad to be here with Senator and Mrs. Gore. Senator Gore, after you spoke and you said you resented the fact that Senator Fulbright was 88 and you were a mere 85½ when you went over to him, I heard him say what the crowd did not. Senator Fulbright looked at him and said, "Albert, if you behave yourself, you'll make it, too." [*Laughter*]

I want to say that it is a deeply humbling experience for me as an American to be here with all these wonderful people. Many people in this audience have made remarkable contributions to our Nation and to the world over the last half century or so. And I thank you all, as part of the contingent of Arkansans who are here who feel very protective of Senator Fulbright and feel that in some ways he is still our own. It's a great pleasure and sense of pride for me to look out and see all of you here.

I also want to say a special word of appreciation to Harriet. You know, when Senator Fulbright announced that he and Harriet were going to be married, all the people from Arkansas started telling cradle robbing jokes. [*Laughter*] And I've got an 88-year-old uncle, and for kicks, he goes out once a week and drives two ladies around. One of them is 91, and one of them is 92. And I asked my uncle, I said, "You like these older ladies?" And he said, "Yes, it seems to me like they're a little more settled." [*Laughter*] I'm glad Bill didn't give into the temptation for being settled and instead found Harriet.

You know, somebody ought to put a little levity into this evening. Senator Pryor and Congressman Thornton are out there, and Jim Blair, who once ran one of Senator Fulbright's campaigns. Those of us who grew up in Arkansas, I have to say, had this incredible image of Senator Fulbright. First of all, if you grew up in our State and you knew anything about politics, it was immensely gratifying after it, to see the way people sort of dumped on our State back in the forties and fifties and said we were all a bunch of back-country hayseeds, and we had a guy in the Senate who doubled the IQ of any room he entered. [*Laughter*] It was pretty encouraging. You know, it made us feel pretty good, like we might amount to something.

When Hillary first came to Arkansas she said, "You know, you all beat better people down here than most States elect." Unfortunately, there were two occasions when that might have applied to me. [*Laughter*] But anyway, Hillary finally developed this theory that the reason all of our good people went into politics is that we couldn't make an honest living in the depressed economy. And it increased the quality of political life.

I say this to try to give you some texture. You know, a lot of people are out here in this audience tonight who worked for Senator Fulbright in his campaigns, worked for Senator Pryor, Congressman Thornton, and worked for me. And some of us have been so controversial that we are, to use the Arkansas colloquialism, we are quite a load to carry. [*Laughter*] And I wish I could take every one of you back tonight to Senator Fulbright's 1968 reelection campaign. I mean, I wish you could have been there. Now remember, here we are, '68: The country is embroiled in the Vietnam war, split right down the middle, except in the South where it wasn't down the middle—more people were still for it than "agin" it. The country was torn up. There had been riots in the streets. There was great division over poverty and race. Everybody was wound tight as a drum. George Wallace was moving through the South faster than Sherman did and carried Arkansas that year. And here we are, all of us kids, trying to reelect Fulbright in this environment, right?

Now, let me give you a flavor. Senator Fulbright had an opponent in 1968 who decided to make trade an issue. Now, the distinguished Japanese Ambassador is here. You know, people write as if we're having bloody fights when we have arguments over trade policy. We didn't have arguments in '68. This guy got up at a

platform and held up a shoe to his opponent, and he said, "This shoe was made in Communist Romania." This is a verbatim account, right? "Communist Romania," he said. "And Bill Fulbright is letting these shoes into your country, throwing our good, God-fearing people out of work to let the Communists from Romania have the job." That's a sample of what we had to deal with. [*Laughter*]

So you know, we worked hard on him, and we got him to wear a checkered shirt. That picture you saw up there in a checkered shirt, that's the only time he ever came home without a necktie. [*Laughter*] So he's wearing this checkered shirt, you know, and we think we finally got him where he can sort of at least tolerate all this insanity that was going on there. All he had to do was kind of halfway be nice to people, and we thought he could get reelected. So, I was driving him around one day, and at the middle of all this tension we come to this little country town in southwest Arkansas, one road in, same road out. And we go into a feed store. And you remember what Lyndon Johnson used to say? If you can't look at a person in the eye and tell whether they're for you or against you, you've got no business in politics. No one could have mistaken the atmosphere in the feed store this day. [*Laughter*] This guy in overalls looked at Senator Fulbright and said, "I wouldn't vote for you if you were the last person on Earth." And Senator Fulbright sat down on this bale of hay or this—it was a big sack of seed, and he said, "Well, why?" And I thought, be nice. The television cameras were on, you know. He said, "Because you're letting the Communists in. They're everywhere. Today it's Vietnam; tomorrow it will be—they're everywhere." And he looked around, and he said, "I didn't see any when I came into town." He said, "Where are they, and what do they look like? I wouldn't recognize one." [*Laughter*]

Well, anyway, he got reelected anyway. I say that because, you know, in all this highfalutin talk, it's important not to forget that the American political system produced this remarkable man. And my State did, and I'm real proud of it.

Senator Fulbright always believed there were some things that he should defer to the judgment of his constituents on, and others that he was charged with knowing more than they were and that he should do what he thought was right. And it did get him into a lot of trouble, but it helped our country get through a lot of rough times.

In addition to those things which have been mentioned and written about, I can't help noting one of the things that drew me to him as a young man, and that is that he stood up to Joe McCarthy, something that meant a lot to a lot of us. The other thing he always tried to do was to get all of us who were around him to look at the other side of an argument. I remember when I was a young man working for him in that campaign, I was driving him around, and sometimes I'd get so exasperated arguing with him because I could never win. We just argued all the time. And one day we were in a town, and I drove back out the same way I drove in. I was going to take us 100 miles in the wrong direction until he corrected me, which meant that the professor was not as absent-minded as the student. [*Laughter*]

But all during this time, it is impossible for me to fully capture for you the impact that he had on young generation after young generation in my State, how he made us believe that education could lift us up and lift this country up, how he made us believe that our obligation was to develop our minds to the maximum of our ability and then to use it, wherever it took us. He believed in reason and argument, and he believed in the end democracy could only prevail if we knew enough and were thoughtful enough to face the truth and try to search it out. It's still a pretty good prescription for what we ought to do. He also deeply believed that the racial, religious, and ethnic differences and the political differences that divided the world so deeply during almost all of his public career were vastly less important than the common bonds of humanity which could unite us if only we could take our blinders off. He was among the first Americans to try to get us to think about the people in Russia as people; he was among the first Americans to try to get us to see people in the Islamic world as people; among the first Americans to try to get us to understand the different and various and rich cultures of Asia, which have now produced some of the most amazing achievements in all of human history. And that is one of the reasons,

I think, Mr. Ambassador, that Japan, thankfully, has become the most outstanding supporter of the Fulbright scholarship program, something for which we are all very grateful.

I close with this thought. About 4 years ago, Senator Fulbright's hometown of Fayetteville, which is the seat of the University of Arkansas where Hillary and I used to teach and where we were married, threw a big party for him and invited me as the Governor to come up and speak. And so I went up there. It was a wonderful day on the square. It was a Saturday. And afterwards the farmers market was there, and I walked around the square and talked to all the farmers. We shot the bull about Bill Fulbright and talked about his career. And then I went up to the hotel room where Senator Fulbright, believe it or not, was watching a football game. And when I walked in and sat down with him—we watched this ball game, and this young man kicked a field goal about 2 minutes after we sat down. He looked at me, and he said, "You know something, I can't believe it's been 64 years since I did that." I say that to make my final point: It doesn't take long to live a life. He made the most of his. And I think his enduring legacy to us is trying to help us all to have a better chance to make the most of ours. Thank you very much.

Sit down; we're going to do one more thing. The job I now have, in the eyes of my mentor, is probably not quite as good a job as being a United States Senator, mostly because I have to take all that criticism. But it does give me some prerogatives. In spite of what you may have seen or heard in the last several days, there are some things I can do without anybody agreeing to it. And tonight, for the first time as President of the United States, I intend to do one of them. And I'd like to enlist the aid of my distinguished military aide. Major Schorsch, would you please read the proclamation.

NOTE: The President spoke at 9:49 p.m. at the ANA Hotel. Following the President's remarks, Senator Fulbright was awarded the Presidential Medal of Freedom.

Remarks at the "Latino USA" Reception
May 5, 1993

Thank you very much. Thank you. I started to apologize for being late, but now I'm glad I am. You're in a good humor. [*Laughter*] I have, as you can tell by my outfit, been somewhere else tonight, but I'm awfully glad to be here. I want to say to Dr. Cardenas and to all of you, happy Cinco de Mayo. *Viva* public radio. And thank you for letting me be here tonight.

There are a lot of friends of mine here, and you see with me Secretary Cisneros and Secretary Peña. They've talked already, I think. I'm very proud of them. I'm very glad they're a part of my administration, along with Regina Montoya, who is my Special Assistant for Intergovernmental Relations. That means when Governors and Mayors are happy, it's her fault. When they're mad, it's because I made a mistake. [*Laughter*] I also would like to thank the Members of Congress who are here: Congressmen Esteban Torres, Carlos Romero-Barceló, Bob Menendez, Solomon Ortiz, Ed Pastor, and Luis Gutierrez, my good friends here. I also want to note the presence here of three people from KUAR–FM in Little Rock, Arkansas: Regina Dean, Ben Frye, and Tim Edwards.

Last year at this time I celebrated Cinco de Mayo on the town square in San Francisco with tens of thousands of people. It was an ecstatic day, 4 weeks from the end of the primary season. I am deeply honored to be here with you tonight to acknowledge this important day, which was a day of victory and a new beginning for the people of Mexico.

Tonight we celebrate another new beginning, and I want to offer my congratulations and best wishes to all who have worked so hard to launch "Latino USA." I believe it will be a new forum for all the diverse voices throughout America's Latino communities and a new way for more Americans to learn more about the importance of the many Latino cultures in the United States and the many leaders who have brought and are bringing hope and inspiration to all Americans. I think tonight I'd like to say that we ought to have a special word of thanks for the life and work of the late Cesar Chavez. [*Applause*]

I want to say a special word of thanks to the Members of the Congressional Hispanic Caucus; I have introduced many of them to you. They have met with me extensively, and they've helped to make me more aware of the needs and opportunities in Latino communities throughout the United States and in Puerto Rico. That's all part of the United States. I'm still for self-determination, by the way. That's my position, and I want to follow it.

I want to say also that the Health Care Task Force, which my wife is chairing, has benefited immensely from the contributions of Latinos in community-based health movements all over the United States who have helped us to understand some of the special needs that we must respond to in putting together a real program to provide health security for all the people of the United States, something that we are determined to do this year. And I want you to support us in that.

I also want you to know that—I don't know if this is a commendation or a condemnation in the world of electoral politics—but my wife and I are NPR junkies. When I was Governor of Arkansas, we woke every morning for more than a decade to the NPR station at home, kicking on at 6 a.m. Our radio would come on, and I would hear some thoughtful news broadcast but desperately want to go back to sleep. But the earnest sincerity of NPR always got me up and got me going. As a matter of fact, I was so impressed with the quality—yes, I am—[*laughter*]—the quality of the programs that I asked NPR's president, Douglas Bennet, to leave his post and join my administration as Assistant Secretary of State for International Organizations. Now, I want you to know that Doug has his hearing on Friday. And after all these years, he's going to get a feel for what it's like to be on the other side of the microphone. That was almost worth making the appointment for. [*Laughter*]

I also want to say a word of congratulations to NPR's news division and its vice president for news, Bill Buzenberg, for "All Things Considered," which celebrated its 22d anniversary on Monday, a great program. I hope that "Latino USA" does for its audiences what programs like "All Things Considered" and "Morning Edition" do for audiences all across America today. Perhaps 22 Cinco de Mayos from today, you too will be able to look back and remember what an important beginning this really was.

And let me say in general, I am trying to make this administration one of new beginnings. I'm doing my best every day to get up and go to work with people like Henry and Federico, knowing that we don't have all the answers and knowing that you can't just turn the ship of state around overnight, but believing that our solemn obligation is to get up every day and try to change this country for the better and try to make it possible for Americans to honestly and maturely and with discipline and vision and

will face our problems and seize our opportunities, trying to make absolutely sure that our diversity is a cause of strength not a source of division so that every person in this country and every child, like that beautiful little girl I held up a minute ago, can grow up and live to the fullest of their God-given capacities. That is our job.

Thank you, and God bless you all.

NOTE: The President spoke at 10:35 p.m. at the Sequoia Restaurant. In his remarks, he referred to Gilbert Cardenas, executive producer of "Latino USA."

Message to the Congress Transmitting Proposed Legislation on National Service and Student Loan Reform
May 5, 1993

To the Congress of the United States:

I am pleased to transmit today for your immediate consideration and enactment the "National Service Trust Act of 1993" and the "Student Loan Reform Act of 1993." These Acts represent innovative public policy founded on traditional American values: offering educational opportunity, rewarding personal responsibility, and building the American community. In affirming these values, the Acts reject wasteful bureaucracy—instead reinventing government to unleash the ideas and initiative of the American people. Also transmitted is a section-by-section analysis.

Throughout the Presidential campaign last year, Americans of all backgrounds and political persuasions responded to national service like few other ideas. The reasons are clear. Higher education is fundamental to the American Dream, but complex procedures and inflexible repayment plans have created serious problems for many students with education loans to pay back. Defaults are too high today—and taxpayers are left to foot the bill. Americans are yearning to reaffirm an American community that transcends race, region, or religion—and to tackle the problems that threaten our shared future.

The two Acts are designed to meet these basic American needs. The National Service Trust Act of 1993 establishes a domestic Peace Corps, offering hundreds of thousands of young people the opportunity to pay for school by

doing work our country needs. The Student Loan Reform Act of 1993 overhauls the student loan system. Through a one-stop direct student loan program, the Act will save taxpayers billions of dollars, lower interest rates for students, and simplify the financial aid system. And through new EXCEL Accounts and other repayment options, the Act will offer borrowers greater choice and lower monthly payments while reducing the chance of defaults.

The National Service Trust Act of 1993 establishes a definition of national service that is clear but broad. National service is work that addresses unmet educational, environmental, human, or public safety needs. It enriches the lives of those who serve, instilling the ethic of civic responsibility that is essential to our democracy. And national service does not displace or duplicate the functions of existing workers.

Building on the National and Community Service Act of 1990 and the flourishing community service programs of nonprofit organizations and States, the initiative rejects bureaucracy in favor of locally driven programs. In the spirit of reinventing government, the Act will empower those with the greatest expertise and incentives to make national service work.

The Act enables citizens of all backgrounds to serve and use their educational awards where they see fit. While many participants will be recent college graduates, Americans will be eligible to enter the program at any time in their adult lives. Both full-time and part-time service will be encouraged. And whatever their education level, those who complete a term of service will receive an award of $5,000. The award will be payable toward past, present, or future educational expenses in 4- and 2-year colleges, training programs, and graduate and professional schools.

The Act demands that programs meet tough guidelines for excellence and requires measurable performance goals and independent evaluations. Within these limits, however, the Act enables the people who run programs to design them. The smallest community-based organizations and largest Federal agencies will be able to compete for funding. A variety of program models will be eligible, ranging from youth corps that enable at-risk youth to meet community needs, to preprofessional programs that give college students ROTC-like training and then placements in specific problem areas, to diverse community corps that involve Americans of all backgrounds in meeting common goals.

With the economic market as a model, there is competition at every level of the system: programs compete for State approval, States compete for Federal approval, and programs at the national level compete against each other and States for Federal approval. To build public/private partnerships that earn support far beyond government, the Act requires programs to make a cash match and to increase nongovernment support as time passes.

The Act is designed to reduce waste and promote an entrepreneurial government culture. The Act establishes a new Government Corporation for National Service that combines two existing independent agencies, the Commission on National and Community Service and ACTION. With flexible personnel policies and a small, bipartisan Board sharing power with a Chairperson, the Corporation will operate as much like a lean nonprofit corporation as a Government agency.

The State level will mirror the Federal level and build a strong partnership between the two. Bipartisan State commissions on national service will be responsible for selecting programs to be funded by States. To ensure genuine Federal/State cooperation, a representative of the Corporation will sit on State commissions and a representative of the States on the Corporation Board.

The National Service Trust Act of 1993 encourages Americans to join together and serve our country—at all ages and in all forms. The Act enhances the Serve-America program for schoolage youth; extends and improves the VISTA and Older Americans Volunteer Programs authorized under the Domestic Volunteer Service Act; supports the Civilian Community Corps and Points of Light Foundation; and pulls these efforts under the new Corporation. The Act will help instill an ethic of service in elementary and secondary school students, encourage them to serve in their college years, and give them further opportunities later in their lives.

The Student Loan Reform Act of 1993 will taken an important first step toward comprehensive reform of the student loan system. It saves money, makes loan repayment more affordable, and holds students more accountable. The measures in no way replace the Pell Grant program, which will remain the cornerstone of financial aid for millions of students.

The Student Loan Reform Act of 1993 replaces the current Federal Family Education Loan program with the Federal Direct Student Loan Program over a 4-year period. By eliminating subsidies to private lenders and making loans directly to students, direct lending will save taxpayers $4.3 billion through Fiscal Year 1998 and still allow interest rates to drop for student borrowers. Many schools will make loans directly to students on campus, though none will be forced to do so. In addition, no institution will service or collect loans. This reform simplifies the system for many students, enabling most to receive all their aid through "one-stop shopping" at their institutions' financial aid offices.

The lending reform expands choice and reduces burdens for all student borrowers by offering a variety of repayment plans—including fixed, extended, graduated, and income-contingent schedules. In the same way that multiple financing options help homeowners, these plans offer real choice to all and lower monthly payments to those who want them. Income-contingent repayments—through the new EXCEL Accounts—also encourage service by students who do not participate in service under the National Service Trust Act. With more manageable monthly payments, more students will be able to take jobs that pay less but do more for their communities, without risking default. And whatever plan they first choose, students will be able to change their repayment schedule as their circumstances change.

The Student Loan Reform Act of 1993 will also reduce default rates. By electing income-contingent repayment schedules, students with lower incomes will be able to repay their loans on a manageable plan, without defaulting. Through cooperation with the IRS, the Act will improve collection and monitoring of student loans. And for those who are able to pay but do not, the Act will give the Secretary of Education authority to require payment on an income-contingent basis.

Opportunity, responsibility, and community go beyond politics. They are basic American ideals. Enactment of these two Acts will express the Nation's commitment to these ideals and to our shared future. I urge the Congress to give the legislation prompt and favorable consideration.

WILLIAM J. CLINTON

The White House,
May 5, 1993.

NOTE: This message was released by the Office of the Press Secretary on May 6.

Remarks to the Export-Import Bank Conference
May 6, 1993

Thank you very much. Good morning everyone. I'm delighted to see all of you here in such large numbers. I want to thank my good friend Ken Brody for inviting me to come and speak with you for a few moments. He's the President-designate of the Ex-Im Bank. That's a delicate way of saying that it takes a long time to get confirmed in today's Washington. [*Laughter*] I know a little about that in another context.

I have thought a good deal about what I wanted to say to you today about the subject which brings you here. I hope you will understand if I ask for a few moments to address the situation in Bosnia first, not only because the national press is here but because you are very much a part of the world which will be affected by what happens there and how that impacts our friends and neighbors in Europe and particularly in the Mediterranean area.

Over the past week we saw some very encouraging progress toward a negotiated settlement of the tragic conflict in Bosnia and Herzegovina. Two of the three Bosnian parties signed the Vance-Owen agreement. The third party, the Bosnian Serbs, signed contingent on approval by their self-styled parliament. Progress unfortunately was stopped by the Bosnian Serb assembly's de facto rejection yesterday of the Vance-Owen agreement. Their action is a grave disappointment to all of us who seek an early and peaceful resolution to what has been a very brutal conflict. It abrogates the earlier approval of

the peace plan by the Bosnian Serb leader Karadzic.

Their call for a referendum on the peace plan can only be seen as a delaying tactic to further consolidate the gains they have made because of the enormous advantage they have in heavy artillery coming as it does from the former Yugoslav army. It ignores the reality that everybody else in the world has recognized: Sooner or later, an enduring peace can only come from good-faith negotiations that lead to a peace plan acceptable to all the parties.

The international community, I believe, must not allow the Serbs to stall progress toward peace and continue brutal assaults on innocent civilians. We've seen too many things happen, and we do have fundamental interests there, not only the United States but particularly the United States as a member of the world community.

The Serbs' actions over the past year violate the principle that internationally recognized borders must not be violated or altered by aggression from without. Their actions threaten to widen the conflict and foster instability in other parts of Europe in ways that could be exceedingly damaging. And their savage and cynical ethnic cleansing offends the world's conscience and our standards of behavior.

Therefore, I have this morning directed Secretary Christopher to continue to pursue his consultations with our allies and friends in Europe and Russia on tougher measures which can be taken collectively, not by the United States alone but collectively, to make clear to the Serbs that we are embarked on a course of peace, and they are embarked on a costly course.

The vote last night simply makes this Christopher mission more important. Secretary Christopher will be insistent that the time has come for the international community to unite and to act quickly and decisively. America has made its position clear and is ready to do its part. But Europe must be willing to act with us. We must go forward together.

Your presence here, your understanding of the importance of exports to America's future, to the blending of our Nation and our culture and our values with those of like-minded persons throughout the world should only reinforce our determination to confine, inasmuch as the international community can possibly confine, savage acts of inhumanity to people solely because of their ethnicity or their religion, and to confine insofar as we possibly can as an international community the ability of one country to invade another and upset its borders, and certainly to try to confine this centuries old series of ethnic and religious enmities to the narrowest possible geographical boundaries.

That is what we seek, not to act alone, not to act rashly, not to do things which would draw the United States into a conflict not of its own making and not of its own ability to resolve but simply concerted action that the international community can and should take to deal with these issues. I'll have more to say about it later, but in view of what happened today, I thought I ought to say this.

For 59 years, since President Franklin Roosevelt created it to help increase foreign aid and trade with the Soviet Union, the Ex-Im Bank has assisted United States companies to sell more than $270 billion in our exports all around the world. And now the Bank's role in helping our economy and helping our exports has never been more important. You are the people who generate an enormous portion of our high-wage, high-growth jobs. Without expanding our exports, this country cannot grow, cannot grow economically and cannot create more jobs.

In the global economy which we now are shaped by we see a critical part of every economy's functioning is related to its level of productivity, especially in the export sector. We also know that America has some special problems entirely of our own making without regard to what we may or may not think of every aspect of our trade policy. We have relatively low savings and investment. We have an enormous budget deficit which we ran up not in investing in productive investments at home that would produce later wealth but largely in increasing consumption. Indeed, for the last 5 years, the spiraling growth of the Government's deficit has been related almost entirely to paying more for the same health care and to bigger and bigger interest payments on accumulated debt. This is a terrible burden on the economic performance of this country as well as on our future.

Finally, we have, as I said earlier, in putting more of our Government's money to health care, we've also seen more private sector dollars go to health care, so that now we are spending 35 percent more of our national treasure on health care than any other nation in the world, imposing significant new burdens on American businesses as they seek to compete within the American market and beyond the American market.

We now, therefore, face an interesting set of challenges, particularly for a country used to looking for simple answers and dealing with one issue at a time. That is, indeed, one of the great debates in which I am engaged here. Some people say, "Well, you just ought to do one thing. Just reduce the deficit, no matter what." For the last 12 years we were on a track that, at least at election time, was focused on one thing: Just lower taxes, no matter what. Never mind what happens to the deficit. Never mind what happens to the investment of the country. Never mind what happens to the long-term economic health.

Do we need to reduce the deficit? Yes, we do. Do we also need a targeted program of investment in the education and training of the American work force and in the technologies that will shape this economy into the future? Yes, we do. Do we have anything so far to replace the steep, steep cuts in defense spending which have gone to the very heart of a lot of our high-wage, high-tech economy, with many spinoffs benefiting the commercial economy to date? No, we don't. But we need a technology policy and a defense conversion policy that attempts to replace that. So we need to bring down the deficit, and we need a targeted program of investments in jobs technology and training.

Thirdly, I would argue that we will never reduce the deficit to zero and never restore fundamental health to this economy until we address the health care crisis in terms of providing security to Americans and controlling the cost. And that is obviously a big part of what we're about up here.

I do not believe we should be forced into the false choice of saying we must do one or the other. In the past, our governments have come to people saying, well, we'll just spend money and solve your problems for you, or we'll just cut taxes and solve your problems for you. Today, we have to have a much more disciplined and coherent approach that says we are going to bring the deficit down, we are going to target investments in technology and training, and we are going to do something about the health care crisis. But we must have an economic policy that is more than investments, that involves doing the right things with technology policy, the right things with defense conversion, the right things with the Ex-Im Bank, the right things to expand our commitment to exports. Indeed, the economy, I think, must continue to be the number one priority of our country, and therefore, the number one priority of this administration.

The work that exporters and the Ex-Im Bank do to expand jobs and growth is fundamentally important, because every time we sell $1 billion of American products and services overseas, we create about 20,000 jobs. In all, more than 7 million Americans clearly owe their jobs to exports. And because those workers in export-related jobs make about 17 percent more than the average worker, we need more of those jobs.

I have this chart here I wanted to show. It's the only one I brought today. I'm trying to resist my policy-wonk impulses. [*Laughter*] But I do want to—you can't see it over there—it shows that in all industries, export-related jobs have average hourly wages of $11.69 as compared with $10.02 for nonexport-related jobs. In manufacturing, the figures are virtually the same, $11.93 to $10.83. And in services, the margin is even bigger, $11.30 to $9.83. It is clear, therefore, that one of the answers to the wage stagnation which has gripped the American economy for almost 20 years now with most hourly wage workers in the country working longer work weeks for stagnant or lower wages—one of the answers to that is to increase our exports.

In the last 5 years, exports have accounted for almost half of our Nation's economic growth. Goods and services exports made up 10.7 percent of our GDP in 1992, up dramatically from only 7.5 percent in 1985, just 7 years earlier.

Your work is important, because if U.S. technology, whether it is related to the environment, energy, transportation, or telecommunications, is to secure its preeminence, it must have a global reach. Only with world markets can we afford the research and development to stay competitive. Export expansion obviously encourages our most advanced industries. I am committed to promoting these exports, and what's where the Ex-Im Bank plays an important role.

In fiscal year 1992, the Ex-Im Bank fostered more than a quarter million American jobs that were an outgrowth of the Bank's support for $14 billion in exports. That's pretty impressive, but it won't be enough just to hold our own ground. I know we can top that by strengthening the partnership between our Government and the private sector through the Ex-Im Bank.

It's helped to send abroad everything from machine tools to computer software. It's been at the forefront of the new export industry that our Vice President has championed, the environmental industry, one that is so important that I have directed Commerce Secretary Ron Brown to work with the Ex-Im Bank, the EPA, and the Department of Energy to craft a national strategy for environmental exports. These efforts will not only help to clean up the planet, they will put a lot more Americans to work.

We have several environmental services exporters with us here today. One of them, Harza Engineering of Chicago, helped a rural community in Venezuela to fight off the threat of cholera and other diseases by channeling a fresh water supply. At the same time it created more than a thousand jobs for Americans. That's just one case among many.

We want to increase exponentially these successes in all areas of exports. We can also make ourselves more competitive by streamlining our programs, an action long overdue. Right now, there are more than 150 different export promotion programs in more than 10 Agencies. They are tangled like a ball of yarn. And our goal is to untangle them. We want to end the duplication and overlap to make sure all these programs are customer-driven. We want our guide to be the needs of the exporters and the lenders.

Our vehicle to a coherent export promotion

plan will be the Trade Promotion Coordinating Committee, an interagency group created by the Congress largely through the efforts of Senator Don Riegle. The Secretary of Commerce Ron Brown chairs the group, which has been meeting daily. And once he is confirmed, Ken will also have hands-on involvement in that effort.

With the Department of Commerce and the Trade Promotion Coordinating Committee, Ex-Im will help lead the way toward developing an export mentality throughout our Government and throughout our Nation. At the same time, the Bank will become more of an active consumer-friendly bank, one that will give more attention to small and medium-sized businesses. For every applicant, the Bank will aim to bypass unnecessary redtape.

Right now, it takes the staff about 6 months to process a preliminary commitment application and only one in six such preliminary commitment leads to an actual export sale. But with new procedures the Bank will be able to respond to most requests within 7 days. Now, that's reinventing Government.

The staff will be able to process more cases and support more real deals. In short, the Ex-Im Bank will use better management measures to do more without spending more. In these days of deficit reduction, the Bank will have to live within its means like all other Government agencies. But Ken has assured me that he has a number of ways to make your tax dollars work harder and more effectively.

What we do domestically and how we do internationally are inseparable. As I said earlier in my remarks, as the Ex-Im Bank builds exports markets abroad, we have to do more to assure that our workers are equipped with the skills that they need. The average worker will now change jobs eight times in a lifetime. We have to do a better job of their education and training.

We need to become better students of economics. The old ways of doing business simply don't translate into reality today. One of the first things I did when I became President was to establish a National Economic Council. It just made good sense to me. We had a National Security Council that met with the President on a regular basis to deal with security issues, but a great deal of our security is in the economic area. And there was no regular discipline mechanism by which all the economic decisions were considered in terms of their impact on one another, and the United States could develop a coherent policy.

Today, we have that mechanism, and it works. It works well, and we're working hard to make it work better.

One of the reasons I was so gratified to get congressional approval of the overall budget plan that I presented in record time—it was the first time in 17 years that Congress had passed a budget resolution within the legal mandate— which reduces the deficit by over $500 billion through spending cuts and tax increases. And there will not be one without the other, I can tell you that; I'm not about to raise your taxes unless the spending cuts are there first. There will be no budget without both.

This is very important in the export area. I can't tell you how many years—you probably know this as well as I do—how many years the United States would show up at some meeting of the G–7 or another international meeting and all of our trading partners would spend all their time telling us that we ought to get our financial house in order, we ought to bring our deficit down, we ought to do something to clean up our own backyard before we lectured our trading partners about changes in policy.

But now we're in a different position. When I go to the G–7 meeting in July in Tokyo, the United States will be a success story in the making. For starters, we have a responsible budget plan that does reduce the deficit. Our interest rates as a result have fallen in many areas to historic lows, allowing American homeowners and businesses to refinance with ways that, if we can keep these rates down for a year, virtually all economists concede will put $100 billion-plus back into this economy, simply because of lower interest rates.

In this room today I bet there are scores of people who have refinanced their home mortgages or been able to have lower business loans as a result of these interest rates. This is the ultimate stimulus for the American economy if we can pass the budget that reduces the deficit and keep these rates down. It is very, very important.

When we can point to these accomplishments it makes it much easier for us to work with the Japanese in getting them to stimulate their economy and buy more exports. It makes it much easier for us to argue to our friends in Germany that it's a good thing to keep bringing interest rates down. It makes it easier to try to help work together with a coordinated economic policy to lift the world out of the economic stagnation that we now see in Europe and the Pacific, as well as in North America.

These things are very, very important. But there is more that we have to do. After 7 years of talks, I would very much like to see a successful completion of the Uruguay round of the GATT by December the 15th. World economic prosperity depends on it. It's the foundation of the global trading system. A few days ago, I met with the Finance Ministers and the Central Bankers of the G–7 nations, and I told them that the United States was prepared to make extraordinary efforts to complete the Uruguay round successfully, that we were willing to go the extra mile in doing that, but we needed their help and support. And I hope we will get it.

The GATT agreement would be a blessing for the United States exporters because it will lower foreign tariffs, curb subsidies that tilt the playing field, and strengthen the protection of intellectual property, the piracy of which costs our companies about $60 billion a year. In the GATT and in all of our trade talks, we have put our trading partners on notice that I expect access to their markets comparable to the access we want to extend to them. But we welcome foreign products and services and investments here, as long as our products, services, and investments have a chance to be welcomed in other countries as well. It's fair, and it's good business.

These are the principles that will underscore not only our multilateral but our bilateral relationships as well. With the right markets at home and the right rules in international markets, our export opportunities are virtually limitless.

I want to say a special word about our opportunities in our own backyard in Latin America. Latin America is reining in its debt and what is emerging from a more stable economy is a populace clamoring for consumer products and entrepreneurs who are shopping for capital goods. It's a market for our exports that is growing at 3 times the rate of any other market in the world. That is why I strongly support the North American Free Trade Agreement, with the supplemental agreements we are presently negotiating with Canada and Mexico relating to labor and the environment.

NAFTA will help us to unlock a market that will create hundreds of thousands of high-paying jobs. And NAFTA, therefore is a high priority for this administration. The reason it is so controversial is that the American people have seen 12 years in which their wages have gone down and 3 years in which we actually have fewer private sector jobs. And everybody is afraid of change. But the only way a rich country can grow richer is by exporting more and by having more partners in economic progress. And if we can make this agreement with Mexico work, then we can move forward to the other market economies of Latin America, to Chile, to Argentina, to any number of other nations who want to be a part of this kind of partnership. I think it is very, very important.

Just listen to this: Exports to Canada already support 1.5 million American jobs. And in the past 5 years, the number of American jobs tied to Mexico have grown from 300,000 to 700,000 jobs, almost exclusively because of the unilateral reduction of trade restrictions by Mexico, which have allowed the volume of trade two-ways to go up and the trade deficit to be erased. These are very encouraging signs. We project another 200,000 good jobs if we can have a successful implementation of the NAFTA process.

Mexico is a valued customer for another reason. We also believe that this new economic thinking, if it works, will help to spread all across the developing world. We know that there are an impressive array of political and economic leaders in Mexico, and I know that the Secretary of Finance Pedro Aspe is with us today. I want to welcome him and extend my best wishes to President Salinas for our emerging partnership.

Outside this hemisphere, I think we have to look increasingly to the newly industrializing countries of Asia. I know we have someone here from Indonesia. Indonesia is the fifth biggest country in the world. Indonesia is now the leader of the nonaligned nations. They have a resolution on Bosnia actually being debated in the Untied Nations today. Maybe they can figure out how to do a better job with this.

We have enormous opportunities there. When I go to the G–7 meeting in Japan, I'm going to meet with the President of Indonesia to send a signal to the nonaligned nations, to the emerging nations of the world, that the United States wants to be their partner in new trade relations, that there are all kinds of things that we can continue to do that we have not done before.

Finally, let me say just a little word about

Russia. The Bank is now setting out to do what it was originally set up to do because Russia may be able to absorb its efforts. To date, the Bank has approved $205 million in final commitments to Russia. It's working on an oil and gas agreement framework that could support as much as $2 billion in American goods and services for Russia's energy sector. As I told President Yeltsin when we met in Vancouver, the United States once had a famous citizen named Willie Sutton who was asked why he was devoting his entire life to robbing banks, and he said, "Because that's where the money is." [*Laughter*] In Russia, energy is where the money is. If we can work it out, we can make a huge partnership there in ways that are enormously beneficial for the American economy and good for the Russians as well.

At different junctures in this century, our country has shown itself to be a catalyst for global reform. We have faced off facism and communism. We helped to build the international institutions after World War II that made so many good things happen in the noncommunist world and now, because of the collapse of communism, are coming into their own with the real potential to fully flower.

The world of tomorrow will reward those of us who not only have the values which made these institutions possible but which behave in ways that will be rewarded in the hard glare of international economic competition.

I just saw today another set of figures showing that in the first quarter of this year, there was another huge increase in productivity in the American manufacturing sector. We want those manufacturers who are increasing their productivity. We want their workers who are the source of that increased productivity to be rewarded. I am convinced that the only way we can do it is by opening markets to the United States and giving the American people the chance to enjoy the benefits, the fruits of their labor and giving other countries the chance to grow through mutual trade and development.

You are on the frontlines of that. I came here to salute you and to assure you that through the Ex-Im Bank and every other means at this administration's command we will do our best to have the kind of trade policy that will grow the American economy and benefit the entire world.

Thank you very much.

NOTE: The President spoke at 11:02 a.m. at the J.W. Marriott. In his remarks, he referred to Radovan Karadzic, leader of the Bosnian Serbs.

Exchange With Reporters on Bosnia
May 6, 1993

Q. Mr. President, the Serbs are now saying that they're going to cut off all but humanitarian supplies to the Bosnians. Do you have any reaction to that?

The President. Well, that would be a good start. We'll see. We're working today on a lot of options. I want to see what happens over the next few days.

Q. Have you gotten back to the Europeans, sir?

The President. Oh, of course.

Q. Today I mean, with either Mitterrand or Major?

The President. I talked with President Mitterrand today.

Q. Mr. President, is military action inevitable at this point? Do you have to do something like that?

The President. I don't want to say anything else. You know what we're doing, and the Christopher mission is proceeding. And I don't have anything to add to what I said earlier except any welcome signs would be welcome. Let's see if anybody changes their conduct.

Q. It doesn't sound like you're getting a lot of welcoming from the Europeans on the Christopher mission.

The President. Oh, I have talked to Mitterrand today. We'll see what happens.

NOTE: The exchange began at 4 p.m. in the Oval

Office at the White House, at a meeting with former baseball player Stan Musial. A tape was not available for verification of the content of this exchange.

Exchange With Reporters on Health Care Reform
May 6, 1993

Q. Mr. Clinton, has your health care program slipped into June?

The President. No. What do you mean "slipped into June"?

Q. The announcement of it.

The President. I don't know when we're going to announce it. We haven't decided exactly. But we're working on it. The most important thing is we're going to finish, outline the details on time. Then we're going to—and one more round of extensive consultations. When we come forward with it depends in part on how we're doing with the consultations. You know, I had lunch today with leading Republican Senators and Members of Congress. We'll just see what happens.

But the critical thing is, we want to introduce it and reveal it in time to make sure it is considered this year. The American people need health security. We need to control the cost of the health care system. We need to be able to guarantee that the American people are not going to lose their health coverage if some misfortune befalls them. And we're going to give the American people that kind of plan. It will be exciting, and it will be dealt with this year.

Q. Do you want to make sure it doesn't get caught up in reconciliation?

The President. Well, I think it's going to be caught up to some extent in it regardless. But I think there is a limit to—I don't think Congress can consider it until they consider the reconciliation. The real issue—it's really almost a technical one—it is at what point in the calendar must a bill be introduced in order to go through all the processes to be considered and voted on by the end of the year. No one thinks it will be considered at the time reconciliation is. The only question is, how quickly do we have to get it in so that it could actually be voted on if we can persuade the Congress to vote on it in this calendar year. That's the issue. And it's almost a mechanical question as much as anything else. But we're going to have a good program. I'm encouraged.

NOTE: The exchange began at 4:25 p.m. in the Oval Office at the White House, at a meeting with the Goodwill Industries National Graduate of the Year. A tape was not available for verification of the content of this exchange.

Remarks on Presenting the Commander in Chief Trophy to the U.S. Air Force Academy Football Team
May 6, 1993

Thank you very much. Please be seated. I want to say what a great pleasure it is for me to welcome the seniors from the United States Air Force Academy football team to the White House to receive the 1992 Commander in Chief's Trophy. With me to honor the Falcons are the Secretary of Defense, Les Aspin, the acting Secretary of the Air Force, Michael Donnelly, General McPeak, the Chief of Staff of the Air Force, and Congresswoman Pat Schroe-

der, Congressman Martin Lancaster, and of course, the Commander of the Joint Chiefs of Staff, General Colin Powell—Chairman—I said the wrong word, didn't I? It's been a long day, folks. We were inside looking at cartoons making fun of the President. That's what General Powell and Secretary Aspin and I were doing. [*Laughter*] It's all I can do to regain my composure here. I also want to welcome the Air Force Academy Superintendent, Lt. General Bradley

Hosmer, and the Academy athletic director, Colonel Ken Schweitzer.

This is my first chance to present the Commander in Chief's Trophy, but I know it's the Air Force's eighth trip to claim it—and the fourth year in a row, something no other team has done. Now, I know the Falcons are smart football players, the epitome of student athletes. But they don't seem to understand the concept of a traveling trophy. I mean the idea is the trophy should travel among the service academies, not for the Air Force to travel with it between Colorado and Washington every year. [*Laughter*]

Of course, the Army and the Navy made it tough this year: both games were hard-fought to the final gun. But the spirit and determination of this team carried the day. Now the class of 1993 has the distinction of being the first service academy class to go undefeated against the other academies. And who would have thought that the Air Force would have accomplished all this with a relentless ground attack?

In the early eighties Air Force's head coach was Ken Hatfield, a native of my State and later the head coach of the University of Arkansas. His offensive coordinator was Fischer DeBerry. When they installed the wishbone offense, they found a winning combination. Since Coach DeBerry took over as head coach in 1984, his teams have won the Commander in Chief's Trophy six times and have earned their way to seven post-season bowl games.

But more importantly than the victories or the trophy are the life lessons Coach DeBerry has taught in word and in deed. In his own inimitable mile-a-minute style, the coach instills the values of discipline, teamwork, and faith that produce success on the gridiron and in life. His guidance and the leadership of the team seniors sustained the Falcons through the challenges and triumphs of a 7–5 season that closed with a heartbreaking loss to the University of Mississippi in the Liberty Bowl.

The University of Arkansas has lost some Liberty Bowl games, too; I know about that. Through it all the 1992 Falcons lived up to their credo: Together, one at a time. Sticking together, believing in each other, taking one game at a time brought them here today. I might add, it will take us as Americans a long way if we can follow those rules.

In honoring the team spirit of the Falcons today I can't overlook one special player, Cadet First Class Carlton McDonald, whose efforts set a standard of All-American excellence at corner back. If you don't believe me, just ask the quarterbacks and the kickers who were terrorized. Whether intercepting passes or blocking kicks, he wreaked havoc on opposing offenses. I'm glad that he will be on our side as an Air Force officer.

In fact, I am proud that in 20 days—26 days and a wake-up—all of you will be commissioned as second lieutenants in the United States Air Force. I encourage you there to carry on your spirit of dedication and selflessness as you become leaders for our Nation.

So now it is with great pride that I present this 1992 Commander in Chief's Trophy to the team captains of the Air Force Academy Falcons, Jarvis Baker, Chris Baker, and Carlton McDonald. Will they please come up, along with the coach?

Let's give them a hand.

[*At this point, the President presented the trophy, and the team then presented gifts to the President.*]

I want you to know that a couple of years ago my wife and daughter went to visit the Air Force Academy, and I think it was one of the most important events of her childhood. She came back with brochures and pictures, and we talk about it all the time. Just last week we had another conversation about it, and she asked me if her eyes were too bad to fly. [*Laughter*] She really loves the Air Force Academy.

I also want to say something to you, coach. I'm glad the Air Force Academy has a coach who doesn't speak with an accent. [*Laughter*]

And I can't close, General McPeak, without a little word of personal pride here. The President's military aide from the Air Force, Major Johnson, over here, was herself a distinguished athlete at the Air Force Academy in basketball. She can still run the President into the dirt on any given morning. [*Laughter*] I thank the Air Force Academy for her, and I thank all of you for being here today. Thank you.

NOTE: The President spoke at 4:44 p.m. in the Rose Garden at the White House.

Nomination for Posts at the Department of State
May 6, 1993

The President named two experienced environmental leaders to Senior Executive Service positions at the State Department today. Rafe Pomerance will serve as Deputy Assistant Secretary for the Environment, Health, and Natural Resources, and Jessica Tuchman Mathews will serve as Deputy Under Secretary for Global Affairs.

"The global environment is one of the most serious issues facing our Nation," said the President. "These two nominees have a lifetime of experience and knowledge in working on this critical issue. I look forward to working with them to attack the pressing problems of global pollution."

NOTE: Biographies of the nominees were made available by the Office of the Press Secretary.

Remarks on Campaign Finance Reform and a Question-and-Answer Session
May 7, 1993

The President. Thank you very much. Mr. Vice President, distinguished leaders of the Congress, ladies and gentlemen from Close Up. I'm delighted to have the Close Up students sitting with us today at the White House. A little more than 30 years ago, when I was about your age, I came here, and the experience changed my life forever in terms of my dedication to try to do more to help our country work. Thirty years from now I hope that all of you will look back on this day and believe that you were witness to an event that helped to change the course of America, for on this day we seek to reform our political process, to restore the faith of the American people in our democracy, and to ensure that once again the voice of the people as a whole is heard over the voice of special interests in Washington.

Today we're announcing the most comprehensive reform of the political system in the history of this country, a proposal that limits spending by candidates for the House and the Senate; a proposal which bans contributions to Members by lobbyists who lobby them; a proposal which curbs the power and influence of political action committees; a proposal that levels the playing field between challengers and incumbents and pays for it by taxing lobbyists and not the American people; a proposal that plugs loopholes in the financing of Presidential campaigns by eliminating so-called soft money contributions.

We take these extraordinary steps in the bill proposed today and commit ourselves to adopting it into law for one fundamental reason. Without fundamental change in the way we finance campaigns, everything else we seek to improve in the lives of our people, from creating jobs to providing a secure system of health care, to educating our people better and enabling us to compete in a global economy, everything will be harder to achieve. Economic reform, health care reform, and political reform must go hand-in-hand. The system has to work to produce good results.

Today, by one estimate, Washington, DC, has at least 80,000 people working directly or indirectly to lobby the National Government, a veritable influence industry. The more we seek to change things, the more we draw lobbyists to Washington to see if they can stop the change. To be sure, these lobbyists often represent points of view that genuinely deserve to be heard, and we in Government often benefit from their views. But there are times when these powerful interests turn debate into delay and exert more influence over decisions in Washington than the people we were elected to serve do.

We're fighting hard to reform our health care system. Soon we'll put forward a plan to ensure health security for every American and to control the exploding costs of health care. Already, some special interests have gone beyond consulting about what the best way to do this is, to preparing to carve the plans to bits to make sure that the present system stays intact, which is good for the people they represent but bad for the public interest.

We're fighting to ensure that the tax burden falls more fairly on those who can afford to pay and less on the middle class, whose incomes went down and tax burdens went up over the last 12 years. And already, special interests are clogging the halls of power, whispering that they deserve to continue the advantages which have pertained for too long.

We're fighting to make it possible for every young person to go to college and to pay back your loans as a percentage of your income after you go to work so that you can never be bankrupted later by heavy student debts today. And already, banks and their allies are out in force, since they profit inordinately from the current system, seeking to frustrate our plans.

It's quite clear, Government will work for the middle class and for the average American only if Washington is free to work for the national interests and not narrow interests. And that won't happen unless we change the way we finance campaigns in this country. It's time to curb the role of special interests and to empower average citizens to have their voices heard once again.

Campaign finance reform is a tough issue to grapple with. It requires those of us who set the rules to change the rules that got us all here. That's not easy to do. Last year, Congress passed a good campaign finance reform bill only to see it vetoed in the past administration. As I promised, we would support campaign reform this year with a bill that is even tougher and better than the bill which passed the Congress and was vetoed last year. Particularly we have taken aim at the lobbyists who symbolize the reason that nothing ever seems to get done here in this city.

And that's why I'm pleased to stand here with these congressional leaders, some of whom have worked for years and years and years on this issue, and others, including the leadership of the House and Senate, who have made it possible to us to bring this bill forward in a way that has a real chance of passage. We're moving forward with this. This bill is for real. Even if special interests object, even if they try to filibuster or delay, eventually I believe we will pass campaign finance reform, and I will sign it, because the people will support it and de-

mand it.

This plan will change the way Washington works, the way campaigns are financed, the way that politics is played. First, the plan will impose strict but voluntary campaign limits on spending in congressional campaigns as required by the United States Supreme Court. Spending has gone up too far and too fast. Last year alone spending on congressional campaigns shot up by 52 percent over the previous election. When campaign spending is out of control, candidates without access to big money simply cannot compete.

Second, this plan will rein in the special interests by restricting the role of lobbyists and PAC's or political action committees. For the very first time, our plan will ban contributions from lobbyists to lawmakers they contact and lobby. It will even bar them from raising money for those officials they lobby. If enacted, this proposal will plainly change the culture in Washington in a very fundamental way. This proposal curbs the role of political action committees. It caps the amount of money any candidate can receive from PAC's. It limits PAC contributions to $1,000 to Presidential campaigns, to $2,500 for Senate candidates. And while it leaves the present limit on the House candidates, it limits the percentage of any candidate's budget which can come from political action committees, a dramatic change in the present system.

Third, our political reform plan will open the airwaves and level the playing field between incumbents and challengers by providing communications vouchers to candidates who agree to the spending limits. This was an important part of my campaign last year. I think we have got to open the airwaves so that there can be honest debate and all the people who run, including challengers, have access to them. These vouchers can only be used to communicate with the voters through broadcast, print, or postage. Let me make clear, these vouchers, no matter what you will hear from the people who want to protect the present special interest system, these vouchers will not be paid for by middle class taxpayers. They will be funded by closing a major tax loophole that allows many businesses to deduct the cost of lobbying and the costs they pay for their lobbyists through repeal of the deductibility of lobbying expenses. Corporate lobbying, believe it or not, has only been deductible since 1962. It's time to close a 30-year-old loophole and instead use the money to give the political process back to the American people. And there will be the voluntary tax checkoff, which will let citizens choose to have $5 of their income tax go to make this system work. It is entirely voluntary, but I think a lot of Americans will like this system better than the one we have.

Our reform plan won't just affect congressional campaigns. During the Presidential campaign, I promised to propose legislation that would shut down the system of soft money that increases spending so dramatically in national campaigns. Today this legislation does exactly that. Make no mistake, this legislation will cost me and the Democratic Party, like the Republican Party, significant sums of money. But it is the right thing to do.

We envision a new Democratic Party and a new party system built on the energy of millions of average citizens who believe that politics is once again a thrilling collective endeavor, who want to give the small amounts of money they can afford to give to the political process and to the party of their choice because they will know that that money will count and will not be overwhelmed by special interests.

This proposal can change the status quo. And the special interests surely will mobilize against it. They don't want to see their ability to give campaign contributions curbed. The status quo suits many of them fine. The problem is that even when a lot of these people are making their voices heard in legitimate ways, the totality of their efforts has served to paralyze this process, to paralyze this city, and to keep meaningful change from occurring long after everybody acknowledges that it has to occur in fundamental areas of our national life, such as economic policy and health care.

I believe the winds of change are too strong. At the beginning of my term, I imposed the strictest ethics restriction ever on my top officials. They'll be prohibited from lobbying their Agencies for 5 years after they leave, and they can never lobby for a foreign government. We've already seen progress in the United States Congress. Earlier this week, the United States Senate passed a historic lobby disclosure bill, a bill which opens the activities of lobbyists to the sunshine of public scrutiny. If this bill passes the entire Congress now, every time a lobbyist spends more than a small amount of money to lobby a bill on any Member, it will all have to be reported. And this is the kind of thing that we ought to be doing.

I worked for this sort of reform for a decade in my own State. I know how hard it is. Finally I had to take my proposals to a vote of the people to pass them. In the Presidential campaign, from the snows of New Hampshire onward, I talked about these kinds of changes. Now we see, from the vote in the Senate yesterday and from the strong support we're receiving on the campaign finance reform bill today, the prospect of real political reform in Washington. I hope the House will act quickly on the measure that the Senate passed yesterday on lobby registration and disclosure.

I believe the season of political reform has finally arrived. Today we are here united in our commitment to enact these kinds of reforms. We need your help, your parents' help, the help of the people that you go to school with, the help of the people that you represent all across this country to overcome the resistance that inevitably accompanies this kind of change. But when we do overcome the forces of inertia, we can once again make our political system work—work more quickly, work more efficiently, work less expensively, and most importantly, work for the people who work hard and play by the rules.

Thank you very much.

[At this point, Senator George J. Mitchell, Speaker of the House of Representatives Thomas S. Foley, Senator David L. Boren, and Representative Sam Gejdenson made statements in support of campaign finance reform legislation, and the Vice President invited questions.]

The President. We'll take some from the students. But I'll take a couple from the press and a couple from the students.

Q. [Inaudible]

The President. As you know, I favor a smaller PAC limit, and I wanted—in our legislation we go to $1,000 in Presidential campaigns, which is more broadly dispersed. I think there were two reasons. One is the House Members believe they have less access to raise funds on a State-wide basis, particularly those who come from very poor congressional districts, and obviously very limited ability to raise money beyond their States. So they were insistent on keeping the limit higher. But they did do something that I never proposed when I ran for President that I think provides an equally important limitation on the influence of PAC's, and that is to set a very strict limit on the percentage of total campaign contributions which could come from PAC's, one which is, as Senator Boren has already noted, is lower than the average that Members of Congress received last time in running for reelection. So they have agreed to dramatically reduce the impact of PAC money on their campaign treasuries over and above what they have been getting. And I thought that was a reasonable agreement.

The Vice President. And the lobby contribution——

The President. And of course, they also, the leadership and the sponsors of the bill, have also agreed to a dramatic change—I want to emphasize this; this is new from the last bill— to say that lobbyists give money to or raise money for Members of Congress whom they have lobbied within the previous year. And if they do that, then they cannot lobby them for a year after this. That is a very significant change. Did you say I got the facts right?

Q. Mr. President, you have no Republicans here. I know you have been trying to get some bipartisan support. Do you think now this is fated to be filibustered and won't——

The President. Why don't I ask maybe one of the Senators to discuss that. Senator Boren and I have already talked about it. Senator Mitchell.

Senator Mitchell. We've reached out to Republican Senators. Senator Boren and Senator Ford have met individually with a large number of Republican Senators. And as you know, yesterday a group of five of them sent me a letter detailing concerns they have and principles they hold with respect to campaign finance reform. And we're going to continue our dialog with them. Having received the letter, it's my hope that we can shortly meet with them, talk with them, and work together to try to achieve a bipartisan bill.

Q. Well, is the issue of public financing negotiable?

Senator Mitchell. Well, we think that the bill the President has presented is the right way to go. Obviously, we're going to listen to, consider thoughtfully and seriously suggestions made by anyone, especially and including the Republican Senators who sent the letter and others. We hope very much that we can reach a bipartisan agreement. We passed this bill last year with Republican Senators' votes. We hope we can do so again this year.

The President. I'd like to make two points,

if I may. First of all, the House Members reminded me in response to the previous question that this bill also does something that we don't do now. This limits the contributions from individuals that House Members can get above $200 to one-third of the total, which is a pretty dramatic change.

Secondly, I think we ought to hone in on the question you just asked, Andrea [Andrea Mitchell, NBC News], in terms of the expressed reservations. And I had talks with Senator Boren and Senator Ford as well as Senator Mitchell before we came out here. The people who will oppose this bill and will say, well, this is public financing, and we're against public financing, and we have so many other needs, how can we spend tax dollars on it—I want to make two points. First of all, this bill will be financed entirely by repealing the lobbyist tax deduction and voluntary contributions from the American people. No taxpayer who's paying anything now will pay any more to finance this bill. No expenditure now going to the education and welfare or national defense of this country will be diverted to pay for this bill, not one red cent.

The second point I want to make is this: If you wish to limit the expenditures on congressional races, as we limit the expenditures in Presidential campaigns, it can constitutionally only be done if it is tied to the receipt of public financing, because the Supreme Court has ruled that a millionaire or a billionaire can spend as much money as they want and that anybody can spend as much money as they can raise on any campaign, unless there is some benefit tied to it. Correct? So there is no way, we will never limit spending in national races unless we can tie it to a broad-based stream of financing, accountable to all the people. That's why some Republicans voted for this bill 2 years ago. They understood this—or last year. And I hope they will again.

Yes, sir.

Q. You're stressing no public support here, but on the Presidential checkoff and presumably the congressional checkoff and also the loss of a deduction of lobbyists, wouldn't that revenue be useful for things such as jobs programs and other areas that you favor? How is it not public support? Could you go into that a little more deeply?

The President. Well, that's only if the individual taxpayers want it to be diverted to that. If they make a decision to do that in the context of a very large budget, it would be a tiny amount that they can divert. But their law-makers will not divert it; the taxpayers can do it. The taxpayers won't pay extra. They can say, well, we'll spend up to $5 of our money on this. But that is their decision. That's not our decision. I like that. I wish we could give people more control over their lives, not less. So I think that's an advance.

Q. Mr. President, on a different subject, now with the Christopher mission over, can you tell us what you and the Europeans have accomplished? The impression is that despite all of his diplomatic skills, that nothing on the ground in Yugoslavia or Bosnia is going to change, at least for the foreseeable future.

The President. I'll be happy to answer that, but if I might, can I just answer—and I'll come back to you before I leave, but could we—if there are any other questions on this subject from the press, on the campaign finance reform. Yes.

Q. Mr. President, how do you intend to convince the public to spend tax dollars on Federal election campaigns? Because, back to Frank's [Frank Murray, Washington Times] question, they haven't been checking off that dollar. One of the reasons it has to be raised to $5 is because the fund is running out of money.

The President. Why don't you answer this?

[*At this point, Representative Gejdenson, Senator Mitchell, and Senator Boren each responded to the question on the voluntary taxpayer check-off, and the Vice President commented on public support for campaign finance reform.*]

The President. One of the reasons that I think people will participate, by the way, is exemplified by the enormous way that lobby registration and disclosure bill carried through the Senate yesterday. I think that when it finally got on the floor it was 95 to 2. The only argument against this will be, well, there's public money involved. But people are smart enough to know that we're paying for it by repealing the lobbyist deduction. The public knows that they're not going to get the money in their back pocket, and they're not going to get the money spent on their favorite program. We're either going to repeal the lobbyist deduction and do this and open up this system, or we're not. And I think we ought to.

Let me also say that I think one reason more people will participate is, they can see some

tangible evidence of political reform which is worth their money. I remind you, we had a big outpouring of voters in the last election. I don't take full credit for it; they voted for all three candidates. But there was a big increase in voter participation, a huge increase in voter participation among young people. This White House has already received more letters in 1993 than came into the White House in the entire year of 1992. People are interested now. They're concerned. They want their country back. They want their Government back. And I think they will seize this opportunity if we give it to them.

Now, we had a couple of young people who had questions there on this. Go ahead.

Q. I was wondering, because incumbents don't have to spend as much money as their challengers, how are you going to make that equal for everyone?

The President. Well, the truth—you can't give the challengers more than the incumbents, but—I have two responses. One, as a practical matter, what often happens is the incumbents hugely outspend the challengers unless the challengers are very well-known or independently wealthy, 4 to 1 is the average. So this will even it up. That's a long way from 4 to 1.

The second thing is that all of us who have run in elections know that there is a core, a threshold amount of money you have to have to make sure your voice is heard. After that, if somebody's got a little more, it's not as important. But this will even up the spending, number one; and number two, it will bring everybody to that threshold where they can be known by the voters and their message can be heard.

Q. My question is this: Do you feel that PAC's like Emily's List that aren't funded by big business and big corporations should be exempt from your proposal?

The President. That's a hot issue up here. The answer is, I don't, from the bundling proposal. The question is whether Emily's List or any other list not tied to a specific interest group like labor or manufacturers or whatever but instead tied to a set of ideas should be able to go and gather up contributions from people all over America and then send them to the candidates of their choice who may or may not be known to the people who gave the money to Emily's List. I can only tell you this bill does not explicitly address that.

My own view is—and I really appreciate the

work that Emily's List has done—is that you can't just make an exemption for Emily's List. Anybody who says, we stand for certain ideas and certain values, whether you like them or not, could do the same thing. So I think there's a way that can be compromised. I think, you know, you might have Emily's List, for example, or any other similar PAC be able to send specific envelopes to their contributors and have the contributors send them directly. But my own personal view is that the law should be the same for everyone.

Q. My question is, with the bill that was passed through the Senate, and if it is passed through the House, would that hurt or will it help your bill if it is passed through legislation?

The President. It will help. Let me tell you what the difference is. The bill that the Senate passed yesterday requires much more extensive registration by people who lobby the Congress, so that the press will be able to find and tell you who is lobbying on what issues, who they are and where they live and what they do. It furthermore now requires the Senate and the House Members who receive any kind of benefit like a trip, a hunting trip or something like that, that is over a certain amount of money, that that has to be disclosed. I think it's over $20, isn't it? Over $20. There has to be a record made of that. That will almost certainly discourage a number of those things. And if they occur, then you'll know what kind of lobbying is really going on. A lot of money is spent on that every year. So getting that into the light of day is a big deal. If that were to pass the House, that would not—I think it would help to pass this, because that bill only deals with the activities of lobbyists. It doesn't deal with the activities of lobbyists and spending limits and political action committees in campaign financing. So I see these two things as going hand-in-hand.

When I ran for President, I said I wanted to have lobby reform and campaign finance reform and motor voter registration and a lot of those things which will all fit together to open the system to the people. So I think it will help. If the Senate bill passes the House, I think it will help campaign finance reform.

That's a very intelligent question, by the way.

The Vice President. They're recommending that you just take one more because of the group from the——

The President. They say I can—go ahead. I

have a crowd waiting for me. I'm sorry. And then I've got to answer your question.

Q. If the bill doesn't pass, what aspects of it would you be willing to change, if any?

The President. Well, I don't want to say that, because if I do that, then the people who don't want it will try to go to the lowest common denominator. Senator Boren I think made the comment, or Senator Mitchell, one of them talked about the letter that was received from the five Republican Senators. So we will see what they have to say as we go along. But let's see, first of all, let's see if it can pass the House. Let's see how the Democrats feel about it and whether there are some Republicans who favor it. And if we can pass it, then we'll go forward.

I think the key thing, frankly, is whether you could say we shouldn't spend taxpayers' money on this when there are so many other needs. If that can really be presented, then the opponents will have won an enormous victory. They will just keep the system just the way it is. When the truth is that we're going to pay for it with voluntary contributions and repealing the lobbyist deduction that they've enjoyed for 31 years. I think if people see this as a way of controlling spending, limiting lobbyists, and limiting PAC's, then the support for it will be overwhelming. And that's why we've been so careful in the way it's been drawn up.

Bosnia

Now, to your question. First, when Secretary Christopher gets back, I expect to see him. I also expect to see Senators Nunn and Lugar at a minimum from the representatives of—the three Republican and three Democratic Senators who have been in the area. Secretary Christopher and I will meet with the other members of our national security group, and we will see where we go from there.

But I've been keeping up with this trip as well as with events and been making some calls overseas myself. I expect we will be able to reach a consensus fairly shortly on which approach to take. And as soon as we do, we will announce it and go forward.

Thank you very much.

NOTE: The President spoke at 9:40 a.m. on the South Lawn at the White House. A part of the question-and-answer session could not be verified because the tape was incomplete.

Exchange With Reporters Prior to Discussions With European Community Leaders
May 7, 1993

Bosnia

Q. Mr. President, what makes you so confident that you're going to get a consensus, and a consensus for what? Air strikes? Lifting the arms embargo?

The President. First of all, I think I should receive a report from Mr. Christopher before I make a final comment on that. The Secretary is coming home, and we're going to meet. We're going to meet with our principals, and we're all going to compare notes. I want to get a good personal briefing from Senator Nunn and Senator Lugar and any of the other Senators who want to talk to me who went on that trip.

I just have the feeling based on my conversations in the last week and the reports I've been getting that we can reach a common policy, particularly in light of the events of the last 2 days. And we'll just see how we do and go forward.

Q. Mr. President, do you feel that you could reach a common policy that would not include military force if the allies are resistant to that but a policy that could still be successful and that wouldn't undermine your authority?

The President. I think we have to turn up the heat and keep the pressure on. You know what our policy has been, what we've been pushing. I think I shouldn't say more until after I see Secretary Christopher.

Q. Mr. President, how does Belgrade's action yesterday change the equation, if at all?

The President. It's hard to say. It was welcome if it's real and if it can be followed through on. But I have to get an intelligence report on what the practical impact of that is. That's one of the things we'll be discussing. Our weekends the last few weeks have been given over to these kinds of matters, and I expect tomorrow morning I'll talk about it quite a bit.

Q. While the deliberations are going on, won't the Serbs be simply confirming their hold on all this land and killing more people? How do you——

The President. We'll have to wait, and we'll have to see. But that will obviously, at least for me, it will affect how I view this and what I will do.

Q. Is it strange to have Milosevic on your side?

The President. Is it strange to what?

Q. To have Milosevic on your side?

The President. Yes, it's an unusual feeling. And I hope he'll stay there.

[*At this point, one group of reporters left the room, and another group entered.*]

Q. Mr. President, do you expect the Europeans to come along now and support the use of force in Bosnia?

The President. Well, I think that we have to take stronger steps. We have to keep turning the pressure up. I think that obviously some of what has been done is having an effect, even though the so-called assembly did not approve the Vance-Owen plan the Serb leaders seem to be in favor of.

I'm going to discuss that with the Prime Minister and with President Delors, and then we're going to talk tomorrow among ourselves. My Secretary of State is just coming home now, and after that I'll have more to say.

Q. Mr. President, do you find Mr. Milosevic's actions and the sanctions against the Bosnian Serbs encouraging?

The President. Yes, I hope it's real. I haven't had time to be advised about the practical impact of it in the short run, but perhaps it will have a psychological impact. I would think these fights between the Serbs and the Bosnia Muslims and the Croats, they go back so many centuries, they have such powerful roots that it may be that it's more difficult for the people on the ground to make a change in their policy than for the leaders. And so I think it may be that over the next several days some change can be effected on the ground. And if it is a genuine effort by Mr. Milosevic, then of course I would be quite happy about that, and we'll see what we can do with it.

NOTE: The exchange began at 10:40 a.m. in the Oval Office at the White House. A tape was not available for verification of the content of this exchange.

The President's News Conference With European Community Leaders
May 7, 1992

President Clinton. Good afternoon, ladies and gentlemen. We have just completed our first meeting of the leaders of the United States and the European Community. I would like to offer a warm welcome to Washington and the White House to Prime Minister Rasmussen and to President Delors.

I had the pleasure of meeting with President Delors earlier, in March, and I'm delighted now to have the opportunity to see the Prime Minister of Denmark and the leader of the EC. Before I comment on some elements of the meeting, I want to describe first the attitude of this administration toward the European Community.

It often seems to be the case that there is a great deal of focus, understandably, on some of the trade disputes that divide us rather than the bonds which unite us. It's useful to recall that our common ground is far, far wider than the areas of disagreement. The United States has long been a strong proponent of European unity and the importance of our transatlantic ties. Thirty-one years ago, President Kennedy made a statement that I believe holds as true today as it did then. He said, "We see in Europe a partner with whom we could deal on the basis of full equality in all the great and burdensome tasks of building and defending a community of free nations." That same vision guides this administration.

The European Community is our largest single trade and investment partner. Our relationships with Europe are directly responsible for an inordinate number of American jobs, and if we cultivate that relationship properly and grow our trade and investment, it will mean more economic opportunities for the American people.

Even more important perhaps is our shared commitment to democratic values, to the protection of basic human rights, and to our collective responsibility to assist others who aspire to those values in their own society. We fully support Europe's efforts toward further integration, and we will work with the European Community to achieve our common goals.

We believe a strong and united European Community as a key partner in the pressing problems around the world is very much in the interests of the United States. I want our partnership to be effective in finding solutions to the problems that we face together and to those few problems which continue to divide us.

Today we agreed to provide leadership to assure a successful conclusion to the Uruguay round. A new GATT agreement could spark economic recovery in Europe and create waves of growth around the world. I have worked quite hard on this in the last several weeks. Just a few days ago I met with the Finance Ministers and the Central Bankers from the G–7 countries. And I said to them what I said today to Prime Minister Rasmussen and what I reiterated to President Delors: The United States wants a successful GATT round, and we are prepared to take a lot of trouble to get it done. We agreed that we would do that. My guests and I are committed to wrapping up these negotiations by the end of the year. We directed our negotiators to proceed urgently with other trading partners to restore momentum to the negotiations. Our aim is to have tangible progress to report when Prime Minister Miyazawa hosts us in Tokyo in July.

We also reviewed the continuing tragedy in the Balkans. We agreed to work closely to avert further aggression against innocent populations. I've already answered some questions about this today, and I think I will let my guests make their statements before we make further comments.

We discussed our common efforts to support democratic reform in Russia, Ukraine, and the other newly independent states of the former Soviet Union. The results of the referendum in Russia clearly indicate support for the approach that we have taken. We agreed that the G–7 summit partners must continue to demonstrate their support for reform in Russia and in these other countries.

I thank the EC leaders for the role they have played in encouraging the Middle East peace talks and the support they have given to the United States in working toward a successful conclusion to those talks. We also had a brief discussion about the growing similarity of our approaches toward protection of our environment and other global problems. These are areas in which we can do more together. I asked the Prime Minister for some advice on health care and how they dealt with that in Denmark. We talked a little bit about the role of training the work force and its impact on productivity and how we need it to make both Europe and the United States more competitive in the global environment. And we agreed that we had a lot of things that we could learn from each other on and work together on.

We believe, finally, that we have proved in Europe and the United States that you can have societies that are diverse and strong, societies that have a rich mosaic of different cultures but band together in common values of democracy and economic freedom and human rights. We know from the hard experiences of this century the importance of collective action in Europe to advance our common security. For all these reasons, I believe today more strongly than ever that we share a future of cooperation and progress.

Thank you both for coming to Washington. I look forward to the progress we can make together in the weeks and months and years ahead.

Mr. Prime Minister.

Prime Minister Rasmussen. Thank you, President. Mr. Prime Minister, ladies and gentlemen, I wish to join the President of the United States in his positive appreciation of the result of this meeting.

We had, throughout, constructive talks. And of all important issues, I think we have been basing our talks on openness and on common ground. In view of the initiative of the Danish presidency to strengthen the transatlantic dialog, I find that the consultations today were most encouraging. May I mention that we have underlined and we did agree today, I think, that the American-EC consensus on the need to strength our cooperation, not least on the economic growth area and the need for creating new employment, is so important that it did play a major role in our discussion. And I feel that we also, as the true upholders of democracy and free markets, have a wide range of jobs to do together.

That leads me, Mr. President, to the subject you mentioned yourself, which I feel that the whole world are waiting upon the next answer to give. We have had an extensive and useful discussion on the tragic conflict in the former

Yugoslavia, in particular in Bosnia-Herzegovina. We both confined and confirmed ourself in having responsibility here. We both agreed upon the need to go forward together. And it is my view that this will happen. On Monday the Foreign Ministers will meet in Brussels of the EC. We have seen some new developments during the last couple of days. Let me mention the most important ones:

The leadership in Belgrade have said they will isolate the Serbs in Bosnia. Consequently, we must keep President Milosevic to his word.

Secondly, this means that the Bosnian Serbs now defy the whole international community's acceptance of the Vance-Owen plan. We, therefore, do not take the so-called Bosnian parliament's "no" for an answer.

And thirdly, I think that the international community, in particular the United States, the European Community, and Russia, is considering ways to increase the pressure on the Serbs in Bosnia. And may I confirm also, Mr. President, that the effectiveness of the sanctions has been a very, very important—has an important effects, and I want to thank you for the effective cooperation on that area also.

Let me finalize my comment about the Bosnian case. We keep all options open. We must continue to follow the path we have taken up until now, namely that any additional measure should be taken and that we should take it together under the auspices of the United Nations Security Council.

Allow me to turn to a few other major issues which I think is important. You mentioned yourself, Mr. President, the revitalization of the war of the economy. I was very happy today to state that after comments by President Delors and yourself, we did confirm each other once more in more detail the progresses on the GATT negotiations and the Uruguay round should be realized and would be realized also so that we together at the G-7 meeting in summer can present some positive results.

I feel also that our discussion about Russia was very promising, and I want to thank you about these interesting positive attitude. And may I finalize by underlining our environmental common issue and goals. Once more I feel that what we have done today is the next important step also in environmental question. What we do in Europe and what you do in the United States do have important issues and effects on both countries and situations.

So what we shall do once more is to cooperate, be it economics, be in foreign policy, be it the tragic war in Bosnia. Thank you so much for a good meeting and very constructive attitude, Mr. President.

President Clinton. Thank you.

Mr. President.

President Delors. President, Prime Minister, just a few words after the declaration of Mr. Rasmussen. My colleagues and myself thank President Clinton to give us the opportunity to discussion. I don't come back on Bosnia, but discussion was very fruitful just before an important meeting of the minister of foreign relations next Monday in Brussels.

On the other subject, we have deepened our discussion on the Uruguay round. And since my first visit to President Clinton, I note that we have made progress together in terms of procedure and also in terms of substance. We concentrate our mind on the market access with the hope to finalize concrete results and to come back to Geneva through a multilateral declaration.

We have also spoken about the economic outlook. For the first time, the Community has taken an initiative at the European level, mixed initiative with Community action and national action to improve the situation of the economy. We expect more growth with this first package, but we intend to rule over the situation and to complete, if possible, this package as far as the room to maneuver of the Community and each country allow the possibility to complete this package.

And we have also discussed about the future framework of the large Europe with the efforts met by the Community to open their market to the Eastern European countries and also to have this country's close cooperation, not only on the economic field but also in the political field.

Thank you.

Bosnia

Q. Mr. President, does this mean that you are closer now to getting the European Community to match up tougher military action in Bosnia?

President Clinton. Well, I think it means that the Prime Minister's words mean exactly what they say. The Prime Minister said to me in our conversation that he thought that some of the reports of the journey of Secretary Christopher across the European capitals had minimized the extent to which European leaders and citizens in Europe feel responsible to do more to try to put an end to the killing and the suffering in Bosnia, and that as long as I was committed to the idea that we ought to do these things together, he thought we would move forward together to take more aggressive steps.

I told you, I can't be more specific than I have been. You know pretty much where I am, but I think I have to wait until Secretary Christopher comes home and gives me his report.

Q. So far, though, they have not gone along with you.

President Clinton. That's not entirely true. There has been a lot of agreement on what should be done. There is still some disagreement around the edges about what the overall specific tactical steps should be, but I think that there is a lot more agreement than you think. And I think in the next few days you will see a common approach emerging.

Q. Mr. President, you talk about a common approach. Does that automatically assume the use of force? And is the United States willing to provide arms to the Bosnians?

President Clinton. I think you know how I feel about that. I think that the imposition of the arms embargo by the United Nations, before actually this country was even created and recognized, had the unintended consequence of giving the Serbs an insurmountable military advantage, which they have pressed with ruthless efficiency.

So I feel very badly about what happened there. I think that's certainly one of the options that we have urged that be considered, and I think it's certainly one of the options that's still on the table. I think we've got to keep the heat on.

Let me ask first—we ought to rotate this. Is there a member of the European press here? Anybody here from Denmark or from the European Community covering the European Community?

Prime Minister Rasmussen. I see a couple of Danes over there.

President Clinton. Could you call on them, Prime Minister? We're going to have some equal opportunity here.

European Community

Q. Mr. President, do you understand the

many things people don't want to join the EC?

President Clinton. Don't want to join the EC?

Q. Yes.

President Clinton. Of course. That's a decision that's up to Denmark, of course. You'll get to vote on the Maastricht Treaty. But I can only—it's not for me to tell the people of Denmark how to vote, but I support the European Community. I support the Maastricht process. I hope it will prevail, but that's, of course, up to you.

Bosnia

Q. Mr. President, it appears, sir, that however things go, you may soon be asking Congress for some sort of approval or authorization for further action in the Balkans. Have you thought through, sir, what form you would want that to take and what it would be?

President Clinton. I have given some thought to it, Brit [Brit Hume, ABC News]. I'm going to be heavily guided there by the leadership, the bipartisan leadership in the Congress and people who care most about these issues. I think that, again, before I make a final decision on that, I'm very, very anxious to talk to Senators Nunn and Lugar and the other four Senators who went across the region and all the way to Moscow in the last week. And obviously, it's important that I have my report from Secretary Christopher, but I've given some thought to it. I think it depends in large measure on the sense of the Congress about how we ought to proceed as well——

Q. Mr. President, our bombing campaign during the Gulf war had only limited effectiveness. The Air Force was unable, for example, to take out the mobile SCUD missile sites. Given that fact, what rationale would there be for going to air strikes in Bosnia which is much more difficult terrain with artillery and installations that could be moved very easily?

President Clinton. Well, let me answer you in this way. If I decide to ask the American people and the United States Congress to support an approach that would include the use of air power, I would have a very specific, clearly defined strategy to pursue and very clear tactical objectives for the use of that air power, which would have a beginning, a middle, and an end, and which not only I but our military advisers had advised me could be achieved.

To be fair to the military in the Gulf, that's exactly what they said. If you remember, we had a different set of objectives in the Gulf

and a very different opponent. The land was more open and easier to bomb, but they also were more heavily armed with missiles. So it was a completely different situation.

I assure you today that if I decide to ask for the authority to use air power from the Congress and from the American people, I will make it very clear what the tactical objectives are, and they will be objectives that our military leaders say can, in fact, be achieved.

Health Care

Q. You said that you asked Mr. Rasmussen about the health care in Denmark. What about social affairs? Could you use anything from Denmark or the Scandinavian welfare system?

President Clinton. Perhaps. One of the things that we talked about, generally, was the extent that which all of our countries are now facing common problems. But each nation in Europe and the United States has perhaps done one thing better or more completely or in a more advanced way than another nation. And I think—something that's important is not to reinvent the wheel.

Yesterday I had a meeting with Republican leaders of the House and the Senate on the question of health care, and one of the things that encouraged me quite a lot is that some of them had actually traveled to Europe to look at some of the health care systems there. I think the more we can share with each other and learn from one another across a wide range, the better off we're going to be.

Andrea [Andrea Mitchell, NBC News].

Bosnia

Q. Mr. President, why do you think the Europeans have been so reluctant on the issue of lifting the arms embargo, whereas they have considered other options, but on that they seem to be fairly well stuck? And then I'd like it if Prime Minister Rasmussen could comment on his views on lifting the arms embargo.

President Clinton. Well, I don't think it's for me to speak for the Europeans. I think the arguments against lifting the arms embargo are fairly clear. You might argue that it will only widen the violence. You might argue that during the time between when you vote to do it and when it has an impact, it will only encourage the Serbs to intensify their efforts to kill and to gain territory. I think you might argue that it might make it difficult in the end to have a settlement. I understand all those arguments. For me, they are outweighed by other considerations. But there are very serious concerns about that.

Q. Mr. Prime Minister?

Prime Minister Rasmussen. Yes. First of all, I think that what the President said, that we want to go together; and that, point two, we haven't closed any options, any options; and point three, I think that the discussion about lifting the weapons embargo, you cannot take that isolated.

You have, as the President said, to evaluate and to take decisions upon the first step, the next step, and the next step. And you have to have clear political goals: what should you obtain, and what is at stake, and what is your means. So, in my mind—and I think we had a quite useful and constructive discussion—in my mind, you cannot exclude any options, which I have underlined, including the question you mentioned. But, on the other hand, I feel that you cannot discuss weapon embargo lifting without placing it in a whole range of issues with other steps. That is at stake in the discussion right now.

The President. Susan [Susan Spencer, CBS News].

President's Approval Rating

Q. A non-Balkan question. We have a poll out tonight that shows that your job approval rating has gone from 64 to 49 percent in the last 2 months, with particular erosion on the economy, which is what most people think you were elected to fix. Why do you think this has happened, and what, specifically, do you think you can do about that?

President Clinton. I think there are two reasons. One is that I've been forced to deal with a lot of other issues. Most voters in this country don't like it when you spend any time on foreign policy because of the economic problems of the country. Secondly, I think even though the voters overwhelmingly supported the job stimulus package, what they really want is for the gridlock to end. And thirdly, I think that there is an inevitable sense that things take—people want things to happen immediately that don't happen immediately. And finally, I think that the stimulus got more publicity than the budget resolution. I think that, for example, I bet not 5 percent of the American people know that we passed a budget which has record-breaking defi-

cit reduction and a long-term investment plan, and it passed at the most rapid point of any budget in 17 years. I bet not 1 in 20 American voters knows that because we did it, and success and the lack of discord is not as noteworthy as failures. So a multi-trillion-dollar budget resolution got—I'm not criticizing you; this is just part of the deal—got less play than a $16 billion stimulus failure. So I think that people only can vote on and express what they know.

I think the other big problem is, I haven't been out there as much as I should have been engaging the American people directly since February. I've been here doing huge, heavy lifting and long meetings on health care and the economy. That's what I've been working on, and I've been forced to deal with a lot of other issues. I think when the American people see that the program that I promised them on February 17th is still intact and on the boards and going forward, when they realize that we are going forward with health care and that that is, notwithstanding, what the perception is, taking the lion's share of my time and attention, and when I get back out there and engage them again on it, I think that those things will turn around.

But you know, you can't operate this job by polls. Anybody who thinks they can be President by polls—I didn't run the Governor's office that way. The only thing that matters is the polls that come around on election day, those are the things that matter. And you have to be willing to take on tough decisions. It takes a certain amount of time to do things, to make difficult decisions and to work through them, and you can't carry on a totally continuous campaign. It's simply not possible.

Middle East Peace Talks

Q. Mr. President, on the Middle East, you mentioned the Middle East talks. Do you think the U.S. should now offer proposals to bridge the gaps? Should the Syrians offer a full peace before Israel agrees to withdraw from the Golan Heights? And could you accept or see a Palestinian state eventually emerging from the talks?

President Clinton. If I answer any of those questions I will undermine the Middle East peace talks. The real answer to that question is, if those parties can agree among themselves in good faith to proposals which will bring an end to the hostilities between Egypt and Syria—

I mean, between Israel and Syria, between Israel and the Palestinians—they can get the multilateral talks going, if they bring in the Jordanians, the Lebanese, that the United States will be prepared to be supportive of their agreements. That is the answer to that. And I hope they can reach them.

Thank you very much.

NOTE: The President's 14th news conference began at 2:03 p.m. on the South Lawn at the White House. In his remarks, he referred to Slobodon Milosevic, President of Serbia.

Nomination for the Board of Directors of the Tennessee Valley Authority
May 7, 1993

The President announced his intention today to nominate two Tennesseans, Johnny Hayes and Craven Crowell, to serve as members of the Board of Directors of the Tennessee Valley Authority. Following his confirmation, Mr. Crowell will be designated by the President as Chairman of the Board.

"The Tennessee Valley Authority is one of the great success stories of the 20th century," said the President. "It transformed the life of an entire region, and still has tremendous impact today. Through their years of service to their State and their Nation, Johnny Hayes and Craven Crowell have proven themselves capable of exercising stewardship over this important institution."

NOTE: Biographies of the nominees were made available by the Office of the Press Secretary.

Nomination for the National Council on Disability
May 7, 1993

The President announced today that he intends to nominate five new members to the National Council on Disability and that he has approved the nomination for reappointment of two others.

"I am pleased to announce these additions to the National Council on Disability," said the President. "With the passage of the Americans with Disabilities Act, people with disabilities are now able to fully participate in our society. These outstanding people will ensure that all Americans are judged by their abilities, not their disabilities."

Among those the President will nominate is Marca Bristo, the president and executive director of Access Living of Metropolitan Chicago. Following her confirmation and appointment, Bristo will be designated by the President as Chair of the Commission.

The other new members the President will nominate are:

Michelle Alioto, television director, producer, writer, and host, and cofounder of the American Paralysis Association

Bonnie O'Day, executive director, Boston Center for Independent Living;

Hughey Walker, chairman, Georgetown (SC) County Council

Katie Pew Wolters, executive director, Steelcase Foundation, and member, Michigan Developmental Disabilities Council

The members being nominated for reappointment are:

John Anthony Gannon, president emeritus, International Association of Fire Fighters, and founder, John A. Gannon and Associates

Lawrence Brown, Jr., business and community relations manager, Xerox, and former running back for the Washington Redskins

The President's Radio Address
May 8, 1993

Good morning. In the early days of our administration we've moved quickly to deal with the problems that concern you most. Our endeavors are ambitious and none will be accomplished easily, some will require time and repeated struggle. But all of them relate directly to improving our economy, to creating more jobs and better incomes and opportunity for hard-pressed working families.

Many of the efforts we're making are opposed by lobbyists, defenders of the status quo and special interests. We're fighting, after all, to do something that no generation of Americans has had to do before: to make dramatic reductions in the Federal deficit, even as we ask for new, very targeted investments in the education and training of our people, in incentives for our industries, in new technologies for new jobs in the 21st century.

Many special interests are trying to stop our every move. They don't believe in a program which cuts spending in areas they don't want to have spending cuts or which raises most of the tax burden from wealthy people whose incomes went up and taxes went down in the eighties, while the middle class paid more in taxes while their incomes went down. We want to reverse that, but most working people don't have lobbyists here to help them.

We're fighting hard to reform our health care system. And soon, we'll put forward a plan to provide real security and health care for every American family. And already, special interests are trying to carve the plan to bits.

We're trying to make it possible for every young person to go to college, to borrow the money that he or she needs and then to pay it back as a small portion of their incomes after they go to work. And already, banks and their allies are out in force since they make enormous profits from the current student loan system, even though it imposes great burdens on many students.

Well, this is what always happens in Washington. Narrow interests exercise powerful influence. They try to stop reform, delay change, deny progress, simply because they profit from the status quo. Because big money and the special access it buys are the problem, we have

to reform the political system even as we try to improve the economy, and open opportunities to all our people.

Unless we change fundamentally the way campaigns are financed, everything else we seek to do to improve the lives of our people will be much harder to achieve. Economic reform and reform of the political system go hand-in-hand. It's time to curb the role of special interests and to empower average citizens in the way our country is governed.

Yesterday I announced a comprehensive campaign finance reform proposal, a proposal to reform the political process, restore faith in our democracy, and ensure once again that the voice of the people is heard over the voices of special interests. The plan will change the way Washington works, the way campaigns are financed, and the way the game of politics is played. Here's how it will work: First, it will impose strict spending limits on congressional campaigns. Spending has gone up too far and too fast. When spending is out of control, candidates who lack access to big money simply can't compete. In the last 2-year election cycle, spending on congressional campaigns increased by 50 percent over the previous 2 years.

Second, this plan will rein in the special interests by restricting the role of lobbyists and PAC's, political action committees. For the very first time, our plan will ban contributions from lobbyists to the lawmakers they lobby. It will bar lobbyists from raising money for the lawmakers that they lobby. If adopted, believe me, this proposal will change the culture of Washington. And it will curb the role of political action committees. We want to cap the amount of money any candidate can receive from PAC's. And we'll limit PAC contributions to $1,000 for Presidential candidates and $2,500 for Senate candidates.

Third, our political reform plan will open the airwaves and level the playing field between incumbents and challengers by providing access to the broad airwaves, for candidates who agree to the spending limits.

Let me make this clear, this broadcast time will not be paid for by middle class taxpayers. It will be funded by repealing a major tax loophole that allows many businesses to deduct the cost of their lobbyists. Corporate lobbying has only been deductible since 1962. We can close that loophole and use that money to open the airwaves to all candidates.

This proposal will change the status quo. And, believe me, the special interests will mobilize against it. They don't want to see their ability to give or to raise campaign contributions curbed. They don't want to see the influence of PAC's curbed. They don't want to see limits on election spending.

But Government will work only for middle class America, if Washington works in the national interest and not just for narrow interests. And that won't happen unless we change the way we finance campaigns in this country.

This political reform bill is for real. It goes hand-in-hand with another bill we're supporting, which has already passed the United States Senate. That bill requires all lobbyists to register and now requires them to report all the money they spend on particular Members of Congress to try to influence or support their causes. And even if the special interests object to these efforts, even if they try to filibuster this campaign finance reform legislation or delay, I believe we will pass it. And I'll sign it because I think you will support it.

When all is said and done, this issue is really about our liberty. It's a matter of preserving our personal freedoms and expanding our opportunity by revitalizing the political freedoms on which they rest. To create jobs, as we must, to increase incomes, to make our health care system better, to open more educational opportunities, we need a democracy where more, not fewer, Americans play a role and have a real say in the decisions that powerfully affect their lives.

Last November, we had a huge increase in turnout, especially among our young people. Since then, I have received more letters in the first 3½ months of my first year than my predecessor did in the entire year of 1992. The American people want to be heard in their political system. If you want to do it, we've got to pass the lobbying bill and we've got to pass this campaign finance reform bill which will pay for equal access through lobbying contributions, control the influence of lobbyists, limit PAC's, and limit campaign spending.

These are changes I'm fighting for. But they won't happen unless you'll fight for them, too. If you'll help we can win this battle and we can keep turning America around.

Thanks for listening.

NOTE: The President spoke at 10:06 a.m. from the Oval Office at the White House.

Remarks to the Community in Cleveland, Ohio
May 10, 1993

Thank you very much. Thank you, Congressman Stokes, Senator Metzenbaum. I want to thank Lou Stokes and Howard Metzenbaum for the support that they have given to this administration to making a new beginning for America, to putting the American people back to work, and to giving Washington back to you.

I also want to say a special word of thanks to my friend Eric Fingerhut for coming here, the leader of the freshmen in Congress and a great Representative, someone who believes in the cause of reform. I want to thank your fine Mayor, Mike White, who labored mightily to try to get some more money for jobs here in Cleveland.

I wish people all over America who think that our cities aren't working would come to Cleveland and see houses being built, the stadium going up, new malls being built, and things happening. I think it is very, very impressive what is happening here under the leadership of Mike White. And I appreciate him very much.

I also want to thank Congressman Hoke for coming here. I'm glad to see a bipartisan Representative. I'm trying to govern in a bipartisan way, and some of those fellows in the Senate don't want me to. But if we get together on America's problems as America, we'd do a lot better than pointing partisan fingers.

Finally, I want to thank attorney general Lee Fisher and your State treasurer, Mary Ellen

Withrow. And I want to say a special word of thanks to Lee for his leadership in our campaign last year. I haven't been to Cleveland since the day before the election—that's right, that's what Lou said. I have been to Ohio once since I've been President. I look forward to coming back.

I want to talk to you a little today about why I came to the middle of the country in the middle of the day to reiterate what is at stake in Washington. I just walked through the Galleria here. I want to thank the people who opened it up to me and Mr. Cleary and Mr. Masters. I want to thank all the store owners who came out to see me. Some of them gave me some things and some of them sold me some things, which is, after all, the most important thing. They did a good job.

I wanted to come back here to remind you that the reason I did all that work last year and came here and asked the people of Ohio and Cleveland to vote for me was not so I could live in the White House but so I could give the Government back to you.

The struggles in which we are engaged now are very important ones. It may seem strange to you, but there are really people in Washington who believe the most important thing we can do is to avoid change at all costs. It may seem strange to you after years of living with a Government where the debt of this country went from $1 trillion to $4 trillion between 1980 and 1992, where unemployment went up and wages went down and we began to lose our competitive position, where we cut defense but had no plan to put our defense workers to work building the domestic economy, with all the troubles we've got, where we've got 37 million Americans with no health insurance and others in small businesses terrified they're going to lose it and people who can't change jobs because they've had somebody in their family sick and they know they can't get health insurance in a new place, it may seem strange to you, but there really are people in the Nation's Capital who say no more change. Well, I think most of you want us to do something, and I think you want us to be bold. I think you want us to try to turn this country around, and I think you would rather see us err on the side of effort than on the side of just preserving the status quo.

You look at these children here, these schoolchildren, or those fine schoolchildren back there or these young naval cadets. This whole deal is about whether they are going to have the American dream, about whether people who work hard and play by the rules are going to wind up better off or worse off.

We've got a lot of complicated problems. I knew when I got there it wasn't going to happen overnight. I tried to make it happen overnight. I've been criticized for doing more than one thing at once. I've always felt—can you do one thing at once? Wouldn't it be nice if all you had to do was go to work and not take care of your family? Wouldn't it be nice if you could pay your bills and not earn any money to pay them? I don't understand this whole—you can't do one thing at once. But anyway, that's what they say.

We are trying to do a lot of things, but they all relate to restoring the economic vitality of this country and restoring the middle class and the values of the middle class to a central part in American life. That is what this whole economic program is about and what I came to talk to you about again today.

No one said it would be easy, but it has been immensely rewarding. In about 110 days, after two vetoes, I can look back and say we signed the Family and Medical Leave Act to guarantee you don't lose your job if you've got somebody sick in your family. We have put forward comprehensive plans to use technology to generate new jobs, comprehensive plans to help move people from defense jobs into domestic jobs and to make sure that our young people who come out of the service after serving this country are not just left out in the cold because of the cutbacks. And we got a record approval of the outline of a budget that cuts the deficit of this country over $500 billion in the next 5 years with over 200 specific budget cuts and, yes, with some tax increases. Seventy percent of them fall on the upper 5 percent of the American people whose taxes went down and whose incomes went up in the 1980's. I think it's a good plan, and it will restore health to the American economy.

You know, we're trying to do something no generation of Americans has ever had to do. I came into office with a record debt. And then after the election I was told the deficit was really about $50 billion higher in 3 of the next 4 years than we'd been told before. And yet, we looked around, and we saw we'd reduced our investment in education and training, reduced our investment in new technologies, had no plan to deal with people who lose their jobs because of defense cutbacks. And so we had to do something nobody had ever done. We had to try to find out how to bring the debt down and invest in our people, their jobs, and their future. I think we have got to do that. If we don't do both, we're going to be in big trouble.

Now look at the result. Since the election, since it became absolutely clear that this administration was dead serious about bringing this deficit down. Interest rates in many areas have hit an all-time low, home mortgages are at a 20-year low. I know there are people in this audience who have refinanced a home mortgage in the last 5 months. I know there are people here who have lower credit card rates, lower business loan rates, lower other rates because of interest rates going down. That's going to put $100 billion back into this economy to spur investment and growth and jobs and income if we bring the deficit down.

Now, we're going to go into a fight where everybody's going to say cut more spending and raise fewer taxes. And you know, what that really says is cut somebody else's spending and raise somebody else's taxes. I wish it were possible for us all to hide behind a tree and point at somebody else. But let's face it, in the last 12 years we got into this mess not overnight and we're not going to get out of it overnight. We also, whether we like it or not, got into it together. We're all in it together, and we'd better get out of it together. We're going to have to climb out of it together, march out of it together, and walk out of it together.

But this plan is fair. This plan has a big increase in the earned-income tax credit to try to relieve families with income of under $30,000 of the burden of the energy tax I proposed, which will raise money and help to clean up the environment. This plan has an increase in this earned-income tax credit so much that if you work 40 hours a week and you've got a child in the home, if you will apply for the tax credit, you will be lifted out of poverty. That is an elemental principle and a fundamental departure in America. We're going to reward work and not welfare for a change. If you work and you've got kids, we're going to lift you out of poverty. This will work. It will bring the deficit down. It will be fairer to working families. It will help us to keep interest rates down. It will help us to grow the economy. And over

the next 5 years, we'll have some money to invest in education and training and new technologies and jobs and trying to help all those people in those high-tech jobs that are losing them, because of defense cutbacks—they can make us strong here at home if we do it right. But we've got to do it as a package.

If everybody goes around saying, "What's in it for me?" instead of what's in it for us, the thing will come apart. That's what paralyzes America. Every time we've got to make a tough decision, somebody says, "Let somebody else do it." There's nobody else to do it but us. We're going to have to lift our country up, and we're going to have to do it together.

One of the things that I do want to do is to repeal the tax breaks that lobbyists get. There are 80,000 lobbyists in Washington making sure that I can't take care of your interests.

One of the things that we also have to do, I think, is to reform the political system. I told you if you would elect me President, I'd do my best to reduce the influence of lobbyists and special interest groups to increase your influence, to make it possible for all of the Members of Congress, without regard to party, at least to feel freer to follow their conscience and their constituents and to listen to them with an open ear and an open heart.

Well, there are two bills moving through the Congress now that will do just that. When I took office the first thing I did was to sign an Executive order saying that people that had top jobs for me couldn't go back into lobbying for 5 years and could never lobby for a foreign government. Then a bill was introduced into the Congress that just passed the United States Senate which, for the first time, requires all the lobbyists to register and requires them to report all the gifts they give to Members of Congress over a small amount, so you'll know.

And at the end of last week we announced a new campaign finance reform bill, which will do this: It will reduce the influence of big money; it will reduce the influence of political action committees; it will reduce the influence of lobbyists; it will give political campaigns back to you. It does it by limiting the amount of money that Members of Congress can take from political action committees by reducing the maximum contribution in many areas. It does it by saying that lobbyists cannot give money or raise money for Members of Congress that they personally lobby. And by repealing the tax exemption that lobbyists get, we're going to take that money and give it to Members of Congress as communication vouchers so we can open the airwaves to honest debate, and nobody is denied the opportunity to be on the television or the radio just because they're not an incumbent or just because they're not wired to the lobbyists. It is a good plan. It will give the Government back to you, the middle class of this country, and we ought to pass it.

There are some other things that I think you need to know about that we're trying to do. We've introduced our plans for national service and to make college available to all Americans, and here's how it works. But I need your help to pass it, because there are interest groups that are against it. There are interest groups against everything.

This plan would say to every American family: You can borrow the money to go to college without fear of going bankrupt because you will not have to pay it back until you go to work. And when you go to work, you can pay it back as a percentage of your income. So that no matter how much you borrow, you can't be required to pay more than a certain percentage of your income; you can't be bankrupted to secure your future.

The bill also will give tens of thousands of young Americans the opportunity to pay their college loan, or a portion of it, off through service to our country as teachers, as police officers, working with kids in trouble. They can earn it before they go to college, while they're in college, or after they get out. But I think people ought to be able to work to make Cleveland and Ohio a better place and pay their college loans off.

And believe it or not, if we just have the courage to change the way we're financing the college loan program, we can pay for most of this, particularly in the early years. Why? Because the way the college loan programs work now, we are losing billions of dollars a year in huge transaction fees to banks and in loan defaults, because the Government guarantees 90 percent of every one of these loans. So what happens? If somebody wants to default on the loan, what incentive does the bank have to go collect it? It would cost you 10 percent to pay the lawyer. So the taxpayers pay. I say let's make the loans direct. Let's cut out all the fat fees. Let's make people pay them back at tax time so they can't beat the bill, more respon-

sibility and more opportunity for everybody.

Let me just make two other points. First of all, while I have proposed over 200 specific budget cuts to take the lead in reducing this deficit by over $500 billion, I want you to know that nothing we can do will reduce this deficit over the long run to zero, which is what we want, until we finally face the fact that the biggest culprit in Government spending today is the exploding cost of health care. If we don't have the courage to try to provide a basic system of health coverage to all Americans, to try to give security to small businesses and working families who have health insurance but are terrified that they're going to lose it—if we don't do that, then you will never get this deficit down to zero because the cost of Government health care is going up by 12 percent a year. And 100,000 Americans a month are losing their health insurance.

Now there is no easy answer to this. If it were easy, somebody else would have done it already. It's hard. Why? Because we're spending too much money on health care, but it's in all the wrong places. And the question is: How are you going to move the money from where it shouldn't be, in administrative costs and extra procedures and duplicated technologies and a lot of other things, to where it should be, covering people who don't have health insurance without bankrupting small business, without imposing undue financial burdens, without imposing new taxes on people that are already paying too much.

Can it be done? You bet it can, but it won't be easy, and it will require people who have been making a killing out of the present system to accept some change. But I'm telling you, the worst thing we can do is to do nothing. When we come out with this plan everybody will say—well, whatever we say to get the money to people who don't have health insurance now or to provide health security to those who can't change jobs now, they'll call that a tax. But when we lower by millions and millions and millions of dollars a year the health insurance premiums of people who are paying too much or the paperwork burdens of the doctors and hospitals who are spending too much money filling out paper, they don't want to count that— the defenders of the status quo—as an offset.

We are going to have to change, folks, but most of what we have to do is to move the money from where it shouldn't be to where it should. We're already spending plenty of money, but we've got to move it around. And you ought to be able to see that not only will it cost some people some more money to have health insurance, but a lot of people who are paying too much will save. And that is what we have to do. If we don't have the courage to change, we will not get the Government budget under control. But most important, working-class families in this country and small business people will never have the health security without which it is virtually impossible to have a good life over the long run. We have got to do this. And I am determined to see that we do.

Let me just close by saying this: This is a difficult time. I told somebody the other day that I was absolutely convinced after 100 days as President that all the easy decisions had already been made by somebody else. Every day I meet with my staff and I say, send me just one easy one. Let's declare a moratorium. We won't talk about anything hard today. Send me an easy one. I'm still waiting. [*Laughter*]

But I want you to know that we can turn this country around; we can secure our future. It is in our power. We can bring the deficit down. We can increase our investment in education and jobs. We can meet the competitive challenges ahead of us. We can face the health care challenge. But we have got to have the courage to change. And we will win if we do that. I wish to goodness I could just say to every one of you, you don't have to do any of this. I'll just go to some other State and make them do it. [*Laughter*] But I can't.

Everybody will always be able to find some fault with every comprehensive proposal like this. There's no such thing as a perfect proposal. I don't like everything about everything that we have presented in the hope of passing and securing change. But the test for this generation, the test for this whole generation is whether we are going to have the courage to make these changes, to rebuild the middle class, and to lift up the economy of this country and to lift up all these children in this audience today. I believe you have that courage, and together we're going to do it.

Thank you, and God bless you all.

NOTE: The President spoke at 11:10 a.m. at the Galleria Mall. In his remarks, he referred to Martin Cleary, president, Richard and David Jacobs Group, and Keith Masters, general manager, Galleria and Tower Erieview.

Remarks to the Cleveland City Club
May 10, 1993

Thank you very much. Well, I don't know what you had for lunch, but I wish I'd had some of it. [*Laughter*] I do want to say I'm delighted to be back in Cleveland and glad to be back at the City Club. And I hold here in my hand a membership to the City Club given to me by Senator Metzenbaum. Now, I'd rather have his vote on all the issues, but I'll take this. [*Laughter*]

Actually, I want to thank Howard Metzenbaum and Lou Stokes and Eric Fingerhut and Congressman Hoke, and all the others who are here, your Mayor, your State treasurer, your State attorney general. I'm delighted to be here with all of you. I saw in the introduction that you mentioned something I was going to say in my own remarks. I very much enjoyed being here last year and having the opportunity to talk in Cleveland about family values.

Two years ago, I came here; the Mayor hosted the Democratic Leadership Council's national convention. And I said at that time that I thought the time had come for us to move beyond the political debate in Washington between one party which seemed to have advocated the politics of abandonment and another which seemed to advocate a politics of entitlement. It seemed to me that time had come for us to face our problems squarely as a country and to try to do something about them, but not to pretend that the Government could give a solution to the American people, solutions to problems that require all of us to give something ourselves and to do more. I feel that even more strongly today.

For 110 days, I have lived and worked in

Washington, DC. I think that all of us would agree that for too long our great Nation's Capital, which is filled with monuments to men and women who have done so much to bring us to this point in history, has practiced more politics than progress. I'm glad to be back here in a place like Cleveland where it's not possible to produce more politics than progress. Here you have to produce steel or automobiles or biomedical technology, real things with real value. This debate in which we are all engaged about America's future should properly take place here in the Industrial Belt and in the Grain Belt and in the Sun Belt and in the Bible Belt, all across America where people live in a world that is determined by consequences and not by talk.

If you're a Mayor in a city like Cleveland, you either provided more houses and people moved into them, or it didn't happen. There either are more economic opportunities, or there aren't. You can measure that. In Washington, we're told that the most important thing to do is not more than one thing at a time. [*Laughter*] And some want you to do one thing at a time because it's easier to stop one thing at a time than it is a whole range of things.

But I would argue to you, my fellow Americans, that the challenges of the moment require both a focus and a discipline on the big problems of our Nation and a determination to face them in a comprehensive way. The challenge of international competition, new technologies, soaring health care costs, defense cuts without an offsetting strategy to invest in America, a global recession, a global inability of wealthy countries to create new jobs in an open and competitive environment, all these things create great new challenges for our country.

Here in the heartland, I've seen you stepping up to the challenges. When the Mayor and I rode in from the airport today, he talked to me about how people were moving from the suburbs back into the cities, how more houses were being built. I looked at some of your economic development projects. I see a partnership between the public and private sector here that does not require someone to check his political label in when you roll up your sleeves and go to work. That is the sort of thing we need to do in Washington and the kind of spirit I hope to be able to bring to our Nation's Capital.

I believe very strongly that in the last 12 years, our Nation's Government has collectively produced two immense problems. Problem number one, obviously, is the enormous explosion of the national debt and the continuing growth of the annual Federal deficit. In 1980, our debt was $1 trillion. Today, it's $4 trillion and rising to about two-thirds of our annual national product, a much bigger percent of our annual deficit than, for example, the debt in Japan is. Now, how did it happen? It happened partly because we liked it when politicians told us what we wanted to hear. It happened because we had big tax cuts and big spending increases at the same time. First the spending increases were in defense. And then when defense began to be cut, they were totally offset, those cuts, by even bigger increases in health care spending through Medicare and Medicaid, the fact that one-tenth of America is now on food stamps, and by huge increases in interest payments on the national debt.

The deficit is also aggravated by the fact that we index both payments to people and income taxes. Now, it's fair to index income taxes. If you get pushed by inflation into a higher bracket, we adjust the brackets upward. For the first time, that's happened in the last few years. No one can doubt that is fair. But consider the impact on that if you offset on the one—hello, Congressman Brown, I didn't see you out there—you offset, on the one hand, your income, and at the same time you promise to pay more out. So everybody that gets a salary or a retirement check, their payments go up with inflation even as your intake comes down with inflation. So these are the two things that have created the kind of problem we have in the budget deficit.

The second thing that happened, interestingly enough, is that that portion of our Government budget which is in partnership with the private sector, making investments in our future and promoting economic growth, actually shrank as a percentage of the whole and often in absolute terms. So that at a time when we are more dependent than ever before on how skilled our work force is, the Federal commitment to education and training of the work force went down, as other nations were exploding their commitment. At a time when we were cutting high technology in the defense sector, the peace dividend was not automatically reinvested in new technologies in the commercial sector and new partnerships. Why? Because, as any Member of Congress here will tell you, the easiest place to cut spending is in that broad category known as discretionary nondefense spending. That doesn't mean anything. That's a lot of gobbledygook. But when you strip it away, a lot of it is our investment in our future. So we wind up with this unusual difficulty: a huge debt, an increasing deficit, and a diminished commitment to invest in our future.

The results have been clear: a limited ability to create new jobs, even when productivity is growing. We're allegedly in an economic recovery of some 17 months in duration, and yet the unemployment rate is higher this month than it was at the depths of the recession. We had a huge increase in productivity in the last 3 months of last year and in the first 3 months of this year, another big increase in output for a person in the manufacturing sector. But that money now is being plowed back into new technologies or kept for profit, not to increase new jobs. As any small business person here knows, it is difficult to increase employment in a small business because of the extra added costs. By the time you pay the Social Security and the worker's comp and all the other costs, you've got more and more small businesses using overtime workers or part-time workers and fewer new jobs being created there.

So here we are. What are we to do? I have asked the United States Congress to adopt a plan that I believe over the next 5 years will do something to make real, measurable change in both those areas. It will substantially reduce the Federal deficit in the most disciplined deficit reduction plan ever presented to Congress, and it will permit some very disciplined, targeted increases in those investments which are critical to our future. We do it by a combination of things: cutting spending, raising taxes, and targeting investment.

Because this involves a whole lot of change, as you might imagine, it challenges a lot of established interests in Washington who would prefer that things go on as they are. Because while as a whole our country is disadvantaged, I would argue, by what we're doing, certain specific groups benefit from everything that is done. Now, the lobbyists are lining the corridors of Washington as never before. There are about 80,000 of them there. And unless all the American people speak out loud and clear, it's going to be hard for us to hold this program together. There are those fighting for the national interests and those who are properly there to be

heard about more narrow interests. There are those who believe we can make things better and those who believe that any change will make things worse for them. There are those who believe we can spend money more productively and less wastefully and others who believe that we ought to just keep on spending it the way we are now.

This is the oldest conflict in our history and the eternal battle of any great democracy. The impetus for inertia is always strong, and very often a country does not have the courage to change until it is almost too late. But I believe with all my heart that the voters said last November—not just those who voted for me, either—but all the voters said, we know this country has got to take a different course. We know we can't keep drifting. We know we can't wander. We have to have a plan; we have to follow it. We have to try to make some things happen that will lift this country's spirits again, lift this country's prospects again, and yes, that will insist that all of us have the discipline and will and vision to change.

Now, I think that there are a lot of, I would call them preachers of pessimism in our Nation's Capital who underestimate the capacity of the American people to know the cost of what is happening to us right now. I readily admit that none of these changes can occur unless a vast majority of us understand the cost of what is happening to us right now: the cost of maintaining this deficit at its present level; the cost of maintaining the present health care system; the cost of maintaining a system which is underinvesting in our future compared to all of our major competitors in a high-wage, high-growth economy; the cost of maintaining the credit crunch on small business; the cost of having no technology policy; the cost of having no plan to convert from a defense to a domestic economy. I would argue that those costs are very high. The cost of having no strategy to put young people to work in our cities, and instead spending money to pay for the cleanup and the consequences of drug problems, gang problems, gun problems—the costs of the status quo are very, very high, even when you don't see it directly attributed on the Government's ledger books. I believe we don't see that enough.

So I think we can do more than one thing at once. I think we can reduce the deficit and provide the opportunity for all of our young people to go to college. I think we can reduce the deficit and provide decent job training and education for our working people when the average worker will change jobs eight times in a lifetime. I believe we can reduce the deficit and put more police on our streets to protect our communities better. I believe we can reduce the deficit and offer more targeted incentives for real investment to American businesses and to their workers. I believe we can reduce the deficit and change the welfare system so that we move people from welfare to work after a certain amount of time. I believe we can do these things. I believe we're strong enough to provide for a budget that reduces the deficit and invests in the future in a prudent way. And I can't help noting that some of those who say that we can't do that are the very ones that brought the debt from $1 trillion to $4 trillion over the last 12 years.

Our greatest Republican President, perhaps our greatest President, Abraham Lincoln, used to tell the story about when he was practicing law in Illinois. It kind of reminds me about some of these folks today talking about the deficit in Washington. He said it reminded him of a man who killed his parents and then threw himself on the mercy of the court because he was an orphan. [*Laughter*] I think we've all got to understand that we didn't get where we are overnight. We have to accept where we are. I don't care about who should bear the blame, but I don't think we should have people pointing fingers who helped to create the current course of events.

We should pull together. My whole approach has been to try to say to the American people, we are all in this together. If we ask, what's in this program for me, instead of what's in it for us, we'll all find something we don't like, including me. If the issue is going to be now, what's in it for me, instead of what's in it for us, we are defeated before we begin. But the what's-in-it-for-me decade didn't work out very well for us over the long run, and I think we can do better.

Now, shortly after I took office I submitted to Congress a blueprint of a budget that makes now over 200 specific budget cuts, reduces the deficit by over $500 billion over 5 years, and refocuses the priorities of our Government from consumption to investment in our future. Both Houses of the Congress passed that blueprint in record time; the first time in 17 years the

budget resolution had passed within the calendar required.

Our commitment to cut the deficit clearly boosted confidence on Wall Street, and it's beginning to be felt on Main Street. It is beginning to change lives for the better already. Starting after the November election, when we announced a clear determination to bring the deficit down, interest rates have been going down. The trend line is steady, with only minor interruptions whenever there's some sense that maybe we won't really reduce this deficit after all. The plan that I announced and the outline that Congress adopted clearly played a major role in bringing interest rates down to historic lows, mortgage rates to 20-year lows. There's been a huge wave of refinancing. I'll bet you anything there are lots of people in this room that since November have refinanced their home mortgages. I know that there are people in every city in America who have gotten business loans, whose consumer loans have gone down, whose costs of car financing have gone down.

It is estimated that in the aggregate, if we can keep these rates down just a few more months, this will lead to enough refinancing of debt that it will release another $100 billion to be reinvested into this economy. That's one and two-thirds percent of our total gross domestic product in a given year. That is a huge impetus to stay on the track we're on to bring this deficit down. According to a bipartisan survey, a poll recently conducted in these conditions, 74 percent of all Americans now believe that homeownership is within reach for most young people. Do you know that it was a year ago? The reverse, 47 percent. The reason for the change is obvious: lower interest rates.

Businesses are paying less to borrow. That means new investments and new jobs. The taxpayers, by the way, are saving billions of dollars in financing the Government debt. We've already brought the deficit down this year because of those interest rates. Along with that, we have launched a real effort to attack the credit crunch in partnership with community banks all across America, and that should mean that farmers, small business people, and homeowners will be able to do even more in the weeks and months ahead. These are things that happen when a people take some responsibility for their financial future. Having passed the budgetary blueprint, the Congress is now about to move into the specifics in what is called the budget reconciliation process. That means they've got to take the targets that were adopted in the budget resolution and specify how we're going to meet those targets: What kind of taxes are going to be raised? What kind of spending is going to be cut? What kinds of investments are going to be made? That is the process now beginning. And that is the kind of thing that will require us all to make tough choices to make good on the results that are being achieved. I've asked Congress to join me in making real spending cuts, and that process is now unfolding.

Our budget contains, as I said, over 200 specific cuts. I thought I should start as President by setting an example. In the new fiscal year we'll be operating the White House with a staff that is 25 percent smaller than my predecessor's. I must say, I made that commitment, and we're going to do all that work. I have to say, in parenthesis, I didn't know that I'd receive more letters in the first 100 days than came into the White House in all of 1992. So if you haven't gotten your letter answered, hold on, I'm coming. [*Laughter*] We're trying to do it. We are going to reduce just in our office alone $10 million in payroll and perks and costs of Government.

In the executive branch, I have ordered over the next 4 years a 14 percent cumulative reduction in the administrative costs of the Federal Government, 100,000 person reduction in the Federal payroll by attrition. That will save well over $9 billion. I have asked the Federal employees to have a pay freeze in this coming year and reduced raises in all the rest of this first term. I just left the Galleria, and right across the street there's a big Federal office building, and a lot of those Federal employees said they weren't looking forward particularly to doing without a raise next year. We have put the clamps on Federal spending, and we have asked Federal employees to make a sacrifice. I didn't see how I could ask people to raise their taxes unless the people who were getting the tax money also made a sacrifice.

I come from a rural State where the Rural Electrification Agency, the REA, has been very important to my family and our people. They have brought life and hope to millions of Americans. But now our country is about 100 percent electrified, and I have recommended that we reduce the interest subsidies to the REA, something that is tough to do for Members of Con-

gress from rural areas and for this President who came from that place. I may get shocked instead of light when I go home. [*Laughter*]

I've asked the Congress to join me in repealing the special interest exemption for lobbying. It's only been in the Tax Code since 1962. Before that, it didn't exist. You had to pay if you wanted to go lobby. Now the taxpayers actually, at large, bear the burden of people's lobbying costs. Now, again, I'm all for people lobbying, and frankly, it's a good thing if it's in balance. But I don't see why the taxpayers should subsidize someone's costs when they go and try to influence the outcome of legislation in Washington.

I've asked to cut urban programs that don't work. While I plead guilty to trying to get more community block grant funds for Mayor White so he could build more houses in Cleveland, I also called for the abolition of a designated project program at the Housing and Urban Development Department because it had no real accountability to the taxpayers and cost over $100 million a year.

I also believe that after all these cuts are in place, if you really expect this deficit to be brought down, we have got to raise some more tax money. And I believe that we ought to do it in a progressive way. I can tell you this just to start out, I have proposed more budget cuts and more taxes than I thought I would when I was running, and the reason is simple: After the election the Government said the deficit was going to be $50 billion a year bigger in 3 of the next 4 years than we thought, and $15 billion in the 4th year. The deficit was announced after the election in each year to be much, much bigger than had previously been forecast.

So we asked for about 73 percent of the money to be paid for by people with incomes above $100,000; the rest to be paid for, 27 percent, by the 93 percent or so of us that are under $100,000. And then there is an exemption in effect for the energy tax burden for lower middle income working people and middle income working people with children up to the levels of about $29,000 by the increase in the earned-income tax credit, which will offset the impact of the energy tax. I think it is a very fair program, and I hope it will be adopted.

We take on the entitlements in this plan. People say, why don't you take on the entitlements? I'll tell you why, because people get mad at you when you do that. We asked Social Security recipients who are in the top 20 percent of income to pay taxes on more of their income than they do today, coming from Social Security. We have done our best to restrain the exploding costs of Medicare. We have taken on these tough issues to cut spending and to raise some money. But I would also argue to you that we must have some disciplined increases in investment. And I'll tell you where my recommendations are.

I recommend, first of all, that we focus on rewarding work, strengthening families, and creating more jobs, especially for the middle class. These ideas include the following—this is where we spend money: First of all, in tax cuts to encourage investments for new jobs. Private enterprise is, after all, the engine of this economy, not the Government, and we need to get it running as close as we can to full throttle. So there are substantial new incentives in this program for both large business and small business to lower their taxes through direct investments. Investments mean lower taxes and more jobs and, therefore, more revenue to the Government by putting people to work if you target it to investment. I think it's very important.

Secondly, we focus especially on the depressed areas of the country, both rural and urban, with establishing a new network of community development banks to make loans to people who want to go into business in these areas with special incentives to get others to do the same thing. With special kinds of enterprise zones, especially in the urban and rural areas which are particularly depressed, that will at least give us a chance to see if free enterprise alone can revive these areas if the Government gives them enough incentives. These are things I believe that will make the private sector work for all Americans.

The plan also strengthens our schools by providing access to Head Start to all children who need it, by setting higher standards throughout the country and enshrining in the law the national education goals and the standards that they will produce. The plan encourages experimentation with things like public school choice and charter schools in public school. It contains a bold national apprenticeship program where the Federal Government is a partner with the private sector and State and local government in helping to retrain the work force for a lifetime. We are the only advanced country, the

only one, that doesn't worry about having a systematic way of training high school graduates who don't go on to college. And yet we now have clear evidence, in the 1990 census, that anybody who graduates from high school but gets no further training or who drops out of high school who goes into the work force is likely to have declining earnings. This is good money, and it will be really shaped by private sector people and public trainers at the local grassroots level, not a national program but a national partnership. And it will really, really increase the productivity of the American work force.

This plan also will open the doors of college education to all Americans by changing the nature of the student loan program. And I want to explain this. Today, the way the student loan program works, you can go down to your bank, you borrow the money, you pay it back based on how much you borrow. If you don't pay it back, the Government gives the bank 90 percent of the loan. That's the way it works. The college dropout rate is more than twice the high school dropout rate, in part because of the cost of a college education. The student loan program is very profitable for many banks and for the national mortgage organization that's behind it. They have made a killing out of it. It's terrible for the taxpayers. Why? Because if somebody defaults on the loan, there's no incentive to go get it because there's a 90 percent Government guarantee. And no offense to all of us lawyers in the crowd, but it's going to cost you more than 10 percent of the loan to pay a lawyer to go get it. Not only that, the repayment terms are often too burdensome.

Here's what we want to do: Set up a system to make the loans directly. Let people pay back the loans only when they go to work, and then as a percentage of their income. So no one will ever not be able to repay, and no one will be discouraged from taking a lower paying but perhaps more rewarding job as a teacher or a police officer or whatever, but collect the money at tax time so you cannot beat the bill. Don't let people welch on their student loan anymore. And we estimate this system can save you $4.3 billion in the next 5 years. That's a lot of money. Let me tell you what we'd like to do with that money, or some of it, anyway. We'd like to give tens of thousands of our young people the opportunity to earn credit against college or pay off their college loan by doing community service before, during, or after they go to college: working with housing projects, working with environmental projects, working to help keep streets safer, working after they graduate as teachers or police officers in underserved areas. We can have a program of national service that is community based that will help us solve so many of our problems.

I got a letter from a friend of mine, with whom I was in grade school, the other day, reminiscing about all kinds of things. And she had a very wise thing in this letter. She said, "You know, somebody came up to me the other day and said, 'How are we going to save all these kids that are in trouble? How are we going to get them back?'." And she said, "Without even thinking I said, 'We're going to get them back just the way we lost them, one at a time'." Now, you think about that. That's what this national service proposal could do. It could give all kinds of young people a chance to do something meaningful to help earn credit to go to college and to help solve the problems of Cleveland and Cincinnati and Columbus and Dayton and every other community in this country. That's the kind of thing that I think is money well spent. And we can pay for it if we just have the discipline to make the student loan program make sense again. I think we have to do it.

Let me say, there are many other issues I could talk about, but I want to mention one other. I have spent a lot of the last 6 years working on the issue of welfare. I have probably spent more time than any elected politician talking to people who live on welfare checks. And I can tell you that nobody likes the system, least of all most people who live on it. But if you want to move people from welfare to work, you have to realize three or four basic things. First of all, you've got to make work pay; welfare can never be a better deal. Secondly, we've got to realize that it's not the welfare check that keeps people on welfare as much as it is the child care and the medical coverage for the children. Most people on welfare have kids. The third thing you've got to realize is that most people, not all but most people on welfare are woefully undereducated and can't claim a very good paycheck in the market that we're in, not all but a lot. So what is the answer? The answer is a comprehensive plan that will empower people to go to work, require them to take jobs when they can, and set a

date certain beyond which no check comes without an effort being made either in a public or a private job. That's what I think should be done. We should do away with the system as we know it forever. It is a shackle on the spirit of millions of Americans, and we can change it.

Now, here's what we're going to propose. One, in this plan, increase the earned-income tax credit. You can fill out a form on your taxes and get money back if you're eligible for the earned-income tax credit. And let's fix it so that any American who works 40 hours a week and has a child in the house is not in poverty. That is a simple, elemental principle that will reduce the incentive of welfare. Second, strengthen the system of child support enforcement. Don't lose $20 billion a year for people who beat their bills and won't support their kids. Let it cross the State lines. Third, provide a system of education and training so that people are empowered to do what can be done in this economy. Fourth, deal with the health care issue through the national health initiative that I'll say more about in a minute. And then finally, set up a system, it will take us a while to do it and to work out the financing, but set up a system so that after a certain amount of time, if there is no private sector job, to keep drawing a check you must make an effort. I think that will be a very good thing. And most people on welfare, once you take care of these other issues, will applaud the American people for changing that system. Nobody likes the system we've got. We've got to have the courage to change it, and I think we will this year.

Finally, let me say a word about the last issue, which incorporates so much of the other. If you want to bring the deficit down to zero, which is what our goal ought to be, over a period of years, we must face the biggest exploder of the deficit and perhaps the biggest human dilemma America faces, and that's the health care crisis.

This year we're going to spend 15 percent of our income on health care. The next nearest country will not spend 10 percent. Now, we should be spending more than everybody else for a number of reasons: Number one, we do more on medical research than any other country. Number two, we rely more on new technologies, and we enjoy that when we need it, as opposed to somebody else needing it. Number three, we have a more diverse population with more poor people than most other advanced countries, more cases of AIDS than most other advanced countries, and we are a more violent country than any other advanced country. So we pay more money, keeping emergency rooms open on the weekend for people getting shot and cut up. [*Laughter*] You can laugh about it; these are true things. Anybody comes and paints some miracle picture on health care without telling you the truth is not credible.

We cannot get our costs down to the level of other nations unless we make changes dealing with these big structural things. We can do something about this violence if we wanted to, and I'll have more to say about that as we go through this term. I've already tried to do too much at once, according to the experts. But let me tell you, we cannot continue to have health care costs go up at the rate of inflation anymore. We cannot do that here. This deficit, no matter how much we bring it down in the next 5 years, will start to go right up again because health care costs are going up at a projected 12 percent a year for the Government. A hundred thousand Americans a month are now losing their health insurance, coming right onto the Government rolls: people giving up jobs because they have sick children; people giving up health insurance to keep the small business from going broke; people giving up health insurance because they have to change jobs, and they have somebody in their family sick.

And there are things that can be done about this. We are spending about 15 percent of every dollar in health insurance on administrative costs and insurance profit. That is exorbitant. It's about a dime a dollar more than any other country in the world is spending. The average doctor in 1980 was taking home 75 percent of all of the money that came into the clinic that he or she brought in, 75 percent. Do you know what it is now? Fifty-two percent; lost 23 cents on the dollar. Why? Because of paperwork. The blizzard of insurance requirements, the blizzard of Government requirements, and a few other things as well. We can do something about this.

Now, the trick is going to be not to spend a lot more money but to move the money from where it shouldn't be to where it should. And some people will have to pay some more. But we are going to do the very best we can to make sure that the people who are entitled to a reduction in their insurance bills start to get it right away, and that we phase in the burdens

of this so that no small business is bankrupt, so that the providers are relieved of a lot of these paperwork burdens, and so that we can actually both lower the costs to the millions and millions of Americans who are entitled to it and stabilize the rate of increase for everybody else.

Now, the nay-sayers can always call any new responsibility that anybody assumes, that they are not assuming now, a tax. Five will get you ten, they'll never want to give any credit for all the cost reductions that will go to the tens of millions of Americans who are paying too much now. We have got to do something about this. We are the only advanced country in the world that has no system for covering everybody, maintaining health security for working families, and trying to keep costs somewhere near inflation. We can do that and preserve everything that is best about the American system, keep spending more than everybody else is, but not run this country into a ditch. And we've got to do it.

In order to do it, all of us will have to take a view about the national interests that will not enable us to say, what's in it for me? We'll have to say, what's in it for us? There are a couple of things moving through the Congress that are very hopeful in that regard. One is the Senate passed a bill this week, that I strongly support, that requires all the lobbyists in Washington to register for a change. Did you know they didn't have to register before? A whole bunch of them never even registered. And limit very strictly the gifts that any Member of Congress can receive without reporting them. They're going to have to report the money that all the lobbyists make, and the lawyers.

And now, we introduced last Friday a new campaign finance reform bill that will limit the cost of congressional campaigns, limit the influence of political action committees, and open the airwaves to challengers and incumbents alike so that the people get a real race every time, and pays for it by repealing the deduction for lobbyist expenses. I hope that those two things can pass. To get economic reform, you're going to have to have political reform. I'm sure of that.

Bring down the deficit; do it with spending cuts and tax increases. No tax increases without the spending cuts. Invest in education and training, new technologies, incentives to business, changing the welfare system. And have political reform; face health care. That is a big agenda, but that is America's agenda. If we're going to bring this country back, that is what we must do. I hope you and every American, without regard to political party, in good faith, will ask the United States Congress to engage these issues this year so that we can move this country in the future.

Thank you very much, and God bless you.

NOTE: The President spoke at 12:45 p.m. at the Statler Tower Building. In his remarks, he referred to Representatives Lou Stokes and Eric Fingerhut.

Question-and-Answer Session With the Cleveland City Club
May 10, 1993

Homosexuals in the Military

Q. Mr. President, based on the congressional hearings so far, how do you expect to resolve the issue of gays in the military this July?

The President. I can only tell you what I think should be done and what my guess is will be done. And I'm glad you asked this question.

Let me say one thing by way of background. The difference between my position and that of many people in the military, including most folks in the military, is over a very narrow category of people, actually. That is, in the last few months, the armed services have, on their own initiative after meeting with me, stopped asking people when they join up whether they are homosexual or not. That is not being asked anymore. For many years that question was not asked. It only started being asked in the relatively recent past. That will solve most of the problems.

I do not propose any changes in the code of military conduct. None. Zero. I do not believe that anything should be done in terms of behavior that would undermine unit cohesion or morale. Nothing.

Here is what this whole debate is about. It is about whether someone should be able to acknowledge, if asked or otherwise, homosexuality and do nothing else, do nothing to violate the code of military conduct and not be kicked out of the service. And my position is yes. Others say no. Others say if you let someone acknowledge it, it amounts to legitimizing a lifestyle or putting it on a par with—I don't see it as that. I just believe that there ought to be a presumption that people ought to be able to serve their country unless they do something wrong. But you need to know, that is it is not such a big difference. That is what we're arguing

about. We're arguing not about any kind of conduct but about whether people can acknowledge that. Like that young man who was the 6th Army soldier of the year and who's now about to be mustered out because he acknowledged being homosexual.

It is not about asking the American people to approve a lifestyle, to embrace it, to elevate it, anything else. The question is if you accept as a fact, as we now know and as the Pentagon has said, there have been many, many thousands of homosexuals serve our country and serve it well with distinction, should we stop asking? They say yes, and I say yes. So we solved most of the issues. They say yes, and I say yes.

Should we change the code of conduct? They say no, and I say no, not at all, not on the base, not any way, no changes in the code of conduct. So the issue is over this: What will happen in this narrow category of cases? And that is what is still to be resolved. I hope my position will prevail. Frankly, I think most people believe as a practical matter, most people who have studied it, that the position I have taken can be worked out and is fairest to the good men and women who serve in the service who have done well. I think they're frankly worried about having that position look like they are embracing a lifestyle or legitimizing a lifestyle they don't agree with. And I keep saying, "That's not what I think we're about." What I think we're about is acknowledging people's right to do right and to be judged by what they do. And that's sort of my position.

Economic Program

Q. Mr. President, as a resident of Ohio, what action can I take, what can I do to express my outrage at Senator Dole and his cohorts who block a legitimate vote like the stimulus package?

The President. Let me make a constructive suggestion. I appreciate your sentiments, obviously, but let me make a constructive suggestion. What I think we need to do is to go on now and pass this budget and then just see where we are.

Let me back up and say what I think happened in that deal. I believe that I won the debate with the American people that we needed more investments to create some jobs now, because this economy is not producing a lot of jobs. On the other hand, the Republicans said, "Well, that's fine, but we ought to pay for it."

Well, I had announced this stimulus program as a part of this 5-year deficit-reduction program. So it had already been incorporated by the financial markets and everybody else who evaluated this. It was paid for in the sense that it was part of the program. But to pass it in time to get the summer jobs and some other things out, we had to, in effect, take it out of sequence, if you see what I mean, to put it up now so we can get the money out to create the jobs in 1993 before Congress could have actually acted on the budget of which it was but a small part.

So what I think, to be constructive, what I think you should do is to do whatever you can to encourage the big budget to pass, long-term deficit reduction, and investment increases. Then let's watch this unemployment rate. And once we have proved that we have the discipline in Washington to cut spending and reduce the deficit, if we don't generate new jobs, if the economy doesn't pick up in terms of employment, then I think we can come back and look at that.

Now, that doesn't solve a couple of the severe problems, like the summer jobs. We're still trying to assess where we are on that. But the larger question of creating jobs is something that I think that we need to recognize is primarily going to be dealt with by the big budget, the big issue. But if we need to come back, then I'll need you and all your folks, because we need to get ahead of the curve on this one. Because we were not trying to increase the deficit, this was part of a big, 5-year plan where we had to take it out of sequence because of the summer jobs issue and because we wanted a lot of these jobs created in 1993.

Thank you for asking.

National Service Program

Q. What is your prognosis for the success of your proposed aid for college students who do public service?

The President. Oh, I think it's got very great prospects of success. We've had wonderful bipartisan support; for several Republican Congressmen in the House of Representatives already asked to be cosponsors. We have at least two supporters, Republican supporters, in the Senate. And as far as I know, virtually every Democrat is for it.

We've worked very hard to try to work out all of the objections, and I think it will be very helpful. We're going to move as quickly as possible. The national service part I think will fly through. The question of cutting down on the cost of the loan program will be more difficult, because many of the bankers and others who like the system as it is will oppose it. But it's unconscionable for us to lose $3 billion a year on loan defaults and $1 billion on transaction fees which could be put into direct loans which could then be collected. So there will be a lot of dispute about the loan issue. But I think the national service part of it will go through. It wouldn't hurt for you to express your support, though, to your Member of Congress.

Thank you.

Environmental Initiatives

Q. Mr. President, what legislations do you hope to pass in order to help protect the environment while cutting the national deficit?

The President. There are several things that we want to do. As you know, the Vice President and I have both worked very hard on this issue since we took office. I want to sign the biodiversity treaty, and I expect to do it, committing the United States to help preserve wildlife species. We want to be part of an international effort to preserve wildlife and plant life in the United States and in the rainforest, especially, around the world. We want to reduce the emissions of greenhouse gases in this country to 1990 levels over this coming decade, which I think we can do.

And we want to invest some of the money that is coming from defense cutbacks into environmental technologies and environmental cleanup here at home, so that those technologies can produce American jobs, many of which can also lead in exporting. The biggest new commercial market in the world in the next 10 years will be the market for various environmental technologies and services. It is a huge gold mine out there waiting to be tapped. When the countries met in Rio last year, regrettably the Germans and the Japanese were much ahead of the United States in total in environmental technology companies and services. But we have a lot of very successful ones here in the United States, and I hope we can galvanize more of them. If we do this right, cleaning up the environment won't cost us jobs, it'll save us jobs. It'll have a big positive impact.

He asked a good question. Give him a hand. Isn't he good. [*Applause*] Thank you.

Health Care Reform

Q. Mr. President, perhaps this is a bit premature. But does your health care program incorporate a focus on wellness as well as merely curing illnesses? And what I mean by wellness is universal immunization, health examinations, and so forth. Or, perhaps Mrs. Clinton might answer that a little bit better. [*Laughter*]

The President. Well, let me say that it will, and that if it were just up to the two of us, it would focus on wellness much more. You may know that, for example, there are a lot of countries, in France for example, where even working-class families get a family allowance when a woman is pregnant. You can only draw the family allowance if the mother can prove that she has followed a certain regime of maternal health designed to produce a healthy baby.

I saw the other day in the paper that some Republican Congressman had suggested that we ought to do the same thing with immunizations, for people on public assistance having to immunize their kids. I thought that was a good idea. I think that we should have a big wellness prevention component of this. That's another point I wish I had made in my remarks. But we are exploring what our options are there.

There will be every effort made to have a strong education and prevention and wellness component of this health care effort. And I might add that if we can have more clinics in chronically underserved areas and more health educators there, I think we can do that. That's one way you can save a ton of money in the system, and I think you must know that or you would not have asked the question.

Thank you.

Taxes

Q. Mr. President, your administration has proposed two new taxes: first, a value-added tax in which goods would be taxed at each stage of production; secondly, an energy Btu tax in which coal, gas, oil, and other forms of energy would be taxed at each stage of use. Are not these taxes inflationary in that they compound at each stage? And secondly, they push up the consumer price index to which wages, prices, and Social Security and other entitlements are indexed to the consumer price index.

The President. Well, first, let me say I have proposed a Btu tax, and I'd like to come back to that. I have not proposed a VAT tax. I have not. There have been a lot of rumors about it.

It's interesting that you should know with whom a VAT tax is popular. Hillary's health care group, the First Lady's health care group, was asked to consider a VAT tax by an unusual coalition of big business and labor interests. Why? Because other countries have a VAT tax. Most other countries have a VAT tax of some kind, and we don't. And a value-added tax is one of the few ways that you can—somebody who advocated it now wants to get off of it. [*Laughter*] Anyway, a value-added tax is one of the few ways that you can avoid taxing your own exports and tax someone else's imports. That is, it is placed on things sold in your country. So when our competitors in Europe, for example, have a value-added tax, when they produce things for sale in the United States, it's not subject to the tax. When we sell our stuff over there, it's already carried the full burden of our taxes, and it gets hit with the VAT.

So there are a lot of business and labor interests who believe that, conceptually, even if we lower some other tax, we should embrace the VAT tax because it helps us in international trade. I had never thought of it as an answer to the health care problem, because I thought it would aggravate the maldistribution of paying for the problem. It would allocate the burden of paying for the problem in ways that I didn't think were particularly fair. But that's what it is.

Now, on the Btu tax, let me say that America taxes energy less than any other country. There were a lot of suggestions for how we might raise funds to reduce the deficit. The energy tax clearly is the thing which, for all kinds of reasons, had the biggest impact on the financial markets.

I was reluctant—there were people who said, "Well, you ought to have a carbon tax. That's the most polluting." I thought that was unfair to the coal-producing States. Then there were people who said, "Well, we have real low gas taxes." We do, but States also set gas taxes. "We have real low gas taxes. You ought to have a gas tax." I thought that was unfair to the rural areas, particularly west of the Mississippi where they have much higher per-vehicle usage.

The reason we decided to go with the Btu tax is that you can put it uniformly on all sources of energy so that it doesn't fall with incredible disproportion on any given sector. Now, the problem is that for the sectors that are especially energy-intensive, it hurts them more than a gas tax. And it hurts people who don't pay anything for their energy now. So farmers, for example, that had a fuel tax exemption are dealing with this burden. And you know, we've tried to come to grips with that. I don't think there is a perfect solution. But I like the Btu tax, because it promotes energy conservation, it's good for the environment, and it's fairer, I think, to every region than any other energy alternative that we could devise.

Let me follow up on that. We tried to increase the earned-income tax credit—that is, the proposal—so that for people with earnings of $29,000 a year or less, $30,000 a year or less with families, the impact of the Btu tax would be offset by the increase they'd get in the tax cut under the earned-income tax credit.

Economic Program

Q. Good afternoon, Mr. President.

The President. Good afternoon.

Q. What I'd like to know is, first of all, your economic plan is twofold. It is to cut spending and, secondly, to encourage more Government spending in the private sector. Well, obviously there's a lot of support for the first part, cutting spending. What I'd like to know is, there seems to be a lack of enthusiasm for the second part. One is: How do you plan to get that through? Basically, how do you plan to garner more support for it? And, once you get your economic package through, how much input are just ordinary people going to have to this? And when will we feel it at our level?

The President. Well, depending on whether you borrowed any money since November, you've already felt it. From the minute Secretary-designate of the Treasury said after the election, Lloyd Bentsen said we were going to attack the deficit and how we were going to do it and what was going to be in it, we began to have pretty steep drops in interest rates. So if you're paying any kind of interest payments, you've already felt it.

The reason I was for the job stimulus program—to go back to the jobs program that the gentleman asked me in the back—is that I wanted to be able to lower the unemployment rate by another half a percentage point this year through an investment program, because all over the world, I will say again, all over the world—Europe's got a higher unemployment rate than we do. Japan has a much lower unemployment rate than we do because it's got a more closed economy, but they also are not creating jobs, and many of their firms are laying off for the first time in modern history. So I wanted to do that.

So you will—let me just tick them off—you should be able—if we pass the budget, I think we will secure a healthier financial environment for the next year, and I think that will help everyone. If we can pass health care, I think, by next year people will begin to feel the impact of greater health security. If we can pass it—it's a big job and it's going to take a lot of work.

The student loan program, if it passes, it will affect people immediately. People will be eligible who are now in college for it, as well as those who would wish to go, the same thing with the apprenticeship program. The welfare reform program should begin to have effect next year. Those are just some of the things that I think will actually touch people's lives and make a big difference.

I think the trick on—to go back to the question the other gentleman asked—to getting people to support the targeted spending for education, training, and technology is to make sure that you lock the spending cuts in first before you do the taxes, and that overall, that the spending increases are small compared to the spending cuts, which they are, in our plan. So I think to me, that's the trick, and that's what I'm trying to achieve, and I hope you'll be with me when we do it.

Thank you.

NOTE: The question-and-answer session began at 1:50 p.m. in the Statler Tower Building.

Nomination for Posts at the Department of Energy
May 10, 1993

The President announced today that he intends to nominate Victor H. Reis to be Assistant Secretary of Energy for Defense Programs and that he has approved the appointment of Michael Gauldin to be Director of the DOE's Office of Public Affairs.

"I am very pleased to be adding these two people to the leadership of the Department of Energy," said the President. "Victor Reis is one of our country's leading defense researchers, and Mike Gauldin has been a valuable aide to me for years. They will each play a key role in helping Secretary O'Leary to meet her goals for the Department of Energy."

NOTE: Biographies of the nominees were made available by the Office of the Press Secretary.

Remarks and a Question-and-Answer Session With High School Students in Bensonville, Illinois
May 11, 1993

The President. Thank you very much, Brian. Thank you, Dr. Meredith. And thank you, ladies and gentlemen. I'm glad to be here at this fine high school. I should also note before I begin that one of many reasons that I decided to come here is that this high school is the alma mater of an important member of my White House staff, Kevin O'Keefe, who graduated from Fenton High School. Where are you? Where's Kevin? Stand up. He didn't have that gray hair when he was here. I met, in addition to your principal and your superintendent, I met Charlotte Sonnenfeld on the way in here, who said she was a teacher of Kevin O'Keefe but was not responsible for him in any way. [*Laughter*]

I also want to thank a number of other people who are here, including several Members of Congress over here to my left, Bobby Rush, Luis Gutierrez, Cardiss Collins, and George Sangmeister. I think they're all here. And I want to thank Richard Dent of the Chicago Bears for coming. Stand up, Richard.

I also want to—is Michael Cruz over there? Is he here? No? Where is he? Here he is. Come here. This young man was on the President's town hall meeting with students. Did any of you see it? Did you see that? And he became a television star because he is a good student. He goes to school in Chicago, and he said he was worried about the safety of the schools and the streets. And he asked the President to try to make all the schools safe for students in every part of America, no matter how tough the neighborhoods were. And I was really proud of him, so I invited him to come here today. I think you ought to give him a hand. [*Applause*]

I know we've got students from other schools here. Where are you, all the students from the other schools that are here?

Audience members. Boo-o-o!

The President. Hey, hey. [*Laughter*] No, no, today's the day when you're supposed to welcome them here.

I want to say how very glad I am to be back in Illinois where I met so many people who shaped the thoughts and the feelings that I carried into the Presidential campaign last year. People who asked me to fight for their families and the future of their children, to help to fix our economy, to create more jobs, to bring the terrible budget deficit down, to deal with the health care and education challenges facing America. A lot of what I learned in that campaign last year I learned from talking to people on the streets in the cities and towns of Illinois, and I'm glad to be back.

This week, some of the Members of Congress whom I hoped would be here are in Washington working on things of importance to you. Your two United States Senators, Paul Simon and Carol Moseley-Braun, are in the Senate today because they're going to vote on the motor voter bill, which will make it easier for young people to register and vote, an issue that's been a big issue for MTV and all the MTV watchers in the country who want to make young people a bigger part of the political process. And Congressman Rostenkowski and the other members of his committee are back in Washington, working on a plan that will help to bring the budget deficit down by over $500 billion over the next 5 years, so that you can grow up in an America that is not paralyzed by a crushing debt, as we have seen in the last 12 years.

But I don't want to talk just about those issues today. I also want to talk about tomorrow, about your tomorrows and about what it will take for you to make the most of the future all of us who have already been in your place and school are trying to make.

I've spent a lot of my time in Washington, in fact, most of my time, working on the economy and the health care crisis today, because I know that unless we can bring the deficit down and invest in jobs and technology and building a strong economy, America can't be what it ought to be. And I believe that unless we attack the problems of health care security and coverage and the enormous contribution that health care costs are making to the financial problems of this country, we can never restore real security to the American family or strength to the American economy or reduce the terrible deficit of this Government so that we can bring our budget into balance. So that's what I spend my time doing.

But I also know that no matter what we do on these issues, unless each and every one of you is a productive, well-educated, well-trained citizen able to take advantage of the opportunities of the world you will live in but also able to meet the highly competitive challenges of people from all over the world who will be struggling for many of the same opportunities that you want, that nothing I can do will change your individual lives. You have to do that. And that's why the provision of excellence in education and real educational opportunities are so important.

Those of you who have been able to go to this school or the other schools here represented can leave your high school with the confidence that you've had the opportunity to get a good education. But you should know that in the world you're living in, the average young American moving into the work force will change work seven or eight times in a lifetime. And more than ever before in the history of the country, what you are able to do in your work life, what you are able to earn, will be directly related not just to what you know today but what you can learn tomorrow. In the last—yeah, you can clap for that. That's a pretty good idea. Thanks. [*Applause*]

Now, in the last 12 years, there has been a dramatic difference, a widening growing-out between the earnings of young people who have at least 2 years of good education after high school in a community college, a good training program, or a 4-year college degree, and young people who drop out of high school or only finished high school. The clear evidence is that in the world in which you will live, you will need not only to make a personal commitment to learning and relearning throughout your lifetime but to getting at least—at least—2 years of education beyond high school and hopefully more.

Now, more and more people have got this figured out. College enrollments have grown up; explosive enrollment increases at 2-year community colleges and technical schools have been seen. Young people have figured that out. But there are still some problems with it, one of which is purely financial. The college dropout rate is more than twice the high school dropout rate, and one big reason is, a lot of people cannot afford to go or, having gone, cannot afford to stay.

How many of you want to go on to some form of further education when you get out of high school? Raise your hand. How many of you think you're going to need to borrow some money or get a scholarship or have some financial help to do it? Raise your hand. [*Applause*] I think it's nice that you can be enthusiastic about that.

You know, last year in Illinois alone, almost 180,000 educational loans were made. Five million educational loans were made in America last year. Higher education is really important. It's important to you economically. It's important for reasons far more important than that, even. It promotes personal growth and gets you in contact with things that have happened in the past and ties you into this great civilization of ours. But it's all academic, to use an appropriate word, if you can't afford to go and stay.

Interestingly enough, the cost of a college education is perhaps the only essential in a family's spending patterns that has gone up more rapidly than health care in the last 10 years. And that's one big reason that the college dropout rate has increased. More and more young people have to deal with this.

On the average, in the country as a whole, tuition fees and room and board cost $5,240 a year at public institutions of higher education and $13,237 at private schools. The cost of these educations has gone up 126 percent in the last 10 years. That means that a lot of people who try to borrow money drop out and then can't repay the debt; others borrow the money and leave college with massive debts and don't know how to repay them. Still others might prefer when they graduate to be a teacher, for example, but they're afraid they can't meet their loan repayment schedule. They might wish to be a law enforcement officer or a police officer; they're afraid they can't meet their loan repayment schedule. That's a bad case of the tail wagging the dog. People actually deciding what to do with their lives based on the crushing burden of debt they have to get an education, the purpose of which was to be free to choose to do whatever you want to do with your life. We can do better than that.

One of the reasons that I ran for President is that I wanted to change that, because I know no economic policy, no health care policy, no reduction in the deficit can change what is in your mind and whether you are able to do well in the world that you will live in. You have to do that. But my generation owes it to you to give you the chance to be able to afford to get a good college education, to go and to stay.

A couple of weeks ago I unveiled a plan to do that based on four simple principles: First, we ought to lower the interest rates on the college loans that you borrow from—that you make. I don't know how many seniors here have already looked into college loans, but if you want a college loan that's guaranteed by the Federal Government, there's a lot of paperwork involved and a lot of hassle. That's because there

are a lot of extra costs in there, from middle men, from banks, and from corporations, who profit from the current loan program.

Your Senator, Paul Simon, was the first person who ever came to see me well over a year ago to say that we ought to make loans directly to students from the United States Government in a financially secure way so that we could cut out paperwork, cut out all the time it takes to apply for them, and eliminate excess profits from middle men. Every student borrower can enjoy a lower rate if we do this. And if we adopt the plan that I have basically developed in cooperation with Senator Simon and others, we can save the American taxpayers $4 billion over the next 5 years and make loans available to you at cheaper rates. I'd say that's a pretty good idea.

The second thing we have to do is make it easier for students to pay the loan back. Today, the loan repayment obligation is directly related to how much you borrow, whether you have a job or whatever your job pays. What I want to do is to give every American young person who borrows money to get a 2-year or a 4-year education after high school the option of paying the money back based on how much you make, so that you can never be saddled with a debt burden greater than a certain percentage of your income. That way, there will never be an incentive not to be a teacher, not to be a police officer, not to work with kids in trouble, not to do whatever you want to do. You will be able to pay your loan back because it will be a percentage of your income. Regardless of how much you borrowed, we'll work it out so that the monthly payment is never too burdensome. That means nobody will be able to say they can't afford a college loan.

The third thing we want to do is to give tens of thousands of you the chance to earn credit against these loans before you go to college or while you're in college or to work them off after you get out of college, not by paying them off but by serving your country in a community service program, working with the elderly, working with other kids, working with housing programs, working with things that need to be done in the neighborhood or in nearby neighborhoods, or if you do it after you get out of college, working as teachers or police officers or in other needed areas in underserved communities in America. Just think of it. We could have tens of thousands of people who could pay off their loans entirely by giving a year or two of their lives to make their countries and their communities better.

Finally—this is the one kicker—I hope you will clap for this, too, because it's important. [*Applause*] Wait until you hear it. [*Laughter*] A lot of people don't pay off their college loans at all. There is an unbelievable default rate. We lose about $3 billion a year from people who don't pay their loans back. Now, there's a reason for that, and I'll explain it more later. But one of the things we do, if we're going to loan you the money directly, we're going to collect the money directly, too, involving the tax records at tax time so you can't beat the bill. People who borrow money, once you make it possible for them to repay it, should not be able to welsh on the loans. That undermines the ability of children coming along behind you to borrow the money. People ought to have to pay the loans back if we make it possible for them to do it. Everybody ought to have to do that.

Now, this will make it possible for millions of young people to borrow money to go to college. I don't propose to weaken the Pell grant programs and the other scholarship programs; we want to keep strengthening them. But this will make it possible for millions of people to borrow money, never have to worry about whether they'll be able to pay it back. You won't have to pay it back until you go to work. When you do go to work, you can pay it back as a small percentage of your income. You will have to pay it back and will do it all at lower cost. This will open the doors of college education to millions of Americans.

Now, you might ask yourself, "Well, if it's that simple, why is this man here talking to me about it? Why don't you just go do it?" Here's why. A lot of people are doing well with the present system. They're making a lot of money out of the present system. There are 7,800 lenders today, people making the student loans. There are 46 different Agencies that guarantee these loans against failure. Then, there are all these people who service the loans and who buy the loans in big packages in ways that you couldn't even begin to understand, probably, but they're all making good money out of the present system. It's confusing and it's costly, and the more money that goes to other things, the less money that's available to provide low-cost loans to the students of America.

Typically, the student takes out a loan from a bank, and then the bank takes the note that you sign when you get the loan and sells it to a corporation. The corporation then makes a profit by packaging the loan to someone else. And the loan is ultimately guaranteed by whom? All of us, the American taxpayers. So nobody can lose any money on it. Now, the biggest middle man in the whole thing is called Sallie Mae, the Student Loan Marketing Association. Last year, lenders made a total profit of $1 billion on student loans. Sallie Mae made $394 million. And between 1986 and 1991—listen to this; this is a group that helps us get student loans, right, which should not be a big profit-making operation—the costs of this corporation went down by 21 percent and its profits went up by 172 percent. But you didn't get the benefits of it; someone else did.

Interestingly enough, banks make more profits and more guaranteed profits on student loans than on car loans or mortgages, but there's no risk. They don't have to worry if the student doesn't pay back the loan. Why? Because the Government will send them 90 cents on the dollar. And as all of you know if you follow this at all, there's not much incentive for a bank to come recover the loan because it costs more than 10 percent of the loan to hire a lawyer and go through a lawsuit and file all the papers and do all that. So every year, the Government just writes a lot of checks to people for the loans that students don't repay. The taxpayers foot the bill, and that's all money that we can't spend loaning money to you and people like you to go to college.

The system is not very good. The lenders do well, but the people who need to borrow the money for a college education are hurt as a result. And the taxpayers get hit coming and going: not enough money made available for student loans, too much money going out to increase the deficit by paying off loans that never get repaid.

So, you might say, "Why don't we change this?" Because in the system we have, the people that are making plenty of money out of the present system will fight it. And they will hire lobbyists who make their money by trying to influence the Congress. No sooner had I even mentioned changing this system than Congress was deluged with lobbyists. The biggest organization, Sallie Mae alone, supposed to be in the business of helping you get money to go to college, has already hired seven of the most powerful lobbyists in Washington to try to stop this process from changing.

Now, there are a lot of people in Washington who want to keep the status quo. A lot of people don't want to lower the deficit, either. How did we get such a big national debt? How did the debt go from $1 trillion in 1980 to $4 trillion in 1992? Because we cut——

Audience member. Republicans.

The President. No, because we did what was popular. It wasn't just the Republicans; they had the White House, but let's be fair. Because how do you run up a big deficit? How do you run up a big deficit? The President proposes, and the Congress disposes. And it's popular in the short run to cut taxes and increase spending, right? I mean, that's popular. It's easy. I'll cut your taxes and send you a check. That's good, right? The problem is, is that at some point you run up debt after debt after debt after debt.

So what am I trying to do? What's not popular? I'm trying to cut spending and increase taxes, mostly on very wealthy Americans but not entirely, because we all have to try to recover our financial future. And I'm trying to do it in a way that preserves some money to invest in your education and new technologies for your jobs. But there are a lot of people who are making money out of a system that cuts taxes and increases spending, and it's not very popular to raise the money and cut the spending. That's the way it is here. There are a lot of people who are doing very well out of this system.

Now, why am I telling you this? Because it is your future on the line, and if you would like to have a system in which it is easier to borrow money to go to college, 2 or 4 years, and which it will be easier to pay it back and in which more of your tax money will be spent to benefit you and your education and your future, then you need to tell your Members of Congress, without regard to their political party, that you would like to have a better future, and this is a change that you want made.

This country is a very great country. It has been around for more than 200 years because every time we had to make real changes, we did it. Now the challenges we face are very much within our borders. It really bothers me that there are so many kids every year who are lost to the future as well as to themselves because of crime and drugs. It really bothers me that so many people drop out of college

and don't get the future that they ought to have just because of the money involved. It bothers me that we spend so much more than any other country in the world on health care, but we don't provide health coverage to all our people, and all the other advanced countries do. And it bothers me that we're not creating jobs for you, but we're piling up debt for your future.

I believe we can do better. But we can only do it if we'll tell each other the truth, keep our eyes wide open, and if you will say, hey, it is my future. Look, I've lived most of my life. Unless I beat the odds and live to be 94, I've lived more than half my life—or 92. I can't even add anymore. I've lived more than half my life unless I live to be 92 years old. It is your life that's on the line. It is your future that's on the line. And our job now is to open it up for you and to face the problems of this time so that you have the same chance to live the American dream that your forebears did. That is our job, and you can help us do it.

Again, let me say, I thank you for letting me come here. I look forward to answering your questions. But when I'm gone, if you don't remember anything else I said, just remember this: There's a plan in Washington to provide more student loans at a more affordable rate so that more people can go to college and stay, but we have to have the courage to change to adopt it.

Thank you very much.

Moderator. Thank you, President Clinton. We understand that you have some time where you could answer some questions from our students. So if you'd have a seat, ladies and gentlemen, and raise your hand, we'll begin by asking you some questions.

Yes?

Student Loans

Q. My name is John Snodgrass. I'm a junior from Fenton High School, and I am wondering what the Government is doing about the families that are defaulting on the student loans?

The President. Well, we try to collect it. But the problem now is that very often the people who don't pay are unemployed, or very often the people who don't pay—there's another problem with this, by the way—are people who got educations from trade schools that couldn't deliver what they promised. That is, they said, "We'll train you, and you'll be able to get a good job, and you'll be able to get a high salary." And a lot of these schools have been able to rip off this system for years because they could charm—they would get all their kids into these programs through student loans, and then they didn't have to worry about whether they finished the program or got jobs, because they already had the student loan money.

So what we're trying to do is, number one, be tougher with the schools. If they're not good schools and they're not really educating the students so the students can repay the loans, we're trying to stop those schools from being eligible for it. Number two, we're looking at ways to toughen up the enforcement.

Here's the way I want to change it so we can collect from almost everybody. If I said to you, look, I'll give you a loan and you don't have to repay it until you actually get a job so you're earning the money. And then you may borrow—let's say you borrow $5,000 and she borrows $10,000 and she borrows $20,000, and you all take jobs earning $30,000 a year, right? The people who borrowed more money would be given the option of paying that loan back as a limited percentage of their income, even though it would take them longer to pay it back. At least they would be able to make the payments, and they wouldn't be defaulting. And then if they didn't pay it back, we would know that they didn't because the Government would have the records, and we would enforce it just like we enforce taxes. In other words, you couldn't beat the bill. If you had a job and you had an income, you would have to pay it back.

But right now, we get the worst of all worlds. We let somebody else make the loan, and we tell them if it's not paid back, we'll pay 90 percent of the loan, and then after all the time goes by, we've got to figure out how to collect it. So we're doing better, but we can do much, much better if we clean out a lot of the system that's there and go at it directly.

Who had a microphone? Anybody? Yes, in the back.

Drug Policy

Q. Going back to that point you made before about drugs, I was wondering which direction the national drug policy is going, whether you want to support more law enforcement in getting drugs off the streets or if you're going to move more towards rehabilitation and education?

The President. Well, I don't think you can do one without the other. But let me say, I believe we need to increase the emphasis on education, prevention, and rehabilitation because we know that's what works. That is, for several years in the 1980's, drug use went down among most groups of young people, largely because they figured out it would kill them. In other words, people decided to change their behavior from the inside out.

Now, that does not—you can't sacrifice law enforcement to that. I think we should do two other things. Let me just run it out real quickly. The second thing we should do is to adopt law enforcement strategies that will reinforce people taking responsibility for themselves and increase the likelihood that they will move off drugs or out of the drug culture. I'll just give you two examples.

One is community policing. Thirty-five years ago there were three policemen on the street in America for every crime committed. Today, there are three crimes for every policeman. It's very hard, therefore, to have enough police to walk the streets, to know the neighbors, to know the kids, and to be a force for preventing crime. Where that has happened, it has worked.

The man I named to be the drug czar in our administration, Lee Brown, was the police chief in Atlanta, Houston, and New York City. And when he left New York, in the areas where they had put in community policing, the crime rate was going down. In some of those neighborhoods, for the first time in 30 years, there had been a reversal in the crime rate. So I think you have to do that.

And the final thing I want to say is we still have a big stake in working with our friends and allies in other countries to try to stop drugs from coming into this country. And we are in the process now of reexamining whether there's anything else we can do to reduce the flow of drugs into the country. But I'll tell you one thing, if we all decided we'd stop taking them, the flow would dry up because there wouldn't be any demand. So we can't just worry about blaming people from outside.

Go ahead. Where's the microphone? Yes?

Defense Spending

Q. A big issue that has been in the newspaper and on the news is military cutbacks. What I'm curious about is, what is being cut back in bases, arms, manpower. My curiosity is because I've enlisted in the U.S. Army. And is it going to effect my future if I decide to use it as a career and go my 20 years or anything like that. Will it affect me?

The President. Can you all hear his question? I'll repeat the question. He said he was concerned about military cutbacks. He wants to know what the nature of the cutbacks are, how far they will go. He's enlisted in the Army. Will that undermine his ability to make the Army a career because of the cutbacks.

Let me say, first of all, you know why the cutbacks are occurring. The cutbacks are occurring because an enormous percentage of our military force was directed against the Soviet Union, and it no longer exists. A lot of our nuclear arsenal was because they had a big nuclear arsenal, and we were positioned against them, and we had planes and ships supporting that, as well as people on the ground with land-based missiles. A lot of our military forces were positioned against all the troops they used to have in Eastern Europe, which have been withdrawn, and the military positioning they had around the world. So we have been able to—in fact, we've been obligated to reduce defense spending, starting in about '86 or '87 because of the receding nature of the threat. And that's good on the whole.

Now, the world is still a pretty dangerous place, and the United States is still the only comprehensive military power. And we have to be careful how we reduce that defense spending and how much we do it.

Right now, we're doing it across the board in three areas: We're reducing military personnel with the view toward going down to a base force of about 1.4 million over the next 5 years, down from over 2.5 million just a few years ago. So that's a lot of people that have been mustered out, including all volunteers, people who wanted to serve their country, many of whom would like to have stayed longer. So the answer to your question is, if we have a smaller base force, it will be more competitive to get into and to stay in the Armed Forces. The recruitment has already been scaled back. So if you've been recruited and if you're going in under the new, smaller recruitment quotas, you'll probably have a reasonable chance to stay in a good, long while if you choose to do it. But not so many good young people will. In that way, it's kind of sad, because the military has done a magnificent job of training and edu-

cating people, of inculcating them with good values and good work habits as well as good education. So that's one of the—kind of the down sides. The second thing we're doing is closing bases, and that's very unpopular. But you can't just cut the forces and not close the bases. And the third thing we've had to do is to cut back on a number of weapons procurements, which cost jobs in the defense industry.

So, on balance, this has been a good thing, but I want you to understand there are some bad consequences to it. And one of the struggles that I expect to have constantly for the next 4 years is to try to convince people in the Congress that as we cut defense we need to be reinvesting that money in education and technology in America to create jobs to replace those lost in defense.

And thank you for being willing to serve your country.

Government Gridlock

Q. Mr. President, I think the American people have become increasingly disenchanted with the lack of progress in our Government. How are you going to convince the American people and all the Members of Congress that your programs are good ones, and how are you going to break the filibusters that have been——

The President. Well, we've only had one. We broke them all but one. Keep in mind that I've just been there 100 days, and I had 12 years of a different direction before I took office. It's hard to turn it around in 100 days. I'm actually quite optimistic.

The Congress passed the outline of the budget I presented which, as I explained earlier, is a very tough thing, you know, to bring the deficit down in a record time, the first time in 17 years under Democrats and Republican Presidents the Congress had ever passed the budget resolution within the time limit. So I think we're moving fairly rapidly.

Just shortly after I took office, Congress passed the Family and Medical Leave Act, guaranteeing people the right to take a little time off from work when they have a sick child or a sick parent or a baby is born, without losing their jobs. That had gone through 8 years of fights and two vetoes. The Congress is trying to pass today this motor voter bill, which would really open up the political process to millions of Americans. So I think we are making progress.

Now, let me also tell you that some of this stuff is really hard. I mean the reason that these things have not been done before is that we've done easy things for 12 years. What I'm asking the Congress to do are things that are really hard, and it may take a while to do it. But I'm not prepared to say, at the moment anyway, that we've lost the battle to gridlock. I don't agree with the minority of Senators who filibustered the jobs bill. But that was not just a political battle; that was an idea battle. A lot of them thought that we shouldn't spend any money on anything until we pass the overall budget which reduces the deficit, even though I knew we were going to.

My view was: We're going to pass this budget, we're going to reduce the deficit, and we've got to get some jobs in this economy. So that was an issue I didn't win on. I'm not going to win every issue I'm fighting. But I believe that we have a real chance to make this Government work, and I'm basically quite optimistic about it.

The one thing I would urge you not to do, any of you, is to put too much faith in just the day-to-day development of the news. You have to take a long-term view of this. And we've had this health care problem for a long time. We've had this economic problem for a long time. And in just a very short time we've been able to put these issues back on the national agenda and move them forward. So I think what you need to do is to remind everybody you can remind—if you want to know what you can do and what the American people can do, it's to try to make everybody think in a less partisan way, not worry about the fights between Republicans and Democrats, and think more every day about what are the problems of this country. And if you don't like what President Clinton says, what's your alternative?

In other words, let's just keep moving the ball forward. What I try to do is to put these problems high on the national agenda and try to ask people to lay down their partisan armor and look at these problems in a new and different way and keep pushing the ball forward. So if you don't like what I want to do about it, then if you're not going to support that, then come up with some alternative so we can do something. The worst thing we can do is stay in paralysis. Let's do something. That, I think, ought to be the message.

Financial Aid for Education

Q. In the past, the financial aid has been based upon a quota system for racial and ethnic minorities. I'm wondering if you're planning to continue this quota system or will it be based on talent and merit and needs straight across the board?

The President. There may be certain minority scholarship programs in certain universities. But the program that I would speak of, both national service and the student loan program, would be available across-the-board. I mean—and I believe—and the student loan program should be available across-the-board virtually without regard to income once you can guarantee that the repayment is going to be there so you don't have to worry about loaning too much money. That's what I think. I favor broad-based and inclusive programs and national service will also be broad-based and inclusive.

I think you have to make efforts to include people from all races and income groups, and I would want to see that done because we have a big stake in making sure that we close the disparity in income and race of people getting an education, because if you come out the other end of the educational system, then the income differences tend to vanish. But I don't think anyone should be excluded, and I don't want to ration this program. I want to open this program to all Americans.

Space Program

Q. Mr. Clinton, I'd like to know what your views are on the space program, if you are in favor of cutting anything or improving anything?

The President. In general, I support strongly the space program and the NASA budget. I have some problems with the space station itself for a couple of reasons. One, it's a hugely expensive program, and there's a lot of debate within NASA itself about whether the old designs should be continued, whether we need that space station design. Secondly, it's had staggering cost overruns. Every time we turn around they're coming back for hundreds of millions of more dollars. And with the deficit the way it is and all these other problems, we can't afford it. So what NASA is doing now is trying to redesign the space station and come up with a multi-year space program that I hope we can get strong bipartisan support for.

I think it would be a big mistake for America

to drastically cut back its role in space. Now I've been criticized for cutting back on the space station, but I haven't cut back the NASA budget. We have cut back the rate of increase that they want to cover all the cost overruns for anything that happens. I just don't think we can do that with the old space station design.

So we're now looking at three alternatives for the space station to take a new and modified course. But I think it would be a great mistake for America to withdraw from space exploration and from work in space. For one thing, it's one of the ways that we may find answers to a lot of our environmental problems as well as to continue to build our scientific and technological base after we cut defense. So I hope we can continue to support it.

Q. Mr. President——

The President. Go ahead. We'll take one more and then I'll take this young man's. Go ahead.

Bosnia

Q. Mr. President, I was wondering with all the news about Bosnia, do you see any differences in sending troops to Bosnia where you were strongly opposed to civil war in Vietnam in the late sixties?

The President. Well, first of all, I do. That's a good question. But I have never advocated the United States unilaterally sending troops to Bosnia to fight on one side or the other of the civil war.

Let me just say what's complicated about it. There plainly is a civil war in Bosnia that is, among other things, a fight primarily between the Serbs and the Muslims but also involving the Croatians. It is complicated by the fact that Serbia, a separate country, has intervened in it, and complicated by the fact that the United Nations before Bosnia, the nation of Bosnia was even recognized, imposed an arms embargo in the area. But the practical impact of the arms embargo that the United Nations imposed was to give the entire weaponry of the Yugoslav Army to the Serbian Bosnians and deprive any kind of equal weaponry to the people fighting against them. So the global community had, not on purpose, but inadvertently, has had a huge impact on the outcome of that war in ways that have been very bad.

My position has been pretty simple and straightforward from the beginning. I think that without the United States unilaterally getting in, or without even—I don't think the United Na-

tions should enter the war on one side or the other. But I think there is much more that we can do to induce the parties to stop the fighting, to do what we can to stop this idea of ethnic cleansing: murdering people, raping children, and doing terrible acts of violence solely because of people's religion. Biologically, there is not much difference between the Muslims, the Croatians, and the Serbians there. The ethnic differences are rooted in religious and historical factors.

Thirdly, we want to try to confine that conflict so it doesn't spread into other places and involve other countries, like Albania and Greece and Turkey, which could have the impact of undermining the peace in Europe and the growth and stability of democracies there.

So I think the United Nations, the world community can do more in that regard. That's quite a different thing than what happened in Vietnam where the United States essentially got involved in what was a civil war on one side or the other. There are some remarkable similarities to it which should give us caution about doing that. There are similarities to that. There are similarities to Lebanon. But that does not mean, just because—I wouldn't propose doing exactly what the United States did in Vietnam. That does not mean that the United States should not consider doing something more, especially if we can get the Europeans who are after all closer to it, who have a more immediate stake in it, to try to help us to stop the ethnic cleansing, the continued fighting, and minimize dramatically the risk of the war spreading.

So that's what we're struggling for an answer to. It's a very, very difficult problem.

Students and the Educational System

Q. Mr. President, what do you feel we as students can do to better the U.S. educational system?

The President. Read more. Read more. I think you can read more. I think you can establish tutoring groups in schools where the students that are doing well help those which aren't. There's a lot of evidence that by the time somebody reaches your age that you all have more influence on one another than I would on any of you. And there's a lot of evidence in schools that are succeeding that when students work with each other either in the same classroom or across grade lines, that the overall performance of the school goes up.

Interestingly enough, there are a lot of studies even showing at elementary schools that this is true and certainly true in high schools. So I think one of the things that I have seen work repeatedly over the last dozen years that I've spent countless hours in schools with students and teachers is that kind of working together.

The third thing that I think you can do is to speak out in a way for a culture of learning and for good values in the schools. I think that's important. I think if the students want a school to be a place where learning is valued and where everybody counts and where violence or drugs or other bad behavior are not tolerated, the students can have more to do with getting rid of it than anything else if it is a bad thing, if everybody looks down on it. And I think that can make a huge difference.

It's so limited what the rest of us can do to help the schools unless there is a right sort of feeling in the hearts of the young people involved. And I think anything we can do to convince all students that they count, that they matter, that we need them all, that they shouldn't drop out, that they can learn, anything we can do in that regard school by school, class by class, year by year, is going to make education in this country a lot better.

The last thing I think you can do is to decide what you think is wrong with education and how we can make it better and tell people like me about it. In other words, tell us from your perspective how we can make your schools a lot better, what you need, how we can give you a better future, what we're not doing that we could be doing. Those are the things you can do.

Moderator. President Clinton, I understand we have time for one more question.

Women in the Armed Forces

Q. Yes. I have a question about women in the military. I heard that they're going to be able to go in combat now. Is it going to become a law that they're going to be drafted also?

The President. I'm sorry I didn't hear you. Go ahead.

Q. I've heard rumors that women are going to be able to be in combat now in the military. So I'm wondering, are they going to be able to be drafted like men?

The President. First of all, men are not drafted. We have an all volunteer service. There are no draftees. Anyone who goes into the service is like this young man. The men or women choose to go. And we have a lot of people who want to go now because of the justifiably high esteem in which our military is held. I can tell you that you can talk to any career service officer, and he or she will tell you that we have the best educated, best trained, best equipped, highest morale military service we have ever had. And it also, by the way, is the most diverse one we've ever had, opening up more opportunities to women and to all members of all races that we've ever had. And yet it's the best educated, best trained, best equipped, best able military service we have ever had although it's under a lot of stress now because of all the downsizing.

The Service Chiefs in the Joint Chiefs of Staff have decided that they ought to open up some more combat roles to women, principally on combat ships. The Navy, for example—I bet a lot of you don't know this—the Navy now has three noncombat ships under the command of women, the United States Navy does.

But Admiral Kelso, the Chief of Naval Operations, had decided that some more combat ship roles should be open to women. And then there was also a decision made that women ought to be eligible to fly combat missions in the face of clear evidence that the airplanes they fly today require not strength so much as response, the capacity for quick and agile response. And there's a lot of evidence that women are at least as good in some of those functions as men, so the Joint Chiefs made that decision. That was a military decision in which I did not intervene at all. I think if the evidence supports it, it's a very good decision. But I want you to know it was made based on the evidence in the case and made by the military, and they deserve the credit.

Well, I could do this all day long. You have been terrific and I'm very proud of you, and you've asked wonderful questions, all of them were very good. I wish you well. Have a good day. And don't stop thinking about these educational issues. Thank you very much.

NOTE: The President spoke at 9:55 a.m. in the gymnasium at Fenton High School. In his remarks, he referred to Brian Shamie, student council president; John G. Meredith, superintendent of schools; and Kevin O'Keefe, Special Assistant to the President. A portion of the question-and- answer session could not be verified because the tape was incomplete.

Remarks to the Leadership Conference on Civil Rights
May 11, 1993

Thank you very much, Mr. Vice President, for that wonderful introduction and for being such a great partner in the campaign of 1992 and in this administration. I think it is fair to say that Vice President Gore has already exercised a larger role in this administration than perhaps any Vice President in the history of this country. And I hope he will continue to do so.

I'm honored to be here with Ralph Neas and with my longtime friend Benjamin Hooks. Don't you just love to hear Ben talk? I mean, really, I could hear him intone those poems from now until tomorrow morning, reminding me of the rhythms of my childhood and the faith of our parents.

I'm proud to be here with all of you tonight not only because of what you have done for the last four decades and more but because of what together we must do now. I'm proud of your commitment to civil rights. I'm proud to be here with our Attorney General, Janet Reno, who is the embodiment of that.

I thank you for the vote of the national board of the leadership conference today to support the nomination of Lani Guinier to be Assistant Attorney General for Civil Rights. I want to say a special word of support for Lani Guinier. I went to law school with her, and I announced at the Justice Department the other day when we announced all of our Assistant Attorneys General that she had actually sued me once. [*Laughter*] Not only that, she didn't lose. And I nominated her anyway. So the Senate ought to be able to put up with a little controversy in the cause of civil rights and go on and confirm her so we can get about the business of America.

I want to say, too, how honored I am to be here with your honorees. My friend Dorothy Height: From the freedom schools in Mississippi to the Black Family Reunion, what a guiding spirit she has been to all of us.

I want to take my hat off to Raul Yzaguirre for his leading voice. Over 20 years ago, I first came in contact with La Raza as a movement and a commitment. And I have watched them over these years help people all across the country with the practical problems of life which give real meaning to the idea of civil rights, when you can actually live in a decent house and have a decent job and know your kids are going to get a decent education and know that you're going to be treated fairly no matter what your race is.

I want to say, too, how very much I admire Justin Dart for all the work that he's done as Chair of the President's Commission on Employment of People with Disabilities and leader in making the Americans with Disabilities Act come to life. You know, Justin, every time we went anywhere in the campaign and had a rally, we always had a section for people with disabilities. Today I went to a suburb north of Chicago, in a heavily Republican community, as it turned out, to meet with a bunch of students from the high school that I was visiting and other high schools and people in the community. And we had a big section there for the students with disabilities. And I was thinking as I was coming over here tonight, a lot of those kids are where they are today because of what you did—and you ought to be proud of that—sitting in the front of the row so they can ask the President their questions and shake hands with the President; instead of being overlooked, being uplifted.

I say that to you to make one introductory point. I've been here for 100 days and a sum, fighting to break the gridlock in Washington. And sometimes I think the biggest gridlock of all is the gridlock in our minds, the hold that foolish notions have on our imaginations. I have been roundly attacked by people on the extreme right trying to make me look like some radical leftwinger because I had this crazy notion that I ought to have an administration that would have some diversity and give women as well as men and people of color as well as people who look like me the chance to serve if they could meet high standards of excellence. And there are people who say, well—and I see these relentless articles in the paper—oh, that's why no appointments are being made. Well, so in 100 days I show up at the Justice Department, and I ask for the totals: Pass me the envelope, please. [*Laughter*] And it turns out that in spite of my commitment to diversity and excellence, after 100 days my predecessor had made 99 appointments, his predecessor, President Reagan, had made 152 appointments, and I'd made 173. Where are they? And I expected to see the shameless right in sackcloth and ashes, saying that we had falsely accused this poor President in promoting gridlock. But they have no shame. [*Laughter*]

Let me tell you something: Today when I was in Illinois, a young, handsome, fine-looking Hispanic man stood up and said, "I have joined the United States Army. And I'm proud that I'm going to serve my country. And I know we've got to cut the military budget, but I want to know if you're going to cut it so much that I can't give my whole career to my country if I want to." And I thought to myself, why doesn't somebody point out to all these people who have attacked us for trying to open the doors of opportunities that the number one, most successful institution in the United States of America for giving opportunities to women and people of color are the United States military branches. They have done it with a commitment to excellence and opportunity. And what we've got to do is to prove that the rest of us can do so as well. And we ought not to make this a partisan issue, and the guardians of gridlock should stop trying to use it to move arguments around that indicate that there's somehow something wrong with the President who believes that everybody who can serve ought to have the chance to do so.

This administration is committed to the enforcement of the civil rights laws. This administration is also committed to programs like national service that give everybody the possibility of being part of a new era of civic responsibility. This administration is committed to guaranteeing that every American is entitled to a fair chance at the brass ring but even more important, to empowering people to seize those opportunities, to moving beyond the incredible gridlock in the mind of this town that you either

have to give somebody something for nothing or take it all off the table.

Why don't we behave in Washington the way people behave in their normal lives? We need opportunity and responsibility. Why don't we stop making these nutty arguments that imply that everything in life is an either-or proposition: We're either going to write somebody a check and bust the Government budget, or we're just going to stick it to them and walk away. That's not the way life works.

You know, civil rights should embody a country that works. We don't want to guarantee everybody equal employment opportunities when there are no jobs. Does that mean that we have to sacrifice one and not the other? No, it means you should have a President who will pursue both, walking and chewing gum at the same time. That's what this is about. Is that right?

We want to guarantee everybody an equal opportunity to get an education, but wouldn't it be nice if the education you're getting is also better? It's not either-or. We want to guarantee everybody the right to health care and family security through health care, but wouldn't it be nice if you live in a rural area or in the heart of a big city if there happens to be a clinic to visit?

I just am amazed after 100 days to find that a lot of the gridlock that has gripped this city for so long is in the imposition of what one writer had called false choices on all of us who are supposed to make policy. It never occurred to me that I should appoint somebody who wasn't qualified to a job. You know, I don't wake up in the morning thinking, you know, I need to find some female Latino who is totally unqualified to put in a job. [*Laughter*] Or neither did it ever occur to me that every white man I appoint is going to hit a home run every day. But that is the kind of rhetoric you see running beneath so much of the characterization when we try to change 12 years of attitudes.

The same people that were criticizing the previous administrations for being insensitive to civil rights immediately turned around and say, "Oh, there's too much, too much attention being given to ethnicity and gender, and that's why no appointments are being made." So the record comes in, and I'm still waiting for the acknowledgement.

I tell you, folks, I refuse to believe that we cannot go forward together, that we cannot set an example, that we cannot make progress. I refuse to believe that you can't be committed to civil rights and to civic responsibility. I refuse to believe that we can't create economic opportunity by empowering people to seize control of their destiny and changing the Government's policies.

I think that if this leadership council should have any mission today, it should be to break through those barriers that push us all into one extreme camp or the other and make us mute in the face of reality and common sense. Surely we can bring the experience of our own lives and the lives of our fellow Americans beyond the borders of this city to the policymaking process that will dominate Washington for the next year. That is what we ought to do if we want civil rights to come alive in this country.

You know, when I ran for this job I spent a lot of time in African-American churches because I always had, and because I felt at home. When I got this job and I sought to protect the religious and civil liberties of every American, it was because I wanted mine protected and because I have a sharp memory of what it was like to live in a society where half the people I knew, because of their color, were treated as second-class citizens.

I also have a sharp memory of those who had the courage to try to change that position. And now that I am President, I want you to know that I'll make my mistakes from time to time, but I'm going to keep trying to move the ball forward. I believe we can make advances. I don't believe that our fights are over.

I know that there are still civil rights battles to be fought, but I know that they need to be fought today in the context of making a real difference in real people's lives. And we should not be intimidated, those of us who believe in the cause of civil rights for all Americans, into thinking that somehow that can be separated from the fight for economic justice and economic progress and making our free enterprise system work better.

We should not let people who basically don't care whether we make progress in civil rights think that you can separate civil rights from the fight for substantive improvements in education and for meaningful advances in health care or any other area of our national life. Let us resolve tonight that we're going to spend the next 4 years breaking down the gridlock by tearing down the artificial barriers in people's minds to bringing us together, saying we don't have a person to waste and lifting up everybody's God-given potential and doing what we can to see that they achieve it.

Thank you very much, and God bless you.

NOTE: The President spoke at 8 p.m. at the Hyatt Regency Hotel. In his remarks, he referred to Ralph Neas, executive director, Leadership Conference on Civil Rights; Benjamin L. Hooks, former executive director, National Association for the Advancement of Colored People; Dorothy I. Height, president and CEO, National Council of Negro Women; and Raul Yzaguirre, president and CEO, National Council of La Raza.

Appointment for Members of the Commission on Presidential Scholars
May 11, 1993

The President today appointed 32 members of the White House Commission on Presidential Scholars. Among them is New Jersey Governor Jim Florio, who will serve as Chair of the Commission.

The Commission on Presidential Scholars is responsible for selecting 141 graduating high school seniors from around the country to become Presidential Scholars, the Nation's highest honor for high school students. The scholars are chosen on the basis of their accomplishments in many areas, such as academic and artistic

success, leadership, and involvement in their schools and communities.

"The Presidential Scholars Program is an important vehicle for recognizing the efforts and accomplishments of our country's young people," said the President. "I am glad that Governor Florio and the rest of this distinguished group of Americans have agreed to serve on this Commission, and I look forward to welcoming the students they choose to the White House."

In addition to Governor Florio, the members

of the Commission are:

Margaret R. Blackshere, Illinois, assistant to the president of the Illinois Federation of Teachers; former elementary school teacher; holds a master's in urban education from Southern Illinois University

Francis J. Bonner, Jr., Pennsylvania, chair of the department of physical medicine and rehabilitation at Mt. Sinai and Graduate Hospitals, Philadelphia, and Sacred Heart Hospital, Norristown

Thomas E. Britton, New Hampshire, chair of the Monadnock Region District School Board; marketing representative for the Millipore Corp. and North American Pharmaceutical Field Marketing

Rev. S.C. Cureton, South Carolina, pastor of the Reedy River Baptist Church; member of the president's executive board of the National Baptist Convention, U.S.A.

John Davidson, New Mexico, member of the New Mexico Commission on Higher Education; shareholder and director in the law firm of Erwin and Davidson

Joseph D. DiVincenzo, New York, commissioner of the Niagara Frontier Transportation Authority; president of DiVincenzo & Associates Insurance Agency; adjunct professor at the Rochester Institute of Technology

Jim R. Fotter, Wyoming, president of the Wyoming Education Association; member of the Education Commission of the States; delegate at the 1992 Democratic National Convention

Susan F. Friebert, Wisconsin, former teacher and currently a high school team leader for guidance counselors and community volunteers to develop and implement programs to direct student academic planning and achievement

Susan E. Gaertner, Minnesota, director of the human services division of the Ramsey County, MN, attorney's office, where she directs legal services for child support enforcement, paternity actions, and civil commitments for the second largest jurisdiction in the State

Felicia Gervais, Florida, president of Leonard L. Farber, Inc., a shopping center development firm; also serves on numerous non-profit boards, including Outreach Broward (a program for troubled adolescents) and Center One (the Nation's first AIDS center)

Freman Hendrix, Michigan, assistant Wayne County executive for legislative affairs; member of many civic groups, including the Northwest Detroit Community Leaders Council

Patricia Jean Henry, Oklahoma, president of the National PTA; member of the boards of the Oklahoma State Chamber of Commerce and the Academy for State Goals; co-founder of Pathway House, a rehabilitation program for drug-addicted children

Barbara Holt, Maine, director of Franklin Pierce College in Portsmouth, NH; served as the chair and director of Victory '92 in Maine

Gloria Jackson, Florida, retired public school administrator in Ft. Lauderdale; alternate delegate to the Democratic National Convention

Nathaniel Hawthorne LaCour, Louisiana, president of the United Teachers of New Orleans; vice president of the American Federation of Teachers; national board member of the A. Philip Randolph Institute; member of the National Board for Professional Teaching Standards

Dhyan Lal, California, principal of Carson High School in Los Angeles; focus of a PBS documentary exploring how a principal communicates with a culturally diverse student population to create a positive learning environment in post-riot Los Angeles

Ronnie Fern Liebowitz, New Jersey, partner in the Newark law firm of Hellring, Lindman, Goldstein & Siegal; former general counsel to Rutgers University

Bill Marshall, Ohio, law professor; served as the Maine State director for the Clinton campaign

Penny Miller, Kentucky, assistant professor of political science at the University of Kentucky; chair of the Kentucky Commission on Women

Sandy Miller, Nevada, First Lady of the State of Nevada; former teacher and advocate for children with learning disabilities

Marilyn Monahan, New Hampshire, secretary-treasurer of the National Education Association

Dan Morales, Texas, attorney general of Texas; first Hispanic elected to a statewide constitutional office in the State of Texas

Daniel Morris, Colorado, former teacher and

president of the Colorado Education Association; former Peace Corps volunteer

Carla Nuxoll, Washington, President of the Washington Education Association; chair of the board of PULSE

James Shimoura, Michigan, former special assistant attorney general for the State of Michigan; shareholder in the law firm of Kemp, Klein, Umphrey, and Edelman

Eddie L. Smith, Jr., Mississippi, former high school teacher; Mayor of Holly Springs, MS

Dawn Steel, California, president of Columbia Pictures from 1987 to 1990, the first woman to head a major motion picture studio

Niara Sudarkasa, Pennsylvania, president of Lincoln University in Chester County, PA;

previously the associate vice president for academic affairs at the University of Michigan, where she was the first African-American woman to receive tenure

Nancy Verderber, Missouri, administrative liaison for disability-related issues for the St. Louis County School Districts; member of the Coalition of Citizens with Disabilities in Greater St. Louis

Margaret M. Whillock, Arkansas, executive vice president of the Baptist Medical Systems Foundation in Little Rock; director of development at the University of Arkansas

Tracey Bailey, Florida, National Teacher of the Year

Nomination for Posts at the Interior and Transportation Departments
May 11, 1993

The President named a total of four officials at the Departments of Transportation and the Interior today. He expressed his intention to nominate Frank Kruesi to be Assistant Secretary of Transportation for Transportation Policy and Ada Deer to be Assistant Secretary of the Interior for Indian Affairs. The President also approved the appointment of Richard Mintz to be the Director of Transportation's Office of Public Affairs, and Patricia Beneke to be Associate Solicitor for Energy and Resources at Interior.

"I am gratified that these individuals will be joining me in Washington," said the President. "Frank Kruesi has been an innovative and successful policy adviser to Mayor Daley. Ada Deer has been a powerful and eloquent voice for changing national Indian policy. Both will be valuable parts of this administration, as will Richard Mintz and Patricia Beneke."

NOTE: Biographies of the nominees were made available by the Office of the Press Secretary.

Interview With Don Imus of WFAN Radio, New York City
May 12, 1993

Mr. Imus. Good morning, Mr. President.
The President. Good morning. How are you?
Mr. Imus. I'm fine. How are you?
The President. I'm all right.

The First 100 Days

Mr. Imus. Let me ask you something. What the hell is going on down there in that White House? What do you mean, you've lost your focus? [*Laughter*]
The President. I haven't lost my focus. You've

just been seeing me through the foggy lens of television instead of the direct one of radio. [*Laughter*] There's a big headline in the Washington Post today, "Clinton Wins Third Major Victory In Congress." I think we're doing fine. You know, we lost one bill, and a lot of people think it's like the last days of Pompeii. I mean, if you're going to fight for change, you've got to be prepared to lose a few as well as win some. But I think we're well on track.

Let me just point out that when the Congress adopted my budget outline, it was the first time in 17 years that they'd adopted it within the legal time limit, faster than they've moved in 17 years. Everybody complained about the appointments process. When 100 days went by, it turned out I'd made more appointments during the period than my two predecessors did. We just passed the motor voter bill yesterday, a big issue for younger voters, making it easier for them to register to vote. We've got the economic program on track. I feel good about the way things are. But you know, change is not easy and people—if you want to keep score after 100 days, where we had 4,500 days of trickle-down economics, you know, I haven't done everything I meant to do in 100 days, but I never promised to do it in 100 days. I think we're doing fine.

Mr. Imus. I think that looked good last night, breaking that Republican filibuster, because it looks like Bob Dole—it's like the "Friday the 13th" movies, you know, where you think you've finished him off and then next thing you know that hand comes popping up out of the lake there and, of course, in this case there was a pen in it. [*Laughter*] But this is an indication that it doesn't look like the Republicans are going to be able to waylay everything you're trying to do, does it?

The President. Well, I don't think so. You know, the filibuster on the jobs bill was an unusual thing, I think, not that they tried to do it but that they never let the majority vote. And I think the American people have got that figured out. And there are always going to be Republicans, or most always, that agree with some aspect of what we're doing. And when you reach out to them and you try to work out compromises, there are, almost always, there are some who want to go for the national interest over the partisanship, and that's what happened here. We worked out some problems with that motor voter bill, and it rolled right through. The same thing with family and medical leave. So I think if we just keep working at it, we'll have some success.

We've had 12 cloture votes—that's the attempt to get 60 percent of the Senate just so a majority can vote their will—12 already in the first 3½ months. So I imagine they'll make us do this a lot, but I think there are always going to be some Republicans who want to be part of a bipartisan movement for change, and

I'm encouraged by it.

Mr. Imus. Or Republicans who want to be President.

The President. There are always going to be people who want to be President, and some days I like to give it to them. But if I did that, at least I'd have a telephone conversation with you before I give it up so you can call me President Bubba. [*Laughter*] See, I've been waiting for this all this time.

The Economy

Mr. Imus. Well, Mr. President, I don't know what you've heard about what's been going on in this program, but it's always been very respectful. And anything you've heard to the contrary would just be further evidence of the collapse of the intelligence community in this country. [*Laughter*] And I mean, these guys didn't even know that the Berlin Wall went down until they saw it on CNN. So you can't trust what you hear from them.

I was talking to my friend Jeff Greenfield over at ABC, and he had a good observation. He said, is this economic program of yours tougher to sell now, you think, because for whatever circumstances you weren't able to run on it?

The President. No, I don't think so. The difference in the program that we're advocating and the one I ran on over a 5-year period is not very great, but what happened was after the election—I want to emphasize this—after the election the Government came out—the previous administration—and said that the deficit was going to be $50 billion a year bigger than they had said before in 3 of the 4 years of the term that I now occupy. So I had to do more to cut the deficit, and we had to put that up front. And it's worked pretty well so far.

You know, ever since we announced serious intentions to cut the deficit and were specific about it, interest rates began dropping very steeply, mortgage rates were at a 20 year low. You're going to have a $100 billion—that's a lot of money—in refinancing of home mortgages and business debt and other things which I think will really help the economy.

But that meant we had to put off some of the plans or scale them back in the early going and put them back into the later years of my term to invest money in things that I think are also important. But we've got to get control of this deficit. It's been spinning out of control now, getting worse and worse for a dozen years, and we don't have the funds we need to invest in jobs to grow the economy, and I think it's very important.

Mr. Imus. I think William Greider pointed it out in Rolling Stone—and you either agree with it obviously or don't—that during the campaign that the focus was on and the debate was on jobs. And it seemed that because of Bush "cooking the books" and not realizing that the deficit was going to be a little bit bigger than it was, that then the agenda switched to this 5-year plan to reduce the deficit. Let me ask you——

The President. But wait, let me make one point. I think they're two sides of the same thing. That is, if I didn't think that reducing the deficit over the long run would help us to create more jobs and if I didn't think we could also get some increased investment in new technologies and education and training and to rebuild our cities and to do these things that have to be done, I wouldn't be doing this.

I think they're two sides of the same coin. I think until we show we can get control over the Government's budget and we can make some spending cuts, as well as restore some of the tax loses that we had in the early years of the trickle-down revolution, I don't think we can get a job program going in the country. So I think this getting the deficit down is part of a long-term job growth strategy. Jobs are the issue; reducing the deficit is a means to get control of our economic future. The whole purpose of it is to put people to work.

Mr. Imus. To talk about it just a second, this economic plan and some of these numbers that we see now suggest that the public is—about half, 50 percent of them don't think it's going to work. And let me tell you what filters down to people like me, you know, aside from the esoteric proposals and figures and stuff that many of us don't understand, but what we hear is that the numbers we hear is that, for every $3 and so in new taxes, we're looking at about a dollar or so in spending cuts. And there are some people that think the ratio's even higher than that. Is that accurate?

The President. No, no. But I'll tell you, if you look at this thing over a 5-year period we have more spending cuts than we do tax increases. And that's true even though we have some targeted increases in investment, in edu-

cation and training, and new technologies. Now, the people who argue this the other way, they play clever games. For example, if you're going to cut a program that's in place, you may have to phase in the cuts over a 5-year period; if you raise a tax, you can raise a tax immediately. You've got to look at this whole budget.

In this budget we have more spending cuts than tax increases. We do have some spending increases, but if you don't believe that there are differences in different kinds of spending, I don't know what we can do. We have some spending increases to give a nationwide apprenticeship program to help retrain the work force. We have some spending increases to get into new technologies to make up for defense cuts because we're losing a lot of high-tech, high-wage jobs.

You know, up in Connecticut we've had a lot of employment dislocation because of defense cutbacks, but you've got a whole high-wage work force that needs to have something else to do. And every other government in the world is investing in new technologies to try to create those jobs for their people. If we don't do it, we're going to be left behind. So we have to target some investments. But this budget has over 200 very specific budget cuts over the last budget adopted in the previous administration. And if you look—it's 5-year budget, that's what the law requires us to do, to adopt 5-year budgets—we've got more spending cuts than tax increases, and we should.

Mr. Imus. Is it important what the ratio is? And if it is, what should it be, do you think? I mean, because that's the—you know, that's kind of the way we relate to it.

The President. Well, the issue is how many cuts can you get without pulling the economy into a recession. What do you have to cut, how many cuts can you get without unfairly cutting the elderly? The same people who say we don't have enough cuts are also often saying we shouldn't cut what we're cutting. And the truth is, if you want to get to a balanced budget through spending reductions, the only way to do it now is to get control of health care costs, and that, basically, in the later part of this decade, if we can adopt a national health system and—you know, Hillary has been working on that with hundreds of others—and we can bring the Government's deficit down to zero, but you can't do that overnight. And the biggest part of our deficit growth now is in health care costs and interest on the debt.

We're not spending a bigger percentage of our income on Social Security—our national income—than we were 10 years ago. We're spending a smaller percentage of our income on Federal aid in education than we were 10, 12 years ago. What's happened now is we started cutting defense, but health care increases overcame the defense cuts. So what I'm trying to do is to cut everything I can now, get health care costs under control and look toward not only cutting the deficit but bringing it down to zero over a multi-year period. You just can't do this overnight.

You know, we took the national debt from $1 trillion to $4 trillion in 12 years with a $300-plus billion a year deficit when I took office. You can't just eliminate that overnight without having serious economic dislocations. You've got to do it in a disciplined way and take it down.

Mr. Imus. There's already been some compromise with some members of your own party in Congress. Do you anticipate any more of that, or is it——

The President. Well, I think there have been some changes that make it better. After all, we put this plan on the table only 30 days after I had taken office, and I invited people to comment on it but to keep its essential features intact. That is, we had to have the spending cuts before I would agree to tax increases. The tax increases had to be largely progressive; that is, they ought to be on people at higher income levels whose tax rates went down in the 1980's while their incomes went up, that we ought to have a earned-income tax credit. That's taxpayer jargon for giving a tax break to working class people with children, particularly who would be especially hard hit by the energy tax, and that affects people with incomes up to about $29,000 a year, where they'll get an offset on their income tax to make up for the energy tax. And there ought to be some incentives for investment in the American economy, either mine or some others. And we emphasize small business, and we emphasize new plant and equipment for big business. And those things are all going to be in the ultimate tax package. So I feel good about it. I think that, you know, the changes that are being made basically, at least so far the ones that have been discussed with me, don't in any way undermine the fundamental principles of the tax program and the spending cut program I laid out.

Bosnia

Mr. Imus. There is a dramatic picture of you and an agonizing Lyndon Johnson on the cover of the current issue of Time magazine asking the question if Bosnia is going to be your Vietnam. One, let me ask you, do you think it has that potential? And two, what is the United States policy in Bosnia?

The President. Well, let me answer the first question. There are similarities to Vietnam in the sense that there is a civil war and there is a national dividing line, that is, between Bosnia and Serbia, which doesn't fully coincide with the ethnic cohesion of the Serbs in Bosnia and Serbia; same thing on the other end of the country with Croatia and Bosnia-Herzegovina. It's a very complicated thing. Those folks have been fighting with each other for a long time.

There are also some differences, however. You have the continuation of a principle of ethnic cleansing that you didn't have in Vietnam, people getting killed or raped just because of their religion, just because they're Muslims and because of their historic conflict in that area. And you have a United Nations resolution which has, in effect, given a military victory to the Serbians. That is, the U.N. imposed an arms embargo which had the effect of opening up for the Serbs the entire arms cache of the Yugoslav Army and denying weapons to the Bosnian Muslims and to a lesser extent, the Croatians. So the international community has been involved. The third and the big difference from the point of view of the average American is, I've made it very clear that the United States, unlike Vietnam, is not about to act alone. It should not act alone. This is a European issue. It's an issue for the world community to address.

We have worked very carefully with our allies to make the sanctions tougher and to keep the pressure on to try to do two things: to try to contain the conflict and to try to put an end to the slaughter. And our policy is that it is in the United States national interest to keep this conflict from spilling over into a lot of other countries which could drag the United States into something with NATO that we don't want and to do everything we can with our allies to stop the slaughter and to end the fighting. And that's our policy. Our policy is not to do what we did in Vietnam, which was to get in and fight with one side in a civil war to assure a military victory. That is not what we're involved in. We are trying to promote a settlement, and we have signed on to a plan—two of the three political factions in that area have signed on to it, and we have committed ourselves to working with our allies. So the policy is very, very different than the policy the United States pursued in Vietnam.

Mr. Imus. Any scenario, anyplace down the road—this may be a dumb question, but I ask a few—that you see ground troops somehow getting involved there? Does it ever reach that point? Say all the allies get on board and——

The President. We believe that there could be a United Nations force which we could take part in that could help to enforce the peace agreement or keep the peace. We've been involved in peacekeeping operations of this kind in many places. But the United States is not going to unilaterally enter the conflict on the side of one of the combatants and do what we did in Vietnam. That is not our policy, and that's not what we're going to do.

Mr. Imus. You know, I agreed with you when you said during the campaign that history has shown that you can't allow the mass extermination of people and just sit by and watch it happen, and that really is driving this, isn't it?

The President. Yes. It is a difficult issue. Let me say that when we have people here who've been involved in many previous administrations that are involved in national security including, obviously, a lot of people who were involved in the two previous ones—everybody I talk to believes that this is the toughest foreign policy problem our country has faced in a long time. And I'm trying to proceed in a very deliberate way to try to make sure there isn't a Vietnam problem here. But also to try to make sure that the United States keeps pushing to save lives and to confine the conflict. I don't think we can just turn away from this. Just because we don't want to make the mistake we did in Vietnam doesn't mean we shouldn't be doing anything. There are things that we can do, and we're trying to do more to try to push this thing toward a settlement.

I also think that in terms of our clear self-interest, in addition to the humanitarian issue, if we can stop this conflict from spreading, and it has powder-keg potential, that that is clearly in our interest.

Media Criticism and President's Agenda

Mr. Imus. You know what I've always wondered, Mr. President, you read the editorials in the Washington Post, the New York Times, and the Wall Street Journal and you read these op-ed pieces—do you ever read one of those and then call Al and say, "Man, that's a good idea. Why don't we do that?"

The President. Often. [*Laughter*] Actually, I do.

Mr. Imus. Do you?

The President. Absolutely, I do. I also often read editorials that question our policies or op-ed pieces that question our policy, and I send it to the Vice President and to other people in the administration, and I say, "If we don't have an answer to this we shouldn't go on. This is the best case against our policy. What's our answer to it?" I think that's important.

You know I don't mind, frankly, I don't mind criticism. In fact, I welcome it when it's rooted in ideas, when people are questioning whether a policy is right or wrong. But what I try to do is to have a new spirit of possibility here. I want a sense that, you know, we stop all this sort of political give-and-take and real harsh partisanship and calculating personal advantage and just talk about the ideas and the issues at stake and try to keep our focus on what's best for the American people. We're really in a new and unchartered time in many ways. It's very exciting. There are all kinds of economic opportunities out there for the United States, but there are also a lot of very, very stiff challenges that we have to meet. And I think in order to do the right thing, we're going to have to keep our minds open and our ears open and be willing to experiment and to try some things until we find a course that will clearly work, that helps to support the security of the American people.

Mr. Imus. You know, I was talking at the beginning of our conversation, Mr. President—I was actually just kidding about this focus issue—but you know, what looked great was when you and Hillary went up to Capitol Hill and when you had that first town meeting in Michigan, and now you are—in Cleveland and Chicago and this telephone call. You know, it began to look for a time—I remember I was watching Willie Nelson and Neil Young out there at Farm Aid, and they were talking about you and Al Gore, and they said, "What change?"

And I think, you know, from the outside looking in, it's like we had 8 years of watching old Reagan get on and off that helicopter, and we wanted to see you do stuff like this. And I think this is great, and I can't tell you how much I appreciate you calling.

But I would say this: Let's not wait until these approval ratings get down to single digits before you call me again, because——

The President. Let me tell you, one of the things I did, though, and you may think this is a mistake, but I mean—put yourself in my position. Partly, when I get out of focus with the people is when I'm not communicating directly with them, when I'm just answering other people's questions, and I'm at the mercy of whatever is on the evening news.

But I came to this city with a determination to work with the Congress and to try to get some things done. In the first 3 months, I thought that, having been out across the country for the last year and a half, I should spend a great deal of time in intense efforts to develop the economic package, a health care package, and to get the basis of our national security and foreign policy down so that I would have a framework to proceed in. Most of the time I've been here, I've spent on the economy and on health care. In other words, my time has been sharply focused. I don't think the American people know that because I haven't been out here talking to you and people like you out there.

But there's been a big difference between the way I've spent my time in the efforts of the administration and, I think, what the perception is. That's my fault, in a way, and I'm going to get out and correct it. But I had to spend a couple of months, I think, just going to work in the office, getting the details down, working through the procedures, making sure I understood how the thing worked. And now I can go back on the road and do the things that I think are important to connect the American people to their Government. And I recognize that that's my responsibility. Only the President can do that, and if I don't do it, it won't be done.

Sports and Physical Fitness

Mr. Imus. I know, Mr. President, you're coming to New York this afternoon. Do you want to go to the Knicks game tonight, or—[laughter]——

The President. You're betraying you're all-sports radio. I know you're trying to convince your listeners that you know something about this. You're trying to get your approval ratings up on sports. I know that.

Actually, I'd like to do it. But I'm going to speak at the Cooper Union this afternoon. And then I'm going to a Democratic Party event tonight. So I can't go to the ballgame, although I'd like to. I'm a big baseball fan, as you know.

Mr. Imus. Well, of course, this would be basketball, Mr. President.

The President. Oh, did you say Knicks? I thought you said Mets.

Mr. Imus. No, nobody wants to see the Mets.

The President. Are you kidding? Let me tell you something. My wife grew up in Chicago as a Cubs fan. Once you get for a baseball team, you can't quit it just because it doesn't win.

Mr. Imus. Well——

The President. I thought you said Mets. No, I'd love to go to the Knicks game, but I'm otherwise occupied. I watched two of those games last night on television. Do you think the American people would think less of me if they thought I stayed up late and watched basketball?

Mr. Imus. No, I don't think that; in fact, I read you've been watching the Houston Rockets and the Clippers.

You know, I'll let you go here. Just one final observation that I thought was kind of funny. Did you see any clips of Strom Thurmond interviewing one of those gay sailors? Here he is—I don't know if you saw this or not, but he was saying, "Have you seen a psychiatrist?"—[laughter]—and I thought, man, if I could be 90 years old and have it that together, there really isn't any other goal. Let's hope the same happens for you, Mr. President.

The President. Since we're on an all-sports network, let me give Senator Thurmond a plug. He still works out for 50 minutes a day, and that's why he's still out there doing it. So if everybody listening to us will start spending 50 minutes a day taking care of themselves, a lot of them will be 90, 91 and still plugging away like Strom.

Mr. Imus. May I ask you a question about your jogging?

The President. Sure.

Mr. Imus. What are your mile splits? We have an estimate here that's right around 12 minutes.

The President. No. When I ran with the Boston Marathon runners, we ran a 5k, and this is allergy time for me so I have to start out slow. We ran the first mile in 9 minutes, the second mile in 8 minutes, and the third mile in 7 minutes.

Mr. Imus. Man, that's a lot faster than I do it.

The President. When I run here in town, I average probably about an 8.5 minute mile. But I can run it faster. On Valentine's Day the Vice President and I did 2.5 miles in a Heart Association run at about 7.5 minutes a mile.

Mr. Imus. That's terrific. Mr. President, thank you very much. Thanks for coming on, and good luck.

The President. Thanks. Talk to you again, I hope.

NOTE: The telephone interview began at 7:38 a.m. The President spoke from the Oval Office at the White House.

Remarks on the Swearing-In of Small Business Administrator Erskine Bowles and Presentation of the Small Business Person of the Year Award
May 12, 1993

Please sit down, ladies and gentlemen. Good morning. It's great to see all of you here in the Rose Garden. I want to thank the Members of Congress who have joined us for this ceremony, and welcome all of you small business people and your families from all across America here to the White House for this important day.

This is an extra special day to celebrate the winners of the small business people of the year awards, because today we're also going to have the oath of office for the new Administrator of the Small Business Administration, Erskine Bowles. I chose Erskine for a very simple reason, because he's a business person and not a politician.

Too often in the past, the SBA has been the province of politics too much and business too little. This man has devoted his life to helping people start businesses, to helping them grow their businesses, to helping them reach out beyond the borders of their communities, to State and regional and national and international markets. He really understands what it's like to start and to keep going a business enterprise. His plans for the Agency include a plan to improve the management and outreach to determine what we can do to actually create more success stories in the small business community.

He's already met, I know, with many of you who are here for this celebration. But that's just the beginning. I think you will see the most energetic, connected, and continuous effort to reach out to small business that the SBA has ever given to the American small business community.

Now, I'd like to introduce Erskine and Judge James Dixon Phillips, Jr., of the Court of Appeals of the 4th Circuit in Durham, North Carolina, who will administer the oath of office. Erskine's wife, Crandall Bowles, will hold the Bible, and then they will take it over from there. Judge?

[*At this point, Judge Phillips administered the oath of office. Mr. Bowles then expressed his gratitude to the President and enumerated his priorities for SBA.*]

Thank you very much. I predict that over the next 4 years, small business men and women in every State in America will come to see Erskine Bowles as the best advocate they ever had. And I assure you that he is going to have a real influence on our economic policy.

Some evidence of that is the presence here today of the two other Members of my Cabinet, Ron Brown, the Secretary of Commerce, and Mickey Kantor, our U.S. Trade Representative. We are going to have a coordinated policy for small business. We have to have the Commerce Department, we have to have the Trade Office, we have to have the Treasury Department if we're going to attack all these issues. And I'm very, very proud of the team that we've got working on it.

Let me just mention one or two other things about the small business economy. We have spent most of our time in the last 3 months or so in meetings in this White House talking about the economy and talking about health care and its impact on the economy. Over and over and over, we come back to a central fact of the American economy in the last 12 years. In every year of the last 12 years, the biggest companies in America have reduced employment in this country, even as they were increasing productivity, even as their profits went up, even as their stock values went through the roof and Wall Street reached all-time highs, in every year.

Some of that is because of being involved in other countries in a global economy. A lot of it is just using the technology of new productivity to have machines do more work, or have people do more work, overtime, and more part-time workers. But the bottom line is, in every year employment has been reduced by the biggest businesses in this country.

In every year until about 3 years ago, the reduction in employment by big business was more than offset by the increase in employment by small businesses in America and by the start-up of new businesses. Then, about 3 years ago, that too came to a halt because of a national and international recession, because of the credit crunch, because of the burgeoning costs of health care on smaller businesses and all the extra additional costs of hiring one more worker, whether it's worker's comp or some other cost or the Social Security costs.

The extra added costs to small business of hiring additional workers meant that, over the last 2 or 3 years, small businesses, even when they were growing, have relied more and more on overtime, more and more on temporary workers, and less on adding to the job base of America. We have talked about this endlessly in these walls here, trying to come up with policies that would address that, trying to reward the spirit, the grit, the entrepreneurialism, the creativity of you and millions of Americans like you all over this country.

I have seen, I suppose, being a former Governor of a small State, as many small businesses up close as virtually anybody who ever occupied this office. I have more than a healthy respect for the fact that you now employ a majority of America's workers and create a huge majority of America's new jobs.

Just a couple of days ago, as I'm sure you all know, I went out to Ohio and to Illinois. And when I finished my speech in downtown Cleveland to the City Club, before we went out to the airport, I told my entourage with no planning that I wanted to go back to a small business that I came across in the primary in Parma, which is a suburb of Cleveland, to visit a woman named Mary Poldruhi, who became a friend of mine in the election. She started a business called Parma's Pierogis. And she did it as a Polish American, and no bank would loan her any money. So she got a telephone book and called hundreds of people in the telephone book with Polish surnames until she found 80 people who agreed to put up $3,000 apiece to start her business, which she runs with her family and a couple of friends and which has done very, very well indeed.

That is the sort of spirit and creativity that I'm sure—I see a lot of you nodding because you identify with that experience in your own lives. I was so impressed with this woman and her family that, literally, I was sitting there in Cleveland—we just decided to go back and see her and see how the business was doing and what could be done to try to stabilize this environment and make it better.

I want to talk about just two or three of the things we're trying to do. Erskine already mentioned the initiative that Secretary Bentsen organized to have the five major financial Departments of the Federal Government work on trying to simplify regulations and end the credit crunch. A lot of business people tell me that it takes a little time for the orders we issue in Washington to manifest themselves in the bank down the street. And if that's not happening, that is one of the things that Erskine Bowles is here to address. We are determined to change the environment which has led to so much withdrawing of capital when it ought to be out there plentiful now, given the economic conditions, for new loans for good prospects.

Secondly, in the proposal that the Congress is now considering to bring the deficit down, there is a sweeping new proposal to provide a huge capital gains cuts for new investments and new enterprises to try to start more small businesses, and I hope it will have your support. We've also asked for an extension of the 25 percent deduction of health care costs for the self-employed, which I think is very important.

Finally, we are in intense negotiations at this moment, as we speak, to guarantee that whatever comes out of the House Ways and Means Committee in the tax bill will include a substantial increase in incentives for small business people to reinvest in their own companies. So these are the kinds of things that I hope will help us to generate more jobs and will support your efforts.

There is also a community development bank initiative and a big enterprise zone initiative that I think will help to spark more small businesses in distressed areas and rural communities and big cities. But over the long run, we also have to have a healthy financial climate in the country. And that means that we must pass a budget this year that takes a strong step to bring this deficit down.

Ever since the election was over when the then-Secretary-designate of the Treasury, Lloyd Bentsen, went on television and said we are going to have a tough deficit reduction plan and outlined some of the elements of it, interest rates have been going down in this country. Mortgage rates are at 20-year lows. The business journals say that if we could keep interest rates down this low for another few months, over $100 billion will be released into this economy through refinancing of home mortgages and business loans and other things for new investment and new opportunities. Now, we know that someday interest rates will go up again, but we want it to happen when the economy starts to boom again. And we want the interest rates to stay down while we refinance and get as much new money as we can at low interest rates back into this economy.

A year ago, only 47 percent of the American people thought, for example, that the next generation of Americans would be able to afford a new home. Just a couple of weeks ago a bipartisan poll said 74 percent of the people now think that, because we're making a strong effort to bring the deficit down to hold the interest rates down. I wish there were easy and painless ways to do that, but it requires cuts and tax increases.

I'm going up to New York after I leave you today to announce at the Cooper Union that I am going to support, strongly, the proposition that we guarantee the American people two things: number one is, no tax increases without the spending cuts, and number two is, that tax increases will go to reduce the deficit, by creating a legally separate deficit reduction trust fund which will tell you where your money is going. I think that this will do as much as anything else we can do to make your lives healthier over the long run.

Let me finally make one last point. We didn't get into our economic difficulties overnight nor

at the hand of any particular party. There is enough blame to go around, and there will be enough credit to go around, if we work our way out of it. I want to reiterate what I have tried to say since the day I became President: I do not seek a Democratic or a Republican resolution of America's problems. I would like for us to define an American solution that goes beyond the paralyzing debates of the past. In spite of the fact that we've had a little of that here, there's also a lot of evidence that we are moving beyond it. We've passed a budget resolution in record time. The Congress passed the motor voter bill yesterday which had strong opposition, but it's a great thing, and the young people of this country are very excited because it will make it easier for them to vote.

In the last election we had more young people voting than any time in 20 years, and there was a sense that we could give our political system back to the people who are the true owners of it. So I think there is every reason to hope that we can still build a sense of possibility and hope and progress among people of good faith in both parties, and I want to encourage that. And it ought to be rooted in ideas and in action, because that's really the sort of thing that brought all of you here today.

I hardly ever have had what you would call a conventional political discussion with a small business person. You know, I mean, if I go in and I talk to somebody about, can you afford health care? What's your coverage? What are the options? What's the matter with the insurance coverage? How big is the pool you're in?— the words Democrat and Republican never come up. Somebody says they went down to the bank, and they couldn't get a loan, and here were the problems, and look at this stack of paper from the Small Business Administration I had to fill out. Nobody ever put a political context on it. And I hope that we can focus our attention here on our problems and ask openly what should be done about them in the same way that you and I would engage if we were just having a personal conversation in your place of business.

The triumphs of the people we honor here today it seems to me, are the triumphs of America. The idea that you've got a right to take a chance. You've got a right to fail so that you have the right to succeed. You're given the opportunity in a free-market economy to bring your ideas to bear and see if people respond.

I have been terribly impressed—I've read the life histories of a lot of the award winners that are here today, and not just the three that we come to recognize. And I wish I could say something about all of you who are represented. But as you know, the purpose of this ceremony is to recognize the second runner-up, the first runner-up, and the Small Business Person of the Year. I just want to say to all the rest of you, we honor your achievements, and we know that these people, in a fundamental and profound sense, are reflective of what all of you have done.

For David Parker, success has been what you might call an open-and-shut case. His Pelican Products of Torrance, California, began as a scuba supply manufacturer but now is best known as a maker of suitcases and containers that are so hardy they're used in the environmental safety industry. They've even survived on a trip to Mt. Everest, something I'm not sure I could do. Now, that is a real climb to success. I want to ask David to come up here and receive our congratulations as a second runner-up in the Small Business Person of the Year.

Carol Rae was hired as a consultant to the Magnum Diamond Corporation. But in no time, she was asked to run the company. Now, I can tell you, as somebody who has fooled with a lot of consultants, that in itself is an incredible compliment. As president of the business, she's made it a leader in surgical tools for eye surgery. The Rapid City, South Dakota company has grown from 7 employees to 68 in about 4 years. That's a very impressive achievement for Carol Rae, our first runner-up. Would you please come forward and be recognized?

Did you hear what she said? "I'm one of his customers." [*Laughter*]

Bill Engler, Jr., is the CEO of Kaytee Products, and that makes him the biggest employer in Chilton, Wisconsin. Kaytee is a case study of making change your friend and not your enemy. The business has been in his family since 1866 when it sold feed and grain, something I know a little about. [*Laughter*] But it wasn't until Bill took over 9 years ago that the business began a growth explosion. Kaytee now sells only wild bird and pet food, and it's gone from 64 employees to 365 workers. Sales went up from $10.6 million to more than $70 million. And for his amazing accomplishments, Bill Engler, Jr., has been chosen the Small Business Person of the Year. Let's bring him up with a hand. [*Applause*]

[*At this point, the President presented Mr. Engler with the award.*]

I want to salute you all. I want to wish you continued success. I want to pledge you continued access to this administration. I want to ask you now as you leave here to give us the benefit of your ideas, your suggestions, your constructive criticisms and help us to bring to the White House the kind of entrepreneurial spirit that you have brought to your businesses and that we must all bring to the United States.

Thank you very much.

NOTE: The President spoke at 11:02 a.m. in the Rose Garden at the White House.

Exchange With Reporters Following the Small Business Person Award Ceremony
May 12, 1993

Bosnia

Q. Mr. President, have you changed your views on the arms embargo at all?

The President. No.

Q. Does the fighting——

The President. I haven't changed my views. I just don't know if I've changed anybody else's, but I haven't changed my views.

Associate Attorney General Nominee

Q. Do you still back Webb Hubbell's nomination?

The President. Of course. Why wouldn't I?

Q. What about the Republican calls for him to resign?

The President. A little inconsistency in their position. Look how they voted on a lot of other people.

Q. Such as who?

Deficit Reduction

Q. Mr. President, why do you feel you have to make this guarantee on deficit reduction?

The President. I just think it will help to reinforce the commitment that we already have: no taxes without spending cuts; all the taxes go to the deficit. I think that's what we ought to do. That's the way we set it up. Now we'll just put it into the law. It will be even better.

Q. What effects do you think it will have on Congress?

The President. It's consistent with what I did as the Governor at home, too. When I raised money at home for education, we put it into education, and it can only be spent on that.

Q. Is it a compromise?

The President. Gosh, no. It makes it better. I mean, I don't know who—compromise—I don't know if anybody's against it. But I think it's the right thing to do.

NOTE: The exchange began at 11:40 a.m. in the Rose Garden at the White House. A tape was not available for verification of the content of this exchange.

Remarks at Cooper Union for the Advancement of Science and Art in New York City
May 12, 1993

The President. Thank you very much. It always seems to be a good thing for me when I'm introduced in New York by Governor Cuomo. [*Laughter*] I must confess to having mixed feelings as I sit on this revered stage with all these distinguished citizens. And President Iselin made his eloquent remarks and then your fine Mayor spoke so forcefully, and the brilliant chairman of the Senate Finance Committee brought us back to Woodrow Wilson. And then Governor Cuomo once again gave me a hard act to follow, and they all left the stage. I thought to myself, pray this is not a metaphor for the battle ahead.

This is the second thing I have had in common with President Wilson. I received a fascinating letter the other day from Johnston and Murphy, the shoe manufacturers from Nashville, Tennessee. They have made shoes for every President going back to the 1850's, so they made a pair of shoes for President Lincoln. And they send you a little catalog, and you pick the shoes you want, and they send them to you with your name in them. It says "Johnston and Murphy—every President served." And so I ordered these rather simple plain black shoes, and they wrote me this wonderful letter in which they said, "We're from Nashville, Tennessee, and we know what's in your heart. So here's an extra pair of shoes." And they sent me a box of blue suede shoes. [*Laughter*]

And then in the letter they recounted the choices of all the previous Presidents. And they said that in one way my choice was not particularly innovative, that five other Presidents had chosen the same style I did, including Harry Truman, which made me very proud. But they said, "You do have the biggest feet of any President since Woodrow Wilson." [*Laughter*] So you had two sets of big feet here from the Presidents.

President Wilson said in an address that Senator Moynihan quoted: "I have been dealing with young men most of my life"—he wasn't so gender-sensitive as he should have been—"and one of the things I have tried most to impress upon them is not to stay young too long, but to take themselves seriously." Now at one level I want us all to stay young forever, but I do think the time has come for us to take ourselves and our purposes more seriously. This celebrated institution and the community of scholars and activists it embraces is the result, as President Iselin said, of Peter Cooper's determination more than 130 years ago to create an institution intellectually vigorous with free tuition, the first nondiscrimination policy in American history, and a genuine commitment to social justice. He believed you could do more than one thing at a time. [*Laughter*]

Here Mr. Lincoln asked our country to confront the cost of the spread of slavery, to ask hard questions about the conditions that had plagued our Nation since its beginning. Remember it was Thomas Jefferson, not Abraham Lincoln—Thomas Jefferson the slave owner—who said, "I tremble when I think of slavery to consider that God is just." There were people who knew in their hearts the truth but had denied it a long time.

Lincoln said that to continue to do that threatened to tear our country apart. He knew the Nation would be destroyed if slavery spread and that unless the country's drifting stopped, the very drift would carry within it the seeds of our destruction. And so, here at Cooper Union he asked those hard questions and gave strong answers. Soon after, he won the nomination of the fledgling Republican Party and went on to win the Presidency by only 39 percent of the popular vote, receiving virtually no votes south of the Mason-Dixon line. Soon after that, the war came, and Lincoln's fight for the Union grew into a determination to abolish slavery.

Several days a week I walk alone into the room in the White House where Abraham Lincoln signed the Emancipation Proclamation and try to remember the purposes of the United States of America. The fight for the Union and the fight against slavery cost Abraham Lincoln his life, as well as the lives of hundreds of thousands of his fellow countrymen. But America prevailed in form and spirit. And America has endured in form and spirit because in times of crisis and challenge, leaders have asked the hard questions and given the strong answers. And the American people have rallied.

Look at the condition of America today. How can we avoid asking those questions? To be sure, we are still the strongest Nation in the world politically, economically, and militarily. To be sure, more than anyone else in the world we have accommodated the incredible diversity of our land with remarkable harmony. When you look at what is happening, the heartbreak in the former Yugoslavia today, where there are three ethnic groups that genetically have no ethnic differences at all but call themselves ethnically different solely because of the accidents of religion and history, it is an incredible tribute that in this country, in this great city and across the country in Los Angeles and in all places in between, that we live together as well as we do with our diversity.

But still we cannot avoid the hard questions. If we're so great, why are most middle class families working longer hours today than they were 20 years ago for wages that in real terms are less than they were a decade ago? Why are one in 10 of our people so impoverished they're on food stamps? Why are over 8 million of us out of work if we're in the 17th month of a recovery? Why are there over 35 million of us without health care and millions more Americans terrified of losing their health coverage, with 100,000 Americans a month losing their health insurance, and millions of others who can never change jobs under the current system because they or someone in their family has been sick and so they have a preexisting condition which makes them unemployable with health insurance elsewhere?

Why? Why that half the people on welfare not get off of it as a safety net after just a few months? Why is there a whole class of new poor people, mostly young women and their little children, many of those children never born into an integrated family? Why? Why was—only 35 years ago, only 35 years ago—there conditions even in New York City in which there were three police officers on the street for every violent crime, and today there are three crimes for every police officer?

Why does the Government fail to deal with the problems that this age has brought to us and engaged the American people in dealing with them? Why have we seen the Government's debt grow from $1 trillion to $4 trillion in the last 12 years, while we reduced our investment in the people of America and their promise and their ability to compete? Why in the world would we reduce all this defense spending, including jobs for engineers and scientists and factory workers, with no plan whatever to put that money back to work to create opportunities for them, cleaning up the environment or exploring the frontiers of technology here at home or helping us to compete with people all around the world?

The American economy finds itself in the middle of a global marketplace, challenged on every hand by nations who have made wise investments in their people, their workers, and their technological edge. Yes, there is today a global recession which is making our problem more difficult. But if you take the long view, those who have made the investments in the eighties and those who are doing so now will be rewarded over the long run. For a decade or more, we have both expanded our debt and reduced our investment in areas key to our future.

We also have in this country a crisis of belief and hope. When President Kennedy took office, younger than I was when I took office, over 70 percent of the American people fundamentally believed that their leaders would tell them the truth and that their system could succeed. Now it seems as if half the people just stand around waiting to be disappointed, waiting to be told what's wrong and who's failed and how the special interests once again have strangled the national interests and why they should go on about their business without believing things can be different. I believe that the nature of our challenge is this: We must both restore our economy and restore the confidence of our people in our democracy. And I do not believe we can do one without the other.

This is a strange and, in a way, wondrous moment in our history when citizens everywhere desperately want things to change but still are wary of it and reluctant to place their faith in anyone's prescription. We must begin with the economy. We must change the way the Government works if we expect the economy to improve. And we must rebuild the confidence of the American people based on the three words which were the watch words of my campaign for President: more opportunity for all, more responsibility from all, and the clear understanding that we are a community and we're all in this together, going up or down together. Whether we like it or not, that is clearly the truth. And we must begin to act as if it were.

How can we reduce the deficit? Let's start with the big problem of the debt. Well, the answer is not popular. To reduce the deficit you have to reverse what produced the deficit. What produced it? Tax cuts and spending increases. Doing what people like. The most popular thing in the world is for me to cut your tax and write you a check. And that was what was done by Government for the American people for 12 long years. I'll cut your tax and I'll write you a check—that's a good deal. It used to be known as a free lunch when I was a kid.

We have to begin to reverse this process. And because Government has been at fault, first you should ask Government to change. So I have asked in Washington that we begin with significant spending cuts below the budget that was adopted last year to reduce the deficit and to free up resources for targeted investment in the future of our economy and of the young people

here present in this hall.

We should look at every program for possible savings, including ones that Democrats have favored for a long time. And there should be no tax increase, not a dollar, without the spending cuts. That is the meaning of the budget resolution that was passed a few weeks ago in record time. It contains the largest deficit reduction proposals in history, over $500 billion in deficit reduction over a 5-year period with more than 200 very specific cuts in programs. Those were tough to make, but necessary in the face of a $4 trillion debt that will continue to grow until the deficit itself is reduced to zero.

That deficit is robbing us of our ability to invest in our future. More and more of our money just goes to pay interest on the debt. If we don't change it, by the end of the decade over 20 cents on every dollar you pay in taxes will go just to service the debt. Now, that is also a redistribution of wealth away from middle class taxpayers to the upper income people who hold the debt, instead of to invest in the jobs and the education and the infrastructure of the future of New York and the rest of America.

We made cuts in Medicare, a thing that is difficult to do. We asked upper income Social Security recipients to pay tax on more of their incomes, a thing that is difficult to do. In spite of the fact that I value public service greatly and I believe public employees too often have been used as whipping boys for the difficulties and frustrations of the moment, still I asked the public employees of the United States of America to have a pay freeze for a year and to keep their wage increases below inflation and cost of living allowances for each of the next 3 years.

I come from a rural State, heavily electrified by the Rural Electrification Agency, but I asked that the subsidies to the REA be reduced. I asked that certain programs that benefit cities but that don't have the accountability of the normal budgeting process also be reduced. All these were not easy. But it seems to me essential, if we're going to ask the American people to sacrifice, that the Government take the lead and show the way.

We're also fighting, however, to do something no Government has done before, to both reduce the deficit and increase targeted investments in areas that are designed to secure the future of this country, in the ones Governor Cuomo mentioned: in Head Start; in the program to get children off to a healthier start in life with immunizations and nutrition; in better programs for apprenticeship training for our work force; in opening the doors of college education to all Americans through reforming the student loan process and a program of national service; in new incentives for our industries to develop new technology. These are things which other countries do as a matter of course and take for granted and which lead to huge increases in productivity. The case for them should be plain in America once inessential spending has been cut.

The cuts, however, must be credible. And credibility is difficult to come by in Washington today. They must be legally enforceable. They must be plain to the American people. After 12 years of rising deficits and Americans feeling deceived about the issue, I don't blame the people of this country for being distrustful about what they hear from Washington when it comes to bringing down this deficit. That is why I have decided today to propose that we establish a deficit reduction trust fund and put every penny of new taxes and the budget cuts proposed in my budget into the trust fund so the American people know that it has to go to deficit reduction.

There are several members of the New York congressional delegation here today. I thank them all for being here, and I thank especially Congressman Schumer for his leadership on this issue. I thank Senator Moynihan for his support of this issue. Senator Moynihan said on the way up here that he thought we ought to do it to win a victory for the clarity of our determination to reduce the deficit. Senator Bradley had an op-ed piece in the paper today endorsing the idea. The time has come to prove that when we say we're going to do something with the people's money, we actually do it.

Let me repeat what this means. We will create a trust fund in which every dollar that is raised will go to deficit reduction and in which all the net budget cuts which have been approved will do so also. This is very important. This seriousness, however, should not relieve us of our obligation to recognize that over the long run we must also bring down the investment deficit in this country. I am as dedicated to that as I ever have been. I know that long-term economic growth depends on high-quality and comprehensive education and training, converting the workers and the investments from

defense that is being cut to new technologies which must be increased, establishing new and innovative partnerships with the private sector and, as I said earlier, opening the doors of college education to all Americans. But bringing the deficit down will give us the freedom to do that.

This budget saves, as I said, about $500 billion. And the trust fund will ensure that we do just that. It will be a change in the way Washington does business. It has broad support. But I also want to emphasize that it will only confirm the direction on which we have embarked. The financial markets here in New York have already understood the seriousness of this administration. Look what's happened to long-term interest rates just since the election, just since the election: mortgage rates at a 20-year low, many other interest rates at record lows. All the analysts say that if this can continue a few more months in this period, we will see about $100 billion freed up for investment in America through people refinancing their home loans and business loans and taking out car loans and consumer loans at lower interest rates. This is a job stimulus program that is big and important. And bringing the deficit down so that the huge overhang of private and public debt of the 1980's can be refinanced is a great strategy to begin the economic renewal of America, and we must stick with it.

More can be done. But to do more we have to actually rethink the whole way the Federal Government operates: How does it operate on its own terms? How does it relate to the States and the private sector? I asked the Congress to give me some more money for technology so I could run the White House with many fewer people than my predecessors had. I asked that we have a 14-percent across-the-board cut in the administrative costs of the Federal Government over the next few years: 100,000 reduction in the payroll by attrition, over $9 billion in savings simply by administrative changes alone. But that is just the beginning.

I have also asked Vice President Gore to head a task force which will reexamine every agency of the Federal Government, every program of the Federal Government, and the whole way it is organized. Every major company in America had to go through a wrenching reexamination process in the 1980's. The Federal Government had many of its Departments cut, but the way it operated continued to be largely unexamined.

It is time that we impose the same sort of reexamination process on the National Government. When we do it, we will find more savings, and more importantly, we will increase the quality of service to the American people.

Finally, I want to compliment the House of Representatives last week on passing a bill with the mind-boggling title of "enhanced rescission." But when you strip it away, what it amounts to is a modified line-item veto, which is enjoyed by most Governors and which will enable the President to strike out spending items that he believes are unnecessary but will give the Congress the freedom to put them back in after voting on them individually so, that the people can make their own judgment and so can the Members of Congress.

These things will make the Federal Government more efficient and will set us on the path to long-term reform. We ought to also think about our partnership with the private sector and our partnership with State and local government. Mayor Dinkins mentioned it. I was gratified to see a couple of mentions in the press recently about the fact that our administration had tried to give cities more relief from unnecessary regulations and States more leeway in promoting various kinds of reform in health care. I just told Governor Cuomo that I was very excited about the health care reform package that he put forward in New York, and Hillary's task force has been very much influenced by the New York reforms.

We believe that a lot of the problems of America can be solved by cities and States if the National Government will have targeted investment and then will give people their head to do what they know needs to be done. You'd be amazed how many programs have quite a bit of money in them, but most of the money, or a great deal of the money, never reaches the ultimate beneficiaries at the State or the city level because of all the layers in between. You'd be amazed. I was in Chicago a couple of days ago, and the Mayor of Chicago told me that there are one or two programs that his staff wouldn't even let him try to get for Chicago because the administrative hassle of securing the funds was so great. We're going to change that. We're going to have a new and different and vibrant process that trusts the people of New York and their elected leaders, and the State of New York and their elected leaders, and people throughout the country to have real

innovation in the same way that I think we want in the private sector in the United States. But finally, let me say—[*applause*]—the Mayor, the lone clapper.

We also have proposed to change the relationship between the Government and the private sector in a tax reform package that Senator Moynihan will soon take up if it passes the House, and I hope it does. There will be significant incentives for businesses, large and small, to increase their investment in this country and to be rewarded for it. We will have initiatives that will empower neighborhoods and give people significant incentives to go into neighborhoods in small towns and rural areas and in big cities to put real investment there to create real jobs. We'll provide people real incentives to end welfare as we know it and require them to move forward with that. We will do things that are different from what either party has done before to try to empower people to live up to their God-given potential in a new and different partnership between the United States and people in the private sector.

When you strip it all away, there's still one more tough question that has to be answered. If you want the deficit brought down, we have to face the fact that in 1981, taxes were cut by 6 percent of the national income of this country, twice what President Reagan originally recommended when he was elected President. And that gap has never been made up.

David Stockman, President Reagan's Budget Director, has an interview in a magazine called the New Politics Quarterly this month in which he says, "I don't agree with all of President Clinton's spending plan, but at least he's telling the truth. You cannot fix the deficit without a tax program, because we cut taxes more than twice as much as we proposed to do it when we came in. We got into a bidding war. We got carried away. What we did was irresponsible. And then all the politicians since then never had the stomach to tell the American people the truth. And it was just more fun to cut taxes and pass out money than to do the reverse." Now, that is the hard truth.

I really believed in the campaign that we could raise revenues modestly on upper income people, close some corporate tax loopholes, and do some other things, do the spending cuts, and bring the deficit down. After I was elected, the Government announced that the annual deficit was going to be $50 billion a year bigger in 3 of the 4 years that I would serve as President, $50 billion a year bigger, and $15 billion bigger in the fourth year. And it became clear to me that under those circumstances we could not begin by cutting anyone's taxes; that we ought to have a responsible, balanced energy tax and that most of the tax burden should be borne by those who had their taxes lowered in the eighties while their incomes went up, people in higher income groups; but that we ought to have a balanced and fair package, not to "soak the rich" but to share the burden, to try to say this is our job.

And so I say to you, yes, I will put this money in a trust fund, but that does not mean the money does not have to be paid. If you want the interest rates to stay down, if you want the profits of lower interest rates, you must undergo the pain of the spending cuts and the tax increases, because that's the only way to really bring the deficit down.

Now, the question is, are we going to do this, or not? Are we going to do this, or not?

Audience members. Yes, we are.

The President. I think we are.

There are some who say no. Today in Washington there are 80,000 lobbyists. It's a growth industry. I'll guarantee you one thing, I created some jobs since I got to be President.

But the Congress is now dealing with two bills which will help to reform the way our politics work. They just passed the motor voter bill, something young people of America really wanted and which I'm very proud of, which I hope and pray will continue the trend of increased voter participation. But now Congress is dealing with two tough other issues. The United States Senate passed last week a bill—finally, believe it or not, in the year 1993—finally requiring everybody who actually lobbies them to register as a lobbyist and requiring that the gifts that they give to Members of Congress or the expenditures they make on trips or whatever all be reported. Believe it or not, they weren't done before now. The Congress passed that with only two dissenting votes—the Senate did. The bill is now going to the House.

In addition to that, last Friday I proposed a comprehensive campaign finance reform law which will lower the cost of congressional campaigns, reduce the influence of political action committees, and open the airwaves to challengers as well as incumbents for more honest debate. It is a tough, good bill. If we can pass these bills, they will help to open the system too.

People are full of hope now. We've received in 3½ months more letters than the White House got in all of 1992. If you haven't gotten yours answered, I hope you'll be patient. We've got over 200 volunteers coming in just to open the mail and trying to sort it and read it. But it is a wonderful reaffirmation, the critical and the complimentary and support letters alike, that Americans really want their system to respond to them again. And we must do that.

If the first issue is the economy—or in the vernacular of my old campaign sign, "It's the economy, stupid"—that means deficit reduction, investment for jobs and technology, and education. It means controlling health care costs and dealing with that crisis. I should tell you that no matter how much we reduce the deficit in the next 5 years, it will go right back up again if we don't address health care costs, because that's the fastest growing part of the Federal budget deficit.

It must include all these things, as well as political reform and changing the way Government works. And change is hard. It doesn't happen overnight. You have to do what Lincoln did: Ask hard questions, give strong answers, and hope the American people rally.

We can move forward. We can have a whole new partnership in this country, one that goes beyond the things that normally divide us, beyond the dividing lines of party, of race, of gender, of region, of income. We can do that. Ideas and energy can replace drift and delay. We can grow in wealth and wisdom and liberty.

But this requires more than good ideas and more than political energy. If I may say, if you don't remember anything else I say, I hope you'll remember this: The human condition in the end changes by faith. And faith cannot be held in your hand. The Scripture that I carry to my place of worship every Sunday says, "Faith is the assurance of things hoped for, the conviction of things unseen." But make no mistake about it, it is by far the most powerful force that can ever be mustered in the cause of change.

Today we are seeing too much cynicism and too little faith, an obsession with the moment, an obsession with the politicians and their wins and their losses, an obsession with blame and division, an obsession with paralysis, an obsession with always pointing out the pain of change and never embracing its promise. Without faith, in the end we always wind up resorting to the easy and the immediate: Tax the other guy; cut that other program, not mine; wait for somebody to deliver the goods to me, or wait for it not to happen till I can blame somebody else for what didn't.

But faith changes all that. Lincoln's cause in 1860 was to keep our house from dividing. Our cause today is to put our house in order. If "a house divided against itself cannot stand," surely a house in disarray will not provide shelter and a home. Surely a house where problems are denied or blamed on someone else in the next room can never be a home for America.

To preserve the American dream in our time and for your future, yes, our leaders must ask tough questions and give strong answers. But people must rally to the cause of change with faith. We have to believe again, believe through the "frustrations and the difficulties of the moment," as Martin Luther King characterized

them, believe through the inevitable rocks in the road to the ends of the journey. We must believe through the smallness and the spite that conflict always brings out in all of us. We must believe through that, to the spirit and generosity and courage that is America at its essence.

Mr. Lincoln closed his Cooper Union speech with the following words: "Let us have faith that right makes might, and in that faith, let us to the end dare to do our duty as we understand it." My fellow Americans, our clear duty is to revive the American dream and restore the American economy. And for as long as it takes, with energy and joy and humility, let us dare to do that duty.

Thank you very much.

NOTE: The President spoke at 3:50 p.m. at the college. In his remarks he referred to Jay Iselin, Cooper Union president; Mayor David Dinkins of New York City; and Senator Daniel Patrick Moynihan, Senate Finance Committee chairman.

Remarks at the Democratic National Committee Presidential Gala in New York City
May 12, 1993

Thank you very much. To Bruce and to Lew, and to all of you, I've had a wonderful time tonight. These lights are so bright. I only know half the people I've shaken hands with. It has been a wonderful time. I want to thank all the people who made this dinner possible, and I want to thank the wonderful entertainment. The choir was terrific. The group doing all the wonderful old songs from Dionne Warwick in the sixties were magnificent.

I was delighted to see Barry Manilow again in such wonderful voice, and grateful for his many contributions to our common efforts. I appreciated Phil Hartman saying he voted for me, but it's not quite enough for all the abuse I've put up with in advance. [*Laughter*] And I want to say to my friend, Whoopi Goldberg: Mayor Dinkins has a telephone call for you over here if you will go over and get it. [*Laughter*]

Ladies and gentlemen, all of you who made this night possible—Lew and Bruce, Bob Rose and the other committee members, Bob Barrie, Bill Boardman, Paul Montrone, George

Norcross, Felix Rohatyn, Ann Sheffer, John Sweeney, and Steve Swid, thank you all. Thank you, Roy Furman. Thank you, David Wilhelm.

A lot of you were here with me a long time ago. I remember once, more than a year ago, when I came to New York and there were hundreds of people here in a hotel for a fundraiser for me. I was dropping like a rock in New Hampshire. All those experts said I was dead. I hear their call again. [*Laughter*] People who couldn't see the long road and didn't want to think of the fight as something that was bigger than any person were all preoccupied. And I just couldn't believe all these folks were even showing up for a dinner in New York. It was so dark in the campaign, I thought, well, people will go ahead and send their checks and then stay home. I imagined going into this vast ballroom and making a speech to eight people.

And I was feeling pretty sorry for myself, frankly. And I told this story many times, but a man stopped me in the hall who was working at the hotel and said that he was a Greek immigrant and he was going to vote for me because his son asked him to—was only 10 years old—that if I got elected, he wanted me to do something for his son. He said, "Where I come from, we were poor but we were free. Here, I make more money, but my boy's not free. He can't go across the street and play in the park without accompaniment from me. He can't even go to his school safely without my going with him. And I want you to work to help make my boy free." And it made me remember what politics was all about. I don't even remember what I said that night, but I know all of a sudden I had forgotten about me and started thinking about the rest of America. And I think that is what we ought to think about tonight.

When we talk about a program, it only counts if there are people behind it. New York City, for all of the problems you may think you have, has registered the first decline in the crime rate in 36 years, because you did something about community policing. So we know now that there is a strategy which can make people freer. That's what personal safety is. And there is no excuse for not doing something about it. And that's what politics is about: focusing on the dreams and hopes and fears and needs of people. Sometimes I think that when we have these wonderful dinners, which are delightful to me, I've gotten to see some of you that I haven't even seen since the election, just to say a simple thank you to you. Remember, we all did it so that we can make a difference in people's lives.

I want to say a special word of tribute here with all the people from New York and New Jersey and Connecticut, and my friend Mayor Rendell and others here from Pennsylvania, and there's even a handful of folks here from my home State. They were the ones who were clapping when Lew Katz gave his Arkansas pander, which I appreciate. I want to say a special word about one person who is here. I want to congratulate my friend Jim Florio on winning the John F. Kennedy Profiles in Courage Award, for facing the financial problems of his State, for facing the educational problems of his State and, yes, for being willing to stand up for the police officers and the people of his cities and State who wanted to be safe from crime, standing up to the gun lobby, and being for safe streets. That's why he got the award, doing real things, even if they weren't so hot in the polls at the time.

Now our country is being called upon to-gether to try to do the things that we just talked about in the campaign. Governor Mario Cuomo said again today when he introduced me at the Cooper Union that we campaign in poetry, but we must govern in prose. It's another way of saying, and a more eloquent way of saying, it's a lot easier to talk about change than it is to do it. I was overwhelmed today to have the opportunity to speak on the same spot where Abraham Lincoln spoke at the Cooper Union in 1860. And I went back and read large portions of Mr. Lincoln's speech. He came to the Cooper Union and catapulted himself into the nomination of the Republican Party, into the Presidency, and into the history and hearts of America. He did it by saying this is a difficult time, we have to ask hard questions and give strong answers. He said that we could not allow slavery to continue to expand; and that if we did, it would destroy the United States. He said in many other places that if the house is divided against itself, it could not stand.

Lincoln went on to become President, and he expanded his vision, and he eventually signed the Emancipation Proclamation abolishing slavery. In the White House we have a painting called "Waiting for the Hour," of black slaves watching a clock at 5 minutes to 12, waiting for the stroke of midnight, January 1st, 1863, for the Emancipation Proclamation to become effective. Several times a week, often late at night, I go alone into the room where Lincoln signed that proclamation, and I remembered what the Presidency is really for: to help the American people move forward.

It is for us now to put this house in order. And the beginning is to stop denying our problems and to accept some common responsibility for solving them. The first thing we have to do is to prove that the Government can be trusted with your money by passing a budget that will bring the deficit down. Look what has happened. Look what has happened just since the election, because finally the country has an administration trying to do that: long-term interest rates going down very low, 20-year low; billions of dollars, tens of billions being recycled into this economy, giving people the opportunity to make new starts. We have got to do that.

We also have to deal with this health care crisis. You know, so many of you said nice things about Hillary tonight, and I want to say I appreciate it, because about every third day she stops speaking to me because I asked her to run the health care project. [*Laughter*] It is the most complex, the most daunting task in our domestic life. But it is also perhaps the most urgent.

If we cannot give working families the security of knowing they're not going to lose their health care, if we can't give businesses the security of knowing that health care doesn't have to go up at 2 or 3 times the rate of inflation, if we can't provide coverage to the 35 million Americans which don't have it, if we can't face the crises of AIDS and the lack of health care in rural areas and big cities, and if we can't invest in research in those things that we have not come to grips with in health care, what can we do as a country? Every other nation has done a better job of many of these things than we do, and so we must.

They say, well, you should only do one thing at a time. "You can't walk and chew gum at the same time in Washington," that's what they say. But I say we will do one thing at a time, but we have to honestly put it all out there. If you want to bring the deficit down, you have to do health care. The only purpose of bringing the deficit down is to make the economy healthy. You have to invest in new technologies and give people incentives to create opportunity for others. It is not so simple as to say, well, just think about this and let another idea cross your mind a year or two from now. We have got to be about the business of rebuilding America. And we can do that if we keep our eyes on the whole picture: bring the debt down, invest in our future, deal with the health care crisis, deal with the special problems of special people in special areas that have been left out and left behind. I believe we can do these things.

I also have to tell you here at this magnificent fundraiser tonight that I am so humbled that so many of you have helped me for so long and asked for nothing in return, and others have done it in spite of the fact that many of the changes that I have advocated are not in your personal, immediate, short-term interest. You ought to be proud of that, because I'm proud of you.

One of the problems that has just killed this country is that all of us have had our blinders on and we've been able to see about 6 inches in front of our eyes. And all of Washington for too long has been dominated by that: 80,000 lobbyists, because of the absence of a compelling national public vision, each picking apart

the public interest. Now I think we have to follow through also on our commitment to political reform, to campaign finance reform, to lower the cost of campaigns, reduce the influence of PAC's, and open the airwaves to challengers. It'll also be nicer for you if you could only go to one dinner a year instead of four or five. It's a good thing. We should do it.

I also believe that we have to continue on this whole reform track. We passed a modified line-item veto in the House of Representatives. The Senate ought to pass it and let the President take the heat for controlling unnecessary spending. We ought to continue to work to open up the political process. Hallelujah, the gridlock was broken yesterday, and the United States Congress passed the motor voter bill to open up the political process to young people all across the country.

These are things that can make a difference. We have to begin to think about America in terms of what's in it for all of us together so that we can move forward together. Let me just mention one or two things tonight. A couple of days ago I was in Cleveland, and on the way out of town, I went by a little pierogi place started by a wonderful young woman who wanted to start her own restaurant, couldn't get a bank loan. She came from a big Polish family, so she just took the Cleveland phone book and called hundreds of people with Polish surnames and asked them to invest in her business until she got 80 folks who'd give her $3,000 apiece, and she's doing real well now. They're the kind of people that we ought to be fighting for.

When I got to another one of my meetings, I saw a woman who had six children and was supporting these children all by herself, making a handsome salary that she had to give up because one of her children was so desperately ill the only way she could afford the child's health care was to become eligible for Government assistance, because we don't have a health care system. And she was there in my speech with her beloved child and their $100,000-a-month medical bills. They're the people who are worth fighting for.

I received a letter yesterday from a wonderful young man and his wife who became friends of mine in New Hampshire and had a desperately ill child who had troubles at birth. And he lost his health insurance and he had to choose between working and not working to get on public assistance, and he struggled on. And the letter says that he just had to file for bankruptcy, but he hasn't given up on himself or his family or his country, and he wants me to keep fighting to make the economy better. That's what this whole effort is all about. There are real people and lives and dramas worthy of the greatest admiration behind so many stories in this room, so many stories in this country.

I ask you for your continued support. I ask you to support the suggestion I made today that we're going to put all this money we're trying to raise into a deficit-reduction trust and say to the American people, every dollar of the tax will go to reduce the debt, and none of the taxes will be raised without the spending cuts. Tell the Congress that we ought to do it, instead of just fooling around with it and talking about it.

But I ask you, finally, to remember that the atmosphere in which we labor, you and I, is still heavily laden with cynicism and skepticism. People have been disappointed on and off for 20 years. I was looking the other night at a little bit of history, an account of the Kennedy administration, reminding me that when President Kennedy was elected, the same sort of time, the same sort of moment, except that over 70 percent of the American people, when he went in, believed that leaders told the truth to the American people and believed they could trust their leaders to do the right thing. We don't have that today. One of the things that those of you who had some personal contact and personal involvement in this administration can do is to help to restore the sense of faith that the American people used to take for granted.

We simply can never succeed, ever, if every step along the way is burdened with people who are denying their own responsibility, waiting for someone to deliver them while making no effort, waiting for someone else to blame, letting the spite that comes out of every conflict overcome the larger vision and purposes that we are about. I am telling you, if we could do one thing tonight that would guarantee the success of everything else we're going to do, it would be all of us in our own way to walk out of here and say, let's try to put aside all of our differences and think about how we can lift up the people of this country. Let us, for a few months, suspend all of our cynicism and instead put our faith in the process that took us to the polls last November. Let us try to

bring out the best in one another even in the most heated debates in the Congress.

I worry from time to time only about one thing, and that is that the people who have to make these decisions will not feel the energy of the American people desperately saying, "Change, have the courage to change. Challenge me, bring out the best in me. Do not give in to the pressures and the temptations of the moment but go forward to a better life."

I ask all of you, too, to remember that I'm going to get up every day and go to work and work hard. Some days I work smarter than other days, but every day I'll work hard. I ask you to remember that one of the great challenges of being President is to try to devote enough time and attention to the job to get the job done and save enough time to stay among the people, selling what you've done and listening and making the proper adjustment when there is something more you need to learn.

I asked so many of you back during the election not to take the election as the end but the beginning of this enterprise. And so I invite you again to be a part of this great enterprise, with your ideas as well as your spirit. We've got 4 years of work to do. We can move this country forward in great ways and in profound ways that will benefit millions, indeed all, of the people of this country. But it's going to take every last good idea, and every last ounce of will and vision, and every ounce of courage and faith.

You have to be a part of that. I want you to leave here tonight knowing that I still want that just as badly as I did in the election. I did not run for this job to move into the White House, as great an honor as that is. I did not run for this job even to have the enormous privilege of standing on Harry Truman's balcony and looking at the statue of Thomas Jefferson every night. I ran for it to be faithful to the tradition they established by making your life better, and you have to help me do that.

Thank you and God bless you all.

NOTE: The President spoke at 9:35 p.m. at the Lincoln Center for the Performing Arts. In his remarks he referred to event chairmen Bruce Ratner, Lewis Katz, and Bob Rose; event cochairmen Bob Barrie, Bill Boardman, and Roy Furman, also Democratic National Committee finance chairman; event vice chairmen Paul Montrone, George Norcross, Felix Rohatyn, Ann Sheffer,

John Sweeney, and Steve Swid; Democratic National Committee chairman David Wilhelm; Edward Rendell, Mayor of Philadelphia and honorary chairman of the event; and Gov. Jim Florio of New Jersey.

Message to the Senate Transmitting the Netherlands-United States Taxation Convention
May 12, 1993

To the Senate of the United States:

I transmit herewith for the advice and consent of the Senate to ratification the Convention Between the Government of the United States of America and the Government of the Kingdom of the Netherlands for the Avoidance of Double Taxation and the Prevention of Fiscal Evasion with Respect to Taxes on Income, signed at Washington on December 18, 1992. An Understanding and exchange of notes are enclosed for the information of the Senate. Also transmitted for the information of the Senate is the report of the Department of State with respect to the Convention.

The Convention replaces the existing income tax convention between the United States and the Kingdom of the Netherlands signed at Washington in 1948 and last amended in 1965. It is intended to reduce the distortions (double taxation or excessive taxation) that can arise when two countries tax the same income, thereby enabling U.S. firms to compete on a more equitable basis in the Netherlands and further enhancing the attractiveness of the United States to Dutch investors. In general, the Convention follows the pattern of other recent U.S. income tax treaties and is based on the U.S. and OECD Model treaties and recent income tax conventions of both parties. It will serve to modernize tax relations between the two countries.

I recommend that the Senate give early and favorable consideration to the Convention and give its advice and consent to ratification.

WILLIAM J. CLINTON

The White House,
May 12, 1993.

Remarks to Small Business Leaders
May 13, 1993

Thank you very much. Erskine's only been here a day, and he's already become one of us. And you just saw an illustration of Clinton's third law of politics: Whenever possible, always be introduced by someone you've appointed to high office. [*Laughter*]

I want to introduce the people who are here with me: first, starting on my left, Frank Newman, the Under Secretary of the Treasury; and Roger Altman, the Deputy Secretary of the Treasury; Laura Tyson, the Chair of the Council of Economic Advisers. You met Erskine Bowles. And next to Erskine is Andrew Cuomo, the Assistant Secretary of the Department of Housing and Urban Development who, among other things, is responsible for developing and implementing our empowerment zone proposal for cities and small towns and rural areas that are economically distressed and that need more free enterprise.

I'd like to thank all of you for coming, but I'd like to also pay a special word of recognition to the smallest entrepreneurs that are here. These young people are from Theodore Roosevelt Elementary School in Houston, Texas. They are second graders. And shortly after I was inaugurated, in February sometime, they sent me this book. I got your book with all their letters, telling me what I ought to be doing. "How are you going to stop the violence and crime? If you will, completely stop it." See, everybody wrote me a letter and there are pictures. "Can you keep companies from making guns so we won't have crime?" And it goes on and on. But the reason they're here is that they are really the smallest entrepreneurs. They sold 22,000 candy bars to raise the money to come to Washington. So I think they deserve a hand. [*Applause*] Thank you.

I want to thank you for taking your valuable time to come here today so that we could talk about the shape of the small business initiatives in the economic program, now well on its way to moving through Congress. So many of you are the best representatives of American small business. For instance, Nancy Alchuleta has led the Mevatec Corporation in Huntsville, Alabama, to compete and win in the world marketplace with a new emphasis on high technology. William Gordon, president of Applied Data Technology—is a high-tech company which has grown from 7 employees in 1986 to over 100 today. Paul Sam, president of Holly Metals—has grown from a custom sheet metal company to the fabrication of metal parts for Boeing and a high-tech composite painting facility.

These are the kinds of things that we need more of in America. As I said yesterday in giving out the Small Business Person of the Year Awards, the United States benefited greatly, particularly in the last 10 to 12 years, from the fact that small business created more jobs than were lost in the large business sector of this economy. It is a little-known fact to most Americans, but in every year of the last dozen, the largest businesses in the country, the Fortune 500, have reduced their employment in the United States by somewhere in the neighborhood of a total of 200,000 jobs. Even as profits increased and productivity increased and stock values increased, the technological advances of productivity led to an actual reduction in the work force, not an increase. For all of the 1980's until the very end of the decade, those reductions were far more than offset by the growing vibrancy of an entrepreneurial economy in America. Indeed, many of the small businesses were contractors and customers and suppliers for the larger businesses in the country.

Then about 3 years ago, the small business job engine began to slow down. And there are any number of reasons why. There was a domes-

tic recession. There is a global recession. The credit crunch in parts of our country plainly contributed to it. The substantial increase in the cost of adding one more employee in terms of Social Security, workers' comp, health care, and other things has certainly led to the use of more part-time employees or asking the existing work force to do more overtime. And you may pay a little more for overtime, but you save all the supplemental costs of hiring the additional employee.

Although things are perfectly rational choices, but what they have meant for the United States is that we've had quite a stagnant unemployment rate, one that mirrors, I might add, every other advanced country in the world. At 7 percent, our unemployment rate is about the same as Western Germany's and still lower than all of Europe; higher than Japan, which has, as you know, a very different sort of economic system than we do. But even there they've had trouble now creating new jobs, and many companies there are having some of the first layoffs they've ever had.

I say that to make the following point: Larger companies, just like the Federal Government, will have no choice but to continue to try to improve productivity and use technology to do more with fewer workers, to increase output per worker. One of the things I'm trying to do here that we're writing into the law, this new budget proposal, is to reduce the size of the Federal Government by attrition by at least 100,000 workers, by increasing productivity and restructuring. But that's what the National Government should be doing.

But if these things are going to occur in our larger organizations, then we have to find a way to preserve the vitality of small business and to increase the capacity of small business to add to the American work force. If everybody in this country who wanted a job had one, we wouldn't have half the problems that we wrestle about all day up here every day. And frankly, you and people like you all over America are the best prospect we have for getting that done. That's why we worked as hard as we could to try to create an economic program that would benefit small business.

Our policy first begins with deficit reduction. The deficit reduction package that the Government has put forward and that the House of Representatives is in the process of coming to grips with now clearly has had a major impact in driving interest rates down over the long run. Since November there has been a dramatic reduction in interest rates. Home mortgage is at a 20-year low, many other interest rates at historic lows. The business analysts estimate that if we can keep these rates down for several more months the impact will be about $100 billion released into this economy, principally through refinancing of home mortgages and business loans and other refinancing as well as the direct benefit of the lower costs of borrowing. That's why I always say the best stimulus program that we can give to this economy just to stimulate growth is to keep these interest, and to keep driving down and to keep driving the deficit down.

Yesterday, in an attempt to build up a sense of real confidence that the administration means business and that the Congress will mean business if they pass this program, I proposed that we put all the taxes raised and the budget reductions into a deficit reduction trust fund so that, number one, no tax increase without budget cuts; number two, no tax increase for anything but reducing the deficit. And putting that in a trust fund, I think, will hammer home the determination that we have to bring the deficit down and to try to keep the interest rates down.

The second thing I think we have to do is to recognize that there are some initiatives which need to be taken to try to improve the access to capital for small business. One of the first things this administration made an aggressive effort to do was to deal with the credit crunch that I heard about all over America but especially in certain parts of the United States. We're trying to make it easier for small businesses to apply for and to obtain loans when they are appropriate and needed to expand and create new jobs.

In March, I announced this plan to ease the credit crunch by reducing some excessively restrictive regulations imposed in reaction to the savings and loan debacle. Our plans strikes a better balance, I think, so that we can have both safety and credit availability. Banks have more leeway now to make character loans based on the reputation of the borrower. We also have moved to ease the paperwork burdens because it shouldn't be as burdensome to get a $25,000 loan as it is to get a $25 million one and it certainly is, in a large measure because of direct Federal rules and regulations.

We have the Treasury and all the financial agencies of the Federal Government working on this. We now have an SBA Director who understands it all too well since before he became SBA Director his job was to help other people start new businesses, which is what he did very successfully.

We also know and we're not naive enough to think that just because we announced the policy in March the practice changed in every community bank and every community in this country. We know that hasn't happened. And I have made an offer, and I make it again here today, of requesting the small business community to tell the Small Business Administrator where the plan for easing the credit crunch is working and where it isn't and what we can do to work through that. The Treasury Department can only do so much until it knows where the backlog and the problems are. So we invite your participation to make the policy we announced in March real in your community as soon as can possibly do that.

The second thing that we have done since we've been here is to try to canvass the small business community about what kind of tax incentive would best serve to help small businesses engage in job creation. Yesterday, the House Ways and Means Subcommittee voted to increase from $10,000 to $25,000 the maximum amount of new investments that a small business can deduct as expenses every year. This means that when you invest so that your company can grow, you can immediately write off $25,000 worth of that investment. If that becomes law, it will be directly because of the input of the small business community to this administration as well as to the Congress.

When I ran for President in 1992, virtually all the small business people I met talked to me about how those which were family-owned businesses and commitments of a lifetime would not have much immediate benefit from the capital gains tax, and they asked for some sort of investment credit. That's why I recommended the permanent small business investment tax credit as compared with a capital gains option. After we got here, the small business organization said that, as a practical matter, we would get more bang for the buck and it would be easier for more small businesses if we simply just increased the expensing provisions to $25,000. That change is directly the result of the input of the small business community in this country. I hope it becomes law, and I hope

Photographic Portfolio

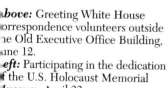

bove: Greeting White House
orrespondence volunteers outside
ne Old Executive Office Building,
une 12.

eft: Participating in the dedication
f the U.S. Holocaust Memorial
Museum, April 22.

bove right: With Vice President
lbert Gore, Jr., and Attorney
eneral nominee Janet Reno in
ne Rose Garden, February 11.

ight: Surveying flood damage in
avenport, IA, July 4.

Above: Holding the children's
town meeting in the East Room,
February 20.
Left: With Supreme Court
nominee Ruth Bader Ginsburg in
the Rose Garden, June 14.
Right: Visiting U.S. troops at
Camp Casey, South Korea, July 11
Overleaf: Walking on the South
Grounds, May 25.

you will do everything you can to see that it does become law.

Now, there is a capital gains provision left in this bill which I think is very helpful. It provides a big exclusion from capital gains taxation to help small businesses get started and to invest in completely new projects. That was one put forward by the American Venture Capital Association and sponsored in the previous Congress, among others, by the senior Senator from my State, Dale Bumpers, who's the chairman of the Small Business Committee. I think that should stay in the law; we're working hard to make sure that it does. I think it now has virtually unanimous support.

Finally, we have decided we should try to offer some very special opportunities in a network of empowerment zones and enterprise communities all across America. In the empowerment zones, we're offering small businesses an employment and training credit of 25 percent of the first $20,000 in wages for employees who live and work in the zones, a targeted jobs tax credit of 40 percent on $6,000 of the first year of wages for these workers, and an increase in the ability to deduct appreciable property.

All these things are our effort to help communities that are willing to help themselves by developing a long-term strategy to grow through private sector and private-public cooperation. To do that, to attract capital in businesses, I am convinced and I think that you are all convinced that with the size of the deficit we have, there is not enough money in America to have a publicly-funded revitalization of America's most distressed communities.

But wherever in America there are people who are underutilized, there is a market opportunity. Because when people are working up to the fullest of their capacity, then they have money to spend and they create jobs for others. So when I look at all these places in America which for too long have been without businesses on their street corners or in their small towns or in their hamlets, I see enormous opportunity. I see in people whose potential is not fulfilled the opportunity to make free enterprise work again.

We all know there are certain considerable barriers to dealing with that. I'm trying to make some of the high-crime areas much more attractive by simply lowering the crime rate. We know we can do that through community policing.

And I've asked the United States Congress to give us some money to put more police on the street in these communities to help make them safer and lower the crime rate. We know that works; there is clear evidence of that. In New York City alone, after the comprehensive community policing program established by the man who is now our drug czar, Lee Brown, for the first time in 36 years the crime rate actually went down in seven major areas. So we know these things can be done.

We know we have responsibilities to make these areas more attractive. But if this empowerment concept can pass, then it will be more attractive for you and people like you all across America to take that extra risk to go into places where there is an enormous prospect of return if a whole lot of people with no income all of a sudden wind up having income and can be customers as well as employees. And I hope all of you will support the empowerment zones.

We've talked and talked and talked about our cities and our drying-up rural communities for years. Democrats and Republicans, they wring their hands every year, and nothing ever happens. I say, let's try this; let's see if it works. Let's see if we can have a public-private partnership that works. If it doesn't work, we'll try something else. But the one thing that we know doesn't work is more words. We've had more words for years. We've had wars of words from people across political and party and regional lines, and that hasn't worked, and that's not ever going to work. So I hope we can try this and see once and for all whether the Government can create an environment which makes it more attractive for free enterprise to flourish in areas where it hasn't.

Finally let me say again, I appreciate the burdens under which you labor. I recognize that some of you, perhaps most of you in this room, would pay higher personal tax rates under the program I have proposed. I hope you will support it anyway because if we do it right, most Americans will save more in long-term lower interest rates than they'll pay in higher taxes. The country will be much better off if we can pass the expensing provisions, the capital gains provisions, the enterprise zone provisions. If we can make our plan to ease the credit crunch work, then small business in the nineties can once again resume its proper role in America as the true engine of our job growth, and there will be more people like you with rewarding stories to tell.

And perhaps most important of all, when these kids grow up, they'll have a chance to be just as entrepreneurial as they have been in getting themselves here today.

Thank you very much.

NOTE: The President spoke at 10:50 a.m. in Room 450 of the Old Executive Office Building. In his remarks, he referred to Erskine Bowles, Small Business Administrator.

Exchange With Reporters Following a Meeting With Small Business Leaders
May 13, 1993

Inflation

Q. Mr. President, could you respond to the inflation numbers out today?

The President. Well, you know, I've looked at them over the last couple of years, and I think we have to watch it closely. But there is, at the present time, no cause for long-term concern. I want to watch it, and we will be watching it. But it could be just a blip. There are lots of things that could have produced it. We'll just have to see. We'll wait for a month or so and see what's going on. Unless there's some underlying change in the economy, it's difficult to imagine how we could have a significant upsurge in inflation.

Deficit Reduction and Taxes

Q. Do you think your deficit reduction trust fund will be able to win support on the Hill despite Domenici and Dole and the other Senators criticizing it as a gimmick?

The President. The people that I'm concerned about are the people who were prepared to vote for responsible deficit reduction all along, the moderate to conservative Democrats who are willing to vote for tax increases as long as they know they're going to go to reduce the deficit. Bill Bradley called for the deficit reduction trust fund also, I noted yesterday. And a whole range of House Members from Charles Schumer to Charles Stenholm did. And I think it will help to—more importantly, I think that in the public mind out there in the country, people will see that it's a double guarantee that the money will go where we say it will go. So I still think it's a very good thing to do.

I didn't expect it to move any of the votes of people who say that they won't vote for a tax increase no matter what. But I must say,

the most encouraging thing on that is the interview that David Stockman, who was President Reagan's Budget Director, did in a magazine called the New Politics Quarterly this month where he basically owns up to the fact that the biggest problem with the deficit is that they cut 6 percent of the national income out of the tax base in 1981 in a bidding war. That was twice the size of the tax cut that President Reagan originally intended to offer to stimulate the economy. And he says the impact of that has never been overcome. So all we're going to try to do is redress that with some tough spending cuts. And I think the public mood will be far more supportive.

Q. Will you go along with a 35 percent corporate tax rate?

The President. If that's what comes out of the Congress. I don't know if the Senate will vote for that. We'll have to see. But the changes made by the House Ways and Means Committee don't reduce the overall contribution from the business sector. They just shift the way it comes. And I think that's okay.

Bosnia

Q. Mr. President, do you hold out any hope that the referendum in Bosnia this weekend might result in some sort of face-saving way to get out of this mess?

The President. The issue is not face saving. The issue is life saving. Face saving has got nothing to do with it. The issue is whether the Bosnian Serbs are ready to have a serious peace process that will save lives, recognize that all those people have some right and some way to live in the piece of land we now know as Bosnia-Herzegovina, and confine the conflict so that it doesn't spill over and cause much more, much more serious political consequences for everybody. And that's what I hope. You know, I wouldn't say I ever have given up hope, but I'm skeptical about it. But it might produce something.

NOTE: The exchange began at 11:24 a.m. in Room 450 of the Old Executive Office Building. A tape was not available for verification of the content of this exchange.

Remarks to the Champion University of Texas Wheelchair Basketball Team and an Exchange With Reporters
May 13, 1993

The President. Ladies and gentlemen, I am honored to be the first President to welcome the national intercollegiate wheelchair champions to the White House. I have to tell you that I am very impressed by this group of fine young men. They've done some amazing things. For the 3d year in a row, the Moving Mavs from the University of Texas of Arlington have brought home a national championship. I hear that they're the pride of UT-Arlington, that their home games are drawing record crowds, and that every time another banner is brought home in Texas Hall the excitement and the enthusiasm of the fans keeps building.

I want to recognize a few of the people who've been instrumental in this team's remarkable success: the driving force behind the Moving Mavs, of course, the coach, Jim Hayes; Ryan Amacher, president of the University of Texas of Arlington; and one of their biggest supporters, my friend Congressman Martin Frost, who just coincidentally happens to represent them. [*Laughter*]

I'm impressed with their winning record and their hard work and determination. I understand that this team really reflects the pioneer spirit of Texas and does not flinch in the face of obstacles. All of them are pioneers not only in wheelchair athletics but in the ongoing struggle in our Nation to obtain equal opportunities on and off the court for all Americans with disabilities, not inabilities.

They display the attributes of strength and determination. They've practiced. They've worked hard. They've produced a championship team in ways that few people ever know. I commend all of you for your unrelenting pursuit of excellence and for your demonstration about what is true in every sport: that as an individual you may star, but as a team you can be champions.

I believe that when people are empowered and when they work together, when they're given the opportunity to make something of themselves by a real community effort, that's when we all achieve the fullest meaning in our lives. If we're going to be a strong America, we're going to have to do more of what you've done with this team, coach.

I'm proud of all of you. I welcome you to the White House. I know the people back home are proud of you, too.

Thank you very much.

[*At this point, Dr. Amacher, Mr. Hayes, and team member Phung Tran presented gifts to the President, and Representative Frost expressed his thanks.*]

The President. Thank you. Thank you very much, all of you, and good luck to all of you. You know, things do get busy around here, but if people like you don't come to see us sometimes, we forget why I'm here. It's easy to get too busy and lose connections with the people in the country. You know, tonight all over this country people will see a picture of you here. And you have no idea whether some young person will see your picture here and be inspired and say, "Well, I can do more with my life. I can make more of myself. There is something else I can do." And I don't think you could possibly underestimate the impact that your achievement will have on others. I really want to encourage you. I also want you to know I don't have the upper-body strength to play basketball. Now, don't run off with that. [*Laughter*]

Tax Legislation

Q. Mr. President, are you satisfied with the way your tax bill came out of the House Ways and Means Committee?

The President. Chairman Rostenkowski called me about an hour or so ago, right after the vote, and based on what I know, I'm very satisfied. I'm immensely pleased. All the basic features of the bill remained intact, and many of the changes that were made I think made it a better bill. So again, I have not had a chance to study all the things that were done today, but based on what I know, I believe it is a very good bill indeed. It still maintains the essential features. The earned-income tax credit is there for people making roughly $29,000 a year or less to basically add fairness to the Tax Code and relieve them of the impact of the energy tax.

The bill is highly progressive, virtually all of the money raised on people with incomes of over $100,000. The immunization program, the family preservation program is intact. The empowerment zone program was endorsed by the committee, and they added quite a bit of money to it so we could encourage more cities to get involved in trying to bring free enterprise into distressed areas. I think that is a very impressive thing. And I think changing the small business incentive to an expensing rather than an investment tax credit is basically a net plus because more small businesses can access it at less hassle. So I feel very good about it—what I know about the bill. You know, like I said, I haven't—but what I know about it is very encouraging.

Q. Why shouldn't the American people regard this as a black letter day with a new tax bill coming their way?

The President. Because all this money is going to go to reduce the deficit. Because we've got interest rates at a 20-year low. Because most Americans have refinanced a home or a business loan, they've already saved more money in interest costs than they will pay in higher taxes. And because if we don't do something to cut spending and increase some taxes we're going to bankrupt the country.

We tried it the other way for 12 years. We tried lowering taxes and increasing spending, and we went from a $1 trillion to a $4 trillion debt; didn't work out very well. And I think the American people want us finally to step up to the bar and reduce this national deficit and get it down eventually to zero and get some economic growth going.

I also believe until we bring the deficit down we won't have any money to invest in education and training and new technologies. We have to prove to the American people first we've got the discipline to spend their money properly and to run this Government properly.

I think it's not a black letter day. It's a red letter day for America. We're finally beginning to face our problems in a mature way. And I'm encouraged. And I applaud the House Committee for what they did today.

NOTE: The President spoke at 4:42 p.m. in the Diplomatic Reception Room at the White House. A tape was not available for verification of the content of these remarks.

Remarks at the National Law Enforcement Officers Memorial Ceremony
May 13, 1993

Thank you very much, Senator DeConcini, Chairman Floyd, President Young, law enforcement officers, and survivors of our fallen brothers and sisters.

America has more than half a million law enforcement officers who serve proudly and bravely. And every day they carry out their sworn duties, risk is a constant companion. No one knows that better than those of you who are here tonight and your families. But I can say that there are very few Americans who owe more to law enforcement officers than do I.

I'm proud to be joined here tonight by three people who have a very important role in the protection of the American people and who have an important role in my administration and my life. I'd like to acknowledge them if I might: the Director of the United States Secret Service, whose members put their lives on the line for the President every day, Mr. John McGaw; the Director of the Office of National Drug Policy and formerly the police chief of the cities of Atlanta, Houston, and New York, Mr. Lee Brown; and Senator DeConcini just mentioned the Attorney General, formerly the prosecutor of Dade County, Florida, Ms. Janet Reno, who just came in. She's somewhere here. I like introducing these people.

I'd also like to thank very much the survivors from Arkansas who came here with me tonight, as well as the law enforcement officials, in particular, the two members of the Arkansas State Police, who for a dozen years worked with me and protected me and my family and stood up to unbelievable pressures from radical fringe groups, from organized rioters, from serious organized criminal efforts, and the day-to-day hazards of law enforcement. I owe them all a great deal, and I'm glad they're here tonight.

More than 13,000 law enforcement officials have fallen in the line of duty. This memorial was dedicated to them a year and a half ago. Tonight we note the names of 328 more who will be newly etched on these marble stones. But our tribute will ring hollow tonight unless we recommit ourselves to do whatever we can to keep the remainder of these stones as smooth as possible, to support the men and women who keep our society more lawful and our lives more secure, to help them as enforcers, and to keep them from becoming victims.

Collectively, we call them our Thin Blue Line. That line is nothing less than our buffer against chaos, against the worst impulses of this society, a shield we may not always think about until it is raised in our own defense. The safety of our citizens in their homes, where they work, where they play, it all depends on that Thin Blue Line. And so it behooves us all to reinforce that line, to make it as strong as we can.

Let us be honest with one another. We know that nothing we do will remove all risk from law enforcement, but we can take steps that will make the profession safer and make ourselves safer as well. We could do that by passing the Brady bill. The American people want it; law enforcement officers have called for it for years. It will save lives, and it would be a tribute to those we honor here tonight.

We can also do that by increasing the number of law enforcement officers on the street. Just a generation ago there were three officers for every serious crime in this country. Today there are three crimes for every officer. It makes police work more dangerous. It makes it more difficult to implement strategies that work like community policing. It makes society less safe. Let us do more to put police officers on the

street, and that will be a tribute to those whom we come here to honor tonight.

Last year Federal, State, and law enforcement officers were killed in substantial numbers, but they say that fewer were killed than at any year since the mid-1960's. Still, one is too many. And statistics, the numbers like 120 people being killed in the line of duty by violent means, they belie the real human stories.

In my State, a 74-year-old sheriff's deputy was beaten to death. That's more than an assault on a law enforcement officer; it's an affront to our common humanity. That officer, R.D. Purifoy, was from a little county next to the one where I was born in Arkansas. He was so dedicated that any time, day or night, for 26 years, he was always there to answer the call. And on the day he died last November, he was simply trying to settle a domestic quarrel.

Then there was Jerry Stallings, a police officer from Barling, Arkansas, in the western part of my State, whose family is here tonight. He was investigating an auto accident when he was struck by a drunk driver. It should have been a routine investigation, but as every law enforcement officer knows, there's no such thing as a routine investigation.

Tonight we honor these men and their families. We honor all those who have fallen throughout our Nation as they carried out their duties to make our lives better and safer: from the officers on the beat and the street, to the patrols on the highways, to the Federal agents in all fields. Tonight we light the darkness with the memories and glories of those who died in the service of their neighbors, their communities, and our Nation. Their brave souls are among us; they are carried brightly in our hearts in gratitude, in joy, in sorrow, yes, but also in the certainty that God looks after those who give such a full measure of their devotion.

We honor these valiant men and women not for dying, because death comes to us all eventually. We honor them for how they died and how they lived. In life they gave us aid when we were helpless, shielded us when we were vulnerable, lifted us when we had fallen, gave us comfort when we were afraid. In rooting out our lawless, they preserved our order. They were our fathers and sons, our brothers and sisters, our mothers and daughters. They were our friends.

Their contribution cannot be measured nor

properly honored by their President or any other citizen except to say a simple thank you and to give a prayer to God for their souls. They will be remembered as all of you knew them, standing tall and ready, the sentinels of our liberty. Let us live in ways that will honor their ultimate contribution to our lives.

Thank you, and God bless you all.

NOTE: The President spoke at 8:40 p.m. at the memorial. In his remarks, he referred to Craig Floyd, chairman, National Law Enforcement Officers Memorial Fund, and Kathleen A. Young, president, Concerns of Police Survivors.

Letter to Congressional Leaders Transmitting a Report on Soviet Treaty Compliance
May 13, 1993

Dear Mr. President: (Dear Mr. Chairman:)
   Enclosed are classified and unclassified copies of the report on Soviet Treaty Compliance required under condition 7 of the Resolution of Ratification for the Strategic Arms Reduction Treaty (START).

   The judgments included in this report are drawn from reports prepared by the Arms Control and Disarmament Agency and submitted to Congress under the provisions of PL 99–145, as amended, and Section 52 of the Arms Control and Disarmament Act.

   Under the terms set forth in the Resolution of Ratification, this report addresses actions of the former Soviet Union which were violations or probable violations of the obligations of the SALT I Interim Agreement, SALT II, ABM,

INF and START Treaties and the ultimate resolution of these issues. This report does not address the actions of the newly independent states which have succeeded the Soviet Union. In contrast to the Soviet Union, the newly independent states have demonstrated a substantially improved willingness to adhere to arms control obligations and to work with us to resolve problems.
   Sincerely,

WILLIAM J. CLINTON

NOTE: Identical letters were sent to Albert Gore, Jr., President of the Senate, and Claiborne Pell, chairman of the Senate Committee on Foreign Relations. An original was not available for verification of the content of this letter.

Nomination for Posts at the Housing and Urban Development, Transportation, and State Departments
May 13, 1993

   The President announced his intention today to nominate G. Edward DeSeve and Nelson Diaz to be Chief Financial Officer and General Counsel, respectively, of the Department of Housing and Urban Development; David Hinson to be Administrator of the Federal Aviation Administration, Department of Transportation; and Peter Galbraith to be Ambassador to Croatia.

   "We are continuing to make real progress in filling key positions in my administration," said the President. "This group of individuals whose appointments we are announcing today have the kind of experience and expertise that our country needs."

NOTE: Biographies of the nominees were made available by the Office of the Press Secretary.

Remarks Honoring Blue Ribbon Schools
May 14, 1993

Thank you very much. Thank you, Secretary Riley. Thank you, ladies and gentlemen.

I want to welcome you all to the White House today on this gorgeous day. I hope you've enjoyed yourselves. The Marine Band has been in especially fine form this morning. I woke up to them; I went jogging to them. I almost felt like a President this morning for sure when I was walking over to the Oval Office. They were playing a march that was written for the coronation of a British monarch, so I almost got myself confused. [*Laughter*]

There are 228 schools here represented today, the winners of the Blue Ribbon Awards this year. And all of you are winners, representing what is best in American education in public and private schools and urban and suburban and rural schools. You all share some common features with all your differences: visionary leadership, a sense of shared purpose, a climate conducive to learning, impressive academic achievement brought on not only by gifted teachers but also by responsible and open student behavior, and real involvement of parents and often the broader community in the life of the school.

I spent a lot of time thinking about these educational issues over the last 12 or so years. I spent more of my time as a Governor on education than on any other single issue except for the economy of my State. I spent hundreds of hours, I suppose, in schools in my State and around the country over the last 12 to 15 years and some time in one of the schools from Arkansas that's being honored today.

A hundred years ago the key to a strong economy was our raw material base. Fifty years ago it was mass production. Now it is clearly the trained human mind. We live in a world where the average person will change work seven or eight times in a lifetime, when the volume of knowledge is doubling every few years. When people in Silicon Valley making new computers and new computer programs tell me their average product life is now down to 18 months, clearly the reasoning, creative, facile but also deep mind is key to the future of the United States. We also live in a time when hardly anybody can get and keep a decent job without more education that too many of our people

lack today.

If we could multiply the grade schools here represented on this lawn all across the country, we could really revolutionize education in America. I must tell you that the most challenging— [*applause*]—give yourselves a hand. That's a good idea. The most challenging thing I ever faced as Governor and the most continually frustrating was going into our schools and realizing that virtually every challenge in American education has been met successfully by somebody somewhere.

There are people succeeding against all the odds and producing magnificent results in extremely difficult circumstances. There are schools producing world-class results by any rigorous measure. The problem with American education is that we have never found an effective way to help replicate success, partly because the magic of education is always what happens in the individual classroom between the teacher and the student, supported by the parents, strengthened by the culture of a school that is set overwhelmingly by a gifted principal. I know that.

But there have to be ways to recognize the plain fact that notwithstanding the funding problems, notwithstanding the inequalities, notwithstanding all the problems of American education, you can find virtually every problem in our country solved by somebody somewhere in an astonishingly effective fashion if you look at enough schools. So the challenge for us here is to figure out how to replicate that. That is what Secretary Riley and I are trying to do with the "Educate America Act," the Goals 2000 act that we presented to the United States Congress, a bill we believe will lead to the creation of world-class learning standards and also help to promote the idea that, clearly, all reforms must occur school by school.

Goals 2000 will, in effect, enshrine the national education goals in the law of the land, raise expectations for all students, and help to enrich the content of our courses, the training of our teachers, and the quality of our textbooks and our technology. Finally, the bill will challenge our schools to show real results. We believe students and schools should have more flexibility in dealing with Federal programs and should be shooting toward real results and clear standards. Goals 2000 is the framework for that educational effort in this administration. It will facilitate fundamental reforms in our schools, and I must say that's probably why some people don't like it all that well, including some members of my own party in the Congress.

But we can't raise standards and achievement either by leaving things the way they are or simply by piling on more particular governmental programs and mandates from Washington. After all, we're only providing about 7 percent of the total financing of public schools today, and while I hope to reverse that trend and over the next 5 years get the percentage back up to somewhere to where it was over the last several years, still the lion's share of the financing and the lion's share of the learning reforms must come from you and people like you. And that means we have to have a different approach in the way the National Government relates to our schools. I hope that the Congress will not dilute the package that I sent to them. I hope we can pass the bill in a way that will represent a real change in the way the National Government relates to the schools and a real increase in confidence in proven local leaders.

I'd also like to say that the private sector in this country has shown an astonishing willingness to become more involved in education ever since the issuance of the "Nation at Risk" report 10 years ago. The New American Schools Development Corporation, on which Governor Baliles serves on the board and which Governor Riley and now Secretary Riley mentioned, has already raised millions of dollars from public spirited business leaders. It has path-breaking design teams which are providing us with valuable lessons about how school innovations all around America can help us to reach world-class standards. And it is trying to help to replicate what works, which I still believe is our most urgent task.

Through these new designs they will be able to provide promising alternatives for schools and States as they work to reinvent their schools with the help of Goals 2000 and other reform efforts that this administration will make. I ask all of you to support this legislation and the work of the New American Schools Corporation. I ask you to support it in the larger context of what we must do as a nation.

Think of what has happened to bring us to

this point where we have come to 17 months in a row with unemployment rate at 7 percent or higher in every month, even though we are allegedly in an economic recovery. What has happened to bring us to a point where most American families are spending more hours on the job than they were 20 years ago with lower real incomes than they made 10 years ago, including some of the families represented in this audience? What has caused that? Our lack of ability to be continuously productive, our lack of ability to create more and more new jobs that will stand the test of the rigorous global economy. What we have to do in our administration and what I earnestly ask for your support in doing is to reverse the trends that have brought us to this past.

Let us first of all bring down the Government deficit that has gotten our debt from $1 trillion to $4 trillion in the last 12 years simply by telling people at election time what they wanted to hear: I'll cut your taxes and write you a check. All the arithmetic teachers in this audience could have figured out that sooner or later that would get us in trouble. Nobody could have passed math in this town in any of your schools in the last 12 years who with a straight face said, "I've got you a deal. I'll cut your taxes, and I'll send you a check."

So it fell to me to try to change that ratio. And the House of Representatives Committee on Ways and Means yesterday reported out a bill which does a lot of that. It restores both spending cuts and tax increases to a proper balance. It will bring the deficit down by $500 billion over the next 5 years. It will provide important new incentives for small businesses and for larger businesses to continue to invest, to create jobs in our country. It provides a real tax break for working families with children with incomes of under $29,000 to offset the impact of the energy tax and reward work so there will never be an incentive for people with families not to work. Because if this tax bill passes, for the first time in our country's history, because of the changes in the Tax Code, we'll be able to say that if you work 40 hours a week and you've got a child in the house, you will not live in poverty. These are important things. And over 70 percent of the money comes from people with incomes above $100,000.

The budget package also over the next 5 years will increase our commitment to Head Start, to apprenticeship training, with partnerships with our schools and our post-high school programs, and opens the doors of college education to everyone through a radical reform in the student loan program and national service. It focuses on, in other words, increasing investment, bringing down the deficit, and bringing us together as a country again. This Goals 2000 legislation is an important part of that. It is our effort to do our job here as well as you do your job back home. If we did our job here as well as you've done yours, then America could celebrate and give itself a blue ribbon in just a few years.

Thank you very much, and God bless you all.

NOTE: The President spoke at 9:51 a.m. on the South Lawn at the White House.

The President's News Conference
May 14, 1993

The President. Good afternoon, ladies and gentlemen. I'm glad the weather permitted us to do this outside.

Three months ago, I presented a plan to our country and to the Congress designed to address what I believe were the significant challenges of this time. For more than 40 years, our country was organized to stand up against communism, to try to help develop the free world, and for most of that time we took our economic prosperity for granted. It is now clear that, at the end of the cold war, we must organize ourselves around the obligation we have to be more competitive in the global economy and to enable our people to live up to their full potential.

That means we have to do a lot of things to turn this economy around, beginning with a serious effort to reduce our national debt, to invest in jobs and new technologies, to restore fairness to our Tax Code, and to make our political system work again.

This week I was able to go back again to the American people to take my case into the country, into Cleveland and Chicago and New York. And here in Washington there were new efforts to break the gridlock and to put the national interests above narrow interests. The results were particularly impressive in the work done by the House Ways and Means Committee, achieving over $250 billion in deficit reduction through spending cuts with $2 in spending cuts for each dollar in new investment, in new jobs, in education. The program provides significantly everything that I presented to the Congress, even though there were some changes. In fact, some of the changes I think made the bill better.

Let me reiterate them: number one, significant deficit reduction; number two, taking on entitlements issues that have for too long been left on the table; number three, real investments for small businesses and for big businesses, incentives to get people to invest money in this economy to create jobs; and perhaps most importantly, a break for working-class families, a huge increase in the earned-income tax credit for people with incomes under $30,000 to relieve them of the impact of the energy tax and to say for the first time, people who work 40 hours a week with children in the home would be lifted above poverty; and finally, of course, the plan was very progressive, 75 percent of the revenues coming from the top 6 percent of the American taxpayers.

I also reiterated that I don't want a penny in taxes without the spending cuts. And I proposed in New York that we create a deficit reduction trust fund into which all the taxes and all the budget cuts could be put and kept for the 5-year life of this budget. This is a very important thing. I realize some have said it is little more than a gimmick, but the truth is there is no legal protection now for the life of the budget for these funds. This will provide it in stone, in law.

In every element of this, there has been some willingness on the part of those who have supported our efforts to take on powerful vested interest in behalf of the national interest, whether it is in repealing the lobby deduction or in going for a direct loan program for college loans that will save $4 billion but which will remove a Government-guaranteed income from several interests who like the system as it is now.

The Congress also moved this week to reinvigorate our democratic process by ending the filibuster and passing the motor voter bill. These are the kinds of changes that the American people expect of us. They do not expect miracles, but they expect solid, steady progress, and I am determined to stay on this course.

It has been a good week, and if we're willing to take more tough decisions, there will be more good weeks for the American people ahead.

Bosnia

Q. Mr. President, you've said that the United States will not go it alone with military action in Bosnia. And yet, the European allies have refused to sign-on to your proposals. If the allies refuse to follow suit, where does that leave the United States?

The President. Let me reiterate what I have said because I think that the United States has taken the right position, and I think that we've gotten some good results. I have said, and I will reiterate, I think that the United States must act with our allies, especially because Bosnia is in the heart of Europe, and the Europeans are there. We must work together through the United Nations.

Secondly, I do not believe the United States has any business sending troops there to get involved in a conflict in behalf of one of the sides. I believe that we should continue to turn up the pressure. And as you know, I have taken the position that the best way to do that would be to lift the arms embargo with a standby authority of air power in the event that the present situation was interrupted by the unfair use of artillery by the Bosnian Serbs. That position is still on the table. It has not been rejected out of hand. Indeed, some of our European allies have agreed with it, and others are not prepared to go that far yet.

But we have to keep the pressure up. And I would just remind you that since we said we would become involved in the Vance-Owen peace process, two of the three parties have signed on. We've gotten enforcement of the no-fly zone through the United Nations. We've been able to airlift more humanitarian supplies there, and we've been able to keep up a very, very tough embargo on Serbia which I think led directly, that and the pressure of further action, to the statement that Mr. Milosevic made to the effect that he would stop supporting the Bosnian Serbs.

Where we go from here is to keep pushing in the right direction. As we speak here, the United Nations is considering a resolution which would enable us to place United Nations forces along the border between Serbia and Bosnia to try to test and reinforce the resolve of the Milosevic government to cut off supplies to the Bosnian Serbs. If that resolution passes, and in its particulars it makes good sense, that is a very good next step. We're just going to keep working and pushing in this direction. And I think we'll begin to get more and more results.

Q. Are you contemplating sending U.S. forces to Macedonia and perhaps to protect safe havens in Bosnia?

The President. On the question of Macedonia, the Defense Department has that and many other options under review for what the United Nations, what the allies could do to make sure that we confine this conflict, to keep it from spreading. I've not received a recommendation from them and, therefore, I've made no decision.

Helen [Helen Thomas, United Press International]?

Q. Mr. President, there is a wide spread perception that you're waffling, that you can't make up your mind. One day you're saying, "In a few days we'll have a decision. We have a common approach." The next day you're saying, "We're still looking for a consensus." Will American troops be in this border patrol that the U.N. is voting on and, you know, where are we?

The President. Well, first of all, I have made up my mind, and I've told you what my position was. And I've made it as clear as I can. But I also believe it is imperative that we work with our allies on this. The United States is not in a position to move unilaterally, nor should we. So that is the answer to your question.

The resolution being considered by the United Nations I think contemplates that the UNPROFOR forces would be moved and expanded and moved to the border. At this time there has been no suggestion that we would be asked to be part of those forces.

Susan [Susan Spencer, CBS News]?

Homosexuals in the Military

Q. A domestic question. Could you tell us how were you affected by the testimony of Colonel Fred Peck, whose son is a homosexual, who said that, nonetheless, he could not in good conscience support lifting the ban?

The President. I thought all the testimony given in that hearing—I saw quite a lot of it from more than one panel—was quite moving and straightforward. I still think the test ought to be conduct.

Q. Does this allow for the possibility of the "don't ask, don't tell"—the compromise that would allow——

The President. You know what my position is. I have nothing else to say about it.

Bosnia

Q. Mr. President, you said last week that if you went to air power in Bosnia you would have a clear strategy and it would have a beginning, middle, and end. What happens, though, sir, if a plane is shot down, if you lose a pilot or a couple of pilots, or if the Bosnian Serbs decide to escalate the conflict, or the Serbians by going into, say, Kosovo?

The President. Well, the Bush administration before I became President issued a clear warning to the Serbs that if they try to occupy Kosovo and repress the Albanians there, that the United States would be prepared to take some strong action. And I have reaffirmed that position. As a general proposition, you can never commit American forces to any endeavor on the assumption that there will be no losses. That is just simply not possible, and as the Pentagon will tell you, we lose forces even now in peace time simply in the rigorous training that our Armed Forces must undertake.

Homosexuals in the Military

Q. In the debate on homosexuals in the military, you use the word "conduct" as though it were an absolute and easily definable term. Do you believe, one, that homosexuals should be celibate, as Schwarzkopf suggested, or could they engage in homosexual activity, consenting, on or off base; or two, should the uniform code be allowed to have any sort of difference between its treatment of homosexuals and heterosexuals?

The President. I support the present code of conduct, and I am waiting for the Pentagon to give me its recommendations.

Brit [Brit Hume, ABC News]?

Lani Guinier

Q. Your nominee to head the Justice Department's Civil Rights Division has expressed what many regard as rather striking views about voting rights and a number of other areas, including expressing some misgivings about the principle of one man, one vote. And I wonder if you are familiar with all these views and if you support them, and if you do not, why you chose her?

The President. I nominated her because there had never been a full-time practicing civil rights lawyer with a career in civil rights law heading the Civil Rights Division. I expect the policy to be made on civil rights laws by the United States Congress, and I expect the Justice Department to carry out that policy. Insofar as there is discretion in the policy, that discretionary authority should reside either in the President or the Attorney General in terms of what policies the country will follow. I still think she's a very well-qualified civil rights lawyer, and I hope she will be confirmed. And I think she has every intention of following the law of the land as Congress writes it.

Carl [Carl Leubsdorf, Dallas Morning News]?

Q. Were you familiar with them when you——

Texas Senatorial Election

Q. Mr. President, as you know, there is a lot of concern in the Democratic Party and in the White House about the upcoming Senate election in Texas. And one of your top political advisers, Paul Begala, is becoming more involved down there. Do you see any expanded role for yourself? Is there anything you can do, or are you all pretty much resigned to losing this seat?

The President. Well, first of all, I'm not resigned to losing it. I think Bob Krueger can still win the race. But it depends on, as with all cases, it depends on how he frames the issues, how his opponent frames the issues, and what happens there. I think he's a good man, and I think he's capable of doing a good job. And I think he could still win the race. But that's up for the people of Texas. You know, in the primary, one of the big problems was 25 percent of the Republicans turned out and only 15 percent of the Democrats did. I don't know what's going to happen there. But I certainly support him, and I hope he will prevail. I think it would be good for the people of Texas and the Congress if he did.

Q. Do you expect to do any more for him and possibly go down there?

The President. No one's discussed that with

me. You know, I don't know. I've always been skeptical about the question of whether any of us could have any impact on anyone else's race. I've never seen it happen up or down in my own State in Arkansas. There may be some ways we can help with fundraising and things of that kind, but all the time I ran at home I never let anybody come in to help me, whatever the national politics were.

Inflation

Q. Mr. President, what would you say or what do you say to Federal Reserve officials who are arguing for a slight rise in short-term interest rates because they're concerned about resurging inflation?

The President. I would say that the month before last we have virtually no inflation, and you can't run the country on a month-to-month basis. You've got to look at some longer trends. There are some clear underlying reasons for this last inflationary bulge which don't necessarily portend long-term inflation. I think it's a cause of concern. We ought to look at it, but we ought to wait until we have some more evidence before we raise interest rates in an economy where industrial capacity is only at 80 percent.

If you look at all the underlying long-term things, long-term trends in energy prices, industrial capacity, the kinds of things that really shape an economy, there is no reason at this time to believe that there could be any cause for a resurge in inflation.

Q. Sir, the argument is made at the Federal Reserve that higher taxes, higher burdens on business through health care fees, or other things like that will indeed raise inflation while the economy stays weak.

The President. Just a few weeks ago some people were arguing that all this would be deflationary and would repress the recovery. So I guess you can find an expert to argue any opinion, but there is no evidence of that. The prevailing opinion at the Fed and the prevailing opinion in the economic community has been that the most important thing we can do is to bring down long-term interest rates by bringing down the deficit. You can't have it both ways. You're either going to bring down the deficit, or we're not. And everything in life requires some rigorous effort if you're going to have fundamental change.

Small Business Exports

Q. I wonder if you ever stop to think that this month we are celebrating two events, Small Business Week and World Trade Week. I wonder do you understand what the importance of the world trade in this week is in the minority and small business people can contribute to export their services and product to the world and mainly to those countries of the former Soviet Union? How do you respond?

The President. How do I want small business to contribute? Well, first of all, an enormous amount of our economic growth in the last 3 years has come out of growth in trade. And one of the problems we're having with our own recovery is that economic growth is virtually nonexistent in Asia and in Europe—at least in Japan and in Europe, not in the rest of Asia. China is growing rapidly.

One of the things that we can do to increase exports is to organize ourselves better in the small business community. The Germans, for example, have enormously greater success than do we in getting small and medium sized businesses into export markets. And one of the charges of my whole trade team is to organize the United States so that we can do that. That's one of the things the Commerce Secretary is working on.

Northern Ireland

Q. Mr. President, you're going to be meeting with the President of Ireland in a little while. And as a——

The President. I'm looking forward to it.

Q. ——as a candidate, you made several promises in regard to Ireland. One of them was to send an envoy, a special peace envoy, and another was that you would not restrict Gerry Adams' admittance into this country. He's the leader of Sinn Fein, and his visa was denied last week. And you promised that as President he would be admitted.

The President. I think you ought to go back and read my full statement that I made in New York about the Adams case. I'll answer that in a minute.

But let me—first on the peace envoy, I talked to the Prime Minister of Ireland, and I will discuss with the President of Ireland what she thinks the United States can do. I am more than willing to do anything that I can that will be a constructive step in helping to resolve the crisis in Northern Ireland.

Q. [*Inaudible*]—whether an envoy is necessary because——

The President. I don't believe the President of the United States should be unaffected by what the Prime Minister or the President of Ireland believe about what is best for Ireland. I don't believe that. I think I should ask them what they believe. I'm not sure I know better than she does about that. And I should listen and should take it into account. I am prepared to do whatever I can to contribute to a resolution of this issue.

On the Gerry Adams question, I said at that time because he was a Member of Parliament, if I were President I would review that. I thought that if there were no overwhelming evidence that he was connected to terrorists, if he was a duly elected Member of Parliament in a democratic country, we should have real pause before denying him a visa. I asked that his case be reviewed by the State Department and others. And everybody that reviewed it recommended that his visa not be granted and pointed out that he was no longer a Member of Parliament.

Wolf [Wolf Blitzer, Cable News Network]?

President's Approval Ratings

Q. Mr. President, in your opening statement, you said this has been a good week for you. But the latest CNN/USA Today/Gallop poll, as you probably saw, shows a 10 percent decline in your job approval rating since the end of April, from 55 to 45 percent. Why do you think that is happening? And is it your fault, and what can be done?

The President. Well, for one thing, I'm trying to do hard things. And I can't do hard things and conduct an ongoing campaign at the same time. You know, I'm doing things that are hard, that are controversial. And anybody who doesn't want to assume responsibility can stand on the sidelines and criticize them. I never expected that I could actually do anything about the deficit without having some hits. I never expected that I could take on some of these interests that I've taken on without being attacked. And whenever you try to change things, there are always people there ready to point out the pain of change without the promise of it. That's just all part of it.

If I worried about the poll ratings I'd never get anything done here. The only thing I'd remind you is for 12 years we've seen politicians and the Congress and the executive branch worry about their poll ratings every month and then at the end of every 4 years things are a lot worse. If things are better at the end of the period that I was given to serve, then the poll ratings now won't make any difference. And if they're not, they won't make any difference. So my job is to do my job, and let the chips fall where they may.

Bosnia

Q. There seems to be a Catch 22 emerging on Bosnia. One would be, you have consistently said that you want to have a consensus with the U.S. allies. But until that consensus is formed, you found it seems very difficult to explain to the American people precisely how that war should be defined: Is it a civil war? Is it a war of aggression? And also not necessarily what the next step should be, but what are the principles, the overriding principles that should guide you as a policy? What can you tell the American people right now about that?

The President. First, that is both a civil war and a war of aggression, because Bosnia was created as a separate legal entity. It is both a civil war where elements of people who live within that territory are fighting against one another. And there has been aggression from without, somewhat from the Croatians and from the Serbs, principally from the Serbs—that the inevitable but unintended impact of the arms embargo has been to put the United Nations in the position of ratifying an enormous superiority of arms for the Bosnian Serbs that they got from Serbia, and that our interest is in seeing, in my view at least, that the United Nations does not foreordain the outcome of a civil war. That's why I've always been in favor of some kind of lifting of the arms embargo, that we contain the conflict, and that we do everything we can to move to an end of it and to move to an end of ethnic cleansing.

Those are our interests there, and those are the ones I'm trying to pursue. But we should not introduce American ground forces into the conflict in behalf of one of the belligerents, and we must move with our allies. It is a very difficult issue. I realize in a world where we all crave for certainty about everything, it's tough to deal with, but it's a difficult issue.

Andrea [Andrea Mitchell, NBC News]?

Q. Mr. President, on the subject of the arms embargo, do you believe that the fighting between the Croats and the Muslims has validated the European objections to your proposal to lift the arms embargo, showing just how complicated it is and how easily those weapons can get into other hands? And, secondly, do you think that you should try to level the playing field by using air strikes alone if your hands are tied on the arms embargo?

The President. I believe that the troubles between the Croatians and the Muslims complicate things, but at least the leaders have agreed on an end to the conflict. On the other issue, I think that the best use of air power is the one that I have outlined, and I don't favor another option at this time.

Norway

Q. The Prime Minister of Norway today announced that Norway is going to resume commercial hunt of the minke whale. How do you react to that? And is the United States going to take any punitive actions against Norway?

The President. It's the first I've heard of it. I'll have to give you a later answer.

White House Staff

Q. One of the charges leveled by critics of you in Arkansas and now at the beginning of your term as President is that you've surrounded yourself with too many young people and put them in too many senior positions. How do you respond to that criticism?

The President. Like Lloyd Bentsen and Warren Christopher? I mean, who are you referring to? Mr. McLarty, Mr. Rubin, Ms. Rasco, and Mr. Lake, to name four, and I are all, I think, older than our counterparts were when President Kennedy was President. There are a lot of young people who work here, but most of the people in decisionmaking positions are not particularly young. And I am amazed sometimes—you think I ought to let some of them go?

I realize that there is this image that the administration is quite young. I think we have one of the most seasoned and diverse Cabinets that anybody's put together in a long time. And we have a lot of people who aren't so young working in the White House. I don't know how to answer your question about it.

Health Care Reform

Q. Mr. President, what will you do to ensure that health care will be accessible geographically to people in inner cities and rural areas, so that cross-town and cross-county travel will not become a barrier to health care?

The President. Well, I haven't received the report, as you know, of the Health Care Task Force yet, but let me say that one of the markers I laid down for them when they began their work was that we didn't need just simply to provide coverage for Americans, but there had to be access in rural areas and in inner city areas, especially. And they are exploring any number of ways to do that.

I spent one afternoon here on a hearing on rural health care, talking about how we could bring health care to people in rural areas and make it economical and available. And I have spent an enormous amount of time in the last 16 months in urban health care settings trying to discover which model—I've done that myself—trying to determine which models can be replicated in other inner city areas. From my experience at home I knew more about rural areas. But the bottom line is you've got to have more clinics in the rural areas and in the inner cities that are accessible and where there is an ethnic diversity, where they are accessible not only physically but in terms of language and culture. And these things can be done. And if you do it right, if they're really comprehensive primary and preventive health care centers, they lower the cost of health care because they keep more people out of the emergency rooms.

Bosnia

Q. Mr. President, the Serbian government has indicated it is going to stop sending arms to the Bosnian Serbs. If they hold true to that, does that then preclude the option of rearming the Bosnian Muslims?

The President. Well, I have two responses. First, I hope the United Nations resolution will succeed so that we can put some U.N. people on the border to determine whether that, in fact, is occurring. Secondly, whether that precludes the rearming option depends really on how many arms have been stashed already in Bosnia, particularly the heavy weapons, the heavy artillery. I think that is the issue. And that's a fact question which we'll have to try to determine.

Latin America

Q. Many people wonder, Mr. President, what your policy in Latin America is going to be.

Your economic team just told us that you want to spend more money in police here in the United States. The past administration spent almost $3 billion in Peru, Bolivia, and Colombia. What is your vision, and how are you going to change that policy?

The President. I think we should continue to support those programs. I can't say that they would be immune from the budget cutting process that has affected almost all of our domestic programs here. We've had such a big deficit, we've got to cut across-the-board. But I believe that those programs have served a useful purpose. I think especially where we have governments with leaders who are willing to put their lives on the line to stop or slow down the drug trade, we ought to be supporting them, and I expect to do that.

David [David Lauter, Los Angeles Times]?

Domestic Priorities

Q. You've been talking a lot recently about deficit reduction, the deficit reduction trust fund. You're talking now about having to stretch out your investment programs, postpone some of the things. What do you say to people in urban areas, some of the liberal Congressmen on the Hill who say, "Wait a minute. We're the ones who elected this guy, and now the programs that have been starved for 12 years that we need aren't going to be able to get money?" What sort of political position does that put you in with your core supporters?

The President. Well, I ask them, first of all, to look at the 5 year budget. The enormous squeeze on domestic spending including investment spending began 12 years ago. I can't turn it around overnight. I asked them to look at the 5 year budget and look at it in light of the fact that the deficit numbers were revised upward after the election by $50 billion a year in 3 of the next 4 years. And I ask them also to consider this: Until we can prove that we have the discipline to control our budget, I don't think we'll have the elbow room necessary to have the kind of targeted investments we need.

I think the more we do budget control, the more we'll be free to then be very sharply discriminating in investing in those things which actually do create jobs. I don't think we have any other option at this time.

Attitudes Toward Change

Q. Mr. President, in your New York speech this past week at Cooper Union, you spoke of a crisis of belief and hope. And earlier Mrs. Clinton in a speech talked about a crisis of meaning. How do you see these crises manifesting themselves? What are the causes of them? And how severe do you see this?

The President. Well, I think they manifested themselves in people's honest feelings that things are not going very well in this country and that they haven't gone very well in a long time and the alienation people feel from the political process and in the alienation they often feel from one another in the same neighborhoods and communities. There are real objective reasons for a lot of these problems. After all, for most people the work week is lengthening, and incomes are declining. The job growth of the country has been very weak. The crime rate is high, and there's a sense of real alienation there. And I don't think we can speak to them just with programs. I think that, in our different ways, that's what both Hillary and I were trying to say.

The thing I was trying to say to the American people at the Cooper Union that I want to reiterate today is that you can never change if you have no belief in the potential of your country, your community, or yourself, and that the easy path is cynicism. The easy path is to throw rocks. The better path is doing the hard work of change.

The thing I liked about what happened in the Ways and Means Committee this week is— not that I agree with every last change they made in the bill, although some of them actually made the bill better, all the fundamental principles were left intact—but we actually did something to move the ball forward, to deal with the deficit, to deal with the investment needs, to deal with—to go back to the other question that Mr. Lauter asked—to deal with the need to get more real investment in the inner cities and the rural areas of the country. We are doing things.

And what I tried to do all throughout the campaign in talking about hope, in talking about belief, in trying to go back to the grassroots was to say to people, the process of change may be uneven and difficult and always controversial, but it has to be buttressed by an underlying belief that things can be made better.

When the election returns in November—that I was not fully responsible for, there were two other candidates in that race—which showed a big increase in voter turnout, especially among young people, that meant to me that we were beginning to see the seeds of a change in attitude. As I said at the Cooper Union, when President Kennedy occupied that office, nearly three-quarters of the American people believed that their leaders would tell them the truth and that their institutions worked and that their problems could be solved. So there was a lot more elbow room there. You know, a year or 2 years could go by, people could be working on something with maybe only slightly measurable progress, but the country felt it was moving forward. That is what we have to restore today, a sense that it can be done. And it cannot be done by the President alone, but the President has to keep saying that, that faith is a big part of this.

Q. And the causes of these crises as you perceive them?

The President. I think the causes of them are the persistent, enduring problems, unanswered, unresponded to, and the absence of a feeling that there is a overall philosophy and a coherent way of dealing with them.

Tax Legislation

Q. Though your tax package has made it through the House Ways and Means Committee, every Republican voted against it. If that happens again in the Senate you could be facing yet another roadblock. How have you changed your legislative strategy to see that you win over a few Republican votes this time?

The President. Well, the budget cannot be filibustered. So in a literal sense, you know, we could pass it without any Republican votes. What I hope is that to show that by a combination of budget cuts and tax increases and the things that have been done to make this program even more attractive. We've got a lot of business people for this program now, a lot of them—that we ought to get some Republican support. But that's a political decision that a lot of those folks are going to make.

I can tell you that one member of the Ways and Means Committee told me yesterday that a Republican member said to him as they were dealing with this, said, "Boy, there's a lot of wonderful stuff in this bill. I didn't know all this stuff was in this bill. This is wonderful." He said, "Well, why don't you vote for it?" He said, "No, we've got to be against taxes." They're going to have to decide what they're

going to do about that.

NAFTA

Q. You talk about being competitive in the world and that, I hope you agree, that involves NAFTA. What would be the priorities of a new ambassador to Mexico, and what is the latest in NAFTA? Do you support tougher sanctions in trade for those that violate the treaty?

The President. I believe the treaty has to have some enforcement provisions. I have not read the last language, but it is my understanding that what the negotiators are working toward is some sort of sanctions for repeated and persistent violations of agreements that the countries involved in NAFTA make. I don't think any of us should make agreements and expect there to be no consequences to their repeated and persistent violation. But I want to say again, I believe that increased trade with Mexico and NAFTA are in the interest of the United States.

The Salinas government, through the unilateral reduction of their own tariffs, has helped to take the United States—and through policies that promoted economic growth, beginning with getting control of their deficit—has taken the United States from a $6-billion trade deficit with Mexico to a $5-billion trade surplus. Mexico just surpassed Japan as our second biggest trading customer for manufactured products. So I think that it's very much in our interest to pass NAFTA, and I hope I'll be able to persuade the Congress to do it when we conclude the agreement.

Q. Would that be a priority of a new ambassador to Mexico?

The President. Absolutely, sure.

Go ahead.

Webster Hubbell

Q. Okay. I'd like to go back to your Justice Department for just a second, Mr. President. Since during the campaign you said it was a mistake and, in fact, apologized for playing golf at an all-white country club in Little Rock, shouldn't it disqualify your nominee for Associate Attorney General, Webb Hubbell? Is there an exception because he's a family friend? And are the local civil rights leaders wrong when they say that his attempts to integrate the club appeared to have been a last-minute political conversion?

The President. Absolutely not.

Q. Are the local civil rights leaders wrong

when they say that his attempts to integrate the club appeared to have been a last-minute political conversion?

The President. No. As a matter of fact, if you go back—first of all, let me—the first question is no, he should not be disqualified. The second question is, is it a last-minute conversion? The African-American who joined the club testified that Webb Hubbell had been trying for years to get him to do it, and he had not agreed. That's what the record shows. Thirdly, my belief is that the overwhelming majority of African-American leaders in my State would very much like to see him confirmed. He has always had a reputation as being a strong advocate of civil rights, whether as Mayor of Little Rock or chief justice of the supreme court of my State. He is a very eminent citizen with a very good background. And I think the vast majority of the civil rights leaders of my State will advocate his appointment based on his record. And I think on the facts of this, I just wouldn't—this last-minute conversion thing just doesn't hold water.

Q. What does it say then, sir, that he should be a member of an all-white country club, as other members of your Cabinet also are or were when it was still all white?

The President. I think he should have either resigned or integrated it. And, of course, he was in the middle. He said, "I tried for years to integrate it, and it took me too long to succeed." What I think is really the case is that some of the other people may have been blocking it. He was trying for years to do it. I know that because I used to hit on him about it for years.

Go ahead, Mara [Mara Liasson, National Public Radio].

Bosnia

Q. Mr. President, I want to go back to a question that Helen asked earlier about your indecisiveness over Bosnia. I'm wondering how you think that's affected perceptions of you as a leader? There is a concern reflected in polls and in some comments from Democratic Members in Congress that you are indecisive and perhaps not tough enough to tackle all the problems.

The President. Well I'd just like to ask you what their evidence is? When "Russia" came up the United States took the lead, and we got a very satisfactory result. When I took office

I said we were going to try to do more in Bosnia. We agreed to go to the Vance-Owen peace process, and two of the three parties signed on. We got enforcement of the no-fly zone. We began to engage in multinational humanitarian aid. We got much, much tougher sanctions. We got the threat of military force on the table as a possible option. Milosevic changed his position. All because this administration did more than the previous one.

And every time I have consulted the Congress they say to me in private, this is a really tough problem. I don't know what you should do but you're the only President that ever took us into our counsel beforehand; instead of telling us what you were going to do, you actually ask us our opinion. I do not believe that is a sign of weakness. And I realize it may be frustrating for all of you to deal with the ambiguity of this problem but it is a difficult one.

I have a clear policy. I have gotten more done on this than my predecessor did. And maybe one reason he didn't try to do it is because if you can't force everybody to fall in line overnight for people who have been fighting each other for centuries, you may be accused of vacillating. We are not vacillating. We have a clear, strong policy.

In terms of the other issues, who else around this town in the last dozen years has offered this much budget cutting, this much tax increases, this much deficit reduction, and a clear economic strategy that asks the wealthy to pay their fair share, gives the middle class a break, and gives massive incentives to get new investment and new jobs in the small business community and from large business as well? I think—I don't understand what—on one day people say he's trying to do too much. He's pushing too hard. He wants too much change. And then on the other day he says, well, he's really not pushing very hard. I think we're getting good results. We've been here 3 months. We've passed a number of important bills, and I feel good about it.

I think the American people know one thing: that I'm on their side, that I'm fighting to change things. And they're finding out it's not so easy. But we are going to get a lot of change out of this Congress if we can keep our eye on the ball and stop worrying about whether we characterize each other in some way or another and keep thinking about what's good for the American people.

Every day I try to get up and think about not what somebody characterizes my action as but whether what I do will or will not help to improve the lives of most Americans. That is the only ultimate test by which any of us should be judged.

Thank you very much.

NOTE: The President's 15th news conference began at 1:05 p.m. in the Rose Garden at the White House. In his remarks, the President referred to President Slobodan Milosevic of Serbia.

Exchange With Reporters Prior to Discussions With President Mary Robinson of Ireland
May 14, 1993

Ireland

Q. Madam President, do you support a peace envoy from the United States to Ireland?

President Robinson. I think it has been very much appreciated, as indeed the Taoiseach said when he met with the President on March the 17th, on St. Patrick's Day, that President Clinton has shown such an interest in and concern for Ireland. That is very well recognized in Ireland itself and that, as President, you have indicated a genuine, a real concern. And I know that when you were discussing with the Taoiseach the idea of a peace envoy that you left open this issue, because it expresses concern, and that you are aware that there are the prospects of resumed talks in Northern Ireland. And I think in those circumstances—and it is appropriate to let those talks take their course.

But the sounding of the concern, the genuine interest, and the fact that you said you were a friend not just on St. Patrick's Day but throughout the year in an interested way, that has struck a very real chord throughout the island of Ireland and an important one. And I think that's very much appreciated, now. So I think that the reality of that concern has created its own very helpful and constructive vibrations.

President Clinton. Thank you.

Perception of the Administration

Q. Mr. President, you sounded a little bit frustrated at the end of your news conference there with the perception of your administration and your Presidency.

President Clinton. I just did what I could to set the record straight. You know, in the end you're measured by whether you act or not and what you stand for and what you don't, and I think the record is pretty clear. This ad- ministration has come out for a lot of bold and comprehensive change and is fighting for it. And if I don't say that, who will?

Q. That may be the question. [*Laughter*]

President Clinton. We haven't lost a majority vote yet. We may before it's over, but we haven't yet.

Ireland

Q. President Clinton, can I ask you a question? Are you going to visit Ireland? You're meeting the President today. Would you like——

President Clinton. I hope so. I told the President I went to Ireland once when I was a young man.

Q. 1969?

President Clinton. It was a great trip.

Q. Do you think you're going to be able to do it?

President Clinton. Did you check my passport files? Is that how you—[*laughter*].

Q. Would you like to visit Ireland?

President Clinton. I would very much.

The First 100 Days

Q. Can I ask you about your first 100 days in office? Have you enjoyed that?

President Clinton. Very much. Even the difficult times have been good. You know, it's an exhilarating thing trying to sort of turn things around, not easy but exhilarating.

Gerry Adams

Q. Mr. President, you've gotten some heat over your Irish problems recently. Do you think looking back on what you said during the campaign and knowing what you know now about, for example, the Gerry Adams status, that you might have rephrased what you were saying?

President Clinton. Well, what I said was— and I did do that—I asked the State Department to review the case and I gave the—and other agencies did so as well. He is no longer a Member of Parliament, which is what I take my statement on. And they unanimously recommended that the visa not be granted. I have no grounds to overrule them.

Lani Guinier

Q. Mr. President, at your press conference today on the Lani Guinier question, you seem to suggest—please correct me if I'm wrong— but that it's simply a matter of Congress confirming her and her doing—or, excuse me, the Senate confirming her and her doing Congress' will as it relates to the Civil Rights Division. But her writings suggest a very interesting interpretation of things like the Voting Rights Act, which she would extend to the executive branch, numerical goals for judicial appointments, which I believe you opposed in your campaign. So what is the Senate, then, to make of the fact that you've sent somebody up there that favors things that you oppose?

President Clinton. Well listen, I would never have appointed anybody to public office if they had to agree with everything I believe in. We wouldn't have a Cabinet. I mean, I take it, based on my personal experience, you will believe me when I say I am confident that she'll follow the Constitution and the laws of the United States. You have to swear an oath of office to that. She may wish the law were different in some areas. But I've had personal experience with her accomplishments as a civil rights lawyer, and I thought we ought to have a distinguished civil rights lawyer as head of the Civil Rights Division. And I say again, the Congress passes the laws and the executive branch enforces them, and when there is a question of policy, that will be resolved by the Attorney General.

Q. Are you disassociating yourself from her writings, sir?

President Clinton. I never have associated myself with all of her writings or all of anybody else's. I even found a word or two in the Vice President's book I didn't agree with. [*Laughter*]

Ireland

Q. President Robinson, what is your message to President Clinton? What is your message to President Clinton today?

President Robinson. Well, it is certainly a very special occasion to come here as President of Ireland and to be welcomed by President Clinton. And I want to reiterate the invitation that has already been extended to him by the Taoiseach to renew his acquaintanceship with Dublin and to come to Ireland on an appropriate occasion. And I want to express appreciation of the fact that President Clinton has clearly signaled an interest in and an active concern for Ireland, for the modern Ireland, the Ireland which I have the honor to represent and that you and your administration are keeping in very close contact, that there is a very open communication and a sense of that, and that has been very consciously realized in Ireland itself and throughout the island of Ireland. And I think it is a very significant and helpful factor in our relations.

NOTE: The exchange began at 4:25 p.m. in the Oval Office at the White House. During the exchange, the following persons were referred to: Albert Reynolds, Prime Minister of Ireland, and Gerry Adams, leader of Sinn Fein. A tape was not available for verification of the content of this exchange.

Message to the Congress Reporting on the National Emergency With Respect to Iran
May 14, 1993

To the Congress of the United States:

I hereby report to the Congress on developments since the last Presidential report on November 10, 1992, concerning the national emergency with respect to Iran that was declared in Executive Order No. 12170 of November 14, 1979, and matters relating to Executive Order No. 12613 of October 29, 1987. This report is submitted pursuant to section 204(c) of the International Emergency Economic Powers Act, 50 U.S.C. 1703(c), and section 505(c) of the International Security and Development Cooperation Act of 1985, 22 U.S.C. 2349aa–9(c). This report covers events through March 31, 1993. The last report, dated November 10, 1992, covered events through October 15, 1992.

1. There have been no amendments to the Iranian Transactions Regulations ("ITRs"), 31 CFR Part 560, or to the Iranian Assets Control Regulations ("IACRs"), 31 CFR Part 535, since the last report.

2. The Office of Foreign Assets Control ("FAC") of the Department of the Treasury continues to process applications for import licenses under the ITRs. However, as previously reported, recent amendments to the ITRs have resulted in a substantial decrease in the number of applications received relating to the importation of nonfungible Iranian-origin goods.

During the reporting period, the Customs Service has continued to effect numerous seizures of Iranian-origin merchandise, primarily carpets, for violation of the import prohibitions of the ITRs. FAC and Customs Service investigations of these violations have resulted in forfeiture actions and the imposition of civil monetary penalties. Additional forfeiture and civil penalty actions are under review.

3. The Iran-United States Claims Tribunal (the "Tribunal"), established at The Hague pursuant to the Algiers Accords, continues to make progress in arbitrating the claims before it. Since the last report, the Tribunal has rendered 12 awards, for a total of 545 awards. Of that total, 367 have been awards in favor of American claimants: 222 of these were awards on agreed terms, authorizing and approving payment of settlements negotiated by the parties, and 145 were decisions adjudicated on the merits. The Tribunal has issued 36 decisions dismissing claims on the merits and 83 decisions dismissing claims for jurisdictional reasons. Of the 59 remaining awards, 3 approved the withdrawal of cases, and 56 were in favor of Iranian claimants. As of March 31, 1993, awards to successful American claimants from the Security Account held by the NV Settlement Bank stood at $2,340,072,357.77.

As of March 31, 1993, the Security Account has fallen below the required balance of $500 million 36 times. Iran has periodically replenished the account, as required by the Algiers Accords, by transferring funds from the separate account held by the NV Settlement Bank in which interest on the Security Account is deposited. Iran has also replenished the account with the proceeds from the sale of Iranian-origin oil imported into the United States, pursuant to transactions licensed on a case-by-case basis by FAC. Iran has not, however, replenished the account since the last oil sale deposit on October 8, 1992. The aggregate amount that has been transferred from the Interest Account to the Security Account is $874,472,986.47. As of March 31, 1993, the total amount in the Security Account was $216,244,986.03, and the total amount in the Interest Account was $8,638,133.15.

4. The Tribunal continues to make progress in the arbitration of claims of U.S. nationals for $250,000.00 or more. Since the last report, nine large claims have been decided. More than 85 percent of the nonbank claims have now been disposed of through adjudication, settlement, or voluntary withdrawal, leaving 76 such claims on the docket. The larger claims, the resolution of which has been slowed by their complexity, are finally being resolved, sometimes with sizable awards to the U.S. claimants. For example, two claimants were awarded more than $130 million each by the Tribunal in October 1992.

5. As anticipated by the May 13, 1990, agreement settling the claims of U.S. nationals for less than $250,000.00, the Foreign Claims Settlement Commission ("FCSC") has continued its review of 3,112 claims. The FCSC has issued decisions in 1,201 claims, for total awards of more than $22 million. The FCSC expects to complete its adjudication of the remaining claims in early 1994.

6. In coordination with concerned Government agencies, the Department of State continues to present United States Government claims against Iran, as well as responses by the United States Government to claims brought against it by Iran. In November 1992, the United States filed 25 volumes of supporting information in case B/1 (Claims 2 & 3), Iran's claim against the United States for damages relating to its Foreign Military Sales Program. In February of this year, the United States participated in a daylong prehearing conference in several other cases involving military equipment. Iran also filed a new interpretative dispute alleging that the failure of U.S. courts to enforce an award

against a U.S. corporation violated the Algiers Accords.

7. As reported in November, Jose Maria Ruda, President of the Tribunal, tendered his resignation on October 2, 1992. No successor has yet been named. Judge Ruda's resignation will take effect as soon as a successor becomes available to take up his duties.

8. The situation reviewed above continues to involve important diplomatic, financial, and legal interests of the United States and its nationals. Iran's policy behavior presents challenges to the national security and foreign policy of the United States. The IACRs issued pursuant to Execu-

tive Order No. 12170 continue to play an important role in structuring our relationship with Iran and in enabling the United States to implement properly the Algiers Accords. Similarly, the ITRs issued pursuant to Executive Order No. 12613 continue to advance important objectives in combating international terrorism. I shall exercise the powers at my disposal to deal with these problems and will report periodically to the Congress on significant developments.

WILLIAM J. CLINTON

The White House,
May 14, 1993.

Nomination for an Assistant Secretary of the Treasury
May 14, 1993

The President will nominate Richard Carnell, the senior counsel of the Senate Banking Committee and former attorney for the Federal Reserve Board, to be Assistant Secretary of the Treasury for Financial Institutions.

"Richard Carnell has been consistently recognized for his expertise in banking law and his

ability to help shape policy decisions," said the President. "I look forward to him playing a key role in shaping banking policy in the next 4 years."

NOTE: A biography of the nominee was made available by the Office of the Press Secretary.

The President's Radio Address
May 15, 1993

Good morning. As we all rejoice in this magnificent spring and the promise of renewal that it brings, we should also feel renewed as citizens, renewed by the progress that is being made in Washington, the progress we are making in strengthening the American economy to help us be more competitive, to grow, to work for the middle class again. Gridlock is on the way out, and our plan to rebuild the economy and restore opportunity for all Americans is moving through Congress.

Look at the progress. Just 3 months ago, I submitted to Congress a balanced economic plan that asked everyone to work together to invest a little more in deficit reduction today, so that we can all enjoy better jobs and higher incomes tomorrow. It says we can do what no generation has ever been called upon to do before, that

we can reduce our deficit sharply and still increase investment wisely in jobs and education and new technology, because we must do both to be a competitive America, to create more jobs and economic growth.

We began by forcing real discipline on the big spenders by making deep and enforceable cuts in the Federal Government in over 200 specific programs. And believe me, these cuts are real. We've taken on spending groups and interest groups that have never been taken on. We've made tough decisions, and now Congress is working with me to make them stick. It wasn't easy.

We'd made major reductions in the so-called entitlement programs like medical care, agriculture, Federal retirement programs. Virtually no area of domestic spending was left un-

671

touched. And we're now on our way to the largest deficit reduction package in American history. And we will not raise taxes without knowing that these spending cuts are part of the project.

These cuts are real, and our plan is fair. The nonpartisan Congressional Budget Office has concluded that 75 percent of all the taxes in this plan fall on the top 6 percent of Americans, those earning $100,000 a year or more. It asked those who got a tax break in the 1980's to pay their fair share in the 1990's. These proposals which reduce the deficit and increase tax fairness were adopted by all the important House of Representatives committees last week.

But I'm asking the Congress to go further. This week I proposed that when we cut programs, we lock the savings up in a deficit reduction trust fund so that you can trust that the money can only be used to reduce the Federal deficit. That's right. No taxes without spending cuts and the spending cuts and the taxes put into a deficit reduction trust fund so that the money must be used to reduce the deficit.

In addition to cutting the spending deficit, the other essential goal of our plan is to create opportunity in our society where hard work is supported and initiative is rewarded. That's why there were important tax incentives added to this plan: increasing the small business expensing provision to $25,000 a year, a goal long sought by the American small business community; a new venture capital gains tax; big investment incentives for larger corporations to invest in new plant and equipment to create new jobs. These and other initiatives to ease the credit crunch and to keep these interest rates at historic lows will mean billions of dollars of new investment into our economy in the near future.

Our economic plan includes also a proposal to create empowerment zones in our most depressed urban and rural communities. We offer significant incentives to those who will go into those neighborhoods and build a business because they will be giving people a chance who haven't had one in a long time. There's not enough Government money in a country to rebuild our cities or our distressed rural areas, but we can do it through free enterprise if we have enough incentive. The Government in the empowerment zones will be the best partner the free enterprise system could have.

This plan also deals with another important problem. No one in America should work hard at a full-time job with children in the home and still live in poverty. But millions of Americans do. Because our economy and our tax system hasn't been working, millions and millions of responsible people are among the working poor who still live below the poverty line. That's the wrong signal to send. That's an incentive to get on welfare, not to get off welfare.

Our plan includes an earned-income tax credit that puts into law this basic principle: If you work 40 hours a week and you have a child at home, you will not be in poverty. This important proposal also is proceeding quickly to congressional approval. The Tax Code was also changed to protect those with incomes of under $30,000 from the impact of the proposed BTU or energy tax, and to phase that tax in so that the average family will pay about a dollar a month next year and about $5 a month the year after, with the full impact of the tax for people with incomes of $40,000 a year or above triggering in at about $16 to $17 a month in 1996.

Just days after we offered our new approach to make college loans available to every qualified American student, regardless of income, this plan was also approved by the House Education and Labor Committee. This is a very important thing. It will save lots of money to taxpayers and make college loans available at lower interest rates and better repayment terms with mandatory repayment to all students in the United States. This is a change that we're working on, cutting wasteful spending, increasing taxes fairly, driving down the deficit while increasing the investment we make through private sector incentives and in education training and technology.

These are the ideas which will make our economy strong and competitive. For every new dollar of investment in America and the American people, there are $3 in spending cuts. This is the right way to go. All told, we've come a long, long distance in the last 3 months, to restoring our economy and reaffirming the values of the middle class and to opening up our democracy again.

I'm especially gratified that just this week we've passed the motor voter bill which will make it easier for people to register and vote. And I fervently hope it will bring more young people into the democratic process. It was the young Americans all across this country who convinced me to redouble my efforts to work hard to pass this bill.

The United States Senate has just passed a lobbying reform bill which will require all of our lobbyists to register for a change and require them to report any gifts beyond a very small amount that they give to any Member of Congress. And I've introduced the toughest campaign finance reform law ever, to lower the cost of campaigns, reduce the influence of political action committees, and open the airwaves to honest debate, all paid for by lobbyists, by repealing the lobbyist tax deduction.

This is a bright and a hopeful day. We've come together not to better one group or one cause but to work together in the common cause of a reinvigorated America. We've been able to bring deep discipline to our budget, positive purpose to our spending, and created the sea change the American people voted for in November, or at least the beginning of that sea change. Now we've got to see through it all the way to the end. The rest of the road won't be easy, just as the last 3 months have not been. But we can do it, and then we'll have something to really celebrate when we've passed the budget, an economic plan, and gotten this country turned around.

Even as we celebrate these changes, let's also remember why we're free enough to make them. May the 15th is Armed Forces Day. And I would like to conclude by honoring those who serve, whose bravery and sacrifice and devotion to country has preserved our liberties and made America the custodian of freedom's dream for the entire world.

I speak for all in my administration in expressing gratitude and profound respect for each member of our Armed Forces, for their supportive families and for their mission. From my first months in office, I can assure you that America has the strongest, best trained, and most faithful Armed Forces in the world, men and women so worthy of the great responsibilities borne by them in our Nation. May God protect them and guide the United States.

NOTE: The address was recorded at 8 a.m. on May 14 in the Map Room at the White House for broadcast at 10:06 a.m. on May 15.

Statement Endorsing the Candidacy of Michael Woo for Mayor of Los Angeles
May 15, 1993

On June 8, Los Angeles voters will select the first new mayor in two decades, a mayor who must reinvigorate the economy and ensure the safety of all communities. I endorse Michael Woo because I believe he is the best person to meet these challenges.

As a councilman, Mike Woo has put people first, consistently fighting for the middle class against the special interests, appealing to our hopes not our fears. He created innovative programs to finance small business, reformed the city's ethics laws, and developed a model community service program. He has fought to get criminals and their guns off the streets.

Early last year, Mike Woo stood with me to support an agenda of change to help working families, rebuild our cities, and bring people together. Mike Woo has dedicated his life to creating jobs in southern California and making government work for all people. The people of Los Angeles can trust Mike Woo to work long and hard to get the job done for them.

As mayor, Mike Woo will be my partner to reinvigorate the southern California economy, put more police on the streets, and inspire the many different communities that comprise Los Angeles to pull together again. I look forward to working with him for change.

Remarks to the Community in Los Alamos, New Mexico
May 17, 1993

The President. Thank you very much. Governor King, Senator Bingaman, Senator Domenici, Congressman Richardson, Congressman Schiff, Dr. Hecker, and the other directors of the other wonderful labs here present, Dr. Narath and Dr. Ruckolls; and my distinguished Secretary of Energy, Hazel O'Leary, who is celebrating her birthday with all of you here in Los Alamos today.

I want to say a special word of thanks to the students from Los Alamos High School here behind us. I love the T-shirts, and I was so gratified to be invited to come to the high school commencement. I didn't make it, but this is almost as good, don't you think? I'm really glad to be here.

I want to say, too, a special word of appreciation to all those who spoke here before me today for what they said. I thought Senator Domenici did a pretty good job of gliding over our differences and getting right in there. I want to tell you how grateful I am for the national leadership that Congressman Richardson has given not only to the Congress but to the efforts I made to become your President. And I can't say enough about the work that Senator Bingaman has done on the issue I came here to talk about today, which is giving us a good high-wage, high-growth future through the wise and sensible investment in technology. You should be very proud of these people, all of whom represent you in the United States Congress. I want to say a special word of thanks to Congressman Schiff. Since he's not here in his home district, he actually gave up the opportunity to speak, which may make him the most popular person here today. You can't tell.

Bruce King told you the truth. We were Governors in the seventies, the eighties, and the nineties. Made an old man of me, but he still looks pretty good. [*Laughter*] He was the first Governor to endorse my campaign, and New Mexico was the next to the last stop I made on election day when I stayed up all night long.

I want to say I've come back here today in the light of day, and a beautiful day it is, to celebrate with the Los Alamos Lab the 50th anniversary of a genuine, remarkable American success story. For the first half century of Los Alamos' service, it was the leading edge of our Nation's security. And now as we go into the next half century, Los Alamos will be, as Senator Bingaman said, the leading edge of our prosperity, developing and nurturing the technology that will put all these young Americans who are here in this great crowd today at the front of a new race, the race to compete and to cooperate in a world that is getting smaller, richer, more diverse, but very, very rigorous in its challenges.

New Mexico should be very proud to be the home of Los Alamos and Sandia. America, indeed the entire democratic world, owes an enormous debt of gratitude to Los Alamos, to Sandia, and to the Lawrence Livermore Laboratory in California. When we needed the military muscle to end a global war, the answer was the Manhattan Project. When we needed the muscle to win the cold war, the long and costly effort to contain and then to triumph over communism, the ideas that made that possible came out of these laboratories. That struggle gave us a focus not just in how we spend our defense dollars but how we invested in everything from our children's education to the Interstate Highway System. These labs were at the core of that effort, providing our nuclear deterrent. From the Berlin crisis in 1948 to the Berlin celebration in 1989 when the Wall came down, the work of this laboratory helped to ensure America's might, America's security, and in the end, a total triumph for democracy and freedom and free-market economics in the cold war. You should all be very proud of that. That's a good 50 years of work if I ever heard it.

Now we are in the post-cold-war effort. Most of the young people here present will live more of their lives in the 21st century than they have in the 20th. And we need a new focus for our efforts. Our job today is to preserve the American dream and America's leadership in the world that America has done so much to make. We have to prove that we can compete and win in this highly complex and rigorous world. We have to do it so that all the young people here will not be the first generation of Americans to grow up to do worse than their parents. We have to do it so that we can continue to be a beacon of hope, so that we can prove that freedom and free enterprise and democracy work.

We have to begin by putting our own house in order, by bringing down our enormous deficit, dealing with our health care crisis which has produced a system that costs way too much and covers too few and leaves too many in the insecurity of daily living, knowing that any moment they might lose the insurance they have. We have to follow policies that enable us to educate and train our people for a lifetime and then promote economic growth so that they will have jobs that they're educated for. These are the things we have to do in this time to be worthy, worthy successors to the American legacy we have inherited.

I've asked the Congress to reduce the deficit by $500 billion over the next 5 years, with a combination of spending cuts and tax increases, none of which are popular, especially, in particular. Everybody's for deficit reduction in general. It's the details that swallow us alive. I have asked that all this money be put into a trust fund by law so that nothing can be done with it but to reduce the debt, so that the children of our country eventually will be able to get out from under the burden their parents and grandparents have left for them. I have committed to all the Members of Congress and to the American people without regard to party that this is just a down payment, that reducing the deficit doesn't begin to bring the debt down until you get it down to zero. And we have to keep working until we do that. We owe that to the young people here.

But we also owe you something more. We have to think about the challenges that are here before us. And when they require us to invest in education and technology and new jobs, we have to do that as well, for we have to remember that the thing which enables us to bring our debt down is the economic strength which reduces working people and incomes from people who then can pay taxes, who can then deal with less Government supports, who don't need the Government spending as much money if they all have jobs and incomes in a strong free enterprise system. That is our obligation to you and to your future.

So the question I came here to discuss today for all of you, and hopefully it will reverberate throughout the United States to people who have never been to New Mexico and may not have even known of the existence of Los Ala-

mos, is what is the opportunity we have right here to revolutionize the economy, not just for those thousands of you who are here but for every American family, for every American young person? Can you affect the future of America as you have the past? I think the answer is a resounding "yes." If we are going to march confidently into the 21st century, we will have to do it on the minds and with the creativity and with the investment represented here in this laboratory and in others like it around the country and with the spirit of partnership between Government and the private sector that pervades so many of the efforts now underway here.

At Los Alamos alone, there are 100 partnerships with industry. Technology has led to the creation of 30 new companies. Before coming here today I took a look at some of the projects underway at a plant facility that handles—listen to this—plasma ion implantation. Now, that sounds like something a plastic surgeon would do, but it has nothing to do with the human body. Instead, it involves a steel vacuum chamber containing high-energy ion which can be pumped into metal surfaces or plastic surfaces and used to harden them so that they will last longer and do better work. This could revolutionize America's ability to manufacture automobiles and other machines to keep going and to have higher productivity longer and lower costs, so we can once again begin to grow high-wage manufacturing jobs. And if it happens, it will happen because of the ideas that started here in the kind of partnerships we need for America's tomorrows. And this technology was a direct outgrowth of the research done on the strategic defense initiative, the so-called star wars initiative, which means that no matter whatever happens there and whatever happens to the final shape of that project, something good came out of it because people were looking to break down frontiers in the human minds and to explore unexplored territory.

This defense technology is now being used as part of a 4-year partnership with General Motors. Another project involves GM in helping to build a clean car. Think of it: What if we could build a car that operated on energy sources provided here in this country, that reduced our dependence on foreign oil, reduced air pollution, increased energy efficiency, and helped us to become a partner in the effort to save the global environment, at the same time exploding American jobs and economic opportunities? If that happens, it will be because of what began here. I saw biomedical technology, analyzing and sorting single biological cells using lasers, with valuable applications for AIDS and leukemia diagnosis, a technology that has already led to an $800-million-a-year business for three new companies. There are projects underway for efficient oil recovery, environmental cleanup, the analysis of air pollution. With these partnerships and others like them, we can find the technology-based answers for the jobs of tomorrow.

In this economic chain reaction, the result will be high-paying jobs here in New Mexico. I saw one project today which is projected to produce 2,000 jobs in New Mexico within the next 3 or 4 years. But there will be jobs all across this Nation, in wide-ranging fields, ever more critical to our future. Supercomputers developed to design nuclear weapons are now being used to improve the fuel efficiency of engines, to help the oil industry find more oil in less time here in the United States at lower cost. They're used to educate youngsters in ways we could never have dreamed of just a few years ago. I met some of those bright students earlier today. They were actually developing programs for energy conservation, using the world's largest supercomputer, having won a contest in the use of computers sponsored statewide in New Mexico and held here at Los Alamos. You could be very proud that you have students like that who can use a facility like this.

We are counting on our Nation's labs to make real contributions in these and other areas of needs that arise out of our energy and national security missions. In these tasks, the laboratories will be helping not only Americans but our fellow citizens around the world. If we can find ways to make the American people healthier and lower health care costs, it will benefit us enormously economically, it will provide personal security to millions of American families. But we will not keep those things as secrets here in our own borders. They will spread around the world and make the world a better and safer and healthier place.

Let me also say that there is still a national defense mission for these labs. We have to continue to maintain the safety and reliability of our nuclear deterrent until all the nuclear weapons in the world are gone. We have to make sure that we can focus on new technologies to counter proliferation of nuclear, biological, and chemical weapons by other irresponsible countries around the world. There are still too many nations who have not learned the lesson of the cold war and how much money was diverted by the United States and the Soviet Union from other important efforts. There are still too many nations who seem determined to define the quality of their lives based on whether they can develop a nuclear weapon or biological or chemical weapons that can have no other purpose than to destroy other human beings. It is a mistake, and we should try to contain it and to stop it.

And so my fellow Americans, there is a peacetime commercial mission for these labs. And there is a national defense mission for these labs. And the line between those two missions is coming down fast. And there is a partnership with the private sector which will spread and grow and strengthen America's support for and understanding of what is done here. These labs are our great national minds' treasure, the world's finest scientists and engineers, more Ph.D.'s per capita here in Los Alamos than any other place on the planet. It's pretty humbling when you're a President and you walk into a room and you realize you're lowering the average IQ of the room just by going in the door. [*Laughter*] You have the world's most powerful computers and lasers and accelerators, some of the world's best materials facilities, the most sophisticated diagnostics. You are our crown jewels in technology and science.

Under the technology policy I have proposed, this lab at Los Angeles—Los Alamos——

Audience members. Boo-o-o!

The President. I'm going there tomorrow, and if I say Los Alamos, will you cheer when I'm in Los Angeles? I owe you one. This lab will work with the Departments of Energy and Defense and Commerce to sustain constant innovation. We're going to have to reorganize a lot of things to get that done. We can't just have the money coming in for specific projects from—some from defense and some from the Energy Department. We'll have all kinds of dislocations. And we had some great conversations today about how we can make a flexible and always available pool of funds there for the kinds of projects that need to be done. And our administration has pledged to do that.

So I say to you again, we must change the whole notion we have of the Federal Government. We're going to have to cut a lot of spending. We're going to have to change a lot of things we have taken for granted. But we will still have to find a way to invest in our future. Our competitors are investing in their futures. There is a race to tomorrow, which is partly cooperation, but make no mistake about it, largely competition. And if we want all of these young people to have the chance to go as far as their efforts and their God-given abilities will take them, we have to do both: We've got to bring this deficit down and sharply invest in things like these laboratories so we can grow the economy for tomorrow.

The reductions in the defense budget, made possible by the end of the cold war, have presented some great challenges to the laboratories, to the defense plants, to the wonderful men and women who have served our Nation in uniform. We owe all of them the opportunity to convert to success in the commercial private enterprise world of America. We have earmarked, this year alone, over $1.7 billion for defense conversion, and I propose to invest about $20 billion in it over the next 5 years. It is a good beginning. It is a good beginning.

I ask you today, as I close, to consider the alternative. If we refuse to bring our deficit down and we still continue to squeeze these areas critical to our investment future, the alternative will be a rising deficit, a declining rate of investment, more unemployment and more stagnant incomes, longer work weeks for less funds, and continued insecurity for America's working families. We must change our priorities no matter how difficult it is. That is the challenge of this day, and we must meet it. As has already been said, President Kennedy stood in this very spot just over 30 years ago and saluted the great patriots of Los Alamos. He said in part, and I quote, "We want to express our thanks to you. It is not merely what was done in the days of the Second War but what has been done since then, not only in developing weapons of destruction which, by irony of fate, helped maintain peace and freedom, but also in medicine and in space, and all the other related fields which can mean so much to mankind if we can maintain the peace and protect our freedom."

Well today, maintaining the peace and protecting the freedom seem more secure than they did when President Kennedy uttered those words. And so, today I come here to thank Los Alamos, not merely for what was done in the cold war and what has been done since but for what you can and will do to secure a stronger, brighter future for all the American people. If we do our job, then perhaps 30 years from now another American President will be able to come to this very site, and some of you who are now children will be here with your children. And you can say, again, thank you, thank you to the labs, thank you to the men and women who used their minds to advance the cause of learning. Thank you for the contributions you have made to the progress of the American dream. May it never stop.

God bless you, and thank you very much.

NOTE: The President spoke at 1:05 p.m. at Los Alamos High School.

Remarks on Arrival in San Diego, California
May 17, 1993

Thank you so much. Let me begin by thanking Lynn Schenk for that vigorous introduction and Bob Filner for what he said. I can tell you, if we had a whole Congress full of people like Lynn Schenk and Bob Filner, we could turn this country around a lot quicker. They have done a wonderful job up there.

I'd also like to thank all the people who came out to see me today and to see my first visit in this county since the election. I want to thank the Mayor of Coronado, the Mayor of San Diego, the State officials who are here, the Lieutenant Governor, the secretary of State, the State comptroller. But mostly, I just want to thank all of you. It is wonderful to be back here again. And I'm happy.

What did you say?

[*At this point, students from Patrick Henry High School greeted the President.*]

You know, I spent a lot of time here during the campaign. I watched people build ships. I listened to people who had lost their jobs. I listened to people who were starting new companies. I listened to people who were prepared to change but who did not understand why the National Government would turn its back on southern California, and on this State which carries with it so much of the hopes and dreams of all of America and so much of the economic future of our entire country.

When I went to Washington, I was determined never to forget the faces that I saw and the stories that I heard and the lessons that I learned. I want you to know that in the last 3½ months we have made a real beginning toward turning this country around. And we are going to stay until the job is done.

You heard Lynn talk about a little of it; you heard Bob talk about a little of it. But let me just repeat: for years and years and years we just saw the Congress and the President fighting against one another, decisions seemed not to be made, the veto pen was used more often, and people worked together. Seventeen days after I took office, I signed the Family and Medical Leave Act to guarantee that working people could have some time off when there's a sick parent or a sick child, without losing their job.

For the first time in 17 years, the Congress passed a resolution on time to set the framework of the budget that we're now working on. And what that means is that we cannot raise your taxes unless we also cut spending, no tax increases without spending cuts to bring the deficit down.

And to all the young people in the audience, we managed to win one for you, too, after years and years of trying. Just a few days ago, the United States Congress passed, and I am about to sign, the motor voter bill, to open up the voting rolls to millions of young people and make it easier for people to register and vote.

But now we must focus on the hard part: How can we do the things that we have to do to turn this country around? How can we open the economy up and give people who are working hard and playing by the rules the chance to have a good future? How can we do these things? Here is what I think we have to do. The first thing we have to do is to pass a budget which does the right things with your money. We have seen the debt of this country

go from $1 trillion to $4 trillion in 12 years. And what did you get out of it? We saw a decline in investment. We saw working people work harder for lower wages. We saw taxes on the middle class go up and taxes on the wealthy go down. Everything was turned around in opposite directions from where we ought to be going.

We are beginning to change that. This budget contains over $250 billion of hard budget cuts. This budget raises most of the money we raise in taxes from people with incomes above $100,000, over 74 percent of it. This budget give a tax break to working families with incomes of under $30,000, to protect them from the impact of the decisions we have to make. And we have proposed to put all the taxes and all the spending cuts into a legally separate trust fund so the money cannot be spent to do anything but bring the debt down. It is time we stopped talking about this and started doing something about it.

And you know, when you hear people say "no, no, no," ask them where they were the last 12 years. Most of the people who say that we don't have a good plan are the very people that drove this country in the ditch in the first place. They took that debt from $1 trillion to $4 trillion. Where were they?

But let me tell you some things you may not know about this bill. When I came here, I said that we had not only to reduce the deficit, we had to provide more incentives for people to invest to create jobs. So this tax bill also gives real incentives to get the real estate markets going here again. It gives small business people a $25,000-a-year expensing provision, 2½ times greater than the present law, so that there will be incentives for small business people to reinvest in their businesses, and put people to work. It gives a big incentive to larger companies located here and throughout the United States to increase in more plants and equipment, to modernize and create jobs, because they can write it off more rapidly. This bill is pro-investment, not consumption. This is a bill designed to create jobs, not take them away. I hope we can pass it in the United States Congress.

And let me say this again: This bill provides for tax relief for the working poor, so that when this bill passes, every American will be able to say with some pride, we're rewarding work and not welfare in this country. Now if you work 40 hours a week and you've got a child in the house, you won't be in poverty anymore. I think that's something that's worth doing. It protects families with incomes of under $30,000 from the energy tax. And for families over $40,000 up to about $100,000, it minimizes the burdens of about $10 to $15 a month. And I think it's worth that to get our country back and get this deficit down and reclaim our financial future. We've got to put our house in order, folks. And if we don't do it, we're going to be paying for it from now on.

But let me tell you what else we are trying to do. It is not just enough to deal with the budget. We have to do things that will create jobs. This county knows, as well as any in America, that it was wrong to cut defense spending as much as we did with no plan to reinvest in a domestic economy. We have in this budget over $1.7 billion this year and $20 billion in the next 4 years to convert from a defense to a domestic economy, to help it go—civilian jobs, commercial jobs, to retrain people, to rebuild communities, to get this country going again. And we must do that.

I also recognize, and I'm sure many of you do, that the financial health of this country will never be assured until finally we join all the other advanced countries with which we're competing and provide health care security with a basic health care for all Americans at affordable cost. And we are coming with a health care plan to do just that. And I hope the American people will support it.

Finally, let me say that California needs an economic strategy that will be built from the grassroots up but that will have a partner in the White House. I have delegated to Secretary of Commerce Ron Brown, the responsibility of representing this administration in this State and developing a coordinated economic policy for the long-term health and welfare of the California economy. And we will not stop until we have turned this State around and moved this State forward.

We have made a beginning in this budget. With all the budget cuts we've got, there is more money in this budget for California and the other States that are hit unfairly by the burdens of large immigration problems and all the costs that go into it. The Federal Government's going to pay more of our fair share in California now and ask you to pay less. We're going to invest more in environmental cleanup,

in the kind of water problems that you have here. We're going to do our part, and we're going to do it right. And most importantly of all, we're going to continue to work on building an economic base that will replace the prosperity you enjoyed in times of high defense spending when the cold war was at its height. It is wrong to let the people who won the cold war lose the peace afterward. It is wrong to turn our backs on the State that moved this country so much in the 1980's. It is wrong not to have a strategy that will not work miracles but that will make progress day in and day out, month in and month out, year in and year out. And I want you to know that we are going to work our hearts out in Washington together in order to move this State forward, and move this country forward. And I want you to help us do it. Will you do it?

Lynn Schenk said it better than I could, but I want to reiterate it: The country went in one direction for 12 years, and it was a popular direction. The most popular thing in the world to do, if you're in public life, is to cut people's taxes and spend more money. But sooner or later, your string runs out. Sooner or later, people look around and they say, "How did we have a $4 trillion debt? How can we be spending over $300 million a year over and above what we're taking in? How can we be working harder for lower wages? Why are these other countries able to invest and create jobs and grow, and we don't have the money?" The reason is because we stopped thinking about the future. We did what was popular in the short run. We took the easy way and the shortcut, and we are paying for it. But I'm telling you, this country is still the strongest country in the world economically, militarily, politically. The fabric of our people, the strength of our families, the will of individuals to succeed is as strong as it has ever been. All we have to do now is to have the courage to face these problems forthrightly. Let's pass a budget that puts our house in order. Let's invest in the education of our people and the new technologies of the future. Let's provide health care to our people. Together we can do it. We need your help. We need your support for people like Lynn and Bob who care about the future and are willing to make the tough decisions. Stay with us and we can turn the country around and

California around together.

Thank you, and God bless you all.

NOTE: The President spoke at 4:55 p.m. at the North Island Naval Air Station.

Remarks at a Town Meeting in San Diego
May 17, 1993

Moderator. Mr. President, these are the people of San Diego. We've got a lot of people out there watching right now that want to hear what you're talking about, and we have a lot of folks here in the studios who want to ask you questions directly.

The President. May I say one word before we start? First I want to thank all of you for being here and to say I think this is probably the second town meeting I've done like this since I have been President, but I want to start scheduling them on a more regular basis now. I'd like just to take a couple of minutes by way of opening statements.

Since I became your President, I have spent most of my time working on two things, the economy and the health care issue. We have worked very hard to present a budget to the Congress and the American people that would do two things, that would decrease the Government's deficit, which is very large as all of you know, and that would provide some targeted money for increases in areas that are very much needed here in southern California, in education and training and new technology, primarily. We also have developed a new policy on defense conversion to try to help provide jobs in areas hit by defense cutbacks, on making the most of our technology in America, and trying to get more jobs from technology. I presented a bill to the Congress, as I pledged in the campaign, to provide for a national service program to open the doors of college education to all Americans. And we will soon present our health care plan to control the cost of health care and provide basic health care to all Americans.

That has been the basic agenda. There are lots of controversies in all these things, and I know you'll ask the questions, but I hope we'll get a chance to talk about what's in the budget and how I proposed a deficit trust fund so that we can't raise any taxes unless we also cut spending. I think that's very important. But I want to answer your questions and spend most of the time talking about what you want to talk about. I just wanted you to know what I've been doing for the last 4 months.

Middle Class Tax Cut

Q. First, President Clinton, let me thank you for giving the opportunity for common folks like us to ask the President of the United States a question in person. It's an honor and a privilege, thank you.

President Clinton, I believe that you were elected largely on the basis of your promise of a middle class tax cut. But for the last 90 days or so, we've seen both you and the Congress transforming that promised middle class tax cut into an unprecedented round of more taxes and new spending. Our county has been in a deepening recession for the last 3 years. There's no end in sight, and a malaise is beginning to set in our county, like the Carter era. Please understand, Mr. President, San Diegans just don't have any more money to contribute to the coffers of Government. My question is, can you name one country that has ever taxed and spent itself back into prosperity? Thank you.

The President. The answer to your question is, I can't. But you can't fairly characterize my program as that. I have cut more spending than my predecessor did. My budget calls for $250 billion-plus in spending cuts net. The first thing I did was cut the White House staff by 25 percent, even though I've already received more mail in 3½ months than came to the White House in all of 1992. If any of you have written me and I haven't answered, that's why. [*Laughter*] I cut the administrative expenses of the Federal Government 14 percent across-the-board. I froze Federal employee pay in the first year and cut back their raises for 4 years. There have been massive spending cuts in this budget. So that's just a big myth that there hasn't been. I also worked hard to pass a budget resolution that would make it clear that we couldn't raise any taxes unless we cut spending.

Now, let me address the middle class tax cut

specifically. Number one, after the election, after the election, the previous administration announced that the Government deficit was going to be $50 billion a year bigger in 3 of the next 4 years, a year, after the election. Therefore, I concluded that I could not in good conscience give anybody an across-the-board tax cut in the first year of my Presidency. I still think there should be an evening-up of the tax burden.

Secondly, it became clear to me that the best thing I could do for the middle class was to bring interest rates down and to try to get control of our budget. So I proposed a plan of budget cuts first and tax increases that are highly progressive. And let me just mention a couple of things that you may not know, having heard the press about the tax program I presented to the Congress. While it does raise about $250 billion over a 5-year period, it also provides significant relief to small business. Expensing provisions in the Tax Code, for example, are raised from $10,000 to $25,000 a year. That will lower a lot of people's tax bills. For people with incomes under $30,000, we increased the earned-income tax credit so much that they will not be affected by this tax increase in any way. And over 70 percent of the money that will be raised in this program will come from people with incomes net above $100,000.

So it's a progressive program; the burden is broadly spread. If we can bring the deficit down, we'll keep interest rates down. I'd just remind you folks that just since the election, when we announced our intention to seriously reduce the deficit, interest rates dropped dramatically. This year, 74 percent of people under 35 in a bipartisan poll said they thought they had a pretty good chance to buy their own home. Last year, the figure was 47 percent. That's because the interest rates are down. That will put another $100 billion back in the economy.

Now, I've got 4 years. Give me 4 years to try to deliver on the middle class tax cut. But the first thing we need to do is drive the deficit down with cuts and some prudent revenue increases. Most of the people paying the taxes are people whose taxes were lowered while their incomes increased in the 1980's. And I think it's very important to get the budget back in balance.

I will also tell you that all of our major competitors impose tax levies at higher rates than we do, and they manage to grow rather briskly.

I don't like taxes. The State I ran, Arkansas, in all the years I was Governor, kept taxes in the bottom 5 of all of the States in the country as a percentage of income. I was very proud of that. I don't like this, but we've got to get a hold of this deficit. It's going to kill us if we don't.

Justice System

Q. Mr. President, it's been more than a year since the first King verdict out of Simi Valley and the riots that followed. Yet the perception lingers that justice is still not being administered evenhandedly in this country. I think that perception is especially strong where the victim or the accused of a crime is a member of a minority group. And this is true in the administration of justice from the streets to the courts. Sir, what specific steps is your administration taking to correct this terrible perception and this dismal reality? And I'd appreciate it if you would include the importance of greater African-American Federal judges and more appointments there, but not limit your response to that issue, sir.

The President. I wouldn't limit it to that. I think, first of all, you can look at the appointment decisions I made. The woman I appointed Attorney General, Janet Reno, was the prosecutor in Dade County, Miami, one of the most ethnically diverse and difficult counties to deal with in the United States. I appointed her because I thought she would understand the importance of having all the communities in this country, including the minority communities, believe in the justice of the justice system. She and the other people we've appointed at the Justice Department I think will change the whole feeling about justice in this country. I think they will vigorously enforce the civil rights laws; I think they will move aggressively against abuse of power.

The second thing we're trying to do is to change the dynamics on the streets in a lot of these communities with about three initiatives. Number one, we are determined to try to put as close as we can to 100,000 more police officers on the street in the next 4 years, sensitive to the community, working in the communities in community policing settings. That leads to less police abuse and stronger relationships. Number two, we intend to spend more money in targeted ways to put our young people back to work and to educate them at the same time, not make-work jobs but really building opportunities. Number three, the empowerment proposal that I have recommended will dramatically increase the incentives that people in the minority and majority communities have to invest in these communities so that they can be brought back into the mainstream. All these things will change the way justice operates at the grassroots level, I believe.

Q. What about more judges?

The President. Well, I'm going to do that. I mean, I think that you've got to appoint judges and U.S. Attorneys that fairly reflect the diversity of America and meet a very high standard of excellence. And I don't think you have to sacrifice one to get the other.

Immigration

Q. I'm a taxpayer. My question is, why are my taxes going to subsidize the health care and the education of illegal immigrants while our own citizens are doing without?

The President. That's a good question. I think there are two answers to that. One, frankly, is a practical one, and that is that the United States does not have the means at the present time to enforce its own immigration laws. And one of the things that I've asked the Attorney General to do is to conduct a nationwide search for the best person to head the Immigration and Naturalization Service, who can really make some changes there and then try to get more border patrol and more ability to enforce the immigration laws. One of the things that was in the jobs package that I proposed—the emergency jobs package that was voted down by the filibuster in the Senate—was money for several hundred more border patrol officers here in California. So we have to deal with that.

The second reason is that the United States Government sets immigration policy but for as long as I can remember has left it up to the States to bear the burden of the immigration costs, or the localities, so that California, Texas, and Florida and, to a slightly lesser extent, New York pay huge bills for national decisions. So in spite of all the budgetary problems we have in this budget, we have recommended several hundred million more dollars to come into the State of California so that your local tax dollars will be freed up for education and for the other needs of the people in California.

It is not fair the way you've been done by the National Government. And given our financial difficulties, we're doing as much as we can to change that. I've got to give a plug to a Californian, Leon Panetta, who's now the head of the Office of Management and Budget. He helped us to redraw the laws so that more of this money for medical care and other health-related and welfare-related costs of immigrants could be borne by the National Government, because it's the national policy. And so your tax dollars here can be freed up for urgent California needs for your own folks.

Welfare Reform

Q. I'm really frustrated with the welfare system. Right now, I'm a single parent, and I just moved into an apartment. Since I moved into the apartment, my benefits have been cut, and I figured I'd try to make a better life for my child and myself, so I started to go to school. Since I've been going to school, I can't get any child care benefits. And the question that I want to ask you: What changes are you willing to make within that welfare system so that people such as myself can make a better life for their child and themselves?

The President. First of all, I'm glad you want to do that. And secondly, I'm glad you're here so that other people who may never have met anybody drawing a welfare check understand that most people on welfare would like to get off.

I've spent an enormous amount of time in the last 6 or 7 years working on this, and I'll bet I have had more personal conversations with people on welfare than any other public official in America. Here's what I think should be done. And you may not agree with all of it, but let me say to you and to everyone here, you just said something that's very important. Most people on welfare do not stay because of the welfare check. They stay because the cost of child care or the cost of medical coverage for their children makes taking a job prohibitive. Because if you don't have a lot of education and you take a low-wage job and no benefits, what you give up is not the check, you give up the child care, because you've got to pay for that, and you give up the health insurance you get out of the Medicaid program. So what I propose to do is the following: I want to change the welfare system so that in any State in America, anybody who is on welfare has to go through an education and training program, then has to take a job, if offered, but gets child care and medical coverage when they do it. And furthermore, I want to make sure work always pays.

So to go back to your question, one of the things we propose to do in this tax bill is to say, for everybody, families with an income of under $30,000, that you get an increase in what's called the earned-income tax credit. And if you're a working poor person, if you work 40 hours a week and you've got children in your house, you would be lifted above the poverty line, so there would never be an incentive not to work.

Now, the flipside of that is if after 2 years on welfare and going through the education program you don't have a job, then everybody under my plan would be required to go to work, either in a private sector job or a public sector job, in order to continue to draw the check. So we would end it, welfare as we know it, but we would give you the tools to succeed in the private sector. The tax system would support it, the child care system would support it, the health care system would support it. If we did that, you'd see a dramatic drop in the number of people on welfare and on food stamps. One in 10 Americans is on food stamps today. That is awful. And a lot of them are working people. So what we need to do is stop penalizing work. We need to reward work, and we need to reward responsible parenting. And I think that these changes will do that.

That bill will be coming up. I'll be introducing that into the Congress sometime in the next few months as we try to work through all the details. But changing the welfare system could do more to strengthen family and work values in this country than just about anything else we could do.

Defense Cutbacks

Moderator. This is a retired Marine Corps general.

Q. Nice to see you.

The President. You should have been with me last week. I was out at the Marine Barracks for the parade.

Q. My son told me.

The President. It was wonderful.

Q. Sir, we're pretty much a service area here, and we're mindful that the United States is famous for building up its military in time of crisis and then dismantling it as soon as the crisis is over, with the result that the next crisis brings a lot of terrible white crosses. And it looks like we're doing that now. I hope that's not true, but it looks like we're doing it. My question is, how do your professional military, your Joint Chiefs of Staff, feel in the light of, first, the crisis that we face and the immense build-down that we're going through now?

The President. Well, let me tell you that I have spent a lot of time with the Joint Chiefs of Staff since becoming President. I've had to, because of the work we've done not only with the defense budget but the crisis in Bosnia, the moving out of our commitment in Somalia—which was a real success—and a lot of other issues. I think it's fair to say that most of them have mixed feelings. They know that we have to reduce defense. They know that we don't need a 2-million or a 3-million-person Armed Forces, but they know there's a limit beyond which we should not go. And I can tell you that in my own mind, I'm very apprehensive about going below where these plans take us. I don't think we should go below about a 1.4-million-person armed services. That will still enable us to have a vibrant and diverse service in all of the service branches to keep them going.

I think there are some weapon systems that we still need to continue to develop. We need more air and sealift capacity, for example, and we will have to do that. And I am very concerned, frankly, that we keep up a vibrant Reserve and Guard component so that if we have to bring people back in in a hurry, we can. But the general feeling is that we're right on the brink of what we can do, and we shouldn't go any further than this budget takes us. And in the foreseeable future, we should really be very reluctant to go much further, unless it is in dropping a particular weapon system that we think we shouldn't have. But we don't need to reduce the uniformed forces, I don't believe, any faster or any lower than this 5-year budget plan, that the Congress is voting on, proposes to do.

A lot of people don't understand this, but the defense budget, which exploded in the eighties, has been going down for about 5 years now. And the reason the deficit keeps getting bigger is that even though defense is going down and we're not spending much new money on other things, you've had an explosion in health care costs, in costs associated with the bottom dropping out of the economy, I mentioned food stamps and interest on the debt.

But there is a limit to how much you can cut defense responsibly.

This country's still the world's only superpower. There are a lot of things only the United States can do. Even our allies in Europe, even the wealthier countries simply cannot do a lot of the things that we might be called upon as a free world to do, not the United States on its own. So I'm glad you asked the question. And we're watching it closely, and I promise you I will watch it every year when I'm there.

Jobs and Training for Youth

Moderator. Mr. President, of course, in all the major cities, San Diego being no exception, crime probably ranks second to the economy right now, and the gang problem specifically. We have with us right now Ariel Zuniga who in San Diego is a gang member.

Q. Mr. President, I live in a gang community, and a lot of gang members want to get out of the gangs, but there's nowhere to go, there's nothing we can do. One big thing that could change a lot of gang members' minds is jobs. If you give us jobs, that will open our minds to live better. Now, that's one way. Do you have any other suggestions for gang intervention or to help gang members go somewhere when they want to get out of the lifestyle?

The President. I'm just glad to hear you say a lot of people want to get out. My own belief is that we do need more jobs and that we do need jobs tied to continuing education and training. And if possible, we need jobs like a lot of the work done by the Los Angeles Conservation Corps, just to mention one example, where people, particularly people who are street-smart, who have been in gangs, can work in community projects with others so that they become accepted by their community, and they become a part of a different kind of gang, if you will. You know, all of us want to be in gangs. We just need to be in positive gangs, good gangs. We want to be part of something bigger than ourselves.

One of the things that I asked for in this emergency jobs package, which was stopped by the minority in the Senate, was enough money for another 900,000 summer jobs, tied for the first time ever, tied to real training programs so that there would be education along with the jobs and tied to an effort to get the private sector into the program so they could match the jobs one for one so that when the summer

was over, all the young people in the gangs, let's say, who had summer jobs would have relationships with people in the private sector who could help to continue to work with them.

I still think these are the best things to do. And I'm going to come back and try to get some more funds for summer jobs, coupled with education. And then we're going to keep working with people all across the country to try to figure out how to create more jobs. I have presented to the Congress a program which doesn't spend a lot of Government money, but which gives real, meaningful incentives to people like the businessman, who was the first person who spoke, and others, whether big or small, to invest in areas to create jobs and then hire people like you and your colleagues. We'll give them big jobs tax credits for hiring you. We'll give them other tax incentives for trying to create economic opportunity.

A lot of these places would not have as many gangs if there were more people who could get up every day and go make a living. And this is a great resource. There are a lot of people out there who have money in these distressed communities, but people wonder whether the streets are safe enough or whether you can really make a return on your investment. So this empowerment zone concept is designed to make sure that there's enough tax incentive in there to give people at least the nudge they need to try to get a return on their investment. And we'll keep working on it.

I also think, frankly, it's not popular to say, but every country in the world now with an advanced economy, except Japan, which is more closed than we are—but if you look at Germany, if you look at Great Britain, if you look at France, you look at all the wealthy countries, they all have high unemployment rates. They're all higher than America's except for West Germany. And we have so many young people that we're going to have to use a Government-private partnership to put people back to work.

You just think about it. I mean, I'm glad you came here. If everybody in this State who wanted a job had one, you'd have about half the problems you have, wouldn't you? But I do think it's important not that you just be given jobs when you're young, but also that we do an honest assessment of everyone's skill level and give them the education and training they need, because the average young person's going to have to change jobs seven or eight times in a lifetime. So it's not just important that you have work but that you be able to get other work. We're going to have to retrain a lot of these defense workers. A lot of them are 50, 55 years old. So that's important, too. It's not just work, but it's education and training.

Q. [*Inaudible*]—summer jobs aren't good enough——

The President. Because they're over, right?

Moderator. You have a more permanent—is that what you're saying?

Q. Yes.

The President. Absolutely, that's what I'm saying. But what we've tried to do with this summer jobs program, let me explain again, is to try to make sure we brought the business community into the program more, so it wasn't just a bunch of Government jobs, and try to make sure we had a good educational component.

And the other thing I want to say to you is that if the national service plan I propose to Congress passes, then all the young people in your neighborhood will be able to earn credit to go to college or a 2-year training program by working in your community. And if you choose, you can borrow all the money you need to go to college and then not have to pay it back until you actually go to work and then at a small percentage of your income, something that we've never done in this country before. So I'll also be able to go in those neighborhoods and say, look, even if you can't get a job in this neighborhood, you can go to college. You can borrow the money to live on and to pay your expenses, and you don't have to pay it back until you go to work. And here's a system that you'll always be able to afford to pay it back. That has also never been the case. A lot of people in this country think they'll never go to college. And even if they go, the dropout rate's more than twice the dropout rate from high school because of the cost. But I don't think there are any easy answers. I think it's work and education. I don't think there's any simple shortcut.

Defense Conversion

Moderator. Mr. President, you mentioned laid-off defense workers. Well, coincidentally, we just happen to have a couple, both of whom are laid-off defense workers.

Q. Before I ask my question, I would like to say, it's a pleasure to be in the same room with the President.

The President. Thank you. I work for you. It's a pleasure for me to be in the room with you.

Q. We've heard of the conversion plan. What is the conversion plan, and how is it supposed to help those of us who are employed? And what is it supposed to convert us into except jobless, homeless, and hungry?

The President. That's a good question. First of all, let me make one thing clear right away, because I owe it to the people of California who had been harder hit by the defense cuts than anyone else—the Marine general, the retired general that was talking about cutbacks. California's been hit hard in two ways: first, by base closing but even harder by cutbacks in contracts so that people who work for defense companies lost their jobs, a lot of our high-wage base manufacturing, and that's you guys.

One of the problems that we have in California is that when we started cutting defense as a nation back in '87, there should have been in place right then a conversion program so that you wouldn't have to wander around for 2 or 3 years out of work with no real strategy. So there is a catchup here to be done. I'm having to play catchup because we're starting in 1993 something that should have been started in 1987.

Now having said that, defense conversion normally means three things, and I'll tell you what we're doing and what I hope to get out of it. Number one, in some cases industries themselves can convert. That is, the employers can find new things to do to keep either all or part of their work force working. The second thing it means is communities converting. That is, communities can figure out how they're going to recruit or start or finance new economic activities which will hire the people who were laid off at the old place. Number three, it means total retraining for workers. I know in my State where an airbase closed and we lost tons of jobs, sometimes people retrained and went to work in the local steel mill or started their own small businesses or started something entirely different.

So when you hear defense conversion, it means three things, not one thing. It means: Can the company do something different and keep you working? If they can't, can the community find a way to start new businesses? And regardless, is there some retraining program that would put you back into the work force fairly quickly at more or less the same income you were making before? Those are the three things.

We have released this year alone $500 million in a technology initiative designed to try to really focus on creating jobs for people on the theory that if the jobs are there, people figure out how to get trained. That's what our focus is. This year we're going to try to spend about $1.7 billion in all three kinds of activities. But California should benefit primarily from the technology focus. There's been a lag time; I admit it. We waited 6 years too late as a Nation to do this. But I think you're going to see an enormous number of jobs created in this State in the next 4 or 5 years in new uses of technology. I mean, right here in San Diego, there is a consortium trying to figure out, for example, how to use old defense technology to build bridges that won't break in an earthquake. If they could do that, you could go through and rebuild or support bridges, create tens of thousands of jobs, not just people working on the bridges but in all the plants making all the materials and designing and everything. That's just one tiny example. There are an unlimited number of things like that, if we will get at it. So that's what we're trying to do.

Economic Redevelopment Strategies

Q. My question is a little bit different. What is available as help for those of us that have been forced into the processes of bankruptcy and foreclosures to stop these proceedings against us and to help us maintain our credibility until we are able to obtain gainful employment?

The President. Well, it's interesting because the bankruptcy laws were, in a way, reformed to make it easier for people to file bankruptcy so they wouldn't lose everything. But the practical matter is if you were basically a wage earner in a factory, it doesn't work that way, as you know. So I'm afraid the answer is right now there isn't anything available. But those are the kind of things we're trying to put in place. That is, we believe that local community groups—and I know you've got somebody working in San Diego on this—that every community that's had a significant displacement because of defense cutbacks should have a community strategy for redevelopment. And among that should be that if you're getting job training and if there's a real effort to create new economic opportunities, then we think at the local level people should be working on creditors to exercise forbearance to try to keep from having people losing their homes and things of that kind. And I believe a lot of that could be negotiated at the local level if people think things are happening.

One of the reasons a lot of people like you are suffering so badly is that people don't sense that they're part of the big plan to turn this whole thing around. So they just treat case by case. And let me say, in an attempt to accelerate that, I've asked the Secretary of Commerce, Ron Brown, basically to head up a team with five or six other Cabinet Departments just to focus on California, because I think if we can turn California around, we can turn the country around. California has 12 percent of the country's population, 21 percent of the defense spending. That will tell you why you boomed in the eighties and why you're getting the shaft in the nineties. Okay, so we're working on things just like that. And if you've got any specific ideas about what we ought to do, maybe you can give them to me after the show. But my thought is that that has to be handled community by community. And what we're going to try to do is make sure every community has a committee that could work with people like you as long as we're moving forward.

Shipbuilding Subsidies

Q. My question kind of relates to the defense cutbacks from a different angle. During that past 10 years, 50 percent of American shipyards have gone away, basically disappeared because of the foreign countries that subsidize their shipyards with billions of dollars. Do you plan in the next 10 years or during your term to allow the remaining shipyards to completely disappear? Are we going to start——

The President. The answer to your question is, I'm going to do what I can to avoid that. It's difficult, with a big Government deficit like we have, to start a subsidy program. But there's no question—if you go back and look at the history of what happened in the eighties—and this is the same thing to me with farmers or anything else—we unilaterally, that is, all by ourselves without asking anybody else to do anything, cut our shipbuilding subsidy. Our major competitors either kept them the same or increased them. So what do you think the result was? I mean, predictably, if the government by artificial means in another country lowers the cost of production and people are going to buy the least expensive ship, America got the shaft.

One of the things that we are doing at the present time is, by the way, reviewing our whole posture on all these shipping issues and especially in connection with California. As you probably know, I was out at the NASSCO yard during the campaign. They turned the whole place out for me—it was wonderful—just because of some specific issues they were interested in that I had taken a position on.

On the question of the subsidy, I think there are two issues here, two possibilities: We can either have some sort of tax incentive for those companies, or in the alternative, we can put the subsidies for shippers on the table when we negotiate with the Japanese, with the other shipbuilders in the other countries. It can be a big issue. You know, I've been criticized for saying I wanted to bargain more toughly with some of our trading partners, but a lot of these folks are doing as well or better than we are now in some of these areas, and I think we have to be pretty firm. We don't have to fall out with the Japanese in the whole range of areas where we share the same values, we have security interests. I admire them and care a lot about them. But I think we have to have tough bargaining on the trade issues with all these countries. So we are trying to decide what the best way to go is. But the answer to your question is, I'll be sick 10 years from now if we're not making any ships in America.

Small Business Loans

Q. Mr. President, availability of funds for minority small businesses through SBA loans and commercial banks is generally agonizing, then followed by defeat. What my question is, is what can you do to change this or to correct this so that we can acquire loans in the future?

The President. I can tell you what we're trying to do. And first, let me say this is a big issue for small business, generally. There has been a credit crunch in California and in New England and in Florida and a lot of other places in the country, but heavily concentrated, which means that small business people, especially people who aren't traditionally good sources of credit or haven't gotten a lot of credit in the past, had real trouble, and that's a nationwide thing.

So we try to basically do three things. Number one, we've got all the financial Agencies, the Treasury Department, Comptroller of the Currency, all those folks together, and we came up with a plan to reduce the credit crunch, to simplify the ability of banks to make character loans to people that look like they'd be good risks. And we're trying to make sure every bank in America understands that there are new rules that they can follow to exercise good sense in doing that.

Number two, I appointed, the first time in a good while, a person to head the Small Business Administration whose job in life before he became head of the Small Business Administration was to start small businesses. That's what he did, he went out and raised money for people who wanted to start small businesses. It was not a political appointment; he was a serious business person. And we are trying now to make the Small Business Administration a real job creator. We have slashed the rules and regulations; it's going to be a lot simpler to apply for loans. It's going to be very different.

The third thing we have to do, and this will affect minority business people especially, I think is to create a national network of community development banks, either within existing banks or separate institutions, that are set up to make loans to people who traditionally have not gotten them but are good risks, modeled on a bank in Chicago called the South Shore Development Bank. And I set up one in rural Arkansas, too. And they made loans to minorities, to women, to low-income people, people who had a good reputation, who had a good product or service, who seemed like a good risk. And they have been quite successful in bringing free enterprise to places where they haven't been.

So, community development banks, a different Small Business Administration, ending the credit crunch, those are the things we're trying to do. I hope it works. Write me in a year and tell me if it is.

POW/MIA's

Q. Mr. President, this is my brother, Colonel Charles Sharpe. He was captured in North Vietnam October 1st, 1965, and I have very good reason he is still alive today. Mr. President, you promised a clean sweep when you became President. The POW families have been stonewalled for more than 20 years by the same people in power. The gridlock continues. And at the same time, the Vietnamese Government, the policy of the Vietnamese Government, "we can keep you forever," continues. But it could end with the removal of the old guard and replacement of a new guard. My question, Mr. President, will you extend this same clean sweep as promised to our POW's, change in the gridlock? And why haven't you signed an Executive order releasing information to the families so the truth can finally be told and to pave the way for the return of our alive prisoners?

The President. Well, I think we have made public a lot of information. And I will go back and check and see what the status of that is. Let me say, first of all, if you have any information about your brother you want to give me, I will do my best to run it down.

Q. I would be happy to, sir.

The President. Secondly, let me say that I have sent or supported a number of Vietnam veterans going over to Vietnam in the last several weeks to try to get more and more information. For the first time, when General Vessey was over there the last time, just a few weeks ago, we actually got a list. They gave us their list, which appears to be a very authentic list of every POW and MIA that they knew and what happened to them, with a lot of information that they had never even revealed that they had before. So I think they are moving forward. Our big stick now is they want to make money, they want to do business with us. And the United States, unlike a lot of other countries—France, which colonized Vietnam and in a way got us into it, is over there doing business with them. The United States has no intention of doing that, at least I don't, until we have a full accounting of the POW's and MIA's.

So I do believe we're making progress. We have more information by far, just in the last few months, than we've ever had before. We are trying to run down all these cases. All I can tell you is, I'm going to do the very best I can to run down every case and to make sure that no family is denied access to reasonable information. And I'll follow up on that last question you made. But if you'll give me whatever information you have, I'll have it run down. We have people going over there all the time now and digging around. And we're doing our best. And they've finally begun to open some files to us that have never before been opened.

Q. Because the right questions have not been asked in the past.

The President. You tell me what questions you want asked, and I'll get them asked.

Q. If you would give the opportunity and promise to go into detail—I've been in this for 27 years with my brother, worked with both Governments and the families and the American Legion and all the friends—if you would take some of our suggestions. Thank you.

Moderator. Mr. President, we've got a very bright young San Diegan who has a question for you.

The President. You've got a nice tie, too.

Moderator. Yes. I think that it rivals the President's tie tonight, don't you think so? He's a sixth grader here in San Diego.

Prospects for the Future

Q. Hello, President Clinton. My question is, my birthday is tomorrow and I'm 12 years old tomorrow, and my question is, what kind of future am I going to have in store for me and the country?

The President. That's a neat question, isn't it? I think you've got a very bright future. The world you will live in will be freer of the threat of total destruction than any world we've ever known. It will be smaller, in the sense it will be in closer touch more quickly with people around the world of all different races and ethnic groups and economic systems. The volume of knowledge will double more quickly. And you will know more and do more with technology than any group of Americans or any group of people ever have. So if you get a good education, by the time you're grown, we will have worked through a lot of the terrible problems we're facing now. And I think you will be part of a new burst of American prosperity, if we fix the problems the country has now.

But our job, my generation's job, is not to leave you saddled with a huge debt, no investment in your future, and an economy that doesn't work and a society that's coming apart, where there's too much crime, too much division, too much violence. If we can simply face our problems today and deal with them like grownups, be honest about them—it's okay to differ, it's okay if we differ about how we should do things, but if we just work on our problems, I think you're going to have a great future. I believe that by the time you get out of high school, that America will really be on the move again and things will be looking great and you'll feel great about your future. That's why I ran for President, to make sure that happens. I'm going to be really disappointed if it doesn't.

Moderator. What kind of a tax rate might he expect to see when he grows older?

The President. I think about what it is now, maybe even a little less, depending. You know, one of the things that we don't know, that we're looking at now, and I meant to go back to the first question you asked, we've got a second round of budgetary changes that I think could come along about September when the Vice President finishes this review I've asked him to undertake about the way Government operates and whether we should just stop doing some of the things we're doing and change the whole way the Government operates. I think that it is conceivable by the time he becomes a taxpayer that technology will render a lot of governmental functions totally irrelevant. And I think that the cost of Government might actually go down.

Now, the cost of health care will be there, the cost of Social Security will be there, and the need to continue to invest in new technologies will be even greater, and the need to educate people will be greater. But a lot of the things that we think of as Government bureaucracy, if this thing is properly managed, could be handled with computers and cards and a lot of the hassle that you think of as Government, everything from waiting for your driver's license to applying for a loan, to dealing with the farm programs, could just be obliterated, if we manage the thing right and get the technology right.

Indian Gambling Rights

Q. Mr. President, the Governor's opposition to the Indian gaming act is full of misinformation. As a former Governor, Mr. President, we know you've heard their side of the issue. Would you be willing, in the next 60 days, to meet with a select group of tribal leaders for a briefing on the matter as it relates to economic impact, jobs, and Native American sovereignty?

The President. Oh yes, I would do that. I have a little different approach to this, and I don't want to take a lot of the program on it because I intended to do that, but I have a little different approach and a little different perspective, I think, than either the Indian tribes or the Governors. The Governors are worried—you all probably don't know what we're talking about. Basically, the Indians who live on Indian lands have been able for many years to have some kind of gambling, like bingo par-

lors. A Federal magistrate ruled several months ago that if any kind of gaming could occur on Indian lands, then all kinds of gaming could, basically, right? So that means that, essentially, if they so chose, that any Indian land could become Las Vegas, could do any kind of gambling. So the Governors are all real nervous about that, partly because they think that they'll have to turn their States into Nevada because the pressure to give the gambling rights to everybody else will get so great, and that the whole thing will get out of hand. So they argue for restrictions which would enable the States to restrict the range of gaming. The Native American tribes don't want that; they want to have this maximum amount of flexibility.

I have a different perspective. I'll just give it to you, but I intend to meet with tribal leaders; I welcome that. I grew up in a town with the largest illegal gambling operation in America when I was a kid. Hot Springs, Arkansas, had the biggest gambling operation except for Las Vegas anywhere in the country. A young man, the age of that fellow that just asked me the question, could walk in any restaurant and put a nickel in a slot machine. There were open casinos. What my belief is, is that it is a lousy basis for an economy, past a certain point. The Indian reservations have been kept dependent for too long, have suffered from the patronizing attitude of the Federal Government, have never been empowered to seize control of their own destiny. And I do not blame the tribes for wanting the maximum possible flexibility on gambling. But what I'd like to see is a whole range of different initiatives so we can have real long-term economic prosperity, because there is a limit to how much gambling the country can absorb. There's a limit to how many Las Vegases can be successful. So we need to talk about it, and I would be happy to see some tribal leaders about it.

Health Care Reform

Q. The finest medicine in the world is practiced in the United States. Eighty-five percent of our population has access to this medical care, either through private insurance, Medicare, or Medicaid. And most of these are very happy with their physician, with the way he works up their problem, and with the outcome of their situation. Fifteen percent of our population, of course, is outside this mainstream. My question to you is, really, how do you want to get that

15 percent into the mainstream, how do you plan to finance it, and what's the way it could be done with minimal perturbations in our current system?

The President. Well, let me first of all say what you already know, which is that the Health Care Task Force that my wife is chairing is, at the moment, trying to finalize their recommendations so they can then take it to the doctors, to the hospitals, the nurses, to the business community, to the labor community, everybody, and try to let them evaluate it and then bring it back to me so I can introduce it in the Congress.

I would like to just reshape what you said just a little bit. I agree we have the finest medicine in the world for people who can access it. I agree that we ought to keep a system where people can have some real choice of their doctors, particularly their primary providers whom they know. I agree that we need to keep medical care in private hands. I think that's all very important. It's a little more complicated than that just 15 percent have no health insurance. About 100,000 Americans a month lose their health insurance and either fall into the category of uncompensated care or onto the Government's Medicare and Medicaid rolls. We also have medical inflation rates at far higher than the world average, and we spend a third more of our income on health care than any other country, even though we don't insure some of our people.

So what I think we need to do is to find ways to reorganize the insurance market so that you can't lose your health insurance if you've had somebody in your family sick and you've got a preexisting condition and you have to change jobs. I think that employers should bear some responsibility for their employees, but I think employees should pay some of their own health care costs, too, because if they don't, there's a tendency to overuse the system, which I'm sure you've seen. It's very important to point out that everybody gets, I'm sure you would acknowledge, everybody gets health care in this country, but it's too late, too expensive, and often at the emergency room. And if the employers who don't do anything for their employees say, well, they shouldn't have to, the truth is that those who do are paying the bill, as you know. Employers who provide health insurance are paying not only for their employees but everybody else, too. And their cost goes

up. So what I want to do is to see a system where we phase in the requirements on employers who don't cover their employees in very reasonable way, where the Government basically provides for the nonemployed uninsured and where we have insurance reforms that will simplify billing and regulation and dramatically reduce your paperwork burden. The average doctor—let me just say another thing—a lot of people complain to me and say, "Well, these doctor fees are going up so fast." You need to know that in 1980—let me just say this, this is real important—in 1980, the average doctor took home 75 percent of all the income that he or she generated into a clinic. In 1992, that figure is down to 52 percent. Twenty-three cents on the dollar gone, mostly to bureaucracy and paperwork and regulation and insurance costs, right?

Q. Right.

The President. So, what I think we have to do is to reorganize the system so it's much more simple from an administrative point of view and so we all take some responsibility for our own health care, including all the employers. But we have to be very sensitive to the small business sector and phase that in. That's basically where we're going with it.

Multilingual Education

Q. Hello. I'm a teacher of English to students who speak another language, and I have observed that those students that do well are those students who feel good about their native language, about being bilingual. I therefore believe that teachers as professionals, as role models, need to be required to have at least a conversational ability in a second language. I'd like you to respond to that.

The President. I think it would be a good thing if all teachers did, but it would take a good deal of time to get that done with the present American teacher corps. And my own view is that that decision should be made at the State level, not nationally. I think the National Government should facilitate and support the development of multilingualism among our teachers. But since over 90 percent of the money is raised for education at the State and local level, I think if there's going to be a regulation about it, it ought to be done at the State or local level. I think the United States should support more language instruction, and I have vigorously done that in my State. We tripled the number of kids in foreign language courses in my State because of the standards we adopted. And I agree it would help if more teachers did it. But I have to tell you, I don't think the National Government should mandate it.

Q. I like your diverse tie.

The President. Thanks. This is the Save the Children tie. I just got it last week. A 12-year-old student designed it.

Endangered Species and the Economy

Q. Mr. President, the economy of San Diego is probably the hardest hit in the country. Our construction industry has an unemployment of about 40, 50 percent, yet the Federal Endangered Species Act has put about 200,000 acres on hold. That could impact about 150,000 jobs, billions of dollars to the economy. And within the last month, three projects were stopped because someone saw or thought they saw a bird, a gnatcatcher, fly through the project area. That eliminated about 200 jobs on the spot and millions of dollars to the economy here in San Diego. What will you do to give us a better balance?

The President. Well, you know, just north of here, I thought the Secretary of the Interior had made an agreement that allowed construction to go forward there. And so what I think we have to do—I'm glad you told me this because I didn't realize there were any issues continuing down here about that. One of the reasons I asked Bruce Babbitt to be Secretary of the Interior is that he'd been a Governor, he had practical sense, he'd been in business, his family had been, and he believed in the environment. But he had common sense about it. And I thought the deal that he hammered out on the gnatcatcher up north, north of here, would have general application and would stop this kind of problem. I didn't know about it. All I can tell you is I'll get on it.

Q. Thank you very much.

The President. I think a lot of these problems—let me say one other thing. I think as long as we have a big and complex society, you can't make all of the problems go away on the front end. But one of the things that I'm trying to do at the White House and one of the reasons I asked perhaps my oldest friend to be my Chief of Staff, a man who made his whole career in business, building new businesses and starting things, is to try to make sure that the White House could maybe be a

place that could break some of these bureaucratic logjams and change things. And I tried to appoint a Cabinet full of really practical people who could solve these kind of problems. You've told me something I didn't know. I'll go to work on it. And if you'll give me a card or something before you leave tonight, we'll get back in touch with you next week.

Immigration

Moderator. Mr. President, we've only got about 3 minutes left. I'd ask you one quick question on my behalf here, something that hasn't been touched on this evening. Our border here with Mexico has become somewhat of a sieve lately. We even have Chinese immigrants trying to get across our border. To what extent do you favor closing off that border, or do you favor it?

The President. I think that the immigration laws, we have to try to enforce them. And let me say, to go back to this lady's question—and if you're going to have laws that you don't even try to enforce, you don't have the resources to enforce, then you shouldn't expect the State to pick up the tab. So even though we're broke and in trouble, I did, as I said earlier, try to get the Federal Government to pick up more of the tab for California this coming year than we did before.

But my own view is that there have to be some limitations on immigration and that once those limitations are concluded, once we agree as a society on whatever they are, then we ought to try to enforce the law, knowing that it's hard to do. And I say that as a person who basically believes America has been greatly strengthened by its immigrants. Almost everybody in this room, except for the Native Americans, were once immigrants. And even most of them had forebears tens of thousands of years ago that came from someplace else, when the land was connected someplace else. So I am basically in favor of a vibrant, diverse immigrant population, but there are limits to what we can afford to do. And once we accept that, then I think we ought to try to enforce the law.

I thought you were going to ask me about the problems with the sewage treatment in Tijuana. I'm also going to try to deal with that. San Diego got the shaft on that in the Congress last year. I'll try to see if I can't fix that this year.

Tijuana Sewage Treatment

Moderator. Real quickly, any suggestions?

The President. On what?

Moderator. On how to fix that.

The President. I just think—it's not that much money, it's about $3 million a year. And we'll just see if we can't, when that particular appropriation comes up, we'll see if we can help on that. I think we should do that. Again, that's something that's not your fault.

Moderator. Mr. President, we're down to one minute, unfortunately.

NAFTA

Q. The question is, with the NAFTA agreement, will you mandate that when a person loses their job as a result of this agreement which our Government entered into, that they would be guaranteed any new job that is created?

The President. I don't think I could do that, but what I think I can do is to identify areas which are likely to be hurt and do more to direct Government investment there and other incentives to hire people back. And I would certainly do that. But I have to tell you, I think California will gain a lot more jobs than you'll lose if we have the right kind of trade agreement. Mexico is now our second biggest purchaser of manufactured products. California wins big on that. I think we will win more than we lose. But some will lose, and we need to have offsetting investments. I agree with that.

Thank you.

Moderator. Thank you very much, Mr. President. The people of San Diego thank you.

The President. Thank you.

NOTE: The town meeting began at 8 p.m. at the KGTV studio. In his remarks, the President referred to Erskine Bowles, Small Business Administrator; Gen. John Vessey, Special Emissary for POW/MIA Affairs; and Thomas F. McLarty, White House Chief of Staff.

Nomination for Posts at the State, Transportation, and Labor Departments
May 17, 1993

The President named four new members of his administration today, announcing his intention to nominate Richard Moose to be Under Secretary of State for Management, Gordon Linton to be Administrator of the Federal Transit Administration, Louise Stoll to be Assistant Secretary of Transportation for Budget and Programs, and Anne Lewis to be Assistant Secretary of Labor for Public Affairs.

"This is a first-rate group of people," said the President. "Richard Moose brings significant experience in both foreign affairs and corporate management to the task of making the State Department work more efficiently. Gordon Linton is a distinguished public servant with an unquestionable knowledge of transportation matters. Louise Stoll has been a leader in both the private and public sectors in managing large endeavors. Anne Lewis has a tremendous sense of the concerns of working Americans. I am honored that all four of them will be joining my administration."

NOTE: Biographies of the nominees were made available by the Office of the Press Secretary.

Nomination for an Assistant Secretary of Labor
May 17, 1993

The President announced his intention to nominate John Donahue to be Assistant Secretary of Labor for Policy. Donahue is an associate professor at Harvard's Kennedy School of Government and an economic and strategy consultant.

"John Donahue is a leading expert on the relationship between business and Government," said the President. "He and Secretary Reich have worked together productively in the past, and I am confident that they will work together now to create policies aimed at giving our coun-

try the most productive, best trained work force in the world."

NOTE: A biography of the nominee was made available by the Office of the Press Secretary.

Remarks and a Question-and-Answer Session at Los Angeles Valley College in Van Nuys, California
May 18, 1993

The President. Thank you very much. I'm delighted to see all of you here, and I'm glad to have the chance to come. I've had a great time touring some of the facilities and seeing some of the programs that are offered here at this college and meeting some of your fellow students. Everybody here is a student, right?

Audience members. Yes!

The President. Everybody back there? I'm glad to see your president, your chancellor who are here, and Mayor Bradley I see back there. Thank you for coming. And I see we have a number of Members of Congress back there. If you've got anything to ask your Congressman, we've got four or five options back there. Will the Members of Congress stand up? Walter and Xavier and Tony Beilenson, Congressmen, it's good to see you all.

I see several State officials back there—the secretary of state, the State comptroller, the insurance commissioner, Michael Woo, Councilman Michael Woo, my friend, a candidate for mayor. Good for you. Good luck.

That "woo" is interesting, isn't it? Makes a good cheer. I like it.

I want to say to all of you, first of all, I am delighted to be back in California; glad to be back in Los Angeles and to Van Nuys and—[*applause*]. Yesterday I was in New Mexico, and I was at Los Alamos, and I said Los Angeles. They all hooted. So I promised them when I got here I'd say I was glad to be in Los Alamos. So there, I did it. [*Laughter*]

I came here for a very specific purpose today, and that is to try to illustrate what the economic efforts that our administration is making will do for you and how your efforts—can we fix this——

[*At this point, a microphone malfunction interrupted the President's remarks.*]

——in the work we're doing to try to turn the California economy around. And I thought that there was really no better place to come than to a college like this where all the people here have already, by definition, taken responsibility for your own future and made a real commitment to do what it takes to be competitive, to develop the skills you need to get a good job, to keep good jobs, and to learn new skills continuously.

I met a very impressive man inside who has got a full-time job, as many of you do, who has been coming back here on his own just to continue to hone his skills, because he says, "What I do requires me to change over and over and over again. So I will always be able to have a good job." And, this is funny, when I was talking to Dan Palmer, who introduced me, he told me that before he was married and began to have children, he was a musician. And he realized that that's not a very solid basis for having job security. I thought about being a musician, too, and I wasn't as good as he was. And I knew I had no job security. So I got into another line of work where I have no job security. [*Laughter*] But, anyway, I understand very much that sort of motivation which I imagine got a lot of you in here.

What I wanted to do was to basically just talk a little bit about our national economic efforts and how it affects California and how what you're doing here is essential if we're ever going to turn the economy of the State and Nation around.

First, when I took office, I found, as you know, a Government with an enormous budget deficit. That is, we were running in the red every year, over $300 billion. Our debt had gone as a nation from $1 trillion to $4 trillion. It's hard to even imagine that kind of money in just 12 years. We were a country for 200 years, we ran up $1 trillion worth of debt. Then in 12, we ran up $3 trillion more.

Why? Because we cut taxes and increased spending. And it was fun for a while. It helped California a lot: cut taxes, people had more money in their pocket; increased spending, mostly in defense; put a lot of people to work in plants out here; put a lot of people to work on and around the bases out here.

In the end, it all catches up to you, and you've seen the last few years what happened: the cold war was over; we began to reduce defense; we had no real plan for dealing with it. And what's happened to your tax money is, the deficit keeps going up even though defense has gone down because of the cost of health care, something that won't surprise any of you.

So what I have tried to do is to come up with a plan that would bring our deficit down, give us control of our budget and your future, get interest rates down so people can refinance their homes and their businesses—and I bet you there are people in this audience today who have refinanced their home loans since last November and saved a lot of money doing it, because we're determined to bring interest rates down—and at the same time, while cutting a lot of spending and raising some taxes, almost all of which—well at least well over 70 percent of it comes from people with incomes above $100,000. And we tried to give a tax cut to people with families with incomes under $30,000 so they wouldn't have to pay a tax increase.

But while doing that, there are some things which we should spend some more money on, and I want to talk about them. We ought to spend some more money on having more programs like this. Why? Because you can have the best economic policies in the world, and if the people don't have the training they need to do the jobs in a global economy, good economic policies don't put people to work.

I'll give you another example: There are also, in this tax bill that I have asked the Congress to pass, there are also big incentives for small businesses and big businesses to reinvest their money to put Americans to work and special programs to induce people to invest in communities that are particularly depressed, more sweeping than anything anybody's ever offered.

Why? Because the Government can't put everybody to work. Most people work in the private sector, and that's as it should be. So we have to find ways to give people special incentives to reinvest their money.

Let's take, for example, a business. If a business goes out and refinances its business loan and gets a lower interest rate, what do you want them to do with the money? Open another business, right? Or expand the business they're doing and hire more people so we can get unemployment down.

So those are the kinds of things we're trying to do. The budget I've asked the Congress to pass has over 200 specific budget cuts. It's got some really tough things in it. We freezed Federal employee pay. We reduced the size of the Federal work force by 150,000 over the next 5 years by attrition, just by not hiring people as vacancies occur. We cut everything from agriculture subsidies to Medicare. We cut a lot of things, starting with the White House staff and the administrative cost of the Federal Government.

We raised the money that I talked about. But we have some targeted increases in investment. So while we're going to bring the deficit down dramatically, we're going to try to get some money for more funds for dislocated workers, more funds for communities that are hurt by base closings or plants being closed because of defense cutbacks, more funds for things like the Red Line Transit System here, where our administration announced over $1 billion in funding to put people back to work and also to have some more stops in the community.

And the thing I want to say to you is that, if we're going to compete, if you're going to be able to have a good job and we're going to turn this community and this area around, we have to have the discipline to cut the things out we don't need to spend money on, to raise some money in order to bring the deficit down, because that means low interest rates, and that's good for the economy. But we also have to invest in people and technology and jobs. We've got to do that.

You know, I got amused when I was on the way in here, people holding up signs, standing together. One of them said, "Don't spend any more money." And another one said, "Close the border to illegal aliens." In the jobs program I presented to Congress, one of the things we had was enough money to hire a lot more border patrol people. You can't have it both ways. If you're going to hire people, you've got to have the money to hire them. And we're going to have to make these kinds of tough decisions.

So I wanted to come here because all of you know this. If you didn't know this, you wouldn't be here. You have this figured out. I mean, maybe not just like I said it, but you've figured it out. The average 18-year-old going into the work force now is going to change work eight times in a lifetime. Eight times. And whether you can get and keep a job now depends as much on what you can learn tomorrow as it does on what you know today. And that's not going to change. The world will get smaller and smaller and smaller, more and more of our economy will depend upon our ability to compete with people around the world. We'll have to trade more. We'll have to sell more to other countries. We'll have to be able to change constantly over and over and over again. And you really are on the cutting edge of that change.

So I wanted to come here to try to illustrate that and to ask you as citizens to support my economic program, to support our efforts to bring the deficit down, to cut spending, to ask wealthy people to pay their fair share, to give people incentives for new jobs, and to invest more in education, training, and technology.

I also want to tell you before I open the floor to questions, I want to introduce one more person. When I was running for President out here——

Audience members. No new taxes!

The President. We tried it their way for 12 years. Look what it got us. You know what the "no new taxes" crowd did for 12 years? They cut taxes on the rich, raised taxes on the middle class, ran the country in a ditch. They had it their way for 12 years. It sounds great, all this talk. They had their chance.

Audience members. You broke your promise!

The President. They had their chance. I broke my promise—you know what else they don't say? Their crowd, what did they do after the election? Oh, after the election they said, "Oh, by the way,"—the previous administration— "Oh, by the way, the deficit is going to be $50 billion a year bigger every year than we told you. But go ahead and do everything you said you were going to do before. Sorry we didn't tell you that."

Audience members. You broke your promise!

The President. What did they say, guys? So the free lunch crowd has had their chance. And I'm telling you there is no free lunch crowd.

And so we'll just have to decide whether we're going to take a different course. I want you to have a chance to do that.

The other thing I want to tell you is, we can't turn this country's economy around unless we lift California up. And so I asked the Secretary of Commerce Ron Brown to head a team in my administration to develop a specific strategy to try to make sure we were doing everything we could do to help to turn this economy around. He has now made, just since I've been President, in 4 months, seven trips to California, meeting with people, working with people, trying to develop a strategy for what our partnership should be. And he came with me today, so I want to introduce him. Ron, stand up, please. He's spending more time here than in Washington.

We're going to work hard, but you've got to do your part, too. And one of the messages that I hope will come out of this event today is that thousands of people in southern California will see you. They will see you and they will think, "I've got to do my part, too. I've got to do something. I have to do something to change what I'm doing. I have to do something to lift up my circumstances." Because I'm telling you, there is nothing the President, nothing the mayor, nothing the Governor, nothing anybody can do for you that you're not prepared to do for yourself. This has got to be a partnership and a two-way street.

Thank you very much.

Who's got a question or a comment?

Q. Hi. First off, I thought you look mighty handsome in that.

The President. I don't know about that, but it's a handsome cap. Thank you.

Voter Registration

Q. I'm a 29-year-old returning student. And I didn't know if you knew, but we are the number one voter registration campus in southern California, LAVC is. I wanted to know, will you support an amendment to your motor voter bill which will allow students to register to vote at the same time they register for classes when they come here to school?

The President. The answer to that is, I support that concept, but it's too late to amend that bill, because we had to fight like crazy just to get it through. You know, it was filibustered once by the minority in the Senate. And finally, we got an agreement and passed the bill, the motor voter bill, after it was passed last year and then vetoed. So it's a great improvement over the present law, the motor voter bill, and so I think that it's unrealistic to think we can amend it.

Now, what I think—as a matter of fact, I want to get it up and sign it before anybody decides to do anything else with it. But what I think you should do, since California has such an incredible array of community colleges and other institutions of higher education, is to try to get a State bill through requiring that to be done here. I mean, that's what I think you should do. I'll bet you could get a lot of help.

And also, I think that the local registrar of voters would probably be happy to do it. And if they're reluctant, then you ought to pursue trying to get a State law passed.

Home Ownership

Q. Mr. President, I still believe in having the American dream. And one of those dreams is to have an education. Another one is to own a home. And I want to know, what do you have in your economic policy that would help me buy a home?

The President. The most important thing that I could do to help you buy a home is to keep the cost of buying a home low. And the best way to do that is to keep interest rates down. Home mortgage rates have been at 20-year lows, 20-year lows. And I want you to understand why. I hope we can keep them down there.

First, interest rates dropped for a long time because of the recession, but they still were pretty high. Then, after the election, I said we were going to bring this deficit down, and I gave a specific outline of how I was going to do it. The rates started dropping rather dramatically.

Last year, a poll was done which said that only 47 percent of the American people under the age of 35 thought they had a real good chance to own their own home. This year, a poll was done that said 74 percent of the people thought they had a chance to own their own home. The only thing that's changed is that the cost of financing a home has gone way down. So the central premise of what we're trying to do in bringing this deficit down is to lower interest rates, lower home mortgage rates, lower credit card rates, lower business rates, lower the car payment rates so that we can help make these things more affordable to average citizens.

In other words, doing the right thing for all Americans will help individual Americans more than any specific program I could have on home-buying.

Now, let me say one other thing. I have also supported having the Federal Government give States the right to issue tax-exempt bonds to provide for lower interest financing for middle class families and for working families with modest means. And again, one of the things that I have tried to do in my program, if it passes, is to make sure that we make that permanent so that every State in America will be able to continue to do what I did vigorously in my State, which is to make available more low-income, low-interest financing to people to buy homes.

Taxes

Q. Mr. President, there are many different claims on how much your economic plan will actually increase middle-income taxes. Can you tell us in very simple, nonpolitical language how much more money middle-income people, those making less than $60,000, will pay in new taxes?

The President. Yes, I'll be glad to. First of all, there is one tax in this program that falls on middle-income people. And that's the so-called Btu tax. It's an energy tax based on, basically, the heat content of various sources of energy.

The purpose of the tax, aside from raising money, is to encourage utilities and industries to shift to the most fuel-efficient and environmentally sensitive forms of energy so that we can do more energy conservation and do more fuel shifting. And we've made some changes in it to try to make sure it works in a more practical way.

But because you consume energy, eventually those things will find their way down to you. That is, some of it will be in the fuel you buy; some of it will be in products you buy that themselves use fuel; a little bit of it would be in anything that's brought to a store by a truck. In other words, ultimately, all people pay these things.

Now, here's how the pricing works. The average family of four, next year will pay virtually nothing. I mean, literally virtually nothing, $1 a month or less. The next year after that, it will be probably about $6 a month. This is $60,000 a year and less. The next year it will be, and the year after that and from then on, it will be someplace between $14 and $17 per month, maximum for a family of four. If you're single, it's much less.

Now, if your income is under $60,000, but is also under $30,000, and especially if you have children, there is a good chance that you will not pay any more money, net, because another provision of this tax bill does something that I personally think is very important; I've wanted to do it for a long time. It increases the earned-income tax credit, which is already in the Tax Code, to the point that we'll be able to say to anybody who works 40 hours a week and has a child in the house, if you do this, you will not be in poverty. In other words, even if we have to give you a tax credit, we're going to lift you out of poverty. We're going to reward work instead of welfare. We're going to say that you'll be out of poverty.

Now again, I want to be very specific. The higher you go toward $30,000, the more likely you are to pay a little bit. But if you have children, you can make maximum use of the earned-income tax credit so that if you've got, let's say, a family of four with an income of $29,000, you will pay nothing or next to nothing on the energy tax, because while you pay it, you'll get an offset on your income tax.

So the lion's share of this, what I told you, $1 a month, $6, $7 a month, up to a maximum of $14 to $17 a month, 3 years, 4 years, 5 years from now, will be paid by people with incomes between $30,000 and really all the way up to about $100,000 a year. Then, it's at that point, when you get to the upper 6 percent of income earners, that the income tax increases trigger in.

So that's what it does.

Illegal Immigration

Q. Mr. President, as Republican filibusters torpedoed your original jobs bill, thereby leaving countless of unemployed and underemployed Americans less hopeful than they were in January, and as the dichotomy between costs and quality in health care and the education system widens, I would like to know what this administration will do to stem the unconscionable flood of illegal aliens that pours virtually unchecked into this country, and that erodes the quality of life for those Americans in the lower economic brackets and must eventually threaten the American middle class?

The President. I'd like to answer the question you asked, and also then make a reference to the other issues you raised on the jobs and the health care issue. The first thing I want to do is to hire a strong, sensible, practical person to be head of the Immigration and Naturalization Service. I have asked the Attorney General, Janet Reno, whom I think has really done a good job, to put a very high priority on selecting a nominee who will be compassionate but also hard-headed. I mean, I think you want somebody who is compassionate, but hard-headed, who is realistic about what we're up against and what we're facing. I think she will make a recommendation to me this week, and we'll resolve that. That's the first thing.

The second thing I think we have to do is to make a better effort to enforce the law that we have. If we've got a law on the books, we ought to try to enforce it, even if it's difficult to enforce. One of the things that was in the jobs program that you referred to that was killed by the filibuster was funds for more border guards to enforce the law. A lot of people don't know that, but that was in there.

So I think we have to find ways to get the resources necessary to do as much as we can to enforce the law that exists. There is a limit to how much any economy can have. You've got the California economy very depressed now. This is a State made by immigrants. It's very important to recognize that. Los Angeles County has people from 150 different racial and ethnic groups. We also will continue to have people who are exiles really from political oppression, and under our law they get a different set of treatment. But I think we have to really roll our sleeves up and do this.

In the meantime, there's something else I think we ought to say. Whatever we do on immigration is a national decision that has uneven impacts. You would admit that, right? It hurts California and Texas and Florida and New York and, to a lesser extent, a handful of other States more financially than it does the rest of the country. But it's a national policy. Or if there's a lack of a policy, it's a national policy. One of the things that has really bothered me, especially as we've seen all these educational cutbacks in California with your economy down after the defense cuts and the other problems, is that the Federal Government has essentially been willing to let you in California eat the cost of the Federal policy. So another thing we have done in spite of all the budget cutting we've done, there are funds in this budget to substantially increase funding to California to deal with the cost of immigration, thereby freeing up other funds in California to be spent on education or jobs or whatever else you all want to do here. I think we need to do more of that.

Now, I don't want to mislead you. There is not as much money here in the budget as a lot of people asked for from California. But there's a whole lot more; I mean, several hundred million dollars more than was previously given. And I just think it is imperative that we have to provide—if the Federal Government is going to have a policy, or lack of it, then the Federal Government ought to pay for the policy, or lack of it, so that the States can be free to spend their money on educating and training and finding jobs for the people who live within the State. That's what I think. So we're going to move toward that.

If I might just make one other comment on what you said earlier. I'm going to try to come back with various pieces of this jobs initiative. I hope we can still get some more money for summer jobs, because we've got the best summer jobs program this country has ever organized. We've worked in partnership with the private sector. We're going to require 90 hours of educational work for people who have summer jobs, hoping that we can actually help people to get full-time continuing jobs and to continue their education, something that's never been done with a Federal summer jobs program before. So we're going to try to get some more.

I also believe very strongly that we need to make a down payment now on the efforts that I'm making to put 100,000 more police officers on the streets so we can have more community-based policing, which means the best of both worlds if you've got the right kind of community policing. It means less crime, tougher law enforcement, and less abuse of authority because you have people working the neighborhoods, knowing their friends and neighbors, and less pressure.

So we're going to start with that and then try to move back toward these other issues.

Financial Aid for Education

Q. Mr. President, I transferred to a State university from here at Valley. I had to drop out of school this semester because I can't afford to go, and I don't qualify for financial aid.

And there are other students that are in my situation. We really want to go back to school. We can't afford the fees. What are you going to do to help us, please tell us. [*Applause*]

The President. I have introduced into the Congress a bill that I do believe will pass with both Republican and Democratic support—two bills—designed to deal with your problem. And let me just talk a little bit about it because you could tell by the clapping that you're not the only person in your fix.

The college dropout rate is 2½ times the high school dropout rate. And an awful lot of people quit because they can't afford to stay. Now, in California this previously was not as big a problem because so many of the institutions were free. But you've got all these economic problems now; that can't be the case anymore. And even if you don't have big tuition you have expensive other—other expenses are significant.

So here are the things we're trying to do. First of all, I've asked the Congress to adopt a national service program which would permit young people to earn up to $5,000 a year in credit either before, during, or after college to pay off loans for college expenses by doing important work in the community. It can be done before, during, or after college. Like after college, if someone agreed to be a teacher, for example, or a police officer in an underserved community, they could get $5,000 a year credit for that to pay off their loans. So that's, in effect, a scholarship program in return for national service.

In addition to that, I've asked the Congress to totally reform the present student loan program. The present student loan program costs $4 billion a year: $3 billion in unpaid debts and $1 billion in fees to banks and to other people who handle the money for the student loan program. It is amazing the money that's in the student loan program. And there is also no incentive for them to collect on people who won't repay, because the Government guarantees 90 percent of it. So if you borrow $20,000 from a bank and you don't repay it, the Government will give them $18,000, and it will cost them $2,000 to go to court and get it, right? So it's not a good system.

What I recommend is that we shift to a system of direct loans by a protected financial entity to be created by the Government to give you lower interest loans, to give you the money you need, and to give it to you on terms that won't frighten you. And here's what I mean—and people would be eligible without regard to their income, and here's how it would work:

If you borrowed the money, you would not have to pay it back until you actually go to work. Then, you would be able to decide how you want to pay it back among two choices: You could pay it back on a regular loan repayment schedule, based on how much you borrowed, or if that was too tough and that scares a lot of people, you could pay it back as a percentage of your income so that you would never be required to pay more than a modest percentage of your income. So there would never be an incentive not to take the loan out, because it would always be an affordable percentage of your income.

The catch is that we can't afford to lose $3 billion a year. So you'd have to pay it back at tax time. So you couldn't beat the bill, but you would always be able to afford to pay it back, and no one would expect you to pay it back unless you were actually working. This will dramatically change the economics of college financing.

Initiatives To Assist the Private Sector

Q. Hi, Mr. President. How are you doing?

The President. I'm fine.

Q. Okay. My question to you, sir, we have a plant in Van Nuys, the GM plant. I notice a lot of businesses such as that went out of State. What can the Government do to motivate big business to invest in the community college as well as State college and major universities?

The President. That's good. Well, I think first of all, most big businesses will invest more in the education of their employees than ever before because it's in their interest to do so. And I think what I should be doing is trying to figure out ways to give businesses incentives to reinvest in America and in putting Americans to work, and also, if possible, to try to make sure that every State has a chance to keep the manufacturing base.

Now, that affects California in two ways; let me just mention them. In the program that I have asked Congress to adopt, in addition to the tax increases, which you were good enough to ask about—and I'm really glad you gave me a chance just to lay it out because it's not near as bad as everybody thinks it is, is it—there is also a lot of incentives for businesses to rein-

vest. Small businesses today can expense or write off $10,000 of expenditures every year on their taxes. We've proposed to take that to $25,000. That's a good incentive for the small businesses to hire maybe one more employee. And most new jobs are created by small businesses. So this is a good thing to do.

Another thing we do is to let larger businesses who make investments in new equipment and modernize write that off more quickly in this Tax Code, which is an incentive to invest more.

The third thing that's real important to California is, at least I have read—you know, you had an economic summit out here not very long ago, and I read that a lot of business people believe that it's harder to keep manufacturing jobs in California because of the costs of the workmen's compensation system. More than half of that—and I'll say a plug for your insurance commissioner, Mr. Garamendi is the first person who ever talked to me about this—more than half the cost of workers' comp comes from health care costs. And in the work that my wife, the First Lady, is doing with the health care commission, one of the things we're trying to come up with is a national system to take the health care portion of workers' comp cost and fold it into a national health system so you lift that burden off of the businesses separately and so no State ever has an advantage over any other State just because of the health care cost of workers' comp. That will also be a huge boost to California and the manufacturing economy of California if we can get it done.

I'll take one more.

Yes, ma'am? I wish I could stay here all day, but I've got to go shake hands with them because they feel deprived. And you. Thanks.

Education

Q. Mr. President, I would like to ask about education. The level of education is declining, the on-campus crime is increasing, and the education budget is decreasing. The percentage of Government expenditure used for education in the United States is 3 to 4 percent. In Japan, it's 7 percent. The California education budget is 85 percent of U.S. average, and it's one-third of New Jersey. So I would like to know what actions are you going to take to solve these kinds of problems.

The President. Well, let me try to reframe a little of what I've said before because I think you've hit it. It would surprise most people to know that while the Government's deficit was going up and the debt was going up in the last 12 years, we were actually reducing the effort the National Government is making to support education and a lot of other initiatives, because all the money was going first to defense and then to health care costs.

What I am attempting to do with my budget and will continue to work on it every year I'm President, is to, every year, to slowly move our spending priorities back toward education, training, and technology.

In this budget, for example, we give more funds to institutions like this for worker training programs. We give much more money for Head Start for preschool kids. We do a lot of things to try to, in other words, let the Federal Government play a bigger role. But another real problem you've got, let me say, in the United States as opposed to Japan where you've got three levels of government that often operate more or less independently, the lion's share of the budget for education always comes at the State and local level.

So then, the other thing I can do is to help alleviate the burdens of the State government. Why is State government spending less on education in California, more on uncompensated care for undocumented people coming into the country, more on exploding health care costs, often mandated by the National Government?

So if I can persuade the Congress, and if we can be wise and good enough to work out a health care program that's good for America, that brings costs in line with inflation, and then if we can compensate the States better for their costs that aren't their fault, like dealing with the immigration issues, then that will free up in California millions and millions and millions of dollars which the State could then turn around and put back into education. So we can help directly some, and we can help indirectly a lot. And I'm trying to do both those things.

Thank you. You were great. I wish I could stay longer.

NOTE: The President spoke at 12:10 p.m. in the courtyard. In his remarks, he referred to Representatives Walter R. Tucker III and Xavier Becerra; Donald G. Phelps, chancellor, and Mary E. Lee, president, Los Angeles Valley College; and Daniel A. Palmer, former student who successfully retrained for a new career.

Remarks Endorsing the Candidacy of Michael Woo for Mayor of Los Angeles and an Exchange With Reporters in Van Nuys
May 18, 1993

The President. Good afternoon, everyone. As you know, a couple of days ago I issued a statement endorsing the candidacy of Mike Woo for Mayor of Los Angeles. I wanted to just amplify a little on that today, make a couple of comments, give Mr. Woo a chance to say something, and then answer a few of your questions.

Let me say that I know it is somewhat unusual for all these national figures to be involved in a mayor's race in Los Angeles. But that's because what happens in Los Angeles matters to America and because we can't really turn America around until we can lift the economy of California up.

I endorsed Mike Woo not because I have something against his opponent; I don't. I just like him, and I like him for some very good substantive reasons. I feel a personal affinity for him because he supported me early in the race for President before the New Hampshire primary. And that's a part of it. But I also have been terribly impressed by what he has said to me in private about this city, about the need to bring people together across racial and ethnic lines, about the need to try some new ideas to get the economy going again.

After the riots last year and long before I was President, I came here and walked the streets of Los Angeles with Mike Woo. And we talked abut the kinds of things it would take to start businesses, to attract investment, to change the framework of people's lives; the kinds of incentives that are embodied in the empowerment zone legislation that I have presented to Congress, which will provide much more dramatic and comprehensive incentives to invest in businesses and jobs and education and anticrime initiatives in our cities than has ever happened before; the kinds of initiatives that are embodied in the national service program that I have presented, that will be embodied in the welfare reform program that is coming forward. I want to do something to help Los Angeles, southern California, and this State revive and come back.

I've assigned the Secretary of Commerce to come out here. He's been here seven times. And I want the best possible partnership to get that done. That's why I endorse Mike Woo. It is 100 percent positive feeling. I have nothing against his opponent. I just care a lot about this community. I care a lot about this State. I want to do everything I can to make it work. I think this will help. And I think the decision was an appropriate one and one I feel very comfortable with.

[At this point, Mr. Woo expressed his appreciation to the President.]

Q. Mr. President, have you ever met Mr. Riordan, and what do you know about him?

The President. I know quite a bit about him. I have met him, and I know a lot of people who are working in his campaign, as you know. And my wife has spent some good time with him. I have nothing against him. I'm for Woo. There's nothing negative here in my feelings about Dick Riordan.

Q. Mr. President, if Dick Riordan does win the election, can Los Angeles count on as close a relationship with the White House as it will have if Mr. Woo——

The President. It won't affect my attitude about Los Angeles in any way. I will work as hard as I can to help the people here, whatever the voters of this city decide to do.

But let me try to reinforce that and put it in what I consider to be the proper framework. Just like I told those students out there today at this college, whatever I do as President, whether this economy works or not depends on their willingness to prepare themselves to compete and win. In other words, they have to do certain things. I'm going to do everything I can. My Secretary of Transportation was out here just a few days ago announcing a $1.4 billion commitment to the Red Line Mass Transit System. We're here for the duration. Ron Brown is going to be here supervising this economic program and our coordinated efforts. But

I think it will work better if there's a mayor who has a lot of good ideas about how to start businesses, how to rebuild communities, how to pull people together. I think Mike Woo's ideas are good. That's my point. It's not anything negative.

Q. Mr. President, is your prestige on the line at all because of this? You know candidates have coattails—sometimes they do, sometimes they don't.

The President. Frankly, I don't know if they ever do. If I have any coattails, it would only be because of the ideas that I share in common with Mike and the things that I hope that we can do together. I was only too happy to do this. Ultimately, in the end, the people of Los Angeles will vote the way people do everywhere. They'll vote on the merits of the issue before them.

The one thing that I hope will happen is that you will have a very good turnout. I hope the citizens of this city realize that this has a lot to do with how things work out in the future. A lot of the things that I want to do—for instance, you take this empowerment zone issue, for example. If we pass this bill through Congress, look what it will do. Say Los Angeles, a big section of Los Angeles, is selected as an empowerment zone. There will be new jobs credits and other new tax incentives for private sector people to invest in these communities and to hire people. There will be all kinds of new initiatives to facilitate investments in housing and in anticrime initiatives, and in education and training initiatives. That's good. But whether it works or not depends on how it's put together once the Federal Government makes the selection. That has to happen from the grassroots up.

So what I would say to the people of Los Angeles is, you need to vote based on what you think is best for you. The reason I think Mike Woo is the better candidate is because I know him, I know how he thinks, and I know he can figure out how to make this stuff work. And in the end, the test of our endeavors is not how well we speak or what we say as much as whether we can change the lives of people. That's the way we ought to ultimately keep score. So that's why I took this position.

Press Secretary Myers. Last question.

Q. *[Inaudible]*—of your administration be coming to Los Angeles and campaign on Mr. Woo's behalf?

Q. [Inaudible]

The President. Well, let me tell you something. When Michael Woo endorsed me, there was not much in it for him. I mean, Michael Woo endorsed me before the New Hampshire primary, and I was still running third in California in June. So there was nothing in it for him. There was never any anticipation that there would be some political payback. He did it because he thought I had good ideas and he thought I'd be a good President.

Do I feel a personal sense of loyalty to him? You bet I do, and I'm not ashamed of that. But would I do it if I thought he wouldn't be a good mayor? Never in a thousand years. I believe he'd be a very good mayor.

Q. Mr. President, will members of your administration be coming to Los Angeles to campaign on Mr. Woo's behalf?

The President. I'm embarrassed to tell you I don't know. I've never even discussed that with them or with him. But I'm strongly in favor of him, and I know Ron Brown feels very positively toward him because we talked about him on the way in here today. This is something I want to do because I believe it's good for the people of Los Angeles. If I didn't think it was, I wouldn't do it.

Thank you.

NOTE: The President spoke at 1:40 p.m. in the courtyard at Los Angeles Valley College.

Remarks to the Community in South Central Los Angeles
May 18, 1993

Thank you. Can Ron Brown shoot a jump shot or what? But I had a good team. I want to tell you, first of all, how happy I am to be here with the Secretary of Commerce and how proud I am of the people who made the Playground a reality. I want everybody in America to know that there are people here is Los Angeles who believe that we can bring business to this area, we can put people to work, we can make things work, if you have the help you need and the support you need to bring this area back.

And I want you know that one of the things that we're working on in Washington is a law that we call empowerment zones that will help to get more people to invest in businesses like this by giving them special incentives to put people back to work where people live. You look at all the people that live up and down these streets. They're a great economic resource. They have the opportunity to spend their money if they have stores here to spend it on. They have the opportunity to support cleaning up these neighborhoods and support it. That's what you can do. I know you can do it.

And I wanted to come here today not just to have a little fun with a basketball, although I did, but to say to you and to all of America: We're going to have to rebuild this country from the grassroots up, with people who want to work and are trying to work but who are going to get a hand up. And that's what this program is all about. We want to create all kinds of opportunities like this not only in Los Angeles but in other cities just like this. We can do it. What we've got to do is to make available money and give people the incentives who have their money to spend it here. This is an incredible untapped resource for America. If everybody in this country who wanted a job had one, we wouldn't have half the problems we've got today.

So when we leave here, Ron Brown and I are going back to Washington to go back to work to try to pass an economic program that will put you back to work. And we need your support. We need your support, but it's going to be a lot easier to be able to go back and say I've been there. I've been there time and time and time again, and I know the people there are willing to work hard and play by the rules if they just have a chance to succeed. These children's future depends upon our being able to bring these communities back. I'm going to do my best, and I need your help to do it.

Thank you, and God bless you all.

I just want to say one more thing. You asked me about a lot of issues. We could talk about them, but I want to say one more thing. I spent a lot of time in Los Angeles, and I came out here to south central L.A. a long time before I ever ran for President, and sat down and met with community leaders before I was ever a candidate, before I ever thought I'd come back here. And I just want to tell you that I believe that we can do this, but we've got to do it from the grassroots up. I can pass all the laws in the world in Washington. And I would be remiss if I didn't recognize all these local leaders that are here, your State senators, county supervisors, and others that are here, and Mike Woo, our candidate for mayor who's here, and all these things.

And one of you said, "What about drugs?" And somebody said, what about something else? Let me tell you just one thing—we don't have time to talk about all of this, but when we start this program I told you about—it's called empowerment zones—the way you can get access to these kind of incentives is that the people at the grassroots level have to put together a plan and say, "Here's what we're going to

do." And it's not just enough to say, "We want all these incentives." You have to show how if we give you more police officers, you'll put them on the blocks and use them to help deal with the drug problem. You have to show how you're going to make the schools better if we give you more money to do that.

So, we're going to deal with all these issues, but you're going to have to say how you would deal with them. That's the way we're going to work it out: a new partnership where you control your destiny and we help you. Instead of telling you what to do, you're going to say what you want to do, and we're going to try to help you. And you'll be able to deal with drugs, with education, with a whole range of issues, but it all starts with finding people who will provide jobs. That's where we're going to begin.

Thank you very much.

NOTE: The President spoke at 3:10 p.m. at the Playground, an athletic wear store.

Nomination for Posts at the United States Fish and Wildlife Service
May 18, 1993

The President announced today his intention to nominate Mollie H. Beattie, the director of a Vermont public policy center and former State natural resources official, to be Director of the U.S. Fish and Wildlife Service, Department of the Interior. In addition, the President announced that his longtime environmental aide Kenneth Smith has been appointed the Fish and Wildlife Service's Deputy Director.

"Secretary Babbitt and I have placed a high

priority on finding new ways to protect biological diversity without endangering economic growth," said the President. "The Fish and Wildlife Service will play a big role in that process. I have full confidence in the ability of Mollie Beattie and Ken Smith to do the hard work and the fresh thinking that needs to be done."

NOTE: Biographies of the nominees were made available by the Office of the Press Secretary.

Exchange With Reporters During a Luncheon With Business Leaders
May 19, 1993

Energy Tax

Q. Mr. President, do you think you can persuade these business leaders that your energy tax is a good tax and that you have enough spending cuts in the budget?

The President. Well, I hope so. Several of

them endorsed this program yesterday. Mr. Chee on behalf of the realtors did, and Mr. Armstrong, he's aircraft. Mr. Wolf did. So I think we're making a real good dent. I think the main reason is that the business leaders who are familiar with what is actually in the program know that there's $100 billion in entitlement cuts there, know that the energy tax is going to work as an important part of getting the interest rates down and having credibility in the markets. So I think we've got a real shot at it.

Health Care Reform

Q. What about an entitlement cap, as some people on the Hill want? Wouldn't that help?

The President. Well, it has to be done in the right way. My view is—and this is a good place to discuss this—the United States Government has already contributed to the rising costs of health care for employers by squeezing Medicare and Medicaid and forcing those costs off onto private employers. So if we have a cap on health care spending, which I'm not opposed to, and it should be done in a right way, it

should be done in connection with the health care plan so that we're helping everybody. If we did it without doing it on the health care, if we did it now, it would run the risk of 2 or 3 years from now having another big increase in their costs, undermining their ability to hire American workers and to keep America competitive. So if we're going to do a health care cap, let's do it with health care. That's the way it should be done.

NOTE: The exchange began at 12:23 p.m. in the Residence at the White House. In his remarks, the President referred to William Chee, chief executive officer, RESCO; Michael Armstrong, chief executive officer, Hughes Aircraft; and Steven Wolf, chief executive officer, United Airlines. A tape was not available for verification of the content of this exchange.

Remarks and an Exchange With Reporters Prior to Discussions With Archbishop Desmond Tutu
May 19, 1993

Angola

The President. It's an honor for me to welcome Bishop Tutu here. As every American knows, he has been a real leader in the fight for democracy and for an end to apartheid in South Africa. Almost a decade ago he won the Nobel Peace Prize for his efforts. And I want to assure him here today that the United States remains committed to the creation of a nonracial democracy in South Africa.

I also want to discuss a decision that I know has been very important to Bishop Tutu and to other leaders for democracy and human rights in Africa. Today I am pleased to announce the United States recognition of the Government of Angola. This decision reflects the high priority that our administration places on democracy.

In 1992, after years of bitter civil war, the people of Angola held a multiparty election that the United States, the United Nations, and others monitored and considered free and fair. Since taking office on January 20th, I have tried to use the possibility of United States recognition as a leverage towards promoting an end to the civil war and hostilities and hopefully the participation of all relevant political groups

in the Government of Angola.

Sadly, the party that lost the election, UNITA, resumed the fighting before the electoral process could even be completed. And UNITA has now refused to sign the peace agreement currently on the table. The Angolan Government, by contrast, has agreed to sign that peace agreement, has sworn in a democratically elected national assembly, and has offered participation by UNITA at all levels of government.

Today we recognize those achievements by recognizing the Government of the Republic of Angola. It is my hope that UNITA will accept a negotiated settlement and that it will be part of this government. I intend to continue working closely with the Government of Angola and with UNITA to achieve a lasting peace settlement and a vibrant democracy there. I hope the efforts of the United States have been helpful. I am confident that the Government of Angola has more than earned the recognition that the United States extends today.

Q. Mr. President, human rights sources are— how do you plan to approach the occupation of East Timor by Indonesia, sir? Could you elaborate on that—how do you plan to approach the problem of the East Timor?

The President. I don't want to talk about it today. We have discussed it, and we may have more to say about it later.

The Vice President. I think just before your question Bishop Tutu was about to say something.

Archbishop Tutu. Well, I just want to say how deeply thrilled I am at the President's announcement, because I have been speaking with the Assistant Secretary of State and Assistant Secretary for Africa yesterday and said I couldn't understand how the United States could not recognize a government that was democratically elected. And they were very cagey in their responses. And I am really over the moon in a sense because I was going to raise this issue with the President in my capacity as President of the All Africa Conference of Churches in our appeal to the administration to reward democracy. And this is happening, and I am certain it will help the process in our continent where not all countries have had a good record on human rights. And I am very, very thrilled. If my complexion was different you would probably see better. [*Laughter*]

Q. [*Inaudible*]—what message are you going to—the President about South Africa—the situation in South Africa today?

Archbishop Tutu. Well, I haven't yet spoken. I would have hoped we would do that and talk with you afterwards because, I mean, I don't think it is fair to say, I am going to say to the President—and I haven't said it yet.

White House Travel Office

Q. Mr. President, can we ask you if you feel you were fair in summarily dismissing some employees of this Government of long standing without a hearing and leaving the impression perhaps that they may have committed criminal acts?

The President. I don't know. I'll have to refer to the Chief of Staff about that.

Q. We're speaking about the Travel Office, sir.

The President. I know. All I know about it is that I was told that the people who were in charge of administering in the White House found serious problems there and thought there was no alternative. I'll have to refer to them for any other questions. That is literally all I know about it. I know nothing else about it.

NOTE: The President spoke at 3:37 p.m. in the Oval Office at the White House. Archbishop Tutu referred to George Moose, Assistant Secretary of State for Africa. A tape was not available for verification of the content of this exchange.

Statement on the Human Rights Situation in Burma
May 19, 1993

I was moved by the stories of individual suffering I heard this afternoon and am deeply concerned by the tragic human rights situation in Burma, as well as by the continued detention of Burmese pro-democracy leader Aung San Suu Kyi, who has been under house arrest since 1989. I strongly urge the Burmese government to release Aung San Suu Kyi and all political prisoners, to respect the results of the May 1990 elections, and to commit itself to genuine democratic reforms.

The Burmese people should know that America stands with them and with others in the international community in the struggle for freedom in Burma.

NOTE: The President issued this statement following a meeting in the Cabinet Room at the White House with a group of Nobel Peace Prize laureates including Archbishop Desmond Tutu, Betty Williams, and Kara Newell, who had traveled to Thailand earlier this year to focus international attention on the human rights situation in Burma.

Statement on the Death of John Wilson
May 19, 1993

As residents of the District of Columbia, Hillary and I mourn the sudden and tragic loss of DC City Council Chairman John Wilson. John was a tremendous individual who devoted his life's work to the empowerment and benefit of the District's citizens.

We know the love that John had for the District of Columbia will be remembered and cherished by all the city's residents as his service and achievements are profoundly appreciated.

Hillary and I will keep his wife, Bonnie, in our prayers.

Nomination for Deputy Administrator of the General Services Administration
May 19, 1993

The President today named nationally recognized Chicago businesswoman Julia Stasch Deputy Administrator of the General Services Administration. Ms. Stasch joins Administrator-designee and former Western Digital CEO Roger Johnson at the head of GSA.

"Julia Stasch is exactly the type of aggressive and innovative business person this administration needs as it seeks to reinvent the way Government works," the President said. "I am confident Julia will work well with Roger Johnson to ensure economy and efficiency are standard rule at the new GSA."

NOTE: A biography of the nominee was made available by the Office of the Press Secretary.

Remarks on Signing the National Voter Registration Act of 1993
May 20, 1993

Thank you very much. Joel, thank you for the T-shirt. In a few moments I'll give out bill-signing pens, but I'd rather have the T-shirt. [*Laughter*]

Getting to know the young people across this country, beginning in New Hampshire, who pushed the motor voter bill, was one of the most rewarding parts of the 1992 campaign. But the effort that we come here to celebrate today has a long and venerable heritage.

A few moments ago, you heard the voice of President Johnson crossing the chasm of time back to 1965 as he signed the Voting Rights Act into law. As a southerner and as President, his words have special significance to me. During my childhood, no family's dinner table, no church congregation, no community, and no place of work was immune from the searing struggle for civil rights. To hear Johnson's voice is to make vivid for me once again those difficult, yet glorious years of struggle, difficult and terrible because so many people gave their lives moving the stone of freedom up the side of a mountain, glorious because the years of contention eventually gave way to an overdue season of reconciliation and renewal, and gave our region and our country a second chance to fulfill our promise.

The victory we celebrate today is but the most recent chapter in the overlapping struggles of our Nation's history to enfranchise women and minorities, the disabled, and the young with the power to affect their own destiny and our common destiny by participating fully in our democracy. When blacks and women won the right to vote, when we outlawed the poll tax and literacy test, when the voting age was lowered to 18, and when finally we recognized the rights of disabled Americans, it was because the forces of change overcame the indifference of the majority and the resistance by the guardians of the status quo. And who prevailed? Brave people working at the grassroots, impatient with an always imperfect democracy and dedicated to widening the circle of liberty to encompass more and more of our fellow citizens.

I have said many times in many places that in this country we don't have a person to waste. Surely the beginning of honoring that pledge is making sure the franchise is extended to and used by every eligible American. Today we celebrate our noble tradition by signing into law our newest civil rights law, the National Voter Registration Act of 1993, which all of us know and love as "motor voter."

An extraordinary coalition of organizations, many of whom played historic roles in our expanding democratic rights, joined many years ago with the hope that they would see this day come. I'm honored to share this podium with representatives with three fighters for freedom: the NAACP, the League of Women Voters, and Human Serve. I want to pay special tribute to Disabled and Able To Vote, to Project Vote, and to Rock the Vote, and literally, the scores of other groups for whom the goal of full voter participation has been a durable and lasting dream. I want to pay special tribute to the young people who lobbied me personally for motor voter and who voted with renewed energy and conviction for their own futures in the election last November.

They all labored hard because this bill was necessary. As many as 35 percent of otherwise eligible voters in our Nation are not registered, and the failure to register is the primary reason given by eligible citizens for their not voting. The principle behind this legislation is clear: Voting should be about discerning the will of the majority, not about testing the administrative capacity of a citizen.

The State of Washington instituted a similar measure during the 1992 election, and their motor voter program registered in that State alone an additional 186,000 people. Motor voter works at registering voters and people who register vote.

With this law and its appropriate implementation by States, voters can register by applying for a driver's license, through uniform mail application, or by applying in person at various agencies designated by the States. As a result, registration for Federal election will become as accessible as possible, while the integrity of the electoral process is clearly preserved.

As I said, I have long supported the idea of motor voter. More than a year ago, I promised as President that I would sign H.R. 2 and fight for its passage. I'm pleased to be able to keep the promise today that I made on this Rock the Vote card which still has my signature back in New Hampshire.

I also want to point out that all the President does is lobby for and sign laws. If the Congress doesn't pass them, they don't get passed. The Rock the Vote card that I signed here says, "Why don't politicians want you to vote?" Well, there are a lot of Members of the Congress here from both parties who do want you to vote, and I want to thank not only those on the platform here but all of those out in the audience who, after all, passed this bill into law. It was their votes that made this day possible.

This bill in its enactment is a sign of a new vibrancy in our democracy. With all the challenges and difficulties, with the years of accumulated economic problems we face, with all the divisions among our people, there is a new determination to make progress. You can see it in many ways: Voter participation was up in November, and after the election it didn't stop. Here at the White House, mail has climbed to unprecedented levels. After I had been in office 14 weeks, the White House had received more mail than was received in all of 1992. We have had the switchboards jammed, the E-mail system full. And if you haven't gotten an answer to your letter, we're working on it. [*Laughter*]

This country is pulsing with the power of individual citizens' ideas in their determination to get something done. The legislators who worked so hard to adopt this bill, the organizations that gave themselves so completely to its endeavor, the young people, the activists, MTV, all of them tapped a powerful current of energy that is still flowing in this country.

The Congress has responded in other ways: the United States Senate passing just a few days ago a lobbying bill requiring registration by all lobbyists and requiring the disclosure of lobbyists' spending on Members of Congress is an example of that. The campaign finance reform which has been presented, dramatically trying to lower the costs of campaigns and reduce the influence of special interest groups, is an example of that.

The current of reform is moving in this country. And those of you who helped to bring this bill to pass can take a large share of credit not only for this bill but for the general movement and energy and involvement and determination of all of our fellow citizens. It was never right to sit on the sidelines of our democracy. And now with motor voter, there will be fewer and fewer excuses for anyone to do so.

Let us remember this in closing: Voting is an empty promise unless people vote. Now there is no longer the excuse of the difficulty of registration. It is the right of every American to vote. It is also the responsibility of every American to vote. We have taken an important step this morning to protect that right. And I want to challenge Joel and all the young people who did so much to register voters for the last election, and all of you who did so much to bring this voting rights bill to law and all the ones that preceded it, to make sure now that

we keep the rights alive by making sure that the responsibility to exercise it is exercised by every eligible American.

When we leave here today, we ought to say: This voting rights bill and the others will not be in vain. Every year from now on, we're going to have more registered voters and more people voting. We're going to make the system work. The law empowers us to do it. It's now up to us to assume the responsibility to see that it gets done.

Thank you very much.

NOTE: The President spoke at 11:32 a.m. on the South Lawn at the White House. He was introduced by Joel Shulkin, University of New Hampshire junior who was instrumental in achieving reform of that State's voter registration laws. H.R. 2, approved May 20, was assigned Public Law No. 103–31.

Exchange With Reporters on the Economic Program
May 20, 1993

Q. Mr. President, can you talk to us?

Q. Can you accept Senator Boren's entitlement cuts?

Q. What's your reaction to Senator Boren's compromise with Danforth?

The President. Well, my first reaction was that it was a huge shift in lowering taxes on people with incomes above $100,000 and hurting people, both elderly people and working people just barely above the poverty line. It's basically a $40 billion shift away from wealthy Americans right onto people just above the poverty line, the elderly and the working poor. So I don't support that. I think that's a mistake.

Q. Would you rule out that kind of compromise to get rid of the energy tax?

The President. I think that that is not a good thing to do if you read the details of it. Obviously, the main purpose of some of them is to do away with the Btu tax, but the mechanics shift over $40 billion away from people with incomes above $135,000 down to elderly and working people just barely above the poverty line. I don't think that's good. There is also

another provision which, if it's implemented in the way they propose, would continue to shift health care costs onto private citizens and private employers, which would hurt the economy and hurt jobs. So those are the two things which concern me.

Otherwise, I'm glad to have people talking and coming up with new ideas. But those are bad things.

Q. [*Inaudible*]—have you essentially heard enough——

The President. I can just tell you what—I've given you my answer. Look, we had 12 years where we made this economy more unequal and unfair. And to move $40 billion off of upper income people to people barely above the poverty line, it seems to me, is not a good way to go.

NOTE: The exchange began at 12:50 p.m. on the South Lawn at the White House. A tape was not available for verification of the content of this exchange.

Remarks on Cuban Independence Day
May 20, 1993

Before I say anything else, I want to acknowledge the presence here of some very special friends of mine, Jorge Perez, Jorge Bolano, and Willie Braceras, who helped me in Miami last year when I hardly knew anyone who lived in south Florida and when I needed to learn a lot about the issues affecting Cuban-Americans. I want to say a special word of thanks, too, to Simon Ferro who helped me to organize this event.

We join all Cubans today in celebrating this, the 91st anniversary of Cuban independence. Just as Cubans struggled for independence nearly a century ago today, a new generation of Cubans in our country and our time are struggling for freedom and democracy. And the American people stand by them and their brothers and sisters in Cuba as they struggle for freedom and democracy.

The people of Cuba deserve to be free and to determine their own future through free elections. They deserve to be free of political abuse and dictatorship. Our administration seeks a rapid and peaceful transition to democracy so that all Cubans can enjoy the fruits of freedom as Cuban-Americans do today. That is why, last year, I was proud to join in supporting the Cuban Democracy Act and why as President I still support it.

I also want to recognize the accomplishments here in the United States of more than one million Cuban-Americans for all they have done not only to rebuild their lives and the lives of their families but to make America a richer, stronger country through what they have done. As I look out on you and I see the great community you represent, I see a real mirror of the American dream. Like others from all over the world you came to our country, or you or your grandparents or parents did, fleeing from oppression, looking for a better life. America offered, in some way, all of us or our ancestors the gift of freedom and opportunity if we would but seize it and exercise it responsibly.

When you came to America, you rolled up your sleeves; you went to work. Many of you work from dawn to dusk, or some of you had to work from dusk to dawn. You were resourceful and talented. You started businesses, entered the ranks of our legal and medical and other professionals. You sent people to Congress and others became artists and athletes and entertainers. You helped to transform the economy of southern Florida so that it now produces more than all of Cuba does under Castro's communism. You've produced musicians like Gloria Estefan, Arturo Sandoval, Celia Cruz, Paquito Rivero; writers, like Herberto Padilla, Liz Balmaseda, Christiana Garcia; prominent citizens like Ramon and Polita Grau, Bishop Augustin Roman, Josefina Carbonell, Orestes Lorenzo; political leaders—and we have in Congress now three Cuban-Americans—Bob Menendez, Ileana Ros-Lehtinen, and Lincoln Diaz-Balart; business leaders, like the distinguished leader of Coca Cola, Roberto Guizueta, and Marcelino Miyares; and educators, like Eduardo Padron. I know you have never forgotten Cuba, any of you, but you have made America a much better place in which to live. And as President of this country, I thank you on this Cuban Independence Day not only for your continuing dreams for the independence of your homeland but your continuing additions to the vitality of the independence and freedom of the United States.

I'd also like to make one final remark. Freedom carries with it not only liberties but responsibilities. And when we neglect our responsibilities as a people, our freedoms erode. That has happened to us in significant measure here in the United States as we have seen, over the last 12 years, our national debt go from $1 to $4 trillion, while our investment in the future and our ability to compete in many areas has declined. I believe I was elected to try to turn that around. I'm doing the best I can to achieve those goals. I hope that all of you will support the efforts that this administration is making to bring our deficit down, to invest in education and technology in the future, and to gain control of our economic destiny again. It can no longer be in the hands of others because we don't have the discipline to control our own direction. I'm very concerned that in the days and weeks ahead the easy path may once again be taken.

Today I heard people talking about an alternative budget that sounded so good. It said less taxes and more spending cuts. Who in the world could be against that? No one. Except when you strip it away there are two things that ought to concern you as Americans first, and second, many of you as business people who have your own health insurance. I'd like to point out what happens when you get into this. Point number one, this so-called alternative proposal today takes $40 billion in tax breaks that it gives to people with incomes above $135,000 and imposes $40 billion in extra burdens on the elderly and working people just above the poverty line. It sounds great to call one a tax cut and the other to call a budget cut, but when you strip all the rhetoric away there's $40 billion worth of burdens on people just above the poverty line and $40 billion less on those of us like me who can afford to do a little more for our country.

The other thing that this alternative budget today presented was a so-called cap on entitlements. Well, in American terms that means one thing: We're going to try to control health care costs. Who could be against that? The problem is that in this proposal we would only control the Government's health care costs. What happens if that happens? If you have private insurance, you know what's happened, you've been paying more than your fair share because if you have health insurance you have to pay for the people who don't have any insurance when they show up and get health care, and they're not paid for, and you have to pay because your Government does not reimburse Medicare and Medicaid at appropriate levels. So if we control the costs of Medicare and Medicaid but we don't reform the health insurance system, that will force the doctors and the hospitals and the

health care providers of this country to explode your health insurance premiums even more in the years ahead than you've experienced in the last 12 years. And that's wrong.

I say let's do it right. Let's control health care costs by doing it for the whole system, reforming the American health care system and reforming the American budget and moving this country forward in a fair and balanced way.

Thank you, and God bless you all.

Now wait a minute, I want to introduce the First Lady for a moment, and let her introduce our wonderful Cuban-American sister-in-law and my brother-in-law, her brother.

[*At this point, Hillary Clinton welcomed participants and introduced Hugh and Maria Rodham.*]

I want to close by acknowledging, in general, the presence in the audience of several members of the Congressional Hispanic Caucus who are not Cuban-Americans but who are here, and other Members of Congress who are here. Could we have all the Members of Congress raise your hand. Senator Connie Mack over there from Florida, thank you for coming. Come on up, Robert. Here's a guy who came from the farthest away. Come up, Bill. Okay, all the Members of Congress come up here. We'll give you a little publicity here.

NOTE: The President spoke at 5:05 p.m. in the Rose Garden at the White House. In his remarks, he referred to Jorge Perez, president and CEO, Related Group; Jorge L. Bolanos, president, Nova Home Health Corp.; Wilfrido Braceras, president, Med-Care Home Health Agency; and Simon Ferro, attorney, Beckers & Poliakoffa, and former Chair of the Florida Democratic Party.

Message to the Senate Transmitting the Mexico-United States Taxation Convention
May 20, 1993

To the Senate of the United States:

I transmit herewith for Senate advice and consent to ratification the Convention Between the Government of the United States of America and the Government of the United Mexican States for the Avoidance of Double Taxation

and the Prevention of Fiscal Evasion with Respect to Taxes on Income, together with a related Protocol, signed at Washington on September 18, 1992. Also transmitted for the information of the Senate is the report of the Department of State with respect to the Convention.

The income tax Convention, the first between the two countries, is intended to reduce the distortions (double taxation or excessive taxation) that can arise when two countries tax the same income, thereby enabling United States firms to compete on a more equitable basis in Mexico and enhancing the attractiveness of the United States to Mexican investors. The Convention is generally based on the Model Treaty of the Organization for Economic Cooperation and Development and recent income tax conventions of both parties.

I recommend that the Senate give early and favorable consideration to the Convention and related Protocol and give its advice and consent to ratification.

WILLIAM J. CLINTON

The White House,
May 20, 1993.

Message to the Congress Transmitting the Report of the Corporation for Public Broadcasting
May 20, 1993

To the Congress of the United States:

In accordance with the Communications Act of 1934, as amended (47 U.S.C. 396(i)), I transmit herewith the Annual Report of the Corporation for Public Broadcasting for Fiscal Year 1992 and the Inventory of the Federal Funds Distributed to Public Telecommunications Entities by Federal Departments and Agencies: Fiscal Year 1992.

WILLIAM J. CLINTON

The White House,
May 20, 1993.

Statement on the Death of Four Marines in the VH–60 Helicopter Crash
May 20, 1993

I am greatly saddened by the news of the death of four Marine servicemen in the helicopter crash yesterday. Hillary's and my thoughts and prayers are with the loved ones of these dedicated airmen. I am sure I speak for all Americans in expressing our Nation's deepest condolences.

Appointment for Members of the President's Commission on White House Fellowships
May 20, 1993

The President appointed 37 members of the President's Commission on White House Fellowships today, including Olympic gold medalist Edwin Moses, chief U.S. district court judge Jose Cabranes, astronaut Sally Ride, actress Cecily Tyson, Maj. Gen. Wesley Clark, and Hawaii Governor John Waihee. The Commission will be chaired by Nancy Bekavac, the president of Scripps College.

The Commission on White House Fellowships provides an opportunity for a select group of men and women to spend a year early in their careers serving as paid assistants to Cabinet-level officials, members of the President's staff, or in the Office of the Vice President. Alumni of the program include the Chairman of the Joint

711

Chiefs, General Colin Powell, and Housing and Urban Development Secretary Henry Cisneros.

"This Commission is comprised of some of the brightest, most talented, and most accomplished people in the country," said the President. "I am confident that they will apply the criteria of achievement, leadership, and promise to select an outstanding group of fellows. I am especially pleased to note the bipartisan nature of this group, which retains several members appointed by my predecessor."

This weekend the Commission will convene in Baltimore to select the 1993–94 class of White House fellows. Approximately 1,000 people applied for the class, and the Commission will choose about 15 fellows from among the 35 who have been chosen as national finalists.

The Commission members are:

Nancy Y. Bekavac (Chair), Claremont, CA: president, Scripps College

Frederick S. Benson III, Washington, DC: vice president, Weyerhaeuser Co.

Marjorie Benton, Evanston, IL: president, Chaplin Hall Center for Children at the University of Chicago

Michael Beschloss, Washington, DC: author and historian

Dr. James E. Bostic, Jr., Atlanta, GA: group vice president, communication papers, Georgia Pacific Corp.

Hon. Jose E. Cabranes, New Haven, CT: chief U.S. district judge, District of Connecticut

Julius L. Chambers, Durham, NC: chancellor, North Carolina Central University; former director-counsel, NAACP Legal Defense and Education Fund

Maj. Gen. Wesley Kanne Clark, Fort Hood, TX: commanding general, 1st Cavalry Division

Clive S. Cummis, West Orange, NJ: chairman, Sills Cummis Zuckerman Radin Tischman Epstein & Gross

Ronald R. Davenport, Pittsburgh, PA: chairman, Sheridan Broadcasting Corp.

Adela de la Torre, Long Beach, CA: economist and chair of the department of Chicano and Latino Studies, California State University, Long Beach

Dr. Anne Cohn Donnelly, Chicago, IL: executive director, National Committee for the Prevention of Child Abuse

Jeri A. Eckhart, McLean, VA: president, Eck-

hart & Co.; president of White House Fellows Foundation and Alumni Association

Carolyn Forrest, Detroit, MI: international vice president, United Auto Workers

Pauline Gore, Carthage, TN: member and managing partner, Peabody Rivlin & Gore; mother of Vice President Gore

Antonia Hernandez, Los Angeles, CA: president and general counsel, Mexican-American Legal Defense and Education Fund

Robert L. Kagen, M.D., Fort Lauderdale, FL: medical director, MRI Scan Center

Hon. James B. King, Ludlow, MA: Director, U.S. Office of Personnel Management

Victor A. Kovner, New York, NY: partner, Lankenau Kovner & Kurtz; former corporation counsel of the city of New York

Robert M. McGee, Bethesda, MD: president, Occidental International Corp.

Dana Mead, Houston, TX: president and chief operating officer, Tenneco, Inc.

Arthur Mitchell, New York, NY: artistic director, Dance Theatre of Harlem

Edwin C. Moses, Laguna Hills, CA: Olympic gold medalist

Faylene Curtis Owen, East Lansing, MI: president and CEO, Mica Consulting Corp.

Jan O. Piercy, Chicago, IL: Deputy Director of Presidential Personnel

Hon. Roger B. Porter, McLean, VA: professor of government and business, Harvard University; Domestic Policy Aide to Presidents Ford, Reagan, and Bush

Professor George E. Reedy, Milwaukee, WI: College of Communications, Marquette University; Press Secretary to President Johnson

Sally K. Ride, Ph.D., La Jolla, CA: professor of physics, University of California at San Diego; former NASA astronaut

Charles T. Royer, Cambridge, MA: director, Institute of Politics, JFK School of Government; former Mayor of Seattle

John Saxon, Birmingham, AL: partner, Cooper, Mitch, Crawford, Kuykendall & Whatley; former counsel to U.S. Senate Select Committee on Ethics, and special counsel to the U.S. Senate Armed Services Committee

Max Starkloff, St. Louis, MO: president, Paraquad, Inc.

Mary Steenburgen, Ojai, CA: actress

Elizabeth Guest Stevens, Washington, DC: editor-at-large, Random House Publishing

Hon. Stansfield Turner, McLean, VA: admiral, U.S. Navy (Ret.); former Director of Central Intelligence

Cicely Tyson, New York, NY: actress

Hon. John David Waihee, Honolulu, HI: Governor of Hawaii

Hon. Robert Yazzie, Window Rock, AZ: chief justice, Navajo Nation

Appointment for the National Transportation Safety Board
May 20, 1993

The President today named Jim Hall, a top aide to Tennessee Senator Harlan Mathews, to be a member of the National Transportation Safety Board.

"Jim Hall has had a distinguished career in Government and in the private sector," said the President. "I am very glad to be appointing him to this Board today."

NOTE: A biography of the appointee was made available by the Office of the Press Secretary.

Statement by the Press Secretary on the President's Meeting With President Askar Akayev of Kyrgyzstan
May 20, 1993

The President and the Vice President met today at the White House with President Askar Akayev of Kyrgyzstan. The President welcomed the Kyrgyz leader, noting his bold support of human rights, democracy, and market reform in the Kyrgyz Republic. During their talks, the President and Vice President discussed a wide range of issues of mutual concern with President Akayev and welcomed the expansion of bilateral ties between our two countries.

The U.S. remains committed to assisting the Kyrgyz Republic in its difficult transition to a democratic and market-oriented system. The President and Vice President congratulated the Kyrgyz leader for being the first of the new independent states of the former Soviet Union to conclude a stand-by agreement with the International Monetary Fund to promote financial stabilization. They singled out Kyrgyzstan as a model for the other new independent states, praising President Akayev for his government's bold pursuit of macroeconomic stabilization and democratic reform.

Exchange With Reporters on Bosnia
May 21, 1993

Q. Mr. President, have you reached agreement with the Russians on a Bosnia policy?

The President. Well, Secretary Christopher is talking to Foreign Minister Kozyrev today, and we will try to reach an agreement about what we do next. As you know, the United States is skeptical that we'll be able to satisfactorily resolve this within the framework that has been proposed, but we do want to work with our allies. And we're trying our best to reach a joint position, and I hope we can do it.

Q. Are you still ruling out safe havens?

The President. Well, I don't want to see the United States get in a position where we are recreating Northern Ireland or Lebanon or Cyprus or anything else. There may be some potential down the road for something to be done in connection with the peacekeeping operation, but I think it's something we have to be very skeptical about. We don't want our people in there basically in a shooting gallery.

Q. [Inaudible]—the issue, though, for now of the land the Serbs have grabbed by force in favor of the idea of this containment?

The President. I will say what I said from the very beginning. Our fundamental interests here, the United States interests, are two. We want the conflict to be contained, and we want the slaughter and the ethnic cleansing to stop.

We believe in order to get that done ultimately there will have to be some reasonable borders, some political solution to this which has a reasonable territorial component. And we'll just have to see what happens over the next few weeks.

NOTE: The exchange began at 10:15 a.m. in the Cabinet Room at the White House, prior to a Cabinet meeting. A tape was not available for verification of the content of this exchange.

Exchange With Reporters Prior to Discussions With President Glafcos Clerides of Cyprus
May 21, 1993

Cyprus

Q. Mr. President, is the United States willing to be a guarantor for Cyprus?

The President. Well, we want to do what we can to promote a good agreement there, and we're going to be actively involved in working toward a peaceful settlement. The talks are just about to start again, and I don't think I should say or do anything which would disrupt them. But I'm glad to have the President here. I really appreciate the attitude he's taken. And I think that we have the best chance we've had in quite a long while to have a peaceful, successful conclusion to these talks.

White House Travel Office

Q. Mr. President, do you think that you have at least the appearance of a problem in firing seven people, five of them apparently without cause, and replacing them with a relative and a major campaign contributor?

The President. Well, I think, first of all, you ought to talk to my staff people who made those decisions. We reviewed the operation of every part of the White House. There was an audit, a review audit by Peat Marwick. It is my understanding that the decision was made based on striving to end inefficiency and mismanagement. And I believe the very first chartered plane flight coming out tomorrow under the new order of things is going to save about 25 percent over the old policy. And we're going to save the taxpayers money and save the press money, something I heard mentioned at the last press

dinner.

So I think what they're trying to do is right. If you have any particular questions about what they did, I would refer you to the people who made the decisions.

Q. Mr. President, Senator Bond has written you a letter saying that there's a pattern of firing experienced public servants and replacing them with young political appointees.

The President. I ask that you look at the facts. Is he defending the practices? Are you defending the practices? We now have a report on this. Do you think it's fine to have no-bid plane rides? At the press dinner there was a complaint about the costs of these plane rides to the press. The very first time in the new regime we go to a competitive bidding, modern system, anything that you would expect done in any sort of private company, and there's a 25 percent savings. Look at the facts, evaluate the facts, and draw your own conclusions.

Q. [Inaudible]—on this issue and the haircut issue?

The President. Not for me. That's what we've got a first amendment for. All I know is the taxpayers save money and the press saves money.

[*At this point, one group of reporters left the room, and another group entered.*]

Cyprus

Q. Mr. President, do you see any room for a direct U.S. involvement in the Cyprus issue?

The President. The President is just about to

start another round of talks, and I don't think I should prejudge the talks. But I have assured him that the United States wants to be active and constructive. And I think we have a reasonable chance to see a successful conclusion of these talks, perhaps the best chance in a long time, not because of me but because of where the parties are and the leadership that will be exercised. And the United States, if we can be helpful, we want to be. But I don't think we should be specific. I think we should let whatever happens come out of these talks and obviously be generated from the parties themselves.

Q. Is your administration prepared to provide some type of guarantee, assurances, resolutions, Mr. President?

The President. Let's see what comes out of the talks and what we're asked to do. Again, I want to be supportive of the process. And I think that if we're supportive of the process, then we're more likely to get a good result. I don't think I should prejudge it or anything we might be asked to do.

NOTE: The exchange began at 5:50 p.m. in the Oval Office at the White House. A tape was not available for verification of the content of this exchange.

Letter to Congressional Leaders Reporting on Iraq's Compliance With United Nations Security Council Resolutions
May 21, 1993

Dear Mr. Speaker: (*Dear Mr. President:*)

Consistent with the Authorization for Use of Military Force Against Iraq Resolution (Public Law 102–1), and as part of my effort to keep the Congress fully informed, I am reporting on the status of efforts to obtain Iraq's compliance with the resolutions adopted by the U.N. Security Council.

My Administration insists on full Iraqi compliance with all U.N. Security Council resolutions. We support Iraqi territorial integrity and will continue to support international efforts designed to ensure that the Iraqi regime does not threaten international peace and security and that it stops the repression of its own people. We continue to work to ensure the integrity of the U.N. sanctions regime, which is the best means to promote Iraqi compliance.

In accordance with U.N. Security Council Resolution 687, the U.N. Special Commission on Iraq (UNSCOM) and the International Atomic Energy Agency (IAEA) have conducted four inspections of Iraq's weapons of mass destruction (WMD) programs since the events described in my last report. Three teams remained in Iraq conducting routine inspection activities: a group at Al Muthanna, where the destruction of chemical munitions continues; a team that is undertaking medium-to-long-term monitoring of missile research and development facilities; and an aerial inspection team.

Ongoing inspections reveal that Iraq still is not complying with applicable Security Council resolutions. In March, UNSCOM #52/IAEA #18 concluded that, of the 242 machine tools at the Hatteen Establishment, a large number should have been—but were not—included in Iraq's December 1991 declaration to the Security Council. U.N. Security Council Resolution 687 required Iraq to provide a comprehensive declaration in April 1991. The IAEA is now deciding what steps should be taken.

Iraqi officials have also balked at moving chemical weapon precursors and associated equipment to Al Muthanna for destruction, despite express instructions from UNSCOM head Rolf Ekeus. Ekeus has given Iraq until May 31 to comply, after which further steps may be necessary.

In addition, Iraq has refused to give details concerning suppliers for its WMD programs, although there have been repeated inquiries. Iraq has continued its refusal to accept a long-term monitoring regime for Iraq's WMD infrastructure. The international community must insist on such long-term monitoring as called for in U.N. Security Council Resolution 715.

United Nations vehicles in Iraq are regularly vandalized, and inspectors' personal property is often stolen. Iraqi officials should take steps to improve the hostile environment, which the U.N. Sanctions Committee has noted is not in accordance with Iraq's obligations. Instead of taking appropriate action, on March 10 Iraqi officials alleged that information from U.N. U2 aircraft had been given to Israel for use in an attempt on Saddam Hussein's life. Iraq called for the end of U2 flights based on this assertion, which is not credible but may be designed to create resentment toward U.N. personnel in Iraq. The flights continue.

I said in my last report that the United States and our allies will not shrink from the use of force in accordance with Security Council resolutions. On two occasions since my last report, force has been necessary. On April 9, an Iraqi antiaircraft site tracked and engaged four U.S. aircraft monitoring Iraqi compliance in the no-fly zone established north of the 36th parallel. Two U.S. aircraft responded by dropping cluster bombs on the target; the site has not since attempted to engage U.S. or Coalition aircraft. On April 18, two Iraqi antiaircraft sites aggressively tracked and illuminated U.S. aircraft monitoring Iraqi compliance with the no-fly zone south of the 32d parallel. One plane fired a missile at one site, which was hit; no electronic emissions have since been detected from either site.

The "no-fly zones" over northern and southern Iraq monitor Iraq's compliance with Security Council Resolutions 687 and 688. Over the last 2 years, the northern no-fly zone has deterred Iraq from a major military offensive against the Kurdish and other inhabitants of the north. Since the no-fly zone was established in southern Iraq, Iraq's use of aircraft in aggression against its population in the region has stopped, as have large-scale troop movements. Nevertheless, evidence continues to mount concerning the massive extent of the Iraqi Government's human rights violations, both before and after the Persian Gulf war. Max van der Stoel, Special Rapporteur to the U.N. Human Rights Commission, has recently developed a plan for the placement of human rights monitors throughout Iraq. We support his proposal and are working to see that it is implemented.

In late April, the United States announced our support for the establishment of a U.N. commission to investigate Iraqi acts of genocide, war crimes, and crimes against humanity. The Commission would prepare information for use in possible prosecution; it would also provide the international community with a thorough, impartial record of atrocities committed by Iraqi officials against the populations of Iraq and neighboring states. We are consulting with our allies on the creation of the commission. In accordance with Security Council Resolution 674, all states and organizations with substantiated information of Iraqi atrocities should provide such information to the United Nations; the United States did so earlier this year.

The International community has continued its efforts, consistent with Security Council resolutions, to alleviate suffering in Iraq. The United States is working closely with the United Nations and other organizations to provide humanitarian relief to the people of northern Iraq in the face of Iraqi Government efforts to disrupt this assistance. We continue to support new U.N. efforts to mount a relief program for persons in Baghdad and the south but must ensure that the United Nations will be able to prevent the Iraqi Government from diverting supplies.

The U.N. sanctions regime exempts medicine and requires only that the U.N. Sanctions Committee be notified of food shipments. In accordance with paragraph 20 of Resolution 867, the Committee received notices of 17 million tons of foodstuffs to be shipped to Iraq through January 1993. The Sanctions Committee also continues to consider and, when appropriate, approve requests to send to Iraq materials and supplies for essential civilian needs. The Iraqi Government, in contrast, has for months maintained a full embargo against its northern provinces and has acted to distribute humanitarian supplies only to its supporters and to the military.

The Iraqi Government has refused to sell up to $1.6 billion in oil, as is provided for in Security Council Resolutions 706 and 712. Iraq could use proceeds from such sales to purchase, under U.N. supervision, foodstuffs, medicines, materials, and supplies for essential civilian needs of its population. Iraqi authorities bear full responsibility for any suffering in Iraq that results from their refusal to implement Resolutions 706 and 712.

Eventually, proceeds from oil sales also would be used to compensate persons injured by Iraq's unlawful invasion and occupation of Kuwait. The U.N. Compensation Commission has received about 800,000 claims so far, with a total of roughly 2 million expected. The Commission's Governing Council, at its last meeting, approved the appointments of three panels, which will begin considering individuals' claims of up to $100,000. The Council also decided to allow governments until October 1, 1993, to file individual claims. The United States Government is prepared to file a fourth set of individual claims with the Commission, bringing U.S claims filed to about 1,000. The Commission's efforts will facilitate the compensation of those injured by Iraq once sufficient funds become available.

Security Council Resolution 778 permits the use of a portion of frozen Iraqi oil assets to fund crucial U.N. activities concerning Iraq, including UNSCOM, humanitarian relief, and the Compensation Commission. (The funds will be repaid, with interest, from Iraqi oil revenues as soon as Iraqi oil exports resume.) Pursuant to Executive Order No. 12817, the United States is prepared to transfer up to $200 million in frozen Iraqi oil assets held in U.S. financial institutions, provided that U.S. contributions do not exceed 50 percent of the total amount contributed. The United Kingdom has recently transferred 1 million pounds sterling to the escrow account, and we have arranged the transfer of the equivalent amount. (The United States previously transferred a total of $50 million to match Saudi and Kuwaiti contributions.) We continue to encourage contributions from other countries.

Iraq has not met its obligations concerning Kuwaitis and third-country nationals it detained during the war. Kuwait has compiled over 600 files on missing individuals. Although Iraq has received this information through the International Committee of the Red Cross (ICRC), it has taken no substantive steps to cooperate fully with the ICRC, as is required by Security Council Resolution 687. Iraq continues to resist unqualified ICRC access to detention facilities in Iraq. Regional organizations have also been engaged—thus far to no avail—in trying to obtain Iraqi compliance on the issue of detainees. We continue to work for Iraqi compliance.

The United Nations has continued its technical task of demarcating the previously agreed Iraq-Kuwait border. The Iraq-Kuwait Boundary Demarcation Commission is expected to submit its final report later this month, notwithstanding Iraq's refusal to participate in the Commission's deliberations. In accordance with Security Council Resolution 806, the United Nations continues to seek the contribution of an armed battalion to the United Nations Iraq-Kuwait Observer Mission (UNIKOM), so that UNIKOM can take necessary actions to prevent violations of the border and the demilitarized zone. The United States and our allies also continue to press the Government of Iraq to return all property and equipment removed from Kuwait by Iraq.

Security Council Resolution 687 required Iraq to renounce all acts, methods, and practices of terrorism. Kuwait has recently arrested 11 people and charged them with participation in an assassination plot against President Bush. We are investigating this matter in cooperation with Kuwaiti authorities.

In late April, Vice President Gore and Secretary Christopher met with representatives of the Iraq National Congress (INC). They stressed the need for full compliance by the government in Baghdad with all Security Council resolutions regarding Iraq. They also emphasized that Iraq could be brought back into the community of civilized nations only through democracy, respect for human rights, equal treatment of its people, and adherence to basic norms of international behavior. A government representing all the people of Iraq, and which is committed to the territorial integrity and unity of Iraq, would be a stabilizing force in the Gulf region. The INC will have the support of the United States in achieving these goals.

I am grateful for the support of the Congress of our efforts.

Sincerely,

WILLIAM J. CLINTON

NOTE: Identical letters were sent to Thomas S. Foley, Speaker of the House of Representatives, and Albert Gore, Jr., President of the Senate.

Appointment for United States Holocaust Memorial Council Posts
May 21, 1993

The President today named Holocaust survivor and businessman Miles Lerman to be Chair of the United States Holocaust Memorial Council and political scientist Ruth Mandel to be the Vice Chair of the Council.

"I was deeply moved when I participated in the opening of the U.S. Holocaust Memorial Museum last month," said the President. "Miles Lerman and Ruth Mandel are charged with keeping the flame of memory alive. I have faith in their ability to do so."

NOTE: Biographies of the appointees were made available by the Office of the Press Secretary.

Appointment for Director of the National Park Service
May 21, 1993

The President announced the appointment of Roger Kennedy as the Director of the National Park Service, Department of the Interior. Kennedy is currently the Director of the Smithsonian Institution's National Museum of American History.

"There are few tasks more serious than the stewardship of our national parks," said the President. "With a record of public service dating back to World War II, Roger Kennedy is more than up to the job of safeguarding these precious resources."

NOTE: A biography of the appointee was made available by the Office of the Press Secretary.

The President's Radio Address
May 22, 1993

Good morning. For the first time in more than a decade, Washington is changing, and we've begun to break the logjam that has kept our economy from growing. We're moving away from trickle-down special interests, anti-middle-class policies, toward fairness and opportunity for all Americans.

Congress is moving our economic plan, which makes real record cuts in the deficit. After a decade of neglect and decline, it also makes carefully targeted investments to create high-skill, high-wage jobs again and to better educate and train our people to fill those jobs so that we can restore our economy now and leave a prosperous America for our children. Our plan challenges the status quo, and this is always hard to do in Washington, especially when there are tough choices involved.

For starters, we take on Government spending, beginning with a cut in the White House staff of 25 percent, a freeze in Federal pay, a reduction of 150,000 in the size of the Federal work force, and cuts in more than 200 specific spending programs, including huge entitlement programs affecting almost every special interest group. These are tough decisions, but they're the right thing to do because they move America forward.

The plan also raises taxes to bring the deficit down. Seventy-four percent of the new revenue comes from people with incomes over $100,000, just 6 percent of the American people, who got most of the tax cuts in the 1980's. The rest comes from the middle class in the form of an energy tax which will help to clean up our environment. What will it cost you? If your income is between $30,000 and $100,000, the energy tax will cost you $1 a month next year, $7 a month the year after, and between $14 and $17 a month, depending on how many kids you have, in the years after that. All the money, the cuts, and the taxes will go into a deficit reduction trust fund. There will be no taxes without the cuts.

Is it worth it? You be the judge. Millions of Americans have already refinanced their home mortgages and business loans. Lower interest rates on car loans and student loans are also coming, because the interest rates are down following our clear determination to reduce the deficit. If you're one of the Americans who has already refinanced a home loan or a business loan, if you're getting lower car loans or student loans, the chances are that this year you will save more than you will pay in 4 years under the economic program in the energy tax.

For example, if you have a $100,000 mortgage on your home at 10 percent, due to lower interest rates we're experiencing that mortgage can be refinanced at about 7.5 percent. What does that mean for you? It means $175 a month or $2,100 a year that you save in interest payments, $2,100 a year in interest savings on home loans alone, just because the interest rates have gone down since we've been working to bring the deficit down.

All told, experts estimate that if we can maintain these lower rates, we can pump another $100 billion into our economy. That means more jobs for Americans, $100 billion more spent on our families, spurring investment, raising incomes. It all creates jobs. That's a definition of a plan that will work.

When you put that with all the incentives we've given to lower taxes for families with incomes under $30,000, increases in small business expensing provisions, investment incentives for bigger businesses, real incentives for people who invest in new businesses, this means more jobs.

The plan is also fair because it asks contributions from everyone while asking the most from people who have the most and who have benefited the most from trickle-down policies. It cuts Medicare costs and some retirement benefits. It does include the energy tax. But it requires the wealthy to pay their fair share and the lion's share of the load.

When I presented the plan to Congress I said then that if the interest groups picked the plan apart the whole principle of shared contribution could be lost. Now, just days before the plan will be voted on by Congress, the opponents and the special interests are trying to get their way. Some of my opponents want to cut Social Security and tax credits to working families with incomes of under $30,000 just to get a tax cut for the rich. The big oil lobby is trying to wiggle out of its contribution to deficit reduction and force senior citizens barely above the poverty line to get lower Social Security benefits and senior citizens who are better off, who are already being asked to pay taxes on more of their income, to pay for a second time.

It's simply wrong for a powerful interest to try and opt out of this program by asking the elderly and the working poor to contribute more so they can contribute less. Making middle America pay more may be business as usual in Washington but to the rest of the Nation it must be unjust, unfair, and unacceptable.

I regret that otherwise good and responsible legislators would even consider this proposal, but I will fight it. The principles of fairness in reducing the deficit, the principle of resisting special interests and having uniform contributions from all, these must be protected to make this plan work.

And if we don't pass the package, what will happen? If we don't continue to cut the deficit, our new and carefully won credibility will crumble as a nation and interest rates will start to rise again, squeezing out the investments we need to make to grow new jobs. And if interest rates take off again, it will further increase the deficit, ultimately consuming not only ours but our children's standard of living.

We can't let this happen. We can't. We have to instead bring the deficit down, keep the interest rates down, make available some funds to invest in new technologies and in helping communities and companies and individuals hurt by defense cuts, doing those things to create jobs and make us competitive.

That's why I need you to raise your voices. Ask Congress to turn down the special interests and to preserve this program that asks fair contributions from everyone so that we can reduce the deficit and create more jobs and provide benefits to everyone.

Together we can all win. In just a few months, working together, we've tackled tough problems with new ideas. And we're stronger for it. Congress has passed laws from family leave to motor voter, long stalled by gridlock, proposals from welfare reform to national service to pay for college education to putting more police on our streets or on deck. But we have to get this economy moving.

The spirit of new hope I believe will prevail. Staying together we can make it work until there is a permanent rebirth of hope in every household across this great Nation. I need your help and so does America.

Thank you very much.

NOTE: The address was recorded at 1 p.m. on May 21 in the Oval Office at the White House for broadcast at 10:06 a.m. on May 22.

Remarks at the New Hampshire Technical College Commencement Ceremony in Stratham, New Hampshire
May 22, 1993

Thank you very much. Madam President, members of the faculty and staff, distinguished Members of Congress and other platform guests, and ladies and gentlemen, and most importantly, the members of this graduating class: To answer the president's question, I came here to address this class because you were the people that I ran for President to serve. It was your America that I hoped to make better.

I'm proud to come back to the State that 15 months ago made me the "comeback kid" in this country. [*Laughter*] On February 7, 1992, when I came to this college, the people I met here asked me about things that matter to mainstream Americans, about jobs and health care and getting the economy moving again and whether the future for our young people would be better than the present. After I finished speaking, one of your students, Greg Fuller, then asked me to come back and speak at this graduation. Stand up, Greg. And then he wrote me a letter to confirm his request. That itself was miracle enough. In 3 months and 2 weeks we had received more mail at the White House than had come in in all of 1992. There may be another letter from Greg somewhere we haven't found yet. [*Laughter*] But I'm delighted to be here.

This is the first graduation ceremony I have addressed as President, and I am told, I don't know, but it may be the first time a President has ever addressed a graduation of a technical college. But I will say this: More colleges like yours should have visits from the President because people who work hard and study hard and who have to raise children and go to work while they go to school and who are really on the cutting edge, up and down, of this economy, you are the heart and soul of our present and our future.

The world in which you—[*applause*]—your families are clapping for you. The world in which you live, to be sure, has been full of bad news here in New Hampshire for the last few years, but it's also a very exciting and challenging place. And it will be different from the world in which I grew up in two very important ways. First of all, more than ever before, Amer-

ica will be captured by the reality of the global economy. More and more of our jobs will depend on trade. And more and more of our future will depend on not only how well we are doing but how well our trading partners are doing. One of our problems today is that Europe and Japan's economies are down, so it's hard for ours to go up. More and more, our national security will depend not just on military power but on our renewal of economic strength. More and more, we'll have to find ways to cooperate as well as to compete with other countries. We'll have to find ways to preserve the global environment and still make it possible for the economies of our world to grow. That's the first thing.

The second thing is something you already know, or you wouldn't be here. We are moving very rapidly in all forms of production and service to a knowledge-based economy in which what you earn depends on what you can learn, not only what you know today but what you're capable of learning tomorrow, and in which every graduate of high school needs at least to go on to 2 years of further education and training. You know that, or you wouldn't be here.

All of you have invested your money, your time, your energy to take personal responsibility for your own lives, developing your own skills and in recognition of this new world reality. Your investment in a way is an act of faith. You know the world is knowledge-based; you know you have to do this. Now having done it, you have to have faith that there will be opportunities for you, that if you have worked hard and played by the rules, you will be rewarded.

As President I share that faith. I believe we can make our system work. I believe we can see our country once again reflect the values with which all of us were raised. I don't think any of us can ever lose sight of that. It's appropriate that I'm at this graduation, because New Hampshire taught me all these things once again. In the fall and winter of 1991 and 1992, when I spent so much time here, I literally, as we say in my part of the country, went to school with you. Two winters ago I came face to face with middle class people who had lost their jobs and their homes and their health care. I met people whose business loans had been canceled, even though they had never missed a payment in their lives. I saw people who went down to the public assistance office and began to draw welfare checks just to make their home payments to keep from putting their kids in the street, middle class people who had had jobs and never thought they'd be unemployed.

Every day when I get up in the White House and go to the Oval Office to work, I think about the people I met here and people like them all over America whose quiet courage and determination inspires me to keep fighting to restore the middle class and the fundamental strength and purpose of this country. I'll never forget people like Ron Macos, Jr., who couldn't get a job with health insurance because his little boy had open heart surgery. And when the First Lady's health care task force presents the national health care proposal in the next few weeks to the Congress, if that proposal passes, the Ron Macoses of this world will be able to keep working and raising their children in the future.

I'll never forget a young woman I met named Emily Teabold, who was a senior in high school when I met her. Her father lost his job in New Hampshire, and he spent her entire senior year in North Carolina, because that's the closest place he could find a job.

I met a man here named David Springs, who was a month away from having his pension vested when he was fired from his company because the people who owned his company sold it out in one of these leverage deals. And they bailed out with a golden parachute to a happy life and left their employees on the rocks.

I remember some stories of courage, too. I went to Clairmont and met the people who were working in the American Brush Company, trying to help revive that community. And I tried to help them find some customers for their products. I remember going to Manchester and visiting a company called Envirotote that made bags that we wound up buying all during the campaign and giving out with our little Clinton-Gore stickers on, all across the country. I saw people who were trying to make this country work again and trying to make New Hampshire a beacon of opportunity again.

Most of the people I saw, for all their hurts, never lost their hopes. And I'm here today to thank you for not losing yours, for going through this program and believing in it. Your president said something I want to reiterate. For most of the 20th century there's been a big division in our minds about what kind of learning counts and what kind of learning doesn't count as much, a big division between what is vocational and what is academic, between what is practical and what is intellectual. In the last few years really smart people realized that that's a bogus distinction and that we have seen all over the world, and especially here in America, the line drawn down between the vocational and the academic, between the practical and the intellectual. All work requires knowledge, and it's not so bad if it has a practical application. That is what you have proved here.

So here we are with you. You have done your job. You have done anything that could be asked of you. Many of you have done this at great personal sacrifice. I wonder how many of you have gotten up in the morning wondering about what you were going to do for child care that day, wondering about whether you should keep doing this given the fact that it costs money and the unemployment rate in the State's above the national average, wondering about all kinds of uncertainties. You have done it. You have done your job. You have now a right to ask what is our job: What can you expect of your country? What can you expect of your Government? What is our job? If you have been responsible, what opportunity should you be able to claim?

Our job is to try to put your values and your dreams into law and into facts. It means we have to have a new economic policy that recognizes that for 20 years, through the administrations of Democrats and Republicans alike, most working people have been working harder for lower hourly pay, one that recognizes that for a long time we have been the only advanced industrial country that didn't provide basic health care to all of our citizens, the only one that puts people in the trap of not being able to change jobs if anybody in their family has ever been sick, because they've got a preexisting condition that will cost them their health insurance if they change jobs. That's a huge handicap in a world where the average 18-year-old will change work eight times in a lifetime and where, because of global competition, most new jobs are created by small businesses that are coming into existence and going out of existence all the time.

And then, for 12 years we have seen our national debt go from $1 trillion to $4 trillion and our national investment in many things that are critical to our future go down. So we're spending less on what we should be spending money on, and costs are exploding.

You have a right to better than that. You have a right to an economic policy that puts our people first, our jobs, our technologies, our education. You have a right to an economic policy that brings this deficit down so that we are not crushed and paralyzed with it, into your children's children's lifetime, with high interest rates and a mortgaged future. You have a right to be treated fairly and to be given a chance to make it. You have a right to live in a country where everybody is given a chance to make it, which is not prejudiced against the wealthy— we'd all like to be that way—but gives those who aren't a fair chance to earn their due.

That is what you have a right to. And that is what you do not have today. We are doing our best in Washington to turn that around, to get control of the deficit, to bring it down, to invest in those things that will create more jobs, and to guarantee over the long run that we'll have jobs and incomes and health care that will justify the efforts you have made by going through this program. That is our responsibility.

I've asked the United States Congress to adopt a program that begins with spending cuts, starting with a reduction in my own staff, a reduction in the size of the Federal Government by 150,000 over the next 4 years, big cuts in the administrative budgets, and asking the Federal employees to accept a wage freeze and lower increases in later years so that we can bring the deficit down. I have asked also that more than 200 other spending programs be cut, including the entitlements that have so much special-interest support.

Second, it is clear to anyone who studies this problem that we need new revenues also to bring the deficit down. I've asked those who can best afford to pay, whose taxes went down in the 1980's, the wealthiest Americans, to pay most of what we need to raise. Over 74 percent of my tax program comes from the top 6 percent of income earners. [*Applause*] A slight clap.

I also have proposed an energy tax which most Americans will pay. It is one called a Btu tax which will help promote conservation and the use of the most clean and fuel-efficient fuels. But listen to the way it works: Because we offer income tax cuts to working families with incomes under $30,000, those will offset the impact of the energy tax. And for larger families under $25,000, there will even be a relief in the tax burden. For people with incomes above $30,000, at $40,000 and $50,000 and $60,000, here's what it costs. You're entitled to know in plain language. Next year it costs a dollar a month per family. The next year after that, $7 a month; and the next year after that, depending on the size of your family, between $14 and $17 a month. You have to decide if it's worth it to bring the deficit down.

But let me tell you, all the tax increases and the spending cuts will be put in a trust fund so that they can't be used to do anything but bring the deficit down. And we can't have the taxes without the spending cut. That's what the budget resolution that was adopted a few weeks ago means. We must cut spending. So we are going to do that, both things.

Now, is it worth it? You have to be the judge. But let me ask you just to consider this. Since November, since we made it clear that we were going to try to attack this deficit, and after the announcement had been made after the election that the deficit over the next 4 years would be over $160 billion bigger than we were told before the election, since November, long-term interest rates have dropped. Millions of Americans have already benefited by refinancing their home mortgages, refinancing business loans. Many others will benefit by lower interest rates on car loans or consumer loans or student loans. If just someone here has refinanced a home loan since November, in all probability, depending on the size of the mortgage, you will save more in 1 year than you will pay in 4 years in the energy tax. I think it is worth it to keep the interest rates down and to drive the deficit down. But you have to decide that.

There's a third way that we're trying to make some fundamental changes. Just as we stop wasting money on things we don't need, I think we do have to invest some in what we do need. A lot of you, just in order to get through this program, had to cut back on some of the things that you would like to have spent money on. A lot of you made meaningful financial sacrifices in your own family life just to get here today so you could wear the cap and gown. I know that. But you've been wise to make that decision. Because of the investments you've made in education and training, in the years ahead you'll be able to do more of the things that you gave up doing in the last 2 years. You'll be able to provide more opportunities for your children. You'll be able to build a stronger family unit with a stronger family future.

That's what we're also trying to do. This program offers dramatic increases in incentives for small businesses to invest money to become more productive and hire new people, to invest in research and development to find new products. It offers dramatic incentives to people to try to end the real estate depression that has gripped New England and southern Florida and California and many other places. It offers real incentives for people to invest in new businesses, the biggest in the history of America, for people to try their hand in starting new businesses. It offers an investment in new technologies, in defense conversion for all these people around America who have lost their jobs because of defense cutbacks. And it attempts to establish a transition from school to work so that everybody, by the time we finish this program, who graduates from high school who doesn't go to a 4-year college would at least have the clear opportunity to move right into a 2-year program like this one, so they don't lose time becoming productive and able to earn the best wages they can earn. I think that is a good investment in our future.

In other words, what I think our Government owes you is to move beyond the two dichotomies that have argued so long in Washington, in what I think is a very stale way. One says, "Well, you're out there on your own, and all we've got to do is make sure we don't spend a nickel to see the cow jump over the moon." The other says, "We'll take care of you. We can do things for you. Don't you worry about it." Neither one of those approaches is right. We can't entitle people to something that they won't work for. But neither can we turn our back on the plain responsibility of the United States to provide opportunity for people who will work for it. We have to empower people to seize what they are willing to seize. You have done your part; now we have to do ours.

I want to emphasize again, for the majority of people who do not go on to a 4-year college, it is imperative that we join the ranks of the other high-wage countries and provide a system by which 100 percent of them at least know they have the opportunity to move into a program like the one that you have been a part of. It is imperative. Why? Because just as what you earn depends on what you can learn, what America does in terms of growing jobs depends on how functional all the people in this country are. We don't have a person to waste. There ought to be twice as many people here today as there are at this graduation ceremony. And if there were, the economy of New Hampshire and the United States would be stronger as a result.

I also believe very strongly that the United States ought to make available, on terms everybody can afford, the funds that people need to borrow to finance their education to 2- or 4-year schools. And we have proposed to change the whole basis of the way the student loan program works: to lower interest rates, number one; and number two, to make available loans and then let people pay them back after they go to work and as a percentage of their income, so that people will not be discouraged from borrowing money today with the fear that they won't be able to pay it back if they get a job, especially if they get a job with a modest wage. You ought to be able to pay it back as a limited percentage of your income. It will make a huge difference.

Now, I believe these policies together will restore the sense of optimism to middle class America that we need: the idea that we can create jobs, that people who work at jobs can raise their incomes over time if they continue to improve their education and their productivity. And if we can do that and deal with the health care issue, we can restore a sense of possibility to America.

I don't pretend that this will be easy, that the progress will be uninterrupted, that nothing bad will happen. As I said at the beginning, some of what happens to us economically here in this country depends on what is happening to all these other countries around the world. A big percentage of the new jobs we've gotten in the last 5 years have come from trade. We won't get many if Europe and Japan are flat on their back.

But a lot of what happens to us depends upon what we do here. And you're entitled, having done your part, to know that your Government has done its part. It may not happen overnight. A lot of these economic trends have been developing for 20 years. The political policies that we seek to change have been developing for a dozen years. And I must say, it is much easier to tell people that I'm going to cut your taxes and spend more money on everything than to say we're going to have to raise some money and spend less money on most things.

A lot of the easy things have been done, but I want you to believe that we can do it. We have made a good beginning. Here's something that can affect you. After years of arguing, we finally passed the family leave bill that says you can get some time off when a baby is born or somebody's sick without losing your job. I signed last week the motor voter bill, which opens up the political process to easier registration, because another young student from New Hampshire got me to sign a card when I was here saying that I'd do my best to pass it if I got elected President.

But changing this economy is a hard job. It requires a lot of discipline, and it requires our patience and concentrated effort, yours and mine, over a long period of time. But we can do it. We can do it.

The work of change is never easy. But you have proved you weren't afraid to change. The average student here is 30 years old. I can remember when I was your age, a lot of people would have been embarrassed to go back to school when they're 30. Now we've got people

going back to school when they're 70. And let me tell you something: You must remain unafraid to change. You must remain unafraid to change. Many of you will have to go through retraining programs when you're in your mid- to late fifties. You should look at that as a great opportunity to live a rich and diverse and interesting life. If we can do what we should do at the national level to reward the efforts you are making, then change can be your friend and not your enemy.

The heartbreaking thing I saw in New Hampshire all during the primary season last year and in 1991 was how many people had been victimized by change. I cannot repeal the laws of change. No person can. Our common challenge is to preserve the values of work and family and community and reward for effort in the midst of all this change.

You have done your part. You should be proud of yourselves today, and you should commit yourselves to continue to work to make sure that change is your friend and that you are rewarded for the extraordinary and courageous efforts you have made.

God bless you, and good luck.

NOTE: The President spoke at 11:05 a.m. In his remarks, he referred to college president Jane Power Kilcoyne.

Remarks on Bosnia and an Exchange With Reporters in Manchester, New Hampshire
May 22, 1993

The President. First of all, I'm very pleased by the agreement that has been reached by Secretary Christopher and the foreign ministers from Russia, France, the United Kingdom, and Spain. I think it puts us back together with a common policy. I think that is a very good thing. I think it does some important work in confining the conflict to Bosnia so it doesn't spread into Macedonia and Kosovo or other places. I think that it takes a step toward ending the ethnic cleansing and slaughter by staking out the safe havens without doing what I was opposed to, which is basically agreeing that those folks were going to be in camps there. In other words, we're still pushing for a political

settlement that has reasonable land for the Bosnian Muslims. So I think it's a real step forward. I think it has a chance to do some good. I'm glad we're working together again, and I applaud all the foreign ministers for this work.

Q. You were a little skeptical yesterday after the meeting with Foreign Minister Kozyrev. Has something happened in the last 24 hours?

The President. Well, what happened was two things. Number one, the safe havens were defined in a way that was clearly designed to end the slaughter, provide safety and humanitarian aid. And number two, they're willing to use the safe havens to build on, that is to build a reasonable territorial settlement instead of just confining folks to camps forever. And finally, they also agree explicitly to leave stronger measures on the table if these fail. So I feel much better about the position than I did yesterday. I applaud Mr. Kozyrev. He's done a lot of work on this. And I will say this: President Yeltsin said to me that after the elections and after they began work on their own constitutional reform, that Russia would come back in and be a full partner in this. And he has kept his word. So we've worked together, and I feel good about it.

Q. [Inaudible]—the risk of the United States forces being drawn into a Vietnam-type quagmire that you're concerned about?

The President. No, it actually decreases that risk. You can see from the statement where we are on this. We have reaffirmed our previous agreement to protect the forces that are there working for the United Nations if they are attacked. We have said explicitly that we would talk to the government in Macedonia about the United Nations strengthening its presence there and about whether it would be advisable for us to have a small force there. We are clearly not going to get involved there either unilaterally or multilaterally in the conflict on one of the sides of one of the combatants in a civil war. That's what happened to us in those other places. So the American people should be reassured that we have limited the possibility of quagmire and strengthened the possibility of ending the ethnic cleansing and the possibility of limiting the conflict. I think this is a significant step. And we're back in harness again, which is where we ought to be. We're all working together. I'm encouraged by it.

Thank you.

NOTE: The President spoke at 5:25 p.m. at the Manchester Institute of Arts and Sciences. A tape was not available for verification of the content of these remarks.

Remarks to the National Commission to Ensure a Strong Competitive Airline Industry
May 24, 1993

Thank you very much. First of all, I want to just thank all of you for your willingness to serve. I think I should say, because of the coverage that this initial meeting is getting, that the American people should know that this is not an ordinary commission; there's only a 90-day time window. It will require an enormous sacrifice of your personal time and effort to do all the massive work that needs to be done, and I very much appreciate your willingness to do it.

I'd also like to say a special word of appreciation to the Congress because of the bipartisan nature of the support that this Commission had. We all made efforts to appoint people without regard to party and instead based upon their knowledge of this issue and their commitment to doing something about it. And I think there is a real consensus in America that the people who make airplanes and equipment and the people who run our airlines are critical to our economic future. It's a big part of our trade surplus. There are millions of people whose jobs depend upon it.

In his most recent book, "Head to Head," the economist Lester Thurow argues that there are seven major areas of technology which will produce the lion's share of the high-wage, high-growth jobs of the 21st century, at least as far as we can see into that century, that aerospace is one of those areas, and that a nation with a stake in any of these technologies gives it up only at its peril.

We have enjoyed an enormously positive position in aerospace for a long time now. But if you look at our airlines, the airlines alone have lost as much money in the last 4 years as they made in the previous 60. We have got to take a look at what that means for us. If you look at the fabulous manufacturers and suppliers that we built up, there's no question that the partnership that those manufacturers were able to develop, not simply with the private airline companies but also with the Defense Department, made the economics of what they were doing work. As we build down our defense budget at the end of the cold war, that imposes major new challenges for the airline manufacturers and for the major component parts suppliers and producers.

So these are difficult issues. There are also serious questions about international competition. What kind of competition do we face, and how can we face it in a way that is fair to the American workers and all the American people whose livelihoods depend on this?

The point I want to make to you is I think that this is one of the major issues involved in shaping our competitive position in the world. Governor Baliles and I were discussing this whole issue 10 days ago. He noted and I will repeat how remarkable it is that almost every major economic issue we face today ultimately comes down to whether we can compete and win in a global economy. And if so, what do we have to do to enable our people to do that, and what kind of partnerships do we need in the public and private sector?

This is an area, I'll say again, where I think we have a major potential for bipartisan agreement to move forward, to protect and promote an enormously significant sector of our economy. I'm very optimistic about what we can do over the long run. A lot of you around this table know more personally than do I what great difficulties we have faced in the last few years and understand there are still some tough challenges ahead. But I feel strongly about this. I think we can do it. I think we have to do it.

If you look at the whole range of challenges facing the United States, the things that I've tried to come to grips with in the last 4 months—trying to get the deficit under control, trying to develop a technology policy, trying to develop a more aggressive way of helping people adjust from the defense to a domestic economy and all the cutbacks that that involves—a lot

of that work will be substantially undermined unless we have a vibrant aerospace sector in our economy. It is critical to building a high-wage future for America not just in the States that are obviously affected, like Washington State—and we have some Members of Congress from Washington on this Committee—but throughout the United States. There's not a State, not a community in this country that won't be better off if we have a strong and vibrant aerospace economy.

Now, having said that, I want to introduce formally, for whatever remarks he might wish to make, Governor Baliles. I asked him to chair this Commission for a number of reasons. I've known him for many years; we were colleagues in the Governors' conference together. In my former life, I had the privilege to serve with about 150 Governors in the seventies, the eighties, and the nineties. If you forced me to make a list of the 10 best I served with, Jerry Baliles would certainly be on the list. He's one of the most intelligent public servants I've ever known. He also has the kind of mind that I think we need to bring to this task. He sorts out the wheat from the chaff pretty quickly, gets to the bottom line, and synthesizes issues remarkably well. I think you will enjoy working with him. I think you will be glad you had the opportunity to do it. And I believe, in no small measure because of the leadership he will bring to your work, there's a real chance that we'll all be very proud of the results that come out.

Thank you very much.

NOTE: The President spoke at 10:20 a.m. in the Indian Treaty Room at the Old Executive Office Building. In his remarks, he referred to Gerald L. Baliles, Chair of the Commission and former Governor of Virginia.

Remarks on the Small Business Administration Microloan Program
May 24, 1993

Good morning. Welcome to the White House, and thank you for coming. A year and a half ago, the Small Business Administration issued the first microloan grants. To date, SBA has

awarded 47 grants. We now more than double the program with 49 new grants. And we believe that 42,000 jobs will be created as a result. This administration is committed to helping entrepreneurs create profits and jobs, and the microloan program is integral to our strategy to make that happen.

I want to thank Senator Pressler and Senator Bumpers for their attendance here today. And I want to say a special word of praise to my State's senior Senator, Dale Bumpers, who sponsored this legislation to create the microloans, something that he learned about as a result of a community development bank operating in our home State. I am very proud of it. It was modeled on the South Shore Bank in Chicago, and when I was Governor, we worked hard to bring the bank there. We know that this concept works. And I appreciate very much the work that Senator Bumpers has done to bring this concept throughout America.

I also want to say that if the Congress, later this year, adopts our proposal for community development banks, then there will be more banks out there supporting the SBA in the work of making microloans. This is very important because an enormous percentage of the jobs in America are now being created by small business people and by people starting up their own businesses and by people who are self-employed. This is an innovative approach which opens the doors of opportunity to Americans who otherwise would find those doors closed. The program enables community-based lenders to expand their reach and to make very, very small loans to entrepreneurs who otherwise simply couldn't find a way to make their ideas real.

Many potential borrowers simply don't meet the credit standards of traditional lenders. Why? Because of a poor credit history or no track record as a borrower, they may simply not have enough collateral. In fact, SBA analysis indicates that many microloans will be made to individuals who are currently on public assistance. By encouraging entrepreneurial instincts, the program will then give them the help they need to take the first steps toward economic independence, not dependence. And in so doing, this could be a very important part of our overall welfare reform strategy to move more Americans from welfare to work.

By using community-based lenders—and some are with us today, and I want to thank all of you who are here for your commitment to this concept—this program relies on the lenders' understanding of the community and helps to empower the community with the needed resources to create jobs and growth. SBA looked

to these lenders for guidance when this program was being designed. It is the lenders' history of investing in their communities that will ensure the program's success.

Gail Miller from Dumas, Arkansas, started her pottery business, Miller's Mud Mill, 8 years ago, intent on making the money to send her sons to college and give them their shot at the American dream. Gail has had good and bad years, but she's learned that 15-hour days and 7-day weeks can produce a profit. In fact, she's had so many orders that she and her two-person staff can't keep up with the demand. Last year their inability to meet the demand cost her $90,000 in lost sales. How many business people in America would love to have that problem? Gail has found the answer, however. The Arkansas Enterprise Group, a microlender from Arkadelphia, Arkansas, knows a good thing when it sees it. Using funds they borrowed from the SBA through the microloan program, the group has granted Gail a $25,000 loan. She's going to use just under 20 percent of the money to buy a version of the machine used by major china manufacturing companies. This increased capacity for production will finally allow her to take advantage of the demand for her product. She'll use the remaining funds for a revolving line of credit.

Denise Cook used to receive welfare benefits through AFDC, but she understands that we all have a responsibility to work for self-reliance. Denise trained herself as a paralegal and put herself through school, working day and night. Eventually, she graduated with a B.A. in criminal justice. She worked for a number of different firms as a paralegal, but her strong desire for independence and a keen interest in forensic research drove her into starting her own business. Self-Help Ventures Fund in North Carolina has a peer-lending microenterprise program that requires training in business ownership, including peer counseling, as a prerequisite for the loan. After she completed the successful training period, Denise received a $500 loan to get her business off the ground. Today she provides investigative legal research to law firms and other clients.

It is exactly these kinds of creative, hard-working people that the microloan program is designed to help. Since June of 1992, the Small Business Administration had awarded about $16 million to lenders who have already made 330 loans to small businesses. Today's awards represent another $16 million. And the Small Business Administration calculates that 42,000 jobs will result.

Small business is the backbone of our economic strength. In the last 10 to 12 years, small business has created more jobs that were lost during the restructuring of the larger businesses of our country. However, about 3 years ago, the small business job engine started to slow down because of the global recession, the credit crunch here in America which we are trying to deal with, the spiraling cost of health care, and other problems. But a lot of it is simply barriers to entry because of the lack of available capital.

To preserve the vitality of small business, and increase their capacity to expand our work force, we need programs like this one. The best route to the American dream is the same route people have trod for many, many years now: through the small businesses. That's why we're expanding the microloan program today. It creates jobs, it relies on the private sector, it rewards drive and creativity.

I want to say a special word of thanks again to the Congress and especially to Senator Bumpers, the chairman of the Small Business Committee, for making this possible. I want Gail Miller to be able to send her sons to college, and this program will give her the tools, and small business men and women like her, to do exactly that.

Now I'd like to introduce two of the success stories here on the program. And I want to introduce all of them, of course: Erskine Bowles, the SBA Administrator, who has already talked; Denise Cook and Gail Miller who will speak;

Geraldine Janes, Chris and Regina Welch are also up here with us, and they may or may not want to say anything. But Denise and Gail have agreed to speak, so I'd like to call first Denise Cook and then Gail Miller. Let's give them a hand. [*Applause*]

[*At this point, Ms. Cook and Ms. Miller discussed their experiences.*]

I want to thank all of you here who are lenders, who have worked on these programs. The folks up here on this platform are the kind of people I ran for President to try to help. And I am deeply moved by what we have seen today. It kind of reinforces my belief that these programs are on the right course and that we can make a huge difference, that there are millions of people our here, literally millions, who could be employed and empowered if we had the systems in place and the people there who felt comfortable making loans and making these kinds of judgments and understood what had to be done.

And I thank all of you for being part of a genuine American experiment. I wish you well. I ask you to redouble your efforts. We'll redouble ours, and I know the Congress will make sure that we get what we need to make these programs succeed. I thank you all. And I thank you, Senator Bumpers, Senator Pressler, for being here. We're adjourned. Thank you very much.

NOTE: The President spoke at 11:05 a.m. in the Rose Garden at the White House. In his remarks, he referred to small business owners Geraldine Janes and Chris and Regina Welch.

Exchange With Reporters Prior to Discussions With President Richard von Weizsäcker of Germany
May 24, 1993

Bosnia

Q. Mr. President, have you been surprised or disappointed by the reaction in Bosnia and Serbia——

The President. You mean, the opposition to it?

Q. The opposition and the initial support from Mr. Karadzic.

The President. No, it's about like I expected it to be.

Q. [*Inaudible*]—U.N. observers into Serbian territory, how does that complicate things?

The President. I don't want to say any more about it now. I want to talk to the President about it. We'll try to just absorb what has been said and make the appropriate decision. But I'm not particularly surprised by the various responses——

Q. Mr. President, do you hope this week goes better than last week?

The President. We had a good week last week. The Ways and Means Committee voted the bill out—signed the motor voter bill.

NOTE: The exchange began at 4:05 p.m. in the Oval Office at the White House. A tape was not available for verification of the content of this exchange.

Message to the Congress Transmitting District of Columbia Budget Requests
May 24, 1993

To the Congress of the United States:

In accordance with the District of Columbia Self-Government and Governmental Reorganization Act, I am transmitting the District of Columbia Government's 1994 budget request and 1993 budget supplemental request.

The District of Columbia Government has submitted a 1994 budget request for $3,389 million in 1994 that includes a Federal payment of $671.5 million, the amount authorized and requested by the Mayor and City Council. The President's recommended 1994 Federal payment level of $653 million is also included in the District's 1994 budget as an alternative level. My transmittal of the District's budget, as required by law, does not represent an endorsement of its contents.

I look forward to working with the Congress throughout the 1994 appropriation process.

WILLIAM J. CLINTON

The White House,
May 24, 1993.

Announcement of Presidential Scholars
May 24, 1993

The President joined Secretary of Education Richard Riley today in naming 141 high school seniors as 1993 Presidential scholars. The scholars, who are recognized for their achievements in academics or the arts, will visit Washington June 19–24 and will be honored at a White House ceremony where each will receive a Presidential scholar medallion.

"These young people represent the best in our country," said the President. "Through hard work and community service they have earned this prestigious award. I look forward to meeting them next month at the White House."

Final selections of the scholars were made by a 32-member Commission on Presidential Scholars chaired by New Jersey Governor Jim Florio. The Commission was appointed by President Clinton earlier this month.

The 141 winners include one young man and one young woman from each State, the District of Columbia, Puerto Rico, and from American families living abroad; 15 at-large scholars and 20 scholars in the arts. Academic scholars were selected on the basis of SAT and ACT scores, essays, school recommendations, and transcripts. Arts scholars were identified through an Arts Recognition and Talent Search program conducted by the National Foundation for Advancement in the Arts.

NOTE: A list of the scholars was made available by the Office of the Press Secretary.

Exchange With Reporters Prior to a Meeting With House Democratic Leaders
May 25, 1993

White House Travel Office

Q. Mr. President, we haven't actually been able to get your view on the dealings the White House had with the FBI on all this travel stuff. Could you tell us what your view of all that is? Was it appropriate? Did you know about it?

The President. The only thing I know is that we made a decision to save the taxpayers and the press money. That's all I know. We saved 25 percent on the first plane ride and saved the taxpayers a bunch of money. Any other questions, I'll just refer you to Mr. McLarty——

Q. Was it your decision to go around the Attorney General and have the FBI issue a very rare statement?

The President. I had nothing to do with any decision, except to try to save the taxpayers and the press money. The press has been complaining for years that they were overcharged by the way the thing was done before. The first trip out we saved 25 percent for the press, and the taxpayers saved a lot of money. That's all I know about it.

NOTE: The exchange began at 8:45 a.m. in the State Dining Room at the White House. A tape was not available for verification of the content of this exchange.

Remarks at the "Drive American Quality" Presentation
May 25, 1993

Thank you very much, Mr. Bieber, and to all of you who are here. I want to say a special word of thanks to Mr. Smith and Mr. Poling, Mr. Eaton and Secretary Brown and Secretary Reich. I see Mr. Bieber just gave Secretary Reich a nightshirt. I also want to thank all the Members of the Congress who are here and for their support of the auto industry in this country.

I grew up as a boy, starting from the time I was about 6 years old, in the back of a Buick dealership. I have been interested in the automobile business all my life. I watched with sadness when it was down, and I feel great elation now that I see it coming back. These cars are what is best about America: increasing productivity, increasing quality, and gaining market share back. The people who make them are the people who deserve our support, and this administration is determined to give it to them. Last year the auto industry production was 5.6 percent of our gross national product. In 1992, vehicle and parts manufacturing directly accounted for 4.6 percent of our manufacturing employment. During the first quarter of this year, the Big Three accounted for two out of three auto sales in the United States, with the American cars gaining market share in 1993. This did not happen by accident. It required investment, it required reorganization, it required some reductions in spending. Over the last 3 years, $73 billion have been invested by the Big Three. Since 1981, quality has dramatically improved. The number of customer-reported defects is down by 80 percent. And many of our American cars, by any quality measure, are better than their foreign competitors today. They are also more fuel-efficient and increasingly so.

Our great challenge now is to produce cars of high quality at affordable costs that are environmentally responsible and that preserve good jobs here in America for those who can compete and win. In order to do that, we have to begin by getting our house in order. In the next few days, the United States Congress will have a chance to adopt the biggest deficit-reduction package in the history of this country, one that asks wealthier Americans—who, I might add, have overwhelmingly been supportive of this—to pay most of the burden of the new taxes, which exempts lower middle income Americans from any burden and which asks the Congress to impose unprecedented cuts, including reducing the Federal work force by 150,000 over the next 4 years and cutting over 200 specific Government programs. This is a balanced program. We also invest in jobs, in technology, and education and training. If we can get our house in order, if we can bring our deficit under control, reduce it, make some room for targeted investments in jobs and people, we can turn this country around.

I think that the auto industry has showed us what it takes. You've seen reduction in spending, you've seen painful cuts, you've seen dramatic increases in investment, you've seen American workers not just working harder but smarter, and you have seen years and years and

years of disciplined effort rewarded by something 5 years ago or 6 years ago most people would tell you would never happen: American-made cars winning the quality race and regaining market share. That's what we're going to do with our country.

Thank you and bless you all.

NOTE: The President spoke at 1:55 p.m. at the National Air and Space Museum. In his remarks, he referred to Owen Bieber, president, United Auto Workers; John F. Smith, Jr., president, General Motors Corp.; Harold A. Poling, chairman and chief executive officer, Ford Motor Co.; Robert J. Eaton, chairman and chief executive officer, Chrysler Corp.

Exchange With Reporters on the Economic Program
May 25, 1993

Q. Mr. President, is the House going to pass your tax bill?

The President. I think they're going to pass the budget bill, yes, which has a lot of cuts in it, and it also has some good things for these folks, good for manufacturing, good for small

business. Good bill.

NOTE: The exchange began at 2 p.m. at the National Air and Space Museum. A tape was not available for verification of the content of this exchange.

Remarks on Signing the Older Americans Month Proclamation
May 25, 1993

Thank you very much, Senator Pryor and Secretary Shalala. Let me also acknowledge in the audience the presence of Senator Bill Cohen from Maine, Congressman Marty Martinez, and Congressman William Hughes. We're glad to see them. And I also want to pay a special word of respect to my good friend, our Vice President's mother, Mrs. Pauline Gore. She's a little too young to be here, but I'm glad to see her here anyway.

You know, Senator Pryor told that story about the 100-year-old man who had been against all the changes he'd seen. One of the things I think that age does for all of us is it gives us the ability to laugh at things that once we would have cried about, something I've needed more

and more as I've taken this job. [*Laughter*]

But David told this story. It reminded me, there's a town in Arkansas that has my name, called Clinton, and I was invited there once to a nursing home to celebrate the 107th birthday of this lovely woman. And I showed up, and she had a beautiful pink dress on. And I said, "Gosh, you're pretty today." And she said, "Don't you go flirting with me. I'm not looking for a husband." [*Laughter*] And so I said, "Well, I appreciate that." I said, "You know, I already have one wife. Don't you think that's enough?" And she said, "I guess so, hard as times are." [*Laughter*] Sometimes I think about that.

This is the 30th anniversary of Older Americans Month. And I can't think of anybody I'd rather be up here with than Secretary Shalala or with Senator Pryor. When I was attorney general and David Pryor was Governor, I just reminded him up here, 18 years ago we sponsored our State's first conference on long-term care and how to provide long-term care for senior citizens. Well, we're still chipping away at it, but I just want you to know at least we've got some credentials for being in the vineyards.

We are committed to keeping faith with the senior citizens of this country, and we are trying to fulfill that commitment in two very important ways that are specific to our senior citizens and one that is very important for the responsibility we all seem to feel for the future. The first is the White House Conference on Aging to discuss providing for older Americans and also for making better use of the time and talents of our senior citizens. I feel very strongly that both those things are important. Most people I know who are in their later years want to be challenged to do more, to bring to bear their energy, their experience, their judgment, and their perspective on a lot of the very thorny problems and challenges we face today. And I hope our administration can do that not only here in Washington but all across America.

I am, in that regard, proud that we have for the first time an Assistant Secretary for Aging in the Department of Health and Human Services, and I'm proud of Dr. Fernando Torres-Gil who was introduced and who received such a warm reception from you.

The second thing that we hope to do is to deal with some of the terrific health care challenges facing our senior citizens while keeping faith with the obligations we now have to maintain the integrity of Social Security. The fastest growing group of Americans are people over 80. The largest number of people I met on the campaign trail last year with really heartbreaking stories were elderly people just above the Medicaid eligibility line who had massive drug bills every month. And literally, I met people in State after State after State that made the weekly choice between food and medicine because they were just above that Medicaid eligibility line and had no way in the wide world to pay for medicine that was absolutely necessary to maintain their health.

So in this health program—I know a lot of you have already heard a speech about this from my wife, and she's gotten a whole lot better

on this subject than I have—but we are committed to a health care plan which will provide coverage for all Americans, which will lower the cost of health care, which will lower the cost of health care for our country in the years ahead—we're already spotting our competitors 35 percent of every dollar spent on health care—and which, at the same time, will begin to address the problems that I saw out there for a wider range of long-term care services and for dealing with the drug problem that our elderly people have who are not Medicaid-eligible. These are the things that we must have in a comprehensive, long-term care package.

I also want to say to you that I believe any responsible health care plan must encourage and indeed have incentives for health care maintenance and for the prevention of bad things happening. With the fastest growing group of people being people over 80, with more and more senior citizens coming into really dominant positions in our country, with the Social Security system starting in a few years to raise the retirement eligibility limit by a month a year, as all of you know, as a part of the 1983 resolution to resolve the crisis that then existed, it is absolutely imperative that we not only think about giving health care services but maintaining strong, healthy people. And that has got to be a critical part of our health care plan, and I know all of you will be out there lobbying for that. We so often strain at a gnat and swallow a camel when we don't have enough prevention and maintenance of healthy people in our health care plans and even in our own daily habits. And so I hope you will all support that.

The last thing I'd like to say is that it seems to me that those of you who represent older Americans are in a unique position, being able to have the benefit of memory, to know what is going to happen to us in the years ahead if we do not move now and move aggressively to get control of this Government deficit, to bring down our interest rates, to enable our economy to grow, to give us some more elbow room. Year-in and year-out for the last several years, my heart has gone out to Members of the Congress in both parties who have struggled to find funds for things they think needed to be funded or to just keep things going along as they are, as we become more and more consumed by an ever-growing deficit, going from $1 trillion to $4 trillion in just 12 years.

I believe, as all of you now know, that we

need to have both spending cuts and tax increases to close this deficit and to bring it down. We could all argue until the cows come home about whether every last decision has been perfectly right, but it is perfectly clear that if you don't do both, you can't get where we're going. And it is absolutely imperative that we send a clear signal not only to the financial markets but to our children and our grandchildren that we are thinking about their future, that we are not going to saddle them with so much debt that we won't be able to finance education and economic growth and the kinds of things that every generation of Americans must be free to spend money on, both private money and public funds. If we don't take that opportunity now, we will have squandered our responsibilities to those who come behind us.

You know, I think more about it with each succeeding year that my daughter grows older. I think about how it won't be so long before she and her generation will be making decisions that now we're wrestling over. We owe it to those kids and to the ones who will follow behind them to provide the freedom of movement that any great society needs to reach the challenges of that time. We today, and this Congress, every Member will tell you, those people who occupy Washington today are hamstrung by a lack of freedom of movement because we have permitted paralysis to drive this deficit up, because we have refused to deal with the health care crisis, we have refused to deal with automatic explosions and things that we could have dealt with. And the time has come to face it and face it squarely. And I hope and pray, for the sake of our children and grandchildren, we are about to do just that in the next few days in the United States of America.

I want to say one thing finally. On the tax side of this plan, 74 percent of the burden falls on the top 6 percent of income earners in America, and a lot of the rest falls on the top 20 percent of Social Security recipients whom we have asked to subject more of their income to taxation so as to avoid reducing cost of living allowances to all the Social Security recipients in the land who need that.

One of the things I think we have not said enough, and I believe most people in the Congress would admit this: We have heard very little opposition from upper income Americans to paying their fair share of taxes as long as they believe we're going to cut spending, bring the deficit down, and provide for the basic needs of this country. And to me, that's been one of the most rewarding things out there. A lot of the opposition is coming from middle class people who think they're going to pay a lot more than they are. But the people who are really going to pay and who know it, by and large, have been immensely patriotic in this last 2- or 3-month period, knowing that they have to make a contribution to securing the future.

All of you here who represent the elderly people of our country, you can reach out and embrace this effort in a way that no other generation of Americans can. This is a difficult time for the Congress, a difficult time for the country. The worst thing we can do is to walk away and do nothing and continue the perilous paralysis of the last few years. So I implore you to shoulder this. Think of our kids and grandkids. Let's move this country forward in a bipartisan and open manner.

Thank you. God bless you. And let's get on with the signing.

NOTE: The President spoke at 5:30 p.m. in the East Room at the White House. The proclamation is listed in Appendix D at the end of this volume.

Exchange With Reporters on the White House Travel Office
May 25, 1993

Q. Mr. President, are you upset by this whole Travel Office mess? And who's responsible for it, sir?

The President. Well, ultimately, anything that happens in the White House is the responsibility of the President. And whenever you've asked me a question, I've told you all I knew about it. All I knew was there was a plan to cut the size of the office, save tax dollars, save the press money. I talked to Mr. McLarty about it this morning. I said, you know, I keep reading this; I know that there is a feeling at least, based on what I've read, that someone in the White House may have done something that was inappropriate or that wasn't quite handled right or something. Mack and I talked about it today. He said he would spend some real time on and look into it, try to ascertain exactly what happened, make a full report to me, which I think is the appropriate thing to do. I simply can't tell you that I know something I don't. I literally don't know anything other than what I've told you. He's looking into it now. He's worked on it quite a bit today. And he's going to make a report to me, and then we will take appropriate steps, including saying whatever's appropriate to you.

Q. Do you think that the White House approached the FBI improperly in this case?

The President. I don't have any reason to believe that. I mean, for example, there are lots of cases where, historically, as nearly as we can determine, the White House, if something happened within the White House, might ask the FBI to look into it. So I don't know that. I don't know that. And I don't have an opinion yet. I have to wait. Mack agreed that he needed to really make sure that he had all the facts down; he needed to know exactly what had happened; he needed to report to me. I said, "Look, this is just a simple case. Let's just follow the do-right rule here, make up your own mind, get the facts, see what you think happened, let me know, and we'll tell the public." I mean, there's nothing funny going on here. We really

were just trying to save money for everybody. That was the only thing I was ever asked about personally. And I don't believe that anybody else had any other motives that I know about. And so I asked him to look into it. When we know more, we'll be glad to say more.

Q. What about Dole saying it has a tinge of Watergate?

The President. There's none of that because, you know, there's nothing like that going on. There's no—no.

Q. Don't you think——

Q. [*Inaudible*]

The President. We're on top of it. We'll——

Q. Don't you think a lot of people were hurt by the way it was handled?

The President. Well, the question is whether the people that were hurt did anything to merit it. We'll just have to see. I mean, I want to get a report, and then I will be glad to tell you whatever I know. But let me find out——

Q. [*Inaudible*]

The President. All those decisions have been made by Mack. We talked yesterday. We talked again this morning. He said, "Look, I just want to get on top of this. I'll tell you exactly what happened. I'll tell you what I think." So I'm waiting for a report. And I don't think I should say anything else until I know more.

NOTE: The exchange began at 5:43 p.m. in the East Room at the White House. A tape was not available for verification of the content of this exchange.

Message to the Congress Transmitting the Notice on Continuation of Emergency With Respect to the Federal Republic of Yugoslavia (Serbia and Montenegro)
May 25, 1993

To the Congress of the United States:

Section 202(d) of the National Emergencies Act (50 U.S.C. 1622(d)) provides for the automatic termination of a national emergency unless, prior to the anniversary date of its declaration, the President publishes in the *Federal Register* and transmits to the Congress a notice stating that the emergency is to continue in effect beyond the anniversary date. In accordance with

this provision, I have sent the enclosed notice, stating that the emergency declared with respect to the Federal Republic of Yugoslavia (Serbia and Montenegro) is to continue in effect beyond May 30, 1993, to the *Federal Register* for publication.

The circumstances that led to the declaration on May 30, 1992, of a national emergency have not been resolved. The Government of the Federal Republic of Yugoslavia (Serbia and Montenegro) continues to support groups seizing and attempting to seize territory in the Republics of Croatia and Bosnia-Hercegovina by force and violence. The actions and policies of the Government of the Federal Republic of Yugoslavia (Serbia and Montenegro) pose a continuing unusual and extraordinary threat to the national security, vital foreign policy interests, and the economy of the United States. For these reasons, I have determined that it is necessary to maintain in force the broad authorities necessary to apply economic pressure to the Government of the Federal Republic of Yugoslavia (Serbia and Montenegro) to reduce its ability to support the continuing civil strife and bloodshed in the former Yugoslavia.

WILLIAM J. CLINTON

The White House,
May 25, 1993.

NOTE: The notice is listed in Appendix D at the end of this volume.

Message to the Congress Reporting on the Federal Republic of Yugoslavia (Serbia and Montenegro)
May 25, 1993

To the Congress of the United States:

On May 30, 1992, in Executive Order No. 12808, President Bush declared a national emergency to deal with the threat to the national security, foreign policy, and economy of the United States arising from actions and policies of the Governments of Serbia and Montenegro, acting under the name of the Socialist Federal Republic of Yugoslavia or the Federal Republic of Yugoslavia, in their involvement in and support for groups attempting to seize territory in Croatia and Bosnia-Hercegovina by force and violence utilizing, in part, the forces of the so-called Yugoslav National Army (57 *FR* 23299, June 2, 1992). The present report is submitted pursuant to 50 U.S.C. 1641(c) and 1703(c). It discusses Administration actions and expenses directly related to the exercise of powers and authorities conferred by the declaration of a national emergency in Executive Order No. 12808 and to expanded sanctions against the Federal Republic of Yugoslavia (Serbia and Montenegro) (the "FRY (S/M)") contained in Executive Order No. 12810 of June 5, 1992 (57 *FR* 24347, June 9, 1992), Executive Order No. 12831 of January 15, 1993 (58 *FR* 5253, January 21, 1993), and Executive Order No. 12846 of April 26, 1993 (58 *FR* 25771, April 27, 1993).

1. Executive Order No. 12808 blocked all property and interests in property of the Governments of Serbia and Montenegro, or held in the name of the former Government of the Socialist Federal Republic of Yugoslavia or the Government of the Federal Republic of Yugoslavia, then or thereafter located in the United States or within the possession or control of U.S. persons, including their overseas branches.

Subsequently, Executive Order No. 12810 expanded U.S. actions to implement in the United States the U.N. sanctions against the FRY (S/M) adopted in United Nations Security Council Resolution No. 757 of May 30, 1992. In addition to reaffirming the blocking of FRY (S/M) Government property, this order prohibits transactions with respect to the FRY (S/M) involving imports, exports, dealing in FRY-origin property, air and sea transportation, contract performance, funds transfers, activity promoting importation or exportation or dealings in property, and official sports, scientific, technical, or cultural representation of the FRY (S/M) in the United States.

Executive Order No. 12810 exempted from trade restrictions (1) transshipments through the FRY (S/M), and (2) activities related to the United Nations Protection Force ("UNPROFOR"), the Conference on Yugoslavia, or the European Community Monitor Mission.

On January 15, 1993, President Bush issued Executive Order No. 12831 to implement new sanctions contained in United Nations Security Council Resolution No. 787 of November 16, 1992. The order revokes the exemption for transshipments through the FRY (S/M) contained in Executive Order No. 12810; prohibits transactions within the United States or by a

U.S. person relating to FRY (S/M) vessels and vessels in which a majority or controlling interest is held by a person or entity in, or operating from, the FRY (S/M), and states that all such vessels shall be considered as vessels of the FRY (S/M), regardless of the flag under which they sail. Executive Order No. 12831 also delegates discretionary authority to the Secretary of the Treasury, in consultation with the Secretary of State, to prohibit trade and financial transactions involving any areas of the former Socialist Federal Republic of Yugoslavia as to which there is inadequate assurance that such transactions will not be diverted to the benefit of the FRY (S/M).

On April 26, 1993, I issued Executive Order No. 12846 to implement in the United States the sanctions adopted in United Nations Security Council Resolution No. 820 of April 17, 1993. That resolution called on the Bosnian Serbs to accept the Vance-Owen peace plan for Bosnia-Hercegovina and, if they failed to do so by April 26, called on member states to take additional measures to tighten the embargo against the FRY (S/M) and Serbian-controlled areas of Croatia and Bosnia-Hercegovina.

Effective 12:01 a.m. e.d.t., April 26, 1993, Executive Order 12846: (1) blocks all property and interests in property of businesses organized or located in the FRY (S/M), including the property of their U.S. and other foreign subsidiaries, that are in or later come within the United States or the possession or control of U.S. persons, including their overseas branches; (2) confirms the charging to the owners or operators of property blocked under this order or Executive Orders No. 12808, No. 12810, or No. 12831 all expenses incident to the blocking and maintenance of such property, requires that such expenses be satisfied from sources other than blocked funds, and permits such property to be sold and the proceeds (after payment of expenses) placed in a blocked account; (3) orders (a) the detention pending investigation of all nonblocked vessels, aircraft, freight vehicles, rolling stock, and cargo within the United States suspected of violating United Nations Security Council Resolutions No. 713, No. 757, No. 787, or No. 820, and (b) the blocking of such conveyances or cargo if a violation is determined to have been committed, and permits the liquidation of such blocked conveyances or cargo and the placing of the proceeds into a blocked account; (4) prohibits any vessel registered in the

United States, or owned or controlled by U.S. persons, other than U.S. naval vessels, from entering the territorial waters of the FRY (S/M); and (5) prohibits U.S. persons from engaging in any transactions relating to the shipment of goods to, from, or through United Nations Protected Areas in the Republic of Croatia and areas in the Republic of Bosnia-Hercegovina under the control of Bosnian Serb forces.

Executive Order No. 12846 authorizes the Secretary of the Treasury in consultation with the Secretary of State to take such actions, and to employ all powers granted to me by the authorities cited above, as may be necessary to carry out the purposes of that order. The sanctions imposed in the order do not invalidate existing licenses or authorizations issued pursuant to Executive Orders No. 12808, No. 12810, or No. 12831 except as those licenses and authorizations may thereafter be terminated, suspended, or modified by the issuing Federal agencies, but otherwise the sanctions apply notwithstanding any preexisting contracts, international agreements, licenses, or authorizations.

2. The declaration of the national emergency on May 30, 1992, was made pursuant to the authority vested in the President by the Constitution and laws of the United States, including the International Emergency Economic Powers Act (50 U.S.C. 1701 *et seq.*), the National Emergencies Act (50 U.S.C. 1601 *et seq.*), and section 301 of title 3 of the United States Code. The emergency declaration was reported to the Congress on May 30, 1992, pursuant to section 204(b) of the International Emergency Economic Powers Act (50 U.S.C. 1703(b)). The additional sanctions set forth in Executive Orders No. 12810, No. 12831, and No. 12846 were imposed pursuant to the authority vested in the President by the Constitution and laws of the United States, including the statutes cited above, section 1114 of the Federal Aviation Act of 1958, as amended (49 U.S.C. App. 1514), and section 5 of the United Nations Participation Act of 1945, as amended (22 U.S.C. 287c).

3. Since the last report, the Office of Foreign Assets Control of the Department of the Treasury ("FAC"), in consultation with the Department of State and other Federal agencies, issued the Federal Republic of Yugoslavia (Serbia and Montenegro) Sanctions Regulations, 31 C.F.R. Part 585 (58 *FR* 13199, March 10, 1993—the "Regulations"), to implement the prohibitions contained in Executive Orders No. 12808, No.

12810, and No. 12831. A copy of the Regulations is enclosed with this report. The seven general licenses discussed in the last report were incorporated into the Regulations. The Regulations contain general licenses for certain transactions incident to: the receipt or transmission of mail and informational materials and for telecommunications transmissions between the United States and the FRY (S/M); the importation and exportation of diplomatic pouches; certain transfers of funds or other financial or economic resources for the benefit of individuals located in the FRY (S/M); the importation and exportation of household and personal effects of persons arriving from or departing to the FRY (S/M); transactions related to nonbusiness travel by U.S. persons to, from, and within the FRY (S/M); and transactions involving secondary-market trading in debt obligations originally incurred by banks organized in Slovenia, Croatia, Bosnia-Hercegovina, and Macedonia.

On January 15, 1993, FAC issued General Notice No. 2, entitled "Notification of Status of Yugoslav Entities." A copy of the notice is attached. The list is composed of government, financial, and commercial entities organized in Serbia or Montenegro and a number of foreign subsidiaries of such entities. The list is illustrative of entities covered by FAC's presumption, stated in the notice, that all entities organized or located in Serbia or Montenegro, as well as their foreign branches and subsidiaries, are controlled by the Government of the FRY (S/M) and thus subject to the blocking provisions of the Executive orders. General Notice No. 2, which includes more than 400 entities, expands and incorporates the list of 284 entities identified in General Notice No. 1 (57 *FR* 32051, July 20, 1992), noted in the previous report.

As part of a U.S.-led allied effort to tighten economic sanctions against Yugoslavia, on March 11, 1993, FAC named 25 maritime firms and 55 ships controlled by these firms as "Specially Designated Nationals" ("SDNs") of Yugoslavia. A copy of General Notice No. 3 is attached. These shipping firms and the vessels they own, manage, or operate by using foreign front companies, changing vessel names, and reflagging ships, are presumed to be owned or controlled by or to be acting on behalf of the Government of the FRY (S/M). In addition, pursuant to Executive Order No. 12846, the property within U.S. jurisdiction of these firms is blocked as direct or indirect property interests of firms organized or located in the FRY (S/M).

The FRY (S/M) has continued to operate its maritime fleet and trade in violation of the international economic sanctions mandated by United Nations Security Council Resolutions No. 757 and No. 787. Operations and activities by Yugoslav front companies, or SDNs, enable the Government of the FRY (S/M) to circumvent the international trade embargo. The effect of FAC's SDN designation is to identify agents and property of the Government of the FRY (S/M), and property of entities organized or located in the FRY (S/M), and thus to extend the applicability of the regulatory prohibitions governing transactions with the Government of the FRY (S/M) and its nationals by U.S. persons to these designated individuals and entities wherever located, irrespective of nationality or registration. U.S. persons are prohibited from engaging in any transaction involving property in which an SDN has an interest, which includes all financial and trade transactions. All SDN property within the jurisdiction of the United States (including financial assets in U.S. bank branches overseas) is blocked.

The two court cases in which the blocking authority was challenged as applied to FRY (S/M) subsidiaries and vessels in the United States remain pending at this time. In one case, the plaintiffs have challenged the application of Executive Order No. 12846, and the challenge remains to be resolved. The other case is presently pending before a U.S. Court of Appeals.

4. Over the past 6 months, the Departments of State and the Treasury have worked closely with European Community (the "EC") member states and other U.N. member nations to coordinate implementation of the sanctions against the FRY (S/M). This has included visits by assessment teams formed under the auspices of the United States, the EC, and the Conference for Security and Cooperation in Europe (the "CSCE") to states bordering on Serbia and Montenegro; deployment of CSCE sanctions assistance missions ("SAMS") to Albania, Bulgaria, Croatia, the Former Yugoslav Republic of Macedonia, Hungary, Romania, and Ukraine to assist in monitoring land and Danube River traffic; bilateral contacts between the United States and other countries with the purpose of tightening financial and trade restrictions on the FRY (S/M); and establishment of a mechanism to coordinate enforcement efforts and to exchange

technical information.

5. In accordance with licensing policy and the Regulations, FAC has exercised its authority to license certain specific transactions with respect to the FRY (S/M) that are consistent with the Security Council sanctions. During the reporting period, FAC has issued 163 specific licenses regarding transactions pertaining to the FRY (S/M) or assets it owns or controls, bringing the total as of April 30, 1993, to 426. Specific licenses have been issued for (1) payment to U.S. or third-country secured creditors, under certain narrowly defined circumstances, for pre-embargo import and export transactions; (2) for legal representation or advice to the Government of the FRY (S/M) or FRY (S/M)-controlled clients; (3) for restricted and closely monitored operations by subsidiaries of FRY (S/M)-controlled firms located in the United States; (4) for limited FRY (S/M) diplomatic representation in Washington and New York; (5) for patent, trademark and copyright protection, and maintenance transactions in the FRY (S/M) not involving payment to the FRY (S/M) Government; (6) for certain communications, news media, and travel-related transactions; (7) for the payment of crews' wages and vessel maintenance of FRY (S/M)-controlled ships blocked in the United States; (8) for the removal from the FRY (S/M) of manufactured property owned and controlled by U.S. entities; and (9) to assist the United Nations in its relief operations and the activities of the U.N. Protection Force. Pursuant to United Nations Security Council Resolutions No. 757 and No. 760, specific licenses have also been issued to authorize exportation of food, medicine, and supplies intended for humanitarian purposes in the FRY (S/M).

During the past 6 months, FAC has continued to closely monitor 15 U.S. subsidiaries of entities organized in the FRY (S/M) that were blocked as entities owned or controlled by the Government of the FRY (S/M). Treasury agents performed on-site audits and reviewed numerous reports submitted by the blocked subsidiaries. Subsequent to the issuance of Executive Order No. 12846, operating licenses issued for U.S.-located Serbian or Montenegrin subsidiaries or joint ventures were revoked and the U.S. entities closed for business.

The Board of Governors of the Federal Reserve Board and the New York State Banking Department again worked closely with FAC with regard to two Serbian banking institutions in New York that were closed on June 1, 1992. Full-time bank examiners continue to be posted in their offices to ensure that banking records are appropriately safeguarded.

During the past 6 months, U.S. financial institutions have continued to block funds transfers in which there is an interest of the Government of the FRY (S/M). Such transfers have accounted for an additional $24.5 million in blocked Yugoslav assets since the issuance of Executive Order No. 12808.

To ensure compliance with the terms of the licenses that have been issued under the program, stringent reporting requirements are imposed. Some 350 submissions were reviewed since the last report, and more than 150 compliance cases are currently open. In addition, licensed bank accounts are regularly audited by FAC compliance personnel and by cooperating auditors from other regulatory agencies.

6. Since the issuance of Executive Order No. 12810, FAC has worked closely with the U.S. Customs Service to ensure both that prohibited imports and exports (including those in which the Government of the FRY (S/M) has an interest) are identified and interdicted, and that permitted imports and exports move to their intended destination without undue delay. Violations and suspected violations of the embargo are being investigated, and appropriate enforcement actions are being taken. There are currently 39 cases under active investigation.

7. The expenses incurred by the Federal Government in the 6-month period from December 1, 1992, through May 30, 1993, that are directly attributable to the authorities conferred by the declaration of a national emergency with respect to the FRY (S/M) are estimated at $2.9 million, most of which represent wage and salary costs for Federal personnel. Personnel costs were largely centered in the Department of the Treasury (particularly in FAC and its Chief Counsel's Office and the U.S. Customs Service), the Department of State, the National Security Council, the U.S. Coast Guard, and the Department of Commerce.

8. The actions and policies of the Government of the FRY (S/M), in its involvement in and support for groups attempting to seize and hold territory in Croatia and Bosnia-Hercegovina by force and violence, continue to pose an unusual and extraordinary threat to the national security, foreign policy, and economy of the United States. The United States remains committed

to a multilateral resolution of this crisis through its actions implementing the binding resolutions of the United Nations Security Council with respect to the FRY (S/M). I shall continue to exercise the powers at my disposal to apply economic sanctions against the FRY (S/M) as long as these measures are appropriate, and will continue to report periodically to the Congress on significant developments pursuant to 50 U.S.C. 1703(c).

WILLIAM J. CLINTON

The White House,
May 25, 1993.

White House Statement on the Situation in Guatemala
May 25, 1993

The President was very disappointed to hear that President Serrano of Guatemala has suspended the Congress and courts and other democratic rights protected by the Guatemalan Constitution. This illegitimate course of action threatens to place Guatemala outside the democratic community of nations. We strongly condemn such efforts to resolve Guatemala's problems through nondemocratic means. We hope the Guatemalan leadership will reverse its course and immediately restore full constitutional democracy.

Appointment for National Railroad Passenger Corporation Posts
May 25, 1993

The President today appointed Robert Kiley, the former chairman of New York's Metropolitan Transportation Authority, and former Ohio Congressman Don Pease to the Board of Directors of the National Railroad Passenger Corporation (Amtrak). The appointments are effective immediately.

"Robert Kiley and Don Pease have both had long and distinguished careers in public service," said the President. "They both will make excellent additions to this important Board."

NOTE: Biographies of the appointees were made available by the Office of the Press Secretary.

Nomination for an Under Secretary of Commerce
May 25, 1993

The President announced his intention today to nominate Dr. Mary Lowe Good, the senior vice president of Allied-Signal, Inc., to be Under Secretary of Commerce for Technology Administration.

"One of the central challenges that we face in the 1990's is making sure that our Nation's technological capacities are developed as fully as possible," said the President. "With a distinguished record of commercial research and of involvement with national technology policy, Dr. Good has what it takes to help ensure that Government does its part to make that happen."

NOTE: A biography of the nominee was made available by the Office of the Press Secretary.

Nomination for Ambassador to Zambia
May 25, 1993

The President today announced his intention to nominate Roland Karl Kuchel to be Ambassador to Zambia. Kuchel, a career foreign service officer, is currently Assistant to the Director General of the Foreign Service.

"I am very glad to be making this nomina-

tion," said the President. "Roland Kuchel has had a long and accomplished career in the Foreign Service."

NOTE: A biography of the nominee was made available by the Office of the Press Secretary.

Remarks and an Exchange With Reporters Prior to a Meeting With the Congressional Black Caucus
May 26, 1993

Budget Proposal

The President. Let me say, what I'm trying to do is pass this program in the House. I do one step at a time. I think it's clearly, of all the things that have been presented, the fairest program. It has significant budget cuts, reduces the size of the Federal Government by 150,000, leaves some room for investment, 74 percent of the tax is paid by 6 percent of the people. It's a fair program. It will cost the average person a dollar a month next year, $7 a month the year after, $15 a month the year after for a family. And it exempts people of incomes under $30,000. It is a fair, balanced program. I'm going to try and pass it.

Q. Sir, what are you telling Members of Congress who are worried that they could lose their seats because of some of the tougher elements of this package?

The President. That all the evidence shows that the more people know about the details of the package, the more likely they are to support it. And that if it becomes a rhetorical battle where anyone says that it's tax-and-spend, well, who's for that? Nobody's for that. But the American people are for bringing this deficit down. They are for investing in jobs and technology. They are for a fairer tax system that asks everyone to pay their fair share. And they are for a system that moves people from welfare to work. This program does all those things. It is a very good program. There is no evidence that once people know the facts that they will do that.

Q. What are you going to do to make sure

they know the facts? Are you going to go on nationwide radio and TV before the House votes?

The President. I don't know that that is possible or that it will be done before the House votes. But what I have told them is that the day that the people had the most detailed knowledge of this plan was February 17th, because I went through the whole thing, chapter and verse. So nothing was hidden from the American people. It was all given out.

What has happened since then is—you know, there's a lot of static and back-and-forth. And the President can't go on television every night for that length of time, but that is clear evidence that the more people know about it the more likely they are to support it. Just today I'm going to see some more of the business executives, who will pay more in this plan, who have supported this. Yesterday, Mr. Rostenkowski listed 50 major companies who are supporting the program. We have small business people all over America who are supporting the program, realtors and others, consumer groups. So the people who know more about the program, the more you know about it the more likely you are to be for it.

Q. But isn't energy the hangup? Mr. President, isn't energy the hangup?

The President. It is a big hangup. And we're working——

Senator Boren's Proposal

Q. And how about Boren? Are you going to be able to work with him?

The President. Well, I hope so. We're working through it. I think that it is now apparent to everyone that there are only two plans on the table in the Senate and that ours is far fairer and better for the economy. I mean, the other plan reduces the tax for the oil interest in Oklahoma and elsewhere, but it does it at the expense of putting a $40 billion burden on Social Security recipients and lower income working people just above the poverty line. It also would shift massive health costs away from the Government on to private employers and employees. I don't think they're for that. So now that we've got an alternative out there, it shows you that our plan is sound and balanced. We're just going to keep working at it.

NOTE: The President spoke at 8:52 a.m. in the Old Family Dining Room at the White House. A tape was not available for verification of the content of these remarks.

Exchange With Reporters During a Luncheon With Business Leaders
May 26, 1993

White House Travel Office

Q. [*Inaudible*]—members of your staff in the Travel Office scandal? Is part of this inquiry going to consider—going to be a chance of shakeups because of the event?

The President. Well, I would like it on the record that one of the things they did was to figure out how to save—how to do the same work with less than half as many people and save you 25 percent on your first flight. I keep hoping I'll read that somewhere in these accounts. I think that ought to be accounted for. I was—the press complained to me repeatedly about being gouged by the White House Travel Office. I kept hearing it everywhere. So we put it out on a competitive bid and saved you 25 percent.

Now, if it wasn't handled right, we'll get to the bottom of it, and we'll straighten that out, and it will be handled right. That's what Mr. McLarty worked on yesterday. And we will do what is appropriate, follow the "do-right rule," and go forward. I don't have anything else to say about it.

Ross Perot

Q. Mr. President, as you meet with these CEO's, your—I put this in quotes—one of your "favorite business guys," Mr. Perot, has been sniping at you again. He told David Frost that you don't have the background or the experience for the most difficult job in the world. How do you deal with this kind of talk from him?

The President. You deal with it. [*Laughter*]

Q. He said you were doing things the Arkansas way.

The President. Well, we know he doesn't like my State. But he spent several million dollars to bad-mouth it last—and it doesn't have much to do with America. We're going to just keep working.

NOTE: The exchange began at 12:25 p.m. in the Old Family Dining Room at the White House. A tape was not available for verification of the content of this exchange.

Announcement of White House Fellows
May 26, 1993

The President today appointed 17 men and women from a variety of backgrounds and across the country to be the 1993–94 class of White House fellows.

White House fellows are a select group of men and women who spend a year early in their career serving as paid assistants to the President, Vice President, or Cabinet-level officials. This class will begin their fellowship year in September. They were selected by a commission appointed earlier this month by the President. It was chaired by Nancy Bekavac, the president of Scripps College.

"This is a group of people of exceptional abilities, strong motivation, and a commitment to serve their country," said the President. "I look forward to their service and am confident they will join the successful ranks of such White House fellowship alumni as General Colin Powell and Secretary Henry Cisneros."

The individuals chosen for this year's fellowships are:

Paul T. Anthony, Washington, DC
Suzanne Rose Becker, Bolton, MA
Christopher Frank Chyba, Ellicott City, MD
Jami Floyd, Oakland, CA

W. Scott Gould, Topsfield, MA
Kevin Vincent Grimes, Mountain View, CA
Suzan Denise Johnson Cook, Bronx, NY
Michael Nathaniel Levy, Washington, DC
Gaynor McCown, New York, NY
Barbara Paige, New York, NY
Raul Perea-Henze, New York, NY
Leslie Ramirez, Evans, GA
Maj. David Rhodes, USAF, Glendale, AZ
Reginald L. Robinson, Lawrence, KS
Martha E. Stark, Brooklyn, NY
Todd Ulmer, San Francisco, CA
Maj. Roderick Von Lipsey, USMC, Philadelphia, PA

NOTE: Biographies of the White House fellows were made available by the Office of the Press Secretary.

Remarks in the "CBS This Morning" Town Meeting
May 27, 1993

Paula Zahn. Here comes President Clinton, cup of coffee in hand—decaf coffee.

The President. Good morning.

Budget Proposal

Ms. Zahn. We wanted to start off by talking about the late night you kept last night. Word of an agreement that was struck between Democratic leaders and conservative members of your party on your economic plan. Do you think you now have the votes to carry this plan through in the House?

The President. I think it will help. This is an agreement that I have wanted for a long time, because I think that the people are entitled to know that if we pass these budget cuts, that they're actually going to be made. I've been concerned, as someone who was a Governor who came from a State with a very tough balanced budget law, I've been very concerned—can you hear me? Can we start again?

Q. You have two mikes on you now, Mr. President.

The President. There was an agreement made last night that I had been supporting for a good long while sponsored by the conservative Democrats essentially to put a mechanism in the budget to force us every year to make the budg-

et cuts that we say we're making in this 5-year budget. That is, obviously it's very hard to predict what will happen in every year for the next 5 years. If you had to do a family budget for 5 years, it might not be possible, or a business budget or a farm budget. So these numbers are as good as we can make them. But this amendment actually says that every year, if we miss the deficit reduction target, the President has to bring in a plan to meet it and the Congress has to vote on it. And if they want to change it some, they can, but we've got to meet the deficit reduction target.

We have been working for days to get this done. And finally, yesterday afternoon they gave up. So I called the folks that had given up, and I said, go back to the table. We've got to have some discipline in this budget, so that if we tell people we're going to make the cuts, we do it. And that's what this amendment says.

Ms. Zahn. What happens if you don't get this through in the House today?

The President. We keep working until we get a budget through. The real problem is, I think, that—there are two problems: One is that the details of the plan have been lost in the rhetoric; the second is that a lot of the Republicans who might otherwise want to vote with us got into a position where they said they wouldn't vote for any tax.

Over 60 percent of this money, of the tax money, over 60 percent comes from people with incomes over $200,000. Seventy-four percent of it comes from people with incomes over $100,000, people whose taxes went down in the eighties while their incomes went up. People with incomes under $30,000 are protected even from the Btu tax. And next year people in the middle will pay about $1 a month, and it goes to $7 a month and then about $15 a month.

We have to get all of our votes apparently from the Democrats this time. I hope it won't happen anymore.

Ms. Zahn. No help from the Republicans?

The President. Well, in the Senate we might get some Republican votes. We're working on it.

[*At this point, the network took a commercial break.*]

Administration Accomplishments

Harry Smith. We are live in the Rose Garden with over 200 people from many States around the country, a couple of foreign countries as well. We're here with President Clinton. We thank you, first, for inviting us in to do this town meeting.

I know you don't pay attention to this sort of stuff, polls. You never pay attention probably, right? The negatives are now higher than the positives in the polls. And I want to tap into something here, because there's a feeling in the country, and I think the people here reflect it. I think people in America want to see you succeed, but I just want to see a raise of hands this morning, and don't be intimidated just because you're in the Rose Garden. [*Laughter*] Do you feel like he could be doing a better job? Raise your hand if you think so. Don't be intimidated. Don't be intimidated. There's a lot of folks who feel that way. Do you feel like there's been a gap between the promises of the campaign and the performance thus far? If you think so, raise your hands. A lot of folks feel that way. What went wrong?

The President. First of all, I don't know that anything went wrong, except I'm glad nobody found our about the manicure I got in California. [*Laughter*]

Ms. Zahn. Let's check it out.

The President. I'll tell you what went wrong.

What went wrong was I was not able to keep the public focus on the issues that we're working on after I gave the State of the Union Address, even though that's what we kept doing.

Now, look, we've been here 4 months, and look what's happened in 4 months—and they give you a 4-year term—look what's happened in 4 months: We had a major foreign policy challenge in Russia right after I got in office. If Yeltsin had gotten beat in Russia and a militant regime had returned, we would have had to turn around with the defense budget and a lot of bad things could have happened to America. The United States went to work, organized the rest of the world, supported Yeltsin. He won the election. We're back on track there making this world a safer place. That's my number one job. I think that's pretty impressive.

The Congress passed a resolution committing to do a budget that reduced the deficit by $500 billion on time for the first time in 17 years. Congress passed the family leave bill they've been fooling around with for 8 years to guarantee people some time off without losing their jobs. They passed the motor voter bill they've been fooling around with for years. No one now asks are we going to reduce the deficit. The question is how much and how. No one now asks are we ever going to do anything about health care. The question is when and exactly what are we going to do. I think that's a pretty good record for 4 months.

Now, if you do a lot of things and you try to change a lot of things overnight, you may break some eggs, and it's not an exact process. And controversy always is better news—you know that—than the lack of controversy. So one of the things that happened—we were laughing about this yesterday—is I'll bet you most people in this audience and most people in this country have no earthly idea that we're going to cut way over $200 billion in spending off of this budget over the next 5 years, because the people who normally fight spending cuts supported it this time, and we rolled through the spending cuts without controversy. So the only controversy is over whether we should raise any taxes and from whom.

Now, I think we're doing pretty well, but I think we've done a lousy job of being able to cut through the fog that always surrounds this town and communicate that. I'll admit that.

Media Coverage

Ms. Zahn. Why? Why have you had a tough time doing that?

The President. Well, you tell me. I don't know. All I know is, I went to Cleveland the other day, and I talked to these four television folks locally. And they said—I'll just lay it out—this guy said, "I was for you, but I'm mad at you because since you've been in Washington, you've spent all your time on Bosnia and gays in the military." I said, "How do you know that?" He said, "I watch the news every night." [*Laughter*] And I said, "Well," I said, "okay, let me tell you," I said, "I just did an analysis of what I did the first 100 days. I spent 25 percent of my time on foreign policy, all foreign policy, including going to Canada to see Mr. Yeltsin. I have to. That's my job. No one else can do that. I spent 40 percent of my office time and about 55 percent of my total time working on the economy and health care"—let me finish—"and 20 percent of the time working on other domestic policies and seeing people and doing that." He said, "How much time have you spent on gays in the military?" I said, "Two and a half hours." He said, "I don't believe that." I said, "That's the truth. You can look at the calendar."

So all I'm saying is controversy gets news. And when we're out here working on things that aren't controversial, it's often not reported in the news. And I have to find a way to do a better job of communicating directly to the American people as well as—I'm not saying we haven't made any mistakes. If you do a lot of things, you're going to make some mistakes. But the major failure since February 17th is not being able to communicate directly what we are doing and answer directly the questions and the criticisms of the American people. That's been the major problem, and I've got to figure out how to do it.

Selection of Attorney General

Mr. Smith. You know what it is, though, I mean, given all of that stuff, motor voter, budget, all that other stuff, on a day-by-day basis, a week barely goes by that there isn't some sort of story that it sounds like—and I think people here would say, is the President on sure footing? One, two, three different choices for Attorney General. Flip-flop: We're going to get tough on Bosnia, and then we're not going to

get tough on Bosnia.

The President. You want to talk about it, we can. See, that's what people do; you can't just lob these things out there.

Mr. Smith. We have 2 hours to talk about all of this. We have 2 hours to talk about all of this, but it seems like a day or a couple of days doesn't go by when they're putting out fires in the White House. And people want to know, do you have this thing under control?

The President. Well, let me just mention the Attorney General thing. First of all, I think I've got a pretty good Attorney General, don't you?

Mr. Smith. I think people would agree with that.

The President. And the country's not—[*applause*]—and I think I did a good job. Secondly, if you look at what happened there, one of the things that no one noticed is that I was the first President since anybody could remember that had every other member of his Cabinet confirmed the day after I took office. So there is another side to this story. That was a manifestation of confidence, getting them all up and getting them all confirmed the next day. That hadn't happened in anyone's memory.

We had some problems with the Attorney General thing, partly because the American people learned about an issue that we're now moving to resolve, this whole business about if you have household help, how you withdraw the Social Security, and what you do. That's a big, tough issue. I'm sorry it happened. I still think Zoe Baird is a fine person who made, obviously, a mistake and paid for it. But thousands of other Americans have, too. And I hope now we're going to get it cleaned up so people will follow the law and the law will be reasonable. But I wound up with an awfully good Attorney General, and I'm proud of her.

[*The network took a commercial break.*]

Health Care Reform and Gridlock

Ms. Zahn. We're back in the Rose Garden now for a 2-hour town meeting with President Clinton. We have your first question now from the audience. Where are you from?

Q. I'm from Milwaukee, Wisconsin. I'm a lab technician.

Ms. Zahn. Fire away.

Q. Well, I think I'll stay with my original question. We've seen a lot of issues being passed lately. We've seen some bills being passed. But the bigger bills, the things that dealt in the economy and jobs creation, along with that, especially this health care thing, they look like they're going to be destined to be locked up in gridlock. Is there some way that we can be confident that things are going to happen in this country?

The President. I think you can be. Let me talk about—let's just talk about health care. And I'd like to talk about health care with this budget. A lot of Americans say to me what I say to myself every morning, which is that after we cut all this spending and raise this money and we reduce the deficit by $500 billion, it's still going to be too big in 5 years because what's driving the deficit now—defense is coming down, we're holding about everything else constant—what's driving the deficit is the exploding costs of health care, the same thing that's hurting a lot of your businesses or maybe your homes or if you buy individual policies.

In the last 4 months we've had hundreds of people here working on this health care task force that my wife is chairing. But we've also really worked hard to reach out to Republicans and Democrats and independents both in the Congress and around the country, people who provide health care, people who insure against health care, all those folks.

I think you're going to see when we get this budget out of the way, which is the toughest thing—everybody wants to reduce the deficit, but everybody's got a different idea about how to do it—when we get that out of the way, I think you'll see an honest debate on health care. Now, keep in mind this health care thing could be the most important thing we've done in a generation to provide security to working families and people who don't have it and people who have to change their jobs.

When President Roosevelt and the Congress put in the Social Security system it took them 2 years to do it. We're going to try to do it in a year. We're going to do our best to do it in a year. And then, of course, we'll have to phase it in over time because of the cost, but I think we can do that.

I wouldn't be too discouraged. What you're seeing now, this fight over the budget and the fight over the emergency jobs plan earlier, is, I hope, the most partisan you will ever see this environment. I am doing everything I can to ask the Republicans to help, to ask people from outside to come in, to open up the process.

I hate all this. I mean, I didn't run for President to get up and fight with the Republicans every day. It doesn't help America, and I don't want to do it. And I believe you will see a much more open process when the health care debate starts.

Now, that's not to say everybody is going to agree with me. They shouldn't. But I believe there's a real chance we'll get health care reform, and it will come with bipartisan support from around the country and within the Congress.

Ms. Zahn. But the fact is you've also had to do a lot of fighting with Democrats of your own party. And I think a lot of people were hoping, with a Democratic President and a Democratic Congress, that things would have gone more smoothly. Do you think issues like the haircut and the problems in the Travel Office have made it harder for you to get this economic plan through?

The President. No. I think this economic plan is—I think it does because if you publicize something like that and people don't know, for example, on my haircut, that I asked whether anybody would be held up or inconvenienced, and I was told no. I asked twice, and I was told no. Now, I'd never do that, not in a hundred years, not ever. I mean, I wasn't raised that way; I've never lived that way. That's not the kind of person I am. So, you know, if something like that happens and it hurts me on a day-to-day basis, it may slow things up.

But the real problem is, if these problems were easy, somebody else would have done them. You try to face difficult things and ask people to take difficult choices and make tough stands; it takes time.

Ms. Zahn. President Clinton, I'm going to have to cut you off. Someone has to pay for the show today.

[*The network took a commercial break.*]

Ms. Zahn. When we left you a couple of minutes ago, President Clinton was addressing the issue of gridlock. Anybody else have some questions here about partisan politics and gridlock? Will you stand up?

Campaign Finance Reform and Gridlock

Q. I'm from Sulphur Springs, Texas. And I do have a question about partisan politics. It seems evident to us voters that when we elect people and send them to State government or to Washington, that they are more interested in the health and well-being of their party then they are the health and well-being of the country in general. And I'm wondering what we can do other than term limits? What can we expect in the next few years to help that situation?

The President. I think there are two things you can do. First of all, you can support some changes in the system that will make it work better. There are two bills here that will help: require all lobbyists to register and report how much money they spend on Members of Congress, and secondly, change the campaign laws. You make the system less partisan if you lower the cost of congressional campaigns, reduce the influence of PAC's, and open the airwaves to honest debate. I think those things would matter.

I think the second thing you can do is to follow up on what this gentleman said. Tell us to get something done here. Tell us, talk less and do more. And I really believe that that mood in the country is going to manifest itself. I've got some friends who are Republican Senators who told me they're not comfortable with this filibuster deal. They want us to get together; they want us to work together. I think you'll see more progress in the months ahead. I really do.

This is the toughest part. The budget is the toughest part. The debt got from $1 to $4 trillion in 12 years. It's hard to turn around. None of the choices are easy. This is the roughest part. I think you'll see it get better. I'm going to do everything I can to reach out to them and to try to depoliticize this atmosphere. But if you change the rules, you'll change that. You will make people closer to their folks and less partisan.

Ms. Zahn. I've got another question here from the audience. Please stand.

National Sales Tax

Q. I'm from Woodlake, CA, and I'm a retired teacher. My concern is about taxes. I'm wondering if you have considered a national sales tax in place of, but not added to, the income tax system we now have. Is it feasible at all?

The President. It is feasible if it's not regressive. In other words, you could lower the income tax and have a value-added tax, so-called national sales tax, but if you did that at a high level, that is, if you're going to replace the income tax or most of it, it would have to—[*in-*

audible]—and you would have to exempt food and housing and the basics of life. It's something that we may look at later on.

Most countries have a small national sales tax to replace part of their income tax. And the reason they do it is it helps your exports, that is, you don't apply it to things you sell to other countries, but you do apply it to things other countries sell in your country. So it helps your exports, and it helps your competitive environment at home more than the system we have. But it's such a big issue, I thought we ought to face the economy and health care first. When that's out of the way there will be plenty of time to debate the tax system. But it is a big change for America. And most Americans don't trust us to fool with their pocketbooks anyway. So it would have to take a big long debate, where people were absolutely concerned that it wasn't going to be regressive and unfair to the middle class.

Ms. Zahn. President Clinton, we're going to take a short break again right now, at 29 minutes after the hour. We'll be back.

[*The network took a commercial break.*]

Mr. Smith. We are back live in the Rose Garden, and we've had a couple of microphone problems which we think we have fixed now. What did you just say?

The President. I said if you were a politician and all these mikes went out, they'd say, are you a failed network, are you a failed newscaster? [*Laughter*]

Ms. Zahn. They will be saying that maybe in a half hour from now.

The President. It's just one of those things. Something always goes wrong.

White House Travel Office

Mr. Smith. You know what, we need to talk about this, "Travelgate." Who knew what when, and why was the FBI called in, and why did you hire your cousin, and why did you have a firm from Arkansas take over this business?

The President. First of all, let's get back to the beginning, okay? Let's talk about my cousin. She's about my fifth or sixth cousin who worked in the campaign and ran the travel operations. We had a very efficient travel operation.

Every operation at the White House was reviewed, because I said I was going to cut the White House staff by 25 percent. That's not easy to do, to run the White House on fewer people than your predecessor. We got more mail in 3½ months than came to the White House in all of 1992. It's tough.

We found out that there were seven people working in the Travel Office, primarily to book travel for the press, and that the press was complaining that the cost was too high. So there were all these recommendations made to change it. But nothing was done until an accounting firm came in and reviewed the operation and found serious management questions in terms of unaccounted-for funds and things like that. So then the person in charge of that made the decision to replace them.

Now, all those questions were raised about whether they all should have been replaced. Mr. McLarty got on it. He did an internal review. He'll fix it. But the issue is: Should we work seven people when three can do the job? And if we saved 25 percent off the cost of the very first plane flight, isn't that a good thing for the press? That's what we're trying to do.

Mr. Smith. And nobody's going to argue with that. But what they are going to argue with is why was the FBI called in?

The President. Oh, the FBI, because—the FBI was called in to look at the auditor's report, not to accuse any of these people of doing anything criminal but because there were sufficient questions raised that there had to be a review of it. And the FBI sounds like a huge deal to you, but when you're in Washington and you're the President, you can't call the local police or the local prosecutor; that's who you call.

Ms. Zahn. But even your own Attorney General is now posing the question about a breach of policy. Is she right or wrong?

The President. Well, to the best of our ability to determine it, there has never been a policy that if the White House had a local internal matter, they had to go through the Attorney General to get to the FBI. The FBI's always been an independent investigative agency. But I have no problem with doing that, because I trust her. I think she's got great judgment.

But the report in the auditor's findings made us believe that someone at least ought to look into this and clear the air. And that's all we were trying to do.

Ms. Zahn. Was Attorney General Reno justified in questioning the process?

The President. She can question whatever she wants to, I think. She's a fine person. I like

her. But I'm just saying, to the best of my knowledge, there has never been a policy that the White House, if they had some internal activity going on here, would clear asking the FBI to look into it through the Attorney General. But I have no problem with doing it. Not with me or anybody else was that the policy before, to the best of my knowledge.

Mr. Smith. But at minimum, it looks like you used the FBI to justify what in turn ended up looking like or was, in fact, an act of cronyism.

The President. No. It may look like that, but the bottom line—it wasn't an act of cronyism. The bottom line is if we can run an office with three that they were taking seven to run, and we can save 25 percent off a trip because we have competitive bidding when they didn't have competitive bidding, the press saves money and the taxpayers save money. That was my only objection. If anything wrong was done, Mr. McLarty will correct it. This is a do-right deal, not a do-wrong deal. Let's not obscure what happened. We were trying to do the people's work with less money.

Mining Reform Legislation

Mr. Smith. Do you have a question?

Q. Yes, I do. I'm from Redwood City, California. I was a Clinton precinct leader in that State, and I'm very happy to see you elected. My question, however, is regarding the environment. I supported you in spite of the issue that Tyson's was one of the major producers of jobs in your State; it's also the major producer of pollution in your State. And I supported you in hope that Al Gore would work on convincing you to be more of an environmental President than George Bush was. However, I noticed that you recently backed down when it came to upping the user fees on mining, grazing, and lumber. This is in spite of the fact that mining, I believe, is fixed at like under a dollar an acre to mine, this based upon a post-Civil-War law, but you've not upped it. I understand that it could contribute——

The President. Let me ask you——

Q. ——$17 billion to the budget.

The President. Okay. No, no. There wasn't $17 billion, I don't think. Do you all know what he's talking about? The Federal Government owns land—that's a very good question. I'm glad you asked it. The Federal Government owns a lot of land on which there are trees, cattle, and minerals to be mined. Most people believe, and it's absolutely true, that essentially people have been permitted to use that land, mostly out west, to cut trees, graze cattle, and mine minerals at lower than a market rate. Now, all the people who do that have good reasons why they think the system is good, and I don't know if we've got any of those folks in the audience, but I feel that the mining fees should be raised.

Originally we had, originally—he's right—we had that in our original budget. And we took it out not to take a dive on it but because, since it's a new issue, under the parliamentary rules of the Senate, we'd be subject to a filibuster. That is, you have to get 60 votes, not a majority, to pass the budget.

So we are moving now a new mining reform law through the Congress which will do exactly what you say. We just had to agree to do it on a separate track. The mining reform is on track. I believe this year I will sign a mining reform law which you will be very proud of, which will require those companies to pay back to the Treasury more nearly the value of what they have gotten from the United States Government, and it will be good for the environment.

It's a good question. It's going through on a separate track, and we had to break it out for parliamentary reasons because of the opposition to it in the Senate.

[*The network took a commercial break.*]

White House Staff

Ms. Zahn. We're back in the Rose Garden live with a 2-hour town meeting with President Clinton. Before we get back to our audience, a quick question to you about staff. There has been a lot of criticism that you've surrounded yourself by young and inexperienced people. There has been talk that maybe there are going to be some major shakeups over the next couple of days. Are you entirely satisfied with the White House staff you have in place?

The President. No, but they're working hard and we've gotten a lot done. I'm glad I got to talk about that. I think there are always going to be—you can't—this is the hardest place in the country to work in some ways. And I think that we've had a period—you know, we came in, most of us were not from here, we were trying to do things differently. And there are a lot of things that we didn't handle as well as could have been handled. This Travel Office

is one. What we were trying to do was good for the country and good for the taxpayers. And there were glitches in it. We are going to fix that. But I think that by and large, we'll——

Ms. Zahn. You're going to fix that by firing——

The President. We have a—well, just watch and see what we do. We're going to——

Ms. Zahn. No hints?

The President. No hints.

But I would also say that I wonder whether people think the staff is younger than it is. I mean, you have the head of my economic team, Bob Rubin, is in his fifties and was one of the most successful people on Wall Street. Our major senior staff, I think, on balance, is slightly older than President Kennedy's were. But there are a lot of young people in other positions here. And sometimes I think that the overall impression is that the staff is quite a bit younger than it is in terms of people that are actually making decisions.

Urban Youth

Q. One of the big things about your campaign was hope for the future and don't stop thinking about tomorrow. My question is about the children in the country, especially in the inner cities. It seems like they've kind of lost hope, and it seems like they don't have a future. And I'm wondering what we can do as a country to instill that back into them.

The President. I think there are some things that I can do as President, but there are also some things that are going to have to be done community by community and block by block.

Let me talk about the things I can do first. My job, I think, for those kids is to try to do as much as I can to make sure they've got a fair chance to make it under difficult circumstances. What does that mean? That they have a healthy beginning, get a good chance to get a Head Start program and decent nutrition, that their schools are as good as we can influence them, that their streets are safer, that they have a chance to work when they're young, at least with summer jobs, and that there's some economic opportunity there.

We have presented initiatives in all this area. We're going to have more police on the street, more investment in Head Start, and a dramatic increase in incentives for business to invest in those areas.

But frankly, I think also, we have to say to

those kids, the only way you can make it is if you play by the rules. And we know it's tougher where there aren't as many intact families. We know it's tougher where there's more violence. But we've got to have more people go in and deal with those kids one-on-one. A friend of mine said the other day—someone asked, "How are we going to rescue all these kids?" And she said, "The same way we lost them, one at a time."

And we've got to have more people interested in these people as people. I'm telling you. I just got back from south central LA. Those kids aren't all that different from everybody else's kids. They just want a chance to live. And if we can give it to them with more personal involvement, I think they can make it.

Mr. Smith. When you talk about one-on-one, are you talking about a giant volunteer corps or are you talking about some kind of system that's going to cost more money to do it?

The President. No, I'm talking about——

Mr. Smith. In 30 seconds.

The President. I'm talking about—the money should be going to the things I mentioned. What we need is for people in each of these communities to be involved with those kids. I can't do that. We need people in these communities sponsoring schools, involved in the schools, working with those kids after school and on the weekends. They're good kids. They just need a chance to make it.

[*The network took a commercial break.*]

Ms. Zahn. Welcome back to Washington and the Rose Garden. We continue our conversation, our town hall meeting, with President Clinton right now. I thought I'd give the folks that have been staring at our back sides all morning a chance to ask you a question.

Sir, your question.

Law Enforcement

Q. My question to you is in regards to a law enforcement issue in this country. We're well aware of the position of the previous administration in regards to the support of law enforcement. My question deals with the fact that I heard you mention earlier about trying to get additional police officers, 100,000 and so forth. We in this city, I believe it was a matter of a couple of weeks ago, went to the Hill to try to get additional funding to keep several segments of our police department run-

ning, mainly one of which is the helicopter unit, which provides a lot of support service for the ground police officers and the Secret Service and ATF. And they were turned down for, I think it was like, they were going for $2 million or something at that rate. But my question to you is, dealing with Congress up there, which it seems they have a problem of partisanism now, like I say, as far as——

The President. Well, let me explain. First of all, let's talk about the bigger issue here, that this gentleman is an example of a major national problem. Thirty-five years ago, there were three policemen in America for every serious crime. Today, there are three crimes for every police officer. And a lot of cities have had to reduce hiring of police officers with budget problems they've got. So one of the things I said in the election was I would try to find a way to put 100,000 more police officers on the street over the next 4 years.

There's a bill moving through Congress right now which makes a down payment on that, and the House passed it late last night. If the Senate passes it, and I think they will this time, it's a smaller bill, but it will permit us to hire another 15,000 or so police officers. And that will start the down payment. Then I'm going to support the crime bill, which includes the Brady bill, to require people to wait so we can check their criminal background before they buy handguns. It will also have more police officers on it.

We're going to give people coming out of the military incentives to go into police work. We're going to give young people the opportunity to pay off part of their college loan by being police officers for a while. So I think we can get this 100,000 figure. And you will be helped by that. But this bill that's going through now should help DC and all the States, because it provides funds specifically for those who want to rehire people who have been laid off as well as hire new police officers. And that should help a lot.

Abortion

Q. Good morning. I'd like to know, is abortion going to be covered under the new health care plan?

The President. I don't think a decision has been made about that. Let me tell you what the problem is. The Congress has historically not permitted public funds to be spent for abortion, except to save the life of the mother. Most private health insurance plans permit some broader coverage for abortion for people who are covered.

So what the health care task force is trying to resolve is how to at least provide for the position that we shouldn't—in solving the national health crisis, we shouldn't take away from people some right they now have in their health insurance plans. And that's what they're trying to work through now. And I'm not sure exactly where they're going to wind up, but I think they're going to try to wind up in a way that either does that or at least makes it possible that that can be done. That's the dilemma here.

Ms. Zahn. You mean the continuation of——

The President. That gives people the right to at least access what they've got now in their health insurance plan, if they're private citizens and they get that, as a result of this change we've got, because what we're trying to do is not run this money for the uninsured through the Government anyway. We want it to be operating outside the Government and the taxpayers.

Ms. Zahn. Harry's working the other side of the audience over there.

Mr. Smith. We've got a 1-minute question.

Immigration

Q. I'm from southern California, and there we have a lot of problem with immigration. I kind of have a question for you. Idealistically, I feel that America should let as many people in as we can. But in our State it's really taking a toll on Medicare, et cetera, et cetera.

The President. Absolutely. You're from California, you know that——

Mr. Smith. Thirty seconds left.

The President. Quick answer. The Nation does not enforce its immigration laws. We should let immigrants come in. It makes us a stronger country. But we can't let everybody in overnight. We should attempt to enforce the laws more rigorously. And when California, Texas, Florida, New York, and other States pay a disproportionate burden, the National Government ought to help them more. We changed the rules to help California more, because it's not fair for you to pay for what the National Government does or doesn't do.

[The network took a commercial break.]

China

Q. I'm from Tarzana, California. I've been going to China since 1980, seven or eight times. I've lived and worked in China for 2 years. I'm very concerned about what you're going to do with the——

Mr. Smith. Most-favored-nation——

Q. ——most-favored-nation. On the one hand, if you don't give them this, you feel that you'll pressure the government into changing their attitude. On the other hand, the people don't want that to happen because they feel that they will be hurt financially. And then when they're hurt economically and financially, then they'll get less rights and privileges.

Mr. Smith. Is this a done deal, your decision on this?

The President. I think it is a done deal for the next year. Let me explain the issue here. In order for a country to trade with us, they have to get what's called most-favored-nation status in order to have big trade. China is a huge trading partner of ours, I think now our second biggest trading deficit, with China just behind Japan. They've got one of the fastest growing economies in the world. They're moving away from communism to market economics very quickly. They still put political prisoners in jail. They still, we think, have used prison labor to make products, and we have some other problems with them.

The issue is should we revoke that or should we put conditions on it. I basically have decided to extend most-favored-nation status for a year because I want to support modernization in China, and it's a great opportunity for America there. But I want to make it clear to them that there has to be some progress on human rights and the use of prison labor. Our trade disputes and our disputes about arms sales I'm going to take out of this issue and negotiate directly with them. I think they will appreciate the gesture I'm making, but I hope they understand that the United States just can't turn its back on the abuse of lots of people and especially the use of prison labor and just choking people off when they say their piece.

The Presidency

Q. I'm from Troy, Michigan. My question, Mr. President, when you wake up in the morning, before you get out of bed, do you lie there and think, what stupid little thing is going to happen today? *[Laughter]*

The President. Some days I do. What I really think of is stupid little things happen to everybody, and I just hope that if some stupid little thing happens to me, it won't overshadow all the big good things I'm trying to do.

But actually, when I get up in the morning, I say a little prayer that I won't make any stupid little mistakes and that I'll do right by America today. That's what I do. Then I go out here and run off old age. I do my best to do that.

Mr. Smith. Here we go, Mr. President.

District of Columbia Statehood

Q. Good morning, Mr. President. I'm president of the Bloomingdale Civic Association here in Washington, and you're welcome to come to our community at any time.

The President. Thank you. I'd like that.

Q. My question basically is, can you express to the American people why it is important for the District of Columbia to have statehood, to have the opportunity to vote for two Senators and Members of Congress?

The President. Well, I think, frankly, I think having the Senators and the Members of Congress is not as important as having control over your own destiny. The District of Columbia now has more people than 5 other States, pays more taxes than 10 other States, and sent more soldiers to fight in the Persian Gulf war than 20 other States. And yet, every time they turn around, Congress can overturn anything they do through their elected officials.

If they became a State, yes, it's true, they would get two Senators and a Member of Congress, just like the other small States. But the main thing is they would have more control over their own destiny. It's very frustrating for the people in the District to know that Congress can do or not do anything, just like this fellow said here, that they can say, "No, you can't have $2 million for police." And they can't do it on their own because they don't have the independence. So that's why I've always supported statehood. Once I saw the facts about the size, the taxes, and the contribution to the national interest, I thought they ought to have the right to be independent.

Mr. Smith. We need to take a break. We'll come back with more live from the Rose Garden.

[The network took a commercial break.]

Mr. Smith. We are live at the White House Rose Garden with President Clinton, the first national network town meeting since you were elected. We appreciate you letting us come in here. We've got lots of questions from more than 200 people in the audience.

Paula.

Ms. Zahn. And this man's been waiting very patiently for the last hour. Please stand, and you can fire away.

President's Haircut

Q. I'm from Montana. I work for the Rural Electric. And my question for you is: With all the troubles in the world going on now, how do you like being on the bubble with your haircut?

The President. I just learn to live with it. I think you've got to learn to laugh at things like that. You know, when little things get made big, and big things get made little, you know, and you make a boner—I mean, I really—I told you the truth earlier. I was really trying to avoid inconveniencing people, not trying to inconvenience people. It just winds out being embarrassing when something like that happens to you. And you just have to laugh it off and go on. If you didn't have a sense of humor in this business, you'd be ground down to nothing pretty quick.

Ms. Zahn. Earlier this morning, President Clinton, you said that you would ask your aides on the plane whether the haircut was going to cause any delays or not, and they said no. There's a piece in the Wall Street Journal——

The President. The Secret Service said no.

Ms. Zahn. The Wall Street Journal is suggesting that maybe the staff members don't have enough of a spine to stand up to you. Can you comment on that report?

The President. Oh, no. The Secret Service asked, and they were told that there would be no delays. It was just a mess-up. I mean, it was just a mess-up. But it's just not——

Ms. Zahn. Do you wish you hadn't gotten that haircut?

The President. Yeah. I mean, look, I wear a $40 watch. Do I look like the kind of guy that would go and sit on an airport—you know, I mean, it was just a blow-up. I'm glad they didn't find out about the manicure. *[Laughter]*

Health Care Reform

Q. Good morning, Mr. President. I am from East Dubuque, Illinois. Tomorrow I'm graduating from medical school and will be going into——

The President. Congratulations.

Q. Thanks—residency training in family practice. I am graduating with over $100,000 in student loans for medical school alone. I am wondering how you anticipate the health care reform will help me to be able to pay back my student loans, as well as the many colleagues that have a similar situation as I do.

Mr. Smith. The fear being that doctors aren't going to make as much money and for folks like this they aren't going to be able to pay the bills, right?

The President. First of all—don't sit down yet, I want to look at you—only about 15 percent of our medical school graduates are now doing what this fine woman is doing, coming out as family practitioners. Most medical school graduates now want to be specialists partly because they want to do it, partly because they can have more control over their hours, partly because they can make more money. What we are going to do is try to create more incentives for people to go into family practice: easier to pay off your loans, have Government-targeted assistance to medical school to lower the cost of medical education, give you more opportunities to be in family practice corps, to bring down the cost of your debt. And I don't think that your income will be constricted. I think there will be more reliance on family practice, and we're going to have to do more in primary preventative medicine in America if we're ever going to bring the cost of health care down.

Ms. Zahn. I have another health care related question for you from back here.

Q. Thanks. I'm from Springfield, Missouri. I'm glad to hear that answer because one of my children is in medical school and going into family health care.

The President. That's great.

Q. I work for a company that has less than 500 employees. I pay $50 a month for a health plan, a dental plan, life insurance. Our health plan is self-insured. I don't want to pay more money for health care individually. I'm concerned that my employer may be taxed and have to pay more money, and I would receive less benefits than I am receiving, as well as I want to keep my self-funded health plan. How would the change in health care affect me as an individual?

The President. Well, let me say first of all, one of the decisions that has not been finalized yet, at least in our original report, is to what extent any companies of any size should be able to, in effect, continue their self-insurance efforts. And that's a tough issue because what we're trying to do is get these pools of insurance big enough for small business to have affordable health care because that's been a back-breaker for a lot of small businesses.

The requirement that they're working on in terms of financial contribution would not be a tax over and above what people are paying now. They're trying to hit the national average, maybe even a little below the national average of what employers are paying now. And many, many employers and employees in this country will actually save money if the health care plan comes into effect.

But if you have a national budget, you have to have some sort of national standard for what the contribution will be by employers, but it's not going to be over and above what people are paying now. They're trying to substitute for it, and they're trying to work out what that number is now. To your point of view, if you have a low-cost self-insurance plan, what we're going to try to do is to make sure that the people with low-cost plans and generous coverage don't have less coverage and higher cost. That's not what we're trying to do. What we're trying to do is to broaden the coverage.

Mr. Smith. Fifteen minutes after the hour. We need to take a break. We'll come back live to the Rose Garden, right after this.

The President. And lower the cost—I'm sorry, I didn't say.

[The network took a commercial break.]

Mr. Smith. It's about a perfect day in Washington, DC. I think the President is probably hoping it's just as nice up the street a little bit in the Congress. But we've got lots of questions from our audience. Go ahead.

Affordable Housing

Q. Mr. President, I'm an architect from Seattle, Washington. And the question I'd like to ask you is what vision do you and your administration have for the revitalization of housing, both in the urban areas and the rural areas?

The President. I think the housing economy, first of all, is a big part of our overall economy. My vision is that we will set in motion market forces—with a little bit of Government support but not a lot—mostly market forces, which will enable us to resume a vigorous homebuilding sector in the American economy. And let me just mention some of the things that are important to that.

The most important thing is to pass a deficit reduction plan that keeps interest rates down. Interest rates, mortgage rates now are about a 20-year low. Last year, only 47 percent of people under 35 thought they were going to be able to own their own homes. This year, about 74 percent do. That's because interest rates are down, because we're trying to bring the deficit down first.

Secondly, I think the low income housing credits, tax credits, should be extended. That's in our tax bill, to give people incentives to build houses in inner cities.

The third thing we need to do is to move aggressively in areas where credit is not available to break the credit crunch. And the Government's working hard on that. There are all kinds of sectors of our country that have had a huge dry-up of credit because of the collapse of the S&L's and because of regional recessions. And we're trying to break that.

And finally, we have a Secretary of Housing and Urban Development in Henry Cisneros, the former Mayor of San Antonio, Texas, who has got a wonderful raft of ideas about how to go into community after community and set up partnerships in rural and urban areas to get people to build more houses. So that's basically what we're trying to do. The dream of home-ownership, and frankly, the importance to the economy are two things that can merge as part of my vision for rebuilding our country from the grassroots up.

Ms. Zahn. President Clinton, we only have a couple of more minutes before we have to take another break. Another quick question for you from over here.

Association With Celebrities

Q. I'm a finance manager from San Jose, California. My perception is that your administration is a little infatuated with Hollywood and celebrities. Is this a valid observation?

The President. No. You know, all these politicians from here run out to Hollywood and have fundraisers all the time. Do you know how many fundraisers I had there before I ran for President? Zero. We've had two meetings here in the White House where groups of people from Hollywood have wanted to come in and talk about health care and the environment. We've

had a couple of people from California who have stayed in the Governor's mansion. When my preacher from Arkansas stayed here, nobody wrote it up. When the guy who ran my campaign in Florida stayed here last week, nobody wrote it up. It's another thing where a little thing becomes big because it makes a good story. It doesn't amount to a hill of beans. There are some people in Hollywood who helped me, who care about the country. I treat them like I do everybody else that was part of the campaign and want to be part of it.

But that is absolutely not true. It is not true now, it's not going to be true, and it's never been true. I like to go to the movies and listen to music. Most of you do, too. And that's about the extent of it.

Ms. Zahn. Are you concerned, though, that when these little stories that you say just simply blow up——

The President. Absolutely. Absolutely——

Ms. Zahn. Let me just ask you this—that people who voted for you in the election and bought into this image of the man from Hope and that maybe stories like the $200 haircut with a guy who has one name might increase their cynicism about what's going on in your administration.

The President. Sure it does. Sure it does, which is one reason they're so overplayed. But that doesn't mean they're valid. What I keep telling everybody here is, we have to realize when you're President, you're a long way from most people in America, and so little things become big. So you have to bend over backwards not to do things that you'd never even give a second thought to if you were a private citizen or a Governor or a Senator because they're going to be taken and blown all out of proportion and your whole image is going to be gnarled by it. So we have to be super sensitive not to do things that we would ordinarily do and not give a second about it because of the way it will be perceived in the country. That's absolutely right. And we haven't been very smart about that on a couple of these occasions. But that doesn't mean——

Ms. Zahn. Whose fault was that?

The President. It means that we have underestimated the fact that the press will play these things big and people will draw those conclusions from it. But she asked me a substantive question, not an image question. She said, has the administration gone Hollywood? The answer to that is, no, heck no, never, no. Never, Never. [*Laughter*] That's a substantive answer.

Ms. Zahn. I think the answer is no.

Mr. Smith. We've got lots more to come live from the White House Rose Garden with President Clinton. We've got questions about defense cuts and what happens to the people who are going to lose their jobs as the defense gets cut. And we're going to come back and get answers to those questions in just a minute.

[*The network took a commercial break.*]

Commemorative Tie

Mr. Smith. I couldn't let this go; you've got to stand up a second. Okay, now, I didn't know this. I knew there were ties like this, but explain—the President of the United States knows that this tie actually means something and what it means.

The President. This tie is part of a series of ties representing Beatles songs. And this one is "Let It Be." And there's Mother Mary here; there's a line in the song that says, "Mother Mary calls to me, whispers words of wisdom, let it be." And here she is with an angel. And so you're supposed to be able to look at this tie and know the Beatles songs. There's a whole bunch of them, and sometimes we give each other tests. [*Laughter*]

Mr. Smith. Do you have a question for the President? Okay.

The Presidency

Q. Yes, I do. It's sort of a change of pace; it's more of a personal question. I was wondering how you felt that you've changed over the last 100 days of your Presidency?

The President. I think I'm a lot more humbled in the face of some of the problems than I was before I became President. I'm still as convinced as I ever was that we can make change. I still think that we can restore a sense of hope and possibility. But a lot of these issues—we talked a little about Bosnia during the break—are very humbling. They're difficult.

And I'm also very mindful that—just what we were saying before—when you're President, everything you do and everything you say and the way you do it and the way you say it and everybody you come in contact with takes on a meaning far bigger than you might have ever imagined as a Governor, a Senator, a candidate for President, a private citizen. And you have to be much more sensitive to that in order to

make sure that the people know you as you really are.

I think those are the two things that I have learned. I also have learned that it's probably the hardest job in the world. And you've got to reach down real deep every day and try to always rise above yourself and not be deterred by the momentary problems or the drops or raises in the polls. Both drops and increases in the polls are illusory in the end. The only thing that matters is, do you do a good job, and are people's lives better off when you finish than they were when you started. And I just have to keep working on that. I think it requires a much stronger character and a much deeper spirit to be President than it does to run for President. And I just try to work on it every day. I try to grow some every day into the job.

Ms. Zahn. President Clinton, you know the tie you just looked at, the "Let It Be" tie? Here's a man that isn't content to let it be. He has a question for you now. Please stand.

Entitlement Programs and Health Care Reform

Q. Mr. President, I'm from Los Angeles. My question is on the entitlement programs. Entitlements are 50 percent of the budget, as you know. And I see the constant growth of these entitlement programs. There's no way, as I see it, to curb the budget deficit without reining in these entitlement programs. And now you are going to propose a health care program, which is another entitlement program.

The President. Well, the answer to your question is, the only way to control the health care entitlements is to get control of health care costs. And the only way to control health care costs in this country, in which we're spending 35 percent more of our income on health care than anybody else, is to provide some way for everybody to have some coverage, not lose it when they change jobs, and control public and private costs the way every other advanced nation has done. We cut a lot on the entitlements, on retirement entitlements, public employee entitlements, and health care. We need to cut much more, and we will.

Ms. Zahn. Thank you, President Clinton. We will be back with a half hour more of our town meeting after this break.

[*The network took a commercial break.*]

Ms. Zahn. Welcome back to "CBS This Morning" and our special 2-hour meeting with President Clinton. We just had to go into a break, and we were talking about the notion of entitlements from this man back here. And his essential question was, with entitlements representing about at least 50 percent of our budget, when is the Government going to get serious about cutting into these programs? Did I paraphrase that correctly?

The President. We have in this budget package that I have presented to the Congress, we have about $100 billion in cuts in various entitlement programs over the next 5 years in Medicare, in agriculture, in veterans programs. But they're still going up very rapidly. The only way ultimately to get control of the entitlements is to control overall health costs and bring them in line with inflation. For example, we could cut health care costs even more, but here's what would happen. If you cut Medicare and Medicaid and you cut what the providers get, the doctors and the hospitals, what do they do? They shift their costs off to you in the private sector. That's been happening for years now. People who have no health insurance get health care in this country. People whose health care is underfunded get health care anyway. And the cost gets shifted onto private employers and their employees in the form of exploding health insurance premiums. So health care cost in the private sector as a whole are going up as fast or faster than health care costs in the Government sector. And the trick is how to get them under control without messing up the programs, like the gentleman over here who has got a good program where they have control of their own costs. That's the trick. But you've got to deal with the private and the public to do that.

Aerospace Industry

Q. The aerospace community is being assailed by the Europeans on the commercial side, and in some respects the defense budget will assail them on the defense budget side. A combination of those two are making aerospace employment a very delicate issue, a lot of unemployment, a lot of people without jobs. How do you think the new defense budget will address that as part of their program?

The President. First of all, I want to answer your question, but I want to make a point since you stood up here, and I appreciate it.

There are budget cuts and budget cuts. Everybody knows we have to bring the defense budget down. And we have cut it a lot. We are right on the edge. We should not cut it more right now. I feel very strongly about that. A lot of the defense cuts are in areas of contracts where people work in America. The question is what are they going to do when you lay them off? Why is southern California in so much trouble? Largely because of all the defense cuts, with no plans to find anything else. We believe very strongly, in this administration, and I personally believe, based on my experience as a Governor trying to put people back to work, that a portion of the defense cuts should be devoted to three things: one, retraining workers if they need retraining; two, helping companies to develop domestic markets to make up for the defense contracts they lost; and three, helping communities that have been devastated to restructure their economies.

In the aerospace industry, I am convinced that the real key there is to try to have a competitive airline industry in America that's healthy and try to make sure the airline manufacturers, the airplane manufacturers and the parts manufacturers, have access to markets at home and abroad. The Commerce Secretary, Ron Brown, has just been around the world doing what he can to open up more markets for aerospace commercially. We cannot afford to lose our world leadership there just because we're cutting back in defense. Aerospace is one of seven areas of technology that will produce most of the high-wage, high-growth jobs for the world in the next 20 years, and we've got to try to maintain our leadership. I just appointed a commission, along with the Congress, completely bipartisan on this issue, to look at ways to revitalize aerospace, and I think we're going to make some progress.

Homosexuals in the Military

Q. Mr. President, I'm the senior pastor at Christ Chapel in Woodbridge, Virginia. And I would like to say that we in the Woodbridge area pray for you and your administration regularly and daily.

The President. Thank you.

Q. And allow me to ask the question, give you 2 minutes in the 2 hours and 31 minutes to talk about the issue of gays in the military, if I may. I'm concerned about the degradation of morality in our Nation, in our society, in the military as a whole, and I'm concerned with the long-term consequences of actions, not only on the issue with gays in the military but also with actions associated with health care in terms of the funding of abortion, issues such as that. The Christian community is very concerned in this Nation about those issues. And I'm somewhat disturbed, particularly, about the policy process for developing these programs.

The President. Let's just talk about the gays in the military, because we don't have a lot of time to go into all of it.

First of all, I think the military has a great moral fabric. We know there are homosexuals in the military and always have been. We know that the Tailhook scandal occurred. I don't think Tailhook reflects on the whole Navy. I think that the military has done more to give people a good, coherent set of values and a way to live and succeed in a very complicated and disintegrating world than most of the institutions in this country have. So I think that you should not worry about that.

Here is the issue: There are and always have been homosexuals in the military. The question is whether they should be kicked out, not because of what they do but because of who they are. My view is people should be judged on their conduct. I have not called for any change in the Uniform Code of Conduct. I simply believe if people work hard, play by the rules, and serve, they ought to be able to serve. That does not imply that the rest of the society agrees with the lifestyle, but you just accept as a fact that there are in every country, and always have been, homosexuals who are capable of honoring their country, laying down their lives for their country, and serving. And they should be judged based on their behavior, not their lifestyle. That's my view: their behavior; it's a behavior test.

Let me say this: We almost have a compromise here. Most Americans believe if you don't ask and you don't say and you're not forced to confront it, people should be able to serve. Most Americans believe that the gay lifestyle should not be promoted by the military or anybody else in this country. The issue is a narrow one: Should you be able to acknowledge, if asked, that you are homosexual? And if you don't do anything wrong, should you be booted from the military? We are trying to work this out so that our country does not—I understand what you're saying—so that our country does not appear to be endorsing a gay lifestyle, but we accept people as people and give them

a chance to serve if they play by the rules. I think that is the tough issue for us, and I think we're very close to resolving it here.

Ms. Zahn. Could you be satisfied with "don't ask, don't tell, don't investigate"? Might that be where you might end up?

The President. Well, we might end up that way as long as it doesn't lead to a whole range of deliberate outings. I mean, we don't want to make it worse. I think we're very close to a compromise along those lines. And I think most Americans will agree when it works out that people are treated properly if they behave properly without the Government appearing to endorse a lifestyle. I think that's what you're concerned about, and it's a legitimate concern. But I have to deal with people as people. And I've had so many people in the military come up to me and say that they have served with homosexuals who served bravely in Vietnam and other places, who were good people, who did not violate any rules. It is them that I am trying to protect.

Ms. Zahn. President Clinton, thank you very much. We're going to take a short break here and be back in just a couple of minutes. Lots more to come on "CBS This Morning."

[The network took a commercial break.]

Mr. Smith. We're back live in the White House Rose Garden. What's your question for the President?

Health Care Reform

Q. Mr. President, one quick question on the health care issue. It does not yet appear what the health care plan is going to look like, but will we be ensured that we know that the less fortunate of this country and the unemployed will have ready access to quality care?

The President. Yes. But it's not just the people who don't have health insurance—the people who have it who are afraid of losing it because somebody in their family's been sick, and they can't change jobs. There are millions of Americans locked into their jobs today because they or someone in their family has a preexisting condition. We need to change the rules so that you can change jobs and you can be unemployed and your business can fail and you don't have to worry about getting health care. I think it's very important. And if we do it right, we can do it and hold down the cost of health care, not drive it up. Keep in mind, your country spends 35 percent more than any other country on Earth on health care, more of our income. We can do this.

Homelessness

Q. I've been visiting Washington, DC, and I've noticed a lot of homeless people on the streets. And it really made me sad and everything. And I was just wondering if you had any plans to help them find jobs and get homes.

The President. We do, actually. The Secretary of Housing and Urban Development, Mr. Cisneros, has just established a commission on homelessness, and they're supposed to give him a report in September about what we can do to change this. It's a very complicated problem. We're now having some people who don't want to go into the shelters at night because they don't think they'll be safe, and they think they're safer on the streets. It's a very sad thing.

It's a question of jobs, of education, of drug treatment often. But we need to do something. I run by, every day when I run out here, I run by about six homeless people who stop and say, hello, Mr. President. And I talk to them, and I look at them and think, you know, I ought to be able to get those people off the street. If I can do anything, I ought to be able to do that. And we're going to try.

Administration Priorities

Q. Hello, Mr. President, I'd like to get back earlier to what we were discussing. You were talking about how you were filtered to the media. And is there a problem with how you're filtered, from the administration's point of view, and your administration? Or is it something with a focus on too many issues at once and not a specific drive, so the public is not confused?

Ms. Zahn. We're really not going to give you much time, 15 seconds, Mr. President. Sorry.

The President. I think we have to do more than one thing. But we need to talk about one thing at a time. There's a difference in—we have to—you can't just shut the whole thing down. If we want to have welfare reform and student loans done 8 months from now, we have to start doing them now. But we need to talk about one thing. I need to get better at that, more disciplined. And I'm really working on it, to try to get through all the fog of all the many stories that are out there.

[The network took a commercial break.]

Ms. Zahn. Welcome back to Washington, in the Rose Garden, where we continue our confrontation with—conversation, not confrontation with—*[laughter]*—conversation, talk with, town hall.

The President. The truth comes out. *[Laughter]*

Meeting With President Kennedy

Ms. Zahn. The President wanted to say something about how it was more than almost 30 years ago that he was standing in this very spot.

The President. This young man asked me where I was standing when I met President Kennedy in the Rose Garden when I was a delegate to the American Legion Boys Nation. He was standing on those steps there, and I was standing here, because they had us lined up in alphabetical order, and I was from Arkansas, and we were at the front of the alphabet. I was also the biggest kid on this side, so when he came over and started shaking hands, I sort—I'm embarrassed to say this, but I kind of elbowed the others out of the way to make sure—*[laughter]*—to make sure if he only shook three hands, at least I get to shake his hand. He was good, he shook hands with everybody on the front row.

The Presidency

Ms. Zahn. So if some wide-eyed kid came up to you from that same position, what would you tell him about being President today and maybe what some of your misconceptions were about the job?

The President. I would tell him it's an incredible challenge, an exhilaration, and a great honor. And if it ended tomorrow, it would be the greatest honor I ever had. You just have to get up every day and do the best you can.

Abraham Lincoln said one time, if he tried to answer all the charges against him, he'd never get anything else done. If the end brought him out wrong, 10,000 angels claiming he was right wouldn't make any difference. And if the end brought him out all right, then everything that was said before wouldn't make any difference. You just have to keep your eye on the ball. The ball is you and your welfare and what happens to you.

Job Training

Q. Mr. President, I'd like to address the issue of employee training. I believe in your campaign that you had stated that employers would be putting forth maybe 1.5 percent towards training. I was wondering, is this going to be mandated for employers to put so much into training, or would it be left up to the voluntary action of employers?

The President. We don't want a mandate. That is about the average of what employers in the country spend. And what we're trying to do is to work out a system of lifetime training that doesn't have mandates on employers but will give them more incentives to do that. You know, there are a lot of employer mandates right now on Social Security and other things that are just very expensive.

Let me tell you where we're beginning. What we're beginning is with the kids who just get out of high school and with older people who come back into 2-year vocational training programs. We're going to try to help to set up a system by putting a little Federal money in and by giving States and localities more flexibility over the money we spend now to guarantee that people will always be able to go back and get at least 2 years of education after high school even if they don't go to college. And then we want to move from there to see what we can do to give the employer community more incentives to do that kind of training or access those things, because the average 18-year-old will change jobs eight times in a lifetime. And if we want to raise incomes in America, we've got to have a very well-trained work force, and people have to think of education as something they do always. We're going to have workers in their sixties going back to school and learning new skills. And if it is a source of security, they will be excited about it. We've got to find a way to make change the friend of Americans, instead of the enemies. That's the idea. But I don't want to mandate it.

Education

Mr. Smith. We have a couple of young women here who are about to become teachers, right?

Q. Correct. The standardized test scores for students in countries like Japan, France, and Canada exceed the ones in America. And as we're going into the 21st century, what changes will you propose to make sure that the students in America—in other words, we become the leader?

Mr. Smith. Competitive, competitive—one

minute.

The President. We are trying right now to write in the national education Goals 2000— [*inaudible*]—law of the land. I then want some national standardized exams that really mean something and aren't bogus and that are updated annually. And we want tougher and higher standards for teachers that have some national credibility, national standards.

I want you to understand, however, we don't go to school as long as a lot of other countries do. And we have a much more economic and social diversity than other countries, more immigrants, a lot more poor people, a lot of differences. But our system can achieve international excellence if we have clear standards and clear ways of training people and then if we judge the schools more based on their results rather than the bureaucratic inputs. So that's basically what we're trying to do.

Mr. Smith. Thank you. We will be back with more live from the Rose Garden and President Clinton in just a second.

[*The network took a commercial break.*]

Mr. Smith. We're back live in the Rose Garden at the White House with President Clinton.

Did you vote for President Clinton?

Q. Yes, I did.

Mr. Smith. And have been worried about him a little bit?

Q. Yes, I have been.

The President. So has my mother. I'm glad you—[*laughter*]——

Q. I'm old enough to be his mother, but I'm the wrong gender. [*Laughter*] No, I was concerned. But frankly, since being here this morning, I am reinforced in my hopes or belief that you'll do a good job. I really am. I think you're on the right track. You've given me a lot more confidence. Thank you.

Health Care Reform

Ms. Zahn. Well actually, I have one question about Chelsea here, but before we get there, before we go off the air, I just wondered if you could give us a little more information on health care this morning. We know that some of your economic advisers have been advising against going with the big bang theory of doing this health care reform all at once. What exactly are their fears? What are they worried about and are those fears warranted?

The President. Well, they're afraid that we

won't be able to get savings out of the system. Basically, to go back to this man's question here on the health care issue, if you look at America compared to other countries, we spend more on insurance and paperwork, Government regulation, and other things than any other country does. What our attempt is going to be is to get savings out of all of that and use that to cover the uninsured and to make it cheaper for farmers, for small business people, and for self-employed people to get insurance. That's the deal. Some of them are afraid we can't get the savings quick enough, so they say we ought to have just a major medical coverage and protect people from disaster. But if you look at the economics, the economics are a disaster. If you have a—I don't know—a $3,000 deductible or something like that, well, what have you got? You don't have much. That's what a lot of people have today. So what I want to do is to phase in the coverage, but when you give it to people, give them something that's worth having, that really gives family security. I think the American people would rather us phase it in and do it gradually and do it right and then give people something that's worth something, than do it overnight but give them something that's not worth a nickel.

Ms. Zahn. Can we talk about a family member now?

The President. Yes.

Chelsea Clinton's Education

Q. Hi. I'm a freshman in high school. My question was, sometime ago you said that our schools were safe. And if so, how come you won't let Chelsea go to a public school?

The President. No, I didn't say our schools are safe, I said they could be. The question of personal safety had nothing to do with it. My daughter was always in a public school, and her public school education is serving her quite well now. She's doing well in the school she's in. She and her mother and I reviewed all the possible schools we could send her to, including—we looked at three private schools and three public schools. We examined, and we thought a lot about it. We decided that this was best for her for a number of reasons. One is my daughter is not a public figure. She does not want to be a public figure. She does not like getting a lot of publicity. And frankly, she has more privacy and more control over her destiny where she is than she would if she were

at the public school that she was also interested in attending. All three of us made a family decision that it would be best for her under these circumstances.

I also think the school that she decided to attend has some very special things about it, including a requirement that children do community service. There's a whole approach that the Friends have to the education system that she was interested in exploring. But it was not a rejection of the public schools. It was a decision that because of who she is and where she is and the circumstance she's in, she would be happier in a—she'd feel that she could be more of a normal kid if she could do that. That's the only reason we did it. We didn't reject the public schools.

Mr. Smith. We've got just a little bit less than a minute right here and a real important question, Mr. President.

Community Involvement

Q. I'm going to ask you the question that President Kennedy admonished us all to ask 33 years ago: What can we do to help our country?

Mr. Smith. And the clock is running, 30 seconds.

The President. You can do what you're doing today. You can keep asking us questions and keep saying to people: Put aside the partisan politics and try to solve the problems of the country. Get something done. You're going to make mistakes if you try to do something, but move us forward. The second thing you can do is to let everybody know that you're willing to do your part if everybody else does theirs, if it's fair. The third thing you can do is to go back home and ask, what problem do we have in this community that Bill Clinton can't do anything about, except maybe set an example, and try to deal with some of these. The family problems we've got, the children's problems we've got, a lot of the value problems we've got, they have to be dealt with one-on-one from the grassroots up. And every American needs to be involved in community service like that. The Government cannot solve some of these problems, and if we did more at the local level our Government would function better.

Mr. Smith. We're going to wrap things up from the White House when we come back.

[*The network took a commercial break.*]

Mr. Smith. We got Josh here from Indianapolis. What's the title of your paper you just wrote?

Q. "Arkansas: The State Where the People Rule."

Mr. Smith. And you don't think you'll get extra credit for getting it signed by the President? [*Laughter*]

Ms. Zahn. This wraps our special 2-hour edition of "CBS This Morning," our town meeting with President Clinton. Thank you so much for your time today.

The President. Thank you very much.

Ms. Zahn. Will you ever invite us back into the Rose Garden here?

The President. Absolutely. I'd like for all of you to come back.

Ms. Zahn. All right. Have a good day everybody. See you in the morning.

NOTE: The town meeting began at 7:03 a.m. in the Rose Garden at the White House.

Interview With Connie Chung and Dan Rather of CBS News
May 27, 1993

Ms. Chung. Good morning, Mr. President.

Mr. Rather. Good morning, Mr. President.

The President. Good morning, Dan. Good morning, Connie.

Ms. Chung. Mr. President, I was watching you on "CBS This Morning," and you were very funny. I think I heard you say that you also had a manicure in California. Is that right?

The President. I was kidding, you know. It was a joke. J-O-K-E. [*Laughter*]

Media Coverage

Ms. Chung. But I also could hear a lot of excuses when you talked about the Travel Office problem, the haircut, the economy, the jobs stimulus program. Why not admit if indeed there was a mistake perhaps with the Travel Office or with the haircut? Why not just say so?

The President. I did say that. I mean, the haircut thing was a boner, but I'm just saying I did ask whether I would inconvenience anybody and was told I wouldn't. It was a mistake. What else is there to say?

The Travel Office thing, obviously I don't think it was handled as well as it should have been, and so I said so. Now that I've said this, I challenge you to tell the American people that I think that we have a right to run an office with three people instead of seven at taxpayers' expense, the primary job of which is to arrange travel for people who travel with me. And I challenge you to tell the American people that we saved 25 percent on the very first flight that we put out for competitive bid. I take responsibility for any mistakes made in the White House, and mistakes were made in the way that was handled, absolutely. But the goal was to save taxpayer money and to save the press money. And the press complained to me about how much the plane rides cost. I'm just trying to fix it. I still think we can achieve the goal and correct the mistakes. We did make a mistake.

Obviously, on the stimulus thing—no one asked me about that—if we would have followed the right strategy somehow we would have won, and we didn't. But if you try to do a lot of things, you're going to make some mistakes. I'm going to admit my mistakes. All I want to do is to have the kind of relationship, with you and others, that will present me as I am to the American people and not as some sort of clay figure that's all pulled out of shape. I'm going to make a lot of—you get out and go to bat every day, you're going to make mistakes. Babe Ruth struck out twice as many times as he hit home runs. And so I expect to strike out. But I'm going to make a few hits too, if I keep going to bat.

Mr. Rather. Mr. President, we will accept that challenge. And Connie joins the "CBS Evening News" next Tuesday night; we hope you'll be watching. She'll accept that challenge and meet what you said.

The President. I think you two will be great together. I'm excited about it.

Mr. Rather. Thank you, Mr. President, thank you.

The President. Bye-bye. Thank you.

Mr. Rather. Mr. President, if we could be

one one-hundredth as great as you and Hillary Rodham Clinton have been together in the White House, we'd take it right now and walk away winners.

As you know, Mr. President, I pride myself on trying to ask the tough questions. So I'm not going to apologize in advance for this question, but I do want to put you on tough question alert.

The President. Go ahead, I'm bleeding already. Go ahead. [*Laughter*]

President's Television Habits

Mr. Rather. You've been through 2 hours of questioning this morning with two of the most insightful questioners on television, Harry Smith and Paula Zahn. Connie came at you there with a substantive question. So here's my question: When you're able to take a deep breath, when you're able to watch television, besides news and sports, what do you like to watch? What do you watch on television?

The President. Besides news and sports? I did watch the NBA playoff game last night while I was calling Congress, asking them to help me in our playoff. I like to watch old movies. After news and sports, my favorite thing to watch are old movies.

Mr. Rather. Could you name two or three that you particularly like?

The President. Yes, I saw "The Maltese Falcon" again on television the other night. I thought that was great. My two favorite movies of all time are "Casablanca" and "High Noon." "High Noon" is my favorite movie. It's a movie about courage in the face of fear and the guy doing what he thought was right in spite of the fact that it could cost him everything. And Gary Cooper is terrified the whole way through. So he doesn't pretend to be some macho guy. He's just doing what he thinks is right. It's a great movie.

Ms. Chung. Are you a channel surfer?

The President. I surf the channels. I do. A lot of times when I come in late at night, I punch that button frenetically just to sort of see what's on. And I like Washington because there are a lot of cable stations here. And I get frustrated, particularly on the weekends if I have a little time, when there's not a single good movie on. But I do like to bump through the channels.

Economic Program

Mr. Rather. Mr. President, we all recognize that you have a kind of "high noon" today with the vote in the House of Representatives. And with that in mind, let's go to our first questioner from among our affiliates, Virgil Dominic from Cleveland.

Q. Good morning, Mr. President.

The President. Hi, Virgil.

Q. Thank you very much for being with us today. We appreciate it so very much. Mr. President, could you please give us more details on the agreement that you and the House leadership and the conservatives worked out early this morning on your economic package that will be going to a vote in the House sometime later today? And specifically, sir, does it include an increase in spending cuts or a lesser increase in taxes or both?

The President. The short answer to your question, or second question, is no. But the agreement that was worked out late last night is an enforcement mechanism to make sure that what happened to the '90 budget agreement doesn't happen this time. That is, this is a mechanism to guarantee that if there's a 5-year deficit reduction target, we meet the targets every year. Because under previous budgets, you could adopt a 5-year budget, but it's hard for CBS or your affiliate or the businesses of anybody represented in this audience today to do 5-year budgets. So this says, after every year, if we miss that deficit reduction target, the President is bound to come in and offer a plan to correct it, and the Congress must vote on it. They don't have to take his ideas, but if they don't do that, they must do something else. This will give the American people the assurance that each year we are going to meet these targets. I think that is very, very important.

Now, let me say one other thing. Most everybody believes that to whatever extent we can, we should have more cuts and less taxes. That's a good thing to do. But when you get to the specifics—if you look at, for example, Senator Boren's plan, which reduces taxes on the wealthy and imposes more burdens on working people and elderly people just above the poverty line, you see how hard the details are.

The Congress will have three more chances to vote to reduce spending. All the appropriation bills are also going through the Congress now, as soon as this is voted on. We're going to have a health care program which will produce savings in the health care area for Congress, the entitlements. And Vice President Gore is going to present a program to reform the way the Federal Government works in September that will give a third chance to cut spending this year. So this is not over. We're going to keep doing things that will reduce unnecessary spending in the Federal Government whatever happens on this bill today.

Mr. Rather. Thank you, Mr. President, and we have another questioner who will identify himself and his station and town.

Q. Good morning, Mr. President. My name is Bill Sullivan from Missoula, Montana.

The President. That's a great town.

Q. Thank you very much. First of all, on behalf of all the CBS affiliates, I want to thank you, and for free broadcasters all over America, for your support of free broadcasting, and also want to say thank you for participating in this town meeting this morning. We were proud to have you on our network.

The President. Thank you.

Pacific Northwest Resource Management

Q. My question, sir: The subject is the Northwest and development and use of the natural resources in the Northwest. The debates have been going on for many, many years. You yourself have been involved in hearings. When is it time to make a decision and let the folks go down the road?

The President. We're going to recommend a resolution to the problems that we found in the timber summit that was held a few months ago, very shortly. We're going to make our recommendation. The Northwest now has a lot of difficult natural resource issues. For example, if you cut all the old-growth forests, you can keep people working for a while, and then you won't have any left at all. You will have lost a lot of not only the biological species there, but there will be more water pollution and the salmon fishermen will be hurt. A lot of these things are very, very complicated. We're going to try to resolve them the best we can and make a recommendation that will preserve as much of the old-growth forests as we can, recognize the importance of maintaining responsible logging practices, and keep the salmon fishers going, and doing as much of those things as we can to balance the economy and the environment.

I understand a little about this because I live in a State that's over half timberland with a lot of national forest land. And I know that these are very tough issues. Probably no one will be happy with the recommendations that our administration will make. But we're going to do our best to be fair and to look at the long view. We have to think about people making a living not just now but also 5 years from now and 10 years from now and how to preserve those essential parts of our environment that are an important part of the character of the Pacific Northwest.

Mr. Rather. Mr. President, thank you very much. We have, I think, time—we want to keep our commitment to you, because we do appreciate very much your doing this. And Allen Howard from KHOU–TV in Houston has a question.

Q. Good morning, Mr. President.

The President. Good morning, Allen.

Campaign Finance Reform

Q. We've heard a lot of comments regarding yet another broadcast campaign reform; 50 percent of lowest unit rate and three commercials are just a couple of the things we've heard. I wonder if you might enlighten us on that, please.

The President. Well, the whole issue of free campaign time from the broadcast networks arose, frankly, as a result of the opposition that some folks have in any public funding of campaigns. The position the administration has taken is pretty simple. I presented a campaign finance reform law to the Congress which lowers the cost of campaigns, lowers the cost of political action committees, and gives people who are candidates for office communications vouchers so they can have access to the airwaves, so the challengers as well as the incumbents, and without regard to party, can have access to the airwaves.

The only discussion about requiring you to offer free air time came about because there are some people in the Congress who are against any public funding of congressional elections. Now, the United States Supreme Court has said that the only way we can lower the costs of campaigns is to tie that to getting some public funding. In other words, the Supreme Court says that if a billionaire wants to run for President, for Senator, for Congress, they can spend all the money they want, they can try to buy the election, they can do whatever they want. We can't stop them, according to the Supreme Court. So the only incentive we have to get people to live within a lower campaign spending limit is to be able to give them some public funding, which I propose to do not in terms of direct money but for communications vouchers so you can only use it to overcome your disability to reach people through communications, either over television or radio or newspaper or mail. So that's how our plan would work.

But you should know that the question you asked about mandatory air time would only come up again, probably, if the public funding portion of this fails. We've got to find a way to guarantee that voters hear an honest debate at an affordable cost, the election should not be bought, and that incumbents should not be insulated from honest debate and challenge.

That's all we're trying to do.

Mr. Rather. Mr. President, thank you very, very much. Our thanks to Virgil Dominic, Bill Sullivan, and Allen Howard. Mr. President, we appreciate more than we can say in a short time both being on "CBS This Morning" and taking the extra time to do this. God bless you. Thank you very much. And tell Mrs. Clinton we respect her and we're pulling for her. Thank you very much.

The President. Thank you very much, Dan.

Ms. Chung. Thank you.

The President. Thank you, Connie. And goodbye.

NOTE: The interview began at 9:05 a.m. The President spoke via satellite from the Rose Garden at the White House. A tape was not available for verification of the content of this interview.

Remarks on House of Representatives Action on the Budget
May 27, 1993

For a long time now, the American people have wondered whether their Government in Washington could ever really work for them again, ever really face the tough problems. Well, tonight the House of Representatives gave America a victory of growth over gridlock. Tonight the House showed courage and conviction. Tonight the House made hard choices: to cut a quarter of a billion dollars in spending; to ask those most able to pay, the wealthy, to do more to reduce our deficit; to increase incentives to invest and create jobs in the private sector; and to provide the incentives to make people at the bottom rungs of the economy prefer work over welfare. Tonight the House said no to gridlock, no to the status quo, and no

to the special interests who worked so very hard to frighten millions of Americans about this program. Tonight the House said yes to jobs, yes to lowering the deficit, yes to lower interest rates, yes to a brighter future.

Tomorrow we go on to the Senate, and we go back to the country. We have broken the gridlock. We are taking responsibility for the future. We are dealing with the tough problems. I am very, very proud of the people who tonight cast a very tough vote in a hard environment for a better tomorrow for America.

Thank you very much.

NOTE: The President spoke at 9:40 p.m. in the Rose Garden at the White House.

Appointment for Posts at the Department of State
May 27, 1993

The President today announced his intention to appoint Molly Raiser to be the State Department's Chief of Protocol. He also intends to

nominate her to the rank of Ambassador while serving in that capacity. In addition, he approved the appointment of Fred DuVal as Deputy

Chief of Protocol.

"Molly Raiser is an outstanding individual who has worked in a variety of ways to make our Nation's Capital a better place to live and to increase the participation of women in American politics," said the President. "Along with Fred DuVal, she will do an outstanding job of ensuring that the diplomatic corps and the many foreign dignitaries who come to Washington each year are given a true American welcome."

NOTE: Biographies of the appointees were made available by the Office of the Press Secretary.

Nomination for Ambassador to Canada
May 27, 1993

The President announced his intention today to nominate former Michigan Governor Jim Blanchard to be the U.S. Ambassador to Canada.

"Our relationship with Canada is absolutely vital," said the President. "They are our largest trading partner and one of our closest neighbors. That's why I am nominating an Ambassador in whom I place such a high degree of trust, my good friend Jim Blanchard. With a voice that will be clearly heard in both Ottawa and Washington, he will ensure that this important relationship continues to be productive for both countries."

NOTE: A biography of the nominee was made available by the Office of the Press Secretary.

Teleconference Remarks With Veterans in VA Medical Centers
May 28, 1993

The President. Vincent Maurio, are you there?

Vincent Maurio. Yes. My name is Vincent Maurio from Philadelphia Nursing Home Care Unit.

The President. And is Eugene Young there?

Eugene Young. Yes, I'm here at Bronx VA Nursing Home Unit.

The President. It's good to hear all your voices. I'm here with Vice President Gore and with Hershel Gober who is the Deputy Secretary of the Department of Veterans Affairs. And as we move into Memorial Day weekend, we just wanted you to know and all veterans like you in hospitals all across America that we're thinking about you, pulling for you. We know you wish you could be home and able to participate in the Memorial Day services. But we're very, very excited about the fact that you have these phones in your rooms now thanks to the PT Phone Home Project.

And I want to say a special word of thanks to Frank Dosio who came up with this idea and to all the people who worked on it: Bell Atlantic, C&P Telephone, NYNEX, and especially the workers, the Communication Workers of America and the International Brotherhood of Electrical Workers. There have been a lot of people who worked on this project, and we wanted to highlight that by talking to you three this morning.

And we thought it was an especially good time to do it as we head into Memorial Day. And I have a few notes about you guys. I know more about you than you know about me now. [*Laughter*] I wanted to say a special word of thanks to all of you. And Mr. Young, I understand you have a couple of sons in the service.

Mr. Young. Yes, I do, sir.

The President. And you ought to be able to talk to them more frequently now. Where are they?

Mr. Young. One, Korea; the other one in Italy in the Army, sir.

The President. Good for you. And you have a third child in college?

Mr. Young. Yes, Queens College.

The President. So, you have one child handy.

Mr. Young. Yes.

The President. Pretty close.

Mr. Young. Yes.

The President. And Mr. Maurio and Mr. Patenaude, both of you are veterans of World War II, is that right?

Mr. Maurio. That's right.

Ken Patenaude. Yes, I am.

The President. Is it nice for you having those phones?

Mr. Young. Very nice.

Mr. Maurio. I think it's an enormous accomplishment, and I think it's going to be great for all of us. It's going to get us easy access to reach our families and friends at home, a greater sense of privacy, and I think it's going to instill in us yet a higher level of self-reliance, which of course in our conditions is very important.

So, I'm fascinated by the incredible technology and the genius that it takes to put this program together and this phone system together. And I've been witness to it all morning long, and it's been extremely fascinating.

The President. Why don't you describe it to us. We can't see it here.

Mr. Maurio. I have surrounding me a bunch of electronic wizards. I don't understand their language completely, but they're absolutely fascinating to listen to. And there's an awful lot of technical equipment here, a lot of apparatus, but I think mainly the most import thing is volunteer efforts of all the people involved. I think that's a little bit of America at work, and it shows what we can do when our minds are set down to it. And I would like to thank all who participated in this wonderful project on behalf of all the patients, the staff, and the administration at both VA Hospital and the Nursing Home Care Unit in Philadelphia. I think it was a marvelous effort on all their parts. They deserve a great deal of credit, and I'm sure you will have to agree with me.

The President. I do. I hope we can get them the credit they deserve by this conversation this morning.

Anyone else have something to say about this?

Mr. Patenaude. Mr. President, this is Ken Patenaude from Albany.

The President. Hi, Ken.

Mr. Patenaude. Never in my wildest dreams did I ever think that I'd be talking to the President. It's an honor.

And I can't believe that this is happening. It's beautiful, the way they have this set up and all the work that these men have put into it. I want to thank all the volunteers from the Communication Workers of America, the VFW, American Legion, and all the employees at the Stratton VA Medical Hospital. This is one of the greatest things that has ever happened in my life.

The President. Well, I think you've earned it. You've served your country well, and I'm just glad to be a small part of this.

Mr. Patenaude. And it's a pleasure to have you on our side.

The President. Thank you. Well, I am. We've got a very good Veterans Affairs Department here headed by two American veterans, Jesse Brown, who's worked for disabled veterans for many years, and my longtime friend Hershel Gober, the Deputy Secretary, who's a Vietnam veteran, also. They are keeping me on the straight and narrow here when it comes to veterans policies. They've got our administration focused on these kinds of problems and a lot of other ones.

And I'm glad to hear you say that. You say you never in your wildest dreams believed you'd be talking to the President. You know there are millions of people who would probably like to give me an earful this morning, and you can do it. So, you've been doing a great job.

Mr. Vice President.

The Vice President. Gentlemen, this is Vice President Al Gore. I just wanted to say that the heads of the labor unions whose members did this on a volunteer basis are here in the Oval Office with us this morning and representatives of some of the companies that made it possible. And I think that what people did in pulling together to make this phone system possible for you really kind of symbolizes the way the entire country feels about your service and about all veterans and what our country owes to you.

The fact that members of organized labor and members of companies in corporate America pulled together with more than 5,000 volunteer hours and huge quantities of donated equipment, volunteers from the VFW and the staff of the VA all working together to make this possible. If the whole country could find ways to express what we feel toward veterans like this, you'd see more of this. Matter of fact, CWA members from other cities have taken up this challenge as a result of what Frank Dosio started there, and now it's beginning to be implemented in other VA hospitals and in other cities.

So, we're really proud of you. We appreciate what you've done. We join you in appreciating what these volunteers have done for you.

The President. I also wanted to note that as we get off the phone here I know that at least in Albany and Philadelphia several hundred other bedside phone units are going to be activated. There must be a lot of folks in those hospitals that want me to get off the telephone so they can use theirs. They're not going to be activated until we finish.

I did want to say one other thing to you. Yesterday morning we had a nationally televised town meeting here in the Rose Garden at the White House with a couple of hundred folks who came from 35 States. One of the people there said, "You know, we're always asking you, Mr. President, what are you going to do and telling you what we think you should do. What do you think we can do for our country to help now?" And I would just kind of like to repeat something that came out of that conversation because I told the woman who asked the question that there are clearly limits to what Government can do as well as great possibilities there. And a lot of the problems that we have in this country have to be dealt with by citizens working together at the grassroots level. And this is a stunning example of that. I mean, just think how many people all across America are going to wind up having telephones in these hospitals because one man had a vision, and his company and his union were willing to support that vision. I mean, that's an example of the kind of things that can be done by American people all over this country working together. Really, he deserves all the credit. I'm just glad to be here with this inaugural telephone kickoff.

Mr. Young, are you going to call your children when we get off the phone?

Mr. Young. I probably will, Mr. President. I'll get the number from my wife, and I definitely will call. And they will be excited like I am. And I would like to say thanks for the opportunity. And like Albany said, I never dreamed that I would be talking to the Presi-

dent of the United States and the Vice President of the United States.

And the Bronx VA Medical Center has some of the best staff there is. And we appreciate their hard labor and the volunteer service. And they're doing a very good job.

The President. Well, we're trying to support your veterans hospital network. Even as tight as the budget is here and as much as we're cutting, we're going to invest some more money in these veterans hospitals next year to try to keep the quality of care up for people like you.

Mr. Young. That's true. Yes—[*inaudible*]—the quality of care for the veterans, allocate more funding, and it will bring better quality care for the veterans which, you know, they deserve. And the staff also.

The President. Well, I wish all of you well. Mr. Young, when you talk to your sons in Italy and Korea, you tell them that we're proud of them on this Memorial Day weekend.

Mr. Young. I sure will, Mr. President.

The President. And when you talk to your child in Queens College, make sure that there's a graduation there. We need all the kids we can get with good educations so they'll support you and I when we get older and have a strong economy.

Mr. Young. That's true, Mr. President. Thank you very much.

The President. Thank you. Vince and Ken, thank you very much.

Hershel, you want to say anything?

Deputy Secretary Hershel Gober. I would just like to say before Memorial Day here for my comrades, fellow veterans, Vince, Ken, Eugene, we're proud of you. And Secretary Brown and I, along with the President and the Vice President, want you to know that we'll provide the support that you need and that you have earned. You have entitlements; you don't receive benefits. And I want you to know that we're thinking about you, and God bless you.

Mr. Young. Thank you very much.

The President. Thank you. Have a good day.

NOTE: The teleconference began at 9 a.m. The President spoke from the Oval Office at the White House.

Exchange With Reporters on Departure for Philadelphia, Pennsylvania
May 28, 1993

China

Q. Heard anything from China, Mr. President? Their reaction, the Chinese reaction?

The President. I don't know what their—I feel very good about our policy. I think it's a good policy. I don't want to isolate China. I want to do what's good for—just the Chinese people. But I think standing up for American values and values in China is the way to go. I think this is the right policy. And we have some very serious issues between us, along with these, a broad range of possibilities. I hope we can work——

NOTE: The exchange began at 10:07 a.m. on the South Lawn at the White House. A tape was not available for verification of the content of this exchange.

Remarks at City Hall in Philadelphia
May 28, 1993

Thank you very much, Rosemary Greco. You know, she's the sort of person that I ran for President to support, a person who started out as a bank teller and became the president of a bank. That's the American dream.

I want to say how glad I am to be here, back in Philadelphia, a city that has been so good to me for so long now, with your Mayor and with Senator Wofford and with the members of the House delegation who are up here on the platform with me and with your State treasurer, Catherine Baker Knoll. I'm glad to be here with all of them. Give them a hand, will you?

My fellow Americans, since I became President I have been working to break the gridlock in Washington, to prove that Government could work for you again. And there have been some impressive examples of success in that regard. The Congress, after 8 years of rankling with the President and two vetoes, voted to pass the Family and Medical Leave Act to guarantee working people a little time off when the baby was born or a parent was sick, and eventually, after years of haggling, voted to pass the motor voter bill to open up the voter registration rolls to millions of Americans and bring them into the political process.

But the real issue was whether we had the courage to come to grips with the economic problems which have paralyzed this country. After years and years and years of gridlock, after years of leaders talking about economic problems and not doing much about them, after years in which we ran our national debt from $1 trillion to $4 trillion and reduced our investment in our people, their jobs, and their future at the same time, last night the House of Representatives gave the American people a victory for economic growth over gridlock.

The plan cuts the deficit by $500 billion, cuts a quarter of a trillion dollars in Government spending, asks the wealthy who can best afford to pay their fair share, invests in education and jobs, and rewards work instead of welfare.

[*At this point, audience members interrupted the President's remarks.*]

Let me tell you something—wait a minute. You know one thing that's wrong with this country? Everybody gets a chance to have their fair say. My budget did more to fight AIDS than any in history, and we're having to put up with this. Tell them to let me talk. If you want to give a speech, go out there and raise your own crowd. We'll be glad to listen to you.

So there were those—I'll make you a deal. I'll ignore them if you will.

There were a lot of people who said we could never change the way things were in Washington, the same sort of people who picked the Phillies to finish last this year. By the way, I think the Phillies are looking pretty good, even that big fellow, Kruk, you know, is a big bat. I wonder who cuts his hair? [*Laughter*]

Let me tell you something, folks, make no

mistake about it, this National Capital of yours is beginning to change. After years in which our house was coming apart with higher deficits and less investment, a Government by special interests instead of the national interests, middle class working harder for less, things are really beginning to change.

After years of a lot of hot air and no responsibility and no willingness to take the tough decisions, yesterday the House began to throw out the economic program that ran our debt to $4 trillion, ran the middle class into the ground, created a new class of poverty, and robbed our country of opportunity and any sense of community. We are now moving forward with a plan that reduces the deficit, asks the wealthy who can pay their fair share, gives the middle class the chance of having a future with real economic growth, and provides profound incentives to prefer work over welfare. These are the kinds of things you elected me to do.

And I want to say one of the most rewarding things is the people who supported this program. I mean, after all, this is a program which asks that 75 percent of the money raised in taxes be paid for by people with incomes above $100,000. And yet, among the strongest supporters were people who had that income who believe their country was more important than their own pocketbook. And we ought to reward that. We had not just labor leaders and small business people and mayors of small and big cities and Governors for this program. There were people who lead some of the biggest companies in this country out there working to give our country a better chance and a brighter future, because they know that we have to stop reducing our investment and running up our debt. We need to reverse our priorities, and now we're on the way to doing it.

A lot of these decisions were not easy, but they had to be made. I tried to set a good example. I reduced my own staff. We've had a reduction in this budget in the Federal work force by attrition, not by laying people off, but we're going to reduce the Federal Government by 150,000 over the next 4 years. That's a lot. That's a lot of Government spending cuts. We cut more than 200 specific programs. We cut $2 in spending for every $1 in new investments and education and jobs and technology.

There were things that had never been really seriously dealt with before, the budget's sacred cows: everything from agricultural subsidies to the REA to other problems that affect the cities; demonstration projects that had never been seriously reviewed; cuts in the Medicare program that couldn't be justified; and the Federal employees perhaps took the biggest hit of all, forgoing a pay raise and having a budget that lowers their raises below the cost of living for 4 years, because most of them agreed that they couldn't ask any of you to pay more, even the wealthiest Americans, unless they took less. That's the kind of spirit it's going to take to turn this country around and move the country forward.

I'll tell you something else. Every dollar in taxes and all the budget cuts have to go into a deficit reduction trust fund. There will be no taxes without the budget cuts, and all the money will go to bringing the debt down. And we will have some left over to do things that need to be done. Here in Philadelphia, you know, because of defense cuts, we need to invest some money to help move our country from a defense to a domestic economy, new technologies for new jobs and new opportunities in the future. Because this debt turned out to be bigger even than we knew before the election, I did ask the Congress to adopt an energy tax, some of which will be paid by middle class Americans. But I want you to know exactly how it works, and you've got to decide whether you think it's worth it.

First of all, we have income tax reductions to protect family incomes below $30,000 from the impact of the energy tax. For people above $30,000 up to $100,000, here's what it costs: $1 a month next year; $7 a month the year after; and if you've got a family of four, $17 a month after that. But consider this: Look how much interest rates have gone down. If we keep interest rates down and people can refinance their homes, get car loans at lower rates, get consumer loans at lower rates, get lower business loans from good bankers like Rosemary, you will save more in interest rates than you'll ever pay in the energy tax, and you'll have a healthier economy and a lower deficit.

Just for example, if someone had a $100,000 home mortgage that was financed at 10 percent, and they refinanced it at 7.5 percent, they'd save $175 a month, a month, not a year. This is going to be good economics. If we can keep interest rates down by bringing the debt down, that will release another $100 billion into this economy this year to put the American people back to work.

Yesterday was a historic day, but it was just the beginning. Now the bill goes on to the Senate. And we must work to pass the bill that meets these principles: The wealthy must pay their fair share; we have to reduce the deficit by $500 billion; we have to keep the incentives for people to invest in our jobs and in our cities; and we've got to give people incentives to move from welfare to work, not the other way around. That's the kind of bill that needs to come to my desk.

There are 80,000 lobbyists in Washington. Many of them don't want Washington to change. Think of that. Maybe some of you all are in the wrong line of work—80,000. Special interests that work in the Senate who have now proposed that we cut Social Security and put more of a burden on the middle class in order to relieve the burden on the wealthiest Americans, when many of them are leading the crusade for change. I think we can do better. I think we can do better. And we're going to do better in the United States Senate with your help.

The process of changing is not easy, not even, and not quick. But we are moving in the right direction. The budget is on the way to being realized. There is a program now in the United States Congress with broad bipartisan support to fulfill the commitment I made to you to open the doors of college education to all Americans and give our young people a chance to pay off their college through national service through their communities here at home.

Very soon the national commission on health care which my wife has chaired will present their plan to provide affordable health care to all Americans and bring down the cost of health care that threatens our economic stability. How many millions of Americans not only lack health insurance but have it and are terrified of losing it because somebody in their family has been sick, and they think they'll never be able to change jobs. We can do better, and we will with your support.

Finally, there are bills in the Congress which will help to change the very way your National Government works: A bill that will require every lobbyist to register and to say how much money they spend lobbying all the rest of us and report it to you—I think that would be a good thing—already passed the Senate; can pass the House.

And Mayor Rendell was talking about the campaign finance reform bill, which at long last will lower the cost of congressional campaigns, limit the influence of political action committees, and open the airwaves to candidates so they can have an honest debate. That bill is in the Congress, and we ought to pass it this year.

When I was running for President, I was profoundly influenced by the series in the Philadelphia Inquirer by Donald Bartlett and James Steele, the stories they made into a book called "America, What Went Wrong?" They said that after 50 years, the middle class and small business had been helped for 50 years, but things began to change about a dozen years ago. About a dozen years ago, the National Government adopted tax policies and economic policies that rewarded those who shut jobs down in America and sent them somewhere else; rewarded those who laid their workers off and bailed out with golden parachutes to better lives. We stopped rewarding responsibility and work and rigged the game of economic life against the broad American middle class. They were right, but we're fighting to change that.

And Americans from all walks of life are helping. I will say again, to me the most moving thing of all has been how many genuinely successful Americans, people this country has been good to, people who have made a lot of money, have come forward and said, "Go ahead and raise my taxes if it will bring the deficit down and put the American people back to work and get this country going again." That's the kind of statesmanship we need everywhere in this country.

Yesterday we began the process of saying no to gridlock, no to special interests, no to the spiraling deficit, no to increased unemployment, no to the conditions which lead so many of you to work harder for lower wages every year. We said yes to a brighter future to America, yes to lower deficits, yes to more jobs, yes to higher incomes, yes to a future in which we have a real chance to compete and win.

Things are going in the right direction. Stay with us. Fight with us. Help to lift this country up, and believe in its future. And we can do it.

Thank you, and God bless you all.

NOTE: The President spoke at 12:19 p.m. in the courtyard. In his remarks, he referred to Edward G. Rendell, Mayor of Philadelphia, and Rosemary Greco, president and CEO, CoreStates Bank.

Statement on Most-Favored-Nation Trade Status for China
May 28, 1993

Yesterday the American people won a tremendous victory as a majority of the House of Representatives joined me in adopting our plan to revitalize America's economic future.

Today Members of Congress have joined me to announce a new chapter in United States policy toward China.

China occupies an important place in our Nation's foreign policy. It is the world's most populous state, its fastest growing major economy, and a permanent member of the United Nations Security Council. Its future will do much to shape the future of Asia, our security and trade relations in the Pacific, and a host of global issues from the environment to weapons proliferation. In short, our relationship with China is of very great importance.

Unfortunately, over the past 4 years our Nation spoke with a divided voice when it came to China. Americans were outraged by the killing of prodemocracy demonstrators at Tiananmen Square in June of 1989. Congress was determined to have our Nation's stance toward China reflect our outrage. Yet twice after Congress voted to place conditions on our favorable trade rules toward China, so-called most-favored-nation status, those conditions were vetoed. The annual battles between Congress and the Executive divided our foreign policy and weakened our approach over China.

It is time that a unified American policy recognize both the value of China and the values of America. Starting today, the United States will speak with one voice on China policy. We no longer have an executive branch policy and a congressional policy. We have an American policy.

I am happy to have with me today key congressional leaders on this issue. I am also honored to be joined by representatives of the business community and several distinguished Chinese student leaders. Their presence here is a tangible symbol of the unity of our purpose. I particularly want to recognize Senate Majority Leader George Mitchell of Maine and Congresswoman Nancy Pelosi of California. Their tireless dedication to the cause of freedom in China has given voice to our collective concerns. I intend to continue working closely with Congress as we pursue our China policy.

We are here today because the American people continue to harbor profound concerns about a range of practices by China's Communist leaders. We are concerned that many activists and prodemocracy leaders, including some from Tiananmen Square, continue to languish behind prison bars in China for no crime other than exercising their consciences. We are concerned about international access to their prisons. And we are concerned by the Dalai Lama's reports of Chinese abuses against the people and culture of Tibet.

We must also address China's role in the proliferation of dangerous weapons. The Gulf war proved the danger of irresponsible sales of technologies related to weapons of mass destruction. While the world is newly determined to address the danger of such missiles, we have reason to worry that China continues to sell them.

Finally, we have concerns about our terms of trade with China. China runs an $18 billion trade surplus with the U.S., second only to Japan. In the face of this deficit, China continues practices that block American goods.

I have said before that we do not want to isolate China, given its growing importance in the global community. China today is a nation of nearly 1.2 billion people, home to 1 of every 5 people in the world. By sheer size alone, China has an important impact on the world's economy, environment, and politics. The future of China and Hong Kong is of great importance to the region and to the people of America.

We take some encouragement from the economic reforms in China, reforms that by some measures place China's economy as the third largest in the world, after the United States and Japan. China's coastal provinces are an engine for reform throughout the country. The residents of Shanghai and Guangzhou are far more motivated by markets than by Marx or Mao.

We are hopeful that China's process of development and economic reform will be accompanied by greater political freedom. In some ways, this process has begun. An emerging Chinese middle class points the antennae of new televisions towards Hong Kong to pick up broadcasts of CNN. Cellular phones and fax machines carry implicit notions of freer communications. Hong Kong itself is a catalyst of democratic values, and we strongly support Governor Patten's efforts to broaden democratic rights.

The question we face today is how best to cultivate these hopeful seeds of change in China while expressing our clear disapproval of its repressive policies.

The core of this policy will be a resolute insistence upon significant progress on human rights in China. To implement this policy, I am signing today an Executive order that will have the effect of extending most-favored-nation status for China for 12 months. Whether I extend MFN next year, however, will depend upon whether China makes significant progress in improving its human rights record.

The order lays out particular areas I will examine, including respect for the Universal Declaration of Human Rights and the release of citizens imprisoned for the nonviolent expression of their political beliefs, including activists imprisoned in connection with Tiananmen Square. The order includes China's protection of Tibet's religious and cultural heritage and compliance with the bilateral U.S.-China agreement on prison labor.

In addition, we will use existing statutes to address our concerns in the areas of trade and arms control.

The order I am issuing today directs the Secretary of State and other administration officials to pursue resolutely all legislative and executive actions to ensure China abides by international standards. I intend to put the full weight of the Executive behind this order. I know I have Congress's support.

Let me give you an example. The administration is now examining reports that China has shipped M–11 ballistic missiles to Pakistan. If true, such action would violate China's commitment to observe the guidelines and parameters of the Missile Technology Control Regime. Existing U.S. law provides for strict sanctions against nations that violate these guidelines. We have made our concerns on the M–11 issue known to the Chinese on numerous occasions. They understand the serious consequences of missile transfers under U.S. sanctions law. If we determine that China has in fact transferred M–11 missiles or related equipment in violation of its commitments, my administration will not hesitate to act.

My administration is committed to supporting peaceful democratic and promarket reform. I believe we will yet see these principles prevail in China. For in the past few years, we have witnessed a pivot point in history as other Communist regimes across the map have ceded to the power of democracy and markets.

We are prepared to build a more cooperative relationship with China and wish to work with China as an active member of the international community. Through some of its actions, China has demonstrated that it wants to be a member of that community. Membership has its privileges, but also its obligations. We expect China to meet basic international standards in its treatment of its people, its sales of dangerous arms, and its foreign trade.

With one voice, the United States Government today has outlined these expectations.

NOTE: The statement referred to Christopher Patten, Governor and commander in chief of Hong Kong. The Executive order and related Presidential determination are listed in Appendix D at the end of this volume.

Letter to Congressional Leaders Transmitting a Report on Most-Favored-Nation Trade Status for China
May 28, 1993

Dear Mr. Speaker: (Dear Mr. President:)

Pursuant to subsection 402(d)(1) of the Trade Act of 1974, as amended, 19 U.S.C. 2432(d)(1) ("the Act"), I hereby submit the attached report concerning the continuation of a waiver of application of subsections (a) and (b) of section 402 of the Act to the People's Republic of China. The report explains my reasons for having determined that continuation of the waiver currently in effect for the People's Republic of China will substantially promote the objectives of section 402. In addition, I am also transmitting herewith for your further information a copy of an Executive Order which enumerates the specific conditions which I have established with respect to a further extension of the waiver next year for the period beginning July 3, 1994.

Sincerely,

WILLIAM J. CLINTON

NOTE: Identical letters were sent to Thomas S. Foley, Speaker of the House of Representatives, and Albert Gore, Jr., President of the Senate. The Executive order and related determination are listed in Appendix D at the end of this volume.

Report to Congress Concerning Extension of Waiver Authority for the People's Republic of China
May 28, 1993

Pursuant to section 402(d)(1) of the Trade Act of 1974 (hereinafter "the Act"), having determined that further extension of the waiver authority granted by section 402(c) of the Act for the twelve-month period beginning July 3, 1993 will substantially promote the objectives of section 402, I have today determined that continuation of the waiver currently applicable to China will also substantially promote the objectives of section 402 of the Act. My determination is attached and is incorporated herein.

Freedom of Emigration Determination

In FY 1992, 26,711 U.S. immigrant visas were issued in China. The U.S. numerical limitation for immigrants from China was fully met. The principal restraint on increased emigration continues to be the capacity and willingness of other nations to absorb Chinese immigrants, not Chinese policy. After considering all the relevant information, I have concluded that continuing the MFN waiver will preserve the gains already achieved on freedom of emigration and encourage further progress. There, thus, continues to be progress in freedom of emigration from China; we will continue to urge more progress.

Chinese Foreign Travel Policies

In FY 1992, 75,758 U.S. visas were issued worldwide to tourists and business visitors from China, a 35 percent increase over FY 1991 and a 76 percent increase over FY 1988. Foreign travel by Chinese-government sponsored businessmen alone increased by 48 percent in FY 1992, reflecting Deng Xiaoping's policies of accelerating China's opening to the outside world.

In FY 1992, 18,908 student visas (including exchange students) were issued, a decline from FY 1991 of 14 percent but still 8 percent greater than FY 1988. The decline was probably the result in part of a recent new directive requiring Chinese college graduates educated at state expense to work for five years before applying for privately-funded overseas study. A drop in funding from recession-strapped U.S. schools and relatives may also have played a role.

Chinese students continue to return from overseas for visits without any apparent problem. With the exception of student activist Shen Tong, we are not aware of any case in which Chinese living in the U.S. who returned to China for visits after June 1989 were prevented from leaving again. Shen was detained in September 1992 and then expelled from China two months later for trying to establish a Beijing chapter of his Fund for Chinese Democracy.

Human Rights Issues

As detailed in the Department's annual human rights report, China's human rights practices remain repressive and fall far short of internationally-accepted norms. Freedoms of speech, assembly, association, and religion are sharply restricted.

China understands that the Clinton Administration has made human rights a cornerstone of our foreign policy. We have already repeatedly raised our concerns with the Chinese authorities and we intend to press at every opportunity for observance of internationally accepted standards of human rights practice.

We have made numerous requests for information on specific human rights cases. China has provided information on some of these cases but further and more complete responses are necessary. The Chinese recently released, prior to completion of their sentences, several prominent dissidents whom we had identified on lists provided to them. These included not only Tiananmen-era demonstrators but also Democracy Wall (circa 1979) activists. We hope this is the first step toward a broad and general amnesty for all prisoners of conscience.

The Chinese promised then Secretary Baker in 1991 that all Chinese citizens, regardless of their political views, have the right to travel abroad. The only exceptions are citizens who are imprisoned, have criminal proceedings pending against them, or have received court notices concerning civil cases. A number of prominent dissidents, despite long delays, have been able to leave China. Some others have not. Those who have been able to obtain exit permits in the past year include labor leader Han Dongfang, writers Wang Ruowang and Bai Hua, scientist Wen Yuankai, journalists Wang Ruoshui, Zhang Weiguo, and Zhu Xingqing, and scholar Liu Qing. Others, like Hou Xiaotian, Yu Haocheng, and Li Honglin, continue to face difficulties in obtaining exit permission, although the Chinese have informed us Hou Xiaotian will soon receive an exit visa. We continue to press the Chinese on these and other cases.

Our goal is the release of all those held solely for the peaceful expression of their political and religious views. In November 1991, the Chinese confirmed to Secretary Baker the release of 133

prisoners on a list presented them earlier in June of that year. Since then, the Chinese have released additional political prisoners, including Xu Wenli, Han Dongfang, Wang Youcai, Luo Haixing, Xiong Yan, Yang Wei, Wang Zhixin, Zhang Weiguo, Wang Dan, Wang Xizhe, Gao Shan, Bao Zunxin, and a number of Catholic clergy and lesser known activists. We continue to press for a general amnesty and for permission for international humanitarian organizations to have access to Chinese prisons. We have also pressed for improvement in the conditions of those in Chinese prisons.

China has publicly acknowledged that domestic human rights policies are a legitimate topic of international discussion. China has hosted human rights delegations from France, Australia, the U.K., and Germany. China sent several delegations to the U.S. and Europe, as well as Southeast Asia, to study foreign human rights practices and issued a "white paper" maintaining that basic human rights are observed in China and arguing that a country's human rights record should be viewed in light of its own history and culture. We reject this limited definition of human rights but believe it is a significant step forward that China is willing to debate human rights issues with its international critics.

The U.S. continually raises with the Chinese government the need for protection of Tibet's distinctive religion and culture. We are concerned about China's heavy-handed suppression of political demonstrations in the Tibetan Autonomous Region. Demonstrations continue to result in instances of brutal beatings and long detentions. China has admitted some foreign observers to Tibet and to the main Lhasa prison. Diplomatic reports state that the Chinese Government is providing funds for rebuilding monasteries and that monks are now provided more leeway in their religious practices. In recent years, an increasing number of Han Chinese have moved to the Tibetan Autonomous Region in search of economic opportunity. We will continue to monitor closely reports that the PRC is encouraging involuntary emigration to areas traditionally settled by Tibetans. So far, we have found no evidence of a Chinese government policy to this effect. This is, however, an area of considerable concern given the relatively small Tibetan population. We join many others in urging the Chinese government to establish conditions under which the unique Tibetan culture and religion will be protected.

Nonproliferation Issues

China's support for global nonproliferation initiatives has increased substantially since the beginning of 1992. In March 1992, China acceded to the Nuclear Non-Proliferation Treaty (NPT) and adhered to the Missile Technology Control Regime (MTCR) guidelines and parameters. In January 1993, Beijing became an original signatory to the Chemical Weapons Convention (CWC). China now is a party to all of the leading nonproliferation agreements. These commitments have influenced Chinese behavior: Beijing has refrained from selling certain sensitive items because of proliferation concerns, and nonproliferation as an issue appears to receive more senior consideration in Chinese policy-making circles.

At the same time, certain sensitive Chinese exports raise questions about PRC compliance with these commitments. At present, the greatest concern involves reports that China in November 1992 transferred MTCR-class M–11 missiles or related equipment to Pakistan. Such a transfer would violate China's MTCR commitment and trigger powerful sanctions under U.S. missile proliferation law. There also are reports that China is exercising inadequate control over sensitive nuclear, chemical, and missile technology exports to countries of proliferation concern. Even if these sales do not violate PRC obligations, they raise questions about China's appreciation of the importance of preventing the proliferation of weapons of mass destruction and their ballistic missile delivery systems.

We are also concerned that China has withdrawn from the Middle East arms control (ACME) talks. The U.S. holds that, as a permanent member of the UN Security Council, China has a special responsibility to continue in these talks.

Seeking full Chinese compliance with multilateral obligations and support for international nonproliferation goals is a top Administration priority. The U.S. is prepared to employ the resources under U.S. law and executive determinations—including the imposition of sanctions—if the PRC engages in irresponsible transfers that violate its commitments.

Trade Issues, Including Prison Labor

Reciprocal granting of MFN tariff status was a key element cementing the normalization of Sino-U.S. relations by providing a framework for major expansion of our economic and trade relations. In 1992, bilateral trade topped $33 billion, with Chinese exports of $25.8 billion and U.S. exports of $7.5 billion. China was our fastest growing export market in Asia in 1992 as U.S. exports to China rose by 19 percent. In turn, the United States remains China's largest export market, absorbing about 30 percent of China's total exports.

China maintains multiple, overlapping barriers to imports in an effort to protect non-competitive, state-owned industries. China also has recognized that its development goals cannot be achieved without gradually reducing protection and opening its domestic market to the stimulus for change brought by import competition.

Our market access agreement, signed October 10, 1992, if implemented by the PRC, will increase opportunities for U.S. exports by phasing-out 70 to 80 percent of China's non-tariff trade barriers over the next four years. The regular consultation process required by this agreement allows us to monitor implementation and take appropriate action should China violate its commitments. Progress has been made in opening the market to U.S. products but we still need to resolve several issues regarding implementation.

Recently, the Chinese have indicated an interest in doing more business with U.S. companies. As U.S. corporate executives are arriving in droves to explore new commercial opportunities in Beijing, at least eight Chinese delegations have been or will soon be dispatched to the U.S. with orders to "buy American". These missions have the potential to generate billions of dollars of exports of aircraft, autos, satellites, oil drilling equipment, aviation electronics, wheat, fertilizer, and other U.S. products.

Still, the large and growing U.S.-China trade deficit is unacceptable. The over $40 billion trade surplus China has accumulated with the United States since June 1989 has been very destructive to American industries, particularly the textile and footwear sectors, resulting in the loss of American jobs. It is therefore essential that the PRC implement the market access agreement we have negotiated, which would produce a much greater equilibrium and fairness in Sino-American trade. It is also important that China liberalize its foreign exchange regime, including a market-determined exchange rate. Regarding the 1992 Intellectual Property Rights (IPR) agreement, the Chinese government has carried out the great bulk of its commitments, although there are some problems that have arisen in implementation.

Prison Labor

China officially banned the export of products produced by prison labor in October 1991. In August 1992, we signed a Memorandum of Understanding under which the Chinese agreed to investigate cases we presented and to allow U.S. officials access to suspect facilities in China.

The U.S. has presented the Chinese government information on 16 cases of alleged use of prison labor. The Chinese have reported back on all 16 cases, admitting that four of the facilities involved have used prison labor for export production in the past. The Chinese maintain that the factories either have ceased exporting, or have removed prisoners from the production line. U.S. officials have visited three prisons and have standing requests to visit five others, including a revisit to one facility.

In the past two years, U.S. Customs has aggressively expanded its enforcement of U.S. laws banning the import of prison labor products. Customs has issued over twenty orders banning suspected Chinese goods from entering the U.S., achieved one court conviction of a U.S. company for importing prison made machine tools and detained suspected equipment in another case. We are actively looking into recent allegations of violations of the prison labor MOU. Talks with China will continue on the full enforcement of the provisions of this agreement.

Conditions for Renewal in 1994

China has made progress in recent years in the areas of human rights, nonproliferation, and trade. Nevertheless, I believe more progress is necessary and possible in each of these three areas. In considering the optimal method of encouraging further progress on these issues, I have decided to issue the attached Executive Order which outlines the areas in the field of human rights with respect to which China, in order to receive positive consideration for a renewal of MFN in 1994, will have to make overall, significant progress in the next 12 months.

In considering extension of MFN, we will take into account Chinese actions with respect to the following:

—Respecting the fundamental human rights recognized in the Universal Declaration of Human Rights.

—Complying with China's commitment to allow its citizens, regardless of their political views, freedom to emigrate and travel abroad (excepting those who are imprisoned, have criminal proceedings pending against them, or have received court notices concerning civil cases).

—Providing an acceptable accounting for and release of Chinese citizens imprisoned or detained for the peaceful expression of their political views, including Democracy Wall and Tiananmen activists.

—Taking effective steps to ensure that forced abortion and sterilization are not used to implement China's family planning policies.

—Ceasing religious persecution, particularly by releasing leaders and members of religious groups detained or imprisoned for expression of their religious beliefs.

—Taking effective actions to ensure that prisoners are not being mistreated and are receiving necessary medical treatment, such as by granting access to Chinese prisons by international humanitarian organizations.

—Seeking to resume dialogue with the Dalai Lama or his representatives, and taking measures to protect Tibet's distinctive religious and cultural heritage.

—Continuing cooperation concerning U.S. military personnel who are listed as prisoners of war or missing in action.

—Ceasing the jamming of Voice of America broadcasts.

The Administration will also use tools under existing legislation and executive determinations to encourage further progress in human rights.

In addition, I wish to make clear my continuing and strong determination to pursue objectives in the areas of nonproliferation and trade, utilizing other instruments available, including appropriate legislation and executive determinations. For example, various provisions of U.S. law contain strong measures against irresponsible proliferation of weapons of mass destruction and nuclear weapons technology. These include missile proliferation sanctions under the National Defense Authorization Act. Using these tools as necessary, we will continue to press China to implement its commitments to abide by international standards and agreements in the nonproliferation area.

In the area of trade, the Clinton Administration will continue to press for full and faithful implementation of bilateral agreements with

China on market access, intellectual property rights, and prison labor. Section 301 of the 1974 Trade Act is a powerful instrument to ensure our interests are protected and advanced in the areas of market access and intellectual property rights. The Administration will also continue to implement vigorously the provisions of the Tariff Act of 1930 to prevent importation of goods made by forced labor.

Remarks Announcing White House Staff Changes and an Exchange With Reporters
May 29, 1993

The President. Good morning, ladies and gentlemen. The objective of this White House and everyone who works in it is to improve the lives of the American people and to change their lives for the better. We have been working on that from the beginning. It takes the right people and the right organization to achieve those objectives. For the last several weeks the Chief of Staff Mack McLarty has been working to make appropriate changes in the White House to strengthen our ability to do our job for the American people.

I am pleased today to welcome to the White House staff one of the Nation's most respected journalists and commentators, David Gergen. I have known David for many years. He is a trusted friend and a dedicated public servant. By agreeing to accept Mack McLarty's invitation to join the White House team he is demonstrating one of the qualities for which he is well known, a sense of patriotism that transcends partisanship.

David Gergen is a Republican, as well as a longtime friend of mine. He is a moderate, prochange, patriotic American. We have shared many ideas over the years and found much agreement in the work I have done as Governor and with the Democratic Leadership Council and in many of the ideas I espoused in the campaign of 1992. I want him to help me make those ideas a reality in the lives of the American people.

The message here is that we are rising above politics. We are going beyond the partisanship that damaged this country so badly in the last several years to search for new ideas, a new common ground, a new national unity.

I am also announcing that my longtime and trusted aide George Stephanopoulos will be working with me more closely, as he did in the campaign, on important matters of policy and strategy and day-to-day decisionmaking, helping me to integrate all the complicated debates that confront my Office. One of the reasons for this move is that I have missed very badly and I have needed the kind of contact and support that I received from George in the campaign, that I think was absolutely essential to the victory that was secured.

I'd now like to introduce the Chief of Staff and thank Mack McLarty for all the hard work that he has been doing, especially in the last few weeks, to try to strengthen the White House and make it able to do the things that we pledged to do for the American people. Mr. McLarty.

[*At this point, Thomas McLarty, David Gergen, and George Stephanopoulos made statements in support of the changes in the White House staff.*]

White House Staff

Q. Mr. President, the decision to bring in a Republican for this key position, does this mean you're going back to your centrist or New Democrat roots that you articulated during the campaign? And what does it mean about some of the more controversial decisions recently that suggested you were moving towards the more liberal wing of the Democratic Party, specifically your civil rights Assistant Attorney General nominee Lani Guinier? Do you still want her to become the Assistant Attorney General for civil rights?

The President. Today I want to talk about David Gergen, George Stephanopoulos, and the White House staff. The announcement that I have made today with Mr. McLarty—it was really his idea; I want to give him the credit for it; I wish it had been mine, but it wasn't— signals to the American people where I am, what I believe, and what I'm going to do.

I did not get into this race for President to divide the American people. I got into the race to unite the American people and to move this country forward. I have always, throughout my public life, had supporters who were independents, who were Republicans, who were interested in ideas and movement and not in partisan gridlock and moving the American people apart. That's what I'm trying to do. That's what I've always wanted to do. And that's what this announcement today means.

President's Priorities

Q. Mr. President, Mr. Gergen talked about scorching partisanship on Capitol Hill and elsewhere in this town. He said that four of the five last Presidents have been broken by the weight of the office that you now hold. Do you feel that you're at that point? Do you feel the weight? And do you feel there's a chance that you, too, could be broken by it?

The President. I don't know about the weight. I feel the responsibility. I have made a deliberate decision to move rapidly to do things which I think need to be done which have been neglected, and to push the agenda forward, especially on the budget. And as you know, we're moving forward in a record pace now with a very tough and difficult set of choices for the American people that I think will allow us to reclaim our destiny.

I believe that, when the history of this administration is written, we will look back and see that taking on the tough decisions early was the right decision for the people of this country. But I have been very concerned that the cumulative effect of some of the things which are now very much in the news has given to the administration a tinge that is too partisan and not connected to the mainstream, prochange, future-oriented politics and policies that I ran for President to implement. And that's what I want to do.

I think that this will help me to be a successful President. But the issue is not whether I'll be a successful President, it's whether we'll have a successful country. And I believe we will. And I think this is one big step toward that today.

Improving Communication

Q. Mr. President, with your public opinion polls fairly low right now, does this change suggest an inability to get your message out so far, or change it?

The President. I don't think that anybody would be surprised to admit that the major work of this administration and the passionate concerns of this administration are not always the things which come to mind in what's being communicated to the American people. So do we want to improve our ability to communicate what we believe and what we're doing? Yes, we do.

When I had the nationally televised town hall meeting here last week and all those people came up to me and said afterward how much better they felt about their country having been here and having had a personal conversation, knowing exactly where I and where my administration is coming from, what our values and objectives are, it made it utterly clear to me that if the American people knew exactly what we were doing, just like they did on the night of February 17th, they would support these tough decisions and these difficult changes.

On the other hand, I think it unrealistic ever to assume you can take on the kind of challenges that we are trying to take on without having some momentary bumps and runs in the public opinion polls. We can't be governed by that. But what I want to know is that the American people at least know me, know who I am, where I'm coming from, and more importantly, know what our administration is about. Then whatever their opinions in the polls will be will actively reflect the reality of who we are and their judgment about it. That's all I want. And I think that's what the communications can do.

President's Priorities

Q. Mr. President, you've made much of cutting the White House staff in an effort to reduce Government spending. With the addition of Mr. Gergen and the rumored addition of others, doesn't that seem out of keeping with a leaner White House staff?

The President. The White House staff is going to be much leaner than it was before, but the number one task that I have is to serve the American people. Let me just give you an example. One of the things we never could have anticipated is that we'd get more mail here in 3½ months than the White House did in all of 1992.

I am cutting the Federal Government. I am cutting the White House staff. We are doing that. But I think our number one objective is to serve the American people well. And that's what we're trying to do.

I have got to go to West Point. I am going to be late, and that would be a terrible mistake. I owe it to the graduating seniors at West Point to get them off on their military careers on time. I'm sorry.

Thank you.

NOTE: The President spoke at 7:30 a.m. in the Rose Garden at the White House.

The President's Radio Address
May 29, 1993

Good morning. This weekend, in solemn ceremonies and joyful gatherings, families will honor the military personnel who have kept us free. In honoring these patriots we honor what is best in the American spirit.

I'll be joining those families at West Point to pay tribute to the officers graduating from the military academy, at Arlington National Cemetery to lay a wreath and pray for the fallen, and at the remarkable memorial to the men and women who died in Vietnam whose names are engraved in its polished walls and whose memories are etched in the hearts of the American people. These are the heroes who have protected our borders, defended our interests, and preserved our values.

Our military strength makes our freedom possible. But our military might depends on our economic strength. Just as our liberty cannot rest upon a hollow army, our strong military cannot rest upon a hollow economy. Our ability to remain strong abroad is founded on our ability to remain strong here at home. For too many years the people in Washington in both parties have permitted our strength to ebb. Government of gridlock and favoritism for the few has caused our economy to lose its historic promise in a time of intense global competition when we have to change and when the status quo isn't enough.

Look at the results of the last several years: middle class families working longer hours for lower wages; economic growth in this recovery slowing to historically low levels; 9 million Americans out of work in the 25th month of what is supposed to be a recovery. Thirty-five million Americans go to bed every night facing a serious illness or injury which could bankrupt their families because they have no health insurance, and many, many millions more fear losing their health insurance if they have to change jobs and they have a sick person in their family or if their company goes down.

In the midst of all of these challenges our National Government too long has given enormous tax cuts to the wealthiest Americans and special interests and, at the same time, reduced investments in areas essential to productivity and security of working families. And in our cities, small towns, and rural areas, look what's happened. In the last 12 years the Government's debt has grown from $1 trillion to $4 trillion, in just 12 years. And what a burden and shackle it has become.

The American economy is in the middle of the global marketplace, challenged by nations who have made wise investments in their people, their workers, and their technological edge, and who have disciplined their own spending on other things. If we don't start getting better, we can fall behind, and the American way of life will be denied to this generation and the next. This is the great struggle of our time. And it is a challenge I am determined our country will meet, a battle we will win.

At stake is whether Washington will stop doing business as usual and put our own house in order and put our people first, whether we will be satisfied with the status quo and let the special interests continue to dictate our country's future, or whether we will expand American prosperity and preserve the American dream.

Just this week, the House of Representatives stepped up to the plate and voted for change, for growth, for renewal. The House voted for an economic program that really reduces the deficit through specific spending cuts that will lead to economic growth. They voted for 200 cuts in old spending programs, $250 billion in deficit reduction through spending cuts alone. We also asked the wealthy to pay their fair share because they are able to pay more and because in the last 12 years taxes have gone down on the wealthy as their incomes have gone up. Of the money we raise in taxes 75 percent of it comes from individuals with incomes above $100,000.

The plan also asks the middle class to make a modest contribution through an energy tax. In 1994, a family making $40,000 a year will pay a dollar a month; the next year, $7 a month; the next year $17 a month when the energy tax is fully phased in.

Our plan for economic growth is serious about deficit reduction, by asking all but the most meagerly supplied working families and the poor to make a contribution. We reduce our deficit by $500 billion. That puts our fiscal house in order. It pays down the deficit, and at the same time, it does something else we have to do: we make a down payment on future economic growth, investing in the work skills, the education standards, the technologies that our people need to be able to compete and win in global markets.

This plan rewards full-time work instead of lifetime welfare. For the first time, this plan will make it possible for us to say to every American family, if you work 40 hours a week and you have children in the home, you won't be in poverty. That means that people will no longer have an incentive to prefer welfare to work. In fact, it will be the other way around.

The House of Representatives deserves our special thanks for passing our plan. Now it's time for the Senators to do the right thing as well. But unfortunately, even well-intentioned and respected legislators are still clinging to the illusions of the past, that somehow there are easy ways out of this and no-pain decisions.

Then other people in the Senate would actually pay for lower taxes on the very wealthy by cutting Social Security benefits for older Americans living barely above the poverty line. And for working Americans living barely above the poverty line, they'd be denied tax benefits so there could be more to upper-income people. If we were to protect interest groups from paying their fair share of taxes by cutting the earned-income tax credit for low-income working Americans, we'd just force millions of low-wage workers back into poverty and force many into welfare.

These ideas would return us to the failed policies of the past, policies that increased our deficit, short-changed our future, and put narrow interests over national interests. But those days are over. Gridlock is out. Growth is in. It's time for the Senate to join the House and get with this program.

This is not about politics. It's about America's future, about rebuilding the foundation of our prosperity, about restoring the confidence of our people in Washington's capacity to deal with our common problems. It's about being strong nationally and about our families being secure and strong in their homes and in their lives.

We're making progress. We're turning things around. We're doing it together like a family. On Memorial Day, let's rededicate ourselves to our Armed Services who are fighting for our national security and to our common economic future which makes that national security possible.

Thanks for listening.

NOTE: The address was recorded at 1:27 p.m. on May 28 in the Wyndham Franklin Plaza Hotel in Philadelphia, PA, for broadcast at 10:06 a.m. on May 29.

Remarks at the United States Military Academy Commencement Ceremony in West Point, New York
May 29, 1993

Thank you very much. Please be seated.

General Graves, thank you for that fine introduction and for your outstanding leadership here. General Sullivan and the distinguished

platform guests, distinguished guests, all the families and guests of this graduating class, and most of all, to the young men and women of the Corps of Cadets, it is a great privilege for me today to join in this celebration of accomplishment.

To the class of 1993, I want to extend my heartfelt congratulations. You've worked hard, and you've well earned the honor bestowed upon you today.

To your parents and your relatives, let me assure you that however often you've wondered about it, you really aren't dreaming. Your sons and daughters, your brothers and sisters really made it. And you can take pride in their graduation and in the strong values that you must have helped to instill in them that made this day possible for them.

To the faculty and staff of this wonderful Academy, let me offer my gratitude for your dedication as this historic institution graduates its 50,000th cadet. It is said here at West Point that much of the history you teach was made by the people you taught. That's true and very much to your credit. The work you and your predecessors have carried forward since 1802 is truly that of nation-building, and today your Nation thanks you once again.

For the class of 1993, today marks the completion of an arduous process. I look out at you and think you endured Beast Barracks. You passed countless PT tests, none of which I could pass anymore. [*Laughter*] You have met high standards for discipline, for physical fitness, for academics, and I must say, I am impressed by your haircuts. [*Laughter*]

No one is perfect, of course, as even the President demonstrates from time to time. I'm reminded that one of your greatest graduates and one of my predecessors as Commander in Chief, General Dwight Eisenhower, was punished as a cadet for such terrible offenses as, I quote, "apparently making no reasonable effort to have his room properly cleaned at a.m. inspection," and—I wonder what a "reasonable effort" is—and second, "being late for breakfast." In the unlikely event that there have been any such breaches of discipline on your part, let me announce today that in keeping with customary practice, I exercise my prerogative as Commander in Chief to grant amnesty to the Corps of Cadets. [*Applause*] I hope the assembled crowd is not too troubled that so many seem to be celebrating. [*Laughter*]

Two centuries ago at this bend in the Hudson River, America's first defenders stretched a chain across the river to prevent British ships from dividing and conquering our new Nation.

Today we add 1,003 new links to that unbroken chain of America's defenders, 1,003 new and solid segments in the Long Gray Line, a line that stretches back 191 years through your ranks and as far into the future as the Lord lets the United States of America exist. The Long Gray Line has never failed us, and I believe it never will.

Like the great chain itself, you have emerged from the forge, tested and tempered, composed of a stronger metal than you brought here. Forty-eight months ago, you came here as young adults. Today when you leave this stadium, you will be officers of the United States Army.

West Point has prepared you for a life of service. And as you well know, West Point's graduates have served America in many, many ways, not only by leading troops into combat but also by exploring frontiers, founding universities, laying out the railroads, building the Panama Canal, running corporations, serving in the Congress and in the White House, and walking on the Moon.

Yet, no service is more important or admirable than your simple decision to put on the uniform of this great Nation and to serve wherever America calls you in defense of freedom. The willingness to serve and sacrifice for the greater good is the ultimate tribute to your character and your efforts. For those services and sacrifices, those that brought you here and those that will take you and our great Nation into the future, you have the appreciation of all the American people.

You have stepped forward not only to serve but to lead. For the hallmark of West Point has been its tradition of growing leaders of character. Whenever the Nation called, members of the Long Gray Line have led the way. Your predecessors led tight-lipped troops into the smoke and flame of battle at Chancellorsville and Gettysburg. They were first out of the muddy trenches into the attack at the Meuse-Argonne. They led the first wave of assaults from Normandy. They held the line at Pusan and were first off the helicopters in the Ia Drang Valley and the Iron Triangle. More recent graduates were among those who jumped into Panama and led the charge into Iraq. And the corps was there as well when the call came from the victims of hunger, when the call came from the victims of Hurricane Andrew. From Florida to Somalia, you have been there.

The 172 battle streamers on the Army flag

commemorate the skill and courage of those who have gone before you. Marked and unmarked graves around the world testify to the corps' selfless devotion to country. Your steadfast commitment to duty, honor, country is our national strength.

My commitment and that of the Congress and the American people is to stand by you. That means before we ask you to put your life and the lives of those whom you command in harm's way, it is our solemn responsibility to take your advice, to give you the tools you need, and then to give you our complete support. That is our pledge to you as you enter this career.

You are pinning on your gold bars at a time of remarkable challenge and change for the United States. On this Memorial Day weekend, we all pray that we have sent America's sons and daughters to war for the last time. Yet, history suggests that during your years of service, we will again need to call upon America's weapons and warriors to defend our national interests.

The changes of recent years allow us to be hopeful. But common sense reminds us to be prepared. One way we must be prepared is by ensuring that our forces have what they need to get the job done, the equipment and the quality people needed to ensure that we can achieve decisive victory should we be called to battle once again. As our forces must change to meet the challenges and dangers of a new world, one need will remain constant, the requirement for leaders of character.

You will be called upon in many ways in this era: to keep the peace, to relieve suffering, to help teach officers from new democracies in the ways of a democratic army, and still to fulfill the fundamental mission which General MacArthur reminded us of, which is always to be ready to win our wars.

But whatever the challenge, I know you will accomplish your mission, not only because of your training but because of your values and character. I will do my part by doing whatever is necessary to keep our forces ready—and to keep our microphones up. [*Laughter*] I will do my part—and I think the Congress will, too—to make sure that our forces are always ready to fight and win on a moment's notice. We ought, really, to meet the standard of one of your classmates, Pat Malcolm, who came in the clutch and delivered the goods for you. If we can do that, you will be able to serve.

If you have the character and will to win, we owe it to you to make you the best trained, the best prepared, the best equipped, and the best supported fighting force on the face of the Earth.

The budget cuts that have come at the end of the cold war were necessary, even welcome, appropriate in light of the collapse of the Soviet Union and other changes. But we must be mindful, even as we try so hard to reduce this terrible national deficit, that there is a limit beyond which we must not go. We have to ensure that the United States is ready, ready to win and superior to all other military forces in the world.

In doing that, we can ensure that the values you learned here and the values you brought here from your families and your communities back home will be able to spread throughout this country and throughout the world and give other people the opportunity to live as you have lived, to fulfill your God-given capacities.

We must also stay prepared by understanding the threats of this new era. We can't predict the future. We cannot tell precisely when the next challenge will come or exactly what form it will take. Yet, we do know that the threats we face are fundamentally different from those of the recent past. The end of the bipolar superpower cold war leaves us with unfamiliar threats, not the absence of danger.

Consider what we witness today in the world you will move into: ethnic and religious conflict, the violent turmoil of dissolving or newly created states, the random violence of the assassin and the terrorist. These are forces that plagued the world in the early days of this century. As we scan today's bloodiest conflicts, from the former Soviet Union and Yugoslavia to Armenia to Sudan, the dynamics of the cold war have been replaced by many of the dynamics of old war. A particularly troubling new element in the world you face, however, is the proliferation around the globe of weapons of mass destruction and the means for their delivery. Today, ambitious and violent regimes seek to acquire arsenals of nuclear, biological, and chemical warfare.

As we discovered in Iraq, surging stocks of ballistic missiles and other advanced arms have enabled outlaw nations to extend the threat of mass destruction a long way beyond their own borders. And meeting these new threats will require a new approach and a new determination shared by all peace-loving nations to oppose the spread of these dread weapons. In the coming months, our administration will address the dangers from growing stockpiles of nuclear materials that could be used in these weapons and the risk of nuclear smuggling and terrorism.

We will soon begin negotiations on a comprehensive test ban treaty which will increase our political leverage to combat this proliferation. We will reform our export controls to keep weapons-related technologies out of the wrong hands, while cutting redtape for legitimate American export activities. And we must make further changes in how we organize the Government to reflect the priority that we place on nonproliferation. For, if we must contemplate the possibility of sending America's men and women once again into harm's way, then we owe it to you to do our best to prevent the proliferation of weapons that could vastly multiply the dangers and the casualties of any conflict.

Ultimately, preparedness lies in strength. And if our Nation is to be strong abroad, it must also be strong at home. It was President Eisenhower who once said, "A strong economy is the physical basis, the physical basis of all our military power."

One of the most potent weapons behind our victory in World War II was the industrial might of the United States. What ultimately enabled us to prevail in the cold war was the simple fact that our free political and economic institutions had produced more prosperity and more personal human happiness than did the confining institutions of communism. In the same way our global era leadership must, must depend on our ability to create jobs and growth and opportunity for Americans here at home who, in turn, will have the finances to make sure we can maintain the world's strongest military.

Unfortunately, for too many years in this new global economy, we have had difficulty maintaining opportunity at home. In the face of intense competition around the world and the now-familiar problems we have in the United States, our debt has grown from $1 trillion to $4 trillion, even as we have reduced military spending and investments in areas that are crucial to our future in new technologies, in education and training, and in converting defense cutbacks into domestic economic opportunities.

Today we face an especially troubling phenomenon that the United States has never faced before at home: slow economic growth which does not create new jobs. We must refuse to accept this as a pattern that will be repeated in the future. Just as our security cannot rest upon a hollow army, neither can it rest upon a hollow economy.

If we are to sustain the American way of life that you have been trained so well to defend, we must do more and do better. We must cultivate the teacher who can hold her class' attention, encourage the entrepreneur who bets his savings on his own ideas. We must do right by the middle class families of this country who work hard and play by the rules. We must pay down the deficit and make downpayments on the future, both at the same time, honoring work, rewarding investment, and sharpening our competitive edge. If you can win on the battlefield, surely America can win in every field of competition we must face as we march toward the 21st century.

That is the great challenge facing our country. And the Congress today is facing that challenge in dealing with the economic plan I have presented. The House of Representatives, led by concerned Americans like Congressman Jack Reed, who is the only West Point graduate in the United States Congress, has sent a plan to the Senate which now must be produced from the Senate in the form of an economic plan to bring this country back.

In this new era, those of us in political life need a new strategy, need sound tactics, need the kind of discipline in implementing it that all of you have learned to provide for our Nation's defense here at West Point. In short, we must approach the job of rebuilding our Nation with the same kind of single-minded determination that you have brought your skills, your dedication, and leadership ability to in these 4 years and that you will bring to the defense of our Nation in the years ahead. We can do no less for you.

Finally, let me say this. Someday, some of you out here will be sitting in the Situation Room at the White House or with the President or with the Secretary of Defense in some other circumstance. At that moment you will be called to give your advice on an issue which may be small but also may be large and of incredible significance to the future of this country. I ask you in all the years ahead to keep preparing for that day throughout your careers by continuing study and continuous listening and continuous absorption of every experience you have.

The world is changing rapidly, and if you do not work to make change our friend, then it can become our enemy. You represent the very best of the American people. It will be your understanding of our Nation's challenges and your embodiment of our Nation's values, enriched by what you have learned here, leavened by the experiences to come, bound by your commitment to "Duty, Honor, Country" which will permit you to make our greatest contribution to the Nation: continuing service. You have earned your turn to lead, to follow in the footsteps of those who have been on the Plain before you.

Over the past 4 years, your Nation has invested heavily in you. The skills and dedication you now bring to the defense of our Nation are more than ample repayment. I am proud of the work you do, honored to serve as your Commander in Chief, confident that all Americans join me in saluting your achievement, and very, very optimistic about the future of our Nation in your hands.

Good luck. God bless you, and God bless America.

NOTE: The President spoke at 10:20 a.m. in Michie Stadium. In his remarks, he referred to Lt. Gen. Howard D. Graves, USA, Superintendent, U.S. Military Academy; Gen. Gordon R. Sullivan, USA, Chief of Staff, U.S. Army; and Pat Malcolm, who kicked the winning field goal in the 1992 Army-Navy football game.

Remarks on the Observance of the 50th Anniversary of World War II
May 31, 1993

Good morning. Please be seated. It's a great honor for the First Lady and for me to have all of you here in the White House today. I want to welcome all of you, and a few by name, beginning with the Secretary of Veterans Affairs Jesse Brown; the Deputy Secretary of Defense Dr. William Perry; Marvin Runyon, the Postmaster General; Lt. General Claude Kicklighter, the Executive Director of the World War II Commemoration Committee; Mr. Roger Durbin, a World War II veteran and the initiator of the World War II Commemorative Coin legislation. Also here with me, representing all World War II veterans, is Admiral Eugene Fluckey. I'd like to welcome Congresswoman Marcy Kaptur from Ohio, an ardent supporter of veterans' cause who heeded the call of her constituent, Mr. Durbin, and took the lead on the legislation to issue the World War II 50th Anniversary Commemorative Coin, to fund a building of the World War II Memorial here in Washington with no net cost to the United States Treasury. I wonder if we might undertake some other programs with that device. [*Laughter*]

I'd like to thank our good friend, Senator Jay Rockefeller from West Virginia, another great advocate for veterans, for being here with us; Secretary Shannon from the Army; Admiral Kelso, wearing both his Chief of Naval Operations and Navy Secretary hats today; Secretary Donley from the Air Force; Admiral Jeremiah, the Vice Chair of the Joint Chiefs; General Sullivan, the Army Chief of Staff who took me to West Point on Saturday for one of the better days of my life, thank you, General; General McPeak, the Chief of Staff of the Air Force; General Mundy, the Commandant of the Marine Corps; and Admiral Kime, the Commandant of the Coast Guard. I'm delighted to welcome the many representatives of veteran service organizations who are here with us today.

I want to say a special word of thanks to the veterans organizations, and the VA particularly, for working with the health care task force that the First Lady is chairing so closely on health care. Hillary visited the Washington, DC, VA medical centers on May 29th, and she talked to me in our brief stay at Camp David for 30 or 40 minutes about how impressed she was about what she saw there. And we are very, very hopeful that we can work with the active military health operations and with the VA in working through this health care issue. I think you have a major role to play.

I'd also like to say a special word of thanks to the people who were involved in the May 28th kickoff of this weekend's Memorial Day remembrances. There I had the opportunity to speak with three VA medical centers, a telephone conversation that initiated a program replacing the old system of isolating veterans in these hospitals from their families and friends by replacing it with a system where telephones are placed alongside their beds and are usable by veterans even with severe disabilities. We now are having five hospitals so equipped, but eventually will have 174 veterans hospitals where veterans will be able to call from their bedside to their families and friends.

This is an important issue. One of the men I talked with in Queens has three children; two of them are in the service and are overseas. And now, even though he is quite ill, he'll be able to talk on this day to both of his children who, like him, are serving in the armed services.

In just a few moments I'm going to sign a resolution and a proclamation designating this May 31st through June 7th as a period of national observance, as part of the 50th anniversary of World War II. But before I do that, and before Postmaster General Runyon and I unveil this year's additions of the World War II Commemorative Stamps, I'd like to say just a few things about the debt that all of us owe to our veterans.

Fifty years ago, the United States and its allies were engaged in a monumental struggle to defeat a totalitarian Axis bent on controlling the world, to preserve the dignity of mankind and to protect individual freedom. Americans from every walk of life were called upon to sacrifice their freedoms and their comforts, to undergo great danger to shore up our Nation's future, and to fight for democracy.

As we observe the 50th anniversary of World War II, our country must remember and honor the million who defended democracy and defeated aggression. We learned from those early defeats in World War II that we must remain vigilant and always prepared to resist future aggression and that all nations dedicated to freedom must stand together. The freedoms we enjoy today are results of our victory over aggression, and the efforts the United States makes today to work with all other nations who love and believe in freedom are a testimony to the wisdom of the lessons learned then.

We must be committed now to leave our children a world free of the horrors of war: hatred, violence, and inhumanity. Franklin Roosevelt once said, "We must cultivate the science of human relationships, the ability of all people to live and work together in the same world at peace." I think Admiral Fluckey, a courageous man, would agree that while courage and deeds of warriors are indeed heroic, the ultimate goal of this courage is to make it unnecessary for future generations.

President Kennedy once said, "It is an unfortunate fact that we can secure the peace only by preparing for war." Our Nation stands committed to defend itself and our allies by remaining strong and vigilant and ready. And therefore, it is very fitting that this week-long period of national observance of the 50th anniversary of World War II begins on Memorial Day, a day when we remember and honor our Nation's war dead. As we work toward a more peaceful future, it is appropriate that we remember and thank the brave and selfless patriots who served our Nation 50 years ago.

During this commemoration, Americans of all ages must also remember those who gave their lives and dedicated themselves in other wars so that our Nation could remain free and strong, so that the deeds, the commitment, and the sacrifice of those who made this commitment will not have been in vain.

I have asked the Secretary of Defense Les Aspin, who is in Brussels today, in conjunction with the Secretary of Veterans Affairs Jesse Brown, to continue coordinating the commemorative events of the 50th anniversary of the Second World War. I want to urge all the veterans, the Government, the civic, the business, and the patriotic organizations to join together in expression so that a grateful Nation will remember. Our Nation will rededicate itself during this time to studying the lessons of the past.

I want to say in closing, again, how grateful I am to have all of you here in the White House today. This is your house. You have paid the price for it, and those whom you represent made the fact that it is still standing possible. We are all very, very grateful to you.

Thank you very much.

NOTE: The President spoke at 9:15 a.m. in the East Room at the White House. H.J. Res. 80, approved May 31, was assigned Public Law 103–34. The proclamation on the national observance of the 50th anniversary of World War II is listed in Appendix D at the end of this volume.

Remarks at a Memorial Day Ceremony at Arlington National Cemetery in Arlington, Virginia
May 31, 1993

Thank you very much. General Gordon, distinguished leaders of the armed services, the Defense Department, the Cabinet, the Congress, the leaders of our veterans organizations here, to all the veterans and their families who are here and to all those here who are family members of veterans buried in this cemetery or in any other place around the globe, and to my fellow Americans: We come together this morning, along with our countrymen and women in cities across the land, to honor those who died that we might live in freedom, the only way that Americans can ever truly live. Today we put aside our differences to better reflect on what unites us. The lines so often drawn between and among us, lines of region or race or partisanship, all those lines fall away today as we gaze upon the lines of markers that surround us on these hallowed hills. The lines of difference are freedom's privilege. The lines of these markers are freedom's cost.

Today Americans all across our land draw together in shared experience and shared remembrance. And whether it is an older veteran in Florida, or a teenager in New Mexico, or a mother in Wisconsin, all today will bow their heads and put hand to heart. And without knowing each other, still we will all be joined in spirit, because we are Americans and because we know we are equal shareholders in humanity's most uplifting dream.

Today, as we fly the American flag, some will recall the pledge we began to recite daily as youngsters in grade school, with solemn faith and awkward salute, some of us even before we learned the difference between our right and left hands. Others will remember the flag waving over public gatherings, large and very small. But on this day, in this serene and solemn setting, conscious of the past, conscious, too, of the perils all too present, what we see most vividly in that flag are the faces of American soldiers who gave their lives in battle and the faces of this generation of young service men and women, very, very much alive, still training and preparing for possible conflicts tomorrow. From the first militiaman downed at Lexington to today's rawest recruit, the flag unites them,

soldiers living and dead, and reminds the rest of us that we are all the inheritors of a sacred trust.

It is with that flag and that trust in mind that we resolve this May morning to keep America free, strong, and proud. We resolve in this era of profound change and continuing peril to be ever vigilant against any foe that could endanger us and against any undercurrent that might erode our security, including the economic security that is the ultimate foundation of our Nation's strength. We resolve, as well, always to keep America's Armed Forces the finest in the world. And we resolve that if we ask them to fight in our behalf, we will give them the clear mission, the means, and the support they need to win.

In honoring those who died in the defense of our country, we must never neglect to honor as well our living American veterans. The Nation owes a special debt to the millions of men and women who took up posts at home or abroad to secure our defenses or to fight for our freedom. Because of what they have done for us, their health and well-being must always be a cause for our special concern.

Here by the Tomb of the Unknown Soldier, we renew our Nation's solemn pledge also to the POW and MIA families from all wars, a pledge to provide not just the prayers and memorials but also to the extent humanly possible to provide the answers you deserve. And we vow, with the new Korean War Memorial project finally underway, that no future conflict, if conflict there must be, must ever be regarded as a forgotten war. The inscription on the Tomb of the Unknown Soldier says that he is, quote, "Known only to God." But that is only partly true. While the soldier's name is known only to God, we know a lot about him. We know he served his country, honored his community, and died for the cause of freedom. And we know that no higher praise can be assigned to any human being than those simple words.

Today we are at peace, but we live in a troubled world. From that flag and from these, our honored dead, we draw strength and inspiration to carry on in our time the tasks of defending and preserving freedom that were so nobly fulfilled by all those we come here to honor in this time. In that effort and in the presence of those buried all around us, we ask the support of all Americans in the aid and blessing of God Almighty. Thank you very much.

NOTE: The President spoke at 11:30 a.m. at the Memorial Amphitheater. In his remarks, he referred to Maj. Gen. F.A. Gordon, USA, commander of the Military District of Washington.

Remarks at a Memorial Day Ceremony at the Vietnam Veterans Memorial
May 31, 1993

Thank you very much. General Powell, General McCaffrey, and my good friend Lew Puller, whom I did not know was coming here today, I thank you so much.

To all of you who are shouting, I have heard you. I ask you now to hear me. I have heard you. Some have suggested that it is wrong for me to be here with you today because I did not agree a quarter of a century ago with the decision made to send the young men and women to battle in Vietnam. Well, so much the better. Here we are celebrating America today. Just as war is freedom's cost, disagreement is freedom's privilege, and we honor it here today. But I ask all of you to remember the words that have been said here today. And I ask you at this monument: Can any American be out of place? And can any Commander in Chief be in any other place but here on this day? I think not.

Many volumes have been written about this war and those complicated times. But the message of this memorial is quite simple: These men and women fought for freedom, brought honor to their communities, loved their country, and died for it. They were known to all of us. There's not a person in this crowd today who did not know someone on this wall. Four of my high school classmates are there. Four who shared with me the joys and trials of childhood and did not live to see the three score and ten years the Scripture says we are entitled to.

Let us continue to disagree, if we must, about the war. But let us not let it divide us as a people any longer. No one has come here today to disagree about the heroism of those whom we honor. But the only way we can really honor their memory is to resolve to live and serve today and tomorrow as best we can and to make America the best that she can be. Surely that is what we owe to all those whose names are etched in this beautiful memorial. As we all resolve to keep the finest military in the world, let us remember some of the lessons that all agree on. If the day should come when our service men and women must again go into combat, let us all resolve they will go with the training, the equipment, the support necessary to win, and most important of all, with a clear mission to win.

Let us do what is necessary to regain control over our destiny as a people here at home, to strengthen our economy and develop the capacities of all of our people, to rebuild our communities and our families where children are raised and character is developed. Let us keep the American dream alive.

Today, let us also renew a pledge to the families whose names are not on this wall because their sons and daughters did not come home. We will do all we can to give you not only the attention you have asked for but the answers you deserve.

Today I have ordered that by Veterans Day we will have declassified all United States Government records related to POW's and MIA's from the Vietnam war, all those records, except for a tiny fraction which could still affect our national security or invade the privacy of their families. As we allow the American public to have access to what our Government knows, we will press harder to find out what other governments know. We are pressing the Vietnamese to provide this accounting not only because it is the central outstanding issue in our relationship with Vietnam but because it is a central commitment made by the American Government to our people, and I intend to keep it.

You heard General Powell quoting President Lincoln: "With malice toward none and charity for all let us bind up the Nation's wounds." Lincoln speaks to us today across the years. Let us resolve to take from this haunting and beautiful memorial a renewed sense of our national unity and purpose, a deepened gratitude for the sacrifice of those whose names we touched and whose memories we revere, and a finer dedication to making America a better place for their children and for our children, too.

Thank you all for coming here today. God bless you, and God bless America.

NOTE: The President spoke at 2:07 p.m. at the memorial. In his remarks, he referred to Lewis B. Puller, Jr., Vietnam veteran and Pulitzer prize-winning author.

Memorandum on Trade Agreements
May 31, 1993

Memorandum for the United States Trade Representative

Subject: Presidential Determination Under Section 1105(b)(1) of the Omnibus Trade and Competitiveness Act of 1988

Section 1105(b)(1) of the Omnibus Trade and Competitiveness Act of 1988 (Public Law 100–48; 19 U.S.C. 2904(b)(1)) ("the Act"), provides that the President shall determine, before June 1, 1993, whether any major industrial country has failed to make concessions under trade agreements entered into under section 1102(a) and (b) of the Act (19 U.S.C. 2902(a) and (b)) which provide opportunities for the commerce of the United States in such country substantially equivalent to the competitive opportunities, provided by concessions made by the United States under trade agreements entered into under section 1102(a) and (b) of the Act, for the commerce of such country in the United States.

Since the United States has not entered into any agreements under section 1102(a) or (b) of the Act, I hereby determine that there has been no failure to make concessions thereunder.

WILLIAM J. CLINTON

Remarks to the Community in Milwaukee, Wisconsin
June 1, 1993

The President. Thank you very much. Senator Kohl, Congressman Barrett, Mayor Norquist, ladies and gentlemen, it's wonderful to be back in Wisconsin and back in Milwaukee again for the first time since I became President. I suppose I ought to begin by thanking the State of Wisconsin for your electoral votes. I'm very grateful for that. I'd also like to thank the Metropolitan Milwaukee Association of Commerce and the Public Policy Forum for hosting this opportunity for me to visit with you, and through you, all the people of Wisconsin, about the economic issues facing our country.

I'd like to introduce some other people who are here, up there somewhere. I asked Senator Kohl where they were, and he said, "Up there somewhere." But it's dark. I can't see. I brought with me the former chancellor of the University of Wisconsin, now the Director of the Department of Health and Human Services, Donna Shalala, who is here; the chairman of the Joint Economic Committee in the House, your Congressman, David Obey, is here with me somewhere there; and we were met at the airport by Congressman Gerry Kleczka, who is here, Gerry; and Congressman-elect Peter Barca, who is also here somewhere. Thank you.

You know, a lot of times when I get out in the country now, people who worked for me—or who didn't, who just feel like they can come up and talk—say, "Well, aren't you worried about getting isolated up there in Washington? I mean, what's the real difference in being President and just being out here living?" And I had one thing happen to me a couple of weeks ago that illustrates the problem of being President or in the Congress or anything else.

I was in the White House and I was up on the residence floor. And I got on the elevator, and I was going down to the first floor where all big—if you've ever taken a tour of the White House, that's where all the big, fancy rooms are that the public tours. But we also use them when they're not open for tours, and I was going to a meeting there. And the young man who was taking me down in the elevator works for the Usher's Office, and of course, they were all hired under my predecessors. He didn't know me very well, and he was a little awkward, you know. So he took me downstairs, and he opened the doors of the elevator, and I found myself immediately in the presence of 30 total strangers who were standing there in front of the elevator. And it turned out that they had been walking out of a meeting with my wife on something entirely different. I didn't know them. They didn't—they knew who I was, but I'd never met any of them. [*Laughter*] And there I was. So I said hello to them, shook hands with them, and they walked by. And I turned around and looked at the young fellow running the elevator, and he was all red-faced. And he said, "Oh, Mr. President," he said, "I'm so sorry I let you out in the midst of all those people." And I looked at him, and I said, "John, that's okay. I used to be one myself." [*Laughter*]

I want to say a lot of things that I'll get into in a moment, but there are one or two things I want to say especially about Wisconsin. First, I was very moved by the drinking water crisis here. And one of the things that we tried to invest in that I don't think is a waste of your money in the next 5 years is more Federal investment in dealing with drinking water problems, waste water problems, and other environmentally related issues. I think that's a good investment of our tax dollars. And I did enjoy my conversation with your Mayor about that.

The other thing I'd like to do is to—[*applause*]. Thank you. I want to say a little more about this in a moment, but since it was brought up, I want to compliment Congressman Barrett and Congressman Kleczka for reintroducing the appropriations to fund the New Hope welfare reform project. It was vetoed last year. And I just want to tell you that, as I said, I want to say a little more about this in my speech, but the idea of giving people the tools they need to move off welfare and then calling a halt to it after 2 years, saying it has to come to an end and people who can should go to work, I think is a good thing. And I think we ought to fund that experiment in Wisconsin and see if it won't work. I think a lot of people will be for it, and I think it will work.

For any visitor who comes here to Milwaukee, as I have many times, the church steeples and the factory smokestacks are a vivid reminder of the faith and the work that made our country what it is today. People from every continent have come to our Nation and come to cities like Milwaukee and Chicago and Detroit without much money in their pockets, but filled with the faith that if they worked hard and played by the rules, they would find a better life for themselves and give their children a better chance.

In my part of the country, in the rural South, when the agricultural economy collapsed in the Depression and then didn't pick up after the Second World War, for 30 years people poured out of the places where my folks farmed in Arkansas and Mississippi and southern States and came up here to the northern cities seeking that same kind of opportunity.

Over the years in different ways our country has dealt with different economic challenges, but we have always tried to keep alive that American dream that if you worked hard and played by the rules you would be rewarded. If you were especially good you could get very, very wealthy, but everyone knew that the country would rise or fall based on the broad middle class, the small business people, the factory workers, the farmers, the people who really lifted the country and made it work.

We have, to a large extent, in the 20th century succeeded in doing that until just recently. Until recently, that is, in the last 20 years, we had succeeded in building the world's most diverse society and keeping it growing together, not coming apart.

Today, we're more diverse than ever before. One county in California, Los Angeles County, has 150 different racial and ethnic groups. Today, we still have the strongest, most vibrant free enterprise economy in the world. We have some of the most productive businesses in the world. But we have serious economic problems, as you all know.

Hard work rewarded by rising living standards is literally at the heart of what it means to be an American. It's at the heart of my family's heritage and probably at the heart of most of your families' heritage. And it's at the heart of the economic philosophy that compelled me to enter the race for President in 1991 and that brings me here again to Milwaukee today.

Once Americans looked forward to doubling their standard of living roughly every 25 years. As I said, that stopped about 20 years ago, as we began to be confronted with the highly competitive global economy and a slower rate of economic growth in our own country. Now, it will take us about 75 years to double our standard of living at the present pace. That means that not only do you have too many people who want to work who can't work, you have too many people working part-time, and you have too many people who are working like crazy and falling further and further behind. Because I believe we can do better, I asked the people of this country to give me a chance to serve as President.

As I said, it's very important to note what happened and when. Our real average hourly wages peaked about two decades ago. And since then, they've either been stagnant or declining as a whole. Indeed, the average working family is spending more hours a week on the job than they were in 1969 for lower real wages than they were making certainly 12 years ago, and in many cases, 20 years ago. This is because, as I said, of changes in the global economy, more competition from people who were either more productive than we are or who work for wages we can't live on, or lack of productivity growth, of efficiency growth in our own country, or other problems with our economy.

Twelve years ago, in 1981, after the Presidential election of 1980—another election conducted in very difficult economic circumstances—the American people decided to give another President the chance to try an approach to deal with this problem. The whole idea of Reaganomics was trickle-down economics, that we should lower taxes on the wealthiest Americans, depend upon them to invest in our economy to grow it; we should reduce domestic spending, but increase defense spending even more than we reduced domestic spending.

Now, in the last 12 years, that philosophy was modified around the edges some, but it maintained itself at the heart of our economic

dealings. Because the taxes were cut so much in '81, they were added back a little bit over the last 12 years, mostly on the middle class. And after a while, defense spending could not be sustained because of the end of the cold war, so it began to be cut. But by the time it was cut, health care costs were exploding. So all the defense cuts were swallowed up by exploding health care costs and interest payments on the debt.

But the fundamental idea remains, that the most important thing was not to worry about investment or the deficit or anything else; the most important thing was to worry about keeping taxes low on upper income people and keeping the Government's hands off the economy, except when it was necessary to invest in defense, and then when it wasn't necessary, to even get out of that.

Now, that was the theory, and we now have had a chance to see how it works. I think it's fair to say that the only reason I was elected in 1992 is that the American people thought that it hadn't worked very well, that there were problems. I say this—as I will make clear in a minute, this is not a partisan criticism, because it took bipartisan agreement at least to go along with the framework of this. But what had happened was that we had a good deal of growth in the early eighties, where we had defense increases and tax cuts, but the deficit got big. Then when the defense business got cut, all we did was pay more for the same health care. No one reinvested in the economy to give those defense workers something else to do, and the deficit got bigger and bigger and bigger.

Now, the American people voted for change. They wanted me to try to rebuild the middle class both in terms of jobs and incomes, to invest in our own people and our jobs, to cut the deficit, to open the doors of education to all, and to deal with the terrible health care crisis, and to make a real dent at welfare reform, removing people from dependence and moving them to independence.

I was sent to the White House, I think, to take on brain-dead politics in Washington from either party, or from both. Some, but not all, in the national Democratic Party have placed too much faith in the whole politics of entitlement, the idea that big bureaucracies and Government spending, demanding nothing in return, can produce the results we want. We know that is simply not true. There is a limit to how much

Government can do in the absence of an appropriate response by the American people at the grassroots level. And there is a limit to how many decisions can be made properly in Washington. And most of our growth has and always will come from the private sector.

On the other hand, some, but not all, in the national Republican Party have practiced the politics of abandonment, of walking away from common concerns like dropping test scores or rising crime rates or an insufficient infrastructure or taking care of the people who won the cold war for us and now don't have anything to do in the wake of defense cutbacks, and in simply insisting that as long as you don't raise taxes on upper income people and don't talk about it when you raise taxes on anybody else, everything's going to be fine. Well, that's not right either. We have to move beyond entitlement and abandonment.

I ran for President basically on the same things that I found had worked for me when I was a Governor, not entitlement, not abandonment but empowerment, the idea of creating a new American community by offering people more opportunity and demanding more responsibility.

I think we have made a real start at that. In the first few weeks of this administration we have passed an important political reform measure, the motor voter bill, and we have moving through the Congress a really tough lobby disclosure bill and a campaign finance reform bill that are the kind of things Wisconsin has been famous for for years.

We have tried to support the middle class in this administration. Only 17 days into the administration, I signed the family leave bill to guarantee that people don't lose their jobs when they have to take a little time off to have a baby or when there's a sick parent. The Congress is now considering our national service legislation, which would open the doors of college education to all, and soon will have a health care program that will provide real security to working families.

For the first time in 17 years the Congress passed the budget resolution, the outline of our deficit reduction plan and our plans to invest in the country, on time, for the first time in 17 years. And that helped to produce the lowest home mortgage rates in 20 years and other low interest rates because people believe we're trying to bring this deficit down. So we have made a good beginning.

But to be fair, the hard work is still ahead. The House of Representatives passed my economic program last week with some minor modifications, many of which made them better, I thought. But the hard work lies ahead. All the difficulties in this world are in the details. We can always agree on generalities. The question is, what are the specifics?

I came here to ask you to join with me in trying to tackle the three deficits that are paralyzing this country today: the deficit of dollars in our Federal budget, the deficit of investment in the private and public sectors, and the deficit of responsibility in our National Government.

Now, let's talk about this deficit, the Government's budget deficit. Our country last ran a balanced budget in 1969. We haven't balanced our national books since then. But to be fair, the deficit was not a serious problem for our economic performance until 1981 when we built permanent deficits into our Federal Government system.

What happened? President Reagan, in the midst of a recession, made what has been a typical proposal by Presidents throughout American history. He said, "We're in a recession. We ought to have a tax cut." The problem was, by the time he and the Congress got through bidding each other up and playing to the American people's hatred of taxes, the tax cut was twice the percentage of our annual income that he originally proposed. And it was adopted anyway. Nobody really thought about what it would do to the structure of the Federal budget.

And ever since then, we've been dealing with the consequences of that, plus increasing spending, as I said, first in defense, and then after defense was cut, an absolute explosion in health care costs, which I'll bet many of you have also experienced in your private health insurance premiums as well as your Government tax dollars.

Listen to this: Over the past dozen years alone, the annual deficit soared from $79 billion to $322 billion. The national debt in 12 years, after over 200 years as a nation, quadrupled from $1 trillion to $4 trillion. While Washington cut taxes on the wealthiest individuals, even after the deficit went up, we had exploding health care costs, exploding costs to pay interest on a bigger and bigger debt. And while the Government was used as a punching bag—everybody talked against big Government—no one ever really did anything fundamentally to reform the way it operates or rein in its unnecessary spending.

As this deficit soaked up more and more of our national savings which could otherwise have been invested in private plant and equipment and human skills, we created a second deficit, an investment deficit. From the 1960's to the 1980's public investment—that is, the expenditure of your Federal tax dollars in education and training, in new technologies for new jobs, and in infrastructure, things like better water systems and bridges and roads and airports— dwindled from 4½ percent to just 2.6 percent of our annual income.

Every time a company can't find qualified workers, every time trucks are rattled by highways riddled with potholes, every time a department store closes because a city is not safe after dark, we see the consequences of the investment deficit. Our income as a nation goes down, and we have fewer jobs as well.

Meanwhile, national policy rewarded companies for their financial strategies, not their investment strategies; for making deals, not products; for seeking new mergers, not new markets. Business investment declined from 7.2 percent of our gross national product in the 1970's to only 5.4 percent in the eighties.

The investment deficit also slows the growth of our workers' productivity. And in a market economy, people get paid by what they can produce by global standards. Compensation per hour, what workers earn in wages and fringe benefits, grew more slowly in the last 20 years than in the previous 100. From 1954 to 1973, hourly compensation grew at over 3 percent per year. The more people produced, the more they earned. But in the last 20 years, as productivity slowed down, compensation increased by less than one percent per year.

This low productivity led to higher unemployment, stagnant wages, and—guess what—lower tax receipts. So the deficit got bigger, because people weren't earning enough money to pay into the Government to keep the deficit down. They relate one to the other.

This was aggravated when we cut the defense budget with no plan to put the defense workers back to work in the new civilian economy. And in some of our biggest unemployment areas, you see, from Connecticut to southern California, you see high-dollar scientific workers, people with advanced degrees and very skilled fac-

tory workers, with nothing else to do because there was no thought given to what these people would do once the defense work was shut down, even though we know there are tens of thousands of jobs waiting to be had in the global economy in new technologies, in aerospace, in electronics, in biotechnology, and environment cleanup, just to name four. We know those jobs are out there. But we know our competitors are working hard in partnership with the government and the private sector to develop them.

At the same time, the exploding costs of health care and education put a crimp not only on the growth of average families' incomes and small business incomes but on the overall health of our economy. Average health costs per family tripled in the last dozen years. Too many middle class people at the same time experienced "job block," that is, they couldn't move jobs because someone in their family had been sick. They had what the insurers call a preexisting condition, meaning that if they wanted to have their health insurance, they had to stay in the job they were in.

Now, we're living in a country, folks, where the average 18-year-old will change work seven or eight times in a lifetime. If you can't change jobs in this kind of an economy, your future is dramatically constricted, all because we are the only nation with an advanced economy that hasn't figured out how to provide basic health care at affordable cost to all of our people.

And look what's happened to education. In the 1980's, the value of an education virtually doubled. By the end of the decade, the average college graduate was earning twice the average high school graduate; the difference between what a college graduate and a high school graduate earned at the end of the decade was twice what it was in 1980 at the beginning. And yet, look what happened to college costs. The cost of public colleges went up by 109 percent and private colleges by 145 percent; college drifting, drifting, drifting out of the reach of ordinary Americans. And the college dropout rate became more than twice as high as the high school dropout rate, either because people were sent unprepared, which was wrong, or they couldn't afford to stay, which happened all too often.

Virtually every economic decision that was made in Washington, or not made properly, sent signals to our people that the old rewards for hard work and playing by the rules and responsibility were declining. Most of the economic gains of the 1980's went to people in the top one percent of the income brackets, and most of them were not those that were producing new products and services but instead were those who were producing financial arrangements, which exploded the cost of paperwork and didn't do much to create more jobs in America.

Too many people who were at the bottom rung of the ladder and working hard to get out, which, after all, is where most of our families started somewhere along the way, found that their hard-earned wages left them below the poverty line and removed even more the incentive to work instead of to be on welfare. If work doesn't pay, why not go on welfare? How many times have we heard that said in the last 10 or 12 years in the city streets and in the rural communities of America?

These are the things, my fellow Americans, that we have to change. This is a historic moment. Now that the House has passed this budget plan to reduce the deficit and to target investments in our future, and it's going to the Senate for further debate, we can make a decision to seize control of our economic destiny. That is why I have asked everyone in Washington to go beyond politics as usual, to forget about partisan divisions, to try to find bipartisan responsibility in place of bipartisan blame and irresponsibility.

Now, the plan that I have proposed cuts $500 billion from the Federal deficit, the largest deficit reduction program in our history. It makes decisions long delayed and avoided. The plan is balanced and fair. About half of the deficit reduction comes from spending reductions and restraints on entitlements; about half comes from tax increases. Entitlements—that is, medical programs, Social Security benefits, agriculture benefits, welfare benefits, food stamp benefits, things you get because of who you are—those things, we rein in spending by $100 billion over the next 5 years. We cut 200 other areas of the budget by more than $150 billion in the next 5 years. We cut some very popular programs in this country, from highway demonstration projects to rural electrification. But that has to be done. We cut about $47 billion directly out of the operations of the Federal Government: freezes in Federal pay, restrictions on Federal retirement, the reduction in the Federal work force by 149,000 people over the next 5 years.

All of that has been written into this budget. The plan imposes new discipline on Government spending: no increases in taxes unless there are cuts in spending, and all of it put into a trust fund that must remain there for the 5-year life of the deficit.

We also adopted a unique mechanism right at the end of the House of Representatives debate which requires every year, if we miss this deficit reduction target—and Congressman Obey got a bunch of charts, I wish he were up here showing them to you, about how the two previous administrations said the deficit would go down to zero three different times, and they never did make a target—if we miss our target, every year now the President is legally bound to come in and offer a correction in the budget to meet that deficit reduction target, and the Congress has to vote on it.

Now, I lead with all this—I dare say that most of you, since all you've heard are about the fights on taxes, didn't know how much spending was cut and probably don't know what incentives are there for investment. I'll get to that in a minute. Some taxes are raised. No less authority than David Stockman, who was President Reagan's Budget Director, was quoted not long ago as saying, anybody, Republican or Democrat, who thinks you can get this deficit down without increasing taxes does not understand what we did to the tax system in 1981.

Now, those are the spending cuts we had. The spending cuts are real. There are more than 200 of them. There are more than I recommended in the campaign because I didn't know in the campaign what happened right after the election, which is that the deficit miraculously was increased by $165 billion, announced by the Government before I took office but after the election. So we cut spending some more.

And there are some more tax increases, too. But look how they fall. Seventy-four percent of the money we raise comes from people with incomes above $100,000. Over 60 percent of this money comes from people with incomes above $200,000. Now, that is not an attack on the wealthy. It is an acknowledgement that people in that income group had their incomes go up and their taxes go down in the eighties. Middle class people had their taxes go up and their incomes go down in the eighties. So we're just trying to redress the fairness of the matter.

Now, let me tell you exactly what you will

pay if you're a middle class American, if your family income is under $100,000. I had wanted, and I advocated in the campaign, tax relief for middle class families, especially those with children. I still want that, and I still intend to propose that before I'm done. But I can't do it now because the deficit is so much bigger than it was when I was making these proposals. It would be irresponsible for me to advocate a very substantial increase on upper incomes and not ask the middle class Americans to make any contribution at all.

But listen to what it costs. First of all, for working families with incomes under $30,000, we have done everything we could to make sure that the energy tax, which is the middle class tax here, will cost nothing by giving an income tax credit to offset the income tax. One fellow out here has been heckling me and saying I'm not telling the truth. So I'll say, Arthur Anderson, which is a fairly reputable firm, hardly packed full of Democrats, has examined my program and says that a family of three with an income of $25,000 a year or less will actually get a tax cut under the Clinton economic plan as it is now. For a family with an income of $40,000 a year, if the energy tax passes just as it is, and if there are four people in the family, the bill will be a dollar a month next year, $7 a month the year after that, and $17 a month the year after that. All of the money, every last red cent of it, will go into a deficit reduction trust fund to bring down the deficit, every penny.

Now, the question is, is it worth it? Is it worth it? And here's my answer to you. You may say it's not worth it, but look what's happened since November. First, when we announced the energy tax and the deficit reduction plan, long-term interest rates started to go down. Second, after I actually presented it to Congress in February, they went down some more. Now, for most of the last 3 months, long-term interest rates have been at their lowest rate in decades: mortgage rates at the lowest rate in 20 years; consumer loans down; college loans down; car loans down; business loans down. Millions and millions of Americans are out there breaking their necks to refinance their home loans and their business loans, so much so that the business analysts say that if we can keep interest rates down at this level for a year, we will put $100 billion back into this economy in lower interest rates because people think we're serious

about bringing the deficit down.

What does that mean? What does that mean? Let's just say if someone had a $100,000 home mortgage financed at 10 percent and they refinanced it at 7½ percent, that would be a $2,000 saving in one year, a $2,000 saving in one year. In other words, there would be more than twice the savings in one year as this program would cost that same family in 4 years if it were passed exactly as it is today.

Now, I think that's pretty good for America. If we don't do something to get the interest rates down, clean the debt out, and get control of our economic destiny, we're going to be in big trouble.

Now, there are also a lot of incentives in this program for people to further save money. Let me just give you a few. Let's take a typical farm family in Wisconsin. The family's income net is under $30,000. They will be eligible for tax credits. A single-family farm under this program for the first time will be able to get a tax deduction for their health insurance premiums, something they haven't been able to do before. The expensing provisions for small businesses and farmers will allow them to write off $25,000, not $10,000, of investment now. So much so that the average Wisconsin farm, even after they pay higher energy costs and have agricultural budget cuts, will wind up with a lower bill rather than a higher bill if this whole program passes.

And I think it's very important to look at the incentives here. We have more incentives for small businesses, an historic incentive for people to invest in new business, real incentives for people to put money into plant and equipment and hire people in America, instead of just put money into financial transactions or invest money overseas. These are incentives that will give the American people the way to lower their taxes by creating jobs here in America, which is what I talked about in the campaign. That's how you ought to be able to lower your tax bill.

Now, let me also tell you that this plan invests some new money. You have to ask yourself whether you think it's worth it. Is it worth it for us to invest enough money at the national level to do the following things: to try to provide some incentives for companies who won't have defense contracts anymore to develop domestic technologies to put those high wage workers back to work. Is it worth it to try to provide jobs in America in areas where America needs work with new water systems and new environmental cleanup systems? Is it worth it to provide a small amount of money to try to see that America joins Germany, Japan, and every other advanced country in saying if you don't go to a 4-year college, at least you ought to have access to 2 years of further education and training so you can get a good and decent job? Is it worth it or not? You have to decide.

Now, if you believe all Government spending is evil and bad, you would say no, it's not worth it. But if you look at our competitors and if you look at what works and what produces growth and the fact that it is clearly the skill levels of our people which will determine as much as anything else the economic future of America, I think you'd have to say yes, it is worth it. We've got too many people who are not competitive in a global economy today.

One final thing: This State has always been a pioneer. People in both parties have always been interested, at least in my experience as Governor, in welfare reform, in moving people from welfare to work. One of the biggest problems with welfare reform is this: If you take somebody off welfare and you put them in a low-wage job because they don't have much education, they have to take that wage and pay for child care out of it, because they're not home taking care of the kids anymore, and they may not have medical insurance. And the earnings are so low there is a big incentive not to do it.

This bill, this economic program, makes a major downpayment on welfare reform, doing what I want to do, which is to change the whole system and say after you get education and training, if after 2 years you don't have a job, you have to go to work in the public or private sector. This bill starts that by saying this: If you work 40 hours a week and you've got a kid in your house, the tax system will lift you out of poverty. We'll give you a tax break so that you will not be living in poverty if you work full-time with children in your home. What else could be more American, and what else would do more to end the welfare dependency we have in this country?

Now, let's talk about where we are with this. This bill's going to the Senate now. Senator Kohl and Senator Feingold are going to get a chance to work on it. And everybody in America—if I said, wouldn't you like it if we did

everything I just said but we did it with more budget cuts and even less tax, and you would say, yes; I would say yes. Who could disagree? Who could disagree? The question is, what are the details?

Let me try to describe to you what's going on. When you hear all this stuff, that this is a tax program, this is not just a tax program. This is a budget cutting program. This is an investment program in your future. This is incentives for the private sector to create new jobs in ways that have never been provided before.

You know, in this bill, if you invest in a new business and it makes money, and you hold that investment 5 years, you cut your tax rate in half under this program. That's a real incentive. Under this bill, if you invest money in a poor neighborhood in Milwaukee, if it gets designated an empowerment zone, you can get all kinds of incentives for private sector investment that have never been available before, ever; never proposed by Republicans or Democrats before to get private sector investment to rebuild. So there's a lot of things in this bill.

But let's just take the rhetoric. Everybody would like to do all this with less tax and more budget cuts. But look behind the rhetoric. For example, when the House voted on my program last week, there was a Republican substitute. The Republican substitute purported to have the same amount of deficit reduction I did with no taxes and all budget cuts. Guess what. More Republicans voted against a Republican bill than Democrats voted against my bill. Why? Why? Because the Republicans who voted against it thought it cut too much out of Social Security, too much out of medical care, too much out of farm programs, too much out of things that are part of the fabric of this Nation's economy or part of our built-in obligation to one another. So they disagreed. They couldn't agree on that.

Let me give you another example. Some define less tax and more cuts as lower taxes on the very wealthy, replaced by reducing the cost of living increase to Social Security recipients barely above the poverty line, or to people barely above the poverty line who are working, they want to reduce the tax credits they get.

Let me give you another example. Others say, "Well, just cut more Medicare costs. Don't give those doctors and hospitals any more money." Now, that's got a lot of appeal to a lot of people. But let me tell you what happens. If you cut

Medicare costs without reforming the health care system, you can do it to some extent, but if you do it too much, you know what will happen? Every one of you who works in the private sector who has a private health insurance policy, will have your premiums go up as a result. Because if the Government doesn't pay for the care that the Government mandates that people get, what do the doctors and hospitals do? They put the cost onto private business, onto private employers and private employees. And your health insurance premiums soar.

One of the reasons a lot of you are paying too much for health care today is that America has 35 million people with no health insurance and other people who are being undercompensated. And as a result of that, you're paying more. Because everybody in this country gets health care, don't they? They just get it when it's too late, too expensive, and at the emergency room. And you get sent the bill if you have health insurance. So it sounds good, but it may not be so good.

I could give you a lot of other examples. The way words are used, for example, the way our adversaries calculate this, if we ask upper income Social Security recipients, who are getting more out of the system than they put in, plus interest, to pay a little more of their income to taxation, then that's a tax. But if we cut the cost of living allowance to the poorest Social Security recipients, that's a budget cut. Right? That's the way they define it.

Now, but most people in this room say, "Well, if you have to do one or the other, better to ask people who can pay and who are getting more back out than they put in plus interest to give a little more than to take it out of the poorest ones who are just above the poverty line." But if you get into these word games, it sounds terrible if it's tax and cut. It doesn't sound so bad when you talk about what it really is.

Here are the principles that I hope the Senate will honor next week:

Number one, we've got to cut the deficit at least $500 billion, and we ought to put it in a trust fund so the money can't be fooled with for the next 5 years.

Number two, because of what happened in the last 12 years, any taxes we raise must, in the end, be progressive. Those who can pay more should pay more, and we should minimize the burden on the middle class.

Number three, don't do anything to the incentive to move people from welfare to work. Let's go ahead and say that if you work 40 hours a week and you have a child in your home, you don't deserve to be in poverty. You've played by the rules, and we'll let you out of poverty.

Number four, keep the incentives for small businesses, for new businesses, for investment in our cities, for housing incentives, for research and development, keep all those tax incentives in there to grow this economy. Don't take them out.

And number five, when we cut spending, and we'll cut some more and raise some, we'll cut the taxes and have more spending cuts next week. But when we do it, let's leave the money in there that will shape these children's economic future. Let's have the money for education and training, for investment in technology, for help for the defense industries that are building down. Let's rebuild the American economy. Because, after all, you can cut all the spending you want, and if people don't have jobs and they aren't earning money, we're still not going to be able to balance the budget. So let's keep the economic future of the country uppermost in our minds.

The last thing I'd like to say to you, my fellow Americans, is that none of this is going to be easy, but you should not be discouraged. After all, these trends, as I said, have gone through administrations of Democrats and Republicans for 20 years now. We are moving away from a set of policies that have been the rule for 12 years. I'm trying to move beyond a bipartisan gridlock which has existed for about a decade.

We are trying to do it in a global economy where other rich nations have unemployment rates as high or higher than ours, and there's a recession all over the world. This is not easy, but it can be done. It can be done if we have the courage to change direction. And if we will listen and look beneath the labels to the facts, I believe we can do it. It is simply a question of asking what we have to do to regain control of our destiny, what we have to do to invest in our people, what we have to do to get jobs and incomes and health security back into this country again.

And let me just say one last thing in closing. When I was a Governor for 12 years, my State in every one of those 12 years had a tax burden—the State and local tax burden was in the bottom five in America. We had one of the toughest balanced budget laws in the country. And when I asked the people of my State for more taxes it was always to pay for something specific, better schools, better roads, more jobs, in a trust fund. I never ever dreamed I would be in a position in my life asking people to pay $1 just to bring the deficit down. But we got ourselves in this fix, folks, over a long period of time. And until we get our interest rates down and regain control of our economic future and show that we have the discipline to handle our affairs, it is going to be very difficult for us to do a lot of these other things that all of us want to do.

These decisions are not easy, but we must make them. So I ask you again, encourage Senator Kohl and all the other people in the United States Senate, encourage Senator Feingold, encourage them all to give me a good budget with less taxes and more spending cuts. But remember the principles: make sure the money goes to deficit reduction; invest some in our economic future, because that's important; make sure the people who can pay do; don't take the welfare reform initiatives out of it; and remember that in the end, the private sector creates the jobs, so leave the incentives in there.

And let me say this: 50 of the 100 biggest companies in this country have endorsed this program. I have been very moved that so many people in upper income groups, who are going to pay the overwhelming majority of these taxes, have endorsed this program, because they know that it is imperative to get control of our future. And I ask you, the people of Wisconsin, to endorse the program for the future of your children and our Nation.

Thank you very much, and God bless you all.

NOTE: The President spoke at 12:10 p.m. in the Milwaukee Exposition Convention Center and Arena. In his remarks, he referred to Milwaukee Mayor John O. Norquist.

Exchange With Reporters in Milwaukee
June 1, 1993

President's Priorities

Q. [*Inaudible*]—view the whole treatment where you basically—first with having to deal day after day with the news accounts that kind of talk about the haircuts and the Travel Office and things? No, no, I'm asking you how important——

Q. That's a cheap shot. That's a cheap shot. You are the President of the United States. You should——

Q. Can I do my job, please?

Q. Get out of here. We don't need those cheap shots. That's a cheap shot. Get out of here.

The President. The answer is, I have to work in Washington, but you have to work outside, too. The real issue is not so much what you said, but the real issue is, I secured agreement early on for about $250 billion in tax cuts, spending cuts, I mean, a little under, about $245 billion. And as a result of that, because they weren't the focus of controversy, no one knows we did it.

And then we got agreement early on for the new incentives, for small businesses and for starting new businesses and for investing in our depressed areas, reviving the housing market. Because there was no controversy, people don't know we did it. So the only controversy has been over the taxes. It's important that people know that there are budget cuts in here. It's important that people know there are real incentives to the private sector in here. It's important that people know what we still spend money on. And it's important for people to know that over 70 percent of the money is being paid by the top 6 percent of income earners. If I don't get out here and do all that work, they won't know it. So that's what I'm doing.

Health Care Reform

Q. Let me follow, sir. Are you going to recommend a tax on hospitals to pay for the health care program on the theory that they're going to have a windfall profit from your reform program?

The President. Well, let me say this, if we

do it right, they will have significantly lower administrative costs. That is, if we do health care right, they will have lower administrative costs. Let me just give you one example: The average American doctor in 1980 took home 75 percent of the income that he or she generated into the clinic. By 1992, that figure had dropped to 52 percent, all the rest of it going to administrative costs caused by insurance companies and the Government just piling on regulations and rules and paperwork and thousands of different insurance costs. If we simplify that, their costs will drop dramatically.

So one of the options that has been recommended is that we leave some of that money with them but have some of that money flow back in to cover the uninsured, which will also help them because that will come right back to the doctors and the hospitals in the form of insurance for the uninsured. So it would be almost like returning the money to them in a different form for services rendered. We'll just have to see whether that works out. No final decision has been made on that.

Q. But you like that idea?

The President. I have made no decision on it. I don't want to flame the story anymore. That is one of the options that has been presented, and one of ones that, frankly, some hospital people have talked to us about.

Q. Are you going to hold off the health plan until the fall, Mr. President?

Q. That's all. You talk——

The President. Hold it off until what?

Q. Are you going to hold off the plan until the fall to let the Congress concentrate——

Q. That's enough.

The President. Oh, no, no, no. I hope we move this budget through in a hurry.

Budget

Q. [*Inaudible*]

The President. [*Inaudible*]—I think he's got some really good ideas. But once he committed himself to cutting as much as he did, he actually lost more Republicans than I lost Democrats.

Q. It's just the issue of party politics that you talked about. The Democrats, I feel, are doing the same thing. So I just think you should address that part of it. The Democrats are doing the same thing.

The President. Well, I didn't let them off the hook.

Q. I'm just bringing up the point because

the people need to know that.

The President. I have nothing to add over and above what's been in the paper already. I mean, the Senators on the Senate Finance Committee have discussed with me and also with the House Members who voted for this program the options that are there within the principles that I established. I always said—on February 17th I said if we can meet these principles, $500 billion in deficit reduction, aggressive taxation, incentives to invest in America, move from welfare to work, lift the working poor out of poverty, and these targeted investments in technology, jobs, and education which will meet those principles, with some less tax and some more spending cuts, I'm for it. And I think that's what we're working toward.

Q. What would you be willing to accept in less taxes——

The President. I'm not going to get into that.

Q. How about——

The President. No, I'm not going to get into it because Congress is on recess and our commitment is twofold, of our administration. One is to work with the Senators of any party who will work with us and, secondly, to make sure the Senate Finance Committee works with all the House Members who voted for this budget with our solemn commitment that we would all work together in the Senate to keep these principles intact and see if these principles can be achieved with less tax and more spending cuts. So that's what we're trying to do.

Q. Good way to sell your plan here?

The President. Oh, I think so. This was terrific. I loved it.

Russia

Q. What's your position on Russia's not paying back your $80 billion in debt, loans that are still outstanding?

The President. They're broke. They can't right now.

Q. What is your feeling on that? Are you looking for them to repay those loans in the next 2 years, or is that part of their plan to balance the budget?

The President. They can't do it right now. They have no money. They're absolutely flat broke. What we ought to do—I think the Russians have now undertaken—their recent credits, in other words, the things that they've gotten since they adopted a free market approach, since they got rid of communism, I think they will honor those debts once they start making money again. But the history is that countries need a few years to basically move from a Communist economy to a free market economy. As they do that and they begin to acquire some success, then I think they'll be able to pay down their debt. But the dilemma now is if we tried to make them pay it off now, we'd just drive them further in the economic hole and run the risk of having them revert to a dictatorship of some kind. And we don't want to do that.

So I wouldn't let anybody off the hook that could pay it back, but the point is for them, they never really—unlike the Chinese, for exam-

ple, who were traders for centuries and had a whole market history, the Russians essentially went from a feudal agricultural economy under the Czars to a Communist economy that then became dominated by heavy industry. And moving into a modern free market economy is very difficult for them.

Q. So we're going to work with them?

The President. Yes, I think we should.

NOTE: The exchange began at approximately 1 p.m. outside the Milwaukee Exposition Convention Center and Arena. A tape was not available for verification of the content of this exchange.

Remarks to Bay View Community Members in Milwaukee
June 1, 1993

The President. Thank you very much. I want to thank Gerry Kleczka and everybody else. But I especially want to thank the Langer family for bringing me to Bay View. I'm glad to be here. When I was on the way out here today the mayor said that he was the mayor of Milwaukee and Bay View and that I needed to know that if I was going to come here. So I'm glad to be here. I also want to introduce to you Wisconsin's newest Member of Congress, Mr. Peter Barca, who just showed up.

I'm sorry you all are in there behind that fence, and I look forward to getting out and shaking hands with you. I just wanted to say one or two things before I do. I was just in downtown Milwaukee, speaking with several thousand people about the economic plan that I have presented to Congress. And there are two or three things that I want to say to you about it so you'll all know, because there are a lot of things that have not been brought out that I think you're entitled to hear.

First of all, this plan has over 200 spending cuts. I see all these signs saying, "Cut spending." Where were you when we cut them? It has a lot of spending cuts in it, over $240 billion.

Secondly, the tax increases in this plan all go to reduce the deficit, and over 74 percent of the money comes from people with incomes above $100,000. Families with incomes below $30,000 pay nothing. The other thing I want to tell you is, if your income is above $30,000

and below $100,000, depending on the size of your family, the energy tax that the House approved costs you a dollar a month next year, $7 a month the year after that, and for a family of four, $17 a month the year after that. All of it goes to reduce the debt.

I think it's worth doing. It's brought interest rates down to a 20-year low. We have interest rates at a 20-year low. That means Americans are going to refinance their homes, get lower car loans, refinance their business loans, get lower consumer loans, lower college loans. It will save $100 billion for American businesses and individuals this year if we can keep those interest rates down. So I want you to support that.

The second thing I want to say about it is this: We have put forward a program which will open the doors of college education to all Americans, just like I promised in the campaign, lower interest loans, better repayment terms, and giving tens of thousands of Americans a chance to pay their college loans by serving their communities here at home, by working to make their communities a better place.

The next point I want to make is that as soon as this budget is over, just like I said in the campaign, we're coming forward with a plan to provide health care security, affordable health care, to the working families of this country, who have been savaged by high costs, insufficient coverage, and the inability to change jobs because somebody in their family has been sick. This administration is about jobs, incomes, health care, education, and training, and bringing this deficit down.

Now, I want to say one last thing. I heard all this talk in the country about how this is a tax program. I just want to make this point. It is not just a tax program. It's an economic program. It is over $240 billion in budget cuts. We're going to reduce the size of the Federal Government by 150,000. We are——

Audience member. Make the cuts first!

The President. We are cutting first. That's what the budget resolution is all about. You can't raise taxes without the budget cuts. It's illegal now. That's the whole point. We won't have the tax increases without the budget cuts. It's all going to be put in a trust fund. And unlike all previous years, if we don't make our reduction targets and reduce that debt, the President by law is now required to come in and fix it, something previous Presidents did not have to do. We have changed the law.

And what you've got to decide is whether you want more hot air, more rhetoric, more politicians up there telling you what you want to hear, or somebody who will tell you the truth, turn the country around, and get the economy

going again. I think that's what you want, and I hope you'll support your Members of Congress and me as we try to do that.

Let me say one final thing. I think that a lot of you before I came here today had no earthly idea that we'd cut all that spending because the Congress didn't fight it; they just did it. I think you did not know also that families with incomes under $30,000 were being held harmless because we had support for that. And you may not know that small businesses like Langer's Pharmacy are going to have tax incentives to reinvest in their businesses that were not there before if this plan passes.

This is a good plan for the economy. It's a fair plan for the middle class. It asks the wealthiest Americans to pay their fair share. And unlike previous plans, it's not a lot of hot air. It will do what it's supposed to do. I think we've had enough hot air for the last 12 years. Let's do something real and strong and move this country forward.

Thank you, and God bless you all.

NOTE: The President spoke at 3:45 p.m. at Jack Langer's Pharmacy. In his remarks, he referred to Representative Gerald D. Kleczka.

Exchange With Reporters Prior to Discussions With Prime Minister Brian Mulroney of Canada
June 2, 1993

Prime Minister's Visit

Q. Is this a hail-and-farewell visit?

Prime Minister Mulroney. I came down to see the President about NAFTA and some trade matters and Bosnia, where we have troops on the ground, and to work with him. We agree with the prudent and thoughtful course he's been pursuing there. And I'd like to talk to him about further engagement at the United Nations and also to say good-bye and to you, Helen [Helen Thomas, United Press International]. After a decade I thought I owed you a trip.

Q. Are you going to miss it?

Prime Minister Mulroney. Pardon?

Q. Going to miss it, aren't you?

Prime Minister Mulroney. Yes. All politicians

suffer from decompression when they leave office.

Bosnia

Q. Do you agree with the Bosnia policy?

Prime Minister Mulroney. Yes, I do. I agree that——

Q. You don't think it should have been more aggressive on the allied part?

Prime Minister Mulroney. Well, I've been astonished by some American commentators and observers asking for an American solution in Bosnia. There's no such thing. There is only a common solution, for all of us have to get into this together and accept our responsibilities. It's unfair to say that, oh, why don't we have an American solution to this intractable problem that's gone on for hundreds of years. It's not available. But there is, perhaps, a better, as the President's pointed out, a better common approach that we can develop at the United Nations Security Council with everybody pulling his weight or her weight. And that's what we're going to talk about today.

Btu Tax

Q. Mr. President, Senator Boren says now that there can be no Btu tax—no longer a compromise, it's now none.

The President. I don't have any comment on that. I had a good visit with him. He called me the other day, said he was encouraged by where we were going, and he thought we would reach agreement. I'm not going to get into a verbal war of words. The Congress is out this week, and we're going to meet next week and try to work it out.

Health Care Reform

Q. Have you decided to push a health care plan?

Q. Are you going to pull the nomination of Guinier?

The President. No, we're working ahead. As a matter of fact, I've got another meeting, a big meeting on the health care issue this week. We are, you know, trying to—we're trying to do two things. We're trying to, first of all, to get as many of the kinks worked out as we can before we go forward. It's an enormously complicated issue. And then we want to make sure that we have, you know, discussed it with as many people as possible, many groups and everything, after we've reached some final conclusions, and that when we present it to the Congress, it's presented at a time and in a way that both the Congress and the American people can focus on it. But there's been no decision for a sustained delay here. I'm focusing right now on passing the budget when the Senate comes back next week.

Q. Will it be released this month?

The President. I don't want to get—I'm not in a time—I don't want to get——

Q. How about Guinier? Are you pulling out the nomination of Guinier?

Prime Minister Mulroney. Bye, Helen. [*Laughter*] On behalf of all Canadians, Helen, good-bye.

Q. Nothing ventured—[*laughter*].

[*At this point, one group of reporters left the room, and another group entered.*]

Public Perception

Q. Mr. President, are you as certain as the Prime Minister that NAFTA will pass? And do you plan on calling on his considerable experience in dealing with the perils of unpopularity?

The President. Well, these things go up and down. I mean, you know, the American people want something done about the deficit but very often don't want to—you know, when the coverage gets negative, because of the pain of it, it's something no one wants to face. I think what I have to do here is do more of what I did yesterday, force, force full coverage of—what's happened in our country is that there has only been discussion about the tax increases in the budget plan. So no Americans really know very much about all the budget cuts that are in there and all the tax incentives that are in there for investment for new jobs. When they know the whole thing and also when the middle class knows how small the burden is on them, then the support for the program and for the administration goes way up. So I'm laboring out there under a general perception that the administration has a tax plan that falls almost entirely on the middle class when, in fact, the administration has a plan for spending cuts, investment incentives to create jobs, and some taxes, which fall almost entirely on upper income people. And that's my problem. It's very difficult in the midst of a legislative debate to keep the public focus on that since the focus is always on controversy. But that's my problem, and I'll fix it.

NAFTA

Q. Why have you not gone out and fought——

The President. On NAFTA I think we can pass it with a very concerted effort if the Congress has some assurances on the environmental and labor issues. Keep in mind, the United States—as far as I know, no country has ever signed a trade agreement which—also an investment agreement, which—at least millions of Americans feel is an investment agreement that would encourage people to invest in another country for production in our market, not in theirs. And so that is the tension here that—I keep arguing to the American people that that could happen anyway, that under our present law, people, if they choose, can go and produce in Mexico for the American market. But that causes great tension here when we've had 20 years of virtually flat wages for middle class working people.

I believe NAFTA will create jobs and raise incomes in both the United States and Mexico, and I think it will help Canada. I have always believed that over the long run, the integration of our three economies and the potential that gave us to continue to move south into other market economies in Chile and Argentina and Venezuela and others was enormous. And I think eventually we'll get there. But it is going to be a very tough fight.

Ross Perot

Q. Why have you allowed Ross Perot to shape the debate on that——
The President. I haven't. I haven't allowed it at all. I don't agree with his position. I don't agree with his assertions, and I don't agree with the evidence that he offers. But you know, in this country we have a free press. I can't control who gets what kind of press coverage. That's what the first amendment is all about.
Prime Minister Mulroney. I saw Ross Perot's appearance on television the other night, and I've heard every single one of those arguments from the Socialists and the protectionists in the Canadian House of Commons. There's not a single word that was new. The fact of the matter is that it's all contradicted by the facts. Canada and the United States entered into a free trade agreement in 1988. We've since been mired in a recession. Even in those 4 difficult years for both countries, American exports to Canada have increased by approximately 25 percent, thereby creating 1.4 million new jobs in the United States. And Canadian exports to the United States have increased by a like amount. Well, this is clear indication that prosperity comes through these lowering of trade barriers and the creating of new pools of common wealth.

What Mr. Perot's argument is—I saw anyway, and I don't know him and he seems to be a fine fellow—is that wage rates alone are a determinant of competitiveness. Wage rates are one of many considerations of competitiveness, cost of capital, infrastructure, education, technology. And if wage rates alone determine the location of industry, Haiti would be the manufacturing capital of the world. Our productivity is so far and ahead above that of Mexico that to make

the argument simply on the basis of wages is misleading in the extreme.

I think the President's point of view is a very valid one. It's one that we support. And the evidence appears to be there that when you lower barriers to trade between and among friendly countries, you create new pools of wealth, and you raise the living standards of everybody affected by it. You don't lower standards. And so these arguments, I have to tell you—Mr. Perot may have some better days. But I want to tell you that his arguments, he might be surprised to find that he's been poaching those arguments from the Socialists in the Canadian House of Commons, and they might sue him for copyright infringement. [*Laughter*]

Q. Mr. President, you that Mr. Mulroney is leaving office——
The President. On NAFTA, let me say one other thing about NAFTA. President Salinas, when he took over in Mexico, unilaterally reduced a lot of very high Mexican tariffs with the consequence that the United States went from a $5 billion trade deficit with Mexico to a $6 billion trade surplus. And last month, Mexico replaced Japan as the second largest purchaser of our manufacturing products. So we are, in effect, opening our trade relationships anyway. It's been, on balance, beneficial to the United States. And I just—if you look at where the world is going, where Europe is going, where Asia is going, there's no question that both Canada and the United States need more trading partners in our own backyard, and we need for them to be richer, to grow, to do more, so they can buy more from us. And I feel very strongly that it's the right thing to do, and I'm going to keep plugging away and hope we can pass it. I think we can.

Haiti

Q. On Haiti, Mr. President. Is it time to show some muscle on Haiti if diplomacy doesn't work?
The President. Well, we thought we had an agreement on Haiti and, of course, it didn't work out, and I'm very disappointed. We worked very, very hard. And I talked to the Prime Minister about this on several occasions. It is time to reexamine our options and consider some others, and I expect the United States will do that.

Prime Minister Mulroney

Prime Minister Mulroney

Q. Mr. Clinton, any parting words for Mr. Mulroney now that he's going to be leaving office?

The President. I wish him well. He served well and for a long time, and I wish him well. And he's given me a lot of very good advice. He's been very helpful.

NOTE: The exchange began at 8:49 a.m. in the Oval Office at the White House.

Remarks and an Exchange With Reporters During a Luncheon With Business Leaders
June 2, 1993

Interest Rates

The President. Let me just make one remark. You know, once a week if at all possible I attempt to have lunch here in the White House with business leaders from around America and solicit their views and their opinions, their suggestions. These lunches have been enormously valuable to me and, I think, are helping us develop the kind of partnership with the private sector we need.

I'd just like to mention two things that I think support the economic position that I have taken and the work we're doing in the Senate. First of all, there were news stories today and yesterday pointing out that long-term interest rates are down again, the stock market is strong again in anticipation of the passage of a real deficit reduction package after the vote in the House. And that means we're taking the right course. And I'm looking forward to working with the Senate when they get back next week.

Secondly, just today we've learned that we had the largest monthly increase in new housing sales in 7 years, which is clearly the result of lower interest rates and proves the point that we've been trying to make that if we can get the deficit down, get the interest rates down, that will be the biggest job stimulus to the economy. It will put another $100 billion back in this economy.

So there are lots of things that we have to discuss and lots of things that perhaps we can all change for the better. But at least the general direction, I think, is clearly right. And I thank these kind business leaders for coming here today, and I look forward to continuing to do this every week as long as I'm President. I think it will be very helpful to the country.

Thank you very much.

Lani Guinier

Q. [*Inaudible*]—nomination, Mr. President?

The President. Well, let me say this, I think that I have to talk to some of the Senators about it because of the reservations that have been raised both publicly and privately. I want to reaffirm two positive things about her. One is everyone concedes she is a first rate civil rights lawyer, and no real civil rights lawyer has ever held that position before, someone who made a career of it.

Secondly, I think any reasonable reading of her writings would lead someone to conclude that a lot of the attacks cannot be supported by a fair reading of the writings. And that's not to say that I agree with everything in the writings. I don't. But I think that a lot of what has been said is not accurate. On the other hand, I have to take into account where the Senate is, and I will be doing that and talking to them. And I think until I do that, I should have nothing else to say.

NOTE: The President spoke at 12:29 p.m. in the Old Family Dining Room at the White House. A tape was not available for verification of the content of these remarks.

Nomination for Ambassador to Mexico
June 2, 1993

The President declared his intention today to nominate Jim Jones, the CEO of the American Stock Exchange and former House Budget Committee chairman, to the position of Ambassador to Mexico.

"A great deal of our economic future," said the President, "is bound up in our relationships in this hemisphere, particularly our relationship with Mexico. That is why I have chosen an Ambassador who is seasoned by years of economic leadership in both the private and public sectors. Jim Jones brings a unique perspective and uncommon talents to the continuing dialog with our Mexican neighbors."

NOTE: A biography of the nominee was made available by the Office of the Press Secretary.

Exchange With Reporters in Frederick, Maryland
June 3, 1993

Economic Program

Q. Mr. President, speaking of construction, should Lani Guinier withdraw?

The President. I'll have more to say about that later. But this is the most important thing I'm working on. This is the illustration of why the economic program is important. Housing sales at a 7-month high last month, creating jobs for people like this because of low mortgage rates. If we can keep the interest rates down by passing the economic program, getting the deficit down, you're going to see a lot more jobs, a lot more homes, a lot of money putting into this economy. That's the real important thing that this administration was elected to do and that's what I'm working on.

NOTE: The exchange began at 11:11 a.m. while the President was touring a house under construction in Fredericktown Village.

Remarks at Fredericktown Village in Frederick
June 3, 1993

Thank you very much. Good morning, ladies and gentlemen, and good morning, boys and girls. It's great to be here in Frederick today. I want to thank Roger Glunt, the President of the National Association of Home Builders, for being here and for his support of our economic program, as well as the support of homebuilders and realtors all across America who understand what we can do for the American economy if we can get interest rates down and keep them there.

I want to thank the Murrays for giving me a tour of their home before it was finished. One of the things I did in my former life, back when I had one—[*laughter*]—when I was a young man, was engage in a little bit of home-building. That's hard work. And I'm glad to see somebody else doing it back there. But they did a great job. I want to say thanks to the Dragers and the Fishmans and the Taylors, the other families here on this circle who showed me their home and talked to me a little bit about their lives. I want to thank Jim Johnson for being here and for the wonderful job that he does at Fanny Mae to help finance homes and make the American dream come real for Americans. And I want to say thanks to Don Meade, the construction site supervisor, who hasn't spoken today. That will make him the most popular person here. I thank him for showing me around.

Ladies and gentlemen, last year when I was

out campaigning for the job I now hold, I think all of us realized that our country was in a period of short-term recession, which it lasted for about 3 years, but of long-term economic problems brought on by some economic competition from other countries around the world and from some problems that we had created for ourselves and that it was impossible to point the blame at one person, that both parties in Washington were to blame, but that it was absolutely clear that we couldn't keep going the way we were going, where the deficit was going up and up and up every year, so our debts were piling higher.

In 12 years, 12 years, we went from a $1 trillion to a $4 trillion national debt. And the deficit was over $300 billion a year. And at the same time, we were reducing our investment in the things that make us a rich country: in incentives for people to build houses, in new technologies to compete with other countries, in the education, and training of our work force.

So what I tried to do was to turn that around. It seemed to me that the faith—we had to begin was to bring down the deficit with a combination of tough spending cuts and tax increases that would be mostly on those who had been more successful, whose taxes had gone down and were in higher income groups.

This plan that I have presented to Congress does that. But I want to emphasize to you— I'll talk a little more about the details in a moment—but why would the homebuilders be here supporting it if it were bad for business and bad for America? They wouldn't be. They're here because all these people building these houses need jobs, and we need more people like them working. And if people can work, we wouldn't have half the problems we've got in this country.

Six million Americans are employed in the housing and related industry. Homebuilding is critical to our future and critical to the dreams of millions of American families. A year ago, less than half of the American people under the age of 35 thought they had a good chance to buy a home. Today, over 70 percent of them do. And there's one clear reason: lower long-term interest rates, which make mortgage rates as low as they've been in 20 years.

If you think about it, mortgage rates currently are at about 7.5 percent. Now, if someone had a home mortgage at 10 percent and they refinance that at 7.5 percent, in the very first year

of the refinancing, they'd save $2,100. That is way over twice as much in one year as the same family, let's say, a family with an income of $40,000 to $60,000 would pay in new taxes under the energy tax in 4 years under our program.

That is the key to this whole thing. A balanced approach, cut spending, raise money from people who can afford it, minimize the burden on the middle class, but ask people to pay something, but give them back low interest rates, more jobs, and a growing economy. That is the idea, and the critical thing is the interest rates.

Every time mortgage rates go down a point, an additional 350,000 people are able to buy homes. In November, shortly after the election, our administration announced a serious attempt to reduce the deficit based on spending cuts, targeted revenue increases. Long-term interest rates started to drop. They've dropped almost one full point since the election. Last week, after the House of Representatives adopted the economic program, they dropped again, and the stock market went up again because people who control these decisions began to believe again that we could take control of our destiny and really move America forward.

You've already heard some of these specific ideas, but let me just reiterate. In this bill there aren't just tax increases; there are spending cuts, $100 billion in the entitlement areas, and another $150 billion in 200 specific cuts in other areas, including a reduction in the size of the Federal Government by 150,000 employees over the next 4 years, an across-the-board cut of 14 percent in the administrative costs of Government, and hundreds of other specific cuts in spending.

But there are also some incentives in this program which are important. The small business community, some of you would be in that, have been asking for years to increase the expensing provisions in the Tax Code so they could write off $25,000 a year, not $10,000 a year, if they invested in their business to make it more productive. That's in this provision.

Larger businesses who invest a lot of money in new plant and new equipment, which put people to work, have been asking for years for us to change the minimum tax provisions so they won't have to pay taxes on investments they make to put people to work. And we did that in this tax bill, and that will put people to work.

People in real estate have been asking for years that they simply be treated on what are called their passive losses, like people in every other business in the United States of America. And that is in this tax bill, and that will put people to work. These things will create jobs.

Maybe most important of all, for something I care a lot about, I'll bet you that more than half the people in this audience from time to time in the last 10 or 15 years, have complained about the welfare system and have said sometimes there seems like there are more incentives to stay on welfare than off. Well, let me tell you something else this bill does. Some people stay on welfare rather than work 40 hours a week, because if they take a minimum wage job and go to work, they've got to pay somebody for child care; they don't have any health insurance, so they go back on welfare; you pay it through Medicaid, and they can stay home with the kids. It's not because the welfare check is big, it's because of the child care and the medical benefits. This tax bill says that, look, we're going to favor work over welfare forever. If you go to work, you work 40 hours a week, you have a child in your house, the tax system will lift you out of poverty. We're going to favor work over welfare. That's a very important thing that this tax bill does.

Now, next week the United States Senate is coming back into session, and we have to pass this bill in the Senate. Many Senators and many House Members and the President would like to pass the bill with even fewer taxes and more spending cuts, and we're going to look for that. But let me remind you, look at the results already. The most important thing is to pass a bill that has real deficit reduction, real spending cuts, put it all in a trust fund so the money can't go to anything else, and no tax increases

without the spending cuts, and keep the interest rates down. That is what is important here.

I have been overwhelmed—yesterday I had lunch again, as I do about every week with a lot of business executives who themselves will have to pay the lion's share of the tax bill. Over 60 percent of this money will come from people with annual incomes in excess of $200,000, over 75 percent of it from people in the top 7 percent of the income bracket. And most of them are willing to pay as long as they know the interest rates will go down because the deficit is going down. So I think it's important to say, yes, let's shoot for more spending cuts and less taxes, but let's pass the bill and get the deficit down.

I want to just leave you with this. New home sales last month reached a 7-year high in April, 7-year high. That's worth doing. Mortgages rates are at a 20-year low. That's worth keeping. Well, I ask you, let's don't take our eye off the ball. It is estimated that in this year alone, if we can keep these interest rates down at this level, it will put $100 billion back into the American economy, in people refinancing their mortgages, refinancing business loans, lower consumer loans, lower college loans, lower car rates. That's what we've got to do.

I ask for your support. I ask for your support not on a partisan basis but to rebuild the American economy. There is no party label; there's just jobs and incomes behind this. We've got to grow this economy.

I thank the people on this stage and all of you for being here today to make that point. Thank you very much.

NOTE: The President spoke at 11:12 a.m. A tape was not available for verification of the content of these remarks.

Exchange With Reporters on the Economic Program in Frederick
June 3, 1993

The President. [*Inaudible*]—deficit down to keep these interest rates low. Here at this place, people understand low deficits means lower interest rates, more jobs and more money in middle class people's pockets. That's what's going to happen.

Q. You seemed more adamant and forceful in your speech today.

Q. Mr. President, why did you come to Republican territory?

The President. This is an illustration of what really counts. Coming here today and being able to put the charts and the words and the numbers with real jobs, real homes, and real people's lives is what really makes this go for me. And this is what I got elected to do. This is why I ran for President. And I'm doing my best to give real opportunity and hope back to the American people.

Q. But Mr. President, why did you come to someplace where you didn't——

Q. [*Inaudible*]—back off with the Btu tax?

Q. It's Republican territory.

Q. Why did you come to someplace where you didn't succeed in November? You only got 32 percent of the vote here.

The President. Doesn't matter, because even here I wanted to make the point that it's not a partisan issue. I mean, I don't know that a majority of the homebuilders in America or a majority of the realtors in America voted for me in November. Most of them were probably Republicans. But the homebuilders and the realtors, as a group, nationwide, are supporting this program because it's good for the economy; it means jobs; it means lower interest payments for middle class people, for businesses; and it means economic opportunities. And I wanted to illustrate that this is not a partisan issue. It's a bipartisan effort to move this economy forward.

Q. Is it still an uphill battle in the Senate, sir?

The President. I'm encouraged. I feel good about it.

Q. Is Lani Guinier a partisan issue, sir?

[*At this point, the President greeted community members before taking further questions from reporters.*]

The President. [*Inaudible*]—and some—if there can be—if there are more cuts, and we're all trying to agree with that.

Q. What's the status——

Q. Do you think that Lani Guinier deserves a public Senate hearing?

The President. I'm here to talk about jobs and the economy today.

Q. Hi. I'm State Senator Jack Derr. We're happy to have you here in Frederick today.

The President. Good to see you.

Q. Are you reconsidering keeping her, sir?

Q. Are you afraid it's going to look like you're cutting and running in the face of Senate opposition?

The President. You can't have it both ways, folks. You can't say that I'm brave to the point of being crazy for offering an economic plan that raises taxes, cuts spending, and changes things, and for taking on issues like gays in the military and then say we're cutting and running. This administration has taken more tough positions on more tough issues earlier than any one I can remember. So I don't think you can have that both ways. This is an idea issue, and I will have more to say about it later.

Q. Are you going to have a speech, Mr. President, this afternoon?

The President. Lower interest rates and real growth. That's what people who don't have jobs are worried about.

NOTE: The exchange began at approximately 11:30 a.m. A tape was not available for verification of the content of this exchange.

Remarks to Central State University NAIA Champion Athletic Teams
June 3, 1993

Thank you. Please sit down, ladies and gentlemen. I want to welcome all of you here and especially say a word of welcome and thanks to Senator Glenn and Mrs. Glenn and their daughter. Senator Glenn made this occasion possible today.

I want to welcome a group of extraordinary student athletes, the Marauders and Lady Marauders of Central State University, winners of the NAIA championships in football as well as

men and women's indoor and outdoor track and field. I want to welcome the Central State president Dr. Arthur Thomas.

These teams have been remarkably successful. First of all, Central State's football team captured the 1992 NAIA Division One national championship with a come-from-behind victory over—what school? [*Laughter*] This was no fluke. For Coach Billy Joe, named Division One Coach of the Year, it was the second time that he's won a national title in 3 years. Coach Joe has guided Central State to the playoffs for the past six seasons and to the finals for the past three. His winning formula: the three D's he preaches to his players, drive, desire, and determination. These are good words to live by not only on the playing field but here in Washington as well. That is surely what drove the senior quarterback, Henderson Moseley, to lead his team to two touchdowns in the second half of the championship, after being carried off in the first half with a severe ankle injury. I've been through that sort of campaign myself. [*Laughter*]

Coach Joe, you've earned a fourth D for the Marauders, dynasty. That's what you've put together. And I must say, I've carried a special interest in this team because you had to run over the University of Central Arkansas a couple of times in playing for these championships. So we followed it very interestingly.

Now, let me move on to track. The Marauders and the Lady Marauders this year swept the Division One national indoor and outdoor track and field championships, making history. I'm told that this is the first time any college in any league has won four outright team championships in track and field in one year. What a sweet victory, especially for Coach Josh Culbreath, a former Olympian who was also named Coach of the Year. Where is he? You come on down here.

Now, I'm told that Coach Culbreath is known as Pop, although he doesn't look old enough to be my pop. [*Laughter*] He came out of retirement 4 years ago to revitalize track and field at Central State. It's amazing what somebody can accomplish in just 4 years.

This was the first national title in both indoor and outdoor track. At the indoor championship, they captured the title by winning the mile relay in the final event. They also swept the 600-yard run behind the winning pace of team member Neil DeSilva. This young man went on to clock winning times in both the 200- and 400-meter dash, to help them win the outdoor championship.

The Lady Marauders took their indoor title and also their first, winning 6 out of 16 events with record-setting performance and double wins by both Carolyn Sterling and Sherdon Smith. Outdoors, the Lady Marauders claimed their third consecutive NAIA championship, a "threepeat." Dionne Hemming set a world record for the 400-meter hurdles on her way to earning the title of Most Outstanding Female Performer. Jumping hurdles can also be a useful skill in this city. But I understand Dionne could not be with us here today because she's in Spain.

On behalf of our Nation, let me salute all of you for your fine performances. You are teams with truly a proven track record. As student athletes at an historically African-American institution, you can be proud of your many achievements. Your drive and your desire and your determination are an example for all Americans.

I want to congratulate both the coaches, give them a chance to say something. And thank you again, Senator Glenn, for bringing them here today to the Rose Garden.

NOTE: The President spoke at 5 p.m. in the Rose Garden at the White House.

Letter to Congressional Leaders on Trade With Albania, Mongolia, Romania, and Certain States of the Former Soviet Union
June 3, 1993

Dear Mr. Speaker: (Dear Mr. President:)

I hereby transmit the documents referred to in section 402(d)(1) of the Trade Act of 1974, as amended (19 U.S.C. 2432(d)(1)) ("the Act"), with respect to a further 12-month extension of the authority to waive sections (a) and (b) of section 402 of the Act. These documents constitute my recommendation to continue in

effect the waiver authority for a further 12-month period, and include my reasons for determining that continuation of the waiver authority and waivers currently in effect for Albania, Armenia, Azerbaijan, Belarus, Georgia, Kazakhstan, Kyrgyzstan, Moldova, Mongolia, Romania, Russia, Tajikistan, Turkmenistan, Ukraine, and Uzbekistan will substantially promote the objectives of section 402 of the Act.

Sincerely,

BILL CLINTON

NOTE: Identical letters were sent to Thomas S. Foley, Speaker of the House of Representatives, and Albert Gore, Jr., President of the Senate. The Presidential determination of June 2 is listed in Appendix D at the end of this volume.

Letter to Congressional Leaders on Trade With Bulgaria
June 3, 1993

Dear Mr. Speaker: (Dear Mr. President:)

I hereby transmit a report concerning emigration laws and policies of the Republic of Bulgaria as required by subsections 402(b) and 409(b) of Title IV of the Trade Act of 1974, as amended ("the Act") (19 U.S.C. 2432(b) and 2439(b)). I have determined that Bulgaria is in full compliance with the criteria in subsections 402(a) and 409(a) of the Act. As required by Title IV, I will provide the Congress with peri-

odic reports regarding Bulgaria's compliance with these emigration standards.

Sincerely,

WILLIAM J. CLINTON

NOTE: Identical letters were sent to Thomas S. Foley, Speaker of the House of Representatives, and Albert Gore, Jr., President of the Senate. The Presidential determination is listed in Appendix D at the end of this volume.

Remarks on the Withdrawal of the Nomination of Lani Guinier To Be an Assistant Attorney General and an Exchange With Reporters
June 3, 1993

The President. Good evening. It is with deep regret that I am announcing tonight the withdrawal of the nomination of Lani Guinier to be Assistant Attorney General for Civil Rights.

Earlier this evening I met with Ms. Guinier to talk through the issues that prompted my decision. I told her that had I known all along the intense controversy this nomination would inspire I would not have asked her to undergo the ordeal, and I am sorry that she has suffered as much as she has.

At the time of the nomination I had not read her writings. In retrospect, I wish I had. Today, as a matter of fairness to her, I read some of them again in good detail. They clearly lend themselves to interpretations that do not represent the views that I expressed on civil rights during my campaign and views that I hold very dearly, even though there is much in them with which I agree. I have to tell you that had I read them before I nominated her, I would not have done so.

Now, I want to make it clear that that is not to say that I agree with all the attacks on her. She has been subject to a vicious series of willful distortions on many issues, including the quota issue. And that has made this decision all the more difficult.

The Lani Guinier I know is a person of high integrity, great intellect, strong character, and a superb civil rights record. That's why I nominated her. I agree with civil rights leaders and members of the Congressional Black Caucus that she is a wonderful lawyer. And I want all of you to know that if this nomination could be fought out on her character or her record as a civil rights lawyer, I would stay with it to the end, if we didn't get but one or two votes in the Senate.

It is not the fear of defeat that has prompted this decision. It is the certainty that the battle would be carried on a ground that I could not defend. The dilemma with which I have struggled basically comes down to this: Should we have proceeded with a confirmation battle that would give her more ample opportunity to clarify her views but would guarantee a bloody and divisive conflict over civil rights based on ideas that I, as President, could not defend.

Because the controversy over her academic writings includes mischaracterizations, this battle, unfortunately, has already polarized our country. My campaign for the Presidency was based on trying to unite Americans on the basis of race, opportunity, and responsibility, the idea that we could all work together to reach common solutions. And I regret very much the bitterness and the divisiveness which has occurred already.

I am well aware that this withdrawal will upset many people in this country who believe in Lani and had hoped that she might be confirmed. I can only pledge to them that I will continue to work, as I have for nearly 20 years, for the cause of civil rights and that I want an administration second to none in its dedication to civil rights.

I will be consulting promptly with the Attorney General and with other Members of the Senate and House committees and with civil rights leaders about a replacement for Lani. I hope to have an announcement in the next few days. In the meantime, I want to again say I take full responsibility for what has happened here. I want to express my sorrow about what has happened to Lani Guinier and to say again I think that she is one of the ablest civil rights lawyers I have ever known, and I wish this battle could be fought over that rather than ideas that I myself cannot embrace.

Q. Mr. President, Attorney General Reno has been a staunch defender of Ms. Guinier. Did she urge you to keep her on, or is she fully on board with your decision to abandon this nomination?

The President. I believe she is. I would urge you to talk to her about that.

Q. Mr. President, could you just give us an idea of what part of her writings you really had trouble with?

The President. Yes, I can give you an idea. In the Michigan Law Review there was an article. Lani analyzed the weaknesses of the present remedies available under the Voting Rights Act—and many of her analyses I agree with—but seemed to be arguing for principles of proportional representation in minority veto as general remedies that I think are inappropriate as

general remedies and antidemocratic, very difficult to defend.

Now, the Supreme Court has obviously changed the law on that, but the whole thrust of that kind of argument, it seems to me, is inconsistent with the arguments that I tried to make to members of all races all during my campaign.

Q. Mr. President, what part did your friendship, yours and Mrs. Clinton's, with Guinier play in your decision to nominate her and perhaps in your decision—or your neglect of her record at the time that you did nominate her?

The President. Well, Hillary played no role in this nomination or this decision and so deserves no blame or credit for it. But the fact that I have known her since law school and had actually seen her in action as a civil rights practitioner played a very large role in my desire to nominate her. That is, I thought it would be not only interesting, but positive to have, for the first time, someone who had been a career civil rights lawyer head that division.

And frankly, I think the fact that I had known her and cared about her and admired her probably contributed to the way this thing has been handled in a kind of a drawn-out fashion. And it may be the adequacy or inadequacy of the briefings I received about this issue is partly based on the assumption that I must have known everything she'd written about since I knew her as a lawyer. I think that's probably true.

Q. Mr. President, there's a perception among some of your critics among the Black Caucus that your move to the center and your desire to have conservative Democratic votes in the Senate for your economic plan, and your health plan to come, played a large role in this. And they are saying—Craig Washington said, for instance, today, that he was with you in the House vote on the economic plan but won't be with you because of your decision to, in his view, cut and run on Lani Guinier. What do you say to those people and how——

The President. I would say two things. Number one, this is about my center, not about the political center. I will say again, I would gladly fight this nomination to the last moment, if nobody wanted to vote her, nobody, if it were on the grounds that I could defend. If somebody said, "You know, she sued the State of Arkansas, and she sued all these other people, and she came out for remedies in her law practice that weren't right, and she ran over this group and that group," I would say, "Fine, let's fight this thing out. You know, I know that. I have personal knowledge of that. You are wrong." And if everybody in the Senate disagreed with me, I would stay with it to the bitter end.

The problem is that this battle will be waged based on her academic writings. And I cannot fight a battle that I know is divisive, that is an uphill battle, that is distracting to the country, if I do not believe in the ground of the battle. That is the only problem. This has nothing to do with a political center. This has to do with my center.

Now, let me say about Craig Washington, whatever he does for the rest of his life, I'll be grateful to him for what he did and what he said in fighting that economic problem through. I know how strongly he feels about it. I can tell you, I received—if any—there's pressure over the issue. I got more pressure to stay with this than to drop it. But in the end, I had to do what I thought was right. Whether I am right or wrong, I tell you tonight, I have done what I think is right.

Q. Mr. President, did she agree with you?

Q. Did she agree with you?

Q. Has she withdrawn or are you withdrawing her?

The President. I am—I think you'd better ask her what she said.

Q. Well, if she comes—have you withdrawn her name?

The President. Well, she's in town and we've—I think she'll probably have a statement later tonight. I have no idea what she will say.

Q. Did she ask you not to withdraw her name, sir?

The President. Well, you know what she wanted. She wanted her hearing. But she was surprised that I felt the way I did. You know, this is the first long, detailed conversation we've had about it. It was a very painful thing between two people who have liked and admired each other a long time. This was one of the most difficult meetings I've ever had in my life. But I did what I thought was right.

NOTE: The President spoke at 9:05 p.m. in the Briefing Room at the White House.

Statement on Sanctions Against Haiti
June 4, 1993

One of the cornerstones of our foreign policy is to support the global march toward democracy and to stand by the world's new democracies. The promotion of democracy, which not only reflects our values but also increases our security, is especially important in our own hemisphere. As part of that goal, I consider it a high priority to return democracy to Haiti and to return its democratically elected President, Jean-Bertrand Aristide, to his office.

We should recall Haiti's strides toward democracy just a few years back. Seven years ago, tired of the exploitative rule that had left them the poorest nation in our hemisphere, the Haitian people rose up and forced the dictator Jean-Claude Duvalier to flee. In December 1990, in a remarkable exercise of democracy, the Haitian people held a free and fair election, and two-thirds of them voted for President Aristide.

Nineteen months ago, however, that progress toward democracy was thwarted when the Hai-

tian military illegally and violently ousted President Aristide from office. Since taking office in January, the United States Government has worked steadily with the international community in an effort to restore President Aristide and democracy to Haiti. The OAS and United Nations Special Envoy, Dante Caputo, has demonstrated great dedication and tenacity. To support Mr. Caputo's effort, Secretary of State Christopher in March named U.S. Ambassador Lawrence Pezzullo as our Special Adviser for Haiti.

We and the international community have made progress. The presence of the International Civilian Mission has made a concrete contribution to human rights in Haiti. Mr. Caputo's consultations with all the parties indicated that a negotiated solution is possible.

Unfortunately, the parties in Haiti have not been willing to make the decisions or take the steps necessary to begin democracy's restoration.

And while they seek to shift responsibility, Haiti's people continue to suffer.

In light of their own failure to act constructively, I have determined that the time has come to increase the pressure on the Haitian military, the de facto regime in Haiti and their supporters.

The United States has been at the forefront of the international community's efforts to back up the U.N./OAS negotiations with sanctions and other measures. Beginning in October 1991, we froze all Haitian Government assets in the United States and prohibited unlicensed financial transactions with Haitian persons. Today, I am acting to strengthen those existing provisions in several ways.

First, I have signed a proclamation pursuant to Section 212(f) of the Immigration and Nationality Act prohibiting the entry into the U.S. of Haitian nationals who impede the progress of negotiations designed to restore constitutional government to Haiti and of the immediate relatives of such persons. The Secretary of State will determine the persons whose actions are impeding a solution to the Haitian crisis. These people will be barred from entering the United States.

Second, pursuant to the authority of the International Emergency Economic Powers Act and the Executive orders on the Haiti emergency, I have directed the Secretary of the Treasury to designate as "specially designated nationals" those Haitians who act for or on behalf of the junta, or who make material, financial, or commercial contributions to the de facto regime or the Haitian armed forces. In effect, this measure will freeze the personal assets of such persons subject to U.S. jurisdiction and bar them from conducting any transactions whatsoever with the individuals and entities named.

Third, I have directed Secretary Christopher to consult with the OAS and its member states on ways to enhance enforcement of the existing OAS sanctions program. And I have directed Secretary Christopher and Ambassador Albright to consult with the U.N. and member states on the possibility of creating a worldwide sanctions program against Haiti.

Sanctions alone do not constitute a solution. The surest path toward the restoration of democracy in Haiti is a negotiated solution that assures the safety of all parties. We will therefore strongly support a continuation and intensification of the negotiating effort. We will impress on all parties the need to take seriously their own responsibilities for a successful resolution to this impasse.

Our policy on Haiti is not a policy for Haiti alone. It is a policy in favor of democracy everywhere. Those who seek to derail a return to constitutional government, whether in Haiti or Guatemala, must recognize that we will not be swayed from our purpose.

At the same time, individuals should not have to fear that supporting democracy's restoration will ultimately put their own safety at risk. Those who have opposed President Aristide in the past should recognize that, once President Aristide has returned, we and the rest of the international community will defend assiduously their legitimate political rights.

It is my hope that the measures we have announced today will encourage greater effort and flexibility in the negotiations to restore democracy and President Aristide to Haiti.

NOTE: The proclamation of June 3 barring the entry of certain Haitian nationals into the United States is listed in Appendix D at the end of this volume.

Letter to Congressional Leaders Reporting Budget Rescissions
June 4, 1993

Dear Mr. Speaker: (Dear Mr. President:)

In accordance with the Congressional Budget and Impoundment Control Act of 1974, I herewith report six proposed rescissions, totaling $176.0 million in budgetary resources.

These proposed rescissions affect the Departments of Housing and Urban Development, Justice, and Transportation. The details of the proposed rescissions are contained in the attached reports.

Sincerely,

WILLIAM J. CLINTON

NOTE: Identical letters were sent to Thomas S. Foley, Speaker of the House of Representatives, and Albert Gore, Jr., President of the Senate. The reports detailing the proposed rescissions were published in the *Federal Register* on June 15.

Statement by the Press Secretary on the President's Task Force on National Health Care Reform
June 4, 1993

On January 25, 1993, the President announced the creation of a Task Force on National Health Care Reform. The President asked the task force to provide him with proposals for comprehensive health care reform. The President also announced on January 25 the creation of an interdepartmental working group that would gather and analyze information and options for the task force.

In over 20 meetings held during April and May, the task force reviewed materials it received from the interdepartmental working group, formulated proposals and options for health care reform, and presented those proposals and options to the President. Each of those task force meetings was noticed in the *Federal Register*.

Having completed its mission, the task force terminated on May 30, as provided in its charter.

The President is now in the process of reviewing the proposals he has received from the task force and choosing from among the policy options that have been presented to him.

The President's Radio Address
June 5, 1993

Good morning. On February the 17th, I presented to our country a national economic strategy to create jobs and increase incomes through investments in our future and bringing our Government's deficit down. This plan is tough, and it requires real contributions from everyone. It was written to improve our economy long-term, but I believed back in February, just as I did in the campaign of 1992, that this plan could produce positive short-term results, and it already has.

Once it became clear that we would take responsibility for bringing our deficit down, interest rates started coming down. Analysts say that if we can keep these interest rates down for a year, we'll put over $100 billion back into this economy. How? Because people will refinance their home loans or their business loans. Many of you listening to this program have already done that and have saved a great deal of money. Think what an extra $100 billion can do, through lower interest rates on consumer loans, car loans, college loans, home loans, and business loans. It means more jobs for ordinary Americans, higher business profits, better consumer confidence, and more consumer spending. All that will grow the economy. It's already beginning to work.

Just yesterday, unemployment fell below 7 percent for the first time in a year and a half. In just the last 4 months, the economy has added 755,000 new jobs. And last month, as mortgage rates hit a 20-year low, new home sales reached a 7-year high. That too means more jobs for ordinary Americans and more Americans realizing the dream of home ownership, building stronger neighborhoods and stronger communities, and making America a better place to live. We're moving on the right track. If we get our priorities right and our Government house in order, more people will be able to order houses for themselves. If we drive interest rates down, jobs and investment will keep going up.

Now the U.S. House of Representatives has acted courageously and decisively to approve our economic growth plan, and it's time for the Senate to do the right thing as well.

In the plan before the Senate, we cut the deficit $500 billion over the next 5 years, the largest reduction program ever proposed by a President. The plan is balanced and fair. About half the deficit reduction comes from spending cuts and restraints in Federal entitlement programs and health care programs, and about half of it comes from new revenues.

Included in the $250 billion of spending cuts are reductions in more than 200 specific programs. We also raised some taxes. But this time, unlike the last 12 years, we're doing it in a fair way. Seventy-five percent of the new money comes from people with incomes above $100,000, people who can better afford it and whose tax rates went down in the 1980's.

Middle class Americans are asked to make a contribution in the form of an energy tax. For families of four with incomes of $40,000 a year or more, that amounts to about $1 a month in 1994, $7 a month in 1995, and no more than $17 a month when the plan is fully in place in 1996 and thereafter. For working families with incomes under $30,000, the income tax system has been changed so that the burden will be virtually nonexistent. And for the working poor, people who are working 40 hours a week or less, we put in place the first big block of our welfare reform program. Because if this plan passes, people who work 40 hours a week and have children in their homes will be lifted above the poverty line for the first time in American history.

Now, no one wants to pay any additional taxes or see anybody else pay taxes. And we're working hard to minimize the tax increases and maximize the spending cuts.

But let me remind you, my fellow Americans, all the people who are out here calling this a tax-and-spend program are the same people who for the last 12 years have lowered taxes on the rich, raised taxes on the middle class, taken the national debt from $1 trillion to $4 trillion, and reduced our investment in our future so that jobs went down and incomes did too. My plan is working to take us in the reverse direction. It does require tough choices. You've had all the easy choices for 12 years and the hidden taxes. We have given you some very simple and open truths. We've got to be tough enough to bring down the deficit, but we have to be smart enough to keep investing in our

people and our technologies to have a growing modern economy.

Next week, the Senate will begin considering this plan for deficit reduction and economic growth. There are principles the Senate should honor when it considers our plan, the things I believe we must have. Number one, we have to cut this deficit by at least $500 billion over the next 5 years. Number two, there could be no increases in taxes before there are real cuts in spending, and all the savings should be locked up in a trust fund for the 5-year life of the plan. Number three, because of what's happened over the last 12 years, those who are successful enough to be able to pay more should pay more, and we must minimize the burden on the middle class and the working poor. Number four, we have to preserve these incentives to reform the welfare system and to encourage people who are working, so that more people will move from welfare to work. And number five, when we cut spending, we still have to leave some investment resources for education and training, for new technologies, for converting from a defense to a domestic economy, and for incentives for businesses and private individuals to invest in communities that are distressed and to create new jobs and new enterprises. These are the steps we must take to rebuild our economy. We can do it.

Although the changes I am asking Congress to approve are difficult, especially after more than a decade of everybody being told exactly what they want to hear while things get worse and worse and worse, these changes have to be made. Our living standards are at stake, and we must rise to the occasion. That is, after all, the promise of America. A community at its best provides a growing measure of prosperity for everyone who works hard and plays by the rules. But our challenge is to fulfill that promise by ensuring that as we expand opportunity and growth, everyone has a shot to earn their share.

In my lifetime, no one has addressed that challenge with greater courage or constancy than the late Senator Robert Kennedy. On Sunday, 25 years after his death, I will be joining his family, their supporters and friends in celebrating his short but exceptional life as one of the most candid and unifying public servants our country has ever known.

At a time when so many citizens feel disconnected from their political leaders, Senator Kennedy had an uncommon feel for what people experienced in their daily lives. He fought to expand economic opportunity, to remind citizens that our rights are accompanied by responsibilities. He sought to close the gap between working class whites and African-Americans when others tried for political advantage to keep them apart.

Most of all, Robert Kennedy reminded us that whatever our differences with our leaders are and our differences with our policies, we can and should all love our country. And that is why, even as we remember his life and mourn his loss, we must celebrate his spirit because his example is what we should be following today.

I will keep fighting for a society filled with opportunity for every American, free of discrimination, full of the hopes and dreams that Bobby Kennedy fought for. Realizing these dreams would be the greatest tribute we could offer him and the greatest gift we could give to our children.

Thanks for listening.

NOTE: The President spoke at 10:06 a.m. from the Oval Office at the White House.

Remarks at the Memorial Mass for Robert F. Kennedy in Arlington, Virginia
June 6, 1993

Father Creedon, Mrs. Kennedy, the children of Robert Kennedy, and the Kennedy family, to all the distinguished Americans here present, and most of all, to all of you who bear the noble title, citizen of this country: Twenty-five years ago today, on the eve of my college graduation, I cheered the victory of Robert Kennedy in the California primary and felt again that our country might face its problems openly, meet its challenges bravely, and go forward together. He dared us all. He dared the grieving not to retreat into despair. He dared the comfortable not to be complacent. He dared the doubting to keep going.

As I looked around this crowd today and saw us all graced not only by the laughter of children but by the tears of those of us old enough to remember, it struck me again that the memory of Robert Kennedy is so powerful that in a profound way we are all in two places today. We are here and now, and we are there, then.

For in Robert Kennedy we all invested our hopes and our dreams that somehow we might redeem the promise of the America we then feared we were losing, somehow we might call back the promise of President Kennedy and Martin Luther King and heal the divisions of Vietnam and the violence and pain in our own country. But I believe if Robert Kennedy were here today, he would dare us not to mourn his passing but to fulfill his promise and to be the people that he so badly wanted us all to be. He would dare us to leave yesterday and embrace tomorrow.

We remember him, almost captured in freeze-frame, standing on the hood of a car, grasping at outreached hands, black and brown and white. His promise was that the hands which reached out to him might someday actually reach out to each other. And together, those hands could make America everything that it ought to be, a nation reunited with itself and rededicated to its best ideals.

When his funeral train passed through the gritty cities of the Northeast, people from both sides of the tracks stood silent. He had earned their respect because he went to places most leaders never visit and listened to people most leaders never hear and spoke simple truth most leaders never speak.

He spoke out against neglect, but he challenged the neglected to seize their own destiny. He wanted so badly for Government to act, but he did not trust bureaucracy. And he believed that Government had to do things with people, not for them. He knew we had to do things together or not at all. He spoke to the sons and daughters of immigrants and the sons and daughters of sharecroppers and told them all, "As long as you stay apart from each other, you will never be what you ought to be."

He saw the world not in terms of right and left but right and wrong. And he taught us lessons that cannot be labeled except as powerful proof. Robert Kennedy reminded us that on any day, in any place, at any time, racism is wrong, exploitation is wrong, violence is wrong, anything that denies the simple humanity and potential of any man or woman is wrong.

He touched children whose stomachs were swollen with hunger but whose eyes still sparkled with life. He marched with workers who strained their backs for poverty wages while harvesting our food. He walked down city streets with people who ached, not from work but from the lack of it. Then as now, his piercing eyes and urgent voice speak of the things we all like to think that we believe in.

When he was alive, some said he was ruthless. Some said he wasn't a real liberal, and others claimed he was a real radical. If he were here today, I think he would laugh and say they were both right. But now as we see him more clearly, we understand he was a man who was very gentle to those who were most vulnerable, very tough in the standards he kept for himself, very old-fashioned in the virtues in which he believed, and a relentless searcher for change, for growth, for the potential of heart and mind that he sought in himself and he demanded of others.

Robert Kennedy understood that the real purpose of leadership is to bring out the best in others. He believed the destiny of our Nation is the sum total of all the decisions that all of us make. He often said that one person can make a difference, and each of us must try.

Some still believe we lost what is best about America when President Kennedy and Martin Luther King and Robert Kennedy were killed. But I ask you to remember, my fellow Americans, that Robert Kennedy did not lose his faith when his own brother was killed. And when Martin Luther King was killed, he gave from his heart what was perhaps his finest speech. He lifted himself from despair time after time and went back to work.

If you listen now you can hear with me his voice telling me and telling you and telling everyone here, "We can do better." Today's troubles call us to do better. The legacy of Robert Kennedy is a stern rebuke to the cynicism, to the trivialization that grips so much of our public life today. What use is it in the face of the aching problems gripping millions of Americans, the American without a job, the American without health care, the American without a safe street to live on or a good school to send a child to? What use is it in the face of all the divisions that keep our country down and rob our children of their rightful future?

Let us learn here once again the simple, powerful, beautiful lesson, the simple faith of Robert Kennedy: We can do better. Let us leave here no longer in two places, but once again in one only: in the here and now, with a commitment to tomorrow, the only part of our time that we can control. Let us embrace the memory of Robert Kennedy by living as he would have us to live. For the sake of his memory, of ourselves, and of all of our children and all those to come, let us believe again, we can do better.

NOTE: The President spoke at 8:13 p.m. at Arlington National Cemetery. In his remarks, he referred to Rev. Gerard Creedon, missionary to the Dominican Republic and celebrant of the Mass.

Remarks to the League of Women Voters
June 7, 1993

The President. Thank you very much, Becky, for that wonderful introduction. I want to thank you and Gracia Hillman and all the leaders of the State and local chapters of the League of Women Voters from around the country who are here. I know there are at least three members from my home State here. I'm glad to see you all. Karen Stevens, Bobbie Hill, and Linda Polk, I thank them for coming. This is your house. And I'm glad to have you back here.

When I ran for President, I did so with the conviction that we had to create a new season of opportunity and a new climate of responsibility in America so that together we could rebuild the American community. And there were some very specific commitments that I made in that regard: an economic program that would be good for America's families and working people;

a health care program that would control cost and provide basic coverage to all Americans; a program of national service and reform of the student loan program to open the doors of college education to all Americans; a program to change the welfare system to move families from dependence to independence; and a program of political reform to open the system of this country so that ordinary Americans could pull the levers of power and have their voices heard.

Your presence here today, for the first time since 1980, after decades and decades, the League of Women Voters coming to the White House without regard to party, in a bipartisan fashion, coming back here for the first time since 1980, is a symbol of the importance of opening the political system to informed citizens to let them have influence over the decisions that are made affecting the lives of ordinary Americans. And I welcome you here today.

Not long ago, as Becky said, we gathered here to sign the motor voter bill—again, a strong priority of the League of Women Voters—without regard to party, opening the franchise more to all Americans and especially to many younger Americans who were so terribly interested in this issue. That was a very, very important day for all of us. It was not only good for voter registration, it was in a very fundamental sense a civil rights law and a real advance for all the people of the United States.

Not long before that, I gathered here with other Americans to sign the family leave bill into law, which is a very important thing because it attempts to unite two of our most important values, work and family, guaranteeing ordinary citizens that if they have to take a little time off for a baby to be born or a parent to be cared for, they won't lose their jobs.

These are the kinds of things that Government ought to do with the American people, not to just do things for people but to empower people to take care of their own business. That's what motor voter does; that's what family leave does. That's what we ought to be about in this country.

Now, we are moving ahead in the Congress with the economic plan, soon to be followed by the health care plan. And there is a very ambitious agenda of political reform before the Congress. I know that's what you're here about, so I'd like to say just a word about that, if I might.

There are actually two important political reform bills in the United States Congress today. And I urge you to embrace them both. The first one you know about and that is the campaign finance reform bill in the United States Senate. The bill does exactly what we ought to do: it lowers the cost of campaigns, reduces the influence of special interest groups, and opens the airwaves to more honest debates so that incumbents are not unduly protected and wealth is not the primary determinant of whether a person can wage a credible campaign. It is a very, very important advance. And we have proposed to—you can clap for that, I like that— [*applause*]—we have proposed to pay for this by repealing a tax deduction that is only 30 years old and that is the tax deduction for lobbying. We've proposed to repeal it and pay for campaign finance reform. No other money will go into campaign finance reform except that which is voluntarily contributed by the American taxpayers if this bill passes as it has been proposed. So I urge you to go up there and plead with the United States Senate and talk to the House Members while you're at it and say, give us a bill we can be proud of to give the election process back to the American people. One of the reasons more people voted in the Presidential election in 1992 than had voted in a long time is because of all the debates, all the town meetings, all the open forums, all the ways that people found to say this is your place, not the politicians' place. This is your country. This is your Government; take it back. And campaign finance reform will help us to do that.

The second bill has already been passed by the Senate and is now in the House. It is a bill long overdue, which will require all people who lobby the United States Congress to register and report and will require the reporting of virtually all funds expended on Members of Congress by lobbyists. It is a very important bill, and I urge you to support that.

Secondly, I appreciate your support for health care reform. Let me say that the First Lady and the hundreds of people who worked on the task force and the people in the administration who are still reaching out over America to the health care providers and the health care consumers and the business community, the labor community, everybody affected by this, deserve a lot of credit. They have done more complex, exhaustive work in less time than any other group like this, I think, in the entire history of the United States. And I'm very grateful to them for that. And soon we will have a health care proposal that I believe will be self-evidently in the interest of the vast majority of the American people, not only to provide universal coverage but to do it in a way which preserves what is best about American health care and brings these costs down before we bankrupt the United States with health care costs and without universal coverage.

Let me say, before we do that, we have got to get the Government's house in order. In 12 years—the 12 years you weren't here; it may be because you weren't here—[*laughter*]—in the 12 years you weren't here, the debt of this country went from $1 trillion to $4 trillion. Our national deficit was over $300 billion this year. We have got to do something about it. But the most frustrating thing of all, it's like health care; we spend 35 percent more than anybody else in the world and do less with it. With our Government's deficit soaring, with our debt exploding, we have reduced our investments in the things that make us a richer, stronger, more productive country and that offer our children the chance to seize the American dream.

We have to put our house in order and reverse a lot of those practices, practices that have, to be sure, the stamp of not only Republican Presidents but also Democratic Congresses, practices born of taking the path of least resistance and telling people what they want to hear. It is always more popular to cut people's taxes and send them more money and deplore the Government every step of the way. But in the end, you have to live with the consequences of what you have wrought. And that is what we are doing today. And we are determined in this administration to change those consequences.

The House of Representatives acted very courageously to pass the largest deficit reduction program ever proposed by an administration. At the same time they did it, I pledged to review the budget to ensure that we maximized our reliance on spending cuts, minimized our reliance on new taxes, and kept the burden on middle class working Americans as light as possible.

As we move into the Senate this week, we will fight for all the $250 billion in spending cuts contained in this program, including $100 billion in reductions in entitlements already in this program. We will fight for the fairness of the program, which has over 60 percent of the new taxes coming from people with incomes above $200,000, over 74 percent coming above $100,000; which costs the average family with a $40,000 or $50,000 income $1 a month next year, $7 a month the year after, and $17 a month at a maximum rate; and which holds harmless working families under $30,000 a year; and which has the first incentive in the history of the United States of America to lift the working poor out of poverty by using the tax system to say if you work 40 hours a week and you have a child in the house, you will not be below the poverty line. If you want welfare reform, that's it.

Now, later today I will meet with Senator Mitchell, the Senate majority leader, and Senator Moynihan, the chairman of the Finance Committee, and I will tell them that I intend to designate the Treasury Secretary, Secretary Bentsen, to work with them to come up with a budget that the American people will accept and that the Congress will pass. As we complete work on this growth plan, I intend to do everything I can to say I welcome additional cuts. But I will fight to protect the most vulnerable people in this country. And I will fight to protect our investments to create jobs. For in the end, this cannot be about passing budgets or reducing deficits. It certainly can't be about raising taxes or even cutting spending. What it is in the end is about giving us control over our destiny again, giving us the ability to create jobs and opportunity and increase incomes for the American people.

And let's not lose sight of what has been done. This program which cuts spending, raises revenues, cuts the deficit, and invests in jobs and technology for the future has already by its advocacy and passing, dramatically contributed to bringing interest rates to their lowest point in 20 years; so that you've got a 7-year high in home buying, unemployment below 7 percent for the first time in a year and a half, and 755,000 new jobs in this economy in the last 4 months. I think that's something to be proud of, and I don't understand why people are not glad that those consequences are flowing from these efforts.

I believe the American people want us to move in this direction. Last week the Home Builders Association endorsed the economic program, not a traditionally Democratic group. [*Laughter*] The Realtors Association has endorsed it. More than half the 100 biggest companies in the United States have endorsed it along with the largest labor organizations in America. This is a program that's good for jobs. The Congressional Black Caucus voted for it unanimously because of the empowerment zones in the program which gives the private sector incentives to invest in putting people back to work in the most depressed areas in America. The business community is pleased because of the incentives for starting new business and for helping small businesses.

If you will look at this program you will see it is no accident why the interest rates are down, the jobs are up, and investment is coming back into America. If we can keep interest rates down, then all this debt that has piled up in the last 12 years at least can be refinanced in terms of home mortgages, business loans, college loans, consumer loans, car loans. And all that lower interest rate will then free up money to invest. That is what is creating these jobs now, and we cannot turn our backs on it.

So I say, let's move on to the Senate. Let's pass the economic program; then let's move on to health care. And let's never forget that it will all work better over the long run if we pass campaign finance reform and lobbying reform and continue to fight to open this system to the American people.

Thank you very much.

Supreme Court Nomination

Q. Mr. President, how close are you to a Supreme Court nomination?

The President. Pretty close. I have not made a decision yet, but I'm working on it, talking to people. I expect a decision very soon.

Q. [*Inaudible*]—spoken to anyone about the decision——

Q. Why are you backing off of Babbitt?

Q. ——any of the potential nominees?

The President. Stay tuned.

Q. Why are you backing off of Babbitt?

The President. I'm not. I've never——

Q. Babbitt's in the race?

The President. I'm not backing off or on anybody. I haven't made a decision yet.

Q. Is he in the race?

The President. I haven't made a decision yet. When I do, I'll tell you. Thanks.

NOTE: The President spoke at 2:23 p.m. in the Rose Garden. In his remarks, he referred to Becky Cain and Gracia Hillman, president and executive director, League of Women Voters of the United States; Karen Stevens and Linda Polk, member and president, Arkansas League of Women Voters; and Bobbie Hill, member of the boards of directors of both the national and Arkansas leagues. The exchange portion of this item could not be verified because the tape was incomplete.

Exchange With Reporters Prior to a Meeting With Senate Leaders
June 7, 1993

Economic Program

Q. How far are you on a compromise on the economics program?

The President. Well, we just started. I have asked Secretary Bentsen to work with Mr. Panetta, to work with the Senate, to basically embody the principles that I think are important. We have to have $500 billion in deficit reduction. We have to have the spending cuts. And no tax increases without the spending cuts. The deficit trust fund is important. The tax burden has to be progressive.

Right now, over 60 percent of this money is coming from people with incomes above $200,000, over 74 percent from people with in-

comes above $100,000. That has to be kept. And then we have to keep the pro-work, pro-jobs portions of this intact. This plan gives the best incentives to small business, to new businesses, and for working poor people to work their way out of poverty, of any tax program we have ever had. And it's not just a tax program. It's an investment program, and it's a spending-cut program. And the whole thing has to be put together. Now, within those principles, these people are going to work out a bill that can pass the Senate, pass the Congress, and can keep the economic growth going.

Keep in mind the main objective is to keep interest rates down, keep the growth going.

We've got 755,000 new jobs since January, a 7-year high in housing starts, first time in 18 months unemployment below 7 percent. This thing is working. We've got to keep it going. That's my concern.

Q. How far are you on a Btu tax? Would you give a little on that?

The President. I want an energy component that promotes energy conservation in clean fuels. That's what I want. I believe that's an important part of our future. Everybody knows that if we're going to have high productivity growth and be a rich country, we have to promote that. That's an important principle to me, too.

Q. [*Inaudible*]—on Senator Boren to get that passed?

The President. I'm promoting the principles. These guys are going to work it out. My job is to advocate for the kinds of product—I want the results. I want jobs and incomes and growth. That's what we're producing now. That's my job. I'm confident they'll produce a plan that will give us that.

NOTE: The exchange began at 5:35 p.m. in the Oval Office at the White House, prior to a meeting with Senators George J. Mitchell and Daniel Patrick Moynihan. A tape was not available for verification of the content of this exchange.

Exchange With Reporters Prior to a Meeting With Congressional Leaders
June 8, 1993

Economic Program

Q. Mr. President, the Republicans have said they won't accept a plan with any taxes. How are you going to bridge that gap with Bob Dole?

The President. I don't know what the bridge will be. Let me just say this, I think it's very important that we move this promptly as possible to pass the economic plan. After the House acted, long-term interest rates dropped again. We now have a 7-year high in housing sales, unemployment below 7 percent—it's the first time in a year and a half—755,000 new jobs since January. And that's because there's a serious attempt to reduce this deficit through a combination of cuts and tax increases, almost all of which come on wealthier individuals. So I think we just need to move forward.

There will be some changes in the Senate, and that is fine. Then we just need to hold to the principles: there ought to be $500 billion in deficit reduction; it ought to be in a trust fund so that neither the taxes nor the spending cuts can be diverted; and the tax burden ought to be progressive, falling largely on the wealthiest Americans; and we ought to keep the incentives for private sector growth in there. We're moving from welfare to work for investing in the depressed areas of the country for starting small businesses. Those are the principles that I have. And the energy tax ought to encourage conservation and the use of cleaner fuels. Those

are the things that I think ought to be done. We'll just see what happens.

Q. Does it have to include—does it have to be a Btu tax, or can you find another energy——

The President. I have delegated to—I don't want to get into the name game here. I'm interested in the principles of the program: deficit reduction, lower interest rates, job growth. We've got job growth coming back into this economy now, and I think we have to continue to do what produces it, which is lower interest rates. The lower interest rates are causing people to refinance all their debt and putting it back into the economy. And that's the thing I'm interested in.

We'll just see. Secretary Bentsen and Mr. Panetta are representing the administration in the conversations with the Senate. And we'll just see what comes out of it.

Q. Do you think you can start over with Bob Dole, after all the bad blood?

The President. I like Senator Dole. I always have. Besides that, he knows more jokes than I do, and I resent it. Get him to share some with you.

NOTE: The exchange began at 9:35 a.m. in the Cabinet Room at the White House. A tape was not available for verification of the content of this exchange.

Statement on Signing the Government Printing Office Electronic Information Access Enhancement Act of 1993
June 8, 1993

It is with great pleasure that I sign into law S. 564, the "Government Printing Office Electronic Information Access Enhancement Act of 1993," which will enhance electronic access by the public to Federal information. Under this Act, the public will have on-line computer access to two of the major source documents that inform us about the laws and regulations that affect our daily lives: the *Congressional Record* and the *Federal Register*. With recent advances in information technology, we can go beyond the costly printing of tons of paper documents without diminishing the quick and accurate delivery of important information to the public.

As Vice President Gore and I announced in our February 22nd statement, *Technology for America's Economic Growth, A New Direction to Build Economic Strength*, we are committed to working with the private sector to use technology to make Government information available to the public in a timely and equitable manner. Federal agencies can make Government information more accessible to the public, and enhance the utility of Government information as a national resource, by disseminating information in electronic media.

For many years, Vice President Gore has been a leader in this area. He introduced the Senate version of this Act last year and worked closely with Chairmen Charlie Rose and Wendell Ford and others on both sides of the aisle to refine the Act.

This important step forward in the electronic dissemination of Federal information will provide valuable insights into the most effective means of disseminating all public Government information. The system to be established by the Government Printing Office (GPO) will complement, not supplant, commercial information services and Federal agency information dissemination programs. Likewise, it should not supplant existing GPO mechanisms of information dissemination to the private sector. Indeed, the lessons learned from this program will be used by Federal agencies to develop the most useful and cost-effective means of information dissemination. To do this, the GPO initiative must be coordinated with related projects in the Executive branch.

WILLIAM J. CLINTON

The White House,
June 8, 1993.

NOTE: S. 564, approved June 8, was assigned Public Law No. 103–40.

Message to the Congress Transmitting the Report of the Federal Council on the Aging
June 8, 1993

To the Congress of the United States:

In accordance with section 204(f) of the Older Americans Act of 1965, as amended (42 U.S.C. 3015(f)), I hereby transmit the Annual Report for 1992 of the Federal Council on the Aging. The report reflects the Council's views in its role of examining programs serving older Americans.

WILLIAM J. CLINTON

The White House,
June 8, 1993.

Nomination for Director of the Trade and Development Agency
June 8, 1993

The President announced his intention to nominate New Hampshire management consultant and political activist J. Joseph Grandmaison to be Director of the Trade and Development Agency, U.S. International Development and Cooperation Agency.

"Joe Grandmaison has many years of experi-

ence in economic development, as well as in civic affairs," said the President. "His knowledge of how the private and public sectors can work together will serve him well in this new position."

NOTE: A biography of the nominee was made available by the Office of the Press Secretary.

Nominations for Posts at the Office of Science and Technology Policy
June 8, 1993

The President today announced his intention to nominate NASA scientist Robert Watson Associate Director for the Environment at the Office of Science and Technology Policy and Mark Schaefer, Washington office director of the Carnegie Commission on Science, Technology and Government, as Assistant Director for the Environment at the OSTP.

"Bob Watson and Mark Schaefer are scientists

who have spent the bulk of their careers studying the connection between science and the environment," the President said. "With their understanding of the important connection between these two fields, I am confident they will ensure American policies work to promote a strong economy and a healthy environment."

NOTE: Biographies of the nominees were made available by the Office of the Press Secretary.

Remarks at the Congressional Barbecue
June 8, 1993

Thank you. Please sit down. Thank you very much. We just want to welcome you here. The big bonus of this evening is there are no speeches and no politics. Hillary and I just want to welcome you here and thank you for coming.

I also want you to know that this tent now has a hallowed heritage. On Saturday night I had my 25th college reunion under this tent, and nobody left until 1:30 a.m. So don't feel bashful if you want to stay awhile.

It is always a privilege to serve our country, but this is a unique time for all of us because of the point in history in which we find ourselves. And I just thought it would be great

if we could get together and enjoy each other's company, get to know each other a little better.

I thank you all for coming, all of you for bringing your spouses, your staff members, your friends, and I hope you enjoy yourselves tonight. This is, after all, your place. I'm just a temporary tenant. I'm glad to be here, glad to welcome you here, and I wanted Hillary to say a word, too, because we're both so pleased to be a part of this evening.

Thank you again for coming.

NOTE: The President spoke at 8:55 p.m. on the South Lawn at the White House.

Remarks and a Question-and-Answer Session With the Business Roundtable
June 9, 1993

The President. Thank you. Thank you, John, and thank you, ladies and gentlemen, for the invitation to come here and speak with you today. I appreciate it not only because of the important things that we need to discuss but because you, as the CEO's of our Nation's top businesses, have a vital role to play in providing what our country needs most now, economic renewal and an honest facing of our real challenges.

In recent years, members of the Business Roundtable have often been among the most enlightened leaders of our Nation, in any walk of life. Many of you have supported the economic program that I have advanced, and for your help I am extremely grateful. All of you know there is a moment in the life of every enterprise when a CEO looks up and realizes that the company has been doing something that simply doesn't work anymore, that the time has come for overhaul and change, and though it will be painful, it has to be done. When that time comes, if you have the courage to do it, you just have to go before the stockholders and tell them that things aren't working, that there's some pain in the short run, but there's a lot of gain in the long run.

Many of you have had exactly that experience in the last 10 to 15 years. You've had to restructure your companies, slim them down, eliminate unnecessary layers of management, embrace quality management, invest more in the training of your work force and in the quality of your equipment and in the competitiveness of your operations.

And as a result of those calls, American companies now are once again the wonder of the world. Detroit turns out much better cars than it did 10 years ago. And guess what? It's gaining market share now in America, something that a lot of people thought would never happen again. Motorola goes head-to-head in Japan and often wins, and manufacturing as a whole has come roaring back. Our workers are proving once again that they are the best in the world. That's exactly what can happen to our Nation as a whole, and what I believe has to happen. If we put our shoulder to the wheel and face the issues squarely, I think it will happen. We'll come roaring back, too.

As a new President, I feel the same as many of you did a few years ago. I look around and I see what I've inherited, and I realize that, just as I said in the campaign, we have been on the wrong track for too long. Just as you've overhauled your companies, we've got to work together to overhaul this country. And I believe that we can. I promise you I'm doing everything I can to get it done.

The people of this country are just like the stockholders in your companies. You can tell them the changes we need. First, the people want to know what's wrong and what the problems are. Then they want to know what the strategy is for solving the problems. And then they want to know what's in it for them, both good and bad. They deserve to have all those questions answered, and I'm doing my best to answer them. They are tough questions but fair ones. They have to be faced.

Four months ago when I came to office, our country was suffering from a long period of economic slowdown, and the Government's deficit figures had been revised upward after the election by $165 billion over the next 4 years. After World War II, the income of the average American family was doubling about every 25 years, an extraordinary feat that created a vast middle class in our country. Everybody thought these good times would go on forever, that the next generation would always be better off than its parents, that the quality of life and of social justice would continue to increase.

But in the early 1970's, that upward escalator came to a screeching halt, brought on by the global economy, its competitive pressures, and a lot of problems we had in our own country which slowed down the productivity growth rate. The incomes of many Americans started falling and average hourly incomes have been stagnant virtually ever since for the Nation as a whole, in spite of the fact that the average family is spending more hours per week at work than it was in 1969.

Now we look forward to a doubling of our standard of living not every 25 years but every

75 years. That is plainly an unacceptable rate. Many unhappy trends accelerated during the 1980's and into the 1990's. Even though the wealthiest Americans consistently did better, middle class incomes stalled and the percentage of people living in poverty exploded, especially the percentage of people working and still living in poverty. Our leaders continued to promise us something for nothing. There was always an easy answer. There was always a slogan that solved the problems. And slogans are always appealing. But as Americans, we can't live like that anymore.

You and I know that a major roadblock to our long-term recovery is the Federal deficit. You and I know that it hasn't been tackled seriously in the past. And I want you to know today that I am committed to tackling this deficit, no matter how much political capital I have to spend to do it, because unless we regain control over our economic destiny, none of the other things that I would hope to do as President will be possible.

What I faced when I came to office was the prospect that unless we acted and acted decisively, deficits would soar out of sight in the 1990's. And notwithstanding the dramatic drop in short-term interest rates, we would continue to have the highest real long-term interest rates of any of our competitors. That would cripple the economy. The United States would relinquish its place of leadership. And most importantly, we would leave our children a mean and surly existence of less economic opportunity and more social division.

That's why I believe so strongly that, as a nation, we have to have the courage to change. And so I spent weeks and weeks working on an economic plan for the Nation, one that would dramatically reduce the deficit while also achieving an equally important aim: investing in a very disciplined way in some of the areas we had neglected in the 1980's but that are critical to our growth and productivity, especially education, training, new technologies for the 21st century, and strategies to ease the transition from a defense-based high-tech economy to one based on a dramatically reduced level of defense spending but increased domestic spending.

Now, when I first presented this plan to Congress and to the American people in February, it received rave reviews. The reaction of the financial markets was immediate and very favorable, just as the reaction to the financial markets

had been favorable right after the election when we said we would come forward with a strong deficit reduction plan.

As the plan has moved its way through Congress, the outline of the budget resolution passing on time for the first time in 17 years, the House of Representatives passing the plan rigorously and quickly under enormous pressure, the financial markets have continued to respond in a very positive way. And many of you have stuck with us because you understand that this is a balanced and fair plan. But most Americans don't know about that because ever since February, the last time I had a chance to discuss it entirely directly with the American people, we have seen a barrage of the same old sloganeering that got us in the fix we're in today. There is an easy answer: Just don't raise taxes and cut spending. It's a simple, unqualified thing. This, from the people who raised all the spending and cut the taxes in the 1980's.

I want to say again how very grateful I am for the people who have supported this program, from the CEO's of companies like Anheuser-Busch, ARCO, Ford, NationsBank, Sara Lee, Tenneco, TRW, Apple, Xerox, and others, to the Home Builders Association, the Realtors Association, the American Electronics Industry Association, and others. I appreciate that.

You might be interested to know that a Congresswoman from California told me that after she spent a week at home, after voting for the plan, in town meetings she met with people who were angry at her and who left supporting the plan for two reasons: Number one, they were astonished to find out what it actually did, since they couldn't tell from the rhetoric of the last 3 or 4 months; number two, they were astonished to know who was for it.

The other day, the Home Builders Association brought their national officers group in to Maryland to meet with me at a homebuilding site to reaffirm their support for the program because we got mortgage rates at a 20-year low and housing sales at a 7-year high.

There has been a calculated effort to distort and to destroy this program by calling it "tax and spend." Never mind that for years the leaders of this effort gave us "borrow and spend." Never mind that they were the architects of a program that took us from a $1 trillion to a $4 trillion debt in 12 years, from an annual deficit of $74 billion a year to over $300 billion a year. Spending increased more than at any time during World War II in the last 4 years, and so did borrowing. And we're in a deep hole. But one more time, the apostles of the easy answers seek to divert the attention of the American people with their simple slogans.

I've been through a lot of political wars in my lifetime. I've, on occasion, gotten knocked down. Sometimes I've knocked myself down. But I always try to come back. And this time the administration is going to come back, because we're telling the truth to the American people, and if we don't face this problem now, we're going to let it get out of hand and lose control of our destiny. That is the big issue, and we've got to have the courage to face it.

Because there have been so many distortions, I'd like to go back through this program one more time, to tell you about the principles that have to be preserved as this plan works its way through Congress. First of all, let's take a look at where the deficit is heading. This is what I found based on the previous actions of the last 12 years. If we fail to act, look at where it's heading and look what the plan now before the Congress will do to bring it under control. That's what this first chart shows.

This is the inherited deficit, even after the 1990 plan, the red line. The deficit, with our budget, is the blue line. I want to come back to that in a minute, but you will see what I want to do with the blue line is take it from where it is in 1997 all the way down to zero. The slight increase in '98 is due to something you all know very well; it's the same thing a lot of you find in your balance sheets. That is health care costs.

If you want to go from where it is in '97 to zero, we have to bring health care costs in the Government as well as in the private sector in line with inflation. That is the sole reason for that line going up. But as you can see, there is a huge difference. That's why there's been a drop in long-term interest rates and mortgage rates are at a 20-year low, the promise of moving this line from red to blue.

There are things that I think can be done that will make a huge difference. Now, how do we get to the red line? First of all, in the 1980's, there was a big tax cut in '81 and a huge increase in national defense. And even though there were some restraints in domestic spending, there was no way in the wide world the domestic spending cuts got even close to the defense increases and the tax cuts.

Then in the mid-eighties, when the defense budget started to go down, by that time, two other bad things had happened from the point of view of the deficit: Health care costs were exploding at 2 and 3 times the rate of inflation, and the interest payments on the debt had become a churning engine that kept going up and up and up and were aggravated by high interest rates, so that we got no benefit from the defense cuts in terms of the deficit because of the health care increase and the rise in interest payments. Interest payments now consume about 15 cents on the tax dollar. And if we don't do anything about the size of the deficit, they will be up over 20 cents on the tax dollar within the next 10 years. These things have to be faced.

Now, let's go to the next chart. My opponents have been distorting the ratio of spending cuts to tax increase in all manner of ways. First they started off saying it was three to one; now they're saying its six to one. Again, I will say that this is the crowd that gave you the deficits of the eighties, and all I used in trying to determine what the ratio of spending to taxes was, was the same thing my predecessors did in defining what was a reduction in Federal spending.

There are some minor differences in the way these things are calculated. Actually, the House Budget Committee has given me more credit for spending cuts as opposed to tax increases than we do. But the rough balance is 50–50. And let me give you an idea of why it's hard to be exact, because of all the word games that are played in Washington. I'll give you two examples: one that arguably redounds to my favor, one that arguably doesn't.

One of the best things about this program is we increased the earned-income tax credit— I'll say a little more about that in a minute— to reward people who move from welfare to work; to say that if you work 40 hours a week and you've got kids in the house, the tax system should lift you above the poverty line. Now, that's a tax cut, right? Because the earned-income tax credit involves an outlay by the Government, some people count it as a spending increase, even though it's a tax cut. I think it's a tax cut. That's the way we count it.

Let me give you another example. Previous Presidents had counted anything that restricted Social Security benefits as a spending reduction in entitlements. Now my adversaries say my proposal to extend income tax consideration to 85 percent of the incomes of the top 20 percent of Social Security earners is a tax increase. In a literal sense, it's a restriction on entitlements and a tax increase. You can argue it either way.

Which is better policy? We could restrain cost-of-living allowances to Social Security recipients, or we could apply taxation to the incomes of upper-income recipients. The fairer way to do it plainly is to ask the people who can afford it to pay more as opposed to holding down the cost-of-living allowances to people just above the poverty line. One is called a tax increase; the other is called a spending reduction. It's six of one and half a dozen of the other.

So there are some arguments around the edges. But basically, this plan is roughly equally divided between spending cuts and tax increases. And as those of you who follow this closely know, we are moving into the Senate where we hope and believe there will be less tax and more spending cuts to further improve the ratio.

But I do want to emphasize that there are significant and very real spending cuts in this program and, as all of you know again, that 75 percent of the new taxes are paid for by people with incomes above $100,000, two-thirds of people with incomes above $200,000, me and everybody else in this room included in that.

The spending cuts I want to talk to you about, they're made in discretionary programs, entitlement programs, and interest payments on the national debt. You can't make cuts of this size unless you basically disappoint every interest group in the Congress. For example, in agriculture, we have made cuts in commodity support, crop insurance, and rural electric. We've asked Federal employees to forego the automatic pay increases tied to inflation they have been getting for years and years and years to the tune of $13 billion. We're trimming 150,000 people from the Federal payrolls by attrition and saving $11 billion in overall administrative cuts.

We're replacing the existing system of guaranteed student loans in a way that will save $4 billion and is wildly unpopular from the people who were making money from the student loan program because it was a Government guarantee with no risk. If you ask about Medicare, there's about $60 billion in cuts from Medicare from the red line I showed you. There are cuts in Medicaid. There are cuts in military and civilian retirement, delaying payments for them to reduce our payments on retirement this year and in the years ahead. No part of the Federal budget has been fully spared.

Of the cuts that are made—I don't think I have a chart on this—but of the cuts that are made, basically we cut over twice as much and apply it to the deficit as we cut and apply to new spending. I've been criticized because I've advocated some new spending programs. I plead guilty to that. But I want you to know exactly what they are.

I plead guilty to believing that it is worth it to have the Government replace some of these defense cuts with investments in domestic commercial technologies and new partnerships with the private sector. That's what our competitors do. I think we have to compete.

I plead guilty to wanting to fully fund the Head Start program, because we've got all these underprivileged kids out there that need to be very privileged and empowered adults, and I think we ought to fully fund the program as part of an overall strategy to meet the national education goals. I plead guilty to that. I think it's worth the money.

There are some targeted and limited funds in there to help every State in the country work with the private sector to set up a system of apprenticeship for all the people who don't go to college and a system of lifetime learning because the average worker will change jobs seven or eight times in a lifetime. It's not a lot of money, but it needs to be spent. I plead guilty. I think it is worth the investment.

These kinds of things matter to a society over the long run. The irony of the last 12 years is that because of, first, our reliance on defense spending to boost the economy, and then when defense spending was cut, our explosion of health care costs and interest payments, we have actually reduced our investments in a lot of the things that make us a richer country, even as this deficit has exploded.

So, those are the things that have been cut. A member of the more liberal wing of the Democratic Party called me the other day and said, "We have done you a terrible disservice. You told us we had to cut this spending, and we did it. And because there was no conflict, there was no publicity on it. Now nobody in America thinks you cut any spending. And you cut retirement; you cut Medicare; you cut Medicaid; you went after Social Security. You cut all these discretionary spending programs, and nobody knows it." Well, I'll predict you'll hear more about it in the days and weeks ahead from the people who feel that they have been rolled and gotten no credit for it. There are a lot of budget cuts in this program, and there will be some more. But the lion's share of the work has been done there.

As I said before and as you can see—and I might as well make full disclosure since I'm here with you—the effect of the new taxes is highly progressive, with almost all the real burden falling on people in the top one percent of the income category and 75 percent of the money being paid for by the top 6 percent. Now, that tracks income growth and tax reductions in the eighties. That is, it reverses the fact of the eighties where middle class taxes were increased through the Social Security tax while middle class incomes declined. But we do ask, through the energy tax, a contribution from virtually all Americans, not including those with incomes under $30,000 with one or two kids in the family. Otherwise, everybody else is asked to pay something.

Now, as I said, I want to mention a couple of other things. In addition to the spending programs, there are some incentives in this program that a lot of people asked for; maybe some of you in this room did. But I want to run through them, because they cost money, too, but I think they're worth it. And you have to decide whether you think they are.

The small business community for years has been asking us to increase the expensing provisions from $10,000 to $25,000 on the theory that they're creating most of the new jobs, and this will help them to do it. So that's what this bill does. The Venture Capital Association for years has been asking us to adopt a venture capital gains tax that would provide huge incentives for people to start new enterprises. We do that in this bill. It costs some money. I think it's worth it.

After the Tax Reform Act of 1986, many businesses, including businesses in this room, said there had to be some changes in the alternative minimum tax provisions of the Tax Code if we wanted people to continue to invest in plant and equipment in this country because of the unfair way the alternative minimum tax works. And we changed it in this Tax Code. We were asked to do it by many people. I think it makes sense. We did it. It's in the Code. It costs money.

For years, Republicans and Democrats alike who actually live out there where people are struggling to make a living have believed that if we wanted to do something meaningful for inner cities and poor rural areas, we had to try to get the private sector more involved, and we had to use market mechanisms. And there are any number of suggestions under the so-called enterprise zone rhetoric about that.

We have, in this proposal, an empowerment zone concept which is by far the most ambitious incentives program ever offered to try to get the private sector involved in distressed areas in America on an experimental basis: to pick 15 or 20 communities and say, "If you hire people from there, you get a credit; if you invest there, you get a permanent credit," and to provide all kinds of other resources in terms of training and support to people who will try to make the private sector work. It's almost 100 percent a private sector initiative. But it costs money.

Is it worth it? I think it is. There's not enough Government money in the world to rebuild south central Los Angeles or some of the most distressed areas in other cities in our country or the Mississippi Delta where I live. But it costs money. But we have to try, I think.

So you have spending reductions. You have tax increases. You have some new spending, and you have a significant amount of private sector incentives in this bill. I think it's all worthwhile.

The most interesting thing is the signals that have been sent to the markets and the result. Now, if I had told you in December—to me this is the most amazing thing of all, and I can't take credit for this. This chart, in some ways belongs to my friend John Scully at Apple Computers. He came in last week, and he said, "Bill, I know you must be low, and I read all the press and the polls and everything." He said, "I am happy as a clam." And I said, "Are you happy as a clam because you're a Republican, and I'm in trouble?" He says, "No, I'm happy as a clam because I'm an American." He said, "If somebody had told you 4 months ago that by June 1st unemployment would drop below 7 percent for the first time in 17 months, that we'd have 755,000 new jobs, over 90 percent of them in the private sector, that we'd have a 20-year low in mortgage rates and a 7-year high in housing sales, and that people would be responding to the program to seriously reduce the deficit and grow the economy, would you have been happy?" He said, "I don't know why everybody's not happy." He said, "I make a living thinking about the long run and thinking about what's happening. This is working."

I believe it's working, too. Now the program is going into the Senate, and they will change it some in cooperation with the House Members, I might add. There's an unusual amount of cooperation here among people who really want to do something. There will be at least one meeting a day between Senators and House Members before the Senate even votes, something that's almost unheard of. People just trying to work together to work this out.

Here's what I think ought to come out of that. There should be some less tax and some more spending cuts. We should have $500 billion in overall deficit reduction, all the cuts in the taxes ought to be in a trust fund so they can't be put anywhere else. There ought to be an enforcement mechanism for the first time that requires the President—because who can foresee what's going to happen 5 years from now? It would be hard for all of you to adopt 5-year budgets with absolute certainty. Nobody can do that. This bill has an enforcement mechanism that says if we miss the deficit target every year, the President has to come in and offer a plan to fix it. Not just shrug your shoulders and say, oh, it's too bad, the economy was down, or something else went wrong, but a plan to fix it, to live with the discipline that the numbers will impose. That's something new, and it ought to stay in there.

The third thing that ought to be in there is the progressivity of this program. Middle class Americans are being asked to pay a modest amount, much less than most of them think now because of the rhetoric of the last few months but a modest amount. It still ought to be progressive because of the tax history and the income history of the last 12 years. So it should be progressive.

We should leave the empowerment initiatives there. The empowerment zones, the small business incentives, the new business incentives, the changes in the alternative minimum tax, in my judgment, ought to be left in there. We should have the targeted investments. And I believe there must be some sort of broad-based energy tax.

I must say that when I first started on this—and my economic adviser over here, Bob Rubin, as most of you know, has laughed a lot when he sees people say, oh, this is such a liberal program—Rubin, Bentsen, and Panetta, my

three deficit hawks, were the people who convinced me that it was worth it even to raise a little more tax if we had to do it to get the deficit down and the interest rates down to get the country going again, not the liberals in my Cabinet who were worried about all of that. The others, the business people did it, the people who understood the financial markets. They said, "We've got to get the interest rates down, and we've got to get the deficit down, even if we have to take a little more heat for the taxes."

So we are trying to come to grips with this. But I know when we started I was told by person after person after person in New York, "If you want to have an influence on interest rates, you've got to do two things: deal with entitlements and have an energy tax, because that looks real to us." Well, we did those things and cut a lot of other spending besides.

So, is this a perfect program? No, there's no such thing. Is it a good one? You bet it is. You can tell by the results. Is the Senate going to work on it? Yes, it is. The Senate will work on it. Then the House and the Senate and the White House will confer. And we'll try to come out with a program which meets these principles. I believe we will.

The main thing I want to say is, it is hard to quarrel with results. And I hope to goodness it is going to be very hard to go back to the same old siren song we've heard time and time again. I've heard all these people say, "Well, just cut spending." It turns out they always want somebody else's spending cut. And we have cut a lot of spending. There are some kinds of spending that everybody in this room wouldn't support. If we don't have it quite right, you can tell us what you think.

Now, let me just also say, the House passed the modified line-item veto. And if the Senate would pass that, I'll give you some more spending cuts. If the Senate will give me that, I'll be happy to give you some more spending cuts and bring it down a little more. And I'm hoping that will come out of this whole budgetary process, so the President can have some more discipline on spending.

But the thing we have to do most of all is to act. We have to act. We have to act, because that is the only thing that will produce results. I believe that we're going to do that. I think you will see the Senate act. I think you will see the Senate and the House come forward with a program that meets the basic principles that I have outlined. I think you will see America in control of its economic destiny. I think interest rates will stay down and growth will stay up, and we'll continue to generate jobs for this economy.

But it requires a lot of courage when all you hear, day-in and day-out, are people trying to paralyze action with the same old rhetoric that put us to sleep for 12 years and got us in the fix that the first chart showed. I like these results better than that first chart. And if you do, I hope you'll support our efforts.

Thank you very much.

Moderator. Mr. President, we thank you for a very substantive and significant speech. The President, ladies and gentlemen, has offered to answer some questions, so I'll turn it over to him for that purpose.

The President. Is somebody carrying a microphone?

Taxes

Q. Mr. President, as one who just refinanced my own home mortgage, I want to thank you for that.

My question really goes to the apparent demise of the Btu tax, which was announced by Secretary Bentsen yesterday, and obviously, the work with Congress that's required in the last administration or this one to make anything really happen. I heard you say that another broad-based energy tax would be recommended. I appreciate any comment you'd have on that and why you think another broad-based energy tax might get more reception or, rather, not have the same treatment that the Btu tax did.

The President. Well, let me say I'm still not sure how it's all going to come out. And let me try to answer this very carefully. Secretary Bentsen did not so much announce as to grudgingly acknowledge—[*laughter*]—the state of play in the Senate. And it's quite interesting, because he's from an energy State, and he came to this Btu tax after going through a lot of other issues.

Let me tell you what the state of play in the Senate is, first of all. You've got essentially a Senate Finance Committee where no Republicans will vote for this bill because they are not going to be for any taxes. And the Boren substitute is a massive shift of the burden to elderly people and the working people just above the poverty line. And if it got on the floor of the Senate, I bet it wouldn't get 20

votes. So there is no other viable alternative out there.

But with an 11-to-9 majority, the Democrats cannot lose any votes on the Senate Finance Committee and get any bill out. Now, Secretary Bentsen had what I thought was a great suggestion for modifying the Btu tax which would essentially have drastically alleviated, all but eliminated, the burden on production, whether industrial or agricultural, but would have otherwise left the tax in shape, so that it applied to all forms of energy and, therefore, was less burdensome to any region of the country but got out of the whole business of whether we were being uncompetitive with people from—when we exported our products or whether imports would acquire a competitive advantage, and whether we were putting too much of a burden on energy-intensive forms of industry which had led the House to make too many exceptions to it. So if you just essentially had a blanket alleviation of the production sector, which is what Secretary Bentsen was talking with them about, it looked to us like that was the best thing.

There had been so much said about the wording of the Btu tax—and, I must say, some legitimate concern about the whole administrative difficulty of starting a new one—the Senate seems disinclined to go forward. That does not mean that the House will give up on a modified Btu tax. I don't know what's going to happen from here on in. And we have not agreed to anything or disagreed with anything. We have been in consultation with the Senate and would go to any meeting they asked us to. But they're going to have to come up with their own program. And they know what the principles I have outlined are. And I just gave them to you. So I don't know what's going to happen now.

Senator Breaux has some ideas that he wants to float, and some others have some ideas. I think you'll have plenty of time to react to them. A lot of them want to rely more on a broad-based transportation tax, but that also has some economic difficulties even if you raise less money.

The number one thing: 100 percent of us agreed and the House Members agreed that we would lower the dollar volume of the energy tax, the total money raised, and make it up in various kinds of cuts. And I think that's where everybody is now. Everybody is there.

And let me just run a few other things out here. There is also a discussion about whether or not there should be a delay in the effective date of the taxes, the income taxes. That's being discussed, the economic grounds for that. And there are all kinds of discussions about that.

I want to red-flag one issue for all of you who provide comprehensive health policies for your employees, though, again, because sometimes things are not what they seem. We cut about $60 billion in Medicare expenditures over and above the red line I showed you. That is, that was a big part of our deficit reduction. There are those who say, "Well, we ought to cut a lot more, and we can freeze provider fees and we can do all this kind of stuff with Medicare." I would urge all of you as employers to look at that very closely because, again, it's a sleight of hand. You know, yes, we can cut the fool out of Medicare. But if we don't have some sort of comprehensive resolution to the health care crisis, what will happen? The same thing that's been happening the last 12 years: All those people will send you the bill.

There will be massive cost-shifting with certain kinds of Medicare cuts unless it is part of an overall health care strategy, which just means a hidden tax on employers and their employees, which is the very thing I'm trying to get away from, anything hidden. And it contradicts one of the essential goals of our long-term strategy, which is to bring health costs in line with inflation and fairly apportion the burden throughout society, which it's not now. Most of you are paying too much and your employees are because of the way the thing is.

So I'm not trying to avoid your question, I'm just trying to tell you I do not know what the Senate will do. My position has been to try to tell them what my principles are; make Secretary Bentsen and Mr. Panetta available to them to discuss everything; ask them to be faithful to the House by involving the House Members in the discussions, because a lot of House Members passed this budget on the understanding there would be some less tax and some more spending cuts and that they would be a part of it. And I don't know what's going to come out of there yet.

Deficit Reduction

Q. My question is this: We in the Roundtable, of course, have made deficit reduction a major issue for a long, long time. And we applaud your efforts in that regard and certainly are

hopeful that the $500 billion sort of reduction over the 4- or 5-year period will be forthcoming. And we're working, as you know, with your administration and Bob Rubin and Leon and others. But even if that objective is achieved, it's clear we have a very significant continuing deficit problem. What is, $1 trillion over the next 4 or 5 years? The deficit only goes from the baseline number of 3.3 percent to about 2.7 percent of GDP. We still have a big, big deficit problem.

My question is, how do you feel about the proposals for process reform that I gather are gaining some currency in the Congress, to put the spending caps on the entitlement programs, the nondiscretionary programs, as well as the discretionary programs, with the fire walls and with the sequestration. How do you look at that whole issue of process reform to deal with this underlying problem of a deficit that doesn't seem to come under manageable proportions?

The President. I want to answer it, but I'd like to ask for—where did those charts go? Are they still up here? I just wanted the first one back to try to highlight the point you're making. Just bring me back the first one, the one with the red and blue lines.

This is what he's talking about. This line here ought to go down to here. And I want to answer your question, but I've got to put it into context. This deficit here is actually about—it's more, it's about—it's over 5 percent of GDP, and we're going to cut it from 5.2 down to about 2.7 or 2.6 here, to a pretty good cut. But it does continue to increase the total national debt by what's down here.

Now, in the mid-seventies, I started looking at what other countries had done on this. This is not an unusual problem for a Western country with a lot of support systems coming out of the Government and difficulty generating jobs and income. I mean, a lot of these Western countries are in the same shape we're in, and I include Japan with that.

Japan had a huge operating deficit in the mid-seventies. And they had a 10-year plan to bring it into balance which they did over a 10-year period, thinking that to rush it any faster might cause a recession, but to delay it would be a terrible mistake. So I thought to myself, maybe we could do it in 8 or 9 or something like—in that range, if we could just deal with this. This is where you have to take the curve down.

Now, to get the curve down, I can just tell

you, we have to do a number of things. But let me say what we cannot do and then what we must do, and then I'll come back to your cap device. There is a limit to how much we can responsibly cut defense within a short time. I think we are right at that edge. I do not want to cut any more in this 5-year budget. Based on what we now know, we are at that limit, unless there—the only other way you can do it that I know of is the Vice President has this reinventing Government task force on. If we can have significant procurement reform, we might be able to have some savings. But in just terms of "slash and burn," we don't need to do any more in my opinion.

Secondly, as I said earlier, there are some things that any government has to do to maintain its competitiveness. And thirdly, there are just human concerns that have to be taken care of, even though they're subject to constraints of the budget. For example, a lot of people don't know this, but actual out-of-pocket costs on welfare and food stamps haven't kept up with inflation in the last 10 or 15 years. The reason those costs have gone up is that there's a whole lot more poor people. You've got 1 in 10 Americans on food stamps now.

But this number, anyway, to go back to his comment, is being driven by two things. One is the entitlements and the fact that things like retirement, wages, Social Security, and whole lot of other things have automatic cost escalators. The one that is not a problem is Social Security. Social Security is no more of our national income than it was 20 years ago, and the tax is higher. And it's producing a $60 billion a year surplus that makes our deficit look smaller than it is. If anything, the payroll tax is too big. But it is producing that.

On the income tax side, what you've got, though—here's the problem with paying for the rest of that stuff that's paid for with income taxes. We are now indexing income taxes, which is fair. That is, people don't get pushed into higher brackets by inflation. But the flip side of that is, if you index income taxes downward and you index income upward for people who are getting tax money, you don't have to be a mathematical genius to realize that there is a conflict there. Then, if you have health care costs increasing at 2 and 3 times the rate of inflation—because you've got more people on the Government rolls, about 100,000 a month losing their health insurance; you have more

people on the Government rolls, prices going up and the ability to churn the system, if there's a fee-for-service system, you've got some real problems.

There are several suggestions which have been made that would essentially require us over the next 5 years to adopt a disciplined system of bringing the cost of entitlements in line with inflation, plus population, to be fair. They're all acknowledging that if there's a growth in poverty or an unexpected downturn in the economy, we would take that into account. I would be open to that as a part of the health care reform issue. That is, what I would like to see is the budgetary discipline on the entitlement issue taken up with health care reform for this reason: If we impose the entitlement caps and we don't face health care reform because it's too controversial or we can't bear to do it, then if the entitlement caps trigger, we will be massively shifting our cost to you, like I said earlier.

The other tough decisions can be made within the budget discipline. But the health care cost issue which is driving it, in my judgment, should be dealt with at the time we impose the overall entitlement restrictions over a 5-year period. That protects the employers and the employees of the country from having mass cost-shifting and forces us to make the tough decisions in Government. But anyway, I know it's a long answer, but I had to explain it in the context that we're operating.

There was a question over here, I think.

Superfund

Q. The Business Roundtable believes that the only way to fix Superfund is to make some fundamental change in the law. If you agree, would you support a legislative fix?

The President. To change the Superfund?

Q. Yes.

The President. Oh, sure I would, but I would want to know what the details are first. But I agree that it needs to be changed, and I'm certainly open to changing it. Lawyers are making more money than cleanup folks are right now.

Let me say as a general proposition on the spending issue, too, there are two other opportunities that the Congress and the President will have to deal with, Government spending and the efficiency of Government programs, this year in addition to this reconciliation process which is going on, and that is that all the appropriations committees are reviewing all their spending.

Keep in mind, what you see now in the budget only includes tax cuts or tax increases and the entitlement programs and the overall spending limits. The specific programs, whether they're cut, increased, or kept the same, that's all handled by the Appropriations Committee, and that's going on now, too. And that will offer other opportunities for dealing with the spending issues.

And the third thing that's going to happen is in September the Vice President is going to come in with this report about reexamining the whole functioning of the Federal Government, and that will open a new avenue of opportunities for dealing with a lot of these issues also.

Is there another question back there? I thought I saw one more hand up. The boss here says we can do one more. Am I going to get out without one more? I accept if—go ahead. I'll do two more. Mr. Morecott once let me play golf with him, so I owe him a question. [*Laughter*]

Trade Negotiations

Q. Mr. President, we heard this morning, some of us, from Mickey Kantor about trade issues, North American trade agreement, Uruguay round, and negotiating with Japan. Can you just comment on those subjects briefly, starting with NAFTA?

The President. Yes. I'm for it, number one. I'm for it.

Number two, we can't pass it in the House of Representatives today, but I think we'll be able to when the time comes.

Number three, the reason we can't pass it and what we're doing with the Mexican and the Canadian Governments are tied together but not—it's not an exact fit, but let me—you know that there's just an awful lot of economic insecurity out there now in this country. And a lot of the Members are rebelling against NAFTA because they see it as the first trade agreement we've ever made where we're making investment easier in another country for the purpose of setting up production to sell in our market, not theirs.

So that's the basic tension, because of the wage differentials. My argument back is the argument that most of you would make, I think, which is that, first of all, you've got a free-market oriented government in Mexico that has unilaterally dropped trade barriers and taken us from a $5 billion deficit to a $6 billion surplus in trade, creating an awful lot of jobs in America.

Secondly, two-thirds of our new jobs in the last 3 or 4 years have come from expansion of trade. Our unemployment problems today are directly related to the fact that our economy, even though it's in a fragile recovery, is in better shape than a lot of other economies which is making our trade situation worse because people don't have the money to buy our products.

What will happen in Asia and in Europe is unpredictable in the years ahead, but we believe we need to establish a relationship not only with Mexico but with the other market economies to the south. Opportunities with Chile, with Venezuela, with Argentina, with all kinds of other countries could open up. So I'm for it.

What Mickey Kantor—he's already talked to you about this—but we're trying to get an agreement on labor standards and the environment with the Mexican and Canadian Governments which would enable us to have some sort of enforcement mechanism, not only if there is one violation but if there is a whole pattern and practice of violations as found by a neutral finder of facts. So that's what we're trying to work out. My gut feeling is that will get worked out pretty soon. We'll go forward with it, and we will pass it. That's what I think will happen.

On GATT, as you probably saw in the press this morning, the French Government has withdrawn some of its objections on the agriculture points of view. That makes me elated. I think that's where—that's a real winner for us and is likely to face less opposition in Congress.

Not very long ago, I met with the central bankers and the finance ministers of the G–7. And I told them that on behalf of the United States I would make exceptional efforts to get a GATT agreement if they would, and I thought we ought to stop talking about it and do it and do it before the year is over because we all needed the global growth. And so I'm hopeful there. And I think the French action is a big plus, and I thank them for that.

On Japan, basically, we're trying to move toward a more results-oriented trade policy with Japan, not to get to the managed trade quota point that they're criticizing us for but in recognition of the fact that there are several areas where by any objective measure we are competitive in price and quality for various products and services. And while they don't have stated tariffs and quotas and barriers that keep us out, we nevertheless aren't in and don't get in and can't get in. And so what we're trying to do is to find our way into dealing with that issue on the theory that it's just—I don't want to close American borders to Japanese products, but I do expect more opportunities for Americans in Japan if we're going to play this.

I know the Japanese have been very harsh in their criticism of our new approach. But that could be because it might work. And I know that they've been harsh in their criticism, but I also know that, notwithstanding all of the problems around, they not only have a massive surplus with us, they're about the only country I know that's got a massive trade surplus with all the Third World countries they deal with, all of them.

So I just think a new approach is called for. And I say that not in the spirit of hostility. I think I probably have more pure admiration for Japan and what they do right and well than any other person that's ever held this job. But I know what's happened to American productivity growth in the last 5 or 6 years. And I know what we can do there if given the chance. And I think we've got to do our best to do it.

If you think we're on the wrong track, feel free to tell us. But I believe we've got to keep pushing forward to try to show you some results from all this talking. We've been talking until we're blue in the face for a long time now. I'd like to show a little bit of result.

Q. That was the question I had.

The President. Let me just say to all of you, we're going to need your help on NAFTA because to pass it, the Congress, and particularly the House, must believe that over the long run it is good for American jobs and incomes. I believe it is. I believe it is. I wouldn't be for it if I didn't think it was. And it just doesn't make sense to me that we can ever grow this economy unless we expand the number of our trading partners and unless we are doing more trade with people whose incomes are rising rather rapidly.

The Mexicans have reached out their hand to us. I want to reach out my hand to President Salinas. And I think we can get over this negotiating impasse we're at now and then go forward. And that's what I intend to do.

Thank you very much.

NOTE: The President spoke at 3:22 p.m. at the J.W. Marriott Hotel. In his remarks, he referred to John Ong, chief executive officer, B.F. Goodrich.

Remarks and an Exchange With Reporters Prior to a Meeting With the Domestic Policy Council
June 10, 1993

Economic Program

The President. I want to make a statement now that we have the Domestic Policy Council here, about what is going on in the Senate.

First of all, I'm very encouraged that the Senate Finance Committee is working hard in trying to push the process forward. I want to reemphasize that, to me, in the end, we have to have certain basic principles satisfied: $500 billion in deficit reduction in the trust fund so that all the spending cuts and taxes have to be protected for that; $250 billion of spending cuts. The taxes have to fall primarily on those best able to pay them. Right now, over two-thirds of the taxes fall on people with incomes above $200,000,

75 percent on people with incomes above $100,000. I want the energy tax to be pro-conservation and as broad-based as possible. And I want the initiatives for growth and jobs in there, the earned-income tax credit to encourage the working poor to move out of poverty, the empowerment zones for investment in our cities, the incentives to create jobs. Those are the principles that I want.

I want to remind you all, too, that the Senate and House will naturally have some disagreements. But when we wind up in conference, we can perhaps get the best bill of all. The main thing, until the Senate acts, we can't go to conference and get a final bill to continue this progress.

What the final shape of the energy portion of this will be no one can now say because that will have to await the conference. But I am very encouraged that progress is being made, and I do appreciate the fact that the Senate began consultations with the House yesterday, which is consistent with the commitments that were made on that.

Q. Where is the progress?

Q. Well, what do you say to Democrats in the House who feel like they walked the plank on the budget for nothing at this point?

The President. They didn't walk the plank on the budget for nothing. Their budget is going to be part of the conference. And they are being consulted now, and no decision has been made by the Senate yet.

You know, Chairman Moynihan and Senator Mitchell started with the Senators who are most hostile to the Btu tax. But they have 11 Senators on a committee they have to satisfy. And then they have to get a majority in the body of the Senate. So no decisions have been made yet. And most of those House Members with whom I talked in the process of passing the bill through the House only wanted to make sure that the House would also be consulted before the Senate committee finally voted. And we took steps to ensure that, and they began the consultative process yesterday.

Q. You've got the Black Caucus apparently so upset that they're not coming to a meeting here. What do you tell those people?

The President. That is not why there's not going to be a meeting here. But the Black Caucus, if they want to advocate for the Btu tax, you know, I like it. I think it's the best and fairest tax. And I think the Secretary of the

Treasury made a very good proposal for a modification of it. But neither they nor I have a vote on the Senate Finance Committee. The Btu levy will be in the conference, and no decision has been made. I have not signed off on any energy proposal in the Senate yet. I believe that the proposal we made is the best one we have. But neither they nor I have a vote on the Senate Finance Committee.

Let me say, in the end, the most important thing is that we bring the deficit down, that we cut spending, that we raise taxes on the wealthy, and that we invest money to grow this economy. That's the most important thing. We've got to find a way to do that consistent with what has happened already. And I'm very encouraged. I don't think—the American people shouldn't be upset by what's going on. They should go talk to their Senators if they have a different view and they want them to take a different view toward these particular taxes. That's what I'm trying to do, is to get the House and the Senate to work together before the Senate Finance Committee even votes.

Former Yugoslav Republic of Macedonia

Q. Why are there troops on the ground in Macedonia, Mr. President?

The President. To limit the conflict. As we said all along, we would support the United Nations in limiting the conflict. It's a very limited thing. No combat but an attempt to limit the conflict.

NOTE: The President spoke at 10:07 a.m. in the Cabinet Room at the White House. A tape was not available for verification of the content of these remarks.

Remarks on Signing the National Cooperative Production Amendments of 1993
June 10, 1993

I want to thank Senator Leahy, Senator Biden, Congressman Brooks, and Congressman Fish for being here today and for their leadership in helping to enact into law the bill I am about to sign. I want to thank the Attorney General for her presence here and for the work

that the Justice Department did on this bill, H.R. 1313, called the National Cooperative Production Amendments of 1993.

This bill was the embodiment of the concept that the Vice President, who has just come in—come on up. Good to see you. He's magical.

I uttered his name, and he appeared. [*Laughter*] This bill is the embodiment of the concept that the Vice President and I strongly espoused during our campaign last year. It will allow American companies, large and small, to pool their resources to compete and win in the international marketplace.

Our Nation leads the world in basic research. We also have to be second to none in moving new technologies from the laboratory to the marketplace. We have to unleash the creativeness and the inventive prowess of both corporate giants and start-up enterprises in order to spur economic growth and new jobs.

The cooperative arrangements envisioned by this legislation will become increasingly necessary as the costs and skills required to develop and manufacture new products exceed the resources of any single company. These alliances will also help our businesses reduce the time required to bring new products to market, which frequently determines who wins and who loses in today's competitive marketplace. Successful companies, in turn, will create high-wage, high-skill jobs that will help to revitalize our economy.

By clarifying and eliminating misapprehensions about antitrust risk, this legislation will allow joint ventures that can increase efficiency, facilitate entry into markets, and create new productive capacity that otherwise would simply not be achieved.

I'm confident this legislation will benefit both the consumers and the workers in the United States by strengthening our industrial base while maintaining a sound antitrust oversight to prevent improper collusion. Now is the time to strip away outdated impediments to economic growth and to our potential and to begin real movement in this last decade of the 20th century.

I'm pleased that the committee report stresses that this legislation is consistent with our international obligations. Our administration will implement this legislation in a way that honors the commitments as set forth in our treaties of friendship, commerce, and navigation, bilateral investment treaties, and free trade agreements, and various organizations for economic cooperation and development.

Again, I want to commend Chairman Brooks, Senator Leahy, Senator Biden, Congressman Fish, and all the other Members of the Congress who worked so hard to make this bill a reality and the leadership of both the House and the Senate. This is an example of how you can have a real bipartisan coalition to make America work again, to help our business and our working people to move forward in the global economy. And I am very excited about it.

And I know that the Vice President joins me in thanking the congressional sponsors for their strong leadership. And I want to thank all the people here around me who helped to make the bill a reality, members of the congressional staffs and of the high-tech community.

NOTE: The President spoke at 5:15 p.m. in the Oval Office at the White House. H.R. 1313, approved June 10, was assigned Public Law No. 103–42. A tape was not available for verification of the content of these remarks.

Remarks on Signing the National Institutes of Health Revitalization Act of 1993
June 10, 1993

The President. Ladies and gentlemen, I want to welcome all those of you who are here today for the signing of S. 1, the National Institutes of Health Revitalization Act of 1993, and to especially recognize the bipartisan coalition which made this bill possible, led by the Senators and the Members of the House of Representatives who are here. I also want to thank the representatives of the groups who are here, including the Women's Health Network, the Juvenile Diabetes Foundation, the American Association of Medical Colleges, the Allen Guttmacher Institute, the Alzheimer's Association, the Human Rights Campaign Fund, the Breast Cancer Coalition, and the National Health Council, and perhaps others. If I've left anyone out, forgive me.

This legislation highlights the importance of

programs administered by the National Institutes of Health, programs vital to our science and biomedical research base. The research carried out at NIH has already led to a healthier and far more productive America. However, there are many challenges still ahead. And this legislation provides the hope that someday we can prevent or cure diseases such as diabetes, cancer, coronary heart disease, AIDS, and Alzheimer's.

I'm particularly supportive of those provisions of S. 1 aimed at improving the health of women and minorities. It's important that we ensure that resources are devoted to increasing our knowledge about conditions which uniquely affect these populations. It's equally important that we expand opportunities and support for the inclusion of women and minorities in research activities.

In the 12 years since AIDS was first reported in the United States, much progress has been made through NIH-supported research. Gains have been made in making available treatment for AIDS and AIDS-related conditions. And clinical trials are underway to test possible vaccines for prevention or treatment of HIV infection.

Someday we're going to have a treatment for all those beepers that go off. [*Laughter*] They have to go to a vote. That's why we're hurrying this up.

We still face, however, an immense undertaking to address the needs of the nearly 300 of our fellow citizens who become infected with HIV each and every day. We must improve the effectiveness of our prevention activity, increase access to early treatment for already infected individuals, and strengthen our research programs. I am pleased to say that S. 1 provides a framework for the increased coordination and direction of AIDS research.

Finally, S. 1 reinforces my action of January 22d to lift the moratorium on Federal funding of transplantation research involving human subjects using fetal tissue from induced abortions. This research has promising application for the treatment of life-threatening conditions including Parkinson's disease, spinal cord injuries, Huntington's, and diabetes. At the same time, S. 1 puts in place important safeguards to ensure against possible abuses by providing a clear separation between research and abortion.

In signing the legislation, I underscore our commitment to address the immeasurable cost to our society and the suffering of our citizens from illness and disability. By strengthening and enhancing biomedical and behavioral research, this National Institutes of Health Revitalization Act is an important step in fulfilling our commitment to promote the health and well-being of all Americans.

And again, let me say a profound thanks on behalf of our Nation to the Senators and Members of Congress who are here and to those not here who provided important leadership in this effort.

[*At this point, the President signed the bill.*]

Q. Mr. President, what about the provision barring immigration by HIV-positive individuals in this bill?

The President. That's the will of the Congress. That's part of the law. I don't think in any way it undermines the overall importance of this law. We have to learn to deal with AIDS better for all of our people and for those who are here within our borders who are not citizens, we've got all we can do to do that. And I think we could benefit people all around if we can make progress in dealing with AIDS.

I think everybody who played a part in the developing of this legislation thinks that it's on balance still a dramatic step forward.

Let me just say on the fetal tissue issue alone, I can't tell you how many people I met all over this country in 1992 from both political parties who came to my campaign and supported me simply because I wanted to put a scientific basis back in our decisions on fetal tissue, I mean, people with parents with Parkinson's, with children with diabetes. One person who became a very close friend of mine and is now in our administration as the Director of the Small Business Administration in part came to my campaign because he had a child with diabetes.

This is a very, very important bill. And I thank all of you for what you did.

NOTE: The President spoke at 5:37 p.m. in the Roosevelt Room at the White House. S. 1, approved June 10, was assigned Public Law No. 103–43.

Letter to Congressional Leaders on the Situation in Somalia
June 10, 1993

Dear Mr. Speaker: (Dear Mr. President:)

On December 10, 1992, President Bush reported to the Congress that U.S. Armed Forces had been deployed to Somalia to assist the United Nations effort to deal with the human catastrophe in that country, to avert related threats to international peace and security, and to protect the safety of Americans and others engaged in relief operations. This action was part of a multilateral response to U.N. Security Council Resolution 794, which authorized Member States, under Chapter VII of the U.N. Charter, to use all necessary means to establish a secure environment for humanitarian relief operations in Somalia. Since that time, my Administration and its predecessor have endeavored, through briefings and other means, to keep you informed about the progress of U.S. efforts in Somalia. I am providing this further report, consistent with the War Powers Resolution, in light of the passage of 6 months since President Bush's initial report on the deployment of U.S. Armed Forces to Somalia.

As you are aware, the U.S.-led operation, known as Operation Restore Hope, was responsible for stemming the tragic situation and saving many lives by ensuring that desperately needed relief efforts in behalf of the civilian population could proceed. Owing in large measure to the success of the U.S.-led Unified Task Force in Somalia (UNITAF), the responsibility for the continuing operation was transferred in an orderly fashion to the operational control of the U.N. Operation in Somalia (UNOSOM II) on May 4, 1993, pursuant to U.N. Security Council Resolution 814. This Resolution similarly invoked Chapter VII of the U.N. Charter and endowed UNOSOM II with the right to use force to ensure that the mandate is implemented.

The United States continues to support U.N. efforts in Somalia by providing approximately 3,000 U.S. logistics and other support personnel under the operational control of UNOSOM II. In addition, approximately 1,100 U.S. troops remain in the area as a Quick Reaction Force (QRF), under the operational control of the Commander in Chief, U.S. Central Command,

for use in emergency situations. The UNOSOM II deputy commander, a U.S. Army general who is the U.S. contingent commander, is authorized to send the QRF into action as may be necessary.

On June 5, 1993, UNOSOM II forces operating in Mogadishu encountered attacks instigated by one of Somalia's factional leaders, resulting in the deaths of 23 Pakistani military personnel. Three U.S. military personnel assigned to UNOSOM II sustained minor injuries. As envisioned in response to such situations, the QRF was called upon to assist in quelling the violence against the lawful activities of UNOSOM II in implementing the U.N. mandate. On June 6, 1993, the U.N. Security Council adopted Resolution 837, reaffirming the authority of UNOSOM II to take all necessary measures against those responsible for these armed attacks.

Our forces will remain equipped and prepared to accomplish their humanitarian mission and defend themselves, if necessary; they also will be provided such additional U.S. support as may be necessary to ensure their safety and the accomplishment of their mission.

I have continued the deployment of U.S. Armed Forces to Somalia pursuant to my constitutional authority to conduct U.S. foreign relations and as Commander in Chief and Chief Executive and in accordance with applicable treaties and laws. This deployment is consistent with S.J. Res. 45, as adopted by the Senate on February 4, 1993, and as modified and adopted by the House on May 25, 1993.

Effective U.S. foreign policy requires close cooperation between the President and the Congress, and this imperative is particularly important regarding issues surrounding the use of our Nation's Armed Forces. I remain committed to ensuring that the Congress is kept fully informed on these matters and that the public good is served through constructive discussions and cooperation between our two branches.

Sincerely,

BILL CLINTON

NOTE: Identical letters were sent to Thomas S. Foley, Speaker of the House of Representatives, and Robert C. Byrd, President pro tempore of the Senate.

Remarks Announcing the Nomination of Walter Mondale To Be Ambassador to Japan and an Exchange With Reporters
June 11, 1993

The President. Good morning. Please be seated. I want to thank all of you for coming here today for the announcement of my nomination of Walter Mondale to be our next Ambassador to Japan. Former Vice President Mondale will succeed Ambassador Michael Armacost, whose service was very valuable. And I want to thank him for it and acknowledge that here today.

This nomination has produced a lot of happiness, not only for me and for our administration but for the people of the State of Minnesota and the people of the United States who have admired Walter Mondale for a very long time.

Fritz Mondale is not only someone I consider a friend but also someone that I and millions of Americans consider a leader of enormous wisdom, courage, compassion, and stature. Like his mentor, Hubert Humphrey, Fritz Mondale is a hero to the people of Minnesota, because he embodies the virtues of the Midwest, because he fought so boldly for those things in the United States Senate, and because he never lost the basic values of his childhood and his adulthood after he became a leader on the national and world stage.

We have a lot in common. We both began our careers as State attorneys general in our home States at a relatively young age. And just as I am the first President from Hope, I am reliably informed that I can assert today that Fritz Mondale is our Nation's first Ambassador to Japan from Elmore.

Fritz Mondale has devoted his entire life to serving our Nation and to building bonds of understanding around the world. He has served our country in the military, as a State attorney general, as an outstanding Senator, and, of course, as Vice President and our party's nominee for President. In all these public roles, as well as in the experience he has gained in the private sector since, he has earned the right to be considered extraordinarily well qualified to assume the task of enhancing our relationship with Japan and projecting American leadership in Asia and the Pacific region.

I also want to say a special word of acknowledgment and appreciation to Joan Mondale, who is here with us today and who I believe will also be an outstanding ambassador for the United States in Japan. [*Applause*] Thank you very much.

Fritz Mondale is no stranger to Japan and her people. He has traveled there often, both in public and private roles. It is moving to recall that as Vice President, Fritz Mondale swore in another Ambassador to Japan who came from the United States Senate and who also served with tremendous distinction, Ambassador Mike Mansfield, and who is here today and who, I might add, at his young age, is probably one of the few people in this audience today who has already walked 5 or 6 miles. [*Laughter*]

Senator Mike Mansfield. Six.

The President. I chose someone of—[*laughter*]—what did he say? Six, he said. [*Laughter*] We never were able to short him.

I chose someone of Fritz Mondale's stature to be my Ambassador to Japan because there is no more important bilateral relationship in the world than that which exists between the United States and Japan. This alliance has supported 50 years of peace and stability in Asia and the Pacific. And the course of economic, political, and security dynamics in the Pacific and throughout Asia will be determined by how well our relationship functions. The challenges and changes facing both Japan and the United States as we move toward the 21st century require us to take a fresh look at our relationships and to take new actions to strengthen the foundations of our alliance.

When Prime Minister Miyazawa and I met here at the White House in April, we agreed to forge a new partnership between our nations aimed at restoring world economic growth, advancing democratic values, and creating the basis for regional peace which can endure well into the next century. To fulfill our shared vision of a new Japan-U.S. partnership, we must sustain our security commitment, work on global problems, and address forthrightly and urgently our often troubled economic relationship. The economic pillar of our relationship needs some repair, and I think we all know that. And Prime Minister Miyazawa and I agreed to give it our personal attention.

It is particularly appropriate that this announcement occurs today, for today we are beginning negotiations with the Japanese to craft the details of an economic framework intended to spur global growth, open markets, and deal with trade and investment issues affecting America's economy and America's workers. This framework, which the Prime Minister and I hope to unveil at our meeting in Tokyo, will get our economic problems out of the headlines and onto the negotiating table where we can best resolve them.

I will look to Fritz Mondale, statesman, negotiator, counselor, and representative of our people, to make the bonds that already exist between our two nations even stronger. Fritz Mondale's skills give me great hope and confidence that my goals with Japan can be achieved in a way that benefits both of our nations and the prospects for worldwide democracy, peace, and global growth.

I don't think our Nation could ask for a more capable representative abroad, and I appreciate the willingness of Fritz Mondale and Joan to accept this challenging assignment. I wish them well, and I know that the people of America, and I believe the people of Japan, are very happy today about this development. Mr. Mondale.

[At this point, Mr. Mondale expressed his gratitude to the President, stated briefly the importance of the relationship with Japan, and answered several questions from reporters.]

Economic Framework

Q. Mr. President, what are the prospects for having this framework ready in time for your meeting in Tokyo next month?

The President. Well, we're working hard. We started the formal negotiations today, and I'm hopeful. If you noticed, I used the word hope. I hope it will be ready to announce in Tokyo. And we've done a lot of preliminary work on it, and I'm encouraged. But I can't say for sure it will be done, because I can't prejudge the outcome of the negotiations. I hope it will be, and a lot of work has been done.

Q. Do you have a Supreme Court Justice today?

Q. Is that possible, sir?

The President. Good morning. [*Laughter*]

Q. It's a daily question.

The President. I don't have anything else to say about it.

Q. [*Inaudible*]—framework?

The President. We want to make some real progress on these very thorny trade difficulties that have proved to be so resistant to change. And you know that the framework of our debate has been pretty well explored in the press. But I think we've got a real shot to reach an agreement here, and we're going to keep working on it.

I think the Japanese are very sensitive about the kinds of economic pressures that are now on them that are somewhat new and different in the last couple of years. And I think both of us recognize that there will have to be an evolution in not only our relationship but in the whole balance of global trade if we're going to have sustained global growth, which is what is in the interest of Japan and the United States. We can't really hope to maintain high levels of growth and high levels of incomes in our jobs unless we get a much more brisk rate of growth throughout the world. And if you look at the whole history of the post-World War II era, it indicates that. If you look at where our jobs have come from in the United States just in the last 5 or 6 years, that's indicated about two-thirds of our new jobs being tied to trade. So it's obvious that we have to have a much higher rate of global growth.

Thank you very much.

NOTE: The President spoke at 10:15 a.m. in the Rose Garden at the White House.

Statement on Nuclear Nonproliferation Talks With North Korea
June 11, 1993

I welcome the successful outcome of talks between the United States and North Korea today in New York, which have led to the agreement of North Korea to suspend its withdrawal from the Non-Proliferation Treaty. This agreement is a first but vital step towards ensuring North Korean participation in a strong international nonproliferation regime, a goal that will benefit all nations.

Preventing the proliferation of nuclear weapons is one of the highest priorities of my administration, and we will continue to press the North Koreans strongly to comply fully with international standards and to move towards the goal of a nuclear-free Korean Peninsula.

The American negotiating team, under the direction of Assistant Secretary Robert Gallucci, achieved this important step not only on behalf of the people of the United States but on behalf of the entire international community.

NOTE: The statement referred to Robert Gallucci, Assistant Secretary of State for Politico-Military Affairs.

Nomination for Five Ambassadorial Posts
June 11, 1993

The President today announced his intention to nominate five career Foreign Service officers to ambassadorial posts. The five are:

William D. Montgomery, Bulgaria
Richard Boucher, Cyprus
Mark Hambley, Lebanon
Roger Gamble, Suriname
Jeffrey Davidow, Venezuela

"Each of these five men has demonstrated the high levels of talent and character required for a sensitive ambassadorial post," said the President. "I salute them for their continuing service to the United States and thank them for taking on these important assignments."

NOTE: Biographies of the nominees were made available by the Office of the Press Secretary.

The President's Radio Address
June 12, 1993

Good morning. Last night the United Nations, acting with American and other coalition forces, successfully attacked the military positions in Somalia of the warlord Mohamed Farah Aideed. Our forces, thankfully, have sustained no casualties.

The U.N.'s action was a response to a savage attack this past week by Aideed's forces carried out on U.N. peacekeepers. Aideed's attack killed 23 Pakistanis and injured 3 Americans serving in the U.N.'s force. It was a cold-blooded ambush on U.N. forces who were delivering food and building peace for the people of Somalia.

The United Nations and the United States refuse to tolerate this ruthless disregard for the will of the international community. Therefore, following a request from the U.N. and pursuant to a U.N. Security Council resolution, I ordered the participation of our troops in this action. I commend the decisive leadership of the U.N. Secretary-General Boutros-Ghali, the commander of the U.N. force, Turkish General Bir, and United States Major General Thomas Montgomery.

With this action, the world community moves to restore order in Somalia's capital and to underscore its commitment to preserve the security of U.N. forces. For if U.N. peacekeepers are to be effective agents for peace and stability in Somalia and elsewhere, they must be capable of using force when necessary to defend themselves and accomplish their goals.

We need to recall why U.S. forces were in Somalia to begin with and how much has been accomplished since they first arrived. Last December the United States first sent troops to Somalia to help the United Nations answer a desperate call for help. By the time we arrived over 350,000 Somalis already had died in a bloody civil war, shrouding the nation in famine and disease. Over 30,000 American men and women, both military and civilian, joined with troops and relief workers from all over the world in an effort to end the starvation and the hopelessness. They worked with courage and dedication to quell the violence, rein in the warlords, and deliver tons of urgently needed food and medicine. That humanitarian effort restored hope, advanced our interests, and represented the very best of America's ideals.

Today in Somalia, crops are growing, starvation has ended, refugees are beginning to return, schools and hospitals are reopening, a civil police force has been recreated, and Somalia has begun a process of national reconciliation with the goal of creating the institutions of democracy. As a result, over recent months, we have been able to reduce our troop presence in Somalia down to fewer than 4,000, a small fraction of the total U.N. force.

While American and U.N. efforts in Somalia have been successful, there remains a small but dangerous minority of Somalis who are determined to provoke terror and chaos. Last night's action was essential to send a clear message to the armed gangs, to protect the vast majority of Somalis who long for peace, to enhance the security of our forces still in Somalia, to hasten the day when they can safely return home, and to strengthen the effectiveness and the credibility of U.N. peacekeeping in Somalia and around the world.

The U.N.'s action holds an important lesson about how our Nation can accomplish our own security goals in this new era. Although the cold war is over, the world remains a dangerous place. The United States cannot be the world's policeman, but we also cannot turn a blind eye to the world's problems, for they affect our own security, our own interests, and our own ideals. The U.S. must continue to play its unique role of leadership in the world. But now we can increasingly express that leadership through multilateral means such as the United Nations, which spread the costs and expressed the unified will of the international community. That was one of the lessons of Desert Storm. And clearly, that was one of the lessons last night in Somalia.

On behalf of all Americans, I am proud of the American forces, who once again have demonstrated extraordinary courage and skill. The world thanks them and all of the U.N. forces in Somalia for their service, for striking a blow against lawlessness and killing, and for advancing the world's commitment to justice and security.

NOTE: The President spoke at 10:06 a.m. from the Oval Office at the White House.

Remarks to Volunteers for Presidential Correspondence
June 12, 1993

Thank you. Good morning. I want to thank you all for coming here and for being willing to help us with what is really a great problem for democracy. But as all of you know, we get a lot of mail at the White House. What a lot of people don't know is we're getting a lot more than anyone ever has. And by the time we had been here 3½ months, more letters had come to the White House than came to the White House in all of 1992.

We're getting about 40,000 letters a day. We are desperately working to try to answer those letters with very limited staff. We've had already about 450 young people from the area agree to come in and help us in the past. But today I'm proud to say that there are over 800 young people who will be working today to help open and staple the mail that comes in here, so that then it can be read and sorted and answered.

We have gotten over 3 million pieces of mail, with more coming. And that's good. But we have to answer all those letters. We have to let the American people know that they are being heard, and we're working very hard on it. And I might say, that's after we opened an E-mail channel, so we've got a lot of people coming in through E-mail. We've got extra phone lines on for people to call in, and we're still getting this much mail.

So you are really going to help make democracy work today. And all over America, people will have their letters read and their letters answered more quickly because you've agreed to come here and help us open and staple the mail so it can all be processed more quickly.

I am personally very, very grateful to you for doing this. You've made a real contribution to helping the White House work for America better. I hope it's also a great fun day for you. And I'm delighted to see all of you here.

Thank you very much. Have a good day. Thank you very much.

NOTE: The President spoke at 11:42 a.m. on West Executive Drive at the White House.

Remarks on Signing the Flag Day Proclamation
June 14, 1993

Good morning. Welcome to the Rose Garden, and thank you for joining us for this observance of Flag Day. As we begin, I want to introduce three children, to my left, to lead us in the Pledge of Allegiance: Christopher Williams, an 8-year-old from Ketcham Elementary School; Delilah Johnson, who is also 8, from Ketcham Elementary School; and Sean Mizzer, 10 years old, from Watkins Elementary School. They are now going to lead us in the pledge.

[*At this point, the students recited the Pledge of Allegiance.*]

Good job. Let's give them a hand. I thought they did well. Thank you. [*Applause*]

Thank you. Please be seated. I want to acknowledge the presence of a few of our guests in the audience today, including Mr. James Kenney, the national commander of AMVETS; Mr. Louis Koerber, the president of National Flag Day Foundation; Mr. George Cahill, the president of the National Flag Foundation; and Mrs. Romaine Thomas, who is the principal of Ketcham Elementary School, where two of these children attend school. Thank you all.

On this day in 1777, the Continental Congress adopted the Stars and Stripes as the official flag of our Nation. Throughout our history, this flag has been a potent symbol of America and what it means to be an American. You can hear America's reverence for the flag in our music from our national anthem, "The Star-Spangled Banner," written by Francis Scott Key in 1814, to George M. Cohan's "You're a Grand Old Flag," to John Philip Sousa's magnificent march "The Stars and Stripes Forever," performed best by his very own United States Marine Band.

We owe a great debt to the members of our armed services, who have defended this flag through two centuries now. The United States Army, coincidentally, also celebrates its birthday today. As we honor the Army's 218 years of history, let us also remember the brave Americans who today are defending the United Nations relief operations in Somalia. Their efforts are a reminder to all of us that we are blessed with enormous freedoms in America.

Think of the pledge we have just made, words we have known since childhood, words that come easily to us, so we often recite them without even stopping to think about their true memory. A "republic" is a government of, by, and for the people. "One Nation": From our myriad diversity, from all of our differences, we still have a deeper measure of unity. "Under God": the reminder that self-government is a sacred trust. "Indivisible": Through a tragic civil war we learned the wisdom of President Lincoln's lesson that "a house divided against itself cannot stand." It is not enough for our house to stand, however. We must remember that a house stands strongest when it stands together. "With liberty and justice for all" is a promise that we must strive to make real, not just in our words but in what we do.

These ideas have brought new Americans to our shores from the beginning of our existence. They make our flag a symbol of hope to people all around the world. To those of you here who are recently naturalized citizens, I say, welcome. A few of you even work here, and we're proud to have you. I'm proud to have you on our staff and more proud to be your fellow citizen and to know that all of you feel as deeply about this country as I do.

Since President Truman's time it has been customary for the President to sign a proclamation designating June 14th as Flag Day in the United States. I want to do that now, and then make a presentation.

[At this point, the President signed the proclamation.]

Since we teach citizenship at an early age, I want to ask Christopher Williams to come up here and to accept on behalf of his school, Ketcham Elementary, this flag which flew above the United States Capitol this morning. Christopher, I want you to take this flag, along with your schoolmates, back to your school and honor it. It symbolizes both your rights and your responsibilities as an American. You should be

very proud of this.

I'd also like any newly naturalized Americans to stand up. Do we have any new citizens here? Let's give them a hand. Look at them. [Applause] Thank you.

Last night when we had the press party here at the White House, perhaps the most moving encounter I had was a couple came through the line; both of them were born in South America. But they had their little child with them who had just been born in the United States, and the child's T-shirt said "Future President" on it. [Laughter] There you are. Look, there he is right there. Give him a hand, the father of the child. [Applause]

This is a special day. The children remind us of it, and so do our new citizens. Thank you all for coming.

NOTE: The President spoke at 10:36 a.m. in the Rose Garden at the White House. The proclamation is listed in Appendix D at the end of this volume.

Remarks Announcing the Nomination of Ruth Bader Ginsburg To Be a Supreme Court Associate Justice
June 14, 1993

The President. Please be seated. I wish you all a good afternoon, and I thank the Members of the Congress and other interested Americans who are here.

In just a few days when the Supreme Court concludes its term, Justice Byron White will begin a new chapter in his long and productive life. He has served the Court as he has lived, with distinction, intelligence, and honor. And he retires from public service with the deep gratitude of all the American people.

Article II, section 2 of the United States Constitution empowers the President to select a nominee to fill a vacancy on the Supreme Court of the United States. This responsibility is one of the most significant duties assigned to the President by the Constitution. A Supreme Court Justice has life tenure, unlike the President, and along with his or her colleagues decides the most significant questions of our time and shapes the continuing contours of our liberty.

I care a lot about this responsibility, not only

because I am a lawyer but because I used to teach constitutional law and I served my State as attorney general. I know well how the Supreme Court affects the lives of all Americans personally and deeply. I know clearly that a Supreme Court Justice should have the heart and spirit, the talent and discipline, the knowledge, common sense, and wisdom to translate the hopes of the American people, as presented in the cases before it, into an enduring body of constitutional law, constitutional law that will preserve our most cherished values that are enshrined in that Constitution and, at the same time, enable the American people to move forward.

That is what I promised the American people in a Justice when I ran for President, and I believe it is a promise that I am delivering on today. After careful reflection, I am proud to nominate for Associate Justice of the Supreme Court Judge Ruth Bader Ginsburg of the United States Court of Appeals for the District of Columbia. I will send her name to the Senate to fill the vacancy created by Justice White's retirement.

As I told Judge Ginsburg last night when I called to ask her to accept the nomination, I decided on her for three reasons. First, in her years on the bench she has genuinely distinguished herself as one of our Nation's best judges, progressive in outlook, wise in judgment, balanced and fair in her opinions. Second, over the course of a lifetime, in her pioneering work in behalf of the women of this country, she has compiled a truly historic record of achievement in the finest traditions of American law and citizenship. And finally, I believe that in the years ahead she will be able to be a force for consensus-building on the Supreme Court, just as she has been on the Court of Appeals, so that our judges can become an instrument of our common unity in the expression of their fidelity to the Constitution.

Judge Ginsburg received her undergraduate degree from Cornell. She attended both Harvard and Columbia Law Schools and served on the law reviews of both institutions, the first woman to have earned this distinction. She was a law clerk to a Federal judge, a law professor at Rutgers and Columbia Law Schools. She argued six landmark cases on behalf of women before the United States Supreme Court and, happily, won five out of six. For the past 13 years she has served on the United States Court of Appeals for the District of Columbia, the second highest court in our country, where her work has brought her national acclaim and on which she was able to amass a record that caused a national legal journal in 1991 to name her as one of the Nation's leading centrist judges.

In the months and years ahead, the country will have the opportunity to get to know much more about Ruth Ginsburg's achievements, decency, humanity, and fairness. People will find, as I have, that this nominee is a person of immense character. Quite simply, what's in her record speaks volumes about what is in her heart. Throughout her life she has repeatedly stood for the individual, the person less well-off, the outsider in society, and has given those people greater hope by telling them that they have a place in our legal system, by giving them a sense that the Constitution and the laws protect all the American people, not simply the powerful. Judge Ginsburg has also proven herself to be a healer, what attorneys call a moderate. Time and again, her moral imagination has cooled the fires of her colleagues' discord, ensuring that the right of jurists to dissent ennobles the law without entangling the court.

The announcement of this vacancy brought forth a unique outpouring of support for distinguished Americans on Judge Ginsburg's behalf. What caused that outpouring is the essential quality of the judge herself: her deep respect for others and her willingness to subvert self-interest to the interest of our people and their institutions.

In one of her own writings about what it is like to be a Justice, Judge Ginsburg quotes Justice Louis Brandeis, who once said, "The Supreme Court is not a place for solo performers." If this is a time for consensus-building on the Court, and I believe it is, Judge Ginsburg will be an able and effective architect of that effort.

It is important to me that Judge Ginsburg came to her views and attitudes by doing, not merely by reading and studying. Despite her enormous ability and academic achievements, she could not get a job with a law firm in the early 1960's because she was a woman and the mother of a small child. Having experienced discrimination, she devoted the next 20 years of her career to fighting it and making this country a better place for our wives, our mothers, our sisters, and our daughters. She herself argued and won many of the women's rights cases before the Supreme Court in the 1970's. Many admirers of her work say that she is to the women's movement what former Supreme Court Justice Thurgood Marshall was to the movement for the rights of African-Americans. I can think of no greater compliment to bestow on an American lawyer. And she has done all of this and a lot of other things as well by raising a family with her husband, Marty, whom she married 39 years ago as a very young woman. Together they had two children, Jane and James, and they now have two grandchildren. Hers is a remarkable record of distinction and achievement, both professional and personal.

During the selection process, we reviewed the qualifications of more than 40 potential nominees. It was a long, exhaustive search. And during that time we identified several wonderful Americans whom I think could be outstanding nominees to the Supreme Court in the future. Among the best were the Secretary of the Interior, Bruce Babbitt, whose strong legal background as Arizona's attorney general and recent work balancing the competing interests of environmentalists and others in the very difficult issues affecting the American West made him a highly qualified candidate for the Court. And I had the unusual experience, something unique to me, of being flooded with calls all across America from Babbitt admirers who pleaded with me not to put him on the Court and take him away from the Interior Department. I also carefully considered the chief judge of the first circuit, Judge Stephen Breyer of Boston, a man whose character, confidence, and legal scholarship impressed me very greatly. I believe he has a very major role to play in public life. I believe he is superbly qualified to be on the Court. And I think either one of these candidates, as well as the handful of others whom I closely considered, may well find themselves in that position someday in the future.

Let me say in closing that Ruth Bader Ginsburg cannot be called a liberal or a conservative; she has proved herself too thoughtful for such labels. As she herself put it in one of her articles, and I quote, "The greatest figures of the American judiciary have been independent thinking individuals with open but not empty minds; individuals willing to listen and to learn. They have exhibited a readiness to reexamine their own premises, liberal or conservative, as thoroughly as those of others." That, I believe,

describes Judge Ginsburg. And those, I too believe, are the qualities of a great Justice.

If, as I believe, the measure of a person's values can best be measured by examining the life the person lives, then Judge Ginsburg's values are the very ones that represent the best in America. I am proud to nominate this pathbreaking attorney, advocate, and judge to be the 107th Justice to the United States Supreme Court.

[At this point, Judge Ginsburg expressed her appreciation to the President and discussed her background and her view of the position.]

Q. The withdrawal of the Guinier nomination, sir, and your apparent focus on Judge Breyer and your turn, late, it seems, to Judge Ginsburg may have created an impression, perhaps unfair, of a certain zig-zag quality in the decision-making process here. I wonder, sir, if you could kind of walk us through it and perhaps disabuse us of any notion we might have along those lines. Thank you.

The President. I have long since given up the thought that I could disabuse some of you of turning any substantive decision into anything but political process. How you could ask a question like that after the statement she just made is beyond me.

Goodbye. Thank you.

NOTE: The President spoke at 2:07 p.m. in the Rose Garden at the White House.

Remarks on the President's Council on Sustainable Development
June 14, 1993

Thank you. Ladies and gentlemen, thank you very much for being here. It has been a year since the Earth summit in Rio. I think you might be interested to know that a year ago at the Earth summit in Rio I placed a call to Senator Al Gore of Tennessee to get a report on the goings-on there from him and from Senator Wirth of Colorado and to begin the process by which we came together as a team. Not very long after that I asked Al Gore to join the Democratic ticket, and the rest was history.

I don't want to make any bones about it. When we had our first very long meeting, one

thing that then-Senator Gore said was that he wanted to be part of a ticket that, if elected, could put the environment back on the front burner in American public life and do it in a way that would be good for the economy, not bad for the economy, do it in a way that would bring the American people together, not divide them. All the policy positions that the Vice President just announced that we have taken to change the direction of the previous administrations and, more importantly, to go beyond politics to embrace a new philosophy of uniting our goals of preserving the environment and promoting economic growth would have been very difficult to achieve had it not been for his leadership and constant involvement and faithfulness to this cause. And the American people owe him a great debt of gratitude.

I would also like to acknowledge the presence of one other person in this audience who has not been introduced and is not up here, but it will become obvious when I say what I want to say. The Deputy Secretary of Education, Madeleine Kunin is here. She is formerly the Governor of Vermont. And as far as I know, she was the only Governor in the country that actually had a sustainable development commission actively operating on the problems of the people of Vermont when she was the Governor. And she in many ways blazed a trail for what we are attempting to do today. And I thank you for that.

A year ago the United States was in Rio fighting the Global Warming Treaty and the Biodiversity Treaty. Our leading economic competitors were at the Earth summit signing off on the Global Warming Treaty, signing off on the Biodiversity Treaty. And while the United States was fighting to water it down, change it, or thwart it, they spent all their time selling environmental technology to other nations in the world, making money while we made hot air.

What a difference a year can make. This morning the Vice President made us all proud in his opening address before the United Nations Commission on Sustainable Development. America is now doing what we ought to do. We're leading again, leading the nations of the world in the pursuit of a great purpose.

This afternoon I am announcing the creation of the President's Council on Sustainable Development to help set policies to grow the economy and preserve the environment for our children and our children's children, bringing together some of the most innovative people from business, from government, from the environmental movement, the civil rights movement, and the labor movement, people who bring a wealth of experience and accomplishment to this mission, people who have developed environmentally sound products, found ways to protect our air and water, and defended communities all across the country against pollution and health hazards.

In the past, many might not have ever had the chance to sit down at the table and work together. But now they are working together. These men and women have real experience

in the real world, and I am counting on them to achieve real results. I am asking them to find new ways to combine economic growth and environmental protection, to promote our best interests in the world community, to bring our people together to meet the needs of the present without jeopardizing the future. I am asking the Council to be guided by three principles that form our environmental policies.

First, we believe a healthy economy and a healthy environment go hand-in-hand. Environmental problems result not from robust growth but from reckless growth. And we can grow the economy by making our people healthier, our communities more attractive, and our products and our services more environmentally conscious.

Second, America must lead the way in promoting economic growth and environmental preservation at home and abroad. We live in an era of global economics, global environmentalism, global epidemics. Our lives and our livelihoods depend upon people throughout the world being healthy and prosperous and respectful of the planet we all share. What is good for the world in this sense is very good for America.

And third, we must move beyond the false choices and unnecessary antagonisms of the past. From American business and American labor to the world's wealthiest nations and the world's poorest, we all share a common interest in economic growth that preserves rather than pollutes our environment. America can set an example by achieving economic growth that can continue through the lifetimes of our children and grandchildren because it respects the resources that make that growth possible.

That is what we mean by sustainable development. That is why I'm asking this Council to promote healthy communities and environmentally sound products and services that will do the best in the world to make our marketplace the best in the world now and well into the 21st century.

When we talk about environmental justice, we mean calling a halt to the poisoning and the pollution of our poorest communities, from our rural areas to our inner cities. We don't have a person to waste, and pollution clearly wastes human lives and natural resources. When our children's lives are no longer cut short by toxic dumps, when their minds are no longer damaged by lead paint poisoning, we will stop wasting the energy and the intelligence that could build a stronger and a more prosperous America.

When we talk about environmentally sound products and services, we mean light bulbs and computers and refrigerators that use less energy and automobiles that produce less pollution. People all across the world want to buy these goods and services, and when we make them in America, that means better paying and more secure jobs and higher living standards for all of our people.

Americans take pride in our know-how, our can-do spirit, and our love of this remarkable land that God has given us. With leaders like the men and women here today, we can put what is best about America to work building a stronger economy and preserving this planet for our children and all generations to come.

Thank you very much.

NOTE: The President spoke at 4:35 p.m. in the Rose Garden at the White House. The Executive order of June 29 which established the Council is listed in Appendix D at the end of this volume.

Exchange With Reporters
June 14, 1993

Senator Arlen Specter's Illness

The President. [*Inaudible*]—and obviously I was very concerned—need for the operation, but our prayers are with him. And we're pulling for him.

Q. Have you spoken to his family at all today?

The President. No, I wanted to wait until, frankly, until I had all this out of the way and until there was time to, you know, get through the operation. Then I thought I'd call them—later. We have a time scheduled to call, but I haven't talked to them yet.

Q. Were you shocked and surprised?

The President. Yes. He was just here last week, and he was—you know, he brought in the family from the Make-A-Wish Foundation. We've had a great visit, and we were talking about a number of different things.

Q. Are you hopeful he'll come back?

The President. Oh, absolutely. And I think he will. We're certainly hopeful.

Supreme Court Nomination

Q. Mr. President, on your nomination, was it tough for you to pass over Judge Breyer and Secretary Babbitt? Was it a hard decision?

The President. Well, it was hard in the sense

that they were all qualified. And there were two or three others I thought were exceptionally well qualified. But once I talked to her, I felt very strongly about her. This is not a negative thing on them. And as I said, out there in the crowd I had a half a dozen people come up to me and thank me for leaving Secretary Babbitt at the Interior Department. They say he's the best Interior Secretary they'd ever seen. So that was a real problem, but I like them all. I thought they were all superbly well qualified. And I think that they will be in the future.

There was no negative—it was a positive position being able to pick the person I thought would be best at this time, a purely positive choice. In that sense it was a joy to make, but not easy. You can see today from—she's an extraordinary woman. She has incredible inner strength and character. And I think it will communicate itself and really help to create a good atmosphere at the Court.

NOTE: The exchange began at 4:55 p.m. in the Rose Garden at the White House. A tape was not available for verification of the content of this exchange.

Statement on the Death of Donald Slayton
June 14, 1993

I was deeply saddened to hear last night of the death of astronaut Deke Slayton, a pioneer in space exploration who helped chart the course for America's pursuit of the New Frontier.

Throughout his career, Deke met adversity with determination, and discouragement with a dedication to never yield his dreams. His commitment to space exploration helped pull the world into an era of new possibilities that grows and expands to this day.

Both Hillary and I extend our heartfelt sympathies to Deke Slayton's family and former colleagues. We mourn his passing, but we celebrate what he stood for and what he accomplished for America.

The President's News Conference
June 15, 1993

Supreme Court Nominee

The President. Thanks for the introduction, Wolf [Wolf Blitzer, Cable News Network]. Good morning, ladies and gentlemen. I'd like to make a couple of opening remarks. First, let me say that this morning I had a good talk with Judge Ginsburg, complimenting her on her very moving statement yesterday. And I assured her that we were moving ahead with this confirmation process. I spoke with Senators Biden and Thurmond and Hatch and asked them to work with me to assure the speediest possible confirmation consistent with the Senate doing its duty. At any rate, I am confident that she will be ready to assume her position on the Supreme Court when the fall term begins in October.

Economic Program

With regard to the economy, we've had, since last Friday, very good reports on low inflation in terms of both producer prices and consumer prices. And in a larger sense, over the last few months, we've seen a continuing reduction in long-term interest rates, which have given us a 20-year low in mortgage rates, a 7-year high in housing sales, and have mightily contributed to the introduction into this economy of 755,000 new jobs, well over 90 percent of them in the private sector.

I am confident that the continuation of this trend depends on our ability to pass a strong economic program through the Congress which reduces the deficit, increases investment in our future, and is fair in terms of requiring a fair apportionment of the burden. The plan that the House passed, that the Senate Finance Committee is now dealing with, for every $10 that the deficit is reduced, $5 comes from spending cuts, $3.75 from upper income people, $1.25 from the middle class, and families with incomes under $30,000 are held harmless.

I hope that the principles I have outlined will be honored as this program moves through the Congress. The Senate Finance Committee has some tough decisions to make. I don't expect to agree with all of them, but I think they will produce a bill. I think the Senate will produce a bill. And then we can go on to conference and see what the final shape of the economic plan that the whole Congress will vote on will be. I'm encouraged, quite upbeat, by the reports I've received from Senator Moynihan, Senator Mitchell, and others about the progress being made there, and I just want to encourage the Senate to move forward.

Campaign Finance Reform

Finally, let me say that the Senate is dealing with another very difficult and very important issue now, and that's campaign finance reform. I have believed for a long time that we can't get thoroughgoing economic reform in our country until we have political reform. That requires the lobby reform legislation that is moving its way through Congress but, very importantly, campaign finance reform to lower the cost of campaigns, reduce the influence of special interests and PAC's, and open the airwaves to more honest debate.

The troubling thing, obviously, is that the Republican Senators have announced that they may yet again filibuster a bill. And the thing that particularly troubles me about this one is that several Republicans voted for a bill not unlike this last year, which contained public financing. If in fact this filibuster occurs, it will be the second time that Republican Senators who voted for a piece of progressive legislation when there was a Republican in the White House have now voted against it and have filibustered it. The first was on the motor voter bill where eventually we were able to work out the problems and get a bill passed. But I think this is very, very important. And I very much hope that the Senators will reconsider and let this bill go forward. We need to pass a strong campaign finance reform bill this year. Political reform and economic reform, in my judgment, over the long run must go hand-in-hand, and time is long since past when we should have campaign finance reform.

Now having said that, I think I ought to give Brit [Brit Hume, ABC News] his followup. [*Laughter*]

Q. I hope you don't mind if I follow up on another subject, sir. In the House——

The President. You know what I'm really upset about? You got a honeymoon, and I didn't. [*Laughter*]

Q. Yes, sir, but you got to end it. [*Laughter*]

The President. Well, let's extend it then. Go ahead.

Economic Program

Q. The House liberals in particular, Black Caucus in particular, seem in a somewhat mutinous mood as they watch the deliberations in the Senate on your economic program. And I'm wondering, sir, what do you say to them to assure them that the tough vote they felt they cast for your program was not in vain and that you haven't really cut the rug out from under them?

The President. Well, I've not cut the rug out from under them at all. I have not agreed to any provision that the Senate Finance Committee is deliberating. There's been no agreement on any issue. I have set out principles: $500 billion in deficit reduction; a deficit reduction trust fund for all the tax increases and spending cuts, at least $250 billion in spending cuts, although I would like some more cuts and some

less taxes. Seventy-five percent of the burden has to fall on upper income people, and we ought to keep the incentives for growth and for empowerment of the working poor and the incentives to move people from welfare to work.

Those are the things that I want to see in the final bill. And what I have assured the Black Caucus—and let me say, I have talked to, oh, probably 15 of the members in the last week or so just in that caucus and many other Members of the House—is that the principles that I outlined are still there and that we'll do our best to articulate those as the Senate deals with this bill.

But the real test will be what happens in the conference and what the final bill looks like that the House and the Senate will vote on. And again, I'm quite encouraged that we'll get a bill out that they'll feel good about. They made it clear to me what they felt most strongly about. And the two things above all were the earned-income tax credit for the working poor, which is an important part of our welfare reform incentive, and the empowerment zones for the depressed urban and rural areas.

And there are all kinds of parliamentary issues that, as you know, the Senate has to consider in all this, but I'm confident that in the end the bill that they vote on in the House to send to me for signature will have those things in it.

Domestic and Foreign Policy Decisions

Q. Mr. President, do you perceive a loss of public confidence in your Presidency because of wavering domestically and in foreign policy? And what do you plan to do about it if——

The President. No.

Q. ——there is such a thing? You don't——

The President. Well, there is no wavering. If somebody had told you at Christmastime, Helen [Helen Thomas, United Press International], that by June 1st we'd have unemployment under 7 percent for the first time in a year and a half, 755,000 new jobs, a 20-year low in interest rates, a 7-year high in housing sales, that the United States would have led a global effort to support Boris Yeltsin, sign the global warming treaty, I mean, the Biodiversity Treaty—that actually happened on June 4th—pass family leave and pass the motor voter legislation, repeal the gag rule and the ban on fetal tissue research to allow more science and less politics in medical research, I'd say most people would think that was a pretty decisive record; that we would have moved this budget through the House of Representatives, sent it to the Senate—much tougher decisions than were required in the Reagan budget in 1981, on a faster track, on a faster track, I think people would have said at Christmastime, that's a pretty good and decisive record.

We haven't solved the problem in Bosnia that has plagued everybody. I concede that. The Europeans wouldn't go along with my proposed resolution. I still think they may be compelled to do that or something very near like it if they want to get anything done over there. And I think we're going forward. I like the Supreme Court judge that I picked. I don't think it shows any wavering at all on that.

Q. You don't think there is a public feeling that you're indecisive? I mean, on the——

The President. Well, all I'm telling you is——

Q. ——highly touted issues, the budget, Bosnia.

The President. Let me tell you something about Bosnia. On Bosnia, I made a decision. The United Nations controls what happens in Bosnia. I cannot unilaterally lift the arms embargo. I didn't change my mind. Our allies decided that they weren't prepared to go that far at this time. They asked me to wait, and they said they would not support it. I didn't change my mind.

And as far as the budget, I don't—how can you say that? No President's budget has been taken seriously in this town for a dozen years. Three-quarters of the Republicans in the House of Representatives voted against President Bush's last budget. I sent a budget up there that passed. A budget resolution passed on time for the first time in 17 years. And we're out here fighting for these tough decisions. How could anybody say—this is the most decisive Presidency you've had in a very long time on all the big issues that matter.

And I might say, all the heat we're getting from people is because of the decisions that have been made, not because of those that haven't.

Somalia

Q. Mr. President, since the United States began bombing in Somalia, the Pakistani peacekeepers on the ground opened fire on civilians. There have been reports that civilians have died as a result of our action. We haven't heard from

you since Saturday on this subject. What is your assessment of the U.N. action there? And how much longer is the U.S. bombing going to go on?

The President. Well, the action that we took was, I think, appropriate in response to what happened, which is that Pakistani peacekeepers were ambushed and murdered. There's no question about that. The action that we took was designed to minimize as much as we possibly could any damage or any injury or any death to civilians.

What happened with the Pakistanis is in some doubt in the sense that they're saying the first time they were ambushed, they were ambushed by people who stood behind women and children and used them as a defense. And as I understand it, the U.N. is trying to get to the bottom of that. I expect them to do it and to take appropriate action and to take every appropriate step to make sure that U.N. peacekeepers do not, do not cause injury or death to innocent people in Somalia. That is the United Nations job, and the United States expects them to do it.

Q. We've also gone from being the heroes in Somalia now to apparently a feeling in the towns themselves of "Yankee, go home." I mean, are you concerned that this action is sort of becoming counterproductive?

The President. I think that on balance, I still believe that most people in the country think that we came in there, we ended starvation, we ended brutalization, we ended violence, we opened up the country again to the beginnings of civilization. I am very sorry about what happened this last week. But we cannot have a situation where one of these warlords, while everybody else is cooperating, decides that he can go out and slaughter 20 peacekeepers. And so, yes, there have been some tensions as a result of that. But we had to take appropriate action. And I hope very much that we can get back to the peacekeeping function as soon as possible.

Q. Mr. President, the attack against the peacekeepers in Somalia raises questions about the safety of U.N. forces everywhere. As you send American troops into Macedonia, how much risk are you exposing them to, and will the United States take action when U.N. peacekeepers are attacked?

The President. The United States has made it clear that we would take action if U.N. peacekeepers were attacked in Bosnia. And obviously, we're going to protect our own soldiers. I believe that the Macedonian deployment carries minimal risk and carries maximum gain in terms of the statement that we don't intend to see this conflict widen. But I think that all Americans know and have to know that whenever we send people around the world, even if they're on peacekeeping missions, there is some risk to them.

Supreme Court Nominee

Q. Mr. President, getting back to Judge Ginsburg for a moment, I know that you're familiar with her Madison lecture and her rather provocative statements about the judicial reach of *Roe versus Wade.* Can you tell me how comfortable you are with her challenge to the whole theoretical construct to that landmark ruling and whether you feel confident that she will, once on the Court, meet what you had said during the campaign was your concerns about continuing——

The President. I think if you read the lecture, she is clearly pro-choice in the sense that she believes the Government should not make that decision for the women of America. She disagrees with the rationale of the decision. I'm not sure I agree with her, as a matter of fact, on that issue, but I thought it was a very provocative and impressive argument. As a matter of fact, I have always thought that *Roe* v. *Wade* was the most difficult case decided in the last 25 years because it was such a difficult issue and that the Court did the best it could under the circumstances. She made a very interesting alternative suggestion, but there is no suggestion in any of her writings that she's not pro-choice. And that was to me the important thing.

Q. Can I follow? How much did you actually discuss legal theory with her? Can you give us some sense of——

The President. I didn't discuss that with her. I'd read the writings, and they'd been widely discussed. When we talked for about an hour and a half, I talked to her a little bit and asked her about a couple of cases that she had been associated with in the business law area and a couple of the cases she fought for women's rights on, just to sort of talk about them, to get a feel for it. And we talked a little bit about one of the religious liberty cases she dealt with involving the right of a soldier to wear a yarmulke. Again, I just wanted to hear her talk about that. That whole issue of religious

freedom is a very big issue in my judgment, and I wanted to hear her discuss it.

Q. Did you discuss homosexual rights with her?

The President. Not at all. It never came up.

Q. And are you at all concerned about some of her rulings in that area?

The President. No.

Space Station and Super Collider

Q. Mr. President, we understand you're about to make a decision on the future of the space station, one way you could quickly cut some Government spending. Could you let us in on your thoughts? We know there are various proposals, big, medium, little, none at all. And also the super collider, since there's a considerable amount of opposition to that as well.

The President. Well, I'll have statements on them in the very near future; if not today, in the next few days. Let me just make one comment about the space station generally. As you know, I have supported both projects in the past. The thing about the space station, first of all, that I want to say is a word of compliment to the Vest Commission that just completed its review, and not only of the space station but of the management structure of NASA and how they interrelate. And they make some very provocative and thought-provoking and, I thought, very important recommendations and suggestions about how not only this project should be dealt with but about how NASA should operate the project and should proceed. So I have them under review.

I do think it's important to recognize that the space station offers us the potential of working with other nations and continuing our lead in a very important area and having a significant technological impact, and that in the aftermath of all the cutbacks in defense and what they mean for science and technology, it is something that we should, in my judgment, consider very carefully. Keep in mind, a lot of the people who say, "Well, I don't like the space station," or "I don't really think the super collider is the best use of our investments in physics," they may be arguing about other investments that they think ought to be made. We're talking here about reducing America's investment in space and science and technology, and that's something I think we need to think about a long time before we do.

Q. It sounds like you're going to continue——

The President. Well, wait and see what I say. I'm going to issue a very careful statement to the Congress in the next few days which will outline my position.

Supreme Court Nomination

Q. In regard to Judge Ginsburg, do you have any regrets about the process that led to her nomination——

The President. I have one big regret——

Q. [*Inaudible*]—Mr. Babbitt and Mr. Breyer's names as frontrunners——

The President. First of all, I strongly dispute that I hung them out. I regret the leaks. But it's not fair to say I hung them out. Any Senator I talked to will tell you, when I called to discuss Judge Breyer, I also said, "I've got someone else I'm looking at." Anybody will tell you that. I told Bruce Babbitt the first day I called him, "I want to know if you agree to be considered, I don't know if the country can afford to lose you as Interior Secretary." The truth is—and I said this yesterday; I will say it again—I've never seen such an outpouring of support for any public official in my adult lifetime as we got for Bruce Babbitt to continue as Interior Secretary while we work through the issues in the Northwest and deal with a lot of these other issues.

I will say again, I think Steven Breyer is superbly qualified to be on the Supreme Court. I think both of them would have been confirmed by very large margins. I have no doubt in my mind of that. I really believe that she was the best candidate at this time. I was immensely impressed with the kind of inner strength and character that she demonstrated out there in the Rose Garden yesterday, and that's why I picked her. But do I regret the fact that there were leaks and that that may have exposed them more than they would otherwise have been? I certainly do. And I'd be happy to—you know, we ought to do better with that. And if somebody's got any suggestions about how I can, I'd like to have them.

Major General Harold N. Campbell

Q. Sir, we have not had the opportunity to ask you your reaction to the derogatory remarks about you that were reportedly made by the Air Force general in Europe. How did you feel when you heard about that? And why have you tolerated it the way you have?

The President. First of all, I have not tolerated it. I have simply permitted the Air Force to handle this in the ordinary course of business, as I thought was appropriate. The Air Force is dealing with this issue. I have been fully briefed on it. I had two feelings about it, frankly. For me personally, I didn't care. People say whatever they want to say about me personally. It had no impact on me. And I thought, well, here's a guy who's served this country, and you know, so what if he doesn't like me. And he doesn't know me from Adam's off ox, so you know, he's just repeating something he's heard.

But for a general officer to say that about the Commander in Chief is a—if that happened—is a very bad thing. And so we are—the Air Force is investigating it. They're going to make a report once they have all the facts, and then there will be some action taken. But I don't think that I should personally intervene as long as the Air Force is doing what is appropriate.

Q. You say you've been briefed on the situation, and we've been told by your folks that this would be resolved by the middle of June. We're at that point now. What have they told you so far?

The President. Just what I told you, that the Air Force felt very strongly that someone should go to Europe, find out exactly what happened, get all the facts, and take appropriate action.

Q. Have they confirmed, though, to you that he said it?

The President. I don't know if the factfinder has come back from Europe. And I have not gotten the final report yet. All I've gotten so far is secondhand stuff.

Bosnia

Q. Mr. President, on Bosnia, could we take your earlier remarks here today to mean that you are now revisiting a tougher policy on Bosnia and that you might go back to the Europeans to try to sell them once again on bombing the Serbs?

The President. I wouldn't characterize it quite that way, but let me restate what I said before. I just want to make it clear that I don't think an unwillingness to move alone in Bosnia on arms embargo issues—and we supported bombing to support, if you will, if you remember—the position we had was that we would support the use of air power to back up a freeze of heavy artillery in place while the arms embargo was equalizing the opportunity that the sides had to work out their business. We thought that would lead, frankly, to a cease-fire and ultimately to a peace agreement.

From the beginning, even after the British and French said, "We don't want to do this right now, and we will not vote for it or support it in the United Nations," and the Russians said the same thing, they all agreed to leave the option on the table if their other efforts failed. What I want to reaffirm to you is that that is still my position. I still think that may be the only way we can get them to have a real meaningful cease-fire and a real meaningful peace agreement. And that option was never taken off the table. The British and French and the Russians never said to me flat out they would never go along. They said they thought they could do better. It seems to me that the political situation has deteriorated since then. And my position has not changed. But I am willing to work with them to do what we can do.

NAFTA

Q. Sir, the NAFTA, the agreement with Mexico, you're going to take jobs down there and plants down—they'll leave the jobs vacant here and take the plants down there. How do you figure that they can make enough goods in Mexico at those low rates and the U.S. brought in plants—how do you figure that they can buy goods up here? We won't have anybody up here to sell—we won't have anybody up here to make goods in our plants, our plants—been gone to Mexico. We won't have anything to sell——

The President. Well, that's the argument against NAFTA, but I don't believe that will happen, and I'll tell you why.

Q. ——you see it?

The President. Yes, I can see it. Look what's happened in the last 5 years. There have been any number of plants that have moved into Mexico. They can continue to do that now under the present law. The *maquilladora* line has been extended well beyond the Rio Grande River. There are lots of plants down there. But just a few years ago we had a $5 billion trade deficit with Mexico. Now we have a $6 billion trade surplus. Last month, they replaced Japan as the second biggest purchaser of our manufacturing products. There are over 80 million Mexicans. As their incomes go up, they will buy more from us. If we can work out an agreement with them, we will then be able to move to similar

agreements with countries even farther from us but in our region in Latin America, like Argentina and Venezuela and other countries, and I believe that that will create far more jobs than it will cost. There will be some changes, but I believe that NAFTA will help us to create jobs.

Now, I promised to hear from you, and then I've got to go. Go ahead.

Economic Program

Q. On the budget, although you are committed, as you say, to a $500 billion deficit reduction package, it appears that you seem to be giving an indirect endorsement to continuing the space station and the superconductor collider. If that be the case, then in a final budget bill are you willing to accept a scaled-down energy tax and some elimination of certain corporate tax incentives, such as suggested by Senator Bradley, specifically a minimum tax, elimination of VAT tax, elimination of expensing provisions in a final bill, particularly if interest rates remain low?

The President. The most important thing is to get the deficit reduction, have the tax burden be very progressive, fall 75 percent on the wealthy, and have at least as many spending cuts as you do tax increases.

Let me answer very specifically your questions. And let me just tell you that in general, first of all, I have an enormous respect for Senator Bradley, and I think the '86 tax reform act did an awful lot of good in eliminating a lot of loopholes, deductions, and things that it's very difficult to argue for and in trying to get rates down.

Now having said that, I still believe that there is a distinction to be made between investment and consumption by businesses and individuals and that the tax system of this country should at the very least not penalize investment. I have favored some changes in the alternative minimum tax because I believe the way it operates now you put people in a very difficult position when they want to go invest in plant and equipment if it triggers the alternative minimum tax burden, even when they're just investing. So, I would like to see some modification in that.

He may have some ideas about how we can have a better modification, or maybe he says we don't need as much money, but I think conceptually it's important. The second thing, the small business community is the major generator of jobs in America, has been for the last 12 years. Their job-generating capacity has slowed recently because it costs a lot of extra money to hire an employee and because of uncertainties in the economy. I believe if we increase the small business expensing provision from $10,000 to $25,000 that for millions of small business people out there who are the backbone of this economy, they will then see the wisdom in continuing to invest, continuing to expand, and a lot of people might hire one more person, two more people, three more people, in ways that will create jobs for the economy.

In the end this is a jobs package. So, there is an expensing provision in the Tax Code right now for small business. I just think it ought to be bigger, and I think it's a job generator.

I'll see you in a couple of days. I'm sorry. Thanks.

Q. In a couple of days?

The President. A couple of months. [*Laughter*]

NOTE: The President's 16th news conference began at noon in the Briefing Room at the White House.

Exchange With Reporters Prior to Discussions With Prime Minister Edouard Balladur of France
June 15, 1993

Cuba

Q. Mr. President, are you willing to talk to the Cubans about improving relations?

The President. I'm here with the Prime Minister of France. [*Laughter*]

Q. [*Inaudible*]—French about the Blair House agreement, Mr. President?

Q. [*Inaudible*]—Cubans' announcement today that they'd like to talk about reparations?

The President. I don't have any reaction at this time.

Trade Negotiations

Q. Do you think you can find common ground with the French about Blair House, sir? About the Blair House agreement?

The President. Well, I was very pleased to see that the oilseeds portion will go forward. But I think the rest of it we need to talk about. The United States supports the Blair House agreement.

[*At this point, one group of reporters left the room, and another group entered.*]

President's Schedule

Q. Mr. President, are you going to France anytime in the near future?

The President. I wish I could go in the very near future, but I suppose that depends on when I can travel again. Of course, I have to go to the G–7 meeting in Tokyo, and that will be my first trip out of the country except for the brief visit to Vancouver with President Yeltsin. I'd very much like to go back. I haven't been in a long time.

NOTE: The exchange began at 3:35 p.m. in the Oval Office at the White House. A tape was not available for verification of the content of this exchange.

Remarks to the College Democrats of America
June 15, 1993

I want to thank Adam Kreisel and Jamie Harmon and Jenny Ritter for this gift and for their leadership in the College Democrats, and I want to welcome all of you here. I know I'm not the first person to speak to you. I've been over lobbying Members of Congress and being lobbied by them about various issues today, and I'm awfully glad to see all of you here.

The first time I came to these grounds was in the summer of 1963, 30 years ago next month, before virtually everybody on these steps was born, long before most of you were born. That visit made a lasting impression on me, and I hope this visit makes a lasting impression on you. I was raised at a time when mothers wanted their children to grow up to be President, and I hope there will be another time when people want their children to grow up to be President. Now there can be daughters as well as sons who can really make a difference in our future.

There is around here a wonderful old photograph of three great Democrats standing on the steps of this building together: President Franklin Roosevelt, who was then a young Assistant Secretary of the Navy, standing next to his President, Woodrow Wilson, and alongside them was William Jennings Bryan, who was then the Secretary of State in the Wilson administration during World War I. Between those 3 men, they represented 9 Democratic Presidential candidacies in 13 consecutive elections. Maybe there's magic on the steps that will rub off on some of you someday. I hope so. I hope some of you will be here.

But I also want to remind you that even though I am profoundly grateful about the help you have given to me and to the Vice President in the past election—and without the young people of this country voting in record numbers, we might not have been able to come here— I remind you that the reason for your party identification and the reason for your work in elections is to change people's lives for the better. That change is, under the best of circumstances, never easy. And after 12 years in which people have been given siren song after siren song after siren song about how evil Government is and all we have to do is just get it out of your lives and everything will go away, all the problems will go away, and every year the problems get worse and worse and worse, still people get used to being told what they want to hear. And now the President is not telling people what they want to hear.

The President is saying we have to bring down the deficit, find some money to invest in jobs and education and our future. We have to be competitive with other nations. We've got to do some tough things. We have to cut spending and raise taxes. But I have given the Congress a proposal that essentially, for every dollar of deficit reduction, takes 50 cents in spending cuts, 37 or 38 cents in taxes on people with incomes above $100,000, and 12 cents in taxes on the middle class, and holds people with incomes of under $30,000 harmless. It's a proposal that puts all the money into a deficit reduction trust fund. It has led to lower interest rates already. The head of the Federal Reserve was in to see me last week saying if we could just keep going and pass an economic program that will keep interest rates down, he believes there will be a significant continuation of our economic recovery.

If someone had told you in December, as you looked forward to the Inauguration of the new President and Vice President, that by June 1st, after 3 years of recession, we would be on our way to passing a budget in record time— the first budget to be seriously considered by the Congress since 1981, presented by a President—if someone had told you that by June 1st, as a result of the serious efforts of this administration to get the economy going and bring the deficit down and to do it in a fair way so that those who benefited most in the 1980's would pay most in our efforts to do this, that we would have a 20-year low in home mortgages, a 7-year high in housing sales, unemployment under 7 percent for the first time in a year and a half, and 755,000 new jobs in the private sector, I think you would think that's a pretty good record.

And let me remind you of what else has already happened. We have passed the family leave bill so people don't lose their jobs when they have to go home for a baby or a sick parent. We overcame a filibuster in the Senate to pass the motor voter bill to open the franchise to more people. After thwarting the attempts to build a responsible global environmental policy for years, on June 4th the United States signed the Biodiversity Treaty and once again resumed its leadership in the effort to promote responsible environmental policies.

And we have introduced into the Congress a vigorous campaign finance reform bill. And I pleaded again today with the Republican Senators who voted for the same sort of bill last year not to filibuster and kill that bill this year. We need to lower the cost of political campaigns, limit the influence of PAC's, open the airwaves to honest debate, and give the American people their political system back. If you want economic reform, we need political reform;

the bill is in the Congress.

And finally, the issue which attracted so many college students to this campaign: The idea that we ought to open the doors of college education to all is making its way through the Congress in two bills. One is the national service bill, which will be marked up tomorrow in both the Senate and the House, with broad bipartisan support, to give more and more young people, tens of thousands of them, the chance to earn credit against college, to work in college, or to work off some of their college loans by giving service to their country here at home to rebuild America. And let me remind you what the other part of that pledge was, because it is also in the administration's economic program. It will save $4 billion over the next 5 years in excessive costs to the present student loan program and make a deal with the students of America. It will say anybody, without regard to income, can borrow the money they need to go to college and pay it back, not based on how much they borrow alone but on what they earn after they go to work. You don't have to pay it back until you go to work, and it's based on your earnings after you go to work. [*Applause*] Yes. Thank you. I think that's a pretty good record for 5 months, don't you?

Yesterday I had an opportunity to do something no Democrat since Lyndon Johnson has done, and that is to nominate someone to serve on the Supreme Court of the United States. I nominated Ruth Bader Ginsburg, a judge on the Court of Appeals here, whose pioneering work for women in the 1970's, taking six cases to the United States Supreme Court and winning five of them, has a lot to do with the fact that all of you will be able to grow up and compete with one another and cooperate with one another on more equal terms in so many ways. She symbolizes, in my judgment, the kind of achievement that we ought to have in this country. When somebody works hard, when they play by the rules, when they are performing at a level of excellence that deserves to be recognized, they ought to be recognized. That should be the rule for everybody in this country.

All of these things that we're talking about today in the end will produce more jobs and higher incomes, will offer more opportunity and demand more responsibility of people, and rebuild the seeds of the American community.

I am tired of our people being divided by race, by region, by income, by party, and every other way. We've got to pull this country together again. But it can only be done when people have a sense that if they work hard and play by the rules, they'll be treated fairly.

I hope that the people who have followed the work of the First Lady and all the health care task force also believe that that is going to be an effort to treat all the American people fairly. She went to the American Medical Association and reached out to the doctors. We've reached out to the hospitals. We've reached out to the people who consume health care, the people who provide it, and all the people in the middle. Let me remind you: If you really want to be able to raise your children in an environment that is free of this awful deficit, where there is still enough money left to invest in our future, we have got to bring health care costs under control, and we have got to restore to the American people a sense of family security. You cannot have millions of people waking up every morning terrified that they're going to lose their health care if somebody in their family gets sick or if they lose their jobs. We've got to do something about that if we really want to build America.

When you leave here I want to ask you to go back home and gin up some support among your people for this economic program. Call the Members of the Senate, without regard to party, and ask them to do it. Tell them we cannot afford to turn away from our obligations to bring the deficit down, increase investment in our future, keep interest rates down, and rebuild the economy.

This administration came to Washington to restore hope and jobs, to demand more responsibility but to reward people if they do it. We have got to do it. And when they ask you what we've done, give them the list I gave you. It's a pretty good list, it's a good beginning, and it justifies the faith you put in Bill Clinton and Al Gore last year. Let's keep working, and we can make the kind of a country we ought to.

Goodbye. Thank you.

NOTE: The President spoke at 5:47 p.m. on the steps of the Old Executive Office Building. In his remarks, he referred to organization officers Adam Kreisel, president; Jamie Harmon, former president; and Jenny Ritter, vice president.

Remarks at a Reception for Members of the Diplomatic Corps
June 15, 1993

Thank you very much. I want to welcome all of you again to the White House, thank the Marine orchestra for providing the wonderful music, and tell you how very glad that Hillary and I are that you could all join us this evening to renew old friendships, begin new ones, and celebrate a new and challenging era in world affairs. I'm especially glad that we could be joined this evening by the Vice President and Mrs. Gore and by Secretary of State and Mrs. Christopher and by the dean of our diplomatic corps, Ambassador and Mrs. Pondi. The gathering of the Washington Diplomatic Corps offers us a good opportunity to become better acquainted and an opportunity to reflect on the state of the world we share.

Standing here, we are within sight, just behind us, of the magnificent memorial to our third President and our first Secretary of State, Thomas Jefferson. He acutely understood the value of diplomacy to the United States. He also is the embodiment of our eternal quest for democracy. His words extolling democracy and human dignity still resonate in the hearts of all Americans and of people around the world.

None of us here this evening can say we represent a nation that has arrived at a perfect solution for the problems of human governance. There will never be a perfect solution for the problems of people who themselves are not perfect. But among the many clear facts of the era we all share is the remarkable worldwide movement toward democracy, from Russia to southern Africa, from Eastern Europe to Central and South America. There is great hope today that governments all around the world, beginning with our own, are becoming increasingly democratic and responsive to those whom they govern. And that is a hope I share. This time of hope is also clearly a time of urgency for the work we will do and must do in the months and years ahead.

Today, billions of people look to us, indeed challenge us, to make progress against one of mankind's oldest enemies: poverty, disease, ignorance, bigotry, or armed strife, and perhaps all of them at once. And they look to us as well to make progress against our new challenges, such as the spread of weapons of mass destruction and the degradation of the global environment. The urgency of these problems is evident, and the complexity and difficulty of them is truly daunting. While none of us has absolute power to make these problems disappear, each of us has far too much power to pretend that we can do nothing or that the problems do not exist. And while each of us here may hold only a piece or two of these troubling puzzles, surely we must remember that together we and the nations we represent hold all the pieces of the puzzles. So this evening, let us talk. And then tomorrow and the months ahead, let us try, for ultimately that is why our nations have sent us here.

I look forward to working with you and the great nations you represent. I thank you again for joining us tonight. And I trust that all of us will always remember that we have been given great obligations and great opportunities and that together we can make a difference for the better.

Thank you very much.

NOTE: The President spoke at 8:01 p.m. on the South Lawn at the White House.

Statement on the Death of John Connally
June 15, 1993

I was saddened to hear of the death today of former Governor and Treasury Secretary John Connally, whose life was one of service to his country and of dedication to the principles in which he so passionately believed. He will be remembered fondly by his State and his country for the work that he did and the person that he was.

Statement on International Broadcasting Programs
June 15, 1993

Today I am pleased to take an important step in the promotion of democracy by putting in place my proposal for strengthening one of the most effective foreign policy tools we have, our international broadcasting programs, for the spread of our values, our ideas, and our democratic way of life can help strengthen our security and support others around the world in their struggle for freedom.

I am pleased to be joined in this effort by the Director of the U.S. Information Agency, Dr. Joseph Duffey, and the Chair of the Board of International Broadcasting, Congressman Dan Mica. These programs have been and will be an essential part of our efforts to promote democracy and advance America's interests abroad.

Our plan proposes a proud rebirth of America's broadcasting programs to reflect this post-cold-war era. Our proposal preserves Radio Free Europe and Radio Liberty, which played such an important role in bringing freedom to Central and Eastern Europe and to the states of the former Soviet Union. It retains our other important broadcasting services, such as Voice of America, Radio Marti, and TV Marti, which have played such an important role in bringing truth and hope abroad. And our plan reorganizes our foreign broadcasting services to make them stronger, more efficient, and more capable of meeting this era's new challenges of fostering democracy and civic reconstruction.

Our victory in the cold war was due not only to the strength of our forces but also to the power of our ideas. While we acted to contain Soviet expansionism, we also sought to inspire freedom's spirit where repression reigned. Voice of America long played an important role in that effort. And to advance that same cause, 40 years ago we began a radio service, Radio Liberty, which aimed to join freedom's advocates behind the Iron Curtain with freedom-loving Americans. The founders of this and the other American radio services understood that truth is one of our most potent weapons in the fight against communism and totalitarianism.

The heroes of the cold war's end, such as Polish President Lech Walesa and Czech President Václav Havel, have often noted the importance they attach to Radio Free Europe and Radio Liberty to their own historic work on behalf of liberty and democracy. Radio Free Europe and Radio Liberty, together with our other broadcasting services, have persistently challenged the ability of repressive leaders to deny history, disfigure truth, and manipulate minds. From Havana to Ho Chi Minh City, from Pretoria to Prague, our foreign broadcast services helped prove a lesson that Americans must never forget: An informed and enlightened populace is the mightiest adversary tyranny can ever face.

Today, the challenges have changed for the states that were once held captive behind the Iron Curtain. Freedom's work is not completed. Most of these states are undergoing a difficult process of consolidating democracy's gains and building prosperity's foundations. The resulting economic and political tensions in many of these nations have bred demagogs and warlords who threaten to reverse democracy's recent progress. These states and many others still need a source of news that is reliably free from the manipulation of their own governments. No nation has more credibility to provide such news than the United States. That is why our radio and other international broadcasting services will continue to be vital as we seek to help strengthen new democracies and bolster the development of democratic institutions where they do not yet exist.

The plan we are announcing today will make those services stronger and better suited to this era:

We will continue the operation of Radio Free Europe and Radio Liberty. Many of our broadcasting services, including both of these radios and Voice of America, will undergo some changes in structure and budget.

We will create a new and independent Board of Governors that will oversee not only Radio Free Europe and Radio Liberty but the Voice of America and other foreign broadcasting services as well. Located within the United States Information Agency, it will replace and perform similar tasks to the Board of International Broadcasting. The new board, which the President shall appoint with the advice and consent of the Senate, will ensure independence, coherence, quality, and journalistic integrity in our surrogate and other broadcast services.

This new board will play an important role in determining the best mix of broadcasting functions: telling America's story to the rest of the world, reporting objective international news, providing accurate in-country news where a free press is not yet developed, and from time to time helping to transmit our Government's official views abroad.

This new board will also take a leadership role in helping to create a new Asian Democracy Radio to provide accurate local and international information for the people of Asia whose governments still suppress the truth.

In addition, we will continue the good work of our important broadcasting services aimed at speeding the arrival of freedom in Cuba, Radio Marti and TV Marti. The current structure of these entities and their boards will remain.

We will encourage the establishment of independent news-gathering and broadcast operations in the countries of Eastern Europe and the new independent states themselves, where they can be rewoven into the fabric of democratic life.

By bringing our broadcasting resources together under one roof, we can achieve substan-tial savings while at the same time providing for greater flexibility to target and shape our broadcasts as may be warranted by changing international circumstances and audience interests. We can also take better advantage of the remarkable technological developments in worldwide broadcasting that are imminent.

The plan we are announcing today was developed through the hard work and cooperation of many individuals, but I particularly want to acknowledge the leadership of Congressman Dan Mica and Dr. Duffey. I also want to acknowledge the high degree of professionalism and dedication among those individuals who have done so much to create the excellence of the Voice of America, Radio Free Europe, and Radio Liberty and our other broadcasting services. They spent years of their lives, and often risked their own lives, to bring accurate news and the message of democracy to people who have been denied both, and we will continue to rely on their excellent service.

I have said that my foreign policy is premised on promoting democracy, improving our security, and revitalizing our economy. The plan we are announcing today assists us in doing all three.

Nomination for an Under Secretary of Commerce
June 15, 1993

The President announced today that he intends to nominate Jeff Garten to be Under Secretary of Commerce for International Trade.

"As we seek to expand free and fair trade with all of our partners around the world, I am very pleased to be naming Jeff Garten to this important post," said the President. "His combination of hands-on business experience, sterling academic credentials, and previous Government service in three administrations amply equips him to tackle the challenges that lie ahead."

NOTE: A biography of the nominee was made available by the Office of the Press Secretary.

Nomination for Ambassador to Italy
June 15, 1993

The President today announced his intention to nominate Reginald Bartholomew, a senior Foreign Service officer with the rank of Career Minister, to the post of Ambassador to Italy.

"Reg Bartholomew has served our country ably in several ambassadorial positions and many other challenging assignments," said the President. "I have full confidence in his ability to maintain our strong relationship with Italy, an important ally whose friendship America highly

values."

NOTE: A biography of the nominee was made available by the Office of the Press Secretary.

Exchange With Reporters Prior to Discussions With President Sam Nujoma of Namibia
June 16, 1993

Economic Program

Q. Mr. President, there are indications that the Senate Finance Committee may not hit your $500 billion target. They may fall short because of this problem on the gasoline tax. Would you accept less than $500 billion, which is one of your main principles?

President Clinton. Well, let's see what they do. I think the—and I think ultimately the conference report will—I think the bill that the Congress ultimately votes on will hit the $500 billion.

Q. If they come out under $500 billion— usually in conference they cut things in half— it would mean that you would get less than $500 billion out of the final product.

President Clinton. I'm not—let's see what they do.

Space Station and Super Collider

Q. Are you going to have a space station decision today—super collider?

President Clinton. There is a deadline sometime in the next 3 days. I don't know exactly when it is, but there's a congressional deadline, and we're working on a statement right now.

Namibia

Q. Do you think Namibia can be a model for South Africa, Mr. President?

President Clinton. I absolutely do. I think it's a model for all of Africa. The reason I asked President Nujoma to come here and be the first African leader at the White House is because of the remarkable success that he and his country have made in promoting democracy and market economies, and they've done it in a multiethnic society with great complications. But they've managed to do it. And I think they're a real shining example for emerging democracies in Africa and on other continents as

well. I'm very excited to have him here today.

Somalia

Q. President Nujoma, are you concerned about the American role in Somalia, Mr. President?

President Nujoma. We are grateful. In fact, I have come to express our gratitude to President Clinton, although the original initial send-up of U.S. troops to Somalia was under the Bush administration—Americans—American President who did that—and when he won in the elections, continued supporting the U.N. action in Somalia, while we were sitting there, while thousands of Somalis were dying every day. And I'm glad that U.S. Government and the President Bush saw the need to quickly move the U.S. troops there to stop the starvation of thousands of Somalis and—the distribution of food to the people who were in need. And that today the Somalis seem like anybody else. And we all see how to us, before the U.S. troops in Somalia, it was terrible. So we certainly hope that other situations, President Clinton and the people of the United States were not to be tired of not making the great efforts either directly or through the auspices of the United Nations to ensure that this—instability throughout the world.

Q. Do you think Aideed, the warlord, should be arrested?

President Nujoma. If he is, he has a hand in committing a crime to ambush and to kill the United Nations peacekeepers, certainly he should be punished for that.

NOTE: The President spoke at 8:40 a.m. in the Oval Office at the White House. A tape was not available for verification of the content of this exchange.

Remarks Following Discussions With President Sam Nujoma of Namibia and an Exchange With Reporters
June 16, 1993

President Clinton. Good morning. Today I am delighted to welcome President Sam Nujoma of Namibia to the White House. Here in this city named after George Washington it is indeed an honor to welcome a person who is known as the George Washington of his country. Three years ago, the world rejoiced at the birth of a new democracy on the African continent. Millions of Americans of all ethnic backgrounds celebrated Namibia's independence as a moment of great joy and real progress. Since that moment, President Nujoma has led his country through one of the most successful political transitions in recent times. I'm particularly pleased to have the President here as the first African head of state received by my administration. It underscores my admiration for what Namibia has accomplished and my commitment to democracy in Africa and elsewhere. Namibia's President and her people clearly share that commitment. Their example inspires the cause of democracy and human rights throughout the continent.

Our meeting today coincides with UNICEF's annual Day of the African Child. A brighter future for those children is a goal we both share. In that regard, I commend the President for his concern for the future of Angola's people as well and particularly her children who have long suffered from that country's civil war. President Nujoma's efforts to bring an end to this conflict have made an important contribution to the cause of peace.

Our meeting today also comes at a time of great promise and challenge for another of Namibia's neighbors, South Africa. I know that I join President Nujoma in hoping that the transition to a nonracial democracy in South Africa can not only come soon but can be as peaceful and successful as the birth of Namibia's own democracy a short while ago. South Africa has seen far too much tragedy and despair for too long. The day is overdue when it would be a welcome time of renewal, of prosperity and hope and peace. With its exemplary experience in recent years, Namibia is truly in a unique position to further the entire region's efforts toward democratization, market economies, con-

flict resolution, and political stability. Namibia's successful transition to a stable, multiparty, multiracial, multiethnic democracy offers hope and optimism for other nations in the region, throughout the continent, and around the world.

I also want to say a special word of appreciation for the work that the President and Namibia have done in promoting their new system of government, promoting education among their people. He has just given me a gift of two games that a young Namibian citizen has developed for the children there, board games on the government and Constitution of Namibia and on the governments of the African continent. And I might point out that Namibia's Constitution also has in it a commitment to preserve the precious ecosystem of that country, a real ground-breaking statement of environmental commitment that I, again, believe will be honored by people throughout the continent and throughout the world.

Again, Mr. President, I'm delighted to have this opportunity to welcome you, a genuine hero of the world's movement toward democracy, and I look forward to working with you on the issues we have discussed and the issues we're about to discuss. The microphone is yours.

President Nujoma. Thank you, Mr. President Clinton. I am particularly grateful that you have extended an invitation to me, and through me to my people, to come and pay an official visit to your great country.

I'm grateful that your Government and your people have decided when the people of Somalia were faced with the tragedy of starvation and death, it was during the Bush administration when President Bush decided to send U.S. troops, before U.N. troops went, to put an end to the civil war and starvation of the people of Somalia. And later on, the U.N. sent its own forces which are still there.

Our continent is faced with turmoils. We have a civil war in Liberia, in Angola, in Somalia, and elsewhere. And I'm appealing to you, Mr. President, and to the people of the United States not to be discouraged but to continue to support the efforts of the United Nations in assisting those who are in need and particularly in preventing further bloodshed and loss of lives and destruction to property in areas such as Angola, Liberia, and others.

Mr. President, after a long bloody struggle for independence, during which there was massive abuse of human rights, Namibia has joined the ranks of free and democratic nations in which the right and dignity of human beings are enshrined in the Constitution of the Republic of Namibia and protected as a matter of policy practiced by my government. Over the last 3 years of its existence as a sovereign state, Namibia has scrupulously observed and upheld political pluralism which—[inaudible]—multipartisan. There are seven political parties represented in our Parliament. All these parties are quite vocal in their criticism of my government. But there has not been a single incident of harassment or intimidation of any one of these parties by my government. Tolerance and accommodation are our guiding principles in this regard.

We are committed to the rule of law, so much so that not a single one of the inhuman apartheid laws, rules, and the regulation has been replaced with undemocratic issues. Our Parliament remains the only legal institution that has the power to repeal, amend, or pass laws to regulate the political and other activities of our society. The separation of powers is the other central principle of our democracy. As such, there has been no interference by the executive branch of the government in the affairs of the judiciary. The judiciary acted independently. Although there were the draconian laws used by the colonial regime to suppress freedom of the press, there is today in Namibia no single law that puts restrictions on that important freedom of the press. Namibia has, therefore, one of the most active and critical press towards the government.

The government of Namibia is committed to a market-oriented economy. As such, there has been no interference by the government in the activities of private sector. Instead, my government is actively creating infrastructures on the joint venture basis, and we intend to leave those infrastructures to the private sector. This is one way we think we can develop our country.

The government is committed to transference in governance. In this regard, there are regular consultations between the government, the private sector, and the civil organizations on issues of national concern. We intend to uphold all these democratic principles because we are convinced that they are essential for the maintenance of peace and stability in our country, as well as for the social economic development of Namibia.

Mr. President, in order to strengthen democracy in Namibia, there is an imperative and urgent need for my government to produce tangible economic results by encouraging private sector investment in the country. Without such a result we cannot say that the future of our democracy is secure. In this connection, my government has just passed incentives which aim at promoting foreign investment. We give a guarantee of repatriation for their dividends and profit. And I hope the U.S. business community members will use the opportunity of coming into Namibia and join us, either on a joint venture basis or just purely direct investment, and make a profit and meanwhile assisting us to develop our country.

I thank you.

President Clinton. Thank you.

Economic Program

Q. [Inaudible]—about whispers that the economic plan will not hit the $500 billion target in the Senate Finance Committee. Despite repeated suggestions by you and your administration and your spokespeople that one of your principles was $500 billion, you didn't seem to clearly rule out taking anything less than $500 billion. Can you rule that out?

President Clinton. No, no. What I mean—let me make it clear. The actual plan I believe the House passed was $496 billion. If it were 497, 498, 495, something in that range, that's not—but if it's considerably below that, I think that would be a mistake. But I have no reason to believe the Senate is going well below that, and I certainly have no reason to believe that the conference report, that is, the final bill in the economic plan, would go well below it. That's the only point I was trying to make.

Foreign Assistance

Q. On a foreign aid question, international aid, some Members of Congress are now saying that because of domestic cutbacks, they may have difficulty in supporting foreign aid. And the question arises, is your Russian aid package in trouble on the Hill?

President Clinton. Well, I would hope not. The United States has some very direct interests in foreign aid. We have shown some real restraint in many of our foreign operations. Yesterday I announced, for example, the reorganization of our broadcasting operations. Even though we want an Asian democracy network along with Radio Free Europe and Radio and TV Marti and our other broadcasting efforts, we're going to reorganize and save some money there. And there are some other cutbacks in our foreign operations. But the United States still needs an aggressive program.

And I would remind you what I have said before about Russia. That is a good investment for America. We're going to make a lot of money out of that over the long run because we'll be able to do joint ventures, because American companies will be able to more securely invest there. Just since we've been working, I can see the obstacles clearing for more investments by American companies there in ways that will benefit Americans. We will see a continued effort to denuclearize the Russian nuclear force which will enable us to continue to do the same thing. So it's a very good investment for the United States. And if democracy were reversed, that would be a bad thing for the United States. So I hope it will pass, and I think it will.

Major General Harold N. Campbell

Q. Mr. President, there is a long tradition of Commanders in Chief, Presidents, firing general officers for gross insubordination. Now that the Air Force has apparently confirmed General Campbell's remarks—I know you told us yesterday you didn't take personal offense. I'd like to know why you don't feel as Commander in Chief you need to take strong action at this time.

President Clinton. Well, what I feel I need to do, sir, is to get a report from General McPeak first. And until I do that, I don't think I should say any more. This thing has proceeded in a very orderly fashion. And I was assured by the Secretary of Defense and by General McPeak that I would get a prompt and timely report, and when I do, then we'll decide what the appropriate thing to do is.

Somalia

Q. Can you clarify for us and maybe for the public what you see as the ultimate goal of the U.S.-led U.N. operation in Somalia? Is it to topple General Aideed? Is it to eliminate all his firepower, to bring him back to talks? What is it that we're doing?

President Clinton. The ultimate goal is to restore the conditions of peace which existed before the Pakistanis were murdered. The ultimate goal is to make sure that the United Nations can fulfill its mission there and continue to work with the Somalis toward nation building and to achieve the objectives that President Nujoma spoke so eloquently about in the Oval Office just a moment ago, to make sure that the human needs of the people can be met and that we can continue to make progress there.

Q. [*Inaudible*]—by his ability to turn this into something of a public relations disaster for the United States?

President Clinton. Well, I don't know that it is that. It may be—the issue is whether the Pakistani soldiers erred, and that's for the United Nations to resolve. And I'm sure that it will. But you can't have these kinds of conflicts and expect them to be brutal and illegal on one side and then have a response and expect that there will be nothing controversial about it. That is not to exonerate or to condemn. The United Nations is looking into the Pakistani conduct. There are, I must tell you, conflicting allegations about what occurred and who was actually responsible for the deaths of all the civilians there, and we need to get to the bottom of it. And if procedures need to be changed, if training needs to be tightened, if discipline needs to be imposed, then I think that can be done. But the fundamental mission of the United Nations in Somalia has not changed. And I still believe it's a very important one.

Congressional Black Caucus

Q. Mr. President, in view of the talks that you had with members of the Congressional Black Caucus, is it still necessary for you to meet with the caucus before your plan goes to the House for a vote?

President Clinton. I honestly don't know. I think I've now talked to probably 15 of them in the last several days. I think that depends, in part, on what the Senate does with the economic plan and what the understandings are about what's going to come out of the conference. So I think we'll have to wait and see what the Senate Committee does and then what the Senate actually adopts on the floor, and then we'll make a decision at that time. And of course, anytime they want to see me they know that there's an open door. But whether a meeting is necessary will depend in large measure, I think, on what the Senate does.

Thank you very much. Thank you, Mr.

Nujoma.

NOTE: The President spoke at 9:10 a.m. in the Rose Garden at the White House.

Exchange With Reporters on Campaign Finance Reform
June 16, 1993

Q. Mr. President, those Senate Republicans, sir, who are now blocking campaign finance reform even though they voted for it before, what do you say to them? I mean, this thing could go down today and be dead.

The President. The real question is what can they say to the American people. What possible reasons can they give other than pure politics for filibustering a bill which they voted for last year? And as I said, this isn't the first time it's happened. It happened on motor voter, but we were able to work that out.

But these are good people, and I think they must be searching their hearts about it and about wondering if they can even begin to defend it on anything other than raw politics. And I'm hoping that there will be some change and some breakthrough. I got some information this morning that it's at least somewhat encouraging, and we'll just keep working on it and hope we can prevail.

Q. Would you agree to give up any public funding? Would that be one way?

The President. Well, the only problem with that is, if you give it all up you have no control on the amount of money being spent. And the argument for the public funding is simply that the Supreme Court has—that unless you give candidates something, you can't condition how much they spend. So if the object is to control the cost of campaigns, as well as to limit the influence of PAC's, and to open the airwaves, it is difficult to meet all those objectives if you don't have some public funding. They're talking about the various compromises. I don't know whether they can reach one, but that's why I hope that Republicans who voted for the bill last year will think about it. It is essential to limit the overall costs of campaigns, and somehow there's got to be a public funding element to it. Thank you.

NOTE: The exchange began at 10:15 a.m. at the North Portico of the White House. A tape was not available for verification of the content of this exchange.

Remarks and an Exchange With Reporters During a Luncheon With Business Leaders
June 16, 1993

Economic Program

The President. I'd just like to make one comment to reinforce the importance of passing this economic plan. We've got interest rates now down to a 20-year low and home mortgage rates. And this new headline, "Inflation Slows, Rates Holding," that's the direction we want. We want a steady recovery. And we have got to pass this economic plan and do it in the near future to ensure that that goes on.

Let me just mention one statistic. In the first

4 months of this administration, we had 130,000 new construction jobs in this country because of low interest rates. That is the largest increase in 9 years in a 4-month period. We can bring this economy back if we pass the plan, get the deficit down, keep the interest rates down, and keep the investment flowing to create jobs in the country. And I think it is terribly important. And I just wanted to emphasize that, to impress upon the country the importance of what the United States Senate is grappling with now.

They simply have to pass this plan and go forward.

Q. Do you think that there will be a deal? And will it have a significant enough——

The President. I'm encouraged.

Q. ——energy tax to make it worthwhile?

The President. Well, it depends on what the—let's look at the final plan. You know, the Senate is going to change the energy tax, but if they have enough deficit reduction and they go to the conference committee, I think that they will come out ultimately with a bill that I'll feel good about.

Supreme Court Nominee

Q. Mr. President, on another subject, were you influenced by the letter writing campaign on behalf of Judge Ginsburg? Did that help persuade you to take another look at her?

The President. No.

Q. Did you read any of the letters?

The President. I read some of the letters that came in on behalf of many candidates. But I was unaware of any big letter writing campaign. I saw seven or eight letters for her.

Q. [*Inaudible*]—influence your decision at all?

The President. No, only that a lot of people thought a lot of her. There were also good letters for, I would say, 10 candidates that I read. I read a lot of letters that came in——

Q. The Marines that are now heading——

Campaign Finance Reform

Q. [*Inaudible*]—campaign financing—the vote on the Hill?

The President. Excuse me?

Q. On the campaign financing, have you heard any more about a possible compromise?

The President. Just what you have, that they're working on it and that they may adopt one which we would find acceptable. But I want to see what they do——

Q. [*Inaudible*]—been in communication with——

The President. A little bit. We know they're trying to work it out. And I'm encouraged. What I said in response, I think, to Andrea's [Andrea Mitchell, NBC News] question this morning, is that I think those five Republican Senators who voted for campaign finance reform last year must surely want to do it again. They know that special interests, financing, and excessive spending have really undermined the public's faith in the political process. So I think we've got a chance to get one.

Q. Mr. President, 2,200 Marines en route to the Somali coast. Can you shed any light on that?

Q. Thank you.

Q. Enjoy your lunch.

The President. Lunchtime.

Q. We don't get any.

The President. You know, I don't believe that. [*Laughter*]

NOTE: The President spoke at 12:40 p.m. in the Old Family Dining Room at the White House. A tape was not available for verification of the content of these remarks.

Letter to Representative William H. Natcher on the Superconducting Super Collider
June 16, 1993

Dear Mr. Chairman:

As your Committee considers the Energy and Water Appropriations Act for Fiscal Year 1994, I want you to know of my continuing support for the Superconducting Super Collider (SSC).

The most important benefits of the increased understanding gained from the SSC may not be known for a generation. We can, however, be certain that important benefits will result simply from making the effort. The SSC project will stimulate technologies in many areas critical for the health of the U.S. economy. The superconductor technologies developed for the project's magnets will stimulate production of a material that will be critical for ensuring the competitiveness of U.S. manufacturers, for improving medical care, and a variety of other purposes. The SSC will also produce critical employment and educational opportunities for thousands of young engineers and scientists around the country.

Abandoning the SSC at this point would signal that the United States is compromising its position of leadership in basic science—a position unquestioned for generations. These are tough economic times, yet our Administration supports this project as a part of its broad investment package in science and technology. Our support requires making sure that the project is well managed and that the Congress is informed of the full costs and anticipated benefits of the program. The SSC previously had an unstable funding profile. The stretched-out funding proposed by our Administration of $640 million in FY 94 will allow better control of project costs. The full cost and scheduling implications of this stretch-out will be complete in the early fall, and will be examined carefully by the Administration at that time.

I ask you to support this important and challenging effort.

Sincerely,

BILL CLINTON

NOTE: This letter was made available by the Office of the Press Secretary but was not issued as a White House press release.

Statement on National Service Legislation
June 16, 1993

I've always said that national service would be America at its best. In reporting out the national service legislation, today two key committees were Congress at its best as well.

National service is not about political partisanship. It is about America and the values that all of us share. National service will do so much that must be done: meeting our country's needs, paying for our children's education, and bringing all of us together in the common work of citizenship.

Democrats and Republicans joined together today in a spirit of service to support this initiative. Senator Ted Kennedy and Representative Bill Ford continued to provide exemplary leadership in moving this legislation forward on a bipartisan basis.

We've known for a long time that national service will bring Americans together. It's good to see that it brings Congress together as well.

Statement on Campaign Finance Reform Legislation
June 16, 1993

I congratulate the Senators from both parties who voted to break the filibuster of campaign finance reform. Today the Senate showed it has heard the American people's demand for change. I have long believed that we will not give the middle class the economic growth and health care reform it needs unless we also reform our political system. Today's vote is a breakthrough in the fight to give the Government back to the American people.

The stage is now set for passage of campaign finance reform legislation that limits spending, curbs the special interests, and opens up the airwaves to greater competition. Make no mistake: This legislation, while it necessarily contains compromises, will change Washington for the better.

This must be only the first step in our effort to ensure that Washington works for the national interest and not narrow interests. I urge the Senate to pass this legislation tomorrow. I urge the House to act quickly on its own campaign finance reform bill. And I urge the Congress to move forward on lobby disclosure legislation that brings the activities of lobbyists into the sunlight of public scrutiny.

Remarks to Representatives From the Central Arkansas Radiation Therapy Institute and an Exchange With Reporters
June 17, 1993

The President. Hi, kids. Please sit down. I want to welcome you all to the Rose Garden and the White House and thank you for coming. Let me say a special word of thanks to Congressman Thornton for being here with his constituents. Senator Bradford, it's good to see you.

Ladies and gentlemen, it seems like just a couple of days ago when Hillary and I were sitting at Trio's Restaurant in Little Rock, talking with Robin Armstrong about how exciting it would be to have the CARTI kids come to the White House. Well, I think maybe they thought we were kidding, but here we all are.

CARTI is the Central Arkansas Radiation Therapy Institute. It's a not-for-profit, freestanding radiation therapy center which in my home State is synonymous with treatment of people with cancer. In its 17 years of service, more than 33,000 people have received treatment there. Today I wanted to especially highlight these young people who are standing behind me. All of them have been fighting difficult battles with great courage and good humor.

I'm proud that my wife and I have long been supporters of CARTI, and our administration was when I was a Governor. In 1977, I addressed the CARTI auxiliary for the first time. And in 1979, in my first term as Governor, our State for the first time supported with State funds radiation therapy, something we continued to do throughout the course of my term as Governor. In 1991, Hillary and I hosted a Celebration of Life picnic at the Arkansas Governor's mansion for more than 1,000 cancer survivors and their families. I'm also proud to say that my mother has received treatment at CARTI and, based on the results, I'd say it's been very good treatment indeed, and I'm very grateful to them.

I'd like now to ask Robin Armstrong to come up here, she's the director of volunteers at CARTI, to introduce you to her kids.

[At this point, Ms. Armstrong introduced the children, who presented the President with several gifts.]

Campaign Finance Reform

Q. Mr. President, is the Senate version of campaign finance reform tough enough?

The President. Well, I haven't had a chance to review it entirely, but I think it is a great advance, and I'm elated that the bill is going on to the House. It reduces the influence of special interests; it lowers the costs of campaigns; it at least provides for some public funding to open the airwaves if one side in an election violates the campaign spending limits.

So I think there's some good things about it. And I'm hopeful that the House will take favorable action, and then we can come back with one common bill that will pass both Houses. Yesterday was a great day for the American people in the Congress, and I was encouraged by that.

Space Station

Q. Mr. President, on the space station, sir, if it came to it, would you be prepared to fight for it and even seek cuts in some of your investment programs to save it?

The President. Well, I have a budget program that includes the space station. We've already cut $4 billion out of it, and I intend to support it. I think it's a very important part of our overall science and technology mission. And if my budget passes, the other investments will be there, too. And if they'll pass all the budget cuts that I've put out there, I think we'll be all right. After all, we've presented 100 budget cuts of more than $100 billion. That's a pretty good clip.

Campaign Finance Reform

Q. The House Speaker is already speaking against your PAC provision in campaign finance. How strong will you fight for that?

The President. I'm going to fight for it hard; I believe in it.

NOTE: The President spoke at 4:05 p.m. in the Rose Garden at the White House. In his remarks, he referred to Arkansas State senator Jay Bradford. The exchange portion of this item could not be verified because the tape was incomplete.

Exchange With Reporters on Somalia
June 17, 1993

Q. Mr. President, are you satisfied with the level of military activity in Somalia, or do we need to add the Marines that are heading that way?

The President. Well, let me just say that for now I think I should say that I've been fully briefed on what has happened to date. I'm en-couraged, and I may have more to say about it this evening.

NOTE: The exchange began at 4:40 p.m. in the Oval Office at the White House, prior to a meeting with White House fellows. A tape was not available for verification of the content of this exchange.

The President's News Conference
June 17, 1993

Somalia

The President. Good evening, ladies and gentlemen. First I want to speak with you about a situation that all of us have followed very closely in the last week, and that is the United Nations action in Somalia.

General Powell reported to me this afternoon that this operation is over and that it was a success. The United Nations, acting with the United States and other nations, has crippled the forces in Mogadishu of warlord Aideed and remains on guard against further provocation. Aideed's forces were responsible for the worst attack on U.N. peacekeepers in three decades. We could not let it go unpunished.

Our objectives were clear: The U.N. sought to preserve the credibility of peacekeeping in Somalia and around the world, to get the food moving again, and to restore security. I want to congratulate the American and the United Nations forces who took part in this operation. In this battle, heroism knew no flag. And in this era, our Nation must and will continue to exert global leadership as we have done this week in Somalia.

Economic Program

Here at home, America is on the move. These past few days have been an impressive and important series of victories for the American people. Congress has taken major steps to limit the influence of special interests and their money in our lawmaking and in our campaigns. Congressional committees have also approved my plan for more college loans for the American people and to enable tens of thousands of them to pay their loans off by community service to their States and Nation. But the most important thing I want to discuss is the progress that is being made, the remarkable progress, on the economic plan.

Last month the House of Representatives passed the plan to reduce the deficit, the first step toward creating jobs and increasing incomes. Yesterday the Senate Finance Committee cleared the way for action by the full Senate. Make no mistake about it, this means that we are putting our economic house in order. Getting the economy back on track depends upon Congress passing this economic plan. It's necessary, it's fair, and it will work.

I propose, indeed I have insisted upon, $500 billion in deficit reduction to be locked away in a deficit reduction trust fund. We will be making historic cuts in the deficit by making historic cuts first in Government spending, then by making high-income Americans pay their fair share so middle class Americans will be treated fairly in the tax burden for a change. Seventy-five percent of the new taxes proposed fall on the top 6 percent of the American people, those with incomes above $100,000. Now, some of the critics of this plan in Congress prefer instead to cut Social Security or health care or tax benefits for elderly people just above the poverty line or working people just above the poverty line so that the wealthy won't pay so much. I'm here tonight to say to you and to the Amer-

867

ican people that I will draw the line here. We have to reduce the deficit by reducing the unfairness of the tax patterns of the 1980's and, once again, asking all Americans to do what is right and fair. We can't simply balance the budget on the backs of the old, the sick, the veterans, and those who work hard but are just barely making ends meet. It's not right.

Let's look at what's at stake here. First of all, this chart shows that if we do nothing, the inherited deficit, what we found when I came into office, will go up by 1998 to about $400 billion a year. If this deficit reduction plan is passed, we will cut $500 billion out of the deficit. That's the difference in this line and that. As all of you know and as you've pointed out in various ways in the last few weeks, I just got here. And I may have a lot to learn, but I didn't create the red line. What I'm trying to do is to change the red line and bring the yellow line in. And let me say, to get the yellow line down here, we have to bring about an affordable health care plan for every American. And that's the next big step.

But look what this deficit reduction plan alone will do. I want to emphasize once again, because there's been so much talk about taxes, that this is the most progressive tax plan this country has seen in decades. Two-thirds of the money will be paid by people with incomes above $200,000. Seventy percent of the economic gains of the last decade went to the top 1 percent of the American people. They are in a position now to pay more to help make this economy move again, and they will.

This is the monthly payment, if my full economic plan is passed, by people with incomes above $200,000. And you can see what happens here to the plan with an actual modest break for people at the bottom end of the income scale. This is a very progressive and fair plan.

Now, finally, let me say there's been a lot of talk about spending cuts here. If you look at this plan, for every $10 in deficit reduction, $5, half of it, comes in spending cuts; $3.75 of the $10 comes in tax increases on the highest income Americans, the upper 6 percent; and $1.25 comes in taxes from the middle class, people with incomes below $100,000 but roughly above $30,000. Families with incomes below $30,000 are held harmless in this program. Now, that's the way this program works. Five dollars in spending cuts, $3.75 in taxes from the wealthiest Americans, $1.25 in taxes from the

middle class. It's fair, and it's balanced. And I hope that the Congress will adopt it.

Let me say that, as I open the floor to questions, the real issue here is whether we will reverse the pattern of the last 12 years where Presidents send budgets to Congress that are never seriously considered and everybody is afraid to talk about taxes because they're afraid, no matter what happens, that will dominate the agenda; nobody will know about spending cuts, nobody will know about deficit reduction, nobody will know about fairness.

I've tried to tell the truth to the American people. And if this plan passes, you will see a continuation of what's happened already in the last 5 months: low interest rates, increased housing sales, more jobs coming into the economy. In the first 4 months of this economy alone we had a bigger growth in construction employment, 130,000 people, than we have had in 9 years. Why? Because we're serious about bringing the deficit down. That's what this last week means. It means continued victory for the American people if we can stay on this road.

Bosnia and NATO

Q. Since Vance-Owen is dead, will the United States approve of a partition of Bosnia if the three factions meeting in Geneva actually approve it? And also, isn't NATO really obsolescent now? I mean, hasn't it outlived—it can't stop the slaughter in Europe, it won't be the policeman in Europe?

The President. There's two separate questions. First of all, as you know, my preference was for a multiethnic state in Bosnia. But if the parties themselves, including the Bosnian Government, agree, genuinely and honestly agree to a different solution, then the United States would have to look at it very seriously.

Secondly, I do not agree that NATO is dead. NATO was limited in what it could do in this instance because there was no agreement among the NATO partners, first of all, and because any organization of states was limited by the rules that the United Nations imposed in the former Yugoslavia, on the arms embargo, for example. The clearest example I know to give you that NATO is not dead was provided by the leaders of all the Eastern European countries that used to be Communist that aren't anymore. When they came here a few weeks ago for the Holocaust dedication, every one of those Presidents said that their number one priority was to get into NATO. They know it will provide a security umbrella for the people who are members. And I think we need to continue to be involved in it.

Q. Who's the enemy?

The President. Well, there will be different enemies. The enemy will be anybody that threatens the security and the peace of the member nations, the values that we hold important. There are all kinds of possible problems in the years ahead, from terrorism, from the proliferation of weapons of mass destruction, from yet unforeseen developments in countries around NATO. So I don't think it's time to dismantle NATO. I think it's very, very important.

Q. Mr. President, doesn't this plan for carving up Bosnia send a dangerous message to separatists around the world, particularly in the former Soviet Union, that military aggression pays?

The President. I think that this plan shows that a civil war which has roots going back centuries, literally centuries, based on ethnic and religious differences, has not been resolved in the way that I certainly would have hoped. I think Serbian aggression has been rewarded to the extent that the United Nations resolution permitted the Serbs to send arms to the Bosnian Serbs and permitted the Croats that were next door to Croatia to have access to more weapons than the Bosnian Government, predominantly Muslim, had. And I think that was a mistake. But I don't think that anybody should overlearn that lesson. Everyone who looks at this concedes that this is perhaps our most difficult foreign policy problem.

Tax Package

Q. Mr. President, getting back to your pie chart, you said that $1.25 from the tax increase will hurt the middle class. During the campaign——

The President. I don't think it will hurt the middle class. I think that it will help the middle class because it will be a way of bringing the deficit down.

Q. A dollar and a quarter out of that tax bite will hit the middle class. In the PBS debate during the campaign, you said, "The only thing Paul Tsongas has recommended that I haven't is a 3- to 5-cent-a-year gas tax increase, and I'll be darned if I understand why we should do that without giving some offsetting tax relief." Then in "Putting People First," which was your

campaign manifesto, you said you opposed a Federal excise gas tax. I quote: "Instead of a back-breaking Federal gas tax, we should try conservation." Why are you now willing to go along with the Senate plan to keep it moving through the Senate for a gasoline tax? Do you think you can defeat it in conference, and if you do, will you try to restore the Btu tax, as your Budget Director suggested today? And if so, won't you then lose Senators Boren and Breaux and all the other opponents when it gets back to the Senate? Isn't it a no-win situation?

The President. First of all, I think it is a win-win situation if the Senate passes a budget that has $500 billion in deficit reduction, locks the spending cuts away in a trust fund, and asks the highest income Americans to pay their fair share. I think that's a win-win situation because I think we'll go to conference and we'll get a plan that will meet those criteria and will also be fairer to middle class people and to the working poor. There's also a lot of important provisions in there that I care about that will help to encourage people to move from welfare to work.

The Senate bill is very different. It does have a 4.3-percent fuel tax in it. That is very different from 3 cents a year, which is 15 cents over 5 years, or 5 cents a year, which is 25 cents over 5 years. A 4.3 percent tax, flat, is not nearly as onerous as that.

I wish we didn't have to do that. But I would remind you that after the election and before I took office, the aggregate deficit over the next 5 years was written up by $165 billion. I'm doing the best I can to use very conservative, hard-headed revenue estimates to get the deficit down, keep interest rates down so that people in the middle class can save more money than they'll pay if they refinance a car loan or a home loan or take out a business loan with lower interest rates. And tonight there will be millions of people who will either watch us or hear about this tomorrow who have refinanced their homes just since November. With interest rates dropping, they'll save more money in 1 year than they'll pay in 5 years under this program. So I still think, on balance, it is the right thing to do.

Somalia

Q. You say this Somalia operation has been a success. Does that mean that the United States and U.N. forces have captured the Somali warlord, General Mohamed Farah Aideed, and his associates, including Colonel Omar Jess? And if you haven't captured them, what are you planning on doing with them if you do capture them? Are they going to be put on war crimes tribunal or anything like that?

The President. No, they have not been arrested. The purpose of the operation was to undermine the capacity of Aideed to wreak military havoc in Mogadishu. He murdered 23 U.N. peacekeepers. And I would remind you that before the United States and the United Nations showed up, he was responsible for the deaths of countless Somalis from starvation, from disease, and from killing.

The military back of Aideed has been broken. A warrant has been issued for his arrest. If he is, in fact, arrested, then the United Nations will have to determine what appropriate action to take. That is the decision the United States is leaving to the United Nations, and one I believe we should.

Health Care Reform

Q. Mr. President, the original deadline for the unveiling of your——

The President. I'm sorry, that's a great tie. I just lost it for a moment there. I wish the American people could see this tie. [*Laughter*] Go ahead. I'm sorry.

Q. Some people believe that that's what the White House press corps is all about—[*inaudible*]—Mickey Mouse. [*Laughter*]

The original deadline for the unveiling of your health care reform plan has come and gone. When will the plan be unveiled? What are the prospects for congressional passage this year? And if you don't get it done this year, won't it be very difficult to do so next year because of the congressional elections?

The President. Let me answer the first question. The task force has made its report to me. They have given me a number of options from which I must choose before I can finalize a bill. The White House is continuing to consult with people who know a lot about this issue. My wife, as you know, went to speak to the American Medical Association just a few days ago.

Is he trying to give me some water? [*Laughter*] Let me answer the question first. Thank you, John. He always wanted to be on television. I hope his mother—[*laughter*].

My wife talked to the American Medical Asso-

ciation recently. We are consulting regularly with both the Democratic and Republican Members of Congress. She also had a long meeting with several Republican House Members just a couple of days ago.

We have determined that, first—and I, personally, am getting quite close to making the final choices from among the options there. I do not believe we can make any serious attempt to go forward with this until the economic plan and the budget is in place; then we will go forward with it. I think because of all the consultation which has been done and all the work that's been done, there's a real shot we can act on it this year. I do not share the view that there's no chance Congress will act next year, although I believe we can do it this year, because I expect a lot of Republican as well as Democratic support for this.

And I think that this issue affects the American people so deeply. There are millions of families out there who are terrified they're going to lose their health insurance; who are terrified they can't afford it; who are terrified because somebody's been sick in their family, if they have to change jobs, they'll be without it; as well as all those who are working for a living without health insurance; as well as all the businesses that are afraid they're going to go broke, that the impetus behind doing something will be very great. I think it will be good, not bad, for the American political system to act on this. So I think whenever the debate really begins in earnest, you will see the prospects of passage intensify, not diminish.

Q. If that does go over until next year, sir, will that become the issue in congressional elections?

The President. I think that and the condition of the economy will be the big issues, and whether we are actually facing up to our responsibilities in this new global economy. But that wouldn't be the worst thing in the world, except I hope and believe that the plan will pass before all that political season starts.

Welfare Reform

Q. Mr. President, Mrs. Clinton recently said that she hopes to tackle welfare reform as her next priority. Will she head the administration's welfare reform effort? And do you expect to get that done this year, too, or is that something that will have to wait until 1994?

The President. Well, that, again, is a subject

that I expect we'll have broad bipartisan support on. And I would expect that all of us will be involved in it. My wife is very interested in this because it affects children.

But let me say that the first big block of the welfare reform package is now being considered by Congress, and that is the earned-income tax credit. Most Americans don't know what that is, but basically it is a change in the Tax Code that will permit us to say to working families, if you work 40 hours a week and have a child in your house, you can be lifted out of poverty. That will remove all the financial incentive to prefer welfare to work, if we can then pass, in the health care reform, health coverage for all children, like every other country does, so we remove that incentive.

But we expect to have a welfare reform package that will literally end welfare as we know it, that will put a time limit on welfare, and after that, people who have been through the education and training programs will have to work. And I, again, would like that if it could be done this year. That will depend on how warmly embraced it is by Congress.

Let me just make one other point. The national service bill, which will provide more college loans and the opportunity to work them off with service, is moving through Congress more quickly than most people thought because we were able to get good bipartisan support and work out a lot of the details. If we can do that on welfare reform, I think we can do it this year.

Economic Program

Q. Mr. President, going back to the budget for a moment, if you manage to get the budget passed, as it seems to be heading, you will have achieved two major objectives: deficit reduction and getting the wealthy to pay a larger share of the cost of Government. But there was a third major objective that you talked about in the campaign and early on in your administration as crucial for the health of the economy, which was your investment package, your new spending that you proposed, which does not seem to be faring well in Congress at all. So you seem to be in a position where you've managed to overturn Reaganomics, but not enact Clintonomics.

So let me ask you two things about that. One is why? What's your analysis of why your spending programs have not been successful? And

second, what do you propose to do about it?

The President. If you look at the budgets, if you look at where we're going with the budgets, we had to cut back all spending in the first 2 years of this 5-year budget period to deal with the fact that the deficit was higher than we thought it would be. And I had to do that as well. But this is a 5-year budget for long-term growth of the American economy. Over the long run, we do have to increase investment. Let me also say that just because we are freezing all domestic discretionary spending for 5 years doesn't mean there aren't changes within those categories. We're cutting a lot of stuff so that we can increase investment in things like Head Start for children and job training for workers and new technologies to help convert from a defense to a domestic economy. A lot of that new investment is in there.

Secondly, I expect this bill to treat the other part of my investment budget, that is, the private sector part, quite well. I think there will be an increase in the expensing allowance for small business, which will really help small business people to hire more workers. I think there will be an empowerment zone proposal in the final bill which will finally test whether free enterprise can go into depressed cities and rural areas and put people to work and invest and start businesses. I believe it can.

I think those are the kinds of things that you will see there. I think the earned-income tax credit again will pass so that we can lift the working poor out of poverty. So I expect a big portion of the investment program to pass, and I'll be surprised if it doesn't.

Q. Mr. President, I'm surprised that for the first 4 months you came into office you were saying how bad the economy was and how important it was for your program to be enacted to grow the economy. Now, we hear you in the last week or so talking up the economy, saying how well things are going, and yet, your program hasn't passed. What are we to make of this? Why have you changed your mind about the economy?

The President. First of all, I think the economy is still bad for most Americans. But the trends are good, and the trends are plainly tied to the determination of this administration to bring the deficit down. We began to see a substantial drop in long-term interest rates after the election when Secretary of the Treasury Bentsen announced that we were going to have a serious deficit reduction plan that would include entitlement cuts, other budget cuts, tax increases on the wealthy, and an energy tax. We saw that. And every student of this, starting with the Chairman of the Federal Reserve, who's testified before Congress to this effect, has said that if we continue and pass this, we will get interest rates down. So those things have been coming down. That's why the Home Builders Association of America—not a Democratic group, presumably largely a Republican group—came from all over the country to Maryland a few days ago to endorse the economic program, because it is already beginning to bring interest rates down.

So are most people affected by the economic recovery? No. But is it a good thing that you have 755,000 private sector jobs in the first 5 months, that you have 130,000 jobs in the construction industry, the biggest gain in a 4-month period in 9 years? Yes, it is. So the point I'm trying to make is we're taking the right direction, but we've still got a lot of changes to make.

Somalia

Q. Mr. President, you said a few minutes ago that you've broken the back of the Somali warlords in Somalia. However, Mohamed Aideed is still at large. This brings to mind the same problem that happened with the previous administration with Saddam Hussein. How can you assure the American people that you're not going to get sucked into an ever-growing vortex of war in Somalia?

The President. Well, there's a big difference there. Aideed is not in control of the government of Somalia. The United Nations force is there; they're still promoting peace. They're now going to be able to deliver food, medicine, do their work, and try to help engage in the long-term process of nation building. And we never, ever, the United Nations and the United States never listed getting rid of Aideed as one of our objectives. In fact, as long as he was willing to cooperate with the United Nations, he was able to live and work in peace right there in Mogadishu.

So what happens, from now on in, will be a function of, number one, what the United Nations thinks is appropriate for his conduct to date and, number two, what he does in the future.

New Zealand

Q. Mr. President, I have an easy problem for you, and it's domestic, too.

The President. There are none. [*Laughter*]

Q. This one's very easy. A lot of Americans are not wildly pronuclear and thought the U.S. may have overreacted in past years in its very heavyhanded treatment of New Zealand. Would you consider meeting now with a New Zealand leader and discussing the situation? Isn't there some way that a compromise can be reached so you can agree to disagree but still restore the political and security relationship?

The President. I've given absolutely no thought to that question. And I'm afraid if I give an answer to it, I'll be in more trouble tomorrow than I can figure out. [*Laughter*]

Economic Program

Q. Mr. President, as you point out, your economic plan would reduce the budget deficit by $500 billion over 5 years, which is a significant improvement over what we've seen in the past. But your critics would point out that the budget deficit would continue to mount by hundreds of billions of dollars a year; and that your attack on the deficit is limited to lowering projected spending increases, rather than taking the much harder tack of making real cutbacks in the budget. Can't you do more to deal with the problem of this deficit and runaway spending?

The President. Let me have the chart again. The answer to that question—first of all, let me answer it. You asked two questions, not one. It is absolutely true that if this whole thing is adopted or any other deficit reduction plan that has been presented to date is adopted, by the fifth year the deficit starts to inch up again, and you don't get down to zero.

Now, that is true, but why is that? That is because primarily of the projected exploding costs in medical care through Medicare and Medicaid and because we have programs like Social Security and other retirement programs where people are given cost-of-living increases year-in and year-out, something that most Americans support. But the prime culprit here is Social Security—I mean, is medical costs, not Social Security. The prime culprit is medical costs. They've been going up way faster than inflation.

Now, I want to make two points. Why do we reduce the deficit only $500 billion over 5 years, even though that's a huge amount? Because it was the considered judgment of the economic team, Secretary Bentsen, Mr. Panetta, Mr. Rubin, that in a recession there was a limit to how fast you could contract the deficit, and that this would be a very rapid reduction of the deficit in a time where there's very slow economic growth around the globe. We think it will actually lead to some expansion of the economic activity. Why? Because there's so much debt built into our system at high interest rates that if people just go refinance all their homes and their business loans, it will give them a lot of cash in their pocket, and that will stimulate the economy to grow.

Secondly, it is our considered judgment that we cannot get the deficit down to zero, which is where it ought to be, until we do something about health care costs, which is why the next big piece of this administration's work is to provide a comprehensive health care plan that will bring health costs in line with inflation. If you do that, then this yellow line here, instead of going up, will keep going down. And since there is no historic precedent in America, let me ask you to go back and look what happened in Japan in the mid-seventies to mid-eighties. They had about the same size deficit we do in the mid-seventies. They decided they were going to wipe it out. They took 10 years to wipe it out, not 5. But they did it. And today, in spite of all their economic problems, they are the only major nation in a surplus position.

We can do it, too, if we do this, then tackle the deficit. And let me remind you of one other thing, in September, the Vice President's task force will make its report on reinventing Government and reorganizing the whole way the Government operates. That will give us another whole shot to deal with this issue.

Media Coverage

Q. Mr. President, John F. Kennedy once said that with the coverage he'd been getting as President, that he'd been reading it more and enjoying it less. And many other Presidents have expressed similar sentiments. Lately, sir, there have been some indications, at least, that you may be experiencing those feelings as well. Can you give us your analysis of that?

The President. I don't think I could say it any better than President Kennedy did. But let me say this: You have to do your job as you see it. And I'm going to do mine the best I can. Everybody in America knows, as I said, that I did not live and work in this city until

I became President. I knew when I came here that there would be things that I would need to learn about the processes and the way things worked. I believed then and I believe now that if I do the big things right and deal with the big issues, that eventually the other things will also work themselves out.

In the meantime, I think the most important thing is that we attempt, you and I, to create an atmosphere of trust and respect and that you at least know that I'm going to do my best to be honest with you. And I think you're going to be honest with me, and I expect you to criticize me when you think I'm wrong. The only thing I ever ask is, if I have a response and I have a side, let that get out, and we'll watch this conflict unfold. I mean, this is nothing new. President Jefferson got a rough press, too.

Haiti

Q. Sir, on Haiti, the Security Council of the U.N. has stated that they're giving Haiti until the 23d of this month before they put real tough petroleum and economic sanctions. Do you think that will solve the problem, or will we see a multinational force in Haiti as we did in Somalia?

The President. As you know, since you asked the question about Haiti, the United States is pushing for the U.N. resolution to strengthen the sanctions to include not simply a freeze on assets and lifting visas but also to include oil. I think it will make a difference. And the Members of Congress who are expert in Haitian affairs and who talk to people in Haiti believe that it will make a difference.

Secondly, I have always assumed that to really facilitate the restoration of democracy in Haiti, there would have to be some sort of multinational force there. But I would remind you that recently when that was proposed with the support of the United States, both sides rejected it. President Aristide rejected it and the de facto government rejected it, which was a disappointment to us. So we decided to go back to the drawing board, look for tougher sanctions.

In the end, since both sides distrust each other to treat each other civilly, even to keep from shooting each other, there in my judgment will never be a resolution of that as long as the main players are who they are, unless we have a multinational peacekeeping force.

Former President George Bush

Q. Mr. President, what have you been told about the plot to assassinate George Bush in Kuwait? How definitive is the chain of evidence against Iraq, and what do you plan to do about it?

The President. I have not received the final report from the FBI, and until I do I don't think I should say what I will or won't do.

U.S. Leadership Role

Q. Mr. President, in Bosnia the Europeans did not want to take action because the United States did not have troops on the ground. In Somalia, although we turned over operations to U.N. peacekeepers about a month ago and it was Pakistani soldiers who were attacked, the forces that went into action were largely American; most of the firepower was American. You were just talking about a multinational peacekeeping force in Haiti. Is the United States now being put in the role of enforcer for the United Nations? And what principles or thoughts do you bring to the table when you consider committing U.S. troops to enforce not something that may be strictly a U.S. interest but something that is the will of the international community?

The President. I think we have to ask ourselves, first of all: What are the interests of the American people? Secondly: What are the values and humanitarian concerns at stake? And thirdly: What is the price of doing what we might be asked to do?

Let me just say on Bosnia, it's not so simple as that. We didn't have an agreement, ever, about what troops would do. I pledged to the American people in the campaign last year, and I reaffirmed repeatedly, that I did not think we had any business sending troops into combat in Bosnia. I also said if there were a cease-fire and a genuine peace agreement and the United Nations had to guarantee the peace agreement, that the United States would participate. I don't think we should minimize the importance of leading the way but also setting an example.

Let me tell you, a lot of other countries—the President of Namibia was here, a very small country; they sent people to Somalia. There are people from all over the world who sent people to Cambodia in very dangerous circumstances. The Pakistanis are the people who were mur-dered in Somalia. So I think this is a very good thing. Yes, America can lead the way. But it is very moving to me to see all these other countries—Ireland sending people, putting themselves on the line, not just government employees but people working through other organizations to try to help solve these problems. There is a remarkable confluence of people trying to promote democracy and human rights and freedom and market economics. And I think that if we can leave that an acceptable price, that is in our narrow interest and it is certainly in our broader human interest.

Space Station

Q. Mr. President, now that you've made your decision about the space station, are you going to appoint a new NASA Administrator? And if you are, when?

The President. I don't have any plans at this time to do that. Let me just make a point about the space station, if I might. As you know, I have always supported the space station; I realize that some people don't. The United States indisputably leads the world in space. It is an important area of science and technology. I think it would be a mistake, after all the work we've done, to scrap the space station.

There is a $4 billion budget cut in my budget for the space station because we're going to redesign it and redesign the management system of NASA. We've brought in all of these scientists to look at it, to tell us exactly what ought to be done and exactly how this thing ought to be run, and we're going to have to make some changes. But I want to tell the American people: We need to stay first in science and technology; we need to stay first in space. We're going to be able to get more people to come in and invest with us, and we're going to have to make some very tough management decisions at NASA to get that done.

Congressional Black Caucus

Q. Mr. President, many African-American leaders have expressed their anger or extreme disappointment with the way you handled the Lani Guinier nomination and with the way you handled the Haiti situation. In addition, the Congressional Black Caucus has said it is very angry with the fact that they voted for your budget package and cast some very politically difficult votes, only to have you negotiate a watered-down package in the Senate. How would you assess your relationship right now with blacks? And what are you doing to mend fences with the Congressional Black Caucus so that they will not vote against the conference report on the budget package?

The President. Well, first of all, I did not negotiate that bill that the Senate passed. That is just inaccurate. I did not do that. And I think you know what I liked about the House bill, and you know where I have been on the issues, and you know what the principles are I've enunciated.

I think Senator Moynihan did a remarkable job to get a bill out that does have $500 billion in deficit reduction, more spending cuts and tax increases, and taxes falling primarily on upper income people. I think to that extent we ought to give him credit. But there has been no negotiations.

Secondly, and quite to the contrary, when members of the Black Caucus came to see me and asked me to pursue sanctions in the United Nations against Haiti that included oil, I examined it, and I agreed to do it. They were the first people who asked me to do it. And very shortly after the meeting I agreed to go forward. But they know, the ones who follow the Haitian developments, that even before that I offered to have the United States participate in a multinational peacekeeping force to restore democracy and to restore President Aristide, and that he rejected that. They know that's a fact.

Thirdly, I don't think my commitment to civil rights is very much open to question. And I think my actions as President and the appointments I've made and the things I've stood for document that. And I believe that over the long run the Black Caucus and the Clinton administration will continue to be very close. And I've talked to any number of them personally, recently.

Campaign Finance Reform

Q. On campaign finance reform, now that most of the public financing provisions have been removed from the Senate bill, how do you convince people that this is truly meaningful campaign finance reform? And also, will you seek at some point in the future perhaps to put that public financing back into another

measure?

The President., First let's see what the House does. Again, this is a bill you're going to have to watch come out of conference. The House will probably adopt a somewhat different bill.

But let's talk about what the Senate bill does do. The Senate bill reduces the influence of PAC's and special interests; it limits the cost of campaigns; it spends public funds, if necessary. If one party violates the spending limits, then the other party can get public funds in the form of communications vouchers so that the airwaves will be open to both parties and people can hear both sides.

So this is a vast advance over the present law in breaking the back of special interest domination of politics and elections. So I like it in that regard. Let's see what the House does. I think we can get a good bill out, and I hope both sides will vote for it.

Tax Package

Q. Mr. President, will you support the Senate's 10 percent increase in the capital gains tax?

The President. They imposed a 10 percent surcharge because there's now a difference between the capital gains rate and the income rate. And as you know, the theory of the Tax Reform Act of '86 was to level them. Let's see what comes out of the conference report. What I want is a tax system where 75 percent of the burden falls on the top 6 percent of the American people, at least that progressive. And if it is that progressive, then I'm open on the details. But I want to see what the final bill is. That's the key thing: Will the wealthy pay their fair share? Will it all be in a trust fund to reduce the deficit? And will the ratio be at least as good as the one I showed—$5 of every $10 in spending cuts; $3.75 in tax increases on upper income people, $1.25 on the middle class.

Thank you very much.

NOTE: The President's 17th news conference began at 8:02 p.m. in the East Room at the White House. Paul Tsongas was a candidate for the Democratic nomination in the 1992 Presidential campaign.

Statement on the Space Station Program
June 17, 1993

At a time when our long-term economic strength depends on our technological leadership and our ability to reduce the deficit, we must invest in technology but invest wisely, making the best possible use of every dollar. That's why I asked for a review of NASA's space station program. Concerns over rising costs and mismanagement raised serious questions about a program vital to our technological leadership. I instructed NASA to redesign the space station program in a way that would preserve its critical science and space research and ensure international cooperation, but significantly reduce costs and improve management.

NASA has met that challenge, offering a plan that will substantially reduce costs to taxpayers, improve management, preserve research, and allow the United States to continue to work with its international partners and keep its international commitments. That was the conclusion of an outstanding panel of independent experts who carefully reviewed NASA's proposals. And that is my conclusion as well, after thoroughly considering their report and recommendations. It will take not just a redesign of the space station but a redesign of NASA itself.

I am calling for the U.S. to work with our international partners to develop a reduced-cost, scaled-down version of the original Space Station *Freedom*. At the same time, I will also seek to enhance and expand the opportunities for international participation in the space station project so that the space station can serve as a model of nations coming together in peaceful cooperation. Finally, I will be directing NASA to implement personnel reductions and major management changes to cut costs, reduce bureaucracy, and improve efficiency. The national performance review team, led by Vice President Gore, has been essential in working with NASA to develop these management proposals. We are going to redesign NASA at the same time that we redesign the space station.

To make maximum use of our investments and meet the scientific goals we have set, the specific design we will pursue will be a simplified version of Space Station *Freedom* recommended by the review panel. We will work with Congress, NASA, and our international partners during the next 90 days to make the very best use of this design. The details of this proposal will be delivered to Congress within the next few days. I have asked Dr. John Gibbons, my Science and Technology Adviser, to transmit a letter to NASA with more detailed instructions for implementing this decision.

The redesigned program will capitalize on the investments we have already made. However, with its deep cuts in future development and operations costs, this redesigned program will save more than $4 billion over the next 5 years, compared with our assessments of what the real costs of funding the planned Space Station *Freedom* would have been. Over the 2-decade life of the program, these savings will grow to more than $18 billion.

There is no doubt that we are facing difficult budget decisions. However, we cannot retreat from our obligation to invest in our future. Budget cuts alone will not restore our vitality. I believe strongly that NASA and the space station program represent important investments in that future and that these investments will yield benefits in medical research, aerospace, and other critical technology areas. As well, the space station is a model of peaceful international cooperation, offering a vision of the new world in which confrontation has been replaced with cooperation.

In making this announcement today, I want to recognize the extraordinary efforts of all those involved. Vice President Gore and Dr. Gibbons assembled an outstanding team of experts, led by Dr. Charles Vest, president of MIT, who assessed several cost-saving options prepared by NASA. This review included not only the design of the space station but also the structure and management of NASA itself. Their work and the work of all those at NASA involved in this project has been invaluable.

Statement on Senate Action on Campaign Finance Reform Legislation
June 17, 1993

Today's vote is a victory for the American people and a setback for the special interests. Government will only serve the middle class if Washington works for the national interest and not narrow interests. By breaking the filibuster and overwhelmingly passing campaign finance reform legislation, the Senate has answered the call for change. This legislation's sponsors and supporters deserve our gratitude.

This bill will end the days when candidates could crush their opponents with unanswered spending by setting voluntary spending limits for candidates. It severely limits PAC's and bans contributions from lobbyists to the lawmakers they contact. It ends the abuses of the "soft money" system. I continue to believe that we should do more to open up the airwaves to candidates. But all in all, this legislation is comprehensive, real reform.

The process of political reform should now move forward quickly. I urge the House of Representatives to enact the strongest possible legislation. Previous Presidents have blocked and even vetoed political reform. I look forward to signing it.

Statement on the Voting Rights Act of 1965
June 17, 1993

The Voting Rights Act of 1965 has been a topic of substantial discussion in recent days. I want to make absolutely clear my full support for the act.

The Voting Rights Act is central to our Nation's efforts to eradicate racial discrimination and secure equal opportunity for all Americans. As I said last month upon signing the motor voter bill, the Voting Rights Act is part of a great tradition of laws that have widened the circle of liberty to encompass more and more of our citizens. This administration remains unwavering in its commitment to effective enforcement of the act and the Nation's other civil rights laws.

The Voting Rights Act was adopted to give reality to the 15th amendment's guarantee of the right to vote, the most basic right of a democracy. When first adopted in 1965, the act responded to long-entrenched barriers that systematically denied voting rights to African-Americans. As more subtle forms of disenfranchisement came to be employed, the Congress, with bipartisan agreement, strengthened and extended the Voting Rights Act in 1982. The Voting Rights Act offers two major protections: It imposes a nationwide prohibition of any electoral process that results in discrimination, and requires that certain specially covered jurisdictions obtain administrative or judicial preclearance before implementing voting changes.

I fully and enthusiastically support Attorney General Janet Reno, and the attorneys of the Civil Rights Division of the Department of Justice, in their efforts to enforce vigorously the Voting Rights Act. Where the Voting Rights Act is violated, this administration will continue, as it has in pending Supreme Court litigation in which the Department of Justice has filed briefs, to seek effective relief by applying the full range of remedies available under law, including remedies that have previously been employed by the Department of Justice or approved by the courts. I also look forward to working with Attorney General Reno and Members of Congress to enact legislation, as needed, to clarify and reinforce the protections of the Voting Rights Act.

In 1965, President Johnson hailed the Voting Rights Act as "a triumph for freedom as huge as any victory that has ever been won on any battlefield." Effective enforcement of the Voting Rights Act will allow us to continue that triumph. Inclusion of all Americans in the political process is necessary if we are to work together as communities, States, and a nation to address the difficult challenges that confront us all.

Message to the Congress Transmitting the Latvia-United States Fishery Agreement
June 17, 1993

To the Congress of the United States:

In accordance with the Magnuson Fishery Conservation and Management Act of 1976 (Public Law 94–265; 16 U.S.C. 1801 *et seq.*), I transmit herewith an Agreement between the Government of the United States of America and the Government of the Republic of Latvia Concerning Fisheries off the Coasts of the United States, with annex, signed at Washington on April 8, 1993. The agreement constitutes a governing international fishery agreement within the requirements of Section 201(c) of the Act.

United States fishing industry interests have urged prompt consideration of this agreement to take advantage of opportunities for seasonal cooperative fishing ventures. I recommend that the Congress give favorable consideration to this agreement at an early date.

WILLIAM J. CLINTON

The White House,
June 17, 1993.

Remarks on the Nomination of Doris Meissner To Be Immigration and Naturalization Service Commissioner and an Exchange With Reporters
June 18, 1993

The President. Thank you all very much for coming. I want to say a special word of thanks to the Members of Congress who are here from both parties, demonstrating a strong bipartisan interest in the subject of immigration. I also want to recognize Admiral John Kime, the Commandant of the Coast Guard, and Admiral Robert Nelson, the Vice Commandant, thank them for coming. And in a moment I'll recognize a couple of other people.

The immigration issue poses real problems and challenges and, as always, provides great opportunities for the American people. It is a commonplace of American life that immigrants have made our country great and continue to make a very important contribution to the fabric of American life. In one of our counties, Los Angeles County, there are today people from 150 different national and ethnic groups. But we also know that under the pressures that we face today, we can't afford to lose control of our own borders or to take on new financial burdens at a time when we are not adequately providing for the jobs, the health care, and the education of our own people. Therefore, immigration must be a priority for this administration.

I am pleased to announce today my intention to nominate Doris Meissner for the position of Commissioner of the United States Immigration and Naturalization Service. I want to say that this nomination has the full support of Attorney General Janet Reno, who could not be here today because of a previous commitment to be at the FBI Training Academy at Quantico. But she has very strongly endorsed and supported Ms. Meissner's nomination.

She has an extensive background in immigration affairs, bringing a unique combination of management and policy experience. She served as Acting Commissioner and in other senior positions in the Immigration and Naturalization Service between 1981 and 1985. She served at the Department of Justice as Deputy Associate Attorney General from 1977 to 1980, and in a variety of other policy positions at the Justice Department where she began as a White House fellow in 1973. Since 1986, Doris Meissner has been senior associate and director of immigration policy project of the Carnegie Endowment for International Peace. She's authored numerous articles on a wide variety of immigration issues and has testified before Congress on many legislative proposals. First and foremost, she is committed to the effective management of the INS and the vigorous and fair enforcement of our country's immigration laws. Her nomination signals my efforts to ensure that we meet the immigration challenges facing our Nation and the world.

Before I call Doris up here, I also want to announce that I have today approved a plan of action to combat the problem of organized crime syndicates trafficking in alien smuggling. The plan involves the coordinated efforts of 12 departments and agencies of the United States Government working in coordination with the White House Domestic Policy Council and the National Security Council. It responds to a major crime problem which has existed for almost 2 years but to date has been dealt with only on an ad hoc basis.

Alien smuggling is a shameful practice of unspeakable degradation and unspeakable exploitation. Migrants and their families must pledge up to $30,000 to come to the United States. Criminal syndicates load these immigrants on ships under conditions that run the gamut from deplorable to life-threatening. The gangs then place arriving immigrants in slave-like conditions of indentured servitude to pay off their debts. Deterring this transport in human cargo and traffic in human misery is a priority for our administration.

The plan I have approved addresses this smuggling in multiple ways. We will strengthen law enforcement efforts in the United States by expanding our investigative efforts and broadening our prosecution strategies. We will go after smugglers and their operations at the source. We will take measures to interdict and redirect smuggling ships when they are in transit. We will expedite procedures for processing entry claims and for returning economic migrants smuggled into the United States. And we will ask Congress to pass legislation to expedite this process further. We will also ask the Congress to increase penalties for alien smuggling to allow us to use the Racketeer Influenced and Corrupt Organizations Act to go after these smugglers and to permit us expanded authority to seize their assets.

With this plan, the United States signals its abhorrence of the trafficking in human beings for profit and its determination to combat this illegal activity. At the same time, we reaffirm our commitment to protect bona fide refugees under our law. This is a good beginning, but there is much more to do.

I'd like now to invite Doris Meissner to say a few words. But before I do, I'd like to ask her husband, Charles, and her daughter, Christine, to stand and be recognized. It's nice to have you with us today.

Chairman Brooks, I want to thank you and all the Members of Congress who are here. And I'd like to now introduce our designate to run the Immigration and Naturalization Service, Ms. Doris Meissner.

[At this point, Ms. Meissner made brief remarks.]

The President. If you have any questions of Ms. Meissner or me, we'll take a couple.

Alien Smuggling

Q. Mr. President, you mentioned that this problem began or has been going on for 2 years. Was there some event that precipitated it?

The President. I just wanted to make it clear that we were aware of this problem before the ship came. And I don't know what event precipitated it. There have been a lot of speculation about the Chinese immigrants themselves and the irony that—it may be that the increasing prosperity in China may have something to do with this because more people at least have the ability to move into the coastal cities and to have a little bit of money to make that first step. No one knows exactly why this happened. We've heard that it may be because certain ships have been diverted from other things, because they couldn't do what they were doing before and now are more available to bring immigrants here. There are all kinds of speculations about what caused it, but that's not important. What's important is that we try to do something about it and bring it to an end.

Q. Mr. President, the Chinese problem is a——

The President. The House Members have to have a vote.

Q. ——Mexican border. What are you going to do about that?

The President. The House Members have to be excused to go to vote.

Go ahead, Sarah [Sarah McClendon, McClendon News], I'm sorry. You're next.

Mexico

Q. Sir, I want to point out to you that for generation after generation, Democrats and Republicans have refused to face the problems of immigration on the Mexican border. And that's where people come through, not only from Mexico. A thousand a night at least get by at one place south of San Diego alone. And that's got to be faced up to. But people come from all over the world to Mexico to come in here. And they don't have to pay $30,000, they just pay the—[*inaudible*]—about $500.

Ms. Meissner. Well, obviously we have a—between the United States and Mexico is a border between countries with the largest income differential of any countries that have a single border. So there's going to be an effort for people to come to the United States. We obviously need to do border control, but we also need to be thinking about development to our south. And the NAFTA that is going to be debated in the next couple of months is a very, very important step in that direction, and I hope that we can support it.

The President. We did not rehearse this, but let me, if I might reinforce that. We have asked for more border guards. I asked for several hundred more in the jobs package that I asked the Congress to pass earlier. And we can do a better job. I think that's clear. We can do a better job if we have more people. But in the end, I think what Ms. Meissner said has to be looked at, the pure economic realities.

One of the arguments for having the right kind of trade agreement with Mexico is to raise incomes in Mexico and create more jobs there. They'll not only buy more of our products, but the incentive to leave home to make a decent living for one's family will go down dramatically. So that's another one of the very important benefits of NAFTA. And I swear we did not coordinate our responses. I didn't know she was going to say that.

Enforcement

Q. Do you think that employer sanctions should be made in order to control better this kind of problem in the United States?

Ms. Meissner. I believe that employer sanctions is an important enforcement tool. I think when the Congress passed employer sanctions in 1986, it realized, and everybody else who was involved in the debate realized, that it was simply a first step at the kind of workplace enforcement that we would need. We may need to look at ways to perfect the law. We certainly need to look at whether we're enforcing it as effectively as we can.

Q. Mr. President, a couple of questions. How much is this going to cost, if you know? And on your list of priorities, and I know you have a lot, where do you place this? Is this close to the top or in the middle or someplace else?

The President. Keep in mind we have a large budget already, and we have a wonderful resource in the United States Coast Guard and a lot of other people who are working in the Immigration and Naturalization Service. So I don't have a price tag for what else it might cost. But let me say that this basically relates to everything else we're working on. What our immigration policy is will affect our ability to create jobs for our people, will affect our ability to provide health care to our people, may affect our ability even to pass a health care program in the United States Congress. This issue will be a priority because it is so integrally a part of so many of the other things that we're dealing with in our effort to revive the American economy and strengthen the lives and the security of the people who live here.

Thank you.

NOTE: The President spoke at 10:49 a.m. on the South Lawn at the White House.

Exchange With Reporters Prior to Discussions With King Hussein of Jordan
June 18, 1993

Middle East Peace Process

Q. Your Highness, what do you think are the prospects for peace soon? Does it look any better to you now?

King Hussein. I believe that some possible ground has been covered. We are still a long

way from getting there, but there is no other alternative. I believe that we must do everything we can not to let the moment pass without——

Q. What's the main stumbling block?

King Hussein. It would complicate, possibly, to attempt to try to explain what the main stumbling block is. I believe that it's one of, hopefully, the Palestinians being able to feel that they are able to speak for themselves and contribute their share in shaping the peace that is comprehensive, that is so very, very important to all of us.

Q. Do you think Israel will be amenable now to recognizing a Palestinian state?

King Hussein. I don't know what Israel would accept or otherwise, but I believe that there is one important element, and that is that people on either side of the divide feel that this is the moment and are determined to continue to move ahead until a comprehensive just peace is—that future generations can enjoy.

Q. That's a pretty subdued tie you have on, Mr. President.

The President. Well, it's not Mickey Mouse. [*Laughter*]

[*At this point, one group of reporters left the room, and another group entered.*]

Q. Mr. President, how do you feel about to-

day's visit and relations with Jordan?

The President. I'm very pleased that the King is here. I have looked forward to this visit for a long time. And I am very, very impressed by the progress which has been made in Jordan moving toward economic reforms, moving toward democracy. And also I am very grateful for the support of the peace process that the King has demonstrated so consistently. I have the feeling that maybe all the parties have now concluded not that they have no difference but that there is no alternative to peace. And if we do see this thing through and find some resolution, that will be in no small measure because King Hussein for so many years has persistently pushed us toward peace. And the United States will do what it can to help achieve that.

NOTE: The exchange began at 11:56 a.m. in the Oval Office at the White House. A tape was not available for verification of the content of this exchange.

Exchange With Reporters Following Discussions With King Hussein of Jordan
June 18, 1993

Budget Proposal

Q. Do you like the budget?

The President. I think in the end, I like it a lot. It's not done yet. We're not even through the Senate yet. We've got a lot of work to do.

Q. Mr. President, what's your reaction to the reprimand accepted by General Campbell?

Q. What do you think about—for Campbell?

[*At this point, one group of reporters left the room, and another group entered.*]

Discussions With King Hussein

Q. What did you accomplish today in the meeting, sir?

The President. Talked a lot about the peace

process. I learned about the King's position; he learned about the United States position. We talked a little about Iraq and the imperative nature of continuing to enforce those sanctions and being very tough on them. We talked about his efforts to democratize the country and to modernize the economy and deal with all the things he's dealt with over the last 40 years and especially the last 3. It was a very, very good meeting.

NOTE: The exchange began at 1:50 p.m. at the Diplomatic Entrance at the White House. A tape was not available for verification of the content of this exchange.

Statement by the Press Secretary on the President's Meeting With King Hussein of Jordan
June 18, 1993

President Clinton and King Hussein of Jordan held a productive meeting which lasted for 2 hours. The two leaders discussed a wide range of issues, including their shared commitment to achieving tangible progress in the Middle East peace process this year.

President Clinton reaffirmed that the United States is committed to serving as a full partner and honest broker in these historic negotiations. He stressed that negotiations are the only viable path to achieve a comprehensive, just, and lasting peace between Israel, the Arab states, and the Palestinians.

The two leaders discussed the importance of strong enforcement of United Nations sanctions on Iraq. The two countries will continue to work closely in pursuit of that goal.

The President and King Hussein also discussed Jordan's progress toward democratization and respect for human rights. President Clinton expressed his support for the courageous efforts of King Hussein in this regard, and noted that this work will encourage long-term stability and prosperity in Jordan.

Message to the Congress Transmitting the Report of the National Endowment For the Humanities
June 18, 1993

To the Congress of the United States:

In accordance with the provisions of the National Foundation on the Arts and Humanities Act of 1965, as amended (20 U.S.C. 959(d)), I transmit herewith the 27th Annual Report of the National Endowment for the Humanities (NEH) for fiscal year 1992. This report was prepared by, and covers activities occurring exclusively during, the previous Administration. It does not necessarily reflect the policies or priorities of my Administration. The Annual Report for 1993, which I will submit next April, will reflect the goals and vision of my Administration for the NEH.

WILLIAM J. CLINTON

The White House,
June 18, 1993.

Nomination for Ambassadors to Iceland and Uruguay
June 18, 1993

The President today announced his intention to nominate Foreign Service officer Parker Borg to be the U.S. Ambassador to Iceland and historian Thomas Dodd to be Ambassador to Uruguay.

"These two outstanding individuals will make fine representatives of our Nation," said the President. "I am very glad to be making these announcements today."

NOTE: Biographies of the nominees were made available by the Office of the Press Secretary.

Nomination for Posts at the Department of State
June 18, 1993

The President announced his intention today to nominate Ed Djerejian, a senior member of the Foreign Service, to be Ambassador to Israel. In addition, Secretary of State Christopher has asked Dennis Ross to be his Special Middle East Coordinator.

"This is a crucial time for the Middle East peace process," said the President. "It is imperative that the United States have talented diplomats working to ensure that the process continues to move forward. Ed Djerejian and Dennis Ross have my complete confidence."

NOTE: Biographies of the nominees were made available by the Office of the Press Secretary.

Remarks on the 40th Anniversary of the Newport Jazz Festival
June 18, 1993

Thank you very much. I can say this, that when she's listening to my jazz she wishes I would practice more. [*Laughter*] I am delighted to have all of you here at this, our first televised concert from the White House. Both Hillary and I are very excited and pleased to welcome you here. It's especially appropriate that we should be together here at America's house to celebrate that most American of all forms of musical expression, jazz.

One of the greatest things that ever happened to jazz was a simple 2-day event that took place in Newport, Rhode Island, way back in 1954. The Newport Jazz Festival was an immediate hit, and it grew and grew. It captured the imagination of young musicians all across the country and eventually across the world. No event has done more to nurture the careers of jazz artists; none has done more to thrill and delight jazz fans. The festival's influence has been truly profound, inspiring more than 2,000 other jazz festivals every year all around the world. Indeed, the French Government recently recognized that impact when it awarded the festival's producer the Legion of Honor.

Tonight we're having our own White House jazz festival as a special tribute to the 40th year of Newport Jazz and, of course, to its founder and its fine producer, George Wein. George, stand up. Where are you? There he is.

You know, jazz is really America's classical music. Like our country itself and especially like the people who created it, jazz is a music born of struggle but played in celebration. This

unique musical and cultural art form is now more than a century old. It's paused periodically in its evolution to give us ragtime and boogie-woogie and swing and bebop and cool and free jazz and fusion, only then to continue its restless rebirth into forms that have yet to be named or even imagined. Original and enduring, adapting and growing, jazz is simply one of our Nation's greatest creations.

Many good people swing to the sound of jazz and rally to its cause, and one of them is our host tonight, the son of a jazz legend. In his father's name, he's established an institute which introduces young people to the beauty of jazz and encourages up-and-coming jazz musicians. And he is a brilliant musician in his own right and a good friend of the President and the First Lady. Ladies and gentlemen, please welcome Thelonious Monk, Jr.

[*At this point, Mr. Monk hosted the musical program.*]

We want to say a wonderful, heartfelt, happy thank-you to all the performers; thank you to Thelonious Monk, Jr., the Thelonious Monk Institute of Jazz, and its executive director, Tom Carter; and a very, very special thank-you to George Wein, the producer of the Newport Jazz Festival. Thank you for the wonderful tradition that you have created.

You know, if you look at the different ages and backgrounds of all the gifted performers assembled on this stage, we're reminded once again that jazz is a true reflection of the American people, a music of inclusion, a music of democracy, a music that embraces tradition and the freedom to innovate. That's a good thought to end on.

Thank you all for coming, and good night;

bless you.

NOTE: The President spoke at 7:45 p.m. on the South Lawn at the White House. He was introduced by Hillary Clinton.

The President's Radio Address
June 19, 1993

Good morning. For 5 months I've been fighting hard for a national economic strategy to build prosperity for all our people. And now America's on the move.

Just this week we scored several significant victories for the American people in the Congress. The Senate passed a campaign finance reform bill that limits the influence of special interests and their money in our lawmaking, and in our campaigns. Congressional committees have adopted my plan to make college loans available to all students at lower interest rates and better repayment terms and to make it possible for tens of thousands of them to pay off those loans through national service to their communities. Most important is the remarkable progress being made on the economic plan to increase growth, jobs, and incomes through bold deficit reduction. Last month the House of Representatives acted courageously to pass this plan, and now the path has been cleared for action by the Senate because the plan has passed out of the Senate Finance Committee.

Make no mistake about it, Washington is finally moving to put our economic house in order. If we want to get the economy back on track, Congress must pass this plan. It's necessary, fair, and it'll work.

When I first presented this growth plan back in February, the financial markets took it seriously, and we saw real improvements in economic fundamentals, like interest rates. We now have the lowest long-term interest rates in 20 years. Mortgage rates are at a 20-year low, and now middle class homeowners are refinancing their mortgages, and some are receiving more than $2,000 in annual savings when they do. Housing sales are at a 7-year high, and employment in the construction industry is up 130,000 people in just the last 4 months. That's the largest increase in 9 years. Inflation is stable,

and more than three-quarters of a million new jobs have been added to the economy in the first 4 months of our administration. Ninety percent of them are in the private sector. And unemployment is finally below 7 percent for the first time in a year and a half.

What explains these optimistic signs? For the first time in many years, we're making tough choices. Our plan makes historic cuts in Federal spending, $250 billion in spending cuts in more than 200 specific programs. We cut virtually every part of the domestic, defense, and foreign aid budgets, including agriculture, veterans, Federal retirement and compensation plans, Medicare, not because we want to but because we have to and because it's the right thing to do.

Because our program is balanced and fair, it also raises taxes to avoid unfair cuts that will damage the elderly, the working poor, and other vulnerable people in our country. But unlike the 1980's, when the rich paid less and the middle class paid more, we're asking the wealthy to pay their fair share to give the middle class a fair shake. Seventy-five percent of the taxes are paid by those in the upper 6 percent of income brackets, those who exceed $100,000 in annual income. Two-thirds of these taxes are paid by individuals whose incomes exceed $200,000. Under this plan, the very wealthiest Americans will pay an additional $1,900 a month, while middle income families will pay only $17 more a month by 1998 and much, much less between now and then.

If you're keeping score, this is how the program works: For every $10 in deficit reduction, we cut $5 in spending, raise $3.75 in taxes from the wealthiest Americans, and ask the middle class for $1.25. Let me say that again: For every $10 in savings, we cut $5 of spending, ask the wealthiest Americans for $3.75, and the middle class for $1.25. This cuts the deficit by $500 billion with all the savings locked up in a trust fund. And unlike some plans, we don't cut the cost-of-living adjustment for Social Security recipients.

Most importantly, if we pass this plan, there will be a big payoff down the road for Americans who work hard and play by the rules. A lower deficit and a healthier economy means more jobs, lower interest rates, more opportunity, and more rewards for your hard work. That's why I'm fighting for this change.

But let's face it, change is hard, and some people do fine with gridlock instead of growth. And nobody likes to make the tough decisions. There are thousands of lobbyists here in Washington who oppose the plan, hoping to force hard-pressed Americans to pay more or give up more so their powerful clients can pay less. Some of the Senate opponents fight the plan because it really raises taxes more on wealthy Americans than they think we should. And some of our adversaries, they don't even have an alternative. They're just playing politics with your economic future, screaming old slogans like "tax and spend" even though they helped to run our debt from $1 trillion to $4 trillion over the last 12 years and helped to bring about a $300 billion annual deficit that I found when I moved to Washington to go to work for the first time back in January. The stakes are just too big to play political games. If our growth plan gets caught in a web spun of gridlock and greed, this historic moment for America to get its fiscal house in order could slip away. You and I can't let that happen.

If Senators are going to oppose my growth plan, they ought to answer these questions:

What programs would you cut more deeply? We've already cut more than 100 programs more than $100 million each. Where are your tough choices? Will you ask the wealthy to pay their fair share, or will you put a higher burden on the middle class? Do you have a real, comprehensive plan to reduce the deficit by $500 billion? Maybe our opponents should listen to Ted Turner's advice: Lead, follow, or get out of the way.

It's time to get America moving again. People don't want 4 more years or 4 more months or 4 more days of politicians telling them what they want to hear while all our problems get worse. It's time instead to make a permanent commitment to a growing economy that produces jobs and a higher standard of living for our people. That's what we're doing.

Where once there was too much spending, there's now a plan with real and deep spending cuts. Where once there were no investments in our people, there's now a plan for college loans, job training and national service, Head Start, and new technologies for those who are losing their jobs due to defense cutbacks. Where once there were tax breaks for the wealthy and tax hikes for the middle class, now there's a plan for tax fairness for all Americans.

Working together, we're making America work again and helping this economy to create jobs again. And soon, if we stay together, we'll make it more prosperous for ourselves and for our children.

Thanks for listening.

NOTE: This address was recorded at 6:45 p.m. on June 18 in the Roosevelt Room at the White House for broadcast at 10:06 a.m. on June 19.

Remarks at the Northeastern University Commencement Ceremony in Boston, Massachusetts
June 19, 1993

Thank you very much. I must tell you, I have marched in many of these processions over the years. I don't think I ever marched in one that made me any happier than when we were coming down this line and all of you were giving me the "high five." And when we arrived here on the podium, I turned to Senator Kennedy,

and I said, "Those are the people I ran for President to help. I'm glad to see them here today."

I want to say a special word of thanks to President Curry, to the faculty and staff for the honorary degree and the invitation to come. To Senator Kennedy and Senator Kerry, Congressman Frank and Congressman Meehan, to Mayor Flynn, and to my good friend Governor Dukakis, and all others who are here, but especially to the graduates and their families, I am so pleased to be here in the Boston Garden with you here today. I'm also glad to be here with someone who's spent a lot of time thinking about the graduates' future, the Secretary of Labor, Bob Reich, whose wife, Clare Dalton, is on the faculty here at Northeastern. Glad to be here.

I know it's warm, and I don't want to prolong the introductory remarks, or any of them, for that matter. But since President Curry mentioned Senator Kennedy's role in student financial aid, I can't help but note that in the last few months, of all the Members in the United States Congress, one stands out at having achieved a phenomenal amount of support from Republicans and Democrats for initiatives to make this country a better place. For out of Senator Kennedy's committee, with big votes from Republicans and Democrats, have come the Family and Medical Leave Act of 1993, to give people the right to have a little time off when a baby is born or a parent is sick; a bill that will require the National Institute of Health to give far greater attention than ever before to issues affecting women's health and their children's; a bill that will enable us to immunize all the children of this country against serious childhood diseases; a bill that will set national academic standards for our public schools, to deal with what the former speaker said we needed to do before you get to college; and finally, the national service and student loan bills, which will open college education to all Americans by providing loans on more generous terms and allowing them to be repaid as a percentage of your earnings, no matter how much you borrow, so you'll never go broke repaying your loans, and allowing more young people to pay them back with service to their communities. All of that came through Senator Kennedy's committee.

I want to congratulate all of you who've survived this 5-year program, and also I want to congratulate you on surviving the Boston traffic jams. That's the second greatest example of gridlock in the United States. [*Laughter*]

I want to say, too, that I treasure a degree from an institution that really exalts public service, not only by elected officials but by private citizens as well. This year I received more than 200 invitations to address graduating classes. But Northeastern stood out to me because I believe you are a symbol of the American dream, built on education and work and community service, blending work and learning, having partnerships with the private sector in this wonderful community of yours to build people, which is, after all, the only real product America has ever been able to depend upon.

When I was working so hard to put together this provision of student aid to make college loans available to all on lower interest rates and better repayment terms and to let more people repay their loans through community service either before or during or after college, it was students like you that I had in mind: hard-working, good people from either middle class families that could otherwise not afford a college education or from poorer families who want to work their way into a better life. You symbolize the very thing that America has always been about and that we must today get back to if we're going to revitalize this great Nation. And I'm very proud to be here with you today.

I can also tell you that I was deeply impressed by Doug Luffborough, and if I could sing like him I wouldn't be up here today as President. I read an article about Doug and his mother and his family and his trials in working his way through college before I came here. In the article he said he planned to invite himself and his mother to the White House. [*Laughter*] Well, I'm going to beat him to the punch. I'd like for Doug and his mother to come to the White House.

If any man in America knows what having a good, hard-working, strong, loving, and disciplining mother can mean, I certainly do. I know it can make all the difference in the world, as it did for Doug and as it has for me. I think it would be appropriate just sort of as a symbol of all the parents who are here if Doug's mother, Mrs. Elsa Luffborough Mensah, would stand up. I think she's over there. Stand up! Give her a hand. See her up there in the white dress? [*Applause*]

I must tell you, ma'am, that there are a lot of people of great and famous achievement who will never know the pride you must have felt when your son stood up here earlier today. I thought it was unbelievable, and I appreciate what you did.

To all of you graduates here at Northeastern, because this is the largest co-op school in the

Nation, you are a breed apart. By having the chance to work for 2 years in your field as you have earned your degree, you have experienced a world that many others of your counterparts all across America only anticipate when they walk up and get their degree. You embody the growing unity in this country between work and learning, based on the clear understanding that the average American must now change work eight times in a lifetime and what you earn depends upon what you can learn. Still, even with the jump your co-op education in this fine place has given you, some of you must be wondering whether you'll be able to find the right job or any job.

I came here to tell you something very simple and straightforward: You have done your part, and you deserve the opportunity to have that job and to make a better life for yourself.

For years and years, the challenges of the global economy and our inadequate responses to them have put unbelievable pressure on middle class families and middle class values. Most people have worked harder for less and paid more for education, for health care, for housing. For most of the 1980's, those with less than 2 years of post-high school education actually saw their incomes drop as they worked longer and longer work weeks. And in the last couple of years, even college graduates have begun to have a difficult time finding good jobs with growing incomes.

Still, we know what works. We know that in this global economy, a good education works. We know that investment in new technology works. We know that when business and workers and Government are cooperating for high productivity, that works. We know that grassroots efforts to build strong and safe communities and to give every person a chance work.

A lot of Americans have worked on that, but we have not done it as a nation. For more than a dozen years we have spent too much time from the top down having our leaders just tell us what we want to hear, that taxes are bad and somebody else's spending is bad, but spending on you is good. And so we've seen the debt go from $1 trillion to $4 trillion, our deficit go from $74 billion to $300 billion a year. And unbelievably, our investment at the national level in the things that make us a rich country has not even kept up with inflation: investment in education, in environmental cleanup, in the new technologies that will permit

us to convert from a defense-based to a domestic high-tech economy. We have not done what we ought to have done there. We have underinvested and still seen much of our future eroded by a massive debt.

We have come to a time, my fellow Americans, when we have to bring to our public life as a nation the same brutal honesty that Doug's mother brought to him when she refused to let his difficult circumstances be an excuse not to succeed. We have to take as a people the same kind of advice your student speaker gave to you. Let's don't say, "I could have. I should have. I would have." Let's say, "We can. We will." And let's get about doing it.

We are beginning to move this country, taking down the obstacles to progress and prosperity, putting our economic house in order, moving toward providing a national plan to provide affordable, quality health care to all of America's families and children, preparing ourselves to compete in the global economy. We have a long road to travel, but we see some hopeful signs.

Because of the progress of the economic plan that I have presented to the Congress to bring down our deficit and increase investment in our people, interest rates have dropped to a 20-year low. That means that when you bring down the deficit and bring down interest rates, you free up money to be invested in productive things. What do lower interest rates mean? They mean lower home mortgages. They mean lower business loans. They mean lower consumer loans and car loans. They mean money that can grow the economy and create jobs. And it also means the Government doesn't have to spend so much of your tax money paying interest on the debt and can pay more financing college loans and an economic future that is worthy of the effort you have made to get here to this place today.

In the first 4 months of this administration, over three-quarters of a million jobs were added to this economy. But we have to finish the job. The United States Senate is now coming to grips with the economic plan. It brings down our national deficit $500 billion over 5 years. And for every $10 we cut that deficit, $5 comes from spending cuts, $3.75 comes from the wealthiest Americans whose taxes were reduced in the 1980's, and $1.25 comes from the middle class. Two-thirds of the tax burden comes from people with incomes above $200,000 because they can best afford to pay.

Now, there are some lobbyists and some legislators who don't like the plan, and they say things that are popular, not the kind of things that your parents told you when you had to kind of take a deep breath and go on but popular. They say, "More cuts, less taxes," but no details. No details. Then when you look at the details, you find that the details hurt the middle class, the working poor, the vulnerable elderly, do less to create jobs and ensure our world economic leadership.

So I say to you, we ought to ask of every American, what is your real alternative, not rhetoric, not chants that sound good, but give the American people as a whole the same sort of truth that every one of your families gave you or you wouldn't be here today. That's what you're entitled to, and that's what I'm determined to give you as President of the United States.

My job is to make your future worthy of the efforts that brought you here today, to try to help to create a national interest that triumphs over anybody's special interests. You have done your part. It is now time for the leadership of this country to do ours.

I ask you only to remember here the lessons you have learned here and the lessons which have already been repeated. Nobody can create for you an opportunity you are not capable of seizing. If you don't continue to learn throughout a lifetime, you can still be left behind. And nobody in this country can fully succeed until more of this country succeeds. We do not walk alone. We walk as families, as communities, as neighborhoods, and as a nation, and we had better start acting like it. We are going up or down together, and we need to go forward.

In 1960, in November, President Kennedy delivered the last speech of his Presidential campaign here in the Boston Garden. He talked of, I quote, "the contest between the comfortable and the concerned, between those who believe we should rest and lie at anchor and drift and those who want to move this country forward." That contest is not over, and it never

will be. But at each critical juncture in our Nation's history, whether we go forward will depend upon whether a new generation of Americans are willing to take up that challenge laid down 33 years ago by President Kennedy.

One of the most distinguished citizens Massachusetts ever produced was Oliver Wendell Holmes. He joined the Massachusetts infantry during the Civil War, and he lived to have a conversation with President Franklin Roosevelt 60 years later. Holmes said that a person must be involved in the action and passion of his time for fear of being judged not to have lived. Well, my fellow Americans, the action and passion of your time is to restore the American dream and to make it real for everyone who is willing to do what you have done in coming here today.

When I was in college—and I just celebrated my 25th reunion—I had a remarkable teacher who said that the most important idea in our culture was the idea that the future could be better than the present and that each of us has a personal moral responsibility to make it so.

And I tell you, when I walked down that aisle today and I saw your enthusiasm, your energy, your intelligence, your love for life, your excitement today, I thought to myself, you deserve that. You deserve that. But only you can provide it. And so I say to you today, let us all, from the President to the students, to the parents, to every person who works in this great land, resolve to do our part to make sure that we have exercised our personal moral responsibility to make your future better than the present.

God bless you, and good luck.

NOTE: The President spoke at 10:55 a.m. in the Boston Garden. In his remarks, he referred to John A. Curry, president of the university, and Douglas Luffborough III, student commencement speaker.

Remarks to the Community in Portland, Maine
June 19, 1993

Thank you very much. Thank you, Senator Mitchell. Thank you, Congressman Andrews.

Thank you, Mayor Pringle. Thank you, ladies and gentlemen, for coming out today in such large numbers. It's good to be back in Maine, and I want you to know I walked down this park in a pair of Dexter shoes made in Maine. I enjoyed it. I also want you to know that Senator Mitchell caught me playing golf in a pair of shoes not made in Maine, and now I have Dexter golf shoes that I wear every time I play golf.

I want to thank the convention and visitors bureau. I want to thank the parks department for hanging the American flag so high today. I want to thank the fire department, and I want to thank all the people who performed before I got here. I'm sorry I didn't hear the Maine humor. I'm sorry I missed the country music. I'm sorry I missed the jazz music. I'm glad I didn't miss you.

I also want to say that behind us there are students from the Reiche School, who won one of our blue ribbon excellence awards. Hear them cheering? Their representatives were in the Rose Garden a few days ago with me and representatives of other distinguished schools all across America. But I know you're proud of your schools and your students, and I did want to say a special word of hello to them because they were with me not very long ago down in Washington.

It is wonderful to be back in Maine. I've been here when it's hot; I've been here when it's cold. This is just about perfect today, and I'm glad to be back.

I want to say a special word of thanks to your Senator, the Senate majority leader and a genuine national treasure, George Mitchell. You know, he said all that about the election being about change and the fact that you gave me your votes in the last election. I'm very grateful for that. But it is hard for a President to make change alone. Some things have to come with the support of Congress. And thanks to the leadership of George Mitchell, just this week the American people had a good week.

First, the Senate passed a campaign finance reform bill that lowers the cost of campaigns, reduces the influence of special interests, and when the campaign limits are broken, helps people who are outspent to get their access to the airwaves, too. It is a good bill, and it's a real advance. And not very long before that, the Senate passed a bill, finally, to require all the lobbyists in Washington to register and say who they are, what they're lobbying for, and to report

any money they spend lobbying the rest of us, which I think is a very good thing to do. That's a message you sent in November. But I can't wave a magic wand and do that. The Congress has to go along. And the Senate has, thanks to Senator Mitchell.

The second thing that happened this week was that the Senate and the House, by significant bipartisan margins, voted out of committee the bills that I have been proposing to open the doors of college education to all Americans. And I want you to know how that will work. We're going to be able to save money by changing the way college loans are given out and provide them to students, without regard to income, at lower interest rates and then give students the chance to pay it back as a percentage of their income, so nobody will ever be discouraged from borrowing money for fear that they'll go broke when they get out of college. And as George Mitchell said, tens of thousands of them will be able to pay it back with service to their communities, whether in big cities or small towns or rural areas, through national service, rebuilding America from the grassroots here at home, a domestic peace corps. That's going to be the best money we ever spent to educate America to compete in the 21st century.

The third thing that happened is that the Senate Finance Committee took action on the economic program that succeeded in passing through the House, thanks to the leadership of the chairman, Senator Moynihan from New York, and Senator Mitchell, who besides being the majority leader is also on the Finance Committee. And next week the Senate will have a chance to vote on this economic program, send it to the House so they can agree on a bill that I think is critical to this country's future.

Now, there's been a lot of talk about this in the last few weeks, and our opponents have said a lot of things about my plan that aren't true. So I want to say to you who gave me a chance to be President, here's my report on what's really in that plan.

First of all, let me tell you, I didn't live in Washington before January, and I didn't take the debt from $1 trillion to $4 trillion or the annual deficit from $74 billion to $300 billion. I was a Governor in a State not very different from Maine, working hard within a balanced budget to provide good educations to our people and good jobs to our people. And I never had to raise any money to pay down a deficit. But the plain fact is that this country is awash in debt. And one of the reasons it is, is that no President's budget has been taken seriously in more than a decade. It's all been political rhetoric.

Last year, my predecessor's budget was voted against by 75 percent of the members of his own party in the House of Representatives. Our party passed the budget in the House, and we're going to do it in the Senate. And we're going to have a comprehensive economic plan to get this country moving again, thanks in no small measure to George Mitchell. And I want you to know what is in it.

First, this plan reduces our deficit by $500 billion over the next 5 years. It begins with $250 billion in spending cuts in everything, in defense, in foreign aid, in veterans benefits, in Medicare. In everything you can conceive of, we have cut across the board, and it is not very easy. But the Democrats have taken the lead in cutting spending. Ask Senator Mitchell how many Republican amendments there were to cut spending in the Senate Finance Committee last week. I'll tell you how many: zero. We cut the spending—we did it—$250 billion.

Do we raise taxes? Yes, we do. But how is it raised? I'll tell you how. Seventy-five percent of the tax money we propose to raise comes from the upper 6 percent of income earners in this country. Over two-thirds of the money comes from people with incomes above $200,000 a year, because their taxes went down and their incomes went up in the 1980's when we gave 70 percent of the gains to the top 1 percent of the population. They can pay now, and they should.

Now, does this plan ask anything of the middle class? Yes, it does. If your income is above $30,000 but below $100,000, we ask for a contribution. Why? Because after the election, lo and behold, the Government says the deficit's going to be $165 billion bigger in the next 5 years than it was going to be before the election, and because if we don't gain our economic destiny back, if we don't get control of our future, if we don't do something about this debt, we're not going to be able to go on to the other challenges facing us. But you have to decide if it's a good deal.

Working families with incomes of under $30,000 are held harmless in this program. And I'll tell you something else that's awfully good

about it. For the first time in history, if this program passes, we'll be able to say that people who work for a living and still live in poverty—and there are millions of them in America—will be lifted out of poverty by the tax system. If you work 40 hours a week and you've got a child in the house, you can get out of poverty if this economic program passes because of the changes in the tax system.

Let me put it to you another way. For every $10 in deficit reduction in this plan, $5 comes from spending cuts, $3.75 comes from the upper 6 percent, $1.25 comes from the middle class with family incomes above $30,000. I think that is fair. I think that is balanced. It will work. And let me tell you why it's important. Why is it important? It's important because when we start to bring down the deficit—and we've been working on this since right after the election—interest rates come down. And when interest rates come down, it puts money back in your pocket, and it puts money back into the economy.

Look what's happened now. We have a 20-year low in mortgage rates, a 7-year high in housing sales, 755,000 new jobs in the economy just since January 20th, 130,000 new construction jobs. That is a 9-year high in construction job growth because of these low-interest rates. And eventually, that's going to help the people making a living out of the wood in Maine and in Arkansas, because they depend upon people building things to make a living. That's why this is important.

Now, do we spend some money in this budget? Yes, we do. You can decide whether you think it's worth doing. This budget increases, for example, the amount of money a small business man or woman can expense every year on the tax return from $10,000 to $25,000. I think it's a great idea. Why? Because small business is the backbone of this economy. Because small business is providing most of the jobs. Because small business stopped providing new jobs to this economy a couple of years ago, and if you take that right off from 10 to 25 grand, a lot of those small business people are going to be able to hire one more person. And if millions and millions of them do it, it will be an awful boon for this economy, and we can get going again. I think it's worth spending that money.

It costs some money to change the Tax Code so that people who work for a living and are still in poverty are lifted above poverty. But I think it is worth it to say it is never a good thing to be on welfare. If you can work, here's an incentive to move from welfare to work and to reward the dignity of work. We're not going to have a tax program grind you into poverty; we're going to have it lift you out of poverty if you're working for a living. It costs some money, but I think it's worth doing.

Maine and Arkansas have some of the poorest rural areas and small towns in the country. I'll tell you something else in this program that costs money. We have some enterprise or empowerment zones in this program that will give real incentives in big cities and in small rural areas for private sector people to come in and invest money to start businesses and put people to work. I've heard Republicans and Democrats talk for 10 years about why we shouldn't give people extra incentives to put private funds into depressed areas, both rural and urban. But nobody's ever tried it. So we're going to try it. There's not enough Government money to rescue the poor and depressed areas in this country. Let's see if we can get the private sector to do it. We've got to give them some incentives. It costs some money, but I think it's worth it. And I think we ought to try it.

And let me say this: Even though overall there's a 5-year freeze on what's called discretionary spending at home, we do spend some more money on Head Start, on education and training, on dealing with the people who have lost their jobs because of defense cutbacks, on trying to develop new technologies so that we can compete and win in this global economy and so that people who lose manufacturing jobs can get them back in a different way, by getting ahead of the curve instead of being behind like we have for the last 12 years. It costs some money. Our competitors are doing it. I think it is worth the money. We can't walk away from what is plainly needed to move this economy forward. We're not in the business of liquidating America; we're in the business of growing America. And we better get about it.

Let me just give you one example that Congressman Andrews has talked to me about. In the last 10 years more than 120,000 American shipbuilders and shipyard suppliers have lost their jobs to foreign competition and cuts in defense spending. And believe me, our competitors subsidize their businesses. Now, our Government didn't do much to help our folks com-

pete in that global economy. And we started cutting defense spending way back in '86 and went for years and never did anything to help the workers and the communities adjust or the businesses get into new lines of production. And we want to change all that. Your Congressman, Tom Andrews, got a bill passed last year—I want to get the formal title here—called the Shipbuilding Promotion Act of 1992, ordering the Federal Government to establish a group to look at threats to shipbuilding jobs. Well, we're doing that. And we're going to do that. And we're going to come back and report and see what we can do about it.

Last year when I was running for President, the Congress passed a bill to appropriate $500 billion to communities that were hurt by defense cutbacks to help the businesses learn to produce new things, to help the workers be trained to do new work, to help the communities redevelop themselves. And when I became President, not one red cent of that money had been released, because they did not believe, the people who were there before, in investing to help people to deal with defense cutbacks. So you had whole areas of State after State after State in terrible economic trouble. Well, we're moving that money.

The Secretary of Labor, Bob Reich, another New Englander, I might add, has approved $3 million for two defense conversion grants just to the State of Maine, $2 million to assist workers at the Loring Air Force Base and $900,000 to assist those being laid off from the Bath Iron Works. And that is a good beginning. But believe me, folks, it is just the beginning of what we have to do.

Now, our opponents chant like a mantra; they say, "Less tax, more cuts; less tax, more cuts." How in the world could anybody be against that? It sounds great, except guess what? There's only been two versions put forward. In the House of Representatives—unlike the Senate, at least the House put a plan out there. And guess what? The House Republican plan, because it was more unfair to the middle class, to the elderly, to the working poor, and to the economic climate of the country, lost more Republican votes than my plan lost Democratic votes. So it sounds great, but when the Republicans looked at it, they didn't like it very well either. And then there was this plan floated in the Senate a few days ago which lowered taxes on upper income people and cut more out of Medicare and did other things that would weaken our economy and be unfair to the elderly and to working people just above the poverty line.

So I say to people: Where is your idea? Senator Mitchell will tell you, this week when the Senate Finance Committee voted that economic plan out, our opponents on the other side, many of whom ought to be helping us, had all kinds of amendments saying let's cut this tax, let's cut this tax, let's cut this tax. Guess what? How many amendments did they offer to cut spending? Zero. And when they were asked, where are your amendments to cut spending, you know what they said? "We don't want to take any politically unpopular votes on spending cuts." Folks, we are telling you the truth for a change. We are telling you the truth. We had 12 years where people said, "We're going to cut your taxes, and we're going to cut somebody else's spending." And what they did was to increase spending, cut taxes on the wealthiest Americans, have back-door tax increases on the middle class, and let the economy go down the tubes. We can do better. And I need your help and support, and so does George Mitchell, in making sure we do better.

And let me tell you, there is more to do. I want to reemphasize, we are not trying to deal with these tough issues just to reduce the debt. When you reduce the debt, you free up money to invest, to create jobs. You think about it. There are people in this audience today who have refinanced their homes since interest rates started dropping so much last November. That's happening to millions of people all across America, and that frees up money. People are getting lower business loans. People are getting lower consumer loans and lower car loans. And over the next year and a half, it will help this economy. It helps the economy if you invest in giving kids a head start, if you retrain workers, if you

invest in helping companies produce things for the civilian market if they don't have a defense contract anymore. It helps the economy if you do what it takes to compete with our foreign competitors everywhere. That's what helps the economy. And that's what we are committed to doing.

And let me say this: After this budget fight is over, as Senator Mitchell just said, I want us to begin in earnest, and we can do it this year if we'll get after it, to provide the security that will come to millions of Americans if we provide affordable, quality health care to every American family. And we can do that, too.

We can pass the national service bill and open the doors of college education to all. We can pass a welfare reform bill that puts people to work instead of maintains them in dependency. We can change the nature of politics. But you have to stay with us. You have to say: We want the House of Representatives to pass campaign finance reform. We want the House of Representatives to tell us where all the lobbyists are and who they're giving money to. We want the whole Congress to pass an economic plan, and we don't want you to stop.

Change is hard and difficult. And it's not easy to get 218 votes in the House and 51 Senators to agree on anything. They all come from different places with different interests. And my job as President is to try to make sure that the national interest overrides the particular interest of anybody and any group in any State, including yours and mine. We have got to pull this country together again and be a family again so we can move forward again.

Thank you very much, and God bless you all.

NOTE: The President spoke at 6 p.m. at Deering Oaks Park.

Remarks at the National Sports Awards Reception
June 20, 1993

Good evening and welcome to the White House, and where appropriate, happy Father's Day. I'm glad all of you could be here with us tonight to celebrate the tradition of sport in American life. Hillary and I are delighted

to be the honorary cochairs of the first annual National Sports Awards and to pay tribute to those outstanding Americans rightly called "the great ones."

Frankly, I'm thrilled to meet these heroes of

sport. And I have to say that of all the perks that have come along with being President of the United States, the best one was being able to play 18 holes of golf with Arnold Palmer this morning. Even if it turned out to be all downhill from here, I could still be on a high. I might say, I'm glad I didn't have to play one on one with Kareem or go 15 rounds with Muhammad Ali to justify the round of golf. [*Laughter*]

It's been said that the athlete does not embark upon a sport but upon a way of life. Tonight we honor five individuals not simply for their athletic superiority but for the special qualities of character and leadership that have earned them the respect and the admiration of our Nation.

Kareem Abdul-Jabbar led every team he ever played for to championships. From Power Memorial High School to UCLA, to the Milwaukee Bucks, to the LA Lakers, he dominated the court for the entire 20 years in the NBA that he played. And he's hailed by many fans and players alike as the greatest center ever to play the game. He led the Los Angeles Lakers to five championships. And his teammates used to call him E.F. Hutton. When Kareem talked, they listened.

When he retired in 1989, he had been a first team all-star 10 times, college player of the year twice, earned 6 world championship rings, 6 MVP trophies, and played more seasons, more games, and more minutes, blocked more shots, and with his elegant trademark "skyhook" scored more points than anybody else who ever played this game. But for all of us who watched him, we know he did something more: He brought a tremendous pride and dignity to a game that will be forever in his debt. And tonight we offer him our highest praise. Congratulations.

Muhammad Ali may be the most widely recognized athlete in the world. He captured the imagination of the world with his distinctive fighting style and with the exhilarating fights he took to places all over the globe. He was the first fighter in history to win the heavyweight title three times. He was a loud, proud poet who told the world he was the greatest and was poetry in motion when he floated around the ring. Sometimes when his opponents couldn't hit him, it was hard to tell whether he was boxing or doing ballet.

He was just as courageous and dignified and mesmerizing a challenger as he was a champion.

And he's a man who has unfailing stood by his principles and his beliefs. It was written of him that he spoke of God before his fights; he spoke of man; he spoke of hungry children. He cared about the sick and the old. He raised the game to drama. And because he stood for something greater, the people who climbed upon their chairs for him felt that they stood, too, for something greater. Congratulations, Muhammad Ali.

Arnold Palmer revolutionized his sport. It's been said that when television discovered golf, the world discovered Arnold Palmer. Fans all over the world grew to love his unique style, his boldness, and his daring. To many he is the American ideal: the perpetual underdog falling behind and then charging down the stretch and tearing up the golf course. I can identify with that. [*Laughter*]

Who could forget the 1960 U.S. Open tournament, where before the final round he trailed in 15th place, and a reporter said he was no more in contention than the man operating the hot dog concession. In one of the most memorable examples of grace under pressure, he birdied the first 6 out of 7 holes and then went on to win the tournament. During the campaign, some people used to call me the Comeback Kid, but I think he deserves that title much more than I ever will. He won the U.S. Amateur, the U.S. Open, the Masters 4 times, the British Open twice, was named Athlete of the Decade in 1970. He is a remarkably gifted man. And we are all in his debt.

I must say, I saw today on the golf course that even today when he tees it up, Arnie's Army is as faithful and enthusiastic as when he marched through Augusta to win his first Masters. We thank him tonight for all he has given us, for all the thrills. And I can tell you that on the basis of a wonderful few hours today, he's just as much of a gentleman and a competitor in private as he always seemed to the public. Congratulations, Mr. Palmer.

Wilma Rudolph had to relearn to walk before she could learn to run. The 20th of 22 children, she suffered a childhood bout with polio, double pneumonia, and scarlet fever, which left her legs paralyzed. But with resilient spirit and undaunted determination, she defied all the expectations and beat the odds to become a great athlete. She was a remarkable star at a fairly early age, although she did not take up track until the ripe old age of 13. Two years later, she won a bronze medal at the 1956 Olympics. She had an extraordinary career at Tennessee State College. She went back to Rome in 1960 and became the first American woman to win three track and field gold medals at one Olympic games. Her trademark composure became familiar to people all over the world. And she became literally an international heroine.

After retiring from track, she continued to dedicate much of her time to working with young athletes. She did more than break world records. She broke barriers for thousands of women competitors and paved the way for those who have followed in her footsteps. Wilma Rudolph, you are a great one.

Our next honoree is not here, but I want you to know a little bit about him. There was a young pitcher new to the major leagues. He was facing a batter by the name of Ted Williams. "Ball three," said the umpire; and the pitcher walked halfway to the plate and screamed, "What was wrong with that pitch?" The umpire dusted off the plate; the young, frustrated pitcher wound up and threw; and once again Ted Williams hit it over the Fenway Park fence. The umpire walked toward the man and said to the rookie, "You see, son, when you throw a strike, you don't have to look to me; Mr. Williams will let you know."

During his 19 seasons with the Boston Red Sox, the Splendid Splinter earned 6 major league batting titles, 2 at the ages of 39 and 40; maintained a batting average of .344, with 2,654 hits, including 521 home runs. These statistics are awesome, all right, but they're even more incredible when you consider that Ted Williams lost most of 5 seasons and hundreds of hits and home runs because he wanted to serve his country. He left baseball twice, first to serve as a fighter pilot in World War II and then to serve again in the Korean war. In 1941, he defied all the laws of baseball when he batted .406. No one has batted .400 since. And talk about grace under pressure, at his very last time at bat in 1960, he hit a farewell home run.

Ted Williams is a great athlete and a great patriot, and I'm proud to honor him tonight, as I know all of you are, for what he's done for his sport and for his country.

Each of you has honored your sport and your Nation and left a legacy of greatness. I hope these National Sports Awards become an American tradition that will honor the legacy of all

those who participate. Today we must look to the future, the idea of service performed by young people all across America.

The funds raised by these awards and this weekend will enable young people dedicated to service to expand their own efforts in rebuilding our more troubled communities, in caring for those unable to care for themselves and transforming the lives of people and cities in need, and in the process, in transforming and improving their own lives.

Some of these young leaders and those who have mentored them into a life of service are here with us. And I urge all of you on the eve of our Nation's summer of service to go forward knowing that you are shining examples of what it means to be a real citizen in our country. You are welcome here, too, tonight. Perhaps there is no way better to honor the athletes tonight than by supporting young people who themselves are dedicated to helping their peers most in need. They are also great ones.

Although we are blessed with the presence of these athletes tonight, we are all, I'm sure, saddened by the absence of another champion, Arthur Ashe, an extraordinary man who lived by the words "thou shalt not close a door behind you." There will be more said about Arthur Ashe tonight at Constitution Hall, but I'm proud that his wife, Jeanne, is here with us tonight. And thank you so much for your presence.

In closing let me just say that I have some people to thank tonight: those who have agreed to serve on the President's Council on Physical Fitness and Sports, including the two cochairs, Florence Griffith Joyner and Tom McMillen, who is standing here and looking short with his friend Bill Bradley as Kareem is up on the platform. They will advise me and the Secretary of Health and Human Services, Donna Shalala, on ways to enhance opportunities for all Americans, not just the young, to participate in physical fitness and sports activities.

Finally, let me say to Kareem Abdul-Jabbar, to Muhammad Ali, to Arnold Palmer, to Wilma Rudolph, to Ted Williams, and to all of you who are here tonight, I thank you for lending your dignity to this occasion and for your service to this country and for your embodiment of the best values of America.

Thank you very much.

NOTE: The President spoke at 6:12 p.m. in the East Room at the White House. In his remarks, he referred to tennis champion Arthur Ashe, who died of AIDS; Olympic track champion Florence Griffith Joyner; and former professional basketball players Tom McMillen and Senator Bill Bradley.

Interview With Michael Jackson of KABC Radio, Los Angeles, California
June 21, 1993

Mr. Jackson. Good morning, President Clinton.

The President. Good morning, Michael. It's nice to hear your voice again. And I enjoyed listening to your callers call in.

Economic Program

Mr. Jackson. Oh, I'm so glad you heard them, sir. I know the budget is the burning issue of the moment. You may have seen a Conrad cartoon; it showed you in caricature, and the caption was "Or maybe you'd like Bush back and another $2 trillion debt." How could we avoid that and make the whole economic climate healthier?

The President. Well, the first thing we have to do is to gain control over our economic destiny again. The deficit is spinning out of control. It was about $74 billion a year in 1980; it's over $300 billion this year. The debt, as you know, has gone from $1 trillion to $4 trillion. And because of that, the money we ought to be investing hasn't been there. You can see that very clearly in Los Angeles and southern California when you had all these defense cutbacks. We should have been reinvesting all that money in domestic technologies to put the people back to work here at home in high-speed rail, environmental cleanup, all kinds of other things. But the debt was so big that the money went to pay interest on the debt and into exploding health care costs.

So our economic plan is terribly important to the people of the United States and the people of southern California because it begins to give us some control back. Already, the fact that the plan is making progress has brought down long-term interest rates. I know one lady who called you said her husband was in construction. Because we are at 20-year mortgage rates lows, there have been 130,000 new jobs come into this economy in construction in the last 4 months. That's the biggest increase in 9 years. Now, it's going to take a while to reach southern California, because that's one of the most distressed areas of our national economy. But it is beginning to turn around.

So you've got to bring the deficit down. You've got to do it in a way that is fair to the middle class, by making upper income people pay the lion's share of the burden. There have to be some incentives in this plan to grow new jobs in the private sector through empowerment zones in our cities and poor rural areas, through new incentives to small business. And there also have to be some targeted investments. Over the next 5 years, we still need to spend some money to try to redevelop the businesses, the communities, and retrain the workers that have been hurt so badly by defense cutbacks.

So this is a good plan, and it's still the only real plan on the table. A lot of people have criticized it, but it's hard to quarrel with the results of it. Just the progress of the plan is bringing down long-term interest rates. We've got three-quarters of a million new jobs in the economy since January 20th, and I am encouraged. We've got a long, long way to go, and we're dealing with some economic trends that have been in place for 20 years in the world economy. But we can turn it around if we will do so with discipline and if we'll stop the delay, if we'll go forward now and pass the plan.

Mr. Jackson. Mr. President, you mentioned critics. Congressman Henry Hyde, speaking for the Republicans, claimed over the weekend that the Senate Democrats are going to agree to a tax-and-spend, tax-and-spend program this summer that will result in another version of the biggest tax hike in history. In a nutshell, by year's end, will the rich be taxed considerably more, heavily taxed? Will the middle class be further hit?

The President. By year's end, if the plan passes, upper income taxes will go up, taxes on the upper 6 percent of the American people; two-thirds of the tax burden would be paid for by people with incomes above $200,000. The tax on the middle class, in the form of an energy tax, would be phased in over a 3-year period and would amount to no more than $17 a month for a family of four with an income of $50,000 to $60,000, by the third year of the plan.

By contrast, families with incomes of under $30,000 would be held harmless, and there would be an incentive in this tax program, for the first time, for people who work 40 hours a week but have children in the home and are still in poverty. The tax system would actually lift them out of poverty.

So it's a very fair tax plan. But the most important thing from my point of view is that there can't be taxes without an equal amount of spending cuts. And there are substantial spending cuts in this program in everything from Medicare to veterans benefits, to agriculture, to all the specific programs, just about, in the Federal Government. People who say there aren't spending cuts just haven't said it right.

And for Mr. Hyde, whom I like a lot, to just get on there and chant their old "tax-and-spend" line, I mean, you know, that's the same crowd that presided over the last 12 years where we went from a $1 trillion to a $4 trillion debt, increased the national deficit every year, and reduced our investment in the future. I mean, they actually set in motion the policies which you see manifest all around you today in southern California. And I don't see how they have any credibility on this.

Last week in the Senate Finance Committee, there were all kinds of amendments by the Senate Republicans. They were all designed to increase the deficit by moderating tax increases with no offsetting cuts. So there just isn't another plan out there. We're either going to have to make up our mind whether to do the tough stuff necessary in terms of budget cuts and fair revenue increases to bring this deficit down and get control of our economic future and keep these interest rates down, or we're not.

And let me just make one other point. For anybody who has refinanced a home loan or refinanced a business loan or gotten a car loan, a consumer loan, a college loan at lower interest rates, a lot of people are going to in the middle class and even some upper income people are going to save more money on lower interest rates than they're going to pay in higher taxes.

That's the key thing. We've got to get the interest rates down. We've got to start investment in this economy again. And if we don't,

we're going to be in real trouble. You had someone call from Orange County; I see what's happened to real estate in Orange County. Our proposal contains significant incentives to get the real estate business in California up and going again and throughout the country.

There are all kinds of things in this plan which are very, very good for business, that the business community has been asking for for years. But we do ask people who are earning income, who have it and whose taxes went down in the eighties while the deficit went through the roof, to pay a fairer share of the tax burden so we can bring the deficit down.

NAFTA

Mr. Jackson. Relating to the calls we received earlier, Mr. President, a blunt question: Does Ross Perot concern you? And I pose it that way because of his stand on NAFTA, the North American Free Trade Agreement. He really is claiming that this country and particularly this State of California is going to lose hundreds of thousands of jobs that would go to Mexico if the agreement should be ratified.

The President. Well, I disagree with him on that issue. There are other issues on which I think we are agreed. We've got a version of the line-item veto in the United States Senate. I very much hope it will pass; I strongly support that. I'm pushing for campaign finance reform to reduce the influence of special interests in campaigns, something that he and I both talked about in the last campaign. We've got that out of the Senate; we need to pass it in the House. We're pushing for lobbying reform, something we both talked about last time. We passed a dramatic increase in the requirements for reporting of lobbyists in the Senate. I hope we can pass it in the House.

But on NAFTA we just disagree. I believe that a country like ours, if we want to generate more jobs, we're going to have to increase the volume of trade. I understand what the concern is with Mexico, but I would say to everyone in California today two things: Number one, something you know perhaps better than other Americans, anyone who wants to shut a plant down and go to Mexico today for low wages can do it. And they'll be able to do it just as well today or tomorrow as they could after NAFTA is ratified. Number two, as you have seen in California, as long as incomes are very depressed in Mexico, you're going to have a bigger and bigger problem with immigration that goes beyond the legal limits of the law. And what I see happening with NAFTA is a Mexico that can buy more American products, where more Mexicans will want to stay home and be near their families because they'll be able to make a living. And Mexico will be the leader of a whole new wave of trading partners for the United States, going down past Mexico into Central America, into Chile, into Venezuela, into Argentina, into other countries. I believe it will create jobs for America. I wouldn't do it if I didn't think so.

And let me also tell you that there's beginning to be a little bit of a chill in the wind of people who think that they ought to just automatically move their plants to Mexico to save money. There's a big story just in the last day or so about General Motors moving 1,000 jobs back from Mexico to the United States to Michigan, a high-cost State with very productive labor, to produce some of their small cars. So I'm very hopeful about this.

And let me make one last point. About 4 years ago we had a $5 billion trade deficit with Mexico. Today, because of the trade barriers that Mexico has lowered, we have a $6 billion trade surplus, which means we've created more jobs because of trade with Mexico than we've lost because of jobs moving down there. So my view is that we can make it a winner.

Now, we don't want to just have a trade agreement with no standards. The Mexican people are going to have to be willing to work with us on environmental standards and on labor standards so we don't just open the floodgates to move jobs to Mexico in ways that won't even raise incomes in Mexico. That would be a terrible thing to do. But if we do it right, it will create jobs for both countries.

International Economy

Mr. Jackson. Mr. President, things are pretty awful all over. I mean, Europe is in the worst recession since the 1930's; Japan has been hit, too. By contrast, aren't things beginning to get better here?

The President. Well, they are beginning to get better here, and they're beginning to get better here basically for two reasons. First off, American industry was really battered here during the entire 1980's and in fact starting back in the mid-seventies. And there has been a determined effort by people running our firms in the private sector to become more competitive, so a lot of them are. And that increased productivity, increasing output per worker, the increasing ability to compete with countries around the world, that is helping things to get better. The second thing that's making things better is that this administration's serious effort to bring the deficit down has helped long-term interest rates to get down to their lowest rate in 20 years, and that's leading people to refinance, freeing up some money, and we're getting some more investment.

But I don't want to mislead anybody. This is still going to be a very tough road back. If you look at southern California, if you look at Connecticut, if you look at some of the States that have been hit especially hard by defense cutbacks of all kinds and other economic problems, we're still going to have to have a very disciplined plan to invest and grow our way out of the problems of the last few years.

But yes, we're in better shape now than Europe and Japan. In fact, if we could get some more growth in those countries, we'd be in better shape because we're not selling as much to them as we would be because of their economic problems. They don't have the money to buy American products. And when I go to Japan in a couple of weeks to talk to the leaders of Europe and Japan, one of the things we're going to be talking about is that America is doing what they asked us to do; we're bringing our deficit down. And we want the Europeans to bring their interest rates down and the Japanese to invest some more money in their economy so they can grow it, because they don't have the deficit we do. And if we can work together, we can grow the world economy and that means jobs for America.

But you're quite right, we're actually in better shape than Japan and Europe is right now, except for unemployment rates. Japan's still got a lower unemployment rate than we do.

Mr. Jackson. Mr. President, thank you very, very much indeed for this, sir.

The President. Thank you, and again, I want to thank your callers for the thoughts they expressed. And I want to encourage them to continue to be active and to question and criticize me when they think I'm wrong but also to support me. I really appreciate the woman who said she didn't vote for me but she's got a stake in the success of this Presidency. We're doing what we can to move this country forward without regard to party or region. And that's the kind of support I need. I'm very grateful for that.

Mr. Jackson. Thank you, Mr. President, very much, sir.

NOTE: The interview began at 12:16 p.m. The President spoke from the Roosevelt Room at the White House.

Interview With J.P. McCarthy of WJR Radio, Detroit, Michigan
June 21, 1993

Mr. McCarthy. Good afternoon, Mr. President. How are you?

The President. I'm great. It's nice to talk to you again.

Mr. McCarthy. I can't hear.

The President. Can you hear me now? I can hear you. Can you hear me?

Mr. McCarthy. Mr. President, I can now. How are you? We haven't talked since very late in the campaign. You were in an automobile someplace, and you were running out of voice. But you were in high spirits, and now we know why. Congratulations.

The President. Thank you very much. It's nice to hear your voice again.

Mr. McCarthy. Nice to hear you.

The President. I got to hear a little bit of your last conversation. That was fascinating.

Mr. McCarthy. With Bob Talbert?

The President. Yes.

Economic Program

Mr. McCarthy. Mr. President, are you going to get your tax bill and your budget bill through the Senate? Carl Levin is on this program a little bit later. We've already taped that segment. He says, "Yes, it will be done." What do you think?

The President. I think it will be done. It's not easy ever to make these kinds of tough decisions. There are $250 billion in budget cuts in that bill that affect everything from agriculture to veterans, to Medicare, to virtually all the specific programs in the Government. And there are some tax increases, as is well-known, two-thirds of them on people with incomes above $200,000, three-quarters of them on people with incomes above $100,000. I think it's fair and balanced. And this will bring the deficit down by $500 billion, and it will keep these long-term interest rates coming down, which is what is so necessary if we're going to have rein-vestment in our country and rebuild the manufacturing sector and get this economy going again.

I think it will pass because, frankly, there isn't another alternative. And those who have tried to fashion other alternatives have come up with programs that hurt the vulnerable in our country and the middle class more and hurt the business economy more. And I think that's why we've had people from companies representing the automakers to high-tech companies in California supporting the program. It's a little-known thing that over half the 100 biggest companies in the country have supported the program, that the labor organizations have supported it, that the home builders organization, a largely Republican group, have supported it because it will bring interest rates down and create jobs and incomes for the American people.

Mr. McCarthy. But if it does pass the Senate, and apparently Senator Levin feels you have enough votes, 50 or more votes, it has to go back to the House. It's been changed significantly from the bill approved by the House. We hear the Black Caucus may be falling out of step. Can it pass the entire Congress?

The President. I think it can. I think what you will see is, when the bill passes the Senate, if we can pass it in the next few days, then there will be a conference of the Senators and the House Members. And they will try to take the best parts of both bills and come up with a bill which has more budget cuts than taxes, fair taxes, but still has some of the incentives we need for small business job creation, for the high-tech job creation, for empowerment zones to get private sector investment into the urban areas and to the poor rural areas, and also some of the money for Head Start education and training and for joint projects with the private sector for new technologies to help to deal with the defense cuts. I think you will see that budget coming out of there. And I expect it to pass both Houses.

Like I said, these are difficult times, because for 12 years the American people have been told one thing and had another thing happen where the debt just kept getting bigger and bigger, and it's eating us alive. And interest rates were high, and we couldn't get investment. We couldn't get jobs. We're going to turn it around, but it's not easy.

Mr. McCarthy. A couple of things started to leak out this weekend on those weekend Washington shows. One item was that entertainers and sports people, people who make big salaries for usually a relatively short period of time, would be exempt from the new higher rate of income tax. Is that true?

The President. Not to my knowledge.

Mr. McCarthy. Apparently it was on "Face the Nation" or one of those shows yesterday. Not so?

The President. No. There aren't any exemptions. I think what you're going to find is that people who make a lot of money for just a couple of years may wind up doing something that many of them already do, by the way, which is structuring their contracts so they get paid over a longer period of years than they play. That's something that's happening now and that may happen. But I know of no exemptions for any high income people.

Mr. McCarthy. And the surtax on the capital gains tax, everyone was figuring maybe there will be a capital gains cut. Maybe that will be a tradeoff, higher income tax rates, lower capital gains. Will there be a surtax on capital gains?

The President. It's hard to say. That's in the Senate bill. But I'm not sure how it will come out in the end. I think one thing you can look forward to is a so-called venture capital gains on new business capital gains tax, where people who put their money into new businesses will be given big incentives to do so. That is, if you take a risk on somebody and you start a new venture and you hire some new people to create new jobs in the economy and you hold that investment for 5 years or more, you'll be able to reduce your tax liability if, in fact, it turns out to be successful. We have to have more people trying to start new businesses. And that's a more hazardous undertaking. So I think you will see that.

Mr. McCarthy. Will there be some incentives for new business? Because I heard from——

The President. Absolutely.

Mr. McCarthy. I asked this morning in my morning show—I mentioned, of course, that I would be talking to you. And I said, "Give me some questions that you'd like me to ask the President." And I heard from several small business people. They said something like this: "Look, I wanted to open two new businesses this year"—this was a fellow who was in the fast-food franchise business, but he said, "With all that's going on relative to the proposed new legislation on taxes, I'm afraid to build any more restaurants." Small businesses are getting hurt. I heard that over and over this morning.

The President. Let me just mention two or three things that should be reassuring to small businesses. If these provisions of my plan pass, first of all, anybody who starts a new venture will be able to get investment for that new venture. And if the investment is held for 5 years or more, the tax rates will be much, much lower than the ordinary income tax rates, if it passes.

Secondly, for ongoing small businesses, today the writeoff for expensing on the tax form is $10,000 per year. We propose to raise that to $25,000. That will be a substantial reduction in the tax burden of most small businesses and will be an encouragement, I think, for them to hire more people.

Thirdly, if someone has a chain of restaurants, for example, like the person who called in, in the plan that I presented to the Congress that the House of Representatives adopted, we have some changes in the alternative minimum tax provisions which operate as real incentives for people to continue to invest their profits in the expansion of their businesses without running up bigger tax bills.

So I would urge the small business people who are listening to us to really look at what is in that House bill. There are a lot of very strong pro-business and pro-small business provisions in the bill that have not gotten a lot of attention. That's why, let me just mention, the National Realtors Association and the National Home Builders Association, two groups not normally associated with the Democratic Party, have already strongly endorsed this economic program because of the incentives for economic growth and because it's bringing down long-term interest rates. That's the last thing I will say. Any business person who has to borrow money in all probability is going to save more money in lower-interest rates than they'll pay in higher taxes.

Mr. McCarthy. Mr. President, one of the thrusts of your campaign was jobs. There would be more jobs. Jobs, jobs, jobs would be created. If the business climate isn't good, if there isn't an opportunity for businesses to do well, to be successful, there will be fewer jobs. I mean, that's just simple economics, isn't it?

The President. That's right, but simple economics dictate that the President of the United States stop telling everybody what they want to hear and start telling the truth. That's what simple economics dictate. I mean, in 1981 we cut taxes and increased spending and nearly bankrupted this country over the next 12 years, and we've been paying for it ever since, so that we had very high long-term interest rates, and credit was expensive, and job generation was weak. That's a problem, by the way, for wealthy countries throughout the world. Even Japan's having trouble creating jobs now. But look what's happened since I announced my plan and it started to pass its way through Congress, just in the last 4 or 5 months. First, we've had 755,000 new jobs in this economy, over 90 percent of them in the private sector, in the first 4 months of this administration. In the previous 4 years, we only had a million jobs. Second, in construction, part of the economy very affected by interest rates, in the first 4 months we had 130,000 new jobs, that's the biggest increase in 9 years. Has that affected every State and every community yet? No, but it shows that we are really moving in the right direction. If we can get everybody in this country to refinance their home loans, their business loans, to take available credit because interest rates

are lower, that will put tens of billions of dollars back into this economy to create jobs.

Mr. McCarthy. What inflation rate, sir—I don't mean to interrupt you, but we're short on time—what inflation rate would you be happy with one year from now?

The President. The lowest possible one. But if we got unemployment down to a very low level and every American had a job, it might be a tad higher than it is now, but right now we think we're in good shape on inflation. What we need in America are more jobs and higher incomes, and that's what we're working on. So, this is a job-creating strategy we're following, and I believe it will work.

Counselor to the President

Mr. McCarthy. How is David Gergen doing in his new job?

The President. He's doing very well. He's a good man. We've been friends a long time and——

Mr. McCarthy. Is the Washington press corps still braying at the moon, sir? *[Laughter]*

The President. I don't even know how to answer that. The moon still comes out here, though, at night, and the sun comes up in the morning.

Mr. McCarthy. President Clinton, a pleasure to talk to you today. Thank you very much for spending the time. I hope you get a chance to visit us.

The President. Me too. See you.

NOTE: The interview began at 12:30 p.m. The President spoke from the Roosevelt Room at the White House. In the interview, he referred to journalist Bob Talbert of the Detroit Free Press.

Interview With Phil Adler of KRLD Radio, Dallas, Texas
June 21, 1993

Mr. Adler. Mr. President, are you there?
The President. I am, Phil.

Economic Program

Mr. Adler. Good morning to you. We think that a lot of people responded to a theme, or at least I think so, in the Presidential campaign of sacrifice to cut the deficit as long as that

sacrifice is equal. The Btu tax was designed originally on the concept of equal sacrifice. But then all of these exceptions were added, and it really makes it appear that it's one of the most complicated proposals ever. Did you make a mistake allowing all the special exceptions to be included in the Btu tax?

The President. Well, I didn't allow them all to be included. Some of them were included in the House of Representatives bill, and I didn't agree with all of them. But let me say what I think was a good criticism of the tax and that is that we wanted the tax to restrain energy consumption in ways that promoted energy conservation and also supported fuel switching to more environmentally beneficial and more available natural gas. That bill, as drawn, would be a big boon to the natural gas industry in Texas and Oklahoma and throughout the United States. And that's one of the things we were trying to do. Now, some of the oil companies didn't like it, but the people that were in the gas business liked it. We had a big Texas gas company, headed by a person who strongly supported President Bush in the last election, endorsed the economic program. ARCO and Sun Oil both endorsed the economic program, including the Btu tax.

So Secretary Bentsen, who, as you know, has represented you in the Senate for a long time, offered the Senate a modified Btu tax which, instead of having all those particular exemptions, would basically have alleviated the burden of the Btu tax on industry and agriculture on the production sector but still given them an incentive to move toward natural gas wherever possible and would also have cut the Btu rate and would have replaced that with more spending cuts.

From my point of view, unfortunately, we couldn't pass that through the committee because Senator Boren had said he wouldn't vote for any tax based on the heat content of fuel. But I still think it was a good concept, and it will be interesting to see what happens if the Senate's version of the economic plan passes, to see what happens in the conference and what we come up with.

Mr. Adler. What we have now is a gasoline tax that's been passed by the Senate committee, and you've called that regressive in the past. How can you sell that, if you have to, to House Members who did risk some political capital by supporting you on the Btu tax?

The President. I think anything that comes out has to be a combination of agreement between the House and the Senate. It's hard to get 218 House Members and 51 Senators to agree on anything that's tough. I mean, everybody can talk about cutting the deficit, but it's one thing to talk about it and quite another

to do. But I think they'll be able to do it. No one was particularly happy with the form of the Btu tax, or very few people were, that passed the House, but everybody thought that Secretary Bentsen could come up with a plan that would make it good for the economy and could achieve what we were trying to do in terms of promoting domestic energy, and I think he did. The Senate preferred a tax that was a gas tax and a tax on some other fuels. It, at least, is small enough so that it is not particularly unfair to people in rural areas. It's not as big as what some had wanted, and certainly I did not want just a big old gas tax. I thought that was unfair.

I also think it's important to point out in Texas, in light of the rhetoric in the recent political campaign, that it is simply not true that there is no spending cuts in this plan. There's $250 billion in spending cuts, and they affect everything. They affect agriculture and veterans and Medicare and the whole range of discretionary spending of the Government. They affect foreign aid; they affect defense. There are sweeping, broad-based spending cuts in this program. And the tax increases, two-thirds of them, fall on people with incomes above $200,000, three-quarters on people with incomes above $100,000. Families of four with incomes below $30,000 are held harmless, and people who work for a living 40 hours a week and have kids in the house who are now in poverty would actually be lifted above poverty by these tax changes in ways that promote the movement from welfare to work. So this is a fair and balanced plan.

It was developed, and in a very aggressive way, by Lloyd Bentsen and by Leon Panetta, who used to be chairman of the House Budget Committee, to be fair, to have equal spending cuts in taxes, and to drive the deficit down so we could bring interest rates down. That's good for Texas, and that's good for everybody in America. And also, it leaves some room for investments that are critical to our future. And as you know, I support—you were implying this before I got on—I support the space station and the super collider projects because I think they're good for America's future. And if you're going to spend money on those things, you have to spend money on them. You can't play games; they do cost some money.

Space Station and Super Collider

Mr. Adler. Mr. President, how long can you guarantee that support for the super collider and the space station? Will they fall if that's the only way to meet your overall deficit reduction goal?

The President. Well, my overall deficit reduction goals can be met in my plan with the space station and the super collider. I do want to emphasize that we've already shaved $4 billion off the 5-year budget for the space station and some money off the 5-year budget for the super collider by redesigning the space station, based on a team of exceptional national experts who analyzed the project and recommended that it be redesigned and also that NASA's management be changed rather dramatically. And we just delayed the implementation schedule on the super collider some, so that none of the opponents of the space station and the super collider could claim that there had been no spending cut there.

So we have done that. But I strongly feel it would be a mistake to abandon those. Now, I would be less than candid if I didn't tell you that there are a lot of people in other parts of the country who want to cut those projects. There was always a lot of opposition to them, and because of the last election and all of the rhetoric and all the claims in Texas that there were no spending cuts in this budget, that has given real energy to the opponents of the space station and the super collider. It wasn't true that there were no spending cuts, but there are a lot of people up there who have been wanting to kill these projects for years who are just gleeful at the way the rhetoric in the last election played out in Texas. They think that they have been given a license by the people of Texas to kill the space station and the super collider. And it's going to be very much harder for me to keep them alive. But I'm doing the best I can.

Mr. Adler. Mr. President, I'm informed that our time has run out, by one of your aides, I believe. Good to talk with you this morning.

The President. Thank you. I enjoyed it.

NOTE: The interview began at 12:42 p.m. The President spoke from the Roosevelt Room at the White House.

Interview With Tim Scheld of WCBS Radio, New York City
June 21, 1993

Mr. Scheld. Good afternoon. President Bill Clinton, joining us from the Roosevelt Room of the White House this afternoon. A good decision, Mr. President, since it is as hot and muggy as you're going to get in New York City today. Be happy you're inside and in Washington, DC.

The President. It's pretty hot and muggy here, too, Tim.

Mr. Scheld. I heard you were jogging this morning in a lot of fog. No fog anywhere in New York City. We're looking for some, so bring some up here, please, next time you come.

The President. I had a great time today, for all the joggers listening to you. I got to run with John Fixx, who is the son of the famous runner Jim Fixx, who died about 9 years ago but made a real contribution to what all of us who love jogging know as the sport.

Mr. Scheld. Yes, but the question now is do you run with Michael Jordan tomorrow?

The President. I'd love to do it if he were willing.

Economic Program

Mr. Scheld. I appreciate you taking the time with us here on WCBS this afternoon. The Senate begins debate on the all-important economic package, but its ultimate shape, as you know, will be determined by the Joint House-Senate Committee probably beginning the 1st of July. Will we see the Btu energy tax proposal be reborn out of that committee, Mr. President? What kind of specific new energy taxes should the American people expect?

The President. Well, first let me say that before we can start that conference, Senator Moynihan has got to shepherd this bill through the Senate, and that's not going to be all that easy. I think we can do it. But there's been so much rhetoric around this economic program and so much inaccurate information put out there that it's not going to be easy to get the Senators to make the tough choices to pass the bill. I think they will do that, and I think in no small measure they will do it because of the leadership of your Senator in leading the Senate Finance Committee.

But after that, the House and the Senate will get together. And I think they'll try to agree on a provision with regard to energy which will do what all of us agreed to do, which is to reduce the energy tax somewhat below where it was in the House version, have some more spending cuts, make it clear to the American people there are more spending cuts than tax increases in this program and that they are fair and balanced.

The Secretary of the Treasury, Lloyd Bentsen, had a good suggestion, I thought, for reducing the Btu tax, reducing its impact on jobs through lowering the industry and agricultural provisions and cutting the rates across the board on middle class Americans but still leaving it in there so there would always be an incentive for energy conservation, environmental cleanup, and switching to American natural gas.

But one of the Senators on the Senate Finance Committee had said he would never vote for a bill based on the heat content of energy, which meant that they had to change the form of the energy levy. And we'll just have to see what comes out of the conference. I don't know what will happen.

Mr. Scheld. This is pretty complicated, but the American people were so well-informed a couple of months ago exactly how much it was going to cost. I think people were—at least in this area, I think we got the impression that people were willing to bite their bottom lip and to pay for deficit reduction. Are you taking that attitude back to the Senate and saying, listen to the American people?

The President. I'm really trying to. And I think what happened was that from the time I gave my speech outlining the plan in February to the American people directly, including telling everybody exactly what we were going to cut and exactly what it would cost, after that the details got lost in all the word games going back and forth and the shouting. And what I tried to do last week by giving a prime-time news conference and doing a number of other things was to let the American people know exactly what was in this bill. Maybe it's worth

restating.

There are $250 billion of spending cuts and $250 billion of revenue increases and $500 billion of deficit reduction in this package. Of every $10 in cutting the debt, $5 comes in spending cuts; $3.75 comes from people with incomes above $100,000; $1.25 comes from people with incomes below $100,000 but above $30,000. People below that are held harmless. That's about how it works.

Mr. Scheld. One Member of Congress over the weekend, I think, was quoted as saying that's engaging in politics of envy, pitting the higher income brackets against those that can't afford it.

The President. No.

Mr. Scheld. Well, what do you say to that?

The President. I have a clear answer to that. I don't seek to punish anybody for their success. But if you look at what happened in the 1980's, we had the reverse of the politics of envy. In the 1980's taxes went up on the middle class while their incomes went down. Taxes went down on upper income people while their incomes went up. This has nothing to do with the politics of envy.

I want it to be possible for people to have more successes. If you look at this bill that is moving its way through Congress, there are big incentives for people to start new businesses, for small businesses to hire extra people, for bigger industries to invest in new plant and equipment, for all private sector people to actually make money by reinvesting in our inner cities and our rural areas again. This is not about the politics of envy. This is about who can afford to pay the freight.

In the last 12 years, we had tax decreases on upper income people and tax increases on the middle class, even though their income trends were just the reverse. So this is nothing but fairness. This is not about class war. This is about fairness.

Health Care Reform

Mr. Scheld. Mr. President, on health care reform, our own Senator Moynihan, you brought up his name, expressed some doubt over the weekend that health care reform would make it to Congress this year. Any update on that?

The President. I still think we can do it this year if we pass the budget in an expeditious way and if the health care reform proposal is perceived as fair by the vast majority of the

American people and if it deals with the problems of the country. That is, can we bring the cost of health care in line with inflation? That's good for business. Can we remove the insecurity that millions of Americans have that they're going to lose their health insurance because of the cost or because somebody in their family's been sick or because they're going to change jobs? Can we provide a way to bring coverage to people who don't have it? Seventy percent of them work for a living. Can we do it in ways that are affordable and balanced, and can we do it in ways that don't in any way affect the right of Americans to choose their doctors or to keep very high quality health care?

If we can do that, then I think you will see a willingness on the part of Congress to take this up, knowing that the whole job can't be done overnight. That is, we could adopt an omnibus bill and still have to phase in the actual practical implementation of it so that if there are problems along the way, they can be corrected.

Senator Moynihan has a lot of experience about how slowly Congress acts, but I think the American people are so hungry and so hurting for something to be done on health care that they'd like to see it dealt with this year, and they'd like to see us at least make a good beginning. I believe with a little luck we can get it done this year.

Henry Leon Ritzenthaler

Mr. Scheld. Mr. President, reading the Washington Post this morning, seeing quotes from a colleague or a friend of yours and someone who I know, Betsy Wright, I'm wondering whether this claim from the Paradise, California, man merits any reaction from you.

The President. I'll be glad to give you a reaction, but let me say I have tried to call him today and have not talked to him yet. And I think I ought to talk to him before I make any public statement. But I'll put out a statement about it later on today.

Former President George Bush

Mr. Scheld. Fair enough, Mr. President. Have you heard from the FBI, by the way, on the inquiry into the alleged plot against former President Bush in Kuwait a couple of months ago?

The President. I have not received a final report from the FBI, and I don't think I should

say anything about what I will or won't do until I do get that report.

Mr. Scheld. So it's either all the wrong questions or all the right questions I get to ask you. [*Laughter*]

The President. No, they're both good questions, and I'm sorry, but it's not in the national interest for me to discuss that until I actually know what I can say about it when I get the report.

President's Visits to New York

Mr. Scheld. Absolutely. One other final question for you here. It concerns when you come to New York, and I'm sure you will be in this area for Governor Florio and for Mayor Dinkins, campaigning; that's my guess, at least. What do you tell the people who are sitting in traffic sometimes because of a Presidential visit? It's a loaded question, sir.

The President. It really bothers me when I come there. I told Mayor Dinkins the last time I was there, I was so concerned that it required so many police officers and firemen. And it seems that the President interrupts the flow of events more coming to New York than any other place because of the density of the population and the traffic. It really concerns me.

One of the things that I can do and one of the things I did do the last time I came was to land at the airport and then take a helicopter in as close as I can to where I'm driving so that really minimizes the disruption to the other people and traffic. You know, I love to come to New York, and I think it's a good thing for the President to be in New York and to be on the streets and to be with the people, and it's such an important part of our national life. There are so many people there I need to talk to and see and listen to. But it bothers me when I inconvenience a lot of people.

Mr. Scheld. Well, we leave you the invitation to always come back here and talk to people, but this is a way to get through to them without causing some traffic problems. But come here anyway. We'd love to see you.

The President. I'd love to do it. Maybe we can do it. Maybe radio can be the best alternative.

Mr. Scheld. Absolutely, sir. Thank you for taking the time this afternoon.

The President. Thanks.

NOTE: The interview began at 12:49 p.m. The President spoke from the Roosevelt Room at the White House. A question referred to newspaper reports that Henry Leon Ritzenthaler might be the President's half-brother.

Interview With Larry King
June 21, 1993

Mr. King. Welcome back to another hour of "The Larry King Show." Great pleasure to have with us—the last time we had him on a radio show he was in a car in Detroit during the campaign, getting to the airport. In fact, he gave us a visual description of the highway. Do you remember that?

The President. I do remember it.

Economic Program

Mr. King. President Clinton, a couple of things. First, Senator Phil Gramm last week on my television show said—the Republican from Texas—anytime, anywhere, anyplace he'll come to the White House, he'll meet with you, he'll sit down to work out a deal on the economy from the Republican Party standpoint. He said, you invite him, he's there. What about it?

The President. I'm always happy to talk to Senator Gramm, but the issue is, what are they for? I mean, there at least was a Republican budget offered in the House of Representatives, and more Republicans voted against it than Democrats voted against my budget. There was a bipartisan budget offered in the Senate Finance Committee which by common consent probably couldn't get 20 votes on the floor of the Senate. So what I want to know is, what are they for? I have met with the Republican Senators completely. I meet with the leadership of the Republicans along with the Democrats all the time. I am always anxious to discuss this. But we need to know what the specifics are. I mean, I put out a plan that has $250 billion in tax cuts in it that affects agriculture, veterans, defense, foreign aid, the Federal employee pay, Federal employee retirement, cuts huge amounts out of all these things. They've been trying to convince the American people that there are no spending cuts. Senator Gramm tried to do it in his own State of Texas in the recent election season.

So, if we're going to have anything to talk about, we've all got to at least say what the facts are. All I'm saying is I'd be happy to have any suggestions he has, but we've got to know where we're going on this.

Mr. King. You're saying it would be pointless to sit down unless they come in with a preagenda?

The President. The Senate Finance Committee met last week on the economic plan and dealt with a lot of Republican amendments after they went all over the country saying the issue was spending. The Republicans tried to lower taxes in a lot of different ways, mostly on upper income folks. And everything they offered would have increased the deficit because they did not introduce one single spending cut amendment, because those are the tough and controversial things, because they know how much we've already cut spending in this budget.

So, all I'm saying is, you know, I'll talk to Phil Gramm; I'll talk to anybody. He may want to talk to me this week because I'm trying to save the space station and the super collider in his State, two things I believe in. After having shaved down the space station by $4 billion and shaved the cost of the super collider some, I believe they're important for America as investments in science and technology. But there are a lot of people who are against these projects who are going to try to take his rhetoric and the rhetoric of the recent Texas election and use it against him because of the things they said. So, Senator Gramm may need me this week because I agree with him on this issue, and I hope we can save them for America's sake. But the political rhetoric of some of the Republicans in pretending that there are no spending cuts has made it tougher.

Mr. King. So in other words, what everybody wants is, they don't want to pay new taxes; they don't want to cut any services. We just want a free ride.

The President. Yes, and we want to do it in a way that looks politically palatable. So they talk about, well, let's put a cap on all this spending or limits on all that and not come up with the specifics. My budget has 200 specific spending cuts over the previous Bush budget. A hundred of them are more than $100 million a piece. And I really have tried to take this thing on. For years we listened to all this rhetoric about how we could cut taxes and increase spending and somehow everything would be all right. And we took the debt from $1 trillion to $4 trillion. We had astronomical long-term interest rates. Ever since we've been trying to bring the interest rates down by bringing the deficit down, you see mortgage rates at a 20-year low, housing starts at a 7-year high; construction employment is increased at the highest rate in 9 years. We've got 755,000 new jobs coming into the economy. Most of them are coming in because people are refinancing their debt and freeing up money to invest in the economy. So we're moving this in the right direction. But of course, it's not popular to do these difficult things.

International Economy

Mr. King. You're going to have to go to Japan in a couple weeks. That's a major economic conference. Let's assume the Senate passes this; then they go to House committee, and that of course won't be settled by the time you go there. And you go to a country where their leadership is going to change. How much of a ball of wax is that?

The President. Well, it's going to be a challenge to get a lot done at this summit. But I'm convinced we can. We have two or three issues that we really need to deal with. We're trying to come to grips with the need for a new trade agreement for the world, which I think is very important, will create more jobs in America. We'd have more jobs today if Europe and Japan weren't in the bad economics conditions they're in. Their growth rates are substantially lower than ours. If they were in better shape, they'd be buying more of our products and we'd have more jobs.

The second thing we're going to try to deal with is what we can do, each in our own countries, to promote global economic growth. The Europeans and Japanese have been telling America for years, "Get your deficit down." So we're doing that. Now they've got to lower their interest rates in Europe so they can grow, and they've got to invest some more money in Japan

so they can grow and buy more of our products. And if we do it together, we can bring this world out of the recession it's in, and that means more jobs for America.

Mr. King. But what part does Japan play if they're lame duck?

The President. Well, I think that depends upon what all the political sides in the country will say about the negotiations that we're on. I mean, it's pretty clear to me that no matter who winds up being Prime Minister of Japan and what faction that person comes out of, that they're going to have to continue to open their economy to our products. And they're going to have to continue to stimulate their economy, because they don't have a budget deficit, they've got a surplus.

What's happening in Japan now I think has more than anything else to do with the legacy of the various political scandals and the political corruption. I think their economic policy is going to have to take the direction that we support almost no matter who gets elected Prime Minister. They can't withdraw from the world or shut us out now. They've got too much at stake in expanding into China and other countries and doing business in a very complicated world that simply won't allow Japan to be the only rich country in the world with $110 billion a year trade surplus.

Mr. King. So you're hopeful, no matter who it is?

The President. Yes, I am. It presents a challenge to get done the things I wanted to get done in Japan at the conference. It will be more challenging, but I still think that we may be able to do that simply because of the limits on their economic options.

NAFTA

Mr. King. During the campaign you told me, in fact, almost the day it happened, when President Bush signed it in San Antonio, you said to me the next day that you supported this fair trade concept with Mexico and Canada on balance. You had some questions. Do you still have some questions?

The President. Yes, but I'm still for it. As a matter of fact, I feel more strongly today, if possible, that it is the right direction for us to take. The trade agreement, I thought, had some weaknesses. It was negotiated with a greater concern for our financial institutions and our intellectual property concerns, that is, patent and copyright concerns, than for new jobs and environmental cleanup, things that I thought were real important.

So we're trying to fix that. We're trying to make sure that this trade agreement with Mexico and Canada has very strong provisions to guarantee appropriate investments in environmental cleanups, so we don't have more pollution in America or we don't have people going down to Mexico just so they won't have to have any antipollution expenses, and so we have some labor protections.

But I think we're getting there. And I believe that the right kind of trade agreement can create jobs in America. I don't agree that it'll cost jobs. If you look just in the last couple of days, there was a notice from General Motors that they're closing an operation in Mexico, bringing it back to the United States, going to create 1,000 jobs in Michigan and higher labor costs because of the productivity and the nearness to the labor parts market, to the auto parts market. And I think you're going to see a lot of that. If anybody wants to shut a plant down and go to Mexico just because they have cheap wages, they can do that today. Nothing is going to change in the NAFTA agreement. But if you have more growth on both sides, then you'll have less illegal immigration from Mexico, more people will be able to get jobs at home and stay with their families, their incomes will rise, and they'll buy more American products. Last month, Mexico replaced Japan as the second biggest purchaser of American manufacturing products. We have a $6 billion trade surplus with them. That means we create jobs out of our trade with them. So I think it's a good deal for America, and I hope we can pass it.

Media Coverage

Mr. King. One other quick thing. L.A. Times Mirror poll out today says 51 percent of the public thinks the press has been unfair to you, more unfair to you than your predecessors. Any comment?

The President. You know, I always trust the people in the end. They pretty well get it right.

Mr. King. You think that's right, about right?

The President. I think the most important thing now is what I said at my press conference last week. The American people know if there's something going on and some tension that is not—doesn't have much to do with their interests. And I think that's what they have perceived here. And so what I have done, clearly, in the last couple of weeks, is to reach out a hand of understanding to the capital press corps here and to ask them not to stop criticizing me, because that's their job when they think I'm wrong or they think there's a story to be pursued, but to approach this whole work that we have to do together with an atmosphere of respect and greater trust. And I pledge to try to do the same thing.

I think the American people want to see the flaws in my proposal, want to see the contradictions if they are there, want to see me subject to honest scrutiny. But they don't like the feeling of feeding frenzy. They don't want that. And so, you know, I've done what I could, and I hope we'll have the kind of response that the American people plainly want.

Chelsea Clinton

Mr. King. Chelsea going to Japan?

The President. Well, I hope so. I think it would be educational for her, although some people have said that, you know, we ought to consider what kind of Asian press coverage she'll get and whether that would prohibit her from learning anything or doing anything there. But there is a lot of precedent for previous Presidents' families going on trade missions. And I'd like to see her do it. I think she'd learn a lot from it if in fact she'll be able to function when she's there. So we're going to try to figure that out in the next few days.

Mr. King. Thanks, Mr. President.

The President. Thanks, Larry.

NOTE: The interview began at 1 p.m. The President spoke from the Roosevelt Room at the White House.

Interview With Bob Levey of WMAL Radio, Washington, DC
June 21, 1993

Mr. Levey. I'm pleased to welcome you to Newstalk 630, WMAL. Thanks so much for joining us.

The President. Glad to do it, Bob.

Economic Program

Mr. Levey. Let's begin with a question about the deficit reduction bill. It passed the Senate Finance Committee last week. Does this now put you on the high road to passage of this bill, or are we still trundling along somewhere below the high road?

The President. Well, I think it is a high road in the sense that that probably was the most difficult committee in the Senate to get such a bill out of. And the fact that they did it and they did it in a timely fashion is encouraging. And I think what we just have to do now is to try to see that the bill—let the bill pass the Senate and send it over to conference, where the Senators and the House Members can discuss what each of them can live with as well as the principles that I have laid down. And I think we can come out of this with a bill which brings the deficit down, requires upper income people, who are in the best position to do so, to pay the lion's share of the taxes, has more cuts than taxes in it, protects the middle class and particularly gives an incentive to the working poor to work their way out of poverty, and has a lot of economic incentives to grow the economy, the kinds of things that have led so many big companies, labor unions, the homebuilders, the realtors, and others to endorse this plan. I think that it is a very good and balanced plan, and I think you'll see that coming out of the session between the Senate and the House, if the bill will be passed in the Senate this week, and of course I'm hoping it will be.

Mr. Levey. Sir, so you know, of course, that the Republicans, cheered up by the results in Texas, are now going around the country saying that you, President Clinton, are doing more for them than they can do for themselves. What's your reaction to that?

The President. Well, my reaction is that it is unfortunate that our side was not, in effect, defended in Texas. Neither of the candidates in the Texas Senate race had voted for or supported my economic program. So the voters of Texas, unfortunately, were permitted to cast their ballots in an atmosphere of unreality, I mean, where one candidate is running saying the issue is spending stupid, and we'd cut $250 billion in spending programs. We'd cut veterans, Medicare, agriculture, foreign aid, defense, just about everything you can see. And it's going to be very interesting now, in light of what happened there, to see the debates that are coming up.

I have been a strong supporter, because I believe in it, of the space station and the super collider. We had a qualified panel of experts. Both those projects are in Texas, you know, super collider entirely in Texas, space station largely in Texas. I had a qualified panel of experts look at the space station. They recommended ways to redesign the project that would save $4 billion and to change the management of NASA in a way that would make the whole space program work better. And we also reduced some spending in the super collider. And I'm hoping I can save those projects now.

But there are strong opponents of those projects in the Congress, and they're saying, "Well, the voters of Texas voted to kill them," because of the unrealistic atmosphere in which that whole election unfolded. And I wish that Lloyd Bentsen, who was Senator from there, had been able to spend full time down there telling the people of Texas he put the program together, and he would not have put a program together which was unfair to Texas, unfair to the middle class, and which didn't have spending cuts.

When you take tough stands and you want to make tough decisions, you have to expect to suffer some unpopularity in the short run as the rhetoric overtakes the reality. But every evidence we have is when the voters know the specifics of the program, that we prevail. In the race in California for Leon Panetta's House seat, where this whole program became the issue, the person who was elected to Congress defended the program, advertised it. Leon got on television and gave the specifics of the program. Our opponent attacked us and said how terrible it was. The voters gave the guy who took my position a 10-point margin. And I thought that in view of all the other problems out there, that was pretty impressive.

Mr. Levey. Mr. President, I thought you got off a good line last week. You said that Washington has become the home of gridlock and greed. Are we really that bad, or is this just political language?

The President. No, I think we're breaking that. I think if this economic program passes, it is fair, it is balanced, and it will bring an end to gridlock. But what I'm saying is it's been more than a decade since a President's budget was even taken seriously by Congress. Nobody ever wanted to talk truth about economics to the American people because the truth is that back in 1981 we cut taxes a bunch, and we increased spending a lot, and we went from a $1 trillion to a $4 trillion debt, and we permitted health care costs to soar out of control. We haven't done anything long-term about our economic health, and now we don't have the money we actually need to be spending on defense conversion, on education and training, on Head Start, on giving people incentives to revitalize our cities.

But if you want to change, it's tough because it means we all have to give up a little something now to get something tomorrow. What we're getting is lower interest rates, more investment, and an economy that will really produce jobs. But to do it we've got to break a mentality of "what's in it for me today." But I think we're on the way to doing that. I think the era of gridlock and greed is fading into the distance, and I'll be surprised if we don't adopt the economic program and a lot of other things that need to be done around this town like political reform, lobbying reform, campaign finance reform, national service. I think we'll get health care reform. I'm hopeful. I'm very optimistic. But I want the people to understand clearly that these things don't happen overnight.

District of Columbia Statehood

Mr. Levey. Sir, speaking of things that need to get done, let's talk for a minute about statehood in the District of Columbia, which you greatly favored and strongly swore that you would lobby for once you got into office. And I have not heard word one from you or from your office about that since you took over. Is this still on your list? And, if so, how high?

The President. Absolutely. I strongly favor it.

I think it ought to be done. Nothing is clearer to me than when you see the Congress still trying to make up their mind what the domestic policy of the citizens of the District of Columbia in non-Federal matters ought to be. I think that the District of Columbia should chart its own course. And I still believe all the concerns are very compelling.

I have to tell you that there has always been substantial opposition in the Congress. And a lot of Members who might ordinarily be strongly for statehood are nervous about whether their own citizens are going to be taxed by the District of Columbia if it becomes a State. I think the question now is, since this is going to be a major debate that will require an awful lot of concentration on the part of the Senators and a lot of focus to work through the issues, when is the appropriate time for it to be brought up to guarantee that it will be seriously considered? Because unless you get serious consideration, it won't pass. That is, the easy thing for a lot of the Members of Congress will be is just to vote no. The only way it can win is if we can bring it up in a relatively calm atmosphere where people can really focus on the practical problems the people living in the District of Columbia face and on the contribution the District of Columbia makes to the country in terms of taxes, people in military service, and in many other ways.

So I still very much believe that this ought to be done. But we have to bring it up at a time when we've got a fair shot to prevail. I mean, I could bring it up and make a speech for it and let it go down. If we want it to pass, we have to bring it up at the right time where people can really focus on it.

President's Priorities

Mr. Levey. Sir, you said the night before you took over, that you did not want to be allowed to become a captive of the White House. You wanted to be the kind of President who got out. Do you think you've succeeded in that?

The President. To some extent. You know, early on here, I have to stay here a lot and just do the work. There's just so much work to be done.

Mr. Levey. I guess so.

The President. If you're trying to change things as much as we are, if you want to put on the Nation's agenda a new economic plan and a new health care plan and then follow that with a plan to open the doors of college education to all, the plan to reform campaign finance and lobbying, a plan for moving people from welfare to work, that requires an immense amount of effort. And then, of course, every President has to spend a significant amount of time on national security and foreign policy issues.

But I have traveled some. I expect to do it more, and I also try to get out and around in DC a lot. You know, one of the reasons I try to jog downtown is just so I can stop and talk to citizens and let them visit with me and kind of make sure I don't lose touch with the real world. I wish I could go——

Mr. Levey. Well, don't jog when it gets humid out there.

The President. It's pretty hot out there.

Mr. Levey. Yes, it is.

The President. But I'm straight. I expect it to be a never-ending struggle, but I hope it's one I can prevail in.

Mr. Levey. Mr. President, we thank you so much for joining us on Newstalk 630 WMAL.

The President. Thank you. I enjoyed it.

NOTE: The interview began at 1:12 p.m. The President spoke from the Roosevelt Room at the White House.

Remarks to the United States-Mexico Binational Commission and an Exchange With Reporters
June 21, 1993

The President. Please sit down, ladies and gentlemen. I want to welcome all of you here to the Roosevelt Room at the White House and say a special word of welcome to our distinguished guests from Mexico.

Today the U.S.-Mexico Binational Commission is holding its 10th meeting at the State Department. I want to say how very proud I am as President to welcome all the participants here. There is no closer partnership between two nations than that which we have with our neighbor Mexico. We share strong ties of history. Our cultures are richly interwoven. Our people are strong in their bonds of kinship and friendship. And the peaceful cooperation of the communities along our 2,000-mile border is not only important but is a real tribute to both our peoples.

An important sign of this close relationship is the Binational Commission itself, which provides a forum for our Cabinets to meet annually to work on issues ranging from the environment to education to telecommunications. Another sign of that partnership is our increasingly close cooperation in world affairs and our commitment to support democracy here in this hemisphere. We worked together to help end the war in El Salvador. Mexico has contributed to the International Civilian Mission of Human Rights Observers in Haiti. Mexico's leadership

in the OAS was critical to the successful collective defense of democracy in Guatemala. And President Salinas speaks with a special authority as one of the world's leading economic reformers when he calls for progress in the Uruguay round to expand world trade.

Mexico and the United States agree that the movement toward open markets and free trade in Latin America is vital for the long term success and strengthening of democracy and human rights in this hemisphere. The countries of Latin American have already made tremendous strides. The emergence of democratically elected governments in this region has permitted Latin America to modernize and to develop. The Latin countries have made enormous progress restructuring and opening their economics, controlling inflation, and increasing the competitiveness of their own productive sectors. In the last 2 years, for the first time in a decade, Latin America has had real growth in per capita income.

Democratic governments have achieved peace, strengthened freedoms, and accelerated the pace of economic integration. With the support of the OAS and the United Nations, internal conflicts in Nicaragua and El Salvador have ended and hopefully will soon end in Guatemala. The OAS routinely observes the freedom of elections across the region. Subregional free trade agreements have emerged throughout the hemisphere. These are points that were recently very well articulated by Foreign Minister Solana at the OAS and those which we in the United States enthusiastically embrace.

Increasingly today, the line has blurred between domestic and foreign policies. What we do abroad directly affects us here at home. And our success at home directly impacts what we are able to do abroad. No relationship illustrates better the strong linkage between foreign and domestic policies than the relationship between the United States and Mexico. The interdependence of our societies and our people are stronger than ever, and they will continue to grow. Domestic policies affect the lives and prosperity of Mexicans, even if they are American domestic policies, in the same way that the domestic policies of Mexico profoundly affect us.

You need only look at the scope and complexity of today's agenda in this meeting to understand how important Mexico and the United States are to each other. We will work to deepen and expand that partnership. One of the most productive areas in which we must work is on trade between our two nations. That has doubled in the last 5 years. This trade is vital to our economic future, to Mexico's economic future, and to our cooperation in every other area of endeavor. It is making both of our economies grow. It is making both of us more efficient and more competitive in global markets. And it adds to the resources we can use to address our common concerns such as the environment.

That is why I am firmly committed to the North American Free Trade Agreement and why the American people and Congress will, I hope and believe, support the NAFTA this year. We are the world's number one exporter. Exports are creating more jobs for us in the last few years than any other source of economic activity. American workers and companies want to be able to compete fully and fairly in global markets. They seek no special advantage, only a level playing field. Mexico has already made important strides in labor rights and in protecting the environment. And when we conclude the side agreements which are now the subject of negotiations, we will have an even broader basis for cooperation and progress and a warmer embrace of the NAFTA here in the United States.

By approving NAFTA, we can cement in place a new source of jobs and economic growth for workers in Canada, Mexico, and our own country. And we'll do more than that. We can send a signal to the nations of the Americas that are on their way to rebuilding their economies, that we are on our way to work with them to build a hemisphere of freer trade, more jobs, and higher growth.

Once again, let me say how very grateful I am to see all of you here. And I know my administration is proud to be a part of these negotiations. I look forward to our continued successes, including the success of NAFTA. I believe that the future belongs to countries committed to democracy, to free markets, and to closer integration of their economies and more trade. That's where the jobs and the incomes are; that's where the hope of a better life lies.

Thank you very much.

[At this point, Foreign Minister Fernando Solana Morales of Mexico made a statement.]

Haitian Refugees

Q. Mr. President, what is your reaction to the Supreme Court ruling on Haitian refugees?

The President. I haven't had a chance to review it. I'm sorry, I haven't had a chance to review it.

NAFTA

Q. Are you frustrated by the fact that these negotiations, the bilateral negotiations, are taking so long and they don't seem to get anywhere yet?

The President. No. I think that everything takes a little longer around here than I think it should. But I think we are getting somewhere, and I think that you will see these negotiations produce successful agreements. And I think we will go forward with the free trade agreement this year. I'm very hopeful.

Q. Can I follow up on that, Mr. President? Don't you think with the full domestic agenda you have and the opposition to NAFTA in the United States, it's more likely to get a ratification, if at all, next year and not this year?

The President. No. Because I think the issue has been, in effect, fully aired and debated before it comes up for ratification. And I think a lot of the questions that have been raised about it in the Congress are the very questions that are being debated and dealt with in the negotiations now going on between the countries. So I would expect that we can get successful consideration of it this year.

And also, you know, I think this is another

one of those battles of ideas in which we're engaged. But I believe very strongly that this will create jobs and increase incomes for people on both sides of the border. And I think if that argument is accepted, it's just as likely to be accepted this year as next year.

Henry Leon Ritzenthaler

Q. [Inaudible]—about the half-brother, is this gentleman your half-brother, do you know?

The President. What did you say, Helen [Helen Thomas, United Press International]?

Q. [Inaudible]—California. Same question, basically.

The President. I placed a call today, but there was nobody home. I don't think I should say anything until after the call takes place.

NAFTA

Q. You do not have the votes in the House right now. Are you planning on launching a campaign in order to push forward for ratification of NAFTA?

The President. I try to win the things that I support. When we can bring it up, we'll bring it up and try to win it. And I have been discussing this quite a bit, actually, in personal conversations with various Members of the House and Senate and getting advice, beginning to plot strategy. But of course, we'll have a campaign to do it. We can't prevail without a campaign; we have to try to win it.

Thank you very much. One person from the Mexican press, we'll take one question. That's only fair.

Drug Policy

Q. Mr. President, do you have a new policy to fight drugs here, or do you have a new policy towards immigration?

The President. We will, but I believe that the announcement of that should involve the drug czar, Mr. Brown, and others. And we will have something to say about that in the future.

Thank you.

NOTE: The President spoke at 2:10 p.m. in the Roosevelt Room at the White House.

Statement on the Meeting of the United States-Mexico Binational Commission
June 21, 1993

Today the U.S.-Mexico Binational Commission is holding its 10th meeting at the State Department. I want to extend a very warm welcome to the members of the Cabinet of President Salinas and to say a few words about our warm friendship with Mexico.

There is no closer partnership between two nations than that which we have with our neighbor Mexico. We share strong ties of history. Our cultures are richly interwoven. Our people share strong bonds of kinship and fellowship. And the peaceful cooperation of the communities along our 2,000-mile border is important to both of our peoples.

An important sign of our close relations is the Binational Commission itself, which provides a forum for our Cabinets to meet annually to work on issues ranging from the environment to education to telecommunications.

Another sign of our partnership is our increasingly close cooperation in world affairs and our commitment to the success of democracy in this hemisphere. We worked together to help end the war in El Salvador. Mexico has contributed to the International Civilian Mission of Human Rights Observers in Haiti. Mexico's leadership in the OAS was critical to the successful collective defense of democracy in Guatemala. And President Salinas speaks with a special authority as one of the world's leading economic reformers when he calls for progress in the Uruguay round to expand world trade.

Mexico and we agree that the movement toward open markets and free trade in Latin America is vital and for the long-term success and strengthening of democracy and human rights in this hemisphere. The countries of Latin America have already made great strides. The emergence of democratically elected governments in the region has permitted Latin America to modernize and develop. The Latin countries have made enormous progress restructuring and opening their economies, controlling inflation, and increasing the competitiveness of their productive sectors. In the last 2 years, for the first time in a decade, Latin America has had real growth in per capita income.

Free trade agreements have contributed to the progress in regional integration. Democratic governments have achieved peace, strengthened freedoms, and accelerated the pace of integration. With the support of the OAS and the U.N., internal conflicts in Nicaragua and El Salvador have ended and hopefully will soon end in Guatemala. The OAS routinely observes the freedom of elections across the region. Subregional free trade agreements have emerged throughout the hemisphere. These are points that were recently well articulated by Foreign Minister Solana at the OAS and that we enthusiastically embrace.

Increasingly today, the line has blurred between domestic and foreign policies. What we seek to do abroad directly affects us at home. No relationship illustrates better the strong linkage between foreign and domestic policies than our relationship with Mexico. The interdependence of our societies and people are stronger than ever and continues to grow. Our domestic policies affect the lives and prosperity of Mexicans in the same way that the domestic policies of Mexico profoundly affect us. You need only to look at the scope and complexity of today's BNC agenda to understand how important Mexico and the U.S. are to each other. We will work to deepen and expand our partnership even further.

One of the most productive areas in which we must work closely together is on the trade between our nations, which has doubled in the past 5 years. That trade is vital to our economic future, to Mexico's economic future, and to our cooperation in every area. It is making both our economies grow. It is making us both more efficient and more competitive in the world market. And it adds to the resources we can use to address common concerns such as the environment.

That is why I am firmly committed to the NAFTA, and it's why I believe the American people and Congress will support the NAFTA this year. We are the world's number one exporter. Exports are creating more jobs than any other source in our economy today. American workers and companies want to compete fairly in the international market. They seek no special advantage, only a level playing field. Mexico has already made important strides in labor rights and in protecting the environment. When we conclude the side agreements, we will have an even broader basis for cooperation and progress.

By approving the NAFTA, we will cement in place a new source of jobs and economic growth for workers in Canada, Mexico, and the United States. And we will do more than that. We will send a signal that the nations of the Americas are on their way to building a hemisphere of freer trade.

Once again, I wish to reiterate my deep personal commitment to continuing the positive, friendly relations between the U.S. and Mexico. I look forward to celebrating together with you the happy occasion of congressional approval of the NAFTA before the end of this year.

Teleconference Remarks With the U.S. Conference of Mayors
June 22, 1993

The President. I'm honored to address all the United States mayors at your conference. I want to thank you first for the strong support that you've given the economic plan I presented to the Congress and to the country. You supported it not only because it's good for the cities but because it's also good for America.

Your president, Mayor Bill Althaus, has certainly earned my respect and support because he's looked beyond party labels to support this plan because it's good for the people of his community. I look forward to having just that good of a relationship with your incoming president, my longtime friend Mayor Jerry Abramson. And I want to say a special word about your host, Mayor Dinkins, a great Mayor of a very great city.

As mayors, more than any other public officials in this country, you have been on the frontlines of public service. Every day you hear from people who have lost their jobs, who live in fear of crime, who desperately want to improve their children's schools and their own way of life. Many of you are trying to reknit a social fabric that has been unraveling for a long time now. From schools with metal detectors to hospital emergency rooms crowded with gunshot victims, to children bearing children, you know what the real problems of America are. I often think that being a mayor today is an act of faith that somehow our cities' problems will not overwhelm their promise. And our cities must always be the centers of commerce and culture, magnets for talent and ambition, places of hope and opportunity. We can't let the problems overcome the promise.

I wish I could be with you today in person, and I will look forward to doing that as you meet in the future. But my first obligation to you and to America is to keep fighting here in Washington for my economic plan. It will create jobs, increase incomes, offer hope and opportunity, and give us the freedom we need to invest in America, in the future.

For 12 years we have seen, all of us, you as mayors and me as a Governor, we saw what happened as we wrestled with many of the problems that grip America everywhere and got a message from Washington, "You're on your own." Washington ran up the national debt from $1 trillion to $4 trillion and still reduced investments in the things that make us stronger and wealthier and more secure as a people. We got make-believe budgets from Presidents and mandates without money from Congress. And Washington never was willing to take responsibility for the future of this country, leaving it to the mayors and the Governors to make all the tough choices.

Well, I don't expect anyone in that room today with you agrees with everything that I'm trying to do as President. But I think all of you understand that because of the massive debt we inherited, I can't do everything that I want to do. But I'll tell you this: I am determined to establish a new relationship, a new partnership with our Nation's cities based on respect and responsibility and an understanding that you ought to have more flexibility to do your work without so much micromanagement and regulation from the National Government. I also want to put the Nation's money where our values are. I want us to invest in rewarding work, strengthening families, and restoring our communities. And I want to set an example of responsibility by making the tough choices that have been avoided and evaded for too long here.

My economic plan is necessary and fair, and it will work. It brings down the national deficit by $500 billion over the next 5 years. For every $10 we cut the deficit, $5 comes from spending cuts; $3.75 from the highest income Americans, those in the upper 6 percent of income brackets; and $1.25 comes from the middle class. Two-thirds of this tax burden comes from people with incomes above $200,000 because they can best afford to pay. And over 100 specific spending cuts are over $100 million each.

Now, it's easy to criticize this plan, maybe just because I've put forward a plan. Most of my critics don't have a plan of their own. Some say they're willing to cut Social Security and Medicare benefits for people just above the poverty line or cut more in veterans benefits than have been cut already or cut tax credits for the working poor just to reduce the tax burden on the wealthy. Well, I draw the line there. I don't think that's fair. I think that we need a fair tax system, not because we want to punish success but because in the 1980's we ran up the deficit while raising taxes on the middle class and lowering them on upper income people.

Now I ask my critics in Congress, where are your tough choices? What are you going to do? If you want to reduce the tax burden on the wealthy, where will you make up the money? What will you do to reduce this deficit? Are you willing to make the same kinds of decisions that I have? I wonder what the middle class, the working poor, the old, the sick, and the veterans will do if the failed policies of the past are not abandoned. I also wonder what they'll do if we don't ask all the rest of us to pay our fair share so that we can still continue to take care of them.

Make no mistake about it, I want to change the way Washington works with people all across this country. I want to move beyond the politics of both parties in Washington, beyond the politics of abandonment, of the politics of entitlement. We've got to have a sense that we're doing this together. We can't do everything for the cities or the people of America, but we can't turn our backs on you either. And frankly, that's what you've had for the last 12 years.

I want a new spirit of empowerment that offers you a hand up, not a handout, that works with you instead of working you over. I want to offer more opportunity and demand more responsibility. And I know the mayors of this country are ready for that kind of arrangement. Just as we need to stop spending on things that don't work, we need to invest more in things that do work.

My plan does cut the deficit, but it finds the money to invest in empowering people to build better lives. I want to empower families to build better lives for their children and am fighting to expand the women, infants, and children's nutrition program so that every expectant mother who needs help can get it. I'm fighting for full funding for Head Start so that every child can start school ready to learn. I want to empower people through education. I'm fighting for tough standards for our students and our schools. I want to give them the resources they need to meet those standards. To offer young people new hope and teach work habits, I'm fighting for summer jobs. Congress has approved 580,000 publicly funded jobs, and we're asking for another 215,000 and challenging the business community to match our commitment. The Labor Secretary, Bob Reich, has been there talking to you about that.

I want to make it possible for tens of thousands of young people to pay off their college loans by serving the communities in which they live. That's the thing your previous speaker was talking about. The National Government can offer you our greatest resource, our people, to work in the streets, in the neighborhoods, in the communities, to work on programs that really change people's lives for the better, programs that you couldn't afford to have as mayors were it not for national service. And I'm proud to say that the national service bill has passed both committees in the House and the Senate just in the last few days with real bipartisan majorities.

To provide new opportunities for young people who aren't going to college, my plan contains the boldest national apprenticeship program our country has ever known, more funds for training in your communities. I want to empower low income people by making work pay. By expanding the earned-income tax credit, we can establish a principle that will be important in every city in this country. If you work 40 hours a week and you have a child at home, you'll no longer live in poverty. We need to encourage full-time work, not lifetime welfare.

I want to empower communities to protect themselves, and I'm fighting for $200 million to help you hire back police officers you've had to lay off. I want to put 100,000 more police officers on our streets and promote community policing programs. That's the best anticrime program we can have.

I want to empower our communities to create new jobs, and I've proposed an empowerment zone program in excess of $5 billion, so that communities can work with the private sector, and we can finally see whether these incentives can attract businesses and create new jobs for people in our distressed inner cities and small towns. I believe they will. We're offering bold, new tax incentives for businesses to create jobs and asking each of you to create a strategy to rebuild your own community. We've learned that Washington can't solve problems from the top down, but that we have to help you. We also know you can't have capitalism without capital. That's why I have proposed a $382 million funding for a network of community development banks all across this country to provide the credit and the banking services that are the lifeblood of local economies and that don't really exist in too many of our communities.

Almost a year ago, I left another convention in New York on a bus tour through America's heartland, to Mayor Althaus's hometown of York, Pennsylvania, to Mayor Abramson's hometown of Louisville, and to many of your own cities and towns. Every day I go to work in the White House, I think about how to create jobs and hope and opportunities for the people I visited on those bus tours. I can't do it alone. I need your support in the tough choices that are coming up in Congress. If you'll stay involved and vigilant and vocal, we can create a vibrant economic growth for every community in this country. We can do it. We can cut the deficit. We can build on the successes we've had.

Just in the last 5 months you see interest rates down, homebuilding up, 130,000 new construction jobs—that's the biggest increase in 9 years—755,000 new jobs in the economy in only 5 months, 90 percent of them in the private sector. This program to bring the interest rates down through deficit reduction is working. And when we do it, we will then have the funds we need to invest in the kind of partnerships that will help us to deal with the problems that all of you face.

So that's what I offer you: a partnership, an economic program that works, and finally, over the long run, the way to deal with a lot of these underlying, deeply seated cultural and social problems that I know have bothered all of you. We have to find new and different ways, one on one, to help to deal with the scourges of drug abuse, of crime, of unsafe streets, and of all these children who are out there having children themselves. But I am very, very hopeful, because I still believe the most creative and innovative leaders in America are those at the grassroots. I'll work with you, and I'll try to be the best partner you ever had in the White House.

Thank you very much.

[At this point, Mayor Althaus thanked the President and introduced Mayor David Dinkins of New York City, who asked the President to implement a more efficient system for distributing Federal funds to cities.]

The President. Mayor, first of all, let me say a word of greeting to Secretary Brown; I see him sitting next to you. I understand five of my Cabinet Secretaries have been there, and I can't find anybody on the phone here in Washington. I hope nothing bad happens while the mayors conference is going on.

I wanted to say just a word about that. As you know, that's a matter that's been debated for years among the mayors, the Governors, and the Congress. We are in the process right now, through the Vice President's task force on reinventing government, of reexamining the way the Federal Government relates to the cities and the States. And if I might make a specific suggestion, I think it would be very helpful if you, or Mayor Abramson, if that's the appropriate person to do it, would designate a group of mayors to make a very specific proposal to our task force because—and obviously, we'll have to invite people who might disagree to do the same thing—but I think it's very important that we examine this because one of the things that I'm concerned about is the colossal amount of money we waste every year trying to micromanage these grants, trying to have extra layers of regulation. And I think that a lot of these things need to be reexamined.

So I think the proper forum for us to do that in is this one. And it's on a very fast track because the report is due in September, so it's not anything we're going to dillydally around

about. And I would like you to make a proposal to our commission.

[Mayor Paul Helmke of Fort Wayne, IN, requested the President's support for legislation to prevent unfunded Federal mandates.]

The President. Well, I haven't reviewed the bill, Paul, but I certainly think that we shouldn't have unfunded mandates. I spoke out against them as a Governor. I told the mayors that I would be opposed to adding to your burdens. I don't believe in that. And I'll review the bill and see whether or not we should support the bill, too. But I have told our administration clearly that I don't want us up there on the Hill supporting bills to load up a bunch of new burdens on the mayors and the Governors when they're broke, when we're not increasing funding to the States and the cities as we should. And I've sent a very clear signal on it. And I will review the legislation.

I also want to thank you and Bill Althaus and many other Republican mayors for supporting the jobs stimulus program. And let me say that I think after we pass this budget we'll be able, together, in a very bipartisan fashion, to try to make the argument that was made there again, which is that there is a difference between investment and consumption spending, and that while the Federal Government may be spending too much on regulation, on the programs of the past, and on uncontrolled health care costs, we are actually not anywhere nearly where we need to be in targeted investments that create jobs and opportunities not only in the public sector but in the private sector. And the mayors were very, very helpful in that regard. I'll never forget what you did. And I don't want you to think that the battle that you waged more ferociously than any other single group in the United States—you did more to try to help that package—and I don't want you to think that the battle you waged was for nothing, because the battle you waged was about an idea that we're still going to have to fight to get back into our national consciousness. Not all Federal spending is the same. Not all taxes are the same. We have to learn to make very rigorous distinctions if we want to grow this economy. And so I do want to thank you for that. And I will review the Kempthorne legislation. Thank you.

Mayor Althaus. Mr. President, I don't know that we've ever been called ferocious before, but we appreciate it. [*Laughter*]

The President. I can't believe you were never called ferocious.

[*Mayor Abramson asked the President to explain his defense conversion plan.*]

The President. Secretary Brown can discuss this in greater detail, but let me say that we have spent a lot of time through the National Economic Council, with all the Departments that you mentioned, trying to make sure that we have a coordinated conversion plan. Some of the work has to be done in the Defense Department. We are shifting more research and development into other areas. We are doing what we can to make sure that the work that is done in Commerce and Energy—Energy has the national labs, as you know—and the Labor Department, that all these things are coordinated and that you will be able to work with the National Economic Council or with any Cabinet Secretary and still have the benefits of all of us working together. We really tried to minimize the turf battles here.

I also asked for quite a large increase in defense conversion funds over the next 5 years, although I don't think it's as much as we need, and I think we'll be asking for more as we go along. And I want to emphasize basically three things because this is not an easy issue. I've done a lot of work on this myself as a Governor. We have to be prepared to retrain workers who can't keep the jobs they have. We have to be prepared to invest in companies to help them find dual-use technologies in the hope that those companies can keep as many workers as possible and can find new products and services they can provide. We also have to be prepared to invest directly in communities that will have to develop all new economic strategies. There are communities which basically don't have a diverse economic base today, where if they lose a base, for example, instead of a plant, that may have great difficulty in redesigning an economic strategy even though they may have the resource of the base right there that they can use. So my view is that there is no silver bullet here. You have to work on the workers, the companies, and the communities. And we've got to keep working on this.

I will say this: I think there is a lot of sympathy and understanding of these problems in the Congress. And I think that the mayors will be able to have some significant successes in the years ahead. If we can go on and pass this economic program, lock down our determination to bring the deficit down, and keep these interest rates down, then I think we'll be able to come back to the Congress on conversion issues and do quite well.

[*Mayor Juanita Crabb of Binghamton, NY, asked the President to meet with mayors and police chiefs to discuss community policing programs.*]

The President. I think that's a good idea, Mayor Crabb. I think the goal can be achieved, but it's important that we achieve it in a way that you feel is maximizing your ability to do a good job and that we do it in a way that achieves the ultimate objective, which is safer streets and more robust and hopeful communities. So I'd like to have the meeting with you and, obviously, representatives of the police chiefs.

There are three or four different avenues that we can pursue to get to our ultimate goal of having 100,000 more police officers. And we really need to talk about what's best for you, what works best, how you can get folks with the maximum flexibility to pursue community policing strategies. I'm very interested in this. This is something that the Attorney General and I have had several conversations about already, and there are a lot of people in the White House itself working hard on this. I think we ought to get our group together and meet with your group and just talk it out, and we can develop a coordinated 4-year plan to get the job done. I'm anxious to do it. It's one thing we can do that will literally change the lives of most Americans who live in the communities affected by it. And we need to continue to work on it until we get the job done.

[*Mayor Althaus again thanked the President and reaffirmed the mayors' support for him.*]

The President. Thank you, Mayor. Goodbye.

NOTE: The President spoke at 10:50 a.m. from Room 459 of the Old Executive Office Building.

Telephone Conversation With the Crew of the Space Shuttle *Endeavour* and an Exchange With Reporters
June 22, 1993

The President. Can you hear me?

Mission Commander Ronald Grabe. Mr. President, I believe we hear you loud, but slightly broken up.

The President. Well, we can hear you, and we are looking at you. And you all look wonderful.

Commander Grabe. Well, you're loud and clear now, Mr. President. That's much better.

The President. We want to congratulate you on a spectacular launch and on looking so happy. The American people are very reassured watching you on television now.

Commander Grabe. Well, thank you sir. It's early in the mission, but we're very excited about the mission. It's certainly a multifaceted one, and it really does show the versatility of the space shuttle. We're doing a little bit of everything on this flight.

The President. I know. I understand one of the things you're doing is chasing down the EURECA satellite that was put up by the shuttle last July. And I'm especially pleased about that because it shows what we can do in the way of international cooperation as well as science. And I want to congratulate you on that and wish you well.

Astronaut Janice Voss. Thank you very much, Mr. President. We've been working very hard for about a year training for this rendezvous and retrieval. And we've had a lot of fantastic support, both in our own country in our own ground support team and the international team all over in Europe, and we're looking forward to bringing back great science in EURECA to the Europeans.

The President. We're looking forward to that, too. I also understand that David and Jeff will be outside the shuttle practicing for the repair of the Hubbell telescope and for the future assembly of the space station. And I thought that maybe one of them or both would like to comment on it so people can get a good look at you now, and when they see you outside in your suits they'll know who they're seeing.

Astronaut Jeff Wisoff. Well, Mr. President, we're looking very forward to the space walk. We feel proud to be able to represent America.

And we're very happy of your support of the space station. We think it represents the best of America and their pioneering spirit. And the NASA team has done a really great job of preparing us for our flight. And I think both Dave and I just can't wait to get there.

The President. Well, we're excited about it. And while you're up there, we're going to be down here trying to support the space program and the space station. As you know, we had a very distinguished commission looking at the whole space station project. They recommended some redesign and some management changes at NASA. But I think this should give us a great deal of credibility. We've got some important votes coming up in the Congress in the next 2 days. While you're up there, we're going to be down here voting on this project. And I very much hope that we can prevail, and I think, frankly, your success and your work will help us to prevail. You're doing as much up there to help us win the votes down here as anyone, and I thank you for that.

Commander Grabe. Well, Mr. President, we're very gratified by your support of the space station. We certainly all consider it to be an immensely important project in continuing our leadership in science and technology.

The President. Thank you. Let me just say one last thing about something that's very important to me. I understand that later in the mission Janice and Brian are going to be talking with schoolchildren around the world. And you may know that my daughter is a big fan of the space program. She's off at summer language camp now. But I want to just tell you how much I appreciate the fact that you're making an international education project out of this mission. That's very important to me.

Astronaut Brian Duffy. Mr. President, we find that using amateur radio is an excellent way of communicating with children all around the world, and we're also able to excite them by using space and science. In letting them see space and science in action, we're able to excite them and hope they'll study harder.

The President. You have no idea. You may be on this mission creating thousands of scientists for the future just by the power of your example and by this direct communication. I think sometimes we underestimate the impact that human contact in an enormously impressive setting like this can have on children all across the world, not only those with whom you'll talk but millions of others who will just see it and know that it happened.

I want to thank all of you for the wonderful job you've done. We're very proud of you, and we're very proud of all the NASA folks down here who are supporting you. I want to encourage you and say again that I'm behind you, this administration is behind you, and I think the American people are behind you.

Astronaut David Low. Mr. President, once again, we thank you very much for your support. It's a real pleasure to be up here at your service.

The President. Thank you. Let's hear from the last astronaut there.

Astronaut Nancy Sherlock. I just wanted to add my thanks for your support. We all feel that the space program has done a tremendous amount for this country, both in promoting inside the country science education and also with the international partners. And it means a lot to us to know that that support still is around and that we're going to have a strong space program in the future.

The President. I'm committed to that. The American people, in watching you today, can see one area of human endeavor in which we are indisputably continuing to lead the world and bringing other countries into partnership. And both leadership in technology and science and partnership with other countries, those are the keys to our future as a people, to our standard of living, to our quality of life, as well as to our ability to continue the American tradition of exploring frontiers. And I'm very proud of you, and I wish you well. And we can't wait until you get home safe and sound. But have a great time up there, and learn a lot, and we'll all learn from you.

Good luck, and God bless you all.

[*At this point, the telephone conversation ended, and the President took questions from reporters.*]

Homosexuals in the Military

Q. Mr. President, there's apparently a memo circulating over at the Pentagon suggesting that gays should be allowed to serve in the military if they simply don't advertise their status. Is that what you're likely to recommend?

The President. I think I should wait until I get the report from the Pentagon. I have not received the report. I talked to Secretary Aspin very briefly just a couple of days ago and asked him to proceed with this and let me know as soon as possible. I think the American people in the military are certainly ready for a resolution. But I can't comment on the specifics until I see it.

Q. Does that sound like a good solution to you?

The President. I want to see what the details are. There's been a lot of very helpful comment I think on this whole issue, finally, in the last few weeks. Senator Dole was very helpful in what he said. I thought some of the people who testified, interestingly enough, on both sides of the issue in the last set of hearings really tried to shed more light than heat, tried to bring down the emotionalism in the debate and get people to look at the facts. So I think we're ready to resolve this and get it behind us. And I hope that it will happen soon. But I don't want to comment specifically until I get a specific recommendation.

Q. But you haven't changed your mind, have you?

The President. Absolutely not. And I don't see this as a liberal-conservative issue. I mean, you've got a core who was in the Reagan administration supporting the idea that there has to be some provisions for people who don't do anything wrong but who are homosexuals serving in the service. You've got Barry Goldwater, you've got a lot of people who served with great distinction in the military who are now in the Congress taking the same position. So I think we're coming toward agreement on it, and I'm hopeful. But I'd like to see it resolved soon.

Henry Leon Ritzenthaler

Q. Sir, have you spoken to this fellow who claims to be your brother—half-brother?

The President. No. I left word on his answering service in California yesterday. I didn't know he was in the air. And I also left word in New York. And I'd like to talk to him, and then I'll have a brief statement about it. But I think I should—I'd like to try one more day to talk to him.

Q. I think he's afraid to call you.

The President. Well, I hope not; I mean, we left word that it would be fine for him to call.

Q. He's showed some reticence.

The President. He's been, I think, very appealing and humble the way he's handled this whole thing. I've been impressed.

Pat Nixon

Q. Any thoughts on the death of Pat Nixon?

The President. Well, I'm very sad, and I intend to try to speak with President Nixon today. I talked with him a couple of times in the last month, once when he was at the hospital and once when he had just come from the hospital in the last month or so, to ask his advice about various things. You know, they had a very long and very close marriage. And this must be a very difficult time for him. I think the American people really appreciate the dignity with which she served as First Lady. And I hope and believe that the Nixon family has the thoughts and prayers of all the American people today.

Q. Is Panetta going to tell us anything we don't know? [*Laughter*]

The President. Well, that's not so much a condemnation of me as a compliment to you. You know everything already. [*Laughter*]

NOTE: The President spoke at 12:45 p.m. in the Oval Office at the White House. The exchange portion of this item could not be verified because the tape was incomplete.

Statement on the Death of Pat Nixon
June 22, 1993

The Nation is deeply saddened today by the loss of former First Lady Pat Nixon.

Patricia Ryan Nixon was a quiet pioneer whose concern for family and country will leave a lasting mark on history. Mrs. Nixon personified a deep reverence for the cherished American traditions of community service, voluntarism, and personal responsibility to one another.

As First Lady, she was indeed a lady of "firsts." She was the first First Lady to represent the President of the United States on an official overseas visit. She was the first incumbent First Lady to publicly support the equal rights amendment. And she was an early advocate of promoting a woman to the U.S. Supreme Court.

While always dignified and gracious, Mrs. Nixon was also a passionate believer in volunteer service and the importance of Americans helping one another. The appearance of the White House today and its accessibility to visitors at special times each year owe themselves in large degree to her generous and creative efforts. During her first Thanksgiving as First Lady she invited 225 senior citizens from area nursing homes to the White House for a special meal. She invited hundreds of families to nondenominational Sunday services in the East Room. And she offered the White House as a meeting place for volunteer organizations dedicated to solving community problems.

Mrs. Nixon, a mother of two, was also a loyal and steadfast believer in family. She traveled extensively with her husband across the Nation and abroad and was widely praised for her diplomatic gestures overseas. As she said in 1971, "We've always been a team." We are heartened that former President Nixon and Mrs. Nixon were able to celebrate their 53d wedding anniversary yesterday. Our thoughts are with Mrs. Nixon's family today as we remember her many accomplishments and contributions to the Nation.

Statement by the Press Secretary on the President's Task Force on National Health Care Reform
June 22, 1993

The United States Court of Appeals for the District of Columbia ruled today that the President's Task Force on Health Care Reform, chaired by First Lady Hillary Rodham Clinton, was not subject to the Federal Advisory Committee Act. The Court of Appeals decision confirms that the task force operated in full compliance with the law.

In reversing the United States district court on this issue, the court of appeals held that Mrs. Clinton is a "full-time officer or employee of the Government" for purposes of the advisory committee act. The court of appeals decision means that the advisory committee act's requirements for open meetings and production of documents did not apply to the task force.

The President announced the creation of the health care task force, as well as interdepartmental working groups, on January 25, 1993. The task force held over 20 meetings in April and May and has presented health care reform proposals and options to the President. The President is now in the process of reviewing those proposals and options and will be preparing a final proposal for delivery to Congress.

The task force terminated on May 30, 1993. There are no plans to reconvene the task force.

White House Statement on the Posthumous Award of the Presidential Medal of Freedom to Arthur Ashe
June 22, 1993

The President awarded a posthumous Presidential Medal of Freedom, the Nation's highest civilian honor, to tennis great Arthur Ashe at the National Sports Awards ceremony at Constitution Hall Sunday night.

Presenting the medal to Ashe's widow, Jeanne, the President noted that Ashe "battled his way to the top rung of international tennis, and he did it with an inner strength and outward dignity that marked his game every bit as much as that dazzling crosscourt backhand."

Appointment for the President's Council on Physical Fitness and Sports
June 22, 1993

The President has appointed Olympic gold medalist Florence Griffith Joyner and former NBA star and Congressman Tom McMillen to be the Cochairs of the President's Council on Physical Fitness.

"It is very gratifying that two such distinguished individuals as Florence Griffith Joyner and Tom McMillen have agreed to join my team as Cochairs of the President's Council on Physical Fitness," said the President. "They are heroes to millions of Americans and deservedly so. I look forward to the advice that they will provide Secretary Shalala and myself on how we can enhance opportunities for all of our people to participate in physical fitness and sports activities."

NOTE: Biographies of the appointees were made available by the Office of the Press Secretary.

Exchange With Reporters on the Economic Program
June 23, 1993

Q. Mr. President, is there any way the Republicans can put a plan together that meets your criteria without taxes?

The President. Well, I don't see how. You know, we've already cut $250 billion in spending. We've cut Medicare, Medicaid, veterans, farmers, defense, foreign aid, every part of the Federal Government. The Republican leader said a couple of days ago he was willing to raise taxes on the wealthy, but apparently the people in his caucus who want to protect high income people and the tax cuts they got in the eighties, while the middle class got a tax increase, are going to win once again. So what he'll have to do is come up with some version of the same plan they have in the House. The Republican plan in the House, I will remind you, lost more Republican votes than the Democratic plan lost Democratic votes. And the reason is it was unfair to the middle class, the working people, the elderly, and to others because it protected upper income people. And I think you're going to see the same thing. We'll see what they have to say, but I can't imagine what else they can do.

We've got a 5-year freeze on domestic discretionary spending. We're cutting defense all we should, in my opinion, and then some. The only thing that's going up in this budget is health care next year. The only thing that's going up is health care. So it's going to be very interesting to see when they have to face the music what they'll say. But we're all eagerly waiting.

Q. When do you think you can get this reconciliation through a conference committee, assuming the Senate passes it?

The President. Well, one step at a time. We have to get it through the Senate first. We have to get the Senate Finance Committee bill on the floor, watch the amendments come forward, see what happens, and try to pass a bill in the Senate to go on to Congress. And then once we do that, we'll talk about the conference committee.

Q. Leon Panetta said yesterday that one of the goals was going to be to restore veterans. How are you going to do that, go more toward the House plan of raising taxes or the Senate plan, which is more cutting entitlements?

The President. We're going to do a good job of that. Just watch.

NOTE: The President spoke at 9:45 a.m. in the Cabinet Room at the White House, prior to a meeting with congressional leaders. A tape was not available for verification of the content of this exchange.

Remarks on the Economic Program and an Exchange With Reporters
June 23, 1993

The President. I just want to make a couple of remarks about where we are in the Congress today. We're at the eleventh hour of this budget debate. It's been going on for months now. And the Republican Senators say finally they're going to offer a plan. The plan clearly, if you look at all the options, will be to protect the privileged and to punish the middle class and the most vulnerable.

The Senate Finance Committee bill which was reported out last week now has 78.5 percent of the burden of new taxes falling on people with incomes above $200,000. All the analysts say that my plan is an honest budget plan, that it will reduce the deficit at least as much, if not more, than we're saying, and it is fair. And we're working hard to pass it in the Senate.

But we ought to have some bipartisan support. We ought to have some Republican support for this. And the fact that the Republican Senators are thinking about coming out with a plan now, calling it a no-tax plan, which is really nothing but a shield to keep the wealthiest Americans from paying their fair share, even though their taxes went down for the last 12 years while the deficit exploded, is a real disservice to this country.

Economic Program

Q. Why, Mr. President, do you think the Republicans want to protect the privileged?

The President. Well, that's what they did. That's what their 12-year economic policy was all about. That's what trickle-down economics was based on, that if you just lower taxes on the wealthy enough and when you have to increase them, increase them on the middle class, and that upper income people, when they get all the economic gains, will then reinvest it, create jobs, and raise incomes. It didn't work. It has never worked in the history of the country.

I want to emphasize, I do not want to punish success. This is not what this is about. I want to reward success. My plan has real incentives for small business, for new business, for new technology. I want to reward success, and I want people to make a lot of money. But we have to have a fair tax system, and this plan should require the vast majority of the new revenues to come from people with incomes above $200,000 because they're the ones that got the benefits of the 1980's.

Q. Do you think their plan will get anywhere? And do you have any Republican support?

The President. No—well, I mean, look at what happened in the House when they had the same sort of thing. The Republican plan in the House lost more Republican votes than the Democratic plan lost Democratic votes.

Q. Are you looking for some kind of middle ground compromise where you might be able to bring on some Republicans?

The President. Well, I'm going to try to pass— what I think we have to do is to get this bill into conference, come out with a bill that meets our objectives: $500 billion in deficit reduction; more cuts than tax increases; progressive tax increases; and then real incentives to reward work, to reward families, to reward investments in this economy. That's what we're trying to do. And I think we're getting close.

Interest Rates

Q. Are you willing to, sir, accept a mild increase in interest rates?

The President. For what?

Q. From the Fed.

The President. Well, whatever they do, I think, long-term interest rates will stay down. That's the key to the economy. But there's no inflation in this economy now that we can see.

Q. So they should not raise rates?

The President. That's a decision they have to make.

NOTE: The President spoke at 12:44 p.m. in the Rose Garden at the White House.

Remarks at the Presidential Scholars Awards Presentation Ceremony
June 23, 1993

I want to thank you all for being here and welcome the Members of Congress who are here and those who were here who had to leave for a vote. I want to say a special word of— it's a good vote—*[laughter]*—I want to say a special word of thanks to the Marine Band for being here to play for us today. Thank you. Since my office is just over there, when they come out here to play for you, they also keep me in a far better frame of mind as I work through the day.

I thank the Commission on Presidential Scholars for all the work that they have put into selecting this year's recipients. I especially want to thank my good friend Governor Florio of New Jersey for his work as Chairman. I asked him to serve as Chairman because I admire the courage and conviction with which he has conducted himself as Governor of New Jersey and particularly the bravery that he showed in dealing with the educational needs of the people of his State.

The Secretary of Education, Dick Riley, for- merly was Governor of South Carolina, and in that connection he labored mightily for years to improve the education of the children of his State and served as a mentor of mine. And I thank him for his leadership.

As I look out at this group today of proud parents and family members and friends and educators, I'm reminded once again of the curious mix of things that produces the sort of achievement that we see embodied in the young people on this stage today. There are, unfortunately, still a lot of people in the United States who believe that how much you learn and how well you do in life depends primarily on your IQ. And yet we know that if you strung all the people on the globe together from first to last by IQ, you couldn't stick a straw between any of the two. A remarkable combination of ability and intangible things like encouragement and love and support as well as personal effort and drive and commitment go into making up really gifted learners who are committed to doing it for a lifetime.

All the young people who have been acknowledged today have great natural talents, and they should be grateful for what God has given them. But every person on this stage today, not only them but me, we're all here because of the people who helped us along the way.

There's a young man who was supposed to be here today named Justin Konrad, from the State of Maine, who on June the 5th was in an automobile accident that claimed the life of one of his friends and claimed part of one of his legs. Today he's in a hospital in Maine recovering from his injuries. I talked to him this weekend when I was up in Maine, and he's already talking about going to Harvard and majoring in government and playing sports. When he gave his—let me see if I can pronounce this—salutatorian's address at his high school graduation, he gave a speech about optimism. And he still has it, and I hope all of you will be able to keep it as you go through college and you pursue your careers. Keeping a positive frame of mind may sound like an obvious and easy thing. It becomes increasingly difficult with a difficulty of circumstances, but more important with every passing day.

Last Saturday, just before I spoke with Justin by phone, I was speaking at the commencement of Northeastern University in Boston, and I met another young student there graduating from college named Doug Luffborough. He was the person who was designated by his fellow students at Northeastern to speak on their behalf. Doug's mother is a cleaning woman who earns $7,000 a year and who, in addition to her regular job, cleans a private school part-time to pay tuition for another of her sons. For a while, the mother and all of her children were actually homeless.

It's remarkable that this young man ever got to go to college at all. The advice he got from one of his counselors was to give it up and start looking for a job. But his mother believed in him and refused to let him aim low. When she couldn't get a babysitter, she took him along to work. And he watched her day-in and day-out never give up hope, and by her example he learned a powerful lesson. When he came to Northeastern University, the school made it possible for him to work part-time while going to school, and his on-the-job experience helped him to get a very good job when he graduated. He's shown an amazing amount of responsibility, but his mother stood by him, his school stood by him, and he had an employer who stood by him.

So no matter how heroic individuals are, they still need help to make it, and support. Chances of success increase dramatically when other people believe in you, give you opportunities, and ask you to take the responsibility to make the most of them. And I want to thank every person here today who made it possible for these young people to be up on this stage and to have the kind of life they're going to have.

I also want to say that this administration is working hard to open the doors of college education to all young people, to make it possible for them to get loans to go to college and to pay them back on much more favorable terms than has been the case in the past. And we are trying to pass, with strong bipartisan support, a national service program which will make it possible for tens of thousands of young people to earn credit against those loans before, during, or after their college years by giving something back to their communities where they live. Vice President Gore has just returned from California where he kicked off our Summer of Service program, which is the beginning of this national service effort.

I know that a lot of you have been involved in service programs. I want to recognize one of the scholars, MarLeice Hyde, from Valley High School in Afton, Wyoming. Where are you? I want to tell you about her. She organized the junior volunteer program at her local hospital, which contributed over 1,000 hours of community service at the hospital, while holding two jobs, attending evening college courses, and meeting the responsibilities that come from being the oldest of six children. Let's give her a hand. [*Applause*] Congratulations.

Finally, let me say a word about our educators. We often spend our time talking about what's wrong with our educational system, but we ought to also acknowledge that there is a great deal that is right with it. And a lot of these young people today might not be here were it not for their teachers, their principals, the people who worked with them and believed in them. We think that the educators of America who are trying to do a good job shouldn't have to go it alone and should have some way of knowing whether they're meeting the competition around the globe. That's why Secretary Riley has worked so hard with his Goals 2000 program and with the legislation now moving through Congress to embrace world-class learning standards that all American schools will be given the opportunity to meet and that all American parents and students can judge their own progress by. I am very encouraged by that work and very grateful for the cooperative spirit that we see now in Washington between everybody involved in the educational endeavor. We think that Goals 2000 will turn a nation at risk into a nation on the move in education.

Let me say in closing that I've thought a great deal about education this summer because I just celebrated under this same tent a couple of weeks ago my 25th college reunion. I saw some of my classmates: One of them runs a refugee center for Palestinians in Jordan; one came all the way back from Cambodia where he had his life at risk monitoring the elections in that troubled country where once so many people were killed by tyranny. Many of them have made incredibly valuable contributions to their lives. And all of us were sitting here 25

years later in this very spot remembering with incredible vividness actual specific things our teachers had said to us in class. We had a contest to remember how many verbatim sentences we could remember from different professors we had. And every one of us concluded at the end that none of our lives would have been possible if we hadn't had the benefit of a world-class education.

I hope this Presidential scholarship brings to all of you on this stage those kinds of memories 25 years from now. I hope you will do everything you can to make the most of the opportunities before you. And I hope you will take some time along the way to enrich the communities from which you came and the people who made it possible for you to be here today.

Thank you all. Congratulations, and God bless you.

NOTE: The President spoke at 4:42 p.m. on the South Lawn at the White House.

Announcement of Senior Executive Service Appointments
June 23, 1993

The President today announced the appointment of a total of 26 Senior Executive Service officials at Departments and Agencies across the Government.

"We are continuing to move forward with the process of filling all of the positions in the Federal Government," said the President. "I continue to be pleased with the excellence of our appointees, the work that is being done across the Government, and the diversity of the administration we are putting together."

The appointees, who do not need to be confirmed by the Senate, are:

U.S. International Development Cooperation Agency

Jill Buckley, Director, Office of External Affairs, Agency for International Development

Department of Commerce

Jill Schuker, Director, Office of Public Affairs
Ellis Mottur, Deputy Assistant Secretary for Technology and Aerospace in Trade Development
Barry Carter, Deputy Under Secretary for Export Administration
Rita Hayes, Deputy Assistant Secretary for Textiles, Apparel and Consumer Goods
Paul London, Deputy Under Secretary for Economics and Statistics
Meredith Jones, General Counsel, National Oceanic and Atmospheric Administration

Department of Defense

Molly Williamson, Deputy Assistant Secretary for Near-East and South-East Asian Affairs
Pat Irvin, Deputy Assistant Secretary for Humanitarian Assistance and Refugee Affairs
Stanley Roth, Deputy Assistant Secretary for East Asian and Pacific Affairs
Jane Mathias, Deputy Director, Office of Legislative Affairs
Gloria Duffy, Deputy Assistant Secretary and Office of the Secretary of Defense Special Coordinator for Cooperative Threat Reduction and Secretary of Defense Representative and Deputy Head to the Safety, Security and Dismantlement Talks
Sarah Sewall, Deputy Assistant Secretary for Peacekeeping/Peacemaking Policy

Brian Sheridan, Deputy Assistant Secretary for Drug Enforcement Policy and Support

Maj. Gen. James Klugh (Ret.), Deputy Under Secretary for Logistics

Louis Finch, Principal Deputy Assistant Secretary for Strategy, Requirements and Resources

Department of Energy

Jack Riggs, Principal Deputy Assistant Secretary for Policy, Planning and Evaluation

Louis Gicale, Deputy General Counsel for Programs

Department of Health and Human Services

John Monahan, Director of Intergovernmental Affairs

Melissa Skofield, Deputy Assistant Secretary for Public Affairs, Policy and Communications

Portia Mittleman, Deputy Assistant Secretary

for Aging

Department of the Interior

Debra Knopman, Deputy Assistant Secretary for Water and Science

National Aeronautics and Space Administration

Jeffrey Lawrence, Assistant Administrator for Legislative Affairs

Department of Transportation

Mark Gerchick, Chief Counsel, Federal Aviation Administration

Department of Veterans Affairs

Dale Renaud, Deputy Assistant Secretary for Intergovernmental Affairs

Edward Chow, Deputy Assistant Secretary

NOTE: Biographies of the appointees were made available by the Office of the Press Secretary.

Remarks to the National Association of Police Organizations and an Exchange With Reporters
June 24, 1993

The President. First, let me welcome you here. And this is our replay from the time we got weathered out in March. And I'm glad you could all come back. I want to thank you for the work you do and for the support that you gave to me last year when I was attempting to become President and for the support you have given so many of our initiatives in the last 5 months.

I have been busily at work for the last several days working with the United States Senate in our attempt to pass our economic plan, which will reduce the national deficit by $500 billion and provide some significant incentives to turn this economy around, including keeping interest rates down, which is critical to our future. We've had a dramatic increase in the number of ordinary Americans, I imagine including some people in this room, who have, for example, refinanced their homes in the last 5 or 6 months, because we've got interest rates at a 20-year low, 130,000 new construction jobs in the economy, 755,000 jobs overall. It is critical that we pass this. And that's what we're primarily involved in today, as I'm sure you understand.

I also asked the Congress to adopt a modified bill for making a down payment on our investment package, which they did, which included, as I'm sure you know, some $200 million for communities to hire police officers. That is a down payment on the campaign commitment I made to empower our communities to hire another 100,000 police officers over the next 4 years, to go to more community policing, to provide for safer streets, and to support you in the work you're doing.

I also want to tell you that the Attorney General and I have been working hard for the last several weeks with interested Members of Congress to bring up a crime bill this year. Sadly, it did not pass last year, for all kinds of reasons. That crime bill is still to be finally defined, but I can assure you it will include the Brady bill; it will include a provision for boot camps as alternative punishment for first-time nonviolent offenders; it will include a continuing effort to hire more police officers on our streets and to expand community policing. I welcome the ideas, the expertise, and the advice of all of you in putting this bill together and in pushing it through the Congress. It will be a high priority for the administration, and I expect it to begin soon.

We can't really revive the whole fabric of our economy until we put the society back together in the places where it's broken. One of the things that we're attempting to do in this economic bill is to finally test the proposition of whether the private sector can revitalize the most distressed areas of our big cities or our small towns and rural areas with an empowerment zone concept that would offer real big incentives for people to go into a lot of the meanest streets in this country and invest their money to put people to work, to start businesses, to try to make those places come alive again in positive ways.

We also, as all of you know, are committed to doing the things that we've been talking about. I think it's worth just closing with the thought that there are a lot of people in this country who are genuinely insecure today. That shooting at the swimming pool here in Washington, DC, that I'm sure all of you read about, is a horrible example of the kind of mindless behavior that is ripping at the fabric of society. And now I think of how many children are afraid to go back to the pool, a place where wholesome recreation will occur, a place where kids can stay out of trouble and in water in the summertime; how many of their parents might be afraid for them to go back.

That is the sort of thing that I hope we can keep in the minds of our policymakers as we deal with the crime bill and deal with these other issues. And I assure you that I welcome your input into all of them.

I think I'd like to close just by saying a special word of appreciation to the Justice Department and the FBI, to the United States Attorney, and to the New York City Police Department for the work that they have done in making the arrests that broke up a terrorist gang in New York. It was a very impressive piece of work and a real tribute to the local folks and to the cooperation that the Federal Government and the local people had. And I thank them for that, and thank you.

Now, the Attorney General and I are here. We're going to answer your questions. But first we're going to answer a few from the press.

Terrorism

Q. Mr. President, can I follow up——

Q. To follow up on that, do you support a Federal law for the death penalty for terrorists? And can you tell us how and exactly when you found out about this plot?

The President. First of all, I support the crime bill. I supported the crime bill last year which expanded the death penalty in many different areas. And as you know, I have a longstanding support for capital punishment.

But let me answer the specific thing. I was briefed about this operation at about the time it was occurring, a little before. I knew that they had been working on it. But all the credit for this goes to the FBI and the local people. They did the work. They've been working on this for some weeks now, and I don't think I should say more about it. The Justice Department will have more to say at an appropriate time.

Q. Can you say whether you believe that everyone has been arrested who was involved in this? And have you had any communication, do you plan to have any communication with President Mubarak or any of the other possible victims?

The President. I have not yet had any communications with any of the people that were on the list. I think any questions about the nature of the conspiracy and the group should be answered by the law enforcement officials, not by me.

Economic Program

Q. Mr. President, do you have the votes yet in the Senate for your budget to pass at this time, now?

The President. I certainly hope so.

Q. Well, I ask the question because your spokesman said earlier that you didn't have them but that you expected to by the end of the day. Do you have them now?

The President. Who did? Who said that earlier?

Q. Dee Dee said that—that you didn't have them this morning, but you expected to have them by the end of the day. Do you have them now?

The President. Senator Mitchell is my ultimate authority on that. We're working our way through these amendments now, and we just had, as I understand it, Senators Harkin, Metzenbaum, and Wellstone just announced their support for the package, pursuant to an agreement to reduce the size of the Medicaid cuts. There are still about $10 billion Medicaid cuts over and above what the House put in, which was about $50 billion.

So that will help, and that puts us three votes closer. And I just don't—I can't say for sure. We're going to have a whole series of amendments which go through today. And then at the end of the day we may find ourselves in a position where some Members want some things which can only come out of the conference, and they may have to just decide whether to let the bill go to conference or not. The House Members had to make the same sort of decision. But I'm hopeful. That's all I can tell you. I'm hopeful. We're working hard, and I'm hopeful.

Q. Does that bring it under $500 billion, sir?

The President. No. Not to my knowledge. The last time I saw it, it didn't, Andrea [Andrea Mitchell, NBC News]. Now, I haven't seen the exact details of the last—the last time I heard about it, about an hour and a half ago, it did not.

Q. What kind of momentum do you want from this vote, and do you see this as a real turning point for your Presidency?

The President. There have been a lot of those lately. [*Laughter*] The vote in the House was, and this will be. We have to go on to conference. If it passes today, this will be a very loud statement. It will say that both Houses of the Congress are committed to the largest deficit reduction program in history, to putting the taxes and the spending cuts in a trust fund, to spending cuts equal to and now greater than the tax increases, and to an extremely progressive program where those who can, best able to pay, are asked to pay. The Senate Finance Committee bill, according to the Congressional Budget Office, distributes 78 percent of the burden to people with incomes above $200,000 whose taxes were lowered in the 1980's while their incomes went up.

So I think that this is a very, you know, it's a very important vote, and I hope we can prevail. But I never count my chickens before they're hatched.

Thank you.

Q. Are you counting any Republicans? Any Republicans, Hatfield or Jeffords?

The President. I've asked; that's all I know.

Q. Did you ask in phone calls?

Q. Mr. President, is the final arrangement on gays in the military going to require them to stay in the closet, sir?

The President. 'Bye, everybody; no more questions. I have to answer their questions.

Thank you.

NOTE: The President spoke at 1:43 p.m. in the Indian Treaty Room of the Old Executive Office Building.

Exchange With Reporters Prior to a Meeting With the University of Arkansas Rollin' Razorbacks Wheelchair Athletes
June 24, 1993

Economic Program

Q. Mr. President, surrounded by all these winners, do you think you can be a winner tonight?

The President. Well, I hope so.

Q. What is your latest assessment?

The President. I feel just the way I did before the House vote. I'm just working. I'm working. We're picking up a few and——

Q. Have you called any Republicans?

The President. I think I should answer that question after the vote tonight.

Q. We don't want to blow their cover.

The President. I think I should answer that question——

Q. Mr. President, in retrospect, do you wish you had reached out more to Republicans early on? Some moderates say they'd be on board if you had.

The President. I don't know. I did call a number of them. And I tried to—after Senator Boren and Senator Danforth announced their little coalition—I don't mean little, I mean their coalition—I also reached out to some Republicans then. And I continue to reach out to some Republicans in the House. It's just rare in these first tough budget votes to get any votes from the other party. And I hope that this will never happen again. I hope that it won't ever happen again.

But you have to understand, we're also trying to reverse 12 years of, basically, people being told the easy thing and letting the country just sort of slowly grind downhill. And we're trying to change it. And these changes are never easy. I never thought they'd be easy. I'm hopeful for tonight.

Q. What would be—in the conference committee, sir?

The President. I'll be glad to answer that question after we see if we're going to have

a conference. First, we have to prevail tonight. Let's try to make sure we win tonight, and then we'll be able to——

Q. Are you—[*inaudible*]

The President. I'm only concerned until there's a vote. We're working hard. I think we'll prevail, but let's wait and see what happens.

NOTE: The exchange began at 5:40 p.m. in the Oval Office at the White House. A tape was not available for verification of the content of this exchange.

Remarks to the United States Academic Decathlon Winners and an Exchange With Reporters
June 24, 1993

The President. I hope you enjoyed your tour of the White House. And I'm sorry we had to start a little late, but as I'm sure you know, a very important debate is now occurring in the United States Senate on the administration's economic plan, and I had to make a call or two.

Congressman Beilenson, it's good to see you. I bet you're glad you're not involved in that this afternoon and glad to be here with your folks.

It's a real honor for me to welcome to the White House a group of true student athletes: the gold, silver, and bronze medal-winning teams in the 1992–93 United States Academic Decathlon. The gold medalists are from Plano East High School of Plano, Texas; the silver medalists from Taft High of Los Angeles; the bronze medal winners of Mountain View High School of Mesa, Arizona.

These students have experienced the excitement of competition and the thrill of victory. And they should be a source of pride for young people all across our country. They've competed for medals in 10 different events, from math and science to language and literature, in an innovative and inclusive program which fosters competition, enhances self-image, and shows how truly exciting the pursuit of knowledge can be.

As I understand it, the team members also are required to give speeches, both prepared

and impromptu—that's a good preparation for being President—write essays and experience interviews. These young people are equipped not with javelins or shotputs but with intellect and knowledge and the ability to think creatively but with discipline.

The importance of this kind of pursuit of educational excellence cannot be overemphasized. We're at a moment in our history when we have to increase the educational ability of all Americans and in which it is not simply important how much our people know but what they are capable of learning and how quickly and well they are capable of thinking through complex problems that may face them tomorrow but are even unpredictable today. Because of these kinds of challenges, we cannot meet our educational excellence goals through Government mandates. We have to meet them through incentives and through environments which promote excellence and leadership from teachers and principals, the kind of group work that we see in this academic decathlon.

I applaud the academic decathlon, its president, John Foley, and its executive director, Ann Joynt. At this time, I want to say a special word of congratulations to the national champions, Plano Senior High School from Plano, Texas— Plano East. They're right behind me, right? In the center. When I was in high school, Plano had a great high school band. Do you still have a good band? It won a lot of national awards.

Of course, that was back in the dark ages, but anyway. Under the coaching of Joyce Gillam and Jack Worsham, Plano East amassed the highest total score, capturing seven gold and five silver medals. One particular youngster, Sunny Chu, deserves special mention. Sunny's father suffered a severe stroke just days before the national competition. Nonetheless, Sunny still managed to win the gold medal for highest overall score in the Nation. And I'm pleased to report that Sunny's dad is back home recovering. Congratulations to you. Let's give him a hand. [*Applause*]

Now, the group from Taft High in Los Angeles. That's you, right? Coached by Michael Wilson, Taft High pulled in seven gold and six silver medals. Mara Weiss achieved the second highest total score in the Nation, earning a gold medal in the essay event and a bronze in fine arts. In fact, I understand Mara recently wrote to my wife expressing her frustration that intellectual pursuits in high school are still seen as the domain of the male student. Mara, where are you? Did you really do that?

Ms. Weiss. Yes, I did.

The President. Good for you. I'll hear more about that as time goes on. [*Laughter*] Let me say that I think that is a real problem. And there is actual documented evidence of that, particularly in the math and sciences areas, as young people move out of grade school into junior high and high school. And you deserve a lot of credit for pointing it out. Just a few days ago in the Rose Garden, however, I appointed another distinguished student and scholar, Judge Ruth Ginsburg, to the Supreme Court. I think those kinds of things should do something to shatter the myth that intellectual pursuits should remain the exclusive domain of men. And I'm sure you'll have a lot to do with that as you go through your life.

I want to congratulate, finally, the Mountain View High School team from Mesa, Arizona. They're here to my left. Under the watchful eye of coach Mary McGovern, Mountain View netted four gold and seven silver medals. Senior Tagg Grant amassed the highest individual point total for his team with the best event being

economics. Where are you, Tagg? I order you to stay here for the next 2 or 3 months. [*Laughter*] This country needs your help.

I understand that the scholarships are awarded to the top three overall medal winners in each of three divisions. It just so happens that eight of those nine scholarship winners are on these three teams. But we've indicted the ninth scholarship winner to be with us today as well. He's Dan Casey, from Lower Merion High School in Bala Cynwyd, Pennsylvania. Where are you, Dan? Welcome. I'm glad they took you in over there. I looked up there and counted; I thought they had an unfair advantage. [*Laughter*] Dan took the silver medal for the second highest point total in the varsity division.

Each of these young people represents our best future, our best hopes. They have proven how much people can do when they put their minds to it, and I am very proud of them.

I'd like now to invite John Foley to say a few words, and then I'd like to have some pictures taken with the teams and say hello to them. But first, Mr. Foley, thank you for your work, and come up and have a platform.

[*At this point, Mr. Foley thanked the President and explained the history of the program.*]

The President. Thank you.

Super Collider

Q. Mr. President, the House has voted to kill the super collider program. Do you have any reaction, sir?

The President. They did last year. Maybe the Senate will save it, and we can save it in conference. I'm not surprised. You know, I'm grateful to them for saving the space station. That was headed for defeat, and we did a lot of work on it, and I'm glad we were able to save it. I always anticipated that if we were going to save the super collider, it would have to come in a conference after the Senate did it. So it's really up to the Senate now to decide on the super collider.

NOTE: The President spoke at 5:33 p.m. in the Rose Garden at the White House.

Statement on Credit Availability
June 24, 1993

Today's announcement by the FDIC is another tangible benefit brought on by the progress of our deficit reduction plan and the lower interest rates it has produced. Fewer bank failures means more and cheaper bank loans to America's businesses and communities. It means billions of dollars more for new jobs, new businesses, and helping families buy new homes. It shows once again how critically important it is for Congress to lock in the benefits of lower interest rates and deficit reduction by approving the Clinton economic plan.

Nomination for Ambassador to Mongolia
June 24, 1993

The President today announced his intention to nominate Donald Johnson, a career member of the Foreign Service, to be Ambassador to Mongolia.

"Donald Johnson has served our country with distinction for almost two decades in the Foreign Service," said the President. "I am pleased that he will be taking this ambassadorial post."

NOTE: A biography of the nominee was made available by the Office of the Press Secretary.

Statement on Senate Action on the Economic Program
June 25, 1993

Tonight the Senate voted for growth over gridlock by passing our plan to cut deficit spending by $500 billion and lock the savings in a deficit reduction trust fund. By rejecting both the trickle-down economics of the 1980's and the tax-and-spend policies of the past, the Senate sent a strong signal to middle class Americans that Washington can work to create jobs, increase incomes, and spur economic growth.

When this debate began, I challenged the Senate to pass a plan that met these principles: It had to reduce the deficit by $500 billion; it had to be balanced between spending cuts and taxes; 75 percent of those taxes had to be paid by the wealthiest 6 percent of the American people; and it had to encourage the creation of jobs and the movement of people from welfare to work. The Senate met these challenges, and that's why this vote is a victory for the American people.

I want to congratulate Senators Mitchell, Sasser, and Moynihan for their leadership, their colleagues for their courage, and the American people for demanding that the deficit come down through tough spending cuts and a Tax Code that asks the most from the people who have the most.

In a matter of days, I will be traveling to Japan to represent the interests of the United States in a summit with our economic competitors. Because we are acting to put our house in order, America will go to that meeting for the first time in years in a strong position to lead the world toward growth.

Remarks on the Appointment of Kristine M. Gebbie as AIDS Policy Coordinator and an Exchange With Reporters
June 25, 1993

The President. Good morning. Thank you very much. First, let me welcome Speaker of the House and other distinguished Members of the House of Representatives here. I appreciate their coming. I understand they were able to get a little more sleep than the Senators were last night. I also want to welcome all the rest of you here.

Before I make the announcement that we're all here to witness and to be a part of, I do want to say a word about the vote that was cast early this morning in the United States Senate to pass a version of the economic plan which I presented to them, which, to be sure, was changed to some extent from the House plan but still reflected, I think, a remarkable degree of courage: $500 billion in deficit reduction in the Senate plan, over 78 percent of the new revenues coming from people with incomes above $200,000, real commitment to significant budget cuts that were slightly greater than the ones in the House plan, and now clearly more budget cuts than tax increases.

The most important thing is that now both Houses of Congress, under very difficult circumstances, with the same old rhetoric of the last 12 years flying at them, had the courage to try to change this country for the better. What this means is incalculable. It means we can now move on to a conference committee with a clear signal to the financial markets that its interest rates should stay down and people should be able to continue to refinance their homes and finance their businesses at lower interest rates and that for the first time in a very long time an American President can go to a meeting of the G–7 nations in a position of economic strength, trying to lead a renewal of growth and opportunity all over the world.

So I very much appreciate that. I want to compliment Senator Mitchell, Senator Sasser, Senator Moynihan, in particular, for their leadership and the courage of the Senators who voted in the way they did, so that we can go forward.

One of the things that was in this budget that has received almost no notice is a real commitment to intensifying our efforts to deal with the AIDS crisis, even in the midst of all the budget cutbacks. One of those important efforts is the naming of a new AIDS coordinator with a higher visibility, a more important policy role, and more influence in the National Government than has been the case in the past.

It is my distinct pleasure today to announce the appointment of Kristine Gebbie as our Nation's first AIDS Policy Coordinator. This position has never existed before, but circumstances now require us to look for unprecedented remedies to an unprecedented problem.

Today, as we toil against one of the most dreaded and mysterious diseases humanity has ever known, we must redouble our Government's efforts to promote research, funding, and treatment for AIDS. The appointment of Kristine Gebbie is part of our pledge to do that. She is a proven health care leader who will bring to the administration years of experience in the AIDS field. I'm confident she'll work hard to ensure that our Nation no longer ignores an epidemic that has already claimed too many of our brothers and sisters, our parents and children, our friends and colleagues.

I'm particularly pleased that Kristine Gebbie is so committed to helping our AIDS effort, for she certainly is no stranger to the field. To begin with, she hails from the Pacific Northwest, one of our country's most progressive regions when it comes to health care. A former nurse, she became the administrator of the Oregon Health Division, a position she held for 11 years, and later served as the secretary of the Washington State Department of Health. Currently she serves as a special consultant to the Department of Health and Human Services. She's also spent a lot of her time and energy on AIDS prevention. Since 1989, she's served as Chair of the Centers for Disease Control Advisory Committee on the Prevention of HIV Infection. She served on the Presidential Commission on AIDS. She was for 3 years a member of the National Academy of Sciences AIDS oversight committee, and she was chair of an HIV committee of State health officials around the United States.

AIDS is terrifying. It inflicts tragedy on too many families. But ultimately, it is a disease, one we can defeat just as we have defeated polio, many forms of cancer, and other scourges in the history of our Nation. How can we do it? With commitment and courage and constancy, and with vocal and responsible leadership from our Nation's Government. Already this administration has requested a large increase in funding for AIDS research and prevention, even in the face of our severe budget cutbacks. We are now moving toward full funding of the Ryan White Comprehensive AIDS Resources Emergency Act. Our budget requested in fiscal 1994 a 78 percent increase in funding for Ryan White, an 18 percent increase for AIDS research, and a 27 percent increase for prevention.

In addition, the upcoming health care reform plan will make sure that AIDS sufferers are not victimized by unfair insurance policies when they seek treatment for their illnesses. AIDS touches all of us, and no single group should be discriminated against on the basis of this disease.

To make Government's role in AIDS more efficient, we're also taking steps to coordinate AIDS policy. On June 10th, I signed into law the National Institutes of Health Revitalization Act that establishes an AIDS research office to coordinate all the AIDS research at NIH. By now appointing an AIDS Policy Coordinator, we will ensure that one person in the White House oversees and unifies Governmentwide AIDS efforts.

Kristine Gebbie will be a full member of the Domestic Policy Council and will work closely with the Department of Health and Human Services—and I'm glad to see Secretary Shalala here today. She has my full support in coordinating policy among all the various executive branch departments.

With the dedication and leadership that she has shown and that she will bring to this effort, I believe we will be able to wage the battle against AIDS with complete resolve. I look forward to working with her as we tackle the challenges that are posed to us. I assure you this is another step in the beginning of our effort, not the end of my personal commitment. This will guarantee the kind of focus this effort has long needed.

Ms. Gebbie.

[*At this point, Ms. Gebbie thanked the President and discussed a coordinated approach to AIDS.*]

The President. Let me also say before we take a question or two, to Mr. Speaker and to Congressmen Studds and Frank and McDermott and Pelosi and Morella and to all the other Members of the Congress who have been willing to support increased efforts for AIDS in the face of these difficult budgetary times, I'm grateful for them, too. Because without the congressional support, we would not be able to make any progress, in my judgment, even with this heightened administrative effort.

Homosexuals in the Military

Q. Mr. President, as you approach your decision on gays in the military, have you reached a conclusion about the directive that says that homosexuality is incompatible with military service? Have you decided——

The President. I have not received any such directive. And until I receive a report from the Pentagon, I have no further comment on this.

Q. Can I just ask you a broader question, then, about this?

The President. I'm not going to discuss it until I receive the report from the Pentagon. I have nothing else to say now.

AIDS

Q. Mr. President, I have a question for Ms. Gebbie, please. During the time that you served in Washington and Oregon on dealing with the AIDS epidemic, what will you bring to this job that you learned there?

Ms. Gebbie. I think one of the biggest things I learned is that people have to be able to hear each other, not just talk to each other but hear each other, and then put that listening into effect, developing policies that work. That's a bit of a global answer, but it really has to be applied to each piece of this puzzle. And it's putting a puzzle together that's developing policy around this disease.

Terrorism

Q. Mr. President, yesterday when the news broke of the terrorist attempts at bombing various points in New York City, a lot of Americans felt an increased sense of vulnerability. I wonder if you would share with us your thoughts when you learned about it, and do you share that increased sense of vulnerability to terrorism in this country?

The President. Any free society has always some exposure to terrorism. I think what the American people should do, though, is to feel an enormous sense of pride in the aggressive work done by the New York Police Department and all the Federal authorities involved in New York. We are working aggressively on this issue. We will continue to work on it in a very tough way, and we will put whatever resources the United States has to put in to combating it.

I think one of the problems that has plagued much of the world in the 1980's is random acts of terrorism. And there is always the possibility with increasing political instability in various places of increased terrorism. But I can tell you that I view the action in New York as reassuring. And all I can tell you is that we're going to do our best to be as tough, as intolerant, as effective in dealing with these kinds of problems consistently as the local and the Federal authorities were in New York.

Economic Program

Q. Mr. President, now that the Senate has voted, can you tell us where you come down on the differences between the House and Senate bills in terms of the gasoline versus Btu tax, in terms of the level of Medicare funding, and the other differences in the bills? And can you tell us, did you win a political victory at the possible expense of your program, in making so many deals that it's just complicated the process of getting things through conference?

The President. Actually, this administration didn't make any deals. The Senate Finance Committee put together a bill that it could get out of the Senate Finance Committee. And then the question was very much whether we would go on to conference. I think there was a great sense in the Senate that they had to go forward with the bill. There were many Senators who told me they liked the House bill better. I mean, there were divisions even in the Senate. There were a couple of Senators who indicated they would have voted for the House bill who did not vote for the Senate bill. There was all kinds of difference of opinion.

I think what happened was there was an institutional feeling there yesterday, which crystallized in the late afternoon, that the worst thing they could do is not to go forward, and that the worst thing they could do is not to break the gridlock, not to find a way to continue to push for real economic reform. And all this happened rather late last evening, and no decisions have been made. I haven't even had an ample opportunity to analyze whatever amendments were made yesterday. But this administration was not nearly as involved in the details of what came out of the Senate as was the case in the House.

I am confident that the conferees will get together, will produce a bill that in some ways is superior to both bills and will have a broader support. That's what I think will happen.

Q. Gas tax, sir?

Q. On the budget, assuming that you want the final bill to resemble your own plan as much as possible, what is your response to Senator Moynihan's observation recently when he said that he felt that directing one-third of all tax increases and spending cuts to investment would be perhaps too excessive?

The President. Well, we'll see. A lot of the Senators who came on to the bill late yesterday were holding out because the investment incentives have been cut back so much by the committee. One of the biggest hurdles was trying to convince some of the Senators that we might increase the investment incentives in the conference. So I can tell you that will be a point of continuing tension. But I expect there will be some real effort to try to get the investment and growth options back in there.

Keep in mind, reducing the deficit helps you by bringing down interest rates. But still in the end if you want to grow the economy, somebody has to invest money and create jobs and put people to work. If the unemployment rate in this country were 4 percent instead of 7 percent, we'd have far fewer problems than we do. And the stagnation worldwide of economic activity, which has been going on for some time now, is holding this country back and requires this country to make extraordinary efforts if we're going to swim against the tide and try to grow more than other nations to increase incentives to invest and create jobs and to grow this economy.

If you take investment out of part of the country as, for example, you see in California with the big cutbacks in defense, there needs to be some offsetting investment. You can't create jobs out of thin air. So I think what we want to see in this economic plan two objectives: really tough deficit reduction, keeping the interest rates down, freeing up money for private sector investment, and increasing incentives by the National Government to get more investment in the economy. And I hope we see it.

Iraq

Q. Mr. President, there seems to be another standoff in Baghdad between U.N. weapons inspectors and the Iraqi Government. This is the first time this has happened on your watch. How serious is this standoff? And what, if anything, do you plan on doing about it?

The President. It's quite serious. And the United Nations—you've already heard the U.N. speak to it, and I would expect that the matter will have to be resolved one way or the other in the fairly near future. I do think that—I don't have much to add to the pronouncements that have come out of the U.N. The United States has to continue to support compliance with the U.N. resolutions as they apply to Iraq.

Economic Summit

Q. Mr. President, you said that this is the first time that we're going to the economic summit in a position of economic strength. Another way to view that is that you had a tie vote in the Senate; that you're caught going into conference between the demands for more social spending, more investment, and those who want more cuts; and that there's no margin for error, which is not a very strong signal of the ability to resolve this and to get anything that will pass finally both Houses——

The President. I don't think any of the people who have looked at this really believe that we won't get a bill out of the conference that will be marginally changed in ways from both the House and Senate bills that will make the bill more passable in the Senate as well as the House. For example, the House wanted basically the incentive package that was there but some less tax and some more spending cuts. That came out of the Senate. The Senate obliged the less tax and more spending cuts but did it at the expense of cutting so much of the investments out, because the energy tax had to be reduced as much as it did, not for the floor of the Senate but to get it out of the Senate Finance Committee.

Now, what will happen now is you'll see a negotiation, and they'll try to bridge those gaps. I don't think they are particularly large. I think it's quite encouraging. And if you look at the level of aggression this country has displayed in trying to do something about its economic circumstances as compared with what is going on in these other nations, the political and the economic problems, I think the United States should be very proud. It is not easy to change.

I mean, we've been on an incredible roller coaster ride for 12 years now, just sort of spending more than we're taking in and living by political rhetoric and hot air. And when you try to change, it's not easy. You know, it's the same—my daughter always says when she is gigging me a little that old line about denial being more than a river in Egypt. I mean, you know, it's not easy to change.

Thank you very much.

NOTE: The President spoke at 8:43 a.m. on the South Lawn at the White House.

Letter to Congressional Leaders on Trade With Mauritania
June 25, 1993

Dear Mr. Speaker: (*Dear Mr. President:*)

I am writing concerning the Generalized System of Preferences (GSP). The GSP program offers duty-free access to the U.S. market for products that are imported from developing countries. It is authorized by title V of the Trade Act of 1974.

Pursuant to title V, I have determined that Mauritania no longer meets the eligibility requirements set forth in the GSP law. In particular, I have determined that it has not taken and is not taking steps to afford internationally recognized worker rights. Accordingly, I intend to suspend Mauritania indefinitely as a designated beneficiary developing country for purposes of the GSP.

This notice is submitted in accordance with section 502(a)(2) of the Trade Act of 1974.

Sincerely,

WILLIAM J. CLINTON

NOTE: Identical letters were sent to Thomas S. Foley, Speaker of the House of Representatives, and Albert Gore, Jr., President of the Senate. An original was not available for verification of the content of this letter. The related proclamation and memorandum are listed in Appendix D at the end of this volume.

Nomination for Posts at the Department of Labor
June 25, 1993

The President announced today that he intends to nominate economists Bernard Anderson and Katharine Abraham to positions at the Department of Labor. If confirmed, Anderson will serve as Assistant Secretary for the Employment Standards Administration, and Abraham will serve as Commissioner of Labor Statistics.

"Applying adequate enforcement standards and tracking the well-being of our Nation's work force are two of the Labor Department's most important responsibilities," said the President. "Bernard Anderson and Katharine Abraham will fulfill them with rigor and integrity."

The President's Radio Address
June 26, 1993

Good morning. I want to talk to you about the battle that I've been waging to fulfill the central commitment of my campaign for President: to make the economy grow, create jobs, and make our Government in Washington work again for all the American people.

But first, let me take just a moment to congratulate the FBI, the New York Police Department, and the United States attorney in New York for breaking up the terrorist ring. The American people need to be reassured by the effectiveness and the determination of our Federal authorities at the national and at the local level to combat terrorism. And the people who would engage in these kinds of acts in this country need to know that we're going to be tough on anyone, anywhere in the world, who threatens or carries out terrorist actions against any American citizen.

Back to the economy. For years, your Government in Washington refused to make the hard decisions necessary for America to compete and win in a global economy. Very often, political leaders told you exactly what you wanted to hear, but they didn't hear your real problems or honor your values. For more than a decade, the National Government borrowed and spent, raised taxes on the middle class, reduced the burden on the privileged, ran up the huge national debt we now have, and discouraged the creation of jobs by reducing our investment. Meanwhile, we ignored problems like health care and the cost and availability of that service and many others.

Now, if we want to preserve the American dream, opportunity for those who work hard and play by the rules, we have to change. And change is hard. For the last 5 months, I've been fighting for a plan to create economic growth, one that reduces the deficit and brings down interest rates and increases investment in education, technology, and jobs. It requires deep spending cuts and some tax increases, asking by far the most from those who have the most to pay.

Congress is rising to the occasion. Last month the House voted for a new direction, and just this week the Senate acted courageously in doing the same. In the next few weeks, representatives from both the House and the Senate will be meeting to reconcile the differences between the two bills. The negotiations will be difficult, but I'm going to work hard to keep the essential characteristics of the economic plan that I believe so deeply in: at least $500 billion of deficit reduction in a trust fund so that the cuts and the taxes can't go to anything else, cuts at least as big as tax increases, if not larger; over three-quarters of the tax increases coming from the top 6 percent of income earners; and real incentives to create new jobs and to encourage the working poor, to move people from welfare to work. We're finally getting our house in order, delivering the changes that America needs.

This program, as I said, reduces the deficit by $500 billion, and you should know again that there are $250 billion of spending cuts in the program, over 100 cuts of over $100 million or more. The revenues that are raised are raised from those who can most afford to pay. This program protects the middle class, something that would not have happened in the 1980's when Washington reduced taxes on the wealthiest Americans and raised them on the middle class. For every $10 in deficit reduction in my plan, $5 comes from spending cuts, $5 comes from new revenues. Of those revenues, $3.75 comes from the wealthiest 6 percent of Americans, almost 80 percent from people with incomes above $200,000 in the Senate plan; and $1.25 comes from the middle class.

All this money is locked up now in a deficit reduction trust fund, which protects the money for the next 5 years for bringing down our deficit. The plan is bold and fair; it'll work. It's a sharp departure from the tax-and-spend policies of the seventies and the trickle-down economics of the eighties. It reduces the deficit; it invests and grows the economy. It's a new direction.

Still, there are some in Washington who use the same old tired rhetoric they used in the eighties to attack this kind of direction, while they followed borrow-and-spend, trickle-down policies. Last week, the only other plan offered to the American people was offered by my Senate opponents. Well, the plan fell more than $100 billion short of the $500 billion deficit reduction bill. And most regrettably, it asks even more of the middle class, of veterans, and millions of elderly people just above the poverty line. It asks those people to do with less in terms of benefits, especially in health care, so that the top one percent of the American people whose incomes went up and whose taxes went down in the eighties could go scot-free in the battle to reduce the deficit, bring down interest rates, and get investment back in the American economy. The plan was defeated and for good

reason. Instead of protecting one group at the expense of others, it's time that everyone made a contribution to help everyone by reducing spending fairly and by investing in the future wisely and by growing the economy.

When the Senate and the House meet to write the final plan, we're all going to work together to set a new course for economic growth. When Congress finalizes the details, I'm going to work as hard as I can to insist that the principles I have talked about repeatedly for 5 months, and indeed during all of 1992 as well, will be followed in shaping this law. We need $500 billion in deficit reduction, in spending cuts, and in taxes which fall almost completely on the wealthiest Americans. We absolutely must put all the net savings from cuts and taxes in a deficit trust fund so the Government can't touch it over the next 5 years. We ought to keep the incentives in my plan for business growth, especially small businesses which create most of the new jobs in America. And finally, we ought to keep our commitment to the 18 percent of the American people who work but are still below the poverty line. Under our plan, if you work full-time and you're still below the poverty line, we will lift you out of poverty by not taxing you and keeping you in poverty.

People who have the courage to change should be rewarded. I know the economy is still struggling, and most Americans are still working too hard for too little. But at least there are some very important economic trends that have begun to move in the right direction. The best news is, new jobs are finally coming back into the American economy. In the last 5 months, as interest rates have dropped to 20-year lows in response to our efforts to bring the deficit down, more than 755,000 new jobs, 90 percent of them in the private sector, have been created. In the first 4 months of this year, more jobs in the construction industry were created than in any similar period in the last 9 years.

These are good and hopeful trends. Our plan builds on this progress. I know we've got a long way to go. But as always, if we'll just act in a way that's consistent with our values and if we'll all pull together, we can move our country in the right direction, meet the challenges of the global economy, and create jobs and opportunity for all Americans again.

Thanks for listening.

NOTE: This address was recorded at 3:50 p.m. on June 25 in the Roosevelt Room at the White House for broadcast at 10:06 a.m. on June 26.

Address to the Nation on the Strike on Iraqi Intelligence Headquarters
June 26, 1993

My fellow Americans, this evening I want to speak with you about an attack by the Government of Iraq against the United States and the actions we have just taken to respond.

This past April, the Kuwaiti Government uncovered what they suspected was a car bombing plot to assassinate former President George Bush while he was visiting Kuwait City. The Kuwaiti authorities arrested 16 suspects, including 2 Iraqi nationals. Following those arrests, I ordered our own intelligence and law enforcement agencies to conduct a thorough and independent investigation. Over the past several weeks, officials from those agencies reviewed a range of intelligence information, traveled to Kuwait and elsewhere, extensively interviewed the suspects, and thoroughly examined the forensic evidence.

This Thursday, Attorney General Reno and Director of Central Intelligence Woolsey gave me their findings. Based on their investigation there is compelling evidence that there was, in fact, a plot to assassinate former President Bush and that this plot, which included the use of a powerful bomb made in Iraq, was directed and pursued by the Iraqi intelligence service.

We should not be surprised by such deeds, coming as they do from a regime like Saddam Hussein's, which is ruled by atrocity, slaughtered its own people, invaded two neighbors, attacked others, and engaged in chemical and environmental warfare. Saddam has repeatedly violated the will and conscience of the international community. But this attempt at revenge by a tyrant against the leader of the world coalition that defeated him in war is particularly loathsome and cowardly. We thank God it was unsuccessful. The authorities who foiled it have the appreciation of all Americans.

It is clear that this was no impulsive or random act. It was an elaborate plan devised by the Iraqi Government and directed against a former President of the United States because of actions he took as President. As such, the Iraqi attack against President Bush was an attack against our country and against all Americans. We could not and have not let such action against our Nation go unanswered.

From the first days of our Revolution, America's security has depended on the clarity of this message: Don't tread on us. A firm and commensurate response was essential to protect our sovereignty, to send a message to those who engage in state-sponsored terrorism, to deter further violence against our people, and to affirm the expectation of civilized behavior among nations.

Therefore, on Friday I ordered our forces to launch a cruise missile attack on the Iraqi intelligence service's principal command-and-control facility in Baghdad. Those missiles were launched this afternoon at 4:22 eastern daylight time. They landed approximately an hour ago. I have discussed this action with the congressional leadership and with our allies and friends in the region. And I have called for an emergency meeting of the United Nations Security Council to expose Iraq's crime.

These actions were directed against the Iraqi Government, which was responsible for the assassination plot. Saddam Hussein has demonstrated repeatedly that he will resort to terrorism or aggression if left unchecked. Our intent was to target Iraq's capacity to support violence against the United States and other nations and to deter Saddam Hussein from supporting such outlaw behavior in the future. Therefore, we directed our action against the facility associated with Iraq's support of terrorism, while making every effort to minimize the loss of innocent life.

There should be no mistake about the message we intend these actions to convey to Saddam Hussein, to the rest of the Iraqi leadership, and to any nation, group, or person who would harm our leaders or our citizens. We will combat terrorism. We will deter aggression. We will protect our people.

The world has repeatedly made clear what Iraq must do to return to the community of nations. And Iraq has repeatedly refused. If Saddam and his regime contemplate further illegal provocative actions, they can be certain of our response.

Let me say to the men and women in our Armed Forces and in our intelligence and law enforcement agencies who carried out the investigation and our military response: You have my gratitude and the gratitude of all Americans. You have performed a difficult mission with courage and professionalism.

Finally, I want to say this to all the American people: While the cold war has ended, the world is not free of danger. And I am determined to take the steps necessary to keep our Nation secure. We will keep our forces ready to fight. We will work to head off emerging threats, and we will take action when action is required. That is precisely what we have done today.

Thank you, and God bless America.

NOTE: The President spoke at 7:40 p.m. from the Oval Office at the White House.

Remarks and an Exchange With Reporters Prior to a Cabinet Meeting
June 28, 1993

The President. First, I want to say that this morning I received a report from the National Security Adviser about the action in Iraq over the weekend, confirming that we did in fact cripple the Iraqi intelligence capacity, which was the intent of the action. Our allies have been quite positive in their response. And I want to say a special word of compliment to Ambassador Albright for the work she did at the United Nations yesterday. I thought it was an excellent job.

I think it's very important today at this Cabinet meeting that we move on to other matters, that we go back to the domestic agenda. We have to prepare for the conference on the budget and the economic plan. We need to think about and talk a little about the upcoming G–7 summit in Tokyo and what that means for our economic prospects here at home. And there are a number of other issues that I want to discuss today, including our efforts to seek rapid passage of the national service act.

So I'm anxious to go forward. I do want to acknowledge, the first time as a confirmed member of this Cabinet, Lee Brown. He was here last time, but he's been confirmed since he was here before. Tom Glynn, the Deputy Secretary of Labor, is here, for those of you who don't know him, because Mr. Reich is moving his family to Washington today. I suppose that means he's going to stay on for a while. [*Laughter*]

Strike on Iraqi Intelligence Headquarters

Q. Mr. President, what kind of message were you sending, first of all, to other terrorist nations, given what we now know about the possibility of Iran and potentially Saddam? And what message do you think this sends also to other countries and to the military here about your resolve in your capacity as Commander in Chief?

The President. Well, the action I took I thought was clearly warranted by the facts. And I think other terrorists around the world need to know that the United States will do what we can to combat terrorism, as I said in my statement on Saturday evening. It is plainly what we ought to be doing.

Q. [*Inaudible*]—the events last week in New York and the attack over the weekend in Baghdad, should the American people be concerned about terrorism on American shores in the next few weeks?

The President. I think the American people should be reassured, in the New York instance, that the Federal authorities and the New York Police Department did a good job. I think the American people know enough about terrorism to know that it is always a potential problem, but we are going to be very aggressive in dealing with it, and we're going to do everything we possibly can to deal with it.

Q. Mr. President, how does the decision to have gone ahead and bombed Baghdad on Saturday, how will this impact your Presidency both in terms of how you're seen domestically and by foreign leaders?

The President. I have no idea. I did my job. It was my job, and I did it the best I could.

Q. Don't you think it will have some political effects——

Q. Any political considerations, Mr. President, at all?

The President. I have no idea. It's my job. I did exactly what I said I'd do in the campaign when confronted by circumstances like this. The evidence was clear. And we took the appropriate action. And it was the right thing to do for the United States, and I feel quite comfortable with it.

NOTE: The President spoke at 10:16 a.m. in the Cabinet Room at the White House.

Letter to Congressional Leaders on the Strike on Iraqi Intelligence Headquarters
June 28, 1993

Dear Mr. Speaker: *(Dear Mr. President:)*

Commencing at approximately 4:22 p.m. (EST) on June 26, 1993, at my direction, U.S. naval forces launched a Tomahawk cruise missile strike on the Iraqi Intelligence Service's (IIS) principal command and control complex in Baghdad. This facility is the headquarters for the IIS, which planned the failed attempt to assassinate former President Bush during his visit to Kuwait in April of this year. This U.S. military action was completed upon impact of the missiles on target at approximately 6 p.m. (EST).

Operating under the United States Central Command, two U.S. Navy surface ships launched a total of 23 precision-guided Tomahawk missiles in this coordinated strike upon the key facilities in the IIS compound. The USS PETERSON (DD 969) launched 14 missiles from its position in the Red Sea, while the USS CHANCELLORSVILLE (CG 62) in the Arabian Gulf launched nine missiles. The timing of this operation, with missiles striking at approximately 2:00 a.m. local Iraqi time, was chosen carefully so as to minimize risks to innocent civilians. Initial reports indicate that heavy damage was inflicted on the complex. Regrettably, there were some collateral civilian casualties.

I ordered this military response only after I considered the results of a thorough and independent investigation by U.S. intelligence and law enforcement agencies. The reports by Attorney General Reno and Director of Central Intelligence Woolsey provided compelling evidence that the operation that threatened the life of

President Bush in Kuwait City in April was directed and pursued by the Iraqi Intelligence Service and that the Government of Iraq bore direct responsibility for this effort.

The Government of Iraq acted unlawfully in attempting to carry out Saddam Hussein's threats against former President Bush because of actions he took as President. The evidence of the Government of Iraq's violence and terrorism demonstrates that Iraq poses a continuing threat to United States nationals and shows utter disregard for the will of the international community as expressed in Security Council Resolutions and the United Nations Charter. Based on the Government of Iraq's pattern of disregard for international law, I concluded that there was no reasonable prospect that new diplomatic initiatives or economic measures could influence the current Government of Iraq to cease planning future attacks against the United States.

Consequently, in the exercise of our inherent right of self-defense as recognized in Article 51 of the United Nations Charter and pursuant to my constitutional authority with respect to the conduct of foreign relations and as Commander in Chief, I ordered a military strike that directly targeted a facility Iraqi intelligence implicated in the plot against the former Chief Executive. In accordance with Article 51 of the United Nations Charter, this action was reported immediately to the Security Council on June 26. On June 27, Ambassador Albright provided evidence of Iraq's assassination attempts to the United Nations Security Council, which had been convened in emergency session at our request.

I am certain that you share my sincere hope that the limited and proportionate action taken by the United States Government will frustrate and help deter and preempt future unlawful actions on the part of the Government of Iraq. Nonetheless, in the event that Iraqi violence, aggression, or state-sponsored terrorism against the United States continues, I will direct such additional measures in our exercise of the right of self-defense as may be necessary and appropriate to protect United States citizens.

I remain committed to ensuring that the Congress is kept fully informed regarding significant employments of the U.S. Armed Forces. Accordingly, I am providing this report on the U.S. military actions of June 26, consistent with the War Powers Resolution. I appreciate your thoughts and continued support as we address these important concerns.

Sincerely,

WILLIAM J. CLINTON

NOTE: Identical letters were sent to Thomas S. Foley, Speaker of the House of Representatives, and Robert C. Byrd, President pro tempore of the Senate.

Statement by the Press Secretary on the President's Telephone Conversation With President Boris Yeltsin of Russia
June 28, 1993

Beginning at about 1:15 p.m. this afternoon, President Clinton spoke with Russian President Boris Yeltsin for 30 minutes. The two leaders exchanged views on issues to be discussed at the G–7 summit in Tokyo. President Clinton described G–7 efforts to develop a program to support the process of democratic reform and development of free markets in Russia and said the U.S. expects the G–7 to move forward with a solid package of assistance.

President Clinton also reviewed progress made in implementing the U.S. bilateral assistance package he announced in Vancouver, noting that the U.S. had already obligated more than half of the $1.6 billion. President Clinton said that the separate and additional $1.8 billion assistance package for Russia has been approved by the House of Representatives and was under consideration by the Senate. He reiterated to President Yeltsin his full support for this effort.

Nomination for the National Labor Relations Board
June 28, 1993

The President announced today that he intends to nominate law professor and arbitrator William Gould to the National Labor Relations Board.

"William Gould has a tremendous amount of both practical and scholarly experience in labor law," said the President, "and stands for the principles I want the NLRB to uphold: the rights of all workers to participate in labor organizations and the need for labor and management to work together to increase our Nation's competitiveness in a global marketplace. I think that he will be an excellent addition to the Labor Relations Board."

NOTE: A biography of the nominee was made available by the Office of the Press Secretary.

941

Nomination for the Corporation for Public Broadcasting
June 28, 1993

The President announced his intention today to nominate University of Arkansas political scientist Diane Blair to be a member of the Corporation for Public Broadcasting.

"Diane Blair is one of the most capable and committed people I know," said the President. "She is one of the most respected people in our State and a dear friend of mine and of Hillary's. I think that she will do an excellent job of maintaining the Corporation for Public Broadcasting's outstanding record."

NOTE: A biography of the nominee was made available by the Office of the Press Secretary.

Remarks at the Democratic National Committee Presidential Gala
June 28, 1993

Thank you very much. Thank you so much. First, let me say a special word of thanks to Scott Pastrick for this wonderful dinner and all those who worked on it, to Roy Furman for agreeing to take on this enormous responsibility in the Democratic Party. I don't think the first time he came to my attention or, rather, I came to his—he hosted me in his office—if he had known then that he'd wind up on this stage tonight, I'm not sure he would have done it. And I thank him. Like so many others, he came into the leadership of this party because of the campaign of 1992.

I thank my dear friend David Wilhelm for his leadership and all of those who work in the vineyards of the Democratic Party. I thank David especially for what he said tonight. Many of the beneficiaries of the efforts we make today are people who may not even understand entirely what we're doing, and they don't have an organized force in the Congress.

I thank the leadership of Congress. Let me say without hesitation that I have literally been awestruck at the demonstration of courage repeatedly by the leadership and by many of the freshmen and by many in between in our party in the United States Congress. And you ought to give them a hand tonight. [*Applause*]

You heard that the Vice President, of course, broke the tie the other night in the Senate on the economic program. What you ought to know is that I was furiously working the phones, and a couple of Senators—Senator Murray from Washington was not well, and so we thought we had enough votes to pass the bill, and so

she stayed home in bed. And two of the people we thought would vote for it said, "Well, I won't let it die, Mr. President, but if the Vice President can break a tie, that's okay with me." So, we were there at the end. And right before the vote came down to the end with the time running off, the Vice President sent a note to Senator Mitchell, our Democratic leader, and he said, "George, I'm wavering." [*Laughter*] But conviction overcame him at the end, and so here we are tonight with a big crowd instead of an empty house.

Let me say to all of you that a lot of speeches have already been made tonight, and the entertainment was marvelous: Little Texas and Whitney Houston and my good friend Kenny G, who let me play with him in the campaign. That was the biggest thrill I got in the whole election. I tell you, I always liked Kenny G because I was running third in the polls when he agreed to play with me in the campaign.

This has been a great night for us and a great night for our party. But I want to remind you that we are engaged on a great struggle to change this country. A year and 8 months ago I entered the race for President when no one thought the incumbent could be defeated and few thought I could be nominated. And I didn't have any idea how it would come out. I just knew that I had a couple of simple convictions. I felt very strongly then that we were not doing what it takes to compete and win in a global economy. I felt very strongly then that we were not facing up to the honest problems we have at home. I felt very strongly that

942

too many people in public life were telling people what they wanted to hear today instead of thinking about how we ought to live tomorrow.

Those things drove me into the race, and they produced in the end, thanks to all of you, a remarkable change in the course of American life. But the details are always more difficult than the rhetoric. Governor Cuomo used to say frequently that we campaign in poetry, but we must govern in prose. And as my daughter likes to remind me of that great slogan the kids are all saying today, denial is not just a river in Egypt. So, when you move from rhetoric to reality, sometimes the going gets tough. I couldn't believe it, we have been ranted and raved against, this administration, as you know; it's all "tax and spend." But we've cut more spending than any administration in history and more than the ones before us. And that's a fact.

And they say, "Well, only the Democrats are voting for this program." But let me tell you, look at the alternatives. In the House of Representatives there was a Republican alternative with no taxes which slashed the middle class, slashed the working poor, slashed the elderly just above the poverty line, and more Republicans voted against it than Democrats voted against our program. In the Senate there was a Republican program, 4 months late, which took $100 billion less off the deficit and was tougher on the middle class and the poor. And in the finance committee, the other party that goes around saying, "It's spending, stupid," you know that great slogan of theirs, guess how many spending cut amendments were offered by the Republicans in the Senate Finance Committee? Zero. Not one.

I say that because it is up to every one of you to go home and tell the people of this country the truth. This is not going to be easy, but it is working. You heard the Vice President; you heard David Wilhelm talk tonight. If anybody had told you on election night in November that by the middle of June unemployment would be below 7 percent, we'd have 755,000 new jobs, a 20-year low in mortgage rates, a 6-year high in housing sales, a 9-year high in construction employment, the family leave bill, the motor voter bill, the Biodiversity Treaty, a

new policy on choice, the most diverse administration in history, an appointment schedule—contrary to what you may have heard—ahead of the last two administrations, you would have felt pretty good about that on election night. And you ought to feel pretty good about it tonight, because this country is on the move.

But never forget this. That sounds good, and compared to the last two administrations it may be, but we've just been here 5 months, and the changes we are trying to make are not in place. We still have to do the economic program and health care and national service and welfare reform. We still have to pass a program that says to people who work 40 hours a week and have children in their homes, you're not in poverty anymore. We still have a lot of work to do. And the things we're doing have still not affected most Americans. We still don't have a serious program for defense conversion, but we're working on that. We've got an airline industry in trouble we're trying to help resuscitate and move forward. We've got all kinds of jobs in this country we have still got to create. We have problems in this country that Government has overlooked for so long, we pretend they're not even there. People say to me, "I am so glad that the Federal Government could help to break up the terrorist ring in New York," or that once again we stood up for our values last weekend. But never forget, in this the Capital City of this country 24 people were killed last week. We have got a lot of work to do, my fellow Americans.

And I'll tell you something. It may not always be easy, and sometimes it may be ragged, but you've got an administration in this town that gets up and goes to work every day and thinks about the problems and the promise of the average people of this country. And we will continue to do it as long as you keep us here.

Thank you, and God bless you all. Thank you.

NOTE: The President spoke at 11:15 p.m. at the Washington Convention Center. In his remarks, he referred to Scott Pastrick, Presidential gala dinner chairman; and Democratic National Committee officers Roy Furman, national finance chairman, and David Wilhelm, chairman.

Remarks and a Question-and-Answer Session With the National Federation of Independent Business
June 29, 1993

The President. Thank you. Thank you very much, and good morning. Please be seated. When Jack Faris came to see me the other day in the Oval Office, he invited me to come over here and speak. And he said the best time to come would be noon. But the President of Argentina will be in the White House at noon, and I couldn't figure out how to explain that to him, that we were going to miss lunch. So then I was invited to come at 9:15, which is okay for me most days. But I'm one of these people who gets up at 6 every morning, and then I wake up about 10:30. [*Laughter*] So if I say anything I shouldn't today, I'll have total deniability since it's 9:15.

I was eager to come by and address you this morning for several reasons: first of all, because your organization is one of this city's most aggressive participants in the economic debate now taking place here and around the country; and because when I was the Governor of my State, I worked very closely with the NFIB on a wide range of issues; and because I know that unless we are firmly and unequivocally committed to private sector job growth, and especially to small business growth, we cannot succeed as a country.

Let me say that when I got into the race for President about a year and 8 months ago, I did so after having worked for nearly a dozen years as a Governor of a State that until the last year I was Governor usually had an unemployment rate above the national average. I spent all my time trying to figure out how to create conditions in which jobs could grow, children could be educated, people could be trained, and folks could be empowered to do what they could do in a very tough global marketplace. I worked year-in and year-out to try to establish partnerships with the private sector. Until I became President, except for one brief interlude when I took office and found an operating deficit as Governor, I had never proposed raising one red cent in taxes to pay down a debt, because my State had a very tough balanced budget law, perhaps the toughest in the country in its practical operation. This has been an interesting and a difficult experience for me

in that regard.

But here's how I see the world: We have now been in a long-term economic slowdown of about 3 years in which our economy is not producing many jobs. We have been in a global economic fight which has caused us grave problems for 20 years. And literally for 20 years most middle class wage earners have worked longer work weeks, and their wages have not kept up with inflation. We have seen an enormous increase in this country, in the 1980's, in the cost of health care, housing, and education, which has far outstripped the earnings of most wage earners and small business people to cope with. And we now find ourselves in the midst of a global recession, as I prepare to go to Tokyo to meet with the leaders of the other G–7 nations—the European nations, Canada, and Japan—in which our economy, though it is weak by our standards, is now perhaps the best performing of all these countries.

During the 1980's, most of our job growth came from two sources. First of all, we had a huge operating deficit that was built into our system because we had a very large tax cut in 1981, twice the original size that President Reagan proposed, when the Congress and the President got into a bidding war, and very large increases in defense spending. So that the deficit, plus investments in defense, especially in defense contracts, as those of you who are from California or Connecticut or Massachusetts who saw it go up and then watched it come down, know that that created a lot of jobs.

The other thing that created a lot of jobs in the 1980's was you, the small business sector. Indeed, throughout the 1980's and every year, the Fortune 500 lowered employment in America, even as income went up, by a couple of hundred thousand people a year. But small business people generated the vast mass of the jobs. In fact, a study by David Birch at the Massachusetts Institute of Technology indicated that about 85 percent of all new jobs were created in units of under 50, and most of those were created by people who themselves were small business persons.

Then about 3 years ago, that stopped. And

we can all argue about why that is, but I think it's clear that there were a couple of reasons. First of all, small business people are not unaffected by slowdowns in the global economy, as well as the domestic economy. Secondly, the extra added cost of hiring one more employee became exponentially greater as health care costs, payroll costs, and other things mounted up, and more and more people, even in the small business sector, turned to overtime and part-time workers.

But the bottom line is we now find ourselves in a world in which there is a global recession, in which we have the lowest unemployment rate of any of our competing wealthy countries, except for Japan which has, as you know, a much different trading system and economic organization, and in which still our unemployment rate is way too high for us. And when we look to the future, it seems to me absolutely clear that we have to find ways to reinvigorate the job machine of America and to restore the health of small business.

The problem is that we have dug ourselves into a number of holes that we have to dig out of, none of which are easy. And all along the way, we have to know that we may not be able to get instant results because what happens in America today is at least to some extent affected by what happens in Europe, what happens in Japan, and what happens in other countries. I know, for example, you had the Trade Ambassador, Mickey Kantor, here yesterday talking about the trade agreement with Mexico. And there's a lot of debate in this country about that. Our administration believes it will create more jobs than it will cost. We feel very strongly about that. We're going to have a debate about it later in the year, but the point is at least it's the right debate. That's the right debate: Is it going to help the American economy? Is it going to create more jobs than it will cost?

Well, it is against that background, anyway, that I became the President: 3 years of slow economic growth, which doubtless contributed to a challenger beating an incumbent; and then a very large Federal debt, having gone from $1 to $4 trillion in 12 years; an annual deficit having gone from $74 billion a year in 1980 to $311 billion projected in 1993; and the deficit for the next 5 years was written up $165 billion, estimated after the election.

And so I was confronted with a very significant problem, one which had very practical impacts on you in at least two ways. First of all, the bigger this debt and the deficit gets, the more of your tax money we have to spend every year paying interest on the debt and the less we have to invest in the future: to finance research and development, to finance new technologies, to finance education and training of the work force, to grow the economy. Second, and even more important for you, America had a historic gap between short-term interest rates and long-term interest rates because of the size of the deficit and because nothing was being done to bring it down. So you had very low short-term interest rates. As you know, they started coming down way over a year ago with the Federal Reserve lowering, lowering, lowering the rates they were charging. But our long-term interest rates, which determine home mortgages, business loan interest rates, consumer loan rates, car loan rates, college loan rates, they were quite high. And the gap between the short and long-term rates was very high.

It was obvious to me that unless we first did something to reassert control over our economic destiny, unless we did something about this deficit first, we would not be able to move forward. And so I proposed a plan to the United States Congress to bring the deficit down by $500 billion over the next 5 years, in roughly equal amounts of budget cuts and tax increases with almost all the taxes, 74 percent of them, falling on the upper 6 percent of income earners, including subchapter S corporations, the upper 5 percent of those, and they were pretty stiff.

But the reason I did it was because it seems to me we had to try to lower the deficit about $500 billion. We imposed what amounted to a 5-year freeze on domestic discretionary spending. That is, we do increase funds for defense conversion to help those poor people that lost their jobs because of the defense cutbacks, for Head Start, for education and training, and for some technologies. But we cut other stuff even more, so there's a decline in defense, a freeze on domestic spending. The only thing that's going up is basically the retirement programs and the health care programs. I'll come back to that. I'll come back to that in a moment. So we had big cuts over the previous budget in everything, all the entitlements: veterans, agriculture, pay of Federal employees, retirement of Federal, civilian, and military employees.

Things that had not been touched in previous budgets we went after, it cut them, locked that down, and then asked for what I thought was a progressive tax package.

But there were also some interesting growth features in the tax program that I proposed that the House of Representatives passed. One was one of your long-time goals, increasing the expensing provision from $10,000 to $25,000 a year. I think that's real important. If we do that, there are hundreds of thousands of businesses in this country that might be able to hire one more person, might be able to get their incomes up by buying another piece of equipment.

The second was something that larger businesses, by and large, wanted, and that was a change in the alternative minimum tax calculations designed entirely for one purpose: to encourage people to invest in more plant and equipment, to become more productive. The third was the small business capital gains tax, designed to encourage people to invest in ventures under $50 million in capitalization and to get a 50 percent cut on the tax due if they held the investment for 5 years. This was designed to get a bunch of new venture capital and private capital into the real job generators of this economy.

The third was a permanent extension of the research and development tax credit. Next, there was changes in the passive loss provisions on real estate designed to get home building and real estate up again, particularly in those regions of the country where it has been so depressed that it's dragged everything else down.

Then we extended the deduction people can take for their health insurance premiums to self-employed people, as well as to other small businesses which already had it, which I thought was very important, a big deal for farmers.

And finally, there were other things, but finally there was a proposal which I think we ought to try to finally test whether the rhetoric that both Democrats and Republicans have been putting out in Washington for years, and in the streets of America, about using the private sector to revitalize the distressed areas of our country could really prove true. We devised an empowerment zone proposal which was an expansion of the enterprise zone proposal that for the last several years had been supported by everybody from Jack Kemp in the Republican Party to Charles Rangel in New York in the Democratic Party. This empowerment zone proposal went beyond anything previously proposed to give really powerful incentives for the private sector to hire people out of depressed cities and small towns in rural areas or to put businesses into those areas. And it seems to me that's very important.

If you look at all the millions of people that live outside the free market economy in America because they live in areas that are so depressed, there is a huge potential market there if the free market system can work. So, those things were also in the bill. In other words, we raised tax rates, but we tried to find ways for people who have been successful, who have money, to lower their taxes but only if they invested in things designed to grow the economy, create jobs, and expand opportunity for all Americans.

Now, when the Senate passed the bill last week there were a lot of things in the Senate bill that were good. They had some less tax and some more spending cuts so that, by any calculation, clearly now the spending cuts exceed the tax increases. But by taking most of the tax cut out of the energy tax and having to make it up to get $500 billion in tax reductions, they reduced the size of the small business expensing from 25 to 20; they eliminated the new business or the small business capital gains tax; they put a surcharge on capital gains, which I think is not well-advised; and made the research and development tax credit temporary. So, we are now trying to resolve the conflicts between those two bills. I know the NFIB will be actively involved in that, but I think it's very important that you understand basically what the tradeoff was made between the Senate and the House bills. The bottom line is both of them reduced the deficit by $500 billion.

You had long-term rates going down again today to a 16-year low, and this has already produced some very significant consequences, if I just might mention a few. From the time Secretary of the Treasury, then designate, Lloyd Bentsen said we were going to have a serious deficit reduction plan and talked about what was going to be in it in November, we've seen long-term interest rates take a dramatic drop. While the economy itself is not recovered by any means, there have been some very significant advances tied directly to the drop in long-term interest rates. And if I might just mention a few, number one, we've had a 20-year low in home mortgages; a 6-year high in housing sales; a 9-year high in increase in construction employment, 130,000 new construction employees in America in a 4-month period; and there have been 755,000 jobs, over 90 percent of which are in the private sector, come into this economy in the last 5 months. That compares with only a net gain of a million over the previous 4 years, all tied to bringing down the long-term interest rates.

There are people in this room today who are responsible for that, directly or indirectly, people who have refinanced their home loans. Most of the real financial gains have come from people who have refinanced their home loans and then turned around and done something else with the money, and that's bumped the economy. But business loans are lower, consumer loans, car loans, college loans, the whole 9 yards. That is the strategy.

It is estimated that if we can pass this deficit reduction plan and keep the interest rates down for a year, that'll put another $110 billion back into this economy. And by the end of the year or next year, that will really begin to produce some job growth, and we'll also begin to produce some real earnings potential.

So that is why we have done what we have done. And I'll say again, as somebody who was a Governor in a State with a very tough budgeting system, it was very painful for me to ask anybody to pay any money just to pay down the deficit. But unless we do something about this, we will never—it's like a bone in our throat as a nation—unless we deal with this, we can't get on to dealing with our other problems. We'll spend all our time in Washington working around the edges of these other problems because we have not faced the problem of the deficit.

Now, let me just make one or two other comments about that. No matter what plan you might embrace to reduce the deficit, and no matter what plan you've read or heard about, every one of them can have our annual deficit go down for 5 years, and then it starts to go up again. Why? Health care costs. We cut $50 billion in the House version, $60 billion in the Senate version off of projected Medicare expenses from the previous year's budget. And it is still estimated that over 5 years, the Medicare budget alone will go up 45 percent. Now, that's better than most of you are doing, right? Most of you are paying more than 9 percent a year in increased premiums. Most of you are

paying almost twice that.

But I say that to try to illustrate the next point. There's been a lot of controversy about the willingness of this administration to try to take on this health issue and whether we're being too comprehensive and what we're going to do and all that. The point I want to make is this: We've got to do something to bring costs within inflation, or it's going to break the country. That's the first thing. You can talk to just about any conservative in Congress of either party, you can talk to the most conservative Republican in the Republican Party, and most of them will tell you now we are not spending enough money on some of the things that will generate jobs in the future. If we don't spend enough money to keep our technology lead over other countries in areas critical to the future, in super computing and electronics and aerospace and these other things, and if we don't really educate and train our people, then our incomes will fall behind. But if we are strangled by rising health care costs, the future can have no lobby in the Congress.

So this budget plan that we presented is great on deficit reduction. It does invest some money in the future, but it doesn't invest anything like what you would want us to invest if we weren't strung up by our heels by the deficit. And there is no answer to it except to get health costs in line with inflation. There is no other answer, because that's the only thing that's eating us alive now through Medicare and Medicaid. It is the same with you.

Now, what we see is people have learned a lot about controlling health care costs, and a lot of big businesses that can self-insure now have their costs in line with inflation. The California public employees system, which is a huge system with bulk purchasing power, this year has a contract which is below inflation. That's great for them. But what does that mean? Even more pressure on you to pay for the uncompensated care bills of people who don't have health insurance if you do. Which means every year more and more small businesses are either dropping coverage—about 100,000 Americans a month lose their health insurance—or they have more limited coverage that may or may not be adequate for the people whom they insure.

So, what I want to say about that is this: It seems clear to me, if you study the Federal budget and you want the deficit down to zero and you want America to invest and grow again, if you look at the private budgets of businesses in this country, that we have to do something to give small businesses bulk purchasing power; relief from all these rules and regulations the Federal Government imposes; relief from the incredible paperwork imposed on health care providers by this country being the only country in the world having 1,500 different health insurance companies, thousands of different policies, a dime on the dollar more in paperwork costs than any other advanced country in the world, a dime on the dollar. And the more big businesses self-insure and control their own costs, the more you're paying the difference. So, we have got to do some things to simplify and make more uniform this system.

Now, the big controversy obviously is over whether there should be a mandate for employers, employees, one or both, to cover people who have no health insurance. Here is the problem, and I invite you to the debate, but here is the problem: Seventy percent of all small businesses have some health insurance. And they're paying out the ears for it. I have to be delicate in my language. [*Laughter*] Seventy percent do. Costs are going up like crazy. For the 30 percent who don't, those folks, if they get sick, will still get health care. Show up at the emergency room, and they will get it. Everybody gets it. But who paid for the emergency room to be there? The rest of you. You built the infrastructure. You financed. You maintain the infrastructure.

The Government should clearly insure the unemployed, uninsured. And my goal has been to do that by managing the system better so we don't have to raise taxes on you to do that, because people who are paying too much already shouldn't pay more to fix the system. But if you look at every system in the world, it is perfectly clear that unless you have some mechanism by which everybody is covered, you cannot control the costs, and you cannot stop the cost-shifting.

Now, nobody wants to do this in a way that kills the only job-generator we've had in America over the last 2 years, which is you. But it's very important to remember that most small businesses do provide health insurance. This is the nub of the economic dilemma. If it were easy, somebody would have done it already, right? I mean, if it were easy, it would already be done. It's not easy. There is no perfect solution. But I assure you that we're all going to

be better off if we enter into an honest debate and try to work through this, and we try to resolve it. The worst thing we can do is to leave it alone, and especially, the worst thing we can do for the small business sector, because bigger employers will figure out how to get managed care, and they'll just go around this whole health insurance system we have today. Everybody else is going to be out there just strung up. So we must face it. And we've got to provide some means of covering people, letting them change jobs, and having people have this without going bankrupt. And that is something that I am deeply dedicated to.

Let me mention one or two other issues that are very important, and then we'll move on to questions. I believe the SBA can be a force for good in small businesses. And I promised myself if I got elected President, when I started, I would appoint somebody to run the SBA who had literally had real experience and was not just a political appointee. Now I plead guilty. Erskine Bowles is a personal friend of mine. His wife went to college with my wife. That does not disqualify him. [*Laughter*] But his wife is a successful business person, and he has spent his lifetime trying to help people like you start your businesses, expand your business, market your business overseas. He actually knows what he's doing. So it seems to me that would be nice to have an SBA director who could do that, who had been through that.

The second thing that I really thought about a lot early in the election because of the experiences I had seen not only in my State but around the country, is that we had to do something to try to deal with the credit crunch. The access to credit is obviously going to have more to do with how a lot of your members do than a lot of other things this Government does. So, early in my administration we brought together all the appropriate banking regulatory agencies and, in what was then an act of unprecedented cooperation, we changed a lot of the restricted regulations that cause so much of the credit crunch. Banks are now clearly empowered to make more character loans based on the reputation of the borrower. Documentation requirements by the Federal Government have been relaxed dramatically, as have regulations regarding appraisals of real estate to secure small business loans. And there will be more flexibility in classifying loans.

Now, that has been done at our level. It takes

more time than I wish it did for all those changes here to actually be felt in every community bank in America. And one of the things that the NFIB needs to do with Erskine Bowles is to let us know in which communities this is working and in which communities there has been no change, because we made a vigorous, clear effort to send this signal out all across America by changing the way we did business with the banks. But it has not changed in every community in America, and a lot of people are still really stung by what happened to them in the eighties. But the banks are in much better shape today than they were 3 years ago. And that's good, that's a good omen for our future. But now that they're in better shape the time has come for them to loan money on good terms, at low interest rates. So we need your help on that.

Next I'd like to say a little something about regulatory reform. Every President talks about it, and almost nothing ever happens. There's a division in our Budget Office that a lot of you probably have never heard of in the Office of Management and Budget called OIRA—that would gag you—OIRA, the Office of Information and Regulatory Affairs. For years, the position of Administrator of this Office, believe it or not, was vacant. But this Office actually has the capacity to rationally review all of these regulations. We have named, and Congress has confirmed, an Administrator for OIRA, and we are going to do our best to see what we can do to reduce unnecessary regulations.

Perhaps more important, I have asked the Vice President as part of his job in reviewing the whole operations of the Federal Government—and by the way, I predict you will be very pleased by the report that is issued by his group in September—we are reviewing the operations of every last part of this Government. Unlike your business, unlike all big businesses, the way we do business in the Federal Government and many of these agencies has been largely unexamined for decades. So that when something new comes along that we have to do, it normally is just added on to what was being done already, instead of being substituted for it. And the whole quality revolution that has engulfed the American private sector and led to rapid increases in productivity has largely escaped Government. And we're trying to change that, too. It escapes nearly every organization that has a mandate for customers and

income, so we're trying to change that. Our goal is pretty simple: We want to avoid regulations that are inconsistent with the goals of jobs and growth; we want to avoid regulations that overlap; we want to create a process that is open and fair, where business has some input, and not just large businesses but also medium and small ones as well; and we want to change the whole way Washington works.

I think these are the kinds of things that you would want us to do, and these are certainly the things that we have to do. I don't plan or pretend that we're always going to agree on all these issues. And I wish that the world looked to me as President just the way it does to you or the way it even did to me as Governor. Like I said, it took a lot of mental gymnastics for me to finally face the hard reality that we had this huge deficit and unless we did something about it, we were never going to be able to do anything else. We'd spend all our time— I spent all my time giving speeches about things we were going to do, and no impact would be felt because we were out of control of our economic destiny. So I hope that you will be supportive, not supportive of me personally so much as supportive of our efforts, common efforts to deal with our common problems. The one thing I made up my mind to do when I won the election in November was at least try to level with the American people about the problems and try to face things that other people in public life had avoided. This is painful. You know, my daughter and the kids her age who get into all this interesting music has got this great phrase. She said, "Dad, denial is not just a river in Egypt." [*Laughter*] And sometimes I think that's probably a good phrase for us to remember in a lot of ways.

But my plain duty to you is at least to try to articulate what these issues are and face them. We tried it the other way. We tried ignoring the deficit. It didn't go away. We tried telling everybody what they wanted to hear, that it could all be done by some sleight of hand, and it didn't happen. And we tried a lot of things about health care in the Federal Government which, frankly, made your problems worse. I could control health care costs without doing anything on the health care system. And what would happen? All the providers, when we just cut Medicare and Medicaid more, all the providers will send you the bill. That's what happens today.

So, I ask you to think about this. Let us face our problems; let us talk about our problems. The first big urgent thing is to pass a deficit reduction plan that keeps as many of these growth incentives as we can possibly have. That was the good thing about the House bill. Then I look forward to engaging in the health debate. I look forward to engaging in the trade debate. I look forward to engaging in the job creation debate. But in the end just remember, every advanced country in the world is having a terrible time creating jobs. We are doing better than most of them because of you, because we have a vigorous small business sector. Unfortunately, a lot of the things that we want to do may help some people and impose burdens on others in the small business sector at the same time, though we know that these big issues will not go away. And we know now after 3 years of stagnation we have to change if we want to grow.

I believe if we do it together the next 20 years can still be the best years this country ever had. We are in a new and unprecedented era. This happens to us about once a generation, and when it happens we have to adjust as a people. That is what we are now trying to do. That's what makes being here so exciting. But I never forget that the thing that's important about it is that what happens here affects what you do there. And what you do there, wherever "there" is, in your hometown, is what really makes America work.

Thank you very much.

Moderator. Mr. President, again we very much appreciate you taking the time to be with us in your remarks today. One of the things the President has asked for and is willing to do is to take some questions from us. I will tell you from the years past, in other conferences with other Presidents who have spoken, this is the first President who has said, "I would like to have questions from the group." And because we have such a large group assembled, Mr. President, what we've done is, we've circulated cards for people to use to ask questions. We've accumulated these, gone through, and picked out the top questions. And we have time for just two or three if we could.

The President. Did you say the tough questions? [*Laughter*]

Moderator. The tough ones, the only kind we have.

The President. I have a feeling when this is over, I'm going to know why my predecessors didn't take questions. [*Laughter*] Go ahead.

Health Care Reform

Moderator. The first one is: I have a small business with two part-time employees. The business is out there for me to expand. However, mandated health care and the present uncertainty has caused me not to hire more people. What assurances can you give me and others in my position that will give me the confidence to hire more people and to create more jobs?

The President. First of all, I think you ought to wait and see what we come out with. I think that most people believe that this plan would be much tougher on small businesses than I believe it will be. But let me put it to you in another way. We have to decide what to do with part-time employees. And either employers will have to make some contribution to their health care. By the way, I think all employees should make some contribution to their health care, because if they don't, they may get to thinking it's free, and overutilization is one of the problems. I mean, everybody should pay something in accordance with their ability to pay. But I have to say this: I believe employers should make some contribution, because I will say again, those who don't pay at all are being supported, even when they don't use the hospital, even when they don't use the clinic, even when they don't use anything, they're being supported by those who do pay something, because they are keeping the infrastructure going. And everybody's bills will be lower over the long run if everyone makes a fair contribution. I think small businesses should really be limited in what they're required to pay by the Government. And also, anything that is done should be phased in so that as we go along the way, if there are mistakes or unanticipated consequences, they can be corrected. We should not wave a magic wand and say, okay, next year the system is going to look like this. We're going to have to phase this thing in so we can all work together and see what the problems are.

But I have to say that I think in terms of job creation over the long run, you're going to have more people working over the long run if we don't have these costs being bounced around and thrown off from one group of employers onto another. The trick is going to be how to keep the questioner's costs low enough, and also what is the fair way to apportion the costs for the part-time workers.

Workers' Compensation

Moderator. Dear Mr. President, as a North Carolina strong Democrat and a strong supporter of the Clinton-Gore campaign, please share your views on reducing the cost of health care and workmen's compensation for my small business.

The President. Well, that's one thing I didn't say. The half of the—is that you? Good for you. This is just like a Baptist church. I figured we've got all the saints on the front row here. [*Laughter*] Let me say, first of all, one of the things that we are seeking to do in this health reform effort is to alleviate the inordinate burden of workers comp on employers by, and I don't want to get and sort of prefigure exactly what this is going to look like, but if you look at the workers comp system it is really three things: it's a health care system, it's a disability payment system, and it's an unemployment system, right? It was created at a time when we didn't have comprehensive systems to do all that. We now have health care systems, a disability program, an unemployment program, and we've got workers comp. And half the cost of workers comp is the health care.

So, what we're going to try to do is to fold the health care costs part of workers comp into this health care program which would dramatically cut the cost of workers comp. Like everything else, it's a little more complicated than it seems. Here is the dilemma. Here's the problem we don't want to do. Most people will tell you who have tried to cut down on abuse of workers comp, that having that health care part of the program out there is one thing that stops it from being abused, because you can prove that people are well; you can say, now you have to go back to work, you have to go to therapy. So, if we merged the cost into a health care program, we don't want to do it in a way that in effect cuts the rest of it loose so people can allege disability in excess of what it is and the abuses that are plain in the present system will be worse instead of less. We have to do this in a way that will reduce the abuses in the present system. So that's the dilemma. It is obviously extremely costly administratively, has a lot of health overlap, to have these duplicated health systems for employees. It's not necessary, and we ought to abolish it, but we need to

do it in a way that doesn't aggravate the disability problem of workers comp. So that's the issue there. I think we can do it.

White House Conference on Small Business

Moderator. Thank you. The national White House Conference on Small Business was scheduled to take place in 1994. Does your administration have a date set for the conference, and will you allow us to assist with issues hitting small business the hardest?

The President. The answer to the second question is yes, we will allow you to assist. The answer to the first question is, do we have a date yet? That was not a yes or a no. He's become a politician. He's just been up here a couple of weeks, and he's already—[*laughter*]—he said that the answer is, it'll be sometime between January and March of 1995. I'm really looking forward to it.

Meetings With Business Leaders

Moderator. We all are. And according to the time that I have, this is the last question. Rather than talk with the CEO's of the Fortune 500 about business matters, why not get a panel of small business members, 50 or less employees, say, 25 from each State, to inform you on a regular basis?

The President. Let me make a suggestion sort of to follow up on that without embracing that specific suggestion, although I think that's about as good as any I've heard. I will hereby, in front of you, deputize Mr. Bowles to work with you to come up with some formula for bringing in a representative group of small business leaders to see me on a regular basis and talk about this. Let me say we'll do that.

Moderator. Thank you.

The President. Let me make one other point about this. Let me say that I have started— and this question may have come from someone who'd seen the press on this. But I have started every week or 2 weeks for the last couple of months, through Alexis Herman, who is my special Assistant for Public Liaison—she works with groups throughout the country and also helped organize my coming here today—having lunch with business leaders from around the country. And we try always to have one smaller business person in with a lot of the big business leaders who come. We have manufacturers, people from finance. We always try to have at least one small business person at the table, or either that or someone who started a business from scratch that may not be so small anymore, but they started—just to try to have the mix. It's been an immensely valuable thing for me just to do this. And we just take an hour-and-a-half informal, off-the-record lunch. We talk about whatever they want to talk about and a couple of things that I'm working on. But it really helps to keep me connected to what's going on out there. It's pretty easy to get isolated, as I'm sure you know, in this town. And so I would embrace this. I'm glad you stood up when I said it, but it will do me more good than it will you. I'll get a lot out of it, and we'll follow up.

Government and the Private Sector

Moderator. Mr. President, your staff says that they will give us time for one more question.
The President. Good.
Moderator. Which we appreciate. Mr. President, thank you for speaking to us. I'm sure you agree that most of our social problems can be eased or solved by putting every capable American to work. What compromises in your social agenda are you willing to make to reduce the burden of Government?
The President. Well, the answer is I'm prepared to do nearly anything to put everybody to work. But let me say again the country with the lowest unemployment rate of all the wealthy countries in the world is Japan. And it would be hard to make a serious case that they have a low unemployment rate because their Government's not involved in their economy. And basically what they have is high productivity for exports and labor-intensive, even not very productive protections for the domestic market, so they can keep unemployment low. It's an interesting system. I'm not suggesting we follow it; I don't think we should. The only point I'm trying to make is that a number of the business leaders who come to see me believe that one of the reasons that we have unemployment as high as it is, is that we had nothing to substitute for the big cutback in defense spending. For example, when Eisenhower was President, we built the interstate highway network. And then we had in the seventies, we had a huge investment in building new water and sewer systems, making environmental investments that had never been made before. And then in the eighties, we had a huge investment in defense industries of all kinds, not just people in the

military but all the contractors.

So my feeling is, what we need to do is to get the Government out of those things where the private sector is doing well and doing better. And I think, as I said, I'm really eagerly awaiting the work the Vice President is doing. He's consulting experts from all over America on what we can do to increase the productivity of the Federal Government. I think the Government does a lot of things that hold back the job engine in the private sector. But there are also some things that Government does well that we're not doing now as much as so many of our competitors are. For example, if you wanted to have a more efficient high-speed rail network in this country, you'd have to have some sort of public input here, just like they do in every other country.

So I think the problem is, we're doing too little of some of the things we do well, and we're doing too much of things that we can't really have much of an impact on except to slow down the job machine. And it's not so much less; we need a lot less in some areas, but we also need to far more sharply define what nearly all of us could agree the Government ought to do as well as what the Government ought not to do. And we're going to have to be much more disciplined about it. I mean, there are lots of departments here in this town that have a good mission. But they also are doing things that they started doing 25 or 30 years ago that may or may not have a credible rationale for continuing now, and we can't afford that anymore.

It's just like you. If you want to increase your impact, and you're not getting any more money, you've got to change what you're doing. You've got to stop doing some things, and you want to start doing others. And the thing I like about this budget that we're about to adopt is that if we want to do new things, it's going to require us to stop doing some old things and will require some real discipline for the first time in a long time. And we'll do our best. And if we set up this consultation process, you can help us along the way.

Thank you very much.

NOTE: The President spoke at 9:15 a.m. at the Hyatt Regency. In his remarks, he referred to Jack Faris, president and chief executive officer of the federation.

Exchange With Reporters Prior to Discussions With President Carlos Saul Menem of Argentina
June 29, 1993

President's Approval Rating

Q. How do you like your new popularity as a result of the attack on Baghdad?

The President. I think there's a lot of evidence that people are learning more about the specifics of the economic program again, too. I think that's a lot of it.

Q. Do you really think that's it?

The President. Absolutely, I do.

Iraq

Q. There were new threats from Iraqi officials this morning, threat of retaliation. Are you concerned about that, Mr. President?

The President. Well, we'll deal with those as they arise.

Haiti

Q. Are you going to discuss the Haitian situation with Mr. Menem?

The President. Absolutely, I will. I want to get his ideas. President Menem has been a real force for democracy and for human rights in our hemisphere. Argentina was extremely helpful in playing a leadership role in the recent Guatemalan crisis. And I want to know what he thinks about Haiti and what we might do.

Q. Are you going to sell him Skyhawks, 36 Skyhawks?

Economic Indicators

Q. [*Inaudible*]—sir, last month after you took great pains to attach the jump to your economic program.

The President. They won't be up every month. But the economy in our country will have great difficulty in totally recovering in any short period of time from the traumas of the last 10 to 12 to 15 years. But I think that it's clear that if we can bring our deficit down, keep our interest rates down, we can get growth up. It's also true that we have to try to work with our trading partners to get growth up. And I might just mention Argentina. Our exports to

Argentina have tripled in the last 4 years. That's the sort of thing we're trying to work on with other countries around the world. And it's not going to be easier quick. We're basically restructuring the American economy at a time when the whole world is in a rebuilding process. But I'm hopeful.

[*At this point, one group of reporters left the room, and another group entered.*]

Argentina

Q. Mr. Clinton, can you tell us what you want to achieve with this visit?

The President. Well, first of all, I want to just get to know President Menem a little better. He is the first Latin American leader I have received here at the White House. I admire very much the program of economic reform that Argentina has pursued under his leadership, their respect for human rights, their support for democracy. I was especially grateful for the position taken in the recent issue with Guatemala. And there are lots of things we have to talk about.

Q. Mr. President, do you agree that Argentina is leading Latin America?

The President. Do I believe Argentina's a leader in Latin America? Absolutely. I hope that we can explore stronger and broader trade relations. I hope that we can continue to work together on the problems in the hemisphere. I'm going to ask President Menem for his views on the situation in Haiti, for example, where I very much want to see democracy restored. And I wanted him to come here and to be the first Latin American leader to come because of the remarkable, some would say astonishing, progress in Argentina in the last couple of years.

NOTE: The exchange began at 11:35 a.m. in the Oval Office at the White House. A tape was not available for verification of the content of this exchange.

The President's News Conference With President Carlos Saul Menem of Argentina
June 29, 1993

President Clinton. Good afternoon, ladies and gentlemen. Today I have the great honor of welcoming President Carlos Menem of Argentina to the White House, the first leader of a Latin American state to visit here since I took office.

Under President Menem's administration, Argentina has become an international leader on the great issues of the post-cold-war era, a leader in this hemisphere in defense of democracy and human rights, a trusted and valued partner and friend of the United States. Together we are constructing a Western Hemisphere community of democracies, interpreted by common political values and growing economic ties. We deeply appreciate President Menem's visit today. He represents a new generation of Latin American Presidents committed to expanding freedom, strengthening democracy, and creating prosperity. His leadership has been bold and his accomplishments truly impressive.

We talked today about Argentina's democratic reforms and the role Argentina has assumed as an international leader. Today, Argentine troops serve with the United Nations peacekeepers in Croatia, in Kuwait, in Mozambique, and in other troubled lands. In the Organization of American States, Argentina consistently takes a strong stand in favor of collective defenses of democracy. With Argentina's support, the OAS has worked to defend democratic institutions in Peru, reverse the coup in Guatemala. And I am confident, together we can restore democracy in Haiti, a subject we discussed at great length today.

Argentina has also confronted crises of recession and hyperinflation and has overcome both. Argentina slashed its tariffs and opened its economy to world markets. It ended its fiscal deficit and created a stable currency. It sold state enterprises and attracted new investment. And as a result, last year Argentina's economy grew 9 percent. I asked him for a few of those points for America today. That was one of the unresolved parts of our discussion. [*Laughter*]

Once Congress successfully ratifies the North American Free Trade Agreement with Mexico and with Canada, we will want to reduce trade barriers with other countries in this hemisphere. Freer trade promotes the kind of economic and democratic reforms we see in Argentina. It clearly benefits our economy as well as that of our neighbors. As I said earlier today, in the last 4 years our trade with Argentina has tripled, accounting for 40,000 jobs in the United States.

Our meeting covered some other areas as well. Argentina's Government has been an important voice in calling for a successful conclusion of the Uruguay round to open the world trading system. Argentina stands among the nations leading the effort to confront the overriding challenge of stopping the spread of weapons of mass destruction. President Menem himself ended a dangerous ballistic missile program, signed important nuclear nonproliferation agreements, placed strong controls on the export of sensitive weapons-related materials and technology, and helped to lead the successful international effort to negotiate the Chemical Weapons Convention.

Argentina has been in the forefront of initiatives to increase the dialog on security issues in its region. Its progress and support for democracy are two reasons why this hemisphere today is more secure and more prosperous today than it was in the past and why it will show the way to a better world tomorrow.

Again, let me say it is an honor for me to welcome the President, whom I admire, whose accomplishments we respect, and whose country will be a great partner for the United States in the years ahead.

Mr. President.

President Menem. Thank you very much, Mr. President. I would like to tell you of my gratitude that is sincere and loyal in the name of my country and of my government for your words. They are the result of a complete knowledge of what is happening in Argentina, in this continent, and in the world.

You may be absolutely sure that Argentina will continue along this road. There is absolutely no possibility of any change in Argentine policies in the field of economics and in the social fields. I always say this is a road that we cannot walk backwards on, and these are the results we are obtaining. If I would have to explain here the achievements obtained, I would have to repeat the same words that you have used, Mr. President, and this would not perhaps be very much in order. But we have talked in an environment of cordiality and affection. We have discussed our relations that are now at their best level ever. We are prepared to improve on them, and I have told the President of the United States that in Argentina he will find a firm and determined ally. And we consider the United States a great ally for Argentina.

Within this framework we have discussed subjects that are related to the consolidation of democracy and freedom, not only within this continent, the issues related to Guatemala, Haiti, Cuba and Peru, but we have also discussed the absolute need for democracy, freedom, the respect of human rights, and all issues related to the environment should become reality in all of this world. We would like to see disappear wherever possible that terrible scourge of war, of any kind of discrimination, international terrorism, drug trafficking. We have not restricted our conversations to a preestablished agenda. We have extended our talks even further.

It is always good to come to the United States of America. I believe it is also good to go to Argentina, and that is why I have invited the President to visit us, because valuable experiences are awaiting in Argentina and this will allow us to make our links even stronger, the links that are joining Argentina to the United States.

Mr. President, once again, thank you very much. Thank you for your gift. He gave me as a gift a basketball signed by all the members of the Chicago Bulls. So, thank you.

Iraq

Q. Mr. President, I'd like to ask you about the bombing. Could the assassination plot against former President Bush have moved forward without the approval of Saddam Hussein? And why did the United States not try to hit closer to home for Saddam Hussein, perhaps his headquarters?

President Clinton. We believe the evidence clearly indicates that the bombing operation was authorized by the Iraqi Government. And it is highly unusual, in the experience of our people—let me recast that—our analysts have no experience of such an operation of that magnitude being authorized other than at the high-

est levels. However, it was thought that under international law and based on the facts of this particular case, that the best possible target was the target of the intelligence headquarters where in all probability the operation itself was planned and that to damage that headquarters significantly would send the appropriate message, given the facts of this case.

Q. But in your mind—*[inaudible]*—did you think Saddam Hussein signed off on this?

President Clinton. I have given you the only answer I think it's appropriate for me to give you.

Q. Mr. President, what do you think you accomplished with the bombing of Iraq and the loss of innocent lives, the destruction?

President Clinton. First of all, we damaged their major intelligence facility quite severely. Secondly, we made it absolutely clear that we will not tolerate acts of terrorism or other illegal and dangerous acts. I think it sent a very important message.

Q. We understand there's been an incident over the no-fly zone in southern Iraq today. A U.S. F–4G Wild Weasel launched a HARM missile against an Iraqi radar installation. What can you tell us about that incident, and secondly, what does it suggest to you that it comes at a time when the Iraqis are still threatening retaliation for the weekend bombing?

President Clinton. The standard rules of engagement for flights in that region are that if radar locks onto our airplanes, our airplanes are authorized to take action against those installations. So this has happened a number of times, and based on the facts that I now have, I wouldn't read too much into it. It's part of the standard rules of engagement.

Q. You said during the transition that you could conceive of a situation where we could have normal relations with Iraq with Saddam Hussein still in power. Given what's occurred, how would you now frame your position on this issue?

President Clinton. What I said or at least tried to say in the transition was that I thought we ought to judge every country based on its conduct. And based on its conduct, I think that the possibility of normal relations is very difficult to conceive, not just in this instance but also in the stubborn refusal of Iraq to comply with the United Nations resolutions.

Q. Mr. President, just now you said that the strike had damaged the intelligence facility. Yesterday you said it had crippled the intelligence facility.

President Clinton. I think it did cripple the intelligence facility. At least the reports that I received from the intelligence services was that 15 of the missiles had hit within just a few feet of where they were exactly programmed, and based on what they knew of the potential for destruction of those missiles, that the facility had been crippled. Those were the exact words I got from the people who briefed me about it.

Q. Was it possible that you were not briefed correctly, because Pentagon officials were saying that Saddam has multiple intelligence facilities and that this was one of three or four and that, in fact, he would be operational without this facility, and especially because he relies so heavily on human intelligence and none of the people were involved——

President Clinton. Well, I didn't mean that they wouldn't have any more intelligence. But I do think the building and whatever resources are in that building, which is plainly the main building, was severely damaged, and that's what our intelligence people told me.

Is there anyone here from Argentina? Yes, a little equal opportunity here.

Terrorism

Q. President Clinton, did President Menem offer you a specific help to combat terrorism? And do you think you have to put more guards on President Menem because there was going to be a plot or something like that from the Arabs?

President Clinton. Well, we try to always provide appropriate security to world leaders who come here. President Menem—perhaps I should let him speak to this—but he was very supportive of the action we took in Iraq and very determined that we ought to stand together with other civilized nations against terrorism everywhere.

President Menem. With more security I would have felt uncomfortable in the United States. I have a very special philosophy in life: Nobody will die the day before his preestablished date. And I rely and trust fully in God. He brought us to this world, and He is to decide the day we leave this world. With a great amount of security around a head of state in general, any terrorist activity may be successful. That is why terrorism has to be fought back without any

kind of compassion. They lack absolutely any kind of compassion since, when they place a bomb, they are prepared to destroy the lives of old people and children. Terrorism is now one of the worst scourges of humanity.

Disarmament and Military Action

Q. Mr. President, the United States speaks constantly of disarmament and world peace, especially after the fall of the Berlin Wall. Your Government, through the Embassy in Buenos Aires, has insisted on this policy of peace and disarmament. Don't you believe that the United States has not given an example to follow this course when bombarding Baghdad as a result of this intelligence information?

President Clinton. No, I disagree. As a matter of fact, the United States has been a leader in disarmament. We have signed significant agreements with first the Soviet Union and now with Russia trying to reduce our nuclear arsenals. We are working very hard to reduce the spread of weapons of mass destruction. And I think what we did last weekend with regard to Iraq is a clear signal that people ought not to use weapons in illegal ways. I would remind you that the action I took was in response to an operation that involved a bomb that, had it exploded in downtown Kuwait City, had a 400-yard radius of lethal destruction. So, I think it was the appropriate thing to do.

Latin America-U.S. Trade Agreements

Q. I have a question for you, Mr. Clinton, and another for Mr. Menem.

First, assuming that NAFTA is approved by Congress, when do you foresee Argentina, or Chile, for that matter, negotiating an agreement with the United States? I'm kind of interested in a timetable. And for Mr. Menem, I would like to get more details on that offer you made yesterday to negotiate between the United States and Cuba to improve relations between the two countries.

President Clinton. I would be prepared to discuss immediately with Argentina, with Chile, with other appropriate nations the possibility of expanded trade relations along the NAFTA model. I have long thought that NAFTA should be a model for embracing all of Latin America's democracies and free market economies. I have no timetable. I think perhaps President Menem would have a better view of that, but my attitude is we ought to get on with it. We ought to try to increase the volume and the variety of trade with the appropriate countries just as quickly as possible.

President Menem. On this issue, we had already discussed this with the President, and I have told him that as a priority so as to be able to start formal talks on the access of Argentina or any other country in the region to NAFTA, it would be fundamental to finish the NAFTA agreement, that on the basis of due legislation this process should come to its end. If NAFTA has been passed and enacted during the first months of the next year or the 1st of January, only then can we start discussing the incorporation of Argentina in NAFTA.

And at the same time, we must remember that we are going through another process of integration within MerCoSur, and we have a commitment with the United States in the four-plus-one agreement as to the possibility of having a free trade area between these four countries of MerCoSur and the United States. This, in the case of coming to understanding, will make it possible not only to Argentina joining NAFTA but also MerCoSur. As the result of the NAFTA agreement coming to its enactment, then the MerCoSur countries could perhaps also be joining NAFTA. This is something that should be discussed between the three other countries that are members of NAFTA.

Cuba

Q. Reuters Agency said yesterday that you were proposing to act as a mediator between the United States and Cuba.

President Menem. As a reply to a question by a journalist when he asked if I would be prepared in participating in any kind of negotiations between the United States and Cuba, I answered: President Bush asked me when we met in Costa Rica for the 100th anniversary of democracy, he asked me to stop over in Nicaragua to ask Daniel Ortega to respect the results of the elections that were to be held a short time after in that country, since doubts existed as to the decision that the people of Daniel Ortega's team would take on this issue. I spent more than 2 hours discussing the subject with Commander Ortega, and he was convinced he would be winning the elections. And finally after 2 hours of discussion he said, "If Mrs. Violeta Chamorro wins the elections, I will give her the government." And if the United States requests it, I am prepared to discuss the issue

with Fidel Castro or with whoever it is necessary. I would like to see Cuba living in democracy as soon as possible.

Patent Protection and Farm Subsidies

Q. This is a question for both of you. Have you discussed pharmaceutical patents and subsidies in agriculture? President Menem first and then President Clinton, please.

President Menem. We have discussed this, and I have told President Clinton what I told Mr. Kantor yesterday. This draft law on patents has been introduced through the Senate to the Argentine Parliament, and we are expecting that it will be passed soon. But the executive power of Argentina has sent this draft law to Parliament.

And on subsidies, this is a subject we discuss constantly not only with the President of the United States but also with the Presidents of the European Community countries since they have taken the more difficult stand on this issue when they are subsidizing agriculture, damaging countries such as Argentina. You must not forget that the amount of subsidies is now exceeding $300 billion. It becomes difficult to compete under these circumstances. And I always tell the people in the United States, the U.S. President, and the Europeans they were the masters in free trade and economic freedom. It is not understandable that they should insist on these attitudes that go against the teachings that they sent to the world at large.

President Clinton. The answer to your question is, just as President Menem said, we discussed the patent protection legislation, and I expressed the hope of the United States that it would pass soon by the legislative body in Argentina.

I also, with regard to agricultural subsidies, pointed out that the United States had reduced agricultural subsidies unilaterally in 1990, that our budget reduces them again this year, and that we strongly support the Blair House accords which were reached last year to reduce agricultural subsidies in the Uruguay round of GATT, and that we are with Argentina on that. Also, having grown up in a farming area, I expressed enormous admiration for the fact that Argentina has the deepest topsoil anywhere in the world. So, if I were in his position, I would be taking exactly the same position. With 20 feet of topsoil he can grow anything and do well.

Yes, one last question, and then we've got

to go.

Iraq

Q. Despite what General Powell said, I don't understand why the United States went after the facility at night, rather than going after the intelligence facility during the daytime when the top people were there. And will you take action if the Iraqis go after the Kurds or the Shiites?

President Clinton. I think we've made it clear to them what our position is on the second question you asked. The reason we went at night was quite simply that we wanted to make a strong point. We wanted to do as much damage to the facility as we could. We wanted to mini-mize the loss of human life because of the nature of what actually happened. I think everyone knows what our military is capable of doing. What we needed to show them was that we were fully possessed of the will to do it under these circumstances. And I think we picked the appropriate target, and I think we did it at the appropriate time under these circumstances.

Thank you very much.

NOTE: The President's 18th news conference began at 1:50 p.m. in the East Room at the White House. President Menem spoke in Spanish, and his remarks were translated by an interpreter.

Message to the Senate Transmitting the Convention on the Marking of Plastic Explosives for Detection
June 29, 1993

To the Senate of the United States:

I transmit herewith, for the advice and consent of the Senate to ratification, the Convention on the Marking of Plastic Explosives for the Purpose of Detection with Technical Annex, done at Montreal on March 1, 1991. The report of the Department of State is also enclosed for the information of the Senate.

The terrorist bombing of Pan Am 103 in December 1988 with the resultant deaths of 270 (including 189 Americans), and the terrorist bombing of UTA flight 772 in September 1989 with the resultant deaths of 171 (including 7 Americans), dramatically demonstrate the threat posed by virtually undetectable plastic explosives in the hands of those nations and groups that engage in terrorist savagery.

This Convention is aimed at precluding such incidents from recurring, as well as others where plastic explosives are utilized, by requiring States that produce plastic explosives to mark them at the time of manufacture with a substance to enhance their detectability by commercially available mechanical or canine detectors. States are also required to ensure that controls are implemented over the sale, use, and disposition of marked and unmarked plastic explosives.

Work on the Convention began in January 1990 under the auspices of the International Civil Aviation Organization (ICAO) on the basis of an initial draft prepared by a special subcommittee of the ICAO Legal Committee. That work was completed, and the Convention was adopted by consensus, at an international conference in Montreal in March 1991. The United States and 50 other States signed the Convention. Early ratification by the United States should encourage other nations to become party to the Convention.

I recommend that the Senate give early and favorable consideration to the Convention and give its advice and consent to ratification, subject to the declaration described in the accompanying report of the Secretary of State.

WILLIAM J. CLINTON

The White House,
June 29, 1993.

Message on the Observance of Independence Day, 1993
June 29, 1993

On Independence Day, we celebrate the birth of the first and greatest democracy of the modern era. The ideals embodied by the Declaration of Independence have served as a guide for our nation and as an inspiration for people around the world. This document delineated the very idea of America, that individual rights are derived not from the generosity of the government, but from the hand of the Almighty. The Founders forever abandoned their allegiance to the old European notions of caste and instead dedicated themselves to the belief that all people are created equal.

The brilliant men who gathered in Philadelphia 218 years ago to declare our nation's independence risked their honor, their fortunes, and their very lives to create a better future for their children and grandchildren. As the inheritors of freedom's legacy, we owe our liberties to the fact that our Founders saw the need for dramatic change and acted upon it.

Today, vast changes are sweeping the globe. Nations that have known only tyranny for centuries are suddenly dedicating themselves to the ideals of freedom and democracy. And wherever freedom is proclaimed, echoes of the American Declaration of Independence can be heard. Thomas Jefferson's words are being spoken in dozens of nations in hundreds of languages.

We are justly proud of the influence that our beliefs have had on the world. But the mission of America is far from complete. While the world is filled with opportunity, it is rife with uncertainty. We must dedicate ourselves to carrying on the dreams of the Founders and adding our own chapter to the unfinished American autobiography. By embracing the changes that are altering the landscape of the world today, we help ensure a brighter, more democratic, and more peaceful world. On this Independence Day, I encourage all Americans to rededicate themselves to the conviction that our heroic journey must go forever upward.

Best wishes to everyone for a wonderful day.

BILL CLINTON

Statement on Flooding in the Midwest
June 29, 1993

I am very concerned about the flooding in the heartland of our country, and I've asked Agriculture Secretary Mike Espy to survey the region and see firsthand what the excessive rains have done to agriculture production there. I also have directed the Federal Emergency Management Agency to keep me fully informed of their activities on behalf of the affected States.

The Mississippi River is closed to navigation over a 500-mile stretch from the Twin Cities in Minnesota to St. Louis. Clearly, this is one of the most significant natural disasters midwestern residents, business owners, and agricultural producers have faced in a very long time. This region of the country is dependent upon agricultural production, and when agriculture faces a disaster like this one, everyone is adversely affected.

Tomorrow Secretary Espy will travel to Iowa, Wisconsin (weather permitting), Minnesota, and South Dakota to view the rain-related damage and talk face to face with farmers and area residents about the damage.

FEMA Director James Lee Witt reports that his Agency already has placed survey teams in the field where they are working with the State emergency operating centers. These teams are laying the groundwork necessary for Federal disaster assistance. We intend to speed the recovery of the affected communities and ensure disaster victims receive the help they need as rapidly as possible.

Upon his return, Secretary Espy will brief me on the condition of the area and make recommendations that will help our fellow citizens living in the region.

As you know, nine counties in southwestern Minnesota were declared disaster areas in late

May. Last week, I granted Governor Arne Carlson's request to extend the incident period to allow for coverage for the torrential rains after May 19th through June.

Wisconsin has been hard hit. The break in the dam at Blackriver Falls has destroyed or damaged over 100 homes. Many of the town's residents have no flood insurance. Governor Tommy Thompson has already asked the National Guard to assist the evacuation of flood victims.

Iowa's Governor Branstad also is using the National Guard to assist flood victims in the eastern part of his State. He has told us that many homes and businesses have been flooded out, and thousands more are at risk if the levee breaks.

The Mississippi River continues to rise in Missouri, threatening towns still dealing with the ravages of the May floods. FEMA teams are in eastern Missouri, continuing to monitor the flooding of the Mississippi. Some areas have been evacuated, and preliminary damage assessment teams are in place for a formal assessment request, pending a call from Governor Mel Carnahan.

I commend the bravery and endurance of the many midwesterners facing torrents of rain and rivers that have not yet crested. We will work together to rebuild your communities as we work together to rebuild America.

Nomination for the Federal Communications Commission
June 29, 1993

The President today announced his intention to nominate attorney Reed E. Hundt as a member of the Federal Communications Commission. Once Mr. Hundt is confirmed as a member, the President intends to designate him Chairman of the FCC.

"Telecommunications innovations are constantly changing the way we as Americans communicate with each other and with the world. With his years of experience, I am confident Reed Hundt will do an excellent job steering the FCC through the challenges it will face over the next 5 years," the President said.

NOTE: A biography of the nominee was made available by the Office of the Press Secretary.

Exchange With Reporters Prior to a Meeting With Congressional Leaders
June 30, 1993

Nuclear Testing

Q. Mr. President, why not resume nuclear testing? There are a lot of people who argue that it's necessary to ensure the safety of the stockpile.

The President. I'll have a statement on that in the next few days. I've been working very hard on it. I will say this then, the story I read about it today is not quite accurate. But I have made a decision, and the administration will have a policy, and we'll announce it sometime in the next few days. We're working out some of the details, and we haven't finished our congressional consultations yet.

Q. You mean if somebody else tests first, you won't then test?

The President. I have nothing else to say about it. I just—I'll talk about it when——

National and International Economy

Q. Mr. President, what do you think of the new economic figures that have come out over the last couple of days?

The President. Well, most of them are pretty discouraging, and some are encouraging. But the most important thing is to look at this thing over the long run. We've had 3 or 4 very tough years. And there's a global recession. Two-thirds of our jobs in the late eighties came from exports, and it's hard to generate jobs from exports when many European countries have actually negative growth and Japan has no growth. And one of the reasons that we're having this meeting today is to talk about what the United States can do at the meeting of the G–7 to try to get growth going in the global economy.

We have low interest rates now; people can invest; a lot of people are refinancing their business and home loans, so there's money out there to invest. But they've got to be able to know that if we create jobs, that people will be able to sell their products and services. And that's why this G–7 meeting is so important, trying to get some growth back into the global economy that will get the export portion of our job growth going again.

Q. And what would you like the other G–7 nations to do, sir?

The President. What would I like them——

Q. Yes, sir.

The President. I think Japan ought to stimulate their economy and open their markets. And the Europeans should resolve their own dif-

ferences about agriculture and other things and help us to sign the GATT agreement before the end of the year. And the Germans have worked very hard, the German Government has, but I think the German central bank should continue to lower interest rates there so that all of us together can expand the economy.

It's very hard for the United States alone to grow jobs without help from other nations. So those are the things that I hope we can keep working on. And if we get a good trade agreement, if we could open the markets of other countries, then I think you'll see some real growth coming into the economy.

Q. Is that possible given the political situation of the leaders?

The President. It's harder, but it's possible.

NOTE: The exchange began at 10:21 a.m. in the Cabinet Room at the White House. A tape was not available for verification of the content of this exchange.

Message to the Congress on Further Sanctions Against Haiti
June 30, 1993

To the Congress of the United States:

Pursuant to section 204(b) of the International Emergency Economic Powers Act (50 U.S.C. 1701 *et seq.*), the National Emergencies Act (50 U.S.C. 1601 *et seq.*), section 5 of the United Nations Participation Act of 1945 (22 U.S.C. 287c), and section 301 of title 3 of the United States Code, in view of United Nations Security Council Resolution No. 841 of June 16, 1993, and in order to take additional steps with respect to the actions and policies of the *de facto* regime in Haiti and the national emergency described and declared in Executive Order No. 12775, I hereby report that I have exercised my statutory authority with respect to Haiti and issued an Executive order that:

—Blocks all property of any Haitian national providing substantial financial or material contributions to the *de facto* regime in Haiti, or doing substantial business with the *de facto* regime in Haiti, as identified by the Secretary of the Treasury, that is or comes within the United States or the possession or control of United States persons. The proposed order de-

fines the term "Haitian national" to mean a citizen of Haiti, wherever located; an entity or body organized under the laws of Haiti; and any other person, entity, or body located in Haiti and engaging in the importation, storage, or distribution of products or commodities controlled by sanctions imposed on Haiti pursuant to resolutions adopted either by the United Nations Security Council or the Organization of American States, or otherwise facilitating transactions inconsistent with those sanctions;

—Prohibits the sale or supply, by United States persons, or from the United States, or using U.S.-registered vessels or aircraft, of petroleum or petroleum products or arms and related materiel of all types, including weapons and ammunition, military vehicles and equipment, police equipment and spare parts for the aforementioned, regardless of origin, to any person or entity in Haiti or to any person or entity for the purpose of any business carried on in or operated from Haiti, and any activities by United States persons or in the United States which promote or are calculated to promote such sale or supply; and

—Prohibits the carriage on U.S.-registered vessels of petroleum or petroleum products, or arms and related materiel of all types, including weapons and ammunition, military vehicles and equipment, police equipment and spare parts for the aforementioned, regardless of origin, with entry into, or with the intent to enter, the territory or territorial sea of Haiti.

I am enclosing a copy of the Executive order that I have issued. The order was effective immediately.

The Secretary of the Treasury, in consultation with the Secretary of State, is authorized to issue regulations implementing these prohibitions.

United Nations Security Council Resolution 841, unanimously adopted on June 16, 1993, calls on all States to adopt certain measures which are included within those outlined above. These measures are called for in recognition of the urgent need for an early, comprehensive,

and peaceful settlement of the crisis in Haiti and in light of the failure of parties in Haiti to act constructively to take steps necessary to begin the restoration of democracy.

The measures we are taking respond to the Security Council's call. They demonstrate our commitment to remain at the forefront of the international community's efforts to back up with sanctions the negotiations process being sponsored by the United Nations and the Organization of American States. These steps also demonstrate unflinching support through our foreign policy of the return of democracy to Haiti.

WILLIAM J. CLINTON

The White House,
June 30, 1993.

NOTE: The Executive order is listed in Appendix D at the end of this volume.

Message to the Congress Transmitting a Report on Aeronautics and Space Activities
June 30, 1993

To the Congress of the United States:

I am pleased to transmit this report on the Nation's achievements in aeronautics and space during fiscal year 1992, as required under section 206 of the National Aeronautics and Space Act of 1958, as amended (42 U.S.C. 2476). Not only do aeronautics and space activities involve 14 contributing departments and agencies of the Federal Government as reflected in this report, but the results of their ongoing research and development affect the Nation as a whole.

Fiscal year 1992 was a significant one for U.S. aeronautics and space efforts. It included 7 Space Shuttle missions and 14 Government launches of expendable launch vehicles (ELVs) carrying a variety of payloads ranging from NASA missions to classified payloads. In addition, there were eight launches of ELVs by commercial launch service providers operating under licenses issued by the Department of Transportation's Office of Commercial Space Transportation. On December 7, 1991, the Air Force achieved initial launch capability for the new Atlas II launch vehicle in a commercial launch

by General Dynamics with support from the Air Force. The Shuttle missions included one using the Atmospheric Laboratory for Applications and Science (ATLAS–1) to study the Sun and our atmosphere, as well as the first flight of the newest orbiter, *Endeavour*, which rendezvoused with, retrieved, and replaced the perigee kick motor of the INTELSAT VI (F–3) satellite that INTELSAT controllers then deployed into its intended orbit.

In aeronautics, efforts have ranged from development of new civil and military aircraft and technologies to research and development of ways to reduce aircraft noise and improve flight safety and security.

One of the major Earth science highlights of the year was the discovery that, like the ozone layer over the Antarctic with its well-documented annual depletion, the ozone layer in the Northern Hemisphere is increasingly vulnerable to depletion by synthetic chemicals. Several Federal agencies have cooperated to study this and other environmental challenges.

Thus, fiscal year 1992 was a successful year

for the U.S. aeronautics and space programs. Efforts in both areas have promoted significant advances in the Nation's scientific and technical knowledge that promise to improve the quality of life on Earth by increasing scientific under- standing, expanding the economy, and improving the environment.

WILLIAM J. CLINTON

The White House,
June 30, 1993.

Letter to Television Networks on Use of Program Violence Warnings
June 30, 1993

Dear Howard:

I applaud the action taken today by CBS and by the other major broadcast networks to begin addressing the problem of violence on television. Millions of parents are rightly concerned that their children are exposed to far too many graphic pictures of murder and mayhem. The announcement of voluntary violence warnings is an important, commendable first step in dealing with this crucial issue.

For the health of our society and the American family, we must continue to find ways to limit the excessive portrayal of violence in our television programming. In the past, the television industry has responded to public concerns and has dealt in a responsible manner with issues such as drug use, alcohol, and smoking. I encourage the broadcast industry, the creators and producers, as well as the advertisers who support network programming, to take full responsibility in limiting the amount of televised violence.

Again, I commend the networks for this initial effort and encourage you to continue to find ways to make your programming suitable for the children and youth of this nation.

Sincerely,

BILL CLINTON

NOTE: This letter was sent to Howard Stringer, president, CBS Broadcast Group. Similar letters were sent to Warren Littlefield, president, NBC Entertainment; George Vradenburg, executive vice president, Fox Television; Thomas S. Murphy, chairman of the board, Capital Cities–ABC; and Ted Turner, chairman of the board and president, Turner Broadcasting System.

Nomination for Posts at the Department of Defense
June 30, 1993

The President today announced his intention to nominate John Hamre to be Comptroller of the Department of Defense. He also announced that he is appointing Mitch Wallerstein to serve at the Pentagon as Deputy Assistant Secretary for Counterproliferation Policy.

"We are continuing the process of putting together a strong and effective staff at the Department of Defense," said the President. "John Hamre and Mitch Wallerstein both bring outstanding academic credentials along with years of hands-on experience to their new positions."

NOTE: Biographies of the nominees were made available by the Office of the Press Secretary.

Nomination for Agency for International Development and Ambassadorial Posts
June 30, 1993

The President announced today that he intends to nominate Richard Holbrooke to be his Ambassador to Germany and Tom Niles as his Ambassador to Greece. In addition, the President announced that he has nominated Robert Houdek to be Ambassador to Eritrea and that he intends to nominate Larry Byrne to be the Associate Administrator for Finance and Administration at the Agency for International Development, U.S. International Development Cooperation Agency.

"The people we are adding to our foreign policy team today are men of tremendous achievement and character," said the President. "I am particularly glad that Richard Holbrooke will be serving our country as Ambassador to Germany. Throughout his years in Government and more recently as a leader in the private sector, he has demonstrated the talents that are needed for an important position such as this one."

NOTE: Biographies of the nominees were made available by the Office of the Press Secretary.

Nomination for Posts at the Housing and Urban Development, Veterans Affairs, and Commerce Departments
June 30, 1993

The President announced his intention today to nominate the following officials:

William Gilmartin, Assistant Secretary of Housing and Urban Development for Congressional and Intergovernmental Relations

Eugene Brickhouse, Assistant Secretary of Veterans Affairs for Human Resources and Administration

Ginger Lew, General Counsel, Department of Commerce

"These three outstanding individuals will make excellent additions to our administration," said the President. "William Gilmartin, Eugene Brickhouse, and Ginger Lew have all proven themselves in their previous Government service. I am grateful that they have agreed to be part of our efforts now."

NOTE: Biographies of the nominees were made available by the Office of the Press Secretary.

Remarks Announcing the Forest Conservation Plan
July 1, 1993

Ladies and gentlemen, this issue has been one which has bedeviled the people of the Pacific Northwest for some years now. It has been one that has particularly moved me for two reasons: first of all, because so many people in that part of the country brought their concerns to me in the campaign on all sides of this issue, the timber workers and companies, the environmentalists, the Native Americans, the people who live in those areas who just wanted to see the controversy resolved, so they could get on with their lives; and secondly, because I grew up in a place with a large timber industry and a vast amount of natural wilderness, including a large number of national forests. So I have a very close identity with all the forces at play in this great drama that has paralyzed the Pacific Northwest for too long.

We're announcing a plan today which we believe will strengthen the long-term economic and environmental health of the Pacific North- west and northern California. The plan provides an innovative approach to forest management to protect the environment and to produce a predictable and sustainable level of timber sales. It offers a comprehensive, long-term plan for economic development. And it makes sure that Federal Agencies, for a change, will be working together for the good of all the people of the region.

The plan is a departure from the failed poli- cies of the past, when as many as six different Federal Agencies took different positions on var- ious interpretations of Federal law and helped to create a situation in which, at length, no timber cutting at all could occur because of litigation, and still environmentalists believed that the long-term concerns of the environment were not being addressed.

The plan is more difficult than I had thought it would be in terms of the size of the timber cuts, in part because during this process the amount of timber actually in the forests and available for cutting was revised downward sharply, in no small measure because of years of overcutting, and in a way that provides an annual yield smaller than timber interests had wanted, and a plan without some of the protec- tions that environmentalists had sought. I can only say that as with every other situation in life, we have to play the hand we were dealt. Had this crisis been dealt with years ago, we might have a plan with a higher yield and with more environmentally protected areas. We are doing the best we can with the facts as they now exist in the Pacific Northwest.

I believe the plan is fair and balanced. I be- lieve it will protect jobs and offer new job op- portunities where they must be found. It will preserve the woodlands, the rivers, the streams that make the Northwest an attractive place to live and to visit. We believe in this case it is clear that the Pacific Northwest requires both a healthy economy and a healthy environment and that one cannot exist without the other.

I want to say a special word of thanks to the Vice President, to the Interior Secretary, Bruce Babbitt, to Agriculture Secretary Mike Espy, to Labor Secretary Reich, Commerce Sec- retary Brown, Environmental Protection Admin- istrator Browner, Environmental Policy Director Katie McGinty, and many others in our adminis- tration who worked together to bring all the forces of the Federal Government into agree-

ment, not because they all agreed on every issue at every moment but because they knew that we owed the people of the Pacific Northwest at least a unified Federal position that would break the logjam of the past several years.

This shows that people can work together and make tough choices if they have the will and courage to do so. Too often in the past the issues which this plan addressed have simply wound up in court while the economy, the envi- ronment, and the people suffered. These issues are clearly difficult and divisive; you will see that in the response to the position that our administration has taken. If they were easy they would have been answered long ago. The main virtue of our plan, besides being fair and bal- anced, is that we attempt to answer the ques- tions and let people get on with their lives. We could not, we could not permit more years of the status quo to continue, where everything was paralyzed in the courts.

We reached out to hundreds of people, from lumber workers and fishermen to environ- mentalists, scientists, business people, commu- nity leaders, and Native American tribes. We've worked hard to balance all their interests and to understand their concerns. We know that our solutions will not make everybody happy. In- deed, they may not make anybody happy. But we do understand that we're all going to be better off if we act on the plan and end the deadlock and divisiveness.

We started bringing people together at the Forest Conference in April. In the words of Archbishop Thomas Murphy then, we began to find common ground for the common good. As people reasoned together in a conference room instead of confronting each other in a court- room, they found at least that they shared com- mon values: work and family, faith and a rev- erence for the majestic beauty of the natural environment God has bequeathed to that gifted part of our Nation.

This plan meets the standards that I set as the conference concluded. It meets the need for year-round, high-wage, high-skilled jobs and a sustained, predictable level of economic activ- ity in the forests. It protects the long-term health of the forests, our wildlife, and our water- ways. It is clearly scientifically sound, eco- logically credible, and legally defensible.

By preserving the forests and setting predict- able and sustainable levels of timber sales, it protects jobs not just in the short term but for years to come. We offer new assistance to workers and to families for job training and retraining where that will inevitably be needed as a result of the sustainable yield level set in the plan, new assistance to businesses and industries to expand and create new family-wage jobs for local workers, new assistance to communities to build the infrastructure to support new and diverse sources of economic growth, and new initiatives to create jobs by investing in research and restoration in the forests themselves. And we end the subsidies for log exports that end up exporting American jobs.

This plan offers an innovative approach to conservation, protecting key watersheds and the most valuable of our old-growth forests. It protects key rivers and streams while saving the most important groves of ancient trees and providing habitat for salmon and other endangered species. And it establishes new adapted management areas to develop new ways to achieve economic and ecological goals and to help communities to shape their own future.

Today I am signing a bill sponsored by Senator Patty Murray and Congresswoman Jolene Unsoeld of Washington and supported by the entire Northwest congressional delegation to restore the ban of export of raw logs from State-owned lands and other publicly owned lands. This act alone will save thousands of jobs in the Northwest, including over 6,000 in Washing-ton State alone.

Today Secretary Babbitt and Secretary Espy are going to the Northwest to talk to State and local officials about how to implement the plan and give to workers, companies, and communities the help they need and deserve. And soon we will deliver an environmental impact statement based on the plan to the Federal District Court in Washington State. We will do all we can to resolve the legal actions that have halted timber sales, and we will continue to work with all those who share our commitment to achieve these goals and move the sales forward.

Together we can build a better future for the families of the Northwest, for their children, and for their children's children. We can preserve the jobs in the forest, and we can preserve the forest. The time has come to act to end the logjam, to end the endless delay and bickering, and to restore some genuine security and rootedness to the lives of the people who have for too long been torn from pillar to post in this important area of the United States. I believe this plan will do that, and this administration is committed to implementing it.

Thank you very much.

NOTE: The President spoke at 10:34 a.m. in Room 450 of the Old Executive Office Building. H.R. 2343, approved July 1, was assigned Public Law No. 103–45.

Exchange With Reporters on Flooding in the Midwest
July 1, 1993

Q. What are you going to do to help the people on the river, sir?

The President. That's what Secretary Espy and I were just talking about. We don't have enough money in the discretionary emergency fund to meet the rather massive losses that a lot of these farmers are facing. And so I expect he will come to me with some legislation in the fairly near future when we have a sense of what the total dimension of the loss was in the corn crop, the soybean crop, and what the other problems are. And he is just briefing me now on what he's seen and where we are. It's a very, very serious thing for the farmers, though. It's the most rain they've had in over 100 years. Right?

Q. Have any idea what the loss would be, I mean, in money?

The President. Well, he's going to brief me as soon as he knows. I think we'll have to watch it. The corn crop is very stunted because of the rain, and this is soybean planting time and coming to the end of it. So there's not a dramatic turnaround in conditions. You saw them drain off the water during—[*inaudible*]—the soybean crop on a lot of that land.

Q. So would there be a disaster declaration, sir, at some point?

The President. We're going to work out exactly what we have to do. It appears that in order to deal with the losses, we'll have to go back to the Congress. I do not believe there are sufficient funds in the discretionary emergency accounts that I have to deal with it. So I think that we'll be going back. And as the Secretary puts together the package, then obvi-

ously he'll share it with you as soon as we know.

NOTE: The exchange began at approximately 11 a.m. in the Oval Office at the White House, during a meeting with Secretary of Agriculture Mike Espy. A tape was not available for verification of the content of this exchange.

Remarks on the Swearing-In of National Drug Control Policy Director Lee Brown
July 1, 1993

The President. Thank you very much. Thank you. Please be seated, and welcome to the Rose Garden. I want to acknowledge the presence in our audience of Lee Brown's children; the Attorney General; the Secretary of Transportation; the Secretary of Agriculture; General Powell, the Chairman of the Joint Chiefs of Staff; numerous other distinguished Americans; and Members of Congress, including Senator Hatch, Senator Dodd, Senator Cohen, Senator Pressler, and Congressmen Rangel, Conyers, Gilman, and Congresswoman Waters. I may have left someone out, and Senator Kennedy just called to say he was on the way. I think that's all a great tribute to Lee Brown.

We are here today to install a uniquely qualified person to lead our Nation's effort in the fight against illegal drugs and what they do to our children, to our streets, and to our communities, and to do it for the first time from a position sitting in the President's Cabinet. When I named Lee Brown to head the Office of National Drug Control Policy, many called that an inspired choice. I would say that is an accurate characterization because Lee Brown brings three decades of experience in highest law enforcement offices in some of the toughest cities in our country, New York and Houston and Atlanta. I know if Mayor Dinkins were here today he would want me to say a special word of thanks for the unique partnership they enjoyed in a safe streets program, which clearly lowered the crime rate in many neighborhoods and many categories of crime in New York City.

Lee Brown's leadership in the cause of keeping our communities and citizens safe is unsurpassed, and now he must bring those skills and all that experience to deal with the destructive

lure of illegal drugs. We know that successful drug control does not take place in a vacuum. This is a many-headed monster. Drugs violate our borders when smugglers bring them in as illegal cargo. Our jails are crowded, and our court system is overloaded with users and dealers. Crime and violence are brought to communities large and small, and random drive-by shootings and deliberate killings as well. Too many young Americans are robbed of their future and many, many of their very lives.

For all those reasons, fighting drugs requires a multifaceted offensive and the maximum use of the resources we have as a people. That's what we've been trying to do in this administration. With all the budget cuts and with a 5-year hard freeze on overall domestic spending, there's a 10 percent increase in the funds in our budget for demand reduction and a dramatic increase in the funds available for community policing, as well as a clear commitment to include drug treatment in the national health care program that our administration will be advancing in the near future.

But most important, we now will have an effort that is coordinated as one, pulled together and anchored by Lee Brown. No longer will the Office of the Director of Drug Policy operate separately from the rest of the Government, consigned just to being a bully pulpit. Now it will work hand-in-hand with the other Cabinet Agencies, and in doing so, our effectiveness will be increased.

Our aim is to cut off the demand for drugs at the knees through prevention. That means more and better education, more treatment, more rehabilitation. At the same time, we want to strangle supplies by putting more officers on the streets, by enforcing the law in our communities, at our Nation's borders, and by helping our friends and allies to do the same thing beyond our borders. We pledge to work with other nations who have shown the courage and the political will to take on their own drug traffickers who destabilize their own societies and their economies.

Our commitment to all these things is personified in Lee Brown. A tough guy might say he's a drug trafficker's nightmare, a cop with a doctorate or a doctor of criminology with a badge. But the most important thing to me is he's got a track record of results. How many law enforcement officers in this country would be proud to look on the record he has amassed of actually reducing the rate of crime in the streets where he has worked.

You know, the insecurity most Americans feel, without regard to income or race, is a truly appalling thing. And anything we can do not only to give lives back to children who might otherwise become involved in drugs but to give the streets and the safety of the streets back to ordinary American families of all kinds is a service well done, and it might mean more to them than anything else this Government could produce during my tenure in office and for the foreseeable future. The work that Lee Brown did in pioneering community policing in Houston and New York is now legendary, with officers on foot patrol knowing their neighbors, working to prevent crime as well as to catch criminals.

This is a fight that surely can unite us all, across the boundaries of party and race and region and income. We are fighting for our families, our children, our communities, and our future. Each and every American, make no mistake about it, also bears a personal responsibility to play a role in this battle. Anyone who thinks that Lee Brown or anyone else can solve this problem for the American people, instead of with the American people, has another think coming. There are people in this audience today whom I know have worked for decades to try to help come to grips with this issue: parents educating their children; teachers working hard to prevent crime; law enforcement officers going into the schools, working in programs like the D.A.R.E. program; people who have worked in drug treatment and know as I do, from our

own family's experience, that it works. All these things are an important part of what we have to do. Make no mistake about it: We've got to try to get the streets back for our kids, too. We ought to have a time in this country when children don't have to be afraid to go down to the neighborhood swimming pool in the summertime.

I am thankful that Lee Brown has taken on this challenge. He'd made the decision to do so at a time in his life when he might have reasonably been expected, for personal and professional reasons, to take a different course. He could clearly be making more money doing something else; he could have far fewer headaches doing something else. He would not have all of us investing so much of our hopes in him if he were doing something else. The simple fact that at this point in his life he resolved to do this says a great deal about him and his character.

I would like now to ask Judge Richard Watson of the U.S. Court of International Trade to join his friend Dr. Brown up here to administer the oath of office, and I would like to invite—James Watson, I'm sorry—and I'd like to invite Dr. Brown's eldest daughter, Torri Clark, up here to hold the Bible for her father.

[*At this point, Judge Watson administered the oath of office. Director Brown then thanked the President and discussed his strategy to solve America's drug problem.*]

The President. Do you have any questions for Dr. Brown?

Q. Mr. President——

The President. We'll take one or two. I just had another press conference.

Q. Do you think an energy tax and small business incentives——

Q. Boo-o-o!

Q. ——should be non-negotiable items of a budget package, which is equally important to the economy as drug control?

The President. Well, we're going to pass a good economic package. I feel confident about that. And we're now trying to work out the differences in the House and the Senate, and I'll have more to say about that in a few days.

NOTE: The President spoke at 11:20 a.m. in the Rose Garden at the White House.

Remarks at a Meeting With Doug Luffborough and an Exchange With Reporters
July 1, 1993

The President. Hello, everybody. Those of you who travel with me regularly will, I think, recognize the young man on my right, Mr. Doug Luffborough. He was the student speaker at Northeastern University in Boston the other day. This is his mother, whom I introduced from the audience; got a big hand. He's here with President John Curry of Northeastern and Senator John Kerry, his Senator. I invited him and his mother to come visit me in the Oval Office, so they didn't wait long to take me up on the invitation. [*Laughter*] I'm glad to see them here today.

You may remember also that he brought the house down. He not only gave a great speech, but he sang at the beginning of his speech. I thought to myself, if I could sing like that I wouldn't be giving speeches today. [*Laughter*]

Mr. Luffborough. Well, it was a wonderful opportunity for me and a wonderful opportunity for my family and especially for my mother. I've been waiting for an opportunity like this, and I'm just really thrilled. And I'm really glad that Northeastern was the place you decided to come. It's been a pleasure and an honor to be here today. Thank you.

Q. Mr. President, what was it about Doug that impressed you so much?

The President. First of all, that he had come from such humble circumstances to go to college and to stay in college and that he had made the most of it. He obviously never felt sorry for himself. He obviously had a mother who helped him to believe in himself, as many others do. And the fact that his fellow students picked him to be the spokesperson for their class showed that they identified with the values and the inner strength and drive that took him to the success that he enjoys. I was very impressed. And I just thought it would be neat if they could come down here and see me.

Vietnam

Q. Sir, what signal do you hope to send by lifting U.S. opposition to international loans to Vietnam?

The President. I haven't made an announcement on that. When I do, I'll be glad to discuss it.

Iraq

Q. Mr. President, Tariq Aziz seems this afternoon to be holding out some type of an olive branch, saying that Iraq will not avenge the attack the other day and also that he hopes for better relations with your administration. What response do you have, if any?

The President. I don't know. I need to be briefed on what he said. But of course, they shouldn't act in revenge. We have evidence that what was done was wrong, and the United States had to respond.

NOTE: The President spoke at 5:03 p.m. in the Oval Office at the White House. A tape was not available for verification of the content of these remarks.

Letter to Congressional Leaders on Somalia
July 1, 1993

Dear Mr. Speaker: (*Dear Mr. President:*)

In my letter to you of June 10, 1993, regarding the deployment of U.S. Armed Forces to Somalia, I reported on the deplorable June 5 attacks on United Nations Operation in Somalia forces (UNOSOM II) instigated by one of Somalia's factional leaders. I also reported to you that on June 6, 1993, the U.N. Security Council adopted Resolution 837, which strongly condemned the unprovoked June 5 attacks that left 23 Pakistani peacekeepers dead. In addition, the Security Council reemphasized the crucial importance of the disarmament of all Somali parties, and reaffirmed the Secretary General's authority under Chapter VII of the U.N. Charter "to take all necessary measures against those responsible for the armed attacks [of June 5], including against those responsible for publicly inciting such attacks, to establish the effective authority of UNOSOM II throughout Somalia, including to secure the investigation of their actions and their arrest and detention for prosecution, trial and punishment."

Since that time, the United Nations has acted resolutely to restore order in Mogadishu and to protect U.N. forces. These actions have ensured that the world community's crucial humanitarian efforts in Somalia and the national reconciliation process in that country will continue to move forward. In view of these developments (in particular the role of U.S. Armed Forces in the recent U.N.-led activities in Somalia), and because of my desire that the Congress be kept fully informed regarding significant deployments of U.S. Armed Forces, I am providing this supplement to my earlier report.

In planning appropriate measures to respond to the violence and to implement the Security Council's mandate, the United Nations was able to draw upon the superb capabilities of the U.S. Armed Forces that remained in Somalia following the transition to UNOSOM II. In addition to the logistics and other support personnel assigned to UNOSOM II, the Quick Reaction Forces (QRF)—under U.S. operational control—was available to assist UNOSOM II during emergencies. At the height of the U.S.-led Unified Task Force (UNITAF) operations, just over 25,000 U.S. Armed Forces personnel were deployed to Somalia. Consistent with U.S. policy objectives, the current smaller U.S. contribution of approximately 4,400 personnel reflects the increased participation by other U.N. Member States.

United States Armed Forces played an extremely important role in the successful efforts of UNOSOM II to restore stability to the area and to enable U.N. humanitarian operations in Somalia to proceed. First, after determining that the leadership of one of Somalia's factions had planned and incited the June 5 attacks on U.N. peacekeepers, UNOSOM II initiated air and ground military operations in the early morning hours of June 12. Primary targets included weapons and ordnance caches and a radio facility that had been used to foment violence towards U.N. forces and opposition to implementation of the Security Council's humanitarian

mandate in Somalia. United States fixed-wing and helicopter aircraft operating as part of the QRF, in support of UNOSOM II, destroyed or disabled those targets in a well-planned effort consistent with the Security Council's disarmament objectives and the mandate to restore security. United States forces sustained no casualties.

On June 17, the Special Representative of the Secretary General, acting pursuant to Security Council Resolution 837, ordered the arrest of General Mohammed Farah Aideed for alleged criminal acts against UNOSOM II peacekeeping forces on June 5. In addition, UNOSOM II forces conducted further coordinated ground and air operations designed to search, clear, and disarm the factional stronghold of General Aideed in south Mogadishu that posed a continuing threat to U.N. operations. Ground and aerial broadcasts warned civilians to leave the area. Targets included weapons and ammunition caches, command and control facilities, and defensive positions. Once again, the U.S. QRF, in support of UNOSOM II, conducted air attacks, followed by search and clearing operations on the ground by non-U.S. UNOSOM II military personnel. Only one U.S. military member sustained minor injury, although there were several deaths and a number of injuries among UNOSOM II forces from other nations due to resistance by militia units and sniper fire. Although Aideed has not yet been arrested, the June 17 operation accomplished the objective of securing Aideed's compound and neutralizing military capabilities that had posed a major obstacle to U.N. efforts to deliver humanitarian relief, facilitate political reconciliation, and promote national reconstruction.

We now see renewed opportunity for UNOSOM II to move forward steadily towards fulfillment of the humanitarian mandate of the Security Council that is shared by the world community. By countering the lawless, unprovoked violence against U.N. peacekeepers, the United Nations has gone far towards preserving the credibility and security of peacekeeping forces in Somalia and throughout the world. United States forces remain on guard along with those of our U.N. partners to counter any threats to the important U.N. mission in Somalia, should they arise.

As before, I remain committed to ensuring that the Congress is kept fully informed on U.S.

peacekeeping contributions and the use of U.S. Armed Forces for these vital purposes. I look forward to continuing discussions and close cooperation with you on these and related issues.
  Sincerely,

WILLIAM J. CLINTON

NOTE: Identical letters were sent to Thomas S. Foley, Speaker of the House of Representatives, and Robert C. Byrd, President pro tempore of the Senate.

Statement on Germany's Reduction of Interest Rates
July 1, 1993

Today's news that Germany has cut interest rates again is welcome news. With over 22 million people out of work in Europe, and our economy at last beginning to create jobs again, Germany's responsible fiscal and monetary actions could not have come at a more critical time for both Europe and the United States. It is also another sign that when America takes the lead in cutting its deficit and getting interest rates down we encourage other major nations to follow our lead in spurring global growth.

By getting our house in order, we have facilitated pro-growth policies in Europe that mean more demand for American products overseas and more jobs and higher incomes for the Americans who make those products here at home.
  Germany has taken an important step toward improved growth, and I look forward to further progress at the G–7 summit in Tokyo.

NOTE: Background information on European interest rates was attached to the statement.

Nomination for the Agency for International Development
July 1, 1993

The President announced today that he intends to nominate Carol Lancaster to be the Deputy Administrator of the Agency for International Development, U.S. International Development Cooperation Agency.
  "An expert in U.S. foreign aid policies, par-

ticularly with respect to Africa, Carol Lancaster will bring a great deal to the management of AID," said the President. "I am grateful for her service."

NOTE: A biography of the nominee was made available by the Office of the Press Secretary.

Nomination for Assistant Secretaries of the Navy
July 1, 1993

The President announced his choices for two top Navy posts today. He intends to nominate Frederick F.Y. Pang to be Assistant Secretary for Manpower and Reserve Affairs and Nora Slatkin to be Assistant Secretary for Acquisition.
  "I am very glad to be adding these two people to my Navy team today," said the President.

"They bring with them lifetimes of dedicated service to their country and years of experience in shaping policies to keep our military the best in the world."

NOTE: Biographies of the nominees were made available by the Office of the Press Secretary.

971

Nomination for an Assistant Secretary of Labor
July 1, 1993

The President announced his intention today to nominate Joseph Dear, formerly director of the State of Washington's Department of Labor and Industries, to be the Assistant Secretary of Labor for Occupational Safety and Health. In that role, he will serve as the Administrator of the Occupational Safety and Health Administration.

"With his experience running a major State agency regulating workplace safety and related matters, Joseph Dear is an outstanding choice for this important position," said the President. "During his tenure in Washington, he turned a deficit into a $350 million surplus in the workers' compensation budget. He established a health care cost containment and quality assurance program and overhauled the workers' compensation system to save the taxpayers money while increasing benefits to workers. That is the kind of leadership I want to have at OSHA."

NOTE: A biography of the nominee was made available by the Office of the Press Secretary.

Nomination for Posts at the Peace Corps
July 1, 1993

The President today announced his intention to nominate former Peace Corps volunteer Carol Bellamy, an attorney and former New York State Senator and president of the New York City Council, as Director of the Peace Corps. The President also approved attorney Brian Sexton as Peace Corps General Counsel.

"Throughout her career, Carol Bellamy has achieved success in both the corporate world and in her own initiatives to improve the lives of those less fortunate," the President said. "I am confident she will use her experience in both of those areas to fulfill the important mission of the Peace Corps."

NOTE: Biographies of the nominees were made available by the Office of the Press Secretary.

Statement by the Press Secretary on Assistance to Haiti
July 1, 1993

On June 25, 1993, the President signed Presidential Determination No. 93–28 on the Haiti Reconstruction and Reconciliation Fund. The determination, signed after careful consultation with the relevant committees of the Congress, waives legal restrictions on providing assistance to Haiti in order to provide up to about $37.5 million from prior year Haiti foreign military financing and development assistance funds and from prior year Bolivia and Peru economic support and foreign military funds.

President Jean-Bertrand Aristide, who requested outside assistance, including for military professionalization, in a letter to the U.N. and OAS Secretaries-General, has indicated his agreement with these broad objectives.

This assistance package is designed to support negotiations to restore democracy to Haiti and the implementation of a phased political solution. Disbursement will be carefully timed to support the negotiations and respond to concrete progress toward restoring democracy. The Department of State is notifying the relevant committees of its intention to carry out the reprogrammings this Presidential determination authorizes and will consult further with the Congress on the military assistance component of this assistance package.

Our current aid program in Haiti of $52 million consists solely of humanitarian assistance, feeding and health activities, funneled through nongovernmental organizations. The new assistance package would provide continued support for the U.N./OAS International Civilian Mission ($10 million), which monitors human rights in Haiti; economic support and stabilization once the democratic government of President Aristide is restored (up to about $12.7 million); the beginning of an administration of justice program to strengthen democratic institutions such as the Justice Ministry ($3 million), and including the creation and training of a new civilian police force ($4 million) as well as a modest, nonlethal military professionalization program to reduce its size and train it to address the needs of Haiti's society and missions set forth in Haiti's Constitution, particularly civic action, engineering, disaster relief, and coastal patrol (about $2.1 million).

NOTE: The Presidential determination is listed in Appendix D at the end of this volume.

Remarks Announcing the Defense Conversion Plan and an Exchange With Reporters
July 2, 1993

The President. Good morning. On Monday, I leave for Tokyo for the G–7 summit, where the world's leading economic powers will seek to build a new era of global growth.

While international summits were once dominated by the drama of the cold war confrontation, today we compete in a quieter field, the world of global economic competition. Now that the cold war is over, we see the opportunity around the world and in this country to reduce defense spending rather dramatically and to devote our attention to rebuilding our country here at home. But we know now clearly, since defense has been coming down since 1987, that this is not an unmixed blessing in the short run for Americans here at home.

Among other things, reduced defense spending means reduced spending on defense contracts. And people, therefore, who work in defense plants are affected by it. And it is impossible to reduce the number of men and women in the armed services without an appropriate reduction in the base structure of the United States at home and abroad.

That is the difficult and painful, but important work the base closing commission has had to do. I have received their latest report, and I have decided to forward that report on to Congress. As I transmit that report to Congress, I am ordering an unprecedented Federal effort in the form of a new five-point program to ensure that when we close these bases we also open a new and brighter economic future for the affected workers and their communities. And this week my administration announced that we were going to shut down not only the bases implied in the base closing commission, but also some 90 bases overseas, to be fair and also because our interests are served by that.

These five points are as follows: First, we will provide an average grant of a million dollars to each community affected by a major base closing. Second, we will establish for the first time a single Federal coordinator for each community so that all the resources and opportunities that attend this reconstruction effort can be made available as quickly as possible. Third, we will establish a fast-track cleanup program for environmental problems. This has been an enormous problem in the past in trying to move bases to commercial uses. Fourth, we will establish a fast-tract disposal of Federal property emphasizing those uses most likely to create new jobs for the communities affected by base closings. And finally, we will have a coordinated effort to pool all Federal resources giving all the affected communities easier access to Federal assistance. Compared to the past, we will respond more quickly, cut redtape more aggressively, and mobilize resources more assertively to help these communities so that when they lose their bases they do not lose their future.

In the past, base closings forced communities to cope with a jarring economic upheaval without tools or resources. Many bases were heavily polluted, the cleanup seemed to take forever.

Redtape and bureaucracy frustrated local officials when they sought help. And people in the community saw an employer of thousands turn into a destroyer of economic security. For communities from coast to coast affected by base closings, the Federal Government will now work aggressively to help these patriotic citizens, cities, and towns prosper. We will help them to use their valuable assets as engines of economic growth.

This Governmentwide effort will cost over $5 billion in the next 5 years. We will respond rapidly and spend money more wisely. Let me give you one vivid example of this new approach. Current law actually requires the Federal Government to charge communities full price for these closed bases if they are used for job creation and economic development. But the Government could give away a base for free for recreational uses. That gets it backwards. I believe if a community has pulled together and produced a real plan for job creation and economic growth, the Federal Government must pitch in by giving that base to the community at a discount or, in some cases, even for free.

Today I am directing the Department of Defense and the National Economic Council to write a legislative proposal within 90 days allowing us to give job creation and economic development the highest priority in the disposition of these assets. This law will be a sizable commitment by the Federal Government. These bases are worth, in some instances, hundreds of millions of dollars. But it's the least we can do for the communities and the people who supported our troops.

To avoid bureaucratic confusion, one week from now we will appoint a team of transition coordinators, senior military personnel who will slash redtape and untangle bureaucracy to help these communities. Cleanup will proceed faster than before. We've increased the size of planning grants to help communities map out their future. And a creative worker training program will visit the bases within the next 2 weeks to let workers know of their opportunities.

Even with all these aggressive efforts the closing of a military base, as with any large employer, will inevitably be traumatic for the host community. And I cannot promise that every job will be saved. But this will be a great test for our Nation. Over the past 50 years these communities have literally hosted millions of American men and women in uniform who were defending our freedom. When we needed them, these cities and towns did their duty. When they need us today, we can do no less. And I am confident that we will be able to make dramatic progress.

I'd like now to introduce the Defense Secretary to make a couple of remarks. I see you raising your hands. We have four other Secretaries who have briefings to give, but after Secretary Aspin speaks, I will take a couple of questions on this subject. You'll have access to me I think later on other matters, but on this subject I will take a couple of questions. But I would like the Secretary of Defense to speak first.

[*At this point, Secretary Les Aspin outlined the defense conversion program.*]

The President. Let me make two other quick comments, and then I'll take a couple questions.

This is one program that I think will benefit from the fact that I was a Governor who managed a base closing from the other end before we went through this. I have had experience with every single problem that this five-point program seeks to address, working with a major base closing that occurred along the Mississippi River in a county that had double-digit employment at the time the base closing was announced. And I believe this is a very practical program that will have a huge practical difference in the lives of these communities, based on my personal experience on the receiving end of the base closing.

The second thing I want to say is, because I won't be here when they speak, is this group of Cabinet officers was here—we had a different group yesterday when we announced our program for the Pacific Northwest. It will make a big difference for people in these communities. Keep in mind a lot of these people have only dealt—the only thing they know about the Federal Government is the Defense Department and the bases. They have never dealt with the Labor Department, the EPA, HUD, Transportation, and Commerce. They don't understand how to deal with all these folks at once. And the fact that we're going to make it possible for them to access the resources of all these Departments at one time and through one person will be a huge boon. It's difficult enough for all of you to figure out your way through the maze of the Federal Government. For a lot of these folks it is an unending nightmare and a practical impossibility. So I did want to make those two points.

Yes, in the back. You had your hand up first. Go ahead.

Defense Conversion Plan

Q. Mr. President, when you go to Asia, how do you plan to alleviate concerns that these closings might restrict the forward basing of air and sea forces?

The President. Well, I plan to make clear statements about our commitment to Asia and our involvement in Asia, in both Japan and Korea. And I think that we will clearly be able to do that, and it will be more explicit when the Secretary of Defense finishes his review.

Q. Will you address the forward basing question, sir?

The President. Yes. Go ahead.

Q. Mr. President, if this is all new money, this $5 billion, and not reprogrammed money, how do you expect to get it from Congress in this budget climate? Your stimulus package got killed. Everything else has been watered down. There isn't money available.

The President. First of all, I think events will prove that I was right to ask for the jobs package.

Q. Such as today's unemployment numbers?

The President. We can't discuss that yet. It's not 9:30 a.m. [*Laughter*] But that's not the point. You can't tell anything from the month's figures anyway. This thing is moving forward in fits and starts, and we're doing a pretty good job of creating jobs, the American economy is now. But the global economy dictates a more aggressive response at this moment from America.

But the reason I think that this will work is I think, first of all, it's a 5-year program. Secondly, keep in mind, we had allocated in the budget, as you remember when we went to the Westinghouse plant, some $20 billion over 5 years that could be used for the total aggregate amount of defense conversion. And some of that money was counted in this. But we allocated another $2 billion to environmental cleanup because that's a huge deal. We can move these bases in a hurry if we can figure out who's responsible for the environmental cleanup and then get about doing it. So, the details can be answered.

I believe the Congress will support this, because I think there's enormous bipartisan under-

standing that you simply cannot take this away from communities without reinvesting something in them. And if it is a net savings to the Government over the long run, we have to invest something back to justify the cut.

Q. How much will you take?

The President. Secretary Aspin knows the number.

Job Creation

Q. Military downsizing in general is getting the blame for the higher unemployment figures which were released an hour ago. Do you worry that you're losing the battle on a broader scale on trying to create jobs?

The President. Well, I think that—let me repeat, there are two things at work here. In any given month, military downsizing—and keep in mind, these decisions we're announcing today will have an impact on the economy a year and a half, 2 years from now, some of them even longer than that, some of them 3 years from now, the base closing commission's recommendations today. So we're giving some advance planning time on that. The military cutbacks that are manifesting themselves in this unemployment rate were based on decisions made a couple of years ago.

Again, I will say you've got two things at work there. Because of the size of the deficit, we are not reinvesting as much as I think we should be reinvesting to generate jobs here at home. But the larger problem is that two-thirds of our jobs in the last 5 years have been generated, or new jobs, have been generated through exports. And with Europe down and Japan down—we've got Europe with the lowest economic growth in 20 years and Japan with the lowest economic growth in longer than that, more than three decades. That's why I'm going to the G–7. Because if we don't find a way for all of us to do things together, it's going to be difficult to sustain jobs.

Now, notwithstanding, the country has produced a substantial number of new jobs in the first 5 months of this year. We're so far behind in coming out of the recession that it's going to be difficult to do unless we can have a global strategy of growth so we can start getting some jobs out of exports again.

Q. What is the economic impact of this overall base closing? You said that you can't guarantee that everybody will get a job. How may people do you—I mean, do you have any estimate of how many people are thrown out of work?

The President. Well, let me say this. What I can tell you based on my personal experience with this is that you've got a lot of very creative, innovative people out there in these communities. And some of these bases have been rumored about now for a couple of years. So in a lot of these communities, as a practical matter, you've had the community leaders out there imagining the worst for a long time, thinking about what they might do, wondering about what they will have to do if something like this happens. I am confident, again based on my personal experience, if we correct the problems and create the opportunities that are embodied in this five-point program, you're going to see a lot of economic growth.

And let me say, the traditional economic analysis is that you can create the same number of jobs in the commercial domestic sector that we create in defense for roughly half the investment. So that if we can get a combination of public effort now and private investment later, we might wind up creating more jobs in some of these communities. Some of these communities, I think, you've got enormous resources out there in these bases, and they'll create more jobs. The only thing I want to say is I don't want to over-promise because I can't foresee the next 5 years with any kind of precision. I just know that this program is going to help these people a lot more than anything that's been done since we started defense downsizing.

President's Tie

Q. On the G–7, as you're about to head off—

by the way, that's a very nice tie. [*Laughter*] I wish the American public could see that tie. [*Laughter*]

The President. This was designed by a 12-year-old. It's a Save the Children tie.

Q. I remember when you spoke about Gene's ties.

Q. Do you want this one?

Q. No, I don't want it.

The President. If it weren't a gift, I would give it to you.

Trade With Japan

Q. Is there any prospect of an agreement with Japan on trade during this G–7 summit?

The President. I don't think I should raise any expectations of that just because it's difficult for us to predict now what will happen. I can tell you this: We're going to keep talking to them, and in the end we're going to get this worked out. I think that the changes now going on in Japan over the long run are going to be good for the Japanese people and good for the American people. It may be painful for them now, but a democracy is an uneven and inexact process. I think that we are moving toward a greater integration of the global economy in ways that will be good for them and good for us. That's what I believe. But this is a transition period for them, and agreements are always more difficult in transition periods.

I'm sorry, I have to go. We have to finish this.

NOTE: The President spoke at 9:15 a.m. in the Briefing Room at the White House.

Interview With Foreign Journalists
July 2, 1993

Economic Summit

Q. What do you expect to be accomplished out of Tokyo summit? And what special roles do you see Japan can play in areas beyond economic constitution in—[*inaudible*]—of global partners with the United States?

The President. First, let me say I think the G–7 meeting will be a very important opportunity for the leaders of the major industrialized

countries of the world to reaffirm their commitment to global growth, to democracy, and to security concerns. I believe there will be serious discussions about three issues on the economic front, one really perhaps for the first time.

The first is that I think there will be a real discussion about how we can coordinate our economic policies in ways that will produce growth. From the first week I was in office, we have spent a lot of time working through the finance ministers, the foreign ministers, and others to talk about how we can coordinate our strategies. For many years, other nations have asked the United States, for example, to lower the budget deficit. And we're working very hard on that, first through this $500 billion deficit reduction program that has now been passed by both Houses of our Congress, then through taking on a health care problem which is the biggest source of our growing deficit. And we need to make sure we are coordinating those policies with things which will produce an overall higher level of growth than we now have. It's a big problem for the United States, because two-thirds of the new jobs we've created here in the last 5 years have come from increased trade with other nations. So if Europe is down economically, if Japan is down economically, it's hard for us to do well here. So I think there will be that.

The second issue I think that we will discuss and, I hope, make some genuine progress on, creating a more open trading system and increasing the chances that we can successfully conclude GATT by the end of the year.

The third thing that I hope to see a very serious discussion on is the microeconomic policies of each of our nations and how we can all do a better job of creating jobs within our economy. Even Japan, with its very low unemployment rate by western standards, is having some trouble now creating new jobs. But it's a very big problem for the United States and for every other country represented around this room today.

And I think that increasingly in a global economy, national policy will have to focus on what the economists call microeconomic policies: What kind of labor support systems do you have; what kind of education and training systems do you have; how do you target investment to create jobs? The west, and increasingly Japan, are having difficulty creating new jobs, even in times of economic growth.

It's quite interesting. If you trace the last 6 or 7 years you can see that in all the western nations, even when there is growth, there is some trouble creating new jobs. So I think that this will all be—we'll deal with this, and I hope in a very informal and forthright atmosphere.

It will be an interesting summit, because there will be several of the people there attending their very first one, first G–7, all at the same time.

The second point you made about Japan's role in the world, I'm going to do what I can while in Japan to strengthen the bilateral relationship between the United States and Japan. In many, many ways it is our most significant bilateral relationship and the key to what happens between the United States and Asia. It's interesting, even though we have incredibly important ties to Europe, economic ties, we have a huge—40 percent of our trade is now with the Pacific. It accounts for almost 2½ million jobs in America, trade with the Pacific. So it's a big issue. And we have major security concerns, as you know, with regard to Japan and with Korea.

So I'm very hopeful that even though Japan is going through a period of political transition, which I hope the Japanese people will view with excitement and interest, not with too much concern, this is a normal thing for a democracy. And periodically you go through these periods of significant change, and I view it as a positive thing for a great country. I think it will leave you stronger and in a better position in the world. So I hope we will discuss a lot of our bilateral economic as well as strategic concerns there. And I hope that when I leave Japan, our relationship will be even stronger than it is when I enter.

NAFTA

Q. Mr. President, there was a court decision this week that's a roadblock to ratification of the NAFTA agreement. Your administration has said that you will go ahead, but you don't appear to have a lot of wiggle room in Congress on some of your other economic initiatives. And I'm wondering, first of all, how you're going to ensure the passage of NAFTA. And secondly, on the eve of the summit, this raises the whole issue of the conflict between environmental concerns and economic growth, and whether it's drift nets in the Pacific or toxic waste in Mexico or the whole problem of aid to the former Soviet Union, that conflict between the environment and economic growth underlies a lot of these issues. And I'm wondering how you see reconciling those issues at the G–7.

The President. Let me mention the NAFTA first and then I'll answer the larger question.

First, on the narrow issue of the lawsuit, we announced within an hour after the court's decision that we would appeal. And we believe we can win an appeal, and we can win it within the appropriate time. There may also be some other avenues which will permit us to do some kind of environmental impact statement and still meet the time limit.

There is a strong opposition to the agreement in some quarters in the United States, and the relative economic problems that we all face now make that more difficult. That is, when unemployment is up and growth is down, people are more insecure. It makes some in Europe less enthusiastic about the GATT now. It's the same reason—it's just—a part of it is almost endemic to the human condition.

I do think we have the votes to pass NAFTA in the United States Senate. And I think that—and we do not have today the votes to pass it in the United States House. But I think we can get the votes to pass it essentially by doing three things:

First of all, by successfully concluding the agreements now subject to negotiation between Canada and Mexico and the United States to strengthen our common efforts at lifting labor standards and environmental quality, particularly along the Rio Grande River, which has been a huge problem.

And I should say by way of background for the rest of you, the reason the labor standards issue is so big is that there was a report issued in this country last year that indicated that the Caribbean Basin Initiative of the United States, where we tried to get investment in Caribbean countries and put plants down there, had not led to increasing the per capita incomes of the people working in those businesses; that because the people were so poor, that a lot of the people who had taken the money that the United States Government had put out had still depressed their wages and increased their profits. So we've given some thought to this labor standards issue here and the environmental issue. So I think if we get those agreements that will help.

The second thing that will help is if—we have to just make the case, you know. Now when we have an agreement, it's a lot easier to defend the jobs argument. Right now there's a simple argument against NAFTA being waged by, articulated by Mr. Perot in this country and others, that you can't make a trade agreement that takes down all the barriers with a country on your border with a per capita income that's only one-eighth as much as yours is. Everybody will take their money and invest in the other country. Well, it has great superficial appeal, but the truth is that anybody who wants to go to

Mexico and invest their money for low wages can do so today. But the market opening measures that have been taken by President Salinas in the last few years have led the United States from a $5 billion trade deficit to a $6 billion trade surplus with Mexico. Mexico is now our second biggest purchaser—manufacturer. And we are in effect—because Canada, as you know, is our biggest trade partner—we are now building this hemispheric economic bloc that we want. And so I think we can refute it on the merits.

The third thing we have to do is ask the economists to consider what will happen if we do not pass the trade agreement. Our relationships with Canada are secure, and we have a bilateral agreement, and that's fine. But we could go back in our relationships with Mexico, which would mean economic problems for Mexico, more trade barriers, fewer jobs in America, more illegal immigration. A lot of problems could develop for the United States if we do not do the NAFTA.

I think when those three things become crystal clear, we will prevail there.

Now on the larger issue, there is no easy or simple answer to the conflict between the environment and the economy in any of our countries individually or in the globe as a whole. However, I believe that our goal ought to be to find ways to make preserving the environment good economics.

At the Rio conference last year, Japan, Germany, and many other European countries were proving that you could do that because they were down there promoting environmental technology while the United States was trying to stop the environmental agreements. I think that our country was not as wise as many of the nations here represented in the way they approached the Rio conference. We have now signed on, the United States has, to the Biodiversity Treaty. And we have basically adopted a policy of long-term environmental preservation with an aggressive effort to figure out how to make jobs and incomes and prosperity flow out of that. And I believe that there are lots of opportunities to do that.

If I might just mention one, our bilateral aid package to Russia that is now making its way to the Congress focuses heavily on what we can do with our technology to help them to reduce the problems that their nuclear industry—and not simply their bombs but their nuclear power plants, for example—present to them, and what else we can do in the area of energy and the environment to help to clean up their environment in ways that are good for their economy and good for ours. So I think there's a lot of opportunity there.

GATT and the G–7

Q. You just said in the beginning, Mr. President, that you hoped that Tokyo would, and I quote you, increase the chances of successfully concluding a Uruguay round by the end of the year. Can I turn that around and say do you think that a failure to do that would seriously jeopardize the whole G–7 process as it currently exists?

The President. Well, there are lots of other nations involved in the Uruguay round apart from the G–7. That was one point that Prime Minister Balladur made to me in our meeting here.

But I think that our job is to lead. And I know it is difficult to lead when you have troubles yourself. All of us have economic troubles. All of us, to a greater or lesser extent, have some political conflict within our countries. But I think that it is very important—and almost to change the atmosphere and the attitudes of the peoples of the G–7. Yes, we're having economic trouble. And the fact that we're all having it should be some indication that there is some sort of historic change going on here and not that there's some character flaw in our people or some great mental breakdown in our countries or something else. This is a tidal wave of global change going on here. But look at the resources we have: We have innovative work forces; we have great bases of technology; we have an understanding of how the world works economically. And I think we have within our power the means to move forward and break out of this problem we're in but only if we have the courage to keep changing.

And so I would say, to try to answer your question directly, there have been debates for years about whether the G–7 process accomplishes anything. But if nothing else, if we can agree among ourselves to take an expansive view of the future and to talk about the strengths of our nations and to recognize that there are only three ways to grow our economies. One is through the changes we make internally, the microeconomic changes; the other is through coordinating our larger macroeconomic policies;

and the last is through creating a more open system of trade so that there is global growth. It's hard for the wealthy countries to grow wealthier unless the people below us are getting wealthier and can buy more of our products. It's not a zero-sum game. And so I feel very strongly that we ought to come out of the G–7 with a more vigorous commitment to get the Uruguay round done.

Now let me just say what I have done in that regard. I have repeatedly said that the United States would bend over backwards to get that done this year, that there are changes that we would like to make. When the G–7 finance ministers and central bank heads were here not very long ago at Blair House across the street, I went over and personally met with all of them and reaffirmed my commitment to this. So I don't know what else I can do, except that I think a lot of this is a matter of attitude. We have to try to lift our own visions and lift the spirits of our people and realize that when you're in difficulty, the worst thing you can do is to hunker down, to withdraw.

When you have difficulties like this with a fundamentally sound system, the time is to change, to be innovative, to be creative, and to reach out. And I think that's what we've got to begin to do at the G–7. The tone, the atmosphere, the ideas that are discussed in that sense may be far more important than anything specific that comes out of the communique. What direction are we going to take the world in?

Global Economy

Q. Mr. President, nobody seems to be happy with the G–7 process, not to mention the results. I wonder if you could define for us—elaborate on what you just said—that the purpose of the G–7 in today's world and tell us what you would like to change.

The President. Well, I don't want to be too presumptuous, since I've never attended one before. I've only read about them before. You know, I always followed them very closely. But what we are striving for—I think the other leaders agree with me, including those like Chancellor Kohl, who's been to many of these. My own view is there ought to be enough time at these G–7 meetings for a serious discussion among the leaders without a lot of bureaucratic procedures and rules and regulations about these big issues. What about the crisis in the wealthy countries creating jobs? What can we do to create more jobs? How do you explain the fact that France, for example—let's take France. France had a productivity growth rate that was the highest in Europe in some of the years of the late eighties and still had relatively high unemployment. The United States, which has far fewer labor supports than most of the European countries do, still has difficulty getting its unemployment rate below 7 percent. We're well into 2 years after the worst of our recession, and yet we are 3 million jobs behind where we would ordinarily be at this point after a recession.

We should discuss these things, and we should think about whether we can learn things from one another about how to create jobs in the west. We should be able to really talk through very frankly what the political and other economic barriers are to getting the GATT done and really think about it and talk about it. It's far more important than what's in the specific words of the communique, whether we come out of there with some sort of commitment to do something, to take action, and to move.

And finally, I think we ought to really focus on how our individual economic strategies may not work as well unless we are coordinated. Let me just give you one example. I'm trying to do something that our country has not done before. We are trying to dramatically cut our Government deficit at a time when our economic growth is slow. Traditional economic theory would say if you have a sluggish economy, you don't cut spending and raise taxes; you might do the reverse, right? Why am I trying to do that? Because we're in a global economy, and the United States deficit caused an imbalance in the global economy, okay? But now, this can work for us for a while just on our own, because we had so much debt in the 1980's accumulated at high interest rates, by bringing down the deficit, interest rates in America have dropped very low. So businesses and homeowners are going out now and refinancing their debt, and that puts a lot of new money into our economy. So I can get a little bit of growth just on what we do here. But in the end, this will only work if there is an expansionary policy in Japan, if Europe is able to resume a higher level of growth so that the system is brought into balance, because what we do has a complementary action in the rest of the G–7.

So these are the things, it seems to me, that really matter. And that's why I think these G–7 meetings can really make a difference. But I think that if we get all hung up on—you know, we all have to have these prepared statements, and we're afraid we're going to say one word out of the way or make one little mistake which makes a huge headline in some country. And then we've got to have every little word right in these communiques. I think that's just— that takes a lot of time and energy away from what we should be doing, which is focusing on how we can make the lives of our people better and fulfill our responsibilities as leaders of the world.

U.S. Leadership

Q. Mr. President, you said earlier, speaking of G–7 leaders, that their job is to lead. Yet there's a broad perception that there is real friction and misunderstanding and doubts about U.S. willingness to lead, not only in the Japan-U.S. relationship, but in the U.S.-European relationship. Why has this happened and what can you do at the summit to clarify U.S. goals and reassure U.S. allies?

The President. Well, let me first of all take issue with you—I mean, not the perception.

The other nations of the world have asked the United States for years and years and years internally to do one thing. The only thing they ever asked of us internally was to do something about our budget deficit, which caused a significant imbalance in the global economic relations. I read about it for years before I became President. And we're doing that, and it is very tough to do in tough economic times. And we're going to wind up with a very tough deficit reduction plan that we believe is good for our economy over the long run. And it's not been easy to do, but we are doing that.

Secondly, the major crisis this world has faced since I've been President, I think, was what would happen to democracy in Russia. And when it became apparent that democracy was in trouble in Russia because of what was happening with President Yeltsin, I immediately publicly supported him. I called every other leader in the G–7 and many others around the world and asked for people to support him. We all did. And I think that we had something to do with the outcome of events there.

I announced a $1.6 billion aid package to Russia, and we have now, by the way, obligated

well over half of that money. And then I announced another $1.8 billion bilateral aid pack-
age to Russia which passed the House of Representatives with 75 percent of the vote almost
last week, bipartisan support. It's going to fly
through the Senate. The IMF gave their first
installment, $1.5 billion, to Russia the day before
yesterday, and we're going to discuss that at
the G–7 summit. I think—and that's a huge
potential market for all of us and a major political issue. And I think that is the big issue we
have faced, and I think we've done it very, very
well.

Now, the only point of contention between
us that I can see—we'll come back to the Japanese issue; you asked that and I haven't forgotten—but the only—in Europe is that we have
not agreed entirely on how to handle Bosnia,
although we've done a lot of work together.
The United States has spent almost $300 million
in humanitarian assistance. We have strongly enforced and pushed for tougher sanctions and
embargoes on Serbia. We believe and the Germans believe the arms embargo ought to be
lifted on Bosnia. France and Britain and Russia
disagree. I understand that. But that doesn't
mean we can't do anything together. We are
trying to work together. And this, I think everyone would admit, is the most difficult international problem that we face. I'm still hopeful
that something humane, decent, and politically
reasonable will emerge from this process before
it's too late. But we all have a disagreement
on that, and I'm sorry we do. But we can't
agree on everything. And this is a very difficult
problem. I still think I was right about what
was the best course. I think events subsequent
to the Athens meeting prove that beyond question. But nonetheless, I don't think that's a reason for us to give up on the European alliance,
give up on NATO, give up on the G–7. This
is a tough problem.

With regard to Japan, I think everyone who
has looked at the problem seriously thought
there would have to be some realignment in
our trade relations. And I think we're going
to work that out. But there are lots of other
things we have in common. Japan has supported
the United States, and the United States has
supported Japan in the things we've done to
support democracy all over the world. Our security relationship is very strong. I intend to reaffirm my commitment to that when I'm in Japan,
and my commitment to Korea and to Asia generally when I'm in Korea.

So I think a lot of this—let me—if I might,
a lot of this uncertainty in Europe, particularly,
is a function of two things. One is the economic
problems that we all have which make people
always just more insecure. And two is, I've only
been President 5 months. And we have a new
Government in France. We have a new Government in Italy. We have a new Government in
Canada. And so a lot of these folks, we don't
all know each other. And I think when people
don't know each other, there is always a—but
you're trying to get to know one another—there
is the temptation to take whatever incident is
in the moment and reach some huge encyclo-
pedia of meaning in it, which may or may not
be accurate.

So I think a lot of these things that you're
talking about will be taken care of by meetings
like this, by trips like this, and by constant working together. I will say—but every opportunity
I've had to work with the other European leaders has been satisfactory. I had good cooperation
between the United States and Italy, for example, when we were trying to reinforce the security of the U.N. forces within Bosnia, because
the U.S. is committed to defend them if they're
attacked, and everybody knows that. So I'm just
a lot more hopeful about this than I think some
are. I think a lot of this is just a function of
economic difficulties and new players who don't
really know each other thoroughly yet.

GATT and Resolution of Trade Issues

Q. Mr. President, if I may go back to trade,
I would like to know what do you say to the
French, who have decided that they won't sign
anything regarding GATT at the Tokyo summit
up until the United States lifted or the Department of Commerce lifted the sanctions of steel,
and we insisted that the United States accept
the principle of multilateral mechanism to solve
commercial conflicts.

The President. Well, those are two different
issues. First of all, the action that was taken
on steel was taken after a lot of deliberation,
most of which was done before I became President, subsequent to United States law, which
is clearly GATT-consistent. So, I think, you
know, if the belief is that the United States
has been wrong on the facts, then we can discuss the facts. But there is nothing wrong with
our law, and it's not that different from the
laws of a lot of other countries that are part

of the world trading system.

Secondly, with regard to the trading mechanism, I have no problem with a multilateral mechanism to enforce trading agreements. But the GATT clearly contemplates that every country in the world, including France, should have the right to act in its own interest if the international system breaks down, which is not to say that you lose some rulings. But if there is no resolution of a crisis, the international system breaks down. All our Section 301 trade law does is to provide for some ultimate reservoir of authority for the United States to act unilaterally if the system itself breaks down. If France, for example, would like to propose a stronger multilateral decisionmaking process as a part of GATT before any country could act on its own, I would be more than happy to discuss that.

I do not see this Section 301 as giving the United States the authority, for example, to decide on its own about all these trade agreements and how they affect us without regard to what other countries want to do. That is not at all the way it is supposed to operate. It's supposed to operate only against countries that are not part of trading agreements at all, so we don't have a trade—countries with whom we have no multilateral agreements, or when there is a total breakdown of the GATT system in this case.

Germany's Interest Rate Reduction

Q. Mr. President, you raised today for the first time, I think, the question and the very important question of the structural impediments to growth. And so far you have and your Government has somehow created the impression that Europe and the difficulties in creating jobs should be loaded at the doorsteps of the Bundesbank. And yesterday you even said, "Well, this is a contribution to global growth." And you raised the expectation and the—that it was just a cyclical problem. Now, why didn't you come out before with this very strong statement that you are looking for structural impediments, that the G–7 should concentrate on doing away with structural barriers instead of pushing all the time the micro question—the macro question, excuse me?

The President. Well, first let me say that I have not criticized Germany in the past, but I have complimented them when the Bundesbank has lowered interest rates. [*Laughter*]

Q. But maybe for different reasons.

The President. And I know that because I realize that, first of all, all nations with independent central banks—and the United States has one, too; that is, the Federal Reserve—independent of the—all nations that have independent central banks are very sensitive about political leaders from within the nation telling them what to do and even more sensitive to suggestions from political leaders outside the nation's borders. And so what I have attempted to do is to say repeatedly, ever since I became President, that I thought that the extent to which we could coordinate the economic policies with Germany and the rest of Europe, and Japan, that that was a good thing. Coordinated economic policies for growth, and expanded trade, and smarter internal, microeconomic policies were all necessary to create jobs and growth in the world.

And when Germany—when the interest rates were lower a couple of days ago, I did applaud that because I think it makes a contribution to growth. But I think—and the only reason that I—and I have done it not to be presumptuous but only to say that the United States was asked for years by its allies to deal with our budget deficit. We are now doing that, and we are getting the results that we hoped we would. We have a 20 year low in long-term interest rates, in home mortgage rates. We've had a 6 year high in housing sales. It's tailing off a little now but good housing sales. We've created more construction jobs in the first 4 months of this year than in any similar period for 9 years.

And the point I'm trying to make here is that there is a limit to what we can do for ourselves, and therefore what we can do for Europe and Japan in terms of buying more of your exports, unless all of us work together to promote growth. And obviously, because of the sheer size of the German economy and the power of Germany as an exporter, the condition of the German economy is critical to what happens to Americans. And you've had a very open trading philosophy. So I thought it was a positive thing, and I thought I should compliment it. But I think it's a delicate thing to talk about, because all of us who have ever suffered from runaway inflation have appreciated some measure of independence in our central banks. And yet all of us know that if the central banks are entirely insensitive to the economic growth needs of the country, we can't coordinate the strategy. So it's a delicate matter. And I don't wish to be seen as interfering, but I think when a bank does something that's clearly a plus for the German people and for all the rest of the world, it's not wrong for an American President to compliment it.

NOTE: The interview began at 10:45 a.m. in the Oval Office at the White House. Journalists par-

ticipating in the interview were Graham Fraser, Toronto Globe and Mail, Canada; Alain Frachon, Le Monde, France; Carola Kaps, Frankfurter Allgemeine Zeitung, Germany; Rodolfo Brancoli, Corriere Della Sera, Italy; Osamu Shima, Yomiuri Shimbun, Japan; Jurek Martin, Financial Times, United Kingdom; and Paul Horvitz, International Herald Tribune. A tape was not available for verification of the content of this interview.

Interview With Foreign Journalists
July 2, 1993

Economic Summit and GATT

Q. Mr. President, I want, first of all, to thank you very much for this opportunity that, let me tell you, we have not had for several years. So, I thank you.

And first of all I want to ask you, this Tokyo trip, it's for you the first appearance on the international scene. But at the same time, the expectations have never been so low for a G–7 summit. You know the difficulties of the different countries and no trade agreement; Soviet aid, we don't know how much, how it will go. So, sir, what do you really think to accomplish?

The President. Well, let me say, first of all, I think the direction of the G–7 meeting is more important than the declaration. I think you put too much, sometimes, stock in the statement. I think it's very important that as world leaders we recommit ourselves to a strategy of global growth, to a strategy of open trade, to seriously examining the problems we are all having with creating jobs, and to dealing with the common security issues that we face. I predict that we will have a very successful meeting as regards Russia. And I still believe that we can make a lot of headway on the issues of trade and global growth.

You know, what we really need to do with all the economic problems our nations have and the political problems is to remind ourselves that these are still very great countries with enormous possibilities and a great future. And we need to sort of lift the spirits of the people and focus on what we can do instead of what we cannot do.

Security Issues

Q. With regard to the political issues, we still, as you said so many times, Mr. President, we live in still a very dangerous world with so many challenges and crises. For example, you probably knew that today three Italian peacekeepers have been killed in Somalia, a dozen injured. Sir, you go to Tokyo; have you some new ideas on how to confront this dangerous world, the challenges?

The President. Well, first of all, let me say that my trip to Tokyo is a trip to the G–7 but also to Japan and to Asia. So one of the things that I intend to do is to make absolutely clear the United States' continuing commitment to engagement in Asia. I hope that we will have some time to talk at the G–7 about some of our other problems. But I would point out that the greatest security challenge we have faced in my judgment in the last 5 months was the threat to democracy in Russia. And the G–7 met the test. We rallied behind Yeltsin. We rallied behind democracy. We supported a free market economic reform in Russia. And I hope we will do so again at the G–7.

We have not solved the problem in Bosnia, and our nations are somewhat divided about it. It is a very difficult problem. But I do have some ideas about those things that I will be discussing with the other leaders.

Japan

Q. Mr. President, let me start my question with your view on Japan. Since you took office you've mentioned Japan several times. At times you were somewhat stern, expressing its remoteness from an open market. At times you were generous for expressing the relationship of the most important bilateral one for the United States. Which of your assessments is true to your feeling?

The President. Both. And let me explain why. First of all, I probably have more admiration for your country in more ways than any President who has ever served. I've had the privilege of traveling to Japan many times. I actively sought Japanese companies to come to my State when I was a Governor. I believe you have a very great country with an even brighter future than your past.

I think that our relationship is based on our ability to stand up for our common security interests, to promote the values of democracy and free markets, and to have a reasonable trade relationship. I think that there are things that we need to do in our trade relationship that will benefit both of us.

I do not want to create American jobs at the expense of Japanese jobs. I think that changing the nature of the trading relationship is in the interest of both countries, and I don't think it's fair for an American President to ask another country to do something that's good for America but bad for the other country. If I didn't think it was good for both of us, I wouldn't push that. But I think we'll work that out.

And the main thing I want to say to the people of Japan is that this period of political turmoil is not a bad thing for Japan. I know it's different from what you've experienced in the last few decades, but Japan has had an astonishing amount of success with the certain political arrangement. But as the global economy changes, as the people of Japan themselves change in their aspirations, the political system will have to alter to reflect that. It is not a bad thing. It is a good thing. And the people of Japan should be, I think, very hopeful about their future.

Q. If I may follow-up, Mr. President, how and how soon this economic present strain be solved do you think?

The President. Well, I think it depends in part on the development of ideas in Japan, both within the government, both elected and civil servant personnel, and among the people themselves. But I think you will see a resolution of this. I'm not pessimistic at all about it, I'm very hopeful that we will work these things out in ways that are good for both countries. I want

to emphasize that.

I've seen some of the press reports in Japan of some of my statements as if I want to protect American jobs and take Japanese jobs away. It's far more complex than that. I think that both of us have to undergo changes. Every nation represented in this circle, with the possible exception of Russia, has hounded the United States, has asked the United States for years to do something about our big Government deficit, saying that that caused a big imbalance in global trade. We are doing that. So we are trying to change. And change is not easy, and I think all of us will have to make some changes.

Q. How soon?

The President. I think it won't be long. I think we'll see—my hunch is that the capacity for adjustment in both countries is greater than we sometimes think, and I think we'll resolve this pretty quickly.

Bosnia

Q. Mr. President, may I begin by asking you about Bosnia? There's an impression that the indecisive way in which you have handled this issue is an illustration of the widening gap of trust between America and Europe. You advocated lifting the arms embargo on the Muslims and striking at some Serbian positions. And then you appeared to back away from that. Then you moved to a compromise plan for setting up safe havens. Now, that's a concept which you, yourself, described as a shooting gallery. My question is this: Are you preparing now to wash your hands of this whole affair and possibly to blame the Europeans for the failure?

The President. No. Neither one. Let me, first of all, point out what the United States has done just since I've been President. We spent a great deal of money on humanitarian aid; we have pushed hard for strengthening the embargo against Serbia; we have pushed for a number of other things to try to help resolve the situation that we have all agreed on.

I did not back away from my position, sir. Britain and France and Russia said they would not support that position within the United Nations. The United States cannot act alone under international law in this instance.

Q. It is their fault?

The President. No, they disagreed with me. It's not their fault. They disagreed. We had an honest disagreement about what the right policy to follow was. I expect as we go through time we'll disagree about other things. I thought I could persuade them that we ought to try this because I was convinced that the reason Milosevic, Karadzic and others were making concessions to try to bring this conflict to an end is because the West was turning the pressure up.

There was an honest disagreement. The leaders of Britain and France and Russia honestly did not believe that lifting the embargo would make things better, would hasten the day of peace. We had an honest disagreement. The German Government agreed with the position I took. But it was an honest disagreement within the most complicated foreign policy problem that any of us have faced in years. I don't seek to place blame anywhere. I don't think that is productive.

When my position did not prevail and when I did not have the power to implement it unilaterally because of the U.N. embargo on arms——

Q. Sure.

The President. ——all I could do is do what we did last week. I voted with many of the nonaligned nations in the United Nations, and we didn't win the battle.

Q. But Mr. President——

The President. But then I went back—when you talk about changing my position, what I did was I went back to the British, the French, and the others and I said, "Okay, what can we agree on? We don't want to say, 'Well, we didn't get our way; so we're going to go home.' We will work with you. What can we agree on?" They proposed a course that we then embarked on, and they agreed not to totally rule out lifting the arms embargo at a later date.

So I, frankly, was pleased to try to work with and to support the efforts of Europe in this regard. I didn't point the finger or blame. But we can't deny the fact that there was an honest disagreement. That doesn't mean that we should all give up.

Q. So may I, as a followup, press you on this? You see, as you say, you voted at the United Nations with Djibouti and Morocco and Pakistan and the Cape Verde Islands on this issue about the arms embargo against Britain and France. Now, the impression still, though, is that nothing very much is happening and that it's felt it's very different when the issue, say, is Iraq when the job can be done with unmanned Tomahawk cruise missiles fired from

a safe distance. There seems to be a difference of emphasis there in the urgency in the way these matters are handled.

The President. Well, I disagree with that. The difference is this: that in Iraq we had clear evidence that the government planned a terrorist attack and an assassination of a former President of the United States for actions he took as President. We clearly had the right to take action under international law, clearly.

Secondly, if you forget about that action and you look at other actions against Iraq, they were taken within the framework of the United Nations and United Nations resolutions. The United Nations operates against, if you will—the governing resolution of the United Nations is against the policy that I have advocated in Bosnia. Therefore, it would take a change in the United Nations posture to effect that policy. The United States cannot go out and violate international law or go out on its own. That is not—we have never been for that.

And we are well aware that even though our military establishment is the biggest and we are the most powerful country in the world militarily, we are well aware that when we commit ourselves to working with our neighbors, through NATO, through the U.N., through the Organization of American States, through any other group, that we have to be prepared not to always have our way just prevail overnight. That's all that happened. I care just as much about those Muslims in the heart of Bosnia as I do about any other group of people in the world. I would give anything to somehow bring an end to the ethnic cleansing, to somehow have a resolution of that. And I think that we are still talking to one another and working in good faith and trying to come to grips with that.

I do not believe, if you meant to ask me this, I do not believe that the United States or Europe should send huge numbers of soldiers there to get involved in a civil war on one side or the other. I do believe that we should use as much muscle as we can muster to try to bring a humane end to the tragedy.

But this is a tough problem. I think that's the real answer here. This is not an easy problem. And I don't want to get into finger-pointing or blame-making; that's not the point. And as far as our willingness to commit troops, you know we put troops into Somalia, and I would say to the people of Italy and to the family members of those three soldiers, you have my gratitude and my deep condolences. But this is a difficult world. A lot of these problems are not going to be easily solved.

Russia

Q. Mr. President, Russian television. It looks like in both of our countries, in the United States and in Russia, what you see over the last few months or maybe in a short time is a growing awareness that, in spite of the fact that the cold war is over, we still have a lot of differences, that our national interests don't coincide as often as somebody would like them to do, to coincide. Now, when you meet President Yeltsin in a few days in Tokyo, on these lines what would your posture be there? How would you address these issues? And let me remind you that our Prime Minister Chernomyrdin was unable to come here because there were some differences unresolved yet.

The President. I would say first, we have a lot more in common than we have which divides us, that I am very proud of the support that the United States and, indeed, that the G–7 gave to the movement toward democracy and the fact that President Yeltsin stood up for the democratic process in Russia. And I'm proud of the courage shown by the Russian people in trying to move toward a market-oriented economy as well as to preserve democracy. And our overriding interests at the G–7 meeting in my judgment is to continue to provide assistance to Russia in that effort. And I will strongly support it.

Now, are we going to have differences of opinion from time to time? Yes, we are. I called President Yeltsin about that matter. We're trying to work it out. I still think we really need this bilateral cooperation. I want the Vice President and Prime Minister Chernomyrdin to meet and to talk about what we can do on cooperating in space, cooperating on nuclear issues, cooperating on environmental issues. And I think that will proceed. I still think all that will be done. But we're going to have differences from time to time. People disagree. That happens in life.

Q. You're talking about support. Can we expect anything significant and concrete at the G–7 concerning the aid to Russia?

The President. I certainly hope so. The United States committed $1.6 billion at Vancouver. Over half that money has now been obligated. We have another bill moving through our Congress that deals largely with energy and nuclear

issues and environmental issues, as well as student exchanges and the attempt to privatize— assistance to privatize industry in Russia. That's $1.8 billion. It has passed one House of our Congress overwhelmingly and will pass the other shortly.

The IMF, 2 days ago, released the first $1.5 billion in authority to Russia. And I think you will see the G–7 agree that we ought all to contribute to a fund to help privatize industry and to start new enterprises and to do things like that. I think this G–7 meeting will be good for Russia.

Q. You think they will be cooperative, the rest of the countries?

The President. Absolutely. We're all having economic trouble, so there won't be probably as much money as I would like because of the economic difficulties that all the nations have. But I think given the problems that the people of these countries have, the commitment to do more for Russia will be clear, substantial, and generous because of all the problems all of our countries have at home.

Economic Summit and GATT

Q. Mr. President, Prime Minister Balladur has warned there will be no world trade agreement unless U.S. penalties on steel are lifted. What can the United States do in Tokyo to try to diffuse the confrontation? And do you think there is any room for a political compromise?

The President. Well, let me say, first of all, the White House had no involvement in that case. That case was developed earlier. We have a process here which is almost like a judicial process in a court for dealing with these things. Clearly, it's legal to have this kind of operation under GATT. So the legality is not in question. If the Prime Minister believes that the facts are different from the facts that were found here, obviously, we can discuss that.

My attitude about that is that all these issues ought to be subject to discussion at the G– 7 meetings. I mean, one of the things that really bothers me about some of these meetings in the past is that we have all been so afraid of making a mistake, that we have all of our aides around, and we've got everything written down on paper. And if you spend all your time trying to avoid making a mistake, it's hard to make anything good happen. And so one of the things that I'm really working for at G–7 is a totally open framework where we can honestly share with each other what we feel and how we can resolve this.

France, if I might say, France has had some truly astonishing economic accomplishments in the last 10 years, many years in which the productivity growth in France was higher than any other European country and higher than the United States' growth. And yet France has had some continuing problems with persistent high unemployment, even with high growth.

So my own view is that it's very much in the interest of France to have a GATT agreement which opens trade and gives the incredible productive capacity of France broader outlets around the world. And I don't want to do anything to stand in the way of that, but we're going to have to work through some of these issues. I think we can.

And I realize how hard it is in France or in any other country with a high unemployment rate to conduct a trade agreement, because people are afraid of change. But when you're in trouble, that's when you need to change. That's the moment when you need to change.

Global Economy

Q. Sir, you've been elected to put America back to work. Do you think the United States has a leadership responsibility in helping the world economy get back to work?

The President. Absolutely. And I do not believe that Americans can go back to work in sufficient numbers until the world begins to work more.

For example, we've created in this country in the last 5 months about 960,000 jobs. That's about the same number we created in the previous 4 years. So it looks pretty good. But our unemployment rate is still quite high here, and the wages are not growing very much. In the last 5 years, two-thirds of our jobs have come from exports, two-thirds. So it is obvious that we can't grow unless Europe grows, unless Japan grows, unless Asia grows, unless Russia becomes a market.

It is not simple generosity. Even though I think it is the right thing to do, it is not simple generosity that prompts me to try to put this money into Russia. I think who is going to be the United States customer in 5 years or 10 years? Who is going to be Europe's customer? Who is going to be Japan's customer? Look at all the people who live in Russia. Look at all the people who live in Ukraine. Look at all

the people who live in the other Republics. My job is not just to go to the G–7 meeting and negotiate for the United States. My job is to try to help us all do something that is good for the world.

U.S. Leadership

Q. Mr. President, during the campaign you talked a lot about American leadership. So far we haven't seen it. Europeans are confused about your direction in foreign policy, Iraq, Somalia, Bosnia. You didn't solve any of these problems really. How would you define your leadership role?

The President. First of all, the central challenge that we have faced since I've been President was the crisis in Russia. And the United States did lead and Europe participated in and Japan participated in an aggressive response from the advanced nations of the world in standing up for democracy and market reform in Russia. That overshadowed every other challenge that we have faced in terms of what it's going to do for our long-term interests.

And let's not be confused about that. Somalia, Iraq, Bosnia, these things are very important. That was the central challenge that will affect our interests. And we did respond, not just the United States, all of us did. And we did the right thing and so far it's had the right consequence.

With regard to Somalia, I frankly just disagree with you about that. I think the United States, under my predecessor—I can't take credit for it—he led the way for a multinational coalition to go into Somalia. We saved hundreds of thousands of lives. We restored order. Children can go to school again. People can eat. They can sleep. There are hospitals. Life is better.

Now, Somalia did not have the infrastructure of a nation. And if we stay there—we are still there; the Italians are there; others are still there—there are going to be problems. Aideed presented us a problem. We did our best to break the back of his military capacity to disrupt Somalia without appearing to go after him personally. And I think that's the right thing to do. I would like it if he were arrested but without trying to just take him out personally. I think we are on the right path in Somalia, but we have to have patience in nation-building.

With regard to Iraq, the action I took in Iraq was specifically designed to respond to the attempt to assassinate President Bush. It was the right thing to do, I think. There are a whole set of other issues which have to do with Iraq's defiance of the U.N. resolutions. The Security Council issued a very stern warning to Iraq, and I think there will either be more compliance or some sort of appropriate action.

But again, I would say to you if you look at Iraq and you say we didn't solve that, it seems to me that the west did the right thing in not being obsessed with deposing Saddam Hussein. We acted against him because he invaded Kuwait. So he was removed from Kuwait and has been confined in a lot of the mischief he might have otherwise have wreaked. So I don't know if you can tout that as a failure.

Bosnia is a disappointment, but it is the most difficult problem, not only in Europe but in the world. We have honest disagreements among ourselves. I still have every hope that something can be done. And I have said repeatedly that the United States would be prepared to contribute to a genuine effort to maintain the peace if an agreement can be signed.

I had thought, as you know, that lifting the arms embargo would accelerate movement to a genuine peace. I still believe that. Others disagreed. That's the way it is in the world we're living in. But I am prepared to make a contribution to maintaining a genuine settlement in Bosnia. I do not believe the West should send in huge numbers of troops to get involved in trying to fight all three sides in a civil war. That's not what I think we should do.

Germany

Q. The German Bundestag decided today that Germans also can stay in Somalia.

The President. I'm very grateful for that.

Q. Do you expect Germany to make their troops available for peacekeeping and peacemaking missions, or is this perhaps the price Germany has to pay for a seat at the Security Council?

The President. Well, as you know, I favor a seat for Germany and for Japan in the Security Council. I think they are great economic powers. I think they have been responsible international political citizens, and they are leaders. I do not think I should involve myself too much in the internal politics of Germany over this issue except to say that as President I am profoundly grateful for the position that Chancellor Kohl has taken on these issues and the willingness of the German people to support involvement

in Somalia, to try to help insofar as they could in Bosnia. And I think it is very hopeful for the future.

I think all of us will have to get into more of these difficult situations like Somalia that have no easy immediate answer if we're going to try to help. If we can reach an agreement in Bosnia and we wind up sending troops there as a result of a peace agreement, there still will be ragged edges to it and difficult moments.

NAFTA

Q. Mr. President, I'd like to turn if I could to the issue of the North American Free Trade Agreement. As you know, there was a U.S. court ruling this week that said that NAFTA could do serious damage to the environment and ordering your administration to conduct an environmental impact review. You've decided to appeal that decision. What happens if you lose the appeal? Are you going to at that point bull ahead with NAFTA and ignore the court order?

The President. Well, in our country we can't ignore court orders. But, first of all, we announced that we would appeal within the hour of the decision. And we believe we will win. We also are exploring other options for compliance that would not delay the treaty, and we are proceeding full-speed ahead.

But the irony of this is that, as you know, this administration has taken some extra time with NAFTA to try to conclude environmental agreements that would make it absolutely clear that the NAFTA agreement would improve the environment on both sides of the border. So this is a delaying tactic but does not square with the facts. NAFTA will help us to improve the environment on both sides of the border. That's what we're negotiating so hard with the Mexicans on, and the Canadians have been supportive of the idea that we ought to try to make sure that there's no environmental degradation. So I still think we can pass it. And we're going to work on it.

Q. In more general terms, I think you'd agree that NAFTA's in considerable trouble in Congress and with American public opinion. At what point are you going to get out and start aggressively selling this agreement, rather than leaving it to Ross Perot and other critics of NAFTA to make the running on it?

The President. Well, first of all, I've had a very consistent and clear public position on it. But I can only undertake one major battle at a time. And right now, I've got to pass this big budget and economic program. It's a dramatic change from the last 12 years of economic policy in the U.S. It's tough. It's controversial. We're going to do it, I think. But that will be over soon.

Then the second thing is, in order to sell it, we have to define exactly what "it" is, which means that we have to conclude our negotiations on the supplemental agreement. We'll do that soon. And then I'll be out there working hard to sell it. We have the votes, I believe, in the Senate to pass it. We do not have the votes in the House to pass it. I think we can get the votes when we point out it will create jobs, not cost jobs. If we don't do it, it will really be difficult. And all the things people worry about, you know, jobs going to Mexico, that

can all happen today. It has nothing to do with NAFTA.

Q. Mr. President, our time is over. We thank you very much.

The President. Thank you.

NOTE: The interview began at 11:30 a.m. in the Roosevelt Room at the White House. In the interview, the President referred to Slobodan Milosevic, President of Serbia; Radovan Karadzic, leader of the Bosnian Serbs; and Somali warlord Mohamed Farah Aideed. Journalists participating in the interview were Hidetoshi Fujisawa, NHK, Japan; Trevor McDonald, ITN, United Kingdom; Sergei Goryachev, Ostankino, Russia; David Halton, CBC, Canada; Jean-Marc Illouz, France TV II; Jochen Schweizer, ARD, Germany; and Giuseppe Lugato, RAI TV I, Italy.

Letter to Congressional Leaders on Trade With Romania
July 2, 1993

Dear Mr. Speaker: (*Dear Mr. President:*)

In accordance with section 407 of the Trade Act of 1974 (Public Law 93–618, January 3, 1975; 88 Stat. 1978), as amended (the "Trade Act"), I am transmitting a copy of a proclamation that extends nondiscriminatory treatment to the products of Romania. I also enclose the text of the "Agreement on Trade Relations Between the Government of the United States of America and the Government of Romania," including exchanges of letters that form an integral part of the Agreement, which was signed on April 3, 1992, and which is included as an annex to the proclamation.

The Agreement will provide a nondiscriminatory framework for our bilateral trade relations and thus strengthen both economic and political relations between the United States and Romania. Conclusion of this Agreement is an important step we can take to provide greater economic benefits to both countries. It will also give further impetus to the progress we have made in our overall diplomatic relations since last year and help to reinforce political and economic reform in Romania. In that context, the United States is encouraging Romania to continue to strive for a democratic, pluralistic society, particularly through the conduct of early,

free, and fair national elections.

I believe that the Agreement is consistent with both the letter and the spirit of the Trade Act. It provides for mutual extension of nondiscriminatory tariff treatment while seeking to ensure overall reciprocity of economic benefits. It includes safeguard arrangements to ensure that our trade with Romania will grow without causing disruption to the U.S. market and consequent injury to domestic firms or loss of jobs for American workers.

The Agreement also confirms and expands for American businesses certain basic rights in conducting commercial transactions both within Romania and with Romanian nationals and business entities. Other provisions include those dealing with settlement of commercial disputes, financial transactions, and government commercial offices. Through this Agreement, Romania also undertakes obligations to modernize and upgrade very substantially its protection of intellectual property rights. Once fully implemented, the Romanian intellectual property regime will be on a par with that of our principal industrialized trading partners. This Agreement will not alter U.S. law or practice with respect to the protection of intellectual property.

On August 17, 1991, President Bush waived

application of subsections (a) and (b) of section 402 of the Trade Act to Romania. He determined that this waiver will substantially promote the objectives of section 402, and, pursuant to section 402(c)(2) of the Trade Act, notified the Congress that he had received assurances that the emigration practices of Romania will henceforth lead substantially to achievement of those objectives.

I urge that the Congress act as soon as possible to approve the "Agreement on Trade Relations Between the Government of the United States of America and the Government of Romania" and the proclamation extending nondiscriminatory treatment to products of Romania by enactment of a joint resolution referred to in section 151 of the Trade Act.

Sincerely,

WILLIAM J. CLINTON

NOTE: Identical letters were sent to Thomas S. Foley, Speaker of the House of Representatives, and Albert Gore, Jr., President of the Senate. The proclamation and related Presidential determination are listed in Appendix D at the end of this volume. The agreement was published in the *Federal Register* on July 7.

Statement on United States Policy Toward Vietnam
July 2, 1993

It has always been my firm belief that America's highest priority in its approach toward Vietnam is to secure a full accounting on our prisoners of war and missing in action. Today I am announcing two new steps toward that goal. The first involves access by Vietnam to the International Monetary Fund. The second is my decision to send a new high-level delegation to Vietnam to press for further progress on unresolved POW/MIA issues. Together, these steps offer the best hope of providing America's POW/MIA families the answers and peace of mind they deserve.

Over the past several months, I have given intense thought to how best to achieve the fullest possible accounting for our POW/MIA's and how to shape U.S. policy toward Vietnam to achieve that goal. I have met with veterans, with the families whose loved ones have not returned, and with Members of Congress who have a strong interest in this issue, including some who were held as prisoners of war.

Last night I met with a group of impressive, dedicated representatives of veterans organizations and families who care deeply about our Government's efforts to achieve the fullest possible accounting of our missing. They share my own belief that our policy toward Vietnam must be driven not by commercial interests but by the overriding purpose of achieving further progress toward the fullest possible accounting of our POW/MIA's. Vietnam has long been a divisive issue for America. It remains so today. I know there is strong disagreement among all those with an interest in the POW/MIA issue on how best to further our mutual goal. Where there is no disagreement, however, is on the need to ensure that any decision taken is made in answer to the only relevant question: Will it help us discover the truth about our missing?

One of the tragedies of this issue is that our own Government has often denied unnecessarily information about this issue to the American public. That is why I have instructed all U.S. Government POW/MIA related documents to be declassified by Veterans Day of this year, except for that tiny fraction that could still affect our national security or invade the privacy of the families. I have also been working to consolidate the POW/MIA agencies and resources to enhance the efficiency of these operations and access by the public. They have a right to know, and I intend to ensure they do.

Since taking office, I have reviewed the progress made to date in resolving unanswered questions concerning the fate of American service personnel who did not return from Vietnam. I have insisted on the fullest possible accounting from the Vietnamese Government and pressed for further progress. As part of this effort, I dispatched Gen. John Vessey to Vietnam last April as my Special Emissary for POW/MIA Affairs to press for further progress. In addition, Members of Congress and representatives of veterans groups have traveled to Vietnam to press for that goal.

In an effort to encourage further progress, it is appropriate at this time to recognize what the Vietnamese have done in our effort to account for our missing. Attached is a summary outlining that progress. Therefore, I have decided to end our opposition to the efforts of other nations to clear Vietnam's arrears in the IMF. I believe, as do former POW's John McCain and Douglas "Pete" Peterson and other veterans such as John Kerry and others in Congress, that such action will best serve the goal of achieving further progress toward the fullest possible acccounting.

Any further steps in U.S.-Vietnamese relations will strictly depend on further progress by the Vietnamese on the POW/MIA issue. We should not be swayed from that course; America owes no less to the brave men and women who fought in Vietnam and to their loved ones. Progress to date is simply not sufficient to warrant any change in our trade embargo or any further steps toward normalization.

In order to press for further progress and send a clear message to the Vietnamese Government, I will send to Hanoi a high-level delegation. The official delegation will include Deputy Secretary of Veterans Affairs Hershel Gober, Assistant Secretary of State Winston Lord, and Lt. Gen. Michael E. Ryan.

I also have invited representatives of the three largest veterans groups to accompany the delegation. The American Legion, the Veterans of Foreign Wars, and the Disabled American Veterans have each agreed to send representatives with the delegation, and I am grateful for their willingness to participate in this important mission. In addition, I have invited the National League of Families of American Prisoners and Missing in Southeast Asia to send a representative. I have also asked our current Ambassador in Thailand, David Floyd Lambertson, who has extensive experience in Vietnam, to assist the delegation.

The delegation will make clear to the Vietnamese that any further steps in relations between our two nations depend on tangible progress on the outstanding POW/MIA cases. We insist upon efforts by the Vietnamese in four key areas:

Remains: Concrete results from efforts on their part to recover remains and repatriate American remains.

Discrepancy cases: Continued resolution of 92 discrepancy cases, live sightings, and field activities.

Laos: Further assistance in implementing trilateral investigation with the Lao.

Archives: Accelerated efforts to provide all POW/MIA related documents that will help lead to genuine answers.

The individuals on this delegation share my own determination to do all we can to find the truth surrounding those who did not come home. They will press hard for results.

The delegation will also raise with the Vietnamese continuing human rights concerns and press for progress in the areas of basic freedoms, democracy, and economic reform.

For many Americans, the Vietnam war left deep wounds that have yet to heal. One of the ways to help the process of healing is to help the friends and families of POW's and MIA's learn the truth. The steps I have outlined today will advance that goal.

Statement by the Press Secretary on the President's Meetings With South African Leaders
July 2, 1993

The President held separate meetings this afternoon with South African State President F.W. de Klerk and African National Congress President Nelson Mandela. The meetings lasted about 30 minutes each.

The two meetings focused on the process of democratic reform in South Africa and how the United States can assist that historic process. The President expressed his appreciation for the leadership demonstrated by both individuals in moving South Africa towards the threshold of a nonracial democracy. He expressed particular admiration to President Mandela for his courage and dignity through decades of struggle and sacrifice against the evils of apartheid and to President de Klerk for his wisdom and determination in moving to dismantle that destructive system. He welcomed the announcement earlier today of the setting of a date for holding the first nonracial elections in South Africa's history and the progress made toward creation of a Transitional Executive Council (TEC) which will help ensure those elections are free and fair.

The President welcomed the progress achieved in the negotiations in the last few days and commended all those working for a peaceful transition to democracy. He pledged that the United States will be a full partner in building democracy in South Africa, including continued support for programs of voter education and training of election monitors. He stressed the need to begin to tackle the cruel legacies of apartheid, including economic inequity, unemployment, inadequate housing, and poor education for South Africa's nonwhite population. He said that the United States will press for a commitment at the G–7 summit in Tokyo next week to reintegrate South Africa into the world economy with agreement on a nonracial democracy.

The President noted that the administration is working with Congress and antiapartheid groups to develop additional support measures

once negotiations have progressed to the point where it is appropriate to lift remaining sanctions. Among these measures are negotiation of an OPIC investment encouragement agreement, a tax treaty, and a housing investment guarantee program. Once the TEC is created, the United States will stand ready to support its institutions designed to facilitate a smooth transition to democracy.

The President also underscored the importance of the private sector in creating growth and equality in South Africa. He looks forward to the day when all South Africans can call for the lifting of remaining economic and financial sanctions, including state and local government sanctions, and hopes that day will come soon.

The President also expressed to President de Klerk the deep appreciation of the United States for the recent decision by the Government of South Africa to forgo development of a space-launch vehicle program. He noted that the United States can now look forward to cooperation with a democratic South Africa on the peaceful uses of space technology.

The President said that he welcomed the opportunity to celebrate our Independence Day by presenting Freedom Awards to Presidents de Klerk and Mandela in Philadelphia on Sunday, July 4.

Nomination for Secretary of the Air Force
July 2, 1993

The President announced his intention today to nominate Sheila E. Widnall, associate provost of MIT and vice chair of the Carnegie Corporation Board, to be the Secretary of the Air Force. Ms. Widnall will be the first woman Service Secretary.

"I am very proud to be making this announcement," said the President. "Sheila Widnall is

a woman of high achievement: a respected scientist, a skilled administrator, and a dedicated citizen. I am confident that she will do an outstanding job of guiding the Air Force through this period of post-cold-war change."

NOTE: A biography of the nominee was made available by the Office of the Press Secretary.

Nomination for Ambassador to South Korea
July 2, 1993

The President announced today that he intends to nominate James T. Laney, the president of Emory University, to be Ambassador to the Republic of Korea.

"As I prepare for my visit to Seoul next week, I am very pleased to make this announcement," said the President. "James Laney is a greatly admired scholar and leader with an understanding and respect for Korea based on more than 45 years experience with the country. He will make an outstanding Ambassador."

NOTE: A biography of the nominee was made available by the Office of the Press Secretary.

Statement on Signing Legislation Extending Fast Track Procedures for the GATT Multilateral Trade Negotiations
July 2, 1993

Today I am pleased to sign into law H.R. 1876, extending legislative "fast track" procedures to conclude the Uruguay Round of multilateral trade negotiations. I want to extend my thanks to the Congress for its broad bipartisan support for this legislation and the Administration's trade policies.

Fast track authority is critical to our effort to complete these important negotiations by December 15, 1993. Fast track procedures give our negotiators the bargaining power they need in Geneva, while at the same time ensuring the Congress' role during the negotiation and approval of a Uruguay Round agreement.

The Uruguay Round is an ambitious effort, involving more than 100 nations, to lower tariff and non-tariff barriers around the world and to strengthen and update a set of rules for international trade that have become increasingly ineffective and obsolete.

Completion of the Uruguay Round would provide a major boost to the world economy at a time when it is crucially needed. As the world's leading exporter—and the world's most open economy—the United States stands to benefit significantly by reducing trade barriers and opening markets around the world for manufactured goods, agricultural products, and services.

We remain committed to completing these important negotiations this year, and we will encourage our trading partners to make their contribution to bringing the negotiations to a successful conclusion.

WILLIAM J. CLINTON

The White House,
July 2, 1993.

NOTE: H.R. 1876, approved July 2, was assigned Public Law No. 103–49. This statement was released by the Office of the Press Secretary on July 3.

The President's Radio Address
July 3, 1993

Good morning. Two hundred and seventeen years ago, our Founding Fathers declared our independence to secure the liberty and prosperity we celebrate every July Fourth. Although our times and challenges are very different from those our founders faced, these issues are still the enduring concerns of the American people today.

In a few days, I will represent the United States in Japan at the annual meeting of the major industrialized nations of the world to work for new global policies that create more American jobs, open markets for our products, and strengthen our security as we embrace the challenges of this new world. America commands respect on the world stage because we have taken aggressive steps to put our own economic house in order at a time when all the advanced nations are having real troubles with the economy.

Here in Washington the House and Senate have both passed versions of my economic plan to promote growth and to reduce the deficit by $500 billion. The plan also has incentives for people to invest more in our economy, to create jobs, and provides money for education and training in new technologies and helps the defense workers who have been laid-off by defense cuts.

We've made a good beginning now. As this plan has progressed through the Congress, interest rates have continued to come down, mortgage rates are now below 7.5 percent, and nearly 1 million new jobs have been added to the economy since January, about the same number as came in the previous 3 years.

Change is hard, though. Many people are still skeptical. Many of the opponents of my plan chant "tax-and-spend." But the truth is, it's not an old tax-and-spend plan. And the people who are attacking it are those who taxed the middle class, cut taxes on the wealthy, borrowed and spent our economy into a $4 trillion debt in the last 12 years. Our plan is fair. It has $250 billion in spending cuts and asks the upper 6 percent of Americans to pay 75 percent of the new taxes. It moves the working poor out of poverty. It enables me to attend this meeting of the other advanced nations with a record of real results that will encourage our competitors to take steps to revive their economies as well. And that's important for every American, because we can't grow the United States economy as we ought to until we have cooperation from other nations, and they're growing. Why? Because since 1987, two-thirds of our new jobs have come from exports. We live in a global economy. We have to compete all over the world, and we have to sell our products and services everywhere.

When we stepped up to the plate here at home to get our own house in order, it enabled us to make the global economy work for the people of the United States if others will do

their part. And that's what we're working on now. As I said, all the nations I'll be meeting with are facing difficult times. Their economies are even slower than ours. But we know that together we can grow, we can have a stronger economy, and we can have more security.

I'd like to talk to you about that for a few minutes. Because of the vigilance, the democratic values, the military strength of the United States and our allies, we won the cold war. Our inheritance, our victory is a new chance to rebuild our economies and solve our problems in each of our countries while we reduce military spending. But our profound responsibility remains to redefine what it means to preserve security in this post-cold-war era We must be strong, we must be resolute, and we must be safe. This great task has certainly changed with the passage of the cold war. The technologies of mass destruction in the hands of Russia and the United States are being reduced. But technologies of mass destruction that just a few years ago were possessed only by a handful of nations, and still are possessed only by a few, are becoming more widely available. It is now theoretically possible for many countries to build missiles, to have nuclear weapons and other weapons of mass destruction. This is a new and different challenge that requires new approaches and new thinking.

During my campaign for President, I promised a wholehearted commitment to achieving a comprehensive nuclear test ban treaty. A test ban can strengthen our efforts worldwide to halt the spread of nuclear technology in weapons. Last year, the Congress directed that a test ban be negotiated by 1996, and it established an interim moratorium on nuclear testing while we reviewed our requirements for further tests. That moratorium on testing expires soon. Congress said that after the moratorium expires, but before a test ban was achieved, the United States could carry out up to 15 nuclear tests to ensure the safety and reliability of our weapons. After a thorough review, my administration has determined that the nuclear weapons in the United States arsenal are safe and reliable. Additional nuclear tests could help us prepare for a test ban and provide for some additional improvements in safety and reliability. However, the price we would pay in conducting those tests now, by undercutting our own nonproliferation goals and ensuring that other nations would resume testing, outweighs these benefits.

I have therefore decided to extend the current moratorium on United States nuclear testing at least through September of next year, as long as no other nation tests. And I call on the other nuclear powers to do the same. If these nations will join us in observing this moratorium, we will be in the strongest possible position to negotiate a comprehensive test ban and to discourage other nations from developing their own nuclear arsenals.

If, however, this moratorium is broken by another nation, I will direct the Department of Energy to prepare to conduct additional tests while seeking approval to do so from Congress. I therefore expect the Department to maintain a capability to resume testing.

To assure that our nuclear deterrent remains unquestioned under a test ban, we will explore other means of maintaining our confidence in the safety, the reliability, and the performance of our own weapons. We will also refocus much of the talent and resources of our Nation's nuclear labs on new technologies to curb the spread of nuclear weapons and verify arms control treaties.

Beyond these significant actions, I am also taking steps to revitalize the Arms Control and Disarmament Agency so that it can play an active role in meeting the arms control and nonproliferation challenges of this new era. I am

committed to protecting our people, deterring aggression, and combating terrorism. The work of combating proliferation of weapons of mass destruction is difficult and unending, but it is an essential part of this task. It must be done.

Americans have earned the right on this Fourth of July weekend to enjoy life, liberty, and the pursuit of happiness in the new era America did so much to create. This moment of opportunity is the reward for our vigilance and sacrifice during the long years of the cold war.

We now have the freedom to concern ourselves not merely with survival but with prosperity for ourselves and our children. We have the strength and the stature to lead the world into a future of greater security and global growth.

Because of the changes we have made, America can now fulfill the dreams and aspirations of the patriots who made our freedom possible more than 200 years ago. We can do them no greater honor than to make the most of what these times have to offer. Working together, we will.

Have a happy and safe holiday, and thanks for listening.

NOTE: This address was recorded at 6:34 p.m. on July 2 in the Roosevelt Room at the White House for broadcast at 10:06 a.m. on July 3.

Statement on Signing the Supplemental Appropriations Act of 1993
July 3, 1993

On February 17, I unveiled my national economic strategy to increase growth and job creation, to reduce the deficit and lower interest rates. The plan reflects my belief that the United States had to address long-standing economic problems so we could expand growth and opportunity for all Americans.

The long-term portion of the plan is nearing completion by the Congress. The House and Senate have adopted versions of the plan that reduce the deficit by $500 billion while providing needed investments in our country's future strength and job creating ability. However, the short-term component, a jobs bill designed to keep the recovery on track, was not adopted

by the Congress.

While there are some optimistic signs—lower long-term interest rates, the lowest mortgage rates in twenty years, and the creation of nearly one million jobs since January—I am not satisfied with the performance of the economy, many Americans are still hurting, and others are uncertain about the future.

Because too many Americans are still without meaningful work, I was pleased to sign into law last night a modest job creating bill, H.R. 2118, the Supplemental Appropriations Act of 1993. This Act funds a variety of critical programs, including key targeted investments that I requested in February. Adoption of this law means that summer jobs will be created, local law enforcement will be able to hire back police laid off during the last recession, and small businesses will be able to expand their payrolls, products, and profits. It also provides funding that will benefit farmers adversely affected by weather conditions in the Midwest.

This bill does not nearly provide what I believe is necessary to help our economy. But every job it creates, every policeman or policewoman it rehires, every farm devastated by weather it assists, and every small business it enables to grow will make a difference to the people and communities served by this legislation.

These are among the provisions of the Supplemental Appropriations Act of 1993:

The Act provides $220 million for summer jobs for youth, including $50 million for the Youth Fair Chance Program. This new program will provide a comprehensive range of services to low-income youth in communities with high concentrations of poverty.

The Act provides $150 million for grants to State and local government to enhance public safety by hiring additional law enforcement personnel. These funds will help fight crime and offset layoffs resulting from fiscal restraints on local governments.

The Act provides $341 million to the Pell Student financial assistance program to help address a shortage of funding from previous years.

H.R. 2118 provides $175 million to support nearly $3.2 billion in SBA loan guarantees. Regular appropriations for SBA's primary lending programs were exhausted in late April, and the program has been shut down since then. The supplemental funds provided for SBA will allow thousands of businesses to receive loans for start-up, expansion, and working capital.

The Act provides $475 million for veterans compensation and pensions, and is necessary to ensure that payments continue to be made to veterans through the end of the fiscal year.

Honoring my commitment to provide additional assistance to victims of Hurricane Andrew, the bill makes available $271 million for disaster assistance through the Departments of Agriculture and Housing and Urban Development.

These funds are to be used to address the destruction caused by Hurricane Andrew, Hurricane Iniki, and Typhoon Omar and, in some cases, other Presidentially declared disasters as well. These funds are necessary to promote rebuilding and to respond effectively to the continuing need for disaster relief. In accordance with the applicable provisions of the Balanced Budget and Emergency Deficit Control Act of 1985, as amended, I join the Congress in designating the $63 million provided by the Act for agriculture disaster assistance as an emergency requirement.

The Act extends Federal crop disaster relief to farmers with disaster-related losses occurring prior to August 1, 1993, without appropriating additional disaster funds. Existing emergency funds are sufficient to pay roughly 15 cents for every dollar claimed. This provision will permit some assistance to farmers impacted by the recent floods in the Midwest. I have directed Agriculture Secretary Espy to submit to me a crop disaster assistance plan to provide additional assistance to these farmers.

The Act support $73 billion in loan guarantee authority to allow the FHA single- and multifamily mortgage insurance programs and the GNMA mortgage-backed securities program to continue operating through the rest of the year. Absent this supplemental, both programs would soon deplete their funding.

Finally, the Act provides $1.3 billion for the Department of Defense and partially offsets the additional funding with nearly $1 billion in rescissions. The additional funds are for the costs of Operation Restore Hope, Operation Southern Watch, and other requirements.

I commend the Congress for developing a supplemental appropriations bill that supports my investment program and meets urgent National needs.

WILLIAM J. CLINTON

The White House,
July 3, 1993.

NOTE: H.R. 2118, approved July 2, was assigned Public Law No. 103–50.

Remarks at an Independence Day Ceremony in Philadelphia, Pennsylvania
July 4, 1993

Thank you very much, President de Klerk, Mr. Mandela, Senator Wofford, distinguished Members of Congress, Mayor Rendell and members of the Philadelphia city government, Judge Higginbotham, Reverend Sullivan, my fellow Americans.

As I flew here today from Washington over the farmlands and the small towns and the cities and I began to land here in Philadelphia, and I could see closely Americans of all kinds enjoying the blessings of liberty and the fruits of their labors, I couldn't help thinking that if the Founding Fathers were with us today, they would be proud of the work that they have done.

I do want to say a special word to two distinguished Pennsylvanians who, but for health reasons, would clearly be here with us today, a word of appreciation to them with whom I talked just a few moments ago, your brave Governor, Bob Casey, engaged in his heroic struggle—we all wish him well—and your distinguished Senator Arlen Specter, who promised me he would be back to work soon. He did not promise me a vote, however. [*Laughter*]

On this, our Nation's birthday in our Nation's birthplace, all of us are part of a truly historic occasion as we welcome these two leaders in the journey to nonracial democracy in South Africa. Here they stand together, the head of state and the former political prisoner. We honor the dedication, the dignity, and the discipline of the ANC president, Nelson Mandela, who walked out of prison after 27 years, astonishingly still unbowed, unbroken, and unembittered. And we salute President de Klerk for his wisdom and his determination in moving to dismantle the destructive system of apartheid and his courage in asking his people to give up something that they have which is not fully legitimate so that they can live together in real harmony, real freedom, and real liberty. That, too, is an act of courage we should honor.

I believe that in their common endeavors they are working together to liberate all South Africans, to restore material wealth, and to bring spiritual health to their beloved country. Many Americans have stood for the cause of freedom in South Africa and now I tell you both: The United States stands ready to help the people of South Africa as they move forward on the journey of democracy.

Here where our own democracy is born, the United States today reaches out a helping hand to those who would build democracy in South Africa. We stand ready to help with voter education. We stand ready to help to heal the cruel legacies of apartheid, from unemployment to poor housing to inadequate education. We want to be your partner. This week when I travel to the summit of the world's leading industrial nations, I will work to include a new and democratic South Africa in the world economy and our common commitment to it.

And closer to home, my fellow Americans, we must rejoice today in the historic accord reached late last evening to restore democracy and its elected leader, President Aristide, to Haiti. This agreement is a tribute to the dedicated efforts of the United Nations, the OAS, and the United States negotiators and to the resilience of the democratic idea and the commitment of the Haitian people to that idea.

I want to say a special word of thanks to all the Members of Congress, including the Congressional Black Caucus who worked so hard to put the United States on the side of democracy in Haiti. This is their victory, too. I called President Aristide this morning to express my congratulations and my appreciation for his signing the peace accord, and he and I agreed that today we could both wish each other happy Independence Day.

Earlier today, as Americans have done for 217 years, I had the honor of participating, with two young children who are direct descendants of our Founders, in ringing the Liberty Bell. When that bell first tolled, it rang with the moral force of the most powerful common idea humanity has ever known: the idea that each of us stands equal before God and must therefore be equal before the law; the idea that our human dignity is given to us not by any government but by God; the idea that we must be citizens, not subjects, proud participants in the democratic process of governing ourselves and building our own future. It is that which we celebrate and hope for in South Africa, in Haiti, and throughout the rest of the world today and that which we must still work to perfect in our own Nation today. Because, even after 217 years, no one would say we have got it entirely right yet.

Still, none can deny that this Nation has survived and succeeded for more than two centuries because at every crucial moment we have had the courage to change, to make difficult but necessary decisions, and still to be faithful to the unchanging ideals which gave birth to us. Thomas Jefferson wrote that blistering Declaration of Independence knowing that his ideals challenged his country to change. He thought of the immorality of slavery in America when he wrote, "I tremble for my country when I reflect that God is just." When Abraham Lincoln wrote the Emancipation Proclamation, he gave our Nation's bloodiest conflict a sacred, moral purpose, to turn the promises of the Declaration and the Constitution and the Bill of Rights into living realities for all our people.

It is a struggle we are still waging. Still, we struggle to live in a way that will please a just God. Still, we struggle to live in a way that we can secure for every American, without regard to race or region or station in life, the blessing of life, liberty, and the pursuit of happiness. Still, we struggle to find ways to extend a helping hand of freedom to people throughout the world. No less than those who founded our Republic or fought to keep it together in the Civil War, we too, must have the vision and courage to change, to preserve our unchanging purposes in a dynamic and difficult world.

This is not just another nation that we live in. It is the noblest effort at self-government and continuous change the world has ever known. Here, people from every continent and every country come, believing that they can build a new life for themselves and a better future for their children. America embodies the idea that a nation can be built by the people of every other nation and still be a beacon of hope and inspiration to the world and still prove that out of all that diversity can become a deeper strength and unity founded on the ideals that we celebrate on the Fourth of July.

To keep that promise, we must continue to lead the world, not only politically and morally but economically as well. And all of you know, my fellow Americans, that is our great challenge today, when most of our people are worried about their own jobs and their own incomes,

the security of their health care, the safety of their streets, the educational future of their children, the challenges to our deepest values here in our own homes, and the challenges to our position around the world.

The brave band who invented our country 217 years ago faced a difficult future with hope. Today, we are bombarded constantly with the magnitude and complexity of our problems, with the foibles of our problem-solvers, with the message that things may not be able to get better. Too many people are gripped by doubt when we need confidence. They are gripped by cynicism when we need hope and faith and conviction.

My fellow Americans, on this Fourth of July look at these two men standing here making world history. Cynicism is a luxury the American people cannot afford. Of course, there is much to question and to worry about. But I ask you to remember here today, this Nation has endured and triumphed over a bloody Civil War, two World Wars, the Great Depression, the civil rights struggle, riots in our streets, economic problems, and social discord at home and great challengers abroad. And we are still here, still leading the way, still looking toward tomorrow. Cynicism is a luxury we cannot afford. It defeats us before we begin. It is our job to carry on this great tradition.

Make no mistake about it, as long as we have faith in the future and the courage to change, our Nation is still unstoppable. I believe we have a future where our ideas continue to be the inspiration for the world, where our system continues to be a model for the world, where our economy, if we do what we need to do, can once again be the envy of the world. All around us, democracy and markets are on the rise, a new global economy is emerging, and we welcome the challenges that it brings. This new economy is built on innovation. But America has always been the home of the great inventors, from Philadelphia's own Ben Franklin to the geniuses today who build new computer hardware and write software in their basements and garages.

The new economy is built on education. And America has always been a home to education, from Thomas Jefferson, from those to the wonderful universities in this great city who educate our young people there and reach out to those in the inner-city schools. The new economy is built on flexibility and change. We are, my friends, a nation born in revolution and renewed through constant change. We can do what we have to do today to renew the American dream.

The genius of our democracy is that we the people are capable of self-government, capable of difficult choices, capable of making the changes that each time demands. Through the miracle of democracy, we are attempting to do just that today, to gain control of our economic destiny, reduce our terrible budget deficit, invest in our future, and do it in a way that is fair and that will work.

In just a couple of days, I will go to Tokyo to represent all of you in a meeting of the world's great industrial nations to work with them to get this economy moving again and to create jobs and opportunity for our people and for theirs as well. We will be able to go there with our heads held high because, for all of our difficult problems, we are moving: almost a million new jobs in 1993, lower interest rates at home, and a sense that things can get better if we keep at it. After long periods of division and denial, we are as a people rising to the occasion to put our house in order. And now we can say with an outstretched hand of friendship to our friends: We have made tough choices; so must you. And together, we can offer opportunity to our people again. Let us stop pointing the finger of blame and assume responsibility and lift the human natures and the human potential of people throughout the world. That is the job we will face in Tokyo.

My fellow Americans, in the shadow of this building let us remember that once, here, patriots and visionaries pledged their lives, their fortunes, and their sacred honor. Today I tell you that we must pledge ourselves to make sure this changing world changes fundamentally for the better. Old injustices are ending; new opportunities and challenges are emerging. And together, we can make the years ahead the best years our Nation has ever had if we can rise above cynicism and doubt, if we can see through the siren's songs of the easy answers of the moment, if we can remember that from the beginning our people have always known that Government could not solve all the problems and that all citizens had to be responsible to build this Nation together.

Today we celebrate these two leaders who have advanced the cause of freedom in South Africa and, to be sure, they have advanced the cause of freedom throughout the world. Tonight, from parks and waterfronts, in backyards, all of us here in America will see our skies brightened by the celebration of our own freedom. It will lift the spirits of people throughout this country and throughout the world who yet yearn to see and breathe and feel that freedom. Let this celebration remind us that democracy is a promise for each of us to keep, a promise to be Americans in the best sense of the word, to be citizens, not spectators, to do the best we can in our families, our jobs, our communities, to shoulder the burden of responsibility, not point the finger of blame. This was the promise our founders made in this place on this day two centuries ago. To keep that tradition, we must be believers and builders. And so must we be every day, starting here, right now, today. Let us resolve to do it.

God bless you, and God bless America.

NOTE: The President spoke at 5:10 p.m. in Independence Hall. In his remarks, he referred to Mayor Edward G. Rendell of Philadelphia; Judge A. Leon Higginbotham, retired, Third Circuit Court of Appeals; and Rev. Leon Sullivan, founder and president of Opportunities Industrialization Center and leader in the antiapartheid movement.

Remarks at a Town Meeting in Eldridge, Iowa
July 4, 1993

The President. Thank you very much. Folks, this is supposed to be informal, so I'm going to sit down if you don't mind. That introduction you just heard is a good illustration of Clinton's first law of politics, which is whenever possible, get somebody you've appointed to high office to introduce you. They'll lie about you every time. [*Laughter*]

I'm glad to be here with your secretary of agriculture, your secretary of state, and your

Governor, my longtime friend. We served together for a long time. And when he got elected Governor, he was 3 months younger than me. He displaced me from being the youngest Governor. Now there are 10 or 12 Governors younger than we are. We've hung around too long and worked ourselves into middle age.

I'm glad to be here with Congressman Jim Leach and with Congressman Lane Evans, who's the Congressman from across the river in Illinois. I want to say we had some contact with Senator Grassley before I came today, and Senator Harkin called me the day before yesterday and gave me a long litany of everything I was supposed to be doing. I said, "Well, Tom, I don't even need to go to Iowa now. I've been educated, you know." [*Laughter*]

It is true that there wasn't much of a sales job to get me to come here. If you could come to Iowa on the Fourth of July or stay in Washington and burn up, what would you do? [*Laughter*] So I'm glad to be back here. The last time I was in this part of Iowa was when I was on my bus trip. And actually, our bus trip went through almost every place that's badly flooded here, starting in northern Missouri and Iowa and Illinois and Minnesota and Wisconsin. And of course, you got some pretty substantial damage in South Dakota also.

I am very glad to be back. I want to thank Secretary Espy for coming out here so promptly. I wish I could have come a few days earlier, but the legislative and other schedules in Washington just wouldn't permit it.

I do want to say that I appreciate, Dale, what you said about Secretary Espy. One reason I asked him to be Secretary of Agriculture is that he represented a district in Congress that bordered my State, and I wanted to appoint somebody Secretary of Agriculture that actually represented farmers and that had seen crops flood and also seen crops burn, often on the same land. If you hang around long enough, you see it on the same land. And we are trying up there to be responsive and to be helpful. And I want to thank all the people here in Iowa and all the people throughout this Mississippi River area who have been very cooperative with us and have helped us.

I came here mostly to listen to you today, but I wanted to talk about—I've got three or four notes here. I want to just make sure I don't forget to say anything. Of the things we already know, we know that the damage from

this flood is going to be somewhere in the neighborhood of a billion dollars. We feel that it is, anyway. I have only $100 million right now in my disaster fund under present law. And I signed a letter releasing that fund before I came out here. There is also a new law which has been passed by the Congress which provides disaster payments for 1993. It's got about $297 million in it. It is on my desk, and I will sign it as soon as I get back. And don't think I'm derelict. You couldn't get get the money even if I signed it yesterday. It'll take a while to get.

So we're still going to be real short of funds. So I'm going to ask Congress on an emergency basis to provide some additional funding, and Secretary Espy is going to be working with the rest of the people in the executive branch and your Representatives from here to put together legislation that will adequately take care of the problems insofar as we can under Federal law.

We are going to ask that the producers here receive the same benefits as the people who were affected by Hurricane Andrew and other major disasters last year, which is something that the congressional delegations and the Governors have asked us to do, and we're going to do that. And we will eliminate the August 1st deadline for disaster filing, which is what's in the present law. We'll present a bill to do that, and I've already talked to the leadership in the House and the Senate on a bipartisan basis from other States. And they don't have any problem with doing that. They know that we need to.

The last thing I'd like to mention before I open it to your comments and questions, because you may have some other specific things we can do, is that I have asked Secretary Espy to work with the other Federal agencies and with the appropriate people in Congress on a long-term reform of the crop insurance system. Any farmer who's ever fooled with it knows it's a good thing if you've got it, if you've got insured what goes wrong, in just the way it's supposed to be. But it's nowhere near what it ought to be. If you don't get your beans planted in the first place, for example, you can't get any insurance on it, even if you pay and pay and pay for years. That's a big issue. I come from a State that has not near as much corn as Iowa, just a little bit of corn, but a whole bunch of soybeans. It's not a program crop, and if you take out crop insurance against it and then it gets wet and you can't plant it at all, under the present system you can't recover. It's just not a very good, comprehensive, or appropriate system in my opinion. So we're going to try to see if we can't get some reforms up that people will agree to.

And there are some other actions that Secretary Espy can take that he may want to talk about or you may want to ask about. But these are the specific things we think we can do. I hope it will be enough so that we don't lose a lot of farmers who are operating on the margins. I went through that whole thing in the 1980's when I was a Governor of a big farm State, and every other day I had a friend who was dropping out of farming. And we're going to do what we can to move as quickly and as aggressively as we can. I hope it will help.

I think it's real, real important to get this long-term reform of the crop insurance system and work it out so that people can access it, and then if they got it, it amounts to something when they suffer a loss. So we're going to do what we can to get that done.

I thank you for spending part of your Fourth of July with me. I know you could be out shooting fireworks, and I'm sorry about all the water. We had a whole lot of my State under water 3 or 4 years ago when the Arkansas River flooded, and we had towns under water, house under water like what I saw today, a town and an awful lot of farmland. I know what you're going through. I'm very sorry. I hope this will help, and I assure you we'll be very diligent in pushing to get this action through Congress. If you have any other ideas or suggestions we would be glad to have them.

And thank you again, Governor. Thank you, Mr. Secretary. Thank you, Madam Secretary. Congressman Leach, I'm glad to be in your district and see you looking so hale and hearty. And thank you all very much for having us.

[At this point, a participant expressed appreciation for the President's visit and discussed severe weather conditions in 1988 and 1991.]

The President. Can I ask just one fact question before we start, just for my interest because we're a little bit further north than my home State. Can you plant soybeans this late here?

Q. This is the cutoff.

The President. You mean 3 weeks from now, if the land dries off, it's too late to plant, isn't it?

Q. Right. Some people have planted as late

as the Fourth of July and get a half a crop. At this point it's not worth the risk of planting a crop. The cost you have of putting it in the ground, you're not going to recover that. So at this point, it's just too late, I think, in the State of Iowa to plant soybeans. There was some corn ground that was switched to soybeans, but it's too late to do that now, too.

Q. Thank you, Mr. President, for your interest in agriculture. I really appreciate it. And my question to you is, will you require repayment of the advance deficiency payments even though the fellow didn't get the corn planted? I would think that would be a very great help to those that didn't get planted to not have that burden of repayment.

The President. I think I'll let Secretary Espy answer that. We talked about that very thing on the airplane when we were about to land, and we saw how much land was under water. It was the first thing that came up when we were looking at the damage.

Secretary Espy. This is something that we've been looking at a lot lately, as you might imagine. And since I returned to Washington from Iowa I've reviewed the law. And any outright waiver of the advance deficiency payment that you've already gotten is going to be really, really difficult to do, certainly if you're not in the program.

But what we want to do is to extend the signing date for program crops, and we'll probably do it until the end of the month, July 31st, so that you can come in and declare your intent to plant another crop, particularly corn. Then you will fall in the 0–92, and then you could keep your advance deficiency payment.

For those farmers that already have the payment, we can't waive it outright, but we'll certainly work with you to make sure we stretch out the payment, or we can go to Congress to ask that we have fallback authority to do some other things.

The President. Under the law, just to flat out do it, we don't have the authority right now. So you either have to change the law or do what Mike said in terms of putting back the filing date and having people come in and make a declaration.

[A participant expressed appreciation for the President's visit and discussed other conditions adversely affecting the crop yield, the special stress the flood places on young farmers, and

the possibility of an assessment fee on commodities traded to be set aside for disaster assistance.]

The President. You know, there's another issue that you alluded to there that I don't have an answer to, but I worked on it quite a lot when I was a Governor, and that is the whole question of the small number of young farmers, unless there are just young farmers that farm their parents' land, and it's all paid for, and they've got their debt paid down. The average age of a farmer is pushing 60, just on the near side of 60. That looks younger to me all the time—[*laughter*]—but still it doesn't quite qualify as young.

We spent a lot of time when I was a Governor trying to work out financing operations and some other things for first-time farmers. Secretary Espy and I spent a good deal of time talking about that. Maybe this is not a discussion for tonight because we're all here worried about the floods, but if you had any specific ideas about kinds of initiatives we might undertake or partnerships for the States for first-time farmers to get young people in or help them get through those first rough years if they've got some accumulated mortgage or other debt, I'd really like to know it, because I think it's a pretty serious social problem for this country to have the average age of farmers going up every year and almost no young farmers coming in.

[*Governor Branstad suggested that a law regarding use of tax-exempt bonds to finance State farm loan programs be made permanent or at least extended.*]

The President. That whole tax-exempt bond law is now part of the discussion now being held on the budget, and I am strongly in favor of extending it. We had a program like that at home. It works, and I'm strong for it. I think it will be extended.

Governor Branstad. It could be made permanent as opposed to extended for a year or so.

The President. I think it will be extended. We're trying to make it permanent, and I hope we can do it.

[*A participant discussed the loss of crops that had not yet been planted and the requirement that a certain percent of any county must be damaged before the disaster assistance program provides assistance. Secretary Espy then advo-*]

cated reform of the crop insurance program.]

The President. Let me just mention one other thing. You asked a question about the county loss thing. That's always been in the Federal law, at least as long as I've been fooling with it. And under normal circumstances it's a pretty good rule of thumb, you know, for example, if there's, I don't know, a tornado or heavy rains that are uniform across the State. But when you have something that comes directly out of the flooding of a river like this, it's possible, depending on the size and shape of the county, that people could be wiped out and could be living just across the county line and their county not trigger.

So what I think we're going to have to do on that—I can't promise, but I'm aware of it because I've been through it before—what we're going to do is wait until all the reports come in, and we can see what the shape of the damage is. And if we've got substantial numbers of people who are really wiped out who are in counties where they don't have the 35 percent county loss for just pure geographical fluke, then we need to make some provisions for that, and I think we'll be able to.

Q. We need to have a crop insurance program with a catastrophic feature to it, and we don't have that now.

Q. I would like to say one thing. I'm from Illinois just across the way here, but I'm not from Iowa, but it's been bad over there, too.

Q. Mr. President, I'm 23 years old, and this is my first year of farming. I had been planning on starting, and I grew up on a farm, but everything I've done I've done myself. And I'm kind of wondering where the money's coming from that you're planning on helping everybody with.

The President. Where's the money coming from, the $850 million?

Q. Exactly.

The President. Well, I don't think we'll have any trouble getting it because this year we're way below the spending targets established by the Congress before I became President. We've got the deficit way down; it's much lower than they thought it was going to be. Our interest payments are much lower because interest payments are down. And I think the Congress, they'll do one of two things: They'll either appropriate it as an extra expense, or they'll just cut the money out of somewhere else and pay it.

Everything we've done so far since I've been there, we've just cut something else and put it into some supplemental bill, which is what we did, for example, to add another 200,000 summer jobs this summer.

So they'll either find something else to cut and pay for it, or they may, because it's a genuine one-time emergency, just appropriate the money since we're well under the spending limits approved by the previous Congress.

Q. In my opinion, what would help us out now and in the future would be not this new tax. We're taxed enough the way it is right now. We only get 50 cents on the dollar. By the time we spend it, I would just as soon be able to spend my money the way I want to spend it.

The President. You won't have to worry about this causing taxes because it's a tiny fraction of a huge Federal budget anyway.

Q. But the whole United States is getting taxed on this, and it's not helping—what percentage of the United States population is farmers?

The President. Three percent, but 100 percent of them eat.

Q. Yes, and 100 percent of them are going to get taxed, too. I would just as soon that you not tax me as a farmer, and I would just as soon if you didn't raise taxes on the rest of the Nation, too.

The President. Well, if we had a decent crop insurance program, we wouldn't have to worry about disaster payments. In other words, if we had one that worked, if there was a system of crop insurance that worked, we wouldn't have to worry about it.

Q. As a farmer we've got enough to gamble on with the weather, let alone gambling on our Government raising taxes. And I remember somebody saying no new taxes about 6 months ago, I believe.

The President. Well, you didn't hear me say no new taxes. I've promised to raise taxes on the wealthy because their incomes were produced——

Q. I'm far from wealthy, Mr. President.

The President. Well, if your income is under $30,000, you'll probably get a tax cut under my plan. If it's between $30,000 and $100,000, according to the Congressional Budget Office, it will cost you a very little amount of money.

Q. Thirty thousand is a wealthy man then?

The President. No, that's not what I said. But

when I took office, sir—let's have a political debate. I didn't think we were going to talk about this, but I'd be more than happy to. Let me tell you something. After the election—not during the election when they had all the figures—the previous government announced after the election that the deficit was going to be $165 billion bigger than they said before the election. We just discovered we're going to have $50 billion more in deficit. This is just for 4 years, not the whole 5-year period.

So my choice was pretty simple. I could ignore that, or I could ask middle class people between $30,000 and $100,000 to pay a modest contribution to the deficit, get almost all the money from people above $100,000, and cut spending by as much as we would raise in taxes, reduce the deficit $500 million, and bring interest rates down.

Let me finish. You've started to talk so you're going to listen to me now. [*Laughter*] Since I became President we dropped long-term interest rates a point; they're at their lowest rate in 20 years, only because there's finally a Government in Washington trying to bring this deficit down. Millions of Americans have refinanced their homes since January, and they've saved more money in one year than they're going to pay in 5 years by far if this small fuel tax passes that the Congress has approved, by far.

The people whose taxes were raised substantially are people whose taxes were lowered in the 1980's while taxes on the middle class were raised. And for every dollar that the taxes were raised, even on the wealthy, we cut spending. We have cut everything in the Federal Government. We have a 5-year hard freeze on all domestic spending which includes the increases we're putting into Head Start, job training, and new technologies. We have slashed spending. We have raised 74 percent of the taxes on people with incomes above $100,000, and we held harmless everybody below $30,000.

I think it's a fair deal. And not only that, if it gets the interest rates down, the country will get more money out of it than they'll pay in taxes. Even the people who don't agree with me admit, right in the Wall Street Journal, if we keep interest rates down this low, it will put $100 billion a year back in the pockets of ordinary Americans to refinance their homes, their business loans, their farm loans, their consumer loans, their car loans, their college loans. And it's because we have let the deficit get out of hand and we're bringing it down. We've got interest rates down. We can turn the country around. I think it is a fair plan. And you may believe you're taxed to death, but our taxes are lower than all of our competitors. And now our interest rates are, too, because we're finally doing something about the deficit.

I might say—all the people who talk about how terrible this was—we just had a hearing in the Senate last week, and it was a straight party line vote voting this bill out of the Senate Finance Committee. But all those people that said the issue was spending in the Senate Finance Committee, you know how many amendments the other side offered to cut spending— they said, you know, "It's spending, stupid. It's not taxes. It's spending"—zero. Not one, not one amendment, because I had taken all these politically tough spending cuts. We slashed education, slashed veterans, slashed—we cut everything in the world in a wide budget.

And I just think it was worth it to get the deficit down. If you don't believe that you should have any tax increase at all, even a very modest one, to reduce the deficit, you're entitled to that opinion. But I think you'll make more money from lower interest rates than you'll pay in higher taxes. And I think it's fair.

Q. Not if I don't borrow money. I've got my money saved from earning it, and I wish the Government could——

The President. Most 22-year-olds don't have that kind of money. Lucky you. I'm proud of you.

[*A participant thanked the President for visiting and advocated action during the G–7 summit to improve market access overseas. He also stated that commodity organizations across the country would support the NAFTA.*]

The President. Thank you. Yes, give him a hand.

If I might, let me just say one thing, to go back to the comment the young man who just spoke made about the taxes. If everybody in this country who wanted to work had a job and we had free and open markets in the world, then we could lower taxes and reduce the deficit. That's the real truth. The real answer to this whole issue is how to get growth back into the economy. That is the ultimate answer. It's not to have the argument he and I just had. But the argument is how can you have more people working and have more markets open.

And if I might just make two comments on that. Since 1987, about two-thirds of the new jobs generated in the American economy have come from expanded trade. That's how you add jobs in a world where you're already a wealthy country and most people are working. I'm glad to hear you say what you did about the North American Free Trade Agreement. I believe that most of the fears the American people have are not well-founded about that. There are some problems with it. We're trying to get side agreements on labor standards and the environment to make sure the Mexican Government strengthens those things. But believe me, folks, anybody who wants to move a plant to Mexico and work people for low wages and export products back in here, they can do that today. In other words, if we don't hit a lick at this NAFTA deal, everything that people are worried about with NAFTA can happen today.

But before Mr. Salinas became President of Mexico, we had a $5 billion trade deficit with Mexico. Today, we have a $6 billion trade surplus. Last month Mexico replaced Japan as the second biggest purchaser of our industrial products. And you know what it does for you folks here and the kinds of crops you raise. It's a good deal.

So we're going to try to pass it. The people who are against it are genuine and passionate, and they represent folks just like you who work hard, play by the rules, and are getting the shaft and are scared to death and are afraid this will make it worse. But I honestly believe it will make it better. If I didn't think it would be more incomes and more jobs and better for the farmers, I wouldn't do it.

And I assure you, when I go to Japan, I'll carry the message you sent me with.

[*A participant supported improved market access through NAFTA and the GATT. Another participant suggested that the Farmers Home reserve be reopened, and Secretary Espy said that would be considered. A participant then discussed the need for adequate drainage of farmland, his view that efforts to save wetlands and ducks had gone too far, and the issue of foreclosure.*]

The President. I don't know—Iowa—is this thing on? I don't know what to say. Where I come from, we grow more rice than anybody else in the country. We're kind of interested in that market access you're talking about. And the rice land floods anyway. So our ducks don't give us that kind of trouble. I never knew I was supposed to be as hard on ducks. I may have to reassess my position on this. I'm not kidding. I mean, I'm really not. Where I come from it's a big deal, but it's not a problem because the rice land's flooded anyway at duck season.

You want to say anything about the other issue?

[*Secretary Espy discussed farm legislation planned for 1995. He announced that based upon the Presidential emergency declaration farmers would be allowed to modify their conserving use acreage and stated that farm foreclosures not presently under purview of the courts would be suspended pending review. Following his remarks, a participant asked if the farm legislation planned for 1995 would provide for increased farm subsidies which would allow farmers a profit margin.*]

The President. If I could just—Mike, you might want to say something about that, but if I could comment on that, just make two points. First of all, on the disaster issue, we're either going to have to have an adequate, reliable, comprehensive disaster program or a decent crop insurance program that works. And if we had one, we wouldn't need the other.

On the question of supports, I can tell you again, the last two farm bills I went through as the Governor, with my farmers on the receiving end of them. As you know because you're a farmer, we had a 20 percent unilateral cut in farm supports in the '90 farm bill. So American farmers have really done their part to reach out to our competitors overseas and ask them to open their markets and stop their supports.

I think it's fair to say that the '95 farm bill, at least from my point of view, since I'm in a different position now, my attitude about it is going to be determined by a couple of things, one of which is, what are these other countries doing? That is, what's it going to take for our people to make a decent living? And if other countries make an appropriate reduction so we got a fair chance to compete in a market system, well, that's one thing. If they don't, then I think we're going to have to take a completely different look at this '95 farm bill about how it's structured. And I think it's fair to say it's up in the air now, and it depends on what happens and what our competitors do. But I'm going

to be very sensitive to people like you because, you know, there's a limit below which we ought not to go in terms of how many farmers we've got in this country as long as we're the most productive in the world. It's just crazy to stay on that trend.

[*A participant suggested that the problems of fuel availability and pollution could be effectively addressed by use of ethanol.*]

The President. I agree with that. Let Mike talk a little about what we're doing.

[*Secretary Espy indicated that the USDA strongly supported the use of ethanol as a viable alternative resource.*]

The President. You know, if I might say, when that whole energy tax issue was being debated, we recommended that ethanol be exempt. And then we had an alternative that was effectively going to just take the tax out of the production sector, out of agriculture and industry altogether. But the Senate decided that rather than do that, they'd go to some more broad-based fuel tax. But if they do it in a way that's consistent with State law, it will still be okay for the farmers, I think.

[*Secretary Espy noted that during the budget process the administration had supported an exemption for ethanol production in the energy tax.*]

The President. Can we take one more question?

[*Governor Branstad said he had testified about ethanol before the Environmental Protection Agency on behalf of a coalition of Governors and expressed his concern about what position EPA would take concerning ethanol. He requested that the President watch the issue to ensure that ethanol production had an opportunity to compete.*]

The President. Yeah, I've noticed them doing that. [*Laughter*] Go ahead.

Q. President Clinton, I'm a local small businessman and employ approximately 30 people. And just to let you shift gears for a second here, can you or would you please tell me something that can alleviate my concerns about the upcoming striker bill. I'm concerned that it will be detrimental not only to the small businessmen but to the economy in general, which again is going to directly affect the farmer.

The President. Well, you know that I have expressed my support for the bill, and I knew you knew that or you wouldn't have asked the question. I don't have any idea of whether it can pass the Senate or whether it will at this time.

Here is the problem. Let's just talk about the problem. For many years the Federal law was that strikers could not be permanently replaced if they went on strike once a group voted to unionize, if the allegation behind the strike was that there had been an unfair labor practice. But if it was just an economic strike, that is, if the strikers say, "We ought to be getting a better deal than we're getting, and we're fighting over this contract," that they could be permanently replaced. That gave the management of unionized firms a little more leverage in dealing with strikes where the argument was wages and benefits instead of, "They did something wrong to us."

And it worked pretty well until the 1980's when the economy became more global and there was more pressure to keep down wages and benefits and when the public mood became decidedly more antiunion in the United States. The reason it worked pretty well is management had the right to do that under a court decision, but they never did it. I mean, it was unheard of. It never happened. For decades no strikes were just broken and people were run off on that account.

Then in the 1980's it started to happen with some significant frequency, and that's what led to the pressure for the striker replacement bill. There was almost a compromise adopted in the—and let me just say that this gentleman's question is related to something else. Very few small businesses in America are unionized. A lot of small businesses believe that maybe they'd be more of a target for a union if people thought they could strike over wages and benefits. I personally doubt that very much because of the relationships most people have with their employees in small businesses. But that's really the fear, I think, behind your question.

But where it is now is that it's passed the House. They don't have the votes in the Senate yet, and we're talking about whether they can get some sort of compromise to deal with the balance issue that I talked about. The people who are for it in the Congress—I don't mean everybody that's supporting it, but the people who are for it in the Congress have no interest in trying to make it either easier or harder than it is right now for people to organize themselves into unions. The question is whether that once the workers vote to join a union, the bargaining process plays out in a fair and balanced way.

And so I think there will be a lot of debate in the next few weeks about whether some compromise along the lines of what they were talking about last time be passed to alleviate some of the fears that you've expressed and still deal with the balance question that came up in the eighties.

[Governor Branstad expressed his appreciation for the President's visit.]

The President. Thank you very much for what you said. I'd like to say one thing in closing if I might. First, I have very much enjoyed being here, and I appreciate your taking some of your family time away on the Fourth of July to come out and visit about these farm issues.

Second thing I'd like to say is I really wish I had more time to do a little town meeting about the larger economic issues like the one the young man raised about the tax issue.

This is a very difficult time for this country. And a lot of the decisions that I have to make as President are not simple or easy. Before I became President I never raised any taxes from anybody to balance a budget or reduce a debt. I lived in a State that had a balanced budget law that made my chief budget officer a criminal if he let 3 months go by where spending outstripped revenues and where I literally had the power to cut spending once a week if I wanted to, to keep the budget in balance. And we did what we did while having one of the fifth lowest tax burdens in the country as a percentage of income. So this whole experience dealing with this deficit has been very painful to me. And I guess we split the difference, he and I did, on what we said.

When I was running for President I said that I thought we ought to raise some taxes to pay the deficit down on upper income people but that we shouldn't raise taxes on the middle class, and I meant it. When the deficit got written up $165 billion, the choice I had was to take the politically difficult decision in the short run to ask for a modest contribution from middle class folks, cut as much as I could in spending without really getting into hurting older people on Medicare or essential investments in education, and take three-quarters of the money from the top 6 percent of the income earners in the country, or stick with literally what I talked about in the campaign and risk not being able to do enough to really get interest rates down and try to get the economy going again.

It's a very tough call. It is not an easy call. But as you will see when you read in the papers about this trip I'm about to take to Japan, as tough a shape as we're in, we're doing better than Europe is. They're having negative growth. Japan's got the slowest growth they've had in 40 years. And all these people have been after us for 10 years to get our deficit down. They said, "If you'll get your deficit down, we'll do some things." And together we can grow the world economy.

So I'm doing the best I can, believe me. You may think I'm wrong, and maybe time will prove me wrong, but I'm trying to make the best decision I can to create jobs and incomes for the American people so that we come out ahead on this deal, not behind. It is a complicated, difficult time that the goal ought to be to ask every question in terms of: Is it good for jobs? Is it good for incomes? Will it help the economy to grow? Will it help people to have security and health care and educating their children and to make this a stronger and better country?

And on this, the Fourth of July, we're always going to have our partisan and philosophical differences, and that's what makes this country wonderful. But if we can always keep that goal in mind, then when we differ, at least we'll be arguing about the right things.

Thank you, and God bless you all.

NOTE: The President spoke at 8:30 p.m. at the Schneckloth farm. In his remarks, he referred to Iowa secretary of agriculture Dale M. Cochran and Iowa secretary of state Elaine Baxter.

Remarks on Departure From Moline, Illinois
July 4, 1993

I want to thank you all for coming out here and for waiting on the Fourth of July. What a wonderful gift it was for me to come back and see all of you here. I couldn't believe it.

As you know, I've been here reviewing the flood damage, meeting the families from both Illinois and Iowa. And I just wanted to tell you first of all, as someone who had grown up in a farming area and has seen this kind of flooding before, I know what it means. I know how hard it is. And we're determined to do everything we possibly can to help the farmers in this area and the communities get through it. And when I get back from my trip to Asia, we'll be pursuing further legislation in the Congress to get some more aid to your farmers and your communities so that we can recover from this and go on. And I'm really appreciative of all the time that the people in this area gave me today to make sure that I understood what was going on.

The second thing I'd like to say to you is that for all the problems this Nation has on the Fourth of July, and we've still got a lot of them—there are an awful lot of people who are worried about their jobs, the security of their health care, the education of their children, the safety of their streets—I'm about to leave to go to a meeting of the world's richest countries where they think we're doing pretty well because our unemployment rate is lower than every country in Europe, we had a million more jobs coming into our economy since the first of the year, and we're finally doing something to bring our terrible Government deficit down and to prepare for our future. And I want you to know that tomorrow when I leave and get on that plane to go to Japan, I'm going to be over there working for things that I think will help to provide jobs and incomes and opportunity and hope for the American people.

These are very difficult and challenging times for our country. A lot of the problems we face are very complicated, and we could argue all day about what the right decisions are. But I promise you this: Every day when I go to work and I fight for our economic plan, which I think is fair and which I know will work, every decision I make I ask myself, is it going to help Americans to have more jobs, better incomes, more security, and a brighter future for their children? And if we could at least ask that question—we can have all of the debates in the world—we'll keep our country going on the right track.

Don't forget this is still the greatest country in the world. And the next 20 years can be the best we ever had, if we have the courage to make the changes we've got to make to deal with all these challenges before us. I think we do. And after spending some time sitting on a bale of hay with a bunch of Iowa farm families tonight, I feel a lot better than I did when I got up this morning on this wonderful Independence Day.

Thank you all, and God bless you. And thank you for coming out.

NOTE: The President spoke at 10:36 p.m. at the Quad Cities Airport. A tape was not available for verification of the content of these remarks.

Remarks to the National Education Association in San Francisco, California
July 5, 1993

Thank you very much. Thank you for the warm reception you gave to the First Lady and to Secretary Riley. Thank you for inviting me back.

You know, last year when we were in Washington I was out in the crowd over there by the Nebraska delegation. Where are the Nebraska teachers this year, over there? And where are the teachers from Arkansas? Over there. Thank you. Always a rowdy group. [*Laughter*]

I want to thank all of you who teach our children, staff our schools, lead our communities, and build our future. I am very grateful for the support you gave in the campaign of 1992, grateful for the support and the work you continue to do as we work our way through the changes this Nation has to make in the Congress and in the country. But most of all, I want to say at the outset, what I tried to say all along the way last year: Perhaps more than any person who ever sought this job, I spent my apprenticeship in the schools of my State, in the schools of this country, listening to teachers talking with children, learning from principals, trying to inspire people everywhere to work together for reform. And I want to thank you most of all for your clear and simple devotion to the work of teaching.

While I was thinking about this speech, I received a quote from the novel, "The Prince of Tides." Secretary Riley gave it to me. I want to give him full credit. He'll probably have to take the blame for a thing or two along the way. [*Laughter*] But I love the "Prince of Tides"; it's my favorite novel I guess I've read in the last decade or so. And the main character

is a teacher named Tom. There's a passage in the book that I remember vividly where he's asked why he chose to, quote, "sell himself short" when he was so talented and he could have done anything with his life. He replied, and I quote from Pat Conroy's eloquence: "There's no word in the language I revere more than 'teacher'. My heart sings when a kid refers to me as his teacher, and it always has. I've honored myself and the entire family of man by becoming a teacher."

I am delighted to be here with so many distinguished Californians, in addition to the teachers: Senator Boxer, Congresswoman Pelosi, Congressman Lantos, Congresswoman Anna Eshoo, Congresswoman Lynn Woolsey, Speaker Willie Brown, controller Gray Davis, secretary of state March Fong Eu, insurance commissioner John Garamendi, Mayor Frank Jordan, Brad Sherman, and many others. To all those folks who are here in our administration and to Keith Geiger and all the people who work for you in Washington, I have a special word of thanks to the NEA for the gift of our Assistant Secretary for the Office of Education and Research and Improvement, Dr. Sharon Robinson, who is also here today.

For the past 5 months all of us have been working hard with you to change our country and to build our future. The film that you so graciously put together shows some of the progress that has been made; the family leave bill; the motor voter bill; a tough ethics set of rules for the executive branch; one House of Congress having already passed finally a lobby reform bill that requires all lobbyists to register and to report what they spend on Members of Congress; and a campaign finance reform bill that lowers the cost of campaigns and opens the airwaves to honest debate and reduces the influence of organized groups; a new environmental policy, which puts the United States at the head, instead of at the rear of the environmental movement that is sweeping the globe. We did reverse the gag rule and the ban on fetal tissue research, which was undermining diabetes and Parkinson's and other medical research so critical to the health and the welfare and the future of the United States.

There is much more to be done. Soon we will pass the economic program. Soon we will begin in earnest an attempt to provide health security and to control health care costs and to provide quality health care to every American family. Soon we will have the Vice President's recommendations on how we can literally reinvent our National Government so that we can reduce the amount of regulation and increase the empowerment we give to people at the local level and free up funds not only to bring our deficit down but to invest in people instead of the constant expansion of yesterday's Government.

These things are very important. And already, in spite of the fact that most Americans are still having a very tough time and are very insecure in this tough global economy, the fact that our economic program is two-thirds home has led to a dramatic reduction in interest rates, which has caused millions of people to refinance their home mortgages and save them a whole lot more money in lower interest than the middle class will be asked to pay to bring this deficit down and leave us some modest funds to invest in education and our future.

We have already seen in 5 months nearly one million jobs added to this economy. It is not enough. It is nowhere near where we should be coming out of the so-called bottom of the recession, now nearly 2 years ago. But it is a beginning, and it indicates that we are moving along the right track.

In a few hours I will be traveling to Tokyo to attend the annual summit of the world's largest industrial nations. A foreign summit with all of its protocol, its interpreters, its communiques, seems awfully remote to most Americans' lives and probably seems remote to the work most of you do in our schools. But in fact, the work that I will be doing in the next

few days and the work that you do every day are closely related, for we have entered an era where the line between our domestic policy and our foreign policy has completely evaporated.

Today I want to take a few moments to explain to you what this trip is about, how it relates to what you do, and the goals that we all share for our country. Like your work in the schools, this trip is about crafting our future. Its goals are our prosperity and security in a tough global economy.

Forty-five years ago at the end of the cold war, President Harry Truman and a generation of visionary leaders realized we had entered a new age that demanded new policies and new institutions. They built NATO to deter Soviet aggression. They created international financial institutions to help to rebuild Europe and Japan and promote global economic growth.

Now our generation after the cold war must create a new vision, new policies, and new agreements to enable the world's nations to prosper. We cannot long continue to promote democracy when Europe is having the slowest economic growth in 20 years, Japan facing the slowest economic growth in four decades, and America over 3 million jobs behind where we ought to be at this point in our development, still with the strongest economy of all these industrialized nations. We can do better, and we must. You think about every one of your schools with every financial problem you've got. If every American who wanted a job had one, and we were growing this economy, the money would be there to pay our teachers, to invest in our schools, to give our kids a better life.

A generation ago, our students prepared themselves for a working world dominated by large corporations and heavy manufacturing industries which competed with each other and the United States, but suffered no foreign competitors and could dominate the international markets they chose to enter. Today they enter a high-tech information revolution spearheaded by flexible entrepreneurial firms, both large and small, that are networked through computers with their suppliers and their customers all around the world. They enter a world where everybody's job, directly or indirectly, is affected by global competition. In this economy, money and management and technology are incredibly mobile, and a nation's well-being depends largely on the skills of its work force and the capacity of the people to adapt and be productive.

A generation ago, students planned for lifetime careers with one company. Today's graduates can expect to change jobs six or seven times in a lifetime, even if they stay with one company. Before they reach retirement, always in conjunction with other workers in the world, they will be in constant competition. And we must face the hard fact that many of the people with whom we compete for the high-wage, high-growth jobs are uniformly more thoroughly prepared to begin their work than our people are.

The European Community will require fluency in two foreign languages for high school graduates by the year 2000. Germany has one of the most well-developed youth apprenticeship programs in the world. The rigor of Japan's public school system is legendary. We know that we, too, have our strengths, and we know that we, too, are challenged in ways that no other nation is. No other nation with which we compete for this future has so many diverse cultures, so many diverse ethnic groups, so many diverse religious groups, and so many poor children that we are trying to educate all the way through high school. No other nation has anything like the system of higher education that we do, and we should be proud of that as well.

But if you look at the challenges we face, if you look at the results faced here in California by big companies and trying to secure qualified employees, if you look at the challenges faced by the children that go to school in this State in some of the toughest neighborhoods in America every day, we still have to say that these things can be challenges to us, but they can never be excuses. For the global economy is here to stay. We can't wish it away. We can't hide from it, and no political leader can promise to protect you from it. We simply have to compete, not retreat, and we have to do it while maintaining our position of world leadership. That means your job and my job are fundamentally intertwined. And unless we both do it very well, this country cannot be what it ought to be.

Now, there are people who believe that the situation is all bad and that our best days are behind us, and we're not going to do what we need to do. I think they're dead wrong. We are better positioned for this new world than most people think. The new economy is built on information and innovation. We are an innovative people with a passion for information technology that dates all the way back to the

first telegraph and the first telephone and is found today in millions of American homes.

The new global economy is built on flexibility and constant change. We are a people whose open society and open political system embrace change more energetically than any other nation. The new global economy is based on interacting and doing business with the people all over the world, understanding their economies, their societies, and their languages. We are a nation of immigrants. We have two centuries of experience in building bridges across the lines of race and religion and culture. One county in this State has people from 150 different racial and ethnic groups. We can meet the challenges of the global economy, and we will.

This new economy is based on high productivity. And after faltering in the seventies and the early eighties, our productivity growth is once again making America the high-quality, low-cost producer in many areas. American automobiles in the last year have been regaining market share in the United States, something people thought would never happen. Why? Because they're the best cars at the most reasonable price. And we can do that in many other areas.

Of course, we have problems. We still lose a stunning number of our children to poverty, to drugs, to violence. Too many of them simply never learn enough to compete and win. Too many, indeed, can barely function in a highly organized and flexible society.

For more than a decade, our policies ignored these problems. We ran up huge deficits, not to invest in our children and our future but huge deficits that mortgaged our future, weakened our economy. And all the while we actually reduced our investments in education and technology and the things that make a country strong. We mortgaged our future by rewarding speculation over savings, by cutting taxes on the wealthy while we raised them on the middle class, by failing to invest in those things which really count in the long run.

But we are turning that around. We are getting our house in order. We are putting the steel back into our competitive edge. But the job that the President has in doing this is no different than the job you have faced in your classroom hundreds, indeed, thousands of times if you've been a teacher long enough. A lot of people don't want to hear what you have to say, to do what it takes to learn what they need to know. [*Applause*] Thank you.

How many times have you been in a classroom when you had to say something that was genuinely challenging and tough to a single student or to a whole class, and they would simply resist and resist and resist it. That's what's going on in this country today, isn't it? Our people have been told what they wanted to hear for so long, instead of what it really takes to make it, that there is a natural resistance, one which I understand and do not begrudge. For 12 years, voters have been spoon-fed pablum. They've been told that there was a free ride. There was a free ride. If only if we would cut somebody else's program, if only we would blame someone else, you can have it all. You can have your lower taxes and all the projects you want, and we'll just cut it somewhere else.

Well, the people of California know better. They know that we had to and we should welcome the opportunity to cut defense spending at the end of the cold war. But that means tough choices like closing bases and reducing contracts. And if there is no plan to invest in the people that are left behind, then an awful lot of unfair harm will be done. So if you're going to make the tough decision, you have to level with the people, and then forge ahead to try to make something good happen.

But I've heard all these siren songs about how "it's spending, stupid." Well, let me tell you something: In our budget, which cuts $500 billion from the deficit, half of it comes from spending cuts. We have a hard freeze on domestic spending over the next 5 years, even though we spend more money in some things you and I care about. We reduced defense spending as much as we should, and we have pushed the limit of that. We have cut and cut and cut the entitlements. We have cut the discretionary programs. We have cut the defense programs.

And when this program came up in the Senate Finance Committee, a fair program that raises 75 percent of its money from the top 6 percent of the income-earners whose taxes were reduced in the 1980's, and has $250 billion in spending cuts, over 100 cuts of $100 million or more—let me ask you a question that you can take home to the classroom of your community: The other side who kept screaming to America, "This is a tax-and-spend program, and the only problem is spending," had their chance to offer spending cuts in the Senate Finance Committee. How many spending cuts do you suppose they offered over and above the tough cuts that I had taken out of agriculture and veterans and every other program? Zero, that's how many. You couldn't find them when it got to be specific.

Let me tell you, for every $10 of deficit reduction in this plan designed to get interest rates down and spur growth, $5 comes from spending cuts; $3.75 from the upper 6 percent of American earners, as I said, whose taxes were lowered in the 1980's; $1.25 comes from the great middle class with incomes of between $30,000 and $100,000. Families under $30,000 are held harmless, and for the first time in the history of this country, if this program passes, people who work 40 hours a week and have children in their homes will be lifted out of poverty. That's the best incentive to get off and stay off welfare I ever heard. That's what's in this plan, and those are the facts.

I challenge you to embrace this issue with exuberance and joy and optimism. The only thing I question about the end of that beautiful film was when everybody said, "We've got to stick with the President, and it's hard to change." It was almost like a burden to carry. This is like teaching a new class to your students. This is no big deal. America will change if somebody will tell the people the truth instead of giving them the same old pablum.

In spite of all the cutbacks, this budget does invest more, in Head Start, in immunizations, in family preservation, in college loans, in national service tuition grants, in school-to-work transition, in defense conversion, to help all those people in the Bay area that are going to lose their jobs because of base closings, and in new technologies to create new jobs for the 21st century to take up for all the defense cuts. It sure does, but we still maintain a freeze on overall spending for 5 years because we've cut so much out of other things.

Now, those are the facts. We need your help to get them out. But most importantly, we need America's help to put this country on the right track. This deficit is like a bone in our throat. It is keeping us from investing in our people, in our growth, and in our future. And you can help to take it out by explaining to the American people what the facts are. This is not about labels and slogans. This is not about tax and spend. It's not about borrow and spend, either, which is what we've been doing for the last 12 years.

And it is not enough to reform our economic

system. We must reform our schools, our welfare system, our health system, and our political system. We have to be about that, too. And we are. We have to do something for all these people who have been hurt by the base closings and the defense contract cutbacks. Here in the Bay area, the people here took the hardest lick from this, the third round of our base closures. They and the people in South Carolina and the people in a part of New York were hardest hit. It is wrong for us not to do something for them. So we propose to spend over the next 4 years $5 billion to speed up the environmental cleanup, to give preference to job-creating strategies around these base closings, to train people, to empower communities, to let people rebuild their lives in a new peace-oriented society where we still value the people who won the cold war. It is worth the money. We have to do that.

Now, what has all that got to do with education, and what has all that got to do with what I'm about to do? That is what I want to say to you in the last portion of my remarks.

I am leaving when I leave you to go to Tokyo to the G–7 summit. This will strengthen my hand, the progress we are making on the economic program. And every one of you, in lobbying your Members of Congress to support it, have helped that. Why will it strengthen my hand? Because for years American Presidents have gone to these meetings, and they have complained that other countries should open their markets to American goods, that other countries should trade with us more fairly. Do you know what the American Presidents have been told? "Don't talk to us about that. Your deficit is so big it is distorting the global economy. It is mandating your big trade deficit. Your Government deficit is messing up the whole works. Don't tell us to change until you change." Well, guess what? I'm going to be able to go for the first time in a decade and say, "We are changing. Now you must change, too. Work with us. Let's put some jobs back into this global economy. We can create more jobs and have more economic growth if we can open everybody's markets and if we can coordinate our economic policies." And now we'll be able to say, "You've been asking us to do this for 10 years. Here we are. Now help. Let's do it."

We cannot grow unless all the world grows. I will say again, Japan has its lowest rate of growth in decades. Europe has its lowest rate

of growth in 20 years. Since 1987, over two-thirds of our new jobs have come from exports. Somebody has to be able to buy from us in order to create jobs that way. This is very important. And by helping us to pass the economic program, you have made a contribution to that.

I also want to say to you very frankly that I am going to challenge the other countries to work with us in a new cooperative effort to tackle the most troubling problem of this new era, and that is the stubbornly high rates of unemployment, even in times of economic growth. Even in times of economic growth. There are European nations that have had big economic growth and have still not been able to get their unemployment rate down below 9 percent.

We're supposed to have been out of the bottom of our recession 2 years ago. And yes, we have nearly a million jobs in the first 5 months of this year, but we're still over 3 million behind where we ought to be based on historical trends. This is a global crisis. The wealthy countries, even when they become more productive, even when they grow, are having trouble creating new jobs. We need to know why. We need to ask new questions, and we need to find new answers. We have to do this. We owe it to you, to your families, and to the future of this country.

Today I am announcing that I have asked my top economic and labor advisers to invite their counterparts from all these nations to come to the United States in the next few months to a meeting in which we search for the causes and possible answers for this stubbornly high unemployment. There are things each of us can do within our Nation, and we do it together, that will help us not just to grow the economy but to ensure that economic growth means more jobs for Americans and more jobs for the world. That is the way we have to do this, and this is a very important advance in the dialog going on among these countries. We've never really discussed this issue before, and we have to face it. I have called several of the other leaders of these other countries, and they are very enthusiastic because they're just as frustrated as I am that no matter what they seem to do for their economy, the jobs aren't coming along. And I will say again, if everybody in every one of your communities who wanted to work had a job, we wouldn't have half the problems we do today.

Finally, I want to emphasize in this area one other issue. I'm not just going to a meeting of the top industrialized nations, I'm taking my first foreign trip to Asia, to send a message that the Asian Pacific region has a very important role to play in your future. After the summit in Tokyo—thank you—[*laughter*]—I'm going to Korea as well. This region today is absolutely bursting with energy and growth. Already, over 40 percent of our trade is with the Asian Pacific region. Last year it exceeded $120 billion and accounted for almost 2½ million American jobs.

Along with Europe and the Western Hemisphere, Asia is where we must find much of our growth in the next few years. In recent years, when we looked across the Pacific, we focused on our trade difficulties with Japan. Well, the trade deficit with Japan is real, unacceptable, and we're working very hard to take some steps with Japan to deal with that. But our relationships with the Pacific for the most part are good for us, and we will benefit from them.

We must never forget how much we've already benefited from all the immigrants who have come to this Nation, many of them to this State, from all the nations of Asia. We can build on that for a brighter future.

I want to lay out ways in which we can make our relationship with Japan, with Korea, and with these other nations stronger. I hope we will have a new global agreement on more open trade before the end of the year. I hope we can coordinate our efforts with these countries because when we do that, it really affects jobs in your community.

These kinds of policies are important, but they're not sufficient, and that's where you come in. Our policies can open the door to new opportunities for the American people, but whether they can walk through the door depends on whether they are educated and trained for the new global economy. Without the knowledge, without the skills, without the temperament, without the drive to capitalize on opportunities, America will still not be what it ought to be.

One hundred years ago our Nation's wealth was based on raw materials. Fifty years ago it was based on the huge capacity we had for mass production. Today it's based on what our people know and what they can learn. That's why the very best investment we can make is in the one resource that remains firmly rooted within our borders, the people who live in the United States of America.

When I was a boy, education was touted, as it always has been, as America's great equalizer. It is still that. But today, it is America's great energizer as well, the best change agent we can possibly have. It binds us together, it draws our youngsters in, it moves them ahead, it builds their self-worth, it instills a sense of pride and civic responsibility. America's public schools have been the cornerstones of progress for over two centuries, from the little red schoolhouses, to land grant colleges, to hundreds of community colleges that gave the children of working parents a chance to make something of themselves. We have seen what education can do.

Now there are school-to-work programs launched in cities and suburbs and rural districts around the country that are giving people the real chance to compete for a lifetime. And now I go into educational settings, and I see people in their twenties, their thirties, their forties, their fifties, their sixties, sometimes their seventies, learning anew for the challenges and opportunities they face.

You know better than anyone else the immense challenges that you face in our schools because they have such ambitious goals and such difficult and challenging obstacles. No other nation, as I said before, tries to teach so many students from so many backgrounds and cultures and languages. You shoulder our country's hardest and most important work. That's why we need to make sure that you and your schools are ready for the 21st century. That's what the national education goals are all about, to ensure that every child enters school ready to learn, to get rid of drugs and violence and make our schools safe. Several weeks ago, our administration's "Safe Schools Act" was introduced into the House and the Senate. It is a good beginning. We cannot expect the students of this country to reach high achievement when their very safety or the safety of their teachers is in danger.

In safe schools, we can make sure our students know what they need to know. We can make sure that our students lead the world in math and science achievement. We can make sure that we can compete in the global economy and live in the global village. As I head overseas, I'm reminded how much more we need to do. We need to give our students a thirst for exploration and a sense of widening horizons. As one college president puts it, we need to acquire global literacy. Our students need to understand not only the meaning of democracy but the spirit of Japanese culture and the richness of African history. We need them to know more about foreign languages than just how to order in a restaurant. Foreign languages in this era aren't simply a sign of refinement, they are a survival tool for America in the global economy.

And while I have said repeatedly all across this country, the magic of education is what occurs in the classroom and what the parents give if they do their job, it is still clear that your National Government has a role to play and must be your partner. Our job is to provide leadership, to set standards, to offer incentives that will help States and local school systems chart their own path to excellence with responsibility and accountability from all in the system. Most of all, we can do that if we are your partners. And I believe that the president of this organization would say we have had the partnership I promised in the campaign of 1992, and we will continue to have it through the work of Secretary Riley and Secretary Reich at the Labor Department and our entire Cabinet. We want the teachers of America to be the engines of reform. And we are convinced that they will be.

Our education agenda is ambitious, and its heart is Goals 2000, which enshrines into law the national education goals and world-class standards. We must reach them by the turn of the century. The legislation we need to make it happen, enshrining Goals 2000, is awaiting action now in both Houses of Congress. It has bipartisan support, thanks in large measure to the Herculian efforts of the Secretary of Education.

Goals 2000 will give parents and students and teachers a clear assessment of classroom performance. It will encourage schools to be more creative in organizing classrooms, training teachers, and motivating students. It will help students to prepare for work after graduation. It will provide funding to support the reform efforts that are blossoming all across America. It will mean that the investments we propose to make in Head Start and other early childhood programs, like immunization, will actually be able to bear fruits so that the gains from preschool will be able to be made permanent instead of being lost if we have the right sort of goals and the right sort of standards and the right sort of partnership and support. That

is what we seek through Goals 2000.

I intend to fight hard for this bill's passage. And I intend to fight hard against anything that will water it down, weaken it, or divert it from its essential mission: partnerships with people at the State and local level. We cannot run the schools of this country from Washington, DC. We need to empower you to run them.

I also want to mention our school-to-work initiative. Today half of America's young people don't go on to college. We know from now the census data in the 1980's that every high school graduate who gets at least 2 years of post-high school education at least has a decent chance to get a good job with a growing income, and that every high school graduate with less than 2 years of post-high school education or every person who drops out of high school has an excellent chance of being unemployed or getting a job with a declining income. I think it is clear what our course should be. Every student ought to finish high school, every high school graduate ought to have at least 2 years of school-to-work transitional education and training so they can successfully learn for a lifetime. That has to be our objective. Our legislation forges a remarkable and heretofore unprecedented partnership between the Departments of Education and the Department of Labor and then working with people at the local level. We must do this.

This is not a controversial issue. It may never blister across the headlines of America. But I'm telling you, if we want to raise the per capita income of Americans, we've got to make every worker literate, we've got to make everybody have the equivalent of a high school degree, and we've got to give people the chance to get at least 2 years of further training. That will raise incomes and increase jobs in the United States.

Now, my fellow Americans, as I leave you and head off to Japan, I want to say again that there is a common challenge that spans your work and mine. For the challenge we face in the global economy is about more than interest rates and trade balances. And the challenge you face in your own classrooms is about more than discrete subjects and SAT test scores. The fundamental question of our time involves a matter of national character, the question of whether we will apply our heritage and values to the demands of a new and rigorous time. I am confident of the answer. I am concerned still that so many of our people seem to lack the same confidence. I know life is tough for most Americans, as much because it is uncertain as because of the real difficulties of the moment. But both are real. Still there is no nation with more resilience, more creativity, more love for freedom and devotion to progress than the United States. So now it is time once again to show what we are made of.

Yesterday in Philadelphia on the 217th anniversary of the United States, I had the astonishing experience of being an American President sitting in the middle of the President of South Africa and the president of the African National Congress, the President of a nation once known as the most vociferous symbol of apartheid in the world and the man who had been the symbol of the struggle against apartheid, having lingered for 27 years in jail as a political prisoner there together to receive in common a political medal from the founding city of the United States of America because they put their differences behind them, agreed on elections, agreed on a nonracial democracy. And by next year we will have that in South Africa. Now, that, that is a symbol. That is a symbol of what people can do when they suspend their cynicism

and they suspend their bitterness and they overcome their difficulties and they act on their beliefs. And what has that got to do with us? Because what is bringing them together are democratic ideals forged in the American Constitution, a commitment to a bill of rights like the American Bill of Rights to protect the rights of minorities as well as majorities and to enable people who are different to live in peace and to pursue progress.

If we can inspire that in that country, how can we not still be a nation of builders and believers here at home. You and I are joined in common cause, and I believe we will succeed. You in the classroom and me in my classroom. And so, now I go abroad grateful for your support, grateful for your commitment to our children, and more confident than ever that together we can do our jobs and make life for all Americans what it ought to be.

God bless you, and God bless America.

NOTE: The President spoke at 10:02 a.m. at the Moscone Center. In his remarks, he referred to Brad Sherman, chairman of the State Board of Equalization, and Keith Geiger, president, National Education Association.

The President's News Conference With Prime Minister Kiichi Miyazawa of Japan in Tokyo
July 6, 1993

Prime Minister Miyazawa. I'm sorry to have kept you waiting. Now I would like to lead off with a brief explanation. I would like to, first of all, extend my warmest welcome to President Clinton and his entourage. And it also is, I believe, most meaningful that President Clinton has chosen Asia as the first overseas visit this time. Of course, his visit is for the summit meeting as well, but he will meet with President Soeharto of Indonesia as well. And I had mentioned, therefore, that I very highly rate the fact that he has visited Asia this time and made the Japan-U.S. leaders meeting as well.

Our relations, the Japan-U.S. relations are built on three pillars: security, global cooperation, and our bilateral economy. In April we said in Washington that we should be establishing a framework for our economy, and both

of us at the working level had been working on this, but time had lapsed. So I sent a personal letter to President Clinton, and today I also received a very kind response to that personal letter. And we wanted on a working level to expedite their work on this matter as quickly as possible. And at the working level, both sides are working. Both of us are determined that a proper framework must be put in place.

And in the summit meetings starting tomorrow, we've agreed that we shall cooperate with each other in bringing the summit meeting to a success.

Mr. President, please.

The President. Thank you very much. First of all, it's very good to see Prime Minister Miyazawa again. We had a fine meeting in Washington in April at the White House, and

I was honored to have the opportunity to come here and meet with the Prime Minister before the beginning of the G–7 summit.

It bears repeating again that the United States has no more important bilateral relationship than our relationship with Japan. We are strategic allies and our futures are bound up together. We have one of the world's most important trading partnerships. We have an array of regional and global alliances. And our historic relationship, as it undergoes change, must also maintain some continuity. I have invested a lot in both the change and the continuity because I think they are terribly important. And I was glad to have the opportunity to discuss a wide range of issues with the Prime Minister today.

We discussed the need for a successful conclusion to the Uruguay round and our hope that we can agree, among the G–7 leaders, on market access, on a range of manufacturing products. We discussed the need to coordinate economic strategies of the world's wealthiest economies in the hope of restoring some growth and job opportunities to our own people and to the global economy.

We discussed the issue which the Prime Minister mentioned on the framework of our own relationships, and I'll have a little more to say about that. But before I do, I want to say something about our security relationship which too often is overlooked.

I emphasized to the Prime Minister that the United States intends to maintain our forward military presence, our presence in Japan, our presence in Korea, and our security agreements in this area. We intend to maintain a full engagement in this region. We discussed some of the difficulties that we face here, but we feel confident, looking toward the future, that our security partnership, which has kept us free of war and which has maintained a strict nonproliferation approach in this region, can continue, and we hope that it will.

I also expressed my support for the extraordinary work Japan has done in supporting the process of reconciliation in Cambodia, in supporting United Nations efforts in Somalia and elsewhere. And I also want to say how much I appreciate the support that Japan has given to the efforts the United States has made with the G–7 to support democracy and market reforms in Russia. I believe that we will see a very positive outcome to those common efforts here at the G–7 meeting.

The primary focus of our relationship was strengthening the economic relationships between our two nations. We are moving away, I hope, from continued tension toward greater shared benefits. The changes I seek in our relationship are not changes that I hope will benefit the United States at the expense of Japan but changes that I believe will benefit the people of both nations. We discussed this back in April. We discussed it again today.

As the Prime Minister said, we reaffirmed our belief in the importance of creating a framework and establishing basic principles for our trading relationships. I remain convinced that we can conclude an important agreement on this issue. The negotiations have not been free of difficulty, but frankly, some significant progress has been made. And we agreed in our private meeting that our respective sides would continue to work in good faith and with real intensity during the next few days to see what we can do.

The best way we can strengthen our historic friendship, as we must, is to make our trade and investment genuinely in the best interests of the peoples of both countries. I hope we will have more trade, not less, more openness, more growth, and more jobs in both Japan and the United States. And I believe we can achieve that with the proper framework.

Finally, let me say that it's a great pleasure for Mrs. Clinton and I both to be back here in Japan. I came here several times when I was a Governor. I suppose, Mr. Prime Minister, I won't have quite the freedom of movement that I once enjoyed as a more private citizen, but on the other hand, I'm being treated to an enormous amount of Japanese hospitality, for which the United States is very grateful, and I look forward to the next few days.

Prime Minister Miyazawa. Thank you very much. Now questions, please.

Framework Agreement

Q. I would like to ask this question of both leaders. I understand from your remarks just now that you have not reached an agreement on the framework which is a matter of focus. I wonder, on these matters of great contention between Japan and the United States like the setting of targets with reduction of surplus, or on the Japanese side, there is a compromise idea for specific sectors, and I wonder if there has been any move closer to each other. If so, how far have you been able to move to each other?

Prime Minister Miyazawa. Well, if you asked, we not reached any agreement, that is wrong. Over the past several days, I myself, and President Clinton have exchanged letters and through that process, the working level of both sides, setting the target of the summit, decided to finalize our work. And that exercise was conducted very intensively, and that effort is continuing.

The President. Let me say that I agree with what the Prime Minister said. Late last week, after the sides had concluded the last round of negotiations without an agreement, the Prime Minister took the initiative and sent me a very thoughtful letter which reached out across the gap between our two positions. I then responded to that letter, and we concluded that both sides should go back to the table. That is where they are.

Differences remain, but enough progress has been made that we believe they should continue to work during this critical period, and that is what they will do. And we have hopes. We don't want to raise false hopes, but we have hopes.

Q. Mr. President, in light of the possible pending changes in the Japanese Government, how crucial is it that this framework is reached at this summit? And how likely do you think that would be? And if I could also ask the Prime Minister if he could help Americans understand what the difficulty is that the Japanese have with the idea of numerical targets.

The President. Well, let me say, if we can get an agreement, the sooner we get it the better. I have been very impressed over the last several days with the terrific amount of energy and engagement that Prime Minister Miyazawa has personally brought to these negotiations and to the openness with which we have discussed these issues and the clear willingness of the Japanese Government and the Prime Minister himself to reach an agreement if we can in good conscience.

There are still issues which divide us. Even if we make an agreement, there will be some issues which divide us. But our purpose is to make progress in dealing with the enormous trade imbalances and also with dealing with the need for our two countries to integrate our economic relationship so that both sides can benefit more. And I believe that it is possible. Conven-

tional wisdom would have it that it would not be possible at such a political moment, but the Prime Minister has defied conventional wisdom. That does not mean that we will get an agreement. We don't know that yet. But at least we are trying, and that's I think a great credit to him.

Prime Minister Miyazawa. Well, both of our countries have a market economy. And even if the government wants to do this or that, that cannot be translated into reality in a market economy. That is what market economy is about.

Now, it is true that the Japanese current account surplus is too large, and we would like to somehow reduce this—work hard at reducing it. There is no doubt about it. But when it comes to suggesting that this surplus should be down to a certain percentage of GDP, you can't control GDP itself. And also since the world trade is free trade, you cannot determine exports and imports. We cannot control either the denominator or the numerator. Therefore, we cannot do that. That's a very simple reason.

Any question from the Japanese side?

Japanese Elections

Q. I would like to ask this question of President Clinton, a question on Japanese politics. In your press conference in Washington, DC, I think you expressed some hope and expectations for Japanese politics. Does that contain your expectations for a change in government? I wonder what sort of expectations do you have of Japanese politics?

The President. First let me say I wish I had been able to answer the previous question a little bit. We have a slight difference of view on that. But my views on the trade issue I think are well-known to the lady in orange. So there's no point in bringing them up again.

I'm glad you asked the question about Japanese politics. The United States takes no position, and I take no personal position on how the people of Japan should vote or will vote. That is a matter for them to decide. What I said and what I believe is that no matter how the vote comes out in terms of the distribution of party preferences for seats in the Diet, this is a period of change and ferment in Japan. It is a period of change and ferment in the United States. It could hardly be otherwise. There is a global crisis of slow growth in the wealthiest countries. There is a global crisis of job growth in the wealthiest countries. Many wealthy countries, even when they have economic growth, are not now creating new jobs.

There is a global feeling among all the democracies of the world that there ought to be more political reform. There is a thirst for political reform in my country, in Japan, in South Korea, in virtually every major democracy in the world. So you see these trends developing around the world.

The point I wanted to make is that, no matter whether the LDP wins the election or there is some different or modified result—however it comes out, this is already a period of change in Japan, and I would hope that that would be viewed with hope and not with fear by the Japanese people. That is a part of the process of democracy, and we can make it a good thing in your country as we are attempting to make it a good thing in ours.

North Korea

Q. Mr. President, last week in an interview with columnists in Washington, you expressed your worst nightmare in Asian security questions would be a North Korea that would have the bomb and be willing to use it. And your second worst nightmare was a Pacific arms race that could lead to—you used the example of development of a nuclear capability by Japan. Could you explain how you feel that might be brought about? And, Prime Minister Miyazawa, would you explain whether you believe that's ever possible under any circumstances, please?

The President. Well, the two were related. I don't think it would ever happen in the absence of the development of nuclear capacity

by North Korea and some retrenchment by the United States.

I want to say again, the United States has no intention at this moment or in the future of weakening its security ties in the Pacific, not to Japan, not to South Korea. We intend to stay engaged, and the security commitments we have given with regard to nuclear and defense issues to Japan are as strong today as they have ever been. And they will so remain.

I very much want North Korea to stay in the NPT and to fully comply with all the requirements of doing so. I think it is in the interest of North Korea to do so. I just simply was recognizing the fact that if North Korea did not do that, that would create a lot of difficulty and concern here in Japan. Whatever North Korea does, the United States will honor its commitments to our allies and friends in this region on the nuclear issue and on security issues generally.

Prime Minister Miyazawa. For Japan, if the people's Democratic Republic of Korea acquire nuclear weapons and also acquires launch capability, that in itself would be a direct threat. It will be a direct threat for Japan. I'm sure you will understand that. We have, obviously, no intention of producing nuclear weapons, and therefore, we will—and definitely we'd be very concerned if we are to be exposed to that sort of threat.

Thank you very much for the press conference.

NOTE: The President's 19th news conference began at 6:04 p.m. at the Iikura House.

Remarks at a Reception for Japanese Leaders in Tokyo
July 6, 1993

Thank you very much. On behalf of Hillary and myself, I want to say how glad we are to be in Japan and how much we appreciate Ambassador and Mrs. Armacost inviting all of you to come here and to meet us.

I want to keep my remarks brief because I hope we can have more time for personal visiting. I do want you to know that I just had a very good meeting with Prime Minister Miyazawa, and we discussed a whole range of

issues. I would say, the most important are that I was able to reaffirm the commitment of the United States to the security relationship that exists between our two nations and the continuing involvement of the United States in a security relationship in Japan and Korea and across a whole broad range of issues that face us as a people.

Secondly, we had a good discussion about our efforts at the upcoming G–7 summit to promote a higher rate of economic growth throughout the globe, to open more markets to trade through the Uruguay round, and finally, to try to secure a democracy and market reforms in Russia, something that Japan has been very helpful to the United States on and for which we are very grateful.

And lastly, we discussed negotiations which are still ongoing in our attempt to establish a framework of basic principles for a new agreement about our trading relationships. Perhaps we can have more to say about that in our personal conversations.

The United States thinks it is absolutely critical for the imbalances to be reduced. We think it is in the interest of both countries for that to happen. We have worked very hard in our Nation on increasing our productivity and our ability to compete in the last several years. And now, as you know, we are taking very, very strong steps to do what our Japanese friends have asked us for years to do, which is to bring down our Government's deficit.

So we come here with an outstretched hand

and the hope that all of the ferment and change and political debate going on in Japan will be a very positive thing for your people and for our relationship. Many of the issues you're debating from political reform to economic issues are also being debated in our country and, frankly, in most other advanced democracies. I think this period of change should be viewed by all of us with hope, with the view that we're going to make something very good come out of it, not only in the election process but in the aftermath.

And there is no more important relationship to the United States than our relationship with Japan. And I intend to keep it on a firm footing, and I hope that our relationship with all of you will contribute to that and, most importantly, to the welfare of the people of Japan and the people of the United States.

Thank you very much.

NOTE: The President spoke at 6:42 p.m. at the residence of U.S. Ambassador Michael H. Armacost.

Remarks and a Question-and-Answer Session at Waseda University in Tokyo
July 7, 1993

The President. Thank you very much. Mr. President, thank you for that introduction, I foolishly came out here without my earphones, so I don't know what he said to make you laugh—[*laughter*]—or what he said about Robert Kennedy. So I should give a speech about how we need to train more Americans to speak good Japanese. Perhaps someday an American President will come here and give a speech to you in your native language. Then I will know we are really making progress in reaching across the barriers that divide us.

It is a great pleasure for me and for the First Lady to be here at this distinguished university today. Waseda is a center of true academic excellence and a training ground for many of Japan's most distinguished leaders. I am proud to be the first American President to visit here.

But as has already been said, 31 years ago another American, whom I admired very much,

Robert Kennedy, spoke in this hall. It was a very different time. The modern economies of Japan and Asia were just emerging. It was the middle of the cold war. Fierce arguments raged here, as in other nations, about where the future lay, with communism or democracy, with socialism or capitalism. On that evening in 1962, those arguments spilled onto this stage. When members of the student Communist movement heckled Robert Kennedy, he challenged their leader to come up and join him. In his characteristic way, Kennedy transformed a diatribe into a dialog and close-mindedness into an open debate.

That is what I hope we will have here today. The exchange that followed was heated, but it demonstrated the best of the values of freedom and democracy that our two nations share. Three decades later, on this day, in this place, the times are very different, but no less challenging. The need for vigorous and open dialog remains. The time has come for America to join with Japan and others in this region to create a new Pacific community. And this, to be sure, will require both of our nations to lead and both of our nations to change.

The new Pacific community will rest on a revived partnership between the United States and Japan, on progress toward more open economies and greater trade, and on support for democracy. Our community must also rest on the firm and continuing commitment of the United States to maintain its treaty alliances and its forward military presence in Japan and Korea and throughout this region.

Is it appropriate? I believe it is, to address these issues here in Japan. The post-cold-war relationship between our two nations is one of the great success stories of the latter half of the 20th century. We have built a vital friendship. We continue to anchor this region's security and to fuel its development. Japan is an increasingly important global partner in peacekeeping, in promoting democracy, in protecting the environment, in addressing major challenges in this region and throughout the world. Because our relationship has been built on enduring common interests and genuine friendship, it has transcended particular leaders in each country, and it will continue to do so.

History has decided the debate that waged here in 1962, a debate over whether communism works. It didn't. Its ruins litter the world stage. Our two nations have proved that capitalism works, that democracy works, that freedom works. Still, no system is perfect. New problems and challenges constantly arise. Old problems deeply rooted in cultures and prejudices remain. To make the most of this new world, we both must change. As Robert Kennedy once noted, "Progress is a nice word, but its motivator is change, and change has its enemies."

The cold war passed from the world stage as the global flow of information pierced the Iron Curtain with news of other ways of living. And the world moved steadily toward a more integrated global economy. Money, management, and technology are increasingly mobile today. Trillions of dollars in capital traverse the globe every day. In one generation international trade has nearly tripled as a percentage of global output. In the late 1980's, increased trade accounted for well over half of the new jobs in the United States.

Meanwhile there have been huge changes in the organization and the nature of work itself. We are moving away from an economy based on standardized mass production to one dominated by an explosion of customized production and services. The volume of information is increasing at an astonishing rate. Change has become the only constant of life. And only firms that are flexible and innovative, with very well-trained people, are doing very well.

The new global economy requires little explanation here in Japan. You have pioneered the modernization of Asia. Now from Taipei to Seoul, from Bangkok to Shanghai, Asian economies are growing at dramatic rates, providing jobs and incomes, providing consumer goods and services to people who could not have even dreamed of them just a generation ago.

To be sure, Asia's progress is uneven. There are still millions in abject poverty. Four of the world's last five Communist regimes and other repressive regimes continue to defy the clear laws of human nature and the future. But the scenes of life in this region paint an unmistakable picture of change and vitality and opportunity and growth.

A generation ago in Singapore, bumboats floated up to the boat quay to unload their cargoes of produce and cloth which were sent out into a labyrinth of smoky shophouses and small family markets. Today such scenes are joined by those of container ships steaming into Singapore's modern port, one every 6 minutes, disgorging their goods into mechanized warehouses and modern supermarkets. In China's Guangdong Province, young entrepreneurs are leaving safe jobs in state-owned enterprises to start their own companies. To describe their daring spirit the Chinese have coined a phrase that literally means "to plunge into the sea." Such images help to explain why Asia likely will remain the world's fastest growing region for some time. Its imports will exceed 2 trillion U.S. dollars. This growth will help to make a tripolar world driven by the Americans, by Europe, and by Asia.

In years past, frankly, some Americans viewed Asia's vibrancy and particularly Japan's success as a threat. I see it very differently. I believe the Pacific region can and will be a vast source of jobs, of income, of partnerships, of ideas, of growth for our own people in the United States, if we have the courage to deal with the problems both of our nations have within and beyond our borders.

Already over 40 percent of American trade is with this region. Last year, over 2.3 million American jobs were related to the $120 billion we exported to Asia. Millions of Asian-Americans in the United States today embody our Nation's devotion to family values, to hard work, to education. In so doing, they have helped to strengthen our cultural ties and our economic ties to this region.

Today, our Nation is ready to be a full partner in Asian growth. After years of difficult transition, our private sector is embracing the opportunities and meeting the challenges of the global economy. Productivity is on the rise. Attempts to pierce overseas markets are more intense than ever. Many of our manufacturing service and financial firms are now the high-quality, low-cost producers in their fields.

At last, our governmental sector in the United States is also moving in the right direction. After years of being urged by Japan and by other nations to do something about the massive American budget deficit, we are on the brink of doing something about it. After years of being urged to do something about improving our education system and making our manufacturing and other sectors more productive and more competitive, we are doing something about it.

We are nearing the adoption of a bold plan to reduce our public deficit by $500 billion over the next 5 years and to increase our investments in education, in technology, and in new jobs for the American people. We are moving to reform our health care system, the world's most expensive, to control costs and provide quality care to all of our people. We are moving to give incentives to the millions of Americans who live in poverty so they will move from poverty into middle class working lives. We too are moving to reform our political system, to reduce the cost of our political campaigns and the influence of lobbyists on our lawmakers. We are moving to face one of our most painful social problems, high rates of crime and violence, with new initiatives to put more police officers on our streets, give better futures to our young people in depressed areas, and keep guns out of the hand of dangerous criminals.

But it is not enough for the United States to change within. To increase the jobs, raise the incomes, and improve the quality of life of the American people, we must also change our relationships with our partners and ask them

to do the same.

Our first international economic priority must be to create a new and stronger partnership between the United States and Japan. Our relationship with Japan is the centerpiece of our policy toward the Pacific community. Our two nations account for nearly 40 percent of the world's output. Neither of us could thrive without the other. Producers in each of our countries are consumers for firms in the other.

We are also joined in our efforts to address global economic problems. We work closely in an effort to move toward a new trade agreement. And I hope Japan will join in the initiative I proposed just 2 days ago in San Francisco: a meeting of the senior G–7 economics and labor and education advisers to look into a new problem with the global economy, stubbornly persistent unemployment in the richest nations of the world, even where there is economic growth, rooted in the inability of so many of these nations to create new jobs.

The economic relationship we have has always benefited both our nations. Americans buy huge volumes of Japanese products. American companies in Japan employ thousands of your citizens. Joint ventures between Japanese and American enterprises advance the economic and other interests of people in both nations. Japanese companies have opened many manufacturing firms, sales offices, and other facilities in the United States. In the 1980's when my country went on a huge debt binge, massively increasing public and private debt, Japanese purchases of much of that debt helped to keep our economy going and helped to prevent our interest rates from exploding.

Still, our economic relationship is not in balance. Unlike our relations with all other wealthy nations, we have a huge and persistent trade deficit with Japan. It usually exceeds $40 billion, with a deficit in manufacturing products in excess of $60 billion in spite of the fact that in recent years our manufacturing productivity has increased very greatly.

It is impossible to attribute this trade imbalance solely to unfair Japanese barriers, from governmental policies to a unique distribution system. Indeed, it is in part simply a tribute to Japanese abilities to produce high-quality, competitively priced goods and to the skill of Japanese businesses in piercing so many overseas markets, including our own. Yet, it is clear that our markets are more open to your products and your investments than yours are to ours. And it is clear that governmental policies consistently promoting production over consumption, exports over domestic sales, and protections of the home market contribute to this problem. The trade deficit is on the rise this year even with the market rise of the yen against the dollar. Though American purchases of Japanese products have remained fairly constant, Japanese purchases of American products have dropped markedly as a consequence of slow growth here in your economy with no offsetting government policies to stimulate demand.

This problem has, as all of you know, fueled resentment in our country both from workers and from businesses who have worked hard to streamline their operations, reduce labor costs, and increase productivity and now want the benefits that can only come from being able to compete and win in a global economy. Our people understand when our Nation has a huge trade deficit with an emerging economy like China. The same was true just a few years ago with Korea and Taiwan. But both those nations have moved closer to trade balance with the U.S. as they have become more prosperous. The same has not happened with Japan.

This persistent trade imbalance has not just hurt American workers and businesses, it has hurt the Japanese people. It has deprived you as consumers of the full benefit of your hard and productive work. For example, partly because of restrictive economic policies, the average Japanese family pays more than twice as much of your income for food as the average American family. And many other consumer products are far, far more expensive here than elsewhere, with these differentials going far beyond what can be accounted for by the transportation costs of bringing products to this market.

Our relationships with Japan have been durable not only because of our security alliance and our political partnership but because our economic relationship has actually served our interests and yours. I believe we must change this economic interest to improve the lives not just of the American people but of the Japanese people as well. It would be wrong for me to come here as President to ask you to embrace changes that would only benefit the people who live in my country. I believe that the changes I advocate will benefit both of us, or I would not be here pushing them.

During my April meeting with Prime Minister Miyazawa, we agreed to build a new framework for trade on macroeconomic, sectoral, and structural issues. Now, I don't know how that translates into Japanese, but the average American has no idea what that means. [*Laughter*] What it means is that we are going to try to deal honestly with the differences we have over our nations' economic policies. We want to talk about the specific sectors of the economy where we believe that more trade is warranted. We want to talk about structural differences between our two countries that operate as effective barriers to finding greater balance and greater volume of trade. Our governments have made progress in these last few days in crafting the basic principles of this new framework. And we will persist until we can produce a sound agreement that is in the interests of people in both countries.

What the United States seeks, let me make clear, is not managed trade or so-called trade by the numbers but better results from better rules of trade. Openness like this cannot simply come from pressure from the United States. That is one reason I wanted so much to be here with you today. A new openness can only come ultimately when Japanese leaders and Japanese citizens recognize that it is in your interests to pursue this course.

So today I would send this message to all of you and to the people beyond the walls here in this hall: You have a common cause with the people of America, a common cause against outdated practices that undermine our relationship and diminish the quality of your lives. The ideas I propose are beneficial to both of us because they will increase the number and lower the costs of the products you are able to buy, the services you are able to access, and they will thereby reward the work, the education, and the skills that you bring to daily life here in Japan. You are entitled to no less, and it will be a part of your role as a great nation for the foreseeable future to have that sort of open relationship. We should take these steps together for ourselves and for future generations. I am optimistic that the people of Japan and the people of the United States can hear the same message and move toward the same goal.

Japan has, after all, a proud heritage of embracing bold change when the times call for it. Much of the success you have enjoyed in recent years comes from a phenomenal ability to adapt to the changing contours of the global economy. And over 120 years ago, the leaders of the Meiji Restoration embarked on a series of rapid and successful initiatives that transformed a feudal Japan into a modern society, making it more open to the West and the broader world, without sacrificing the uniqueness of the Japanese culture.

On this campus today, there is a statue honoring one of the great statesmen of that period, this school's founder, Count Okuma. In his exhaustive narrative of the Meiji Restoration, Okuma attributes the period's reforms, and I quote, to "thoughtful and farsighted Japanese leaders." And he concludes, "Even as the spirit of liberality has animated the Japanese race during the past half-century of its remarkable progress, so it will ever impel its march along the paths of civilization and humanity." To keep the country's doors wide open is a national principle to which Japan has attached the greatest importance from its earliest days. I believe and hope that spirit still prevails and that a stronger Japan-U.S. economic relationship, driven by mutual wisdom, can power our new Pacific community well into the next century.

The second building block of that community must be a more open regional and global economy. That means that together we must resist the pressures that are now apparent in all wealthy countries to put up walls and to protect specific markets and constituencies in times of slow growth. We must resist them because the only way wealthy countries can grow richer is if there is global economic growth and we can increase trade with people who themselves are growing more prosperous. An essential starting point is the successful completion of the Uruguay round of the General Agreement on Tariffs and Trade. I am committed to doing that by the end of this year, and I hope that your government is also. I believe we should also work to reduce regional trade barriers. That is what we in the United States are attempting to do in negotiating an agreement with Mexico and Canada not to close North America to the rest of the world but to open it up. And perhaps we should consider Asian-Pacific trading areas as well.

The most promising economic forum we have for debating a lot of these issues in the new Pacific community is the Organization for Asian-Pacific Economic Cooperation, APEC. The 15 members of APEC account for nearly half of the world's output and most of the fastest growing economies. This fall, we will host the APEC ministerial meeting in Seattle. I will speak at that meeting to signal America's engagement in the region. But I hope we can go beyond it. I am consulting with the leaders of APEC at this moment on a proposal that they join me in Seattle in an informal leadership conference to discuss what we can do to continue to bring down the barriers that divide us and to create more opportunities for all of our people. In addressing common economic challenges we can begin to chart a course toward prosperity and opportunity for the entire region.

Of course, the purpose of meetings like this is not simply more meetings and communiques, it is to improve our people's lives, not just the lives of those who dash around financial districts in Tokyo or New York with cellular telephones in their pockets but the millions of people in my country and the billions of people on the Earth who work hard every day in factories and on farms simply to feed their families and to give their children a better life than they have enjoyed. It will make a world of difference to them if our leaders can set pro-grow policies, dismantle trade barriers, and get government out of the way. Expanded trade and more open economies will not only enrich people, they also empower them. Trade is a revolutionary force that wears down the foundations of despotic rule. The experiences of the Philippines, Taiwan, Korea, and others prove that the move toward more open economies also feeds people's hunger for democracy and freedom and more open political systems.

This then should be our third priority in building a new Pacific community: to support the wave of democratic reform sweeping across this region. Economic growth, of course, can occur in closed societies, even in repressive ones. But in an information age, it cannot ultimately be maintained. People with prosperity simply crave more freedom. Open societies are better able to address the frictions that economic growth creates and to assure the continuance of prosperity. A free press roots out corruption, even though it sometimes aggravates political leaders. The rule of law encourages and protects investments.

This spread of democracy is one of the best guarantees of regional peace and prosperity and stability that we could ever have in this region. Democracies make better neighbors. They don't wage war on each other, engage in terrorism, or generate refugees. Democracy makes it possible for allies to continue their close relations despite changes in leadership. Democracy's virtues are at the core of why we have worked so hard to support the reforms and the reformers in Russia, which is now on a path toward becoming one of the Pacific's great democratic powers.

The movement toward democracy is the best guarantor of human rights. Some have argued that democracy is somehow unsuited for Asia, or at least for some nations in Asia, that human rights are relative and that they simply mask Western cultural imperialism. I believe those voices are wrong. It is not Western urging or Western imperialism but the aspiration of Asian peoples themselves that explain the growing number of democracies and democratic movements in this region. And it is an insult to the spirit and hopes and dreams of the people who live here to assert that anything else is true.

Each of our Pacific nations must pursue progress while maintaining the best of their unique cultures. But there is no cultural justification for torture or tyranny. We refuse to let repression cloak itself in moral relativism, for democracy and human rights are not occidental yearnings, they are universal yearnings.

These, then, are the economic essentials for this new Pacific community, one in which most of you, being so much younger than I am, will spend far more of your lives in than will I. A better U.S.-Japan relationship, more open economies and trade, more democratic governments, these things will make your lives better. I will pursue these goals vigorously. You will see that commitment reflected in what our administration does. Together we can make this decade and the coming century a time of greater security, democracy, prosperity, and personal, family, community, and national empowerment.

So today, on this holiday of Tanabata, a holiday of joining together and hopeful wishes, let us wish for a new Pacific community, built on shared effort, shared benefit, and a shared destiny. Let us write out our brightest dreams for our children on pieces of paper as bright and differently colored and numberless as are the peoples of the Asian-Pacific region. In the spirit of this holiday, let us fly those dreams from bamboo poles that are as high as our hopes for the era, and then, together, let us dedicate ourselves to the hard work of making those

dreams come true. Senator Kennedy was right when he said that change has its enemies. But my friends, we can make change our friend.

Thank you very much.

Now, I'm going to take some questions, and I think I'm supposed to go down here. So I will try to go down there without breaking my leg, and then we'll take some questions.

Japanese Imperial Family

Q. Thank you for giving me a chance to ask you a question today. The wedding ceremony of the Crowned Prince and the Princess Masako Owada was held recently. What did you think of the ceremony? And also, what do you think of the Imperial Family, which you don't have in the United States?

The President. Well, the Imperial Family is an important part of your culture. We do not have one in the United States, as you know. That's because when we broke off from England, they had a king, and so we thought we had to behave differently. So we elected our Presidents, and then over 100 years later we decided they could only stay for 8 years. And then when times got tough, most of them found it was difficult even to stay 8 years. [*Laughter*]

But let me say, I'm very interested in the Imperial Family. We followed the marriage with great interest, my wife and I, and discussed the marriage and how impressed we were with the Princess and with the devotion of the Prince who pursued her. I have invited the Emperor and the Empress to visit the United States next year, and we are hopeful that they will come sometime in the late spring or the early summer and that they will have a very good trip. We are eager to receive them.

Q. Thank you very much.

Iraq and Bosnia

Q. With regard, Mr. President, to the Iraq retaliatory attack. Of course, this took place, and there was no military mobilization that took place on the part of Iraq. However, this attack did take place. And I'm just wondering what your thoughts are on this situation.

The President. You mean the attack that I ordered on Iraq?

Q. With regard to this attack, of course, there are criticisms that are launched by the Middle Eastern countries that perhaps this might be a discriminatory measure that was taken by the United States society which still has as the majority the white people. And in the United States, of course, despite that fact, it's an ethnically mixed group of people who live there, and you have your own special situation. However, there is this criticism that has been launched by the Middle Eastern countries that this is, in fact, nationalism where, perhaps, discrimination on the part of the United States against Iraq. And then, of course, there is also the issue of the ethnic cleansing that is taking place in Bosnia that I would also like to have you address.

The President. First, let me talk about Iraq, and then I will discuss the other issues. There was no discrimination involved. Our intelligence and law enforcement agencies conducted an investigation on the people who were arrested in Kuwait and charged with bringing in a very dangerous bomb for the purpose of assassinating former President Bush because of actions he took as President in the Gulf war. I was advised that they believe that that in fact occurred, that a plan devised by the Iraqi Government was attempted to be carried out in Kuwait to kill former President Bush with a bomb that had a lethal radius of about 400 yards. That is, it could have killed people within 400 yards around where it exploded. So I took what I thought was appropriate and perfectly legal retaliatory action, basically as a deterrent to further behavior of that kind. It had nothing to do with any racial or religious distinction. And indeed, Iraq's closest neighbors, Kuwait and Saudi Arabia, applauded the action that was taken.

Secondly, with regard to Bosnia, the United States has spent hundreds of millions of dollars in humanitarian aid. It is prepared to do more and advocated, along with the nonaligned nations and most of the Muslim nations of the world, lifting the arms embargo on the Bosnian Government and giving the Bosnian Government time to implement the arms embargo with standby air power. That position did not prevail in the United Nations because others were against it. That's what I thought the right thing to do was.

The United States also was involved in helping people in Somalia. We were actively involved in the agreement announced just last weekend to restore Father Aristide to Haiti within 4 months.

There was no racial or religious or ethnic discrimination involved in the Iraqi action. It

was, I believe, clearly the right thing to do. But we are reaching out to Muslim peoples all across the world with our friendship with Turkey, our friendship with many of the newly independent states of the former Soviet Union, and elsewhere, people who share our values. We respect their religious and their cultural traditions. We want stronger ties. And I very much hope that the multiethnic government in Bosnia can survive.

Q. Thank you.

Korean Reunification

Q. I am a student, Mr. President, from South Korea, and I would like to ask you a question about the Korean Peninsula. As you are aware, sir, South Korea and the DPRK are, in fact, not reintegrated. We are the last two states in the nation that need to be reintegrated. And I'm wondering if you have any prospects, if you have any thoughts on when the reintegration of South Korea and North Korea might take place.

The President. Well, I think that that is a matter for the Korean people themselves to decide. And we will obviously support the decision that they make. I have to tell you that my hopes for an early reintegration have been dampened somewhat by the recent controversy over whether North Korea would withdraw from the NPT regime, not allow the international inspectors to continue to inspect the sites to ensure that North Korea does not become a nuclear power. That would be a very grave development, not just for South Korea but for Japan as well and for all of Asia.

I think the most important thing I can do as President to speed the day of reunification on terms that are humane and decent and honorable is to maintain a strong presence in the area, to honor our security commitments, and to do everything I can to deter the development of nuclear potential in North Korea. These two nations should unite again based on shared culture and family ties and common economic interests and a common interest in a peaceful future, not trying to be a nuclear power at a time when Russia and the United States, for example, are trying to reduce their nuclear arsenals. We need fewer nuclear weapons, not more. That's one reason I announced that we would not resume nuclear testing a few days ago, in the hopes that we could, together with the other nuclear powers, continue to discourage the development of nuclear weapons and other weapons of mass destruction.

Q. Thank you.

Human Rights

Q. Mr. President, you mentioned the importance of human rights, and I understand that recently you've submitted some international conventions to the Senate for consideration, including the convention on torture. Does this indicate a change in policy from previous administrations concerning human rights, and do you have any plans to submit any other human rights conventions to the Senate?

The President. Well first of all, I want to see how we do with the ones we submitted. I think they will be ratified. I wouldn't rule out the submission of others. It does recommend a change in policy. Our administration has been very forceful in its advocacy of human rights. The Secretary of State gave a very eloquent speech in Vienna recently advocating the universality of human rights and rejecting the idea that there were some cultural relativism involved. And I think you can look forward to the United States standing up for human rights on every continent, in every way that we possibly can. I will say that it is very rare for me to have a discussion with any leader from any other country in which I do not bring the subject up. And we work at it steadily every day.

Q. Thank you.

Q. We will end this program because of your schedule.

The President. I would stay all day if I could. I like this.

Hillary Clinton and the Role of Women

Q. In Japan there are many people who think that women should not work, have a job, especially after marriage. But in the United States, I heard that feminism is more accepted in people, and there is less discrimination. Actually, there are many working women like Mrs. Hillary Clinton. And then I want to ask you two questions. How do the American people think about Mrs. Hillary Clinton acting or making political speeches in official situations? And second, what do you yourself think of her as your political partner?

The President. Well, first of all, most American women, even with young children, are in the work force now. More than half of them, even with children under 6, are in the work force. That presents us with a great source of wealth and talent to strengthen America. It also presents us with challenges, providing adequate care for the children, trying to provide adequate time for the parents to be with the children. After all, raising children is still the most important work of any society, and it should not be minimized. But I strongly believe that women should have equal opportunities with men in all areas. We have many women in the United States Senate, we have many women Governors of States, and someday before long I think we'll have a woman President.

As you noted, my wife is a lawyer. We're both lawyers, and most people who know us think that she is the real lawyer in our family. So I like it when she gives political speeches, when she works as she is now as the head of our task force to reform our health care system. I asked her to do it because I thought she had more ability than anyone else I knew to do that job. And if we get that done for the American people, that will be perhaps the most important social reform in America in a generation. And so I think I would be irresponsible as the President of the United States not to use the talents of someone I know can serve the American people. It's very simple to me; it's a straightforward thing.

Now, having said that, this issue is still—it's not as controversial perhaps as in Japan, but it's still a controversial issue at home. There are still people who have some reservations about the role of women in various areas of our life. There are still people who have certain reservations about whether a spouse of a political leader should make speeches, have opinions that are expressed, and do this kind of work. I might say that most of the people who say that my wife shouldn't be doing this really disagree with our position. They're saying she shouldn't be doing this, but most of them just don't agree with what we're trying to do. So there is some controversy in the United States about it, but I think most people, and I know most women, respect the fact that the First Lady is functioning as a full citizen and as a partner, as a part of this administration. I am ultimately responsible for the decisions that the President must make. There are all kinds of things that we never even talk about. But to ask her to do something she is clearly competent and able to do seems to me is the right thing to do for America.

If you look at the population trends in Japan, your rather low birthrate but your phenomenally high life expectancy, so that most Japanese couples will have literally decades after their children have left the home, it seems to me that your country will have to take advantage of the brains and the education and the skills and the capacities of women in order to be what you ought to be and do what you have to do. I think you will have to do that.

Do I have to leave, Mr. President?

Q. Thank you very much.

The President. Thank you very much.

NOTE: The President spoke at 9:29 a.m. in Okuma Hall.

The President's News Conference With Prime Minister Carlo Azeglio Ciampi of Italy in Tokyo
July 7, 1993

The President. Good morning. I have just finished my first personal meeting with Prime Minister Ciampi, and I enjoyed it immensely. The close ties between the United States and Italy will stand us in good stead as we try to meet the common challenges that we face. I told the Prime Minister that I admire very much the economic reforms and the political reforms that he and his government are undertaking and the impressive results they are producing.

I also mentioned that in appointing one of the United States finest professional diplomats, Mr. Reg Bartholomew, Ambassador of Italy, I have tried to send a signal of the enormous importance of that bilateral relationship to the United States. The fact that Mr. Bartholomew grew up in the United States speaking Italian at home reinforces that tie.

In addition, I invited the Prime Minister to come to the United States some time in the next couple of months for a personal visit at the White House so that we might discuss the issues of common concern further.

We talked a good deal today about economic issues and the importance of the G-7 reaffirming our support for a conclusion of the Uruguay round this year. This has gone on entirely too long. With recession in Europe, slow growth in Japan and the United States, it is imperative that we send a signal of economic expansion and hope. And both of us, I think it's fair to say, support that approach.

We also discussed the foreign affairs issues which concern us both, including Somalia and Bosnia, and I was very impressed with the comments and the points that the Prime Minister made.

I want to close by thanking Italy for its renewed effort in global problem-solving; the humanitarian and peacekeeping assistance in Bosnia, Albania, Somalia, Mozambique; its mediation efforts in the Nagorno-Karabakh. The United States highly values this as well as the critical partnership we have enjoyed with Italy in NATO, and we look forward to the NATO summit coming up in the next few months to reaffirm that partnership.

Again, let me say, I thank the Prime Minister for his time today. It was very enlightening for me. I learned a good deal, and I look forward to a continued warm and constructive relationship between the United States and Italy.

Mr. Prime Minister.

Prime Minister Ciampi. First of all, I would like to thank the President for having invited me to visit Washington. This invitation I accept with great pleasure. I would also like to add that our talks today were very cordial and positive. And despite our age differences, the spirit was the same.

I tried to illustrate to the President the great changes that are underway in Italy right now. But I also made it a point to emphasize that, despite these changes, one thing will not change, and that is our foreign policy. Italy will continue, as Italy has continued to do, to give its full consent to future problems, the most important problems which affect the world scene. It is important that this summit concludes by giving clear signals to the operators in the world. This clear-sent message would be to enhance a recovery of—to enhance the Uruguay round negotiations which have dragged on for too long. This would help to contribute our energies to overcome the recession that we are going through now and to develop the economy in the world and to create new jobs.

We also discussed the issues which directly affect the U.S. and Europe and the U.S. and Italy. We have also exchanged our opinions on the two most crucial issues of the day, which are Bosnia and Somalia. As far as Somalia is concerned, the most important thing is that we cannot forget what our priority goal is. And the goal is to normalize the political and social situation in the country, which has undergone domestic strife and which has prevented the distribution of food to the starving population. And in undertaking our military action, we must never forget the political action which, of course, must be supported by the military action. And I have found a full understanding on the President's part as far as Italy's request to have a greater presence of the Italians in Somalia.

And in conclusion, I must again thank the President of the United States, Bill Clinton. This is our first meeting, although we have spoken on the phone before in a very cordial and practical conversation. The fact that we have finally met personally reinforces in me the sensation that the President is a very agreeable person and that we can work out our problems together.

Political Reform

Q. Mr. President, in your university speech, you appeared to be going over the head of the Japanese Government when you made this direct appeal to the Japanese consumers for open markets. Now, with Japanese elections only two weeks away, why shouldn't the Japanese see this as intervention in domestic politics? And given the uncertainty of the political situation right here now, isn't that somewhat of a political gamble on your part?

The President. No, because I was not trying to interfere in domestic politics. I thought I owed it to the Japanese people and especially to the young people who were largely the audience today to make the case of the United States directly to them. I wanted them to understand clearly that the things that we advocate in terms of changing the trade relations between our two countries are things which I believe are in the interest of the Japanese as well as American workers.

And just to reinforce the point about not wanting to interfere into the domestic politics,

keep in mind, a major part of this election is being argued out on questions of domestic political reform. Italy is dealing with issues of domestic political reform. The United States is dealing with campaign finance reform and lobbying reform. This whole issue of political reform is very much alive in most of the advanced democracies today. The point of that is this: It is impossible for the United States to know with any real certainty what outcome of the election might produce a government more responsive to the arguments we're making.

The present government has reached out to us in good faith to attempt to negotiate the principles behind a basic framework for new trade relations. Those negotiations are going on right now. So I want to make it clear—I'm very glad you asked the question—we are not, in any way, trying to influence the outcome of the election in terms of who wins what seats in the Diet. That is up to the people of Japan. But I owe it to the people of Japan, since there is no more important bilateral relationship than the relationship between the United States and Japan, to make the United States case directly to them, and that's what I was trying to do today.

Somalia

Q. Did you discuss the possibility that Italy gets a higher post in the high command militarily, and did you discuss the restarting of the negotiation towards national reconciliation in Somalia?

The President. We discussed the former, but not the latter, expressly. The Prime Minister did say, and he's absolutely right, that the ultimate purpose of our presence in Somalia is to restore normal conditions of life and to try to help to build the nation there so that people can engage in self-government. Because of the intervention of the United Nations, people were saved from starving, medicine was provided, schools were reopened, the conditions of normal life have returned for most people. The present tension, occasioned by the action of General Aideed and then our reaction to that, is really the sort of thing people assumed would happen at the beginning of the United Nations intervention. But in the end, as the Prime Minister said, we have to try to have a political resolution of this.

Now, with regard to the fact that the major elements there in terms of military forces are

Italian, Pakistani, and American—of course, there is unified United Nations Command under General Bir, something that we supported. How all the forces relate to General Bir is ultimately a matter for the United Nations Command to resolve. But I thought that the Prime Minister raised some serious questions and some legitimate issues, and I pledged to discuss those with our defense people and to get back to him and also to discuss it with the U.N. people. We didn't resolve it, and I can't say the United States has a position now, because this is the first opportunity I've had to discuss it. But he made a very important case that every nation with a substantial military presence there should at least have its views heard in some organized way. Perhaps he would like to comment, but I think that's a fair statement of where we were.

Prime Minister Ciampi. I've little to add. It's very clear what I said, and it's very clear what President Clinton said.

Japanese Elections

Q. Mr. Clinton, I recognize that you weren't trying to interfere in Japanese politics. You did talk in the speech at Waseda about change. Do you see a linkage between the kind of change you're talking about and the kind of proposals being offered by the opposition parties?

The President. Well, let me say again the question of political reform is one that every mature democracy has to face. But what I was talking about today is the necessity of changing the nature of the economic relationships. The opposition parties are in different places on a lot of those issues, and the incumbent government in the form of a personal letter from the Prime Minister has reached out across a gap to us within the last week that has not been bridged in years. So I will say again, I have no way of predicting what kind of election outcome would produce a government most likely to pursue this course that I am advocating, this new partnership with us. My belief is that no matter who wins the election, in the end, history is on our side and will require a change in the relationships.

So I want to say again, I maintain a strictly neutral position about the people who are running and who should win. That is a decision for the Japanese people to make. I am generally supportive of the notion of political reform. I have generally tried to reassure the people of Japan that I do not think they should be too

filled with anxiety in the face of these changes. This is the sort of thing that is happening in many, many countries, including the United States. But they will have to decide which party and which individual candidates and which leaders are best for them. That is not for the United States to say.

Electoral Reform and Unity in Italy

Q. Mr. President, you spoke about changes in democracies. But in Italy these changes have been fairly dramatic. There has been fear of separation between north and south. There have been proposals for the introduction of direct election of the government. Do you share those fears that a separation could be possible? And do you think the political change could happen fast? And do you think that works better where democracy is a direct election of the government?

And just for Mr. Ciampi, you spoke about the need from the G–7 of getting clear messages for the markets. Don't you think that the markets are expecting clear messages from Italy that something more should be done? Will you go back to Italy proposing the more comprehensive plan for restructuring the political and economic systems of the country?

The President. It is inappropriate for me to express a firm opinion about the questions you ask since the Italian people will have to resolve that for themselves, just as the Japanese people will have to resolve their questions of political reform. But I would make two observations.

First is that the differences in economy and culture between the north and the south in your country have some analogy in our country. That is, we have some places in our country that are far wealthier than others. We have places in our country that are far different culturally than others. And that is a continuing challenge. My own view is that we're much better facing those things together and trying to create a community of interest than we would be if we were to split up. I realize the challenge it presents to Italy; I spent time in southern Italy; I spent time in northern Italy. I'm well aware of the fact that some parts of northern Italy achieve per capita incomes higher than the Federal Republic of Germany before the merger of West and East Germany. But I think that these are the kinds of challenges that would have to be faced, regardless, and the heritage of Italy as a united country is a very old one indeed.

With regard to the electoral system, at various times the people in democracies, when times are tough, tire of the system they have. In our country, for example, we had a third party candidate get the highest percentage of the vote that a third party candidate has gotten since the beginning of this century.

On the other hand, I believe that the two-party system and the fact that we have roughly centrist parties with majority rule, right of center, left of center a little bit, but roughly centrist parties, has stabilized our political system over the years. Sometimes, people have been disappointed that there weren't clear-cut differences and ideas throughout American history in the parties, and then sometimes there are. But if you have a majority rule system, you tend to have more compromise and more stability. Sometimes people grow tired of it, and they look for other options. It has happened to us three or four times in our history where a new party has come up, and one of our existing parties has disappeared over 217 years. But it has served us well, I believe, on balance. Nearly any student of American history would say that we have been served well by that system. Now,

whether it will work in Italy is a decision you'll have to make.

Prime Minister Ciampi. First of all, I would like to add a few points, Mr. President, and they will be very brief and very clear. First of all, no new party in Italy or no party at all questions the unity of Italy. The second point is that the Italian Parliament is currently studying electoral reform to solve the institutional problems of Italy. Second of all, the Italian Government—and I would hope that you would read the relative documentation—is fully supporting the electoral reform and is making it the number one priority.

The President. Thank you very much.

Q. Progress on trade talks?

The President. You know, I was out at the university, and then I came directly back here to meet with the Prime Minister. So I've received no report. I can't say.

NOTE: The President's 20th news conference began at noon in the Wakakusa Room at the Okura Hotel. Prime Minister Ciampi spoke in Italian, and his remarks were translated by an interpreter.

Exchange With Reporters Prior to the Opening Session of the Economic Summit in Tokyo
July 7, 1993

Trade Negotiations

Q. Mr. President, what do you hope to accomplish at this first summit meeting?

The President. My spokesperson over there, she has my proxy. [*Laughter*]

Well, we're off to a good start. We hope to get the Uruguay round going again, and we have very encouraging news on that. We hope we can promote growth in our economies and jobs for our people, all of us do. And I think we will do what we can to support reform in Russia. So there are lots of things——

Q. Do you think there will be success on the Uruguay round, sir?

The President. I certainly hope so. I think there will be an announcement on that later today.

Prime Minister Miyazawa. [*Inaudible*]—made great headway.

Q. Great headway, did you say, Mr. Prime Minister?

Prime Minister Miyazawa. Yes.

The President. Our people worked almost all night last night. A great advantage for the Americans, since they couldn't sleep anyway. [*Laughter*]

[*At this point, one group of reporters left the room, and another group entered.*]

Q. Mr. Prime Minister, do you have any message—world community as you lead this meeting?

Prime Minister Miyazawa. [*Inaudible*]—contribute to the prosperity—of the whole world.

[*At this point, the second group of reporters left the room, and a third group entered.*]

Q. Is there progress on the Japanese trade

talks, Mr. President?

The President. They're working hard. I think the big news today will be on the manufacturing goods in the GATT round, and we'll have an announcement about that later today. It will be a big deal for Americans, lots of jobs involved

if it works. And we're hopeful.

NOTE: The exchange began at approximately 2:15 p.m. at the Akasaka Palace. A tape was not available for verification of the content of this news conference.

Nomination for Ambassadors and U.S. Attorneys
July 7, 1993

The President has announced his intention to nominate the following to the position of U.S. Attorney: John W. Raley, Jr., of Oklahoma; Charles R. Tetzlaff of Vermont; and William D. Wilmoth of West Virginia.

The President also intends to nominate Walter Carrington to be Ambassador to Nigeria and Theodore E. Russell to be Ambassador to the Slovak Republic.

"With these U.S. Attorney appointments we will continue to place skilled and dedicated professionals in the Justice Department," the President said. "With the addition of Charles Tetzlaff and William Wilmoth and the reappointment of

Attorney Raley, I believe the American public and the judicial system will be well served."

The President called Walter C. Carrington "a career professional whose affiliation with several renowned international agencies, including several associated with African issues, makes him a sound choice for the Nigerian post."

"Theodore Russell," the President said, "has demonstrated a talent and dedication for foreign service throughout his career, and I will be pleased to make his nomination official."

NOTE: Biographies of the nominees were made available by the Office of the Press Secretary.

Remarks on the Market Access Agreement and an Exchange With Reporters in Tokyo
July 7, 1993

The President. Ladies and gentlemen, I want to read a statement about the market access agreement that was reached. Ambassador Kantor, I know, has already been down here answering your questions, and Secretary Christopher and Secretary Bentsen are here.

I want to try to explain why I can't take a broad range of questions on the G-7 summit. Under the rules of the summit, we can't discuss what's going on while it's going on unless we get an exemption. Since we've actually made an agreement on this, I can make the following statement.

The breakthrough achieved today in the international trade talks is good news for America and good news for the world. It means more jobs and higher incomes for our people. While there are difficult negotiations ahead, today's

agreement on manufactured goods breaks the logjam in the Uruguay round. For years, talks in that round have languished. G-7 leaders have emerged from these summits pledging renewed commitment to complete the round. Their pledges have gone unfulfilled. But this year, we have recaptured the momentum.

If we can complete the Uruguay round by the end of this year, and I believe we can now, then this agreement will bring the largest tariff reductions ever. It will lower duties on 18 categories of manufactured goods from paper to chemicals to electronics. It eliminates tariffs entirely, that is, it creates global free trade for eight major sectors including farm implements, steels, and pharmaceuticals. This agreement means new jobs and new growth in the United States and in other nations. It proves that government can be a productive partner with business, helping to open markets and create jobs.

Special praise is due to the European Community, to Canada, and to Japan, who joined with us in this effort; to our negotiator, Ambassador Mickey Kantor; and to the United States Congress which voted last week to renew my fast track authority to complete this round.

With today's accord, I am more determined than ever to press ahead with the Uruguay round by the end of this year. This really can mean an enormous number of jobs to the American people. When we came here, frankly, we did not know whether we could get an agreement on market access for manufactured goods. It is a very, very good sign that the agreement was achieved not only because of the jobs that this holds for Americans but because of the promise it holds to actually complete the Uruguay round.

G–7 Meetings

Q. Mr. President, could you just tell us whether you're getting to know the other leaders and what the mood was at the meetings?

The President. Good mood. It was a good mood. Of course, I know—I have spent time with several of them already. But so far it's been a very good mood. We had over 3 hours

all alone where we just talked about various things. And I'm looking forward to more of this time. It's very valuable, actually, getting to know them because there are so many things we have to do together.

Q. What about the Japanese agreement?

Q. Do you feel, Mr. President, that they're trying to size you up, take your measure?

The President. I don't know. I'm getting to know them. I'm having a good time.

U.S. Leadership

Q. Does it answer any of the questions about leadership, America's leadership?

The President. Well, I think Mr. Kantor probably told you how this agreement came about and what the sequence of events was. But I don't think there's any question that our country played its appropriate role in getting this agreement.

Q. Any closer to the agreement guidelines for the Japanese?

The President. Bye.

NOTE: The President spoke at 7 p.m. at the Okura Hotel. These remarks were released by the Office of the Press Secretary on July 8. A tape was not available for verification of the content of these remarks.

Radio Address to Midwest Flood Victims
July 8, 1993

This is President Clinton. Although I'm in Japan at a meeting of our economic allies, I'm deeply concerned about the disaster hitting many of you in the Midwest. As the waters continue to rise, I'm keeping in touch through Vice President Gore and Federal officials in Washington. My direction to them is simple, urgent, and clear: All Federal agencies delivering services to you must coordinate their actions. Teamwork is the order of the day.

I want the services you need to be delivered responsibly, efficiently, and without delay. And most of all, I want you to be treated the way every American would ask to be treated if they were on the receiving end of this disaster, with compassion and effectiveness as neighbors and friends.

When I was Governor of Arkansas, I worked with farmers in my State through a number of natural disasters, including very serious floods. What I saw in Iowa last weekend when I was there with Secretary Espy were conditions as bad as I've ever seen. That's why I'm determined to have a Federal response that rises to the occasion and deals effectively with the problems you're facing.

Before I left for Japan, I asked Vice President Gore to monitor actively the efforts to deal with this disaster. With his leadership and the hard work of a number of dedicated Federal officials, relief and response efforts are already underway. We're organizing the appropriate Federal agencies to ensure that they work together as a team. The Federal Emergency Management Agency,

FEMA, is working around the clock, cooperating with each of the affected States and managing our coordinated response. FEMA personnel are in five States now, assisting State governments with preparedness and recovery efforts. And FEMA's in close coordination with other States.

Where disasters are declared, FEMA will set up facilities called "disaster application centers" to provide a speedy and efficient one-stop process for recovery. It's also providing an 800 number for victims of the flooding which allows for rapid application for aid by telephone. The Department of Transportation is monitoring the conditions of barge traffic and damage to highways. The Army Corps of Engineers and the National Guard are out fortifying levees and flood walls, providing security and traffic control and simply doing their best to stop or alleviate water damage wherever they can. The Department of Agriculture is making shelter available, helping farmers with their loan obligations, and working to alleviate crop losses and losses farmers experience when they can't plant their crops. The Emergency Broadcast System is being used throughout the region to provide notifications of flash floods, evacuations, and tornadoes.

Efforts are being made now to remove debris in Minnesota, to provide sandbags in Iowa and Illinois, to guard against public health problems, and to provide potable water where needed. I've asked our Budget Director, Leon Panetta, to begin assembling a funding bill that will provide emergency assistance to the region. We'll be working with Congress early next week to get this process underway. We'll ask for Federal funds on an emergency basis to help pay for crop losses and damage to homes, businesses, and public property.

Times of turmoil and trouble bring out the best in Americans. This flood has been no exception. Members of the Red Cross and the Salvation Army are doing what these organizations have always done, bringing comfort to people of your region who have had their lives turned upside down by this flood. National Guard personnel have been mobilizing, filling sandbags and providing assistance wherever they can. Some of them have canceled vacations to come home and help the people of their communities, strangers and friends alike. These are good people, and I'm thankful to them for all they're doing.

In closing, let me ask each of you to take heart and have faith. As hard as these times are, you know that the waters will soon recede and the work of recovery will begin. The people who grow our food and the communities that surround and support you are central to the American way of life. Just as we depend upon you for the harvest, you can depend upon us for support at this critical moment in your lives. For that is the American way.

Thanks for listening, and God bless you all.

NOTE: The President spoke at 11:06 p.m. from the Okura Hotel in Tokyo for broadcast in the United States.

Remarks to the American Chamber of Commerce in Tokyo
July 9, 1993

The President. I would like to resume the discussion because I want to have as much time as possible just to listen and learn today. Let me say that in my former life I came here several times and met with business leaders on behalf of the interests of my State.

I'm sure that the people who have spoken before me have basically outlined the strategy we are attempting to pursue back home. But essentially what we're trying to do is to deal with the major problems of America at home and then try to get ourselves in a better position to do what we can to be a good partner for the private sector in competing in a global economy.

We are well on the way to passing a record-breaking deficit reduction plan that has great credibility in the financial markets. And we've got a big decline in long-term interest rates at home, which I think is quite good. For all the economic softness, and it's quite considerable at home, we have over 950,000 new jobs in the economy in the last 5 months. That's about as many as the United States produced in the previous 3 years.

We've got a serious attempt going on to bring health care costs under control, which as all of you know is one of the major causes of America's lack of competitiveness. We're over 14 percent of GDP in health care; nobody is over 9 except Canada, and they're barely over 9. And we're working on significant changes in our policies with regard to technology, defense conversion, and trade, among other things.

So, that's a basic outline of what I've been trying to do for the last 5 months. I wanted to come here and just listen to you today because you've been able to do something that I think is very important, which is to operate in Japan to create opportunity. And I just want to know what you think we should be doing and how we can do more to help you and to create more people like you.

I didn't hear what Mr. Fallon said, but if the Ambassador fairly characterizes it, and he's pretty good at doing that, my attitude about this is that I prefer an open trading system. I don't think a wealthy nation can grow wealthier unless there is global economic growth. There are all kinds of challenges to that. Now, I think the environmental movement that is sweeping the globe actually gives us a chance to create more jobs, not lose them, if we do it in an intelligent way.

But my view is also that the United States should try to get better rules but play by the rules that are in play. That's sort of always been my attitude. I could never have won an election if I wanted the rules to be different from those that obtain at the time. You can always try to improve the rules. We're trying to have a different campaign finance reform system, we're trying to have a different lobby reform system in America, but meanwhile we all play by the rules that are there. So, that's my attitude about that. I wish I'd heard exactly what you had to say but I think—I get criticized in some quarters for saying that, but normally when you show up for a game you've got to play by the operative rules, not the ones you wish were in play.

[*At this point, panelists discussed problems and successes unique to operating an American business in Japan.*]

The President. I was just going to make one other comment about this. You made a very perceptive observation when you said the Justice Ministry only has this issue to negotiate and we've got nothing to give back because they can't imagine why Japanese lawyers would set up offices in New York to do business or anything like that. I mean, I can understand that. Most people just assume when they go to another country they'll use lawyers who understand the law and practice in those countries. But one of the big problems we've got in America, as I'm sure you know, is that we don't have enough lawyers who are facilitators and we have too many who are, in effect, litigators. We have too many who slow down the operations of the private sector rather than who speed it up.

And there may be a little something we can do on the political side by indirection, by, you know, by sort of saying that Japanese companies doing business in America—one of the things that this administration is looking at in the whole productivity mix is how we can reduce the cost of litigation and the cost of decision making and the delays there. And there may be some merit in our taking some initiative to bring some Japanese lawyers who do business work to the United States to work with American lawyers, to work with American businesses to see if we can kind of change the culture a bit and maybe some of the laws in our country. That is a little something we could give back, and it wouldn't do us any harm to do that anyway.

Q. There are some who are there already. And they can do that. We can't do the same thing here.

The President. I know but, I mean, if they thought they were going to, their companies operating in America——

Q. I'm talking about the lawyers.

The President. Yes, I know, but if they thought their companies in America were going to get something out of it, it might help us to get a little more leverage here. And we'll pursue that. You made a very compelling point.

NOTE: The President spoke at 8:10 a.m. in the Akebono Room at the Okura Hotel.

The President's News Conference With Prime Minister Kim Campbell of Canada in Tokyo
July 9, 1993

The President. Good afternoon. I have just spent a very rewarding hour and a half with Prime Minister Campbell and members of her government. After a very impressive career in other posts in government and a very rapid rise to the leadership of her country, I must say I have been very impressed with the contributions that she has made to this summit and with the conversations that we have had all along, but especially today.

The relationship that we have with Canada is really unique in all the world. It is our largest trading relationship. We are each other's largest trading partners. And even though we have disputes from time to time, when you consider the volume and diversity of trade between us, those disputes are remarkably few and narrow in scope.

Canada has been a very strong security partner of the United States. And while we share a lot in common, we also are very different and distinctive countries, and I think we have a lot to learn from one another.

I might just mention with regard to two specific issues that we discussed, first, I reaffirmed to the Prime Minister my commitment to successfully concluding the side agreements to the North American Free Trade Agreement and to then moving forward to successful passage of that agreement in the United States Congress. As you know, it has passed the Canadian Parliament pending its ratification by Congress. And secondly, I asked the Prime Minister for her support in our attempts to fulfill the agreement signed just a few days ago by President Aristide and General Cedras to restore democracy in Haiti. Canada has been one of the United States' best friends on the Haitian issue, with a substantial Haitian population and a lot of French-speaking people who can make a unique contribution to this restoration process. So for both those things, I am grateful for our common positions, and I appreciate her support.

I think I'll turn the microphone over to Prime Minister Campbell now, and then we'll be glad to answer some questions.

Prime Minister Campbell. Thank you very much, Mr. President.

I'd simply like to reiterate that we had a very fruitful discussion, and I think as two novices in the summit process, we both enjoyed participating very much. I'd like to thank the President for responding very quickly to a request that we have made, and that is that he designate someone in the White House to be a point of contact for us in managing a variety of issues that arise between our two countries, and particularly some trade dispute issues. And the President has agreed to do that, and we're looking forward to having that person designated.

I also want to take this opportunity to congratulate the President and his Government on the resolution of the situation in Haiti. I think without the United States' involvement, we would not have that kind of happy resolution. And I confirm Canada's willingness and commitment to be supportive to the followup process in Haiti.

Economic Summit and Japan-U.S. Trade

Q. Mr. President, how important is it for you and Prime Minister Miyazawa to wrap up this summit with a bilateral U.S.-Japanese trade agreement? Will the summit be detracted if you fail to achieve this agreement, given the fact that when you met in April, both of you indicated that you would achieve this agreement by now?

The President. No, it will not, because I think everybody concedes that the summit has far exceeded expectations for it before we began, for two reasons: first of all, the market access agreement on manufactured goods, which is the biggest tariff reduction agreement among nations in 7 years—the jobs, the implications of that are staggering if we can, in fact, conclude the trade agreement by the end of the year; and secondly, because of the size and scope of the aid package to Russia which is very much, as I have said repeatedly, in the interest of the United States and every other democracy in the world—continuing to denuclearize Russia, continuing to develop a free market economy that can interact with the rest of us. So this has been an extremely successful summit.

We should be driven in our negotiations with

Japan by one simple question: Is this a good agreement or not? Will it advance our common interests in reducing the imbalances in our relationship? And if the answer is yes, we should go forward; and if it's not, we shouldn't. And that's what we're going to do. I don't think it has anything to do with the way the summit comes out. It's been a huge net plus.

Q. Mr. President, there seems to be a new optimism today about seeing such an agreement, and are you willing to compromise on the numerical targets or the basic issues enough to bring about an agreement?

The President. Well, I hope there will be an agreement, and I hope I can answer yes to the question that I just posed. I don't think I should say much more about it now. They're talking——

Q. But there is a new optimism?

The President. I don't want to characterize it. I think anything I say to characterize it, up or down, may be wrong. We just have to wait and see what happens.

Q. Mr. President, the economic declaration that you just approved today said that in the future the summits should be more informal, and they should have fewer documents and declarations. And given that this one was a lot less specific in terms of the commitments to growth and stimulus than you had originally wanted, have you given any thought to doing away with this declaration in the future? Did this have any purpose at all?

The President. No, I like this political declaration. Actually, I think both the declarations that we issued here are briefer than they have been in the past, and they're quite specific and, I think, quite good. But we tried very hard not to make them unrealistic, that is, not to have the nations commit to things they had no intention of doing or, perhaps more to the point, no capacity to do.

So I feel pretty good about that. I think what the people who've been here for many years said was that they liked the fact that we were moving back toward a more informal summit process where we focused on one or two big issues, where we tried to get one or two things done, and we didn't overly bureaucratize it. And I think our commitment was to go to Italy next year with smaller operations, more streamlined, even less bureaucracy but focusing on intense, very honest and open interchanges among the leaders, and then try to get one or two specific

things done.

Anyone from the Canadian press?

Canada-U.S. Trade and Strike on Iraq

Q. For your benefit, Mr. President, I'll put my question in English. I would like to know, Mrs. Campbell, in what terms you did talk to the President about trade disputes between Canada and the United States. And I'd like to know as well if you asked him that the next time the United States launches an attack somewhere, if Canada would like to be informed before the event instead of after?

Prime Minister Campbell. Well, in answer to your second question, the answer is yes.

In answer to the first question, I raised a number of the issues that are outstanding between us. Now, obviously we weren't in a position to resolve them here. A number of my provincial colleagues also raised concerns, and so I discussed the irritants that are between us, particularly wheat, sugar, softwood lumber. And I'm very pleased that we will be pursuing those, but more importantly, that we now will have someone in the White House who will be designated as someone that we can be in touch with to help manage those particular irritants between us.

The President. Let me answer—if I might answer that question. The Prime Minister mentioned wheat, sugar, lumber, and beer. We talked about those issues. She also brought to my attention, frankly, something that I have to admit I think she's absolutely right on, that Canada should have been notified at the time we took the action in Iraq. Let me tell you, there was a very tight time window there because of the coincidence of the time when I received the final report from my intelligence and investigative agencies and when the trial started again and getting past the Sabbath in the Islamic countries, the day of worship. That's something that we should have done then and that we will do in the future. Canada has been a good strategic ally of the United States. It's absolutely pivotal in any number of ways. And it was a very legitimate issue to raise.

Another question from the Canadian press?

Trade With Japan

Q. Prime Minister, President Clinton has been pressed from the Japanese to reduce their trade deficit. Are you not afraid that such pressure might result in Japanese investment in Canada being reduced and siphoned off to the United States?

Prime Minister Campbell. Well, there is already a competitive environment for investment. I think the challenge for us is to be an attractive investment environment. And right now there are no guarantees. So I don't see that that's necessarily going to result in the future. I think what the Americans are most concerned about is not simply the flow of investment from Japan to North America but the opening of the Japanese market to goods that are made in North America. And I think that's the significant part of that, of the concern that the United States has raised with Japan. So the short answer to your question is no, I don't see that as a problem in either the short or medium term.

The President. If anything, it might increase Japanese investment in both the United States and Canada so that market share could be maintained while abating the trade deficit. So I wouldn't worry about that at all. I think if anything happens on the investment side, it will encourage more investment in our continent.

Q. Prime Minister, do you support numerical trade targets with Japan the way the United States is seeking at the moment?

Prime Minister Campbell. Well, I think it's up to the United States and Japan to find the mechanism that will work best to meet their goals. I made the point both to the President and to the Prime Minister of Japan that it is in Canada's interest that they resolve those problems because when the United States and Japan have a trade dispute, it is very often Canada that gets sideswiped by the remedies.

So it is very much in Canada's strategic interests that those issues be resolved. As to which mechanism is used, I think that's up to the United States and Japan to determine. But we very much support the resolution of that dispute.

The President. Thank you all very much.

NOTE: The President's 21st news conference began at 2:23 p.m. at the U.S. Ambassador's residence. In his remarks, he referred to Gen. Raoul Cedras, commander of the Haitian military.

The President's News Conference in Tokyo
July 9, 1992

The President. Good evening. The summit we have concluded today sends a message of hope to America and to the world. Some have called this a jobs summit, and they are right because the creation of new jobs in the United States and in all the other countries here present was at the center of all of our discussions.

All of us are mindful that we have a long way to go to restore real growth and opportunity to the global economy, but we have made a serious start. We reached an agreement here that can open manufacturing markets to American products and to all other products in ways that we have not seen in many years. Indeed, the agreement if finally concluded could bring the largest reduction in tariffs in world history.

While tough negotiations still remain, this world trade agreement captures the momentum that we have needed in these negotiations for a long time. We now can move toward completion of a broader trade agreement that could spur the creation of hundreds of thousands of jobs over the next decade in the United States and millions throughout the world.

We also agreed that the other industrialized nations will send their top education, labor, and economic ministers to Washington in the fall for a serious conference on the creation of jobs. All the advanced nations are having difficulty creating new jobs even when their economies are growing. This was a constant cause of concern in all of our conversations, and we are now going to make a serious effort to examine the problem from every angle and to try to come up with new and innovative solutions which can be helpful in the United States and throughout the G–7 countries. We have to figure out how to unlock the doors for people who are left behind in this new global economy.

I want to say a special word of appreciation that the other industrial nations expressed their support and praise for the United States' economic plan to reduce our deficit dramatically and invest in our future.

Ever since 1980, whenever these meetings have occurred, the statements issued at the end have either explicitly or implicitly criticized the United States for our budget deficit. This statement explicitly supports the United States for our effort to bring the deficit down and to bring growth and investment back into our economy.

Other nations clearly welcome our resolve. I might note that the fact that both Houses of Congress had passed the economic plan greatly strengthened my hand in the discussions and the negotiations which have taken place here this week.

This summit also held out fresh hope for other peoples of the world, especially those involved in democratic reform in Russia, led by President Yeltsin who joined us here today. The $3 billion program we announced here to help Russia move to a market system will not only bolster prospects for freedom there, it is a very solid investment for the United States. Funds to move state-owned industries to private hands to make the free enterprise system work, funds to make available operations for new enterprises, funds from the World Bank, and funds for credits for export, all these things will help Americans to do more business in Russia and will help Russia to succeed in a way that will continue the path charted by the end of the cold war, fewer nuclear weapons, fewer defense investments, more opportunities to invest in people and jobs and a peaceful future.

American leadership has been indispensable to growth and to freedom throughout this century. In partnership with others, we will now be able to continue to meet that responsibility in the years ahead. I have said before and I will say again, I came to this summit in the hope that we could get an agreement to open more markets to manufactured products, in the hope that we could get a strong program for Russian aid, in the hope that together we would demonstrate resolve to restore the ability of all of our countries to create jobs and opportunities for our people. I believe those objectives were achieved. And I am pleased at the first of these G–7 meetings which I was able to attend.

Helen [Helen Thomas, United Press International].

Japan

Q. Mr. President, a host of Presidents have tried to convince Japan that trade is a two-way street. What makes you think you can con-

vince them? What is the chance of getting an agreement on trade talks? And what did you learn at the summit that you didn't know before?

The President. You ask a lot of questions. What did you say? You have a followup? [*Laughter*] No, Brit [Brit Hume, ABC News], you get the followup.

I think we do have a chance to get an agreement, and I think in part it is because we are coming to a common understanding that the serious imbalance in trade between our two nations cannot continue and that, in the end, it is not in the interest of either country.

I met this morning with several hundred members of the American Chamber of Commerce here in Tokyo, people who are selling their products and services in this country. They pointed out and illustrated to me once again why more sales of American products in the Japanese market would be good for both countries. When these people come here, they hire Japanese people. They create jobs here in Japan. But as the market is opened up, the price of products and service and their variety is dramatically expanded—the price is driven down; the variety and number of services and products are expanded. So the Japanese people will win if we can correct this imbalance. And of course, the American people will win. It will mean lots more jobs for our folks.

That's what I tried to say at Waseda University. I think that we are now coming to a common understanding that it is in the interest of both countries to change this policy. I think we're also coming to a common understanding that we have to try some new approaches, that Americans have had real increases in productivity and quality—we are now the high-quality, low-cost producer of many products and services—and that that alone is not going to be sufficient to change the market imbalance. And I think those two realizations give us a shot. And I'm hoping that we can move forward.

What did I learn that I didn't know when I got here? I learned a lot more about the other world leaders. I got to know them all better. I got to understand more about where they're coming from, what their countries' problems and opportunities are, and what we can achieve together. I'm, frankly, more optimistic about our potential for common action than I was before I came here.

I also feel much better about our long-term

capacity to make some progress in our relationships with Japan. I was glad to be the first American President ever to address a university audience and to answer questions there. And I feel much more positively about that relationship than I did when I came here. And it is, perhaps, our most bilateral relationship. So that's very good.

Russia

Q. Mr. President, Boris Yeltsin said today that sooner or later Russia would make the G–7 a G–8. My question is why not sooner than later? What are the arguments against keeping Russia out of the G–7?

The President. Well, I don't want to make the argument against keeping Russia out of the G–7. I do believe that you will see him here every time we meet as long as he is President of Russia, which I think will be quite a while. And I think that's a very good thing.

I think that when the G–7 was organized, it was organized as a group of the world's most powerful economic interests and not just political interests. And I think that there will come a time when Russia will probably join this group when there is a consensus that that time has come.

To be fair to all the people who are here, there was really no serious discussion of that. But for the first time, President Yeltsin was invited to come next year before he ever even made a statement. That was part of the Chairman, Prime Minister Miyazawa's opening statement, to make sure he would know that he was going to be invited to come and participate in next year's meeting in Italy.

Brit.

Multilateral Trade Negotiations

Q. Mr. President, you mentioned that further negotiation must be done toward a new world trade agreement. One of the major sticking points for a number of years has, of course, been the issue of agriculture subsidies and agriculture generally. I wondered what, if anything, you may have heard here from your counterparts from Europe and the EC and from Japan that renews your hope, if it does, that such a thing may be possible by December, as you've suggested.

The President. Well, if all the Europeans will adhere to the Blair House accords, I think there's a good chance we can have an agricul-

tural agreement.

As you know, France has some problems with it and has expressed those. And it was an issue in the last election in France. But as I pointed out, the United States cut our agricultural subsidies unilaterally and substantially in 1990, and we have proposed further reductions this year as part of the deficit reduction package. If we were to reopen the Blair House accord, our farmers would want us to go in the opposite direction on these issues from the direction that some of the European interests would take.

Because the European Community is made up of diverse nations, they have a mechanism within the Community to make adjustments among the countries if they adhere to an agreement like an agricultural agreement that affects some countries more adversely than others. So I'm still hopeful that as these negotiations resume—and they will resume in Geneva soon—that the Blair House accord will stand and that we'll be able to work out a balance of trade agreements that will enable it to stand.

If that happens, then much of what we need to do in agriculture will have been done. This market opening agreement, if it can be embraced by the other nations at the GATT, will be nailed down, and then we'll just have a few issues left to go. I remind you the majority of the issues have been resolved although some of the tough ones remain.

Andrea [Andrea Mitchell, NBC News].

North Korea

Q. Mr. President, a week ago before leaving for Asia, you said that North Korea was perhaps the scariest place in the world. And many analysts including Larry Eagleburger have said that North Korea already has the bomb; others believe that it is at least very close to having the bomb. Would you consider a preemptive strike? Would you rule that out? And what message do you want to send in your trip to South Korea about our military interests in the region and about the role of our American troops?

The President. Well, first of all, I don't answer hypothetical questions, especially as they relate to national security, for obvious reasons. But the message should be clear. Even as we move into and through the 6th year of defense cuts, we are not reducing our base presence in Japan; we are not reducing our base presence in Korea. We are strengthening our military presence in Asia and in the Pacific, and we reaffirm our security commitments to Japan and to Korea and to all our other allies in this region. And we intend to press to see that the Non-Proliferation Treaty's regime is fully observed, including having the international observers there.

That is the position that the United States takes. And I think we have to adhere to it very firmly.

Susan [Susan Spencer, CBS News].

Q. So what should we do about North Korea, sir?

The President. Well, we don't—North Korea has not yet declined to comply. And we're going to have to—let us continue the negotiations. Until there is a rupture that seems final, I don't think we should talk about what would happen at that point.

Approval Ratings and the Economic Summit

Q. Sir, before the summit started it was noted widely that your own approval ratings, as unhappy as you may sometimes be with them, were higher than those of any other political leader here. Virtually all of these people are either on the way out or in some great difficulty at home. How did that diminish this summit? And having been to one now and seen how bureaucratic they can be, do you really think in these days of modern communications that these sorts of extravaganzas are necessary at all?

The President. Well, first of all, I think that it did not diminish the summit. In fact, there was more done here and there was more energy and more zip in it than I thought there would be. And I think part of it was, apparently, this summit is less bureaucratic than its predecessors. We ended two of our meetings an hour early, which I liked awful well. And there was an amazing amount of open, free flow of honest exchange. It was very, very good.

I think that any time you have the major economies of the world in the doldrums, combined in some of these countries with a real impetus toward political reform and a felt need of the people to make their political systems work better, you can't expect to see high poll numbers. When people are having a tough time making ends meet, they don't tend to be very happy with their political leaders. So that is a given.

Notwithstanding that, this summit produced real substantive benefits for the people who sent these leaders here.

Now, there was a reaffirmation, a unanimous

reaffirmation on the part of the heads of state in this meeting to make this process less bureaucratic, less expensive, and less cumbersome. And I think you will see an even more streamlined summit next year in Italy, one in which all the delegations are smaller and in which there is more flexibility. I hope that something was learned out of this summit, that if you focus on one or two objectives and really work at it and work at it, you can get something done.

Wolf [Wolf Blitzer, Cable News Network] and then David [David Lauter, Los Angeles Times].

Iraq

Q. Mr. President, even as you were meeting here with these other world leaders, there seems to be another standoff in Baghdad with U.N. weapons inspectors and the Iraqi Government. Double-pronged question: How serious is this, and what, if anything, is the U.S. prepared to do? Is there a unilateral response, or would it be only multilateral this time?

The President. First of all, I think it is serious. And secondly, the response should be a multilateral one. The action we took in response to the plot to assassinate President Bush was a unilateral one, and it should have been, clearly provided for under international law. This action is a violation of the United Nations resolutions, and we are going to keep pushing on it. Hopefully, the Iraqis will relent. If they don't, then we'll go back to the U.N., to the Security Council, and decide where to go from there.

David.

Economic Summit and Job Creation

Q. Mr. President, if I could follow up for a moment on your answer to Susan's question, I wonder, given that these things tend to be very scripted and set out ahead of time, was there any moment in this thing, any event that happened over the last few days that told you something that you didn't know, that presented things in a new light that might give us some insight into how this process works?

The President. Well, first of all, there were moments that were not at all scripted. The first time we met everybody went around the table and sort of described the condition of the economy in each country and what the government was attempting to do about it. And that was somewhat scripted in the sense that everyone was told in advance we'd be asked to do that. After that, only the topics were basically scripted. Very few of us carried a lot of notes around. Very few people referred to them. We really talked about these issues.

I think the thing that impressed me the most—maybe it's just because what I'm most concerned about—was the high level of rather sophisticated knowledge that all these people had about the stagnation of their own economies when it comes to creating jobs. For example, it was pointed out that the French economy was actually, by every other measure, very, very strong in most years of the eighties and several years had a higher growth rate than the German economy. And they still never got their unemployment rate below 9.5 percent, even when they were just really chugging along. The Japanese economy which still enjoys quite a low unemployment rate, in part because of the structure of this economy, still is having quite a lot of difficulty creating jobs.

Most of these countries have very low population growth rates, rapidly aging population, and they're very worried that unless they can turn this situation around that 10 years from now they're going to have two people working for every person that's retired. And they're really quite concerned about it. I think the fact that they're all thinking about it and they all had a little bit different take on it, gave me some hope that we might be able to find some solutions.

Q. Did anyone offer solutions?

The President. Well, there were lots of different solutions offered. But one of the things— Helmut Kohl is a very wise man, I think, and one of the things he said that was interesting was that if we could come to grips with this in the same way we try to come to grips with trade problems, for example, that if there are tough decisions to be made, it will be easier for each country to make them if the people who live in each country are aware that this is a worldwide problem and that there have to be some new and different directions taken.

Hillary Clinton

Q. Mr. President, your wife, Hillary Rodham Clinton, has caused quite a stir in Japan, and yet she's followed a very traditional wives' schedule here which, frankly, doesn't seem much like her. I wonder if she's been muzzled here perhaps to avoid offending Japanese sensibilities?

The President. No, she did what she wanted to do. She thought about it quite a lot, and

I've been, frankly, impressed and gratified by the response that she's gotten from just the people in the street, especially the young working women as well as the students at the university the other day. And I think it's a real indication of the aspirations of younger Japanese people to see that everybody here has a chance to live up to their potential. I was really very pleased by it.

Economic Program

Q. You return home in a few days. You're going to be facing kind of a do-or-die situation with the budget bill which got you so much play here. How do you relate your accomplishments from this week to what faces you when you get back next week?

The President. Well, it certainly ought to strengthen the resolve of the Congress to carry through on this. There's no question that the other countries were very much encouraged by the determination of the United States to reduce its deficit, that they believe that's one of the things that has distorted the world economy for the last several years.

And likewise, there is no question that some of our job growth we're going to have to do on our own. So a lot of these investments, both the private and the public investments in the economic plan, to create jobs should be adopted.

So I am hoping that what happened this week will strengthen the resolve of the Congress to go ahead and pass the economic plan and to do it in short order so that we can go on to other things. We all, after all, have a lot of other things to do. We have to get the health care cost controls in and provide basic health care security to American families. We have to continue to deal with the transformation from a defense to a domestic economy and try to help people accommodate all those changes. We've got an enormous amount of work to do. We've got a crime bill we need to pass. We've got a lot of other things on the agenda. So we've got to get this economic plan passed.

Q. Mr. President, you came here——

The President. Go ahead. I'll take both of you. Just stand there. That's called splitting the difference.

Go ahead.

Korean War

Q. Mr. President, with regard to your forthcoming trip to Korea, I wondered, first of all, do you have any personal recollections of the war? I know you were quite young when that happened. And secondly, knowing your views on the Vietnam war, is the Korean war one that you would have felt comfortable fighting in, where you were not so with Vietnam?

The President. Absolutely. We did the right thing there, and I don't really think we had any choice, given the way it began. And I think the years and the aftermath have certainly validated the decision which was made to contest the forces of communism where we did and when we did.

And yes, I do have quite a vivid memory. I remember mostly, even though I was very young, President Eisenhower's campaign and what he said about going to Korea. It's almost my first political memory, that campaign.

Yes, go ahead.

Russian Nuclear Powerplants

Q. Mr. President, we were told that you came to this summit with growing concerns about the condition of former Soviet nuclear powerplants that are deteriorating. Will you broach this personally with Yeltsin tomorrow? Is there another Chernobyl out there? In other words, how imminent of a crisis is this, and what's the West going to do about it?

The President. Actually, we talked about it today at some great length. And there were two issues raised. The first is, President Yeltsin thanked the West for the assistance which has already been given to try to help them make those plants either safer or decommission them. What he called the first generation of their nuclear plants, they're actually trying to decommission them all, just take them out of commission so they won't run the risk of another Chernobyl. He said they had virtually completed that task. And he talked a little bit about his plans for energy and for nuclear power specifically. And I think the conversation was quite reassuring to the others who were there. I say to the others because I had talked about it a little bit with him before.

The second thing that came up, which I was very impressed by, raised by President Mitterrand, was the question of whether the Russian plans for decommissioning these plants, as well as technical assistance to do it ought to be made available to other Republics of the former Soviet Union who had similar plants, and he agreed

to do that. He said that if other Republics that had these kind of nuclear plants wanted the plans and wanted the technical assistance, he would be very happy to do it. And the rest of us said we'd be glad to support that. So that was the resolution that I thought quite good.

Unemployment

Q. Do you have any concern that the jobs summit may turn to looking like it's a union-bashing event in that a lot of the work rules that are established in Europe that a lot of people think caused the problems are, in fact, union related?

The President. They could, but there's a serious factual problem, if that's the total slant on it, which is the experience of Germany before the East was integrated into it. That is, if you split out East Germany from West Germany and you look just at the unemployment rate in West Germany for the last year or two, you'll see that's the only country in Europe with an unemployment rate as low as ours. Ours is too high. And their is too high, but theirs is much lower than all the other European countries. And yet they have very high costs in terms of mandatory vacations, in terms of mandatory worker retraining, in terms of general education investment in workers, in terms of mandatory health care coverage. Although their health care is much less expensive than ours, all employers have to undertake it.

So it's a hard case to make in the case of Germany where they have rather high labor costs and manufacturing wage costs, higher than the United States on average, terrifically productive workers, and they have managed to keep their unemployment fairly low. Now their overall unemployment is higher because of the very high unemployment in East Germany.

So we're going to have to be a little more sophisticated than that. I mean, there are some things that may add to unemployment or may prohibit job creation and some that aren't.

Bosnia

Q. Mr. President, you said in your political communique that stronger measures could be taken against Serbia to end the war in Bosnia, but you didn't say what those measures were, nor under what conditions they might be taken. Given your inability to bring the Europeans along on your efforts before in the fighting there regarding air strikes and lifting the arms embargo, why should we think that action will now be taken as a result of your communique?

The President. The discussions that I had at this meeting about Bosnia were almost all, not all but almost all, one-on-one with other leaders. And frankly, I counseled against raising hopes unnecessarily and focusing more on what we might do and saying less until we were prepared to do something.

I will say this: The one new statement that is in this policy that I am absolutely convinced that all the leaders of the other countries meant, that should have some impact on the situation, was the one proposed by Chancellor Kohl which says that, essentially, that if Serbia and Croatia carve up Bosnia in the absence of an international peace agreement to which the Bosnian Government freely subscribes, that the rest of us have no intention of doing any business with either of them if that happens.

That would have a very serious detrimental economic consequence on both Croatia and Serbia. And it had never been said exactly like that before, particularly as it relates to Croatia. So I think that is the new part of this statement. Yes.

Japan

Q. Mr. President, the last time an American President was in this city the Japanese Prime Minister said he pitied the United States. It was a remark you cited often in the campaign. In your talks with the Prime Minister did you detect any change in that attitude, or did you think there's still pity for the United States?

The President. I did detect a change. But I have to tell you, I have tried very hard to move this dialog into a constructive frame of mind. When I spoke at Waseda University, I acknowledged that one of the reasons that there was such a big trade deficit with Japan in the

1980's was that we had such a huge Government deficit, we needed a lot of Japanese money to pay for our debt, to keep our interest rates down.

In other words, I tried to go beyond the rhetoric and finger-pointing of both sides. I also pointed out, however, that we have now had 10 years of high manufacturing productivity growth, that we really are the high quality, low cost producer of many goods and services, and that we have to recognize we have to have a new relationship.

I think we should focus on things that are positive for both of us and be very, very firm about the need to change. But I don't sense a lot of ridicule here. And as a matter of fact, what I was hoping was that the Japanese would not be too concerned about all the changes going on in this country. A lot of the political changes are without precedent in the postwar era, post-World-War-II era. But they are the inevitable part of growing in a democracy and changing. And I sense a real sense of anticipation and openness here that's perhaps a little greater than it has been in past years and pretty uniformly throughout the people that I met and talked with.

I must say a special word of appreciation to our host, Prime Minister Miyazawa, who, even though his party is facing elections, as you know, in just a few days, displayed a great vigor and willingness to discuss a lot of these issues and to try to bring them to closure, and clearly had to sign off on the market access agreement and had to make some changes to do so in his government's position.

Thank you very much.

NOTE: The President's 22d news conference began at 8:10 p.m. in the garden of the U.S. Ambassador's residence.

Exchange With Reporters in Tokyo
July 9, 1993

Aid to Russia

Q. Mr. President, we wanted to ask you about Russian aid. Is there any sense of disappointment that there isn't more cash, less credit, that

this isn't helpful enough to Yeltsin? What is your take on it?

The President. No. As a matter of fact, I think, based on where we were 5 or 6 weeks ago, this is a real success. I'm very pleased.

I came here with the hope of getting $500 million in a privatization fund to help convert these government-owned industries to private sector industries. And the Europeans have really come forward. I talked to a lot of them in the last week, and it appears to me that we'll have at least $500 million in that fund and an aid package that will probably be somewhere in the neighborhood of $3 billion. So that is very good. It's also very good for America. I mean, there's a lot of business to be done in Russia by Americans to create American jobs, business and energy and natural resources, in environmental technologies, in all kinds of consumer operations. This is a huge new market for American goods and services.

It's also good news because it will end—a lot of this money will enable us to continue to denuclearize Russia, that is, to dismantle their nuclear weapons and to help to deal with the aftermath of that. And that is very, very important in terms of making our country and our world more safe and helping us to continue to manage these defense reductions. So I'm very happy about that.

Q. What did President Yeltsin tell you tonight? What was his reaction, do you know?

The President. Well, he's in a good humor tonight, but we just had dinner together. It was a formal dinner, so we didn't have much time to talk business. I'm going to see him tomorrow, and I'm looking forward to visiting with him again. But he is in very good shape now, since the election. The process of political reform is continuing in Russia, and I feel good about it. And also, one thing I really appreciate about President Yeltsin is that he encouraged us to set up an operation in Moscow to make sure that our money was not wasted, which I was very impressed with. And so I've been working for months now to try to get agreement among all these countries about exactly what mechanism we'll have to monitor the expenditure of this money. And we've achieved agreement on that. So I'm very encouraged about that.

Trade Negotiations

Q. Mr. President, do you expect any more breakthroughs at this summit, I mean, in terms of Japanese trade rules and so forth? Or are we just flailing?

The President. No, we're not just flailing. But I don't know. I mean, if that were to happen it would be a good thing, as long as it's a good agreement for America. But I don't want to raise any false hopes. We were able to get this huge breakthrough on the trade in manufactured goods with these other nations, which could lead to a huge number of new jobs for America. The same thing could happen if we could get a breakthrough in our trade relations with Japan. But our job is to negotiate firmly in the interests of the United States, and we're doing that. And we'll just have to see what happens.

Russian Role in Economic Summit

Q. Mr. President, why is the G–7 not disposed to make themselves the G–8 and include Russia?

The President. Well, I think you will see more and more involvement by Russia over the next couple of years. President Yeltsin's coming here; I expect he'll be with us next year. And I don't think that this group is wedded to any particular membership. But I'm not sure it's the right time to discuss a formal expansion. But he's going to have a major role in this meeting tomorrow, and I expect him to be here next year.

Q. Isn't the statement on Bosnia somewhat disappointing?

Japan-U.S. Relations

Q. Will you have dinner tonight with Mr. Miyazawa? And what do you read into the fact that he wants to see you again for a trade agreement or——

The President. I think they are interested in moving our relationships forward. To me, it was encouraging that he invited me to dinner because we've already been together once. And I think it indicates that the Japanese do understand there has to be some change in the relationship between the United States and Japan, in both our interests.

Whether we can agree on exactly what the shape of that should be at this time, I don't know. And I'm doing the best I can to represent the interests of our country. But as I said in my speech yesterday to the university students, I also believe that the position I've taken is in the best interests of Japan. I know it's in the best interests of Japanese consumers, but it's going to help to stabilize this economy, too, if they can open their markets more and not be driven by the desire to maintain these massive trade surpluses. So we'll work at it. But I was gratified that he invited me to dinner, and I'm going to go.

Q. Wasn't there something good to tell you?

Q. Wasn't the statement on Bosnia——

Economic Summit

Q. You had expressed some frustration with the sort of formal, stilted nature of these things, sir. Did you feel you're making any progress towards getting them——

The President. A lot. A lot.

Q. How is that working out?

The President. Well, we finished an hour early today, partly because of the extra informality. The reason we finished an hour early today is because we discussed a lot of what was on the agenda today, yesterday, when we had a more unstructured 3-hour meeting and last night during our dinner. And we agreed this afternoon to make next year's session even more informal so that we could focus on a few big things, cut out a lot of the bureaucracy and all the other stuff that goes with these summits, and really try to get a few big things done in a very informal way. So I feel good about it.

Q. Aren't you disappointed on Bosnia, Mr. President? Isn't it sort of a weak statement on Bosnia?

Japanese Crown Prince and Princess

Q. How did you like the Crown Prince?

Q. No, let me just ask—let me ask——

Press Secretary Myers. He's done.

Q. How did you like her?

The President. A lot. I had dinner with her. I liked her a lot. I liked him a lot.

Q. What did you talk about?

Press Secretary Myers. Okay, thanks, you guys. Everybody out. Come on.

Q. Give us some color.

Midwest Flooding

Q. What did they tell you about the flood——

The President. I think they've crested at the upper level. But there will be rolling floods all the way down the Mississippi. We'll just have to see what happens.

NOTE: The exchange began at 11:30 p.m. in the President's suite at the Okura Hotel.

Letter to Congressional Leaders on the Former Yugoslav Republic of Macedonia
July 9, 1993

Dear Mr. Speaker: (*Dear Mr. President:*)

On June 18, 1993, the U.N. Security Council adopted Resolution 842, expanding the size of the U.N. Protection Force (UNPROFOR) in the former Yugoslav Republic of Macedonia. The Security Council acknowledged the important contribution of the existing UNPROFOR presence to stability in the region and welcomed the addition of a U.S. peacekeeping contingent to UNPROFOR in Macedonia. I have since ordered the deployment of U.S. Armed Forces to Macedonia for these purposes and am providing this report, consistent with Section 4 of the War Powers Resolution, to ensure that the Congress is kept fully informed about this important U.S. action in support of United Nations efforts in the region.

After the adoption of U.N. Security Council Resolution 795 (1992), which established the UNPROFOR Macedonia mission under Chapter VI of the U.N. Charter, UNPROFOR deployed a Nordic battalion composed of some 700 military personnel to Macedonia in early 1993. This peacekeeping force has been stationed along the northern Macedonian border with the mandate of monitoring and reporting any developments that could signify a threat to the territory of Macedonia. Norway, Finland, and Sweden have contributed infantry companies to this battalion, which is under the U.N. command of a Danish Brigadier General.

Over the past several days, we have begun implementing plans to augment UNPROFOR Macedonia with U.S. Armed Forces, consistent with Security Council Resolution 842 and as part of the U.S. commitment to support multilateral efforts to prevent the Balkan conflict from spreading and to contribute to stability in the region. At my direction, the Chairman of the Joint Chiefs of Staff through the Commander in Chief, U.S. European Command, ordered the deployment of Company C, 6th Battalion, 502nd Infantry Regiment of the Berlin Brigade to Macedonia. On July 3, advance parties and support elements began transporting equipment into Macedonia by U.S. C–141 aircraft. The main body of this unit began arriving by U.S. C–5 aircraft on July 7. The unit's equipment, including M–113 Armored Personnel Carriers (APCs), has also been delivered to the operating area. It is expected that the full contingent of U.S. military personnel, numbering approximately 350, will be in place and equipped by July 12.

The U.S. contingent will serve under the operational control of UNPROFOR Macedonia and will conduct missions as directed by the U.N. commander. Although UNPROFOR Macedonia is a U.N. peacekeeping force under Chapter VI of the Charter and has not encoun-

tered hostilities to date, our forces are fully prepared not only to fulfill their peacekeeping mission but to defend themselves if necessary.

This deployment is important to our foreign policy and natural security interests and has been directed in accordance with Section 7 of the United Nations Participation Act and pursuant to my constitutional authority as Commander in Chief and Chief Executive. I will continue to keep you informed about the progress of this and other U.S. efforts towards peace and stability in the vital Balkan region.

Sincerely,

BILL CLINTON

NOTE: Identical letters were sent to Thomas S. Foley, Speaker of the House of Representatives, and Robert C. Byrd, President pro tempore of the Senate.

Nomination for Posts at the Commerce and Transportation Departments
July 9, 1993

The President has announced his intention to nominate David Barram to the position of Deputy Secretary at the Department of Commerce and Steve Palmer to be Assistant Secretary for Governmental Affairs at the Department of Transportation.

"These appointments are a continuation of our efforts to nominate accomplished and dedicated professionals to important Government positions," the President said.

The President said that Mr. Barram's private

sector experience will be a valuable asset at the Commerce Department. "His professional background combined with his extensive community service will add an important perspective."

"Steve Palmer," said the President, "has lengthy experience in Federal Government which makes him especially qualified for this post."

NOTE: Biographies of the nominees were made available by the Office of the Press Secretary.

The President's News Conference with President Boris Yeltsin of Russia in Tokyo
July 10, 1992

President Clinton. Good morning. I want to make just a couple of brief remarks and let President Yeltsin make a couple of remarks, and then we'll take a few questions.

Since I last met with President Yeltsin in Vancouver, the Russian people have voted in an historic referendum to continue their march to-

ward democracy and toward a free market economy. They've taken bold steps to create a new constitution.

We have now obligated over two-thirds of the funds that we promised to contribute to Russia's march toward democracy and free markets at Vancouver. We are delivering the promised humanitarian food shipments. We have provided substantial support for Russia's efforts to privatize state-owned industries. Loans to create new Russian businesses and jobs will soon be on the way through our Russian-American Enterprise Fund. And just this week, the United States Export-Import Bank signed a $2 billion oil and gas framework that will help to revitalize Russia's energy sector and provide for expanded sales of American equipment and services.

As I have said to the American people from the very beginning, an investment in Russia's future is good for the American people as well as good for the Russian people.

I want to mention a special project in particular that Hillary has been involved with. She discovered that Mrs. Yeltsin has a special interest in improving the dental health care of Russia's children, and she was able to arrange the delivery of surplus American military equipment for two dental clinics in Moscow. I very much appreciate Mrs. Yeltsin's efforts in this regard.

I've also been working, as all of you know, with the congressional leadership and members of both parties to pass a second round of Russian aid through the Congress, as well as to eliminate obsolete cold war restrictions that still impede our trade, scientific, and cultural contracts with Russia. I expect those will be successful also.

We discussed a lot of issues here today, but the bottom line is we believe we have a good partnership. We think it is working in the interests of the people of Russia and the people of the United States. And we intend to keep it going.

Mr. President.

President Yeltsin. Thank you.

After the Vancouver meeting, President Clinton and I have established a relationship over months that have been replete with significant work. It was President Clinton's purpose to ensure that Congress adopt the package of agreements that we had set. I, for my part, had to win the referendum and also ensure that we prepare ourselves for the adoption of our new constitution. And I think both parties, the two Presidents, have resolved these matters.

And today we had an opportunity of checking up on time limits, what has been accomplished since the Vancouver meeting, what has been failed in a sense, and it's like answering to the test that you have to undergo at school. And I think that, in a sense, well, I think that we

managed to clear about 25 questions together. And this, of course, concerned bilateral relations and also international matters, starting with the Asian and the Pacific region, the Middle East, and also general problems or world problems that we share in connection with the military.

Now, I'd like to say that I'm happy with our meeting here. And I think that our partnership and our friendship is strengthening day by day, and this is indeed the guarantee of further developments and progress.

Thank you.

Russian Military Sales

Q. Were you able to persuade Mr. Yeltsin to cancel the sale of Russian missile technology to India and Libya? Did you discuss that, and where does that stand now?

President Clinton. We discussed the outstanding differences of opinion, and we agreed to continue the negotiations intensely and immediately. And I think you may have some sort of answer at least on the ongoing status of the negotiations next week.

Russia–U.S. Relations

Q. How do you evaluate the level of Russian and American relations in terms of dealing with problems? Are they at the level of mutual understanding or shall we say there is certain interaction, and how far are we getting in the relations between the two countries?

President Clinton. Is that for me or for President Yeltsin?

Q. Both.

President Clinton. I think we have forged a remarkable partnership. We have worked together on any number of issues including this G–7 summit we just completed, including our efforts to avoid the problems that would be created if North Korea were to withdraw from the nonproliferation regime, and a whole range of other issues.

I think it has been a remarkable partnership. Are there differences between our two countries and between our positions? Of course there are. Can we resolve every issue? Of course we can't. We represent two great countries that are now very much more alike than they have ever been in their histories but still have some differences. But I think the peoples of our nations should feel very good about the level of cooperation that we have and the deep bonds of partnership that we have formed.

President Yeltsin. I'd like to say that we do have a very good partnership, and I think that we're developing relations and more than that. Earlier, we used not to discuss matters of local conflicts within the Community of Independent States. But this time we have touched on matters concerning Georgia, the situation in Georgia, and we've also covered the Baltic States and a number of other aspects and issues. So indeed, we have started tackling specific issues. And so we have brought the oppositions closer, and there is a lot that is in parallel, so to speak.

Ukraine

Q. This is a question for both Presidents. Ukraine has said that it wants to be a nuclear power, and it does not want to give up its weapons. What do you think of that?

President Clinton. Well, there are different voices in Ukraine. Ukraine is also committed to join the NPT and to ratify START I and to go on to START II. We have a lot of outstanding negotiations with Ukraine. We are now trying to negotiate a comprehensive agreement for the disposition of highly enriched uranium in Ukraine and Kazakhstan, as well as in Russia. There are lots of things that we have going on.

And I can only tell you for my part that I hope that there will be a nonnuclear Ukraine, that the commitments the Government has made will be kept. And I hope the United States can be engaged with Ukraine in a positive way so that they will feel that it is very much in their interests to do that. And I think President Yeltsin feels the same way.

President Yeltsin. Yes, indeed, I agree with you. And we've agreed today to supply certain ideas so that the concept of a trilateral agreement for Ukraine—let's say, Ukraine, U.S.A., and Russia.

Russia-U.S. Trade

Q. I heard—[*inaudible*]—yesterday that some 300 legislative acts in the United States discriminatory towards Russia would be lifted within 2 years or so. What can you say on that, and how soon Russia is going to get the most favorable nation status? Thank you.

President Clinton. First of all, I think that many of those acts discriminatory against Russia that date back to the cold war period will be removed from the books of Congress in this year. We have compiled quite a long list of them that we think cannot be justified anymore. And there is a strong base of support in both political parties in the United States Congress to remove those laws. So we will, as soon as I go home, we will begin to put in motion the process of removing many of those statutes.

As to the second question you mentioned, we are working also on the possibility of the graduation out of the Jackson-Vanik restrictions for Russia. And the President and I discussed a couple of items outstanding on that. And we made an agreement about how we would proceed with them. And I think if we can resolve them, you will see that moving forward as well.

Thank you very much.

Visit to Moscow

Q. Are you going to have a meeting in Moscow?

President Clinton. It's possible. I hope so. We didn't set a definite date, but I accepted President Yeltsin's invitation.

Q. This year?

President Clinton. I hope it will be this year. That depends on what we do at home, you know. But I hope so.

NOTE: The President's 23d news conference began at 9:17 a.m. at the U.S. Ambassador's residence. President Yeltsin spoke in Russian, and his remarks were translated by an interpreter.

Remarks With Prime Minister Kiichi Miyazawa of Japan in Tokyo
July 10, 1993

Prime Minister Miyazawa. President Clinton and I were able to agree upon the establishment of the Japan-U.S. framework for a new economic partnership. This agreement comes at a time to coincide with the Tokyo summit, which symbolizes the cooperation and coordination between the G–7 partners in the international society in the post-cold-war era.

This framework is something that President Clinton and I agreed to establish in our bilateral summit meeting held in last April. President Clinton and I share the views that establishing such a new framework and stabilizing Japan-U.S. economic relations from the medium- to long-term perspective and managing our bilateral economic relationship constructively are extremely important not only to the enhancement of the national life of our two countries but also to the maintenance and strengthening of the free trading system of the world.

The negotiating teams of our two countries, based on those perspectives, the negotiating teams of both countries made serious negotiations both in Washington and Tokyo. And they made further negotiations on the occasion of President Clinton's visit, and subsequently, they have succeeded in reaching an agreement.

Let me share you the gist of this framework in a few words. This framework aims at facilitating frank and broad exchange of views between our two countries, and aims at resolving the economic issues between our two countries based on the spirit of joint exercise between the two largest free market economies that are the United States and Japan, and also aims at advancing our cooperation on issues such as environment and technology which have significance. More concretely, under this framework we will operate on the principles of two-way dialog and limiting our consultations to matters within the scope and responsibility of government.

Under those principles, we will deal with the following: to Japan's efforts at reducing the current account surplus and the reduction of the American Federal budget deficit, in the macroeconomic area. In sectoral and structural area we will deal with government procurement and deregulation, et cetera. And on our common task for cooperation on global perspective, we will deal with issues such as environment and technology. And we will announce the achievements regarding these issues at our biannual bilateral summit meeting.

Furthermore, let me share with you that Japan intends to take measures on its own initiative to further expand its market access, to enhance its transparency, and promote deregulation, all along with our objective to achieve better quality of life. And I expect and hope that

in the United States as well the U.S. Government will make progress in reducing the Federal budget deficit and in strengthening international competitiveness.

Through the efforts of our two governments, we would like to contribute to the strengthening of Japan-U.S. economic relations and also to contribute to the development of world economy in the future.

Thank you, Mr. Clinton.

The President. Thank you. Thank you very much. Today's agreement is an important step toward a more balanced trade relationship between the United States and Japan, but it also benefits the world trading system.

For years we have had trade agreements that have failed to reduce our chronic trade deficits. Those agreements have not worked because they lacked a commitment to tangible results and they provided no way to measure success. This has caused resentment to build over time on both sides, threatening our vital friendship.

This framework agreement we are announcing today takes a different approach. As I said in my speech at Waseda University earlier this week, we are not interested in managed trade or trade by numbers but better results from better rules of trade. This framework launches us on that road.

As the Prime Minister said, we will negotiate a series of agreements under this framework, some to be completed within 6 months, the rest within a year, that will allow greater penetration of the Japanese marketplace in specific areas of the economy. And these new agreements will include specific timetables and objective criteria for measuring success. These results-oriented agreements can create bigger markets for key U.S. industries, including the automotive industry, computers, telecommunications, satellites, medical equipment, financial service, and insurance. If we are successful, we will create benefits for citizens in both the United States and Japan: more jobs and opportunities for America's workers and businesses, new choices and lower prices for Japanese consumers, and new jobs for Japanese citizens in business establishments located in Japan but owned by citizens of other countries.

Again, as the Prime Minister said, this framework also includes a basic bargain. We agree that the United States will significantly cut our budget deficit, which has clearly slowed the growth of the global economy. And we will continue our efforts to improve our competitive position, to be the high-quality, low-cost producer of more and more goods and services. In return, the Japanese agree to what the agree quotes as highly significant reductions in their trade surplus and increases in their imports of goods and services from the United States and other countries. In other words, both nations have made some tough choices.

We should have no illusions. We announced today a framework to govern specific agreements yet to be negotiated. Negotiating those agreements will surely be difficult. But now, at least, we have agreed what the outcome of these negotiations needs to be: tangible, measurable progress.

I have said for some time that the United States and Japan, the two largest economies of the world, must strengthen our friendship. Our political relationship is strong; our security relationship is firm. These trading disputes have been corrosive, and both of us are called upon to change. It is essential that we put this relationship on a footing of mutual respect and mutual responsibility. This framework is a good beginning.

As the Prime Minister said, many people worked very hard on these negotiations. And before I conclude my statement, I would like to express appreciation to people on both sides. I want to thank on the American side Mr. Bo

Cutter, who was our lead negotiator and is the Deputy Director of the National Economic Council; Charlene Barshefsky, the Deputy U.S. Trade Representative; Roger Altman, the Deputy Secretary of the Treasury; and Joan Spero, the Under Secretary of State. They did an excellent job. They worked many long hours with their Japanese counterparts. I also want to thank the Japanese negotiating team, and I want to say a special word of appreciation to Prime Minister Miyazawa for his leadership here at the G–7 summit and his constant attention to these bilateral negotiations while they were going on. He has shown wisdom, determination, and genuine leadership.

Perhaps only I and a few others know how difficult these negotiations have been, how many late night discussions have been involved, how hard so many people have tried for our two countries to reach across the divide that has separated us on this issue. I do not believe that this day would have come to pass had it not been for Prime Minister Miyazawa, and I thank him in a very heartfelt way. I think he has done a great service today for the people of Japan, the people of the United States, and for the principle of a free world economy.

NOTE: The remarks began at 10 a.m. at the Okura Hotel. A tape was not available for verification of the content of these remarks.

Remarks and an Exchange With Reporters Following Discussions With President Kim Yong-sam of South Korea in Seoul
July 10, 1993

President Kim. Today President Clinton and I had very useful discussions of the wide-ranging issues of mutual concern for about 1½ hours. I was deeply impressed by President Clinton, who is playing leadership role in maintaining world peace and coping with new challenges in the post-cold-war era.

In today's meeting, President Clinton and I discussed current international political situation, including new post-cold-war situation in northeast Asia. We also had wide-ranging consultations on how to further develop the Korea-U.S. partnership in the areas of politics, security, economy, and trade.

In particular, we had an indepth discussion on North Korea's nuclear development program. And we shared the view that this issue poses a serious threat not only to peace on the Korean Peninsula but also to the security of northeast Asia and the world as a whole. Also, we expressed our satisfaction over the close coordination between our two countries in dealing with the North Korean nuclear issue. Most importantly, we confirmed that, through this process, we should continue to encourage North Korea to remain within the nuclear nonproliferation regime and to implement faithfully these inspection responsibilities with the IAEA mechanism.

We also reconfirmed that through effective mutual inspections by the two Koreas themselves, the denuclearization declaration should be fully implemented, leading eventually to the resolution of North Korea's nuclear issue.

We will, therefore, continue our efforts to persuade North Korea to remove suspicion over its nuclear program. The next round of U.S.-North Korean contacts will be held in a few days. And at the same time, we will keep the door open for South-North dialog. In case, however, North Korea does not demonstrate different attitudes toward the resolution of the nuclear issue, in spite of our sincere efforts, then the international community will inevitably have to come up with appropriate countermeasures to deal with the issue.

President Clinton renewed firm commitment of the United States to the defense and security of the Republic of Korea and reassured that any further reduction of U.S. forces in Korea would be made only after the uncertainties surrounding North Korea's nuclear program has been thoroughly examined.

President Clinton and I noted with satisfaction the amicable trade relations between our two countries and concurred that the measures the Korean Government is taking to liberalize and internationalize this economy under the new economic policy will help further expand and develop our bilateral trade relations. More specifically, President Clinton and I agreed on the need to develop a future-oriented economic partnership between our two countries. And for this purpose, we have agreed to launch a new bilateral forum for consultation, named the Dialogue for Economic Cooperation. Within this framework, the two countries will discuss various ways to enhance bilateral economic cooperation and address the issues of economic deregulation as it affects economic relations between our two countries. Also, we shared the hope that the Uruguay round of multilateral trade negotiations should be concluded before the end of this year to help revitalize the world economy. And we have agreed to work together to achieve that goal.

As staunch friends and allies, the Republic of Korea and the United States have maintained a close and cooperative relationship during the last several decades. Our countries will continue to expand this relationship to make it into a lasting and comprehensive partnership based upon the common ideals of democracy in the fields of politics, national security, economy, trade, culture, and academic exchanges.

I'm entirely satisfied with the result of our today's summit meeting, and I'm fully convinced that today's meeting will mark the first of many fruitful occasions of such consultations between President Clinton and me in the future. Thank you very much.

President Clinton. Thank you very much. First, let me thank President Kim for his warm welcome and for his very accurate summary of the discussions that we have just held. I would simply like to highlight a couple of points.

First, we reviewed our mutual efforts to ensure the security and peace of the people living on the Korean Peninsula. And I reassured President Kim of my commitment to ensure that the United States continues to play its historic role. We devoted particular attention to the issue of North Korea's nuclear program and agreed to continue our very close cooperation in dealing with this matter. This program is of great concern not only to the United States and the Republic of Korea but to all in this region. We agreed to consult closely on our joint efforts to achieve a full resolution of this issue, and we are resolute to take additional steps if they are required. I did reaffirm my strong intention to have no further reduction in our military presence in this region as long as there is any outstanding question of security regarding this issue.

President Kim and I also discussed the importance of working together to expand trade through the Organization on Asian Pacific Economic Cooperation and the meetings we will have there in Washington this fall.

I thanked President Kim for his support of the results of the G–7 conference just concluded in Tokyo, his support of the Uruguay round of the world trade negotiations, and for the announcement of the new Dialogue for Economic Cooperation to resolve the outstanding issues between our two countries and to build an even stronger economic cooperation between us.

Finally, I want to express my appreciation to President Kim for his personal lifetime devotion to the cause of democracy and for the very good example that the anticorruption and deregulation campaigns here set for all of Asia and indeed for budding democracies throughout the world. I believe that this is the sort of example we need more of.

And finally, let me say I appreciate the visit

that we had. I think we established a very good personal relationship and a very good bond between our two countries. I look forward to further talks, and the President has accepted my invitation to visit the United States later this year, so we will have another chance to work on these issues personally.

North Korean Nuclear Development

Q. Mr. President, in case North Korea doesn't show sincere efforts to solve their nuclear problem, then the Republic of Korea will react with appropriate countermeasures to deal with the issue. Is there any time scale in your plan to deal with this issue, and what is the most appropriate measures to be taken towards it?

President Kim. I do not necessarily think that it is desirable to give you any time scale or any concrete appropriate actions to be taken. But what is most important, what is most clear, is that with regard to this issue we had a very close consultation with the United States, and we will continue to do so in the future.

China

Q. President Clinton, what role can China play in trying to be helpful, if at all helpful, in this? Do you see China as being instrumental in trying to persuade the North Koreans to follow the treaties?

President Clinton. I do believe China can play a constructive role. When the United States and South Korea were attempting to discourage North Korea from withdrawing from the NPT, China was quite helpful. I think the Chinese Government is very interested in supporting the position we have taken here. They have stronger and stronger trade relations with South Korea. And they obviously are more and more interested in becoming a commercial power of the future rather than a military power of the past. And so, we will both—we agreed today that we would continue to inform the Chinese of what we were doing, and we will certainly ask for their support in our efforts.

Dialogue for Economic Cooperation

Q. President Clinton, there was an announcement today that the Dialogue for Economic Cooperation will be launched from today. At the same time, there is an expectation that the Uruguay round of negotiations, multilateral negotiations, will come to conclusion, at latest, before the end of this year. Now, there is, however,

a concern that perhaps the launching of this new Economic Cooperation Dialogue is a means for the United States to press ahead with its own idea of economic relationship with the United States in a bilateral sense. Does it carry any truth, or do you have any comment on this?

President Clinton. First let me say that is a very good question. I do not see our efforts to get an agreement in the Uruguay round and this announcement today as in conflict. Between any two nations that have as many trade relations as the United States and the Republic of Korea, there will always be issues outstanding that need to be discussed.

Obviously, if by the end of the year we can conclude a successful Uruguay round, that may resolve some of the issues between our two countries. But still there will be other issues in terms of the practical openness of our markets, what we can do to encourage more investment, how we enforce the laws that we all agree should be on the books. There are lots of questions like this that in good faith two friends ought to discuss. And so, we're very hopeful that that is what we can do.

I should say, too, as much for the Americans as for the Koreans here, that just a few years ago Korea had a very large trade surplus with the U.S. In the last 2 or 3 years, it's been a very small trade surplus, and this year we might actually have a small surplus with Korea. So our trade is more or less in balance, and the problems we have relate to the way we implement certain things. So I don't think you should be concerned. We are going to go forward with the Uruguay round, and we won't do anything in this context that is in conflict with the desire to get a world trade agreement.

North Korean Nuclear Development

Q. President Clinton, you mentioned being resolute to take additional steps to stop North Korea's nuclear program. What are the carrots and sticks that you could apply to make North Korea comply with the IAEA safeguards?

President Clinton. First, let me say that the talks will resume in a few days. I think it is obvious that the most important carrot out there is the one that President Kim has articulated when he described the conditions under which the two nations might move toward reunification with various confidence-building measures and other steps along the way. The economic success of South Korea and the prospect that North Korea might one day have a cultural unity again and an economic success must be the greatest carrot of all. The sticks I think are obvious, but I think, again, I would support what President Kim said. We should not be discussing at this point what we might do if all our other efforts fail.

Thank you.

NOTE: The remarks began at 4 p.m. at the Blue House. President Kim spoke in Korean, and his remarks were translated by an interpreter.

Remarks to the Korean National Assembly in Seoul
July 10, 1993

Thank you very much, Mr. Speaker, leaders of the National Assembly, members of all political parties here present joined together in our common devotion to democracy.

It is a great honor for me to be here today with my wife, with the United States Secretary of State, the Secretary of Defense, with other military and political leaders from our Government in this great hall of democracy.

I first visited your beautiful capital city 5 years ago. Since then, Korea's energy and culture have shown themselves in many new ways: Your bustling capital has continued to grow. Your economy has continued to expand. Your nation hosted the Olympics and has taken its place as a full member of the United Nations. You have established new ties to Russia and to China. But no achievement is more important than the consolidation of your democracy with the election of a bold democrat, President Kim Yong-sam.

Geography has placed our two nations far apart, but history has drawn us close together. Ours is a friendship formed in blood as our troops fought shoulder to shoulder in defense of freedom. Then as Korea's economy became the "miracle on the Han," we built an economic partnership that today exceeds $30 billion in fairly well-balanced trade. Today, Korea's democratic progress adds yet another bond of shared values between our two peoples.

When President Truman sent American troops to Korea's defense 43 years ago, he said he aimed to prove that, and I quote, "Free men under God can build a community of neighbors working together for the good of all." Our efforts together since then have benefited all our peoples, not only the people of our own countries but in the Asian Pacific region, all who seek to live in peace and freedom. Our relationship has made this region more secure, more prosperous, and more free. Now with the cold war over and profound changes sweeping throughout your country, this whole populous region, and indeed throughout the world, we must create a new vision of how we as a community of neighbors can live in peace. I believe the time has come to create a new Pacific community built on shared strength, shared prosperity, and a shared commitment to democratic values.

Today I want to discuss the fundamentals of security for that new Pacific community and the role the United States intends to play. I had the opportunity just a few days ago at the G–7 summit in Tokyo to travel to Waseda University to talk about the economic aspects of that new partnership. And I think clearly all the economic reforms that we can make will benefit a great market system like Korea.

But we must always remember that security comes first. Above all, the United States intends to remain actively engaged in this region. America is, after all, a Pacific nation. We have many peoples from all over Asia now making their home in America, including more than one million Koreans. We have fought three wars here in this century. We must not squander that investment. The best way for us to deter regional aggression, perpetuate the region's robust economic growth, and secure our own maritime and other interests is be an active presence. We must and we will continue to lead.

To some in America there is a fear that America's global leadership is an outdated luxury we can no longer afford. Well, they are wrong. In truth, our global leadership has never been a more indispensable or a more worthwhile investment for us. So long as we remain bordered by oceans and powered by trade, so long as our flag is a symbol of democracy and hope to a fractious world, the imperative of America's leadership will remain.

I believe there are four priorities for the security of our new Pacific community: first, a continued American military commitment to this region; second, stronger efforts to combat the proliferation of weapons of mass destruction; third, new regional dialogs on the full range of our common security challenges; and last, support for democracy and more open societies throughout this region.

The bedrock of America's security role in the Asian Pacific must be a continued military presence. In a period of change, we need to preserve what has been reliable. Today we therefore affirm our five bilateral security agreements with Korea, with Japan, with Australia, with the Philippines, and with Thailand.

Those agreements work because they serve the interests of each of the states. They enable the U.S. Armed Forces to maintain a substantial forward presence. At the same time they have enabled Asia to focus less energy on an arms race and more energy on the peaceful race toward economic development and opportunity for the peoples of this region.

The contribution Japan and Korea make to defray the cost of stationing our forces underscores the importance of that presence to both of those countries. There is no better example of that commitment than our alliance with your nation.

As the cold war recedes into history, a divided Korea remains one of its most bitter legacies. Our nation has always joined yours in believing that one day Korea's artificial division will end. We support Korea's peaceful unification on terms acceptable to the Korean people. And when the reunification comes, we will stand beside you in making the transition on the terms that you have outlined. But that day has not yet arrived. The demilitarized zone still traces a stark line between safety and danger. North Korea's million men in arms, most stationed within 30 miles of the DMZ, continue to pose a threat. Its troubling nuclear program raises questions about its intentions. Its internal repression and irresponsible weapons sales show North Korea is not yet willing to be a responsible member of the community of nations.

So let me say clearly: Our commitment to Korea's security remains undiminished. The Korean Peninsula remains a vital American interest. Our troops will stay here as long as the Korean people want and need us here.

We lost tens of thousands of America's best in Korea's mountains and mud and sky. But Korea lost millions. That sacrifice affirmed some old truths: Vulnerability invites aggression; peace depends upon deterrence. We cannot forget those lessons again.

And so it is throughout the region. Our commitment to an active military presence remains. Our mutual agreement with the Philippines to close our bases there should not be cause for Asian alarm. The larger picture tells a different story. We have obtained increased access for our forces throughout Southeast Asia to facilitate our presence and, if necessary, to project our forces beyond the region.

Here in Korea we have frozen American troop withdrawals and are modernizing Korean and American forces on the peninsula. We have deployed to Japan the Belleau Wood Amphibious Group and the U.S.S. *Independence* Battle Group, the largest and most modern in the world. These are not signs of disengagement. These are signs that America intends to stay.

The second security priority for our new Pacific Community is to combat the spread of weapons of mass destruction and their means of delivery. We cannot let the expanding threat of these deadly weapons replace the cold war nightmare of nuclear annihilation. And today, that possibility is too real. North Korea appears committed to indiscriminate sales of the SCUD missiles that were such a source of terror and destruction in the Persian Gulf. Now it is developing, testing, and looking to export a more powerful missile with a range of 600 miles or more, enough for North Korea to threaten Osaka or for Iran to threaten Tel Aviv.

We have serious concerns as well about China's compliance with international standards against missile proliferation. And since both you and we are attempting to engage China in a more extensive trade relationship, I hope together we can have a positive influence against that development.

The Pacific nations simply must develop new ways to combat the spread of biological, chemical, and missile technologies. And in the coming weeks, the U.S. will propose new efforts aimed at that goal. But no specter hangs over this peninsula or this region more darkly than the danger of nuclear proliferation. Nearly 160 nations have now joined to resist that threat through the Nuclear Non-Proliferation Treaty, the most universally supported treaty in all history.

Now, for the first time since that treaty was open for signatures, one of its members has threatened to withdraw. Our goals remain firm. We seek a nonnuclear Korean Peninsula and robust global rules against proliferation. That is why we urge North Korea to reaffirm its commitment to the Non-Proliferation Treaty, to fulfill its full-scope safeguards obligations to the International Atomic Energy Agency, including IAEA inspections of undeclared nuclear sites, and to implement bilateral inspections under the South-North nuclear accord.

Our goal is not endless discussions but certifiable compliance. North Korea must understand our intentions. We are seeking to prevent aggression, not to initiate it. And so long as North Korea abides by the U.N. Charter and international nonproliferation commitments, it has nothing to fear from America.

The U.S. has worked to bring North Korea back within the fold of nuclear responsibility. But your nation, too, has a critical role to play. The future of this peninsula is for you and North Korea to shape. The South-North nuclear accord you negotiated goes even further than existing international accords. It not only banishes nuclear weapons from the peninsula, it also bans the production of nuclear materials that could be used to make those weapons. We urge full implementation of this path-breaking accord which can serve as a model for other regions of nuclear tension.

Even as we address immediate concerns such as proliferation, we must also have a vision of how we will meet the broader challenges of this era. That is what I sought to create during the recently concluded G–7 talks, for example, by proposing new ways to focus on new problems such as the slow pace of job creation in the G–7 countries. And it is why I have proposed a NATO summit so that we can adapt that institution to new times and new challenges.

In both Asia and Europe the dominant unitary threat of Soviet aggression has disappeared. In both regions, the end of the cold war has allowed a host of problems to emerge or to reappear, such as ancient ethnic rivalries, regional tensions, flows of refugees, and the trafficking of deadly weapons and dangerous drugs.

In Europe these changes require us to adapt an existing security institution, NATO. In the Pacific no such institution exists. Moreover, since the Asian Pacific face a unitary threat, there is no need for us to create one single alliance. The challenge for the Asian Pacific in this decade, instead, is to develop multiple new arrangements to meet multiple threats and opportunities. These arrangements can function like overlapping plates of armor, individually providing protection and together covering the full body of our common security concerns.

Some new arrangements may involve groups of nations confronting immediate problems. This is the model we pursued to address North Korea's nuclear program. Our two nations worked not only with each other but also with Japan and with others who could bring their influence to bear. Other arrangements may involve peacekeeping, such as the massive and promising U.N. effort to support reconciliation in Cambodia. Still others may pursue confidence-building measures to head off regional or subregional disputes.

We also need new regional security dialogs. This month's ASEAN post-ministerial conference in Singapore, which the United States will attend, offers an immediate opportunity to further such a dialog. Korea can play a vital role in the region's new arrangements, for it stands at the center of northeast Asia, within 2 hours by air from Singapore, Tokyo, Beijing, and Vladivostok.

The many economic discussions within the region also can play a role. By lowering barriers to trade and investment, we can generate jobs, ease regional tensions, and thus enhance regional security. That is why I welcome the new dialog for economic cooperation our two nations are launching on this visit. And that is why I announced in Japan that I would like to host an informal economic conference among APEC's leaders following the ministerial meeting in Seattle, Washington, this fall.

The goal of all these efforts is to integrate, not isolate, the region's powers. China is a key example. We believe China cannot be a full partner in the world community until it respects human rights and international agreements on trade and weapon sales. But we also are prepared to involve China in building this region's new security and economic architectures. We need an involved and engaged China, not an isolated China.

Some in the U.S. have been reluctant to enter into regional security dialogs in Asia. They fear it would seem a pretext for American withdrawal from the area. But I see this as a way to supplement our alliances and forward military presence, not to supplant them.

These dialogs can ensure that the end of the cold war does not provide an opening for regional rivalries, chaos, and arms races. They can build a foundation for our shared security well into the 21st century.

Ultimately, the guarantee of our security must rest in the character and the intentions of the region's nations themselves. That is why our final security priority must be to support the spread of democracy throughout the Asian Pacific. Democracies not only are more likely to meet the needs and respect the rights of their people, they also make better neighbors. They do not wage war on each other, practice terrorism, generate refugees or traffick in drugs and outlaw weapons. They make more reliable partners in trade and in the kind of dialogs we announced today.

Today, some argue democracy and human rights are somehow unsuited to parts of Asia or that they mask some cultural imperialism on the part of the West. My ear is drawn instead to more compelling voices: the Chai Ling, who proclaim democracy's spirit at Tiananmen Square; to Aung San Suu Kyi whose eloquent opposition to repression in Burma has stirred the entire world; to Boris Yeltsin who is leading Russia toward becoming a great democratic power on the Pacific; and to your own President Kim and others in this multiparty assembly who have helped democracy flower here in the Land of the Morning Calm.

You are truly an example to people all over the Asian Pacific region because you have had the courage to confront the issues of political reform and economic reform; to ask the hard questions of yourselves; to have the public debates necessary when people honestly seek to improve and open their society and move forward. And I salute you on behalf of freedom-loving people everywhere in the world.

To be sure, every nation must retain its own culture, and we will all struggle about what it means to define that. But Korea proves that democracy and human rights are not Western imports. They flow from the internal spirit of human beings because they reflect universal aspirations.

Now we must respond to those aspirations throughout this region. We must support the nongovernmental organizations that seek to strengthen Asia's building blocks of civic society, such as open elections, trade unions, and a free press. And we must deploy accurate news and information against Asia's closed societies. I have proposed creating an Asian democracy radio for this purpose, and I look forward to its establishment in the near future.

Two hundred seventeen years ago, America's founders declared the rights of self-government to be God-given, and therefore inalienable. Today, here on Asian soil, let us together reaffirm that declaration, not only as an article of faith but as a sturdy building block in our region's shared security.

This, then, is our Nation's vision for security in the new Pacific community: a continued United States military presence, new efforts to combat proliferation, new regional security dialogs, and vigorous support for democracies and democratic movements. These elements of security can help create a Pacific region where economic competition is vigorous but peaceful; where diverse nations work as partners to improve their shared security; where democracy, as well as balanced military strength, takes its place as a guardian of our security.

We will not realize every aspect of that vision overnight, nor will the new Pacific community come to pass without great effort. But neither of our nations is a stranger to hard work.

I think in particular, of the image of your great long-distance runner, Hwang Yung Cho, who endured the final steep hill in Barcelona to capture the gold in the marathon in the 1992 Olympics. His energy and perseverance captured the spirit of the Korean people who have not only endured but prospered through a long, hard, and challenging history. We respect that spirit. We honor your values. We have stood shoulder to shoulder with you in days past, and so it shall be in the days ahead. The struggle for freedom and democracy and opportunity is, indeed, a marathon. Let us run the race together.

Thank you very much.

NOTE: The President spoke at 5:33 p.m. in the National Assembly Hall. In his remarks, he referred to Park Jyun Kyu, Speaker of the National Assembly.

Remarks at a State Dinner in Seoul
July 10, 1993

President and Mrs. Kim, distinguished guests: First let me, on behalf of my wife and all the Americans here present, thank you for the warm hospitality we have already received. I had a very fine meeting today with President Kim and then had the opportunity to be the guest of the Speaker at the National Assembly.

Tonight we celebrate the warm friendship between our two nations. Forty-three years ago America and the Republic of Korea joined forces to preserve freedom on the peninsula. The times then were perilous, and few could have imagined just how successful those efforts would be. Your nation's remarkable development has made Korea a model today for other nations seeking to join the ranks of the developed world. And your rising prosperity is now complemented in the leadership of President Kim by a second "miracle on the Han," the flowering of democracy. President Kim, you have been an eloquent voice for democracy when democracy was not an easy thing to advocate. Your values and your valor have led the people of Korea to a new level of freedom.

And so I come, along with our party, to Korea to discuss, in the spirit of friendship, the challenges that lie ahead; to continue a dedicated partnership between our two peoples; to affirm our resolute commitment to Korea's security; and to begin a personal partnership with you, Mr. President, which I know will flourish in the years ahead.

In our separate Inaugural Addresses, Mr. President, we each invoked the image of a season of rebirth. You heralded the hope of a new spring, and I suggested a new spring of hope. Now as we enter the summer months, let us celebrate the meeting of our minds and rejoice in the warm friendship between America and Korea.

With great respect, I ask everyone here to join me in a toast to you, Mr. President, and to the Republic of Korea for peace, for democracy, for eventual unification, and for continued prosperity.

NOTE: The President spoke at 8:45 p.m. at the Blue House.

The President's Radio Address
July 10, 1993

Good morning. This week I've been in Tokyo attending the annual summit of the world's seven major industrial nations. This year we devoted most of the time to an issue critical to most Americans, how to create more jobs and more prosperity.

In this era, our standard of living is increasingly linked to other countries. The more other nations lower their trade barriers, the more American firms can export. And the more we export, the more jobs we'll create. The more the economies of other nations expand, the more their people can buy our products, creating even more American jobs. Our exports to other countries account for some 7 million American jobs. And most of our job growth over the last decade has come from increases in our sales overseas.

For some weeks, I've been saying that the more we get our own economic house in order, the more we can get our trading partners to open up their markets and expand their own economies. That was clearly true this week. My hand was strengthened in these meetings with other world leaders because of everything the American people have been doing: calling for change, pushing the Congress to cut the deficit and increase investment in American jobs, demanding that we reform our campaign laws, our Government, and our health care system. In these meetings I was able to say to the world's other leaders, "The American people are willing to make some tough choices, and now your nations must do the same thing so that together we can get the world's economy growing again."

For over 10 years, every time a American

President came to one of the meetings, the leaders of the other nations of the world said, "Before we can straighten out this economy, America has to reduce its deficit and invest more in the education and training of its people." Now we're doing that, and we can ask the other nations to play their part as well.

This has been a good week for the American people. I'm going home with some tangible agreements that can make life better for our workers and our businesses. Let me give you one example. After years of deadlock at these summits over the world trade agreement, we were able to get the world's major trading powers to agree on a plan that will dramatically lower tariffs on manufactured products. This agreement covers everything from paper to chemicals to electronics. For several groups of products, including steel, farm equipment, and pharmaceuticals, our agreement will eliminate tariffs entirely. This plan could mean the biggest reduction in tariffs in history. Now, how does this affect American workers? Well, the lower the tariffs, the lower the price on American goods when they hit the market in another country. And the lower the price, the more we sell and the more jobs we create back home.

This agreement has added momentum to our efforts to achieve a large global trade agreement by the end of the year, an agreement that could create hundreds of thousands of export-based American jobs and dramatically rebuild the manufacturing sector in America. These jobs will be the better, higher paying jobs.

Agreements like this are a good start to get our economy moving again. But there's still a lot of work ahead of us. For example, over the next few weeks we still need to get Congress to take the final steps to pass the budget and deficit cutting plan. If you haven't said anything to your Member of Congress to let them know how you feel, please pick up the phone first thing Monday morning and do that. We've got to keep bringing our deficit down so we can keep these interest rates down and get our economy moving again.

Meeting with the world's other leaders this week drove home another important point. The challenges facing our Nation are also facing most other nations as well. Workers in every advanced country are coping with increased foreign competition. Communities in every major nation are frustrated by stubbornly high rates of unemployment. Overseas, as in the U.S., there is a tremendous thirst for political and economic reform so people can have more control over their own lives, their jobs, and their governments.

The changes you and I are pursuing in our businesses, in our communities, in our Government, are making America stronger. But they're also having an impact on other countries in ways we usually don't even think about. We're showing people the world over that the challenges of this new era can be met. As the American people have done in so many other times, we're setting an example, offering hope, and providing inspiration. Our country has never shied away from challenges. After this week, I am more confident than ever we're going to make the world's new economy work for us.

Before I sign off this morning, I want to say a word about a continuing tragedy I've followed closely while I've been overseas: the terrible flooding that has hit the Midwest in and near the Mississippi River Valley. On Sunday I went to speak with some of the families who have been hit by the rising waters in Iowa and Illinois. As someone who grew up in farm country, I was stunned by the devastation—houses, businesses, farms, in some cases whole communities, all under water.

I want the people in these communities to know that my thoughts have been with them. Before I left the country, I asked Vice President Gore to take personal charge to make sure that all the emergency services available get to those who need them. I know that people all over America have been offering their help and support to these flood-ravaged cities and towns. All our prayers are with the people of the Midwest as they face the task of rebuilding their communities, their farms, and their lives. When hard times hit, the American people stand by each other. Even in this new era, I don't think that will ever change.

Thanks for listening.

NOTE: This address was recorded at 11:55 p.m. on July 9 at the Okura Hotel in Tokyo, Japan, for broadcast at 11:06 p.m. on July 10 from Seoul, South Korea.

Exchange With Reporters in Seoul
July 11, 1993

South Korea

Q. What do you think of Korea?

The President. It's a terrific country. It's amazing all the things that have been done in such a short time. And the vibrancy of the democracy is really amazing. To think that President Kim just a few years ago was under house arrest and then he winds up being the President of the country; it's a real tribute to the people here as well as to their leaders.

North Korea

Q. What do you hope to accomplish with your visit to the DMZ this afternoon?

The President. First of all, since I'm in the country, I want to go up there and see our forces and tell them how much I appreciate what they're doing. Secondly, I want to reinforce the message that I issued yesterday in my meeting with President Kim and in my speech to the National Assembly.

Q. Why do you feel North Korea needs the message right now?

The President. Because they are not fully in compliance with the NPT.

NOTE: The exchange began at 9:55 a.m. at the Blue House. A tape was not available for verification of the content of this exchange.

Remarks to the American and Korean Chambers of Commerce in Seoul
July 11, 1993

Really, I came here mostly to listen. And I'm very delighted to be here. I'm glad to have this opportunity. You may know that the Secretary of State and the Secretary of Treasury and I met with the U.S.-Japan Chamber of Commerce in Tokyo the other day. We had about 375 people there, and it was very interesting. We had a roundtable, and they had a panel, sort of like you. And I just listened and asked them what we could do to help.

Let me just make a couple of observations. First of all, this has been, I think, from an economic point of view, quite a successful trip for the United States. The G–7 summit produced an agreement by the G–7 members on market access which would, if incorporated into the final General Agreement on Tariffs and Trade, would be the biggest reduction in tariffs in 7 years and have a huge market-opening impact on manufactured goods throughout the world. I also think it will give some real impetus as we go back to Geneva to complete the Uruguay round this year. So I feel good about that.

The second thing the G–7 did was to adopt a $3 billion, 18-month grant and loan assistance package to Russia, anchored in a $500 million fund to help to privatize more of their state-

owned industries more rapidly. That comes just after the United States Export-Import Bank has approved $2 billion in credits for energy operations.

So I think we're really moving quite well in our partnership with Russia. I feel much better about the stability of the political climate and the capacity for economic change than I did even after the election there. There's been a lot that happened that is basically quite encouraging.

Then thirdly, at 2 a.m. in the morning on the day that I left, the United States and Japan reached agreement on a framework for changing our trading relationships, which is quite encouraging. We committed to work toward some specific agreements in specific areas that will have some real targets, measurable progress for change in objective ways, and commits our relationship to a results-oriented basis for the first time in a way that I think is quite good. So this was a good trip.

Back home, let me just observe that the problems in America are well-known, and they are basically faced by every wealthy country in the world today. We have modest growth; we're behind where we ordinarily would be in job growth after the bottom of a recession, and the incomes for most working people have remained pretty stagnant for more than a decade. And it's all part of this global slowdown that you're all very familiar with.

The positives are that, because of the progress of the deficit reduction package, we've got long-term interest rates down now to a 20-year low, tens of billions of dollars being generated back into the economy through refinancing of homes and business loans, about a million new jobs coming into this economy in the first 6 months of this year as compared with about a million in the previous 3 years.

So, even though the job engine is still slow, it's picked up markedly in the first 6 months of this year. And I think, clearly, largely because of the low interest rates and the refinancing, so that we're shifting not so much from debt to equity but from high-cost debt to lower cost debt, and the difference is being freed up for some new investment. And we can work that for a year, or maybe a year and a half, because there's so much accumulated high-interest debt in the American system.

The strategy we are seeking to follow at home is one that brings the deficit down, increases investments both public and private, and the generation of new jobs and new technologies addresses some of the real distortions in the American economy, such as the exploding cost of health care and the fact that we spend 30 percent more on it than anybody else does, and attempts to develop policies for defense conversion, technology, and trade which will hook us into the global economy in a better way.

We also tried to achieve an agreement at GATT toward more coordination of our economic policies to produce higher levels of global growth. And there was some modest success.

For the first time in a decade, GATT did not criticize America's trade—I mean, budget deficit. They complimented us for trying to get it down, which is nice.

But we also got an agreement, I think, to continue to work with the Europeans and the Japanese, but there are domestic political considerations which limit what they can do. The Germans are bringing their interest rates down, but they're also tightening up their economy. The Japanese are stimulating their economy, but not as much as we wish they were. Nonetheless, I think on balance things are going in the right direction at home, and the G–7 was a big, big plus for the concept of an open trading system and for the promise of future growth.

Now, having said that, obviously there are a lot of differences between words that are spoken by people in political life, and even that are put down on paper, and the way things operate in fact. So I'm here today as much as anything else for an hour now just to listen to you, to ask you how we can help to support your mission here. America had a 20-year high in productivity increase in the last quarter of last year. There are many, many areas of the world now where in products and services we are the high-quality, low-cost producer. And there are all kinds of opportunities for us around the world that we need a good partnership between the United States and the private sector to achieve.

And so unless we know what you're thinking and what we're supposed to do, it will be hard to do that. And that's why the Secretary and I and all the folks on the wall are here today, and the rest of this hour belongs to you.

NOTE: The President spoke at 10:40 a.m. at Yongsan Army Base.

Exchange With Reporters at the Demilitarized Zone in South Korea
July 11, 1993

Q. So what do you think?

The President. I think anyone who sees this would understand how important it is for us to stay strong on the issue of North Korea staying in the NPT and allowing those atomic energy inspectors back in there. And I think anyone who sees this would be proud of these young men in uniform for being here.

NOTE: The exchange began at 1:45 p.m. at a lookout post near Camp Bonifas.

Exchange With Reporters at the Demilitarized Zone
July 11, 1993

North Korea

Q. How many more years do you think this line will hold?

The President. I don't know. I hope it won't be long. But in the meanwhile, I'm glad these people are here. All these young men are doing something very important. And when you see, as I said, when you see the way North Korea's been behaving, their presence here is even more important. The American people should be very proud of them. They are making a major contribution to the defense of freedom and also to the spread of freedom. And in the end our side of that bridge will prevail.

Q. Do you think they know you're here?

The President. I imagine they do. They were certainly looking. And someday they'll be able to——

Q. Menacingly?

The President. Well, I hope someday they'll just be able to walk on over here in peace.

Q. Knowing what you know now, do you think they're more likely or less likely, the North Koreans, to comply with the treaty?

The President. Well, I don't know. They've been rather calm in response to my trip here. And that is somewhat encouraging. But it doesn't make any sense. When you examine the nature of the American security commitment to Korea, to Japan, to this region, it is pointless for them to try to develop nuclear weapons because if they ever use them it would be the end of their country. All they have to do is read our security agreements.

So I hope that this trip will serve to get things back on track. And I hope they will comply. The President of South Korea, President Kim, has laid out a long-term gradual way of reunification that is clearly in the interest of the people on both sides of this great divide. But we can't even resume that until they make it clear that they're going to stay in the Non-Proliferation Treaty regime, they're going to allow the inspectors back in, they're not going to try to become a nuclear power. That's the major issue for this day. And until that happens, we just need to redouble our resolve and make it clear where we are.

Q. Well, weren't they moving toward rapprochement, and all of a sudden something happened, they were really——

The President. They seemed to be. And, as I said, President Kim reached out to them. And it's clear that the people of South Korea would like reunification to be possible, if you can preserve democracy and freedom.

So we'll just have to see. The wisdom of what our country has done for 40 years is basically demonstrated by this abrupt change in North Korean policy. We know what works. If we just stay strong and we stay resolute and we stay firm, we know that will work. And eventually, we have to hope that they will take the sensible course and that we can then resume the thaw that was in place before this last unfortunate development.

Thank you.

NOTE: The exchange began at 2:55 p.m. at the Bridge of No Return.

Remarks to the Troops at Camp Casey, South Korea
July 11, 1993

The President. Thank you. Thank you very much. Thank you, General Abrams. Thank you, Sergeant Corley, for the tomahawk.

Audience members. Oooh.

The President. He looks to me like he could use it. [*Laughter*]

I want to say how glad I am to be here today. I want to introduce a couple of the people who came with me: the Secretary of State Warren Christopher; your Secretary of Defense, Les Aspin; I think you know General Luck. And I thank you already for the welcome to me and my wife, the First Lady.

I see some of the young women soldiers

jumping up and down here in the back. We'll do that better—that's good.

I want to say to all of you, it is a great privilege for me to be here on the frontier of freedom with the warriors of the 2d Infantry Division. You are a very critical part of the finest Armed Forces the world has ever seen.

I'm sorry to be a little late, but I think you all know that because of the rains we couldn't take the helicopters today, and we drove to the DMZ.

Audience members. Woo! Woo! Woo!

The President. It was the first opportunity I had ever had to be along the DMZ. And I understand that I was in a more forward position than any President had been before. When I stood on the Bridge of No Return and looked over with my binoculars at those young North Korean soldiers, I thought to myself, I wish they were free to walk across this bridge and be with us in peace and freedom. And because of you, someday they will be, because of you.

For 40 years American soldiers like you have stood shoulder to shoulder with our Korean allies, providing South Korea with security against attack and the opportunity to flourish first as a great economy and now as a great democracy. I want every one of you to know whatever you do here, if you carry a rifle or drive a truck or repair a helicopter, whatever you do, your work is vital. And I admire your service, and believe it or not, so do millions of Americans you will never see or meet and may not even know exactly what you do. All of them know they live a little freer and a little better because of you and your sacrifice and your service.

All of you know that this is a challenging time to be in the military. Because the cold war has ended, some people think the threats to our country have ended, but you know better. You know that there is a reduced need for certain missions and forces around the world, but many threats continue.

Just a few weeks ago I ordered an attack on Baghdad, and you know why: because we concluded that Iraq had staged a plot to assassinate former President Bush while he was in Kuwait. And they were under the illusion that we treat our political leaders like they treat theirs. This is America. We honor everybody who has served this country, and we stick together. But when I gave that order, I did it with the confidence that we had the best military in the world, equipped with the finest technology in history. And after that action was over, I felt more strongly than ever before that we must continue to have the best military in the world and the finest technology in the world.

For 6 years now, force levels have been lowered, budgets have been reduced, bases have been closed. These changes are unsettling and difficult, but I tell you that still we must maintain our readiness and we must make these cutbacks gradually and with a real feeling for the men and women who have won the cold war and deserve their country's best efforts to help them maintain successful lives.

And even in this time of transition, we must remember that we have to show foresight and caution in reducing our defenses. North Korea's stubborn refusal in recent months to fully comply with the requirements of the Nuclear Non-Proliferation Agreement is the most urgent example of this. And in this new round of military cuts, I know that you all noticed no cuts were made in troop levels in Korea or Japan, and we beefed up our naval presence in the Pacific because that is what the national security requires.

You know, too many times in the past, in the absence of an overpowering threat, our country has forgotten just how badly we need people like you, with the morale and energy and vigor and determination that you're all demonstrating today. In 1945, before any of you were born, we won the Second World War. And just 5 short years later, we were involved in another conflict here in Korea. But by then we had diminished our strength so much that we entered the conflict inadequately prepared, without enough equipment or training, without enough strength. We must not ever make that mistake again.

So I say to you that, while over the next few years we will continue to reduce defense expenditures where appropriate and acknowledge that in many cases that may be desirable, there is clearly a line below which we cannot go. Our Armed Forces must still be able to fight and win on a moment's notice.

Let me make this last point: To do that, of course, we have to provide you with the most sophisticated precision-guided weapons we can. To do that, of course, we have to provide you with all the support we can. But in the end, you will make the difference: your discipline, your character, your will to win, your love for your country, your ability to get up day-in and day-out and feel the way you are manifesting your feelings for your country and your duty today. That is America's winning edge, and that is what we must never lose.

Let me say in closing, I know that what you do is difficult and sometimes dangerous and often very lonely. You're a long way from home. When I was up on the DMZ, I met three people from my home State, a long way from home. You, too? And I want all of you to know that your demonstration of your professionalism and your dedication means that you and America really are second to none. What I want you

also to know is that I can see from my perspective sometimes something you may not be able to see, and that is, these pictures of you here saying what you're saying, doing what you're doing, being who you are, give great pause to the enemies of freedom and great heart to our allies and to all the American people.

Thank you, and God bless you all. Thank you.

NOTE: The President spoke at 5:10 p.m. In his remarks, he referred to Brig. Gen. John Abrams, USA, commanding general, 2d Infantry Division, Camp Casey, and Gen. Gary E. Luck, USA, commander in chief, U.S. Forces, Korea.

Remarks at the U.S.S. *Arizona* Memorial in Honolulu, Hawaii
July 11, 1993

Admiral Larson, ladies and gentlemen, it's a great honor for me to be here, not for the first time but for the first time as President, to honor the memory and the service of those who were killed 52 years ago on a Sunday morning like this in the service of their country. During December of 1941, Americans throughout our Nation were going about their business aware that much of the rest of the world was already embroiled in a conflict but hopeful that America would not be forced into it, that somehow by standing apart we might keep America's shores and our sons and daughters safe from the strife that had then engulfed much of the rest of the world.

Much has changed since that fateful Sunday morning in 1941. The United States no longer faces the threat of an expansionist Germany or Japan. Indeed, I have just met with the leaders of those two nations and four others in an attempt to increase the prosperity and opportunity of all the peoples who live within our nations. The expansionist Soviet Union, which sprung up after the Great War, was dismantled in the failure of communism in the last few years. And at this same meeting in Tokyo, the new democratically elected President of Russia, Boris Yeltsin, came and talked to us about how together we might build a brighter and freer and more prosperous future for his people.

Our closest friends now are those with whom we fought a half a century ago. And yet, it

is still as clear now as it was then that the United States cannot disengage from the world. To be economically and physically secure, we must continue to be strong. In visits to Japan and to Korea I have reaffirmed the commitment of the United States to the security of our allies and friends in the Pacific, beginning with a continuing military presence made possible by the men and women who serve our Nation here at Pearl Harbor and throughout the region. As we honor those who gave their lives a half century ago, let us also honor those who guard our security today.

I had breakfast with some of the young men and women of the Pacific Command this morning. And Admiral, I thank you very much for that opportunity. I was profoundly impressed by their energy, their discipline, their knowledge, their commitment, their willingness to do their jobs. I met with other members of our Armed Forces in Korea yesterday, including in the DMZ, where I was able to take the most forward position that any American President has ever enjoyed, standing on the Bridge of No Return about 10 yards from the dividing line which still separates us from what is perhaps the most anachronistic Communist regime remaining in the world.

I believe more strongly than ever before that the world has never had a better fighting force than the men and women who serve in the military service of our country. We are all in

1063

their debt for their service and their dedication. We are all proud of what they do for us.

So in the presence of this memorial to those who gave their all in 1941, looking across the harbor at our magnificent fleet of 1993, let us resolve today to honor their sacrifice and their service by maintaining the best prepared and best equipped force in the world, always ready to meet any challenge, always worthy, and receiving our full support.

Thank you very much.

NOTE: The President spoke at 10:15 a.m. In his remarks, he referred to Adm. Charles R. Larson, commander in chief, U.S. Pacific Command.

Remarks to the Community in Honolulu
July 11, 1993

The President. Thank you. Thank you very much. Thank you so much. Thank you, Mayor Fasi, Congressman Abercrombie, Congresswoman Mink, Senator Akaka, my longtime and good friend Governor Waihee. When I look out here at this wonderful scene tonight, it is almost impossible for me to remember that in the snows of New Hampshire in 1992, when many people thought I had no chance to be elected President, John Waihee left this scene and came to that snow to campaign for me, and I'll never forget it. Thank you very much.

I want to thank all of you for coming out and all the people behind me. I can't turn around and face them or the sound will go off. I am so glad to be home. How's this? [*Applause*] Like that. [*Applause*]

It is wonderful to be home after my first trip overseas as your President. I went to Asia to a meeting of the world's seven great industrial nations. I also went to meet in Japan and Korea and here today in Hawaii with the people who are in charge of the national security interests of the United States in Asia and the Pacific region. This morning I ended that trip with a visit to the *Arizona* Memorial and a briefing by the commander in chief of our forces in the Pacific and his senior officers.

As Hillary said, yesterday we were in Korea along the Demilitarized Zone. And I walked out further than any American President ever had onto the Bridge of No Return, about 10 yards from the line separating South and North Korea. And with my binoculars I looked into the other side, and I saw some young North Korean soldiers looking back at me. And I thought to myself, I wish you could walk over this bridge, and I hope it won't be long until you can, until we put down the threat of nuclear war and open up the hand of friendship.

You would be very proud if you could see what I saw in Korea, in Japan, see the young men and women who voluntarily have joined our Nation's Armed Forces and gone there and represent us with great ability and enormous enthusiasm, I might add, young people from every State in this country. And I was proud of them, and you can feel better about your country just seeing and knowing that they're there.

The other thing I did on this trip was to worry about what I could do abroad to help our economy here at home. There is a direct connection, as the people of Hawaii know as well as any people in America, between how well America does and how well the rest of the world does. We have been in a period of slow economic growth with great problems in creating new jobs, in raising incomes. But I went to Japan, which is having its lowest period of economic performance in 20 years, to meet with leaders from Europe, where every nation has a higher unemployment rate than we do and many countries are in their lowest period of economic performance in 30 or 40 years. There is a global economic slowdown, and we have to turn it around to open opportunities for Americans.

To be sure, there are things we can do here, and we have made a beginning, a serious beginning at bringing the terrible budget deficit down and spending less on things we shouldn't spend on and investing more in education, in technology, in defense conversion, and building a stronger future for the American people.

We are building new partnerships with people

in their private capacities. Something I did as President when I was overseas was to meet with over 350 Americans representing business interests in Japan and then meeting with the executive board of the American Chamber of Commerce in Korea to talk about what we could do together to create opportunities for American businesses and American workers.

And we are making some progress. We have interest rates at a 20-year low, millions of people refinancing their homes and their business loans, almost one million new jobs in the American economy since January. That compares with only a million new jobs in 3 years before then. We are making some progress, but we've got a long way to go.

I want to tell you what this trip meant for America and what it means for Hawaii. First of all, we agreed among ourselves, these seven nations, that we would support the reduction in tariffs in the trade of manufacturing goods all across the world on a level that we have not seen in many years. That could mean literally millions of jobs in the global economy, hundreds of thousands of jobs in the American economy where manufacturing is coming back. We are now the high-quality, low-cost producer of many products and services again. Our automobiles are regaining market share here in America and are more attractive than they have been in decades.

The second thing we did was to agree to invest some money, including some of your money, to keep democracy and a free market going in Russia. Why? Because it's in our interests for them to reduce their nuclear arsenals instead of build them up, because it's in our interests for all those people over there to become customers for United States products and travelers to Hawaii someday.

And finally, in what could prove to be an historic breakthrough, we agreed on a framework to change the terms of trade between the United States and Japan. The Japanese made a good-faith commitment to bring down the enormous trade surplus between the United States and Japan and to help work with us to sell more products and more services and to equalize the imbalance in the global economy. They have been saying to us for 10 years, "You've got to bring your budget deficit down." I went to Japan and I said, "OK, we did that. Now bring your trade surplus down." And they said yes. They said yes.

And let me say again, this can affect you. No State is more closely tied to Japan than Hawaii. How many Japanese visitors come to these shores every year? If we have a more open economic system and consumer goods and services cost less in Japan, then the Japanese people will have more of the benefits of their hard work and their efforts, their incomes will go further, and more of them than ever before will be able to travel to the United States of America and to Hawaii, to integrate the global economy in a way that is positive and good.

That is what we were doing. Two-thirds of the jobs that have been created in the United States of America since 1987 have come from trade. We are in an increasingly smaller global economy, and we have to find ways to live together on this planet in ways that help us all. That is what I was trying to do, to help America by going to Japan. And I believe it was a good trip.

Finally, since Presidents don't often come to Hawaii, let me make a couple of remarks about this wonderful State. Let me say first, thanks for the support you gave to me and to the Vice President in the last election. Thank you for setting a model for health care and in many other areas. And let me say that I have been benefited enormously by the work that your congressional representatives have done in informing me about issues of concern to Hawaii. And I want to just mention two, if I might.

Number one, my wife, as she said, is going to Kauai to view the hurricane damage in a couple of days. Just a few days ago, I signed a bill to provide $40 million in extra assistance to the victims of the hurricane in Hawaii. And I have instructed the Secretary of the Department of Housing and Urban Development to devote an enormous amount of his time to work to repair the damage here. And he will be doing that as well as taking some of the money that they have to rebuild some of the houses on that troubled island. So we hope we can be good partners with you in rebuilding Hawaii.

The next thing I would like to say is that, as Governor Waihee said, this is the 100th anniversary of the overthrow of the Hawaiian monarchy. Your Governor has talked to me for months and months, going way back last year, about issues of concern to native Hawaiians. And I pledge to you that I will work with him, with Senator Inouye, with Senator Akaka, with Congressman Abercrombie and Congresswoman

Mink to address these concerns in a positive way. We will not forget them.

Finally, let me say that, as Hillary said, we have learned a lot from Hawaii's health care system, but you should know that your Governor has asked us to give him permission to do some more things to fully cover all Hawaiians and to manage this system better.

And so I want to close with this thought: We will never bring the Government's budget deficit down to zero, we will never restore full health to the American economy until we find a way to provide basic health security to all American families and bring the cost of health care in line with inflation. It is the single biggest long-term drag on our budget deficit and our economic performance. And I pledge to you, building on the example of Hawaii, preserving the right of people to choose their doctor and to keep the medical system that works so well, we will find a solution to this problem, and we will begin soon. We must do it to bring the American people together and restore the economic health of America.

Audience members. Justice for Hawaii! Justice for Hawaii! Justice for Hawaii!

The President. I hope we can provide it.

Thank you for being here in such numbers. We want to get out and visit with you. This is probably the longest political speech any of you ever listened to on a vacation in your lives.

So to close, I'll give you a laugh. I told my mother about this trip, and I said, "You know, Mother, when we come back we pick up 19 hours, and I'll have two whole Sundays." And she said over the phone, "Son, you need it." [*Laughter*]

Thank you all, and God bless you. I'm glad to see you.

NOTE: The President spoke at approximately 6:30 p.m. at the Hilton Hawaiian Village. In his remarks, he referred to Mayor Frank F. Fasi of Honolulu.

Letter to Congressional Leaders on Economic Sanctions Against Libya
July 12, 1993

Dear Mr. Speaker: (Dear Mr. President:)

I hereby report to the Congress on the developments since the last report of December 30, 1992, concerning the national emergency with respect to Libya that was declared in Executive Order No. 12543 of January 7, 1986. This report is submitted pursuant to section 401(c) of the National Emergencies Act, 50 U.S.C. 1641(c); section 204(c) of the International Emergency Economic Powers Act ("IEEPA"), 50 U.S.C. 1703(c); and section 505(c) of the International Security and Development Cooperation Act of 1985, 22 U.S.C. 2349aa–9(c).

1. There has been one amendment to the Libyan Sanctions Regulations, 31 C.F.R. Part 550 (the "Regulations"), administered by the Office of Foreign Assets Control ("FAC") of the Department of the Treasury, since the last report on December 30, 1992. The amendment, published on March 10, 1993, 58 *Fed. Reg.* 13198, added an interpretation of the Regulations' prohibition against the exportation of services to Libya from the United States, and a general license and statement of licensing policy concerning the provision of certain legal services. A copy of the amendment is attached to this report.

The prohibition against exportation of services to Libya contained in section 550.202 of the Regulations is interpreted in new section 550.422. Services (including legal services) are considered to be exported to Libya if their benefit is received in Libya and the services are performed (1) in the United States; (2) by an entity located in the United States, including its overseas branches; or (3) outside the United States by an individual U.S. person ordinarily resident in the United States. The benefit of services performed anywhere in the world on behalf of the Government of Libya, including a controlled entity or Specially Designated National of the Government of Libya, is presumed to be received in Libya. Legal services performed by U.S. persons outside the United States with respect to property interests of the Government of Libya are prohibited pursuant to section 550.209, which prohibits U.S. persons from dealing in any property (including contracts) in which the Government of Libya has an interest. Section 550.205, which prohibits performance by U.S. persons of any contract in support of an industrial or other commercial or governmental project in Libya, may also be applicable in these instances. For example, sections 550.205 and 550.209 of the Regulations, taken together, prohibit U.S. persons from representing a foreign entity in contract negotiations, contract performance, or arbitration with the Government of Libya. Such representation may be authorized only by specific license from FAC.

New section 550.517 of the Regulations states that the provision of legal services to the Government of Libya or to a person in Libya generally requires the issuance of a specific license, and that the receipt of compensation for such legal services must, in all cases, be specifically licensed by FAC. However, the provision of the following legal services to the Government of Libya or to a person in Libya (but not receipt of compensation for those services) is generally licensed: (1) the provision of legal advice and counselling to the Government of Libya or to a person in Libya on requirements of and compliance with U.S. law, provided that such advice and counselling are not provided to facilitate transactions in violation of the Regulations; (2) representation of the Government of Libya or of a person in Libya when named as a defendant in domestic U.S. legal, arbitration, or administrative proceedings; (3) initiation of domestic U.S. legal or administrative proceedings in defense of property interests subject to U.S. jurisdiction of the Government of Libya that were in existence prior to January 8, 1986, or of a person in Libya; (4) representation of the Government of Libya or of a person in Libya before any Federal agency with respect to the imposition, administration, or enforcement of U.S. sanctions against Libya; and (5) provision of legal services in any other context in which prevailing U.S. law requires access to legal counsel at public expense. The enforcement of any judgment, decree, attachment, or lien through execution, garnishment, or other judicial process purporting to transfer or otherwise alter or affect a Government of Libya property interest is prohibited unless specifically licensed.

2. During the current 6-month period, FAC made numerous decisions with respect to applications for licenses to engage in transactions under the Regulations, issuing 60 licensing de-

terminations—both approvals and denials. Consistent with FAC's ongoing scrutiny of banking transactions, the majority of the determinations (51) concerned requests by non-Libyan persons or entities to unblock bank accounts initially blocked because of an apparent Libyan interest. Three determinations involved license applications for export sales transactions from the United States to Libya. Four determinations concerned registration of individuals pursuant to a general license authorizing travel to Libya for the sole purpose of visiting close family members. Finally, FAC has also issued two licenses authorizing U.S. landlords to liquidate the personalty of the People's Committee for Libyan Students, with the net proceeds from the sale paid into blocked accounts.

3. During the current 6-month period, FAC has continued to emphasize to the international banking community in the United States the importance of identifying and blocking payments made by or on behalf of Libya. The Office worked closely with the banks to implement new interdiction software systems to identify such payments. As a result, during the reporting period, more than 44 transactions involving Libya have been blocked.

The proactive compliance programs initiated by FAC have resulted in the imposition of substantially fewer civil penalties for banks' failure to block payments in which an interest of the Government of Libya exists. Since December 30, 1992, FAC has collected $140,000 in civil penalties for violations of U.S. sanctions against Libya. Fewer than one-third of the violations involved the failure of banks to block funds transfers to Libyan-owned or -controlled banks, with the remainder about equally divided between violations involving merchandise transshipment and illegal representation of the Government of Libya.

Various enforcement actions carried over from previous reporting periods have continued to be aggressively pursued. Several new investigations of potentially significant violations of the Libyan sanctions have been initiated by FAC and cooperating U.S. law enforcement agencies. Many of these cases involved complex conspiracies to circumvent the embargo through the use of international diversionary shipping routes to and from Libya. For example, during the current reporting period, a U.S. citizen was indicted for his employment as a manager at a German oil refinery, Holborn Europa Raffinerie GmbH, which dealt primarily in Libyan crude oil and and in which the Government of Libya had acquired a majority ownership interest. In addition, a foreign national and two foreign firms for whom that individual acted as agent were indicated by a Federal grand jury for illegally transshipping agricultural equipment from the United States to Libya.

FAC has worked closely with the Departments of State and Justice to identify several U.S. persons who had entered into contracts or other agreements with the Government of Libya, or other third-country parties, to lobby United States Government officials and to engage in public relations work on behalf of the Government of Libya without obtaining FAC authorization, in violation of the Regulations. In one such case, FAC levied civil penalties totaling $35,000 against three individuals who had engaged in such activity.

In addition, during this reporting period, FAC blocked a foreign merchant vessel under the management and control of a Specially Designated National of Libya, following the vessel's unauthorized entry into a U.S. port. FAC imposed and received a civil penalty in the amount of $10,000 from agents of the shipping company prior to authorizing release of the vessel and its departure from the U.S. port.

FAC has continued to pursue its Operation Roadblock initiative, issuing an additional 70 warning letters and demands for information during the reporting period to persons believed to have travelled to and worked in Libya, or made travel-related payments to Libya in violation of U.S. law. To date, Operation Roadblock's ongoing investigative efforts have resulted in one criminal conviction and several civil penalty assessments. In addition, these investigations have yielded substantial information concerning alleged criminal violations of the embargo by businesses and individuals. FAC is aggressively pursuing its investigations of such suspected violators in cooperation with other agencies of the United States Government, including the Departments of State and Justice, the Treasury Department's Financial Crimes Enforcement Network (FinCEN), the Federal Bureau of Investigation, and the U.S. Customs Service.

4. The expenses incurred by the Federal Government in the 6-month period from January 7 through July 6, 1993, that are directly attributable to the exercise of powers and authorities conferred by the declaration of the Libyan national emergency are estimated at approximately $2.7 million. Personnel costs were largely centered in the Department of the Treasury (particularly in the Office of Foreign Assets Control, the Office of the General Counsel, and the U.S. Customs Service), the Department of State, and the Department of Commerce.

5. The policies and actions of the Government of Libya continue to pose an unusual and extraordinary threat to the national security and foreign policy of the United States. I shall continue to exercise the powers at my disposal to apply economic sanctions against Libya fully and effectively, so long as those measures are appropriate, and will continue to report periodically to the Congress on significant developments as required by law.

Sincerely,

WILLIAM J. CLINTON

NOTE: Identical letters were sent to Thomas S. Foley, Speaker of the House of Representatives, and Albert Gore, Jr., President of the Senate.

Letter to Congressional Leaders on Economic Sanctions Against Haiti
July 12, 1993

Dear Mr. Speaker: (Dear Mr. President:)

1. In December 1990, the Haitian people elected Jean-Bertrand Aristide as their President in a free and fair election. The United States applauded this remarkable achievement and actively supported the new government. However, Haiti's progress toward democracy was thwarted in September 1991, when the Haitian military illegally and violently ousted President Aristide.

2. The United States, on its own and with the Organization of American States ("OAS"), immediately imposed sanctions against the illegal regime. The United States has also actively supported the efforts of the OAS and the United

Nations to restore democracy to Haiti and return President Aristide through negotiations between the Haitian parties. In March, Secretary of State Christopher named Ambassador Lawrence Pezzullo as our Special Envoy on Haiti. In addition the United States and the international community offered material assistance to facilitate the return to democracy, build constitutional structures, and foster economic well-being.

3. When the *de facto* regime rebuffed the international community's efforts, I ordered several measures to increase our pressure on it. On June 4, I barred the entry into the United States of individuals associated with the *de facto* regime who have been impeding a settlement. I also ordered that their assets under U.S. jurisdiction be frozen and that transactions with them be prohibited. With strong U.S. backing, the OAS voted to tighten its embargo. We took the lead in the successful effort to have the United Nations Security Council adopt mandatory oil, arms, and financial sanctions on Haiti on June 16; these came into effect June 23.

4. On June 30, 1993, I issued Executive Order No. 12853, which broadens U.S. authority to block all property of and prohibit transactions involving Haitian nationals providing substantial financial or material contributions to, or doing substantial business with, the *de facto* regime in Haiti. The Executive order also prohibits the sale or supply from the United States of petroleum, petroleum products, arms, or related materiel of all types. The order also prohibits the carriage on U.S.-registered vessels of petroleum or petroleum products, or arms and related materiel, with entry into, or with the intent to enter, the territory or territorial waters of Haiti.

Issuance of this Executive order demonstrates continued U.S. leadership of the international community's use of strong sanctions to reinforce the negotiations process being sponsored by the United Nations and the OAS.

5. This report details the measures we have instituted and enforced pursuant to the requirements of the International Emergency Economic Powers Act. I am committed to the restoration of democracy in Haiti, and I am confident that the measures we have taken will help achieve that outcome.

6. On October 4, 1991, in Executive Order No. 12775, President Bush declared a national emergency to deal with the threat to the national security, foreign policy, and economy of the United States caused by events that had occurred in Haiti to disrupt the legitimate exercise of power by the democratically elected government of that country (56 *Fed. Reg.* 50641). In that order, the President ordered the immediate blocking of all property and interests in property of the Government of Haiti (including the Banque de la Republique d'Haiti) then or thereafter located in the United States or within the possession or control of a U.S. person, including its overseas branches. The Executive order also prohibited any direct or indirect payments or transfers to the *de facto* regime in Haiti of funds or other financial or investment assets or credits by any U.S. person or any entity organized under the laws of Haiti and owned or controlled by a U.S. person.

Subsequently, on October 28, 1991, the President issued Executive Order No. 12779, adding trade sanctions against Haiti to the sanctions imposed on October 4 (56 *Fed. Reg.* 55975). This order prohibited exportation from the United States of goods, technology, and services, and importation into the United States of Haitian-origin goods and services, after November 5, 1991, with certain limited exceptions. The order exempts trade in publications and other informational materials from the import, export, and payment prohibitions and permits the exportation to Haiti of donations to relieve human suffering as well as commercial sales of five food commodities: rice, beans, sugar, wheat flour, and cooking oil. In order to permit the return to the United States of goods being prepared for U.S. customers by Haiti's substantial "assembly sector," the order also permitted, through December 5, 1991, the importation into the United States of goods assembled or processed in Haiti that contained parts or materials previously exported to Haiti from the United States. On February 5, 1992, it was announced that specific licenses could be applied for on a case-by-case basis by U.S. persons wishing to resume a pre-embargo import/export relationship with the assembly sector in Haiti.

7. The declaration of the national emergency on October 4, 1991, was made pursuant to the authority vested in the President by the Constitution and laws of the United States, including the International Emergency Economic Powers Act (50 U.S.C. 1701 *et seq.*) ("IEEPA"), the National Emergencies Act (50 U.S.C. 1601 *et seq.*), and section 301 of title 3 of the United States Code. The emergency declaration was re-

ported to the Congress on October 4, 1991, pursuant to section 204(b) of IEEPA (50 U.S.C. 1703(b)). The additional sanctions set forth in the Executive order of October 28, 1991, were imposed pursuant to the authority vested in the President by the Constitution and laws of the United States, including the statutes cited above, and represent the response by the United States to Resolution MRE/RES. 2/91, adopted by the Ad Hoc Meeting of Ministers of Foreign Affairs of the OAS on October 8, 1991, which called on Member States to impose a trade embargo on Haiti and to freeze Government of Haiti assets. The current report is submitted pursuant to 50 U.S.C. 1641(c) and 1703(c), and discusses Administration actions and expenses since the last report that are directly related to the national emergency with respect to Haiti declared in Executive Order No. 12775, as implemented pursuant to that order and Executive Order No. 12779.

8. On March 31, 1992, the Office of Foreign Assets Control of the Department of the Treasury ("FAC"), after consultation with the Department of State and other Federal agencies, issued the Haitian Transactions Regulations ("HTR") (31 C.F.R. Part 580 *Fed. Reg.* 10820, March 31, 1992), to implement the prohibitions set forth in Executive Orders No. 12775 and No. 12779. Since the last report, there has been one amendment to the HTR and one policy statement issued concerning the HTR.

On January 13, 1993, FAC, in consultation with the Department of State and other Federal agencies, amended section 580.510 of the HTR (58 *Fed. Reg.* 4080) to provide general authorization for the commercial exportation from the United States to Haiti of medicine and medical supplies. New section 580.517 of the HTR also provides for specific licensing on a case-by-case basis authorizing the exportation of (1) personal hygiene items and ingredients used in the manufacture of medicines; (2) paper and school supplies; and (3) generators and generator parts intended for use in humanitarian projects. A copy of the amendment is attached to this report.

Early in the embargo an exception to the export ban had been made with respect to medicines and medical supplies. Prior to the recent amendment, such exportations could be authorized only by specific licenses issued on a case-by-case basis. The general license provided by the amendment applies only to finished medi-

cines and medical supplies. The exportation to Haiti of components and materials used in the manufacture of medicines and medical supplies, and personal hygiene items, requires specific licensing on a case-by-case basis.

Although significant quantities of school supplies have been donated to Haiti by various U.S. organizations since the inception of the embargo, supplies of many basic items have remained chronically low. Applications for specific export licenses are carefully screened to ensure that goods intended primarily for entertainment and other non-educational uses are denied authorization. Qualifying shipments of paper are limited to paper that will be used as writing paper, notebooks, tablets, and texts.

In order to operate medical apparatus, refrigeration units, and communications devices, hospitals, schools, and various charitable and religious organizations require alternative energy sources to augment the often intermittent supply available from the government-run utility. To meet this need, specific licenses are issued for generators and generator parts and only where the humanitarian application of the equipment is definitively established.

9. On January 8, 1993, FAC published a policy statement extending all then-current licenses issued under section 580.515 of the HTR (58 *Fed. Reg.* 3228). Those licenses, which authorize transactions in connection with both the exportation to Haiti of articles containing specified parts or materials, and the importation into the United States of specified articles assembled in Haiti containing materials or parts exported from the United States, were extended to January 31, 1994. The policy statement also clarified reporting requirements pursuant to these licenses. A copy of the policy statement is attached to this report.

10. In implementing the Haitian sanctions program, FAC has made extensive use of its authority to specifically license transactions with respect to Haiti in an effort to mitigate the effects of the sanctions on the legitimate Government of Haiti and on the livelihood on Haitian workers employed by Haiti's export assembly sector having established relationships with U.S. firms, and to ensure the availability of necessary medicines and medical supplies and the undisrupted flow of humanitarian donations to Haiti's poor. For example, specific licenses have been issued (1) permitting expenditures from blocked assets for the operations of the legiti-

mate Government of Haiti; (2) permitting U.S. firms with pre-embargo relationships with product assembly operations in Haiti to resume those relationships in order to continue employment for their workers or, if they choose to withdraw from Haiti, to return to the United States assembly equipment, machinery, and parts and materials previously exported to Haiti; (3) permitting U.S. companies operating in Haiti to establish, under specified circumstances, interest-bearing blocked reserve accounts in commercial or investment banking institutions in the United States for deposit of amounts owed the *de facto* regime; (4) permitting the continued material support of U.S. and international religious, charitable, public health, and other humanitarian organizations and projects operating in Haiti; and (5) authorizing commercial sales of agricultural inputs such as fertilizer and foodcrop seeds.

11. The widespread supply of embargoed goods, particularly petroleum products, to Haiti by foreign-flag vessels led to the adoption on May 17, 1992, by the Ad Hoc Meeting of Ministers of Foreign Affairs of the OAS of Resolution MRE/RES. 3/92 urging, among other things, a port ban on vessels engaged in trade with Haiti in violation of the OAS embargo. There was broad consensus among OAS member representatives, as well as European permanent observer missions, on the importance of preventing oil shipments to Haiti. Vessels from some non-OAS Caribbean ports and European countries have been involved in trade, particularly in oil supplies, that undermines the embargo. As previously reported, section 580.211 was added to the HTR (57 *Fed. Reg.* 23954, June 5, 1992) prohibiting vessels calling in Haiti on or after the effective date from entering the United States without authorization by FAC.

Strict enforcement of the vessel regulation issued to implement Resolution MRE/RES. 3/92 has benefitted from the close coordination between FAC, the U.S. Embassy at Port-au-Prince, the U.S. Customs Service, the U.S. Navy, and the U.S. Coast Guard in monitoring vessel traffic to and from Haiti.

This coordination has resulted in the identification of some 60 vessels involved in the shipment or transshipment of unauthorized goods to or from Haiti. Enforcement coordination with the U.S. Customs Service in Miami has led to increased inspection of all outbound vessels to Haiti, thus preventing as many as 20 unauthorized shipments. Three vessels, large quantities of motor oil, electronics equipment, and miscellaneous cargo have been seized.

More than 60 cases, some involving ships flying foreign flags-of-convenience of at least 9 countries, have been referred to FAC for investigation during the reporting period. These cases involve a variety of illegal trade transactions, including third-country transshipments. Among these is one criminal case involving the shipment of petroleum products. Enforcement efforts have identified a number of transshipment routes utilized by violators throughout the Caribbean. Numerous illegal shipments have been deterred as a result of heightened scrutiny of vessels bound for suspect destinations. One such route has been successfully terminated as a result of intensified activity and close coordination among enforcement agencies.

Similarly, enforcement efforts have curtailed the previously widespread practice of mixing unauthorized goods with licensed or exempted merchandise. Many shipments, nearly all originating in Miami and fraudulently described as "humanitarian goods," were found to be commercial in nature. The legitimacy of recipients of identified donated goods is now verified, and use of this ruse has been significantly reduced. This unified enforcement effort on the part of numerous Federal agencies has been a deterrent to would-be violators.

To further strengthen the economic sanctions, on June 4, 1993, FAC issued General Notice No. 1, announcing the names of 35 entities and 83 individuals who have been determined to be Specially Designated Nationals of the *de facto* regime in Haiti. The persons identified have been so designated for one or more of the following reasons: (1) they seized power illegally from the democratically elected government of President Jean-Bertrand Aristide on September 30, 1991; (2) they are substantially owned or controlled by the *de facto* regime in Haiti; or (3) they have, since 12:23 e.d.t., October 4, 1991, acted or purported to act directly or indirectly on behalf of the *de facto* regime in Haiti or under the asserted authority thereof. This listing is not all-inclusive and will be updated from time to time.

U.S. persons are generally prohibited from engaging in transactions with these entities and individuals unless the transactions are authorized by FAC. Additionally, all assets within U.S. jurisdiction owned or controlled by these entities or individuals are blocked. U.S. persons are not prohibited, however, from paying funds owed to these entities or individuals into the blocked Government of Haiti account at the Federal Reserve Bank of New York, or, pursuant to specific licenses issued by FAC, into blocked accounts held in the names of the blocked parties in domestic U.S. financial institutions.

12. Since the last report, two penalties have been collected from U.S. banks for violations involving unlicensed transfers from blocked Government of Haiti accounts or failure to block payments to the *de facto* regime, and a penalty of $40,000 has been assessed and paid by a corporate entity for other violations of the HTR. As of March 16, 1993, payments of penalties assessed against the masters of vessels for unauthorized trade transactions or violations of entry restrictions totalled about $48,000, bringing total collections for the period to nearly $93,000.

As an enforcement initiative devised in response to the U.N. oil embargo against Haiti, FAC's civil penalties staff has developed an expedited procedure for the processing of administrative civil monetary penalties with respect to Haiti. The primary subject civil penalty actions under the Haitian Transactions Regulations will be vessels used in Haitian trade in violation of the embargo and the Regulations.

13. The expenses incurred by the Federal Government in the 6-month period from October 4, 1992, through April 3, 1993, that are directly attributable to the authorities conferred by the declaration of a national emergency with respect to Haiti are estimated at about $2.1 million, most of which represent wage and salary costs for Federal personnel. Personnel costs were largely centered in the Department of the Treasury (particularly in FAC, the U.S. Customs Service, and the Office of the General Counsel), the Department of State, the U.S. Coast Guard, and the Department of Commerce.

14. The assault on Haiti's democracy represented by the military's forced exile of President Aristide continues to pose an unusual and extraordinary threat to the national security, foreign policy, and economy of the United States. The United States remains committed to a multilateral resolution of this crisis through its actions implementing the resolutions of the OAS with respect to Haiti. We are unequivocally committed to the early return of constitutional democracy and President Aristide to Haiti. The United States has launched an energetic diplomatic campaign to help accelerate the momentum of the ongoing United Nations/OAS negotiations to achieve peaceful restoration of democracy. The United States is prepared to consider additional tougher sanctions should the negotiations stall. These measures include, but are not limited to, targeted sanctions against particular intransigent groups, a further tightening and globalization of the trade embargo, and even more vigorous enforcement measures against violators. I shall continue to exercise the powers at my disposal to apply economic sanctions against Haiti as long as these measures are appropriate, and will continue to report periodically to the Congress on significant developments pursuant to 50 U.S.C. 1703(c).

Sincerely,

WILLIAM J. CLINTON

NOTE: Identical letters were sent to Thomas S. Foley, Speaker of the House of Representatives, and Albert Gore, Jr., President of the Senate.

Nomination for Asian Development Bank Executive Director and an Assistant Secretary of State
July 12, 1993

The President announced his intention today to nominate Linda Tsao Yang to be Executive Director of the Asian Development Bank and Robert Gelbard to be the Assistant Secretary of State for International Narcotics Matters.

"As I return from my successful trip to Asia, I am pleased to make these two significant foreign policy nominations," said the President. "Linda Tsao Yang will bring impressive skills in capital development and a strong knowledge of Asia's economy to her post at the Asian Development Bank. Robert Gelbard has the strength, skill, and knowledge to make a real difference in fighting the international drug trade. I am proud of both of these choices."

NOTE: Biographies of the nominees were made available by the Office of the Press Secretary.

Nomination for Resolution Trust Corporation Chief Executive Officer
July 13, 1993

The President announced today that he will nominate Florida businessman Stanley Tate to be the Chief Executive Officer of the Resolution Trust Corporation.

"Under the leadership of Deputy Treasury Secretary Roger Altman we have instituted a program of reforming RTC's operations that is already beginning to take hold," said the President. "With his deep understanding of real estate markets and abiding commitment to public service, Stanley Tate will continue that process of saving the taxpayers money."

NOTE: A biography of the nominee was made available by the Office of the Press Secretary.

Nomination for Director of the National Science Foundation
July 13, 1993

The President announced his intention today to nominate Dr. Neal F. Lane, the provost of Rice University, to be the Director of the National Science Foundation.

"By providing financial support to our Nation's scientists and engineers, the National Science Foundation fuels the engine of creativity that helps us to increase our economic potential and our base of knowledge," said the President. "Neal Lane, with his considerable experience as a scientist and administrator, will provide the leadership necessary to foster the great talent, ingenuity, and potential of the American research community."

NOTE: A biography of the nominee was made available by the Office of the Press Secretary.

Nomination for United States Representative to the European Community
July 13, 1993

The President nominated Washington lawyer Stuart E. Eizenstat today to be the Representative of the United States to the European Community, with the rank of Ambassador.

"Stuart Eizenstat has been an important and highly respected voice in national and international policy debates for many years, and I have frequently found his advice to be invaluable," said the President. "As our country's representative to the European Community, he will ensure that our interests are well represented as the process of change continues on that continent."

NOTE: A biography of the nominee was made available by the Office of the Press Secretary.

Remarks and an Exchange With Reporters at a Water Distribution Site in Des Moines, Iowa
July 14, 1993

The President. Thank you very much. Let me just say, first of all, how very appreciative I am for the incredible work that has been done here in the last several days by the people of this State. I'm very proud of the contribution that has been made by all of the Federal Agencies, working in partnership with the people of Iowa, and I want to say a special word of appreciation for the Federal Emergency Management Agency and its Director, James Lee Witt, but also to the Agriculture Department. Secretary Espy is here with me for the second time in only 10 days, and I think his third trip to Iowa, and Mr. Witt is here. And your Senators and your congressional delegation, they're all here with us today. And Governor Branstad and I took a helicopter flight over the major portions of Des Moines and the surrounding area that have been hurt so badly.

Because I come from a State that's not all that different from Iowa, I have seen whole towns flooded, I have seen massive amounts of farmland flooded, but I've never seen anything on this scale before. And certainly, in my lifetime, anyway, to my knowledge there's never been an American city without water that was this large for this long a period of time.

I'm here today to view this damage, to talk to the members of the congressional delegation, to talk to the Governor and the other State officials of the people who are here working, and to do what I can to assure you that the victims of this disaster—and insofar as I, as President, can guarantee it—will be treated just like the victims of Hurricane Andrew or Hugo or the terrible devastation in Hawaii that my wife is visiting today from just several months ago. This is a very profound problem.

As you know, we have five States now, Minnesota, Wisconsin, Illinois, and Missouri, along with Iowa, that have been declared disasters. We have our Federal folks in South Dakota, which has had extensive crop damage, Kansas, and Nebraska, reviewing those States. We will present today a bill to the Congress for emergency assistance based on our best estimates of the damage reports that have been filed to date. But we know there will be several more

in, in the next few days, and I expect we'll have to revise all those numbers upward. We want to get the bill in today just to start movement on the bill. But as the damage reports come in over the next 4 to 5 days, I expect you'll see some revision upward in the numbers that the administration has asked for, both in the House and the Senate. And I want to say again, I'm going to do my best to make sure that the full reach of Federal assistance comes to the people of Iowa and to all the victims of this flood, and I'll be working closely with your congressional delegation to get that done.

But in the end, this is really a triumph of the spirit of the people of this State. I've been very moved by what I have seen not only from the helicopter but here in this parking lot today. And I want to say a special word of thanks to all those who have volunteered their time and who have come forward to help people in times of need, because that's really what America is all about. We've seen once again that we are capable of being a very strong family when we need to be, and it's a great tribute to your people. Thank you very much.

Q. Mr. President, there's a lot of desperate people here in Iowa, and Minnesota, Missouri, throughout the Midwest. What kinds of words on a personal level, words of encouragement, can you give them?

The President. Well, I can tell them that I have seen this sort of thing happen before in my own State. I've lived through this. I've seen people wiped out of their homes. And I talked to a lot of people here today who have lost everything they had in their homes, their businesses, their crops. And what I would say to them is we'll do what we can to help. But in the end, it is the inner strength of people and the support of the communities and families that will bring us through. But this will pass, and we have to keep looking to the future. That's what I sense in this crowd today, people who are willing to do that. I will do everything I can to make sure that this country does not forget about the people of Iowa and the other victims of the disaster, but we've just got to go on. We've got to pick up the pieces and go on. That's what Americans do, and that's what we're going to have to do.

Q. Can you help out, Mr. President, without busting the budget?

The President. Oh, I think so. Keep in mind all these emergency appropriations do come as emergencies, that is, outside the budget. But you should be encouraged that since January because of our efforts to reduce the deficit in the next 5 years, because they've been successful, long-term interest rates have dropped rather dramatically. And our deficit this year is more than $20 billion less than it was estimated to be when I took office.

So while a few billion dollars will add to it in this year, it will still be lower than everyone thought it was going to be, and it will not in any way affect the 5-year deficit reduction program now moving through Congress. So the people of Iowa don't need to feel guilty about taking this money; that's what it's there for. We've always done this. I think there is enormous bipartisan support in the Congress for this. There is no sense that this is something that should be held hostage to the budget negotiations. And we're going to do just fine on that,

I think.

Q. Mr. President, you were here 10 days ago. What are the differences now than 10 days ago when you were in Davenport?

The President. A lot more water over more of the State and a lot of residential and business damage in addition to the agricultural damage. It is very substantial, and it changes the mix of what our responsibilities are. It also makes it a little more difficult to calculate right now, so we will ask in this bill that will go before the Congress for a significant amount of money, several hundreds of millions of dollars in contingency appropriations, over and above anything we've proved in direct damages, because we can't know for sure at this moment, and we won't know next week, although we care for every last eligible disaster loss. And that's very different from the way it was before.

Thank you very much.

NOTE: The President spoke at 11:33 a.m. at the HyVee Food and Drug Store in the South Ridge Shopping Center. A tape was not available for verification of the content of these remarks.

Interview With Jan Mickelson of WHO Radio in Des Moines
July 14, 1993

Midwest Flooding

Mr. Mickelson. Mr. President, 1040 WHO Radio, KLYF–FM, and TV–13 welcomes you to Iowa and the Nation's heartland. Thank you for coming.

You spent the morning and the midday touring the wreckage and the damage, flood damage. Give us some of your impressions, sir.

The President. I did have the opportunity to tour, first of all, by helicopter. I spent about a half an hour flying over the Des Moines area, and then I stopped in a supermarket lot where water was being distributed. I talked to people who had lost everything in their houses, they've lost their businesses, people who obviously have had their farms flooded out. It was a very moving thing. I talked to parents who were worried about their children and whether they could get adequate water and how they were going to do that safely. And some of them had been

able to send their children to relatives in other communities; some had not.

But the spirit of the people seemed pretty undaunted. Several people broke down, and they were very choked up, but they were resolute. And I think that, as terrible as these things are, in some ways they bring out the best in people. I saw an enormous number of people who had just stopped their lives and come in to volunteer and help other people deal with their problems.

I will say this: This is a different sort of emergency than I saw 10 days ago when I came to Iowa and Illinois. It's gone beyond the flooding of farmland, obviously, to the destruction of a lot of homes and businesses and the public safety issue here with the water. Your people I think have done a very good job working with the Federal agencies and the State people, and I was very impressed by that.

I guess we ought to just do a rundown, since we have people listening to us from other States. We know now that there have been five States declared disaster areas: Iowa, Illinois, Missouri, Wisconsin, and Minnesota. We also have Federal officials in South Dakota, Kansas, and Nebraska reviewing the damage there.

A lot of people here are clearly and justifiably concerned about these losses. And I want to make just two or three comments about that. First of all, just before I came on this program I talked to the Director of our Office of Management and Budget, Leon Panetta, and authorized him to send today to the Congress a bill to provide emergency help to the families, the farmers, the businesses, and the communities who have been hurt by the rains and the flooding along the Mississippi River and its tributaries.

The bill will initially ask for about $2.5 billion in disaster funds, based on preliminary estimates of damages and several hundred million dollars in what are called contingent appropriations. That is, if the damages come through, the money can be released; if not, then it's not released and doesn't go against the spending. We expect that the damages, frankly, the compensable damages will be greater than that. And in the next 4 or 5 days we expect to be modifying that bill some. But we felt it was very important to go ahead and get the bill in, start it through the congressional process. And over the next 4 or 5 days we'll be getting more hard estimates of damages in, and it can be modified, first in the House and then in the Senate. After that, if further modifications are needed, we will be able to go back and ask the Congress to do more.

The principle, the operative principle here, ought to be that the people who have been hit by this disaster should not be treated any differently than people who were victims of Hurricane Andrew, Hurricane Hugo, the terrible devastation on the island of Kauai in the State of Hawaii. We ought to treat everybody the same.

Let me just make one other point in addition to the aid. I want to compliment the work that has been done at the local level and by the Federal agencies here. The Secretary of Agriculture, Mike Espy, has been here three times. The Director of the Federal Emergency Management Agency, James Lee Witt, has been here extensively. He was just complimented at the Hy-Vee parking lot here because the hospital needed some water purification equipment, and he produced it within 24 hours.

You've got the Departments of Transportation and Commerce and Housing and Urban Development, Health and Human Services, the Small Business Administration, the Corps of Engineers, and the Coast Guard, and National Guardsmen from all over working hard here. So I have been very impressed with that, and we're going to keep doing that.

I want to say a special word of commendation to FEMA and to the Director, James Lee Witt, because they have really worked hard to cut through the redtape. I got asked a lot of questions in the crowd today at the parking lot, and there must be people all over this Mississippi River area asking those questions. So let me say that you can go to a disaster assistance center set up by FEMA, and they'll give you one-stop shopping. That is, if you have some problem that is not necessarily covered by the Federal Emergency Management Act, if you just show up there, they'll work you through the system and what's there. We're going to have, I think, a coordinated and effective as well as a compassionate effort.

So those are the two things I wanted to say. For the people here who still have questions about where they are and what they need, go to the disaster assistance center. Secondly, I'm going to send the bill up to the Congress this afternoon and urge them to move in a speedy way. When I say $2.5 billion, let me emphasize there's probably another $1 billion in ongoing appropriations of the Congress which can be used to deal with the agricultural and other losses here, just money that's already out there that we'll just reprogram for the hard-hit areas. And as we get more disaster estimates in over the next couple of days, if it's warranted—and I think it will be, based on what I've seen and heard—we will modify the figures upward.

But I want to say, again, I've been very impressed. This has been a particularly moving experience for me and for the Vice President and for our families because so many of these towns that were hit were on the bus tour that we took last year. And when I've looked at these towns and I've seen what's happened, so many of them, you know, particularly along the river, in East St. Louis and Hannibal and Wayland and Keokuk and Fort Madison, Burlington in this State, Muscatine, Davenport, Bettendorf—

we visited all those places. We visited Prairie du Chien and La Crosse in Wisconsin. So I've met a lot of the people that have been hurt by this flood, and I just want you to know that we're going to do everything we can to be there and be a good partner. And if there are more things that should be done. I want the people to let us know through FEMA.

Mr. Mickelson. I had a chance to speak with one of Iowa's congressional delegation last night, Senator Grassley, who was most appreciative that this has been a bipartisan effort, and he wanted to have me make certain to pass on to you how much he appreciated being included today, as well as the Republican side of the aisle.

The President. It rains on all of us, you know.

Mr. Mickelson. Yes, on the just and the unjust, I think the Good Book says. [*Laughter*]

The President. That's right.

Mr. Mickelson. The second thing is, this $2.5 billion you're talking about—and you implied that it will be left somewhat open-ended—we won't even know for sure the extent of the damage, especially the crop-related damage, until fall when we figure out what is left of the wreckage. Will that also be included as part of this package?

The President. Well, some of that will be. Some of the fall's money, I think, will have to come out of the next fiscal year, maybe. But keep in mind, that may be a wash on the Federal budget, because the more crop land that's taken out of production, the more you'll have some upper pressure on prices, and probably less crops in the loan program. So while we'll spend more Federal money in some senses on these crop losses, we'll spend somewhat less in other areas. And we're just going to have to work that through as we go along.

Some of that money will be covered under existing Federal law. Some of it will be covered probably by the next fiscal year. Some of it, we may have to come back in for another supplemental appropriation. We're just going to have to play it by ear because we literally won't know. Senator Grassley and Senator Harkin were both commenting, along with your congressional delegation today and of course Governor Branstad, who is a farmer, they were all saying we won't know the full extent of the farm losses until the fall. And so we'll play it by ear, and as they become evident, we'll do what's appropriate.

Mr. Mickelson. The way it was handled in Hurricane Andrew, we'll try to duplicate that? Some cases, the matching funds, requirements from the States and localities was waived in the case of Hurricane Andrew. Will that be the case here in Iowa?

The President. In some cases they were, on a case-by-case basis. I've asked the FEMA Director, James Lee Witt, to look at that. FEMA has gotten some good publicity for a change, and I'm glad to see that in the course of this. Part of it is, the Director was not only the director of emergency assistance in our State, but before that he was a local official. So I think we're pretty sensitive about what can and can't be paid. We're prepared to look at that, but we should look at it under the law. We have to look at it on a case-by-case basis, and we will.

Mr. Mickelson. Mr. President, joining us via our live line from the scene of more flood damage around and along the Mississippi River is Anne Keith from KMOX Radio in St. Louis. Anne, we'd like to welcome you to WHO and to our listeners.

Anne Keith. Good afternoon, and good afternoon, Mr. President.

The President. Good afternoon, Anne.

[*At this point, Ms. Keith asked about flood insurance reform and the length of the response time.*]

The President. The consensus is that we've had a more rapid response this time than in previous ones. And I think the reason is that we do have a very high level of coordination here among the agencies. We do have some problems with flood insurance. We've got some real problems with crop insurance, and I think there's a real consensus about the fact that we have to reform the crop insurance system and some of what ought to be done about it. On the flood insurance, I think that's something else we'll have to look at. But I think that we're getting pretty good marks this time for getting out ahead of the curve on the disaster coordination. And if you have any other specific ideas about what we should do, I'd be glad to have them.

Mr. Mickelson. Also joining us from our live line from Minneapolis from radio station WCCO is Steve Murphy. Steve?

[*Mr. Murphy asked for assurance for farmers*

that Government relief would be adequate.]

The President. I think we know enough about what the size of the problem on the farm side's going to be that I can clearly give you that assurance. The real problem we've got is that the crop insurance program itself has some serious shortcomings. And we're going to have to move in and reform that and, in the meanwhile, try to hold as many of these farmers short of total destruction as we can. We're working on it very, very hard.

Secretary Espy has used and will continue to use every bit of flexibility that he has under the present law to try to save as many farmers as possible and to try to deal with the individual situations that we face. As I said earlier, a lot of the people working on this disaster have dealt with this kind of thing, flooded farms and flooded towns and these kinds of problems. And Mike Espy represented a farm district in Mississippi before he became Secretary of Agriculture.

We are determined to do everything we can to minimize the damage and to try to keep these farmers farming. And we're going to do the best we can.

Mr. Mickelson. Do you visualize a formula?

The President. What do you mean?

Mr. Mickelson. Is it possible for the Federal Government to restore everything 100 percent?

The President. Well, I don't think so. It's not possible to restore everything 100 percent because some of these programs are loan programs. But there are a lot of things that can be done. I believe, with the flexibility the Secretary has asked for that will keep these people farming. And that's our goal now, to try to help put people's lives back together and keep the farmers farming. And I think we'll do that.

Mr. Mickelson. We want to include our listeners in this mix, Mr. President, and we have asked our listeners to call us from all over the State with questions, flood related. But I'd like to just use the privilege I have as a talk show host to ask you a personal question of my own, if you don't mind. What gives you your greatest pleasure as a President, flying around in Air Force One or being able to preempt Rush Limbaugh, as we're doing right now?

The President. Oh, the latter. That's not even close. [*Laughter*]

Mr. Mickelson. I figured it wouldn't. Let's talk to some of the——

The President. Actually, my greatest pleasure being President is when you do something that you think affects people's lives in a positive way. There is so much in public life——

Mr. Mickelson. Would you include category B in that category? [*Laughter*]

The President. Perhaps only because of the purpose for which I'm here today.

[*At this point, a participant asked how disaster assistance costs would affect deficit reduction.*]

The President. Well, I think this particular one has a fairly happy answer, but let me give you the general argument. The thing that has gotten our budget in trouble are ongoing trends. Particular disasters that do, frankly, increase spending on a one-year basis have not contributed in any significant way at all to the Government's deficit problem. And I think that there is a general feeling in the country, and certainly in Washington among people of both parties, that when something like this happens you have to put the people first.

Now, in this particular case, while I will ask for $2.5 billion in budget authority, and it may go up based on the real losses, it's happening in this budget year where our deficit is more than $20 billion less than we thought it was going to be in January. Because there's been a serious debate in the Congress and an effort that is progressing to bring the deficit down dramatically, long-term interest rates have dropped. And as they have dropped, the cost of carrying the debt has gone down. And some other expenses we thought we would have, have not materialized. We've had about one million new jobs in the economy, for example, since January. So our deficit this year is projected to be over $20 billion less than we thought it was going to be, so that while this will cut into that, at least we'll still wind up way short of where it was projected in January.

Mr. Mickelson. Every county in the State of Iowa is on your list now, eligible for disaster relief.

The President. Every one.

Mr. Mickelson. I can't remember that ever occurring in midwestern history. What about you, sir? This is just——

The President. It's very——

Mr. Mickelson. ——devastating.

The President. We've never had a time, for example, in my State—which has more tornadoes per capita than any State and where we've had a lot of flooding—we've never had all our counties on disaster relief. And this is highly unusual.

[A participant asked if Federal troops could help with sandbagging and water relief efforts.]

The President. Well, if we need them, we can provide some, certainly. But so far, it's my understanding that the National Guard and the other human resources are sufficient for that at this time. If we need more, we can provide more. We've made it clear. The FEMA Director, James Lee Witt, knows that basically that's a high priority, and if they need more bodies, more help, that we'll try to provide it.

[A participant asked if water levels set by the Corps of Engineers could be changed to prevent future floods.]

The President. Mitzi, let me just say for the benefit of the listeners, Lake Ouachita and Lake Hamilton are two of the three lakes around Hot Springs where I grew up. So she and I are from the same place more or less.

The answer to your question is, yes, some more can be done for some of these communities, but a lot of this flooding occurred in the 100-year flood plan, that is in areas that are projected to flood only once every 100 years. And the Governor told me today that some of this water was 4 feet above the 100-year level. It is often very difficult and quite expensive to protect beyond the 100-year flood plain.

But I do believe what should happen is that, as we get the water down and we manage that process, all the communities affected need to look at what their flood protection is and to analyze whether more needs to be done. There clearly are some communities that had virtually no protection at all and that were vulnerable well below the 100-year flood level. And I think that just needs to be a community-by-community assessment. And we, of course, will work with all of them.

So my short answer to you is yes, I think the Corps can help some of the communities, but I do not believe that any reasonable effort would have forestalled all of the damage here. This was an unusual flood. It will be more than a century in all probability before anything remotely like this occurs again.

[A participant asked how soon Congress would act on disaster legislation and suggested an investigation of Corps of Engineers water manage-

ment practices.]

The President. Thank you. Let me answer you the first question first. I think that Congress will move very quickly on this. As I said, I authorized the bill to be sent up there today to start the legislative process. We want it frankly, to take a few days because we want to get the latest damage estimates. We'll know a lot more about 6 days from now than we know today. So if that bill needs to be amended in any way, we can amend it in the process. But by starting today, we ought to be able to move it through, I would say, in just a couple of weeks, and then the money would be released virtually immediately.

Also keep in mind, some of the funds which are emergency funds, like emergency help to people who have lost everything, been wiped out of their homes, that come through the FEMA programs, there's already money associated with that. I want to emphasize that again. A lot of the money that can be used to deal with this emergency may be already appropriated and in that sense may not in any way increase the deficit or cause any problems. But a lot of the funds will have to be done over and above that.

Now, with regard to the Corps of Engineers, let me say that you're the first person who has mentioned that to me. I'll be happy to look into it. We had a horrible flood in my State and lost a couple of little towns completely. I mean, they were totally underwater, and they lost a lot of farmland a couple of years ago. And there were all kinds of questions about whether the Corps of Engineers back up the river had managed the dams properly. But I had——

Mr. Mickelson. Same questions are occurring now.

The President. Same questions. And they're legitimate questions, and they can be looked into. But I have to tell you again, I want to say that when water gets 4 feet higher than the 100-year flood plain, it's almost impossible to conclude that some technical decision back up the river could have made a big difference. I think that it's worth looking at. I think we should look at all aspects of this. But I think that it is unlikely that that made a major contribution to this problem.

[A participant asked about the Red Rock area and about assistance for people in the restaurant

business.]

The President. First of all, I didn't go down that far, but I did talk to some people about it. There are a couple of problems. One is how to manage the outflow of water from the dam. The other is, to the extent we have any control over it, how to drain all this flooded farmland between here and the Mississippi River. See, you've got these tributaries that cause all the flooding around Des Moines, but you've got about a—well, from here to the Mississippi River you've got a whole swath of land that is totally flooded. So it's like you've got another big lake here that's 3 miles wide at its widest point. And to whatever extent we can control that, that needs to be drained in a way that doesn't just throw all the water back in at once and then down on the folks down river. So all that will have to be managed very carefully and by people who are expert in doing it.

Secondly, with regard to the restaurant business, for the people who work there and the people who own it, you should check in at the disaster assistance centers and ask essentially about two things. One is what kind of Small Business Administration programs are there to help you, because there are some, and they are pretty significant. I think you'll find them pretty significant. And secondly, for the people who work for you who may have lost everything in terms of their ability to earn any income for a significant period of time, there are some individual disaster assistance programs that might be available to help them. And at the disaster assistance center, they can give you all that information.

Mr. Mickelson. The cliche question is like this, Mr. President: Could you please cut spending first right after you send us the $3 billion? Talk to us about this. How will you be able to justify this level of expenditure to people who live in New Jersey?

The President. Because it might happen in New Jersey someday, Because it happened in Florida and Louisiana and South Carolina with Hurricanes Andrew and Hugo. Because you just can't stop nature from taking its course, and we can't afford to paralyze the American people on this.

And let me just back up and say I don't want to get into a political discussion on the budget today unless you wish to do so. I'll be happy to. But let me just point out to the American people who are listening to this, over the next 5 years, if this budget passes, we will have a hard freeze on non-health-care-related domestic spending. That means every dollar we increase Head Start by or we spend more on technology or spend to help people in California, for example, to convert from defense cuts to domestic economy and opportunities, will be made up for by cuts everyplace else. We have cut agriculture. We have cut veterans costs. We've cut all kinds of things in this budget to actually flatten that spending.

So you've got a decline in defense spending, flat domestic spending. The only increases in this whole budget for the next 5 years net are increases in Social Security and other income-related programs and increases in health care costs, which are still going up at 9 percent a year while inflation is about 3 or 4. And that's the next big challenge for our administration. But believe me, we've got $250 billion plus in cuts there now, and we ought to keep them there. But we can't not deal with this disaster or some other disaster for fear of having it go up just a little bit.

[*A participant requested cooperation from private lending institutions in the coming years to help farmers recover from their losses.*]

The President. Well, let me make two points, if I might. First of all, you characterized what happened in the eighties rather well. We had a lot of droughts in the eighties, but we also had, as you well know, a huge amount of farm debt out there which had been taken out when there was inflation, rising prices, rising land prices, and high interest rates. And then when commodity prices collapsed in the eighties, a lot of farmers couldn't finance that debt. And it took about 5 years for the Federal Government to agree on a bipartisan basis on a farming refinancing system, which then the private lending institutions could plug into. I think that provided for forbearance, for example, and other things.

I think you've got a lot of that out there now. There are also some real options that every farming State in this country has to try to help the lending institutions deal with the farmers. We won't go through all the details, but we do.

The next thing I would like to say to you, however, is that we are working aggressively to try to change the regulatory environment in which small business and agriculture live and relate to the federally insured financial institutions, the private banks. And I think that over the next year you will see a significant increase in credit offered to businesses and to agriculture because of this changing regulatory environment.

Mr. Mickelson. Mr. President, we're out of time here. On behalf of KMOX Radio in St.

Louis, WCCO Radio in Minneapolis, WHO Radio here in Des Moines, along with KLYF–FM and TV–13, thank you for coming and sharing your thoughts and visiting the heartland. I appreciate it.

The President. Thank you.

NOTE: The interview began at 1:30 p.m. at WHO Studios.

Interview With Wolf Blitzer of CNN in Des Moines, Iowa
July 14, 1993

Economic Summit

The President. [*Inaudible*]—revised upward in about 5 days.

Mr. Blitzer. Significantly?

The President. Could be.

Mr. Blitzer. And tomorrow you're supposed to go up to Capitol Hill to meet with some Members of the House and Senate, I take it, to discuss this issue or the whole G–7 Tokyo summit?

The President. Well, I will certainly give them a briefing on this issue, and I want to talk about what happened on our trip and what happened at the Tokyo summit and how important it is for us now to pass this budget. This is our part of the bargain. We got a new trade agreement with Japan. We got an agreement to lower tariffs historically with the other major industrialized countries. We're trying to restore growth to the world economy, but to do it we've got to bring the American budget deficit down, too.

Mr. Blitzer. You come to this area here—helicopters are flying overhead even as we speak—to see the devastation. The G–7 summit must seem like 100 years ago, doesn't it?

The President. It's a long way away, but the focus of those high-flung summits is to affect the lives of people like the folks on this street for the better. So in a way, it's a good way to come home, and I should be here.

Midwest Flooding

Mr. Blitzer. Now, as a former Governor, you seem to be so comfortable dealing with these natural disaster type of situations, and you get really immersed into it right away. Am I wrong? Is that just my impression?

The President. No, you're right——

Mr. Blitzer. In certain areas you seem uncomfortable, but in this kind of area you seem very comfortable.

The President. Well, I think in every new job there's a learning curve, but I don't have much of one here. Most people who would become President, who would come out of the Congress, for example, might not have anything like the experience that I've had dealing with disasters. But my State, on a per capita basis, suffers from tornadoes more than any other. We've had major floods. We've had huge droughts. I've dealt with a lot of these, and I know what's been wrong in the past. And I'm glad that a lot of people think we're trying to put it right here. I feel good about it.

Mr. Blitzer. You're going to go back to Washington tonight. Any plans to come back to this area, visit other devastated areas in the Midwest?

The President. Well, I don't want to rule it in or out. I've got to go back and see where we are, first of all, on the aid package, and secondly, where we are with the budget negotiations, and thirdly, where we are in dealing with the States and the localities. That's the big issue. That's the thing we're trying to do a better job of, make sure everybody is sort of on board and we're all doing things together, singing out of the same hymnal. And I wouldn't rule it out, but I don't want to commit yet. I've got to go back and see what the job is, what we have to do in Washington.

Homosexuals in the Military

Mr. Blitzer. And on top of everything else, this week the Pentagon is supposed to give you its recommendations on the whole issue of gays in the military.

The President. They are.

Mr. Blitzer. What's your sense? Is it falling into place right now?

The President. My sense is there's still some difference of opinion even among the service chiefs about what they want. But I hope they'll come up with something that everyone can agree is fair and we can all live with. We'll just have to see.

Mr. Blitzer. How much after you get that recommendation do you think you will finally act on some decision?

The President. Oh, I won't take long, won't take long at all. No, I won't take long.

Mr. Blitzer. Have you basically made up your mind already?

The President. Well, I want to see what they say first. I think they're still debating it a little among themselves, and I want to see what they say.

Mr. Blitzer. Okay, Mr. President. Thank you very much once again for joining us.

The President. Thanks, Wolf. Thank you.

Mr. Blitzer. Pretty devastated area.

The President. It is.

NOTE: The interview began at 3:20 p.m. at the intersection of Fleur and Valley Drives. A tape was not available for verification of the content of this interview.

Letter to the Speaker of the House on Flood Disaster Assistance
July 14, 1993

Sir:

I ask Congress to consider expeditiously the enclosed requests for emergency FY 1993 supplemental appropriations. These requests provide for emergency expenses arising from the consequences of the recent heavy rains and flooding along the Mississippi River, particularly in the Upper Midwest. I ask further that the legislation in which these funds are provided be kept free of extraneous matters in order that there may be a minimum of delay in providing necessary funds to the disaster areas.

I hereby designate the following requests as emergency requirements pursuant to the Balanced Budget and Emergency Deficit Control Act of 1985, as amended:

- Department of Agriculture, Commodity Credit Corporation, Commodity Credit Corporation fund: $600,000,000;
- Department of Agriculture, Agricultural Stabilization and Conservation Service, Emergency conservation program: $20,000,000;
- Department of Agriculture, Soil Conservation Service, Watershed and flood prevention operations: $25,000,000;
- Department of Defense—Civil, Corps of Engineers, Flood control and coastal emergencies: $45,000,000;
- Department of Housing and Urban Development, Community Planning and Development, Community development grants: $3,000,000;
- Department of Transportation, Federal Highway Administration, Federal-aid highways: $100,000,000;
- Department of Transportation, United States Coast Guard, Operating expenses: $5,000,000;
- Small Business Administration, Disaster loan program account: $70,000,000; and
- Federal Emergency Management Agency, Disaster relief: $550,000,000.

The details of these requests are set forth in the enclosed letter from the Director of the Office of Management and Budget. I concur with the Director's comments and observations.

Sincerely,

WILLIAM J. CLINTON

Statement on the Death of Patrick Lippert
July 14, 1993

I am deeply saddened by the untimely death of one of America's brightest young leaders, Patrick Lippert. An activist for many years, most recently Patrick launched Rock the Vote, an organization that reinvigorated an entire generation's interest in our democratic process by rallying them to vote in the past election, many for the first time. Rock the Vote will continue to serve as a political forum for countless new generations of young Americans to come, thanks in large part to Patrick.

Many remarkable Americans have accomplished far less than Patrick did in his 35 years.

As executive director of Rock the Vote, he helped to conceive of and then to pass the motor voter bill, which will make registering to vote much easier for millions of Americans. I was honored to have Patrick at my side 6 weeks ago as I signed the bill into law.

Patrick's friends knew him as a tireless and selfless fighter for the rights of people he never even knew. His concern for people and for his country was profound. He will be sorely missed by all of us who were inspired by his relentless fight for change. His passing should serve as a reminder that we must rededicate ourselves to the ideals he stood for.

Nomination for Posts at the Department of Defense
July 14, 1993

The President announced today that he intends to nominate R. Noel Longuemare to be the Deputy Under Secretary for Acquisition and Gilbert F. Casellas to be General Counsel of the Air Force.

"Today we are naming two more people to our Pentagon team," said the President, "both of whom are respected professionals who have achieved high levels of achievement in the private sector. I am grateful to both of them for coming into public service."

NOTE: Biographies of the nominees were made available by the Office of the Press Secretary.

Nomination for Posts at the Department of Labor and the Federal Mediation and Conciliation Service
July 14, 1993

The President announced his intention today to nominate Martin Manley to be the Assistant Secretary of Labor for the Office of the New American Workplace and John Calhoun Wells to be Director of the Federal Mediation and Conciliation Service.

"Martin Manley and John Calhoun Wells have both spent much of their lives trying to bring labor and management together in partnerships for growth," said the President. "That is exactly the kind of person that we need in these important positions. I am confident that they will bring that same spirit of cooperation to their work in my administration."

NOTE: Biographies of the nominees were made available by the Office of the Press Secretary.

Remarks Announcing the Community Development Banking and Finance Initiative
July 15, 1993

Thank you very much. I want to say to Joe and Beverly and Tim, they have stated more eloquently the case than I ever could for the work we are here to begin today. I thank them for their presence here and for their fine presentations.

I want to acknowledge, too, the presence in the audience of so many people who have been involved in community development financing for a long time. I thank all of you for coming from all over America. We have a remarkable group of people here from the United States Government from the executive branch today: Secretary Bentsen and Under Secretary Newman from the Treasury Department; Secretary Espy and Under Secretary Bob Nash from the Agriculture Department; Under Secretary Terry Duvernay and Assistant Secretary Cuomo from HUD; the SBA Administrator, Erskine Bowles; the Comptroller of the Currency, Gene Ludwig; the Federal Reserve Board Governor George Lindsey; the Acting Director of the Office of Thrift Supervision, Jonathan Fiechter; the FDIC Acting Chair, Andrew Hove, and many, many others, showing that this administration has worked together to try to come up with this proposal.

I'd also like to say that we have some specific Members of Congress who are here today whom I will acknowledge, but just for the rest of you who have been working in this field for a long time and who have felt left out, I'm going to do something I don't think I've ever done before. I'm going to ask every Member of Congress who is here to stand so you can see what support you have in the United States Congress. Would you all please stand? By my quick count, there are 41 or 42 Members of the Congress here, a very significant representation of people who asked me actually to—they felt so strongly about coming here—to delay the start of our ceremony this morning for a few moments so that they could complete their votes and still come up here.

I'm particularly pleased that the House and Senate Banking Committee chairs have agreed to sponsor this legislation and shepherd its package through Congress. Representative Henry Gonzalez and Senator Don Riegle have both long been champions of reinvesting in our communities.

The Senate Banking Committee will hold its hearing on this bill this afternoon at 2 p.m. The subcommittee chairs of the House, Congressmen Neal, Kanjorski, Kennedy, Frank, and Flake, have all joined to make sure this bill will receive consideration by the full House Banking Committee within the next few weeks.

There are four Members of the House I would like to pay some special recognition to. First, Representative Joe Kennedy of Massachusetts, who has worked to make the Community Reinvestment Act a reality for all Americans in all communities. And I thank you for that. Second, Representative Floyd Flake of New York, who has worked to provide innovative ways to spur reinvestment by major financial institutions in communities and has actually tried to do something with his ideas in the private sector as well as with his work in Congress. I thank him very much for his efforts. Next, Representative Maxine Waters of California, who has been the conscience that has kept community development banking and strengthening the CRA on the Nation's legislative agenda. Thank you very much, Maxine. And finally, Congressman Bobby Rush of Illinois, who has forged a coalition of more than 70 cosponsors for a community development financing institutions bill that shares common ground with my initiative. I look forward to working with him in Congress and across the country to champion reinvesting in all of our communities, and I thank him for mobilizing 70 Members of the House of Representatives in this cause. Thank you, Bobby.

I'd also like to pay some recognition to a person here who has for many years, more than I can remember, pointed out to the American people that most poor folks in this country and most people who have been left outside of the mainstream want a hand up, not a handout, Reverend Jesse Jackson. Thank you for being here.

Ladies and gentlemen, as you know, I have just returned from the summit of the world's seven industrial nations in Tokyo. What I saw there indicated to me that, from Harlem to the south side of Chicago, to south central Los Angeles, there is a feeling shared from Tokyo to Toronto: People want more control over their lives, their families, their communities, and their countries. The movement for political reform is running in high gear in all these countries because there is such a demand for economic opportunity so that people can live up to their God-given abilities.

This administration has tried to pursue this demand in two ways: first of all, to have a good overall economic policy, a policy for bringing the deficit down, a policy for increasing investment in our country, a policy for broadening the rules of trade in ways that help Americans who are working for a living. But secondly, we have to recognize that there are certain specific problems that are unique to our country, unique to our States, unique to our communities. And they require a specific response. And so we have developed a technology policy, a policy for defense conversion for communities and people who have been hurt by cutbacks in defense spending. We have sent to the Congress a proposal to create empowerment zones which will complement this effort, to encourage people to invest in distressed rural and urban communities in this Nation. And today we take up the community financing issue.

A few days ago when I was in Japan working to build a new global economy, my hand was strengthened because of the progress that has been made in Congress in dealing with these larger issues, reducing the deficit and investing more in education and training. It enabled me to ask our friendly competitors to lower their trade barriers so that we can increase American jobs and American exports, to work with us to increase economic growth, keep interest rates down, and make common cause to battle high unemployment, which is a problem in every advanced nation in the world today.

Today I will report to a bipartisan leadership meeting of the Congress on the achievements of this summit. But I will also have to tell them that the challenge remains. We can only enjoy the fruits of the opportunities created at the Tokyo meeting if we follow through on the commitment to pass the economic plan now before the Congress and if we take the initiatives like the one we're here to celebrate today.

To those who would do nothing or let us slide back into the status quo, I would say that we must go forward. We must adopt the largest deficit reduction plan in our history. Look how low the long-term interest rates are now because of the efforts that are being made. We must adopt these strategies to bring jobs to America. We must maintain our Nation's leadership in the global economy. On the issue of whether there must be economic change in a nation desperate for jobs and growth, there can be no doubt of the answer.

Today I am sending to Congress an innovative proposal that will bring new life and new opportunity and new directions to communities all over America that lack capital and credit, the kinds of basic banking services that these three fine people needed so badly and had to look so long for. This proposal creates a fund to provide grants to new and existing community-based lenders. The fund will provide about $400 million over 5 years and will employ a number of measures to increase significantly the total money provided to communities through these community institutions.

Under this plan every dollar the fund provides to a community development bank must be matched at least by another dollar of private capital. Other community development financial institutions will also be required to match assistance as well. The Treasury Department predicts that this matching requirement and the leverage provided by the institutions will produce at least $2 billion in additional investment.

If you look at the size of the average loan in these kinds of institutions leading to the number of jobs created that are represented by the three fine people on this platform today, the potential for creating new jobs in America through this initiative is absolutely enormous. And they can be created in places where people have long given up on the free enterprise system simply by making the free enterprise system work for a change for those people.

These institutions come in a wide variety of sizes and shapes. They are banks with a special commitment to community development. They are community development banks set up for that purpose only. They are credit unions. They are microenterprise loan funds. I can tell you this, most of the enterprises that we are talking about helping, that were in existence in the 1980's that made loans to poor people who lived in their community or to struggling small business people had a lot lower failure rate than some of the high-flown financial schemes that were subsidized by other Government policies in the last decade.

Because of the commitment and understanding of people in all different kinds of financial institutions, every type of community development financial institution will be eligible for assistance under our program. The existing network of community lenders have demonstrated that when there is a constant commitment to this kind of development you can produce growth and jobs.

Many of you with us today, from Chicago's Shore Bank to North Carolina's Self-Help Credit Union to Arkansas' Elkhorn Bank—which Mack McLarty and the First Lady served on the board of, and which I helped to raise funds for when I was in a previous position—understand how economic growth is built from the grassroots. It works in urban areas. It works in rural areas. We were wondering when we set up this bank in Arkansas whether small towns and rural areas really could benefit from the kind of strategy that had worked so brilliantly for the South Shore Bank in Chicago, and the answer turned out to be a resounding yes.

The Government's role in this is crucial, but limited. The real solutions must come from the community, from the people who live there who know their neighbors. It is our job to empower those communities with the tools they need to generate growth and jobs, and then let the hard work and the determination of the people pay off.

At the same time, I recognize that without the involvement and investment of major banks, low and moderate income communities will still be deprived of a full range of economic opportunity. The Community Reinvestment Act of 1977 requires that banks and thrifts meet the credit needs of the entire community in which they do business. And while the CRA has played an important role in making credit available to underserved urban and rural communities, I think we would all admit that it hasn't lived up to its potential. The current enforcement system relies too much on public relations documentation and not enough on real lending performance.

This has been a pain for everybody involved: too much paperwork for the banks and not enough investment for the communities. That's why I am sending a memorandum to the four Federal banking regulators that requires them to implement a series of reforms around CRA,

designed to increase investment in communities that need it, while simultaneously streamlining and clarifying the regulatory process. The policy will be good for banks, good for communities, good for borrowers, and it represents real change.

These actions today fulfill a commitment I made during the last campaign when I promised that we would work hard to unlock the energy and the entrepreneurship that lies latent in the hearts and souls of men and women in this country in every community. This proposal will enable them to take a small loan and start a business, to turn their dreams into storefronts and then expand those storefronts into chains, creating jobs for their neighbors and bringing opportunities to their neighborhoods. It will make them a part of the movement for democratic capitalism and growth that is reshaping the entire world but has left too many Americans behind.

Now, I'd like to introduce three people who are going to help us carry out these commitments: Hugh McColl, the CEO of NationsBank; Irving Henderson, the chair of the National Community Reinvestment Coalition; and Ron Grzywinski, the chairman of Shore Bank in Chicago.

[*At this point, Mr. McColl, Mr. Henderson, and Mr. Grzywinski spoke on community development banking.*]

I'd like to conclude this morning's ceremony just by saying again, as I did when I opened, that I know that every one of you who's worked in this field for any length of time has a story or personal stories that you could tell. And I just want you to know that I am grateful for the work that you have done and the role that each of you have played in bringing this bill to its present point.

I got on this issue as Governor when I saw so many needs that were unmet, and when the now Under Secretary of Agriculture for Community Development, Bob Nash, and I worked hard to use our existing authorities to help people who couldn't have access to credit. I learned about the South Shore Development Bank. And through them I met a remarkable man named Mohammed Yunis, who told me how he, through the Grameen Bank, had made market rate interest loans to poor village women in Bangladesh, and over 95 percent of them had actually paid the loans back.

And then, this became part of our reinventing Government initiative of the Democratic Leadership Council and then an idea that the Vice President championed in his efforts to examine what we're doing here. A lot of you have helped me in my understanding of this. Floyd Flake showed me the businesses around his church. Hugh McColl stayed up half the night one night talking with me about the Community Reinvestment Act and how we could make it work. My friend, Charles Stith there, from Boston, has spent years on this.

To all of you who have played any role on this, I thank you very much. And I ask you now to work with this wonderful representation from Congress to make sure we get the job done and do it in a hurry. Thank you. We're adjourned.

NOTE: The President spoke at 12:12 p.m. on the South Lawn at the White House. In his remarks, he referred to Timothy Bazemore, founder and president, Workers Owned Sewing Co.; Beverly Ross, owner, Lakeview Stables; Joseph Holland, owner, Ben and Jerry's Ice Cream Franchise of Harlem, New York, NY; Lawrence B. Lindsey, Federal Reserve Board Governor; and Rev. Charles R. Stith, national president, Organization for a New Equality (ONE).

Message to the Congress Transmitting Community Development Banking and Finance Legislation
July 15, 1993

To the Congress of the United States:

I am pleased to submit to the Congress the "Community Development Banking and Financial Institutions Act of 1993". This legislative initiative will promote the creation of community development financial institutions that will empower individuals and communities and provide for greater economic opportunity. Also transmitted are a statement of the Administration's principles embodied in this proposal and a section-by-section analysis.

In too many urban and rural communities, there is a lack of capital and credit. Lending in distressed communities, particularly to small businesses, can be complicated. It may require special expertise and knowledge of the borrower and the community, credit products, subsidies, and secondary markets. Community development financial institutions—including community development banks like South Shore Bank in Chicago, community credit unions such as Self-Help in North Carolina, community development corporations, micro-enterprise loan funds, and revolving loan funds—have demonstrated that they can provide capital, credit, and development services in distressed areas and to targeted populations.

The bill proposes establishment of a Community Development Banking and Financial Institu- tions Fund that would support a program of investment in community development financial institutions. The Fund would provide financial and technical assistance to, and serve as a national information clearinghouse for, community development financial institutions.

This initiative reaffirms my commitment to helping communities help themselves. By ensuring greater access to capital and credit, we will tap the entrepreneurial energy of America's poorest communities and enable individuals and communities to become self-sufficient.

My Administration is also committed to enhancing the role of traditional financial institutions with respect to community reinvestment. As a complement to the community development financial institutions initiative, we will adopt regulatory changes to more effectively implement the Community Reinvestment Act of 1977. These changes will replace paperwork with performance-oriented standards and will include tougher enforcement measures for noncompliance.

In order to secure early enactment of legislation in this crucial area, I urge the Congress to consider the Community Development Banking and Financial Institutions Act of 1993 as a discrete bill, separate from general issues of financial services reform and any other non-germane amendments.

WILLIAM J. CLINTON

The White House,
July 15, 1993

Remarks and an Exchange With Reporters Following a Meeting With Congressional Leaders
July 15, 1993

The President. I wanted to just make a brief opening statement and then take a couple of questions. I had the opportunity today to brief the bipartisan leadership group in Congress about the trip to Japan and Korea in terms of what was achieved at the G-7 meeting and what was achieved in the new breakthrough on our trade relations with Japan and the national security issues, reaffirming America's role as a Pacific power and our commitment to the security of Japan, Korea, and our other allies in the region.

I have just come from a bipartisan meeting of House Members and Senators from the States affected by the floods. And I was grateful to see the committee leaders there, even though many were from States not affected by the flood. I think it's fair to say that based on the leadership luncheon, or meeting, and the meeting I just came from, that there is a bipartisan commitment in the Congress to aggressively push the flood relief package. And for that I am grateful to Senator Mitchell and to Senator Dole and to the Speaker and Mr. Gephardt and Mr. Michel and the others. I think there's a real feeling that this is something we ought to do together as a nation. And I appreciate that.

I want to reiterate that we will be aggressively working in the next few days with the Governors and the others in the respective States to work through the practical problems, as well as to get the most up-to-date damage estimates in the event that the bill moving through the Congress needs to be modified in its appropriations amounts.

If there are any questions, I'd be glad to take them.

Disaster Assistance

Q. Mr. President, you've asked Congress for $2.5 billion in disaster relief. And yesterday the Director of FEMA and others have put that figure—[*inaudible*].

The President. First of all, let me emphasize a couple of things. The Federal Government does not reimburse 100 percent of the losses of these programs. Some of that has to be done from private sources; some of it has to be done from local match. Secondly, the ongoing budgets of many of these Departments, the Agriculture Department, for example, and FEMA, for another, contain funds which will be in the ordinary course of business directed to the area where it's most needed. So some of the ongoing budget will take care of this.

Now, in answer to your specific question, I have consulted with the leadership about that. The 1990 budget bill plainly concede of genuine emergencies being funded outside the budgetary process. And I think it's almost universally acknowledged now that even though we don't have the specific figure, this year's deficit will be quite a bit lower than it was estimated to be in January because we're working so hard at reducing the deficit that interest rates are down and therefore the cost of servicing our debt is down. So I think we can handle this.

I have heard the general principle advanced, it would be nice if we paid for it all with offsets, but I haven't seen any specific suggestions. And in the absence of those, I think we should just take the '90 law and proceed as is. If Senator Mitchell or the Speaker or Mr. Gephardt or anyone else has a different idea, of course, I'd be glad to hear it. The most important thing is that we get the aid out to those folks as quickly as possible.

Economic Program

Q. [*Inaudible*]—and what advice are you giving to the leaders about how to resolve the——

The President. What was that last question?

Q. What advice are you giving to the leadership about——

The President. Well, first of all, there is a general consensus that we ought to make this the biggest deficit reduction package the country's had, and that means hard numbers and good figures. The number that was adopted in 1990, I think, is now generally conceded was not as firm as it might have been. And also there was a big economic slowdown, and the health care cost increases were greater than originally thought. But I think this is going to be a more solid plan.

How it's resolved is something that the conference will have to work out. I'm going to be giving them some advice, but it won't be inconsistent with what I've said before. I want a very progressive plan. I want the deficit reduction. I want people who can afford to pay, whose taxes went down in the eighties, to pay their fair share now. I very much want some of the incentives in this plan that were in the House bill. I hope some of them can be put back in the Senate bill. I think that it's important that people who work 40 hours a week and have children in the home be able to be lifted out of poverty rather than taxed into it. I think it is very important that we have incentives to grow the high-technology sector of our economy, that's the R&D and the new venture capital-gains tax that Senator Bumpers has long championed, along with others. There are several things in there. The empowerment zone issue is very important to me. It goes very closely with the community development bank proposal we made today to generate jobs and growth.

Keep in mind the ultimate purpose of deficit reduction is to improve the economy by getting interest rates down, freeing up tax funds that we would otherwise have to spend on serving the debt, and improving the climate for new jobs. It's also clear that we have to have some investment incentives. People have to take this money that we're going to save through reducing the deficit, turn around and invest it in the economy. And if you raise tax rates on upper income people and then you provide only a very targeted way to in effect lower their tax burden by having them create jobs, then you win either way, because either way you reduce the deficit and you improve the economy. That's what we're going to try to do.

Q. [*Inaudible*]—part of the reason you supported obviously is for the—[*inaudible*]. You haven't talked very much about other reasons

why you might want—[*inaudible*]. What are the other reasons——

The President. Well, I think it's sound policy. We have the world's lowest energy levies. And we're trying to promote conservation and a pure and cleaner environment, which is the reason we proposed it in the first place. But it was proposed, obviously, to help close the gap to meet our deficit reduction targets also. And the conferees know how I feel about it.

But the number one thing is we have got to produce a growing economy. And the deficit reduction package is absolutely critical to that. Let me back up and say this is the first time in 10 years plus, the first time since 1981 an American President has gone to a meeting of the world's seven great industrial powers and not been criticized because of the American budget deficit. This time the statement complimented the United States for taking aggressive action to bring down the deficit and acknowledged the responsibility of other nations to try to help us grow the global economy. That would not have happened if the House and the Senate hadn't passed versions of this deficit reduction package.

And that is the central message out there. People think, who have observed things for years, that we are doing something serious to change the climate in Washington, to improve the economy, and to move us off dead center. I don't want to say too much to prejudge the enormously difficult work the conferees have to do to reconcile the differences between the Senate and the House version. I want to see how they can do. And I will give them my advice, but I think the more, right now, they can be left free to do their work and consult with me, the better off we'll be.

Disaster Assistance

Q. Mr. President, a followup on both the numbers. On the flood bill, you all sent up a package of $2.5 billion but concede it will go much higher. Now, the new numbers are $5 billion, as high as $10 billion. Are you all working with a new number?

The President. Those numbers are numbers for estimated aggregate damage in the area. Let me say again, point one, the Federal Government has never compensated natural disasters a dollar-for-dollar for every kind of disaster loss. There are some personal losses, for example, that you can only have low-interest loans for, the actual out-of-pocket costs of which are less than the loan. There are other costs that have to be matched by State and local government, although the Federal Government has the power under certain extreme circumstances to waive some or all of it. There are other losses that simply aren't covered by any Federal law. So there is a big distinction to be drawn between the aggregate loss and what is normally compensable by our Federal programs. The second thing I want to emphasize in this, that some of these losses can be covered by the ongoing

programs in the Federal Government. And I guess I should add a final point, which is that we won't know the total dimensions of the Federal—excuse me, the agricultural losses, until very near the beginning of the next fiscal year. So some of them may come in the next fiscal year as well.

Thank you very much.

NOTE: The President spoke at 5:20 p.m. at the Capitol. A tape was not available for verification of the content of these remarks.

Nomination for Posts at the Environmental Protection Agency
July 15, 1993

The President announced his choices for five key positions at the Environmental Protection Agency today, declaring his intention to nominate Jonathan Cannon to be the Assistant Administrator for Administration and Resources Management and the Chief Financial Officer; Elliot Laws to be Assistant Administrator for Solid Waste and Emergency Response; Mary Nichols to be Assistant Administrator for Air and Radiation; Robert Perciasepe to be Assistant Administrator for Water; and Shelly Metzenbaum to be Associate Administrator for Regional

Operations and State/Local Relations.

"This outstanding group of people, added to the already strong team at EPA, will work together with Administrator Carol Browner to continue building a stronger and more vibrant Agency," said the President. "Each of these five individuals has expertise in environmental issues, meaningful Government experience, and most importantly, a strong commitment to protecting our Nation's precious natural resources."

NOTE: Biographies of the nominees were made available by the Office of the Press Secretary.

Nomination for Posts at the Department of Energy
July 15, 1993

The President announced today that he intends to nominate Martha Krebs and Corlis Moody to senior positions at the Department of Energy. Krebs will be Director of the Office of Energy Research, and Moody will be the Director of the Office of Minority Economic Impact.

"It gives me great pleasure to announce these nominations today," said the President. "Martha Krebs has demonstrated tremendous leadership

capacity as an administrator of one of our country's most important research facilities and a senior congressional aide. As for Corlis Moody, Secretary O'Leary knows better than anyone the high quality of work that she has done in the past and is capable of doing at the Department of Energy. I welcome both of their service."

NOTE: Biographies of the nominees were made available by the Office of the Press Secretary.

Nomination for Posts at the Agency for International Development
July 15, 1993

The President today announced his intention to nominate Margaret Carpenter, Assistant Administrator for Asia and Douglas Stafford, Assistant Administrator for Food and Humanitarian Assistance at the Agency for International Development, U.S. International Development Cooperation Agency.

"With their dual experience in the field of foreign affairs and understanding of the good global assistance can do, I am certain both Margaret and Doug will work hard to fulfill AID's mission of providing economic and humanitarian assistance to the developing world," the President said.

NOTE: Biographies of the nominees were made available by the Office of the Press Secretary.

Nomination for Inspector General of the United States Information Agency
July 16, 1993

The President today announced his intention to nominate attorney Marian Bennett as Inspector General at the United States Information Agency.

"I am pleased today to name Marian Bennett to this important post at USIA," the President said. "I am certain she will work hard to ensure USIA is a tight-run operation up to the task of its mission to promote democracy and freedom abroad."

NOTE: A biography of the nominee was made available by the Office of the Press Secretary.

Interview With WGEM Radio, Quincy, Illinois
July 17, 1993

Disaster Assistance

Q. Good morning, Mr. President.

The President. Good morning.

Q. How are you, sir?

The President. I'm fine. As you know, I'm now on Air Force One, on my way to St. Louis to a meeting with the Governors of all the affected States and a number of Cabinet-level officials. I think we have about seven or eight going down today, as well as a number of Members of Congress who have jurisdiction over the committees that are writing the relief legislation.

I wanted to call you, because your radio station has done such a remarkable job of kind of coordinating the information and keeping people in touch and keeping them up in the middle of this. I really respect what you've done, and I appreciate it very much.

Q. Mr. President, this is Steve Cramblit. The people that have really done the work are the people who have been at the levees slinging the sandbags on the Mississippi River water out of their homes and out of their agricultural lands. They're really the heroes in all of this.

The President. Yes, I've seen a lot of them working, as you know, on my two previous trips. It's been an amazing effort. And of course we're not out of the woods yet. I know you lost a dam there last night, and a lot of people on the other side of the river had to evacuate. And then the county down from that, Pike County, I think the name of it is, is really concerned. So we've got a few anxious days left to go.

Q. Mr. President, this is Jeff Dorsey with you now, and I was down in the Pike County area yesterday. Are there any words that you can give them, something to pick up their spirits at this point after 3 weeks of fighting the Mississippi off? Can you tell them anything? They're all listening out there to you right now, sir.

The President. Well, first of all, let me say that I think, you know, we may have a few more days of this, but I think in a few days it will be over. And as tough as things are, we are doing everything we can to make sure that we've got in place emergency relief help and that we are planning for the long run to stay with this process, the long run, to help people get back on their feet and go on with their lives. I've seen an awful lot of brave people in the Midwest in the last 2½ weeks, and I just would urge the folks to hang in there and not expect the worst but to prepare for it, and then we'll deal with whatever comes.

Q. Mr. President, this is Bob Turek. You have already asked for $2.5 billion, and we understand that Senator Paul Simon and some of the others are saying that damage might be a lot higher. Are you going to try and seek—allow for emergency relief?

The President. Yes. As the evidence comes in to support it, we decided that we really needed to get a bill up to the Congress and start moving it through. Now can you hear me? We decided we needed to get a bill up to the Congress and start moving it through. But as we get new damage estimates, we'll be giving them to the congressional committees, and the bill can be amended in the House and in the Senate to reflect the new damage estimates. And then if something comes in later, we can take new legislation up there.

But we felt very strongly that we needed to start getting the help out there just as quickly as possible and that we ought not to wait another month or so to present a bill. So that's why we're doing what we're doing. And I think it's the right thing to do. But it's not the end of the road. The bill we presented will be modified, I think, in the Congress, if the evidence comes in to support the need for more aid. And I think we'll fulfill our responsibilities. We just want to be quick about it so that we can really give people help, and they don't get caught in the bureaucratic delay.

Q. Mr. President, this is Rich Cain. We've had a number of listeners who are very concerned over the National Guard troops who have been in the area for quite some time now who are becoming somewhat fatigued and have been, in battling this fight, as well as a number

of volunteers. The question is, Mr. President, is there any consideration towards possible activation of troops on the Federal level?

The President. That's one of the issues that I want to talk to the Governors about today. I'm concerned that in some of the States involved, they have used all their available Guardspeople and they may be exhausted. Some of them have been working virtually around the clock. And I think that we need to look at either bringing in Guard folks from other States or maybe activating some Federal troops if, in fact, all of the State resources have been exhausted. And I'm going to take that up with the Governors today.

I know you're going to carry the meeting live on your radio station, which is something I very much appreciate, and so we'll get some answers from them and then I'll give an appropriate response. But I appreciate your bringing that up and I will check into it—in particular, in your area.

Q. Mr. President, we appreciate taking your valuable time, and I know that you are preparing for that meeting today. We thank you very much. And would you give us one final word to the people of this area from the President of the United States?

The President. I just want you to know that we're thinking of you, we're praying for you, we're pulling for you, and we're working. All of us are working as hard as we can with your Governors and your local representatives to try to make this crisis pass as quickly as possible. We're not in control of this situation entirely, because Mother Nature is having its way with us, as periodically happens. But I do believe that we're going to be able to get our way through this, and the courage and the good humor of the people of the Midwest has been the key element, if we can keep people thinking positively, looking toward the future, preparing for whatever might happen. We'll do our best to be there as your partners. And the rest of the country is thinking about you and really is determined, I think, to have the National Government do what it takes to help you put your lives back together and get back on track here.

Thank you so much. Goodbye.

[*At this point, the telephone interview ended, and the President then took questions from reporters aboard Air Force One.*]

Q. What are the chances of Federal troops?

The President. I need to ask. It's something I thought about in Iowa the other day, where the Guardsmen there obviously have been working around the clock. What we need to do— of course the folks there, we have no way of knowing whether they are—have they mobilized the entire State Guard, can they send other Guardsmen there? You know, I need to ask about the facts, but I will, because they brought it up and because they also brought it up in Des Moines last week. We will raise that with the Governors today in the meeting. But I don't think it's appropriate for me to make that decision. They may have a lot of other Guard troops within the States that can be mobilized.

Q. What's the—[*inaudible*]—decisions?

The President. I have nothing to add to what's been said or speculated about. I think the Attorney General—I would refer you to her on that.

NOTE: The President spoke at 9:30 a.m. from Air Force One en route to St. Louis, MO. A tape was not available for verification of the content of this interview.

The President's Radio Address
July 17, 1993

Good morning. These past 2 weeks as I've traveled across our Nation and our world, I've been reminded that Americans can rise to any challenge. The Vice President and I have visited communities in the Midwest where floodwaters have destroyed farms and businesses and homes, reaching historic levels. We've seen much that is heartbreaking but also a lot that is heartlifting.

The natural disaster is bringing out the best in our people. I saw that when I visited Des Moines on Wednesday. People there have been going without tapwater, but they still remember what it means to be Americans. Volunteers from all over the State and around the country are there distributing food and water, filling sandbags, and helping older people, the sick, and neighbors whose livelihoods have been washed away.

Already I've declared disaster areas in Iowa, Illinois, Missouri, Wisconsin, and Minnesota. And Federal officials are now in South Dakota, North Dakota, Kansas, and Nebraska, reviewing the extensive flood damage in those States. I've directed all the appropriate Federal agencies to work together as a team to help the victims of these floods. And I've been especially pleased with the work of Secretary Espy and the Agriculture Department and the sterling efforts of the Federal Emergency Management Agency and its Director, James Lee Witt.

Now I'm asking Congress to approve emergency assistance to help the families, farmers, businesses, and communities who've been hurt.

And today I'll be heading back to St. Louis to meet with Governors from the Midwest and several Members of the Congress to plan short-term disaster relief and long-term economic recovery. At a time like this, people who have worked hard all of their lives deserve a helping hand. With that helping hand, the people of the Midwest will get back on their feet. After all, they're Americans. They're facing this crisis with grit and courage and generosity.

That indomitable American spirit is recognized as far away as Tokyo and Korea. In Tokyo, I attended a summit of the world's seven leading industrial nations. In Korea, I visited our service men and women serving along the Demilitarized Zone and standing up to the nuclear threats that the North Koreans have presented to us in the last several weeks.

In Tokyo, at the economic summit, my hand was strengthened because of everything the American people have been doing, working to change our economic policies and pushing to cut our deficit and increase investment in American jobs. For the first time in more than a dozen years, an American President was able to go to one of these summits and look at the leaders of the other great economic powers and say, "We are putting our own house in order." Your commitment to change has helped me to come home with job-creating agreements to lower trade barriers worldwide and to reduce our trade deficit with Japan. These agreements will make life better for America's workers,

America's businesses, and our families.

After years of deadlocked talks with the world's leading trading powers, we negotiated a plan that will dramatically reduce tariffs on manufactured products, from chemicals to electronics, from pharmaceuticals to farm equipment. When other countries lower their tariffs, more consumers all across the world will buy our products. That means more manufacturing jobs here in America, high-skill, high-wage jobs with a future, and jobs that create other jobs back home.

I could not have persuaded our trading partners to reach these agreements without having made the progress we've made at home on our economic plan. For years other nations have come to these meetings and said the same things to an American President: We can't have a healthy economy in the United States or the world until America cuts the deficit, invests in education and technology, and is able to compete and win again.

Well, from the bargaining table at Tokyo to our factory floors here at home, we are on the move again, stepping up to the plate, taking responsibility, making the tough choices, and building our economic strength, not borrowing from it. America is now the high-quality, low-cost producer of many products and services that can compete in any market in the world.

And our economic plan answers the call that other world leaders have made for years, and now that the American people are making, for historic change. It has the largest deficit reduction in history, $500 billion over 5 years. It has historic spending cuts, more than 200 specific cuts that save more than $250 billion from this budget. And it makes an historic shift from trickle-down economics, where taxes were lowered on the wealthy and raised on the middle class, because more than three-quarters of the new taxes in this plan will be paid by the wealthiest 6 percent of Americans. In fact, for every $10 that we cut the deficit, $5 comes from spending cuts, $4 comes from taxes on the wealthiest 6 percent, and only a dollar comes from the middle class. Working families with incomes under $30,000 are held harmless. The working poor, those who work 40 hours a week, have children in the home, and are still in poverty, will get tax relief so that no American who's working full time with children in the home will live in poverty.

A majority of our small businesses, where the jobs are mostly created in America these days, will actually get a tax cut because of the job-creating incentives in this plan. The plan is fair, it's balanced, and it will create new jobs, permanent, productive, private-sector jobs. With this plan in place, the American economy can produce 8 million jobs over the next 4 years, 8 million new jobs.

As the economic plan has progressed through Congress, the financial markets where long-term interest rates are set have responded. Long-term interest rates have declined to historic lows; mortgage rates are at 20-year lows. Now, if we can keep interest rates at this low level for the rest of the year, people refinancing their home loans or taking out new business loans will pump $100 billion of new capital back into the economy, because they'll have lower interest payments and then they'll have money to consume or to invest.

On top of that, the new business incentives, especially those for small businesses, will create new jobs. There will be new incentives for people to move from welfare rolls to payrolls. That means more jobs and new opportunities for young people to serve their communities while they finance their college education and become more employable in a tough global economy.

The House and the Senate have both passed versions of this plan, and now they're meeting to write a final proposal. With your help we can make sure that Congress says no to gridlock and yes to growth, yes to change, and yes to what is best in the American spirit.

Throughout the natural disaster in the Midwest I've been profoundly impressed by how our people have pulled together as a family. From the Congress to the Governors, to the community leaders in our cities and towns, to the volunteers, and to the people who have been dispossessed, Americans have risen above their divisions and their personal concerns to help people in trouble. In times of crisis we're not Democrats or Republicans, we are Americans.

Today I ask all of you to show that same spirit in responding to our economic problems. To those who would do nothing or slide back into the status quo of the last several years, I say we must go forward with a plan that grows the economy, reduces the deficit, creates jobs, and restores fairness.

I say to my friends in the other party in Congress, just as you have worked with me and the people of the Midwest together to help the people dig themselves out of a natural disaster, so should you join us in digging America out of the legacy of two decades of declining growth, declining productivity, growing deficits, and economic crisis. We are Americans; we can pull together. And together we can make the historic decisions to build a new generation of prosperity for ourselves, our children, and our children's children.

Thank you for listening.

NOTE: This address was recorded at 5:27 p.m. on July 16 in the Roosevelt Room at the White House for broadcast at 10:06 a.m. on July 17.

Remarks at a Roundtable Discussion on Flood Relief in Arnold, Missouri
July 17, 1993

The President. Thank you all for coming. As you know, we're starting just a bit late because we all had to come down from the airport, and we came in different ways. I do want to thank everyone for being here and say this is a rather extraordinary meeting of Federal, State, local, and private sector emergency response people. We're going to try to get through a very busy agenda today, and it will be my job to try to keep us more or less on schedule. So I hope we can, because there are an awful lot of issues that have to be dealt with.

I'd like to thank the Governors who are here: Our host, Mel Carnahan, of Missouri. Terry Branstad of Iowa I think is here—there he is; I missed him when I went around—who hosted me on a trip to Iowa, two trips to Iowa recently. Is Governor Thompson of Wisconsin here? I think he's coming. Governor Edgar of Illinois, Ben Nelson of Nebraska, Ed Schafer of North Dakota, Arne Carlson of Minnesota, and Walter Miller of South Dakota. I think that is all the Governors who are here.

I'd also like to thank the Members of Congress who are here or who are scheduled to come. We have Senator Barbara Mikulski at the table, whose committee has jurisdiction over the operations of emergency management; Senator Kit Bond from Missouri, our host; Senator Bill Bradley is here somewhere or on the way, whose family farm in Missouri is apparently under water. He may be here in his private capacity rather than as United States Senator.

We're delighted to be in the host district of the majority leader of the United States House of Representatives, Dick Gephardt, and I want him to say a word in a moment, since we're camped out here in his backyard. Congressman Bruce Vento from Minnesota; Congressman Peter Hoagland from Nebraska; Congressman Minge; Congressman Volkmer is coming, I think; and Congressman Pomeroy is here. And I think Senator Wellstone from Minnesota is scheduled to come.

Let me also tell you, all of you from all these States, that the Vice President and I and our administration team had an extensive meeting yesterday in Washington with the congressional delegations from all the affected States. And you would be very interested to know that not only did virtually every Member of Congress from every State here represented show up, but there was also a rather substantial representation from interested Members of Congress from other States who just wanted to be there, get a briefing, and know what they could do to help. It was a very, very large and very impressive turnout. And I told them all we were coming here today. I invited them here, but most of them did their work on this issue yesterday at that meeting. Did I recognize Congressman Wheat? I don't know if I did, but he's here. Thank you.

I also want to say that the heads and Secretaries of 10 Federal Departments or Agencies in our administration are here working together. And I'd like to briefly acknowledge them so you'll know who they are and ask them to at least raise their hands: James Lee Witt, the Director of FEMA; the Secretary of Agriculture, Mike Espy; Secretary of Transportation, Federico Peña; Secretary of Commerce, Ron Brown, who just became a grandfather to twins. He's only 35 years old. We can't figure out how it happened. [*Laughter*] The Secretary of Health and Human Services, Donna Shalala; Secretary of Housing and Urban Development, Henry Cisneros; Secretary of Labor, Bob Reich;

head of the Corps of Engineers, General Williams; the Commandant of the Coast Guard, Admiral Kime; and the head of the National Weather Service, Dr. Joe Friday, is also here. And he and the Vice President had a very interesting conversation about what caused this flood. They're going to talk a little in a minute. The Director of the Office of Management and Budget, Leon Panetta. And I'd also like to recognize in the audience the head of the American Red Cross, Elizabeth Dole, who flew down with us. And the Red Cross has done wonderful work, and we thank you for being here.

Now, I'd like to ask Congressman Gephardt if he'd like to say anything on behalf of his district. And then I want to recognize the Vice President for opening remarks.

[*At this point, Representative Gephardt thanked the President and members of the administration for their visit.*]

The President. Thank you very much. I would just like to say in response to that, I think it's fair to say that all of us in the administration who have been to this region have been very moved by what we have seen, both the pain that people have experienced and their enormous courage and often their great good humor in dealing with this crisis.

I also want to thank the people in the rest of the United States who have sent help of all kinds. We even have seen help coming in from South Florida, which suffered so much from Hurricane Andrew last year.

I do want to say, too, we are here to deal with basically two great issues. One is, what are we going to do right now, while everybody is up to their ears in alligators? And the second is, how are we going to keep this effort going over the long run, so that we can see these areas through to full recovery? There has been a disjuncture in the past, I think, between what happens in the short run—there's all kind of questions about whether we've had enough coordination or not; I think we've really worked through that this time—but also whether the Federal Government can stay in the long run. And there is an almost collective emotional process that people go through when it first hits. Folks are brave and good humored and courageous, but then the reality of the losses that sink in, and a grief takes over. And then, if everyone is not at least doing their best, a lot of anger can come in the wake of that.

And our goal is to just be a good partner and to sensitively know that people will have to go through an emotional cycle, and the whole States will go through an emotional cycle. But we don't want people to think that they have been abandoned when the immediate emergency is over. So we're going to start this meeting with a discussion of the present conditions and what we can do in the short run. Then we're going to go to a discussion of long-term relief. And then at the end of the discussion, we're going to move to the legislation that is now moving through Congress, what it means and where we go from here.

Let me just introduce the Vice President with this thought. I read the other day that a 61-year-old retired State police officer in Quincy, Illinois, was fighting to save that bridge up there. And as you know, unfortunately the Fabius Levee broke in spite of their best efforts, and the bridge has now been closed. So there's no link for about 200 miles now across the Mississippi River. But this police officer said it's a shame the rest of the country can't come together like this to solve its problems. I thought that was such a simple and yet brilliant statement. I hope that we can come away from this with a sense that we've all done our very best to work together to solve this problem and that we will take the powerful example of human courage that we have seen in countless places across these States to follow that.

Again, I want to say to all of you, I thank you for taking your time to come today. We will run through a rather brisk schedule. And I want to begin with the Vice President, who has been to this region twice and who I think has done a very good job, especially when I was away on the G-7 meeting. And I'm very grateful to him. But he has a little insight on exactly what the scope of the damage is and how it all came about. And I think it would be good to sort of set the stage with his remarks.

Mr. Vice President.

[*The Vice President, using satellite images, discussed the unusual weather patterns that led to the flooding.*]

The President. Thank you very much. I'd like to now call on the White House Chief of Staff Mack McLarty to make a few remarks. I have asked Mack to oversee the White House coordination of this to ensure that it receives the best possible attention within the White House and that we continue the very close coordination we've had with all these Government Departments represented here today.

Mack.

[*Mr. McLarty discussed the administration's commitment to provide adequate and effective assistance.*]

The President. Thank you very much. Before we begin to call on the Governors, I'd like to ask Secretary Espy and our FEMA Director, James Lee Witt, to just briefly, for about 5 minutes each, review the current situation in the region and an overview of the present Federal response. They have spent more time here personally by quite a long ways than anyone else in our administration. And I think it's important that their views get out and that they have a chance just to make a few introductory remarks.

So I'd like Mr. Witt and Secretary Espy to talk in whatever order they have decided to speak.

[*Director Witt explained FEMA's efforts to assist flood victims. Secretary Espy then described the damage to the agricultural community and discussed USDA assistance efforts, including offices in FEMA disaster centers.*]

The President. Thank you very much, Mr. Secretary.

With regard to the co-location of offices, I also want to point out that FEMA has brought in 20 SBA specialists into the tele-registration center, and there are small business people who are now filling out the applications for aid by telephone. This is also something that has really been without precedent, particularly between the SBA and FEMA.

I neglected to introduce earlier, in that regard, the Director of the Small Business Administration, Erskine Bowles, from North Carolina, and also Congressman Talent. I apologize for that. And Governor Thompson, I introduced you before you got here, but we're glad to see you.

I'd like to now ask our host Governor, Governor Carnahan—we're going through a whole series of issues here. And if you don't feel something is adequately discussed, feel free to interject. But I think it's important that we try to stay on the agenda. And I'd like to ask Governor Carnahan to begin by discussing short-term emergency response and public assistance delivery.

[*Governor Carnahan discussed the damage and assistance needs in Missouri.*]

The President. Thank you very much, Governor. A little later in the program, I'm going to ask the Secretary of Labor, Bob Reich, to talk about the dislocated worker issue. It is a major issue.

But before we move this topic, I'd like to ask General Williams from the Corps of Engineers if you have anything you want to say about the emergency work, work to repair the public and private facilities and what you're doing to try to minimize the damage.

[*General Williams discussed Corps of Engineers disaster relief and water management efforts.*]

The President. Let me ask you one quick followup question. When Governor Branstad and I were in Iowa the other day and we saw this vast lake that essentially went from Des Moines all the way to the Mississippi River—the kind of thing the Vice President was talking about there—and one of the people who was there with us said that we had to be very careful how we drained off this water in order not to aggravate the problems of the rivers being too high. Is that a serious issue?

[*General Williams said the Corps will continue efforts to coordinate water levels in both tributaries and main rivers to prevent further damage.*]

The President. With regard to the issue that Governor Carnahan raised, this is not exactly responsive, because you talked about farm losses. But I do think it's important to point out that FEMA does have a modest program to deal with personal losses of families. And I thought I'd let Mr. Witt just briefly state that again so people who have been wiped out of their homes or jobs and don't have anything would know about it. Would you just briefly say what it is.

[*Director Witt said flood victims might be eligible for grants to cover personal losses.*]

The President. I'd like to, if I might, move on to another issue, which affects more people in Iowa than any other place, but that's the lack of potable water. And I'd like to ask Governor Branstad to talk to us a little about that. I live in a State where I've seen whole little towns flooded out and gone. I don't believe there's been another time in my lifetime when so many Americans in one place have been without drinking water, bathing water, any kind of water as are the people who live in and around Des Moines. And I'd like for Governor Branstad to discuss how they're managing that and how they're dealing with the public health risks that are posed by that.

[*Governor Branstad described water distribution efforts and infrastructure damage in Iowa.*]

The President. I just want to throw out something; I don't need a response now, but I invite any of the Governors who choose to respond. I spoke this morning to the people who are constantly on the air at that wonderful radio station in Quincy, Illinois, that's served as sort of the informal headquarters and information source for people on both sides of the river, on this part of the flooding. They're, by the way, broadcasting this whole hearing live. But one of the things that I was asked on the radio was whether or not the National Guard resources of the States were being stretched too thin, whether or not the Guardsmen and women were in need of some relief, and whether I had thought of sending in any regular personnel.

Let me just say to all of the Governors, we have no way of knowing what percentage of your National Guard force you have deployed to do this. But if you do feel you need some relief from resources outside the State Guard, I hope you will feel free to let me know, and we'll try to deal with that.

General Williams, did you have a question?

[*General Williams and the Vice President commented on the National Guard's role in relief efforts. Governor Branstad then commented on State, local, Federal, and private sector cooperation in Iowa.*]

The President. Thank you. Before we move off the public health issues, I'd like to ask Secretary Shalala to comment about a number of issues. The obvious one is the water situation and with regard to potable water. But there are some other issues here: Are there any risks of disease from other flooded facilities, water facilities or treatment facilities or flooded fields washing pesticides? Are there environmental risks there? What about the damage sustained that we are aware of by Federally supported public health facilities? And so a lot of public health issues here, and I'd like for Secretary Shalala to just make whatever comments she'd

like to make about that.

[*Secretary Shalala discussed cooperative public health efforts concerning infectious diseases and mental health.*]

The President. Thank you very much. If I might just respond to two other issues Governor Branstad raised, first with regard to the National Guard. I don't know what this country would do without them. Anybody who has ever served as a Governor knows that you literally couldn't function, the Governor's office could not function in most major problem areas, without them.

The second thing, with regard to your request for a waiver of the local match, I have asked James Lee Witt, since he obviously had experience in his former life as the director of emergency services at the State level in our home State, to work with the Governors on that and to try to make a reasoned judgment about what can and can't be done. There is some precedent, as you know, for waiving all or part of the match. There's also a big precedent for the match. And we have to be very careful about how we handle this. Where there is a genuine problem, we want to be responsive. But we want everybody to kind of work with us and work through the facts on it, and we will try to make a humane as well as a clearheaded decision.

I'd like to ask Governor Edgar from Illinois now to talk about the current situation in terms of its impact on the farmers. We've heard Mike Espy talk about it, but I think it would be helpful to have a Governor of a great farm State just to start and discuss a little about how the impact is in Illinois.

[*Governor Edgar requested that the National Guard postpone other duties in order to help damaged areas rebuild. He then discussed the damage and assistance needs in Illinois. Secretary Espy then stated that financial assistance would be provided as quickly and in as flexible a manner as possible and promised to work on crop insurance reform.*]

The President. Let me say, if you have any other specific suggestions on this, this is an important issue that Governor Edgar has raised and that the Secretary has responded to. As we look at the crop insurance reformation issue, if there are other areas of flexibility you believe ought to be given to the Secretary of Agriculture to help deal with this and subsequent crises, it's very important that you get them to us now

while the Congress is focused on this issue.
Yes?

[Governor Branstad expressed concern that the amount of disaster assistance allocated for farmers would not be adequate.]

The President. Senator Bond and Congressman Gephardt, the administration, I think, in 1992 presented a revised downward formula. It used to be two-thirds of two-thirds, didn't it, something like that? And it was revised downward because of the magnitude of the losses in Andrew and the side problem with the deficit, is that right? I wasn't here so I don't know.

Senator Bond. Mr. President, in the 1990 farm bill we authorized a very complicated formula for people with crop insurance. It was essentially 65 percent of 65 percent. As a result of OMB actions during some of the disasters, they cut what is effectively 42 percent by a half, and thus the proposal is about 21 cents on the dollar. We had a chance to discuss and several of the Members of Congress discussed with you our strong desire and our hope that OMB and you will support, and we can encourage Congress not to cut that 42 percent in half, because for most farmers that represents their out-of-pocket costs of feed, fertilizer, and fuel to put the crop in.

The President. We're going to review that. We presented that under the terms of—the same thing that happened with Hurricane Andrew. And I frankly was not even aware of it being a problem until the Congressmen from the affected States brought it up to me in large numbers and on a bipartisan basis yesterday at our big meeting. And so we're going to review that.

[Governor Branstad thanked the President for agreeing to review assistance for farmers.]

The President. I think it's very important that, even under the formula adopted in 1990, everyone understands it's not a question of whether you're holding people harmless but whether you're at least giving them enough help to have a fair chance so that they'll be able to continue in farming.

Let me just mention two other things quite quickly. I got a note on this local match issue. Secretary Shalala sent up a note that said we need to get rid of the State match on VETRA control so we can quickly put in a multistate strategy on mosquitoes. If we have time I'll tell you a story one time when I gave a speech when a swarm of mosquitoes came up in a rice field. The speech lasted 20 seconds, and I never lost the county again. *[Laughter]* I could have used that swarm of mosquitoes in later points in my life. *[Laughter]*

I want to say one other thing. Yesterday Congressman Harold Volkmer, who is not here today, told me about an incident involving FEMA and State emergency people that affects environmental and health issues that I thought I should repeat in the event that it happens to any of you, so you know that this capacity is there.

There was a pesticide and herbicide storage area at Hannibal, Missouri, that was threatened. And immediately FEMA and the State emergency people were able to put divers into the area, and the divers actually helped to shore up the area and keep that from being threatened. If that storage area had been overrun, obviously you would have had a huge amount of very toxic materials, not very much diluted, to which people would have been exposed. So I think it's important that we try to identify that. Every time I fly over one of these sewage treatment facilities or something else where there's water all around it, I just get the willies thinking about what could happen. And I think that it's important to know that we do have this dive capability. And if something like that you think might happen, you need to call FEMA to try to put together a dive team and a reinforcement team so that we avert those kinds of possibilities.

I'd like now to talk about individual assistance and small business assistance. And I'd like to ask Governor Thompson of Wisconsin to talk about it. The worst of his flooding, we hope, is behind us, although after the Vice President's weather forecast today, I'm not sure. But we hope that it's true. And as people begin to look about getting back on their feet, I'd be interested in knowing how you think this assistance program is working, how adequate is it, what's your assessment of both the individual and the SBA programs.

[Governor Thompson discussed the damage and assistance needs in Wisconsin.]

The President. Thank you very much. I'd like to ask the SBA Director, Erskine Bowles, to comment briefly on the SBA programs and how they're being implemented here. Erskine.

[*Administrator Bowles discussed SBA disaster assistance programs and promised the Agency's cooperation. Mr. McLarty mentioned USDA loan programs to complement those of SBA. Administrator Bowles then stated that some checks had already been delivered.*]

The President. Believe it or not, we're almost back on schedule. Before I move away from the short-term to the long-term issues, I think it would be a mistake not to at least acknowledge the efforts of the private volunteers, the people who came on their own, the people from the Salvation Army. I saw a lot of Salvation Army people in Iowa, and I was deeply moved by them. They even showed up, some of them, in their uniforms. I couldn't believe they could bear to work in their uniforms, as hot and difficult as it was. And of course, the Red Cross, where I think, Governor Branstad, the largest employer in your State gave, I think, $100,000 to the Red Cross while I was there to do their work.

Since Mrs. Dole is here, I thought, if there's any comment you'd like to make about the volunteer efforts, what we're doing, where we're going, we'd be glad to hear from you. And I think it might be nice if you came down and sat in Senator Wellstone's chair, and then we'll take a picture of you there with his name and send it to the Senate minority leader for his— [*laughter*]. There's a certain sweet irony there— my photographer to take a picture of Senator Wellstone as she speaks.

[*Mrs. Dole praised the spirit of the volunteers.*]

The President. Thank you. I also think it's fair to say, though, that all those volunteers have to be coordinated. And we really appreciate the work that's been done there.

James Lee, did you want to say something about that?

[*Mr. Witt praised the Red Cross and other volunteers. The Vice President and Governor Branstad then discussed FEMA's coordination of the distribution of donated goods.*]

The President. Since we're talking about this, I want to get in a plug for my pet project. Some of our national service volunteers this summer have come to the flooding areas and are working as volunteers. And Senator Durenberger and Congressman Vento from Minnesota have suggested that we actually have a little modest appropriation to get some more of these

young people who are in the national service program just physically to the affected States. Bruce, you might want to say a word about that, but I really——

[*Representative Vento encouraged the involvement of youth in relief efforts. Representative Minge then requested flexibility in banking and crop insurance requirements.*]

The President. Thank you very much. As I said, we do intend to review the agricultural rules. Let me comment very briefly on the bank loan issue. Along with a number of other farm State Governors, back in the mid-eighties we had a meeting in Chicago—I never will forget this—Governor Edgar's predecessor hosted it, and we tried to work through reform in the farm financing system. Congress acted on that, substantially what we recommended, but it was 4 years later and 255,000 farmers later. I believe that the regulators have the authority to give the banks the flexibility to do what you suggest, but I will check to make sure.

[*Representative Minge expressed congressional support for the administration's efforts.*]

The President. Let me make one other comment on the crop insurance issue. There are deficiencies in the crop insurance program all right for the catastrophic losses. The main problem we've got in this instance is that this flood occurred a heck of a lot further north on the Mississippi than floods normally occur. And by the time the land drains off, it'll be too late to plant soybeans. I mean, that's the main problem we've got. So unless you sort of threw the beans in the ground to create a fiction, you know, a falsehood, to claim your crop insurance, you can't cover it. That does not mean that, at least I could, in good conscience, to ever advise any farmer not to ever buy crop insurance. It does do some good, and I do think that, in effect, the preference in the law for people who have some insurance is a pretty good thing, still, but we do need to drastically reform the crop insurance program.

[*Representative Minge predicted long-term reductions in the cost of farm programs.*]

The President. Thank you very much. I want to move on, if I might, and talk about—he meant 10 cents, Jim—I want to move on to discuss, if I might, some of the long-term issues here and ask Governor Miller of South Dakota to begin by just discussing the impact of the flood on jobs. That will take us back to the job training remark made by Governor Carnahan at the end of his remarks. But I'd like for Governor Miller to talk a little bit about the job impact on this flood.

[*Governor Miller discussed the damage and assistance needs in South Dakota.*]

The President. Thank you. Mr. Bowles has already discussed the SBA programs which would be relevant here. And the Secretary of Agriculture has talked about the farm programs a little. I'd like to ask the Secretary of Labor, Bob Reich, to talk about the job training elements of this issue.

[*Secretary Reich discussed the availability of disaster unemployment insurance and funding for jobs in the cleanup effort. He then gave checks to some of the Governors present.*]

The President. You're the only guy in my administration with any money. How can you do that?

Yes, Governor Schafer.

[*Governor Schafer asked for information on the disaster unemployment assistance program, and Secretary Reich gave a brief explanation.*]

The President. I think that's important. Terry's going to say something, but when I was in Iowa the other day, it's very interesting that you discussed this because there are more people than you would think affected by this who aren't in the normal unemployment insurance pool. And I had two or three people come up to me just when I was in Des Moines to talk about it.

Terry, what were you going to say?

[*Governor Branstad expressed concern for the rebuilding needs of small businesses.*]

The President. Given the—no one has ever mentioned this to me. You know, when you get to be President, you're supposed to never say anything off the top of your head. But given the problems we've got with the budget and the difficulty of dealing with that issue, I think it would be virtually impossible that the Congress would adopt any new program in that regard.

The one thing I would ask the Governors to consider among yourselves about this is whether or not you would want to ask us, the Federal Government and the Congress, for some sort of modification of the law affecting how you can invest your community development block grant funds for a year or so because that's something that—I mean, I know that that program is not real popular with every Member of Congress, but it's real popular with me because I was a Governor. And I know how much good it can do, and I think there's very little— at least in my State there was very little waste in it. But I think that if you have the flexibility to allocate some of that money to job creation or job preservation under emergency situations for a year or two, that might make a significant difference. So let me just suggest that that's something you all might want to put your heads together about and get back to us on.

Ron, what were you going to say? Secretary Brown.

[*Secretary Brown discussed the need for a long-term economic development plan.*]

The President. Let me just follow up on that very briefly and say that I think that that is very good. I'd like to ask you to examine, given the specific questions you've heard today, what you think the EDA could do and the Department of Commerce. And at the end of the session here, I want to talk a little about long-term planning. And I think that you should really work with the Secretary of Agriculture to make sure that every State knows that they have available the resources of Commerce to develop this kind of economic plan.

And meanwhile, I think the Governors ought to look at this community development block grant option. I think it's got some legs. And I don't know, but Des Moines may get CDBG directly; does it? It may be of sufficient size to get it. So that would also be quite helpful there.

I'll call on Bruce Vento, and then we've got to go. We're getting behind.

[*Representative Vento expressed concern about long-term unemployment among agriculture-related workers in urban areas and among migrant workers.*]

The President. Thank you.

We have a few other topics I think it's really important that we cover today: shipping and commerce, housing, and infrastructure for sure. I'd like to ask Governor Carlson and Governor Schafer to comment on the issues of shipping and commerce, the impact of the flood on shipping and commerce over the long run.

[*Governor Carlson expressed his support for crop insurance reform and more flexibility in banking regulation and his concerns regarding insurance for development on flood plains. He also commended efforts to open global markets to U.S. agricultural products. Governor Schafer then discussed long-term difficulties in storage and shipment of agricultural products as a result of flood damage.*]

The President. Thank you. I'd like to ask Secretary Peña to comment on this issue, as well as on the infrastructure damage generally.

[*Secretary Peña discussed the extraordinary impact of the flooding on both regional and national transportation systems.*]

The President. Thank you very much. Before we move on to discussing the actual aid legislation, I'd like to talk about one or two other issues. I'd like to ask Governor Nelson of Nebraska to talk about the question that many of the Governors are facing, which is what happens to people who are displaced from their houses, and then I want to ask Secretary Cisneros to comment on that. And you might feel free to comment on any of the other long-term economic issues of concern to your people. Thank you.

[*Governor Nelson discussed wind losses in Nebraska, suggested the use of community development block grants for housing assistance, cautioned against downsizing the National Guard to the point of limiting its emergency response capability, and questioned the relocation of homes out of proximity to cropland and agricultural jobs.*]

The President. Thank you.

Secretary Cisneros, we flew over a lot of people that don't have their homes anymore today.

[*Secretary Cisneros discussed use of community development block grants for immediate cleanup and reconstruction work including waivers to permit use for public facilities and services, elimination of matching fund requirements for the home program, easing of FHA and HUD mortgage foreclosure practices, and assistance through other FHA and HUD programs.*]

The President. Thank you very much. That's very encouraging. And I know all the Governors listened closely to it. I'm going to wait to hear

from you, from the Governors, about exactly how you would advise me to proceed on the CDBG issue and the waivers. You can be in touch directly with us or Secretary Cisneros. But I thank him for that very comprehensive discussion.

We need now to have a brief presentation from Mr. Panetta about the legislation now pending in the Congress. We are running about 30 minutes behind. We're actually only about 10 minutes behind because we started 20 minutes late because of the transportation. I think that's remarkable. But I would like to ask Leon just to run briefly through a summary of where we are right now and what the sort of timetable is for the movement through Congress as well.

[*Director Panetta said he expected a House vote on disaster assistance legislation by July 22 and rapid Senate action as well. He then listed specific elements of the package.*]

The President. Thank you very much.

Before we close out this section, and there are a couple of other things that we need to do, but I would like to thank and recognize and give an opportunity to speak to Senator Mikulski. She has come all the way from Maryland—this is not in her district or State—because of her profound and longstanding concern about the operations of FEMA which fall within the jurisdiction of her committee. I thank her for coming, and I hope she will be graceful enough, Governor Carlson, not to mention the Orioles' victory over the Twins last night. It was a very exciting game that I watched at the end.

[*Senator Mikulski said Congress would act quickly on the legislation. She then praised State, local, and volunteer disaster workers and congratulated the President for leading a quick and comprehensive Federal response.*]

The President. Thank you. I like that line. I don't know about being "Commander in Chief of disasters." I'm afraid I may live to hear that again before long. [*Laughter*] But thank you very much, Senator Mikulski. That was a wonderful statement, and thank you for your work.

We have to wrap up, but Governor Edgar has asked for the floor.

[*Governor Edgar expressed concern that the $2.5 billion requested would not be enough.*]

The President. I want to make two points

here. First, as we get more information in over this legislative process, we will ask that the bill be amended, wherever it is, if it's in the House or in the Senate. But in order to keep faith with the Members from all the other States, all of whom themselves might have disasters someday—many of whom do—but who are also charged along with me with, you know, maintaining the discipline of the budget, it's very important that when we plug a number in we have some research basis, some factual basis for it. But we intend to modify this as the information comes in on the losses. If the bill passes and there's still things that aren't dealt with that should be dealt with under Federal law, we will go forward with seeking more assistance. I want to make that absolutely clear.

Let me make one final comment about the substance here. Many of you have made the same observation that Senator Mikulski did about the importance of the ongoing effort, and that's really where I began my remarks.

In other contexts I have asked a member of the Cabinet to supervise. I asked Secretary Cisneros, for example, almost the week after we took office, to go down to Florida and supervise the long-term effort in the aftermath of Hurricane Andrew so that they would know that we were still in there. I asked Secretary Brown to go to California and to try to supervise a long-term effort to deal with the collapse of the economy of that State rooted very largely in the dramatic reductions in defense spending without any kind of off-setting plan for defense conversion.

And I think we ought to do that here. And so, because so many of these States are farming States and because so much of this is agricultural loss, I've asked Secretary Espy to coordinate the long-term Federal response in the flooded area here, and he has agreed to do that. So he will be working with all the suggestions made by the Governors today and by the suggestion made by Secretary Brown for economic development plans and others as well as with the FEMA Director, James Lee Witt, who may well have another emergency to deal with

before we work our way out of the long-term problems here, which is why I've asked Secretary Espy to do that.

Let me also thank all of our hosts from Missouri: Mr. Wheat, Mr. Talent, Senator Bond, Majority Leader Gephardt, and Governor Carnahan. And before we break from here, I want to talk about the very important sessions coming up. I want to ask Mr. McLarty to describe very briefly what happens now.

[*Mr. McLarty gave instructions to the participants for the afternoon session.*]

The President. I want to give our hosts here, Mr. Gephardt and Mr. Carnahan, a chance to wrap up if they like, or Senator Bond. But before I do, let me say that Governor Finney from Kansas could not be here today, but she is ably represented by her Chief of Staff, who also happens to be her daughter, and we're glad to see you here. And I thank all the rest of you from around the room for being here. I hope the afternoon sessions are valuable. I think this has been quite important.

Not long after I became President I met with the Governors, and I asked the Governors on a bipartisan basis to make sure that we kept our administration rooted in the real problems of real people. This is not exactly what I had in mind, but it certainly does qualify. And I thank you all for being here and for the contribution you've all made.

[*Governor Carnahan, Representative Gephardt, and Governor Bond expressed their appreciation to the President.*]

The President. Governor Branstad wants a last word. He's earned it, since he's down to taking a shower every other day.

[*Governor Branstad presented the President with a T-shirt.*]

The President. Thank you.

NOTE: The President spoke at 10:22 a.m. at Fox Senior High School. A portion of this item could not be verified because the tape was incomplete.

Teleconference Remarks to the National Association of County Officials
July 19, 1993

The President. Good morning. I'm honored to address the National Association of County Officials today and very, very grateful for the strong support you've given to our economic plan. It's good for the counties of this country; it's good for America; it's good for the working people of this country.

I very much appreciate that nice introduction by your president and my long-time friend, John Stroger. He's been a valuable part of our team and a very effective advocate for county government. As Cook County Commissioner, he also represents one of the legendary counties in America. That was true even before my wife was born there. [*Laughter*]

Let me say just a few words about the terrible flooding throughout the Midwest. There's been extraordinary damage done to crops and homes and businesses, but not to the spirit of our people or to our commitment to join them as neighbors to help them to rebuild each of those communities.

As county leaders, you know more than most about the hopes and problems of families. For many, the efforts of local government represent the best ideals of America. But for too many years, since Washington has spent too much and invested too little and refused to make the tough decisions necessary to keep our economy healthy, the only clear message local leaders got from Washington was, "You're on your own. And by the way, here are a few more burdens." Washington gave you make-believe budgets and mandates with no money. They drove up the debt from $1 trillion to $4 trillion and still invested less in the things that make our communities stronger.

Well, you've been at the forefront of trying to change this. You know that we must create high-wage, high-skill jobs again so there will be less crime, fewer transfer payments, and more revenues to support businesses and institutions that are the foundation of all stable communities.

I wish I could be with you in person today, and I'm looking forward to doing so when you have future meetings. But as you know, my first obligation to you and to our Nation is to keep fighting for change right here in Washington

and for an economic plan that creates jobs and raises incomes, that invests in a stronger tomorrow and brings this terrible deficit down.

This economic plan is good for the country and the economy and good for the forgotten middle class. It contains the largest Federal reduction of the deficit in history, with over $250 billion of dramatic cuts in spending. It finally begins paying down the deficit and shifting the budget away from waste and toward sound investments in job creation and entrepreneurship, in new technologies, and in the health and education of our people. There couldn't be a more profound change from the old ways and the failed policies of the past to a new direction that will make our economy work again.

For starters, we make more than 200 specific cuts that slash over $250 billion from this budget. For the first time, we secure the savings from both tax increases and spending cuts in a trust fund so they can't be touched. While the old ways favor those at the very top income brackets, our plan asks the most from those who are most able to give. At least 70 percent of the new taxes in this plan will fall on those making over $200,000 a year, while millions of families earning below $30,000 will actually get a tax break. And those who work full-time and have children at home will be lifted out of poverty. Over 90 percent of the small business who are unincorporated will have the opportunity for a reduction in their taxes through increasing their expensing provisions. So working families and the middle class, after 12 long years of being ignored, win in our program.

The old ways ignored the business incentives and the investments in technology and infrastructure that will allow our economy to create growth in a tough global economy. And while my plan does cut the deficit dramatically, it also empowers families and businesses to build better lives and stronger communities.

This plan reforms the student loan program, saving billions of dollars and making it easier for millions of our young people to pay for college. It creates a program of national service to allow young people to pay for college by serving their Nation in communities like yours. And for the majority who don't attend college, we've funded the boldest national apprenticeship program ever. Educating and training young people is the best investment we can make, and it's time we committed ourselves to doing that.

We empower communities to protect themselves by providing more funds for police officers. It empowers creditworthy small businesses to a new network of community development banks and creates empowerment zones to bring to bear the full power of free enterprise on our poorest large and small areas. And because I believe new environmental technologies and improved water systems and better roads and incentives for the private sector will mean more jobs and more growth, our plan creates a greater commitment to each.

I'm excited about our future. I know this plan will work. It's already beginning to work. In the last 5 months, as we have moved to reduce this deficit and to increase business incentives, interest rates have hit record lows. That will add billions to our economy as millions of Americans, including many in your audience, I bet, refinance their homes or their business loans or buy cars or borrow for college or consumer loans at much lower rates. In the last 5 months, the economy has been creating private sector jobs at 7 times the rate of the last 4 years. And inflation is flat.

Now, make no mistake about it, we still have a lot to do. Economic growth is still way too slow and too uneven. But putting our economic house in order is beginning to bring prosperity here at home and helping America to gain a new competitive edge in the global economy, as I learned at the Tokyo talks among the large seven industrial powers last week.

Because the American people are having the courage to change and because Congress is really moving to reduce the deficit and to invest in jobs, my hand was greatly strengthened at that meeting in Tokyo. Negotiations that had gone extremely slowly for years suddenly opened up, and we struck a new agreement to dramatically lower and in some cases to completely eliminate tariffs on a variety of manufactured products. That can mean hundreds of thousands more jobs for American workers in manufacturing areas with high wages and more growth for American companies, if we can now move to get that agreement accepted by all the other countries in a general agreement before the end of the year. I'm very excited about the prospect.

Our commitment to a balanced plan of deficit reduction and economic growth simply has raised our stature among the community of nations. This, combined with a pledge to fundamentally reform health care, which will be extremely significant for our counties in reducing our deficit and in helping our economy to recover, gave us the right to demand that the world's major trading countries take new steps themselves to create jobs and growth and to open their markets to our products.

After the meeting in Tokyo I am more confident than ever that we can make the world's new economy work for us. But we can only enjoy the opportunities created in Tokyo if we follow through on our own responsibilities to bring our deficit down, to invest in our people, to be more competitive. There is still a lot of work ahead of us. This economy has been in the doldrums for years. We have been following the wrong policies for more than a decade. We have to have the patience and discipline and conviction it takes, all of us, to do our fair share to move this thing forward.

If you haven't said anything to your Member of Congress to let them know how you feel, now is the time. Without regard to party, I ask for your help and your active involvement. There are some who are standing on the sidelines who must be convinced to join with us. This is bigger than party or politics. Bringing down America's deficit, investing in America's future, helping us to open new trade opportunities and new investment opportunities and new job-creating opportunities at home and abroad, these things should be beyond politics.

So please pick up the phone and lend your voice to the call for change and jobs and growth that is beginning to make life better in America. Together we can build prosperity and hope again. Let's capture the spirit of our mighty Midwesterners, who for 2 weeks have refused to relinquish their dreams in the face of this terrible flooding and who have proven that nothing is impossible when we all pull together. In a few weeks, let's give ourselves a vote we can look back on with pride because together we helped to create a new era of American greatness.

Thank you very much.

Asia-U.S. Trade

Q. Good morning, Mr. President.
The President. Good morning.

Q. We're really glad that you could join us today. I'm from Florida, and we recently opened a trade office in Singapore, so I was particularly interested in your remarks relating to opportunities to participate aggressively in the global economy. What types of changes do you think we should have in our international policy so that we as a nation can expand our opportunities in all the countries in the Pacific Rim?

The President. Let me, first of all, say to all of you present that your county has done a smart thing, and I think that other counties should consider following suit. Forty percent of American trade is now with the Pacific region. It's the fastest-growing part of the economy in the world. About 2.5 million American jobs now depend upon trade with the Pacific. It's very, very important.

I would say there are three things that we should be doing at the national level. First, we need to complete an agreement before the end of the year on the General Agreement on Tariffs and Trade, the new world trade agreement. The meeting of the G–7 in Tokyo made that much more possible by having the big countries agree to reduce tariffs and to eliminate them entirely. A good study here in this country says that we could add $6 trillion to the world economy by the next decade if we would simply conclude this agreement. That will open a lot of new jobs for Americans in manufacturing and in agriculture and in services.

The second thing we need to do is to build stronger ties to these countries. I'm very proud that in the fall of this year I will host a meeting in Seattle, Washington, for the Organization of Asian Pacific Economic Cooperation. All these nations are coming here, and after the ministers meet, the next day many heads of state will meet with me.

The third thing we need to do is to redefine our trading relationship with Japan. And as I'm sure you know, at the very end of the G–7 meeting, the Prime Minister of Japan and I agreed to and announced a framework for a new trade relationship in which Japan pledged for the first time to substantially reduce its trade surplus with the United States and to have measurable objective measures of progress in several important areas of our trading relationship.

Now, even if we do all that, we still need more local governmental units and especially more American business men and women who are willing to aggressively exploit opportunities in the Pacific area. Americans have got to be better traders and more interested in selling their products and their services around the world. Even small businesses have to do a better job of that.

So we're going to do those big three things, but we need more folks like you who are interested in taking advantage of the global economy. Over half of our jobs in the last 5 years have been related in some way to trade and a lot of them to the Pacific. So that's what I think we should do in the Pacific region.

Unfunded Federal Mandates

Q. [*Inaudible*]—Texas, one of the poorest counties in the Nation. I also am a member of NACO board of directors and serve as—[*inaudible*]. We need your help, Mr. President. Every year Congress passes new laws that require us to provide new services or to meet new standards. But rarely does Congress appropriate the dollars to meet this mandate. We have to raise our county local taxes to meet these costs and these new mandates. What can your administration do to help us?

The President. Well, first of all, you've asked a great question. As a Governor for 12 years in one of the poorer States in America, I understood the burden of unfunded mandates very well. And I'm familiar with your county in Texas, and I hear your message loud and clear.

The first thing we can do is to do no harm. The first thing we can do is to be the first administration in a long time not to load any more unfunded mandates on you. And that is a commitment I will do my best to keep. The second thing we can do is to review the present pattern of Federal regulation and requirements as it affects local government. Vice President Gore, at my request, is heading a commission on reinventing the role of the Federal Government and we are examining everything we do from top to bottom to see how we can better serve the American people, either with greater efficiency or with lower costs or both.

And if there are some things that NACO specifically feels ought to be changed in terms of giving the counties greater flexibility in the way certain rules and regulations are applied, I want to invite you as an organization to make those recommendations known to the Vice President. I know you've been consulted on this. But those are the two things I think you can do and I hope that we can do, and we're going to do our best to do them.

Health Care Reform

Q. Mr. President, counties spend over $30 billion a year on health care. We own and operate more than 4,500 health facilities. We, in essence, take care of the uninsured in this country. What role do you see for county officials in your proposed health reform plan?

The President. I think the counties that are providing health care services may well continue to do so and will do so much more happily than they do now if our health reform plan passes, for a couple of reasons. First of all, we are looking for ways now, and I think we've found some, to provide basic health insurance to the uninsured, unemployed. If we do that, then as you provide those health services to those folks, you'll get a more reliable stream of income. And the only monies that will have to be matched at the State and local level are those that are now matched under the Medicaid program.

Secondly, the proposal that we will make will cut out a lot of the redtape, a lot of the regulation coming from the Government, coming from the way the insurance markets are now organized. And local public health units will be able to do much more with the money that they've got to serve people in ways that are more flexible and more creative.

So I would think that you will like this very much. People will be able to do this. If any of the counties want to get out of the business because there won't be anybody without basic insurance and think they can be handled in some other way, the counties will also have that option. But the counties that want to stay in the business will be able to do it with a much more reliable funding stream, in more innovative and comprehensive ways.

Welfare Reform

Q. Now Mr. President, when you've discussed the Nation's welfare system, you have pledged to end welfare as we know it. And as you know, many county governments contribute to AFDC programs, and many also administer their own general assistance programs. We have supported the welfare reform for years and actively supported the creation of the 1988 Family Support Act. My question is, Mr. President, what guiding principles will your working group operate under

to ensure the end to welfare as we know it, that reform will in fact achieve the desired results?

The President. Thank you very much, Mr. Williams, and thank you, too, for the special leadership role that San Diego County has played for years in the whole area of welfare reform. As you know, San Diego is repeatedly cited in every study as one of the places that's proved that we can move people from welfare to work. So you have a lot of credentials to ask that question. And I also appreciate the support you gave to the Family Support Act of 1988, which I as a Governor had a big hand in trying to fashion.

Let me tell you what the principles that animate us are and what we're doing about them. Number one, we need to make work pay. We need to make work pay. That means that as a starting point we should adopt the provision in the economic plan I presented to Congress which will use the earned-income tax credit to lift the working poor out of poverty if they have children in the home. Eighteen percent of America's workers today are working and still living below the Federal poverty line. An enormous number of working parents go home at night to children, having worked a full day and a full week, and still live below the poverty line. I believe we should change the tax system so that anybody who works 40 hours a week and has children in the home is lifted out of poverty. That rewards work and not welfare. It removes a dramatic incentive to stay on welfare and gives people an incentive to go to work and stay there.

Second, we need to have tougher child support enforcement. We are losing billions of dollars a year because people who can afford to pay something for their children do not do it. And we need to have a much stronger system. We have proposed that, and some of that program is now working its way through Congress.

Third, we need to fully implement the education and training aspects of the Family Support Act of 1988. As you know, that act has never been adequately funded in its education and training provisions so that we empower people to move off welfare.

Fourth, we need to pass a health care reform bill so that people are not without health insurance when they lose their jobs, or if they take jobs where the employer presently doesn't provide health insurance. The welfare check itself is no longer an incentive to stay on welfare. The real value of a welfare check in almost every place in America is far lower than it was 20 years ago. What keeps people on welfare is the cost of health care and child care for their kids and the inability to get a good job because of a lack of education and training. So we've got to have health care reform.

Finally, having put all that in place, I think we should move to a system in which if there's no incentive not to work, if people get education and training, if the children are covered with health insurance, if you have tough child support enforcement system, you shouldn't be able to stay on welfare without working for more than a couple of years. After that, you should have to work and earn income just like everybody else. And if you put the building blocks in, you can have a 2-year limit on welfare as we know it. You would end the system as it now exists. It would be temporary for everybody who is able-bodied.

Improved FEMA Performance

Q. First, on behalf of Iowans everywhere, I'd like to thank you for your efforts and your encouragement during the devastating floods that are occurring across Iowa and other midwestern States. The outpouring of help and support from our county colleagues and people throughout the U.S. is deeply appreciated, and we really do thank you.

My question relates to one of prevention. In the past, NACO has called for increased professionalism at FEMA, making it comparable to other Federal public safety agencies such as the FAA and the Centers for Disease Control. Your new Director, Lee Witt, has acted quickly in this crisis. But I'm wondering if you are going to propose any statutory changes that would allow FEMA to become more proactive and to increase that level of service.

The President. First, let me thank you for what you said about the work done by Mr. Witt and FEMA. And let me also say again how very sorry I am about what's happened and pledge our best efforts to stay in touch and keep working with you in the aftermath. As you know, Iowa's got a big clean-up job to do now. We still don't have—we don't have water back in Des Moines; we've got a lot of continuing problems.

With regard to the specific question you asked, we're going to review FEMA's operations

to see what needs to be done to strengthen them. From the point of view of the Governors and the people at the local level, one of the biggest criticisms has been that FEMA has to go through this long approval process with the Governor asking for emergency aid. And we're looking at what can be done to maybe pre-position people and move this whole process faster.

With regard to the question of the professionalization of the Agency, Senator Mikulski has a bill now in the Senate that she's been working on. We are discussing it with her, we are working with her, and I want to evaluate it as we go along, as I'm sure you do.

This is very important to me. I live in a State, or I did before I became President, lived in a State that had the highest tornado occurrences per capita in America, that regularly had floods and ice storms and drought. I've been through a lot of experience with FEMA. And I think the American people are entitled to an emergency management agency that is as good and quick and competent and professional as possible.

Let me just mention one other issue that we have to really think through, and that is that FEMA is essentially set up to act quickly with problems that are immediate. But these disasters often leave a long rebuilding period in their wake. You can't just turn these things around overnight. Now, one of the things that we've tried to do is to set up a set of de facto solutions to this. For example, when I became President, I asked Henry Cisneros, the HUD Secretary, to take over coordinating the long-term response to Hurricane Andrew in Florida. I have asked Secretary Espy, the Agriculture Secretary now, to take over the long-term management of our commitment in the Midwest in the aftermath of the flood. But that also needs to be thought through because a lot of these problems we're going to be dealing with in the fall and the winter and next year as well. Senator Mikulski came to St. Louis with me last Saturday when we met with the Governors and other emergency personnel from all the States affected by the flood. And we're going to be talking about what else we need to do legally.

Thank you.

John Stroger. Thank you, Mr. President. And frankly, as a fellow Arkansan, I can't think of a better time to be president of the National Association of Counties and have this opportunity to work with you. And I know that you're very sensitive, concerned. You're imbued with a sense of fairness for all Americans. And working with us here at NACO and with other groups of Americans like us, you're going to help us make America really, really great. So we stand here with you ready to face the challenges together and build on America's already greatness. Thank you very much, and God bless

you. And I hope he continues to allow you to be strong to carry forth your charge.

The President. Thank you, John. God bless you. Thank you, ladies and gentlemen.

NOTE: The President spoke at 11:34 a.m. via satellite from Room 459 of the Old Executive Office Building. A tape was not available for verification of the content of these remarks.

Remarks Announcing the New Policy on Homosexuals in the Military
July 19, 1993

Thank you very much. Secretary Aspin, General Powell, members of the Joint Chiefs, Admiral Kime, to our host, Admiral Smith, ladies and gentlemen, I have come here today to discuss a difficult challenge and one which has received an enormous amount of publicity and public and private debate over the last several months: our Nation's policy toward homosexuals in the military.

I believe the policy I am announcing today represents a real step forward, but I know it will raise concerns in some of your minds. So I wanted you to hear my thinking and my decision directly and in person because I respect you, and because you are among the elite who will lead our Armed Forces into the next century, and because you will have to put this policy into effect and I expect your help in doing it.

The policy I am announcing today is, in my judgment, the right thing to do and the best way to do it. It is right because it provides greater protection to those who happen to be homosexual and want to serve their country honorably in uniform, obeying all the military's rules against sexual misconduct. It is the best way to proceed because it provides a sensible balance between the rights of the individual and the needs of our military to remain the world's number one fighting force. As President of all the American people, I am pledged to protect and to promote individual rights. As Commander in Chief, I am pledged to protect and advance our security. In this policy, I believe we have come close to meeting both objectives.

Let me start with this clear fact: Our military is one of our greatest accomplishments and our most valuable assets. It is the world's most effec-

tive and powerful fighting force, bar none. I have seen proof of this fact almost every day since I became President. I saw it last week when I visited Camp Casey, along the DMZ in Korea. I witnessed it at our military academies at Annapolis and West Point when I visited there. And I certainly relied on it 3 weeks ago when I ordered an attack on Iraq after that country's leadership attempted to assassinate President Bush.

We owe a great deal to the men and women who protect us through their service, their sacrifice, and their dedication. And we owe it to our own security to listen hard to them and act carefully as we consider any changes in the military. A force ready to fight must maintain the highest priority under all circumstances.

Let me review the events which bring us here today. Before I ran for President, this issue was already upon us. Some of the members of the military returning from the Gulf war announced their homosexuality in order to protest the ban. The military's policy has been questioned in college ROTC programs. Legal challenges have been filed in court, including one that has since succeeded. In 1991, the Secretary of Defense, Dick Cheney, was asked about reports that the Defense Department spent an alleged $500 million to separate and replace about 17,000 homosexuals from the military service during the 1980's, in spite of the findings of a Government report saying there was no reason to believe that they could not serve effectively and with distinction. Shortly thereafter, while giving a speech at the Kennedy School of Government at Harvard, I was asked by one of the students what I thought of this report and what I thought of lifting the ban. This question had never before been presented to me, and I had never had the opportunity to discuss it with anyone. I stated then what I still believe, that I thought there ought to be a presumption that people who wish to do so should be able to serve their country if they are willing to conform to the high standards of the military and that the emphasis should be always on people's conduct, not their status.

For me, and this is very important, this issue has never been one of group rights but rather of individual ones, of the individual opportunity to serve and the individual responsibility to conform to the highest standards of military conduct. For people who are willing to play by the rules, able to serve and make a contribution, I believed then and I believe now we should give them the chance to do so.

The central facts of this issue are not much in dispute. First, notwithstanding the ban, there have been and are homosexuals in the military service who serve with distinction. I have had the privilege of meeting some of these men and women, and I have been deeply impressed by their devotion to duty and to country.

Second, there is no study showing them to be less capable or more prone to misconduct than heterosexual soldiers. Indeed, all the information we have indicates that they are not less capable or more prone to misbehavior.

Third, misconduct is already covered by the laws and rules which also cover activities that are improper by heterosexual members of the military.

Fourth, the ban has been lifted in other nations and in police and fire departments in our country with no discernible negative impact on unit cohesion or capacity to do the job, though there is admittedly no absolute analogy to the situation we face and no study bearing on this specific issue.

Fifth, even if the ban were lifted entirely, the experience of other nations and police and fire departments in the United States indicates that most homosexuals would probably not declare their sexual orientation openly, thereby making an already hard life even more difficult in some circumstances.

But as the sociologist Charles Moskos noted after spending many years studying the American military, the issue may be tougher to resolve here in the United States than in Canada, Australia, and in some other nations because of the presence in our country of both vocal gay rights groups and equally vocal antigay rights groups, including some religious groups who believe that lifting the ban amounts to endorsing a lifestyle they strongly disapprove of.

Clearly the American people are deeply divided on this issue, with most military people opposed to lifting the ban because of the feared impact on unit cohesion, rooted in disapproval of homosexual lifestyles and the fear of invasion of privacy of heterosexual soldiers who must live and work in close quarters with homosexual military people. However, those who have studied this issue extensively have discovered an interesting fact. People in this country who are aware of having known homosexuals are far more likely to support lifting the ban. In other words, they are likely to see this issue in terms of individual conduct and individual capacity instead of the claims of a group with which they do not agree and also to be able to imagine how this ban could be lifted without a destructive impact on group cohesion and morale.

Shortly after I took office and reaffirmed my position, the foes of lifting the ban in the Congress moved to enshrine the ban in law. I asked that congressional action be delayed for 6 months while the Secretary of Defense worked with the Joint Chiefs to come up with a proposal for changing our current policy. I then met with the Joint Chiefs to hear their concerns and asked them to try to work through the issue with Secretary Aspin. I wanted to handle the matter in this way on grounds of both principle and practicality.

As a matter of principle, it is my duty as Commander in Chief to uphold the high standards of combat readiness and unit cohesion of the world's finest fighting force, while doing my duty as President to protect the rights of individual Americans and to put to use the abilities of all the American people. And I was determined to serve this principle as fully as possible through practical action, knowing this fact about our system of government: While the Commander in Chief and the Secretary of Defense can change military personnel policies, Congress can reverse those changes by law in ways that are difficult, if not impossible, to veto.

For months now, the Secretary of Defense and the Service Chiefs have worked through this issue in a highly charged, deeply emotional environment, struggling to come to terms with the competing consideration and pressures and, frankly, to work through their own ideas and deep feelings.

During this time many dedicated Americans have come forward to state their own views on this issue. Most, but not all, of the military testimony has been against lifting the ban. But support for changing the policy has come from distinguished combat veterans, including Senators Bob Kerrey, Chuck Robb, and John Kerry in the United States Congress. It has come from Lawrence Korb, who enforced the gay ban during the Reagan administration, and from former Senator Barry Goldwater, a distinguished veteran, former chairman of the Senate Armed Services Committee, founder of the Arizona National Guard, and patron saint of the conservative wing of the Republican Party.

Senator Goldwater's statement, published in the Washington Post recently, made it crystal clear that when this matter is viewed as an issue of individual opportunity and responsibility rather than one of alleged group rights, this is not a call for cultural license but rather a reaffirmation of the American value of extending opportunity to responsible individuals and of limiting the role of Government over citizens' private lives.

On the other hand, those who oppose lifting the ban are clearly focused not on the conduct of individual gay service members but on how nongay service members feel about gays in general and in particular those in the military service.

These past few days I have been in contact with the Secretary of Defense as he has worked through the final stages of this policy with the Joint Chiefs. We now have a policy that is a substantial advance over the one in place when I took office. I have ordered Secretary Aspin to issue a directive consisting of these essential elements: One, service men and women will be judged based on their conduct, not their sexual orientation. Two, therefore the practice, now 6 months old, of not asking about sexual orientation in the enlistment procedure will continue. Three, an open statement by a service member that he or she is a homosexual will create a rebuttable presumption that he or she intends to engage in prohibited conduct, but the service member will be given an opportunity to refute that presumption; in other words, to demonstrate that he or she intends to live by the rules of conduct that apply in the military service. And four, all provisions of the Uniform

Code of Military Justice will be enforced in an even-handed manner as regards both heterosexuals and homosexuals. And thanks to the policy provisions agreed to by the Joint Chiefs, there will be a decent regard to the legitimate privacy and associational rights of all service members.

Just as is the case under current policy, unacceptable conduct, either heterosexual or homosexual, will be unacceptable 24 hours a day, 7 days a week from the time a recruit joins the service until the day he or she is discharged. Now, as in the past, every member of our military will be required to comply with the Uniform Code of Military Justice, which is Federal law, and military regulations at all times and in all places.

Let me say a few words now about this policy. It is not a perfect solution. It is not identical with some of my own goals. And it certainly will not please everyone, perhaps not anyone, and clearly not those who hold the most adamant opinions on either side of this issue.

But those who wish to ignore the issue must understand that it is already tearing at the cohesion of the military and it is today being considered by the Federal courts in ways that may not be to the liking of those who oppose any change. And those who want the ban to be lifted completely on both status and conduct must understand that such action would have faced certain and decisive reversal by the Congress and the cause for which many have fought for years would be delayed, probably for years.

Thus, on grounds of both principle and practicality, this is a major step forward. It is, in my judgment, consistent with my responsibilities as President and Commander in Chief to meet the need to change current policy. It is an honorable compromise that advances the cause of people who are called to serve our country by their patriotism, the cause of our national security, and our national interest in resolving an issue that has divided our military and our Nation and diverted our attention from other matters for too long.

The time has come for us to move forward. As your Commander in Chief, I charge all of you to carry out this policy with fairness, with balance, and with due regard for the privacy of individuals. We must and will protect unit cohesion and troop morale. We must and will continue to have the best fighting force in the world. But this is an end to witch hunts that spend millions of taxpayer dollars to ferret out individuals who have served their country well. Improper conduct, on or off base, should remain grounds for discharge. But we will proceed with an even hand against everyone, regardless of sexual orientation.

Such controversies as this have divided us before. But our Nation and our military have always risen to the challenge before. That was true of racial integration of the military and changes in the role of women in the military. Each of these was an issue, because it was an issue for society as well as for the military. And in each case our military was a leader in figuring out how to respond most effectively.

In the early 1970's, when President Nixon decided to transform our military into an all-volunteer force, many argued that it could not work. They said it would ruin our forces. But the leaders of our military not only made it work, they used the concept of an all-volunteer force to build the very finest fighting force our Nation and the world have ever known.

Ultimately, the success of this policy will depend in large measure on the commitment it receives from the leaders of the military services. I very much respect and commend the Joint Chiefs for the good-faith effort they have made through this whole endeavor. And I thank General Powell, the Joint Chiefs, and the Commandant of the Coast Guard for joining me here today and for their support of this policy.

I would also like to thank those who lobbied aggressively in behalf of changing the policy, including Congressman Barney Frank; Congressman Gerry Studds; and the Campaign for Military Service, who worked with us and who clearly will not agree with every aspect of the policy announced today, but who should take some solace in knowing that their efforts have helped

to produce a strong advance for the cause they seek to serve.

I must now look to General Powell, to the Joint Chiefs, to all the other leaders in our military to carry out this policy through effective training and leadership. Every officer will be expected to exert the necessary effort to make this policy work. That has been the key every time the military has successfully addressed a new challenge, and it will be key in this effort, too.

Our military is a conservative institution, and I say that in the very best sense, for its purpose is to conserve the fighting spirit of our troops, to conserve the resources and the capacity of our troops, to conserve the military lessons acquired during our Nation's existence, to conserve our very security, and yes, to conserve the liberties of the American people. Because it is a conservative institution, it is right for the military to be wary of sudden changes. Because it is an institution that embodies the best of America and must reflect the society in which it operates, it is also right for the military to make changes when the time for change is at hand.

I strongly believe that our military, like our society, needs the talents of every person who wants to make a contribution and who is ready to live by the rules. That is the heart of the policy that I have announced today. I hope in your heart you will find the will and the desire to support it and to lead our military in incorporating it into our Nation's great asset and the world's best fighting force.

Thank you very much.

NOTE: The President spoke at 2:36 p.m. at the National Defense University at Fort McNair.

Remarks on the Dismissal of FBI Director William Sessions and an Exchange With Reporters
July 19, 1993

The President. Good afternoon. In recent months, serious questions have been raised about the conduct and the leadership of the Director of the FBI William Sessions. Among other matters, the Department's Office of Pro-

fessional Responsibility has issued a report on certain conduct by the Director. I asked the Attorney General, Janet Reno, to assess the Director's tenure and the proper response to the turmoil now in the Bureau. After a thorough review by the Attorney General of Mr. Sessions' leadership of the FBI, she has reported to me in no uncertain terms that he can no longer effectively lead the Bureau and law enforcement community.

I had hoped very much that this matter could be resolved within the Justice Department. The Attorney General met with Judge Sessions over the weekend and asked him to resign, but he refused. In accord with the recommendation of the Attorney General, with which I fully agree, I called Director Sessions a few moments ago and informed him that I was dismissing him, effective immediately, as the Director of the FBI.

We cannot have a leadership vacuum at an agency as important to the United States as the FBI. It is time that this difficult chapter in the Agency's history is brought to a close. The FBI is the Nation's premier investigative and enforcement agency. Law-abiding citizens rely on the FBI to handle a wide array of complex and sensitive matters, to protect our shores against terrorism, our neighborhoods against the scourge of drugs and guns, our public life against white-collar crime, corruption, and crimes of violence. The Agency's brilliant detective work in the wake of the World Trade Center bombing has shown even in a time of difficulty the men and women on the street and in the labs have continued to give their country their best. With a change in management in the FBI, we can now give the crimefighters the leadership they deserve.

Tomorrow I expect to make an announcement about my nominee to be the next Director of the FBI. In the meanwhile, the Attorney General and I have asked Floyd Clark to serve as Acting Director of the Bureau.

Q. Mr. President, are you—what did he do wrong? And are you confident that there was not an internal vendetta against Judge Sessions because he wanted to broaden the look of the FBI, take in more Hispanics, blacks, and women?

The President. Well, let me answer the second question first. I think that will be remembered as the best thing about his tenure. And he deserves the support and thanks of the American people for trying to broaden the membership of the FBI to make it look more like America and to follow the lead of some other agencies and the United States military.

Now, but beyond that, if you read the report

of the Office of Professional Responsibility and you do what the Attorney General did, if you look at that and all of the other circumstances and you assess the capacity of the present Director to lead or the incapacity of the Director to lead, she reached the judgment, which she communicated to me, that he ought to resign. And I fully agreed with that judgment. There are lots of reasons for it.

Q. Mr. President, do you think that this will in any way create the impression that the FBI is being politicized and hurt the longstanding tradition that the FBI not be subject to political pressure?

The President. Absolutely not. As a matter of fact, that's one of the reasons we have taken the amount of time that we have. The Attorney General, when she took office, was asked by me to review this matter. Both of us agreed that in the normal course of events, the Director of the FBI should not be changed just because administrations changed, even when, perhaps even especially when, there's a change of political party in the White House. So the Attorney General was very deliberate, very thorough in this, and I think has gone out of her way to avoid the appearance of political impropriety.

Homosexuals in the Military

Q. Mr. President, won't your new policy on homosexuals in the military require gays in the military to stay in the closet? And do you hope that the courts will take this policy further?

The President. No, it will not necessarily require them to stay in the closet. The policy as written gives people a limited right, obviously, to express their sexual orientation. But if they do so, they are at risk of having to demonstrate in some credible way that they are observing the rules of conduct applied in the military service. That is much more than they had before.

Over and above that, the investigative rules, which are part of the policy, go far beyond anything that was written in law before in terms of respecting the privacy and associational rights of homosexuals in the military service and others, and nonhomosexuals, heterosexuals, in the military.

Q. Mr. President, you said in your speech that you thought you had done what was right. You had earlier said that what was right was lifting the ban. How did you reach the decision not to stick with your guns, go ahead, lift the ban, take the heat? This is going to be decided in the courts anyway. Why not stand by your principles?

The President. First of all, I think I did stand by my principles. Under this policy, a person can say, "I am a homosexual, but I am going to strictly adhere to the Code of Conduct." If you go back through every statement I have made, I never said that I would be in favor of changing any of the rules of conduct. I said I did not agree with the whole policy. The only part of this policy with which I do not agree is that the rebuttable presumption, in effect, puts the burden on the service member to demonstrate credibly that he or she understands the rules of conduct and is going to adhere to them. That is the only part of it with which I do not agree.

On the investigative rules governing conduct, there is more protection for privacy rights and for associational rights than I ever discussed in the campaign, than I have ever discussed as President. And it is a significant change, significant in the policy operations of the United States military. So from the point of view of homosexuals who wish to serve honorably, I think it was a substantial advance. That's one answer.

The second point is, I think it is very important for the President, whenever possible, to work with the military services who will have to carry out the policy in a way that maintains the kind of cooperation manifested today. I think all of you who know anything about this issue know that the Joint Chiefs moved a very long way from where they were today, compared to where they were when I first met with them after I became President.

The third issue—there's one last issue—the third issue is that had I done that, that position would have faced certain swift and immediate defeat in the United States Congress because of the opposition of the Joint Chiefs, which they are by law required to give if asked in congressional testimony.

Q. Do you have a sense now that Senator Nunn will not bring about that result by virtue of what he tries to enact? Have you talked to him?

The President. Well, I hope he doesn't. We have been in regular contact with him. Since I basically was not involved in the negotiations of the policy until just a couple of days ago, the Secretary of Defense, at my instruction, was in regular and almost constant contact with Sen-

ator Nunn and with some others. And I hope very much that he won't.

There were some changes, a few minor changes and one that was important to me, made in the last few days at my suggestion. But the Joint Chiefs signed off on them. It seems to me that their judgment, given the fact that they were all opposed to the changes which we are now making—they've worked through these things; they've looked at the legal, at the practical, at the factual situations that we face— it seems to me that their judgment ought to count for a great deal and that we should not get in the business of legislating every personnel policy. I would hope that Senator Nunn would support this policy.

One more.

Q. Mr. President, how does what people do in private, whether they're gay or straight, have any bearing on their fitness to serve in the military?

The President. Well, you know that I don't believe it does, but today—now, wait a minute, go back and read the policy. Read the policy. Today the Joint Chiefs took the position that any violation of the Code of Conduct must be applied in an even-handed way as it reflects heterosexuals and homosexuals. And you have to go back and read the whole Military Code to understand the significance of that, but it is quite a significant statement by them.

Thank you very much.

FBI Director

Q. One for the Attorney General?

Q. Attorney General Reno, there have been sort of two tracks in terms of the allegations against the FBI Director: one, the ethical problems that were in the original report that was carried over from the Bush administration. The other is that in the months since, he has lost the confidence of his Agency and, therefore, the ability to do his job effectively. For which of those two things is he being dismissed?

[At this point, Attorney General Reno read the letter she sent to the President recommending the dismissal of Mr. Sessions.]

Q. Mr. President——

Q. Does that mean it was both?

Q. Mr. President——

Q. Let me follow up for just a second, Sarah [Sarah McClendon, McClendon News Service]. Did you find that he did violate any laws or

Government regulations as charged in the original report? And where did that fall in terms of the confidence that members——

Attorney General Reno. I concluded that, based on the report and the responses to the report, that the Director had exhibited a serious deficiency in judgment regarding matters in the report.

Q. Mr. President, we have seen here an Agency maneuvering the White House, the press, the public, and getting their own head of the Agency that they want. We have seen them push out a man here, and let me tell you—don't you think it's about time to protect American

people from any actions, operations of the FBI, that we should write a charter for them in Congress? They only exist by an Executive order which Teddy Roosevelt wrote in 1908.

The President. Well, I don't agree with the characterization you made of what has occurred. So I can't comment on it. I flat disagree.

Q. Would you look into that, because you obviously have not looked into that?

The President. No, I just disagree.

NOTE: The President spoke at 4:15 p.m. in the Briefing Room at the White House.

Exchange With Reporters Prior to a Meeting With Congressional Leaders
July 19, 1993

Q. Mr. President, have you given up on a utility tax, and how much of an increase would you take on a gas tax? And besides that——

The President. Well, I'm just sitting here meeting with the chairmen, and I'm going to also, you know, keep working through this with the conferees. And we're going to see what we can do. But we're just beginning our conversa-

tions, so I can't answer those questions.

Q. Sir, what qualifications will the new FBI Director have?

The President. Good ones.

NOTE: The exchange began at 5:06 p.m. in the Oval Office at the White House. A tape was not available for verification of the content of this exchange.

Nomination for General Counsel of the Environmental Protection Agency
July 19, 1993

The President announced today that he intends to nominate Jean Nelson to be General Counsel of the Environmental Protection Agency.

"Through her service as a law enforcement official and environmental activist, Jean Nelson has been consistently recognized for her

achievements," said the President. "I am confident that her service at the EPA will be marked by the same level of excellence as her previous work."

NOTE: A biography of the nominee was made available by the Office of the Press Secretary.

Remarks Announcing the Nomination of Louis Freeh To Be FBI Director
July 20, 1993

Good morning. Please sit down. Mr. Vice President; Attorney General Reno; the Acting

FBI Director, Floyd Clark; former Director of the FBI, Judge William Webster, we're delighted to have you here. Senator D'Amato; Judge Robert Bonner, the DEA Administrator; the representatives of all the law enforcement agencies who are here and the friends and family of the nominee to be the next Director of the FBI.

The Federal Bureau of Investigation is the Federal Government's cutting edge in the fight against crime. Its agents are the best trained in the world. Its sophisticated technology enables law enforcement agents to catch criminals with a fragment of a fingerprint. As we saw only recently in the remarkably swift arrest in the World Trade Center bombing, the Agency continues its preeminent place in the law enforcement world. The Agency itself must clearly adapt to new times. It must continue the progress of opening its ranks to minorities and to women that began in recent years. It must work cooperatively with other agencies in the United States and in international partnerships against crime with police forces of other nations.

Yesterday I announced my intention to appoint a new Director of the FBI. Today I am pleased to nominate a law enforcement legend to be the Director of the FBI, Judge Louis Freeh. Judge Freeh knows the FBI. He is a highly decorated former agent and supervisor. He has investigated and prosecuted some of the most notorious and complex crimes of our time. He is experienced, energetic, and independent. He will be both good and tough, good for the FBI and tough on criminals.

It can truly be said that Louis Freeh is the best possible person to head the FBI as it faces new challenges and a new century. He has spent his career in the Federal justice system. After working his way through law school, he became an FBI agent. He knows the Agency as only an agent can, working the dangerous streets. He helped lead the waterfront investigations that led to the criminal convictions of 125 people, including leading organized crime figures.

From the FBI, Judge Freeh became a Federal prosecutor in New York City. He prosecuted and won convictions against the leaders of what was then the largest heroin importation case in our history, the legendary "Pizza Connection" case. The trial lasted over a year. Among other defendants, Judge Freeh sent the head of the Sicilian mafia to jail. Observers were dazzled. He was called, and I quote, "one of the Government's toughest investigators, a ram-

rod-straight and ferocious crusader against the mob, an investigative genius."

Three years ago, as Judge Freeh neared the end of his work as a prosecutor, the Department of Justice selected him to head a special task force in one of the most notorious and difficult criminal cases of our day. A mysterious bomber was at work in the South, mailing parcels that killed Federal Judge Robert Vance near Birmingham, Alabama, and civil rights leader Robbie Robinson in Savannah, Georgia. Many predicted that the case would never be solved. But led by Louis Freeh, the task force tracked down the bomber, and Freeh himself prosecuted the case and obtained convictions. The bomber is now serving seven life terms in prison. In recognition of his service to the law, President Bush appointed Louis Freeh to the Federal bench. Now Judge Freeh has agreed to leave that lifetime post to serve his Nation once again in a difficult new job. There are few jobs in our Government that are more important.

Our Federal law enforcement agencies face an ever-changing array of threats. Drugs continue to ravage our young people and our streets. Law-abiding citizens can be caught in the crossfire between gangs, today equipped like armies. White-collar swindlers practice inventive forms of what Al Capone once called "the legitimate rackets." And our Nation, so long immune from the terrorism that has plagued the world, now faces that threat, too.

With Attorney General Janet Reno, Drug Policy Coordinator Lee Brown, and now, we hope, FBI Director Louis Freeh, our administration has a street-smart front line against crime. These law enforcers did not learn about crime in theory books, they learned about it on the streets and in the courtroom. And they have learned the best lessons of State and local enforcers. With all of their hard-won experience, this crimefighting team can work hard every day to protect the American people's right to safety in their homes and in their communities.

I must tell you that I am very proud and very grateful that Judge Freeh was willing to leave his lifetime appointment on the Federal bench for the somewhat less secure work that the rest of us find in the executive branch. [*Laughter*] I hope the American people will be grateful as well, and I look forward to his speedy confirmation.

NOTE: The President spoke at 9:27 a.m. in the Rose Garden at the White House.

Exchange With Reporters Prior to a Meeting With Congressional Leaders
July 20, 1993

Representative Dan Rostenkowski

Q. Mr. President, do you think that Chairman Rostenkowski's legal problems will have any effect on the budget process?

The President. No. We've got a lot of work to do. Chairman Rostenkowski's done a great job with this budget so far, and we've worked very closely together. And we're going to work today. I don't know anything about the rest of it. I just know that we're going to work. That's what we all got hired to do, and we're going to do our job.

Energy Tax

Q. Are you ready to give up on an energy tax?

The President. No.

Q. Does an energy tax have to be part of the program? There's a lot of move on Capitol Hill against it.

The President. I know it. But if you look at all the numbers, it's hard to get there without it. So, I think we ought to——

NOTE: The exchange began at 12:41 p.m. in the Old Family Dining Room at the White House. A tape was not available for verification of the content of this exchange.

Remarks to Democratic Members of the House of Representatives
July 20, 1993

Thank you very much, Mr. Vice President, Mr. Speaker, Mr. Leader. Ladies and gentlemen, as all of you know I have just spent several days away from Washington, stopping along the way to look at the floods in Iowa and going through California to meet with the National Education Association and then on to Japan where I met with the leaders of the seven large industrial nations of the world, which included an agreement to reduce tariffs by historic rates, agreed to continue our common efforts to promote democracy and economic progress in Russia, and reached an agreement with Japan that, for the first time, convinced the Japanese explicitly to reduce dramatically their trade surplus with us and to work with us with specific numerical objective criteria to deal with that problem. Then I went to Korea to see our young men and women in uniform there defending freedom at a distant outpost. I got within about 10 yards of the dividing line between North and South Korea, the Bridge of No Return,

then flew back through Hawaii to see the many, many thousands of sailors there at Pearl Harbor along with the leaders of our military in the Pacific Command. And then I came back with Leader Gephardt on Saturday to go to St. Louis to visit the Governors who have been victimized by the floods, and their people have.

All these trips have a common thread, as disparate as they were. I had an opportunity to see people who were serving this country and people who are living here and working hard, making our jobs possible. And I was immensely moved, as I always am, by the incredible character and courage and good common sense of the American people.

Now, we come here at a difficult time for the country and for the world. The world is in a significant economic crisis. All the wealthier countries of the world are facing difficulties in creating new jobs. For a very long time there has been a kind of political paralysis in this country where we always knew what we had to do, but we could never quite bring ourselves to do it. And because we had divided Government, it was always possible for one branch to blame the other one for what did not get done. And the worse the problem got, the more painful their solutions became. That is always the way in human life, not just in Government but in every part of our lives.

Now, because of your help and the leadership and the raw courage many of you have demonstrated, we've brought our country to the verge of fundamental economic change. In just 6 months we have certainly changed the nature of the economic debate here in our Nation's Capital. The new direction that I discussed with you in February in the State of the Union Address is at hand. Once, a President joked that the deficit he created was big enough to take care of itself. Now no one jokes about it, and no one doubts that we are about the serious business of reducing that deficit and the stranglehold it has on our ability to create better times now and to provide a better future for our children.

Rather than debating whether to ignore the deficit, we have now begun a serious discussion about how to really bring it down. That is leading change, not going along with events. Where once Presidents sent you budgets that were not worth the paper they were printed on, now we have a real economic plan that, for all the controversy, is moving through Congress at a record pace.

I am amused now when I read that the difficult tough choices that I have asked the Congress to make are passing with narrow margins in our majority party when last year 75 percent of the House Members of the other party voted against their own President's budget and for years Presidential budgets have been political documents, not serious attempts to turn this country around.

Now we are involved in a serious attempt to do that, you and I leading the change. Where once the other party taxed middle class people so that those in upper income groups would not have to pay even their fair share, we have a plan that asks those that benefited most in the 1980's and whose taxes went down then to pay their fair share, not because we want to punish success but because it is the American way to ask everyone to pay according to their ability to do so. That is what the middle class demands, and that is a change we are making.

Where once National Government had slogans for small business, we now have an economic plan that actually provides target incentives to business to create real jobs, something we have needed for a long time. And this effort to pass this plan as it has moved through the Congress has clearly, as the Chairman of the Federal Reserve said not very long ago, been the major force in driving interest rates to their lowest level in 20 years, something that is leading to a huge amount of refinancing of home loans, business loans, something that clearly will act in a positive way that will manifest itself in new investment today and new jobs in the near future. Where once Government spending soared even as investment in the future decreased, we now have an economic plan that dramatically shifts spending priorities away from wasteful cuts and still with some prudent, wise investments.

Once, our economic planners in the White House focused on quick fixes for the next election. Every budget document that came up to this Hill for years was discarded by serious people in both parties. You know it as well as I do. It's just a political document to make sure that the President can stay in good graces with the American people, instead of telling the truth and making the tough choices.

Now there is an economic plan before you that looks at the long term, not the next election. We look at the next generation, hoping that by the next election the American people will see that as exactly what has been done. Where once the other party used welfare as a whipping boy without doing anything to move a single person from welfare to work, we now have an economic plan that is step one of a long-term strategy to end welfare as we know it. The earned-income tax credit in this plan will save everybody who works 40 hours a week with children in the home. If you do that, that's work, we're going to reward it, and we will lift you out of poverty. It's one of the most significant social reforms enacted in this country in a generation. And we do it through the tax system, rewarding work.

Where once a President had to go to international economic conferences like the one I just attended with their hats in their hand and sit there while people from other countries criticized the United States relentlessly, saying, "How can you expect us to grow the world economy when you have a big deficit and you, a wealthy country, soak up savings from all over the world, financing half of your public and private debt, or one-third of it, anyway, from foreign sources?", I had the privilege of going to a G–7 meeting which, for the first time in a decade, did not criticize the United States but complimented the United States for a serious attempt to reduce the deficit. And make no mistake about it, that is what gave me the leverage, your action to reduce this deficit gave me the leverage to argue that the time had come to reduce these tariffs and to take it back and make it part of an international agreement on trade that will create hundreds of thousands of manufacturing jobs in this country in the next few years.

This is an agreement that we made that will create manufacturing jobs in America. There is no doubt about it. Everyone can see it, everybody who has ever studied it. It is not like many of the issues we have around here where there's a lot of debate and argument. Everyone knows that this is a good deal for America. We have to make it part of the global trade agreement by the end of the year, and we have a good chance to do it now because the agreement at the G–7 would never have happened if you hadn't passed the budget in the Senate and the House and given me the leverage to say we're doing our part, now you do yours.

Make no mistake about it, we would never, never have reached this agreement with Japan to change the nature of our trading relationships had I not had the leverage to say, I know that during the 1980's you took the trade surplus you had and turned it into an investment deficit by sending a lot of your money back to this country to help us to finance our deficit and keep our interest rates from absolutely exploding, but we are taking care of that. We're doing what you asked us to do. We're bringing our deficit down, investing more in our economy, our productivity is going up. We can compete again. Now we have to change the trade rules. If you hadn't passed, each House, a version of that budget, we would not have been able to do that. That is what is happening today.

Yes, it is painful. Yes, it is difficult. But it is progress. It is change. It will make a difference. And it is focused on the long-run interests of the people of this country. We have come this far. This is no time to turn back. We have been bold. This is no time to be timid. We have faced this crisis squarely. This is no

time to blink.

We can come out of this conference with a plan that can pass the Congress and, most importantly, can pass the critical judgment of the American people if we make sure they know what is in it. As you work through the myriad of important details in this massive economic conference, we would do well to keep in mind that history will not note who wins in the technical detailed arcana that may consume much of the debate. But our children and our grandchildren will remember whether we were bashful or bold. They will remember whether we showed courage or whether we turned away from this challenge. They will remember whether we gave in to gridlock in the kind of easy rhetoric that has come to dominate our politics of the last few years or whether we govern.

I understand and appreciate the fact that compromise and consensus and conciliation will have to be the order of the day. Nothing this difficult and complex can be accomplished without listening to different voices and different ideas. But I have no illusions about the challenges that lie before us.

Of course, this is politically difficult and institutionally demanding. But that, again, makes it a challenge worth accepting. Remember this: None of it will be worth anything if at the end of the day, we provide something less than fundamental change. From the beginning of this process, that is what I have tried to argue. Yes, there will be changes around the edges. Yes, there have been already changes around the edges. But we must provide fundamental change. What are elements of that change? First, we have to seize control of our economic destiny, put our fiscal house in order.

This deficit is the bone in the throat of America. And we ought to deal with it by passing a plan that reduces it by $500 billion, putting it in a trust fund so the American people know, because they don't trust anyone in politics, that the money will be used to reduce the deficit and having an enforcement mechanism that says if we miss the targets, because no one is smart enough to foresee everything that will occur over the next 5 years, the President does have to come forward with a plan to set it right every year. That is the first thing we ought to do to establish credibility with the American people.

Second, we ought to return to the fundamental notion of fairness. Those who have the most should pay the most. We did the reverse in the 1980's, and it didn't work out very well. Every serious study shows that most of the economic gains of the last decade went to the top one percent. The people who put those policies forward said you ought to do that because then they will create more jobs. But we created jobs at a slower pace, at a slower pace. We are over 3 million jobs behind where we ought to be today at this point in a so-called economic recovery. Why? Because the policy doesn't work. Because of the changes that have been made in this program, that have been moved through the Congress with some more spending cuts and some less tax increases that were originally proposed, I can now say to you that we ought to require that at least 70 percent of the tax burden of this plan fall on people with incomes above $200,000—that is now possible because of the changes which have been made—and that there will be no increases on working families unless their incomes are well above $100,000 a year.

Third, we must keep faith with the hard-working middle class families who have worked hard and paid more for the last 12 years. They are the backbone in the country, and the economy is not working for them. Many of them work harder every year for less, and many of them are afraid of losing their health insurance. Many of them are afraid that the Government will never again do anything that really makes a difference. But if we take action to remove the uncertainty that they have and to clear the cloud of rhetoric that they've heard with our adversaries who don't want to do anything, trying to convince them that they're going to pay the lion's share of the tax load, we can again not only gain their confidence but, even more important, do something that is very much in their interest by passing this program.

Because you have been pressing, you especially in the leadership, for deeper spending cuts and for different tax proposals that, in the aggregate are less, we can now say, looking at the proposals on the table, that we will not need to ask the average working family to pay more than about $50 a year to contribute to this plan. That is a reasonable thing.

You cannot make me believe, once you get out there and tell the truth to the people in any district represented in this room, that the average middle class family with incomes above $30,000 a year and below the income tax increase threshold wouldn't pay a buck a week to get this deficit down. I don't believe it. I think they would. And I think they expect to do something to contribute to the future of this country as long as they know it's fair and we're not going to squander the money. And that's the opportunity we're going to be given, to demonstrate to them that fact during this conference and in the weeks ahead.

Fourth, we cannot ignore the fundamental economic reality that a lot of Americans are still left out and left behind in this weak economy. We have got to have incentives in the final bill to spur growth, to create jobs, to deal with the fact that no industrial country is now able, even in times of economic growth, to generate very many new jobs. We have got to try some new things. That's why I'd like, for example—I don't want to start listing them, because you may think I've left something out I'd want in—but just for example, that's why I think we ought to try that venture capital gains tax that is in the House bill that was, by parliamentary accident, taken out of the Senate bill. We've got to try some different things to create new jobs. And while I feel very strongly that we ought to create the empowerment zones in the inner cities and the small towns and the poor rural areas to see if we can make free enterprise work in these places, there's not enough Government money to go in and recover the fortunes and the futures of the people who live there. We've heard our adversaries on the other side talk about this concept for years. Why don't we do it and do it right and see if it works? This is a good proposal. Let's try it.

While we're at it, let me say one other thing. In the plans adopted by both the Senate and the House, without respect to all this hot air and rhetoric I've heard about how tough it is on small business, the hard, cold truth is that both these plans will give a tax cut to 90 percent of the small businesses in the United States of America that spent one red cent reinvesting in their business, because we doubled or more the expensing provision without raising their income tax. How can the small business associations of this country come out against this proposal when we are lowering taxes on 90 percent of their members? And the Wall Street Journal has got an article today documenting that fact. That ought to stay in the plan, even if the leadership opposes it.

Finally, I am for the cuts that have been

made. But we have to recognize that there is a limit to how much, particularly in this reconciliation process, we can cut beyond where we are without hurting the elderly, the working poor, and the middle class. There is a limit to what we can do.

As you know, almost all the increases left in this budget are in health care. And I am committed to coming up with a solution to this process which brings the problem—it gets health care costs in line with inflation. That's the way to deal with that. But you cannot just arbitrarily cut it out. I do not believe we should cut Medicare more, at least than the Senate number. I just don't believe we should. There is a limit to how much we should cut it unless we are solving the problem. We can cut it more when we solve the problem. We have to do this first, and then we can do that. Let's fix the budget first.

Now, if we meet these requirements, we will have produced a plan that delivers on economic renewal, that looks to the long run, not just the short term, that gives the American people a sense that we are rewarding and honoring the values and the vision of the people who work hard and play by the rules: work, family, education.

I believe these requirements can unite this conference. Of course, in some ways, even though our opponents have had some near-term rhetorical success, I think they have done something to unite us as well by serving as the implacable guardians of an indefensible status quo, against governing, in the favor of gridlock or the short-term fears that keep us from facing our problems instead of courage to seize control of our destiny and our future. Their policies ought to give us courage. After all, they had the ball for 12 years, and look what they did with it.

Now, I said on February the 18th in the State of the Union Address that I was not interested in blame, and I'm still not. And there's enough blame to go around, and there still is, not just among people in both parties of the Congress but among people who were Governors, mayors, and judges back then. That's fine. But there is blame to go around if you don't take responsibility now towards the future.

Just a few days ago there was a remarkable article in the Wall Street Journal, hardly an organ of the national Democratic Party—[laughter]—which said that Republicans' response to

the budget crisis and the economic crisis of the country represented, and I quote, "no new anything." That should unite us. On every important test, their alternatives have come up short. In both the House and the Senate, they offered much less deficit reduction and yet more pain to the average people in this country. They didn't lock their savings into a trust fund or have a real mechanism to enforce it. They weren't willing to stand up and ask their powerful and privileged and well-to-do and successful to pay even their fair share. In fact, they weren't willing to ask those people to pay anything at all. But they were more than happy to ask people on Medicare and the veterans and others to pay even more after we had already cut all those programs, again, saying the burden ought to be borne by the elderly, the working poor, and the middle class.

Our plan supports growth and fairness, and theirs is another victory for special interests. They refuse to even close loopholes for three-martini lunches or CEO salaries out of line with performance or the loophole that subsidizes the very lobbyists who write the loopholes. I read their plan. They didn't want to do that. They have no targeted incentives for businesses to create jobs in a global economy where plainly new strategies are called for, no targeted investments for growth; just taking more from health care, from veterans, from everything else that helps the average people in this country, just so the well off don't have to pay one red cent in new taxes.

Frankly, folks, I'm tired of what is sort of cold-blooded being passed off as courageous, just because of the sloganeering. The slogans are easy: "tax and spend," "cut spending first," "it's spending, stupid." They all sound so good, so that they mask the reality. The reality is, this budget cuts $250 billion in spending, over 200 specific spending cuts, not the general we'll-take-care-of-it-later of our opponents, the Vice President talked about, over hundreds of specific budget cuts in excess of $100 million apiece. That's what it does. There is nothing to be ashamed of here except somehow we haven't found a way to take a big old knife and cut through the rhetorical fog that has been blanketing our efforts in this town for the last several months. But I assure you, we're going to do it in the days ahead.

You know, in the Senate Finance Committee, there was an interesting little drama that played itself out after we heard all this stuff about "tax and spend" and "it's spending, stupid" and "we're going to cut spending". When the bill got down to the lick-log in the Senate Finance Committee, how many spending cuts do you think were offered by the other side, over and above the tough ones we had already put in place? Zero. Not one. Not one red cent. When it came down to getting away from this general stuff and to the specifics, nothing. Why? Because nobody wants to say anything hard. Because, sure, it is always the best thing in the heat of the moment to tell everybody just what they want to hear, but all of the easy things have been done. That's why we're in the fix we're in. And we have to do some things that are difficult.

Let me say, it grieves me in some ways that this has become a partisan fight. I did not seek that. I still have some hope that some of the genuinely conscientious and responsible Members on the other side, when this conference report emerges, will vote for it. I know many of them think there are many good things in it. And we have done some changes, frankly, that moved this bill in the direction that the more moderate and responsible Members have asked for on the other side. But I will not shrink from defending what I know in my heart will help the economy when it is subjected to untrue and unfair attacks. This is the nature of our profession, I guess, but somewhere along the line, what's really in the interest of the American people ought to count, too.

The last thing I want to say is that if you know you have to go this alone, and we don't get much help from the other side, there's an awful temptation, I guess, to do nothing, or at least to do nothing for a while. And I can tell you the cost of doing nothing is far higher in both political and economic terms than paying the price of progress today. We were elected to govern. We were elected to end gridlock. I don't know how many people I heard last year tell me, "Even if you make me mad, do something. Do something. Move this thing. Break us out. Get something going." If we flinch or fail to get our mandate for a moment, the reaction to that would be far greater than any particular unpopularity of this effort.

When we succeed and set our Nation on a new direction, and it will begin the day after both Houses vote for a combined plan—there will be a surge in conference—people will then see the facts, not the fog but the facts of what was in this program. The reality will take over. Then we will be on our way to building an economy which once again restores the American dream. We have been seeing it slip away for literally 20 years now. The peak of middle class prosperity in this country occurred 20 years ago in 1973. Ever since then, all new additions to earnings have come from people working longer hours or more people in the same family working. Ever since then, for 20 years, we have had different but inadequate responses to the challenges of the global economy. And then for the last 12 years, we tried trickle-down economics, which was shove it all up and hope it gets invested back down and it will work out fine.

Now, I believe that the truth is somewhere between and beyond, more importantly, the old paradigms of Government. We cannot spend our way out of this crisis. The Government cannot work the American people, alone, out of this crisis. But neither can we ignore our fundamental responsibilities to put our house in order, invest in our people, and have the kind of program that will move us into the 21st century.

This country is doing a lot of good things that often get lost because of the momentary insecurities. There has been a huge increase in productivity in the private sector. Your country is the high-quality, low-cost producer of hundreds, indeed thousands of goods and services that can help us if we can open markets and if we can get our house in order here and if we can continue to improve the skills of our people and if we can deal with the particular problems of various areas of the country and various parts of our economy. We can move this thing. We do not need to stay in the rut we're in. But we have been on this path in one way or the other for two decades. We cannot expect to move out of it in 6 months. But we will never move out of it unless we move. We can't just sit around and pray for rain. It doesn't work that way.

Let me close with just this personal indulgence, if I might. Thirty years ago today, I visited Washington, DC, for the first time in a now rather well-known encounter I had with President Kennedy in the Rose Garden. I had hardly ever been out of Arkansas, and I wasn't sure where I was or what I was seeing. But I knew one thing in the week I spent here: I had no doubt whatever that the Congress of the United States and the President of the United States could solve whatever problem and could meet whatever challenge we were facing. Now people all over America don't believe that anymore. Thirty years ago when I was here, I didn't have an instant of a doubt. And it was an incredible honor to be in this place, because this is where my country's business was done. Four months after I was here, of course, President Kennedy was assassinated, and the pain of that still lives on in this country and perhaps was the beginning of the slow undoing of our collective confidence in ourselves and our institutions. But you know, if you remember all the wonderful things that John Kennedy said, I think in some ways my favorite line was that "We must always remember that here on Earth, God's work is truly our own." The only way to ever honor any memory of something gone is to do something today which reinforces the validity of that memory in our hearts.

This day, it's far more important in our Nation's history for another reason, not because of my first trip here but because it was on this day in 1969 that an astronaut fulfilled one of President Kennedy's greatest dreams, when Neil Armstrong became the first person ever to walk on the Moon. When John Kennedy directed our attention to the heavens and inspired our notion of expanding knowledge, he saw it not as a test of our capacity, if you will remember, but of our character. He said, and I quote, "We choose to go to the Moon in this decade

and to do the other things not because they're easy but because they're hard. Because the challenges are one we are willing to accept, one we are unwilling to postpone, and one we intend to win."

So I say to you: I ask for your support, your unfailing efforts, your courage, your energy, because it is time to meet that kind of challenge. I know this is hard, more than anything else because it's been so hard in the last 2 months to get the facts out to the people. Every single piece of evidence shows that when people know what we're trying to do and what the details of this plan is, whether it's a Senate plan, a House plan, or something in between, a majority of the American people will see it as fair, sensible, and progressive. We are being not by the specifics, but by the rhetoric that has enveloped the fog of this town. I am telling you, once we act, we can make it go away because then the reality will begin to hit people's lives.

And so I ask you in this place in time to remember the challenge that John Kennedy laid down in deciding to go to the Moon. This should be one we are willing to accept, one we are unwilling to postpone, and one we intend to win. Thank you, and God bless you.

NOTE: The President spoke at 3:02 p.m. at the Cannon House Office Building. A tape was not available for verification of the content of these remarks.

Interview With the Wisconsin Media
July 20, 1993

The President. I'd like to make just a brief opening statement, and then I'll be happy to answer your questions. As you know, the designated committees from the Senate and the House are about to take up the conference process on the economic program I have presented to the Congress. I'd like to make a few comments about it and then answer your questions.

I have just returned from a meeting of the world's seven large industrial nations in Tokyo. At that meeting, two significant decisions were made that could dramatically improve the economy of the United States in the years ahead and obviously will be very good for Wisconsin.

The first decision was an agreement among the seven nations to lead an effort to dramatically reduce tariffs on manufactured goods across a whole range of services. It is estimated that if we can put this into a world trade agreement by the end of the year, it would add hundreds of thousands of jobs to the manufacturing economy in the United States over the next decade. The second agreement was an historic agreement with Japan in which, for the first time, the Japanese agreed to reduce their trade surplus with the United States and to be accountable in specific ways for reducing that trade surplus in specific areas. Again, that means more jobs for Americans.

Neither of these agreements would have been possible were it not for the progress we are making toward enacting the economic plan which reduces the deficit by $500 billion over the next 5 years. For 10 years American Presidents have gone to these meetings and been criticized because the United States would not assume any discipline over its budget. This is the first time leaders of other nations have complimented instead of criticized the United States. None of it would have happened had it not been for the Congress making progress on this plan.

Now, there is a great deal of misinformation in the minds of many Americans about what is actually in this plan, thanks largely to the rhetorical attacks on the plan by its opponents, most of them in the other party. I'd just like to point out five critical facts about this plan which, to me, make it fair and good for the people of the United States and the people of Wisconsin.

Number one, it has about $500 billion in deficit reduction locked in a trust fund so that over the next 5 years all the spending cuts and all the new taxes are saved for deficit reduction. It has a mechanism of enforcement so that if, because of economic developments, we miss the deficit reduction target in any given year, the President must come right back to the Congress and give adjusted suggestions for how to meet that target, and the Congress has to vote on them. The spending cuts have to equal or outweigh the tax increases. So that's the first thing, the $500 billion cut.

Secondly, for the first time in more than a decade, the plan asks the wealthiest Americans to pay their fair share. Thanks to the changes which have been made in the last couple of weeks in the area of more spending cuts, I can now say to you that the plan which comes out will have at least 70 percent of the new taxes paid for by people with incomes above $200,000. That's about the top 1.2 percent of the American people.

Thirdly, it is fair to working Americans, to the middle class. It asks people with incomes of between $30,000 and $180,000 in family incomes now to pay an energy tax which amounts to about $50 a year. That is about $1 a week for families of four with incomes in the $30,000 to $180,000 range. For working families with incomes below $30,000, there is no tax increase.

Fourth, the plan really supports economic growth. And this is very important. And this will be a matter of contention between the Senate and the House because the House plan has more incentives for economic growth. But I think they are very important: a new business capital gains tax, an expensing provision for small businesses which will give—and I want to say this very clearly so everyone understands it—which will give over 90 percent of the small businesses in America a tax break under this bill, not a tax increase but a tax break if they invest more money in their business.

And finally, the plan is fair to the elderly, to the middle class, to the working poor in contrast to the Republican alternatives which refuse to tax the wealthy but have less deficit reduction and take more out of the hides of people who are most vulnerable.

So I hope we can get the facts out. I hope it will pass. I think it will make a big difference. I know it will make a difference in terms of seizing control of our economic destiny and promoting economic growth for the United States. And so I wanted to give you in Wisconsin and I'll be giving people from other States a chance to ask me questions directly about this and other issues of concern to the folks back home.

Midwest Disaster Assistance

Q. Good afternoon, Mr. President. Thank you for being with us this afternoon. As you know, flooding continues to be a problem here in Wisconsin and throughout the Midwest. Tens of thousands of people have suffered some very real damages. And we're wondering what assurance you can give those people that they'll be receiving some real assistance from the Federal Government, and what form might that take, sir?

The President. Well, it will take several forms. First let me say that, as you know I think, I have made three trips to the Midwest since the flooding began and last Saturday met for about 2½ hours with the Governors of eight of the nine affected States, including Governor Thompson.

We have asked, last night actually, for another substantial increase in flood relief aid. The package that we're asking for the Congress to adopt is now up to about $2.9 billion. And let me just run through some of the kinds of relief available.

For individuals who have been thrown out

of work and who don't have enough money to live on—and there are many hundreds of them that are flooded out that badly in the Midwest—FEMA takes disaster applications and can provide cash funds for living expenses as well as emergency unemployment, even for self-employed people and other contractors who are not eligible for unemployment normally.

Secondly, for small businesses, they are available for small business disaster loans, and the SBA is working now with FEMA to handle a lot of those applications even over the phone. Of course, the agriculture programs are, I think, quite well-known by the farmers, and they understand them. There are some operational problems with those agriculture programs based on the way they were handled, I think, after Hurricane Andrew that we're trying to work out.

And finally, there will be some direct aid to communities who have been hurt, who have lost public facilities and roads and bridges and things of that kind. The Federal programs cannot and are not designed to absolutely make whole every loss from every individual business or community. But they will make a big difference. And I think that the general consensus is that our administration has been more aggressive and more coordinated and more prompt in dealing with this than has been the experience in the past. And we're going to continue to try to do that.

Defense Cuts

Q. Mr. President, I attended a make-believe budget-cutting public hearing Monday night in Madison in which some 80 Madison area citizens were asked to write their own Federal budget. Some of the trimmers favored President Bush's defense cuts because they dealt with some specific high-profile weapons: a cap on B-2 bombers, cancellation of the Seawolf submarine, and a new air defense system—forego a new air system. While your defense budget requests go far beyond the $97 billion that Mr. Bush recommended, I wonder if you could spell out some of the specific cuts that you propose to make in the defense budget.

The President. Yes, sir, I can. First of all, we kept the B-2 bombers at the level recommended last year, so that is something we did. The Seawolf program is phased out, and other weapons systems are scaled down, including Star Wars, rather dramatically. Over and above that, we plan to reduce the aggregate

size of the armed services by about 200,000 more than in the last Bush budget, and we asked the employees of the Department of Defense, both military and civilian, to take the same reductions in pay that other Federal employees are going to take.

Those are the three areas which we make up the basic difference between the budget we presented and the last budget presented by President Bush. Let me say, we do not reduce our presence in Asia at this time, and I do not think we should because of the ongoing controversy we're having over North Korea and whether they're going to withdraw from the regime which commits them never to develop nuclear weapons. Until that is resolved, I think we have to maintain a strong presence in Asia. But otherwise, we're having substantial cuts in troop levels in Europe and some in the United States.

Welfare Reform

Q. I'd like to ask you about welfare reform. When you were in Milwaukee on June 1st, you made a passing favorable reference to the notion of eliminating welfare benefits after 2 years, limiting the time on welfare to 2 years. It was something you had talked about in the campaign last fall. Now Governor Thompson of Wisconsin, a Republican as you know, has suggested a pilot program of that sort in Wisconsin, and he has asked for waivers from your Department of Health and Human Services. I have a twofold question: Are you in favor of the waiver to start the Wisconsin pilot program, and as a concept, do you really, Federally or in Wisconsin, intend to kick people off welfare after 2 years, even if they are able-bodied and refuse to work? If you do that, what happens to them?

The President. Let me answer the second question first. Yes, I want to end welfare as we know it, and if people are able-bodied, able to work and there's a job available for them, and they refuse to work, I think they should live with the consequences. I don't think many people will refuse to work. The evidence is that most people on welfare, once their children are taken care of, are eager to go to work if they have the skills necessary to succeed in the work force.

I want to back up in a minute and tell you the sequence of events that we intend to follow here to put us in a position to end welfare as we know it. But let me answer your specific question now on the Wisconsin program. I talked with Governor Thompson about this briefly, not when I saw him on Saturday but the last time I saw him when I was in Wisconsin. And I urged him to put the plan together and get it through and send it to us. And I assured him that we would give it quick consideration. I can't commit to support something the details of which I have not reviewed, but in general I've been very favorable to pilot projects in the welfare reform and in the health care reform area.

Now, let me back up very briefly and tell you what I think we have to do to end welfare as we know it, if I might. Number one, you've got to make work pay. That's one of the most important parts of this economic program. Under our economic program, we use something called the earned-income tax credit which basically is a tax credit which can even lead to a refund to people. If they work 40 hours a week and have children in the home, we don't believe people should live in poverty. This is a dramatic improvement in promoting work over welfare. So if the budget passes, you'll have a principle that has to be established: If you work 40 hours a week, you have children in the home, you won't be in poverty. Number two, we have to toughen child support enforcement dramatically. Wisconsin has done a lot of good work on that, and we're going to build on that and the work of other States to do that. Number three, we have to pass a health reform plan that guarantees that the children in this country will have health care. A lot of people don't leave welfare for work because they think their kids will lose their health care coverage. Number four, we've got to make sure we educate and train workers. And then, five, if we're going to call an end to welfare after 2 years, we have to know that there will be work available. So if there is not a private sector job we're going to have to offer work as an alternative to welfare. Those things will be done in order, and as they are done, we literally will change the whole focus of this social program from welfare to work, from dependence to independence.

NAFTA

Q. Mr. President, the North American Free Trade Agreement is on the minds of every union member. And Milwaukee has lost thousands of good-paying jobs to Mexico. Recently, the manufacturing policy project, which was funded by U.S. businesses, did a study that said Wisconsin can expect to lose 178,000 more manufacturing jobs. How do you reconcile these facts with your support of NAFTA, and what happens to these people?

The President. Well, first of all, I just don't agree that NAFTA is going to cost us a lot of jobs if we do it right. Secondly, if we don't conclude the trade agreement, anybody who wants to move their manufacturing facility to Mexico to get lower wages can do it now. There is absolutely no restriction at this moment on moving a plant to Mexico. The purpose of NAFTA is to lower Mexican and United States tariffs—the Mexican tariffs are even higher—so we can sell more products to Mexico from the United States.

And let me just make two points, if I might. Point number one, 5 years ago we had a $500 billion trade deficit with Mexico. Now we have a $6 billion trade surplus because we have lowered tariffs. So that even though we've lost jobs in America, we've gained more jobs than we've lost because our trade has gone from a deficit to a surplus position. Secondly, people are going to find out, who want to go to Mexico just for low wages, that good transportation, well-trained and skilled workers, and high productivity are more important. General Motors just the other day announced that they were going to close a plant in Mexico and move it back to the United States and put 1,000 Americans to work because they weren't having the success they needed in Mexico. When I was Governor of Arkansas, we had one or two small plants—I can't remember whether it was one or two—close down and do the same thing, because they'd had an unsuccessful move.

Now, there are some problems with this trade agreement which I am trying to fix right now through negotiations to get the Mexican Government to agree to higher labor standards, tougher environmental standards, and to work with us on dealing with these common problems, and a consequence if the standards they agree to are not observed. But my own view is that America has to have more exports in order to create more manufacturing jobs.

As I said, if we make this deal with the world trading powers to lower tariffs all across the world on manufacturing products, it will create U.S. manufacturing jobs. So my opinion is if we don't have NAFTA, people who want to chase low-wage jobs, will still move their jobs to Mexico, just like they're doing today. If we do have it, we'll create more jobs than we'll lose. And for those who lose their jobs, let me say, I do have a plan. I have a plan to improve education and training and community economic development, and that's a big part of this program. That's part of what I've been criticized for. While I have cut spending dramatically in some areas, I recommend spending more in education and training, on defense conversion and new technologies so we can deal with people who lose their jobs.

Economic Program

Q. Mr. President, thanks for making yourself available. As to why we're here, though, today, how worried are you about losing support in the Wisconsin congressional delegation for the deficit reduction package you're talking about? Is it Senator Kohl in the Senate, Representative Barca? Who are you trying to get us to jawbone, so to speak?

The President. Well, you don't have to jawbone anybody. I want the people of Wisconsin to know directly from me what I think is good about this program and why I think it's important. And I think it's support that I owe to any Member of Congress that I would ask to vote for this.

But let me just say, Senator Feingold has made it clear to me that he supports our objectives and in general that he is very supportive of the program. Senator Kohl has said he is generally supportive of the program, but is worried about the fuel tax at any level. And my view is that when you tell working families with incomes between $30,000 and $180,000 that you're asking them to pay $50 a year, but that 70 percent of this program will be paid for by people with incomes above $200,000 and that over half the money will come from spending cuts, that folks will think it's fair and will want to make a contribution to bringing this terrible deficit down.

Welfare Reform

Q. Mr. President, if I could, I'd like to return just a moment to a question that was asked earlier and drive a little closer to the answer, perhaps.

I had lunch today with a man from Milwaukee you've just hired to come into Washington to work with Donna Shalala. He has a lifetime of experience in community service work, and he said that he is concerned that in the process of welfare reform what's going to happen is 500,000 or so people are going to drop off the bottom of the page because they are not going to have jobs no matter what happens at the end of 2 years, they are just going to be out there. And I suggested to him, well, maybe they'll turn to crime or maybe they'll just quietly starve to death. And he said, "Well, I'll tell you they won't quietly starve to death." So just to reiterate a question asked earlier, what happens to those people who don't have jobs? You have said—if there aren't jobs for them, well, what happens to them then?

The President. I think we have to provide community service type jobs if there are no private sector jobs available in order to justify cutting off the benefits. I don't think you can do it in any other way. You can't tell people they have to work if there are no jobs. Once they get into the work force, then if they lose their jobs and get them back, they'll be like other people, they'll have access to unemployment. But for people who have not been in the work force, I think there has to be some sort of access to community service jobs if the private sector jobs aren't there.

Economic Program

Q. Mr. President, many of our readers are the people you are addressing, the middle class. But a good number of them are what many people call upper middle class, and it's a group that is—it's just not fashionable right now in Washington, or maybe among this group here, to speak in any way in favor of them. But they tell us in letters to the editor, in stories to reporters, that they are very concerned about, well, taxes.

Their point is this: They've put in the hours to get where they are now. They've worked the 70, 80, sometimes 90 hours a week. You understand those hours, sir. Why should they be singled out? And I don't know the ceiling you're putting on, your definition of upper middle class or wealthy. We're speaking about people who make maybe $90,000 to $100,000 combined, have a house, have a family, paying off the mortgages, paying off the cars and the bills and the property taxes which in this area are going up. Why should they be singled out after putting in those many hours for so many years to see it taken away so easily?

The President. First of all, if it's a family with a joint income of $100,000, they won't have an income tax increase. Under this plan they would pay the fuel tax, which will be about $50 a year for normal fuel usage for a family of four. The income taxes trigger in at adjusted gross income of roughly $180,000 per couple and about $40,000 less than that for individual. Taxable income is somewhat lower, but even taxable income for individuals is above $100,000 and about $140,000 per couple. But in terms of salary, net income, the way people think of their incomes, it's about $180,000 when the taxes trigger in.

Why should they pay? A lot of those people work hard and got themselves to a point of success. We do not seek to punish success, we just seek to balance the scales. If you go back through the 1980's you will see that what happened in the eighties was that middle class incomes—that is, people with incomes from, let's say, $20,000 to $90,000 or $70,000—basically were stagnant, but their taxes were raised at the national, State, and local level. Upper income people, who got most of the gains of the 1980's, actually had their taxes lowered by the National Government.

So I'm not trying to punish anybody, even people with incomes above $200,000 who will pay 70 percent of the cost of this program and virtually 100 percent of the income taxes. I'm not trying to punish them, I'm just trying to balance the scales to get a little back to where we were a few years ago when we were generating plenty of jobs and growing. No one seriously disputes the fact that a major cause of the Federal deficit being as big as it is, is that there was a huge cut in income taxes on upper income people, which has to be addressed if we're going to get this deficit down. Even then, I think those folks are entitled to know that there will be spending cuts at least equal to if not greater than the tax increases.

Let me make one last point. Since we started working to bring the deficit down, long-term interest rates have dropped. Alan Greenspan, the Republican Chairman of the Federal Reserve Board, has acknowledged that the primary reason that long-term interest rates have dropped is the administration's serious attempt to cut the deficit. And many of these same people have refinanced their homes or their business loans or taken advantage of low-interest rates in ways that will give them more gains

from lower interest rates than they will pay in higher taxes. And that's a very important point, I think, that has to be driven home.

Presidential Leadership

Q. Mr. President, rightly or wrongly, public opinion polls have suggested that a number of people see you as not being a strong leader. They also see your position on gays in the military as having been a bit of a compromise. Would you expect to continue to compromise on important issues in the future, or do you see yourself as becoming a stronger leader on those key issues?

The President. Let me tell you, I regret those opinion polls. I think they have something to do, frankly, with the way you folks discuss these issues. Now, let me just run through this. I am the first President in a decade who has had his budget considered seriously by Congress. After Ronald Reagan's first budget, every budget that he and George Bush presented was laughed off as a political document. Seventy-five percent of the Republicans in the House of Representatives—the Republicans in the House of Representatives—voted against the last Bush budget. This one is being taken seriously. I am the first President in a decade that was complimented, not criticized, at the recent meeting of the world's great industrial countries, because we're doing something serious about our economy. I immediately organized the G–7 nations to support Boris Yeltsin when he was in the ropes last spring. That's not a sign of weakness. And we had a major role in the preservation of democracy in Russia. We passed the family leave bill, the motor voter bill through Congress quickly. We have three major pieces of political reform moving through Congress, already passed one House: campaign finance reform, lobby reform, and the line-item veto. I don't think that is a sign of weakness.

When you live in a democratic society and you're elected President, you are not a dictator. The resolution we had on the gays in the military, which was worked out by Les Aspin from Wisconsin, was a slight compromise from my position in this way: If it were up to me alone, I would say that a person could acknowledge being gay openly, clearly, but say that he or she was completely conforming to the Military Code of Conduct and be able to serve. In this policy, if a person does that, that raises the presumption that the person intends to do something that the Code of Conduct forbids. But then the service man or woman is given the opportunity to demonstrate that he or she will abide by the code. That's the rule. The second thing this policy does, which goes well beyond anything I discussed in the campaign, is to provide very explicit, explicit, protections for privacy and associational rights by service members without regard to their sexual orientation, going well beyond anything I ever discussed in the election.

I am the first President who ever took on this issue. Is that a sign of weakness? It may be a sign of madness, sir, but it is not a sign of weakness. And I think that we need to get our heads on straight about what is strong and what is weak. When a President takes on tough issues, takes tough stands, tries to get things done in a democracy, you may not get 100 percent. Was I wrong to take 85? What would have happened if I had just put my campaign pledge into play? What would have happened?

You know and I know and Les Aspin will tell you, the United States Congress would immediately have reversed it. So I would have the great good fortune of being able to say I'm "Simon Pure," and the people in the military who are serving well and honorably who happen to be homosexual would not be one step further ahead than they were when I got elected. They're much better off today because we took an honorable compromise.

That's what democracy is about. Read the United States Constitution. It's about honorable compromise. And that is not weakness if you're making progress.

Q. Mr. President, thank you for answering questions from reporters from Wisconsin.

The President. Thank you.

NOTE: The President spoke at 5:05 p.m. via satellite from Room 459 of the Old Executive Office Building.

Interview With the Louisiana Media
July 20, 1993

The President. Good afternoon. I understand that I can't see you because you're having a rainstorm down there, and I'm sorry that we can't have a two-way, at least visual communication. But I'm glad that you can hear and see me.

First, let me thank you for giving me the opportunity to speak through you directly to the people of Louisiana. I want to say a few words in opening about the economic program that I have presented to Congress, which is now being debated between the Senate and the House. There are some differences between the two plans, but the essential features are common, and I'd like to review them and what they could mean to Louisiana.

First of all, the plan has $500 billion in deficit reduction over the next 5 years. That is equally divided between spending cuts and tax increases. It's in a trust fund so that the money cannot be squandered on anything else. And if we don't make our targets, the President has a legal obligation to come forward and do some more cutting to make sure we do bring this deficit down.

Secondly, the plan asks the wealthiest Americans, whose taxes went down as their incomes went up in the 1980's, to pay most of the load. And let me be quite specific. The income taxes of Americans do not go up until they have adjusted gross income of $180,000 per family, $140,000 per individual. That means that 70 percent of this tax load will be paid by people with incomes above $200,000, the top 1.2 percent of the American people.

Thirdly, the plan is fair to the middle class and to the working poor. I want to emphasize that. The fuel tax in the plan, now at about 4.3 cents, amounts to about a $50-a-year tax to a family of four with an income of $40,000 to $50,000. That's less than $1 a week directed and dedicated to bringing down your country's enormous deficit. For families with incomes of $30,000 or less—I think that's right at a majority in Louisiana—they will be held harmless or actually get a tax reduction from this plan.

Fourthly, the plan has important incentives for business growth: incentives for people to invest in new businesses and other small businesses; incentives for larger companies to buy new plants and equipment, to put people to work; incentives for research and development in new technologies to help to create new jobs for the 21st century. And perhaps most importantly, it doubles the expensing provision for small business, which means that 94 percent, let me say that again, 94 percent of the small businesses in the entire United States of America will not only get no income taxes increase from this plan but will be eligible for a tax break if they invest in their businesses.

Finally, unlike the Republican alternatives, this plan cuts the deficit more but does it in a way that is fairer to the elderly, to the working poor, and to the middle class. The Republican alternative cuts the deficit less but takes more out of the hides of the folks on Medicare, takes more from the veterans, takes more from agriculture, cuts things that have already been reduced dramatically.

So this plan, once the details are known, I think, clearly is good for America and good for Louisiana. It has already brought interest rates down dramatically. It is leading many, many people to refinance their homes and their cars and their businesses in ways that are putting money in Americans' pockets, not taking them out. And there's no question that without the progress this budget plan has made through the Congress, I would not have been able to lead an effort by the industrialized nations of the world in Tokyo to agree to reduce tariffs on manufactured products, to agree to reduce the Japanese trade imbalance with the United States in ways that will mean hundreds of thousands of manufacturing jobs to America.

So I believe if we can get the facts out there, I can persuade the Congress to adopt the plan, and we can put it behind us, seize control of our destiny, stop letting the deficit eat us alive, and start putting America back to work. That's the key thing.

Approval Ratings and Accomplishments

Q. Mr. President, recent polls nationally and here in Louisiana have indicated that a lot of Americans have already lost enthusiasm with your administration, a perception of indecisiveness if you will, a perception of someone who may be a little bit more tax and spend, the traditional liberal Democrat, than the moderate image he sold the American electorate. Why do you think you've suffered so much in the

public opinion arena in so short a period of time? And considering you've got Democratic majorities in both the House and Senate, Mr. Clinton, why do you think you've gotten so little accomplished in terms of what people expected of the Clinton era?

The President. Well, first of all, let me say I think the public opinion polls are obvious. And that's because the only news coverage we get out of this town is over the fight over taxes, so that the American people, literally by huge majorities, do not have any idea what is in this program. They don't know there's any deficit reduction. They are not aware that there are any spending cuts. They are certainly not aware that 70 percent of the new taxes fall on people with incomes above $200,000. In Louisiana, I'm certain they're not aware that families of incomes of $30,000 or less pay no tax and, in fact, many will get a tax break under this, and that all the working poor, people who work with children in the home still below the poverty line, will get a significant tax relief under this program. They don't know the facts because the only coverage is over where the fight is, and that's been over the taxes. So the Republicans can scream "tax and spend" and all this label stuff, and if the people don't have the facts before them, all they can do is operate on what they know.

Now, secondly, I just want to take issue with you. I, frankly, think that one of the reasons the American people are disappointed about—you said the slow pace of progress—is because they haven't been told the truth about that. Do you know that if the Congress passes this budget on or before August the 5th when they go on recess, it will be the fastest they have acted in a very long time?

And in terms of the difficulty I'm having getting this through, this is tough stuff. You've been sold syrup and sugar for years. But let me give you an example. Most of the Democrats voted for my program. In the last year of President Bush's administration, 75 percent of the Republicans in the House of Representatives—not the Democrats, the Republicans—voted against his budget. Why? Because no President has tried since 1981 to seriously engage the Congress in a budget that will turn the economic fortunes of the country around. Presidents don't want to be criticized for failing or for compromising, so they have played these political games, sent budgets up to the Hill that they knew had no chance of passing the Congress, and made speeches to the American people. I have gone to work.

Now, I ask you to compare what has actually been done in the first 6 months of this administration with what any previous administration has done in 6 months. We have put a serious budget on the table which will bring the deficit down and which has already brought interest rates down. We led an effort in the world's nations to save democracy in Russia, which will help America by enabling us to reduce defense and define new markets for our goods. We passed the family leave bill to protect families when their jobs require them to leave because they've got somebody sick in the family. We passed the motor voter bill, which will make it easier for people to register and vote. We have passed in one House of the Congress campaign finance reform, lobbying restrictions, and the line-item veto.

We are moving forward with a welfare reform proposal. We are moving forward with a national service plan, which I talked about repeatedly in Louisiana—it's going to be passed in one House this week, and it's going to be law very soon—which will open the doors of college education to millions and millions of young people who can't afford to go now with lower interest loans, and allow many of them to work that off with community service. Now, that is the record of this administration.

I just came back from the most successful meeting of the world's great industrial powers in years, because the United States, for the first time in 10 years, was not attacked at that meeting for its outrageous Government deficit. Instead we were complimented, and we got the other nations to agree to bring down tariffs and open up markets for American manufactured products, which means more jobs for Louisiana.

I would like for you to go back and analyze the first 6 months of the previous administrations and tell me who got more done in 6 months. If you can tell me, I'll be glad to hear it. If there isn't anybody you can find who's done more, then we need to examine why the American people don't know that.

Gridlock

Q. Mr. President, you came to Washington promising to get things moving, and you hit a brick wall of entrenched interests from all sides. Were you surprised by the intensity of the resistance? And what needs to be done so Government can respond quicker and better?

The President. Excuse me. My microphone fell.

Well, first of all, I want to say again, changes don't happen overnight. This country has been losing its economic position for 20 years. We've been with trickle-down economics for 12 years. It's been a great deal. The idea was: Give special interests and the wealthiest Americans whatever they want. Don't do too much to the middle class. Tell everybody what they want to hear, and hope nobody notices that we're running up a deficit that is keeping interest rates high, weakening the country, and not generating jobs. Now, that's been going on for a long time. So when you try to make tough decisions, it's not going to be easy to change.

I knew it would not be easy to change. No one can turn a country around overnight. I'm, frankly, reasonably pleased with the pace of change, but the one thing that has surprised me and deeply disappointed me is that the people in the other party have been so bitterly partisan about this. Many of them have come to me privately and said, "You're doing a good job. We agree with a lot of these things, but you know, our party just is going to oppose you." And so I'm hoping that we'll have more bipartisan support when we try to provide affordable health care to all American families and open the doors of college education than we have on this budget. And on welfare reform I think we'll get some Republican support.

Now, you asked me specifically what needs to be done. Congress needs to pass three bills that have only passed one House. One, campaign finance reform: Lower the costs of campaigns for Congress, reduce the influence of special interests through political action committees, open the airwaves to honest debate. Two, restrict the influence of lobbyists—do for people who lobby Congress what I've already done in my administration: Say that anybody who spends any money on a Member of Congress has to report what they spend and what it's for, eliminate the tax deduction for lobbying, and open the process more so that people know what is being done. The third thing that ought to be done is that the Senate should pass the modified line-item veto that the House has already passed, which gives the President the power to cut extra unnecessary spending.

Those three things would go a long way toward reforming the political process. I have already restricted by Executive order the ability of people in my administration to become lobbyists, especially those in high positions, to ever lobby for foreign governments. So if you deal with lobbyists, campaign finance, and the line-item veto, those things I think would help the system to move along faster. But keep in mind, any time you have to make tough decisions after people have been fed sugar for a long time, it's not going to be easy.

Energy Tax

Q. Mr. President, on the chance that congressional negotiators cannot agree on either a Btu tax or motor fuel tax, do you have any alternative measures that you would try to push to fill the resulting revenue gap?

The President. Well, let me say right now what I want to do is to stick with my program, and that's what I expect to do to the end. I expect to pass this program. I don't think that there will be a Btu tax, although the Btu tax alternative that the Secretary of the Treasury had ready to go would have exempted everything that the people in Louisiana I talked to were concerned about, agriculture, industry. Nonetheless, I think that that is unlikely. I think we'll be much closer to the fuel option that the Senate adopted.

But as I said, I think if we put a ceiling of $50 a year on it for the average family of four, that is, somebody with an income of $40,000 to $50,000, and if we hold working families under $30,000 a year harmless, and we don't kick the income taxes in on families with incomes of less than $180,000 or individuals under $140,000, I think that's pretty fair. And I think, again, it's a question of perception over reality. If we can cut through all this heavy rhetoric fog, I think we can get something done.

Now, let me just mention one other thing. I want to say again, over the previous budget adopted by President Bush and the Congress, there are $250 billion in spending cuts, 100 cuts of over $100 million apiece, over 200 specific ones. When my bill came up in the Senate Finance Committee, the Republicans in the Senate Finance Committee offered all kinds of arguments about why we should cut taxes, mostly on the wealthy. They had a chance to say, "Well, we're for spending cuts." You know, that's what they've been saying: "The President wants to raise taxes; we're for spending cuts." Do you

know how many spending cuts were offered by the Republicans in the Senate Finance Committee? Zero. Not one. Not one. And the spending cuts put in their bill in the Senate included over $60 billion of unspecified we'll-figure-it-out-later cuts. So that we are the ones who are cutting spending. But I do think it is reasonable to ask people who are going to benefit from lower interest rates and more jobs to pay something that amounts to less than $1 a week to help to bring this deficit down.

Economic Program

Q. Mr. President, why proceed with higher consumer taxes in your deficit reduction package when the growth of the economy appears to be flattening out? Won't that worsen things?

The President. I think that the worst thing that could happen that could really flatten this economy is if we weaken the deficit reduction package and interest rates went back up. There is a general consensus, even reinforced by Alan Greenspan, the Republican who heads the Federal Reserve Board, that the efforts we have made to bring this deficit down are mostly responsible for bringing long-term interest rates down. There are lots of folks in Louisiana who will be listening to this or who will read what you say who have refinanced their homes or refinanced their business loans or gotten lower interest car loans or consumer loans since the first of the year because interest rates are at a 20-year low. If we were to dramatically reduce the amount of deficit reduction, it would be fine if it had no other economic impact, but it will have an economic impact. It will lead to higher interest rates. And if the interest rates go back up, then people will lose more on interest rates than they would pay on this modest fuel tax.

Let me say one other thing: We want to add something to what the Senate did, though. We want to put back some incentives for people to pay lower taxes if they invest in jobs and growth. And this is a very important point. A lot of these taxes can be avoided by people if they invest in jobs and growth. That is, if you increase the small business expensing provision, if you have opportunities for big companies to invest in new plant and equipment, if you have opportunities for individuals to put their savings into new businesses, and if you don't tax activities of that kind, in fact, you give a big tax break to it, then that will mean that people will say, "Hey, I don't have to pay more taxes if I invest in things that will generate jobs for people in my State and my country." That is the really key thing. We've got to get the job incentives that I originally proposed back into the final bill. And if we do, most folks are going to come out well ahead and this economy is going to grow more.

Q. Hi, Mr. President. Could you repeat again exactly how your plan will affect lower income families, particularly those who aren't working now? Will enough jobs be created for them to get into the job market, have more money to spend in the economy?

The President. Absolutely. There are two kinds of low-income people in the economy. There are those that are working and those that aren't. Believe it or not, about 18 percent of all working people are still below the Federal poverty line. And I want to emphasize how they will both be affected.

Number one, people who are working but are still in poverty will benefit from a change in this law called the earned-income tax credit. It will be increased to the point that we'll be able to say to a working person in a family of four, let's say, that if you work for a living and you have children in your home and you're still in poverty, you will get a tax credit, a refundable tax credit from the Federal Government which will lift you out of poverty. That will mean more money in their pockets, they'll spend more, they'll boost the consumer economy, and that will be very good. It will also be a real incentive for people to move from welfare to work.

For people on welfare, that is, people who want to work but aren't working or people on unemployment, we estimate that this plan will create another 89,000 jobs in Louisiana, which will mean more jobs for unemployed people. For people on welfare, we will have a welfare reform program which will emphasize education and training and will eventually require people who can work to take jobs instead of staying on welfare. So this whole program is designed to help low income people whether they're working or not working. But it's important, especially in a place like Louisiana or my home State to your north, Arkansas, to note that most low income people work.

The last point I want to make is people with family incomes under $30,000 are held harmless in this program because they'll be eligible for an income tax cut to offset the gas tax increase. So most people in Louisiana will come out the same or ahead on the tax side, but they'll win big time when we reduce the deficit, invest some more in education and training, in jobs and new technologies, and grow this economy.

Energy Tax

Q. Mr. President, the Btu tax is something that everybody is watching very closely here. You read one day that the thing's dead and one day that it's getting resurrected. What is the status with the Btu tax at this point?

The President. I think there is virtually no chance that the committee will report out a Btu tax. Let me back up and say everyone had decided earlier that the tax ought to be modified so as not to affect any kind of manufacturing and agricultural operation. But I think now that is gone, basically because of the work that Senator Breaux did in the Senate Finance Committee in his efforts to try to have a different sort of tax that was more focused on transportation. So that's where we are now.

I think there is virtually no chance that the transportation tax will be raised much above what would be—it may be raised a tad above where it is now in the Senate. But as I said, I think the goal we're all shooting for is about a $50 bill for a family with an income of between $40,000 and $50,000 a year. So $50 a year would be about a buck a week. I think that's about what you're looking at.

Louisiana Democratic Party

Q. Mr. President, one question I would like to ask is what is your opinion of the Louisiana Democrats here who supported you so wholeheartedly during your Presidential election, John Breaux and J. Bennett Johnston, yet those individuals who, in essence, left the flock of the Democratic Party when it came time to the energy bill that was in your package that you brought before the Congress. I'd like to know what you think of the Democratic Party here in Louisiana. And a followup question, if I may: Is this perhaps the reason why we haven't seen any of Louisiana natives appointed to high positions in your administration?

The President. Well, the answer to the second question is no. And I expect you will see some distinguished Louisianians appointed before long. That has nothing to do with it.

Let me say first, Senator Breaux, in my judgment, played a very constructive role in this whole process. He wanted to pass a budget that was fair to Louisiana and also fair to the United States. And he voted for the passage of the Senate budget. So I have absolutely nothing negative to say about him. You've got to give him credit for trying to work out a program that he thought was better for Louisiana than the original proposal I had made but would also meet our objectives. And the budget that he worked on and that he voted for plainly does that.

Senator Johnston was very candid. You know, he went through a tough campaign, and he's very worried about the ability of the facts of this budget to be misrepresented. I mean, John Breaux told me the other day that he cannot believe that people in Louisiana have bought all the negative rhetoric about the budget when most Louisianians either would get no tax increase or would actually get a tax decrease because this program emphasizes help to the working poor and the small businesses. Let me just give you one example, once again. Ninety-four percent of the small businesses in the United States will not have income tax increase under this plan. And every one of them will be eligible for a tax cut if they invest more money in their own business. Now, that is a stunning statistic. I'll bet you not 5 percent of the people in Louisiana know that. Why? Because it hasn't been a source of controversy.

So I think Senator Johnston, if he knew for sure that the people in Louisiana knew what was in this program, would feel more comfortable about voting for it. He's getting a lot of negative feedback. I understand that. But the facts are that this is a very good program for Louisiana and Louisianians, and I don't think people know the facts. We find that over and over again, that not since I laid out the program on February 17th, when over 60 percent of the American people said they were for it, had they been given the details of the program. All they have heard since February the 17th is a endless litany on the part of people who are against it, largely Republicans, about taxes that they say are damaging to the people and to the economy. If you look at the facts, it's good for Louisiana, and it will be good for the future of the State.

Super Collider

Q. Mr. President, in my neck of the woods, the superconducting super collider project would mean more than 1,000 jobs in our immediate vicinity. Yet, on the two most recent occasions, the Senate has all but killed the matter. Are you still supporting it, number one? And number two, do you believe it's going to come out of Washington intact as proposed now?

The President. Yes, I do support it, and I support it strongly. And I'm very glad you asked me about it. The superconducting super collider was defeated soundly in the House, and its fate is in danger in the Senate. But I want you to know why. You know, it's been in some trouble in the last few years, but I want you to know why. You know, most of the project is in Texas. The people of Texas just voted in the Senate race overwhelmingly for a new Senator who basically said that the issue was "spending, stupid," and accused the Congress of making no spending cuts. When the House of Representatives was voting just a couple of weeks ago on the superconducting super collider, which benefits overwhelmingly the State of Texas, the two United States Senators from Texas were outside on the steps with Ross Perot telling the House they ought to cut spending and attacking them for not doing it. In fact, it wasn't true. We've cut spending $250 billion below the last Bush budget. We've cut over 100 things over $100 million apiece.

But I, frankly, think a lot of people got sick and tired of hearing that. And I hate to say it, because I am for the superconducting super collider. It is a good science project. It is good for America's high-tech employment. It is good for our future. And I strongly support it. But it is difficult to get these other Members of Congress from other States that do not benefit from it to vote for it when the people from the States that do benefit from it will not stand up and take the same kind of votes, and instead engage in rhetoric which is simply not true.

Now, if you want to know the truth, that's why it's in so much trouble up here. I hope I can save it. I'm doing what I can to save it. I'll keep doing what I can to save it. But it would certainly help if the people who are going to benefit immediately from it would stop saying things which drive the rest of the Congress up the wall, because they're not true.

Q. Mr. President, thank you for being with us.

The President. Thank you. I've enjoyed it.

NOTE: The President spoke at 5:30 p.m. via satellite from Room 459 of the Old Executive Office Building. A tape was not available for verification of the content of these remarks.

Statement on the Anniversary of the Arrest of Aung San Suu Kyi of Burma
July 20, 1993

Today, July 20, marks the 4th anniversary of the arrest and detention of Aung San Suu Kyi, the courageous Burmese opposition leader and Nobel Peace Prize laureate. The overwhelming mandate won by her party in the 1990 elections remains unfulfilled. This is a tragedy for Burma and a cause for outrage in the international community.

Despite her isolation, Aung San Suu Kyi is not forgotten. An authentic voice of Burmese democracy, she remains a symbol of hope to the people of her country who yearn for rep-

resentative government and an inspiration to all who are striving for freedom and democracy elsewhere in Asia and throughout the world.

Today I renew my call to Burma's military rulers to release unconditionally Aung San Suu Kyi and all other prisoners of conscience, to respect the results of the 1990 elections, and to undertake genuine democratic reforms. History is on the side of freedom throughout the world, and I remain confident that the aspirations of all Burmese people for basic human rights and representative government will ultimately be fulfilled.

Message to the Congress Transmitting the Notice on Continuation of Iraqi Emergency
July 20, 1993

To the Congress of the United States:

Section 202(d) of the National Emergencies Act (50 U.S.C. 1622(d)) provides for the automatic termination of a national emergency unless, prior to the anniversary date of its declaration, the President publishes in the *Federal Register* and transmits to the Congress a notice stating that the emergency is to continue in effect beyond the anniversary date. In accordance with this provision, I have sent the enclosed notice, stating that the Iraqi emergency is to continue in effect beyond August 2, 1993, to the *Federal Register* for publication.

The crisis between the United States and Iraq that led to the declaration on August 2, 1990, of a national emergency has not been resolved.

The Government of Iraq continues to engage in activities inimical to stability in the Middle East and hostile to U.S. interests in the region. Such Iraqi actions pose a continuing unusual and extraordinary threat to the national security and vital foreign policy interests of the United States. For these reasons, I have determined that it is necessary to maintain in force the broad authorities necessary to apply economic pressure to the Government of Iraq.

WILLIAM J. CLINTON

The White House,
July 20, 1993.

NOTE: The notice is listed in Appendix D at the end of this volume.

Message to the Congress Transmitting a Report on Most-Favored-Nation Trade Status for Bulgaria
July 20, 1993

To the Congress of the United States:

On June 3, 1993, I determined and reported to the Congress that Bulgaria is in full compliance with emigration criteria of the Jackson-Vanik amendment to, and Section 409 of, the Trade Act of 1974. This determination allowed for the continuation of most favored nation (MFN) status for Bulgaria without the requirement of an annual waiver.

As required by law, I am submitting an updated formal Report to Congress concerning emigration laws and policies of the Republic of Bulgaria. You will find that the report indicates continued Bulgarian compliance with U.S. and international standards in the areas of emigration and human rights policy.

The Administration intends to propose legislation, which would let me terminate the application of Title IV of the Trade Act of 1974 to Bulgaria.

WILLIAM J. CLINTON

The White House,
July 20, 1993.

Message to the Senate Transmitting the Amendment to the Montreal Protocol on Ozone-Depleting Substances
July 20, 1993

To the Senate of the United States:

I transmit herewith, for the advice and consent of the Senate to ratification, the Amendment to the Montreal Protocol on Substances That Deplete the Ozone Layer ("Montreal Protocol"), adopted at Copenhagen on November 23–25, 1992, by the Fourth Meeting of the Parties to the Montreal Protocol. I am also enclosing, for the information of the Senate: the adjustments, also adopted November 23–25, 1992, that accelerate the respective phaseout schedules for substances already controlled under the Protocol (chlorofluorocarbons (CFCs), halons, other fully halogenated CFCs, methyl chloroform, and carbon tetrachloride); and the report of the Department of State.

The principal feature of the Amendment that was negotiated under the auspices of the United Nations Environment Program (UNEP), is the addition of new controlled substances, namely hydrochlorofluorocarbons (HCFCs), hydrobromofluorocarbons (HBFCs), and methyl bromide. The Amendment, coupled with the adjustments, will constitute a major step forward in protecting public health and the environment from potential adverse effects of stratospheric ozone depletion.

The Amendment will enter into force on January 1, 1994, provided that 20 Parties to the Montreal Protocol have deposited their instruments of ratification, acceptance, or approval. Early ratification by the United States is important to demonstrate to the rest of the world our commitment to protection and preservation of the stratospheric ozone layer and will encourage the wide participation necessary for full realization of the Amendment's goals.

I recommend that the Senate give early and favorable consideration to the Amendment and give its advice and consent to ratification.

WILLIAM J. CLINTON

The White House,
July 20, 1993.

Message to the Congress Transmitting the 1990 Report of the Commodity Credit Corporation
July 20, 1993

To the Congress of the United States:

In accordance with the provisions of section 13, Public Law 806, 80th Congress (15 U.S.C. 714k), I transmit herewith the report of the Commodity Credit Corporation for fiscal year 1990.

WILLIAM J. CLINTON

The White House,
July 20, 1993.

Message to the Congress Transmitting the 1991 Report of the Commodity Credit Corporation
July 20, 1993

To the Congress of the United States:

In accordance with the provisions of section 13, Public Law 806, 80th Congress (15 U.S.C. 714k), I transmit herewith the report of the Commodity Credit Corporation for fiscal year 1991.

WILLIAM J. CLINTON

The White House,
July 20, 1993.

Interview With Larry King
July 20, 1993

The Presidency

Mr. King. Good evening. Back in Louisville, about 3 days before the election, President Clinton said on this program, "I'll come on every 6 months." This is the 6-month anniversary. The timing is perfect. Tonight is 6 months in office for Clinton-Gore.

Before we get into some—what we'll do is cover some current issues, talk about the budget, take calls. OK? But first, there's no way you could plan for this job, so what about it surprises you the most?

The President. It's hard to say. I've learned a lot in the last 6 months, and as much as I have followed this over 20 years, I think there are some things that you could not have anticipated. I think the thing that has surprised me most is how difficult it is, even for the President, if you're going to take on big changes and try to make big things happen, to really keep communicating exactly what you're about to the American people.

Mr. King. And why is that hard?

The President. I think because there's so much else in the atmosphere, first; and secondly, because when you do something like this big economic plan we're pushing, only the controversy is newsworthy at a time when there's so much else to cover. So I'm trying always to remind people, look, we've got as many spending cuts, or more, than tax increases; that the upper income people, people over $200,000, are paying 70 percent of the burden, and that the middle class is paying very little; the working poor are paying nothing. All the details I try to get into.

But it's very difficult. And we found that the American people knew the most on February 17th, the night I announced the plan and went through it point by point, and that since then, the sort of yelling and rhetoric and screaming and back and forth, that I have lost the ability to make sure everybody knows the things I want them to know. And I feel very badly about that.

Mr. King. Is that everybody's fault? I mean,

is it your fault? Media fault?

The President. I think certainly so. I mean, I'm not trying to shift responsibility away from myself. But you asked me. That's been a real surprise to me because when I was a Governor in a smaller place where lots of people knew me, even if I were doing something that was quite unpopular with the media, say, and they were criticizing me, I could always get my side out there, my points. The essential facts would be out there. And that, to me, has been the most frustrating thing.

And also when you're President, you have to make a lot of tough decisions. You just have to keep lining them up and making them, whether it's base closings or the very difficult problems in the Pacific Northwest with the forests or the whole litany of things that we've done here: the POW/MIA issue and how we're going to deal with Vietnam, the FBI, the gays in the military, you name it. And they keep coming in quick succession. You can't just say, "Okay, stop the world. I'm going to just work on this. I'm not going to make these other decisions." You have to keep going.

Mr. King. We were talking before we went on about Elvis Presley and isolation. And I was saying that I thought he had a more isolated life than you do. But this is an isolated life in here, isn't it?

The President. It can be very isolating.

Mr. King. Do you have to fight it?

The President. I fight it all the time. And it can be isolating for two reasons. One is there is so much to do that you have to be very disciplined about your time. And I think the more I've been in this office, the more conscious I've become of it and, I think, the more disciplined I've become about my time. But discipline means deciding things you won't do, people you won't see, calls you won't make.

The second problem is, frankly, the security problem. The——

Mr. King. How so?

The President. Well, I think the Secret Service do a very, very good job. But if your job is to keep the President from being harmed in a world full of people who may have some reason to do it, may have the means to do it, obviously the best thing would be if you put him in a bulletproof room and walked out, if you see what I mean.

Mr. King. You couldn't stand that.

The President. No, I couldn't stand that. So

they do a terrific job. But we've worked out our accommodations so that I can at least run every day. I run different routes, and we do different things. And I try to get out and see the people when I can.

Mr. King. Is it hard to understand their job for you?

The President. It's much easier now. I really respect them; they've got a very tough job. And I make it harder because I'm a real people person, you know. I like to be out there. But I think it's an important job. But if you don't spend some time with just ordinary people who tell you what they think, hey, you almost forget how to hear and how to listen and how to speak and the way that most people live.

Mr. King. By the way, have you seen "In the Line of Fire"?

The President. Yes, I watched it last night.

Mr. King. What did you think?

The President. I thought Eastwood was terrific. I thought he was good in "Unforgiven." I think he's good in this. I think he's making the best movies he's ever made.

Mr. King. Did you like the movie?

The President. I liked the movie very much.

Mr. King. Was it realistic?

The President. I think it was as realistic as it could be and still be a real rip-roaring thriller, you know. [*Laughter*]

Homosexuals in the Military

Mr. King. We helped their business a lot. Let's touch some other bases. Okay. First, today Secretary of Defense Aspin appears with what looked like the entire military in the world before Senator Nunn's committee. And Senator Nunn finishes by saying he still wants to go to Congress, but he's inclined to support it. Is this a plus for you today?

The President. I think it is a plus. The Joint Chiefs came a long way on this policy from where they were back in January when we talked.

Mr. King. When they were almost totally against it, period.

The President. Completely against changing it at all; grudgingly said, "Well, we'll stop asking," and none of the things that were in this policy except for that. And I commend them. They really tried hard to come to grips with this. And they know that there are and always have been homosexuals in the service who served with real distinction. They and the Secretary of Defense deserve a lot of credit. But also, frankly, the people who argued for an even broader policy deserve a lot of credit: the Campaign for Military Service, Congressman Studds, Congressman Frank. They worked hard to try to come to grips with this. I don't think anyone was fully satisfied with the result, but I believe it's the best we can do right now.

Mr. King. Were you in a no-win?

The President. Well, I don't know. I don't view it that way. It depends on what the standard is. I was in a no-win if the only way I win is to do exactly what I think is right and——

Mr. King. Which would have been, sign them and let them in, right?

The President. Yes. But I think it's very important when you hear the criticism of it from the left, if you will. What I said was that I thought that status should be the judge—should not be the judge. It ought to be conduct, not your orientation. That's what the policy is now. I further said that I thought a person ought to be able to say, "I'm gay." And as long as they didn't do anything that violated the rules, they should be able to stay.

Mr. King. That's now true.

The President. That's only true in a restricted way. Now if you say it, it creates a presumption that you're going to do something wrong while you're in the military, but you are given the opportunity to present evidence that you won't, to convince, in effect, your commander that you will observe the rules. But I never promised to change the rules of conduct. That's in the Uniform Code of Military Justice. That's the way it is.

Now, to be fair to the Joint Chiefs, they agreed to go further on matters of privacy and association than I ever discussed in the campaign. So this provides dramatically increased protection and a range of privacy for present and future soldiers who happen to be homosexuals but happen to be good military people.

Mr. King. So in other words, you filled your promise.

The President. I did, except for the fact that we were not able to do precisely what I wanted, which was to give people the freedom to acknowledge their sexual orientation as long as they were following the rules of conduct. Today if you do that, it can get you in trouble, but you have the option to convince your commander that you really are following the rules. So I don't think it goes quite as far as I wanted

on statements. On the other hand, it goes quite a bit further to protect private conduct on the rules of investigation than I anticipated.

Mr. King. What do you make of Senator Nunn in all of this?

The President. I think first of all, he doesn't agree with my position, but I think he's worked hard, too, to try to come to grips with the reality of this, to open his mind and heart to the arguments on both sides. And I think he feels a special stewardship for the military. He's been chairman of the Armed Services Committee for a long time. He wants to make sure that if this is going to be the policy and he's going to support it, that it is legally defensible. And I think he's doing what he thinks is his job.

Mr. King. Do you think it will pass in the Senate?

The President. I do. I think if I had done what I wanted to do, the Senate and the House would have reversed it.

Reaction to Criticism

Mr. King. How do you take—before we take a break, and then we're going to get to the economy—bashing? You know, the heat that a President takes, and you've been taking a lot of it. How do you deal with that?

The President. Well, it's all part of it.

Mr. King. It rolls off you?

The President. Most of it rolls off of me; not all of it. If I think something is particularly unfair—the only thing that really bothers me, if you want to know the truth, is when I think that the bashing is in some area that prevents the American people from focusing on what we're doing about the things they care about that are most important, or if it undermines my ability to get things done.

The criticism is a part of the job, and, frankly—you know Benjamin Franklin said a long time ago, "Our critics can be our friends, for they show us our faults." Sometimes our critics show us our faults, and I try to listen and learn from my critics. But if I think they're diverting the attention of the American people from the real issues or the whole thing is undermining my ability to do what I was elected to do, that bothers me. But just to be criticized, shoot, that's part of it.

[*At this point, the stations took a commercial break.*]

Midwest Disaster Assistance

Mr. King. We're back with President Clinton. A couple of other bases, then the economy. Where do you get your money for the floods? Where does that come from?

The President. It comes from emergency appropriations. That is, we just add it to our spending this year. That's the way we've traditionally handled emergencies in America. And this year, thankfully, our deficit is well down because the interest rates have come down so much that we expect a big drop in the deficit over and above what we thought it would be.

Mr. King. So it's going to be $2.5 billion almost in some States——

The President. Well, we have upped our request to almost $3 billion now, and it may have to be revised upward again. Keep in mind, we can't hold harmless everybody from every loss, but there are programs to help businesses, farms, communities, and individuals who are out of work and who have no means of support.

Mr. King. Can you waive the State matching funds?

The President. I can do it. I can waive it, or we can write it down some.

Mr. King. What are you going to do?

The President. It depends on what the facts of each State are, how much problem they've got, how much of a burden it would be.

Mr. King. It'll be State by State?

The President. Yes, we'll have to look at it on a State-by-State basis, I think. I think that's the only fair way to do it.

FBI Director

Mr. King. Was it hard to fire Mr. Sessions?

The President. It was not hard, but it was sad for me. I admire the FBI greatly. I had a lot of contact with former FBI officers, had several of them in my administration. My criminal justice adviser was once the number two man in the FBI. My chief of staff for some time was a retired FBI agent. I love the FBI, and I hated to be the first President ever to have to fire a Director. But he said that that's the way he wanted it. He refused to resign, and I felt I had no choice.

I do think that Louis Freeh, the Federal judge whom I appointed today, will be a sterling FBI Director.

Mr. King. The word is, this guy, where's he been? This guy is, like, flawless.

The President. Well, he's an amazing man.

I mean, he grew up in a working-class family in Jersey City. He married a wonderful girl from Pittsburgh, whose dad was a steel worker. He worked his way through law school. He's my kind of guy, you know, just from the heartland.

Mr. King. That "flawless" is the quote from the guy who did the investigation.

The President. Absolutely. Well, then he was a great FBI agent, and then he was a prosecutor. He did the Pizza Connection case which was then the biggest heroin ring ever broken in the United States. He investigated a seafront corruption and brought indictments against 125 people. And then that awful mail bombing— two murders in the South, the Federal judge, the civil rights leader—he broke that case when people thought it could never be broken, and then he prosecuted it himself. He has really been an amazing success, and as you know, President Bush made him a Federal judge. And I think it's really a testimony to his character that he was willing to leave a lifetime job to be Director of the FBI, because he knew the Agency needed him.

Mr. King. He's also very big in the area of civil rights, is he not?

The President. That's right. That was a big thing with me. I wanted somebody who was tough on crime, but who knew the FBI had to bring in more women and minorities. They've been behind on that. And they're moving, and I want to give Judge Sessions credit for that. He did a good job on that, trying to open the Bureau, and Judge Freeh said he'd continue it.

Supreme Court Nominee

Mr. King. Do you expect Judge Ginsburg to be approved easily?

The President. Yes. I'm very proud of her, and she did real well today, I think. She's an extraordinary woman, as a real pioneer in women's rights, but also, I think, has been a judge in the best sense. She's very hard to categorize as liberal or conservative, but she'll take a tough decision when she thinks it's right.

Mr. King. On your key issue, though, which you said in the campaign, of freedom of choice, you think she'll come through?

The President. Yes. Well, she's got a real record of statement there. I didn't give her any kind of litmus test in the interview; I didn't think it was right.

Mr. King. You didn't?

The President. No. But I was familiar enough with her rulings and her speeches and her statements to know how she felt about that issue.

Surgeon General Nominee

Mr. King. And Dr. Elders—standing with her?

The President. Absolutely.

Mr. King. Were you at all dismayed by some of the things she said, "enemy of the fetus" and——

The President. Well, she's a very passionate woman. But I think you have to understand where she came from. I mean, Joycelyn Elders grew up as one of seven children in a cotton field in South Arkansas. She came from nowhere, economically anyway. Her brothers and sisters worked hard to help her get through medical school. She married a man who later became the most successful high school basketball coach in our State, very much a beloved man. And she was a doctor, a professor in the medical school when I finally, after three times, talked her into becoming the health department director.

And she said, "What do you want me to do?" I said, "I want you to fight teen pregnancy, I want you to fight AIDS, I want you to do something about environmental health, and I want us to get infant mortality down." And she found that her passion, in effect, drove her. I mean, she's a very passionate woman. And sometimes she says things in stark and blunt terms that make people draw up. But I think it's fair to say that in our State, which is a pretty old-fashioned, conservative place, she was very popular because people believed she was fighting for children, she was fighting to reduce infant mortality, she was fighting to reduce teen pregnancy. She was not pro-abortion. And, as a matter of fact, in many years I was Governor, the number of abortions performed dropped over the previous years.

Mr. King. So you're not—are you surprised that the far right has kind of taken off on her?

The President. No, because she is a lightning rod. They sort of took off on her in Arkansas for a while. But in the end she prevailed because people believed she cared about people. She was trying to save these kids from having babies. She was trying to reduce the infant mortality rate. She was trying to force people to do things—to change their behavior so AIDS wouldn't be communicated.

Mr. King. Will she prevail here, too? Will she be confirmed?

The President. I think she's an extraordinary woman. I'll be very surprised if she's not confirmed.

Representative Dan Rostenkowski

Mr. King. Dan Rostenkowski gets into trouble on the eve of maybe the most important time for him in your administration, because he's the spear carrier for the House side for the economic plan. How do you feel about that? What happens if he is indicted? That's a fair question because there's the possibility he could be indicted.

The President. Well, first, about that, of course, I can't comment. I'm not involved, and I shouldn't be, and I can't comment. I can only tell you that I've worked very closely with him and with Senator Moynihan. And he was here today continuing to work. I think, like every other American, he should be given the presumption of innocence.

Mr. King. But what happens if this——

The President. But all I can tell you is his backbone has been a mile wide and awful stiff in this whole thing. He's been a major force in pushing for changes that will finally get this deficit under control and help us to turn our economy around. And I'm going to keep working with him as long as he's here.

Mr. King. Have you asked him about this incident at the post office?

The President. No.

Mr. King. If something were to happen, do you have another point man in mind? I mean, will this hurt the chances of a compromise if Rostenkowski's stature is limited?

The President. Well, I don't even know how to comment on that. All I can tell you is that if he keeps working at it like he has, he's going to make a positive difference.

Mr. King. We'll be right back with President Clinton.

[The stations took a commercial break.]

Mr. King. Our guest is President Clinton. We're in the Library. We're ready to go to your phone calls. We ask that you get right to the point so we can reach as many people as possible.

Orlando, Florida, hello.

Defense Base Closings

[*A participant asked why the Orlando Training Center was selected for closure.*]

The President. I understand. Let me say, first of all, I think it is a good training center. For all of our listeners, the Orlando Training Center in Florida was one of the bases recommended by the Joint Chiefs of Staff and by the Secretary of Defense for the base closing, and the Commission voted to do that, to close the Orlando Center.

One of the biggest problems when you close a big military base is that many military bases have people retired around them who used to be in the military who use the medical facilities, and therefore, in the aftermath, that's often one of the toughest issues.

Let me answer those two things separately, if I might. First of all, I can't answer why the Orlando Training Center was picked by the Joint Chiefs. That process began before I became President. They sent the recommendation to the Secretary of Defense, who sent it to the Base Closing Commission. They thought that it should be closed, and they approved it. They sent the whole list to me, and I either had to sign on or off. And I concluded that I had no basis to reject the whole package, so I approved it, and it went to the Congress.

Now, let me make just one important point about that. It's very tough when you close these bases. I know it. But we have taken the military down from about 2.5 million people, going down toward 1.6, then 1.5, then 1.4. You can't reduce the military by 40 percent and only reduce the base structure by nine. Most of the bases that are recommended for closure are in Europe, some in the United States. But we have to reduce the base structure because otherwise we won't have enough money to train the personnel and to keep developing the smart weapons and the important technology that keep our people the best fighting force in the world and keep them safe.

Now secondly, let me just say on the health issue, when the First Lady agreed to take up the health issue and her task force began to work, one of the things I asked her to do is to look into health care for military retirees around military bases and look into those facilities. That is one of the things that that task force has done. They are looking at those facilities, asking: Can they be open, can they be

reopened, should they be reopened, should they be military facilities, should they be available for military and civilian personnel, what's going to happen in terms of the availability of health care? So that's something that the commission is looking on, and I expect that I'll get some recommendations on that that we'll know about pretty soon when we announce the health care plan.

Mr. King. To St. Louis, Missouri, with President Clinton. Hello.

National Lottery

[*A participant asked if the President had considered a national lottery to reduce the deficit.*]

Mr. King. It's been proposed for years.

The President. Yes. Let me say, it has been proposed, a national lottery to reduce the deficit. And every time I have seen anybody talk about it, the conclusion has been that we probably shouldn't do it for two reasons. Number one, it would probably not raise an enormous amount of money. And number two, it might dramatically eat into the proceeds that are now going to the States who have lotteries. Most States have lotteries now, and that money generally goes to the education of our children or, in the case of Pennsylvania, the care of elderly citizens. And the Federal Government, I think, would get a lot of opposition from the States if it appeared that we were going to take away their efforts to educate people to pay down the debt.

I have to say, finally, I personally have always had some reservation about the lotteries because, disproportionately, the people who play them tend to be on the lower income scale. But even if you put that to the side, for the other two reasons I think it is probably not a very good idea.

Mr. King. It is voluntary taxation.

The President. It is absolutely voluntary. And that's the best argument for it. The best argument for it is it's absolutely voluntary. And if it raised $1 billion, it's $1 billion we wouldn't have otherwise. So there are some arguments for it. But the two I mention are the reasons I think that it's never been adopted.

Economic Program

Mr. King. We have to take a break, but quickly, why did you have to change your mind on the tax rates for middle income?

The President. Because after the election was

over, the government of the previous administration revised upward the deficit by, oh, about $50 billion a year in each of the next 3 years.

Mr. King. So you had no idea of that when you were running?

The President. No, I didn't know it would be revised upward. So the decision I had to make was, well, are you going to live with a bigger deficit and less deficit reduction, or should you ask the middle class to pay a little?

I also, frankly, did something else I didn't like. I revised upward the tax burden on the wealthiest Americans, and I think there's a limit beyond which you don't want to go on them either.

Mr. King. We're going to break. We'll pick up on that.

[The stations took a commercial break.]

Mr. King. We're back in the Library with President Clinton, and before we take our next call we want to pick up where we left off on, because he's taken a lot of shots on this, and it would be interesting to hear it in this setting, the other side.

The President. I just want to say that when I became President and the deficit had been estimated upward since the election quite a bit, over $125, $130 billion, I decided that we were going to have to cut more spending and raise more revenues than I had thought to get the deficit down to a point that it was manageable and to keep long-term interest rates coming down.

I think that it's very important to hammer home that there's a real connection between an effort to reduce the deficit and getting these long-term interest rates down. Before the election, basically you had short-term interest rates brought way down by the Federal Reserve Board but a big gap between them and the long-term rates. And that's what determines mortgage rates, business loans, and a lot of other things. So we decided that it would be worth it to really take a tough stand to raise some more money, most of it from upper-income people but a modest amount from middle-class people, and cut more spending.

And let me show you what the difference is. If you look at this chart here, if I had just stayed with the budget that I found when I took office, that is, the one adopted in the last year of President Bush's term, here's what happens to the deficit.

Mr. King. That's the inherited deficit?

The President. This is the inherited deficit. With our plan, here's what happens to it over 5 years. Now, what you see down here is the real hitch—we can come back to this later—and that is that with all of our cuts and with the revenue increases, health care is still going up at 9 percent a year. Until we bring health care costs in line with inflation, we can't go down to zero. When we do, we can get down to zero and balance this budget. That's why health care reform is so important.

But look at the difference here. Now, let me just show you one other thing. Even though I did decide to ask for a modest tax increase on the middle class, let me just say exactly what this is.

Here is a deficit reduction plan. For every $10, $5 comes in spending cuts, $4 comes from people with incomes above $100,000; that's the top 6 percent. Of this $4, seven-eighths of that comes from people with incomes above $200,000. And then $1, 1 in 10, comes from people with incomes between $30,000 and $100,000. Families with incomes below $30,000 are held harmless.

So I think it is a fair and balanced package. Now, this portion, the portion the middle class pays, if anything near what the Senate bill does passes, will be about $50 a year for a family of four with an income of, let's say, between $40,000 and $50,000 a year, or about a buck a week. And all this money—all this money goes into a trust fund for 5 years to pay down the deficit. It has to be used for that. And if we miss our targets of paying down the deficit, that is, if we miss my line back here any year, I have to come back in and give new cuts, new ways to meet the deficit reduction.

Now, what does this mean for the average American? It means that, as we have made progress on this, we've got the lowest interest rates in 20 years. So millions of people are refinancing their homes, refinancing their business loans. They're going to take out lower college loans, car loans, consumer loans. Millions of Americans will save far more in interest rates than they will pay in this modest tax package, even upper income people.

Let me just make a couple more points. Ninety-four percent of the small businesses in this country will pay no income tax increase and will have the opportunity to get a tax cut if they simply invest more money back in their business and create jobs, because we more than double the expensing provision for small business.

One final thing that's important. I just got back from this G–7 meeting, the meeting of the world's great industrial powers. For 10 years, at every meeting the United States didn't have much influence because we were attacked over having such a big deficit and being greedy, taking money from all around the world to pay for it. This year, for the first time in a decade, we were complimented, not criticized, and that's why—the progress of this economic plan is why at this meeting we were able to get an agreement to lower tariffs on our manufactured products. It means hundreds of thousands of jobs for Americans if we can get all the countries in the world to agree to change the trade agreement, like the big countries have. And we've got a new trade deal with Japan where the Japanese for the first time agreed to dramatically reduce the trade deficit.

Economic Summit

Mr. King. By the way, did you expect that going there?

The President. No, but I hoped for it. I had an instinct that both those things could happen. Everybody said nothing is going to happen at this meeting because all of these countries are in terrible economic shape, all their leaders are unpopular. Well, they are. We've got a global economic crisis, and when people can't make a living, when they're insecure, they're worried about losing their health care, their benefits, the ability to raise and educate their children, leaders aren't going to be popular.

But what happened was, there was a sense that we owed it to the people we represent to do something, to try to move this economy and create jobs and get some things going. And that spirit sort of overtook the meeting. I called several of them before we met, and I said, "Everybody says we're not going to do anything, but why is that? Why don't we go and do something? We're actors; we want to get something done." And I was very pleased with it.

Mr. King. Los Angeles, as we go back to calls for President Clinton. Hello.

Economic Program

[*A participant asked about tax increases.*]

The President. Well, the deficit has dropped this year about $25 billion or so below where

it was estimated to be when I took office because interest rates have dropped. Therefore, what we have to pay on the accumulated debt of the country has gone down. The only reason interest rates have dropped is because we've got a serious attempt to reduce the deficit.

And, again, let me just reiterate what the facts are: Seventy percent of the new taxes will be paid by people who make incomes above $200,000. No income tax increases will be paid by people who have adjusted gross incomes—individuals below $140,000, couples below $180,000. There will be no tax increase at all for people with incomes below $30,000. And this modest fuel tax will amount to about $50 a year for families with incomes of about $50,000. Now, I think that is a very modest price to pay, especially when we have spending cuts that are equal to—in fact, they'll be slightly greater than, I believe, the tax increase.

Q. What kind of fuel are you going to tax? Which are we going to go with, the House or Senate, do you think?

The President. I think something closer to the Senate version. They haven't been finally settled on but——

Mr. King. Gas tax?

The President. Closer to that. There's less opposition to it.

Mr. King. Copenhagen, Denmark. Hello.

Bosnia

[*A participant asked about U.S. troop participation in peacekeeping efforts.*]

The President. Well, let me remind you, sir, that we have had several thousand troops in Somalia. We have contributed hundreds of millions of dollars in humanitarian aid to the former Yugoslavia. We have done airdrops of supplies. We have always been committed to use our air power to protect your troops and any other troops. We have not wanted to get the Untied States involved in the conflict there unless there was a settlement. I have always said that we would send appropriate military personnel to be part of a United Nations enforcement of the settlement.

Let me also say that the closest we ever were to settling that was when the Serbs and the Croats thought that the Europeans were going to go along with my proposal to lift the arms embargo and to make available standby air power to enforce no use of the Serbian artillery against the Muslim, the Bosnian government there while the arms embargo was being lifted. When it became obvious that I could not prevail in the United Nations because of the opposition of some of the European nations, that's when things began to deteriorate again instead of move toward peace.

So I had a policy. I'm disappointed that it was rejected by some of the European countries. I'm grateful that the Germans and some others supported it. But we are prepared to do our part to try to resolve this. We are working weekly on it. I feel terrible about it. But I do not believe the United States needs to send a lot of troops there which might get involved in a civil war on the ground when we had a plan—which would have led, I'm convinced, to a settlement—which was not accepted. If we get a settlement, as we might now under other conditions, we are prepared to do our part through the U.N. to help to enforce it.

Mr. King. We'll be back with President Clinton.

[The stations took a commercial break.]

Mr. King. This is funny, folks, what happens behind the scenes, so we'll make it public for you. We had arranged with President Clinton's staff that we would finish at 10 p.m. Eastern time, one hour, and the staff had arranged it with our producers. And then President Clinton just said to me, "Could we go a little longer?" And I said, "Sure, if you want to go a little longer, we can go another half hour." And he said he'd be happy to.

So we didn't do it, and I just want the staff to know that we didn't do it. If you would like to do it, we would be happy to accommodate you.

The President. You offered us the opportunity this afternoon and I think at that time we didn't know whether we could or not. But I'd like to do it.

Mr. King. You're feeling refreshed?

The President. Yes, and I like answering the questions. I think that's important.

Mr. King. By the way, before we take our next call, he did give credit to Mr. Eastwood. We did add on the break that he also wanted to give credit to John Malkovich in "In the Line of Fire."

The President. He's a great villain, isn't he? I mean, he was fabulous.

Mr. King. I haven't seen it yet, but they tell me it's unbelievable.

The President. Unbelievable. Rene Russo was good, too, and I'd only seen her in that Mel Gibson movie.

Mr. King. You are a movie buff, right?

The President. I love the movies. I love the movies.

Mr. King. What's it like when you order them here in the White House?

The President. Well, you know, they send in movies on a regular basis, so I get to see a lot of movies here. Normally, what we do is on Friday night—I normally work pretty late on Friday night, till 7, 7:30 p.m. Last Friday I worked till 8:30 p.m. And then we gather up whoever is still working late in the White House, and Hillary and I and, when Chelsea's here, Chelsea would come down and watch the movie. We like that.

Economic Program

Mr. King. We're ready to go back to more phone calls for President Clinton. Again, when you come on the line, please make the question or comment right to the point. And before we take our next call, I also want to give him a chance to expound on the lady who did call. I think he looked a little—when the lady who said——

The President. She said, well, if the deficit is down, why do you need to raise any taxes. Keep in mind, we went from a $1 to a $4 trillion national debt—that's the annual deficits added up—in only 12 years, from 1980 to 1992. And we need to get that deficit down to zero as quickly as we can without collapsing the economy. You can't do it overnight, but we have to do it over a period of years.

And as we do it, that's less money we have to spend on interest on the debt and more money we can invest in creating jobs, business incentives, and education and training and new technologies, and building roads and bridges and airports and things that make a country rich and competitive in this world. So even though we're getting a break on the deficit, we're getting a break on the deficit because the financial markets are responding to our efforts to bring the deficit down. And so we can't back up. We don't want to overdo it because that will slow the economy down, if you take too much money out at one time. But if we do it too little, then the interest rates will go up and we'll be in trouble on that score again.

Mr. King. Montreal, Quebec, Canada. Hello.

Homosexuals in the Military

[*A participant asked why the President did not act on the issue of homosexuals in the military the same way President Truman had concerning desegregation of the military.*]

The President. Well, first of all, let's talk about what I did do, and then I'll tell you why the argument you made is not analogous.

What I did do was to give instructions to the Secretary of Defense to promulgate a policy which permits gays to serve for the first time and judges them like other service men and women on their conduct, not their sexual orientation. That is a big change. They're not going to be asked about their sexual orientation. Their privacy, including their rights of association, are going to be protected. That is, if they are seen going into a gay bar, that will not lead to an investigation of their sexual orientation. The laws against sexual misconduct will be enforced clearly and unambiguously in an even-handed way against heterosexuals and homosexuals. And if a gay person says that he or she is homosexual, while that can create a presumption that they are doing something that is prohibited and lead to their separation from service, they will be given an explicit opportunity to argue that they are honoring the code of conduct. Now that is a big change.

Now, how is that different from the situation with President Truman? The real thing you ought to ask is how long did it take before African-Americans, in this case, were treated fully equally in the service? It didn't just happen snap with Truman's order. It didn't happen after Truman's order, and it developed a long time before Truman's order. There was an explicit open involvement of the military culture with blacks in a segregated way for a very long time before this order was issued.

The same thing happened with women. One of the things that's achieved almost no notice is that during my administration the Pentagon has voted to dramatically expand the role of women in the military services, make available far more roles for them than were available before. But it didn't happen overnight. It happened over a period of years as the military culture adapted to it.

Now, if I had done what you suggest, if I had just said that gays could serve and whatever

they do in private is their own business—which I never committed to do in the campaign—I'll tell you exactly what would have happened. Congress would have overturned it immediately and done it on the defense bill and in ways that would have been difficult, if not impossible, for me to veto.

So the situations simply aren't analogous. Congress has no intention of overturning President Truman's position, and it's something that had built up over a long period of time, not something that just entered the public debate, in effect, about a year ago.

Mr. King. St. Thomas, the Virgin Islands. Hello.

Puerto Rico and the District of Columbia

[*A participant asked about voting rights for residents of Puerto Rico.*]

The President. Well, it would take a legal change. I'm embarrassed to tell you I don't know if it would take a change in the Constitution. I'd like to invite you to write me about it, and I'll commit to you I'll look into it. I know that in the case of Puerto Rico, they did have a Presidential primary, which I was very active in. And the people there were very good to me, and I'm grateful for that.

I have strongly supported, in the case of Puerto Rico, self-determination. That is, if they have a referendum there and they vote to continue their commonwealth status or to become independent or to become a State, whatever they decide I will support.

Mr. King. You also support statehood for Washington, DC?

The President. I do. And I didn't, frankly, until about a year and a half ago when a number of people, including Jesse Jackson, who is one of the shadow Senators for DC, pointed out to me that this community, which was once a Federal preserve entirely, now has more people than 5 States, pays more taxes than 10, and sent more soldiers into harm's way in the Persian Gulf than 20. So I think there are ways you can carve out a Federal enclave here that's still separate and apart and let the rest of those folks become a State. There are some complicated issues there. I think there's a lot of—if you had the first city-state, they try to tax people from other states, and we'd have to work though all that. And if——

Mr. King. And if Puerto Rico wants statehood,

you'd be happy to welcome them as number 51?

The President. If that's what they vote for. I think they, the people of Puerto Rico, should decide.

Mr. King. We'll be back with President Clinton.

[*The stations took a commercial break.*]

Mr. King. We're back on "Larry King Live." Now, you would think these are two pretty powerful—the President of the United States. We're doing all right. The President had another commitment he didn't know about, right? So he'll be with us until the top of the hour. However, every 6 months we have a kind of rotating date, right, as promised during the campaign?

The President. And I owe you a half an hour now.

Mr. King. And he'll owe us a half an hour, so the next appearance will be 90 minutes in 6 months. Or 2 hours, as pointed out by Atlanta—they never stop—2 hours, OK. But we do thank—there was another appointment which he was unaware of and we were unaware of. So we'll get to some calls quickly, and he will be returning every 6 months. He promised it during the campaign; this is the 6-month anniversary.

Arlington, Virginia, with President Clinton. Hello.

President's Domestic Priorities

[*A participant asked what the President would like his legacy to be.*]

Mr. King. Is it too early to have a legacy?

The President. No, I'd be happy to tell you that. Number one, I'd like to get this economy moving again, get the deficit down and start creating jobs and seeing working Americans have their incomes go up.

Number two, I'd like to provide health security for all Americans. I'd like for us to join all the other advanced countries in the world and provide a system of affordable health care to all of our people.

Number three, I want my national service plan to pass. It will open the doors of college education to millions of Americans for lower interest loans and give many, many of them the chance to work those loans off through service at their communities.

Number four, I strongly want to pass a welfare reform bill that will move people from welfare to work and end welfare as we know it.

And five, I want to reform the political system. We have already passed the motor voter bill that makes it easier for people to register and vote. Three other bills that I care very deeply about have passed one House of Congress, but not both: one, a campaign finance reform bill to lower the cost of political campaigns, reduce the influence of PAC's, and open the airwaves to debate; two, a bill that drastically opens up lobbying behavior, restricting some lobbying behavior and requiring them to report what they spend on members of Congress; and three, the modified line-item veto, which I think will help discipline spending. So those are the things; I would like those things to be my legacy.

NAFTA

Mr. King. Want NAFTA to pass, too?

The President. Very much. I strongly support—I think it means more jobs, not less. Let me just make——

Mr. King. You disagree with Mr. Perot?

The President. I do, because keep in mind, anybody who wants to go to Mexico because they have low wages and send the products back here can do that today. Mexican tariffs on American products on average are higher than American tariffs on Mexican. Because of what President Salinas has done in lowering those tariffs in the last few years, we've gone from a $5 billion trade deficit to a $6 billion trade surplus with Mexico. They now have displaced Japan as the second biggest purchaser of American manufactured products. So I think a wealthier Mexico means more products going down there and more jobs for America.

Mr. King. A quick call, last call. Paris, France, hello.

Terrorism

[*A participant questioned U.S. policy toward Iran.*]

The President. The answer is we are doing everything we can to impose restrictions on trade with Iran. We are pressuring our allies and friends all the time not to support any government, including Iran, that supports terrorism and assassination.

I'm glad you brought it up. I think it's a very significant problem. I hope you will press this hard in Paris as you are pressing Washington, because that is something that all the West should be sensitive to. We must not allow Iraq, Iran, and other agents of terrorism and assassination to dominate the world politically and to terrorize innocent people. I think you're absolutely right.

Mr. King. Thanks very much, Mr. President.
The President. Thank you.

NOTE: The interview began at 9 p.m. The President spoke from the Library at the White House.

Statement on the Death of Deputy White House Counsel Vincent Foster, Jr.
July 20, 1993

It was with deep sadness that I learned of the death of Vincent Foster, who served ably and with distinction as Deputy White House Counsel and was my friend for over 40 years. Hillary and I love his wife Lisa and their three children, and we want to draw them close to our hearts and keep them in our prayers in this painful moment of grief. His family has lost a loving husband and father, America has

lost a gifted and loyal public servant, and Hillary and I have lost a true and trusted friend. My deepest hope is that whatever drew Vince away from us this evening, his soul will receive the grace and salvation that his good life and good works earned.

NOTE: Information regarding the circumstances of Mr. Foster's death was included with this statement.

Excerpts of Remarks in a Meeting With White House Staff on the Death of Deputy White House Counsel Vincent Foster, Jr.
July 21, 1993

First of all, I want to tell you how very glad I am to see all of you here today. I thought it was important that we come together for a few minutes. Forty-two years ago, when I met Mr. McLarty in kindergarten, I lived with my grandparents in a modest little house around the corner from Vince Foster's nice, big, white brick house. And our backyards touched. Yesterday, last night when I finished the Larry King show and I was told what happened, I just kept thinking in my mind of when we were so young, sitting on the ground in the backyard, throwing knives into the ground and seeing if we were adroit enough to make them stick.

When I started my career in Arkansas politics, he was there to help me. When I decided to run for attorney general, he was the first lawyer in Little Rock I talked to about supporting me. When the Rose law firm hired Hillary after I moved to Little Rock, Vince Foster and Webb Hubbell became her closest friends. I have two things to say about that: One is, he was a per-

fectly wonderful man on whom I relied and on whom I put a lot for a very long time. The second thing is, for all of you who are especially younger, you will find the longer you live, the more you mark the shape of your life by the people you have truly loved who, for whatever reason, aren't around anymore.

And so, I want you to think about the following: In the first place, no one can ever know why this happened. Even if you had a whole set of objective reasons, that wouldn't be why it happened, because you could get a different, bigger, more burdensome set of objective reasons that are on someone else even in this room. So what happened was a mystery about something inside of him. And I hope all of you will always understand that.

And the last thing I want to say is that all of us who loved him also did a little bit of laughing last night. Just as it is wrong to try to explain or understand something that cannot be grasped, it is very wrong to define a life like his in terms only of how it ended. And anybody in this room could be proud to have raised the children, done the work, been the friend that he was. God bless you.

NOTE: These remarks follow the text as released by the Office of the Press Secretary. A tape was not available for verification of the content of these remarks.

Remarks on the Death of Deputy White House Counsel Vincent Foster, Jr.
July 21, 1993

The President. Good afternoon. I have just met with the White House staff to basically talk with them a little bit about the death of my friend of 42 years, Vince Foster. It is an immense personal loss to me and to Hillary and to many of his close friends here and a great loss to the White House and to the country.

As I tried to explain, especially to the young people on the staff, there is really no way to know why these things happen, and it is very important that his life not be judged simply by how it ended, because Vince Foster was a wonderful man in every way and because no one can know why things like this happen.

I also encouraged the staff to remember that we're all people and that we have to pay maybe a little more attention to our friends and our families and our coworkers and try to remember that work can never be the only thing in life and a little humility in the face of this is very, very important.

I also pointed out that we have to go on. We have the country's business to do. I am keeping my schedule today except for the public events. I'm keeping all my appointments, and I expect to resume my normal schedule tomorrow. And then, of course, when the funeral is held, Hillary and I will go home and be a part of that. But otherwise, we will go on with our schedule and keep doing our work.

Q. Mr. President, do you have any idea why he might have taken his life? There's no indication——

The President. No. I really don't. And frankly, none of us do. His closest friends sat around discussing it last night at some length. None of us do. For more years than most of us would like to admit, in times of difficulty he was normally the Rock of Gibraltar while other people were having trouble. No one could ever remember the reverse being the case. So I don't know that we'll ever know. But for me, it's just important that that not be the only measure of his life. He did too much good as a father, as a husband, as a friend, as a lawyer, as a citizen. And we'll just have to live with something else we can't understand, I think.

Q. There's some feeling that he might have felt the guilt or blame for things that went wrong in the White House during the first 6 months.

The President. I don't think so. I certainly don't think that can explain it, and I certainly don't think it's accurate.

Thank you.

NOTE: The President spoke at 12:50 p.m. in the Rose Garden at the White House.

Interview With the Alabama Media
July 21, 1993

The President. First of all, let me thank you for coming, and thank you for understanding why we didn't do the entire hour today. I'll be happy to answer any questions you have. And I have reviewed your schedule. I hope you found it helpful coming here, and I'm very glad to see you. I saw some of you walking across the street today.

Go ahead, sir.

Economic Program

Q. The Vice President was just talking about Senator Dole's alternative plan, and your administration's spokesman has been very critical and much more so of Republicans in recent days, what they've put forward. He used the phrase that the Republicans didn't have the guts to make the tough choices. I was just curious whether you would extend that characterization to Senator Shelby, the cosponsor of that Republican plan.

The President. Well, let me characterize the plan. I mean, what bothered me about the plan was that it seemed to me to run the risk—I thought there were two things wrong with it. First of all, it had a lot less deficit reduction in it than our plan does. Secondly, under the guides of not taxing the middle class, it imposed no new revenues on the people who were paying 70 percent of our load, that is, people with incomes over $200,000 a year. That group of people, the top one percent of Americans, derived, according to all serious, studies, about 70 percent of the gains, economic gains of the 1980's, and their taxes were reduced while middle class Americans had their incomes stagnant and their taxes increased in the aggregate in the 1980's. The third problem that I saw with it was that even the deficit reduction figure that they alleged was actually quite a bit smaller because they had what we call a plug in it. And I think that must be what the Vice President must have referred to. That is, there was, I don't know, $65 billion, $70 billion, something like that where they said, "Well, we'll cut this, but we'll tell you later how we're going to do it. We'll figure that out somewhere down the road."

Our plan really from the beginning was dedicated toward being taken seriously by the experts in this field who very often have almost made fun of Presidential budgets, so that it could really make a contribution to lowering interest rates as well as lowering the deficit. The budget expert for Price Waterhouse, for example, was quoted recently in a Philadelphia Enquirer piece as saying I had the much better side of the argument on deficit reduction as compared with Senator Dole and that it was the first genuinely honest, credible budget to

be presented by a Chief Executive in a decade, and that, in fact, the only thing that I have understated was the amount of deficit reduction in it, that it would probably reduce the deficit considerably more than we had claimed.

So that's all I can say. I don't want to get into characterizing Senator Dole or Senator Shelby except to say I know these are difficult decisions. But this is not a narrow dispute over whether we should have some sort of energy tax, which I think we should because the energy tax, let me say, essentially permits us to fund some mechanisms for people to avoid paying the higher taxes through tax incentives but only if they're trying to create jobs.

And I'd like to just make that point, if I might, very quickly. This bill also has—I think it will have in its final form, it did in the House version and I think will in the final form in the Senate, an increase in the expensing provisions for small businesses. It will more than double under either provision. And what that means is—and I want to hammer this home, because this affects Alabama—this means over 90 percent of the small businesses in the country, the Subchapter S corporations, that is, that's in the small businesses in the Tax Codes, over 90 percent of them will not only pay no tax increase under the income tax provisions but, in fact, will get a tax break if they simply reinvest more in their companies because of this Code. Now, no one has been saying that except me. But it's a fact. The Wall Street Journal yesterday had a great article on that issue.

Secondly, the new business and small business capital gains provision enables people to cut the tax they would pay on their gains from investments in companies with a capitalization of $50 million or less when those investments are held for 5 years or more. That is a huge tax break designed to create jobs. Similarly, we do much more for research and development tax credit, for the education and training workers by employers, for investments to get the real estate and home building market going again, all those things. So that even those Americans, that top one and a half percent or so that will be affected by these income tax raises, the substantial income tax raises, they can lower those rates if they'll just simply turn around and invest their money in creating jobs in America. So that's why I wanted this plan and why I still think it's way the best.

Yes?

Q. We have heard the figure all day of 82,000 new jobs for Alabama. When you're talking about a State, though, that has in some counties people with less than a seventh grade education, they're not trained to do the type of technical jobs that you're talking about. What kind of jobs—and I've been trying to pin this down all day—what kind of jobs are Alabamans trained to handle that would bring in these 82,000 new jobs for our people?

The President. Well, first of all, I would make two observations to that. You're asking me a Governor's question now. It's something I know a little bit about. And I guess I need to back up and tell you a story. Let me just give you a two or three-sentence story about my State.

When I became Governor of Arkansas in January of 1983, we had an unemployment rate 3 percentage points above the national average. We had a State that, compared with what was working for America in the eighties, was too poor, too undereducated, too rural, too oriented toward production as opposed to services. We just didn't fit very well. And we embarked upon a long-term strategy to make ourselves fit with the global economy.

During the entire term of my service, our unemployment rate dropped below the national average only one time for 1 month until 1992, when it dropped well below it. And today it's about a point below the national average, even though for 5 years running we created jobs at a more rapid rate than the national average. In other words, we had to change the job mix of the State and the skill mix of our people. And you can't do that overnight.

But the point I want to make is it can be done. And we have seen it. So the President and the Congress cannot do everything. We have to have a partnership. Your new Governor, Governor Folsom, was up here the other day going around and visiting people in our Government who might be in a position to help change both the job mix and the skill mix of the Alabama economy. And we can be partners there, but a lot of that work has to be done at the State and local level.

Now, let me give you the two examples to get to your point. Don't forget that Alabama today has an enormous technological base around, let's say, your medical facilities, your distinguished medical school and your medical facilities in the Birmingham area, or in terms of the space operations in the northern part

of your State, where a cousin of mine for many years was a career NASA scientist. You have, in addition to that, a lot of industries that have gone through all the things the American industry went through in the 1980's to become far more competitive in the global economy in traditional industries, which may not require people with college educations but almost certainly require people who can read at the high-school-graduate level and who can have up to 2 years of further training.

So I would say, therefore, that what you should be looking to us for is help in the whole area of defense and military conversion and help in the whole area of trying to get more private sector dollars into distressed areas and then hooking into the efforts that we're going to try to establish to have a national system of training, which includes more aggressive efforts in the literacy area and in development apprenticeship programs that are partnerships with the private sector. All of the small town and rural south has been involved in an aggressive effort, in effect, to be a better fit with the global economy.

But I would say that there are lots of jobs. First of all, not all the jobs that will be created—if you create a manufacturing job, let me just give you another example, if you create a few thousand more manufacturing jobs, there will be about one and a half other jobs created, many of which don't require many skills at all, for every manufacturing job you create, because that's the way that works. I would be looking at a State strategy to hook into the national strategy, which would take advantage of lower interest rates, the specific programs of the administration, and which would focus on those two areas: changing the skill mix, changing the job mix.

Yes?

Space Station

Q. Mr. President, we've talked about the space station funding with several people today. A lot of people in north Alabama depend on the space station program and, of course, NASA for their livelihood. This administration is committed to funding right now. Is it committed, say, next year? The following year?

The President. Absolutely.

Q. Or should those NASA workers look for other jobs?

The President. No. I feel passionately myself,

as does the Vice President, about the space program and about this project as redesigned. I want to have a very candid conversation with you about this. I mean, I want to say things, and I don't want you to overdraw the political implications. But I want to just try to describe to you the situation I found. When I was elected President, I was elected saying that we were going to have to cut the deficit and cut a lot of spending but that a lot of the targets for spending cuts I did not agree with. In other words, there was a big constituency in the Congress last year for eliminating the space station and eliminating the superconducting super collider. I thought the space station was very important technology, and I thought the super collider was very important science, and I still do.

I also think that with regard to the space station, you have to see the validity of the space station not only in terms of its own merits but in terms of what we have already done to the science and technology base of the country by cutting the defense budget since 1987—which is not just closing bases, it's shutting down contracts—without aggressively implementing a defense conversion strategy until about 4 months ago when we started in earnest to spend funds that had lain dormant up here in Washington for a year almost. So there are two reasons, I think, to go forward.

It was obvious to me that the space station was in trouble on management grounds, design grounds, and because the political constituency for it had gotten too narrow, that it was too narrowly focused around Alabama and Florida and Texas and California where the jobs were. We can't afford to start voting in the Congress based on that alone. If it's in the national interest, we should continue it. So we got this eminent body, as you know, to review the whole space station project, to look at the budget constraints, and to design a program that we could continue in good faith.

As you know, the program only survived by one vote the first time in the House. And two friends of mine, who were part of a group that had voted to kill it, stayed until the end and changed their votes and voted to put it over. And I was immensely gratified by that. I think we have the votes in the Senate to continue it, and I am passionately committed to it. I believe in it very strongly. So I can tell you, I'll be there.

I also want to say to you, though, that one of the problems is that when people who advocate the space station at the same time say things like, "Well, it's just spending, stupid. If we just cut more spending, we wouldn't have to raise any revenues," and try to falsely give the impression that all these taxes are going to come on the middle class and that it's not going to go to deficit reduction, and imply that there is no spending cut in the program as it is when that's not true, that creates a problem. I'll give you an example in the case of the super collider just so you'll see how sharply it is. At the very moment the super collider, which I was strongly supporting, came up for a vote in the House of Representatives, on the steps of the Capitol were standing—and the super collider is in Texas, you know, primarily, a little bit in Louisiana—the two Republican Senators from Texas and Mr. Perot from Texas, saying, "We've got to cut more spending." So they send the message to the House, and the thing loses by 70 votes more in the House than it did last year. They just—"Well let's just lob them one then."

In other words, it is very difficult, when all these other people from other States are getting nothing out of this budget, if the people from the States that have massive Federal projects won't help to bring the deficit down and make the tough choices. It makes it harder to keep it alive. Now, that's just a fact. Consider how you'd feel if you were a Member of Congress from Iowa where we've cut farm programs, from the Rocky Mountain West where we have restrained the Government subsidies of a lot of the resources in the West, and you're being asked to keep alive the space station or the super collider, and the people who represent those States are screaming at you that if only you'd cut more spending you wouldn't have to raise these taxes. Now, that's really the political problem.

I can do a couple more. Go ahead.

Military Base Closings

Q. Mr. President, in our area in southern Alabama, in Mobile, people have said, the economic plan—we'd like to support it, but, on the other hand, we see the Federal Government do things like build a brand new home port and then within a couple of years decide to close something that hasn't really had a chance to even rust. How do you instill confidence in—

The President. You mean because of the base closing operation?

Q. Yes, exactly.

The President. Well, let me say, first of all, I can't either defend or criticize every particular decision of the base closing commission. I have to tell you that they have a very difficult job. The Joint Chiefs of Staff made recommendations to them, passed on by the Secretary of Defense. They reviewed it, and they modified it to some extent to try to ease the unemployment impact in some areas. But here is the fundamental problem, and I'll come back to your specific case.

The fundamental problem is that we are going in rather rapid succession from a military with about 2.5 million people in 1987 to one with somewhere between 1.6 million and 1.4 million people at the end of this decade. Now, as we do that, we were looking at projected downsizing of the military force by 40 percent, with a base structure downsized by only 9. If you do that, that means you're going to have a lot of base structure and capacity you can't use. And what will happen is you will have to cut contracts for these weapons that are so important to us. For example, in the attack on Iraq where we sent the cruise missiles in, it's very important that we continue to modernize those things, make them more accurate, continue to develop weaponry. You have to cut more of that if you don't cut bases and structure appropriately. So, in general, I had to approve that.

Now, my argument to the people in Mobile is that there are long lead times in defense expenditures. The decision to build that facility, to modernize it, was made probably in the early eighties before we could have anticipated the end of the cold war, the collapse of the Soviet Union, the need to redesign this whole national security system. And that should not be viewed as a waste.

On the other hand, what ought to be done is the Government should have a significant burden to work with the people of Alabama to figure out what can be done to turn that to a valuable commercial use. How can this be used to create jobs and opportunity for Alabama? How can this be turned into a real asset for your State? That is my commitment. My problem with this whole defense downsizing all along is there are all these economic studies which show that you can create about as many jobs in civilian life as you can in defense for

about half the money. But if you don't spend any of the money and if you don't work at it, then you'll never get that done. So that's the only answer I can give you.

I'll take another couple. Go ahead.

NASA and Senator Richard Shelby

Q. I've been getting shrugs all day to this question, Mr. President. Let's try once more. It was the biggest story in Alabama politically all year. About 5 months ago, Mr. Panetta gave a directive to NASA to transfer the external tank project out of Huntsville. The press was told this was done to punish Mr. Shelby for his criticisms of your economic program. NASA has written back to you 2 months ago saying this is a dumb idea, it's not safe, it doesn't make economic sense, and we can't guarantee the safety of future shuttle flights if you separate the management team from the engineers they manage. What is the status of what we call the "Shelby sanction"?

The President. Well, first of all, you just told me something I didn't know. I had no idea that NASA had written to me about that, and I will take it up immediately.

Secondly, let me tell you, you can go back through my whole career as Governor, which was a pretty successful one, and I got a lot done, and I went through a whole lot of tough decisions, usually with the same sort of criticism I've been getting early on here. When you start something tough and you start pushing rocks up a hill, you know, sometimes you have to settle for 85 percent of what you ask for. But if you advance the ball, that's the game.

I have to tell you, I have not had any personal criticism of anyone for their opposition to my plans. The thing that I thought was wrong about what Senator Shelby did was that he launched his criticism in a very personal way against the Vice President after the television cameras showed up, and I thought that was wrong. I thought it was insensitive to a new Vice President and President. I didn't like that.

I have tried to have, and I want to have, a good relationship with Senator Shelby. I have a very good relationship with several Republican Senators who rarely vote with me. But there are all kinds of other issues. This is not the end of the world. This economic plan—after we finish this, we've got to pass national service, which is being debated, which was one of the heartland provisions of my campaign. We've got to deal with the health care crisis, and we're going to have some bipartisan support on that. We've got to take up a crime bill in an environment which is very troubling in America today. We've got a whole lot of other fish to fry for the American people. And I do not want to have any kind of bad relationship with any Member of Congress I can avoid. So I want to have a good relationship with Senator Shelby. And I have to tell you, that was my only personal regret. The fact that he stood up against my program is a decision for him to make. But I did not know what you just told me about that letter, and I will get it and review it and get a report back from the NASA Director.

Yes?

Unfunded Federal Mandates

Q. Mr. President, one of the questions that we raised earlier—being from Montgomery, we're very sensitive to the fact that over the years the Federal Government has mandated programs and then has asked the States to pay more along the way, something that you can relate to from your days in Arkansas. Is there any encouragement from your administration toward the new administration of Governor Folsom——

The President. Absolutely. Absolutely. I just talked to the National Association of Counties this week, and I reiterated what I said in my 3-hour work session with the Governors earlier this year. We are going to do everything we can to stop this practice of nonfunded mandates.

One of the charges I gave the Vice President when he undertook this reinventing Government project, which I think will be very exciting to you and to the people of Alabama when we recommend some pretty fundamental changes in the way the Federal Government operates, is to try to get out of this business of rulemaking against the States and the local governments that cost money without paying for it.

Now, I have to say, I want to give just this little window here. There are times when the Congress passes laws that the President is not in a position to veto. For example, sometimes the Congress will put a little mandate in a huge budget bill that you simply cannot veto, because you have to let the agencies go forward. But the Congress, the Democrats who have been involved in this in the past clearly know of my position on this and my strong conviction. I think it's wrong.

I'll take one last question. Go ahead.

Q. Mr. President, I've been told I can't return to Alabama until I ask you: Who's going to win the next Alabama and Arkansas game?

The President. Well, all I can say is after I went to the last one I predicted that Alabama would win the national championship. And I hope we'll be more competitive next year. I think we probably will be.

Thank you.

NOTE: The President spoke at 4:55 p.m. in the Roosevelt Room at the White House.

Remarks Prior to Discussions With President Jean-Bertrand Aristide of Haiti and an Exchange With Reporters
July 22, 1993

The President. Let me make a brief statement, and then I can answer some questions.

First of all, it's a good pleasure for me to have President Aristide back here in the White House. I want to commend him on the progress that has been made and the courage he showed in signing the Governor's Island agreement which set a process and a timetable for his return as President of Haiti by October 30th and for the parliamentary agreement. We're here to talk about what our next steps are.

I want to compliment, again, the United Nations envoy, Mr. Caputo, and our Ambassador, Mr. Pezzullo, for the wonderful work they have done in trying to restore democracy and Father Aristide to the Presidency. So we're going to have a good meeting this morning and talk about the next steps, naming the Prime Minister, getting the international police force in place, and going forward. I'm excited about this process. It's a major potential for a victory for democracy.

Haiti

Q. Is President Aristide ready to accept 300 American troops to train his military force and carry out all the provisions of the agreement?

President Aristide. We are doing our best to do that and also to have what we call the four points of—[*inaudible*]—plan: professionalization of the army, a new police force, reform of the judicial system, and the economic package for having something for every single citizen of the country.

Economic Program

Q. Mr. President, on the budget, Senator Boren wants more cuts; Congressman Rangel wants more taxes for more investment programs. How do you bridge this kind of gap?

The President. I don't know. That's what they're working on now. Senator Boren voted with some enthusiasm for the bill when it came out of the Senate. We'll be glad to work with him. But we'll just have to see what happens.

Q. And are you leaning toward a higher gasoline tax than the 4.3 percent? There are indications from your people on the Hill that you are.

The President. Let's see what happens there in the budget process. I went up there and talked to the conferees, and I told them what I thought the principles and the guideposts ought to be, and they're working on it.

Q. How about——

The President. They may discuss a lot of different things. Let's just see what happens.

Q. Are you thinking of 5 cents, 5 cents a gallon?

Bosnia

Q. Have you given up on Bosnia?

The President. No. That's not true. Those stories are not accurate.

Q. That's the way Secretary Christopher's remarks were interpreted.

The President. I disagree that that's what they said. I realize that that's how one or two sentences were interpreted, but that's not so. We have aggressively committed ourselves to the process in Geneva. And if the Bosnian Government voluntarily signs an agreement, we have made it clear that we were prepared to participate in the enforcement of it. And we are continuing to work with the Europeans on other options. So you know what the United States believes, that an opportunity was lost shortly after Athens because our position did not prevail with the Europeans. But that is not true that we have given up on it. We are continuing to work.

NOTE: The exchange began at 9:40 a.m. in the Oval Office at the White House. A tape was not available for verification of the content of this exchange.

Statement by the Press Secretary on the President's Meeting With President Jean-Bertrand Aristide of Haiti
July 22, 1993

President Clinton held a cordial and constructive meeting this morning with President Jean-Bertrand Aristide of Haiti. The meeting lasted about 30 minutes. This was their first meeting since the signing of the so-called Governors Island agreement on July 3, although they spoke by telephone on July 4.

The President commended President Aristide on his signing of the agreement, which establishes a sound timetable for the restoration of democracy and for Aristide's return to Haiti on October 30, just 100 days from now. The President described the agreement as an historic step forward for democracy, economic prosperity, and freedom for Haiti. He reaffirmed that the United States will continue to play a leadership role with the international community in helping foster a better life for the Haitian people.

The President and President Aristide discussed the steps that need to be taken to fulfill the terms of the agreement, including the naming of a new Prime Minister by President Aristide in consultation with members of the Haitian Parliament.

Remarks at a Communications Technology Demonstration
July 22, 1993

Thank you very much. Distinguished Members of Congress, FCC Commissioners, Mrs. Graham, distinguished members of the high-tech community and communications industry who are here today, I thank all of you for coming, and I appreciate your sitting through my education here. I hope it isn't too warm. We've gotten a little bit of break in the weather. I got to send the Vice President that message over there, and it's nice to know he'll be able to stop the rains in the Midwest within a few moments, remote control. [*Laughter*]

Just beginning by building on what the Vice President said, it is perfectly clear that in our Nation we need an economic strategy that deals with a lot of our larger structural issues, particularly the deficit, but also recognizes that creating jobs today in a global economy requires us to make the most of the assets we have and to find a way once again to make sure that technology continues to be a net generator, not a net reducer, of jobs. We are here today to celebrate one of those opportunities. In recent years, we haven't done enough to control our larger economic issues, nor have we done enough to seize these particular opportunities. We want to reverse both these trends and ignite growth.

The economic plan that I have presented to the Congress, as all of you know, offers $500 billion worth of deficit reduction divided equally between spending cuts and revenue increases, with most of the revenue increases coming from people with incomes well above $200,000 and the spending cuts coming across the board in virtually every area of our national life.

The Chairman of the Federal Reserve, Alan Greenspan, in testimony to the House Banking Committee on Tuesday said that the reason long-term interest rates were at a 20-year low is because, and I quote, "of the expectations of a significant, credible decline in the budget deficit." And he pointed out that if we did not act now and significantly, those good trends and long-term interest rates being down—which are leading millions of Americans to refinance their homes, I would imagine including some people here in this audience today, refinance business loans, and otherwise move in ways that are advantageous to themselves and the economy—

that if we did not do that, we would be in trouble. He further pointed out that if we resolved the budget issue and dealt with our health care cost problems, the United States economy could, quote, "emerge healthier and more vibrant than in decades." That is what we're talking about, the future of this country. And I think that is what we must focus on.

Part of this economic plan is the "Emerging Telecommunications Technology Act" introduced by Senators Hollings, Inouye, Stevens of Alaska, Congressman Dingell of Michigan, Congressman Markey of Massachusetts, who is here with us. It's been called the information equivalent of the Alaskan oil strike or the California gold rush. It offers great opportunities for people to create new jobs, start new businesses, invest in people. And it will reduce the deficit, according to Congressional Budget Office estimates, by something over $7 billion. It's a great deal for all of us.

In this plan we allow for 200 megahertz of the electromagnetic spectrum now used by Federal Agencies to be licensed to the private sector by the Federal Com- munications Commission. For the few nonphysicists in the audience, the spectrum is the airwaves that transmit communication signals. The additional 200 megahertz of the spectrum would be capable of adding the equivalent of 33 television channels in every market in the United States. A decade ago, as the Vice President said, the U.S. cellular telephone industry was launched on only 50 megahertz of the spectrum. At that time, experts said the industry would have slightly less than a million subscribers by the year 2002. Well, those initial licenses leveraged $11 billion in private investment that grew into more than 11 million subscribers, $3 billion in exports, and 100,000 jobs in 1992. When the FCC reallocates the spectrum for personal communication services alone, it is estimated that another 300,000 jobs could be added to the American economy in the next 10 to 15 years. And that doesn't take into account what will be done with the remainder of this 200 megahertz allocation.

This plan creates the infrastructure to develop the most advanced commercial wireless communication networks the world has ever known.

It will allow an industry to grow by tens of billions of dollars by the end of the decade, producing hundreds of thousands of new high-skill, high-wage jobs. It will close our Federal budget deficit, or certainly help to, while correcting America's investment deficit at the same time, a win-win scenario for our taxpayers, our workers, our Government, and our entrepreneurs, an investment of historic proportions.

We have entered a new era of human communications where wireless technologies become information skyways, a new avenue to send ideas and masses of information to remote locations in ways most of us would never have imagined, and as we've just seen in all these demonstrations, also provides new ways to improve people's lives in very practical ways, and perhaps to save lives in remote areas or emergency circumstances where once that was simply impossible. Wireless hand-held computers and phones will deliver the world to our fingertips, wherever we may be, with speed and flexibility.

Only last week the FCC reallocated emerging technology spectrum for the kinds of services and benefits we've seen here today. When a natural disaster hits, this technology can come to the rescue. When an emergency medical vehicle has a patient and the only hospital is a long way away, it can mean the difference between life and death, as we've seen this morning. In schools where wires may be too costly to run, this technology can link students with other students, with libraries in other schools. In manufacturing, this technology can give our companies the extra speed and production that today may make all the difference between staying ahead of the competition and going under.

When the race toward innovation knows no boundaries, this economic plan can keep America ahead of our competitors with information highways and skyways second to none and the best educated, best trained, and best equipped work force in the world. That's what this economic growth strategy is all about: historic change, more growth, more free enterprise, more innovation to put the American people to work and give them the future they deserve.

Thank you very much.

NOTE: The President spoke at 11:13 a.m. on the South Lawn at the White House. In his remarks, he referred to Katharine Graham, chairman of the board, Washington Post Co.

Interview With the New York and New Jersey Media
July 22, 1993

The President. Thank you very much, Mr. Vice President.

I'm sorry we are a little bit late. We had an unavoidable problem come up in the office a few minutes ago that we had to deal with. But I do want to echo a couple of things the Vice President said and make one or two specific points.

On Tuesday, the Chairman of the Federal Reserve Board, Alan Greenspan, appeared before the House Banking Committee. And in his testimony he said the most important thing we could do would be to urgently pass this plan for deficit reduction because there's no question that it is the primary thing driving down long-term interest rates and that the economy could absorb $500 billion in deficit reduction. And that plus trying to do something about the ever-increasing costs of health care to the Government budget and to the American people generally were two things which could give us a very vibrant economy. And I think he used the phrase, something like we could have more prosperity than we'd had in decades.

But I just want to emphasize that when you get outside of the political arena and you analyze this thing, there are Republicans as well as Democrats; there are small-, medium-, and large-sized businesses. Yesterday I had lunch with a significant number of small business people from around America, because most of the vocal support we had gotten for the economic plan had come from bigger businesses. And they were supporting the plan because of the capital gains incentives for investment in new businesses, enterprises that are capitalized at $50 million a year or less. They were supporting it because of the emphasis on research and development. They were supporting it because, frankly, over 90 percent of the small businesses in the country are in a position to get a tax cut under this bill with the expensing provisions, which says that if you invest more you pay less tax. They pay no income tax increase, and they can reduce their tax burden if they invest more. Now, you never get any of that in the rhetoric of our opponent, but that is the fact.

Let me make one other point. There's a lot of talk about spending cuts and people saying, well, there ought to be more spending cuts. Well, there are 200 specific spending cuts in this program, over 100 of them in excess of $100 million apiece. And when the Senate Finance Committee took up this economic plan and dealt with the spending cuts that were on the table, the Republicans on the committee did not offer one single spending cut in addition to the ones that we had put on the table. Not one, not one red cent. So it is very easy to talk in general terms about cutting spending and capping this and "We'll figure out something else later," and quite another thing to say, "This is where we're going to cut the spending." And that's what we have done. And therefore, I think we put together a good and balanced plan.

I'm encouraged by the progress of the conference so far. There are still some difficult issues ahead and a lot of vote-getting to do, but the main thing is we have to resolve the uncertainty, keep the interest rates down, bring the deficit down, and get this economy moving again.

And that's why we're doing a whole series of these, and I'm glad to have so many of you from New York and New Jersey here. And if you have questions, I'll try to answer them.

Economic Program

Q. This scenario, as we heard today, to paint the picture of not passing this an economic catastrophe, is that your strategy for the next couple of critical days or critical weeks?

The President. No, I think we are going to pass it. But I think that if you look—there was an article in either the Times or the Wall Street Journal today, I can't remember which, which said there was a little bump up in the long-term interest rates yesterday because the bond markets, the people who set these interest rates were afraid that maybe the Congress wasn't serious. I think they are serious. I think they will pass it. There is not a serious alternative. And

there is no question that the failure to pass the budget would be a destabilizing effect on the economy. It would lead to an increase in long-term interest rates, there's no question about that. But I'm not trying to talk in terms of Armageddon. I want the Congress to do something that will move the country forward, that'll get energy back in.

I feel, frankly, quite good about what's happening. These are tough decisions. You know, the easy decisions had all been made by the time we got here. Anybody can write you a check and run the deficit up. It's quite another thing to try to have a disciplined plan to cut spending, increase revenues in a very fair way, and have a very targeted increase in investments in areas that will generate jobs. That's a much tougher thing to do.

Q. In our briefings today we were led to believe that you are moving towards the Senate version of this plan. Is that accurate?

The President. No, not quite. I think what is fair to say is, I think that any energy tax that comes out will be closer to the Senate version, not only in form but in dollars. It will be closer to the Senate version. But the House version has a lot of very important economic initiatives in it and one very important pro-work, pro-family provision that I believe should be in the final bill. And if I might, I'd like to just mention them very quickly, the things in the House bill which I believe should be either in the final bill, or the final bill should be more like the House bill than the Senate bill.

Number one, both bills dramatically increase the earned-income tax credit, which is, in effect, a tax reduction for people of middle incomes and lower incomes who work and therefore earn income and pay income taxes. It was appropriate for the Senate to lower the earned-income tax credit a little bit, because the energy tax was lower and it was really designed to make sure that nobody with a family income of $30,000 a year or less would pay any new taxes under this program. But the other major thing is that we want to be able to say that anybody who works 40 hours a week and has children in the home will not be in poverty after this plan passes, that we're going to reward work, we're going to encourage people to get off welfare. And the way it starts is by saying if you do work 40 hours a week, if you have a child in the house, you won't be in poverty. Let me give you an idea of why that's so significant.

Eighteen percent of the American people in the work force today are living below the Federal poverty line. So I want some adjustment in the number that came out of the Senate so we'll be able to achieve that goal.

The second thing is, I think the House bill had a lot of economic incentives that ought to be in there. By the way, the ones I mentioned, you shouldn't infer from that that anything I forget to mention, I don't care about whether it gets in. I can't remember every issue, but let me just give you a few. I'm confident that the conference report will include the new business, small business capital gains tax. It's been pioneered by the chairman of the Senate Small Business Committee, Senator Bumpers, from my home State, and others. It is not particularly expensive, but it gives a very significant incentive for people to invest in enterprises capitalized at less than $50 million a year. I think they will take the surcharge off capital gains, which I hope will be done. I think they will do more on the research and development tax credit and more to revitalize the real estate markets than the Senate bill does. I think all those changes will come in, and I think that will give more of a pro-growth, pro-investment, pro-business, and pro-jobs shape to the final bill.

After all, keep in mind, the way the bill was structured was not simply to impose virtually all of the taxes on people with incomes above very high levels—now, the bill will clearly have 70 percent or more of the tax burden on people with incomes above $200,000—the bill also was designed to say to those people, "But you can ease that tax burden if, but only if, you turn around and invest in job-generating activities in the American economy."

Yes, sir. You had a question back there.

Energy Tax

Q. There's a report out this morning from the Heritage Foundation that says the gas tax would affect eight or so States, in particular, New Jersey among the hardest. There are other statistics that a Senator like Frank Lautenberg looks at and says——

The President. How could the gas tax affect New Jersey hardest? It's the most densely populated State in the country.

Q. If you drive between Philadelphia and New York, I guess.

The President. More single-car commuters?

Q. I haven't seen the report myself. But at any rate, Senator Lautenberg takes this and says that this plan is a bad deal for New Jersey. Is there any response that you have to that?

The President. Yes, I do have a response to that. Let me say, first of all, Senator Lautenberg's position is premised on two arguments. One is that New Jersey has a high per capita income. The second is that New Jersey gets a low per capita return in Federal aid. But the point I want to make to you is that those two things are inextricably related. That is, if New Jersey is the second highest State in the country in per capita income, obviously you will pay more taxes to the Federal Government, and you will get less Federal money in the income-based programs. Keep in mind, an awful lot of Federal money is spent on Social Security, Medicare, Medicaid, food stamps, and a lot of other things that are tied to income. So the richer you are, the lower you're going to be on the Federal payroll unless you happen to have a huge defense establishment. And even that, of course, is now ratcheting down.

But look at it the other way. New Jersey also has a lot of high-tech companies, a lot of entrepreneurs, a lot of people who are trying to make the future. Frank Lautenberg himself created a high-tech company and became a very successful person financially by creating a company with an idea and with technology. This is the most protechnology economic plan I think our country has ever adopted. We just had a press conference out here this morning with people in the communications industry on the plan that's in this economic program to auction 200 megahertz of communications in the spectrum, to open that up to commercial development. It's going to generate $7 billion to reduce the deficit and create up to 300,000 jobs in the next 10 years. The new business capital gains tax, the expensing provision for small business, more on research and development, the probusiness, pro-job growth aspects of this program, I think, have been largely lost. And to the extent that New Jersey has a better economic infrastructure than other places and an artificially high unemployment rate—both of which are true now, right?—historically low unemployment now high, strong economic infrastructure, New Jersey should do quite well from these economic incentives.

So I don't believe in terms of private sector job growth that the State will be hurt. But I understand the force of his argument, and I understand that it has a lot of appeal to voters, too, the first time they hear it.

Drug Policy Director

Q. Mr. Clinton, I wonder whether we could move to another subject on the minds of a great deal of New Yorkers just for a moment.

The President. We'll answer any questions. Let's let the plane go over. Thank you.

Q. That's best for us because we're television. The State report on the Crown Heights riots was released earlier this week, which greatly criticized the performance of your now drug czar, Lee Brown. And we were wondering, first, whether you were worried that it may have damaged his credibility as drug czar. And also, as a secondary question, I was wondering what your general feelings are on the issue of the riots in New York and whether you might be paying a visit to perhaps help your embattled friend, Mayor Dinkins, there.

The President. Well, I haven't had any conversations about that issue one way or the other. I'll tell you about the Lee Brown issue. The report obviously came in an extended period of time after the riots themselves occurred. And I have not read it or reviewed it. I know generally what its conclusions were. If you read it in the light most unfavorable to Lee Brown, in other words if you say, "Well, they said that he didn't do a good job managing a riot with a police force," that wouldn't be the first police chief about whom you could say that. And it would do absolutely nothing to undermine the irrefutable facts that he did a good job as police chief in Atlanta and Houston and in New York and that because of the intense and increased neighborhood policing systems that were inaugurated during his tenure, the statistics show that there was a drop in crime in many major categories for the first time in more than three decades during the time that he served. So I think, on balance, the people of New York were still much better off having had him as police chief, even if you read the report in the light most unfavorable to him. Whether the report is accurate or not, I just have no way of knowing.

Yes, sir.

Energy Tax

Q. Two questions, if you will, back on the economic subject. One is, by saying a moment ago that you think that any energy tax that

comes out of this conference will be closer to a Senate version, are you saying that you're now ready to accept a gasoline tax?

The President. I'm saying just exactly what I said. I think that the dollar value and perhaps the form, but certainly the dollar value, of the tax that comes out of that conference will, I believe, be closer to the Senate version. And I think it should be now, because we've got some more spending cuts that we've put into the bill.

Yes, go ahead.

Terrorism in the U.S.

Q. The World Trade Center bombing brought a lot of attention to our political asylum laws. That was several months back. Since then there's been a lot of speeches made. But still, if someone arrives at JFK this afternoon, the situation is the same. What can you say to the people of the metropolitan area that are worried about this?

The President. That they are right to be worried. We need to change. And just in the next few days we will have an announcement on that. We've had some people working on it for several weeks now. When I went to the G–7 summit in Tokyo, I asked the Vice President to try to coordinate their efforts a little better to make sure that we speeded up the process. And we'll have an announcement on that quite soon. That was a very good—it's very important.

I'll take a couple more. Go ahead, and then we'll do a couple more.

Campaign Promises

Q. Mr. President, one of the issues that's come up with gays in the military resolution and on this issue of the gas tax or Btu tax is when is a compromise appropriate and prudent? When is it a broken promise? And I'm curious to hear you talk a little bit about, in terms of judging your Presidency, should it be judged anymore on "Putting People First" and on all 232 pages there, what you fulfilled? When is a compromise, in your mind, on those issues legitimate? When is it a broken promise? And how does one judge a Presidency like your own?

The President. Well, the only commitment that I have myself abandoned on my own initiative was the one that I went before the American people and told them about on February 17th, and that was the commitment not to have any sort of tax burden on the middle class.

We're now down to about $50 a year. And I explained to the American people why I did that: because the deficit was written up so much bigger after I got elected, and because I thought it was important to get the deficit down, and I thought they'd be better off over the long run, and that I still believe that the tax system ought to be changed to be more fair to middle class families, especially those with children, and I had a 4-year term to try to get it done. And I think when a President has to break a campaign commitment, the best way to do it is to go before the American people and say, "Here's what I had to do and why."

Now, we also, frankly, clearly delayed what I said I would do on immigration of Haitians. And I've already explained why on that. But we are working through this whole immigration policy in a way that I think will allow us to return to the policy I advocated in the campaign.

When you compromise, I think the question is almost always: What are your alternatives, and are the people you're trying to help and the objectives you're seeking to further better off? I can hardly add anything to what Barney Frank said in his op-ed piece on the gays in the military, for example, in the Washington Post, I mean, the idea that no President in the history of this country has ever tried to take on this issue, no candidate running for President had ever really spoken to the issue before I did. I don't ask for any kudos for that, that's just a fact. I think the consciousness of the American people is different and broader as a result, and I think that the question of the compromise here is a pretty clear one.

If you look at it in words, the compromise is more restrictive than what I wanted and what I would like to do today. I think people ought to be able to say they're gay and serve and obey all the rules. But I couldn't get that past the Joint Chiefs, who are bound to follow my orders, but they're also bound by law to tell the Congress the truth about what they think when asked by Congress. That's also the law of the land, and that would have led to a certain reversal of the policy by the Congress. Everyone who lives in this town knows that. So—let me finish—on the other hand, as a practical matter, the Joint Chiefs and the Secretary of Defense, working together and then with me, agreed to provide much more practical protection for the privacy and associational rights of all members of the armed services, without regard to their sexual orientation, than existed before in ways that will clearly advance the cause that we all know is a fact: that there are homosexuals who serve in the Armed Forces with great distinction.

So the question is: Was it a good compromise or an abandonment of principle? Should I have made everybody feel better for a day and then watch their hopes dashed and see Congress maybe even return to the status quo ante, which was—the first battle we won on that was getting the Joint Chiefs to stop asking at the beginning of the year. Is it better off? I have nothing to add to what Barney Frank said. I think that it was an honorable compromise by honorable people, and we did the best we could.

And on the economic plan, what I said about that in the campaign, and the only thing I ever said about that with regard to the gas tax, was that I thought raising the gas tax a nickel a year in a 5-year budget plan was too much. And I still believe that. The gas tax now being debated is a lower tax on fuel than the Btu tax which passed the House. It is a lower tax on fuel than the Btu tax that passed the House. Therefore, there is nothing dishonorable or dishonest about what would happen.

I think if you look at what this administration has done—we've taken on the deficit; we're taking on health care; we're taking on welfare reform. We're about to get national service, being debated in both Houses today. We passed a campaign finance reform bill, a lobby bill, and the line-item veto, all things I advocated, through one of the two Houses of Congress. If you go back to the last several years, it would be hard to find a 6-month period early in a Presidency in which more had been done on more issues to fulfill the specific commitments I made in the campaign and to actually get things done that will change the lives of the American people.

So I think it is indeed a strange measure of the progress of our administration that these negative comments would come out. I mean, my predecessor had been Vice President for 8 years and didn't announce a foreign policy until August. You know, I got out here, and I got up here every day and went to work, and that's what I'm going to keep doing. But anyway, that would be my distinction between those two things.

Business Entertainment Deduction

Q. Some may think the business reduction tax is elitist. But in New York City, that is the heart and soul of New York. Some analysts say that over 1,000 jobs may be lost, and these are middle class jobs.

The President. The business entertainment tax, you mean?

Q. Yes. And these are middle class jobs.

The President. Absolutely they are.

Q. Busboys, dishwashers, waiters. How can you do something in such a town that really needs this? We're in the middle of a recession in New York. We're not slipping into one; we are in a recession.

The President. First of all, New York needs a lot of things. And my own judgment is—not just New York, New Jersey, Arkansas, you name it. California is in terrible shape. We've got a lot of things to do in this country.

My response would be twofold. Number one, I think that New York will gain far more from a stable, credible deficit reduction plan and the other business incentives that we are putting into the law than you will lose by a restriction on the entertainment deduction. Number two, when the entertainment deduction was reduced before from 100 to 80 percent, the same claims were made against the reduction. And afterward a study concluded there was no loss of jobs. I believe the American people will continue to travel, and I believe more and more American people will continue to eat out as more families have two income earners and work longer hours. I think there are large social forces at work here which make it highly unlikely that a job loss will occur.

Yes, sir.

Deficit Reduction

Q. Chairman Greenspan the other day said that $500 billion of deficit reduction was about the right size as a first installment, that you have to revisit this issue. Do you expect to be proposing another deficit reduction plan of this magnitude in your first term here?

The President. Well, I think that we will point the way toward eliminating it altogether. And let me explain what I mean by that. Chairman Greenspan and I have discussed this at great length, and we discussed whether there was an analogy here to what Japan did from the mid-seventies to the mid-eighties when they had a comparable operating deficit to ours. And they

took it down to zero and actually began to run a surplus. But they took, as I recall, somewhere between 9 and 11 years to do it. I can't remember exactly. But I saw a chart in one of the papers here represented, I just can't remember which one, which showed how long they took.

I believe that in order to move the deficit down beyond where it is now, if you look at it, it's clear what you have to do. You have to pass a health reform plan that brings health care costs in line with inflation plus population growth. That's what you have to do. If you go back and look at this budget, if you look at discretionary domestic spending, it's flat for 5 years now. That is, everything we increase in education, in technology, in defense conversion, we cut in some other area. Defense goes down. The only thing that's really going up in this budget besides cost-of-living increases for Social Security and much more modest pay increases for military and civilian employees, is a 9 percent increase in health care costs, which is down from the projected 12 percent per year increase in the budget before I took office. So Greenspan is right. If you want to get this deficit down, the next thing is to bring health care costs down to inflation plus population.

The other point I would make is there is the chance that this deficit reduction will be greater than we think because of lower interest rates, if we can keep them down long and if we can have good economic growth. I noticed the other day in an article in the Philadelphia Inquirer, a lot of budget analysts were interviewed on the validity of this plan, and the one for Price Waterhouse said that this was the most honest budget plan presented to the Congress in more than a decade, and the only thing I might be off on is it might well produce more deficit reduction. So we just don't know.

Deputy Counsel Vincent Foster, Jr.

Q. Can we just ask you about Mr. Foster? Is there anything more——

The President. No.

Q. Have you learned anything at all?

The President. No, and I don't think there is anything more to know. His family, his friends, his coworkers, we've been up real late two nights in a row now, remembering and crying and laughing and talking about him. I don't think there is anything else.

NOTE: The President spoke at 3:54 p.m. in the East Garden at the White House. He was intro- duced by the Vice President.

Remarks to the American Legion Girls Nation
July 22, 1993

The President. Thank you very much. Thank you. Please be seated. It's wonderful to have you in the Rose Garden today. As I think all of you probably know, I, myself, owe a great deal to the American Legion for sponsoring this wonderful program that teaches our young people so much about our country and the responsibilities of citizenship. Boys Nation made a major impact on my life and very much inspired the career that I subsequently pursued in public service. Like many of you, I was just a high school student from a fairly small town—I had never been to Washington before, and I never knew whether I'd ever get to come—when I stood here, right over there in that corner 30 years ago this week and had the opportunity to hear President Kennedy speak.

I was reviewing an article in a paper from that week before I came out here to speak with you, and I noted that when President Kennedy spoke to our group, he actually got into some hot water by saying that our group, in adopting a civil rights resolution in the early sixties, had acted more responsibly than the Nation's Governors who were meeting at the same time. He said we had shown more initiative than the Governors. Well, we loved it, but somehow the Governors didn't.

And so I would say to you, I don't want to make any other group mad, but I hope you today will leave here with a real sense of initiative. It's very important not only that we have convictions and feelings and concerns but that we act on them. Every program that I have pursued, every challenge I have laid down has been animated by a desire to get the American people to assume more responsibility for themselves and their neighbors, to offer more opportunity to all people, and to rebuild a sense of community, a sense that we are all in this together, that we share a common destiny, and that we will be more likely to achieve our individual capacities if we work together.

With the help of young people all across the country, we were able to pass and we had a wonderful signing ceremony on the motor voter bill, which many of you will be familiar with, which makes it much easier for people to register and vote. Together with other groups of young people, again from all over America, we are on the verge of passing an historic bill for national service that will make it possible for millions of young people to get much lower interest college loans and pay them back on more favorable terms and, over the next few years, for hundreds of thousands of them to work off a portion of their loans by giving some service to their community, either before, during, or after college. This will help to build America by strengthening the bonds of community, offering people the chance to take more responsibility for their own lives, and really creating opportunity that wasn't there before.

We're also trying to improve your future by cutting the Federal deficit by $500 billion over the next 5 years. In 1980, the entire debt of our country amassed since George Washington became President was $1 trillion. From 1980 to 1992, that debt grew to about $4 trillion, quadrupling in only 12 years. Now, when a problem like this gets that severe, you can't solve it all at once. The spending cuts and tax increases it would take just to do away with the deficit in 4 years would be so severe as to undermine our economic recovery. But we're in a box. If we don't move on the deficit now, we can't have any economic recovery, either. And because of the progress which has been made, interest rates are coming down, and we're moving forward.

You should know that you're not only moving into a time when the global economy offers you unparalleled, exciting opportunities but where it also presents some mysteries to us that no one quite understands. For example, almost all of the wealthy countries are having difficulty creating new jobs, even when their economy is growing and certainly when the economy is not. And so this economic program that I have offered not only seeks to reduce the deficit by cutting spending and raising taxes, 70 percent of which will fall on people with incomes above $200,000, it also seeks to help people to create jobs. Ninety percent of the small businesses in America will be eligible for a tax cut in this plan if they invest more money in their businesses to create jobs—new opportunities for people to avoid higher income taxes, but only if they invest in companies that will create jobs. We have got to find a way to make sure that if all of you go to college and all your classmates go to college and everybody plays by the rules, there will be something for them to do when the effort is over.

Thirty years ago, when the delegates from Girls Nation came to the White House in the same summer that I was here, my next-door neighbor represented our State at Girls Nation. It was a great thrill for me, and she's still one of my closest friends. Just last week when I went home, she got some of our high school friends together, and they and all their children, there must have been 30 of us in her home having dinner together. And when she was here where you are, President Kennedy told the young women there assembled that it might be possible for one of them to become President, but it was not likely. And almost as a consolation prize, he said, "At least I'm sure I'm talking to a future First Lady." Well, today a lot of things have changed. First of all, I think that it is a very honorable thing to be the First Lady. Some day there will be a First Man. And I think it is not unlikely that 30 years from now the delegates from Girls Nation may well be in the Rose Garden being addressed by a woman President who is in this crowd today.

Again, let me wish you well, and thank you for coming here. Let me tell you that the 30 years that have passed since I sat where you are today have passed in the flash of an eye, that I hope for all of you a rich and full life, and I would encourage you to focus on the point I made earlier: You came here to learn about your country, your history, your opportunities, and your responsibilities as citizens. None of it matters very much unless you not only think and feel but also act.

Good luck, and God bless you.

Let me also say, I'm going to embarrass somebody who's here maybe a little bit. There are other things in life after a Girls Nation or Boys Nation than being President. I just learned that my military aide came to Girls Nation. Raise your hand. This is Major Michelle Johnson, the United States Air Force. She is from Iowa, graduate of the Air Force Academy, Rhodes scholar, terrific athlete. I told her someday I was sure I'd be saluting her and calling her General. So that also is something that you might do with your life that you couldn't have done perhaps a few years ago.

I'd like to now ask Joann Cronin to come up and take over the program.

[At this point, the President was presented with gifts, including bills and resolutions passed by Girls Nation.]

I saw the first resolution was the sex education one. That's one I said I was for. You may know that tomorrow the hearing begins on the appointment I made of an African-American doctor, the director of the department of health in my home State, to be the Surgeon General of the United States. And we caused a lot of controversy because we tried to promote comprehensive family education, parenting education, and we did our best to reduce the scourge of teenage pregnancy in our State, not by denying it but by embracing the challenge. And I appreciate the resolution that you sent. I will also review the other resolutions.

On Saturday—you mentioned 30 years from now—Saturday your counterparts from Boys Nation will be here, and we're going to have a 30-year reunion of my class Saturday at noon when they're here. So I'm looking forward to it. One of the things that happens when you run for President is that the people you haven't seen in a long time show up, and that's mostly good. So I'm looking forward to it.

Now are we going to take a picture? Is that the way we're going to do it? And then aren't we going to take a group photo also? Okay, great.

NOTE: The President spoke at 4:47 p.m. in the Rose Garden at the White House. In his remarks, he referred to Joann Cronin, national Girls State director.

Exchange With Reporters Prior to a Meeting With Chairman Stanislav Shushkevich of Belarus
July 22, 1993

Surgeon General Nominee

Q. Mr. President, are you confident that Dr. Elders has the answers to the questions she'll be asked tomorrow?

The President. I think she'll do very well.

Let me also say while Chairman Shushkevich is here that I am very honored to have him here in the White House. And I want to thank him publicly for the support his country has given to the nonproliferation regime and to START I. We're going to have a good partnership. I look forward to its development. And I very much appreciate the fact that he has come here off of a successful commitment by his nation to be nonnuclear. And it means a lot to the United States and to the world.

Midwest Disaster Assistance

Q. Are you concerned about getting the flood money from the House, sir?

The President. No, not from what I heard about that. I think it's okay.

NOTE: The exchange began at 5:40 p.m. in the Oval Office at the White House. A tape was not available for verification of the content of this exchange.

Statement by the Press Secretary on the President's Meeting With Chairman Stanislav Shushkevich of Belarus
July 22, 1993

In an Oval Office meeting, President Clinton today congratulated the head of state of Belarus, Stanislav Shushkevich, for the historic decision his country has taken to join the Non-Proliferation Treaty (NPT). The President praised Chairman Shushkevich for the support Belarus has given to the cause of nonproliferation.

The President noted that Belarus is the first of the newly independent states of the former Soviet Union to fully honor its commitments under the Lisbon Protocol to ratify START and accede to the NPT. He applauded this courageous step, stating that under the leadership of Chairman Shushkevich, Belarus has been in the forefront of the global effort to safeguard mankind from the threat of nuclear destruction.

The President announced that this week our countries have signed three agreements providing for $59 million in assistance under the Nunn-Lugar legislation for projects aimed at dealing with the legacy of nuclear weapons in Belarus. We expect to be working closely with Belarus in the near term to develop additional projects.

President Clinton also stressed the strong interest of the U.S. in expanding economic ties with Belarus, particularly in trade and investment opportunities for American and Belarusian firms. He expressed his hope that the U.S. and Belarus will conclude soon a bilateral investment treaty, a tax treaty, and a Peace Corps agreement.

Chairman Shushkevich's visit to Washington represents the President's first official meeting in the United States with the head of state of one of the newly independent states.

Letter to Congressional Leaders Reporting on Iraq's Compliance With United Nations Security Council Resolutions
July 22, 1993

Dear Mr. Speaker: (Dear Mr. President:)

Consistent with the Authorization for Use of Military Force Against Iraq Resolution (Public Law 102–1), and as part of my effort to keep the Congress fully informed, I am reporting on the status of efforts to obtain Iraq's compliance with the resolutions adopted by the U.N. Security Council.

Over the last several months, we have seen more examples of the Iraqi Government's refusal to comply with relevant Security Council resolutions and international law. In May I reported on our investigation of allegations that Iraq attempted to assassinate former President Bush during his recent trip to Kuwait. We uncovered compelling evidence that the Iraqi Intelligence Service directed the attempt. I concluded that there was no reasonable prospect that new diplomatic initiatives or economic measures could influence the current Government of Iraq to cease planning future attacks against the United States and that a continuing threat was posed to the United States. Accordingly, I ordered a precise and limited strike against the headquarters of the Iraqi Intelligence Service in the exercise of our inherent right of self-defense under international law. In accordance with the Charter of the United Nations, we reported our actions to the Security Council immediately.

We will strive to use law enforcement and international cooperation to prevent the Iraqi regime from once again killing innocent people in pursuit of its ends. It should be clear, however, that we will strike directly at those who direct and pursue Iraqi policies when it is necessary to do so in our self-defense.

Also, on June 19, a U.S. aircraft fired a missile at an Iraqi anti-aircraft site that had displayed hostile intent. The site has not been active since the attack.

Inspections by the U.N. Special Commission on Iraq (UNSCOM) and the International Atomic Energy Agency (IAEA) to date have forced Iraq to disclose, destroy, or render harmless all the major nuclear weapons facilities and equipment of which we are aware. Along with damage inflicted in combat, these inspections have effectively put the Iraqi nuclear weapons program out of business in the near-term and have substantially impaired Iraq's other weapons of mass destruction (WMD) programs.

Over the long-term, however, we believe that Saddam Hussein is committed to rebuilding his WMD capability, especially nuclear weapons. UNSCOM and the IAEA are therefore developing a program of long-term monitoring in accordance with Security Council Resolution 715. Iraq has refused to accept that Resolution, blocking UNSCOM from installing cameras to monitor Iraq's compliance with restrictions on long-range missiles and from sealing missile sites. The Security Council has declared these actions, along with Iraq's failure to comply with demands related to its chemical weapons program, to be a material and unacceptable breach of Resolution 687 and has warned Iraq of "serious consequences" if it fails to comply. Discussions between UNSCOM and Iraq on these issues are currently underway.

Iraq depicts itself as seeking consultations, rather than confrontation, in complying with Security Council resolutions. Iraq, however, has attempted to obstruct even the clearest Security Council requirements. In June, Iraq missed two deadlines to deliver equipment for producing chemical weapon precursors to UNSCOM for supervised destruction. UNSCOM has reported the matter to the Security Council, which has the matter under consideration. Iraq still refuses to divulge information indicating the foreign companies from which it purchased equipment and materials. Accurate information is integral to a workable and realistic mechanism for import control, as required by Security Council Resolution 715.

Iraq has also tried to restrict the exercise of UNSCOM's aerial inspection rights, impose limits on the duration of inspections and the size and composition of inspection teams, required advance notice of inspection activities, and limit inspectors' rights to take photographs. Vandalism, harassment, and theft have continued against inspectors and U.N. property. Iraq is responsible for improving this hostile environment.

We have received reports of Iraqi forces shooting at Saudi border guards across the Iraq-Saudi border. These acts appear to violate paragraph 3(a) of Security Council Resolution 686, which demanded that Iraq cease hostile or provocative acts against other states. These incidents are the first of their kind since the ceasefire and further call into question Iraq's intention to live in peace with its neighbors.

The "no-fly zones" over northern and southern Iraq permit the monitoring of Iraq's compliance with Security Council Resolutions 687 and 688. Over the last two years, the northern no-fly zone has deterred Iraq from a major military offensive in the region. Since the no-fly zone was established in southern Iraq, Iraq's use of aircraft against its population in the region has stopped, as have large-scale troop movements. However, the no-fly zone has not prevented the Iraqi army from conducting an ongoing campaign against Iraqi Shias in the southern marshes, involving the recent burning of several villages. We are continuing to work toward the placement of human rights monitors throughout Iraq as proposed by Max van der Stoel, Special Rapporteur to the U.N. Human Rights Commission, and to work for the establishment of a U.N. Commission to investigate and publicize Iraqi war crimes and other violations of international humanitarian law.

The international community has continued its efforts, consistent with Security Council resolutions, to alleviate suffering in Iraq. The United States is working closely with the U.N. and other organizations to provide humanitarian relief to the people of northern Iraq, in the face of Iraqi Government efforts to disrupt this assistance. We continue to support new U.N. efforts to mount a relief program for persons in Baghdad and the South and will ensure that the U.N. will be able to prevent the Iraqi Government from diverting supplies.

The U.N. sanctions regime exempts medicine and requires only that the U.N. Sanctions Committee be notified of food shipments. In accordance with paragraph 20 of Resolution 687, the Committee received notices of 20 million tons of foodstuffs to be shipped to Iraq through June 1993. The Sanctions Committee also continues to consider and, when appropriate, approve requests to send to Iraq materials and supplies for essential civilian needs. The Iraqi Government, in contrast, has maintained a full embargo against its northern provinces and has acted to distribute humanitarian supplies only to its supporters and to the military.

The Iraqi Government has so far refused to accept U.N. conditions for selling $1.6 billion in oil as previously authorized by the Security Council in Resolutions 706 and 712, although talks between Iraq and the United Nations on implementing these resolutions were resumed in New York on July 7 for the third time in two years. Iraq could use proceeds from such sales to purchase foodstuffs, medicines, materials, and supplies for essential civilian needs of its population, subject to strict U.N. monitoring of sales and the equitable distribution of humanitarian supplies (including to its northern provinces).

Proceeds from oil sales also would be used to compensate persons injured by Iraq's unlawful invasion and occupation of Kuwait. The U.N. Compensation Commission has received about 800,000 claims so far, with a total of roughly two million expected. The U.S. Government has filed a fourth set of individual claims with the Commission, bringing U.S. claims filed to about 1,100. The Commission's efforts will facilitate the compensation of those injured by Iraq once sufficient funds become available.

Security Council Resolution 778 permits the use of a portion of frozen Iraqi oil assets to fund crucial U.N. activities concerning Iraq, including humanitarian relief, UNSCOM, and the Compensation Commission. (The funds will be repaid, with interest, from Iraqi oil revenues as soon as Iraqi oil exports resume.) The United States is prepared to transfer up to $200 million in frozen Iraqi oil assets held in U.S. financial institutions, provided that U.S. contributions do not exceed 50 percent of the total amount contributed. We have arranged a total of over $51 million in such matching contributions thus far and anticipate making another matching contribution of just over $40 million.

Iraq still has not met its obligations concerning Kuwaitis and third-country nationals it detained during the war. Iraq has taken no substantive steps to cooperate fully with the International Committee of the Red Cross (ICRC), as required by Security Council Resolution 687, although it has received over 600 files on missing individuals. Regional organizations have also been engaged—thus far to no avail—in trying to obtain Iraqi compliance on the issue of detainees. We continue to work for Iraqi compliance.

The United Nations has completed its technical task of demarcating the previously agreed Iraq-Kuwait border, and the President of the Security Council accepted its work. Iraqi Government officials have refused to recognize the boundary, despite the requirement to do so under Security Council Resolution 687. In accordance with Security Council Resolution 806, which responded to Iraqi disruptions on the border, the U.N. continues to seek the identification and deployment of an armored battalion to the United Nations Iraq-Kuwait Observer Mission (UNIKOM), so that UNIKOM has sufficient force to take necessary actions to prevent violations of the border and the demilitarized zone. The United States and our allies also continue to press the Government of Iraq to return all property and equipment removed from Kuwait by Iraq.

Iraq can rejoin the community of civilized nations only through democratic processes, respect for human rights, equal treatment of its people, and adherence to basic norms of international behavior. A government representing all the people of Iraq, which is committed to the territorial integrity and unity of Iraq, would be a stabilizing force in the Gulf region. The Iraqi National Congress (INC) espouses these goals and our support for the INC is a signal of the future we seek for Iraq.

I am grateful for the support of the Congress of our efforts.

Sincerely,

WILLIAM J. CLINTON

NOTE: Identical letters were sent to Thomas S. Foley, Speaker of the House of Representatives, and Robert C. Byrd, President pro tempore of the Senate.

Remarks on National Service Legislation and an Exchange With Reporters
July 23, 1993

The President. Good morning, everybody. Before I leave I'd like to make a couple of comments, if I might.

First of all, I was frankly somewhat disappointed yesterday at the delay in the progress of the national service legislation in the Senate. This is one idea that all Americans should be able to agree on. We know we have broad bipartisan support. Several Republican Senators have told us that they like the bill and intend to support it. And I very much hope that next week whatever considerations were moving the Republican Senate toward filibuster will evaporate.

Mr. Segal and all the people supporting national service have worked hard with Republicans and Democrats from the inception of this legislation. We have a very large number of Republican supporters in the House of Representatives, as well as the Democrats, and significant support in the Senate. And this is not the bill to delay. America needs this. It's a very important part of our efforts to open the doors of college education to all Americans and give hundreds of thousands of young Americans over the next few years a chance to serve their country while earning credit against their college costs. I think it's very important that we move on it.

The next thing I would like to say is I'm very encouraged and I have very positive feelings about the progress made in the conference on the budget plan. The conferees are obviously determined to move toward the largest deficit reduction package in history and to do it in a way that promotes growth and jobs. I was quite encouraged that some of the provisions that were agreed on yesterday were those that I think are important to encourage people to invest in new jobs in this country, including the provision long championed by Senator Bumpers to give a significant tax break to people who make investments of 5 years or longer in new businesses and smaller businesses in this country. So I think we're off to a good start on that, and I'm very hopeful about the spirit that is prevailing in the conference today.

Deputy Counsel Vincent Foster, Jr.

Q. Mr. President, do you have any update on the Park Police or the Justice Department on Vince Foster and the investigation?

The President. No. It's just a normal, routine

thing that would be done. I don't think anything's going to come out other than what you already know.

Q. What will you say about your friend in Arkansas?

The President. That he was a wonderful person. That I don't think that any of us will ever know exactly why his life ended the way it did. But today I think that we should all determine not to judge his life by the way it ended solely. He was a terrific friend, a great father, a great husband, a great lawyer. He was one of the ablest and best people I ever knew in my life. That's what makes this day the more painful. But we have to accept the fact that there are many things we're not in control of, many things we don't understand, and we have to be grateful for what his life was.

Thank you.

Midwest Disaster Assistance

Q. The floods—what about the funds, and

are they playing politics on the flood issue?

The President. Who?

Q. The House?

The President. I don't think we should read too much into that. Let's wait and see what happens next week. There are people in the House that have very strong feelings about the procedures by which matters should be brought to vote and debated, and I think that's what's going on. I wouldn't read too much into that one way or the other. Let's wait and see what they do. I think they'll work through it next week.

Thank you.

NOTE: The President spoke at 8:15 a.m. on the South Lawn at the White House prior to his departure for Little Rock, AR. A tape was not available for verification of the content of these remarks.

Exchange With Reporters in Hope, Arkansas
July 23, 1993

Q. How are you feeling?

Q. Can you tell us—what are these watermelons?

The President. They're the best. It's a little early yet. They'll be big in about a month. Four weeks from now we're going to have the watermelon festival here. And I used to come down here every year and run in the 5K run and enter the cow chip throwing contest, which I won one year, I'm embarrassed to say. The year I won it they said I shouldn't be rewarded because I have an unfair advantage, since politicians do it for a living. [*Laughter*] That's what they said.

But anyway, they're pretty good yet, but it's a little early in the season, and we need a little more rain.

Q. Is this your first trip back to Hope since the Inauguration?

The President. Yes. Yeah.

Q. How is Mrs. Foster doing, Mr. President?

The President. I think they're doing pretty well. You can see they've got a very wide circle of friends here in this State, up in Little Rock and here. I think it will really help them a

lot.

Q. How are you doing?

The President. I'm all right. I'm pretty sad, but I'm all right.

Q. Does it help you to come home?

The President. Oh, a lot. We were all standing out there at the cemetery today, and all these people showed up we went to kindergarten and first grade with and people that all of us have shared the last 20 or 30 years with. It helped them a lot, I think, and it helped me. And then getting to go by and see my uncle meant a lot to me. He'll be 89 in December. Yes, he's a remarkable man, remarkable man.

Q. He's 89?

The President. December. He's 88; he'll be 89 in December. He had lung cancer like 15 years ago, had a lung taken out, and just rolled right on. He lost his wife a couple of years ago.

Q. Your mother wasn't in that picture?

The President. Yes, she had to go back. She's doing something now.

Q. Did he have any advice for you?

The President. He said, "You remember at

Christmas," he said, "I told you you were grabbing hold of a big hog by the tail." He said, "The problem with grabbing hold of a big hog by the tail is a hog's tail gets smaller and smaller and smaller. You just can't let one start to get away from you." [*Laughter*]

Q. What does that mean?

The President. It means hold tight, I think.

Q. You're not really going to have a haircut on Air Force One, are you?

The President. No. No, but my barber, he's going to cut my hair.

Q. You're going to him? What time?

The President. I'm going to meet him somewhere, wherever he says to meet. I told him I'd either come there, or he could come to me. He's going to decide. He's closing up at 6 p.m. He ends at 6 p.m. on Saturday. He works all day Saturday because it's convenient for working people to go in there. So when we get back, he'll have been down about 30 minutes, so we're just going to go wherever he says go.

Q. Were you surprised the limo was down when you went out to the house today? Did you expect to spend 15 minutes in the street there?

The President. Oh, I didn't know whether they were back or not, but I knew I'd have to spend a little time with the neighborhood kids anyway, so it was fine. And then a lot of people came up that don't live in the neighborhood that I knew. That was Win Rockefeller, you know, came up——

Q. I saw, yes.

The President. He's an alltime, longtime friend of mine and Hillary's. I reappointed him the State police commissioner. Senator Pryor put him on the State police commission.

Q. It's the only Corvette police car in the country.

The President. Yes. He loves the State police. He did when I first met him in 1969, when his father was the Governor and he and I were students. And I was fixin' to go—I had been in England, and he was fixin' to go. He was already in love with the State police. It was his number one passion even when he was a young boy. So it was nice to see him.

Q. Are we going to get some of these watermelons——

The President. You bet.

Q. ——back to Washington?

The President. Everybody on the plane. You're on the plane, aren't you?

Q. Oh, absolutely.

Q. I didn't realize they had yellow meat. I think of watermelons as just red.

The President. Yes, you can breed them for yellow, too. The seeds—yeah.

Q. Are they sweeter?

The President. They're sweeter. You'll see. They're going to load up. I'm going to ask Jack how many yellow-meated ones he put on. But I had him put one or two on.

Q. They just filled the van up right behind you.

The President. I had him put one or two yellow-meated ones on so everybody could get a chance to taste them.

Q. Yes, I've never had one.

The President. Now, in August, when they start having the contest for the biggest melon, they're really not much. They don't taste very good after they get about 65 pounds or bigger than that, they've got so much water in them. But you can almost literally watch them grow. I mean, they get up to 50, 60, 70 pounds. And you just have to keep pouring water—and they grow in real sandy soil—and pour water in them. The stalk is there, and it just sucks the water out of the ground, literally, like a vacuum cleaner. The water will go in and just suck it back out into the melon. It is amazing.

Q. It looks kind of dry here, Mr. President.

The President. Yes, it's been dry. We may not get many big melons this year. A lot of it is the seeds and the sand, the seeds and the soil and just proper care. It's really interesting to watch them get into the contest the last week or two because if the skin splits at all, if there's the tiniest rend in the fabric of the skin, then the melon is disqualified from the contest. It doesn't matter how much it weighs. It has to have a uniformly smooth skin, and yet the water is just bursting at it, you know. So they get down—it's really scientific—you thump it, you just have to have a—you have to know when to quit. General rule of life.

Q. I guess that's it.

Q. I still like your uncle's advice about the hog by the tail.

The President. He said a lot of smart things to me. When I was in my first term as Governor, the one I lost, he told me I was in a world of trouble. He called me one day, the only time he ever called me the whole time I was in public life. He said, "People are mad at you for raising car licenses." I said, "They said they wanted the road fixed." He said, "They didn't mean it." He said, "Most people like me," he said, "I don't give a rip about politics, as long as I can go hunting, fishing, rivers are clean." He said, "They did want it, but not"—he said, "It just didn't work." He said, "You need to undo it." He's really smart. He's a very smart guy.

Q. Has he figured out the deficit?

Q. Are you sure you don't need him in Washington?

The President. He's like a lot of people down here. He's got a high IQ and not a lot of formal education but a world of horse sense. I mean, he's really a smart man. And when I was a child living down here and then after I moved to Hot Springs when I was 6, I used to get on a bus, a Trailways bus, and take the bus back down here—stop at every little town along the way, you know—and come down and spend a weekend with him. He and his wife, they would feed me. And Chelsea wasn't in that house 10 minutes till he had her in the back giving her peanut brittle.

Q. See, that's what the world is all about.

The President. Yes. But I loved to go down here.

Q. We passed the house they said you were born in.

The President. Well, I was actually born in a hospital, which, funny, was torn down before the election. Somebody of little faith put an office building up there. Now they wish they didn't. But that's where I lived. And my mother, of course, was widowed by then, so my grandparents lived in that house. And my grandmother was a private-duty nurse. She lived down the block, and my granddaddy had a little country store out across from the other cemetery where Mack's father and my father are buried. It's parallel to the road we're taking now. I think Mack went over there today—and where my grandparents are buried. But anyway, my granddaddy had a store out there, and my grandmother walked down the street to work every day. And Mother and I lived there. And then when I was 2, she went away to get her nurse's training finished.

But Vince Foster's house was around the corner. It was that sort of nice brick house around

the corner. I don't know if you noticed, but it had two-tone brick. It's kind of ugly now, but when he lived there they painted it white and it was perfectly beautiful. And for some reason—I never have understood why they took the white paint off, because it's not near as pretty now. But anyway, that's where Vince lived, around the corner.

Q. But that white house that's being worked on is the one where you lived when you were little?

The President. Yes. When my mother left the hospital with me, we went there. We lived there until I was 4. When I was 4, my mother remarried Roger Clinton, and we moved out on the other side of town, a little bitty house on 13th Street. And I understand they've got a sign out front of that, too.

Q. I want to know why she let you play with knives at the age of 4, Mr. President. [*Laughter*]

The President. I don't think they knew. I'm not sure they knew. It was a dull knife. It was a dull knife.

Q. Mr. President, what have you learned about life this week?

The President. I think what I said in the service and what I said to my staff: There are a lot of things that we're not in control of and a lot of mysteries we don't understand. And I think all of us need to work a lot harder not to be so pressured by whatever we're doing that we don't pay enough attention to ourselves, our families, and our friends, people we work with. I think we all need to not deaden our sensitivities by working too hard. It undermines how well you work for the people, and it obviously undermines the quality of life.

No one will ever know whether there was anything any of us could have done to avoid this, but it certainly gave me a lot of renewed sense of humility about how we should all conduct ourselves and what we should do.

But Vince Foster had a lot of friends. You can see that today. A whole lot of people really cared a lot about him.

Ready to go? We got it? Let's roll.

NOTE: The exchange took place in the late afternoon at Jack Still's watermelon stand. A tape was not available for verification of the content of this exchange.

The President's Radio Address
July 24, 1993

Good morning. Six months ago this week, I took office as your President. And together we dedicated ourselves to fulfilling a vision of change for our country, change that would set us firmly on the path to growth, to progress and prosperity based on some old-fashioned principles and some new ideas.

The principles are that we all ought to be able to take more responsibility for ourselves, our families, and our neighbors; that we ought to have more opportunity in this country; and that together we can make a stronger American community so that all of us as individuals can do better.

We decided to begin with an economic plan which puts aside trickle-down economics and emphasizes bringing down this deficit and investing in our people and our economy; to be followed by an effort to control health care costs and provide affordable health care to all Americans; a welfare reform plan to move people from welfare to work; the national service program to open the doors of college education to millions of young people and give many, many of them a chance to pay their college loans back through service to their communities; a tougher crime bill; and a bill to reform the political system itself, to reduce the influence of big money and lobbyists and to open the process to the influence of ordinary people.

We're making progress on all these efforts, but for the centerpiece, the economic plan, the moment of truth is almost at hand. Lawmakers on Capitol Hill are working on a final version of our budget plan, and in the next couple of weeks when your Senators and Representatives vote on this plan, they will determine whether we will reduce the deficit, rebuild our economy, and recharge our job-creating machine.

This morning I want to talk to you again about that plan and the new jobs it will create. This is our historic opportunity for getting our economic house in order. If we pass the plan, we'll be on the way to reducing the deficit by $500 billion over the next 5 years, to putting millions more Americans to work, and providing middle class Americans and businesses with the tools they need to compete and win in the global economy.

This plan represents fundamental change, and that's why we're not without our critics in Washington. The problem is that most of what the critics have told you about the plan, that there are no budget cuts, there's no deficit reduction, it's all a big tax increase on the middle class, all those things are absolutely untrue. The fact is, we're cutting $250 billion in spending, and a lot of those spending cuts are not popular. Over 100 of those cuts exceed $100 million each.

The second thing is that there are as many spending cuts as tax increases in the plan, and all the cuts and the tax increases will be put into a deficit reduction trust fund so they can't be touched for any other purpose but bringing down our debt.

And another thing you won't hear from the critics of the deficit reduction plan is that 70 percent—that's right, 70 percent—of the new taxes will be paid by the richest Americans, the 1.2 percent of us with incomes of $200,000 a year or more.

Now, these things are very important. But it's also important what you will have to do, if you're a member of the middle class or the working poor. The middle class will be asked to make a contribution but a very modest one. A family of four with an average income of $50,000 will be asked to pay about $50 a year in an energy tax, that's less than $1 a week, to help ensure the future of our children and our grandchildren. Working families with incomes of under $30,000 will be held harmless. And the working poor, for the first time in the history of this country, will be helped through the tax system to move out of poverty. That's right. We'll be able to say for the first time if you work full time and you have children in your home, you won't be poor any more. That's the biggest incentive to ending welfare as we know it that I can imagine. At the same time, this plan helps businesses with special incentives to create new jobs.

Over 90 percent of the small businesses in this country will be eligible for a tax cut if they invest in their businesses to improve their productivity and to make it possible for them to grow. That's right. There is no income tax on over 90 percent of the small businesses in this country, and all of them will be eligible for a tax reduction if they invest more money in their businesses. There are special incentives to get people to invest in new businesses, to support research and development, to encourage our bigger companies to employ their resources for new plant and equipment so they can hire new people, to revitalize the real estate industry. There is a provision here that in new communication technology alone can create 300,000 jobs in the next 10 years.

Yesterday the Treasury Department issued a new State-by-State study of the jobs the economy has projected to create over the next 4 years if the Congress passes the economic plan. Based on projections from several leading independent analysts, this report says that over the next 4 years the economy will create 8 million jobs. The Treasury also reports that in the first 5 months of this administration, there have been 740,000 private sector jobs created, about 150,000 a month. That's over seven times the rate of job creation during the previous administration.

These forecasts indicate that individual States should show dramatic improvements compared to the previous 4 years. For example, California's projected to create nearly 2 million new jobs, more than 10 times the number created during the last administration; Georgia, about 400,000 jobs, more than 10 times the number created during the previous years; and Massachusetts projected to create about 100,000 jobs. That's very important there, because in the late 1980's and early 1990's, Massachusetts actually lost over 180,000 jobs. We can help these States with our economic plan and all the others as well, helping to get America moving again, generating permanent, productive private sector jobs.

In the meantime, we're already seeing the dividends from our commitment to fix the economy. As the Chairman of the Federal Reserve Board, Alan Greenspan, reported to the House last week, confidence that we're going to reduce the deficit through this budget plan has inspired those people who determine what the interest rates in our country are, so that now we have the lowest long-term interest rates in 22 years. As a result, many of you listening today may be thinking of refinancing your home, or maybe you're one of the millions of homeowners who have already done it or all the people who are refinancing their business loans. If you do that, you can save a whole lot more on lower interest rates than you'll be asked to pay in higher taxes to make this plan work.

None of this would have been possible without the determination of our administration to reduce the deficit and to rebuild the economy. We've all gotten an earful from our opponents who would really rather just leave things the way they are. They've misrepresented who is paying the taxes and how much the budget cuts are and the fact that small businesses by and large are getting a tax cut, not a tax increase.

You may recall that I've asked those critics to come up with an alternative. Because let's face it, if there's a better way than the way I've proposed to fix the mess I inherited, I'm sure I want to hear it and you do too. So our critics came up with a plan. And if you have a problem remembering the details, there's a good reason. There weren't a lot of details in the last Senate Republican plan on reducing the deficit. You see, it reduced the deficit a lot less than our plan; $66 billion of the so-called spending cuts weren't even specified. They said, "Well, trust us. We'll come up with that for later." And as for burden-sharing, they didn't ask the wealthiest Americans, whose taxes went down while their incomes went up in the 1980's, to pay one red cent. They just wanted to cut more in Medicare for the elderly, in programs for the working poor and the middle class. It was burden-shirking, not burden-sharing.

In sum, our opponents' plan was a rerun of the same old trickle-down economics we tried in the 1980's. We've all seen that movie before. They said, "It's spending, stupid." But when they had their chance, when our budget was before the Senate Finance Committee, the Republicans on the committee did not offer one red cent in specific spending cuts.

Someone once said that the truth is like a torch that glows in the fog. Well, I want that torch to burn brightly, to burn away all the fog that's surrounded the debate on this economic program and let the real picture of positive change for America shine through. Make no mistake about it, we're on the verge of doing something historic for our country. It'll be a challenge, but we always welcome a challenge.

This week, on the 24th anniversary of the first walk by an American on the Moon, we should remember the challenge laid down by President Kennedy. He said, and I quote, "We choose to go to the Moon and to do other things not because they're easy but because they're hard, because the challenges are ones we are willing to accept, unwilling to postpone, and ones we intend to win."

We should be willing to accept this challenge, unwilling to postpone it, and let's intend to win.

Thanks for listening, and God bless you all.

NOTE: The address was recorded at 8 p.m. on July 22 in the Oval Office at the White House for broadcast at 10:06 a.m. on July 24.

Remarks to the American Legion Boys Nation
July 24, 1993

The President. Thank you very much, and please be seated. I told the Vice President what I was about to do, and he wanted to come out and say hello to you. But he has another meeting; he's trying to pass our economic plan, so he has to go. He just wanted to say hello. So I'm going to let him come up here and say a few words to you, so he can go back to work while I have a good time with you.

The Vice President. Thanks very much. I know this is a very exciting day for all of you. And I want to wish you well. And if there is anyone here who has in the back of his mind any notion at all of going into public service or politics, I only have one word of advice. If you can manage somehow to get a picture of you shaking hands with President Clinton here today, it might come in handy later on. [*Laughter*]

The President. Thank you very much, and welcome. I want to acknowledge the presence here of the national commander of the American Legion, Roger Munson; and the national chaplain, James Wagner; the executive director, John Sommer; and the director of activities, Jack Mercier, who was at Boys Nation 30 years ago when I was here—he started I think 31 years ago; George Blume, the legislative director; and a number of people here from my time of involvement, including one Member of Congress, a Republican from Minnesota, Congressman Jim Ramstad. Where are you? Stand up there. I think all of you know that we're also having a 30-year reunion here this weekend, those of us who were here with me. And the organizer of that was Judge Pete Johnson from Alabama. Pete, where are you? Stand up over there. Gary Sammons, the chair of the National American-ism Commission, is here, the policymaking body that oversees Boys Nation. He was a Michigan Boys Stater in 1963. And I'm just curious.

Would all the people who are here from our reunion class of '63 please stand up. See, they look pretty good, don't they? None the worse for the wear. [*Applause*] Thank you.

Let me say to all of them, we're going to have this ceremony, I'm going to take pictures with the young men who are here as delegates, and then afterward I hope all of you here for the reunion will hang around a little and we'll have a chance to visit, too.

For those of you who are here, I say welcome, and those of you who were here 30 years ago, I say welcome back. All of us share a common bond. We owe a great deal of gratitude to the American Legion for the exceptional chance they have given us and so many others over the last many, many years to learn so much about the responsibilities as well as the rights we have as American citizens.

Three decades to the day have passed since my group and I were here in the Rose Garden to meet President Kennedy. But I think that all of us probably remember exactly how we felt then. It was a very different time for America. There was virtually no cynicism. None of us had any doubt that our country could solve its problems, meet its challenges, bridge its gaps. Nor did we have any doubt that our President, our Congress, the people whom we elected, could faithfully and fully represent us in meeting the great challenges of that day.

One of the most important moments at Boys Nation is the debate about resolutions. And 30 years ago when we were here, believe it or not, we always assumed that President Kennedy would be running for reelection, that Senator Goldwater would probably be his opponent, although there was a lot of turmoil within the Republican Party at that time about who the nominee would be, and that the great issue would be civil rights. Our Boys Nation group passed a resolution against racial discrimination. Many of us had grown up in segregated societies. We understood the pain, the cost, the incredible waste in human potential that that had caused. And so we voted for it.

I was very proud to be one of the southerners that voted for it, and I think that two others that I remember were my two colleagues from Louisiana. I think they're both here today, and they both voted for it. I remember clearly the discussions we had late at night in the dorms discussing it.

The Nation's Governors had just met that week, and they broke up their resolution conference so they wouldn't have to deal with civil rights. So when we showed up here, President Kennedy said that we had shown more initiative than the Nation's Governors. Now, we loved it, but the Governors didn't like it very much. And it got him in a lot of hot water with them.

Sixteen weeks later, President Kennedy was taken from us before he was able to fulfill his commitments in civil rights. But when President Johnson and the civil rights movement carried it through, it was the greatest domestic achievement of my lifetime, and it helped to make possible so many good things for so many people over the last 30 years, even though, to be sure, the work is nowhere near over.

Most of you now attending Boys Nation were born in 1976, the bicentennial year of our independence. And you will live your entire lives in the third century of America's life. I think about that often because my daughter will soon be your age, and everything that we are working on that really matters is designed as much to help you and your tomorrows as to improve the lives of Americans today.

We have a covenant with you which requires us to make some very tough choices. We have some of the same problems we had in 1963 but some very different ones as well. From the time we became a nation until 1980, we had amassed over that entire life of this country a national debt of only $1 trillion. As a percentage of our income, it seemed to be quite manageable, and we were still free to invest in those things we ought to invest in. In the last 12 years, partly because of misguided policies, partly because of gridlock, partly because of people trying to outbid one another, we have gone from $1 to $4 trillion in national debt. The estimated annual deficit when I took office was well over

$300 billion, although we've gotten it down some this year. And clearly, we have unmet needs that we don't have the money to invest in.

As compared with many other nations, just for example, we spend too little money on new technologies for the 21st century which will shape the jobs that you and your colleagues will have. We spend too little money on the continued education and training of our work force. We have all kinds of other challenges occasioned by the builddown of the reduction in defense spending. We owe it to the people who worked hard to help us win the cold war not to leave them out in the cold, and yet we don't have all the funds we need to spend on that. And yet, we have this enormous debt. It is a terrible dilemma for this country.

We have whole sections of America where unemployment is too high and poverty is too high and the major source of income is drugs and the major organizations that works in society are gangs. We have to change all that. But we have to also free ourselves economically of the paralysis that this enormous annual deficit and the accumulated debt impose. And so we are trying to do that here for you as well as for your parents and your grandparents.

In your lifetime, communism, the great threat of my childhood, has been defeated. I can still remember going to high school assemblies and junior high school assemblies and sitting there being given instructions about how to find the nearest bomb shelter and what we would do if a nuclear war occurred. I can still remember hearing people speak about what communism was like in the Soviet Union and how there would be a lifelong struggle between the forces of freedom and the forces of communism. Well, in 1989 when the Berlin Wall fell, it was a stunning reaffirmation of America's commitment to freedom and democracy and to free market economics and the right of individuals to seek their own way as long as they didn't hurt their communities. That is an incredible achievement. In all probability, you will be able to raise your children without any threat of the annihilation of this society or this globe on which we live.

On the other hand, as we have learned from every source of wisdom beginning with the Scriptures, there will never be an end to problems, never be an end to challenges. It is part of human nature that as new opportunities develop, new problems do, too. We have to do something about our debt here. We have to invest. We have to compete. We have to create opportunities for your future. We also have to recognize that the world remains a dangerous place, and there are people running governments who desperately want to develop weapons of mass destruction and have very little concern what is done in retaliation to their own citizens. That is a deeply troubling thing. We still face the threat of terrorism from people who honestly believe that the best way to achieve their political objectives is to kill, even if they kill innocent people. And we still have the terrible, terrible burden of knowing that in spite of all the progress we have made, there are millions of Americans who do not have the chance to grow up to live to their God-given potential. And until that happens, we will never be as secure, as strong, as full as we need to be.

We are trying, among other things in this administration, to make people believe again that their collective efforts can make a difference. Until the American people can overcome their cynicism and believe that if they act, it can matter, it is going to be very difficult for us to solve the problems of this country. I believe that every Member of Congress, without regard to party, would admit that the National Government has a responsibility to set up a framework within which opportunity can be seized, but that many of our problems have to be dealt with person to person, family to family, school to school, job to job, community to community, at the grassroots level. We have to create a climate in which people are challenged to take responsibility for themselves, their families, and their communities; given as many opportunities to do so as possible. But the nature of the problems we have today require the concerted action of millions of Americans.

The good news about that is that all of you can make a difference. That's why I have worked so hard since becoming President to create this program of national service, which would open the doors of college education on better terms to millions of Americans and then give hundreds of thousands of them—hundreds of thousands of people like you, I hope—the opportunity to pay all or a portion of their college loans back with work for their country, in their communities or in other communities here at home, rebuilding America from the grassroots up and doing it either before, during,

or after college. This national service program can make a fundamental difference to the way we view ourselves and our country. It can make more and more people have the same kind of enthusiasm I saw on your face when the Vice President and I walked in here today. We know you're connected to America. We need to connect everyone else to America, as well.

Right now there's a little bit of political maneuvering going on in the Congress about national service. It's sad to me because we have good Republican and Democratic support for this bill. And I earnestly hope that this whole idea will be saved from becoming a political football. It is too important to America. It has nothing to do with partisan politics and everything to do with giving people a chance to serve their country and, in so doing, to help to build a belief in their country again.

People my age remember President Kennedy starting the Peace Corps. Our fathers and mothers remember when President Roosevelt launched the Civilian Conservation Corps during the Great Depression and gave people a chance to build their way out of that depression. In my State I could take you to community after community after community where there are still CCC projects that older people today point to with pride, their hearts swelling, because they, with their own hands, at a time when 25 percent of the American people were unemployed, were given a chance to rebuild their country. We just had a big reunion out in California of the Peace Corps volunteers, and I have named a former Peace Corps volunteer to be the first ex-Peace Corps person to run the Peace Corps. They are swelling with pride to this day for what they did 25 and 30 years ago. And so it will be with national service if we can do it.

I want to say one last thing to all of you. Thomas Jefferson, whose memorial is right back over there and was built 50 years ago this year, was fond of saying that the Earth belongs to the living in trust; that all of us have to balance our lives between doing what is good for us today and what is good for our country, our families, our friends, and our children and grandchildren tomorrow. That means that for all the opportunities you will have, and you young men will have more than most Americans, you have an immense responsibility to give something back to your country. One day you will understand that even more clearly than you do today, although I wish that Americans twice your age understood it as well as you clearly do at this moment.

Regardless of what you do, remember this: It is not enough in life to have feelings. It is not enough in life to have convictions. You must act on them. You must act on them. You must move. You must do. You must make things happen. That is surely the ultimate lesson of Boys State and Boys Nation. We were given a system by the Founding Fathers which permitted people in every generation of Americans to the end of time to join together and to act, to deal with the challenges, seize the opportunities, and beat back the problems of the day. That is the legacy that you have been given. And that is the responsibility that you must assume.

I can tell you that, to me, it seems only yesterday that I was your age, standing here. It doesn't take long to live a life. But it can be very rewarding if you have convictions, if you believe in your feelings, and if you act.

I wish you well, and God bless you. [*Applause*] Thank you. Thank you. Thank you very much.

I'd like now to ask Roger Munson to come forward, and ask the rest of you to sit down. It won't be much longer. I know it's hot out here. When Girls Nation was here a couple of days ago, it wasn't so warm. But it's still a nice day.

[*At this point, Arkansas delegates Traftin Thompson and James Welch presented the President with a 1963 photograph of himself with President Kennedy.*]

Thank you very much. I think now we're going to take the pictures over here. Is that right? No, we're going to do—we've done that. Oh, they're coming to speak? One of the things that happens to you when you become President is you sometimes don't get good instructions.

[*Laughter*] Then you just have to fall on the sword.

Who am I supposed to introduce? Pete, are you coming up here? And Jeff Keyes, is he here? Come on.

Let me say, I saw Pete again during the course of the Presidential campaign. And until that happened, I had one Boys Nation person who went to Georgetown with me who was in my class; the two guys from Louisiana, one who went to Georgetown with me, one who went to law school with me, those two guys I had stayed in close touch with; and one other person who was a delegate from Virginia who I stayed in touch with over the years. Now, when I ran for President, I met so many of them again.

And I wanted to make one other point. It wasn't in my notes, but I'd be remiss if I didn't. It is a very great thing to be given the chance to serve this country as President. But it is a very great mistake to think that that is the thing that counts the most in America. The thing that counts the most in America is the contributions that are made by all Americans who work hard, play by the rules, raise their children well, make their communities stronger. And I was so terribly impressed by learning about the life stories of the other people with whom I was here, the struggles that they'd had, the tragedies they'd faced, the triumphs that they had created. And I want you to remember that, too. Each of you has to serve, and each of you can serve, and each of you can make a difference. And the collective efforts we make are far more important than the individual achievements of any person.

NOTE: The President spoke at 11:11 a.m. in the Rose Garden at the White House. Following his remarks, 1963 Boys Nation delegate Jeff Keyes presented him with a plaque and a second photograph with President Kennedy.

Remarks to the Conference on the Future of the American Workplace in Chicago, Illinois
July 26, 1993

The President. Thank you very much. Senator Simon, Senator Moseley-Braun, Mayor Daley, President Gross, and my friends and colleagues

Secretaries Brown and Reich, and to all of you in the audience, my old colleague Governor Caperton and the distinguished business and labor leaders from all across America.

This has already been a little bit of fun for me. I never thought I'd see Carol Moseley-Braun blush. [*Laughter*] But I will say this: You can call me anything you want as long as you don't take out after me like you did Jesse Helms the other day. [*Laughter*]

I want to say a special word of appreciation to Mayor Daley for talking about the Chicago Laboratory for Change, because it really is sort of symbolic of what we're trying to do all across the country, the kind of partnership between government and business and labor and social service agencies to try to put low income people into the work force, into independence, and away from dependence. And I'm very excited about that.

I talked to President Gross before we came in about the history of Roosevelt University, a very appropriate place to be cosponsoring this event. I'd also be remiss if I didn't thank Adele Simmons, the president of McArthur Foundation, for that foundation's support for this conference and the Joyce Foundation for supporting the conference. I'd like to acknowledge in the audience—I believe she's here—the Reverend Willie Barrow, the chairwoman of Operation Push. They held a conference on economic empowerment this week here, and I want to talk a little more about that later, but until we find a way to reward the working poor and to move people from welfare to work and to make it attractive for people to invest in distressed areas of this country, our economic recovery is going to be limited. Finally, let me say a special word of appreciation to Secretaries Brown and Reich for their work on this conference.

And there's one group of American workers I really want to acknowledge today. This is the third anniversary of one of our most important civil rights laws, the Americans with Disabilities Act. For more than 40 million people, this law is clearing the barriers to full participation in American life, making real the whole pledge that we often say that we don't have a person to waste. This morning in Washington I ran a 5K race with a group of astonishingly able disabled Americans: two who raced in their chairs who had raced all over the world; one marathon runner who happened to be blind; one woman who had MS and made a terrific race around the 5K track, kept the pace all the way; one amputee who had once run a 62-mile race in one

day on a prosthesis and today made the 5K around on his crutches just to prove he could do that, too. The kinds of achievements that these people have demonstrated athletically are demonstrated even more profoundly in the work force every day. We need them, and I am proud of that law.

I am glad to be here in Chicago to discuss this subject today—the city that works, the city of big shoulders, all that. You need to know why I'm glad to be here, because in a very real way, I would not be here as President if it weren't for Chicago. And the economic forces that bring us here to discuss this subject today help to explain that.

I was once at a meeting here in 1988 over at the South Shore Development Bank, and I discovered that three city councilmen, two or three Democratic ward chairs, and a significant portion of the business community in this city came from Arkansas, and it was no accident. If you've ever read Al Hawkis—you ought to read John Johnson's autobiography here, which might be subtitled, "How I Escaped the Abject Poverty of Arkansas City and Came to Chicago and Became a Big Cheese." [*Laughter*] It is a story that has millions of replications: people in the South who couldn't make a living in the Great Depression leaving in massive numbers from the farms and small towns; coming to Chicago, coming to Detroit; finding a way to get into the factories or start a business, at the least; becoming middle class Americans; earning a decent wage with a rising paycheck and a good retirement and health care benefits and enough to buy a home and take a vacation and send your kids to college.

It was the American dream. And when I began running for President I found myself deluged with people in Chicago who had roots in my hometown, in my home State. We had two delegates here, two who were born in the same little town in Arkansas that my Chief of Staff and I were born in, in the Chicago delegation. There's a whole town in Michigan where 90 percent of the people who live in this little town were born in my State. They all came looking for a different life. And that's what basically worked for us. Then eventually, the industrialization which bloomed first here spread back to the South.

In the year I was born, my home State's per capita income was only 56 percent of the national average. Mississippi's was only 48 percent.

The postwar economic boom of America by the late seventies had taken the entire South to about 87 percent of the national average in per capita income. And it was projected that the region would equal or exceed the national average of per capita income by the turn of the century. But then the economic slowdown of the last 20 years hit everywhere and hit those who were less well-educated, more rural, less able to compete in the global economy, even harder.

And I say that's what's important to bring us here today because I got to this job by being a Governor for 12 years in a State where I focused almost exclusively on the subjects and the triumphs and the tribulations that will be discussed here today, on jobs and education and partnerships and productivity. And when I became Governor for my second term in 1983, my State's unemployment rate was almost 3 points higher than the national average. In every month but one until 1992, we were above the national average in unemployment. Then in 1992, we were first or second in job creation. And in 1993, the State enjoys an unemployment rate that I think is still too high but is well below the national average.

The point I want to make is this: The issues we are discussing today in terms of the big, sweeping developments in America have been of at least 20 years in building. The policies we need to change have been in place for a good long while nationally. You know what works in the workplace. You know that partnership works. You know that investment in new technology works. You know that flexibility works. You know that being competitive works. You know that treating people like assets instead of something that is expendable is very important. We need to figure out how to write that large in national policy and then be better partners with you in what you do.

And one of the things that I understand very clearly because I have been a Governor is that nothing I do as President can be fully successful unless it makes sense and works with what all of you are doing. And what I want to talk to you about today is how we can be better partners and what we can do to meet the challenges of this time, because it's much more complex than it was after the Great Depression and after the Second War, when people at least, even though it pained them to do so, could leave their little farms in Texas and Arkansas and Ala-

bama and Mississippi and come to Chicago or come to Detroit or go to Pittsburgh or go out to California, and know they could get a job and hope that when they retire they could come home.

Now the whole country is caught up in a global economy which, to be sure, is always affecting different States and communities in different ways, but essentially has some broad, sweeping characterizations that we have to work to reverse. And to make it more complicated, all over the world the wealthiest countries are having many of the same problems we are. I just returned from Tokyo from a meeting of the great industrial powers of the world. And we find that all of them are having trouble promoting economic growth, all of them are having trouble generating new jobs, and in the 1980's, all of them found an increase in inequality of income and greater difficulty in creating new jobs, even when their economies were growing. So that it is clear that we are dealing with a very complicated issue and that no one has all the answers.

Still it is clear that some things have to be faced. We know that every nation competes in a global marketplace where money management and technology are increasingly mobile. We know that increased productivity and new technologies often mean that more output can be produced with fewer people and that not always now, as was in the case for the last four decades—when that happened before, it was always new and different jobs waiting for those people, so that technology was always a winner. Productivity was always a winner. It always was a net expansionary force. We've always had changes. People have always been moving in and out of jobs. No one can freeze-frame any form of human work and make sure it will always be there in just that way forever. But we know now that for the last 20 years we have seen a steady erosion of the security of average middle class people who work hard and play by the rules, because we have not been able to make the adjustments necessary in this new and different global economy.

We know that we can only meet the challenge if we begin with a very basic fact, the one that you are here to celebrate today and to elucidate: The most precious asset any nation has is the people who live there and that as long as the people who live there are willing to do what it takes to learn more, to do better, to be smarter, to stay ahead of the curve, there are going to be opportunities. We also know that most jobs in every society now are going to be created by the private sector and by what people do or do not do to be more productive, to reach out to new markets, to develop new products and services. And the third thing we know is that Government policy makes a difference at home and abroad. It does make a difference.

For more than two centuries our country has built prosperity by investing in our people and our technology and our future. We have, in other words, followed the policy that I have called putting people first. We invested in our skills through a public school system, through the land grant colleges, through expanding opportunities through the GI bill after the war, our investments in canals and in railroads and highway systems and mass transit, all of these things have helped to make us more productive. We've developed cutting-edge technologies through national defense; through the space program; and to a lesser extent in the past, but it must be more in the future, toward civilian partnerships for new technologies.

But for 20 years we still have seen most Americans working harder for less money. And we have not developed an adequate response to the new global economy. For at least a dozen years, our country has pursued policies that are popular in the short run but very limiting in the long run. We have, to be popular in the short run, reduced taxes and increased the deficit in a way that has taken our national debt in 12 years from $1 to $4 trillion and our annual deficit from about $73 to a projected $311 when I took office.

At the same time, we have miraculously managed to reduce our national investment in the education skills and technology that our people need to grow in the future, a mathematical sleight of hand that is almost inconceivable when I tell people about it, but it's true. Why? Because we keep spending more on the same health care and more on interest on the debt. So that the people you think of in Washington as being to blame for big spending and big deficits because they're spending more on programs are, in fact, by and large, spending less on programs that would help you to do your job better. But because there has not been a disciplined effort to bring down the deficit, a disciplined effort to bring health care costs in line with inflation, which would bring interest

rates down there and then reduce what we have to spend servicing the debt, we are actually spending more and getting less for it, the worst of all worlds.

This has continued the downward pressure on wages and job growth. And every working family in America has felt its impact. Between 1972 and 1992, while the work year got longer for Americans, average hourly wages actually dropped by 10 percent. The 75 percent of our workers who don't have 4-year college degrees felt it most profoundly. For those who began but didn't complete college, wages fell 10 percent from 1979 through 1991; for those who didn't go on to college, wages fell 17 percent; for those who left high school, wages dropped 24 percent.

It is, of course, perhaps enough to say to explain this, that as we move into a global economy where what you earn depends on what you can learn, many of those people could not command more in a global labor marketplace. But that is an insufficient response if you want to keep the American dream alive, you want to keep the morale and the spirit of America moving forward, and those of you who are employers want to be in a workplace where people are productive because they are happy and constructive and an important part of a team. In other words, it is not enough just to say that we're in this terribly difficult period that it took 20 years to build and that no one knows exactly what caused it. We simply cannot go gently into a good night of limited economic expectations, slow growth, no growth in living standards, and a lesser future for our children. It is not the American way.

We know that it may take us a good deal of time to work out of this, and we know there may be no simple answers or silver bullets, but we have got to do better at building a future for ourselves. Of course, we have a rare opportunity to do it because the cold war is over; because democracy and free markets are in favor and flower throughout the world; because a global economy creates opportunities as well as challenges and hazards for us because there are new things which have to be done. We have to find a way, for example, to make money out of the global environmental crisis and make jobs out of it, and I believe we can. And in many ways, the challenges we face today are ready-made for Americans, with our love of learning, our proven genius at innovation, our far greater flexibility than any of our competitors, and our capacity for communicating with people among different cultures. After all, we have at least one county in this country with people from 150 different racial and ethnic groups. It need not be a weakness; it can be an enormous asset for us as we move into a global society.

But we know we have to stop doing some things and to start doing some other things. Put simply, we have to stop borrowing so much from our future and start investing more to build it again. We need fundamental changes, and we have to do a lot of things at once. And therefore, our administration is trying to do a number of things in a short time: to reduce the deficit, to improve education through our schools, through opening the doors of college, through reforming the system by which we support those of you who want to train your own workers. We need to reward work and reform welfare. We cannot continue to spend 30 percent more than any other country in the world of our income on health care.

Many of you today here work in companies or represent workers who do not have jobs who would have jobs if we simply had been able for the last 12 years to keep health care costs in line with inflation plus population growth. Many of you do. So all these things are related. When people say to me, well, you know, why don't you just reduce the deficit and forget about the rest of it? I'll tell you why. Because 5 years from now, no matter who does what with the deficit, it goes up again if you don't bring health costs in line with inflation plus population growth. They say, well, why don't you just not spend a nickel on anything? I'll tell you why. Because look at California if you want to see the consequences of 6 long years of cutting the defense budget and letting the people who won the cold war go out in the cold and giving no thought to what we're going to do with the scientific and technological base and the workers there and whether there is not some new partnership that would give them something to do.

So we have to do things in order, and we have to begin by bringing the deficit down and putting our financial house in order. But we also have to think anew. All these partnerships you've got going in your businesses, if somebody came to work one day and said, "OK, we're going to forget about these 12 things and just

do this one," a lot of you would go broke if you did that. You do not have the luxury of ignoring some problems if you have the means at all to deal with them. And I would argue that we don't either. But there needs to be one overriding purpose for this country, and that is returning us to a path in which we can build a high-skill, high-wage, high-growth society in which people who work hard and play by the rules will be rewarded with decent work and an opportunity to raise a strong family in a safe neighborhood.

Let me say very briefly that the essentials of the economic plan that the Congress is wrestling with—and I mean that literally, "wrestling with." I feel since I'm here in Chicago I have to say this. Chairman Rostenkowski and Senator Moynihan from New York are obviously the lead conferees on our budget, and they're working through some very difficult and complex issues today, and I compliment them for their enormous labors and for what they're doing. But the elements of the plan are clear: We want to bring the deficit down by $500 billion over 5 years. We want to make at least as many cuts as we raise taxes, if not more. There are 200 cuts with more than $250 billion in them if the Congress will adopt them. We want to restore some fairness to hard-working middle class families, and we want to reward work over welfare.

For every $10 in the plan I presented to the Congress, and this is true in both the House and Senate version, $5 comes from spending cuts, $4 from new revenues from people in the upper 6 percent of earning brackets, $1 from the middle class. Families with incomes under $30,000 are held harmless. The working poor for the first time are lifted out of poverty by not taxing them into poverty if they work hard. This is a very big deal in America. Eighteen percent of the people who work full-time in this country are living below the Federal poverty line. It is hard to lecture people, to say, "Well, don't be on welfare; go to work," if you don't reward work. That is something the Government can do that I think all Americans should support.

Now, I want to say something else today, because we're celebrating partnerships here. The tax part of this program does not impose 70 percent of its burden on people with incomes above $200,000 to soak the rich or promote class warfare. I want to reward success. The tax burden is the way it is because we seek to reverse what happened in the 1980's, where taxes went up on the middle class and down on the wealthiest Americans. Payroll taxes went up, and the Government shoved more and more off on the State and local government, and almost all the revenues they adopted hit the middle class disproportionately. This has nothing to do with class warfare. It has to do with opportunity and fairness. And I think it will rebuild a sense of teamwork and a spirit of partnership and cooperation.

I also want to point out that if we can continue to bring this deficit down, you will see the continuation of the last 5 months of a big drop in long-term interest rates, which is causing millions of people to refinance their home loans or their business loans or take out other forms of credit in ways that will save them far more money than they will pay in new revenues. If we can keep interest rates down for over a year at this level, it is estimated from a low side of $50 to a high side of $100 billion will be released to be reinvested back into this economy to jumpstart the economy again. I think it is terribly important.

The second element of this plan, in addition to deficit reduction, is incentives for people and companies to invest more. That is, nothing would please me more than if people who would be pushed in the higher income brackets by this plan would lower their tax burden by turning around and reinvesting the money in creating jobs here at home. And this plan gives the opportunity to do that. We double the small business expensing provision. We have a new business capital gains that anybody that invests in a company capitalized at $50 million or less and holds the investment for 5 years or more will cut their tax burden in half. We extend the research and development tax credit. We do some other things to revitalize the home building industry and the real estate sectors of our economy. All these things will give opportunities for people who have funds to invest and to create jobs as they do. I think that is very important.

I want to say I'm very grateful for the fact that at least 50 of the 100 biggest companies in the country have endorsed this program, partly because the changes in the alternative minimum tax lets them invest in new plant and equipment, to mitigate the impact of the taxes, and to create more jobs and productivity. I'm

grateful for the support we've received from the high-tech community, and I'm grateful that finally we're getting out the facts that 90 percent plus, that's right, over 90 percent of the small businesses in America actually get a tax cut under this plan if they simply invest more money in their business because the expensing provision has been doubled, and their income taxes don't go up, something that you haven't been reading a lot about in the press. But it is true, and I am glad to see it coming out. And it's very important, because most of our jobs are created by smaller firms, and that needs to be emphasized.

The third element of this plan is investments to empower people to compete and win. Every child born in this country should be able to grow up to be successful. But you and I know that we have a far higher percentage of people living in unhealthy, disadvantageous environments than most of our wealthy competitors. We have proof; we have evidence. No one disputes it that if you invest in child nutrition, immunization, and preschool education, and they're good programs, the programs pay for themselves many times over: The taxpayers win, productivity goes up, and you have people who can learn when they get into school. So yes, we do spend some more money on that. We also have a program of modest cost but enormous impact called Goals 2000 coming out of the Department of Education, designed to set national standards by which all schools and students can be evaluated. And that is important in a global economy. And we have, as has already been said by Senator Simon and others, a really ambitious and I think quite wonderful program to open the doors of college education to all Americans by lowering the costs of loans, making their terms of repayments better, and giving thousands of them the opportunity to pay back their college loans through service to their communities, rebuilding them. And I might say some of those young people in our experimental program for the summer have helped people to try to deal with the aftermath of this terrible flood in the Midwest. That is just one example of what we can do if we have the right kind of incentives.

Finally, we very much want to create a program of training for people who don't get 4-year college degrees, that merge the partnership and efforts of the private sector, the education system, and the Government. Everybody in this country who doesn't go on to a 4-year college needs to finish high school and get at least 2 years of further training, either in a school, on the workplace, or in the service. Everybody. All the demographic figures are clear now from the '90 census. All the people in this country who have high school plus 2 years, if it's good, are highly likely to get jobs with growing incomes. Those who have less are highly likely to get jobs with shrinking incomes. You know, you don't have to be Einstein to figure out we should do what is likely to give people jobs with growing incomes and that, in the aggregate, it's better for you in the workplace and better for the country as a whole. So we're trying to do that.

And lastly, let me say, we've got to provide markets for all these people's labor in products or services. We simply have to continue to expand the frontiers of the global economy. A wealthy country cannot grow richer unless there is a higher rate of global growth. We cannot do it by simply drawing within. And perhaps the most important thing that happened at the G–7 meeting in Tokyo was that the seven industrial powers agreed among themselves to a dramatic reduction, in many cases, to outright elimination of tariffs, that every analyst says will dramatically increase the number of manufacturing jobs in the United States of America between now and the end of the decade if we, the larger countries, can get the other countries to agree to it by the end of the year in a world trade agreement. No analyst has disputed this. It has the potential of being the most important thing we've done in a long time to revitalize manufacturing in America. And of course, when you rebuild manufacturing, you get more service jobs, you get a lot of other support jobs. It is very, very important.

Let me also say that I think it's important that we not forget about the Americans who are working hard and are struggling along. I mentioned this earlier. The most revolutionary social aspect of this economic plan is that instead of spending a lot of money to hire people to work for the Government to go out and help people who are in trouble, we invest a lot of money in this program in lowering the taxes of people who work 40 hours a week and are still in poverty. What better thing could we do to reward work and family than to be able to say for the first time that in this country if you work 40 hours a week and you've got a

child in your house, you're going to be lifted out of poverty, not by something the Government does but by your own labor. We'll just change the tax system to take you out of poverty. It is a profoundly significant thing, and it should not be watered down in this conference. We ought to do enough to be able to say that to all Americans.

Let me just say that the one thing that's happened in the last 4½, 5 months is that interest rates have started coming down as it became serious that we were trying to bring the deficit down. And there has been a beginning of reinvestment. A lot of that is coming out of the private sector. Last year, in the last quarter, we had the biggest increase in productivity in 20 years in America, thanks to a lot of you in this room. Those two things together mean that in this economy we have seen in the first part of the year about 150,000 new private sector jobs a month being created—that is as compared with 20,000 a month in the previous 4 years—so that we are moving in the right direction. But that's all we're doing, is moving in the right direction. That is nowhere near enough, and there is still a great cloud of uncertainty out there.

So I think today we need to have three challenges. One is, the Government needs to pass this budget and get on with the rest of the business. Hanging out there, debating it, dragging it out for weeks and weeks, will only make it worse. There comes a time when delay to get a slightly better decision is worse than action to get a pretty good decision. We have reached that time. We don't need to do that. We've got other things to do. And you need to know what the rules are going to be, what the deal is, and we need to go on with our lives.

The second challenge is to you in business. If we can get the cost of capital low, if we are doing our part, then the savings must be used to put more people first, to create jobs, to train employees, not just the executives but the workers as well, to have other companies in this country learn from those of you in this room that you can grow and prosper by treating workers like indispensable partners. Companies like Motorola outside Chicago, which Secretary Brown visited recently, and L. S. Electro Galvanizing in Cleveland, which Secretary Reich visited recently, and all the many that I have had the privilege to visit over the last several years can show that.

And the challenge to labor is clearly the same thing. This is an opportunity we have to seize. There is no way we can ever see wages grow and jobs increase in this country again unless there is an emphasis on education and training, flexibility in the workplace, partnership and responsibility by everybody for improving quality. But if the labor people do it, then Government ought to do right by them and by business, and business should do right by their workers. There is no easy answer here, but we all know, I think, that if we treat each other better we're going to come out ahead, and that insofar as we drive up unemployment and run people off, we also diminish the number of customers with money in their pockets to make the American economy go. We are truly in this together.

Now, let me just say one more word about this. I don't think the fight in Washington should be about Republicans and Democrats. I think most of the arguments we have to have are about issues that don't have an easy partisan tent. The world is a very different place than it was when most of the party lines were drawn 10 and 20 and 30 years ago. This really is about growth against gridlock, decision against delay, change against the status quo. And you have got to demand that we do something.

I mean, you know, this gridlock thing is amazing. Let me just give you an example of how bad it gets sometimes with Congress. I had my nominee for Surgeon General up there in the Congress—Senator Braun was sitting with her; I appreciated that—a woman that grew up in a cotton field in Arkansas. Her brothers and sisters put her through medical school. And maybe there were people who don't agree with her and didn't want to vote for her, but through some parliamentary maneuver, they tried to put off the whole hearing. The country needs a Surgeon General. Thanks to Senator Kennedy, the chairman of the committee, they went back and had the hearing. He told them they were going to stay there 'til kingdom come, 'til they finished. But if somebody wants to vote against her, let them vote. But let's get on with it.

Let me give you another example. There is now a filibuster in the Senate against the national service plan. We have worked our hearts out with the Republicans and the Democrats. We have lots of Republican cosponsors in the House and a few in the Senate. They just want to delay it. Why? Why shouldn't we send a signal to America's young people that we want

you to work in your community to make it a better place? Why shouldn't we say we want to open the doors of college education to everybody? Look at the figures from the '90 census.

Last week there was even a filibuster or a delay in the House against flood assistance to Illinois and to Iowa and to Kansas and South Dakota and North Dakota and Minnesota and Missouri. Why? Got me. There is ample precedent for emergency action here. We do not need to raise a tax to pay for flood relief; because interest rates have come down, the deficit is already going to be much lower this year than anybody thought it was. And here are these people out here up to their ears in tragedy, wondering when Congress is going to get around to passing the flood relief. There is a point at which we need to learn what we're talking to you about. We need to work together and make decisions.

How many of you could stay in business if either management or labor said when you started a new path, "Well, I think I'm going to call a filibuster and wait 3 or 4 weeks to make up my mind whether to do this?" Your bills still come in. You still have to pay the payroll. Let's vote. I don't have to win them all, but let's make decisions. This institutionalized delay and gridlock is bad for America.

In just a couple of weeks——

Q. How can you talk about a Democratically controlled Congress? The Democrats have controlled Congress—talk about gridlock. Why don't you take leadership?

The President. Now, wait a minute. Whoa!

Q. You're the one that talks about——

The President. Do you want me to answer the question?

Q. Yes. You're the one——

The President. Wait, wait, wait, wait, wait. Most people, sir—no, wait a minute. Are you going to let me answer the question?

Q. [*Inaudible*]—Congress and you won't——

Audience members. Quiet!

The President. Are you going to let me answer the question? This is not your meeting, sir. And most people have better manners than to interrupt somebody giving a speech. I might say that's another thing that's wrong with this country, there's not enough civility in how we treat one another.

But the answer to your question, which is good Civics 101, is that the Democrats do not control the Congress when 41 Republicans want to vote to keep anything from being voted on in the Senate. That is the answer. They do not. The filibuster rule means you have to have 60 votes to bring anything to a vote except for this budget. Everything else requires 60 votes. But it's not a party deal, it's a question of whether we should make decisions. I say, if they want to vote against me, fine; let's make a decision and go on to something else. Let's just move. I think that's the issue.

Let me just say one last thing. I believe that this works. I came here basically to highlight what you're doing and to support it and to ask

you to tell me what I can do to help it be better at the national level. But in the end, if this kind of attitude that you are here to celebrate, this whole new idea of a partnership for productivity and leaving behind all the sort of labeling that has shackled us for too long, if this doesn't take over the private sector, nothing the President can do can revitalize America. You have to carry it. And I believe you will.

Thank you, and God bless you all.

NOTE: The President spoke at 1:15 p.m. at the Sheraton Chicago Hotel.

Remarks in a Conference Panel Discussion in Chicago
July 26, 1993

Once again, let me say how delighted I am to be here and to see all of you here and how pleased I am to see the Secretaries of Labor and Commerce working together. We're trying to build some teamworks in our Cabinet that have not historically been there. And I think that this is a good example.

I understand that this morning's panels were quite interesting, and I got a play-by-play description for a few moments when we were taking a break in there. So far you have focused on what we mean by the new American workplace and the problems and barriers that companies and workers must struggle with in redesigning their organizations.

I, frankly, am learning how hard this can be myself, because we have a very serious project underway now in the Federal Government in trying to reinvent the Federal Government. The project is headed by the Vice President. We have sought out the opinions of a number of people in this room that I recognize here today. But I think that next month—or, excuse me, in September—when we announce the report of the reinventing Government task force, you will be very pleased to see that we're trying to take another page out of your book to make the Government more efficient and to work better.

Our responsibility, it seems to me, as I said in my speech, is to create the most favorable economic conditions. Sometimes that means reducing the deficit; sometimes it means specific incentives or programs; other times it means just getting out of your way and deregulating. The Government's relationship to the private sector are changing the nature of that relationship.

There are challenges that are clearly unique to the workplace, outside the realm of Government, that you have to meet by yourselves but with our encouragement and without our interference. Those are the things we're going to focus on now. The purpose of this panel is to focus on why companies and public institutions are literally reinventing themselves organizationally by asking such questions as what benefits workers receive from new workplace organizations; why unions should support these practices; how companies' bottom lines are affected; and how moving to high-performance work can help improve our Nation's economic performance. We can begin to establish high-performance workplaces as the models, the rules, if you will, for our country's new economy.

NOTE: The President spoke at 2:24 p.m. at the Sheraton Chicago Hotel.

Interview With the Indiana Media in Chicago
July 26, 1993

The President. Thank you very much. Please sit down. Sorry the conference ran a little late, but there was a lot of enthusiasm up there.

Let me just make a very brief opening statement. I want to give most of the time over to you for questions. I am doing a series of press conferences like this with representatives of the press from various States around the country, trying to do as many as I possibly can, the Vice President is doing others, to answer questions directly about the economic plan now before the Congress and any other issues that you would like to raise. It's not possible for the President, at least during the budget time, to travel the country as much as I would like to, so this gives me a chance as nearly as possible to communicate directly with the people whom you report to.

I want to emphasize just one or two things, if I might, about this economic plan. More than any other one which has been presented by any party, it reduces the deficit in a way that is fair to all the American people; that balances spending cuts and tax increases; that asks the middle class to pay a very small percentage of the overall burden in what amounts to about, at the most, $50 a year, a little less than a dollar a week; holds working families with incomes of under $30,000 harmless; and actually gives over 90 percent of the small businesses in the United States a chance to reduce their tax burden because they have no income tax increases. And they're given a chance to reduce their tax burden because the expensing provision which rewards them with lower taxes if they reinvest in their businesses is doubled under this plan.

This is a plan that will promote jobs, bring the deficit down, keep interest rates down, and enable us to move ahead with our business as a country. I think it is imperative that it pass. The most important thing is the Congress needs to pass a budget and to do it quickly so we can get on to other matters and start doing the other things that need to be done to grow the American economy as well.

If there are questions, I'll be glad to take them.

Yes, sir.

Taxes on Small Business

Q. Mr. President, the majority of jobs in Indiana are from small businesses, and you indicated that also in your address at noon today—Sub S corporations. A lot of the business people we talked to are really frightened that the tax package or the budget package would increase their taxes to the point where they're afraid they're going to have to cut back, lay off people, maybe some even go out of business. What assurance can you really give Hoosier business men and women that this plan is good for them?

The President. Well, there are 7 million Subchapter S corporations in America. Of those 7 million, 400,000, or far less than 10 percent, will have any income tax increase at all under this program. All of them, if the program passes, will have the expensing provisions of the Code, that is, they'll be able to just immediately write off $20,000 rather than $10,000 of expensing. So I will say again, over 90 percent of the small businesses in this country will get a tax break under this program.

To those who will pay higher taxes because the income taxes on the upper 6 percent of the country are going to be raised—it will be roughly small businesses with an income above $140,000 adjusted gross income—to them, I would say there are ways to avoid that through reinvestment, just as there are for individuals. Keep in mind, this plan also leaves the rates where they are for capital investment, so if you reinvest in a business, your tax rates don't go up. If you invest in a new business or a small business with a capitalization of $50 million a year or less, and you hold the investment for 5 years, your tax rates go way down under this plan.

We also extend the tax incentives for research and development, which the Republican plan did not do, so that you can take your taxes down if you do more R&D expenditures, which is what keeps the economy growing.

Another thing that we do I think is very important is to revitalize the real estate and home-building sectors of the economy by returning to the incentives which exist there. That's why the homebuilders and the realtors, two groups that normally are associated, frankly, more with the Republican Party than the Democratic Party, nationally are supporting this plan, because it's good for that sector of the economy—again, something not in the Republican plan.

And one final thing I would say is that we extend the tax credit for health insurance for self-employed people, something that was not done under the Senate Republican plan. So in effect, all those people would have had a tax increase if the Republican plan had passed.

So I think if you look at the small business sector—and I want to compliment the Wall Street Journal. They've run a number of stories, factual stories, in the last week which have analyzed the facts of this economic plan as against the outrageous and inaccurate attacks being made on it which sort of show this. I mean, one of the people who was testifying against our plan for some group was given the facts of her business, and she said that's not what they told me this did. And it turned out she got a tax decrease instead of a tax increase.

Economic Program

Q. Well let's talk about, Mr. President, that for a second if you could. Senator Dan Coats' office this morning is saying they admire your sophistication of going to the local media, but the facts are taxes outstrip cuts two to one in this proposal. And they point out that among Hoosier voters, even something like a cigarette tax, your friend Governor Evan Bayh couldn't get it passed in Indiana—make the case to Hoosiers for what the Republican Senators are just calling a tax package.

The President. Well, first of all, they're wrong. They're wrong. Go back and look at what they said about the budget program they voted for in 1990, which had taxes and budget cuts in it and which had an outrageous estimate of economic growth in it, so much so that they changed their own program. They wrote it down by about a third within 60 days after passing it. I mean, the things I call tax increases and spending cuts are the same things that Ronald Reagan and George Bush and the Republicans in the Senate call tax increases, spending cuts.

They say that if they, under the budget they passed in 1992, were going to raise Medicare expenses 12 percent a year, and we cut it back to 9 percent a year, shaving $50 billion off the deficit and now almost $60 billion from what it would have been under their last budget, that that doesn't count as a cut. They say that it's

not a cut. I think it is. They say if we reduce interest costs to the Federal deficit, which we have done, by the way, already—the deficit this year is going down because we're bringing the deficit down, because the markets have brought long-term interest rates down because they see finally there's somebody serious about bringing the deficit down—they say that doesn't count as reducing the deficit. They're playing word games. All of a sudden they've got a whole new dictionary now that they're out of power. I'm using exactly the same calculations that they used for 12 years on what increases the deficit, what reduces the deficit.

Defense Cuts

Q. Mr. President, let's talk about some jobs in Indiana that are scheduled to go out of business on your watch. The White House the other day put out a list of all the jobs that were lost under the Bush administration. The 2,800 jobs I'm referring to are at the Military Finance Center at Fort Benjamin Harrison, which as you know, was one of a number of finance centers across the country scheduled to be consolidated, this one to be closed in 1995. Indianapolis, we're told, was one of the 20 finalists to retain those jobs and pick up some more and then one of the 5 winners. And then at the very last minute, Defense Secretary Aspin stopped the ballgame and said we're going to start the process all over again. What can you say about the fairness of changing the rules at the end of the game, and what can you say to these 2,800 workers whose lives have been on a yo-yo?

The President. First of all, the decision that was made to close those facilities was made, as you know, in the previous administration, not under my administration. Secondly, it's just not true that there were five finalists picked. I mean, at least I couldn't find it. I asked the Defense Department to tell me where we were on this issue when I became President, and they said, here are the 20 finalists. And I said, has the decision been completed? They said, no, we're still at the 20 finalists. And I said, what are the criteria? And we talked about it.

And interestingly enough, the only thing I said about it was that I felt very strongly that one of the criteria should be how badly a community or a State had been hurt by other defense cutbacks, because I was worried that those States or communities that had been hurt more by defense cutbacks might have less ability, in effect, to put up their own financial incentives to get the financial accounting centers there. That is, I didn't think that we ought to reward people who could, in effect, buy the Senators by putting up a whole lot of money up front or who couldn't afford to compete because they had lost a lot of defense jobs. And I didn't even ask them to go back and start the whole thing all over again. I just said I'd like that factored in, that I thought that was something the American people would want us to do— would want us to take account of where all these defense cuts had hurt people the worst. And so they said they would work up that, and go back and do it.

And my own impression is that the finalists from the first round are still in very, very good shape. That's at least the indication I have and that the Defense Department will be ready to make a recommendation to me pretty soon. But I did want to say that's the only role I had in it, was I was assured that there was no decision made. They were still at 20 finalists. I asked only that the burden those communities and States had borne in the defense cutbacks since 1987 should be able to be a factor to be taken into consideration. And that was it.

Q. [*Inaudible*]—that the list is up to 100 cities again, 100 contestants——

The President. Well, there may be 100 who comply, but it has to be that the people who did well the first time would be in good shape to do well the second time. I was astonished that they reopened it. They seemed to think that if they changed one criteria they had to, at least in theory, reopen it.

Q. One of the concerns that people in Indiana have is that those final centers are going to be chosen based on their political connections to you. Can you guarantee that that won't happen?

The President. That won't happen. You know, during—you might say that, but let me say this: It was interesting to me that during the last election, right before the election, conveniently it was leaked by the Defense Department that the centers were going to be perhaps in this city, that city, the other city, and, quote, "someplace in Indiana," which didn't exactly sound like the most meritorious decision in the world at the time it was leaked.

So all I can tell you is I'm telling you just like it is. I asked for one thing to be taken into account. I said, "I don't think we ought to let these things get bought by communities that are already wildly successful without any consideration being given to the communities that have been hurt most economically by the defense cutbacks." That's the only thing I ever asked them to do. Yes.

Steel Industry

Q. Mr. President, a question about northwest Indiana. I noticed that the chairman of Inland Steel, Robert Darnall, was present at your conference today. And I was wondering what kind of job security you can offer steel workers, particularly those in the Gary area where over 30,000 steel jobs have been lost since the 1980's.

The President. Well, I'll tell you what I think will happen in steel. I think you're going to see a big increase in the number of steel jobs if we have flexibility and competitiveness and if two other things happen: if we move at the national level to bring health care costs under control and if we can continue the work we're doing now to bring tariffs down in worldwide manufacturing trade.

And let me just mention those two things specifically. The most important thing for average Americans that happened at the Tokyo meeting of the G–7 was the agreement that we made among ourselves to try to drastically reduce tariffs on manufactured products and to eliminate them in whole classes of products with the view toward getting the other countries to agree to do that, because we were taking the lead by the end of the year and having a new world trade agreement. It's not like NAFTA. There's some difference of opinion, as you know, about NAFTA. And I'm for it, a lot of people aren't. But there's a difference. On the agreement we made at Tokyo everybody concedes that if we can make that a part of the world trade law, it will lead to hundreds of thousands of manufacturing jobs coming into the United States.

Meanwhile, the steel companies I think will tell you that our administration has been much more vigorous in trying to protect them from unfair trade practices from other countries than any administration in a very long time. I think every steel executive, if you called him, would tell them that, that we have worked with them. We've tried to make sure that the investments they've made and the productivity they've achieved will result in more secure jobs by giving them a fair deal.

Now, the second thing I want to say is this: steel and automobiles, among others, but they're really out there on the cutting edge, have enormous, enormous health care costs, spending often 15 percent or more of payroll on health care costs. The work that we have been doing to try to bring health costs in line with inflation and at the same time find the mechanism for all Americans to have health security will help heavy industry as much as any other section of our economy. It is very difficult for them to compete in a global economy where they're spending 35 or 40 percent more on health care than any of their competitors. So I can't promise anybody that's in a tough global economy job security. I can tell them that the things we're doing will make them more likely to succeed.

NAFTA

Q. Mr. President, what can you tell the people of Indiana who—for instance, I do a talk show in South Bend, and many of my callers are very concerned about NAFTA as it is. You mentioned NAFTA a minute ago. What solutions are there for those people who are out there that are out of work and they're losing their homes, they're losing their cars, they're losing their identity because of their companies that have pulled out or are pulling out of the country?

The President. First of all, that's the initial point we ought to make. And let me back up and say this. This is a little background. For 12 years I was Governor of a State that had plants shut down and go to Mexico. Before I quit we had one or two of them come back, just like that General Motors plant. I don't know if you saw that, it was announced they were going to shut down 1,000 jobs and bring them back to Michigan because they thought they could achieve higher levels of productivity. The point I want to make to you about NAFTA is this—I want to make two or three points about it. Number one, if we don't do it, let's say we don't do it, anybody who wants to shut a plant down in America and move it to Mexico for lower wages can do that anyway within the so-called *maquilladora* zone, right? And what upsets people is they move jobs down there, then they produce products and bring it back here, okay? What NAFTA does primarily with regard to that is to move the line back down toward Mexico, throughout Mexico. It makes the whole country eligible. But if you wanted to

go to Mexico for low wages to produce for America, you would stay as close to the border as you could to cut your costs down. If you go to Mexico City, in all probability you're going down there to produce for the Mexicans in Mexico City. So if we do nothing, what people really hate about this can continue and will.

Secondly, I think the people will be better off because I don't intend to sign this agreement or send it up to Congress until we get some agreements on the part of the Mexican Government to lift labor standards and to lift environmental standards there which will lower the wage gap and the cost-of-production gap, increase incomes from Mexican people, and enable them to buy more of our products.

Thirdly, 5 or 6 years ago Mexico had a $5 billion trade surplus with us because they had more tariffs on our products than we had on theirs, 5 or 6 years ago. Now, we've got a $6 billion trade surplus with them because President Salinas had lowered these tariffs. So I believe that if we go forward with the agreement, if the Mexican incomes rise, they will be able to buy more American products, and it will create more jobs than it costs. If I didn't think that, I wouldn't be for this. And I think everything that's bad about it is going to happen anyway and even more so if we don't do anything. That's what I believe. That's the reason I'm for it. Yes.

Defense Cuts

Q. I want to go back really quickly—[*inaudible*]—association. Evansville, Indiana, with which I am a reporter from, was one of the 20 finalists. You mentioned that——

The President. There were two or three cities in Indiana, weren't there, in the finalists?

Q. Indianapolis and Evansville were the 2 on the list of 20. You mentioned that you thought that the incentive program was not a good idea. Evansville——

The President. No, I do think it's a good idea. No, I think it's a good idea, the incentive program. I do not believe that there should be no consideration—under the previous formula, no consideration was given to the harm done to communities by defense cutbacks. So, no, I didn't ask them to take the incentive out. I think they should leave that in. I just didn't want to eliminate any considerations for the harm done to communities.

Go ahead.

Q. Evansville submitted a bid that would have cost the Government $1 a year in operating costs. Now, since Indianapolis has lost Fort Benjamin Harrison, which has been closed down, would that give Indianapolis a more favorable advantage over Evansville and the southern half of the State?

The President. It depends. It doesn't mean that the Indianapolis bid would prevail, it just means that they would get some credit, and it would be dependent on how much they've been hurt by it.

Q. Local officials have enacted a tax increase in Evansville to help fund this center, or try to work with the department of revenue to have it repealed in—Vanderburgh County in Evansville. Should local officials give up and have this tax repealed, or is there still a chance?

The President. Absolutely not. No. I'm telling you, no decision has been made about any of this stuff. And I was really stunned—the question that he had. I'm going to go back and check this out. I asked point blank—because if the whole process was over, I was just going to announce it and go on.

Q. [*Inaudible*]—has on good authority that there were five and Indianapolis was one of them.

The President. Well, all I can tell you is I asked where they were going, and they said here are 20 cities, and the 5 haven't been decided yet.

Q. When will a decision be made on this?

The President. Well, I hope in a hurry. Actually, I asked a couple of days ago, and I was supposed to get a report this week about when the whole thing will be completed.

Q. I talked with several workers who are being hired part-time, but they're actually doing full-time work just because the company doesn't want to pay for the benefits, i.e., retirement and health insurance. What can you do to make these companies do what's right for these people?

The President. Well, first of all, I think the only way that's ever going to happen under the circumstances we're living under today is if you have a system like every other advanced country does which has some provision for adequate health care for all workers and requires everybody, including the workers themselves, to assume some responsibility for their health care and the employers. I mean, look at the system, we're the only country, the only advanced country that does what we do. Germany doesn't do this and Japan—no other country does this, where basically if you want to take care of your workers you can, and if you don't, you don't have to. And so it's just up to what you think is better—either more humane or better for your productivity.

In the 1980's, the cost of health care went up by more than twice the rate of inflation because, again, we were the only advanced country that had no system for trying to rein it in. So that if you're employer X and you're competing with employer Y and they don't do it, and you do, what kind of a disadvantage do you have? That's why we have to have a systematic response to this, and why I think it is so important—let's just go back to the deficit reduction. Under any conceivable deficit reduction plan, including mine, which I think is the best, you can bring the deficit down for 5 years and then it starts to go up again in the sixth year. Why? Because of health care costs.

So the answer to your question is we've got to have a national response. About 100,000 Americans a month are losing their health insurance now because of the phenomenon you asked. If it's just a dog-eat-dog world, there has to be some law that requires coverage, but does it in a way that doesn't bankrupt small business. And it's clearly possible to do.

We were just out in Hawaii. I went there to review the Pacific Fleet and to meet with our military leaders in the Pacific on the way back from Asia. And then Hillary spent a day there looking at the health care network. And virtually every employer in Hawaii insures their employees, including the smallest ones. The premiums are slightly below the national average. They've done it for 20 years now. They've managed the system quite well. It can be done.

Yes? Nice tie. [*Laughter*]

Gridlock

Q. I wanted to ask you about actually the subject you came here to push, the budget. You talked a little bit about the political problems Republicans have caused for you, but you have some problems in your own party. On the deficit reduction package last year, two Democratic Members of the Indiana congressional delegation voted against it. Given the election results in Texas and California, what kind of leverage do you have to influence people in your own party who are in vulnerable districts?

The President. Well, the mayor's race in California didn't have anything to do with it. There has only been one race in this whole country which was a referendum on my economic plan. That is, an honest referendum. That is, where both sides were debated and then three House races, all of which the Democrats won. But the only one where a Democratic candidate decided to defend and, more importantly, to explain the budget proposal was in the race for Leon Panetta's old seat where, by the way, there were a lot of upper income constituents who had to pay higher taxes. And the guy won by nine points. And he did things that I never asked him to do. I wasn't even particularly involved. He ran my picture in his brochures, and he said, "This is right for America, and here's why I'm for it." And he had advertisements saying, "No matter what you've heard, here's what the truth is." And we won the race by nine points.

There was no fight in Texas. I mean, there was no issue. But let me just tell you what happened as a result of that. On the day that Senator Hutchinson from Texas went out on the steps of the Capitol with Senator Gramm from Texas, talking about how no taxes are needed, and all we need to do is cut spending— she was standing there with Ross Perot—the word spread in the House of Representatives they were out there. And so the House voted on the superconducting super collider, a project I have supported, and defeated it by 70 more votes than they defeated it last year and just lobbed it over to them. I said—because it's all in Texas, right? So, I mean, I think it's in the national interest to pursue it, myself. I think it's crazy for us to just dismantle our science and technology system and the kind of high-tech investments that make us a strong country.

But the only place we've had a debate where the voters heard the other side was in that district in California. Even in the Wisconsin-Mississippi races, that was not the issue.

Q. We have time for one more question.

The President. Go ahead.

Economic Program

Q. A followup—why are you having some trouble persuading—[*inaudible*]

The President. Because it's tough. All the easy decisions have been made, because the American people have been fed pablum for 12 years. Because it's easier to cut taxes and spend more money than it is to spend less money and raise taxes and because the rhetoric is unfavorable. But the specifics show every single solitary focus group or poll where the people have been sat down and go through the specifics, shows that the people will support the program. It's the generalities and the desperate looking for the easy answer. Look, in 1980 we had a $1 trillion national debt piled up since we became a country. Now it's $4 trillion. Something went wrong.

David Stockman, who was Ronald Reagan's budget director, right, was not a liberal Democrat, gave an interview a few weeks ago in which he said that it was folly to believe that this whole thing could be solved by spending cuts alone, that they meant to cut taxes 3 percent of the gross national income in 1981, and they got into a political bidding war, and they got to liking it, and they just got carried away, and they lost control, and they cut taxes 6 percent of income.

But I can understand; look, most middle class people are working harder for less money, and they didn't get a tax cut. Their Social Security taxes went up at the national level, and State and local taxes went up at the local level as the Federal Government threw more stuff off on State and local government throughout the 1980's. I lived through that as a Governor.

And any mention of taxes is always unpopular. But I can tell you—I ought to have some credibility on this—my State had the toughest balanced budget law in the country. We were always in the bottom five in the percentage of income going to State and local taxes. I never raised any taxes to balance the books. I did raise some money to build roads and educate kids. We ran our business in order. But the truth is this country's out of control financially. But the easy decisions have been made. The only ones that are left are tough.

And let me say this: I have a lot of sympathy with the Democratic Members of Congress from Indiana because they come from districts that are just like my State. They're fiscally conservative. They want their money spent right. They're tired of the money being wasted. And they don't believe anything anybody says in Washington. I understand that. But I don't think we've done too badly. Let me just give you one comparison. In 1992, 75 percent of the House Republicans, not Democrats, Republicans, voted against President Bush's last budget. I mean, this is a serious budget.

Let me just make one last plug, because a lot of this stuff operates at a rhetorical level. If we have to do—is get in a shouting match as sort of like as we would on a Rush Limbaugh show or something like that—[*laughter*]—it's hard for the responsible position to win. But if you have to get to beyond the rhetoric to the facts, I think we can win.

And let me just give you one last thing. The Philadelphia Inquirer went out and actually interviewed people who are experts on the budget who don't have an ax to grind, budget analysts with big accounting firms, for example. And the budget analyst for Price Waterhouse is a person obviously, I don't know, never met him—said that my budget was the most honest budget in 10 years and that the only thing that was not accurate about my budget is that it would produce more deficit reduction than I said it would. It would bring the deficit down more. And we can get you a copy of the article if you'd like to see it.

I mean, I was a Governor. With all the unmet needs this country has and all the other things we need to be addressing, from health care reform to welfare reform to a new policy to revitalize the workplace—the thing we met here about—to the crime bill I want to bring up, all these things I'm interested in—spending 8 months or 7 months doing nothing but this is not my idea of recreation. But we have lost control over our financial affairs. And this deficit is like a bone in our throat, and we have to take it out. And I don't know any other way to do it. If I could think of any other way to do it, I would do it. I also think to get it down to zero, which is really important, over a fixed period of time, you've got to deal with the question of exploding health care costs. But the fair way to do that without bankrupting hospitals or being unfair to providers or to elderly people is to overhaul the entire system.

Yes, sir?

Agriculture Assistance

Q. Mr. President, a lot of people downstate are involved in agriculture, and many are having a tough time making ends meet. Some of them are even going out of business, going bankrupt. What type of hope can you offer them?

The President. Well, first of all, we're going to rewrite the farm bill, as you probably know. We have to do that for 1995. And one of the things that I've asked the Secretary of Agri-

culture to do is to examine whether or not the bill that was done in 1990 has done enough to help family farmers stay in business and whether or not we need to look at the farm finance issue even more than the crop price supports, as well as to look at what we can do to help younger people get into farming. And that's all separate from what we need to do for the farmers that lost money in the flood, you know, in the Midwest.

Just in my lifetime, and especially in my tenure as a Governor of a farm State where most of the farmers were family farmers, I watched the number drop drastically. I think that we are looking at a period, if they can hang on another year or so, where just looking into the future you're going to have pretty stable markets for American agricultural products, in fact, ones that might grow and where, if we can put in place some systems in this new farm bill to help the family farmers deal with the radical swings in income caused by the weather, caused by markets, caused by other things that the big corporate farms can endure, I think that the future of the people now farming can be pretty solid. But I do think with the average age of the farmer being about 58 and a half now, we're going to have to do something to help ease the financial barriers to getting young people into farming.

Q. Thank you.

The President. Thanks.

Health Care Reform

Q. My only question is you talked about how health care is going to be such an integral part of reform in labor and in farming. So how much is the Government going to be involved in whatever health care reform package there will be? And how soon will that happen?

The President. Well, I think we'll have to phase some parts of it in over a period of years, but I want to come forward with a program as soon as we get the budget out of the way.

I'd like for the Government to take care of insuring the unemployed, uninsured, and to make sure that people can change jobs even if someone in their family has been sick—you know, today you've got millions of people locked into the jobs they're in because they've got a sick husband, wife, child, or something, and they can't change—and mandating reform of the insurance markets so that small businesses don't get busted just to buy health insurance—and self-employed people.

But I think that the providers system we have in America is very good now. And I think we ought to leave the doctors, the hospitals, all the private providers and private choice in providers intact, but we'll have to do some more in rural areas especially, and in inner cities to provide for some assistance just to get doctors and nurses and clinics out there in places that are terribly isolated. But the fundamental system is sound. It's the insurance and the coverage that is messed up. The delivery system—if you've health care in America, you're getting pretty good health care.

Thank you. I've got to go, sorry.

Representative Dan Rostenkowski

Q. Could you comment on Chairman Rostenkowski's situation? The buzz among Indiana Republicans that I spoke to today was that that's the real story. It's not policy, but it's practical politics, and if he's indicted you're really dead

in the water.

The President. Well, I don't agree with any of that, but I can't comment on something that hasn't happened. I have no way of knowing, and I think it would be irresponsible for me to do that. I mean, I'm a public official. I don't know what the facts are. We'll just have to see what happens, and I have no reason to believe that the conference won't proceed and produce a report and the Congress won't vote on it no matter what.

Q. [*Inaudible*]—Stevens says that you are holding up the whole investigation to get the budget over with.

The President. Well, you know that's not true, don't you?

Q. Well, of course, I know that's not true. We have to ask.

NOTE: The interview began at 4:07 p.m. at the Sheraton Chicago Hotel.

Exchange With Reporters Prior to a Meeting With Congressional Leaders
July 27, 1993

Economic Program

Q. Mr. President, are these your "delay in gridlock" friends?

The President. These are my friends. This group had always supported an aggressive approach to deficit reduction, the balanced approach.

Middle East Peace Talks

Q. Are you sure?

Why is Secretary Christopher coming back?

The President. Because I want to talk with him about the Middle East before he goes there.

Q. Do you think the peace process is in jeopardy, sir?

The President. Well, I hope not. I certainly

have no reason to believe that it is, but obviously I'm concerned about it. I think the Syrians have shown commendable restraint so far. And I don't think we should let Hezbollah and all these groups that don't want anything good to happen in the Middle East derail the peace process by what they do. I don't think we should, any of us, should allow that. I mean, I really want something to happen there. So I'm very hopeful. But I thought that in view of the events there, that he ought to come home, and we ought to have a conversation about it before he goes to the Middle East.

NOTE: The exchange began at 10:20 a.m. in the Roosevelt Room at the White House. A tape was not available for verification of the content of this exchange.

Remarks and an Exchange With Reporters on Immigration Policy
July 27, 1993

The President. Thank you very much, ladies and gentlemen. I'd like to say a special word of thanks to the large number of Members of Congress who are here today. I think I have the entire list. If I don't, the Vice President will amend it when I finish. But I see Senator Kennedy, Senator Simon, Senator Feinstein, Senator Boxer, Senator Graham and Congressmen Brooks, Mazzoli, Schumer, Bryant, Fish, Kennedy, Lantos and Gilman. I think that's every Member of Congress here. Did I miss anyone? I missed Congressman Gallegly; I'm sorry.

Several weeks ago, I asked the Vice President to work with our Departments and Agencies to examine what more might be done about the problems along our borders. I was especially concerned about the growing problems of alien smuggling and international terrorists hiding behind immigrant status, as well as the continuing flow of illegal immigrants across American borders.

Following several weeks of intense efforts, including his personal involvement in resolving the recent alien smuggling incident with Mexico, the Vice President presented me with a report spelling out what we might do. I have reviewed that report and approved it. We have spoken to Members of Congress, including those who are here today and others. I want to particularly acknowledge Senator Kennedy, Senator Simpson, Congressmen Brooks and Mazzoli for all their work on this issue over many, many years. We're also in debt to Senators Feinstein and Boxer for their aggressive work in trying to deal with the growing problem, especially in the State of California, and I want to state publicly how much I appreciate the work the Hispanic Caucus has done to ensure that a balanced approach is adopted in dealing with this issue.

The simple fact is that we must not, and we will not, surrender our borders to those who wish to exploit our history of compassion and justice. We cannot tolerate those who traffic in human cargo, nor can we allow our people to be endangered by those who would enter our country to terrorize Americans. But the solution to the problem of illegal immigration is not simply to close our borders. The solution is to welcome legal immigrants and legal legitimate refugees and to turn away those who do not obey the laws. We must say no to illegal immigration so we can continue to say yes to legal immigration.

Today we send a strong and clear message. We will make it tougher for illegal aliens to get into our country. We will treat organizing a crime syndicate to smuggle aliens as a serious crime. And we will increase the number of border patrol, equipping and training them to be first class law enforcement officers. These initiatives for which I am asking the Congress for an additional $172.5 million in 1994 are an important step in regaining control over our borders and respect for our laws. When I made a commitment to combat this problem on June 18th, I announced a plan of action. This is the next step in fulfilling that commitment.

Some will worry that our action today sends the wrong message, that this means we are against all immigration. That is akin to America closing its doors. But nothing could be further from the truth. Let me be clear: Our nation has always been a safe haven for refugees and always been the world's greatest melting pot. What we announce today will not make it tougher for the immigrant who comes to this country legally, lives by our laws, gets a job, and pursues the American dream. This administration will promote family unification. We will reach out to those who have the skills we need to make our nation stronger, and we will welcome new citizens to our national family with honor and with dignity. But to treat terrorists and smugglers as immigrants dishonors the tradition of the immigrants who have made our nation great. And it unfairly taints the millions of immigrants who live here honorably and are a vital part of every segment of our society. Today's initiatives are about stopping crime, toughening penalties for the criminals, and giving our law enforcement people the tools they need to do their job.

I'm also taking steps today to address the long-term challenges of reforming our immigration policy. I intend to appoint a new chair to the congressionally mandated Commission on Immigration Reform and to ask the Congress to expand the Commission to include senior administration officials. I'm also asking our Attorney General, Janet Reno, and the INS Commissioner-Designate, Doris Meissner, to make sure the INS is as professional and effectively managed as it can be. Under their leadership, I have no doubt that it will be. With these efforts, I hope that we can begin a broad-based national discussion on this important issue and move toward significant resolution of the problems that plague all Americans.

Now, I'd like to ask the Vice President to come forward with my thanks for his outstanding work to discuss the specifics of the initiative.

[*At this point, the Vice President outlined the immigration policy. The Attorney General then discussed what enforcement measures would be taken.*]

Q. With all due respect, sir, all of this has been tried previously. The Simpson, Romano, Mazzoli bill did make a similar attempt to this by increasing penalties, they increased funding, they increased border patrols, they increased penalties to employers, and yet, nothing happened. What leads you to believe that this time something might really happen?

The President. I want to give them a chance to answer this. It's not true that all these things have been tried before. First, Senator D'Amato, I'm glad to see you. Thank you for coming.

It's not true that all these things have been tried before, and it's certainly plain to anybody with eyes to see that the border patrol is drastically understaffed, breathtakingly understaffed. But there are also some new elements in this, and I think I'd let the Vice President and the Attorney General address them.

The Vice President. Yes, the change in the exclusion provisions is brand new. The change in the investment in the information systems that will avoid a repetition of what happened when the sheik applied for a visa and then the office didn't have the information because even though the State Department did, it didn't have the information system to display it, a lot of these things are brand new. They've never been done before, and it is a coordinated approach involving all of the players involved and the full keyboard, if you will. Every part of the issue is being addressed here.

Now, there are some things that are not addressed and the procedure the President outlined for addressing the longer term problems

is going to work just as well as this procedure worked. It's going to take more time, though.

Q. How much of this counterterrorism provision was sparked by the World Trade Center bombing, and how confident are you that the borders will be safe now from terrorists getting into the United States, if this proposed legislation is enacted?

The President. I can answer the first part; maybe I should invite the Attorney General to comment on the second. There's no question that the World Trade Center bombing has caused us to review a whole range of issues, not just involving immigration, in terms of our ability to deal with the whole threat of actual or potential terrorism. And when that happened, we began in earnest to review not only this issue but the capacity of our law enforcement agencies to deal with it, and we will continue to do that. I think that I owe that to the American people, and that clearly had something to do with it.

Attorney General Reno. With respect to the second part, no one can ensure anything, except that we are going to try our best. When I came into office, I found a service that too often did not communicate with law enforcement and vice-versa, that too often was not in communication with other Federal Agencies. I think it's imperative that we bring everyone together to communicate to do everything that we can to address the critical issue of terrorism and to be as vigilant as possible. To ensure our borders at this day and time is a very difficult task, but it is one that is of the highest priority of this administration.

Q. Mr. President, on the question of the reason illegal Chinese immigrants—obviously, they involve three parties: the United States, China, and Taiwan, because some of the ships are from Taiwan. So I wonder, are you planning to personally discuss with leaders of China and Taiwan, maybe, in November APEC meeting in Seattle?

The President. Well, let me say, first of all, I just talked to the Secretary of State last night, and he raised these issues personally in his conversation with the representative of the Chinese Government recently. And we have enjoyed good relations with Taiwan, also. We intend to raise it with them. We intend to raise it at the highest levels with both countries and to seek their active and consistent cooperation. And I think, as you point out, without that cooperation, we will continue to have greater difficulties on this end. But I think they will help us more, and I have no reason to believe that they won't. We're just going to have to work on it. We're going to have to have their help to do better.

Q. Are you inviting them to the APEC meeting? Are you inviting President Li Teng-hui to the APEC meeting?

The President. We also are discussing how we're going to deal with the APEC meeting, who is going to come from all the 15 countries. And of course, who comes will be in part, I think, determined by how much we'll want to pursue this discussion there. But in terms of who will be there, that hasn't been finalized from their point of view.

Go ahead.

Q. Mr. President, how do you depoliticize the asylum process? Because in the Reagan years, anybody from El Salvador was not considered to have a bona fide claim of asylum. In the Bush years, Chinese fleeing birth control policies were deemed to have a good claim for asylum. How do you make this more rational so that the American people and the foreigners both know what qualifies as asylum?

The President. That's a very good question. I'm so glad you asked it. I think the answer is that we have to have criteria for enforcing this law that grows out of our laws that are based on policies rooted in laws enacted by the Congress. I think that is the answer. Obviously, if Congress and the administration work with the Congress, if we decide that there's some policy that's so important for other reasons, for our other foreign policy concerns, our human rights concerns, you name it, that we want to root that in our legal policy, then no one can accuse us of being arbitrary, because we will have gone through a deliberative process. The Congress will have made a judgment; we will all be on public record.

But I do think it's very important that immigrants from the world looking at us and governments from the world looking at us, not believe that the President will wake up someday and decide that for some arbitrary reason we will enforce the immigration laws of the country in

one way or another. Perhaps the Vice President and the Attorney General would like to make a comment about that, also.

The Vice President. I'd like to add one brief point. This proposal does take the partisanship and the politics out of it. This is a bipartisan initiative. Republicans as well as Democrats are here from both the Senate and the House. And if I could summarize the basic tone of this initiative, I would use the words of Doris Meissner, who is the designee to head up INS, when she said not long ago, we want to stop illegal immigration so that we can continue opening our country to legal immigration. The two go together, and that's what this proposal is designed to do.

The President. I think we've answered about all the questions we can. I'd like to close by reemphasizing that point. When I ran for President, I think in some ways the most rewarding part of the experience was having the opportunity to see just how many different countries and how many different ethnic groups have contributed to making America what it is today. We don't want to do anything to interrupt that. But we cannot continue to progress as a country unless we have a more vigorous response to this problem, and we don't want to cloud the two. This has nothing to do with our support for keeping the rainbow and the melting pot of America going and growing and enriching and strengthening this country.

But the kinds of practices that are manifest in who can get into this country on an airplane, what kind of illegal smuggling can go on, and the fact that our borders leak like a sieve, those things cannot be permitted to continue in good conscience. It's not good for the American immigrants who are here legally in this country, for the American economy, for the cohesion of our society, or for the rule of law worldwide. And we're going to try to do better. This is a very good first step.

Thank you very much.

NOTE: The President spoke at 11:38 a.m. in Room 450 of the Old Executive Office Building.

Message to the Congress Transmitting Proposed Legislation on Illegal Immigration
July 27, 1993

To the Congress of the United States:

I am pleased to transmit today for your immediate consideration and enactment the "Expedited Exclusion and Alien Smuggling Enhanced Penalties Act of 1993." This legislative proposal is designed to address the growing abuse of our legal immigration and political asylum systems by illegal aliens holding fraudulent documents and by alien smugglers. Also transmitted is a section-by-section analysis. The proposal is part of a larger Administration initiative that I announced on June 18, 1993, to combat the illegal entry and smuggling of aliens into the United States.

The use of fraudulent documents by aliens seeking to enter the United States has increased dramatically. This proposal would expedite the exclusion and return of certain undocumented and fraudulently documented aliens who clearly are ineligible for admission to the United States, while ensuring that persons who have legitimate asylum claims receive full and fair hearings. In addition, the bill would increase the ability of the Immigration and Naturalization Service (INS) to prosecute alien smugglers and enhance the penalties for alien smuggling.

The expedited exclusion procedures would apply to an alien who, for example: (1) attempted to use a fraudulent passport to enter the United States; (2) came to the United States by commercial airplane and did not present a visa upon arrival; or (3) was encountered by the Coast Guard on the high seas and brought to the United States. To apply for asylum, these aliens first would have to establish that they had a credible fear either of persecution in the country from which they had departed or of return to persecution. If an asylum officer determined that the alien had such a credible fear, the alien then could apply for asylum. If the alien did not have the requisite fear of persecution, the alien would be subject to an immediate order of exclusion barring him or her from entering the United States. The bill would limit judicial review of such an exclusion order.

Alien smuggling has become an increasingly pervasive problem, as seen in the current wave of Chinese aliens being brought to the shores of this country by unscrupulous criminal organizations. These organizations seek to profit both from transporting these aliens and from their labors once in this country. The number of alien smugglers arrested in the past 3 years has tripled, and the number of smugglers convicted has doubled.

Alien smuggling not only violates our criminal and immigration laws, but it also takes a terrible toll on the lives of the aliens illegally brought into this country. Many of these individuals transfer their entire life savings and pledge thousands of additional dollars to smugglers. These aliens are often placed in deplorable conditions amounting to indentured servitude until they can pay the debts incurred for their passage to America. Moreover, organized criminal syndicates are becoming more frequently associated with this highly profitable traffic in human cargo.

The bill's criminal provisions are vital to help apprehend offenders and deter future criminal activity in this area. Under this proposal, the maximum penalty imposed against certain smugglers would be increased from 5 to 10 years in prison for each individual smuggled. Since clandestine means of investigation are often needed to build cases against alien smuggling rings, the bill would authorize INS to conduct wiretaps for alien smuggling investigations.

Finally, the Racketeer Influenced and Corrupt Organizations statute would be amended so its penalty and forfeiture provisions could be used against alien smuggling organizations. The proposal also would expand the ability of law enforcement personnel to forfeit the proceeds of illegal alien smuggling, such as cash and bank accounts.

In addition to this bill, our efforts to combat alien smuggling include strengthening law enforcement efforts and attacking smuggling operations at the source. The Federal Government already has begun interdicting and redirecting smuggling ships, where feasible, in transit to the United States. INS is detaining aliens who enter the United States in conjunction with criminal smuggling activities. The Department of Justice, consistent with due process and existing laws, is expediting the adjudication of entry claims raised by migrants who are the victims of organized criminal smuggling schemes.

All of these actions, taken together, signal the United States abhorrence of the trafficking in human beings for profit and our determination to combat this illegal activity. At the same time, they reaffirm our Nation's commitment to safeguarding the protection of bona fide refugees.

I urge the prompt and favorable consideration of this legislative proposal by the Congress.

WILLIAM J. CLINTON

The White House,
July 27, 1993.

Exchange With Reporters Prior to a Meeting With Midwestern Governors
July 27, 1993

Disaster Assistance and Economic Program

Q. Mr. President, do you have any problem with Senator Boren's idea for a budget summit?

The President. Let me make a statement, first of all, about what we're here for.

I want to welcome the Governors from the States afflicted by the floods to Washington, and I'm very encouraged by the work they've been doing here today. Of course, we hope the legislation will pass the House today, and if it does then when it moves on to the Senate it is our intention, as I indicated when I was in St. Louis, based on Mr. Panetta's figures, to ask that the relief package be increased by another $1.1 billion which will take us to just slightly above $4 billion. And of course, we're still collecting damage estimates. It may get worse because it's still going on in some places. But I'm very hopeful that we can push this through and work this through. And of course, there are a lot of other issues the Governors want to talk about and deal with that we're going to try to help them on some. I'm encouraged by that.

In terms of the other question you asked me, go back to 1990. You know, I will say again, that the strongest reaction I got yesterday in Chicago with that highly bipartisan crowd was when I said we need to make a decision and go on with other things.

If you look at what happened in 1990, there was this sort of delay. If you delay it a couple of months you're going to have less deficit reduction, higher interest rates, more fragility and uncertainty in the economy, more consumer confidence going down. We have been working on this.

We have other things to do. The American people want us to solve the health care crisis, deal with welfare reform, to pass a crime bill. We have a whole range of other issues out there. The Congress is strangled from doing anything else until we put this budget issue behind us. So the time has come to act. We just need to move and go on and almost everything else that needs to be done, I hope and believe we'll have bipartisan support and we'll meet the needs of this country. Nobody wants to reduce the deficit because—the reason it got so bad as it did is that there were tough decisions required to turn it around. And I think to delay it while we nibble around the edges would be a serious error.

NOTE: The exchange began at 1:54 p.m. in the Cabinet Room at the White House. A tape was not available for verification of the content of these remarks.

Remarks on the Anniversary of the Americans with Disabilities Act
July 27, 1993

It is great to see all of you. You know, I heard Tom's speech outside, and I want to say, first of all, how grateful I am, as an American, to Tom Harkin and Steny Hoyer and all of you who made the Americans with Disabilities Act a reality, but how much I owe, as a public servant, to Senator Harkin personally. You know, when we were on the campaign trail together, he made his brother the most famous brother in America in a very beautiful way. And you need to know when he was up here speaking we've been killing time because his brother, Frank, is on the phone, and he doesn't have time to talk to me right now. [*Laughter*] His line is busy. This is true. His line's busy. We've been trying to call him which is great. It's great. It means that the thing is working. [*Laughter*] This is—yesterday, I guess, was the effective date when the telephone service had to be provided. So I'm so excited about that.

While we're waiting for the line to clear, let me just—if I might make a few points. First, I want to reaffirm strong support of our administration for implementing and enforcing the act. Yesterday, the Attorney General and a number of other Cabinet members conducted some activities designed to clearly remove any ambiguity about that and to reinforce our commitment on that issue.

The second thing I want to do is to—I know that Roy's already introduced them, but to say a special word of thanks to Americans with disabilities who happen to be part of this administration and to those who will be, including some in this room and some who are not in this room.

Finally, let me say, we need your help because you have become a very powerful force. We need your help to pass this economic plan so we can get on with the rest of the business of the country, and then so we can get on the

health care and try to deal with the issues of long-term care and personal services and empowerment, the kinds of things that are so important to—I heard Tom talking about the inclusion, independence, and empowerment. There are a lot of Americans who need that, not just Americans with disabilities. And we have to go forward.

And I know a lot of people, but none more than you, are eager to see this debate on health care begin. It cannot begin until we have a budget and economic plan in place. And there are many more things that we have to do which are also of interest to you that are especially important. We need a new crime bill. We need a bill that reforms the welfare system. It also works on empowerment. We need a whole series of things that we are eager to get on with doing. But first we have to nail this budgetary issue.

I am especially interested in the health care debate, as you know. And I spoke with the First Lady this morning, as I do on most mornings—[*laughter*]—and we were reviewing our days, and I told her that Tom and I were going to be here with you today. And she was very interested in, you know, the fact that we were going to do this and asked me to give you her best and to thank those of you who have been involved already with her in the health care task force in trying to work through these issues.

NOTE: The President spoke at 2:50 p.m. in the Roosevelt Room at the White House. A tape was not available for verification of the content of these remarks.

Remarks in a Telephone Conversation With Frank Harkin
July 27, 1993

The President. Hello?

Operator. Yes, hello. Good afternoon. This is Agent 218 of the Federal Information Relay Service.

The President. May I speak with Frank now?

Operator. Yes, he's on line standing by for your conversation.

The President. Frank, this is Bill Clinton. I'm really glad to be able to talk with you now

that the text telephone system is in place nationwide. And I'm here with your brother, Tom, who just gave a great speech.

If it hadn't been for you, I don't think he would have had all those great speeches. I just told the crowd here that he made you the most famous brother in America last year.

Mr. Harkin. Gee, thanks.

The President. He said, "Gee, thanks."

Mr. Harkin. Thanks for saying that.

The President. "Thanks for saying that."

What we all want to know is whether you are wet or dry.

Mr. Harkin. It is a great moment to talk to you, Mr. President.

The President. Frank, what we all want to know here is whether you are wet or dry. I've been to Iowa twice, and I know how much flooding you've had. So tell us how it is around where you live.

Mr. Harkin. Today it is humid and muggy. I did watch on TV when you were in Iowa.

The President. Well, I just had the Governors of six States, including Iowa, in to see me to talk about how we could help people get over the flood damage, and I certainly hope we can do a good job of that.

Mr. Harkin. Hopefully you will do your best.

The President. I want you to tell all the people here with me how you like this communications system.

Mr. Harkin. It is wonderful—have a TV crew from Des Moines in my house.

The President. Well, now I want you to say a word to your brother. You have proved that you are a person of fewer words than—[*laughter*]—than the President or your brother. Congratulations.

NOTE: The President spoke at 3:09 p.m. in the Roosevelt Room at the White House. The conversation took place during a ceremony commemorating the anniversary of the Americans with Disabilities Act.

Interview With the Georgia Media
July 27, 1993

The President. Well, first of all, I want to thank you for coming. Welcome. As you probably know, we've been doing a whole series of these press conferences, both when I'm out and when I'm here and also some of it electronically, but as much in person-to-person as possible. And I would like to give as much time as possible to answer your questions.

But I think I should begin with a story that Charles Stenholm told this morning. He's the chairman of the Conservative Caucus in the House who, by the way, thinks we should make some changes in the program during the conference. But he acknowledged today that—he said every time someone calls me criticizing this program, they've normally had their heads filled full of misinformation by people who are criticizing them without telling everything. And every time I talk somebody through it, they wind up thinking it's not so bad.

Last night Leon Panetta went to a Maryland district that's fairly representative of the United States with Congressman Cardin and went through the whole program. And afterward the Congressman asked the people, "Do you want me to vote for this, or do you want me to delay it 60 days more or just let it to go to pieces and see what happens?" And three to

one, they wanted him to support it.

Then the Wall Street Journal last week finally began something that has not happened up here. This is not your issue but ours in Washington. They actually went around and started asking people who said they were with small business groups opposed to this plan if they knew what was in it, and it turned out they didn't. And over 90 percent of the small businesses in America will actually be eligible for a tax reduction under this program, because they have no tax increase on the income taxes, and we doubled the expensing provisions for small businesses.

So the program—I just want to emphasize again—is the only program presented that provides $500 billion of deficit reduction, an equal balance between spending cuts and tax increases. For every $5 in spending cuts, there are $5 in tax increases; $4 of those come from people with incomes in the upper 5 percent of the income brackets; $1 comes from the middle class. Working families with incomes of under $30,000—and there are a bunch of them in Georgia—are held harmless in this program. An average family of four with an income of $50,000, we're looking at a ceiling of about $50 a year, which is less than a buck a month to get the deficit down and provide some of the economic incentives to grow some jobs, which I think is very, very important. So I think it's a balanced plan. I think it's a fair plan. And if you look at the alternative that was presented in the Senate, it's the only serious plan so far that's been up that really has big deficit reduction in a fair way.

Questions? Go ahead.

Georgia Congressional Support

Q. As you're meeting with us, obviously, some of this is directed at reaching our congressional delegation as well. We had conservative Democrats in the House, and obviously Senator Nunn in the Senate, who had voted against the plan. How are you approaching our delegation? Are you meeting with them personally? How are you lobbying them? Are you disappointed that you haven't had them with you? And do you think you can turn them around?

The President. First of all, we got a good number of votes from Georgia for which I am very grateful. But let me tell you how I'm doing it generally. I'm trying to meet with the House Members in the big caucuses first: the Conservative Caucus; the Mainstream Forum, which is sort of the DLC group; the Black Caucus; the Hispanic Caucus; the Women's Caucus. I've met with all of them, except I'm meeting with the Mainstream Forum tonight, and then talking to individual Members about individual concerns.

In the Senate we pretty well know the 10 or 15 Senators that could go either way and what the issues are for them, and so I'm trying to talk to each of them individually about their concerns. I met with four Senators over the weekend, and I have talked to a number of others over the phone.

The concerns basically are twofold. They break down into two broad categories. Some are just worried about a political reaction. And many of them have said to me, "Look, if our constituents knew what was in this, we know they would support it."

This is the only political issue in my lifetime where people have known less about it as it's gone on; that is, known less about the issue as time has gone on. The night I gave the State of the Union Address when there was a great deal of support for this was really the time when people had the largest number of facts. And then all the groups that ginned up opposition to it—it's like this spokesperson for a small business group last week ran a car washing service;

turned out she got a tax reduction, not a tax increase out of this plan, and she didn't know it. And the people that had gotten her to stand up and speak against something she didn't know what was in.

So for those folks we have really got work on just making sure that they understand, that we now have an aggressive effort to get the evidence out that this is fair, progressive, real deficit reduction and real job creation. It's going to keep interest rates down and get jobs up. I mean, that's just a—that's reality, and I think that's important.

To the second argument is that the country wants us to make a decision and go on about other things. They don't want us to fool around for 60 more days without a budget. They want us to make a decision and then deal with health care, the crime bill, the welfare reform bill, all the other issues out there facing us.

Now, there's another group of people who basically didn't like either the bill that passed the Senate or the bill that passed the House but are more than prepared to take the political heat associated with serious deficit reduction if they can get a bill that they agree with. Senator Nunn, for example, told me that there were basically two big issues for him. And he told me that he might have reluctantly voted for the House bill because the House bill addressed one issue, which is that we need some more incentives in the Tax Code for people to invest their money in job-creating activities. And in the House, you know, we had incentives for new and small business capital gains tax. You invest your money in a business capitalized at $15 million a year less; if you hold it for 5 years, you cut your tax rate in half on the gain.

By raising personal income tax rates, we created a significant incentive to halve capital gains generally by investing in new businesses. We had some new incentives for new plant and equipment. We had new incentives to revive real estate and homebuilding. We had incentives to do more research and development.

When the Senate passed its bill to move from the Btu tax down to the fuel tax at 4.3 percent, one of the ways they did it was just to eliminate all that stuff, as well as the empowerment zones to try to get free enterprise into the depressed urban and rural areas. They cut that way, way back, so—no, they eliminated it in the Senate bill.

So, I believe that that concern will be addressed in the conference report. That is, I think the final bill will, through a combination of other spending cuts and maybe some just minor modifications to the revenue package, put a lot of those job incentives back in there.

The other issue that Senator Nunn raises is one with which I am very sympathetic but one that I am absolutely convinced we cannot deal with right now but that we have to deal with. And that is that there needs to be some limits, some discipline on the growth of entitlement spending. Let me just give you an example. The budget that was passed last year before I became President had an estimated 12 percent a year increase in health care costs, Medicare and Medicaid, 12 percent a year. Now, the rolls were growing some, but most of it was just inflation, paying more for the same health care.

We cut that back to 9 percent a year and saved $55 billion or so off the previous budget, a big shave. But still if you look at this budget now, you've got defense going down, many domestic programs going down, and an overall freeze on domestic spending. That is, for all the increases we have in Head Start and worker training and new technologies and defense conversions, we have offsetting decreases in something else. And the only thing that's really increasing in this budget are the retirement programs, Social Security cost-of-living increases, which are at least covered by the Social Security tax, and other cost-of-living increases on retirement programs and health care. That's what's going up.

So Senator Nunn and others believe, and I do, that you have to find a way to control health care costs. Otherwise, you're going to give the whole budget over to health care. You wind up cutting defense too much, and you don't have enough money left to spend where you ought to spend it, which is in revitalizing this economy. The problem is that if you put a cap on health care costs in this budget without reforming health care, which is the next big issue I want Congress to take up, if you did that, then all that would happen is you'd impose a hidden tax on every American with health insurance. Because what happens is if you just quit paying doctors and hospitals at the Federal level, then they just send a bill to your employers and to you if you pay part of your health insurance.

And that's why I don't think we can pass this cap now. I think we can pass the controls on health care costs by the Government if we reform health care. So anyway, that's a long answer. But you're interested in the Georgia politicians. I'm dealing with the political concerns and the substantive concerns as they come up.

Senator Sam Nunn

Q. Can I follow up? Why could you not convince Nunn of that, given the fact that here's a guy who supported you in the campaign and sold you, in effect, to Georgia voters in campaign ads? And it would seem like, this being as important to you as it is, that you would be able to persuade him to accept the logic of that and wait for health care reform down the road.

The President. I'm not sure he won't. I mean, he told me clearly that he found that he thought the Senate was wrong to take out all the job incentives, and of course, I did, too. But my argument to him was don't let the thing get defeated. Let's send it to Congress and see if we can put them back in. But you know, he and Senator Domenici worked for years on this program of strength in America. I think he's got a lot vested in it. He's got some very strong convictions about it. But all of us, including the President, in order to get anything done in a tough time, we've got to be willing to compromise some. And I hope we will get his support at the end.

But I just wanted to tell you what I think the roots of it are. I think they're—and that I'm very sympathetic with a lot of what he was saying. And I think in the end we'll get where he wants to go.

Let me just mention one other thing I have to tell you. If you get the budget out of the way and you start health care reform, which is the only way to ever get the deficit down to zero, by the way—I'm not satisfied with going down to $200 billion a year and then going back up again in 5 years; we've got to do something about health care to move it to zero. Then the other big issue that's coming up this fall that I think is terribly important is the Vice President's report on reinventing the Government. That's been a big issue that Senator Nunn and I worked on through the Democratic Leadership Council. He is going to offer some very controversial but very important suggestions to cut the overhead costs of the Federal Government and make it more efficient, make it more user-friendly to the taxpayers, and free up some money which can itself be used to reduce the deficit or to invest in our future. So all these things have to be seen together.

And the argument I have to make to Senator Nunn—and I'm trying to make to some others, and a lot of the moderate Republicans who basically think they ought to support me if they could get out from under the partisan deal—is that you cannot solve every problem with the Federal budget with this act. We cannot solve all the problems. But if you put the budget and economic program with the Gore reinventing Government initiatives, with health care reform, you can bring this deficit down to zero, and you can really revitalize the economy, and you can do it in a way that's fair to all the American people. But you can't do it in one bill. And I guess that's the—a lot of the people who are holding out are saying, "Well, we want it to be perfect." Well, it can't be perfect. It's just got to be a big advance. It's given us the dramatically lower interest rates, and it's a good thing.

Q. Can you tell us a little about your relationship to Senator Nunn? I'm belaboring the point a little bit, but we have watched this over the last 6 months. How often do you talk with him? How is your personal relationship, despite all of the thing with gays in the military——

The President. Probably—I don't know—anyway, often. I talk to him often on the phone. And I see him with some frequency, and I hope to see him again pretty soon to discuss this. But you know, it's not unusual for me every week, a time or two, to pick up the phone and call him on something.

Q. Are you frustrated with him?

The President. No. No, I mean, I think—you know, I don't agree with the decision he made on the budget bill. But I agree with the reasons he had for not liking the way it came out. I didn't like the way it came out. But I think we should have kicked it into the conference—the Senate did the right thing—so we could keep the process going. Because the Republicans have not offered any credible alternatives, so there's no basis for us to build a bipartisan coalition. I hope we never have another bill without a bipartisan coalition, because I'm not comfortable with that. But in general I think it's going pretty well. I mean, the other issues—you know, he never made any pretense. He never agreed with me on the gays in the

military issue. He made it clear in the campaign. He made it clear during the transition. He made it clear after the election. And we wound up—he wound up in a place where I don't think he expected to wind up either. I mean, I think we moved this thing quite a long way.

As a practical matter, if you read this policy, it differs from what I said in the campaign in only one respect: You still can't openly declare your homosexuality without some fear of being severed from the service. If you do that, the burden is then on you to demonstrate you are not going to violate the Code of Conduct. But I never said one word, not a word, about changing anything about the Code of Conduct. And yet the military leaders themselves decided to go further than they had ever gone in protecting the privacy and association rights of all members of the military in ways that Colin Powell summed up as a policy of "live and let live." That goes well beyond anything I even talked about in the campaign. Senator Nunn endorsed that. The Joint Chiefs endorsed that. The House leadership yesterday endorsed that. So I'm very encouraged about where we are on it.

Economic Program

Q. I've asked this question of a couple of your people, and I'd really like to hear your response on it as well. You last week released the jobs State by State that you think the plan will generate. Now, this morning in a session, Roger Altman's staff basically said, "Gee, we probably shouldn't have been so specific. We should have rounded these numbers a little bit. We're not going to create 238,416, or whatever, for the State of Georgia."

The President. It might be more; it might be less. I think everybody knows projections are approximations.

Q. But the choice was to release very specific numbers and now to round them. And now the administration is getting some criticism for that. Do you not think it may have been a mistake to have tried to put such specific numbers together in an attempt to sell this plan?

The President. Well, it may have been, but let me tell you why we did it. What we're trying to do is to avoid—frankly, the main reason we did it was to avoid overpromising, because I don't believe that this plan alone can restore America's health. I just think it is the critical, it is the critical first step. Without it I think you have total uncertainty; you have chaos; you have interest rates going back up again, and you have a Government that can't get anything done.

With it you begin the march to progress. I think to get total economic health you have to do something about the health care crisis, do something about the way the Government does its business, deal with the welfare reform issue. And then there has to be a whole set of other economic strategies to help people convert from a defense to a domestic economy, continue the education and training of the work force, open new markets, all those other things.

So I think what they were trying to do was to say yes, it will do something, but we don't want to overpromise. Here's a model we ran through, and this is where we got. It may or may not have been a mistake, but we were trying to give people a sense of what our own research had produced.

Media Coverage

Q. Could I ask a followup please? One of the reasons for days like today is that people acknowledge that you have been misunderstood to some extent in terms of this plan. As you well know, there's been a fairly constant sense among some people in the administration, and sometimes you're one of them, that you've been misunderstood a lot on issues like gays in the military and what you first meant and what you really meant and on the economic plan, that sort of thing. Why, now that you've been here for a while, do you feel there is something systemic that's wrong with the way the media covers the White House? Why have you been so misunderstood by the people who cover this administration?

The President. Oh, I don't know. I think that for one thing if you throw something really controversial out there, and are new and different, it is very difficult for anything but the controversy to get constant coverage. And I don't say this so much about you but I mean, just in all the stories that compete for time on the national news. For example, let's suppose you're—and this is not a criticism more than an observation—suppose you are the producer of ABC News or wherever. You've got to put the flood on, right? The Israelis bomb the Bekaa Valley or attack the—you've got to put that on. So instead of, I mean, you can't go back through every night all the essence of the economic plan. And if our adversaries decide just to scream,

"taxes," it's just easier to cover that story and to get it in the timeslots you can cover it.

I think that a big part of it is when there is just a huge volume of news and you've got somebody like me who's very much into trying to solve problems and get them out of the way, whether it's the test ban issue or the POW issue or the Northwest United States forest issue, I just try to take all these things and move through them. If you get something really controversial like gays in the military, it's not as if I had a chance to sit in the home in a fireside chat with the American people and walk them through my position and then walk them through why we came up with this compromise and why I think it is the principled, right thing to do.

And on the economic plan, I think it's just clear, I think—let me just give you—Bernie Sanders from Vermont is an independent from Vermont, the only independent in the Congress. He called me the other day and he said, "I have done you a terrible disservice." I said, "What do you mean? You voted for me on everything." He said, "That's what I'm telling you." He said, "If the progressives in the Congress had burned you in effigy for all these spending cuts, then America would know you had made spending cuts. But because the entire Democratic Party and I rolled on the spending cuts, it was never newsworthy." They weren't newsworthy. The newsworthy thing was the fight over the taxes, so that even when the Republicans—they were so smart about it—when the Republicans in the Senate Finance Committee offered all kinds of things to water down the tax program, but they did not offer one, not one red cent in spending cuts, because they didn't want to take any tough decisions. They knew we already made a lot of spending cuts, and they just wanted a lot of attacks on the taxes.

So I think, frankly, anytime you do hard things and you try to change, you have to expect to be misunderstood. But when you've got more than one thing out there at once, you have to really work on talking it through, which is why I think I should have been doing this from February the 18th until today, not just for the last month or so.

Q. But is any of this your fault, sir?

The President. Sure it is. Sure it is. I mean, I'm sure it is. I've got to learn—you know it is. But I'll tell you this, I've got an administration that's tried to face the problems of this country. Everybody up here is trying to do right by America. We get up every day and go to work, and we have taken on things that have been ignored for a long time. And I do not believe, frankly, that the evaluation of the administration by the press or the people has fairly compared us with what got done in previous administrations. I mean, I could have been, I guess, immensely popular if all I'd done is make speeches for the last 6 months and not try to do anything.

Taxes

Q. Mr. President, this goes to what you've already been saying about American taxpayers. There are many people who have the perception that you are a taxaholic, that you didn't get the message that many people in this country want you to cut spending first, get rid of the bloat in the Federal Government and then talk about tax hikes.

The President. But we are cutting spending. And if all you had was spending cuts, you would have a deficit reduction package in the neighborhood of $250 billion to $260 billion which no one—which the financial markets would not take seriously and interest rates would be 2 percent higher and all these people refinancing their home and saving a ton of money on it wouldn't be saving it.

In other words, let me give it to you in another way. We are cutting spending. We're going to cut more spending. But you'd be amazed how many of those same people, when you say, "Okay, all the growth is in Medicare and Medicaid. You want me to cut Medicare?"—they say, "No, don't do that." I mean, there are people who believe that all the Federal budget goes to welfare and foreign aid— which is something we cut, by the way, foreign aid—which is a tiny percentage of the total overall budget of the Federal Government.

We are—this administration, not the two previous ones—that's really got the serious attempt going to reduce the Federal bureaucracy and to change the way the Federal Government relates to people. That's what the Vice President is working on, and we'll have our report out next month. But we don't have time to fool around.

Let me just make one final point about this. David Stockman, who was Ronald Reagan's Budget Director when the '81 tax cuts were enacted, gave an interview last month in which he said it was folly to believe we could balance the budget on spending cuts alone, because in 1981 President Reagan intended to cut taxes 3 percent of national income. And by the time he and the Congress got through with their bidding war, they had cut them 6 percent of national income, so much that some companies couldn't even handle all their tax cuts. They were selling them to others. And he said, "That has to be reversed." That's what I'm trying to do.

And you know, let me just point out for all those people who think I'm a taxaholic, for 12 years I was Governor of a State that was always in every year in the bottom five of the States in the country in the percentage of income going to State and local taxes, in every year. We had the toughest balanced budget law in the country, and the only time we raised money was when a majority of the people of my State supported it, and the money went to schools or roads. We didn't do anything but education and jobs with new taxes. In the late eighties, the percentage of our income going to taxes in Arkansas was the same as it was in the late seventies when I became Governor.

But when you get up here, you see the problems we've got and you see how long they've been ignored. And keep in mind, families with incomes under $30,000 are going to be held harmless. Families with incomes between $30,000 and $140,000 are going to be asked to pay very modest amounts. The average payment for a family of four with a $50,000 income is $50 a year. To get this deficit under control, I think it's worth it. If the people don't think so, they can tell their Congressman. But the idea that there are no spending cuts in this thing is simply not true. The spending cuts have not been controversial, so they have not been reported, so people don't think they exist. But they do exist.

Legislative Action

Q. Mr. President, what are the consequences of your not getting this budget plan passed as you want it by the August recess?

The President. Well, the consequences of not passing a budget plan—it won't be exactly as everybody wants it. That's what a democracy is about. People get together and work through. But if they don't pass the budget plan by the August recess, what will happen is we'll flail around here for a couple of months. You'll see interest rates start to go up again. Uncertainty will get worse, and you'll wind up with less deficit reduction. Politics will take over, and you'll wind up with less deficit reduction. So the thing we need to do is to make a decision and get on with it. I mean, we've been fooling around with this for long enough.

I realize that we're keeping a pace that's faster than normal for Washington; but for America, they want something done. It's time to do something. It means that if you fool around with it, it means we don't deal with health care; we don't deal with welfare reform; we don't deal with the crime bill; we don't deal with all these other issues that are out there crying for attention in America. Eight months is long enough to make a decision about a budget and an economic plan. It's just long enough.

Q. Are you worried you're not going to be able to get it?

The President. Well, I think in the end they will do it because I think that all the Republican Members have gone on strike basically. We've reached out to them. We've tried to negotiate with them. And they have basically said, you know, they don't want to talk unless we're willing to do things that aren't real, adopt these amorphous caps and slash Medicare even for middle class people, and I'm not willing to do that.

Q. Did you talk to Senator Coverdell?

The President. Yeah, I've met with the whole Republican caucus. And I meet with the Republican leadership, with the Democrats every other week.

Q. What have you learned about your ability to rally your own troops? You talked about under Republican resistance, but some of the strongest resistance has come within the party.

The President. Well, I think you should not assume—the Democratic Party, first of all, is much more diverse than the Republican Party but, secondly, has been much more unified with me than the Republicans were with President Bush.

That's another thing. Look at the historical perspective. Here's a little question: There was a Republican House budget plan and my plan voted on back to back in the House. There are more Democrats than Republicans, right?

Now, the Republican plan was no tax increases, the Kasich plan. He lost more Republicans for his plan than I lost Democrats for mine because it was so unfair to the elderly, the poor, the middle class. That was the other plan in the House. Last year, 1992, when the Bush budget came up in the House of Representatives, 75 percent of the Republicans, not the Democrats, the Republicans, voted against it. Why? Because it was a political document. I mean, I have given them a real budget, and it's tough.

Let me just say one thing in closing. The reporter for the Philadelphia Inquirer, the political reporter, went out and did something that we should have arranged. I wish I had thought about it, but he did it about 2 weeks ago. He interviewed all these budget experts who work for private companies but whose job it is to know about the Federal budget. And he wrote an article which said that the consensus was that my claims were accurate and that Senator Dole's attacks were not. And the budget expert for Price Waterhouse, not an employee of my administration, said that the budget we had presented was the most honest budget in more than a decade and the only thing that was wrong with it was that it would produce more deficit reduction than I was claiming. And we can get you a copy of the article. It was very impressive.

But I think the Democrats, when you think about the withering attack that they have been under, constant misinformation, and almost no way to get the facts out except through their newsletters—and we have begun to run ads for some of them now, those that have been subject to ad attacks—I think there's been a remarkable cohesion in a very diverse party because there is now a consensus that the time has come to do something about the deficit and to try to grow some jobs. And that's what we're trying to do. And I think they'll do it before August 5th. I'll be very surprised if they really want to go to an August recess, have all this unresolved, and come back here and fool around in September and October and not deal with the other problems of America. I think it will be a mistake, and I don't think they'll do it.

Thanks.

NOTE: The interview began at 3:59 p.m. on the South Lawn at the White House.

Remarks to the National Conference of State Legislatures
July 27, 1993

The President. Thank you very much, Art. Thank you for your leadership of the National Conference of State Legislatures, and thank you for your friendship to me. And most of all, thank you for giving me the chance to speak with all of you by satellite today.

It wasn't very long ago that you and the other leaders of the National Conference of State Legislatures came here to Washington along with some State legislators from California to speak about the specific problems of their State. I understand your incoming president, Senator Bob Connor from Delaware—perhaps he remembers, as I do so well, stopping in Wilmington last fall when my voice was so bad I could barely speak. I hope you're all able to hear me a little better today.

And to all my friends from Arkansas, let me say I do miss you, and there are plenty of days when I would trade with you. But after all, I asked for this job, and most of the folks in the Congress do want to move this country off dead center and move it forward, and I'm convinced we're going to break the gridlock and go forward with your help.

President Franklin Roosevelt once said that, "What this country needs is bold, persistent experimentation." As a former Governor who has worked with you to redefine how our Government can best meet the needs of our people, I think I know what that means. Most of you in this audience and most of the Governors with whom I work really have worked hard for a long time now to represent the laboratories of reform, whether in the cause of reinventing Government or controlling health care costs and providing health care to people who don't have it or giving people the dignity to move from welfare to work or to build an ambitious set of national goals for education or to devise State strategies for generating jobs and income.

For more than a decade, I have worked on these reforms with you. Now, as President, my administration aims to establish an historic partnership between the White House and the statehouses to give you the freedom to experiment in bold and innovative ways to meet the unique needs of people in your own States. The first order of business, as you know, must be to

reclaim control of our economic destiny. Here in Washington, I put forward an ambitious economic plan that finally does something serious about the deficit, reducing it by $500 billion to be locked away in a deficit reduction trust fund, the largest deficit reduction program in history, with $250 billion net in real, enforceable spending cuts. This plan restores tax fairness. For every $10 we reduce the deficit, $5 comes from spending cuts, $4 comes from taxes on the wealthiest 6 percent of Americans, and only $1 from the middle class, with working families under $30,000 held harmless.

This plan keeps faith with the hard working middle class, because over the course of a year, the average middle class family of four would pay about $1 a week. The plan is designed to restore our economic greatness by cutting the deficit and by getting on with the business of investing in our future. And you at the State level know that we have to do both. You couldn't run your State budgets with the kind of deficits we have, but if you didn't invest and give incentives to the private sector to invest, you know you wouldn't be able to meet the global competition.

So indeed, we must invest more to start new businesses, to create new jobs, to rebuild our infrastructure, to train our workers for the jobs of tomorrow. Our plan invests in our people and their education and their training as workers and new police officers on the streets and in new technologies that will boost economic growth and help to put our defense workers back to work. And analysis shows that this plan will create in California alone roughly 1.9 million jobs by 1996. As Government borrows less, interest rates will go down, and America will invest more.

Since I was elected President and it became clear that Washington would now be serious about deficit reduction, the financial markets have reduced long-term interest rates to historic lows. That means lower mortgage payments for middle class homeowners, particularly in California where property values are so high, and better loans for small business entrepreneurs who create a majority of our new jobs. It also means lower interest rates for cars and consumer loans.

1207

I'll bet there are people here at this convention who have refinanced your own home in the last 6 months and are saving a lot more money in lower mortgage rates than you'd be asked to pay in the modest fuel taxes. If we can keep these interest rates down for a year, this economic plan will pump between $50 billion and $100 billion of new private investment back into the economy by the end of the year. In the end, it all comes down to this: a choice between change for the better or more of the same.

We've seen the cost of gridlock, and the price is simply too high. We cannot afford for Washington to put off the hard choices or pass them on to people like you in the States any longer. It's time for us to act to get our own house in order.

We have to keep pace with the economic changes that are going on in the world. We have to decrease the deficit, lift the skills and wages of workers, open opportunities for young people who work hard and play by the rules.

I know you've got some questions for me, and I want to get to them in a moment. But first, let me tell you about one more issue, an announcement I made just a few hours ago with Vice President Gore and Attorney General Reno. I know it concerns people in San Diego a great deal, and it concerns many of the States which you represent.

Earlier today, our administration took new critical steps to control the growing problem of illegal immigration. America will continue to welcome new citizens into our family with honor and with dignity. But we will not allow terrorists and smugglers to dishonor the millions of immigrants who live here lawfully and contribute to the vitality of our society.

We will, first, expedite the process to exclude undocumented aliens without credible claims to asylum. Second, toughen penalties in law enforcement efforts to crack down on gangs of so-called "coyotes," or organized crime syndicates who smuggle illegal aliens to America by boat. And third, increase funding for up to 600 additional border agents and the training and technology they need to be effective.

We will not surrender our borders to those who wish to exploit America's history of freedom and justice, to engage in terrorism against Americans or traffic in human cargo. By correcting the system, by moving against those who traffic in cargo, and trying to make it far more difficult for terrorists to travel to this country, we will

also protect the immigrant who comes to America legally to live by our laws, work for a living, and to pursue the American dream.

I'm very grateful to the Vice President for coordinating these initiatives since we began this effort on June the 18th. And I also want to thank California Senators Feinstein and Boxer and the Hispanic Caucus and Congress for their aggressive work in trying to resolve this difficult issue through a balanced approach.

Now, I know you have some questions, and I want to answer them. I ask, finally, for your partnership: passing this economic plan, moving forward to the reinventing Government program, to a new health care program which will alleviate enormous pressures on your budget as well, and to helping you fight the battles against crime and for welfare reform, and to open the doors of college education to the citizens in your State. All that awaits the successful conclusion of the struggle in which I am now engaged and for which I seek your help.

The floor is yours. Thank you.

Unfunded Federal Mandates

Arthur M. Hamilton. Thank you, Mr. President. Our first question will be offered by State Senator Robert Connor of Delaware, president-elect of NCSL.

Mr. Connor. Good afternoon, Mr. President.

The President. Good afternoon, Bob.

[*Mr. Connor thanked the President and asked if he planned to relieve the burden of unfunded Federal mandates.*]

The President. Yes, I can. First, I have to be careful what I say because I've promised the Vice President faithfully that we would not dribble these recommendations out a little at a time but instead we'll try to present them in a package.

But I'd like to mention just two things if I might and to offer you an invitation. First, I want a part of this reinventing Government to be a reaffirmation of the idea that the Federal Government should not continue to put unfounded liabilities on the States. Second, I would like this report to also specifically outline some areas in which we can deregulate our relationships with the States and with local communities as well, where we can provide the funds that come from the Federal Government and the partnership that comes from the Federal Government without so much front-end regulation but instead evaluating whether these programs work after you've been given a chance to implement them. I hope both those things will be a part of the final report.

In that connection, I want to invite you again, and I know you've been consulted before, to give us collectively or any individual in this audience to present to us any specific recommendations you have for the kinds of things we could do that might save the taxpayers money, save you bureaucratic headache, and still put more funds or other resources into your hands so that you can actually solve the problems of the people that you are closer to than we are here in Washington. And I want to invite you to do that. We still have a few weeks left before we finalize the program, and any specific suggestions you have will be most welcome.

Energy Tax

Mr. Hamilton. Mr. President, thank you. Our next question comes from Karen McCarthy, representative from Missouri, vice president, National Conference of State Legislatures.

[*Ms. McCarthy asked if the proposed gas tax would be dedicated to the highway trust fund.*]

The President. Well, that's a subject, actually, that is now being discussed in the conference. It was raised with me for the first time today, actually, and I say that because you have given me a little impetus now to get more involved in this question. As you know, when I proposed the Btu tax, I thought the compromise would be one that saved the Btu tax without imposing it on production. I still think that was a better alternative. But the Senate fuel tax proposal seems destined to, in some form or fashion, become a part of the conference. And I will take that issue up with them. I want to make sure you understand, however, that even if it is put into the trust fund for the period of the deficit reduction, it still has to go to that. Of course, after that, it could then be freed up for the original purpose for which it was intended if we had done what we ought to do by then, which is to control health care costs and otherwise change the Government so we're moving toward a zero deficit, which is what our ultimate goal ought to be. But I will consider that. I never even thought about it until the last day or so, and I appreciate you bringing it to my attention.

Block Grants

Mr. Hamilton. Mr. President, our next question comes from Senator Bud Burke, president of the senate in Kansas and the immediate past president of NCSL. Bud.

[*Mr. Burke asked if the President would support legislation to consolidate Federal programs into flexible grants.*]

The President. Senator, let me ask you a question. Have you presented that specific proposal to the Vice President's task force on reinventing Government? Do you know the answer to that?

Mr. Burke. Yes, we have. And we've also discussed this proposal with congressional leaders over the past 3 years.

The President. Let me tell you that, generally, I am very favorable to that sort of approach. I must say I was disappointed when we were trying to pass the emergency jobs package earlier in the year, that there seemed to be so much resistance or at least so little enthusiasm among Members of the Congress in both parties for the community development block grant program. I don't know what your experience has been in Kansas, but in Arkansas, I can tell you that if it hadn't been for the CDBG funds and the flexibility they gave us, it would have been very difficult for us to have the kind of aggressive economic development program we had when I was Governor.

So I am generally very favorably inclined toward consolidating specific programs into larger block grants. I will look at the specific proposal; I will review it; I will discuss it specifically with the Vice President about in terms of what role it should have in his final recommendations.

But I have to say that we're going to have to do a little work on Members of Congress from both parties to increase their enthusiasm for the block grants. I don't quite know what the problem is, because it seems to me that the evidence is clear, at least based on my personal experience, that Federal money goes farther, does more good, has a bigger impact if we stop trying to micromanage it and overregulate it and instead let it be spent where the people and the problems are. So I'm very sympathetic, but I want to be candid. I think we've got a little work to do to bring the Congress to where we are.

Banking and Community Development

Mr. Hamilton. Mr. President, our next question comes from Assemblywoman Gwen Moore of California, who is a majority whip of the California Assembly.

[*Ms. Moore asked if the President opposed efforts to preempt State laws related to interstate branch banking and community reinvestment.*]

The President. Let me first, if I might, make a comment in reference to the first thing you said about California, because we now have legislators from all over America there. I want to make it clear that I got hired by all the American people to revitalize the whole American economy. But we can't get there unless something is done about California.

California has 12 percent of the country's population, 21 percent of the country's defense budget, took about almost 40 percent of the cuts in the last round of base closings, has taken a huge percentage of the cuts of defense cutbacks, and therefore is a net drag on the whole rest of the country when we have to pour money in for welfare, for food stamps, for unemployment, for maintenance programs, instead of having California do what it has done for much of the last 20 years, which is to lead the vibrant economic growth of America. So it is critical to all of you in the audience, whether you're from California or not, that something be done to deal with what is otherwise the world's sixth biggest economy.

Now, to go back to your community development question. I'm from Arkansas; my people have an interest in this. Everybody does. Now, let me say about the community involvement issue, I believe strongly that the Federal Community Reinvestment Act should be easier to follow and more clearly enforced. There is a way that we can make it less bureaucratic and still more easily enforced.

I believe that we ought to create partnerships, as you know, for community lending institutions all across America. There is clear evidence in the South Shore Bank in Chicago, in the Southern Development Bank in Arkansas, in the community initiatives in North Carolina and a lot of other places in this country, that you can make loans to poor people in distressed areas and make free enterprise work, create jobs, and move people from welfare to work. That clearly mostly is going to have to be done by people at the local level working in partnership with the bankers. Therefore, I do not see any need to preempt whatever State laws might be also

adopted with regard to community investment priorities or initiatives.

In terms of interstate banking, the other question you asked, that hasn't come up yet. I know of no reason that we would want to do that, and I certainly won't make any move or make any final decision on it without consulting you and the Governors and others at the State level who have an interest in this.

Ms. Moore. Thank you very much.

Health Care Reform

Mr. Hamilton. Mr. President, our last question will be offered by Senator Don Wesely of Nebraska, who is chair of our assembly on the legislators.

[*Mr. Wesely asked when the President would announce his health care reform package and if it would allow States to continue experimenting with their own programs.*]

The President. We expect to come forward with a package after the budget passes, that Congress has made it clear that they do not want to deal with an issue as major as health care while the budget was still on the griddle.

I think that it's also clear that we're going to be able to do far more at lower burden than had originally been assumed in terms of providing basic coverage for the unemployed, uninsured, locking in people to some coverage even if they have some preexisting health condition or someone in their family does, and promoting some significant insurance reforms and Government reforms to simplify the administrative costs.

I think there needs to be a sort of baseline comprehensive care package that every American has access to. But I also believe the States should be left a considerable amount of freedom to experiment with whether they want to provide other services or alternative delivery networks or alternative financing systems. So I think you can look forward to seeing a fairly significant amount of State flexibility here.

It's interesting, if you go back and look at the Canadian system, they've started that in one Province. We now have a lot of States trying different things. Hawaii, for many years, has provided some health insurance to virtually all their employees, although not all children were covered. But they did more sooner than anybody else. Now you've got Washington State, you've got Minnesota with new plans, you've got Kentucky and Vermont with plans on the griddle, a lot of other things being considered. So I think we need to maintain the elbow room and the creativity of the States in solving some of these problems, but there needs to be enough of a framework so that no one fears being left out and so that there's enough systematic change to bring these cost increases down. We have got to get health care costs down closer to inflation, plus population growth, or we're never going to turn this economy around in the long run. We're spending 14 percent of our income on health care, and only one other nation in the world, Canada, is even over 9 percent of income, and they're just barely over.

So we are going to have to have some uniformity, but I want the private system to remain in place, and I want as much flexibility for the States as possible.

Mr. Wesely. Thank you, Mr. President.

[*Mr. Hamilton then thanked the President for participating in the program.*]

The President. God bless you, Art. Thank you all, and goodbye.

NOTE: The President spoke at 5:10 p.m. in Room 459 of the Old Executive Office Building. A tape was not available for verification of the content of these remarks.

Exchange With Reporters at a Meeting With Democratic Members of Congress
July 27, 1993

Flood Relief Legislation

Q. Mr. President, the flood aid bill, sir? Your response to the House—overwhelmingly passed the flood aid bill?

The President. I'm elated. I'm elated. I think it's a wonderful thing. We had, as you know, the Governors from the flooded States, and they're real grateful. And we just have to see quick action from the Senate. There are still a lot of problems out there, a lot of things that could still go wrong. And the front needs to break up so the South and East can get some rain, or we're going to have some agricul-

tural disasters there.

Q. Would it help with the chances in the Senate that Kansas has had some pretty severe flooding at this point?

The President. I don't think that has anything to do with it. I think the Senate will support it on a bipartisan basis and without regard to where they're from.

NOTE: The exchange began at 7:26 p.m. in the State Dining Room at the White House. A tape was not available for verification of the content of this exchange.

Statement on the Death of Matthew Ridgway
July 27, 1993

There can be no greater tribute for a patriot than to say he spent his life serving his nation. General Matthew Ridgway was such a patriot. He fought for our liberty and in opposition to tyranny through two great conflicts, World War II and the Korean conflict. Through his efforts, General Ridgway became one of our most venerated military leaders. His greatest legacy is

the freedom his tireless work helped preserve and promote.

Hillary and I wish to extend our condolences to Mrs. Ridgway and the rest of his family. We all owe a debt of gratitude to Matthew Ridgway, soldier and patriot.

NOTE: The related proclamation of July 29 is listed in Appendix D at the end of this volume.

Exchange With Reporters on Bosnia
July 28, 1993

Q. Mr. President, are you going to send air power to Bosnia?

The President. Let me say, I saw the stories this morning. The position of the United States has long been that if the United Nations troops were attacked there, we would do our part to protect it and by making available air power. We have not yet been asked to do that. If we are asked, that's something we'll give good consideration to. But we have not been asked to do it, and I——

Q. The French did not ask you?

The President. Not yet. But we've had some conservations with them. I'm very upset by the shelling of Sarajevo. And we're going to take a look at what the situation is and what the options are. But they have not formally asked yet.

Q. Does that mean the answer could be— a request is made that the answer will be yes, sir?

The President. It means just what I said. It means that the United States has always had the public position and the private position— we've made it very clear that if the United Nations operations in Bosnia were attacked, we would be prepared to defend them with air power. And we have not been asked yet. If we are asked, that's something we will seriously consider.

Q. You certainly are expecting it, aren't you? I mean, Bosnia has been attacked and they are on the——

The President. We'll just have to see. I am going to be reviewing it in the next couple of days. I asked the Secretary of State to come home to discuss the Middle East before he goes to the Middle East. So he will be here. We'll have a chance to discuss it, and as soon as we make a decision we'll let you know.

NOTE: The exchange began at 8:34 a.m. in the State Dining Room at the White House, prior to a meeting with freshman Democratic Members of Congress. A tape was not available for verification of the content of this exchange.

Remarks Following a Luncheon With Business Leaders and an Exchange With Reporters
July 28, 1993

The President. Thank you very much. Please be seated. First let me thank all the business leaders who are here: Felix Rohytan, John Johnson, Ron Hall, Harry Buckley, and Mike Walsh for the fine words that they said but all those who are also on this platform behind me today. They represent companies of all sizes and shapes from Main Street to Wall Street.

They're here united in an unwavering desire and commitment to the health of the American economy over continued political rhetoric, to productivity over politics, to action over gridlock. They are here, just as I am, not because anyone agrees with every last line and jot and tittle of this economic program as it will doubtless come out of the conference, but because of what it does and because it does far more good than harm; because it brings down the deficit by $500 billion; because it has an equal apportionment of cuts and new revenues; because the revenues are fairly apportioned. And I was very proud of the speakers because the people who are up here with me are the ones who are really going to pay all the revenues that others are complaining about. And they have determined that they will do it to bring the deficit down, to keep interest rates down, to restore the stability and health of the American economy.

We talked a lot today about a few other issues at lunch, and I just would emphasize what I have tried to emphasize before, which is that over 90 percent of the small businesses in this country will be eligible for a tax cut if this plan passes; that working families with incomes under $30,000 will be held harmless; the working poor with children in their homes who spend 40 hours a week on the job will, for the first time, be able to work themselves out of poverty; that we have new and important incentives for high tech companies, extension of the incentives for research and development, and a real commitment to grow this economy.

I want to say again, as I have on so many other occasions, that for every $10 of deficit reduction, $5 is in spending cuts; $4 in new revenues from the upper 6 percent of the American work force; and $1 from middle class families with incomes of between $30,000 and $140,000.

The people on this platform today represent what makes America work—the fact that they have become more involved in this, that they are willing to put their own names on the line. And many of them are Republicans; some are Democrats; some are independents. They're all united here because they're Americans, and they know that we've neglected our problems long enough.

I thank them for their presence here, for their willingness to lobby the Congress. And I assure them that together our best efforts, I believe, will produce a victory in this economic battle.

Thank you very much.

Bosnia

Q. Mr. President, if I could turn your attention to the situation in Bosnia. The United States has long promised to provide air support if U.N. peacekeepers are threatened. French peacekeepers have now been fired on for 2 days in a row. Are you now prepared to deliver your air power, and would that alone be enough to deter Serbian aggression?

The President. We are prepared to fulfill our commitments, yes. The procedure is as follows: The United Nations forces in Bosnia must ask the Secretary-General of the United Nations for assistance. He will then relay that request to NATO, and we would act through NATO. And the answer to your question is, we are prepared to move if we are asked to provide that assistance by the Secretary-General.

Will it be enough to deter aggression, to stop the shelling of Sarajevo, to bring the parties to the peace table? I don't know. But we are prepared to do our part.

Q. Mr. President, do you feel that the United States and its NATO allies already have the assets in place, the air power and the air traffic

controllers to go ahead with these kinds of air strikes? And what does your gut tell you? Do you think the U.S. and its allies will be bombing Serbian targets in Bosnia within the next few days?

The President. There are a few questions on which a President's conversation with his gut should not be made public until the facts present themselves. [*Laughter*] Let me say this: If the request comes, we certainly can be prepared. NATO can be prepared within a very brief time span.

Middle East

Q. [*Inaudible*]—bombing—near silence of the United States during this fourth day of bombardment of Lebanon—the civilians being driven from—is being interpreted in the Middle East as supportive of these assaults. What are you going to do to stop the bombing, and would Christopher really be welcome in these outraged capitals?

The President. The reason I asked—well, I didn't ask; Secretary Christopher and I had a conversation, and we agreed that he should come home—is because we are so concerned about what is going on in the Middle East. I think Hezbollah should stop its attacks, and I think Israel should stop the bombardments. I think that Syria should go from showing restraint to being an active participant to try to stop the fighting. And we ought to do whatever we can to stop the fighting as quickly as possible.

Economic Program

Q. Mr. President, on the subject of the budget, at least eight Democratic Senators, possibly as many as 10 or 12, have said that they are leaning against voting for it. And five Democratic Senators have written to the conference committee chairman and have said that they do not want the gasoline tax or any form of energy tax. Do you believe you will have to make major compromises, such as eliminating the gasoline tax entirely, in order to get it past the Senate? How do you propose to get Senator——

The President. I don't.

Q. ——Boren and Senator Nunn——

The President. I don't, because I haven't—no one's answered the question that—almost all the ones who say that also say I want $500 billion in deficit reduction and, by the way, put all the economic incentives for growth in. It becomes an arithmetic problem at some point. And that's really basically what it is. The fuel tax that's in there now is modest. It will not promote a great deal of energy conservation. It has very little environmental significance. The real question is, is it necessary to get $500 billion in deficit reduction to have real tax fairness in terms of what's provided in terms of the earned-income tax credit and to have the economic incentives. And no one so far has been able to give a credible alternative. So I would say to you I think our plan is still the best one on the table.

Q. You've been meeting one-on-one with them. Have you been able to persuade any of the opponents to switch?

The President. Let me say this: The atmosphere and discussions here is not as bad as—if anything, it's a little better than it was before the initial votes were taken in the Senate and the House. We'll just have to see. I mean, I think in the end a lot of them, whatever the situation is, they're going to have to make up their minds whether the consequences of voting no for the country are graver than the consequences of voting yes. If that's the question, they'll all vote yes.

Bosnia

Q. Mr. President, I just want to clarify on the Bosnia situation. Is it your interpretation that if we do engage in air strikes there, that we will go not after the source of fire if it can be identified but also, if necessary, against other Serbian targets, headquarters, or logistical sites? And just as a followup to that, if I could, are you concerned that in doing this that we'll send a signal possibly to the Moslems that it could be overinterpreted by them that the cavalry is coming and maybe now they should hang back a little bit?

The President. Let me try to answer both questions. First of all, I have not yet had a meeting with the Secretary of Defense and the Chairman of the Joint Chiefs. I have not been briefed on our options. And I don't think I should comment on that at this time.

Secondly, we have, at the request of President Izetbegovic, agreed to have Reg Bartholomew go and participate in the discussions about whether a peace agreement can be reached. We have made it clear to all the parties all along that we would never seek to impose an agreement on the Bosnian Government. We've also made it clear to the Bosnian Government that we think that they should always be willing to talk, but we're not going to try to impose a settlement on them. I think that they know that our position would be that we should continue to discuss a peaceful resolution to this.

Middle East

Q. Do I detect correctly, sir, a slight shift in your attitude towards Syria, which you commended yesterday for its role in the current trouble in the Middle East? And do you think you might have been too hasty yesterday and have you changed your mind?

The President. No. I don't think anybody thought that Syria was exactly behind Hezbollah. I just believe that they could do more. I think it's now time for all the players to do more to bring an end to the fighting. I think Syria, and Israel, Jordan, the Palestinians, and the Lebanese, everybody except these political groups that make their living from the continued misery of the Palestinians, everybody else has a vested interest in continuing the Middle East peace process, and I hope that we can get it going again.

NAFTA

Q. On the free trade agreement, you are coming to the end of the collateral negotiation with Canada and Mexico. I understand they'll be meeting here tomorrow—country are talking about—deficit reduction. What new facts are you getting from them on the free trade agreement, are they backing you on that?

The President. I think most of them are for it. I certainly hope they are, and I believe they are. I'll take one more.

Bosnia

Q. Mr. President, Boutros-Ghali has said in the last few hours that he thinks the NATO air cover should be able to start early next week. Based on what you know about it now, and this plan has been around since May, how do you calculate the risk? Do you feel like you have any obligation to go to Congress before that first plane takes off or to go to the public with this?

The President. I think I should wait. I asked the Secretary of State to come home to discuss the Middle East. He is now home. I want to talk about Bosnia with him, with the Secretary of Defense, with some others, before I decide on what next has to be done. I think that the commitment that we have had all along to defend the United Nations forces there if they were attacked is, I think, fairly clear and has been highly publicized. But of course, if we have to take any action, I will have appropriate consultations with Congress and appropriate conversations with the American people.

Thank you.

NOTE: The President spoke at 2:12 p.m. in the East Room at the White House. In his remarks, he referred to Felix Rohytan, senior partner, Lizard Freres; John Johnson, chairman and chief executive officer, Johnson Publishing Co.; Ron Hall, president and chief executive officer, Citgo Petroleum Corp.; Harry Buckley, president and chief executive officer, H&R Block Tax Services, Inc.; Mike Walsh, chairman and chief executive officer, Tenneco, Inc.; and Alija Izetbegovic, President, Republic of Bosnia-Herzegovina.

Interview With the Texas Media
July 28, 1993

The President. It's nice to see you all here. And I know you've all received other briefings today. And so I think that probably the best thing to do would be to start, and I'll answer your questions.

Texas Senatorial Election

Q. [*Inaudible*]—we are aware of the fact that did carry the State in the election last year. And more recently Texas rejected the Democratic-appointed Senator in what some people, such as Senator Gramm, characterized as repudiation of you and your policies. So to paraphrase Admiral Stockdale, why are we here?

The President. [*Inaudible*]—several others who wanted to support it and felt that there had never been an adequate defense made in Texas. I thought, given the fact that I had two Texas opponents, I did rather well there in the last election. And I don't, with all respect, I don't think the Senate race in Texas was a referendum on our program, because nobody defended it; nobody said what was in it.

There have been four special elections in the Congress: three in the House, one in the Senate. The Democrats won all three in the House. But frankly, only one of those races was a referendum on the program, because it was the only place where the Democrat on his own initiative defended the program—without my even knowing it, put my picture in his brochures, ran television ads explaining to the people what was in the program. And he won the race by nine points in a district in which a lot of upper income people live who would have to pay the higher taxes.

So you can't have a referendum on a program if the people don't know what's in it. If anything, if I've made any mistake in this, it is that this is the only issue in my lifetime where the people knew less about it as time went on. That is, on February the 18th when I spoke to the country, I actually went through chapter and verse factually all the things that were in this program and how they fit with what we wanted to do in health care, welfare reform, the crime bill, all the things that are coming afterward. But I said who was going to pay the taxes, what the spending cuts were going to be.

After that, because there was no fight over the spending cuts, people were not told there were any, and the rhetoric against the program took over. So I think I owe it to the people of Texas to at least put my case out there. And I certainly owe it to the Members from Texas who supported the program because they think it's the right thing.

Taxes

Q. [*Inaudible*]—Corpus Christi. It's a community that's just now coming out of recession, and they're doing it, probably they're diversifying. What can you say to reassure folks who have been hearing about this gasoline tax, people who are in the tourism industry who depend on people driving to come see us and our attractions, people who in the refinery industry who are dependent on—and the people, the trucking industry, agricultural and so forth? What can you say to them that will put them at ease about what may be coming out of this conference committee?

The President. I don't think the conference committee is going to adopt anything in the range of a dime, nine cents, eight cents, anything like that. I think, first of all, gasoline is at its lowest real price adjusted for inflation in more than three decades. I think that any tax they put on it will be modest and will amount to no more than $50 a year for a family of four with an income of $50,000 a year, about $1 a week to help to pay down the deficit. All the money will be put in a trust fund and can only be spent to reduce the deficit.

And I think that it is a bearable burden. It was not, as you know, my first choice. We had a compromise Btu plan that was never really considered that exempted agriculture, exempted all production, and broadened the base of the tax to even it out a little. But I think that this is something that we can clearly manage given the fact that gasoline is at it's lowest real price in 30 years.

Q. [Inaudible]

The President. Well, I told you what it will amount to. It can amount to about a dollar a week for a middle income family, a family with an income of $40,000 to $50,000 a year. I don't think that will be a significant burden.

And in terms of the energy industry, we had people from three energy companies here today, ARCO, Sun Oil, and Citgo, as well as the CEO of Tenneco here supporting the plan because they believe that bringing the deficit down, keeping interest rates down, which the deficit reduction plan is doing, enabling people to refinance their homes and business loans, and stabilizing the economy will do far more good than this will do harm. And I believe that, too.

Super Collider

Q. I know you support the SSC, but about a week and a half ago, you strongly criticized Senator Gramm and Senator Hutchinson for calling for spending cuts while the House vote was going on. I think yesterday Senator Gramm sent you a letter urging you to pick up the pace of your support for the SSC. Can you get together with them and keep this project——

The President. I'm a strong supporter of that project. And I worked it in the House. But, you know, the timing was amazing. I mean, I couldn't believe that they would walk out on the steps of the Capitol with Ross Perot and begged the Congress to cut spending more and rail against taxes and give people the impression that there was some huge middle class tax burden in this thing, which is false. After the Senate Finance Committee had met and the Republicans offered not one single specific spending cut in the Senate Finance Committee—not one, not one dollar—and then, they go out on the steps of the Capitol, while we're doing our best not to get beat too bad in the House, hoping we can do what we did last time, pass it in the Senate and save it in the conference.

You know, this is tough. I mean, you've got all those Congressmen from California. They took 40-something percent of the base-closing cuts this time, a State with second highest unemployment rate in the country. They take 40-something percent. Their Congressmen line up and vote for this program to benefit Texans with lower interest rates and a more stable economy. You know, and they say, "Here's a State with a space station. Here's a State with all the benefits from the super collider." All they want to do is gain the political benefits of all this Federal spending and the political benefits of railing against the taxes and not have to take responsibility for proposing specific spending cuts. And it's just a little too much to swallow. You've got to put yourself in the position of people from other States. And so, they said, "Let's just lob them one." And so we lost by this breathtaking margin, far worse than we lost last year.

And then, of course, they want to disclaim any responsibility for that. I don't blame them, but I'm telling you—put yourself in the—suppose you were from Idaho or Utah, or someplace that had hardly any of this stuff. Nobody's writing you Federal checks every month. You don't have hundreds of scientists and engineers and high-tech employees. It's just difficult for these Members that I'm lobbying to take.

We came very close to losing the space station in the House. And two supporters of mine who were in a group that had already come against the space station stood down there in the well and waited until the last votes, and they realized that it could not prevail unless they changed their votes, and so they went down and voted for it.

And that's how we saved the space station in the House. So, all I'm saying is, I believe in the super collider, and I believe in the space station. I believe we have now saved the space station, and I feel very good about it. And now I can sort of gin up my efforts on the super collider. We've got to pass it in the Senate to have any hope of getting it out of conference. All I can tell you is, you have to put yourself in the position of people from other States who have been asked to take the tough votes, take the hits, who've already voted for $250 billion of spending cuts, and then they're told by people who stand on the steps of the Capitol they hadn't cut spending. It just was difficult for them. And I thought it was kind of an interesting irony that at least they could have waited a day to do it, you know. They could have had the good grace to wait instead of just rubbing the Congress' face in their rhetoric.

Media Coverage

Q. Why not talk about the economy if learning about the economy and learning about the problems with the economy and how deficit reduction can help the economy? Why not talk to the whole country about the economy, rather than each State individually?

The President. Well, I intend to do that also. But one of the problems is that, as those of you who are in this town know, what really makes news is controversy. I mean, the President can't just go talk to the country whenever he pleases. Last time I talked to the country, this program had good support because I was able to give out all the information. Since then, it's just been rhetoric, 10-second sound bites, taxes, or "it's spending, stupid," or something like that. And the whole facts don't get out.

So one of the things I can do to reach the whole country is to spend more time with media from many States. We're doing this with a lot of States. I will, I hope, have the chance to address the country again. But I tried to do this in a national press conference, and only CNN and one network covered it. And by the way, the research showed that the people who saw it on the network that covered it had their attitudes markedly altered about the economic plan. So I'm doing the best I can to get information out.

NAFTA

Q. [*Inaudible*]—Corpus Christi. But we live in an area, because we're so close to the border that if things go sour in the U.S., we get hit; and if things happen in Mexico we feel it also. So we're looking at the North American Free Trade Agreement. Can you bring us up to date on that one?

The President. Yes. We're making good progress on our efforts to achieve agreements relating to the environment and labor standards. The last reports I have are quite good. And I think that when those agreements are finalized and announced that we will really diminish at least the fervor of some of the opposition to NAFTA. We're also making good progress in getting a broad base of support for it. And I still believe we can go forward with it and pass it this year. There is an awful lot of opposition to it in the House and some in the Senate. You may have seen recently that some Congressmen were asking me virtually to delay consideration indefinitely. But we have to take it up this year. And I expect to do that.

And I think the more we talk about it—I think the important thing with NAFTA is to try to—as I believe with a lot of these things, by the way. And because NAFTA will have bipartisan support and bipartisan opposition, we may be able, funny enough, to have a calmer conversation. We may be able to talk to each other as if we're all in the family.

I mean, one of the things that I tell people about NAFTA, is I was Governor of a State where people shut their plants down and moved it to Mexico. I know a lot about that. But the point—if we have no NAFTA, as you well know, that will continue or could continue. NAFTA is not about stopping that or accelerating that. That is virtually irrelevant to what we're trying to achieve. And I think it's quite important.

So we're making good progress. I expect to go forward. I have high hopes. We've got a lot of opposition, but I think if we can really be calm and talk each other through it, we can make it.

Deputy Counsel Vincent Foster, Jr.

Q. We've heard conflicting stories about—this is on another subject. On the telephone call that you made to Mr. Foster, we heard at one point it was made on Sunday, then we heard it was made on Monday. And we heard, oh, it was just a routine call, because you talk all the time. And then we heard it was to buck him up. Can you sort of set the record straight?

The President. I called him Monday night because at the last minute—Hillary was gone, was still in Arkansas with our daughter. And I decided to watch a movie, and Webb Hubbell was still hanging around here. And I hadn't seen Vince in a while, and I called him. I didn't—

unlike some other people, who did know that he'd been quite distressed, I was not really aware of that. But I knew I hadn't seen him in a while, and I just kind of got lonesome. Webb Hubbell and I and one or two other people were going to watch a movie. So I just wanted to watch the movie. I called him and we talked for, I don't know, 20 minutes or so. We talked about what he'd done the weekend before, talked about some things he was concerned about on the job, but it was just the sort of thing we'd always talk about. He was real work-oriented. And we agreed to meet on Wednesday. And that was it.

House Budget Language

Q. There has been a difference between the House and Senate on capping entitlement programs. What is your position on that?

The President. You mean because the House version has stronger language in it?

Q. Right.

The President. Well, I'm glad you asked that. Now, here's something you all can help on. The House version, first of all, has some disciplined language in there with dealing with the entitlements and also has some language which says that—well, first let me say, we adopt 5-year budgets around here. I think you know—all of you, or the groups that you work for—it's very hard to adopt a 5-year budget with exactitude. I mean, nobody can see the 5 years with absolute precision.

So what this House bill does that had never been done before is not only to put all this money in a trust fund so it can't be spent on anything else but to say if we miss the target in any year, in any of these areas—you know, the targets on discretionary spending, entitlements, or revenues—whatever reason, we don't make our deficit reduction target, under this bill, the President must propose a plan to correct it, to meet the target, and the Congress must vote on it. Now, the Congress, obviously, wouldn't have to do exactly what I wanted. They could amend it, you know, but at least there's a process there for addressing the fact that we're missing the deficit reduction target.

I feel very strongly that that should be a part of the final package. You need to know what the problem is. Under the rather arcane rules of the Senate, this reconciliation, economic budget plan, is just about the only thing—I think the only thing that does not require—

it's not subject to a filibuster. So if you get one more vote than half, you win, and it can't be filibustered, because the country has to have a budget.

But if there is any subject in this reconciliation bill that does not directly relate to the budget itself, it can be challenged and then, in effect, you can require 60 votes to put it in there. This mechanism has been challenged by the Republicans in the Senate, even though I believe 100 percent of them are for it. I mean, I believe 100 percent of them honestly want to get the deficit down and believe that this discipline ought to be in there, and they're still fighting it because it's another way to derail what we're trying to do. So the way to get it in there is for at least four or five of them to let that go in the law because it's good Government. It doesn't have anything to do with party.

Bosnia

Q. Regarding the situation in Bosnia, now that you have met with Secretary Christopher, can you tell us a little bit about your options in the air strikes?

The President. Well, we expect the U.N. forces there in Bosnia to communicate—the commander there to communicate to Boutros-Ghali what the situation is and what he wants, and then the Secretary-General of the U.N. will either make or will not make a request to NATO. And all this will unfold over the next few days during which time the Serbs, Bosnian Serbs, either will or won't stop shelling Sarajevo and will pull back. And we'll just have to wait and see what happens.

But the United States is bound—we are committed to come to the aid of the United Nations forces as a part of NATO if they are attacked, and they have been. So we're just going to have to wait and see what happens.

NAFTA

Q. On NAFTA, are you telling all the Members of Congress what will happen to us if we have a disagreement with Mexico about rates and about products? And isn't it true that panels of young lawyers from Europe could come over here and decide questions of difference between us and Mexico about the operation of NAFTA?

The President. You mean under the agreements now being negotiated?

Q. ——and come back, and regardless of

what our laws were, they would be the ones to decide whether we were fair or not. And if they decide we were not fair, even if it was something that conflicted with our laws, they would prevail.

The President. Well, I haven't agreed to any specific enforcement mechanism. But one of the things that has been of some controversy is the—obviously the Mexicans have not wanted to accede control of their national sovereignty to the United States and vice versa. So the Mexican, Canadian, and American negotiators have been struggling to find a way to adopt an agreement that had some teeth in it, that has some enforcement provision, at least if there were a pattern and practice of violation on their part or on ours. And I don't think they have finalized that. Until they do, I can't really say more.

Q. [Inaudible]—the Republicans in the House are saying that our sovereignty would go and you all would have to, under the rules, that you would have to give in to this panel of lawyers from outside the country who would decide these matters.

The President. Well, I can't comment on that because I don't know what they are finally going to agree to. But I think that the most important thing from my point of view is that we have some way of knowing that whatever we agree to is going to be observed by all countries and that it is not a violation of our sovereignty to be held to the agreements, to be held to keep our word. And we'll have to find some sort of mechanism to see that we do it and to see that the Mexicans do it. Nobody has discussed the option you just described to me, and I can't comment on it until I know whether it's a live option.

Economic Program

Q. Back to your economic plan. The conservative Democrats on both Houses are the ones who are really key to you. One of those conservatives is a key player, Charlie Stenholm, who was visiting with you last night. He came out saying that he still is unalterably opposed to the gasoline tax. What can you tell those conservative Congressmen, many of whom come from Texas, what basically can you give them to get their vote?

The President. Well, let me tell you what they say. I mean, it's interesting what a lot of them say who aren't for the gasoline tax. They think

that it raises so little money that it's not worth the political heat. A lot of them are basically tired of the partisan beating up they've gotten for trying to do something responsible about the deficit. They are frustrated that all of their attempts to put in more spending discipline—and Charlie Stenholm has done, I think, a brilliant job of that—has not generated any willingness on the part of Republicans to support any kind of reasonable budget package.

And so they're saying that this is a pure matter of public perception: "Why for a relatively small amount of money should we have any gas tax at all since it is a modest one and give the Republicans something else to beat us over the head? Why don't we just keep the upper income taxes and the spending cuts and go on?" Here's the answer to that, and it's the question I pose to them. In other words, there's no—it's just not like the Btu tax. You can't make a claim that it's promoting great energy conservation or it's good for the environment or anything. It's just a very modest attempt to raise some funds to pay down the deficit and monies which someday might go into road building after the end of the deficit reduction period but not any time in the foreseeable future.

The answer is this: If we have to pass this bill with only Democrats, there are other conservative and moderate Democrats who don't object to the gas tax but would object if we took out the economic growth incentives. And let me just mention some of them. And there are others who would object if we didn't reduce the deficit by $500 billion or some figure very close to it. So then the issue is, if you take out the gas tax, what do you replace it with? If you just say, "Well, we'll just reduce the deficit by that much less," then you have all these people who say, "Well, you lose me because we're not reducing the deficit enough." Or do you say, "We'll take out the gas tax and we won't have any economic growth incentives." Now, let me mention some of them to just give you an example. Over 90 percent of the subchapter S, the small businesses in this country, will be eligible for a tax cut under this program because we double the expensing provisions. So any small business with adjusted gross income of under $140,000, which is 94 percent of them, will be eligible for a tax cut under this program. They generate a lot of the jobs in America. That's a job program.

We've got a provision in here to provide capital gains treatment—big break in people who invest for 5 years in companies that capitalize at $50 million a year or less. We took out the surcharge on capital gains to give people incentives to invest so they can earn investment income at lower rates than the personal rates. We have increased the research and development tax credit. We've increased the incentives for investing in getting real estate and homebuilding going again. That's one reason the national realtors and the homebuilders have endorsed this plan, two predominately Republican groups.

If you take all that out, you know, to keep the deficit number up, to get rid of the gas tax, then you lose a whole different group of Democrats. Then there are those who say, "Well, we don't need the earned-income tax credit. Get rid of that and get rid of the gas tax." The problem is if you do that, you lose people who represent huge numbers of working poor. Eighteen percent of the work force in this country now, including a whole lot of folks in Texas, work 40 hours a week and still live below the poverty line. That's a stunning statistic.

Perhaps the most important social policy, if you will, that I would think virtually all Americans could agree on that this plan furthers is that this says, if you're one of those folks and you have children in your home, and you work 40 hours a week, the tax system will lift you above poverty so that nobody who works with children will be in poverty if this plan passes, once we get it fully phased in.

So if you take that out, then you lose all those Democrats that represent that. So the real problem is it's really an arithmetic problem. If you want the pro-growth, pro-jobs incentives and you want to support work instead of welfare and you want to stay at $500 billion of deficit reduction or awfully close, how do you do it without this modest fuel tax?

The only other option that was given is further cuts in Medicare, which in my opinion, again, would lose you a lot of Democrats, both people who are concerned about middle class elderly people on Medicare and people who are concerned about doctors, hospitals, home health providers, and others who are under reimbursed now and who just have to shift their costs onto the private sector.

So if someone could solve that problem— I wouldn't say that problem couldn't be solved—

but I think it is highly unlikely that a resolution of that—I'm sympathetic with Charlie Stenholm. He has been very courageous. He has been very helpful. He has done as much as any Member of the Congress in either party to really control the deficit. And nobody has a better record than he does in trying to control spending and control the deficit. And he's made a very compelling case, but I don't know how to solve it.

Q. Given the fact that if your plan passes— it will probably do so without a single Republican vote—do you think it would be fair for the American people to give your administration all the credit or all the blame with the economic condition of the country over the next 3½ years?

The President. No, but it'll probably happen anyway. [*Laughter*] That is, it will be fair to give the administration and those who voted for it the credit or the blame for whatever impact this has. And I think it will be basically positive. We know it will keep interest rates down. I mean, you've got Alan Greenspan, who's the Republican head of the Federal Reserve Bank, who has constantly told the Congress they need to do a deficit reduction package in this range, and they need to do it immediately to keep interest rates down and to help the economy to recover.

But let me make two points. Just a substantive point—I don't want to talk about politics but just the substance of it. Number one, the country has been in an economic difficulty on and off for 20 years. The high water mark of American economic dominance was about 20 years ago. Since then the pressures of a global economy, which have punished the relatively undereducated, the relatively rural, the people that didn't fit very well in the global economy, have been building up and basically real wages of working people have been stagnant or declining, and the work week has been increasing for 20 years.

For 12 years we have followed a path that worked in the short run but caused us great grief in the long time. That is, supply-side economics, which basically says we're going to cut taxes and increase spending, took us from a $1 trillion to a $4 trillion deficit—debt, a huge deficit. In the short run, we came out of the recession of '81–'82 after we cut taxes and increased spending and kind of kept the lid on inflation. But in the long run we have dug ourselves into a hole now where we—for example, we actually—almost anybody—Charlie Stenholm said the other day, "We need to be spending more money helping places like California and Connecticut and some other places to convert from a defense to a domestic economy. But we don't have the money. We need to do whatever we can to train our non-college educated workers better. We don't have the money. We've got a lot of things we need to do. We can't and we're paralyzed". So I would say to you that we didn't get into this mess overnight. We're not going to get out of it overnight.

The second thing I want to say is, we need to bring the deficit down to zero. To do that, we have to pass health care reform. Then to make people more productive we need to pass our education bill and the welfare reform bill, and we need to pass a lot of other things. There's lots of work we need to do here to open new markets—you asked the NAFTA question—to get this economy turned around. But I expect to be held accountable. I just would tell you, this bill is important. Without it, we can't go forward. But it is not the end-all and the be-all.

Cuba and Vietnam

Q. One of the cornerstones of your whole program is to stimulate business growth. I'm just curious, do you believe that lifting the trade embargo against Vietnam at this time would benefit the economy? And a part two to that question: Do you believe that lifting the embargo against Cuba and allowing American businesses to trade in both Vietnam and Cuba would be good for the economy of this country?

The President. I believe if the embargo were lifted, some businesses would clearly benefit. I think it would be a marginal benefit to the economy in the short run because the economies of both those countries are so small compared to ours. I don't think it would have a major impact. But I don't support it for different reasons. I think the embargo against Cuba should stand until there is a real movement toward freedom and democracy. I think the embargo against Vietnam should not be lifted until we have even more assurances that they are doing everything they can to help us with the POW/ MIA issue.

As you doubtless know, or you wouldn't have asked the question, I did remove the objections of the United States to letting Vietnam participate in International Monetary Fund financing,

which will help them to improve, because they have taken a lot of steps since I've been President and since before I became President, starting right before I became President, to open up the country, to help us try to find the answers about our POW and MIA personnel. But I'm not confident that everything that should be done, has been done. And until I am, I can't support lifting that embargo.

Q. I've talked to a couple of business people who say that telephone lines are burning up at the Commerce Department—[*inaudible*]— business people all over the country. I was in Vietnam and I met American business people who were there able to initial business contracts but couldn't sign them. I would just like to know, how much pressure are you getting from American businesses to lift the embargo?

The President. Not much. Some. A lot of the business people want to do it, but I would hope that the business community would also understand that we have a lot of families out there, a lot of relatives, a lot of friends, and a lot of supporters of the people who have served who have never been accounted for. And that while we have gotten an awful lot of information in the last few months, even that has raised questions in some people's minds as why are we just now getting it, you know, and all of that.

I think we are now getting real access to the country. We are making real progress. I just wrote a letter to the President in Vietnam, in response to a letter he wrote me, encouraging him to continue on this path. I know a lot of American businesses want to do business there, but that cannot be the sole criteria of what we do. And our first concern has to be for the POW's and the MIA's. We are moving in the right direction. Let's just hope it continues so we can continue to make progress.

Taxes

Q. The American people are now being taxed in local and State and national levels up to 50 percent of what they are making. And we look back at the serfs in Europe, and they only had to give up 30 percent of their income, and we looked at them as slaves. Why are we any better than the serfs? And why have you been so loyal to promises to the homosexual community, but not quite so loyal with your tax cut promises to the middle class of America?

The President. First of all, what you've said

is not accurate. All major Western countries have higher tax rates than we do. You know, it does not serve the public debate to tell people that Germany has had a higher growth rate than America because they have lower taxes. It's simply not true. It is absolutely untrue. National tax rates in Japan are much higher than they are here. And aggregate corporate rates in Japan at all levels of government will be higher than they are here even if my plan passes. And if you look at the percentage of income going to taxes in America, with the exception of some very high taxed urban areas, where the cost of living is very high, we compare very favorably, if this plan passes in toto, with the tax rates in all the countries with which we are competing. The problem with it is that we're not spending money on the right things. We're spending too much on interest on the debt. We're spending too much on health care. We're spending too little on things that create jobs and growth and opportunity. Nevertheless, I did not raise taxes happily here.

I was Governor of a State that was always, always, every year I was Governor, was in the bottom five States in America in the percentage of people's income going to taxes. Always. And after I had been Governor 10 years, the same percentage of income was going to taxes that was going 10 years before. I never raised taxes to balance the books. The only times we ever raised taxes in Arkansas was for schools and roads and had the support of big majorities of the American people.

I don't like this. I made it very clear why I decided to ask for a modest contribution from middle class families with incomes over $30,000, but under $140,000; no income tax increases until families who were basically families, if you had two earners above $180,000. And the reason is that after the election, the Government—the previous Government, not mine—estimated the deficit over the next 5 years to be about $150 billion bigger than they said it was before the election.

So I had to face a decision. Was I going to try to do more on deficit reduction and try to deal with this and get these interest rates down, based on changed circumstances, minimizing the tax burden all I could and still asking the top—really over two-thirds of this burden will come from the top one percent of taxpayers, who got two-thirds of the benefits the last 12 years. Or was I going instead to do what was

more politically popular and consistent with what I honestly believed in the campaign but not what I thought was best for Americans. And I decided the best thing to do would be to try to take account of the fact that the deficit was $150 billion bigger than we thought and to try to respond to it. The American people will have to decide whether they think that's right or wrong.

Now, I have done my best to make the tax system fairer. I have done something for working families under $30,000 a year. They've all been held harmless. We've done something significant for the working poor. And I have 4 more years to try to deal with further inequalities in the tax system, which I plan to do. But I think this deficit has to be attacked first, and I think I did the right thing.

Space Station and Super Collider

Q. From a scientific standpoint, do you think the collider and space station are of equal merit? And would you be prepared to veto an energy and water preservation bill if it's not included in the collider funding?

The President. Well, I don't know if I would be prepared to veto it. Nobody has ever asked me that, and I don't know what the consequences of that would be. I think that they are different, entirely different. The space station is important technologically, and it's important for our country's continued leadership in space, which is very important. It also has enormous international implications in terms of potential partnerships with Russia and with a lot of other countries.

If we back off of this space station, other countries will move into the breach, they will push us out of an area that we plainly dominate the international economy in. They will make those partnerships, and we will be left, I think, without the leadership that we need and deserve and without the potential to create enormous economic opportunity, as well as political cooperation in the years ahead.

It's interesting, and I'm glad you mentioned it. One of the things that is very important and quite apart from the technology is that the promise of cooperation between the United States and Russia, and perhaps with other countries just emerging, is one of the main carrots we have if you will—not a stick but a carrot—to discourage countries from doing irresponsible things with nuclear weapons, with other weapons of mass destruction, discourage them from selling them to other people. So I think that's very, very important.

Now the super collider is different. The space station is a technological wonder that maintains our leadership in an area we have already fleshed out. The super collider is science. It's research. Therefore, it is, by definition, less certain. But this country has gotten a long way throughout its history by taking a chance on things that might not be certain that promised enormous potential benefits. So the possible benefits of the super collider, the possible implications of it, in any number of areas of technology in the future, are absolutely staggering.

Sure, it might not work. It's like any investment of this kind. But that's what science is. This is scientific research. This is an attempt to break down barriers of knowledge, to see the world in a whole different way, to unlock all kinds of secrets. And we have made a major investment in this. We also, by the way, can

get some other countries to invest in it, but not if they have to sit around every year waiting to see if we're going to chuck it. I mean, one of the biggest problems we've had in getting these other countries who said they'd invest in it, is they don't know from one year to the next whether we're going to keep it. And one of the things that I hope we can do this year, if we can get it passed in the Senate, get it in the conference, is to get a commitment for a multiyear continuation of it.

Now, it is more difficult to save than the space station simply because it's science instead of technology, if you see what I mean. It is by definition more theoretical. But I still think it's quite important, and I am hoping we can save it.

Thank you.

NOTE: The interview began at 5 p.m. in the State Dining Room at the White House.

Statement on House of Representatives Action on National Service Legislation
July 28, 1993

By approving my national service plan today with overwhelming support, the House proved that Government can work, without partisan rancor, in a spirit of community, and for the common good.

Now that House Republicans and Democrats have joined in this great act of civic service, I urge Republican Senators to put partisan politics aside and do what is right for this country.

House Members showed the spirit of service

that we need in our politics and around the country. Members of both parties recognized that national service isn't Democratic or Republican. It's just plain American, helping young people who help America. The bill embodies principles that Americans from every political viewpoint share: community, responsibility, and opportunity. House Republicans put service ahead of politics. I urge Senate Republicans to do the same.

Nomination for Chief Financial Officer at the Department of Education
July 28, 1993

The President today announced his intention to nominate financial expert Donald R. Wurtz as Chief Financial Officer at the Department of Education. Wurtz is director of the General Accounting Office unit charged with cracking down on high-risk areas of waste, abuse, and

fraud in the Federal Government and has worked extensively on problems involving the Education Department's guaranteed student loan program.

At the Education Department, Wurtz will be charged with improving accounting and financial management. He also will play a key role in implementing the direct student loan program.

"Throughout his career, Don Wurtz has worked to uncover and correct the abuse and mismanagement that is too common in the Federal Government," the President said. "As CFO at Education, Don will work with Secretary Riley to ensure that the tax dollars of hardworking Americans are not wasted, but instead directed 100 percent to bettering education in America."

NOTE: A biography of the nominee was made available by the Office of the Press Secretary.

Memorandum on Excused Absence for Federal Employees in Disaster Areas
July 28, 1993

Memorandum for the Heads of Executive Departments and Agencies

Subject: Excused Absence for Employees Affected by the Flooding of the Mississippi River and Its Tributaries

I am saddened by the devastating losses caused by the flooding of the Mississippi River and its tributaries and the impact on the well-being and livelihood of our fellow Americans. Many parts of the Federal Government have been mobilized to respond to this disaster and to begin a massive effort to recover from the ravages of this flooding.

As part of this effort, I request heads of executive departments and agencies who have Federal civilian employees in the areas designated as disaster areas because of the flooding to use their discretion to excuse from duty, without charge to leave or loss of pay, any such employee who is faced with a personal emergency because of the flooding and who can be spared from his or her usual responsibilities. This policy should also be applied to any employee who is needed for emergency law enforcement, relief, or clean-up efforts authorized by Federal, State or local officials having jurisdiction.

WILLIAM J. CLINTON

NOTE: This memorandum was released by the Office of the Press Secretary on July 29.

Remarks on the Earned-Income Tax Credit and an Exchange With Reporters
July 29, 1993

The President. I don't want them to miss the vote. [*Laughter*] This is what is known as an excused absence for the Congress. I want to say a warm welcome and a word of thanks to the Risners, the Dorseys, and the Dikemans, all of them, for coming here. They're not used to being public speakers, but I think they did a fine job, don't you?

I'd also like to say a special word to Mr. Dorsey. When I was a boy, I cut lawns for a living, too, and nobody ever gave me more than I charged. You're either a better salesman, a better grass-cutter, or you had better customers. [*Laughter*]

I am so glad to have these families here today because they emphasize that a pivotal part of this economic plan is increasing the earned-income tax credit which, more than anything else we could do, will reward work and family and responsibility and make a major downpayment on welfare reform.

You heard Robin make that point. There are so many Americans in this country who want to work, who want to be independent, who want to support themselves, and who find themselves in a position of not being able to make ends meet, not being able to cover basic costs. The earned-income tax credit can help them do that.

It is a terribly important part of this overall plan, which not only reduces the deficit by $500 billion, but also does it in a fair way. Half of the reduction comes from budget cuts; four-fifths of the rest comes from taxes on the upper income people in this country, the upper 6 percent; one-fifth from taxes on families with incomes above $30,000 and below, for couples, $180,000.

But the most important thing of all to reward work is that this will be the first time in the history of our country when we'll be able to say that if you work 40 hours a week and you have children in your home, you will be lifted out of poverty. It is an elemental, powerful, and profound principle. It is not liberal or conservative. It should belong to no party. It ought to become part of the American creed. It's not about more governmental or social workers or more services. It's about more groceries and a car, more school clothes for the kids, and more encouragement and hope to keep doing the right thing. These families have made it clearer than I ever could.

One of the things that I want to emphasize is that if we ever want to really restore the health of the American economy, it won't be enough just to bring down the budget deficit or just to have good economic policies. You have to find a way to tell people that if they work hard and play by the rules they'll be able to make it, they will be rewarded. The incentive system in America has worked against that for too long.

You know, it's amazing to me how many American families still live in poverty. About 18 percent of the work force, nearly one in five families, have a worker and still do not reach the Federal poverty line. There are 36 million, approximately, low-income Americans; about 20 million of them live in a family that works, with someone working at least part of the year; 6 million live in families where someone works all year round, full-time, and the family is still in poverty. And as I said, where there is a family of four, about one in five, or 18 percent, have insufficient incomes to lift them above the Federal poverty line.

So in spite of all the pro-family rhetoric of our National Government for years, our policies haven't worked. In fact, they've been going in the wrong direction. We need every American who can to work if we're going to compete and win in the global economy. And more than

ever, we need strong families. This is, as you can see, not just a pro-work policy, it is a pro-family policy. We shouldn't make it harder to work and support a family. We ought to make it easier, and the people who do it should be lifted up as examples of the American ideal, not punished because they're trying to do the right thing. That's what the EITC does.

We ought to have two principles that operate in this country: People who can work should work, but if they do work, their families at home shouldn't be poor.

Today I also want to announce that the IRS will begin an aggressive outreach campaign to reach all Americans who are entitled to the credit. This will make it easier for them to receive benefits they have earned by working. It will also help us to educate them about the advantage of getting an advanced EITC, rather than having to wait an entire year. All these folks figured out how to work the system. But there are a lot of people out there, just like them, who haven't and who deserve the same incentive for work and for family.

We know that this program works. We know it's a lifeline for semi-skilled workers who are working to improve their education and training. We want Robin to get home in time for the test, and we want her to make a good grade. And we want that, also, to be a symbol for all the people in this country who are struggling to do the same thing.

We know that the vast majority of all those who benefit from the EITC work very long hours for a very modest compensation in jobs that very often have inadequate benefits, either for themselves or for their children. These are just three of the millions of stories we might have heard today from a part of America we almost never see on the evening news.

Every time you see a crime story reported in a tough neighborhood, remember that most people in that neighborhood, no matter how tough it is, work for a living, do their best to raise children, never break the law, and are struggling, struggling against odds that are enormous to make it and to make the American dream real for themselves and their children.

It is time we acted to support those people. In some ways, they may be the most heroic of all Americans today. If we really want to rebuild family life in America, if we want to recognize the realities that nearly everybody has to work to make ends meet, and more and more families have to have both parents working if they're in the home, even if they have four children and two of them are as young as those two youngest boys, we have got to say to those people: We are on your side. Your country is for you. You have done what all of the speechmakers talk about, and it's time the people who make the speeches had policies that reward you for doing what people have been pleading for Americans to do for years and years now.

That's why I think this is a critical part of this economic package. Make no mistake about it: If the people who favor the "no-new-anything approach," as the Wall Street Journal characterized the opponents of our plan, prevail, Americans will lose the pro-work, pro-family, pro-responsibility element of the earned-income tax credits, the largest single expansion in an effort to help the working poor in over two decades.

We can't let this happen. This is just one more reason why we have got to act, and act now on this economic plan. This is not about numbers and digits and accountants' gimmicks; it's not about arguments about who perceives or feels what about this economic plan. This is about how the low-interest rates, deficit reduction, the business incentives and, most important today, the earned-income tax credit will affect the real lives of real people and help them to live and succeed in the way that we always speak as if we want them to be able to live and succeed. This is the real world. You met it today. I hope the Congress will make it possible in the next few days to have more families like this with more success stories. Thank you very much.

We can take a couple of questions.

Economic Program

Q. Mr. President, what do you think is the chance of your budget getting through?

The President. Good.

Q. We understand it's in deep trouble in the Senate.

The President. I think it's good. You have to listen not only to what's being said but how it's being said. You know, as more information gets out, it's just like I've always said, rhetoric was our enemy and reality is our friend. There's a story in the Wall Street Journal today that once again Americans are hearing the facts instead of the rhetoric and the bad-mouthing and the negativism of our opponents and people are saying, "Let's give the President's plan a chance," and more likely to support Members of Congress who support it than they are Members who oppose it. They're beginning to learn again that over 70 percent of the taxes now fall on families with incomes above $200,000, the top 1.2 percent of the population, and that this attack that the Republicans have used to try to convince ordinary Americans that they're being soaked, that there's no deficit reduction, is all a bunch of hooey. And I think we've got to get this out. So I'm feeling much better about it.

Q. Mr. President, that same survey shows that despite all the time you've spent on the economy, more people give you high marks for foreign policy than for handling the economy. Why do you think that's the case?

The President. Because they're still worried about their economic circumstances. And because they want results. And because the Congress hasn't passed the plan yet. We need to begin to do things. But if we pass the economic plan, if we move on the health care to welfare reform, deal with the crime bill, if the Senate will not filibuster the national service bill and open the doors of college education to all Americans and give people a chance to serve their country, then people will believe that Washington will do better. Also, the ratings of the Congress will go up. People want things done. They didn't hire us to come up here and give speeches. We've tried the speechifying for a good long while; it didn't work very well. They want things to be done. I think the American people are very patient in terms of knowing we've been getting into economic trouble for 20 years, and we followed a certain economic policy that I want to change for 12, and it's not going to turn around in 6 months or a year, that we've got a lot of effort to make. But they want to know that we're at least moving, that we're moving from talk to action.

And that's why I wanted these families to come here today, to point out that this really will affect people's lives. There was another article I saw in one of the papers this morning interviewing very small business people who had been told on the talk shows and from other sources that they were about to get whanged by this plan, and all of a sudden now they've realized they're going to get their expensing provision doubled, and over 90 percent of the small businesses in this country will have an opportunity to lower their tax burden if, but only if, they invest. So I think that reality is creeping back in, and that's a healthy thing always.

Iraq

Q. Mr. President, the Pentagon says that U.S. naval aircraft have again bombed Iraqi missile sites. Could you update us and tell us what exactly is going on?

The President. There is nothing out of the ordinary about what happened. It was not part of any new initiative. It was part of the old understandings under which our planes operate in that area and circumstances under which they respond.

Entitlements

Q. Mr. President, another controversial aspect of your plan deals with entitlements. A few days ago, Congressman Tim Penny said that you're considering issuing an Executive order to curb entitlements. My understanding is it would be modeled after the Stenholm entitlement budget provision in the House. Can you comment?

The President. The Stenholm provision basically imposes discipline on our budget. It says that if we miss the deficit reduction target in any given year in any given category, whatever the category is, whether it's general expenditures, revenues, or entitlements, that the President will have to come back in with a plan to meet the deficit reduction target, and the Congress must vote on it. They don't have to vote specifically for that, but they must vote for something. They have to vote on it. In the rather arcane rules of the Senate, there is some question about whether that provision can go on this budget bill without triggering a filibuster and, therefore, requiring 60 percent to approve that provision.

Now, I believe every Republican Senator is for the Stenholm amendment, in his or her heart. I believe that, because it is what they always say they want: spending discipline. And yet they are threatening to filibuster it. Why? Because it makes our bill stronger, because it's a real deficit reduction, because it undermines the ability to give speeches instead of doing something.

And so if they don't let the Stenholm provision go on the budget, then I will do my best to, by Executive order or through a separate bill or through some other measure, to get as much of that discipline as I can. I think we should every year—nobody, nobody running a business can foresee what's going to happen for 5 years. The networks represented here can't do a 5-year budget and estimate with absolute exactitude what their revenues are going to be and who will watch what and all that sort of stuff. And you ought to make corrections every year, and this is the first time the Government's ever committed itself to that. I like it.

Bosnia

Q. Mr. President, are you considering the use of war planes over Bosnia, not just to protect U.N. peacekeeping forces but also to keep the supply lines going and perhaps to stop some of the shelling in Sarajevo?

The President. The best way for me to answer that today is to say that nothing has changed since I was asked that question and others yesterday. We're still waiting to hear from the U.N. When we do, when we make a decision, then I will respond.

NOTE: The President spoke at 12:02 p.m. in Room 450 of the Old Executive Office Building. In his remarks, he referred to participant Robin Dikeman. A tape was not available for verification of the content of these remarks.

Interview With the Nevada Media
July 29, 1993

The President. It's nice to hear your voice. I want to thank all of you for participating in this radio press conference or town hall meeting or whatever we want to call it. I'm glad to have the chance to talk with you.

Let me just say very briefly by way of summary, the Senate and the House are meeting today, trying to agree on a final version of the economic program which could then be presented for a vote next week. Obviously, I'm trying to secure passage of the program. I believe it is very important. I want to emphasize, if I might, some of the major features.

First, this is the largest program for deficit reduction in the history of the country, $500 billion. Of every $10 of deficit reduction, half of it is in spending cuts, very significant ones in nondefense as well as in defense, including 150,000-person reduction in the Federal work force and big cuts across the board in many other programs.

Second thing I want to say is that of the $5 in new revenues, about 80 percent of them come from the top 5 percent of the American work force. There are no income tax increases on couples with incomes below $180,000 a year.

Third thing I want to say is that in addition to reducing the deficit and imposing a fair tax burden, this program does an awful lot to promote job growth. It holds families with incomes of under $30,000 a year harmless. It doubles the expensing provision of small business and makes over 90 percent of the small businesses in America eligible for a tax reduction if they invest more in their businesses. It has a very innovative capital gains tax for investment in small new companies that are capitalized at $50 million a year or less, which should benefit a fast-growing State like Nevada. It has any number of other very important things that could help the technology jobs in your State, including an extension of the research and development tax credit, as well as real initiatives to revive homebuilding and real estate which is why the National Home Builders and the National Realtors, two groups not normally associated with Democratic Party initiatives, have endorsed this program.

Yesterday we had almost 70 business executives from all over the country, including 4 big energy company executives, about half of them Republican and of course the other half Democratic, endorsing the program and saying it was important because we had a 20-year low in interest rates, and we had to restore certainty to the economy, keep these interest rates down because we're bringing the deficit down, and get on with other business. We've got a health care issue to deal with, a crime bill to deal with, welfare reform to deal with, all these things that have to be done but can't be done until we first pass the economic plan.

With that, I'll be glad to take as many questions as we can.

Economic Program

Q. Thank you, Mr. President, for allowing us this opportunity. Why have you had such a tough time selling your economic plan to not only Congress but to the American public?

The President. I think until the last couple of weeks, the opposition did a better job than we did because they had a simpler job of selling it. We had some overtures to the Republicans, and especially in the Senate, before I even unveiled this program about whether there was a possibility of a real bipartisan effort to deal with this deficit. And we were basically told that if we were going to have any taxes on upper income people, they weren't interested. And they basically wanted to take it all out of Medicare and other things that we think there's a limit to how much you can cut. And we've cut Medicare as much or more than they have in the past but not as much as they wanted.

So when you've got a program of spending cuts, tax increases that are overwhelmingly on the wealthy with an enormous number of economic incentives to grow, you'd think it would be quite popular. In fact, it is when people know the details of it. But what happened is, you had everybody from the Republican Senators to a lot of the House Members to Rush Limbaugh just trying to convince the American people that there were no spending cuts, no deficit reduction, and no taxes on anybody but the middle class. None of that was true. But it's a lot easier to bad-mouth something like that and just scream "taxes" than it is to deal with the specifics.

Let me just give you one example. Just in the last couple of weeks, it's been very impressive to me that the Wall Street Journal, a newspaper that's not editorially on my side often, that their news columns have repeatedly shown how most small businesses benefit from this program, but most of them didn't know. Their communications job, those that are against us, was simpler than ours, and we've only begun to do what we should in the last couple of weeks.

But the more people know about this, the more likely they are to support it. The details of the plan are friendly to support; it's all this rhetoric that's hurt us so bad.

Taxes

Q. Mr. President, I am here, and on behalf of our audience in northern Nevada, I would like to thank you for this opportunity. We've had quite a lot of interest at our station today particularly in the subject of the cost of your economic program to our people here in northern Nevada. Mr. President, the deficit is something that most people cannot reach out and touch or feel, and yet taxes, whether we're talking income taxes, a gas tax, a value-added tax, those are very real to our people here in northern Nevada. Is there too much emphasis in your program on reducing the deficit through taxes and not enough on cutting the burden to the American people?

The President. Well, let's talk about that. I think from the day I made it clear that we were going to bring down the deficit and then the Chairman of the Federal Reserve Board, a Republican, Alan Greenspan, came out and supported it, long-term interest rates began to drop. When the House passed my bill, they dropped some more. When the Senate passed my bill, they dropped some more.

So here's why average people should be for bringing the deficit down. Number one, that's the way to keep long-term interest rates down. That means you can refinance your home or your business loan or take out a car loan, a consumer loan, or a college loan at lower interest rates. Millions and millions of Americans have refinanced their homes just in the last 5 or 6 months with these lower interest rates that are a direct result of our serious attempt to bring the deficit down. And if we pass the program, the interest rates will stay down until the economy really, really starts to boom again. That's good news.

Here's another reason ordinary people should be for bringing the deficit down. We are spending more and more of taxpayers' money just to pay interest on the debt. In 1980 our debt was $1 trillion. By 1992 our debt was $4 trillion. Today every Nevadan puts 15 cents of every tax dollar to the Federal Government just to pay interest on the debt. That means middle class people are paying interest payments to upper income bond holders who hold that money, instead of using the money to educate their children or to build roads or otherwise develop the economy of Nevada.

The third thing I would say is that this deficit has clearly made our economy weaker. It is one reason we cannot grow jobs and increase incomes. Now, Nevada has been the fastest growing State in the country for new jobs for the

last 6 or 7 years. But even that cannot go on forever.

Finally, let me say, let's talk about what this burden really is. Keep in mind that half of this deficit reduction is coming from spending cuts. Of the taxes which will be paid, basically, for a family of four with an income of $50,000 or $60,000 or what we're talking about today, the costs will be no more—and this is the outside—than $50 a year, or less than a dollar a week. For a family with income of under $30,000, they'll be held harmless. And the income tax increases only trigger on people whose taxes were lowered in the 1980's while middle class taxes went up, families in the upper 6 percent of the income earners. So I think it is a fair and balanced program.

Q. Thank you, Mr. President.

Q. Good afternoon, thank you.

The President. Thanks.

Senator Richard Bryan

Q. Are you speaking to residents of the Silver State today mainly at an attempt to change Senator Richard Bryan's opposition to your deficit reduction plan?

The President. Yes, but not only that, also to point out why Senator Reid and Congressman Bilbray voted for it. They've all been good friends of mine. And Senator Bryan has some very legitimate concerns which I've tried to address, and I think when this conference report comes out, that is, the final form comes out, the bill will be more to his liking.

One of the things that Senator Bryan, himself, thought the Btu tax was a little better than the gas tax. He also felt very strongly that we ought to have more economic growth incentives in this bill than the Senate originally provided. And we're putting some of those growth incentives that I proposed in the beginning back in there: the new business capital gains tax, the incentives to rebuild the homebuilding industry in America, the incentives for industry to invest in new plant and equipment, doubling the expensing provision for small business, more incentives for research and development, the things that will cause business and individuals to invest to grow jobs. Dick Bryan said he thought that too much of that had been taken out when the Senate bill passed, and I agree with him. And I hope when we get this final bill out there he'll see it as a pro-jobs bill that will be good for Nevada, and then he'll feel that he can vote for it.

Job Creation

Q. We seemed to be losing jobs nationally faster than they can be generated: last week Procter & Gamble, this week IBM, not to mention the jobs that have been lost through the cutback in the Sears catalog stores. How do you propose to reverse that process, and is there something specific that the private sector can do to help?

The President. Yes, there are some specific things that the private sector can do, and let me make two comments, if I might, to the statement you made by way of introduction. Number one, every rich country in the world is now having trouble creating jobs, even when they're having economic growth. We've seen that in Germany. We've seen it in France. We've seen it in Japan. That's cold comfort for America, but our unemployment rate is actually lower than all those countries now, as tough as it is here.

Number two, in our country and in all other advanced countries, big, big companies like IBM, Procter & Gamble, Sears are going through a process of restructuring where they're eliminating middle layers of management, getting rid of unprofitable businesses, and cutting down so they can be more flexible and so they can compete. That is very tough, and it's tough for our economy.

So how are we going to generate more jobs? These are the things that have to be done. First of all, what can the private sector do? They can invest more, create more jobs here, and sell more products and services at home and abroad.

What is the Government going to do to help them do that? The first thing I want to do is get the deficit down so we can keep interest rates down. The second thing I want to do is to change the Tax Code so that we favor investment for jobs, that we give people ways to lower their tax burden by investing to create jobs. The third thing I'm trying my heart out to do is to open new markets for our American products and services around the world. If we do those three things and we provide a better system for educating and training the work force, control health care costs, which is a big problem for a lot of these big companies—a lot of them are going into real trouble because they can't control health care costs—and then have a bet-

ter system for developing our people's ability to work, reducing the welfare rolls, increasing the work rolls, training people better, those are the kinds of things that will change the future of this country. And that's what my economic plan is designed to do. The deficit reduction program and the jobs incentives, that's only the first step. We've still got to do these other things as well.

Economic Program

Q. Of all the things in the budget and the deficit reduction package, several of the things which seem to hurt Nevada the most—we're basically a service economy; we depend on tourists arriving here. We're not a manufacturing State; we're not really an agricultural State; we don't export a lot of things anywhere. And yet, the proposal for a nickel more a gallon on gas—the Btu tax may or may not be dead—all of those things would tend to drive down tourism, the very thing that Nevada thrives on. What is there in your program, since we're already the second fastest growing State job-wise and we have among the highest in new construction and what have you in our State—what is there specifically in your plan that will actually be of benefit and not of cost to the people of Nevada?

The President. Well, first, let me make a comment about—there will not be a Btu tax. If it is an energy tax, it will only be the fuel tax. I think it will pass at a low enough level so that it will not burden travel any. Keep in mind that gasoline in America is the cheapest of any country in the world, and gasoline is now at its lowest price in 30 years in America when you make adjustments for inflation. So we've got very low fuel costs, and we're proposing a very modest gas tax, not a big one.

Secondly, there are a lot of things that are good for Nevada, are the incentives to revitalize the homebuilding and real estate—homebuilding's slow everywhere, just about—the incentives for all small businesses to invest more, to increase their profitability and their employment, which is a dramatic thing. We've qualified over 90 percent of the small businesses in this country for a tax break. And then the incentives for new high-tech industry and research and development and investment in new companies, that's very important, because among other things, we're trying to find alternative developments uses for the nuclear test site while we've got this moratorium on nuclear testing. You've got a big sort of technology-based infrastructure up there because of the past nuclear tests, and the Governor's economic development task force is working with us now to determine whether there are alternative uses and projects and spin-offs. And this would help a great deal because it would make this kind of investment more attractive to more capital by giving tax incentives to attract it.

So all those things are important. And in the end, I'll say every State in the country will have a more attractive, effective economy if the deficit stays down and we can keep interest rates down. Low interest rates for a sustained period of time will make available more money to more business people and lower cost in every State in America, and that's very, very important. That's a big issue in every State.

We can take a few more questions if you like. Let me go back to the top.

Federal Lands

Q. Yes, sir. Mr. President. Do you see there being increases in grazing fees for public lands, and also on mining royalties?

The President. I think the Congress will pass some increase on mining royalties with a bipartisan consensus that has some support from the West this year. I think they will be pretty modest and the subject of a lot of discussion. But it appears to me that they're going to pass a bill to do that.

With regard to the grazing issue, Secretary Babbitt has visited Nevada as part of his western swing to talk to people about that. What we had hoped to do is to turn that whole issue into an environmental one, that is, to give ranchers incentives to continually restore the ranchland as a way of avoiding higher fees and also to make sure that any fees that were imposed were not economically crippling to the people involved.

As you may know, if you've been reading the press back East, that we took a lot of criticism, Secretary Babbitt and I did, from a lot of legislators from places other than the West who wanted to mandate by law much, much higher grazing fees. And we took the position that the Secretary ought to go out West, ought to sit and visit with the ranchers and cattlemen and talk to them about what we could do to make sure we're being environmentally responsible with this Federal land and how we can use

the grazing fee structure in a way that would encourage that. So that's where that issue is now.

Energy Tax

Q. A fuel tax increase will not only be felt at the gas pumps, sir, but in people's pocketbooks as well, in regard to the price of goods and services at the consumer level. Now, the Fed has indicated that interest rates will be raised if inflation starts to rise. How do you justify a double whammy or a double blow like that? How can that be good for the economy, sir?

The President. Well, the Fed has basically indicated that they're going to raise interest rates if this deficit reduction package doesn't pass. Alan Greenspan has repeatedly told the Congress that the size of the Federal deficit and the accumulated Federal debt from the last 12 years was the biggest threat to the health of the American economy. And he was up there just last week saying that if this plan is derailed and we don't, in fact, come up with a plan for just about $500 billion of deficit reduction, that in his view interest rates are going to go up, and that will cripple the economy.

As I said, everybody we have talked to has suggested that this level of fuel tax increase will be very modest and have virtually no impact on the economies of the various States in the country. Virtually all States in America have raised fuel taxes more than this for their road programs over the last 10 years without adverse economic impact.

Q. Early on in the proposition on the Btu tax, you mentioned that one of the reasons for such a tax was to provide an incentive for alternate energy sources. Now, Nevada has tremendous geothermal energy resources here that are being developed on a somewhat small scale. Without that Btu tax and that incentive, what kind of an incentive are you going to provide down the road for developing alternative energy such as geothermal?

The President. We're going to have to come up with another approach. The reason I liked the Btu tax is that it promoted the development of American clean energy: natural gas, geothermal, methane, ethanol, solar energy, all kinds of things which would have led to big investments in the West particularly to try to develop the technologies. But there was so much misinformation and such an effective special interest campaign carried out against the Btu tax that it was killed. We just had no way to save it.

I will say this in response to the gas tax question: The fuel tax now being considered is a smaller amount per gallon than the Btu tax was. But Nevada would have gotten the benefit of having a greater economic incentive to develop geothermal and alternative sources of energy. I haven't given up on that, but I can't do everything in this bill. In order to get on to energy policy, control of health care costs, which is a huge economic issue for America, welfare reform, all these other issues, we've got to pass the economic plan first.

Federal Employees

Q. We hear again and again how we all must make sacrifices to bring the deficit under control. What about the salaries and benefits that Federal employees earn? Will they too be asked to sacrifice?

The President. Absolutely. First of all, let me repeat again, I recommended, number one, that we reduce the Federal work force by now a figure that is now 150,000, and I think it will be bigger before we finish, that is, I have another report coming out on this next month; number two, that we freeze the pay of Federal employees of next year, and for the next 5 years we not give them the cost-of-living increases that they got all during the eighties, that we give them less than the total cost-of-living increase.

I think you can make a compelling argument that Federal employees are making from a percentage point of view, the biggest contribution to deficit reduction of any single group in America. And by and large, interestingly enough, they've been pretty supportive of this. They've recognized it that they have jobs with the Federal Government, that we've got to downsize the Government, and that they need to show some restraint, if other Americans are going to be asked to pay $50 a year in a fuel tax, that they need to show some restraint on their pay. But if you look at the automatic cost-of-living increases they've been getting for the last 12 years, it will cost them a lot more than $50 a year, this program will, before we're done, and they'll pay a much bigger share. But I think that's right; the Government should make a bigger sacrifice than the taxpayers. I believe that they should, and I believe they are.

Line-Item Veto

Q. Our Senator Harry Reid recently had a small success in getting the 100-year-old Tea Tasting Board abolished and the funds for that. He proposes sunset legislation that would cut off funding for all programs after 10 years without a review, and President Bush and several others have proposed the line-item veto, something that the State Governors, many State Governors have. Why haven't we heard anything about that? It would seem to me and to many that it would be a way to cut a lot of pork out of the various national budgets.

The President. I'm strongly in favor of it, and we have actually passed it through one House of the Congress already. A strict line-item veto would probably require a constitutional amendment. We had to modify it some to meet the requirements of the Federal Constitution, but we've passed a strong bill out of the House. It's in the Senate now. I think both Senator Reid and Senator Bryan support it, and I very much hope that we can pass it. If I had the line-item veto, I assure you that I would, myself, be able to deal with things like the Tea Tasting Board and some of the other subsidies.

You know, Senator Bryan has proposed eliminating the mohair subsidy, which goes back to the Korean war, which was a pretty gutsy thing for him to do, but it passed the Senate last week. So both Harry Reid and Dick Bryan have been working on this cost-cutting in the Senate. I want the line-item veto very badly. I pushed it as hard as I could. We got it through the House, and I think that the Senate will pass it, but everything is on hold while they deal with the budget. But you're absolutely right, it ought to be passed.

As far as the sunset review goes, we had such a law in my State, and we tried to use it. My own experience would indicate that the Government could eliminate an agency a year and never miss it. That's basically what we'd try to do. Every time our legislature met every 2 years, we'd just try to eliminate a government agency. We did it, oh, three or four or five times, and I never heard any complaint from the taxpayers if it was something we didn't need anymore.

So I think there is more specific cutting that we can do, but I would remind you that next month the Vice President is going to reveal his report on reinventing Government, and we'll have a lot more recommendations for further cuts in there.

Let me take one last question—oh, they say I have to quit. I'm sorry. I'm having a good time, and I wish I could talk to you some more, but I've got to go to another meeting.

Let me say how much I appreciate your giving me this opportunity to speak directly to the people of Nevada, and how much I hope that they will encourage their Senators and Congressman Bilbray to support this plan. It's clearly good for America. There is an enormous bipartisan support from people who know how badly this huge deficit has hurt our country and how much we need some more incentives in the Tax Code for people to invest where the new jobs are being created, in small businesses.

We have done our best to ease the impact of this on middle class families and on any given State. Like Nevada, I live in a State with a high amount of gasoline usage. But the price of gasoline now, plus the relatively modest amount of the fuel tax, it seems to me is a small price to pay to get this Federal deficit under control and keep these interest rates down.

So I hope you will support the plan. And we need it. And most importantly, I hope you will support the fact that your Senators and your Congressmen are up here in Washington really trying to honestly cut this budget and make some tough decisions, and I think they deserve support in that effort.

Thank you very, very much.

NOTE: The interview began at 4:43 p.m. The President spoke via satellite from the Roosevelt Room at the White House. A tape was not available for verification of the content of this interview.

Remarks on Presenting the Young American Medals for Service and Bravery
July 29, 1993

The President. Thank you very much. Ladies and gentlemen, especially to our honorees, I want to welcome you to the White House and say I hope you had a wonderful day in Washington. I know you've been over to the Justice Department with the Attorney General. I want to thank her for her service to America and for her introduction and to recognize some others who are here: Floyd Clarke, the Acting Director of the FBI; Robert Bonner, the Administrator of the Drug Enforcement Administration; Henry Hudson, the Director of the U.S. Marshals Service; S.S. Ashton, Jr., of the Office of Justice Programs; and Ellen Wesley, who coordinates this program at the Department of Justice. I'd also like to recognize at least four Members of the Congress who are here: Senators Kent Conrad and Byron Dorgan from North Dakota, and Senator Larry Pressler from South Dakota, and Congressman Tim Johnson from South Dakota. I want to thank you for coming.

The Young American Medal for Service and the Young American Medal for Bravery are awarded to a young person whose deeds, in a very real way, represent the best our Nation can offer. At a time when we hear too much about self-interest and not enough about what each of us can do to advance the common good of all Americans, seven young people here being honored, with their families, are role models for all the rest of us. Their selfless acts of service to their neighbors remind us of our own responsibilities to our communities and to our Nation.

As extraordinary as the courage and initiative of all these young people has been, we must remember, too, that every American can contribute. Look how the American people are responding to the challenge presented by the horrible floods in the middle of the country or how they responded to Hurricane Andrew last year. Most Americans want to do more and will every day if they're given a chance to do it.

The medals we award today honor special acts. And in the same spirit, I have tried to launch in the Nation's Capital for young people throughout the country a program of national service that will give people the opportunity to help people day-in and day-out, and to earn some money as well against their college education.

The plan was passed yesterday by the House of Representatives, and we are one vote shy of ending the filibuster in the Senate. I hope that will happen tomorrow, and millions of young people over the next umpteen years will be given the opportunity to serve in a very real and compelling and human way in their own communities.

Lately we hear a lot about the things like cost-effectiveness and efficiency, and those are very important things, but they sound sort of bureaucratic. Today we honor things that matter more, the potential of the human heart and the courage of even the very young, what the great American writer from my part of the country, William Faulkner, called the truths of the heart: love and honor and pity and pride and compassion and sacrifice. When an emergency struck, the young people we honor today didn't wait, they acted. When a need arose, they didn't question whether they would succeed in the end, they simply went to work. We have a lot to learn from the young people we honor today.

Now I'd like for each of them to come up on the stage and receive his or her medal as I call their names, and then we have a place for them to stand. I'd also like for their parents and family members to stand as I read a few words about them.

The Young American Medal for Bravery is presented to Waylon Dean Bertsch of Buchanan, North Dakota. I'd like the people who are here with Waylon to stand up. Anybody here? There they are, back there. When Waylon was 10 years old, his 5-year-old sister, Andrea, fell through the ice in a river near their home. He sent for his parents and then went to his sister's rescue. After falling through the ice himself, he kicked to keep his body and his sister above water. It worked. When their parents arrived, they pulled both of them out alive. Good for you.

Christopher Paul Erichs, Rapid City, South Dakota. Stand up. Give him a hand. [*Applause*] A student at Christopher's school entered a classroom with a sawed-off shotgun, ordered the teacher to leave, and took 22 students hostage over a 2½-hour standoff with professional negotiators. As the gunman moved to light a cigarette, Christopher snatched the shotgun from his hands, calmly freed the other hostages, and called in the police. Let's give him another hand. [*Applause*]

Jessica Ann Johnson of Elliott, Iowa. Who is here with you? Look, you've got plenty of folks here with you. Jessica was just 7 years old on her family farm when she heard the screams of her 4-year-old brother. He had crawled into a pigpen and was attacked, trampled, and bitten by 450-pound sows. She went into the pen with the sows, dragged her brother to a safe spot, went back through the pen and went to her mother for help.

I can only tell you that this is something I have a limited, similar experience with. When I was 6, I was attacked by a ram on our farm, and I was darn near killed. I know how terrifying it is when you're that age to be attacked by an animal that can take your life. To think that this young girl at her age, to have that amount of courage to save a member of her family is really astonishing. Let's give her a hand. [*Applause*]

After I got bloodied by that ram, I got into politics thinking I wouldn't get knocked around so much. I think you ought to stay on the farm. [*Laughter*]

The Young American Medal for Service is presented to Kelly Elizabeth Broxton from Gaithersburg, Maryland. Who's here with you? They couldn't contain themselves. They started clapping early. Stand up. This is great. Kelly taught over 300 students about basic first aid, certified first aid training, and how to get treatment for substance abuse. She also organized a youth council that recruited students from 19 other schools to perform community service projects. Good for you. Congratulations.

Dennis Chisholm, Jr., of Winston-Salem, North Carolina. Your family is standing. Give them a hand. [*Applause*] Dennis volunteered his many talents during the school year and 5 days a week in the summer to work in a center for children with disabilities. He helped other children develop motor skills and build their self-esteem through a range of physical and creative activities, including music and even computers.

I think that I should note that we have just celebrated this week the 3d anniversary of the Americans with Disabilities Act, a major piece of civil rights legislation. But like every other piece of civil rights legislation we ever signed, it can only work if there is change in the hearts and minds of the rest of the American people. And this young man has helped other people to see the abilities of people with disabilities.

We're all in his debt.

Another person who has done much the same is Sarah Elizabeth Greensfelder of Baltimore. Sarah has taken part in all kinds of community service programs: at blood drives, the Special Olympics, Johns Hopkins Pediatric Center, in nursing homes, or with housebound senior citizens. When she was selected for this medal she had volunteered over 900 hours for helping others, the equivalent of working full-time for half a year. Let's give her a hand. [*Applause*] Where's your family? They should stand, too. Let's give them a hand. [*Applause*] That's good. Look at that. You've got a whole back row. Thank you.

Now I'd like to ask—I'm not going to leave you over there—Gennie Sue Sluder of Clatskankie, Oregon—did I say it right?

Ms. Sluder. No. [*Laughter*]

The President. How do I say it? Say it.

Ms. Sluder. Clatskankie.

The President. Clatskankie, Oregon—[*applause*]—stand up. Gennie started a program called Help Hungry Kids. She went to the school board and managed a statewide campaign that asked students at all 235 high schools in Oregon to donate $1 and two cans of food apiece for needy children. Now she's at George Fox College, and she's working at two jobs to put herself through school. But when she was in high school she thought of a way to organize a plan for every person her age in the State to help children who were less fortunate. A very impressive accomplishment.

I want to say again on behalf of all the people of the United States, it is a great honor to have these fine young people, their families, friends, and supporters in the White House today. They've made us all very proud, and they've reminded us again of what is most important about our citizenship, our roles in our families and in our communities, and in a very real sense, what it means just to be a person. They're great. Let's give them one more hand. And thank you all for being here.

NOTE: The President spoke at 6:05 p.m. in the East Room at the White House. A tape was not available for verification of the content of these remarks.

Remarks in the Flood Aid Telethon
July 29, 1993

The President. I have made three trips now to the Midwest during this flood. My Secretary of Agriculture and the Director of FEMA have been there many, many more times. We've seen so many people who have lost their homes, their farms, their businesses, but they are carrying on very, very bravely.

Here in Washington, we're working hard to get a multibillion dollar emergency aid package through the Congress to help rebuild the communities, the businesses, the homes, to help to provide basic assistance. But the Federal Government can't do it all. Our country always has had a system in which the National Government would come to the need of States and communities and citizens when they needed help, but we've never been able to cover all the costs, and we won't be able to now. That's why we need your help.

The Red Cross has done a magnificent job; so has the Salvation Army; so have the churches and the other community groups; so have thousands of people, young and old and all in-between, who have come to help. But we need your help. And I hope that you, too, will contribute whatever you can afford to help these wonderful Americans put their lives back together. They need your encouragement and your support. We'll do our part. We need you to help, too.

Q. [*Inaudible*]

The President. The aid should be there very soon. Of course, some of the emergency aid is there now. The Federal Emergency Management Agency and the Department of Agriculture have been giving cash and food stamps to people who are totally out of all resources and money. But the big aid will be there just as quickly as we can get it through the Congress. I think it will happen very soon. And we're all set up to move the checks out very quickly, I think within a couple of weeks after I can sign the bill. And that should be just in the next day or so.

In terms of the long run, we've already got a group established to look at that. I met with the Governors of the affected States here in the White House just a couple of days ago, and we're going to work hard in the long run, too. I don't want this to happen again to you or to anybody else.

Q. [Inaudible]

The President. There is an 800 number that gets several thousand calls a day just from Iowa, down in Texas. If you don't have it, I will arrange to have it called in while the telethon is going on. We've tried to set up a one-stop telephone so that all Americans who are affected by the flood could call. We're going to do our best, as I said, to take care of this and also to take care of the long-term problems. I can't control the weather, but we're going to work hard to help you.

NOTE: The President spoke at 8:15 p.m. via satellite from the Library at the White House. A portion of these remarks could not be verified because the tape was incomplete.

Remarks in the Missouri-Kansas Flood Relief Telethon
July 29, 1993

The President. My fellow Americans, I want to thank you for watching this program tonight and for your concern for those who have been victimized by this awful flood. I've been to the Midwest three times myself. I've met with the Governors of the affected States here in the White House. Our people are there every day working hard to try to help put the lives of the folks back together who have been so hurt.

We have an emergency aid package moving through Congress which should be signed very shortly, and then the money will begin to flow to the Midwest. But under our system, the Federal Government can only do so much. We also need your help. The Red Cross has been magnificent. So has the Salvation Army. So have the churches and the other volunteer groups and people of all ages from all over America. But we now need to fill the gap left by Federal assistance, and left by the limits that people have in their own bankbooks, with private donations to help people put their lives back together. I hope you will help, too, so that together we can restore the people who have been so hurt and help them to rebuild their lives and our Nation.

Q. [Inaudible]

The President. I think the bill will pass the Congress in the next couple of days and come right to me for my signature. The people in our administration believe that we'll be able to have checks flowing out there within 2 weeks after that bill is signed. I have told them to be ready and to work hard. We also have an 800 number which any citizen can call, which I'll provide to your station, to provide specific information about farm aid, small business aid, personal assistance, what can happen to the communities. We're working very hard to be ready, to be aggressive, to be fast.

Q. [Inaudible]

The President. I think we lost a day we should not have lost, but I think now you will see the thing move very, very quickly indeed. And they'll bring it to me. And as soon as it comes, I'll sign it, and we'll move the money out. I think no more than a day has been lost. There was an honest debate here about how we're going to pay for emergency assistance over the long run, but we couldn't afford to let that take away from the urgent need to help the people in the Midwest. And that's the program everybody's on now, without regard to party and without regard to which House of Congress. I think you'll get it in a hurry.

Q. [Inaudible]

The President. The Small Business Administration has an emergency program to provide very, very long-term, very, very low-interest loans to help people get back on their feet. In addition to that, for people who have been totally wiped out and have no assets left, there is some emergency financial aid available through the Federal Emergency Management Agency. So between the two of them, I think we can go forward. As I said, one of the things

I hope you'll do tonight is put our 800 number up. A person can call that number and get information on all the programs from all the agencies. You don't have to go to the hassle to call first one place and then another.

Q. [Inaudible]

The President. I was very moved by it. When I went to Iowa and to Illinois and to Missouri and everyplace I went, there were just literally thousands of people who just showed up to help and to pour out their concern and to break their backs, frankly, to help their fellow Americans. It was our country at its best. And that's what I hope that this telethon will prove to be, too, asking for help and giving people a change to participate in the reconstruction of millions of lives.

Q. [Inaudible]

The President. Well, for one thing, the Government programs have never been designed to cover 100 percent of the losses. We simply can't do that. We are going to help the cities, we are going to help as many farms and business people as we can, but there will be some gaps

in this coverage. And those gaps have to be filled by private citizens.

For another, Americans have always rallied to one another in times of real need. And if we can do that now in this place for these people, just as we did about a year ago for the victims of Hurricane Andrew, then who knows when Americans in another State—people listening tonight who think nothing like this could ever happen to them, they may need the help of the folks in the Midwest. So if we help each other, we can put our lives back together and our whole country will be stronger, believe me. Someone in Utah or Texas or my home State of Arkansas, their economies will be weakened by the fact that the Midwest has been hurt by this flood. But if we all work together and rebuild the region, then that helps everybody in every State in America.

NOTE: The President spoke at approximately 8:30 p.m. via satellite from the Library at the White House. A tape was not available for verification of the content of these remarks.

Message to the Congress Transmitting the United States Arctic Research Plan Revision
July 29, 1993

To the Congress of the United States:

Pursuant to the provisions of the Arctic Research and Policy Act of 1984, as amended (15 U.S.C. 4108(a)), I hereby transmit the third biennial revision (1994–1995) to the United States

Arctic Research Plan.

WILLIAM J. CLINTON

The White House,
July 29, 1993.

Nomination for Administrator for Federal Procurement Policy
July 29, 1993

The President today announced his intention to nominate Steven Kelman, a Harvard professor and advocate for cutting Government waste through better purchasing policies, as Administrator for Federal Procurement Policy at the Office of Management and Budget.

"With his background and commitment to making the Government more efficient, I know

Steven Kelman will ensure Government purchases are made economically and with care," the President said.

NOTE: A biography of the nominee was made available by the Office of the Press Secretary.

Nomination for Ambassador to Jamaica
July 29, 1993

The President today announced his intention to nominate former Congresswoman Shirley Chisholm to be the U.S. Ambassador to Jamaica.

"Shirley Chisholm is a true pioneer of American politics whose passion for social justice is unparalleled," said the President. "I am honored that she will be my Ambassador to Jamaica and confident that she will do an outstanding job in that position."

NOTE: A biography of the nominee was made available by the Office of the Press Secretary.

Interview With the Arizona Media
July 30, 1993

The President. Thank you for joining me by satellite. I'm glad to have the opportunity to speak with you and through you to the people of Arizona. I'd like to make a brief opening statement and then preserve as much time as possible for your questions.

The Senate and the House conferees are nearing agreement on a budget program which preserves the essential principles that I began with in this whole endeavor back in February.

First, it will reduce the deficit by about $500 billion with divisions equally between spending cuts and revenue increases.

Secondly, it will restore fairness to the Tax Code by asking 70 percent or more of the burden of the new revenues to be borne by people with incomes above $200,000, the top 1.2 percent of our country, the people who received most of the economic gains of the last 10 years and got a tax reduction during that period.

Third, the burden on the middle class, people with incomes above $30,000 for family incomes, but less than $180,000, will be asked to pay a modest fuel tax, about 4.3 cents, which will be less than $50 a year on average for the average family.

Fourth, for the first time ever, we will be able to say to working people with children that if they work 40 hours a week, if they play by the rules, they will not be taxed into poverty but lifted out of it because of a dramatic expansion in the earned-income tax credit. This is an essential downpayment on welfare reform, really rewards work and family, and it's very, very important.

And finally, and perhaps most important of all, this plan brings down the deficit and keeps interest rates down and at the same time provides important new incentives for business investment and job growth and new incentive to invest in small businesses capitalized at $50 million a year or less, very important to the high-tech community; a huge increase in the expensing provision for small businesses, meaning that 90 percent of the small businesses in America will actually be eligible for a tax reduction under this program if they reinvest in their businesses; third, an expansion of the research and development tax credit, very important to the growing economy; and fourth, something that will affect Arizona because you've got a lot of new people coming in there, some real incentives to revitalize homebuilding and real estate in ways that will generate a lot of a new jobs.

So for all these reasons, I very much hope that this plan will pass. The more the American people know about it, the more they are likely to support it. Almost all of the opposition has been generated by false claims that this plan has no deficit reduction, no spending cuts, and too much of a tax burden on the middle class. All three of those things are wrong.

And finally, let me say just one other point, because I've had this conversation with Senator DeConcini so often. There's a difference in this plan and the plan that passed in 1990, which didn't produce deficit reduction. First, we don't have unrealistic revenue forecasts. We have cold-blooded, hard facts in our projections that are agreed to by all the expert analysts. Secondly, all this money goes into a trust fund and can only be spent for deficit reduction. Thirdly, under the House version of the bill, there is an actual enforcement mechanism so that if we miss our deficit reduction target in any of the next 5 years, the President would be legally bound to correct the miss on the target, because nobody can foresee the future with absolute precision, and the Congress legally bound to vote on it or vote on another proposal to do the same thing.

So we have some protections here that have not been there before, that will bring this deficit down, revitalize our economy, and enable us to go on to the other crucial issues facing this country, including health care, welfare reform, the crime bill, the immigration issue, a lot of the other things we need to face. And I hope that your Members of Congress will support it. I thank Representative English for doing so the first time around. I'll be glad to answer your questions.

Deficit Reduction

Q. Mr. President, thank you very much for being with us by satellite this afternoon. And as we begin in the interest of fairness and full disclosure to the viewing audience and to the people listening on the radio, I think it's important to point out that the White House has imposed a ground rule here today that there will be no followup questions from reporters.

That being said, Mr. President, it's clear that most Americans do want to see a deficit reduction here. The plan which is likely to come out of the Senate Conference Committee, maybe even yet today, is somewhat short of your $500-billion-dollar-over-5-year target. Arizona Senator Dennis DeConcini, whom you talked about just a moment ago, says that he can't vote for it when it comes up for a full Senate vote because there are, quote, no assurances that new taxes will be used for deficit reduction—[*inaudible*]—retire the debt. Those words were spoken by him this morning.

Now, I understand what you just said, but obviously, he doesn't believe it's going to reduce the deficit far enough. What's your response to that?

The President. I have a twofold response. First of all, they are arguing about the details. They are talking about a deficit reduction package somewhere in the range of $490 billion to $496 billion or $497 billion; anything in that range would be 98 percent of where we are.

Secondly, the taxes will not legally be able to be spent on anything other than deficit reduction. They will be put into a trust fund which must be spent on deficit reduction. They can't legally be spent on anything else.

Now, Senator DeConcini wants a strong budget control mechanism to go into the plan. But as he pointed out to me, I supported his amendment, too, which is very much like the one we passed in the House. The only reason that the DeConcini amendment did not pass in the Senate is that all the Republicans voted against it because they don't want us to have good budgetary control. I don't know why; you'll have to ask them. But I'm going to have the strongest possible controls to guarantee that all the tax money goes to deficit reduction. If you put it into a trust fund and if we have to make annual corrections if we miss the targets, that's about as well as we can do, I think.

Senior Citizens' Investments

Q. Mr. President, the readers of my newspaper are nearly all senior citizens. They've seen the returns on their nest eggs decline considerably in recent years. Will your economic plan strengthen their investments, and if so, how?

The President. I think it will strengthen their investments by promoting economic growth. A lot of senior citizens who have their investments in primarily interest-earning accounts have had earnings drop as interest rates have gone down. But that's one of the reasons that you've had in Arizona, for example, a big increase in home-building and more people working in construction.

But I think what you will see over the long run is a very strong stock market, highly reliable bonds, and interest rates that will be lower as long as we can keep inflation low, but that will grow with the economy. And I think over the long run, what the senior citizens need is stable economic growth. They may have to balance their investment portfolios more between equities and plain bonds that depend on long-term interest rates. But I think all of us are helped over the long run if we can keep long-term interest rates down.

Economic Program

Q. Mr. President, why did you decide to do this in Arizona this afternoon? Is it because your tax plan is in trouble here? Is it because this morning Dennis DeConcini said again he wouldn't vote for it and because the Republicans are busy running a bunch of radio ads encouraging Karan English to vote against it?

The President. Well, it's because I think that I ought to answer these questions directly and because, frankly, the Republicans have willfully misrepresented the truth and the facts about this all over the country and especially in Arizona. I have been doing this, however, in many other States. You've actually—you helped to support the Republican rhetorical campaign by just what you said.

This is not a tax plan. This is an economic plan. Fifty percent of the deficit reduction is in spending cuts. We're cutting the Federal work force by 150,000. We're cutting everything from agriculture and veterans benefits to all kinds of other programs, all across the board. We have asked the wealthiest 1.2 percent of the American people who got big tax cuts during trickle-down economics to pay over 70 percent of the tax burden. We've held families with incomes under $30,000 a year harmless. We have actually rewarded the working poor of whom there are many in Arizona with a change in the Tax Code so that they'll be lifted out of, not kept in, poverty by taxes. And we've got big incentives for small business investment.

I will say this again: The Wall Street Journal has now run three articles in the last 2 weeks pointing out how a lot of these lobbying groups have willfully misrepresented the facts of this program to the small business community. Over 90 percent of the small businesses in the United States of America will be eligible for a tax reduction under this program if they reinvest in their businesses.

And I think when people know the facts— Senator DeConcini pointed out to me in my conversation with him 2 days ago—he said it's really too bad that people don't know the facts. He said, "This program had real support on February the 18th when you spoke to the Nation and went through the facts, point by point by point." And now the program is even better for average Americans than it was then. We've improved it. But all they've been told by the Republicans is, no deficit reduction, all taxes.

Let me just point out one other thing for all the Republican ads that are being run. When this budget came up in the Senate Finance Committee and the Republicans, with all their talk about needing more budget cuts, were given their chance, the Republicans did not offer one

nickel in budget cuts over the ones that I had already offered, not one red cent.

When Senator Dole presented his plan in the United States Senate it was a joke, from people who thought we ought to have $500 billion of deficit reduction. He had $100 billion less than I did, and $66 billion of his spending cuts were, quote, unspecified, meaning, "Trust me, I'll figure that out later. I don't want to make anybody else mad."

Now, if you look at my spending cuts, they're specific. There are 200 of them. We've got a plan. All I want the people of Arizona to know is the truth. When they get the facts, they can make their own conclusions.

Small Business

Q. Mr. President, in the past week we've heard from several small business groups who say increasing taxes on the most successful small businesses, which according to figures are 4 percent, would hurt those who are providing all of the new jobs, especially here in Arizona. I want to know your response to that.

The President. My response is that there are 700,000 small businesses that are organized and pay taxes under the Tax Code as individual taxpayers. Of that, 94 percent of them will have no income tax increase but will be eligible for a very big increase in their expensing provisions, which means they'll be eligible for a tax cut.

I think for the top 6 percent to say they should have no responsibility in paying down the deficit is wrong. And for them to say they're the only ones creating new jobs is wrong. All of them, anybody that's that big has the option of converting to the regular corporate status, and regular corporations don't pay a tax increase in this until they have taxable income in excess of $10 million. But people who get the benefits that come from being taxed as individual taxpayers should be taxed as individual taxpayers. They also have options to reinvest in their businesses and get tax benefits down the road, I might add.

Economic Program

Q. Mr. President, in the past few weeks we've had interviews with Al Gore, with Bruce Babbitt, with David Wilhelm. All were sent out to Arizona or called on the telephone to talk about this program. And now today we're getting to speak with you. You seem to be expending a tremendous amount of political capital over this program. I know you don't like to think about this, but I wonder, if the worst happens and this package loses, how big of a setback will it be for your administration?

The President. It will be a big setback for America. Let me remind you—this is an interesting thing—that we had 67 business executives here in the White House a couple of days ago endorsing this plan. About half of them were Republicans. We had the heads of four energy companies here. Lod Cook, who was one of President Bush's cochairs in 1992, was here endorsing our economic program.

This is not a partisan issue. Alan Greenspan, a Republican who is head of the Federal Reserve Board, has repeatedly said if we don't pass this deficit reduction plan, it means higher interest rates, a weaker economy, more uncertainty for America. What I'm trying to do is to cut through the incredible partisan fog that our adversaries have created and look at the facts. Republican business people who have looked at the facts are overwhelmingly supportive of this program. The Republican head of the Federal Reserve Board is supportive of this program.

When I represented the United States in Tokyo recently and got an agreement from other countries to lower tariffs on our manufactured products which, if we can get everyone in the General Agreement on Trade to sign off on by the end of the year, will put hundreds of thousands of manufacturing jobs into America. I got that agreement because we were bringing down our deficit. It was the first time in 10 years the leaders of the other industrialized countries had not attacked America in their statement, instead, they complimented us.

This has nothing to do with party or with me personally. Look, I want to get on to other things. I'll tell you what will happen if we don't do that. We'll spend 60 days or 90 days fooling around with this. You'll get less deficit reduction. You'll get higher interest rates. And the United States Congress will not go on to deal with health care, which every American has a stake in seeing resolved so that we can stabilize and make secure health care for all Americans and bring costs within inflation. We won't go on to welfare reform. We won't go on to the crime bill. We'll just sit here and flail around, and it'll be bad for America. I'll get up and go to work the next day, try to get the Congress to do its part. But I don't think that's going

to happen. I don't think the United States Congress is going to let interest rates go up because of the fog of misinformation that's put out here. I think they're going to trust their people, go home and tell them the truth. And I'll tell you something else: I think the Republicans will begin to vote with us on other issues. You can already see it now on national service. We're going to pass the national service program I campaigned so hard on next week with broad, bipartisan support because people are tired of all this partisanship.

Q. I'd like to go back to the question we talked about a moment ago, and that is why we're doing this. Half of our congressional delegation clearly will not vote for the plan, and three of the Democrats either will not or may not. I think we would all learn a little bit from the kind of personal interaction you're having with DeConcini, Coppersmith, and English to try to get them to be on your side.

The President. Well, I've asked them all to vote for the program, and I've told them that I would do what I could to get the facts out. But let me say this: There are two categories of people who are holding out now and trying to make up their mind how to vote. There's one group of people who desperately believed that this program ought to pass, but they're simply afraid that they'll never be able to convince their own voters, because of all the sort of rhetoric that's come out of the Republicans, that it's good for them. That is, I don't know how many Members of Congress have said to me, "This is a good deal for the people of my district. If they knew the facts, they would like the program. I don't know if I'll ever be able to get them the facts because of the dominance of the sort of 'tax, tax, tax' attack on it." So I think for those folks, I have to get out there and give them the facts. That's what I'm trying to do here today with you.

There are others who have certain specific objections that I have tried to meet. One of them is the objection that Senator DeConcini always raises, that we can't go back to 1990. If we have a deficit reduction package, the taxes have to go to reduce the debt, and we have to have an enforcement mechanism. And we have done that, and we will do that.

Let me assure you: I'm doing this with a lot of other States, too, for the same reasons. I want to try to at least explain to people directly what the issues are and what the facts are so they can make up their own minds. And I believe that, as President, I should be directly accountable not only to the people but also to press out in the country and not just depend upon whatever the nightly controversy is that dominates the evening news and the political press corps here to get the information out, to you. I think I owe you more than that, and I'm just trying to do my job.

Manufacturing

Q. Mr. President, much of the economic projections we hear about have to do with growth in the services industry. And yet many of the economists tell us that America only moves its engine forward when industry prospers, when manufacturing is doing its thing. What plans do you have for rejuvenating and improving the manufacturing engine of the United States?

The President. Good question. Let me mention, if I might, three things. First, let me compliment you on the question. I do think that services are important, but no great nation can give up its manufacturing base. I'm working on three things.

First of all, in this economic program, there are plain incentives for manufacturers, tax incentives, to invest in new plant and equipment to be more competitive, or to start new businesses, especially in the high-tech area.

Secondly, in the budget we are actually spending more on a couple of things. One of the most important things is more money on defense conversion to try to take advantage of the incredible skills of these companies that have lost their defense contracts but have the capacity to produce for the high-tech, nondefense economy of the world.

The third thing we're trying to do is to find more markets for our manufactured products. The most important thing I did at Tokyo was to get these other countries to agree to drop their tariffs, in many cases eliminate their tariffs on everything from pharmaceuticals to electronics so that Americans can sell more abroad. And I might say that there is virtually no disagreement on this. Everybody agrees that if the big seven nations can get what we agreed to into a world trade agreement by the end of the year, it will bring hundreds of thousands of manufacturing jobs back to the United States. So those are the three things we're really trying to hammer.

Economic Program

Q. Mr. President, given the job that the opponents of this economic package have done in selling it here in Arizona and elsewhere as a tax-and-spend plan, and we have two freshman Democrats who are sort of laying their careers on the line if they vote for this, what specifically can they tell their constituents, not in general terms but in very specific terms, what can they tell their constituents is in this package for them?

The President. First of all, they can tell their constituents that almost every small business in their district will be eligible for a tax reduction if they invest more in their business.

Secondly, they can tell their constituents that California is a growing State with a vibrant population where a lot of new businesses will be started. And this plan has dramatically increased incentives for getting capital for new businesses.

Thirdly, they can tell their constituents who are working hard for limited wages that this plan holds them harmless if they're families with incomes of less than $30,000 a year, and actually if they're at a low income and still working full time, they'll get a tax break out of this. Those are personal, immediate benefits.

And finally they can say that all of them will benefit from low interest rates. How many Arizonans have refinanced their homes since we've been able to bring interest rates down by taking on this deficit? How many more will be able to do it in the next few years or get a lower business loan or a lower car loan or a consumer loan or a college loan? These are personal, immediate, tangible benefits.

The other thing they can say is that when they do pay taxes to the Federal Government, we won't have to spend so much of it paying interest on the debt. We can spend more of it investing in the future of Arizona and America. These are things that I hope your freshman Congressmen can say.

But let me say that the opponents have a lot easier case. If you don't care what the facts are and you just want to say "tax and spend," it's an easy task. But let me just point out, it was under Republican Presidents that the debt of this country went from $1 trillion to $4 trillion. And you can look at the evidence. The Congress actually appropriated slightly less money than those Presidents asked them to spend over the last 12 years.

And a lot of the people that are raising all this cain now helped us to get in the fix we're in. I was a Governor during that period, and you look at my record. My State was always in the bottom five States in the country in the percentage of income going to State and local taxes. We never had to raise any money to pay off a debt. I don't like this. I hate the idea of raising taxes to reduce the deficit. But no one seriously believes that we can do what we need to do unless we reverse some of the things that happened during the trickle-down years of the eighties. I'm doing the best I can to take the tough decisions now to free up our economy as we move toward the 21st century. And I hope that Republicans, independents, and Democrats in Arizona who can think about that in terms of the future will be supportive.

Health Care

Q. Good afternoon, Mr. President. This question maybe is not related to the budget plan, but it's so important to the Hispanic community. Three days ago, you asked the Congress for $172 million in order to reinforce the immigration law and reduce the number of people that is coming illegally to this country. The majority of these people, Mr. President, are not criminals but working people. They are paying taxes. And they need medical care. My question, Mr. President, is, in your health care reform, is going to protect community health centers who right now treat illegal aliens here in Arizona? They are the only one. Are you going to protect these centers?

The President. The final shape of the health care reform has not been decided. But I believe that the likelihood is that American citizens will be individually covered but that public health centers will also be funded and that people who come into their doors will be eligible for care. That's what I think will happen. I think that is the likelihood.

I don't think you can see that sort of entitlement, the health care card that Americans might get otherwise, will go to illegal aliens. I think that is probably not going to happen. But I do think we will continue to fund public health facilities, and I think we must. I think that there are a lot of American citizens who would otherwise have no access to health care if we did not do so, particularly in urban areas that are quite poor or rural areas without access to other health care.

Consumer Confidence

Q. Mr. President, I guess I want to go back to something you said just a moment ago. You said no one believes that we can change things unless we reverse the policies of the eighties, to paraphrase what you said. But there's something I don't understand, and that is why most Americans or many Americans at least don't seem to agree that the consumer outlook, the economic outlook, is good. The consumer confidence level has dropped to its lowest point in 10 months this July. And more importantly as they look out over the next 6 months, consumers, according to most of the surveys, aren't very optimistic about the economy and things improving even with your economic plan.

The President. I think there are—[*inaudible*]—reasons for that. First of all, keep in mind, America's economic difficulties that most Americans face—that is, most people are working harder for lower wages and not keeping up with inflation, while health care and education and housing costs have outstripped inflation—those trends have been in the making for 20 years and are a function of our inability to adjust as well as we should have over those 20 years to the new challenges of the global economy. Secondly, there was a great deal of optimism right after I was elected, but you can't expect results overnight. These forces have been in play for years and years. You can't turn them around overnight. Thirdly, most of these people have been given an enormous amount of misinformation about what is actually in the economic plan. And finally as I tried to say in response to a lot of the very good questions which have been asked, this economic plan alone is not the answer. It is an essential first step. We still have to have a more aggressive trade policy to sell our products. We've still got to reinvest in the skills of our people. We've still got to have a good defense conversion policy. We've cut all these defense workers out without reinvesting in their potential to contribute to the economy.

So there are many other things we have to do. But once we do this, I think you'll see an upturn in confidence: We can move on the health care; we can move on the other job-creating policies; we can move on to welfare reform. And those things together will make a real difference in the economy and a real difference in the outlook for most Americans.

But most folks in this country have had a

pretty tough time for 20 years now. And I want to turn it around, but it is not going to happen overnight. And we have to have the courage and the fortitude and the constancy to take on a whole lot of issues and not expect a silver bullet or an easy answer.

Q. Mr. President, I wish we had more time, but thank you very much for being with us.

The President. Thank you, sir—[*inaudible*]—

and thank you, ladies and gentlemen.

NOTE: The interview began at 4:44 p.m. The President spoke via satellite from Room 459 of the Old Executive Office Building. In his remarks, he referred to Lodwrick M. Cook, chairman and chief executive officer, ARCO, and David Wilhelm, chairman of the National Democratic Committee.

Interview With the California Media
July 30, 1993

Q. I know you'd like to start out this afternoon with an opening remark, sir.

The President. I would, and thank you very much for allowing me to join you in this way. I hope I'll get back to the Central Valley in person before long. I had some wonderful times there during the election, and I'm glad to have the chance to visit with you directly.

As you know, in the next few days the Congress will take up a final vote on the economic plan, which they have been debating now since February. So far the Congress has moved with great speed in trying to deal with this plan and trying to keep its essential features intact. I want to just review those features today and why I think it's important as a first step in our long-term efforts in redeveloping the American economy and the California economy.

First, the plan will reduce the deficit by very close to $500 billion, equally divided between spending cuts and revenue increases, put in a trust fund so that the money cannot legally be spent on anything else but deficit reduction.

Secondly, the plan will ask of the tax increases that 70 percent at least of those come from people with incomes above $200,000, the top 1.2 percent of our economy, people who got most of the economic gains and a tax cut in the 1980's.

Thirdly, the middle class burden will be quite modest. I wish there didn't have to be any middle class tax, but the deficit has gotten much larger just since the election, and we have to address it now. And that burden will be for a middle class family of four with an income of between $40,000 and $60,000, less than $50 a year. Next, the plan holds working families

with incomes of under $30,000 a year harmless and gives the working poor, those who still live below the poverty line, actual tax relief so that we'll be able to say for the first time, if you work 40 hours a week and you have children in your home, you'd be lifted above the poverty line. This is a profoundly important thing.

And next, and perhaps most important for California, the plan has real incentives for private sector business growth: Incentives that the high-tech community in California wanted very badly for investments in new companies with $50 million a year or less in capitalization, big cuts for them; an increase in the expensing provision for small business that will give over 90 percent of the small business operations—and farms that qualify, too, I might add—a tax benefit, not a tax increase but a tax benefit when they reinvest in their businesses; next, an increase in the research and development tax credit; and finally, some incentives to invest in areas that are traditionally underdeveloped, both rural and urban areas, to get free enterprise in there to do that job.

So for all these reasons, this economic plan is good for the country, and it's good for California. It is not the end-all and be-all. We have to move on to health care. We have to move on to a trade policy that enables us to sell more of our products and services abroad. We have to move on to welfare reform. We have a crime bill. We have an immigration initiative up. All these things are important.

Secretary Babbitt is working with the farmers in your area to resolve some of your water problems. But all these things cannot be brought to fruition completely until we pass an economic plan and a budget and get this country moving again, keep the deficit down, and keep the interest rates down.

Let me finally say that this plan has the support of an enormous number of Republicans and independents who are not politicians and have no stake in misrepresenting the facts. Earlier this week, about 67 business leaders from around the country, including the heads of four energy companies, equally divided pretty much between Republicans and Democrats, endorsed this plan. And one of the people who endorsed it was Lod Cook, the chairman of ARCO, who was a cochairman of President Bush's campaign. So this is not a partisan effort on my part. It's just a tough decision to deal with problems that developed in Washington long before I showed up. And I hope the people of California and the Central Valley will support it.

I'll be glad to answer your questions.

Immigration

Q. Mr. President, you mentioned just a moment ago immigration. I'd like to ask you about that. As you know, we in California are struggling with the problem of immigration, both legal and illegal. One-third of all new arrivals in the United States wind up in California. I know you've asked for additional funds to speed up asylum processing and hearings and also border patrol, but we're wondering if $172 million in new dollars is enough. Can you offer any specific additional Federal help for California alone to try and deal with the immigration problem?

The President. Well, I'm glad you asked that. Let me, first of all, just reiterate very briefly what you said. We're trying to deal with, in effect, three different problems. We're trying to deal with the problem presented by the fact that our airports are too porous and terrorists or potential terrorists can get in, and we're trying to tighten up all those procedures in foreign airports and here. We're trying to deal with the problem of alien smuggling, which is something California is familiar with, by tightening the control procedures and also increasing penalties for that. And finally, we're trying to deal with illegal aliens coming into the country generally. We do have more border patrol people coming in, 600 of them. California will get a good number of them. And Senator Feinstein and Senator Boxer were both particularly active in this regard.

The second thing that I want to mention is that before any of this was done, we had changed some Federal laws in this economic plan to give California some more money under existing laws because it has a disproportionate burden of immigrants. So we'll be giving you some more money over and above this to handle the immigrant burden that's already there. That will free up some of your State money for other problems there in California.

I know you've had a lot of terrible budget problems. So we changed the formula by which the Federal Government gives money to the States to deal with immigration, to put more money into California because of your extra problems. And Leon Panetta, who, as you know, used to serve California in the Congress and is now my Budget Director, had a lot to do with that. I hope that will help. I believe it will.

Water Management

Q. Mr. President, I wanted to know—you mentioned a moment ago Secretary Babbitt coming to the Central Valley to talk about water issues. And one of the big water issues for us down here is the Endangered Species Act. What I wanted to know is, is the Act going to be changed at all in the next year or so to allow for economic burdens that are being suffered on the west side of the valley?

The President. Well, let me say first of all, the Act as it's presently written has an economic impact provision, which has not been used very often but which plainly can be used. Secretary Babbitt asked me before we commit to make any changes in that to give him the chance to work out the problems that the farmers had. As you know, we've had a drought for many years and the allocations this year, given the amount of water that's out there since the drought went away, has not satisfied a number of the farmers. And we know there are some other distributional issues. Some of them involve the Endangered Species Act, but Bruce Babbitt believes, anyway, that he can work out a fair treatment for the farmers without an amendment to the Act. And I think I ought to give him a chance to continue to work with the farmers before I commit to change it. So that's the position I'm going to take. I want to wait and see how he does with his negotiations with the farmers first and how they come out.

Crime

Q. Mr. President, we in Los Angeles, of course, have been crippled in terms of quality of life, and also economically, by burgeoning crime and not enough more police to fight it. Our new Mayor, Richard Riordan, was recently in Washington, as was police chief Willie Williams, both of them begging for assistance. Is there anything that your administration can do to help?

The President. Absolutely, there is. We intend to push a crime bill which, along with some other legislation we're pushing, will have the Federal Government help local communities to put up to 100,000 more police officers on the street in this country over the next 4 years.

This summer I got an emergency bill through Congress which will provide funds to Los Angeles and other cities to rehire police officers that have been laid off and otherwise staff up a little bit. It's a down payment on that. As soon as this budget—economic plan—is over in the Senate and in the House, I will be developing a crime bill which will provide more funds to local communities for this purpose. We have got to get some more police officers on the street.

When your new chief was a police chief in Philadelphia, he had some real success in lowering crime rates in very tough neighborhoods by adopting community policing strategies that included people actually walking beats that previously had only been driven. I know this can work. I actually walked down some of those streets that the chief helped to change in Philadelphia, and I talked to the people who live in the houses there. So I know it can make a difference. I saw play yards that had formerly been taken over by gangs and were unsafe for children now open for basketball for the kids.

We can do this. We're going to have to have more police. I hope that the crime bill will enjoy broad bipartisan support. We can bring it up if we can get this budget business done.

Agricultural Subsidies

Q. Mr. President, what farm policy have you and Secretary Espy outlined or are outlining? And would you consider any reductions or elimination of farm subsidies and irrigation subsidies?

The President. Well, let me say, first of all, if you look at our budget this year, because there are $250 billion in spending cuts over the previous budget, we have reduced some of the agricultural programs along with everything else. We've cut just about everything, so there is some reduction in agriculture. But I don't think we should do any more until we have an agreement on world trade. That is, I am reluctant to have more unilateral reduction in agricultural programs because I think that hurts our competitive position. If we can reach agreement on a new trade agreement with our competitors in which those nations that subsidize agriculture much more than we do also reduce their subsidies, then I would also support doing something here at home, because I'm convinced that on a level playing field our farmers can compete with anybody in the world.

So my answer to you, sir, would be I'm hoping we can get a new trade agreement by the end of the year which will permit some reduction in agricultural subsidies but only because our competitors will be reducing them even more. Otherwise, I think we'll have to wait 'til we reauthorize the farm bill in 1995 to look at these issues.

I come from a farming State, and I really want to see us maintain our competitive position in agriculture. I had to cut agriculture some this year. I cut everything, but I don't want to cut it so much we are at a competitive disadvantage.

1990 Deficit Reduction Program

Q. Mr. President, I was wondering if you believe that the deficit reduction plan of 1990 was successful in its goal of slashing the deficit. And if not, how can you assure America that this year's plan will work any better? What are the differences between the two plans?

The President. There are several differences. First of all, the 1990 plan was not completely successful for a couple of reasons, and I'd like to point out what was wrong with it. I'd also like, in fairness, to tell you a couple of good things about it.

The main thing that was wrong with it is that the administration and its supporters in Congress, the people who were in Washington then, made too many claims for it. That is, they said it would reduce the deficit by $480 billion, and they based that on wildly optimistic revenue growth forecasts. We have based our plan on very conservative revenue forecasts, so that when the recession continued, they didn't get the money they thought they were going to get out of any of the new revenues.

The second problem they had was that health

care costs in particular increased at a far more rapid rate than they had projected. We have attempted to deal with that by having some stricter controls on health care costs.

So those are the two things that really got them in trouble. The third thing, of course, was the economy just stayed in a slump for a long time. Now, the one thing they did right that we're also doing, except we're doing it even tougher, is they had some pretty stiff caps on spending programs, domestic spending programs. So there were some greater controls on spending after 1990 than had been the case in the past. I think I ought to give them credit for that, and we're trying to live with those now.

But we think we can do better. This plan you have more specific budget cuts, better controls on health care spending, and more realistic revenue estimates. And you've got all this money being put in the trust fund, and furthermore, another big difference is I will be under the obligation if we miss the deficit reduction target to come in on an annual basis and say, "Hey, we missed it a little. Here's my plan to make sure we make it. Here's where you've got to cut more. Here's what else you have to do." We're going to do that every year.

I think all Americans know it would be hard for any business to estimate for 5 years in advance exactly what will happen, but we haven't had to correct ourselves. Now we're going to do that.

I will say this. Let me say this in my own behalf. A reporter for the Philadelphia Inquirer a couple of weeks ago went around to all the budget experts for big private companies like big private accounting firms, and asked them what they thought of this. And the consensus was that we had a very good chance to meet our deficit reduction targets. The budget analyst for Price Waterhouse, the big accounting firm, said that it was the most honest budget presented to the Congress in more than a decade and that the only thing he thought I was wrong about is he thought we'd actually have more deficit reduction than we're projecting.

So let's hope he's right. We've done our best to be very tough about this.

Health Care

Q. Mr. President, you mentioned the importance of health care in the budget situation as we went through the nineties and into the early

nineties we're in now. I'm wondering what specifically we can look forward to as regards to health care reforms within the next 6 to 8 months.

The President. You can look forward to a plan which will, first of all, protect the health care benefits that Americans enjoy now and enable people to move their jobs without losing their health coverage. One real problem we've got now is millions of Americans locked into their jobs because somebody in their family's been sick. So I think you can look forward to ending the job lock. People will be able to move jobs. We'll have a system that will enable people to keep having health care for their families if they lose their jobs through no fault of their own.

If all the plan passes, we will reorganize the insurance markets so that farmers and self-employed people who are in nonfarm jobs will be able to purchase health insurance at lower rates, more generous insurance because they'll be able to purchase it more on terms that people who work for big employers purchase it today.

And we'll also have a system that, if it all goes through, will actually dramatically lower the rate of increase of health care. You know, health care costs have been going up at roughly twice the rate of inflation or 3 times the rate of inflation, and we've got to bring that within inflation plus our population growth. And that will be good for business, good for agriculture, and good for individual Americans. So those are the main things we're going to try to do. I think we'll be able to do it. It's very, very important.

Let me say that if you look at the American budget now, the only thing that's really going up a lot in the Government's budget is health care costs for Medicare and Medicaid. The only way we can take this deficit from where it is now down to zero, which is where I want it, is to do something to control health care costs. This plan will lower it for 4 or 5 years, after which it starts to go up again, unless you control health care costs. That is the thing that is strangling the American economy long-term. And I believe we can do better. That's what the health care plan is designed to do. And as soon as the economic plan is over, we'll be able to begin a great national discussion about that.

Jobs

Q. Mr. President, Governor Wilson predicts that in the next 2 years this State is going to— rather, in the next 5 years, this State is going to lose 2 million jobs. Your economic plan is boasting 1.9 million jobs, yet we're seeing an exodus of manufacturing jobs from the Central Valley. What is your plan proposing to do to try to keep some of these companies from leaving not only the State but the country and taking jobs elsewhere? And what's also being done in your plan to put more Californians to work?

The President. Let me talk about manufacturing specifically, if I might, about what we can do and what you have to do. And I'd like to establish my credentials. I was Governor of Arkansas for 12 years. When I became Governor of my State, we had an unemployment rate nearly 3 percentage points above the national average; we were losing manufacturing jobs rapidly, plants closing down like crazy. And we devised a plan to retrain our work force and to make our State more attractive to manufacturing. At a time when they said we were going to lose manufacturing jobs, we didn't even need to try that. We were able to increase the percentage of our work force involved in manufacturing.

For the last 4 or 5 years we were among the Nation's leaders in job growth. In 1992 we ranked first or second in every month. And now the State has an unemployment rate of about 5.2 percent. It took about 8 years to do that. But we did it, and it worked. So you can increase your manufacturing base. Now, what does the United States have to do to help California do that? I think in your case, three things. Number one, we've got to do something to help you with all these people who have been laid off or lost their jobs because of defense cutbacks. We started defense cuts in America in 1987. I wasn't in Washington when it started, but it was unconscionable to start cutting all these contracts with no plans for conversion to help companies, to help individuals, to help communities to maintain a manufacturing base in nondefense areas. We have an aggressive defense conversion plan that, if it's done right, will be greatly beneficial to California. We have already begun working on that.

Number two, our economic program has some significant incentives to promote manufacturing: incentives for bigger companies to invest in new plant and equipment, incentives to start and capitalize smaller manufacturing operations.

The third thing we're doing is finding new markets for American manufacturing. When I was in Tokyo recently, the world's seven industrial powers agreed to lower or eliminate tariffs in a sweeping fashion, more than has been done in years and years. And every independent analysis says that if we can get all the countries of the world that are in our trading group, the General Agreement on Tariffs and Trade, to accept this by the end of the year, it will put hundreds of thousands of manufacturing jobs back into the American economy in the next few years.

Now, if we do all that, that will help California. California also has to examine its situation. Why would someone close a plant down in California and move it to another State? What do you have to do to make the State more attractive? There are some things we can do on that. Our apprenticeship programs, our worker training programs will help California. Our health care cost control programs may help you not only with health care but with the enormous cost of worker's comp out there.

But a lot of these decisions need to be asked and answered in California. If California is losing manufacturing jobs to other States, you need to think through what changes can be made there to make you more competitive.

Small Business

Q. Mr. President, you said that your economic plan will provide most small businesses with a tax break. Won't these breaks be offset and surpassed by what you're going to ask small business to pay to support your new health care plan, and what kinds of increases can small business expect?

The President. No, well, let me answer—the short answer is no. Seventy percent of the small businesses in this country are providing some health coverage for their employees. Many of them may wind up with lower costs because of the insurance reforms that we'll recommend. Many of them are paying way too much for limited coverage.

For those who provide no coverage at all, I think there will be some requirement that they make a contribution to the coverage of their employees and that the employees provide a contribution, too. But the burden is likely to be far more modest than anything I've been reading about. I've not signed off on all the final provisions yet, but we're really working hard to make sure anything we do is phased in and the burden is kept as light as possible on small businesses to help them maintain their ability to generate jobs.

But let me just point out to you that everybody in this country can eventually get some health care, even if they have no health insurance. But if they don't have any health insurance, they often get it when it's too late and too expensive and when it's paid for by someone else. We are the only advanced nation that does not have some system by which all people are covered for health care. Most countries require some contribution by employers and employees across the board. We are also the only advanced nation in the world that spends more than 10 percent of its income on health care. We spend over 14 percent of our income on health care. Only one other nation, Canada, is over nine. Our major competitor, Germany, is just over 8 percent of their income. That means of every dollar made by anybody in this country, we're putting 6 cents more into health care. That is a phenomenal amount of money that might be reinvested to create manufacturing jobs, to strengthen agriculture, to strengthen small business.

So I believe the small business community as a whole will be dramatically strengthened by this, and I'm going to do everything I can to minimize the burden on those that presently offer nothing to their employees. But it is not responsible for those who offer nothing to ask everybody else to pay for the hospitals, the clinics, the infrastructure of health care that they then get to take advantage of when they need it.

California Recovery

Q. Mr. President, you talk about economic growth by creating new jobs in California. And we're seeing, like we said earlier, we're seeing a lot of jobs leaving the State. But from where you stand and from some of the things you pointed out, do you see a turnaround at all for California in the next year?

The President. I do for a couple of reasons. I think there will be a turnaround. I don't want to pretend that this is going to be an easy, quick miracle. I think there are some things that are going to have to be done to preserve your manufacturing base. I already said that.

But I think the likelihood is good that California will turn around for a couple of reasons. First of all, you have enormous human and physical resources. That is, a lot of these people who have lost their jobs are very well-trained,

very well-educated people, are highly productive workers, even if they don't have a lot of formal education. And have a huge infrastructure that can be revitalized, that was built up in part by defense developments in the 1980's.

Secondly, more than any other State involving trade, California's tied not only south of our border but also to the Pacific, and the Pacific is the area of the world most likely to revitalize its economy quickest. One of the things that's hurting you in California is that it's hard to make a lot of money off manufacturing and service jobs tied to trade when Japan's in a recession, when Europe's in a recession. For the last 5 years, more than half of our new jobs in America have been tied to trade. And if everything is flat everywhere else, it's hard for us to grow when they're not. It is more likely that the Pacific will grow more quickly and come out of this recession more quickly than the rest of the world. And that will disproportionately benefit California.

So for all those reasons, I think there'll be some turnaround by next year. But I don't want to kid you. The California economy was built up over the last 20 years, with some things that will carry you right into the next century and other things, like the defense base, which have to be refigured if you're going to have those folks doing well and making a contribution to your economy.

So we're going to have to make some changes. We can do it. But the intrinsic health of the California economy, I think, is still there.

One last point about that. We're also going to have to make an extra effort to help the areas that have been really hurt by base closings. The Bay Area, for example, which took a big hit, I think that they'll wind up net economic winners because of the enormous resources there.

But we're going to have to plan to do that. And we're going to have to have incentives to invest in places like the distressed areas of Los Angeles to bring free enterprise in there. And I've offered a dramatic plan to create those kinds of enterprise zones. I call them empowerment zones. It goes far beyond what previous administrations have recommended. That plan is working its way through Congress, and I think that will help.

Job Creation

Q. To go back to jobs, you're promising 8

million jobs nationwide and about 1.9 million in California. Smaller citywide programs like Build in Baltimore cost millions and failed miserably, creating low-paying temp jobs with no benefits. How is your plan going to succeed? What kind of jobs are going to be created? And do you have a timetable for the job creation?

The President. Most of the jobs that we believe, based on our economic analysis, will be created are private sector jobs that will be fulltime jobs. The private sector has got to be the engine of economic growth. If you look at this economic plan, we do invest some more money in partnerships for new technologies and in defense conversion and to help companies train their workers. But most of the new jobs are going to be created by the private sector. We want to invest in more jobs, in infrastructure building, road-building, and things of that kind.

But the great vast bulk of these jobs will be private sector jobs. Let me just give you some examples of how they'll be created. First of all, to keep interest rates down, you'll create more jobs. Secondly, this plan provides economic incentives for people to invest in new plant and equipment, for people to invest more in their small businesses, for people to do more research and development. All those things are directly related to job development. If you have more investment in the private sector, you will have more job development. So I see this as a private sector job initiative.

And exactly on what timetable these jobs will be created depends on the general recovery not only of the American economy but of the global economy. The one thing that could prevent us from meeting this goal is if the other countries of the world don't join us in a new trade agreement and pursue foolish economic policies and collapse their own economies. In order to grow the American economy, we need a growing world economy. But I think we're going to have some good success in coordinating our economic policies to generate more jobs.

Let me just say this. In spite of all the fits and starts in the economy since the beginning of the year, through the first 6 months, we've had about 900,000 new jobs created, over 90 percent of them private sector jobs. And I hope that we can accelerate that pace in the months and years ahead. I think we can if we can get this economic plan passed and put the health care plan out and, to respond to one of the earlier questions, to allay the fears of some of the people in the business community about the health care plan so they can see it will be good for business, not bad for business. Then I think you'll see a lot more investment coming out of the lower interest rates.

But most of this job growth is going to have to come in the private sector. The Government can't do it.

Q. Thank you, Mr. President. We've flat run out of time. We were going to try and squeeze in another couple of questions, but I guess we can't do it.

The President. I'll stay if you can.

Q. Well, hey, we'll stay. We'll stay all night. No satellite. We lost the satellite.

The President. They say we're going to lose the satellite. I'm sorry.

NOTE: The interview began at 5:20 p.m. The President spoke via satellite from Room 459 of the Old Executive Office Building.

Statement on Surgeon General Nominee Joycelyn Elders
July 30, 1993

I am pleased that the Senate Committee on Labor and Human Resources has recognized the talents and capabilities of Dr. Joycelyn Elders. As Surgeon General, she will be an effective advocate for clinical and educational programs to address the fundamental health and social problems that affect all Americans. I am especially grateful to Chairman Kennedy for his steady leadership during the committee's consideration of Dr. Elders' nomination. I look forward to her speedy confirmation by the full Senate.

Statement on Ending the Filibuster on National Service Legislation
July 30, 1993

By breaking the gridlock and ending the filibuster on national service today, the Senate scored two victories. It won one for the American people, but it also won one for the Senate itself, showing that when Democrats and Republicans work together, we can move America ahead.

National service will be America at its best, energizing our youth, meeting our Nation's needs, and reuniting all of us in the common work of citizenship. This legislation joins our Nation's finest traditions of building community, rewarding responsibility, and offering opportunity.

I want in particular to thank those Republicans who found the courage and vision to support this landmark legislation. When we put partisanship behind us and work together, we really can change America.

Remarks on the Economic Program
July 31, 1993

Good morning, and welcome to the Rose Garden.

My fellow Americans, 5 months ago when I addressed the Congress in my State of the Union Address, I pledged to the American people that I would do my best to change the way Washington works; to revive our economy by reducing our deficit; cutting spending; reversing trickle-down economics and asking the wealthiest Americans to pay their fair share of our tax burden; increasing incentives to business to create new jobs; helping the working poor to stay out of welfare and stay in the work force; and renewing the skills and productivity of our workers, our students, and our children. I presented to Congress an economic plan designed to achieve those objectives.

Now the Members of both Houses of Congress are close to deciding on a final version of an economic growth plan that meets these objectives. The plan will contain the largest deficit reduction plan in our Nation's history, about $500 billion, with nearly a quarter of a trillion dollars in real and enforceable spending cuts. The plan creates a trust fund in which all the spending cuts and all the tax increases are placed and dedicated by law for 5 years only to reducing our Nation's debt. Every new dollar of taxes will be matched by a dollar of spending cuts. And now, thanks to the efforts of the last few weeks, 80 percent of the new taxes will come from individuals earning over $200,000 a year, the top 1.2 percent of our income bracket, people who got most of the economic benefits of the 1980's and, unlike most Americans, also received tax cuts in that decade. No working family earning less than $180,000 will pay a penny more in income taxes. That will be a real change from the trickle-down economics of the past dozen years.

Average families, that is, people with family incomes above $30,000 and below $180,000, will be asked to pay but one tax, less than a dime a day, or about now $33 a year, in an energy tax devoted entirely to reducing our deficit. I believe that is a modest and fair price to pay for the change we seek and the progress it will bring. I pledged always in the beginning of this program to seek the least possible burden on middle income taxpayers, and I believe this is the least possible burden we can have and still achieve meaningful deficit reduction.

Because we need the private sector to grow, we also recommended investing in the job creating capacity of American business and in the education and skills of our people. This plan offers 90 percent of the small businesses in the United States of America the chance to actually reduce their tax burden if, but only if, they invest more in their businesses to strengthen their businesses and their capacity to hire new people. The plan offers new incentives, especially to high-tech, high-growth companies, to invest more in research and development. It offers incentives to larger companies to invest more in new plant and equipment. It gives a groundbreaking new incentive to people of all kinds to invest in new companies to help them grow the economy. A significant percentage of new American jobs come from the creation and expansion of new enterprises. And this plan will open the door of college education to millions of Americans by dramatically changing the way the student loan programs works.

And next week when the national service plan passes, these two plans together will enable us to say to the young people of this country: If you want to go to college now, you need not fear the costs. You can borrow the money, but you won't have to pay it back until you actually have a job. And if the job is a lower paying job, you will not be asked to pay more than a certain fixed percentage of your income in paying back the loan. But this time, you will have to pay it back, because the tax system will be used to help collect the loan. And if you want to work the loan off, you can do some of that by participating in a program of service to your community before, during, or after college. That will give us the chance to solve a lot of America's problems and educate a whole new generation of young Americans. All this is done without imposing harmful cuts on older Americans. We build a better future for our children without asking unreasonable sacrifice from their grandparents.

It is time for Congress to pass this plan. It is time for Washington to show the courage to change. It is time for the Members of Congress to roll back the fog of misinformation that has shrouded this whole debate for the last 5 months. To the people who have told the American people there is no deficit reduction, there are no spending cuts, and the burden is on the middle class, the facts of this plan stand in stark contrast. This plan will keep interest rates down and grow the American economy.

This week I had the honor of meeting with many Americans from all walks of life who are taking personal responsibility for their families, their workplaces, and their country. On Monday, I attended a conference that our administration sponsored in Chicago where workers and managers talked about how they could work together to improve the quality of their goods and services and increase the security of their jobs and incomes. I met an executive from Missouri who turned around a failing plant by sharing information and giving a sense of ownership to workers who previously had been totally shut out of all those decisions. Once he did that and the employees understood the big picture, they did better at their jobs, they turned the company around. Their jobs and incomes were more secure, and they're making money. I met a widow from Detroit with no prospect of a job, thinking she would have to go on welfare because of her children, perhaps forever. Instead, she found a job as a machinist after enrolling in a 6-year advanced training program. When she completes that program, instead of being on welfare she'll have the equivalent of a master's degree in engineering.

On Wednesday, I met with more than 60 corporate executives from all over America, from all kinds of companies. Many of these executives were Republicans who will have to pay higher taxes under this plan. But they had made the hard-headed decision that it was important to pass this economic plan because they knew that their companies, their shareholders, and their country would be better off if we reduced the Federal deficit, kept interest rates down, and got investment going back into the American economy. As the chief executive officer of one of these corporations said, it's time to quit fooling around and act.

And I want to tell you about one more group of people who are quiet heroes of this economy. On Thursday, I met with three families who work hard for low wages from the States of Georgia, Kentucky, and Oklahoma. Thanks to the earned-income tax credit in our Tax Code, which reduces the tax burden on low income workers, they are supporting their children instead of going on welfare. Now, this is very important, because 18 percent, almost one in five, of American workers today actually work for wages that will not support a family of four above the poverty line. This plan has a revolutionary expansion of the earned-income tax credit so that for the first time ever, we can say to American workers: If you work full time and you have children in your home, you will not live in poverty. The tax system will lift you out of poverty, not drive you into it. This is the biggest incentive for people we have ever provided to get off welfare and go to work, to reward work and family and responsibility. It is not a partisan issue; it is an American issue. And it will empower all kinds of Americans to seize a better life for themselves.

I'm proud a lot of Americans have decided to do what is right for themselves and their families. They're looking for new skills, looking for new ways to work with their bosses in the workplace. They're choosing work over welfare. I'm proud so many people now are tired of the old divisions in our country. They don't want to see this country divided between labor and management or Democrats and Republicans. They want us to unite as Americans.

As your Senators and Representatives conclude work on this budget, I'd like to say a special word to those of you here in the Rose Garden and all of those listening to me across the country. The time has come to act. Unless the Congress acts on this budget, we cannot remove the uncertainty that exists in the economy, we cannot continue to bring interest rates down, and we cannot possibly move on to the other challenges that await us. We still have to provide security and health care to all Americans and bring the cost of health care down within inflation. We still have to face the fact that we have to reform our welfare system. We still have to pass a crime bill to put 100,000 more police officers on the streets over the next 4 years. There are many challenges awaiting this Congress and our Nation, and we cannot move

on unless we pass this plan. And most importantly, we will not have a framework within which we can work for jobs and higher incomes for the American people.

If you believe we ought to do it, now is the time to make your voices heard. Your Senators and Representatives have been subject to an amazing amount of unfair pressure and flat wrong and false information. I need your help. Tell your Senators and your Representatives if they have the courage to finally bring this deficit down and turn the country in the right direction and create jobs, you would appreciate it, you will support it, and you will stand with them. Now is the time to act. We have talked and dawdled for long enough.

In 1980, this country had a $1 trillion national debt after 200 years. Today, it is $4 trillion. We have got to turn this around for our children, for our grandchildren. And funny enough, this is something that will help us all today, right now, too. I need your help, and I hope you'll tell your Senators and your Representatives the time has come to move forward.

Thank you, and good morning.

NOTE: The President spoke at 8:52 a.m. in the Rose Garden at the White House.

The President's Radio Address
July 31, 1993

Good morning. Five months ago in my State of the Union Address to Congress, I pledged to the American people that I would do my best to fulfill the campaign commitment of 1992 to change the way Washington works. That means reviving our economy by reducing our deficit; cutting spending; reversing trickle-down economics by asking the wealthiest Americans to pay their fair share of taxes; increasing incentives to business to create new jobs; helping the working poor; and renewing the skills and productivity of our workers, our students, and our children.

Now the Members of both Houses of Congress are preparing to decide on a final version of my economic growth plan that meets the objectives I discussed when I presented it 5 months ago. This plan will contain the largest

reduction in our deficit in the Nation's history. With nearly one quarter of a trillion dollars in real, enforceable spending cuts, every new dollar of taxes will be matched by a dollar of spending cuts. And 80 percent of the new taxes now will be raised from individuals earning over $200,000 a year. No working family earning less than $180,000 will pay more in income taxes. That will be a real change from the trickle-down economics of the past dozen years. The average family will pay only one tax, less than a dime a day in an energy tax devoted entirely to deficit reduction. That's about $33 a year for a family of four with an income of $40,000 or $50,000 a year. I think that's a modest and fair price to pay for the change we seek and the progress we're making. We pledged to have the lightest possible burden on the middle class; and I think that, we have done.

Because we need the private sector to grow, the plan provides investments in job-creating capacities of American business and in the education and skills of our people. For example, the plan supports small business by dramatically increasing the tax incentive they get to invest in their own operations. Under this plan, more than 90 percent of the small businesses in America will actually be eligible for a reduction in their taxes. The plan also gives other incentives to business for new plant and equipment, to invest in research and development for high-tech firms, to invest in new fast-growing firms that create so many of our jobs. And perhaps most important to many middle class families, this plan opens the doors of college for millions of families by reforming the student loan program and making college affordable again to all Americans.

We do all this without imposing harmful cuts on programs that benefit older Americans, and building a better future for our children without asking unreasonable sacrifice from their grandparents. It's time for Congress to pass this plan. It's time for Washington to show the courage to change, just as people all across America are showing that kind of courage.

This week I had the honor of meeting with many Americans who are taking personal responsibility for making their lives and our country even better. On Monday, I attended a conference in Chicago where workers and managers talked about how they can work together to improve the quality of their goods and services, increase the strength and security of their own jobs and incomes. I met an executive from Missouri who turned around a failing plant by sharing information with employees about the company's performance. When the employees understood the big picture, they did even better at their jobs. And I met a woman from Detroit who got a job as a machinist after enrolling in a 6-year advanced training program. When she completes the program, she'll have the equivalent of a master's degree in engineering.

On Wednesday, I met with more than 60 corporate executives who support my economic growth plan. Many of them are Republicans who will have to pay higher taxes under the plan. But they made the hard-headed economic decision that their companies, their shareholders, and their country will be better off with this

economic plan because it means lower deficits, lower interest rates, and a more stable environment to grow. As the chief executive officer of one of these corporations said, it's time to quit fooling around and pass the plan.

And I want to tell you about one more group of people who are quiet heroes in our economy. On Thursday, I met with three families who work hard for low wages. Thanks to the earned-income tax credit, which under this plan reduces the tax burden on low income workers, they can support their children without going on welfare. This plan increases that earned-income tax credit so that we can finally tell every working parent in America: If you work full time and you have children at home, we will lift you out of poverty. This will have more to do with encouraging people to get off welfare and go to work than anything else we've done.

I'm proud that so many people have the courage to learn new skills, to choose work over welfare, to look beyond the old divisions between labor and management, between Democrats and Republicans, to the things that unite us as Americans. These people are ready to change.

As your Senators and Representatives conclude work on our budget, I'd like to say a special word to each of you listening to me today. There's been a lot of misinformation about this economic plan. Now you know the truth: $500 billion in deficit reduction, equally divided between cuts and revenues; 80 percent of the new revenue is going to the top 1.2 percent of our people; a trust fund so that all the money goes to reduce the deficit; real investments to help the working poor, to help middle class families sending their children to college, without undue cuts on the elderly.

This is a new economic direction for our country. If you want it, if you want the jobs it will provide and the growth for our economy, you must make your voices heard. Tell your Senators and Representatives that this plan, with its deficit reduction, with its lower interest rates, with its investment in private sector jobs, means more jobs and a better future for America, and it is time to pass it.

Thank you for listening.

NOTE: This address was recorded at 8:40 a.m. in the Oval Office at the White House for broadcast at 10:06 a.m.

Statement on the Death of Representative Paul B. Henry
July 31, 1993

Hillary and I received the news of Congressman Paul Henry's passing with deep sadness. It's tragic when such a productive and promising life is cut short so much before its time. His personal courage and bravery will be an inspiration for us. Our thoughts and prayers are with his family.

Appendix A—Digest of Other White House Announcements

The following list includes the President's public schedule and other items of general interest announced by the Office of the Press Secretary and not included elsewhere in this book.

January 20

Following the Inaugural luncheon at the Capitol, the President and Hillary Clinton went by motorcade along the parade route to the White House, where they viewed the Inaugural parade from the reviewing stand. In the evening, they attended several Inaugural balls.

January 21

In the morning, the President and Hillary Clinton held an open house for the American people in the Diplomatic Reception Room at the White House.

In the afternoon, the President met with senior staff members in the Roosevelt Room, after which he and Hillary Clinton hosted a reception in the State Dining Room for their family and friends from Arkansas.

January 22

In the morning, the President attended a reception for Cabinet members.

January 23

In the morning, the President had telephone conversations with President Boris Yeltsin of Russia and Prime Minister Yitzhak Rabin of Israel.

The President later met with Chairman of the National Economic Council Robert E. Rubin.

January 25

In the afternoon, the President met at the White House with the Joint Chiefs of Staff.

The President appointed John D. Hart as Deputy Assistant to the President and Deputy Director of the Office of Intergovernmental Affairs, and Arthur Jones and Lorraine Voles as Deputy White House Press Secretaries.

January 27

In the afternoon, the President met with Democratic congressional leaders.

January 28

In the morning, the President met with Federal Reserve Board Chairman Alan Greenspan, Secretary of the Treasury Lloyd Bentsen, and Chairman of the National Economic Council Robert E. Rubin.

Later in the morning, the President and Hillary Clinton attended funeral services at the Washington National Cathedral for Justice Thurgood Marshall.

In the afternoon, the President met with:
—Susan Maxman, president, American Institute of Architects, and Kevin Roche, recipient of the 1993 medal of the American Institute of Architects;
—Richard English, a participant in the Make-A-Wish Foundation, and his family.

January 29

The President met at the White House with the Vice President and Senator George J. Mitchell. Later, he met with economic advisers.

January 30

In the morning, the President and Hillary Clinton went to Camp David, MD, for a retreat with the Cabinet and White House senior staff members.

January 31

In the afternoon, the President and Hillary Clinton returned to the White House from Camp David, MD.

February 2

In the morning, the President met with Democratic congressional leaders at the Capitol. In the afternoon, he met with economic advisers at the White House.

February 4

In the morning, the President met with House Democratic leaders at the Capitol.

In the afternoon, the President met at the White House with:
—Girl Scouts from Los Angeles, CA;
—women athletes representing the Women's Sports Foundation on National Women and Girls in Sports Day;
—freshman Members of Congress.

February 5

In the afternoon, the President met in the Blue Room with representatives of the American Association of Retired Persons.

The President designated the following persons for the positions indicated:

James H. Quello, Chair of the Federal Communications Commission on an interim basis;
Elizabeth Anne Moler, Chair of the Federal Energy Regulatory Commission on an interim basis;
Gail C. McDonald, Chair of the Interstate Commerce Commission on an interim basis; and

John A. Gannon, Acting Chairperson of the National Council on Disability.

February 8

The President appointed Kathleen McGinty as Deputy Assistant to the President and Director of the White House Office on Environmental Policy.

February 10

In the afternoon, the President traveled to Detroit, MI, where he attended private receptions at WXYZ-TV. He returned to Washington, DC, in the evening.

February 11

In the morning, the President met with:
—the Washington, DC, Mardi Gras queen;
—the Vice President, for lunch;
—congressional leaders.

February 12

In the morning, the President and Hillary Clinton toured the Fenwick Center health clinic in Arlington, VA.

February 14

In the morning, the President went to Haines Point in East Potomac Park, where he signed the proclamation designating February as American Heart Month and then ran in the American Heart Association's Run for Heart.

February 15

In the morning, the President had a telephone conversation with President François Mitterrand of France.

February 16

In the afternoon, the President toured a road construction site at South Dakota Avenue NE and met with construction workers.

February 17

At noon, the President had lunch with news media anchors. In the afternoon, he met with Secretary of State Warren Christopher and later had a telephone conversation with Ross Perot.

February 18

In the afternoon, the President traveled to St. Louis, MO. In the evening, he traveled to Chillicothe, OH.

February 19

In the morning, the President held interviews with local TV stations in Chillicothe.

In the afternoon, the President traveled to Hyde Park, NY, where he visited the Franklin D. Roosevelt Library and held interviews with local media before returning to Washington, DC, in the evening.

February 20

The President announced that he will nominate Mary Jo Bane to be Assistant Secretary of Health and Human Services for Children and Families.

February 21

In the morning, the President traveled to Santa Monica, CA, and in the afternoon, he traveled to Los Angeles and San Jose.

In the evening, the President had dinner with chief executive officers of California-based companies in Los Gatos, CA.

February 22

In the morning, the President toured Silicon Graphics in Mountain View, CA. In the afternoon, he traveled to Everett, WA, and he returned to Washington, DC, in the evening.

The President announced his nomination of Frank Wisner to be Under Secretary for Policy at the Department of Defense. He also announced his intention to nominate the following individuals for the posts listed:

Department of Defense

John Deutch, Under Secretary for Acquisition

Department of Energy

Thomas P. Grumbly, Assistant Secretary for Environmental Restoration and Management

Susan Fallows Tierney, Assistant Secretary for Domestic and International Energy Policy

Department of Health and Human Services

Walter Broadnax, Deputy Secretary

David Ellwood, Assistant Secretary for Planning and Evaluation

Jerry Klepner, Assistant Secretary for Legislation

Avis LaVelle, Assistant Secretary for Public Affairs

Harriet Rabb, General Counsel

Fernando Torres-Gil, Commissioner on Aging, Administration on Aging

Department of the Interior

Robert Armstrong, Assistant Secretary for Land and Mineral Management

Jim Baca, Director, Bureau of Land Management

Bonnie Cohen, Assistant Secretary for Policy, Management and Budget

George Frampton, Assistant Secretary for Fish and Wildlife and Parks

John Leshy, Solicitor

Elizabeth Reike, Assistant Secretary for Water and Science

Leslie Turner, Assistant Secretary for Territorial and International Affairs

Department of Labor

Geri Palast, Assistant Secretary for Congressional and Intergovernmental Relations

Thomas Williamson, Jr., Solicitor

Department of the Treasury

Peggy Richardson, Commissioner of the Internal Revenue Service

Jeffrey Shafer, Assistant Secretary for International Affairs

February 24

In the evening, the President had a working dinner with Prime Minister John Major of the United Kingdom.

February 25

In the morning, the President met at the White House with:

—Representative Eva Clayton;

—representatives of the Business Council.

In the afternoon, the President met at the White House with:

—the crew of the space shuttle *Endeavour*;

—members of the Wine Institute;

—members of Future Farmers of America;

—congressional leaders.

February 26

In the late morning, the President attended a reception at American University.

The White House announced that the President has invited the following world leaders to the White House for working visits: NATO Secretary General Manfred Woerner (March 2), President François Mitterrand of France (March 9), Prime Minister Yitzhak Rabin of Israel (March 15), President Jean Bertrand Aristide of Haiti (March 16), Prime Minister Albert Reynolds of Ireland (March 17), Chancellor Helmut Kohl of Germany (March 26), and President Hosni Mubarak of Egypt (April 6).

The White House announced the following departmental appointments:

Diana Josephson, Deputy Under Secretary for Oceans and Atmosphere, Department of Commerce;

Stephanie Solien, Assistant to the Secretary for Congressional and Intergovernmental Affairs, Department of the Interior;

Judy Feder, Deputy Assistant Secretary for Planning and Evaluation, Department of Health and Human Services; and

Anne Lewis, Deputy Assistant Secretary for Public Affairs, Department of Health and Human Services.

March 1

In the morning, the President traveled to New Brunswick, NJ, and he returned to Washington, DC, in the afternoon.

March 2

In the morning, the President went to the Capitol, where he met with House Republican leaders and then attended a luncheon with Senate Republican leaders in the afternoon.

Later in the afternoon, the President met with the National Association of State Treasurers and with the National Association of Counties.

The White House announced the following departmental appointments at the Environmental Protection Agency:

Loretta Ucelli, Associate Administrator for Communications, Education and Public Affairs; and

Robert Hickmott, Associate Administrator for Congressional and Legislative Affairs.

March 4

In the afternoon, the President met at the White House with:

—the Vice President, for lunch;

—former President Jimmy Carter;

—DC public school students;

—Westinghouse Science Talent Search finalists.

The President declared that a major disaster existed in the State of Washington and ordered Federal aid to supplement State and local recovery efforts in areas struck by severe storms and high winds on January 20–21.

The President declared that a major disaster existed in the State of Georgia and ordered Federal aid to supplement State and local recovery efforts in areas struck by tornadoes, high winds, and heavy rain on February 21–22.

March 5

The White House announced that the President transmitted to the Congress the 1993 Trade Policy Agenda and the 1992 annual report on the Trade Agreements Program.

March 8

The President had a telephone conversation with former President George Bush to discuss the situation in Russia.

In the afternoon, the President met with members of the House Budget Committee. In the evening, he met with former President Richard Nixon.

March 9

In the afternoon, the President met with Democratic Senators.

In the evening, the President attended a birthday party for Senator Strom Thurmond at the J.W. Marriott Hotel.

March 11

In the morning, the President traveled to Linthicum, MD, where he toured the Westinghouse Electronic Systems plant. In the afternoon, he returned to Washington, DC.

Later in the afternoon, the President met at the White House with:

—departing White House military personnel;

—Special Olympics international athletes;
—recipients of the Presidential Secondary Awards for Excellence in Science and Mathematics Teaching.

March 12

In the morning, the President traveled to the U.S.S. *Theodore Roosevelt* at sea, where he toured the ship. He returned to Washington, DC, in the afternoon.

The White House announced that Prime Minister Giuliano Amato of Italy will meet with the President at the White House on April 26.

The President announced his intention to nominate Kenneth S. Apfel to be Assistant Secretary for Management and Budget and Philip R. Lee to be Assistant Secretary for Health at the Department of Health and Human Services.

March 15

The White House announced that Prime Minister Kiichi Miyazawa of Japan will meet with the President at the White House on April 16.

The President appointed Mary Ann Campbell as Chair of the National Women's Business Council. She is currently a member of the Council.

March 16

In the morning, the President met with Senators from Western States.

March 17

In the morning, the President met with the governing board of the Electronics Industry Association.

In the afternoon, the President and Prime Minister Albert Reynolds of Ireland attended the Friends of Ireland St. Patrick's Day luncheon at the Capitol.

The President announced his approval for the following departmental appointments at the Department of the Interior:

Brooks Yeager, Director of Program Resources Management;
Kevin Sweeney, Director of Communications; and
Thomas Williams, Deputy Assistant Secretary for Fish, Wildlife, and Parks.

The President announced his intention to nominate the following individuals for the posts listed:

Eugene Branstool, Assistant Secretary of Agriculture for Marketing and Inspection Services;
Lionel Skipwith Johns, Associate Director for Technology, Office of Science and Technology Policy;
Daniel Beard, Commissioner, Bureau of Reclamation, Department of the Interior;
Mary Lou Keener, General Counsel, Department of Veterans Affairs;
Edward Scott, Assistant Secretary of Veterans Affairs for Congressional Affairs; and
Joe Shuldiner, Assistant Secretary of Housing and Urban Development for Public and Indian Housing.

March 18

In the morning, the President met with Democratic Senators. Later, he toured the Department of the Treasury.

In the afternoon, the President had lunch with the Vice President and afterwards met with the Black Publishers Association.

In the late afternoon, the President met with the President of the Commission of the European Communities, Jacques Delors, and then with recipients of the White House News Photographers Association awards.

In the evening, the President attended the Radio and Television Correspondents Association dinner at the Washington Hilton.

The White House announced that the President has invited the President of the European Council, Prime Minister Poul Nyrup Rasmussen of Denmark, and the President of the Commission of the European Communities, Jacques Delors, to the White House for the biannual Presidential consultations between the European Community and the United States on May 7.

March 19

In the morning, the President traveled to Atlanta, GA, and he returned to Washington, DC, in the evening.

March 21

In the morning, the President traveled to Little Rock, AR.

March 22

In the evening, the President returned to Washington, DC.

March 24

In the afternoon, the President met with Gov. Pedro J. Rossello of Puerto Rico.

March 25

In the afternoon, the President had lunch with the Vice President. He then met with:
—Foreign Minister Anatoliy Zlenko of Ukraine;
—Easter Seal Society representatives;
—the University of Alabama Crimson Tide football team.

In the evening, the President hosted a working dinner for Members of the House of Representatives.

March 26

In the afternoon, the President hosted a White House tour for Chancellor Helmut Kohl of Germany.

In the evening, the President hosted a working dinner for Members of the Senate.

The White House announced that the President has assigned Secretary of Commerce Ronald H. Brown to lead a Cabinet-wide effort on the application of the President's national economic strategy to the specific economic problems of California.

March 27

In the evening, the President attended the Gridiron dinner at the Capital Hilton.

March 28

In the morning, the President traveled to Little Rock, AR.

March 30

In the afternoon, the President returned to Washington, DC.

The White House announced that the President made available fiscal year 1993 emergency appropriations for the Departments of Agriculture and Education to provide assistance to victims of recent natural disasters.

April 1

In the morning, the President traveled to Annapolis, MD, where he had lunch with U.S. Naval Academy midshipmen.

In the afternoon, the President traveled to Portland, OR.

April 2

In the evening, the President met at the Oregon Convention Center in Portland with a group of Governors who attended the Forest Conference.

The President declared that major disasters existed in New York, following the February 26 bombing of the World Trade Center, and in Nebraska, as a result of severe March flooding and ice jams. The disaster declarations allow the Federal Emergency Management Agency to provide public assistance grants to affected municipalities in the two States.

The President announced that he intends to nominate the following individuals for the posts listed:

Victor Jackovich, Ambassador to Bosnia and Herzegovina;

Walter Slocombe, Deputy Under Secretary of Defense for Policy; and

Ellen Haas, Assistant Secretary of Agriculture for Food and Consumer Services.

The President designated William Hathaway to be Chair of the Federal Maritime Commission.

The President appointed William Timbers as Transition Manager at the U.S. Enrichment Corporation.

April 3

In the morning, the President traveled to Vancouver, Canada, where he met with Prime Minister Brian Mulroney at the residence of the president of the University of the British Columbia. Later in the morning, President Clinton and President Boris Yeltsin of Russia attended a luncheon hosted by Prime Minister Mulroney.

In the afternoon, President Clinton and President Yeltsin toured the Museum of Anthropology.

In the evening, President Clinton hosted a working dinner for President Yeltsin.

April 4

In the morning, the President attended Palm Sunday services at the First Baptist Church in Vancouver.

April 5

In the early morning, the President returned to Washington, DC, from Vancouver, Canada.

The President approved the designation of Tony E. Gallegos to chair the Equal Employment Opportunity Commission on an interim basis. He is currently a member of the Commission.

April 6

The President announced his approval of the appointments by Secretary of Commerce Ronald H. Brown of Kent Hughes as Associate Deputy Secretary and Wilbur Hawkins as Deputy Assistant Secretary for Economic Development.

April 8

In the morning, the President met with Secretary of Defense Les Aspin and the Joint Chiefs of Staff at the Pentagon.

Later in the morning, the President and Hillary Clinton traveled to Little Rock, AR.

April 9

In the afternoon, the President and Hillary Clinton attended a memorial service for her father, Hugh Rodham, at the First United Methodist Church in Little Rock.

The White House announced that the President would send to the Congress proposed legislation to extend congressional fast track procedures to conclude the Uruguay round of the multilateral trade negotiations.

April 10

In the morning, the President and Hillary Clinton traveled from Little Rock, AR, to Scranton, PA, where they attended funeral services for her father. In the evening, they traveled to Camp David, MD, for the weekend.

The White House announced that the President has asked Gen. John W. Vessey, Jr., to travel to Vietnam on April 18–19 to assess Vietnamese cooperation on accounting of American POW/MIA's and to seek further progress.

April 12

In the morning, the President and Hillary Clinton returned to the White House from a weekend stay at Camp David, MD.

April 13

In the afternoon, the President attended the "Especially Arkansas" exhibit at the Willard Hotel.

In a ceremony on the State Floor, the President received diplomatic credentials from Ambassadors Ricardo Luna Mendoza of Peru, Siragatour Ibrahim Cisse of Mali, Teboho Ephraim Kitleli of Lesotho,

Mohamad Al-Sabah of Kuwait, Jorge Montano of Mexico, Fayez Tarawneh of Jordan, Henrik Liljergren of Sweden, Ojars Kalnins of Latvia, Helmut Turck of Austria, Hafiz Pashayev of Azerbaijan, Itamar Rabinovich of Israel, and Sheikh Abdulrahman al-Thani of Qatar.

April 15

In the morning, the President met with Gen. John W. Vessey, Jr., Special Emissary for POW/MIA Affairs. In the afternoon, he had lunch with the Vice President.

April 16

The White House announced the President's initiative on telecommunications encryption technology.

April 17

In the morning, the President traveled to Pittsburgh, PA, and he returned to Washington, DC, in the afternoon.

April 19

In the evening, the President toured the U.S. Holocaust Memorial Museum.

The President announced his intention to appoint Beth Nolan, currently serving in the White House Counsel's Office, to the National Commission on Judicial Discipline and Removal.

April 20

In the morning, the President went jogging with Senator Harris Wofford and members of the District of Columbia National Service Corps.

The President appointed James A. Baker III to lead the Presidential delegation to the state funeral of President Turgut Ozal of Turkey in Ankara on April 21.

April 21

In the morning, the President went jogging with Boston Mayor Raymond Flynn and six winners of the Boston Marathon. Later, the President met with Gen. John W. Vessey, Jr., Special Emissary for POW/MIA Affairs.

In the afternoon, the President met at the White House with:

—President Lech Walesa of Poland;
—President Chaim Herzog of Israel;
—President Mario Soares of Portugal;
—President Franjo Tudjman of Croatia;
—President Ion Iliescu of Romania;
—President Zhelyu Zhelev of Bulgaria;
—President Arpad Goncz of Hungary;
—President Milan Kucan of Slovenia;
—President Václav Havel of the Czech Republic;
—President Michal Kovac of the Slovak Republic;
—Prime Minister Aleksandr Meksi of Albania;
—Prime Minister Andrei Nicholas Sangheli of Moldova.

In the evening, the President and Hillary Clinton hosted a private reception at Blair House.

April 23

The President announced his intention to nominate the following individuals for the posts listed:

Robert Nordhaus, General Counsel at the Department of Energy;
Robert Hunter, Ambassador to NATO; and
Bruce Lehman, Assistant Secretary of Commerce and Commissioner of Patents and Trademarks.

The President appointed Nan Hunter to be Deputy General Counsel at the Department of Health and Human Services.

The President announced his intention to nominate Secretary of Housing and Urban Development Henry G. Cisneros, Assistant to the President Alexis M. Herman, and Secretary of Agriculture Michael Espy to serve on the Martin Luther King, Jr., Federal Holiday Commission.

The President designated Secretary of Commerce Ron Brown to serve as Vice Chair of the National Women's Business Council.

April 24

In the morning, the President and Hillary Clinton traveled to Jamestown, VA, where they went sightseeing with several family members. Later, the President traveled to Williamsburg, where he attended the Senate Democrats Conference.

April 25

In the morning, the President traveled from Williamsburg, VA, to Boston, MA. In the evening, he returned to Washington, DC.

April 26

The President announced the establishment of a National Biological Survey, to be created by reorganizing and upgrading current biological research programs within the Department of the Interior.

April 27

In the afternoon, the President met with congressional leaders.

In the evening, the President attended a reception honoring Joe Moakley at the Hyatt Regency Hotel and later attended the National Endowment for Democracy reception at the Capitol Hilton.

The President declared that major disasters existed in the following States:

—Oklahoma, as a result of severe storms on April 24;
—Oregon, as a result of an earthquake on March 25; and
—Iowa, as a result of severe storms and flooding on March 26.

In addition, the President approved expanded emergencies in Alabama and North Carolina, following severe snowstorms on March 15 and March 13–17, respectively.

April 28

In the afternoon, the President had lunch with the Vice President. In the evening, he hosted a working dinner for Members of the House of Representatives.

April 29

In the afternoon, the President and Hillary Clinton met with King Juan Carlos I and Queen Sofia of Spain.

In the evening, the President attended a reception for representatives of G–7 member nations at Blair House.

April 30

In the morning, the President traveled to New Orleans, LA, and he returned to Washington, DC, in the evening.

May 1

In the evening, the President attended the White House Correspondents' Association dinner at the Washington Hilton.

The White House announced that the President has appointed Secretary of Health and Human Services Donna E. Shalala to head the delegation to the funeral of African National Congress leader Oliver Tambo in Johannesburg, South Africa, on May 2.

May 3

The President announced that he has selected Adm. David E. Jeremiah, Vice Chairman of the Joint Chiefs of Staff, as his special representative to the Australian-American Friendship Week activities in Canberra, Australia, from April 30 to May 8.

May 5

In the afternoon, the President hosted a working lunch for a group of Democratic Senators.

The White House announced that the President has asked Robin L. Raphel, a career Foreign Service officer, to be his personal representative at the funeral of slain Sri Lankan President Ranasinghe Premadasa in Colombo, Sri Lanka, on May 6.

May 6

In the afternoon, the President hosted a working lunch for a group of Republican Senators. In the evening, he met with members of the Senate Finance Committee.

May 7

In the evening, the President and Hillary Clinton attended a reception in honor of the Commander in Chief and a Marine Corps evening parade at the Marine Barracks.

The President designated Securities and Exchange Commission member Mary Schapiro as Acting Chair of the SEC pending the confirmation of Chair-designate Arthur Levitt, Jr.

May 8

In the morning, the President met with national security advisers.

May 9

In the afternoon, the President and Hillary Clinton toured an exhibit of French paintings at the National Gallery of Art.

May 10

In the morning, the President traveled to Cleveland, OH, and Chicago, IL.

May 11

In the afternoon, the President returned from Chicago, IL, to Washington, DC.

May 12

In the afternoon, the President traveled to New York City, and he returned to Washington, DC, in the evening.

The White House announced that the President transmitted to the Congress amendments to fiscal year 1994 appropriations requests for the Departments of Education and Agriculture.

May 13

In the afternoon, the President had lunch with the Vice President. He then met with members of the National Association of Private Enterprise and a group of departing White House military aides.

The President announced his approval of the following departmental appointments:

John Horsley, Deputy Assistant Secretary of Transportation for Governmental Affairs;

Kathryn Kahler, Director of Communications at the Department of Education;

Ken Thorpe, Deputy Assistant Secretary of Health and Human Services for Planning and Evaluation; and

Susan Levine, Deputy Assistant Secretary of the Treasury for International Development and Debt Policy.

The President declared the following States major disaster areas:

—Vermont and Maine, as a result of lake and river flooding caused by heavy rain and melting snow;

—Oklahoma, as a result of storms, tornadoes, and flooding;

—Missouri, due to damage resulting from heavy and continuous rainfall; and

—Iowa, due to severe storms and flooding.

May 14

In the afternoon, the President met with President Mary Robinson of Ireland.

The President appointed Clifton H. Hoofman as a member of the National Council on Surface Transportation and Frances M. Visco as a member of the President's Cancer Panel.

May 15

In the afternoon, the President and Hillary Clinton attended the U.S. Air Force Thunderbirds aerial demonstration at Andrews Air Force Base in Camp Springs, MD. Later, they traveled to New York City, returning to Washington, DC, late that night.

May 16

In the afternoon, the President and Chelsea Clinton attended a family picnic at Sidwell Friends School. Later in the afternoon, the President attended a health care meeting.

May 17

In the morning, the President traveled to Los Alamos, NM, where he toured the Supercomputer Center and the Plasma Implantation Facility at the Los Alamos National Laboratory. In the afternoon, the President traveled to San Diego, CA.

May 18

In the morning, the President traveled from San Diego to Los Angeles, CA, where he toured a laboratory at Los Angeles Valley College.

In the afternoon, the President visited a sporting goods store in south central Los Angeles, where he played basketball with community members. In the evening, he returned to Washington, DC.

May 19

In the morning, the President met with members of the Democratic Caucus and Democratic leaders on Capitol Hill.

The White House announced that the President has invited President Sam Nujoma of Namibia to meet with him in Washington, DC, on June 16.

May 20

In the afternoon, the President had lunch with the Vice President.

May 22

In the morning, the President traveled to Stratham, NH, and he returned to Washington, DC, in the evening.

May 25

In the morning, the President met with freshman Democratic Members of Congress.

May 26

The President appointed Norman R. Augustine as Chair and William T. Esrey as Vice Chair of the President's National Security Telecommunications Advisory Committee (NSTAC). He also named Joseph T. Gorman and Albert F. Zettlemoyer to the NSTAC.

May 27

In the afternoon, the President had lunch with the Vice President. He then met with winners of the U.S. FIRST science competition.

May 28

In the morning, the President traveled to Philadelphia, PA, where he attended private receptions, and he returned to Washington, DC, in the evening.

May 29

In the morning, the President traveled to West Point, NY, and he returned to Andrews Air Force Base, MD, in the afternoon. The President and Hillary Clinton then traveled to Camp David, MD, for the weekend.

May 31

In the morning, the President and Hillary Clinton returned to the White House from Camp David and had breakfast with representatives of veterans groups. Later in the morning, the President visited Arlington National Cemetery, VA, where he placed a wreath at the Tomb of the Unknowns. In the afternoon, the President participated in a wreath-laying ceremony at the Vietnam Veterans Memorial.

June 1

In the morning, the President traveled to Milwaukee, WI, and he returned to Washington, DC, in the evening.

The White House announced that the President signed H.R. 1378, Making Technical Corrections in Defense-Related Laws.

June 2

In the morning, the President participated with former Georgetown University classmates in a clean-up project sponsored by the Marshall Heights Community Development Organization at Watts Branch Park.

June 3

In the morning, the President traveled to Frederick, MD, and he returned to Washington, DC, in the afternoon.

June 4

In the afternoon, the President met with:
—the Vice President;
—Justice Department officials;
—civil rights leaders.

The White House announced that the President sent to the Congress requests for fiscal year 1993 supplemental appropriations.

June 5

In the evening, the President hosted a reunion gala for former Georgetown University classmates.

June 6

In the evening, the President attended a reception at Hickory Hill, the Kennedy estate in McLean, VA.

June 9

In the morning, the President and Hillary Clinton attended Chelsea Clinton's eighth grade graduation ceremony at Sidwell Friends School.

June 10

In the afternoon, the President met with:
—Jean Nickel, winner of the National Multiple Sclerosis Society's Mother of the Year award;
—Bob Jester, winner of the National Multiple Sclerosis Society's Father of the Year award;
—Dana Stephenson and Beth Troutman, recipients of America's National Teenager Scholarship Program;
—Gabrielle Fleekop, a participant in the Make-A-Wish Foundation program.

The President announced his intention to appoint Merrill D. Peterson, Thomas Jefferson professor of history emeritus at the University of Virginia, as Chairman of the Thomas Jefferson Commemoration Commission. The President also named the following persons as Commission members:

John T. Casteen III, president, University of Virginia;
James K. Golden, professor emeritus, Ohio State University;
H. Draper Hunt, professor of history, University of Southern Maine;
Russell E. Dickenson, former director, National Park Service;
James R. Thompson, former Governor of Illinois; and
George Taylor Stewart, president, the Foundation for Jefferson's Poplar Forest.

June 11

In the afternoon, the President had lunch with Judge Stephen Breyer.

Later in the afternoon, the President received diplomatic credentials from Ambassadors John de Chastelain of Canada, Rouben Robert Shugarian of Armenia, Edmond A. Mulet Lesieur of Guatemala, Mukhamed Bobir Malikov of Uzbekistan, and Amos Bernard Muvengwa Midzi of Zimbabwe.

The White House announced that the Domestic Policy Council has formed a Working Group on Welfare Reform, Family Support, and Independence to be chaired by Bruce Reed, Deputy Assistant to the President for Domestic Policy; David Ellwood, Assistant Secretary of Health and Human Services for Planning and Evaluation; and the Assistant Secretary of Health and Human Services for Children and Families, after a nominee for that position is confirmed by the Senate.

June 12

The President declared that a major disaster existed in Minnesota following severe storms, flooding, and tornadoes on May 6–19.

June 13

In the evening, the President and Hillary Clinton hosted a reception for members of the White House press corps.

June 14

The White House announced that the President has directed Secretary of Energy Hazel Rollins O'Leary to perform the duties of the Office of the Nuclear Waste Negotiator.

The White House also announced that the President will visit Seoul, South Korea, on July 10–11 to meet with President Kim Yong-sam and visit American troops stationed at the DMZ.

June 15

The White House announced that the President sent to the Congress amendments to the fiscal year 1994 appropriations requests for international development assistance, the Legal Services Corporation, and the Department of Justice.

The President announced the selection of physicists Leon M. Lederman, Harold Brown, and John S. Foster, Jr., as winners of the 1992 Enrico Fermi Award.

June 17

In the afternoon, the President had lunch with the Vice President.

The President announced the appointment of Jody Greenstone as Special Assistant to the President and Deputy to the Counselor to the President.

June 19

In the morning, the President traveled to Boston, MA. In the afternoon, he traveled to Portland, ME, and he returned to Washington, DC, in the evening.

June 23

In the afternoon, the President had lunch with business leaders.

In the evening, the President received diplomatic credentials from Ambassadors Mohamed Benaissa of Morocco, Roberto Mayorga-Cortes of Nicaragua, Thomas Kahota Kargbo of Sierra Leone, Li Daoyu of China, Han Sung-su of the Republic of Korea, and Adriaan Pieter Roetert Jacobovits de Szeged of The Netherlands.

June 24

In the afternoon, the President had lunch with the Vice President. He later met with Joe Louis Barrow, Jr.

In the evening, the President hosted a reception for congressional leaders.

June 25

In the afternoon, the President had a telephone conversation with Henry Leon Ritzenthaler.

June 28

The President announced his intention to nominate Einar Dyhrkopp of Shawneetown, IL, to be a member of the U.S. Postal Service Board of Governors.

June 30

In the evening, the President, Hillary Clinton, and Chelsea Clinton attended a performance of "The Phantom of the Opera" at the John F. Kennedy Center for the Performing Arts.

July 1

In the afternoon, the President had lunch with the Vice President.

In the evening, the President and Hillary Clinton had dinner with Senate Republican leader Robert Dole and Ambassador and Mrs. Robert Strauss.

July 2

The President announced his intention to nominate career Foreign Service officers Edward Perkins and Victor Tomseth to be Ambassador to Australia and Ambassador to Laos, respectively, and Toby Gati to be Assistant Secretary of State for Intelligence and Research. In addition, the President has accorded the personal rank of Ambassador to Robert Gosende in his capacity as Special Envoy for Somalia.

The President announced his approval of the following Senior Executive Service appointments at the Department of Defense:

V. Larry Lynn, Deputy Under Secretary for Advanced Technology;
Maj. Gen. Frank Horton, Principal Deputy Assistant Secretary for Command, Control, Communications, and Intelligence; and
Mari-Luci Jaramillo, Deputy Secretary for Inter-American Affairs.

July 4

In the afternoon, the President traveled to Philadelphia, PA, where he participated in a Liberty Bell ringing ceremony. Later in the afternoon, he traveled to Eldridge, IA, where he surveyed damage caused by severe flooding.

In the evening, the President traveled to San Francisco, CA.

July 5

In the afternoon, the President and Hillary Clinton traveled from San Francisco, CA, to Tokyo, Japan.

July 6

After arriving in Tokyo in the late afternoon, the President met with Prime Minister Kiichi Miyazawa of Japan at the Iikura House.

July 7

In the morning, the President met with President Soeharto of Indonesia at the U.S. Embassy. In the afternoon, he met with Prime Minister John Major of the United Kingdom at the Okura Hotel.

In the evening, the President attended a working dinner at the residence of Prime Minister Miyazawa.

July 8

In the morning, the President attended sessions of the economic summit and a working luncheon at the Akasaka Palace. In the late afternoon, he met with Chancellor Helmut Kohl of Germany.

In the evening, the President and Hillary Clinton attended a dinner hosted by Emperor Akihito at the Imperial Palace.

July 9

In the morning, the President attended sessions of the economic summit at the Akasaka Palace.

In the afternoon, the President attended a working luncheon with Prime Minister Kim Campbell of Canada at the residence of the U.S. Ambassador. He then returned to the Akasaka Palace to attend final sessions of the economic summit.

The President named Gerald Corrigan, president and CEO of the Federal Reserve Bank of New York, as Chairman of the Russian-American Enterprise Fund.

July 10

In the late morning, the President and Hillary Clinton traveled from Tokyo, Japan, to Seoul, South Korea.

July 11

In the morning, the President had breakfast with President Kim Yong-sam of South Korea in the Blue House garden.

In the evening, the President and Hillary Clinton traveled to Honolulu, HI, crossing the international dateline and arriving in Honolulu on the morning of June 11.

After arriving in the early morning, the President had breakfast with servicemen at the Pearl Harbor Naval Base. After the breakfast, the President and Hillary Clinton participated in a wreath-laying ceremony at the U.S.S. *Arizona* Memorial. The President then attended briefings at the CINCPAC headquarters at Camp H.M. Smith.

In the evening, the President and Hillary Clinton attended a dinner for Gov. John Waihee of Hawaii.

July 13

In the late evening, the President traveled from Honolulu, HI, to Des Moines, IA.

July 14

Following his arrival in Des Moines in the morning, the President took a helicopter tour of areas damaged by severe flooding in Iowa. In the evening, he returned to Washington, DC.

The President announced the addition of 87 more counties in the State of Iowa to the Presidential major disaster declaration of July 9, allowing flood victims to be eligible for Federal assistance. The additions brought to 99 the number of counties in Iowa eligible for Federal assistance to affected residents and businesses.

July 15

In the afternoon, the President had lunch with the Vice President.

The President announced his intention to nominate Joseph Swerdzewski to be General Counsel of the Federal Labor Relations Authority and Alice Dear to be Executive Director of the African Development Bank, and to renominate William Hathaway as a member and Chair of the Federal Maritime Commission.

July 17

In the morning, the President traveled to St. Louis, MO, where he took a helicopter tour of areas damaged by severe flooding.

In the afternoon, the President traveled to Little Rock, AR.

July 18

In the afternoon, the President returned to Washington, DC, from Little Rock, AR.

July 19

The President declared that major disasters existed in Nebraska and South Dakota as a result of severe storms and flooding and ordered the Federal Emergency Management Agency to provide assistance to affected individuals and communities in those States.

July 22

The White House announced the President will travel to Chicago, IL, on July 26 to address the Conference on the Future of the American Workplace sponsored by the Departments of Commerce and Labor

The President declared that a major disaster existed in Kansas as a result of severe storms and flooding and ordered the Federal Emergency Management Agency to assist individuals and families in a five-county area.

The President announced the following Senior Executive Service appointments:

U.S. International Development Cooperation Agency
Richard McCall, Jr., Chief of Staff, Agency for International Development

Department of Commerce
Will Martin, Special Adviser for International Affairs, National Oceanic and Atmospheric Administration

Department of Defense
Keith Gaby, Director of Intergovernmental Affairs
Jonathan Spalter, Special Assistant to the Principal Deputy Under Secretary for Policy

Timothy Connelly, Principal Deputy Assistant Secretary for Special Operations and Low Intensity Conflict

Carol DiBattiste, Principal Deputy General Counsel of the Navy

Sandra Stuart, Assistant to the Secretary for Legislative Affairs

Todd Weiler, Deputy Assistant Secretary of the Army for Training

Wade R. Sanders, Deputy Assistant Secretary of the Navy for Reserves

Joseph J. Kruzel, Deputy Assistant Secretary, European and NATO Policy

Department of Education
Howard Ray Moses, Deputy Assistant Secretary for Special Education and Rehabilitative Services

Raymond C. Pierce, Deputy Assistant Secretary, Office of Civil Rights

Thomas R. Wolanin, Deputy Assistant Secretary, Office of Legislation and Congressional Affairs

Department of Energy
Dan W. Reicher, Principal Deputy Assistant Secretary, Office of Environmental Restoration and Waste Management

Terry Cornwall Rumsey, Director, Office of Scientific and Technical Information

General Services Administration
Patrick Dorinson, Assistant Administrator for Public Affairs

Emily Clark Hewitt, General Counsel

Kenneth Kimbrough, Commissioner of Building Services

Department of Health and Human Services
Anna Durand, Deputy General Counsel

Ann Rosewater, Deputy Assistant Secretary for Policy and External Affairs, Administration for Children, Youth and Families

Department of the Interior
Robert L. Baum, Associate Solicitor (Conservation and Wildlife)

Anne H. Shields, Deputy Solicitor

Department of Justice
Samuel J. Dubbin, Deputy Assistant Attorney General, Office of Policy Development

George Havens, Special Assistant, Office of the Attorney General

Sheldon C. Bilchik, Assistant Deputy Attorney General

Robert Brink, Deputy Assistant Attorney General, Office of Legislative Affairs

Department of State
Barbara Mills Larkin, Deputy Assistant Secretary for Legislative Affairs

Valerie A. Mims, Deputy Assistant Secretary for the Bureau of Legislative Affairs

Department of Transportation
Theodore A. McConnell, Chief Counsel, Federal Highway Administration

Department of the Treasury
Fe Morales Marks, Deputy Assistant Secretary (Financial Institutions)
Mozelle Willmont Thompson, Deputy Assistant Secretary, Government Finance
David A. Lipton, Deputy Assistant Secretary for Eastern European and Former Soviet Union Policy

Office of the United States Trade Representative
Irving A. Williamson, Deputy General Counsel
Jennifer Hillman, Chief Textile Negotiator

July 23
In the morning, the President traveled to Little Rock, AR, where he and Hillary Clinton attended the funeral service for Deputy White House Counsel Vincent Foster, Jr., at St. Andrew's Cathedral. In the afternoon, they traveled to Hope, AR, where they attended the burial service at Memory Gardens Cemetery.

July 24
In the early morning, the President and Hillary Clinton returned to Washington, DC, from Little Rock, AR.

July 26
In the morning, the President went jogging with the Achilles Track Club. He then traveled to Chicago, IL.

In the evening, the President attended a Democratic National Committee dinner at the Chicago Historical Society and then returned to Washington, DC.

The President declared that a major disaster existed in North Dakota due to excessive rainfall and flooding beginning June 22.

July 28
In the evening, the President met with the Democratic Study Group on Capitol Hill. He then had dinner with House Members in the House Longworth Cafeteria.

July 29
In the afternoon, the President had lunch with the Vice President. He then met with recipients of the Enrico Fermi Award.

July 30
The White House announced that the President added $1.3 billion to his request for supplemental appropriations to cover emergency expenses related to the Midwest flooding.

Appendix B—Nominations Submitted to the Senate

The following list does not include promotions of members of the Uniformed Services, nominations to the Service Academies, or nominations of Foreign Service officers.

Submitted January 20

Warren Christopher,
of California, to be Secretary of State.

Lloyd Bentsen,
of Texas, to be Secretary of the Treasury.

Les Aspin,
of Wisconsin, to be Secretary of Defense.

Zoe Baird,
of Connecticut, to be Attorney General.

Bruce Babbitt,
of Arizona, to be Secretary of the Interior.

Mike Espy,
of Mississippi, to be Secretary of Agriculture.

Ronald H. Brown,
of the District of Columbia, to be Secretary of Commerce.

Robert B. Reich,
of Massachusetts, to be Secretary of Labor.

Donna E. Shalala,
of Wisconsin, to be Secretary of Health and Human Services.

Henry G. Cisneros,
of Texas, to be Secretary of Housing and Urban Development.

Federico Peña,
of Colorado, to be Secretary of Transportation.

Hazel Rollins O'Leary,
of Minnesota, to be Secretary of Energy.

Richard W. Riley,
of South Carolina, to be Secretary of Education.

Jesse Brown,
of the District of Columbia, to be Secretary of Veterans Affairs.

Madeleine Korbel Albright,
of the District of Columbia, to be the Representative of the United States of America to the United Nations

with rank and status of Ambassador Extraordinary and Plenipotentiary, and the Representative of the United States of America in the Security Council of the United Nations.

Carol M. Browner,
of Florida, to be Administrator of the Environmental Protection Agency.

Michael Kantor,
of California, to be United States Trade Representative, with the rank of Ambassador Extraordinary and Plenipotentiary.

Leon E. Panetta,
of California, to be Director of the Office of Management and Budget.

Laura D'Andrea Tyson,
of California, to be a Member of the Council of Economic Advisers.

Roger Altman,
of New York, to be Deputy Secretary of the Treasury.

Hershel Wayne Gober,
of Arkansas, to be Deputy Secretary of Veterans Affairs.

Madeleine Kunin,
of Vermont, to be Deputy Secretary of Education.

Alice Rivlin,
of the District of Columbia, to be Deputy Director of the Office of Management and Budget.

Clifton R. Wharton, Jr.,
of New York, to be Deputy Secretary of State.

R. James Woolsey,
of Maryland, to be Director of Central Intelligence.

Submitted January 25

John Howard Gibbons,
of Virginia, to be Director of the Office of Science and Technology Policy, vice D. Allan Bromley, resigned.

Withdrawn January 26

Zoe Baird,
of Connecticut, to be Attorney General, which was sent to the Senate on January 20, 1993.

Submitted January 28

Lloyd Bentsen,
of Texas, to be U.S. Governor of the International
Monetary Fund for a term of 5 years; U.S. Governor
of the International Bank for Reconstruction and Development for a term of 5 years; U.S. Governor of
the Inter-American Development Bank for a term of
5 years; U.S. Governor of the African Development
Bank for a term of 5 years; U.S. Governor of the
Asian Development Bank; U.S. Governor of the African Development Fund; and U.S. Governor of the
European Bank for Reconstruction and Development.

Submitted February 23

William J. Perry,
of California, to be Deputy Secretary of Defense, vice
Donald J. Atwood, resigned.

Frank G. Wisner,
of the District of Columbia, to be Under Secretary
of Defense for Policy, vice Paul Dundes Wolfowitz,
resigned.

Submitted February 26

Peter Tarnoff,
of New York, to be Under Secretary of State for
Political Affairs, vice Arnold Lee Kanter, resigned.

Janet Reno,
of Florida, to be Attorney General.

Submitted March 4

Russell F. Canan,
of the District of Columbia, to be an Associate Judge
of the Superior Court of the District of Columbia
for the term of 15 years, vice Ronald P. Wertheim,
retired.

Submitted March 5

Terrence R. Duvernay, Sr.,
of Georgia, to be Deputy Secretary of Housing and
Urban Development, vice Alfred A. DelliBovi, resigned.

Submitted March 8

James B. King,
of Massachusetts, to be Director of the Office of Personnel Management for a term of 4 years, vice Con-
stance Berry Newman, resigned.

Jean Nolan,
of Maryland, to be an Assistant Secretary of Housing
and Urban Development, vice Mary Shannon Bru-
nette.

Withdrawn March 9

The following named persons to be Commissioners
of the Copyright Royalty Tribunal for terms of 7 years,
which were sent to the Senate on January 5, 1993:

Edward J. Damich, of Virginia.
Bruce D. Goodman, of Pennsylvania.

Submitted March 15

Strobe Talbott,
of Ohio, to be Ambassador at Large and Special Adviser to the Secretary of State on the New Independent States.

Harriet C. Babbitt,
of Arizona, to be the Permanent Representative of
the United States of America to the Organization of
American States, with the rank of Ambassador.

Stephen A. Oxman,
of New Jersey, to be an Assistant Secretary of State,
vice Thomas Michael Tolliver Niles, resigned.

Submitted March 16

Joan E. Spero,
of New York, to be Under Secretary of State for
Economic and Agricultural Affairs, vice Robert B.
Zoellick.

James Lee Witt,
of Arkansas, to be Director of the Federal Emergency
Management Agency, vice Wallace Elmer Stickney,
resigned.

Submitted March 17

Robert M. Sussman,
of the District of Columbia, to be Deputy Administrator of the Environmental Protection Agency, vice
Frank Henry Habicht II, resigned.

Thomas E. Donilon,
of the District of Columbia, to be an Assistant Secretary of State, vice Margaret DeBardeleben Tutwiler,
resigned.

Submitted March 22

Jack R. DeVore, Jr.,
of Texas, to be an Assistant Secretary of the Treasury,
vice Desiree Tucker-Sorini, resigned.

Frank N. Newman,
of California, to be an Under Secretary of the Treasury, vice Jerome H. Powell, resigned.

Leslie B. Samuels,
of New York, to be an Assistant Secretary of the
Treasury, vice Fred T. Goldberg, Jr., resigned.

George Edward Moose,
of Maryland, a career member of the Senior Foreign Service, class of Minister-Counselor, to be an Assistant Secretary of State, vice Herman Jay Cohen, resigned.

Thomas P. Grumbly,
of Virginia, to be an Assistant Secretary of Energy (Environmental Restoration and Management), vice Leo P. Duffy, resigned.

Submitted March 25

John M. Deutch,
of Massachusetts, to be Under Secretary of Defense for Acquisition, vice Donald Jay Yockey, resigned.

Submitted March 26

Eugene Allan Ludwig,
of Pennsylvania, to be Comptroller of the Currency for a term of 5 years, vice Robert Logan Clarke.

Jamie S. Gorelick,
of Maryland, to be General Counsel of the Department of Defense, vice David Spears Addington, resigned.

Submitted March 29

Ronald K. Noble,
of New York, to be an Assistant Secretary of the Treasury, vice Peter K. Nunez, resigned.

Thomas R. Pickering,
of New Jersey, a career member of the Senior Foreign Service, with the personal rank of Career Ambassador, to be Ambassador Extraordinary and Plenipotentiary of the United States of America to the Russian Federation.

Submitted March 30

Roberta Achtenberg,
of California, to be an Assistant Secretary of Housing and Urban Development, vice Gordon H. Mansfield, resigned.

Submitted April 1

Leslie M. Turner,
of New Jersey, to be an Assistant Secretary of the Interior, vice Stella Garcia Guerra, resigned.

Avis LaVelle,
of Illinois, to be an Assistant Secretary of Health and Human Services, vice Alixe Reed Glen.

Susan Fallows Tierney,
of Massachusetts, to be an Assistant Secretary of Energy (Domestic and International Energy Policy), vice John J. Easton, Jr., resigned.

Submitted April 2

Harry J. Gilmore,
of Virginia, a career member of the Senior Foreign Service, class of Minister-Counselor, to be Ambassador Extraordinary and Plenipotentiary of the United States of America to the Republic of Armenia.

Patrick Francis Kennedy,
of Illinois, to be an Assistant Secretary of State, vice Arthur W. Fort, resigned.

Geri D. Palast,
of California, to be an Assistant Secretary of Labor, vice Frances Curtin McNaught, resigned.

Steven Alan Herman,
of New York, to be an Assistant Administrator of the Environmental Protection Agency, vice Herbert Tate.

David Gardiner,
of Virginia, to be an Assistant Administrator of the Environmental Protection Agency, vice J. Clarence Davies.

Submitted April 5

J. Brian Atwood,
of the District of Columbia, to be Administrator of the Agency for International Development.

Jerry D. Klepner,
of Virginia, to be an Assistant Secretary of Health and Human Services, vice Steven B. Kelmar.

Elizabeth Ann Reike,
of Arizona, to be an Assistant Secretary of the Interior, vice John M. Sayre, resigned.

Submitted April 7

Webster L. Hubbell,
of Arkansas, to be Associate Attorney General, vice Wayne A. Budd, resigned.

Drew S. Days III,
of Connecticut, to be Solicitor General of the United States, vice Kenneth Winston Starr.

Marshall Fletcher McCallie,
of Tennessee, a career member of the Senior Foreign Service, class of Counselor, to be Ambassador Extraordinary and Plenipotentiary of the United States of America to the Republic of Namibia.

Harriet S. Rabb,
of New York, to be General Counsel of the Department of Health and Human Services, vice Michael J. Astrue, resigned.

Robert Armstrong,
of Texas, to be an Assistant Secretary of the Interior, vice David Courtland O'Neal, resigned.

Bonnie R. Cohen,
of Massachusetts, to be an Assistant Secretary of the
Interior, vice John Schrote, resigned.

Submitted April 19

Mark Johnson,
of Montana, a career member of the Senior Foreign
Service, class of Minister-Counselor, to be Ambassador
Extraordinary and Plenipotentiary of the United States
of America to the Republic of Senegal.

Marilyn McAfee,
of Florida, a career member of the Senior Foreign
Service, class of Minister-Counselor, to be Ambassador
Extraordinary and Plenipotentiary of the United States
of America to the Republic of Guatemala.

William Thornton Pryce,
of Pennsylvania, a career member of the Senior Foreign Service, class of Minister-Counselor, to be Ambassador Extraordinary and Plenipotentiary of the
United States of America to the Republic of Honduras.

E. Allan Wendt,
of California, a career member of the Senior Foreign
Service, class of Minister-Counselor, to be Ambassador
Extraordinary and Plenipotentiary of the United States
of America to the Republic of Slovenia.

Eric James Boswell,
of California, a career member of the Senior Foreign
Service, class of Minister-Counselor, to be Director
of the Office of Foreign Missions, with the rank of
Ambassador.

Mary A. Ryan,
of Texas, to be Assistant Secretary of State for Consular Affairs, vice Elizabeth M. Tamposi, resigned.

Conrad Kenneth Harper,
of New York, to be Legal Adviser of the Department
of State, vice Edwin D. Williamson, resigned.

Margaret Milner Richardson,
of Texas, to be Commissioner of Internal Revenue,
vice Shirley D. Peterson, resigned.

Kay Casstevens,
of Texas, to be Assistant Secretary for Legislation and
Congressional Affairs, Department of Education, vice
B. Robert Okun.

Norma V. Cantu,
of Texas, to be Assistant Secretary for Civil Rights,
Department of Education, vice Michael L. Williams.

Jim Baca,
of New Mexico, to be Director of the Bureau of
Land Management, vice Delos Cy Jamison, resigned.

Alicia Haydock Munnell,
of Massachusetts, to be an Assistant Secretary of the
Treasury, vice Sidney L. Jones, resigned.

Alvin P. Adams,
of Virginia, a career member of the Senior Foreign
Service, class of Minister-Counselor, to be Ambassador
Extraordinary and Plenipotentiary of the United States
of America to the Republic of Peru.

James R. Lyons,
of Maryland, to be an Assistant Secretary of Agriculture, vice James R. Moseley, resigned.

Richard E. Rominger,
of California, to be Deputy Secretary of Agriculture,
vice Ann M. Veneman, resigned.

Richard E. Rominger,
of California, to be a member of the Board of Directors of the Commodity Credit Corporation, vice Ann
M. Veneman, resigned.

John A. Rollwagen,
of Minnesota, to be Deputy Secretary of Commerce,
vice Rockwell Anthony Schnabel, resigned.

Sheila Foster Anthony,
of Arkansas, to be an Assistant Secretary of Commerce, vice Mary Jo Jacobi, resigned.

Clarence L. Irving, Jr.,
of New York, to be Assistant Secretary of Commerce
for Communications and Information, vice Gregory
F. Chapados, resigned.

D. James Baker,
of the District of Columbia, to be Under Secretary
of Commerce for Oceans and Atmosphere, vice John
A. Knauss, resigned.

Victor Marrero,
of New York, to be the representative of the United
States of America on the Economic and Social Council
of the United Nations, with the rank of Ambassador.

Victor Jackovich,
of Iowa, a career member of the Senior Foreign Service, class of Counselor, to be Ambassador Extraordinary and Plenipotentiary of the United States of
America to the Republic of Bosnia and Herzegovina.

Bob J. Nash,
of Arkansas, to be Under Secretary of Agriculture
for Small Community and Rural Development, vice
Roland R. Vautour, resigned.

Bob J. Nash,
of Arkansas, to be a member of the Board of Directors
of the Commodity Credit Corporation, vice Roland
R. Vautour, resigned.

Judith Heumann,
of California, to be Assistant Secretary for Special Education and Rehabilitative Services, Department of Education, vice Robert Refugio Davila, resigned.

Arati Prabhakar,
of Texas, to be Director of the National Institute of Standards and Technology, vice John W. Lyons.

Wardell Clinton Townsend, Jr.,
of North Carolina, to be an Assistant Secretary of Agriculture, vice Charles R. Hilty, resigned.

Submitted April 20

Wendy Ruth Sherman,
of Maryland, to be an Assistant Secretary of State, vice Janet Gardner Mullins.

Douglas Joseph Bennet, Jr.,
of Connecticut, to be an Assistant Secretary of State, vice John R. Bolton, resigned.

John Howard Francis Shattuck,
of Massachusetts, to be Assistant Secretary of State for Human Rights and Humanitarian Affairs, vice Patricia Diaz Dennis, resigned.

Alexander Fletcher Watson,
of Massachusetts, a career member of the Senior Foreign Service, class of Career Minister, to be an Assistant Secretary of State, vice Bernard William Aronson, resigned.

Nicolas P. Retsinas,
of Rhode Island, to be an Assistant Secretary of Housing and Urban Development, vice Arthur J. Hill, resigned.

Submitted April 21

Eugene Branstool,
of Ohio, to be an Assistant Secretary of Agriculture, vice Jo Ann D. Smith, resigned.

Eugene Branstool,
of Ohio, to be a member of the Board of Directors of the Commodity Credit Corporation, vice Jo Ann D. Smith, resigned.

Kenneth D. Brody,
of New York, to be president of the Export-Import Bank of the United States for a term of 4 years expiring January 20, 1997, vice John D. Macomber, resigned.

Sally Katzen,
of the District of Columbia, to be Administrator of the Office of Information and Regulatory Affairs, Office of Management and Budget, vice S. Jay Plager, resigned.

Philip Lader,
of South Carolina, to be Deputy Director for Management, Office of Management and Budget, vice Francis S.M. Hodsoll, resigned.

Submitted April 22

Pamela Harriman,
of Virginia, to be Ambassador Extraordinary and Plenipotentiary of the United States of America to France.

James S. Gilliland,
of Tennessee, to be General Counsel of the Department of Agriculture, vice Alan Charles Raul, resigned.

Thomas P. Glynn,
of Massachusetts, to be Deputy Secretary of Labor, vice Delbert Leon Spurlock, Jr., resigned.

Stephen H. Kaplan,
of Colorado, to be General Counsel of the Department of Transportation, vice Walter B. McCormick, Jr., resigned.

John D. Leshy,
of Arizona, to be Solicitor of the Department of the Interior, vice Thomas Lawrence Sansonetti, resigned.

Michael A. Stegman,
of North Carolina, to be an Assistant Secretary of Housing and Urban Development, vice John C. Weicher, resigned.

Submitted April 27

Kenneth S. Apfel,
of Maryland, to be an Assistant Secretary of Health and Human Services, vice Arnold R. Tompkins, resigned.

Walter D. Broadnax,
of New York, to be Deputy Secretary of Health and Human Services, vice Kevin E. Moley, resigned.

Jean E. Hanson,
of New York, to be General Counsel for the Department of the Treasury, vice Jeanne S. Archibald, resigned.

Bruce C. Vladeck,
of New York, to be Administrator of the Health Care Financing Administration, vice Gail Roggin Wilensky.

Jeffrey Richard Shafer,
of New Jersey, to be a Deputy Under Secretary of the Treasury, vice Olin L. Wethington, resigned.

Michael B. Levy,
of Texas, to be a Deputy Under Secretary of the Treasury, vice Mary Catherine Sophos, resigned.

Joan E. Spero,
of New York, to be U.S. Alternate Governor of the International Bank for Reconstruction and Development for a term of 5 years; U.S. Alternate Governor of the Inter-American Development Bank for a term of 5 years; U.S. Alternate Governor of the African Development Bank for a term of 5 years; U.S. Alternate Governor of the African Development Fund; U.S. Alternate Governor of the Asian Development Bank; and U.S. Alternate Governor of the European Bank for Reconstruction and Development, vice Robert B. Zoellick.

George Edward Moose,
an Assistant Secretary of State, to be a member of the Board of Directors of the African Development Foundation for the remainder of the term expiring September 27, 1997, vice Herman Jay Cohen.

David T. Ellwood,
of Massachusetts, to be an Assistant Secretary of Health and Human Services, vice Martin H. Gerry.

Lorraine Allyce Green,
of the District of Columbia, to be Deputy Director of the Office of Personnel Management, vice Bill R. Phillips, resigned.

Elinor G. Constable,
of the District of Columbia, a career member of the Senior Foreign Service, class of Career Minister, to be Assistant Secretary of State for Oceans and International Environmental and Scientific Affairs, vice E.U. Curtis Bohlen, resigned.

Jerry W. Bowen,
of Arkansas, to be Director of the National Cemetery System, Department of Veterans Affairs, vice Allen B. Clark, Jr., resigned.

Mary Lou Keener,
of Georgia, to be General Counsel, Department of Veterans Affairs, vice James Ashley Endicott, Jr., resigned.

Edward P. Scott,
of New Jersey, to be an Assistant Secretary of Veterans Affairs (Congressional Affairs), vice Sylvia Chavez Long, resigned.

D. Mark Catlett,
of Virginia, to be an Assistant Secretary of Veterans Affairs (Finance and Information Resources Management), vice S. Anthony McCann, resigned.

Charlene Barshefsky,
of the District of Columbia, to be a Deputy U.S. Trade Representative, with the rank of Ambassador, vice Julius L. Katz.

Kathryn D. Sullivan,
of Texas, to be Chief Scientist of the National Oceanic and Atmospheric Administration, vice Sylvia Alice Earle, resigned.

Mortimer L. Downey,
of New York, to be Deputy Secretary of Transportation, vice Arthur J. Rothkopf, resigned.

Rufus Hawkins Yerxa,
of the District of Columbia, to be a Deputy U.S. Trade Representative, with the rank of Ambassador.

Marshall S. Smith,
of California, to be Under Secretary of Education (new position).

Augusta Souza Kappner,
of New York, to be Assistant Secretary for Vocational and Adult Education, Department of Education, vice Betsy Brand, resigned.

Thomas S. Williamson, Jr.,
of California, to be Solicitor for the Department of Labor, vice Marshall Jordan Breger, resigned.

Submitted April 28

Karl Frederick Inderfurth,
of North Carolina, to be the Alternate Representative of the United States of America for Special Political Affairs in the United Nations, with the rank of Ambassador.

Erskine B. Bowles,
of North Carolina, to be Administrator of the Small Business Administration, vice Patricia F. Saiki, resigned.

Michael P. Huerta,
of California, to be Associate Deputy Secretary of Transportation, vice Robert E. Martinez, resigned.

Rodney E. Slater,
of Arkansas, to be Administrator of the Federal Highway Administration, vice Thomas D. Larson, resigned.

George J. Weise,
of Virginia, to be Commissioner of Customs (new position).

George T. Frampton, Jr.,
of the District of Columbia, to be Assistant Secretary for Fish and Wildlife, vice Mike Hayden, resigned.

Daniel P. Beard,
of Washington, to be Commissioner of Reclamation, vice Dennis B. Underwood, resigned.

Eugene Moos,
of Washington, to be Under Secretary of Agriculture for International Affairs and Commodity Programs, vice Richard Thomas Crowder, resigned.

Eugene Moos,
of Washington, to be a member of the Board of Directors of the Commodity Credit Corporation, vice Richard Thomas Crowder, resigned.

Maria Echaveste,
of New York, to be Administrator of the Wage and Hour Division, Department of Labor, vice Paula V. Smith, resigned.

Ruth R. Harkin,
of Iowa, to be President of the Overseas Private Investment Corporation, vice Fred M. Zeder II, resigned.

Thomas W. Payzant,
of California, to be Assistant Secretary for Elementary and Secondary Education, Department of Education, vice John T. MacDonald, resigned.

David A. Longanecker,
of Colorado, to be Assistant Secretary for Postsecondary Education, Department of Education, vice Carolynn Reid-Wallace, resigned.

Roger W. Johnson,
of California, to be Administrator of General Services, vice Richard G. Austin, resigned.

Daniel K. Tarullo,
of Massachusetts, to be an Assistant Secretary of State, vice Eugene J. McAllister, resigned.

Submitted April 29

Sheila Foster Anthony,
of Arkansas, to be an Assistant Attorney General, vice W. Lee Rawls, resigned.

Frank Hunger,
of Mississippi, to be an Assistant Attorney General, vice Stuart M. Gerson, resigned.

Eleanor Acheson,
of Massachusetts, to be an Assistant Attorney General, vice Stephen J. Markman, resigned.

Walter Dellinger,
of North Carolina, to be an Assistant Attorney General, vice Timothy E. Flanigan, resigned.

Anne Bingaman,
of New Mexico, to be an Assistant Attorney General, vice James Franklin Rill, resigned.

Lani Guinier,
of Pennsylvania, to be an Assistant Attorney General, vice John R. Dunne, resigned.

Steven S. Honigman,
of New York, to be General Counsel of the Department of the Navy, vice Craig S. King, resigned.

Joseph Shuldiner,
of California, to be an Assistant Secretary of Housing and Urban Development, vice Joseph G. Schiff, resigned.

Ashton B. Carter,
of Massachusetts, to be an Assistant Secretary of Defense, vice David S.C. Chu, resigned.

Edwin Dorn,
of Texas, to be an Assistant Secretary of Defense, vice Christopher Jehn, resigned.

Edward L. Warner III,
of Virginia, to be an Assistant Secretary of Defense, vice Colin Riley McMillan, resigned.

Anita K. Jones,
of Virginia, to be Director of Defense Research and Engineering, vice Victor H. Reis, resigned.

The following named persons to be members of the Federal Energy Regulatory Commission for the terms indicated:

James John Hoecker, of Virginia, for the remainder of the term expiring June 30, 1995, vice Branko Terzic, resigned.
William Lloyd Massey, of Arkansas, for the remainder of the term expiring October 20, 1993, vice Martin Lewis Allday, resigned.
William Lloyd Massey, of Arkansas, for the term expiring June 30, 1998 (reappointment).
Donald Farley Santa, of Connecticut, for the term expiring June 30, 1997, vice Charles A. Trabandt, term expired.

Ellen Weinberger Haas,
of New York, to be an Assistant Secretary of Agriculture, vice Catherine Ann Bertini, resigned.

Ellen Weinberger Haas,
of New York, to be a member of the Board of Directors of the Commodity Credit Corporation, vice Catherine Ann Bertini, resigned.

Marilynn A. Davis,
of New York, to be an Assistant Secretary of Housing and Urban Development, vice Jim E. Tarro, resigned.

Aida Alvarez,
of California, to be Director of the Office of Federal Housing Enterprise Oversight, Department of Housing and Urban Development, for a term of 5 years (new position).

Withdrawn April 29

Sheila Foster Anthony,
of Arkansas, to be an Assistant Secretary of Commerce, vice Mary Jo Jacobi, resigned, which was sent to the Senate on April 19, 1993.

Submitted May 7

Joseph D. Duffey,
of West Virginia, to be Director of the United States
Information Agency, vice Henry E. Catto, resigned.

Karen Beth Nussbaum,
of Ohio, to be Director of the Women's Bureau, Department of Labor, vice Elsie V. Vartanian, resigned.

Philip Benjamin Heymann,
of Massachusetts, to be Deputy Attorney General, vice
George J. Terwilliger III, resigned.

Douglas Kent Hall,
of Kentucky, to be Assistant Secretary of Commerce
for Oceans and Atmosphere, vice Jennifer Joy Wilson,
resigned.

Submitted May 10

Vicky A. Bailey,
of Indiana, to be a member of the Federal Energy
Regulatory Commission for the term expiring June
30, 1996, vice Jerry Jay Langdon, term expired.

Submitted May 12

Christopher Finn,
of New York, to be Executive Vice President of the
Overseas Private Investment Corporation, vice James
David Berg, resigned.

Submitted May 14

Philip R. Lee,
of California, to be an Assistant Secretary of Health
and Human Services, vice James O. Mason, resigned.

Penn Kemble,
of New York, to be Deputy Director of the United
States Information Agency, vice Eugene P. Kopp, resigned.

Submitted May 17

Andrew M. Cuomo,
of New York, to be an Assistant Secretary of Housing
and Urban Development, vice Skirma Anna Kondratas.

Submitted May 18

James Richard Cheek,
of Arkansas, a career member of the Senior Foreign
Service, class of Minister-Counselor, to be Ambassador
Extraordinary and Plenipotentiary of the United States
of America to Argentina.

Archer L. Durham,
of Maryland, to be an Assistant Secretary of Energy
(Human Resources and Administration), vice William
H. Young, resigned.

William J. Taylor III,
of Texas, to be an Assistant Secretary of Energy (Congressional, Intergovernmental, and International Affairs), vice Greg Ward, resigned.

William H. White,
of Texas, to be Deputy Secretary of Energy, vice
Linda Gillespie Stuntz, resigned.

Harold P. Smith, Jr.,
of California, to be Assistant to the Secretary of Defense for Atomic Energy, vice Robert B. Barker, resigned.

Submitted May 19

John Francis Maisto,
of Pennsylvania, a career member of the Senior Foreign Service, class of Minister-Counselor, to be Ambassador Extraordinary and Plenipotentiary of the
United States of America to the Republic of Nicaragua.

Deborah Roche Lee,
of Maryland, to be an Assistant Secretary of Defense,
vice Stephen M. Duncan, resigned.

Emmett Paige, Jr.,
of Maryland, to be an Assistant Secretary of Defense,
vice Duane Perry Andrews, resigned.

Walter Becker Slocombe,
of the District of Columbia, to be Deputy Under
Secretary of Defense for Policy, vice I. Lewis Libby,
Jr., resigned.

Submitted May 20

Chas. W. Freeman,
of Rhode Island, to be an Assistant Secretary of Defense, vice James Roderick Lilley, resigned.

Olena Berg,
of California, to be an Assistant Secretary of Labor,
vice David George Ball, resigned.

John D. Donahue,
of Indiana, to be an Assistant Secretary of Labor,
vice Nancy Risque Rohrbach, resigned.

Lee Patrick Brown,
of Texas, to be Director of National Drug Control
Policy, vice Bob Martinez.

Albert J. Herberger,
of New York, to be Administrator of the Maritime
Administration, vice Warren G. Leback, resigned.

William Christie Ramsay,
of Michigan, a career member of the Senior Foreign
Service, class of Minister-Counselor, to be Ambassador
Extraordinary and Plenipotentiary of the United States
of America to the Republic of the Congo.

Sharon Porter Robinson,
of Kentucky, to be Assistant Secretary for Educational Research and Improvement, Department of Education, vice Diane S. Ravitch, resigned.

Judith A. Winston,
of the District of Columbia, to be General Counsel, Department of Education, vice Jeffrey C. Martin, resigned.

Lionel Skipwith Johns,
of Virginia, to be an Associate Director of the Office of Science and Technology Policy.

Submitted May 24

Everett M. Ehrlich,
of Pennsylvania, to be Under Secretary of Commerce for Economic Affairs, vice Jose Antonio Villamil, resigned.

Mary Jo Bane,
of Massachusetts, to be Assistant Secretary for Family Support, Department of Health and Human Services, vice Jo Anne B. Barnhart.

Submitted May 28

Thomas J. Downey,
of New York, to be a member of the Defense Base Closure and Realignment Commission for a term expiring at the end of the first session of the 103d Congress, vice Arthur Levitt, Jr., resigned.

Submitted June 1

Jean Kennedy Smith,
of New York, to be Ambassador Extraordinary and Plenipotentiary of the United States of America to Ireland.

Submitted June 7

William H. Dameron III,
of the District of Columbia, a career member of the Senior Foreign Service, class of Counselor, to be Ambassador Extraordinary and Plenipotentiary of the United States of America to the Republic of Mali.

Peter W. Galbraith,
of Vermont, to be Ambassador Extraordinary and Plenipotentiary of the United States of America to the Republic of Croatia.

Benjamin Leader Erdreich,
of Alabama, to be a member of the Merit Systems Protection Board for the term of 7 years expiring March 1, 2000, vice Daniel R. Levinson, term expired.

Benjamin Leader Erdreich,
of Alabama, to be Chairman of the Merit Systems Protection Board, vice Daniel R. Levinson.

Tara Jeanne O'Toole,
of Maryland, to be an Assistant Secretary of Energy (Environment, Safety and Health), vice Paul L. Ziemer, resigned.

Victor P. Raymond,
of the District of Columbia, to be an Assistant Secretary of Veterans Affairs (Policy and Planning), vice Jo Ann Krukar Webb.

Doug Ross,
of Michigan, to be an Assistant Secretary of Labor, vice Roberts T. Jones, resigned.

Withdrawn June 7

Lani Guinier,
of Pennsylvania, to be an Assistant Attorney General, vice John R. Dunne, resigned, which was sent to the Senate on April 29, 1993.

Submitted June 8

Robert E. Hunter,
of the District of Columbia, to be U.S. Permanent Representative on the Council of the North Atlantic Treaty Organization, with rank and status of Ambassador Extraordinary and Plenipotentiary.

June Gibbs Brown,
of Hawaii, to be Inspector General, Department of Health and Human Services, vice Richard P. Kusserow, resigned.

Bruce A. Lehman,
of Wisconsin, to be Commissioner of Patents and Trademarks, vice Harry F. Manbeck, Jr., resigned.

Withdrawn June 8

John A. Rollwagen,
of Minnesota, to be Deputy Secretary of Commerce, vice Rockwell Anthony Schnabel, resigned, which was sent to the Senate on April 19, 1993.

Submitted June 15

Robert Riggs Nordhaus,
of the District of Columbia, to be General Counsel of the Department of Energy, vice John J. Easton, Jr.

Submitted June 16

Raymond Leo Flynn,
of Massachusetts, to be Ambassador Extraordinary and Plenipotentiary of the United States of America to the Holy See.

Joseph A. Saloom III,
of Virginia, a career member of the Senior Foreign Service, class of Minister-Counselor, to be Ambassador

Extraordinary and Plenipotentiary of the United States of America to the Republic of Guinea.

Dennis C. Jett,
of New Mexico, a career member of the Senior Foreign Service, class of Counselor, to be Ambassador Extraordinary and Plenipotentiary of the United States of America to the Republic of Mozambique.

Steven E. Steiner,
of Maryland, a career member of the Senior Foreign Service, class of Minister-Counselor, for the rank of Ambassador during his tenure of service as U.S. Representative to the START Joint Compliance and Inspection Commission.

Jolene Moritz Molitoris,
of Ohio, to be Administrator of the Federal Railroad Administration, vice Gilbert E. Carmichael, resigned.

Submitted June 17

Laurence Everett Pope, II,
of Maine, a career member of the Senior Foreign Service, class of Minister-Counselor, to be Ambassador Extraordinary and Plenipotentiary of the United States of America to the Republic of Chad.

Howard Franklin Jeter,
of South Carolina, a career member of the Senior Foreign Service, class of Counselor, to be Ambassador Extraordinary and Plenipotentiary of the United States of America to the Republic of Botswana.

Zachary W. Carter,
of New York, to be U.S. Attorney for the Eastern District of New York for the term of 4 years, vice Andrew J. Maloney, resigned.

The following named persons to be members of the Board of Directors of the Tennessee Valley Authority for the terms indicated:

Johnny H. Hayes, of Tennessee, for the remainder of the term expiring May 18, 1996, vice Marvin T. Runyon, resigned.
Craven H. Crowell, Jr., of Tennessee, for the term expiring May 18, 2002, vice John B. Waters, term expired.

Submitted June 18

Alan S. Blinder,
of New Jersey, to be a member of the Council of Economic Advisers, vice David F. Bradford, resigned.

Joseph E. Stiglitz,
of California, to be a member of the Council of Economic Advisers, vice Paul Wonnacott, resigned.

Submitted June 22

Ruth Bader Ginsburg,
of New York, to be an Associate Justice of the Supreme Court of the United States, vice Byron R. White, retired.

Andrew J. Winter,
of New York, a career member of the Senior Foreign Service, class of Minister-Counselor, to be Ambassador Extraordinary and Plenipotentiary of the United States of America to the Republic of The Gambia.

David Laurence Aaron,
of New York, to be the Representative of the United States of America to the Organization for Economic Cooperation and Development, with the rank of Ambassador.

G. Edward DeSeve,
of Pennsylvania, to be Chief Financial Officer, Department of Housing and Urban Development (new position).

Susan Gaffney,
of Virginia, to be Inspector General, Department of Housing and Urban Development, vice Paul A. Adams, resigned.

Submitted June 23

Patrick H. NeMoyer,
of New York, to be U.S. Attorney for the Western District of New York for the term of 4 years, vice Dennis C. Vacco, term expired.

Mary Jo White,
of New York, to be U.S. Attorney for the Southern District of New York for the term of 4 years, vice Otto G. Obermaier, resigned.

Submitted June 24

Ramon C. Cortines,
of California, to be Assistant Secretary for Intergovernmental and Interagency Affairs and for Human Resources and Administration, Department of Education.

Victor H. Reis,
of the District of Columbia, to be an Assistant Secretary of Energy (Defense Programs), vice Richard A. Claytor, resigned.

Robin Lynn Raphel,
of Washington, a career member of the Senior Foreign Service, class of Counselor, to be Assistant Secretary of State for South Asian Affairs (new position).

Submitted June 29

Loretta L. Dunn,
of Kentucky, to be an Assistant Secretary of Commerce, vice Mary Jo Jacobi, resigned.

James Patrick Connelly,
of Washington, to be U.S. Attorney for the Eastern District of Washington for the term of 4 years, vice William D. Hyslop, resigned.

John Thomas Schneider,
of North Dakota, to be U.S. Attorney for the District of North Dakota for the term of 4 years, vice Stephen D. Easton, resigned.

Alan H. Flanigan,
of Virginia, a career member of the Senior Foreign Service, class of Minister-Counselor, to be Ambassador Extraordinary and Plenipotentiary of the United States of America to the Republic of El Salvador.

Robert Gordon Houdek,
of Illinois, a career member of the Senior Foreign Service, class of Minister-Counselor, to be Ambassador Extraordinary and Plenipotentiary of the United States of America to Eritrea.

John T. Sprott,
of Virginia, a career member of the Senior Executive Service, to be Ambassador Extraordinary and Plenipotentiary of the United States of America to Swaziland.

Roland Karl Kuchel,
of Florida, a career member of the Senior Foreign Service, class of Minister-Counselor, to be Ambassador Extraordinary and Plenipotentiary of the United States of America to the Republic of Zambia.

Richard Scott Carnell,
of Florida, to be an Assistant Secretary of the Treasury, vice John Cunningham Dugan, resigned.

Submitted June 30

David Russell Hinson,
of Illinois, to be Administrator of the Federal Aviation Administration, vice Thomas C. Richards, resigned.

Arthur Levitt, Jr.,
of New York, to be a member of the Securities and Exchange Commission for the term expiring June 5, 1998, vice Richard C. Breeden, resigned.

Ada E. Deer,
of Wisconsin, to be an Assistant Secretary of the Interior, vice Eddie F. Brown.

Submitted July 1

Janet Ann Napolitano,
of Arizona, to be U.S. Attorney for the District of Arizona for the term of 4 years, vice Linda A. Akers, resigned.

M. Joycelyn Elders,
of Arkansas, to be Medical Director in the Regular Corps of the Public Health Service, subject to quali-

fications therefor as provided by law and regulations, and to be Surgeon General of the Public Health Service, for a term of 4 years, vice Antonia Coello Novello.

Gordon J. Linton,
of Pennsylvania, to be Federal Transit Administrator, vice Brian W. Clymer, resigned.

Submitted July 13

James J. Blanchard,
of Michigan, to be Ambassador Extraordinary and Plenipotentiary of the United States of America to Canada.

Walter C. Carrington,
of Maryland, to be Ambassador Extraordinary and Plenipotentiary of the United States of America to the Federal Republic of Nigeria.

Jeffrey Davidow,
of Virginia, a career member of the Senior Foreign Service, class of Minister-Counselor, to be Ambassador Extraordinary and Plenipotentiary of the United States of America to the Republic of Venezuela.

Thomas J. Dodd,
of the District of Columbia, to be Ambassador Extraordinary and Plenipotentiary of the United States of America to the Oriental Republic of Uruguay.

Stuart E. Eizenstat,
of the District of Columbia, to be Representative of the United States of America to the European Communities, with the rank and status of Ambassador Extraordinary and Plenipotentiary.

James E. Hall,
of Tennessee, to be a member of the National Transportation Safety Board for the term expiring December 31, 1997, vice Christopher A. Hart, term expired.

Donald C. Johnson,
of Texas, a career member of the Senior Foreign Service, class of Counselor, to be Ambassador Extraordinary and Plenipotentiary of the United States of America to Mongolia.

Richard Menifee Moose,
of Virginia, to be Under Secretary of State for Management, vice J. Brian Atwood, resigned.

George Munoz,
of Illinois, to be an Assistant Secretary of the Treasury, vice David M. Nummy, resigned.

George Munoz,
of Illinois, to be Chief Financial Officer, Department of the Treasury, vice David M. Nummy, resigned.

Mary M. Raiser,
of the District of Columbia, for the rank of Ambassador during her tenure of service as Chief of Protocol for the White House.

Louise Frankel Stoll,
of California, to be an Assistant Secretary of Transportation, vice Kate Leader Moore, resigned.

Stanley G. Tate,
of Florida, to be Chief Executive Officer, Resolution Trust Corporation, vice Albert V. Casey, resigned.

Charles Robert Tetzlaff,
of Vermont, to be U.S. Attorney for the District of Vermont for the term of 4 years, vice George J. Terwilliger III, resigned.

William David Wilmoth,
of West Virginia, to be U.S. Attorney for the Northern District of West Virginia for the term of 4 years, vice William A. Kolibash, term expired.

Submitted July 15

Aurelia Erskine Brazeal,
of Georgia, a career member of the Senior Foreign Service, class of Minister-Counselor, to be Ambassador Extraordinary and Plenipotentiary of the United States of America to the Republic of Kenya.

John S. Davison,
of Maryland, a career member of the Senior Foreign Service, class of Minister-Counselor, to be Ambassador Extraordinary and Plenipotentiary of the United States of America to the Republic of Niger.

James Robert Jones,
of Oklahoma, to be Ambassador Extraordinary and Plenipotentiary of the United States of America to Mexico.

Nelson A. Diaz,
of Pennsylvania, to be General Counsel of the Department of Housing and Urban Development, vice Francis Anthony Keating II, resigned.

Submitted July 16

Mollie H. Beattie,
of Vermont, to be Director of the United States Fish and Wildlife Service, vice John F. Turner, resigned.

Mary Lowe Good,
of New Jersey, to be Under Secretary of Commerce for Technology, vice Robert Marshall White, resigned.

J. Joseph Grandmaison,
of New Hampshire, to be Director of the Trade and Development Agency, vice Jose E. Martinez, resigned.

Donald J. McConnell,
of Ohio, a career member of the Senior Foreign Service, class of Minister-Counselor, to be Ambassador Extraordinary and Plenipotentiary of the United States of America to Burkina Faso.

Submitted July 20

Louis J. Freeh,
of New York, to be Director of the Federal Bureau of Investigation for the term of 10 years, vice William S. Sessions.

Gaynelle Griffin Jones,
of Texas, to be U.S. Attorney for the Southern District of Texas for the term of 4 years, vice Ronald G. Woods.

Karen Elizabeth Schreier,
of South Dakota, to be U.S. Attorney for the District of South Dakota for the term of 4 years, vice Philip N. Hogen.

Judith Ann Stewart,
of Indiana, to be U.S. Attorney for the Southern District of Indiana for the term of 4 years, vice Deborah J. Daniels.

Walter Michael Troop,
of Kentucky, to be U.S. Attorney for the Western District of Kentucky for the term of 4 years, vice Joseph M. Whittle.

Submitted July 22

Graham T. Allison, Jr.,
of Massachusetts, to be an Assistant Secretary of Defense, vice Stephen John Hadley, resigned.

Robert T. Watson,
of Virginia, to be an Associate Director of the Office of Science and Technology Policy, vice Donald A. Henderson, resigned.

Sheila E. Widnall,
of Massachusetts, to be Secretary of the Air Force, vice Donald B. Rice, resigned.

Frank Eugene Kruesi,
of Illinois, to be an Assistant Secretary of Transportation, vice Stephen T. Hart.

Jay E. Hakes,
of Florida, to be Administrator of the Energy Information Administration, Department of Energy, vice Calvin A. Kent, resigned.

Submitted July 23

Walter F. Mondale,
of Minnesota, to be Ambassador Extraordinary and Plenipotentiary of the United States of America to Japan.

Submitted July 29

Richard Holbrooke,
of New York, to be Ambassador Extraordinary and
Plenipotentiary of the United States of America to
the Federal Republic of Germany.

James T. Laney,
of Georgia, to be Ambassador Extraordinary and Plenipotentiary of the United States of America to the
Republic of Korea.

Eric Himpton Holder, Jr.,
of the District of Columbia, to be U.S. Attorney for
the District of Columbia for the term of 4 years,
vice Jay B. Stephens, resigned.

Stephen Charles Lewis,
of Oklahoma, to be U.S. Attorney for the Northern
District of Oklahoma for the term of 4 years, vice
Tony Michael Graham, resigned.

Vicki Lynn Miles-LaGrange,
of Oklahoma, to be U.S. Attorney for the Western
District of Oklahoma for the term of 4 years, vice
Timothy D. Leonard, resigned.

Thomas Justin Monaghan,
of Nebraska, to be U.S. Attorney for the District of
Nebraska for the term of 4 years, vice Ronald D.
Lahners.

John W. Raley, Jr.,
of Oklahoma, to be U.S. Attorney for the Eastern
District of Oklahoma for the term of 4 years.

Randall K. Rathbun,
of Kansas, to be U.S. Attorney for the District of
Kansas for the term of 4 years, vice Morris Lee
Thompson, resigned.

Frederick W. Thieman,
of Pennsylvania, to be U.S. Attorney for the Western
District of Pennsylvania for the term of 4 years, vice
Thomas W. Corbett, Jr.

Michael Joseph Yamaguchi,
of California, to be U.S. Attorney for the Northern
District of California for the term of 4 years, vice
Joseph P. Russoniello, resigned.

Anne H. Lewis,
of Maryland, to be an Assistant Secretary of Labor,
vice Steven I. Hofman, resigned.

Submitted July 30

Jeffrey E. Garten,
of New York, to be Under Secretary of Commerce
for International Trade, vice John Michael Farren,
resigned.

Appendix C—Checklist of White House Press Releases

The following list contains releases of the Office of the Press Secretary which are not included in this book.

Released January 21

Transcript of a press briefing by Director of Communications George R. Stephanopoulos

Released January 22

List of Cabinet members to be sworn in

Transcript of a press briefing by Director of Communications George R. Stephanopoulos

Released January 23

Transcript of a press briefing by Press Secretary Dee Dee Myers

Released January 25

Transcript of a press briefing by Director of Communications George R. Stephanopoulos

List of participants in economic policy meeting

Advance text of remarks at a meeting of the health care working group

Statement by Director of Communications George R. Stephanopoulos on the President's meeting with the Joint Chiefs of Staff

Released January 26

List of participants in meeting with congressional leaders

Transcript of a press briefing by Director of Communications George R. Stephanopoulos

Released January 27

Transcript of a press briefing by Director of Communications George R. Stephanopoulos

Transcript of a press briefing by Press Secretary Dee Dee Myers

Released January 28

Transcript of a press briefing by Press Secretary Dee Dee Myers

Transcript of a press briefing by Director of Communications George R. Stephanopoulos

Released January 29

Transcript of a press briefing by Director of Communications George R. Stephanopoulos

Released February 1

Transcript of a press briefing by Director of Communications George R. Stephanopoulos

List of participants in meeting with National Governors' Association members

Announcement of Medicaid waiver streamlining directives

Released February 2

Transcript of a press briefing by Director of Communications George R. Stephanopoulos

Transcript of a press briefing on welfare reform by Deputy Assistant to the President for Domestic Affairs Bruce Reed

Transcript of a press briefing by Press Secretary Dee Dee Myers

Released February 3

Transcript of a press briefing by Director of Communications George R. Stephanopoulos

Transcripts of two press briefings by Press Secretary Dee Dee Myers

Released February 4

Transcript of a press briefing by Director of Communications George R. Stephanopoulos

Transcripts of two press briefings by Press Secretary Dee Dee Myers

Released February 5

Transcript of a press briefing by Director of Communications George R. Stephanopoulos

List of participants in meeting with mayors

Released February 7

Transcript of a press briefing by Director of Communications George R. Stephanopoulos

Text of a letter from Kimba Wood to the New York Times

Released February 8

Transcript of a press briefing by Director of Communications George R. Stephanopoulos

Transcript of a press briefing by Press Secretary Dee Dee Myers

Background information on unemployment insurance extension

Fact sheet on the new environmental policy

Released February 9

Transcript of a press briefing by Press Secretary Dee Dee Myers

Transcript of a press briefing on White House reorganization by Chief of Staff Thomas F. McLarty III

Fact sheet on White House reorganization

Transcript of a press briefing by Director of Communications George R. Stephanopoulos

List of participants in meeting with Boy Scouts of America representatives

Released February 10

Transcript of a press briefing by Director of Communications George R. Stephanopoulos

Transcript of a press briefing by Press Secretary Dee Dee Myers

Released February 11

Transcript of a press briefing by Director of Communications George R. Stephanopoulos

Transcript of a press briefing by Press Secretary Dee Dee Myers

Released February 12

Transcript of a press briefing by Director of Communications George R. Stephanopoulos

Released February 15

Transcripts of two press briefings by Press Secretary Dee Dee Myers

Transcript of a press briefing by Director of Communications George R. Stephanopoulos

Released February 16

Transcript of a press briefing by Press Secretary Dee Dee Myers

Transcript of a press briefing by Director of Communications George R. Stephanopoulos

Released February 17

Transcripts of two press briefings by Press Secretary Dee Dee Myers

Transcript of a press briefing on the President's economic program by Director of the Office of Management and Budget Leon E. Panetta, Secretary of the Treasury Lloyd Bentsen, and Chairman of the Council of Economic Advisers Laura D'Andrea Tyson

Announcement of travel schedule for Cabinet members to promote the economic recovery program

List of participants in meeting with congressional leaders

Released February 18

Transcript of a press briefing by Press Secretary Dee Dee Myers

Released February 22

Statement by Press Secretary Dee Dee Myers announcing the President's meeting with United Nations Secretary-General Boutros Boutros-Ghali

Outline of the President's comprehensive new technology initiative

Released February 23

Joint statement with United Nations Secretary-General Boutros Boutros-Ghali

Biographies of nominees for 21 sub-Cabinet posts

Transcript of two press briefings by Press Secretary Dee Dee Myers

Transcript of a press briefing by Director of Communications George R. Stephanopoulos

Transcript of a press briefing on technology policy by Assistant to the President for Science and Technology Policy John H. Gibbons and Deputy Assistant to the President for Economic Policy W. Bowman Cutter

Released February 24

Transcript of a press briefing by Press Secretary Dee Dee Myers

Transcript of a press briefing by Director of Communications George R. Stephanopoulos

Released February 25

Transcripts of two press briefings by Press Secretary Dee Dee Myers

Transcript of a press briefing by Director of Communications George R. Stephanopoulos

List of Philadelphia and Houston business and labor leaders endorsing the President's economic program

Announcement of the President's planned meeting with space shuttle *Endeavour* astronauts

Released February 26

List of American business and labor leaders endorsing the President's economic program

Statements by American business and labor leaders supporting the President's economic program

Transcript of a press briefing by Director of Communications George R. Stephanopoulos

Released March 2

Transcripts of two press briefings by Press Secretary Dee Dee Myers

Transcript of a press briefing by Director of Communications George R. Stephanopoulos

Statement by Press Secretary Dee Dee Myers on the President's meeting with NATO Secretary General Manfred Woerner

Released March 3

Transcripts of two press briefings by Press Secretary Dee Dee Myers

Transcript of a press briefing by Director of Communications George R. Stephanopoulos

Released March 4

Transcript of a press briefing by Press Secretary Dee Dee Myers

Transcript of a press briefing by Director of Communications George R. Stephanopoulos

Transcript of a press briefing on the inner-city crisis by former President Jimmy Carter

Released March 5

Transcripts of two press briefings by Press Secretary Dee Dee Myers

Transcript of a press briefing by Director of Communications George R. Stephanopoulos

Released March 8

Transcripts of two press briefings by Press Secretary Dee Dee Myers

Transcript of a press briefing by Director of Communications George R. Stephanopoulos

Released March 9

Transcript of two press briefings by Press Secretary Dee Dee Myers

Transcript of a press briefing by Director of Communications George R. Stephanopoulos

Released March 10

Transcript of a press briefing by Press Secretary Dee Dee Myers

Transcripts of two press briefings by Director of Communications George R. Stephanopoulos

White House statement announcing the Forest Conference

Released March 11

Transcript of a press briefing by Press Secretary Dee Dee Myers

Transcript of a press briefing by Director of Communications George R. Stephanopoulos

Transcript of a press briefing on defense conversion by Gene B. Sperling, Deputy Assistant to the President for Economic Policy; Dorothy Robyn, Special Assistant to the President for Technology Policy; Steve Jones, Director for Defense Policy, National Security Council; Don Gessaman, Deputy Associate Director for National Security, Office of Management and Budget; and David Lane, Director for Defense Conversion Policy, National Security Council

Released March 15

Transcript of a press briefing by Press Secretary Dee Dee Myers

Transcript of a press briefing by Director of Communications George R. Stephanopoulos

Released March 16

Transcript of a press briefing by Press Secretary Dee Dee Myers

Transcript of a press briefing by Director of Communications George R. Stephanopoulos

Released March 17

Transcripts of two press briefings by Press Secretary Dee Dee Myers

Transcript of a press briefing by Director of Communications George R. Stephanopoulos

Released March 18

Transcript of a press briefing by Press Secretary Dee Dee Myers

Transcript of a press briefing by Director of Communications George R. Stephanopoulos

Released March 20

Transcript of a press briefing by Director of Communications George R. Stephanopoulos

White House statement on President Boris Yeltsin of Russia

Released March 22

Transcripts of two press briefings by Press Secretary Dee Dee Myers

Transcript of a press briefing by Director of Communications George R. Stephanopoulos

Released March 23

Transcript of a press briefing by Press Secretary Dee Dee Myers

Released March 24

Transcript of a press briefing by Press Secretary Dee Dee Myers

Transcript of a press briefing by Director of Communications George R. Stephanopoulos

Released March 25

Transcripts of two press briefings by Press Secretary Dee Dee Myers

Transcript of a press briefing by Director of Communications George R. Stephanopoulos

Released March 26

Transcript of a press briefing by Press Secretary Dee Dee Myers

Transcript of a press briefing by Director of Communications George R. Stephanopoulos

List of working group members for the President's Task Force on National Health Care Reform

Released March 29

Transcript of a press briefing by Press Secretary Dee Dee Myers

Transcript of a press briefing by Director of Communications George R. Stephanopoulos

Released March 30

Transcripts of two press briefings by Press Secretary Dee Dee Myers

Transcript of a press briefing by Director of Communications George R. Stephanopoulos

Released March 31

Transcript of a press briefing by Press Secretary Dee Dee Myers

Transcript of a press briefing by Director of Communications George R. Stephanopoulos

Released April 1

Transcript of a press briefing by Press Secretary Dee Dee Myers

Fact sheet on the "Comprehensive Child Immunization Act of 1993"

Advance text of remarks to the American Society of Newspaper Editors

Released April 2

Transcript of remarks by the Vice President on opening the Forest Conference in Portland, Oregon

Released April 3

Transcript of a press briefing by Director of Communications George R. Stephanopoulos

Released April 4

Vancouver Declaration: Joint Statement of the Presidents of the United States and the Russian Federation

Fact sheet on humanitarian/health assistance and food sales to Russia

Fact sheet on private sector development in Russia

Fact sheet on the Democracy Corps initiative for Russia

Fact sheet on the officer resettlement initiative for Russia

Fact sheet on the energy and environment initiative for Russia

Fact sheet on trade and investment in Russia

Fact sheet on Food for Progress credit sales to Russia

Fact sheet on Russia and the GATT

Fact sheet on the Generalized System of Preferences

Fact sheet on the Safe, Secure Dismantlement (SSD) Initiative with Russia

Fact sheet on the Safe, Secure Dismantlement (SSD) Initiative with Belarus, Kazakhstan, and Ukraine

Fact sheet on the START I/NPT (Lisbon Protocol)

Released April 5

Transcript of a press briefing by Director of Communications George R. Stephanopoulos

Released April 6

Transcript of a press briefing by Press Secretary Dee Dee Myers

Released April 7

Transcript of a press briefing by Press Secretary Dee Dee Myers

Transcript of a press briefing by Director of Communications George R. Stephanopoulos

Released April 8

Transcript of a press briefing by Press Secretary Dee Dee Myers

Transcript of a press briefing by Director of Communications George R. Stephanopoulos

Transcript of a press briefing on the budget by the Vice President, Secretary of the Treasury Lloyd Bentsen, Director of the Office of Management and Budget Leon E. Panetta, and Chairman of the Council of Economic Advisers Laura D'Andrea Tyson

Released April 9

Transcript of a press briefing by Press Secretary Dee Dee Myers

Released April 10

Statement by Press Secretary Dee Dee Myers announcing a mission to Vietnam by the President's Special Emissary for POW/MIA Affairs

Released April 12

Transcript of a press briefing by Press Secretary Dee Dee Myers

Transcript of a press briefing by Director of Communications George R. Stephanopoulos

Released April 13

Transcript of a press briefing by Press Secretary Dee Dee Myers

Transcript of a press briefing by Director of Communications George R. Stephanopoulos

Released April 14

Transcript of a press briefing by Director of Communications George R. Stephanopoulos

Office of Media Affairs press releases sent to Pennsylvania, New York, Maine, Vermont, Oregon, and Missouri media on jobs directly created by the stimulus plan

Released April 15

Transcript of a press briefing by Press Secretary Dee Dee Myers

Transcript of a press briefing by Director of Communications George R. Stephanopoulos

Statement by Press Secretary Dee Dee Myers announcing the President's trip to Pennsylvania

Statement by Director of Communications George R. Stephanopoulos on the President's Federal income tax return

Released April 16

Transcript of a press briefing by Press Secretary Dee Dee Myers

Transcript of a press briefing by Director of Communications George R. Stephanopoulos

Statement by Press Secretary Dee Dee Myers announcing the President's initiative on telecommunications encryption technology

Released April 17

Statement by the President on the jury verdict in the Rodney King case

Released April 19

Transcripts of two press briefings by Press Secretary Dee Dee Myers

Transcript of a press briefing by Director of Communications George R. Stephanopoulos

Released April 20

Transcript of a press briefing by Press Secretary Dee Dee Myers

Transcript of a press briefing by Director of Communications George R. Stephanopoulos

Released April 21

Transcript of a press briefing by Press Secretary Dee Dee Myers

Transcript of a press briefing by Director of Communications George R. Stephanopoulos

Fact sheet on the "Goals 2000: Educate America Act"

Released April 22

Transcript of a press briefing by Press Secretary Dee Dee Myers

Transcript of a press briefing by Director of Communications George R. Stephanopoulos

Released April 23

Transcript of a press briefing by Press Secretary Dee Dee Myers

Released April 26

Transcript of a press briefing by Press Secretary Dee Dee Myers

Transcript of a press briefing by Director of Communications George R. Stephanopoulos

White House statement on the establishment of a National Biological Survey

Released April 27

Transcript of a press briefing by Press Secretary Dee Dee Myers

Transcript of a press briefing by Director of Communications George R. Stephanopoulos

List of Members of Congress meeting with the President on Bosnia

Released April 28

Transcript of a press briefing by Press Secretary Dee Dee Myers

Transcript of a press briefing by Director of Communications George R. Stephanopoulos

Released April 29

Transcript of a press briefing by Press Secretary Dee Dee Myers

Transcript of a press briefing by Director of Communications George R. Stephanopoulos

Transcript of a press briefing on Bosnia by Chairman of the Joint Chiefs of Staff Gen. Colin Powell

Transcript of a press briefing on Bosnia by Secretary of State Warren M. Christopher

Released May 1

Statement by Press Secretary Dee Dee Myers on the delegation to attend the funeral of African National Congress leader Oliver Tambo on May 2

Transcript of a press briefing on Bosnia by Secretary of State Warren M. Christopher

Released May 3

Transcript of a press briefing by Press Secretary Dee Dee Myers

Transcript of a press briefing by Director of Communications George R. Stephanopoulos

Statement by Director of Communications George R. Stephanopoulos on the President's remarks concerning Senator Dole at the White House Correspondents' Association dinner

Released May 4

Transcript of a press briefing by Press Secretary Dee Dee Myers

Transcript of a press briefing by Director of Communications George R. Stephanopoulos

Released May 5

Transcript of a press briefing by Press Secretary Dee Dee Myers

Transcript of a press briefing by Director of Communications George R. Stephanopoulos

Released May 6

Transcript of a press briefing by Press Secretary Dee Dee Myers

Transcript of a press briefing by Director of Communications George R. Stephanopoulos

Released May 7

Transcript of a press briefing on campaign finance reform by Special Assistant to the President for Policy Coordination Michael Waldman

Statement by Director of Communications George R. Stephanopoulos on Ross Perot's remarks concerning the President's decisions on Bosnia

Released May 8

Transcript of a press briefing by Director of Communications George R. Stephanopoulos

Released May 12

Transcript of a press briefing by Press Secretary Dee Dee Myers

Released May 13

Transcript of a press briefing by Press Secretary Dee Dee Myers

Transcript of a press briefing by Director of Communications George R. Stephanopoulos

Released May 14

Transcript of a press briefing on the economic program by Director of the Office of Management and Budget Leon E. Panetta, Secretary of the Treasury Lloyd Bentsen, and Chairman of the Council of Economic Advisers Laura D'Andrea Tyson

Released May 17

Announcement of Presidential Faculty Fellows Program award recipients

President's financial disclosure report

Released May 19

Transcript of a press briefing by Press Secretary Dee Dee Myers

Released May 20

Transcript of a press briefing by Press Secretary Dee Dee Myers

Transcript of a press briefing by Director of Communications George R. Stephanopoulos

Released May 21

Transcript of a press briefing by Director of Communications George R. Stephanopoulos

Statement by Director of Communications George R. Stephanopoulos on White House travel services

Announcement of President's Task Force on National Health Care Reform audit and list of participants

Released May 24

Transcript of a press briefing by Director of Communications George R. Stephanopoulos

Released May 25

Transcript of a press briefing by Director of Communications George R. Stephanopoulos

Statement by White House Counsel Bernard W. Nussbaum on the White House Travel Office

Released May 26

Transcript of a press briefing by Press Secretary Dee Dee Myers

Transcript of a press briefing by Director of Communications George R. Stephanopoulos

Released May 28

Transcript of a press briefing on most-favored-nation trade status for China by Assistant Secretary of State for East Asian and Pacific Affairs Winston Lord

Released May 29

Transcript of a press briefing on White House staff changes by Chief of Staff Thomas F. McLarty III and Counselor to the President David R. Gergen

Released June 1

Statement by Press Secretary Dee Dee Myers on the President's signing of H.R. 1378, Making Technical Corrections in Defense-Related Laws

Announcement by the Office of Presidential Correspondence on public access to the White House electronic mail system

Released June 2

Transcript of a press briefing by Senior Policy Adviser George R. Stephanopoulos

List of business leaders attending a luncheon with the President

Released June 3

Statement by Press Secretary Dee Dee Myers on the President's planned meeting with Lani Guinier

Released June 4

Transcript of a press briefing by Senior Policy Adviser George R. Stephanopoulos

Announcement of transmittal of supplemental appropriations requests

List of officials and civil rights leaders meeting with the President

Released June 7

Transcript of a press briefing by Counselor to the President David R. Gergen and Director of Communications Mark D. Gearan

Transcript of a press briefing by Press Secretary Dee Dee Myers

Statement by Chief of Staff Thomas F. McLarty III on White House staff changes

Released June 8

Transcript of a press briefing by Press Secretary Dee Dee Myers

Statement by Press Secretary Dee Dee Myers on the President's meeting with Federal Reserve Board Chairman Alan Greenspan

Released June 9

Statement by Press Secretary Dee Dee Myers on Kuwait's lifting of the boycott of companies dealing with Israel

Transcript of a press briefing by Press Secretary Dee Dee Myers

Transcript of a press briefing on the President's economic program by Director of the Office of Management and Budget Leon E. Panetta

Released June 10

Transcript of a press briefing by Press Secretary Dee Dee Myers

Fact sheet on the National Institutes of Health Revitalization Act

Announcement of appointment of Chairman and members of the Thomas Jefferson Commemoration Commission

Released June 11

Transcript of a press briefing by Press Secretary Dee Dee Myers

Statement by Press Secretary Dee Dee Myers on the establishment of a working group on welfare reform, family support, and independence

Released June 15

Announcement of international broadcasting reorganization

Announcement of scheduled courtesy calls by Judge Ruth Bader Ginsburg

Released June 16

Transcript of a press briefing by Press Secretary Dee Dee Myers

Released June 17

Announcement of the space station *Freedom* redesign decision

Fact sheet on the space station *Freedom* program redesign

Released June 18

Transcript of a press briefing by Press Secretary Dee Dee Myers

Fact sheet on the alien smuggling policy

Released June 21

Transcript of a press briefing on the economic program by Secretary of the Treasury Lloyd Bentsen

Released June 22

Transcript of a press briefing by Press Secretary Dee Dee Myers

Released June 23

Transcript of a press briefing by Press Secretary Dee Dee Myers

Transcript of a press briefing on the economic program by Director of the Office of Management and Budget Leon E. Panetta

Released June 24

Transcript of a press briefing by Press Secretary Dee Dee Myers

Released June 25

Transcript of a press briefing by Press Secretary Dee Dee Myers

Announcement of nomination for two U.S. Attorneys

Statement by Chief of Staff Thomas F. McLarty III on White House staff changes

Released June 28

Transcript of a press briefing by Press Secretary Dee Dee Myers

Announcement of nomination for two U.S. Attorneys

Released June 30

Transcript of a press briefing by Press Secretary Dee Dee Myers

Transcript of a press briefing on the court decision requiring a NAFTA environmental impact statement by U.S. Trade Representative Mickey Kantor

Statement by U.S. Trade Representative Mickey Kantor on the court decision requiring a NAFTA environmental impact statement

Released July 1

Transcript of remarks by the Vice President, Secretary of the Interior Bruce Babbitt, Secretary of Agriculture Mike Espy, Secretary of Labor Robert B. Reich, Secretary of Commerce Ronald H. Brown, and EPA Administrator Carol M. Browner in an announcement of the Forest Conservation Plan

Transcript of a press briefing on the economic summit by Secretary of the Treasury Lloyd Bentsen

Released July 2

Transcript of a press briefing on the White House Travel Office management review by Chief of Staff Thomas F. McLarty III

Transcript of a press briefing on the economic summit by Secretary of State Warren M. Christopher

Announcement of nomination of Janet Napolitano to be U.S. Attorney for the District of Arizona

Released July 3

White House statement on U.S. policy on nuclear testing and a comprehensive test ban

Released July 6

Transcript of a press briefing on the economic summit by Secretary of State Warren M. Christopher and Counselor to the President David R. Gergen

Released July 7

Transcript of a press briefing by Counselor to the President David R. Gergen

Transcript of a press briefing on the economic summit by Secretary of State Warren M. Christopher and Secretary of the Treasury Lloyd Bentsen

Transcript of a press briefing on the economic summit by U.S. Trade Representative Mickey Kantor

Released July 8

Transcripts of three press briefings by Counselor to the President David R. Gergen

Transcript of a press briefing on aid to Russia by Secretary of the Treasury Lloyd Bentsen

Released July 9

Transcript of a press briefing on the President's visit to Japan and the economic summit by Counselor to the President David R. Gergen, Under Secretary of State Joan E. Spero, Under Secretary of the Treasury Lawrence H. Summers, and Special Assistant to the President Bob Fauver

Transcript of a press briefing on the President's visit to Japan and the economic summit by Counselor to the President David R. Gergen

Announcement on implementation of Vancouver initiatives

Announcement on U.S.-Russia expanded bilateral cooperation

Announcement on the Russian-American Enterprise Fund

Released July 10

Transcript of a press briefing on the Japan-U.S. economic framework agreement by Counselor to the President David R. Gergen, Deputy Assistant to the President for Economic Policy W. Bowman Cutter, Deputy U.S. Trade Representative Charlene Barshefsky, Under Secretary of State for Economic and Agricultural Affairs Joan E. Spero, Deputy Secretary of the Treasury Roger C. Altman, and Under Secretary of the Treasury for International Affairs Lawrence H. Summers

Released July 12

Statement by Press Secretary Dee Dee Myers on the Presidential delegation to Vietnam

Released July 15

Statement by Press Secretary Dee Dee Myers on Surgeon-General-designate Joycelyn Elders

Transcript of a press briefing by Press Secretary Dee Dee Myers

Transcript of a press briefing on deficit reduction by Director of the Office of Management and Budget Leon E. Panetta and Deputy Secretary of the Treasury Roger C. Altman

Released July 16

Transcript of a press briefing by Press Secretary Dee Dee Myers

Released July 17

Joint Statement Between the United States and Russia on Cooperation in Space

Released July 19

Transcript of a press briefing by Press Secretary Dee Dee Myers

Announcement of nomination for four U.S. Attorneys

Directive by Secretary of Defense Les Aspin on the policy on homosexuals in the Armed Forces

Released July 20

Transcript of a press briefing by Press Secretary Dee Dee Myers

Released July 21

Transcript of remarks by the Vice President to small business owners in Clinton, MD

Transcript of a press briefing on the economic program by Small Business Administrator Erskine B. Bowles

Transcript of a press briefing by Chief of Staff Thomas F. McLarty III and Director of Communications Mark D. Gearan

Statement by Chief of Staff Thomas F. McLarty III on the death of Deputy White House Counsel Vincent Foster, Jr.

Obituary of Deputy White House Counsel Vincent Foster, Jr.

Transcript of remarks by White House Counsel Bernard W. Nussbaum at a White House staff meeting

Released July 22

Transcript of a press briefing by Press Secretary Dee Dee Myers

Joint declaration on relations between the United States and the Republic of Belarus

Released July 23

Transcript of a press briefing on the economic program by the Vice President, Chairman of the Council of Economic Advisers Laura D'Andrea Tyson, Secretary of the Department of Labor Robert B. Reich, and Secretary of Commerce Ronald H. Brown

Released July 26

Transcript of a press briefing by Press Secretary Dee Dee Myers

White House statement on the arrangement by the Presidential Inquiries Branch with U.S. Soldiers' and Airmen's Home to continue processing White House mail

Released July 27

Transcript of a press briefing by Press Secretary Dee Dee Myers

Fact sheet on the "Expedited Exclusion and Alien Smuggling Enhanced Penalties Act of 1993"

List of participants in meeting with Conservative Democratic Forum members

Released July 28

Statement on the signing of the Liberia peace agreement

Released July 29

Transcript of a press briefing by Press Secretary Dee Dee Myers

Announcement of nomination for eight U.S. Attorneys

Statement on the request for additional funding for Midwest disaster assistance

Released July 30

Transcript of a press briefing by Press Secretary Dee Dee Myers

Transcript of a press briefing on national service legislation by Assistant to the President for National Service Eli J. Segal

Appendix D—Presidential Documents Published in the Federal Register

This appendix lists Presidential documents released by the Office of the Press Secretary and published in the Federal Register. The texts of the documents are printed in the Federal Register (F.R.) at the citations listed below. The documents are also printed in title 3 of the Code of Federal Regulations and in the Weekly Compilation of Presidential Documents.

PROCLAMATIONS

EXECUTIVE ORDERS—Continued

OTHER PRESIDENTIAL DOCUMENTS

Subject Index

Abortion—7-11, 131, 278, 749, 835, 850
Academic Decathlon, U.S.—929
Acquired immune deficiency syndrome (AIDS). *See* Health and medical care
ACTION—575
Administration. *See* other part of subject
Adult Learning Center, New Brunswick, NJ—217
Advisory committees, Federal. *See* Government agencies and employees
Aeronautics and Space Administration, National—621, 850, 874, 876, 902, 908, 918, 920, 962, 1153
Aerospace industry. *See* Aviation industry
AFL-CIO. *See* Labor & Congress of Industrial Organizations, American Federation of
Africa. *See* specific country
African-American History Month, National—28
African Development Bank—1267
Agency. *See* other part of subject
Aging, Administration on. *See* Health and Human Services, Department of
Aging, Federal Council on the—820
Aging, White House Conference on—732
Agricultural Stabilization and Conservation Service. *See* Agriculture, Department of
Agriculture
  Crop insurance system—1000, 1077, 1098, 1100
  Disaster assistance—959, 966, 996, 1000, 1032, 1074, 1077, 1082, 1099, 1103, 1125
  Farm financial assistance—1080, 1192
  International government subsidies—957, 1005, 1039, 1246
  Water management—1245
Agriculture, Department of
  Agricultural Stabilization and Conservation Service—1082
  Assistant Secretaries—256, 264, 1260, 1261
  Budget—1263
  Commodity Credit Corporation—1082, 1137
  Deputy Secretary—256
  Disaster assistance funding—1261
  General Counsel—284
  Meat inspection, role—80
  Rural Electrification Administration—119, 606
  Secretary—68, 80, 546, 959, 966, 996, 1000-1002, 1004, 1005, 1032, 1076, 1078, 1097, 1098, 1103, 1108, 1192, 1235, 1262
  Soil Conservation Service—1082
  Under Secretaries—256, 264
AID. *See* Development Cooperation Agency, U.S. International
AIDS. *See* Health and medical care
AIDS Policy Coordinator, Office of the National—932
Air Force, Department of the
  See also Armed Forces, U.S.

Air Force, Department of the—Continued
  Air Force Academy, U.S.—582
  General Counsel—1083
  Homestead Air Force Base, FL—77, 287, 288
  Investigation of major general's remarks—851, 862
  Secretary—992
  Thunderbirds precision flying team—1264
Airline Industry, National Commission to Ensure a Strong Competitive—412, 416, 539, 725
Airline industry. *See* Aviation industry
Alabama
  Governor—1151
  News media—1149
  Snowstorms—1262
Alabama, University of—1260
Albania
  Prime Minister—1262
  Trade with U.S.—807
Alcohol, Tobacco and Firearms, Bureau of. *See* Treasury, Department of the
Ambassadors. *See* specific country
American. *See* other part of subject
American University—206
Amtrak. *See* Railroad Passenger Corporation, National
Angola, U.S. recognition—704
APEC. *See* Asia-Pacific Economic Cooperation forum
Architects, American Institute of—1257
Arctic Research Plan, U.S.—1237
Argentina
  Arms control negotiations and agreements—954
  President—953, 954
  Trade with U.S.—953, 954
  U.S. Ambassador—366
Arizona, news media—1238
Arkansas Land and Farm Development Corp.—482
Arkansas, President's visits—367, 1169, 1261, 1267, 1268
Arkansas, University of—511, 928
Armed Forces, U.S.
  See also specific military department; Defense and national security
  Assignment of women—623
  Ban on homosexuals in the military—13, 18-20, 23, 74, 78, 153, 337, 338, 352, 511, 610, 756, 919, 1109, 1113, 1138, 1146, 1161, 1203
  Base closings—77, 288, 292, 296, 300, 301, 973, 1012, 1142, 1153, 1187, 1189
  Health care—8, 11
  International role. *See* specific country or region
  National Guard—1033, 1092, 1093, 1098
  Personnel reduction—286, 973
  POW's/MIA's—491, 688, 786, 990, 1221, 1261, 1262
  Radio address—283
Armenia
  Ambassador to U.S.—1265

Name Index

Aaron, David Laurence—515, 1278
Abdul-Jabbar, Kareem—893
Abercrombie, Neil—1065
Abraham, Katherine G.—936
Abramson, Jerry—913, 916, 917
Acheson, Eleanor Dean—536, 1275
Achtenberg, Roberta—36, 1271
Adams, Alvin P.—313, 1272
Adams, Gerry—663, 668
Adler, Phil—900
Aideed, Mohamed Farah—839, 862, 867, 870, 872, 970, 987, 1028
Akaka, Daniel K.—1065
Akayev, Askar—713
Albright, Madeleine K.—6, 465, 486, 505, 939, 940, 1269
Alchuleta, Nancy—649
Ali, Muhammad—893
Alioto, Michelle—596
Allen, James—308
Allison, Graham T., Jr.—370, 1280
Althaus, Bill—558, 913, 916, 917
Altman, Roger—318, 1050, 1269
Alvarez, Aida—354, 1275
Alvarez-Machain, Humberto—529
Amacher, Ryan—653
Amato, Giuliano—1260
Anderson, Bernard—936
Anderson, Bette B.—539
Andrews, Thomas H.—891
Angelou, Maya—472
Anthony, Paul T.—742
Anthony, Sheila Foster—100, 536, 1272, 1275
Apfel, Kenneth S.—1260, 1273
Archbishop Desmond Tutu—704, 705
Archbishop Iakovos—357
Aristide, Jean-Bertrand—55, 56, 85, 162, 231, 290, 309, 489, 810, 873, 875, 972, 997, 1025, 1035, 1068, 1071, 1154, 1155, 1259
Armacost, Michael—837
Armstrong, Michael—703
Armstrong, Robert—1258, 1271
Armstrong, Robin—866
Asad, Hafiz al- —408
Ashe, Arthur—61, 894, 921
Aspin, Les—8, 20, 233, 270, 288, 289, 293, 296-301, 317, 337, 338, 439, 505, 511, 784, 919, 974, 1110, 1111, 1114, 1128, 1142, 1146, 1153, 1161, 1214, 1261, 1269
Atwood, J. Brian—368, 1271
Augustine, Norman R.—1264
Aung San Suu Kyi—705, 1056, 1135
Avent, Loretta—250, 435
Aziz, Tariq—969

Babbitt, Bruce—68, 469, 691, 844, 846, 851, 965, 966, 1231, 1244, 1245, 1269
Babbitt, Harriet C.—1270
Babbitt, J. Randolph—539
Baca, Jim—1258, 1272
Bai Hua—773
Bailey, Tracey Leon—460, 628
Bailey, Vicky A.—422, 1276
Baird, Zoe—5, 7, 8, 65, 94, 744, 1269
Baker, Chris—583
Baker, D. James—100, 1272
Baker, James A., III—773, 1262
Baker, Jarvis—583
Baliles, Gerald L.—539, 658, 726
Balladur, Edouard—853, 979, 986
Bane, Mary Jo—1258, 1277
Bao Zunxin—773
Barclay, Charles M.—539
Barram, David—1046
Barrett, Bill—788
Barrow, Joe Louis, Jr.—1265
Barshefsky, Charlene—321, 1050, 1274
Bartholomew, Reginald—505, 858, 1027, 1214
Bartlett, Donald—769
Baum, Robert L.—1267
Baylor, Don—403
Beard, Daniel P.—1260, 1274
Beattie, Mollie H.—703, 1280
Becker, Suzanne Rose—742
Bekavac, Nancy Y.—712, 742
Bellamy, Carol—972, 1176
Benaissa, Mohamed—1265
Beneke, Patricia—628
Bennet, Douglas Joseph, Jr.—247, 573, 1273
Bennett, Marian—1091
Benson, Frederick S., III—712
Benton, Marjorie—712
Bentsen, Lloyd—13, 89, 120, 187, 213, 318, 319, 417, 494, 613, 635, 817-819, 827-829, 833, 871, 873, 901, 903, 908, 946, 1031, 1059, 1132, 1257, 1269, 1270
Berg, E. Olena—460, 1276
Bernthal, Frederick M.—420
Bertsch, Waylon Dean—1234
Beschloss, Michael—712
Betts, Ginny Trotter—567
Biden, Joseph R., Jr.—96, 278, 833, 847
Bilbray, James H.—1229
Bilchik, Sheldon C.—1267
Bingaman, Anne K.—536, 1275
Bingaman, Jeff—674
Bir, Cevik—565, 839, 1029
Birch, David—944
Bishop, Ann—73

Document Categories List